MW00446448

The Complete Guide to Human Resources and the Law

2018 Edition

by Dana Shilling

The Complete Guide to Human Resources and the Law is an invaluable tool for the HR professional who needs to place legal principles and developments in the context of the practical problems he or she faces every day. The law as it relates to human resources issues is an ever-growing, ever-changing body of information that involves not just court cases but also statutes and the regulations of administrative agencies. In 2017, administrative regulations, and judicial and congressional responses to administrative regulations, took on a much higher profile than usual.

The Complete Guide to Human Resources and the Law brings you the most up-to-date information as well as practical tips and checklists in a well-organized, easy-to-use resource.

Highlights of the 2018 Edition

The 2018 Edition provides new and expanded coverage of issues such as:

- Near the end of the Supreme Court's 2016–2017 term, Judge Neil Gorsuch of the Tenth Circuit was confirmed , by a 54-45 vote, bringing the Supreme Court back to a full bench of nine Justices. Previously, confirmation of a Supreme Court Justice required 60 votes, but the Senate rules were changed to permit confirmation by a simple majority, abolishing the filibuster for Supreme Court nominations.

- In March 2017, the Supreme Court restricted the president's ability to make administrative appointments without Senate advice and consent. A "PAS position" is one that must be filled by presidential appointment, confirmed by the Senate. To prevent abuse, the Federal Vacancies Reform Act of 1998 (FVRA) provides several ways for the president to make PAS appointments. The default is for the first assistant to the former holder of the job to take over as acting holder of the position. The FVRA also allows the president to appoint, as acting official, a senior employee at the same agency or someone who has already been nominated and confirmed for a job at another federal agency. Theoretically federal law limits how long a person can serve in an acting capacity, but in practice many appointees served longer. The FVRA invalidates certain actions taken by acting officers who were not validly

appointed. Lafe Solomon, a senior National Labor Relations Board (NLRB) employee, was appointed by then-president Obama as NLRB acting general counsel. Obama later nominated Solomon to hold the job permanently, but the Senate did not act on the nomination. Richard Griffin was confirmed as general counsel in November 2013. A company that faced NLRB charges challenged Solomon's actions taken when he was acting general counsel between June 2010 and November 2013. The Supreme Court held in early 2017 that it violated the FVRA for Solomon to serve for so long, and that a person nominated to fill an office permanently cannot hold the office as an acting official: *NLRB v. SW General*, 137 S. Ct. 929 (2017). [§ 30.01[A]]

- The 21st Century Cures Act, Pub. L. No. 114-255, signed December 13, 2016, waived the excise tax penalty on stand-alone HRAs (reimbursement by employers of the premiums on individual health policies owned by employees) until December 31, 2016. The legislation also allows Qualified Small Employer Health Reimbursement Arrangements (QSEHRAs) to be adopted starting January 1, 2017 by employers with fewer than 50 employees who do not have a group health plan. The employer pays the full cost of the QSEHRA, which reimburses premiums or actual medical expenses. The maximum permitted QSEHRA reimbursement is $4,950 (employee-only coverage) or $10,000 for family coverage; these amounts will be indexed for inflation in later years. IRS Notice 2017-20 gives small employers extra time to give notice to employees of how the QSEHRA works and how QSEHRA coverage affects their compliance with the individual mandate to maintain health insurance: 21st Century Cures Act, Pub. L. No. 114-255; Notice 2017-20, 2017-11 I.R.B. 1010. [§§ 2.01[A], 18.18]

- The Department of Labor (DOL) finalized a regulation, intended to increase eligibility for overtime pay, in May 2016. The regulation was supposed to take effect in December 2016. However, 21 states (Alabama, Arkansas, Alaska, Georgia, Indiana, Iowa, Kansas, Kentucky, Louisiana, Maine, Michigan, Mississippi, Nebraska, Nevada, New Mexico, Ohio, Oklahoma, South Carolina, Texas, Utah, and Wisconsin) and more than 50 business groups sued in the District Court for the Eastern District of Texas in September 2016, alleging that the rule was unconstitutional and was not properly adopted. The district court issued a nationwide preliminary injunction that kept the overtime rule from being implemented. Before President Trump's inauguration, the DOL appealed the injunction; after the injunction, the case was deferred for the new administration to formulate a policy about defending the rule. Because the rule had not taken effect before the initial suit was filed, the DOL has the power to repeal and replace the rule by publishing a *Federal Register* notice with a new comment period for a redrafted rule: *State of Nevada et al. v. United States Dep't of Labor*, No. 4:16-CV-00731 (E.D. Tex. Nov. 22, 2016) [preliminary injunction]; (E.D. Tex. Aug. 31, 2017) [final order]; *Nevada v. DOL*,

No. 16-41606 (5th Cir. Feb. 22, 2017). On August 31, 2017, the district court held that the overtime rule was invalid because it exceeded DOL's authority. The salary level was set so high that in effect entitled a large segment of the workforce to overtime pay purely because of their compensation, without considering the mandatory component of what their duties are. [§§ 1.05, 1.15]

- A bill to repeal and replace the Patient Protection and Affordable Care Act (PPACA), the American Health Care Act (AHCA) was drafted in early 2017, but was not brought to a vote because it was predicted that it would not attract enough votes to pass. However, Congress continued to consider various approaches to health insurance reform. [§ 18.01]

- With respect to the Equal Employment Opportunity Commission's (EEOC's) investigations, the Supreme Court ruled that when the EEOC issues a subpoena in a case, and a district court either enforces the subpoena or quashes it, then if the district court's decision is appealed, the appellate court will analyze whether the district court abused its discretion. The validity of the decision will not be reviewed de novo. Decisions about subpoenas issued by other agencies, such as the NLRB, are also reviewed for abuse of discretion. *McLane Co., Inc. v. EEOC,* 137 S. Ct. 1159 (2017). [§§ 34.01, 41.01]

- The Fair Pay and Safe Workplaces Rule, an Obama Executive Order, was eliminated pursuant to the Congressional Review Act (CRA). The House of Representatives passed Joint Resolution 37, and the Senate passed S.J. Res. 12, to overturn the regulation. It was signed by the president on March 27. Under the CRA, Congress has veto power over regulations adopted at the end of the previous legislative session, as long as both houses pass the resolution and the president signs it. (If the president refuses to sign the resolution, it can be re-passed by a two-thirds vote of each house.) When a regulation is eliminated under the CRA, the agency that issued it will need specific authorization from Congress to issue a substantially similar rule in the future. President Trump also signed an executive order revoking three Obama-era Executive Orders dealing with pay issues. [§§ 1.04[A], 25.07, 30.01, 40.06[A], 41.01]

- On January 13, 2017, the Supreme Court granted certiorari in three consolidated cases, in order to resolve the circuit split as to whether employers can impose waivers of class actions: *NLRB v. Murphy Oil,* No. 16-307, *Epic Systems Corp. v. Lewis,* No. 16-285 and *Ernst & Young v. Morris,* No. 16-300. It was expected that a decision would be rendered by the end of June 2017, but oral arguments were delayed until the October term, which means that the decision will not be rendered until late 2017 or even 2018. [§§ 30.01, 40.04]

- The DOL published the controversial "fiduciary rule" in April 2016. The rule imposes fiduciary duty on brokers who are paid to provide guidance on retirement accounts and IRAs. The rule requires the advisers to act solely in the best interests of the investor when they make recommendations. This is stricter than the previous rules, which merely required recommendations to be suitable for the client. Under the fiduciary rule, compensation to an adviser must be paid pursuant to a written contract. The adviser must represent that the investment is appropriate, the fees are reasonable, and the adviser must disclose any conflicts of interest. Compliance with this rule was supposed to be phased in until January 1, 2018. [81 Fed. Reg. 20945 (Apr. 8, 2016)]

- A February 3, 2017 memorandum from President Trump directs the DOL to re-examine the fiduciary rule to determine if it should be maintained; maintained but with changes; or rescinded: Presidential Memorandum (Feb. 3, 2017), available at <https://www.whitehouse.gov/briefing-room/disclosures>. The DOL published a document in the *Federal Register* on April 7, 2017, Doc. No. 2017-06914, 82 Fed. Reg. 16902 (Apr. 7, 2017) extending the applicability date for 60 days. Instead of certain provisions taking effect on April 10, 2017, as originally scheduled, the date was extended until June 9, 2017. Other provisions are scheduled to take effect on January 1, 2018. [§§ 4.01[D], 6.08[A], 15.02[A]]

- Immigration is a particular focus of the Trump administration. A draft of an executive order, "Protecting American Jobs and Workers by Strengthening the Integrity of Foreign Worker Visa Programs," was circulated; if adopted, it would affect many kinds of non-immigrant visas, in order to protect wages of U.S. workers by making it more difficult for businesses to hire non-U.S. workers. Changing the number of visas available under a particular program requires congressional action: the president cannot make the determination alone. [§ 23.11[B]] See 81 Fed. Reg. 92398 (Nov. 18, 2016) for Obama-era final regulations increasing portability of H-1B visas, and giving employment-based immigrant workers more time to enter and leave the United States before or after a work assignment [§ 23.11[E]]

LATE-BREAKING NEWS

Certain developments occurred too late to be reflected in the body of the text:

- Hurricane Harvey, one of the worst disasters in U.S. history, struck in late August, 2017, with effects on the economy and the legal system that will be difficult to remedy or even calculate. Most of the economic losses are uninsured. Employers affected by the storm will have to make sure their pay and other labor practices satisfy federal and state requirements. To assist them, agencies such as the IRS, DOL, and PBGC issued relief provisions waiving penalties for missed deadlines.

- The DOL published a proposed regulation to extend the compliance date for the central provisions of the fiduciary rule for an extra 18 months, until July 1, 2019. [82 Fed. Reg. 41365 (Aug. 31, 2017)]

10/17

For questions concerning this shipment, billing, or other customer service matters, call our Customer Service Department at 1-800-234-1660.

For toll-free ordering, please call 1-800-638-8437.

THE COMPLETE GUIDE TO HUMAN RESOURCES AND THE LAW

2018 Edition

Dana Shilling

Published by Wolters Kluwer in New York.

Wolters Kluwer Legal & Regulatory U.S. serves customers worldwide with CCH, Aspen Publishers and Kluwer Law International products.

Printed in the United States of America

ISBN 978-1-4548-8430-9

1 2 3 4 5 6 7 8 9 0

About Wolters Kluwer Legal & Regulatory U.S.

Wolters Kluwer Legal & Regulatory U.S. delivers expert content and solutions in the areas of law, corporate compliance, health compliance, reimbursement, and legal education. Its practical solutions help customers successfully navigate the demands of a changing environment to drive their daily activities, enhance decision quality and inspire confident outcomes.

Serving customers worldwide, its legal and regulatory portfolio includes products under the Aspen Publishers, CCH Incorporated, Kluwer Law International, ftwilliam.com and MediRegs names. They are regarded as exceptional and trusted resources for general legal and practice-specific knowledge, compliance and risk management, dynamic workflow solutions, and expert commentary.

WOLTERS KLUWER SUPPLEMENT NOTICE

This product is updated on a periodic basis with supplements and/or new editions to reflect important changes in the subject matter.

If you would like information about enrolling this product in the update service, or wish to receive updates billed separately with a 30-day examination review, please contact our Customer Service Department at 1-800-234-1660 or email us at: *customer.service@wolterskluwer.com*. You can also contact us at:

Wolters Kluwer
Distribution Center
7201 McKinney Circle
Frederick, MD 21704

Important Contact Information

- To order any title, go to *www.WoltersKluwerLR.com* or call 1-800-638-8437.

- To reinstate your manual update service, call 1-800-638-8437.

- To contact Customer Service, e-mail *customer.service@wolterskluwer.com*, call 1-800-234-1660, fax 1-800-901-9075, or mail correspondence to: Order Department—Wolters Kluwer, PO Box 990, Frederick, MD 21705.

- To review your account history or pay an invoice online, visit *www.WoltersKluwerLR.com/payinvoices*.

Wolters Kluwer

CONTENTS

*A complete table of contents for each chapter
appears at the beginning of the chapter.*

Chapter 12
PLAN DISTRIBUTIONS

Chapter 13
PROCESSING AND REVIEWING CLAIMS AND APPEALS

Chapter 14
AMENDING A PLAN

Chapter 15
ENFORCEMENT AND COMPLIANCE ISSUES
FOR QUALIFIED PLANS

Chapter 16
EFFECT OF CORPORATE TRANSITIONS ON PENSION AND BENEFIT PLANS

Chapter 17
PLAN TERMINATION

PART IV
BENEFIT PLANS

Chapter 24
RECORDKEEPING

Chapter 25
CORPORATE COMMUNICATIONS

Chapter 26
PRIVACY ISSUES

Chapter 27
THE ROLE OF THE COMPUTER IN HR

Index

PREFACE

This book, originally published in 1998, is reissued each year, in revised form, to deal with the cases, statutes, and administrative rulings affecting HR issues. This 2018 edition went to press in April 2017, so it reflects events from mid-2016 to mid-2017.

The election of Donald Trump as the 45th president, with both houses of Congress controlled by Republicans, led to a high volume of pro-business and anti-regulatory activity.

The Congressional Review Act of 1996 (CRA) allows the House and Senate, by a simple majority vote, to overturn agency rules passed in the last 60 legislative working days of the previous administration. In the case of the Obama-to-Trump transition, that means agency rules adopted after June 2016. Acting under the CRA, both houses of Congress passed a joint resolution to nullify the Fair Pay and Safe Workplaces rule (House Joint Resolution 37, Senate S.J. Res. 12). The CRA has seldom been used in the past, because if Congress is controlled by the President's party, Congress probably will not want to reverse the administration's orders. But Congress now has a Republican majority with incentives to reverse Obama-era regulations.

The CRA was also used under H.J. Res. 83 (passed by the House on March 1, 2017 and the Senate on March 22) to eliminate OSHA's *Volks* rule, which extended the length of time when OSHA could impose citations. The CRA was also used to eliminate rules to encourage states and cities to create savings programs similar to IRAs for employees who do not have employer-provided pension coverage, although some of the programs continued despite losing exemption from ERISA requirements.

An Executive Order was issued on January 30, 2017. Reducing Regulation and Controlling Regulatory Costs requires any new costs added by newly adopted regulations to be offset by eliminating the costs associated with at least two existing regulations. The director of the Office of Management and Budget issued guidance on February 2, 2017, explaining that this requirement applies to significant regulatory actions taken between January 20, 2017 and September 30, 2017 (actions likely to affect the economy by $100 million a year or more; that materially harm public health, safety, or a sector of the economy; that interfere with another agency's action; or that raise novel issues). Agencies planning to propose regulations during fiscal 2017 are required to name two other regulations to be eliminated.

On March 1, 2017, the House passed the SCRUB (Searching For and Cutting Regulations That Are Unnecessarily Burdensome) Act. If it becomes law, it would create a commission to recommend regulations for repeal and create procedures for executive agencies to repeal regulations identified by the commission. Regulations would be recommended for repeal based on, e.g., if the objectives of the regulation have been met, if the regulation is unduly expensive, or if the rule is ineffective or anti-competitive. Agencies would be forbidden to reenact regulations that are substantially similar to, or manifest the same problems as, a repealed regulation.

Just as the 2018 edition went to press, Judge Neil Gorsuch of the Tenth Circuit was confirmed as a Supreme Court justice.

The American Health Care Act, a statute to repeal and replace PPACA, was supposed to be voted on in March 2017, but was withdrawn from consideration before a vote was taken. It is unclear what changes will be made to federal healthcare law in the future. The Senate version, the Better Care Reconciliation Act, did not pass before Congress' 2017 summer recess.

The 2018 edition is divided into 43 chapters, in eight parts:

1. Part I: Pay Planning, including compensation planning, bonuses, severance pay, and tax issues.

2. Part II: Pension Law, comprising basic pension concepts, defined benefit plans, and the transition from the predominance of defined benefit plans to the rise of defined contribution and 401(k) plans; cash balance plans; nonqualified plans; and plans for early retirement and retiree health benefits.

3. Part III: Pension Plan Administration, going from the adoption of a plan to disclosures to plan participants, handling claims and appeals, amending the plan, complying with the Employment Retirement Income Security Act (ERISA) and tax rules, handling plans in the context of corporate transitions, such as mergers and acquisitions, and terminating a plan.

4. Part IV: Benefit Plans, such as health plans, continuation coverage and portability requirements for health insurance, plans that provide insurance coverage and disability plans.

5. Part V: The HR Function, including hiring and recruitment, HR computing, recordkeeping, corporate communications, employee privacy rights, diversity issues, and work-family issues.

6. Part VI: Employee Relations, not only the major topic of labor law but also occupational safety and health, unemployment insurance, and workers' compensation.

7. Part VII: Substantive Laws Against Discrimination, focusing on Title VII (and sexual harassment, which is considered a form of sex discrimination), age discrimination, disability discrimination, the Family and Medical Leave Act, and wrongful termination suits.

8. Part VIII: Procedure for Handling Discrimination Charges, not only in the context of lawsuits brought by the Equal Employment Opportunity Commission (EEOC), by state regulators, or by private individuals, but by using arbitration and other alternative dispute resolution methods to resolve problems without going to court.

NOTE ON WEB SOURCES: Several Websites that are frequently cited, such as benefitslink.com, plansponsor.com, and Lexology.com, use very long URLs that are hard to cite. Therefore, for convenience, citations to cases and articles appearing there are simply cited; do a search for the name of the article if you'd like to retrieve it. I cite to online editions rather than print editions of the New York Times and Wall Street Journal.

For older online references, wherever possible I include the latest update of the resource, and the date I accessed it—a date on which the resource was available online. Unfortunately, the URL may change, or the item may no longer be available online, or may be behind a paywall when you attempt to access it.

PART I

PAY PLANNING

CHAPTER 1

PAY PLANNING

§ 1.01 INTRODUCTION

Since 2008, employers have been facing problems of managing HR functions in a recession. It has often been necessary to lay off workers, let positions go unfilled by attrition, or cut back on benefits. The 2016 presidential election triggered major changes in federal treatment of pay planning issues. In this election, a number of states also adopted relevant provisions.

One of the most significant pay planning issues is the determination of which workers are properly classified as independent contractors, and which ones are common-law employees. For common-law employees, one of the most significant issues is which of them are entitled to receive overtime, and which ones are exempt from overtime requirements because, for example, they are administrative workers or managers. Many cases have been litigated alleging that major corporations have failed to pay overtime required by law—perhaps by classifying individuals whose jobs are routine as supervisors who are not entitled to overtime. There has also been extensive litigation about whether employees receive the rest and meal breaks as required by law and whether "donning and doffing" time (putting on and removing protective clothing; traveling to and from the work station) must be compensated. It is also common in wage and hour litigation for plaintiffs to allege that they were required to "work off the clock" (be paid for less time than actually worked).

In mid-2015, the Department of Labor (DOL) issued major statements about employee classification and overtime. In mid-2016, the DOL attempted to make major changes to pay planning by publishing regulations making millions more employees eligible for overtime by greatly increasing the salary thresholds for the white collar exemption and the highly compensated employee exception. But these regulations did not take effect as scheduled, and it is likely that they will be overturned as a priority of the Trump administration. See §§ 1.08 and 1.15, below.

State laws about how often employees must be paid vary, and many states make this a strict liability offense; double and treble damages are common. Class actions are a real possibility. Usually, weekly pay is required in the northeast, but it is lawful to pay employees only once a month in some of the western states. In 19 states, semi-monthly pay is required. (Semi-monthly pay, e.g., on the first and fifteenth of the month, provides 26 paydays a year, whereas bimonthly pay provides 24 paydays a year). [Hannesson Murphy, *Are You Paying Your Employees Frequently Enough?*, Barnes & Thornburg LLP (May 8, 2014), available at Lexology.com. This article includes a state-by-state chart of minimum pay requirements.]

Although it is not required under federal law, most states require the final paycheck to be delivered promptly to a terminated employee—usually before the next payday, sometimes even faster. Massachusetts, Connecticut, and Washington, D.C. require delivery the day of termination or the next business day. Most states permit payment by the next payday if the employee quits rather than being fired. Most states impose a fine for violation, perhaps double or treble the employee's daily pay for each day of violation, and a few states make the violation a criminal offense. [Elizabeth K. Acee, *Final Paycheck Laws—Getting It Right (Part II)*, LeClairRyan (Apr. 24, 2014), available at Lexology.com]

The California Labor Code requires payment within 72 hours of all wages due to an employee who quits—or at the time the employee leaves, if he or she gave 72 hours' notice. Employers who violate this provision can be penalized up to 30 days' wages. In mid-2016, the California Supreme Court held that the legislature intended that retirement be treated as quitting for this purpose, so the timing requirement must be satisfied. [*McLean v. State of California DOJ*, **Docket No. S221554,** 2016 Cal. LEXIS 8192 (Cal. Aug. 18, 2016); see David D. Kadue & Michael A. Wahlander, *California Supreme Court Says Retiring Employees Must Be Paid Promptly,* Seyfarth Shaw LLP (Aug. 22 2016), available at Lexology.com; Monica Rodriguez & Justin T. Curley, *Prompt Payment Required— Doesn't Matter If Fired, Retired, or Resigned,* Seyfarth Shaw LLP (Aug. 24, 2016), available at Lexology.com]

Minnesota has a similar statute, calling for penalties of up to 15 days of the employees' salary if the employer does not make proper payment of wages and commissions already earned at the time of separation from employment. However, penalties are not imposed unless the employee's claim is greater than the amount already paid in good faith by the employer. In 2016, the Minnesota Supreme Court held that non-wage-related amounts that the employee owes to the employer cannot be offset against wages or commissions to determine if penalty should be assessed. In this case, the plaintiff sued his ex-employer and was awarded more than $100,000 in disputed commissions, but the employer won $800,000 from the employee in an unrelated judgment. The Minnesota Supreme Court decided that the state legislature did not intend offsets to be available in this situation. [*Toyota-Lift of Minnesota, Inc. v. American Warehouse Systems, LLC,* 886 N.W.2d 208 (Minn. 2016); see Michael T. Miller, *Minnesota Supreme Court Affirms Wage Claim Penalties*, Briggs and Morgan (Nov. 28, 2016), available at Lexology.com]

There are also issues to be considered in making a final payment after an employee dies. Generally, state law must be consulted. The basic rule is that payment of final wages goes to the decedent's estate, but many states allow part or all of the last paycheck to be distributed directly to the surviving spouse (especially if the employee died intestate). When there is no surviving spouse payment would probably go first to adult children then parents or siblings. When the estate is small (e.g., under $30,000), direct payment to surviving spouse or other family member may also be required or allowed. Very large amounts of wages may have to be paid to the estate instead of the spouse. It is common for state probate laws to prescribe a form for surviving spouses to send an affidavit or demand to the employer for the final payment. If the final payment occurs in the year of the employee's death, the Federal Unemployment Tax Act (FICA) and the Federal

Unemployment Tax Act (FUTA) should be withheld from the final wage payment, but income taxes should not be withheld, but if the payment is in the next year, FICA, FUTA, and income tax withholding do not apply. The company should issue a Form 1099-MISC to the survivor or the estate receiving the distribution, with the amount of gross wages reported in Box 3 as "other income." [Aurelio J. Perez, *The Dear Departed: Making Final Wage Payments for Deceased Employees*, Littler Mendelson PC (Feb. 29, 2016), available at Lexology.com]

Early in 2010, in a suit alleging unpaid overtime and benefits, the Supreme Court ruled that a corporation's principal place of business is its executive office, not where its products are sold. The effect is that fewer cases can be filed in state court—and state courts are less hostile to class actions than federal courts.

Previously, federal courts used various tests. Before 1958, a corporation was only a citizen of its state of incorporation. Congress did not want local businesses to be able to escape state court suits by incorporating out of state, so the federal rules of civil procedure were amended to make a corporation a citizen both of its state of incorporation and where it had its principal place of business. However, the statute did not define the company's principal place of business, and the Courts of Appeals had different standards. [*Hertz v. Friend*, 559 U.S. 77 (2010)]

In March 2010, as part of the economic recovery effort, the Hiring Incentives to Restore Employment (HIRE) Act was enacted, with a 6.2% payroll tax incentive (the employer's share of FICA tax was waived for the period February 3, 2010–January 1, 2011). Employers could also receive a general business tax credit of up to $1,000 per worker if the worker remained on the payroll for at least a year. [Rebecca Moore, *New Law Offers Tax Incentives for Hiring*, plan sponsor.com (Mar. 18, 2010)]

In late 2010, Congress took another approach to using tax incentives to increase hiring: reducing the employee's, but not the employer's, FICA rate. The Tax Relief, Unemployment Insurance Reauthorization, and Job Creation Act of 2010, Pub. L. No. 111-312 set the employee FICA rate at 4.2%, with the employer rate reverting to 6.2%, plus Medicare tax at a rate of 1.45% each for employer and employee. The Making Work Pay credit expired December 31, 2010. The Temporary Payroll Tax Cut Continuation Act retained the 4.2% FICA rate for employees through the end of February 2012. This statute imposed a 2% recapture tax (capping the amount of wages eligible for the payroll tax cut at $18,350). A subsequent statute, the Middle Class Tax Relief and Job Creation Act of 2012, enacted February 22, 2012, Pub. L. No. 112-96, retained the 4.2% employee rate—a payroll tax cut that was estimated to benefit 160 million workers—and repealed the $18,350 limitation. However, the payroll tax cut was permitted to expire.

High-income employees ($250,000 income on a joint return, $200,000 for single, head of household, surviving spouse with a dependent child, $125,000 for married persons filing separately) are subject to additional Medicare tax; this portion of the tax is applied only to the employee, with no employer match.

The 2017 taxable wage base is $127,200. The additional Medicare tax is not indexed for inflation, so the amounts did not change. [Marjorie Martin, *Social Security Benefits and Taxable Wage Base to Increase for 2017,* Xerox HRLaws (Oct. 18, 2016) (benefitslink.com)] In 2017, the Social Security tax rate is 6.2% each for employer and employee, up to the wage base. The Medicare tax rate is 1.45% each on employer and employee. [IRS.gov, *Publication 15 (Circular E), Employer's Tax Guide for Use in 2017,* <www.irs.gov/publications/p15/index.html> (Dec. 19, 2016) (last accessed Mar. 27, 2017)] The American Health Care Act, the proposed "repeal and replace" bill to eliminate the Patient Protection and Affordable Care Act (PPACA) (see § 18.19[N]), would have eliminated the additional Medicare tax, but the bill was withdrawn from consideration in March 2017. At press time in 2017, it was unknown whether another repeal bill, perhaps of more modest scope, would be introduced and, if so, if it would pass.

In March 2014, the Supreme Court reversed the Sixth Circuit and held that the severance payments constituted FICA wages. The Supreme Court held that severance payments are made only to employees, and they are made because of service to employers because "service" is defined broadly as the entire relationship between the employer and employee. However, severance payments made for disability retirement are exempt. The Supreme Court said it would not be necessary to specify this exemption if severance pay in general did not constitute FICA wages. Code § 3401(a), dealing with income tax withholding, also has a broad definition of taxable wages, subject to a list of exemptions. The list says that Supplemental Unemployment Benefits are treated as if they were wages: see § 3402(o). [*United States v. Quality Stores Inc.,* 134 S. Ct. 1395 (2014)]

FICA does not apply to work done by "students" who work for their educational institution. A 2004 Treasury regulation says that a full-time employee is not considered a student, even if the work has a training aspect. The regulation uses medical residents as an example of trainees who are considered full-time workers subject to FICA rather than students. The Mayo Foundation for Medical Education and Research sued to challenge the application of this rule to medical residents who are scheduled to work more than 40 hours per week. The Supreme Court upheld the rule, treating it as a reasonable construction of the statute. [*Mayo Found. for Med. Research v. United States,* 562 U.S. 44 (2011)] See 1.07[A] for discussion of the pay planning implications of internships.

Because participants in a top hat plan earn more than the FICA wage base, they do not have to pay FICA on their non-qualified plan benefits or contributions. The "non-duplication rule" says that if FICA tax is withheld when the benefits or contributions become vested, FICA tax is not due when the benefits are paid. Current and former employees of Henkel who participated in a non-qualified deferred compensation plan sued Henkel because the employer did not withhold FICA taxes when the contributions were made and vested. The result was that the recipients had to pay FICA taxes on the benefits. Many of the recipients were retired, with earnings below the FICA wage base. In early 2015, the District Court for the Eastern District of Michigan granted summary judgment for the plaintiffs, holding that the employer violated the plan by committing a FICA error. [*Davidson v. Henkel Corp.*, No. 12-cv-14103, 2015 U.S. Dist. LEXIS 722 (E.D. Mich. Jan. 6, 2015)] The case was settled in late 2015 and the district court approved the $3,350,000 settlement, which includes attorneys' fees, litigation expenses, and the award to the lead plaintiff. The retirees received a 40% gross-up of benefit distributions to cover taxes. [*Davidson v. Henkel*, No. 12-cv-14103-GAD-DRG (E.D. Mich., settled 2015)]

Traditional methods of distributing pay—whether cash in a pay envelope or paychecks—are not necessarily practical in the twenty-first century and employers are using new modes of payment. Direct deposit is efficient and inexpensive for the employer—but does not work for employees who do not have bank accounts. Payroll cards, like direct deposit, reduce employers' payroll costs, and it is faster to make a final payment to a terminated employee by adding value to a card than by overnight mailing a check.

More than half the states (27) have enacted laws regulating paycards. [John L. Litchfield, *Paycard Use Comes with Convenience, Regulation*, Foley & Lardner LLP (Nov. 17, 2014), available at Lexology.com] Some states require employees to be given at least a minimum number of free ATM withdrawals with payroll cards; others merely require the employee to be able to access the full wage amount in one lump sum without a fee, perhaps by getting cash from a bank teller or getting a courtesy check. Some states forbid employers to derive benefit from payroll card fees; a commission or even reduction in payroll costs might be deemed to fall into this category. [CFPB Bulletin 2013-10, available online at <www.consumerfinance.gov/f/201309_cfpb_payroll-card-bulletin.pdf>]

[A] SEC Regulation of Compensation

In 2006, the SEC required public corporations to disclose information about the compensation of top managers. The final rule requires publication of both tables of top management compensation and narrative disclosure of three years' worth of compensation. Public companies must use the Compensation Discussion and Analysis (which will be filed with the SEC, so the CEO and CFO must certify it) to disclose the compensation for top management. The value of equity-based awards such as stock options must be disclosed, and the SEC required disclosure of timing of option grants, as a way to deter back-dating. A similar disclosure format is required for compensation of directors. Public companies must disclose the extent to which directors are independent, and must reveal more about officers' and directors' holdings of the company's own stock. [SEC Press Release, *SEC Votes to Adopt Changes to Disclosure Requirements Concerning Executive Compensation and Related Matters*, <http://www.sec.gov/news/press/2006/2006-123.htm> (July 26, 2006), finalizing provisions proposed in Rel. Nos. 33-8655, 34-53185, and IC-27218 (2006).]

Dodd-Frank Act § 953(a)(1) requires the SEC to issue rules requiring "reporting companies" (companies that have to make financial reports to the SEC) to report pay for performance figures for their top managers. The SEC published a proposal on April 29, 2015, to carry out this mandate. Under the proposal, the companies must include a table in their proxy statements, using the SEC's standardized format, giving the actual pay of the CEO, average actual pay for other top officers, the company's total shareholder return, and total shareholder return for the company's competitors. The purpose of the table is to allow shareholders and potential investors to see if the company's pay to top management reflects the managers' success in maintaining or improving the return to the company's shareholders. For this purpose, "executive compensation actually paid" includes more than cash salary. The equity awards granted that year are subtracted, but the fair value of equity vesting in the fiscal year is added back in, and adjustments are made for changes in actuarial present value of defined benefit and pension plans. [SEC Release No. 34-74835 (Apr. 29, 2015), available at <http://www.sec.gov/rules/proposed/2015/34-74835.pdf>; see Frederic W. Cook & Co., *SEC Proposes Pay-for-Performance Disclosure Rules* (May 1, 2015) (benefitslink.com)]

Early in 2011, the SEC published the shareholder Say on Pay rules required by the Dodd-Frank Act (Pub. L. No. 111-203). The shareholder vote is non-binding, but the intention is that corporations would be too embarrassed to continue a policy that was disapproved by its stockholders. The rules also allow shareholders to vote on certain golden parachutes in connection with mergers and acquisitions, and require the corporations to make more extensive disclosures about the compensation packages for top executives. [Rebecca Moore, *SEC Adopts Say on Pay Rules*, plansponsor.com (Jan. 25, 2011)] The compensation packages nearly always obtain shareholder approval.

In 2016, the sixth year when Say on Pay was required, most companies received shareholder approval of 90% or more for their compensation practices. [Mike Rourke, *2016 Trends and Developments in Executive Compensation*, Meridian Compensation Partners, LLC (May 5, 2016) (benefitslink.com)]

Before the shareholder vote, the company should decide how it will disclose a negative shareholder vote, and what will be said in the Form 8-K that discloses the results of the vote. If the vote is negative, some or all independent directors could be directed to examine executive pay, and stock awards and options could be made contingent on performance.

On August 5, 2015, the SEC adopted a "pay-gap" rule (implementing a Dodd-Frank Act requirement). Companies must disclose the difference in median pay between the CEO and rank and file workers under Regulation S-K Item 402. Disclosure is required on Forms 10-K, registration statements, and proxy statements. This is a controversial measure certain to lead to litigation. The rule applies to large public companies, although smaller companies and some foreign-owned companies are exempt. Up to 5% of employees who work outside the United States can be excluded from the calculation. The employer is permitted to calculate the median based on the total employee population, statistical sampling, or other reasonable method of the employer's choice. The ratio has to be re-calculated every three years. For this purpose, the employee population includes all full- and part-time employees, including temporary and seasonal employees. The initial compliance date is the fiscal year beginning on or after January 1, 2017; for calendar-year companies, that would be the 2018 proxy season. [SEC press release, *SEC Adopts Rule for Pay Ratio Disclosure* (Aug. 5, 2015), available at <http://www.sec.gov/news/pressrelease/2015-160.html>]

In early 2017, the SEC asked for comments about the disclosure rule. There was a chance that Dodd-Frank would be repealed in whole or in part. At that time, the SEC had only two of five commissioners; both commissioners would have to approve any changes to the rule. Many Republicans oppose the disclosure rule, arguing that it is outside the SEC's mission of providing investors the information they need to make investment decisions. [Tatyana Shumsky, *SEC Says Conflict Minerals, Pay Ratio Rules Remain in Force*, WSJ.com (Feb. 24, 2017)]

In mid-2011, the D.C. Circuit vacated Rule 14a-11, the proxy access rule, which would have permitted some shareholders to write in their nominees for the board of directors. The D.C. Circuit found that the SEC exceeded its discretion in adopting this rule. [*Business Roundtable & Chamber of Commerce v. SEC*, 647 F.3d 1144 (D.C. Cir. 2011)]

The Financial Accounting Standards Board (FASB) issued guidelines for proper accounting treatment of stock-based compensation in March 2015, and then updated them in late 2016. Under the update, employers that make grants of stock to employees will be permitted to make a one-time election to calculate liability-based awards at their intrinsic value, using the Current Value Method (CVM), rather than at fair market value. CVM relies on current share price, without considering potential exit scenarios. The American Institute of Certified Public Accountant's (AICPA's) position is that this methodology is appropriate for companies that are close to an exit event. [Amy Thomas & Rick Schwartz, *New Private-Co. Stock-Based Compensation Rules Analyzed*, www2.cfo.com (Dec. 30, 2016) (benefitslink.com). See also Wilson Sonsini Goodrich & Rosati, *FASB Updates Accounting Standards for Stock-Based Awards* (May 2, 2016) (benefitslink.com). For the fiscal years of public companies that begin on or after December 15, 2016, there are no adverse accounting consequences when employers impose withholding when they settle stock-based awards such as options and restricted stock units at up to the maximum individual tax rate. Employees who get these grants are likely to be in the top tax bracket, so withholding at a lower rate could understate the employee's tax liability.]

[B] Section 162(m) and Clawback

Restrictions on executive pay were first imposed by the Emergency Economic Stabilization Act of 2008 (EESA) Pub. L. No. 110-343, which set up a program for the federal government to purchase troubled assets from financial institutions. Institutions that transferred "toxic" assets to the federal government under the Troubled Asset Relief Program (TARP) had to agree to limits on deductions for compensation and bonuses for their top managers. Companies participating in TARP could not use certain types of golden parachutes; had to restrict their severance arrangements for top managers; and had to seek "clawback" (repayment) of certain sums paid to top managers if the payments were based on incorrect financial figures. The TARP program ended in October 2010.

Additional restrictions were imposed by the American Recovery and Reinvestment Act of 2009 (ARRA), Pub. L. No. 111-5. Limits were imposed on top management's bonuses, retention awards, golden parachutes, and incentive compensation. [74 Fed. Reg. 28393 (June 15, 2009)]

Public companies are subject to the requirements of Code § 162(m). The general rule is that only $1 million in compensation is deductible for the company's CEO and each of its four other highest-compensated officers. The $1 million limit does not apply to qualified performance-based compensation, that is only paid if the payee meets at least one objective performance goal that was set in advance. The performance-based compensation must have been ordered either by the company's board or a compensation committee consisting of outside directors, and the terms of the plan are disclosed to, and approved by, the shareholders in advance.

To make sure that § 162(m) rules for performance-based compensation are satisfied, each year, the compensation committee must certify in writing that performance goals were satisfied before a bonus is paid. Performance goals must be set in the first 90 days of a performance period; for calendar-year plans, this means by March 16. Most incentive compensation plans do not use a formula; they specify objective criteria for calculating performance-based compensation. But if the compensation committee makes awards based on actual targets, the performance criteria and the maximum award any individual can receive must be approved by the stockholders every five years. [GTLaw.com, *Section 162(m): Actions That Should Be Taken by March 30, 2016, and/or in This Year's Proxy to Avoid the $1,000,000 Deduction Limitation* (Mar. 22, 2016) (benefitslink.com)]

Under final regulations published in early 2015, a plan under which an option or stock appreciation right (SAR) is granted must state the maximum number of shares with respect to which options or SARs can be granted to "any individual." Prior law required disclosure of the maximum number of shares with respect to which stock options and SARs could be granted. T.D. 9716 adds restricted stock, restricted stock units, and other equity-based awards. If the corporation goes public, the § 162(m) deduction limit does not apply to restricted stock units (RSUs) that are paid—not just granted—before the earliest transition event listed in the IRS regulations. [T.D. 9716, 80 Fed. Reg. 16970 (Mar. 31, 2015). See Sally P. Schreiber, *Qualified Performance-Based Compensation Rules Are Finalized*, J. of Accountancy (Mar. 31, 2015) (benefitslink.com).]

The Sarbanes-Oxley Act, EESA, and AARA also call for "clawback": companies must recover from the payee any bonus or incentive compensation that was paid to a top executive on the basis of false financial reporting, and compensation plans must not encourage future false reporting that would lead to higher compensation. The Treasury has the authority to review bonuses, retention awards, etc., paid to top management. If the Treasury deems the payments to have been inconsistent with the purposes of the TARP program, it can negotiate with the company and the recipients of the compensation about appropriate reimbursement to the U.S. government.

In mid-2016, the Ninth Circuit became the first court of appeals to rule that Sarbanes-Oxley § 304 permits clawback of certain CEO and CFO compensation even if the officers were not personally at fault in the events that triggered the clawback. The Ninth Circuit also ruled that Exchange Act Rule 13a-14 gives the SEC a cause of action against a CEO or CFO who certifies false or misleading statements; the court rejected the argument that clawbacks are only proper for failure to certify, not false certification. The Ninth Circuit ruled that corporate officers should not be permitted to benefit if other people within the corporation commit misconduct. [*SEC v. Jensen*, 835 F.3d 1100 (9th Cir. 2016); see Alexander Song, *Ninth Circuit Holds That SOX 304 Clawback Applies to Executives That Are Not at Fault*, Employment Matters Blog (Sept. 14, 2016) (benefitslink .com)]

According to Audit Analytics, in 2016, public companies filed 737 restatement disclosures (far fewer than the peak of 1,851 disclosures filed in 2006). But not all of those companies were obligated to claw back compensation. SEC proposed rules require clawback only in case of a "reissuance" restatement, not a minor revision that corrects immaterial issues in a previous statement that do not require the past statement to be reissued. [Winston.com, *Clawbacks, Clawbacks Everywhere Nor any Moment to Think* (Oct. 18, 2016), available at Lexology .com]

On July 1, 2015, the SEC proposed that national securities exchanges amend their listing standards to require clawback policies. The new rule, proposed '34 Act Rule 10D-1, requires that when a listed company makes an accounting restatement, current and former executive officers must repay incentive-based compensation they would not have received if the company had stated its financial figures properly. This is a no-fault requirement: it applies not only when there was deception, but also when there were mistakes. The rule applies to all incentive-based compensation that reflects accounting-related metrics, total shareholder return, or stock price, received in the three fiscal years before the year of the restatement. "Executive officer" means corporate policy-makers such as the president, CFO, principal accounting officer, or VP in charge of a business unit, division, or function. [SEC Release 2015-136, *SEC Proposes Rules Requiring Companies to Adopt Clawback Policies on Executive Compensation* (July 1, 2015), available at <http://www.sec.gov/news/pressrelease/2015-136.html>]

Additional Dodd-Frank clawback rules were released by six federal agencies, including the SEC, that supervise the financial services industry. The rules, which were published in April 2016, apply not only to the top management of major financial institutions, but to executives who are "material risk-takers" at those institutions. Certain stock-based bonuses must be deferred for four years. If the institution restates its financial results (i.e., the earlier results were incorrect), then clawback is required over a seven-year period. [<http://online.wsj.com/public/resources/documents/WallStreetCompensation2016-04-21.pdf>; see Nathaniel Popper, *Wall St. Regulators Propose Stricter Pay Rules for Bankers*, NYTimes.com (Apr. 22, 2016)]

§ 1.02   DECISION FACTORS IN SETTING COMPENSATION

A business's compensation policies reflect many factors:

- What the business can afford to pay;

- Competitive factors (other local companies competing for workers, prevailing wages, state or local minimum wage requirements, unemployment rates);

- Impact on cash flow (until recently, cash-poor companies with bright prospects often relied heavily on stock options and/or the potential for an IPO as elements of compensation);

- Effect on future financing (venture capitalists who expect one-third of the shares in a new business, or a business receiving later rounds of funding, will not want too many of the shares to be assigned to employees);

- The compensation package favored by the kind of workers the employer wants to attract. If the objective is to minimize turnover, for instance, workers with families will place a high value on health benefits, whereas more mobile younger workers will tend to favor higher cash compensation and pension portability;

- Tax factors for both employer and employee; the objective is for the employer to get the highest permissible deduction and for the employee to retain as much as possible after taxes.

The Wall Street Journal found that the biggest rewards went to a handful of executives, but pay did not necessarily correlate with the corporation's size or financial results. The top 10% of CEOs earned 23% of CEO compensation. The DOL said that in 2013, wages and salaries for all private-sector workers rose an average of 1.8%, whereas CEO pay rose a median of 5.5% to $11.4 million, but almost two-thirds of CEO compensation was performance-linked. [Theo Francis and Joann S. Lublin, *CEO Pay Rises Moderately; A Few Reap Huge Rewards*, WSJ.com (May 27, 2014)]

The Census Bureau reported that in 2015, women earned 79 cents for every $1 earned by men (based on median salaries for full-time workers). This is much higher than the 53 cents per $1 earned by men in 1963, although there has been little progress in the twenty-first century. Even within the same occupation, pay gaps occur. For example, female surgeons earn 71 cents for every $1 earned by their male counterparts; women food preparers earn 87% as much as male counterparts. The gap is not completely explained by any economic measure such as education, experience, hours worked, or time off. The pay gap shrinks when salaries are published. Some companies that learn of the difference take measures to equalize pay and improve promotion opportunities for women. Men are much more likely to negotiate salaries—and even when women do negotiate, they ask for less than men do. Starting salaries have implications throughout the career. One reason is that men are respected for negotiating, women are depreciated. To promote equality, companies can set a salary range for the job and make non-negotiable offers or reduce or eliminate reliance on past salary, which disadvantages women who were previously underpaid, or who took time off to raise a family, or who previously worked in lower-paid public sector or nonprofit jobs. [Claire Cain Miller, *How to Bridge That Stubborn Pay Gap*, NYTimes.com (Jan. 17, 2016)]

Some states have passed legislation to address the pay gap between the sexes. Effective January 1, 2016, California's Fair Pay Act forbids paying members of one sex less than rate paid to other sex for substantially similar work. It is not mandatory to pay everyone the same for substantially similar work—but the burden is on the employer to show that any discrepancy results from a seniority or merit system, earnings measured by quantity or quality of production, or a bona fide factor other than sex. All of the employer's locations (even those outside California) are covered. Violations are punishable by awards of twice the back pay and interest. Employers must retain records about the terms of employment, including wage rates, for at least three years. Employers are forbidden to retaliate against employees for disclosing their own wages, inquiring about or discussing the wages of others, or encouraging co-workers to exercise rights under the law. [Jennifer B. Rubin and Brent M. Douglas, *California Expands Gender-Based Wage Protections by Adopting "Substantially Similar" Test and Requiring Employers to Justify Wage Discrepancies*, Mintz Levin Cohn Ferris Glovsky and Popeo PC (Oct. 8, 2015), available at Lexology.com; Lauren Weber, *For Bosses in California, a Tough New Fair-Pay Law*, WSJ.com (Dec. 29, 2015). This statute is part of a package of eight bills dealing with pregnancy and family status discrimination.]

New York also has an Equal Pay Act. When women are paid less, the employer is required to prove a bona fide factor other than sex exists that is both job-related and consistent with business necessity—e.g., education, training, and experience. If the employer raises this defense, the employee can rebut it by showing that the firm refused to use an available alternative employment practice that would satisfy the same business purpose without disparate impact. Successful plaintiffs can recover up to 300% of unpaid wages for willful violations, plus attorneys' fees. Like the California statute and the federal Executive Order, the New York law forbids retaliation against employees who discuss or disclose compensation. Employers cannot forbid employees to discuss or disclose compensation. [Lauren Helen Leyden et al., *New Women's Equality Act Legislation Raises Bar for New York Firms*, Akin Gump Strauss Hauer & Feld LLP (Oct. 26, 2015), available at Lexology.com. The New York statute also forbids family status discrimination and requires reasonable accommodation of pregnancy-related conditions.]

The Maryland Equal Pay Act has been significantly expanded, effective October 1, 2016. Gender-based pay discrimination is forbidden, and employees must be permitted to discuss pay disparities without reprisals. It is unlawful to provide less favorable employment opportunities (such as career tracks and access to information about promotion opportunities) on the basis of sex or sexual orientation. Nebraska passed a pay equity law in March 2016 expanding coverage of the statute from companies with 15 or more employees to companies with two or more employees. [Matthew Durham et al., *Maryland Enacts Pay Equity Legislation Joining Growing List of States Enacting Pay Fairness Laws*, Winston & Strawn LLP (June 13, 2016), available at Lexology.com]

Massachusetts amended its equal pay law on August 1, 2016, making the Massachusetts law one of the most stringent in the United States. The law now requires equal pay for comparable work (work that requires substantially similar effort, skill and responsibility) even if the jobs are not the same. It is a defense that a difference in compensation reflects seniority (but time spent on pregnancy leave, parenting leave, or the Family and Medical Leave Act (FMLA) leave does not reduce seniority), a merit system, education or training, or is based on travel requirements. The statute also includes an unusual requirement: employers cannot ask job applicants for their salary history unless the applicant voluntarily raises the issue. (The intention is to protect female applicants who have been underpaid in the past.) Employers must also allow employees to disclose and discuss how much they earn. The law does not take effect until 2018. [Barry J. Miller, Daniel B. Klein and Hillary J. Massey, *Massachusetts Governor Signs Stringent Pay Equity Requirements, Effective in 2018*, Seyfarth Shaw LLP (Aug. 1, 2016), available at Lexology.com] The states of Delaware and Oregon, and a number of cities (e.g., Boston, New Orleans, New York, Philadelphia, and Pittsburgh) limit employers' ability to ask job applicants about their salary history or research what they earned in the past. Many of these statutes allow inquiries after a job offer has been accepted, to confirm what the applicant said he or she earned. Bills like this have been introduced in the legislatures of 26 states. [Amanda Van Hoose Garofalo and Amy J. Traub, *Employers Will No Longer Be Permitted to Ask About Previous Pay in New York City*, Baker & Hostetler LLP (Apr. 16, 2017), available at Lexology.com; Cody Emily Schvaneveldt, *Oregon Enacts New Equal Pay Law That Includes Salary History Inquiry Restrictions*,

Littler Mendelson PC (June 1, 2017), available at Lexology.com; Michael L. Stevens, *Delaware Becomes the "First State" to Enforce Ban on Employer Requests for Salary History,* Arent Fox LLP (June 29, 2017), available at Lexology.com; Alif Mia and Amber M. Rogers, *San Francisco Bans Employers from Asking Job Applicants About Salary History, 26 States Considering Similar Legislation,* Hunton & Williams LLP (July 20, 2017), available at Lexology.com; Daniel J. Clark and Michael C. Griffaton, *Delaware Becomes the Latest State to Ban Salary Inquiries,* Vorys Sater Seymour and Pease LLP (Aug. 9, 2017), available at Lexology.com]

However, the Ninth Circuit ruled in mid-2017 that it does not violate the Equal Pay Act to pay men and women different amounts for the same work—if the differential is based on earnings in their former job. (Since this case was decided, California adopted AB 1676, which allows plaintiffs charging pay inequality to argue based on substantially similar comparators even if they are not completely identical, and allows the entire corporation, not just one establishment, to be analyzed). [*Rizo v. Yovino,* 854 F.3d 1161 (9th Cir. 2017); see James McDonald Jr., *An Old-School Approach to Equal Pay at 9th Circ.,* Fisher Phillips (May 26, 2017), available at Lexology.com]

For discussion of the federal Equal Pay Act (29 U.S.C. § 206), see § 34.06[C].

[A] Coping with the Downturn

Since the stock market crash of 2008, many businesses looked for ways to cut the size of their workforce, and to reduce the number of hours worked (e.g., by implementing furloughs).

Non-exempt workers do not have to be paid during furlough periods because they are paid only for hours actually worked. But the Fair Labor Standards Act (FLSA) provides that if an exempt employee does any work in any part of a week—including making phone calls and checking e-mails—then the employee must receive full salary for the week. There are exceptions for bona fide sick leave or voluntary absences (e.g., the employee is granted extra time off at the end of a vacation).

Exempt employees do not have to be paid for weeks in which they do not work at all, whether the absence is voluntary or involuntary, but partial-week furloughs create difficulties. An employee might cease to be exempt if the employer fails to pay full salary for the week when it is due—but the exemption will not be lost for an inadvertent, isolated violation that is corrected by reimbursing the employee for improper deductions.

The Middle Class Tax Relief and Job Creation Act of 2012 provided federal funding so states could expand their STC (short-time compensation) work sharing programs. To receive funding, state programs must require

employers to maintain benefits for workers whose hours are reduced, and partici-
pating workers' hours cannot be reduced by more than 60%. In 2016, there were
STC programs in Arizona, Arkansas, California, Colorado, Connecticut, the
District of Columbia, Florida, Illinois, Iowa, Kansas, Maine, Maryland,
Massachusetts, Michigan, Minnesota, Missouri, Nebraska, New Hampshire, New
Jersey, New York, Ohio, Oregon, Pennsylvania, Rhode Island, Texas, Vermont,
Virginia, Washington, and Wisconsin. Table 4-5 in this document summarizes the
duration of the approved plans, maximum benefits (usually 26 weeks, but some
states allow 52 weeks), and the required reduction of work hours to participate).
[DOL, *Comparison of State Unemployment Insurance Laws*, <http://www
.unemploymentinsurance.doleta.gov/unemploy/comparison2016.asp> (reflecting
laws current as of Jan. 1, 2016) (accessed Jan. 28, 2017)]

§ 1.03   BENEFITS AS AN ELEMENT OF COMPENSATION

The accepted rule of thumb is that the cost of benefits adds about one-third
to the employee's stated salary.

The size of the benefit package is often directly related to the size of the
company. Generally, for any particular benefit, the percentage of companies offering that benefit increases with the size of the workforce, and it is also often true
that larger companies offer a more generous benefit package.

In general, unionized workers have access to more benefits than non-
unionized workers, and pay and benefits tend to be lower in the South than in
other regions.

In March 2017, 70% of civilian workers had access to retirement and medical care benefits; 94% of unionized workers did. Among nonunion workers, 66%
had access to retirement benefits, 67% to health benefits. Access to retirement
benefits varied by industry: from 42% in service occupations to 82% for managers and professionals. Among full-time workers, 91% had access to paid vacations, and 90% to paid holidays. [BLS.gov news release USDL-17-1013,
Employee Benefits in the United States (July 21, 2017), available at <https://
www.bls.gov/news.release/ebs2.nr0.htm>]

Willis Towers Watson reported in mid-2017 that the cost of employee benefits rose 24% between 2001 and 2015, largely because health care costs doubled.
In 2001, all employer-provided benefits equaled 14.8% of pay; in 2015, they were
18.3% of pay. Health care costs for active employees went from 5.7% to 11.5%
of pay in this period, although retirement costs actually went down (from 9.1% to
6.8% of pay), largely because of the shift from defined benefit to defined contribution plans. [S. Miller, *Employers' Benefit Costs Have Risen 24% Since 2001,*
shrm.org (July 27, 2017) (benefitslink.com)]

On July 22, 2016, BLS said that 64% of workers had access to at least one
day of paid sick leave, which was the highest level ever reported—a percentage
that has grown 7% in a decade. However, high-wage workers were 2.2 times more

likely to have access to paid sick leave than low-wage workers. [Heidi Shierholz, *Record Share of Private Industry Workers Have Paid Sick Leave*, blog.dol.gov (July 26, 2016) (benefitslink.com)]

Paid sick leave is required by the states of California, Connecticut, Massachusetts, Oregon, Vermont, and Washington, D.C. These statutes typically require very small employers to provide unpaid sick leave, and larger employers to permit employees to accrue a certain amount of paid sick leave each week. A number of cities, such as New York City, Chicago, Minneapolis, Saint Paul, San Francisco, and Philadelphia have their own paid sick leave requirements. [Jennifer Cerven, *Chicago Workers to Earn Paid Sick Leave as Trend Continues in Big U.S. Cities*, Barnes & Thornburg LLC (June 24, 2016), available at Lexology.com]

In the November 2016 elections, Arizona, Louisiana, Vermont, and Washington State voters approved paid sick leave requirements. The Arizona statute, effective July 1, 2017. requires companies with 15 or more employees to permit accrual of up to 40 hours of paid sick leave per year. Smaller employers are not exempt, but they are only required to allow accrual of 24 hours per year. Washington State Initiative 1433 (which also increased the minimum wage), effective January 1, 2018, applies to all employees covered by the minimum wage law. Employees accrue one hour of paid leave for every 40 hours of work, with no limit on total accruals. Neither the Arizona nor the Washington law requires terminated employees to be compensated for accrued unused sick leave—but the leave becomes available again if the employee is rehired. Erin Denniston Leach, *Workplace Word—Just Like the Flu, Paid Sick Leave Laws Don't Seem to Want to Go Away*, Snell & Wilmer (May 1, 2017) (benefitslink.com); Adam T. Pankratz, *Washington State Approves Paid Family and Medical Leave: What Employers Need to Know*, Ogletree.com (July 7, 2017), available at Lexology .com]

As of January 1, 2018, New York requires paid family and medical leave, funded by employees through a payroll deduction starting July 1, 2017. The paid leave requirement is phased in over a four-year period. [The ABD Team, *ABD Compliance Alert—New York to Offer Paid Family Leave in 2018; DC Law to Take Effect in 2019* (June 1, 2017) (benefitslink.com)]

However, the trend of expanding access to paid sick leave is not universal. Many states (e.g., Alabama, Arizona, Florida, Georgia, Indiana, Iowa, Kansas, Louisiana, Michigan, Mississippi, Missouri, North Carolina, Ohio, Oklahoma, Oregon, South Carolina, Tennessee, and Wisconsin) have adopted statutes that forbid local governments to adopt paid sick leave laws. [Rachel Emma Silverman, *Varying Sick-Leave Laws Vex Some Employers,* WSJ.com (Sept. 27, 2016);Towerswatson.com, *Voters in Arizona and Washington Approve Paid Sick Leave Mandate* (Feb. 23, 2017) (benefitslink.com)]

The South Carolina law was signed April 5, 2017. The Minnesota legislature passed a similar bill, but it was vetoed by the governor—and in fact Minneapolis and Saint Paul adopted paid sick leave requirements. [Matthew K.

Johnson, *South Carolina Prevents Local Municipalities from Passing Paid Leave Requirements,* Ogletree.com (Apr. 14, 2017) (benefitslink.com)]

Executive Order 13706, signed on Labor Day 2015, takes effect in 2017. It requires federal contractors to allow employees to accrue at least one hour of paid sick leave for every 30 hours they work. Sick leave entitlement carries over from one year to the next. Unused leave does not have to be cashed out when the employee terminates employment, but it must be restored if an employee is rehired. [Whitehouse.gov, *Executive Order—Establishing Paid Sick Leave for Federal Contractors* (Sept. 8, 2015); see <https://www.white house.gov/the-press-office/2015/09/08/executive-order-establishing-paid-sick-leave-federal-contractors>. DOL's paid leave resources page is <www.dol.gov/featured/paidleave>]

The rule was finalized on September 29, 2016. The final rule applies to any new federal contract, including replacement contracts, entered into after January 1, 2017. Subcontracts are covered. The rule does not apply to certain employees covered by a Collective Bargaining Agreement (CBA) that was ratified before September 30, 2016, that entitles them to at least seven days or 56 hours of paid sick leave per year. The final rule, unlike the proposal, does not require employers to notify employees of balance of leave they have accrued with every paycheck. The notice only has to be given once a pay period or month (whichever is shorter) and when the employee separates from service. [Joshua D. Seidman, *DOL Publishes Final Rule on Federal Contractor Paid Sick Leave Requirements*, Seyfarth Shaw LLP (Sept. 29, 2016), *available at* Lexology.com]

At press time in 2017, the Trump administration had not taken specific action on this order, so it took effect for most federal contracts issued or renewed in 2017. However, it was likely to be overturned in the future. [Anne G. Bibeau, *U.S. Department of Labor Issues Final Rule on Mandatory Paid Sick Leave for Federal Contractors*, Vandeventer Black LLP (Feb. 3, 2017), available at Lexology.com; Ben Penn, *Obama's Sick Leave Order Survives Under Trump, For Now*, bna.com (Apr. 17, 2017) (benefitslink.com)]

Some states (e.g., Connecticut, Hawaii, Illinois, New York, Oregon, and Rhode Island) have laws protecting victims of domestic violence in the workplace: e.g., forbidding discrimination and/or requiring time off to make court appearances and otherwise deal with domestic violence. California requires reasonable accommodation, such as changing the employee's telephone number or office location to hinder stalking. [Susan Gross Sholinsky, *Take 5: Views You Can Use: Labor and Employment*, Epstein Becker Green (Nov. 12, 2013), available at Lexology.com]

See Chapter 38 for a discussion of the Family and Medical Leave Act, which requires eligible employers to provide 12 weeks of unpaid leave for specified medical and family needs.

On September 30, 2014, the Sixth Circuit held that a Wisconsin law, requiring employers that provide paid disability leave to provide disability leave to new mothers (or six weeks of unpaid leave if there is no disability plan) is preempted by the Employment Retirement Income Security Act (ERISA). The court found preemption, because plans are required to provide benefits to women who do not fit the plan's definition of short-term disability. The Sixth Circuit permanent enjoined enforcement of the state law. [*Sherful v. Newson*, 768 F.3d 561 (6th Cir. 2014); Jacklyn Wille, *Divided Sixth Circuit Rules That ERISA Bars Wisconsin Law on Maternity Leave*, Bloomberg BNA (Oct. 1, 2014) (benefitslink.com)]

The Massachusetts Maternity Leave Act (MMLA) was signed January 7, 2015, with an effective date of April 7, 2015. Previously, women workers in Massachusetts were entitled to eight weeks of job-protected leave for the birth or adoption of a child. This law extends the leave entitlement to men and covers leave for placement of a child under a court order. Non-birth parents can take leave to bond with the child. However, if both parents work for the same employer, they must share the eight weeks of parental leave. If the employer agrees to grant more than the required eight weeks of leave, the employer cannot deny reinstatement after the leave ends unless the employer gave written notice, before the leave was taken, that taking additional leave could result in denial of reinstatement. [Jackson Lewis PC, *Massachusetts Enacts Parental Leave Law, Giving Leave Rights to Male Employees* (Jan. 14, 2015) (benefitslink.com)] See 28.01 for discussion of maternity and parenting leave.

On October 11, 2015, California amended the "kin care" provision of Labor Code § 233, which allows employees to use half of their accrued sick leave to care for a family member. The definition is very broad, including grandparents, grandchildren, and siblings, in addition to children, parents, spouse, or domestic partner. Caregiver leave can be taken for preventive care as well as diagnosis or treatment and for some domestic violence/sexual assault/stalking events. [Angie Brown, *California Kin Care Amendment Effective January 1st, 2016*, Claim Vantage (Nov. 10, 2015), available at Lexology.com Georgia also requires employers with 25 or more employees to allow employees who have access to paid sick leave to use up to five days a year for "kin care": Shella B. Neba and Blaze R. Douglas, *Georgia Enacts Kin Care Law*, Little Mendelson PC (May 15, 2017), available at Lexology.com]

In mid-2016, the Society for Human Resources Management (SHRM) reported that employers are reducing their commitment to wellness programs (see § 18.19[G]) because these programs did not provide the expected reductions in the costs of maintaining a health plan. In 2015, almost half of survey respondents offered health coaching, a percentage that declined to 37% in 2016. Provision of flu vaccination fell from 61% to 54%. The SHRM monitors 330 benefits, versus only about 60 benefits 20 years earlier. [Rachel Emma Silverman, *Employers Cut Down on Wellness Benefits*, WSJ.com (June 20, 2016)]

A new benefit is emerging: assistance with repaying student loans. So far, only 3% of employers offer these plans, but this could expand greatly in the future. A total of $1.3 trillion in student loan debt is outstanding, an average of $30,000 per student. The rationale for employers to offer benefits that are not mandated by law is to attract valuable employees, so employers compete by offering benefits that are valued. In a recent survey, three-quarters of respondents said that their willingness to accept a job offer would be decided or strongly affected by the availability of student loan repayment assistance, and having such a plan promotes loyalty and reduces turnover. Employers that offer repayment benefits could provide a flat monthly amount or amount per paycheck (e.g., $50 to $200), a bonus at certain milestone anniversaries such as the first or fifth year of employment, or an arrangement to allocate amounts between the employee's 401(k) plan and his or her loan repayment. For example, the consulting firm Bright Horizons' EdAssist plan includes a repayment program; contractors such as Tuition.io provide interfaces for handling payments and taxes (such arrangements are taxable to the employee). [Bobbi Kloss, *A New Important Benefit Consideration: Student Loan Repayment,* The Institute for HealthCare Consumerism (Aug. 8, 2016) (benefitslink.com); Jared Bilski, *The Next 401(k)? Why Student Loan Repayment May Soon Be a Standard Benefit,* hrbenefitsalert.com (July 19, 2016) (benefitslink.com)]

IRS proposed and temporary regulations issued in mid-2016 generally prevent partners from participating in employee benefit plans that cover the employees of a "disregarded entity" (a type of related business). The regulations were issued to clarify that partners who provide services to a disregarded entity cannot be treated as employees of that entity. IRS reaffirmed its position: bona fide partners are not employees of their partnership for the purposes of FICA, FUTA, or income tax withholding. A partner who works in the conduct of the partnership's trade or business, or provides services to the partnership as an independent contractor, is treated as a self-employed individual and not as an employee. The temporary regulations apply to any qualified plan, health plan, or cafeteria plan sponsored by the disregarded entity. [Sullivan & Cromwell LLP, *Treasury Clarifies That Partners Working for a Disregarded Entity Owned by a Partnership are Self-Employed* (May 3, 2016), available at Lexology.com]

§ 1.04 AVOIDING DISCRIMINATION

The gender pay gap is small when employees are first hired, but grows over the next two decades—the late 20s to mid-30s, when many female employees have children. The gender wage gap is smaller for unmarried, childless women than for married women and especially married women with children. College-educated women earn 90% as much as college-educated men at age 25, but only 55% as much at age 45. A recent article estimates that 73% of the pay gap is attributable to women getting fewer raises and promotions than men, rather than to taking time out of the workforce to raise children. [Clair Cain Miller, *The Gender Pay Gap Is Largely Because of Motherhood,* NYTimes.com (May 13, 2017)]

The Equal Employment Opportunity Commission (EEOC) Compliance Manual contains a section dealing with compensation issues in the context of various antidiscrimination statutes. The EEOC's position is that antidiscrimination laws apply to all aspects of compensation, including salary, overtime, bonuses, options, profit sharing, fringe benefits, and expense accounts. The agency says that employers are never justified in taking race, color, sex, national origin, religion, age, or disability into account in setting compensation.

The EEOC says that equal severance benefits are required for all similarly situated employees, regardless of age. Employers may not deny severance because the employee is eligible for a pension, although sometimes pension benefits can be offset against the severance pay. Denying recall rights to older workers operates as involuntary retirement. Because the cost of providing severance pay does not rise with the employees' ages, employers are not allowed to assert an equal cost defense.

However, retiree health benefits can legitimately be offset against severance if the retiree is eligible for an immediate pension; if he actually receives health benefit coverage; and the retiree benefits are at least comparable to Medicare in type and value. If the retiree is over 65, benefits must be at least comparable to one-fourth the value of Medicare benefits. The offset itself must be reduced by any percentage by which the pension is reduced for retirement before normal retirement age, and by any percentage of the premium that the retiree has to pay for retiree health coverage.

The Compliance Manual says that "if the employer provides additional pension benefits that are enough, or are higher than those necessary to bring an employee up to the level of an unreduced pension, the employer can offset the full amount of those benefits. On the other hand, if the employer offers benefits that are insufficient to raise the employee to an unreduced pension, the employer cannot claim any offset at all."

Employers that need to cut costs often use a Reduction in Force (RIF) for this purpose. However, RIFs must be handled carefully to avoid findings that they were used selectively to eliminate employees who were the victims of discrimination. In order to carry out a Reduction in Force that complies with applicable laws, employers must document the preliminary steps to cut costs that were taken before the RIF. Increasing the compensation and benefits of top management when jobs are being cut looks suspicious. Discretionary spending on items such as office parties and corporate jets should probably be reduced before a RIF is instituted.

There are also alternatives such as hiring freezes, shorter workweeks, and furloughs. Management should document the steps that were taken, and that alternatives were considered but were not adopted for reasons that are fully documented. Voluntary exit programs can be used as an alternative to layoffs—either company-wide, in a particular division or unit, or a voluntary early retirement program could be offered to employees with a certain amount of age and service.

(The risk is that employees the company wants to retain might opt for early retirement.) The economic necessity for a RIF should be documented (e.g., industry conditions, loss of a major contract, so fewer workers are required).

A furlough (where workers are still employed but their hours have been reduced, or they are on unpaid leave until there is work for them) is different from a layoff, where employees are terminated. Group policies, including medical stop-loss insurance for employers that self-insure health care, might impose eligibility or "actively at work" requirements that rule out furloughed employees, placing the employer at high risk if it must pay even one large claim to a furloughed employee with heavy medical expenses.

Benefit plans frequently specify eligibility criteria that include minimum hours worked. In some companies, the benefits department is not even aware of which employees have been furloughed, if HR did not inform them. Employees who lose health coverage during a furlough are COBRA-eligible.

Income protection plans (life insurance, Accidental Death & Disability, and disability plans) pay for loss of life, ability to work, or other event affecting an employee's ability to work. Most plans require active employment or minimum number of hours for coverage, so a furloughed worker will eventually lose eligibility. The employer must consider what will happen when the employee returns to normal work after a furlough. Employees whose furlough lasts more than a certain amount of time generally must satisfy a waiting period and give evidence of insurability. The policy may allow employees whose coverage is lost to convert the policy to individual coverage, within a certain period of time.

With respect to 401(k) plans, furloughs have limited effect. The furloughed employees have not been terminated, so they are not eligible for distributions from the plan. However, they are no longer accumulating hours of service toward vesting credit (which has limited effect if the employee has already fully vested). Furloughed employees cannot contribute to the 401(k) plan or get employer matches because they do not have income. It is possible that they will default on outstanding plan loans, if the plan has no arrangements for collecting repayment from non-active employees. A default could lead to the loan being taxed as a distribution, which is particularly difficult for employees who are not earning income to offset the additional tax liability. Employees will be required to repay the defaulted loan when they are reinstated. If the employer does not deduct loan repayment from the income of an employee who defaulted, the plan makes an ineligible distribution—an operational failure that must be corrected or the plan will be subject to penalties, fines, and perhaps even disqualification. [Steve Goulet, Justin Elmore and Robert Massa, *The Impact of Furloughs on Benefit Plans*, ascenda.com (Feb. 18, 2016) (benefitslink.com)]

The Age Discrimination in Employment Act (ADEA) provides a safe harbor for early retirement programs that are truly voluntary, but suits might still be filed if a participant claims the program was not really voluntary or if it is not consistent with the purposes of the ADEA. It is important to train managers not to make statements that could be interpreted as threatening to employees who are reluctant to retire. The most common employee claims about layoffs involve age discrimination, so the employer must be prepared to prove what the criteria were for selecting employees for RIFs, and that the criteria were appropriate and job-related. The least problematic structure is work elimination (eliminating an entire department or function) because personal selections are not made. A number of cases say that it is impossible to prove a prima facie case of discrimination when a whole job or department is eliminated.

If individual selections for RIF are made, there must be well-defined selection criteria that are uniformly applied within a department or group. In unionized businesses, it may be necessary to observe seniority. Performance ratings seem to be objective, but employees can argue that the evaluators were biased in rating performance. It is wise to train line managers not to assume that employees close to retirement age intend to retire, and it is not good practice to ask them about their retirement plans (in case they think they are being forced out of the company). Line managers should document their selection criteria and how employees were chosen for RIF or retained.

Mass layoffs may require notice under the Worker Adjustment and Retraining Notification (WARN) Act (see § 30.10) or its state counterparts. In unionized businesses, it is an Unfair Labor Practice for management to act unilaterally about wages, hours, and other terms and conditions of employment; it is necessary at least to bargain to an impasse before making changes. The National Labor Relations Board's (NLRB's) position is that a layoff for economic reasons (rather than layoffs based on a fundamental change in the organization's business) require prior bargaining about the decision and its implementation.

[A] Fair Pay and Workplace Safety Executive Order

Executive Order 13665 (April 8, 2014), "Non-Retaliation for Disclosure of Compensation Information," was promulgated to forbid federal contractors to retaliate against employees for disclosing their compensation, or discussing compensation with co-workers. The order says that ordering employees not to talk about compensation prevents applicants and employees from negotiating knowledgeably, and makes it harder to detect and punish discrimination in compensation. The order took effect immediately. [*Non-Retaliation for Disclosure of Compensation Information*, 79 Fed. Reg. 20749 (Apr. 8, 2014)]

Executive Order 13665 was supplemented by the "Fair Pay and Workplace Safety" order, Executive Order 13673 (July 31, 2014), covering about 24,000 federal contractors. The order affects contractors and bidders on contracts worth more than $500,000. Businesses subject to the order must disclose their violations of employment law. Bidders must self-report all civil judgments, administrative merits determinations, and arbitration awards against them in the preceding three years under 14 labor laws, including the FLSA, Davis-Bacon Act,

OSHA, the NLRA, FMLA, ADA, VEVRA, Rehab Act, and Title VII. Serious infractions can result in termination of a current contract or debarment from federal contracting. The disclosures must be renewed every six months. Contractors must investigate the practices of their subcontractors, and report violations. [Katharine Parker, *Contractors Face Uncertainty Amid New Labor Law-Related Requirements*, N.Y.L.J. (Oct. 20, 2014) (law.com)]

Executive Order 13673 has been nicknamed the "contractor blacklisting rule" because violators can be debarred from holding federal contracts. On October 24, the day before the scheduled effective date of Executive Order 13673, the District Court for the Eastern District of Texas issued a nationwide injunction. The district court held that the rule conflicts with laws that require a full hearing and a final adjudication to debar a contractor. The opinion centered on the disclosure requirements obligating federal contractors to self-report if they had violated 14 employment-related statutes. In the district court view, the plaintiffs demonstrated that they would suffer immediate and ongoing injury if the rule took effect. The district court said that contractors should not be disqualified based on administrative merits determinations that are not final agency findings. Executive Order 13673 also contained a ban on mandatory predispute arbitration clauses relating to Title VII and sexual harassment claims, which was also enjoined. [*Associated Builders & Contractors, et al. v. Rung*, No. 1:16-CV-425, *2016 U.S. Dist. LEXIS 155232, 167 Lab. Cas. (CCH) P36,481; 100 Empl. Prac. Dec. (CCH) P45,671* (E.D. Tex. Oct. 24, 2016); see Gerald F. Lutkus, *Down to the Wire: DOL's "Blacklisting Rule" Enjoined*, Barnes & Thornburg LLP (Oct. 25, 2016), available at Lexology.com; James J. Murphy and Hera S. Arsen, *Contractor Blacklisting Rule Enjoined at the Last Minute*, Ogletree Deakins (Oct. 25, 2016,) available at Lexology.com; Roger V. Abbott, *Federal Court Repudiates the Most Significant Provisions of the New DOL Rules*, Mayer Brown LLP (Oct. 27, 2016), available at Lexology.com]

On January 29, 2016, the Obama administration issued rules requiring companies with 100 or more employees to report to the federal government about pay, analyzed by race, gender, and ethnicity, on the EEO-1 form. The employer must report the number of workers in each sex, race, or ethnic group, in 10 job classifications, and in 12 wage bands ranging from $19,239 to compensation exceeding $208,000. The EEOC said that this information will "inform our investigations." [Julie Hirschfeld Davis, *Obama Moves to Expand Rules Aimed at Closing Gender Pay Gap*, NYTimes.com (Jan. 29, 2016). The initial rules were published at 81 Fed. Reg. 5113 (Feb. 1, 2016). They were amended on July 14, 2016, to reduce the burden on employers., and the first filing deadline was postponed until March 31, 2018. Manatt Phelps & Phillips LLP, *EEO-1 Forms Final, Employers Must Report Pay Data in 2018* (Oct. 25, 2016), available at Lexology.com] The EEO-1 report is unpopular with employers, many of whom said that collecting the broad data required would be difficult and expensive, and does not offer clear gains in improving pay equality. In February 2017, acting EEOC chair Victoria Lipnic said that she was interested in reconsidering the

EEO-1 requirement, but, as of mid-2017, had not taken steps to alter the requirement. [David J. Goldstein, *Revised EEO-1 Report—Where Does It Stand?*, Littler Mendelson (July 31, 2017), available at Lexology.com]

In early 2017, when the Fair Pay and Safe Workplaces Rule remained in limbo in the courts, Republicans in the House of Representatives initiated a "joint resolution of disapproval" under the Congressional Review Act (CRA). The House passed Joint Resolution 37 to disapprove the rule on February 2; the Senate passed an identical resolution, S.J. Res. 12. The CRA is a 1966 statute that gives Congress a limited amount of time to overturn a regulation; in effect, it is a legislative veto. The joint resolution must pass both houses, and must either be signed by the president or re-passed by a two-thirds vote of each house. If this occurs, the rule does not take effect—and the federal agencies require specific authorization to issue a substantially similar rule in the future. The statute has only been used once: to annul OSHA's ergonomics rule in March 2001, but many Obama-era regulations are vulnerable: all those adopted after June 2016. [Heidi Wilbur, *Fair Pay & Safe Workplaces Rule Is on the Chopping Block*, Constangy Brooks Smith & Prophete LLP (Feb. 1, 2017), available at Lexology.com; Richard W. Arnholt, *Congress Acts to Rescind the Already-Enjoined Fair Pay and Safe Workplaces Regulation and Other Last-Minute Obama Administration Rules*, Bass, Berry & Sims PLC (Feb. 6, 2017), available at Lexology.com; Eric Morath and Natalie Andrews, *Senate Votes to Overturn Obama-Era Workplace Rule*, WSJ.com (Mar. 6, 2017); Joy Sturm, Michael D. McGill and Allison Pugsley, *Congress Invalidates Controversial Fair Pay and Safe Workplaces Regulations*, Hogan Lovells (Mar. 9, 2017), available at Lexology.com]

President Trump signed the joint resolution on March 27, 2017 rescinding the whole Fair Pay and Safe Workplaces Rule. In addition, he issued a new EO, Revocation of Federal Contracting Executive Orders, revoking EOs 13673 and 13738, thereby eliminating the entire Fair Pay and Safe Workplaces Rule structure, including rules about disclosure of pay and restrictions on pre-dispute arbitration mandates. Approval from Congress would be required for the DOL to enact similar rules in the future. [Michael J. Schrier, *Fair Pay and Safe Workplaces Regulations and Executive Orders Are Rescinded*, Duane Morris LLP (Mar. 28, 2017), available at Lexology.com]

§ 1.05   VARIABLE PAY

A variable pay system makes part of the compensation dependent on meeting goals or targets. Because these plans are supposed to create incentives for better work, communication is key. Formal annual review explaining how the award was calculated is useful to pinpoint areas in which employees succeeded and those in which more work is necessary. The most effective plans had "moderate stretch" (i.e., they asked employees to achieve targets that were not impossible, but were not comfortably in view either).

It is important to make it clear whether the variable compensation is a commission on sales or a bonus, and whether the employee is entitled to a specific amount or percentage, or whether the variable pay award is discretionary with management and whether it is contingent on anything (e.g., continued employment with the same company). In some states, sales commissions are considered vested and must be paid when the employee quits or is terminated. [Rebecca E. Ivey and Rebecca Williams Shanlever, Troutman Sanders LLP, *Easy Come, Easy Go: State Rules on Post-Termination Forfeitures of Bonuses and Commissions* (Apr. 12, 2010) (benefitslink.com)]

In mid-2010, the Connecticut Supreme Court ruled that an attorney's year-end bonus was not "wages" as defined by the Connecticut Wage Act, so statutory double damages and attorneys' fees were not available. An amount is treated as wages if entitlement is based on specific definable goals such as billing a certain number of client hours per year—but does not constitute wages if payment of the bonus is discretionary and based on something like the employer's determination that it has had a financially successful year. [*Ziotas v. Reardon Law Firm PC*, 296 Conn. 579 (2010)]

In 2012, the New York Court of Appeals held that a job offer to a financial services executive included an oral promise of a guaranteed $175,000 bonus, so when he was fired, the bonus constituted "wages," and he could collect attorneys' fees under the New York statute that calls for an award of attorneys' fees when "wages" are not paid on time. [*Ryan v. Kellogg Partners Institutional Servs.*, 19 N.Y.3d 1 (N.Y. 2012)]

Some states continue to maintain "blue laws" that require premium pay when hourly employees work on Sundays or holidays. This is true in Massachusetts and Rhode Island; these laws forbid discrimination against employees who refuse to work on Sundays or certain holidays. [Robert T. Quackenboss & Anna P. Lazarus, *Blue Laws May Require Extra Pay for Non-Exempt Retail Employees During Holidays*, Hunton & Williams LLP (Dec. 9, 2016), available at Lexlogy.com]

§ 1.06 WAGE AND HOUR ISSUES

The HR department's many and varied responsibilities probably include handling (or outsourcing and supervising) payroll matters, including paying employees subject to the appropriate deductions.

See § 2.01[A] for a fuller discussion of FICA tax. Note that in late 2015, a suit was settled for $3.5 million (including fees and costs) when non-qualified plan participants sued their employer for failure to handle FICA to reduce the participants' taxes. The court held that even though the taxes were required, the employer could lawfully have structured the plan for the participants' benefit. [*Davidson v. Henkel*, No. 12-cv-14103 (E.D. Mich., settlement approved Dec. 8,

2015); see Angela M. Bohmann, *FICA Lawsuit Settles for Over $3 Million*, Stinson Leonard Street LLP (Feb. 11, 2016), available at Lexology.com]

The Protecting Americans From Tax Hikes (PATH) Act (2015), Pub. L. No. 114-113, reinstates the expired tax credit for research and development (R&D), and makes it permanent. The statute also allows some small businesses to claim the R&D credit to reduce their share of FICA tax. For tax years beginning after December 31, 2015, a qualified small business can elect for any taxable year to take part of the R&D credit to reduce its share of FICA. The IRS's consent is required to revoke the election. A qualified small business is a new business, organized as a partnership or corporation (either C or S) with gross receipts under $5 million for the taxable year and that did not have gross receipts for more than five taxable years before the present one.

A sole proprietorship can be treated as a qualified small business if it meets the criteria, but a tax-exempt organization cannot be. The R&D tax credit amount that can be applied to FICA tax is the smallest of an amount (up to $250,000) elected by the taxpayer; the R&D tax credit for that year; or the amount of general business tax credit carryforward for that tax year. (A partnership or S Corporation cannot take the carryforward option). A qualified small business can only make this election for five years. Making the election depends on whether the business will pay less tax if it uses the R&D credit or reduces its FICA tax; if the business has employees but no taxable income, the FICA option is clearly more advantageous. [Douglas W. Charnas, *PATH Act Allows R&D Credit to Reduce FICA Taxes for Certain Small Businesses*, McGuireWoods LLP (Feb. 9, 2016), available at Lexology.com]

The Fair Labor Standards Act (FLSA) [29 U.S.C. §§ 201–219 and 251–262] regulates wages and hour matters. The FLSA forbids sex discrimination in compensation, sets a minimum wage, requires extra pay when a "non-exempt" worker puts in overtime hours, and sets standards for record keeping and record retention. The Department of Labor's Wage and Hour Division is responsible for administering the FLSA.

David Weil, head of the DOL's Wage and Hour Division (WHD), says that wage theft is facilitated by changes in business structure: more use of temporary agencies, franchises, and subcontractors makes it easier for employers to deny knowledge of wage violations. The WHD has uncovered close to $1 billion in illegally unpaid wages since 2010; immigrants are at special risk of experiencing wage theft. The New York attorney general has recovered $17 million in wage claims over a three-year period. [Steven Greenhouse, *More Workers Are Claiming "Wage Theft,"* NYTimes.com (Aug. 31, 2014)]

Wage enforcement takes place at the state level as well. Although the New York Industrial Board of Appeals has awarded five- or six-figure amounts to many low-wage workers for wage theft (sometimes for theft persisting over several years), the employees frequently are unable to collect. A coalition of labor and public interest groups, including the Legal Aid Society, the Urban Justice Center, and the National Center for Law and Economic Justice published a report calling for changes that would make it easier to enforce these judgments. The report says that at least $125 million in judgments and orders has been granted. Some employers do not have the funds to pay; others have concealed assets. For example, workers at the Babi nail salons were awarded $474,000 for retaliatory discharge and wage theft at a time when the owners had millions of dollars in assets, including $400,000 in cash. However, because the plaintiffs could not attach the defendants' assets before the trial, they collected only $110,000. A bill has been introduced in New York to permit wage liens, to parallel mechanics' liens, and to allow the civil court to attach assets in a pending case based on the plaintiffs' showing of likelihood of success. The bill would also make it easier to hold the primary shareholders of corporations personally liable for unpaid wage judgments. [Jim Dwyer, *Awarded Stolen Wages, Workers Struggle to Collect*, NYTimes.com (Feb. 19, 2015); Sarah Maslin Nir, *Workers Find Winning a Wage Judgment Can Be an Empty Victory*, NYTimes.com (Apr. 14, 2017). Maryland adopted a lien provision for unpaid wages in 2013, for employees who can prove, by a preponderance of the evidence, that they were denied wages. The lien is enforceable for 12 years against the employer's real or personal property: Rebecca Landon Tzou, *Maryland's New Lien for Unpaid Wages Law—A Reasonable "Stick" Or an Inequitable Bludgeon?*, Kelley Drye & Warren LLP (Aug. 29, 2013), available at Lexology.com.]

˙As of January 2014, the IRS classifies automatic gratuities (e.g., 18% service charge for party of 8 or more) as service charges, which are regular wages, subject to payroll withholding, rather than as tips, which employees must report as income. As a result, some chain restaurants stopped including automatic gratuities on the bills of large parties. Many employees opposed the IRS ruling, preferring to receive tips at the end of a shift to waiting two weeks for a paycheck. [Julie Jargon, *Tax Change Affects Restaurant Tips for Large Groups*, WSJ.com (Sept. 4, 2013)]

FLSA § 203(m) permits employers to take a tip credit against the minimum wage of tipped employees, as long as the employee is aware of the credit and is permitted to keep all the tips. The FLSA also allows pooling of tips among employees who customarily and regularly receive tips.

A mid-2016 Fifth Circuit decision does not permit the employer to take the full tip credit if it takes a deduction that exceeds the actual credit card fees on credit card tips. The employer deducted 3.25% from tips charged on credit cards, claiming that it needed to have cash on hand to process the credit card tips each day. However, the Fifth Circuit said that tips do not have to be paid out each day; they can be settled each pay period. The desire to keep cash on hand was an internal business decision, not a necessary cost of accepting credit cards. Because of the impropriety, the Fifth Circuit would not permit the use of the tip credit at all. [*Steele v. Leasing Enters., Ltd.*, 826 F.3d 237 (5th Cir. 2016); see David B. Jordan, *Fifth Circuit Declines to Broaden Permitted Deduction of Credit Card Fees from Tips*, Littler Mendelson PC (June 30, 2016), available at Lexology.com]

The Department of Labor's took the position in 2011 that tipped employees are entitled to keep all their tips whether or not the employer takes the tip credit. The Ninth Circuit has upheld this regulation. The Tenth Circuit held that the DOL had no authority to adopt the regulation, and employers can legitimately retain tips as long as they pay the full minimum wage and overtime. [*Marlow v. The New Food Guy, Inc.* No. 16-1134 (10th Cir. June 30, 2017); see Adam J. Rocco and Michael C. Griffaton, *The Ninth and Tenth Circuits Split on Tip Credits,* Vorys Sater Seymour and Pease LLP (July 13, 2017), available at Lexology.com] The Ninth Circuit case is *Oregon Rest & Lodging Ass'n v. Perez,* 816 F.3d 1080 (9th Cir. 2016); a petition for en banc rehearing was filed Apr. 6, 2016.] However, in the OMB's semi-annual agenda of regulatory actions published July 20, 2017, the DOL proposes to rescind the current restrictions on keeping tips when employers pay the minimum wage. [Jackson Lewis PC, *Department of Labor to Rescind 2011 Tip Pooling Regulation* (July 20, 2017), available at Lexology.com]

Sometimes plaintiffs argue that assigning tipped employees to do "side work" (such as wiping tables in a restaurant or cutting fruit for garnishes in a bar) prevents the employers from taking the tip credit because it means that the employee in effect has two jobs, one of which is covered by the regular minimum wage. However, the Seventh Circuit rejected this argument, holding that it was proper to apply the tip credit to time spent on side work. Even if the tasks in question are performed by non-tipped employees at other restaurants, they are not necessarily unrelated to the tipped occupation. [*Schaefer v. Walker Bros. Enters.,* 829 F.3d 551 (7th Cir. 2016); see Gerald L. Maatman, Jr. & Jennifer A. Riley, *Seventh Circuit Serves Up Employer-Friendly Recipe for Compensating Tipped Employees,* Seyfarth Shaw LLP (July 22, 2016), available at Lexology.com] The Tenth Circuit's analysis was that a person can engage in both tipped and non-tipped work for the same employer, and is entitled to the normal minimum wage while doing non-tipped work. Tips received at a time when a person is not a tipped employee do not count as FLSA wages—and therefore do not count toward determining if the worker received the minimum wage. [*Romero v. Top-Tier Colorado LLC,* No. 16-1057 (10th Cir. Mar. 7, 2017); see Michael D. Thompson, *Tips Do Not Count Towards the Minimum Wage Unless a Worker Qualified as a "Tipped Employee,"* Epstein Becker Green (Mar. 29, 2017), available at Lexology.com]

The Fifth Circuit held that tip pooling is permitted only among employees who customarily receive at least $30 a month in tips. DOL rules require a tipped employee to have more than de minimis interaction with customers who leave tips that are not allocated to particular individuals. The Fifth Circuit reversed the district court's grant of summary judgment for a restaurant that included its barista in a mandatory tip pooling arrangement with waiters, busboys, and bartenders. The barista was paid $10 per station per shift rather than receiving a share of the tips. The waiters sued, alleging that it was illegal to make them share tips with the barista, who worked in the kitchen and did not serve customers. The Fifth Circuit found that there was a genuine issue of material fact as to the status of the baristas. [*Montano v. Montrose Rest. Assocs., Inc.,* 800 F.3d 186 (5th Cir. 2015)]

The Ninth Circuit held in 2010 that an employee's property right to tips under the FLSA only attaches if the tip credit is taken by the employer. In 2015, the Fourth Circuit also held that FLSA §§ 216(b) and 203(m) do not create a free-standing cause of action for lost tips, so employees can only sue for misappropriation of gratuities if the employer used the tip credit. Under this interpretation, adding ineligible employees to a tip pool, and/or failing to inform employees of the tip pooling policy does not create an FLSA cause of action when employees merely sue for the tips without raising a minimum wage or overtime claim. [*Trejo v. Ryman Hospitality Props.*, 795 F.3d 442 (4th Cir. 2015)]

In 2016, the Ninth Circuit held that the DOL has jurisdiction in cases alleging improper tip pooling. [*Cumbie v. Woody Woo, Inc.*, 596 F.3d 577 (9th Cir. 2010); *Oregon Rest. & Lodging Ass'n v. Wynn Las Vegas LLC*, No. 13-35765 (9th Cir. Feb. 23, 2016); see Jonathan R. Tung, *9th Circuit Expands Dept. of Labor Power into Tip-Pools*, Findlaw 9th Circuit Court of Appeals Opinion Summaries Blog (Feb. 26, 2016)]

According to the DOL, a tipped employee is someone like a waiter, valet, or bartender who regularly and customarily gets more than $30 a month in tips. The employer must notify the employee that the tip credit applies; the notice should be in writing and, preferably, should be signed by the employee. The tip credit cannot exceed the actual amount of tips received; that the employee retains all of his or her tips unless there is a valid tip pool; and the tip credit does not apply unless the employee receives the notice. (If the employer fails to give proper notice, it cannot take the tip credit, and must pay the regular minimum wage— and can be required to pay back pay.) The employer must make up the difference if the employee fails to earn tips equal to the tip credit in a particular week. If the employee earns tips that at least equal the tip credit, the employer is not permitted to retain any part of the tips or take deductions for uniforms or other work-related items. If a tip is paid by credit card, the employer is permitted to deduct a percentage of the tip equal to the card issuer's transaction fee. (This is the DOL's position; the Fifth Circuit disagrees—see above.) A tipped employee's compensation is not affected if he or she must perform activities that are not directly related to serving customers (e.g., folding napkins or preparing garnishes for the bar) if these activities do not take up more than 20% of the work time in the work week. But if these activities exceed 20%, the employee is considered to have two jobs and the tip credit applies only to the tipped portion. Many states set higher minimum wages or impose special rules for tipped employees. [Elizabeth S. Washko, *FAQs on Compliance with the Federal Tip Credit*, Ogletree Deakins (Nov. 3, 2014), available at Lexology.com]

Tip pooling cases raise broader questions of who can be considered a "supervisor." In mid-2009, the California Court of Appeal held that shift supervisors should not be considered agents of the owner because they usually do the same work as the baristas and can keep individual tips, so they should be allowed to share in the tip pool. [*Chau v. Starbucks Corp.*, 174 Cal. App. 4th 688 (Cal. App. 2009)]

The First Circuit affirmed class certification and an award of over $14 million in damages ($7.5 million in damages plus 12% prejudgment interest per year, plus $6.6 million treble damages with respect to tips collected by shift supervisors contrary to the July 12, 2008 amendments to the Massachusetts Tips Act) in a suit about Starbucks' policy on tip pooling. The Massachusetts Tips Act forbids having waitstaff share their tips with anyone who is not a member of the waitstaff. The Tips Act says that the waitstaff are workers who do not have any managerial responsibilities. Starbucks took the position that shift supervisors do not have managerial responsibility and spend 90% of their time doing the same work as other baristas, so they are entitled to share the tips. The First Circuit rejected this argument: shift supervisors have to open and close the store, account for cash, and supervise baristas' break schedule. [*Matamoros v. Starbucks*, 699 F.3d 129 (1st Cir. 2012)]

Instead of settling the question of whether assistant store managers should share in the Starbucks tip pool, the Second Circuit certified the question to the New York Court of Appeals. [*Barenboim v. Starbucks/Winans v. Starbucks*, 698 F.3d 104 (2d Cir. 2012)] The New York Court of Appeals' answer, in 2013, was that shift supervisors, as workers with some supervisory duties, but who primarily serve customers, might be entitled to share in the tip pool. However, assistant managers are not entitled to share tips, because they have too much managerial authority. [*Barenboim v. Starbucks Corp.*, 21 N.Y.3d 460, 995 N.E.2d 15 (N.Y. 2013)]

California's Labor Code § 351 makes tips the sole property of the employee or employees for whom the tip was left, and it is illegal for employers to take the gratuity. However, California has ruled that this prohibition does not extend to tip pooling required by the employer. A card dealer brought a class action against a casino challenging a mandatory tip pool. The California Supreme Court ruled that there is no private cause of action to sue under Labor Code § 351—enforcement can only be done by the Department of Industrial Relations charging the employer with a misdemeanor. [*Lu v. Hawaiian Gardens Casino, Inc.*, 50 Cal. 4th 592 (2010)]

A 2010 New York statute, the New York State Wage Theft Prevention Act (S. 8380), amending New York Labor Law § 195 with respect to wage notice requirements, took effect April 9, 2011. It requires employers to give employees written notice (when they are hired and each year thereafter) of matters such as their regular payday, regular pay rate, overtime rate, commissions, etc. Employees can sue if they do not receive the required notice, and the Commissioner of Labor can also enforce the statute; criminal penalties are possible. Furthermore, the Commissioner can impose a civil penalty of up to $10,000 for retaliation, and retaliation is a misdemeanor. [John P. Furfaro, *New State Laws Cover Wage Notices, Tips, Independent Contractor Status*, N.Y.L.J. (Feb. 4, 2010) (law.com)]

In a FLSA/New York Labor Law action, the Second Circuit affirmed certification of a class of waiter/captains who alleged that they were forced to share their tips with employees who were not eligible for tips and that they were not given the required extra hour's pay for working over 10 hours in a shift. (New York law limits the tip credit to $2.25; the FLSA allows the employer to take a credit of up to 50% of the minimum wage—but not more than tips actually received. The FLSA forbids use of the tipped credit if tipped employees must share tips with non-tipped employees.)

FLSA collective actions are opt-in, and New York class actions are opt-out, so the issue in this case was whether it was proper for the federal court to hear the New York claims at the same time. The Second Circuit held that the cases could be combined because they involved the same basic facts. The Third, Seventh, Ninth, and D.C. Circuits have allowed federal courts to combine state class actions with an FLSA collective action. [*Shahriar v. Smith Wollensky Rest. Grp.*, 659 F.3d 234 (2d Cir. 2011). See also *Knepper v. Rite Aid Corp.*, 675 F.3d 249 (3d Cir. 2012); *Ervin v. OS Rest. Servs. Inc.*, 632 F.3d 971 (7th Cir. 2011); *Wang v. Chinese Daily News*, 623 F.3d 743 (9th Cir. 2010), *vacated on other grounds*, 132 S. Ct. 74 (2011) and 709 F.3d 829 (9th Cir. Mar. 4, 2013). The March 2013 decision was replaced in September. The Ninth Circuit applied *Dukes* to reverse certification of a (b)(2) class, because monetary relief was requested, and remanded for the district court to reconsider whether there were class-wide issues. The Ninth Circuit said that first the district court must determine commonality under (a)(2); if it is found, the district court should consider whether (b)(2) certification for injunctive relief can be sustained. None of the named plaintiffs is a current employee of the defendant, so none has standing to pursue class-wide injunctive relief, but the Ninth Circuit held that certification for injunctive relief might survive if there are still-employed identifiable class members: *Wang v. Chinese Daily News Inc.*, 737 F.3d 538 (9th Cir. 2013).]

The Sixth and Seventh Circuits use different standards for certifying FLSA collective actions. The Sixth Circuit says the question is whether the plaintiffs are similarly situated; the stricter Federal Rules of Civil Procedure Rule 23 requirement of predominance of shared over individual issues should not be applied. Thus, the Sixth Circuit certified a collective action of cable technicians with similar job duties, under the same compensation plan, using the same timekeeping system. The Seventh Circuit, however, said that it was illogical to have different standards for collective actions and Rule 23 class actions. [Compare *Monroe v. FTS USA, LLC*, 815 F.3d 1000 (6th Cir. 2016) with *Espenscheid v. DirectSat USA, LLC*, 705 F.3d 770 (7th Cir. 2013); see Gary C. Ankers, *Sixth Circuit Refuses to Apply Stricter FLSA Collective Action Certification Standard*, Littler Mendelson PC (Mar. 10, 2016), available at Lexology.com]

The FLSA says that suit may be maintained in either state or federal court. In mid-2003, the Supreme Court interpreted this to mean that an FLSA suit for unpaid wages, liquidated damages, interest, and attorney's fees can be removed by the defendant employer from state to federal court. Just because the suit may be maintained in either system doesn't prevent removal, or require a case to remain in the same system from beginning to end. [*Breuer v. Jim's Concrete of Brevard Inc.*, 538 U.S. 691 (2003)]

Employees have a private right of action (that is, they can sue their employers) for unpaid minimum wages and/or overtime, plus liquidated damages, attorneys' fees, and court costs. Courts have the power to order legal and equitable relief against employers who fire employees, or otherwise discriminate or retaliate against them for making an FLSA complaint or participating in a Wage and Hour Division proceeding. [29 U.S.C. § 216] The Eleventh Circuit held in mid-2017 that a plaintiff who receives at least the minimum wage plus overtime does not have a cause of action under the FLSA based on a charge that the employer misappropriated the employee's tips—although a cause of action may be available under state law. [*Malivuk v. Ameripark, LLC,* No. 16-16310 (11th Cir. June 9, 2017); see Allan Bloom, *11th Cir Denies Private Federal Right of Action for Withheld Tips,* Proskauer Rose LLP (June 12, 2017), available at Lexology.com]

Not only can employees sue their employers, the Secretary of Labor has the power to sue for unpaid minimum wages and overtime. The funds go directly to the employees who should have received them, not to the Department of Labor (DOL). The court can enjoin the employer against committing any further violations. Willful violations of the FLSA are criminal rather than civil in nature, so prosecution by the federal Attorney General's office is possible, in addition to DOL actions or civil suits by the employees.

The Third Circuit joined several other circuits in 2015 holding that employees who receive the predominant benefit of a meal break cannot treat the time as FLSA work time. The test is whether the employee is primarily engaged in work-related duties during the meal period. The plaintiffs were prison officers who received a one-hour meal period, 45 minutes of which was paid. The plaintiffs said they should be paid for the full hour because they had to stay in uniform, remain near emergency response equipment, and remain on call. However, the Third Circuit said that they were allowed to eat away from their desks and could get permission to leave the worksite. The CBA also provided for overtime pay for meals interrupted by work. [*Babcock v. Butler Cnty.,* 806 F.3d 153 (3d Cir. 2015)]

After nine years of litigation, the California Supreme Court ruled in April 2012 that employers must provide meal and rest breaks for employees but they are not obligated to make sure that employees actually take the breaks instead of continuing to work. However, this decision was not entirely an employer victory: the California Supreme Court held that workers are entitled to more frequent rest breaks than the employers contended. A concurring opinion points out that class actions remain viable for pressing wage and hour claims. [*Brinker Rest. v. Superior Court (Hohnbaum),* 53 Cal. 4th 1004 (Cal. 2012). Note that the statute of limitations for claims of denial of meal breaks is three years: *Murphy v. Kenneth Cole Prods. Inc.,* 40 Cal. 4th 1094 (Cal. 2007).]

Subsequently, the California Supreme Court ruled that an employer must either permit its employees to have rest breaks with no assigned duty, or pay them for an extra hour of straight time. The case was brought by security guards who said they were required to stay on call, with cell phones or pagers, in case they were needed; the employer argued that in practice the rest breaks were seldom disturbed. However, the supreme court read the state law to require rest breaks with no duties assigned. [*Augustus v. ABM Security Servs., Inc.*, No. S224853, 2016 WL 7407329 (Cal. Dec. 22, 2016); see David E. Amaya, *A Break Is a Break: California Supreme Court Rules That Rest Breaks Must Be Duty Free*, Fisher Phillips (Dec. 22, 2016), available at Lexology.com]

Wal-Mart has frequently been accused of labor law violations, such as denying employees legally mandated breaks and forcing them to work off the clock. Such cases raise important issues of when employees' claims are sufficiently similar to justify a class action. A class action involving three million Wal-Mart employees, the largest wage and hour class action ever reported, was settled in 2009; the District Court for the District of Nevada's approval also resolved 39 class actions in several states. [Rebecca Moore, *Wal-Mart Wage-and-Hour Settlement Approved in NV*, plansponsor.com (Nov. 4, 2009)] On May 1, 2012, Wal-Mart agreed to pay $4.8 million in back wages and damages to those who received between $30 and $10,800 each, plus $464,000 in civil penalties. The Department of Justice found that more than 4,500 workers were improperly denied overtime, and security guards and vision-department managers were misclassified as exempt between 2004 and 2007. [Shelly Banjo, *Wal-Mart to Pay $4.8 Million in Back Wages, Damages*, WSJ.com (May 1, 2012)]

The District Court for the District of Massachusetts denied a defense motion to compel plaintiffs to respond to written discovery about their immigration status—and ordered a restaurant to answer written questions about potential class members. The plaintiffs claimed that they routinely worked 60–80 hours a week and were not paid for all the hours they worked, and in fact earned less than the minimum wage and did not receive overtime. The court ruled that *Hoffman* does not affect illegal immigrant workers' right to receive back pay, because they are still employees for FLSA purposes. The DOL position is that allowing illegal workers to recover is compatible with federal immigration policy. [*Lin v. Chinatown Rest. Corp.*, No. 1:09-cv-11510-GAO (D. Mass. Mar. 23, 2011). The Eighth Circuit held that the FLSA applies to hiring of illegal aliens; employers are not permitted to profit by knowingly hiring employees who are not authorized to work in the United States: *Lucas v. Jerusalem Cafe LLC*, 721 F.3d 927 (8th Cir. 2013).]

The District Court for the District of Arizona held that undocumented workers can recover liquidated damages. The district court said that enforcing the FLSA undercuts IRCA in some ways—but still promotes immigration objectives overall—by removing the incentive to hire illegal workers in order to underpay them. The FLSA liquidated damages provision involves compensation for work already done, which avoids the *Hoffman* problem. The district court said that employers are excused from statutory liquidated damages only if they show good faith and lack of willfulness in wage violations. [*Vallejo v. Azteca Elec. Constr.*, No. CV-13-01207-PHX-NVW 2015 U.S. Dist. LEXIS 11780 (D. Ariz. Feb. 2, 2015)]

The Seventh Circuit interpreted the FLSA regulations to mean that employees are not doing compensable work merely because they are subject to callout (i.e., being summoned back to work with a phone or beeper to respond to emergencies)—their activities are not restricted as long as the employer has a way to reach them. The court also found that the class action brought by utility workers was inappropriate because the class was not homogenous enough. Either classes should be certified containing similarly situated employees, or the lunch break grievance should be handled through arbitration. [*Jonites v. Exelon Corp.*, 522 F.3d 721 (7th Cir. 2008)]

The prevalence of electronic devices, such as pagers and increasingly sophisticated cell phones, raises questions about the status of workers who are on call, or who can be contacted when they are not in the workplace.

The Sixth Circuit ruled that meal breaks for casino security guards, who were required to remain onsite and monitor their two-way radios, were not compensable. Plaintiffs alleged that the mandatory 15-minute roll call before each eight-hour shift entitled them to 1.25 hours of overtime. However, the Sixth Circuit ruled that the breaks were not predominantly for the employer's benefit. Monitoring the radio and being available to respond to emergencies was de minimis, not a substantial job duty. [*Ruffin v. MotorCity Casino*, 775 F.3d 807 (6th Cir. 2015)]

The Seventh Circuit held that the city of Chicago was not liable for after-hours work (monitoring and responding to e-mails) that police officers did on their BlackBerrys. Although the court held that the work was substantial enough to be otherwise compensable, and employers have to pay for work that they did not ask for or even want, the city did not have to pay because it did not know, and did not have reason to know, that the work was performed. [*Allen v. City of Chicago*, No. 16-1029, 2017 U.S. App. LEXIS 14230 (7th Cir. Aug. 3, 2017); see Jeffrey W. Brecher and Eric R. Magnus, *City of Chicago Not Liable for Police Officers' After-Hours Smartphone Use, Seventh Circuit Affirms*, Jackson Lewis PC (Aug. 7, 2017), available at Lexology.com]

A controversial early 2015 California decision requires that security guards assigned to 24-hour shifts (8 hours for sleep) must be paid for all 24 hours—even though their contract says that sleep time is not compensable. The California Supreme Court said that on-call hours were compensable and sleep time payment cannot be excluded by agreement. Factors in the decision include whether the employees were required to live on premises; if their movements were restricted; if the fixed time for responding to calls was unduly restrictive; if employees were permitted to swap shifts; if the restrictive nature of the assignment could be reduced by using pagers; and whether employees actually engaged in personal activities during on-call time. Other courts have also considered whether time is spent primarily for the benefit of the employer and the employer's business. The California Supreme Court did not make its order prospective only, leaving open the possibility of cases seeking back pay. [*Mendiola v. CPS Security Solutions, Inc.*, 182 Cal. Rptr. 3d 124, 340 P.3d 355 (Cal. Jan. 8, 2015)]

It is often alleged by wage and hour plaintiffs that their paychecks are not correct: they have been forced to work additional, "off the clock" time, sometimes without compensation at all, or sometimes they receive their regular compensation, but say they are not paid overtime for overtime hours. These cases raise important legal questions of what constitutes an adequate complaint and what constitutes adequate proof, especially since the plaintiffs are often in the position of challenging the validity of payroll records submitted by the employer-defendant. Employers often introduce evidence of their official policies, requiring reporting of all hours worked and forbidding off-the-clock work.

In a 2015 Eleventh Circuit case, plaintiff Bailey alleged that he was not paid for overtime during his year of employment. He said he worked off the clock and his supervisor changed his time records. The employer, TitleMax, said that it was a violation of company policy to fail to report hours properly, and he should have complained about his supervisor's unethical conduct. The Eleventh Circuit rejected the defendant's "unclean hands" defense, holding that TitleMax knew or should have known that the plaintiff worked overtime because his supervisor encouraged false timekeeping. Merely introducing the formal policies did not prove that employees were not coerced into off-the-clock work. Presenting credible evidence that managers changed the time sheets was a question of fact that could go to the jury as to whether the employer was aware of the unpaid work. [*Bailey v. TitleMax of Georgia*, 776 F.3d 797 (11th Cir. 2015)]

[A] FLSA Litigation

Employers face not only class actions from groups of dissatisfied employees (asserting claims of discrimination and/or violations of state wage and hour laws), but also a special kind of "collective action lawsuit" authorized by FLSA § 216. There are many technical legal differences between class actions and FLSA collective actions.

An FLSA § 216(b) collective action can be brought by one or more employees on behalf of themselves and similarly situated employees; to join, similarly situated employees must opt in. Commencing a collective action requires the plaintiff to show that there is a similarly situated group of employees, although the FLSA does not contain a statutory definition of how similar the group must be. If the court grants conditional certification, it determines whether other similarly situated employees should be notified. The more significant differences appear among the opt-in plaintiffs, the less likely it is that the employees in the group are truly similarly situated.

Settlement terms were negotiated in a FLSA class action in the District Court for the Western District of Kentucky alleging unlawful off-the-clock work and violations of the rules about tip pooling. However, the defendants learned that a state intermediate appeals court, in a different case, ruled that class actions are not available under the state wage and hour act. The defendants moved to stay the court's approval of the settlement. The district court denied the motion and approved the settlement. The defendants moved to decertify the class based on the other decision. The district court held that the settlement agreement was a binding contract so it refused to decertify the class. The Sixth Circuit held that a settlement does not become invalid as a result of a later change in the law; the federal class action rules do not protect litigants who make a bad bargain. [*Whitlock v. FSL Mgmt., LLC*, 843 F.3d 1084 (6th Cir. 2016); see Jeremy Gilman, *In a Scorching Opinion, Sixth Circuit Refuses to Undo Class Action Settlement*, Benesch Friedlander Coplan & Aronoff LLP (Dec. 27, 2016), available at Lexology.com]

The Federal Judicial Center said that 8,781 FLSA cases were filed in 2015, significantly more than the 8,160 filings in 2014. The year 2016 was predicted to be an active one in FLSA litigation because of changes in the white collar exemption and the DOL regulations on this topic released mid-year. Suits about misclassification of workers as independent contractors rather than employees were also predicted to soar (See § 1.08.) [Richard L. Alfred, *FLSA Suits Continue to Skyrocket: New Record High in 2015, More Than 9,000 Expected in 2016*, Seyfarth Shaw LLP (Nov. 20, 2015), available at Lexology.com]

FLSA suits are popular with plaintiffs and the plaintiffs' bar because there are no administrative prerequisites for filing the suit and the burden of proof is on the employer. Prevailing plaintiffs are usually entitled to attorneys' fees. To avoid suits, employers can require employees to sign their time sheets, certifying that the records are accurate, and that there was no off-the-clock work. There should be regular wage and hour assessments and audits of timekeeping practices. Employees should be made aware that there is an effective procedure for reporting complaints about wage and hour issues. [Aaron Zandy and Jessica Walberg, *Innovative Strategies for Defending Against the Rising Tide of Wage and Hour Class Actions*, FordHarrison LLP (Sept. 24, 2014) (benefitslink.com)]

Expensive restaurants have frequently been the target of FLSA suits. In the federal courts nationwide, the number of such suits doubled between 2005 and 2015, and the number of suits during this time almost tripled in New York City. A 2014 DOL study said that in New York State, wage violations cost workers $10–20 million a week, with the hospitality industry the worst offender. In the first seven months of 2015, New York State recovered $11.6 million in unpaid wages in New York City. The prestigious restaurant Per Se settled in July 2015 for $500,000 for two years of improper seizure of employees' tips. The star chef Daniel Boulud agreed to a $1.4 million settlement with employees. [Thomas MacMillan, *More Employees Sue Restaurants in Wage Disputes*, WSJ.com (Aug. 17, 2015)]

For the FLSA's anti-retaliation provision [§ 125(a)(3)] the Ninth Circuit refused to use a bright-line test of whether the plaintiff is considered a manager. In the First, Fifth, Sixth, and Tenth Circuits, there is a specific legal standard for managers: to engage in protected activity, the employee must not represent the company and must exercise FLSA rights by filing or threatening to file an action adverse to the employer or actively help other employees assert FLSA rights. The

Ninth Circuit used a generalized fair notice standard, under which managerial status is only one element the fact finder considers. The Ninth Circuit said that an entry-level employee's report that someone was underpaid would be an FLSA complaint but the same report could just be part of the duties of a manager responsible for FLSA compliance. [*Rosenfield v. GlobalTranz Enters.*, 811 F.3d 282 (9th Cir. 2015). See also *Greathouse v. JHS Security Inc.*, 784 F.3d 105. (2d Cir. 2015): under the FLSA anti-retaliation provision, a retaliation case does not require a complaint to a government agency.]

However, the FLSA anti-retaliation provision only applies to complaints about violations of substantive provisions of the FLSA; general complaints about working conditions are not protected. Thus, complaining about not getting breaks was not protected because the FLSA did not mandate breaks for the employee. [*Richard v. Carson Tahoe Regional Healthcare*, 2016 U.S. App. LEXIS 3932 (9th Cir. Mar. 2, 2016); see Noel P. Tripp, *Ninth Circuit Affirms: Not All Complaints About Work Policies Relating to Hours "Protected Activity" Under the FLSA*, Jackson Lewis PC (Mar. 11, 2016), available at Lexology.com]

Recent cases make it clear that plaintiffs must provide specific information about their claims, even at the earliest stages of the case. The Third Circuit, like the Second Circuit, requires FLSA plaintiffs to provide more than generalized allegations of hours worked in order to satisfy the standards for what constitutes an adequately pleaded federal complaint. A statement that a hospital did not compensate the plaintiff for hours over 40 a week, work during meal breaks, training, and outside scheduled shifts, was inadequate. [*Davis v. Abington Mem. Hosp.*, 765 F.3d 236 (3d Cir. 2014)]

The Second Circuit ruled that, to state a valid overtime claim that satisfies federal pleading requirements, the plaintiff must allege that he or she worked 40 hours in a given week, plus some uncompensated additional time. The case was dismissed because the plaintiff's complaint merely rephrased the FLSA and did not estimate her hours or provide a factual context for the number of hours worked. [*DeJesus v. HF Mgmt. Servs., LLC*, 726 F.3d 85 (2d Cir. 2013)]

A Time Warner business unit used an online timekeeping platform and rounded employees' time stamps to the nearest quarter hour. Federal regulations allow the employer to record start and stop times to the nearest five minutes, one-tenth of an hour, or quarter hour. Rounding is permitted as long as it does not lead to failure to compensate workers properly over time. The Ninth Circuit held that rounding regulations do not have to apply individually to each employee to make sure that no compensation is ever lost. A neutral rounding policy must allow employers to round both up and down, so that compensation averages out over the long term, not necessarily in a particular pay period. The Ninth Circuit found the rounding policy to be neutral on its face because time was rounded to the nearest quarter-hour, which could favor either the employer or the employee. The plaintiff sought compensation for a minute each shift spent logging on to the tracking program, but the court treated this as de minimis. [*Corbin v. Time Warner Entm't-Advance/Newhouse P'ship*, No. 13-55622, 2016 WL 1730403 (9th Cir.

2016); see Liebert Cassidy Whitmore, *Neutral Time-Rounding Policies Do Not Violate the FLSA* (June 13, 2016), available at Lexology.com]

In June 2012, the Supreme Court ruled that drug "detail" representatives are exempt from overtime because they fall under the exemption for "outside salespersons." [*Christopher v. SmithKline Beecham Corp.*, 132 S. Ct. 2156 (2012)]

The Ledbetter Act extends the statute of limitations for some Fair Pay Act claims, in that each new paycheck affected by discrimination starts the clock running. Davis went on disability-related leave. She was demoted to a different job, with lower pay, because she failed a physical/eye test for returning to her former job. Davis alleged that demoting her violated the ADA. The claim would have been time-barred, but she argued that the Ledbetter Act applied because each paycheck was smaller because of discrimination. The Second Circuit ruled in mid-2015 that the Ledbetter Act did not cover her claim because the Ledbetter Act is limited to discriminatory compensation decisions, not to other employment decisions. The Act would cover a charge that the company paid disabled employees less than similarly situated employees who are not disabled, but would not apply to a claim of a discriminatory transfer to a different job that paid less. The Second Circuit said that Davis' reduction in pay was directly related to her demotion, which was a discrete act that started the statute of limitations. [*Davis v. Bombardier Transportation Holdings, Inc.* 794 F.3d 26 (2d Cir. 2015)]

Although *Dukes* and other recent cases make class certification more difficult, some district courts allow class certification when plaintiffs can show a class-wide employment policy and a damages model that applies to the whole class. *Leyva v. Medline Industries*, 716 F.3d 510 (9th Cir. 2013) allows class certification in some cases where damages have to be calculated individually as long as the plaintiffs can show that the employer damaged the proposed class the same way (e.g., failure to calculate overtime properly and provide wage statements). But other cases reject class certification when there is no common formula for damages: e.g., *Roach v. T.L. Cannon Corp.*, No. 3:10 Civ. 0591 (TJM), 2013 WL 1316452 (N.D.N.Y. Mar. 29, 2013); *Cowden v. Parker & Assocs.*, No. 5:09-323-KKC, 2013 U.S. Dist. LEXIS 72253 (E.D. Ky. May 22, 2013). Plaintiffs might be able to use Rule 23(c)(4) to certify a class as to liability only, with damages computed by an individualized showing by each plaintiff. [See *Comcast v. Behrend*, 133 S. Ct. 1426 (2013), a non-employment case requiring that, in a (b)(3) case, damages must be capable of measurement on a class-wide basis.]

In early 2016, the Ninth Circuit held that employees who had the authority to edit their time entries could not satisfy the commonality requirement for a wage-hour collective action. The plaintiffs alleged that the employer habitually forced hourly employees to delay or skip meal breaks or take shorter breaks than they were legally entitled to. The case alleged that the employer only paid the premium required by California law when the timecard showed the meal break was not taken at all. The district court said that there was no policy or practice of denying premium pay: employees could correct entries that they believed to be incorrect. The Ninth Circuit said that proof of commonality would require a common practice of denying breaks, not just failure to pay the wage premium. [*Coleman v. Jenny Craig, Inc.*, 649 Fed. Appx. 387 (9th Cir. 2016); see Daniel L. Messeloff, *Ninth Circuit Affirms Dismissal of Wage-Hour Class Action Where Employees Could Edit Their Own Time Entries*, Jackson Lewis (May 26, 2016), available at Lexology.com]

When the putative class representative in an FLSA case makes a colorable showing that there is a class of similarly situated employees, conditional certification helps the court find them and then process the case based on a known class. Some courts do not require much evidence to conditionally certify a class, so employers may face extensive litigation even if the actual claims are weak. There is no equivalent under the FLSA of FRCP Rule 23(f), which allows interlocutory appeal of decisions on conditional certification. In a recent Third Circuit case, a class of employees said the University of Pittsburgh Medical Center denied them breaks and meal periods. After conditional certification, about 4,000 employees opted in. The defendant's motion to decertify the class was granted. The plaintiffs said that dismissal of their claims made the order to decertify the class a final, appealable order. However, the Third Circuit held that dismissal deprived the Third Circuit of jurisdiction over the case, because the dismissal terminated not only the plaintiffs' individual claims but their interest in representing co-workers. [*Camesi v. University of Pittsburgh Med. Ctr.*, 729 F.3d 239 (3d Cir. 2013)]

Late in 2003, the Eleventh Circuit held that once a named plaintiff in an FLSA collective action settles his own claims, he will not be allowed to continue the action and notify other class members of a potential case. The Eleventh Circuit distinguished between the FLSA collective action form and the Rule 23 class action, where class members can opt out and the representative plaintiff has the status of a private Attorney General to pursue grievances. [*Cameron-Grant v. Maxim Healthcare Servs. Inc.*, 347 F.3d 1240 (11th Cir. 2003) Another Eleventh Circuit case, *Prickett v. DeKalb Cnty.*, 349 F.3d 1294 (11th Cir. 2003) rules that, if an additional claim is added to an FLSA collective action for overtime pay, workers who opted in initially are not required to opt in again, because it cannot be concluded that they agreed only to the specific claims initially asserted.]

The Supreme Court decided a case about FLSA collective actions. The plaintiff sued on behalf of herself and similarly situated employees. However, the defendant made a settlement offer; the plaintiff ignored it. The Supreme Court held that, since no other employees joined the suit, and the settlement offer would have fully resolved her complaint, the Federal Rules of Civil Procedure required dismissal of the case. There was no longer an active case, because the plaintiff had no personal interest in representing other employees. The Supreme Court drew a distinction between the procedural rules for FLSA collective actions and the rules for class actions. [*Genesis Healthcare Corp. v. Symczyk*, 133 S. Ct. 1523 (2013)]

The Seventh Circuit ruled that there is no hard-and-fast rule against certifying a Rule 23(b)(3) class action involving state-law claims in a case that also includes an FLSA collective action, because the FLSA's legislative history does not show an intention to replace other legal procedures. The case was brought by tipped employees who said that Outback Steakhouses maintained policies that violated the FLSA and state wage and hour laws dealing with tips, and employees were not paid for all hours worked. The district court said that a (b)(3) class action, which includes class members unless they opt out, cannot be combined with an FLSA collective action (which required potential plaintiffs to opt in to the action), but the Seventh Circuit disagreed. [*Ervin v. OS Rest. Servs. Inc.*, 632 F.3d 971 (7th Cir. 2011)] In addition to arbitration agreements and class action waivers, some employers use contracts to alter other legal issues, e.g., shortening the statute of limitations. FedEx's employment agreement required suits against the employer to be brought within six months. The Sixth Circuit allowed a suit under the FLSA and Equal Pay Act to proceed: it was brought more than six months after the event, but within the statutory statute of limitations. The court said that reducing the statute of limitations would deprive the plaintiff of legal rights. The Sixth Circuit drew a distinction between Title VII rights, which can be waived, and FLSA rights to minimum wage, overtime, and liquidated damages, which cannot be waived because employers profit directly from such violations. [*Boaz v. FedEx Customer Info. Servs., Inc.*, 725 F.3d 603 (6th Cir. 2013)]

In mid-2012, the Third Circuit rejected class certification and dismissed the Racketeer Influenced and Corrupt Organizations Act (RICO) and false imprisonment claims brought by illegal immigrants hired by Wal-Mart contractors and subcontractors to clean Wal-Mart stores. The plaintiffs alleged that Wal-Mart exercised enough control to be their employer, and knowingly hired contractors who employed illegal workers. The plaintiffs worked in other places, not exclusively for Wal-Mart, and Wal-Mart hired other contractors and also assigned store employees to cleaning jobs. The Third Circuit held that an FLSA collective action requires that the plaintiffs be similarly situated, as determined on a case-by-case basis, using all the relevant factors (similar claims; working in the same corporate location, division, or department; similar compensation and circumstances of employment; whether they all seek similar relief). The Third Circuit did not find enough similarities to certify a collective action: the plaintiffs worked in 180 different stores in 33 states, and the 70 contractors and subcontractors, not Wal-Mart, set wages and hours. [*Zavala v. Wal-Mart*, 691 F.3d 527 (3d Cir. 2012)]

Sometimes the term "severance pay" is used to refer to legal obligations, sometimes to obligations under benefit plans, Collective Bargaining Authority (CBAs), or employer polices. In a 2014 Sixth Circuit case, plaintiff McCarthy was given two choices when she was facing involuntary layoff: either retire with a lump sum, or continue working for 85% of her prior wage. She chose to keep working. She brought an FLSA suit, alleging that the payments were a preexisting severance obligation rather than wages, so she was forced to work without compensation. The Sixth Circuit dismissed her case: even if she was fraudulently induced to accept the arrangement, her fraud claim could not be imported into an FLSA claim. [*McCarthy v. Ameritech Publ'g*, 763 F.3d 488 (6th Cir. 2014)]

Settling a Rule 23 opt-out class action is straightforward: the parties seek the court's approval of a Rule 23(e) settlement class. If the class is not approved, the parties return to the pre-settlement status quo. The FLSA opt-in rules are more complicated. Courts take different approaches to settling putative collective actions. Some follow the Rule 23 model; some require stipulated notice first, so class members get a chance to opt-in, without prior approval of settlement; others say that a purported settlement moots the case and forecloses notice. The FLSA opt-in requirement was enacted in the Portal-to-Portal Act to limit private FLSA plaintiffs to persons asserting claims in their own right, rather than in representative actions. FLSA compliance is facilitated if each Rule 23 class member who did not opt out gets a check that says that cashing the cash not only releases all FLSA claims but confirms the person's decision to opt in. In an FLSA-only case, the complaint has to be amended to add Rule 23 classes under state law, such as state wage and hour law or common-law breach of contract or unjust enrichment claims, creating complete preclusive effect: the settlement binds all class members who didn't opt out. [Phillip H. Wang, *Innovations in Settling Wage Hour Class/Collective Actions*, DLA Piper LLP (Sept. 8, 2015), available at Lexology .com]

For about 30 years, it was assumed that, to be enforceable, FLSA settlements would have to be approved by the DOL or by a court—creating problems for employers that wanted the settlement to be kept confidential. (Settlements of employment cases often include a release of all claims and a confidentiality clause forbidding the plaintiff to discuss the terms of the settlement.) Several cases suggest that private settlements might be enforceable, although it is a risk to settle an FLSA claim without court or DOL approval when there is a chance that the plaintiff(s) will later try to invalidate the settlement. [See, e.g., *Martin v. Spring Break '83 Prods., LLC*, 688 F.3d 247 (5th Cir. 2012). According to *Fernandez v. A-1 Duran Roofing, Inc.*, No. 12-CV-20757, 2013 WL 684736 (S.D. Fla. Feb. 25, 2013), court approval is not necessary, although courts can grant motions to approve an existing settlement.]

In the Second Circuit, FLSA settlements are unenforceable unless they are approved by either a judge or the DOL. [*Cheeks v. Freeport Pancake House, Inc.*, 796 F.3d 199 (2d Cir. 2015)] The Eastern District of New York held that the FLSA is a uniquely protective statute, so requiring court or DOL approval of a settlement is consistent with the statutory objective [*Martinez v. Ivy League Sch., Inc.*, No. 2:15-cv-07238-DRH-GRB (E.D.N.Y. June 18, 2016); see Robert S. Whitman, Howard M. Wexler and Meredith-Anne Berger, *District Court Turns the Other "Cheeks" on Parties' Proposed Stipulation of Dismissal*, Seyfarth Shaw LLP (July 11, 2016), available at Lexology.com. The District Court for the Southern District of New York also requires court approval to settle an FLSA claim via Rule 68, citing the risk of abuse: *Mei Xing Yu v. Hasaki Rest., Inc.*, No. 16-CV-6094 (JMF) (S.D.N.Y. Apr. 10, 2017); see Brett C. Bartlett and Samuel Sverdlov, *SDNY Pancakes Parties' Attempt to Bypass Cheeks: Requires Approval of Rule 68 Settlement,* Seyfarth Shaw LLP (May 1, 2017), available at Lexology.com]

In the Fifth Circuit, an FLSA claim can be settled privately, but enforcement is limited. To be valid, an FLSA claim release must discuss the employee's claim and the settlement and release must resolve a bona fide dispute about FLSA liability. In a case about unpaid overtime, the Fifth Circuit held that a generic release dealing broadly with state court claims (about alleged violations of non-compete, non-disclosure, and non-solicitation settlements) did not resolve subsequent FLSA claims because it was not reached in a bona fide FLSA dispute. The settlement negotiations never mentioned the FLSA, so FLSA claims were not resolved. [*Bodle, et al. v. TXL Mortgage Corp., et al.*, 788 F.3d 159 (5th Cir. 2015)]

Even if there is no legal requirement of DOL or court involvement, attempts to settle without lawyers can create difficulties, as a recent Eleventh Circuit case shows. A motel desk clerk accepted an offer of about $3,000 to withdraw her suit; she was homeless and urgently needed the money. The offer was made by her ex-employer, who did not have a lawyer. The clerk signed a voluntary dismissal with prejudice (which could have prevented her from re-filing the suit). The Eleventh Circuit held that the district court erred by approving the settlement; it was not a "stipulated judgment" as defined by the Eleventh Circuit in *Lynn's Food Stores* because the clerk did not propose the settlement to the court. [*Nall v. Mal-Motels Inc.*, 723 F.3d 1304 (11th Cir. 2013). See *Lynn's Food Stores v. United States*, 679 F.2d 1350 (11th Cir. 1982).]

The Fifth Circuit does not allow punitive damages or damages for pain and suffering in ADEA cases. However, the ADEA's provisions about remedies derive from the language of the FLSA, and the Fifth Circuit wants to interpret those two statutes consistently. In late 2016, the Fifth Circuit reaffirmed that pain and suffering and punitive damages are unavailable in ADEA discrimination or retaliation cases—but a different Fifth Circuit panel granted emotional distress damages in an FLSA retaliation case. [Compare *Pineda v. JTCH Apartments, LLC*, 843 F.3d 1062 (5th Cir. 2016) [FLSA] with *Vaughan v. Anderson Regional Med. Ctr.*, 843 F.3d 1055 (5th Cir. 2016); see W. Stephen Cockerham & Leslie Brockhoeft, *Are Pain and Suffering and Punitive Damages Recoverable Under the ADEA and FLSA? The 5th Circuit Issues Inconsistent Decisions*, Husch Blackwell LLP (Jan. 13, 2017), available at Lexology.com]

A plaintiff cannot receive an award of liquidated damages under both the FLSA and the New York Labor Law for the same violation. The Second Circuit held that the New York legislature did not adopt a provision for cumulative liquidated damages, and double recovery is generally disfavored. The two statutes have similar language and serve similar purposes, so a federal award of liquidated damages carries out the New York statutory objective. [*Chowdhury v. Hamza Express Food Corp.*, 666 Fed. Appx. 59 (2d Cir. 2016); see Allan S. Bloom, *Recovery of Liquidated Damages Under Both FLSA and State Law Improper, Says Second Circuit*, Proskauer Rose LLP (Dec. 12, 2016), available at Lexology.com]

The Second Circuit held that successful plaintiffs in an FLSA case are not entitled to an award of expert witness fees because these items are not mentioned in the statute, and do not fit under the statutory definition of "costs." [*Gortat v. Capala Bros. Inc.*, 795 F.3d 292 (2d Cir. 2015); see Matthew J. Thomas, *Expert Fees Not Recoverable Under FLSA Fee-Shifting Provision*, Jenner & Block (Aug. 31, 2015), available at Lexology.com]

[B] Arbitration

Frequently, employees asserting FLSA violations will be subject to mandatory pre-dispute arbitration—and many of those employees will also be subject to requirements that they pursue their claims as individuals rather than bringing a collective or class action.

The law firm Carlton Fields Jorden Burt reported that, in 2012, 16% of survey respondents used arbitration agreements with class action waivers—a percentage that rose to 43% in 2014, in the wake of *Concepcion*. [*AT&T Mobility v. Concepcion*, 131 S. Ct. 1740 (2011)] Employment lawyers say that this has greatly reduced the number of suits against employers. Carlton Fields reported that in 2011, 28% of all class actions dealt with employment matters, but only 23% did in 2014. Recoveries also fell: $598.9 million in 2011, $462.8 million in 2014. In 2011, Cornell University researchers found that employers were more likely to prevail in arbitration cases than in suits, and employees who did win got lower awards from arbitrators than from juries or judges. [Lauren Weber, *More Companies Block Employees from Filing Suits*, WSJ.com (Mar. 31, 2015)]

In 2004, the Fifth Circuit confirmed that FLSA claims can be the subject of a compulsory pre-dispute arbitration agreement: there is nothing in the FLSA that requires the court system rather than arbitration to resolve disputes. The limitations on discovery in arbitration do not deprive plaintiffs of substantive rights under the FLSA. [*Carter v. Countrywide Credit Indus. Inc.*, 362 F.3d 294 (5th Cir. 2004); see also *Adkins v. Labor Ready Inc.*, 303 F.3d 496 (4th Cir. 2002) (there is no inherent conflict between the FLSA and the Federal Arbitration Act, and FLSA claims can be subject to mandatory arbitration because the FLSA's statutory language is similar to that of the ADEA, and ADEA claims are subject to mandatory arbitration)]

The Eleventh Circuit held that the right to bring FLSA collective actions is not a substantive right that can never be waived. Therefore, it upheld an arbitration agreement forbidding FLSA class claims. The Eleventh Circuit did not find any Congressional intention under the FLSA to overrule the Federal Arbitration Act's (FAA's) strong support of arbitration. [*Walthour v. Chipio Windshield Repair*, 745 F.3d 1326 (11th Cir. 2014). The Second, Fourth, Fifth, and Eighth Circuits had already taken this position.]

The Ninth Circuit permitted an employer to compel individual arbitration after a class had been certified and a wage and hour class action had been in progress for several years. The Ninth Circuit held that *Italian Colors* requires enforcement of arbitration agreements, even in cases charging violations of federal statutes, and found the waiver of class arbitration to be valid. [*Richards v. Ernst & Young, LLP*, 734 F.3d 871 (9th Cir. 2013)]

A recent article suggests that an employer that maintains an arbitration clause should move quickly to enforce the arbitration clause before the process of class certification begins and should draft the agreement to include a delegation clause. The first stage of an FLSA class action is considering whether the claims are similar enough to notify potential class members nationwide. After discovery, the second stage rules on whether the claims are similar enough to continue in a single action. A Fifth Circuit case alleged failure to pay overtime to bank tellers. The bank's dispute resolution policy included an arbitration provision, which only permitted class actions on agreement of all parties. The Fifth Circuit ruled that the issue of whether the case should go to arbitration should be decided well before nationwide notification was issued. In the Fifth Circuit's view, the delegation provision of the arbitration clause gave the arbitrator authority to decide gateway questions of arbitration, including whether the agreement covers a particular controversy. It also gave the arbitrator sole authority to resolve disputes about the interpretation or formation of the arbitration policy. [*Reyna v. International Bank of Commerce*, 839 F.3d 373 (5th Cir. 2016); see Daniel S. Klein, *Fifth Circuit Holds Bank Overtime Claims Should Be Arbitrated, Providing Guidance on Employer-Friendly Delegation Clauses*, Kane Russell Coleman & Logan PC (Oct. 13, 2016), available at Lexology.com]

In 2013, the California Supreme Court reversed its earlier position (that arbitration agreements waiving employees' right to make wage claims at administrative hearings are void and unenforceable). The California Supreme Court ruled that changes in federal precedent meant that the FAA preempts any state rule that waivers of administrative hearings are invalid. [*Sonic-Calabasas v. Moreno II*, 57 Cal. 4th 1109, 163 Cal. Rptr. 2d 269, 311 P.3d 184 (Cal. 2013)]

California's Private Attorney General Act (PAGA) allows employees to bring suits if they are unable to get the California labor regulators to investigate their allegations. Successful PAGA plaintiffs receive 25% of any civil penalties imposed on the employer; the balance goes to the state. Although several California cases found class action waivers unconscionable and therefore unenforceable, in mid-2014 the California Supreme Court ruled that an employment agreement that waives the right to arbitrate grievances on a class basis is valid. However, arbitration agreements cannot make employees waive the right to bring PAGA actions. [*Iskanian v. CLS Transportation Los Angeles LLC*, 59 Cal. 4th 348 (Cal. 2014), *cert. denied*, 135 S. Ct. 1155 (2015)] Therefore, California employees can continue to bring PAGA suits but employers are permitted to draft arbitration clauses that forbid class arbitration. [Michael W. Kelly, *United States Supreme Court Declines to Review California Supreme Court Decision Erecting*

Barriers Against Arbitrating Private Attorneys General Act Claims, Squire Patton Boggs (Jan. 21, 2015), available at Lexology.com] However, this is a California state decision. In contrast, the District Court for the Central District of California compelled arbitration and enforced a PAGA representative action waiver, finding that FAA preemption is a federal issue, so the California Supreme Court ruling was not binding. [*Fardig v. Hobby Lobby*, No. SACV 14-00561 JVS, 2014 WL 4782618, 2014 U.S. Dist. LEXIS 139359 (C.D. Cal. Aug. 11, 2014)]

Litigation continued on this issue: see Chapter 40. In March 2017, the Ninth Circuit held that federal courts can compel arbitration of PAGA claims. *Valdez* says federal courts can compel arbitration of PAGA claims (in this case, alleging failure to provide rest and meal breaks, make timely wage payments, or provide accurate pay statements). The Ninth Circuit held that *Iskanian* forbids complete, categorical waivers of the judicial forum; it allows a generally applicable contract defense that applies whether or not the waiver is expressed in an arbitration agreement or another type of contract. But an individual employee can be required to arbitrate a PAGA claim as long as there is no complete, categorical waiver of the right to sue. A recent article points out that PAGA claims are not subject to a jury trial requirement and judges have complete discretion over penalties, so employers may not be at risk of runaway jury verdicts even if a case is tried in court when arbitration cannot be compelled. [*Valdez v. Terminix*, No. 15-56236, 2017 U.S. App. LEXIS 3881 (9th Cir. Mar. 3, 2017); see Barbara I. Antonucci, *California Corner: Employers Can Compel Arbitration of PAGA Claims, Ninth Circuit Says (But California Courts Beg to Differ)*, Constangy Brooks Smith & Prophete LLP (Mar. 14, 2017), available at Lexology.com]

The Sixth Circuit refused to enforce a waiver of class/collective actions included in the severance agreements for about 70 employees who were terminated in connection with restructuring. Some of them filed an FLSA collective action seeking overtime. The Sixth Circuit held that the arbitration clause was not contained in the severance agreement so cases about collective action waivers in arbitration agreement were not relevant. [*Killion v. KeHE Distributors, Inc.*, 761 F.3d 574 (6th Cir. 2014); see *Boaz v. FedEx Customer Info. Servs., Inc.*, 725 F.3d 60 (2013)]

Ex-employees of a pizzeria brought an FLSA collective action. The defendant implemented an arbitration policy covering current employees that forbade active employees to join the collective action. The district court enjoined the employer from enforcing the arbitration agreement against active employees who chose to join the suit—but the Eighth Circuit reversed, finding that the ex-employees did not have standing to challenge the arbitration agreement affecting the current employees. [*Conners v. Gusano's Chicago Style Pizzeria*, 779 F.3d 835 (8th Cir. 2015); see Paul G. Williams and Kristin Ann Shepard, *Circuit Courts Address Impact of Arbitration Agreements on Labor Class and Collective Actions*, Carlton Fields Jorden Burt (Mar. 27, 2015), available at Lexology.com]

§ 1.07 MINIMUM WAGE

. In 2017, the federal minimum wage remained unchanged at $7.25/hour ($2.13/hour for tipped employees). The Department of Labor, under Executive Order 13658 and regulations at 29 C.F.R. Part 10, is required to re-set the minimum wage for employees of federal contractors. The 2017 level is $10.20/hr, or $6.80/hr for tipped employees. [81 Fed. Reg. 64513 (Sept. 20, 2016); see Caroline J. Brown, *2017 "Contractor Minimum Wage" Rate Released*, Fisher Phillips (Sept. 20, 2016), available at Lexology.com; Sarah J.Gorajski, *Department of Labor Issues Notice of 2017 Minimum Wage Increase for Federal Contractors*, Littler Mendelson PC (Sept. 20, 2016), available at Lexology.com]

In 2016, minimum wage increases were adopted in 17 states and the District of Columbia, with four additional increases enacted by the November elections (in Arizona, Colorado, Maine, and Washington State). In 2017, the minimum wage in Alaska rose to $9.80; Arizona to $10 (except small businesses); Arkansas $8.50; California $10.50; Colorado $9.30, phasing up to $12 over a four-year period; Connecticut $10.10; the District of Columbia $12.50; Florida $8.10; Hawaii $9.25; Maine $9.00; Maryland $9.25; Massachusetts $11; Michigan $8.90; Missouri $7.70; Montana $8.15; New Jersey $8.44; New York $9.70 (as of December 31, 2016), $10.40 (December 31, 2017); Ohio $8.15; Oregon $10.25; South Dakota $8.65; Vermont $10; Washington $11. [Charles E. McDonald, III, *Employer Alert: Many State Minimum Wages to Increase in 2017*, Ogletree Deakins (Dec. 19, 2016), available at Lexology.com; it includes a table of tip credit amounts and exemptions. Eric Morath, *Minimum-Wage Votes Show Worker-Friendly Policies Gaining Momentum*, WSJ.com (Nov. 9, 2016); Mark B. Wiletsky, *Colorado Minimum Wage Hike Passes*, Holland & Hart LLP (Nov. 9, 2016), available at Lexology.com]

Florida adopted a constitutional amendment setting a statewide minimum wage, which is recalculated every year on September 30. [Edmund J. McKenna, *Florida's Minimum Wage to Increase on January 1, 2017*, Ogletree Deakins (Oct. 20, 2016), available at Lexology.com] Washington, DC's "Fair Shot Minimum Wage Amendment Act of 2016" increases the minimum wage from $10.50 to $11.50 in July 2017, rising about 70 cents a year until 2020, when it reaches $20/hr, with future increases for inflation. California law phases in a $15/hour minimum wage in 2022. The $15 minimum wage has been enacted first for New York City, then later for the rest of the state. [Mary Kate Nelson, *D.C. Home Care Workers Win $15 Minimum Wage* (June 29, 2016), available at homehealthcare-news.com; Robert Turk, *A Penny for Your Thoughts . . . A Nickel for Your Minimum Wage*, Stearns Weaver Miller Weissler Alhadeff & Sitterson PA (Oct. 19, 2016), available at Lexology.com] In November 2013, the New Jersey constitution was amended by referendum, requiring an annual review of the minimum wage. Both houses of the state legislature passed an increase to $15 by 2021, but the legislation was vetoed by Gov. Christie.[Richard J. Cino & Justin B. Cutlip,

New Jersey Minimum Wage to Increase in 2017, Jackson Lewis PC (Oct. 4, 2016), available at Lexology.com]

On February 18, 2016, the Oregon legislature adopted a unique tiered minimum wage to balance the needs of farming community against conditions in the metro Portland area. The minimum wage went from $9.25/hour to an amount based on which of three tiers a location falls within. Between July 1, 2016 and July 2018, the minimum wage ranges from $9.50 to $9.75, increasing gradually until June 2019, when the minimum wage ranges from $10.50 to $12 an hour depending on location. [Michael C. Griffaton, *Oregon Enacts a First-Of-Its-Kind Tiered Minimum Wage*, Vorys, Sater, Seymour and Pease LLP (Feb. 22, 2016), available at Lexology.com]

In eleven states (Arizona; Colorado; Florida; Missouri; Montana; Nevada; New Jersey; Ohio; Oregon; South Dakota; and Washington), the minimum wage must be examined each year and potentially increased. [R. Brian Dixon and Sebastian Chilco, *Minimum Wages, Maximum Challenges in 2016 (2017, 2018 . . .)*, Littler Mendelson (Dec. 11, 2015), available at Lexology.com]

On March 14, 2017, the Arizona Supreme Court upheld Proposition 206, which was passed at the November 2016 election, increasing the minimum wage and requiring paid leave. It was estimated that about 700,000 of Arizona's 2.5 million workers would benefit by the minimum wage increase, and 900,000 workers would gain access to paid leave. The plaintiffs challenging Proposition 206, the Arizona Chamber of Commerce and other business groups, contended that the increases violated the state constitutional requirement that ballot measures that require the state to spend more money must provide a revenue source such as a tax increase. Although Proposition 206 does not directly affect state employees, some private firms with state contracts, such as home health agencies, are paid under contracts negotiated before Proposition 206 passed, and a higher minimum wage increases the state's payments to these contractors. The Arizona Supreme Court ruled that this is not the kind of direct cost increases contemplated by the state constitution. [Howard Fischer, *Supreme Court Affirms Arizona's Higher Minimum Wage,* Tucson.com (Mar. 18, 2017) (benefitslink.com)]

Five states, including Alabama, do not have a state minimum wage. A number of cities adopted their own minimum wages—but Alabama, Michigan, and Missouri have state laws that forbid cities to adopt their own minimum wages. Alabama's bill was passed after Birmingham adopted a $10.10/hour minimum wage—the first local minimum wage adopted in a Southern state. A bill like this was passed in Montana but was vetoed by the governor. The National Employment Law Project said that, in effect, over a dozen states forbid the adoption of local minimum wages. [Alan Blinder, *When a State Balks at a City's Minimum Wage*, NYTimes.com (Feb. 23, 2016)]

The Kentucky Supreme Court held that the city of Louisville did not have authority to set a minimum wage, rendering the increased minimum wage unenforceable. [*Kentucky Rest. Ass'n v. Louisville Metro Council*, 501 S.W.3d 425 (Ky. 2016); see Catherine Salmen Wright & Amir J. Nahavandi, *Kentucky*

Supreme Court Strikes Down Minimum Wage Ordinance, Dinsmore & Shohl LLP (Oct. 21, 2016), available at Lexology.com]

Fast-food workers and civil rights advocates in Birmingham, Alabama sued Governor Robert Bentley to overturn the state law that forbids cities from raising their minimum wages. The complaint alleges that the disparate impact on black workers shows racial animus. [Melanie Trottman, *Workers Sue Over Alabama Wage Law, Citing Civil Rights*, WSJ.com (Apr. 28, 2016)]

The Seattle minimum wage is scheduled to reach $15 gradually. Franchisees objected, asserting that it discriminates against interstate commerce. The case reached the Ninth Circuit, which held that there was no interference with interstate commerce, because the negative effects (higher payroll costs) applied to the franchisees in Seattle, not franchisors elsewhere. The Supreme Court denied certiorari. [*International Franchise Ass'n v. Seattle*, No. 15-35209 (9th Cir. Sept. 25, 2015), *cert. denied*, No. 15-958 (May 2, 2016). See Brent Kendall and Eric Morath, *Supreme Court Turns Away Challenge to Seattle Minimum Wage Law*, WSJ .com (May 2, 2016).]

California's Governor Brown signed two wage law bills in August 2014. AB 2074 clarifies the statute of limitations for suits for liquidated damages for violation of the minimum wage requirements. Under prior law, employees could sue for unpaid compensation, with liquidated damages equal to the unpaid wages plus interest, if they alleged that they were paid less than the California minimum wage. AB 2074 allows the liquidated damage suit to be filed at any time before the statute of limitations runs on the underlying underpayment claim; this is generally three years. The statute was necessary because at least one California Court of Appeal decision sets the statute of limitations at one year. The other bill, AB 2743, extends existing civil penalty and suit provisions for entertainment industry workers whose CBA imposes a time limit for wage payment upon discharge or layoff, in cases where wages are not paid according to the schedule in the CBA. [Koryn M. McHone, *California Governor Signs Bills Impacting California Wage Suits*, Barnes & Thornburg LLP (Aug. 22, 2014), available at Lexology.com]

In addition to changes in law and by regulation, some major employers announced a voluntary policy of paying more than the minimum wage: e.g., Wal-Mart, Target, and TJX (the parent company of T.J. Maxx, Marshalls and HomeGoods). [Paul Ziobro, *Target to Increase Wages to At Least $9/Hour for All Workers in April*, WSJ.com (Mar. 18, 2015); Chelsey Dulaney, *TJX to Boost Pay for U.S. Employees to $9 an Hour*, WSJ.com (Feb. 25, 2015)]

Low wages were especially common in the restaurant industry. Almost 15% of the 2.4 million waiters and waitresses live in poverty, versus 7% of all workers. Waiters and waitresses are more likely than other workers to receive public assistance, and to lack sick leave and health benefits. In seven states, including California and Alaska, tipped employees must receive the regular minimum wage (New York has proposed doing this), and a further 24 states require employers to pay more than the federal tipped minimum wage. According to the BLS, the median wage for waiters and waitresses is $8.94 an hour including tips, whereas the median wage for other workers is $15.84. However, the National Restaurant Association disputes this, and says servers earn more than that. [Jo Craven McGinty, *Tips Don't Add Up for Most Waiters and Waitresses*, WSJ.com (Aug. 8, 2014); Sophia Hollander, *Minimum-Wage Boost for Tipped Employees*, WSJ.com (Feb. 24, 2015)]

The political movement to increase the minimum wage began with New York City fast food workers, but it has spread nationwide and to other industries, and is a major issue in the 2016 presidential campaign. The campaign seeks a $15/hour minimum wage. Cities with a local minimum wage higher than the federal (and state minimum if there is one) include NYC, Seattle, Portland, Maine, Oakland, Chicago, Kansas City, Missouri, Washington, D.C., San Francisco, Los Angeles, Santa Fe, and San Diego. Business owners say that they may have to cut jobs if there are increases. [Patrick McGeehan, *Push to Lift Minimum Wage Is Now Serious Business*, NYTimes.com (July 24, 2015)]

Many day laborers are undocumented immigrants who are vulnerable to being cheated by employers. A Queens immigrant rights group, New Immigrant Community Empowerment (NICE) (part of the nationwide National Day Laborer Organizing Network), created a smartphone app ("Jornalero") for day laborers. They can rate their employers, log hours and wages, take pictures of job sites to identify bad employers, and send warnings to other workers. The advocacy group uses the information to work with lawyers to collect stolen wages. The Worker Institute, part of the Cornell University School of Industrial and Labor Relations, ran forums in NYC to find out what workers wanted to see in an app. They wanted to be able to track payments, share pictures to ID employers, and record unsafe conditions—anonymously. Workers save hours and wages in a profile, with a phone number but no name, linked to the database. NICE contacts employers when there is a report of wage theft; if necessary, a lawyer from the monthly Urban Justice Center monthly clinic helps recover the wages. [Liz Robbins, *New Weapon in Day Laborers' Fight Against Wage Theft: A Smartphone App*, NYTimes.com (Mar. 2, 2016)]

As our population ages, the question of how to compensate home care workers becomes more salient. Traditionally, home care workers were held to be providing "companionship," rather than health care services. In 1974, although Congress extended the FLSA to protect domestic service workers, they were excluded from minimum wage and overtime protection. A DOL regulation, 27 C.F.R. § 552.109(a), held that home care workers who provide companionship services to the elderly and infirm are not covered by the FLSA's minimum wage or overtime provisions, whether they were officially employed by the person receiving the care, the person's family, or a third-party agency. The Supreme Court upheld this regulation in mid-2007. [*Long Island Care at Home v. Coke*, 551 U.S. 158 (2007)]

The DOL reversed its course in September 2013, adopting a final rule granting minimum wage and overtime protection to more than two million home health and personal care workers who are employed by an agency rather than working directly for a patient or his or her family.

When the rule was adopted, 15 states (e.g., Nevada, Montana, Illinois, Minnesota, Pennsylvania, and New York) already required minimum wage and overtime protection, and another six states plus the District of Columbia already required payment of the minimum wage. [DOL regulations: 78 Fed. Reg. 60454 (Oct. 1, 2013)]

The District Court for the District of Columbia ruled in December 2014 in suits brought by home care provider trade groups, that DOL's 2013 rule is invalid because it violates *Coke*, and the way it was adopted violated the Administrative Procedure Act. The exemption was applied both to home care workers directly employed by patients and their families and to home care workers employed by an agency. [*Home Care Ass'n of Am. v. Weil*, No. 14-cv-967(RJL) (D.D.C. Dec. 22, 2014)]

Subsequently, however, the D.C. Circuit ruled in August 2015 that third-party agencies providing companionship services or live-in care must pay their employees minimum wage and overtime. The D.C. Circuit found that the regulations were consistent with the FLSA and Congress authorized the DOL to determine whether it was reasonable to deny the exemption to third-party agencies. Although the DOL altered a policy that had been in effect for 40 years, the D.C. Circuit ruled that the change was not arbitrary or capricious because it reflected major changes in the home care industry. [*Home Care Ass'n of Am. v. Weil*, 799 F.3d 1084 (D.C. Cir. 2015), certiorari was denied in mid-2016: No. 15-693 (June 27, 2016).]

In mid-2016, the District Court for the Eastern District of New York refused to certify a collective action sought by 5,000 home care workers. The district court held that overtime and misclassification claims citing the FLSA companionship services exemption are not suitable for collective action. The claims required proof that the plaintiffs devoted more than 20% of their workday to non-exempt general household work; the court said that the plaintiffs performed different tasks reflecting their clients' differing needs. [*Cowell v. Utopia Home Care, Inc.*, No. 14-CV-736 (LDW)(SIL) (E.D.N.Y. Aug. 8, 2016); see Vincent M. Avery, *Hope for Employers: Court Says Home Health Aides Can't Bring Collective Action*, Akerman LLP (Sept. 12, 2016), available at Lexology.com]

The Illinois Domestic Workers' Bill of Rights, signed August 21, 2016, (effective January 1, 2017) amends four state laws to apply to domestic workers entitling them to minimum wage and overtime protection and either one day off a week or overtime for time voluntarily worked on the scheduled day off. The legislation affects about 35,000 workers in-state; there are about two million domestic workers nationwide. New York, in 2010, became the first state to enact a bill of rights for domestic workers, entitling them to overtime and either a day off or overtime payment for working on the rest day. The New York statute created a special cause of action for sexual harassment of domestic workers. California, Connecticut, Hawaii, Massachusetts, and Oregon enacted similar overtime laws; all except California forbid discrimination or harassment of domestic workers. However, the Oregon law does not apply to independent contractors or home care workers who take care of senior citizens or persons with disabilities [Melissa L. McDonagh and Angelo Spinola, *Illinois Becomes Seventh State to Expand Employment Rights to Domestic Workers*, Littler Mendelson PC (Sept. 23, 2016), available at Lexology.com]

Franchise workers in Seattle, including home health workers, are entitled to receive the city's minimum wage, which phases up to $15 by 2018. The International Franchise Association and some businesses challenged the statute's requirement that local franchises of corporations be treated as part of the parent company—not entitled to the small-business exception that defers the $15/hour minimum until 2021. The Supreme Court denied certiorari. However, the Missouri Department of Health and Senior Services proposed a wage increase for home care workers, but the legislature blocked the increase in February 2016; the governor vetoed the legislation, but the legislature overrode the veto. [Tim Mullaney, *Home Care Franchises Lose Battle Over Seattle's $15 Minimum Wage*, Home Health Care News (May 4, 2016), available at homehealthcarenews.com]

The District Court for the Eastern District of Pennsylvania held that home care companies were entitled to a refund of employment taxes, because they had a reasonable basis under the § 530 safe harbor (see § 1.12[B]) for describing the workers as independent contractors. The company consistently filed returns characterizing them as independent contractors, and relied on legal precedents for this characterization. The business was registered as a home care registry which, according to mandatory training required by the state, is a registry that refers independent contractors. [*Nelly Home Care, Inc. v. United States*, **185 F. Supp. 3d 653** (E.D. Pa. 2016); see John B. Waters, *Home Care Company Had Reasonable Basis for Treating Home Care Workers as Independent Contractors and Was Entitled to a Refund of Employment Taxes*, Roetzel & Andress (Sept. 23, 2016), available at Lexology.com]

[A] Interns and Volunteers

Internships, unpaid or with a small stipend, are replacing traditional entry-level jobs for many recent college graduates. The Department of Labor permits unpaid internships for trainees, so the trainees can acquire usable job skills. The DOL has set out criteria for acceptable internship programs: for example, the real benefit of the training is to the trainee, not the employer; the training is similar to the curriculum of a vocational school; and trainees do not replace regular employees. The DOL has stepped up investigations, as some companies try to take advantage of the recession by obtaining unpaid labor from "interns."

In 2011, two interns working on the film "Black Swan" sued for back pay. The district court ruled in their favor, using the DOL's 2010 six-factor test, e.g., the work is similar to school classes; is performed for the benefit of the intern, and does not displace paid workers. However, the Second Circuit reversed, holding that Fox Searchlight Pictures correctly classified the plaintiffs as interns and not employees. The Second Circuit used the primary beneficiary test—someone is an employee only if the employer benefits more from the relationship than the worker does. The case was remanded. [*Glatt v. Fox Searchlight Pictures Inc.*, 791 F.3d 376 (2d Cir. 2015)]

In early 2016, the Second Circuit amended its *Glatt* decision to add a third salient feature to the "primary beneficiary" test: that the intern expects training or education, not a conventional employment relationship. The amended opinion is limited to internships, not all kinds of training programs, and requires consideration of the internship program as a whole rather than the experiences of a particular intern. [*Glatt v. Fox Searchlight*, 811 F.3d 528 (2d Cir. 2016); see Robert S. Whitman and Adam J. Smiley, *Second Circuit Leaves Interns in the Cold—Again*, Seyfarth Shaw LLP (Jan. 25, 2016), available at Lexology.com. A preliminary settlement was reached in mid-2016, for about $600,000 (including $260,000 in attorneys' fees); most intern plaintiffs received $495, but the lead plaintiffs were awarded between $3,500 and $7,500 each: Robert S. Whitman and Adam J. Smiley, *That's a Wrap: Fox Reaches Deal with Unpaid Interns*, Seyfarth Shaw LLP (July 14, 2016), available at Lexology.com.]

In mid-2016, the Southern District of New York applied the primary benefit test and once again held that unpaid interns at Hearst magazines were not entitled to wages under either the FLSA or the New York Labor Law. They knew they would not be paid for their work and were not guaranteed a paid job. They benefited by learning skills of the industry they were interested in. Only the six named plaintiffs remained in the suit after the Second Circuit's July 2015 denial of certification of a class or collective action. [*Wang v. Hearst Corp.*, No. 12-CV_ 0793 (JPO), 2016 U.S. Dist. LEXIS 113191 (S.D.N.Y. Aug. 24, 2016); see Robert S. Whitman, *In Final Exam, Court Rejects Hearst Interns' Pay Claims*, Seyfarth Shaw LLP (Aug. 26, 2016), available at Lexology.com]

The Eleventh Circuit also adopted a "primary beneficiary" test for interns. The plaintiffs were students in a master's program to become registered nurse anesthetists. The program required them to participate in at least 550 clinical cases. The plaintiffs said that they were really employees. The Eleventh Circuit rejected the DOL's six-factor test, on the grounds that it is not a regulation and is not necessarily entitled to deference. The Eleventh Circuit found the six-factor test to be too rigid. [*Schumann v. Collier Anesthesia*, 803 F.3d 1199 (11th Cir. 2015)]

The District Court for the Northern District of California ruled that cosmetology students were not employees of the defendant's beauty school, even though customers paid for their services. The plaintiffs did not show a lack of educational benefit or a requirement of performing extensive non-cosmetology menial tasks. The district court said that a control test would be irrelevant because schools typically exercise significant control over students without becoming their employers. [*Benjamin v. B&H Educ., Inc.*, Case No. 13-cv-04993-VC, 2015 U.S. Dist. LEXIS 144351 (N.D. Cal. Oct. 16, 2015)]

Sirius XM Radio settled with a class of 1,852 interns, for a reported $1.3 million; the interns raised allegations of lack of training, entitlement to minimum wage and overtime coverage. [*Tierney v. Sirius XM Radio Inc.*, No.14-cv-02926 (S.D.N.Y., settled Aug. 2015)]

New York state, Illinois, Maryland, Oregon, California, and the city of New York adopted statutes extending the protection of anti-discrimination laws to unpaid interns. [Jose Perez, *Unpaid Interns Are Now Protected Against Discrimination and Harassment*, Proskauer Rose LLP (Sept. 12, 2014), available at Lexology.com; Winston & Strawn LLP, *Illinois Extends Employment Protections to Unpaid Interns* (Aug. 29, 2014), available at Lexology.com; Guy Brenner and Alex C. Weinstein, *Maryland Passes Bill Protecting Interns from Employment Discrimination*, Proskauer Rose LLP (Apr. 24, 2015), available at Lexology.com]

However, the Wisconsin Supreme Court found that unpaid interns cannot bring anti-discrimination suits, because they are not "employees" who are subject to disciplinary action. [*Masri v. State Labor & Indus. Review Comm'n*, 356 Wis. 2d 405, 850 N.W.2d 298, 2014 WI 81 (Wis. 2014); see Sandra R. King et al., *Courts, Lawmakers Consider Employment Protections for Interns*, Manatt Phelps & Phillips LLP (Aug. 6, 2014), available at Lexology.com]

Particularly in the nonprofit sector, a great deal of work is done by volunteers. The "threshold remuneration" test of employee status, which is friendly to employers, primarily considers whether any compensation was provided or intended for the work. The Sixth Circuit rejected this test, preferring a balancing test involving all common-law agency factors. Commentators say that providing benefits to volunteers can create problems, because, unless the benefits are available to the public at large, they suggest that the volunteers are actually employees. A clear path from volunteering to paid employment also suggests an employment relationship. Two nuns volunteered for the Red Cross and the Ross County Emergency Management Agency. They alleged that they were fired because of their religious beliefs. The Sixth Circuit held that, because they were not employees, they could not pursue discrimination claims. [*Marie v. Am. Red Cross*, 771 F.3d 344 (6th Cir. 2014)]

§ 1.08   DETERMINING WHO IS AN "EMPLOYEE"

There are many reasons why it becomes necessary to determine if a particular person who performs services is an independent contractor or an employee of the company for which the services are performed. For example, employment status is involved in determining who is allowed to participate in pension and benefit plans; who is entitled to overtime; who is entitled to unemployment benefits and Worker's Compensation; and who can sue under antidiscrimination laws. Although similar factors are used in analyses for different purposes, it is possible that someone will be considered an employee for some purposes but not for others.

If the individual is an employee, the employer will be responsible for paying FUTA taxes and its own share of FICA, and will have to withhold income taxes. In contrast, independent contractors are responsible for their own tax compliance.

Clearly, the company saves money if it can characterize workers as independent contractors, because it saves on taxes and benefits (even if the cash compensation is the same). To prevent abuses, this is an area where the IRS and other regulators are active in determining whether the so-called independent contractor is really an employee.

The involvement of staffing firms makes it difficult to determine the number of independent contractors. The BLS considered about 14% of the U.S. workforce, approximately 20.2 million people, to be "professional and business service" workers in 2016, versus 9.9% in 1990. Professors Lawrence Katz and Alan Krueger estimated in 2016 that the percentage of workers hired out by contracting companies to a single client was 0.6% of the workforce in 2005, rising to 2% of the workforce in 2015. Their estimate is that another five million people, about 3.1% of the workforce, work on-site but for more than one client. Data is hard to obtain, because it is typical to include outsourcing contracts with a company's general and administrative expenses rather than breaking them out. [Lauren Weber, *Counting Up Contractors Is a Tricky Business*, WSJ.com (Feb. 2, 2017)]

The distinction between employees and independent contractors comes from New Deal legislation; it has been suggested that it does not work in the digital age, especially for the "App Economy," in which smartphone apps are used to match up businesses or people needing services with "app-enabled" workers such as drivers or housekeepers. Former NLRB chair Wilma Liebman suggested adopting the category of "dependent contractor" now in use in Canada and Germany. David Cameron, the prime minister of the United Kingdom, appointed a "freelance czar" to recommend how to handle non-traditional work assignments. Business owners treat the workers as "micro-entrepreneurs," but many suits have been filed by "flexible laborers" who charge that they must accept contracts that transfer the personal and financial risk to them in exchange for inadequate rewards [Lauren Weber and Rachel Emma Silverman, On-Demand Workers: *"We Are Not Robots,"* WSJ.com (Jan. 27, 2015); Lauren Weber, *What If There Were a New Type of Worker? Dependent Contractor*, WSJ.com (Jan. 27, 2015)]

Arizona's "Declaration of Independent Business Status" (DIBS) law took effect in August 2016. It is the first law to specify a way to confirm independent contractor status. An independent contractor can sign a "DIBS," which must be signed and dated, to acknowledge that the person operates an independent business, is not entitled to unemployment benefits, must pay all taxes, and secure any necessary licenses. The DIBS form must state that worker meets six of ten status criteria, such as not being covered under the employer's health plan or Worker's Compensation policy; being expected to work for other people, not just one employer; and that the independent contractor is not economically dependent on the hiring organization. The DIBS document creates a rebuttable presumption that the signer is an independent contractor. [Guy Brenner and Carolyn M. Dellatore, *New Arizona Independent Contractor Law Now in Effect,* Proskauer Rose LLP (Aug. 22, 2016), available at Lexology.com]

The Third Circuit allowed franchisees of commercial cleaning franchises to pursue a class action under Pennsylvania state law after their franchises failed. The Third Circuit held that the franchise agreement gave the franchisor significant control over the franchisees. The defendant had previously won a very similar case under California franchise law, which requires proof that the franchisor exercised control over and above what is required to protect its trademark, trade name, and goodwill. [*Williams v. Jani-King of Philadelphia, Inc.,* **837 F.3d 314** (3d Cir. 2016); see Donald S. Prophete & Jeffrey M. Rosin, *Court Misses Chance to Clarify Conflict Between Franchise, Employment Law—But Dissent Gets It Right,* Constangy Brooks Smith & Prophete LLP (Sept. 28, 2016), available at Lexology.com]

Although generally speaking it is the employer who agrees to pay money to settle a case, in September 2015, the DOL agreed to pay Gate Guard $1.5 million to settle claims that the DOL acted in bad faith when investigating whether gate attendants were misclassified as independent contractors. First, the district court awarded $565,000 in attorneys' fees to Gate Guard under the Equal Access to Justice Act, finding that the DOL's actions were not substantially justified but the agency's conduct was not bad enough to justify an award of damages for bad faith. On appeal, the Fifth Circuit found that the DOL's conduct was frivolous, egregious, and lacked legal support. The investigation violated the DOL's internal guidelines and was unethical. The investigator, who was not properly trained, destroyed evidence and sought a grossly inflated penalty. The DOL's litigation conduct was also improper. Specious motions were filed, the agency refused to answer questions, and falsely claimed that witness statements were privileged. The DOL also continued to litigate after discovering authority supporting Gate Guard's classification of the workers. Shortly after the case was remanded for the district court to set the award, the DOL settled. [Erin Fowler, *DOL to Pay $1.5 Million to Employer for Bad Faith Investigation,* Franczek Radelet (Sept. 24, 2015), available at Lexology.com]

The Internal Revenue Code specifically identifies some groups as statutory employees, and others as statutory non-employees. [I.R.C. §§ 3121, 3401, 3306, 3508]

The categories of statutory employees are:

- Agents or commission drivers who deliver food products, laundry, or dry cleaning;

- Full-time traveling salespersons who solicit orders for merchandise to be delivered later;

- Full-time life insurance salespersons;

- Corporate officers;

- People who work in their own homes, but under the supervision of someone who supplies the materials to be used in work (e.g., assembling clothing components).

The Fifth Circuit held in early 2016 that independent contractors can bring Rehab Act § 504 discrimination suits against a federally funded programs. Flynn was a contract doctor for the Air Force. She was diagnosed as being on the autism spectrum, which explained her allegedly erratic behavior around patients, which led to complaints. The officer in charge of her contract with the base recommended that she be removed from providing services, which happened. She asked to be reinstated with accommodations; her request was denied. The district court said that independent contractors cannot sue under Rehab Act, but the Fifth Circuit reversed. The language of 504(a) is very broad, and any federally funded program can be sued, not just an employer. [*Flynn v. Distinctive Home Care Inc.*, 812 F.3d 422 (5th Cir. 2016)]

The Ninth Circuit affirmed the NLRB's determination that cab drivers were employees and not independent contractors, because of the substantial evidence of control over their means and manner of performance, and the non-entrepreneurial nature of the job. [*NLRB v. Friendly Cab Co.*, 512 F.3d 1090 (9th Cir. 2008)]

The traditional model of providing rides through taxi services has been supplemented by car services and ride-sharing services. The ride-sharing services Uber Technologies and Lyft are part of the "app economy," which does not fit well into existing categories. [Rachel Emma Silverman, *Judges Skeptical of Uber-Lyft Claims in Labor Cases*, WSJ.com (Feb. 2, 2015)]

According to Uber, regulators in Indiana, Georgia, Pennsylvania, Colorado, Texas, Illinois, New York, and California have found their drivers to be independent contractors. However, in August 2015, the California Employment Development Department ruled that an ex-driver qualified for unemployment benefits based on Uber's high degree of control. [Mike Isaac, *California Agency Says Former Uber Driver Was an Employee*, NYTimes.com (Sept. 10, 2015); Douglas MacMillan, *Another Uber Driver in California Ruled an Employee, Not Contractor*, WSJ.com (Sept. 10, 2015); Mike Isaac and Natasha Singer, *California Says Uber Driver Is Employee, Not a Contractor*, NYTimes.com (June 18, 2015)]

Shortly before the scheduled start of a trial on the issue of the status of Uber drivers, the parties reached a deal under which approximately 100,000 California and Massachusetts drivers would have been treated as independent contractors. However, the District Court for the Northern District of California rejected the settlement for failure to be fair, adequate, and reasonable. The court stated that the $84 million that Uber agreed to pay was only 10% of the non-PAGA claims raised by the plaintiffs. (The drivers had agreed to waive claims under PAGA, which raised an issue of whether they could do this or whether they had a duty to other aggrieved workers.) The district court said that the offer of a $16 million add-on payment if Uber made an initial public offering was illusory. The case was stayed, pending interlocutory appeal. [*O'Connor v. Uber Techs., Inc.,* No. 13-cv-03826-EMC, 2016 U.S. Dist. LEXIS 110368 (N.D. Cal. Aug. 18, 2016); see Manatt Phelps & Phillips LLP, *Judge Puts the Brakes on Uber's $100M Settlement* (Oct. 11, 2016), available at Lexology.com; Mike Isaac, *Judge Overturns Uber's Settlement With Drivers,* NYTimes.com (Aug. 19, 2016)]

In early 2017, Uber settled a federal case on the same day it was filed by the FTC for $20 million to be distributed to drivers who were paid less than the advertised average pay. In some cities, fewer than 10% of drivers earned the advertised amounts. Uber did not admit wrongdoing. [FindLaw Technologist blog, *Uber Settles FTC Case for $20 Million* (Jan. 26, 2017), available at FindLaw.com]

Early in 2016, Lyft agreed to pay $12.25 million to settle a California federal court case about classification of drivers—but refused to change the classification going forward. The settlement fund was supposed to go to class members, based on hours worked. However, Judge Vince Chhabria of the Northern District of California rejected the settlement, holding that the amount was inadequate because it severely undercompensated drivers for their mileage expenses. [*Cotter v. Lyft,* No. 3:13-cv-04065-VC (N.D. Cal. Feb. 11, 2016 and Apr. 7, 2016); see Stanley W. Levy, *Misclassification Suit Against Lyft Brakes into Settlement Deal,* Manatt Phelps & Phillips LLP (Feb. 10, 2016), available at Lexology.com; a subsequent proposal more than doubled the offer, to $27 million. Lawyers for the Lyft drivers estimated they would get more than $6,000 if the new offer is approved—significantly less than the $8,000 drivers received in the Uber settlement noted above: see Douglas MacMillan, *Lyft Agrees to $27 Million Settlement with Drivers,* WSJ.com (May 11, 2016).] On March 16, 2017, the $27 million settlement was approved; the judge said that this was a better deal for drivers than the earlier rejected settlement but the status of Lyft drivers under California law remains unsettled. Without a resolution, drivers may continue to apply for unemployment benefits (which have been granted to some former Lyft drivers in California and Florida). [Richard R. Meneghello, *Latest Misclassification Settlement Fails to Lyft Sharing Economy Companies,* Fisher Phillips (Mar. 20, 2017), available at Lexology.com; Findlaw.com Technologist blog, *Judge Approves $27 Million Lyft Settlement* (Mar. 23, 2017), available at FindLaw.com]

In 2017, the Second Circuit applied economic reality analysis to rule that drivers of "black cars" for a conventional car service were independent contractors, not employees: some of them bought franchises (at widely varying prices), others did not; the terms of their agreements with the car service differed; they could and did drive for other services as well; they set their own schedules; and their earnings varied widely. [*Saleem v. Corporate Transportation Grp. Ltd.,* No. 15-88-cv (2d Cir. Apr. 12, 2017); *see* Richard J. Reibstein, *Black Car Drivers in*

New York City Held Independent Contractors By Federal Court of Appeals, Pepper Hamilton LLP (Apr. 13, 2017), available at Lexology.com]

The Fifth Circuit focused on economic reality in deciding whether an insurance company's "sales leaders" were independent contractors: whether the worker is economically dependent on the company it calls an employer, based on the degree of control over the worker, the relative investment by the worker and the company, the degree to which the potential employer determines the worker's opportunity for profit or loss; the permanency of the relationship; and the skill and initiative needed to perform the job. In this case, the insurer controlled the meaningful economic aspects of the business by hiring, firing, and assigning the agents who worked for the sales leaders (most of the sales leaders' income came from a share of the agents' commissions), so not being able to make personnel decisions limited the sales leaders' control over their income. The insurer also assigned geographic territories and controlled sales leads. The Fifth Circuit discounted the fact that the plaintiffs had signed independent contractor agreements: their subjective beliefs about their status could not overcome economic reality. [*Hopkins v. Cornerstone Am.*, 545 F.3d 338 (5th Cir. 2008)] Under I.R.C. § 414(n), a long-term leased employee may have to be counted in testing pension and benefit plans for discrimination. A safe harbor is permitted when a company gets less than 20% of its non-highly compensated employees through leasing services, and if those services provide adequate pension coverage for their employees.

Bronk v. Mountain States Telephone & Telegraph Inc. [140 F.3d 1335 (10th Cir. 1998)] holds that, although the Employment Retirement Income Security Act (ERISA) [29 U.S.C. §§ 1001 *et seq.*] forbids excluding employees from the plan once they have satisfied minimum age and service requirements, it is permissible to draft the plan to deny participation to leased employees, even if they are common-law employees of the sponsor company. The Tenth Circuit position is that I.R.C. § 414(n)(1)(A) merely requires that leased employees be treated as employees; it doesn't require them to be offered plan participation.

Independent contractors can be considered "beneficiaries" under ERISA plans and therefore a suit by a commodities trader that made state insurance and tort law claims about the denial of disability benefits was preempted by ERISA. [*Shyman v. Unum Life Ins. Co.*, 427 F.3d 452 (7th Cir. 2005); see *Ruttenberg v. U.S. Life Ins. Co.*, 413 F.3d 652 (7th Cir. 2005) (another case involving floor traders, for the proposition that independent contractors can be beneficiaries of ERISA plans)]

In 2010, the Eighth Circuit ruled that firing an independent contractor marketing representative and replacing her with a younger common-law employee did not violate the ADEA. The Eighth Circuit held that all factors must be considered to determine if a person is an independent contractor or an employee; the Darden factors are non-exhaustive, and no one factor is decisive. [*Ernster v. Luxco, Inc.*, 596 F.3d 1000 (8th Cir. 2010)]

The NLRB's position is that independent contractor status is analyzed using common-law agency principles; there is no single determining factor. The worker's opportunity for gain or loss should be examined based on actual rather than theoretical opportunities. The NLRB tries to determine if the worker actually is operating an independent service business. In a union petition alleging that 20 FedEx Home Delivery drivers were employees, the NLRB's regional director said they were employees who could unionize, whereas the D.C. Circuit ruled that drivers performing the same job at a different facility were independent contractors. [Brian Schwartz and Robert T. Zielinski, *NLRB Clarifies Independent Contractor Standard*, Miller Canfield PLC (Oct. 8, 2014), available at Lexology.com]

In 2010, 42 MDL cases on this issue were decided in favor of FedEx Ground. However, the Ninth Circuit reversed [*Alexander v. FedEx Ground Package Sys.*, 765 F.3d 981 (9th Cir. 2014)], finding that the right of control is the primary determinant of employee status, rejecting the D.C. Circuit's "entrepreneurial opportunities" test. A smaller class action, brought by 360 Oregon drivers, holds that the FedEx contract with its drivers, and its written policies and procedures, made the drivers employees under Oregon and California law. [*Slayman v. FedEx Ground Package Sys., Inc.*, 765 F.3d 1033 (9th Cir. 2014)]

Missouri state law permits employees who were misclassified as independent contractors to recover monetary damages based on the value of the ERISA plan benefits they were denied. A group of full-time delivery drivers charged FedEx with misclassification, and alleged they were entitled to coverage under the company's welfare benefit, pension, and 401(k) plans. The District Court for the Eastern District of Missouri held that the state law is not preempted by ERISA. ERISA § 514(a) says that, except as limited by § 514(b), ERISA preempts state laws relating to benefit plans. The plaintiffs were not trying to recover plan benefits or enforce rights under the plan, they were seeking damages for misclassification. If they won the case, the damages would be paid by the employer, not the plan, so the state-law claims would have no impact on the plan. They sued as employees, not plan participants, so the case did not affect plan administration. [*Gray v. FedEx Ground Package Sys., Inc.*, No. 4:06-CV-422-JAR, 2014 WL 4386739 (E. D. Mo. Sept. 5, 2014)]

However, FedEx has prevailed in cases that found single-route Ground Division drivers to be independent contractors under the National Labor Relations Act (NLRA). The D.C. Circuit refused to enforce an NLRB decision requiring FedEx to bargain with a Teamster Union local representing such drivers. In early 2017, the D.C. Circuit once again reversed the NLRB, requiring the same result to apply in another suit between the same parties about the same issue. [*FedEx Home Delivery, an Operating Division of FedEx Ground Package System, Inc. v. NLRB*, 849 F.3d 1123 (D.C. Cir. 2017); see Richard J. Reibstein, *FedEx Succeeds Again on Appeal of an NLRB Ruling on Independent Contractor Misclassification*, Pepper Hamilton LLP (Mar. 7, 2017), available at Lexology.com; Steven M. Swirsky, *D.C. Circuit Rejects NLRB Finding That FedEx Drivers Are Employees, Not Independent Contractors and Raises Doubts as to Board's Joint Employer*

Test, Epstein Becker Green (Mar. 10, 2017), available at Lexology.com. See <https://independentcontractorcompliance.com/legal-resources/ic-diagnostics/>, for a proprietary tool that applies the tests of contractor status in the applicable jurisdiction.]

Sometimes a person will be considered an employee under federal law but not under state law, or vice versa. Early in 2015, the New Jersey Supreme Court rejected the "economic realities" test of the FLSA. Instead, the court applied the "ABC test" from the state's unemployment compensation act. The ABC test presumes that a worker is an employee and the burden of the proof is on the employer to show that the person is free from control or direction in the performance of work (both in formal contract terms and in reality); the work is outside the usual course of business or performed away from all of the potential employer's places of business; and the worker customarily engages in an independent profession, trade, or business. The case began as a federal suit brought by mattress delivery drivers. The district court said the drivers were independent contractors. When the case was appealed to the Third Circuit, the Third Circuit certified a question to the New Jersey Supreme Court. [*Hargrove v. Sleepy's*, 106 A.3d 449 (N.J. 2015)]

At the end of 2016, the Fifth Circuit joined the Sixth and Seventh Circuits in holding that emotional distress damages are available in FLSA retaliation actions—but the plaintiff must be a true employee, not an independent contractor. [*Pineda, et al. v. JTCH Apartments, L.L.C*, 843 F.3d 1062 (5th Cir. 2016); see Nicole Eichberger & Minia Bremenstul, *Fifth Circuit Joins Sister Circuits in Holding That Employees May Recover Emotional Distress Damages in FLSA Retaliation Suits*, Proskauer Rose LLP (Dec. 21, 2016), available at Lexology .com]

§ 1.09 STAFFING ARRANGEMENTS

The U.S. workforce can no longer be divided simply into full-time and part-time workers, or permanent workers and "temps." Many other arrangements have evolved, although, as noted above, the employer's characterization of the arrangement is not always accepted for tax and other legal purposes. Some of the possibilities are:

- Workers who are actually employed by a temporary agency that recruits, trains, and sends workers to companies that are clients of the agency;

- Long-term temporary assignments—where the temporary worker stays at one location for weeks or months, instead of being hired on a daily basis;

- Payrolling—a company wants to hire a specific person, and therefore arranges for a temporary agency to hire that person and be responsible for payment, taxes, and other employment-related matters;

- Part-time workers;

- Independent contractors—who are genuinely self-directed; have clients rather than employers who control their work; and are responsible for their own tax compliance;

- Contract workers—an arrangement usually made with technical workers who are formally employed by a technical services firm. This arrangement is often used for long-range projects, including those that require the contract worker to relocate to the employer's site;

- Leased employees—who are paid by the leasing company, which also handles administrative tasks like tax and Worker's Compensation compliance;

- Outsourcing—delegating a function such as payroll processing, guarding a worksite, or operating an employee cafeteria to a company that specializes in that function.

[A]   PPACA and Staffing Arrangements

At press time in 2017, the ongoing status of PPACA was uncertain, so this discussion is couched in the past tense. For periods of time when PPACA was in full effect, workers had to be characterized, using terms such as "seasonal worker" and "seasonal employee." The PPACA regulations use the terms "temporary staffing firm," "professional employer organization" and "staffing firm" rather loosely and not necessarily in conformity with industry usage. The 20-factor test was used to determine if workers were common-law employees, no matter what the staffing services agreement said. The PPACA regulations included anti-abuse provisions when the same worker was partially employed both by a staffing firm and a client firm. [79 Fed. Reg. 8544 (Feb. 12, 2014)]

§ 1.10   SIZE OF THE CONTINGENT WORKFORCE

Clearly, many ways to work have evolved. The BLS uses more than one definition for "contingent workers," the broadest of which is workers "who do not expect their current job to last." The BLS also collects information about "alternative" work arrangements (employment can be both contingent and alternative at the same time).

The Department of Commerce set out a four-part definition for "digital matching firms": these companies 1. use technology such as mobile apps to facilitate peer-to-peer transactions; 2. employ a quality control system based on user ratings; 3. workers decide their typical schedule; 4. workers use their own assets or tools (e.g., cars they own) to provide a service. More than a dozen states and cities have adopted regulations governing ride-sharing services. [Eric Morath, *A*

Tricky Task: Government Tries to Define the Gig Economy, WSJ.com (June 27, 2016)]

DOL discontinued its Contingent Worker Supplements (CWS) to the Current Population Survey in 2005, for funding reasons, but announced in late 2016 that it would revive the Contingent Worker Supplements (CWS), to gather information about the number of contingent workers. The May 2017 population survey included new questions about usage of mobile apps to perform work online or find customers; how on-demand workers connect with customers; and whether the work is a primary or secondary source of income. [Ilyse W. Schuman and Michael J. Lotito, *DOL Moves Forward with Plan to Determine Size of the Gig Economy,* Littler Mendelson PC (Sept. 30, 2016), available at Lexology.com]

Since its April 2013 announcement of an initiative to protect temporary workers, OSHA has published three guidance bulletins explaining when staffing agency and host employer are joint employers; the two most recent deal with Personal Protective Equipment (PPE) and whistleblower rights. When PPE is necessary, the host employer must provide and maintain it and train employees, but the staffing agency must monitor the host employer's compliance and assess potential hazards. If a host employer wants a temporary worker removed from its site for raising health or safety concerns or reporting an injury, the staffing firm can be liable for retaliation. Temporary workers can file an OSHA retaliation complaint against staffing agency and/or host employer. [OSHA Temporary Worker Initiative Page, <https://www.osha.gov/temp_workers/index.html> (last accessed Jan. 28, 2017)]

Women are more likely to have part-time jobs than men: 24% of working women, 13% of working men. The number of people working several jobs has declined steadily since the 1990s but, in all age groups, women are more likely to have multiple jobs than men, especially women 20–24, 6.7% of whom had more than one job (while 4.6% of men did). The retail workforce is 62% female, and less than half work full-time. [Anna Louie Sussman, *Is the "Gig Economy" a Thing? Ask Women*, WSJ.com (July 27, 2015)]

A 2016 study says that 4.2% of adults earned sharing-economy income at some point in three years. In September 2015, according to JP Morgan Chase, almost 1% of adults earned income from a sharing/gig economy firm, but usually as a supplement rather than replacement for full-time work. In October 2012, only 0.1% of adults had gigs. The sharing labor force is 2.5 million, or about the number of public school employees. The average monthly income for gig participants was $533, one-third of their total income. Only 40% of gig economy earners sold services or labor; the rest used capital such as renting their apartments on AirBnB. [Eric Morath, *Gig Economy Attracts Many Workers, Few Full-Time Jobs*, WSJ.com (Feb. 18, 2016)]

About 20 million low-wage workers, most of them female, and many of them in the food service or retail industries, are at risk of having unpredictable schedules, making it difficult to plan in advance or earn a consistent income when the number of hours worked fluctuates. Economics Professor Lonnie Golden says that between 10 and 20% of workers have on-call or irregular schedules. One survey showed that almost 20% of survey respondents said they had a day or less of advance notice of their schedule, almost 20% reporting a day or less of advance notice of schedule, another 12% said they had two to three days' notice, and 12% four days to a week. [Teresa Tritch, *Unpredictable Work Hours, Chaotic Life*, NYTimes.com (Aug. 10, 2015)]

Under the FLSA, employees are entitled to pay when they are on call if the wait time is predominantly for the employer's benefit, and the employee cannot effectively use the time for his or her own purposes. See § 1.14 for more discussion of this issue. [Graydon Head & Ritchey LLP, *On-Call Shifts Cause Headaches for National Retailers* (Nov. 13, 2015), available at Lexology.com]

A few states, including New York and California, have statutes that mandate payment of at least four hours at the minimum wage to employees who are sent home when they report for a scheduled shift. Legislation (the Schedules that Work Act) has twice been introduced in Congress, without success, and about a dozen other states have proposed bills. [Lauren Weber, *Abercrombie to End Contentious On-Call Scheduling*, WSJ.com (Aug. 6, 2015)]

§ 1.11 CO-EMPLOYERS

It's not always possible to say that one company is the employer and the other has no responsibility. Sometimes two companies (such as a leasing company and the company where the individual actually performs services) will be jointly liable—e.g., if the individual is injured at the workplace or harms someone else. Plaintiffs' attorneys are raising new theories of employer liability for wage and hour class actions: for example, citing defendants as joint employers who are responsible for the actions of their contractors, subcontractors, and temporary employment agencies.

Wage liability in joint employer cases is potentially imposed on anyone who makes key decisions about the economic realities of the employment relationship: e.g., corporate entities, officers, perhaps even board members. Shared or leased employees can create wage and hour duties even if the sharing or leasing employer believes that proper payments have been made. Under DOL regulations, joint employment exists when two or more employers appear to share an employee, act in each other's interests with respect to the employee, or multiple employers have common control. In most circuits, a four-factor economic reality test is applied: (1) direct or indirect power to hire, fire, discipline, or change working conditions; (2) ability to set compensation and means of payment; (3) maintenance of employment records; and (4) direct or indirect supervision and control of work schedules or conditions of employment. The recent trend is for courts to consider additional factors, such as resource sharing by employers; whether an entire business is shifted between primary and secondary employers; and whether original and secondary employers share business purpose, management, and staff.

[Natasha Dorsey, *FLSA Liability Issues and Influence over the Employment Relationship*, Foley & Lardner LLP (Nov. 11, 2013), available at Lexology.com]

California AB 1897, signed September 28, 2014, holds companies that use workers supplied by a labor contractor jointly liable for payment of wages and income tax withholding, and for failure to secure Worker's Compensation coverage. But it does not apply to workers who are exempt under the administrative, executive, and professional exceptions. As a result, non-exempt workers from a staffing company do not have to prove joint employer status to collect from a contracting company, but they are required to give notice to the company at least 30 days before filing a civil action naming the company as liable. AB 1897 does not apply to companies with fewer than 25 employees, including those supplied by the staffing company, or companies that have fewer than five employees supplied by a staffing company at a given time. [Baker & McKenzie, *Certain California Employers Who Use Staffing Agencies and Contractors Statutorily Liable for Wage and Hour and Safety Violations* (Dec. 26, 2014), available at Lexology. com]

In 2000, the NLRB ruled that temporary workers could be included in the same bargaining unit as permanent employees, provided that the characteristics of the jobs were similar. But in 2004, the NLRB overturned this decision and ruled that the consent of both the agency supplying the workers and the company where the services are performed is required before temporary workers can be made part of the bargaining unit. [*M.B. Sturgis Inc.*, 331 N.L.R.B. 173 (Aug. 25, 2000), overruled by *Oakwood Care Center*, 343 N.L.R.B. 76 (Nov. 19, 2004)]

In an important ruling from mid-2015, the NLRB found Browning-Ferris Industries and Leadpoint to be joint employers. Leadpoint supplied workers to Browning-Ferris to sort materials at Browning-Ferris' recycling plant. The contract designated Leadpoint as the employer, and it was in charge of hiring and payroll, But Browning-Ferris had a contractual right to set working hours and processes and sometimes could reject workers supplied by Leadpoint. The NLRB rejected a 30-year-old standard, and returned to the traditional common-law test of joint employment (as expressed in the Restatement (2d) of Agency: sharing or co-determining the essential terms and conditions of employment—even if the contractual right of control is never exercised. [*Browning-Ferris Indus. of California, Inc.*, 362 N.L.R.B. No. 186 (Aug. 27, 2015); see James J. Long et al., *Franchise, Antitrust, Distribution and Dealer Newsletter*, Briggs and Morgan (Oct. 30, 2015), available at Lexology.com. See also Steven M. Swirsky and Daniel J. Green, *Does the NLRB's New Joint-Employer Standard Mean That a Corporate Social Responsibility Policy Can Turn a Customer Into a Joint Employer?*, Epstein Becker Green (Aug. 30, 2016), available at Lexology.com: maintaining a corporate social responsibility policy governing the labor policies of suppliers and affiliates might result in being treated as a joint employer based on exercise of control over the supplier's or affiliate's policies.]

A mid-2016 NLRB decision finds a construction company and temp agency to be joint employers because of their potential for future joint projects: the construction company placed conditions on hiring and the characteristics of workers assigned to it. [*Retro Environmental, Inc./Green JobWorks, LLC*, 364 N.L.R.B. No. 70 (Aug. 16, 2016); see Kathleen M. Tinnerello, Howard M. Bloom & Philip B. Rosen, *NLRB Finds Joint Employers Despite Speculative Future Relationship*, Jackson Lewis PC (Sept. 6, 2016), available at Lexology.com]

For three decades (since 1984), the NLRB only imposed liability based on direct control, such as sharing or co-determining hiring, firing, and discipline. In 2014, however, the NLRB took a new tack, examining the extent to which franchised operations (e.g., McDonald's) are responsible for labor conditions at franchise locations. Courts may refuse to find a franchisor liable if it does not have authority over key aspects of employment; giving advice to franchisees does not mean that the advice can be enforced. [Jeffrey S. Klein, Nicholas J. Pappas and Sarah Martin, *Claims Against Franchisors as Alleged "Employers,"* Weil Gotshal & Manges LLP (Oct. 22, 2014), available at Lexology.com. See, e.g., *Orozco v. Plackis*, 757 F.3d 445 (5th Cir. 2014)]

Mid-2016 marked the first time in which a class action was certified in a McDonald's pay equity case. The suit, filed in 2014, alleges deliberate, systematic underpayment of employees at five McDonald's restaurants owned by the same franchisee in Northern California, in the forms of unpaid overtime, deliberate mis-recording of time on time cards, failure to pay minimum wage, and failure to pay accrued wages to employees who quit or were fired. Millions of dollars are at stake, given the allegations relate to approximately 500 employees. The franchisee settled the case for $700,000, leaving open the question of McDonalds' liability as parent corporation. On the issue of unpaid overtime, the judge said that McDonalds' argument that it was not liable "bordered on the specious." The franchises received overtime tracking software from McDonald's. The suit alleged that the software was programmed to treat overnight shifts and day shifts worked by an employee as occurring on two different days, even if the employee actually worked more than eight hours in a 24-hour period. [Editorial board, *A Step Forward for Fair Pay at McDonald's*, NYTimes.com (July 15, 2016)]

Later in 2016, McDonald's agreed to pay $3.75 million to settle a suit about McDonald's status as joint employer with respect to alleged wage and hour violations at a Bay Area franchise location. This was the first time McDonald's agreed to pay a franchisee's liability. [FindLaw Employment Law News blog, *McDonald's Settles with Franchise Workers for $3.75 Million* (Nov. 15, 2016), available at FindLaw.com]

After *Browning-Ferris*, some states are passing statutes to clarify the status of franchisors, focusing on control a company could potentially exert over the employees of another company. Georgia, Indiana, Louisiana, Michigan, Texas, Tennessee, Utah, and Wisconsin have passed legislation to protect franchisors from joint employer treatment and California, Colorado, Massachusetts, Oklahoma, Pennsylvania, Vermont and Virginia have introduced similar legislation.

The Texas statute provides that a franchisor is only considered the employer of the franchisee's employees for purposes of employment discrimination, health and safety, wage and hour, or Worker's Compensation claims if a Texas court finds that the franchisor exercised an unusual degree of control over the franchisee or its employees. [Jonathan J. Spitz, Jason R. Carruthers and Kathleen M. Tinnerello, *New Georgia Law Says Franchisors Generally Not Employers of Franchisees or Franchisees' Workers*, Jackson Lewis PC (May 5, 2016), available at Lexology.com; Sheila Raftery Wiggins et al., *More States Enact Laws: Franchisors Are Not "Joint Employers,"* Duane Morris LLP (May 10, 2016), available at Lexology.com]

In the IRS's latest compliance initiative, most companies with leased employees were found to be in compliance with the rules. The few exceptions often used Employee Plans Compliance Resolution System (EPCRS) to correct their failures, so there were few enforcement actions against non-compliant plans. Leased employees must be treated as common-law employees under the minimum participation, minimum coverage, vesting, nondiscrimination, and other pension rules.

The IRS says that there are four requirements for being a leased employee:

1. An agreement between a recipient company and a leasing organization to use the person's service, with a fee to the leasing organization;

2. The worker provides substantially full-time services for at least one year for the recipient, at least 1,500 hours in any 12-month period;

3. The recipient company has primary direction or control over services performed, such as when, where, how, in what order, and by whom services will be performed;

4. Considering all facts and circumstances, the leasing company is the common-law employer of the worker. [Guest Article, Deloitte's Washington Bulletin, *IRS Compliance Initiative Finds Most Plan Sponsors Are Correctly Applying the Leased Employee Rules* (Jan. 17, 2012) (benefitslink.com)]

The First Circuit dismissed a sexual harassment case against a parent corporation, on the grounds that the plaintiff was actually employed by a subsidiary corporation. The First Circuit held that the subsidiary, not the parent, issued the plaintiff's W-2 form and had its own accounts, records, and payroll. [*DeLia v. Verizon Commc'ns Inc.*, 656 F.3d 1 (1st Cir. 2011)]

In early 2017, the Fourth Circuit applied a six-factor test, holding that neither the employers' good faith nor the legitimacy of the business relationship between employers determines if they are joint employers for FLSA purposes. In this reading, there is joint employment when multiple entities share, allocate responsibility for, or otherwise codetermine the essential terms and conditions of employment (whether this is done formally or informally, directly or indirectly), as long as the worker is an employee and not an independent contractor. This test, which focuses on the relationship between the two employers, may be less favorable to many employers than the economic reality test that the Fourth Circuit rejected. [*Salinas v. Commercial Interiors Inc,* 848 F.3d 125 (4th Cir. 2017); see Molly Hughes Cherry, *Fourth Circuit Pronounces Joint Employer Test Under FLSA,* Nexsen Pruet (Feb. 1, 2017), available at Lexology.com; Brian E. Spang, Bruce M. Steen & Michael D. Mandel, *"Not Completely Disassociated": 4th Circuit Creates New FLSA Joint Employer Test,* McGuireWoods LLP (Feb. 2, 2017), available at Lexology.com]

The Fourth Circuit rendered another joint employment decision on the same day. Independent contractors working for an intermediary sued DIRECTV and the intermediary under the FLSA, asserting that they were actually employees of both as joint employees. Here, too, the Fourth Circuit found joint employment because the two potential employers were "not completely dissociated" with respect to the workers. [*Hall v. DIRECTV LLC,* 846 F.3d 757 (4th Cir. 2017). See Richard R. Meneghello, *Joint Employment Jolt: Federal Appeals Court Creates New and Troubling Standard,* Fisher Phillips (Jan. 30, 2017), available at Lexology.com.]

The District Court for the Northern District of Texas applied a hybrid test, involving both economic realities and common-law control (right to hire, fire, supervise, and schedule work), with the most important factor being the alleged employer's right to control the employee's conduct. The suit was brought by the EEOC against a cell phone repair company that allegedly discriminated against two deaf applicants. The defendant argued that the plaintiffs did not apply to the defendant but rather to the staffing agency that the defendant used to find contingent workers. The district court allowed the case to go to trial. [*EEOC v. S&B Indus.,* Civil Action No. 3:15-CV-0641-D, 2016 U.S. Dist. LEXIS 169483 (N.D. Tex. Dec. 8, 2016); see Jeff Barnes, *A Contingency Plan for a Contingent Workforce: Ensuring Workplace Protections for Staffing Agency Workers,* Fisher Phillips (Feb. 1, 2017), available at Lexology.com]

The Eleventh Circuit reversed the NLRB's finding that stagehands were employees of a referral service. The NLRB held a union election and certified a union as the stagehands' bargaining representative. The Eleventh Circuit held that the stagehands were independent contractors, so the NLRB did not have jurisdiction. The stagehands' work was controlled by event producers and touring crews, not the referral company, which did not control the details of their work. The referral company did not withhold taxes; the stagehands signed contracts as independent contractors; they used their own tools; and their insurance came from the customers, not the referral service. [*Crew One Productions Inc. v. NLRB,* 811 F.3d 1305 (11th Cir. 2016); see John T.L. Koenig, *11th Circuit Overturns NLRB: Finds Atlanta-Area Stagehands Are Independent Contractors,* Barnes & Thornburg LLP (Feb. 4, 2016), available at Lexology.com]

A plaintiff, Thompson, was hired by a company, but trained by its sister company. After a year, she was told to fill out an application to work at the second company. From then on, the second company issued her paychecks but there was no change in her job duties, job location, pay, or supervisors. She resigned and sued both companies under the FLSA. The defendants said that her original employer was no longer in existence. Thompson said that the second company was responsible for the FLSA violations as a successor. The Third Circuit agreed that the second company could be sued as a successor, using federal rather than state law on issues such as continuity of operations and whether the alleged successor was on notice of the violations. [*Thompson v. Real Estate Mortg. Network*, 748 F.3d 142 (3d Cir. 2014)]

The Third Circuit held that a company that uses temporary employees from a staffing agency can be sued under Title VII if racial discrimination occurs during the assignment. The decision factors are the hiring party's right to control the manner and means of performing the work. In this case, the company made payments to the staffing agency, but the payments were the equivalent of direct compensation based on the number of hours worked. [*Faush v. Tuesday Morning, Inc.*, 808 F.3d 208 (3d Cir. Nov. 18, 2015)]

§ 1.12 APPLICABLE TESTS

[A] The 20-Factor Test

Determining employee status is not a simple matter. The test an employer will be subject to depends on whether the issues arises in the context of the Internal Revenue Code, the Fair Labor Standards Act, or other labor law, and whether the employer is asked to redress underpayments and pay fines to the government and/or pay damages in an employee's civil suit.

The internal IRS documents used to train tax auditors set out 20 factors to be used to determine if income tax withholding is required:

1. If the employer gives instructions that the employee has to follow;

2. If the employer trains the employee;

   ■ **TIP:** Don't assign independent contractors to take training sessions with employees!

3. If the person renders services that are specific to him or her and can't be delegated to someone else;

4. If the employer provides whatever assistants are needed for the work (someone who provides his own assistants is more likely to be an independent contractor);

5. Whether the services are integrated into the employer's ordinary work, or are separate;

6. If the work relationship continues over time;

■ **TIP:**   Independent contractors should not be asked to be on call.

7. If the worker is subject to a shift system or other established, structured work hours or work schedule;

8. If the employer demands the worker's full-time commitment;

9. If the worker works for other companies at the same time (if the answer is "yes," it tends to imply independent contractor status, although part-time common-law employees may hold more than one job);

10. If work is done on the employer's premises;

11. If the employer determines the order or sequence of tasks to be done to accomplish the overall task;

12. If the worker has to submit regular oral or written reports;

13. If payment is by time (hour, week, or month) rather than project;

14. If the employer supplies tools and materials;

15. If the worker has to make a significant financial investment to accomplish the tasks;

16. If the employer pays business and travel expenses;

17. If the worker has a profit-and-loss interest in the underlying business of the employer;

18. If the worker gets paid by the employer's customers;

19. The employer's right to fire the worker (as distinct from carrying out the termination provisions of a contract, or refusing to renew the contract) tends to imply employee status;

20. The possibility of the worker's becoming liable to the employer if he or she quits suggests independent contractor status, because this is consistent with remedies for breach of contract.

At a minimum, if the IRS examines records and determines that common-law employees were incorrectly treated as independent contractors, the employer will have to make up the employment taxes that should have been paid but were not. Additional penalties may also be imposed. If the employer filed the required information returns (W-2s and 1099s) and did not intentionally misclassify the worker, then the penalty will be limited to 1.5% of the employee's wages, plus 20% of the FICA taxes that went unpaid because of the incorrect classification.

Those penalties are doubled if the information returns were not filed (unless there was no willful neglect, and there was reasonable cause for failure to file). Even heavier penalties are assessed if the employer not merely was mistaken about filing responsibilities, but deliberately attempted to avoid taxation.

The IRS's Topic 762, Independent Contractor vs. Employee says that evidence for characterization falls into three categories: Behavioral Control (the right, via instructions, training, etc., to direct or control how the work is done); Financial Control (whether business expenses are reimbursed; worker's investment in facilities to do the work; how the worker is paid; extent to which the worker can gain profits or risk losses); and the relationship between the parties (e.g., written contract terms; worker's ability to work for others as well; presence or absence of employment-type benefits). [<http://www.irs.gov/taxtopics/tc762.html> (revised Dec. 30, 2016) (last accessed Jan. 28, 2017). See also IRS Publication 1779, *Independent Contractor or Employee*.]

Either the worker or the firm can file IRS Form SS-8, available from <http://www.irs.gov/pub/irs-pdf/fss8.pdf> (revised May 2014) (last accessed Jan. 28, 2017) to obtain an IRS determination (for federal income tax and withholding purposes) whether an individual is an employee or an independent contractor. It calls for information such as the firm's business, what the worker does (and his or her job title), and if there is a written service agreement. Part II of the form assesses behavioral control, Part III financial control, and Part IV the relationship between company and worker. Part V assesses the working conditions of salespersons and those who provide services directly to customers. In 2011, the IRS created a new program, the Voluntary Classification Settlement Program (VCSP), under which employers can voluntarily re-classify workers to resolve past issues instead of waiting to be audited.

The VCSP was expanded in 2012 so more businesses, especially large employers, can use an inexpensive option to re-classify workers. Even employers that are being audited by the IRS (other than employment tax audits) can use the VCSP. In general, employers will be ineligible for VCSP if they did not file the required 1099s for the past three years for the workers whom they wish to reclassify, but this requirement was waived until June 30, 2013. The employer must consistently have treated the workers in question as non-employees. The ordinary payroll tax statute of limitations applies, whereas participants used to be subject to a special six-year statute of limitations. Application is made on Form 8952 at least 60 days before the employer intends to treat the workers in question as employees. Employers in the program pay about 1% of the reclassified workers' wages for the previous year, without interest or penalties. [Announcement 2012-45, 2012-51 I.R.B. 724, Announcement 2012-46, 2012-51 I.R.B. 725, discussed in *Voluntary Classification Settlement Program*, <http://www.irs.gov/Businesses/Small-Businesses-%26-Self- Employed/Voluntary-Classification-Settlement-Program> (Sept. 14, 2016) (last accessed Jan. 28, 2017)]

[B]   Safe Harbor Treatment

In 1979, Congress passed a safe harbor provision, Section 530 of the Revenue Act of 1978. Under this provision, if an employer treats someone as an independent contractor, the IRS will not be able to reclassify that person as an employee (and will not be able to assess back taxes and penalties) as long as the employer made the characterization reasonably and in good faith. Employers can also apply for a refund of penalties that they believe were improperly assessed.

There are three safe harbor tests for reasonableness:

1. The court system or the IRS has created published authority (e.g., decisions, IRS rulings, or IRS Technical Advice Memorandums) that justifies independent contractor treatment in similar situations;

2. The IRS has already audited the employer, and the audit did not uncover any problems of worker characterization;

3. There is an established practice, within a significant segment of the employer's industry, of treating people who do similar work as independent contractors.

To use the safe harbor, the employer must have treated the person consistently as an independent contractor, including filing Form 1099 as necessary. If the person was treated as a common-law employee at any time after December 31, 1977, the safe harbor will not be available.

See Publication 1976, "Section 530 Employment Tax Relief Requirements," <http://www.irs.gov/file_source/pub/irs-pdf/p1976.pdf> (last accessed Jan. 28, 2017), for relief for businesses with reasonable basis for saying a worker is not an employee.

[C]   Other Tests of Employee Status

The fundamental test is ability to control work behavior, both as to methods and as to results. This is the test used to determine employee status for ERISA purposes.

State unemployment insurance coverage typically depends either on the common-law right of control, or supplying a worker with a workplace, tools, and materials in addition to control. Most states use an "ABC test": someone who performs services is an employee, and the employer must pay unemployment insurance premiums for that person, unless:

-   the person is customarily engaged in an independent trade, business, profession, or occupation;

-   no direction or control is given in performing the services;

- the services are not performed in the usual course of the employer's business, or are not performed within any regular business location of the employer.

The employer must pay unemployment insurance plus penalties and interest for misclassified workers.

The FLSA test is based on economic reality. In other words, someone who is not economically dependent on a company, and is not an integral part of its operations, would not be an employee. Factors in the decision include:

- The worker's investment in facilities or equipment;

- Presence or absence of opportunity to earn profits or suffer losses due to managerial or special skills;

- Degree of control others have over the person's work;

- Permanence of the work relationship;

- Skill required to perform the services.

In this case, misclassification can lead to a duty to pay any unpaid minimum wages and overtime, plus liquidated damages, attorneys' fees, and court costs.

A Nevada statute (Rev. Stat. SSR 224), signed June 2, 2015, establishes a conclusive presumption that a person who meets certain conditions is an independent contractor and not an employee. A person is conclusively presumed to be an independent contractor if the contract with the principal requires the person to hold state or local business licenses and to be insured or bonded, and if the person meets at least three of five criteria. The criteria are having control and discretion over the means and manner of work and the results; control over the time the work is performed; the person is not obligated to work exclusively for the employer; the person can hire assistants; and the person has a substantial capital investment in the business. [Rick D. Roskelley and Kathryn B. Blakey, *Nevada Establishes Conclusive Presumption for Independent Contractor Status*, Littler Mendelson (June 10, 2015), available at Lexology.com]

Dancers, exotic and otherwise, have been plaintiffs in a number of employee classification cases.

The District Court for the Northern District of Georgia rejected the argument that male strippers were exempt from the FLSA as creative professionals, which would require invention, originality, or talent in a recognized field or artistic or creative endeavor. The court noted that original choreography was not required and the strippers were hired based on their looks; no dance training was required. [*Henderson v. 1400 Northside Drive*, 110 F. Supp. 3d 1318 (N.D. Ga. 2015); Briggs and Morgan, *Are Male Strippers Exempt from the FLSA as Creative Professionals?* (June 30, 2015), available at Lexology.com]

A New York federal judge awarded over $10 million in back pay to approximately 2,000 current and former exotic dancers in a class action against Rick's Cabaret for unpaid wages between 2005 and 2012. In September 2013, the court found that the dancers were employees and not independent contractors and, consequently, were covered by the New York Labor Law as well as the FLSA, [*Hart v. Rick's Cabaret Int'l*, 967 F. Supp. 2d 901 (Sept. 10, 2013); the case settled in 2015 for $15 million (including both payments to the dancers and to class counsel), No. 09-CV_3043 PAE/RLE (S.D.N.Y. 2015).

Six exotic dancers were awarded $196,956 in unpaid minimum wages and overtime by a jury, and the judge added $68,230 in liquidated damages (because of employer bad faith), for a total recovery of $265,276. The plaintiffs alleged that they were mis-classified as independent contractors. The judge found that the dancers were employees because their performances were integral to the clubs' business. The Fourth Circuit affirmed in mid-2016. [*McFeeley v. Jackson Street Entm't LLC et al.*, No. 8:12-cv-01019 (D. Md. Feb. 9, 2015), *aff'd*, 825 F.3d 235 (4th Cir. 2016). Adult entertainment dancers have been found to be employees rather than independent contractors in, e.g., *In re Penthouse Executive Club Compensation Litig.*, Master File No. 10 Civ. 1145 (KMWV), 2014 U.S. Dist. LEXIS 5864 (S.D.N.Y. Jan. 14, 2014); *Stevenson et al. v. The Great Am. Dream, Inc.*, No. 1:12-CV-3359-TWT (class certified, N.D. Ga. Aug. 14, 2014); see Joshua F. Naylor and Jessica Perry, *Strippers and the Fair Labor Standards Act: Lessons for All Employers*, Orrick (Jan. 22, 2014), available at <http://blogs.orrick.com/employment/2014/01/22/strippers-and-the-fair-labor-standards-act-lessons-for-all-employers/> (last accessed Aug. 11, 2017)]

The District Court for the Western District of Virginia held that strippers who are required to dance to music streamed over the Internet are employees covered by the FLSA. FLSA coverage can be individual (because a worker engages in interstate commerce or production of goods for interstate commerce) or enterprise coverage, where employees engage in commerce in an enterprise with annual gross volume of $500,000 or more. The district court held that the dancers were required to use an instrumentality of interstate commerce—the Internet. [*Foster v. Gold & Silver Private Club, Inc.*, No. 7:14CV00698, 2015 U.S. Dist. LEXIS 165217 (W.D. Va. Dec. 8, 2015)]

Professional cheerleaders have brought wage theft suits against five NFL teams, charging misclassification as independent contractors. Cheerleaders say they worked long hours without overtime, for less than minimum wage, were fined for minor infractions, and had to work while injured. Cheerleaders claim that they also had to make weight requirements and were sexually harassed. The Oakland Raiders and Tampa Bay Buccaneers have settled suits for over $2 million in back pay. [Nily Rozic and Lorena Gonzalez, *Cheerleaders, Until They See Their N.F.L. Paychecks*, NYTimes.com (Sept. 12, 2015)]

California adopted legislation in July 2015, effective January 1, 2016, making cheerleaders for professional sports teams employees who are eligible for minimum wage, overtime, Worker's Compensation, and paid sick leave. Comparable legislation was introduced in New York, and suits were filed in Florida, New York, and Ohio. [Sharon B. Bauman et al., *Something to Cheer About: Cheerleaders Declared Employees in California*, Manatt Phelps & Phillips LLP (Aug. 7, 2015), available at Lexology.com]

The New York Court of Appeals held that certain yoga instructors were independent contractors. The studio had some teachers on its staff, who were employees, and some non-staff teachers. The state Unemployment Insurance Appeal Board found the studio liable for unemployment insurance contributions for the non-staff instructors, whom the board treated as employees. But the Court of Appeals held that the studio did not exercise enough control over the results and the means to achieve them to treat the non-staff teachers as employees. They set their own schedules; decided if they would be paid by the hour or take a percentage of fees paid for the class; they were at financial risk because they were not paid unless a minimum number of students took the class; and they were allowed to teach at other studios. [*Yoga Vida NYC, Inc. v. Commissioner of Labor*, 64 N.E.3d 276 (N.Y. 2016); see Allan S. Bloom, Carolyn M. Dellatore & Guy Brenner, *Yoga Instructors Can Be Independent Contractors, Says NY Court of Appeals*, Proskauer Rose LLP (Oct. 28, 2016), available at Lexology.com]

§ 1.13 BENEFITS FOR CONTINGENT WORKERS

This issue came to prominence in connection with Microsoft "perma-temps" who were characterized by the company as freelancers and independent contractors, paid through invoices submitted to the accounts payable department rather than through the payroll process. The IRS ruled that these people were really common-law employees. They sued to be held eligible to participate in Microsoft's savings and employee stock ownership plans.

The Ninth Circuit ruled that eligibility for participation depends on being a common-law employee; the form in which payment is rendered is not relevant. The court also rejected the agreement signed by the workers, characterizing them as ineligible for plan participation, on the grounds that an agreement of this type cannot alter employee status. [*Vizcaino v. Microsoft Corp.*, 97 F.3d 1187 (9th Cir. 1996), *aff'd*, 120 F.3d 1006 (9th Cir. 1997), *cert. denied*, 522 U.S. 1088 (1998)] In 1999, the Ninth Circuit held that temporary agency workers can participate in the stock plan if they satisfy the common-law control test.

In December 2000, Microsoft agreed to pay $96.9 million to settle the *Vizcaino* case and another pending case.

In March 2003, the Third Circuit decided an important case, holding that to draft a benefits plan to exclude hourly employees does not violate ERISA. [*Bauer v. Summit Bancorp.*, 325 F.3d 155 (3d Cir. 2003)] In this analysis, ERISA allows the employer to deny participation for any reason, as long as ERISA's age and length of service requirements are respected. Of course, if the employer wishes to draft the plan to cover hourly as well as salaried workers, this is permissible.

The Tenth Circuit held that it was reasonable for a pension plan administrator to rely on the method of payment, the plan provisions, and payroll data to deny coverage to a contract worker who was not on the corporate payroll. [*Scruggs v. ExxonMobile Pension Plans*, 585 F.3d 1356 (10th Cir. 2009); see Mercer Select, *Contractor Isn't Eligible "Employee" Under Pension Plan, Appeals Court Says* (Nov. 19, 2009) (benefitslink.com)]

As the proportion of gig workers (i.e., those undertaking tasks on demand, often through an online marketplace) increases, competition for their services increases. Employers want to be considered a preferred client of gig workers. According to a report by Upwork, *Freelancing in America,* almost two-thirds of independent workers they surveyed say their freelance out of choice, not necessity; 79% prefer freelancing to full-time work; and 52% say they have the right amount of work (averaging 36 hours of work a week). Gig workers want portable benefits, and availability of benefits can guide their choice of assignments. Gig workers value being respected, being paid on time, and not having to complete too much paperwork—all things that do not cost the employer anything to provide.

However, gig workers' strongest preference in benefits is for health insurance—but covering them under an Employee Group Health Plan (EGHP) creates a serious risk that the worker will be considered a common-law employee and not an independent contractor. Uber and Etsy have an arrangement under which Stride Health acts as a health insurance broker, offering gig workers health plans that the workers pay for themselves. Gig workers often feel valued if they are included in company activities or programs—but the employer should consider whether this will lead to their being characterized as employees. [mark@trampsteamer.com, *What Benefits Can Companies Offer Gig Workers?*, shrm.org (Mar. 21, 2017) (benefitslink.com)]

§ 1.14 WORK SCHEDULING

[A] Overview

To an ever-increasing extent, new (and usually longer) schedules are replacing the conventional nine-to-five or eight-to-four workday. Some employees will have to work overtime and weekend hours occasionally. Some will have to work unconventional hours as a long-range or permanent condition of employment. As business becomes more international, it becomes necessary to be able to deal with customers during their workweek—which may occur on a very different schedule from the traditions of the U.S. workplace.

The FLSA allows employers to define the workweek as seven days starting on any day and any time of day—but, once the schedule is established, non-exempt employees must be paid overtime for work in excess of 40 hours per week. The FLSA workweek is not necessarily the same as the calendar week or the business' scheduled or pay week. Workers who are assigned to work, and do work, four 10-hour days in the same workweek are not entitled to overtime under the FLSA. However, if the employee actually works 42 hours in that week, two hours of overtime pay is required even if the employee was not scheduled for the extra work. [John E. Thompson, *The Legal Implications of Nontraditional Workweeks*, Workforce Mgmt. Online (October 2008) (benefitslink.com)]

"Flextime" is a schedule under which employees commit to working at least a certain number of hours per day, week, or month, and also agree to be present at certain agreed-upon times (e.g., for the weekly staff meeting or when customer demand is highest), but otherwise set their own hours to complete their assignments. Flextime can be an Americans with Disabilities Act (ADA) "reasonable accommodation" and can also be used by employees taking FMLA leave. [BLR/HR Daily Advisor Employee Fringe Benefit Survey Series: *Telecommuting, Flextime and Dress Code Practices* (2010) (benefitslink.com)]

There is a basic division between hourly workers, who get more pay if they put in longer hours, and salaried workers, whose compensation does not vary with the number of hours worked. Controversial 2016 DOL rules would have greatly expanded the availability of overtime, but the regulations did not take effect.

It is customary, although not legally required, for hourly employees to clock out when they leave the workplace (e.g., for lunch breaks or to do personal errands). They are not normally paid for this nonwork time. Salaried employees are usually not charged for such nonwork time, although personal time is sometimes charged against their sick leave. In a unionized workplace, the Collective Bargaining Agreement (CBA) determines issues like scheduling of meal breaks and when employees have to punch in and punch out.

See § 1.06 above, for discussion of meal and rest breaks.

Most of the states require employees to be given time off to vote and protect them from retaliation for taking time to vote. The time may be limited (e.g., two hours of paid leave), and/or the employer may get some input into when in the day the employee can take such leave. However, time off to vote is not required in Connecticut, the District of Columbia, Indiana, Louisiana, Maine, Michigan, Mississippi, Montana, New Hampshire, New Jersey, North Carolina, North Dakota, Oregon, Pennsylvania, Rhode Island, South Carolina, Vermont, and Washington. [Constangy Brooks, Smith & Prophete LLP, *Employer's Guide to State Voting Laws 2016* (Oct. 10, 2016) (benefitslink.com)]

San Francisco was the first city to adopt a "secure scheduling" law; several other cities subsequently adopted these measures. For example, Seattle requires that large retail and food service establishments provide their hourly, non-exempt employees with a good-faith estimate of the work schedule for the job when they are hired. The estimates must be updated each year or when the business model changes significantly. Under the Seattle law, work schedules, including on-call shifts, must be conspicuously posted at least 14 days in advance. Employees must be informed of changes in the schedule, and have a right to turn down work hours that were not in the original schedule. Employees are entitled to 10 hours of rest between shifts, unless they agree to return to work sooner (when they must be paid time and a half for the shortfall). [Guy Brenner and Elaine H. Lee, *Seattle Becomes Second City to Pass "Secure Scheduling" Ordinance*, Proskauer Rose LLP (Nov. 30, 2016), available at Lexology.com; Melanie Trottman, *Local Governments Arrive on Schedule to Buttress Part-Time Workers*, WSJ.com (Nov. 26, 2016)]

In mid-2017, Oregon became the first state to adopt a law requiring large employers (500 or more employees) to give hourly employees advance notice of their schedules, with additional compensation for last-minute changes. Employees are entitled to overtime pay for hours subtracted from their schedule at short notice. [Roman D. Hernandez and Samuel Hernandez, *Oregon Is Set to Become the First State in the Nation Requiring Employers to Give Hourly Employees Advance Notice of Their Work Schedules*, K&L Gates (July 13, 2017), available at Lexology.com]

[B] Telecommuting

To an increasing extent, employees are working from home or from other remote locations by "telecommuting," working on a computer and dealing with other employees and clients or customers by telephone or e-mail. Although telecommuting was hailed as a way to save money, save gasoline, and improve productivity, 2013 saw something of a reversal, with a growing belief that employees are not just more productive but more innovative when they collaborate face-to-face with co-workers. Large corporations such as IBM, Yahoo, Bank of America, and Aetna have ordered employees to reduce telecommuting, or work at the office all the time. Sometimes this is a concealed RIF—when the employer knows that the employee will not be willing to go back to full-time office work. Some employers say that remote work did not save the company as much money as anticipated. However, remote work is extremely popular with employees, and restricting it can cause tensions. [John Simons, *IBM, a Pioneer of Remote Work, Calls Workers Back to the Office*, WSJ.com (May 18, 2017) and *The Boss Wants You Back in the Office*, WSJ.com (July 25, 2017); Christopher Mims, *Why Remote Work Can't Be Stopped*, WSJ.com (June 4, 2017)]

A Gallup survey comparing 2012 and 2016 trends found more people working remotely, and for longer periods, in the later year. In 2016, 43% of employed Americans spent at least some time working remotely—4% more than 2012. Employees who work three to four days a week off-site feel the greatest sense of engagement with their work. [Niraj Chokshi, *Out of the Office: More People Are Working Remotely, Survey Finds,* NYTimes.com (Feb. 15, 2017)]

The 2010 Telework Enhancement Act, Pub. L. No. 111-292, requires federal agencies to establish telework policies (including policies dealing with disaster recovery) and determine which employees can telework. [Fred Schneyer, *President Signs Federal Telework Legislation*, plansponsor.com (Dec. 13, 2010)]

There are many practical steps that a company can take to make the arrangement smoother and more productive. The "teleworkers" should sign written agreements clarifying whether they are independent contractors or common-law employees; who they will report to; whether the telework assignment is expected to be temporary or permanent; how often they will be expected to go to the office; how many hours they will work; their work schedule; and promotion possibilities. Telework is most suitable for clearly defined projects with easily measured milestones.

Telecommuting relies heavily on electronics, so it's important to safeguard hardware and data, with backup equipment and an efficient source of online or other data storage.

Make sure the telecommuter has homeowner's insurance (if necessary, in the form of a rider or a separate policy) that covers the computer equipment against theft and damage. This is especially important if the employer supplies the equipment. A "consequential damages" provision that covers lost data and business opportunities is hard to find, but a valuable addition to the policy.

At first, Ford Motor Company obtained summary judgment in a suit brought by the EEOC. However, the Sixth Circuit reversed and reinstated the suit, holding that a steel buyer who had irritable bowel syndrome was otherwise qualified, either because her physical presence in the office rather than at home was not required, or because she requested reasonable accommodation for her disability. The Sixth Circuit three-judge panel held that, given technology's role in reducing the importance of a centralized workplace, the question was whether it was truly essential for the plaintiff to work at the office rather than at home [*EEOC v Ford Motor Co.*, 752 F.3d 634 (6th Cir. 2014)] The case was reheard en banc and reversed: the enc banc court found that presence in the office and face-to-face interaction with customers were an essential part of the job. [*EEOC v. Ford Motor Co.*, 782 F.3d 753 (6th Cir. en banc 2015)]

In mid-2015, the D.C. Circuit held that telecommuting was not a reasonable accommodation for a budget analyst who frequently missed work because of hypothyroidism, depression, and migraine. After she used up her FMLA leave, she requested being allowed to arrive at work at 11 a.m. (the other workers arrived between 6 a.m. and 8 a.m.) and telecommuting. The D.C. Circuit held that the job required being present in the office, on the regular schedule. [*Doak v. Johnson*, 798 F.3d 1096 (D.C. Cir. 2015)]

In a case about telecommuting by a pregnant employee, the trial court ruled for the employer; the Second Circuit reinstated part of the case but affirmed the dismissal of the counts under New York State human rights law. The plaintiff quit her job and moved from New York to Los Angeles when her husband got a new job. Her supervisor suggested that she continue to work but to use the bank's alternative work arrangement policy. The bank's policy treats failure to resume a traditional work schedule or location when an alternative arrangement is terminated as a voluntary quit. After the plaintiff started working in California, the bank placed all remote assignments under review. The next day, the plaintiff notified her supervisor that she was pregnant. The bank required all team leaders to be at the Buffalo office at least two days a week. She submitted a doctor's note saying she should not travel. Management said that there was not enough remote work, so she had to either return to Buffalo within 30 days, take short-term disability leave, or be terminated with 11 weeks' severance pay. She rejected the offer and got a lawyer. The bank agreed that she could continue to work remotely for the rest of her pregnancy, but reinstatement was conditioned on waiving claims for money damages. She sued under Title VII, the FMLA, and New York and California law. The Second Circuit upheld dismissal of many of the claims, but allowed the New York claims to continue. [*Sheng v. M&TBank Corp.*, 848 F.3d 78 (2d Cir. 2017); see D. Sharmin Arefin, *2nd Cir. Reverses Judgment in Favor of Bank Employer on "Remote Work" Pregnancy Discrimination Claims*, Maurice Wutscher LLP (Feb. 27, 2017), available at Lexology.com]

New York ruled in 2003 that a former telecommuter who lived in Florida and submitted work to a Long Island company over telephone lines was not entitled to New York unemployment benefits when the arrangement ended and the employer was no longer willing to allow her to work from home. The "work" occurred at her Florida home. [*Allen v. Comm'r of Labor*, 100 N.Y.2d 282 (N.Y. App. 2003)]

New York found that 100% of the earnings of a computer programmer who lives in Tennessee and spends only a quarter of his time in New York were taxable in New York, because he worked at home for his own convenience and not that of his employer. [*Matter of Huckaby v. State Div. of Tax Appeals*, 4 N.Y.3d 427, *cert. denied*, 546 U.S. 976 (2005)]

The District Court for the Eastern District of Louisiana ruled in mid-2016 that the FMLA threshold (50 employees) was satisfied because the plaintiff, who telecommuted from Louisiana, reported to an office in Florida with 50 or more employees: the relevant worksite was the place she reported to. However, she was unable to sue under the Louisiana Employment Discrimination Law, which excludes companies with fewer than 20 employees in Louisiana; her employer had only four employees within the state. [*Donahoe-Bohne v. Brinkmann Instruments*, No. 16-2766, 2016 U.S. Dist. LEXIS 77934 (E.D. La. June 15, 2016); see Dave Strausfeld, *For Telecommuter, FMLA 50-Employee Threshold Measured by Office to Which She Reported*, WK WorkDay Blog (June 23, 2016) (benefitslink .com)]

The Seventh Circuit affirmed dismissal of an FMLA interference claim but upheld the retaliation claim. The plaintiff was initially granted permission to work at home two days a week to care for her autistic son. When the employer ran into financial trouble, work-from-home arrangements were terminated suddenly. The HR department incorrectly told the plaintiff that she could not use FMLA leave to care for her son. The Seventh Circuit also upheld the award of liquidated damages, finding that the employer did not act in good faith when it misinformed the plaintiff. [*Wink v. Miller Compressing Co.,* No. 845 F.3d 821 (7th Cir. 2017); see Katrin Schatz, *A Cautionary Tale: How Sudden Changes to Intermittent FMLA Can Cost You,* Jackson Lewis PC (Jan. 17, 2017), available at Lexology.com]

See <http://www.eeoc.gov/facts/telework.html> (last accessed Jan. 28, 2017) for the EEOC's fact sheet on using telework to promote full employment opportunity for people with disabilities; how to supervise telecommuters; and the extent to which offering telework options is a reasonable accommodation to disability. But it has generally been held that the ADA does not require employers to grant permission to work at home as an accommodation to disabled employees. However, terminating a telework arrangement could be problematic. According to the D.C. Circuit, permitting a worker disabled by injuries to work at home for up to two days a week could be a reasonable accommodation. Therefore, a new managers' revoking permission to telecommute was discrimination. [*Woodruff v. Peters,* 482 F.3d 521 (D.C. Cir. Apr. 6, 2007)]

[C] Integrated Time Off

An integrated time-off system is an attendance policy that gives the worker the right to take a certain number of days off per year, no matter what the reason for being away from work. The value to the employer is that it keeps people at work because they no longer have an incentive to take sick days for every minor illness just because otherwise they would lose the time. A common system is to provide a certain amount of paid vacation (e.g., one to three weeks a year), six to eight paid holidays, and six sick days a year. Employers vary as to whether they allow unused sick days to be carried over from year to year, or impose a "use it or lose it" rule.

A PTO (Paid Time Off) program integrates vacation and sick days. An Integrated Disability Program (also known as "24-hour coverage") adds disability benefits to the mix. State law determines whether the employer must cash out unused PTO upon termination. If the employer has an established policy, it must be observed; changes in time-off policy must be posted, or employees must be given written notice. The plan must specify whether PTO accrues all at once at the beginning of the year or by the month, week, or pay period. Some state laws treat accrued PTO as vested, so forfeitures are illegal.

The policy should also explain the increments in which PTO can be taken—a full day only, or half days or less? For exempt employees, deductions for personal, vacation, and sick leave can be taken only as full days, and the employer is forbidden to make deductions that exceed the time actually taken. [See Rev. Rul. 2009-31, 2009-39 I.R.B. 35 and Rev. Rul. 2009-32, 2009-39 I.R.B. 398]

According to Mercer Absence and Disability Management Survey, in 2016, 63% of organizations had PTO plans—far more than the 38% level in 2010 and 50% level in 2013. However, 44% of survey respondents said that their employees took less than 80% of the PTO available to them. [Wolters Kluwer Law & Business, *Use of PTO Plans Continues to Increase* (Dec. 27, 2016) (benefitslink .com)]

The purpose of maintaining a PTO bank is to allow employees to decide how to use their time off, in the hope that they will appreciate this flexibility. Mercer's annual absence/disability management study showed the usage of PTO banks went from 38% of respondent employers in 2010 to 63% in 2015. Note that states that mandate paid sick leave do not forbid PTO banks, but administration becomes more complex because employees are entitled to a certain amount of sick leave. PTO banks are also vulnerable to abuse if sick employees insist on coming to work to preserve their days off for more enjoyable usage. Some risks of abuse can be mitigated by having PTO accrue over time, for example, two days a month rather than a block of 24 days a year. Employers considering implementing a PTO bank should consider whether employees will be allowed to roll over unused time to the next year and, if so, if limits will be imposed such as if employees can cash out unused time and keep the money or deposit it in a 401(k) plan or HSA. The payroll and HR systems must be capable of administering the plan and management must explain it to employees. Success will depend on managers being sympathetic and willing to adjust work schedules to employees' PTO utilization. [Joanne Sammer, *Employers Are Banking on Paid Time Off*, shrm.org (Jan. 9, 2017) (benefitslink.com)]

Some companies have adopted a flexible strategy called "unlimited PTO," "open vacation" or "flexible vacation" instead of limiting vacation days, to show their commitment to equality, or to reduce administrative work. (The theory is that, when no one accrues vacation time, it is not necessary to track the accrual.) However, companies that adopt such a strategy must be sure to obey state law. In California, "use it or lose it" vacation policies are forbidden, so the employer might have to make a large payout when an employee leaves. Other states, such as Texas and New York, allow the employer some discretion in making the final payout. To be sure to conform to all requirements, multistate companies often adopt nationwide policies of distributing pay for accrued vacation time in the final paycheck. A late-2014 article says that best practice is to limit unlimited vacation to exempts; a timekeeping system is already in place for hourly workers, who are not allowed to work off the clock or on vacation days. An unlimited vacation policy does not alter the employer's obligations to provide leave under, e.g., the FMLA or ADA. When there is mandatory paid sick leave, the employer cannot take away accumulated sick leave and sick leave must continue to accrue in the future. If employees are granted unlimited vacations, vacation time already accrued under the previous system can either be cashed out or the accruals can be exhausted gradually over time (which requires ongoing monitoring). [Susan F.

Eandi and Teresa Burlison, *Singing the Siren Song of Unlimited Vacation Policies*, Law360 (Oct. 15, 2014) (benefitslink.com)]

The Society for Human Resources Management reported in mid-2015 that about 3% of U.S. companies have some kind of unlimited vacation policy. The policy works best if employees already have flexible hours and a high degree of autonomy. If employees need a supervisor's permission to take vacation time, the company must ensure that it is enforced fairly and consistently, without favoritism. The company can require management or the HR department to approve more than a certain number of consecutive days off and vacation usage can be limited during especially busy periods. Controls should be imposed to reduce the number of employees who are on vacation at the same time. [Annie Lau, *Is an Unlimited Vacation Policy Right for Your Workplace?*, Fisher & Phillips LLP (July 1, 2015), available at Lexology.com]

[D]   Coping with Absenteeism

Employers must cope both with absenteeism (employees calling in sick when they are not sick enough to stay home) and presenteeism (when genuinely sick—and perhaps infectious—employees insist on coming to work). Epidemiologists suggest that a person with a contagious illness stay home for at least 24 hours after the fever and symptoms abate, About half (51%) of respondents to SHRM's survey said that they maintain a paid time-off bank, giving employees access to a specified number of days off for all reasons, up from 42% in 2009. When a flu or other epidemic occurs, some employers temporarily allow employees additional sick leave without reducing their vacation entitlement. [Sue Shellenbarger, *The Art of Calling in Sick—Or Toughing It Out*, WSJ.com (Oct. 23, 2012)]

EEOC technical guidance, *"Pandemic Preparedness in the Workplace and the Americans With Disabilities Act,"* permits employers to ask employees if they have cold or flu symptoms such as fever, sore throat, or chills; this is not a disability-related inquiry. It is also permissible to send employees home if they have symptoms. It is permissible for employers to adopt workplace infection control practices such as those set out on the OSHA Web page, "Workplace Safety and the Flu." [Melanie Trottman, *Flu Season Amplifies Calls for Paid Sick Leave*, WSJ.com (Feb. 22, 2013)]

[E]   Catastrophe Planning

Employers must be prepared for a variety of adverse events, including the man-made (terrorist attacks) and natural (weather events and epidemics). In addition to practical questions such as determining when the business will be able to open and assembling the necessary staff (when travel conditions may be difficult), the disaster will have employment tax consequences, and many other laws may be invoked as well.

IRS Notice 2006-59 permits creation of a disaster leave donation program: other employees donate leave time for the benefit of co-workers who miss work because of a presidentially declared disaster that causes severe hardship to the employee or family. The leave must be used in connection with the disaster, and the severity of the disaster determines the reasonable period of time during which leave can be taken. At the end of the specified post-disaster period, any unused leave must be returned to the donor. [Peter Alwardt, *Tax Considerations in Implementing Donated Leave Policies*, Eisner Amper (Jan. 14, 2013) (benefitslink .com)]

A natural disaster can require the employer to take steps under many different statutes. Under the FLSA, if the worksite is open but an exempt employee chooses to remain at home for weather-related reasons, the DOL considers this a personal absence. These rules were developed before the 2016 rules expanded overtime eligibility; probably, a new set of rules will evolve accordingly. For full days when an exempt employee did not report to work, the employer can treat it as unpaid leave or subtract it from the employee's accrued vacation time. If an employee is absent for one or more full days for personal reasons, the employee is still deemed to be salaried (rather than paid by the hour) if salary deductions are made on account of the absence—but the employer must deduct full days, not partial days. The employer is permitted to deduct partial days from the employee's leave bank, but if the leave bank is exhausted, it is not permissible to make salary deductions. Once exempt employees return to work, they can be required to make up the lost time. Non-exempt workers can be required to "catch up" only if they are paid overtime for hours over 40 per week. Employees who are on call and not free to leave (such as maintenance workers assigned to remain onsite during a disaster to perform emergency repairs) must be paid even if they are not given any work assignments. Employees must also be compensated if they are required to wait (e.g., stay in the workplace waiting for power to be restored).

There is a WARN Act exception for closings or layoffs caused by disasters, although the employer must still give as much notice as possible and must explain why less than 60 days' notice was given. USERRA forbids taking adverse employment action against a person (e.g., a National Guard member) who is called up for active duty during an emergency. The employer is entitled to timely notice of the call-up, although it can be given in writing or orally, and can come either from the service member or from an officer.

Employers must make decisions about benefit coverage. If coverage will continue during a plant closure, the employer should consult its benefits vendor. If the plan is subject to COBRA, the plan administrator must be notified if any employees lose coverage because they are not working. At that point, the administrator must provide COBRA notice; in practical terms, the notice may not be received if the employee has had to evacuate from the last known address on file with the employer. (The legal obligation is simply to send notice to the last known address.) Someone who is physically or emotionally injured by the disaster may also be entitled to ADA reasonable accommodation, as long the accommodation does not impose undue hardship on the employer.

OSHA obligates employers to protect employees from unreasonable dangers in the workplace, which could mean keeping them out of harm's way before, during, and after a disaster. Employees who are forced to work under unsafe conditions, or who suffer retaliation for refusing or reporting unsafe conditions, may be entitled to whistleblower protection. The National Labor Relations Act may require changes in a workplace that has become unsafe. Refusing to work under dangerous conditions might constitute protected concerted activity, even if only one employee is acting on behalf of others.

Unionized employers may be subject to force majeure clauses in the CBA that explain rights and duties in emergencies. If the disaster causes enough damage to force the employer to go out of business, the employer does not have an obligation to bargain with the union about the decision to go out of business—but effects bargaining will be required. A number of states provide that the employer's Unemployment Insurance experience account will not be charged for layoffs caused by a natural disaster. The Disaster Unemployment Assistance program helps people, including farm owners and the self-employed, who lost jobs as a direct result of a declared disaster. [Brooke Duncan III, *Addressing Employment Concerns in a Disaster*, Adams and Reese LLP (Aug. 19, 2016), available at Lexology.com]

Employees who check work-related e-mails or make telephone calls probably are entitled to be paid as if they had reported to work, even if the employer did not request that they work at home. Exempt employees are not entitled to extra pay if they are required to work longer hours as a result of disaster-related issues. Non-exempt workers must be paid for all time worked, although the employer can require approval for reporting to work before normal hours or staying later. Nevertheless, employees must be paid for time actually worked, even if contrary to directions. Commuting time is not compensable, so neither is extra commuting time caused by disaster conditions. [Robert Bernstein, *Taking Care of Business When Hurricanes, Storms, and Natural Disasters Hit*, Greenberg Traurig LLP (Oct. 7, 2016), available at Lexology.com]

Under Code § 139 and IRS guidance, when a disaster occurs, the employer can provide cash or benefits to assist employees affected by it. These payments are exempt from federal income and employment tax, and are deductible by the employer. Code § 139(a) provides that qualified disaster relief payments are not included in the employee's gross income; § 139(b) defines a qualified disaster relief payment as one that pays or reimburses personal, family, living, or funeral expenses caused by a disaster. A disaster, in turn, is defined as a presidentially declared disaster, a disaster caused by a common carrier accident, terrorism, military action, or anything else determined by the Secretary of the Treasury to be a catastrophic event. Recipients will probably not be taxed on amounts paid by a federal, state, or local government agency. But amounts are excluded from income only to the extent that the same expense is not already covered, e.g., by insurance.

Also covered are the repair or rehabilitation of the employee's personal residence (whether owned or rented) and repair or replacement of the contents of the personal residence required by the disaster. See IRS Publication 3833. However, replacement of lost wages or other income is not considered a qualified disaster relief payment. [Mary Hughes, *Employers May Provide Tax-Free Relief to Employees Hit By Storm, Attorney Says*, Human Resources Report (Nov. 5, 2012) (benefitslink.com)]

Severe weather conditions in recent winters highlighted the need for companies to maintain a policy about when employees are required to come to work despite weather problems; when they can work at home; and if they will be paid if it is impossible to get to work. (Another option is to give employees a choice between extra pay and comp time if they are able to come to work despite severe weather conditions.) When a storm is forecast for the next day or day after, advise employees to take work home with them, but let employees wait to come in until after the roads have been plowed. Sometimes it is worthwhile to make a deal with a local hotel near the workplace, where key employees can stay and avoid commuting problems. However, the workload is also likely to be low—if employees can't get to work, neither can customers. [Sarah E. Needleman, *It's Snowing. Do We Get the Day Off?*, WSJ.com (Feb. 4, 2011)]

NIOSH has a summary of cold stress conditions, with suggestions about protecting outdoor workers: scheduling maintenance and repair for the warmer months, or at least the warmer part of the day; provide extra or relief workers for long jobs; provide warm drinks in heated break areas; train employees about appropriate dress and how to recognize cold damage; provide extra socks and blankets; and keep a thermometer and chemical hot packs in the first aid kit. OSHA forbids retaliation against workers who reject unsafe work assignments. OSHA fall protection requirements are in effect if employees are ordered to the roof to remove snow. Also see OSHA's hazard alert about falls during snow removal. The NLRA also allows workers to refuse to work in unsafe conditions but, unless the employer agrees that driving is too dangerous, it is lawful to fire employees who refuse to drive to work in difficult conditions.

If the workplace does not open, or shuts down early for weather and sends non-exempt workers home in the middle of the shift, they are only entitled to pay for time actually worked. But some states, such as California Connecticut, Massachusetts, New Hampshire, New Jersey, New York, Oregon, Rhode Island, and Washington, D.C., have report-in laws requiring payment when employees are scheduled to work but are sent home early (A call-in pay requirement might be waived based on the employer's good-faith attempt to give reasonable advance notice to employees that they should not report.) [Alexander J. Passantino, *Juno How to Pay When Your Facilities Close for Weather-Related Reasons?*, Seyfarth

Shaw LLP (Jan. 26, 2015), available at Lexology.com—the title is a reference to 2015's Winter Storm Juno]

If exempt employees work at all, they must be paid for the full week, because the regulations do not include weather closures in circumstances permitting pay deductions. But if the business was closed for the entire week, and exempt employees did not work at all, the employer is not obligated to pay them. Exempt employees can be required to use paid time off such as vacation or personal time. If an employee has used up all paid time off, the employer is not permitted to take a salary deduction. If the business is open and an exempt employee chooses to stay home, accrued leave can be deducted from the individual's leave bank. If paid leave has been exhausted, pay can be reduced for full days of absences (see 29 C.F.R. § 541.602(b)(1)). If the employer knows that employees are working from home, they should be compensated for work time. [Sara H. Jodka, *Oh the Weather Outside Is Frightful! How Employers Can Handle the Impact of Inclement Weather (Polar Vortex Anyone?) and What NIOSH, OSHA, the NLRA and the FLSA Have to Say About It*, Porter Wright Morris & Arthur LLP (Jan. 6, 2014), available at Lexology.com]

An effective policy for inclement weather will specify who is authorized to decide whether to close the facility so employees will know whom to ask. There are several ways to notify employees of closings, early closings, or delayed opening—for example, recorded messages, phone trees, e-mail, social media, the company's Website and intranet, and voicemail, although some of these will not function if there is a power outage. Consider if employees will be permitted to bring their children to work if schools and daycare facilities are closed but the workplace is open. The employer should indicate how to report work and record hours for work at home.

A "state of emergency" is an officially declared request that people stay off the roads or that businesses close; it does not affect pay planning or make absences excused. However, non-emergency employees should not be disciplined for not coming to work during a state of emergency. [Diane M. Saunders, *Effective Inclement Weather Policies—Top 10 Factors to Consider*, Ogletree Deakins (Feb. 11, 2015), available at Lexology.com]

In 2009, in response to pandemic flu, the EEOC issued ADA guidance, which is also relevant to Ebola virus. Unless there is a direct threat, employers cannot ask employees or applicants about their exposure to Ebola or require a medical examination because this is considered a disability-related inquiry for ADA purposes. The employer can ask about exposure based on a reasonable belief, stemming from objective evidence, that the employee poses a direct threat or his or her job functions will be impaired. When employees return from travel during a pandemic, employers can legitimately ask about exposure before employee develops symptoms. It is also permitted to ask about exposure during personal travel to high-risk areas. Telework and leave are reasonable accommodations to control spread of infection. Employees can be required to use infection control tactics in the workplace, such as hand washing and proper disposal of tissues. [Phyllis Cheng, *Ebola: Best Practices for US Employers—6 Questions to Ask*, DLA Piper LLP (Nov. 12, 2014), available at Lexology.com]

In 2016, the newsworthy epidemic was the Zika virus, which is spread by mosquitos; by mothers to babies; and by contact with body fluids. OSHA's general duty clause requires employers to provide a safe and healthful workplace and protect employees against recognized hazards. Employers may have an obligation to develop a plan to protect employees who are likely to be exposed to Zika, for example through work travel to affected regions. The employer must track infections and provide medical surveillance for infected employees. Occupational Zika illnesses must be reported on the OSHA 300 log. A pregnant employee has the right to refuse an assignment that could result in Zika exposure and retaliation for turning down the assignment is unlawful. An employee who contracts Zika through occupational exposure can be entitled to temporary total disability benefits to replace the lost wages, plus medical expenses and an award reflecting any resulting permanent disability. Because Zika symptoms are typically mild, the disease might not be a serious health condition for FMLA purposes, but if it is, then leave must be provided. Zika itself is probably not an ADA disability but complications might produce a disability. [For general information about Zika, see <http://www.cdc.gov/zika/> (last updated Jan. 26, 2017) (last accessed Jan. 28, 2017); see Mark A. Lies II, Patrick D. Joyce and Adam R. Young, *Zika—Employer Liability Issues*, Seyfarth Shaw LLP (Feb. 11, 2016), available at Lexology.com]

§ 1.15 OVERTIME AND OVERTIME PLANNING

[A] Generally

One of the major functions of the FLSA is to require "time and a half for overtime" to be paid to certain employees who work more than 40 hours in a work week. They must receive 150% of their normal pay rate for the additional hours.

Traditionally, it was clear that blue-collar workers paid by the hour would qualify for overtime, and this is still true. Before DOL regulations were finalized in May 2016, many white-collar workers were exempt from overtime, either because of their duties or because they earned more than a specified amount. The 2016 rule greatly increases the amount, and shifts the focus to earnings and away from the employee's duties. However, because the rules have not yet come into effect, because they may be struck down legislatively or by court decisions, and because it takes many years for cases to go through the court system, the earlier rules will continue to have an impact in some contexts.

According to the D.C. Circuit, the FLSA does not require employers to pay overtime when a worker puts in more than eight hours in a particular day, as long as his or her hours for the week as a whole do not exceed 40. The plaintiff alleged that her CBA required payment of overtime, but even if that is true, the court ruled that it did not have federal subject matter jurisdiction over a contract interpretation claim. [*Fernandez v. Centerplate/NBSE*, 441 F.3d 1006 (D.C. Cir. 2006)]

The Tenth Circuit upheld the employer's contention that a plaintiff was salaried, holding that an isolated deduction does not prevent the employee from being salaried. Ellis was a store manager, who was paid $600, later increased to $625, and was classified as exempt. She was expected to work at least 50 hours a week. In a week when she reported only 40.91 hours, her check was reduced $31.20 for a partial day absence. The court said that even though there were 13 occasions when she worked less than 50 hours a week, this was the only time she was docked. The handbook had a mechanism for refunding improper deductions that were made in good faith. The Tenth Circuit also allowed the employer to use the "window of correction" defense: the exemption can be maintained by reimbursing employees for isolated or inadvertent incorrect deductions. It doesn't have to be both isolated and inadvertent. [*Ellis v. J.R.'s Country Stores, Inc.*, 779 F.3d 1184 (10th Cir. 2015)]

The Fifth Circuit ruled that it is permissible for an employer to structure the workweek in the way that requires the least overtime, even if it does not follow the employee's understanding of the workweek. The plaintiffs worked seven consecutive 12-hour shifts in each two-week pay period, which ran from Thursday to Wednesday. The plaintiffs said that the FLSA required calculation of overtime to use the Thursday-Wednesday workweek, but the employer calculated overtime on a Monday-Sunday pay period. As a result, the employees received less than 10 hours overtime per pay period; they asserted that they were entitled to 40 hours of overtime. The Fifth Circuit held that the workweek need only be a fixed, regularly recurring period of seven consecutive 24-hour days; it does not have to be a calendar week. [*Johnson v. Heckmann Water Resources*, 758 F.3d 627 (5th Cir. 2014)]

Certain categories of employees are exempt from the FLSA's minimum wage and overtime provisions. [29 U.S.C. § 213(a)(1)] The major exempt categories are executives, administrators, professionals, and outside salespersons.

Exempt workers do not have to be paid for weeks in which they do not work at all, but otherwise 29 C.F.R. § 541.118(a) provides that their salary cannot be reduced based on the number of hours worked or the number of hours of absences. The employer cannot reduce the wages of exempt employees for absences that were caused by the employer or the operating requirements of its business. Nor can the employer take deductions to penalize an exempt worker for work place infractions, other than violations of major safety rules.

Specifically, docking a worker's pay for "variations in quantity or quality of work" is appropriate for workers who are entitled to overtime, but not for exempt workers. The real test, however, is whether reductions are ever taken. In 1997, the Supreme Court ruled that police officers were exempt salaried employees, even though the employee manual said that pay could be docked for various disciplinary infractions: the mere possibility didn't make them nonexempt. [*Auer v. Robbins*, 519 U.S. 452 (1997)]

[B] Categories of Exempt Employees

The FLSA defines executives, professionals, and other categories of workers, based on their main responsibilities. However, the statute left many important questions unresolved, and furthermore the existing regulations expressed obsolete concepts about the workplace and the economy.

Until a final rule was promulgated in 2004, the minimum salary test for the white-collar exemption under the FLSA had remained pegged at $155 a week since 1976.

The final rule that took effect August 23, 2004 (69 Fed. Reg. 22122) provided for two exemptions from overtime eligibility for white-collar workers. The general test for exemption, for anyone earning $23,660 or more a year, was based on duties performed. A subsidiary test made a highly compensated employee earning $100,000 or more a year exempt from overtime.

In March 2014, the Obama administration issued an Executive Order directing the DOL to revise the overtime rules for white-collar employees. DOL issued proposed rules in mid-2015. Final rules were published May 18, 2016. The proposals made major changes in the treatment of employee compensation, treating a white-collar worker earning less than $913 a week, $47,476 a year, as eligible for overtime. The test for highly compensated employees was also amended, to $134,000 a year. The final rule does not include a "duties" test (e.g., that a person claimed to be exempt as a manager must spend at least 50% of work time on exempt duties). [Notice of Proposed Rulemaking: 80 Fed. Reg. 38515 (July 6, 2015); final regulation, 81 Fed. Reg. 32391 (May 23, 2016). See Marlene M. Nicolas and Evan C. Mix, *DOL Makes Last-Minute Tweaks to New Overtime Exemption Rules*, Sheppard Mullin Richter & Hampton LLP (May 19, 2016), available at Lexology.com.]

The DOL regulation was finalized in May 2016, with an intended final effect in December 2016. The regulation was supposed to make 4.2 million people, earning $47,476 per year or less, eligible for overtime pay in weeks where they worked over 40 hours. [Melanie Trottman and Eric Morath, *Businesses Assess Effects of New Overtime-Pay Rule,* WSJ.com (May 18, 2016)]

However, 21 states and over 50 business groups, led by the U.S. Chamber of Commerce, filed suits in the District Court for the Eastern District of Texas in September 2016. The attorneys general of Texas and Nevada asserted that the rule is unconstitutional and exceeds Congress' authority. The attorneys general alleged that the automatic update of the compensation threshold every three years was adopted without the mandatory rule-making process, denying stakeholders a chance to express their concerns. The district court issued a nationwide preliminary injunction that prevented the overtime rule from being implemented. [Melanie Trottman, *Group of 21 States Sues U.S. Over New Overtime-Pay Rule*, WSJ.com (Sept. 20, 2016); Melanie Trottman, *Court Halts Overtime Rule, Leaving Employers in Limbo*, WSJ.com (Nov. 22, 2016). The states that sued are Alabama, Arkansas, Alaska, Georgia, Indiana, Iowa, Kansas, Kentucky, Louisiana, Maine, Michigan, Mississippi, Nebraska, Nevada, New Mexico, Ohio, Oklahoma, South Carolina, Texas, Utah, and Wisconsin.]

The Department of Labor appealed the injunction to the Fifth Circuit prior to President Trump's inauguration. The state plaintiffs asked the Fifth Circuit to affirm the injunction, arguing that the DOL violated the statute by defining overtime eligibility by salary level rather than by job duties. [*State of Nevada et al. v. United States Dep't of Labor,* No. 4:16-CV-00731, 2016 U.S. Dist. LEXIS 162048, **167 Lab. Cas. (CCH) P36,489** (E.D. Tex. Nov. 22, 2016) (preliminary injunction); *Nevada v. DOL,* No. 16-41606 (5th Cir. Feb. 22, 2017) (DOL motion for 60-day extension of time to file reply brief, until May 1, 2017, granted); see Melanie Trottman, *Labor Department Appeals Injunction on Overtime-Pay Rule,* WSJ.com (Dec. 1, 2016); Jeffrey W. Brecher, *State Plaintiffs Urge Fifth Circuit to Affirm Nationwide Injunction Blocking DOL Overtime Rule,* Jackson Lewis PC (Jan. 17, 2017), available at Lexology.com]

On June 30, 2017, the DOL informed the Fifth Circuit that it will abandon the 2016 rule, but wants to re-start the rulemaking process, using the principle that the salary level needs to be updated, but using a lower salary, perhaps around $30,000–$35,000. The DOL said it would not re-propose the rule until the Fifth Circuit issued a decision that the agency has the authority to set a salary level at which overtime pay is required. [Donald P. Lawless, *U.S. Department of Labor Abandons Obama Overtime Rule,* Barnes & Thornburg LLP (July 11, 2017), available at Lexology.com] Under the pre-2016 rules, which are likely to be applied if the 2016 rules are definitively struck down—and which apply to cases working their way through the legal system when the 2016 rules were adopted—a worker is an exempt executive, not entitled to overtime pay, if:

- The person's primary duty is management either of the entire enterprise that employs him or her, or a recognized subdivision or department of the enterprise.

- He or she "customarily and regularly" directs the work of two or more fellow employees (or two full-time equivalents in an enterprise that has some part-time workers).

- He or she has hiring and firing authority, or can make suggestions that "are given particular weight" with respect to (29 C.F.R. §§ 541.100, 541.102).

The C.F.R. defines "management" as activities such as hiring and training employees, appraising their work performance, assigning tasks, budgeting, and complying with legal requirements. If a person otherwise qualifies as an executive, he or she remains exempt despite the performance of concurrent duties (nonexempt work such as waiting on customers, stocking shelves, or cleaning business premises, undertaken by a person whose primary duty is management). However, a person such as a factory supervisor whose main duties are nonexempt does not become an executive merely because he or she occasionally has to make discretionary decisions.

In late 2015, the First Circuit vacated summary judgment for the employer in an FLSA case brought by former managers of Dunkin' Donuts stores. The First Circuit said that a person who does some manual work can nevertheless be considered a manager. The plaintiff alleged that 90% of his time was spent on non-managerial work, and it impaired his ability to manage. This was enough to defeat summary judgment. [*Marzuq v. Cadete Enters., Inc.*, 807 F.3d 431 (1st Cir. 2015)]

The Eighth Circuit ruled in mid-2016 that an employee can be exempt as an executive even without final authority over hiring and firing; the Eighth Circuit found that the weight given to the plaintiff's hiring and disciplinary recommendations made her an executive. [*Garrison v. ConAgra Packaged Foods*, 833 F.3d 881 (8th Cir. 2016); see Michael C. Wilhelm, *Do Employees Need to Have Final Hiring and Firing Authority to Qualify for the FLSA's Executive Exemption?*, Briggs and Morgan (Aug. 22, 2016), available at Lexology .com]

A "business owner" (29 C.F.R. § 541.101) owns a bona fide equity interest of 20% or more in the business that employs him or her, and who is actively employed in the management of the business. A business owner is considered a manager and therefore is not entitled to overtime, even if he or she earns less than $455 a week.

An exempt administrative worker is primarily engaged in "work directly related to the management or general business operations" of the employer company or its customers. See 29 C.F.R. § 541.201—work in "functional areas" such as purchasing, marketing, HR, public relations, etc. The employee must be required to exercise discretion and independent judgment on significant matters. 29 C.F.R. § 541.203 provides examples of the administrative worker exemption, e.g., insurance claims adjusters; financial services employees who collect and analyze information about customers' income, assets, and investments; and executive assistants and administrative assistants. There is a specific provision (§ 541.203(e)) clarifying that personnel clerks are typically not exempt from overtime, but human resources managers "who formulate, interpret or implement employment policies" are exempt. A number of cases have been decided on the administrative worker exemption.

Insurance claims adjusters are exempt because they exercise discretion and make independent judgment after, e.g., investigating and settling claims and making repair adjustments: *Robinson-Smith v. GEICO*, 590 F.3d 886 (D.C. Cir. 2010); *Roe-Midgett v. CC Services, Inc.*, 512 F.3d 865 (7th Cir. 2008); *Miller v. Farmer's Insurance Exchange*, 466 F.3d 853 (9th Cir. 2006), amended 481 F.3d 1119 (9th Cir. 2007); *Harris v. Superior Court (Liberty Mutual Insurance Co.)*, 53 Cal. 4th 170 (Cal. 2011). However, in late 2015, the Fourth Circuit held that employees who reviewed potentially fraudulent claim referrals and gave adjusters information about whether to pursue a fraud case were not exempt, despite GEICO's argument that they did the same work as claims adjusters. [*Calderon v. GEICO Ins. Co.* 809 F.3d 111 (4th Cir. 2015); Chris Lauderdale and William Robert Gignilliat, IV, *Fourth Circuit Holds Insurance Fraud Investigators Are Not Exempt from Overtime Pay, Creating Circuit Split*, Jackson Lewis PC (Apr. 5, 2016), available at Lexology.com. But see *Foster v. Nationwide Mutual Ins. Co.*, 710 F.3d 640 (6th Cir. 2013), holding that the fraud investigation function is directly related to insurers' general business operations.]

The Seventh Circuit held that an insurance company employee who was the expert on particular insurance products and trained sales staff about them, was an exempt administrative employee. He characterized himself as a salesperson who did not use discretion or independent judgment, but the Seventh Circuit held that he used discretion and independent judgment to assist salespersons. [*Blanchar v. Std. Ins. Co.*, 736 F.3d 753 (7th Cir. 2013)]

In 2006, DOL defined mortgage loan officers as exempt administrative workers, describing their primary duties as administering financial transactions, not making sales. In 2010, the DOL issued a new interpretation, stating that the loan officers are non-exempt because they primarily sell financial products. The Supreme Court decided a case on this issue in early 2015, rejecting the banking industry's challenge to the DOL regulation holding the loan officers can be entitled to overtime. The Supreme Court ruled that the DOL is permitted to change its position without soliciting public comments—reversing a long-held doctrine that federal agencies must use the notice and comment procedure before changing the definitive interpretation of a regulation. [*Perez v. Mortgage Bankers Ass'n/Nickols v. Mortgage Bankers Ass'n*, 135 S. Ct. 1199 (2015); see Brent Kendall, *Supreme Court Leaves Amtrak Authority Unsettled*, WSJ.com (Mar. 9, 2015)]

Residential loan underwriters filed a class action stating that they were entitled to overtime because their job was not administrative. The Sixth Circuit held that they were administrative employees because they helped to operate or service a business. This is different from the Second Circuit test, which holds that residential loan underwriters are exempt because their duties do not impinge on a production activity. [*Lutz v. Huntington Bancshares*, 815 F.3d 988 (6th Cir. 2016); see Justin Jennewine, *Sixth Circuit Tackles Administrative Exemption Under the FLSA*, Squire Patton Boggs (Mar. 4, 2016), available at Lexology.com] The Ninth Circuit also held that mortgage underwriters are not exempt—it is production work, not administrative work, because the work is not related to the employer's management or general business operations. [*McKeen-Chaplin v. Provident Sav. Bank FSB,* No. 15-16759 (9th Cir. July 5, 2017)]

The Ninth Circuit held that "service advisors" in auto dealerships were not exempt even though the FLSA has an exemption for "salesmen," "partsmen," and "mechanics" in car dealerships. The job of the service advisors was to greet potential customers, determine what was wrong with their cars, recommend the repair work to be done, and write up an estimate. If the customer agreed, the repairs would be done by a mechanic. The service advisors were paid only a commission, not a salary or hourly wages. This contradicts the rulings in the Fourth and Fifth Circuit, which found that service advisors were exempt from the overtime requirements. Because there was more than one reasonable way to define "salesman," the Ninth Circuit deferred to the DOL's interpretation (that the exemption is a narrow one—a salesman is someone who sells cars, not repair services). Therefore, the Ninth Circuit held that the service advisors were entitled to overtime. [*Navarro v. Encino Motorcars, LLC,* 780 F.3d 1267 (9th Cir. 2015)]

The Supreme Court reversed the Ninth Circuit, in mid-2016, in a decision that deals with administrative law as well as the specific question of overtime eligibility. The Ninth Circuit deferred to a DOL regulation, but the Supreme Court said that the text of the statute is more significant than the administrative regulation. The Supreme Court said that the regulation was not entitled to controlling weight because the DOL did not give an adequate explanation for changing its position between 2008 and 2011 as to whether service advisors are entitled to overtime. [*Encino MotorCars, LLC v. Navarro,* No. 15-415 (U.S. June 20, 2016); see Tawny L. Alvarez, *Service Advisor Question Sent Back to Ninth Circuit,* Verrill Dana LLP (June 21, 2016), available at Lexology.com]

On remand, the Ninth Circuit reversed the district court's dismissal of the federal overtime claim, holding that service advisors are not subject to the "salesman, partsman, or mechanic" exemption but affirmed the dismissal of the other federal claims. The Ninth Circuit reversed the dismissal of the state claims. As a result, there is still a circuit split, with the Ninth Circuit contradicting the Fourth and Fifth Circuit rulings. [*Navarro v. Encino Motorcars, LLC,* 845 F.3d 925 (9th Cir. 2017); see Jeffrey W. Brecher, *Ninth Circuit Reaffirms Service Advisors Eligible for Overtime, Setting Up Second Potential Trip to Supreme Court,* Jackson Lewis PC (Jan. 10, 2017), available at Lexology.com]

Yet another overtime exemption applies to those employed in "a bona fide professional capacity," defined by 29 C.F.R. § 541.300 either as work requiring advanced knowledge acquired by formal education, or "requiring invention, imagination, originality or talent in a recognized field of artistic or creative endeavor." In addition to the traditional "learned professions" (e.g., medicine, law, engineering, teaching, pharmacy), registered nurses, registered or certified medical technicians, and physician's assistants, and dental hygienists are considered to be professionals. 29 C.F.R. § 541.302 defines creative professionals as those whose primary work requires creativity and artistry, e.g., in music, writing, acting, or graphic arts—work that cannot be done by a person with only general "manual or intellectual ability and training."

The District Court for the Southern District of New York ruled that a contract attorney doing litigation document review was in fact practicing law and was not entitled to overtime. The work is nevertheless the "practice of law," requiring exercise of judgment, no matter how routine and boring it may be. [*Henig v. Quinn Emanuel Urquhart & Sullivan, LLP*, No. 1:13-cv-01432, 2015 U.S. Dist. LEXIS 172823 (S.D.N.Y. Dec. 30, 2015)]

The Second Circuit held that entry-level accountants were not entitled to overtime; they were learned professionals. They said that this category did not apply to them because they got their training while working for KPMG, not from previous intellectual instructions. They also said that their routine, low-level jobs did not permit consistent exercise of professional judgment. The Second Circuit held that "professional judgment" is not applied the same way in this exemption as "discretion and independent judgment" in the administrative exemption. Learned professionals do not have to have managerial authority, it is only required that they use intellectual judgment in the domain of their particular expertise. [*Pippins v. KPMG LLP*, 759 F.3d 235 (2d Cir. 2014)]

The final white-collar exemption, for Outside Sales staff, is defined by § 541.500 as workers whose primary duty is making sales or getting orders or contracts. The mainstay of such an employee's work is performed outside the employer's place of business. This category does not include mail, telephone, or online sales unless these media are only used to set up a personal appointment. When it comes to "drivers who sell" (§ 541.504), the test is whether sales predominates over delivery (thus making the person exempt) or whether delivery predominates (making him or her eligible for overtime).

The Supreme Court resolved a circuit split about the proper treatment of drug "detailers" in June 2012. The Supreme Court ruled that these pharmaceutical representatives are outside salespersons exempt from overtime. [*Christopher v. SmithKline Beecham*, 132 S. Ct. 2156 (2012)]

Christopher was cited in a mid-2016 Eleventh Circuit case, for the proposition that the FLSA is not intended to protect highly paid employees. There is an overtime exemption for computer professionals earning more than $27.63 an hour. Plaintiff Pioch was a software engineer, paid $50 to $85.40 per hour; he was not paid overtime for hours over 40 a week. He quit after an internal investigation accused him of receiving almost $150,000 in improper per diem payments. His final paycheck of $13,367.20 for three weeks' work was withheld. He sued for violation of the FLSA's minimum wage and overtime requirements. The Eleventh Circuit held that he earned far more than the computer professionals exemption and the propriety of withholding his final paycheck had to be addressed via a state contract suit, not under the FLSA. [*Pioch v. Ibex Eng'g Servs., Inc*, 825 F.3d 1264 (11th Cir. 2016); see Jeffrey L. Glaser, *The Spirit of the FLSA Haunts a Highly Paid Employee*, Seyfarth Shaw LLP (June 20, 2016), available at Lexology.com]

The 2016 Final Rule was not intended to affect the eligibility of blue-collar workers for overtime pay. Its examples of blue collar workers are construction workers, carpenters, electricians, plumbers, laborers, etc. (69 Fed. Reg. 22122; 29 C.F.R. § 541.3). As a general rule, public safety workers (e.g., police officers, fire-fighters, paramedics, Emergency Medical Technicians) are also entitled to over-time. Employers continue to be bound by whatever overtime arrangements they have entered into under Collective Bargaining Agreements, and state laws that are more protective of workers are not preempted by the Final Rule (29 C.F.R. § 541.4). However, the Sixth Circuit held that police officers on airport duty did not prove that they were entitled to overtime pay for times when they were required to wear pagers and stay within a set radius of the airport in order to report when summoned for an emergency. The Sixth Circuit said that the test of whether comp time has to be granted is whether off-duty time is so severely burdened that workers cannot control their use of the time (29 C.F.R. § 553.221(d)). [*Adair v. County of Wayne*, 452 F.3d 482 (6th Cir. 2006); see Fred Schneyer, *Detroit Cops Lose OT Court Fight*, plansponsor.com (July 11, 2006)]

A group of current and former fire captains sued the county that employed them for denial of overtime. Some of the plaintiffs were shift commanders and safety officers; the others were station commanders and EMS supervisors. The district court granted summary judgment for the county, concluding that the cap-tains were exempt from overtime because they were executives and the C.F.R. provision about first responders is limited to blue-collar workers. The Fourth Cir-cuit held that 29 C.F.R. § 541.3 does not apply to firefighters (of any rank or pay level) who fight fires and rescue people: their primary duty is firefighting, not management. The Fourth Circuit said that the nature of emergency response is that more time will be spent waiting for calls than handling them. The captains are paid about the same as non-exempt lieutenants one level down the hierarchy; they have no input on budget, hiring, or firing; and they are supervised by others. The Fourth Circuit considered the importance of exempt duties versus other duties; the amount of time spent on exempt work; degree of freedom from direct supervision; and how salaries compare to those earned by non-exempt employ-ees. [*Morrison v. County of Fairfax, Va.*, 826 F.3d 758 (4th Cir. 2016); see Alison R. Kalinski, *The Fourth Circuit Holds That Fire Captains Are Non-Exempt Employees Under the FLSA Because Their Primary Job Duty Is Being a First Responder*, Liebert Cassidy Whitmore (July 13, 2016), available at Lexology .com. The suit was settled at the end of 2016 for $7.95 million: see Curt Varone, *Fairfax County Settles FLSA Suit with Fire Captains for $7.85 Million*, Fire Law Blog (Dec. 4, 2016), available at <http://www.firelawblog.com/2016/12/04/fairfax-county-settles-flsa-suit-fire-captains-7-85-million/>]

Professional motor carriers are generally exempt from overtime but there is an exemption for drivers whose vehicles weigh less than 10,000 pounds. McMas-ter worked for an armored courier company. Her vehicle assignment was vari-able, based on business needs, but she spent 51% of total work days driving vehicles over 10,000 pounds. She was paid by the hour, including overtime, and frequently worked more than 40 hours a week. She sued, seeking overtime for all hours over 40. A class of similar employees was certified. The Third Circuit held that the plaintiff was eligible for overtime, even though she worked on lighter vehicles less than half the time. [*McMaster v. Eastern Armored Servs.*, 780 F.3d 167 (3d Cir. 2015)]

Illinois' governor Rauner vetoed the state's Senate Bill 261 on January 27, 2017, so home care workers will not receive overtime pay. The bill would have prevented the state from limiting the number of hours worked in a week by an individual home care worker. The bill reflects the governor's attempt to cut state spending. [Alana Stramowski, *Illinois Home Care Workers Say Goodbye to Overtime Pay* (Jan. 31, 2017) (benefitslink.com)]

[C] Payment of Overtime

Nonexempt employees must be paid time-and-a-half (150% of their normal pay rate, including commissions) when they work more than 40 hours in any work week. Work time is all the time when the employer controls the employee's actions, including times the employee is required to be on duty or at a prescribed place. However, bona fide meal periods are not considered work time. Ordinary commuting to work is not work time, Work-related travel, such as an assignment to deliver something or go to a meeting at a client's office, is work time.

These are some items that may require compensation or overtime:

- Rest breaks under 20 minutes;
- Down time or on-call time that prevents the employee from carrying out personal business;
- Preparation before shift or clean-up after shift;
- Mandatory classes, meetings, or conventions;
- Travel time other than normal commuting.

The workweek doesn't have to be Monday–Friday, 9–5: it can be defined as any 168 consecutive hours, starting any time. It doesn't have to be the same as the payroll period. Different work groups or individuals can have different work-weeks. Usually, once an employer sets a workweek, it has to abide by it—but a permanent change that is not a subterfuge to evade the FLSA's overtime requirements is permitted. [See 29 C.F.R. § 778.104, averaging a long and a short week to see if overtime is payable is not allowed]

Some employees have two jobs, only one of them exempt: for example, a non-exempt school employee who is also an exempt sports team coach, or an exempt administrator who drives a bus. The FLSA regulations say that an employee cannot hold multiple statuses and is either exempt for all duties or non-exempt for all duties. The test is the employee's primary duty, based on the job as a whole. An employee whose primary duty is non-exempt even when performing duties that would be exempt, and vice versa. The percentage of time spent on each category of activities is important but not dispositive. [Douglas A. Hass, *Working Two Jobs to Make Ends Meet: Paying Employees Working Exempt and Non-Exempt Jobs*, Franczek Radelet PC (Oct. 6, 2014), available at Lexology.com]

Non-exempt engineers who worked at remote locations were paid an hourly wage, overtime, and a per diem expense reimbursement because they worked remotely. The plaintiffs said that the per diem was based on the number of hours worked, making it a shadow wage that should have been included in overtime calculations. The First Circuit held in 2014 that the regular rate of pay does not include travel expenses or "supper money" when the employee is away from the regular workplace. However, expenses normally incurred by employees for their own benefit, such as buying lunch, are included in the regular rate. The First Circuit agreed with the plaintiffs that the per diems were partially based on hours worked, so they should have been included in the regular rate to calculate overtime. [*Newman v. Advanced Tech. Innovation Corp.*, 749 F.3d 33 (1st Cir. 2014)]

The "fluctuating work week" method of paying overtime involves paying the worker a salary covering all hours worked in each regular work week. Overtime compensation is due only on hours worked over 40 in a week. If the employee earns $20 an hour for regular work, plus $30 an hour for overtime hours, an additional 10 hours of work would add $300 to the compensation for the week. Under a fluctuating workweek calculation, an employee whose salary is $800 and who works 50 hours, overtime is calculated by dividing the $800 salary by the 50 hours worked, resulting in $16 per hour. The employer must pay an additional $8 for each of the 10 overtime hours—$880, rather than $1,100 that would be due if this method were not used. However, some state statutes forbid this method: e.g., it cannot be used by restaurants in New York. [Jeffrey H. Ruzan and Peter M. Panken, *Coping With the New Definition of Exempt Employees: The Proposed New Salary Test May Not Benefit Currently Salaried Employees*, Epstein Becker Green (Aug. 19, 2015), available at Lexology.com]

The FLSA requires overtime (for employees entitled to overtime) to be based on the regular rate of pay. The computation of the regular hourly rate must include all remuneration for employment, so most bonuses must be included. If the bonus is defined as a predetermined percentage of the employee's pay (straight time plus overtime), it is not necessary to calculate additional overtime on the bonus, because it has already been factored in. For example, if an employee earns a 5% bonus for excellent performance over a period of four full workweeks, and the employee earned $2,400 straight time, $900 overtime in that period, the bonus can be $165, 5% of the combined wages. If there is a fixed bonus pool, the total straight time plus overtime worked by the pool participant is divided, with each participant receiving the stipulated percentage of total wages (including overtime) for the bonus period. DOL cautions that a bonus is an extra reward, and the term should not be used for a portion of regular wages that the employee is entitled to receive under the ordinary terms of employment. [John E.

Thompson, *What Is a "Percentage Bonus"?*, Fisher & Phillips LLP (Jan. 11, 2016), available at Lexology.com]

The Ninth Circuit ruled that 29 U.S.C. § 207(e) provides that, when calculating overtime pay, all compensation is included in the regular rate unless it is specifically excluded. Therefore, cash payments made in lieu of health benefits must be included in the regular rate. [*Flores v. City of San Gabriel*, No. 14-56421 (9th Cir. June 2, 2016)*cert. denied* No. 16-911 (May 15, 2017); see Lisa S. Charbonneau, *The Ninth Circuit Holds That Cash Payments Made to Employees in Lieu of Health Benefits Must Be Included in the Regular Rate for Overtime Purposes Under the FLSA*, Liebert Cassidy Whitmore (June 3, 2016), available at Lexology.com]

According to the Third Circuit, paying workers for lunch breaks does not prevent the employer from having to pay overtime for work done before and after the employee's shift. The case was brought under the FLSA to recover donning and doffing time and compensation for "shift relief" (discussing work issue with the incoming shift of workers) before and after the scheduled shift. According to the plaintiffs, these tasks consumed 30–60 minutes per day. The employee handbook said that employees who are required to do shift relief are paid for lunch as part of their shift. Both sides agreed that the workers received paid break time that exceeded the time spent on donning/doffing and shift relief. The Third Circuit held that employees would be shortchanged if time used to calculate their regular pay for the first 40 hours was also credited against overtime. The Third Circuit reads the FLSA to allow certain compensation already paid to offset overtime liability—but it must be premium-rate extra compensation of at least 150% the normal rate, paid under a CBA or for weekends and holidays. In this case, the pay for meal breaks was part of regular compensation, so it could not be deemed "extra compensation." [*Smiley v. DuPont,* **839 F.3d 325** (3d Cir. Oct. 2016); see Manatt Phelps & Phillips LLP, *Employer Can't Offset Overtime Work With Paid Lunch, Breaks* (Oct. 25, 2016), available at Lexology.com; see Scott A. Ohnegian et al., *Paid Meal Breaks May Not Be Used to Offset Overtime Obligations*, Riker Danzig Scherer Hyland & Perretti LLP (Nov. 2, 2016), available at Lexology .com]

The Sixth Circuit held that an employer has constructive knowledge (reasonable cause to believe) of a fact when the employer should have discovered the fact by exercising reasonable diligence. There is no violation if the employer was not aware that overtime was worked, particularly if the employee concealed it. Employers are not liable if they maintain a reasonable time-reporting procedure but the employee fails to use it. However, there are two exceptions to this rule: if the employer prevents employees from reporting all the hours worked or if the employer learns that employees are not reporting all the time worked, but does nothing about the situation. [Philip C. Eschels, *Employers in the Sixth Circuit Must Use "Reasonable Diligence" to Avoid Liability for Unreported Overtime*, Bingham Greenebaum Doll LLP (Aug. 15, 2016), available at Lexology.com]

Once it is determined that employees have been misclassified as exempt, the question arises whether they are entitled to time and a half for overtime hours or only to the half time premiums.

The Supreme Court has held that the employer could use a fluctuating work week (FWW) calculation, becoming liable for only the half time premium. A 2012 Seventh Circuit case also upholds this methodology. For example, a misclassified employee who worked 50 hours a week would receive time and a half for 10 hours a week, at a rate of the weekly salary divided by 40, under the time-and-a-half methodology. The FWW calculation would entitle the employee to the weekly salary divided by 50, with the half-time premium paid on this lower rate. In 2013, the Fifth Circuit applied the FWW method for 16 store managers, holding that the correct formula was their weekly salary divided by the number of hours worked, plus half time for hours worked in excess of 40 a week. [*Ransom v. M. Patel Enters., Inc.*, 734 F.3d 377 (5th Cir. 2013). See also *Overnight Motor Transp. v. Missel*, 316 U.S. 572 (1942); *Urnikis-Negro v. Am. Family Prop. Servs.*, 616 F.3d 665 (7th Cir. 2012)]

In 2016, many federal agencies imposed significant increases in penalties, making up for many years when penalty levels remained the same despite inflation. Effective August 1, 2016, the DOL increased FLSA penalties for violations occurring after November 2, 2015. A monetary penalty of up to $1,894 can be assessed for each repeated or willful violation of minimum wage or overtime rules (the previous maximum was $1,100). A violation can be treated as a repeated violation even if it is not factually or legally the same as the earlier violation, and the DOL can assert the penalty for willfulness if the employer either knew it violated legal requirements, or acted in reckless disregard as to whether or not it violated the requirements. [Interim Final Rule, 81 Fed. Reg. 43430 (July 1, 2016); see Caroline J. Brown, *FLSA's Civil Money Penalties to Increase*, Fisher Phillips (July 8, 2016), available at Lexology.com]

In early 2017, DOL announced a second round of penalty increases, the second in less than a year. The latest schedule of penalties applies to penalties assessed after January 13, 2017, for predicate violations that occurred after November 2, 2015. At one time, the FLSA § 16(e)(2) penalty for repeated or willful violation of minimum wage or overtime requirements was $1,100. In August 2016, it rose to $1,894, and then in January 2017 it rose to a new maximum of $1,925. Generally, this penalty is imposed per person, times the number of employees who did not receive proper pay. A violation can be considered repeated for penalty enhancement purposes even if it is not factually or legally the same as an earlier violation (e.g., a minimum wages and an overtime violation). Under the latest rules, a violation is deemed willful if the employer knew that it violated the law or acted with reckless disregard as to compliance. The penalty for employing a person under age 18 in violation of the FLSA child labor rules, which rose to $12,080 in 2016, is now $12,278. If the child labor violation causes a child worker's death or serious injury, the civil penalty could be as high as $55,808—doubled, in case of repeat or willful violations. [John E. Thompson, *FLSA*

Civil Penalties to Increase Again, Fisher Phillips (Jan. 17, 2017), available at Lexology.com]

A Connecticut statute signed June 23, 2015, effective October 1, 2015, makes employers subject to double damages if they fail to make required payments to employees. The award of double damages, plus court costs, is mandatory upon a finding of failure to pay wages or fringe benefits, violation of minimum wage or overtime laws, or failure to satisfy an arbitration award; a showing of bad faith or unreasonable conduct is not required. [Jason R. Stanevich and Sharon B. Bowler, *Connecticut Imposes Double Damages for Failure to Pay Proper Minimum Wage Or Overtime*, Littler Mendelson (June 25 2015), available at Lexology.com]

[D]   Case Law on Overtime

In a shaky economy, FLSA litigation (and employment discrimination litigation) predictably increases, because many potential plaintiffs are no longer employed and do not fear that filing suit will lead to their discharge. Employers often take the position that the FLSA rules are outdated, and fail to represent the current realities of the workplace, because the statutory categories represent outmoded categories.

Issues often raised in litigation include misclassification of workers as exempt and demands that workers (especially in the retail and restaurant industries) work "off the clock."

Many important cases have reached a verdict or settlement, although employees frequently lose overtime cases.

The Seventh Circuit ruled that time (including travel time) spent attending counseling sessions mandated by the employer pursuant to a fitness for duty examination was work time compensable under the FLSA. [*Sehie v. City of Aurora*, 432 F.3d 749 (7th Cir. 2005)]

In a suit for the recovery of unpaid overtime, the California Supreme Court ruled that individual officers, directors, and shareholders were not personally liable. Corporate directors can be jointly liable with the corporation if they personally direct or participate in tortious conduct, but the court declined to impose personal liability in *Reynolds v. Bement* because failure to comply with statutory overtime requirements is not tortious, and there was no allegation that the officers or directors retained the unpaid overtime compensation for their own benefit. [*Reynolds v. Bement*, 36 Cal. 4th 1075 (Cal. Sup. 2005)]

The Supreme Court ruled in March 2011, that it is unlawful to retaliate against an employee who complains about an FLSA violation—even if the complaint is made orally, not in writing, and is made to the employer rather than to a government agency. [*Kasten v. Saint-Gobain Performance Plastics Corp.*, 131 S. Ct. 1325 (2011)]

In a 2014 Sixth Circuit case, the plaintiffs were mortgage loan officers who were not paid overtime because they were classified as independent contractors. They filed a class/collective action under the FLSA and the Ohio Minimum Fair Wage Standards Act. The Sixth Circuit held that the employer could compel individual arbitration, even after the expiration of the plaintiffs' employment contracts. The contracts contained an arbitration clause, but did not specify whether class arbitration was available, so the Sixth Circuit held that class-wide arbitration is available only if the agreement specifically permits it. [*Huffman v. The Hilltop Cos.*, 747 F.3d 391 (6th Cir. Mar. 27, 2014). It was already clear that CBA disputes must be arbitrated even after the expiration of the CBA: *Litton Financial Printing v. NLRB*, 501 U.S. 190 (1991). See also *Reed Elsevier, Inc. ex rel. LexisNexis Div. v. Crockett*, 734 F.3d 594 (6th Cir. 2013): when the contract is silent on the issue of class arbitration, class arbitration is not available.]

Recent cases stress that FLSA overtime plaintiffs must do more than merely state they worked unpaid overtime. See *Lundy v. Catholic Health System of Long Island*, 711 F.3d 106 (2d Cir. 2013): to survive a motion to dismiss, the plaintiff must at least allege 40 hours of work in a particular workweek plus uncompensated time.

The Fifth Circuit held that an employer has the right to forbid overtime and make employees abide by the policy. The Fifth Circuit rejected the plaintiff's claim that the employer had constructive knowledge of the extra hours based on her computer usage report: mere access to information is not the same as constructive knowledge. The plaintiff claimed that she did not get authorization for overtime or report the overtime because there was a company policy against working overtime; the Fifth Circuit refused to reward an intentional flouting of company policy. [*Fairchild v. All American Check Cashing*, 811 F.3d 776 (5th Cir. 2016); see Noel P. Tripp, *Fifth Circuit: Employer Has Right to Mandate Employee Compliance with Overtime Reporting Procedures and Is Not Liable When Employee Fails to Follow*, Jackson Lewis PC (Jan. 27, 2016), available at Lexology.com; Michael C. Griffaton, *Court Finds That a Company's Clear Wage-Hour Policy Defeats a Claim for Unpaid Overtime*, Vorys, Sater, Seymour & Pease LLP (Mar. 15, 2016), available at Lexology.com]

Nevertheless, in a case where the plaintiff had no corroborating evidence of his contention that he worked an average of 65–68 hours a week and the employer submitted time sheets and pay stubs showing that he seldom worked more than 30 hours a week, the Sixth Circuit reversed the district court's grant of summary judgment for the employer. The Sixth Circuit said that it was up to the jury to decide who to believe. [*Moran v. Al Basit LLC.*, 788 F.3d 201 (6th Cir. 2015); see Daniel L. Messeloff, *Sixth Circuit Makes It Harder for Employers to Defeat "Bald Assertions" of Wage Violations in Collective Actions*, Jackson Lewis PC (Sept. 4, 2015), available at Lexology.com]

[E]   Scheduling Workers for Overtime

Sometimes, the employer will have to provide additional incentives, such as meal vouchers or free meals in the employee cafeteria or transportation home, for overtime work. But it is more common for employees to compete to be able to put in extra hours at the higher overtime rate. It is legitimate to assign overtime in order of seniority: to let employees bid for overtime work, with priority to the most senior.

In a unionized workplace, the CBA determines how much notice the company must give when overtime will be required; the extent to which overtime is assigned and when it is voluntary; who gets to bid on it; maximum overtime hours; and meal and rest breaks during overtime. If the employer assigns overtime, the disciplinary procedure should be drafted to specify that refusal to work mandatory overtime is a legitimate subject for discipline.

The FLSA allows employers to maintain a policy under which overtime work must be authorized. (Otherwise, employees would have an incentive to goof off during the day and catch up during better-paid overtime hours). But overtime pay is required if the employer permits or even is aware that nonexempt employees are working more than 40 hours a week.

■ **TIP:**   The amount of overtime can be reduced by

- Planning further in advance;
- Being more realistic about deadlines;
- Coordinating tasks better, so materials and intermediate products are available when the production cycle requires them;
- Coordinating vacation and leave schedules so there will be enough employees available and it won't be necessary for a few workers to put in extra hours to cover for those who are absent.

[F]   Donning and Doffing; Preliminary and Postliminary Activities

The Portal-to-Portal Act makes the FLSA applicable to the employee's "workweek": the time when he or she is engaged in the principal activities of the job. Walking around within the workplace is not considered to be work time, and neither are "preliminary" and "postliminary" activities prior to and after the employee begins to work.

However, it is often necessary to determine whether "donning and doffing" (putting on and removing required uniforms, equipment, and safety gear) time constitutes work time. This is an issue that the Supreme Court has continued to revisit.

In November 2005, the Supreme Court ruled that putting on and taking off gear that is integral to work is compensable as part of the work day, as is walking between the production area and the area where protective clothing is put on and removed. However, the time employees spend waiting to put on their protective gear is not compensable because it is not closely enough related to the principal activities of the job. [*IBP v. Alvarez*, 546 U.S. 21 (2005)]

According to the Supreme Court, principal work activity includes anything integral and indispensable to that activity. Donning and doffing can qualify if predominantly performed for the benefit of the employer. If changing clothes on the employer's premises is required by law, the employer's rules, or the nature of the work, it is integral. When time to change clothes is compensable, so is time going to and from the changing room. Under FLSA § 203(o), a CBA can be drafted to make changing time non-compensable, but some jurisdictions make walking/ waiting time compensable even if changing time is not. The critical issue is employer control over the process, not whether changing clothes constitutes enough effort to be deemed "work": *De Asencio v. Tyson Foods*, 500 F.3d 361 (3d Cir. 2007). The employer must inform employees what equipment is mandatory and what is provided for the comfort and convenience of employees.

The Supreme Court held in early 2014 that, in a unionized operation, it is up to the collective bargaining agreement whether employees will be paid for donning and doffing time. The case, a class action, was brought by steelworkers who alleged that they were entitled to pay for time spent changing in and out of work clothes and walking from the locker room to their work stations. The Supreme Court held that changing into the required safety gear was defined as "changing clothes"—which is rendered not compensable by FLSA § 203(o). [*Sandifer v. U.S. Steel*, 134 S. Ct. 870 (2014)]

A unanimous Supreme Court ruled at the end of 2014 that a temp agency did not have to pay workers at an Amazon warehouse for the time spent waiting to go through security screening at the end of the day. The court said that the screenings were not integral and indispensable to the job of packing orders and they could have performed their work if the employer had eliminated the screening requirement. According to the plaintiffs, Amazon had an obligation either to pay for the time or to speed up the process by hiring more screeners or staggering the end of the work shift; Amazon said that the screening took only a few minutes. [*Integrity Staffing Solutions v. Busk*, 135 S. Ct. 513 (2014)]

After the Supreme Court *Busk* ruling, the plaintiffs amended their complaints to assert claims under the laws of Nevada and Arizona, the location of the warehouses. They lost again, because the Nevada and Arizona laws (like the laws of most states except California) are worded similarly to the FLSA. [*In re Amazon.Com Inc., Fulfillment Ctr. FLSA Litig.*, MDL Docket No. 2504 (W.D. Ky. June 7, 2017); see Gregory V. Mersol, *Time Spent in Post-Shift Security Checks Once Again Held Not Compensable,* Baker & Hostetler LLP (June 12, 2017), available at Lexology.com]

While *Busk* was pending, the District Court for the Southern District of New York approved a $910,000 settlement of a class action alleging that employees should have been paid for waiting for the changing room and putting on their uniforms. Damages ranged from $5 (for new hires) to about $4.50 a week for more experienced employees. [*Trinidad v. Pret A Manger (USA) Ltd.*, No. 12-6094, 2014 WL 4670870 (S.D.N.Y., order entered Sept. 19, 2014)]

In March 2016, the Supreme Court returned to the question of how to prove damages in FLSA class actions. The Supreme Court allowed the introduction of expert witness testimony about the length of time spent on donning and doffing prepared by viewing videotapes of workers. The Supreme Court said that the standard is the same in class and individual actions: whether the statistical evidence is relevant and has probative effect. Tyson Foods objected to introduction of the testimony because the workers' experiences were not uniform, and some workers did not qualify for any overtime pay. The Supreme Court said that the workers should not be penalized because their employer did not have accurate records of the time spent; they should be able to offer evidence to create reasonable inferences about the amount of time they spent. As a result, the $5.8 million jury verdict will stand. The court's ruling on the use of statistics will also be important in other kinds of class action cases. [*Tyson Foods, Inc. v. Bouaphakeo*, No. 14-1146 194 L. Ed. 2d 124 (2016); see Adam Liptak, *Supreme Court Upholds Worker Class-Action Suit Against Tyson*, NYTimes.com (Mar. 23, 2016); Jess Bravin, *Supreme Court Upholds Employee Class Action Against Tyson Foods*, WSJ.com (Mar. 23, 2016)]

In mid-2016, the Arkansas Supreme Court held an employer liable for about $3 million in unpaid overtime and interest for failure to pay production workers for 14–20 minutes donning and doffing time per shift. According to the court, the state's minimum wage law, unlike the FLSA, does not provide an exemption for compensation paid in compliance with a CBA. [*Gerber Prods. Co. v. Hewitt*, 492 S.W.3d 856 (Ark. 2016); see Brent I. Clark, Benjamin D. Briggs & Craig B. Simonsen, *Food Manufacturer Found Liable in Donning and Doffing Case*, Seyfarth Shaw LLP (June 7, 2016), available at Lexology.com]

The Connecticut Supreme Court ruled in 2014 that a plumbing foreman was not entitled to compensation for time spent commuting to and from job sites at the beginning and end of the workday, even though he used a company vehicle and carried company tools. The court applied the federal definition; the Connecticut DOL's test for the compensability of travel is more favorable to employees. The court held that the Portal to Portal Act preempts the state regulations on travel time. The plaintiff failed to show that driving the car and carrying the tools was more than a minimal burden. [*Sarrazin v. Coastal, Inc.*, 89 A.3d 841 (Conn 2014)]

In contrast, the Ninth Circuit held that an employee might be compensated for commuting in a company vehicle when the employee is responsible for the theft or damage to the vehicle or work tools kept there. Hobart allowed technicians either to drive home in company vehicles or leave the vehicles at the branch office overnight. Plaintiff Alcantar said that leave the car at the office was not feasible because of the lack of secure parking and the risk that up to $80,000 worth of tools could be stolen. The Ninth Circuit held that a reasonable jury could agree with this, and reversed denial of class certification because there was a common question capable of class-wide resolution. [*Alcantar v. Hobart Servs.*, 800 F.3d 1047 (9th Cir. 2015)]

In an FLSA collective action brought by over 400 iron foundry employees who claimed overtime for time spent showering and changing at the end of the shift, the Seventh Circuit held that summary judgment for the employer was inappropriate. The employees said that they were exposed to chemicals at work, so showering and changing clothes protected their health. The district court held that, because there is no OSHA standard requiring foundry employees to shower or change on site, the activities were not necessary. The Seventh Circuit reversed, holding that the court should be able to rely on scientific testimony about the necessity of these activities. [*DeKeyser v. Thyssenkrupp Waupaca, Inc.*, 735 F.3d 568 (7th Cir. 2013)]

The Eighth Circuit reversed two wage and hour class action judgments against Tyson Foods: one for $18.7 million, the second for $4.96 million. Meat processing plant workers sued under Nebraska state wage payment law, alleging that they were not properly compensated for "K-Code Time" (pre-and post-shift activities including donning and doffing, cleaning the equipment, and walking between their lockers and the production line). State laws often allow plaintiffs to claim "gap time" (non-overtime hours for which they were not paid). The Eighth Circuit reversed the judgments, holding that the FLSA cannot be used to support a state-law claim. Under the FLSA, wages can only be recovered if the employer agreed to pay, and there was no proof that Tyson agreed to pay for the K-Code time. [*Acosta v. Tyson Foods Inc.*, 800 F.3d 468 (8th Cir. 2015); *Gomez v. Tyson*, No. 13-3500 (8th Cir. Aug. 26, 2015)]

To "preserve the appearance of the workplace," Securiguard Inc., required security guards to leave their work stations for meals and breaks. It could take 10–12 minutes to get to a place to take a meal break. The Fifth Circuit held that the off-the-clock meal periods might be compensable, because a reasonable jury could believe that the transit time predominantly benefited the employer. Although the trip to the break area was short enough to be de minimis, if the lunch break was shortened enough to become a compensable meal break, the FLSA requires the employees to be paid because the employer benefits from a more rested workforce. [*Naylor v. Securiguard, Inc.*, 801 F.3d 501 (5th Cir. 2015)]

Holding regularly scheduled "pre-shift" meetings can be valuable to give employees announcements and set the tone of the workday. However, an employer that holds such meetings can be liable if time spent this way is not accurately recorded as work time for non-exempt employees. The FLSA requires pay for every hour employees are allowed to work. Activities before the official start of the shift are compensable if they include the tasks the employees are paid to perform or that are an integral and indispensable part of the job, such as setting up a cash register, collecting supplies, or taking a hand-off from the previous shift. Several cases hold that a roll call meeting reviewing policies and getting assignments is compensable. The de minimis rule relieves employers from recording small amounts of time, but the FLSA does not define any period of time that can arbitrarily be ignored. Some courts reject the de minimis rule as an obsolete relic of the days of manual timekeeping. It is definitely unlawful to set up a time clock to adjust the time the employee actually clocks in (e.g., 7:55) to the scheduled start of the shift (e.g., 8 a.m.). Best practices for employers include reminding supervisors that employees are not allowed to work before clocking in; the time recording must be accurate; and pre-shift meetings must be accounted for, perhaps in a special log that records the time and duration of meetings. If there is an employee handbook, it should instruct workers not to work off the clock—and to report to HR if they are ever told to work off the clock. [Allison Kheel, *"Pre-Shift" Does Not Mean "Before-Shift": Are Your Pre-Shift Meetings Violating The FLSA?*, Fisher Phillips (Mar. 1, 2017), available at Lexology.com]

§ 1.16 VACATIONS AND VACATION PAY

On the average, U.S. workers get less vacation than European workers. Furthermore, U.S. workers may feel that if they take their scheduled vacation time, they will not be able to complete all the work that falls to them in a downsized workplace.

In the private sector, about three-quarters of workers receive paid vacation time; 23% do not. But for the lowest-paid employees, only 34% receive paid holidays and 23% do not get paid vacation time. In the top 10% of the income distribution, 93% of employees get both paid holidays and paid vacation. [epi.org, *Millions of Working People Don't Get Paid Time Off for Holidays or Vacation* (Sept. 1, 2015) (benefitslink.com)]

In 2015, over half of U.S. employees (55%) left some vacation time unused. Between 1976 and 2000, workers took an average of 20.3 vacation days a year, falling to 16.2 days in 2015. Fifty-five percent did not use all of their days. Of 658 million unused days in 2015, 222 million were forfeited because the employees were not entitled to roll them over or receive cash payment. More than two-thirds of survey respondents entitled to paid time off said that their bosses are negative, send mixed messages, or say nothing about using vacation time—whereas managers tend to remember that they encouraged employees to use their vacation days. [Melanie Trottman, *More Than Half of U.S. Workers Are Leaving Some Vacation Days Unused*, WSJ.com (June 14, 2016); John Simons, *Bosses Are to Blame for Unused Vacation Time*, WSJ.com (Oct. 11, 2016)]

■ **TIP:** Audit requirements may actually require employees with access to the firm's cash and books to take at least two consecutive weeks of vacation. An employee who never uses his or her full allotment of vacation time could be a conscientious person who wants to cope with a backlog, a workaholic who really needs to "get a life" outside the office, a subpar employee who needs extra time to make up for incompetence, or an embezzler who has to hang around to prevent crooked schemes from unraveling!

The federal Davis-Bacon Act requires government contractors to pay for unused vacation days when an employee terminates but there is no general FLSA provision covering other situations. Most of the states impose a similar requirement for state government employees, but not in the private sector. Some states, however, have rules about this.

Federal law doesn't require celebration of holidays, and does not require holiday pay, although some states impose special requirements for employees who do work on a holiday. However, once a company adopts a holiday policy, it must continue to follow it; failure would constitute not paying all wages due. The policy must explain who is entitled to holiday pay and what happens if the holiday coincides with a day when the workplace is closed. Generally, payment is required only for hours actually worked plus any holiday supplement promised to the employees. Comp time is another possibility, but it must be spelled out. [John Donovan, Fisher & Phillips LLP, *Solutions at Work, Does Your Holiday Policy Need a Tune Up?* (February 2011) (benefitslink.com)]

§ 1.17 GARNISHMENTS AND DEDUCTIONS FOR SUPPORT ORDERS

[A] Assignments versus Garnishments

There may be instances in which the HR department is asked to apply some of an employee's wages to a debt, such as consumer debts, student loan debt, and the obligation to support children, and/or an ex-spouse.

An "assignment" is an action undertaken by an individual to direct some of his or her future compensation to creditors. A "garnishment" is a deduction from wages made pursuant to a court order. Federal law doesn't say anything about wage assignments, although many states limit the amount or percentage of each paycheck that can be assigned, permit assignments only for certain classes of debts, or require the spouse's consent to the assignment.

According to payroll preparation firm ADP, in 2013, 7.2% of employees had wages garnished for all causes (taxes, child support, student loans, or debts). Garnishments are most common in the Midwest and in the manufacturing industry because of the economic doldrums there. Employers that commit administrative errors when complying with state garnishment laws are at risk of default judgments for the full amount of the unpaid debt—even if the debtor is not an employee. State law determines the disclosures the employer must make, as well as how long garnishment lasts, the definition of earnings and disposable earnings, and what to do when garnishment ends. [Martin C. Brook, *Wage Garnishments—A Big Problem with Solutions on the Horizon*, Ogletree Deakins (Sept. 16, 2014), available at Lexology.com]

The Uniform Law Commission published its Uniform Wage Garnishment Act (UWGA) although, at press time in 2017, it had been introduced in the Nebraska legislature but had not yet been adopted by any state. The UWGA offers nationwide uniformity in garnishment procedures and forms, and relieves employers of some expenses and efforts. Under the UWGA, a garnishment action is initiated in the state where the employee works. (Prior law allows a garnishment action to be initiated in any state where the employer is present, no matter where the employee works.) The garnishment motion is served by the creditor on the employer's registered agent for service of process. The motion must give the name of the employee, the amount that the creditor claims is owed, enough information to identify the judgment on which the action is based, and a notice for the employee disclosing the amount owed and what the employee's options are. The UWGA forbids employers to take adverse employment action because employees have a garnishment or attempted garnishment. Compensation of independent contractors is also subject to garnishment under the UWGA. The statute provides for employers to receive notice of failure to comply with a garnishment, so they can comply before penalties are assessed. The penalty on the employer is limited to one day's garnishment amount. The UWGA permits employers to receive upfront fees from the judgment creditor for managing the garnishment. Prior law based priority among garnishments on the order in which they were served. The UWGA changes this by providing that the maximum garnishment amount (under the relevant federal or state statute) will be equally shared by each creditor who has served a garnishment order on the employer. [<http://www.uniformlaws.org/ LegislativeFactSheet.aspx?title=Wage%20Garnishment%20Act> (last accessed Jan. 28, 2017); see Manatt Phelps & Phillips LLP, *Uniform Law Commission Finalizes Wage Garnishment Act* (July 28, 2016), available at Lexology.com; Martin C. Brook, *Uniform Wage Garnishment Act Approved by Commission*, Ogletree Deakins (July 14, 2016), available at Lexology.com]

An employer that receives a writ of garnishment has 20 days to file a written response with the issuing court informing the court and the parties to the case how much the employee is paid and how much will be withheld in each pay period pursuant to the writ. The employer is entitled to receive $100 from the court plus $5 for the first withholding and $2 for each subsequent withholding. The employer is required to sequester the withheld wages until it receives a court order explaining how to handle the funds. An employer that fails to remit the funds becomes responsible for paying the debt, up to the amount that the employer owes the employee. A "head of family" exemption is from garnishment is available in some states, such as Florida; it is not clear, but probably true that income tax refunds, deferred compensation, and severance payments are not subject to head-of-family exemptions or caps on the amount that can be garnished. A bonus based on a formula about work performed is probably deemed to be wages and subject to a cap on garnishment, but a strictly discretionary bonus is probably subject to garnishment. [Marissa D. Kelley, *The Writ (and Wisdom) of Wage Garnishments*, Stearns Weaver Miller Weissler Alhadeff & Sitterson PA (June 20, 2016), available at Lexology.com]

The federal bankruptcy reform law, Bankruptcy Abuse Prevention and Consumer Protection Act (BAPCPA), made it harder for many consumer debtors to file for bankruptcy protection. Although the lesser of 75% of wages, or 30 times the minimum wage, is exempt from garnishment, the minimum wage has not kept up with inflation, with the result that only $217.50/week is exempt from seizure under the federal rules. (Some states exempt larger amounts.) Losing 25% of income may make it impossible for the low-wage debtor to pay bills. [Sidney Jones, *More Struggling Borrowers Face Pay Garnishment*, NYTimes.com (Apr. 2, 2010)]

Pensions cannot be assigned before they are received (except through a Qualified Domestic Relations Order (QDRO) see § 12.08). Once a pension payment is made, the recipient can do whatever he or she wants with it, but the "anti-alienation" rules of ERISA prevent advance assignment.

The federal Consumer Credit Protection Act (CCPA) [15 U.S.C. §§ 1671 *et seq.*] puts limits on garnishment. Generally, the maximum permitted garnishment will be 25% of the employee's "disposable" earnings, with stricter limits on garnishments for very low-income workers. "Disposable earnings" is defined as approximately equal to gross income minus Social Security taxes and withheld income taxes. Health insurance premiums and spousal and child support are not deducted, even if the support is ordered by a court. Thus, serious problems can occur if the same individual is subject to garnishment both for consumer debt and support payments.

Garnishment for support rather than consumer debt can be higher [15 U.S.C. § 1673]:

- 50%, if the employee is supporting a spouse or child other than the subject of the order, and the garnishment order covers less than 12 weeks' worth of arrears;

- 55%, if conditions are the same but more than 12 weeks of arrears are involved;

- 60%, if the employee does not have a new family to support, and arrears are 12 weeks or less;

- 65%, if there is no second family and arrears exceed 12 weeks.

There is no limit on garnishments that respond to an order issued by a Chapter 11 or Chapter 13 bankruptcy court, or on a debt due for any state or federal tax. The general rule against alienation of plan benefits doesn't prevent the IRS from garnishing a taxpayer's (or rather, nontaxpayer's) vested interest in qualified benefits when the agency has a judgment for unpaid taxes.

There is a split among bankruptcy courts as to whether a bankrupt employee's automatic stay prevents enforcement of a garnishment. At least some creditors will agree to forego garnishment but, if the creditor does not provide guidance, the employer is at risk of liability. The bankruptcy automatic stay does not apply to domestic support orders or to certain taxes. Employers should have a protocol in place for handling garnishments of wages of bankrupt employees with agreement from the creditor, debtor, and/or bankruptcy trustee as to how to handle the situation. [Hunton & Williams LLP, *Employee Pay and the Bankruptcy Stay—Potential Pitfalls Part 2: Garnishment Issu*es (Aug. 1, 2016), available at Lexology.com]

The CCPA says that, if state law limits garnishment more than the federal law does, employees are entitled to the protection of the stricter state-law limits. In other words, the garnishment is limited to what is permitted by state law. Under the CCPA, it's illegal to fire an employee for having one garnishment, but it's lawful to fire if additional garnishments are imposed. [16 U.S.C. § 1674] Willful violation of this provision can be punished by a $1,000 fine and/or one year's imprisonment.

It should be noted that qualified plan benefits can be garnished to collect a criminal restitution order under the Mandatory Victims Restitution Act of 1996 (MVRA), which provides restitution for property losses. Restitution orders have the same status as tax liens, for which plan benefits can also be garnished. [*United States v. Novak*, 441 F.3d 819 (9th Cir. 2006)]

The District Court for the Western District of North Carolina held in mid-2015 that a retirement plan balance can be garnished for debts to the federal government. The anti-alienation provisions of ERISA and the Internal Revenue Code do not prevent enforcement of restitution against a criminal defendant under the MVRA. The MVRA exempts property that is exempt from an IRS levy but restitution orders are treated as a lien on a par with a tax lien. (Defendant Wilson was ordered to pay about $850,000 in restitution when he was convicted of a mortgage fraud scheme.)

Employers should never ignore garnishments (which are court orders) even if the subject of the order is not an employee or does not appear to earn enough money to satisfy the judgment. A few states require disclosure at the end rather than the beginning of garnishment, and a garnishee who does not respond is liable for the amount that would have been withheld from wages. In Georgia and Wisconsin, a default is automatically entered against an employer that fails to answer a garnishment order, but has 15 days to re-open the default by paying costs. If the order is not reopened, default judgment can be entered for the full amount of the outstanding debt even if the debtor is not—or never was—an employee of that employer. [Martin C. Brook, *Tips for Garnishee Employers, Part One: The Perils of Ignoring Garnishment Orders*, Ogletree Deakins (Jan. 10, 2014), available at Lexology.com]

Tennessee law requires answering the garnishment within 10 business days, stating whether the employer holds the employee's property or owes the employee any money. If the employer fails to answer in time, the employee's judgment creditor can move for a conditional judgment making the employer responsible for the entire amount of the debt, but even a late answer will prevent issuance of a conditional judgment. If a conditional judgment issues, the employer can appear in court and explain why it is not responsible for the debt. [John Paul Nefflen, *I Forgot to Respond to a Garnishment. Now What?*, Burr & Forman LLP (Feb. 8, 2016), available at Lexology.com]

Texas requires all deductions from wages, other than payroll taxes and court-ordered garnishments, to be authorized in writing by the employee. Texas employers therefore should get a wage deduction authorization agreement at the time of hiring. It can be signed in conjunction with acknowledgment of receipt of the employee handbook, authorizing deductions for wage overpayments, unreturned property (e.g., company phones), uniforms, and vacation days taken in advance. [Monica Velazquez, *Employee Final Pay: Don't End Up Like Jaime Lannister*, Strasburger & Price LLP (June 5, 2014), available at Lexology.com]

The federal Fair Debt Collection Practices Act (FDCPA) [28 U.S.C. § 3001] lets the federal government collect its judgments by garnishing property held by a third party on the basis of the debtor's "substantial non-exempt interest" in the property. According to the Sixth Circuit, tax levies do not violate ERISA's anti-alienation provisions. [*United States v. Sawaf*, 74 F.3d 119 (6th Cir. 1996)]

The Seventh Circuit held in mid-2016 that a wage garnishment under Illinois law is not a legal action against a consumer for FDCPA purposes. As a result, it does not have to be brought in the judicial district where the debtor lives or where the debtor signed the debt agreement (15 U.S.C. § 1692i(a)(2)). Although it is clearly a legal action, the Seventh Circuit held that it is not an action against a consumer because the focus of the Illinois garnishment system is the third-party employer, not the judgment debtor. The summons is served on the employer, who must answer interrogatories under oath. The employee merely receives notice by mail and a copy of the employer's answers and is not obligated to do anything (although the debtor can contest the employer's answers). Penalties for noncompliance with the garnishment order are imposed on the employer, not the judgment debtor. [*Etro v. Blitt & Gaines PC*, 833 F.3d 860 (7th Cir. 2016); see Richard Payne, *7th Cir. Rejects FDCPA Claims That Illinois Wage Garnishments Are Actions "Against Consumer,"* (Aug. 22, 2016), available at Lexology .com]

In mid-2010, the Pension Benefits Guaranty Corporation (PBGC) revised its regulations on debt collection, to add salary offset and administrative wage garnishment to the acceptable methods of collecting non-tax debts owed to the PBGC. Administrative offset is the process of having amounts that are owed to a business (such as a government contractor) paid to the PBGC instead, to pay the business' debts to the PBGC. Salary offset is withholding of up to 15% of a federal employee's disposable pay to collect debts. Administrative wage garnishment is withholding of wages of a former federal employee who now works for a non-federal employer. The PBGC has to inform debtors of the amount and type of the debt (such as an employer's failure to pay PBGC premiums, or amounts that the PBGC overpaid to an employee), how the PBGC intends to collect the debt, what happens if the debt is not repaid, and how the debtor can make alternate arrangements if the business or individual objects to the PBGC's proposed collection efforts. Under limited circumstances, the PBGC can waive interest, penalties, and administrative costs—but federal law forbids certain types of waivers. [PBGC Proposed Rule, *Debt Collection*, 75 Fed. Reg. 42662 (July 22, 2010)]

Georgia's garnishment statute was held to be unconstitutional by the District Court for the District of Georgia on the grounds that the statute does not require creditors to notify debtors about the types of property (such as Worker's Compensation and Social Security benefits) that are exempt from garnishment. The plaintiff, Strickland's, bank account holding his Worker's Compensation settlement was garnished by a credit card company. As a result, Strickland had to delay cancer surgery by more than five months. Strickland was not given notice or an opportunity to claim the exemption before the garnishment occurred. [*Strickland v. Alexander*, No. 1:12-CV-02735-MHS, 2015 U.S. Dist. LEXIS 121958 (N.D. Ga. Sept. 8, 2015)]

[B]   Student Loan Garnishments

There are separate federal rules at 20 U.S.C. § 1095a with respect to garnishment to repay student loans. Up to 10% of disposable earnings can be garnished to repay those loans. The employee can sign a document agreeing to a higher garnishment level. Before the garnishment order is submitted to the employer, the employee has the right to contest the garnishment and suggest a voluntary repayment schedule. If a person is fired or laid off from a job, and is rehired (by the original employer or someone else) within 12 months after termination, student loan garnishment is deferred until the person has been back in the workforce for 12 months.

The federal provisions do not require employers to change or depart from their normal payment mechanisms to comply with student loan garnishment orders, but if they fail to comply with the order entirely, employers can be penalized by the amount that should have been withheld to satisfy the garnishment, plus costs, fees, and punitive damages.

Federal law forbids an employer to discharge, refuse to hire, or discipline a person because he or she is subject to a student loan garnishment. Employers that violate this rule can be ordered to reinstate the affected employee with back pay, and can also be ordered to pay punitive damages and attorneys' fees.

[C]   Child Support Collection

State governments are heavily involved in child support enforcement, to prevent children from becoming welfare recipients because their parents do not support them. The federal government also requires state governments to take this enforcement role. Under a federal statute, the Child Support Enforcement Amendments of 1984 [Pub. L. No. 98-378], states can lose federal funding if they do not enact laws requiring wage withholding for support arrears. States must also have a procedure for Qualified Medical Child Support Orders (QMCSOs) under which parents who are covered by an Employee Group Health Plan (EGHP) are required to take steps to enroll their children under the plan.

Federal law also requires state-court child support orders to contain a withholding provision, so a withholding order can be issued as soon as a parent falls behind on support, with no need for separate court proceedings. The state child support enforcement agency notifies the employer that a particular employee has child support arrears. The employer is obligated to impose withholding as of the first pay period after 14 days of the date the agency mailed its notice. Once withholding begins, the employer has an obligation to notify the child support agency promptly if the employee quits or gets fired. The notice should give the termination date, the employee's last known address, and the address of the new employer (if known).

The CCPA percentage limits discussed above apply to child support orders. Depending on circumstances, up to 65% of disposable income may be subject to withholding for support. The Child Support Enforcement Amendments allow states to impose a late payment fee of 3 to 6% of the overdue support. Support withholding takes priority over other legal processes (e.g., for consumer debts or student loans) applying to the same income.

Employers must also submit data about newly hired employees to the state unemployment insurance agency within 20 days of hiring. The information is aggregated into a National Directory of New Hires that is used to track down "deadbeat parents" who fail to pay child support.

The basic federal report (which can be made by mail or magnetic tape; state support enforcement agencies can accept telephoned, faxed, and e-mailed reports) consists of:

- Employer's name, address, and Taxpayer Identification Number;
- Employee's name;
- Employee's address;
- Employee's Social Security number.

States may impose additional requirements, such as telephone numbers, driver's license number, and information about the group health plan (to be used in conjunction with a QMCSO). The employer also has to make a quarterly report of wages paid, for use in instituting withholding orders. Failure to make a required report can be penalized by $25 per employee, or $500 for conspiracy with an employee to avoid the requirement.

§ 1.18   USERRA

Under the Uniformed Services Employment and Reemployment Rights Act (USERRA) [38 U.S.C. §§ 4301 *et seq.*], employers have obligations toward their employees who temporarily leave employment to fulfill a military commitment. After the armed service member, reservist or National Guard member returns to civilian life, the employer is obligated to re-employ the person. USERRA requires the employee to give the employer advance written or verbal notice of leave, unless this would be impossible, unreasonable, or precluded by military necessity. The statute requires the employer to reinstate the service member after discharge, in the job he or she would have achieved but for the period of military service, applying the "escalator principle" to seniority, status, compensation, and other seniority-related rights. Furthermore, the employer is not obligated to offer the returned service member a job at the same location, and federal law does not require the employer to pay the service member during military leave. The employee can elect to use accrued vacation or other paid leave while he or she is serving, but employers are not allowed to require the service member to use accrued paid leave.

The employer is obligated to make a reasonable effort to provide training to refresh or upgrade the returning service member's skills. Employees who cannot qualify for their former job must be placed in an alternative position. However, re-employment is not required if circumstances have changed so much that it would be impossible, unreasonable, or impose an undue hardship to do it. When active duty lasted 181 days or more, the re-employed person can be fired only for cause during the first year of reinstatement (and only for cause in the first six months after re-employment following service of 30 to 180 days).

If the service member was on active duty for 30 days or less, USERRA requires him or her to report back to work after active duty on the next regular workday. If the military commitment was 31 to 180 days, the general rule is that USERRA requires the employee to apply for re-employment within 14 days of finishing the military commitment. The period to re-apply stretches to 90 days if the service member was on active duty for over 180 days.

Under USERRA, the employer must treat a period of military duty as active service with the employer for eligibility, vesting, and benefit accrual purposes. However, once the service member returns to work, he or she is entitled to benefits attributable to employee contributions only to the extent that he or she actually made such contributions. The employer is not obligated to make contributions to a 401(k) plan while the employee is on active service, but when the service member is re-employed, the employer must make whatever employer contributions would have been made if the service member had continued at work.

Veterans with service-connected disabilities are covered both by USERRA (enforced by the Department of Labor) and the ADA (enforced by the EEOC). Both statutes impose an obligation of reasonable accommodation on employers;

the USERRA obligation is broader, because it requires employers to make efforts to assist returning veterans to become qualified, e.g., by training or retraining. Some service-related disabilities qualify for accommodation under USERRA even though they are not ADA-level disabilities.

Employer Support of the Guard and Reserve (ESGR), <www.esgr.mil> (last accessed Jan. 28, 2017), is a Department of Defense unit, staffed by over 900 volunteers, to provide liaison between Reservists and their civilian workers on USERRA issues. The Website American Heroes at Work, <http://www.dol.gov/vets/ahaw/> (last accessed Jan. 28, 2017), jointly managed by the DOL Office of Disability Employment Policy and the Veterans' Employment and Training Service, provides resources in toolkit form for employers when veterans with traumatic brain injury or post-traumatic stress disorder (PTSD) return to work. The site covers, e.g., implementing accommodations at work and services for veterans.

Creditors are legally obligated under USERRA to reduce interest rates to 6% or less on debts owed by those entering military service. The statute allows plan fiduciaries to petition the relevant court to maintain a higher interest rate, based on a showing of the servicemember's ability to pay. USERRA also allows (but does not obligate) the plan to suspend the obligation to make regular payments of plan loans during the term of military service. The Service Members Civil Relief Act, Pub. L. No. 108-189 clarifies that the 6% interest rate ceiling only applies to obligations incurred prior to entering military service. Therefore, a plan loan made to a plan participant who is already on military duty can charge the plan's normal interest rate. But interest over and above the permitted 6% level must be forgiven, not merely postponed until the servicemember returns.

Under federal law, USERRA leave does not have to be paid leave (although some state laws do impose a requirement of a period of paid leave). The federal statute allows employees, at their option, to use accrued vacation or other paid leave while they are on active duty, but the employer is not permitted to force them to do so if they prefer unpaid leave and preservation of their leave accrual.

There is no requirement that employers provide pay supplements to prevent servicemembers from suffering a loss of income when they lose their civilian paychecks and get military pay (often much lower). However, some employers elect to do so as a patriotic statement of support for the troops. The time periods vary from three months to several years. The GAO studied past military operations, and concluded that 41% of reservists lost income when called up for active duty, 30% experienced no change, and 29% actually had higher income post-call-up.

In addition to the federal requirements, a number of states (e.g., California, Illinois, Indiana, Maine, Minnesota, Nebraska, New York, Rhode Island, and Washington) have enacted statutory employment rights for servicemembers. [See George P. Kostakos and Stephen T. Melnick, *New Rhode Island Law Grants Military Families Unpaid Leave*, Littler Press Releases, Media Advisories, and Newsletters (July 2008) (benefitslink.com)]

Being called for active service is also a COBRA event, requiring notice and giving the service member and family the option of continuing coverage in the employer's plan for up to 24 months by making premium payments. After a service member is deactivated, he or she and family members can also do a kind of reverse-COBRA election by choosing to remain within the TRICARE system for a period of time. [GAO-03-549T, *Military Personnel: Preliminary Observations Related to Income, Benefits, and Employer Support for Reservists During Mobilizations* (Mar. 19, 2003), <http://www.gao.gov/new.items/d03549t.pdf> (last accessed Jan. 28, 2017)]

The reverse claim has also been made: a reservist sued his ex-employer under USERRA, including a claim that the employer improperly continued the plaintiff's health coverage while he was on military leave; he said that continuation was unnecessary because he had military health care coverage. (Funds were deducted from his Paid Time Off account to pay the premiums.) The employer said that it continued coverage because the employee did not ask to discontinue it. The District Court for the Western District of Michigan said that USERRA deals with the right to maintain coverage during deployment, not the right to suspend it. The employer returned the deductions to the PTO account and billed the employee directly. The district court ruled that the employer did not violate USERRA. [*Eichaker v. Village of Vicksburg*, No. 1:12-cv-01350, 2015 WL 113902 (W.D. Mich. Jan. 8, 2015)]

As of 2009, two Circuit Courts (the Fifth and Sixth Circuits) had ruled that USERRA cases fall under mandatory arbitration clauses, finding that statutes that provide for lawsuits do not thereby rule out mandatory arbitration of discrimination claims. However, two District Courts have held that USERRA claims are not subject to mandatory arbitration, because the USERRA provision that says the law preempts state laws that eliminate, reduce, or limit USERRA rights forbid mandatory arbitration because the arbitration requirement limits servicemembers' rights under USERRA. [Compare *Landis v. Pinnacle Eye Care*, 537 F.3d 559 (6th Cir. 2008) and *Garrett v. Circuit City Stores*, 449 F.3d 672 (5th Cir. 2006) with *Lopez v. Dillard's, Inc.*, 382 F. Supp. 2d 1245 (D. Kan. 2005) and *Breletic v. CACI Inc.*, 413 F. Supp. 2d 1329 (2006).]

In late 2016, the Ninth Circuit joined the Fifth and Sixth Circuits in finding USERRA claims to be subject to mandatory arbitration pursuant to a clause covering "employment-related" claims. The Ninth Circuit held that arbitrating a case does not force the veteran to forfeit substantive rights under USERRA and USERRA does not overrule the FAA. Ziober said that the USERRA statute creates a right to sue in federal court that outweighs arbitration, but the Ninth Circuit said that arbitration doesn't forfeit substantive rights, and USERRA doesn't overrule the FAA. [*Ziober v. BLB Resources*, 839 F.3d 814 (9th Cir. 2016); see Kimberlee W. DeWitt, *Ninth Circuit Joins Sister Circuits in Holding That Employees May Be Required to Arbitrate USERRA Claims*, Hunton & Williams LLP (Nov. 4, 2016), available at Lexology.com]

In mid-2016, the Eleventh Circuit enforced an arbitration clause even though some of its provisions (reducing the statute of limitations; allowing the employer to apportion attorneys' fees and costs) violated USERRA. The Eleventh Circuit upheld the district court's decision to sever the invalid provisions and compel arbitration. The Eleventh Circuit held that USERRA's "non-waiver" provision, forbidding contracts that limit USERRA rights, does not automatically invalidate a non-compliant agreement, and reforming a contract is consistent with the FAA. [*Bodine v. Cook's Pest Control Inc.,* 830 F.3d 1320 (11th Cir. 2016); see Robert Scavone Jr. & Juan C. Enjamio, *Eleventh Circuit: Arbitration Agreement Enforceable Despite Terms That Violate USERRA,* Hunton & Williams LLP (Aug. 18, 2016), available at Lexology.com]

Note, however, that the California Court of Appeal ruled in late 2007 that USERRA rights cannot be waived by contract. Therefore, a release of rights under a severance agreement could not be enforced to the extent it dealt with allegations that a Marine Reserve captain was terminated because of his military status. (He was fired the day after he returned to work from Reserve duty.) 38 U.S.C. § 4302(b) provides that USERRA supersedes any state law or contract that reduces, limits or eliminates any USERRA right; the court interpreted this to cover suits for wrongful termination and breach of an oral employment contract. [*Perez v. Uline,* 157 Cal. App. 4th 953 (Cal. App. 2007)]

The Sixth Circuit reached a different conclusion in mid-2010, finding that a veteran of the war in Afghanistan could not sue his former employer, IBM, under USERRA, because he negotiated an Individual Separation Allowance Plan under which he received $6,000 for release of all of his employment-related claims. The Sixth Circuit enforced the release because it was knowing and voluntary; the release form was not ambiguous; and there was no evidence of fraud or over-reaching. [*Wysocki v. IBM,* 607 F.3d 1102 (6th Cir. 2010)]

The Supreme Court denied certiorari in the Sixth Circuit case of a Nashville police officer who charged that imposing a three-week delay in reinstating him after his discharge from the Army Reserves violated USERRA. The Sixth Circuit ruled in his favor because he satisfied the conditions for reinstatement (discharge under honorable conditions; military service lasting less than five years; prompt request for re-employment), even though the Nashville police department said that its internal policies called for the delay, and the plaintiff was charged with violating Army regulations. The Sixth Circuit held that USERRA rules prevail over internal employment policies. [*Petty v. Metropolitan Gov't of Nashville,* 538 F.3d 431 (6th Cir. 2008), *cert. denied* as *Metropolitan Gov't of Nashville v. Petty,* 556 U.S. 1165 (2009)]

The Eighth Circuit held that the purchaser of a business did not meet its USERRA obligations when the plaintiff, who was deployed in Iraq, was not included in the list of active employees. The purchase agreement required reasonable efforts to offer employment to the list of employees furnished by the selling company. Everyone on the list was hired, but the plaintiff was not rehired when he returned from deployment in December 2008. (He was eventually hired in

April 2009.) He sued his ex-employer, which said that it was not obligated to rehire him because going out of business constituted changed circumstances. The Ninth Circuit held that an employee on military leave is entitled to the same rights and benefits as comparable employees without military commitments. Employers have better records than employees, so it was up to the seller corporation to explain whether employees on long-term non-military leave were included on the hire list when the plaintiff was not. [*Dorris v. TXD Servs., LP*, 753 F.3d 740 (8th Cir. 2014)]

Retaliation claims are one of the largest portions of the employment discrimination caseload, and retaliation allegations are also raised in the USERRA context. A California jury awarded $275,000 to a police officer who charged USERRA retaliation. The District Court dismissed the jury award, but the Ninth Circuit reinstated it. [*Wallace v. City of San Diego*, 460 F.3d 1181 (9th Cir. 2006)]

A "cat's paw" is a tool used by someone to accomplish his purpose. In the employment law context, this theory imputes one person's discriminatory animus to the decision-maker, if the decision-maker was influenced by the other person. The Supreme Court allowed "cat's paw" liability to apply in a USERRA case: the plaintiff alleged he was fired because of his military history. The plaintiff charged that the hospital scheduler exerted influence to get him fired. The employer is liable because its agent, pursuing discriminatory animus, intends to and does cause an adverse employment action. [*Staub v. Proctor Hosp.*, 131 S. Ct. 1186 (2011)]

[A] Regulations

Although USERRA is a 1994 statute, the first proposed regulations were not issued until September 20, 2004, by the Department of Labor's Veterans' Employment and Training Service (VETS). A few months later, on December 10, 2004, President Bush signed the Veterans Benefits Improvement Act of 2004, Pub. L. No. 108-454, amending USERRA Title 38 § 4317 to allow servicemembers to elect and pay for continuation coverage. Another statute, the Heroes Earned Retirement Opportunities Act, Pub. L. No. 109-227, allows active servicemembers to treat combat pay as compensation that can be contributed to an IRA.

The Heroes Earnings Assistance and Relief Tax Act (HEART Act, Pub. L. No. 110-245) provides financial flexibility for servicemembers, in the form of special options in health care FSAs and Qualified Reservist Distributions. Notice 2010-15, 2010-6 I.R.B. 390, explains that differential pay provided to employees on active service must be included in pension calculations. Funds can be withdrawn without an early withdrawal penalty from defined contribution plans by a person on active duty for at least six months. Survivors of deceased servicemembers can make tax-free rollovers of the military death benefit and life insurance to a Roth IRA or education savings account. Military service is not a break in service when it comes to participation, vesting, or benefit accruals. Joint employers are covered by USERRA, and so are a company's successor in interest, even if unaware of the servicemember's re-employment claims (20 C.F.R. §§ 1002.35–.37). Temporary, part-time, laid-off and seasonal employees, job applicants, and employees who are on leave are protected by USERRA, but independent contractors are not. If the employer offers more than one type of non-military leave, military leave must provide the same benefits as the most generous of those (20 C.F.R. § 1002.149). The employer must be prompt about re-employing a returned servicemember. Unless there are unusual circumstances, re-employment should occur within two weeks of the application, and for weekend National Guard duty, it should occur on the next regularly scheduled work period (20 C.F.R. §§ 1002.180–.181).

One acceptable alternative is for the employer to use the "escalator principle" and grant the re-employed employee the raises and benefit increases that were reasonably certain to have occurred if he or she had not been called to duty. However, the regulations permit other alternatives, such as returning the employee to the position held before deployment; giving him or her a comparable position to the pre-service or elevator position; or making the nearest possible approximation to one of those. If the person would have been laid off if he or she had remained at work, re-employment to layoff status is permitted (20 C.F.R. § 1002.194).

The appropriate placement of the employee depends on factors such as length of service, the employee's qualifications, and any extent to which military service caused or aggravated an existing disability (20 C.F.R. §§ 1002.196–.197). Sections 225 and 226 require the employer to make reasonable efforts to accommodate disability of persons seeking re-employment and to help the applicant become qualified to perform the duties of the offered job.

[B]   Recent Cases

USERRA has generated a number of important cases.

The First Circuit ruled that USERRA protects servicemembers who have not actually been recalled to active duty, but who have expressed a definite intent to return to active service in the near future. [*Vega-Colon v. Wyeth Pharm.*, 625 F.3d 22 (1st Cir. 2010)]

A surgeon who was employed for only a brief period before deployment was not entitled to be reinstated. He refused a permanent job so he could keep his options open. His 30-day assignment was extended several times and then he signed a one-year contract that either side could terminate on 90 days' notice. His employer sent him a termination agreement when he was in Iraq because it wanted a permanent employee. The Sixth Circuit held that USERRA contemplates permanent rather than temporary employment. [*Slusher v. Shelbyville Hosp. Corp.*, 805 F.3d 211 (6th Cir. 2015)]

The Eleventh Circuit held that the Alabama Department of Mental Health violated USERRA by failing to rehire servicemember Roy Hamilton on a timely basis after return from his 2003 deployment. While he was on active duty, the facility where he had worked was closed. The Eleventh Circuit said that Hamilton's rejection of a transfer to a different city, for family reasons, did not prevent him from being entitled to reemployment. The Eleventh Circuit upheld the jury's $25,000 award for lost pay and benefits. The court held that the department was not entitled to sovereign immunity, because the suit was brought by the Department of Justice rather than by a private individual. [*United States v. Alabama Dep't of Mental Health & Mental Retardation*, 673 F.3d 1320 (11th Cir. 2012)]

USERRA has a for-cause standard for returning veterans. That is, veterans who served for 30–180 days cannot be discharged other than for cause for six months after their return. Those who served more than 180 days are similarly protected for a one-year period. The employer has the burden of proving not only that the veteran's discharge was reasonable but also that the employee was on notice that his or her conduct could lead to discharge. In a recent Tenth Circuit case, the plaintiff was fired after three instances of failing to provide notice that he would be late for his shift, as required by the employer's written policy. However, the plaintiff's manager told him that it would be acceptable to give an explanation the next day. The Tenth Circuit held that a reasonable jury could find that the supervisor's statement deprived the plaintiff of notice that he could be fired for violating the policy. [*Starr v. QuikTrip Corp.*, **655 Fed. Appx. 642** (10th Cir. 2016); see Christopher Wilkinson, Mark R. Thompson & Joshua F. Naylor, *Veterans Returning to Work After Military Service May Not Be Discharged Except "For Cause,"* Orrick, Herrington & Sutcliffe LLP (July 28, 2016), available at Lexology.com]

Two Chicago police officers seeking promotion to sergeant sued under USERRA. The promotion exam was scheduled for March 25, 2006, when the plaintiffs were on active duty. They took the test outside the United States; passed; and were placed on the eligibility list. They sued when the person with the highest score was promoted. The plaintiffs alleged that they would have scored higher if they had not had to travel long distances to take the test, and they should have been given a chance to take the promotion exam at the bases where they were stationed. The Seventh Circuit ruled that USERRA § 4311 does not require accommodation, and the plaintiffs were not entitled to better treatment than employees who were in Chicago on the test date. [*Sandoval v. City of Chicago*, 560 F.3d 703 (7th Cir. 2009)]

In a failure to promote suit, the Third Circuit held at the end of 2016 that plaintiffs do not have to plead or prove their objective qualifications for the promotion to satisfy their initial burden of proof. However, the employer can asset lack of qualifications as a defense against the USERRA charge. [*Carroll v. Delaware River Port Auth.*, 843 F.3d 129 (3d Cir. 2016)]

The First Circuit held in 2013 that when an employee is reinstated after active service USERRA requires the employer to consider whatever non-automatic discretionary promotions the employee might have received in addition to the "escalator position" reflecting automatic promotions such as those based on seniority. The First Circuit read the regulations to require promoting the employee to the position that would have been held, with reasonable certainty, absent active military service. [*Rivera-Melendez v. Pfizer Pharm., LLC*, 730 F.3d 49 (1st Cir. 2013)]

The Fourth Circuit held in late 2016 that reinstating the plaintiff would have been futile. The employer had already compensated her for lost wages and benefits, and the plaintiff did not allege that the USERRA violation was willful. [*Butts v. Prince William Cnty. Sch. Bd.*, 844 F.3d 424 (4th Cir. 2016)]

The Veterans' Benefit and Improvement Act of 2008, Pub. L. No. 110-389, eliminated the statute of limitations on USERRA claims. However, this law is not retroactive. For cases before it took effect, the statute of limitations is four years. Therefore, a plaintiff who did not file his case within four years was time-barred. Even if the running of the statute of limitations was tolled (suspended) while he was on active duty, he still missed the deadline. There was no evidence of wrongdoing by his employer that would justify equitable tolling. [*Baldwin v. City of Greensboro*, 714 F.3d 828 (4th Cir. 2013)]

CHAPTER 2
TAX ASPECTS OF PAY PLANNING

§ 2.01 INTRODUCTION

One reason why corporations adopt pension and benefit plans is that, under appropriate circumstances, the employer will get a tax deduction, and the employee will receive valuable benefits—but the employee will not have immediately taxable income as a result of the benefits (or only part of the benefit will generate taxable income). At press time in 2017, corporate tax reduction was a priority for the Trump administration but no specific measures had been adopted or proposed. Lower tax rates make it less attractive to the corporation to provide benefits that it can deduct and lower individual rates could make employees more interested in receiving a higher cash salary rather than benefits because cutting the tax bill is less imperative.

Pay planning requires the employer to determine what portion of each employee's compensation is taxable, and performing tax withholding, depositing taxes, issuing information returns, and maintaining tax records. In most years, at least one tax bill is enacted that affects employers' tax responsibilities; in some years, there are several bills. In recent years, changes in FICA rules have been especially notable. See § 2.01[A] for a narrative account of recent tax changes.

The pace of change can be fast enough to make it difficult to keep up with current tax rules—and, in fact, there may be several tax rules that apply in the same year, depending on the effective date of the statutes passed during that year.

The basic tax rule is that everything received is taxable income, unless there is a specific exclusion. Therefore, the tax definition of "wages" includes vacation pay, commissions, bonuses, and some fringe benefits, not just straight salary. Severance pay is considered taxable wages, but payments for cancellation of an employment contract are not wages.

These items have been granted exclusions from taxable income:

- Worker's Compensation benefits;

- The employer's contributions to qualified pension plans (but the employee's pretax deferrals placed into 401(k) plans are the Federal Unemployment Tax Act (FUTA) and the Federal Insurance Contributions Act (FICA) wages);

- Up to $50,000 in § 79 group-term life insurance coverage. Additional coverage is taxable income that must be reported on the W-2 form, but income tax withholding is not required. The excess coverage is not subject to FUTA, but is subject to both the employer and employee share of FICA;

- Certain fringe benefits, e.g., employee discounts, working condition and de minimis fringes, qualified transportation fringes, qualified dependent care assistance within limits, etc.

The IRS issues annual updates of its Publication 15-A, Employer's Supplemental Tax Guide and Publication 15-B, Employer's Tax Guide to Fringe Benefits. See <http://www.irs.gov/pub/irs-pdf/p15a.pdf> (version for preparing 2016 taxes last accessed Jan. 31, 2017) and <www.irs.gov/pub/irs-pdf/p15b.pdf> (last accessed Jan. 31, 2017) respectively.

When a new employee is hired the employer must use Form I-9 to verify immigration status and that the person can lawfully work within the United States. [See § 23.11 for more information about immigration issues in hiring.]

For a life insurance contract on the life of an employee (including a highly compensated employee or a 5% owner of the business) to qualify for exclusion from income tax (see § 21.02[A]), notice and consent requirements must be met. Before the contract is issued, the employee must be given written notice that the policyholder intends to insure the employee's life and the maximum face amount of such insurance. The employee must be informed that the insurance could be maintained even after the employee terminates employment, and that, when the insured employee dies, the insurance proceeds are paid to an applicable policyholder. If the insured is still alive, the employer might be able to cure a failure before the return is due for the year in which the policy was issued, by having the employee sign a consent form furnished by the insurance agent or drafted by the employer's attorney. [Steve Gorin, *How to Avoid Tax Traps in Life Insurance*, Thompson Coburn LLP (Jan. 10, 2017), available at Lexology.com]

Employer Group Health Plans (EGHPs) that fail to satisfy certain federal requirements must pay excise taxes, which are reported on IRS Form 8928; at press time in 2017 it was possible that these requirements would be repealed. Self-reporting is required for compliance with the Comprehensive Omnibus Budget Reconciliation Act (COBRA) requirements (including the subsidy program); the Health Insurance Portability and Accessibility Act (HIPAA) rules; benefits for childbirth, mental health parity, and Michelle's law; and the Genetic Information Nondisclosure Act.

If the employer fails to make contributions to Medical Savings Accounts (MSAs) or Health Savings Account (HSAs) that are comparable as between rank and file and highly compensated employees, the excise tax generally equals 35% of aggregate employer contributions to all employees' MSAs and HSAs for the year. In this situation, Form 8928 is due by the fifteenth day of the fourth month of the year after the year in which a non-comparable contribution was made. An excise tax is imposed for failure to comply with a variety of requirements (dealing with, e.g., pre-existing condition limitations, nondiscrimination in enrollment, minimum hospital stay for childbirth, mental health parity). But the excise tax is waived if the responsible person did not know, and could not have known with due diligence, of the failure; or the failure was reasonable, not caused by willful neglect, and was corrected within 30 days. There are additional penalties for late returns and late payments. [IRS Instructions for Form 8928, <http://www.irs.gov/instructions/i8928/ch01.html> (last accessed Jan. 31, 2017)]

When a plan complies with Patient Protection and Affordable Care Act (PPACA) and covers participants' adult children until their 26th birthday that coverage is tax-free for federal purposes—but not necessarily under state law. If state law does not track the federal law, then it may be necessary to report the fair market value of the coverage for state tax purposes.

The employer mandate under PPACA, also known as the "pay or play" rules, requires Applicable Large Employers (ALEs) to offer at least a basic package of affordable health insurance to their employees—or pay an excise tax penalty. Companies with under 50 employees are not subject to these requirements. Notice 2015-87, 2015-52 I.R.B. 889 provides that for 2015, the penalty for failure to offer minimum essential coverage to all full-time employees is $2,080 (2015) and $2,160 (2016). The corresponding penalty is $2,260 for 2017. The penalty for failure to offer minimum value, affordable coverage to any employee is $3,120 (2015), $3,240 (2016), and $3,390 (2017). [Lyndsey R. Barnett, *The IRS Finally Confirms Penalty Amounts for the Pay or Play Penalties for 2015 (and 2016)*, Graydon Head (Dec. 17, 2015), available at Lexology.com]

Notice 2015-87 also provides that, for tax years beginning in 2015, coverage is considered "affordable" if it does not cost more than 9.56% of household income; the corresponding 2016 percentage is 9.66%, and 9.69% for 2017. [Kathleen Reilly Barrow and Stephanie O. Zorn, *Late-Breaking Benefits News for 2016*, Jackson Lewis PC (Dec. 30, 2015), available at Lexology.com] As with all PPACA figures, however, the potential for repeal must be considered.

It used to be common for employers to maintain an "employer payment plan," (EPP) under which employees were reimbursed for the premiums of health insurance policies they purchased individually. In 2013, the IRS determined that these plans are group health plans that must satisfy PPACA requirements or be subject to penalties under § 4980D ($100 per employee per day); DOL penalties under ERISA were also a possibility. [Notice 2013-54, 2013-40 I.R.B. 287] Small employers were given transition relief, until June 30, 2015, under Notice 2015-17, 2015-28 I.R.B. 67. [Wolters Kluwer Law & Business, *IRS Transition Relief for Small Companies Offering Employer Payment Plans Ends on June 30* (June 13, 2016) (benefitslink.com)]

The IRS's position, since Notice 2015-87, 2015-52 I.R.B. 889, is that some "opt-out payments" (made by employers to employees who turn down medical coverage from the employer) could be considered part of the employee's cost of obtaining coverage. The IRS proposed regulations in July 2016 stating that an unconditional payment that the employee could obtain merely by opting out of the employer group health plan (EGHP) was an employee cost, and, therefore, a salary reduction paid by the employee. This characterization could mean that the coverage failed to satisfy the PPACA affordability standard, exposing the employer to penalties under the employer mandate. However, the IRS considers an "eligible opt-out arrangement" to be a conditional opt-out based on proof that the employee and dependents have other coverage, so it is not an employee cost even if the employee takes the coverage. The IRS first granted interim relief to employers who adopted an opt-out arrangement before December 16, 2016. Opt-out payments did not have to be taken into account until final regulations were issued, which was supposed to occur on January 1, 2017. However, this did not occur, so the IRS extended relief for plans adopted before December 16, 2015, until further regulations are issued. Of course, if the employer mandate is repealed, the issue will become moot. [Jason T. Froggatt et. al., *Update #2: Relief Extended for "Opt-Out" Payments for Health Coverage*, Davis Wright Tremaine LLP (Jan. 23, 2017), available at Lexology.com]

The PATH Act (Protecting Americans From Tax Hikes; Pub. L. No. 114-113) delays the "Cadillac tax" on high-value employee group health plan coverage until 2020 (it was originally scheduled to take effect in 2018). The PATH Act also makes any Cadillac tax eventually imposed a deductible business expense. The PATH Act also repeals the PPACA rule that would have required employers with more than 200 employees to automatically enroll employees in their health plans. The Cadillac tax is likely to be repealed, although this had not occurred as of this 2018 edition.

In addition to welfare benefit plans that provide health insurance, some employers include health insurance coverage as a part of their retirement plans. T.D. 9665 provides that, starting with the 2015 tax year, most payments by qualified retirement plans for accident or health insurance will be taxable to the plan participants. There are exceptions for retiree health benefits and amounts used to pay disability insurance premiums. If the disability insurance replaces plan distributions when the participant is disabled, the premiums will not be taxable income for the employee, as long as the aggregate contribution for benefits is not greater than 25% of total plan contributions. [T.D. 9665, 79 Fed. Reg. 26838 (May 12, 2014)]

Medical flexible spending accounts, also known as Flexible Spending Accounts (FSAs) and flex accounts, permit employees to save up to $2,500 a year pre-tax (adjusted for inflation). Initially, sums were forfeited to the extent they were not used for medical expenses during the plan year. Recently, the IRS has permitted a grace period for reimbursement of expenses incurred in the two-and-a-half months after the end of the plan year. In late 2013, the IRS allowed employers to choose between offering either this grace period or a $500 carryforward of unused funds at any time during the next plan year. The Treasury said that rule changes under PPACA, altering the amount that can be contributed to an FSA (the 2013 limit is $2,500; the 2015–2016 limit is $2,550), there is less need to prevent excess sheltering of funds in FSA accounts. [Notice 2013-71, 2013-47 I.R.B. 532; Rev. Proc. 2015-53, 2015-44 I.R.B. 615] The 2017 limit is $2,600. [Rev. Proc. 2016-55, 2016-45 I.R.B 707. See Haynes and Boone LLP, *Health Care FSA Contribution Limit Increased for 2017* (Nov.10, 2016), available at Lexology.com.]

In early 2017, the IRS proposed amendments to the definition of qualified matching contributions (QMAC) and qualified nonelective contributions (QNECs), for 401(k) plans. [See § 6.04 for more discussion of 401(k) plans.] The proposals would allow employer contributions to be treated as QMACs or QNECs if they satisfy requirements for non-forfeitability and distributions at the time of allocation to participants' accounts—not when contributed to the plan (i.e., they don't have to satisfy the requirements at the time of contribution). The practical effect is that forfeitures can be used to fund QMACs and QNECs. [Rebecca Moore, *IRS Proposes Changes to QMAC, QNEC Definitions*, plansponsor.com (Jan. 17, 2017)]

IRS proposed and temporary regulations adopted in the spring of 2016 generally prevent partners from participating in employee benefit plans that cover the employees of a "disregarded entity" owned by the partnership. To oversimplify somewhat, a disregarded entity is a Limited Liability Company owned by a partner who provides services to the partnership; it is "disregarded" because he is not an independent taxpayer. The IRS's position is that partners who provide services to a disregarded entity are not employees of that entity. Bona fide partners are not employees of a partnership for purposes of FICA, FUTA, or income tax withholding. A partner who works in the conduct of the partnership's trade or business, or who offers services to the partnership as an independent contractor, is a self-employed person, not an employee. [Sullivan & Cromwell LLP, *Treasury Clarifies That Partners Working for a Disregarded Entity Owned by a Partnership are Self-Employed* (May 3, 2016), available at Lexology.com; Reginald J. Clark et. al., *Neither a Partner nor Employee Be: Treasury and the IRS Issue Regulations Clarifying the Employment Tax Treatment of Partners in Partnerships,* Sutherland Asbill & Brennan LLP (May 5, 2016), available at Lexology.com]

[A] Changes in Tax Statutes

Although the tax bills since 2005 have not made tremendous changes in the employment tax picture, nevertheless they have made some modifications that are worth noting. The various tax bills since have made changes—often subtle—in employment-related taxes.

Small and medium-sized businesses often forgo targeted tax incentive tax breaks, because they are too hard to understand, cost too much to implement, or risk pushback from the IRS. According to tax consultants, eligible businesses claim only about 5% of the tax breaks they are entitled to. [John D. McKinnon, *Firms Pass Up Tax Breaks, Citing Hassles, Complexity*, WSJ.com (July 22, 2012)]

As of January 1, 2010, eligible rollover distributions paid directly to a non-spouse beneficiary are subject to 20% mandatory withholding (not 10% voluntary withholding for non-periodic payments) if the amount is not directly rolled over to an IRA. [Elizabeth Thomas Dodd, Groom Law Group Memorandum to Clients, *RE: IRS Pension Distribution Reporting Changes for 2010* (Mar. 3, 2010) (benefitslink.com)]

The Heroes Earnings Assistance and Relief Tax Act (HEART Act, Pub. L. No. 110-245) allows servicemembers to take qualified reservist distributions, cash distributions from their FSAs that are taxable income but do not trigger the 10% penalty, and provides financial flexibility for servicemembers. See Notice 2008-82, 2008-41 I.R.B. 853 [JP Morgan Compensation & Benefit Strategies, *IRS Releases Guidance on Health FSA Distributions Under the HEART Act* (Oct. 10, 2008) (benefitslink.com)]

The American Recovery and Reinvestment Act of 2009 (ARRA; Pub. L. No. 111-5) enacted a temporary premium subsidy for COBRA premiums, but it was permitted to expire.

The Patient Protection and Affordable Care Act, Pub. L. No. 111-148 (PPACA), the health care reform bill, includes a number of tax-related provisions to finance the expansion of health insurance coverage.

PPACA §§ 1421 and 10105 provide a tax credit for small employers. The credit can be claimed for tax years beginning after December 31, 2009, if the employer makes non-elective contributions that cover at least half the premium for covering participating employees. A small employer is defined as an employer that maintains a qualified health arrangement, and that has up to 25 full-time equivalent employees (FTEs), whose average wage is not more than twice the dollar amount prescribed for the tax year. The credit is reduced based on the number of employees and their average compensation, and is eliminated at 25 FTEs.

For tax years 2010–2013, the credit is 35% of the employer's total non-elective contributions on behalf of employees to pay premiums for qualified health coverage. However, the credit is capped at the amount that HHS determines is the average small-group premium for the relevant market. That is, employers who pay above-average premiums cannot claim the credit on the full amount paid.

For tax years that begin in 2014 or later years, the maximum credit is 50% of the premiums that the small employer pays on behalf of employees who get their health coverage through the Small Business Health Options Program (SHOP) exchange. [IRS, *Small Business Health Care Tax Credit Questions and Answers: Who Gets the Tax Credit,* available at <https://www.irs.gov/uac/small-business-health-care-tax-credit-questions-and-answers-who-gets-the-tax-credit> (updated Dec. 23, 2016) (last accessed Mar. 28, 2017)]

The small business health care credit is claimed on Form 8941. Qualifying employers have fewer than 25 employees, average wages under $50,000 per employee, and the employer pays at least half the premium for health insurance for enrolled employees. The employer can claim the credit for only two consecutive years beginning in or after 2014. [EBIA Weekly, *IRS Releases 2013 Form 8941 and Instructions for Claiming Small Business Health Care Tax Credit* (Jan. 16, 2014) (benefitslink.com)]

Very few employers used the SHOP exchange: as of January 2017, only 7,554 employers, with 38,749 employees, had coverage under the federally facilitated SHOP exchange, and 19,651 employers with almost 200,000 covered persons had coverage under state SHOP exchanges. Because the tax credit could be claimed for only two years, probably most eligible employers had already exhausted it by 2017. CMS announced that, as of the end of 2017, the federally facilitated SHOP exchange would be phased out. Employers can enroll directly with insurers or use agents or brokers. The state SHOP marketplaces can either continue providing enrollment online or refer businesses to agents and brokers. [Timothy Jost, *CMS Announces Plans to Effectively End the SHOP Exchange*, Health Affairs (May 15, 2017), available at healthaffairs.org]

The original text of PPACA called for the imposition of a "Cadillac tax" starting in 2018, on high-value plans whose premium exceeds $10,200 for individuals, or $27,500 for family coverage (with higher limits for non-Medicare-eligible retirees over age 55, and employees with certain high-risk jobs). [Brian Faler, *"Cadillac Tax" the Next Big Obamacare Battle*, Politico (Apr. 6, 2015), <http://www.politico.com/story/2015/04/obamacare-health-care-cadillac-tax-116659>]

However, in 2015, the PATH Act (Protecting Americans Against Tax Hikes; Pub. L. No. 114-113) deferred the starting date for the Cadillac tax two years, until 2020. It is likely that the Cadillac tax will be repealed in 2017 or 2018.

PPACA § 9002 requires that, employers must disclose the aggregate cost (employer share plus employee share) of employer-sponsored coverage on Form W-2 The costs of long-term care insurance, accident & health, disability income insurance, fixed indemnity insurance, and coverage limited to a specified disease are not included in this figure. [See IRS, *Form W-2 Reporting of Employer-Sponsored Health Coverage*, <http://www.irs.gov/uac/Form-W-2-Reporting-of-Employer-Sponsored-Health-Coverage> (last updated Nov. 2, 2016) (last viewed Jan. 31, 2017)]

Code § 6056 requires employers to report both to employees and the IRS. The reporting obligation was delayed several times because of problems launching health care reform, but finally took effect as of January 1, 2015. Employers that have 100 or more full-time equivalent employees in 2015, or 50 or more full-time equivalent employees in 2016 and later years, must report information so the IRS can determine if they offered PPACA-compliance coverage to at least 70% of qualifying employees (for 2015) and 95% of qualifying employees in subsequent years. Self-funded plans are also subject to reporting requirements for administration of the individual mandate (the obligation imposed on certain individuals to maintain coverage). Reporting employers must report coverage on a month-by-month bases and use Form 1094C and 1095C to report information relevant to the "pay or play" penalty and the individual mandate. Insurers and self-insuring companies that are not applicable large employers use Forms 1904B and 1095B. Information about employee and individual coverage can be reported to employees, retirees, and COBRA beneficiaries on Forms 1095B and 1095C, although employers can use other formats as long as the necessary information is conveyed. The due date for these forms is the same as for Form W-2, and employee statements can be provided with the W-2. Reports to employees are due by January 31 of the year after the year for which figures are reported. Reports to the IRS are due February 28—or March 31 if they are e-filed. [Brown, Todd, *Month by Month, Employers Must Track Employees in 2015 for Required Reporting Under Health Reform Rules*, Brown Todd (Jan. 15, 2015) (benefitslink.com)]

The penalties for failure to provide proper information returns were raised by the Trade Preferences Extension Act. Penalties for information returns (including W-2 as well as 1094-B, 1095-B, 1094-C and 1095-C) increase from $100 to $250 per return. The cap on penalties goes from $1.5 million to $3 million, and all the penalties are doubled if the failure involves both a payee statement and an information return submitted to the IRS. Furthermore, the penalty is $500 per return, not $250, for each failure caused by intentional disregard of the law, and there is no cap. [Trade Preferences Extension Act, Pub. L. No. 114-27; see Elizabeth Vollmar, *New Trade Bill Escalates ACA Reporting Penalties, Resuscitates Health Coverage Tax Credit*, Lockton (July 2015) (benefitslink.com)]

On November 18, 2016, the IRS announced a 30-day extension of the time to furnish 2016 Form 1095-Cs to employees, making the due date March 2, 2017. The announcement itself does not extend the deadline for the 1094-C and 1095-C forms, but an automatic 30-day extension can be obtained by filing Form 8809. The IRS will not impose penalties for incorrect information, such as date of birth or Social Security Number, if the employer made a good-faith effort to comply, and forms were distributed and filed no later than the applicable deadline. [Jennifer Bibart Dunsizer et. al., *Labor and Employment Alert: 30 Extra Days to Distribute 2016 Form 1095-Cs to Employees*, Vorys Sater Seymour and Pease LLP (Nov. 26, 2016), available at Lexology.com]

Starting January 1, 2013, PPACA imposes higher Medicare payroll taxes on high-income persons. Instead of 1.45%, the employee share of Medicare tax is 2.35% for high-income persons. The employer's share of the Medicare tax does not increase. High-income persons also pay a Medicare surtax on their investment income other than tax-exempt bond interest and profits on sale of their principal residence. The tax applies to persons whose wages, compensation, or self-employment income exceed $250,000 (joint returns), $125,000 (married persons filing separately), $200,000 (single persons, heads of household, and qualifying widow(er)s with one or more dependent children). The employer must withhold the additional tax from wages over $200,000 paid to anyone, irrespective of the recipient's filing status or wages paid by other employers. The employer cannot modify its withholding of additional Medicare tax. However, a person who expects to owe more than the amount withheld by the employer can increase withholding on the W-4 (e.g., a joint return where neither spouse earns over $200,000, but the total is over $250,000).

The 3.8% investment surtax applies to gains on nonqualified stock options when they are issued. The surtax also applies to restricted stock when it vests. For high-income taxpayers, tax treatment of dividends depends on whether or not a Code § 83(b) election to accelerate income tax has been made. If there has been an election, the dividends are subject to the 3.8% tax; if not, the dividends are subject to the 0.9% tax. Taxable fringe benefits are also subject to the 0.9% tax. [Final regulations: T.D. 9645, 2013-51 I.R.B. 738.] Although the American Health Care Act (AHCA) would have repealed these surtaxes, at press time in 2017 the AHCA had been withdrawn from consideration before Congress could vote on it, and a related Senate bill also failed..

On a related issue, see T.D. 9659, clarifying what constitutes "substantial risk of forfeiture" when stock that constitutes employee compensation under § 83 is transferred. [T.D. 9659, 2014-12 I.R.B. 653; see *Austin v. Comm'r*, 141 T.C. No. 18 (2014), finding that the discharge-for-cause provision in the taxpayer's employment agreement created a substantial risk of forfeiture]

It is common for employees who get restricted stock awards to file an election as to the awards to start the clock for long-term capital gains. The IRS eliminated the requirement of submitting a copy of the § 83(b) election with the income tax return. The IRS's rationale is that the previous requirement prevented people in this situation from e-filing their returns, because commercial tax filing software has no way to attach the election. The employee files the election with the IRS separately, within 30 days after the property is transferred to the employee. For transfers on or after January 1, 2016, the IRS will scan the election form, keep it on file, and associate it with the tax return. [80 Fed. Reg. 42439 (July 17, 2015); finalized in T.D. 9779, 2016-33 I.R.B. 233. *See* Crescent Moran Chasteen, *IRS Simplifies Section 83(b) Election Process*, Nutter McClennen & Fish LLP (Aug. 3, 2016), available at Lexology.com]

The 2013 FICA base is $113,700, the 2014 base is $117,000, and the 2015–2016 base is $118,500. The 2017 base is much higher: $127,200.

The IRS view is that severance payments are subject to FICA but some Supplemental Insurance Benefits (SUB payments) are not. Termination benefits that are excluded from FICA probably will not affect the recipient employee's eligibility for state unemployment benefits. A SUB plan is a severance plan to help employees after their involuntary termination. SUB payments supplement state unemployment benefits. To receive SUB pay, the employee must apply for and be granted state unemployment benefits and must verify each week that he or she is still unemployed but is available for work. A traditional SUB plan terminates benefits when the employee gets another job or otherwise ceases to be eligible for state unemployment benefits. SUB benefits must be paid weekly or with each payroll; they cannot be distributed as a lump sum. Unless state law forbids it, SUB pay can be paid from the employer's general assets. If state law does forbid it, the employer can create a trust for the SUB plan. The trust can be—but is not required to be—a tax-exempt 501(c)(17) trust or a Voluntary Employees' Beneficiary Association (VEBA). [Vicki M. Nielsen, *The Advantages of Offering*

Supplemental Unemployment Benefits Instead of Severance, Part I: FICA Taxes and More, Ogletree Deakins (Aug. 26, 2013), available at Lexology.com]

FICA taxes are owed on the exercise of nonqualified options or Stock appreciation rights (SARS), or when restricted stock vests. For compensation deferred in 401(k) or nonqualified deferred compensation plans, FICA is owed at the time of deferral even though income tax is not owed until the funds are removed from the account. Nonqualified stock options can be exercised without FICA tax consequences on income recognized at exercise if the employee's compensation for the year exceeds the FICA base. Medicare tax and additional Medicare tax are due on all compensation, with no limit. Therefore, 2012 was a good year to exercise nonqualified stock options, because of the payroll tax cut and because the extra Medicare tax had not yet taken effect. [MyStockOptions Blog, *Social Security Yearly Income Cap Will Rise in 2013: Impact on Stock Comp and NQDC* (Oct. 17, 2012) (benefitslink.com)]

For an account balance non-qualified plan, FICA is due when benefits are credited to the account or when they vest, whichever is later. For a non-account balance plan, FICA is due at retirement on the present value of the entire benefit, because that is when the deferred amount is both reasonably ascertainable and vested.

Participants in Henkel Corporation's Supplemental Executive Retirement Plan (SERP) brought a class action when the plan started withholding FICA tax from distributions to participants in a non-qualified deferred compensation plan. Top hat plan participants almost always earn more than the FICA wage base, so FICA is not due on non-qualified plan benefits or contributions. If FICA tax is withheld when the benefits or contributions vest, the "non-duplication rule" provides that FICA tax will not be due when the benefits are paid.

The PPACA also imposes a small fee on self-insured plans and issuers of health insurance policies, for plan years that end on or after October 1, 2012 and before October 1, 2019. (The fee will be used to fund research into which treatments are the most effective.) The sponsor of a self-insured plan, or the insurer of a policy covering an insured plan, must pay $1 per person covered under the plan for the first year, and $2 per person for the second year, with subsequent inflation adjustments. The 2016 fee is $2.17; Notice 2016-64, 2016-46 I.R.B. 626 sets the 2017 fee at $2.26. The fee is paid on IRS Form 720.

PPACA retains the ability of corporations to receive federal subsidies tax-free if they provide prescription drug coverage for their retirees. The subsidy is 28% of the cost of coverage, subject to a cap of $1,330 per retiree. However, PPACA provides that the subsidy amount will no longer be deductible, starting in 2013. [Kris Maher, Ellen E. Schultz, and Bob Tita, *Deere, Caterpillar: Health-Care Law to Raise Expenses*, WSJ.com (Mar. 26, 2010)]

Stimulus efforts continued with the enactment of the Hiring Incentives to Restore Employment (HIRE) Act, Pub. L. No. 111-147, in March 2010; there was a temporary payroll tax incentive for hiring unemployed workers if hiring occurred between February 3, 2010 and January 1, 2011. [Rebecca Moore, *New Law Offers Tax Incentives for Hiring*, plansponsor.com (Mar. 18, 2010)]

This was replaced by another payroll tax incentive, a cut in employees' FICA rates. The Temporary Payroll Tax Cut Continuation Act, Pub. L. No. 112-78 (Dec. 2011) reduced the employee FICA rate to 4.2% (or 10.4% for self-employed persons) but subject to a wage cap of $18,350. The Middle Class Tax Relief and Job Creation Act of 2012, Pub. L. No. 112-96, enacted February 2, 2012, extended the 4.2% FICA rate for workers until the end of 2012, and repealed the cap. [<http://www.irs.gov/pub/irs-pdf/f941.pdf>] However, there were no further extensions of the FICA cut after the end of 2012.

The Small Business Jobs and Credit Act, Pub. L. No. 111-240 (SBJCA), also includes some miscellaneous employment-related provisions. Retirees can access income from part of an annuity, keeping the rest invested; and if a plan includes a Roth 401(k) feature, eligible rollover distributions can be transferred from regular to Roth 401(k) plans. (The transfer is taxable, but opens the way to eventually taking funds from the Roth 401(k) tax-free.) [Laura Saunders, *Tax Report: Surprise New Tax Breaks*, WSJ.com (Sept. 25, 2010)]

The SBJCA increased the penalty for failure to file Form 1099-series on time. The penalty, up to $100 per form (2011) was adjusted for inflation in 2012 and will be adjusted every five years after that. [McKay Hochman Company, Inc. E-Mail Alert 2010-16, *Form 1099 Series Penalties Increased* (Oct. 15, 2010) (benefitslink.com)]

The Tax Relief, Unemployment Insurance Reauthorization, and Job Creation Act of 2010 (TRUIRJCA), Pub. L. No. 111-312, was signed December 17, 2010. It provided for a one-year cut in payroll tax, an extension of the Work Opportunity Tax Credit, and an ongoing exclusion of the gain on qualified small business stock.

In November 2011, the VOW to Hire Heroes Act (Pub. L. No. 112-56) was enacted, including a new tax credit for hiring veterans, up to a maximum of $9,600 per veteran, available for hires until January 1, 2013. [Notice 2012-13, 2012-9 I.R.B. 421]

The "fiscal cliff" tax bill, the American Taxpayer Relief Act of 2012 (ATRA; Pub. L. No.112-240) set the employer's share of FICA tax at 6.2% of income up to $113,700, and made it easier to convert defined contribution accounts to Roth status. See Notice 2013-74, 2013-52 I.R.B. 819, for guidance on in-plan Roth rollovers (rollovers within a 401(k) plan to a designated Roth account within the same plan). Under Code § 402A, designated Roth contributions are elective deferrals to a retirement plan that the participant elects to include in gross income, although they would otherwise be excludable. Designated Roth contributions and their earnings must be maintained in a separate account within the plan. Distributions from an individual's account in a retirement plan other than a designated Roth account can be rolled over to the participant's designated Roth account in the same plan. When in-plan Roth rollovers were first permitted by the Small

Business Jobs Act, rollovers were limited to amounts that were otherwise distributable (e.g., the participant had reached age 59½ or terminated employment).

Notice 2013-74 explains that elective deferrals, matching contributions, and non-elective contributions can be rolled over to the Roth account. But amounts rolled over to a designated Roth account remain subject to the distribution restrictions applicable to the amount before the rollover. [Lisa A. Berkowitz Herrnson, *IRS Provides New Guidance on In-Plan Roth Rollovers*, Proskauer Rose (Dec. 17, 2013), available at Lexology.com]

At the end of 2013, a number of business credits were allowed to expire, such as the credit for research and experimentation, the work opportunity tax credit, and certain corporate charitable donation provisions. The 100% exclusion of gain on sale of small business stock expired, but for 2014, 50% of gain is excludable from taxable income. In general, the 50% additional first-year depreciation rule has been eliminated (except for some transportation assets and some long-production-period property placed into service before January 1, 2015). The ability to expense assets under Code § 179 greatly decreased. [Joint Committee on Taxation JCX-1-14, *List of Expiring Federal Tax Provisions 2013-2024*, <http://www.jct.gov> (Jan. 10, 2014); David S. Lionberger, *Numerous Federal Tax Provisions Will Lapse in 2014*, Hirschler Fleischer (Jan. 13, 2014), available at Lexology.com]

As a result of the passage of the Trade Preferences Extension Act of 2015, the Health Coverage Tax Credit (HCTC), which expired January 1, 2014, has been restored for all eligibility coverage months beginning before January 1, 2020. The HCTC is a refundable credit equal to part of the premiums paid for health insurance (including COBRA coverage) for themselves and families. The HCTC covers 72.5% of eligible healthcare costs for workers who lose their jobs because of foreign competition. Plans can also voluntarily participate in the federal HCTC program, under which the federal government pays part of the premiums. [Trade Preferences Extension Act of 2015, Pub. L. No. 114-27; see Segal Consulting Update, *Restoration of the Health Coverage Tax Credit* (Oct. 5, 2015) (benefitslink.com)]

The Protecting Americans From Tax Hikes (PATH Act; Pub. L. No. 114-113) expanded the definition of targeted individuals for whom a Work Opportunity Tax Credit (WOTC) can be claimed. IRS Notice 2016-22, 2016-13 I.R.B. 488 notes that the IRS modified Form 8850 to be used to request WOTC certification for qualified long-term unemployment recipients. The deadline for Form 8850 was extended until June 29, 2016, for hiring long-term unemployment benefit recipients that occurred between January 1, 2016 and May 31, 2016. The expanded definition is retroactive, so the Form 8850 deadline was also extended for hiring other targeted individuals in the period January 1, 2015–May 31, 2016. [Steptoe & Johnson LLP, *IRS Issues Work Opportunity Tax Credit Guidance and Transition Relief* (Mar. 7, 2016), available at Lexology.com]

In addition, the PATH Act retroactively renews and extends certain tax provisions that expired December 31, 2014, and makes them permanent. The Code § 1202 100% exclusion of gain from the sale of certain Qualified Small Business stock held for more than five years has been made permanent for all qualified stock acquired after September 27, 2010. [David J. Sorin et.al., *Qualified Small Business Stock Tax Incentives Made Permanent*, McCarter & English LLP (Dec. 22, 2015), available at Lexology.com]

The PATH Act reinstates the Research & Development (R&D) tax credit and makes it permanent; it is one of the 36 credits that make up the general business credit. It also provides that certain small businesses can use the R&D credit to reduce the employer share of FICA. A qualified small business can elect for any taxable year beginning after December 31, 2015, to use part of the R&D credit to reduce the employer's FICA obligation. IRS consent is required to revoke an election once it is made. A qualified small business is one that is less than five years old and whose gross receipts were less than $5 million for the taxable year for which the election is utilized. The maximum amount that can be applied to FICA tax is $250,000. In effect, the business must decide whether it obtains more tax benefits by using the R&D credit to reduce income tax or FICA tax; for a new business with little or no income, reducing FICA tax will be more beneficial. [Douglas W. Charnas, *PATH Act Allows R&D Credit to Reduce FICA Taxes for Certain Small Businesses*, McGuireWoods LLP (Feb. 9, 2016), available at Lexology.com]

The 21st Century Cures Act, Pub. L. No. 114-255, was signed by then-president Obama on December 13, 2016. The Cures Act suspends the applicability of the § 4980D excise tax to stand-alone HRAs (employer reimbursement of premiums on individual health policies maintained by employees) a second time, until December 31, 2016. Furthermore, the Cures Act allows QSEHRAs (Qualified Small Employer Health Reimbursement Arrangements) to be maintained starting January 1, 2017. A small employer (under 50 employees) that does not offer an EGHP can establish a QSEHRA. The QSEHRA can only reimburse actual medical expenses or premiums, and the employer pays the full cost—employee contributions are not permitted. All employees must have access to the plan on the same terms, but it is permissible to exclude employees who have not yet completed 90 days of service, employees under age 25, part-time and seasonal employees, or employees covered by CBAs. It is permissible to vary the benefit on the basis of the employee's age or family size, if this affects the premium. The maximum reimbursement under the plan is $4,950 (employee-only coverage) or $10,000 for family coverage. These amounts will be indexed for inflation in later years. [Vorys, Sater, Seymour and Pease LLP, *21st Century Cures Act* (Dec. 16, 2016) (benefitslink.com)]

Notice 2017-20, 2017-11 I.R.B. 1010, gives small employers additional time to comply with the QSEHRA notice requirements. Employers seeking to implement a QSEHRA must notify employees of the effect of QSEHRA coverage on

their compliance with the individual mandate; the extent to which employer contributions to the QSEHRA might constitute taxable income for employees; and
how the QSEHRA might affect eligibility for tax credits for purchasing health
coverage on an Exchange. Generally speaking, the notice must be given at least
90 days before the beginning of the year in which the QSEHRA will take effect,
but there is a transition rule allowing notice for 2017 QSEHRAs to be given
within 90 days after the IRS issues additional guidance on Notice 2017-20 topics.
[Kenneth A. Mason, *IRS Extends Deadline for Providing Small-Employer HRA
Notices*, Spencer Fane LLP (Feb. 28, 2017), available at Lexology.com]

[B] Tax Implications of Same-Sex Marriage

In mid-2013, the Supreme Court struck down the federal Defense of Marriage Act (DOMA). DOMA defined marriage, for federal purposes, as a union of
one man and one woman. Because the Supreme Court found this statute unconstitutional (on due process and equal protection grounds), same-sex married
couples are entitled to file joint income tax returns. There are many other federal
consequences, including military spousal benefits and estate tax status as a surviving spouse. [*United States v. Windsor*, 133 S. Ct. 2675 (2013); *Hollingsworth
v. Perry*, 133 S. Ct. 2652 (2013)]

On June 26, 2015, the Supreme Court's *Obergefell v. Hodges*, 135 S. Ct.
2584, decision required all the states to recognize same-sex marriage. See further
discussion in § 18.06. As a result, the employer's procedures for updating
employee's records, and adding spouses to plans or designating them as beneficiaries, apply to same-couples as well as male/female couples.

On October 21, 2015, the IRS issued proposed regulations reflecting
Obergefell, indicating that the IRS recognizes any marriage for federal tax purposes if it is recognized by any state. The terms "husband" and "wife" include
same-sex spouses. Registered domestic partnerships and civil unions are not
deemed to be marriages for tax purposes. IRS says for federal tax purposes, same-
sex marriages are treated the same way as mixed-sex marriages. Marriage is recognized for federal tax purposes if it would be recognized by any U.S. state,
possession, or territory. Marriage doesn't include civil union or registered domestic partnership. [REG-148998-13, <https://www.irs.gov/irb/2015-45_IRB/ar09
.html>]

§ 2.02 THE COMPENSATION DEDUCTION

Internal Revenue Code § 162 allows a corporation to deduct its ordinary and
necessary business expenses, including reasonable salaries in exchange for personal services rendered to the corporation. Salaries are only reasonable if the person hired is qualified to perform the services, and actually performs them. If

vacation pay is treated as deferred compensation, it is not deductible until the year it is actually paid. [See I.R.C. § 404(a)(5)]

For public corporations, § 162(m) does not allow a deduction for over $1 million in compensation paid to "covered employees"—certain senior executives. However, the cap does not apply to "performance-based compensation"—compensation payable solely because the payee has achieved an objective goal (or goals) set in advance. [See Rev. Rul. 2008-13, 2008-10 I.R.B. 518, tightening up the rules for performance-based compensation.]

Under Rev. Rul. 2012-19, 2012-28 I.R.B. 16, to qualify for exemption from the $1 million limit, dividends on restricted stock and restricted stock units (RSUs) can only be payable if the payee meets performance goals. However, the performance goals for this purpose do not have to be the same ones for granting the underlying restricted stock or RSUs. T.D. 9716, 80 Fed. Reg. 16970 (Mar. 31, 2015) finalizes 2011 proposed regulations under § 162(m)(4)(c).

A plan under which an option or stock appreciation right (SAR) is granted must state the maximum number of shares with respect to which options or SARs can be granted to "any individual." Prior law required disclosure of the maximum number of shares with respect to which stock options and SARs could be granted. A 2015 set of final regulations, T.D. 9716, 2015-15 I.R.B. 863, adds restricted stock, restricted stock units, and other equity-based awards. If the corporation goes public, the § 162(m) deduction limit does not apply to RSUs that are paid—not just granted—before the earliest transition event listed in the IRS regulations. [See Sally P. Schreiber, *Qualified Performance-Based Compensation Rules Are Finalized*, J. of Accountancy (Mar. 31, 2015) (benefitslink.com).]

There is an IPO exception for new public companies: the $1 million limit on deductions does not apply to compensation paid under a plan that existed before the IPO, but the exception is limited to a transition period that ends when the plan expires, all the stock under the plan is distributed, or the first annual meeting is held after the end of the third calendar year after the year of the IPO. [Mark Kelly, *Final Section 162(m) Regulations Clarify Exceptions to $1 Million Deduction Limit*, King & Spalding LLP (Aug. 28, 2015), available at Lexology .com]

Section 162(m) compliance also requires the compensation committee to make an annual written certification that performance goals were satisfied before a bonus is paid. (It is common for the committee to use this meeting to set per-formance goals for the current year.) Performance goals must be set in the first 90 days of the performance period: i.e., by March 16 each year for a calendar-year plan. For awards that are based on actual targets, the performance criteria and the maximum award that can be granted to any individual must be approved by the stockholders every five years. [GTLaw.com, *Section 162(m): Actions That Should Be Taken by March 30, 2016, and/or in This Year's Proxy to Avoid the $1,000,000 Deduction Limitation* (Mar. 22, 2016) (benefitslink.com)]

SEC Form 8-K might have to be filed only four days later. Annual bonus awards and targets set in 2017 for payout in 2018 or later years do not have to be disclosed in SEC Form 8-K if they are consistent with prior years' awards and targets. Bonuses paid in 2017 for 2016 performance don't have to be disclosed if consistent with awards previously reported. [Winston.com, *Incentive Bonus Reporting on Form 8-K* (Jan. 16, 2017) (benefitslink.com)]

The Supreme Court refused to review the Eighth Circuit's decision that cash distribution dividends paid to redeem stock held in an Employee Stock Ownership Plan (ESOP) are not deductible—Code § 162(k)(1) provides that there is no § 404(k) deduction available for amounts paid to an ESOP trust to redeem shares of the parent company's stock, and the facts in this case were fairly similar. [*Nestle Purina Petcare Co. v. Commissioner of Internal Revenue*, 594 F.3d 968 (8th Cir.), *cert. denied*, 131 S. Ct. 86 (Oct. 4, 2010); *General Mills, Inc. v. United States*, 554 F.3d 727 (8th Cir. 2009)]

Allen Sloan's article, "The Executive Pay Cap that Backfired" [ProPublica, Feb. 12, 2016] says that § 162(m) backfired by having little or no effect on corporate behavior. In 1992, Congress was concerned with income inequality, and limited the deduction for compensation other than qualified performance-based compensation. ProPublica and the Washington Post commissioned research into the top 50 companies within the S&P 500, but excluding companies that were not reporting companies just before § 162(m) was adopted.

In 1992, 35% of covered executives were paid over $1 million in income subject to deductibility limits; 95% were in 2014, but there had been decades of inflation to explain part of the change. But between 1992 and 2014, compensation per executive in limited deductibility categories rose 650% (from $1.1 million to $8.2 million) vs. 350% in categories, e.g., stock options and incentive pay, that are not subject to deductibility limits ($970,000 to $4.4 million). Compensation subject to limits went up almost twice as fast as compensation that was not subject to limits. Sloan's article concludes that compensation committees weren't very concerned with deductibility; the lost deduction had no effect on corporate profits. The "gnat" can easily be swatted away. When originally proposed, § 162(m) would have denied a deduction for any employee compensation if executive compensation was more than 25 times the pay of lowest-paid employee; the provision that was adopted is much milder. [Cydney Posner, *Is Section 162(m) Just "A Gnat On An Elephant"?*, Cooley LLP (Feb. 18, 2016) (benefitslink.com)]

§ 2.03 INCOME TAX WITHHOLDING

[A] Calculation

Taxpayers can obtain Employer Identification Numbers (EINs) online in real time, by going to <http://www.irs.gov>, accessing the Internet EIN System, and entering the required fields. A permanent EIN is issued for immediate use if the data passes automated validity checks. Employers whose application is rejected can correct the information and then re-submit the application. Once the application is complete, the taxpayer can view, print, and save the confirmation notice rather than having it mailed. At the time of hiring, the employer must also have the employee submit Form W-4 (Employee's Withholding Allowance Certificate) to indicate the filing status (married filing a joint return, married filing a separate return, single, head of household) and the number of withholding allowances that he or she claims. The more withholding allowances, the less that will be withheld from the employee's paycheck.

Although there are other methods, the amount of income tax to be withheld is usually calculated under either the percentage method or the wage bracket method. (The calculations will be done by the payroll preparation contractor, if the employer outsources this function.)

Under the percentage method, the IRS tables are used. The number of allowances claimed is multiplied by the amount from the allowance table; the result is subtracted from the employee's wages. The wage rate table gives the actual dollar amount to be withheld.

Under the wage bracket method, tables are used to compute withholding per weekly, semiweekly, or other pay period, based on wage level, marital status, and number of claimed exemptions.

There was a "Making Work Pay" credit of up to $400 for an individual, $800 on a joint return. It was enacted by ARRA (Pub. L. No. 111-5) but expired at the end of 2010. For income tax purposes, "supplemental wages" means compensation other than, or in addition to, ordinary cash compensation. Bonuses, commissions, overtime pay, severance pay, back pay, taxable fringe benefits, and payments for accumulated sick leave are all supplemental wages.

For payments made after 2004, once a person's supplemental wage income exceeds $1 million, the employer must withhold on the supplemental income at the highest income tax rate (currently, 35%). Employers have an obligation to keep a cumulative record of this income so that they will be aware when the $1 million threshold is crossed.

T.D. 9276 clarifies that compensation can be treated as "supplemental" even if the payee had no regular wages for the year. The category of supplemental wages also includes nonqualified deferred compensation that is included in wages, imputed income when a non-dependent (e.g., a same-sex partner) receives health coverage, and income due to lapse on restrictions on property transferred from employer to employee. Commissions, bonuses, and taxable noncash fringe benefits cannot be treated as regular wages. Under the proposed regulations, commissions could be treated as regular wages if the employee did not receive any other compensation, but T.D. 9276 eliminates this option. [T.D. 9276, 2006-37 I.R.B. 423]

Rev. Rul. 2008-29, 2008-24 I.R.B. 1149, provides guidance under the supplemental wage regulations for signing bonuses and various kinds of commissions. For severance pay, the employer can either add supplemental wages to regular wages and use the tax tables, or can withhold at a 25% flat rate. Central to the tax treatment of settlements and damages employees obtain from suing the employer is whether the money replaces compensation that the employee would have earned absent the factors that led to the suit.

The Second Circuit held that back pay is defined as the wages the plaintiff would have earned from the date of discharge to the date of reinstatement, plus lost fringe benefits, whereas front pay is awarded for lost compensation either instead or reinstatement or running from the judgment to the time of reinstatement. A former New York State employee was awarded back and front pay by the jury. State and federal taxes were deducted. The Second Circuit held that, even without direction from a court to deduct the taxes, the New York State Office of Comptroller was correct to do so: Back pay and front pay are wages subject to FICA and income tax withholding. [*Noel v. New York State Office of Mental Health Cent. New York Psychiatric Ctr.*, 697 F.3d 209 (2d Cir. 2012)]

The Second Circuit held that settlement proceeds in an Age Discrimination in Employment Act (ADEA) suit were wages subject to FICA. The agreement expressly permitted the employer to deduct and withhold all sums subject to withholding under applicable laws and regulations, but did not state how the $250,000 settlement proceeds would be treated for tax purposes. A court analyzing a settlement payment looks first to the nature of the claim that was settled, then remedies under governing law, then to the parties' intention. In ADEA cases, the remedies are lost wages, liquidated damages, and equitable relief—but not pain and suffering or emotional distress damages (which would probably not be treated as wages). [*Gerstenbluth v. Credit Suisse*, 728 F.3d 139 (2d Cir. 2013)]

The Tax Court reaffirmed that emotional distress damages are taxable income for recipient. Agreements are analyzed according to their express language. A settlement described as covering emotional distress results in taxable income, even if there are physical manifestations of emotional distress. [*Sharp v. Comm'r*, T.C.M. 290 (2013), Docket No. 21332-12, 106 T.C.M. (CCH) 700 (T.C. Dec. 23, 2013)]

The withholding system must distinguish between compensation paid to the employee and reimbursement of legitimate business expenses that the employee incurred on the employer's behalf (reimbursement is not taxable income).

For tax purposes, expense accounts are either "accountable" or "non-accountable" plans. Amounts paid under an accountable plan are not wages for the employee, and therefore are not subject to FICA or FUTA. Withholding is not required. Employees must meet two tests under an accountable plan:

- They paid or incurred deductible expenses in the course of employment;

- They are required to provide adequate accounts of the expenses within a reasonable time of incurring them.

If they receive any amount over and above the expenses, they have an obligation to return it within a reasonable time. The general tax rule is that it is reasonable for employees to be reimbursed within 30 days of spending money; to provide an expense account within 60 days of spending the money; and to return excess amounts within 120 days of the initial advance.

Accounting for a per diem or a fixed allowance (e.g., X cents per mile for business travel) is considered adequate as long as the payment is no higher than the government per diem rates for meals and lodging (see IRS Publication 1542) and the standard mileage rate for travel. [IRS Publication 553]

If these tests are not met, the money is treated as if it were paid under a nonaccountable plan (one which does not require documentation of expenses). Expenses reimbursed under a nonaccountable plan are considered wages, included in income and subject to withholding in the first payroll period after there has been a reasonable time to return any excess funds.

Form 2106 is used for employees to claim business expense deductions for work-related travel, transportation, meals, or entertainment if the employee was reimbursed for deductible work-related expenses. The simplified Form 2106-EZ can be used by employees who use the standard mileage rate for vehicle expenses and who do not receive any expense reimbursement that is not reported as taxable income. The "accountable plan" rules relieve employees from tax on business expense reimbursement if the expenses are business-related, adequately substantiated, and the employee returns any amount of reimbursement that exceeds the expenses. If the reimbursement is less than the actual expense, an employee who can substantiate the actual amount can take a deduction on Form 2106 for the difference.

The optional 2017 standard mileage rate for business use of a vehicle is 53.5 cents per mile; the rate for driving in connection with a work-related move is 17 cents per mile. Depreciation of an automobile used for business is 25 cents per mile. Under a Fixed and Variable Rate (FAVR) plan, the maximum standard cost is $27,900 for cars, $31,300 for trucks and vans. [Notice 2016-79, 2016-52 I.R.B. 918]

The rules for employer-provided fringe benefits for parking and mass transit assistance have fluctuated frequently. The PATH Act of 2015, Pub. L. No. 114-113, made the parity between the two benefits permanent. The 2015–2016 amount is $255. When first enacted, the transit benefit was lower than the parking benefit. Between 2009 and 2013, the two benefits were equal. The parking benefit is indexed by statute; changes in the transit benefit are up to the IRS. [Rev. Proc. 2016-14, 2016-9 I.R.B. 365; see Gary B. Kushner, *Transit Pass Parity with Parking Benefit Starting in 2016*, Kushner & Co. (Dec. 21, 2015) (benefitslink.com)]

All of the employee's taxable income is subject to income tax withholding, except to the degree that a withholding exemption is available. FICA (Social Security) taxes are imposed on the employee's taxable income, up to a certain amount ($118,500 for 2015–2016, $127,200 for 2017) each year's wage base must be published in the *Federal Register* no later than November 1 of the preceding year. The employer and employee are each taxed at a rate of 6.2% on income up to the limit, and Medicare taxes are imposed on all compensation.

AJCA § 251, affecting I.R.C. § 13121(a), 421(b), 423(c), provides that for FICA and FUTA purposes, the definition of "wages" does not include remuneration from exercising an Incentive Stock Option (ISO) or option to buy stock under an employee stock purchase plan.

Quality Stores went through Chapter 11 bankruptcy. Terminated employees received severance benefits that were not tied to the receipt of state unemployment benefits. The payments varied based on the employee's job duties and length of employment. At first, Quality Stores withheld FICA taxes on these amounts. Then the company decided that the payments were not FICA wages, so it sought a tax refund for itself and about 1,850 ex-employees who received payments. In March 2014, the Supreme Court held that the severance payments constituted FICA wages. The Supreme Court held that severance payments are made only to employees, and they are made because of service to employers because "service" is defined broadly as the entire relationship between the employer and employee. The court noted that the FICA statute provides a list of exemptions from the general rule that all compensation constitutes FICA wages. One of the exemptions is for severance payments made for disability retirement. The Supreme Court said it would not be necessary to specify this exemption if severance pay in general did not constitute FICA wages. Code § 3401(a), dealing with income tax withholding, also has a broad definition of taxable wages, subject to a list of exemptions. The list says that Supplemental Unemployment Benefits are treated as if they were wages: see § 3402(o). Quality Stores interpreted this to mean that, although SUB payments are treated "as if" they were wages, they are not wages for this purpose or for FICA purposes. However, the Supreme Court traced this provision to the history of tax withholding, when Congress wanted to relieve terminated workers from the burden of year-end tax liability. [*United States v. Quality Stores Inc.*, 134 S. Ct. 1395 (2014)]

The Supreme Court held, early in 2011, that medical residents working over 40 hours a week are not "students" for FICA purposes. Therefore, their compensation is subject to FICA tax. [*Mayo Found. for Med. Educ. & Research v. United States*, 562 U.S. 44 (2011)]

Deferred compensation is frequently payable to the deceased employee's beneficiary or estate when the employee dies. This occurs, for example, in traditional defined contribution plans, incentive arrangements, and stock awards. The terms of the plan govern what payments will be made to survivors. Taxation is governed by Rev. Ruls. 71-456 and 86-109. For income tax purposes, post-death compensation is not considered wages, so payments to beneficiaries or the estate are not subject to income tax withholding. The FICA rules are different and vary depending on whether the payment is made in the same calendar year as the death or in a later year. Section 3121(a)(14) makes amounts paid in the year of death FICA wages that are subject to Social Security and Medicare tax withholding.

This is not true of amounts paid in a subsequent year. Amounts earned but unpaid when the person died are reported on Form 1099-MISC as non-employee compensation, reflecting any FICA withholding. The net amount of the distribution (i.e., net of FICA) is reported in Box 3 of a 1099-MISC (Other Income) which is issued to the beneficiary or the estate.

If withholding is required, the employer should issue a Form W-2 in the name of the decedent with the decedent's SSN covering only the FICA wages and withholding. The compensation distributed goes in Box 3 (Social Security wages) and Box 5 (Medicare wages and tips). The employee share of Social Security tax withheld goes in Box 4, and the employee Medicare tax withheld goes in Box 6. But if the payment is made after the year of death, neither income tax nor FICA is withheld and no W-2 is issued. The full amount of distributions to the estate or beneficiary is reported in Box 3 of Form 1099-MISC. [Rebecca L. Hudson and Arthur Hundhausen, *Tax Reporting for Deferred Compensation Payments Following Death of Employee: Are You Reporting Correctly?*, Holland & Hart LLP (Sept. 22, 2016), available at Lexology.com]

[B] Withholding on Pensions

The general rule is that income tax withholding is required when a plan makes payments to retired employees. There are circumstances under which the retirees can elect to waive withholding, but there are other circumstances in which withholding is mandatory.

For ordinary pension payments in annuity form, the plan can use its regular withholding procedures, based on the number of withholding exemptions on the retiree's Form W-4P. If no W-4P is submitted, the plan should withhold as if the retiree were married and claimed three withholding allowances.

However, if the distribution is a lump sum or other nonperiodic payment and not an annuity, the question is whether it is an "eligible rollover distribution." If it is not, the basic requirement is to withhold at a 10% rate, although the person receiving the lump sum can use the W-4P to claim exemption from withholding. If the recipient of the lump sum expects to be in a high tax bracket, the person can ask for withholding at a rate higher than 10%.

An eligible rollover distribution is an amount that could be placed in the retiree's IRA, Roth IRA, or transferred to another qualified plan. Any such amount that is not rolled over is subject to withholding at a rate of at least 20%. The recipient of the distribution can increase the withholding rate, but cannot lower it below 20% or claim a withholding exemption. See Code § 3405 and the instructions for Form 1099-R. The Pension Protection Act also permits a non-spouse beneficiary of a qualified plan account to roll over inherited funds to his or her own IRA.

Withholding from lump-sum pension distributions is not reported on Form 941. Instead, Form 945 (Annual Return of Withheld Federal Income Tax) is used. The pension withholding amounts should be combined with the other Form 945 amounts, but for nonpayroll withholding only, not payroll taxes. [See Form 945 instructions.] The recipient of the distribution receives a Form 1099-R (Distributions from Pensions, Annuities, Retirement or Profit-Sharing Plans). [See Chapter 12 for further information on distributions from qualified plans.]

The rules for Roth 401(k) rollovers were made more taxpayer-friendly in September 2014. Previously, when funds were deposited in a new plan or IRA directly, rather than via trustee-to-trustee transfer, rollovers that included both pre-tax 401(k) contributions and Roth contributions had to allocate a pro rata share of both types of funds to each destination account. The result was that employees either had to wait until they got a new job whose plan allowed Roth contributions, leave the money in the former employer's plan, or carry out a direct rollover. But Notice 2014-54 removes the pro rata requirement for distributions on or after January 1, 2016. [Winstead.com, *Simplified 401(k) Roth Rollover Rules Finalized* (May 19, 2016) (benefitslink.com)]

§ 2.04 FUTA TAX

FUTA (Federal Unemployment Tax Act) taxes are paid entirely by the employer, on the first $7,000 of the employee's wages that are subject to FUTA. The FUTA tax form is Form 940. IRS discontinued the previous Form 940-EZ (short form) in 2007, but redesigned Form 940 to be more logical and easier to use.

Employers are subject to FUTA tax if they paid wages of $1,500 or more to all employees in any calendar quarter in 2015 or 2016, and if they had at least one employee for at least part of a day in 20 or more different weeks in 2015 or 2016. The base FUTA rate is 6.0% of the first $7,000 in wages, but employers receive a credit of up to 5.4%, with the result that the net rate paid by most employers is 0.6%. See below for variations in state rates; in a "credit reduction state" (which has borrowed money from the federal government and is not current in repayment), employers get a smaller or no credit, so they must pay more FUTA tax.

The FUTA tax return, Form 940, is filed annually. The due date is January 31, but employers that deposited FUTA tax as it came due have until February 10 to file. If an employer's FUTA liability is at least $500 for the full year, the employer will have to make at least one quarterly deposit of FICA tax. If the liability for a given quarter is under $500, the employer carries it forward to successive quarters until it reaches $500. FUTA deposits are made by electronic funds transfer, usually through the Electronic Federal Tax Payment System (EFTPS). [IRS Topic 759, *Form 940: Employer's Annual Federal Unemployment*

(FUTA) Tax Return—Filing and Deposit Requirements, <http://www.irs.gov/taxtopics/tc759.html> (revised Dec. 30, 2016) (last accessed Feb. 1, 2017)]

Taxpayers must file Schedule A of Form 940 if they paid wages to employees in more than one state—or if they paid wages in any credit reduction state.

On November 10, 2014, DOL posted the results of its review of state unemployment trust fund loan status. In some states, employers' FUTA taxes are increasing between $84 and $119 per employee—far more than the standard $42/employee tax. The FUTA tax is 6.0%, but a credit of up to 5.4% is available in states that do not have outstanding loans. The credit is reduced if the state has an outstanding balance at the beginning of two or more consecutive years, if all advances are not repaid before November 10 of the taxable year. January 31 is the date for the final payment of the previous year's FUTA taxes. The BCR Add-on (see FUTA § 3302(c)(2)(A)) is imposed on states that pass a fifth consecutive year with an outstanding loan balance, although 20 C.F.R. § 606.25 permits waivers under some circumstances—but not if there is a net decrease in the state UI trust fund's solvency.

In 2016, California, Connecticut, and Ohio were subject to a FUTA credit reduction of 1.8% for failure to repay outstanding advances. [See DOL, *Potential 2015 Federal Unemployment Tax Act (FUTA) Credit Reductions*, available at <http://oui.doleta.gov/unemploy/docs/trustFundSolvReport2016.pdf> (last accessed Mar. 11, 2016)]

The Supreme Court seldom tackles employment tax issues, but see its 2001 decision in *United States v. Cleveland Indians Baseball Co.* [532 U.S. 200 (2001)] If an employee settles an employment case and receives back pay, for FICA and FUTA purposes the money is taxed in the year in which the wages were actually paid and not the year in which they were earned—whether the tax rates in the year of payment were higher or lower than the rates for the year in which the money was earned.

§ 2.05 TRUST FUND TAX COMPLIANCE AND THE 100% PENALTY

The FICA tax withheld from employees' salary (both the old age, survivor and disability insurance (OASDI) and the Medicare components) is called a "trust fund tax." (Although the employer must pay its FICA share, and must pay FUTA, these are not trust fund taxes.)

Frequently, the employer will collect employee FICA tax from each payroll, but will not have to deposit the tax until the end of the quarter. A cash-strapped company's temptation to "borrow" that money for its own immediate needs is strong. To reduce the temptation, I.R.C. § 6672 imposes a 100% penalty that cannot be discharged in bankruptcy on "responsible persons" who willfully fail to submit the withheld trust fund taxes to the government. The 100% penalty means that the penalty is as large as the amount of taxes that were not properly paid.

Furthermore, all of the personal assets of the responsible party can be attached to satisfy the debt.

Tax law creates a very large class of responsible persons, including the corporation's officers, shareholders, and directors, based on their level of responsibility within the corporation. The factors include authority to hire and fire; to decide which creditors will be paid and in what order, control over payroll, and power to deposit federal tax amounts. Top managers will probably be liable because of their degree of control over corporate financial managers. Lower-level managers probably will not be liable unless their duties include actually writing checks (and thus actual knowledge of amounts disbursed or not disbursed). Even parties outside the corporation, such as its bankers and its accountants, can be liable if they have the real control over corporate funds. In an appeal from a conviction for willful failure to pay over payroll taxes, the Ninth Circuit held that "willful" is defined as a voluntary, intentional violation of a known legal duty. [*United States v. Easterday*, 539 F.3d 1176 (9th Cir. 2008)]

The IRS assessed a trust fund recovery penalty against a taxpayer who was the wife of a passive investor in the employer corporation. She had only ministerial duties, such as opening the company's bank account when it started up, although she was authorized to sign checks. She was not an officer, had no ownership interest in the business, did not control its financial affairs, and did not have the power to hire or fire employees. In late 2016, the Tax Court exonerated her, holding that she was not a responsible person. The company had a professional payroll service that was supposed to deposit the trust fund taxes. When the company was in financial trouble, the payroll service stopped depositing taxes—although the taxpayer was not aware of that fact. The company's president and general manager previously prevailed in IRS administrative proceedings about their liability. The Tax Court said that this taxpayer could not have willfully failed to deposit the taxes because she had no knowledge that they were not paid properly. [*Fitzpatrick v. Commissioner*, T.C. Memo. 2016-199; see Douglas W. Charnas, *Tax Court Case Demonstrates IRS' Vigorous Pursuit of Trust Fund Recovery Penalty*, McGuireWoods LLP (Nov. 7, 2016), available at Lexology.com]

When a penalty is due, the government can either collect all of it from one responsible person or divide it among several. To avoid liability, an individual has to prove that he or she was incorrectly characterized as a responsible person, or that the failure to pay over the money was not willful. In this context, "willfulness" only means knowledge that the taxes were not submitted, and a failure to correct the situation. If a responsible person finds out that, a payment was missed in one-quarter that creates a duty to investigate to find out if other payments were missed as well.

The responsible person's duty is to use all of the corporations "unencumbered funds" to pay trust fund taxes. Unencumbered funds are those not already assigned to a debt that existed before the tax liability arose.

Thanks to the Taxpayer Bill of Rights 2 [Pub. L. No. 104-168] a responsible person is entitled to notice before the IRS imposes the 100% penalty. The notice must also give the names of other responsible persons, the IRS's collection efforts against them, and the success of those efforts. (The other responsible parties who actually pay the IRS can sue other responsible parties to make them pay their fair share.) The recipient of the notice can pay the penalty and sue for a refund, or contest the penalty in federal court. Collection efforts will be suspended until the case is resolved.

T.D. 9356, 2007-39 I.R.B. 675 took effect Jan. 1, 2009. From that date, Subchapter S corporation subsidiaries, Limited Liability Companies, and certain single-owner entities are required to file employment tax returns and make payments separate from the business owner's return. (Under prior law, the taxpayer could handle all the employment obligations for the employees of a disregarded entity as if the business owner was their employer.) Under the new procedure, taxes paid by the owner are treated as overpayments (although they are not always fully refundable), but the business entity remains liable for the unpaid taxes, penalties, and interest. If no tax return is filed, the statute of limitations never begins to run, so the potential liability extends indefinitely.

IRS policy is to avoid assessing the § 6672 penalty against a responsible person as long as a corporate debtor complies with the terms of its bankruptcy payment plan. However, the IRS might depart from this policy close to the end of the statute of limitations, when failure to enforce might make the debt uncollectable.

Underpaying taxes creates an obligation to catch up on the payments, plus interest. Penalties may also be assessed for, e.g., failure to file, late filing, or serious understatement of the amount of tax.

Code § 6690 imposes a penalty of $50 per failure to furnish a statement required under § 6057(e) to a participant, or for willfully furnishing a false or fraudulent statement. Section 6693 imposes the same penalty for improprieties in connection with statements relating to IRAs, MSAs, or HSAs. Failure to keep records necessary for § 6047(d) reporting is penalized by $50 per person, up to a maximum of $50,000 a year. The administrator of a defined benefit plan who fails to file the actuarial report required by § 6059 is subject, under § 6692, to a penalty of $1,000 per failure (unless reasonable cause for the failure can be shown).

In December 8, 2015, the IRS announced the Early Interaction Initiative, a program to notify employers that they might be behind in paying employment taxes or failing to account for and remit withheld trust fund taxes—even before the Form 941s are filed for the quarter. The IRS monitors payment patterns to find employers who used to pay by the month, to see if they are at risk of default. [Findlaw.com blogs, *IRS Has a New Program to Help Employers Stay on Top of Payroll Taxes* (December 2015), available at <http://blogs.findlaw.com/in_house/2015/12/irs-has-a-new-program-to-help-employers-stay-on-top-of-payroll-taxes.html?DCMP=NWL-cons_humanresource>]

Furthermore, criminal liability can be imposed in five situations:

- Willful failure to collect or pay over federal tax;

- Willful failure to pay tax, make a return, keep records, or provide mandated information to the IRS is a misdemeanor (not a felony);

- Willful furnishing of a false or fraudulent tax statement, or willful refusal to furnish a required statement;

- Willful tax evasion;

- It is perjury to willfully sign a return or other tax document that the signer knows to be false or inaccurate.

In March 2016, the Justice Department announced that it will increase investigations and prosecutions for failure to submit trust fund taxes. Larry Thornton, the owner of two companies, plead guilty to failing to submit over $6.8 million in trust fund taxes. He agreed to pay over $10,8 million in restitution and could be sentenced to up to five years in prison. [Devlin Barrett, *Justice Department to Get More Aggressive in Employment-Tax Fraud*, WSJ.com (Mar. 29, 2016)]

Although the statutory penalties are heavy, in practice the IRS often attempts to collect civil penalties instead of criminal ones, because it's easy to prove that taxes were not paid as required, but hard to prove the state of mind of the person or organization who was supposed to make the payment.

The Voluntary Classification Settlement Program (VCSP) has been expanded so more businesses can clarify the status of their workers as employees or independent contractors and, therefore, report and pay employment-related taxes correctly.

Even employers being audited by the IRS (except for employment tax audits) can use VCSP. An employer is eligible to use VCSP for a particular worker if the employer is currently treating the worker as a non-employee; has consistently treated the worker that way, including filing 1099s; if that worker's status is not the subject of a current IRS payroll tax audit, or a DOL, or state agency labor audit; and the worker's status is not currently being contested in court. Under prior law, a special six-year statute of limitations applied to classification cases, but VCSP participants are subject to the regular statute of limitations for payroll taxes. The application is made on Form 8952 and must be made at least 60 days before the employer wishes to treat the worker as an employee. Employers that participate in VCSP have to pay 10% of the employment tax that would have been due on the worker's compensation for the most recent tax year, but using reduced rates under Code § 3509(a). No interest or penalties are imposed. The employer will not be audited for payroll taxes for those workers for the past year. [*Voluntary Classification Settlement Program (VCSP)*, <http://www.irs.gov/Businesses/Small-Businesses-&-Self-Employed/Voluntary-Classification-Settlement-Program> (updated Sept. 14, 2016) (last viewed Feb. 2, 2017)]

As Chapter 1 shows, the "gig" or "on-demand" economy creates many questions about whether workers under these arrangements are employees or independent contractors. Ride-sharing companies such as Uber and Lyft have been involved in many suits, as have many technology companies. [Robert S. Whitman and Adam J. Smiley, *"On-Demand" Litigation Heats Up This Summer*, Seyfarth Shaw LLP (July 13, 2015), available at Lexology.com] In mid-2016, the IRS published a new web page for tax compliance in the gig, sharing, on-demand, or access economy containing simplified options for some deductions, such as standard mileage rates for drivers. The IRS recommends using IRS Direct Pay or Treasury's Electronic Federal Tax Payment System to pay, or increasing withholding if the gig worker also holds a conventional job. [<https://www.irs.gov/businesses/small-businesses-self-employed/sharing-economy-tax-center>; see IR-2016-110, *IRS Launches New Sharing Economy Resource Center on IRS.gov, Provides Tips for Emerging Business Area* (Aug. 23, 2016), available at <https://www.irs.gov/uac/irs-launches-new-sharing-economy-resource-center-on-irsgov >> (last accessed Mar. 28, 2017)]

The District Court for the Eastern District of Pennsylvania held that a home care company was entitled to refund of employment taxes for home care workers because the company had a reasonable basis for treating the workers as independent contractors under the Code § 530 safe harbor (see § 1.12[B]). The company consistently filed returns treating the workers as independent contractors; there was legal precedent for this position; and it was consistent with practices of other home health agencies. Several years before the agency was audited, the IRS audited the business owner's personal return, when she was working as a home health aide, and did not question her independent contractor status. The business was registered as a home care registry. Mandatory training materials issued by the state defined a home care registry as a business that refers independent contractors for work. [*Nelly Home Care, Inc. v. United States,* **185 F. Supp. 3d 653** (E.D. Pa. 2016); see John B. Waters, *Home Care Company Had Reasonable Basis for Treating Home Care Workers as Independent Contractors and Was Entitled to a Refund of Employment Taxes,* Roetzel & Andress (Sept. 23, 2016), available at Lexology.com]

Non-qualified deferred compensation (NQDC) plans can create some issues of FICA compliance. Deferred compensation must be included in income for FICA purposes when it vests (when there is no longer a substantial risk of forfeiture). Frequently, vesting will occur long before the money is actually paid. Income tax will probably not be due until the recipient gets the money, but the FICA rule is different. The vested amount is added to FICA wages for the year. Because NQDC plans usually cover highly paid executives, it is likely that the total amount will exceed the FICA wage base for the year (in 2017, the wage base is $127,200), but the entire amount is subject to Medicare tax. See I.R.C. § 3121(v)(2). [E. Drew Cheney, *Non-Qualified Deferred Compensation Plans,* BNN Benefits Blog (Aug. 23, 2016) (benefitslink.com)]

§ 2.06 W-2s AND OTHER TAX FORMS

The W-2 form, used to report employee compensation, is a multipart form. Forms are sent to the IRS and to state tax authorities (and city authorities, in cities that impose their own income tax). The employer must also furnish the employee with copies that the employees can use to prepare their tax returns. Of course, the fact that the employer submits the same information to the taxing authorities makes it harder for employees to omit employment income from their tax returns.

T.D. 9730, 2015-35 I.R.B. 223 provides final and temporary regulations revoking the automatic extension of time to file W-2 series forms (other than Form W-2G). Only one, non-automatic, 30-day extension is available. The IRS adopted this policy to accelerate submission of the forms so that the IRS will have more time to detect identity theft and refund fraud. [Steptoe & Johnson LLP, *IRS Releases Final and Temporary Rules on Form W-2 Filing Extensions* (Aug. 12, 2015), available at Lexology.com]

For distributions in 2009 and later years, IRS Announcement 2008-56, 2008-26 I.R.B. 1192 requires employers to report the dividends on employer securities distributed from an ESOP on a Form 1099-R that does not report any other distributions. (If the plan makes distributions that are not 404(k) distributions, they must be reported on a separate Form 1099-R.) ESOP distributions that are 404(k) dividends are not subject to the 10% excise tax under Code § 72; not subject to withholding; and are not eligible for rollover. [Announcement 2008-56, Rebecca Moore, *IRS Changes Reporting Requirements for Dividends on ESOP Distributions*, plansponsor.com (June 10, 2008)]

IRS Forms 3921 and 3922 are used for reporting information about exercise of Incentive Stock Options and options under an ESOP—e.g., grant and exercise dates and fair market value of shares at relevant times.

Between 2015 and any date at which PPACA repeal takes effect, companies with 50 or more employees are subject to requirements to report the cost of health care coverage on employees' W-2 forms. In this time period, employers must issue Form 1095-C (to employees) and Form 1094-C (to the IRS) reporting information about whether the health coverage offered to employees satisfies the federal minimum requirements, and also meets the definition of affordability. See § 18.19 for more detailed discussion, and § 2.01[A] for enhanced penalties for failure to report under the Trade Preferences Extension Act of 2015. [See IRS, *Form W-2 Reporting of Employer-Sponsored Health Coverage*, <http://www.irs. gov/uac/Form-W-2-Reporting-of-Employer-Sponsored-Health-Coverage> (last updated Nov. 2, 2016) (last accessed Feb. 1, 2017) which includes a chart of types of health coverage that must be reported: major medical coverage, hospital indemnity or specified illness insurance paid by the employer or through pre-tax salary reduction, EAPs, wellness programs, and on-site medical clinics but only if the employer charges a COBRA premium.]

In mid-2017, the IRS Office of Chief Counsel issued two letters confirming that, until Congress repeals PPACA, the employer and individual mandates are still in effect. [OCC Letters 2017-0010, 2017-0017 (Apr. 14, 2017); see Winstead PC, *IRS Confirms ACA Tax Assessable Payments Still in Effect* (July 19, 2017) (benefitslink.com)]

§ 2.07 TAX DEPOSITS

Employment taxes (withheld income taxes, FICA) are usually remitted by the employer either once a month or every other week. The schedule for reporting depends on the size of the employer's tax obligation for the previous year; the IRS notifies employers every November which category they will fall into for the next year. [See Treas. Reg. § 31.6302-1]

The basic reporting form is the quarterly Form 941, but income tax and back-up withholding on nonpayroll amounts are reported once a year on Form 945—Annual Return of Withheld Federal Income Tax. The IRS will notify small employers if they qualify to use Form 944, the annual federal tax return; qualifying employers can, nevertheless, elect to continue to file Form 941. See IRS Publication 15, Employer's Tax Guide for details on filing and reporting.

Penalties of between 2%–15% are imposed for late deposits (rising with the extent of the delay), with the highest penalty imposed on continuing failure to deposit after a demand from the IRS. A failure-to-deposit penalty of 10% is imposed on employers who had an obligation to use EFTPS and did not.

Employers whose annual employment tax liability does not exceed $1,000 do not have to file a quarterly Form 941, and most employers in this category will not have to make monthly or semi-monthly payments. However, the IRS estimates that employers will qualify only if their wage payments are less than $4,000 a year. The IRS created an invitation program under which it notifies very small employers that they can file Form 944 rather than 941. (If they prefer, qualifying employers can still file Form 941.). Employers can request to participate in the Form 944 Program, but they must get the IRS permission before moving to annual filing and once they enter the program, they must file a Form 944 each year until a request to return to filing Form 941 has been made and granted, or until they no longer qualify for the 944 program. Qualifying employers are those whose annual employment tax liability (including FICA, Medicare, and federal income tax withholding) is very small: less than $1,000 for the calendar year. However, agricultural employers and employers of household employees (e.g., nannies, housekeepers) do not qualify. [T.D. 9566, 76 Fed. Reg. 77672 (Dec. 14, 2011)]

Form 944 and associated tax payments are due January 31 of the year after the year for which the return is filed, but employers who have paid all employment taxes accrued to date get an extra 10 calendar days to file. Employers can find out if they qualify by calling (800) 829-0115. New employers who expect tax liability below $1,000 a year can apply to the IRS and indicate on their Form

SS-4 that they project a minimal tax liability. If their actual liability exceeds $1,000, they should file Form 944 and then file Form 941 in the future.

§ 2.08   TRANSITION TO ELECTRONIC FILING

For many years, the IRS has been developing rules for electronic filing of tax forms. According to the agency, more than eight million business returns were electronically filed in 2005, with a 99% accuracy rate. By 2006, most business and employment tax returns (including information returns) could be filed electronically. (The TeleFile program, which allowed some forms to be filed over the telephone, was discontinued in mid-2005.)

Business taxpayers can pay all of their federal taxes online or by phone using the Electronic Federal Tax Payment System (EFTPS). EFTPS does not impose any fees. EFTPS is set up to facilitate transmission and processing of tax information submitted by corporations. Payments are made by electronic funds transfer. EFTPS is a highly secure site, using the highest available level of encryption. Users have to enroll on Form 9779, and need a Taxpayer ID, a PIN, and an Internet password to log on. EFTPS users go online or make a phone call at least one calendar day before the due date of a return to input the tax information for their accounts; then the taxpayer directs movement of funds from an approved bank account to the U.S. Treasury account. (Payments can be scheduled in advance, and taxpayers can check the status of any payment made in the preceding 16 months.) [See Publication 966 (business and individual e-filing rules), <https://www.irs.gov/pub/irs-pdf/p966.pdf> (revised Mar. 2012) (last accessed Feb. 1, 2017)]

T.D. 9363 created the modern electronic filing system. Mid-size and large corporations (with assets of $10 million or more and at least 250 returns—including income tax returns, employment tax returns, and information returns—filed per year) are required to file their Forms 1120 and 1120-S (corporate tax returns) electronically. The IRS has revamped its corporate electronic filing system, known as Modernized e-file (MeF). Large corporations must either register with the IRS as a "Large Taxpayer" that prepares their returns in-house or work with an e-file service provider approved by the IRS. [IRS, *E-File for Large Business and International*, <https://www.irs.gov/Businesses/Corporations/e-file-for-Large-Business-and-International-%28LB&I%29> (updated Jan. 25, 2017) (last accessed Feb. 1, 2017)]

IRS Publication 1220 gives the specifications for e-filing Forms 1097, 1098, 1099, 3921, 3922, 5498, and W-2G for 2016 tax years. [<http://www.irs.gov/pub/irs-pdf/p1220.pdf> (revised Dec. 2016) (last accessed Feb. 1, 2017)]

See "Electronic Filing Options for Business and Self-Employed Taxpayers," <https://www.irs.gov/tax-professionals/e-file-providers-partners/electronic-filing-options-for-business-and-self-employed-taxpayers> (revised Aug. 23, 2016) (last accessed Feb. 1, 2017) for links to the Employment Tax e-file System, which is available to "Reporting Agents," IRS-authorized service providers who file Forms 940, 941, and/or 944 electronically for their clients. Business taxpayers can also file online with the 940, 941, and 944 online filing programs, and all federal tax payments can be made by electronic funds transfer or by credit card. W-2 forms can be submitted electronically, although the Social Security Administration rather than the IRS site is the proper place of filing. The Social Security Administration has online help for employers who file W-2 forms electronically.

§ 2.09 BANKRUPTCY ISSUES

In April 2005, the Supreme Court decided that IRA balances are exempt from creditor claims in bankruptcy because the right to receive IRA funds is "on account of age." Although IRA funds can be withdrawn at any age, there is a substantial penalty on withdrawals prior to age 59½ unless another exemption is available. The Supreme Court resolved a circuit split under which the Second, Fifth, Sixth, and Ninth Circuits took the position eventually adopted by the Supreme Court, but the Eighth Circuit deemed IRA account holders to have unlimited access to their funds, so creditors should be able to reach the funds. (It is likely that the Supreme Court accepted the policy argument that IRAs often receive rollovers from qualified pension plans.) [*Rousey v. Jacoway*, 544 U.S. 320 (2005)]

However, a mid-2014 Supreme Court decision says that creditors can assert claims on IRAs that are inherited by a non-spouse beneficiary (in this case, the daughter of the deceased account owner). [*Clark v. Rameker*, 134 S. Ct. 2242 (2014)]

The Sixth Circuit held that income available to Chapter 13 debtors after repaying a 401(k) loan is projected disposable income that must be paid to unsecured creditors. If the bankruptcy trustee objects, the debtors will not be permitted to use it to make voluntary contributions to the plan. The Bankruptcy Abuse Prevention and Consumer Protection Act of 2005; Pub. L. No. 109-8 (BAPCPA) provides a limited exclusion for amounts withheld by an employer from an employee's wages for contributions to a qualified plan, so the Sixth Circuit held that plan loan payments are excluded from debtor's disposable income, but voluntary contributions to a 401(k) plan are not. The Sixth Circuit said that contributions are only excluded from the bankruptcy estate if they were made before the date of the petition. [*In re Seafort*, 669 F.3d 662 (6th Cir. 2012)]

Although the primary impact of BAPCPA is on individual filings, this legislation has some provisions that affect employment tax planning:

- Clarification that a broad range of retirement savings vehicles will be excluded from the individual debtor's bankruptcy estate—not just government plans and private employer plans subject to ERISA Title I, but also tax-deferred annuities under 403(b) plans, health insurance plans regulated by state law, IRAs (including education IRAs), and funds placed in a § 529 (tuition savings program) a year or more before the bankruptcy filing. In general, the IRA exemption is limited to $1 million, but qualified rollovers into the IRA are not counted for this purpose. Furthermore, protection is granted to employee contributions even before they are deposited into the plan. This wide scope of protection applies even if the debtor is an insider of the employer corporation, and whether the debtor elects the state or federal exemption scheme.

- BAPCPA alters the previous treatment of plan loans. It is not a violation of the automatic stay to withhold a debtor-employee's wages to repay a plan loan from a qualified plan.

- Pre-BAPCPA, wages, salaries, and commissions for services rendered filing of the bankruptcy petition generally could be paid and claimed as administrative expenses. BAPCPA strictly limits payments of retention bonuses and severance payments to corporate insiders.

BAPCPA extends the avoidance period (i.e., makes it easier for the bankruptcy trustee to reverse payments) with respect to transfers made to insiders—including certain transfers made under employment contracts that are not in the ordinary course of business.

§ 2.10 THE INTERACTION BETWEEN §§ 409A AND 415

The general tax rule is that payments made after an employee's separation from service are not compensation for § 415 purposes. The practical effect is that after an employee is terminated, he or she can no longer defer funds (e.g., severance benefits) paid by the ex-employer by depositing them in a 401(k) or 403(b) or 457 account. However, under IRS rules, a payment made within the 2½-month period after separation can be deferred in two situations. Either the payment would have been made anyway, even if employment had not terminated, or the payment relates to bona fide vacation, sick leave, or other leave the employee would have had access to if employment had continued.

The Code § 409A provision governing nonqualified plans also has implications for the taxation of post-severance compensation (see § 8.02[D] for a more detailed discussion). "Separation pay" is the term used in § 409A for severance pay. It is regulated as defined compensation if there is a legally binding right to payment in a future year—even if there is a substantial risk of forfeiture. Section 409A applies to all legally binding rights to deferred compensation, not just salary reduction and salary deferral plans, but also severance agreements and informal bonus programs. Elective deferrals such as salary deferrals are always considered vested. However, noncompete agreements do not defer vesting. However, if the payment is entirely at the payor's discretion, there is no legally binding right to payment, so § 409A will not apply. Under the current regulations, payment of current compensation in exchange for nonqualified deferred compensation to be paid in the future can be treated as impermissible acceleration of the compensation that violates § 409A.

Failure to comply with § 409A has serious consequences. The executive covered by the arrangement will be taxed in the year that the compensation vests, whether or not it is paid in that year. The executive is also liable for the 20% excise tax on noncompliance nonqualified deferred compensation, plus interest on the late payment. [Lori Jones, *Section 409A: Top 10 Rules for Compliant Non-Qualified Deferred Compensation,* Thompsoncoburn.com (July 28, 2016) (benefitslink.com)]

Regulations under § 409A explain when either an employee or independent contractor has "separated from service." For an employee, separation occurs when no further services will be performed after a certain date, or the level of bona fide services is permanently reduced to 20% or less of the previous average level of services (e.g., the person works one day a week or less). There is a rebuttable presumption that there was no separation if services continue at 50% or more of the prior level. For independent contractors, separation from services usually means expiration of all contracts, leading to good-faith termination of the contractual relationship.

On July 14, 2015, the SEC released a proposed rule requiring publicly traded companies to have a "recovery policy" of clawing back incentive-based compensation that was paid to executives if the compensation reflects metrics that were revised in the company's financial statements because they were overstated. If the recovery policy provides for clawback from nonqualified deferred compensation before it becomes payable, the executive could experience high liability under § 409A. If the employee has already paid taxes, the SEC rule requires the clawback to equal the pre-tax bonus amount, not the net amount. A company's ability to claw back from deferred compensation that is not yet payable violates the § 409A anti-acceleration rule of § 409A, so it is wise to draft the recovery policy to claw back the compensation from sources other than deferred compensation subject to the anti-acceleration rule. [Securities Law Insider, *SEC Clawback Rules Have Executive Tax Consequences* (Oct. 5, 2015) (benefitslink .com)]

Section 409A greatly increased IRS scrutiny of deferred compensation plans. In mid-2014, the IRS launched a formal audit program to determine if employers satisfy operational and document requirements. The first audits were limited to the 10 highest-compensated employees at each of 50 very large companies. The focus is on executives' initial and subsequent deferral elections, and corporate compliance with distribution requirements. The results will determine if the IRS will expand or modify the program. [David C. Strosnider, *IRS Begins Code Section 409A Audit Program*, Roetzel & Andress (June 18, 2014) (benefits link.com); William E. Wright, *On the Section 409A Hunting Trail*, Womble Carlyle Sandridge & Rice LLP (June 16, 2014), available at Lexology.com]

In June 2015, the IRS released new audit guidelines for nonqualified deferred compensation plans, e.g., top hat plans; excess benefit plans (plans providing benefits that would otherwise be ruled out by the § 415 limitation); restricted stock unit plans; bonus deferral plans. The guidelines state that amounts in these plans cannot be protected from the employer's creditors and participants can be taxed on amounts that are constructively but not yet actually received. Constructive receipt might occur as a result of deferred compensation accounts such as checkbooks, debit cards, or credit cards. The cash equivalence doctrine says that if a solvent obligor makes an unconditional, assignable promise to pay that is not subject to setoff, and the promise is of a type that is frequently transferred to lenders or investors, the promise is the equivalent of cash. For purposes of FICA and FUTA tax, non-qualified deferred compensation is taxable when the amounts vest, not when they are distributed. [Mark S. Weisberg and Linda Lemel Hoseman, *Nonqualified Deferred Compensation Plan Update*, Thompson Coburn LLP (Oct. 30, 2015), available at Lexology.com]

Proposed Regulations under § 409A issued in mid-2016 impose stricter rules for correcting nonqualified deferred compensation arrangements that fail the requirements of § 409A. The proposal says that if there is a specified correction method in IRS guidance about the particular error, the employer must use it—and must apply it to all other similar errors. The same correction requirements apply to distributions payable on the death of a participant or the death of a beneficiary. However, certain delays in payment will be allowed, if they are necessary to avoid violating applicable laws (such as federal securities laws). [81 Fed. Reg. 40569 (June 22, 2016); see Anthony G. Provenzano and Nicholas P. Walmsley, *Proposed Section 409A Regulations Make Several Notable Changes*, Millerchevalier.com (June 29, 2016) (benefitslink.com)]

Mid-2016 regulations use a single rule for all purposes: a payment is made when it yields current taxable income. A transfer of restricted stock or other unvested property is not a payment unless the service provider elects under § 83(b) to include it in income. Theoretically, the § 409A rules permit payment at death, including acceleration of payment, but this provision can create administrative problems because the employer might not know about the death until after the § 409A deadline has passed. The 2016 proposed regulations allow payment until December 31 of the calendar year after the calendar year in which death occurs, when designated by the payor or payee. Employers can amend their plans to conform to this rule without having to satisfy the § 409A rules for changes in the timing of payments. The 2016 proposal also allows the payment-at-death rules to be extended to payments at the death of the beneficiary, or to payments based on the beneficiary's disability or unforeseen emergency. Prior law exempted stock rights from § 409A only if they were granted to someone who provides services to the issuer or its subsidiary on the date of the grant. However, the proposal extends the exemption to grants to someone who has not yet started work, but who was reasonably expected to start work within 12 months and actually did so.

However, this is a tax rule. Securities law limits the ability to offer equity to persons who have not yet been hired and the rules for Incentive Stock Options also refer to grantees who are employed as of the grant date. The proposed rules also address the treatment of transaction-based compensation (stock or stock value awards) when a company is acquired. The 2016 proposed rules also give examples of unacceptable practices that will bar relief and require penalties for noncompliance.

The proposed rule exempts severance pay when a person is hired and fired in the same calendar year. Payments that otherwise qualify can be considered exempt short-term deferrals if they are made after the normal 2½ month limit, if the employer reasonably believed that making the payment on schedule would violate a law (e.g., a requirement of securities law). [Ropes & Gray LLP, *Updates to the 409A Rules* (June 27, 2016), available at Lexology.com]

For ISOs exercised in 2016, and 2016 transfers of shares that were purchased under a tax-qualified employee stock purchase plan (ESPP), an annual information statement was required to be furnished to participants by January 31, 2017. Information returns were due to be filed with the IRS by February 28, 2017 (for paper documents) and March 31, 2017 (e-filing). Companies that file 250 or more ISO or ESPP returns must e-file, using IRS's FIRE system. A 30-day automatic extension is available based on filing Form 8809. For ESPPs, the company must report the first transfer of legal title to shares purchased under the plan, if the price was lower than the Fair Market Value (FMV) on the date of the grant (or was not fixed or determinable at that time). ISO data is reported on Form 3921, ESPP data on Form 3822. However, the forms must be ordered from the IRS. The forms are posted online but are not acceptable for filing. The same forms can be used to provide the statements to participants, but employers can also draft their own forms that include the same information. A separate Form 3921 or 3922 must be filed for each transaction; multiple transactions by the same employee cannot be consolidated. The penalty for failure to furnish a required statement, or for issuing an incomplete or incorrect statement, can be as much as $260/statement, subject to a cap of $1,072,500 for a small business, $3,218, 500 for a large business. Penalties are enhanced for intentional failure to submit statements to the IRS.

The payor company is obligated to report the ordinary income that optionees recognize when they make a disqualifying disposition of ISO shares (i.e., sale before two years after the grant or one year after the exercise, whichever comes later, has passed). Reporting is done on Box 1 of the W-2 form. A company that fails to report the income will not be able to deduct the income produced by the disqualifying disposition, and reporting penalties might be due. The first time ESPP stock is transferred is also reported in Box 1 of the W-2. [Orrick.com Insights, *Annual Reporting Requirements for Incentive Stock Options and Employee Stock Purchase Plans* (Jan. 20, 2017) (benefitslink.com)]

Small closely held companies, especially start-ups, use stock options as an incentive to executives and to save cash that can be invested in the business. However, Code § 409A applies to stock options and SARs, which determines the exercise price and requires a valuation of the business to set the price. The IRS has consistently taken the position that discounted stock options are deferred compensation subject to § 409A. This makes the options less attractive to employees because they cannot control the timing of income recognition by controlling the timing of the exercise. ISOs under Code § 422 and stock options issued under an ESOP pursuant to § 423 are exempt from the § 409A regulations as long as they continue to be qualified. [Peter Alwardt, *Discounted Stock Options are Subject to 409A*, Eisneramper.com (Oct. 22, 2015) (benefitslink.com)]

Under mid-2016 proposed regulations, a stock right that does not otherwise provide for deferral of compensation is not deemed to defer compensation merely because the amount payable when an executive is fired for cause, or is terminated based on a condition within the service provider's control, is based on a calculation that is less than fair market value. [Rebecca Moore, *Proposed Rules Issued About Application of 409A to NQDC Plans,* plansponsor.com (June 23, 2016)]

The golden parachute rules of Code §§ 280G and 4999 impose a 20% excise tax on certain payments made to top executives based on corporate change of control. Payments subject to the golden parachute rules are not deductible by the payor corporation. These rules apply to officers; the highest-paid 250 employees within the employer's controlled group of corporations (or the highest-paid 1% if there are fewer than 25,000 employees in the controlled group) if their annual compensation is higher than the threshold amount for that year. The rules also apply to employee-shareholders who own more than 1% of the fair market value of the outstanding shares of all classes of the employer's stock. The excise tax applies if the executive receives payments and benefits due to the change in control that are at least three times the base amount. The base amount is three times the executive's average annual compensation for the past five years. Employment agreements can be drafted to avoid application of the golden parachute rules— e.g., by reducing payments to the maximum that does not trigger the excise tax. The Code § 409A rules about nonqualified deferred compensation must also be consulted. A gross-up provision calls for reimbursing the executive for the excise tax incurred. But the payor corporation cannot deduct gross-up payments, and shareholders may be angered about this use of corporate funds. [PLC Employee Benefits & Executive Compensation, *Addressing Sections 280G and 4999 in Executive Employment Agreements* (Apr. 16, 2013) (benefitslink.com)]

CHAPTER 3

BONUSES AND SEVERANCE PAY

§ 3.01 INTRODUCTION

Although regular compensation and benefits are the main focus of compensation planning, there are two important types of nonrecurring compensation that also play an important role: bonuses and severance pay.

The 2005 Bankruptcy Reform Act (Pub. L. No. 109-8) limits the ability of a company that is a Chapter 11 debtor to offer retention bonuses and/or severance pay and then claim these payments as an administrative expense in the bankruptcy case. A retention bonus or severance payment to a director, officer, partner, or control person is allowed only if the fact and amount of the payment are both reasonable.

A retention bonus to an insider is allowed only if the insider has, in fact, received a bona fide job offer elsewhere paying at least as much as the insider's job, preventing the insider from taking the offer is essential to the business's survival, and the amount of the bonus is limited to either 10 times the average retention payment made to rank-and-file employees or 25% of any similar payment made to or on behalf of the insider in the previous calendar year. Severance payments to insiders are allowed only as part of a program covering all full-time employees, and insiders must not receive severance that exceeds 10 times the average severance payment to the rank and file.

[A] Limitations on Executive Pay

After many years of assuming that the setting of pay was purely a discretionary act on the part of the paying corporation, limitations began to be imposed: such as § 162(m) limitations on the tax deduction for compensation (see § 3.03[G], below), and restrictions on "shutdown benefits."

Even outside the bankruptcy context, a plan that is "at risk" (i.e., significantly underfunded) may be barred by the Pension Protection Act of 2006, Pub. L. No. 109-280, from providing "shutdown benefits"—payments to employees who are losing their jobs when an operation is shut down. In some cases, the employer will be permitted to make the payments if the employer makes an additional contribution to shore up the plan.

Companies that received Troubled Asset Relief Program (TARP) bailout payments under the Emergency Economic Stabilization Act of 2008 (EESA), as amended by the American Recovery and Reinvestment Act of 2009 (ARRA), were subject to limits on bonuses, incentive compensation, and retention awards as long as they had any outstanding obligations to the federal government. (The TARP program ended in 2010.)

Companies receiving TARP assistance were also forbidden to make "golden parachute" payments to top executives leaving the company. See § 3.03[D] below. EESA and AARA also required "clawback": companies receiving assistance had to recoup bonuses and incentive compensation paid to top executives as a result of false financial reporting.

The Virginia Supreme Court ruled that, when a change in a business' relationship with government regulators (e.g., under TARP regulations limiting parachute payments) makes it impossible to pay severance, the business can use the contract-law defense of "impossibility of performance" to avoid making the payment. The plaintiff, a bank president, had a contract that entitled him to three years of salary if he quit within six months after a material change in control; his bank merged into another bank. He sued his ex-employer when he did not receive a parachute payment that was forbidden by TARP. [*Hampton RoadsBankshares, Inc. v. Harvard*, 781 S.E.2d 172 (Va. 2016); see Virginia Whitehill Guldi, *Can Government Regulation Make It Impossible to Pay Severance?*, Zuckerman Spaeder LLP (Feb. 8, 2016), available at Lexology.com]

The Dodd-Frank Act, Pub. L. No. 111-203, was passed to prevent future economic meltdowns. "Clawback" is also required by the Dodd-Frank Act. On July 1, 2015, the SEC proposed rules for national securities exchanges ('34 Act Rule 10-D), mandating that all listed companies have clawback policies. The policies force executive officers to repay the company if they received improperly awarded incentive-based compensation, and the company makes an accounting restatement. The purpose of this provision is to deter executives from taking imprudent steps in order to increase their income. Former as well as current executive officers must repay any incentive-based compensation (e.g., bonuses) that they would not have received if the initial statement of financial results had been accurate.

Recoupment is required for all incentive-based compensation that reflects accounting figures, total shareholder return, or the company's stock price, if the compensation was received in the three fiscal years before the year of the restatement. It is a no-fault provision; it is not necessary that the restated figures were deceptive, only that they were incorrect. Executive officers are top corporate policy-making officials, such as the company's president, CFO, principal accounting officer, or any vice president in charge of a business unit, division, or function. [SEC Release 2015-136, *SEC Proposes Rules Requiring Companies to Adopt Clawback Policies on Executive Compensation* (July 1, 2015), <http://www.sec.gov/news/pressrelease/2015-136.html> (last accessed Feb. 2, 2017)]

In mid-2015, the SEC released a proposed rule requiring publicly traded companies to have a recovery policy. The companies must "claw back" incentive-based compensation that was paid to executives, if the payment was based on overstated metrics that the company had to revise in its financial statements. [Securities Law Insider, *SEC Clawback Rules Have Executive Tax Consequences* (Oct. 5, 2015) (benefitslink.com)]

The SEC and five other agencies that regulate the financial services industry issued additional proposals under the Dodd-Frank Act in April 2016. Under these proposals, clawback can occur as much as seven years after the inappropriate transaction or reporting. The highest-paid employees at major financial institutions such as large banks would have to wait at least four years to receive part of their compensation, in case clawbacks are required after the pay is earned. [<https://www.ncua.gov/About/Documents/Agenda%20Items/AG20160421 Item2b.pdf>; see Nathaniel Popper, *Wall St. Regulators Propose Stricter Pay Rules for Bankers*, NYTimes.com (Apr. 22, 2016); Donna Borak, Andrew Ackerman and Christina Rexrode, *New Rules Curbing Wall Street Pay Proposed*, WSJ.com (Apr. 22, 2016)]

In mid-2016, the Ninth Circuit ruled that Sarbanes-Oxley § 304 permits clawback of certain compensation paid to CEOs and CFOs, even if the officers were not personally at fault in the events triggering the clawback. [*SEC v. Jensen*, **835 F.3d 1100** (9th Cir. 2016); see Alexander Song, *Ninth Circuit Holds That SOX 304 Clawback Applies to Executives That Are Not at Fault*, Employment Matters blog (Sept. 14, 2016) (benefitslink.com)]

Dodd-Frank Act § 951 requires public companies to allow their shareholders a "say on pay": input into the compensation process for top executives. Shareholders have the right to cast advisory (i.e., non-binding) votes on executive compensation and golden parachutes. As of January 21, 2011, proxy statements must include say on pay resolutions—and a vote on how often say on pay votes will be conducted.

Exchange Act Rule 14a-21(b) requires public companies to hold a say on pay vote at least once every six years as to whether the actual vote will be held every two or every three years. Shareholders must be given a vote on golden parachutes, and parachute arrangements for top executive officers must be disclosed. A separate vote is not required if the golden parachute has already been the subject of a say on pay vote. [Text of rule: <http://www.sec.gov/rules/final/2011/33-9178.pdf>; SEC press release: <http://www.sec.gov/news/press/2011/2011-25 .htm> (Jan. 25, 2011)]

Consulting firm Willis Towers Watson reported that approximately half (47%) of respondents to their survey said that the effect of the say on pay requirement has been very or generally positive. Only 10% said it has had a negative effect and only 4% advocate repealing say on pay. Most respondents said that they might even continue to hold say on pay votes even if Dodd-Frank were repealed because institutional investors and proxy advisors might oppose the re-election of directors where there was no say on pay vote. Eighty-three percent of respondents have some kind of clawback policy. [S. Miller, *Top Executives Get Performance Bonuses Despite "Tepid Growth,"* shrm.org (Jan. 4, 2017) (benefitslink.com)]

In mid-2011, the D.C. Circuit vacated Rule 14a-11, the proxy access rule, which would have permitted some shareholders to write in their nominees for the board of directors. The D.C. Circuit found that the SEC exceeded its discretion in adopting this rule. [*Business Roundtable & Chamber of Commerce v. SEC*, 647 F.3d 1144 (D.C. Cir. 2011)]

The SEC took additional actions related to executive pay in 2015. Dodd-Frank Act § 953(a)(1) requires the SEC to issue rules requiring reporting companies to disclose the relationship between top management pay and corporate financial returns. The SEC published a proposal, Release No. 34-74835, on April 29, 2015 to carry out this mandate. The proposal calls for inclusion of a table in each proxy statement, in a standardized format prescribed by the SEC. The table gives the actual pay of the CEO, average actual pay for other top officers, the company's total shareholder return, and total shareholder return for the company's competitors. The metrics in the table are intended to let shareholders and potential investors track whether top-management pay reflects the managers' success in improving shareholder return. [SEC Release No. 34-74835 (Apr. 29, 2015), available at <http://www.sec.gov/rules/proposed/2015/34-74835.pdf> (last accessed Feb. 2, 2017)]

In response to criticisms about income inequality, on August 5, 2015, the SEC adopted a "pay-gap" rule requiring large public companies to disclose the difference in pay between the CEO and rank-and file-workers, with the pay ratio re-calculated every three years. Compliance is required as of fiscal years beginning on or after January 1, 2017, with extra time allowed for smaller or emerging growth companies. [SEC press release 2015-160, *SEC Adopts Rule for Pay Ratio Disclosure* (Aug. 5, 2015), available at <http://www.sec.gov/news/pressrelease/2015-160.html> (last accessed Feb. 2, 2017)]

In early 2017, the SEC asked for public comments on the pay ratio rule. At that point, there was significant interest in Congress in repealing the Dodd-Frank Act or modifying its requirements. Opponents of the pay ratio rule say that it lies outside the SEC's authorized mission of providing investors with the information they need to make investment decisions. [Tatyana Shumsky, *SEC Says Conflict Minerals, Pay Ratio Rules Remain in Force*, WSJ.com (Feb. 24, 2017)]

§ 3.02　BONUSES

For many years, the compensation of executives and professionals was enhanced by bonus amounts—often much greater than their salaries. This was especially true in technology, Internet companies, and financial services firms. Bonus practices became controversial in a recessionary environment, with widespread layoffs and benefit cuts. Many companies increased the extent to which executive compensation is linked to corporate performance.

Willis Towers Watson reported in early 2017 said that 36% of companies surveyed expect to pay annual bonuses greater than 110% of the target; 35% expect to pay 90% of target or less; and 29% expect annual incentives to be close to target. Willis Towers Watson found these results surprising because revenue and earnings growth in many industries has been tepid. [S. Miller, *Top Executives Get Performance Bonuses Despite "Tepid Growth,"* shrm.org (Jan. 4, 2017) (benefitslink.com)]

Many compensation plans provide that a bonus is not earned if the employee is no longer employed on the schedule date of payment (e.g., December 31). However, some states forbid forfeiture provisions. Other states distinguish between commissions on sales already made (which cannot be forfeited) and bonuses (based on performance figures for the person or the company as a whole). As a general principle of contract interpretation, ambiguous provisions will be construed against the party that drafted the agreement (and could have made it clearer)—so it is vital to make sure that the contract clearly sets out the intended terms.

Under the Fair Labor Standards Act, overtime calculations must include all remuneration for employment, so most employee bonuses are included. Bonuses that are defined as a predetermined percentage of the employee's straight time and overtime for the period do not require additional overtime to be calculated on the bonus because it has already been factored in. If there is a fixed bonus pool, the total straight time plus overtime of all participants is divided, with each participant receiving that percentage of total wages (including overtime). The DOL's position is that a bonus is an extra reward and the term should not be used for a portion of the regular wages the employee is entitled to receive under his or her regular working arrangement. [John E. Thompson, *What Is a "Percentage Bonus"?*, Fisher & Phillips LLP (Jan. 11, 2016), available at Lexology.com]

A 2010 Connecticut Supreme Court case draws a distinction between bonuses that are recoverable as wages under the Connecticut Wage Act (including statutory double damages and attorneys' fees) and discretionary bonuses that are not subject to the wage law. The court found that an attorney's year-end bonus was not "wages" because it was discretionary and not premised on specific, definable goals (such as number of hours billed). [*Ziotas v. Reardon Law Firm P.C.*, 296 Conn. 579 (2010)]

Termination of a bonus plan, even if the employer reserved the right to terminate, could lead to liability for breach of contract if the employer violates the implied covenant of good faith and fair dealing. The Seventh Circuit held in mid-2013 that an employer carrying out an express contract provision can still breach the contract if it exercises discretion in a manner contrary to the reasonable expectations of the parties. The plaintiff, Wilson, was a recruiter who found students to enroll in CEC's culinary arts college. The bonus plan paid representatives a bonus for each student recruited over a threshold number, if the student graduated or completed at least a year of study. However, when representatives are terminated, they are only entitled to bonuses for students who have already completed a year or graduated, not those enrolled. In October 2010, the federal Department of Education issued regulations forbidding such bonus plans, effective July 2011; CEC said that bonuses would not be paid after February 2011. [*Wilson v. Career Educ. Corp.*, 729 F.3d 665 (7th Cir. 2013)]

Employers are not required to pay bonuses that are based on a goal, if the employee missed the goal as a result of taking the Family and Medical Leave Act

(FMLA) leave. 29 C.F.R. § 825.215(c) permits the employer to deny the bonus—unless the bonus was paid to employees who took equal amounts of non-FMLA leave. "Goal-based" is defined broadly to include attendance, safety, sales, and production bonuses but not holiday or similar bonuses that are paid to all employees. If the leave has an impact on the bonus, the regulations do not state whether or not prorate is required. [Jeff Nowak, *FMLA FAQ: Is an Employer Required to Pay a Prorated Amount of Annual Bonus After Employee Takes FMLA Leave?* (Dec. 23, 2014) (benefitslink.com). See, e.g., *Sommer v. Vanguard Grp.*, 461 F.3d 397 (3d Cir. 2006)]

The Second Circuit (joining the D.C. Circuit) said that reducing a discretionary bonus can be an adverse employment action, although the Seventh Circuit disagrees. The plaintiff received a $1,000 bonus for student achievement, rather than the $3,000 the other teachers received; Davis received a smaller bonus because she took several months of unpaid medical leave to recover from an automobile accident. She brought an Americans with Disability Act (ADA) suit, which the district court dismissed on the grounds that there was no adverse action because her employer had the discretion to determine the amount of the bonus. The Second Circuit held the mere fact that the bonus was discretionary did not mean that cutting it was not an adverse action. But nevertheless, the court affirmed dismissal of the suit for failure to prove that disability discrimination was a motivating factor in the bonus decision. [*Davis v. New York City Dep't of Educ.*, 804 F.3d 231 (2d Cir. 2015)]

Sometimes C corporations try to avoid income tax by "zeroing out" the corporation's taxable income. All of the income is listed on W-2 forms for shareholder/employees as "bonuses." Sometimes the money does not even change hands because the shareholders are deemed to lend the money back to the corporation. The tax court rejected this tactic in a case where the corporation did not have enough cash on hand to cover the check. Vanney Associates paid its founder $20,000 a month in wages. Each year, the company paid off its bills, gave bonuses to employees, and distributed whatever was left over to founder Vanney as a year-end bonus. His 2008 bonus was $815,000. Taxes were withheld, and he was issued a $464,000 check that he "loaned" to the corporation instead of cashing. The tax court disallowed the bonus on the grounds that Vanney and his wife (the company bookkeeper) knew or should have known that the check could not be honored because the business did not have enough funds to cover it. [*Vanney Assocs., Inc.*, T.C. Memo 2014-184]

The 2016 proposals adopted by federal agencies that regulate financial services require certain bonuses to be deferred for four years; the restriction applies to executives who are major "risk takers" who could get the employer into trouble if they engage in financially hazardous transactions to earn large bonuses. [<https://www.ncua.gov/About/Documents/Agenda%20Items/AG20160421 Item2b.pdf>; see Nathaniel Popper, *Wall St. Regulators Propose Stricter Pay Rules for Bankers*, NYTimes.com (Apr. 22, 2016); Donna Borak, Andrew

Ackerman and Christina Rexrode, *New Rules Curbing Wall Street Pay Proposed*, WSJ.com (Apr. 22, 2016)]

§ 3.03 SEVERANCE PAY

[A] Generally

There is no federal law requiring that employees receive severance pay, but nevertheless it is very common for employers to provide this type of compensation (unless the employee was fired for misconduct). Severance pay is often defined as a certain number of days or weeks of pay for every year of service with the employer.

The most important characteristic of severance pay is that it is over and above the normal salary or wages earned for past services. Severance payments are by and large discretionary, unlike payment for past services, which must be made when employment terminates. If the employer enters into an express or implied contract to provide severance benefits that contract can be enforced. However, employers typically retain the right to alter their severance pay plans, and this is sometimes done just before a major layoff. Employers may also provide benefits to only certain persons affected by a mass layoff, claiming that the others were terminated for poor performance.

The term "severance pay" can mean statutory obligations or obligations created by a benefit plan, Collective Bargaining Agreement (CBA), or employer policies. New York does not require severance as a matter of state labor law, but employers who have such programs must be consistent with wage and hour law. In a Sixth Circuit case from 2014, plaintiff McCarthy was given two choices when she was faced with involuntary layoff: retiring with a lump sum or continuing to work at 85% of her previous wage. She chose to keep working. She brought a suit to collect the minimum wage, asserting that, because the payments she received were a preexisting severance obligation, she worked without compensation. The Sixth Circuit held that even if she was fraudulently induced to accept the lower-paid job, she could not import her fraud claim into a Fair Labor Standards Act (FLSA) claim. [*McCarthy v. Ameritech Publ'n*, 763 F.3d 469 (6th Cir. 2014)]

Employees of companies in bankruptcy are at especially high risk of losing severance. Severance payments by bankrupt companies require court approval (and 2005's bankruptcy reform legislation limits payments to insiders), and must compete with other creditor claims.

The Equal Employment Opportunity Commission (EEOC) and National Labor Relations Board (NLRB) review severance agreements, with particular attention to waivers and releases of claims, confidentiality requirements, and non-disparagement clauses. The agencies disfavor clauses that seek to limit the right to file an administrative charge, communicate with regulators, or participate in agency investigations. It is permissible to make employees give up the right to individual relief but there should be a carve-out permitting employees to participate in agency investigations. Payment of severance should not be conditioned on withdrawal of a pending agency charge, but if the employee does withdraw the charge, the employee should be required to inform the agency of the severance agreement. [Debra A. Mastrian, *Tips for Drafting Severance Agreements to Avoid Scrutiny from the EEOC and NLRB*, SmithAmundsen LLC (Oct. 7, 2015), available at Lexology.com]

There are two basic kinds of severance plan: the traditional plan, funded through the employer's general assets or with a trust, and Supplemental Unemployment Benefit (SUB) plans. SUB plans provide additional payments to supplement state unemployment insurance benefits. To receive SUB payments, employees must be eligible for state unemployment benefits, and must verify each week that they continue to be eligible and to look for work. Design changes can save money. A SUB plan resembles unemployment benefits in many ways. Employees have to be eligible for state unemployment to get SUB and they have to verify each week that they're eligible and looking for work. The benefit is often defined as a multiplier of years of service: for example, one to two weeks of benefits for each year that the employee worked for the company. Setting the appropriate level of benefits available under the plan depends on what the company's objective is in adopting the plan: to help employees bridge an income gap until they get a new job? To improve the company's profile after a layoff? There is a potential for a windfall if the employee gets a new job before the severance period ends; SUB plans eliminate this problem because they coordinate with state unemployment benefits, which end when the claimant gets another job. [Philip Parker, *Severance Plans: The Promise and the Savings*, Benefits Quarterly (Second Quarter 2012) (benefitslink.com)]

If the employee turnover is caused by a corporate transition (see Chapter 16), severance-related benefits can be provided under three main structures: a change in control agreement; a severance plan; or a change in control protection plan. Generally, individual agreements will be offered if the intent is to protect only selected executives, whereas a formal plan should be adopted if there is a broader-based group that might receive severance. (A formal plan will almost certainly be subject to the Employment Retirement Income Security Act (ERISA).) For a change in control provision or retention agreement, the most important questions are which executives are significant enough to be awarded protection, and what will trigger benefits (Termination without cause? Resignation for good cause? Resignation during a window period following a change in control?) The usual term is one to two years after the change in control occurs. For the employee, the most favorable provision is for the employer to reimburse the employee for golden parachute tax penalties imposed under Code § 4999; the intermediate position is for the company and the executive to divide the payment;

and the least favorable is for the employee to forfeit severance benefits in any situation in which the employer would lose the deduction as a result of § 280G.

Departing executives often have access to special terms that are not offered to rank-and-file employees: for example, keeping them in active status in the employer group health plan (EGHP) while they are receiving severance or paying their Comprehensive Omnibus Budget Reconciliation Act (COBRA) premiums after termination. These special terms are usually set out in a severance agreement. However, if the employer maintains a self-funded group health plan, it is subject to the Code § 105(h) nondiscrimination requirements and it is forbidden to maintain eligibility provisions that discriminate against non-HCEs. Therefore, § 105(h)(7) will probably require the market value of continuation coverage for departing executives to be treated as taxable compensation. [E is for ERISA Blog, *Special COBRA Coverage Terms for the Departing Executive: Pitfalls to Avoid* (Dec. 12, 2011) (benefitslink.com)]

Section 105(h) does not apply to after-tax payment of premiums, so giving the employee additional cash solves this problem and the employee can choose between COBRA and marketplace coverage. COBRA notices should be updated to discuss this issue. [Richard J. Birmingham, *What Everyone Needs to Know About the Coordination of Severance Benefits, COBRA, and the ACA*, Davis Wright & Tremaine (June 9, 2014) (benefitslink.com)]

Providing subsidized health coverage can create COBRA problems. The company might provide three months of "garden leave" before termination, with the company continuing to pay health insurance premiums during the leave. COBRA entitlement dates from the qualifying event, even if coverage is not lost until later. Plans are permitted to extend the COBRA period until coverage is actually lost. For example, it is common to treat terminating employees as covered by the plan until the end of the month in which they are terminated, with COBRA starting on the first day of the next month. Under such an arrangement, employees might argue that they are entitled to six months of paid premiums.

A reduction in work hours is only considered a qualifying event if it results in loss of coverage. The employer could specify that coverage ends on the last day of work, with the employer subsidizing the cost if the employee makes a COBRA election. The plan could also make the COBRA period concurrent with the extended, subsidized coverage—in which case, COBRA notice of the qualifying event should be given. The insurer's consent might be required to provide more coverage than the COBRA minimum. [Michael Lane, *Did You Consider the COBRA Implications of Your Severance Arrangement?*, Thompson Coburn LLP (Nov. 2, 2016), available at Lexology.com]

If there is a formal plan, the employer can protect itself by reserving the right to amend or terminate the plan. If there is a dispute about an informal arrangement, it will probably end up in state court, with the court having broad scope to review the plan administrator's decision. If there is an ERISA plan, then participants must exhaust their administrative remedies within the plan before bringing suit; the suit will have to be filed in federal court; and jury trial will not be available. If the plan document gives the administrators discretion to interpret the plan, the court will review the decision deferentially and is likely to uphold the administrator's decision unless it was arbitrary and capricious. It is permissible to have multiple benefit formulas, as long as the plan does not discriminate in favor of employees in protected classes. A formal plan can be a morale-building tool, because employees know in advance what to expect.

However, the disadvantage is that a formal plan results in loss of flexibility. Individual negotiations with employees are ruled out. The plan requires more administrative time than occasional individual negotiations. It is possible that different treatment of employees will result in discrimination allegations, so it is vital to be able to show a rational business reason for the distinctions. ERISA compliance can be time-consuming and costly.

Furthermore, even if the intention is to avoid maintaining an ERISA plan, a de facto plan might be found based on oral representations made to employees; the employer's intention (as manifested by, for example, past practices or maintaining a fund or account to pay benefits). If the plan is deemed to be an ERISA plan even though this was not the employer's intention, penalties might be imposed for reporting and disclosure violations. [Sandra W. Cohen and Carol Buckmann, *ERISA Considerations for Severance Pay Policy Checklists* (February 2011) (benefitslink.com)]

A 2014 article gives some drafting advice:

- If there is a significant gap between notice and the last day of work, is the executive expected to keep working? Would a later termination date permit any benefits or awards to vest? The company might be liable for the executive's actions between the time he or she was informed of termination and the actual date of departure, so it might be worthwhile reducing the length of the gap period to reduce the risk; benefits might also be contingent on signing a second release on the actual departure date.

- If there is a dispute about the amount of compensation, it could give rise to state-law wage claims, so the separation agreement should clarify that the dispute has been compromised by agreeing on a fixed payment. If state law requires distributing all earned compensation no later than the last day of employment, be sure to comply.

- The separation agreement should address whether severance is provided in a lump sum or as continuing payments. In a change of control situation, clarify whether the buyer or seller is responsible for the payment.

- Set out what non-cash benefits will be made available (e.g., outplacement assistance; favorable or at least neutral recommendations; outplacement services).

- Define the forum and choice of law; this is important because state laws vary so much—although a choice of law clause that is favorable to the employer might be denied enforcement if the forum state has no connection to the executive or his or her work.

- If an Alternative Dispute Resolution (ADR) is desired, specify the types of claims covered; include a waiver of class arbitration if this is the intent. [Renee Inomata, *10 Most Overlooked Executive Separation Agreement Clauses—Part 2*, Burns & Levinson LLP (Sept. 9, 2014), available at Lexology.com]

When a termination event does occur, severance benefits can be conditioned on the departing employee signing a covenant not to compete, and not to solicit the ex-employer's customers. Some severance agreements are subject to Code § 409A and its standards for "separation pay arrangements." A plan that is limited to paying lump sums after there has been a termination without cause, with payments completed within two-and-a-half months of termination, would probably be exempt from § 409A. There are § 409A exemptions for collectively bargained plans; plans that are not created under a CBA, and that pay less than twice the participant's annual compensation, with payments completed by the end of the second post-termination calendar year. Benefits that add up to less than $5,000 and are not a substitute for other § 409A benefits are also exempt, as are vacation and sick leave, disability pay, tax-free health benefits, benefits under a qualified retirement plan, and rights accrued and vested before January 1, 2007 and not substantially modified since October 3, 2004. However, it is unusual for separation pay benefits to vest, because they are generally subject to a substantial risk of forfeiture.

In general, an agreement for severance benefits can permit payment at any time within the 90-day period following the event, but only if the employee cannot make a direct or indirect election about when compensation will be paid within this period. The IRS says a release condition in an agreement violates § 409A if the condition operates as an indirect election by the employee about benefit timing. The Age Discrimination in Employment Act (ADEA) requires 45 days' notice for an employee to consider a release and gives him or her seven days after signing to revoke a release, so severance payments are generally not made until after the revocation period has elapsed. Problems can arise if a release is offered late in a year—but not signed until the following year.

IRS Notice 2010-6, 2010-3 I.R.B. 275, says that § 409A is triggered by this "straddle," and it is a major issue in 409A audits. A mid-2011 article suggests drafting releases to provide that if benefits could be paid in two different tax years depending on when the release is signed, benefits will automatically be paid in the later year. [McGuireWoods LLP, *Employee Release Provisions Present Section 409A Trap for the Unwary* (Aug. 31, 2011) (benefitslink.com)]

A Final Rule, 72 Fed. Reg. 16878 (Apr. 5, 2007) addresses the treatment of certain severance benefits vis-à-vis the § 415 limitations on the amounts employers can contribute to qualified plans and the amounts that plan participants can receive under the plan. Under the final regulations, certain amounts paid within two-and-a-half months after severance from employment are considered compensation under § 415 (which means that the employer may be able to deduct them). Payments also qualify if they represent sick leave, vacation days, or other leave that the employee would have been able to take if he or she had continued to be employed. An amount can still qualify as § 415 compensation if it is paid later than 2½ months post-termination, as long as it is paid by the end of the plan's limitation year that includes the date of termination. However, for the employer to take advantage of this rule, the plan must state explicitly that the post-termination payments are included in compensation.

"Terminal leave" can be used if the employer is willing to stretch out a termination date—for example, to allow further vesting of retirement benefits or stock awards, or to extend the period before COBRA starts, perhaps with the result that the terminating employee will be eligible for Medicare once COBRA ends. However, terminal leave can create problems with insurers if they insist that coverage is limited to current active employees—or with the IRS, which might say that § 409A has been triggered. On the other hand, the employer might want to accelerate the termination date so that there is no gap period after an employee's signing a release, and during which further claims might arise.

"Garden leave" is a term used for a transition period during which the employment relationship continues in some way, and the employee is not permitted to get another job; in effect, the employee is paid to stay home. The employee is not expected to work, but must be available or able to be contacted as long as the period continues. Garden leave is common in, e.g., England and the European Union, where there is a legal requirement of continuing wages during the notice period, and is gaining popularity in the United States. It can be an attractive option for an employer that seeks to protect confidential information or relationships with clients or suppliers. The provision could be structured to provide a fixed number of days of continuing salary and benefits followed by severance pay subject to a release of claims and agreements to maintain confidentiality and not to compete, or to solicit the employer's other employees. Executive stock awards, incentive compensation, and supplemental retirement benefits could be restructured into a post-termination package contingent on loyalty agreements. [Anthony Lieu, *What is Gardening Leave?*, LegalVision (Jan. 25, 2017), available at Lexology.com]

A departing employee might sign a release in exchange for severance—without leaving right away. In general, no one is permitted to release future claims, so a release will be effective only up through the date of the release. The employer might be exposed to claims that arise between the date of the release and the departure date. This risk can be addressed by getting a "back-stop release," a second release covering the interim period. [Neal T. Buethe, *The "Back-Stop" Release*, Briggs and Morgan (June 20, 2016), available at Lexology.com]

In mid-2009, the EEOC updated its guidance document, "Understanding Waivers of Discrimination Claims in Employee Severance Agreements," covering ADEA and Older Workers' Benefit Protection Act (OWBPA) implications of layoffs. The Guidance says that an employee can file an EEOC discrimination charge, even if the employee signed a waiver, because the EEOC still has the power to investigate and pursue such claims. The EEOC's position is that the employee does not have to return severance pay before filing a discrimination charge with the EEOC. It is settled law that severance does not have to be returned in ADEA cases, but less clear for other statutes. The Guidance says that if an employee challenges the validity of an age discrimination waiver in court, the employer must continue complying with its obligations under the severance agreement, including making any ongoing payments still due. [<http://www.eeoc.gov/policy/docs/qanda_severance-agreements.html> (July 15, 2009) Appendix B, dealing with releases in group layoffs of persons over 40, was revised in April 2010, last accessed February 2, 2017. See *EEOC v. Watkins Motor Lines, Inc.*, 553 F.3d 593 (7th Cir. 2009) on the EEOC's right to proceed after a waiver by the complainant.]

The Fourth Circuit ruled that sex discrimination in severance packages is unlawful. It reversed the district court's finding that there can be no "adverse employment action" because severance is paid after employment terminates: the plaintiff charged that she was fired only after rejecting a discriminatory severance package, so she was employed at that time. [*Gerner v. County of Chesterfield*, 674 F.3d 264 (4th Cir. 2012). *Hishon v. King & Spalding*, 469 U.S. 69 (1984) stands for the proposition that discrimination must be avoided in all benefits in the employment relationship.]

[B]   Severance Arrangements as ERISA "Plans"

ERISA is not involved in an employer's one-time decision to grant or enhance severance benefits. Nor is there an ERISA component to an employer's payroll practices or payments of extra money for active workers' overtime or holiday work. However, ERISA does come into play if severance payments are made in connection with a "plan," and even an unwritten or informal arrangement might constitute a plan.

Once the severance payment comes within the ambit of ERISA, the degree and nature of regulation depend on whether the plan is characterized as a pension plan or a welfare benefit plan. The arrangement will not be a pension plan (and therefore will not be subject to the stringent rules imposed on pension plans) if:

- Payments are not contingent on the recipient's retirement—i.e., the recipient can retain the payments even if he or she gets another job;

- The total payments do not exceed twice the recipient's compensation for the year just before the termination;

- The payments are completed within 24 months of the termination. If the termination is part of a "limited program of terminations" then payments can be completed within 24 months of the time the recipient reaches normal retirement age, if that is later.

[See DOL Reg. 29 C.F.R. §§ 2510.3-2(b) and 2510.3-1(a).]

The Eighth Circuit ruled in mid-2011 that a one-person employment contract is not an ERISA plan. However, the case was remanded to the district court because the federal system might still have had jurisdiction over part of the complaint. The plaintiff, Schieffer, had an employment contract. Shortly before a merger obtained regulatory approval, Schieffer was terminated without cause, triggering the payment of a lump-sum severance payment. Schieffer alleged that he did not receive all the benefits he was entitled to and moved for arbitration. His employer moved to enjoin arbitration, arguing that the employment agreement was an ERISA severance plan so ERISA preempted the demand for arbitration. The Eighth Circuit held that the employment contract was not an ERISA plan because it covered only one person, not a class of employees. However, the other benefits he sought might have been promised by ERISA plans, so the Eighth Circuit sent the case back to see if those demands were preempted by ERISA. [*Dakota, Minn. & E. Railroad Corp. v. Schieffer*, 648 F.3d 935 (8th Cir. 2011)]

The case was remanded to determine whether the contract operated as an amendment to an ERISA plan, or a promise to pay ERISA plan benefits in the future. In 2013, The Eighth Circuit rejected both of these possibilities. The severance agreement only came into operation when the ex-CEO had ceased to be a plan participant. It was also a free-standing agreement; although the amount to be paid was determined by reference to an ERISA plan, the benefits came from the employer's general assets, not plan assets; and making the payments would not affect the administration of ERISA plans. The arbitration demand did not seek benefits due under an ERISA plan—which meant that the determination of underlying rights had to be done by an arbitrator, not the federal courts. When the case got to arbitration, the state law claims (including the double damage claim) could be heard because ERISA preemption did not occur. [*Dakota, Minn. & E. R.R. Corp. v. Schieffer*, 711 F.3d 878 (8th Cir. 2013)]

The Fifth Circuit held that a severance plan was governed by ERISA, and state contract law was preempted, because the plan involved ongoing administration and discretion over eligibility decisions. Nevertheless, the Fifth Circuit upheld the decision to deny severance benefits to a terminated employee who deleted computer files from his company laptop after he signed a severance agreement that required return of all company property. According to the ex-employee, he was concerned about security; the employer said that he destroyed the only copies of the data supporting his final assignments. [*Gomez v. Ericcson, Inc.*, No. 15-41479 (5th Cir. July 8, 2016); see Lorene D. Park, *ERISA Governed Severance Plan Which Properly Denied Benefits to Employee Who Didn't Return Property*, WK WorkDay Blog (July 12, 2016) (benefitslink.com)]

In August 2016, BlueLinx agreed to pay $265,000 to the SEC for violating SEC Rule 21F-17 by requiring departing employees to waive their rights to SEC whistleblower awards. Rule 21F-17 was adopted in 2011; it forbids impeding anyone from communicating directly with the SEC's staff. The SEC treats denying the right to receive awards as an impediment to communications with the agency. [Brian P. Morrissey and Benjamin M. Mundel, *SEC Fines Company That Used Severance Agreements to Discourage Whistleblowing*, Sidley Austin LLP (Aug. 15, 2016), available at Lexology.com.]

In the same month, HealthNet agreed to pay $340,000 to settle Rule 21F-17 charges relating to its severance agreement. The company revised its agreement; the SEC ordered the company to make reasonable efforts to contact people who signed severance agreements between August 12, 2011, and October 22, 2015, to inform them that they can apply for SEC whistleblower awards. In April 2015, KBR Inc., agreed to pay a $130,000 penalty because of restrictive language in its confidentiality agreements that allegedly deterred reporting to the SEC. [<https://www.sec.gov/news/pressrelease/2016-164.html>; see Lloyd B. Chinn, Harris M. Mufson and Esther Y. Pak, *SEC Continues to Scrutinize Separation Agreements*, Proskauer Rose LLP (Aug. 17, 2016), available at Lexology.com]

[C] Case Law on Other Severance Pay Issues

In a highly anticipated March 2014 decision, the Supreme Court resolved a Circuit split. Reversing the Sixth Circuit, the Supreme Court held that the severance payments in question constituted the Federal Insurance Contributions Act (FICA) wages. The Supreme Court held that severance payments are made only to employees, and they are made because of service to employers because "service" is defined broadly as the entire relationship between the employer and employee.

The court noted that the FICA statute provides a list of exemptions from the general rule that all compensation constitutes FICA wages. One of the exemptions is for severance payments made for disability retirement. The Supreme Court said it would not be necessary to specify this exemption if severance pay in general did not constitute FICA wages. Code § 3401(a), dealing with income tax withholding, also has a broad definition of taxable wages, subject to a list of exemptions. The list says that Supplemental Unemployment Benefits are treated as if they were wages: see § 3402(o). Defendant Quality Stores interpreted this to mean that, although SUB payments are treated "as if" they were wages, they are not wages for this purpose or for FICA purposes. However, the Supreme Court traced this provision to the history of tax withholding, when Congress wanted to relieve terminated workers from the burden of year-end tax liability. If the Supreme Court had decided the other way, corporations would have been entitled to billions of dollars in tax refunds. [*United States v. Quality Stores Inc.*, 134 S. Ct. 1395 (Mar. 25, 2014)]

Although in general the Federal Arbitration Act (FAA) is interpreted to mean that class action waivers are enforceable, and class arbitration is only available if the agreement specifically states that it is (see § 40.07[D]), there are some Sixth Circuit cases saying that agreements limiting FLSA rights might not be enforceable, if the agreements are included in an ordinary employment or separation agreement rather than in an arbitration agreement. The Sixth Circuit refused to enforce a class/collective action waiver that was included in the severance agreement for about 70 employees who were terminated in connection with restructuring. Some of those employees brought an FLSA collective action to recoup unpaid overtime. The court equated the right to participate in a class action with the right to bring a suit within the statute of limitations, and a 2013 Sixth Circuit case says that the statute of limitations cannot be shortened by private contract. [*Killon v. KeHE Distributors*, LLC, 761 F.3d 574 (6th Cir. 2014); see also *Boaz v. FedEx*, 725 F.3d 603 (6th Cir. 2013)]

For high income executives, FICA tax on severance has little impact if the layoff occurred after the executive had already earned the FICA maximum; the only practical effect is on Medicare tax. Laid-off workers should ask if their former employer is pursuing FICA refunds. The company does not have to inform them until the IRS accepts the claim. At that point, the employer will ask the former employees for consent to include their refund claim. When the IRS refunds the FICA amounts, the employer will distribute the employee share to the former employee. If the employee believes that a refund is due, but the employer did not file for one, the employee may be able to file Form 843 to seek a refund, but this must be done before the statute of limitations expires. Generally this will be three years after the due date for the tax return covering the year the severance was received. If the IRS does make a refund, it will not be taxable to the employee. [Laura Saunders, *Tax Report: When Severance Pay Is Subject to Payroll Tax*, WSJ.com (Oct. 26, 2012)]

The Seventh Circuit had to decide whether DHL violated the WARN Act in connection with its November 10, 2009 announcement that five out of its six Chicago-area facilities were going to close. Although the CBA did not provide severance benefits, the Teamsters Union negotiated severance benefits. On December 5, 2008, each bargaining unit received a severance agreement. Receiving severance was conditioned on waiving all claims, including WARN Act claims. Approximately 500 employees took a severance package, receiving either four or 10 weeks' pay. Workers who did not take a severance package retained seniority and recall rights—and the right to sue the former employer. Two laid-off workers sued. The Seventh Circuit held that there was no plant closing because employees who accepted severance should not be counted; without them, the number of layoffs did not reach 33% of the workforce. Under the WARN Act, a voluntary departure is not an employment loss requiring notification. Voluntariness is determined based on whether employees were forced out or coerced. The plaintiffs argued that employees resigned under extreme economic uncertainty and pressure from the employer. The Seventh Circuit said that, although the situation was not perfect, the severance agreements were still voluntary. The agreements and the release were negotiated by the union; were not ambiguous; and informed employees of their right to consult an attorney. [*Ellis v. DHL Express Inc USA*, 633 F.3d 522 (7th Cir. 2011)]

Employees often argue that a covenant not to compete is unenforceable because there was no consideration for the agreement (see § 25.02[C]). However, many states, including Tennessee, treat continued employment as consideration for the agreement. Tennessee also held that continued employment allows an employee to enforce a severance agreement. Plaintiff Hensley, who had worked for Cocke Farmer's Cooperative for 28 years, signed a severance agreement in 2010. The agreement ran until 2024 and called for paying the employee's current salary and health insurance premiums from the date of termination until 2024, unless termination was caused by death, disability, merger, or a criminal conviction related to employment. But shortly after the agreement was signed, Hensley was terminated without cause. The employer refused to pay the severance benefits. The Tennessee Supreme Court held that continued employment constituted consideration for the agreement and ordered the employer to pay $380,000 in severance benefits and $6,125 a month in health insurance premiums. [*Hensley v. Cocke Farmer's Cooperative*, No. E2014-01775-SC-R11-CV, 2016 Tenn. LEXIS 71 (Tenn. Jan. 21, 2016); see John Paul Nefflen, *Continued Employment Is Enough for a Severance Agreement*, Burr & Forman LLP (Feb. 9, 2016), available at Lexology.com]

An employee signed a severance agreement waiving FMLA claims. She subsequently sued her ex-employer for FMLA interference and retaliation, arguing that either those claims were prospective claims that could not be waived or that the agreement violated public policy and her acceptance was not knowing and voluntary. The Eleventh Circuit said that the legal distinction is between future violations and those that have already occurred. The release was not prospective, because it referred to the latter. The record showed that the plaintiff signed voluntarily, and the public policy argument was waived because it was raised too late. [*Paylor v. Hartford Fire Ins. Co.*, 748 F.3d 1117 (11th Cir. 2014)]

A 2010 Sixth Circuit case permits enforcement of a clearly written release of Uniformed Services Employment and Reemployment Rights Act (USERRA) claims that was part of a severance package, finding that the release was knowing and voluntary and was not obtained by overreaching. The Sixth Circuit allowed USERRA to be released on the same terms as any other employment-related claim. [*Wysocki v. IBM*, 607 F.3d 1102 (6th Cir. 2010); but see *Perez v. Uline*, 157 Cal. App. 4th 953 (2007) holding that USERRA claims cannot be waived by a written release.]

When Allstate moved its agents from employee to independent contractor status, more than 6,200 agents were terminated. They were offered four severance options, three of which required releases of claims (including ADEA claims). The fourth option, known as the "base option," did not require release of claims—but provided only 13 weeks of severance, and employees who took this option had greater noncompete and nonsolicitation obligations than those who took the other options. More than 400 former agents sued Allstate, alleging ADEA violations. Allstate said these claims were barred by valid ADEA releases. The District Court for the Eastern District of Pennsylvania held that ADEA releases can be invalidated even if they satisfy the Older Workers' Benefit Protection Act (OWBPA; see § 25.13) because that statute furnishes a minimum, not a maximum, requirement. The district court found that the waivers were not voluntary: the severance options forced the ex-agents to sign waivers to provide for their financial security. They had invested in their agencies, and would have lost their investment if they refused to sign releases and were fired. Taking the option that did not require waiver of ADEA claims would reduce the amount of severance while burdening them with greater nondisclosure and noncompete requirements. [*Romero v. Allstate Ins. Co. et al.*, No. 01-3894, 2016 WL 2619853 (E.D. Pa. May 4, 2016); see Colton D. Long, *What Is Knowing and Voluntary? One Court's Take on the Enforceability of ADEA Waivers,* Ogletree Deakins (June 10, 2016), available at Lexology.com] All state ended this long-running litigation by settling the case, agreeing to pay $125,000 to the plaintiffs: See *Romero v. Allstate,* No. 5:16-cv-04037 (3d Cir. June 15, 2017).

Questions often arise as to whether a person who receives severance pay qualifies for unemployment benefits. As a general rule, employees who are in the position of voluntarily quitting their jobs will not be eligible for unemployment; those who receive severance when they lose their jobs through no fault of their own probably will be eligible.

To avoid having to cover $200,000 in loan interest to fund the state's unemployment insurance trust fund, New York made major reforms to its unemployment insurance system. As of January 1, 2014, an offset is imposed: an employee who receives "dismissal pay" (severance pay, or payment other than pension, accrued leave, or SUB, made on account of separation) within 30 days of dismissal is not eligible for unemployment benefits for weeks during which severance exceeds the maximum weekly benefit ($405 until October 2014, when it rises to $420). For severance paid in a lump sum, New York State allocates it on a weekly basis. Once severance pay is exhausted, the individual can collect benefits for the remaining weeks of benefit eligibility. Disqualification applies only to benefit claims filed after January 1, 2014, not previously filed claims. However, an ex-employee can receive unemployment benefits immediately if the initial payment or lump-sum severance payment is made more than 30 days after the last day of employment. [Barbara E. Hoey and Mark A. Konkel, *Severance Payments Offset NY Unemployment Insurance Benefits as of January 1, 2014*, Kelley Drye & Warren LLP (Feb. 11, 2014), available at Lexology.com]

A company in Chapter 7 bankruptcy negotiated an agreement to pay $375,000 in severance to a terminated corporate officer to make sure that firing him did not disrupt negotiations for $80 million in financing. The officer agreed to resign and support the company publicly. The officer filed a $135,000 claim in the bankruptcy proceeding, including $10,950 in wage claims as a priority employee. The Chapter 7 bankruptcy trustee tried to set aside the deal as a fraudulent transfer to a corporate insider. The Tenth Circuit held that the negotiations resulted in the debtor receiving reasonably equivalent value, so it was not a fraudulent transfer. Moreover, a person who knows he is about to be fired does not have the close relationship, or control over the company, to be an insider. [*In re Adam Aircraft Indus., Inc.*, 805 F.3d 888 (10th Cir. 2015)]

[D] Parachute Payment Law and Regulations

A specialized form of severance, the "parachute" payment comes into play in the course of a hostile takeover or takeover attempt. The best-known form is the "golden parachute" for executives—the counterpart of the "golden handcuff" compensation packages that are supposed to keep top managers from leaving companies that depend on their services. A golden parachute arrangement is supposed to deter unwanted takeover attempts, because so much cash severance (and other benefits, such as stock, enhanced pension benefits, and insurance) is owed to the top managers that the acquisition becomes even more expensive—perhaps prohibitively so. A few states mandate the payment of "tin parachutes" to rank-and-file employees when they lose their jobs during a corporate transition.

A "single-trigger" golden parachute agreement gives the executive the right to additional compensation whenever the employer company merges or is acquired. A "double-trigger" agreement doesn't become effective until there has not only been a corporate transition, but the executive has been demoted or terminated and therefore has a real economic injury.

A mid-2015 article reports that golden parachutes (also known as severance affected by Change in Control, or CIC) are still part of the mergers and acquisitions process but, in recent years, they have changed to be more favorable to the corporations' stockholders. Most (340) of the Fortune 500 companies offer CIC severance, usually in the form of individual severance. As a result of pressure from shareholders, 95% of these companies use double-trigger plans, where both a CIC event and termination of employment is required for a parachute payment. The most popular duration is termination within two years of the CIC event; only one Fortune 500 company still has a single-trigger parachute plan. A few companies have a modified single-trigger plan that gives the executive a window to resign after a CIC (7% for the CEO, 3% for other named executive officers). These plans are unpopular with shareholders because they put the executive in control of the payout. The most popular payment method is payment of a lump sum, usually two to three times covered compensation for most named executive officers.

Covered compensation includes both salary and bonuses for 94% of CEOs, 92% of other named executive officers. Nearly all (95%) of plans provide post-termination medical coverage for named executive officers, usually lasting for as many years as the plan provides a multiple of compensation but ending when the person gets coverage from a new job. Outplacement benefits for a period of months is also routine. The biggest change is reduction in the popularity of tax gross-ups, a provision that shareholders never favored and can now be reflected in say on pay votes. In 2015, less than half of the Fortune 500 companies with CIC provisions retained a gross-up provision (i.e., the benefit is increased to reflect the tax the recipient must pay). Between 2012 and 2015, 25 Fortune 500 CEOs were involved in mergers. Their median golden parachute was $24 million. [Cody Nelson, *The Changing Landscape of Golden Parachutes in a Say-on-Pay World*, Towers Watson (May 28, 2015) (benefitslink.com)]

Golden parachute rules under Code §§ 280G and 4999 were enacted to prevent large payments to top executives when a change in control occurs. Certain change in control payments are subject to a 20% excise tax, and are not deductible to the employer. Compensation subject to these rules can include bonuses, accelerated vesting or payment of equity awards, severance pay, and post-termination benefits.

The provisions generally apply to officers; the 250 highest-paid employees within the employer's controlled group (the highest-paid 1% if the controlled group has fewer than 24,900 employees), if their annual compensation exceeds the threshold amount, which is indexed annually. Employee-shareholders who own more than 1% of the fair market value of all classes of employer stock are also included. The rules are triggered if the aggregate value of payments and benefits to the executive as a result of the change in control is equal to or greater than three times the base amount (the executive's average annual compensation for the past five years). The amount that exceeds the base amount is taxed and is not deductible by the employer.

There are many ways to draft employment agreements to escape these rules. A safe harbor cutback provides that payments and benefits will be reduced to the maximum amount that will not trigger the excise tax. Drafters must consider § 409A: the employer's or executive's ability to elect which payments to change may constitute a late deferral election or accelerated payment for § 409A purposes.

A valley provision, also known as a better-off cutback, reduces the payment to the maximum amount that will not trigger the excise tax—unless the executive would be better off on a post-tax basis by receiving the payments and paying tax on them. Such a provision benefits the employee, but the employer loses the tax deduction, and § 409A issues might arise.

A full gross-up reimburses the executive for excise tax incurred, but this can be costly for the employer, particularly since the gross-up is not deductible. Shareholder advocates tend to oppose gross-ups, which can be a problem for public companies. A modified gross-up gives the executive a full gross-up unless reducing payments by a specified amount would avoid the excise tax. [PLC Employee Benefits & Executive Compensation, *Addressing Sections 280G and 4999 in Executive Employment Agreements* (Apr. 16, 2013) (benefitslink.com)]

On August 4, 2003, the IRS issued final regulations dealing with golden parachutes. [68 Fed. Reg. 45745 (Aug. 4, 2003)] A corporation is exempt from the rules about excess parachute payments if, just before control of the corporation changed, the corporation was not publicly traded and holders of at least 75% of the voting power of the corporation approved the payment. Furthermore, only one change in ownership or control will be deemed to have occurred with respect to any transaction, even if the language might make it appear that there were multiple changes.

The final rule takes the position that accelerating the vesting of a stock option creates value that counts toward determining whether there has been a parachute payment.

The excise tax on excess parachute payments can be prepaid either in the year of the change in control or any later year—as long as the amount, form, and commencement date of the payments is already known and is reasonably ascertainable under the Code § 3121(v) rules on FICA taxation of nonqualified deferred compensation. However, the excise tax cannot be prepaid on any part of an excess parachute payment that is attributable to continuing to provide health benefits to the recipient of the parachute payment.

[E] Parachute Payment Cases

Eligibility to participate in the plan providing parachute payments was the issue in *Habets v. Waste Management, Inc.* [363 F.3d 378 (5th Cir. 2004)] The Fifth Circuit ruled that once the company's Board of Directors exercised its discretion to decide who was a participant in the parachute plan by removing the plaintiff from the list of eligible persons (after he lost his officer status in a corporate restructuring), the plaintiff was no longer entitled to receive parachute payments. Under the plain language of the agreement, only corporate officers were entitled to parachute payments, so termination of his officer status also terminated eligibility for the payments.

Golden parachutes have been included in say on pay votes since 2011. M&A lawyer Regina Olshan told the *Wall Street Journal* that the golden age of golden parachutes has ended: investors and regulators are scrutinizing executive pay packages, especially when the package is not performance-based. Golden parachute defenders say that the parachutes benefit investors too, because they prevent chief executives from blocking deals that are good for stockholders but would reduce the executive's payout. Once, it was common for cash severance to be more than three times annual salary and bonuses but now the cash aspect has been reduced and gross-ups are less common. Shareholders are also driving a shift to golden parachutes that are only available when the executive is fired after a merger, not when there is a merger but the executive remains employed. [Liz Hoffman, *Investors Close Golden Parachutes*, WSJ.com (June 5, 2014)]

In mid-2016, the Federal Circuit considered whether the Housing and Economic Recovery Act of 2008's ban on golden parachute payments was a "taking" of the former employee's property interest, thus violating the Fifth Amendment. The executive, Piszel, sued the government rather than his ex-employer. The Federal Circuit ruled that he had a cognizable Fifth Amendment interest and did not have to bring a private suit before suing the government. However, the Federal Circuit held that Congress did not forbid all golden parachute arrangements and allowed the FHA to issue regulations. Therefore, Piszel's claim against his employer was subject to his employer's argument that it was impossible to pay his golden parachute without violating the law. [*Piszel v. United States*, **833 F.3d 1366** (Fed. Cir. 2016); see Michael S. Melbinger, *Clawbacks: Can a New Statute or Regulation Override an Existing Employment Agreement?*, Winston & Strawn LLP (Oct. 6, 2016), available at Lexology.com]

[F]   "Separation Pay" Under § 409A

Under § 409A, which was designed to be a comprehensive regulation of deferred compensation, the IRS calls severance (which was not previously analyzed as deferred compensation) "separation pay." Separation pay is regulated as deferred compensation if there is a legally binding right to payment that arises in one tax year and is paid in a future year, even if there is a substantial risk of forfeiture. The exception is a payment entirely in the discretion of the payor (so there is no legally binding right to receive the funds). A binding contract between employer and employee could give rise to deferred compensation where the employer promises to pay a defined amount when the employee separates from service. But there is no deferred compensation if the employer offers to trade an immediate lump sum for a release, because the right to payment and taxation occur in the same year.

Section 409A regulates non-qualified deferred compensation (NQDC) plans, including severance agreements and informal bonus programs. Noncompliance with § 409A requirements makes the recipient employee taxable on the deferred compensation in the year it vests, whether or not it has been paid. The employee is also subject to a 20% excise tax on noncompliant NQDC, and perhaps to penalties and interest for failure to report or pay taxes on the noncompliant NQDC. Short-term deferrals are exempt from § 409A; a short-term deferral is paid within 2½ months after the end of the plan year in which entitlement to the compensation vests. But if the plan allows the possibility of payment after the 2½-month period, the payment is not treated as a short-term deferral even if in fact actual payment occurs within the 2½-month window. Section 409A is difficult to apply because of its idiosyncratic terminology: for example, it says that there is a separation from service if, and only if, the employee does not work for any member of the employer's controlled group (but with special rules for consulting relationships). Noncompete agreements do not delay vesting. Payment of NQDC to key employees of publicly traded companies must not begin for at least six months after separation from service. [Lori Jones, *Section 409A: Top 10 Rules for Compliant Non-Qualified Deferred Compensation,* Thompsoncoburn.com (July 28, 2016) (benefitslink.com)]

Separation pay can be provided without triggering § 409A, for example, by using the short-term deferral and safe harbor exceptions; "stacking"; and integrating the payments with release of claims. Separation pay, for this purpose, is defined as amounts payable only because of separation from service, such as negotiated departure agreements, severance plans, and individual severance plan agreements. Payments are not considered deferred compensation if they are made within 2½ months of the end of the year in which the right to payment vests. "Stacking" means arranging separation pay so that some fits under the short-term deferral rule, some qualifies for the safe harbor, and some is deferred compensation that complies with § 409A. However, amounts that are not deferred compensation cannot be substituted for amounts of deferred compensation.

In public companies that are required to "claw back" incentive-based compensation after restating financial statements, where nonqualified deferred compensation is clawed back before it became payable, the recipient could experience significant liability under § 409A. If the employee has already paid taxes, the SEC's July 2015 proposed regulations require the clawback to equal the pre-tax bonus amount, not the net amount. Note that drafting a clawback provision to encompass deferred compensation before it is payable violates the § 409A anti-acceleration rule; recovery policies should be drafted to obtain the clawback from sources that are not subject to the anti-acceleration rule. [Securities Law Insider, *SEC Clawback Rules Have Executive Tax Consequences* (Oct. 8, 2015) (benefits link.com)]

The § 409A correction program was originally set up in Notice 2008-113. Notice 2010-6, 2010-3 I.R.B. 275 extends this program to correct document failures as well as operational failures. Correction is required based on certain arrangements that condition separation pay or other forms of severance on employment-related actions that make the separation pay subject to § 409A, such as releasing claims or signing a noncompete agreement. There are limited situations under which separation pay is exempt from § 409A. Even when there is no exemption, the employer can address an existing arrangement without violating § 409A. For example, if the agreement has either a 21- or 45-day period for the employee to complete the employment-related action, followed by a seven-day revocation period, the payment date could be set more than seven days after the end of the revocation period. If the agreement does not provide for payment subject to employee action, it must provide for payment only on a fixed date of either 60 or 90 days after the occurrence of the permissible payment event. [Jeff Minzel, Kurt Linsenmayer and Susan J. Daley, *In 2010 Employers Should Respond to New Developments for Existing and Future Separation Arrangements*, Perkins Coie News (Oct. 29, 2010) (benefitslink.com). Also see mid-2016 Proposed Regulations that narrow the options for correcting nonqualified deferred compensation arrangements that violate § 409A. The regulations clarify that it is permissible to delay payment if the delay is required by another law, such as federal securities law: 81 Fed. Reg. 40569 (June 22, 2016); see Anthony G. Provenzano and Nicholas P. Walmsley, *Proposed Section 409A Regulations Make Several Notable Changes*, Millerchevalier.com (June 29, 2016) (benefitslink.com)]

[G] Section 162(m) Issues

Code § 162(m) limits (to $1 million) the compensation that a public company can deduct for any executive's compensation in any one year. This general rule is subject to some exceptions—for example, performance-based compensation can be deducted even if it exceeds $1 million. The statutory definition of performance-based compensation is money payable solely as a result of achieving established, objective performance goals set by the company's compensation committee. Compensation will also be considered performance-based if there is a potential for it to be paid on the basis of death, disability, or change in control, but if compensation is in fact paid on such a basis, it will not be considered performance-based. See 76 Fed. Reg. 37034 (June 24, 2011), IRS proposed regulations setting requirements for stock option and stock appreciation awards to qualify as performance-based compensation; these regulations were finalized at 80 Fed. Reg. 16970 (Mar. 31, 2015).

The payor may have to file Form 8-K four days after performance goals are set for the current year. Annual bonus awards and targets set in 2017 for payout in 2018 or later years do not have to be disclosed in an 8-K if they are consistent with awards and targets in prior years—a change from bonuses paid in 2017 for 2016 performance, which were exempt from disclosure if they were consistent with previously reported bonuses. [Winston.com, *Incentive Bonus Reporting on Form 8-K* (Jan. 16, 2017) (benefitslink.com)]

Final regulations published in March 2015 provide that stock options and SARs automatically qualify as performance-based compensation without being subject to separate performance goals, as long as the equity plan is approved by shareholders and includes a limit per employee on the number of options or SARs that can be granted to an employee during a specified period. Section 162(m) provides an IPO exception for new public companies: the $1 million limit on deduction does not apply to compensation paid under a plan that existed before the IPO. However, the exception is limited to a transition period that expires when the plan expires, is materially modified, all the stock or other compensation under the plan is distributed, or first annual meeting to elect directors after the end of the third calendar year after the calendar year of the IPO is held. Under the final regulations, Restricted Stock Units and phantom stock arrangements are not treated like stock options for the IPO exception; they only qualify under the exception if the awards are actually settled or paid during the transition period. But this rule is prospective only, applying to grants on or after April 1, 2014. [80 Fed. Reg. 16970 (Mar. 31, 2015)]

However, Notice 2007-49, 2007-25 I.R.B. 1429 provides that CFOs are never subject to § 162(m), even if they are among the corporation's highest earners.

Part II
PENSION LAW

CHAPTER 4

BASIC PENSION CONCEPTS

§ 4.01 INTRODUCTION

This chapter provides a summary and overview of the major ERISA and tax issues that help shape plan design. Many of these subjects are taken up in greater detail in the other chapters in this part of the volume. At press time in 2017, it was evident that the Trump administration intended to make major changes in the regulation of retirement plans, although these changes will develop over time, with input from the executive, judicial, and legislative branches.

In the private sector, employers make part of the employee's compensation available immediately in cash. The employee's total compensation package also includes benefits such as health insurance and fringe benefits, plus deferred compensation that will eventually provide a lump sum or income at the time of the employee's normal, disability, or early or late retirement. The subject of pensions and benefits is an important one.

In March 2017, 70% of civilian workers (94% of union members) had access to retirement and health benefits sponsored by their employers. Looking at private-industry workers (as compared to government workers, who typically have higher benefits), 66% had access to retirement benefits, and 50% participated in these plans, so the take-up rate was 75%. Access to retirement benefits varied greatly by occupation, from 82% for management and professional workers to 42% for service occupations. Participation in retirement benefits was 82% for workers in the top 10% of compensation, but only 58% for workers in the bottom 10%. [BLS.gov, *Employee Benefits in the United States—March 2017* (July 21, 2017), available at <https://www.bls.gov/news.release/ebs2.nr0.htm>]

The total cost of employee benefits rose 24% between 2001 and 2015, largely because the cost of providing health care benefits doubled. However, retirement costs dropped 25%, falling from 9.1% of pay in 2001 to 6.8% of pay in 2015; the shift from defined benefit to defined contribution plans drove this trend. Defined benefit plan costs declined by 2.9% in this period, and defined contribution plan cots rose 1.6%, but starting from a much lower base than defined benefit plan costs. [S. Miller, *Employers' Benefits Costs Have Risen 24% Since 2001,* shrm.org (July 27, 2017) (benefitslink.com)]

At the end of the fourth quarter of 2016, the average 401(k) account balance was $92,500—a record ($4,300 more than the year before). Fidelity reported that the average contribution to a 401(k), including employer matches, was $10,200, also a record. Only 21% of participants had outstanding loans—the lowest proportion since the fourth quarter of 2009. [Lee Barney, *401(k) Balances, Contributions Reach Record Highs in 2016, Fidelity Reports*, Plansponsor (Feb. 2, 2017)]

Because of the high risk of improprieties or mistakes in handling the funds that the employees rely on for future security, pension plans are administered by fiduciaries. A fiduciary is an individual or institution that takes care of the property of others, and therefore must be held to the highest standards of ethics and prudence. In 1974, Congress, concerned about potential abuses of pension plans, passed the Employee Retirement Income Security Act (ERISA). ERISA provides very detailed rules for how pension plans must be administered; how they must accumulate funds for later benefit payments; who qualifies for various kinds of benefits; how those benefits are to be distributed; and how the plan must keep records and communicate with its participants and beneficiaries. ERISA governs not only how ongoing plans operate, but how they can be created and how they can change form by merging with other plans or undergoing termination. See § 4.25, below, for the vicissitudes of the "fiduciary rule" that would have subjected certain financial advisers to fiduciary standards.

Furthermore, ERISA establishes pensions and benefits as an entirely and inherently federal area of jurisdiction. States are forbidden to legislate in this area, so the question of whether "ERISA preemption" has occurred is an important one.

The bulk of ERISA deals with pension plans, although the statute has less extensive provisions dealing with other types of plans including profit-sharing plans, stock bonus plans, and welfare benefit plans such as health plans, vacation plans, and cafeteria plans.

The legal definition of a pension plan describes it as a plan established and maintained primarily to pay definitely determinable benefits to participants— usually monthly for the rest of the retiree's life, although lump-sum payouts and annuities for a term of years are also permissible. Unlike profit-sharing plans, pension plans normally make distributions only on the basis of retirement, death, disability, or term of employment; hardship distributions are usually not available.

Traditionally, the IRS has relied on its program of "determination letters" to ascertain whether pension plans are operated in accordance with the qualification requirements of Code § 401(a). However, in mid-2015, the IRS drastically curtailed the determination letter program. Determination letters will still be issued for certain new plans, but employers will no longer get IRS reviews every five or six years. Plan sponsors will therefore have less certainty that their plan amendments are valid. In the mergers and acquisitions context, both buyers and sellers have more risk if they do not have IRS approval of the plan's structure and operations. [Announcement 2015-19, 2015-32 I.R.B. 157; see Practical Law, *Employee Benefits & Executive Compensation, Expert Q&A on the Impact of Downsizing the IRS Determination Letter Program* (Oct. 12, 2015) (benefitslink.com). See §§ 10.02 and 14.02 for more discussion of plan amendments and determination letters.]

Rev. Proc. 2016-37, 2016-29 I.R.B. 136 explains that, as of January 1, 2017, an individually designed plan can only get a determination letter when it initially qualifies; when it terminates; or in exceptional circumstances (e.g., when the plan cannot adopt a pre-approved plan). However, the six-year remedial amendment cycle for pre-approved plans remains in effect. For individually designed plans, the IRS will publish a list of required amendments each year. [Rebecca Moore, *IRS Officially Ends Determination Letter Program*, plansponsor.com (June 30,

2016); Bradley Arant Boult Cummings, *IRS Issues Guidance on Determination Letter Program* (July 5, 2016) (benefitslink.com); Raymond P. Turner, *Determination Letter Rationing: IRS Reveals the Brave New World*, Jackson Lewis PC (July 10, 2016), available at Lexology.com]

Sponsors of individually designed plans are no longer required to follow the Rev. Proc. 2007-44 procedure for adopting interim plan amendments for adoption dates on or after January 1, 2017. The remedial amendment period for disqualifying provisions identified in Rev. Proc. 2007-44 (i.e., provisions that make a plan non-compliant with the Internal Revenue Code as amended) for a new plan is the later of the fifteenth day of the tenth month after the end of the plan's first plan year, or the modified § 401(b) expiration date, which is generally the due date of the tax return. For ongoing plans, the remedial amendment period for disqualifying provisions listed in Rev. Proc. 2007-44 is extended from December 31, 2016 to December 1, 2017 (except for provisions on the 2016 Required Amendments List). To replace the previous procedure, IRS will publish an annual Required Amendments List, starting with changes in qualification requirements that take effect on or after January 1, 2016. As an aid to sponsors, the IRS will issue an Operational Compliance List each year to explain changes in qualification requirements taking effect during the year. Employers must nevertheless comply with all relevant qualification requirements even if they are not on the list. [Katuri Kaye, *Internal Revenue Service Provides Guidance on the Scope of the New Determination Letter Program for Individually Designed Plans*, Truckerhuss.com (Aug. 4, 2016) (benefitslink.com)]

An Operational Compliance List was published on February 27, 2017, including proposed regulations about using forfeitures to fund defined contribution plans; qualified matching contributions; and qualified non-elective contributions. The IRS extended the temporary nondiscrimination relief for closed defined benefit plans and explained how to distribute partial annuities from defined benefit plans for employees going through phased retirement. The Operational Compliance List also includes final regulations on the rate of return to be used in cash balance plans. The IRS warned that plans must satisfy all qualification requirements, even if they are not on the list. [Sheila Ninneman, *The 2017 Operational Compliance List,* findleydavies.com (Mar. 15, 2017) (benefitslink.com)]

The IRS encourages employers that have individually designed plans to convert the plans to pre-approved (PA) plans. Rev. Proc. 2017-41, 2017-29 I.R.B. 92, combines the existing programs of master and prototype plans and volume submitter plans into a single program of pre-approved plans. There are two types of PA plans: standardized and non-standardized. Both defined benefit and defined contribution plans can use either of these types. Employers adopting a standardized plan have to use the IRS forms without changes; a non-standardized plan allows the sponsor some flexibility. The period for submitting PA plan documents runs from October 2, 2017 to October 1, 2018. [Susan E. Stoffer et. al., *IRS Reorganizes Pre-Approved Plan Opinion Letter Program,* Nelson Mullins Riley & Scarborough LLP (July 12, 2017), available at Lexology.com]

The mid-2006 passage of the Pension Protection Act (PPA), Pub. L. No. 109-280, enacted immense changes. Although the legislation focuses on shoring up the soundness of defined benefit plans, the PPA also has significant provisions about defined contribution and cash balance plans. As it turned out, however, this statute was passed shortly before the economy soured, and the PPA was modified to relieve some of the burden on already hard-pressed employers in stimulus legislation such as the Emergency Economic Stabilization Act of 2008 (EESA), the Worker, Retiree, and Employer Recovery Act of 2008 (WRERA), and the Preservation of Access to Care for Medicare Beneficiaries and Pension Relief Act of 2010. The Moving Ahead for Progress in the 21st Century Act (MAP-21; Pub. L. No. 112-141) gives the sponsors of defined benefit plans interest rate relief: by allowing them to assume higher interest rates, they can lawfully reduce their contributions to their plans. See § 4.01[B] below.

As a general rule, the employer's tax deduction is taken on a cash basis—for the year in which money was contributed to a qualified plan. Employers that maintain nonqualified plans instead of, or in addition to, qualified plans do not get a deduction until the employee receives benefits from the nonqualified plan and includes them in income.

One of the most important criteria for plan qualification is that the plan must not discriminate in favor of highly compensated employees (HCEs). For the years 2006–2007 HCEs earned $100,000 or more; for 2008, rising to $115,000 in 2012–2014 and $120,000 in 2015, 2016, and 2017. (Because of low inflation, many official figures did not change between 2015 and 2017.) Yet many companies identify a need for additional benefits to stay competitive in the executive recruiting stakes. It is legal to maintain nonqualified plans limited to, or offering superior benefits for, HCEs (see Chapter 8 for more discussion), but the expenses associated with these plans will not be federally tax deductible.

One of the most important questions in plan administration is the standard of review that will be applied when a decision (e.g., denying benefits; altering the terms of the plan) is challenged. In April 2010, the Supreme Court ruled that as long as the plan gives its administrators the power to interpret the plan, then courts must review plan administrators' decisions deferentially—as long as the decisions are reasonable. [*Conkright v. Frommert*, 559 U.S. 506 (2010)]

The case continued to be remanded, appealed, and remanded again. In late 2013, the Second Circuit sent the case back to the District Court for the Western District of New York for the third time. The latest version of the suit holds that the district court erred by denying the plaintiffs discovery on the plan administrator's conflict of interest. The Second Circuit found that the suit was meritorious, and the proposed offset was unreasonable because it led to an absurd, contradictory result. The Second Circuit also found the Summary Plan Description (SPD) inaccurate, because it said that the lump sum "may" reduce the benefit, not that it would. However, the Second Circuit found that, this time, the district court properly applied the *Firestone* standards, and its refusal to re-open discovery was not an abuse of discretion. [*Frommert v. Conkright*, 738 F.3d 522 (2d Cir. 2013)]

Xerox was subsequently required to pay almost $4.9 million in attorneys' fees and costs to plaintiffs; 2011 billing rates were used, not later rates that the district court found excessively high. [*Frommert v. Conkright*, No. 00-CV-6311L, **2016 U.S. Dist. LEXIS 17147** (W.D.N.Y. Dec. 12, 2016)]

Every ERISA retirement plan, of any size, has to file Form 5500 with IRS; the forms are shared with DOL. The due date is seven months after the end of the plan year, which is July 31 for calendar-year plans. A 2½ month extension can be obtained by filing Form 5558 before the due date. However, Form 5500 is a basic information-gathering form, not a tax return. Generally speaking, the form is prepared by the plan's Third-Party Administrator or recordkeeper, but it must be signed by the plan administrator under penalty of perjury. Plans that have 100 or more participants at the start of the plan year must attach an audited financial report of plan assets to the form. (Form 5500-EZ can be used by plans for a self-employed person who has no employees and when plan assets do not exceed $250,000; a plan with fewer than 100 employees can file the 5500 Short form). [Editors, *The Basics About Form 5500s*, plansponsor.com (Jan. 23, 2017)]

In mid-2016, the Pension Benefits Guaranty Corporation (PBGC) proposed a rule that would expand its "missing participants" program (those for whom the plan does not have contact information) to terminated defined contribution plans such as 401(k) and profit-sharing plans, and some plans that would not otherwise be covered could opt in. Under the program, a plan that undertakes a diligent search and then pays a small fee to the PBGC would be able to transfer the account balances or accrued benefits of missing participants to the PBGC, which maintains a searchable online directory of missing participants and makes periodic attempts to find them and distribute their balances. [81 Fed. Reg. 64699 (Sept. 20, 2016); see Haynes and Boone LLP, *PBGC Missing Participant Program to Include 401(k) Plans and Certain Other Plans That Terminate After 2017*, Haynes and Boone LLP (Sept. 30, 2016), available at Lexology.com]

[A] PPA Changes

The PPA is a wide-ranging statute, and is referenced many times in this book. The major provisions of the PPA (some of which have been amended in light of economic factors) include:

- "At-risk plans" (defined benefit plans that fail to meet the PPA's new standards for adequate funding) are restricted in their ability to make certain types of distributions. If the risk is especially severe, the plan will be required to cease further accruals unless the employer makes additional contributions. The at-risk rules do not apply to plans covering fewer than 500 employees.

- The concept of the "minimum funding standard account" has been replaced by the "basic minimum funding contribution," and a new Code § 430 has been enacted for the purpose; the basic minimum funding contribution is calculated by adjusting the "target normal cost."

- The employer's tax deduction for plan contributions is capped.

- For 2008 and later plan years, plans must set their interest rate assumptions based on corporate bond yields. This requirement has caused compliance problems since the 2008 recession began; it has been the subject of several federal laws providing relief for plan sponsors.

- For plan years beginning after 2007 (collectively bargained plans: 2008) married participants must be given the option of a joint and 75% survivor annuity as well as the well-established joint and 50% survivor annuity. This is referred to as a Qualified Optional Survivor Annuity (QOSA);

- A court order allocating employee benefits order can be a Qualified Domestic Relations Order (QDRO) even if it issued after or revises an earlier order.

- Phased retirement is permitted—a plan can start pension distributions for a person who has reached age 62, but has not reached the plan's Normal Retirement Age, and who works a reduced schedule.

- Congress has given its approval to cash balance plans, but has imposed compliance requirements for new cash balance plans and conversions after mid-2005. The PPA provisions do not retroactively authorize cash balance plans created or converted earlier, and some courts find them age-discriminatory.

- Starting in 2015, PBGC premiums will be due at the same time, irrespective of the size of the plan; under prior law, the due date depended on plan size. [79 Fed. Reg. 13547 (Mar. 11, 2014); see Rebecca Moore, *PBGC Finalizes Premium Changes*, plansponsor.com (Mar. 10, 2014)]

- The obligations of communicating with plan participants have been increased, starting with the 2008 plan year: defined benefit plans must give their participants an annual funding notice no later than 120 days after the end of the plan year. At-risk plans have to give additional disclosures.

- Starting in 2010, companies with fewer than 500 employees can maintain "eligible combined plans," a new type of plan that combines defined benefit and 401(k) components.

As for defined contribution plans, under the PPA:

- Employers are encouraged to implement automatic enrollment in their 401(k) plans.

- The defined contribution plans of publicly traded companies must offer the opportunity for participants to diversify their 401(k) accounts (to avoid excessive concentration of employer stock), and must be notified of this right.

- It is easier for employers to maintain automatic-enrollment 401(k) plans, as long as the participants are fully vested within two years of enrollment. Immediate participation is not required.

- If the employer/plan sponsor is a public corporation, and the plan holds employer securities, participants must be given at least three other investment options, and must be notified of their right to diversify out of the employer's stock.

- It is not a prohibited transaction for fiduciaries of 401(k) plans to give investment advice to participants, subject to some conditions.

PPA § 303 amends Code § 415(b), so that plan distributions other than straight life annuities are adjusted actuarially to see if they satisfy the assumptions of § 415(b). Pre-PPA, the interest rate assumption for the adjustment could not be lower than the rate specified in the plan or the § 417(e)(3) rate—whichever was lower.

As of August 17, 2006, 401(k) plans can allow distributions for health, tuition, or funeral expenses relating to a "primary beneficiary": that is, a person who is named as a plan beneficiary and has an unconditional right to part or all of the account balance when the plan participant dies. The hardship distribution must be necessary to satisfy the financial need. A § 409A plan can treat a beneficiary on a par with a spouse or dependent to decide whether the participant has incurred an unforeseeable financial emergency.

For distributions after December 31, 2006, PPA § 820 amends Code § 402(c)(11) so that a direct trustee-to-trustee transfer to the IRA of a non-spouse beneficiary can be treated as an inherited IRA and a direct rollover of an eligible rollover distribution, and will not be gross income for the recipient in the year of the distribution. To qualify, the rollover must be made to an IRA established on behalf of the designated beneficiary. Plans are not obligated to offer direct rollovers of distributions to non-spouse beneficiaries, but if they are offered, it must be on a nondiscriminatory basis.

Under pre-PPA law, a defined contribution plan satisfied the § 411(a) minimum vesting rule for employer non-elective contributions as long as vesting occurred on a five-year cliff, or three-to-seven-year graded vesting schedule. PPA § 904, however, requires faster vesting: for plan years beginning after December

31, 2006, vesting must occur vis-à-vis employer non-elective contributions on a three-year cliff or two-to-six-year graded schedule. Plan amendments that change the vesting schedule accordingly must satisfy § 411(a)(10). The plan can maintain separate vesting schedules for employer non-elective contributions, depending on whether or not they are subject to § 411(a)(2)(B).

PPA § 1102 permits notices under §§ 402(f), 411(a)(11), and 417 to be given as much as 180 days before the annuity starting date. However, the plan must revise its 411 notice to take the PPA rules into account. The notice must describe the increase in benefits under a defined benefit plan if receipt is deferred; a defined contribution plan notice must explain the plan's investment options (including associated fees) if distributions are deferred. The notice for either type of plan must reproduce any part of the SPD that contains special rules that could have a material effect on the decision to take benefits right away or defer them.

Mortality tables are used to estimate the number of participants in a plan will die in a given year. Projections about longevity affect the length of time that a plan must pay lifetime benefits to retirees, or how large a lump sum must be paid to equal the value of receiving an ongoing stream of pension benefits.

A small plan (one with under 500 participants) can use a single blended static table for all participants. The PPA also allows certain large employers with adequate experience (at least 1,000 deaths for each sex over a five-year period) to use individualized plan specific tables that accurately reflect the plan's experience. [Steptoe & Johnson LLP, *Static Mortality Tables for Pension Plans Updated* (July 31, 2015), available at Lexology.com]

In October 2014, the Society of Actuaries (SOA) gave its final approval of the first new mortality tables since 2000. The SOA predicted that the liabilities of the typical pension plan would increase 4%–8%, because of the greater longevity figures. [Rob Kozlowski, *Moody's: New Mortality Tables Will Increase Pension Liabilities by $110 Billion*, Pensions & Investments (Nov. 3, 2014) (benefitslink .com)]

This was followed up in late 2016, with the release of the annual mortality improvement scale, MP-2016, reflecting Social Security Administration mortality data for 2012–2014. The life expectancy of a 65-year-old male declined from 86.2 years (under MP-2015) to 85.8 years; the life expectancy for a 65-year-old female fell from 88.2 to 87.8 years. [Plansponsor staff, *SOA Publishes Update to Mortality Improvement Scale*, plansponsor.com (Oct. 20, 2016)]

Notice 2016-50, 2016-38 I.R.B. 384, provides the updated static mortality tables for use under ERISA § 303(h)(3)(A)/Code § 430(h)(3)(a) for calendar 2017 calculations such as the funding target ratio. The notice also includes a modified unisex table for determining minimum present value of lump-sum distributions (ERISA § 205(g)(3)/Code § 417(e)(3)). There are no major changes for 2017; the tables continue to use 2000 as a base year. The IRS announced in advance that a draft of the 2018 tables would be released shortly thereafter and commentators assumed that some form of the Society of Actuaries (SOA) RP-2014 table would be adopted. [Rebecca Moore, *IRS Updates DB Plan Mortality Tables for*

2017, plansponsor.com (Sept. 6, 2016); Matt Klein, *Mortality Table Update,* Finleydavies.com (Sept. 9, 2016) (benefitslink.com)]

Regulations were proposed at the end of 2016, updating the mortality tables for setting minimum required contributions to single-employer plans, based on the RP-2014 table; projected mortality improvements are based on the MP-2016 scale. Plan sponsors can use either a generational table or separate static tables for annuitants and non-annuitants. A small plan (500 participants or under) can use a static table combining annuitants and non-annuitants. If a small plan lacks fully credible mortality data, it can use a weighted average of the standard table and an evidence-based substitute table that it could create if it had fully credible data. However, a small plan that does not have at least 100 deaths for one sex over a five-year period cannot use a substitute mortality table. [81 Fed. Reg. 95911 (Dec. 29, 2016); see Javier Simon, *IRS Releases Proposed Mortality Tables for DB Plans*, plansponsor.com (Dec. 29, 2016); P-Solve USA, *IRS Mortality Tables- . . . Finally!* (Jan. 9, 2017) (benefitslink.com)] The IRS decided in mid-2017 to delay implementation of the RP-2014 table until 2018. As a result, for the second half of 2017, plan funding status was slightly better, and valuation of employer liability for purposes of minimum required contributions, PBGC variable-rate premiums, and lump-sum distributions to terminated plan participants is somewhat lower than it would have been if the new tables were in force. However, the plan's auditors may still require use of the RP-2014 table to update the assumptions in the plan's financial statements for accounting purposes. [Greg Meila and Justin Teman, *Thought Mortality Was Dead? Considerations for Pensions Given the IRS's Delay in Implementing RP-2014,* Cambridgeassociates.com (June 1, 2017) (benefitslink.com); Michael Katz, *IRS' Delay in Implementing Mortality Tables Affects Pension Decisions,* ai-cio.com (June 15, 2017) (benefitslink.com)] Changes in the mortality tables provided incentives for a number of major companies, such as Motorola, GM, and Verizon Communications to transfer risk to insurers by purchasing group annuity contracts. Doing so greatly reduces the company's retirement obligations, but this tactic is potentially risky for plan participants and beneficiaries because the new arrangements are not guaranteed by the PBGC. [Dan Fitzpatrick, *Rising U.S. Life Spans Spell Likely Pain for Pension Funds*, WSJ.com (Oct. 27, 2014)] It is also problematic for the PBGC if the companies that engage in "risk transfer" are fairly stable and probably would not require rescue by the PBGC. [Vipal Monga, *Pension Dropouts Cause Pinch,* WSJ.com (Oct. 6, 2014)]

Out of approximately 3,600 large plans examined by the PBGC's actuaries, more than 500 had risk transfer events in a five-year period, with more than a million participants leaving the plans. Almost 400 events were lump-sum payments, the rest annuity purchases. [PBGC Blog, *Retirement Matters Risk Transfer Activity Significant; Over One Million People Affected,* <http://pbgc.gov/about/who-we-are/retirement-matters/post/2015/12/09/Risk-Transfer-Activity-Significant;-Over-One-Million-People-Affected.aspx> (Dec. 9, 2015)]

In mid-2015, the Fifth Circuit held that decisions to amend a plan and transfer assets to an annuity contract were settlor and not fiduciary functions, resulting in dismissal of a class action about Verizon's purchase of an annuity from Prudential to settle $7.4 billion in liabilities. [*Lee v. Verizon*, 623 Fed. Appx. 132 (5th Cir. 2015); see Rebecca Moore, *Court Affirms Dismissal of Verizon Pension Risk Transfer Suit*, plansponsor.com (Aug. 21, 2015)]

Then, in mid-2016, the Supreme Court granted certiorari and vacated the Fifth Circuit's decision about the de-risking transaction and remanded the case for reconsideration on the issue of whether a plaintiff has standing if the only concrete harm the plaintiff has suffered is violation of a private right conferred by a federal statute. In the interim, the Supreme Court had decided the *Spokeo* case [***Spokeo, Inc. v. Robins*, 136 S. Ct. 1540** (2016)] which makes it more difficult for potential plaintiffs to assert standing to sue. [*Pundt v. Verizon*, No. 15-785 (Aug. 17, 2016); see Rebecca Moore, *Supreme Court Revives Part of Verizon PRT Challenge*, plansponsor.com (May 23, 2016)]

On remand, the Fifth Circuit once again held that the de-risking decision was lawful and Pundt did not have standing to sue because he did not experience actual injury: his benefits were not threatened. [The case was re-titled as *Lee v. Verizon Commc'ns, Inc.*, 837 F.3d 523 (5th Cir. 2016); see Jacklyn Wille, *Verizon Victory Not Changed by Recent Supreme Court Case*, bna.com (Sept. 19, 2016) (benefitslink.com); Rebecca Moore, *5th Circuit Again Dismisses Verizon Pension Buyout Lawsuit*, plansponsor.com (Oct. 14, 2016)]

Starting in mid-2015, the IRS limits "de-risking" tactics. (See § 5.03[A] for more detailed discussion of de-risking measures.) As of July 9, 2015, employers can no longer offer lump-sum benefit windows to participants who have reached age 70½ and are receiving installment payments. The Notice forbids changing the form or period of distributions that have already commenced. (The new rule does not apply to lump-sum risk-transfer programs that were already in place on July 9, 2015.) [Notice 2015-49, 2015-30 I.R.B. 79; see Rebecca Moore, *IRS Announces Halt to Certain Lump-Sum Offerings*, plansponsor.com (July 10, 2015)]

The ASPPA, looking back after a decade of the PPA, concluded that in the low-interest, post-2008 environment, pensions are in trouble. The defined contribution landscape has changed significantly. Automatic enrollment became extremely popular, especially among large employers. Perhaps the greatest improvement is the rapid expansion of Qualified Default Investment Alternatives (QDIAs), putting a great deal of money under professional management. The PPA also made EGTRRA's incentives for retirement savings permanent, such as greater portability, higher contribution limits for IRAs and Roth 401(k)s, and reduced administrative burdens for plan sponsors. The PPA also made the Saver's Credit permanent, clarified the status of cash balance plans, and required publicly traded sponsors to allow their employees to diversify out of investments in the employer's stock. [ASPPA.org, *Pension Protection Perspective* (July 22, 2016) (benefitslink.com)]

[B] Changes Under Recovery Statutes

The PPA was drafted during what, in retrospect, was a robust economy, where employers would be able to shoulder short-term burdens in order to maintain the long-term stability of the pension system. Financial events soon made it necessary to trim the PPA's remedial scheme. The PPA called for plans to become 100% funded within seven years. Congress voted in December 2008 for plans with large investment losses to comply without reaching 100% funding within the seven-year time frame. [Mary Williams Walsh, *Pensions Get a Reprieve in Congress*, N.Y. Times, Dec. 12, 2008]

Congress responded to corporations' pleas for relief by enacting the Preservation of Access to Care for Medicare Beneficiaries and Pension Relief Act, Pub. L. No. 111-192, allowing employers to pick two years to pay only the interest on the funding shortfall, or to amortize the funding shortfalls for any two plan years between 2008 and 2011 over an extended (15-year) period. [See Rebecca Moore, *Obama Signs Pension Relief Bill*, plansponsor.com (June 25, 2010); Gina Chon, *Private-Firm Pensions Face Deadline for Funding Level*, WSJ.com (Apr. 1, 2010)]

The Pension Protection Technical Corrections Act of 2008 (part of the Worker, Retiree and Employer Recovery Act, or WRERA, Pub. L. No. 110-458 (Dec. 23, 2008)) provided several kinds of relief to pension plans. For the year of 2009 only, participants in defined contribution plans and IRAs were not required to take minimum distributions (because they might have had to sell securities at a loss to satisfy the minimum distribution requirements). Plans were given extra time to phase in the funding target percentage. Some "smoothing" was allowed (plans got 24 months to recognize unexpected gains or losses, rather than having to account for them in the year they occurred). Accrual requirements were loosened. The rules about vesting and interest crediting in plans covered by CBAs were delayed. [Fred Schneyer, *Pension Relief Bill with RMD Moratorium Slides Through U.S. Senate*, plansponsor.com (Dec. 11, 2008)]

In addition to PPA technical corrections, WRERA includes relief provisions for employers. The WRERA includes both PPA technical corrections and relief provisions. The PPA introduced the concept of the "target normal cost." WRERA allows expenses paid directly by the plan to be included in calculating the target normal cost; this is elective for 2009 but mandatory for later years.

WRERA requires the same interest rate assumptions to be used to calculate the funding target and the target normal cost. WRERA gives the IRS expanded authority to issue guidance about determining funded status for years before 2008—which is important for seeing if a plan is at risk.

The PPA includes provisions about cash balance and other hybrid plans (age discrimination rules, conversions, and the whipsaw calculation). WRERA limits the applicability of the new vesting requirements for cash balance plans (such as 100% vesting after three years of service). [Deloitte's Washington Bulletin, *PPA*

Technical Corrections Affecting Defined Benefit Plans, <http://benefitslink.com/articles/guests/washbull090112.html> (Jan. 12, 2009) (benefitslink.com)]

MAP-21, signed in July 2012, extends the period for calculating interest rates to 25 years—making recent years, when rates were very low, less influential in the calculation. For 2012, the plan's interest rates must be within 10% of the average benchmark bond rates for the previous 25 years.

The Highway and Transportation Funding Act of 2014, Pub. L. No. 113-159 (HATFA) includes "rate smoothing" provisions, allowing employers to use more favorable interest rates to calculate the minimum funding obligation. For calendar years 2012–2017, the "corridor" is a minimum percentage of 90%, a maximum percentage of 110%. For 2018, the corresponding figures are 85% and 115%; for 2019, 80% and 120%; for 2020, 75% and 125%; after 2020, 70% and 130%. However, these smoothing rules do not apply to bankrupt companies: see Code § 463(d)(2) for benefit restrictions. [Vipal Monga, *Welcome to the World of "Pension Smoothing,"* WSJ.com (Aug. 11, 2014)]

[C]   "Cromnibus" and Later Legislation

The Consolidated and Further Continuing Appropriations Act of 2014, Pub. L. No. 113-483, is nicknamed the "Cromnibus" bill. It provides that § 4062(e) [permitting the PBGC to collect downsizing liability payments from the plan sponsor] applies only if there is a permanent shutdown, and it affects 15% or more of all of the sponsor's employees. (Prior law measured the percentage based on employees enrolled in the plan.) Under the Cromnibus Act, there is no § 4062(e) event unless employees actually lose their jobs, not merely go to work for another company. If there is a § 4062(e) event, the Cromnibus bill substantially reduces employer liability.

If a plan adopted an Normal Retirement Age (NRA) on or before December 8, 2014, as the earlier of an age permitted by current law, or age plus completing a number of years of service (at least 30), the plan will not fail to comply merely because the rule applies to only certain participants.

In general, the coverage of this book is limited to single- rather than multi-employer plans. However, the Cromnibus bill includes the MPRA (Multi-Employer Pension Reform Act of 2014), which makes changes to the rules about multi-employer plans that are so significant that they deserve a mention here—especially if they are later adopted to cover single-employer plans as well.

The MPRA sets out a structure of rules under which multi-employer plans that are in critical and declining status will be permitted to reduce benefits. (As a tradeoff for the liberalized rules, the PBGC premium for multi-employer plans doubles, from $13 to $26 per participant.) The premium rose again, to $27, in 2016.

The problems of the multi-employer plan sector are very serious. In 2016, Moody's reported that out of 10.4 million participants in all multi-employer plans, 3.7 million were receiving benefits, and another 2.9 million were eligible for benefits in the near future, so underfunded plans would soon face major liabilities. The 124 multi-employer plans that Moody's studied had a $337 billion shortfall at the end of 2014. The 2008 recession caused a 25% loss of assets, some $80 billion, for multi-employer plans. In response, some plans adopted high-risk asset strategies—making the risks even greater. [Tatyana Shumsky, *U.S. Pension Funding Levels to Deteriorate, Moody's Says*, WSJ.com (July 13, 2016)]

For this purpose, a plan is in critical and declining status if its funded percentage is under 65%, and it is projected to become insolvent within 15 plan years—or within 20 plan years if plan has more than two inactive to every active participant, or the plan's funded percentage is under 80%. Plans that otherwise could not satisfy PPA requirements get an indefinite extension of amortization periods; the extensions can be considered in determining when the plan can exit critical status. A plan that leaves critical status can re-enter critical status in any later plan year. Plans in endangered status use a special method of determining their targeted funded percentage. The federal government will provide assistance to help endangered plans merge to avoid or at least postpone insolvency.

The most innovative feature of this legislation is that certain troubled multi-employer plans that could not otherwise avoid insolvency will be permitted to reduce benefits. Plan trustees are allowed to suspend accrued benefits if the plan is at risk of being unable to pay 100% of vested benefits within the next 10 to 20 years and insolvency is inevitable despite all reasonable measures having been taken. Benefits cannot be reduced below 110% of the PBGC monthly benefit. Participants over age 80 or who are disabled cannot have their benefits reduced at all and reductions are limited for people over age 75. Trustees are permitted to impose greater benefit cuts on retirees than on active workers. After benefits are suspended, they do not have to be returned to their previous levels even if the plan's financial condition improves. Trustees who want to suspend benefits must apply to the Treasury, which consults with DOL and PBGC. If the agencies approve the proposal, it is submitted to the participants and beneficiaries for a vote. If the plan is considered systematically important: that is, if the PBGC could have to pay $1 billion to prop up the plan, then the Treasury has the right to either modify the plan or implement the trustees' proposal. [Michael I. Richardson and Trevor W. Holmes, *New Federal Spending Bill Includes Extensive Pension Related Provisions*, Franczek Radelet PC (Dec 19, 2014), available at Lexology .com; see Rev. Proc. 2015-34, 2015-27 I.R.B. 4, for proposed, interim and temporary regulations about plan partition and suspension of benefits.]

The PBGC's annual report for fiscal 2016 shows that the deficit in the single-employer program declined from $24.1 billion in 2015 to $20.6 billion in 2016, There were fewer plan terminations than expected. At the end of fiscal 2016, the single-employer program's assets were $97.3 billion, with liabilities of

$117.9 billion. The agency paid out $5.7 billion in benefits in 2016, to approximately 840,000 retirees in more than 4,700 single-employer plans. In 2016, the PBGC assumed responsibility for 46,000 additional people in 76 single-employer plans. In contrast, multi-employer plans are in serious trouble. The deficit of the PBGC's multi-employer plan program rose to $58.5 billion, not only because of low interest rates but because of the increase in the number of plans expected to default within 10 years. [Rebecca Moore, *PBGC Multiemployer Program Deficit Nearly $60 Billion*, plansponsor.com (Nov. 16, 2016)]

According to Segal Consulting, two-thirds of calendar-year multi-employer plans surveyed were in the "green zone" as defined by the PPA and MPRA. Of the rest, 11% were in the yellow zone, 25% in the red zone (15% in critical status, 10% in critical and declining status). In 2015, the calendar-year plans had a funding percentage of 88%, declining slightly to 87% in 2016. Eight plans moved from yellow or red to the green zone by improving their funding; three plans declined from green to yellow status, two from yellow to red. In some industries (e.g., transportation, manufacturing, and service industries) more than half of the plans are in the red zone. About half the plans that are now in critical and declining status now were in the red zone even before the 2008 crash and may have to suspend benefits or be partitioned in order to survive. [John Manganaro, *Multiemployer Plans Are Predominantly in Green Zone*, plansponsor.com (Aug. 3, 2016); Plansponsor staff, *Multiemployer Plans' Zone Status Remains Stable*, plansponsor.com (Jan. 19, 2017)]

The PBGC announced in 2016 that, without additional increases in premiums, the multi-employer program had a 43% probability of becoming insolvent within 10 years, and 93% probability within 20 years, even if no plans suspend benefits or receive financial assistance. However, raising the premiums would make insolvency much less likely: a 31% probability of insolvency within 10 years if the premium rose to $39, 20% if it were increased to $52 (double the current level). Instead of raising the general premium, the PBGC could take other steps to remain insolvent, such as imposing fees specifically on large troubled plans. [Richard Teitelbaum, *PBGC Raises Possibility of Program Insolvency*, WSJ.com (Mar. 31, 2016)]; Tatyana Shumsky, *U.S. Pension Insurer Projects $53.4 Billion Deficit for Multiemployer Program By 2025*, WSJ.com (June 17, 2016)

Additional Treasury regulations were proposed in February 2016 for multi-employer plans in critical and declining status when an employer has completely withdrawn from the plan, paid full withdrawal liability, and assumed liability under a Collective Bargaining Agreement (CBA) to provide benefits to participants and beneficiaries. The regulations reflect the relationship between United Parcel Service (UPS) and the Central States, Southeast and Southwest Pension Fund and explains how the fund should treat the benefits of non-UPS versus UPS participants; cuts to "orphan plans" whose employers have withdrawn must be at least as great as cuts to UPS participants and beneficiaries. [81 Fed. Reg. 7253 (Feb. 11, 2016); see Morganlewis.com, *Treasury Releases Proposed Regulations*

Clarifying the UPS Rule Under MPRA (Feb. 2016) (benefitslink.com)] These regulations were finalized in May 2016. [81 Fed. Reg. 27011 (May 5, 2016). See Steptoe & Johnson LLP, *IRS and Treasury Issue Regulations Regarding Suspension of Pension Benefits* (May 3, 2016), available at Lexology.com.]

See Rev. Proc. 2017-43, 2017-31 I.R.B. 153 for the procedures to be used, for applications submitted on or after September 1, 2017, to seek permission to suspend benefits under a multi-employer defined benefit plan that is in critical and declining status.

The PBGC published proposals in June 2016 explaining steps the PBGC can take (such as training, technical assistance, and mediation) to facilitate mergers between troubled multi-employer plans, when a merger is in the best interests of the participants and beneficiaries of at least one of the plans, and will not be harmful to the participants of the other merging plan(s). [81 Fed. Reg. 36229 (June 6, 2016); see Robert F. Schwartz and Alex E. Trabolsi, *Pension Benefit Guaranty Corporation Issues Proposed Rule for Multiemployer Plan Mergers and Transfers*, Truckerhuss.com (June 2016) (benefitslink.com)]

Local Ironworkers 17, of Cleveland, Ohio, was the first union to approve pension cuts. Less than half of the 2,000 participants voted, but of those who voted, two-thirds voted in favor of the cuts. [Frank T. Mamat, *Union Retirees Cut Their Own Pension to Forestall Doomsday Scenario,* Foster Swift Collins & Smith PC (Feb. 6, 2017), available at Lexology.com]

Although more than a dozen applications were rejected in the interim, it took until July 20, 2017, for the second application to be approved: the United Furniture Workers Pension Fund A received conditional approval to divide the plan into an original and a successor plan, with the PBGC assisting the successor plan. [<https://www.treasury.gov/services/Responses2/UFW%20Notification%Letter.pdf>; see David B. Brandolph, *Treasury Department Gives Thumbs Up to Second Pension Rescue,* bna.com (July 21, 2017) (benefitslink.com). For background, see Bury Pensions, *Breaking News: Fifteenth Union Plan Files* (Apr. 18, 2017) (benefitslink.com)]

The Bipartisan Budget Act of 2015, Pub. L. No 114-74 (BBA) relaxed minimum funding requirements for single-employer defined benefit plans, increasing federal revenue, and potentially lowering the amount of deductions employers can take when they reduce their pension contributions and thereby report higher income. The BBA also permits greater flexibility in setting mortality assumptions.

PBGC premiums have been a constant arena for change. The BBA also increases PBGC premiums once again, reflecting the assumption that more and more plans will exit the system, leaving fewer and weaker plans to pay premiums. This was not the last premium increase: see <https://www.pbgc.gov/prac/prem/premium-rates.html>. For 2016, the BBA sets the per-participant flat-dollar premium at $64, rising to $69 in 2017, $74 in 2018, and $80 in 2019, and then indexed for inflation. This is a much higher rate of increase than wage growth. For 2016, the Variable Rate Premium level is $30; for 2017, it is $34; $38 for

2018; and $42 for 2019. The variable-rate premium is subject to a cap of $517 per participant (2017–2019).

The original plan under the PPA was to determine pension liabilities based on the average of corporate bond rates over the previous 24 months, but this has been modified many times. In 2012, MAP-21 granted relief to plan sponsors by artificially increasing interest rates, and therefore reduced the size of the minimum required contribution. As originally enacted, these rates were supposed to phase out by 2016, but relief was continued by HATFA. The BBA once again extends the relief, this time until 2024, with interest rates for the interim years higher than they would have been under HATFA. However, this BBA provision is limited to determination of the minimum required contributions, not the maximum contribution that can be deducted, plan termination costs, or PBGC premiums, all of which are based on actual interest rates. [Ekon Benefits, *The Bipartisan Budget Act of 2015: The Impact on Single-Employer Pension Plans* (Nov. 2015) (benefitslink.com)]

[D] Trump Administration Initiatives

The "fiduciary rule," a controversial DOL final rule published in April 2016, imposes fiduciary duty on brokers who are paid to offer guidance on retirement accounts and IRAs, requiring them to act solely in the best interests of the investor when they make recommendations. This is more stringent than the previous rule, which merely required recommendations to be suitable for the client (even if the advisor suggested investments based on how much the adviser earned, when better investments were available). DOL was particularly concerned about the selection of investments when assets are rolled over from 401(k) plans or other employer-sponsored plans to IRAs.

Under the fiduciary rule, compensation to an adviser must be paid pursuant to a written contract. The adviser must represent that the investment is appropriate, the fees are reasonable, and the adviser must disclose any conflicts of interest. Compliance with this rule was supposed to be phased in until January 1, 2018. [81 Fed. Reg. 20945 (Apr. 8, 2016); see Jason Zweig, *New Government Rule Rewrites Retirement Savings*, WSJ.com (Apr. 4, 2016); Plansponsor editors, *Final Fiduciary Rule Includes Requested Changes*, plansponsor.com (Apr. 6, 2016)]

On October 27, 2016, the DOL issued initial guidance on the fiduciary rule, in the form of FAQs. In these FAQs, the DOL said that any broker-dealer or financial intermediary that suggests how a retirement investor should invest could be a fiduciary, as could individual financial advisers or registered representatives employed by financial institutions. In April 2016, DOL released two new exemptions: the BIC (Best Interest Contract) and Principal Transactions exemptions. They require the institution and the financial advisors to satisfy impartial conduct standards. They must act in the best interest of the retirement investor; must refrain from unreasonable charges; and must disclose all material facts, including all fees and material conflicts of interest. Reasonableness depends on what investors receive for their money. The FAQs say that the BIC Exemption can apply to all categories of assets. It is permissible for financial institutions to manage some accounts on a level-free basis, while collecting commissions on other accounts. [Hillel T. Cohn, *DOL Issues First Guidance on Fiduciary Rule*, Morrison & Foerster LLP (Oct. 28, 2016), available at Lexology.com]

As soon as the rule was promulgated, suits were filed to challenge the rule, arguing that DOL exceeded its powers and did not follow proper administrative procedures. [See Russel H. Hirschhorn and Benjamin Saper, *Update on Lawsuits Challenging the U.S. Department of Labor's Fiduciary Rule*, Proskauer Rose LLP (July 14, 2016), available at Lexology.com]

In late 2016 and early 2017, several court decisions upheld the fiduciary rule. The District Court for the District of Columbia ruled in favor of the DOL, dismissing the National Association for Fixed Annuities' challenge to the conflict of interest rules and the exemptions related to it. The ruling was appealed to the D.C. Circuit, which also rejected the challenge. The D.C. Circuit ruled that the National Association for Fixed Annuities did not satisfy the stringent rules for obtaining an injunction pending appeal. [*National Ass'n for Fixed Annuities v. Perez*, Civil Action No. 16-1035 (RDM), 2016 WL 6573480 (D.D.C. Nov. 4, 2016); see Russell I. Hirschhorn and Benjamin Saper, *DOL Prevails in First Challenge to the Conflict of Interest Rule and Related Exemptions*, Proskauer Rose LLP (Nov. 18, 2016); John Hilton, *DC Circuit Court Rejects DOL Rule Injunction* (Dec. 16, 2016) (benefitslink.com).]

Similarly, in February 2017, the District Court for the District of Kansas granted summary judgment for the DOL, holding that the agency had the power to issue the rule. [*Market Synergy Grp., Inc. v. U.S. DOL*, No. 16-cv-4083, **2017 U.S. Dist. LEXIS 23155 (D. Kan. Feb. 17, 2017)**]

The District Court for the District of Texas denied the Chamber of Commerce's motion for summary judgment, and granted the DOL's motion for summary judgment. This decision was appealed to the Fifth Circuit on February 25, 2017, seeking an emergency request to prevent the rule from taking effect before the appeal was denied. [*Chamber of Commerce of the United States v. Hugler*, No. 3:16-cv-1476-M, **2017 U.S. Dist. LEXIS 17619 (N.D. Tex. Feb. 8, 2017), 2017 U.S. Dist. LEXIS 39806** (Mar. 10, 2017). See Thinkadvisor.com, *Emergency Request to Block DOL Fiduciary Rule Filed in Texas Court* (Mar. 14, 2017) (benefitslink.com).]

On April 4, 2017, the Fifth Circuit refused to enjoin the fiduciary rule from taking effect: *Chamber of Commerce of the United States v. Hugler*, No. 17-10238. Oral argument in the underlying case about the validity of the rule was heard on July 31, 2017; at press time in September 2017, the decision had not yet been announced.

However, although the rule was successful within the court system, it was not successful in Congress or the Executive Branch. On February 3, 2017, President Trump sent a memorandum to the secretary of labor ordering re-examination of the April 2016 fiduciary final rule, with consideration of whether the rule should be revised or rescinded. The president's memorandum tells DOL to analyze whether the rule harms investors' access to retirement advice and products; whether it would disrupt the retirement services industry in a manner detrimental to retirees and/or investors; whether the rule is likely to increase the cost of retirement services; and whether it is likely to promote additional litigation. [Spender Fane Blog, (no title) (Feb. 6, 2017) (benefitslink.com)]

The DOL published a notice in the *Federal Register* on April 7, 2017, delaying the implementation of the fiduciary rule and the related PTE exemptions, for 60 days. Without further postponements, the fiduciary rule took effect on June 9, 2017 (with some provisions involving brokers and insurance agents taking effect January 1, 2018), although the DOL continued to consider modifying or terminating the rule in the future. As of June 9, 2017, financial advisers will be subject to the requirement to make recommendations only in their customers' best interests, avoid misleading statements, and charge reasonable compensation. [82 Fed. Reg. 16902 (Apr. 7, 2017); see Lee Barney, *DOL Moves Forward with 60-Day Fiduciary Rule Delay,* plansponsor.com (Apr. 5, 2017)]; Plansponsor editors, *No More Delays for DOL Fiduciary Rule*, plansponsor.com (May 24, 2017); Lisa Beilfuss, *"Fiduciary" Rule to Take Effect June 9 with No Further Delay*, Labor *Secretary Says*, WSJ.com (May 22, 2017)

§ 4.02 EXTENT OF COVERAGE

In the more than 40 years since ERISA took effect, the pension sector of the economy has grown mightily, but has changed its characteristics very significantly. There has been a tremendous shift from plans in which the employer makes the contributions, decides how contributions will be invested, and takes the investment risk to plans in which employees bear a far greater burden of making both contributions and decisions. One of the major objectives of the PPA is to improve the soundness of the surviving defined benefit plans by requiring more realistic funding and reporting, although some of the more stringent rules were relaxed by 2008–2009 federal legislation.

According to LIMRA, in 2015 there were 49.5 million retirees in the United States, making up 15% of the total population. In 2014, retirees received a total of $1.3 trillion in income. Of this amount, 42% of total income came from Social Security, and 30% from traditional pension and retirement plans. The majority of Americans (57% of men, 64% of women) claimed Social Security benefits in 2014 before full retirement age, so they received less than the full benefit that would have been available later. [LIMRA, *Fact Book on Retirement Income 2016* (Oct. 25, 2016) (benefitslink.com)]

Analyzing the retirement plan field requires looking at both access (whether a worker could potentially participate in a retirement plan) and participation (whether the person does in fact participate in the plan). A plan's take-up rate is the percentage of eligible workers who participate. In 2016, the take-up rate for defined benefit plans was 85%; the take-up rate for defined contribution plans was 69%. The discrepancy occurred because defined benefit plans are usually funded only by employer contributions, whereas defined contribution plans depend on employee contributions. Furthermore, although now some defined contribution plans have automatic enrollment (employees who do not wish to participate can opt out), traditionally employees had to make an affirmative choice to participate in defined contribution plans and might have preferred to receive the funds immediately instead of deferring them even if deferral gave them tax advantages. [John J. Topoleski, *Worker Participation in Employer-Sponsored Pensions: A Fact Sheet,* Congressional Research Service No. R43439 (Feb. 27, 2017)]

In 2016, according to the Bureau of Labor Statistics (BLS), 44% of private industry workers participated in defined contribution plans. In that year, 63% of management/professional/related workers participated in defined contribution plans, as did 46% of sales and office workers but only 19% of service workers. In 2015, almost three-quarters of private industry workers participating in defined contribution plans participated in savings and thrift plans (plans where the employee places a predetermined amount of earnings in an individual account, usually receiving an employer match; in 2015, 62% of such plans included an employer match).

Half of the plans matched up to 6% of earnings or employee contributions, and the others had a lower ceiling, typically 3%–4%. It is common for participants in savings and thrift plans to be allowed to make traditional and/or Roth 401(k) contributions. In 2015, all savings and thrift plans allowed pre-tax contributions, and half permitted post-tax contributions.

Deferred profit-sharing plans generally do not require employee contributions. The employer contributes either fixed or discretionary amounts to employee's accounts; the amounts reflect company profits. Contributions can be equal for all employees, or allocated by salary. In 2015, 19% of private industry workers in defined contribution plans participated in deferred profit-sharing plans. In companies with 1–99 workers, 21% of workers participated in deferred profit sharing, but in establishments with 100 or more, 17% participated in deferred profit sharing.

A money-purchase plan allocates fixed employer contributions, generally defined as a percentage of employee earnings to individual employee accounts each year. An employer maintaining an ESOP pays a designated amount into a fund that is typically invested in company-related stock. Funds are distributed to retirees in accordance with a formula. A SIMPLE plan, which can be part of a 401(k) plan or administered via IRAs, is a small business plan that sets up individual accounts for employees. The employer contributes a set amount per hour worked. Usually the employer has fewer than 100 employees and no other qualified plan. Retirees get funds distributed according to a formula. [Eli R. Stoltzfus, *Defined Contribution Retirement Plans: Who Has Them and What Do They Cost?*, BLS (Dec. 2016) (benefitslink.com)]

A Census Bureau survey, based on Form W-2 tax data from 2012, raises concerns. It shows that two-thirds of Americans do not contribute at all to 401(k)s or other employer plans. Either they do not have access to a plan, or they do not contribute to an available plan. [Ben Steverman, *Two-Thirds of Americans Aren't Putting Money in Their 401(k)*, Bloomberg.com (Feb. 21, 2017) (benefitslink.com)]

§ 4.03   EFFECT OF DEMOGRAPHICS ON PLANS

The Baby Boom, people born after World War II, are the largest age cohort in U.S. history. The oldest boomers are already eligible for reduced-level Social Security benefits. That means that soon, employers will not only face the challenge of paying pensions to a very large group of retirees—they will have a smaller group of active workers to generate corporate income and profits. Furthermore, retirees may take priceless and irreplaceable skills and work ethics with them when they leave the workforce.

The population is aging, and the fastest-growing demographic group is the "old old": people over age 85. Senior citizens consume more health services than younger people, so retiree health benefits (see Chapter 9) and the Medicare system will be severely strained.

In the mid-1980s, labor force activity among older Americans began to rise because of changes in Social Security law, the shift to 401(k) plans, and better health, longevity and education. However, those factors have achieved their maximum impact and have been fully phased in. [Alicia H. Munnell, *The Average Retirement Age—An Update*, Center for Retirement Research IB #15-4 (Mar. 2015) (benefitslink.com)]

In mid-2016, the Insured Retirement Institute (IRI) reported that 81% of today's retirees receive at least some pension income. For 42% of them, the pension provides at least half of their retirement income. But among persons currently employed, only 24% participate in a defined benefit plan. The IRI predicts that up to 56 million Baby Boomers will not receive pension income—and a future retiree will need more than $400,000 in savings to make up for those losses. Over one-third (40%) of retirees have undergone a major health event, such as a heart attack or stroke, and 25% needed money for a major non-medical event such as home repair. More than a quarter of survey respondents (27%) moved when they retired, 60% for a better lifestyle, 30% to save money. [Lee Barney, *As Pensions Fade, Retirees Will Need More Savings*, plansponsor.com (Sept. 26, 2016)]

The PPA provides approval for plans to make in-service distributions starting at age 62, i.e., a person who reduces work effort can continue to draw both a reduced salary and a pension. [*Retirees Continue Working but Not for the Reason*

You Think, plansponsor.com (Feb. 24, 2006)] See T.D. 9235, 2007-24 I.R.B. 1386, for Final Regulations defining "Normal Retirement Age" in connection with in-service distributions and phased retirement; issues of early retirement, including phased retirement, are discussed in Chapter 9.

The tax rules for retirement plans have been modified, effective July 2, 2014, to permit employees to buy longevity insurance inside retirement plans. They can purchase a deferred income annuity by exchanging a lump sum for a stream of guaranteed lifetime income to begin later, possibly in their late 70s or in their 80s. Under prior law, these annuities were uncommon, because the Required Minimum Distribution (RMD) rules required withdrawals to begin no later than age 70½. The 2014 rules, however, permit the use of part of a retirement account to buy annuities that begin by age 85. The participant can invest up to 25% of the account balance, or $125,000 (whichever is less) to purchase the annuity. The *New York Times* said that deferring annuity payments means that those who survive long enough to collect will get larger payments than those who invested in immediate annuities. For example, a 68-year-old man would have to pay about $170,000 to purchase an immediate annuity paying $12,000 a year. But a 58-year-old man who purchased an annuity at age 58 and deferred benefits until age 78 would have to pay only $40,000 for the right to receive annual income of $12,000. [T.D. 9673, 2014-30 I.R.B. 212]

Notice 2016-39 provides IRS guidance on when payments made to employees from a defined benefit plan during phased retirement are considered taxable annuity payments from the plan. The notice explains the present value factors used to determine a basis recovery fraction for each payment (i.e., to determine how much of the payment derives from amounts that have already been taxed). [Notice 2016-39, 2016-26 I.R.B. 1068; Lee Barney, *IRS Guidance Explains Annuity Taxation During Partial Retirement*, plansponsor.com (June 14, 2016)]

§ 4.04 INVESTMENT FACTORS

For many years, the strong investment climate allowed plans to reduce or even suspend their contributions to defined benefit plans, because the plans were ample to satisfy the obligation to make future payments.

In the 1990s, many companies found that their investment experience was so favorable that they were able to suspend contributions to their plans, because the plan was already fully funded. This trend later reversed. [John D. McKinnon, *Warning of Pension-Plan Shortfall Raises Pressure for Financial Fix*, Wall St. J., Sept. 5, 2003, at A1] Then, in 2000 and 2001, the dot-com bubble collapsed; the September 11 attack and the Enron scandal also damaged investment results.

The 2008–2009 declines in the real estate market and financial markets, in conjunction with business problems caused by lack of access to borrowing, placed pension plans under great stress, leading to many plan freezes, plan terminations, and reductions or elimination of employer matching contributions. [Alicia H.

Munnell, Jean-Pierre Aubry and Dan Muldoon, *The Financial Crisis and Private Defined Benefit Plans*, No. IB#8-18, Center for Retirement Research at Boston College]

According to Mercer, the funded status of the largest U.S. corporate pension plans was about the same in 2015 and 2016. The funding ratio for S&P 1500 plans was 81.8% at the end of 2015, 81.9% at the end of 2016. The S&P 1500 had $1.81 trillion in pension assets on December 31, 2016, 0.56% more than on the same date a year earlier. The aggregate deficit for these plans increased $4 billion, reaching $408 billion. [Meaghan Kilroy, *Corporate Funded Status Sees Little Change in 2016—3 Reports*, pionline.com (Jan. 5, 2017) (benefitslink.com)] The Aon Hewitt Pension Risk Tracker reported in March 2017 that the funded status of S&P 500 companies declined $15 billion in the year to date, but the funded ratio was 80.9%; Aon Hewitt reported that there were $41 billion in asset gains year-to-date, and an increase in liabilities of $26 billion. [Lee Barney, *Pension Funded Status Down $15B YTD*, plansponsor.com (Mar. 6, 2017)]

Freezing or terminating a defined benefit plan can have unforeseen consequences for the sponsor's profit sharing plan, especially if the plan is top-heavy or uses the cross-testing method (for example, a professional firm's cash balance plan). For top-heavy or cross-tested plans, minimum benefits must be provided to non-key, non-HCE employees.

If the defined benefit plan is terminated and its assets distributed, the defined benefit amounts for active employees are still considered in the top-heavy determination for the remaining plans for up to five years. Although the ability to reduce the minimum profit-sharing benefit is good for the employer, it will probably have a negative effect on employee motivation, so the employer might choose to keep the profit-sharing rates stable at first and decrease them over time. [Mark Schulte, *Employers Need to Understand Minimum Profit Sharing Benefits for Frozen/Terminated Defined Benefit Plans*, VIA Retirement Plan Blog (Nov. 9, 2011) (benefitslink.com)]

Many pension plans reacted to the financial downturn by freezing defined benefit plans or ceasing or reducing contributions to defined contribution plans—or both. Many employers maintain plans of both types.

§ 4.05 DEFINED BENEFIT/DEFINED CONTRIBUTION

The traditional kind of pension plan, the one usually in effect when ERISA was passed, is the defined benefit plan. In a plan of this type, the employer agrees to provide benefits according to a formula. A typical formula would set the pension level as x% times the number of years the employee worked before retirement times the employee's average pay for his or her last five years working for the employer—or perhaps the average of the three years in which he or she earned the most.

The employer's contributions for all employees go into a single account or trust for the entire plan. However, there must be a separate account balance for each participant who makes voluntary contributions. [I.R.C. § 411(b)(2)(A)]

In some ways, this arrangement is problematic both from the employer's and the employee's point of view. When employees retire, they receive a fixed pension that will probably not be inflation-indexed and will not offer cost of living adjustments. In a highly inflationary environment, they will find that their pension buys less and less over time. Nor will their pension increase if the investment climate is favorable.

From the employer's point of view, defined benefit plans carry heavy burdens, including uncertainty. The employer's commitment is to contribute enough to the plan each year to ensure that the participants will receive the promised level of benefits. Not only does this require elaborate (and expensive) actuarial calculations, it places the investment risk on the employer, who will have to make larger contributions in years in which the value of the plan's securities portfolio declines.

A defined contribution plan is a different, and much simpler, structure. The employer establishes a separate account for each employee who has satisfied the criteria for plan participation. If the plan requires or accepts employee contributions, there will usually be separate subaccounts for employer and employee contributions, but this is not a legal requirement.

The employer's commitment is to contribute the amount required by the plan formula—generally a simple percentage of compensation. ERISA § 404(c) permits the plan to give control over the assets to the participant. If this is done, the plan's fiduciaries will not be liable for losses that result from the control exercised by the participants.

A "brokerage window" is similar to conventional brokerage account; it permits participants in a 401(k) plan to buy a wide range of securities, while the number of funds in the central menu is reduced. The advantage to employees is access to a greater variety of choices, but at the risk of higher fees. A $50 annual maintenance fee is typical, plus commissions of about $10 per stock trade. In 2011, 29% of large employers included a brokerage window in their 401(k) plans, a percentage that increased to 40% in 2015. Only a small minority of 401(k) participants (about 1%–4%) enroll in a brokerage window; they are usually older and more affluent than other employees. The sponsor's fiduciary obligation to select and monitor the core investment menu does not apply to investments that employees choose for themselves through a brokerage window. In 2015, participants in brokerage windows had a 5.5% decline in account value—whereas those who invested in the core funds lost only 1.9%. [Anne Tergesen, *Why More 401(k) Plans Offer "Brokerage Windows,"* WSJ.com (July 1, 2016)]

There is no limit on the number of plans a particular employer can maintain, and it is not uncommon for an employer to maintain both defined benefit and defined contribution plans. Under prior law, § 415(e) imposed a limit on benefits from a combination of defined benefit and defined contribution plans, but that limitation was repealed for limitation years beginning on or after January 1, 2000.

ERISA § 404(c) also requires the plan to give participants adequate information about the investment options they have for their accounts. The plan must offer at least three diversified investment types, with materially different characteristics with respect to risk and return.

A major economic trend over the last several decades has been the movement from conventional, defined benefit pension plans to 401(k)s and other defined contribution plans. However, approximately since 2010, there has been some movement back in the other direction, out of concern for whether workers with only 401(k) plans will have enough money in retirement.

The Plan Sponsor Council of America's 59th annual survey, published in late 2016, showed that in 2015, the average contribution rate for employees was 6.8% of gross annual pay. The average company contribution was 3.8% for 401(k) plans, 5.4% for combination defined benefit/defined contribution plans. In 2015, 57.5% of plans had automatic enrollment. 401(k), profit sharing, and combination plans offered an average of 19 investment options. Three-quarters of plans have QDIAs; 75% of those plans used a target date fund as the default. In 2015, 81.9% of eligible employees contributed to their plan. More than half of plans (59.5%) permitted Roth 401(k) contributions; 20% of employees who had access to Roth 401(k) contributions made such contributions. [Meaghan Kilroy, *Employee Contributions Rise in 2015—PSCA Survey,* Pionline.com (Dec. 19, 2016) (benefitslink.com)]

The Employee Benefits Security Administration's (EBSA's) analysis of 2014 Form 5500s finds that the number of defined benefit plans grew 1.6% in 2014. Defined contribution plans remained dominant, although they grew only 0.5%. Assets of all plans rose 5.5%, reaching $8.3 trillion: defined benefit plans increased 4.2% to approximately $3.0 trillion, defined contribution assets rose 6.3% to $5.3 trillion. However, in 2014, 21.4% of all defined benefit plans were fully frozen, and 14.9% of all defined benefit plan assets were subject to a freeze. There were 89.9 million active participants in private-sector retirement plans in 2014: 75.4 million in defined contribution plans, 14.5 million in defined benefit plans. In that year, contributions to defined contribution plans were up 7.0%, reaching $403.5 billion, whereas defined benefit plan contributions declined 13.9%, to $97.9 billion. Retirement plans disbursed a total of $650 billion in 2014, either directly to participants and beneficiaries or to insurance carriers. Of this amount, $428.4 billion came from defined contribution plans (11% higher than the year before), and $221.6 billion from defined benefit plans (3.5% less than the year before). However, both types of plans disbursed more than they received: defined benefit plans disbursed $123.7 billion more than they collected in contributions, defined contribution plans $24.9 billion more than they collected. [Rebecca Moore, *DB Plans Are Not Totally Disappearing,* plansponsor .com (Oct. 31, 2016)]

Although it is more common for defined benefit plans to be terminated and replaced by defined contribution plans, a transition in the other direction is also a possibility. The PBGC published a proposal in April 2014 to facilitate rollovers from defined contribution to defined benefit plans. PBGC director Josh Gotbaum said that annuities offer greater retirement security, so participants who have rollover options would be allowed to transfer between plans. Rolled over benefits would not be subject to the PBGC limit on the amount of benefits guaranteed when benefits increase within five years before plan termination. [79 Fed. Reg. 18737 (Apr. 3, 2014)] It was finalized in November 2014, effective December 26, 2014. [RIN 1212-AB23, 79 Fed. Reg. 70090 (Nov. 25, 2014)]

Concerns have been raised about the ability of current institutions to provide retirement security, especially for low-wage workers or those with intermittent work histories. Only half of private sector workers have any kind of employer-sponsored retirement plan, so about a third of households have no coverage during worklife and no retirement income other than Social Security. Even employees with access to 401(k) plans often fail to accumulate significant amounts of savings, because they have a median job tenure of four years.

President Obama signed a presidential memorandum on January 29, 2014, directing the Department of the Treasury to create a new "myRA" savings program for people who lack access to an employer-sponsored plan. The new accounts would be similar to Roth IRAs: contributions can be withdrawn tax-free at any time, but withdrawals of earnings will be taxed. The Roth IRA income limits apply (for 2017, $133,000 for single persons, $196,000 for married persons filing joint returns). The only permitted investment would be a variable-rate fund that invests in Treasury bonds. Once the balance reaches $15,000, or after 30 years, the myRA balance must be rolled over to a regular IRA; the owner can roll it over at any time. [Anne Tergesen and Colleen McCain Nelson, *Obama Signs Order for New myRA Retirement Accounts*, WSJ.com (Jan. 29, 2014)]

According to DOL, one-third of American workers do not have a retirement savings plan at work. California, Connecticut, Illinois, Maryland, and Oregon have adopted automatic savings plans and other states have marketplaces or voluntary plans.

California's law, SB 1234, was signed September 29, 2016, effective January 1, 2017. It calls for automatic payroll deductions at private-sector companies with five or more employees that do not have a current retirement plan. The deductions are channeled into IRAs. The level of the automatic deduction is 3% of payroll, but employees can change the deferral level or opt out entirely. Connecticut HB 5591, signed May 27, 2016, rolls out in 2018. Covered employees at companies with five or more workers get Roth IRAs, with a default 3% contribution which can be changed or opted out of. The Illinois program, under SB 2758, requires setting up an IRA trust no later than June 1, 2017. Covered employers have been in business for at least two years and have 25 or more employees, although smaller employers can voluntarily opt in. Maryland's SB 1007/HB 1378, signed May 10, 2016, took effect July 1, 2016. Oregon HB 2960 set up a retirement savings board required to set up the program by July 1, 2017. Massachusetts, New Jersey, and Washington have voluntary programs. Massachusetts HB 3754 covers small nonprofits; New Jersey A4275 and Washington SD 5826 create marketplaces but do not prescribe a specific program. [Alicia H. Munnell, Anek Belbase and Geoffrey Sanzenbacher, *Issue Brief: State Initiatives to Cover Uncovered Private Sector Workers*, Center for State & Local Government Excellence (Mar. 2016), available at <http://crr.bc.edu/wp-content/uploads/2016/02/IB_16-4-1.pdf> (last accessed Feb. 6, 2017); Nancy Ober and Sean Brown, *Mandatory Payroll Deduction Savings Programs Are on the Rise*, Littler Mendelson PC (Nov. 7, 2016) (benefitslink.com)]

In mid-February 2017, the House of Representatives passed a resolution under the Congressional Review Act (see § 4.01) to overturn this DOL rule. [Yuka Hayashi, *House Votes to Scrap Rules on State Retirement Plans*, WSJ.com (Feb. 15, 2017)] Congress used the Congressional Review Act procedure to pass H.J. Res. 66 and H.J. Res. 67, eliminating DOL regulations that granted state and local retirement plans that auto-enroll employees exemption from ERISA, and President Trump signed the resolutions. EBSA accordingly removed the regulations from the Code of Federal Regulations. [Removed rules: 81 Fed. Reg. 59464 (Aug. 30, 2016), removed by 82 Fed. Reg. 29236 (June 28, 2017). See Rebecca Moore, *Trump Signature Overturns DOL Rule for Government-Run Auto-IRAs*, plansponsor.com (Apr. 14, 2017).]

However, at that point, California, Illinois, New Jersey, and Oregon had already created programs, and some of them said they would keep the programs open even though they would no longer have ERISA immunity. At least 20 state legislatures considered bills in 2017 to establish such programs. [Anne Tergesen, *States Press on with Retirement Programs, Despite Losing Regulatory Cover,* WSJ.com (May 8, 2017); Rebecca Moore, *Oregon State-Run Retirement Plan for Private Sector Opens Soon*, plansponsor.com (June 19, 2017)]

In a sense, the Social Security system is a kind of pension plan. Both employers and employees pay Federal Insurance Contributions Act (FICA) taxes to fund retirement benefits. Although all earned income is subject to Medicare taxes, the FICA tax phases out at a figure that changes every year. (For 2012, only the first $110,100 is subject to FICA tax; for 2013, the applicable amount is $113,700, for 2014 it is $117,000, and for 2015–2016 it is $118,500; for 2017 it is $127,200.) The employer makes FICA contributions on all or nearly all of rank-and-file workers' pay, but only on a smaller proportion of the compensation of top earners. The Tax Relief, Unemployment Insurance Reauthorization, and Job Creation Act of 2010, Pub. L. No. 111-312 reduced the employee's share of FICA taxes (but not the employer's share) for 2011 only. [Plansponsor staff, *Principal Says Tax Holiday an Opportunity to Save*, plansponsor.com (Dec. 17, 2010)] PPACA also imposes additional Medicare tax on high-income earners.

The Temporary Payroll Tax Cut Continuation Act, Pub. L. No. 112-78, extended the 4.2% FICA rate but subject to a cap of the first $18,350 of compensation. The Middle Class Tax Relief and Job Creation Act of 2012, Pub. L.

No. 112-96, enacted February 2, 2012, extended the 4.2% rate until the end of 2012, and removed the cap.

The Internal Revenue Code contains "permitted disparity" rules for "integrating" a qualified plan with Social Security (disparities are not permitted in 401(k) plans). Within limits, the employer can reduce its plan contributions on behalf of rank-and-file employees to compensate for the employer's FICA contributions. As long as the permitted disparity rules are satisfied, the plan will remain qualified, and will not be considered discriminatory—even though the practical effect is to cut down on contributions and lower the pension the rank-and-file employees will eventually receive. The 2016 table of covered compensation with respect to permitted disparities appears at Rev. Rul. 2016-5, 2016-8 I.R.B.

§ 4.06 OTHER PLAN TYPES

An Employee Stock Ownership Plan (ESOP) provides employees with shares in the employer company as a form of deferred compensation. Sometimes ESOPs purchase the company. Commentators noted that ESOPs can provide tax and financing advantages that surpass other takeover alternatives. The transaction involves large-scale loans; as the company repays the loans, the interest is tax-deductible and may be large enough to significantly reduce or even eliminate taxable income for the business. The business is also exempt from capital gains taxation on purchases of certain securities that are retained within the ESOP for three years or more—provided that the ESOP owns at least 30% of the employer stock.

The National Center for Employee Ownership said that an average of 229 new ESOPs were created each year between 2010 and 2017. In 2014, the 6,717 ESOPs in the United States held assets of more than $1.3 trillion, and had 14 million participants (10.6 million of them active participants). There were 5,533 stand-alone ESOPs and 1,184 KSOPs (ESOPs with a 401(k) feature). [Rebecca Moore, *ESOPs Still a Significant Share of Retirement Plans*, plansponsor.com (July 24, 2017)]

Employers interested in succession planning may be interested in creating an ESOP, so the business can eventually be owned by employees—who have a personal interest in its prosperity. However, setting up an ESOP is complicated, and usually costs $150,000–$250,000, a large amount for a small company. To be practical, an ESOP conversion probably requires at least 40 employees and annual sales over $5 million. Lawyers, a valuation expert, and an ESOP trustee will be required. There are also ongoing compliance costs. There must be good succession management and a training program to develop managers for the long haul. Some successful ESOPs took years or even decades for full transition to employee ownership. The deal can be structured to give the ESOP an initial minority position, so the deal can be reversed if it is not successful. [Josh Patrick, *The Questions to Ask Before Adopting an ESOP*, NYTimes.com (July 11, 2013)]

Employees are at high risk if their individual pension accounts are heavily invested in employer stock—and the stock does poorly. Because of the ESOP's mission of investing in employer stock, participants have generally been unsuccessful in challenging ESOP fiduciaries when the value of the stock falls. (See § 15.03[C] for discussion of "stock drop" suits in general.)

On November 16, 2009, the IRS released updated ESOP regulations, increasing the flexibility for satisfying the requirements of § 423 (favorable tax treatment for stock acquired under an ESOP option). To qualify for favorable treatment, the employee must hold the stock for at least two years from the grant, and one year from exercise of the option. For nonqualified options, the employee has ordinary income at the time of exercise, equal any excess of fair market value over the exercise price. To be a § 423 plan, the ESOP plan, including the maximum number of shares available, must be approved by the company's stockholders within a period of 12 months before or after the date the plan was adopted. In general, all employees of the corporation must be granted options. Up to $25,000 worth of stock can be optioned for each year the option is outstanding, whether or not the option is exercisable. The exercise price must be at least 85% of the fair market value at the time of grant or exercise. [Sonnenschein Nath & Rosenthal LLP, *IRS Releases Final Regulations on Employee Stock Purchase Plans* (Nov. 17, 2009) (benefitslink.com)]

Hybrid plans are defined benefit plans whose benefits accrue under the formula set by the sponsor rather than as a monthly payment. The benefit is usually defined as a lump-sum account balance and not an annuity benefit payable at NRA. Employers who adopt hybrid plans often do so because funding is predictable and the plan design is easier for employees to understand than other types of defined benefit plans.

Most hybrid plans are cash balance plans, with the benefit based on a percentage of pay credited annually each year with interest determined based on the plan's interest crediting rate.

In mid-2016, the consulting firm Kravitz reported that there was a 2% increase in cash balance plans over the year before, and a 19% increase in new cash balance plans. IRS regulations in 2010 and 2014 broadened investment choices for cash balance plans, enhancing their popularity. The cash balance plan market hit a total of $1 billion in total invested assets. In 2001, cash balance plans made up 2.9% of defined benefit plans, a proportion that increased 10-fold, reaching 29% in 2016. In 2014, the last year for which complete IRS data are available, there were 15,178 cash balance plans, 91% of them maintained by firms with fewer than 100 employees. [John Manganaro, *Cash Balance Plans Continue to Be Attractive Option for Employers,* plansponsor.com (July 7, 2016)]

Another plan design, the Pension Equity Plan (PEP) posts percentage credits to the employee's account each year. The lump-sum balance at retirement is the total of the percentages times the employee's final average pay.

Typically, hybrid plans increase the rate of pay credits as age and/or service increase. To avoid back-loading, IRS rules mandate crediting a minimum interest rate. Employees generally must meet age and service requirements to participate in hybrid plans, such as one year of service plus reaching age 21. The pension can be computed based on salary alone, or salary plus overtime and commission, but most plans include all compensation including overtime, bonuses, and commissions. In late 2010, the IRS issued final and proposed regulations for hybrid retirement plans, including cash balance plans, and PEPs. The 2010 final regulations deal with subjects such as age discrimination, vesting, conversions from conventional defined benefit plans, and safe harbor rates for crediting interest.

Each participant has a hypothetical account that is credited with the employer's hypothetical contributions based on compensation credits (the participant's eligible compensation) plus interest credits (the hypothetical earnings on the account). Usually, compensation credits are defined as a percentage of eligible pay, although the formula may factor in age and years of service. The interest credits can operate as a fixed rate or be based on an extrinsic interest. Compensation credits end when the participant stops working for the employer, but interest rates generally continue until the pension is distributed. The PEP benefit equals a percentage of the final average pay, with the percentage set based on points earned each year by participants.

Under the final regulations, the entire accrued benefit for a plan using a hybrid formula must vest no later than three years of service. The final regulations provide an Age Discrimination in Employment Act (ADEA) safe harbor: the accumulated benefit of any participant must not be less than the accumulated benefit of any similarly situated younger participant. Whether two participants are similarly situated depends on their period of service, their job, compensation, date of hire, and work history. A hybrid plan that does not qualify under the safe harbor must satisfy the general age discrimination rule of Code § 411(b)(1)(H)(i).

To prevent wearaway, the final regulations provide that if an amendment adopted and effective on or after June 29, 2005, eliminates or reduces future benefit accruals, and part or all of the benefit is determined based on the statutory hybrid formula, the benefit after the conversion amendment must at least equal the accrued benefit on the conversion date plus the accrued benefit after the conversion, with no offsets between the two.

The PPA requires hybrid plans to credit interest at a rate that does not exceed a market rate of return. The final regulations define a market rate as a rate that does not exceed the rate on long-term investment-grade corporate bonds, the rate on certain Treasury bonds; or the actual rate of return on plan assets, if the benefits are indexed; or the rate of return on annuities issued by an insurance company. The rate of benefit accrual can increase as participants earn more, but any year's accrual rate must not exceed one-third more than the previous year's rate.

[75 Fed. Reg. 64123 (Oct. 19, 2010) (final regulations), 75 Fed. Reg. 64197 (Oct. 19, 2010)]

Final and proposed regulations on hybrid defined benefit plans, covering changes made by the PPA and WRERA, were published in September 2014 as T.D. 9693, 2014-41 I.R.B. 596. The 2014 final regulations permit the 133 1/3% rule of § 411(b)(1)(B) to be used for defined benefit plans that adjust benefits with a variable rate that could be negative for plan years beginning on or after January 1, 2012. T.D. 9693 also expands the types of interest crediting rates that will be allowed and changes the treatment of certain benefits paid before NRA.

Additional PEP regulations were released in late 2016. Notice 2016-67, 2016-47 I.R.B. 751 explains the treatment of interest rate credits in two kinds of PEPs: implicit interest and explicit interest. The notice concentrates on the former: plans that calculate benefits by applying a deferred annuity factor to the accumulated benefits, rather than adjusting the benefit with interest credits. [Rebecca Moore, *IRS Clarifies Interest Crediting Rules for Pension Equity Plans*, plansponsor.com (Nov. 7, 2016)]

[A] Money Purchase Plan

A money purchase plan provides definitely determinable benefits, funded by fixed employer contributions made in accordance with a single allocation formula for all participants. Money purchase plans are subject to the I.R.C. § 412 minimum funding standard. The plan must offer Qualified Joint Survivor Annuities (QJSAs) and Qualified Preretirement Survivor Annuities (QPSA)s. [See §§ 12.05, 12.06] Money purchase plans can accept employee contributions and make plan loans to participants.

[B] Profit-Sharing Plan

A profit-sharing plan must have a definite formula, set in advance, for allocating the employer's total contribution among the various plan participants, and for distributing the account money to participants. Distributions can be made after the funds have been in the account for a certain length of time (ERISA requires this to be at least two years), attainment of a stated age (which does not have to be retirement age) or an event such as retirement, termination, illness, or disability. Profit-sharing plans have to have formulas for allocating and distributing employer contributions, but the corporation's Board of Directors can legitimately be given discretion to set the level of contributions each year. Since 1986, it has not been necessary for the contributions to be made from corporate profits, or only in a year in which there are profits. The maximum contribution that the employer can deduct is 15% of the participant's contribution for the year. Profit-sharing plans are allowed to make plan loans.

[C] Target-Benefit Plan

A target-benefit plan is a money purchase plan (and therefore subject to the defined contribution rules), but contributions are calculated to fund a specified level of retirement benefits at normal retirement age. The participant receives the aggregate of all contributions plus their earnings, although the actual benefit may be either higher or lower than the target, depending on investment results. The IRS treats these plans as defined contribution plans with respect to the Rev. Proc. 2007-44 filing deadlines. Therefore, opinion and advisory letters for PPA restatements of prototype or volume submitter plans had a January 31, 2012 deadline. Rev. Proc. 2011-49, 2011-44 I.R.B. 608 requires master or specimen plans to have at least 30 sponsors registered as adopting that plan word for word. The only exception is for money purchase plans (when only 10 adopters required). Target benefit plans do not qualify for this exemption. [Suzanne L. Wynn, *Target Benefit Plans: On the Edge of Extinction*, Pension Protection Act Blog (Dec. 13, 2011) (benefitslink.com)]

[D] Floor-Offset Plan

A floor-offset plan is a hybrid plan, where the defined benefit portion of the plan guarantees a minimum level of benefits, offset by the annuity the retiree could purchase at retirement with the balance in the defined contribution portion of the plan. *Lunn v. Montgomery Ward & Co. Retirement Security Plan* [166 F.3d 880 (7th Cir. 1999)] holds that an employee who retired four years after normal retirement age was not entitled to additional retirement benefits to make up for the reduced duration of benefits. The court upheld the idea of floor-offset plans, finding that this type of plan does not violate ERISA benefit accrual requirements or anti-forfeiture provisions.

[E] New Comparability Plan

A new comparability plan is a special type of defined contribution plan (or combination of defined contribution and defined benefit plan) that can increase the allocation for HCEs without violating the antidiscrimination rules. See § 4.22.

The plan document can define the classes used to group the employees in various ways, although a plan amendment is required to change the number or definition of classes, and this cannot be done retroactively. A class could be specified, for example, as all employees born before a certain date, those hired after a certain date, those with a certain number of years of service, those working in a particular department, those with a stated title or type of job, or those assigned to a named region. [Mark Papalia, *Class-Based Pensions: A Cost-Saving Alternative for Companies of All Sizes*, J. of Accountancy (Jan. 2005) (no longer available online)] New comparability plans are also called cross-tested plans. Cross-tested plans are the opposite of safe harbor plans, where contributions are uniform for all participants. This plan design can be attractive if the employer wants to make larger contributions for valued older employees who have fewer years until retirement for contributions to be made. A cross-tested plan can be paired with a cash balance plan. If the employer contributes 7.5% to the cross-tested and cash balance plan, the employer will be permitted to exclude the lower of 50 employees or 40% of the workforce from the cash balance plan. [Plansponsor editors, *New Comparability Plans Allow the Employer to Reward Older Employees and Owners,*   plansponsor .com (July 27, 2017)]

[F] SEP

A SEP (Simplified Employer Pension) is an IRA sponsored by the employer, under a written plan whose contribution formula does not discriminate in favor of HCEs. For 2009–2014, the § 402(k)(2)(C) compensation amount is $550; it is $600 for 2015–2017. For 2009–2011, the SEP annual compensation limit (§ 408(k)(3)(C)) is $245,000, rising to $250,000 in 2012, $255,000 in 2013, $260,000 in 2014, $265,000 in 2015–2016, and $270,000 for 2017. IR-2015-118, *IRS Announces 2016 Pension PlanLimitations; 401(k) Contribution Limit Remains Unchanged at $18,000 for 2016,* <https://www.irs.gov/pub/irs-news-IR-15-118.pdf>; Notice 2016-62, 2016-46 I.R.B. 725] For 2016–2017, the elective deferral limit is $18,000. The defined contribution limit is $53,000 for 2016, $54,000 for 2017. The catch-up contribution limit is $6,000 for both years. [*401k and Retirement Plan Limits for the Tax Year 2016,* 401khelpcenter.com (undated, last accessed Aug. 5, 2016) (benefitslink.com)]

[G] SIMPLE

A Savings Incentive Match Plan for Employees (SIMPLE) plan, available only to companies with 100 or fewer employees, involves employer contributions to employees' own IRAs. The SIMPLE IRA offers tax advantages for both employer and employees in small companies, and is easier and less expensive to administer than a 401(k) plan. As a general rule, the company cannot offer any other retirement plan, and all participants must have earned at least $5,000 per year from the company in any two previous years, and expect to earn $5,000 in the current year. The employer can elect two kinds of plan. The most common plan form requires the employer to match employee contributions up to 3% of compensation. The 2015 limit is $12,500; the maximum catch-up contribution is $3,000. These figures remain unchanged for 2016 and 2017. (The limit is subject to the aggregate dollar limit of $18,000 for all elective contributions made by a person to all employer-sponsored plans.) The general rule is that the employer can deduct its contributions to the SIMPLE IRA plan. [IRS Publication 560, *Retirement Plans for Small Business (SEP, SIMPLE, and Qualified Plans)* for 2016 returns, available at <https://www.irs.gov/pub/irs-pdf/p560.pdf> (last accessed Feb. 5, 2017)]

[H] Cafeteria Plans

The underlying purpose of all employee benefits is to motivate employees to do better work. Employees differ in their characteristics and priorities, and it is reasonable to assume that employees will be most strongly motivated by benefits that fit their individual needs. Hence, the Internal Revenue Code, at § 125, regulates "cafeteria plans," giving employees choices from a "menu" of taxable and non-taxable benefits. In the summer of 2007, the IRS withdrew a number of earlier proposals and offered new guidance about cafeteria plans (general rules about qualified and nonqualified benefits in these plans; rules for elections; Flexible Spending Account (FSA) plan rules; nondiscrimination; substantiating expenses for qualified benefits).

A cafeteria plan must be set out in writing. The written plan document must explain:

- How to make elections

- The employer's contributions under the plan

- The maximum salary reduction permitted under the plan, either as a maximum percentage of contribution or a maximum dollar amount

- The plan year (unless there is a valid business purpose for a shorter plan year, it must be 12 consecutive months)

- If the plan covers paid time off, ordering of non-elective and elective paid time off

- Rules for any Flexible Spending Account included in the plan

- If there is a Health Savings Account, who is eligible to contribute

- Grace period (if any) for health FSA or dependent care assistance

All reimbursements under the plan must be individually substantiated by someone other than the employee. If the cafeteria plan discriminates in favor of highly compensated employees, the HCEs have income for tax purposes equal to the highest value of the benefits they could have elected. The Proposed Regulations incorporate some of the safe harbor testing rules of Code § 410(b), with an objective test to determine when the actual election of benefits is discriminatory: when HCEs have higher benefits, measured as a percentage of compensation, than non-HCEs.

PPACA creates a new form of cafeteria plan available to small employers (an average of 100 or fewer employees in either of the previous two years) starting in 2011. Like the Simple 401(k) and Simple IRA plan, the Simple Cafeteria

Plan insulates small employers from nondiscrimination problems that might otherwise occur. If a company grows in size, it can keep its Simple Cafeteria Plan until the end of the plan year in which it reaches 200 employees.

All qualified employees must be eligible to participate if they had at least 1,000 hours of service in the previous plan year. Highly compensated and key employees can participate in the Simple Cafeteria Plan, but the plan must avoid discrimination in their favor in eligibility and benefits. All eligible employees must be allowed to elect any benefit in the plan under the same terms and conditions as all other participants.

The employer maintaining the Simple Cafeteria Plan must make a minimum contribution that the participant can apply toward any benefit within the plan. For non-HCEs, the minimum is at least 2% of compensation, an employer match of double the employee contribution, or 6% of compensation. See Notice 2013-61, 2013-44 I.R.B. 432 and Notice 2014-1, 2014.2 I.R.B. 270, explaining the cafeteria plan rules and rules about Health Savings Accounts (HSAs) as they apply to same-sex married couples. Under IRS REG-148998-13, 80 Fed. Reg. 64378 (Oct. 23, 2015), the general rule is that same-sex marriages have the same tax implications as male/female marriages, and a marriage is recognized for federal tax purposes if it would be recognized in any U.S. state. However, domestic partnerships and civil unions are not deemed to be marriages.

[I]   QLACs

The Department of Treasury noted the role of "longevity risk" in the need for retirement income. A 65-year-old woman has a 50-50 chance of living past 86; a 65 year-old man has an equal chance of living past 84. The replacement of defined benefit plans by defined contribution plans as the predominant form leaves many people at risk of outliving their funds.

IRS final regulations on the purchase of Qualified Longevity Annuity Contracts (QLACs) with pre-tax amounts in defined contribution plans, IRAs, and §§ 403(b) and 457 plans were published in mid-2014. The regulations do not cover defined benefit plans but the preamble to the regulation seeks comments about the desirability of permitting defined benefit plan beneficiaries to elect QLACs. The final QLAC regulations permit narrow modification of the minimum distribution rules with respect to amounts used to purchase qualifying deferred annuities that begin payments at an advanced age. Combination options are also allowed—that is, the employee accesses part of a § 401(k) plan distribution as a lump sum, and annuitizes the rest. Before annuitization, the value of the QLAC is excluded from the amount taken into account in calculating the required minimum distribution. The final regulations provide the QLAC disclosure requirements. When the contract is issued, the employee must be informed that the contract is a QLAC. The issuer must report annually to the employee and the

IRS (e.g., how to contact the issuer; information about premium payments and contract payments). [T.D. 9673, 2014-30 I.R.B. 212]

Under prior law, it was difficult to have a split distribution because the statutory interest rates and mortality tables had to be used for both the lump sum and the annuity, precluding the plan from using its own figures in the annuity calculation. The new rules allow the use of the statutory assumptions for the lump sum only, with the plan's regular conversion factors for the partial annuity.

Prior law also worked against longevity annuities, because the minimum distribution requirements impose penalties if the entire account is not distributed over the individual's predicted life expectancy—which means that people who outlive their predicted life expectancy will have exhausted their accounts. The new rules allows 401(k) (and IRA) plans relief from the minimum distribution requirements for annuities that cost less than the smaller of $100,000 or 25% of the account balance and that start by age 85. This type of distribution is referred to as a QLAC, or "qualified longevity annuity contract." The annuity will be disregarded for RMD purposes until its benefits begin. Longevity annuities must satisfy some requirements for death benefits and cash-out to ensure that they are used only to hedge against longevity risk, and full disclosure of the annuity terms is required.

Rev. Rul. 2012-4, 2012-8 I.R.B. 386 explains how an employer that offers both defined contribution and defined benefit plans can permit 401(k) plan participants who are ready to retire to roll over part or all of the 401(k) account balance to the defined benefit plan receiving an immediate annuity under the defined benefit plan. The plan must use the same actuarial assumptions (such as interest rates and mortality tables) for annuitized rollovers as for defined benefit distributions.

Mid-2014 IRS regulations facilitate accepting rollovers from other qualified plans or IRAs by granting safe harbors to administrators—as long as they ascertain that the contribution consists only of valid rollover distributions from an eligible plan. [Eugene S. Griggs, *Accepting Rollover Contributions Now Easier—and Less Risky—for Retirement Plans*, Poyner Spruill LLP (Aug. 7, 2014) (benefitslink.com)]

To encourage the provision of lifetime income, the PBGC published a final rule for transferring defined contribution plan accounts to defined benefit plans. The rules provide that rollovers will not be lost if the PBGC takes over the plan, even if the maximum guarantee would otherwise apply. Under the five-year phase-in rule, defined benefit increases in the five years prior to termination must be phased in over five years after termination. This rule exists to deter plans from increasing benefits when they know they are in trouble. However, the 2014 final rule exempts rollovers that derive from employee contributions from the five-year phase-in rule. [79 Fed. Reg. 70090 (Nov. 25, 2014)]

§ 4.07   IRA/QUALIFIED PLAN INTERFACE

As the name suggests, an Individual Retirement Arrangement (IRA) is maintained by an individual on his or her own behalf, not by a corporation. However, the two types of plan interact when an IRA is used as a "conduit" for a transfer of funds between two qualified plans, or when distributions from a qualified plan are sheltered from immediate taxation by being rolled over to an IRA.

Employers can maintain a program under which employees authorize payroll deductions to be invested in either regular or Roth IRAs. Such arrangements do not constitute ERISA plans (and therefore do not subject the employer to regulation or potential supervision) if:

- The employer doesn't make any contributions;

- Employee participation in the arrangement is completely voluntary;

- The employer's sole involvement is letting employees participate (without endorsing participation), making the payroll deductions, and forwarding the amounts to the IRA sponsor.

The employer can collect reasonable reimbursement for its services in connection with the employees' IRAs, but no other compensation. The employer can provide educational materials about IRAs and the value of saving for retirement, but must make it clear that the employer's role is purely administrative and does not involve contributions to the plan. It's also permissible for the employer to distribute literature prepared by the IRA sponsor, and even to display its own logo on the materials.

Either the employer can choose a single IRA sponsor or inform employees of criteria for choosing a sponsor. However, it is not permitted for the employer to negotiate special terms for its own employees that are not available to everyone who buys IRAs through that sponsor. The employer should inform employees that there are other ways to fund IRAs; that IRAs are not a suitable investment for everybody; and that IRAs work the same way whether the employee authorizes a payroll deduction or submits the contribution directly to the IRA sponsor.

The Economic Growth and Tax Relief Reconciliation Act (EGTRRA) increases the maximum amount that can be contributed to an IRA (especially by persons over 50) and institutes a tax credit for low-income IRA investors, so IRA options will be more attractive than ever before. Active servicemembers can also base IRA contributions on combat pay.

EGTRRA also creates another option, the "deemed IRA," for plan years beginning after December 31, 2002. A qualified plan can permit employees to contribute to a separate account within a qualified plan. If the separate account meets the criteria for being either a conventional or a Roth IRA, it is treated as an IRA and not a qualified plan—and the employer's qualified plan won't lose its qualified status just because of the IRA subaccounts. The difference between a deemed IRA and the payroll deduction plan described above is that the employer, not the employee, sets up the account, although deemed IRAs can take payroll deductions.

Deemed IRAs are considered IRAs rather than qualified plans, so it is not necessary to satisfy ERISA's coverage and nondiscrimination rules. However, deemed IRAs are subject to ERISA's fiduciary and enforcement provisions, including the requirements for processing claims. Each deemed IRA must be held in a separate account or separate annuity under the plan, and the plan must provide separate accounting for the IRS contributions and earnings.

Under the final rule published in 2004, the deemed IRA account must satisfy the rules for either a traditional or Roth IRA. SEP and SIMPLE IRAs cannot be used as deemed IRAs. Because the employer's qualified plan and the deemed IRA are treated as separate entities, rules such as the minimum distribution requirements must be satisfied separately for each.

For 2016, the amount for determining the deductible portion of an IRA contribution made by taxpayers who are active participants in a plan is $98,000 (joint return or qualifying surviving spouse); $61,000 for other returns, but $0 for a married person filing separately. The corresponding 2017 figures are $99,000, $62,000, and $0. The applicable dollar amount for a taxpayer who is not a plan participant, but who is married to one, is $184,000 for 2016, $186,000 for 2017. For Roth IRAs, entitlement to contribute phases out at adjusted gross income of $184,000–$194,000 (joint returns, 2016), $186,000–196,000 (joint returns, 2017) or $117,000–$132,000 (single or head of household returns for 2016, $118,000–$133,000 for 2017); the range for married persons filing separate returns is very limited, topping out at $10,000 (2015–2017 figures). [IRS.gov, IR-2015-118 (Oct. 21, 2015), available at <https://www.irs.gov/pub/irs-news/IR-15-118.pdf>; Notice 2016-62, 2016-46 I.R.B. 725)]

The Saver's Credit, also known as the retirement savings contributions credit, applies to individuals and married persons filing separate returns with incomes up to $30,750 (for 2016), joint returns with income up to $61,500, and heads of household with income up to $46,125. The corresponding 2017 figures are $31,000, $62,000, and $46,500. The person claiming the credit must be over 18, not a full-time student, and not the dependent of another taxpayer. The credit is a percentage of the amount contributed, with the highest percentage at the lowest income level. The credit is reported on Form 8800, Credit for Qualified Retirement Savings Contributions. [IRS Publication 560, *Retirement Plans for Small Business (SEP, SIMPLE, and Qualified Plans for 2016 returns)*, available at <https://www.irs.gov/pub/irs-pdf/p560.pdf> (last accessed Feb. 6, 2017)]

The American Taxpayer Relief Act of 2012 authorizes in-plan Roth conversions of defined contribution accounts that are not otherwise distributable, with no income limitation. Under prior law, only amounts that were distributable (e.g., to a participant who had reached age 59½) could be converted to Roth form. Although the provision is effective January 1, 2013, prior account balances can be converted. [Rebecca Moore, *Fiscal Cliff Deal Extends Roth Conversions*, plansponsor.com (Jan. 3, 2013)]

Roth 401(k) plans (i.e., plans that do not give rise to tax benefits at the time funds are deferred, but from which funds can be withdrawn tax-free at retirement) are another option. [See § 6.04[E]] Roth 401(k) plans were first authorized in 2006. There is no income limit on who can contribute. Account-holders do not get a tax deduction for their contributions, but they can withdraw funds from the account tax-free after retirement. Therefore, these plans are best for people who expect to be in a higher tax bracket after retirement than before—although it is very difficult to predict tax trends. If a Roth 401(k) account contains pre-tax matching contributions from the employer, these contributions must be kept in a separate sub-account, and will be taxable when they are withdrawn. Sponsors of prototype Roth IRA plans who wish to accept rollovers from Roth 402A accounts are required to amend their IRA documents. See Final Regulations covering 401(k), 403(b), and Roth IRA plans. [Fred Schneyer, *IRS Puts Out Roth IRA Rollover Final Regs*, plansponsor.com (June 4, 2007)]

The PPA increases the extent to which non-spouse beneficiaries will be able to roll over inherited benefits to an IRA, subject to most of the same rules as other eligible rollover distributions. The plan must permit the non-spouse beneficiary to make a direct rollover (a trustee-to-trustee transfer) of the eligible rollover distribution to an inherited IRA. The plan administrator must provide the non-spouse beneficiary with a written notice explaining the direct rollover rules and mandatory 20% withholding if amounts eligible for rollover are not rolled over. The non-spouse beneficiary cannot contribute to the inherited IRA, cannot roll other amounts into or out of the inherited IRA, but can perform a trustee-to-trustee transfer to another inherited IRA in the name of the decedent with the same beneficiary. [CCH Pensions & Benefits, *IRS Explains Requirements for Nonspousal Distributions* (Jan. 5, 2010) (benefitslink.com). Notice 2009-68, 2009-39 I.R.B. 423, includes sample notice forms]

§ 4.08 INCIDENTAL BENEFITS

A qualified plan is permitted to offer incidental benefits such as disability, Social Security supplements for early retirees, lump-sum death benefits, incidental death benefits, or 401(h) retiree health benefits. Life insurance can be provided as an incidental benefit as long as the death benefit does not exceed 100 times the estimated monthly retirement benefit under the qualified plan it supplements. However, offering other benefits, such as other medical benefits or layoff benefits, is forbidden, and can lead to loss of plan qualification.

The Tenth Circuit ruled in 2009 that the anti-cutback rule does not apply to a death benefit, or a plan feature that pays a lump sum at retirement that is the actuarial equivalent of a death benefit, so it could lawfully be terminated. The Tenth Circuit ruled that the death benefit was not an accrued benefit, because the plan's definition of accrued benefit excluded death benefits. It could not be a retirement-type subsidy because that means only benefits that continue after retirement. [*Kerber v. Qwest Pension Plan*, 572 F.3d 1135 (10th Cir. 2009)]

T.D. 9665 sets out the rules, starting in 2015 tax years, for taxability of payments for accident and health insurance to participants of qualified retirement plans. Participants will not be taxed on retiree health benefits or costs of disability insurance coverage. [T.D. 9665, 79 Fed. Reg. 26838 (May 12, 2014)]

§ 4.09 STRUCTURE OF ERISA

ERISA is not an easy statute to understand. A vast variety of plan provisions can legally be embodied in qualified plans, and many of these provisions depend on complex mathematical formulas. Furthermore, ERISA is both a labor law and a comprehensive and difficult piece of tax legislation.

Title I of ERISA, also referred to as the labor title, covers issues such as plan structure, fiduciary conduct, and prohibited transactions. Title II is the tax title, covering the requirements for plan qualification and tax deductions. The Title II provisions are duplicated in the Internal Revenue Code. There is some overlap between the two titles. For instance, prohibited transactions are defined in Title I, but the excise tax penalty is imposed under Title II.

Many of the provisions that are most significant for plan administration are found in Title I, Subtitle B. This subtitle is divided into six parts:

- Part 1: Reporting and disclosure;
- Part 2: Participation and vesting standards;
- Part 3: Funding standards;
- Part 4: Fiduciary responsibility;
- Part 5: Administration and enforcement;
- Part 6: Continuation coverage for health insurance.

The Fifth Circuit ruled that a company's Wealth Accumulation Plan (WAP) was an ERISA pension plan because participants could defer distributions until termination. The plan provided for mandatory and voluntary deferrals by participants and matching contributions to be distributed to the participant when they vested. Participants could defer their distributions until termination or for a later in-service distribution. Plaintiffs who forfeited WAP benefits when they were terminated sued, alleging that the WAP's forfeiture provisions violated ERISA. The defendants said that the plan was not a pension plan and accordingly was exempt from ERISA, but the Fifth Circuit found that there was a plan, and it was not a top hat plan. [*Tolbert v. RBC Capital Mkts. Corp.*, 758 F.3d 619 (5th Cir. 2014)]

Although there are some exceptions, the safest way to operate is just to assume that all benefit plans will be subject to at least some ERISA requirements. For example, a welfare plan (one that provides nonpension benefits such as healthinsurance or severance pay) is subject to most of the rules on reporting and disclosure, and the fiduciary, administration, and enforcement rules of Parts 4 and 5, but does not have to satisfy the participation, vesting, or funding standards.

§ 4.10   REQUIRED PROVISIONS FOR ALL QUALIFIED PLANS

Although within these confines a tremendous number of variations can be created, ERISA and the I.R.C. impose certain obligations on all qualified pension plans:

- The plan must be in writing [ERISA § 402(a)(1)];

- The employer must intend the plan to be permanent (although mergers and terminations are permitted under appropriate circumstances) [Reg. § 1.401-1(b)(2). Annuity, profit-sharing, and stock bonus plans are also subject to this requirement];

- The plan must provide a procedure for amendments and must indicate who has the authority to amend the plan [ERISA § 402(a)(1)];

- Plan funds must be managed through use of a trust [ERISA § 403(a), I.R.C. § 401(a)], unless they are held in a custodial account that is invested and managed by someone other than the account custodian.

- The plan must be operated for the exclusive benefit of its participants and their beneficiaries. [I.R.C. § 401(a)(2)] If the employer attempts to violate this rule by obtaining reversions of plan assets, an excise tax will be imposed under I.R.C. § 4980 unless an exception to the general rule applies. Even on termination, defined contribution plans generally cannot return any assets to the employer. Independent contractors must not be allowed to participate, because they are not considered employees;

- The plan must have a published funding policy [ERISA § 402(b)(1)];

- Contributions made to the plan, or benefits received under the plan, are subject to the limitations of the I.R.C.;

- Benefits must not be decreased when Social Security benefits increase;

- Employees must be permitted to participate in the plan as soon as they satisfy the plan's minimum participation standards [I.R.C. §§ 401(a)(3), 410];

- The plan must satisfy minimum coverage requirements, and defined benefit plans must satisfy a minimum participation rule;

- Employee contributions and salary deferrals intended for 401(k) plans must be deposited into the plan as soon as possible, always within 90 days [DOL Reg. § 2510.3-102];

- The plan must not discriminate in favor of highly compensated employees (HCEs);

- The plan's vesting schedule must satisfy federal standards—and if the plan is top-heavy (concentrates its benefits on the highest-paid group) it must vest even faster than the basic rule [I.R.C. §§ 401(a)(7), 404(a)(2), 411(b)] EGTRRA, the 2001 tax law, also increased the speed with which employer matching contributions must vest, and the PPA sped up the vesting schedule for employer's non-elective contributions;

- Benefits must be distributed only to participants and their beneficiaries (including "alternate payees" under Qualified Domestic Relations Orders). This is known as the "anti-alienation" rule. In particular, creditors cannot reach pension benefits before they have been distributed;

- Pension benefits must start within 60 days of the end of the plan year in which the individual reaches the plan's normal retirement age (NRA), reaches age 65, terminates service or has 10 years of service—whichever occurs last;

- The plan must furnish Summary Plan Descriptions (SPDs), Summaries of Material Modifications (SMMs) and other disclosure documents [see Chapter 11];

- The plan must designate at least one fiduciary who is responsible for management. Named fiduciaries are allowed to delegate certain plan responsibilities to other people, such as investment managers—but only if the plan specifically permits such delegation;

- The plan must have a procedure for making claims and appealing denials of applications. The claims procedure must be disclosed in the Summary Plan Description [see §§ 10.05, 11.02] but need not be included in the plan document itself;

- Defined benefit plans must pay premiums to the Pension Benefits Guaranty Corporation (PBGC);

- Transfers of assets between plans, and mergers and terminations of plans, are also regulated. [See I.R.C. § 411(d)(3)]

In response to the low level of savings by plan participants, many industry figures recommended that pension plans be permitted to enroll employees automatically in 401(k) plans, so that employees who did not wish to have amounts deducted from their salaries to save for retirement would have to opt out, rather than employees needing to make an affirmative commitment to open 401(k) plan accounts. Automatic enrollment began in the 1990s, and was popularized by the PPA. To make it easier to design and administer automatic enrollment plans, the DOL issued final rules in 2009.

The 2009 final rules cover Qualified Automatic Contribution Arrangements (QACAs; for single-employer plans) and Eligible Automatic Contribution Arrangements (EACAs; the counterpart for multi-employer plans). The final rules allow employers to increase the percentage rate for automatic contributions during the plan year, not just at the beginning of the plan year, to reflect salary increases or performance evaluations—as long as the increase applies uniformly to all employees.

In a QACA, the employer's safe harbor contribution must be 100% vested after two years of service. Either the contribution must be 3% of pay for all eligible employees (whether or not they contribute), or the employer must match 100% of the first 1% deferred plus 50% of the next 5% deferred, up to a maximum of 3.5% of compensation. Employees must receive notice of automatic enrollment in a plan not less than 30 and not more than 90 days before they become eligible, and before the beginning of each plan year. However, if it is not practicable to give notice on that schedule (e.g., participants are eligible under the plan as soon as they are hired) then the employer can simply give notice as soon as it is practicable. Safe-harbor non-elective and matching contributions under a QACA are not eligible for hardship withdrawals. The QACA rules apply to plan years that begin on or after January 1, 2008; the EACA rules apply to plan years beginning on or after January 1, 2010. [T.D. 9447, 2009-12 I.R.B. 694]

Contributions to a QACA or EACA are invested in the QDIA (Qualified Default Investment Alternative), selected not just to preserve the safety of the invested capital, but to provide appreciation for participants' long-term retirement needs. Employees must be given notice about the QDIA, and how they can change the investment of their funds.

After earlier proposals about investment advice to plan participants were withdrawn, DOL returned to the subject in 2010, proposing a revised rule limited to implementation of the PPA statutory exemption for certain limited forms of investment advice. Under the 2010 revision, advice can be given two ways: through the use of an unbiased computer model, or when the adviser's fees do not vary no matter what investments the participants choose. The computer model or level fee arrangement has to be chosen by the fiduciary, independent of adviser and its affiliates; qualifications set for the investment expert who certifies the model; investment advisers can't get compensation from affiliates on the basis of their recommendations; and advice arrangements have to be audited each year. Additional requirements, including fee disclosure, are imposed. [Proposed rule, 75 Fed. Reg. 9360 (Mar. 2, 2010)]

As the value of pension accounts declined, there was increasing attention to the subject of fees. In good times, high fees often are not noticed—or are accepted as a fair exchange for the excellent investment results obtained. But fees are more noticeable when account balances drop—and it is harder to argue that the mutual fund or other investment vehicle was successful enough to be entitled to high fees.

In 2010, the Supreme Court held that, in a case charging that excessive fees were imposed, the correct legal standard is whether the fees were so excessive that they must have reflected manipulation—they could not have been the result of arm's length bargaining. [*Jones v. Harris*, 559 U.S. 335 (2010)] However, the Supreme Court refused to hear the appeal of dismissal of another Seventh Circuit case about excessive 401(k) fees. [*Hecker v. Deere & Co.*, 556 F.3d 575 (7th Cir. 2009)]

The Supreme Court vacated an Eighth Circuit decision about whether mutual fund fees violated Section 36(b) of the Investment Company Act. The Eighth Circuit had relied on the marketplace to prevent excessively high fees from being imposed. However, the Supreme Court remanded the case to comply with *Jones v. Harris*. [*Ameriprise Fin. Inc. v. Gallus*, 130 S. Ct. 2340 (2010)] On remand, the Eighth Circuit held that the plaintiffs did not show that the fees were so unreasonably high that they could not have been the product of arm's length bargaining. [*Gallus v. Ameriprise*, 675 F.3d 1173 (8th Cir. 2012)]

In mid-2008, the DOL proposed regulations requiring the fiduciaries of individual account plans to provide specific disclosures about the plan's investment options—and the fees for these plans: see 73 Fed. Reg. 43014 (July 23, 2008). It was the third set of regulations about defined contribution plan fees—the previous ones were published at 72 Fed. Reg. 64710 and 64731 (Nov. 16, 2007), dealing with Form 5500 reporting requirements, and 72 Fed. Reg. 70988 (Dec. 13, 2007), requiring fiduciaries to obtain specific information about fees, compensation, and conflicts of interest from their service providers.

DOL published regulations in October, 2010, governing disclosure of fees to plan participants: see 75 Fed. Reg. 64910 (Oct. 20, 2010). Originally, these regulations were scheduled to take effect July 16, 2011, but to give employers more time to update their systems, and to conform to regulations about cost disclosure to the plan itself, their effective date was delayed until April 1, 2012; see 76 Fed. Reg. 42539 (July 19, 2011).

Another question is the extent to which an account is invested in the employer's securities—a matter that often becomes controversial if the stock price falls, and the value of the account falls with it. T.D. 9484 [2010-24 I.R.B. 748, 75 Fed. Reg. 27927 (May 19, 2010)], effective for plan years beginning on or after January 1, 2011, provides Final Regulations under Code § 401(a)(35), a diversification requirement enacted by PPA § 901. Defined contribution plans subject to these requirements must give each participant who has at least three years of service (and beneficiaries of such participants and of deceased participants) the right to divest employer securities in their accounts and re-invest these amounts. The plan must offer at least three diversified investment options other than employer stock. Divestment/reinvestment must be allowed at reasonable intervals, at least quarterly. "Stock drop" suits are discussed in more detail in, e.g., § 15.03[C] and 15.09[A].

§ 4.11   NORMAL RETIREMENT AGE

Many ERISA and tax rules depend on the concept of drawing a pension at, before, or after the plan's Normal Retirement Age (NRA). The standard NRA remains 65, although perhaps this will change not only as life expectancies increase, but as the Social Security system phases in a higher age for receiving unreduced benefits. (The basic Social Security retirement age is gradually being increased from 65 to 67.)

However, a plan can set the NRA either higher or lower than 65. The plan can choose an NRA lower than 65 if this is customary for the company or for its industry—as long as this choice is not a device to accelerate funding. If the NRA is very low—below 55—I.R.C. § 415(b) requires that maximum pension payable under the plan be reduced, in light of the large number of payments that will be made. However, a profit-sharing plan is allowed to have an NRA lower than 55, even if this is below the industry average.

Form 5300 (application for determination letter) was revised in December 2013, to include a new Line 5. Defined benefit plans (including cash balance plans) must indicate if the plan had an NRA lower than age 62 at any time since May 22, 2007. If so, the employer (or the trustees, if it is a multi-employer plan) must indicate whether they made a good-faith determination that the NRA was reasonably representative for the industry. The IRS will no longer issue a private letter ruling as to whether an NRA below 62 is acceptable. [Form 5300: <http://www.irs.gov/pub/irs-pdf/f5300.pdf> (revised Jan. 2017) (last accessed Feb. 6, 2017); see Julie Koos, *Pension Plan Sponsors Must Justify the Reasonableness of Normal Retirement Ages Under Age 62*, Prudential Compliance Advisory (Feb. 2015) (benefitslink.com)]

> ■ **TIP:** If the plan does not specify an NRA, the NRA will be deemed to be the age at which accrued benefits no longer increase solely on account of age or service.

If the plan sets the NRA above 65, or if there is no definition in the plan, then each participant will have an individual NRA. It will be either his or her 65th birthday or the fifth anniversary of plan participation, whichever comes later.

See T.D. 9325, 2007-24 I.R.B. 386, for Final Regulations giving rules for determining whether a plan's NRA is valid if the plan makes in-service distributions under a phased retirement program. In general, the NRA must be set at least as high as the industry standard, although there is a safe harbor if the NRA is at least 62, or is between 55 and 62 and the employer makes a good-faith determination that the NRA is appropriate for the industry.

T.D. 9693, 2014-41 I.R.B. 596 changes the age discrimination rules for plan years beginning on or after January 1, 2016. If the annual benefit payable before NRA is greater for a participant than the benefit for any similarly situated older person who is at or before NRA, the excess is not considered part of the subsidized portion of an early retirement benefit and is not disregarded for age discrimination testing purposes.

The Multi-Employer Pension Relief Act of 2014 says that if a plan adopted an NRA on or before December 8, 2014, as the earlier of an age permitted by current law, or age plus completing a number of years of service (at least 30), the plan will not fail to comply merely because the rule applies only to certain participants.

The Supreme Court declined to review the Seventh Circuit's *Fry v. Exelon* decision from 2009. The Seventh Circuit ruled that a plan sponsor could define NRA other than as a specific age. In that case, Fry took a lump sum in 2003 from a cash balance plan, and later challenged the plan's definition of NRA, saying that it violated ERISA because it was used to avoid the whipsaw calculation. (This was pre-PPA, so there had not yet been a definitive statement that whipsaw is not required.) [*Fry v. Exelon*, 571 F.3d 644 (7th Cir. 2009), *cert. denied*, 130 S. Ct. 1504 (Feb. 22, 2010)]

However, in 2013, the Second Circuit held that PriceWaterhouseCooper's cash balance plan did not define NRA appropriately. The plan defined NRA as five "years of service." The Second Circuit held that NRA must be defined as an age, so "five years of service" is not a valid NRA, and the five-year requirement does not reflect expectations about when average persons will retire. [*Laurent v. PricewaterhouseCoopers LLP*, No. 14-1179, 2015 WL 4477191 (2d Cir. July 23, 2015). Certiorari was denied on the issue of whether ERISA requires NRA to be based on the typical age at which the employer expects participants would retire: *PricewaterhouseCoopers LLP v. Laurent*, No. 15-638 *cert. denied* (Jan. 25, 2016)]

In mid-2012, the Fourth Circuit held that increases in benefit accruals to participants who have reached NRA do not violate ERISA's prohibition against backloading in later years of service. (The plan defined NRA as the earlier of age 64 or 60 months of vesting service.) The 133 1/3% test forbids accrual of benefits more than one-third greater than the annual rate of accrual in the previous year. This rule was adopted to prevent employers from skimping on accrual rates in the early years of service, when turnover is highest. The Fourth Circuit held that anti-backloading rules no longer apply after the participant reaches NRA. [*McCorkle v. Bank of Am. Corp.*, 688 F.3d 164 (4th Cir. 2012)]

§ 4.12 NORMAL RETIREMENT BENEFIT

The NRB, or Normal Retirement Benefit, is a related concept. It is either the benefit commencing at the NRA or the early retirement benefit (if the plan provides one)—whichever is greater. The early retirement benefit is not adjusted actuarially for this purpose, even though it will be paid for more years than if benefits had commenced at the NRA. Early retirement subsidies are not counted if they continue only until the retiree becomes eligible for Social Security, and if they do not exceed the Social Security benefit.

Not everyone retires on the anniversary of plan participation. If benefits depend on average compensation for, e.g., three or five years, then Treas. Reg. § 1.411(a)-7(c)(5) mandates treatment of the last partial year of service as a full year.

§ 4.13   PARTICIPATION AND COVERAGE

Both defined benefit and defined contribution plans are subject to "minimum coverage" rules under I.R.C. § 410(b). Remember, one of the main motives in passing ERISA was to prevent plans from concentrating unduly on providing benefits to stockholders and managers. However, it can be difficult to satisfy the various tests in a small company (see § 4.14[A] for top-heavy plan rules) or in a company where there is a great disparity between managers' pay and rank-and-file pay, or where there is a stable group of HCEs but heavy turnover in rank-and-file employees.

To satisfy the minimum coverage rules, the plan must either cover a percentage of the rank and file that is at least 70% of the percentage of highly compensated employees covered by the plan; or the plan must cover a reasonable classification of employees that is not discriminatory. Furthermore, the contributions made on behalf of, or the benefits provided to, the rank-and-file must equal at least 70% of those made or provided to the highly compensated.

Defined benefit plans are subject to a minimum participation rule. On each day of the plan year, the plan must benefit either 40% of all the company's work force, or 50 people, whichever is less. However, plans that are not top-heavy and do not benefit any highly compensated employee or former employee are exempt from the minimum participation rule.

The I.R.C. does not require qualified plans to cover all employees from the time of hiring. It is permissible for a plan to require employees to be at least 21 years old and to have completed one year of service before being eligible for participation. Part-time employees must be covered if they can work 1,000 hours within a 12-month period. If plan benefits become 100% vested after only two years, a qualified plan (other than a 401(k) plan) can require two years of service for participation.

§ 4.14   VESTING

[A]   Generally

Participation in a plan is only the first step toward eventually receiving a pension. Vesting is the process of the benefits becoming nonforfeitable. ERISA includes detailed vesting rules to prevent earlier abuses, under which plans were often drafted so that so many years of service were required to achieve a pension that many rank-and-file employees would end up forfeiting their pensions (with the forfeitures going to swell the accounts of highly compensated executives and stockholders).

The normal benefit must always be nonforfeitable at the normal retirement age. It is not required that employees immediately gain 100% ownership of their defined contribution accounts, or the amounts contributed on their behalf to a defined benefit plan. Vesting is the process of moving toward 100% ownership. The Code prescribes minimum funding schedules; employers are always permitted to give employees faster vesting. "Cliff vesting" means that, for a period of time, the employee is not vested at all—but at a certain point, the entire account becomes vesting at once. "Graded vesting" means that part of the account vests each year, until 100% vesting is attained.

There are only two basic vesting schedules allowed by I.R.C. § 411(a):

- Five-year cliff vesting: participants are not vested at all for the first five years of service, but then they are immediately 100% vested as to employer contributions;

- Three-to-seven graded vesting: no vesting at all for three years, but full vesting by seven years of service, increasing proportionately in years 4, 5, and 6.

Top-heavy plans must provide even faster vesting—three-year cliff or six-year graded—but plans with a lot of participants usually are not top-heavy.

The PPA required cash balance plans to provide 100% vesting after three years of service—but WRERA suspended this requirement.

For an example of how vesting works, if a participant leaves employment at a time when he or she is 60% vested, then a participant in a defined contribution plan will be entitled to $60 of every $100 in his or her individual account. A participant in a defined benefit plan will be entitled to an annuity of $60/month for every $100/month that would have been payable if he or she had remained at work until becoming 100% vested.

EGTRRA, the 2001 tax legislation, provides even faster vesting for employer matching contributions (as distinct from the employer's own contributions). Vesting for matching contributions must be either three-year cliff vesting or graded vesting over two to six years (20% in the second year of service, 40% in the third year, etc.). Under the PPA, employer non-elective contributions made for years beginning after December 31, 2006 must satisfy either three-year cliff or two-to-six-year graded vesting.

[B]   Vesting on Termination

All qualified plans must provide that, if the plan is completely or partially terminated, all affected participants immediately become 100% vested. [I.R.C. § 411(d)(3)] For plans that are not subject to the minimum funding standard of I.R.C. § 412 (for instance, profit-sharing and stock bonus plans), 100% vesting must also occur when the employer completely ceases to make contributions to the plan. A profit-sharing or stock bonus plan is deemed terminated on the day when the plan administrator notifies the IRS of the cessation of contributions.

[C]   Vesting and Service

For vesting purposes, a year of service is a period of 12 consecutive months during which the employee performs at least 1,000 hours of service. Plans are not required to provide fractional years of service credit—i.e., if someone works only 500 hours, the employer does not have to credit half a year of service.

For the purposes of vesting or participation for accrual purposes, a year of service can be any period of 12 consecutive months that the employer designates. But a year of service for plan eligibility purposes must start on the first day of employment. A plan can have more than one vesting year. If the plan selects a single vesting year for convenience, it doesn't have to be the same as the plan year.

§ 4.15   BREAK-IN-SERVICE RULES

For some pension-related purposes, it makes a big difference whether the individual has been continuously employed by the employer sponsoring the plan, or whether employment has been interrupted: whether the person has been laid off and then recalled, for instance. Interruption of continuous employment is called a "break in service"—a concept that has many implications.

A one-year break in service has occurred when a person renders 501 or fewer hours of service for the employer in a particular year. If someone works more than 501 but less than 1000 hours for the employer in a given year the employer does not have to credit a year of service, but cannot penalize the employee for the break in service.

After someone has had a one-year break, the employer can disregard service before the break for vesting purposes until the employee has come back to work and completed a year of service. After there have been five consecutive one-year breaks in service, a defined contribution plan, or some insured defined benefit plans, can treat the vested benefits as forfeited, and allocate them to other participants.

If the participant was 0% vested before the break in service, the "Rule of Parity" requires the plan to add up the number of years of service before the break. If the number of consecutive one-year breaks is at least five, or is greater than or equal to the aggregate number of pre-break years of service (whichever is greater), the rule allows the pre-break years to be disregarded for vesting purposes, even if the participant is later rehired.

However, under the Retirement Equity Act of 1984 [Pub. L. No. 98-397], a break in service that is caused by parenting leave probably cannot be counted against the employee. A reservist who is called to active military duty does not have a break in service during the active-duty period. [See § 1.18, *supra*, for more about the employment law implications of call-ups of reservists and members of the National Guard.]

§ 4.16   PLAN LIMITS

One of the basic purposes of ERISA is to prevent plans from unduly favoring executives, managers, and other highly paid employees. One of the ways ERISA furthers this objective is by placing limits on the amount that can be contributed each year to a defined contribution plan, deferred in a 401(k) plan, or provided as a benefit under a defined benefit plan.

The underlying principle is that plan limits are adjusted annually. The adjustment reflects changes in the Consumer Price Index. Starting in 2003, the changes are to be rounded down in $5,000 increments; previously, changes were adjusted in $10,000 increments.

Before 2000, I.R.C. § 415(e) imposed a combined limitation on the allocations to defined contribution plans plus accrued benefits from defined benefit plans. However, as of 2000, plans are permitted to—but not obligated to—impose a combined limitation with respect to employees who participate in both types of plans. Defined benefit plans are allowed to increase benefits (for retirees as well as active employees) to reflect repeal of the combined limitation. See Notice 2007-28, 2007-14 I.R.B. 880, for post-PPA application of the combined limit, and its effect on the employer's maximum deduction.

For 2016–17, the elective deferral limit is $18,000. The defined contribution limit is $53,000 (2016) and $54,000 (2017). The catch-up contribution limit is $6,000 for both years. In 2017, the maximum annual benefit under a defined benefit plan is $215,000. A "highly compensated employee" as defined by § 414(q)(1)(B) is one who earns $120,000 or more. The maximum amount of annual compensation that can be taken into account in making calculations under §§ 401(a)(17) and 404(l) is $270,000. [*401k and Retirement Plan Limits for the Tax Year 2016*, 401khelpcenter.com (last accessed Apr. 10, 2016) (benefitslink .com); Debra J. Linder, Thomas B. Henke and James B. Platt, *Benefit Plans: 2017 COLAs,* Fredrikson & Byron PA (Oct. 27, 2016), available at Lexology.com]

§ 4.17 EMPLOYEE CONTRIBUTIONS

Although 401(k) plans get their basic funding from employees' deferred salary (and may get matching contributions from the employer), pension plans work the other way around. They get their basic funding from the employer, but some plans require and other plans permit employees to make additional contributions to the plan. Internal Revenue Code § 411(c)(2) characterizes employee contributions as mandatory if making the contribution is a precondition of the employer match.

> ■ **TIP:** The Bankruptcy Abuse Prevention and Consumer Protection Act of 2005 (BAPCPA; Pub. L. No. 109-8) gives employees additional protection against their contributions being seized by their employer's creditors, when the employee has made the contribution but the employer has not yet deposited it into the plan.

Employee contributions are also important in determining whether or not a plan discriminates in favor of highly compensated employees. I.R.C. § 414(g) contains the formula for testing whether the employer's aggregate contributions to the plan on behalf of HCEs are too high. If the plan fails to satisfy the requirements of this section, it will be disqualified, unless the excess contributions made on behalf of the HCEs, plus the earnings on the excess contributions, are returned to the company's employees by the end of the plan year after the year of the excess contribution. A 10% excise also applies to excess employee contributions (e.g., made by HCEs) that are not distributed within two-and-a-half months of the end of the plan year.

Benefits attributable to employer contributions cannot be assigned or anticipated before they are received, except in the form of a QDRO. But employees can withdraw some or all of their voluntary contributions while continuing to be employed and to participate in the plan. Employees must always have the right to withdraw their own voluntary contributions to the plan at any time, without the accrued benefits attributable to employer contributions becoming forfeitable. [I.R.C. § 401(a)(19)] However, if the plan mandates employee contributions, I.R.C. § 411(a)(3)(D) allows the plan to provide that employer contributions will be forfeited if a participant withdraws any mandatory employee contributions at a time when he or she is less than 50% vested. If the benefits are repaid within five years after the withdrawal, or two years after the employee returns to participation under the plan (whichever comes first), the benefits must be restored.

Employees are always 100% vested in their own voluntary contributions to a pension plan. When an employer matches these voluntary contributions, EGTRRA requires vesting in the employer's matching contributions to occur either on a three-year cliff schedule, or a six-year graded schedule, beginning with 20% vesting in the second year of the employee's service.

§ 4.18 PLAN LOANS

Under the right circumstances, plans are permitted to make loans to participants. These loans can be a useful resource if, for instance, a plan participant wishes to buy a house or pay a child's tuition. Loans to rank-and-file participants are usually permitted. However, a direct or indirect loan to a "party in interest" or a "disqualified person" is a prohibited transaction, unless a prohibited transaction exemption is available to justify the loan.

Under I.R.C. § 72(p), the general rule is that plan loans are treated as distributions—in other words, taxable income to the recipient. But there are certain exceptions. A loan will not be treated as a distribution if it does not exceed $50,000 or half the present value of the employee's nonforfeitable accrued benefit under the plan (whichever is less). (The employee can borrow up to $10,000, even if this amount is more than half the value of the accrued benefit.) Where the participant's account balance is the only security, the loan is theoretically not permitted to exceed half the pledged amount. The DOL Regulations dealing with plan loans do not forbid participants from borrowing funds from their accounts, pledging 50% of the account, and then taking hardship withdrawals, even though these steps have the effect of reducing the security below 50% of the account. [See Reg. § 2550.408-1(f)(2)]

The agreement to take a loan from the plan must call for repayment within five years, in payments made at least quarterly, with level amortization. Plans are permitted to impose variable interest rates on plan loans.

■ **TIP:** BAPCPA (Pub. L. No. 109-8), the 2005 bankruptcy reform statute, makes it clear that when an employee files for bankruptcy protection (even a Chapter 13 wage-earner plan), it is not a violation of the automatic stay for the employer to withhold from the employee's wages in order to repay a plan loan from a qualified plan. Plan loans do not qualify for the automatic discharge provision of Bankruptcy Code § 523, and bankruptcy plans are not permitted to materially alter the terms of a plan loan. However, amounts that an employee uses to repay plan loans are not considered "disposable income" and therefore cannot be reached by the employee's other creditors.

For reservists and National Guard members on active duty, federal law limits interest rates on all loans to the service member (including plan loans) to 6%. However, plan fiduciaries have the right to petition the relevant court to permit a higher interest rate. Under USERRA (See § 1.18, *supra*), a pension plan is allowed—but not obligated—to suspend the obligation to make regular repayments of plan loans during active military service.

Publicly traded companies must also be aware of the Sarbanes-Oxley Act [Pub. L. No. 107-204] ban on loans made by such companies to their directors and executive officers; this prohibition took effect on July 30, 2002, although loan arrangements already in effect on that date are exempt as long as their terms are not materially modified after July 30, 2002.

Plan loans made to parties in interest are likely also to constitute prohibited transactions for ERISA fiduciary purpose, subject to a 15% excise tax.

Early in 2009, amendments to Regulation Z were published, exempting most retirement plan loans from the Truth in Lending Act (TILA). To qualify for the exemption, which takes effect July 1, 2010, the loan must be made to a plan participant, from fully vested funds in the participant's account, and the loan must comply with Internal Revenue Code requirements, including Code § 72. [Federal Reserve Reg. § 226.3(g), Document E8-31185, 74 Fed. Reg. 5244 (Jan. 29, 2009)]

Under Federal Reserve Board regulations revised July 1, 2010, loans to plan participants made from fully vested funds in the participant's account in a qualified plan are exempt from TILA, but loans to beneficiaries and QDRO alternate payees require disclosures. The TILA exemption is also unavailable for loans that violate Code § 72(p)—e.g., those that have a term greater than five years, exceed the maximum loan amount, or are not repaid in equal installments. If the plan is subject to the ERISA disclosure requirements, the SPD must disclose the fees or charges that can be imposed on plan loans. [Deloitte's Washington Bulletin, *Most Plan Loans Now Exempt from Truth-in-Lending Act Disclosures* (Aug. 9, 2010) (benefitslink.com)]

§ 4.19 EMPLOYER'S DEDUCTION

An employer that maintains a qualified defined benefit plan is entitled to deduct the greatest of these three amounts:

- The minimum funding standard as provided by I.R.C. § 412;

- The amount necessary to fund the cost of covering all the employees for their projected future service;

- The amount necessary to fund present and future costs, which may include liabilities stemming from service performed before the plan was established.

In 2007, the IRS published Q&A on the PPA's rules for the employer's deduction for contributions to the retirement plan (Code § 404). If the plan year is not the same as the employer's tax year, the employer can choose to use the deduction limit for the plan year that begins in the tax year; the plan year that ends in the tax year; or a weighted average of the two. For calculating the combined limit when an employer sponsors both defined benefit and defined contribution plans, and the employer's contributions to the defined contribution plan exceed 6% of compensation, the employer contribution to the defined compensation plan minus 6% of compensation is applied to the combined limit. [Notice 2007-28, 2007-14 I.R.B. 880]

§ 4.20 REVERSIONS

If there were no statutory ban, unscrupulous employers might raid pension assets when they needed cash, or might terminate plans merely to recoup assets or excess assets. To prevent this, defined contribution plans (including profit-sharing and stock bonus plans) usually cannot return any assets to the employer under any circumstances. Even forfeitures (amounts contributed on behalf of employees whose employment terminates before they become vested) are to be allocated to other participants in the plan.

Under appropriate circumstances, employers can receive reversions from a defined benefit plan after satisfaction of all obligations under the plan to employees. Nor may the employer lawfully transfer assets from an overfunded plan to an underfunded plan.

Internal Revenue Code § 4980 imposes an excise tax on the amount of assets reverting to an employer from a qualified plan. The tax rate, for reversions occurring after September 30, 1990, is at least 20%. The rate rises to 50% unless the employer either transfers 25% of the assets in question to a qualified replacement plan, or increases the benefits under the terminating plan to the extent of 20% of the previous benefits to participants. A qualified replacement plan covers at least 95% of the active employees from the terminated plan who continue to be employed.

§ 4.21 FORFEITURES

Depending on the plan, at least some employees—and perhaps the vast majority of the rank-and-file workforce—will terminate employment before they become vested. The contributions made on account of such employees are known as forfeitures.

Under I.R.C. §§ 401(a)(8) and 404(a)(2), defined benefit plans are required to provide that forfeitures will not be applied to increase the benefits any employee would otherwise receive. Instead, favorable plan experience when it comes to forfeitures (or mortality or employee turnover) reduces the amount the employer has to contribute to the plan. In contrast, defined contribution plans are allowed to—and usually do—allocate forfeitures to the accounts of other participants.

If someone leaves employment, and is later rehired by the same company, the eventual retirement benefit must be adjusted actuarially to reflect both periods of employment (unless the break-in-service rules make this unnecessary). Another option is for the plan to give timely notice of its provisions for suspension of benefits, so there is no forfeiture. [Treas. Reg. § 2520.203-3(b)(4)]

When an employee dies, the plan can impose forfeiture of his or her unvested benefits, except if a Qualified Preretirement Survivor Annuity (QPSA) is required. [See § 12.06]

Mishandling of forfeitures is a common target of IRS audits. The IRS requires forfeitures to be used or allocated for the plan year in which they arise— or, in appropriate circumstances, in the following plan year. Forfeitures can be used to pay reasonable administrative expenses of the plan; to reduce the employer's contribution; to restore previously forfeited participant accounts; or to provide additional contributions to participants. Placing the forfeited amounts into a suspense account is not permitted. For two years after the error, mistakes in handling forfeitures can be corrected with the IRS's Employee Plans Compliance Resolution System (EPCRS), a program that allows plans to return to compliance on easy terms. After the two-year period, voluntary correction program (VCP) must be used unless the failure is considered insignificant. VCP must be used if the terms of the plan are incorrect and a retroactive plan amendment is required to correct them. [Chadron J. Patton, *Common Plan Mistakes: Failure to Timely Allocate Forfeitures*, Spencer Fane (Nov. 16, 2012) (benefitslink.com)]

Regulations proposed in early 2017 would allow employer contributions to 401(k) plans to be treated as Qualified Matching Contributions (QMACs) and qualified nonelective contributions (QNECs) if they satisfy the requirements of non-forfeitability and distributions at the time they are allocated to participants' accounts, even if they do not satisfy the requirements at the time they were contributed. The practical effect is that forfeitures can be used to fund QMACs and QNECs. [Rebecca Moore, *IRS Proposes Changes to QMAC, QNEC Definitions*, plansponsor.com (Jan. 17, 2017)]

§ 4.22 DISCRIMINATION TESTING

One of the most basic plan concepts is that a plan must be operated for the exclusive benefit of its participants and beneficiaries. Furthermore, one of the main reasons for the creation of ERISA, and its elaborate structure of rules, is to prevent plans from being administered so that company owners, or major executives, get generous benefits while rank-and-file workers get little or nothing. A qualified plan must be "tested" for "discrimination." In this context, discrimination does not mean discrimination on the basis of sex, race, nationality, and so forth; it means allowing a disproportionate share of plan benefits to go to Highly Compensated Employees (HCEs).

Although actual nondiscrimination testing is usually done by a plan's TPA or recordkeeper, the sponsor must nevertheless understand how the tests work, the kinds of contributions tested, and the consequences of failure. ERISA requires several tests a year to show that a 401(k) plan does not discriminate in favor of higher-income employees. There are several kinds of nondiscrimination rules: the § 410(b) coverage test; the actual deferral percentage (ADP) test; the ACP test (actual contribution percentage); and test to see if the plan is top-heavy (more than 60% of the plan's overall assets are attributable to key employees). A plan that fails the § 410(b) coverage test must be brought into retroactive compliance by the end of the plan year, either by covering more non-highly compensated employees, changing contribution allocations or benefit accruals—or the HCEs will have to report their vested accrued benefits as income. A plan that fails either the ADP or ACP test has 12 months after the end of the plan year either to make a qualified non-elective contribution to all eligible non-HCEs to raise the percentages or distribute the excess contributions to the HCEs. [Noel Couch, *401(k) Nondiscrimination Tests Explained*, plansponsor.com (Dec. 1, 2014)]

A pension, annuity, profit-sharing, or stock bonus plan can lawfully favor HCEs in terms of contributions or benefits, but not both. [See I.R.C. §§ 401(a)(4), 404(a)(2)] Internal Revenue Code § 414(q) says that, for plan years after 1996, an HCE is defined as someone who owned 5% or more of the employer company's stock in either the current or the preceding year—or someone whose compensation for the preceding year was at least $80,000, as adjusted for inflation. For 2013–2014, the adjusted figure is $ $115,000; for 2015–2017, it is $120,000. The employer has the right to choose to use an alternative definition, under which HCEs are those who not only earn more than the adjusted amount, but are also in the top 20% of earners in the company.

The Code used to contain rules called "family aggregation rules" (nicknamed "aggravation rules" because of their complexity) under which the compensation of several members of the family owning a family business had to be combined for purposes including discrimination testing. However, effective for plan years beginning on and after January 1, 1997, the family aggregation rules were abolished by the Small Business Job Protection Act (SBJPA) of 1996. [Pub. L. No. 104-188]

It does not violate the antidiscrimination rules for a plan to be "integrated" with Social Security within limits set by the "permitted disparity" rules of Code § 401(l). In effect, the employer can treat the employee's Social Security benefit (which was partially funded by the employer's FICA contributions) as part of the pension, or the employer can treat its FICA contributions as pension contributions.

The Code includes "safe harbor" provisions for discrimination testing. Plans are not obligated to follow the safe harbor rules; they can set their own formulas. But if they do follow the safe harbor rules, they are sure not to be challenged by the IRS on this issue.

In a "soft freeze," a defined benefit plan is closed to new hires, but accruals continue for workers hired before the freeze. Often, the employer adopts a new defined contribution plan for new hires, or enhances benefits under an existing defined contribution plan. Notice 2014-5, 2014-2 I.R.B. 276 provides temporary relief for satisfying the § 401(a)(4) nondiscrimination requirements by defined benefit plans that have been closed to new hires. On its own, the frozen defined benefit plan might not pass § 410(b) coverage testing, because there is more turnover among non-HCE participants than HCEs. The frozen defined benefit plan will therefore have to be aggregated with the defined contribution plan for coverage testing; if the plans are aggregated for coverage testing, they must also be aggregated for nondiscrimination testing, which many defined contribution plans will fail because HCEs have a higher normal allocation rate. Notice 2014-5 provides temporary relief for plan years beginning before January 1, 2016 for defined benefit plans that were amended to exclude new hires before December 13, 2013. The defined benefit plan must be part of an aggregated plan that either is primarily defined benefit in character, or the defined benefit plan passed nondiscrimination testing on its own, without aggregation, for the plan year beginning in 2013. [Paul Hamburger and Lisa A. Berkowtz Herrnson, *IRS Issues Temporary Non-Discrimination Testing Relief for Closed Defined Benefit Plans and Request for Comments*, Proskauer's ERISA Practice Center Blog (Dec. 20, 2013) (benefitslink.com)]

§ 4.23   LEASED EMPLOYEES

Leased employees (hired by a company from an agency that supplies workers) play a significant role in the economy. However, it is often the case that the treatment of a particular individual varies depending on the context. It is simplistic to say that a person is just an employee or a non-employee. Internal Revenue Code § 414(n) requires some people to be treated as employees eligible for plan participation even though they are formally employed by a leasing company rather than by the company for whom they perform services each day.

Section 414(n) refers to "leased employees," who are nominally employed by a "leasing organization" (e.g., an organization that furnishes temporary and contingent workers) but who "perform services" for a "service recipient." Instead of paying the leased employees directly, the service recipient pays the employees' wages (and an agency commission) to the leasing organization, which handles payroll functions including tax withholding.

However, the leased employees will be treated as employees of the service recipient when it comes to determining whether the service recipient's pension plans discriminate in favor of highly compensated employees. If the leasing organization maintains a pension plan for the employees it leases out, its contributions or benefits are treated as if they came from the service recipient for the service recipient's discrimination tests. The leasing organization's plan must count all service by leased employees for the leasing organization (even when they're leased out to a service recipient) with respect to coverage, vesting, contributions, and benefits under its own plan.

Service recipients have to count leased employees when they test their plans under the minimum participation, age and service, vesting, and top-heavy rules. They must be taken into account when computing limits on compensation and benefits and whether contributions to the plan are deductible. Furthermore, the leased employee will be treated as an employee under the Code's rules for fringe benefits such as group term life insurance, accident and health insurance, cafeteria plans, and dependent care assistance. Leased employees also have COBRA rights (they can elect continuation of health coverage).

For I.R.C. § 414(n) purposes, leased employees are those who provide services that last more than a year to a service recipient in conformity with the service recipient's agreement with the leasing organization. As a result of amendments made by the Small Business Job Protection Act of 1996, the test for 1997 and later years is whether the service recipient provides the primary direction or control for the work. (Service for related companies, such as the service recipient's controlled group of corporations, is aggregated with service for the service recipient.)

These rules relate to "substantially full-time service," which is defined as 1,500 hours of service in a 12-month period, or a job that is equivalent to 75% of the hours that the service recipient's actual employees put in during a 12-month period. In other words, after a year of the recipient's full-time work, the leased employee is treated as the service recipient's employee for pension testing purposes. However, if the worker is a common-law employee for other purposes, this safe harbor cannot apply.

Even if leased employees have to be counted in determining whether the service recipient's pension plans are discriminatory, they do not have to be offered participation in the plan until they satisfy any conditions for plan participation lawfully imposed by the plan (e.g., if the employer imposes an age-21 minimum for participation, and a leased employee starts working for the employer at age 19, completing a year of service at age 20, participation can be delayed until the leased employee reaches 21).

To qualify for the safe harbor, the service recipient must get 20% or less of its rank-and-file workforce (that is, workers who are not HCEs) through leasing—and the leasing organization must have its own qualified pension plan that fits particularly stringent criteria. The leasing organization's plan must be a money purchase plan. It must not be integrated with Social Security. The leasing organization's employees must be able to participate as soon as they are hired by the organization. They must be fully vested immediately. Furthermore, the leasing organization must contribute at least 10% of compensation for each plan participant.

Although it is good practice to have individuals you believe to be independent contractors sign waivers agreeing that they are not entitled to participate in pension and benefit plans, these waivers are not sufficient if, under otherwise applicable legal principles, they really are common-law employees.

See § 1.11. for additional discussion of issues of shared employment.

§ 4.24 COMMUNICATING WITH EMPLOYEES

The subject of communications and notification to employees rates a chapter of its own (see Chapter 11), so here it will merely be noted that the plan administrator is responsible for reporting and disclosure, and can be held liable if appropriate disclosures are not made.

ERISA permits three methods of communication:

- Giving each employee a copy of the plan itself;

- Giving each employee a booklet containing the Summary Plan Description (SPD), describing the features of the plan in understandable language;

- Posting a notice on the bulletin board to inform employees that the company has adopted a plan, and where copies of the plan documents can be consulted.

Nearly all plans adopt the second alternative. The actual plan document is a lengthy, highly technical legal document, and doesn't do much to inform the average employee about rights and obligations under the plan.

To an ever-increasing extent, employers are permitted to use e-mail and secure Websites to deliver information to employees.

Under the PPA, the requirement that defined benefit plans issue Summary Annual Reports (SARs) was replaced by the requirement of a different disclosure document, the Annual Funding Notice. (Defined benefit plans such as owner-only plans and professional service company plans that are not insured by the PBGC do not have to issue Annual Funding Notices.) EBSA final rules published February 2, 2015, cover the annual notice of funded status for defined benefit plans. About 27,000 plans are subject to this regulation; they have about 43.7 million participants and beneficiaries. The annual notices must disclose the benefits eligible for PBGC guarantees; limitations on the guarantee; and when those limitations apply. Single-employer plans must summarize the plan termination rules. Multi-employer plans must summarize the insolvency rules. In general, notices must be furnished within 120 days of the end of the plan year, but plans with 100 or fewer participants can defer the notice until the filing date (as extended) for the annual report. The final rules include one model notice for single-employer plans and one for multi-employer plans. [80 Fed. Reg. 5625 (Feb. 2, 2015)]

Plan administrators of individual account plans (e.g., 401(k) plans) informed EBSA that it was difficult to make the mandatory disclosures on an annual basis. In response, the rule was changed to allow the "annual" investment and plan-related information to be given to participants in participant-directed individual account plans such as 401(k) plans at least once in any 14-month period. The actual disclosures remain unchanged; all that has changed is the schedule. However, EBSA will withdraw this rule and issue another final rule if the comments are negative. [Direct Final Rule, 80 Fed. Reg. 14301 (Mar. 19, 2015); see EBSA News, *US Labor Department Announces Additional Flexibility to 401(k) Plans Furnishing Annual Investment Information to Workers,* <http://www.dol.gov/ebsa/newsroom/2015/ebsa031815.html> (Mar. 18, 2015)]

PPACA mandates that certain employers provide a Summary of Benefits and Coverage (SBC). In early 2017, although it was anticipated that a bill to replace PPACA would be voted on in Congress, it was withdrawn shortly before the scheduled vote.

§ 4.25 FIDUCIARY DUTY

A fiduciary is anyone who has charge of someone else's property or finances. Fiduciaries have legal duties to act honestly, prudently, and in the best interests of the owner of the assets. Pension plan fiduciaries have a duty to invest intelligently, selecting a diversified portfolio of appropriate investments that do not involve an excessive degree of risk.

ERISA obligates fiduciaries to administer the plan exclusively in the interests of plan participants and their beneficiaries. Specifically, if there is a situation in which one strategy would be most beneficial to the participants and another strategy would be most beneficial to the corporation sponsoring the plan, the fiduciaries must choose the first course of action, not the second.

If the plan has more than one named fiduciary, they are jointly and severally liable. Someone who alleges fiduciary impropriety can sue any one fiduciary, all of them, or any combination, and can collect the entire amount of liability from each one or from any combination of fiduciaries—no matter which fiduciary was actually at fault. The harshness of this high standard is relieved somewhat by the fact that fiduciaries who are sued can bring fiduciaries who weren't sued into the lawsuit, and can make them pay their fair share.

In recent years, fiduciary liability has been one of the most active areas of employment-related litigation (see Chapter 15 for details). See § 6.08 for discussion of DOL's attempt to treat retirement advisors as fiduciaries. In particular, allegations of breach of fiduciary duty have often been made against plan administrators and plan investment committees based on a theory that it was imprudent to retain employer stock as a plan investment, or to fail to warn employees of various factors contributing to decline in the value of the stock. However, these allegations are very seldom successful.

In a mid-2014 Supreme Court case, plaintiffs charged that fiduciaries of an ESOP plan, who invested primarily in employer stock, violated their duty of prudence. According to the plaintiffs, they should have known that investing in employer stock was too risky—not only because of their status as officers, but because of publicly available information. The Supreme Court rejected the presumption of prudence that had generally been applied in "stock drop" cases. The

Supreme Court held that ESOP fiduciaries have the same duties as other fiduciaries, although they are relieved of the obligation of diversifying the plan's portfolio. The Supreme Court held that, to make out a claim of breach of the duty of prudence, the complaint must plausibly allege a lawful alternative course of conduct that would have yielded better results. Fiduciaries never have an obligation to violate securities laws by using inside information. [*Fifth Third Bancorp et al. v. Dudenhoeffer*, 134 S. Ct. 2459 (2014). The case was settled in March 2016. The settlement, which received preliminary approval of the district court, calls for six million dollars to be placed into an account to be distributed to class members. The Fifth Third Stock Fund will be frozen, with no new contributions accepted. Participants who are 20% or more invested in that fund will be notified about the benefits of diversification: *Dudenhoeffer v. Fifth Third Bancorp*, No. 1:08-CV-538-SSSB (Stipulation of settlement, S.D. Ohio Mar. 15, 2016); see Rebecca Moore, *Famous Fifth Third Stock Drop Suit Reaches Settlement*, plansponsor .com (Mar. 24, 2016)]

Since the Supreme Court *Dudenhoeffer* decision, the National Center for Employee Ownership's review of litigation about employer stock choices shows a major decline in litigation. Only 21 new cases were decided, 17 of them about ESOPs. Few of these cases offered significant new guidance to planners:

- *Tatum v. R.J. Reynolds Tobacco Co.*, No. 1:02-cv-00373-NCT-LPA, 2016 U.S. Dist. LEXIS 19536 (M.D.N.C. Feb. 18, 2016): rules for the employer, finding that the fiduciaries acted reasonably under any standard of review; The Fourth Circuit affirmed in 2017, holding that the same standard applies for investment and divestment: *Tatum v. R.J. Reynolds Tobacco Co.*, No. 16-1293 (4th Cir. Apr. 28, 2017).

- *Coburn v. Evercore Trust Co., N.A.*, 160 F. Supp. 3d 361 (D.D.C. 2016): trustees are not required to guess, on the basis of publicly available information, if a stock was over- or underpriced

- *Amgen v. Harris*, 136 S. Ct. 994 (2016) (per curiam): the Supreme Court once again reversed the Ninth Circuit's decision about the prudence of continuing to hold employer stock. When the case was remanded from the Supreme Court's earlier decision, the Ninth Circuit held that the fiduciaries should have removed employer stock from the plan, which would have had the same effect on the market as disclosing information about business problems. The Supreme Court held in 2016 that the complaint did not allege a breach of the duty of prudence.

- *Allen v. GreatBanc Trust Co.*, 835 F.3d 670 (7th Cir. 2016): the Seventh Circuit did not require plaintiffs to satisfy the *Dudenhoeffer* standard, and permitted them to continue their suit. [Plansponsor editors, *Key Recent Decisions in Employer Stock Plan Litigation*, plansponsor.com (Sept. 6, 2016)]

- In another much-litigated case, the district court held that fiduciaries breached their duty. On appeal, the Eighth Circuit held that the district court erred by not evaluating different methods of measuring the loss due to the breach. At an earlier stage of the case, the Eighth Circuit proposed an alternative calculation for comparing the funds in the plan to allegedly superior choices. On remand, the district court felt obligated to use that method but, on appeal, the Eighth Circuit held that the district court should have evaluated several possible ways to measure the plan's losses before selecting one. [*Tussey v. ABB, Inc.*, 850 F.3d 95 (8th Cir. 2017); see Practicallaw.com, *Eighth Circuit Remands Tussey v. ABB, Inc. for a Second Time, Instructing District Court to Evaluate Methods of Measuring Plan Losses Caused by Fiduciary Breach* (Mar. 14, 2017) (benefitslink.com)]

§ 4.26 BANKRUPTCY EFFECTS

Confusion may arise because the Bankruptcy Code uses the term "plan" to refer to the reorganization plan resolving creditors' claims, and not to ERISA plans. A Chapter 11 filing, in which the debtor continues to do business while reorganizing, sometimes affects ERISA plans, and sometimes does not; it is common for employers to modify or terminate ERISA plans as part of the reorganization process. Employee benefit claims against a bankrupt employer may include unpaid wages, vacation pay, severance pay, Worker's Compensation, insurance, and retirement benefits. Claims against the bankruptcy estate for wages and pension or welfare benefits are unsecured claims, and are paid according to the Bankruptcy Code's system of priorities. Administrative claims, including wages, salaries, and commissions for services performed after the bankruptcy filing receive second priority.

Before the 2005 bankruptcy reform legislation was passed, each employee was entitled to a third priority claim of up to $4,925 for wages, salaries, commissions, vacation, sick leave, and severance pay relating to the period 90 days before the bankruptcy filing or 90 days before the cessation of the employer's business—whichever came first. The Bankruptcy Abuse Prevention and Consumer Protection Act of 2005 (BAPCPA), Pub. L. No. 109-8, increased the amount to $10,000 and the period to 180 days before the filing or cessation of business, but makes it a fourth priority claim. This amount is inflation-indexed; the 2015 level is $12,475 and the 2016 amount is $12,850.

Defined benefit plans, including 401(k) plans, are treated the same way as other employee benefits when priorities are set, based on whether the contributions relate to pre- or post-petition services. However, to motivate employees, employers often petition the bankruptcy court for permission to make contributions that were pending at the time of filing such as deferrals withheld from paychecks but not yet deposited into the 401(k) plan trust.

Bankruptcy Code § 1114 provides special protection for retirees' non-pension benefits (health coverage, life insurance, disability insurance). In effect, they become super-priority administrative expenses and a court order is required for the debtor or bankruptcy trustee to modify them. [Kenni B. Merritt, *Employee Benefits in Bankruptcy: The Employer's Perspective and the Employee's Perspective*, Oklahoma Bar J. (Jan. 2005) (benefitslink.com)]

The IRS finalized regulations under the Code § 411(d)(6) anti-cutback rules, effective for plan amendments adopted and effective after November 8, 2012. A single employer defined benefit plan subject to ERISA § 4021 can be amended to eliminate lump sum or other optional forms of benefit that accelerate payment after bankruptcy. The PBGC and the bankruptcy court must determine that the plan would go through a distress or involuntary termination without the elimination of the optional benefit. The PBGC must also determine that the plan isn't sufficient for guaranteed benefits. If the sponsor eliminates an optional form of benefit under these regulations, and the plan does not offer other options with substantial survivor benefits, the sponsor can add other options to provide those benefits as part of the amendment that eliminates the lump-sum distribution option. The entire plan amendment is considered together in determining if the amendment can take effect in accordance with § 436(c). [Kristen Heinzinger, *IRS Finalizes Relief for Bankrupt DB Sponsors*, plansponsor.com (Nov. 8, 2012)]

In late 2012, the DOL proposed to extend its Abandoned Plan Program to permit Chapter 7 bankruptcy trustees to distribute assets from bankrupt companies' individual account retirement plans. The proposal sets out streamlined provisions for terminating such plans and distributing their benefits. The Abandoned Plan Program was created in 2006, but applied only to financial institutions holding the assets of abandoned plans. [DOL/EBSA, *Fact Sheet: Proposed Amendments to Abandoned Plan Program* (Dec. 2012) (benefitslink.com)]

There are two kinds of bankruptcy that may have an effect on pension plans: the employer's or an employee's. If the employer is one who seeks bankruptcy protection, an argument could be made under Bankruptcy Code § 547 that the employer's contributions to a qualified plan during the 90 days before the bankruptcy filing are "preferential transfers," and therefore should be returned to the bankruptcy estate and preserved so that creditors can make claims on them.

When it comes to the employee's bankruptcy, a highly relevant case is *Patterson v. Shumate* [504 U.S. 753 (1992)], which provides that ERISA plan law constitutes "applicable non-bankruptcy law" that will permit amounts in the plan to be excluded from the bankruptcy estate. The Supreme Court also held, in its 2005 *Rousey v. Jacoway* decision [544 U.S. 320 (2005)], that IRAs are more akin to qualified plans than bank accounts from which withdrawals may be freely made. Therefore, the Supreme Court extended the exemption of qualified plans from the bankruptcy estate to IRAs. But this is only true of the debtor's own IRA, or an IRA inherited from a spouse. IRAs inherited from someone other than the debtor's spouse (e.g., a parent or sibling) are subject to claims of the debtor's creditors. [*Clark v. Rameker*, 134 S. Ct. 2242 (2014)]

BAPCPA contains a number of provisions affecting both employer and employee bankruptcies:

- Makes the employee's interest in qualified plans and IRAs exempt from the bankruptcy estate. The IRA exemption (which includes both conventional and Roth IRAs) is limited to $1 million—but the $1 million figure does not include amounts rolled over into an IRA from a qualified plan;

- As noted above, limits severance and retention payments to corporate insiders and makes it easier for the business' bankruptcy trustee to set aside preferential payments made to insiders;

- Increases the employer's ability to continue to collect repayments of plan loans from employees who have sought bankruptcy protection;

- Gives the bankruptcy court the power to cancel the employer's modifications of its retiree health benefits made during 180 days before filing of a bankruptcy petition, although if the court is persuaded that the balance of equities favors leaving the modifications in place, they can be affirmed.

Internal Revenue Code § 401(a)(33) forbids certain plan amendments if the plan is covered by ERISA § 4021. Plan benefits may not be increased while the plan sponsor is a bankruptcy debtor. The plan cannot be amended to increase the plan's liabilities because of an increase in benefits, any change in the accrual of benefits, or any change in the rate at which benefits become nonforfeitable. The ban applies only if the amendments in question take effect before the effective date of the employer's plan of reorganization.

The restrictions do not apply if the plan would otherwise have a funded current liability percentage of at least 100%; if the IRS determines that the amendment is reasonable and increases benefits only slightly; or if the amendment is actually required to conform to changes in tax law. The PPA's limitations on activities of "at risk" plans will also affect many companies that are contemplating bankruptcy or have already filed for protection.

§ 4.27 FACTORS IN CHOOSING A PLAN FORM

In deciding which form of plan to adopt, or whether to convert a plan or terminate an old plan and adopt a new one, the employer must balance many considerations, including financial and tax factors and the expected effect of a plan in motivating employee behavior (including retiring at the time most convenient for the employer).

Participants in a defined benefit plan know what their eventual pension will be if they stay with the plan until normal retirement age. If they terminate employment earlier, the vesting rules also control the size of the pension that will be paid later on, when they reach retirement age. This degree of certainty is valuable, but retirees have the problems caused by having a fixed income that does not reflect investment results.

In contrast, defined contribution plan participants know how large their account is at any given time. They can make projections of how large it will grow, based on predictions about interest rates and stock market trends. Market risk shifts from the employer to the employee and future retiree. Defined contribution plans also offer more portability: the contents of the employee's account from Plan A can simply be rolled over to Plan B when the employee stops being a Company A employee and is hired by Company B.

Before the 2008 recession began, there had been a very large-scale shift from defined benefit to defined contribution plans. One effect of the recession, however, was to increase interest in defined benefit plans and in features such as automatic enrollment and investment advice to participants that make defined contribution plans work more like defined benefit plans.

Defined benefits, but not defined contribution plans, are covered by the Pension Benefit Guaranty Corporation's (PBGC's) insurance program. The PBGC insures that employees will receive their pension benefits, at least the part that does not exceed a maximum figure. In exchange, employers must pay insurance premiums to the PBGC. If an underfunded defined benefit plan is terminated, the PBGC takes over part of the obligation to pay benefits.

About 85% of retirees who receive their benefits from the PBGC receive the full amount of benefit they were promised. For 2015–2016 (because of low inflation, there was no increase in 2016; PBGC increases are tied to Social Security COLAs, and there was no 2016 COLA), the PBGC's maximum guaranteed monthly benefit for a 65-year-old retiree is $5,011.36 a month for a straight life annuity, $4,510.22 for a joint and 50% survivor annuity (if both spouses are the same age; otherwise, actuarial adjustments are made); for a 75-year-old, it is $15,234.53 (one life), $13,711.08 (joint and survivor). At younger ages, the maximum monthly guarantee is $3,257.38 (one life), $2,931.64 (joint and survivor). The lowest age given in the PBGC's table is 45, when the one-life maximum guarantee is $1,252.84, and joint and survivor is $1,127.56 a month. [PBGC, *Maximum Monthly Guarantee Tables*, <http://www.pbgc.gov/prac/mortality-retirement-and-pv-max-guarantee/present-guarantee.html#2016>; see Hazel Bradford, *PBGC Maximum Guarantee Unchanged for 2016*, PIOnline .com (Oct 29, 2015), available at <http://www.pionline.com/article/20151029/ONLINE/151029823/pbgc-maximum-guarantee-unchanged-for-2016>]

For 2017, the guarantee rose 7.1% over 2015–2016 levels. The maximum single life annuity at age 55 is $28,994 and the maximum joint and survivor annuity (where both spouses are the same age) is $26,095. At age 60, the corresponding figures are $41,881 and $37,693. At 65, the figures are $64,432 and $57,989, and at 70 it is $106,957 and $96,261. The guarantee for the multi-employer plan program is not indexed, so it is unchanged. For 20 years of service, the limit is 100% of the first $2,640 of benefit, 75% of the next $7,920, yielding a maximum of $8,580. For 35 years' service, it is 100% of the first $4,620, and 75% of the next $13,860, for a maximum of $15,015 a year.

In late 2016, the PBGC reported that more than 40 million people in private sector plans were covered, and the PBGC pays benefits to about 1.5 million people in failed pension plans. [PBGC.gov, PBGC No. 16-16, *PBGC Guarantee Limit for Single-Employer Plans Increases for 2017* (Oct. 28, 2016) (benefitslink .com). Full table is available at <http://www.pbgc.gov/wr/benefits/guaranteed-benefits/maximum-guarantee.html?source=govdelivery&utm_medium=email& utm_source=govdelivery>.]

In early 2017, the PBGC announced that it was taking over the Road Carriers Local Pension Fund, a multi-employer plan. The PBGC warned that there are more than a million participants in about 200 plans that are expected to go broke over the next 20 years. PBGC Director Tom Reeder estimated that the insurance program covering insolvent multi-employer plans would itself run out of money by 2025. If and when the program does run out of money, its only source of income will be incoming premiums, so it will have to reduce benefit payments severely. The Local 707 Fund benefits were cut back to the PBGC guarantee limit. The average guaranteed monthly benefit was $570, versus a $1,313 average under the plan. [Rebecca Moore, *Benefit Cuts Could Hit More Than One Million Multiemployer Plan Members,* plansponsor.com (Mar. 2, 2017); Meep, *When Multiemployer Pensions Fail: Teamsters Local 707,* Stump (Feb. 28, 2017) (benefitslink.com)]

See § 17.01[B] for discussion of suspension of benefits under the Multi-Employer Pension Relief Act (MPRA).

Before the PPA, a number of companies adopted cash balance plans (which combine some features of defined-benefit plans with some features more typical of a defined-contribution plan) even though the tax status of these plans was ambiguous, and it was uncertain whether they violated the Age Discrimination in Employment Act. The PPA makes it clear that cash balance plans (as long as they are operated in accordance with the rules!) are tax-compliant and do not discriminate against older workers. (See Chapter 7.) However, this favorable treatment is prospective only. Most courts have ruled in favor of cash balance plans established before the PPA took effect—but some have found ERISA and/or ADEA violations.

An early 2012 article suggests that a company that has maxed out its 401(k) plan but still has steady cash flow and discretionary income that could be used for benefits might consider implementing a cash balance plan. For plan participants in their fifties who got a late start on retirement planning, even if they make catch-up contributions, they could not save as much in a 401(k) plan as in a cash balance plan. A cash balance plan can also be used as a mechanism for a young partner to indirectly buy out an older partner who wants to retire. [Tom Sigmund, Kegler, Brown, *How To Determine If a Cash Balance Pension Plan Is Right for Your Company,* Hill & Ritter Smart Business (Jan. 3, 2012) (benefitslink.com)]

In 1981, Herbert Whitehouse (then an HR executive at Johnson & Johnson) was one of the first advocates of 401(k)s. He thought the plans would be useful supplements to defined benefit plans and did not anticipate that cost-cutting companies would use 401(k) plans to replace pensions. Whitehouse, and some other people who helped popularize 401(k) plans, now regret the results, saying that they were too optimistic and did not intend 401(k) plans to be the primary source of retirement income. Some of the early backers now favor either forced savings or requiring employers to contribute more.

The conventional assumption during the bull market in the 1980s and 1990s was that workers could safeguard their retirement by placing 3% of their compensation into a 401(k) account because investment returns would be around 7%—a level that has proved to be unrealistic, especially when the impact of fees and costs is included, and after recessions in the 2000s. [Timothy W. Martin, *The Champions of the 401(k) Lament the Revolution They Started*, WSJ.com (Jan. 2, 2017)]

CHAPTER 5

DEFINED BENEFIT PLANS

§ 5.01   INTRODUCTION

This chapter deals, in detail, with issues that are specific to defined benefit plans. See Chapter 4 for background issues on pensions, Chapter 6 for defined contribution plans and 401(k) plans, and Chapter 7 for cash balance plans.

One of the most important changes in the employment/retirement landscape has been the transition from the defined benefit plan to the defined contribution plan. Major legislation, the Pension Protection Act (PPA; Pub. L. No. 109-280), has been passed to improve the stability of the remaining defined benefit plans.

However, due to financial problems occurring after the passage of the legislation, it was deemed necessary to relax some of the more onerous requirements, by passing the Worker, Retiree, and Employer Recovery Act of 2008 (WRERA; Pub. L. No. 110-458); the Preservation of Access to Care for Medicare Beneficiaries and Pension Relief Act of 2010 (PRA; Pub. L. No. 111-192), the Moving Ahead for Progress in the 21st Century Act, aka MAP-21 (Pub. L. No. 112-141); the Highway and Transportation Funding Act of 2014 (HATFA) (Pub. L No. 113-159); and the Consolidated and Further Continuing Appropriations Act, aka "Cromnibus" (Pub. L. No. 113-483).

The Employee Benefits Security Administration's (EBSA's) analysis Form 5500 data from 2014 shows that there were 89.9 million active participants in qualified plans, but only 14.5 million of them were in defined benefit plans. In that year, the number of defined benefit plans increased 1.6% but defined contribution plans, which grew by only 0.5%, remained the dominant plan form. In 2014, defined benefit plans had assets of about $3.0 trillion, 4.2% higher than in 2013. Contributions to defined benefit plans fell 13.9%, to $97.9 billion. In 2014, all retirement plans disbursed $650 billion, $221.6 billion of which came from defined benefit plans (either going directly to participants and beneficiaries or to insurers in de-risking transactions). Disbursements were 3.5% lower than in 2013. However, defined benefit plans disbursed $123.7 billion more than they collected in contributions, exacerbating their financial problems. [Rebecca Moore, *DB Plans Are Not Totally Disappearing,* plansponsor.com (Oct. 31, 2016)]

At press time in 2017, shortly after President Trump's inauguration, the administration's pro-business initiatives included a freeze on new regulations and a directive to eliminate large numbers of existing regulations.

The Wall Street Journal reported in 2014 that pension plans are facing a "double whammy": a significant increase in the cost of regulatory compliance (e.g., much higher Pension Benefit Guarantee Corporation (PBGC) premiums), and increasing life expectancies (requiring more years of pension payments). The article predicts a life expectancy of 87.9 years for male retirees and 90.1 years for female retirees by 2029. These factors help explain the shift away from defined benefit plans. In 1979, 38% of private sector workers were covered by a defined benefit plan; in 2011, only 14% were. Aon Hewitt estimated that increasing life expectancy will require the sponsors of defined benefit plans to increase the pension obligations on their balance sheets by some 7%. Some employers that still have defined benefit plans are taking steps like freezing the plan, moving workers to defined contribution plans, or buying annuities to satisfy defined benefit obligations. [Vipal Monga, *Pension Plans Brace for a One-Two Punch*, WSJ.com (Mar. 24, 2014)]

Hybrid plans are defined benefit plans that accrue benefits under a formula, but define the benefit as a lump sum (the account balance) and not as a monthly payment after retirement. Funding of hybrid plans is predictable for the employer, and some employees find them easier to understand than traditional defined benefit plans. Cash balance plans (see Chapter 7) are the most popular type of hybrid plans. The benefit is based on a percentage of pay credited each year, plus interest at the plan's interest crediting rate. A Pension Equity Plan (PEP) posts percentage credits to the employee's account each year, defining the lump-sum balance at retirement as the total of the percentages multiplied by the employee's final average pay. Final regulations on hybrid plans were published in 2010: see 75 Fed. Reg. 64123 (Oct. 19, 2010).

Additional guidance was furnished in September 2014 by T.D. 9693 and final and proposed IRS regulations about hybrid defined benefit plans were published in September 2014 explaining the changes required by the PPA and WRERA. (A hybrid defined benefit plan is a defined benefit plan that expresses a participant's accrued benefit as the balance of a hypothetical account for the participant, or the current value of an accumulated percentage of the participant's final average compensation.) T.D. 9693 has added some new rates that satisfy the market rate of return requirement.

The September 2014 regulations address issues that were not covered in T.D. 9505. T.D. 9693 allows the 1331/3% rule of Code § 411(b)(1)(B) can be used by defined benefit plans that use a variable rate (possibly negative) to adjust benefits to be applied for plan years beginning on or after January 1, 2012. The taxpayer can also elect to apply an earlier date.

The age discrimination rules change for plan years that begin on or after January 1, 2016. If the annual benefit payable before Normal Retirement Age (NRA) is greater for a participant than the annual benefit for the corresponding form of benefit for any similarly situated older person who is at or before NRA, the excess benefit is not considered part of the subsidized portion of an early retirement benefit and is not disregarded for purposes of determining if age discrimination has occurred.

Related proposed regulations were released at the same time explaining that when a hybrid plan fails to satisfy § 411(b)(1)(H), the rules that forbid reduction of benefit accrual because of attainment of any age, where the plan's interest rate credit exceeds a market rate of return and the amendment decreases a participant's accrued benefit. An amendment that eliminates or reduces an early retirement benefit or optional form of benefit for service before the amendment is deemed to reduce the accrued benefit. The proposals note that the rules governing market rate of return conflict with the anti-cutback rule, so the IRS will permit a plan whose interest crediting rate is non-compliant to be amended as to benefits already accrued, so the interest crediting rate can be brought into line. [T.D. 9693, 2014-41 I.R.B. 596]

As Chapters 10 and 14 show, the IRS is reducing the scope of situations in which it will issue determination letters; this is a powerful incentive for employers to adopt pre-approved plans. See Rev. Proc. 2016-37, 2016-29 I.R.B. 136: as of January 1, 2017, most individually designed plans will only be able to obtain a determination letter on initial qualification, on termination, or in unusual circumstances. The six-year cycle for making amendments to pre-approved plans is not affected by this change. [Rebecca Moore, *IRS Officially Ends Determination Letter Program*, plansponsor.com (June 30, 2016); Bradley Arant Boult Cummings, *IRS Issues Guidance on Determination Letter Program* (July 5, 2016) (benefitslink.com); Raymond P. Turner, *Determination Letter Rationing: IRS Reveals the Brave New World*, Jackson Lewis PC (July 10, 2016), available at Lexology.com]

IRS's pre-approved plan program has been expanded to include cash balance plans. Employers with individually designed plans should use IRS Form 8905, Certification of Intent to Adopt a Pre-Approved Plan, if they want to switch to a pre-approved cash balance plan. [Rev. Proc. 2015-36, 2015-27 I.R.B. 20; IRS Employee Plan News No. 2015-6 (June 10, 2015); see ERISA Lawyer Blog, *Employee Benefits-IRS Announces That Its Pre-Approved Plan Program Is Expanded to Include Cash Balance Plans and ESOPs* (June 2015) (benefitslink .com)]

The IRS continued to provide guidance on the transition. Rev. Proc. 2016-37, 2016-29 I.R.B. 136 explains how IRS will handle the changes required by law: the IRS will publish a Required Amendments List each year, and will publish guidance throughout the year, including model amendments. The IRS will also publish an Operational Compliance List highlighting changes in the law that plans must comply with before the deadline for plan amendments, but the IRS will no longer require interim amendments to reflect the items on the list. Terminating plans must be amended reflecting all changes in the law as of the time of termination, whether or not the item is on the Required Amendments List. Announcement 2016-32, 2016-40 I.R.B. 434 calls for comments about what IRS should do to improve compliance in the post-determination-letter environment when the program ends; Rev. Proc. 2016-51 explains how the Employee Plans Compliance Resolution System (EPCRS) of correcting plan failures (see § 15.19), which previously operated based on determination letters, will function going forward. [Lois Wagman Colbert et. al., *IRS Provides Guidance for the Post-Determination Letter Era*, Kilpatrick Townsend (Oct. 19, 2016), available at Lexology.com]

The IRS launched a program for pre-approved (PA) plans, combining Master & Prototype Plans and Volume Submitter Plans in a single program that can be used by either defined benefit or defined contribution plan sponsors. PA plans can be either standardized plans, requiring use of the IRS documents without alterations, or non-standardized plans with some design flexibility. PA plans are considered qualified during the six-year remedial amendment period that runs from February 1, 2017 to January 31, 2017. [Rev. Proc. 2017-41, 2017-29 I.R.B. 92; see Susan E. Stoffer et al., *IRS Reorganizes Pre-Approved Plan Opinion Letter Program,* Nelson Mullins Riley & Scarborough LLP (July 12, 2017), available at Lexology.com; Groom Law Group, *IRS Revamps Pre-Approved Qualified Plan Program,*(July 27, 2017) (benefitslink.com)]

As a result of PPA § 504, employers must post actuarial information about the funding status of defined benefit plans on their corporate intranet (if they have one; it is not necessary to create an intranet just for this purpose). The posting must include basic information about the plan, and the actuarial information about the plan. However, if the employer chooses to post the entire form rather than just the mandatory information, Form SSA should be removed, because it contains the Social Security numbers of plan participants. The DOL informally indicated that the requirement does not apply to defined contribution plans such as 401(k)s. [Timothy D.S. Goodman, Dorsey & Whitney LLP Resources, *New Law Requires Employers with Defined Benefit Plans to Post Information on Their Intranet* (Nov. 2, 2009) (benefitslink.com)]

[A] PPA and Later Changes

Although it contains other types of provisions, the Pension Protection Act (PPA; Pub. L. No. 109-280) takes defined benefit plan reform as its central mission. Major changes wrought by the PPA include:

- Changing the rules for the interest rate assumptions sponsors must use in plan funding and operations.

- Amending the funding rules, so that plans will have to be 100% funded (earlier law allowed funding at a 90% level). This change is being phased in gradually to give plan sponsors time to adjust.

- Sponsors must meet "funding targets" by making at least the "minimum required contribution" required for the plan, a calculation involving the plan's "target normal cost."

- Contributions over and above the minimum required contribution give rise to "credit balances" which can be applied toward the required minimum contribution for later years.

- Valuation of plan assets can either be at fair market value or "smoothed" over a 24-month period, but values must always fall within 90%–110% of FMV.

- Special rules are imposed on the activities of "at-risk" plans (i.e., those that are at risk of becoming unable to pay benefits as they come due). Plans with fewer than 500 participants are exempt from the at-risk plan rules.

However, these requirements were increasingly burdensome in light of economic conditions in 2008 and later, so a number of relief provisions have been adopted.

President Bush signed WRERA, the Worker, Retiree, and Employer Recovery Act of 2008, Pub. L. No. 110-458, on December 23, 2008. WRERA provides PPA technical corrections and relief from some of the more onerous PPA requirements. The PPA required plans to become 100% funded within seven years. Businesses asked for temporary relief, but Congress made it permanent, allowing companies with major investment losses to come into compliance without reaching the 100% level within the seven-year time frame. [Mary Williams Walsh, *Pensions Get a Reprieve in Congress*, <http://www.times.com> (Dec. 12, 2008)]

The PPA replaced the concept of the funding standard account with a requirement that contributions each year must be at least as great as the target normal cost (the cost of the benefits that accrued during the year) plus the amount needed to amortize the funding shortfall, as it stood at the beginning of the year, over a period of approximately seven years. Tougher funding requirements were imposed on at-risk plans.

WRERA provides that expenses paid directly by the plan are included in the target normal cost. Under the PPA, the plan's contributions and distributions had to be included in the calculation; WRERA also allows consideration of expected earnings. WRERA requires the same interest rate assumptions to be used to calculate the funding target percentage and the target normal cost.

WRERA expands the IRS's authority to issue guidance about how to determine the plan's funded status for years before 2008, which is important for determining if plan is at risk.

As a result of WRERA, the restrictions on lump-sum distributions do not apply to mandatory cash-out of de minimis amounts under $5,000. To determine whether benefit accruals must cease in 2009, the plan can use either its 2008 or 2009 AFTAP—whichever is greater.

Section 415(b) requires benefits that are not in the form of a life annuity beginning between age 62 and age 65 to be converted to that form using actuarial assumptions prescribed by the IRS. The PPA said that the § 415(b) mortality assumptions would be based on the standard table for group annuity contracts, but WRERA requires instead that the table for converting benefit accruals to lump sums under § 407(e) must be used. [See also T.D. 9467, 2009-50 I.R.B. 760, dealing with post-PPA funding requirements for single-employer defined benefit plans.]

In mid-2010, with financial conditions still hazardous, Congress provided additional relief for defined benefit plans. The Preservation of Access to Care for Medicare Beneficiaries and Pension Relief Act (PRA; Pub. L. No. 111-192) gives employers two choices. The employer could select two years in which to pay only interest on the plan's funding shortfall (rather than contributing enough to actually reduce the shortfall as required by the PPA), or amortize the shortfall for any two plan years between 2008 and 2011 over 15 years. [Rebecca Moore, *Obama Signs Pension Relief Bill*, plansponsor.com (June 25, 2010). See also Notice 2011-3, 2011-3 I.R.B. 324 (Dec. 22, 2010)]

Important defined benefit plan provisions were included in MAP-21, the Moving Ahead for Progress in the 21st Century Act. [Hazel Bradford, Pensions & Investments, *Congress Passes Pension Changes in Highway Package* (June 29, 2012) (benefitslink.com)]

MAP-21 extends the period used to calculate interest rates to 25 years, so the recent period, with extremely low interest rates, has a lesser impact on the calculations. The interest-rate change is expected to save the typical defined benefit plan 15%–25% of its contribution requirement. MAP-21 also increases the PBGC premiums and allows overfunded plans to transfer money to a 401(h) plan providing either health benefits or group-term life insurance for retirees. [Rebecca Moore, *Congress Passes Bill with Pension Funding Relief*, plansponsor.com (June 29, 2012); Buck Consultants FYI, *2012 Pension Plan Funding Stabilization Finally a Reality* (July 6, 2012) (benefitslink.com)]

Mid-2014 legislation, the Highway Transportation Funding Act of 2014 (Pub. L. No. 113-159) continues the MAP-21 relief by continuing to permit "pension smoothing," a form of stabilization. Smoothing reduces the employer's obligations with respect to minimum funding by adjusting the interest rates used to calculate the minimum funding obligation. The practical effect is that sponsors' contributions can be calculated based on average interest rates for a longer period of time, not just the most recent years, when interest rates were very low. The lower the interest rates, the more the employer must contribute to satisfy its funding obligations.

Under the 2014 legislation, for calendar years 2012–2017, the "corridor" is a minimum percentage of 90%, a maximum percentage of 110%. For 2018, the corresponding figures are 85% and 115%; for 2019, 80% and 120%; for 2020, 75% and 125%; after 2020, 70% and 130%. However, these smoothing rules do not apply to bankrupt companies: see Code § 463(d)(2) for benefit restrictions. [Groom Law Group Benefits Brief, *Extension of Pension Interest Rate Smoothing Relief Clears Congress Before August Recess*, <http://www.groom.com/media/publication/1444_Extension_of_Pension_Interest_Rate.pdf> (Aug. 1, 2014); Vipal Monga, *Welcome to the World of "Pension Smoothing,"* WSJ.com (Aug. 11, 2014)]

Final regulations, at 81 Fed. Reg. 15432 (Mar. 23, 2016) change the name "FTAP" to "4010 funding target attainment percentage." The regulations also state that the plan's funding target for § 4010(d) reporting purposes is calculated without using the MAP-21, HATFA, and BBA 2015 stabilized interest rate rules. These regulations modify the situations in which plans must make reports to the PBGC of their financial and actuarial data. Reporting is not required for smaller plans, some plans with statutory liens, and some plans that have obtained waivers from the minimum funding requirements. [Cheiron.us, *PBGC Revises Annual Financial and Actuarial Information Reporting for Single-Employer Plans* (June 8, 2016) (benefitslink.com)]

[1] Cromnibus 2014 and BBA 2015

The "Cromnibus" (Consolidated and Further Continuing Appropriations Act), the federal spending bill lasting through September 2015 makes some changes in the rules governing defined benefit plans. If, on or before December 8, 2014, the NRA for a defined benefit plan was the earlier of an age allowed by law, or the age when a defined number of years of service (at least 30) has been completed, the plan will not be disqualified merely because the NRA rule applies only to certain participants or only to the employees of certain employers. The Cromnibus bill limits the circumstances under which the PBGC can impose liability on an employer that downsizes: see § 5.10, *infra*, for discussion of Employment Retirement Income Security Act (ERISA) § 4062(3) reporting, for events occurring on or after December 16, 2014.

> ■ **TIP:** Do not confuse "multi-employer plans," (maintained by several employers and one or more unions, under a Collective Bargaining Agreement (CBA)) with "multiple-employer plans," defined benefit plans operated by two or more employers that are legally unrelated and are not treated as a single employer.

The Cromnibus bill also includes the Multi-Employer Pension Reform Act of 2014 (MPRA; also known as the Kline-Miller Act). Although in general discussion of multi-employer pension plans is outside the scope of this book, this legislation makes major changes in the regulation of multi-employer plans, which can be summarized as follows:

- The amount of information the plans must disclose is increased
- The PBGC premium doubles, from $13 to $26 per participant (It has subsequently been increased.)
- Plans that merge to avoid or postpone insolvency get government assistance

- A formal procedure is created for partitioning eligible multi-employer plans

- Multi-employer plans that would otherwise fail to satisfy PPA requirements are entitled to indefinite extension of amortization periods

- Plans that are projected to reach critical status in the future can elect to be in critical status for the current plan year

- Extensions of amortization periods can be considered in determining when a plan can leave critical status

- A plan that has left critical status can go back to critical status for any later plan year

- The method of determining the targeted funded percentage for plans in endangered status has been changed

- When a plan is in critical or endangered status, benefits cannot be improved; contributions can be reduced, and certain employees can be excluded

Certain seriously troubled plans that could not otherwise avoid insolvency will be permitted to cut back their benefits, and will not be considered to violate the anti-cutback rule. Plan trustees can suspend accrued benefits if the plan is at risk of being unable to pay 100% of the vested benefits in the next 10 to 20 years. The trustees must show that insolvency is inevitable, and all other reasonable measures have been tried and failed. A plan is deemed to be in critical and declining status if its funded percentage is under 65%, and the plan is projected to become insolvent within 15 years—within 20 years, if it has more than two inactive participants to every active participant, or its funded percentage is under 80%. Benefits must not be reduced below 110% of the PBGC-guaranteed monthly benefit. Benefits cannot be reduced for participants who are 80 years of age or older or for disabled participants; the reduction must be smaller for participants who are between 75 and 80 years of age than for younger participants. However, the MPRA gives trustees some discretion as to how benefit cuts will be structured. They are permitted to favor active employees over retirees by imposing greater cuts on retirees (up to age 75). Suspensions must be distributed in an equitable fashion, based on factors such as life expectancy, length of time in pay status, and the extent to which the benefit was subsidized.

Once benefits have been suspended, the MPRA does not require them to be reinstated if the plan's financial situation improves. After the trustees approve suspensions, they must apply for approval from the Department of the Treasury, in consultation with DOL and PBGC. If the agencies approve, the participants and beneficiaries get to vote on whether benefits can be reduced. But the Treasury can overrule a vote against reductions, if the plan is "systematically important" (i.e., the PBGC's potential exposure is $1 billion or more). If the vote is over-ruled, the Treasury can either force implementation of the trustees' proposal, or issue a modified plan. If, on or before December 8, 2014, the NRA for a defined benefit plan was the earlier of an age allowed by law or the age when a defined number of years of service (at least 30) has been completed, the plan will not be disqualified merely because the NRA rule applies only to certain participants or only to the employees of certain employers. [*"Cromnibus Act" Changes for Multiemployer and Single-Employer Defined Benefit Pension Plans* (Dec. 26, 2014) (benefitslink.com)]

The MPRA created a new way for troubled multi-employer plans to eventually pay full benefits. Previously, the PPA set up a zone system for rating the financial health of multi-employer plans as green, yellow, or red based on current status and expectations of future solvency. The MPRA says that plans in the red zone (critical status) that are also in declining status can reduce some benefits, including some benefits in pay status. The MPRA calls this "suspension" of benefits, because the benefits could be reinstated if funding status improves. The process requires a vote of approval by a simple majority of the plan population. The MPRA allows the government to override a no-vote by the plan, but only if the plan's insolvency would cost the PBGC more than a billion dollars. The IRS created a three-step process. First, ballot materials are distributed to eligible voters. Then they vote, and votes are tabulated. The Treasury determines if there has been a majority vote authorizing suspension. The plan sponsor provides a list of voters eligible to receive ballots, and must give each eligible voter an individualized explanation of how his or her benefits will be reduced, within seven days of the date the Treasury approves the application to suspend benefits [Editors, *IRS Offers Up Rules for MPRA-Related Benefit Reductions*, plansponsor.com (Sept. 1, 2015)]

Before the MPRA, the PBGC could only partition a plan that was in bankruptcy. Participants' benefits were reduced to the level of the PBGC's payment to multi-employer plans. For most employees, the maximum payment from the PBGC would be less than $13,000 a year after 30 years' service. The MPRA allows the PBGC to take on some benefit liabilities to preserve a plan that otherwise would run out of money within 20 years. Benefits can be maintained at 110% of the PBGC guaranteed amount.

In 2014, there were 1,427 multi-employer defined-benefit plans, with aggregate assets of $431 billion. Up to 10% of those plans are likely to become insolvent; most will require both partition and suspension of benefits. The PBGC's estimate is that about 1.5 million participants are covered by multi-employer plans that are expected to be insolvent by 2023. Suspensions could preserve payments to 600,000 participants; the other 900,000 could receive more benefits than the regular PBGC guarantee.

In a partition, the plan isolates a group of participants, and the PBGC provides financial assistance to a new successor plan, with the original plan remaining intact. The best candidates for partition are plans where benefit cuts by themselves would not allow the plan to survive. The plan must undertake all reasonable measures to remain solvent, including seeking the Treasury's permission to reduce benefits to 110% of the PBGC guarantee (although benefits are preserved for aged or disabled participants). The PBGC cannot assume plan liabilities until the Treasury grants permission. The PBGC must certify that participating in a partition will not impair its ability to help other multi-employer plans. In June 2015, the PBGC estimated that it had the capacity to make up to $60 million in payments and process up to six applications a year. [Hazel Bradford, *Multiemployer funds, PBGC Face Hurdles with Partition*, Pionline.com (July 13, 2015) (benefitslink.com)]

The IRS and PBGC issued Rev. Proc. 2015-34, comprising proposed, interim, and temporary regulations about MPRA benefits suspensions and partitions. The MPRA changed the funding rules for multi-employer plans as well as specifying how plan can apply to suspend benefits.

Rev. Proc. 2015-34 explains how to apply for a suspension, and includes a model notice to participants. Participants, beneficiaries of deceased participants, and alternate payees have to be notified of suspension. The sponsor must make reasonable efforts to communicate the information; mailing to the last known address is not sufficient. If the request for suspension is approved, the sponsor must make an annual re-determination that all reasonable measures have been taken to avoid insolvency, and suspension remains necessary to avoid insolvency. If the re-determination is not done, the suspension expires at the end of the year. Systematically important plans may have to submit individual participant data to the Department of Treasury. If the plan applies for partition as well as suspension, the suspension cannot take effect until the effective date of the partition.

Rev. Proc. 2015-34 includes a model notice to disclose estimates of individual effects of the proposed reduction, a submission checklist, and a sample power of attorney. Under ERISA § 4233, the PBGC will only authorize partition if the PBGC's costs will be reduced, and the plan can stay solvent. A plan applying for partition must submit complete data about the plan, its finances, and projected financial condition; identify which participants will be removed from the plan; how they were chosen; and what it will cost the PBGC to provide their guaranteed benefits. [Rev. Proc. 2015-34, 2015-27 I.R.B. 4]

See Rev. Proc. 2017-43, 2017-31 I.R.B. 153, for the revised procedures that must be used to apply for suspension of benefits from a multi-employer defined benefit plan in critical and declining status for applications submitted on or after September 1, 2017. Projected payments attributable to prior withdrawals must be separated from projected payments attributable to expected future withdrawals. [Rebecca Moore, *IRS Updates Procedure for Applying for Suspension of Benefits*, plansponsor.com (July 13, 2017)]

A final rule for partition of multiemployer plans, reflecting comments, was published at the end of 2015. It makes small changes to the 2015 Interim Final Rule, about information requirements, the timing of the PBGC's initial review of partition applications, and the coordinated application process for both partition and suspension of benefits. These amendments apply to applications for partition submitted on or after January 22, 2016. [80 Fed. Reg. 79687 (Dec. 23, 2015); see Rebecca Moore, *PBGC Issues Final Rule for Multiemployer Plan Partitions*, plansponsor.com (Jan. 11, 2016)]

A mid-2016 PBGC proposed rule explains how the PBGC will use its power under ERISA § 4231 to facilitate mergers between troubled plans. The PBGC has the power to provide training, technical assistance, and mediation. First, the PBGC analyzes whether a proposed merger is in the best interests of the participants and beneficiaries of at least one of the plans, and the merger is not likely to harm the participants and beneficiaries of the other plan(s) involved. The PBGC also has a fund for providing financial assistance to plans in critical and declining status that are expected to become insolvent within 14–19 years. The PBGC cannot grant financial assistance when the grant would impair other PBGC financial obligations. [81 Fed. Reg. 36229 (June 6, 2016); see Robert F. Schwartz and Alex E. Trabolsi, *Pension Benefit Guaranty Corporation Issues Proposed Rule for Multiemployer Plan Mergers and Transfers*, Truckerhuss.com (June 2016) (benefitslink.com)]

Local Ironworkers 17 (in Cleveland) became the first union whose members voted to approve drastic pension cuts. Less than half of the plan's 2,000 participants voted but two-thirds of voters approved of the cuts, which took effect February 1, 2017. About one-sixth of the participants would incur substantial cuts in their benefits; the rest would have lesser cuts. (The Pension Rights Center reported that before this, four applications for pension cuts were denied and another four were under review.) [Rebecca Moore, *First Multiemployer Plan to Make Benefit Cuts Under MPRA*, plansponsor.com (Jan. 27, 2017); Frank T. Mamat, *Union Retirees Cut Their Own Pension to Forestall Doomsday Scenario*, Foster Swift Collins & Smith PC (Feb. 6, 2017), available at Lexology.com]

Although over a dozen applications were submitted by troubled multiemployer plans, the Treasury did not approve another application until July 2017. The United Furniture Workers Pension Fund was given permission to submit its plan for partition to the members. If the members approve, the PBGC will provide assistance to one of the partitioned plans. The plan would allow almost three-quarters of participants to get full benefits, and only 6% would have cuts over 10%—but a small sub-group (295 participants) would lose 30% or more of their pensions. [<https://www.treasury.gov/services/Responses2/UFW%20Notification%20Letter.pdf >(July 20, 2017); see David B. Brandolph, *Treasury Department Gives Thumbs Up to Second Pension Rescue*, bna.com (July 21, 2017) (benefitslink.com)]

§ 5.02   BENEFIT LIMITS

The limit on the maximum benefit that anyone can receive from a qualified defined benefit plan in a year is set by I.R.C. § 415(b)(1). The limits remained the same in 2016 as in 2015.

For 2015–2016, the defined benefit limit on the annual benefit is $210,000, rising to $215,000 for 2017; the annual compensation limit is $265,000 (2015–2016) and $270,000 (2017); and an HCE is a person who earns at least $120,000 (unchanged from 2015 to 2017). [IR-2015-118, *IRS Announces 2016 Pension Plan Limitations; 401(k) Contribution Plan Limit Remains Unchanged at $18,000 for 2016* (Oct. 21, 2015), <https://www.irs.gov/pub/irs-news/IR-15-118.pdf>; Notice 2016-62, 2016-46 I.R.B. 725]

As a result of the PPA, underfunded plans are restricted in their benefit distribution options: see § 5.10.

§ 5.03   BENEFIT FORMS FOR DEFINED BENEFIT PLANS

All pension plans must provide the basic payment form: a life annuity for single participants, and a QJSA (qualified joint and survivor annuity) for married participants. The basic form of QJSA provides a certain level of benefits while both the former employee and spouse are still alive. When one of them dies, the payment is cut in half, because only one person remains to be supported. Although employers are allowed to offer 50% survivor annuities, they are also allowed to subsidize the survivor annuity so that it is more than 50% of the initial payment, or even so that the payment does not decline when one payee dies. As a result of the Pension Protection Act, employers must now offer married participants not only a choice between a joint and 50% survivor annuity and a single-life annuity, but a choice between a survivor annuity at the 50% level and at the 75% level (Qualified Optional Survivor Annuity, or QOSA).

Internal Revenue Code § 401(a)(25) says that a plan that provides for alternative benefit forms (annuity, installment, lump sum, early retirement) must specify, in a definite form that precludes employer discretion, what actuarial assumptions (such as interest rates and mortality assumptions) are used to calculate equivalencies among different benefit forms. This disclosure obligation does not, however, extend to the plan's funding assumptions.

In a flat benefit plan, the pension is defined as a certain number of dollars per month, or a percentage of average annual compensation or average compensation for the "high three" years. A unit benefit plan defines the pension as compensation times years of participation times a percentage rate. Some plans of this type increase the accrual rate in later years, or are calculated using a "high five" or "final average pay" (the average of the last three years of work, when presumably earnings will be at their peak).

The IRS has ruled frequently on when and how plans can eliminate benefit forms that are hard to administer and are rarely chosen by participants, but the theme of all these rules is that the core benefit forms must remain available to participants. Final Regulations were published under § 411(d)(6) on August 11, 2005, further explaining the benefits and redundant payment forms that can be eliminated from defined benefit plans. The IRS also published proposals in the same document, allowing elimination of benefits that fail a utilization test.

Any benefit outside the core options can be eliminated after four years. The core options are defined as the straight life annuity; the 75% joint and contingent annuity; the 50%/100% joint and contingent annuity; the 10-year certain and life annuity; and an option such as a lump sum or a survivor annuity that would be valuable for a participant with a short life expectancy. [T.D. 9219, 2005-38 I.R.B. 538; see also 71 Fed. Reg. 45379 (Aug. 9, 2006)]

IRS Regulations proposed at 70 Fed. Reg. 31214 (May 31, 2005), finalized at 72 Fed. Reg. 16878 (Apr. 5, 2007) unify and systematize the § 415 rules, explaining how to calculate the maximum permitted benefit when a retiree has multiple annuity start dates and how to calculate qualified joint and survivor annuities when the benefit is partly taken as a lump sum and partly in annuity form. In 2012, proposals were published to encourage plans to offer a Qualified Longevity Annuity Contract (QLAC), a partial lump sum calculated using the statutory actuarial assumptions, combined with an annuity using the plan's regular conversion factors, [IRS Proposed Rules, 77 Fed. Reg. 5443 and 5454 (Feb. 3, 2012)]

In the IRS's view, many participants are better off if they can accelerate part of the benefit and receive a lump sum, while receiving the balance of the benefit in annuity form. That way, they are bolstered against longevity risk (if the annuity payment continues for life) but receive a lump sum that they may be able to invest for a higher return than the plan would provide. T.D. 9783 is a final rule that modifies the minimum present value requirement for partial annuity distributions from defined benefit plans.

It amends the regulations under § 417(e) to simplify the treatment of certain optional forms of benefit paid as a combination lump sum and annuity. The § 417(e) and Reg. § 1.417(e)-1(d) minimum present value requirements only apply to the lump sum part of the benefit. If the plan provides an early retirement benefit, a retirement-type subsidy, or an ancillary benefit that applies to only part of the benefit, the plan must identify what part of the benefit is paid out with the lump sum.

T.D. 9783 applies to annuity starting dates that occur in plan years that begin on or after January 1, 2017. [T.D. 9783 (81 Fed. Reg. 62359, 2016-39 I.R.B. 396 (Sept. 9, 2016)); see Rebecca Moore, *IRS Issues Final Rule on Requirements for Partial Annuities in DB Plans*, plansponsor.com (Sept. 9, 2016); Sally P. Schreiber, *Defined Benefit Plan Participants Can Receive Lump Sum and Annuity Under New Rules*, J. of Accountancy (Sept. 2016) (benefitslink.com);

Octoberthree.com, *IRS Finalizes Partial Annuity Regulation* (Oct. 6, 2016) (benefitslink.com); Xerox FYI, *IRS Proposes More Changes to Minimum Present Value Calculations* (Dec. 1, 2016) (benefitslink.com)]

Further guidance was offered by Notice 2016-39, explaining when payments to employees from defined benefit plans in conjunction with phased retirement (working part-time while collecting a partial pension) are considered taxable annuity payments from the plan. Generally, the payments will be taxable in the year of distribution; the Notice explains the factors used to determine which part of each payment is recovery of basis. [Notice 2016-39, 2016-26 I.R.B. 1068; see Lee Barney, *IRS Guidance Explains Annuity Taxation During Partial Retirement*, plansponsor.com (June 14, 2016)]

In 2008, the Northern District of Illinois held that Verizon was bound by the language in its defined benefit plan document even though a drafting error had possible consequences of $1.67 billion. The cashout value of interests in the predecessor plan was incorrectly drafted, calling for multiplying the balance twice by a variable transition factor based on age and years of service. However, on reconsideration, the Northern District held that the error was an honest mistake, and other actions in administering the plan showed an intent to use the multiplication factor only once. Judge Denlow said that employers would be discouraged from adopting plans at all if they feared that mistakes could have catastrophic consequences that could not be corrected. The Seventh Circuit affirmed in mid-2010 and the Supreme Court denied certiorari. [*Young v. Verizon's Bell Atlantic Cash Balance Plan*, 615 F.3d 808 (7th Cir. 2010), *cert. denied*, 131 S. Ct. 2924 (May 23, 2011), *reh'g denied*, 132 S. Ct. 47 (July 25, 2011)]

[A] De-Risking

Defined benefit plans, in response to investment volatility, changing rules, and longer-lived participants, are looking for "de-risking" strategies; a popular strategy is to purchase annuity contracts to fulfill payment obligations, while transferring the decisions about how to invest the funds to the annuity seller. The trend for Pension Risk Transfer (PRT) activity was popularized in 2012 when General Motors and Verizon announced PRT activities. Bristol-Meyers Squibb, Motorola, Newell Rubbermaid, E.W. Scripps Co., and Kimberly-Clark engaged in major PRT deals in 2014–2015. At first, most bulk buyouts were part of plan termination but the current trend is for the plan sponsor to buy out retirees only.

The sharp increase in PBGC premiums also increased sponsor interest in de-risking. The persistent low-interest-rate environment meant that sponsors had to pay more to meet their funding obligations. Sponsors were also concerned about the expected effect of new mortality tables requiring greater funding to support increased longevity. [Ellen Shaer, *Pension Plans: To Terminate or Not to Terminate*, captrustadvisors.com (Feb. 29, 2016) (benefitslink.com)]

An employer engaging in a pension risk transfer turns over assets to an insurer to back up the obligations, plus payments to the insurer (generally in the "mid single digits" as a percentage of the assets). State regulators require the insurer to set aside capital, typically 5%–10% of the transaction, in case the financial projections for the deal are incorrect. Pension risk transfer is expected to transform pension management by greatly reducing exposure to volatility in the stock and bond markets. It also gives insurance companies a source of growth at a time when some of their traditional businesses are not prospering. Rising interest rates make it cheaper to engage in a risk transfer. Prudential is the leader in this market, holding 10 jumbo deals covering more than 320,000 people and $45 billion in corporate pension obligations. MetLife and the U.S. unit of Britain's Legal & General are also market leaders. [Leslie Scism, *Your Pension Check May Soon Be Coming from an Insurance Company*, WSJ.com (Mar. 12, 2017)]

A PBGC study of defined benefit plans with over 1000 participants found that more than half (534) engaged in some kind of risk transfer activity during the period 2009–2013, including 145 cash balance plans and 135 collectively bargained plans. The activities resulted in over a million participants leaving the plans. Of those 534 plans, 50 went through a standard termination. Approximately 400 of the activities were lump-sum buyouts, the rest annuity purchases. The PBGC's conclusion was that the sponsor's financial condition did not determine risk transfer activity. Union and non-union plans were equally likely to offer risk transfers, but fewer union members accepted them. [PBGC Blog: *Retirement Matters Risk Transfer Activity Significant; Over One Million People Affected*, <http://pbgc.gov/about/who-we-are/retirement-matters/post/2015/12/09/Risk-Transfer-Activity-Significant;-Over-One-Million-People-Affected.aspx> (Dec. 9, 2015)]

Data from LIMRA's Secure Retirement Institute show that single-premium plan pension buyout sales were close to $3 billion in the third quarter of 2016. This was the largest third-quarter sales figure since 1990. By the end of the third quarter, 225 sponsors had converted their defined benefit plans to group annuity contracts, and the group annuity risk transfer market held $141 billion in assets. Smaller companies were beginning to adopt pension buyouts. LIMRA attributed the increase in buyout activity to low interest rates and rising PBGC premiums. [LIMRA.com, *LIMRA Secure Retirement Institute Survey: Single Premium Pension Buy-out Sales Nearly $6 Billion in the Third Quarter 2016* (Nov. 29, 2016) (benefitslink.com); John Manganaro, *DB Pension Buyouts Reached a Milestone in Q1*, plansponsor.com (June 1, 2016)]

For 2016, LIMRA reported that single-premium pension buyout sales were $13.7 billion, up about 1% over the year before. [LIMRA.com, *U.S. Single Premium Pension Buy-Out Sales Top $13.7 Billion in 2016, LIMRA Secure Retirement Institute Reports* (Mar. 1, 2017) (benefitslink.com)]

In mid-2015, however, in Notice 2015-49, 2015-30 I.R.B. 79, the IRS narrowed the exemption granted to pension amendments that increase benefits. The IRS said that the § 401(a)(9) regulations have been amended to rule out amendments to adopt lump-sum windows for retirees. The IRS says that sponsors who engage in de-risking by offering lump-sum windows have treated the right to convert current annuity to immediate lump sum as an increase in benefits. But as of July 9, 2015, the IRS says the only permitted benefit increases are those that increase ongoing annuity payments, not those that accelerate payments. Lump-sum windows remained acceptable for participants not yet in pay status, and the amendments to the regulations do not apply to lump-sum risk transfer programs that were already in place before July 9, 2015, if they were required by a CBA; if the plan amendment adopting de-risking was approved by a board or committee; if the IRS issued a favorable PLR on the transaction; or the participants were notified in writing of the company's intention to implement a de-risking program.

As of July 9, 2015, employers can no longer offer lump-sum windows to participants who are receiving installment payments and have reached age 70½. The Required Minimum Distribution requirements mandate distribution either of the entire interest by the Required Beginning Date, or distributions over life of employee or lives of employee and designated beneficiary. Notice 2015-49 forbids changing the period or form of distributions once they commence. Notice 2015-49 does not say whether the prohibition applies to participants who are getting pensions but have not reached age 70½, or whether it applies to terminating plans (some plans with only a few pensioners want to buy them out on termination instead of buying a small number of annuities.) [Edward R. Mackiewicz and Edward Thomas Veal, *IRS Moves to Increase (Slightly) the Cost of Pension De-Risking*, Steptoe & Johnson LLP (July 13, 2015), available at Lexology.com]

The Fifth Circuit upheld dismissal of a suit brought by 41,000 Verizon management retirees who opposed Verizon's plan to replace $7.4 billion in pension obligations with purchase of a single-premium group annuity from Prudential. The district court held that ERISA § 510 was not violated, because the annuity payment was the equivalent of the current pension benefit. The Fifth Circuit held that decisions to amend a plan and transfer assets to an annuity contract were settlor and not fiduciary functions (the decision to amend a plan involves the plan design; fiduciary duties are triggered by the administration of plan assets). Therefore, the class action about the purchase of the annuity was dismissed. Some of the plaintiffs had benefit liabilities that were transferred to Prudential; the liabilities of others remained in the plain. The Fifth Circuit said that the non-transferee class did not prove individual harm, so they did not have standing to sue. The transferee class alleged that the SPD failed to disclose that Verizon's benefit obligations might be converted to an annuity. The Fifth Circuit held that the SPD disclosed that Verizon had retained the right to amend the plan, and SPDs do not have to describe future actions. [*Lee v. Verizon*, 623 Fed. Appx. 132 (5th Cir. 2015); see Rebecca Moore, *Court Affirms Dismissal of Verizon Pension Risk Transfer Suit*, plansponsor.com (Aug. 21, 2015)]

The Supreme Court granted certiorari in mid-2016, vacating the Fifth Circuit decision and remanding it for the Fifth Circuit to reconsider whether the plaintiffs had standing to sue, when the only concrete harm they alleged was violation of a private right under a federal statute. [*Pundt v. Verizon*, No. 15-785, *cert. granted* (May 23, 2016); see Rebecca Moore, *Supreme Court Revives Part of Verizon PRT Challenge*, plansponsor.com (May 23, 2016)] When the case returned to the Fifth Circuit, the court once again upheld the legality of the de-risking decision and also found that Pundt did not have Article III standing, as defined by the Supreme Court's *Spokeo* decision, because he did not allege that he was at imminent risk of loss of benefits due to plan default. [*Lee v. Verizon Commc'ns, Inc.* **837 F.3d 523** (5th Cir. 2016); see Jacklyn Wille, *Verizon Victory Not Changed by Recent Supreme Court Case*, bna.com (Sept. 19, 2016) (benefitslink.com); Rebecca Moore, *5th Circuit Again Dismisses Verizon Pension Buyout Lawsuit*, plansponsor.com (Oct. 14, 2016)]

[B] Transfers Between Plans

Recent IRS and PBGC guidance deals with important issues of moving funds from defined contribution to defined benefit plans, and creating a safe harbor for movement of funds from one qualified plan to another, or from an IRA to a qualified plan. These measures are important in a mobile society, where plans often change form and many employees move between jobs.

The PBGC published a final rule for transferring assets from defined contribution plans to defined benefit plans. The rule is effective December 26, 2014. The PBGC wants to encourage the provision of lifetime income to plan participants by making it easier to make such transfers without worrying that the portion of the rollover that exceeds the maximum PBGC guarantee might be lost if the PBGC takes over the plan. The final rule says that the "five-year phase in rule" does not apply to rollovers that derive from employee contributions. This rule provides that defined-benefit increases added to the plan in the five years before termination must be phased in over a five-year post-termination period at a rate of 20% per year. The PBGC said that the benefit based on the rollover is added to the PBGC maximum guarantee for the single-employer plan. The rollover amounts include salary deferrals made by the participant, plus any other employer contributions to the defined contribution plan. Lifetime income purchased with a rollover contribution is a Category 2 priority benefit, just after voluntary account benefits. When a plan goes through a distress termination, the participant's rollover account cannot be distributed as a lump sum. [RIN 1212-AB23, 79 Fed. Reg. 70090 (Nov. 25, 2014)]

Guidance was necessary because some plans refused to accept rollovers from other qualified plans or from IRAs because handling rollovers was so cumbersome. The IRS introduced a streamlined process in mid-2014 for validating rollovers from qualified plans and IRAs. However, not all distributions can be rolled over. For example, hardship withdrawals cannot be rolled over, so the plan administrator must determine that the contribution includes only valid rollover distributions from eligible plans. A plan is entitled to relief if it accepts what it reasonably believed to be a valid distribution, and returns the amounts to the employee within a reasonable time of the discovery of the invalidity. There is a safe harbor for contributions that the administrator believed were valid (and had no evidence to the contrary) if the check for the distribution is payable to the plan and the administrator receives a copy of the transferor plan's Form 5500. The administrator must check the DOL database (<http://www.efast.dol.gov>) to make sure that Code 3C, Line 8a of the Form 5500 is not checked, which would indicate that the plan is not qualified. For IRA rollovers, the administrator can rely on the check coming from the IRA, plus the employee's certification that the roll-over does not include any after-tax amounts, and the employee will not reach age 70½ by the end of the year. [Eugene S. Griggs, *Accepting Rollover Contributions Now Easier—and Less Risky—for Retirement Plans*, Poyner Spruill LLP (Aug. 7, 2014) (benefitslink.com)]

§ 5.04 MORTALITY TABLES

Before 2002, the IRS required defined benefit plans to use the 1983 Group Annuity Mortality (83GAM) table for making the actuarial calculations for the value of accrued benefits. [I.R.C. § 417(e)] The mortality tables must be used to make sure that the value of a lump-sum benefit is at least as great as the predicted value of an annuity.

Defined benefit plans also have to calculate adjustments of the plan limita-tions, as required by I.R.C. § 415(b), when the benefit under the plan is paid in any form other than a QJSA, or when the employee retires before age 62 or after age 65.

The PPA imposed additional § 412 funding requirements for defined benefit plans that have unfunded current liability (§ 412(l)(8)). Current liability is deter-mined using the mortality table prescribed by the Secretary, who is required to update the table at least once every 10 years. Additional tables are prescribed for disability retirees whose disability satisfies Social Security Act Title II standards: a table for disability occurring before January 1, 1995 and a table for disabilities with later onset. Under § 412(l)(7)(C)(ii)(III), the tables have to be reviewed at least once every five years to reflect trends in mortality rates. The mortality tables have been updated for use in 2014 and 2015: see Notice 2013-49, 2013-32 I.R.B. 127. [T.D. 9310 RIN 1545-BE72 72 Fed. Reg. 4955 (Feb. 2, 2007); Rev. Proc. 2008-62, 2008-42 I.R.B. 935]

Under the PPA, a defined benefit plan must provide that the present value of an accrued benefit, and the amount of any distribution (lump sum or other-wise) must be at least the amount calculated using the Regulations Section

1.417(e)-1(d) appropriate interest rate for the month and the prescribed mortality table.

The Society of Actuaries (SOA) approved revised mortality tables in late 2014, predicting that as a result of increases in longevity, the typical pension plan would experience a 4%–8% increase in liability. [Plansponsor staff, *Updated Mortality Tables Increased Pension Liabilities by $100B*, plansponsor.com (Feb. 12, 2015)]

See Notice 2015-53, 2015-33 I.R.B. 190 for the updated static mortality tables. The notice also includes modified unisex tables to calculate minimum present value under Code § 417(e)(3) and ERISA § 205(g)(3), for distributions with annuity dates in stability periods that begin in 2016 calendar years. [John Manganaro, *IRS Unveils Mortality Tables for 2016 Pension Funding*, plansponsor.com (Aug. 5, 2015)] In September 2015, the IRS decided to delay until 2017 the requirement of using the 2014 mortality tables to calculate pension obligations. [Vipal Monga, *Moody's: IRS Mortality Decision to Save Corporate Pensions $18B in 2016*, WSJ.com (Sept. 2, 2015)]

The IRS published mortality tables to be used for minimum funding requirement calculations and lump-sum distributions in 2017, in Notice 2016-50, 2016-38 I.R.B. 384. There are no major changes over the previous set of tables, and 2000 is still the base year. The IRS gave advance notice of its plans to release a draft of the 2018 tables. Important changes were expected, presumably as a result of adopting some form of the SOA RP-2014 tables. [Matt Klein, *Mortality Table Update,* Finleydavies.com (Sept. 9, 2016) (benefitslink.com); Rebecca Moore, *IRS Updates DB Plan Mortality Tables for 2017,* plansponsor.com (Sept. 6, 2016)]

Shortly afterwards, the SOA released a mortality improvement scale, MP-2016, including Social Security Administration mortality data from the 2012–2014 period, giving a life expectancy of 85.8 years for a 65-year-old man, 87.8 years for a 65-year-old woman. [Plansponsor staff, *SOA Publishes Update to Mortality Improvement Scale,* plansponsor.com (Oct. 20, 2016)]

Then, in mid-2017, the IRS decided to delay the date when the new tables would be required, until some times in 2018. As a result, employers had a period when they could provide smaller lump-sum pension payouts than will be required when the tables are finally adopted. However, some plans' auditors required the plans to base their financial statements on the updated assumptions under the new tables. [Greg Meila and Justin Teman, *Thought Mortality Was Dead? Considerations for Pensions Given the IRS' Delay in Implementing RP-2014,* Cambridge Associates (June 1, 2017) (benefitslink.com); Michael Katz, *IRS' Delay in Implementing Mortality Tables Affects Pension Decisions,* ai-cio.com (June 15, 2017) (benefitslink.com)]

§ 5.05 FUNDING THE DEFINED BENEFIT PLAN

[A] Funding Requirements

The process of funding a defined contribution plan is quite simple. The employer simply determines a percentage of compensation, and as long as the contribution does not exceed the Code maximum, then there are no further problems. No discretion is involved.

In contrast, funding a defined benefit plan requires subtle decisions about long-range economic and employment trends in order to deposit enough money to yield the correct stream of future benefits to plan participants and their beneficiaries.

Defined benefit, money purchase, and target benefit plans (but not profit-sharing plans, stock bonus plans, or plans under I.R.C. § 412(i) that are exclusively funded by the purchase of individual insurance or annuity contracts) are subject to a "minimum funding" requirement under I.R.C. § 412. Before the PPA, the benchmark was the status of the plan's "minimum funding standard account," but the PPA enacts a new Code § 430, setting out the requirements for "basic minimum funding contributions."

An excise tax of 10% is imposed by I.R.C. § 4971 for failure to meet the minimum funding standard. The excise tax rises to 100% of any deficiency that remains uncorrected a reasonable time after the plan receives notice of deficiency from the IRS.

According to the Supreme Court case, *United States v. Reorganized CF&I Fabricators of Utah Inc.* [518 U.S. 213 (1996)], the 100% assessment is a penalty (and therefore an ordinary unsecured claim) and not an excise tax entitled to seventh priority, if the company subject to it files for bankruptcy protection.

According to Mercer, the funded status of the largest corporate pension plans was about 82% in both 2015 and 2016; The plans in the S&P 1500 had $1.18 trillion in pension assets as of December 31, 2016, which was 0.56% more than the previous year, but the aggregate deficit of these plans rose $4 billion, to $408 billion. [Meaghan Kilroy, *Corporate Funded Status Sees Little Change in 2016—3 Reports*, pionline.com (Jan. 5, 2017) (benefitslink.com)] In March 2017, the Aon Hewitt Pension Risk Tracker reported the funded status of the S&P 500 companies as declining $15 billion year-to-date, with a funded percentage of 80.9%. Aon Hewitt said that these plans gained $41 billion in assets, and their liabilities increased $26 billion, in the first quarter of 2017. [Lee Barney, *Pension Funded Status Down $15B YTD*, plansponsor.com (Mar. 6, 2017)]

Underfunding has other implications. The PPA imposes limitations on benefits. If the plan is covered by PBGC insurance, the PBGC must be notified whenever the minimum funding standard is not met. If the plan is terminated (see Chapter 17), then underfunding can make the plan liable to the PBGC for accumulated funding deficiencies.

However, complying with the minimum funding standard doesn't solve all of the employer's problems, because I.R.C. § 4972 also imposes an excise tax on excess contributions to a defined benefit plan.

Therefore, the employer should make sure that its contributions to the defined benefit plan fall within the acceptable range. Contributions should not be small enough to constitute underfunding—especially not small enough to trigger PBGC termination of the plan. But the employer will not want to contribute more than can be deducted, and will particularly want to avoid the excise tax on excess contributions.

[B] Deduction Limit

The funding standard serves another purpose: it sets an upper limit on the amount that the employer can deduct under I.R.C. § 404. If the employer overstates its pension liabilities by 200% or more, and therefore takes too large a deduction, with the result that its income taxes are underpaid by 20% or more, then a 20% accuracy-related underpayment penalty can be imposed under I.R.C. § 6662. The penalty will be suspended if the pension overstatement was less than $1,000, or if the plan relied on substantial authority such as Revenue Rulings or IRS Notices.

Pensions are a form of deferred compensation, and any form of compensation is deductible only if it is reasonable and constitutes an ordinary and necessary business expense. Part of the compensation of particularly highly paid employees may have to be disregarded for certain tax-related purposes.

For example, under I.R.C. § 401(a)(17) only $200,000 of compensation (adjusted for inflation in increments of $5,000) can be taken into account. In 2015–2016, the amount is $265,000; for 2017, it is $270,000. Even legitimate compensation may have to be deducted over a span of several years, not all at once.

[C] Calculating the Contribution

Before the PPA, defined benefit plan actuaries used two basic methods (each of which had variations): the accrued benefit method and the projected benefit cost method. Contributions were made for each participant based on "normal cost" (the actuarial value of benefit units for that year) plus "supplemental liability" (adjustments for service before adoption of a plan, or after a plan is amended). The PPA approach starts with the "target normal cost" and, as [D], below, shows, this is the point of departure for various adjustments.

[D]   From the Minimum Funding Standard Account to the Minimum Required Contribution

Pre-PPA law required that a "minimum funding standard account" be maintained in all plan years until the end of the year in which the plan terminates. [See I.R.C. § 412(b) and ERISA § 302(b)] Under the pre-PPA rules, the minimum funding standard is met when there is no accumulated funding deficiency at the end of the year. There is no deficiency if, for all plan years, the credits to the funding standard account are at least equal to the total charges.

The minimum funding standard account consists of charges for normal costs, past service liabilities, experience losses in investments, and funding deficiencies. The general rule is that experience losses and funding deficiencies have to be amortized, not deducted currently. The charges to the account are offset by credits for, e.g., the employer's contributions to the plan, investment experience gains, and funding deficiencies that are waived by the IRS. WRERA provides (as an option for 2008, but mandatory for later years) that expenses paid directly by the plan are included in the target normal cost. Under the PPA, the plan's contributions and distributions had to be included in the calculation; WRERA also allows consideration of expected earnings. WRERA requires the same interest rate assumptions to be used to calculate the funding target percentage and the target normal cost.

Internal Revenue Code § 412(l) imposes additional obligations on single-employer plans with 100 or more participants whose "funded current liability" percentage falls below 80% for the current year when it was below 90% for the preceding year. The funded current liability percentage equals the value of the plan assets divided by current liabilities. The underfunded plans are obligated to notify their participants and beneficiaries of the funding deficiency, and must pay an additional PBGC premium. In egregious cases, the PBGC may be able to bring a civil suit against the plan.

The PPA introduced several new concepts and new requirements. The employer's obligation is now the "minimum required contribution," defined as the amount the employer must contribute each year to fund benefits that will be paid in that year, as well as phasing out any existing funding shortfall over seven years. If the plan's assets are lower than its funding target, the minimum required contribution for the year is the "target normal cost" plus the amount needed to amortize the funding shortfall over seven years. The "funding target" is the accrued liability to date: the sum needed to pay all of the claims of participants and beneficiaries, as of the valuation date. The target normal cost, in turn, is defined as the benefit liabilities accruing in the current year, including past service benefits that increased reflecting the employee's higher compensation in the current year. A funding shortfall is any difference between the funding target and the plan assets. The "shortfall amortization installment" is the payment due in each of the seven years to close the gap. However, if the employer contributes more than the required amount, a credit balance is created that can be applied toward the required contribution for later years.

The carried-over balance is also credited with interest, but at the rate used to calculate the plan's liabilities, not the actual interest rate that the plan earns on its investments.

A degree of temporary relief from the requirements for amortizing the shortfall was provided by the Preservation of Access to Care for Medicare Beneficiaries and Pension Relief Act of 2010, which allowed employers to elect to pay only the interest on their shortfall for two years, or to amortize the shortfall in any two plan years between 2008–2011 over 15 rather than seven years.

T.D. 9732, published in September 2015, provides final regulations under § 430 for determining the required minimum contribution for single-employer defined benefit plans requiring annual contributions to the plan to at least equal the normal cost (expected benefit accruals during the year) plus enough money to amortize any funding shortfall over seven years.

The funding shortfall is the difference between the value of accrued benefits at the beginning of the year and the plan assets. The required minimum contribution must be made within eight-and-a-half months after the end of the plan year. If there is a funding shortfall for earlier years, it must be amortized over a period of seven years. The plan must make quarterly payments of 25% of the required annual payment, which is the smaller of 90% of the required minimum contribution for the current year or 100% of the required minimum contribution for the previous year, without considering any § 412(c) funding waiver for that year. Quarterly installments paid after the due date are subject to interest at the plan's effective interest rate plus five basis points. For plans with unpaid contributions, payments are applied first to the earliest plan year for which there is still an unpaid minimum required contribution.

T.D. 9732 also explains how to calculate the § 4971 excise tax for failure to satisfy the requirements. The excise tax is 10% of the total unpaid minimum required contributions for all years remaining unpaid at the end of any plan year. There is also a 10% excise tax, under § 4971(f)(1) on the liquidity shortfall for any quarter that is not paid by the due date for that quarter's installment payment; § 4971(f)(2) imposes the excise tax if there is a liquidity shortfall at the end of five consecutive quarters.

The year in which a plan is terminated is treated as a short year, ending on the termination date, and amortization is prorated to reflect the short year. [T.D. 9732, 2015-39 I.R.B. 371]

[E] Full Funding Limitation

Before 2004, it was necessary to calculate a "full funding limitation" (FFL) because excise taxes could be imposed if the employer's contribution fell below that amount. The Economic Growth and Tax Relief Reconciliation Act

(EGTRRA) reduced the full funding limitation for 2002 and 2003 and provided that the percentage test would expire in 2004, when the FFL would be the difference between the plan's accrued liability and the value of its assets.

[F] Funding Procedures

Actual funding of the plan is done by the employer's contributing cash, non-cash property, or its own securities. The valuation of cash is simple; for property and securities, it can be difficult. The prohibited transaction rules (see § 8.03) must be consulted to make sure that contributions do not violate these rules. Wherever possible, transactions should be structured so that the plan trust will not have Unrelated Business Taxable Income (UBTI). In general, plan trusts are not subject to income tax—unless they have unrelated income.

Wherever possible, the employer should avoid contributing depreciated property to the plan. That's because I.R.C. § 267(b)(4) provides that the employer will have taxable gain (capital or ordinary, depending on the facts) if it contributes appreciated property to the plan. But losses on contributions of depreciated property are not recognized, because there is a transfer between the trust grantor and the trust's fiduciary.

■ **TIP:**   An employer that wants to use depreciated property in funding can sell the property to a third party, recognize the tax loss, then contribute the cash proceeds of the sale.

The PPA provides that most plans must make their required contribution no later than 8½ months after the end of the plan year. Some plans, however (those with more than 100 participants, and that had a funding shortfall in the previous year) will have to make quarterly contributions (April 15, July 15, October 15, January 15) instead of being permitted to make the whole year's contribution at once. The quarterly installment must equal 25% of the lesser of 90% of the minimum required contribution for the current plan year, or 100% of the minimum required contribution for the previous year.

[G] Liens Based on Funding Failures

Under I.R.C. § 412(n), a lien can be imposed against the employer, and in favor of the plan subject to PBGC jurisdiction, if the employer fails to make a required contribution to the plan when it is due.

■ **TIP:**   The person responsible for making the payment that was missed has an obligation to inform the PBGC within 10 days of the due date that the payment was missed.

The lien covers all of the employer's real and personal property. The lien can be imposed if the plan's funded current liability percentage fell below 100% and the unpaid balance, plus interest, was more than $1 million. It starts on the date the payment should have been made, and runs to the end of the plan year in which the liabilities go over the $1 million mark.

The PBGC can sue in federal district court under ERISA § 4003(e)(1) to enforce the lien against the employer. This power can be exercised at any time until three years after the PBGC knew or should have known of the failure to make the necessary payment (extended to six years if the employer committed fraud or concealment), or for six years after the due date from the payment.

[H] Plan Valuation Issues

An actuarial valuation must be performed at least once a year to determine the assets, liabilities, and contribution level for plans subject to I.R.C. § 412. (EGTRRA gives the Treasury the power to adopt regulations that call for even more frequent valuations.) The information is also used to prepare the Schedule B for the 5500-series form.

The basic factors in setting assumptions include:

- Employee compensation;

- Early retirement rate;

- Employee turnover;

- Disability and mortality rates (both before and after retirement);

- (For QJSAs) Life expectancy of employees' spouses;

- Expected percentage return on the plan's investments (interest assumptions may have to be adjusted in the future to reflect the plan's investment record);

- Administrative expenses, defined either as dollars per participant or a reduction in the plan's rate of return.

Within the limits set by I.R.C. § 412 and other relevant provisions, the size of the contribution can be increased or decreased somewhat based on corporate needs. However, the plan's actuarial assumptions must always be reasonable—each individual assumption, not just the aggregate. Courts have the power to overturn a plan's actuarial assumptions, even if the assumptions are not unreasonable. This is especially likely to happen if the plan has applied its own assumptions inconsistently.

■ **TIP:** In general, the valuation date has to be within the plan year for which the assets are being valued, or within a month before the start of the plan year—but EGTRRA § 661(a) creates an exception under which the valuation date can sometimes be in the previous year. This exception can only be used if the plan assets, valued as of the prior plan year's date, is at least 125% of the plan's current liability.

ERISA § 302(c) provides that a plan covered by PBGC termination insurance requires IRS approval to change its actuarial assumptions, if the aggregated unfunded vested benefits of all underfunded plans maintained by the employer, or members of the same controlled group, exceed $50 million. Approval for the change is also required if the change in the assumptions raises the unfunded cumulative liability for the current plan year by more than $50 million, or more than $5 million, if this is 5% or more of the current liability.

Before the PPA, plans could use "smoothing" to cope with changes in the valuation of plan assets over time. The PPA requires plans either to value their assets at fair market value (FMV) or to restrict "smoothing" to a 24-month period, during which values fall within the range of 90–110% of FMV. (See § 5.05[I] immediately below for further discussion of smoothing.)

A Pension Equity Plan (PEP) is a defined benefit plan that expresses accumulated benefits as the current value of a participant's final average compensation, highest average compensation, or highest average compensation in a period of years. Notice 2016-67, 2016-47 I.R.B 751 explains the market rate of return limitation rules for PEP plans, especially "implicit interest PEPs" that determine the benefit by applying a deferred annuity factor to the accumulated benefits. (An "explicit interest PEP" adjusts the benefit with interest credits at the annuity starting date after principal credits cease.) Notice 2016-67 says that implicit interest PEPs do not have to amend the deferred annuity factors to reduce the preretirement interest rate. [Rebecca Moore, *IRS Clarifies Interest Crediting Rules for Pension Equity Plans*, plansponsor.com (Nov. 7, 2016)]

[I]   Interest Rates

Internal Revenue Code § 412(l)(7)(C)(i) sets the parameters for the interest rates used to determine the employer's contributions and the plan's current liability.

Under pre-PPA rules, the Department of the Treasury has the power to issue Regulations that lower the permissible range [see I.R.C. § 412(b)(5)] but it is not allowed to fall beneath 80% of the weighted 30-year average Treasury rate.

Factors in the interest rate assumption include:

- The economic components of interest rates;

- Current long-term interest rates;

- The plan's individual actuarial and investment factors;

- Long-range economic trends, especially in the money supply and interest rates throughout the economy.

The basic principle under the PPA—that the present value of a plan's current liabilities must be calculated with an interest rate based on corporate bonds, not Treasury bills—survives. However, the lower the interest rates applied to the calculation, the more the employer must contribute to fund the plan. Congress permitted some funding relief in 2012, under the MAP-21 (Pub. L. No. 112-141). Defined benefit plans consider interest rates stretching back 25 years, so the recent, very low rates, will have less impact on the calculation. For 2012, the interest rates used in the calculation must be within 10% of the average of benchmark bond rates for the previous 25 years.

Employers are allowed to use two approaches to calculate the present value of future pension benefits. The future expected payments can be discounted using a yield curve based on corporate bond data published by the Treasury. The other approach is to use segment rates based on averages from the most recent two years of yield curves. For each year, MAP-21 specifies the range of rates that can be used.

MAP-21 requires plan administrators to disclose additional information if the plan had 50 or more participants on any day of the preceding plan year; the stabilized funding target is less than 95% of the regular funding target; and the plan would have a funding shortfall of $500,000 or more absent stabilization. If all three of those factors are present, the plan's Annual Funding Notice must disclose that the law has changed reducing the employer's contribution. The notice must include a table showing the MAP-21's effect on funding requirements, plan's funding shortfall, and the minimum contribution for the current year and the two years before. [Rebecca Moore, *Congress Passes Bill with Pension Funding Relief*, plansponsor.com (June 29, 2012); Buck Consultants FYI, *2012 Pension Plan Funding Stabilization Finally a Reality* (July 6, 2012) (benefitslink .com)]

Pub. L. No. 113-159, the Highway and Transportation Funding Act of 2014 (HATFA), extends the ability of pension plan sponsors to reduce their contributions, probably until 2020. The PPA required calculations to reflect the average corporate bond yield going back only 24 months; MAP-21 allowed a corridor within a 25-year average. MAP-21 provided for the corridor to expand each year, so that, as of 2016, MAP-21 relief would phase out and PPA principles would once again be in force. But the 2014 statute keeps the 2014 corridor figure in effect until 2017. For calendar years 2012–2017, the "corridor" is a minimum percentage of 90%, a maximum percentage of 110%. For 2018, the corresponding figures are 85% and 115%; for 2019, 80% and 120%; for 2020, 75% and 125%; after 2020, 70% and 130%. Note that bankrupt companies cannot take advantage of this relief. [John Dowell, *Pension Funding Relief: What's in It for My Plan?*, Nyhart Actuary & Employee Benefits (Aug. 15, 2014) (benefitslink.com)]

IRS guidance on HATFA says that the corridor for segment rates has been reduced again. For plan years 2012–2017, the segment rates fall between 90% and 110% of corresponding 25-year average segment rate, increasing gradually in later years. For plan years beginning after 2020, the corridor is 70%–130% of the segment rates. A plan sponsor can elect not to apply modifications of minimum funding requirements for any plan year beginning in 2013, either for all purposes or only for determining the AFTAP for the year. [Notice 2014-53, 2014-43 I.R.B. 739]

New market rate of return rules were adopted by the IRS in November 2015 for hybrid pension plans (defined benefit plans, such as cash balance and pension equity plans, that use a benefit formula based on lump sums) and other plans whose formulas have a similar effect. Under these rules, the sponsor of an applicable defined benefit plan whose rate of return exceeds the market rate is permitted to adopt a lower, permissible rate without violating the anti-cutback rule. These regulations are generally applicable to plan amendments on or after September 18, 2014, or an earlier date elected by the plan. However, the rules are scheduled to expire for amendments made on or after the first day of the first plan year that begins on or after January 1, 2017. [T.D. 9743, 2015-48 I.R.B. 679]

The higher the discount rate, the higher the growth rate over the annuity period, so the present value of a lump sum will be lower. A lower discount rate requires a higher lump sum. In a class action about the discount rates used by a pension plan to convert a straight life annuity to a lump sum, the Seventh Circuit ruled in 2013 that the pension plan's segment rate of approximately 5.4% was acceptable. Under the PPA, discount rates can be increased retroactively; this is not a cutback. The plan forbade reduction in accrued benefits (the value of the straight life annuity), it did not forbid a retroactive reduction in the benefits of participants who took a lump-sum distribution. [*Dennison v. MONY Life Ret. Income Security Plan*, 710 F.3d 741 (7th Cir. 2013)]

[J] Funding Changes

Rev. Procs. 2000-40 and -41, 2000-42 I.R.B. 357 and 371, provide the procedures under which the sponsor or administrator of a defined benefit plan subject to I.R.C. § 412 or ERISA § 302 can get the Secretary of the Treasury to approve a change in the plan's funding method under I.R.C. § 412(c)(5)(A)—e.g., changing the method of valuing assets, the plan year, or the valuation date.

The IRS has jurisdiction to review the appropriateness of any change that significantly affects the plan's minimum funding requirement or full funding limitation. The agency will approve a change in funding method only if the proposed new method and the form of the transition are both acceptable. The due date for a request is the end of the plan year in which the change will be effective. The IRS has discretion to extend the due date by up to two-and-a-half months if the plan submits a statement giving adequate reason for the delay.

[K]   Minimum Funding Waivers

Waivers from the minimum funding standard are governed by Code § 412(c). The current (i.e., post-PPA) version allows a waiver of all or part of the minimum funding standard if the employer would not be able to satisfy the minimum funding standard without encountering temporary substantial business hardship—and the plan participants would be worse off if the plan were compelled to meet the standard. However, a plan cannot get waivers for more than three years in any 15-year period, and amounts attributable to a waived funding deficiency in one year cannot be waived in the next. For a single-employer plan, if a waiver is granted, the minimum required contribution under § 430 is reduced by the amount of funding deficiency that is waived; this amount is amortized under § 430(e).

Factors in determining whether the employer is undergoing temporary substantial business hardship include whether:

- The company is operating at a loss;

- The industry is experiencing substantial under- or unemployment;

- The industry's sales and profits are declining or already reduced;

- The waiver is the only way for the plan to continue.

The plan can be required to give security for the waiver, to be enforced by the PBGC. The waiver application must be made not later than the fifteenth day of the third month beginning after the end of the plan year. The company applying for the waiver must prove that it has notified affected parties (e.g., plan participants and beneficiaries) of the application.

The notice must be given within 14 days before the date of the application for the waiver, and must disclose the sponsor's name; the year for which the waiver is requested; the FMV of plan assets; the present value of vested benefits under the plan; the present value of all benefits if the plan terminated; and the interest rate used in the calculations. Plan participants and beneficiaries must be informed that they can get a copy of the plan's latest annual report, and can submit comments about the waiver application. [IRS EP Examination Process Guide § 9, <http://www.irs.gov/Retirement-Plans/Retirement-Plan-Participant-Notices-Request-of-a-Waiver-of-the-Minimum-Funding-Requirement> (updated Aug. 18, 2016) (last viewed Feb. 7, 2017)] Plans that have obtained a waiver are not permitted to adopt amendments that increase benefits, change accrual of benefits, or change vesting schedules—unless the amendment is required for compliance, repeals another amendment that would be problematic, or is reasonable and has only a minimal effect on plan liabilities.

See 78 Fed. Reg. 20039 (Apr. 3, 2013) for PBGC proposals greatly reducing the number of situations in which "reportable events" must be reported to the PBGC, but application for a minimum funding waiver would continue to be a reportable event.

[L] Pension Freezes

A frozen plan is a defined benefit plan that either has ceased benefit accruals for all employees, or accrues benefits for current employees but does not accept new entrants. A frozen plan with 50 participants and $500,000 in underfunding would see heavy increases in PBGC premiums, The new mortality tables (see § 5.04) could increase plan liabilities by 6%–8%, and the amount needed to cash out participants with lump sums could increase by 7%–15% depending on a participant's age and retirement date. As research by the Center for Retirement Research at Boston College shows, since the mid-2000s, pension freezes have been common even in plans maintained by companies that are financially sound. Previously, it was very rare for defined benefit plans to be frozen, and then usually in association with bankruptcy or serious financial problems. The researchers attributed the increased acceptability of freezes to:

1. Reducing workers' compensation to be able to compete in the global market.

2. Cutting back pensions because health costs had soared.

3. Financial risks (such as stock market exposure) that made funding defined benefit plans unattractive.

4. Upper management's lack of interest in rank-and-file pensions because so much of their compensation came from nonqualified plans.

The researchers identified three forms of plan freezes:

1. Closing the plan to new hires;

2. A partial freeze that covers new hires and some current employees; or

3. A total freeze that affects all employees.

[James Willhite, *Pension Terminations May Spike in the Near-Term*, WSJ. com (Nov. 12, 2013)]

U.S. Steel froze its defined benefit plan for non-union participants, effective December 31, 2015; they were moved to a defined contribution plan. [Barry B. Burr, *Pension Pioneer U.S. Steel Joins Corporate Wave*, Bloomberg (Sept. 15, 2015) (benefitslink.com)]

Whether it is more cost effective to terminate or immunize a frozen defined benefit plan depends on factors such as how much it would cost to buy annuities for the participants and how much management time is needed to administer the plan. (Immunization means buying assets to secure benefit payments, such as long-term, high-rated bonds that generate income in amounts and at the time needed to pay benefits.) The PPA, by allowing plan sponsors to make lump-sum calculations based on higher interest rates, reduces the size of lump-sum payments, and, therefore, makes it easier to terminate plans than under prior law.

The demographics of the plan's participants greatly affects the decision. In most plans, liability is fairly equal for active participants, ex-employees who terminated when they had vested benefits, and retirees. A young plan is one where liabilities are concentrated on funding future benefits for active employees; a mature plan already has a high volume of retirees receiving benefits. The authors of the article concluded that termination is probably less expensive than immunization in a young plan, but costs are fairly similar for termination and immunization in either a typical or a mature plan.

Employers received temporary relief, for years before 2017, under Notice 2014-5, 2014-2 I.R.B. 276, and Notice 2015-28, 2015-14 I.R.B. 848.

Additional relief was provided in early 2016 when employers made certain allocations to replace defined benefit plans. If a plan that transfers defined benefit funds to defined contribution plans and the plan includes a closed plan, certain discrimination testing rules are relaxed if the closed plan was in effect for five years before the closure, without significant changes. [81 Fed. Reg. 4976 (Jan. 29, 2016); see Rebecca Moore, *IRS Proposes Nondiscrimination Relief for Closed DBs*, plansponsor.com (Jan. 28, 2016) See also Announcement 2016-16, 2016-1 I.R.B. 697, discussed in Prudential Compliance Advisory, *IRS Proposes New Nondiscrimination Rules* (June 2016) (benefitslink.com)]

Notice 2016-57, 2016-40 I.R.B. 432, extends the relief for another year, for defined benefit plans that were soft-frozen via amendments adopted prior to December 13, 2013, because the IRS did not anticipate it would be able to publish final regulations before the relief expired. The objective was to allow closed defined benefit plans to satisfy anti-discrimination requirements as grandfathered employees accrue more seniority and earn more than the younger workers entering the transferee defined contribution plan. [Marjorie Martin & Joanne Jacobson, *IRS Extends Temporary Nondiscrimination Relief for Closed DB Plans Through 2017* (Sept. 19, 2016) (benefitslink.com); Rebecca Moore, *IRS Extends Nondiscrimination Relief for Closed DBs*, plansponsor.com (Sept. 21, 2016)]

The § 4043 reporting rules continue to apply until the plan is fully terminated and all assets have been distributed. Failure to comply can be penalized by up to $1,100 a day. Even after a plan has been frozen, most reportable events can still occur and the PBGC reporting and liability rules under § 4063 can be triggered by a permanent substantial cessation of operations at any of the sponsor's facilities if it results in substantial job loss. [Vivian S. McCardell, *Pension Plan Sponsors: Whether Your Pension Plan Is Frozen, Partially Frozen Or Freeze*

Dried, Don't Forget Those PBGC Reportable Events, Morgan Lewis & Bockius LLP (Aug. 11, 2015), available at Lexology.com] On § 4043 reportable events in general, see 80 Fed. Reg. 54979 (Sept. 11, 2015).

The Bank of America/Merrill Lynch suggested tactics in 2016 for managing frozen plans. They call for a four-step process. The first is evaluating the goals of the plan, including setting a time horizon, assessing costs, and considering the implications for corporate earnings. The second step is understanding liability risks, including potential liability in connection with future termination of the plan. The third step is to consider the assets that must be invested. The article warns that overfunding the plan is wasteful, because it is difficult to remove the extra funds from the plan without becoming liable for excise taxes. The final step is carrying out the strategy, reviewing it periodically to make sure goals are being met. [Bank of America/Merrill Lynch, *A Road Map for Effectively Managing a Frozen Pension Plan,* Retirement & Benefit Plan Services (Apr. 2016) (benefitslink.com)]

[M]   The Annual Funding Notice

Most plans that are subject to PBGC jurisdiction must provide participants and beneficiaries with annual funding notices—the document that replaced the SAR. PPA § 501(a) amended ERISA § 101(f) to require all PBGC-insured defined benefit plans to provide an annual funding notice to each participant and beneficiary, any unions for the workplace, and to the PBGC. Defined benefit plans that are not subject to the PBGC's jurisdiction (e.g., government plans; church plans; plans of professional service employers with 25 or fewer employees) must still file the SAR.

The annual funding notice must be provided to each participant, beneficiary, union, and the PBGC. The DOL will not take action against single-employer plans with liabilities under $50 million for failure to give notice to the PBGC, as long as they respond to the PBGC's request for the information within 30 days. [See 74 Fed. Reg. 17 (Jan. 2, 2009) for the EBSA final rule imposing civil penalties of up to $1,000 per day for each violation of ERISA § 101 or 514(e)(3) committed by not furnishing the annual funding notice, and 75 Fed. Reg. 70625 (Nov. 18, 2010).] The penalty for failure to notify participants and beneficiaries of benefit restrictions under Internal Revenue Code § 436 is much higher: as of August 1, 2016, it is $1,632 a day. See § 5.08[D] below for the 2016 increases in many ERISA penalties.

The 2012 pension funding relief bill, MAP-21 (Pub. L. No. 112-141), requires some plans to provide additional information in their annual funding notices. The requirement applies to plans that had at least 50 participants at any time in the previous year; the stabilized funding target is less than 95% than the regular funding target; and, without the relief provided by MAP-21, the plan would have a funding shortfall of $500,000 or more. Plans subject to the requirement must disclose that the law has changed, reducing the employer's required contributions. The funding notice must include a table showing the effect of the law on required contributions and the funding shortfall.

EBSA issued final regulations about the ERISA § 101(f) annual funding notice requirements for defined benefit plans, incorporating the MPRA disclosure requirements for multi-employer plans in critical and declining status. Approximately 27,000 plans, with about 43.7 million participants and benefits, are subject to the rule. However, certain terminating single-employer plans are excused from furnishing the funding notice. If a material event that would otherwise require disclosure is not known to the plan administration until 120 days or less before the due date of the funding notice, the event can be omitted from the notice. A funding notice need not be provided for a plan year if the notice's due date is on or after the date of filing the PBGC Form 500 (standard termination notice)—as long as final distribution of plan assets to satisfy benefit liabilities occurs pursuant to ERISA § 4014(b). Multi-employer plans that have terminated by mass withdrawal, and § 412(e)(3) plans, have alternative methods of compliance: see ERISA § 4014A(a)(2). Small plans (100 or fewer participants on each day of the previous year; single- or multi-employer) must provide the notice on the later of the date the annual report is filed, or the date of the extension granted to the plan.

In general, the annual funding notice must provide information about the plan's assets and benefit payments; PBGC guarantees; and possible benefit reductions. Notice must be sent to every participant who was covered under the plan on the last day of the notice year; every beneficiary; every alternate payee; every labor organization, as well as to the PBGC. Notice must also be given to every employer that is a party to the CBAs under which the plan is maintained—or who might otherwise be liable to withdrawal liability under ERISA. These final regulations are effective March 4, 2015, for notices relating to years beginning on or after January 1, 2015. [80 Fed. Reg. 5625 (Feb. 3, 2015); Appendix A provides a model notice for single-employer plans, Appendix B for multi-employer plans.]

§ 5.06 BENEFIT ACCRUALS

Another issue in plan administration and compliance is the schedule on which benefits are contributed on the individual's behalf, being added to the pension account so that eventually the participant will receive his or her defined benefit. Vesting is a separate but related concept. Vesting determines the extent to which employees will be entitled to receive the accrued benefit when they retire or employment otherwise terminates.

Defined benefit plans must accrue benefits using one of the three permitted mechanisms:

1. The 3% rule: at all times, the accrued benefit must be at least 3% of the maximum benefit calculated under the plan's formula, multiplied by the number of years of participation.

2. The 133.5% test: the accrued benefit payable at Normal Retirement Age equals the normal retirement benefit, and accrual in any plan year does not exceed 133.5% of the accrual for any prior year. In other words, benefits must accrue in a fairly level manner in each year.

3. The fractional rule: the annual benefit an employee has accrued at the time of separation from service must be proportionate to what he or she would have received by remaining employed until normal retirement age.

Under § 412(i), insured plans whose accrued benefit is always at least equal to the cash surrender value of the insurance are exempt from the minimum funding rules.

The Second Circuit ruled in early 2006 that Xerox unlawfully reduced the pension benefits of persons who left the company and were rehired. Xerox used a "phantom account offset" system under which the lump sum received when the individual left the company for the first time was used to cut the benefits at eventual retirement. The Second Circuit ruled that a plan amendment occurs not when the plan administrator changes the way the plan operates, but when the employees are properly informed of the change. The court ruled that proper information was not provided until 1998, so applying it to anyone who was rehired before that date would be a violation of the anti-cutback rule. [*Frommert v. Conkright*, 433 F.3d 254 (2d Cir. 2006); the same offset method was also disapproved in *Miller v. Xerox Corp.*, 464 F.3d 871 (9th Cir. 2006), *cert. denied* (Mar. 19, 2007)] In its April 21, 2010 decision in this case [559 U.S. 506], the Supreme Court strongly affirmed the powers of plan administrators. According to the Supreme Court, the basic principle comes from *Firestone Tire & Rubber v. Bruch.* [489 U.S. 101 (1989)]

When the plan documents delegate the power to interpret the plan to the administrators, courts will uphold the administrator's interpretation of plan terms if it is reasonable. The Supreme Court sent the case back to the Second Circuit, which sent it back to the District Court for the Western District of New York. In December 2013, the Second Circuit held that the suit was meritorious. The proposed offset method was unreasonable and the SPD was not accurate because it did not clearly disclose that the lump-sum distribution would reduce benefits. [*Frommert v. Conkright*, 738 F.3d 522 (2d Cir. 2013)]

Later, the Western District of New York ruled that the notice violations justified imposing an equitable remedy of re-calculating the benefits when the plaintiffs were rehired as if they were new hires. [*Frommert v. Becker,* No. 00-CR-6311L (W.D.N.Y. Jan. 5, 2016); a later order with the same case number, dealing with pre-judgment interest, was issued on November 3, 2016.]

A mid-2012 Fourth Circuit decision holds that increased benefit accruals to participants who have reached normal retirement age (NRA) do not violate the prohibition against backloading in later years. The 1331/3% test forbids accrual of benefits more than 1/3 greater than the annual rate of accrual in the previous year. The rule was adopted to prevent employers from offering inadequate accrual rates in the early years of employment (when turnover is highest). In this case, the NRA was defined as the earlier of age 64 or 60 months of vesting service. The Fourth Circuit held that ERISA anti-backloading rules no longer apply once the participant reaches NRA. [*McCorkle v. Bank of Am. Corp.,* 688 F.3d 164 (4th Cir. 2012)]

§ 5.07 NOTICES OF REDUCTION OF BENEFIT ACCRUALS

Defined benefit plans (and other plans subject to the I.R.C. § 412 full funding rules) have an obligation under ERISA § 204(h) and I.R.C. § 4980F (a new provision added by EGTRRA) to provide notice of plan amendments that significantly reduce future benefit accruals. The notice must contain the text or a summary of the plan amendment, and the effective date of the amendment. Notice must be given at least 15 days before the effective date of the plan amendment.

Not only is an excise tax imposed on the failure, but in "egregious" cases (where the employer intentionally refused to give notice, or failed very badly to disclose the needed information) the plan amendment will not be given effect. Therefore, participants will be entitled to the unreduced benefit that was in effect before the plan was amended. See T.D. 9052, RIN-1545-BA08 2003-19 I.R.B. 879. The plan is required to provide notice to plan participants when the rate of future accrual is significantly reduced, or when an early retirement subsidy is modified in a way that operates as a reduction in the rate of future benefit accruals.

In general, the notice must be given at least 45 days before the effective date of the change, but the notice can be as short as 15 days before the effective date for certain merger and acquisition-related transactions of small plans. Also in connection with mergers and acquisitions, where there is a plan-to-plan transfer or merger that affects only the early retirement benefit or subsidy, notice can be given after the effective date of the amendment, but no more than 30 days later.

The notice must be given in a form that is understandable to the average plan participant, providing enough information to understand the effect of the amendment. It is not necessary to give participants a § 204(h) notice with respect to PPA amendments reflecting mandatory changes in interest rates or mortality assumptions. Nor is a 204(h) notice required for changes to benefits that are not protected benefits, or to protected benefits that can be altered in accordance with § 411(d)(6), or for adoption of a retroactive amendment to comply with PPA § 1107. [T.D. 9472, 2009-51 I.R.B. 850]

Code § 4980F(e)(3) requires notice to be provided within a reasonable time before the plan amendment takes effect. In general, that means 45 days before the effective date (15 days for small or multi-employer plans). The First Circuit held that it was permissible for an employer to eliminate participants' option to move defined contribution plan assets to a defined benefit plan. Although an accrued benefit was diminished, the anti-cutback rule was not violated because ERISA permits this type of benefit to be eliminated. [*Tasker v. DHL Ret. Sav. Plan*, 621 F.3d 34 (1st Cir. 2010)]

In another case involving the same plan, the Ninth Circuit joined the First Circuit in holding that it is not a cutback for an employer to eliminate a transfer provision in a plan that allows employees to move assets from a defined contribution to a defined benefit plan. The IRS regulations say that a plan "may be amended to eliminate provisions permitting the transfer of benefits between and among defined contribution and defined benefit plans." When DHL bought Airborne Express Inc., and merged the two companies' retirement plans, it removed the transfer option from the Airborne plan. [*Andersen v. DHL Ret. Pension Plan*, 766 F.3d 1205 (9th Cir. 2014)]

The Eleventh Circuit, noting that Social Security integration (reducing the benefit to coordinate the Social Security benefits the participant receives) is permitted by 29 U.S.C. § 1056(b)), held that it did not violate the anti-cutback rule for a frozen plan to adopt amendments that changed the Social Security integration formula for people who had not yet reached the plan's early retirement age. The change could not affect future benefit accruals because the plan was frozen and there would be no more benefit accruals. The test of an accrued benefit is what a participant would receive by terminating employment at that point, and the plaintiff here was younger than 52, the earliest age at which benefits were available. The right to a future benefit accrual based on additional service is not an accrued benefit, so changing it does not violate the anti-cutback rule. [*Cinotto v. Delta Air Lines Inc.*, 674 F.3d 1285 (11th Cir. 2012)]

In late 2012, the IRS finalized regulations under the § 411(d)(6) anti-cutback rules effective for plan amendments adopted and effective after November 8, 2012. Single-employer defined benefit plans that are subject to ERISA § 4021 can be amended to eliminate lump sum or other optional forms of benefit that accelerate payment after bankruptcy. The PBGC and the Bankruptcy Court must agree that the plan would go through a distress or involuntary termination if the optional benefits are not eliminated. The PBGC must also determine that the plan is not sufficiently funded to provide the guaranteed benefits. If an optional benefit form is eliminated, and the plan does not have other options with substantial survivor benefits, the same amendment that eliminates the lump-sum distribution option can also adopt other options to provide survivor benefits. The entire amendment is considered together in determining if the amendment can take effect in accordance with § 436(c). [T.D. 9601, 77 Fed. Reg. 66915 (Nov. 8, 2012), finalizing proposals at 77 Fed. Reg. 37349 (June 21, 2012)]

For example, the bankruptcy court permitted American Airlines to eliminate optional lump sum and installment forms of benefit payments, on the grounds that so many pilots would retire if they could get a lump sum when the airline emerges from bankruptcy that it would be difficult to adequately staff the schedule. [Rebecca Moore, *American Allowed to Eliminate Lump Sums*, plansponsor.com (Dec. 14, 2012)]

§ 5.08 PBGC COMPLIANCE

[A] PBGC Organization

Formally speaking, the Pension Benefit Guarantee Corporation (PBGC) is organized as a corporation, but it's really a quasi-governmental agency that draws its powers from ERISA § 4002. The PBGC's Board of Directors consists of the Secretaries of Labor, Treasury, and Commerce. The federal court system gives the agency special deference, by giving its cases the earliest possible calendar dates. Employers sued by the PBGC in connection with a plan termination can be required to pay part or all of the agency's litigation costs.

According to the PBGC's 2015 annual report, in fiscal year 2015, the PBGC paid $5.6 billion in benefits to 826,000 retirees from terminated single-employer plans, slightly more than $5.5 billion paid the year before. In FY 2015, the PBGC assumed responsibility for 25,000 more people in 65 trusteed single-employer plans. The PBGC received $4.1 billion in premiums under the single-employer program, but its investment income was only $324 million. The single-employer plan program's deficit increased from $19.3 billion in 2014 to $24.1 billion in 2015. The multi-employer plan program's problems got much worse, in part because changes in the annuity marketplace led to changes in the interest factors that the PBGC uses to value its liabilities. The multi-employer plan deficit was $42.4 billion in 2014 and $52.3 billion in 2015. A further 17 multi-employer plans were identified as newly terminated or projected to run out of money within 10 years. At that point, no plan had completed the process for reducing benefits, so the PBGC's results did not reflect any such activity. [PBGC press release No. 15-12, *PBGC Paid Nearly $6 Billion in Pension Benefits to Retirees in FY 2015* (Nov. 17, 2015) (benefitslink.com); For full analysis of 2014 statistics, see <http://www.pbgc.gov/prac/data-books.html>; see Rebecca Moore, *PBGC Data Tables Show Serious Underfunding*, plansponsor.com (May 31, 2016)]

The 2016 annual report showed a decline in the deficit of the single-employer program, from $24.1 billion to $20.6 billion, and there were fewer plan terminations than were expected. At the end of fiscal 2016, the single-employer program had $97.3 billion in assets, $117.9 billion in liabilities. The agency paid out $5.7 billion in benefits to close to 840,000 retirees in more than 4,700 single-employer plans—slightly more than the $5.6 billion paid to 826,000 retirees the previous year. The PBGC took on responsibility for more than 46,000 more people in single-employer plans in 2016. [Rebecca Moore, *PBGC Multiemployer Program Deficit Nearly $60 Billion*, plansponsor.com (Nov. 16, 2016)]

PBGC's FY 2014 Projections Report delays projected insolvency date for the multi-employer program (which covers over 10 million people) for three years (2025 rather than 2022), thanks to new premium revenues provided by the MPRA. [Judy Faust Hartnett, *PBGC Issues New Solvency Projections*, plansponsor.com (Sept. 28, 2015)]

The main task of the PBGC is to guarantee that participants in defined benefit plans will receive a basic benefit even if their plan is insufficiently funded, or if it is terminated. See § 5.01[A][1] for the PBGC's role when multi-employer plans are partitioned or permitted to reduce benefits.

Most qualified plans are required to file Form 5500, which goes both to the DOL and the IRS, to report about plan finances and operations. DOL proposed changes in mid-2016 to improve the collection of plan data, increase the amount of compliance information available to the agencies, and make it easier to analyze the data electronically. The proposal also applies to Form 5500-SF for small plans. The changes generally apply to the 2019 plan year, but employers are permitted to adopt them voluntarily for earlier years. [81 Fed. Reg. 47533 (July 21, 2016); see Carly E. Grey, *DOL Proposes Major Changes to Form 5500*, Morgan Lewis & Bockius LLP (July 20, 2016), available at Lexology.com]

The PBGC maintains a Missing Participants program that finds participants who are entitled to plan benefits. The existing program covers certain defined benefit plans (single-employer plans insured by the PBGC). In mid-2016, the PBGC proposed to expand the program to additional types of defined benefit plans (e.g., terminating multi-employer plans; small professional service organization plans)—and to terminated defined contribution plans. The plans would transfer amounts owed to the missing participants to the PBGC, which would retain the money until the participant could be located by periodic searches of the PBGC's database of missing participants. The PBGC expected to implement the proposal in 2018. [PBGC.gov, *Proposed Expanded Missing Participants Program* (Sept. 19, 2016) (benefitslink.com)]

For at least 30 years, the PBGC's general position was that buyers of a business' assets are not liable for termination liabilities of the seller's plan. Some courts have held that a buyer that has notice of the liability, and that has substantial continuity of operations with the seller, can be liable. However, the PBGC changed its position and argued that an asset buyer was liable as successor for the seller's unfunded defined benefit plan liabilities. This argument was unsuccessful in a 2017 Northern District of Ohio case. The district court refused to apply federal common law, holding that ERISA has a specific statutory scheme that must be followed. A recent article notes that it is possible—but not certain—that in a bankruptcy situation, Bankruptcy Code § 363(f) will protect asset purchasers from successor liability when liability is imposed for withdrawal from a multi-employer plan. [*PBGC v. Findlay Indus., Inc.*, 2016 WL 7474404 (N.D. Ohio 2017); see Eric Keller, *PBGC Attempts to Hold Asset Buyer Liable for Seller's Underfunded Single Employer Pension Plan Termination Liabilities*, Paulhastings.com (Feb. 2, 2017) (benefitslink.com)]

[B] PBGC Premiums

The PBGC stays afloat by charging premiums to employers who maintain defined benefit plans. There are three types of premium: the flat-rate premium; the variable-rate premium (VRP) imposed on insured single-employer plans that have unfunded vested benefits; and a one-time termination premium In recent years, premiums have increased significantly, not only administratively but under the Moving Ahead for Progress in the 21st Century Act (MAP-21; Pub. L. No. 112-141), the Bipartisan Budget Act of 2013, Pub. L. No. 113-67, HATFA, the MPRA and the Bipartisan Budget Act of 2015.

An additional premium of $1,250 per participant is imposed when a single-employer plan is terminated under ERISA § 4041(c)(2)(B) or 4042. If the plan is terminated while the sponsor's Chapter 11 bankruptcy case is pending, the special premium is not due until the sponsor's bankruptcy discharge or until the bankruptcy case is dismissed.

For plan years that begin in 2016, the flat rate premium is $64 for single-employer plans, $27 for multi-employer plans. For single-employer plans, the variable rate premium for 2016 is $30/$1000 unfunded vested benefits, capped at $500 times the number of participants. (Certain plans with fewer than 25 employees may qualify for a lower cap.) All of these amounts are scheduled to be indexed after 2016. [PBGC.gov, *Premium Rates 2016*, <http://www.pbgc.gov/prac/prem/premium-rates.html> (last accessed Aug. 4, 2016)]

The Bipartisan Budget Act of 2015 [BBA 2015; Pub. L. No. 114-74] provides for ongoing future increases in PBGC premiums, and accelerates the pace of increases in the premium. Minimum funding requirements were relaxed, which tends to lower the amount of pension contributions that employers can deduct thereby increasing federal revenues from corporate taxes. Before BBA 2015, PBGC premiums were scheduled to increase based on growth of average wages, but BBA 2015 calls for much greater increases: a single-employer flat-rate premium of $69 in 2017, $74 in 2018, $80 in 2019, and then indexing for inflation. The VRP was also supposed to increase in line with wage growth, but BBA increases the VRP to $37 in 2018 and $41 in 2019, although the cap amount remains $500 per participant, and the flat rate premium for multi-employer plans remains $27 for 2017–2019. [Ekon Benefits, *The Bipartisan Budget Act of 2015: The Impact on Single-Employer Pension Plans* (Nov. 2015) (benefitslink.com)]

Premiums increased once again, in 2017, when the single-employer premium was $69 but the multi-employer plan premium rose to $28 and the VRP was $34 per $1,000 of unfunded vested benefits, capped at $517. The premium payment instructions for 2017 include a new section for calculating premiums for a year in which the plan is involved in a merger, consolidation, or spinoff. The MyPAA web portal is used for electronic payment of premiums. Filings can be made by using the portal's data entry screens, or compatible private-sector software. See the Where to File section for due dates. The filing requirements for 2017 are largely unchanged from those for 2016. [<http://www.pbgc.gov/Documents/2017-Premium-Payment-Instructions.pdf>; see John Manganaro, *2017 Premium Filing Instructions Updated by PBGC,* plansponsor.com (Jan. 6, 2017)]

Until 2014, the due date for paying the PBGC premium depended on whether the plan was small (under 100 participants). However, a new rule was phased in starting in 2014, with phase-in complete by 2015: now the due date for all sizes of plan is the fifteenth day of the tenth full calendar month that begins on or after the first day of the premium payment year. Therefore, for calendar year plans, the premium due date is October 15, 2015.

A terminating plan must continue to make premium filings, and pay premiums, up through the year in which any of these events occurs:

- All of the plan assets have been distributed to satisfy liabilities;
- A trustee has been appointed under ERISA § 4042;
- All of the plan's assets and liabilities have been distributed to another plan or other plans in connection with a merger or consolidation;
- The plan is no longer a covered plan under ERISA § 4021;

until all of the plan assets have been distributed to satisfy liabilities; [<http://www.pbgc.gov/prac/prem/filings/2015-premium-payment-instructions .html> (Aug. 8, 2015)]

Defined benefit plans are obligated to pay PBGC premiums within nine-and-a-half months of the beginning of the plan year (this means October 15 for calendar-year plans). Before 2016, the penalty for late payment was 1% of the late payment per month, capped at 50%, if the premium underpayment was corrected before the plan received notice from the PBGC, In April 2016, regulations were proposed, and finalized in September 2016, reducing penalties for late payment of premiums for both single and multi-employer plans. The PBGC was concerned that high penalties would give sponsors an additional incentive to terminate their plans. In 2015, approximately 2,000 plans were subject to late payment penalties, for a total of $7 million. Premiums have risen more than 80% between 2012 and 2016, and the penalty for underfunding has more than tripled. PBGC's final rule on penalty relief cuts late payment penalties in half. Penalties are reduced by 80% if the plan has a good history of compliance (either timely payments or all penalties waived for the previous five years) and pays promptly after receiving notice of underpayment from the PBGC. The September 2016 rule does not affect penalties for late payment of the special premium imposed on a terminating plan. [81 Fed. Reg. 65542 (Sept. 23, 2016); see Marjorie Martin and Joanne Jacobson, *PBGC Finalizes Reduced Late Premium Payment Penalties*, HRC FYI (Sept. 22, 2016) (benefitslink.com); Cheiron.us, *PBGC Issues Final Rule for Premium Penalty Relief* (Oct. 4, 2016) (benefitslink.com); Vipal Monga, *Pension Insurer Moves to Ease Burden on Defined Benefit Providers*, WSJ.com (Sept. 22, 2016)]

The IRS's Employee Plans Compliance Unit (EPCU) launched a Form 5500 non-filer project late in 2011, sending compliance check letters to plan sponsors for whom there is no record of a 5500 or 5500-SF filing with the DOL, or 5500-EZ with the IRS after six to nine months have elapsed since the due date of the return. EPCU asks the sponsor to either file the return or explain why it was not necessary. If a form was required, the IRS sends out a CP 403 Notice (delinquency notice) seeking a response within 30 days. EPCU does not analyze whether employers' explanations for nonfiling are reasonable, although the IRS or the DOL may waive or reduce penalties on a showing of mitigating circumstances that reduced the plan's ability to file the return. [IRS Employee Plans News, Issue 2011-7 (Oct. 12, 2011)]

A plan's failure to make a timely Form 5500 annual report filing can be penalized under both the Code and ERISA. Previous IRS guidance said that correcting the late filing under the DOL's Delinquent Filer Voluntary Compliance Program (DFVC) program could relieve the plan of both IRS and DOL penalties. However, the IRS announced in mid-2014 that avoiding IRS penalties requires a separate filing. This requirement applies retroactively to all DFVC filings made since 2009. Before 2009, plan administrators reported about terminated participants with vested benefits on Form 5500, Schedule SSA. The IRS's transition to electronic filing included replacing Schedule SSA with Form 8955-SSA, which is filed only with the IRS. In 2013, the DOL required e-filing of all DFVC reports using the EFAST2 program. At that point, DOL stopped accepting Form 8955-SSA, with the result that the information that the IRS requires no longer can be submitted under the DFVC program.

IRS's Notice 2014-32 creates a relief program for years in which the plan administrator satisfies the DFVC requirements, and also files a complete Form 8955-SSA for the year no later than December 1, 2014—or 30 days after the DFVC filing. However, the Form 8955-SSA filed for this purpose must be on paper, not electronic. [Notice 2014-35, 2014-23 I.R.B. 1072. Notice 2014-35 does not apply to Form 5500-EZ or 5500-SF filers, because those forms are filed by non-ERISA plans.]

All premium information required by ERISA § 4007 must now be e-filed. The plan can file by entering data directly into MyPAA, by uploading data from proprietary software, or by importing data into the MyPAA data entry screens from approved software. MyPAA accepts credit cards, electronic checks, and Automated Clearing House transfers; payments can also be made outside MyPAA. The PBGC recommends using <http://www.pay.gov>, a free federal website for making secure payments to the PBGC and federal government agencies. See the 2015 instructions; Appendix 3 explains the payment options in detail.

Under proposed regulations effective for plan years beginning on or after January 1, 2014, administrators of plans such as 401(k)s would have to file Form 5500 and Form 8955-SSA electronically or on specified magnetic media if the employer files at least 240 returns of any type, including income tax returns, W-2 and 1099 forms, and employment tax returns. The proposals deal with the tax requirements, which are separate from the ERISA reporting requirements. Failure to file electronically when this is mandatory is considered a failure to file. , According to EBIA, the proposals do not impose significant changes, because DOL already requires Forms 5500 and 5500-SF to be e-filed and Form 8955-SSA could already be e-filed with IRS's FIRE system. But the e-filing obligation has been extended to the limited number of 5500-EZ filers who are required to file more than 250 returns a year. [*Employee Retirement Benefit Plan Returns Required on Magnetic Media*, 26 C.F.R. Part 301, 78 Fed. Reg. 53704 (Aug. 30, 2013)]

[C] Accounting Issues

On March 10, 2017, the Financial Accounting Standards Board (FASB) issued Accounting Standards Update No. 2017-07, Topic 715: *Improving the Presentation of Net Periodic Pension Cost and Net Periodic Postretirement Benefit Cost,* to increase transparency of information about defined benefit plans that is published in an employer's financial statements. Under Generally Accepted Accounting Procedures (GAAP), defined benefit pension cost and net benefit cost (the post-retirement pension cost) must be aggregated for reporting on financial statements. FASB made these changes because commenters asserted that reporting defined benefit cost on a net basis requires aggregation of dissimilar elements, forcing users to spend more to analyze financial statements. Under the new standard, service cost components must be broken out from other components of net benefit costs. The FASB standard explains how service costs (which can be capitalized) and other components of the net benefit cost (which cannot) should be presented in the income statement. The new standard requires breaking out service cost component from other components of net benefit cost. The standard explains how to present the service cost component and other components of the net benefit cost in the income statement. The standard is effective for public companies for annual periods beginning after December 15, 2017. [Kenneth Tysiac, *FASB Changes Presentation of Defined Benefit Costs,* journalofaccountancy.com (Mar. 2017) (benefitslink.com)]

On the fifteenth of every month, the PBGC updates its Website [<http://www.pbgc.gov/prac/interest.html>] to give the interest rates that should be used in that month for:

- Valuation of lump-sum payments made by the plan;

- Variable rate premiums;

- Valuation of annuity benefits;

- PBGC charges imposed with respect to employer liability, unpaid contributions, and unpaid premiums.

PBGC staff can be reached by e-mail to answer compliance questions about:

- Premium calculations and payments: premiums@pbgc.gov;

- Coverage and standard terminations: standard@pbgc.gov;

- Distress terminations: distress.term@pbgc.gov;

- Early Warning Program: advance.report@pbgc.gov;

- ERISA § 4010 reporting: ERISA.4010@pbgc.gov;

- Reportable events: post-event.report@pbgc.gov;

- General legal questions: AskOGC@pbgc.gov;

- Problem resolution officer: practitioner.pro@pbgc.gov;

- Other: Ask.PBGC@pbgc.gov.

[D] Penalty Increases

The Bipartisan Budget Act of 2015, Pub. L. No.114-74, ordered federal agencies to make up for decades without increases in civil penalties. As a result, civil penalties increased greatly, often to two or three times the earlier level. The DOL published interim final rules at 81 Fed. Reg. 29765 (May 12, 2016) and 81 Fed. Reg. 43429 (July 1, 2016), increasing the penalty levels under many ERISA provisions. It is important to note that these regulations do not use a simple formula such as "all penalties that were $1,100 are now $2,063," and that these regulations do not cover all ERISA penalties. The first set of penalty increases applied to ERISA violations that occurred after November 2, 2015, and for which penalties were assessed after August 1, 2016. Because penalties are now increased annually, additional increases were adopted for penalties assessed on or after February 3, 2017, for violations occurring after November 2, 2015. [Xerox FYI, *DOL Increases Penalties for ERISA Compliance Violations* (July 18, 2016) (benefitslink.com); 82 Fed. Reg. 8813 (Jan. 31, 2017); see Conduent FYI, *DOL, PBGC and HHS Increase Penalties for Violations* (Feb. 10, 2017) (benefitslink .com)]

The new maximum penalties include (with the second set of increases after the slash):

- Failure to furnish statement of benefits to ex-participants, or failure to maintain retirement plan records (ERISA § 209(b)): $28 per employee/ same

- Failure or refusal to file Form 5500, or multi-employer plan's failure to certify endangered status (§ 502(c)(2)): $2,063 per day/$2,097 per day

- Failure to notify single-employer plan participants of benefit restrictions; failure to furnish multi-employer plan documents on request from a participant or union; failure of a multi-employer plan to give an employer an estimate of its withdrawal liability (§ 502(c)(4)): $1,632 per day/ $1,659 per day

- Failure to comply with a DOL request for employee benefit plan documents (§ 502(c)(6)): $147 per day, capped at $1,472 per request/$149 per day, capped at $1,496 per request

- Making a prohibited payment from a defined benefit plan at a time that the plan has a liquidity shortfall (§ 502(m)): $15,909 per prohibited payment/$16,169 per prohibited payment.

§ 5.09 REPORTABLE EVENTS

The PBGC doesn't want to be caught by surprise when a plan fails. To this end, plan administrators have a duty to report unusual events to the PBGC that might eventually require the agency to take over payment of pensions. See ERISA § 4043 and the regulations at 29 C.F.R. Part 4043. Depending on the seriousness of the event, the PBGC might merely maintain a watchful attitude; or it might seek the appointment of a temporary trustee to manage the plan, or even go to the appropriate federal District Court to seek authority to terminate the plan.

Between 2009 and 2015, the PBGC made a number of changes in what constitutes a reportable event, with the final result that far fewer events must be reported, and reporting waivers have become much more freely available.

Final rules were published in September 2015. [80 Fed. Reg. 54980 (Sept. 11, 2015)] Failure to provide a required Form 10 notice can be penalized by up to $1,100 a day.

The new waiver structure is primarily based on the company's financial strength in order to identify companies likely to default. The sponsor company decides whether it qualifies for a safe harbor and does not have to inform the PBGC of the determination. For five events (extraordinary dividend or stock redemption; change in controlled group; reduction in active participants; distribution to a substantial owner; transfer of benefit liabilities) reporting is waived based on criteria such as financial soundness (low risk of default); favorable debt: earnings ratios; no loan defaults within the previous two years; and no missed plan contributions within the previous two years (unless reporting was waived). A waiver is also available if the plan did not owe a variable-rate premium for the plan year before the year of the reportable event. There are event-specific waivers. Reporting of a missed required contribution is waived as long as the deficiency is made up within 30 days, and the only reason for missing the deadline was the sponsor's failure to make a timely election to use the funding balance to satisfy the funding requirement. Small plans can get a waiver for missing a quarterly installment. The PBGC can also waive reporting of any event on a case-by-case basis.

A waiver is available if any contributing sponsor of the plan is a public company that disclosed the event on a timely SEC Form 8-K. (However, this exception does not apply to disclosures under Item 2.02, Results of Operations and Financial Condition or Item 9.01, financial statements and exhibits.) The September, 2015 regulations continue several waivers from the old rules: for small plans, de minimis segments, and foreign entities.

However, these regulations make some changes in the definition of reportable events. Bankruptcy filing is no longer a reportable event. The previous regulations treated all reductions in active participants the same way. Sponsors had to track the participant count on each day of the plan year. The 2015 rules differentiate between events from general attrition and single-cause events such as a reorganization or mass layoff. Single-cause events must be reported within 30 days of the event. For attrition, the report can be made when the PBGC premium is paid. The reportable event for benefit liability transfer has been re-drafted to exclude cash-outs and de-risking by purchasing annuities. The previous rules required reporting when a loan payment was over 30 days late, the lender accelerated the loan, or a written notice of default based on serious conditions was issued. The 2015 rule requires reporting of any default, or whenever a lender waives or amends any covenant in a loan agreement that corrects or avoids a potential default.

Most extensions of the 30-day post-event reporting deadline have been eliminated, but the PBGC will grant extensions on a case by case basis. The penalty for violating the rules remains $1,100 per day. [TowersWatson Global News Briefs, *U.S.: PBGC Creates Reportable Event Waiver Structure* (Oct. 2015) (benefitslink.com); MWE.com, *Reportable Event Changes for Pension Plans Effective January 1, 2016* (Dec. 1, 2015) (benefitslink.com)]

ERISA § 4010 is the section mandating reporting of actuarial and financial information by employers whose single-employer pension plans are significantly underfunded—the funding target attainment percentage is below 80%. Final § 4010 regulations were issued in March 2016, reflecting changes made by MAP-21, HATFA, and BBA 2015. Originally, the PBGC planned to permit a waiver of reporting for plans with less than 500 participants and whose underfunding did not exceed $15 million. However, in response to comments, the IRS decided to allow a waiver as long as the shortfall for all plans within a controlled group is not over $15 million. There is also a waiver if all of the plans within a controlled group have a total of fewer than 500 employees and a waiver for reporting a statutory lien for missing contributions over $1 million or outstanding minimum funding waivers greater than $1 million. [81 Fed. Reg. 15432 (Mar. 23, 2016); see Xerox FYI, *PBGC Finalizes Changes to 4010 Annual Financial Reporting* (Mar. 23, 2016) (benefitslink.com); Practicallaw.com, *PBGC Issues Final Regulations on Pension Plan Reporting Under ERISA Section 4010* (Mar. 29, 2016) (benefitslink.com)]

Submission of Form 10 and Form 200 to report events is done through the PBGC's e-filing portal, <https://efilingportal.pbgc.gov/e4010>, which was launched on December 9, 2015. Using the portal requires having an e-4010 account. E-filing under the ERISA § 4043 regulations can also be done on the portal: see <http://www.pbgc.gov/documents/2015-22941.pdf>. The e-filing portal provides a multi-employer plan module which is mandatory for some notices and applications and permissive for others. However, MyPAA, and not this portal, is used to file Form 5500.

After almost 19 years and five appeals, the *Matz* case returned to the Seventh Circuit, which affirmed the dismissal of the case. In 2004, the Seventh Circuit adopted a rebuttable presumption that a 20% or greater reduction in census was a partial termination, but a reduction of less than 10% was conclusively not a partial termination. In Rev. Rul. 2007-43, the IRS adopted the 20% presumption but not the 10% non-presumption. The Seventh Circuit's 2014 opinion says that the period over which reductions occur can be aggregated to see if there was a partial termination generally will be one plan year. However, related significant corporate events that occur over a multi-year period can be combined to measure the percentage reduction, because it is not always possible to complete a complex transaction within a year. In this case, even if the employees of all seven subsidiaries were aggregated, the percentage terminated would be 17%—so it would not be conclusive that a partial termination had occurred. [*Matz v. Household Int'l Tax Reduction Inv. Plan*, 774 F.3d 1141 (7th Cir. 2014); see Jerry R. Capwell, Larry R. Goldstein, *Seventh Circuit Again Considers Partial Terminations of Retirement Plans* (Jan. 8, 2015) (benefitslink.com)]

At the beginning of 2015, the PBGC premium filing procedure was revised to require reporting of pension risk transfer actions such as annuity purchases and lump-sum windows. These transactions must be reported because the PBGC is concerned that many financially sound companies will engage in risk transfer actions—leaving only a smaller, less financially stable group of companies to pay PBGC premiums. [Maria P. Rasmussen and James P. McElligott Jr., McGuire Woods LLP, *PBGC Wants Reporting on Lump-Sum Pension Cash-Outs and Annuity Purchases* (Jan. 16, 2015) (benefitslink.com); Rebecca Moore, *PBGC to Begin Requesting Pension Risk Transfer Information*, plansponsor.com (Jan. 13, 2015)]

In addition to the required report to the PBGC, whenever a defined benefit plan fails to satisfy the minimum funding standard, and there has been no waiver of minimum funding granted, then participants must be notified. Form 200 must be filed with the PBGC within 10 days of the time a failure to meet the minimum funding standard involves $1 million or more. For the evolution of these rules, see 74 Fed. Reg. 11022 (Mar. 16, 2009) [final regulations for ERISA § 4010 reporting]; and 78 Fed. Reg. 20039 (Apr. 3, 2013). [reduction in reporting requirements]

The § 4010 report is due 105 days after the end of the information year (i.e., April 15 of the following year, for calendar-year plans). PBGC's Technical Update 14-2 provides guidance about the effect of the HATFA on § 4010 reporting. HATFA extends the MAP-21 relief, so defined benefit plans can discount their future benefit payments to present value using a 25-year rather than a two-year average of bond rates. Plans have the option of applying MAP-21 rates for the 2013 plan year and HATFA rates for 2014. [PBGC Technical Update 14-2; see Rebecca Moore, *PBGC Issues Guidance About Funding Relief Effect on Reporting*, plansponsor.com (Oct. 20, 2014)]

A related form of reporting is the "4063 notice" that must be submitted by the administrator of a single-employer plan when an employer who is a contributing sponsor ends operations at a facility, resulting in job loss for more than 20% of the plan participants. A 4063 notice is also required if a substantial employer withdraws form a multiple employer plan. The 4063 notice does not replace any Reportable Event notice that is required by § 4043.

At press time in 2016, there was no official PBGC form for the 4063 notice; employers who are required to report should send the notice within 60 days of the event—either by mail to the PBGC's Corporate Finance & Restructuring Department, 1200 K Street NW, Washington, DC 20005-4026, faxed to (202) 842-2643, or e-mailed to 4063.report@pbgc.gov. [PBGC, *Section 4063 Notices* <http://www.pbgc.gov/prac/reporting-and-disclosure/section-4063-notices.html> (viewed Feb. 7, 2017)]

The Early Warning Program (EWP) for single-employer defined benefit plans is intended to avoid plan termination by working with the sponsor to create protective devices before losses become irreparable. In December 2016, the PBGC's Website was updated to add two more events to the list of transactions monitored by the PBGC: deterioration in the sponsor's credit rating, and downward trends in financial factors such as cash flow.

The PBGC identifies about 300 transactions and trends that could imperil plan security; if necessary, it intensifies its review to find about 100 early warning cases a year. Possible concerns are changes in the plan's controlled group (the group of companies with potential responsibility for the plan); spin-offs and split-offs that could lead to a plan remaining with, or being transferred to, a less financially stable company. Transfer of significantly underfunded pension liabilities in connection with the sale of a business is also an issue. A major divestiture, while retaining significantly underfunded pension liabilities, could result in remaining entities that do not have enough revenue to cover the plan. A leveraged buyout that adds major secured debt is also a risk. The new debt related to the buyout has higher priority in bankruptcy than unsecured obligations such as pension funding—or the PBGC's claim for underfunding. A large dividend paid to shareholders could prevent the sponsor from funding the plan.

If a plan is found to be at risk, the PBGC can take steps such as requiring higher plan contributions, making the plan sponsor get a letter of credit or grant a security interest in specific company assets for security, or getting an affiliate to give a standby guarantee to take over the plan or pay any unfunded liabilities that the sponsor is unable to pay. Theoretically, the PBGC can terminate risky plans, but PBGC says that it seeks protection in only about five cases a year (under 2% of those monitored). [Harold J. Ashner and Deborah West, *PBGC Expands Scope of Early Warning Program,* Bloomberg BNA Pension & Benefits Daily (Jan. 10, 2017); Rebecca Moore, *PBGC Lists Triggers for Early Warning Program,* plansponsor.com (Jan. 17, 2017) (benefitslink.com); Towerswatson.com, *PBGC Adds to List Of Early Warning Factors* (Feb. 2017) (benefitslink.com)]

§ 5.10 SPECIAL RULES FOR AT-RISK PLANS

The PPA creates a new category, the "at-risk" plan. Plans with under 500 participants are exempt. The determination of risk assumes that all participants who are eligible for benefits in the current plan year or the following 10 years retire as soon as they can and opt for the subsidized early retirement benefit (the benefit with the highest present value of liabilities). A plan is at risk if, in the previous plan year, it was less than 80% funded using the general funding rules and less than 70% funded using the tougher actuarial assumptions for at-risk plans. The 80% requirement is phased in gradually between 2008 and 2011. Plans that were at risk for two of the previous four years must make their calculations subject to an added load factor of $700 per participant, 4% of the funding target and target normal cost.

For at-risk plans, the controls depend on the "adjusted funding target attainment percentage," the ratio of plan assets to the plan's funding target. The funding target is calculated as if the plan had purchased annuities for every participant who was not a Highly Compensated Employee for the two years before the year of the calculation.

At-risk plans are restricted vis-à-vis benefit increases, payments, accruals, and shutdown benefits. The plan cannot be amended to increase benefits if the adjusted funding target attainment percentage is lower than 80%, or if the amendment has the effect of reducing the percentage below 80%. An exemption is available if the plan sponsor makes additional contributions or provides security to bring the plan up to the 80% funding level. The rule is not applied during a plan's first five years in existence. Amendments that increase benefits under a formula that is not based on compensation, and where the increase is not more than the average wage increase for plan participants, are exempt. So are cost of living increases in flat-dollar plans.

If the plan's adjusted funding target attainment percentage is below 60%, or if it is below 100% and the sponsor is bankrupt, then benefits must be paid in life annuity rather than lump-sum form. (This restriction does not apply to plans that were frozen as of September 1, 2005, and continues frozen.) Plans whose adjusted funding target attainment percentage is somewhere between 60%–80% are allowed to make a one-time lump-sum payment, limited to the present value of the maximum amount guaranteed by the PBGC to the participant, or 50% of what would otherwise be paid—whichever is smaller. When the adjusted funding target attainment percentage is below 60% (except in the first five years of a new plan's operations), all future benefit accruals must be frozen unless the sponsor makes contributions or gives security to bring the funding up to the 60% level. Shutdown benefits, and other benefits based on an unpredictable contingent event, are forbidden when the target attainment percentage—before or after payment of the benefit—is below 60%.

Plan participants must be notified if funding deficiencies result in restrictions on benefits.

The benefit restrictions do not apply if the plan is fully funded: that is, if they satisfy the percentage requirements of the PPA as modified by WRERA.

The PBGC publishes tables for defined benefit plans to use to administer the partial restrictions imposed on lump-sum distributions by Code § 436(d)(3) and ERISA § 206(g)(3)(C) that are made by plans that fall in the range of 60%–80% funded. The PPA limits lump sums and other accelerated distributions to the lesser of 50% of the benefit otherwise payable or the present value of the participant's maximum guarantee from the PBGC. The PBGC determines the present value under ERISA § 4022 each year. For annuity starting dates in 2017, the present value limit runs from $153,783 (age 25) to $352,104 at age 45, $579,776 at age 55, $913,208 at age 65, to $6,321,974 at age 85. [PBGC, *Present Value of PBGC Maximum Guarantee*, <http://www.pbgc.gov/prac/mortality-retirement-and-pv-max-guarantee/present-guarantee.html#main-content>; <http://www.pbgc.gov/prac/mortality-retirement-and-pv-max-guarantee/present-guarantee.html#2017> (Dec. 2, 2016).] See also Table I-17, indicating the likelihood of distress or involuntary termination, based on the plan's monthly benefit; the table runs from 2018 to 2027. [81 Fed. Reg. 83137 (Nov. 21, 2016); see Plansponsor editors, *PBGC Issues New Table for Use by Involuntarily Terminating DBs*, plansponsor.com (Nov. 22, 2016)]

In March 2011, the PBGC proposed a rule under PPA § 403, making the phase-in period for guarantee of benefits that are contingent on an unpredictable contingent event begin no earlier than the date of the event. (The example used in the proposal is a plant shut-down.) The rule was necessary because PBGC's guarantee of new pension benefits and benefit increases phases in over a five-year period starting with the later of the date of adoption or the effective date of the change, so the PBGC wanted to protect itself against plans adding new benefits when they knew they were about to terminate. [ERISA § 4022(b)(8); see PBGC Proposed Rule RIN 1212-AB18, 76 Fed. Reg. 13304 (Mar. 11, 2011). See also PBGC Final Rule, 75 Fed. Reg. 33688 (June 15, 2010) providing that there is no guarantee of benefits earned between the time an employer files for bankruptcy and the date the PBGC takes over the plan; in a bankruptcy situation, benefits are guaranteed only if they were nonforfeitable as of the bankruptcy filing date.]

The rule was finalized in May 2014. The final rule provides that an Unpredictable Contingent Event Benefit (UCEB) is a benefit payable solely because of an event like a plant shutdown, or a non-event occurrence (such as reaching an age or length of service) that triggers benefit eligibility. The most common UCEB allows a person to collect a full, unreduced benefit earlier than it would have been available if the Unpredictable Contingent Event (UCE) had not occurred. The PBGC determines the date of an UCE by consideration of all facts and circumstances, including the plan provisions, the level of activity in the facility that is being shut down, and the permanence of the situation. The provisions of the plan determine whether the determination is made for the entire facility; on a participant-by-participant basis; or otherwise. When an employer establishes a new pension benefit or increases a current benefit, the PBGC guarantee is generally phased in over a five-year period. This is done to protect the PBGC against adoption of benefit increases in anticipation of termination. Phasing in of a UCEB guarantee starts on the date the UCEB provision was adopted; the effective date of the provision; or the date of the event—whichever comes last. This rule implements the PPA, so it is effective for UCEBs payable as a result of a UCE occurring after July 26, 2005—this is not a typo for 2015! [79 Fed. Reg. 25667 (May 6, 2014)]

Some employers who downsized were pursued by the PBGC under ERISA § 4062(e), which gives the agency the power to require immediate escrow payments or posting of bond when cessation of operations results in separation from service of over 20% of participants in a defined benefit plan. Regulations were published in 2006, creating potential liability even on plans that did not terminate, and allowing the PBGC to demand that the plan place funds in escrow or purchase a bond to guarantee payments if an involuntary or distress termination occurred later. Additional regulations were proposed in 2010 expanding the definition of "substantial cessation of operations" and explaining the calculations involved. [PBGC, *Liability for Termination of Single-Employer Plans; Treatment of Substantial Cessation of Operations*, FR Doc 2010-19695, RIN 1212-AB20, 75 Fed. Reg. 48283 (Aug. 10, 2010)]

In late 2012, the PBGC proposed to concentrate its enforcement efforts under § 4062(e) on the few plans that are at greatest risk. Under the new policy, the PBGC would not take action under § 4062(e) against small (fewer than 100 participants) or credit-worthy companies. [R. Randall Tracht, Brian J. Dougherty, Lisa H. Barton and Eric P. Sarabia, *PBGC Changes Enforcement Policy Under ERISA Section 4062(e)* Morgan, Lewis & Bockius (Nov. 13, 2012) (benefitslink .com)]

In mid-2014, the PBGC announced a moratorium on § 4062(e) enforcement, until the end of 2014. The PBGC said it would use the time to work with stakeholders to determine when pensions are genuinely at risk. The PBGC directed businesses to report new § 4062(e) events as they occur, but reassured them that no enforcement action would be taken on those events in 2014. [PBGC Press Release No. 14-09, *PBGC Issues Moratorium on 4062(e) Enforcement*, <http://www.pbgc.gov/news/press/releases/pr14-09.html?cid=CPAD01PRJUL0 820141> (July 8, 2014)]

The moratorium was ended by the Cromnibus bill, which redefines ERISA § 4062(e) events for events occurring on or after December 16, 2014. Plans with fewer than 100 participants are exempt, as are plans that are at least 90% funded. Now, § 4062(e) events are limited to permanent shutdowns, involving 15% of all of the sponsor's employees who are eligible to participate in any pension plan, including 401(k) plans, maintained by members of the employer's controlled group. (Under prior law, the test was 20% of participants in the defined benefit plan.) The Cromnibus Act provides that there is no § 4062(e) event unless the shutdown is substantial relative to the size of the employer's entire operation. Generally speaking, there is no § 4062(e) event unless employees actually lose their jobs, not just go to work for someone else.

Even if there has been a § 4062(e) event, the Cromnibus Act reduces the penalties. The employer can satisfy its § 4062(e) liability by contributing one-seventh of the unfunded vested benefits, times the percentage reduction in the number of active participants, in each of seven years. Each installment is also capped. Installments do not have to continue after the plan's unfunded vested benefits are at least 90% vested, and do not have to resume if the percentage later falls below 90%. [PBGC, *Important Changes to ERISA Section 4062(e)*, <http:// www.pbgc.gov/about/faq/pg/important-changes-to-erisa-section-4062(e).html> (undated, viewed Mar. 14, 2016)]

If the employer responsible for maintaining a defined benefit plan is part of a controlled group, all members of the group are jointly and severally liable for funding. If the sponsor is no longer able to pay benefits, the PBGC can terminate the plan and require the sponsor and the controlled group to submit the unfunded benefit liabilities. The Eleventh Circuit considered whether the trustee of a bankrupt sponsor can sue the ex-owner of the corporation as a former member of the controlled group to recover the liabilities on behalf of the bankruptcy estate and the unsecured creditors.

The Eleventh Circuit ruled that the trustee of a reorganizing corporation cannot sue the ex-owner on behalf of the estate for termination liabilities. ERISA provides that once a plan is terminated, all parties except the PBGC are limited in the relief they can obtain from either the current or former controlled group. The PBGC can get legal or equitable relief from the controlled group for failure to fund the plan—but anyone else is limited to equitable relief. The Eleventh Circuit held that whether the trustee's intended relief was legal or equitable, it did not have a cause of action to recover funds for the bankruptcy estate to satisfy the PBGC claim. The ERISA duty of controlled group members to pay unfunded benefit liabilities runs to the plan's beneficiaries, not the unsecured creditors of the bankrupt sponsor. A complicating factor in this case was that the statute of limitations had run, so the PBGC could not sue the controlled group for termination liability. [*Durango-Georgia Paper Co. v. H.G. Estate LLC*, 739 F.3d 1263 (11th Cir. 2014)]

The PBGC announced in March 2017 that it was taking over the Road Carriers Local 707 Pension Fund, which will require the PBGC to spend $1.7 million a month to provide benefits. (In the single-employer program, the PBGC actually takes over administration of insolvent plans, but in the multi-employer program, the existing administrators retain control, but the PBGC provides funding.)

The PBGC warned that more than a million people are participants in plans that are expected to become insolvent over the next 20 years. Financial factors such as deregulation that led to industry restructuring, reductions in demand, and a poor investment climate for plans made many plans unstable. If companies involved in a multi-employer plan go out of business, that shifts the entire burden to the remaining employers, who may be financially insecure themselves. This in turn stresses the PBGC's already underfunded multi-employer pension program; if the program itself becomes insolvent, then plan participants' benefits will have to be cut drastically because the PBGC's only source of funds will be current premiums. [Rebecca Moore, *Benefit Cuts Could Hit More Than One Million Multiemployer Plan Members,* plansponsor.com (Mar. 2, 2017); Meep, *When Multiemployer Pensions Fail: Teamsters Local 707,* STUMP (Feb. 28, 2017) (benefitslink.com)]

CHAPTER 6

DEFINED CONTRIBUTION AND 401(k) PLANS

§ 6.01 INTRODUCTION

As explored in Chapters 4 and 5, the defined benefit plan not only places the investment risk on the employer (because the employer must adjust its contributions to provide the promised level of benefits—and if the value of the plan's assets declines, and its investment return goes down, the employer must supply additional funds) but also subjects the employer to complex and expensive administrative requirements.

In the 1990s, therefore, the trend was to shift from defined benefit to defined contribution or 401(k) plans. The 401(k) plan form grew fast, because (although employer matches are permitted) the predominant form of funding for these plans is deferral of employee compensation.

In recent years, court cases and regulations have centered on economic factors. Many disappointed plan participants have charged that they were not given adequate investment alternatives, or that they lost potential appreciation because excessive fees were charged. In general, however, these suits have been unsuccessful—although in mid-2014, the Supreme Court held that, in "stock drop" case (where the value of plan participants' accounts falls) fiduciaries are not entitled to a presumption of prudence when they are accused of retaining employer stock as a plan investment for too long. [*Fifth Third Bancorp et al. v. Dudenhoeffer*, 134 S. Ct. 2459 (2014). In March 2016, the case was settled, and the settlement obtained preliminary approval from the district court. The settlement calls for distribution of $6 million to class members; the Fifth Third Stock Fund was frozen and ceased accepting new contributions; and participants who invested 20% or more of their balances in that fund were sent notices about the importance of diversification: *Dudenhoeffer v. Fifth Third Bancorp*, No. 1:08-CV-538-SSSB (Stipulation of settlement, S.D. Ohio Mar. 15, 2016); see Rebecca Moore, *Famous Fifth Third Stock Drop Suit Reaches Settlement*, plansponsor .com (Mar. 24, 2016)]

Federal regulators responded to these concerns by increasing the amount of disclosure required in connection with defined contribution plans. Service providers (e.g., investment advisors; recordkeepers) must give the plan detailed information about the services they render the plan—and the cost of those services. The plan, in turn, must disclose information about investment costs to plan participants. Under appropriate conditions, service providers can render not just advice to the plan as a whole, but individual advice to plan participants.

The Employee Benefits Security Administration (EBSA) analyzed 2014 Form 5500s (the latest year for which complete data is available) and found that defined contribution assets represented $5.3 trillion of the $8.3 trillion universe of plan assets. There were 89.9 million active plan participants, 75.4 million of whom were enrolled in defined contribution plans. Defined plan contributions for the year were $403.5 billion, 7.0% higher than the year before. Defined contribution plans disbursed $428.4 billion to participants, beneficiaries, and insurance carriers—11% more than the year before. [Rebecca Moore, *DB Plans Are Not Totally Disappearing,* plansponsor.com (Oct. 31, 2016)]

In 2016, 44% of workers in private industry participated in defined contribution plans, but there were wide variations by type of work: 63% of managers, professionals, and related workers were defined contribution plan participants, as were 46% of sales and office workers—but a mere 19% of service employees. In 2015, about three-quarters of private-industry participants in defined contribution plans (74%) participated in savings and thrift plans—i.e., plans where the employee contributes a predetermined amount of pay into an individual account, generally receiving an employer match up to a percentage of earnings (e.g., 6%). [Eli R. Stoltzfus, *Defined Contribution Retirement Plans: Who Has Them and What Do They Cost?,* BLS (Dec. 2016) (benefitslink.com)]

The Plan Sponsor Council of America's 59th Annual Survey showed that in 2015, the average contribution rate for employees was 6.8% of gross annual pay. The average employer contribution to 401(k) plans was 3.8%; the average contribution for combined plans was lower: 5.4%. In 2015, 57.5% of plans provided automatic enrollment. About one-fifth of assets (19.8%) were invested in target date funds; 21.4% of assets were invested in active domestic equity funds, 12.4% in domestic equity index funds. The average number of investment options offered by 401(k), profit sharing, and combination plans was 19. Three-quarters of plans surveyed offered QDIAs (default investments)—and 75% of those plans used a target date fund as the default. In 2015, more than half of plans (59.5%) allowed Roth 401(k) contributions, a slight decline from the 62% proportion in 2015. In 2015, only 20% of employees who were permitted to make Roth contributions actually did. [Meaghan Kilroy, *Employee Contributions Rise in 2015—PSCA Survey,* Pionline.com (Dec. 19, 2016) (benefitslink.com)]

Traditionally, the IRS required plans to obtain "determination letters," and to renew them periodically to show that the plan continued to be operated in accordance with current law and rules. As §§ 10.02 and 14.02 explore in more depth, the IRS is now restricting the determination letter process, exposing plan sponsors to greater uncertainty as to whether their plans are compliant.

Rev. Proc. 2016-6, 2016-1 I.R.B. 200 is the annual revenue procedure about issuing determination letters, which has been updated to reflect the phase-out process. The latest schedule of user fees appears in Rev. Proc. 2016-8, 2016-1 I.R.B. 243. See Notice 2016-3, 2016-3 I.R.B. 278. The IRS wants to encourage sponsors to adopt pre-approved plans that use language that the IRS has already cleared. Sponsors were given an extension of time until April 30, 2017 to adopt a pre-approved defined contribution plan. [Lori L. Shannon and Monica A. Novak, *But Wait . . . There's More . . . Additional Revisions to the Employee Plans Determination Letter Program,* Drinker Biddle & Reath LLP (Jan. 19, 2016), available at Lexology.com; Randal M. Limbeck, *Deadline for Restating Your 401(k) Plan May Be Around the Corner,* Jackson Lewis PC (Nov. 10, 2015), available at Lexology.com]

Further guidance for the phase-out process was published in July 2016. As of January 1, 2017, an individually designed plan can only get a determination letter when it initially qualifies; upon termination; or, at the IRS's discretion, in exceptional circumstances. Instead of reviewing individual plans and informing sponsors if they are compliant, the IRS will publish an annual list of required amendments. However, the six-year remedial amendment cycle for pre-approved plans remains in effect. For individually designed plans, the IRS will publish a list of required amendments each year. [Rev. Proc. 2016-37, 2016-29 I.R.B. 136; see Raymond P. Turner, *Determination Letter Rationing: IRS Reveals the Brave New World*, Jackson Lewis PC (July 10, 2016), available at Lexology.com]

In mid-2017, the IRS announced a PA (pre-approved) plan program, covering both Master & Prototype and Volume Submitter plans. Both defined contribution and defined benefit plans can use the PA program. The IRS accepts both standardized PA plans that use the IRS model documents without modification, and non-standardized plans that can adapt the model documents somewhat for their individual needs. [Rev. Proc. 2017-41, 2017-29 I.R.B. 92; see Susan E. Stoffer et. al., *IRS Reorganizes Pre-Approved Plan Opinion Letter Program*, Nelson Mullins Riley & Scarborough LLP (July 12, 2017), available at Lexology.com]

§ 6.02 DEFINED CONTRIBUTION PLANS

The 401(k) plan, also known as a CODA (Cash or Deferred Arrangement) is the most popular type of defined contribution plan, but a variety of defined compensation plan designs can be used, e.g., profit sharing; money purchase; target benefit; Employee Stock Ownership Plan (ESOP); leveraged ESOP; new comparability plans, as stand-alones or in conjunction with 401(k) plans.

The profit-sharing plan is the most basic defined contribution plan design. The employer does not have to have profits to make contributions, nor is it required that contributions be made whenever there are profits. Allocations can be made by a fixed formula such as a specified percentage of pay; as a flat dollar amount; a formula tied to age and/or years of service (such as X% of pay until the sum of age plus service reaches a certain amount, then a different percentage); a formula related to corporate profits; pro rata contributions by pay, or a completely discretionary amount. A profit-sharing plan can be integrated with Social Security benefits, so that the contribution percentage rises after the participant's income hits the Federal Insurance Contributions Act (FICA) contribution base. In practice, most sponsors of profit-sharing plans do not actually make profit-sharing contributions; the plan is a vehicle for attaching 401(k) savings and matches.

Money purchase pension plans are defined contribution plans that are also pension plans. The formula must be fixed, not discretionary; the Employment Retirement Income Security Act (ERISA) rules apply; and the sponsor must meet a minimum funding standard. The contributions can be related to pay, be a flat amount, follow an age-plus-service formula, or other variations. Money purchase pension plans used to be fairly popular, especially among companies that wanted to offer very generous defined contribution plans—more than the 15% of eligible contribution that was once the limit for defined contribution plans. However, true money purchase plans are now obsolete, because a profit-sharing plan contribution can be as much as 25% of compensation.

A target benefit plan is a special money purchase pension plan that mirrors the accruals in a defined benefit plan, reflecting the underlying defined benefit plan formula—but each participant has an account balance which determines the eventual benefit. Target benefit plans were never very popular, and almost no new ones have been created since 1986, when that year's tax bill imposed anti-discrimination regulations that made it difficult to operate a target benefit plan.

An ESOP is a money purchase plan designed to invest primarily in employer securities. This was a popular plan design in the 1980s, but heavy investments in employer stock are now extremely controversial. A Leveraged ESOP (aka LESOP) is partially or wholly financed with loans that the plan sponsor obtains from banks or other lenders. Employees get shares allocated to their LESOP accounts (and can also diversify their investments), then receive shares or cash representing their vested balance when employment terminates. [JP Morgan Compensation & Benefit Strategies, *Rediscovering Defined Contribution Plans—Design Basics*, plansponsor.com (Nov. 13, 2008)]

According to the National Center for Employee Ownership, in 2014 there were 6,717 ESOPs in the United States (5,533 stand-alone plans, 1,184 "KSOPs" that have a 401(k) feature), holding more than $1.3 trillion in assets for their 10.6 million active and 3.4 million retired participants. An average of 229 new ESOPs were added each year from 2010 to 2014.

[Rebecca Moore, *ESOPs Still a Significant Share of Retirement Plans*, plansponsor.com (July 24, 2017)]

The shift to defined contribution plans also endangers the financial position of workers with disabilities because it is only since mid-2014 that long-term disability insurance could cover retirement plan contributions. (The change occurred as a result of T.D. 9665, 79 Fed. Reg. 26838 (May 12, 2014), which exempts the purchase of long-term disability insurance within a defined contribution plan that covers contributions to the plan that are lost due to disability.) The change was necessary because defined benefit plans were usually drafted to continue to accrue benefits for disabled employees, but defined contribution plans lacked comparable protections. The disability insurance is considered an investment of the plan, so the premiums and benefit payments are not taxed to the plan participant until they are withdrawn. [David C. Kaleda, Emily R. See and Matt Schoen, *Addressing the Risk of Long-Term Disability on Retirement Income*, 42 J. of Pension Planning & Compliance No. 4 (Winter 2017) (benefitslink.com)]

The maximum employer contribution to a defined contribution plan is $50,000 for 2012, $51,000 for 2013, $52,000 for 2014, $53,000 for 2015–2016, and $54,000 for 2017. The accrued benefit for a participant in a defined contribution plan equals the balance in the account. The balance, in turn, consists of employer contributions, any mandatory employee contributions that the plan requires, plus any voluntary contributions that the plan permits and the employee chooses to make. Defined contribution plans usually maintain separate subaccounts for the employer and employee component of each employee's account, but this is not a legal requirement.

Early in 2009, amendments to Regulation Z were published, exempting most retirement plan loans from the Truth in Lending Act. Effective July 1, 2010, qualifying loans are made to a plan participant, from fully vested funds in his or her account, complying with all tax requirements including the § 72 annuity rules. [Rebecca Moore, *Plan Loans Exempt from Truth-in-Lending Disclosure Requirements*, plansponsor.com (Mar. 13, 2009)]

In 2015, 25% of plan participants had plan loans—many more than the 14.6% who had loans in 2014. The average loan as a percentage of total assets was 1.6%. The average loan was also much higher: $6,216 in 2014, $8,380 in 2015. [Meaghan Kilroy, *Employee Contributions Rise in 2015—PSCA Survey*, Pionline.com (Dec. 19, 2016) (benefitslink.com)]

The Sixth Circuit held that income available to Chapter 13 debtors after repaying a 401(k) loan is projected disposable income that must be paid to unsecured creditors. The debtors will not be permitted to use it to make voluntary contributions to the plan. The 2005 bankruptcy reform law, Bankruptcy Abuse Prevention and Consumer Protection Act (BAPCPA), provides a limited exclusion for amounts withheld by an employer from an employee's wages for contributions to a qualified plan. The Sixth Circuit held that plan loan payments are excluded from debtor's disposable income, but voluntary contributions to a 401(k) plan are not. Contributions are only excluded from the bankruptcy estate if they were made before the date of the petition. [*In re Seafort*, 669 F.3d 662 (6th Cir. 2012)]

ERISA § 404(c) allows the participant to control the assets in a defined contribution account, including directing the investment of the account. If the participant assumes control, the plan's fiduciaries will not be liable for losses that result from participant control over the funds. Section 404(c) requires the plan to disclose adequate information about their investment alternatives. The plan must offer at least three diversified investment types, with materially different risk and return characteristics. Intent to use the § 404(c) safe harbor for part or all of a plan must be disclosed on Item 8a on the plan's Form 5500—and the form is signed under penalty of perjury. Participants must be allowed to change their portfolios at least once a quarter—more often if volatility requires. Participants must be given the mandatory disclosures (that the plan is a § 404(c) plan; that fiduciaries can be relieved of liability; what the plan's investment options are; and how to give investment instructions for the account). Participants can also request additional information, such as the annual operating expenses for each investment option, copies of financial statements and prospectuses, and the description and value of the assets in the portfolio.

If § 404(c) is satisfied, the fiduciary is not liable for losses resulting from the participant's or beneficiary's exercise of control over the assets in the account. However, the fiduciary has a duty to monitor ongoing compliance with 404(c); this generally does not require monitoring of individual investment decisions. But there is a residual obligation to monitor the ongoing prudence of including particular funds in the menu. Sponsors usually think of the menu as including four categories: the default investment; core funds that let the participant decide basic asset allocation; company stock or stable value funds; and other funds. The criteria for prudence are performance, cost, competence of management, and suitability. [Octoberthree.com, *The Fiduciary Duty to Monitor 401 K Plan Investments* (Aug. 12, 2015) (benefitslink.com)]

Plan administrators informed Employee Benefit Security Administration (EBSA) that it was difficult to make the mandatory disclosures on an annual basis. In response, the rule was changed to allow the "annual" investment and plan-related information to be given to participants in participant-directed individual account plans such as 401(k) plans at least once in any 14-month period. The actual disclosures remain unchanged; all that has changed is the schedule. However, EBSA will withdraw this rule and issue another final rule if the comments are negative. [Direct Final Rule, 80 Fed. Reg. 14301 (Mar. 19, 2015)]

The Seventh Circuit agreed with the Fourth Circuit (and the Department of Labor): choosing investment options for the plan, and deciding to retain an investment within the plan, are fiduciary acts that are not entitled to § 404(c) immunity because § 404(c) protects fiduciaries from being blamed for decisions over which they did not have control. However, the Seventh Circuit found for the plan: the stock fund was not worthless, and was not so risky that retaining it in the plan was imprudent. The plan was diversified and offered many other options. [*Howell v. Motorola Inc.*, 633 F.3d 552 (7th Cir. 2011); *Lingis v. Dorazil*, 633 F.3d 552 (7th Cir. 2011)]

The Third Circuit, relying on decisions in the Seventh and Eighth Circuits, allowed dismissal of a breach of fiduciary duty claim alleging that funds with excessive fee profiles (e.g., retail mutual funds) were included in the plan—as long as the fiduciary selected a broad enough range of funds with varying fee characteristics. At the time the complaint against Unisys was filed, the 401(k) plan had 73 different investment options, including 67 individual retail mutual funds with varying characteristics. However, the Third Circuit did not consider whether the 404(c) safe harbor was available, on the grounds that the complaint was properly dismissed so it didn't matter if the safe harbor would have applied. The Third Circuit treated Fidelity as a directed trustee with no contractual authority to control investment options—therefore, it was not a fiduciary for this purpose.

All claims against Fidelity were dismissed, because Fidelity did not have knowledge of Unisys' process for selecting investment options. [*Renfro v. Unisys Corp.*, 671 F.3d 314 (3d Cir. 2011)]

But if the § 404(c) safe harbor is not available, a fiduciary can be liable for allowing participants to invest in company stock when it was manifestly imprudent to let them. A Seventh Circuit case held that the plan made no effort to show § 404(c) compliance, and the plaintiff remained 98% invested in employer stock, while its profit margins declined 70–80% over five years. [*Peabody v. Davis*, 636 F.3d 368 (7th Cir. 2011)]

DOL's FAB 2009-03 (September 2009) permits the Summary Plan Description (SPD) to be used to satisfy the requirements of Employee Retirement Income Security Act (ERISA) § 404(c), the provision that relieves fiduciaries of liability for investment losses in self-determined accounts, by the sponsor providing a copy of the most recent prospectus close to the time of an initial investment in a registered security. The SEC published a summary prospectus form that can be used for this purpose.

Late 2008 Department of Labor (DOL) regulations create a safe harbor when the fiduciary performs a thorough, objective search before selecting an annuity provider and compares the total cost of the annuity to the benefits of the deal. [DOL Reg. § 2550.404a-4, 73 Fed. Reg. 58447 (Oct. 7, 2008); Amendment to Interpretive Bulletin 95-1, 73 Fed. Reg. 58445 (Oct. 7, 2008); Amendments to DOL Reg. §§ 2550.404a-3 and 2578.1, 73 Fed. Reg. 58459 (Oct. 7, 2008); Amendment to PTE 2006-06, 73 Fed. Reg. 58629 (Oct. 7, 2008)]

[A] § 415 Regulations

In 2005, the IRS proposed regulations to update the § 415 regulations first published in 1981. The regulations were finalized in 2007. Plans can provide that payments in any limitation year will not exceed the § 415(b) limit as of the annuity starting date, and increased pursuant to § 415(d); if this is done, the plan does not require actuarial adjustments for automatic increases unless the benefit is subject to § 417(e)(3).

Under the PPA, compensation used to calculate the "high 3" years does not have to be earned while the employee is an active plan participant. In general, the "high 3" is calculated subject to the annual compensation limit of § 401(a)(17), but the Final Regulations allow grandfathering-in of some additional compensation based on plan provisions that were in effect before April 5, 2007.

In general, money received after severance from employment is not considered § 415 compensation, but the Final Regulations allows inclusion of certain payments under bona fide sick or vacation leave plans—even if the payments are made more than 20½ months after severance from employment or the end of the year.

The Final Regulations allow some payments from non-qualified plans to be treated as § 415 compensation, as well as certain payments to disabled participants. The IRS announced its intentions to revise the rules covering multiple annuity starting dates. Various technical changes are made in the way that defined benefit payouts are adjusted when payment begins between age 62 and age 65. [Final Rule, 72 Fed. Reg. 16878 (Apr. 5, 2007)]

[B] Pension Protection Act (PPA) Changes

As Chapter 5 shows, the PPA was intended in part to improve the stability of defined benefit plans. Nevertheless, there are important PPA provisions that will affect the operation of defined contribution plans.

One PPA focus is protecting plan participants against excessive risk from declines in the value of the employer's stock. If the employer corporation's stock is publicly traded, then defined contribution plan participants must be given at least three investment options other than employer stock, and participants must have a right to diversify out of their holdings in employer stock—and must be notified of this right. (Because ESOPs are intended to hold employer stock, they are exempt from these requirements.)

The fiduciaries of 401(k) plans are permitted to give investment advice to participants: a prohibited transaction exemption is available if banks, insurance companies, broker/dealers, or registered investment advisers give advice after December 31, 2006. To qualify for the exemption, the adviser either must use an independently verified computer model to make recommendations, or the adviser's compensation must not vary based on the participant's investment choices. The PPA doubles the size of the bond (from $500,000 to $1 million) that fiduciaries must post if the plan they administer holds employer securities.

The PPA also gives small employers (fewer than 500 employees) a new option: maintaining an eligible combined plan that has some features of a defined benefit and some features of a 401(k) plan. An eligible combined plan must comply with the rules for both plan types. The eligible combined plan rules are effective starting in 2010. The plan consists of a single trust, with its assets allocated between a defined contribution plan such as a 401(k) plan, and a defined benefit plan.

§ 6.03 NEW COMPARABILITY PLANS

On October 6, 2000, the IRS published Proposed Regulations at 65 Fed. Reg. 59774-59780 setting the nondiscrimination requirements for "new comparability plans." The regulations were finalized by T.D. 8954, 66 Fed. Reg. 3435 (June 29, 2001). These are defined contribution plans that are allowed to perform cross-testing and demonstrate nondiscrimination under Treas. Reg.

§ 1.401(a)(4)–(8) by reference to their benefits rather than the employer's contributions, although they must satisfy a "gateway" requirement preserving at least a minimum rate of accrual for non-HCEs. In practice, this is usually done by finding a defined benefit equivalent for the allocations and then arranging them in rate groups.

The plan document can specify the classes in many ways—by age, hiring date, length of service, type of job, or the location in which they work, for example. The number or definition of classes can only be changed via plan amendment, and the changes must be prospective only, not retroactive. [Mark Papalia, *Class-Based Pensions: A Cost-Saving Alternative for Companies of All Sizes*, J. Accountancy (Jan. 2005) (benefitslink.com)]

New comparability plans are also known as cross-tested plans. These plans are sometimes adopted to increase the contributions that can be made for older employees who have fewer years until retirement. The rules allow new comparability plans to be combined with cash balance plans, and for the combination to exclude up to 50 employees or 40% of the workforce from the plan if the employer's contributions meet the required level. [Plansponsor editors, *New Comparability Plans Allow the Employer to Reward Older Employees and Owners*, plansponsor.com (July 27, 2017)]

§ 6.04   401(k) PLANS

[A]   Overview

The Cash or Deferred Arrangement (CODA), also known as the 401(k) plan, has achieved prominence as one of the leading forms of plans for providing post-retirement income. Such plans were authorized by a 1978 amendment to the Internal Revenue Code and first became available in 1981. Although 401(k) plans are subject to the rules for defined contribution plans, strictly speaking 401(k)s are not conventional pension plans. In a 401(k) plan, the employee agrees to have part of his or her salary, up to the limitation provided by the plan (which, in turn, is subject to limitations under the Tax Code) deferred and placed into an individual account instead of being paid in cash as it is earned. The advantage to the employee (apart from the forced savings aspect) is that the appreciation in value of the account is not taxed until withdrawals begin.

At the end of the fourth quarter of 2016, the average 401(k) balance was $92,500—the highest ever recorded and $4,300 more than the previous year. Fidelity reported that the average 401(k) contribution in 2016 was also a record: $10,200. Only 21% of participants had an outstanding plan loan, the lowest percentage since the fourth quarter of 2009. [Lee Barney, *401(k) Balances, Contributions Reach Record Highs in 2016, Fidelity Reports*, Plansponsor (Feb. 2, 2017)]

Many 401(k) plans feature an "employer match" (the employer contributes a percentage of what the employee contributes) but this is not a mandatory feature of this type of plan.

IRS proposed regulations from early 2017 would change the definition of Qualified Matching Contributions (QMACs) and Qualified Nonelective Contributions (QNECs) for 401(k) plans. Under these proposals, employer contributions could be treated as qualified matching or non-elective contributions if they satisfy the requirements for non-forfeitability and distributions at the time they are allocated to participants' accounts rather than when they are contributed to the plan. The practical effect is that employers can use forfeitures to fund these contributions. [Rebecca Moore, *IRS Proposes Changes to QMAC, QNEC Definitions*, plansponsor.com (Jan. 17, 2017)]

President Obama signed a presidential memorandum January 29, 2014, directing the Department of the Treasury to create "myRA" accounts as a savings vehicle for the workers (approximately half the workforce) who do not have access to 401(k)s or other retirement accounts.

Under this plan, money is contributed to the account on an after-tax basis, and investment gains and withdrawals are tax-free. The only investment option permitted for myRAs is a variable-rate Treasury bond carrying the same interest rate as the Thrift Savings Plan Governmental Securities Investment Fund for federal workers. When a myRA account reaches a balance of $15,000, it must be rolled over to a regular IRA. However, the myRA is strictly an opt-in account, and employees cannot be automatically enrolled. [Anne Tergesen and Colleen McCain Nelson, *Obama Signs Order for New myRA Retirement Accounts*, WSJ .com (Jan. 29, 2014)]

In mid-2017, the Department of the Treasury closed down the myRA program, on the grounds that the low demand for the program made it uneconomical. About 30,000 people (20,000 of them enrolled in 2016) signed up for the plan. They were informed by e-mail that they could transfer their deposits to a Roth IRA account. [Tara Siegel Bernard, *Treasury Ends Obama-Era Program to Help Workers Save for Retirement*, NYTimes.com (July 28, 2017); Kate Davidson, *Trump Administration to Wind Down Obama-Era myRA Retirement Program*, WSJ.com (July 28, 2017)]

Seven states, including California, Illinois, New Jersey, Oregon, and Washington State, adopted programs to provide retirement savings for workers who do not have access to an employer-sponsored retirement plan. Similar legislation was introduced in many of the other states. Under these programs, employees without employment-related access are automatically enrolled in IRA programs, but can opt out if they do not want to participate. EBSA guidance published in 2016 said that these plans, as well as similar plans adopted by municipalities, would be exempt from ERISA. The exemption would have made the plans much easier and less expensive to administer. However, Congress passed, and President Trump signed, two resolutions under the Congressional Review Act, H.J. Res. 66 and 67, removing the exemption and making these plans subject to ERISA requirements.

[Yuka Hayashi, *Senate Votes to Undo Rule Aimed at Helping Private-Sector Workers to Save for Retirement,* WSJ.com (Mar. 30, 2017); Rebecca Moore, *Trump Signature Overturns DOL Rule for Government-Run Auto-IRAs,* plansponsor.com (Apr. 14, 2017); Anne Tergesen, *States Press on with Retirement Programs, Despite Losing Regulatory Cover,* WSJ.com (May 8, 2017)]

Oregon decided to roll out its OregonSaves plan despite the loss of the exemption, and the California and Illinois plans were expected to begin in 2018. [Rebecca Moore, *Oregon State-Run Retirement Plan for Private Sector Opens Soon,* plansponsor.com (June 19, 2017); Anne Tergesen, *For Workers Without Retirement Plans, States Step In,* WSJ.com (Aug. 16, 2017)]

Notice 2014-37, 2014-24 I.R.B. 1100 states that a qualified 401(k) plan remains qualified if it adopts a midyear amendment to comply with Notice 2014-19, 2014-17 I.R.B. 989 (benefits for same-sex spouses). Q&A 8 of Notice 2014-19 sets the deadline to amend the plan for this purpose as December 31, 2014 or the deadline under the successor to Rev. Proc. 2007-44—whichever comes later. Rev. Proc. 2007-44 provides that, when plan qualifications change in a way that affects the plan document, an interim amendment must generally be adopted by the later of the end of the plan year in which the change takes effect or the due date of the employer's tax return for the year in which the change takes effect. But, because this could violate the restriction on midyear amendments of safe-harbor 401(k) plans, Notice 2014-37 clarifies that adopting the mid-year amendment does not make the plan unqualified. [Sally P. Schreiber, *Notice Clarifies Midyear Amendment of Certain Retirement Plans Post-Windsor,* AICPA (May 15, 2014) (benefitslink.com)]

A "brokerage window" resembles a conventional brokerage account; it allows plan participants to invest in a broad range of securities—although it also increases their exposure to fees. In 2011, 29% of large employers maintained a brokerage window, a proportion rising to 40% in 2015. A plan that maintains a brokerage window can limit the number of mutual funds in its central menu. Only a small percentage (1%–4%) of 401(k) participants use brokerage windows; usually they are older and more affluent than the average participant. More than half (60%) of plans that have brokerage windows charge maintenance fees, e.g., $50 per year, with commissions on each stock trade, so this form of investment is usually more expensive than using the core fund options. The sponsor does not have fiduciary obligations with respect to investments chosen by participants in self-directed brokerage windows. [Anne Tergesen, *Why More 401(k) Plans Offer "Brokerage Windows,"* WSJ.com (July 1, 2016)]

[B] Deferral Limits

Thanks to the Economic Growth and Tax Relief Reconciliation Act (EGTRRA), and as carried forward by the PPA, the amount that employees can defer will increase after 2001. EGTRRA also includes other novel 401(k) provisions. Participants in 401(k) plans who are over 50 are permitted to make additional "catch-up" contributions, and low-income plan participants are allowed to take a tax credit and not a mere deduction in connection with part of their 401(k) deferrals.

Participants in 401(k) plans are always 100% vested in their deferrals at all times. Employees must be allowed to participate in the cash or deferred part of the plan starting with the first entry date after they have one year of service with the employer. Participants must be re-admitted to the plan immediately if they terminate their jobs but are re-employed at the same company before they have undergone a one-year break in service. For 2015–2016, the defined contribution plan limit is $53,000 and the 2017 limit is $54,000; the 401(k) plan contribution limit is $18,000, with a catch-up contribution limit of $6,000. [IR-2014-99, *IRS Announces 2015 Pension Plan Limitations; Taxpayers May Contribute Up To $18,000 to Their 401(K) Plans in 2015*, <http://www.irs.gov/uac/Newsroom/IRS-Announces-2015-Pension-Plan-Limitations-1> (Oct. 23, 2014); IR-2015-118, *IRS Announces 2016 Pension Plan Limitations; 401(k) Contribution Limit Remains Unchanged at $18,000 for 2016* (Oct. 21, 2015), <https://www.irs.gov/pub/irs-news/IR-15-118.pdf>; Notice 2016-62, 2016-46 I.R.B. 725]

[C] Catch-Up Contributions

EGTRRA added a new I.R.C. § 414(v), which allows employees who are age 50 or older to order additional deferrals, over and above the normal limits. These additional amounts are referred to as catch-up contributions. The intent is to make sure that older employees will come closer to getting the same benefit from the enhanced opportunities for deferrals over the course of their careers as younger employees who can make the greater deferrals for a greater number of years. Catch-up contributions can be made for taxable years beginning after December 31, 2001. The maximum catch-up contribution rose from $5,000 in 2006–2008, reaching $6,000 in 2015–2017. [IR-2014-99, <http://www.irs.gov/uac/Newsroom/IRS-Announces-2015-Pension-Plan-Limitations-1> (Oct. 23, 2014), IR-2015-118, *IRS Announces 2016 Pension Plan Limitations; 401(k) Contribution Limit Remains Unchanged at $18,000 for 2016* (Oct. 21, 2015), <https://www.irs.gov/pub/irs-news/IR-15-118.pdf>; Notice 2016-62, 2016-46 I.R.B. 725]

EGTRRA § 631 provides that, if all employees who have reached age 50 are permitted to make catch-up contributions, the amount of the catch-up contributions will not be used in calculating the contribution limits. Nor will the catch-up amounts be used in nondiscrimination testing.

A plan participant is eligible to make catch-up contributions as of January 1 of the calendar year in which he or she reaches age 50—irrespective of the plan year.

[D] Other EGTRRA 401(k) Changes

Low-income 401(k) plan participants are entitled to a tax credit for their deferrals, for tax years beginning after December 31, 2001. The lower the income, the larger the percentage of the deferral can be claimed as a credit (10%, 20%, or 50%), but after an income limit is reached, the credit is unavailable. This "saver's credit" was made permanent by the PPA. The figures for 2016 are: $61,500 for joint returns, $46,125 for heads of households, $30,750 for single persons and married persons filing separate returns. [IR-2015-118, *IRS Announces 2016 Pension Plan Limitations; 401(k) Contribution Limit Remains Unchanged at $18,000 for 2016* (Oct. 21, 2015), <https://www.irs.gov/pub/irs-news/IR-15-118.pdf>] For 2017, the corresponding figures are $62,000, $46,500, and $31,000. [IRS Special Edition Tax Tip 2014-22, <https://www.irs.gov/uac/save-twice-with-the-savers-credit> (revised Jan. 27, 2016) (last accessed Feb. 9, 2017)]

Under current law, a small (under $5,000) balance can be "cashed out"— i.e., even if the employee wants the money to remain within the plan, the employer has the right to close out the account and send such small, hard-to-administer sums to the account owner's last known address. (Tax should be withheld, and an early distribution penalty should be taken if the person is under age 59½.)

[E] Roth 401(k)s

Yet another EGTRRA legacy is I.R.C. § 402A, which authorizes "qualified plus contribution programs"—in effect, 401(k) accounts that operate like Roth IRAs. An employee can make an irrevocable designation of part or all of the employee's elective salary deferral as designated Roth contributions. Employees' elective salary deferrals are taxed when they are placed in the account, but can be withdrawn tax-free as long as they have remained in the account for five years and the person withdrawing is at least 59½ or disabled (or the withdrawal is made by the estate of a deceased account holder).

A person who cannot contribute to a Roth IRA because of excess income can nevertheless contribute to a Roth 401(k). Furthermore, the maximum contribution to a Roth 401(k) is the normal 401(k) maximum, which is much higher than the Roth IRA maximum contribution. Roth 401(k) plans are subject to the minimum distribution rules. [Rev. Proc. 2006-53, 2006-48 I.R.B. 997]

Employers are not permitted to offer a 401(k) plan that accepts only designated Roth contributions: contributing employees must be given a choice between making pre-tax elective contributions and designated Roth contributions.

Employer matches are not permitted, although employers can use automatic enrollment in a Roth 401(k) plan. Designated Roth contributions can be treated as catch-up contributions, and can be collateral for plan loans to participants. [T.D. 9237, RIN 1545-BE05, 4830-01-p, 2006-6 I.R.B. 394]

Designated Roth contributions are aggregated with all other 401(k) and 403(b) contributions, so for 2015– 2017, the maximum Roth 401(k) contribution is $18,000; the catch-up contribution maximum is $6,000. [IR-2015-118, *IRS Announces 2016 Pension Plan Limitations; 401(k) Contribution Limit Remains Unchanged at $18,000 for 2016* (Oct. 21, 2015), <https://www.irs.gov/pub/irs-news/IR-15-118.pdf>; Notice 2016-62, 2016-46 I.R.B. 725]

An in-plan Roth rollover is a rollover within a 401(k) plan to designated Roth account in the same plan. Designated Roth contributions and their earnings must be maintained in a separate account under the plan. Code § 402A defines designated Roth contributions as elective deferrals to a retirement plan that would otherwise be excludable from gross income, but the plan participant elects to include them in gross income.

The Small Business Jobs Act of 2010, Pub. L. No. 111-240, allows in-plan Roth conversions for 401(k)s, effective on signing of the bill (September 27, 2010). Employers can amend their plans to permit Eligible Rollover Distributions (ERDs) to be transferred to a designated Roth account in the plan. If the plan did not already offer Roth accounts, the plan must be amended, and the payroll system updated accordingly. This provision benefits sponsors who were concerned about large balances being taken out of the plan, but does not make a major change for participants, who already had the option of rolling over the funds to a Roth IRA. [*New Law Allows In-Plan Rollovers to Designated Roth Accounts*, <http://www.irs.gov>]

The American Taxpayer Relief Act of 2012 (ATRA; Pub. L. No. 112-240) enacted Code § 402A(c)(4)(E), which permits in-plan Roth conversions of defined contribution accounts that would not otherwise be distributable, with no income limitations, as of December 31, 2012. Under prior law, only amounts that were immediately distributable (e.g., to a participant who had reached age 59½) could be converted to Roth status. The provision is effective January 1, 2013, but account balances in existence on that date can be converted. [Rebecca Moore, *Fiscal Cliff Deal Extends Roth Conversions*, plansponsor.com (Jan. 3, 2013)]

Some 401(k) plans allow additional after-tax contributions, up to the maximum contribution for the year. The additional contributions do not reduce taxable income but tax on the earnings is deferred until withdrawal. A 2014 IRS ruling makes it easier to convert these after-tax contributions to Roth IRA funds at retirement or other termination of employment. For example, assume a 45-year-old employee in a plan that allows both pre-tax and after-tax 401(k) contributions. The employee contributes the pre-tax maximum of $18,000 and receives a $7,000 employer match (for a total of $25,000). This employee can contribute up to $28,000 to reach the $53,000 maximum addition to a defined contribution account. If he or she then leaves the company after five years, he or she will have $140,000 in after-tax contributions, eligible for a tax-free rollover to a Roth IRA. The rest of the 401(k) balance can be rolled over to a traditional IRA. This strategy is different from using a Roth 401(k); Roth 401(k) contributes are made with after-tax funds, but are subject to the 401(k) annual limit. [Notice 2014-54, 2014-41 I.R.B. 670]

Before Notice 2014-54, when funds were deposited in a new plan or IRA (instead of being moved with a trustee-to-trustee transfer), rollovers that included both pre-tax 401(k) contributions and Roth contributions had to allocate a pro rata share of both kinds of funds to each destination account. As a result, employees either had to wait until they were hired by a company whose plan permitted Roth contributions; maintain the funds in their former employer's plan; or perform a direct rollover. The rules of Notice 2014-54 were finalized, effective for distributions on or after January 1, 2016; the final rules are identical to the proposed rules except for a few clarifications. [Winstead.com, *Simplified 401(k) Roth Rollover Rules Finalized* (May 19, 2016) (benefitslink.com)]

§ 6.05 401(k) ANTIDISCRIMINATION RULES

Understandably, highly compensated employees (HCEs) are in a better position to bypass immediate receipt of part of their salaries than rank-and-file employees. Therefore, the Internal Revenue Code includes detailed provisions for determining whether the plan is excessively unbalanced in favor of deferrals by HCEs.

A person is an HCE if he or she earned more than $115,000 in 2012 or 2013, or $120,000 in 2014–2017—or owned more than 5% of the company, irrespective of income. In most cases, the actual nondiscrimination testing is performed by the plan's third-party administrator or recordkeeper, but the sponsor must be aware of how the tests work to avoid adopting policies that result in failing the tests. The employer can elect to measure the top 20% of employee ranked by compensation.

There are three kinds of nondiscrimination rules: to see if there is broad coverage of employees; whether the plan is top-heavy; and whether the actual deferral percentage and actual contribution percentage unduly favor HCEs. If a plan fails the § 410(b) coverage test, the plan sponsor gets until the end of the plan year to bring the plan into compliance. Either the plan must become more generous to non-HCEs, or the HCEs must report their vested accrued benefit as income. If the plan's deferral or contribution percentage does not conform to the rules, the plan has 12 months after the end of the plan year to take corrective action, either by making a qualified non-elective contribution to all eligible non-HCEs or distributing the excess contributions to the HCEs by March 15 of the following year. Excess matching contributions that are not 100% vested are forfeited. [Noel Couch, *401(k) Nondiscrimination Tests Explained*, plansponsor.com (Dec. 1, 2014)]

The IRS Website includes a chart of potential mistakes that 401(k) plans can fall into, but that can be retrieved by going through a correction program such as SCP, VCP, or Audit CAP.

1. Is the plan document updated to reflect changes in the law? (The IRS suggests establishing a tickler file to ensure annual review).

2. Is the plan operated in accordance with the plan document? (Due diligence to make sure plan terms are followed is suggested.)

3. Does the plan define compensation correctly for deferrals and allocations?

4. Did the employer make matching contributions for all eligible participants?

5. Does the plan satisfy the applicable nondiscrimination tests?

6. Were all eligible employees given a chance to opt for elective deferrals? (The plan sponsor must monitor employee census information and apply the participation requirements correctly.)

7. Are elective deferrals kept within the § 402(g) limit for the year, with any excess deferrals promptly distributed to resolve the problem?

8. Are employee elective deferrals promptly deposited?

9. For top-heavy plans, were required minimum contributions made? The IRS says plans should be tested each year to see if they are top-heavy.

10. Were hardship distributions made properly?

11. Did plan loans to participants satisfy the requirements under the plan and Code § 72(p)?

12. Was Form 5500 filed for the plan for the year? [IRS chart, *401(k) Plan Fix-It Guide*, <https://www.irs.gov/retirement-plans/401k-plan-fix-it-guide> (updated Apr. 19, 2017) (last accessed Aug. 11, 2017).]

There are two antidiscrimination tests: the ADP test (Actual Deferral Percentage) and the ACP test (Aggregate Contribution Percentage). A full discussion is beyond the scope of this book; you should just be aware that the 401(k) plan will be scrutinized for compliance with at least one of these tests.

The employer can correct the situation in three ways:

- Distributing the excess contributions (and the income allocated to them) out of the plan before the end of the following plan year;

- Recharacterizing the excess contributions as after-tax contributions;

- Making qualified nonelective or qualified matching contributions.

Given the complexity of these rules, the IRS has recognized various safe harbor mechanisms that employers can use to simplify compliance. Companies that use the safe harbor are required to give plan participants notice that is accurate and comprehensive enough to inform them of their rights. The notice must be given a reasonable period (30–90 days) before the beginning of the plan year. Therefore, in a calendar year plan, notice is required on or before December 1 of the previous year.

The Voluntary Correction Program (VCP) component of Employee Plans Compliance Resolution System (EPCRS) permits a plan sponsor to pay a fee and submit corrections for IRS approval. Forms in the 14568 series are used to submit standardized corrections. Sponsors submit a Compliance Statement summarizing the submission. The IRS signs and returns this statement if it approves the VCP submission.

The general rule is that sponsors of preapproved defined contribution plans were required to adopt new plan documents on or before April 30, 2016, incorporating the changes mandated by the PPA. Failure to do can result in loss of qualification. However, correction is permitted under the IRS's VCP and, if the VCP submission is approved, the plan's favorable tax status is renewed. The user fee can be anywhere from $500 to $15,000, depending on the number of participants. If the VCP submission is made to the IRS by April 29, 2017, the general user fee is cut in half, provided that the failure to adopt the documents restated to comply with the PPA is the only reported failure. [Meredith R. Fergus, *Did Your Company Fail to Adopt a New Preapproved Defined Contribution Plan by the April 30th Deadline? The IRS Has a Solution for You,* Jackson Lewis PC (May 22, 2016), available at Lexology.com]

Another option for employers who do not want to commit to using the safe harbor, but who want to make non-elective contributions, is to give notice, again by December 1 of the preceding year, that the plan may be amended in the next calendar year to provide for safe harbor non-elective contributions, and that the employees will receive a further notice explaining their rights if such an amendment is adopted.

The IRS will generally treat a plan as having lost its status as a 401(k) safe harbor plan if it fails to provide a timely annual safe harbor plan notice for a year. If this status is lost, the plan must satisfy the nondiscrimination requirements from which it was exempted. This could limit HCEs' ability to defer compensation, or could require the plan sponsor to refund some amounts already deferred. Penalties could also be imposed for failure to provide the automatic enrollment or Qualified Automatic Contribution Arrangement (QACA) notice. Failure to give timely Qualified Default Investment Alternative (QDIA) notice forfeits fiduciary protection of the sponsor, plan administrator, or investment company for investment loss. Protection is only restored for amounts invested in the QDIA after compliance with the notice requirements. [McKenna Long & Aldridge LLP, *2011 Year-End Disclosure Reminders for Qualified Defined Contribution Plan Sponsors* (Nov. 2011) (benefitslink.com)]

§ 6.06 DISTRIBUTIONS FROM THE 401(k) PLAN

[A] General Rule

Pre-tax deferrals from a 401(k) plan cannot be distributed to the participant until:

- Retirement,
- Death,
- Disability,
- Separation from service (see below for the abolition of the "same desk" rule),
- Hardship,
- The participant reaches age 59½.

Although profit-sharing plans can make distributions purely because of the number of years the participant has worked for the employer, or the number of years the funds have remained in the account, these are not acceptable rationales for distributions from a 401(k) plan. [I.R.C. § 401(k)(2)(B)(ii)]

EGTRRA enacted § 411(d)(6)(E), providing that the accrued benefit is not reduced by elimination of a form of distribution—if the participant can receive a single-sum distribution at the same time as the eliminated form of distribution, and the single-sum distribution is based on at least as great a portion of the account as the form of distribution that was eliminated. A plan amendment under the Final Regulation can apply only to distributions whose annuity starting date occurs after the adoption of the amendment, not to distributions that have already commenced.

The Heroes Earnings Assistance and Relief Tax Act (HEART Act; Pub. L. No. 110-245) also revives an expired provision that allows reservists called for at least six months of active duty to take money out of their 401(k) and other defined contribution plans before age 59½ without having to pay the 10% penalty for early withdrawals. Employers must also recognize differential pay to called-up employees when they calculate pension benefits. The HEART Act includes the HEROES Act, which protects the (employment-related) survivor's benefits for survivors of servicemembers killed in the line of duty. [Rebecca Moore, *Reservist Benefits Bill Signed into Law*, plansponsor.com (June 19, 2008)]

The Second Circuit required a profit-sharing plan to give a participant over $1.5 million in assets, earnings, and interest that were wrongly transferred to his ex-wife—even though the plan did not recoup the money from the ex-wife. (The Northern District of New York granted a judgment for the plan against the ex-wife, but the money was not recovered.) The Second Circuit found a legal duty to reimburse the plan participant, finding that undistributed funds held in trust are not considered benefits for purposes of the ban on alienating plan benefits. Furthermore, plan assets can be used to satisfy a judgment against the plan itself. [*Milgram v. Orthopedic Assocs. et al.*, 666 F.3d 68 (2d Cir. 2011)]

Similarly, according to the Tenth Circuit, the ERISA ban on forfeitures does not make the plan liable for third-party wrongdoing. It was not a forfeiture when the plan incorrectly paid benefits to a participant's ex-wife instead of to him. It was the participant's fault that he did not give the plan his current address. His ex-wife learned how to access the benefits, got a user ID, changed the account password, filed a change of address form listing her P.O. box as an address, and withdrew all the money from the account. The participant did not sue his ex-wife; he sued the plan under ERISA § 1132(a)(1)(A) for refusing to distribute the plan funds to him. [*Foster v. PPG Indus. Inc.*, 693 F.3d 1226 (10th Cir. 2012)]

A couple who had been married to and divorced from each other twice before marrying for a third time signed a prenuptial agreement both before and after the third wedding. The wife waived rights to the husband's 401(k) plan. He named his parents as beneficiaries. The husband died after there had been a filing for a third divorce. Both his wife and his parents attempted to collect the 401(k) balance. The Eighth Circuit ruled for the wife: the prenuptial agreement was not an effective waiver of the wife's interest, because the agreement did not clearly disclose that spousal rights were being waived. The agreement seemed to contemplate execution of an additional waiver in the future, but that never occurred. [*MidAmerican Pension & Emp. Benefits Plans Admin. Comm. v. Cox*, 720 F.3d 715 (8th Cir. 2013)]

Although some employers have added annuities as defined contribution plan options, others are reluctant to do so because there has not been strong demand for them from participants. Young workers are often not interested in annuitizing. The current uncertainty in the market also deters some participants from accepting market risks by taking a lump sum that then has to be invested. There is also a concern about lack of portability: if a plan participant invests in a deferred annuity product, changes jobs, and rolls over the money, expenses already paid may be lost. If, instead of rolling over the amount, the employee leaves the funds in the original plan, he or she will have to manage and track multiple plans. There are also concerns about the size of the fees and charges associated with annuities. [Sharon F. Fountain, *"Annuitizing" a 401(k)—Options for Plan Sponsors and Participants*, Bloomberg BNA (Nov. 30, 2012) (benefitslink.com)]

On the tax front, the Treasury and DOL are working to reduce the risk of employees outliving the balances in their defined contribution plans. Two Revenue Rulings and two Proposed Regulations from 2012 make it easier for plans to offer full and partial lifetime annuities. Rev. Rul. 2012-3, 2012-8 I.R.B. 383, allows defined contribution plans to offer deferred annuities as investments without forcing the entire plan to comply with the QJSA/QPSA (Qualified Joint and

Survivor Annuities/Qualified Preretirement Survivor Annuities) rules—as long as the deferred annuity contract is accounted for separately. When the tax-deferred annuity reaches pay status, only that investment requires a QJSA. But if the plan permits the participant spouse to waive the QPSA the non-participant spouse must receive disclosures and must give notarized consent to the waiver.

In late 2014, the PBGC published a final rule (effective December 26, 2014) for transferring defined contribution plan assets to defined benefit plans. The PBGC wanted to encourage such transfers because they promote lifetime income for plan participants. The final rule eliminates concerns that rolled-over funds could be lost if the PBGC later takes over the defined benefit plan if the balance exceeds the maximum guarantee. The "five-year phase in" rule says that if benefits under a defined benefit plan are increased in the five years before the plan terminates, the increase must be phased in over a period of five years post-termination. The 2014 final rule exempts rollovers from employee contributions from this rule. When the assets are allocated, the benefits go into the second highest priority category. In general, if a plan goes through a distress termination, participants will not be able to take a lump sum to recoup mandatory employee contributions attributable to rollover amounts. [RIN 1212-AB23, 79 Fed. Reg. 18483 (Nov. 25, 2014). Previously, Rev. Rul. 2012-4, 2012-8 I.R.B. 386 dealt with rollovers from defined contribution to defined benefit plans.]

Many employers have closed their defined benefit plans to new hires, although they usually provide a defined contribution plan for new employees. Over time, it becomes harder for the closed defined benefit plan to satisfy the minimum coverage test because the grandfathered-in employees build seniority and earn more than the younger workers in the defined contribution plan. In early 2016, the IRS published a relief proposal. If a combination of defined contribution and defined benefit plans includes a closed plan that was in effect for more than five years before closing, and has not been significantly amended since then, discrimination testing can be done in a way that favors the plan. [81 Fed. Reg. 4976 (Jan. 29, 2016); see Rebecca Moore, *IRS Proposes Nondiscrimination Relief for Closed DBs*, plansponsor.com (Jan. 28, 2016), available at Lexology.com]

Regulations proposed in 2012, and finalized in mid-2014, add the possibility of using a QLAC (Qualifying Longevity Annuity Contract). As the name suggests, this tool provides lifetime income even if the plan participant survives to an advanced age. Plan participants in 401(k) plans and IRAs are not required to take RMDs on amounts used to purchase the QLAC between age 70 and the deferred start date of the annuity: for example, at age 80 or 85. The final rule, T.D. 9673, limits the amount of the account balance used to purchase the QLAC to $125,000 or 25% of the balance, whichever is less. Annuity payments must begin no later than when the annuitant reaches age 85 (but this age limit will be adjusted actuarially to reflect increasing lifespans). The annuity must not be variable or indexed, and cash surrender provisions are forbidden. [T.D. 9673, 2014-30 I.R.B. 212]

[B] Hardship Distributions

Treas. Reg. § 1.401(k)-1(d)(2)(i) defines hardship as an immediate and heavy financial need that cannot be satisfied by reasonable access to the participant's other assets. The hardship withdrawal from the plan must not exceed the amount of the need plus any taxes and penalties that the participant can reasonably expect to incur. Note that, post-PPA, hardship distributions can also be made based on the needs of plan beneficiaries as well as of plan participants.

Certain categories have been identified as automatically satisfying the financial needs test:

- Medical expenses of the employee, spouse, and dependent children;

- Purchase of a principal residence (but not routine mortgage payments);

- Staving off eviction or foreclosure of the mortgage on the principal residence;

- Tuition, room, board, and related expenses for the next 12 months for post-secondary education of the employee, spouse, or dependents.

Employees are expected to seek insurance reimbursement wherever it is available to cope with financial hardship; to liquidate their other assets to the extent this is reasonable; to cease further elective contributions to pension plans; to seek other distributions and nontaxable loans from employer plans; and to engage in commercial borrowing on reasonable terms, before they take hardship distributions from their 401(k) plans.

2016 IRS FAQs state that if a plan permits hardship distributions, it must use objective, non-discriminatory standards to determine what constitutes a hardship. Some expenses are presumed to be immediate and heavy, such as critical medical expenses, purchase of a principal residence, avoiding eviction from a principal residence, certain repairs (e.g., after a natural disaster), education costs, and funeral or burial expenses. The hardship distribution must not exceed the need (although this is measured taking into account the taxes and penalties on the distribution). The maximum amount of elective contributions that can be distributed from a 401(k) plan as a hardship distribution equals the employee's total elective contributions (including designated Roth contributions) minus any previously distributed elective contributions. All hardship distributions except designated Roth contributions are included in gross income. Employees who take hardship distributions cannot repay them (unlike plans loans), so taking a hardship distribution has the effect of permanently reducing the account balance. Employees are not allowed to roll over hardship distributions to IRAs or qualified plans. Unless special legislation is passed (e.g., for Hurricane Katrina), the regular hardship distribution rules apply to distributions to repair a principal residence damaged by a natural disaster. [<http://www.irs.gov/Retirement-Plans/Retirement-Plans-FAQs-regarding-Hardship-Distributions> (Jan. 23, 2017) (accessed Feb. 9, 2017)]

Under the Final Regulations, 69 Fed. Reg. 78143 (Dec. 29, 2004), a hardship distribution must satisfy both the "events test" (the participant has an immediate and heavy financial need) and a "needs test" (the distribution must be necessary to satisfy the need). A hardship distribution for medical expenses is limited to expenses that would be deductible as medical care under I.R.C. § 213(d), although the 10% (or 7.5% for senior citizens) of adjusted gross income (AGI) limit does not apply. The Final Regulations add two new grounds for distributions: funeral or burial expenses within the immediate family, and expenses for repairs to the principal residence.

[C] Elimination of "Same Desk" Rule

One basis on which employees can get distributions from a 401(k) plan is separation from service—i.e., ceasing to be an employee. Before EGTRRA was passed, the "same desk" rule was applied. Under this rule, a person would not be considered separated from service if the original employer had gone through a merger, consolidation, or liquidation, but the employee continued to carry out the same job for the successor company, and thus would not be entitled to a distribution from the plan.

EGTRRA provides, for distributions made after December 31, 2001, that if a corporation sells "substantially all" (defined as 85% or more) of its business assets to an unrelated company, or sells a subsidiary to an unrelated person or company, the selling company's employees have separated from service even if, in practice, they carry out the same tasks for the new employer. [See also Rev. Proc. 2000-27, 2000-21 I.R.B. 1016]

[D] "Orphan" Plans

In addition to plan freezes (see § 5.05[L]), problems arise because of "orphan" or "abandoned" plans—plans in which the sponsor went out of business, without making arrangements to terminate the plan and distribute benefits. The DOL estimates that roughly 1,650 401(k) plans are abandoned each year (about 2% of the total), affecting approximately 33,000 workers and balances of about $850 million. One advantage of a defined contribution plan over a defined benefit plan is that defined contribution plans are designed to be portable. But participants in these "orphan" plans, although they retain ownership of their accounts, often have difficulty in accessing them, because under previous law, if there was no representative of the sponsor company available, the financial institution could not release funds until DOL appoints an independent fiduciary to supervise the distribution. The DOL issued rules to permit financial institutions holding assets from the defunct plans of bankrupt companies to roll over the 401(k) balances with no requirement of court approval. The rules create a procedure that financial institutions can use to terminate the plan and distribute the benefits; enact a safe harbor for fiduciaries who distribute funds from orphan plans; and a format for filing a terminal report for an orphan plan. [71 Fed. Reg. 20820 (Apr. 21, 2006)]

EBSA's Abandoned Plan Program provides standards for determining if a plan is abandoned (e.g., no contributions or distributions for at least 12 consecutive months; the sponsor cannot be located by reasonable effort, no longer exists, or is unable to maintain the plan), with streamlined shut-down and distribution procedures. A Qualified Termination Administrator (QTA), qualified to serve as trustee and hold the assets, determines if the plan is abandoned. The QTA is not required to file Form 5500 on behalf of the abandoned plan, but is obligated to file a summary terminal report. [FAQs on the program: <http://www.dol.gov/ebsa/faqs/faq-abplanreg.html> (undated, accessed Mar. 15, 2016)]

DOL FAB 2014-01 (Aug. 14, 2014) explains how fiduciaries should search for missing participants and beneficiaries of terminated defined contribution plans and how to distribute the account balances of missing participants so that the assets are no longer considered plan assets and the person is not longer a participant. At least four steps must be undertaken, and the fact pattern (the size of the account balance; the cost of further search) may require additional steps. The four required steps, which can be performed in any order, are sending notice of plan termination (by certified mail); searching the plan's and employer's records for updated addresses; contacting the designated beneficiary to see if the beneficiary knows the participant's whereabouts; and making reasonable use of free Internet tools like search engines, public records, social media, and obituaries.

If those steps are unsuccessful, possible subsequent steps include paying for credit reports or employing commercial locator services or information brokers. The fiduciary is permitted to charge reasonable search expenses against the account. If, after making a reasonable effort, the fiduciary still cannot locate the participant, the account balance must be distributed. The preferred option is a direct rollover to an IRA, because this is the most beneficial to the missing person. ERISA § 404(a) creates a safe harbor for fiduciaries who send notices to participants or beneficiaries, but no form of distribution is elected within 30 days of the notice. Balances distributed to individual accounts must be invested in a low-cost product that preserves principal while producing a reasonable rate of return. If direct rollover to a plan is impossible or inadvisable, the funds can be transferred to a federally insured bank account or the state unclaimed property fund. The latter has bad tax consequences for the recipient, so it could breach fiduciary duties unless other factors outweigh the tax problems. [Austin K. Stack, *DOL Issues Guidance on Missing Participants in Terminated Plans*, Holland & Knight (Nov. 3, 2014) (benefitslink.com)]

In September 2016, the PBGC proposed to expand its Missing Participants Program, which was originally limited to single-employer defined benefit plans, to include additional plans, including terminated defined contribution plans. Under this program, plans transfer benefits to the PBGC, which retains the funds until they can be distributed by locating the participant in the PBGC's database. Otherwise, the plan would have to establish an IRA to hold the money; the account is depleted by the ongoing need to pay fees. [PBGC.gov, *Proposed Expanded Missing Participants Program* (Sept. 19, 2016) (benefitslink.com)]

At the end of 2012, the DOL announced its intention to extend the Abandoned Plan Program to help trustees in Chapter 7 bankruptcy cases when they act as plan administrators for companies that have made Chapter 7 filings. Under this proposal, the bankruptcy trustee can terminate and wind up the plan or appoint an eligible financial institution to do so. If collecting the delinquent contributions costs less than the amount to be collected, the trustee must pursue it. [DOL/ EBSA, *Fact Sheet: Proposed Amendments to Abandoned Plan Program* (Dec. 2012) (benefitslink.com)]

§ 6.07 ADMINISTRATION OF THE 401(k) PLAN

Defined contribution plans must give their participants a variety of notices:

- Safe harbor 401(k) plan's annual notice about the features of the plan, such as the safe harbor non-elective contribution or matching contribution of the plan; this must be given 30–90 days before the beginning of the plan year;

- Qualified Automatic Contribution Arrangement (QACA) safe harbor 401(k) plans must provide an annual notice on the same schedule;

- Qualified Default Investment Alternative (QDIA) notice of rights and obligations, such as the participant's right to transfer the account to other investments, and when funds will be invested in the QDIA; must be provided at least 30 days before the beginning of the plan year;

- 401(k) automatic enrollment notice, providing information such as deferrals made without an affirmative election, and how the plan invests contributions where there is no election; must be provided 30–90 days before the beginning of the plan year;

- Employer stock diversification notice: information about the right to transfer the participant's investment from employer stock into other investments (if the employer's stock is publicly traded). The notice must be given no later than 30 days before the first date that diversification rights can be exercised.

- Participant-level fee disclosure, providing information about fees and expenses, so employees can make intelligent choices about the investment of their accounts. The notice is due before an employee enrolls in the plan, and then must be repeated each year.

In general, two or more notices can be combined into a single document as long as the time requirements are satisfied. Electronic distribution is permissible if the electronic disclosure requirements are satisfied—but the defined contribution plan requirements cannot be satisfied in the SPD even if it is distributed annually. [McKenna Long & Aldridge LLP, *2011 Year-End Disclosure Reminders for Qualified Defined Contribution Plan Sponsors* (Nov. 2011) (benefitslink .com)]

In late 2015, the DOL sent letters to plan sponsors who reported failures to make timely 401(k) deposits on their annual return. To reduce the risk of audit, the sponsor should make a Voluntary Fiduciary Correction Program (VFCP) filing to correct the problem. Participant contributions, including any amount withheld from wages by the employer, plus elective deferrals, loan repayments, and voluntary after-tax contributions, become plan assets as of the date they can reasonably be segregated from the employer's general assets. DOL regulations say that they become plan assets on the fifteenth business day of the month after the month in which the contribution was received, if that is earlier than the time of segregation. Employer contributions become plan assets when contributed. Plans with fewer than 100 participants at the beginning of the plan year are entitled to a safe harbor if segregation occurs within seven business days of the date the funds were withheld from wages (or otherwise received, for example, as a voluntary after-tax contribution). The safe harbor operates on a payroll-by-payroll basis, so failure in one pay period does not disqualify other pay periods.

Late transmittal is corrected by transferring funds from the employer's general assets into the plan trust as soon as possible after detecting the error and replacing the lost earnings on the late deposits. It is useful to complete the correction before the plan's Form 5500 is filed because the annual report will show that the failures have been corrected, reducing the risk of audit. Failure to make deposits on time is a prohibited transaction, violating Code § 4975, so excise tax penalties can be imposed. The employer becomes a disqualified person that is deemed to use the plan assets deriving from participant contributions for its own business purposes. The penalty, paid to the IRS on Form 5330, is at least 15% of the lost earnings associated with the late deposit. The DOL can impose additional penalties. ERISA penalizes fiduciary breaches by 20% of the amount recovered in a judgment or settlement, but this is waived if there is voluntary reporting and correction under VFCP. [Susan Quintanar, *Late Deposits—A Timely Topic*, Trucker Huss (Dec. 2015) (benefitslink.com)]

[A] Automatic Enrollment

Even prior to the recession beginning in 2008, there was concern that many employees would not have a secure retirement because many workers would refuse or neglect to take the affirmative steps necessary to open a 401(k) account, select investments, and have the necessary discipline to save part of their compensation. (It also became clear that even workers who faithfully saved their money were at the mercy of market forces that could greatly reduce the value of a 401(k) account.)

In 2000, the IRS gave its blessing for 401(k) plans to operate by automatically enrolling eligible workers rather than by permitting participation only by those workers who took steps to opt in: Rev. Rul. 2000-8, 2000-7 I.R.B. 617.

An automatic plan sets a default savings rate such as 2% to 3% of pay and establishes a default investment, such as a money market or stable value fund. Usually only about 4% of eligible opt out; Hewitt Associates estimates that in a plan where opting in is required, 30% of eligible workers never join. A step-up program gets the employee's advance consent to increasing his or her contributions as income increases.

The PPA makes it easier for employers to operate 401(k) plans that automatically enroll employees and then permit them to opt out, rather than requiring employees to choose to participate in the plan. Automatic-enrollment plans must have employer matches (and the PPA contains a schedule for calculating the required match). Participants in an automatic enrollment plan must be 100% vested after two years, although the employer is not required to offer immediate participation in the plan.

Final Regulations, effective December 24, 2007, were published at 72 Fed. Reg. 60452 covering investments in QDIAs for participants who do not direct the investment of their accounts. Under the Final Regulations, fiduciaries are not liable for losses on amounts invested in a QDIA, and the plan's fiduciaries are not liable for decisions made by the managers of the QDIA. A QDIA can mix equity and fixed income investments—for example, in a life cycle or targeted retirement date fund; it can also be a balanced fund or a professionally managed fund. However, a capital preservation fund or other stable value fund can be a QDIA only for the first 120 days after a participant's first elective contribution.

The IRS Website includes a sample automatic enrollment notice for a hypothetical QACA: <http://www.irs.gov/pub/irs-tege/sample_notice.pdf> (last accessed Feb. 9, 2017), and the DOL announced that using this notice also complies with ERISA. Employees are fully vested in employer matching contributions in two years. Participants can choose among the various investment funds available, but funds are invested in the QDIA if there is no direction, and absent an election, 3% of eligible pay will be deposited into the account. The employer match is dollar-for-dollar up to 1% of eligible pay and 50 cents per dollar for employee deferrals of 1%–6% of eligible pay. DOL says that using this notice also complies with ERISA.

Final IRS rules in T.D. 9447 (2009-12 I.R.B. 694) permit employers to add an automatic enrollment feature to 401(k) plans without performing nondiscrimination testing, but the plan must be a QACA or an EACA (Eligible Automatic Contribution Arrangement—the equivalent for multi-employer plans). T.D. 9447 reflects changes in the law under the Pension Protection Act of 2006 and The Worker, Retiree and Employer Recovery Act (WRERA; Pub. L. No. 110-458).

QACA plans must automatically enroll all employees, with contributions beginning at 3% of salary, rising 1% a year until they reach 6%. An employee who opts out can withdraw from the plan and have contributions end within 90 days. The distribution from the plan is taxable to the employee, but is not subject to the 10% penalty tax on premature withdrawals. The Final Regulations apply to plan years beginning on or after January 1, 2008. [Joanne Wojcik, *IRS Rules on 401(k) Will Help Some Employers*, Business Insurance (Feb. 25, 2009) (benefits link.com)]

For QACAs and EACAs, the employer is permitted to increase the percentage of automatic contributions in the middle of the plan year, not just at its beginning, in order to reflect salary increases or performance evaluations, as long as the increases are uniformly applied. Employees must be notified of their automatic enrollment in the plan before they become eligible and at the beginning of each plan year. The QACA rules apply for plan years beginning on or after January 1, 2008; the EACA rules apply to plan years beginning on or after January 1, 2010. See 74 Fed. Reg. 17 (Jan. 2, 2009): for plan years beginning on or after January 1, 2008, civil penalties of up to $1,000 per day can be imposed for failure to inform participants of their rights with respect to automatic contributions.

The safe harbor rules allow employers to avoid some of the most stringent non-discrimination standards, on condition that they make minimum contributions on behalf of all eligible employees. Final regulations were published in late 2013, dealing with permitted midyear reduction or suspension of safe harbor nonelective and matching contributions, making it easier for financially troubled companies to reduce their contributions. The regulations permit employers to suspend or reduce safe harbor contributions when running at a loss, or if the annual safe harbor notice discloses that the plan can be amended to reduce or suspend safe harbor contributions. The notice must be given 30 days in advance, telling employees the effective date of the amendment, how it works, and how they can change their elective deferrals. [T.D. 9641, 78 Fed. Reg. 68735 (Nov. 11, 2013)]

[B] Fees

Plan participants disappointed in the returns of their accounts often charge the fiduciaries of the plan with breach of duty, and often the claims include a charge that the fiduciaries allowed the plan to pay excessively high fees, e.g., to brokers and mutual funds. See §§ 15.03[C], 15.15, and 15.17. Plaintiffs frequently allege that retail mutual funds are an unsuitable plan investment; the plaintiffs say that these funds charge fees that are inappropriate when there is little marketing or administration that must be done.

In the decade 2006–2016, there have been over 75 suits filed alleging excessive fees on defined contribution plans. The suits were filed first against large plans, then moved to smaller plans and nonprofits. There are three main categories of suits. The first is the general excessive-fee case, which blames the plan sponsor for getting revenue-sharing payments or choosing investments poorly. In these cases, the plaintiffs allege that the investment options are imprudent because they were too expensive and performed worse than other available choices. The second general type of case is brought against plan service providers, on the theory that they should be treated as "functional fiduciaries" of the plan and that revenue sharing should be treated as a prohibited transaction. The third type of suit targets financial institutions that are also plan sponsors, alleging that they engaged in self-interested actions that breach their fiduciary duty. [<http://www.groom.com/media/publication/1636_401k_Fee_Cases-Detailed_Chart__September27_2016_.pdf>; see Groom Law Group, *Excessive Fee Litigation* (Oct. 26, 2016) (benefitslink.com)]

In 2010, EBSA issued "participant-level fee disclosure" rules, mandating that fiduciaries of 401(k) plans offer disclosure of the investment alternatives that the plan offers, including the fees and expenses associated with each alternative. Participants are entitled to get the statement before they are enrolled in the plan and then at least once a year after that. In 2015, a two-month grace period was enacted, allowing any plan to provide the disclosure statement within a 14-month period. [80 Fed. Reg. 14334 (Mar. 19, 2015); see DOL Fact Sheet, *Direct Final Rule Provides Flexibility for the Timing of Annual Disclosures to Workers in 401(k)-Type Retirement Plans*, <http://www.dol.gov/ebsa/newsroom/fsdirectfinalrule.html> (undated, accessed Feb. 9, 2017)]

[1] Case Law

Dozens of suits about plan fees have been filed. The earliest suits were brought by plan participants against the sponsors, alleging that revenue-sharing with service providers was a breach of fiduciary duty because it required participants to pay excessive fees. Then broader challenges were brought about, for example, using actively managed funds in plans; funding plans with retail shares; using unitized stock funds that imposed "transaction drag"; using a service provider who bundled services; or the fiduciaries' alleged failure to obtain additional revenue streams for the plan's benefit. Sometimes the service providers have been sued on the theory that they are functional fiduciaries whose revenue sharing activities are prohibited transactions. [Groom Law Group, *401(k) Fee Litigation January 2015* (Feb. 2, 2015) (benefitslink.com)]

A mid-2017 summary says that there were 25 suits filed in 2016 to challenge 401(k) fiduciary conduct—the largest number in any single year. There were some major settlements, like the $22 million settlement American Airlines agreed to pay for offering expensive mutual funds from an investment company affiliated with the airline. Northrup Grumman agreed to pay $16.75 million to settle allegations of self-dealing (that two 401(k) plans were improperly required to pay the sponsor for administrative services). Merrill Lynch paid $25 million to settle allegations that it charged excessively high fees to small 401(k) plans for mutual fund shares that it allegedly should have offered at a discount.

However, there were also notable defense victories, such as the District Court for the District of Massachusetts' dismissal of a suit against Putnam Investments because the plaintiffs failed to show that the defendant advanced its own interests improperly. The District Court for the Northern District of California found that the choice of funds in Chevron's 401(k) plan did not require participants to pay excessive fees, and the plaintiffs failed to show that Chevron obtained any benefits from its relationship with Vanguard. [Anne Tergesen, *Latest Wave of 401(k) Suits Yields Big Wins, and Big Losses, for Plaintiffs*, WSJ.com (July 13, 2017). See, e.g., *Brotherston v. Putnam Invs.*, No. 1:15-cv-13825 (D. Mass. June 19, 2017); *In re Northrop Grumman Corp. ERISA Litig.*, No. CV 06-06213 MMM (JCX) (C.D. Cal., settled Mar. 17, 2017) discussed in John Manganaro, *Sponsor Settles Northrop Grumman ERISA Suit*, plansponsor.com (June 13, 2017); *Fernandez v. Merrill Lynch, Pierce, Fenner & Smith Inc.*, No. 1:15-cv-22782-MGC (S.D. Fla., settled June 8, 2017), discussed in Carmen Castro-Pagan, *Merrill Lynch to Pay $25M in Lawsuit Over Fees in Small 401(k)s*, bna.com (June 9, 2017) (benefitslink.com); *White v. Chevron*, No. 4:16-cv-0793-PJH (N.D. Cal. May 31, 2017)]

The Supreme Court held that the correct legal standard in an excessive fund fee case was whether the fees were so disproportionately large that they could not have been the product of arm's length bargaining (the standard used by most federal courts). [*Jones v. Harris*, 559 U.S. 335 (2010)]

However, the Supreme Court refused to hear the appeal of the dismissal of another Seventh Circuit case about excessive 401(k) fees: *Hecker v. Deere & Co.* [556 F.3d 575 (7th Cir 2009); see Fred Schneyer, *U.S. Supremes Turn Away Hecker Fee Case Appeal*, plansponsor.com (Jan. 19, 2010)]

The Supreme Court vacated an Eighth Circuit decision about whether mutual fund fees violated Section 36(b) of the Investment Company Act. The Eighth Circuit had relied on the marketplace to prevent excessively high fees from being imposed. However, the Supreme Court remanded the case to comply with *Jones*, where the standard is whether a fee is so unreasonably large that obviously there was no arm's length bargaining between the fund and its clients. [*Ameriprise Fin. Inc. v. Gallus*, 130 S. Ct. 2340 (2010)] On remand, the Eighth Circuit found that the plaintiffs did not demonstrate a breach of fiduciary duty; the fees were not so high that they fell outside the range of reasonable fees that could have been negotiated at arm's length. [*Gallus v. Ameriprise*, 675 F.3d 1173 (8th Cir. 2012)]

Participants in a 401(k) plan sued under ERISA and the Investment Company Act, alleging that the fees on their annuity insurance contracts were excessive. The district court dismissed the Investment Company Act claims, requiring an ownership interest to bring a derivative suit—the plaintiffs were no longer investors in those funds. The district court also dismissed the ERISA claims because the plaintiffs did not make a pre-suit demand on the plan's trustees to make them correct the problem, nor were the trustees named as parties to the suit. The Third Circuit affirmed the Investment Company Act ruling, but reversed on the ERISA question, deciding that ERISA does not require a pre-suit demand, and trustees do not have to be named as parties. [*Santomenno v. John Hancock Life Ins. Co.*, 677 F.3d 178 (3d Cir. 2012)]

In subsequent proceedings, the Third Circuit held that the 401(k) plan service provider was not a fiduciary when it selected the mutual fund menu (concentrating on its own proprietary funds). The plan trustees picked a smaller menu of funds, which were actually offered to participants. Because of the trustee's final authority over fund offerings, the Third Circuit held that the service provider was not a fiduciary. Certiorari was denied in May, 2015. [*Santomenno v. John Hancock Life Ins. Co.*, 768 F.3d 284 (3d Cir. 2014), *cert. denied*, 135 S. Ct. 1860 (2015)]

In 2015, the District Court for the Central District of California refused to certify a class action alleging that service providers charged excessive fees to plans because the accounts invested in publicly available mutual funds and the defendants provided no services on those accounts but, in 2016, certification was granted with respect to allegedly improper fees: No. CV 12-02782 DDP (MANx), 2016 U.S. Dist. LEXIS 40468 (C.D. Cal. Mar. 14, 2016). The district court said that class adjudication would be inefficient because class claims did not predominate when determining the reasonableness of the fees paid by each plan versus services received. [*Santomenno, et al. v. Transamerica Life Ins. Co., et al.*, 310 F.R.D. 451 (C.D. Cal. 2015)]

Exelon employees charged that their plan, offering 32 funds (24 retail mutual funds) generated excessive fees. The Seventh Circuit held that fiduciaries are not obliged to include only the lowest-cost funds, and noted that the fees were set competitively for the retail funds. The Seventh Circuit rejected the argument that institutional funds are always superior to retail funds; institutional funds might offer less liquidity or transparency than retail funds. [*Loomis v. Exelon*, 658 F.3d 667 (7th Cir. 2011)]

The Eighth Circuit upheld an award of $14.3 million against a 401(k) plan sponsor for breaching the fiduciary duty to control the costs of recordkeeping. The Eighth Circuit found that it was acceptable to pay for recordkeeping through revenue sharing and bundled service agreements—but the fiduciaries failed to investigate adequately before incurring the costs. However, the Eighth Circuit remanded a separate award of $21.8 million in alleged financial losses that were calculated by comparing the investment results of one of the plan's investments in a mutual fund to the returns of a different mutual fund; the Eighth Circuit held that the hindsight calculation was too speculative. The Eighth Circuit also reversed $1.7 million against Fidelity; the district court found that Fidelity breached its fiduciary duty when it failed to pay "float" income (interest earned before plan assets were transferred from one account to another) to the 401(k) plan. The Eighth Circuit held that these amounts did not constitute plan assets. As a result, Fidelity could not be liable for attorneys' fees or costs in the litigation. [*Tussey et al. v. ABB*, 746 F.3d 327 (8th Cir. 2014) *reh'g denied* (May 20, 2014)]

On remand, the district court for the Western District of Missouri found for the defendant, despite a holding that changing the investment selection was a breach of fiduciary duty because the plaintiff did not use the appropriate calculation of damages and did not offer evidence about the performance of funds whose performance would have been better. [*Tussey v. ABB*, No. 2:06-cv-04305-NKL (W.D. Mo. July 9, 2015)]

The evergreen case went back to the Eighth Circuit, which ordered yet another remand. The Eighth Circuit held that the district court used the alternative calculation proposed by the Eighth Circuit (comparing the performance of Fidelity funds with the worst funds in the plan) as if the Eight Circuit had mandated this approach. The Eighth Circuit said that the remand was ordered for the district court to evaluate several methods of quantifying losses before choosing one to apply. [*Tussey v. ABB, Inc.*, **850 F.3d 95** (8th Cir. 2017); see Practicallaw .com, *Eighth Circuit Remands Tussey v. ABB, Inc. for a Second Time, Instructing District Court to Evaluate Methods of Measuring Plan Losses Caused by Fiduciary Breach* (Mar. 14, 2017) (benefitslink.com)]

The Ninth Circuit applied a six-year statute of limitations, starting when the decision was made, to include allegedly improper investments in a plan, to a case where the plaintiffs challenged the selection of funds in a 401(k) plan. The Ninth Circuit held that the 404(c) safe harbor does not apply to designating investment options. The Ninth Circuit said that revenue sharing is not a prohibited transaction, in light of the prohibited transaction exemption stating that revenue sharing is not "consideration" given to fiduciaries. This opinion holds that, in general, including retail funds in the portfolio is not per se imprudent, and the portfolio can also include short-term funds—but, because the plan failed to do a proper analysis, it was imprudent to include two of the retail funds. The fiduciaries still had an obligation to consider all available share classes, even though they used a consultant. Then the Ninth Circuit amended its opinion, holding that the decision to retain a stock in the plan is not entitled to deference if the decision promotes the interests of anyone except the plan's beneficiaries. [*Tibble v. Edison Int'l*, 711 F.3d 1061 (9th Cir. 2013), amended 729 F.3d 1110 (9th Cir. 2013)]

Certiorari was granted in October, 2014 but limited to the issue of whether participants can challenge decisions that were made more than six years before their suit was filed, if the decisions could have been reconsidered during the six-year period. The Supreme Court held in May 2015, that 401(k) plan sponsors have an ongoing duty to monitor trust investments and divest imprudent ones (for example, retail mutual funds when less expensive institutional alternatives were available). This duty is separate from the duty of prudence in selecting investments. The case also affects the calculation of timeliness: the six-year ERISA statute of limitations does not necessarily begin with the purchase of an investment, so cases can be timely if they refer to decisions about retaining investments. [*Tibble v. Edison Int'l*, No. 13-550 (U.S. May 18, 2015)]. On the latest remand, the District Court for the Central District of California ruled in August 2017 that it was imprudent to invest in retail funds instead of institutional shares from the same funds. Plaintiffs are only entitled to damages for wrongdoing occurring within the statute of limitations which, in this case, meant the ongoing duty to monitor the appropriateness of plan investments. The court held that reasonable fiduciaries would have known at all times that institutional shares were available. Both sides stipulated that the damage calculation would begin with $7.5 million of profits the plan lost by investing in retail shares. The court gave the parties four possible methods of calculating the actual damages and ordered that, if they cannot agree, they submit their proposed calculations to the district court. [*Tibble v. Edison Int'l*, No. CV 2007-0539-SVW-AGR (C.D. Cal. Aug. 16, 2017); see Nevin E. Adams, *Tibble's Trials Near the End with a Win*, NAPA Net (Aug. 17, 2017) (benefitslink.com)]

The case returned to the Ninth Circuit, which dismissed the suit, holding that, although the Supreme Court imposed an ongoing fiduciary duty to monitor investments, the plaintiffs waived that argument by failing to raise it at the district court level. [*Tibble v. Edison Int'l*, No. 10-56406 (9th Cir. Apr. 13, 2016); see Daniel Wiessner, *Edison International Wins Dismissal of U.S. Lawsuit Over 401(k)*, Reuters (Apr. 13, 2016) (benefitslink.com)] However, en banc rehearing was granted on August 5, 2016. [*See* Jacklyn Wille, *Edison 401(k) Case Will Be Reheard by Ninth Circuit*, bna.com (Aug. 8, 2016) (benefitslink.com)]

At the end of 2016, the en banc Ninth Circuit vacated the district court's judgment for the defense. The en banc court held that the "ongoing duty to monitor" argument was not forfeited at the district court or Ninth Circuit level. In fact, the defendants waived the argument by failing to raise it in time. The en banc court used trust law to determine the scope of fiduciary duty to monitor and concluded that investments must be reevaluated periodically, especially when comparable products were available at lower cost. The en banc court remanded yet again for the district court to re-evaluate the award of costs and attorneys' fees in light of the Supreme Court decision and en banc remand decision. [*Tibble v. Edison*, 843 F.3d 1187 (9th Cir. en banc 2016); see John Manganaro, *Plaintiffs Still Pushing Tibble vs Edison Through Federal Courts*, plansponsor.com (Dec. 16, 2016)]

After the Supreme Court's *Tibble* decision, the Eleventh Circuit vacated and remanded two decisions that dismissed cases as untimely. The Eleventh Circuit applied the continuing duty standard for monitoring plan investments: a case is timely if it is brought within six years of an alleged breach of this duty, rather than within six years of the investment's initial selection. [*Stargel v. Sun Trust Bank Inc.*, 791 F.3d 1309 (11th Cir. 2015)]

The case of *Spano v. Boeing*, dealing with whether it was a breach of fiduciary duty to allow 401(k) plan participants to be charged excessive fees; whether the retirement plan of imprudently retained funds; and whether Boeing had a conflict of interest, was settled in August 2015. Boeing agreed to pay $57 million but did not admit liability. Boeing's 401(k) plan, which has $44 billion in assets, is the second-largest in the United States (IBM's is the largest). Previously, Lockheed Martin had paid $62 million, and CIGNA had paid $35 million, to settle similar claims [*Spano v. Boeing*, No. 06-0743-DRH (S.D. Ill., settled Aug. 26, 2015)]

A long-running suit against State Street Bank about the handling of General Motors' 401(k) ESOP plan was dismissed in late 2015. The Sixth Circuit held that, after *Dudenhoeffer*, State Street's actions were reviewed under a "prudent process" standard. A plaintiff alleging that an ESOP's investment in a publicly traded security was imprudent must show special circumstances to survive the defendant's motion to dismiss. The Sixth Circuit found that State Street engaged in a prudent process of decision because it repeatedly discussed whether the investment remained prudent: more than 40 meetings were held in a period of less than nine months. [*Pfeil v. State Street Bank & Trust*, 806 F.3d 377 (6th Cir. 2015); Certiorari was denied in mid-2016: No. 15-1199 (June 27, 2016). See Rebecca Moore, *Court's Decision About State Street's Handling of GM Stock Stands*, plansponsor.com (June 27, 2016).]

The Second Circuit held that participants in Lehman Brothers' retirement plan did not prove a fiduciary breach in connection with employer stock in the plan. Although ESOP fiduciaries are not entitled to a special presumption of prudence, plaintiffs must allege special circumstances to contend that fiduciaries should have recognized from publicly available information that the market under- or over-valued a stock. For claims based on non-public information, plaintiffs must plausibly allege an alternative course of action fiduciaries could have taken that would have benefited the plan. [*Rinehart v. Akers (In re Lehman Bros. Sec. & ERISA Litig.)*, No. 15-2229, 2016 U.S. App. LEXIS 5114 (2d Cir. Mar. 18, 2016); see Rebecca Moore, *Lehman Again Granted Victory in Stock Drop Suit*, plansponsor.com (Mar. 23, 2016). Certiorari was denied in February 2017 (*Rinehart v. Lehman Bros. Holdings*, **137 S. Ct. 1067** (2017)); see John Manganaro, *Lehman Stock Drop Suit Passed Over by Supreme Court*, plansponsor.com (Feb. 23, 2017)]

Many of these cases were brought by plan participants; a recent Eighth Circuit case was brought by the plan sponsor. The Eighth Circuit dismissed a plan sponsor's suit against a service provider charging that fees were excessive. The Eighth Circuit held that it was not acting as an ERISA fiduciary when it contracted to offer separately managed accounts for the plaintiff's retirement plan. The participants paid the defendant's management fees and operating expenses;

the fees were a percentage of the assets invested in a separate account, varying by the mutual fund adjusted by the account. The sponsor said that the defendant exercised discretionary authority over plan administration and management, imposing a fiduciary duty to charge reasonable fees. The Eighth Circuit, however, said that there is no fiduciary duty when a service provider carries out the terms of an agreement that was negotiated at arm's length with its client. [*McCaffree Fin. Corp. v. Principal Life Ins. Co.*, 811 F.3d 998 (8th Cir. Jan. 8, 2016); see Rebecca Moore, *Excessive Fee Claims Against Principal Dismissed*, plansponsor.com (Jan. 11, 2016)]

New York Life Insurance settled a class action for $3 million in 2016, without admitting liability. The plaintiffs are participants in two 401(k) plans who alleged that the plans offered an index fund that was costlier than comparable index funds, so the plan should have selected a cheaper index fund. [*Andrus et al. v. New York Life Ins. Co., et al.,* No. 1:16-cv-o5698 (S.D.N.Y, settled 2016); see Robert Steyer, *New York Life Settles Lawsuit Over Alleged Excessive Fees in Its 401(K) Plans*, pionline.com (Feb. 17, 2017) (benefitslink.com)]

> In mid-2016, fees on 401(k) plans declined, and many employers shifted costs to employees. According to Deloitte Consulting LLP, about 18% of total fees are for recordkeeping and disclosure to participants, and the rest are investment-related. In 2006, the median administrative fee per participant was $118, which dropped to $70 in 2014 and reached an all-time low of $64 in 2015. Many plans, especially mid-sized and large plans, explicitly impose separate administrative fees instead of using mutual fund fees under revenue-sharing to cover the administrative expenses. However, if the plan includes both index funds (which have very low fees) and actively managed funds that include administrative expense fees, the cost burden falls on participants who opt for actively managed funds. The form of the fee determines how the total costs are allocated among the participants. If the plan charges a flat fee per year, the fee represents a higher percentage of small than of large accounts. If the fee is a percentage, e.g., 0.1% of assets, then small accounts pay less.

[Anne Tergesen, *401(k)s Tweak How They Charge for Expenses*, WSJ.com (May 20, 2016)]

[2] Regulations

In late 2010, EBSA published a final rule dealing with disclosure of investment options, including the fees imposed on employees in participant-directed individual account plans. The final rule says that investing plan assets is a fiduciary act subject to ERISA § 404(a)(1), requiring fiduciaries to be prudent and act solely in best interests of plan's participants and beneficiaries. Plan administrators are not liable if they rely, reasonably and in good faith, on information given by a service provider. The plan administrator must make sure that participants and beneficiaries who have investment responsibilities are informed of their rights and responsibilities in connection with their accounts. They must be given the fee and expense information they need to make informed decisions.

Participants must receive performance data, such as one, five, and 10-year historical returns. If the investment does not pay a fixed rate of return, the total annual operating expenses as a percentage of assets, and as a dollar amount per $1,000 invested, must be disclosed. For investments with a fixed rate of return, fees and any restrictions on ability to purchase or withdraw investments must be disclosed. The mandatory information must be given to participants on or before the first date they can direct their investments, then annually thereafter. They must receive general information about the structure and mechanics of the plan, how to give investment instructions, a list of the current investment choices, and fees and expenses for general plan services that can be charged to the account. Participants must receive statements, at least quarterly, showing the dollar amount of fees and expenses actually charged to their accounts, with a description of the services rendered.

This information must be provided in a chart or similar comparison format; DOL drafted a model chart. The final rule differs from previous law by entitling participants to disclosures no matter the size of the plan; previous law applied only to plans with 100 or more participants. Fee disclosure for individual plans extends beyond the fees charged for the plan's investment options, and includes general administrative services such as recordkeeping, accounting, and legal services. Participants must be advised whether the fees are charged pro rata or per capita, so they can determine if some participants pay more than their fair share. Benchmark returns must be compared with a broad-based market index that is not affiliated with the investment firm. [Final Rule, *Fiduciary Requirements for Disclosure in Participant-Directed Individual Account Plans*, 75 Fed. Reg. 64910 (Oct. 20, 2010). The model disclosure form is at <http://www.dol.gov/ebsa/participantfeerulemodelchart.doc> (last viewed Feb. 9, 2017).]

A final rule requiring service providers to report the direct and indirect compensation paid by plan sponsors for account services was published in February 2012. The rule applies to service providers who are expected to receive $1,000 or more in compensation from defined benefit or defined contribution plans, for providing services or furnishing investment options in connection with brokerage or recordkeeping. The disclosures, on paper or electronic, must be given to the plan fiduciary. The final regulation is effective July 1, 2012, for both existing and new contracts. [77 Fed. Reg. 5632 (Feb. 3, 2012)]

A Notice of Proposed Rulemaking (NPRM) was published in the *Federal Register* for March 12, 2014, proposing to require a guide to be provided to disclosures by covered service providers that appear in multiple or lengthy documents. The guide assists plan fiduciaries in locating specific items of information that relate to their contracts with the service provider—e.g., the services that will be provided, if the provider has fiduciary status, how much the service provider will be paid, plus required investment disclosures for fiduciary, brokerage, and recordkeeping services (e.g., total annual operating expenses). [FR Doc 2014-04868, 79 Fed. Reg. 13949 (Mar. 12, 2014)]

§ 6.08 INVESTMENT ADVICE FOR PARTICIPANTS

PWBA Advisory Opinion 2001-09A [(Dec. 14, 2001), <http://www.dol.gov/ebsa/programs/ori/advisory2001/2001-09A.htm>] says that it would not be a prohibited transaction for a company that provides financial services to retain an independent professional to use computer modeling and modern portfolio theory to offer discretionary asset allocation services and recommended asset allocation services in connection with individual account plans—i.e., 401(k) plans. Participants will be given advice about how to allocate assets within their accounts, but would be permitted to either accept or reject the advice.

In effect, this was the approach adopted by PPA Title XI (§§ 601–625). It is not a prohibited transaction for a plan to provide plan participants with investment advice as long as the plan fiduciaries' fees for providing the advice do not vary based on the actual recommendations. There is also a safe harbor for investment advice that is generated by a valid computer model.

In early 2008, the Supreme Court ruled that the purpose of ERISA is to safeguard benefits. Therefore, although the general rule is that ERISA § 502(a)(3) can only be used to provide remedies for the plan as a whole, in a defined contribution plan, a participant can bring suit charging that fiduciary misconduct reduced the value of his or her plan account. [*LaRue v. DeWolff, Boberg & Assocs., Inc.,* 552 U.S. 248 (2008)]

In 2010, the DOL withdrew an earlier, controversial rule and replaced it. Under the revised rule, advice can be given two ways: through the use of an unbiased computer model, or when the adviser's fees do not vary no matter what investments the participants choose. The computer model or level fee arrangement has to be chosen by the fiduciary, independent of adviser and its affiliates; qualifications set for the investment expert who certifies the model; investment advisers can't get compensation from affiliates on the basis of their recommendations; and advice arrangements have to be audited each year. Additional requirements, including fee disclosure, are imposed. [Proposed rule, 75 Fed. Reg. 9360 (Mar. 2, 2010). The earlier rule was RIN-1210-AB-13, *Investment Advice: Participants and Beneficiaries*, 74 Fed. Reg. 23951 (May 22, 2009).]

Late in 2011, the DOL finalized the ERISA § 408(g) regulations that say it is not a prohibited transaction for fiduciary advisors to give individualized investment advice to participants in individual account plans. Fiduciary advisors qualifying for this exemption include broker-dealers, registered investment advisors, banks, and insurance companies. The effective date is December 27, 2011.

The DOL's Fact Sheet on the regulations estimates that about 134,000 defined contribution plans having 17 million participants and beneficiaries will contract with 16,000 investment advisory firms under these rules, and an estimated 3.5 million participants and beneficiaries will access the advice.

Advice must be based on generally accepted investment theories considering historic returns of different asset classes over time, plus information about the individual's age, life expectancy, current investments, assets and income, and investment preferences. The adviser's direct or indirect compensation must not vary based on which options the participant selects. Asset allocations in a computer model must be based on objective criteria, and must not be based on the size of the fee the advisor receives. Before a computer model is used, an eligible investment expert has to certify that it satisfies the requirements.

To use an eligible investment advice arrangement, the plan must have express authorization from a fiduciary. At least once a year, the arrangement must be audited by an independent auditor. The advisor must retain its records for at least six years after furnishing advice. [76 Fed. Reg. 66637 (Oct. 7, 2011)]

Some commentators predicted that "robo-style" automated investment services would gain an increasing role in the 401(k) market for small businesses. According to the GAO, about one-third of private-sector workers, some 42 million employees, work for small businesses (100 employees or fewer), but only 14% of small businesses sponsor retirement plans. The robos offer low-cost indexed investments (e.g., index mutual funds and Exchange Traded Funds) and operate online. For plans with assets over $1 billion, the average fee is 0.26% of assets, whereas some small plans pay 1.5% of assets in annual fees. The rise of robos reduced fees in general. Between 2009 and 2013, the average fee paid by small business plans with $1 million to $10 million in assets dropped from 1.21% to 1.06%. [Anne Tergesen, *New Online 401(k) Plans Disrupt Retirement Market*, WSJ.com (July 31, 2016)]

[A] DOL Fiduciary Rule

When ERISA was adopted in 1975, the Internal Revenue Code was amended to provide fiduciary rules and bans on self-dealing that were almost identical for tax and ERISA purposes. In 1978, IRS and the DOL agreed that DOL would have jurisdiction to issue regulations that apply under both the Code and ERISA, covering qualified plans and IRAs. Between 1975 and mid-2016, DOL used the ERISA § 3(21) five-part test of fiduciary status: e.g., advice is given on a regular basis, as the primary basis for an investment decision. At that time, however, defined benefit plans predominated and the defined contribution plans then in existence seldom allowed participants to direct investments; this is now common.

The DOL published final regulations in April 2016, defining those who give investment advice to retirement plan sponsors or participants as fiduciaries. The DOL also issued rules for complying with the Prohibited Transaction Exemption that allows a vendor to be paid for rendering investment advice. Although the regulation had a nominal effective date of June 7, 2016, DOL agreed to delay implementation until April 10, 2017. If the rule had been implemented as scheduled, its impact on plan sponsors would have been fairly small, because they have always been considered fiduciaries, but it would have had a significant impact on the operations of the financial service industry.

The DOL believed that plan participants and IRA investors need help understanding the relationship with advisors. The DOL said that a fiduciary relationship exists if someone recommends the purchase, sale, or retention of an investment; recommends someone to give investment advice; or makes a specific individual recommendation about the handling of IRA distributions, rollovers, or transfers. The DOL final rule does not require a regular pattern of advice or a mutual understanding on how the advice will be used. The advice does not have to be the primary basis for an investment decision. The final rule does not apply to benefit plans funded with insurance or other assets that do not have an investment component. Education and general communications that are not tailored to a particular recipient are not advice.

The DOL issued new Prohibited Transaction Exemptions, including the Best Interest Contract (BIC) exemption which imposes a best interests of the client standard for fiduciaries who are paid by a third party (e.g., under a revenue sharing arrangement) or whose compensation varies based on the actions taken (e.g., commissions and 12b-1 fees). This requirement applies to "retail advice": advice to participants of defined contribution plans who direct their own investments or have the power to make decisions about distributions; to IRA owners or beneficiaries; to plan fiduciaries who manage less than $50 million in assets; or to plan sponsors who do not make investment decisions or whose plan has less than $50 million in assets. The BIC exemption requires a written contract. All financial institutions involved have to adopt an anti-conflict procedure that is posted online. Specific disclosures of services, fees, and compensation are required. The service provider must forbid compensation that is unreasonable for the services provided and must not use bonuses or other incentives that encourage advisors to make recommendations that are not in their clients' best interests.

The customer must receive a written disclosure statement at the beginning of the relationship disclosing the fees or compensation of the advisor; links to additional online disclosures; contact information for complaints; and the extent to which recommendations are limited to proprietary products and/or products that pay fees to the advisor. Class action waivers are forbidden, although the contract can waive the right to receive punitive damages. Even if disclosure is adequate, the BIC exception is not available for transactions where the advisor's compensation is unreasonable. DOL's position is that, because plan sponsors have a duty to monitor their service providers, the plan sponsor might become liable as a co-fiduciary if a vendor consistently violates the rules. [81 Fed. Reg. 20945 (Apr. 8, 2016); see Frost Brown Todd, *The DOL's New Fiduciary Rules: What They Will Mean for Retirement Plan Sponsors* (Sept. 6, 2016) (benefitslink.com)]

In mid-2016, business and financial groups including the U.S. Chamber of Commerce sued in the Northern District of Texas to strike down the fiduciary rule. The plaintiffs alleged that the rule increases costs, limits access to professional financial advice, and reduces retirement choices. The plaintiffs said that the rule was invalid because the DOL did not have congressional authority to adopt it. In early 2017, the District Court for the Northern District of Texas ruled that the DOL had authority to implement the fiduciary rule. The district court held that Congress had never ratified the previous ERISA fiduciary standard, so plaintiffs could not argue that the test had been ratified as part of ERISA: inaction does not prove Congress' intent. [*Chamber of Commerce of the U.S. v. Perez*, Civil Action No. 3:16-cv-1476-M, **2017 U.S. Dist. LEXIS 17619** (N.D. Tex. Feb. 8, 2017); see Andrew Ackerman, *Groups Sue Obama Administration Over "Best Interest" Rule for Retirement Advice*, WSJ.com (June 2, 2016); Russell L. Hirschhorn & Benjamin Saper, *Update on Lawsuits Challenging the U.S. Department of Labor's Fiduciary Rule*, Proskauer Rose LLP (Oct. 26, 2016), available at Lexology.com; John Manganaro, *DOL Fiduciary Rule Wins Another Court Victory*, plansponsor .com (Feb. 9, 2017). See also *Thrivent Fin. for Lutherans v. Perez*, No. 0:16-cv-03289 (D. Minn., filed Sept. 29, 2016) challenging the BIC exemption as exceeding the DOL's statutory authority for requiring disputes to be resolved in federal court rather than through arbitration, which Thrivent says is required to preserve Thrivent's fraternal relationship to its members.]

As of August 2017, the case (now re-titled as *Thrivent Fin. for Lutherans v. Hugler*) was still pending, as was a similar case in the District Court for the District of Minnesota: *Thrivent Fin. for Lutherans v. Acosta*, No. 0:16-cv-03289. On August 9, 2017, the DOL notified the Minnesota court that it had submitted amendments to the Office of Management and Budget that would delay the effective date of the BIC Exemption and two other PTEs until July 1, 2019. See Shearman & Sterling LLP, *DOL Seeks Further Delay of "Fiduciary Rule" Exemptions* (Aug. 10, 2017), available at jdsupra.com]

In November 2016, the District Court for the District of Kansas sided with the DOL and refused to impose a preliminary injunction to prevent the fiduciary rule from taking effect. The District of Kansas said that Congress gave the DOL the power to decide what was in the public interest in this context. When the case proceeded, the district court upheld PTE 84-24 with respect to Fixed Indexed Annuities, holding that DOL did not violate the APA or the Regulatory Flexibility Act and that the DOL gave fair notice of the changes and had statutory authority to make them. The district court ruled that it was not arbitrary to treat Fixed

Indexed Annuities differently from other annuities, because of their greater risks. [*Market Synergy Grp. v. DOL*, No. 5:16-cv-04083, **2017 U.S. Dist. LEXIS 2315** (D. Kan. Feb. 17, 2017); see John Hilton, *Kansas Judge Rejects DOL Rule Injunction*, insurancenewsnet.com (Nov. 29, 2016) (benefitslink.com); Employee Benefits Alert, *Kansas Court Again Upholds Fiduciary Rule as Department of Labor Seeks to Delay Implementation*, Millerchevalier.com (Feb. 22, 2017) (benefitslink.com)]

The District Court for the District of Columbia granted DOL's motion for summary judgment, and dismissed the National Association for Fixed Annuities' challenge to the conflict of interest rule and related exemptions .The district court held that DOL is empowered to interpret ERISA and impose conditions for PTEs. It was not arbitrary and capricious to apply the BIC Exemption to fixed index annuity sales, and DOL performed an adequate regulatory analysis of the impact of the rule on small business before issuing it. [*Nat'l Ass'n for Fixed Annuities v. Perez*, No. CV 16-1035 (RDM), 2016 WL 6573480 (D.D.C. Nov. 4, 2016); see Russell L. Hirschhorn and Benjamin Saper, *DOL Prevails in First Challenge to the Conflict of Interest Rule and Related Exemptions*, Proskauer Rose LLP (Nov. 18, 2016), available at Lexology.com; Sandra Cohen, *Fiduciary Rule Survives First Court Challenge—Will Other Courts Follow?,* cohenbuckmann.com (Nov. 14, 2016) (benefitslink.com)]

Similarly, in February 2017, the District Court for the District of Texas denied the Chamber of Commerce's motion for summary judgment, and granted the DOL's motion for summary judgment. This decision was appealed to the Fifth Circuit on February 25, 2017; an emergency request to prevent the rule from taking effect before the appeal was denied. [*Chamber of Commerce of the U.S. v. Hugler,* No. 3:16-cv-1476-M, **2017 U.S. Dist. LEXIS 17619** (N.D. Tex. Feb. 8, 2017, **2017 U.S. Dist. LEXIS 3980** (Mar. 20, 2017). See Thinkadvisor.com, *Emergency Request to Block DOL Fiduciary Rule Filed in Texas Court* (Mar. 14, 2017) (benefitslink.com)]

At the beginning of 2017, Republican Representative Joe Wilson of South Carolina introduced legislation to delay implementation of the fiduciary rule by two years. [Lisa Beilfuss, *Fiduciary Rule Guidance Unveiled as Implementation Deadline Looms*, WSJ.com (Jan. 13, 2017)]

Elimination of the fiduciary rule is one of the Trump administration's priorities, as part of an overall reduction in regulation of business. On February 3, 2017, President Trump directed the DOL to review the fiduciary rule; the acting Secretary of Labor announced that the department will consider what its statutory options are for delaying the effectiveness of the rule. [<https://www.white house.gov/the-press-office/2017/02/03/presidential-memorandum-fiduciary-duty-rule>]

The memorandum says that the rule could significantly alter the availability of financial advice. The memorandum directs the DOL to examine the rule to see if it impairs access to retirement information and financial advice. DOL is directed to prepare an updated legal and economic impact analysis as to whether the rule would reduce access to offerings, products, or information about retirement savings; whether it has disrupted the industry in a way that could harm retirees or investors; and whether the rule is likely to lead to more litigation and higher prices. If the DOL makes such findings or otherwise finds that the rule is inconsistent with Trump administration priorities, it is directed to publish a proposed rule rescinding or revising the fiduciary rule.

The OMB characterized the effort to stop the fiduciary rule as economically significant, which is defined as a regulatory action with an effect on the economy of $100 million a year or more, or materially affecting the whole economy or part of it, or influence on productivity, competition, jobs, the environment, public health or safety, or state or local governments or communities. A regulatory action is also deemed significant if it interferes with another agency's actions, makes a material change in the budgetary impact of fees, grants, or entitlement programs; or raises novel legal or policy issues. Significant regulatory actions require the compilation of a cost-benefit analysis. [John Manganaro, *Trump Administration Hits Hurdle in Fiduciary Fight*, plansponsor.com (Feb. 28, 2017)]

The DOL published a rule in the *Federal Register* on April 7, 2017. This rule delays implementation of the most significant aspects of the fiduciary rule (requirement to act in the clients' best interests by making only objective recommendations; avoiding misleading statements; reasonable compensation for services) for 60 days, until June 9, 2017. Procedural portions of the rule, such as disclosure requirements, are scheduled to take effect on January 1, 2018. The DOL solicited comments to assist its reconsideration of the fiduciary rule, which could be modified or withdrawn after DOL's review. [82 Fed. Reg. 16902 (Apr. 7, 2017); see Lee Barney, *DOL Moves Forward With 60-Day Fiduciary Rule Delay*, plansponsor.com (Apr. 5, 2017)]

However, although the DOL continued to review the rule, asked for public comments, and might eliminate the rule in the future, the fiduciary rule took effect without further delays on June 9, 2017. [Lisa Beilfuss, *"Fiduciary" Rule to Take Effect June 9 With No Further Delay, Labor Secretary Says*, WSJ.com (May 22, 2017); Plansponsor editors, *No More Delays for DOL Fiduciary Rule*, plansponsor.com (May 24, 2017)]

The fiduciary rule included a private right of action, under which customers could bring class actions against brokers who allegedly failed to act in the customers' best interests. This was intended to be the main enforcement mechanism for the rule. Under prior law, dissatisfied investors who charged violation of the suitability standard would probably have been required to press the claim through FINRA arbitration. It is likely that the cost-benefit analysis of the fiduciary rule will show that this provision increases litigation, so one possible outcome is that the fiduciary rule will survive, but in modified form, without the class action provision. [Lisa Beilfuss, *As Fiduciary Rule Gets Reviewed, Class-Action Provision Is Under Microscope*, WSJ.com (Mar. 15, 2017)]

§ 6.09 401(k) PLANS RESPOND TO THE ECONOMY

[A] Market Effects

In the 1990s, 401(k) plans rose to prominence. Employers wanted plan participants to be able to benefit from the bull market—and employers were also concerned about the complexity and investment risk involved in operating a defined benefit plan.

The recession caused significant losses to 401(k) accounts, even those managed by reputable firms. A 2012 article [Steven Greenhouse, *Should the 401(k) Be Reformed or Replaced?*, NYTimes.com (Sept. 11, 2012)] suggests what would once have been a ludicrous suggestion: for many years, 401(k)s were acclaimed as a solution for both employers' and employees' needs. Now some commentators are questioning whether the 401(k) form has failed or is so questionable that it requires major changes—if it can or should survive at all.

In 1981, Herbert Whitehouse (then an HR executive at Johnson & Johnson) was one of the first advocates of 401(k)s; he thought that they would be used to supplement, rather than replace, defined benefit pensions. Thirty-five years later, he is one of many original proponents of the 401(k) form who now regret that 401(k)s came to dominate the retirement landscape because participants are vulnerable to investment risks and high fees. In the 1980s–1990s bull market, the conventional assumption was that employees could fund their retirement by saving 3% of compensation in a 401(k), with investment returns of 7% a year. That level is now generally unattainable, especially if the account is subject to high fees. Now some commentators favor either higher employer contributions or forced savings.

According to the Employee Benefits Research Institute (EBRI), only 61% of eligible workers are currently saving for retirement, and few understand that they would need at least eight times their annual salary for comfortable retirement. But for workers in the 50–64 age cohort and the bottom half of earnings, their median income is $32,000 but their median retirement assets are only $25,000. For the middle 40% of the earnings distribution, they earn a median of $97,000, with median savings of $121,000, whereas the top 10% earn a median of $251,000 but still have savings of only $450,000. According to the National Institute on Retirement Savings, almost half (45%) of households have no retirement savings at all. EBRI and the Investment Company Institute (ICI) note somewhat more optimistically that people in their sixties who have been contributing to 401(k) plans for decades have average balances of $304,000. [Timothy W. Martin, *The Champions of the 401(k) Lament the Revolution They Started*, WSJ.com (Jan. 2, 2017)]

Since the 2008 recession, savings in defined contribution plans have risen. According to the Profit-Sharing Council of America (PSCA), 99% of full-time employees are eligible to participate in their companies' plans, and half of the plans allow participation by part-time workers. About 88% of eligible plan participants have an account balance, and 80% contribute to the plan. Deferral rates have increased: in 2013, the average deferral rate was 5.3% of pay, whereas it was 5.8% in 2015 for lower-paid employees. In 2008, utilization of plan loans peaked but in 2015, the percentage of participants holding loans, and the percentage of plan assets loaned out, were at their lowest rate in a decade. In 2015, 14.6% of participants had a loan balance, and only 0.7% of plan assets were in loans. [PSCA press release, *Participant Deferral Rates the Highest in Years and Loan Usage the Lowest, According to PSCA's 58th Annual Survey* (Jan. 11, 2016) (benefitslink.com)]

[B] Employer Stock and Diversification

During the bull market, publicly traded companies had very strong incentives to use their own stock to compensate employees. Not only could they save cash by offering stock or stock options, but distributing stock to employees reduces the risk of unfriendly takeovers, increases employees' stake in the company and therefore at least theoretically their loyalty, and gives employees the chance to benefit from increases in the value of the stock. The problem is that, in a bear market, employees suffer correspondingly as a result of decreases in the value of the stock. Diversification is a basic principle of investment theory. By law, defined benefit plans cannot be more than 10% invested in the employer's stock; however, employees, especially those who get employer matches in the form of the employer's stock, often have more than one-quarter of their account invested in employer stock. As Chapter 15 shows, many suits have tried (generally unsuccessfully) to penalize plan fiduciaries for retaining employer stock as an investment for an unduly long period.

Removing company stock from the plan is not the only possible response. A third-party fiduciary can be involved to determine the role of employer stock in the plan. The most common cap is 20%.

Pensions & Investments reported in mid-2015 that company stock represented 19.4% ($207.5 billion) of the total of $1.07 trillion in defined contribution plan assets in the 100 largest corporate plans. These major plans hold about one-quarter of all 401(k) plan assets. [Robert Steyer, *Company Stock Still a Corporate DC Staple*, pionline.com (June 29, 2015) (benefitslink.com)]

PPA §§ 507 and 901 enacted a new Code § 401(a)(35) and a related ERISA provision at 204(j), explaining diversification rights for publicly traded employer securities held by a defined contribution plan. Participants (and some beneficiaries) are entitled to notice of the right to diversify their elective deferrals and after-tax contributions. Plans must offer at least three other investment options, with materially different risk and return characteristics. (Because ESOPs are designed to invest in employer stock, they are exempt from these rules.) Plan administrators must notify participants of their rights to divest at least 30 days before the first date the right to divest can be exercised. [IRS Notice 2006-107, 2006-5 I.R.B. 1114 (Nov. 30, 2006)] Failure to provide the statement is penalized per day elapsed without providing the required statement. The penalty rose to a maximum of $131 a day as of August 1, 2016: see 81 Fed. Reg. 42491 (June 30, 2016).

All defined contribution plans must issue a statement at least annually, and quarterly statements are required for individual account plans (e.g., 401(k)s) whose participants can direct the investment of their account balances. The quarterly statement must disclose:

- The total account balance;

- The amount that is vested; if none is, the earliest vesting date for the participant;

- A breakdown of the value of each of the investments within the account;

- Whatever limitations or restrictions are placed on the right to direct investments by the terms of the plan;

- An explanation of why diversification is important;

- URL for the DOL Website containing investment information;

- (For profit-sharing plans integrated with Social Security) an explanation of plan integration.

Employers can use the general DOL and IRS procedures for distributing statements in electronic rather than hard-copy form. The information can be provided on a secure Website as well as through individual e-mails. But if the sponsor chooses to use a Website to distribute the information, participants and beneficiaries must be given a written notice explaining how to access the information online—and that they can get a free paper copy if they prefer.

Individual account plans that do not permit individuals to direct the investment of their accounts must also furnish annual statements within 45 days of the end of the year. The statements are similar but need not include information about restrictions on investments or the explanation of the importance of diversification. The information can be furnished on a secure Website. [Gregory B. Kuhn, *New Benefit Statement Requirements for Retirement Plans*, <http://www.utz miller/benefitstatement.pdf?> (Mar. 16, 2007). The DOL URL is <http://www.dol.gov/ebsa/investing.html> (last viewed Mar. 21, 2015)]

Regulations proposed in early 2008 were finalized in July 2010, explaining the diversification requirements imposed on plans that invest in publicly traded securities of the employer. Under the Final Rule, a participant who has at least three years of service (or the beneficiary of such a participant, or the beneficiary of a deceased participant) must be given a chance at least every quarter to diversify out of employer securities held in that person's account. The plan must offer at least three investment options other than employer stock, and those three must be diversified and must have materially different risk and return characteristics. [T.D. 9484, 75 Fed. Reg. 27927 (May 19, 2010)]

As § 15.03[C] shows, a number of "stock drop" cases have been filed over the years. That is, plaintiffs whose account value has declined significantly because they invested in employer stock that declined in value frequently bring suits alleging that the plan's fiduciaries were imprudent to retain employer stock as a possible investment. Most of these cases have been dismissed. Many plans removed employer stock as an investment alternative, heading off suits. Improvement in the stock market climate also reduces the number of suits because there are fewer employer companies whose stock shows a sharp decline.

The *Wal-Mart v. Dukes* Supreme Court ruling (see § 42.06[A]) creates problems for class certification in stock drop cases, although *Dukes* is an employment discrimination case. *Dukes* increases the evidence requirement for certifying a class action. In the stock drop context, the problem is that the plan participants have different experiences based on investing for different periods of time.

In mid-2013, the Seventh Circuit permitted 401(k) class actions for investment losses due to imprudent plan investment options, although in this case the plaintiffs said that the stable value fund's choices were imprudent not because they were too risky, but because too many money market funds were included, making it difficult to keep up with inflation. The plaintiff class was defined as 56,000 plan participants who invested in the stable value fund. [*Abbott v. Lockheed Martin Corp*, 725 F.3d 803 (7th Cir. 2013)] The *Moench* presumption is a legal theory that fiduciaries are presumed to be prudent when they keep employer stock as a plan investment. The nature of a presumption is that it can be rebutted if the plaintiffs produce enough evidence. The presumption stems from a 1995 Third Circuit case [*Moench v. Robertson*, 62 F.3d 553 (3d Cir. 1995)]; in the 1990s and 2000s, it was adopted by many other courts: the Second, Fifth, Sixth, Ninth, and Eleventh Circuits, although they differed on the technical legal rules for applying the presumption.

However, in 2014, the Supreme Court rejected the presumption in a case involving an ESOP that invested primarily in employer stock. According to the plaintiffs, the fiduciaries were imprudent to retain the stock in the plan, because their status as officers—and publicly available information—should have made them realize that the investment was too risky. The Supreme Court held that ESOP fiduciaries are subject to the same standard of prudence as other fiduciaries, except that ESOP fiduciaries do not have a duty to diversify the plan's investment portfolio; ESOPs are supposed to invest heavily in employer stock. The Supreme Court remanded the case to determine if the plaintiffs had pled their case adequately. The Supreme Court held that it is generally not enough for plaintiffs to charge that the market either over- or undervalued publicly traded stock. To assert a tenable claim for breach of the duty of prudence, the complaint must plausibly allege a superior alternative that the fiduciaries could have adopted— without breaking the law. It is never imprudent for fiduciaries to refuse to trade on non-public information. Furthermore, it might have violated fiduciary duty if the ESOP trustees had disposed of the employer stock, because it could have caused the stock's value to decline even further. [*Fifth Third Bancorp et al. v. Dudenhoeffer*,134 S. Ct. 2459 (2014)]

Because of *Dudenhoeffer*, the Ninth Circuit revised its ruling in a stock-drop suit. Previously, the Ninth Circuit reversed the dismissal of the case based on the presumption of prudence for investments in company stock. The Ninth Circuit's latest decision still reverses the dismissal and remands for further proceedings—but holds that ESOP fiduciaries are not presumed prudent, although they are not obligated to diversify the plan's holdings. The defendants said that divestment would have forced the collapse of the stock price, but the Ninth Circuit said that the fund could have been removed as an investment option without harming the participants; the fund would not be liquidated even though it was no longer an investment option for the plan. The Ninth Circuit said that the issue was failure to disclose required information to the public, rejecting the defense argument that it would violate securities law to remove the fund based on undisclosed material information. [*Harris v. Amgen*, 770 F.3d 865 (9th Cir. 2014). Rehearing en banc was denied on May 26, 2015. The effect of the denial is that the case returned to the district court, for reconsideration in light of *Dudenhoeffer*, and without applying a presumption of prudence: *Harris v. Amgen*, No. 10-56014, *reh'g en banc denied* (May 26, 2015). See John Manganaro, *9th Circuit Confirms Stock Drop Remand*, plansponsor.com (June 30, 2015)]

In 2016, the Supreme Court revived securities claims against Amgen, remanding the case once again to the Ninth Circuit. The Supreme Court held that the Ninth Circuit did not evaluate the complaint properly, and did not find enough facts and allegations to support a claim for breach of the duty of prudence. [*Amgen v. Harris*, No. 136 S. Ct. 758 (2016); see Barbara Leonard, *9th Circuit Handed New Reversal on Amgen Case*, Courthouse News Service (Jan. 25, 2016) (benefitslink.com)]

Although it was anticipated that, by removing the presumption of prudence, *Dudenhoeffer* would make it easier for stock-drop plaintiffs to be awarded damages, that has not played out in practice because of the difficulty of pleading an alternative action that would have had a better result. For example, in an early 2017 case, the D.C. Circuit rejected the argument that an ESOP case was about the sponsor's failure to understand how risky an investment was, not the sponsor's valuation of the price, because the D.C. Circuit said that risk analysis is based on market valuation. The D.C. Circuit also held that claims of imprudence based on publicly available information require special circumstances, such as fraud. [*Coburn v. Evercore*, **844 F.3d 965** (D.C. Cir. 2016); see *Plansponsor* editors, *D.C. Appellate Court Affirms Employer Win in Stock Drop Suit*, plan sponsor.com (Jan. 5, 2017)]

The Fifth Circuit affirmed a $6.5 million judgment about an ESOP's mishandling of an $18.4 billion stock purchase: the fiduciaries relied on inaccurate valuations from an appraiser. The fiduciaries did not investigate the appraiser's background and did not discover that he had a fraud conviction. Nor did the fiduciaries give the appraiser enough information about the company's risk factors; they did not double-check the appraiser's conclusions; and they ignored evidence of his collusion with the company's attorneys. [*Perez v. Bruister,* **823 F.3d 250** (5th Cir. 2016); see Jacklyn Wille, *Labor Secretary Wins 5th Circuit Battle Over Employer Stock,* bna.com (May 5, 2016) (benefitslink.com). For the attorneys' fee phase of the case see. **653 Fed. Appx. 811** (5th Cir. 2016)]

J.C. Penney agreed to pay $4.5 million to settle a suit about retaining company stock in the plan once it was no longer prudent. Preliminary approval was granted. There was no admission of liability. The settlement class includes people whose accounts held shares in the Penney Common Stock Fund during the period from November 1, 2011 to May 31, 2016. [Rebecca Moore, *J.C. Penney to Settle Stock Drop Suit,* plansponsor.com (Jan. 10, 2017)]

In a "reverse stock drop case" (alleging that it was a breach of duty for fiduciaries to get rid of employer stock too quickly), the district court ruled for the plan and the 401(k) plan committees. The Fourth Circuit reversed, finding that the district court applied the wrong legal standard. After Nabisco spun off its tobacco business, the new 401(k) plan maintained two Nabisco single-stock funds as frozen funds: participants could retain existing investments but could not add to them. Later, when Nabisco shares were at their lowest point, the funds were divested from the plan. Then a takeover offer led to a bidding war and a spike in Nabisco's stock price. The Fourth Circuit said that the defendants had the burden of proof as to whether the decision to divest the funds was objectively prudent. The standard is whether fiduciaries use appropriate methods to investigate the value of an investment; use reasoned processes consistent with what a prudent man in the same capacity would do; and monitor to make sure that the decision remains in the best interests of participants. Under this standard, the Fourth Circuit found that the fiduciaries violated their duty. The amendment to the plan was invalid. There was no evidence that the fiduciary committee analyzed the elimination of the funds and management knew that a letter sent to participants saying that it would be illegal to maintain the funds was incorrect. [*Tatum v. RJR Pension Inv. Comm.,* 761 F.3d 346 (4th Cir. 2014). Certiorari was denied, as No. 14-656, on June 29, 2015. See Jill Cornfield, *SCOTUS Won't Hear Reverse Stock Drop Case,* plansponsor.com (June 30, 2015)]

On remand from the Fourth Circuit, the district court held that a hypothetical prudent fiduciary would have divested the Nabisco company stock funds from the plan. Therefore, the fiduciaries were not personally liable for damages. The Fourth Circuit used the standard of whether a hypothetical prudent fiduciary would have made the same decision, not the standard of whether the fiduciary would be excused from liability if a prudent fiduciary could have made the same decision. On remand in 2016, the district court said that the prudence of a divestiture decision depends on whether the duty of monitoring the fund would have required a change in strategy when circumstances changed. The district court said that it was not foreseeable that the Nabisco stock would recover from its "tobacco taint" and rise in price. [*Tatum v. R.J. Reynolds Tobacco Co.*, No. 1:02CV00373, 2016 WL 660902 (M.D.N.C. Feb. 18, 2016); see Practical Law Employee Benefits & Executive Compensation, *On Remand, Plan Fiduciaries' Decision to Divest Nabisco Stock Fund Found Prudent* (Feb. 23, 2016) (benefitslink.com); Rebecca Moore, *RJR Handed a New Win in Stock Divestment Decision*, plansponsor.com (Feb. 22, 2016)]

The Fourth Circuit rendered yet another decision in April 2017. This time, the Fourth Circuit reaffirmed that if a fiduciary's process for making an investment decision was not prudent, the fiduciary will be liable unless it can show by a preponderance of the evidence that a prudent fiduciary would, more likely than not, have made the same decision. But the Fourth Circuit held that RJR did satisfy this standard. The Fourth Circuit applied the same standard to divestment as to the initial choice to add an investment to the plan. [*Tatum v. RJR Pension Inv. Comm.*, 855 F.3d 553 (4th Cir. 2017); see John Manganaro, *RJR Wins Third Appellate Decision in ERISA Case,* plansponsor.com (May 2, 2017); Paul J. Ondrasik Jr. and Edward Thomas Veal, *"Coulda, Woulda, Shoulda": Fourth Circuit Re-Revisits a Controversial Position on ERISA's Prudence Standard,* Steptoe & Johnson LLP (June 7, 2017), available at Lexology.com]

The Sixth Circuit held that an employee who sold most of her shares of employer stock at a time when she alleged the share price was artificially inflated by the company's financial misconduct did not have standing to maintain a stock-drop suit. She had no actual injury: if anything, the so-called misconduct benefited her by increasing the price she received for selling the stock. [*Taylor v. KeyCorp.*, 680 F.3d 609 (6th Cir. 2012)]

[C] Blackout Periods

In certain instances, often associated with corporate mergers and acquisitions, or with the release of corporate earnings and other financial statements, a "blackout period" is imposed, and ordinary activities in connection with plan accounts are suspended. Because of concerns that rank-and-file employees are at risk of losing money during blackouts, the Sarbanes-Oxley Act [Pub. L. No. No. 107-204] not only limits the trading activities of corporate insiders, but also obligates the corporation to provide notice of future blackout periods to the employees at large.

A blackout period, according to § 306(a)(4) of the Act, means a period that lasts more than three consecutive business days, during which at least 50% of the plan's participants or beneficiaries' ability to trade in the employer company's stock is affected. An "individual account plan" means a retirement plan that has more than one participant, and where each participant has his or her own separate account. For instance, a 401(k) plan is an individual account plan, but a defined benefit pension plan is not, because the whole plan has only one account from which benefits are paid.

Certain events that affect trading are not considered blackout periods, so the notice requirement doesn't apply. Under the legal definition, blackout periods are only temporary, so if rights are permanently amended or eliminated, this does not constitute a blackout period, and notice will not be required.

Furthermore, if the plan imposes regularly scheduled blackouts—for instance, every quarter at the time that earnings figures are released—and if the scheduled blackouts have been disclosed to participants and beneficiaries in the Summary Plan Description (SPD) or other plan communications, notice will not be required.

Finally, an event is not a blackout period if it is imposed just because someone becomes—or ceases to be—a participant or beneficiary in an individual account plan because of a corporate merger, acquisition, or divestiture. Limitations on just one person's account (relating to a divorce-related court order or a tax levy, for instance) are not considered blackout periods either, because a blackout period is a mass rather than an individual event.

[D] Changes in the Employer Match

Under prior law, the sponsor of a safe harbor 401(k) plan could eliminate or reduce matching contributions under certain circumstances, but could only suspend or cut non-elective contributions by terminating the plan. Proposed regulations published in mid-2009 [74 Fed. Reg. 23134 (May 18, 2009)] allow plan sponsors to reduce or suspend their safe harbor non-elective contributions during a plan year in which they encounter a substantial business hardship. The eligible employees must be notified of the reduction or suspension, and the plan must be amended to provide that anti-discrimination tests must be satisfied for the whole plan year. Substantial business hardship means that the sponsoring corporation is operating at a loss; unemployment or underemployment is common in the sponsor's industry; the industry as a whole is depressed or in a decline; and it is reasonable to predict that the plan cannot be continued without reducing or suspending non-elective contributions. The rules are complex, so sponsors must get legal advice before attempting to alter plan contributions. [See Towers Perrin Governance and Compliance Advisory Insight, *New IRS Regulations Allow Safe Harbor 401(k) Plans to Suspend Non-Elective Contributions* (May 2009) (benefitslink.com)]

The regulations were finalized in late 2013: 78 Fed. Reg. 68735 (Nov. 15, 2013). The final rules make it somewhat easier for the employer to show entitlement to suspend or reduce the contributions during a plan year. The final regulations generally apply to amendments adopted after May 18, 2009; they apply for plan years beginning on or after January 1, 2015 with respect to mid-year reductions or suspensions.

Seven circuits (the Third, Fourth, Fifth, Sixth, Ninth, Tenth, and D.C. Circuits) have held that beneficiaries of an ERISA plan do not have to exhaust administrative remedies before bringing a suit, as long as the suit asserts ERISA violations rather than claims for benefits. (However, the Seventh and Eleventh Circuits disagree.) The most recent, Sixth Circuit, case deals with Cumberland University's defined contribution plan. In 2009, the university adopted a 5% match (i.e., employee contributions to the plan were matched, up to 5% of the employee's salary). The plan was retroactively amended on October 9, 2014, changing to a discretionary match set by the employer each year. The university announced that there would be no matching contributions for the period 2013–2015. A class action was filed on November 12, 2015, asserted wrongful denial of benefits, violation of the anti-cutback provision, notice failure, and breach of fiduciary duty. The District Court for the Middle District of Tennessee reversed and remanded, holding that the plaintiffs charged that their benefit was properly calculated, but under illegal plan terms. The Sixth Circuit said that the legality of the plan amendment fell within the expertise of the court system, and it would be a waste of legal system resources to make the plaintiffs exhaust administrative remedies that would have been futile. [*Hitchcock v. Cumberland Univ.*, **851 F.3d 552** (6th Cir. 2017); see gtlaw.com, *Sixth Circuit Joins Six Other Circuits in Ruling Exhaustion of Plan's Administrative Procedures Not Required When Asserting Statutory Violations* (Mar. 23, 2017) (benefitslink.com)]

CHAPTER 7

CASH BALANCE PLANS

§ 7.01 INTRODUCTION

A cash balance plan is a hybrid pension plan that shares features of a conventional defined benefit plan with characteristics more like a profit-sharing or 401(k) plan. Cash balance plans are subject to the defined benefit plan rules.

The IRS's definition of a cash balance plan, found at 64 Fed. Reg. 56579, is "a defined benefit pension plan that typically defines an employee's retirement benefit by reference to the amount of a hypothetical account balance." In a typical cash balance plan, this account is credited with hypothetical allocations and interest that are determined under a formula set out in the plan.

The plan is drafted so that the corporation's books reflect an individual account for each participant. The employer funds the plan each year, based on a percentage of pay, and subject to the I.R.C. § 415 limit on employer contributions. The pension the employee will eventually receive reflects two elements: an annual benefit credit (a percentage of pay) and annual interest credited at the rate specified by the plan. Because cash balance plans provide individual accounts, the plans are more portable than ordinary defined benefit plans.

At retirement, the employee's retirement annuity is based on the vested account balance. In practice, although in most defined benefit plans accrual is greatest in the later years of employment, in cash balance plans accrual is greatest in the early years. Defined benefit plans often provide early retirement subsidies; cash balance plans seldom do.

The consulting firm Kravitz said that, in 2016, the cash balance plan market achieved the level of $1 trillion in total invested assets. In 2001, cash balance plans represented 2.9% of all defined benefit plans—rising to 29% of defined benefit plans in 2016. In 2014, the last year for which complete IRS data is available, there were 15,178 cash balance plans in existence, nearly all (91%) in firms with fewer than 100 employees. Nearly half of those plans—8,000—were created post-2014 to be able to take advantage of the 2010 and 2014 regulations that permit broader investment choices for cash balance plans. [John Manganaro, *Cash Balance Plans Continue to Be Attractive Option for Employers,* plansponsor.com (July 7, 2016)] Hybrid plans accrue benefits under the fixed formula set by the employer; see also Kravitz' *2017 National Cash Balance Research Report* (Sept. 12, 2017) (benefitslink.com)]

A hybrid defined benefit plan usually defines the benefit as a lump-sum account balance rather than an annuity benefit payable at age 65. Cash balance plans are the most popular type of hybrid plans. The account balance is the sum of periodic pay credits (a percentage of pay) plus interest credits reflecting the interest rate chosen by the employer.

The employer's discretion is not infinite: an April 7, 2017 IRS memorandum warns that a cash balance plan that gives the employer discretion to include only part of annual compensation, a special bonus, or only the pay above a certain dollar amount could violate the requirement that amounts used in defined benefit plan calculations be "definitely determinable." [Roberta P. Granadier,

New Cash Balance Retirement Plan Guidance, Dickinson Wright (May 15, 2017), available at Lexology.com]

Historically, cash balance plans were not allowed to use preapproved plans, but Rev. Proc. 2015-36, 2015-27 I.R.B. 20, allows them to use prototype or volume submitter plans. The IRS has also released sample language that drafters can use. However, cash balance plans cannot use preapproved plan documents if they were converted from defined benefit plans and if they use certain benefit formulas; if they allow plan participants to choose the investments on which their interest accumulation rate is based; or use the Code § 411 accrual rates. [Ferenczy Benefits Law Center Flash Point, *Well, They've Done It: The IRS Jettisons the FDL Program* (July 24, 2015) (last accessed Feb. 11, 2017) (benefitslink.com)]

Notice 2016-67, 2016-47 I.R.B. 751, explains how to apply the market rate of return limitations to a Pension Equity Plan (PEP)—a defined benefit plan that expresses accumulated benefits as the current value of an accumulated percentage of the participant's final average compensation, highest average compensation, or highest average compensation in a period of years. An explicit interest PEP adjusts the benefit with interest credits to determine the amount payable at annuity starting dates after the principal credits cease. The interest credits are subject to the market-return limitation under the 2015 hybrid plan regulations. Therefore, amendments to make the interest crediting rate compliant with the hybrid plan rules must be made before the start of the first plan year beginning on or after January 1, 2017. However, Notice 2016-67 focuses on implicit interest PEPs—plans that determine the benefits by applying a deferred annuity factor to the accumulated benefits. "Implicit" refers to the preretirement interest being implicitly reflected in the deferred annuity factor. The preretirement interest implicit in applying the deferred annuity factor to the accumulated benefit is not defined as an interest credit because the accumulated benefit remains a constant percentage of average compensation and is not adjusted with interest credits after the principal credits end. The IRS says that the hybrid plan regulations do not require amending the deferred annuity factors to reduce the preretirement interest. [Rebecca Moore, *IRS Clarifies Interest Crediting Rules for Pension Equity Plans,* plansponsor.com (Nov. 7, 2016)]

The legal status of cash balance plans was highly ambiguous until the Pension Protection Act of 2006 (PPA; Pub. L. No. 109-280) made it clear that a cash balance plan that satisfies the statutory criteria will not be considered discriminatory. (See § 7.07.) However, this relief is prospective only, and cash balance conversions that occurred before June 29, 2005 are not affected by the legislation. As § 7.04 shows, although most courts have ruled in favor of cash balance plans, a few cases have found the cash balance form in general, or specific plans and plan provisions, to violate the Employment Retirement Income Security Act (ERISA) or discriminate against older workers.

Although plan amendments cannot reduce benefits earned before the conversion, some conversions have the effect that employees who already earned benefits do not earn additional retirement benefits for varying periods of time after the conversion. This effect, often referred to as "wearaway" or "benefit plateau," continues until the employee's benefit under the ongoing cash balance formula catches up with the employee's protected benefit.

The ERISA Advisory Council defines wearaway as an effect of plan transitions. The employee can get either the frozen benefit under the old plan formula or the total benefit under the cash balance plan—whichever is greater. But for employees who are close to early retirement age, the frozen benefit may be so much larger than the accruals under the new cash balance formula that, in effect, little or nothing will be accrued for a long time, until the benefit under the old rules is "worn away."

In late 2015, the District Court for the Southern District of New York ordered Foot Locker to reform its cash benefit plans to disclose the period of wearaway, so accrued benefits would be calculated the way the participants expected. The plan used the defined benefit plan balance as the beginning balance, applied a 9% discount rate and had a mortality discount. After the conversion, account balances were credited with pay credit and an interest credit at a fixed 6% rate. The employer knew that for a period of years, most participants' account balances would be lower than they were under the defined benefit plan. To avoid the anti-cutback rule, the plan gave retiring employees the greater of the accrued benefit under the defined benefit or cash balance plan. [*Osberg v. Foot Locker*, No. 07-cv-1357, 2015 U.S. Dist. LEXIS 132054 (S.D.N.Y. Sept. 29, 2015). The Second Circuit affirmed in mid-2017, holding that the district court had the power to order reformation of the pension plan to conform to the plaintiffs' mistaken—but reasonable—expectations: *Osberg v. Foot Locker Inc.*, No. 15-3602 (2d Cir. July 6, 2017)]

Although it is a cash balance plan case, the Supreme Court's mid-2011 decision in *Amara v. CIGNA* has much broader implications for ERISA enforcement, looking at the remedies plan participants can receive based on the traditional "equitable" suits that descend from medieval English church court practice. In this case, CIGNA performed a cash balance conversion of its plan. CIGNA distributed summaries and the Summary Plan Description (SPD) stating that the new plan provided an overall improvement in retirement benefits, and that the participants' opening account balance equaled the full value of their accrued benefits. Plan participants filed a class action charging that many participants were subject to wearaway; that the opening account balance did not reflect the early retirement subsidy, so it offered less than full value; and that the employer saved $10 million a year as a result of the conversion. (CIGNA eventually conceded the last point, but said that it spent the money on other benefit plans.)

In 2011, the Supreme Court held that the SPD merely communicates about the plan, and the terms of the SPD are not part of the plan itself. The settlor of the plan sets the terms of the plan; the plan administrator is responsible for communicating with participants. This decision wipes out a long line of cases that hold that, if the SPD conflicts with the plan terms, the SPD should be enforced because it is the document that the beneficiaries saw. The Supreme Court also said that plaintiffs cannot use ERISA § 502(a)(1)(B) to enforce a contract claim for benefits. Asserting a likelihood of harm to a class is not enough to support relief, and (a)(1)(B) does not give courts the authority to reform the terms of a plan.

However, with regard to what constitutes appropriate equitable relief under ERISA § 502(a)(3), the Supreme Court left open the possibility of getting the plan reformed, seeking equitable estoppel, or even getting the trustee to reimburse the plan ("surcharge"). In general, plaintiffs do not have to prove detrimental reliance in equitable proceedings for reformation or surcharge. To win, plaintiffs must show actual harm (e.g., that they lost money), and that the defendants' actions caused the harm. However, they do not have to prove that they actually relied on the provisions of the SPD. The case was remanded for further proceedings. [*Amara v. CIGNA*, 131 S. Ct. 1866 (May 16, 2011)]

On remand, in late 2012, the District Court for the District of Connecticut ordered additional benefits as appropriate equitable relief, and reformed the plan terms. Although the Supreme Court applied trust law concepts, the district court used a contract-based analysis. The district court ordered that the plaintiffs receive full benefits under both plans. [*Amara v. CIGNA Corp.*, No 3:01-cv-2361, 2012 U.S. Dist. LEXIS 180355 (D. Conn. Dec. 20, 2012)]

The case was appealed to the Second Circuit, which found that the district court had discretion to reform the plan, because CIGNA engaged in fraud or comparable inequitable conduct. Even plaintiffs who received the same amount as they have under the old plan, the Second Circuit held that they were still misled about the risk that fluctuating interest rates would cause wearaway. [*Amara v. CIGNA*, 775 F.3d 510 (2d Cir. 2014)]

The case was sent back to the District Court for the District of Connecticut once again, which ordered changes in the benefit calculations in early 2016. The 2016 decision forbids discounting the opening account balances and changes the company's calculation of the offset for Social Security benefits. Because of CIGNA's misrepresentation of the effects of the conversion and failure to keep adequate records, the district court resolved ambiguities in the participants' favor. CIGNA was ordered to produce records to prove its contention that more than 9,000 members of the class were not entitled to any relief. [*Amara v. CIGNA Corp.*, No.3:01-cv-02361-JBA (D. Conn. Jan. 14, 2016); see Jacklyn Wille, *Judge Nixes Cigna's Pension Math in Long-Running Case*, BNA Pension & Benefits Daily (Jan. 19, 2016) (benefitslink.com)]

In October 2011, the Pension Benefit Guarantee Corporation (PBGC) proposed a rule to implement PPA provisions for allocating assets and determining the amount of benefits when a cash balance or other statutory hybrid plan terminates. The PBGC's intention was to give participants more certainty about their benefits when a plan is terminated and trusteed by the PBGC. An applicable defined benefit plan must have provisions for plan termination. If the interest crediting rate is variable, the interest rate applied to accrued benefits at termination is the average of interest rates for the five-year period ending on the date of termination. The interest rates and mortality tables as of the termination date are used to compute plan benefits that are payable as annuities at normal retirement age. Any variable rate must be the average of the five-year period ending on the termination date.

For distress terminations, the proposed termination date determines the benefits. If the proposed termination date is delayed, benefits accrued between the proposed and actual termination dates are recalculated using the interest rate that would have applied before the actual date of termination.

The PPA provides that a defined benefit plan fails to meet accrual requirements related to age if the plan provides for an interest credit in any plan year that exceeds the market rate of return. A plan satisfies the present value requirements if the present value of any participant's accrued benefit equals either the balance in the participant's hypothetical account, or an accumulated percentage of final average compensation.

Under the PBGC's proposed rule, some benefits are calculated differently for valuation than for payment purposes. The PBGC determines if a benefit can be cashed out (i.e., is small enough to be distributed in a lump sum). If, after August 17, 2006, the plan made lump-sum payments based on the hypothetical account balance without regard to the present value rules, the PBGC makes a de minimis lump sum determination using the same method as the plan did. The proposed rule says that Category 3 benefits for participants who were eligible to retire three years before plan termination or the sponsor's bankruptcy, but did not retire, are determined based on the account balance and interest rate that would have applied if the person had retired before the applicable date.

For bankruptcy terminations in general, the PBGC determines the hypothetical account balance as of the bankruptcy filing date using the actual crediting interest rate for interest between the bankruptcy filing date and the date of termination. For credits after the plan's determination date and before Normal Retirement Age (NRA) or the annuity start date, the rate in effect on the termination date is used. [76 Fed. Reg. 67105 (Oct. 31, 2011)]

The Consolidated & Further Continuing Appropriations Act. Pub. L. No. 113-483 (aka "Cromnibus Act"), provides that if, on or before December 8, 2014, the NRA for a defined benefit plan was the earlier of an age allowed by law or the age when a defined number of years of service (at least 30) has been completed, the plan will not be disqualified merely because the NRA rule applies only to certain participants, or only to the employees of certain employers. [PBGC Fact Sheet, "Multiemployer Pension Reform Act of 2014 FAQs," <http://www.pbgc .gov/prac/pg/mpra/kline-miller-multiemployer-pension-reform-act-of-2014-faqs .html> (accessed Feb. 11, 2017)]

§ 7.02   CASH BALANCE PLANS: PROS AND CONS

The PPA provision authorizing cash balance conversions was adopted because many employers had already converted their plans to cash balance form, or showed an interest in doing so. Employers wanted to keep the difference between the plan's actual investment return and the rate of return promised to employees. They hoped that the plan could become self-funding without additional employer contributions if the difference were large enough. Perhaps ironically, the development of a positive body of decisions and regulations supporting cash balance plans and cash balance conversions has occurred when financial conditions are not necessarily suitable for conversions.

Cash balance plans, like defined benefit plans but unlike 401(k) plans, cover all employees—so employees will get some employer contributions in a cash balance plan even if they would not get an employer match in a 401(k) plan if they could not save enough money to fund a 401(k) account. Combining a cash balance plan with a defined contribution plan places some of the risk on each. [Plansponsor staff, *New Regs May Warrant Reconsidering Cash Balance*, plan sponsor.com (Mar. 25, 2011)]

§ 7.03 "WHIPSAW" AND FINANCIAL FACTORS

The "whipsaw" issue arises because I.R.C. § 417 specifies the interest and mortality assumptions that must be used in converting from annuity to lump-sum payment. When a worker covered by a defined benefit plan terminates employment, the sponsor must calculate the present value of any lump-sum distribution.

This is done by projecting the account balance that would be available at normal retirement age, using PBGC-authorized interest rate assumptions. The next step is to find the value of the annuity that could be purchased with that sum. Finally, the PBGC interest rate assumptions are used again, to reconvert the annuity to a lump sum that represents the present value of the participant's account.

Applying this so-called whipsaw calculation to some cash balance plans increases the lump sum available to some plan participants. The participants who benefit naturally argue that the calculation has to be applied—and plan sponsors want to argue that they can bypass the whipsaw calculation. The higher the interest rates used, the less likely participants are to complain. Therefore, the whipsaw problem is most acute for disputes about plan actions taken before 1995, because in 1994 the PBGC raised its interest rate assumptions significantly.

The PPA avoids the whipsaw problem by requiring the lump-sum distribution to equal the hypothetical account balance, and by specifying the range of interest rates. See § 7.07, below.

The Sixth Circuit held in April 2007 that although the whipsaw calculation is not required after the PPA took effect, it was required before that, and therefore upholds an award of $46 million in benefits and prejudgment interest to a class of 1,250 former employees who retired early and received lump-sum distributions. [*West v. AK Steel Corp.*, 484 F.3d 395 (6th Cir. 2007), *cert. denied*, 129 S. Ct. 895 (Jan. 12, 2009)]

The Sixth Circuit held that 92 plan participants had the right to file a claim against the plan, charging that their payments were incorrect because the plan administrators did not use the whipsaw calculation. The Sixth Circuit upheld the district court's grant of about $3 million in unpaid benefits. The named plaintiff, Schumacher, brought suit in October 2009, asking for a whipsaw calculation of benefits for 92 participants excluded from the *West* case. The Sixth Circuit held that the *Schumacher* suit was timely because ERISA suits borrow the most analogous state statute of limitations, which in this case could be as much as 15 years. The Sixth Circuit held that the plaintiffs' severance agreements mentioned "claims" in general terms but did not specifically address ERISA or pension claims, so the agreements did not prevent the plaintiffs from maintaining their suit. [*Schumacher v. AK Steel Corp. Ret. Accumulation Pension Plan & AK Steel Corp. Benefit Plans Admin. Comm.*, 711 F.3d 675 (6th Cir. 2013)]

The Seventh Circuit held, in late 2011 that, when a district court creates a remedy for participants who were subjected to impermissible whipsaw calculations that did not add future interest credits to their lump-sum distributions, the court does not have to defer to the plan's preferred method for recalculating the lump sums. The plan conceded that unlawful whipsaw had occurred but said that the suit was time-barred or, as an alternative, that the plan's method of calculation should be used. The Seventh Circuit said that the unlawful calculations were part of the plan, so the plan's fiduciaries did not engage in any interpretive discretion to which the court could grant deference. [*Thompson v. Retirement Plan for Employees of S.C. Johnson & Son, Inc.*, 651 F.3d 600 (7th Cir. 2011)]

The Fourth Circuit rejected claims that the Bank of America violated the anti-backloading provision by defining the NRA as the earlier of the first day of the calendar month after the participant reached age 65 or having 60 months of vesting service. The court held that it was not necessary for every employee to have the same NRA and it was permissible to set the NRA on the basis of vesting service to prevent some participants from being entitled to whipsaw distributions. In the Fourth Circuit view, the backloading rules cease to apply once a plan participant reaches NRA. [*McCorkle v. Bank of Am.*, 688 F.3d 164 (4th Cir. 2012)]

The Sixth Circuit held that an ex-employee who challenged the calculation of her lump-sum distribution from a cash balance plan was not required to exhaust her administrative remedies under the plan—an appeal would have been futile. According to the Sixth Circuit, participants can go straight to court when they challenge the legality of a plan's entire methodology. The plaintiff admitted that she received the proper amount under the plan's method of calculation—what she objected to was the method. [*Durand v. The Hanover Ins. Grp.*, 560 F.3d 436 (6th Cir. 2009)]

§ 7.04   CASE LAW ON CASH BALANCE PLANS

The fundamental age discrimination issue is how ERISA § 204(b)(1)(H)(i) and Code § 411(b)(1)(H), which forbid terminating benefit accrual or reducing the rate of accrual because of a plan participant's attainment of any age, define "rate of accrual." If the rate of accrual is the change, from year to year, in the annuity that the participant can expect at age 65, then cash balance plans are inherently age-discriminatory because of the greater number of years over which younger participants can accrue interest credits. However, if it is merely the pay and interest credits to the hypothetical account, then cash balance plans are not discriminatory, they merely reflect the basic economic concept of the time value of money. By mid-2008, five of the courts of appeals (Second, Third, Sixth, Seventh, and Ninth) had already ruled that cash balance plans are not inherently discriminatory against older workers. These courts generally held that the higher balance for younger workers was a simple effect of the time value of money. [*Hurlic v. Southern California Gas Co.*, 539 F.3d 1024 (9th Cir. Aug. 20, 2008) (allowing, however, maintenance of a claim that the plan violated ERISA's notice requirements by not providing notice of wearaway); *Hirt v. Equitable Ret. Plan for Emps., Managers & Agents*, 533 F.3d 102 (2d Cir. 2008); *Register v. PNC Fin. Servs. Grp., Inc.*, 477 F.3d 56 (3d Cir. 2007); *Drutis v. Rand McNally & Co.*, 499 F.3d 608 (6th Cir. 2007), *cert. denied*, 555 U.S. 816 (2008); *Cooper v. IBM Personal Pension Plan*, 457 F.3d 636 (7th Cir. 2006), *cert. denied*, 549 U.S. 1175 (2007)]

Verizon Communications' cash balance plan document included a drafting error (a transition factor for calculating opening balances was used twice instead of once). According to the Northern District of Illinois, the plan's administrative committee should have gone to court to reform the plan documents to correct the mistake; it did not have the power to reform the plan. However, it was not an abuse of discretion to use 120% of the PBGC interest rate instead of 100% to calculate the opening account balance. [*Young v. Verizon's Bell Atlantic Cash Balance Plan*, No. 05 C 7314 (N.D. Ill. Aug. 28, 2008); see Fred Schneyer, *Verizon Hit for Cash Balance Conversion Error*, plansponsor.com (Sept. 2, 2008)] The Northern District re-heard the case in 2009 and ruled that Verizon could correct the error, holding this time that requiring the language to be applied literally would give participants a $1.67 billion windfall. Magistrate Judge Morton Denlow said that employers would be discouraged from adopting plans if they suffered unduly harsh penalties for mistakes. The Seventh Circuit affirmed in 2010. The Supreme Court refused to review the case. [*Young v. Verizon's Bell Atlantic Cash Balance Plan*, 615 F.3d 808 (7th Cir. 2010), *cert. denied*, 131 S. Ct. 2924 (May 23, 2011), *reh'g denied*, 132 S. Ct. 47 (July 25, 2011)]

The Eighth Circuit held in 2009 that a defined benefit plan that converted to cash balance form in 2000 (i.e., long before the PPA took effect) did not reduce accrued benefits when the discount rate it used to calculate the accrued benefit portion of the opening account balance was 8% at a time when the § 417(e)(3) rate was slightly over 6%. A lower discount rate would have yielded a higher opening balance, and therefore a larger lump sum. At the time of the cash balance conversion, ERISA did not include a definition of "opening account balance." The Eighth Circuit held that using the statutory discount rate to determine the opening balance would have given participants a windfall. However, since the PPA, § 411(b)(5)(B)(iii) has provided that the benefit under the converted plan must be at least as great as the accrued benefit under the old plan, plus the accrued benefit since the conversion. [*Sunder v. U.S. Bancorp Pension Plan*, 586 F.3d 593 (8th Cir. 2009)]

The Seventh Circuit affirmed certification of a Rule 23(b)(2) ERISA class action with more than 4,000 current and former participants in a cash balance plan. The plaintiffs made cutback, whipsaw, and wearaway claims covering a 23-year period. The district court certified 10 subclasses. The employer challenged class certification, arguing that *Dukes* (see § 42.06) rules out (b)(2) class actions for monetary, declaratory, or injunctive relief. The employer argued that certification of a (b)(2) class is appropriate only if a single injunction or declaratory judgment could provide relief to all the subclasses. The employer also argued that claims for monetary relief were inappropriate in (b)(2) cases, at least where they are not incidental to injunctive or declaratory relief. The Seventh Circuit rejected these arguments, reading *Dukes* to mean that the requirement of a single injunction or declaratory judgment does not apply where each member in a subclass has the same claim. The Seventh Circuit held that the plaintiffs were seeking a declaration of rights under the plan and reformation of the plan to follow the declaration—any monetary relief would be incidental. It was too early to determine if individualized proceedings would be required at a later stage, but the Seventh Circuit held that it might be possible to bifurcate the case, with subclasses that obtained Rule 23(b)(2) declaratory relief following up with an opt-out (b)(3) proceeding to set relief for the individual members of the class. [*Johnson v. Meriter Health Servs. Emp. Ret. Plan*, 702 F.3d 364 (7th Cir. 2012)]

The suit was settled in 2014; Meriter Health Services agreed to pay $82 million to settle a class action suit by cash balance plan participants. [*Johnson v. Meriter Health Servs.*, (7th Cir., settled Sept. 17, 2014), <http://www.plan sponsor.com/uploadedFiles/Plan_Sponsor/news/Rules,_Regs/JohnsonvMeriter Heatlhsettlement.pdf>]

The Fourth Circuit permitted participants in the Bank of America's cash balance plan to sue for illegal transfers of 401(k) balances to the cash balance plan. In 1998, the bank amended its 401(k) plan to permit eligible participants to transfer account balances to the cash balance plan. Participants chose a hypothetical portfolio, and their account was credited with what those investments would have earned. But the actual investments were selected by the bank, which kept the difference if the actual investments earned more than the hypothetical portfolio. In 2005, the IRS ruled that transfers between 1998 and 2001 violated the Code and regulations; the bank settled with the IRS for $10 million and a special 401(k) plan to restore the accounts.

The Fourth Circuit found that the plaintiffs had standing to sue under ERISA § 502(a)(3). The Fourth Circuit said that the transfer violated the anti-cutback provision, and transferring the Bank of America's profits on the transferred assets to the plaintiffs constitutes appropriate equitable relief. The Fourth Circuit said that the relevant statute of limitations was the 10-year statute of limitations under North Carolina trust law; the first transfer was in 1998 and suit was filed in 2004, so it was timely. [*Pender v. Bank of Am. Corp.*, 788 F.3d 354 (4th Cir. 2015); see Rebecca Moore, *4th Circuit Revives Case Over Transfers to Cash Balance Plan*, plansponsor.com (June 10, 2015)]

§ 7.05 THE CONVERSION PROCESS

At least 15 days' notice must be given in advance of adoption of a plan amendment that significantly reduces the rate of benefit accruals in the future. [See § 11.05 for a discussion of EGTRRA rules increasing the amount of disclosure that participants are entitled to in this situation.] The plan may also have to issue a revised SPD and/or a Summary of Material Modification in connection with the conversion.

EBSA's cash balance plan FAQ [<http://www.dol.gov/ebsa/faqs/faq_consumer_cashbalanceplans.html> (Jan. 2014) (last accessed Feb. 11, 2017)] says that neither ERISA nor the Tax Code obligates employers who convert to a cash balance plan to give employees the option of remaining in the old plan. The employer can simply replace the old formula with the new formula for all participants, as long as the benefits already accrued as of the date of the conversion are not reduced. Or the employer can keep current employees under the old plan formula, applying the new formula only to those hired after the change. Another option is for some employees to be "grandfathered in," or allowed to receive their pensions under the old formula.

The first suit under the Lilly Ledbetter Fair Pay Act (Pub. L. No. 111-2) was filed eight days after the bill was signed. The case involved the El Paso pension plan's cash balance conversion. The plaintiff sought to reverse a January 21, 2009 decision that his age discrimination charge against the conversion was untimely. (The Ledbetter Act provides that an unlawful practice occurs when a violative plan is adopted, when the plaintiff became subject to the practice, or each time the plaintiff was affected by that practice.) [Suzanne L. Wynn, Pension Protection Act Blog, *And the Lilly Ledbetter Litigation Begins* (Feb. 11, 2009) (benefits link.com)]

In 2011, the Tenth Circuit held that the wearaway provision of Tomlinson's cash balance plan did not violate the Age Discrimination in Employment Act (ADEA) § 4(i) accrual requirement, because credits were posted to the accounts of both young and older employees in a nondiscriminatory manner. Many employees were subject to wearaway because it took several years after the cash balance conversion for the minimum benefit to exceed the former benefit, especially for older employees. (The conversion occurred in 1997; wearaway was not forbidden until June 29, 2005.) The Tenth Circuit said that § 4(i) requires equality in inputs (benefit accruals) rather than outputs (accrued benefits), agreeing with the argument that the effect of the time value of money cannot be treated as age discrimination. The Tenth Circuit held that, absent deceit by the employer or failure to explain how the benefits are calculated, an SPD will not be invalidated for failure to inform employees about a wearaway period. [*Tomlinson v. El Paso*, 653 F.3d 1281 (10th Cir. 2011)]

[A] The 204(h) Notice Requirement

ERISA § 204(h), nicknamed the "anti-cutback rule," imposes notice requirements: plan participants and beneficiaries must be informed of plan changes that significantly reduce their entitlement to benefits. T.D. 9472, 74 Fed. Reg. 61270 (Nov. 24, 2009) is a final rule covering the 204(h) notice requirements for plan amendments that reduce accrued benefits. It provides that the effective date of an amendment that is adopted retroactively is the date the amendment goes into effect on an operational basis.

The Tenth Circuit upheld Solvay Chemicals' cash balance conversion, and said that the ERISA § 204(h) regulations did not mandate telling employees in either percentage or dollar terms that the conversion would reduce their future accrual rates. It was permissible to use tables of hypothetical benefit figures, because the data would allow employees to estimate their benefits, and it was clear from the tables that most employees were worse off after the conversion. The Tenth Circuit held that the cash balance plan did not violate the ADEA and satisfied ERISA requirements. However, the Tenth Circuit sent the case back to the district court to determine whether participants could use the information they were given to understand how the early retirement subsidy was calculated, or whether the company committed an egregious failure. [*Jensen v. Solvay Chems. Inc.*, 625 F.3d 641 (10th Cir. 2010)]

The district court found that there was no egregious failure under either standard. The plaintiffs appealed to the Tenth Circuit once again; the Tenth Circuit found no reason to disturb the district court's finding. [*Jensen v. Solvay Chems., Inc.*, 721 F.3d 1180 (10th Cir. 2013)]

§ 7.06 DECEMBER 2002 REGULATIONS: PROPOSAL AND WITHDRAWAL

In December 2002, the IRS published a set of Proposed Regulations, REG-209500-86, at 67 Fed. Reg. 76123 (Dec. 11, 2002), while the moratorium on cash balance plan conversions was in effect. The proposal created the concept of an "eligible cash balance plan," for which the rate of benefit accrual includes additions to the participant's hypothetical account for the plan year, but not previously accrued interest credits. The Proposed Regulations stated that merely converting a defined benefit plan to an eligible cash balance form plan would not make the plan fail under Code § 411(b)(1)(H) as long as there was no wearaway. Under the proposal, plans could not stop or reduce accruals on the basis of age after NRA.

However, this proposal was politically controversial, and was withdrawn in mid-2004 by Announcement 2004-57, 2004-27 I.R.B. 15. Eventually, however, the PPA gave approval to the cash balance form.

§ 7.07 CASH BALANCE PLANS UNDER THE PPA AND WRERA

In 2006, Congress resolved legal uncertainties going forward, by providing rules under which cash balance plans can be created, or existing plans can be converted. However, the PPA specifically provides that it does not govern the validity or propriety of cash balance plans already in existence on June 29, 2005, so sponsors who "jumped the gun" by adopting cash balance plans, or making cash balance conversions, in the absence of guidance, could find themselves vulnerable in court. See § 7.04, above.

The statute uses the term "applicable defined pension plan" to refer to cash balance plans. Because other PPA provisions restrict the extent to which pension plans can "smooth" their investment results over several years, many sponsors will have to increase their contributions to defined benefit plans accordingly—a further incentive to convert to cash balance form.

A cash balance plan adopted or converted on or after June 29, 2005 will not be considered discriminatory if participants are 100% vested after three years of service. The plan must calculate interest credits with a rate of return that is not higher than market rates. The rate of return can be set as the greater of a fixed or a variable rate of return, and plans can implement a guaranteed minimum rate of return as long as it is reasonable.

No matter what their ages, all similarly situated employees must have equal accrued benefits. Participants are similarly situated if they have the same position, compensation, date of hire, and terms of service, and differ only in age. This provision adopts the argument that effects of the time value of money do not constitute age discrimination.

The PPA forbids the use of wearaway (adjusting plan formulas in a way that harms long-standing participants) under any plan amendment adopted after June 29, 2005. When a defined benefit plan is converted to a cash balance plan, each participant must receive the benefit accrued before the conversion, calculated under the pre-conversion formula, plus the benefit accrued after the conversion using the cash balance plan formula. Wearaway is also forbidden if a company freezes its defined benefit plan and adopts a cash balance plan. Qualifying participants must be permitted to receive early retirement subsidies.

The PPA eliminates whipsaw by mandating that the lump-sum distribution from the plan must be equal to the hypothetical account balance. Cash balance plans are allowed to use a variable interest crediting rate, but the rate must not be higher than the market rate of return, and must be at least zero. Therefore, the account balance never falls below the cumulative total of pay credits. See proposed regulations about Code § 411 minimum vesting and accrual requirements, because cash balance plans are considered defined benefit plans. [NPRM REG-104946-07, 2008-11 I.R.B. 596]

According to retirement consultant Alan Glickstein, plan sponsors liked CB plans in the 1980s because of the simplicity and transparency of knowing how much is in the account. PPA clarified that age discrimination does not occur as long as the rate of interest does not exceed a market rate. PPA also eliminated the issue of whipsaw for plans with rates that do not exceed market rates. PPA solved the problem of wearaway by requiring the frozen benefit to be converted to the account balance plus new accruals for all participants each year. However, even after the PPA, suits can still be brought about failure to communicate with participants when their plan is converted to cash balance form. [Plansponsor editors, *PPA Reduced Lawsuits Against Cash Balance Plans*, plansponsor.com (Aug. 12, 2016)]

The Worker, Retiree and Employer Recovery Act (WRERA), the relief bill for employers harmed by the economic downturn, signed December 23, 2008, eases the PPA's provisions dealing with such matters as age discrimination, conversions, and whipsaw, for cash balance and other hybrid plans. Although the PPA required 100% vesting in cash balance plans after three years of service, WRERA says this only applies if the participant has at least one hour of service after the effective date of the new rules. As a result of WRERA, the whipsaw rules are not applied in determining whether a participant is subject to mandatory cashout; it depends on the balance in the hypothetical cash account. In mid-2008, The IRS proposed regulations allowing the same relief permitted by Rev. Rul. 2008-7, to clarify how defined benefit plans, especially hybrid plans that use a "greater of" benefit formula, can satisfy the anti-backloading test. In general, they can test each formula separately. This is useful for employers who want to convert defined benefit to cash balance plans, but still provide pensions for older employees that are more generous than the required transitional relief. [NPRM, *Accrual Rules for Defined Benefit Plans*; RIN 1545-BH50, 73 Fed. Reg. 34665 (June 18, 2008)]

[A] 2010 Final and Proposed Regulations

In late 2010, the IRS issued final and proposed regulations for hybrid retirement plans, a category that includes not only cash balance plans but Pension Equity Plans (PEPs). In the 1990s, hybrid plans grew in popularity, but also attracted a number of lawsuits, generally charging age discrimination, challenging the calculation of lump sums, or challenging wearaway within the plan. The IRS issued proposed regulations implementing the PPA in December 2007. The 2010 regulations deal with age discrimination, vesting, conversion from defined benefit to cash balance form, and safe harbor interest crediting rates (final regulations) and alternative rates that constitute a "market rate of return" (proposed regulations).

In general, a hybrid plan can be described as one that calculates accumulated benefits with a hybrid formula. Each participant has a hypothetical account, which is credited with the employer's hypothetical contributions based on "compensation credits" (reflecting the participant's salary) plus "interest credits" (hypothetical earnings from investing the account). PEPs define the benefit as a percentage of final average pay, with participants earning points each year to set the percentage. Compensation credits are usually defined as a percentage of the employee's eligible pay, possibly adjusted based on age and years of service. When the participant stops working for the employer, compensation credits end. Interest credits usually continue until the benefits are distributed.

The 2010 final regulations require the entire accrued benefit of hybrid plans to vest in no more than three years of service (with an exception for the traditional defined benefit portion of a floor offset arrangement that combines a defined benefit plan and a separate hybrid plan). The 2010 final regulations include an ADEA safe harbor, as long as the accumulated benefit of any participant is not less than the accumulated benefit of any similarly situated younger participant (similar in terms of date of hire, work history, compensation, and job duties). A hybrid plan that does not satisfy the safe harbor must satisfy the general Code § 411(b)(1)(H)(i) age discrimination rule. The final regulations say that the safe harbor can be used if the plan gave the participant a choice between a traditional defined benefit plan and the hybrid plan at the time of conversion; the safe harbor is not limited to plans that used a sum-of or greater-of formula at conversion.

The final regulations protect benefits against wearaway if a defined benefit plan is converted to a hybrid plan by an amendment adopted and effective on or after June 29, 2005. If the amendment eliminates or reduces future benefit accruals, and part or all of the benefit is determined based on a statutory hybrid formula, then the post-amendment benefit must be at least as great as the accrued benefit as of the conversion date plus the accrued benefit after the conversion, with no integration of the two.

The PPA forbids crediting interest at a rate greater than a "market rate of return"; the 2010 regulations use the rate of return on investment-grade long-term corporate bonds, certain Treasury bonds, the actual rate of return on plan assets, and the rate of return on an annuity contract for an employee as benchmarks.

It is permissible for the rate of benefit accrual to increase as participants earn more, as long as any year's accrual rate is not more than one-third higher than the previous year's rate. [Final regulations: 75 Fed. Reg. 64123 (Oct. 19, 2010); proposed regulations, 75 Fed. Reg. 64197 (Oct. 19, 2010).]

The Moving Ahead for Progress in the 21st Century (MAP-21) Act, Pub. L. No. 112-140, allows plan sponsors some relief from interest crediting rules that can make defined benefit and cash balance plans unduly expensive. [Mark L. Lofgren, *Cash Balance Plans IRS Further Delays Reasonable Interest Rate Rules and Provides Guidance for Plans with Rates Affected by Map-21*, Groom Law Group (Sept. 17, 2012) (benefitslink.com)]

Subsequent legislation, the Highway Transportation Funding Act of 2014, Pub. L. No. 113-159, allows employers to continue making use of smoothing to reduce the amount that they must contribute to their plans; the statute prescribes rates to be used until 2017. [Vipal Monga, *Welcome to the World of "Pension Smoothing,"* WSJ.com (Aug. 11, 2014)]

[B] T.D.s 9693 and 9743

IRS final regulations for hybrid plans (including cash balance plans), published in September 2014, elaborate on the 2010 final regulations by expanding the hybrid plan formulas that will qualify for relief. The 2014 regulations include special rules for variable interest crediting rates and age discrimination in light of the need to use market rates of return in plan administration. The market rate requirement prevents cash balance plans from discriminating against older workers by crediting interest at an unreasonably high rate. "Market rates" are defined as the actual rate of return on plan assets; the segment rates set out in Code § 430(h)(2)(C); or a fixed rate of up to 6%. (This is a change from the 2010 proposed regulations, which allowed a fixed rate of up to 5%.) The plan can also use a minimum annual rate associated with a rate based on federal government bonds. A COLA-based variable rate of up to 5%, or a minimum rate of up to 4% associated with a rate based on investment-grade corporate bonds, can also be used. If the plan uses rates based on investments or bonds, it can use a cumulative 3% minimum rate.

The final rules are generally applicable to plan years beginning on or after January 1, 2016. The IRS continued to study whether self-directed investments should be allowed in hybrid plans.

At the same time, the IRS published a proposed rule allowing a hybrid plan that used a rate of return greater than the market rate to adopt a permitted interest crediting rate without violating the anti-cutback rule. The proposal deals with the situation in which a plan had conflicting obligations: to satisfy the market rate of return rule, and to avoid reducing benefits. The proposal gives adjusting the rate of return higher priority. [T.D. 9693, 2014-41 I.R.B. 596]

New market rate of return rules were adopted by the IRS in 2015 for hybrid plans. The rules are generally applicable to amendments on or after September 18, 2014 (or an earlier date elected by the plan), a sponsor of a plan that does not satisfy the market rate of return requirements can amend the plan to adopt a permissible rate without violating the anti-cutback rule. The relief does not apply to amendments adopted on or after the first day of the first plan year beginning on or after January 1, 2017. [T.D. 9743, 2015-48 I.R.B. 679, 80 Fed. Reg. 70680 (Nov. 16, 2015)]

CHAPTER 8

NONQUALIFIED PLANS

§ 8.01 INTRODUCTION

[A] Generally

One of the most important aspects of maintaining a qualified plan (and therefore obtaining a tax deduction for related costs) is satisfying the Internal Revenue Code's tests for nondiscrimination.

However, it is not illegal for an employer to set up a discriminatory plan, and in fact many types of nonqualified plans have evolved for companies that want to recruit, retain, or motivate senior management and/or persons who own significant amounts of stock in the corporation. Nonqualified plans are also used to provide post-retirement income higher than the levels that can be generated through a qualified plan. Unlike qualified plans, which are subject to detailed funding and operational requirements under the Employment Retirement Income Security Act (ERISA), nonqualified plans need not be funded in advance. Payments to distribute benefits can be made as they come due, out of the employer's general assets instead of from a special trust. Insurance policies, and other investments that would not be permissible in an ERISA plan, can also be used to fund nonqualified plan benefits.

Since 2004, sponsors have faced a new set of tax challenges for nonqualified plans under the American Jobs Creation Act of 2010 (AJCA), Pub. L. No. 108-357, which enacted Code § 409A, and under the Pension Protection Act of 2006 (PPA), Pub. L. No. 109-280.

A deferred compensation plan is a plan or individual agreement to pay compensation to one or more employees in one or more later years for services rendered. Such plans can be taxable or tax-exempt. A nonqualified plan is exempt from most ERISA and IRS requirements, but at the cost of foregoing the tax deductions available to sponsors of qualified plans.

Yong Lee, the COO of MullTBG, says that there are four main areas for sponsors of nonqualified deferred compensation (NQDC) plans to consider:

- Do they understand the regulatory consequences of the plan?

- In light of what the regulations permit, how do they want to design the plan?

- How do they want to finance the plan?

- How can participants be educated about the plan? Older employees may prefer paper documents and face-to-face meetings; younger employees often prefer online delivery, but Webinars appeal to both groups.

According to Lee, plans are usually financed with taxable securities, such as mutual funds or Company-Owned Life Insurance. [Kevin McGuinness, *Ensuring Best Practices for NQDC Plans*, plansponsor.com (Feb. 13, 2014)]

The general practice is for the payor corporation to record the expense on its books when the compensation is earned, even if the tax deduction is not available until a much later year. The general rule of § 409A is that elective participant deferrals are irrevocable, and the election must be made before the beginning of the calendar year in which the services commence. The election must identify the amount to be deferred; the length of the deferral period; and the form of payment. However, for performance-based compensation for services performed over a period of 12 months or more, the initial deferral election can be made at any time up through six months before the end of the performance period. Payments to key employees of public companies triggered by separation from service (other than in case of death, disability, or similar event) must be delayed at least six months after separation. The Code § 83 economic benefit doctrine makes income taxable upon grant if the executive receives tangible, quantifiable value, and there is no substantial risk of forfeiture.

To escape taxation under theories of constructive receipt and economic benefit, benefits under a nonqualified plan must be funded and must be subject to the claims of the corporation's general creditors. If the company becomes insolvent or bankrupt, the executive's right to payment cannot be greater than the right of any other general unsecured creditor.

Corporations with NQDC plans usually engage in informal funding, e.g., by setting money aside in trusts such as rabbi trusts to cover future payments under the plan. The trusts are assets of the corporation and can be reached by its creditors. Section 409A accelerates income tax and imposes penalties if assets are transferred outside the United States, or if benefit payments are triggered by the corporation's financial problems (i.e., if executives are insulated against the consequences of the company's financial difficulties).

Penalties are also imposed on key executives if the employer sets aside assets to pay NQDC when the corporation is bankrupt, within six months of termination of an underfunded plan, or if the plan is "at risk" as defined by the PPA and is funded below the 80% level. In many instances, registration exemptions will be available, but absent an exemption, an employee's interest in an elective deferred compensation arrangement is a security that will have to be registered. "Blue sky" compliance (with state securities laws) may also be required. [David Wang and Melissa Rasman, *Elective Nonqualified Deferred Compensation Plans—A Primer*, Hay Group's Executive Edition Newsletter (Feb. 1, 2008) (benefitslink.com)]

In a qualified plan, a "bad boy" clause (one that removes entitlement to benefits) is allowed only for fraud or abuse of fiduciary duty. In a nonqualified plan, benefits can be forfeited by an executive who leaves the company.

Under a qualified plan, the employer gets a current deduction each year as it makes contributions to the plan. The employer's deduction for nonqualified plan expenses is not available until the year in which the participant receives money from the plan and includes it in income. The corporation's general creditors are entitled to make claims against reserves set aside to pay nonqualified plan benefits, but the qualified plan trust is protected against creditors' claims.

The Fifth Circuit deemed RBC Capital Markets Corp.'s Wealth Accumulation Plan (WAP) to be an ERISA pension plan because participants could defer distributions until termination of employment. Although the express purpose of the WAP was not to provide retirement income, the plan's statement of purpose described the WAP as a deferred compensation plan. The plan provided mandatory and voluntary participant deferrals. Matching contributions could be distributed to participants when they vested, but the participant could also defer distribution for a later in-service distribution or distribution at termination. The plaintiffs forfeited their WAP benefits when they terminated and sued, claiming that the WAP's forfeiture provisions violated ERISA. The Fifth Circuit held that pension plans must either satisfy the ERISA and Code requirements for qualified plans or operate as top hat plans (unfunded; maintained by the employer primarily to provide deferred compensation to a select group of managers or HCEs; not subject to ERISA funding requirements). [*Tolbert v. RBC Cap. Mkts. Corp.*, 758 F.3d 619 (5th Cir. 2014). On remand, the District Court for the Southern District of Texas included all employees of the plan sponsor and its participating subsidiaries, because that was the definition in the plan terms: *Tolbert v. RBC Capital Mkts. Corp.*, No. CIV.A H-11-0107, 2015 U.S. Dist. LEXIS 55196 (S.D. Tex. Apr. 28, 2015)]

The Ninth Circuit held in mid-2016 that Booz Allen Hamilton's Stock Rights Plan, offered to certain employees, is not an ERISA plan. Participants were expected to hold their shares as long as they were employed but could sell paid-up stock back to the firm at any time. The Ninth Circuit said that the mere potential for deferring income did not subject the plan to ERISA. [*Rich v. Booz Allen Hamilton*, **823 F.3d 1205** (9th Cir. 2016) *reh'g denied* (July 1, 2016); *see* Rebecca Moore, *Court Finds Equity Compensation Plan Not an ERISA Plan,* plansponsor .com (June 30, 2016)]

It is also possible that a plan benefiting a corporation's executives will be a welfare benefit plan for ERISA purposes, and that Form 5500 will have to be filed for the plan. A "funded" plan either receives employee contributions, or holds plan assets in trust; welfare benefit plans that use insurance to pay benefits are treated as funded plans. Unfunded plans pay all benefits from the employer's general assets. For executive life or disability plans, Form 5500 is not required if the plan covers fewer than 100 employees, and is unfunded or solely insurance-funded. But large plans, whether funded or unfunded, and small plans that are funded, including those that use insurance to pay benefits, are subject to the Form 5500 filing requirement.

Some top hat plans are not required to file Form 5500. Exempt top hat plans must make a limited filing, reporting the plan's name, address, and Employer Identification Number, the number of plans and the number of employees each covers, and a statement that the plan primarily provides non-qualified deferred compensation. The filing is required within 120 days of the time the plan becomes subject to ERISA. Missing the filing deadline requires the plan to file each year.

If the plan has 100 or more participants, it is also obligated to perform audits. [Samuel A. Henson and Jason Maples, *Executive Benefits: Exempt, But Perhaps Not from Reporting*, The Beacon (undated) (benefitslink.com)]

[B] Structures for Nonqualified Plans

Various structures and funding mechanisms have evolved for providing non-qualified plan benefits to executives, managers, and other favored corporate employees. Objectives include providing incentives for managers by providing generous deferred compensation, and protecting entitlement to these sums against the corporation's creditors.

The most popular structures for nonqualified plans include SERPs, QSERPs, top hat plans, rabbi trusts, and secular trusts, as discussed below. Other structures used for nonqualified plans include:

- Excess benefit plans: plans that provide benefits higher than those permitted by Code § 415. Unfunded excess benefit plans are exempt from ERISA Title I, but that renders them vulnerable to state regulation;

- Integrated plans provide benefits over and above 401(k) plan benefits, using the same investment options and subject to the same employer match rules. The deferral percentage is set by the plan participant. Transfers of both elective deferrals and employer matches are made first to the qualified plan, then to the nonqualified plan;

- Tandem plans combine with qualified plans to accrue more savings for retirement-but usually offer features and investment choices that are different than those offered under the regular qualified plan;

- Wrap plans collect funds throughout the year on behalf of top executives. Once a year, the maximum amount that can be transferred for those executives without violating the nondiscrimination rules is transferred to the qualified plan; the rest is placed in a nonqualified plan.

[1] SERP

A Supplemental Executive Retirement Plan (SERP), also known as an excess benefit plan, can be used to defer amounts that exceed the qualified plan limits on behalf of executives. Hay Group says that the most popular formula aims to 60% of the executive's pre-retirement income, which would be impossible under most qualified plans. A performance-based SERP makes accrual of benefits dependent on achievement of one or more performance measures. The measures could be the ones used in the company's incentive programs (e.g., revenues, profitability, or earnings), or could be personalized (a sales target or profitability goal for a particular corporate unit) or depend on other goals or events (developing a product; successful bankruptcy reorganization).

The Sixth Circuit held that claims by executives of Metaldyne corporate executives' claims about cancellation of their SERP plan could be tried in state court. Metaldyne was once partially owned by Heartland Industrial Partners, LP, an investment firm. In mid-2006, Heartland agreed to sell its Metaldyne stake to another investment firm. The SERP included change in control provisions under which Metaldyne would owe the plaintiffs about $13 million. The Metaldyne board canceled the SERP to avoid this obligation. The SERP participants sued in state court for tortious interference with contractual relations. The Sixth Circuit found that these claims were not preempted by ERISA because the state court would not have to interpret the SERPs, just calculate damages if the plaintiffs proved that canceling them violated state law. [*Gardner v. Heartland Indus. Partners*, 713 F.3d 609 (6th Cir. 2013)]

In late 2016, the District Court for the Northern District of California permitted ERISA § 502(a)(3) to be applied to enforce provisions of a top hat plan. The president/CEO of Mechanics Bank was fired. He was given a separation agreement releasing the bank from all claims, including ERISA claims. The plaintiff had several retirement plans, including a SERP. Accrual of new SERP benefits was frozen in 2008; a new Executive Retirement Plan (ERP), in which Buster also participated, was adopted. An agreement called for a $1 million lump-sum "retirement pay" payment to Buster on termination, plus $1.8 million under the ERP and a one-year severance payment of about $1 million—total $3.8 million. The agreement didn't mention the SERP. Buster said that a board member told him that this agreement didn't affect his SERP, 401(k), or pension benefits. He said he signed the agreement in reliance on that representation. In May 2015, he asked for an estimate of retirement benefits. He was told that because of the agreement he wasn't entitled to SERP benefits; he sued in March 2016 for denial of benefits under ERISA, seeking equitable estoppel, and reformation of the agreement. The district court said that ERISA exempts top hat plans from some Title I requirements. An administrator of a top hat plan is exempt from ERISA fiduciary duties, and the SERP's terms were unambiguous. The plaintiff didn't ask for equitable relief for the SERP; he wanted equitable estoppels and reformation of the agreement, which the defendants said waives SERP benefits. The court found that it was plausibly ambiguous whether agreement's provision concerning "claims arising under ERISA" encompassed claims for benefits from an ERISA plan, and an e-mail about Buster's SERP benefits makes it more plausible that he was told the agreement didn't affect his SERP benefits. The court said that § 502(a)(3) appropriate equitable relief can extend to remedying inequities an vis-a-vis an alleged waiver of plan rights; the administrator of a top hat plan is not immune from equitable remedies under § 502(a)(3) just because the plan is exempt from the fiduciary standard of care; and, for top hat plans, there are equitable remedies for breach of contract law's general standard of good faith.

[*Buster v. Mechanics Bank*, No. C16-01146 WHA, **2016 U.S. Dist. LEXIS** (N.D. Cal. Aug. 26, 2016); see Plansponsor editors, *Court Finds ERISA Can Be Used to Enforce Top-Hat Plan Terms*, plansponsor.com (Nov. 9, 2016)]

Because a SERP is a top hat plan, it is not protected against the claims of the employer's creditors, even if the employer includes an anti-alienation provision in the SERP agreement. Therefore, at least 25% of a bank executive's SERP was subject to garnishment by a creditor of the bank. The state's garnishment law was not preempted by ERISA, because it was a law of general application not related to employee benefit plans. The state Consumer Credit Protection Law protects 75% of a pension or retirement benefit from garnishment, so the judge reserved decision on the fate of 75% of the executive's SERP. [*Sposato v. First Mariner Bank*, No. 1:2012-cv-01569, 2013 WL 1308582 (D. Md. Mar. 28, 2013)]

In the Second Circuit view, early retirement benefits from a SERP are not severance payments that get "administrative expense" (i.e., high) priority in bankruptcy, because the benefits accrue over the entire course of employment—they are not a new benefit earned at termination, and only new benefits can be administrative expenses. [*In re Bethlehem Steel*, 479 F.3d 167 (2d Cir. 2007)]

[2] QSERP

A Qualified Supplemental Executive Retirement Plan (QSERP) is a qualified plan used to enhance retirement benefits for executives. The plan must satisfy nondiscrimination requirements and is subject to the I.R.C. § 415 limits. However, the employer's contributions can be integrated with Social Security, reducing the amount the employer has to contribute on behalf of lower-paid employees. To adopt a QSERP, the employer corporation can simply amend the plan documents to include an annual list of people or job titles entitled to additional benefits of $X/year. Usually, QSERP amounts are subtracted from the amounts that would otherwise be payable under nonqualified plans. Because the QSERP is a qualified plan, the employer gets a current deduction, and the employee is not taxed until benefits are actually paid (and the employee has some certainty that they will be paid because of prefunding). If the QSERP is a defined contribution plan, it is subject to the overall limitation on contributions to all defined contribution plans; if the employer is already making close to the maximum contribution under other qualified plans there is little leeway for the QSERP. [Mark E. Carolan, *The QSERP Gaming the Nondiscrimination Rules to Provide Larger Qualified Benefits for Executives* <http://www.thefreelibrary.com/The+Q SERP%3a+gaming+the+nondiscrimination+rules+to+provide+larger . . . -a0235 406866> (June 22, 2010) (accessed Apr. 7, 2015)]

For the executive, having a QSERP provides the advantage of securing the benefit (although PBGC limits will apply if the plan sponsor goes bankrupt). QSERPs are not subject to § 409A. Blogger John Lowell, pointed out advantages of QSERP. While the benefit remains in the plan, there has been no constructive receipt under § 83. Benefits payable in lump-sum form can be rolled over to an IRA, further deferring taxation. The executive can wait until just before the benefit commencement date to choose the time and form of benefit distribution. Shareholders benefit because the QSERP is income-neutral or income-positive, and it protects the company from cash flow demands of having to make large payments. [Michael S. Melbinger, *Another Blogger Sings the Praises of QSERPs*, Winston & Strawn LLP Executive Compensation Blog (Sept. 19, 2011) (benefitslink.com)]

Nondiscrimination testing is the highly technical art of determining whether a qualified plan discriminates excessively in favor of highly compensated employees. The process is even more difficult when the employer maintains an "aggregated" plan (combining a defined benefit plan with a defined contribution plan). The IRS has allowed sponsors of aggregated plans some relief from formulas that would otherwise apply: see Notice 2015-28, 2015-14 I.R.B. 848, extending the relief to 2016. However, the formula must be reasonable, based on objective business criteria for selecting employees to benefit. QSERPs may have to be amended to satisfy this requirement. [Xerox FYI, *IRS Nondiscrimination Proposal Limits QSERPs, Adds Cross-Testing Option and New Closed Plan Relief* (Feb. 4, 2016) (benefitslink.com)]

In early 2016, the IRS proposed regulations that could make it harder to maintain a QSERP that covers only one person who is identified by name. Historically, the IRS has opposed benefit formulas for individual employees, and these regulations deal with the application of nondiscrimination rules to these plans. The proposal did not forbid QSERPs or plans that name an Highly Compensated Employee (HCE). But if the benefits or contributions for a named executive are determined under a formula that applies only to the named executive, the ratio percentage would have had to be at least 70% to pass nondiscrimination testing.[81 Fed. Reg. 4976 (Jan. 29, 2016); see Hansonbridgett.com, *Is the QSERP Dead? Proposed Rules Target Individual Benefit Formulas* (Feb. 2016) (benefit slink.com); Plansponsor editors, *IRS Proposal Would Change Rules for QSERPs*, plansponsor.com (Mar. 22, 2016)]

Then, just a few months later, the IRS withdrew the proposal, stating that more time was needed to consider the issues. [Announcement 2016-16, 2016-18 I.R.B. 697; see John G. Ferreira, Brian J. Dougherty and Timothy Kennedy, *IRS Withdraws Proposal Targeting QSERPs*, Morgan Lewis & Bockius LLP (Apr. 15, 2016), available at Lexology.com]

[3] Rabbi Trust

A rabbi trust (so-called because the first one was created by a synagogue for its clergyman) sets aside assets in an irrevocable trust to pay the benefits, although the corporation's creditors can reach the assets. The assets in the trust cannot revert to the employer until all of the obligations to pay deferred compensation have been satisfied. Executives are not taxed until they receive benefits from the trust, because of the risk that creditor claims will prevent benefit payments. A "springing" rabbi trust is set up with only minimal funding. However, if the control of the corporation changes (for instance, because of a merger or acquisition), then the trust provides for funding for payment of benefits. The rabbi trust will not be considered "funded" for ERISA purposes just because it has a spring provision.

A rabbi trust furnishes the greatest permissible degree of protection for participants in deferred compensation plans. Many such trusts are set up with a directed trustee, who follows directions from the sponsor or a committee, and has no discretion over the trust or the plan. A few plans give the trustee full discretion, or discretion for some services. Another option is to increase the trustee's discretion over benefit decisions after a change in control, to relieve participants' anxieties about whether new management will pay the benefits promised by the predecessor. Depending on circumstances, the trustee may have to issue a W-2, Form 1099-R or Form 1099-Misc when the rabbi trust makes distribution. [No by-line, *Special Report: Deferred Compensation: Change Management*, plan sponsor.com (magazine article, June 2006)]

A commentator suggests that one way to make sure that nonqualified plan benefits are paid to the executives is to put the money in an irrevocable rabbi trust, separate from the corporation's general assets. Rabbi trust assets are subject to the claims of the corporation's general creditors if the company becomes insolvent but are protected in other situations—including the case of a new or successor employer that does not want to pay the benefits. [Michael S. Melbinger, *How Can SERP and Non-Qualified Plan Participants Protect Themselves Against the Loss of Benefits?*, Winston & Strawn LLP Executive Compensation Blog (Mar. 20, 2011) (benefitslink.com)]

State Street Bank was the trustee of a top hat plan covering special retirement benefits for Chrysler Automotive assets. In 2008, when Chrysler was facing bankruptcy, the company used $200 million of rabbi trust funds for company operations, depleting the accounts of approximately 400 retired executives, including ex-chairman Lee Iacocca. The reorganization proceedings did not provide any relief for them. The retirees sued State Street and Chrysler's parent company, Daimler A.G. The Sixth Circuit held that state-law claims of fraud and fiduciary breach were preempted by ERSIA—but ERISA breach of fiduciary duty claims would be futile because the top hat plan had no bankruptcy protection for retiree accounts. The court found no violation of the plan documents and ADEA claims were time-barred. [*Pfeil v. State Street Bank*, **806 F.3d 377** (6th Cir. 2016), *cert. denied.* **136 S. Ct. 2511** (2016); see Wilber H. Boies and Andrew C. Liazos, *Second Court of Appeals Win for State Street Bank in $200 Million Chrysler "Top Hat Plan" Class Action*, McDermott Will & Emery (Dec. 7, 2016), available at Lexology.com]

One of the effects of the AJCA (see § 8.02[D]) is to ban offshore rabbi trusts.

[4] Secular Trust

A secular trust is an irrevocable trust whose assets cannot be reached by the employer's creditors, including its bankruptcy creditors. It offers more protection to the executive's right to receive deferred compensation than a rabbi trust, but has less favorable tax consequences. The price of increased protection for the employee is that the employee has taxable income (taxed using the I.R.C. § 72 annuity rules) equal to the employer contributions to the trust on the employee's behalf. The employer can deduct its contributions to the trust, to the extent they are ordinary and necessary business expenses, in the tax year in which the contributions become taxable income for the employee.

Secular trusts gained in popularity because of economic conditions and the difficulties of complying with § 409A. In general, nonqualified benefits offered through a secular trust are immediately taxable to the employees, but the trust assets are protected from the company's creditors. Rev. Rul. 2007-48, 2007-30 I.R.B. 129, tended to promote the use of secular trusts simply because it was clear what the rules are.

This ruling states that a participant in a secular trust does not have gross income on account of an interest in the trust until accrued benefits vest. The gross income for a given year is the fair market value of the vested part of the account as of the last day of the trust's tax year (whether or not this amount is distributed), plus the amount distributed to the participant during the participant's tax year, minus the participant's investment in the contract (the fair market value (FMV) of the vested portion of the account at the end of the trust's previous tax year), because the participant has already been taxed on the investment in the contract.

The secular trust must maintain separate accounts for each participant (although there can be multiple accounts in one trust). The sponsor corporation can deduct its contributions in the corporate tax year in which the recipients include the funds in the gross income. The income of a secular trust is taxed to the trust itself, not to the sponsor, and the trust can deduct trust income that vests in the participants during the tax year even if the income is not actually paid. [Michael Melbinger, Winston & Strawn LLP, *Protecting Non-Qualified Deferred Compensation—The Secular Trust* (June 9, 2009) (benefitslink.com)]

[5] Top Hat Plan

A top hat plan is an unfunded deferred compensation plan limited to managers and/or HCEs. An unfunded top hat pension plan is not subject to the ERISA participation, vesting, funding, or fiduciary responsibility rules. The plan must have a claims procedure. Even the modest role that ERISA plays in regulating top hat plans is probably enough to preempt state law, so suits cannot be brought in state court involving claims against top hat plans.

Employers that contribute to NQDCs typically set a vesting schedule at least as strict as the schedule for the qualified plan. It may even be stricter—e.g., a "bad boy" clause that denies payments to persons who are terminated for cause or who breach a noncompete agreement. Courts will uphold these stricter requirements only if the NQDC plan is a top hat plan that is exempt from ERISA. Relevant factors are whether eligibility is limited to a select group of management or highly compensated employees; what percentage of employees are eligible; how the compensation of eligible employees compares to the workforce as a whole; the titles and duties of covered employees; and the extent to which covered employees have influence over management decisions. [Michael S. Melbinger, *Follow-Up on Top Hat Plan Testing/Review*, Winston & Strawn Executive Compensation Blog (Dec. 12, 2013) (benefitslink.com)]

In late 2014, DOL proposed to require electronic filing of top hat plan statements. To remain exempt from the ERISA reporting and disclosure rules, the top hat plan must file a simple statement with the DOL within 120 days of the date the plan starts. The statement requires disclosure of contact information about the employer, the number of plans, and the number of employees covered. There is no specific penalty for failure to file—but failure to file means that the plan will be subject to ERISA's reporting and disclosure requirements. After the filer clicks the "submit" button, the filer receives a confirmation number and a downloadable PDF of the filing that can be saved or printed, as well as a confirmation e-mail containing the same information. The plan must make a new filing, even if it has already made a top-hat filing, if a new top hat plan is adopted. However, a new filing is not required if an existing plan is amended to add a new, separate class of participants. Mistakes can only be corrected by filing an amended statement using the confirmation number of the earlier, erroneous filing. Filed statements are open to the public, and will be posted on the DOL Website. [EBSA, *Top Hat Plan Statement*, <http://www.dol.gov/ebsa/efiletophatplanfilinginstructions.html> (expires Dec. 13, 2017) (accessed Feb. 11, 2017)]

In mid-2008, the Second Circuit ruled that it did not violate ERISA or the Age Discrimination in Employment Act (ADEA) for a company (that had reserved the right to terminate) to terminate its top hat plan, even if the plaintiff relied on the representations made in his early retirement package. The plan had become financially untenable, so it was not arbitrary or capricious for the board of directors to terminate it.

The Second Circuit pointed out that many ERISA provisions, such as the fiduciary duty provisions, do not apply to top hat plans. However, the ERISA administration and enforcement provisions do apply to top hat plans, so state law claims such as breach of contract, bad faith, and negligent misrepresentation were preempted. [*Paneccasio v. Unisource Worldwide*, 532 F.3d 101 (2d Cir. 2008)]

DOL has not provided any guidance about what constitutes a select group of management or highly compensated employees, although there are a few illustrative court cases. The DOL focuses on the extent to which employees covered by the plan have the power to influence management decisions, but this has not greatly influenced court decisions. The courts of appeals that have examined this issue differ on how to define a top hat plan. Courts tend to focus on five factors: the percentage of the total workforce covered by the plan (rather than the percentage of eligible employees who participate); the number of employees covered by the plan; the compensation of the lowest level of employees covered by the plan, and how it relates to compensation trends in the business' geographic area; the titles and job duties of covered employees; and whether employees are automatically covered if they satisfy the plan's definition versus whether they are selected by management or the company's board of directors. [Michael S. Melbinger, *So, What the Heck Is the Standard for Determining Top Hat Status?*, Winston & Strawn LLP (Mar. 14, 2016), available at Lexology.com]

To determine whether a plan coves a "select group," courts consider objective factors like the percentage of the workforce covered by a plan, and how their compensation compares to the average for the company. There is no set figure for what constitutes a small percentage of the workforce, but the smaller the percentage, the more likely that the plan covers a small group. If participation in the plan is optional, courts will probably calculate the percentage based on all employees invited to participate. But if in realistic terms, only the highest-paid employees can participate, then only the actual participants are counted. Sometimes former employees will also be included in the calculation.

For a recent example, in May 2015, the DOL filed an amicus brief in the Fourth Circuit case of *Bond v. Marriott International Inc. Stock & Cash Incentive Plan*. The district court had ruled that Marriott's plan of making deferred stock bonus awards was a top hat plan and, therefore, exempt from the ERISA minimum vesting requirements. The DOL's position is that the "select group" exception applies only if the plan consists solely of managers or HCEs. [The case is No. 15-1160(L), 2016 U.S. App. LEXIS 1499 (4th Cir. Jan. 29, 2016). See John McGuiness and Kelly Geloneck, *View from Groom: DOL Weighs in Again on Select Group Requirement for Top Hat Plans*, Bloomberg BNA Pension & Benefits Daily (Sept. 2, 2015) (benefitslink.com)]

The District Court for the Southern District of California said that plans restricting participation to 15% or less have consistently been treated as top hat plans. [*Callan v. Merrill Lynch & Co.*, No. 09 CV 0566 BEN (BGS), 2010 U.S. Dist. LEXIS 89997 (S.D. Cal. Aug. 30, 2010)]

The Sixth Circuit reversed the district court's decision that a nonqualified plan was an ERISA plan but not a top hat plan. Apparently, the plan was intended to be an unfunded top hat plan; the author of the article said that an ERISA plan that was not a top hat plan would create a "tax debacle." The Sixth Circuit ruled that the district court should have remanded the matter to the plan administrator to expand the administrative record. [*Daft v. Advest*, 658 F.3d 583 (6th Cir. 2011)]

The District Court for the Western District of Pennsylvania held in late 2015 that a plan was a top hat plan because it covered only 68 participants (0.2% of the employer's work force) and their average compensation was $500,000. The district court rejected plaintiff Sikora's argument that the plan was not a top hat plan because its participants did not have enough bargaining power with the plan to be able to do without ERISA protection. The district court said that ERISA does not prescribe a "bargaining power" test. [*Sikora v. UPMC*, No. 2:2012cv01860, 2015 U.S. Dist. LEXIS 170717 (W.D. Pa. Dec. 22, 2015); see John D. Martini et. al., *Courts Reject ERISA-Based Participation and Vesting Challenges to Top Hat Plans*, Reed Smith LLP (Mar. 18, 2016), available at Lexology.com. This case was appealed to the Third Circuit on February 7, 2017: see <https://www.pacer monitor.com/public/case/20545951/Paul_Sikora_v_UPMC,_et_al>]

In a class action about the discount rates used by a top hat plan and a pension plan to convert straight life annuities to lump sums, the Seventh Circuit upheld the lower court's grant of summary judgment for the plan. The top hat plan used a 7.5% discount rate (the pension plan used a rate of approximately 5.4%). As a nonqualified plan, the top hat plan was not subject to the PPA cap on discount rates. The plan terms permitted a 7.5% discount rate to be used by any nonqualified plan, and top hat plans are by definition nonqualified. [*Dennison v. MONY Life Ret. Income Sec. Plan*, No. 710 F.3d 741 (7th Cir. 2013)]

Participants in a top hat plan could not recover under ERISA § 502 from the company that bought all of the assets of the bankrupt company that formerly maintained the plan. The buyer did not assume any of the sponsor's liabilities under the plan. At that point the seller was a shell company with no assets, so it was unable to pay benefits. The Seventh Circuit rejected the plaintiffs' arguments that the buyer was a de facto plan administrator, holding that the buyer did not connive with the seller to cheat plan participants, and that the buyer was not just a continuation of the seller. Therefore, the buyer did not have to acquire the liabilities of the unfunded top hat plan, and the buyer did not violate ERISA § 510 either—it did not interfere with the attainment of ERISA benefits. In the Seventh Circuit view, § 510 refers to employment actions, and many of the plan beneficiaries were former employees or non-employees of the seller. [*Feinberg v. RM Acquisition, LLC*, 629 F.3d 671 (7th Cir. 2011)]

§ 8.02 TAXATION OF NONQUALIFIED PLANS

[A] General Considerations

Nonqualified plans can create some subtle tax problems for plan participants. The mere fact that the employer promises to pay benefits in the future doesn't create income for the plan participants, until plan benefits are either actually or constructively received. Constructive receipt is a tax concept roughly equivalent to deliberately turning down money that the taxpayer is entitled to.

Employees are taxed on benefits from nonqualified plans as they are distributed. To the extent that the employee already had to pay tax on amounts not yet distributed, employees are entitled to compute an exclusion ratio (percentage of a distribution that has already been taxed and will not be taxed again).

Nonqualified plan participants are taxed in the year in which rights to property become transferable, or the substantial risk of forfeiture ends, whichever comes first. Sometimes, property rights depend, directly or indirectly, on the plan participant continuing to perform services for the employer. If there is a covenant not to compete, however, property rights might depend on not performing services! Under the IRS Regulations, the facts of each case must be examined to determine whether there is a substantial risk of forfeiture because of a requirement of continued employment or noncompetition.

As for the trust income, there are complex factors (centering around the extent of the employer's contributions and degree of control) that determine ownership of the trust, and therefore whether the employer, the employee, or the trust itself should be taxed on income earned by a secular trust arrangement.

The 2014 Federal Insurance Contributions Act (FICA) base is $ 117,000; the 2015–2016 base is $118,500; and the 2017 base is $127,200.

FICA issues must be considered when managing an NQDC plan. Deferrals are included in income for FICA purposes at the time of vesting. A typical NQDC arrangement gives senior executives the right to one or more payments on retirement, death, or disability. Usually payments are considered vested (i.e., there is no longer a substantial risk of forfeiture) long before the payment is actually made. A properly constructed plan can permit deferral of income tax until the amounts are paid—but FICA tax will be due based on the vesting date. See § 3121(v)(2) for NQDC FICA rules. The vested amount is added to the FICA wages for the year. It is often the case that, in the year of vesting, the executive's compensation exceeds the FICA base, so the vested amount is only subject to Medicare tax (which applies to all compensation). For an account balance plan (i.e., a plan whose benefit is the principal amount credited to the employee plus income on that principal), the taxable amount for FICA purposes is the amount contributed to the account, whereas a non-account balance plan's FICA taxable amount is the present value of the vested future payment. [E. Drew Cheney, *Non-Qualified Deferred Compensation Plans*, BNN Benefits Blog (Aug. 23, 2016) (benefitslink.com)]

NQDC distributed after a participant's retirement is not taxed the same way as retirement income from defined benefit or 401(k) plans. The distribution is generally reported on Form W-2 as supplemental wages, not on Form 1099-R for retirement income. (However, some non-employees, such as directors of the company, independent contractors, or beneficiaries of a participant, may be entitled to receive NQDC; such payments are reported on Form 1099-MISC.) Because NQDC fits under the heading of supplemental wages, it is necessary to use the different formulas for supplemental wages under $1 million and above $1 million. A recent article suggests keeping the NQDC participants in the payroll system even after they leave the company. Current addresses and other payroll information must be retained, not least so that the employer can substantiate deductions of NQDC as it is distributed. If the recipient moves after retirement (e.g., to a warmer climate) then it may be necessary to withhold income taxes to the state where the compensation was earned and/or the state where it is paid. [Bank of America/Merrill Lynch, *Managing Nonqualified Deferred Compensation Distributions: What Employers Need to Know* (Oct. 2015) (benefitslink .com)]

See T.D. 9645, 2013-51 I.R.B. 738, for final regulations on the additional Medicare tax that PPACA imposed on high earners, irrespective of the recipient's filing status or wages paid by other employers. The employer cannot modify its withholding of additional Medicare tax. However, a person who expects to owe more than the amount withheld by the employer can increase withholding on the W-4 (e.g., a joint return where neither spouse earns over $200,000, but the total is over $250,000). [IRS, *Questions and Answers for the Additional Medicare Tax*, available at <https://www.irs.gov/Businesses/Small-Businesses-&-Self-Employed/Questions-and-Answers-for-the-Additional-Medicare-Tax> (Dec. 6, 2016) (last accessed Feb. 11, 2017)]

The rules for income tax and FICA treatment of NQDCs are different. Generally, income tax applies at the time the benefits are paid or made available to the individual—but FICA applies at the earlier of the time the amounts vest or are paid. If NQDC vests at retirement age, FICA tax applies to the present value of the entire benefit. Thus, if the employee has already reached the FICA wage base, he or she will only have to pay the Medicare portion of the FICA tax (which is not capped). FICA regulations require the employer to withhold FICA from each deferred compensation payment as it is made.

Participants in Henkel Corporation's SERP brought a class action when the plan started withholding FICA tax from distributions to participants in a NQDC plan. Top hat plan participants almost always earn more than the FICA wage base, so FICA is not due on nonqualified plan benefits or contributions. If FICA tax is withheld when the benefits or contributions vest, the "non-duplication rule" provides that FICA tax will not be due when the benefits are paid. FICA tax was not withheld by Henkel over the course of employment, so when the benefits were paid FICA taxes were due; by then, many recipients had retired and earned less than the FICA maximum, so they were subject to tax. The District Court for the Eastern District of Michigan granted summary judgment for the plaintiffs, holding that that the employer was obligated to withhold FICA tax either when tax withholding was done, or when the employer matching contribution was credited to the account. Commentators suggested that this case shows that employers have an obligation to operate the plan to give the employees the best tax consequences. [*Davidson v. Henkel Corp.*, No. 12-cv-14103, 2015 U.S. Dist. LEXIS 722 (E.D. Mich. Jan. 6, 2015)]

Henkel settled the suit for $3,350,000, including attorneys' fees, an award to the lead plaintiff and litigation expenses. The retirees receive a 40% gross-up of the benefit distributions to cover taxes, and plan participants are indemnified against FICA tax assessments. The settlement was approved by the district court. [*Davidson v. Henkel*, No. 12-cv-14103-GAD-DRG (E.D. Mich., settled 2015).]

An employee of NCR Corp., became a participant in its top hat plan for senior employees. He retired in 2006 with a joint and survivor life annuity paying about $29,000 a year. In 2013, NCR terminated the plan, paying Taylor a $440,000 lump sum for the actuarial net present value of the annuity. After taxes, he received $254,063. The plan documents allowed the plan to be terminated as long as accrued benefits were not adversely affected. Taylor sued, pointing to the plan's choice of discount rate as a factor in halving his benefit. The District Court for the Northern District of Georgia dismissed, holding that the plan document permitted termination of the plan; beneficial tax impact is not an ERISA-protected benefit; and it was reasonable for the plan to use a discount rate to calculate present value, so there was no reduction in benefits or impairment of accrued benefits. [*Taylor v. NCR Corp.*, No. 1:14-cv-2217-WSD (N.D. Ga. Sept. 23, 2015). Note, however, that an unpublished Second Circuit case, *Gill v. Bausch & Lomb*, 594 Fed. Appx. 696 (2d Cir. 2014), holds that it violated plan terms to terminate a rabbi trust and distribute the benefits as a lump sum; the participants were awarded $730,106 in damages and attorneys' fees.]

Under Code § 415, "compensation" includes any NQDC under § 409A that is includible in the employee's income. [Final Regulations, 72 Fed. Reg. 16878 (Apr. 5, 2007)]

[B] I.R.C. § 83 Issues

Tax planning for nonqualified plan participants also requires a look at I.R.C. § 83, which sometimes requires employees to include in income amounts that have not been distributed from the nonqualified plan. Section 83 provides that whenever property is transferred to anyone except the employer for the provision of services, the employee's taxable income includes the fair market value of the transferred property, minus any amount paid for the property.

Section 83 doesn't apply to transfers to qualified plan trusts, or to a deferred compensation arrangement that gives the employee a mere contractual right to receive compensation in the future. Many stock option transactions are also exempt from this section. However, § 83 does apply to assets set aside in trusts, escrows, or similar arrangements that are not subject to the claims of the corporation's general creditors.

Where § 83 applies, the employee's tax is based on the value of the employee's income on the plan trust at the time of taxation, and not on the fair market value of the employer's contributions from the trust.

For example, assume that a startup company grants an employee 100,000 shares of stock, which vests at the rate of 25,000 shares at the end of each 12-month period after the grant date. The fair market value (FMV) of the shares is five cents per share at the time of grant, reaching 75 cents in Year 2, $2.00 in Year 3, and $5 in Year 4. Section 83(a) requires the equity grant to be taxable on the FMV as of the vesting date, not the grant date. If the employee's effective federal tax rate is 30%, the grant will require the employee to pay $60,000 in federal income tax. But when property is subject to a substantial risk of forfeiture, or is non-transferrable restricted property, the employee does not recognize income until vesting, when the restrictions lapse.

An election is available under § 83(b) to accelerate the taxable event to the date of the grant, recognizing as income the FMV of all granted shares as of the grant date. The election makes the employee the owner of the restricted property, so vesting is not a taxable event. Generally speaking, a § 83(b) election will be favorable to the employee. In the example above, the FMV on the grant date is 5 cents a share, or $5,000 for all 100,000 shares; at the 30% rate, the tax is $1,500. The § 83(b) election has to be made within 30 days after grant date. If the employee paid FMV for the property, he or she would have no taxable compensation at the grant date; but if the restricted property was received free or at a discount, the difference between the FMV and the price paid constitutes compensation.

When the property is disposed of, any appreciation in value since the grant date is generally capital gain rather than ordinary income. If the employee makes a § 83(b) election and holds the restricted property for at least a year from the grant date, the gain is generally long-term capital gain; if held less than a year, it is short-term capital gain, taxed at the same rate is ordinary income. However, the § 83(b) election is irrevocable. If the employee forfeits the property, or the value of the property falls, the employee will not be able to obtain a refund of the tax already paid. There might be a capital loss in the year of forfeiture, but the employee might not be able to use it to reduce taxes. [Timothy E. Glasgow, *Taking Advantage of the Section 83(b) Election*, Bryan Cave LLP (Nov. 4 2015), available at Lexology.com]

A § 83(b) election can be made to treat restricted stock as received on the grant date. The value at the time of the grant, minus any payment made for the stock, is ordinary income to the recipient. When the stock is disposed of, any post-grant appreciation is taxed as capital gains. However, when the recipient of a non-qualified stock option exercises the option, there is an ordinary income equal to the fair market value at the time of exercise minus the exercise price. If restricted stock on which a § 83(b) election was made is forfeited, the taxpayer has a capital loss, which might not fully offset the previously recognized ordinary income. A restricted stock unit (RSU) plan provides that the cash (for a cash-settled plan) or stock is only delivered after vesting conditions are satisfied. No compensation is issued before vesting, so there is no chance to make a § 83(b) election. [Hoon Lee, *Stock Options, Restricted Stock and Restricted Stock Units*, Hoon Lee Law PLLC (Jan. 17, 2017), available at Lexology.com]

In early 2014, the IRS finalized regulations to clarify when there is a "substantial risk of forfeiture" on transfer of stock that is treated as employee compensation under § 83. Substantial risk of forfeiture can be established only through a service condition or a condition related to the purpose of the transfer (e.g., achieving a performance goal). A service condition means that the employee's rights are contingent on performance or refraining from performance—such as under a noncompete agreement. In determining substantial risk based on a condition related to the purpose of the transfer, both the likelihood of the event occurring and the likelihood of the forfeiture being enforced must be considered. In general, transfer restrictions such as lock-ups, bans on insider trading, and blackout periods, do not create a substantial risk of forfeiture. But if the stock cannot be sold because of Securities Exchange Act § 16(b)'s short-swing profit rules, unless the taxpayer elects under § 83(b) to be taxed when the stock is issued, the stock is considered subject to a substantial risk of forfeiture. [T.D. 9659, 2014-12 I.R.B. 653, finalizing proposed regulations at 77 Fed. Reg. 31783 (May 30, 2012)]

IRS's § 83 regulations provide that a provision calling for forfeiture of stock if the employee is discharged for cause or for committing a crime does not create a substantial risk of forfeiture. Nevertheless, in 2014 the Tax Court held that the discharge for cause provision in the taxpayer's employment agreement did create a substantial risk of forfeiture. The clause permitted termination for cause for several reasons, including failure to perform his duties diligently and adhere to the employment agreement. The Tax Court said that the regulations, as interpreted, focus on termination for committing a crime, which is unusual enough not to constitute a substantial risk. In this case, however, the Tax Court believed that the broader terms in the taxpayer's employment agreement did create a substantial risk of forfeiture. [*Austin v. Comm'r*, 141 T.C. No. 18 (2014)]

In mid-2016, the IRS made it easier to e-file tax returns, by eliminating the prior requirement of filing a paper copy of the § 83(b) election with the tax return. The employee can submit the copy to the IRS separately, within 30 days of receiving § 83(b) property; the IRS scans the paper forms and links them to the Form 1040 when it is received. [T.D. 9779, 2016-33 I.R.B 233; see Crescent Moran Chasteen, *IRS Simplifies Section 83(b) Election Process*, Nutter McClennen & Fish LLP (Aug. 3, 2016), available at Lexology.com]

[C] Employer's Tax Deduction (Pre-AJCA)

Before the AJCA was enacted, the employer's deduction, as provided by the texts of Code sections 404(a)(5) and 404(d)(2) was not available if the plan provided deferred compensation for shareholders who were not employees of, or independent contractors to, the employer corporation. The employer's deduction for paying deferred compensation occurred in the year the employee received the compensation, not the year of the contribution. Each employee covered by funded, NQDC arrangements had to have a separate account. Distributions from nonqualified plans were FICA and Federal Unemployment Tax Act (FUTA) wages, but I.R.C. § 3121(v)(2) provided that amounts deferred under a NQDC plan were taken into account only once—at the later of the time services were rendered, or when there ceased to be a substantial risk of forfeiture of the amounts.

[D]   AJCA and § 409A

The American Jobs Creation Act of 2004 (AJCA), Pub. L. No. 108-357, adds new I.R.C. § 409A to the Internal Revenue Code. It is effective for amounts deferred after 2004. There is no requirement of common-law employment, so deferred payments to independent contractors and outside directors are also subject to these rules. The I.R.C. § 409A rules supplement those already in place governing economic benefit and constructive receipt of deferred compensation. In effect, amounts deferred under a nonqualified plan are included in the recipient's gross income unless they were previously included in his or her income, or unless they are subject to a substantial risk of forfeiture. Compensation is taxed when I.R.C. § 409A is triggered, or the previous rules apply—whichever comes first.

Compliance with I.R.C. § 409A is critical because the AJCA carries a big stick: unless its requirements are satisfied, all compensation deferred under the nonqualified plan for all taxable years is included in the participant's gross income for the current year, plus interest and a penalty of 20% of the compensation included in gross income. Penalties are also imposed if plan assets are placed into a trust outside of the United States, whether or not the assets are available to satisfy the claims of creditors. Another creditor protection measure applies the penalties if plan assets are placed in a domestic trust triggered by the employer's financial condition.

A plan is considered a NQDC plan if it is not a qualified pension or welfare benefit (e.g., vacation, sick leave, disability pay, death benefit plan, HSA, HRA, medical reimbursement plan). Whether an option plan is subject to I.R.C. § 409A depends on the terms of the arrangement. If the exercise price for the option is at least as high as the underlying stock's fair market value on the date of the grant, then the option is not considered deferred compensation unless it includes some deferral feature over and above the ability to exercise the option in the future. There is a statutory exemption for ISOs and employee stock purchase plans. By and large, Stock Appreciation Rights (SARs) will be subject to I.R.C. § 409A, although a SAR, that has a fixed payment date, or a non-discounted publicly traded SAR, will be exempt.

I.R.C. § 409A requires elections to defer compensation to be made on or before the end of the taxable year before the year in which the compensation will be earned. For performance-based compensation (e.g., sales commissions) based on services rendered over a period of 12 months or more, the election can be made within the six months before the end of the service period.

Distributions to key employees cannot be made earlier than six months after separation from service, or upon the key employee's death. A key employee is one covered by I.R.C. § 416(I)(l)(c). Distributions from a deferred compensation plan can be made only when the person earning the money is separated from service, dies, when a specified time is reached (or when a specified schedule begins), when the corporation changes control, the participant becomes disabled, or there is an unforeseeable emergency; otherwise, elective withdrawals are forbidden, even with a penalty. Even if an unforeseeable emergency has occurred, the amount of the distribution must not exceed the amount needed to cope with the emergency and pay the taxes on the premature distribution. Nor can distributions be made if the hardship could be handled through insurance reimbursement or liquidation of the participant's other assets.

Changes in the form of distribution that have the effect of accelerating payment of deferred compensation are forbidden to the same extent as acceleration of the distribution. However, I.R.C. § 409A is not violated merely because a plan provides a choice between cash and taxable property, if the same amount of income is included in income in the same year irrespective of the participant's election. Therefore, the plan can provide for a choice of a lump sum or a fully taxable annuity contract without falling afoul of I.R.C. § 409A.

The initial election to defer must specify the form of any payment that is supposed to be received at a specified time or on a specified schedule. Exceptions are made to this general rule for payments under a QDRO, payments made to comply with federal conflict of interest requirements, amounts needed to pay FICA taxes, and amounts withheld when there has been an I.R.C. § 457(f) vesting event. A lump sum payment of up to $10,000 is also permitted to a terminated employee.

If an election is made to defer distribution past its original date, the election must be made 12 months before the scheduled distribution date, and must defer payment for an additional five years.

A payment (e.g., a bonus) is not subject to I.R.C. § 409A as long as the employer makes the payment no later than the next taxable year after the amount ceases to be subject to a substantial risk of forfeiture. The payment must be made within two-and-a-half months after the end of the employer's tax year or the end of the employee's tax year in which the condition lapses—whichever is later.

I.R.C. § 409A does not apply to payments when all the taxpayers involved use the accrual method. Nor does it apply to payments made to someone who is actively engaged in providing non-employee or non-director services to two or more unrelated recipients. An entity is deemed related if the service provider owns at least a 20% interest in it. Property (such as restricted stock) that is subject to I.R.C. § 83 is not subject to I.R.C. § 409A, but a service provider's enforceable right to receive property in a later year (e.g., under an RSU plan) can be subject to I.R.C. § 409A.

Under an RSU plan, the stock (or cash, in a cash-settled plan) is only delivered after vesting conditions are satisfied. No stock is issued before vesting, so there is no chance to make an 83(b) election. That can simply administration of the RSU plan—but employees must consider the § 409A implications of the timing of award payments on vesting, [Hoon Lee, *Stock Options, Restricted Stock and Restricted Stock Units,* Hoon Lee Law PLLC (Jan. 17, 2017), available at Lexology.com]

It does not constitute prohibited acceleration for a company to waive or accelerate the satisfaction of a condition that is a substantial risk of forfeiture, as long as the other conditions of I.R.C. § 409A are satisfied. Plans can also be amended so that the entire interest under a future deferral will be distributed in a lump sum whenever the participant's interest in the plan falls below the *de minimis* amount specified by a plan when a distribution event occurs. It is also permissible to accelerate distributions to someone other than the participant to satisfy a Qualified Domestic Relations Order (QDRO); to the participant to pay FICA and income taxes under § 3121(v); or to a participant to the extent required to pay income taxes generated by a § 457(f) plan's vesting event.

Deferred compensation payments can be accelerated in connection with a change in control (change in ownership or effective control of the company); the change-in-control event must be objectively determinable.

Under § 409A, disability can trigger deferred compensation; many plans provide for 100% vesting on disability. Even if the plan does not make disability a payment trigger, the onset of disability can affect vesting and the timing of payments made for separation from service. If disability leads to full vesting but does not affect the actual payment, then the plan can use any definition it wants and need not satisfy standards under § 409A. [Randy L. Gegelman, The Law Firm of Faegre & Benson LLP, *Practical 409A: The Impact of Disability on Non-Qualified Deferred Compensation Under Code § 409A* (Mar. 23, 2009) (benefits link.com)]

For § 409A purposes, merger or acquisition of a company's equity usually does not constitute a separation of service for employees who continue to be employed after the transaction. If there is an asset sale or transfer, someone who leaves the seller's employ and goes to work for the buyer generally does have a separation from service. But if the transaction is a transfer of substantial assets, such as substantially all of a business' assets, then the buyer and seller can make an election as to which employees who go to work for the buyer have a separation from the seller's service. The election must be set out in a written document created before the transaction closes, the document must be the product of bona fide, arm's-length negotiations, and all employees must be treated consistently for this purpose. [Will Fogleman and John McGuiness, *Separation Anxiety: Analyzing Separations from Service Under Section 409A,* Bloomberg BNA Pensions & Benefits Daily (Dec. 23, 2014) (benefitslink.com)]

Section 409A greatly increased IRS scrutiny of deferred compensation plans. In mid-2014, the IRS launched a formal audit program to determine if employers satisfy operational and document requirements. [David C. Strosnider, *IRS Begins Code Section 409A Audit Program,* Roetzel & Andress (June 18, 2014) (benefitslink.com)]

In mid-2015, the IRS released new audit guidelines for non-qualified deferred compensation (NQDC) plans. The guidance defines NQDC plans as the following:

- Salary reduction arrangements, where the participants have their current salary reduced, but replaced by an equivalent amount payable in the future. These arrangements resemble 401(k) plans, but the employer does not get a current deduction, and the employee could lose the deferred amounts if the employer becomes insolvent.

- Bonus deferral plans, which are similar but involve bonuses rather than salary; a plan can also cover both salary and bonuses.

- Top hat plans, maintained primary for a select group of managers or highly compensated employees. Note that this requirement is under the jurisdiction of the DOL rather than the IRS.

- Excess benefit plans, providing benefits greater than the § 415 limitations allow for qualified plans.

- Phantom stock plans, also known as restricted stock unit plans.

The IRS guidelines say that the audit issues include funding (amounts must not be protected from claims of the employer's creditors). The guidelines say that many constructive receipt issues were eliminated by the enactment of § 409A, but constructive receipt might occur in connection with devices like checkbooks and debit/credit cards tied to deferred compensation accounts that give the employer a high degree of control over the account. The IRS also recognizes the "cash equivalence doctrine": if a solvent company makes an unconditional, assignable promise to pay that is not subject to set-off and the promise is of a kind that is frequently transferred to lenders or investors, for tax purposes, the promise is the equivalent of cash. The guidelines say that the employer company cannot deduct interest or earnings credited to deferred compensation until the deferred compensation is taxable to the participants.

For FICA and FUTA purposes, NQDC is taxable when the amounts vest, not when they are distributed. Plan sponsors should also be aware that employers are not permitted to condition any other benefit, including participation in the NQDC plan, on participating or refraining from participating in the company's 401(k) plan. [<https://www.irs.gov/Businesses/Corporations/Nonqualified-Deferred-Compensation-Audit-Techniques-Guide> (updated June 6, 2016) (last accessed Feb. 11, 2017)]

The choice between options and restricted stock involves many considerations, such as dilution of the holdings of existing shareholders. On the date of the grant, restricted stock may have value that accrues to the holder, whereas that value does not accrue to the holder of a stock option. Therefore, less restricted stock, which creates less dilution, can be issued to yield the same amount of compensation as stock options. Restricted stock is typically not subject to § 409A. If the exercise price of stock options is at least FMV, the options will also be outside § 409A, but there could be § 409A penalties if it is later determined that the exercise price was lower than the stock's value at the time of the grant. [Hoon Lee, *Stock Options, Restricted Stock and Restricted Stock Units*, Hoon Lee Law PLLC (Jan. 17, 2017), available at Lexology.com]

[E]   The PPA, 2005 Proposals, and 2007 Final Rules

In 2005, the IRS issued a lengthy and detailed set of proposed regulations [70 Fed. Reg. 58930 (Oct. 4, 2005)] dealing with many aspects of nonqualified plans: valuation; severance pay plans; initial elections to defer compensation; performance-based compensation; commissions; and rules for distributing deferred compensation, including relief for certain delays in distribution.

The basic rule is that a nonqualified stock option is not subject to § 409A if it is granted for at least the FMV of the stock on the date of the grant; it is taxable under § 83; and the option does not have the effect of deferring compensation. Generally speaking, SARs are treated like stock options.

However, Code § 409A applies to stock options and SARs, which determines the exercise price and requires a valuation of the business to set the price. The IRS has consistently taken the position that discounted stock options are deferred compensation subject to § 409A. This makes the options less attractive to employees because they can't control the timing of income recognition by controlling the timing of the exercise. ISOs under Code § 422 and stock options issued under an Employee Stock Option Plan (ESOP) pursuant to § 423 are exempt from § 409A regulations as long as they continue to be qualified. To be exempt under § 409A, nonqualified options must satisfy several basic requirements. The exercise price must at least equal the fair market value (FMV) of the underlying shares as of the grant date. Public companies must base FMV on a reasonable method using actual sales of their common stock, whereas private companies must reasonably apply valuation methods that reflect the relevant factors. The stock must be eligible common stock. The stock option must not provide for deferral of delivery of the shares when the option is exercised, nor can the option be exchanged for other deferred compensation. If an existing grant is materially modified, it will be treated as a new grant subject to § 409A. If any § 409A requirement is violated, the Nonqualified stock Options (NQSOs) or SARs are immediately taxable or taxable on vesting, when the option is no longer subject to a substantial risk of forfeiture. The grantee has ordinary income equal to the excess of the FMV on December 31, minus the exercise price and the amount paid for the option when it was granted. This compensation is also subject to a 20% penalty tax. [Peter Alwardt, *Discounted Stock Options Are Subject to 409A*, Eisneramper.com (Oct. 22, 2015) (benefitslink.com)]

A major principle of § 409A is that any legally binding right to deferred compensation constitutes NQDC, so informal bonus programs and severance programs are affected and non-executive employees and independent contractors are covered if they receive NQDC. A mid-2016 article points out that § 409A is hard to apply because it uses idiosyncratic definitions of common terms. In the § 409A context, "plan" means all plans of the same type covering an individual. Separation from service occurs only if the employee no longer works for any member of the employer's controlled group (with special rules about consulting). Noncompete agreements do not delay vesting. [Lori Jones, *Section 409A: Top 10 Rules for Compliant Non-Qualified Deferred Compensation,* Thompsoncoburn.com (July 28, 2016) (benefitslink.com)]

Severance pay plans are exempt from § 409A if they are collectively bargained; if they are broad-based (i.e., not limited to key employees); or if payments are made within two years after the year of termination of employment. There is a special exception for severance payments that would not otherwise be exempt, but are made within 2½ months of the end of the year of termination of an employee who was involuntarily terminated. An initial election to defer severance resulting from involuntary separation from service can be made at any time before the employee has a legally binding right to the payment, as long as the severance pay is the subject of bona fide arm's-length negotiations. For severance payments under a window program, the initial election to defer the payment can be made until participation in the program becomes irrevocable.

Distributions made to a key employee of a public corporation cannot be made because of separation from service until at least six months have elapsed since the separation.

The plan must have a schedule for making the distribution (e.g., three months after the participant becomes disabled). Employees must make their initial election to defer compensation under a nonqualified plan by the end of the year preceding the year in which the compensation subject to deferral is earned.

The Pension Protection Act of 2006 had a seismic impact on many aspects of the pension and tax world—and nonqualified plans did not escape this phenomenon. Section 116 of the Pension Protection Act (PPA; Pub. L. No. 109-280) amends § 409A to add new categories of compensation that are taxable to the recipient of deferred compensation.

When a defined benefit plan is "at risk," there will be a "restricted period" during which transfers of funds to a trust or other arrangement in order to pay NQDC to a "covered employee" will result in the employee being taxed on the amounts transferred, and also on the value of plan assets that are restricted to providing NQDC. Not only are the assets in question taxable to the employee, the employee will have to pay a 20% excise tax. In some instances, the employee will also have to pay interest on underpayments of tax resulting from this inclusion in income. Furthermore, if the transferred or restricted assets increase in value or accrue earnings, those additional amounts are simply treated as more property transfers taxable to the employee. For this purpose, it is irrelevant whether the assets used for deferred compensation are subject to the claims of the sponsor's general creditors—so rabbi trusts do not protect the employee against taxation.

The definition of covered employees comes from § 162(m)(3) and includes the CEO and the four highest-paid executive officers other than the CEO plus officers, directors and 10% stockholders, because the definition incorporates the Securities Exchange Act § 16(a) definition as well. The restricted period means any time when the sponsor company is bankrupt, when its defined benefit plan has at-risk status (see § 4.01[A]) and a 12-month period measured as the six months before and the six months after an involuntary or distress termination of any defined benefit plan maintained by the sponsor. If the payor corporation is publicly traded, it may be subject to SEC rules about management compensation. If the company received federal "bail-out" funds, it may also be subject to limitations on executive compensation, including incentive and deferred compensation. See § 1.01[B].

A plan is considered at risk if its funding status falls below 70% (considering various factors set out in the PPA) and below 80% (when these factors are not considered).

If the employer provides a gross-up (i.e., indemnifies the employee for the extra tax burden), payments of this type will be treated as taxable income to the employee, plus a 20% penalty. The employer will not be permitted to deduct the gross-up payment on its own income tax return. [This issue is discussed, in Gardner Carton & Douglas Client Memorandum, *Pension Protection Act Restricts Funding of Certain Nonqualified Deferred Compensation Arrangements*, <http://www.gcd.com/PPARestrictsFunding.pdf> (Sept. 2006)]

In April 2007, reflecting public comments as well as the PPA, the IRS published final regulations, defining the types of plans (e.g., short-term deferral of compensation; Stock Appreciation Rights; some health reimbursement arrangements) that are exempt under § 409A. Qualified plans, welfare benefit plans (e.g., disability plans, sick and vacation leave plans) are exempt from § 409A coverage, as are ISOs and other statutory stock options and ESOPs.

The plan must be in writing and must disclose the payment schedule, trigger events for payments, amount to be paid, and conditions imposed on making elections under the plan.

The prior regulations did not have a uniform rule for determining when a payment has been made, with the result that certain events were "payments" for some purposes but not others. June 2016 proposed regulations specify a single rule for all purposes: when the event yields currently taxable income. A transfer of unvested property such as restricted stock is not a payment unless the service provider makes a § 83(b) election to include it in current income.

The previous rules exempt from § 409A severance payments that do not exceed the smaller of two amounts, one of which is the person's pay for the previous year. The 2016 proposal allows a payment that does not exceed the annualized current-year pay, if the person did not have a prior year's pay (e.g., was hired and fired in the same calendar year). The 2016 proposal allows a payment to be treated as an exempt short-term deferral if it is made later than the usual 2 ½-month period—if employer reasonably anticipated that making payments on schedule would violate securities or other law.

The § 409A rules allow payment, including acceleration of payment, at death but this creates plan administration problems because the employer might not learn about an ex-employee's death until after the § 409A deadline has passed. The proposed rules allow a payment at death to be made whenever designated by the payor or payee, up to and including December 31 of the calendar year after the calendar year of death. The payment at death rule also applies to payments premised on the death of the beneficiary, or a disability or unforeseen emergency affecting the beneficiary. The proposed rules amend the previous ban on mandatory repurchases of stock options and SARs based on measures other than fair market value. This raised concerns that the ban could impair forfeitures and clawbacks for violating a noncompete. The 2016 proposal copes with this problem by allowing relief when a service provider is terminated, or based on events within the service provider's control such as breach of a restrictive covenant.

Prior law exempted stock rights from § 409A only if granted to someone providing services to the issuer or its subsidiary on the date of the grant. The proposal exempts grants to someone who has not yet started work, if he or she is reasonably expected to start within 12 months when the shares were granted—and actually does. However, this relief has limited applicability, because securities law limits the ability to offer equity to future employees, and the ISO rules also require grantees to be employed on the grant date.

Parties to an acquisition transaction frequently want to change the payment terms of the target company's incentive-based pay arrangements, especially arrangements based on stock value, to align the treatment of transaction-based compensation (stock or stock value awards) with the treatment of ordinary shareholders. If the transaction-based compensation is subject to § 409A, the altered terms may fail to satisfy the general § 409A limits on changing the terms of deferred payments. The previous regulations treated revised payment terms for transaction-based compensation as § 409A-compliant as long as payments reflect the payment terms for shareholders and do not extend the payments for more than five years after the transaction. However, it was not clear under the prior rules whether relief applied to otherwise exempt stock rights (for which extensions are harder to obtain). The June 2016 proposed regulations allow relief in this specific case, but do not allow restructuring of stock rights as unvested promises to cash out or RSUs that make payments over the original vesting term of the award.

A stock right that does not otherwise defer compensation is not deemed to defer compensation merely because an amount that is payable on involuntary termination for cause or due to a condition that is within the service provider's control, is based on a measure that is less than fair market value. [81 Fed. Reg. 40569 (June 22, 2016); Anthony G. Provenzano and Nicholas P. Walmsley, *Proposed*

Section 409A Regulations Make Several Notable Changes, Millerchevalier.com (June 29, 2016) (benefitslink.com); Andrew C. Liazos and Allison Wilkerson, *Proposed Changes to §409A Regulations: Greater Clarity and Better Planning Alternatives,* The Practical Tax Lawyer (Spring 2017) (benefitslink.com)]

Some inadvertent errors can be corrected using IRS correction programs; for the year of a corrective plan amendment, the tax return should include a note that the amendment was adopted in reliance on the correction program. The June 2016 proposals specify that a § 409A failure can be corrected if the arrangement is modified before the year of vesting (i.e., when there was still a substantial risk of forfeiture). If the IRS provides guidance about specific correction methods, all similar errors must be corrected in the same way.

Not only is § 409A an issue in the corporation's dealings with individual executives, but also it must be considered when there is a change in control of the corporation—for example, in a merger or takeover, when many employees are involved. Section 409A potentially applies to many compensation arrangements in change-of-control situations, such as severance arrangements, stock options, and incentives. Violating the rule leads to accelerated inclusion in income, and a 20% federal penalty. California imposes its own 20% penalty.

Alternative payment methods for a double-trigger severance plan (see § 3.03[D]) could violate § 409A. Some employers fail to realize this because the pre- and post-change severance provisions are found in different documents, such as a company-wide severance plan and an individual change-in-control agreement with a key executive. A double-trigger arrangement typically falls under § 409A if its "good reason" payment trigger is excessively broad—for example, if the executive can resign and collect severance based on a minor reduction in pay or duties, or if the installment payments exceed $490,000 (as indexed for inflation) or extend more than two years after separation from service. An installment or lump sum double trigger violates § 409A unless the definition of change in control complies with § 409A, and it often does not. To avoid this problem, the plan can be structured to make pre- and post-change in control payments in the same way.

§ 8.03   PROHIBITED TRANSACTIONS AND CORRECTIONS

Section 409A requires nonqualified plans to provide for payment only on a permitted event, for example death, disability, or separation from service. They must specify that the date of the event is the payment date or specify a fixed schedule or a different payment date that is objectively determinable and not discretionary. A nonqualified plan can also provide that payment is determinable and non-discretionary when it is made, but only if the period begins and ends in the same tax year for the employee or the period is not more than 90 days and the employee does not have the right to designate the taxable year of the payment. (It is common for plans to call for payment within a period of time after an event, because it can be inconvenient to make the payment exactly on the day of the event.)

As a result of these requirements, a nonqualified plan may discover that it has created additional tax liability for the plan and for its beneficiaries.

Notice 2010-80, 2010-51 I.R.B. 853, offers additional relief for § 409A plans—more types of plans will be eligible for relief under Notice 2010-6, 2010-3 I.R.B. 275 (corrections of plan document failures); a new correction method is permitted when there is a failure of payment at separation of service subject to a requirement to release claims.]

In mid-2015, the SEC proposed a rule requiring publicly traded companies to maintain a "recovery policy" under which they "claw back" incentive-based compensation that has been paid to executives, if the compensation reflects figures that had to be restated in the company's financial statements. (That is, if an executive's pay is based on the corporation's revenue, income, or profits, and those figures were inaccurate, then the company must claw back that part of the executive's pay.). The policy might call for clawback of nonqualified deferred compensation before it becomes payable—which would subject the executive to significant liability under § 409A. If the employee has already been taxed on the compensation, the SEC rule requires the clawback to equal the pre-tax bonus amount, not the net amount. If the recovery policy provides for clawback from nonqualified deferred compensation before it becomes payable, the executive could have a lot of § 409A liability. A company's ability to claw back from deferred compensation that is not yet payable violates the § 409A anti-acceleration rule, so recovery policies should be drafted to recoup the funds from sources other than deferred compensation subject to the anti-acceleration rule. [Securities Law Insider, *SEC Clawback Rules Have Executive Tax Consequences* (Oct. 5, 2015) (benefitslink.com), Clawback is only required if there was a "reissuance" restatement, not a minor revision restatement that reflects correction of immaterial errors in a previous statement that were corrected in the current report: Winston.com, *Clawbacks, Clawbacks Everywhere Nor any Moment to Think* (Oct. 18, 2016), available at Lexology.com]

Nor are tax problems the only potential issues for nonqualified plans. ERISA § 502(i) gives the DOL power to assess a civil penalty against a "party in interest" who engages in a prohibited transaction with a nonqualified plan. The penalty, which is usually assessed in connection with top hat plans, is 5% for every year or partial year in which the prohibited transaction continues in effect. There is an additional 100% penalty if the DOL issues a notice of violation, but the violation is not corrected within 90 days (or whatever extension of time the DOL grants).

CHAPTER 9

EARLY RETIREMENT AND RETIREE HEALTH BENEFITS

§ 9.01 INTRODUCTION

The timing of retirement is an individual choice, but employers can take steps to make early retirement either more or less attractive. Sometimes employers pursue early retirement incentives because they find it less expensive to encourage retirement than to maintain a large payroll. At other times, employers want to encourage older, skilled, and experienced employees to remain in the workforce—or they do not wish to devote funds to paying incentives to retire early!

Without careful planning and drafting, early retirement programs can also have a legal downside. The employer must make sure that incentives are available without unlawful discrimination. Furthermore, although it makes sense to ask early retirees to waive their claims against the employer, the waiver must be drafted with due attention to the Older Worker's Benefit Protection Act (OWBPA).

An early retirement program can create risks from two directions. Employees who are eligible may charge that the plan is a subterfuge for forcing them into involuntary retirement. On the other hand, employees who are not offered the incentives can charge that the unavailability of the program was the result of discrimination against them. Furthermore, if the early retirement program changes over time, employees who accepted a first offer may claim that the company should have informed them of the potential for getting a better offer by waiting longer. [This topic is discussed in more detail in Chapter 15, § 15.07, as an issue of fiduciary responsibility to make full disclosure to plan participants]

The questions of early retirement programs and retiree health benefits need to be examined in tandem, because one of the most important questions in deciding whether to retire early is the availability of health coverage. Medicare eligibility depends on age (65 or over) or disability, not employment status. (However, it is possible that the Medicare system, like the Social Security system, will be altered to increase the age of eligibility.) Furthermore, the Medicare system does not provide spousal benefits: each spouse must qualify independently. Therefore, a potential early retiree who is younger than 65 will need retiree health coverage, Comprehensive Omnibus Budget Reconciliation Act (COBRA) coverage, or private insurance.

Health-Related Arrangements (HRAs) and Health FSAs (see § 18.19[F]) are considered group health plans for Patient Protection and Affordable Care Act (PPACA) purposes. A standalone HRA that covers only retirees is not subject to PPACA's market reforms, but constitutes minimum essential coverage. Hence, retirees who participate in the HRA cannot get a premium tax credit for the purchase of Exchange coverage. (See § 18.19[J][1].) [Notice 2013-54, 2013-40 I.R.B. 237 and DOL Technical Release 2013-03] As with all discussion in early 2017 of PPACA issues, the strong possibility of repeal must be taken into account.

PPACA reduced the desirability of covering retirees in the same plan as active employees because PPACA mandates, such as the ban on dollar limits, are often incompatible with the provisions of the retiree health plan. The ban on benefit limits makes stand-alone HRAs impossible for active employees, but not for retirees. However, the PPACA restrictions do not apply to plans with fewer than two active employees as participants, so stand-alone retiree health plans are not subject to PPACA requirements. One option is to spin off a separate retiree medical coverage plan, with separate plan documents, separate Summary Plan Descriptions (SPDs), and perhaps a separate Form 5500. If the medical benefits are funded by a trust, there should be separate sub-accounts containing contributions for active employees and retirees. Insurance policies or self-insured plan documents should be amended to specify that retirees are covered; otherwise, the insurer might deny claims for retirees—in effect, forcing the employer to self-insure. [Erik D. Vogt, *Compliance Checkup: Does Your Company's Retiree Medical Coverage Get a Passing Grade?*, Foley & Lardner LLP (Apr. 7, 2014), available at Lexology.com]

Note that a person who was retired for the whole year is not an "employee" for whom reporting is required under PPACA with respect to minimum essential coverage, but reporting is required for retirees under age 65 who worked full-time for at least one month of the year. [Lois Mathis-Gleason, *Retirees Receiving Health Coverage: Must We Report Them?*, IFEBP.org (Aug. 18, 2015) (benefits link.com)]

However, if an employee retires and becomes covered by a retiree-only plan, but is rehired by the same employer, difficulties are likely to arise. If the rehired person is incorrectly characterized as an independent contractor, the employer might have to pay for all medical claims that arose during the time the rehired person should have been covered by the Employee Group Health Plan (EGHP). A September 2015 article advises employers to consider five factors when deciding whether to rehire a retiree: first, suspend the retiree health benefits as soon as someone is rehired; second, coordinate welfare plans so the same claim cannot be covered under both active and retiree plans; third, determine if the plan calls for suspension of pension payments when a person enrolls in the EGHP; fourth, assess the effect of temporary employment on future retiree medical plan eligibility and review eligibility under the cafeteria plan (it is common for plans to provide that someone rehired within 30 days of the termination of initial employment is limited to the previous plans and coverage; someone rehired after a longer absence is typically treated as a new hire); and fifth, coordinate benefits with Medicare, which is only the secondary payor. A rehired employee must either suspend retiree coverage and enroll in active coverage, or waive employer-sponsored coverage and rely on Medicare, and any Medicare Part B subsidies from the employer must end. [April A. Goff, *Employing Retirees Part 2: Take Steps to Avoid Problems with Health & Welfare Plans*, Warner Norcross (Sept. 29, 2015) (benefitslink.com)]

In the second quarter of 2017, close to 19% of people aged 65 and over worked at least part-time—the highest level in 545 years. About one-third (32%) of people aged 65–69 were employed, as were 19% of people aged 70–74. According to the Employee Benefit Research Institute (EBRI), 79% of active workers expect to supplement their retirement income with paid work—but that is not always possible. Sixty-one percent of retirees surveyed said that they retired earlier than they planned (often for health reasons), and only 29% found paid work at some point in their retirement. Furthermore, it is common for retirees who re-enter the workforce to move from full-time to part-time or contingent work, at much lower pay rates. [B. Steverman, *Working Past 70: Americans Can't Seem to Retire*, Bloomberg.com (July 10, 2017) (benefitslink.com)]

After 2000, employment rose among senior citizens: about one-third of people aged 65–69 were in the workforce in 2016, as were about one-fifth of people aged 70–74, and even 8.4% of people aged 75 and over. The decline of defined benefit pensions means that fewer people have an incentive to stop work because their pensions are "maxed out" and they will not accrue any additional pension benefits. Early retirement reduces the eventual pension benefit, and for life, not just until the person reaches full retirement age. The AARP's estimate is that a woman entitled to a $1,500 monthly benefit at full retirement age would get a pension of only $1,125 if she retired at age 62, but would receive $1,980 if she delayed retirement until 70. [Paula Span, *Of Retirement Age, but Remaining in the Work Force*, NYTimes.com (Aug. 2, 2016)]

A strong majority (70%) of active employees say they plan to work as long as possible after their formal retirement and only 25% intend not to work at all post-retirement. Of those planning to work after retirement, 38% say they like to work, 35% cited financial motives, and 27% said both motives were involved. Forty-seven percent of retirees were somewhat or very worried about outliving their savings. [Rebecca Moore, *Money Not the Only Reason for Delaying Retirement*, plansponsor.com (Sept. 7, 2016)]

Worries about the need for additional funds for health care are very reasonable. Many people underestimate the amount of money they will require for post-retirement health care. Medicare covers about 62% of seniors' health costs, so the retirees must pick up the other 38%, and Medicare premiums and copayments and Medigap insurance are ongoing costs. A mid-2016 estimate is that a single woman who was age 65 at that time would spend $135,000 during retirement on health care; a 65-year-old man would spend $125,000. The difference relates to women's greater life expectancy: 87 years for women, 85 for men. According to Fidelity, a 65-year-old couple would have to set aside $260,000 for Medicare premiums and other out-of-pocket costs during retirement: this figure does not include long-term care. [Ben Steverman, Retirees *Need $130,000 Just to Cover Health Care, Study Finds*, Bloomberg.com (Aug. 16, 2016) (benefitslink.com)]

HealthView Services/ 2016 Retirement Health Care Costs Data Report's estimate is even higher, projecting that a healthy 60-year-old couple retiring in 2016 would spend $288,400 in 2016 dollars on Medicare Part B, Part D, and

Medigap insurance during their remaining life spans. Adding in out-of-pocket expenses such as dental, hearing, and vision care raises the total to $377,412. A 66-year-old couple retiring in 2016 would have to devote 57% of their Social Security benefit to health costs. Assuming a 3.1% cost-of-living adjustment (COLA) in 2017 and 2.7% a year after that, a 55-year-old couple expecting to retire 10 years later would need to allocate 88% of their Social Security check— and these amounts would represent 116% of a 45-year-old couple's projected Social Security check. If, as expected, the Medicare program is significantly contracted and Social Security benefits are cut, the planning process will become even more difficult. [Rebecca Moore, *Retirement Health Care Costs Could Top $375K*, plansponsor.com (May 18, 2016)]

Pew Research Center said that older people do not necessarily remain in the workforce merely because they need the money. Highly educated baby boomers have had access to jobs that are not physically demanding. In a work-identified culture, many people do not want to give up work. [John Hanc, *Workers Are Working Longer—and Better*, NYTimes.com (Mar. 2, 2017)]

A study by the San Francisco Federal Reserve found that policies favoring later retirement are hampered by discrimination, especially discrimination against older women. The study's conclusion is that changing employers' attitudes toward older and female workers would be more effective than supply side reforms like raising the Social Security retirement age. The researchers sent out 40,000 fake applications for fairly low-skilled jobs like retail sales worker, administrative assistant, and security guard with the hypothetical workers at a range of ages in 12 cities. For all kinds of jobs, the percentage of the fabricated resumes getting a callback was higher at ages 29–31 than for ages 49–51 or 64–66, especially for women. The difference was most pronounced for retail sales jobs. [Harriet Torry, *Ageism Thwarts Policies to Boost the Senior Workforce, Study Finds*, WSJ.com (Mar. 2, 2017)]

There are reasons why a business might want to retain its older workers to transmit their skills. The LIMRA Secure Retirement Institute reported that 92% of employers are taking action to keep older workers in the workforce; 80% of survey respondents said that the organization loses institutional knowledge and experience when older workers leave. Two-thirds offer flexible hours, 42% offer flexible location such as working remotely. Job training and job sharing are also common. However, older workers increase health costs. Half of the respondents said they were going to absorb the costs, 40% said they would pass them along to the employees. [Rebecca Moore, *Firms Want to Keep Older Workers, but Cite Challenges*, plansponsor.com (Aug. 11, 2015)]

The National Institute for Occupational Safety and Health (NIOSH) launched the online National Center for Productive Aging and Work, a virtual center promoting safety and well-being at all ages, as well as productive aging. The center's mission is to research the best practices for aging-friendly workplaces, including fall prevention and universal design. [<http://www.cdc.gov/niosh/topics/productiveaging/?s_cid=3ni7d2ncpaw10132015> (accessed Feb. 12, 2017)]

PPA § 841 amends Code § 420: a plan whose assets are at least 120% of current liability is permitted to fund a 401(h) plan with at least two years' worth of estimated retiree health costs. However, a sponsor that chooses to do so must keep the plan funded at a level of at least 120%; if funding drops below this level, the sponsor must withdraw funds from the 401(h) plan until the plan's funding level returns to at least 120%. The PPA also permits transfers to fund the expected future costs of retiree health benefits under a Collective Bargaining Agreement (CBA), as long as the employer used at least 5% of its 2005 gross receipts for the purpose of providing retiree health benefits. The interim highway funding bill, HR 3038, signed July 31, 2015, extends Code § 420(h)'s authorization of 401(h) plans until 2025. [Pensions & Investments, *Use of Excess DB Plan Assets for Health Care Extended to 2025* (July 31, 2015) (benefitslink.com)] See § 9.13, below, for more discussion.

§ 9.02 ADEA ISSUES OF EARLY RETIREMENT INCENTIVES

At what point does an incentive provided to motivate early retirement turn into pressure that adds up to "constructive discharge" (the equivalent of firing the employee)? The relevant statute is the Older Worker's Benefit Protection Act, which allows voluntary early retirement incentives but only if they satisfy the objectives of the Age Discrimination in Employment Act (ADEA): promoting employment opportunities for qualified and willing older workers.

The OWBPA allows employers to subsidize early retirement via flat dollar benefits, extra benefits, or percentage increases. Employees who retire early can be offered a more favorable benefit formula (e.g., adding a certain number of years to the number of years actually worked). It does not violate the OWBPA to impose a "window" period that is the only time that the incentive is available. HHS published an Interim Final Rule, implementing the reinsurance program, on May 5, 2010: see 75 Fed. Reg. 24450 (May 5, 2010).

A defined benefit plan can pay a "Social Security supplement" starting at the date of early retirement, extending until the first date the retiree will be able to receive reduced Social Security benefits—or, if the employer prefers, until the retiree will be eligible for a full unreduced Social Security benefit.

■ **TIP:** The employer can amend the pension plan to raise the Normal Retirement Age (NRA) from 65 to 67 (a change that the Social Security Administration is gradually implementing), as long as accrued early retirement benefits, including subsidies, are preserved.

In September 2014, the IRS released final and proposed regulations on hybrid defined benefit plans (including cash balance plans), altering the age discrimination rules for plan years that begin on or after January 1, 2016. If the annual benefit payable before NRA is greater for a participant than annual benefit for the corresponding form of benefit for any similarly situated older person who is or could be a participant and who is at or before NRA, the excess is not deemed to be part of the subsidized portion of an early retirement benefit and is not disregarded when determining if age discrimination has occurred. A plan fails § 411 if an amendment decreases a participant's accrued benefit, including by eliminating or reducing an early retirement benefit.—But a plan whose interest crediting rate is noncompliant can be amended with respect to benefits already accrued, to bring the interest crediting rate into compliance. [T.D. 9693, 2014-41 I.R.B. 596]

The Multi-Employer Pension Reform Act (MPRA; part of the late 2014 spending bill, Pub. L. No. 113-235) also says that if a plan adopted an NRA on or before December 8, 2014, as the earlier of an age permitted by current law, or age plus completing a number of years of service (at least 30), the plan will not fail to comply merely because the rule applies to only certain participants. [Michael I. Richardson and Trevor W. Holmes, *New Federal Spending Bill Includes Extensive Pension Related Provisions*, Franczek Radelet PC (Dec. 19, 2014)]

The Supreme Court denied certiorari in early 2016 on the issue of whether ERISA requires the definition of NRA to be based on the typical age at which the employer expects participants to retire. [*PricewaterhouseCoopers LLP v. Laurent*, 136 S. Ct. 981 (2016)]

A university offered early retirement incentives to both tenured professors and top-level administrators. The North Dakota district court said (and the Eighth Circuit agreed) that payments to the faculty members were not "wages" (and therefore not subject to Social Security taxes) because the payments were made in exchange for property rights in university tenure. The payments to administrators, although similar, were subject to the Federal Insurance Contributions Act (FICA), because the administrators were at-will employees, whereas the tenured faculty could only be dismissed for grave cause. [*N.D. State Univ. v. United States*, 85 A.F.T.R.2d ¶ 2000-332 (D.N.D. Nov. 19, 1999), *aff'd*, 255 F.3d 599 (8th Cir. 2001)] The general rule is that lump-sum severance payments will be treated as FICA wages: *United States v. Quality Stores*, 134 S. Ct. 1395 (2014).

§ 9.03 DISCLOSURES TO EMPLOYEES

An employee can't make a meaningful decision about whether or not to retire without understanding the choices that will be available in the near future. If the terms of the early retirement program change, people who were not eligible for the improved terms, or who elected early retirement without knowing that they could have gotten a better deal by waiting longer, may charge the employer with fraud, and may charge various parties involved with the plan with violations of fiduciary duty.

The Third Circuit announced a rule in *Fischer v. Philadelphia Electric Co.* [96 F.3d 1533 (3d Cir. 1996); see also *Bins v. Exxon Co.*, 189 F.3d 929 (9th Cir. 1999), on rehearing, 220 F.3d 1042 (9th Cir. 2000)], that a revised early retirement incentive has received "serious consideration," and therefore must be disclosed to potential early retirees, once senior managers discuss the proposal for purposes of implementation.

The First Circuit held that the Employment Retirement Income Security Act (ERISA) preempts state-law claims of negligence, equitable estoppel, and negligent misrepresentation made by an early retiree who blamed his employer's erroneous estimate of his benefits for inducing him to retire early. The plaintiff said that he was not suing over plan administration issues that would be preempted by ERISA, only about the employer's legal obligations to keep proper records. He also said that he sought damages for the employer's negligence, not plan benefits. The First Circuit did not accept this argument, holding that resolution of the claim would require determining whether the plan complied with the record requirements imposed by ERISA. [*Zipperer v. Raytheon Co.*, 493 F.3d 50 (1st Cir. 2007)]

It is a breach of fiduciary duty to inform potential early retirees that lump-sum payouts are available, without also disclosing the I.R.C. § 415 limitations on rollovers and explaining the tax consequences. [*Farr v. U.S. West Commc'ns, Inc.*, 58 F.3d 1361 (9th Cir. 1998)] Given that the fiduciaries' common-law duty of loyalty requires them to deal fairly and honestly with plan participants, it is a violation to give them incomplete information.

Gearlds alleged that his employer negligently induced him to take early retirement by promising health benefits. The district court dismissed the case, arguing that all he asked for was compensatory damages (past and future medical expenses, attorneys' fees, and costs), which are not an available equitable remedy. However, the Fifth Circuit said that *Amara* [*CIGNA Corp. v. Amara*, 131 S. Ct. 1866 (2011)] allows relief that makes a plaintiff whole for losses caused by breach of fiduciary duty. [*Gearlds v. Entergy Servs. Inc.*, 709 F.3d 448 (5th Cir. 2013)]

To assist older employees in making decisions about Medicare Part D (the prescription drug program that took effect in 2006), employers are required to issue a notice to all Part D-eligible employees (with disclosure to the Center for Medicare and Medicaid services as well) informing them as to whether there is prescription drug coverage under the employer's plan, and whether that coverage is creditable or non-creditable. [See § 9.10[B].]

§ 9.04   EEOC MANUAL ON EARLY RETIREMENT INCENTIVES

Late in 2000, the Equal Employment Opportunity Commission (EEOC) updated Section 3 of its Compliance Manual to deal with benefits. [No. 915.003 (Oct. 3, 2000), <http://www.eeoc.gov/policy/docs/benefits.html>] As of press time in 2017, this section of the manual had not been updated. The agency's position is that an early retirement incentive (ERI) program is lawful as long as it's voluntary. The EEOC will not get involved if the employer chooses to:

- Set a minimum age or minimum number of years of service for employees who participate;

- Have a window (i.e., the incentive is only available for a limited time period);

- Limit the ERI to a manager, a department, a particular facility, etc.

However, ERI benefits can't be reduced or denied for older employees versus similarly situated younger employees unless the employer qualifies for one of five defenses:

- Equal cost;

- Subsidizing a portion of the early retirement benefit;

- Integrating the incentives with Social Security;

- (For a university) incentives for a tenured faculty member;

- The plan is consistent with the objectives of the ADEA.

The equal cost defense probably will not be available in connection with ERIs, because the cost of early retirement benefits generally does not increase with the employee's age.

The EEOC allows the employer to limit the ERI or pay higher ERI benefits to younger employees where the benefits are used to bring early retirees up to the level of the unreduced pension they would receive at the NRA from a defined benefit pension plan. But the subsidized pension can't be greater than the pension of a similarly situated older employee who has reached NRA.

It is also permissible to offer an ERI to bridge the gap to Social Security eligibility, for a person who has not yet reached the Social Security early retirement age (currently slightly over 62). The supplement can't exceed the Social Security benefit that the employee will eventually receive as an early or normal age retiree.

According to the EEOC, equal severance benefits are required for all similarly situated employees irrespective of their age. Employers may not deny severance on the grounds that the employee is eligible for a pension, although sometimes pension benefits can be offset against the severance pay. Denying recall rights to older workers operates as unlawful involuntary retirement. The cost of providing severance does not rise with the employees' age, so employers are not allowed to assert an equal cost defense in this context.

Retiree health benefits can legitimately be offset against severance if the retiree is eligible for an immediate pension; the retiree actually receives health benefits; and the retiree benefits are at least comparable to Medicare in type and value. If the retiree is over 65, the benefits must be at least comparable for one-fourth the value of Medicare benefits. The offset itself must be reduced by any percentage by which the pension is reduced for retirement before the NRA, and any percentage of the retiree health coverage premium that the retiree has to pay.

In the EEOC view, an ERI ignores age as a criterion (and therefore is consistent with the ADEA's objectives) as long as it gives all employees above a certain age:

- A flat dollar amount (e.g., $20,000);
- Additional service-based benefits, for instance, $1,000 for each year of service;
- A percentage of salary;
- A flat dollar increase in pension benefits, such as an extra $200 a month;
- A percentage increase (e.g., 10%) in pension benefits;
- Extra years of service and/or age used in pension computations.

§ 9.05   ERISA ISSUES

[A]   Generally

Because one of the primary purposes of ERISA is to make sure that retirement benefits will be paid in accordance with the terms of the plan, ERISA issues often arise when early retirement plans must be construed. Sometimes, ERISA welfare benefit plans will also be involved.

[B]   Preemption

It is very likely that ERISA will be held to preempt state-court cases about group health plans. In its June 2004 decision in the consolidated cases of *Aetna Health Inc. v. Davila*, and *Cigna Healthcare of Texas, Inc. v. Calad*, 542 U.S. 200 (2004), the Supreme Court found that ERISA § 502(a) completely preempts state-law claims alleging that managed care plans improperly denied care (in one case, it was claimed that the plaintiff was injured by taking a lower-cost drug rather than the safer, more expensive drug that was not covered by the plan; in the other case, alleged premature discharge from hospitalization). [See § 15.18.] Preemption is much less likely to be found in the early retirement context. According to the Sixth Circuit, ERISA does not preempt age discrimination claims merely because the plaintiff had already retired and was collecting a pension as of the time of the suit. [*Warner v. Ford Motor Co.*, 46 F.3d 531 (6th Cir. 1995)]

The 1996 case of *Lockheed v. Spink* [517 U.S. 882 (1996)] found (among other issues) that it is not a prohibited transaction (as defined by ERISA § 406) to establish an early retirement program that is conditioned on waiving enforcement of employment claims. Under this analysis, paying benefits under any circumstances shouldn't be treated as a prohibited transaction.

[C] Fiduciary Duty

Persons dissatisfied with the terms of an early retirement plan, or the way those terms are applied, often bring suit for breach of fiduciary duty. Whether a breach will be found depends on factors such as whether potential retirees received materially misleading information—possibly whether or not intent to mislead, or even negligence, was present. It does not violate ERISA to deny early retirement to employees who are deemed especially valuable to the company, if the plan gives management discretion as to whether early retirement is in the company's best interests. [*McNab v. Gen. Motors*, 162 F.3d 959 (7th Cir. 1998)] Another General Motors case says that the Labor Management Relations Act (LMRA and National Labor Relations Act (NLRA) do not preempt an early retiree's state-law claims that the employer fraudulently induced acceptance of early retirement. [*Voilas v. Gen. Motors*, 170 F.3d 367 (3d Cir. 1999)]

In the fourth opinion in this case, rendered October 2009, the Third Circuit found that it was a breach of fiduciary duty to give employees the impression that their retiree health benefits would continue for life when, in fact, the employer had the power to terminate the benefits at any time. In this view, employees received "at best a half truth" when the company did not disclose the power to amend the plan. Although the SPD disclosed the right to amend, the Third Circuit said that this was irrelevant because it was not distributed until after the plaintiffs retired, so it could not have affected their knowledge of the plan. The Third Circuit upheld the injunction issued by the district court, because the injunction corrected a violation of fiduciary duty, and the specific provisions in ERISA dealing with equitable relief outweigh the general principle that ERISA does not regulate settlor activity. [*In re Unisys Corp. Retiree Med. Benefits ERISA Litig.*, 579 F.3d 220 (3d Cir. Oct. 19, 2009), *cert. denied*, 559 U.S. 940 *sub nom. Unisys Corp. v. Adair* (Feb. 22, 2010)]

[D] Anticutback Rule

ERISA § 204(g) forbids cutbacks in benefits. On June 7, 2004, the Supreme Court ruled that it is a violation of the anti-cutback rule to amend a plan to further restrict the type of work that retirees can do without forfeiting their pensions, if the result of the amendment is that early retirement benefits that were already accrued would be suspended. (The plan ruled out benefits for retirees who engaged in post-retirement work as "construction workers"; the plaintiffs were "construction supervisors." Then the plan was amended to rule out benefits for anyone who did any work at all in the construction industry.) [*Central Laborers' Pension Fund v. Heinz*, 541 U.S. 739 (2004)]

The Ninth Circuit held that it was an abuse of discretion for plan trustees to forbid participants to work certain post-retirement jobs if they wanted to collect pension benefits. The trustees identified post-retirement jobs as traffic flagger and snowplow driver as falling within the same classification as their pre-retirement union jobs as skilled mechanics. The plan allowed early retirement at age 52 with 10 or more years of credited service. Early and normal-age retirees can collect retirement income while working, as long as they do not have more than 51 hours of post-retirement service in any month in their former job classification and in the industry in which the employers are involved. The trustees called the post-retirement jobs similar in duties, skills, and general competencies to the pre-retirement jobs; the Ninth Circuit said the post-retirement jobs were unskilled roadwork. [*Tapley v. Locals 302 & 612 of the Int'l Union of Operating Eng'rs*, 728 F.3d 1134 (9th Cir. 2013)]

Participants must receive a "§ 204(h) notice" informing them in plain English if there has been a significant reduction in the rate of future benefit accrual, or whenever an early retirement benefit or early retirement subsidy has been eliminated. Although the basic rule is that notice must be given at least 45 days before the effective date of the amendment, small (under 100 participant) plans can comply by giving notice at least 15 days before the effective date. Amendments relating to mergers and acquisitions can also give only 15 days notice. If the amendment significantly reduces an early retirement benefit or subsidy, but does not significantly reduce the rate of future benefit accruals, the notice can even be given after the effective date of the amendment, as long as it is within 30 days after the effective date.

A plan administrator's plan interpretation, reducing certain employees' pension benefits, violated the plan terms. Therefore, it was a cutback that violated ERISA § 502(a)(1)(B) and the anti-cutback rule. Cottillion left employment before the defendant's NRA of 65. The plan administrator interpreted the plan to offer an unreduced pension benefit commencing before age 65. The plan was subsequently restated to add a provision expressing that benefits were actuarially reduced for commencement before NRA. The plan's actuaries said that paying unreduced pensions endangered the plan's qualification. The administrator told people who had already retired that their benefits would be actuarially reduced and told people already in pay status that benefits would be reduced to account for future actuarial reduction and to recoup overpayments already made. The Third Circuit held that the plan document before the amendment called for an unreduced pension, so the new interpretation did not get deference and members of the class were entitled to unreduced benefits. The change was a cutback that violated § 204(g). [*Cottillion v. United Ref. Co.*, 781 F.3d 47 (3d Cir. 2015)]

The Tenth Circuit found that converting a defined benefit plan to cash balance form had the effect of depriving employees of early retirement subsidies. The Tenth Circuit remanded the case to the district court for consideration of remedies for the plaintiffs—bearing in mind that remedies for § 204(h) notice failures are available only if the employer's failure to give notice was egregious. An egregious failure means that the circumstances were within the employer's control, and the employer nevertheless intentionally failed to give notice after discovering an unintentional past failure to satisfy the § 204(h) requirements. In this case, the Tenth Circuit ruled that there were no egregious circumstances, only a forgivable omission in the course of drafting the complex notice required by ERISA. [*Jensen v. Solvay Chems.*, 721 F.3d 1180 (10th Cir. 2013)]

T.D. 9601, 77 Fed. Reg. 66915 (Nov. 8, 2012) permits a bankrupt sponsor to amend its plan to eliminate optional forms of benefits that accelerate payment after bankruptcy. Approval by the PBGC and the bankruptcy court is required.

[E] Other ERISA Issues

The Seventh Circuit ruled that it was not an abuse of discretion for the district court to approve a settlement of an ERISA class action about severance benefits that was less favorable to early retirees than to other members of the class. The Seventh Circuit had already ruled that a defined benefit plan with a COLA must provide the actuarial equivalent of the COLA to participants who receive lump-sum benefits. The Seventh Circuit ordered the district court to draft a damage award. The plan argued that the early retirees were not entitled to damages. The Seventh Circuit ruled that the settlement award was fair to the early retirees because it balanced their risk of continuing to litigate a case where they might lose. [*Williams v. Rohm & Haas Pension Plan*, 658 F.3d 629 (7th Cir. 2011)]

The Pension Benefit Guaranty Corporation (PBGC) publishes a table every year in November or December, most recently Table I-17, <http://www.pbgc.gov/prac/mortality-retirement-and-pv-max-guarantee/erisa-section-4044-retirement-assumptions/retirement-rate-category-tables-2017.html> (last accessed Feb. 12, 2017), for plans with valuation dates in 2016, which estimates the probability that a person will retire early from a plan that is being terminated by the PBGC, or in a distress termination initiated by the employer. The table is used to determine the total value of the benefits under the plan by computing the value of early retirement benefits. The likelihood of early retirement is considered low if the monthly benefit is below a certain amount, high if it exceeds a certain amount, and medium if it falls in between.

The table is based on the monthly benefit the worker will receive at "URA" (Unreduced Retirement Age)—either the plan's Normal Retirement Age or the age at which the worker could first receive a benefit that is not actuarially reduced to account for early retirement.

For example, if the participant reaches URA in 2017, the likelihood of early retirement is considered low if the benefit is under $631 a month; medium, if the benefit is between $631 and $2,665; and high if it exceeds $2,665. The table includes figures for retirement in or after 2027, at which time likelihood is considered low if the benefit is under $631 a month, high if it exceeds $3,268 a month, and moderate for amounts in between. [81 Fed. Reg. 83137 (Nov. 21, 2016); see Plansponsor editors, *PBGC Issues New Table for Use by Involuntarily Terminating DBs*, plansponsor.com (Nov. 22, 2016)]

§ 9.06   PHASED RETIREMENT

In many instances, the needs of both employer and employee would be well served by the option of "phased retirement" (a gradual transition out of the workforce) rather than a bright-line test of being either fully active or retired. Employers would certainly save money if they could reduce the full-time payroll yet continue to receive part-time services from older workers, instead of offering them early retirement subsidies.

For many years, phased retirement was quite difficult to implement because of rules limiting "in-service" distributions, other than those made on account of hardship, from defined benefit or 401(k) plans. Many commentators have raised the question of how to structure phased retirement equitably, e.g., by determining that a person is 50% retired, and therefore paying him or her 50% of the salary for the position, and also 50% of the retirement benefits that would be available if the person had completely retired.

Many pension plans (perhaps deliberately to encourage early retirement or as an unintended result of other design features) in effect grant the most rapid accrual of pension benefits when workers are in their fifties; between their mid-fifties and retirement, workers may find that pension accrual is actually negative. That is, even though they will eventually qualify for a larger pension because they work longer, they also receive the pension for one year less for each additional year worked.

The Pension Protection Act of 2006, Pub. L. No. 109-280, includes two major provisions dealing with early retirement and retiree health issues. PPA § 905 amends ERISA § 3(2)(A) and the corresponding Code § 401(a)(36) to permit plans to retain qualification even if they make in-service distributions for the phased retirement of persons aged 62 or older who continue to work on a reduced schedule. This is true even if the recipient of the distributions has not reached the plan's Normal Retirement Age.

2007 final regulations concentrate not on whether the plan's NRA is a subterfuge to avoid qualified plan requirements, but whether it is at least as high as the typical age for the industry. If the NRA is set between 55 and 62, the employer's good-faith determination that the NRA falls within industry norms will be given deference if it is reasonable in light of the facts and circumstances. An NRA below 55 is presumed unreasonable, although not if the employer can prove the contrary. Note that an NRA of 50 will be considered reasonable for public safety employees like police or firefighters. [T.D. 9325, RIN 1545-BD23, 2007-24 I.R.B. 1386]

In mid-2016, the IRS offered guidance on the tax treatment of payments to employees from defined benefit plans during phased retirement, explaining when the amounts are deemed taxable annuity payments from the defined benefit plan. The IRS defined phased retirement as an arrangement for receiving part of the retirement benefit while continuing to work part time. Payments are generally taxable in the tax year in which they are distributed. The notice explains the present value factors used to determine a "basis recovery fraction" for each payment, and when to calculate this amount. [Notice 2016-39, 2016-26 I.R.B. 1068; see Lee Barney, *IRS Guidance Explains Annuity Taxation During Partial Retirement*, plansponsor.com (June 14, 2016)]

Subsequently, in T.D. 9783 (81 Fed. Reg. 62359, Sept. 9, 2016), the IRS explained how it has modified the minimum present value requirement for defined benefit plans, to make it easier for the plans to distribute benefits partly as a lump sum and partly as an annuity.

Expected retirement ages are rising and retirement is not defined as a single event, rather it's a transition between full-time work and full-time retirement. Most companies with 50 or more employees maintain some kind of flexible work options, generally through informal programs, but usually they are not available to everybody.

The Society for Human Resources Management (SHRM) reported that in 2012, 10% of U.S. companies had formal or informal phased retirement programs, a proportion that rose to 14% in 2016. The program could be contingent on older workers mentoring younger workers. Steelcase requires employees to make a business case for their phased retirement applications, saying what they want to do for a period of six months to two years of reducing their hours—and how that plan helps the company. [Carol Hymowitz, *A Way to Ease into Retirement That's a Win-Win for Managers and Employees,* Bloomberg.com (Dec. 16, 2016) (benefitslink.com)]

Transamerica's Aegon Center for Longevity and Retirement reported that over half of employees age 55 and over (55%) would prefer gradual retirement, but only 27% said their employers offered a transition to retirement through part-time work. Amazon's pilot program allows certain employees to work a standard reduced schedule of four hours a day from Monday to Thursday, plus additional flexible hours for a total of 30 hours a week. An effective phased retirement program requires clear criteria for which employees (perhaps selected by job title or length of tenure) can use the program and explains how the reduced hours affect compensation (including benefits such as insurance, pensions, and vacation time). It can be helpful for the program to set a firm date for the employee's full retirement; otherwise, employees who like the reduced schedule could overstay their welcome. This can be done by asking for a post-dated letter of resignation. [Joanne Sammer, *Taking Phased Retirement Options to the Next Level*, shrm.org (Feb. 7, 2017) (benefitslink.com)]

§ 9.07 RETIREE HEALTH BENEFITS: INTRODUCTION

At one time, it was very common for part of the incentive for early retirement to come in the form of health benefits to replace the employer's group health plan. Employers often promised "lifetime health benefits at no cost." However, health care costs rise significantly every year, and employees in poor health are more likely to be interested in health benefits than employees in good health. Therefore, a retiree health benefit program can become a major burden on the employer.

According to the Employee Benefits Research Institute (EBRI), the prevalence of retiree health benefits began to diminish seriously in December 1990. One of the precipitating factors was the Financial Accounting Standards Board's (FASB's) release of a standard called SFAS 106, requiring employers to record their unfunded retiree health benefit liabilities on their financial statements—with the result that corporate earnings decreased.

In response, some employers stopped providing retiree health benefits altogether; others put their plans on a defined contribution basis, added age and service requirements, or maintained the level of benefits for current retirees but reduced the benefits that would eventually be available to people retiring in the future.

The Kaiser Family Federation reported that in 2015, 23% of companies with 200 or more employees provided retiree health coverage—versus 66% in 1988. Even retirees who have coverage are likely to get their coverage under private health exchanges, where the risk of premium increases falls on the retirees. [Mark Miller, *Employer Health Benefits for U.S. Retirees Keep Declining*, Reuters (Apr. 14, 2016) (benefitslink.com); Rebecca Moore, *Fewer Retirees Have Employer-Sponsored Coverage*, plansponsor.com (May 10, 2016)]

FASB's SFAS No. 158 (generally effective for fiscal years ending after December 15, 2006) requires the funded status of all post-retirement plans— including retiree health plans—to be recorded on the company's balance sheet, not just included as a footnote to the financial statements. This FASB document does not require prefunding of retiree health liabilities, but the reporting obligation might provide an incentive to do so.

Among companies continuing to provide some kind of retiree health plans, there has been a strong trend to shift more and more of the costs to the retirees. To reduce the cost of the plan, many employers adopted caps, i.e., maximum amounts that they will devote to retiree health benefits; if costs increase past this point, the additional cost will be entirely passed along to the participants. Another tactic is to impose a combination of age and service requirements for participation in the retiree health plan, e.g., limiting it to persons over 55 with 10 years' service. Or, the amount of financial contribution an employee is expected to make to the retiree health plan could be made proportional to length of service. Or, retirees can be placed into a separate risk pool rather than a shared risk pool with active employees; premiums can be set higher for one group of retirees than another. [Ellen E. Schultz, *Conquering Retirement: When Retirees Face Health-Plan Cuts*, WSJ.com (Apr. 20, 2012)]

The Early Retirement Reimbursement Program (ERRP), created by PPACA, reimbursed employers for claims incurred by retirees over 55 who are not Medicare-eligible, or incurred by their dependents of any age. Five billion dollars was appropriated to fund the program. It was scheduled to last until January 1, 2014 or when the money ran out.

As expected, the money ran out, and the termination of the ERRP program on January 1, 2014 was announced. [78 Fed. Reg. 23936 (Apr. 23, 2013); see Kevin McGuinness, *ERRP Will Sunset at Start of 2014*, plansponsor.com (May 17, 2013)]

§ 9.08 THE RIGHT TO ALTER OR TERMINATE RETIREE HEALTH BENEFITS

At one time, it was common for employers to promise their employees that, after the employees retired, they would receive lifetime health benefits without cost. Economic developments in the interim have led many employers to terminate their retiree health plans, or to impose premiums and copayment requirements, or increase retirees' financial responsibilities. It is also common for retirees to sue their ex-employer to roll back these changes.

The general rule is that, as long as the employer drafts the plan to provide that the employer retains the right to amend, modify, or terminate the health benefits, the employer can do so unilaterally. ERISA has rules about vesting of pension benefits (i.e., the circumstances under which the right to a pension becomes nonforfeitable) but ERISA does not provide for vesting of welfare benefits such as retiree health benefits. Furthermore, ERISA preempts state law on this subject, so the states do not have the power to impose vesting requirements. [See, e.g., *Gen. Dynamics Land Sys. Inc. v. Cline*, 540 U.S. 581 (2004) (terminating retiree health benefits did not violate the ADEA)]

The Supreme Court returned to the subject of welfare benefit vesting in early 2015. The court permitted cuts in retiree benefits—reversing the Sixth Circuit holding that the benefits vested for life. All of the justices joined in the result: that retiree health benefits are not deferred compensation and the ambiguous provisions of the plan did not create a lifetime promise. The case was remanded for the Sixth Circuit to apply contract-law principles to see if the CBA granted free lifetime health benefits. The Supreme Court majority opinion said that when a contract is silent on the duration of retiree benefits, a court cannot draw an inference of lifetime vesting. [*M&G Polymers USA v. Tackett*, 135 S. Ct. 926 (2015)]

The case was sent back to the Sixth Circuit to apply contract-law principles to interpreting the agreement. The Sixth Circuit sent the case back to the district court once again, directing the district court to apply the Supreme Court decision to analyze the parties' intention without implying lifetime benefit entitlement. [*Tackett v. M&G Polymers USA*, 811 F.3d 204 (6th Cir. 2016); see Findlaw Sixth Circuit blog, *Retiree Benefits Case Goes Back to Trial Court for the 3rd Time* (Jan. 2016), available at FindLaw.com. See also *Gallo v. Moen Inc.*, 813 F.3d 265 (6th Cir. 2016), also holding that contractual obligations end with the termination of the CBA, and applying the same contract-law principles to both collectively bargained and other contracts about retiree health benefits.]

For post-*Tackett* cases holding that retiree health benefits were not vested for life, see, e.g., *Grove v. Johnson Controls, Inc.*, No. 12-2622, 2016 WL 1271328 (M.D. Pa. Mar. 31. 2016); *Sloan v. BorgWarner, Inc.*, No. 09-cv-10918, 2016 U.S. Dist. LEXIS 167588 (E.D. Mich. Dec. 5, 2016); *Watkins v. Honeywell Int'l, Inc.*, No.3:16-cv-01925, 2016 U.S. Dist. LEXIS 174222 (N.D. Ohio Dec. 16, 2016). These cases are discussed in Proskauer's ERISA Practice Center Blog, *District Court Rules Johnson Controls Retirees Not Entitled to Lifetime Health Benefits* (July 11, 2016) (benefitslink.com); Rebecca Moore, *Retirees' Claim for Lifetime Health Benefits Denied*, plansponsor.com (Jan. 4, 2017). *Barton v. Constellium Rolled Prods.-Ravenswood LLC*, 851 F.3d 349 (4th Cir. 2017), discussed in Madeline C. Rea, *Fourth Circuit Rejects Retirees' Claim for Vested Health Benefits*, Proskauer Rose LLP (Mar. 29, 2017), available at Lexology.com, holds that, under the CBA and SPD, retiree health benefits did not vest. The SPD, like most SPDs, said that pension benefits vest; in the Fourth Circuit's view, stating this but not stating that health benefits vest expressed an intention not to vest health benefits.

However, *Cooper v. Honeywell* [No. 1:16cv00471 (W.D. Mich. Dec. 14, 2016)], enjoined cuts to Honeywell retiree health benefits from Michigan plants, and a suit was allowed to proceed about retiree benefit cuts at Honeywell's Greenville, Ohio plant. [See Jacklyn Wille, *Honeywell's Retiree Health Cuts Divide Federal Judges*, bna.com (Dec. 20, 2016) (benefitslink.com). Honeywell retirees could not compel arbitration of disputes over retiree health benefits. The District Court for the Southern District of Ohio held that Honeywell only agreed to engage in arbitration with employees and unions, not retirees or ex-employees: *Fletcher v. Honeywell Int'l, Inc.*, 207 F. Supp. 3d 793 (S.D. Ohio 2016); see Jacklyn Wille,

Honeywell Won't Have to Arbitrate Retiree Health Cuts, bna.com (Sept. 16, 2016) (benefitslink.com)]

Retirees from Sprint-Nextel Corporation, Embarq Corporation, and predecessor companies sued after changes to, or elimination of, retiree health and life insurance benefits. The plaintiffs used an ERISA theory: that there was a contractual obligation to provide vested health and life insurance benefits. However, the Tenth Circuit ruled that these are welfare benefit plans. They are not subject to the ERISA vesting rules. Unless there is clear and express language in the plan documents (the SPD is considered a plan document for this purpose), the employer can unilaterally modify or eliminate the benefits. In this case, the documents did not include express vesting language, so the employer could change or end the benefits unilaterally. [*Fulghum v. Embarq Corp.*, No. 778 F.3d 1147 (10th Cir. 2015)] On remand, the District Court for the District of Kansas held that the plan documents do not grant a right to lifetime benefits. The district court granted the defendants' motion for summary judgment and denied the plaintiffs' motion for summary judgment. [*Fulghum v. Embarq Corp.*, No. 07-2602-EFM, 2015 U.S. Dist. LEXIS 76141 (D. Kan. June 10, 2015). The Tenth Circuit granted rehearing by the panel on April 27, 2015, but denied en banc rehearing: 785 F.3d 395 (10th Cir. 2015).]

However, there are circumstances under which an employer's promise of retiree health coverage will become an enforceable contract. Under the "promissory estoppel" theory, if the employer makes an unambiguous promise of lifetime benefits, it will no longer be permitted to change the plan.

Another argument that employers can make to cut back or eliminate retiree health benefits is that the benefits were provided under a particular collective bargaining agreement and do not survive the expiration of that agreement unless the agreement specifically calls for their survival. Retirees are no longer employees, and therefore are not part of the bargaining unit. The bargaining agent does not have a duty to represent retirees—and there is a real potential for conflict of interest between current employees and retirees. Retiree benefits are not included among the mandatory subjects of bargaining. [See § 30.07[A].]

In April 2017, the Sixth Circuit applied the analysis of *Tackett* to decide three cases about retiree health benefits under United Auto Workers CBAs. The Sixth Circuit found that the retiree health benefits had vested in two of the cases. The CBA was ambiguous, so the court looked at extrinsic evidence and found that company officials had frequently promised employees lifetime retiree health benefits. However, the third CBA, for Meritor, Inc., was not ambiguous, and included a general "durational" clause showing that the retiree health benefits were intended to end with the expiration of the CBA defining them. [*United Autoworkers v. Kelsey-Hayes Co.*, No. 15-2285 (6th Cir. Apr. 20, 2017); *Reese v. CNH Indus. N.V.*, No. 15-2382 (6th Cir. Apr. 20, 2017); *Cole v. Meritor, Inc.*, No. 06-2224 (6th Cir. Apr. 20, 2017). See Jacklyn Wille, *Trio of Retiree Health Benefit Decisions Delivered by 6th Cir.*, Bloomberg BNA (Apr. 21, 2017) (benefitslink.com); Wolters Kluwer Legal & Regulatory, *Retirees of Automotive*

Manufacturer Established Entitlement to Lifetime Health Benefits (May 8, 2017) (benefitslink.com).]

A class of 277 plaintiffs worked for Westinghouse before Siemens purchased the unit where they worked in late 1997. The Westinghouse plan said that benefits would not be payable to employees who were hired by a purchaser or if their employment ended after 1998. Under ERISA § 208, plan participants cannot be denied benefits when their plan consolidates with another plan or transfers its assets and liabilities to another plan. In this case, however, liabilities were transferred, but ERISA does not provide an entitlement to benefits that did not exist under the original plan. ERISA § 204(g) does not protect the cutback of an early retirement benefit for someone who has not satisfied the conditions for receiving the benefit. These plaintiffs were offered employment by the successor, so they did not qualify. The Third Circuit said that, because Siemens did not establish or maintain the plan, it could not be liable for benefits. [*Shaver v. Siemens Corp.*, 670 F.3d 462 (3d Cir. 2012)]

§ 9.09 TAX ISSUES FOR RETIREE HEALTH BENEFITS

Internal Revenue Code § 419A(c)(2) permits the employer to deduct the cost of retiree health benefits as part of a nondiscriminatory funded welfare plan. Key employees' retiree health benefits must be drawn from separate accounts, not the main account. Failure to maintain the separate accounts, or discrimination in furnishing retiree health benefits, is penalized by the 100% excise tax on disqualified benefits imposed by I.R.C. § 4976.

A funded welfare plan can maintain a reserve for future retiree health benefits, funded over the work lives of employees, without violating the account limit. The reserve must use a level-basis actuarial determination, making use of reasonable assumptions and current medical costs.

The Voluntary Employees' Beneficiary Association (VEBA) [I.R.C. § 501(c)(8)] is a possible funding vehicle for retiree health benefits. Caution must be exercised. The VEBA is a tax-exempt organization, so its investment income is subject to taxation. VEBAs are required to use current health costs to calculate the contributions to be made for future retirees. So if costs increase more than anticipated, or if retirees use more health care than expected, the VEBA may be exhausted.

One of the most important functions of ERISA is to make sure that pensions are properly funded in advance of the time that benefits must be paid. However, with respect to retiree health benefits, prefunding is allowed but not required. An argument can be made both for prefunding and for keeping the benefits unfunded.

Unfunded benefits are unsecured and can be changed at any time. They give rise to a large annual expense under the FASB rules. This expense generally increases over time, and can be higher than the pension expense precisely because of the mandate of prefunding pensions. There will also be a large accrued liability on the corporate books. The income received on sums that remain general assets of the corporation (because the money is not dedicated to prefunding retiree health benefits) is taxable. The employer's income tax deduction attributable to the retiree health plan is limited to the annual cost of benefits actually paid in that year.

In contrast, if the plan is funded, the money dedicated to this purpose is protected from diversion. Therefore, the plan is not very flexible. However, the corporation can accelerate its tax deduction, and there is more opportunity to manage the tax deduction. The corporation receives the investment income of a 401(h) account tax-free. Such income reduces the operating expenses of the plan and helps level out the future expenses. That makes the plan's accounting results look more favorable—and therefore the company will have less incentive to cut the benefits in the future.

§ 9.10 MPDIMA AND THE MEDICARE INTERFACE

[A] In General

There are two ways a person can qualify for Medicare: either being completely and permanently disabled for a period of at least two years—or reaching age 65. Income and assets are irrelevant—and so is employment status. In other words, people who are still working can be entitled to Medicare benefits (although the employer's group health plan will usually be the primary payor) but a person under 65 who is not disabled will not qualify for Medicare merely because he or she is retired. Nor does Medicare provide benefits for the under 65 spouses of retirees (or retirees' dependent children, if the unusual case but not impossible case that they have any).

The Medicare system includes "secondary payor" rules under which retirees can elect to make Medicare the primary payor for their medical care, with the employer group health plan merely the secondary payor. However, the employer does not have this option, and is not permitted to draft the health plan to make Medicare the primary payor.

Because of its role as secondary payor, Medicare is entitled to seek reimbursement from any entity (including Medicare beneficiaries, health care providers and suppliers, and attorneys) that has received payment from a primary payor. Rules published in 2006 clarify the statutory definitions, including the legal basis for recovery when Medicare paid first although it should have been secondary. If the primary payor is an EGHP or large group health plan, all of the employers that sponsor or contribute to the plan must reimburse Medicare, whether the plan is insured or self-insured. [71 Fed. Reg. 9466 (Feb. 24, 2006)]

If the EGHP fails to make primary payments for active employees of Medicare age, or the Medicare-age spouse of a plan participant, double damages under the Medicare Act or treble damages under the False Claims Act can be imposed. However, the EGHP is exempt from the secondary payor rule if it has fewer than 20 employees; if the participant receives treatment for End Stage Renal Disease; or if the participant is in a large group health plan is disabled. Effective January 1, 2009, the Medicare, Medicaid, and SCHIP Extension Act of 2007 (SCHIP Act; Pub. L. No. 110–173) imposes new Medicare Secondary Payor reporting requirements. EGHPs must find out which participants are Medicare-eligible, and report to CMS for use in the agency's enforcement efforts. Failure is subject to a CMP of $1,157 per day (for penalties assessed after January 13, 2017 for violations occurring after November 2, 2015) as well as the regular Medical Secondary Payer (MSP) penalties such as the excise tax. [The current penalty level can be found at 82 Fed. Reg. 8813 (Jan. 31, 2017)]

An active employee's becoming entitled to Medicare is usually not a COBRA qualifying event because Medicare is the secondary payor to the EGHP. If the employer offers retiree health coverage as a non-COBRA alternative to COBRA coverage, the retirees are still covered employees for COBRA purposes. It is permissible for an EGHP to terminate or reduce coverage when a retiree becomes entitled to Medicare. If this results in loss of coverage for the retiree's spouse and dependents, the spouse and dependents have had a COBRA qualifying event and they can elect up to 36 months of continuation coverage, running from the date of Medicare entitlement. [Jennifer Carsen, *How COBRA Intersects with Medicare and Retiree Health Plans*, HR Daily Advisor (Dec. 27, 2016) (benefitslink.com)]

Medicare is only a secondary payor, and not a primary payor, with respect to Worker's Compensation, so employers and insurers must also report WC claims involving Medicare beneficiaries to CMS. If Medicare pays medical expenses for such a worker, it is entitled to be reimbursed if there is a recovery from an insurer or tort defendant. The claims that must be reported are those involving a Medicare beneficiary who has received a settlement, judgment, award, or other medical expense reimbursement on or after July 1, 2009.

An increasing number of employers have adopted High-Deductible Health Plans (HDHPs) combined with Health Savings Accounts (HSAs). In many companies this is the sole health benefit. There can be knotty problems of coordinating HDHP/HSAs and Medicare. Only eligible individuals are allowed to contribute to HSAs or have contributions made on their behalf by employers. An eligible individual is one who is enrolled in an HDHP with no other health benefit coverage before the HDHP deductible has been satisfied. Therefore, Medicare is disqualifying coverage because it would pay benefits before the statutory minimum HDHP deductible was satisfied. Mere eligibility for Medicare does not affect a person's eligibility, but once someone applies for Medicare coverage and has coverage in effect, that person loses HSA eligibility on the first day of the month when entitlement begins. A person becomes entitled to Part A coverage either automatically when he or she applies for Social Security benefits (which can be done while the person is still working), or by making a separate application. But a person who receives Social Security benefits cannot waive Medicare Part A coverage. To remain eligible under the HSA, the retirement application must be withdrawn and any Medicare or retirement benefits already received must be repaid. An individual is only allowed to withdraw one application and the withdrawal request must be made within 12 months of the person being found Medicare-eligible. A person who doesn't understand these rules and makes improper HSA contributions can be subject to a 6% excise tax on the improper contribution unless it is removed promptly. Some employers might offer HDHP coverage to people who retire before age 65 and continue to fund their HSAs.

In most cases, retirees will not be able to contribute to their HSAs through a cafeteria plan, so the employer's contributions must satisfy the HSA comparability rules. In other words the employer must make comparable contributions (measured as the same amount or the same percentage of the applicable deductible) to the accounts of all comparable participating employees. [Leslye Laderman and Mary Harrison, *Older Workers and Retirees: Avoiding HSA Pitfalls*, Conduent FYI (Feb. 9, 2017) (benefitslink.com). For further details on HSA contributions, see IRS Publication 969.]

[B] MPDIMA Statute and Regulations

The Medicare Prescription Drug, Improvement and Modernization Act of 2003 (abbreviated MPDIMA) [Pub. L. No. 108-173], in addition to creating the Health Savings Account plan type discussed in § 18.09, and including provisions for the Medicare Advantage managed-care system to replace the existing Medicare + Choice plans, also enacted the Medicare Part D prescription drug insurance program. Congress passed a subsidy program benefiting employers who provide prescription drug coverage that is "actuarially equivalent" to the Medicare coverage.

Part D is voluntary: Medicare beneficiaries decide whether or not to enroll. They pay a monthly premium (e.g., $30 a month), then are responsible for an annual deductible and copayments for certain drug costs. Until 2020, there is a "doughnut hole": a level of drug spending after which Part D beneficiaries pay the full cost of their drugs. But if spending reaches a specified higher level, Part D will pay the full cost of drugs used by the Part D beneficiary. Employers can coordinate with Part D in several ways—by paying retirees' Part D premiums, or by providing supplementary coverage when retirees pay their own Part D premiums. [Kin Chau and Richard Stover, *CMS Releases 2016 Medicare Part D Benefit Parameters*, Buck Consultants FYI (July 31, 2015) (benefitslink.com)] For 2017, the deductible is $400, the initial coverage limit is $3,700, the out-of-pocket threshold is $4,950. The minimum copayment for the catastrophic benefit increases to $3.30 for generic/preferred drugs, $8.25 for other drugs. [Xerox FYI,

CMS Releases 2017 Medicare Part D Benefit Parameters and Proposes Lower Payments to EGWPs, <https://hrlaws.services.xerox.com/wp-content/uploads/sites/2/2016/03/hrc_fyi_2016-03-22.pdf> (Mar. 22, 2016) (last accessed Feb. 12, 2017)]

MPDIMA requires the plan sponsor to attest to the Department of Health and Human Services at least once a year (more often if the agency requests it) that the actuarial value of the prescription drug coverage under the plan is at least equivalent to Plan D coverage. HIPAA disclosures must be made to both the qualified covered retirees and to HHS as to the extent to which the employer's plan offers creditable coverage (see § 19.05).

Disclosure is made by e-filing at <http://www.cms.gov/Medicare/Prescription-Drug-Coverage/CreditableCoverage/index.html> (last updated Apr. 5, 2013) (last accessed Feb. 12, 2017). Disclosure to CMS must be made within 60 days after the start of the plan year; for calendar year plans, the CMS filing was due on February 29, 2016. The plan must inform CMS of the number of prescription drug options offered to Medicare-eligible persons, and how many of them are creditable. The employer must estimate the number of people eligible for Part D expected to enroll in the employer's creditable coverage, and its non-creditable coverage. Notice to CMS is also due within 30 days after termination of a prescription drug plan, or when the status of the employer's drug coverage as creditable or non-creditable changes.

Part D notices of creditable coverage must be issued to employees before October 15 of each year. Part D participant notices are often included in plan enrollment materials but under PPACA, the Part D annual enrollment period runs from October 15 to December 7, so this is not always practical. See the CMS site for the Creditable Coverage Model Notice Letter. [Marsh Consulting Group, *October 15th Deadline for Medicare Part D Creditable Coverage Notices* (Dec. 15, 2016) (benefitslink.com); Cowden Compliance Bulletin, *Medicare Part D Disclosures Due by March 1, 2017 for Calendar Year Plans* (Jan. 11, 2017) (benefitslink.com)]

PPACA, the health care reform bill, maintains the subsidy for companies that provide retiree prescription drug benefits. However, it provides that, starting in 2013, the subsidy will no longer be tax-deductible. [Kris Maher, Ellen E. Schultz and Bob Tita, *Deere, Caterpillar: Health-Care Law to Raise Expenses,* WSJ.com (Mar. 26, 2010)]

In 2017, eligible employers can be reimbursed 28% of prescription drug expenses in the range of $400–$8,250 per retiree, making the theoretical maximum subsidy per retiree $2,198. [Xerox FYI, *CMS Releases 2017 Medicare Part D Benefit Parameters and Proposes Lower Payments to EGWPs,* <https://hrlaws.services.xerox.com/wp-content/uploads/sites/2/2016/03/hrc_fyi_2016-03-22.pdf> (Mar. 22, 2016) (last accessed Aug. 8, 2016)]

[C]   Accounting Issues Under MPDIMA

As noted above, PPACA removes the corporate tax deduction, as of 2013, for the retiree health benefit prescription drug subsidy. David Zion, a Credit Suisse analyst, said that the S&P 500 companies will suffer a $4.5 billion loss in first quarter earnings. Large companies said that the loss of this deduction would have a severe negative impact on their earnings. Some of them took a charge against earnings in 2009 to reflect the unavailability of this tax deduction in the future. John Deere & Co. took a $150 million one time charge because of the loss of deduction; Caterpillar Inc. took a $100 million charge (about 40,000 retirees receive drug benefits from the company), and AK Steel took $31 million. The companies say they need the charge now to reflect future tax deductions that will not be available. [Kris Maher, Ellen E. Schultz and Bob Tita, *Deere, Caterpillar: Health-Care Law to Raise Expenses*, WSJ.com (Mar. 26, 2010)]

[D]   *Erie* Issues

The Third Circuit in *Erie County Retirees Ass'n v. County of Erie* [220 F.3d 193 (3d Cir. 2000)] ruled that the ADEA applies to retiree benefits, including health benefits. Therefore in this reading, an employer violates the ADEA by offering Medicare-eligible retirees health benefits that are inferior to those offered to employees who are not yet eligible for Medicare, unless the employer can demonstrate that it incurred equal costs or provided equal benefits for both retiree groups. On April 16, 2001, when the case was remanded to the lower court, the Western District of Pennsylvania decided that the plan did not satisfy the equal cost/equal benefit test. [*Erie Cnty.*, 140 F. Supp. 2d 466 (W.D. Pa. 2001)]

Although at first the EEOC adopted the Third Circuit's position, in July, 2003, the EEOC proposed "anti-Erie" regulations allowing employers to reduce or eliminate retiree health benefits when a retiree becomes eligible for Medicare. [68 Fed. Reg. 41542 (July 14, 2003), adding 29 C.F.R. § 1625.32]

The EEOC proposal soon became the subject of litigation. American Association of Retired Persons (AARP) sued the EEOC, and the Eastern District of Pennsylvania permanently enjoined implementation of the regulations in March 2005, holding that the EEOC's rule was not entitled to deference because the EEOC violated the plain language and Congressional intent of the ADEA.

Then Judge Brody reversed her earlier decision, in compliance with a Supreme Court ruling, in an unrelated case, that federal administrative agencies' regulations are entitled to a high degree of deference. In June 2007, the Third Circuit affirmed the District Court's change of policy, and ruled that the EEOC had the power to enact the regulation permitting reduction of retiree health benefits for Medicare-eligible retirees, under the section of the ADEA that allows the EEOC to grant exemptions from ADEA requirements. [*AARP v. EEOC*, 489 F.3d 558 (3d Cir. 2007)] In August 2007, the Third Circuit announced its refusal to review its ruling, [Jerry Geisel, *Review of Retiree Health Care Bias Ruling Denied*, Business Insurance (Aug. 22, 2007) (benefitslink.com)] and in March 2008, the Supreme Court refused to hear an appeal of the Third Circuit decision. [*AARP v. EEOC*, 128 S. Ct. 1733, *appeal dismissed* (Mar. 24, 2008)]

In December 2007, the EEOC issued a final rule, permitting coordination of retiree health benefits with Medicare. However, the rule affects only the ADEA, not other issues (such as the status of Medicare as secondary payor for Medicare beneficiaries who continue to be employed). [EEOC Final Rule, 72 Fed. Reg. 72938 (Dec. 26, 2007)]

A group of people who retired from working for a county, then were subsequently rehired, sued under the Age Discrimination in Employment Act (ADEA) and the equal protection clause of the Fourteenth Amendment, after the county stopped paying for their Medicare supplement (Medigap) insurance. The insurer said that the people who were rehired were not eligible for Medigap insurance, so the plan would lose its federal exemption if they remained in the plan. That would lead to even higher insurance costs for the already cash-strapped county. The county decided to fire the rehired retirees. The Seventh Circuit, noting that retiree-only plans are exempt from many HIPAA and PPACA requirements, ruled for the county. The Seventh Circuit held that the ADEA case failed because the plaintiffs did not show that they were treated worse than comparable younger workers, and they did not demonstrate disparate impact from any facially neutral employment practice. The Fourteenth Amendment case failed because their age was not the cause of their termination: the employer had a rational financial reason for firing them, to prevent adverse financial impact from higher insurance premiums. [*Carson v. Lake Cnty., Ind.*, No. 16-3665 (7th Cir. July 26, 2017); see Greg Grisham and Frank Day, *Seventh Circuit Holds Distressed County Did Not Violate ADEA When It Terminated Rehired Retirees to Preserve Supplemental Health Coverage and Avoid Additional Costs,* Fordharrison.com (July 26, 2017) (benefitslink.com)]

§ 9.11 SOP 92-6 REPORTS

The American Institute of Certified Public Accountants (AICPA) requires health and welfare benefits to prepare SOP 92-6 reports. SOP stands for "Statement of Position." [See the online newsletter by the Segal Company, *Timing Is Everything: Anticipating and Preparing for Higher Retiree Health Expenditures* (June 2001), <http://www.segalco.com/publications/newsletters/june01.pdf>]

The cash flow projections for the 92-6 project the amount of money needed every year to pay health costs. Although prefunding of welfare benefits is not required, it is often a good idea to create an asset pool (e.g., using a VEBA) to generate tax-free investment income that can be used for future costs.

The 92-6 report deals with issues such as the number of active employees, retirees, spouses, and surviving spouses covered by the plan; the cost of plan benefits; and projections of the cost of providing benefits in the future.

§ 9.12 IMPLICATIONS OF THE EMPLOYER'S BANKRUPTCY

Retiree benefits are often central to bankruptcy cases, because the high cost of providing such benefits adds to the financial stress on the company.

The basic rule, as created by *In re White Farm Equipment Co.* [788 F.2d 1186 (6th Cir. 1986)] is that vesting of welfare benefits is not automatic. It is a subject of bargaining, to be contracted for. In that case, the bankrupt company maintained a no-contributory, non-collectively bargained plan that provided retiree benefits. The plaintiffs were retirees who wanted a declaratory judgment (an official statement) that their claims were both valid under ERISA and allowable as bankruptcy claims.

They also asked the court to order the employer to reinstate the plan retroactively and to resume funding it. But the court found that employee benefits regulation is strictly a federal concern. Furthermore, the employer had reserved the power to terminate the plan and could do so at that time.

Ironically, retirees of bankrupt companies may have more protection for their benefits than retirees of solvent companies. Conversely, bankruptcy may solve some of a company's problems while creating others.

Under 11 U.S.C. § 1113, a company that has filed for Chapter 11 status can ask the bankruptcy court for the right to reject an existing collective bargaining agreement, including provisions covering retiree health benefits. The company must disclose the relevant information to the union and bargain in good faith about the termination.

If the company in Chapter 11 was already paying retiree benefits, the Retiree Benefits Bankruptcy Protection Act of 1988 (RBBPA) [Pub. L. No. 100-334] requires medical and disability payments to retirees to continue, on their original terms, either until the parties agree to modify the benefits or the bankruptcy court orders a modification.

The Act includes standards for bankruptcy courts to use in deciding whether a modification is appropriate. Any modifications proposed by the bankruptcy trustee must be equitable, not just to current and former employees, but also to the company's creditors. The retirees must not have had good cause to reject the proposals. The proposed modifications must be necessary to permit the employer to reorganize in bankruptcy on fair terms.

The RBBPA also requires the employer to negotiate with retiree representatives and to disclose the best available information about the employer's financial condition. Generally speaking, the union will serve as the representative of the retirees, unless the union refuses to do so or unless the court rules that a different representative should be appointed. Any party can petition the court to appoint a committee of retirees to represent benefit recipients who are not covered by a collective bargaining agreement.

The court considering the trustee's proposal does not have the power to order benefits lower than the proposed schedule. Once the parties reach an agreement, or once the court orders changes in the benefits, the authorized representative of the retirees can petition the court for an increase, which will be granted if it appears clearly just to do so.

> ■ **TIP:** The RBBPA's protection does not apply to retirees, their spouses, or dependents if the retiree's gross income was $250,000 or more in the year before the employer's bankruptcy petition. The only exception is retirees who can prove they are unable to get comparable individual health care coverage. Nor does the RBBPA require bankrupt employers to maintain retiree health benefits that were provided by the union, not the employer, prior to the bankruptcy.

Congress returned to the subject of protection of retiree health benefits when the employer files for bankruptcy protection in the 2005 statute, the Bankruptcy Abuse Prevention and Consumer Protection Act (Pub. L. No. 109-8). Section 1403 of this statute amends Bankruptcy Code § 1114. If the corporation, at a time it was insolvent, modified retiree benefits during the 180-day period before the bankruptcy filing, then any party in interest has the right to move for a court hearing. After the hearing, the bankruptcy court is required to order reinstatement of the provisions that were altered—unless the court finds that the balance of the equities clearly favors the modification. That is, if the modification is challenged, it is up to the employer to prove that the modification is fair; the opponents of the change don't have to prove its unfairness.

Under Bankruptcy Code § 1114, first the debtor must try to negotiate or get an agreement to modify the benefits from a union or a court-appointed committee representing the retirees. All affected parties must be treated fairly and equally. The debtor must propose only modifications that are necessary to permit its reorganization. The debtor must release relevant information to the representatives of the retirees, and must bargain with them in good faith.

The bankruptcy judge allowed a coal company in liquidation to reject two CBAs and terminate its retiree benefit obligations in order to assist in pending sale of the mining operations to a coalition of lenders that agreed to forgive $1.25 billion in debt and pay $5.4 million in cash. Walter Energy owes benefits to over 3,100 union retirees and spouses, with almost $580 million in unfunded liabilities. The sale is contingent on court approval of rejection of CBAs. The buyers refused to take over the plan; the PBGC announced that it would assume responsibility on January 1, 2016. [*In re Walter Energy Inc.*, No. 15-02741 (Bankr. N.D. Ala. Dec. 28, 2015)]

Certain retirees of bankrupt companies have or have had access to the Health Coverage Tax Credit (HCTC), which paid. 72.5% of health insurance premiums for retirees after a PBGC takeover of their pension plan. Those eligible were employees aged 55 to 64, enrolled in a qualified health plan for which they paid more than 50% of the cost. [IRS, *Health Coverage Tax Credit*, available at <https://www.irs.gov/credits-deductions/individuals/hctc> (updated Feb. 1, 2017) (last accessed Mar. 30, 2017)]

The HCTC expired at the end of 2014, but was reinstated, for all eligibility coverage months that begin before January 1, 2020, by the Trade Preferences Extension Act. [Trade Preferences Extension Act of 2015, Pub. L. No. 114-27; see Elizabeth Vollmar, *New Trade Bill Escalates ACA Reporting Penalties, Resuscitates Health Coverage Tax Credit*, Lockton (July 2015) (benefitslink.com)]

In 2007, the Supreme Court ruled that a bankrupt company does not have a fiduciary duty to consider merging its pension plan into a multi-employer plan. It is not a violation of ERISA to shut down the plan using a standard termination and to purchase annuities to satisfy payment obligations. [*Beck v. PACE Int'l Union*, 551 U.S. 96 (2007)]

In mid-2015, the Sixth Circuit held that GM was not required to contribute $450 million to fund retiree health benefits for United Auto Workers (UAW) members. The court said that the latest UAW contract extinguished the obligation to contribute. After an earlier suit to recover retiree health benefits and a bankruptcy reorganization, GM agreed to make a one-time $450 million contribution to the trust. GM made a Chapter 11 filing and sold all its assets and liabilities to "New GM." New GM entered into a settlement with the UAW but the settlement did not refer to the $450 million amount. The UAW tried to collect the money; GM said that it was not obligated to pay. The Sixth Circuit held in mid-2015 that, although the payment obligation survived the reorganization (because the purchase agreement also transmitted all liabilities under the CBA with the UAW), New GM did not have to make the payment because the subsequent settlement covered all obligations. [*Int'l Union United Auto., Aerospace & Agric. Implement Workers of Am. v. Gen. Motors, LLC*, 2015 WL 223950 (6th Cir. May 14, 2015)]

A company purchased another company under an asset purchase agreement that included a promise of retiree health benefits for the employees of the acquired company. The benefit could not be reduced or premiums increased without the written consent of the seller—who refused to consent. The purchaser company reorganized in bankruptcy, leading to the rejection of the asset purchase agreement. The purchaser company said that the agreement was no longer in force, so retirees' health premiums could be increased substantially. The retirees sued alleging that the asset purchase agreement amended the retiree health plan and the amendment remained valid after the bankruptcy. The Fifth Circuit held that the asset purchase agreement amended the plan, because any writing that follows certain formalities can amend an ERISA plan. The plan survived bankruptcy, and its terms could only be changed with the consent of the seller company. [*Evans v. Sterling Chems., Inc.*, 660 F.3d 862 (5th Cir. 2011)]

§ 9.13 401(h) PLANS

[A] Basic Principles

The basic principle is that assets must remain within a qualified pension plan until they are distributed to participants or beneficiaries. However, the Code permits transfers of certain assets of overfunded plans to special funds known as 401(h) plans that are segregated to provide retiree health benefits.

A 401(h) plan is a pension or annuity plan that also provides incidental health benefits for retirees: benefits for sickness, accident, hospitalization, or medical expenses. The health-type benefits must be subordinate to the plan's main business of offering retirement benefits. The incidental (insurance and health) benefits must not cost more than 25% of the employer's total contributions to a defined benefit plan.

An employer that maintains a 401(h) plan must maintain separate accounts for retiree health benefits and pension benefits. The transfers are not treated as reversions to the employer, so the § 4980 excise tax is not imposed. The employer must make reasonable and ascertainable contributions to fund the retiree health benefits. These contributions must be distinct from the contributions to fund pension benefits. At first, Code § 420(b)(5) allowed one transfer a year to a 401(h) account for tax years beginning between January 1, 1991–December 31, 2005; this was extended until December 31, 2013 by the Pension Funding Equity Act of 2004, Pub. L. No. 108-218.

Before making a transfer to a 401(h) plan, the plan administrator must give the DOL at least 60 days' notice, and must also notify participants, beneficiaries and any union representing the participants.

The American Jobs Creation Act of 2004 (AJCA) amends I.R.C. § 420, so that, for tax years after the date of the AJCA's enactment, the determination of whether a 401(h) plan satisfies the minimum cost requirements during the five years after a transfer of pension assets permits the employer to reduce costs only as much as they would have been reduced if the employer had used the maximum amount permitted under current Regulations. In effect, overall benefit costs for all retirees can be cut by the same amount that would have been saved by reducing the number of retirees. [Ellen E. Schultz, *More Retirees May See Health Cuts*, Wall St. J., Oct. 14, 2004, at A5]

The Pension Protection Act of 2006, Pub. L. No. 109-280, permits a plan whose assets are at least 120% of current liability to transfer at least two years' worth of estimated retiree health costs to the 401(h) plan. However, for the year of the transfer, the employer must either make plan contributions sufficient to keep the plan funded at the 120% level, or must recoup money from the 401(h) plan until the 120% level is reached. Transfers to fund the expected cost of retiree health benefits that must be paid in the future under Collective Bargaining Agreements are also permitted, as long the employer used at least 5% of its 2005 gross receipts to provide retiree health benefits.

[PBGC Proposed Rules, *Pension Protection Act of 2006; Conforming Amendments; Reportable Events and Certain Other Notification Requirements*, RIN 1212-AB06 74 Fed. Reg. 61248 (Nov. 23, 2009)]

The Moving Ahead for Progress in the 21st Century Act (MAP-21; Pub. L. No. 112-141) extends the authorization of 401(h) plans, which was supposed to expire in 2013, until December 31, 2021. Plans that achieve more than 125% of their funding target and target normal cost are allowed to transfer excess funds to a 401(h) plan covering either retiree health benefits or retiree group-term life insurance (generally limited to $50,000 per person). The provision for life insurance benefits is added by MAP-21. Life insurance assets must be kept in a separate account within the plan, separate both from the retiree medical account and from the defined benefit plan. A further extension, until 2025, was provided by the 2015 interim highway funding bill, HR 3038 (signed July 31, 2015). [Pensions & Investments, *Use of Excess DB Plan Assets for Health Care Extended to 2025* (July 31, 2015) (benefitslink.com)]

[B] Final Regulations

Effective June 19, 2001, the IRS issued final regulations on the I.R.C. § 420 minimum cost requirements. [T.D. 8948, R.I.N. 1545-AY43] An employer that significantly reduces its retiree health coverage during a cost maintenance period does not satisfy the I.R.C. § 420(c)(3) minimum cost requirement. The Uruguay Round Agreements Act of 1994 [Pub. L. No. 103-465] shifted the focus in regulating 401(h) plans from health costs to health benefits, allowing the employer to take into account cost savings recognized in managing retiree health benefit plans, as long as the employer keeps up substantially the same level of coverage for the four years after the transfer as for the year of the transfer itself and the year before the year of the transfer.

PART III

PENSION PLAN ADMINISTRATION

CHAPTER 10

ADOPTING AND ADMINISTERING A PLAN

§ 10.01 INTRODUCTION

The process of creating a plan and getting it approved by the IRS and Department of Labor is exacting. Many alternatives are permitted, and choosing one of them requires projections about the future of the business, the future of the workforce, trends in the economy as a whole, and the laws, court decisions, and regulations that will come into effect in the future. For plans that are subject to the Employment Retirement Income Security Act (ERISA) Title I, the Department of Labor must be notified. The IRS does not have to be notified of the intention to adopt a qualified plan, unless and until a determination letter is sought. The employees must always be notified of the adoption of a plan.

Once the plan is in operation, its activities are subject to regulation both on the ERISA and on the tax front. See § 10.02 below: as the IRS reduces the availability of determination letters for ongoing plans, sponsors face greater uncertainty as to whether their plans remain compliant.

An ERISA employee benefit plan requires several elements. At a minimum, there must be an intended benefit, an intended beneficiary or group of beneficiaries, a source of financing, a procedure for claiming benefits, and an ongoing administrative scheme.

Plan administration is difficult, painstaking, and mistakes can incur heavy penalties. For these and other reasons, it is common for tasks to be delegated to service providers. Because the term "third-party administrator" (TPA) does not have a uniform definition, it is difficult to estimate how many TPAs there are. An estimate from early 2012 is that about half of all workers covered by private industry plans are covered by plans with some degree of TPA involvement in administration, although some TPAs carry out quite sophisticated tasks, whereas others just process clerical transactions. [Fred Hunt, *Numbers: How Many TPAs Are There? Explanation and Legal Liability Factors*, Society of Professional Benefit Administrators (Jan. 2012) (benefitslink.com)]

The IRS introduced a streamlined process for validating rollovers, to encourage plans to accept rollovers from other qualified plans or from IRAs. A safe harbor is available, freeing plan administrators from the need to obtain proof of the other plan's qualified status. Because not all distributions can be rolled over (rollovers of hardship withdrawals are forbidden), the plan administrator must determine that the contribution includes only valid rollover distributions from an eligible plan. The safe harbor protects plans that erroneously accept what they reasonably believed to be eligible distributions. Once the error is discovered, the invalid amounts and their earnings must be returned to the employee within a reasonable time. Plan administrators are permitted to rely on the transferor plan's validity if the transferor plan provides a copy of its Form 5500 and makes the check payable to the transferee plan. However, the administrator must search the <http://www.efast.dol.gov> database to make sure that Form 5500, Line 8a, Code 3C [plan that is not intended to be qualified] is not checked. Administrators can rely on checks from an IRA if the employee certifies that the rollover does not include any after-tax amounts, and the employee will not reach age 70½ by the end of the year (i.e., a required minimum distribution does not have be taken). [Eugene S. Griggs, *Accepting Rollover Contributions Now Easier—and Less Risky—for Retirement Plans*, Poyner Spruill LLP (Aug. 7, 2014) (benefitslink .com)]

Rules adopted since 2012 make sweeping changes in the Pension Benefit Guarantee Corporation (PBGC) reporting obligations; overall, the number of situations requiring reporting has decreased, and the reporting process itself is streamlined.

See Accounting Standards Update No. 2017-07, Topic 15, *Improving the Presentation of Net Periodic Pension Cost and Net Periodic Postretirement Benefit Cost* for Financial Accounting Standards Board's (FASB's) requirements for improving reporting of defined benefit plan information in the employer's financial statements. [Kenneth Tysiac, *FASB Changes Presentation of Defined Benefit Costs,* journalofaccountancy.com (Mar. 2017) (benefitslink.com)]

[A] Plan Expenses

Running a qualified plan is a difficult business involving the input of many people, including professional advisors. Not all expenses of administration can be paid from the assets of an employee benefit plan. The decision to use plan assets to pay expenses if a fiduciary decision, subject to ERISA fiduciary enforcement.

As long as the plan document allows, or at least does not prohibit, the use of plan assets for this purpose, ERISA allows payment of reasonable administrative expenses. (If the plan document is silent, expenses can be paid by the plan unless the document requires the employer to pay the expenses.) If the employer has retained the right to amend the plan, a prospective amendment can be made to allow payment of expenses from plan assets.

Individual account plans can set out a method for allocating the expenses paid by the plan to participants' accounts. Any allocation method described by the plan is a settler decision, and plan fiduciaries must abide by it. If the plan is silent or unclear, the fiduciaries must select a reasonable method of allocation.

Because businesses are not required to have pension or benefit plans at all, ERISA permits (within limits) the plan to be established, amended, or terminated as the sponsor wishes. Such activities are settlor functions. However, if the employer administers the plan, it acts as a fiduciary. Although settlor decisions are not subject to fiduciary standards, expenses for settlor activities must be paid by the employer—and plan assets cannot be used for this purpose.

Settlor functions include setting up, amending, and terminating a plan, so it is improper for the plan to pay for, for instance, plan design studies, drafting of discretionary plan amendments, determining if the employer satisfies financial accounting standards, and negotiating with a union about proposed plan amendments.

If the plan pays legal expenses, the person who receives the advice will probably find it impossible to deny that the advice was received in a fiduciary capacity—which could make lawyer-client privilege unavailable.

Plan-wide basic administrative services can be paid from the assets of an ERISA plan, because they are fiduciary rather than settlor expenses. Expenses that probably can properly be paid from plan assets include:

- Providing required disclosures to participants, including Summary Plan Descriptions (SPDs), Summary Annual Reports (SARs), required benefit statements, and complying with disclosure requests from participants,

- Communicating with participants about issues such as benefit windows. (Allocation is required if the communication relates to more than one plan, or combines plan and non-plan information),

- Making calculations to implement a plan merger or spin-off,

- Maintaining tax-qualified status (applying for a determination letter; performing nondiscrimination testing; drafting plan amendments needed to comply with ERISA or Internal Revenue Code changes),

- TPA expenses,

- PBGC premiums,

- ERISA bond,

- Fiduciaries liability insurance for the fiduciaries of the plan—but only if the policy gives the insurer recourse against the fiduciary for losses due to breach of fiduciary obligations,

- Making legally required reports, such as Form 5500,

- Enrollment and claims processing,

- Management fees and sales charges for the plan's investments,

- Recordkeeping, including preparing audited financial statements,

- Investment management and advice.

The plan can pay the cost of drafting any legally required amendment, but the general rule is that the employer must pay for drafting discretionary amendments, including amendments that relieve the employer of the obligation to pay plan expenses.

Sanctions and penalties can be paid out of plan assets if they were imposed on the plan—but not if they were imposed on a plan administrator in his personal capacity. Sanctions for late payment of PBGC premiums can be paid from plan assets (as long as the plan is not involved in a distress or involuntary termination)—but correction costs under the Voluntary Fiduciary Correction Program cannot be. [Andree M. St. Martin and Jennifer E. Eller, *Paying Employee*

Benefit Plan Expenses Chart, Practical Law Co. (undated) (benefitslink.com) (a chart giving the source for the treatment of various items)]

§ 10.02 DETERMINATION LETTERS

A "qualified plan" (i.e., one that is qualified under the various tax rules for plans) receives many tax advantages. Employees are not taxed on contributions to the plan, or the appreciation in value of the contributions, until the benefits are distributed. The employer is entitled to a tax deduction for various amounts spent on the plan. However, qualified plans are also subject to many stringent requirements (about eligibility, vesting, and nondiscrimination, for example), and the rules change frequently, requiring formal plan amendments as well as changes in the way plans are managed. There are major negative consequences, including tax liability and tax penalties, if a plan is disqualified.

Traditionally, the IRS issued "determination letters" stating that a proposed plan was a qualified plan. For plans operated through plan trusts, the determination letter also states that the plan trust is qualified. A plan that has obtained a determination letter and is amended on a timely basis to conform to changes in the law will probably be able to defend itself against an IRS attempt to retroactively disqualify the plan. After obtaining the initial determination letter, plans had to apply for renewed determination letters every few years, on a schedule determined by the plan's tax identification number.

Plans can be categorized as Master & Prototype and volume submitter plans, and individually designed plans (created for a particular employer's needs). Master & Prototype plans are published by the IRS, offering guidance about compliance requirements. Volume submitter plans are drafted by financial service providers, which are responsible for getting IRS approval of the plan and amending it to reflect changes in the law. Master & Prototype and volume submitter plans are usually reviewed by the IRS once every six years. Individually designed plans had a five-year remedial amendment cycle, where one-fifth of the plans applied for determination letters in each year, based on the last digit of the company's employer ID number (EIN). Plans whose EINs end in 1 or 6 are in Cycle A, EINs ending in 2 or 7 are in Cycle B, 3 or 8 in Cycle C, 4 or 9 in Cycle D, and 5 or 10 in Cycle E. See § 10.03 below for 2017 changes.

When defined benefit plans apply for determination letters, they must indicate if the plan has maintained a Normal Retirement Act (NRA) lower than age 62 at any time since May 22, 2007. The IRS will not issue private letter rulings on the acceptability of NRAs lower than 62. [See Julie Koos, *Pension Plan Sponsors Must Justify the Reasonableness of Normal Retirement Ages Under Age 62*, Prudential Compliance Advisory (Feb. 2015) (benefitslink.com)]

In mid-2016, the IRS announced that the cover letter or an attachment to the application for a determination letter for a defined benefit plan must state whether the plan includes lump-sum risk transfer language (i.e., if the plan can reduce its liabilities by arranging for an insurance company to pay annuities to plan participants). If so, the applicant must state whether the plan complies with Notice 2015-49, 2015-30 I.R.B. 79. If the plan includes risk transfer language but does not comply with that Notice, then the IRS will not grant a determination letter until the risk transfer language is removed. For all other defined benefit plans, the determination letter will include a caveat that the plan does not rely on any risk transfer language that has obtained IRS approval. [IRS.gov, *New Process for Defined Benefit Determination Letter Applications* (June 29, 2016) (benefitslink .com)]

The previous practice was that, every year, the IRS published a cumulative list of items that it considers when reviewing documents for individually designed plans; these items often reflect new developments in the law, such as new federal statutes offering relief to plan sponsors, or major Supreme Court decisions such as the ones recognizing same-sex marriage. The IRS adopted a major policy change in 2015. It announced that, to conserve its limited resources, it would eliminate the five-year determination letter cycle for individualized plans. Effective January 1, 2017, individually designed plans will only be reviewed when they initially qualify and then when they terminate. Off-cycle applications (i.e., those not made at the time required for all the plans in the same cycle) will no longer be accepted, as of July 21, 2015.

The new rules are effective January 1, 2017. To the extent that determination letters will still be issued, and what their significance is, see IRS Publication 794, *Favorable Determination Letter* (Nov. 2016), available at <www.irs.gov/ pub/irs-pdf/p794.pdf>.

The IRS will still audit plans for compliance, so plans will have to undertake greater due diligence to make sure that they keep up with changes in the law, because the security of having a determination letter will no longer be available. This is particularly bothersome for mergers and acquisitions, because the lack of a determination letter requires the buyer to assume additional risks about tax qualification, and it becomes more likely that the seller could violate representations and warranties that the plan is tax-compliant. [Announcement 2015-19, 2015-32 I.R.B.154]

In 2016, the IRS issued several guidance documents about the transition to the system in which determination letters are the exception rather than the rule. Because the five-year cycle has been eliminated, determination letters no longer have an expiration date. An update about the process of issuing determination letters appears in Rev. Proc. 2016-6, 2016-1 I.R.B. 200. The schedule of user fees for 2016 appears in Rev. Proc. 2016-8, 2016-1 I.R.B. 243. Rev. Proc. 2016-37, 2016-29 I.R.B 136, provides further details.

As of January 1, 2017, an individually designed plan can get a determination letter upon initial qualification or at termination; otherwise, determination letters will be issued only in exceptional circumstances. The IRS will publish a list of required amendments each year. Generally, the amendments must be made by the end of the second calendar year after the year in which the list was published. The IRS said that items would not be placed on the list unless IRS guidance was available on the issue. The IRS said that it would consult employee plan stakeholders about what constitutes an issue requiring clarification. [Rebecca Moore, *IRS Officially Ends Determination Letter Program*, plansponsor.com (June 30, 2016); Raymond P. Turner, *Determination Letter Rationing: IRS Reveals the Brave New World*, Jackson Lewis PC (July 10, 2016), available at Lexology.com]

Rev. Proc. 2016-37 says that the deadline for amendments to conform to the list is generally last day of the second plan year after the year in which the item first appeared on the list (although the list itself can set a different deadline).

Notice 2016-80, 2016-52 I.R.B. 918, is the IRS's first Required Amendments List, of statutory and administrative changes in the requirements for plan qualification. There is only one item on this initial list: restrictions on accelerated distributions from underfunded collectively bargained single-employer defined benefit plans of bankrupt employers. Terminating plans have to be amended for all changes in law as of time of term, whether or not the item is on the Required Amendments List. Generally, IRS will only put items on the Required Amendments List after issuing regulations and/or model amendments on the changes. [Haynes and Boone LLP, *IRS Publishes First Required Amendments List* (Dec. 30, 2016), available at Lexology.com]. *See also* Notice 2017-37, 2017-29 I.R.B. 92, for the 2017 cumulative list of changes for pre-approved defined contribution plans.

The IRS will also publish an Operational Compliance List of changes in the law that plans have to comply with before the deadline for amending the plan. The IRS will no longer require interim amendments to conform to the items on the list. Discretionary amendments (such as design changes, or other things not required by changes in the law) must be adopted by the end of the year in which the plan amendment takes effect. A plan that already has a determination letter can continue to rely on it with respect to legal provisions that are not subsequently changed. [Lois Wagman Colbert et. al., *IRS Provides Guidance for the Post-Determination Letter Era*, Kilpatrick Townsend (Oct. 19, 2016), available at Lexology.com]

The initial Operational Compliance List was published on February 27, 2017. The IRS warned that plans must satisfy all relevant qualifications even if they are not on the list. The 2017 document covers proposed regulations about using forfeitures to fund matching contributions and qualified nonelective contributions in defined contribution plans; extension of temporary nondiscrimination relief for frozen defined benefit plans; partial distribution options for defined benefit plans; and final regulations on the market rate of return requirements for hybrid plans, including cash balance plans. [Sheila Ninneman, *The 2017 Operational Compliance List*, findleydavies.com (Mar. 15, 2017) (benefitslink.com)]

Termination of an individually designed plan generally ends its remedial amendment period, so retroactive remedial plan amendments, or other required amendments must be adopted in connection with the termination even if they do not appear on the Required Amendments List. The sponsor should include the amendments with the Form 5310 filing. [Katuri Kaye, *Internal Revenue Service Provides Guidance on the Scope of the New Determination Letter Program for Individually Designed Plans*, Truckerhuss.com (Aug. 4, 2016) (benefitslink .com)]

Most plans use preapproved documents, but this is not an option for every plan. Historically, cash balance plans and Employee Stock Ownership Plans (ESOPs) were not allowed to use preapproved plans, but Rev. Proc. 2015-36, 2015-27 I.R.B. 20 allows some cash balance plans and ESOPs to use prototype or volume submitter plans, starting on February 1, 2017. The IRS has also released sample language that drafters of these plans can use. The IRS's intention was to reduce its own review costs, while also making it less expensive to adopt an ESOP because custom documents would no longer be required. A preapproved ESOP cannot have a money purchase feature, but it can be a "KSOP" that includes a 401(k) feature. To adopt a preapproved ESOP, a plan must complete Form 8905, Certification of Intent to Adopt a Preapproved Plan, showing intent to transition from an individually designed to a preapproved plan. However, union plans and Taft-Hartley multi-employer plans, target benefit plans, plans with 401(h) retiree health accounts, variable annuity plans, and defined benefits plans whose benefit accrual is based on the rate of return of identified assets cannot use preapproved plans. [Rebecca Moore, *IRS Expands Pre-Approved Plans Program*, plansponsor.com (June 9, 2015); Jason C. Ray, *IRS: Prototype ESOP Documents Now Allowed*, Morgan Lewis & Bockius LLP (Oct. 29, 2015), available at Lexology.com]

§ 10.03 PROTOTYPE AND MASTER PLANS

Until 2017 there were two categories of preapproved plans: master and prototype (M&P) and Volume Submitter (VS). An M&P plan consists of a basic plan document with mandatory provisions, an adoption agreement (which can include optional provisions chosen by the employer) and a trust or custodial account to fund the plan. A prototype plan has a separate funding mechanism for each employer; a master plan has a single funding mechanism (such as a trust) that covers multiple employers.

The IRS defines a "mass submitter" of an M&P plan as a business that submits applications for opinion letters for at least 30 unrelated sponsors that have adopted the plan word-for-word. An M&P sponsor is a business that has, as clients, at least 15 employers that the sponsor reasonably expects to adopt the plan drafted by the sponsor. A VS submits applications on behalf of at least 30 unrelated practitioners who sponsor the same plan and have at least 15 clients apiece who will adopt the specimen plan or one that is substantially similar to it. [IRS, *Types of Pre-Approved Retirement Plans*, <https://www.irs.gov/Retirement-Plans/Types-of-Pre-Approved-Retirement-Plans> (Oct. 6, 2016) (last accessed Feb. 13, 2017)]

Rev. Proc. 2017-41, 2017-29 I.R.B. 92 creates a new category of pre-approved (PA) plans, including both master and prototype and volume submitter plans. There are two kinds of PA plans: standardized and non-standardized, and either defined benefit or defined contribution plans can use either one. Adopting a standardized plan requires using the terms and language prescribed by the IRS without modifications. Employers are permitted some flexibility in how they draft non-standardized plans, especially with respect to defining compensation and adopting administrative and safe harbor provisions. PA plans are subject to a six-year remedial amendment period: a PA plan that has an opinion letter is considered qualified between February 1, 2017 and January 31, 2013. To be considered "on cycle," defined contribution sponsors plans must apply for determination letters between October 2, 2017 and October 1, 2018. Applications can be made at other times, but "off cycle" applications are subject to limitations. The next cycle for defined benefit PA plans begins February 1, 2019 and ends January 31, 2025. The IRS wants employers with individually designed plans to convert them to PA plans, but acknowledges that this could be difficult in some cases. PA plans cannot be used for multi-employer plans, collectively bargained plans, some kinds of ESOPs, and some kinds of hybrid plans. [Rev. Proc. 2017-41, 2017-29 I.R.B. 92; see Susan E. Stoffer et. al., *IRS Reorganizes Pre-Approved Plan Opinion Letter Program*, Nelson Mullins Riley & Scarborough LLP (July 12, 2017), available at Lexology.com; Groom Law Group, *IRS Revamps Pre-Approved Qualified Plan Program* (July 27, 2017) (benefitslink.com)]

§ 10.04 ROUTINE TAX COMPLIANCE

[A] Necessary Forms

Day-to-day administration of a plan involves creation of tax records and submission of many forms to the IRS and state taxing authorities.

One of the most important forms is Form W-2, disclosing compensation paid to each individual employee. The form must be submitted to the IRS and also to the employee. The normal due date for employee W-2s is January 31 following the end of the year of employment. However, employees who leave during the year have a right to demand that they get a W-2 form within 30 days of the last paycheck (or of the request, if made at a later date). The employer can use IRS Form 8809 to request additional time to file W-2s.

One of the requirements of the health care reform bill, the Patient Protection Affordable Care Act (PPACA), is that employers provide information reporting on Form W-2 of the cost of health coverage provided by the employer. This amount is not taxable, but it is relevant to the determination of whether the employer provides adequate coverage, whether it is subject to penalties, and whether the employee is entitled to a subsidy if he or she obtains health insurance through an Exchange. [See § 18.19[K] for more discussion of these issues.]

Employers must report to the IRS about their compliance with the employer mandate ("pay or play" requirement; Code §§ 6055 and 6056). Notice 2015-87, 2015-52 I.R.B. 889 says that, for 2015, the penalty for failure to offer minimum essential coverage to all full-time employees is $2,080; the penalty for failure to offer minimum value, affordable coverage to an employee is $3,120. The 2016 amounts are $2,160 and $3,240 respectively; the 2017 amounts are $2,260 and $3,390. At press time, efforts were underway in Congress to repeal PPACA and replace it with a superior program or to repair the defects of PPACA, although over time, this effort became politically more complicated. [Lyndsey R. Barnett, *The IRS Finally Confirms Penalty Amounts for the Pay or Play Penalties for 2015 (and 2016)*, Graydon Head (Dec. 17, 2015), available at Lexology.com; Hinkle Law Firm LLP, *Affordable Care Act Compliance Update*, <http://www.hinklaw. com/alerts/affordable-care-act-compliance-update-employer-pay-or-play-penalties-and-affordability-percentages-both-increased-for-inflation-2/> (undated; last accessed Feb. 13, 2017)]

In 2015, Applicable Large Employers (ALEs) must offer PPACA-compliant coverage to 70% of full-time employees. In 2016 and later, they must cover 95% of full-time employees. (A company is an ALE if it has 50 or more employees who work 30 or more hours a week; hours for employees who work less than 30 hours a week are amalgamated to determine if the employer has the equivalent of 50 full-time employees.) ALEs must file an information return in 2016, reporting the health coverage offered to their employees in each month in 2015. ALE employers report both pay or play and individual mandate information on Forms 1094-C and 1095-C. Insurers and non-ALE self-insured employers use Forms 1094-B and 1095-B. Reporting of information to employees, Comprehensive Omnibus Budget Reconciliation Act (COBRA) beneficiaries, and retirees can be done on Forms 1095-B and 1095-C, but the employer can elect other formats for reporting.

The standard due date for these forms is the same as for Form W-2 and statements to employees can be provided with the W-2. Reports to employees are due January 31 after the year of the events; reports to the IRS are due February 28 (if filed on paper) or March 31 (if e-filed). [*Month by Month, Employers Must Track Employees in 2015 for Required Reporting Under Health Reform Rules*, Brown Todd (Jan. 15, 2015) (benefitslink.com); Jackson Lewis PC, *Health Care Reform: Employers Should Prepare Now for 2015 to Avoid Penalties* (Aug. 8, 2014) (benefitslink.com)]

In mid-2017, the IRS Office of Chief Counsel sent out several information letters to relieve some of the confusion about PPACA's future. On January 20, 2017, President Trump issued an Executive Order (EO) directing HHS and other federal agencies to provide relief from PPACA burdens until the statute can be repealed and replaced. The EO told the agencies to waive, defer, or grant exemptions from PPACA requirements that could be economically burdensome to employers. The IRS said that until Congress enacts new legislation, PPACA provisions such as the employer shared responsibility payment and individual mandate remain in effect—and so do the penalties for noncompliance unless an exemption applies. On July 28, 2017, the IRS released drafts of the 1094- and 1095-series forms to be used for 2017 reporting; they are substantially similar to the 2016 forms. [Information Letters 2017-0010, 2017-0013 (Apr. 14, 2017), available at <https://www.irs.gov/pub/irs-wd/17-0010> and <https://www.irs.gov/pub/irs-wd/17-0013.pdf>; see Burnhambenefits.com, *Pay or Play Mandates, Employer Reporting, and Health Insurance Fee* (Aug. 16, 2017) (benefitslink .com)]

The Trade Preferences Extension Act of 2015, Pub. L. No. 114-27, enacts heavy increases in penalties for failure to provide correct information returns. The penalty for failure to provide proper W-2, 1094-B, 1095-B, 1094-C, and 1095-C forms increases from $100 to $250 per return. The penalties are doubled if the failure involves both the payee statement (to employees) and the information return submitted to the IRS. There is a cap on the amount of penalties a company can be required to pay; this legislation doubles the cap, from $1.5 million to $3 million. But if the failure is caused by intentional disregard of the law, the cap does not apply, and there is no limit on the penalties. The penalty is $500, not $250, per return for intentional disregard. For the first year of PPACA filings, the IRS will waive penalties for employers who can show that they made a good-faith attempt to comply with the new, and confusing, requirements. [See Elizabeth Vollmar, *New Trade Bill Escalates ACA Reporting Penalties, Resuscitates Health Coverage Tax Credit*, Lockton (July 2015) (benefitslink.com)]

Penalties for failure to file returns or furnish statements were increased in late 2016, and can be as much as $260/violation, capped at $3,218,500 a year (or a lower maximum for small business). The penalty is lower if correction is made before August 1, and lowest of all if the failure is corrected within 30 days of the required filing deadline. [Rev. Proc. 2016-55, 2016-45 I.R.B. 707]

Other forms include:

- Form W-3: a transmittal form filed with the Social Security Administration consolidating all the W-2 and W-2P forms for the entire company. The regular due date for any year's W-3 is February 28 of the following year;

- Form W-4P: is used by employees to opt out of withholding or increase withholding on their pension and annuity payments. This form goes straight from employer to employee, no IRS filing is required;

- Forms 941/941E: these are the forms for quarterly returns of federal income tax. Form 941 is used if there are Federal Insurance Contributions Act (FICA) taxes withheld or paid, 941E otherwise. The due date is the end of the month after the close of the calendar quarter being reported on. However, some employers can file an annual Form 944 in lieu of quarterly 941s, if their annual employment tax liability, including income tax withholding, FICA, and Medicare tax, is under $1,000 for the calendar year: [T.D. 9566, 76 Fed. Reg. 77672 (Dec. 14, 2011)]

- Form 945: the report on withheld taxes that are not payroll taxes (e.g., withholding on retirement plan distributions);

- Form 1041: trust income tax return, required if the plan's trust becomes disqualified (or otherwise does not operate as a tax-exempt organization) and if it also has income equal to or greater than $600. The due date is the fifteenth day of the fourth month after the end of the trust's tax year;

- Form 1099-R: 1099-series forms are used to report miscellaneous sums that might otherwise escape the attention of the taxing authorities. The 1099-R is used to report lump sums and periodic distributions. The entire group of a company's transmittal forms requires its own transmittal form, Form 1096. The filing is due by February 28 each year for the preceding year;

■ **TIP:** Within two weeks of making a distribution, the plan administrator must provide each recipient with a written explanation of the tax consequences of taking a lump sum, including how to elect lump-sum tax treatment and how to roll over the sum to another qualified plan or to an Individual Retirement Arrangement (IRA).

- Form 5308: form filed in connection with a change in the tax year of a qualified plan or trust;

- Form 5330: excise tax form for failure to meet the minimum funding standard, or for receipt of an impermissible reversion of plan assets. Disqualified persons who engage in prohibited transactions are also required to file this form. There is no fixed due date: the timing depends on the nature of the transaction subject to excise tax. Form 5558 is used to request additional time to file this form;

- Form 8109: the quarterly estimated tax return when a plan trust has unrelated business taxable income (UBTI) [see I.R.C. § 512(a)(1)] from operation of an unrelated trade or business. UBTI is limited to business net income (after deducting the costs of generating the income). It does not include dividends, interest, annuities, loan fees, or royalties;

- Form 8928: used (starting with the 2010 plan year or taxable year) by employers to self-report and pay excise taxes for certain compliance failures of Employee Group Health Plans (EGHPs)—COBRA requirements (including the American Recovery and Reinvestment Act (ARRA)) premium subsidy, HIPAA rules, mental health parity, the Genetic Information Nondiscrimination Act, and failure to make comparable contributions for all employees if there is a Health Savings Account (HSA) or Medical Savings Account (MSA) plan. [74 Fed. Reg. 45994 (Sept. 8, 2009)]

- Form 8955-SSA, replacing Form 5500 SSA to report information about participants who had deferred vested benefits when they separated from a plan. Unless an extension is granted, Form 8955-SSA must be filed by the last day of the seventh month after the last day of the plan year: July 31 for a calendar-year plan. Form 8955-SSA is filed only with the IRS (the predecessor form reported to both the IRS and DOL). Therefore, some plans attempting to correct failure to file timely Form 5500 annual reports will have to file both with the IRS and with DOL—including retroactive filings going back to 2009. [Notice 2014-35, 2014-23 I.R.B. 1072] The IRS notes that there are four possible penalties that could be imposed in connection with Form 8955-SSA. Failure to file an annual registration statement for all required participants is subject to a penalty of $1 per person per day, capped at $5,000. Failure to file notification of a change in the status of the plan (e.g., termination of the plan; change in the identity or address of the plan administrator) is penalized by $1 per day up to $1,000. Willful failure to furnish the Form 8955-SSA statement to an affected participant, or willful provision of a false statement, is penalized by $50 per failure. Late filing (unless there is reasonable cause for lateness) is penalized at $25 per day of failure. [IRS, *Penalties Related to the Filing of Forms 8955-SSA*, available at <https://www.irs.gov/Retirement-Plans/Penalties-Related-to-the-Filing-of-Forms-8955-SSA> (July 5, 2016) (last accessed Feb. 13, 2017)]

In late 2015, DOL proposed regulations extending some of the PPACA procedural protections and safeguards in the claims process required of EGHPs to stand-alone disability benefit plans and pension plans that provide disability benefits (such as payment of all accrued benefits when a person becomes disabled). For example, people who make claims decisions must be independent; claimants are entitled to more disclosure about adverse benefit determinations, and are entitled to present evidence during the review process. The regulations had not been updated since 2001. However, compliance will not be required until after final regulations are issued. [80 Fed. Reg. 72014 (Nov. 18, 2015); see Towerswatson.com, *DOL Updating Employer Disability Benefit Claims and Appeals* (Jan. 7, 2016) (benefitslink.com)]

On December 8, 2015, the IRS announced Early Interaction Initiative, a program to notify employers that they might be behind in paying employment taxes or accounting for and remitting withheld trust fund taxes. The problem is that employers that fail to remit taxes on time generally use the money to satisfy immediate cash flow needs—but their financial situation continues to deteriorate, and the debt increases. The IRS program is intended to inform employers even before the due date of the Form 941 for the quarter. Although it is permissible to pay the taxes in a lump sum, the IRS tracks payment patterns to see if a company alters its previous pattern of monthly deposits. [IR-2015-16, *New Early Interaction Initiative Will Help Employers Stay Current with Their Payroll Taxes,* (Dec. 8, 2015, updated Nov. 2, 2016) (last accessed Feb. 13, 2017)]

The IRS's project of moving all business tax form filing online is well underway. (The next important planned step is the integration of federal and state tax filings through a coordinated electronic system.) (The TeleFile program, allowing telephone filing of many forms, was discontinued in mid-2005.)

Business taxpayers file taxes via the Electronic Federal Tax Payment System (EFTPS), a highly secure encrypted Website. [See <http://www.irs.gov/efile> and IRS Publications 4132, 966, 4169, 4321, 4130, 4276, and 4048.] For tax years ending on or after December 31, 2005, corporations with assets of $50 million or more that file at least 250 returns a year, including income and employment tax and information returns, are required to file their 1120 and 1120-S forms electronically. The next year, the electronic filing requirement is extended to corporations with assets of more than $10 million who file 250 returns a year. To file electronically, large and mid-size corporations must use the IRS e-file system Modernized e-File (MeF). W-2 forms also can be submitted electronically, although those forms must be filed with the Social Security Administration rather than the IRS.

In 2014, IRS regulations for filing certain plan statements, returns, and reports on magnetic media (e-filing and other permitted filing) were finalized, effective for plan years beginning on or after January 1, 2014, for filings whose deadline, not including extensions, occurs on or after July 31, 2015. For returns and reports required under Code §§ 6057–6059, the regulations apply for plan years beginning on or after January 1, 2015, whose deadline, not including extensions, is after December 31, 2015. Plan administrators who file at least 250 returns of all types per calendar year must submit the Form 5500 annual report and related documents electronically. As an alternative, they can use IRS-permitted magnetic media for statements and notifications required under Code § 6057. The Form 8955-SSA, reporting the plan's separated participants who have vested benefits, must be filed using the IRS's FIRE system. A one-participant plan that is eligible to file Form 5500-EZ can use EFAST2 without satisfying the requirements for filing attachments. The Treasury said that economic hardship waivers from the e-filing requirement will only be granted in exceptional cases. [<http://www.gpo.gov/fdsys/pkg/FR-2014-09-29/pdf/2014-23161.pdf>]

On the subject of routine compliance under non-routine circumstances, see Rev. Proc. 2005-27, 2005-20 I.R.B. 1050 for a list of 32 employee benefit issues that are affected automatically whenever the President declares a disaster.

A mid-2013 IRS phone forum described some factors triggering IRS audit of a retirement plan. Plans are at above-normal audit risk if they have many separated participants who are not 100% vested; if a high percentage of plan assets are described as "other" rather than discussed in detail; the income statement shows significant distributions; or a 401(k) plan or plan for a self-employed individual is top-heavy.

If the contributions to the plan reflect an incorrect amount of compensation, there will be an operational failure, because the operation of the plan will not conform to its terms. A plan is not required to use the same definition of compensation for all types of contributions. For example, discretionary contributions might be allocated based only on base salary, but salary deferral contributions could reflect all compensation, including bonuses and commissions. Compensation errors occur when a payroll processor or TPA does not know the plan's various definitions of compensation, or is not alerted to plan amendments, or if payroll systems are not updated.

The Employee Plans Compliance Resolution System (EPCRS); see IRS's summary at <http://www.irs.gov/Retirement-Plans/EPCRS-Overview> (updated Nov. 1, 2016) (last accessed Feb. 13, 2017) can be used to fix the mistakes, under either the self-correction program (SCP) or Voluntary Correction Program (VCP). Self-correction without IRS approval is permitted for insignificant errors, or for significant errors that are corrected within two years. However, a plan sponsor is only entitled to self-correct if it has implemented practices and procedures that promote overall tax-law compliance. EPCRS allows correction of qualification failures via SCP or VCP.

The VCP can be used to correct errors, with IRS approval. The VCP submission should explain the plan failure and the proposed correction, including the corrective contributions to be made, and the plan's proposal for improving administration to prevent future errors. The correction method should restore participants to the status they would have been in if there had been no error (for example, making larger contributions, or distributing excess amounts from the plan). If too much compensation was included in the calculations, the correction consists of distributing the excess elective deferrals and earnings to the affected participant, with excess discretionary contributions forfeited as required by the plan document. Forfeitures should either be reallocated to participants based on correct contributions, or transferred to an unallocated account that reduces future contributions.

Conversely, if the error was omitting some forms of compensation from elective deferrals, matches, or discretionary contributions, corrective contributions must be made for the affected participants. For missed salary deferrals, the amount of omitted compensation should be multiplied by the deferral percentage specified in the employee's salary reduction agreement. The missed deferral opportunity is equal to 50% of the omitted compensation. The missed deferral opportunity should be contributed to the employee's account, plus earnings up to the date of the corrective contribution. If discretionary contributions were made to participants for a plan year, the same percentage of omitted contribution should be contributed, plus earnings to the date of correction.

IRS published a new VCP Submission Kit in mid-2015, used to correct contribution failures for money-purchase and target benefit pension plans. If a sponsor did not make the contributions required by Code § 412 in a timely manner or did not operate the plan in accordance with written document, there has been an operational failure that can lead to disqualification. Master & Prototype or target benefit plan can correct under EPCRS by submitting to VCP. The kit includes a list of documents to submit, information for completing the forms, and instructions for calculating the fee. [<http://www.irs.gov/Retirement-Plans/VCP-Submission-Kit-Failure-to-Make-Timely-Required-Contributions-to-a-Money-Purchase-or-Target-Benefit-Plan> (updated Oct. 4, 2016) (last accessed Feb. 13, 2017)]

EPCRS previously relied on the determination letter program, so it has been amended to remove those references. SCP eligibility was contingent on having a favorable determination letter; that is still the case, but it is no longer necessary to have a current letter because the surviving determination letters no longer have an expiration date. Also note that, starting in 2017, the fees for VCP will be published in IRS's annual guidance on user fees, not as part of the annual EPCRS revenue procedure. [Rev. Proc. 2016-51, 2016-42 I.R.B. 465; see Lois Wagman Colbert et. al., *IRS Provides Guidance for the Post-Determination Letter Era,* Kilpatrick Townsend (Oct. 19, 2016), available at Lexology.com]

Audit CAP sanctions are no longer limited to a negotiated percentage of the maximum payment amount: the maximum payment amount is only one factor to be considered. Generally, Audit CAP sanctions will be at least as high as the VCP fees. [IRS.gov, *Updated Retirement Plan Correction Procedures* (Oct. 3, 2016) (benefitslink.com)]

For VCP fees for submissions made on or after January 1, 2017, see IRS.gov, *Voluntary Correction Program (VCP) Fees,* <https://www.irs.gov/retirement-plans/voluntary-correction-program-fees> (revised Jan. 12, 2017) (last accessed Feb. 13, 2017). The general fee is $500 if 20 or fewer participants were affected by the failure; $750 if 21–50 participants were affected; $1,500 if 51–100 were affected; $5,000 if 100–1,000 were; $10,000 if 1,001–10,000 were; and $15,000 if over 10,000 participants were affected. However, specific fees apply to certain categories of failures. If the only failure was late adoption of an interim or optional amendment, the fee is $375; the general fee is cut in half if a single failure to adopt amendments on time is submitted on Form 14568-B. Operational failures with respect to required minimum distributions are $500 if under 150 participants were affected, $1,500 if 151–300 participants were affected. (The general fee applies if more than 301 participants were affected by a required minimum distribution failure.) The fee may be waived for a terminating orphan plan that makes a written request for waiver in the VCP submission. Adjustments are made if there are multiple failures, but they are eligible for fee reduction. Fees must be paid in full with a check payable to the United States Treasury, accompanied by Form 8951, the User Fee Application for Voluntary Correction Program (VCP).

To be allowed to self-correct plan failures, the sponsor must maintain practices and procedures that are reasonably designed for Code compliance. Prior law said that this was true if excess annual additions were regularly corrected within 2½ months of the end of the limitation year. Rev. Proc. 2015-27 extends that to 9½ months after the end of the limitation year.

VCP is an IRS program; its DOL counterpart is the VFCP (Voluntary Fiduciary Correction Program). EBSA received 1,643 VFCP applications in 2014 and more than 24,000 annual reports were filed for correction of violations. [EBSA Fact Sheet, *EBSA Restores Over $599.7 Million to Employee Benefit Plans, Participants and Beneficiaries* (Jan. 13, 2015) (benefitslink.com). See <http://www. dol.gov/ebsa/
calculator/main.html> for a VFCP calculator (accessed Aug. 17, 2017)]

The DOL sent letters to plan sponsors whose annual returns reported failures to make timely 401(k) deposits. In this situation, the DOL recommends correcting the problem with a VFCP filing to reduce the risk of audit. Plans with fewer than 100 participants at the beginning of the plan year are entitled to a safe harbor if deposit occurs within seven business days of the time amounts are withheld from wages or received by the employer as voluntary after-tax contributions. Late transmittals are corrected by transferring funds from the employer's general assets to the plan trust as soon as possible after the error is detected—including interest on the late deposits. The best practice is to make the correction before filing Form 5500. Delinquent deposits create a § 4975 prohibited transaction, subject to excise taxes of at least 15% of the lost earnings associated with the late deposit. The employer becomes a disqualified person that is deemed to use the plan assets for its own business purposes. The excise tax is paid to the IRS on Form 5330, although sometimes VFCP will allow waiver of the excise tax. Making a VFCP submission assures the applicants that DOL will not recommend an audit for fiduciary breaches associated with the delinquent deposits. Normally, DOL must impose a civil penalty for fiduciary breach equal to 20% of the amount recovered in a suit or settlement—but this is waived if a voluntary report is made and VFCP is used for correction. Excise tax relief for this prohibited transaction is available if the delinquent deposits were made up within 180 calendar days of the payroll withholding date, and VFCP excise tax relief was not also obtained in the three years before the VFCP submission. [Susan Quintanar, *Late Deposit—A Timely Topic*, Trucker Huss (December 2015) (benefitslink.com)]

Nine schedules were published in January 2014 by the IRS, for submission of standardized corrections to plans under the VCP component of EPCRS. See the Form 14568 (January 2014) version. Forms 14568-A and -B are used to report failures to amend the plan on time. Forms -C and -D are used for corrections to SEPs, SARSEPs, and SIMPLE IRAs. Form 14568-E is used for plan loan failures in qualified plans; -F is used by an employer not entitled to maintain a 401(k) plan. Form 14568-G corrects failures to distribute elective deferrals that exceed the § 402(g) dollar limit, -H is for correction of failures to make timely Required Minimum Distributions. Form 14568-I is used for plan errors that can be corrected by amendment as described in Rev. Proc. 2013-12, Appendix B. [IRS Form 14568 series (Jan. 2014)]

> ■ **TIP:** The IRS processes VCP and determination letter applications separately, so overlapping documents should be filed in duplicate with each application. [Elizabeth Thomas Dold, *Plan Corrections Take on a Slightly New Look with Revenue Procedure 2013-12*, Journal of Pension Benefits (December 2013) (benefitslink.com)]

Plans can submit voluntary closing agreement requests to VCP, for issues where the Rev. Proc. 2013-12 version of EPCRS is unavailable. The IRS decides whether a closing agreement is appropriate. The sponsor submits a detailed letter explaining the problem, how it occurred, the number of employees and the amount of money involved, how the sponsor will correct the problem, and how the tax, interest, or penalties were calculated. Issues that can be resolved under VCP should be resolved that way; if a case has mixed issues, the IRS may accept a closing agreement, but the VCP-eligible issues will be resolved under Rev. Proc. 2013-12.

The request for a closing agreement will not be considered if the plan or sponsor is under investigation by the IRS or has an appeals or Tax Court matters pending. The IRS may refuse to enter into a closing agreement if the plan, its sponsor, or any other party to the closing agreement was a party to an abusive tax avoidance transaction. A closing agreement generally is not appropriate if there was a willful or intentional plan to evade or avoid taxes.

Plans subject to ERISA Title I should use DOL's VFCP before requesting a closing agreement from the IRS, and all actions described in the agreement must be completed before signing the agreement. Closing agreements cannot be used to address future events or seek guidance about retirement plan issues or actions. For the agreement to be worthwhile for the IRS, the sponsor should be prepared to show that it will document its tax liabilities; that the agreement is in the best interests of the IRS and the federal government in general; and if there was any violation or tax deficiency, it was unintentional.

The request for a closing agreement must be made by an authorized employee of the plan or its sponsor, or a representative who is authorized to sign Form 2848. The request is submitted to Internal Revenue Service TE/GE:EP:VC Group 7554: Request for Voluntary Closing Agreement. 9350 Flair Drive, 3rd Floor El Monte, CA 91731 [IRS, *Employee Plans Voluntary Closing Agreements*, <http://www.irs.gov/Retirement-Plans/Employee-Plans-Voluntary-Closing-Agreements> (updated Oct. 17, 2016) (last accessed Feb. 13, 2017)]

Previously, sponsors often used the IRS letter forwarding service to find payees of benefits. For requests postmarked on or after August 31, 2012, however, Rev. Proc. 2012-35, 2012-37 I.R.B. 341 announces that the IRS no longer considers finding missing persons a "humane purpose." Employers must therefore devise other means of finding the payees. The DOL's suggestions are Internet searches, credit reports, and commercial locater services. The Social Security Administration's forwarding service is still available, but at a cost of $25 per letter, whereas the IRS service was free for up to 50 participants. If the plan is terminating, it can use the PBGC's missing participants program, which requires the employer to submit the amount of the benefit to the PBGC, which looks for participants in connection with the termination. The Pension Protection Act mandated that the PBGC extend the program to non-defined benefit plans (e.g., 401(k)s) that terminate, but the PBGC never issued implementing regulations. [Rebecca Moore, *IRS Updates Compliance Resolution System*, plansponsor.com (Jan. 3, 2013)]

An "operational error" is a failure to comply with the terms of the plan. Often this can be corrected without IRS involvement and without penalties to the plan. The sponsor must put the plan and its participants in the position they would have been in if there had been no error. However, if correction requires a plan amendment, then it will probably be necessary to use EPCRS, and to file under the Voluntary Correction Program.

However, there are five situations under which a sponsor can use the Self-Correction Program (SCP) to adopt a retroactive corrective amendment without making a VCP filing. The first is making a hardship distribution from a plan lacking a hardship distribution option. The second is making a plan loan without an option. The third is allowing participation by an employee who has not yet satisfied eligibility requirements. The fourth is allocating a contribution to correct a violation of the compensation limit under § 409(e)(17), and the last is correcting a discrimination testing failure via a Qualified Nonelective Contribution (QNEC) that would not otherwise be available under the plan.

The plan must comply with the requirements of Code §§ 401(a), 410(b), and 411(d)(6). If the correction is a retroactive amendment to allow hardship distributions or loans, the best practice is to make sure that enough non-highly compensated employees (NHCEs) had access to them to satisfy the nondiscrimination rules. Amendments to change eligibility dates should also predominantly benefit NHCEs. [Raymond P. Turner, *The Retroactive Amendment Fix for Plan Operational Failures*, Jackson Lewis PC (July 15, 2015), available at Lexology.com]

A forfeiture generally occurs when a participant leaves the employer before becoming fully vested for matching or other employer contributions. The rules permit forfeiture of the non-vested portion, although in practice many plans do not call for forfeiture until there have been five consecutive one-year breaks in service. Mishandling of forfeitures is a common target of IRS audits. The IRS requires forfeitures to be used or allocated for the plan year in which they arise— or, in appropriate circumstances, in the following plan year. Forfeitures can be used to pay reasonable administrative expenses of the plan; to reduce the employer's contribution; to restore previously forfeited participant accounts; or to provide additional contributions to participants. The IRS's position is that forfeitures cannot be used to fund 401(k) safe harbor contributions, because these contributions have to be 100% vested when they are made. Placing the forfeited amounts into a suspense account is not permitted. The most common reasons for not allocating forfeitures on a timely basis are:

- Failure by the sponsor or TPA to monitor the forfeiture account to make sure the allocations are proper;

- Where the plan has both a sponsor and a TPA, each one thinks the other one is monitoring;

- When the plan sponsor incorrectly believes it has more discretion to apply forfeitures than the rules allow;

- When the plan terms do not explain how to handle forfeitures;

- When the sponsor elects not to make discretionary contributions for the plan year; with no contributions to be offset by the forfeited amount, the sponsor does not allocate them;

- When the sponsor does not think of using forfeitures to pay administrative expenses.

In the first two years, mistakes can be corrected with EPCRS. After two years, the VCP must be used unless the failure is considered insignificant. The VCP must be used if the terms of the plan are incorrect and a retroactive plan amendment is required to correct them. [Chadron J. Patton, *Common Plan Mistakes: Failure to Timely Allocate Forfeitures*, Spencer Fane (Nov. 16, 2012) (benefitslink.com)]

The IRS's Operational Compliance List, published February 27, 2017, lists qualification rules that plans must meet. One item on the list is recent proposed regulations about using forfeitures to fund defined contribution plan qualified matching contributions and qualified nonelective contributions. [Sheila Ninneman, *The 2017 Operational Compliance List*, findleydavies.com (Mar. 15, 2017) (benefitslink.com)]

A 2015 article points out that, although the IRS has not published any formal standards for approving a retroactive plan amendment to correct operational failures, the IRS requires the plan to submit convincing documentation to show that the actual operation of the plan reflected the way that the sponsor and any relevant service providers believed the plan was drafted. [Raymond P. Turner, *The Retroactive Amendment Fix for Plan Operational Failures*, Jackson Lewis PC (July 15, 2015), available at Lexology.com]

In recent years, IRS audits of 401(k) plans often ask the employer for evidence that participants were given the safe harbor notice. Plans that cannot produce this evidence are often asked for corrections and perhaps subjected to a closing agreement sanction. To avoid this problem, the plan should keep a dated copy of the notice and the cover letter sent with it (or a list of recipients and a dated copy of the e-mail used to furnish notice electronically). Failure to give the safe harbor notice is considered failure to comply with the terms of the plan, not just a failure to satisfy the statutory requirements of § 401(k). It is an operational failure that can be corrected under the VCP, although it is not included in EPCRS. If the participant was aware of his or her eligibility to defer, the employer can correct the failure by giving the notice, even if it is late, and improving its procedures in the future. But if the participant was not aware of the option to defer, the employer must treat the employee as improperly excluded, and make a contribution equal to 50% of the missed deferral, plus any employer match required by the plan and an additional amount to compensate for lost earnings on the amount that should have been contributed. [SunGard Relius, *Failure to Provide Safe Harbor Notice Correction* (Nov. 30, 2012) (benefitslink.com)]

[B]   Investment-Related Costs

The DOL undertook several measures in 2009–2011 to increase the transparency of defined contribution plan fees. The first step was the new Schedule C requirements that took effect in 2009, enhancing the disclosure that has to be made to the federal government about indirect compensation (revenue sharing) paid to service providers.

The second step was a rule released in July 2010, requiring providers to report to plan sponsors on direct and indirect compensation that the sponsors paid for account services. [EBSA press release, *U.S. Department of Labor Announces Intention to Extend Applicability Date of Section 408(b)(2) Fee Disclosure Regulation* (Feb. 11, 2011) (benefitslink.com); Plansponsor staff, *DoL Extends Applicability Dates for Fee Disclosure Rules*, plansponsor.com (July 13, 2011)] The rule was finalized in early 2012, effective July 1, 2012, requiring service providers to give the plan written disclosure of compensation and other information about the arrangement under which services are provided to a defined contribution plan. EBSA published a sample guide to disclosure. [77 Fed. Reg. 5632 (Feb. 3, 2012); DOL Fact Sheet, *Final Regulation Relating to Service Provider Disclosures Under Section 408(b)(2)* (February 2012) (benefitslink.com)]

The DOL requires fiduciaries to be prudent in choosing a fiduciary investment adviser, and must monitor their abilities and qualifications periodically (including whether the adviser continues to comply with securities laws, compliance with the terms of engagement), but the plan's fiduciaries are not obligated to oversee the provision of specific advice. The advisers should be chosen based on an objective process analyzing qualifications, quality of services offered, and the reasonableness of fees. The process must be free of self-dealing, conflict of interest, and improper influence. Advice should be based on generally accepted investment theories. The Pension Protection Act of 2006 (Pub. L. No. 109-280 § 601) adds a prohibited transaction exemption under Code § 4975(d)(17) and ERISA § 409(b)(14) for advice from a fiduciary adviser under an investment advice arrangement. (Note that this requirement is not the same as the controversial "fiduciary rule" about advice given to plan participants and IRA holders: see §§ 4.01[D] , 4.25, and 6.08[A].)

The DOL published Final Regulations on the selection of annuity providers for individual account plans in late 2008, pursuant to the PPA. Including the option of distributing an individual account plan by purchasing an annuity contract does not trigger the "safest available annuity" standard of Interpretive Bulletin 95-1, but other fiduciary standards apply. Fiduciaries qualify for a safe harbor when they adopt annuities as a distribution method if the provider is selected after an objective investigation. To qualify for the safe harbor, the fiduciary must also retain an appropriate expert to monitor compliance, although the fiduciary is not required to perform ongoing review of the appropriateness of the initial selection. [DOL Reg. § 2550.404a-4, 73 Fed. Reg. 58447 (Oct. 7, 2008); Amendment to Interpretive Bulletin 95-1, 73 Fed. Reg. 58445 (Oct. 7, 2008); Amendments to DOL Reg. §§ 2550.404a-3 and 2578.1, 73 Fed. Reg. 58459 (Oct. 7, 2008); Amendment to PTE 2006-06, 73 Fed. Reg. 58629 (Oct. 7, 2008)] See also §§ 6.07[B], 15.15, and 15.17 for discussion of cost issues in the plan context.

Dozens of suits about plan fees have been filed. The earliest suits were brought by plan participants against the sponsors alleging that revenue-sharing with service providers was a breach of fiduciary duty because it required participants to pay excessive fees. Then broader challenges were brought about, for example, using actively managed funds in plans; funding plans with retail shares; using unitized stock funds that imposed "transaction drag"; using a service provider who bundled services; or the fiduciaries' alleged failure to obtain additional revenue streams for the plan's benefit. Sometimes the service providers have been sued on the theory that they are functional fiduciaries whose revenue sharing activities are prohibited transactions. [Groom Law Group, *401(k) Fee Litigation January 2015* (Feb. 2, 2015) (benefitslink.com)]

[C]　Satisfying PPA Requirements

The Pension Protection Act (PPA), Pub. L. No. 109-280, although primarily focused on improving the stability of defined benefit plans, has had important effects on other types of plans as well.

Rev. Rul. 2007-67, 2007-48 I.R.B. 1047, held that it does not violate the anti-cutback rule to adopt a plan amendment that adopts the PPA amendments to § 417(e)(3) [actuarial assumptions used in calculating the minimum present value of the accrued benefit]. Accordingly, in the spring of 2008, the IRS proposed amendments to Code § 4980F and ERISA § 204(h), under which a 204(h) notice would not be required if the effect of complying with PPA changes in actuarial assumptions is to reduce a lump-sum distribution from a defined benefit plan. [EB095625, REG-110136-07, RIN 1545-BG48, 73 Fed. Reg. 15101 (Mar. 21, 2008). See also Notice 2007-86, 2007-46. I.R.B 990.] However, some cash balance plans must issue 204(h) notices if an amendment to eliminate whipsaw also has the effect of reducing lump-sum distributions, and T.D. 9472, 2009-51 I.R.B. 850.

Notice 2014-37, 2014-14 I.R.B. 1100 states that a qualified 401(k) plan remains qualified if it adopts a midyear amendment to comply with Notice 2014-19, 2014-17 I.R.B. 979 (benefits for same-sex spouses). [Sally P. Schreiber, *Notice Clarifies Midyear Amendment of Certain Retirement Plans Post-Windsor*, AICPA (May 15, 2014) (benefitslink.com)]

Only about two-thirds of eligible workers participate in 401(k) plans; the PPA promotes automatic enrollment, on the theory that very few workers would actually opt out of a plan once enrolled in it. In September 2006, DOL proposed a regulation explaining the PPA safe harbor for default investments by fiduciaries who have not been instructed by plan participants.

Under the PPA, a plan participant or beneficiary is deemed to have exercised control over the account (thus exonerating the fiduciary) if the fiduciary invests in a "qualified default investment alternative" (QDIA) in a situation where the participant or beneficiary had the opportunity to give investment directions but did not. Notice must be given 30 days before the first investment, and 30 days before each subsequent plan year, explaining the circumstances under which assets will be invested in a QDIA. If the investment gives the plan any materials (e.g., prospectuses for securities), it must be passed along to the participants and beneficiaries.

The participant or beneficiary must be permitted to remove and redirect QDIA funds as often as other plan investments without incurring a penalty—at least quarterly. The plan must offer the broad range of investment alternatives in addition to the QDIA, as required by the ERISA § 404(c) regulations. The QDIA must be diversified, and must be managed by an investment manager or a registered investment company. The QDIA is forbidden to directly invest participant contributions in the employer's stock, and money market and stable value funds are not suitable because their rate of return is too low to provide reliable retirement security. However, life cycle funds, targeted retirement date funds, balanced funds, and professionally managed accounts are all permitted. [<http://www.dol. gov/ebsa>, Fact Sheet, *Proposed Regulation Relating to Default Investment Alternatives Under Participant Directed Individual Account Plans* (Sept. 26, 2006)] If all of these requirements are satisfied, the fiduciary then qualifies for safe harbor relief. However, the selection of the default investments remains a fiduciary decision—which, in turn, must be prudent, considering fees and expenses. Once selected, the default arrangement must be monitored for continued appropriateness. [EBSA FAB 2007-1, discussed in Fred Schneyer, *DOL Sets Out Fiduciary Adviser Selection/Monitoring Guidelines*, plansponsor.com (Feb. 2, 2007)]

Fiduciaries are not liable for losses on amounts invested in a QDIA, and the plan's fiduciaries are not liable for decisions made by the managers of the QDIA. A QDIA can mix equity and fixed income investments—for example, in a life cycle or targeted retirement date fund; it can also be a balanced fund or a professionally managed fund. However, a capital preservation fund or other stable value fund can be a QDIA only for the first 120 days after a participant's first elective contribution.

The DOL announced a final rule on improving access to financial advice for 401(k) and IRA accounts in January 2009, but this rule was withdrawn and replaced by a proposal published in March 2010. Under the March 2010 proposal, advice can be given two ways: through the use of an unbiased computer model chosen by the fiduciary, or when the adviser's fees do not vary no matter what investments the participants choose. Additional requirements, including fee disclosure, are imposed. [Proposed rule, 75 Fed. Reg. 9360 (Mar. 2, 2010). For history of the rule, see 74 Fed. Reg. 11847 (Mar. 20, 2009) and 74 Fed. Reg. 23951 (May 22, 2009)]

Final IRS rules in T.D. 9447 (2009-12 I.R.B. 694) permit employers to add an automatic enrollment feature to 401(k) plans without performing nondiscrimination testing, but the plan must be a Qualified Automatic Contribution Arrangement (QACA) or an Eligible Automatic Contribution Arrangement (EACA) (the equivalent for multi-employer plans). A QACA is a Cash or deferred Arrangement (CODA) that satisfies the 401(k)(13) rules about notice, automatic deferrals, and matching or nonelective contributions. A QACA must begin automatic contributions at 3% of salary, adding 1% a year until reaching 6%. Company matches and mandatory nonelective contributions vest in two years. If an employer offers a QACA, all employees must be automatically enrolled. If the employer withholds excess contributions from employees who opt out of coverage, the employer must make a corrective distribution by June 30. An employee who opts out can withdraw from the plan and have contributions end within 90 days. The distribution from the plan is taxable to the employee, but is not subject to the 10% penalty tax on premature withdrawals. The Final Regulations apply to plan years beginning on or after January 1, 2008. [Joanne Wojcik, *IRS Rules on 401(k) Will Help Some Employers*, Business Insurance (Feb. 25, 2009)]

Late in 2011, the DOL finalized the ERISA § 408(g) regulations, so it is not a prohibited transaction for fiduciary advisors to give individual account plan participants individualized investment advice—as long as the advice is based on generally accepted investment theories considering the individual's investment characteristics as well as the performance of various asset classes over time. Either the adviser's remuneration must be independent of the choices made by the individual, or the advice must be rendered based on a valid computer model. [76 Fed. Reg. 66637 (Oct. 7, 2011)]

Economically targeted investments (ETIs) base their decisions on ESG standards (environmental, social, or governance). DOL Interpretive Bulletin 2015-01 discusses the fiduciary process that a plan committee should use to decide whether to adopt ETIs as plan investments. DOL says that ETIs are not inherently suspect and do not require special scrutiny. Plan committees can legitimately contemplate ESG considerations as primary factors in choosing investments where those considerations affect investment returns. ESG features can be secondary factors to break ties between equivalent prudent investment choices. However, the committee must only select ETIs that are expected to perform as well as investments with similar risk characteristics; it is not prudent to accept a lower rate of return, although where rates of return are comparable, the ETI can be chosen as a tie-breaker. It also is acceptable to use a brokerage or mutual fund window that allows participants to invest in ETIs. [C. Frederick Reish, Bruce L. Ashton and Joshua J. Waldbeser, *"Socially Responsible" Investing Under ERISA: New DOL Guidance*, Drinker Biddle (Nov. 18, 2015), available at Lexology.com]

§ 10.05   ERISA COMPLIANCE ISSUES

Many compliance issues (e.g., payment of premiums; reporting events that may imperil a plan's future; terminating a plan) involve interaction between plan sponsors and the PBGC. PBGC.gov has been updated, to make the site run faster and make it easier to search.

The Summary Plan Description (SPD) for a newly created plan must be filed with the Department of Labor within 120 days of the plan's adoption. (If this is later than the date of establishment, filing must be made within 120 days of the first time the plan covers common-law employees and therefore becomes subject to ERISA Title I.) It is wise to include a disclaimer in the SPD, to the effect that the plan instrument and not the SPD will govern in case of conflict.

ERISA § 104(a)(4)(A) gives the DOL the power to reject an incomplete SPD filing. The plan administrator has 45 days to file again to answer the DOL comments. If the second filing is not made, DOL has the power to sue for legal or equitable relief, or any other remedy authorized by ERISA Title I.

According to EBSA, it is a violation of ERISA's "exclusive purpose" rule for fiduciaries to use plan assets to advance proxy resolutions for political or policy issues that are not connected to increasing the value of the plan assets. Fiduciaries are barred from accepting higher expenses, lower investment returns, or risks to the security of the plan's assets in order to advance any goals that are not directly related to the plan. [EBSA Advisory Opinion 2007-07A; see Rebecca Moore, *Use of Plan Assets for Non-Plan Related Political Issues Violates ERISA*, plansponsor.com (Jan. 3, 2008)]

DOL published a final rule on January 14, 2010, creating a safe harbor for small plan (under 100 participants). The safe harbor explains when funds received from participants or withheld from their wages for contribution to a pension or welfare benefit plan become plan assets under ERISA Title I. In 1988, DOL ruled that the contributions became plan assets on the earliest date they could reasonably be segregated from the employer's general assets, but in any case within 90 days of the employer's receipt of the funds. A 1996 rule reduced the period to the fifteenth business day of the month after receipt. The 2010 rule deems a contribution timely if it is placed into the plan no later than the seventh business day after the employer received it—even if it would have been possible to deposit it faster. [Transamerica Center for Retirement Studies 2010-01, *Department of Labor Final Rule on Definition of Plan Assets—Participant Contributions* (Jan. 22, 2010) (benefitslink.com); the proposed rule was published at 73 Fed. Reg. 11072 (Feb. 29, 2008)]

In 2015, approximately 2,000 plans were liable for late premium payment penalties, for a total of about $7 million, out of $4.3 billion in premium income received by the PBGC.

In April 2016, the PBGC published a proposal to reduce the penalties for late payment of premiums, in order to assist plans that are struggling financially. Premiums in 2016 were over 80% higher than in 2012. The previous rule used a two-tier structure. Tier 1 imposed a penalty of 1% per month on late payments corrected before the PBGC notified the sponsor of the deficiency. Tier 2 raised the penalty to 5% if the PBGC notified the sponsor. The Tier 1 penalty was capped at 50% of the overdue amount; the Tier 2 penalty was capped at 100% of the overdue amount. The 2016 proposal, which applies to both single- and multi-employer plans, cuts the penalties in half—or reduces them by 80% if the sponsor otherwise has a good payment history and responds to a notification of late payment by making a prompt catch-up payment. The proposal applies to premium payments for 2016 and later plan years. [81 Fed. Reg. 25363 (Apr. 28, 2016); see PBGC Press Release No. 16-05, *PBGC Takes Steps to Reduce Premium Penalties* (Apr. 27, 2016) (benefitslink.com)]

The rule was finalized in September 2016, with limited changes. However, penalties for late payment of the termination premium are not affected by this rule. [81 Fed. Reg. 65542 (Sept. 23, 2016); see Cheiron.us, *PBGC Issues Final Rule for Premium Penalty Relief* (Oct. 4, 2016) (benefitslink.com); Marjorie Martin & Joanne Jacobson, *PBGC Finalizes Reduced Late Premium Payment Penalties*, HRC FYI (Sept. 22, 2016) (benefitslink.com); Vipal Monga, *Pension Insurer Moves to Ease Burden on Defined Benefit Providers*, WSJ.com (Sept. 22, 2016)]

The PBGC premiums have frequently been increased to reflect the PBGC's needs for financial stability as increasing demands are placed on it. Increases were adopted by the Moving Ahead for Progress in the 21st Century Act (MAP-21); the Bipartisan Budget Act of 2013; the "Cromnibus" legislation; and most recently by the Bipartisan Budget Act of 2015, Pub. L. No. 114-74. At press time in 2017, the premiums for 2016 and scheduled increases for later years were:

- Flat-rate premium: $64 per participant in 2016 for single-employer plans, $27 per participant in multi-employer plans; for 2017, the flat-rate premium is $69 for single-employer plans, $28 for multi-employer plans. The projected premiums for single-employer plans are $74 for 2018 and $80 for 2019, with the multi-employer plan premium remaining $28.

- Variable-rate premium: for 2016, $30 per $1,000 in unfunded vested benefits, capped at $500 per participant, for single-employer plans, increasing to $34 in 2017, capped at $517; $38 in 2018, capped at $517; and $42 in 2019, capped at $517. (There is no variable-rate premium for multi-employer plans.)

. No additional increases have been legislated after 2020, but indexing applies to all amounts. [PBGC, *Premium Rates*, <http://www.pbgc.gov/prac/prem/premium-rates.html> (last accessed Feb. 13, 2017)]

Every ERISA retirement plan, of any size, must file Form 5500 with the IRS. The IRS shares data with the DOL. The form is due seven months after the end of the plan year. For a calendar-year plan, this means July 31. A two-and-a-half month extension can be obtained by filing Form 5558 before the due date of the return. Form 5500 is not a tax return per se; it gathers information about the plan. 5500 forms are usually prepared by the plan's recordkeeper or TPA, but the plan administrator must sign the form under penalty of perjury. On the form, the plan's asset value, liabilities, contributions, fees, changes in net assets, and participant count must be reported. Plans with 100 or more participants at the beginning of the plan year must attach audited financials. Smaller plans may be able to file Form 5500-EZ or the short form 5500 rather than the full long form, which requires submission of multiple schedules. [Editors, *The Basics About Form 5500s*, plansponsor.com (Jan. 23, 2017)]

DOL released 2015 Form 5500, including 5500-SF, in late 2015. There are only minor changes since the 2014 form. But IRS added a series of compliance questions to Schedule R of the Form 5500-SF and EZ, dealing with, e.g., discrimination testing for 401(k) plans and coverage requirements. Two specific IRS questions were added to the compliance questions on Schedules H and I of the SF and EZ, dealing with unrelated business taxable income and in-service distributions. [2015 Form 5500 and instructions, <http://www.dol.gov/ebsa/5500main.html#2015>; see EBIA Weekly, *Form 5500 for 2015 Plan Year Released, Including New IRS Compliance Questions* (Dec. 3, 2015) (benefitslink.com)]

In mid-2016, the DOL proposed changes to Form 5500 (and the Form 5500-SF for small plans) with the intention of improving the collection of plan data and reporting of plan compliance. The agency also wanted to gather more information about fiduciary fees, and maintain all data in a form amenable to data mining. Generally, the changes are required for 2019 plan years, but plans can adopt them voluntarily before that. Under this proposal, health and welfare benefit plans with fewer than 100 participants would no longer be exempt from reporting. All health and welfare plans, of any size, would have to complete the new Schedule J disclosing their claim payment policies, enrollment data, and their cost sharing and wellness practices. The DOL said that this information is needed to enforce PPACA and the mental health parity requirement. Additional changes call for defined contribution plans to report more information about their investment offerings, and whether they offer Roth features, a qualified default investment, and/or investment education for participants. All qualified plans must disclose if they have invested in derivatives, hedge funds, or other hard-to-value vehicles. Additional information is required about distributions to terminated participants. Schedule S now has additional questions about participation rates and employer matching contributions to defined contribution plans, and about nondiscrimination testing. All indirect compensation to service providers must be reported on Schedule C. The 2016 proposal also reinstates Schedule E (ESOPs) that was removed in 2009. [81 Fed. Reg. 47533 (July 21, 2016); see Carly E. Grey, *DOL Proposes Major Changes to Form 5500*, Morgan Lewis & Bockius LLP (July 20, 2016), available at Lexology.com]

Also in late 2015, the IRS released a draft of Form 5500-EZ for some one-person plans. On June 3, 2015, the IRS announced that relief for late filing of Form 5500-EZ had been made permanent. (Form 5500-EZ filers are not eligible for relief under DOL's DFVC program, because they are not ERISA Title I plans.) A plan seeking relief must file paper returns for each year for which relief is sought; there is a penalty of $500 per delinquent return per plan, capped at a maximum of $1,500 per plan. The penalty is paid with Form 14704. [Rev. Proc. 2015-32, 2015-24 I.R.B. 1068]

At the beginning of 2015, the PBGC premium filing procedure was revised to require reporting of pension risk transfer actions such as annuity purchases and lump-sum windows. These transactions must be reported because the PBGC is concerned that many financially sound companies will engage in risk transfer actions—leaving only a smaller, less financially stable group of companies to pay PBGC premiums. [Maria P. Rasmussen and James P. McElligott Jr., McGuire Woods LLP, *PBGC Wants Reporting on Lump-Sum Pension Cash-Outs and Annuity Purchases* (Jan. 16, 2015) (benefitslink.com)]

The PBGC also changed the payment procedure, making it simpler and more uniform. As a result of Executive Order 13563, "Improving Regulation and Regulatory Review," effective for plan years beginning on or after January 1, 2014, the PBGC has eliminated the requirement that plans with 500 or more participants pay their estimated flat-rate premiums early in the plan year (February 28). The new rule is that flat-rate premiums are due on October 15 in a single payment, with no need to make estimated payments—and the flat-rate premium is due on the same date as the variable-rate premium. The same date applies to plans of all sizes, with the result that plans with fewer than 100 participants now must file earlier, on the date that already applied to mid-sized plans, whereas large plans get more time to file. [79 Fed. Reg. 13547 (Mar. 11, 2014); see <http://www.pbgc.gov/prac/prem/filings/2017-premium-payment-instructions.html> for the 2017 payment instructions, using the MyPAA web portal.] Filers can use either the portal's data entry screens or compatible private-sector software. The instructions include a new section on how to calculate the premium in the year a spinoff, merger, or consolidation occurs. The PBGC suggests that filers consult the Premium Payment Instructions and Addresses section of the instructions each year; the 2015 rules for payments, including mailing addresses for paper checks and wire transfer instructions were changed for 2017. [<http://www.pbgc.gov/Documents/2017-Premium-Payment-Instructions.pdf>; see John Manganaro, *2017 Premium Filing Instructions Updated by PBGC,* plansponsor.com (Jan. 6, 2017)]

Small plans are also permitted to use either current-year or prior-year figures to compute the variable-rate premium. (Some small plans determine their funding levels late in the year, so they do not have current-year figures available at the new due date.)

In mid-2016, the PBGC, the DOL, and the IRS jointly issued revisions to Form 5500, but compliance will not be required until Form 5500s are prepared for the 2019 plan year.

The revisions update reporting requirements for fees and expenses and improve compliance by adding new questions about plan operations, service provider relationships, and financial management.

Schedule C is used to report information about service provider fees and other compensation if the provider receives more than $5,000 from the plan. It has been revised to align with ERISA § 408(b)(2) fee disclosure requirements. Schedule C also reports termination of plan accountants or actuaries. Exemption of small pension and welfare plans from Schedule C filing has been eliminated.

Schedule E (ESOPs) was eliminated in 2009 when mandatory e-filing was imposed, but it has been reintroduced, calling for information that was transferred to Schedule R, plus new questions about whether the sponsor is an S Corporation and whether the plan made prohibited allocations.

Schedule H has been re-drafted to improve the transparency of disclosure of "other" assets reported on the balance sheet, such as alternative and hard-to-value assets. More detailed reporting is required for, e.g., salaries, audit fees, legal fees, trustee expenses, and valuation fees. For merged or terminated plans, additional information is required, such as the date of transfers of assets or liabilities. Terminated defined contribution plans must provide disclosures so missing participants can locate assets that have been transferred to financial institutions.

Additional compliance questions have been added to Schedules H and R, such as whether anyone whose criminal convictions disqualify him or her under ERISA § 411 provided services to the plans; if administrative expenses were paid but not reported; and whether the plan sponsor or its affiliates received compensation for providing services to the plan. Additional information is required from participant-directed plans, such as the number of designated investment alternatives and, if participants receive the disclosures mandated by the DOL.

In 2009, when e-filing became mandatory, many IRS-specific questions were removed from Form 5500. In 2015, certain questions were returned to the form—but the IRS directed plans not to answer them. Starting with the 2019 form, additional tax-related information will be required, such as the name of trustees, if the plan is a 401(k) plan or a preapproved plan; how nondiscrimination and coverage testing are performed; the date of any favorable determination letter obtained by the plan; if any phased retirement distributions have been made by defined benefit or money purchase plans; and if a defined participation plan satisfies the minimum participation rules.

Under the revision, all group health plans covered by ERISA Title I will have to file Form 5500, regardless of their size or insured status. However, small, fully insured plans will only be required to submit basic information. The revision adds a new Schedule J, information about PPACA and COBRA coverage, if retirees and dependents as well as active employees are covered; the types of group health benefits offered; how the benefits are paid; if the plan qualifies as an HDHP, health FSA, or HRA; rebates, including medical loss ratio rebates, received from service providers; details on claims payments including claims denials and appeals. Welfare benefit plans with fewer than 100 participants are no longer permitted to use Form 5500-SF. [Frost Brown Todd, *Form 5500 Updates and Increased ERISA Penalties* (Oct. 5, 2016) (benefitslink.com)]

A terminating plan must continue to make premium filings, and pay premiums, up through the year in which any of these events occurs:

- All of the plan assets have been distributed to satisfy liabilities;

- A trustee has been appointed under ERISA § 4042;

- All of the plan's assets and liabilities have been distributed to another plan or other plans in connection with a merger or consolidation; and

- The plan is no longer a covered plan under ERISA § 4021.

- Until all of the plan assets have been distributed to satisfy liabilities. [<http://www.pbgc.gov/prac/prem/filings/2017-premium-payment-instructions.html>] The final premium for a terminating plan is due no later than the filing of the post-distribution certificate. This rule was adopted because the final premium was sometimes forgotten in standard terminations when the due date was months later than the plan closed its books. Furthermore, plans will generally be exempt from the variable-rate premium for the year in which a standard termination is completed and small plans may be exempt from the variable-rate premium for the first year of coverage.

All premium information required by ERISA § 4007 must now be e-filed. The plan can file by entering data directly into MyPAA by uploading data from proprietary software or by importing data into the MyPAA data entry screens from approved software. MyPAA accepts credit cards, electronic checks, and Automated Clearing House transfers; payments can also be made outside MyPAA. The PBGC recommends using <http://www.pay.gov>, a free federal Website for making secure payments to the PBGC and federal government agencies. The instructions explain the payment options in detail.

EBSA announced in early 2013 that migration to the fully electronic EFAST2 system is complete for all filing years and paper filings will no longer be accepted. See the DOL Website for an explanation of which version of the Form 5500/5500SF is required for your plan, and which schedules to use. The announcement, which primarily deals with the Delinquent Filer Voluntary Compliance Program (DFVCP), says that although DFVCP does not offer relief from late filing penalties under the Code or ERISA Title IV, the PBGC has agreed to provide some ERISA § 4071 penalty relief for delinquent filings of annual reports if the conditions of the DFVCP are satisfied. The IRS announced that it would issue separate guidance on penalty relief for Form 5500/5500-SF delinquencies where both DFVCP and IRS requirements are met. [Notice: <http://www.dol .gov/find/20130128>, FAQs at <http://www.dol.gov/ebsa/faqs/faq_dfvc.html> (updated Jan. 28, 2015) (both last accessed Feb. 13, 2017)]

The DFVCP allows plan administrators to pay reduced civil penalties if they make the required filings before the DOL gives the administrators written notice of their failure to file a timely Form 5500 (the ERISA Title I annual report). (Form 5500-EZ filers and filers of Form 5500 for plans without employees are not eligible for DFVCP because they are not subject to ERISA Title I.) The plan administrator is personally liable for ERISA § 502(c)(2) civil penalties, which cannot be paid from plan assets.

If, during the period when the reports were not filed, the plan went from small to large, the large-plan penalties apply. A plan that has received an IRS late-filer penalty letter can participate in DFVCP, but a plan that has received a DOL Notice of Intent to Assess a penalty cannot. [DOL/EBSA, *FAQs About the Delinquent Filer Voluntary Compliance Program*, <http://www.dol.gov/ebsa/faqs/faq_ dfvc.html> (last accessed Feb. 13, 2017)]

In September 2015, the IRS Employee Plans Compliance Unit announced a project to identify non-filers of Form 5500 by comparing payroll and plan data to DOL records. The IRS contacts plans that apparently failed to file. If they do not respond explaining why filing was not required, then it is on record that they were informed of the potential penalties. [Christopher M. Allesee, *New IRS Project Sets Its Sights on Form 5500 Non-Filers*, Graydon Head & Ritchey LLP (Sept. 3, 2015), available at Lexology.com]

Starting January 1, 2012, Forms 5500 and 5500-SF must be signed electronically by the employer, plan sponsor, or plan administrator. The signer must have a valid EFAST2 user ID and personal ID. If the electronic signature is rejected by the online filing system, it may be necessary to get new credentials. Forms that do not have an electronic signature will not be processed, and the plan might be penalized. Forms that have an invalid electronic signature will be characterized as "processing stopped." Forms can also be signed by an authorized plan service provider (APSP) who has specific written authorization from the plan administrator, including the plan administrator's manual signature on a paper copy of the form. A PDF of the first two pages of the manually signed form must be attached to the filing, so the DOL can add an image of the manual signature to its online database. [John Iekel, *Electronic Signatures for Forms 5500 and 5500-SF Mandatory Jan. 1*, Smart HR (Dec. 21, 2011) (benefitslink.com)]

Code § 6057(a) requires reporting of certain information about participants who separate from service with deferred vested benefits. Until 2009, this was done on Schedule SSA of the Form 5500. IRS and SSA developed Form 8955-SSA, which is filed directly with the IRS for plan years beginning on or after January 1, 2009.

The information reported on the new form is similar to the Schedule SSA information: participants separated from service when entitled to a deferred vested benefit. The Social Security Administration uses this information to tell retirees who are applying for Social Security what pension plan benefits are available to them. [Jeffrey Ashendorf, *Legal Alert: IRS Replaces Schedule SSA* (Mar. 4, 2011) (benefitslink.com)]

ERISA § 412 requires all plan officials who handle the plan's money or property to carry a bond of at least 10% of the amount the manager handles, with a minimum of $1,000. The maximum bond required of a plan is $500,000 per plan official—rising to $1 million per official for plans that hold employer securities. EBSA's Field Assistance Bulletin (FAB) 2008-04 provides guidance about the bonding requirements, such as how to calculate the amount of a bond covering multiple plans; if the $1 million maximum for bonds applies; if the plan holds employer securities only because it invests in pooled investment funds; and when third-party service providers that handle plan funds must be bonded. [Rebecca Moore, *EBSA Provides Guidance on Plan Official Bonding Requirements*, plan sponsor.com (Nov. 25, 2008)]

Many penalties imposed by federal agencies went for years or even decades without being increased. In May 2016, the PBGC increased the penalties for failure to provide certain ERISA notices from $1,100 to $2,063, and raised the penalty for failure to provide multi-employer plan notices from $110 to $275. [81 Fed. Reg. 29765 (May 12, 2016); see David B. Brandolph, *PBGC to Double Penalties for Failing to Give Notices*, bna.com (May 13, 2016) (benefitslink.com)]

The Federal Civil Penalties Inflation Adjustment Act, which is part of Pub. L. N. 114-74, not only imposed major increases in civil penalties, but provides that, in 2017 and afterwards, penalties must be adjusted for inflation each year. Additional increases in ERISA penalties were published in 81 Fed. Reg. 42491 (June 16, 2016). [See DOL Fact Sheet, *Interim Final Rule Adjusting ERISA Civil Monetary Penalties for Inflation* (June 30, 2016), available at <http://www.dol.gov/ebsa/pdf/fs-interim-final-rule-adjusting-erisa-civil-monetary-penalties-for-inflation.pdf> (last accessed Feb. 13, 2017).] Penalties were increased once again in early 2017, pursuant to the requirement of inflation adjustment. [Conduent FYI, *DOL, PBGC and HHS Increase Penalties for Violations* (Feb. 10, 2017) (benefitslink.com)]

In this list, the first set of figures applies to maximum penalties under the June 2016 regulation, for penalties imposed after August 1, 2015, for violations committed after November 2, 2015. The second set of figures applies to penalties assessed after January 13, 2017, also for violations committed after November 2, 2015. The section numbers are ERISA sections:

- Failure to maintain records, or failure to provide benefit statements (§ 209(b)): $28 per employee/$28 per employee

- A plan's failure or refusal to file Form 5500, or failure to a multi-employer plan to certify its endangered or critical status (§ 502(c)(2)): $2,063 a day/$2,097 a day

- Failure to notify participants of Code § 436 limitations on benefits, or to provide financial and actuarial reports of multi-employer plans (§ 502(c)(4)): $1,632 a day/$1,659 a day

- Failure to answer an information request from the Secretary of Labor (§ 502(c)(6)): $147 a day, capped at $1,472 per request/$149 a day, capped at $1,496 per request

- Failure of the sponsor of a multi-employer plan to take steps appropriate to the plan's financial condition; failure to meet rehabilitation benchmarks (§ 502(c)(8)): $1,296 a day/$1,317 a day

- Making a prohibited distribution (§ 502(m)): $15,909 per distribution/$16.169 per distribution

- Failure to give EGHP participants a Summary of Benefits Coverage (ERISA § 715): $1,087 per notice failure/$1,105 per notice failure.

[A] Reportable Events

The PBGC's model of operations requires the agency to be aware of events that could lead a plan to terminate, or be taken over by, the PBGC. Therefore, certain business and financial events are designated as "reportable events" about which a plan sponsor must advise the PBGC. [See 29 C.F.R. § 4043.23 *et seq.*] Some events are reportable in advance; others, promptly after they have occurred. This has been a volatile area, with the PBGC frequently changing the rules generally to make them simpler and easier to comply with. For earlier steps in the evolution of these rules, see PBGC Technical Update 13-1 [78 Fed. Reg. 20039 (Apr. 3, 2013)]

In September 2015, the PBGC issued final rules for reportable events, continuing the stress on the few plans or sponsors that are at greatest risk of default. In response to comments, PBGC increases sponsors' flexibility in determining whether a waiver applies. The final regulations took effect January 1, 2016. The PBGC explained that its objective was to require reporting only of the information the PBGC actually needs to carry out its mission. The PBGC estimated that the final regulations would entitle 82% of plans with 100 participants or more to use a reporting waiver.

The final rule says some waivers are based on risk of not being able to maintain the plan—unlike previous rules, which only focused on funding levels.

The PBGC's FAQ analyze the reportable events into two groups. One group is corporate events (issuing an extraordinary dividend; change in controlled group; insolvency or similar settlement—but not bankruptcy, which is not considered a reportable event; loan default; and liquidation).

The second group is plan events (reduction in the number of participants; distribution to a substantial owner; transfer of benefit liabilities; missing a required contribution; applying for a minimum funding waiver; and inability to pay benefits when due). Usually, if an event must be reported, the report is due within 30 days of the event ("post-event reporting"). But some of these events also require advance reporting 30 days before the event.

ERISA gives the PBGC the power to waive reporting requirements for any reportable event. Small plans (under 100 participants) are entitled to waivers. For five events (extraordinary dividend, change in controlled group, reduction in active participants, distribution to a substantial owner, transfer of benefit liabilities), the PBGC will waive the reporting requirement if the company's financial figures show that it is unlikely to default; if the plan is sufficiently funded not to have to pay a variable-rate premium; or if the company is publicly traded, and the event has already been reported on SEC Form 8-K. For missed contributions, reporting is waived for small plans if the missed contribution was a quarterly installment; for other plans, reporting is waived if the contribution was made up within 30 days, or the sponsor failed to make a timely election to apply the plan's credit balance to the funding requirement.

Reporting is done using the revised Form 10, for post-event reporting of events occurring on or after January 1, 2016. There is a new Form 10-Advance for reports expected to take effect on or after January 31, 2016—i.e., for which reports are due on or after January 1, 2016. Large unpaid contributions ($1 million or more) must be reported on new Form 200, if the aggregate value of the unpaid contributions reaches $1 million on or after January 1, 2016. These forms must be filed electronically. [80 Fed. Reg. 54980 (Sept. 11, 2015); PBGC, *Reportable Events FAQs*, available at <http://www.pbgc.gov/prac/reporting-and-disclosure/reportable-events-faqs.html> (Jan. 2015) (last accessed Feb. 13, 2017)]

The Early Warning Program is another facet of the PBGC's supervision of plans. This program identifies about 300 plans a year and requests additional information about their operations. About 100 plans are subjected to deeper review. When the PBGC identifies a risky plan, it might require the sponsor to increase its plan contributions, ordering the sponsor to obtain a letter of credit or grant a security interest in specified corporate assets as security, or obtaining a guarantor. The PBGC has the power to terminate risky plans, but this is very much a last resort. [Towerswatson.com, *PBGC Adds to List of Early Warning Factors* (Feb. 2017) (benefitslink.com)]

In December 2016, the PBGC added two events to the list of monitored transactions (deterioration in credit rating or financial metrics), but in May 2017, the PBGC updated its website and removed these factors from the list. However, the PBGC still considers credit ratings in its analysis, and change in a company's controlled group, a major divestiture such as a leveraged buyout, or substituting secured for unsecured debt can still trigger an investigation. The May guidance includes a sample information request businesses can consult, and explains the PBGC's process of negotiating with a company from which information is sought. [Groom Law Group, *PBGC Walks Back Early Warning Program Expansion* (May 11, 2017) (benefitslink.com)]

Notice 2012-46, 2012-30 I.R.B. 86, effective November 1, 2012, gives the ERISA § 101(j) notice requirements for single-employer plans subject to benefit limitations under § 436. When the funding status of a single-employer plan falls below a certain level, the administrator has 30 days to provide notice to participants and beneficiaries. The DOL can collect a penalty for each participant who should have been, but was not, notified. The notice must be in plain English and must include the plan name, its EIN and plan number, and a general description of the payment limitation. The prohibited benefits must be described in detail. The notice must explain when the limitation will cease to apply (e.g., when the AFTAP rises to at least 80%). Once the limitations cease to apply, participants will be entitled to additional forms of distributions, so the plan administrator must distribute a § 101(j) notice within 30 days of the date the limitations cease to apply. The notice must be written, but can be given electronically if it is reasonably accessible to the participants who are entitled to notice. [McGuireWoods LLP, *IRS Provides Guidance on Notices for Funding-Related Pension Plan Benefit Limitations* (Aug. 28, 2012) (benefitslink.com)]

ERISA § 4062(e) requires reporting of certain substantial cessations of operations by employers who maintain single-employer plans. Originally, reporting was required if cessation of operations at a facility caused more than 20% of participants to be separated from employment. An employer subject to § 4062(e) must either post bond or place a specified amount in escrow; these funds are applied toward underfunding if the plan terminates within a five-year period. However, § 4063(e) authorizes the PBGC to waive this liability if the sponsors of the plan have an appropriate indemnity agreement, and the PBGC can make alternative arrangements to satisfy the obligation (see § 4067). [RIN 1212-AB20, 75 Fed. Reg. 48283 (Aug. 10, 2010)]

However, in 2012, the PBGC announced that it would concentrate its enforcement efforts on plans that are truly at risk. Therefore, there was a moratorium on enforcing § 4062(e) against small companies (under 100 participants) or credit-worthy companies that were not considered highly risky. [R. Randall Tracht, Brian J. Dougherty, Lisa H. Barton, and Eric P. Sarabia, *PBGC Changes Enforcement Policy Under ERISA Section 4062(e)*, Morgan, Lewis & Bockius (Nov. 13, 2012) (benefitslink.com)]

For the second half of 2014, the PBGC suspended § 4062(e) enforcement. Businesses were told to report new § 4062(e) events as they occurred, but the PBGC said no action would be taken on the reports at least until the end of the year. The PBGC needed the extra time to work with stakeholders to determine which plans are genuinely at risk. [78 Fed. Reg. 20039 (Apr. 3, 2013); PBGC Press Release No. 14-09, *PBGC Issues Moratorium on 4062(e) Enforcement*, <http://www.pbgc.gov/news/press/releases/pr14-09.html?cid=CPAD01PRJUL08 20141> (July 8, 2014)]

The moratorium was ended by the Cromnibus bill, which redefines ERISA § 4062(e) events for events occurring on or after December 16, 2014. Plans with fewer than 100 participants are exempt, as are plans that are at least 90% funded. Now, § 4062(e) events are limited to permanent shutdowns involving 15% of all of the sponsor's employees who are eligible to participate in any pension plan, including 401(k) plans, maintained by members of the employer's controlled group. (Under prior law, the test was 20% of participants in the defined benefit plan.) The Cromnibus Act provides that there is no § 4062(e) event unless the shutdown is substantial relative to the size of the employer's entire operation. Generally speaking, there is no § 4062(e) event unless employees actually lose their jobs, not just go to work for someone else.

Even if there has been a § 4062(e) event, the Cromnibus Act reduces the penalties. The employer can satisfy its § 4062(e) liability by contributing one-seventh of the unfunded vested benefits times the percentage reduction in the number of active participants in each of seven years. Each installment is also capped. Installments do not have to continue after the plan's unfunded vested benefits are at least 90% vested, and do not have to resume if the percentage later falls below 90%.

The administrator of a single-employer plan is obligated to submit a § 4063 notice when an employer who is a contributing sponsor ends operations at a facility, resulting in job loss for more than 20% of the plan participants. A § 4063 notice is also required if a substantial employer withdraws from a multiple employer plan. The § 4063 notice does not replace any Reportable Event notice that is required by § 4043. At press time in 2016, there was no official PBGC form for the § 4063 notice; employers who are required to report should send the notice within 60 days of the event—either by mail to the PBGC's Corporate Finance & Restructuring Department, 1200 K Street NW, Washington, DC 20005-4026, faxed to (202) 842-2643, or e-mailed to 4063.report@pbgc.gov. [PBGC, *Section 4063 Notices*, <http://www.pbgc.gov/prac/reporting-and-disclosure/section-4063-notices.html> (last viewed Feb. 13, 2017)]

[B] Annual Funding Notice

Defined benefit plans are subject to an annual funding notice requirement (ERISA § 101(f)). In early 2015, about 27,000 plans, with approximately 43.7 million participants and beneficiaries, were subject to this requirement.

In general, the annual funding notice must provide information about the plan's assets and benefit payments; PBGC guarantees; and possible benefit reductions. The notice explains the rules about plan terminations (single-employer plans) or insolvency (multi-employer plans). Notice must be sent to every participant who was covered under the plan on the last day of the notice year; every beneficiary; every alternate payee; every labor organization, as well as to the PBGC. Notice must also be given to every employer that is a party to the CBAs under which the plan is maintained—or who might otherwise be liable to withdrawal liability under ERISA. EBSA issued final regulations in early 2015 reflecting the Multi-Employer Pension Reform Act (part of Pub. L. No. 113-235) requirements for additional disclosures by multi-employer plans that are in critical and declining status. These final regulations are effective March 4, 2015 for notices relating to years beginning on or after January 1, 2015. Certain terminating single-employer plans are not required to provide this notice if the plan distributes the plan assets to satisfy its liabilities, as prescribed by ERISA § 4014(b). [80 Fed. Reg. 5625 (Feb. 3, 2015); Appendix A provides a model notice for single-employer plans, Appendix B for multi-employer plans.]

The funding notice need not be provided for a plan year if the notice's due date is on or after the date of filing the PBGC Form 500 (standard termination notice)—as long as final distribution of plan assets to satisfy benefit liabilities occurs pursuant to ERISA § 4014(b). Multi-employer plans that have terminated by mass withdrawal and § 412(e)(3) plans have alternative methods of compliance. [See ERISA § 4014A(a)(2)]

See T.D. 9732, 2015-39 I.R.B. 371 for final regulations for calculating the minimum required contributions for single-employer defined benefit plans. The required minimum contribution must be paid by eight-and-a-half months after the end of the plan year. Any funding shortfall for earlier years must be made up through quarterly payments of 25% each of the required annual payment—the smaller of either 90% of the required minimum contribution, or 100% of the previous year's required minimum contribution.

T.D. 9732 also deals with the § 4971 excise tax for failure to satisfy the minimum funding requirements. The excise tax is 10% of the aggregate unpaid minimum contributions for all plan years remaining unpaid at the end of the plan year. A 10% tax is also imposed on the liquidity shortfall for a quarter that is not paid by the due date for that quarter's installment, or if there is a liquidity shortfall at the end of each of five consecutive quarters. T.D. 9732 allows employers to elect to apply a credit balance to quarterly contributions, which reduces the paperwork burden. Employers can adopt a formula, which gives much more flexibility than designating a dollar amount.

[C]   § 4010 Reporting

Certain underfunded defined benefit plans are also required to make another type of annual report to the PBGC. Reporting is required under ERISA § 4010 about the plan's financial and actuarial information, such as its funding target attainment percentage (FTAP) and the funding target determined as if the plan had been at risk for five years. The report is due 105 days after the end of the information year (i.e., April 15 of the following year, for calendar-year plans).

In late 2015, the PBGC created a portal for e-filing 4010 reports, <https://efilingportal.pbgc.gov/e4010>. To use the portal (which is separate from MyPAA), practitioners must obtain an e-4010 account from the PBGC. The portal can also be used to make ERISA § 4043 filings, and for certain multi-employer plan notices and applications (e.g., the annual funding notice and notice of critical or endangered status). [The PBGC's web page for § 4010 reporting can be found at <https://www.pbgc.gov/prac/reporting-and-disclosure/4010-reporting.html> (last accessed Feb. 13, 2017)]

PBGC's Technical Update 14-2 provides guidance about the effect of the Highway and Transportation Funding Act of 2014 (HATFA) on § 4010 reporting. HATFA extends the MAP-21 relief so defined benefit plans can discount their future benefit payments to present value using a 25-year rather than a two-year average of bond rates. The Bipartisan Budget Act of 2015, Pub. L. No. 114-74, allows continued use of rate stabilization under HATFA until 2023.

Further final regulations were issued in 2016, changing the requirements for waivers of § 4010 reporting. Reporting is waived if the aggregate funding shortfall for an employer is less than $15 million, but the shortfall is measured using the non-stabilized rates that prevailed before HATFA. Because of this requirement, the figures used for § 4010 reporting might be different from the ones used to prepare Form 5500.

The 2016 final regulations add three new funding waivers. One is for controlled groups that have fewer than 500 employees in all their plans (including exempt plans), no matter how great the underfunding. Reporting is also waived if there is a statutory lien of more than $1 million because of missed required contributions, or because the plan's minimum funding waivers exceed $1 million—but this § 4010 waiver applies only if these events are reported to the PBGC as "reportable events." Note that the PBGC now refers to what was known as the FTAP (Funding Target Attainment Percentage) as the "4010 funding target attainment percentage." [81 Fed. Reg. 15432 (Mar. 23, 2016); see Xerox FYI, *PBGC Finalizes Changes to 4010 Annual Financial Reporting* (Mar. 25, 2016) (benefitslink.com); Practicallaw.com, *PBGC Issues Final Regulations on Pension Plan Reporting Under ERISA Section 4010* (Mar. 29, 2016) (benefitslink,com)]

CHAPTER **11**

COMMUNICATIONS WITH EMPLOYEES AND REGULATORS

§ 11.01 INTRODUCTION

Although the Employment Retirement Income Security Act (ERISA) does not require corporations to have employee benefit plans at all, if they choose to implement plans, there are many rules that must be followed, including procedural rules. Plan participants must be given enough information from the plan itself to understand their benefits—especially benefits available in multiple forms—so that informed choices must be made. In addition to their ERISA obligations, plans are also subject to extensive disclosure requirements under the Internal Revenue Code.

The Summary Plan Description (SPD) is the main document for communications between the plan and its participants, although other documents may also be required, for example when the terms of the plan are altered. If the plan is materially modified, or if there are changes in the information given in the SPD, the plan administrator has a duty to give participants a Summary of Material Modifications (SMM).

For a calendar-year plan that has undergone a material modification, the SMM must be sent to participants and beneficiaries by July 27 of the following year. Fiscal-year plans have until the 210th day after the end of the plan year.

The due date for the Form 5500 is July 31 (calendar-year plans) and the last day of the seventh month of the plan year after the plan year being reported, for plans that have a fiscal year. This is also the reporting schedule for individual statements of deferred vested benefits, to be sent to plan participants whose employment terminated during the plan year and who were entitled to deferred vested benefits at the time of termination.

For defined benefit plans only, the Pension Benefit Guaranty Corporation (PBGC) Form 1 is due on September 15 (calendar year plans) or eight-and-a-half months after the close of the plan fiscal year being reported on. For most defined benefit plans, the PPA has replaced the former requirement of issuing a Summary Annual Report with an Annual Funding Notice, see § 11.03, below.

The IRS analyzes the required notices that plan administrators must provide as two groups: participant events and plan events. The IRS also summarized the rules for providing notice in electronic form.

Notice of participant events are:

- Information provided at plan enrollment (e.g., enrollment package, SPD, salary deferral elections, beneficiary designation).

- Notice of automatic enrollment, given 30–90 days before automatic enrollment of an employee in either an Eligible Automatic Contribution Arrangement (EACA) or Qualified Automatic Contribution Arrangements (QACA) plan (see § 6.07[A]). This notice can be provided on the hiring date, if employees are immediately eligible to participate in the plan.

- Individual benefit statement, furnished on termination of employment or on the employee's written request. (Only one request per year has to be honored.) If the participant's account is not directed by the participant, notice of benefits must be given once a year; if it is self-directed, quarterly notice is required, because participants may wish to adjust their investment choices based on this information

- QJSA (Qualified Joint and Survivor Annuity) notice, given 30–180 days before benefits are paid; the notice explains the terms and conditions of the QJSA, what happens if a different payment form is elected, and the rights of beneficiaries to refuse to waive the QJSA.

- QOSA (Qualified Optional Survivor Annuity) notice, also given 30–180 days before benefits are paid. This notice explains the terms and conditions of the QOSA, effect of waiver, and spousal rights.

- QPSA (Qualified Preretirement Survivor Annuity) notice, given to the participant when he or she is in the age range 32–35 (or within a year of participation for people hired after age 35), disclosing terms and conditions, waiver rights, and effect of a waiver.

- Rollover eligibility notice, given 30–180 days before a participant receives a lump-sum plan distribution that is eligible for rollover. (The notice is given to the beneficiary if the distribution is made on account of the participant's death.) The notice explains the differing consequences of rolling over and not rolling over the distribution.

- Notice upon termination of employment, given within 90–180 days of resignation or retirement, explaining the right to defer receipt of the account balance—and the consequences of taking an immediate distribution.

- Notice of suspension of benefits, required when retirement benefits are suspended because the individual continues to work after normal retirement age.

The notices of plan events are:

- Annual funding notice (defined benefit plans), given within 120 days of the end of the plan year, describing, e.g., value of the plan's assets and liabilities, and its funding percentage.

- Notice of failure to make a required contribution (defined benefit plans), given within 60 days of the time when the employer failed to make a required quarterly funding contribution.

- Notice of request for a waiver of the minimum funding requirement (defined benefit plans), due within 14 days after the waiver application is filed with the IRS.

- Section 436 notice (defined benefit plans), issued within 30 days of the time a funding-based limitation on benefit accruals and distributions takes effect.

- Notice to interested parties, including plan participants, given 10–24 days after the plan applies for a determination letter about the plan's status as a qualified plan (including termination of the plan).

- Notice of a blackout period in an individual account plan, when the participant's ability to direct investments, get loans, or take plan distributions is temporarily suspended.

- Notice of adoption of a SIMPLE IRA plan.

- Safe harbor notice for 401(k) plans, explaining the employer's matching or non-elective contributions and the amount of compensation that can be deferred. (This notice must be given 30–90 days before each plan year).

- Notice of standard termination, given to plan participants, deceased participants' beneficiaries, Qualified Domestic Relations Order (QDRO) alternate payees, and unions.

- Notice that a terminated plan has been abandoned, informing participants of their account balance and requesting that they designate a form of distribution.

- Notice of significant reduction of future benefit accruals caused by a plan amendment or other employer action (e.g., a merger), explaining that benefits are eliminated or how they have been modified. The due date is 45 days before a benefit reduction takes effect, 30 days for modification of an early retirement subsidy because of a merger or acquisition, or 15 days for other merger-related event, or events involving small pension plans.

- Critical and endangered status notices (multi-employer defined benefit plans), informing participants, Collective Bargaining Agreement (CBA) parties, the Pension Benefit Guaranty Corporation (PGBC), and the DOL within 30 days of the time the plan's actuary certifies that the plan is in critical or endangered status.

- The IRS points out that notices given in electronic form must be as understandable as those provided on paper. The recipient must give consent to receiving electronic notice, after receiving disclosure of the consequences. All electronic notices must inform the recipient of the right to request hard-copy notices at no charge. [Notices in general, available at <http://www.irs.gov/Retirement-Plans/Plan-Participant,-Employee/Retirement-Topics-Notices> (updated Jan. 30, 2017) (last accessed Feb. 14, 2017)]

The DOL's *Reporting and Disclosure Guide for Employee Benefit Plans* [<http://www.dol.gov/ebsa/pdf/rdguide.pdf>; see also <http://www.dol.gov/ebsa/pdf/troubleshootersguide.pdf> (last viewed Feb. 14, 2017)] is a 30-page booklet that, for a variety of documents, lists in tabular form the kind of information covered; who receives it; and when it must be provided. The guide deals with the disclosure requirements that are common to pension plans and welfare benefit plans, as well as requirements specific to pension plans and those relating to group health plans. The guide also explains the reporting and disclosure requirements, administered by the PBGC, for defined benefit pension plans that are governed by ERISA Title IV. The last chapter of the guide explains annual reporting on Form 5500. It also includes links to Employee Benefit Security Administration (EBSA) and PBGC information resources.

The DOL documents should be read in conjunction with the IRS's updated guide to reporting and disclosure, which covers Form 5500, Form 5330, forms for reporting distributions made from the plan, and safe harbor notices. [<https://www.irs.gov/pub/irs-tege/irs_reporting_disclosure_guide.pdf>; see John Manganaro, *IRS Updates Reporting Disclosure Guide*, plansponsor.com (Mar. 3, 2017)]

Magistrate Judge Denlow allowed Verizon relief from the consequences of a typographical error that led to a class claim of $1.6 billion. When Verizon acquired Bell Atlantic, the new plan was incorrectly drafted: the lawyer drafting the plan included a multiplier in the middle of a sentence, and forgot to delete it from the end of the sentence, so that plan participants argued that they were entitled to have the multiplier applied twice. The magistrate judge allowed correction of the "scrivener's error" because applying the multiplier twice would give plan participants a windfall. His decision was affirmed by the Seventh Circuit in mid-2010. [*Young v. Verizon's Bell Atl. Cash Balance Plan*, 615 F.3d 808 (7th Cir. 2010), *cert. denied*, 131 S. Ct. 2924 (2011), *reh'g denied*, 132 S. Ct. 47 (2011)]

Previously, sponsors often used the IRS letter forwarding service to find payees of benefits. For requests postmarked on or after August 31, 2012, however, Rev. Proc. 2012-35, 2012-37 I.R.B. 341 announces that the IRS no longer considers finding missing persons a "humane purpose." Employers must therefore devise other means of finding the payees. The DOL's suggestions are Internet searches, credit reports, and commercial locater services. The Social Security Administration's forwarding service is still available, but at a cost of $25 per letter, whereas the IRS service was free for up to 50 participants. If the plan is terminating, it can use the PBGC's missing participants program, which requires the employer to submit the amount of the benefit to the PBGC, which looks for participants in connection with the termination. The Pension Protection Act mandated that the PBGC extend the program to non-defined benefit plans (e.g., 401(k)s) that terminate, but the PBGC never issued implementing regulations. [McDermott Will & Emery, *IRS Eliminates Use of Letter Forwarding Service to Find Missing Participants and Beneficiaries* (Sept. 27, 2012) (benefitslink.com)]

See DOL FAB 2014-01 (Aug. 14, 2014) for the four minimum steps that fiduciaries must use to try to find missing participants and beneficiaries of terminated defined contribution plans and how to distribute missing participants' account balances. At a minimum, the fiduciaries must send notice of termination by certified mail; search plan and employer records for a current address; ask the designated beneficiary where the missing participant is; and use free Internet search tools. Depending on the facts of the case, it may be necessary to use paid commercial locator services or information brokers. The preferred method of distributing the account balance is a direct rollover to an individual retirement account or annuity, but a safe harbor is available if proper notice is given and 30 days elapse without instructions from the participant about how to handle the funds. If a direct rollover is not possible or is not prudent, the DOL permits the fiduciary to transfer the funds to a federally insured bank account, or a state unclaimed property funds. [Austin K. Stack, *DOL Issues Guidance on Missing Participants in Terminated Plans*, Holland & Knight (Nov. 3, 2014) (benefits link.com)]

Plan documents should state whether it is permissible to pay plan expenses out of the plan's assets. If the document does not give this information, then it is allowable to use plan assets to pay plan expenses unless the plan document obligates the employer to pay the expenses. However, an employer that retained the right to amend the plan can adopt an amendment allowing payment of expenses in the future. An individual account plan can specify the way to allocate expenses paid by the plan to the participants' accounts. An allocation method described in the plan is a settlor decision, so the fiduciary must abide by it. If the plan does not specify, or if it is unclear, the fiduciaries must adopt a reasonable allocation method.

Assets of an ERISA plan can be used to pay expenses that are considered "fiduciary" expenses, but not those considered to be "settlor" expenses. For example, the plan can pay for recordkeeping, accounting, legal services dealing with fiduciary issues, trustee services, custodial services, annual or other periodic compliance audits, completion of legally mandated forms such as Form 5500, processing claims, and communicating with participants, including furnishing required disclosures such as SPDs and benefit statements and furnishing documents requested by plan participants and beneficiaries. Expenses for investment advice, educational seminars, and providing electronic access to plan information can also be paid out of plan assets. So can management fees and sales charges for plan investments.

However, settlor expenses that cannot be paid out of plan assets include, e.g., legal services for setting up a plan; costs of plan design; legal fees for plan termination; and most actuarial services used for planning.

A recent GAO report, *Participants Need Better Information When Offered Lump Sums That Replace Their Lifetime Benefits*, says that many employees do not get the information they need to make an informed decision. Since 2012, there is a trend among large employers to give some workers and retirees a chance to take a lump-sum benefit. Generally, there is a limited "window," e.g., one month, to exercise the option. The GAO says that this is legal, but participants may not have enough information. The GAO reviewed 11 information packets from lump-sum offers affecting close to 250,000 participants, and said that the packets were consistently unclear or deficient in key information—e.g., the value of the lump sum often was not compared to value of the lifetime monthly benefit; mortality assumptions and interest rates often were not explained; and PBGC guarantees (and loss thereof) were not explained clearly—although many people interviewed by the GAO said that they wanted a lump sum because they were afraid the plan sponsor would default. The GAO's recommendation is that eight kinds of information must be disclosed for participants to make an informed decision—and recommended that DOL and Treasury oversee lump-sum offers. [<http://www.gao.gov/assets/670/668106.pdf> (last accessed Feb. 14, 2017)]

[A] Communications Requirements Under PPACA

The health care reform act, the Patient Protection and Affordable Care Act of 2010 (PPACA) adds a number of communications and compliance requirements, covering both data that must be provided to plan participants and data to be submitted to regulators. Many of the provisions of PPACA require notices to be furnished, either to specific participants, or as a part of the plan's general benefits materials. Many plans include these notices in the annual enrollment package or the plan's SPD. As of August 2017, a bill to repeal and replace PPACA had been drafted but was withdrawn from consideration. If PPACA is eventually repealed under a different bill, then these requirements will no longer apply, although if there is a replacement plan, it is likely that employers will have to communicate the statutory changes to employees when replacement occurs, and will probably have ongoing communication obligations.

All plans, including grandfathered plans, must offer a one-time special enrollment period for adult children who were not covered because of age, or who aged out of the plan, and for persons who lost coverage because they reached the plan's maximum coverage, and notice must be given of the special enrollment period.

PPACA also requires notices of:

- Grandfathered status.

- Patient Protection Model Notice: If the plan requires participants to designate a primary care provider, how to choose one; notice that female enrollees can see an OB/GYN without prior authorization or referral. (Not required for grandfathered plans.)

- Explanation of the external review process; many plans include this in the SPD. (Not required for grandfathered plans.)

- Notice of internal adverse benefit determination.

- Advance notice that coverage will be cancelled or rescinded. [Christy Tinnes and Brigen Winters, *What Notices Are Required by PPACA?*, plansponsor.com (Sept. 21, 2010)]

Another PPACA requirement is notifying all eligible employees of their right to maintain Employee Group Health Plan (EGHP) enrollment of their children up to age 26. In order to remain grandfathered, a grandfathered plan must include an explanation of why the plan is grandfathered in all plan materials that are distributed to existing employees, new hires, and the Comprehensive Omnibus Budget Reconciliation Act (COBRA) beneficiaries. The notice must be repeated for each year that the plan maintains grandfathered status, although it can be incorporated into the open enrollment materials furnished to employees and COBRA beneficiaries.

The PPACA requires the employer to give each employee a summary of benefits and coverage (SBC) that explains (in understandable form) the covered benefits, exclusions, cost sharing, and continuation coverage aspects of the plan. SBCs must use the official template, <http://www.dol.gov/ebsa/pdf/correctedsbc template2.pdf> (accessed Feb. 14, 2017). There is an official Uniform Glossary of health plan terms, <http://www.dol.gov/ebsa/pdf/SBCUniformGlossary.pdf> (accessed Feb. 14, 2017). The SBC must be given along with the enrollment materials, and when coverage is renewed or reissued. If employees request another copy, it must be provided within seven days. Participants and beneficiaries must be notified, no later than 60 days after a material modification takes effect, of how the modification changes the terms of the plan. A penalty of $1,000 per violation is imposed for noncompliance with this disclosure requirement. (increased to $1,087 pursuant to the Bipartisan Budget Act of 2015: see 81 Fed. Reg. 42491 (June 30, 2016)).

A new SBC template was issued in April 2016, for use in plan years starting on or after April 1, 2017. Plans that maintain an open enrollment period are required to start to use the new templates on the first day of the first open enrollment period that begins on or after April 1, 2017, with respect to coverage for years beginning on or after that date. Plans without an annual open enrollment period are required to use the new template on the first day of the first plan or policy year beginning on or after April 1, 2017. The final template is five pages long, a page shorter than the previous edition. The disclosures about continuation coverage and appeal rights have been revised. [EPIC Compliance Alert, *New Summary of Benefits and Coverage (SBC) for 2017* (Aug. 31, 2016) (benefitslink .com)]

Under PPACA, the employer (not the health welfare benefit plan) is also required to inform all employees every year that they may qualify for premium subsidies for child health care; the DOL has published a model notice that can be used for this purpose, at <http://www.dol.gov/ebsa/pdf/chipmodelnotice.pdf>

(last accessed Feb. 14, 2017). If the EGHP includes a wellness program that offers rewards in exchange for meeting a condition, the plan must inform employees of options for waiving the condition or qualifying in an alternative way. Plan participants and beneficiaries have the right to request notices explaining the mental health parity rules (see § 18.03[E]). ERISA § 502(c)(9)(A) requires the employer to inform employees of the eligibility requirements for child health care; the penalty for failure to give this notice rose from a maximum of $110 per day of failure per employee to $112. [Conduent FYI, *DOL, PBGC and HHS Increase Penalties for Violations* (Feb. 10, 2017) (benefitslink.com)]

If a mental health or substance abuse claim is denied, the participant or beneficiary can request a notice explaining the reason for the denial. If the plan asserts an increased-cost defense for not providing parity in benefits for mental health/substance abuse claims, notice must be given to participants, beneficiaries, EBSA, and state regulators. [DOL's *Reporting and Disclosure Guide for Employee Benefit Plans*, <http://www.dol.gov/ebsa/pdf/rdguide.pdf> (Sept. 2014) (last viewed Feb. 14, 2017)]

Final Regulations on the Code § 6055 requirements for minimum essential health coverage were published on March 10, 2014. The regulations explain the requirements imposed on companies with 50 or more full-time employees to report to the IRS and to employees about health care coverage available to employees. The requirements will be used by the IRS to enforce the pay-or-play mandate once it takes effect, and to administer the tax credit that certain individuals will receive for buying health care coverage on an Exchange under Code § 36B.

Information is reported to employees on Form 1095-C, then transmitted to the IRS on Form 1094-C. E-filing is mandatory for employers who are required to file 250 or more tax returns. Notice to employees can be given electronically if the employees agree. Employers that sponsor self-funded plans can use Form 1094-C to combine reporting for §§ 6055 and 6056.

Failure to satisfy these reporting requirements can be penalized under § 6721 (failure to file required information returns) and § 6722 (failure to provide payees with reports). However, if there is reasonable cause, § 6724 may offer relief by waiving penalties. [79 Fed. Reg. 13220 (Mar. 10, 2014)]

An information return is prepared for each employee, then the returns are transmitted to the IRS. For insured plans, the insurer prepares Form 1095-B (for individuals) and Form 1094-B (transmission form to the IRS). Self-insured small employers also use these forms, whereas applicable large employers with self-insured health plans use Form 1095-C to report to employees and Form 1094-C as a transmittal form.

An applicable large employer is one that had at least 50 full-time or full-time equivalent employees in the year before the year of the report. The Form 1095-C contains information that the IRS uses to determine whether the employer met the requirement of offering its employees adequate coverage (i.e., satisfying the standards not only for adequacy of benefits, but for affordability).

The basic due date for giving employees the appropriate 1095-series form is January 31. If the employee agrees, the statement can be sent electronically rather than in hard copy. [Bill O'Malley and Jill Harris, *New Information Reporting Requirements Under the Affordable Care Act*, McGladrey Tax Alert (Aug. 7, 2014)]

For the 2016 reporting forms, see Form 1094-B: <https://www.irs.gov/pub/irs-pdf/i109495b.pdf>; Form 1094-C: https://www.irs.gov/pub/irs-pdf/f1094c.pdf; and Form 1095-C: <https://www.irs.gov/pub/irs-pdf/f1095c.pd>. The 2016 forms are very similar to the previous editions, but two new codes have been added to Form 1095-C dealing with conditional offers of coverage to employees' spouses. The general due date for individual 2016 statements was January 31, 2017; IRS returns were due February 28, 2017 (paper) and March 31 (electronic filing). The penalties for failure to file increased, to $260 per violation, capped at $3,193,000 per year (or less, for small business). [Chelkogroup.com, *Final Forms for ACA Reporting Released* (Oct. 4, 2016) (benefitslink.com)]

The Summary of Benefits and Coverage can be distributed electronically to plan participants and beneficiaries who are already covered by an EGHP. DOL electronic disclosure requirements must be satisfied. For eligible people who are not yet enrolled (e.g., newly hired employees), the SBC can be distributed electronically in a readily accessible format, but the plan must make free hard copies available on request. If the electronic distribution occurs via a Website, then the employer must send written notice or e-mail to give the URL for the site and tell employees that they can request free hard copies. [Tracey Giddings and Birgit Anne Waidmann, *Administration Issues Final Rules on PPACA Summary of Benefits and Coverage*, PricewaterhouseCooper HRS Insight No. 12/06 (Feb. 14, 2012) (benefitslink.com)]

PPACA included a deferred requirement that, as of January 1, 2014, large employers would have to automatically enroll employees in the EGHP, giving employees reasonable notice of the coverage options available to them, including the possibility of opting out of the plan. However, the requirement was repealed by the Bipartisan Budget Act of 2015, Pub. L. No. 114-74. For plan years beginning on or after January 2, 2014, EGHPs may not impose waiting periods that exceed 90 days.

Starting with January 1, 2011, administrators of self-insured plans (and health insurers) must report to the HHS on the "loss ratios"—the amount of premiums devoted to paying claims rather than administrative expenses. In the large group market, if the loss ratio falls below 85%, the plan must give each enrollee a pro rata rebate each year.

Another implication of PPACA is that employers have a duty to inform laid-off employees that they can purchase health insurance on the Exchange instead of making a COBRA election. Individuals can purchase Exchange coverage outside the open enrollment period if they undergo an event affecting their insured status, such as job loss. However, employees who want to keep the same doctors might prefer COBRA coverage to Exchange coverage. Another factor is that low- or moderate-income individuals may qualify for a federal subsidy if they purchase Exchange coverage. [Louise Radnofsky, *Employers Must Notify Laid-Off Workers of Health Care Options, New Rule Says*, WSJ.com (May 2, 2014)]

[B]   Cromnibus Changes

The "Cromnibus" (Consolidated and Further Continuing Appropriations Act; Pub. L. No. 113-235) legislation is a spending measure lasting through September 2015. It also addresses pension issues, especially for vulnerable multi-employer plans, which may be permitted to suspend benefits under certain conditions. Trustees of a plan that intends to suspend benefits must give notice of the proposed suspension to participants, employers, unions, and the Department of the Treasury. Suspension requires the secretary of the treasury to rule that the suspension satisfies the statutory requirements. The suspension must also be submitted for a vote by participants. The Cromnibus legislation expands the ERISA requirements of information disclosure: for example, plans that are in critical or endangered status must disclose their rehabilitation plan or latest funding improvement plan. [*"Cromnibus Act" Changes for Multi-employer and Single-Employer Defined Benefit Pension Plans* (Dec. 26, 2014) (benefitslink.com)]

> ■ **TIP:** These Cromnibus rules primarily deal with "multi-employer plans," which are different from "multiple-employer" plans. A multi-employer plan is operated by several employers and one or more unions, pursuant to a collective bargaining agreement. A multiple-employer plan is a defined benefit plan operated by two or more unrelated employers, that are not so closely related as to be treated as a single employer.

§ 11.02   SUMMARY PLAN DESCRIPTION (SPD)

[A]   Basic Requirements

ERISA § 102 imposes a duty on the plan administrator to furnish a copy of the Summary Plan Description (SPD) to each participant and to each beneficiary receiving benefits under the plan. The SPD must be furnished within 90 days of the time a person becomes a participant or first receives benefits. (For a new plan, the SPD can be furnished within 120 days of the time the plan comes under Title I of ERISA, if this is later than the 90-day period.)

ERISA § 102 requires the SPD to be written in a way that can be understood by the average plan participant. The document must be accurate and comprehensive enough to inform them of their rights and obligations. ERISA requires the following items to be included in the SPD:

- The formal and common names of the plan;
- The name and address of the employer (or of the organization maintaining a collectively bargained plan);
- The employer's EIN and the plan's IRS identification number;
- What kind of plan it is;
- How the plan is administered—e.g., by contract or by an insurer;
- The name and address of the agent for service of process (the person designated to receive summonses, complaints, subpoenas, and related litigation documents);
- A statement that process can be served not only on this designated agent, but also on the plan's administrator or trustee;
- The name, address, and title of each trustee;
- Disclosure of whether the plan is a collectively bargained plan, and a statement that the participant can examine the collective bargaining agreement or get a copy of the agreement from the plan administrator;
- Rules of eligibility for participation;
- The plan's normal retirement age;
- Circumstances under which plan benefits can be altered or suspended;
- How to waive the normal payment mechanism (the Qualified Joint and Survivor Annuity) and elect a different payment form, such as a lump sum;
- Procedures for QDROs and Qualified Medical Child Support Orders (QMCSOs), either through a description in the SPD itself or disclosure that a free copy of a separate document will be provided on request;
- A description of the circumstances under which the plan can be terminated, the rights of participants and beneficiaries after termination occurs, and the circumstances under which benefits can be denied or suspended; what will happen to the plan's assets upon termination. (All amendments must be made with the necessary corporate governance steps, such as adoption of a resolution by the Board of Directors);
- If the plan benefits are insured by the PBGC; if they are not, the reason why insurance is not required; if they are, a disclosure that PBGC insurance is in place, how it works, and where to get more information (from the plan administrator or the PBGC; the PBGC's address must be given in the SPD);

- An explanation of the plan's rules for determining service to calculate vesting and breaks in service;

- Do the contributions to the plan come exclusively from the employer, or are employee contributions accepted or mandated?

- Method of calculating the contribution. (A defined benefit plan is allowed to simply say that the amount is "actuarially determined");

- The funding medium and entity for the plan. Usually this will be a trust fund, but sometimes an insurance company is involved;

- The plan's fiscal year;

- How to present a claim for plan benefits;

- If the plan will use the "cutback" rule to change the vesting or accrual rules described in the SPD, participants must be informed which provisions of the plan are subject to modification; when modified, the nature of the modification must be explained;

- Remedies that are available if a claim is denied;

- A statement of the rights of participants and beneficiaries and what protections are available for those rights. A model statement that can be used for this purpose is published at 29 C.F.R. § 2520.102-3.

After reviewing public comments, EBSA decided that the current disclosure requirements give enough information about cash balance conversions and operations, so it was not necessary to impose any special requirements.

SPDs must be given to participants and beneficiaries within 90 days after they achieve that status. For a new plan, all participants must get an SPD 12 days after the plan becomes subject to ERISA reporting and disclosure requirements. If a company offers different benefits to different groups of SPDs, the company can issue a separate SPD for each group.

■ **TIP:**   If a significant percentage of the participants in a plan are not literate in English, but are literate in the same non-English language, the SPD must include a notice in that language offering assistance in understanding the English SPD. In this context, a significant percentage means over 25% of the participants in a plan with fewer than 100 total participants, or the lesser of 10% of the participants or 500 people in a large plan.

Nevertheless, the District Court for the District of Maryland ruled in mid-2014 that failure to provide a Spanish-language SPD did not violate ERISA. ERISA does not explicitly require multiple-language SPDs, but the English SPD must include a prominent notice in the employees' prevailing language offering help, if a plan has under 100 participants 25% or more of whom are literate only in the same non-English language, or, for a larger plan, that at least 10% of all participants or 500 employees are literate in the same language. The district court said that there is no private cause of action for violation of the right to receive SPDs within 90 days of becoming plan participants. However, one plaintiff was awarded up to $400 (up to four days of statutory damages at $100/day) for documents received more than 30 days after the document request. [*Melendez v. Hatfield's Equipment & Dedication Servs., Inc.*, No. 1:13-cv-03684, 2014 U.S. Dist. LEXIS 110974 (D. Md. Aug. 12, 2014)]

The best distribution methods are handing the SPDs to the employees at the workplace, or mailing them to employees' homes. It is not enough to put them out in the workplace, because there's no guarantee that employees will take them.

The SPD can also be distributed as an insert in an employee periodical such as one published by the company or the union. If you choose this option, be sure to put a prominent notice on the front page of the periodical, stating that this issue contains an insert that has important legal consequences, and that it should be retained for reference and not discarded.

■ **TIP:** The statement of participant rights required by ERISA can be incorporated into the SPD.

If a plan is amended—and most are, sooner or later—the plan administrator must issue an updated SPD every five years (measured from the time the plan first became subject to ERISA) reflecting the changes of the past five years. Even if there are no changes at all, the administrator must provide an updated SPD to all participants every 10 years.

If there are any false statements in the SPD, ERISA disclosure regulations have been violated, and the employer could face penalties from the Department of Labor. Most plan participants never see the trust documents for the plan, so they get their information from the SPD.

A three-judge panel of the Ninth Circuit held in 2016 that, if a claimant for benefits makes a prima facie case that he or she is entitled to the benefits but does not have corporate information that is needed to substantiate the claim, the burden shifts to the defendant employer to produce the information. When the claimant asked for documents, the plan administrators provided some documents, but not a copy of the SPD. The Ninth Circuit said that, although in most situations (for example, proving disability under a Long-Term Disability plan) the burden of proof falls on the plaintiff, but when the defendant is the only party with the information and the plaintiff has no other way to get it, the burden was on the employers, who had the information about the plaintiff's work record and who had copies of the SPD. [*Barton v. ADT Sec. Servs. Pension Plan*, 820 F.3d 1060 (9th Cir. 2016); see Practicallaw.com Employee Benefits & Executive Compensation, *In the Ninth Circuit, a New Burden of Proof for Employers in Benefits Litigation* (Sept. 22, 2016) (benefitslink.com)]

Until mid-2011, there was a split in authority about which provisions should prevail if the SPD contradicted the plan terms. The Supreme Court settled the question in the very important mid-2011 *Amara v. CIGNA* decision, holding that the terms of the plan prevail over the SPD, because the plan terms reflect the intentions of the settlor that adopted the plan. [*Amara v. CIGNA*, 131 S. Ct. 1866 (May 23, 2011), *on remand*, 925 F. Supp. 2d 242 (D. Conn. 2012). The case continued to be litigated; see, e.g., No.3:01-cv-02361-JBA (D. Conn. Jan. 14, 2016), but that phase of the case deals with other issues. See, however, *Koehler v. Aetna Health Inc.*, 683 F.3d 182 (5th Cir. 2012) holding that even post-*Amara*, SPDs must be drafted so participants can understand them—so ambiguities in the plan and SPD must be resolved in favor of the plan participant.]

The Sixth Circuit held that a claim for equitable relief is allowable when the SPD conflicts materially with the plan even without other elements, such as reliance. The plaintiff was offered a buyout package shortly before Chrysler's bankruptcy filing. He turned down the offer, and was then fired for improper use of company vehicles. Before his termination, he was eligible for a supplemental benefit providing an additional stipend until he became eligible for Social Security, but he lost eligibility for this benefit because of his termination. He claimed that the SPD, which did not say that terminated employees were ineligible, controlled. The Fifth Circuit held that the plan did not allow this "30 and out" benefit, so recovery under ERISA § 502(a)(1)(B) was unavailable. But the Sixth Circuit said that the district court should have allowed him to amend his complaint to add equitable claims for reformation, estoppel, and surcharge because a material conflict between plan terms and SPD can give rise to equitable relief. In this interpretation, *Amara* means that under ERISA § 502(a)(1)(B), conflicts between the plan documents and the terms of the SPD must be resolved in favor of the plan document. Nevertheless, ERISA § 502(a)(3) permits equitable relief for violations of ERISA. [*Pearce v. Chrysler Grp. LLC Pension Plan*, No. 15-0459, 2015 WL 3797385 (6th Cir. June 18, 2015)]

[B] Health Plan SPDs

ERISA § 104(b)(1)(B) requires that plan participants and beneficiaries be notified within 60 days of a material reduction in the services provided under an Employee Group Health Plan (EGHP). Or the plan sponsor can simply provide notices at regular intervals, not more than 90 days apart, of changes in the interim. The SPD for an EGHP must indicate if a health insurer is responsible for financing or administration (including claims payment). If an insurer is involved, the insurer's name and address must appear in the SPD.

Group health plans SPDs must include the following:

- Participants' responsibility for cost-sharing (premiums, deductibles, coinsurance, copayments);

- Lifetime or annual caps on plan benefits; any other benefit limits;

- Procedures for Qualified Medical Child Support Orders (QMCSOs);

- Coverage of preventive services;

- Coverage (if any) of established and new drugs;

- Coverage of medical tests, devices, and procedures;

- Which health care providers are part of the network, and how the network is created;

- Circumstances under which network providers must be used; coverage, if any, for out-of-network services;

- How primary care and specialty providers must be selected;

- Conditions for getting emergency care;

- Requirements for preauthorization of treatment and utilization review;

- Information about the required length of hospital stays for childbirth, including descriptions of the federal law and any additional protection furnished by state law;

- Either a description of claims procedures or a statement that a free copy of the claims procedure is available on request;

- The role of health insurance in the plan; the EBSA says "particularly in those cases where the plan is self-funded and an insurer is serving as contract administrator or claims payor, rather than as an insurer";

- Extent to which the sponsor has the right to eliminate benefits or terminate the plan;

- Participants' rights under ERISA.

The SPD can include only a general description of the provider network, as long as the SPD explains that a separate document, available without charge, lists all the network providers. If the plan requires participants and beneficiaries to designate a primary care provider, the SPD must inform participants how to do this, and must explain how to designate a provider for a child; see model language at <http://www.dol.gov/ebsa/patientprotectionmodelnotice.doc> (last accessed Apr. 11, 2016).

A health plan's SPD must describe employees' and their families' COBRA rights:

- What constitutes a qualifying event;

- Premiums ex-employees must pay for continuation coverage;

- Notice procedures;

- How to make a COBRA election;

- How long coverage will last.

The SPD for an EGHP must either describe the plan's procedures for validating Qualified Medical Child Support Orders (QMCSOs), or must inform participants that a free copy of the plan's QMCSO procedures is available on request. The description should be complete enough to assist potential alternate payees in asserting their rights.

A welfare benefit plan that is not an EGHP must also have an SPD, containing information such as:

- Plan name;

- Employer's name and address;

- EIN and plan number for annual reporting purposes;

- Contact information for the plan administrator;

- Information about the trustees;

- Who is eligible to participate in the plan;

- Claims procedure;

- Statement of participants' rights under ERISA;

- Where to serve process;

However, welfare benefit plan participants are entitled to SPDs only if they are "covered by the plan," which happens on the earliest of these dates:

- The date the plan says participation begins;

- The date the person becomes eligible to receive a benefit subject to contingencies such as incurring medical expenses;

- The date of the initial voluntary or mandatory plan contribution.

Therefore, SPDs (and SMMs) must be furnished to employees; retirees covered under the plan; the parent or guardian of a minor child who is the "alternate recipient" under a QMCSO; and spouses or other dependents of deceased participants. Although ERISA doesn't say this, some court decisions require SPDs to be furnished to guardians or other representatives of incapacitated beneficiaries.

Health plans must inform the Centers for Medicare and Medicaid Services (CMS), which plan participants and beneficiaries are eligible for Medicare; and whether the plan offers prescription drug benefits that are at least actuarially equivalent to the coverage under Medicare Part D, the prescription drug program. Actuarially equivalent benefits are referred to as "creditable coverage." (Employers that offer an actuarially equivalent plan may also be able to collect a federal subsidy; see Chapter 9.) The notice must be given at least once a year, before the start of the annual Medicare enrollment period, which is now October 15–December 7 of each year. (The period was extended and moved to earlier in the year by the PPACA.)

Notice must also be given when an employee who is eligible for Medicare enrolls in the health plan, although this can be included in the new-hire package; on request; and when the plan's coverage either becomes creditable or ceases to be creditable.

An EGHP's SPD made references to the "plan document," although no separate plan document existed. Traditionally, EGHP plan booklets included the relevant provisions about benefits and claims that would appear in an SPD, but often failed to include other essential provisions such as appeals procedures and explanations of how the plan was funded. In this case, the SPD could serve as the plan document because it included all of the requirements for a written plan document. The Fifth Circuit held that the participants were not harmed by the absence of a separate plan document. [*Rhea v. Alan Ritchey, Inc., Welfare Benefit Plan,* No. 16-41032 (4th Cir. May 30, 2017); see *Fifth Circuit Confirms a Summary Plan Description May Also Act as the Plan Document Under ERISA,* Haynes and Boone LLP (June 7, 2017), available at Lexology.com]

§ 11.03 SUMMARY ANNUAL REPORT (SAR)/ANNUAL FUNDING NOTICE

Before the Pension Protection Act (PPA) took effect, both defined contribution and defined benefit plans were required to distribute Summary Annual Reports (SARs) to beneficiaries, based on information from the plan's annual report (Form 5500). As a result of the PPA, SARs are still required for defined contribution plan participants; for defined benefit plans covered by ERISA Title IV, it has been replaced by the Annual Funding Notice. The administrator has nine months from the end of the plan year (or two months after the end of the extension, if an extension was granted for filing the underlying Form 5500). DOL regulations [29 C.F.R. § 2520.104b-10(d)] provide a simple "fill in the blanks" form that must be used for the SAR.

The SAR form consists of a basic financial statement about the plan and its expenses, the net value of plan assets, and whether the plan's assets appreciated or depreciated in value during the year. If the plan is subject to the minimum funding standard, the plan must disclose either that contributions were adequate to satisfy the requirement, or the amount of the deficit. Participants must also be informed of their right to receive additional information, including a copy of the full annual report, a statement of the plan's assets and liabilities, or a statement of the plan's income and expenses. Plans that have simplified reporting requirements can use alternative compliance methods to satisfy the SAR requirement.

The annual funding notice is required from most defined benefit plans that are subject to PBGC jurisdiction; certain government and church plans and small professional service corporation plans are not insured by the PBGC and continue to issue the SAR. Before the PPA, multi-employer plans had to issue annual funding notices, but single-employer plans did not.

Notice must be given within 120 days of the end of the plan year (for plans with 100 or more participants) or by the extended date for filing Form 5500 (for smaller plans), to each participant and beneficiary and union, and to the PBGC. However, the PBGC will not take enforcement action against a plan whose liabilities exceed its assets by $50 million or less, as long as the plan provides the mandatory information within 30 days of a request from the PBGC.

EBSA issued a final rule in February 2015 about the annual notice of funded status under ERISA § 101(f). The annual notice discloses the benefits eligible for the PBGC guarantee, the limitations on the guarantee, and when the limitations apply. Single-employer plans must summarize the rules about plan termination. Multi-employer plan notices must summarize the rules about insolvency.

The regulations incorporate the MPRA disclosure requirements for multi-employer plans that are in critical and declining status. If there is a material event that would require disclosure, but the plan administrator does not become aware of it until 120 days or less before the due date of the funding notice, it can be omitted from the notice. Multi-employer plans that have terminated by mass withdrawal, and § 412(e)(3) plans have alternative methods of compliance: see § 4014A(a)(2). Generally, the notices are due within 120 days of the end of the plan year but plans with 100 or fewer participants have until the filing date of the annual report (as extended) to issue the notices. The regulation provides model notices for single- and multi-employer plans, although plans can draft their own forms if they prefer. The regulations are effective March 4, 2015, for notices for years beginning on or after January 1, 2015. [80 Fed. Reg. 5625 (Feb. 2, 2015)]

The Moving Ahead for Progress in the 21st Century Act (Pub. L. No. 112-141, aka MAP-21) helps the sponsors of defined benefit plans by allowing them to calculate their contributions using more favorable interest rate assumptions. However, plans that take advantage of this assistance have additional disclosure obligations. MAP-21 requires plan administrators to disclose additional information if the plan had 50 or more participants on any day of the preceding plan year; the stabilized funding target is less than 95% of the regular funding target; and the plan would have a funding shortfall of $500,000 or more absent stabilization. If all three of those factors are present, the plan's Annual Funding Notice must disclose that the law has changed reducing the employer's contribution. The notice must include a table showing MAP-21's effect on funding requirements, plan's funding shortfall, and the minimum contribution for the current year and the two years before.

The Highway & Transportation Funding Act of 2014, Pub. L. No. 113-159, extends the period for which defined benefit plan sponsors can get relief from the implications of low interest rates; this legislation does not alter the employer's disclosure obligations. The Consolidated and Further Continuing Appropriations Act, Pub. L. No. 113-235, requires multi-employer plans to increase disclosure to plan participants, informing them of potential suspensions of benefits and giving them a chance to comment.

§ 11.04   INDIVIDUAL ACCOUNT PLAN DISCLOSURES

Defined contribution plans must give their participants a variety of notices:

- Safe harbor 401(k) plan's annual notice about the features of the plan, such as the safe harbor non-elective contribution or matching contribution of the plan; this must be given 30–90 days before the beginning of the plan year;

- Qualified Automatic Contribution Arrangement (QACA) safe harbor 401(k) plans must provide an annual notice on the same schedule;

- Qualified Default Investment Alternative (QDIA) notice of rights and obligations, such as the participant's right to transfer the account to other investments, and when funds will be invested in the QDIA; must be provided at least 30 days before the beginning of the plan year;

- 401(k) automatic enrollment notice, providing information such as deferrals made without an affirmative election, and how the plan invests contributions where there is no election; must be provided 30–90 days before the beginning of the plan year;

- Employer stock diversification notice: information about the right to transfer the participant's investment from employer stock into other investments (if the employer's stock is publicly traded). The notice must be given no later than 30 days before the first date that diversification rights can be issued.

In general, two or more notices can be combined into a single document as long as the time requirements are satisfied. Electronic distribution is permissible if the electronic disclosure requirements are satisfied—but the defined contribution plan requirements cannot be satisfied in the SPD even if it is distributed annually.

EBSA published a direct final rule in the *Federal Register* on March 19, 2015, amending the rules about "participant-level fee disclosure" that were promulgated in 2010. The disclosure rules require the fiduciaries of 401(k) plans to provide a disclosure statement about the investment alternatives offered by the plan. Participants are entitled to get the statement before they are enrolled in the plan, and then at least once a year after that. EBSA interprets the "once a year" requirement to mean that second and subsequent disclosure statements must be provided within 12 months of the disclosure provided upon enrollment. The 2015 rule allows any plan—calendar- or fiscal-year—to provide the disclosure statement at least once in any 14-month period. In other words, there is a two-month grace period for furnishing the annual statement. [80 Fed. Reg. 14334 (Mar. 19, 2015); see DOL Fact Sheet, *Direct Final Rule Provides Flexibility for the Timing of Annual Disclosures to Workers in 401(k)-Type Retirement Plans*, <http://www.dol.gov/ebsa/newsroom/fsdirectfinalrule.html> (undated, last accessed Feb. 15, 2017)]

The IRS will generally treat a plan as having lost its status as a 401(k) safe harbor plan if it fails to provide a timely annual safe harbor plan notice for a year. If this status is lost, the plan must satisfy the nondiscrimination requirements from which it was exempted. This could limit highly compensated employees' ability to defer compensation, or could require the plan sponsor to refund some amounts already deferred. Penalties could also be imposed for failure to provide the automatic enrollment or QACA notice. Failure to give timely QCIA notice forfeits fiduciary protection of the sponsor, plan administrator, or investment company for investment loss. Protection is only restored for amounts invested in the QDIA after compliance with the notice requirements. [McKenna Long & Aldridge LLP, *2011 Year-End Disclosure Reminders for Qualified Defined Contribution Plan Sponsors* (Nov. 2011) (benefitslink.com)]

In 2008–2009, during the financial crisis, interim regulations were adopted allowing employers to reduce or suspend non-elective contributions due to substantial business hardship. Before the interim regulations were adopted, the employer could not reduce or eliminate elective contributions to safe harbor plans in mid-year, although it was permissible to suspend or reduce matching contributions in mid-year on 30 days' notice to participants.

The final regulations published in late 2013 define substantial business hardship as operating at an economic loss; notice to employees is still required. Before these rules were published, many employers thought they could only use the safe harbor if they were bankrupt or close to bankruptcy. As of January 1, 2015, a company operating at a loss can suspend its matching contributions in mid-year. Such contributions can be reduced in mid-year even if the employer is not suffering economic hardship, as long as the right to reduce contributions is reserved in the annual safe harbor notices given to participants. Employers could suspend safe harbor non-elective contributions as soon as the final regulations took effect. The 30 days' notice to employees must inform employees of the effective date of the plan amendment, how the amendment works, and how they can change their elective deferrals. [John Manganaro, *IRS Revises Safe Harbor Plan Rules*, plansponsor.com (Nov. 15, 2013)]

Failure to give the safe harbor notice is an operational failure that requires correction under the IRS Self Correction Program; the Employee Plans Compliance Resolution System is not available. Plans that cannot provide the evidence are required to engage in corrections and possibly pay closing agreement sanctions. Plans should protect themselves by keeping dated copies of the notice and cover letter (for electronic communications, the e-mail, the date it was sent, and a list of addressees). If the plan cannot provide the evidence, the IRS is requiring corrections and perhaps a closing agreement sanction. [SunGard Relius, *Failure to Provide Safe Harbor Notice Correction* (Nov. 30, 2012) (benefitslink.com)]

The modern trend is for plans to provide participants with a greater degree of control over the way their pension plan accounts are invested. DOL Reg. § 2550.404c-1(b), dealing with "participant directed individual account plans" (profit-sharing, stock bonus, and money purchase plans) obligates plans to offer at least three diversified categories of investments, with materially different risk and return characteristics, so that overall the participant can choose the balance between risk and return that he or she prefers. Plan fiduciaries are not liable if the participant's own investment choices result in losses, unless obeying the participant's instructions violates the terms of the plan.

Participants are entitled to receive a great deal of information in connection with individual account plans. The burden is on the plan to supply the information, not on the individual participant to request it. The mandated disclosures include:

- A description of the available investment alternatives available under the plan; the general risk and return characteristics of each, including the composition of each portfolio and how they are diversified;

- The designated investment managers for each alternative;

- When and how participants can give investment instructions; any limitations imposed on those instructions (for instance, only four changes in investment per year);

- Fees and expenses that affect the participant's account balance;

- Contact information for a fiduciary (or designee of a fiduciary) who can provide additional information about plan investments on request;

- The fact that fiduciaries are not liable if they follow the participant's investment directions, even if losses result;

- (If participants can invest in securities of the employer) Procedures to maintain confidentiality about the participant's voting and tendering shares of employer stock, and contact information for the fiduciary who monitors the confidentiality provisions.

EBSA published an Advance Notice of Proposed Rulemaking (ANPRM) on May 5, 2013, dealing with lifetime income illustrations in defined contribution plans' periodic pension statements. EBSA sought comments on how to present accrued benefits as an estimated lifetime stream of benefits as well as an account balance. EBSA's position is that disclosing the lifetime income stream will help employees prepare for retirement. [EBSA.gov, *Fact Sheet On Lifetime Income Illustration* (May 7, 2013) (benefitslink.com). A calculator for lifetime income streams under these rules was published at <www.dol.gov/ebsa/regs/lifetime incomecalculator.html> (last accessed Feb. 15, 2017).]

When a participant invests in publicly traded securities and other assets subject to the Securities Act of 1933 [15 U.S.C. § 77a], the participant must be given a prospectus for the investment either before or right after making the investment. If the plan "passes through" to participants the rights to vote and/or tender the shares, the plan must provide the participant with the proxy materials and other relevant documents, and must provide instructions on how to exercise the rights.

The plan further has a duty to disclose, based on the latest information available to the plan, at least this much information (either to all participants, or on request by a participant):

- For each investment alternative, the fees and operating expenses as a percentage of the average net assets of the investment alternative;

- Whatever prospectuses, financial statements, and reports the plan has about the investment alternative;

- A description of the portfolio of each alternative;

- The value of shares in each alternative;

- The current and past performance of each alternative, net of expenses, calculated on a "reasonable and consistent basis";

- The value of the shares in the individual participant's account.

Since 2010, the DOL has been issuing regulations on two important topics: the information that service providers (such as brokers and investment advisers) must give qualified plans about their fees and services—and the way the plan must disseminate this information to plan participants and beneficiaries. This obligation is separate from the "fiduciary rule" about paid advisors to retirement plan participants and IRA owners that was under attack by the Trump administration in early 2017: see § 6.08[A].

A 2010 EBSA final rule says that investing plan assets is a fiduciary act subject to ERISA § 404(a)(1), requiring fiduciaries to be prudent and act solely in best interests of plan's participants and beneficiaries. If the participants and beneficiaries have investment responsibility for their own accounts, the plan administrator has a duty to ensure that they are informed of their rights and responsibilities in connection with the investments in their accounts, including fee and expense information.

Participants must be given plan-related information before the first date on which they can direct investments, and then on a regular basis afterward. Participants must also receive a statement, at least quarterly, disclosing the dollar amount of plan-related fees and expenses actually charged to their accounts, and why. They must receive one-, five-, and ten-year performance data for their investments. Any fees or restrictions on their ability to purchase or withdraw from an investment must be disclosed. Information must be disclosed in a chart or similar format that facilitates comparisons; the final rule includes a model chart that can be used for this purpose. Participants must also be given whatever materials the plan receives with respect to voting, tender, or other rights with respect to the investment.

On request from a participant, the plan administrator must furnish prospectuses, financial reports, and statements of asset value for that particular investment option. The general disclosure rules at 29 C.F.R. § 2520.104b-1, including the electronic disclosure rules, also apply to material furnished under this final rule. [EBSA Fact Sheet, *Final Rule to Improve Transparency of Fees and Expenses to Workers in 401(k)-Type Retirement Plans* <http://www.dol.gov/ebsa/pdf/fsparticipantfeerule.pdf> (Feb. 2012) (last accessed Feb. 15, 2017)]

Under DOL's final regulations on disclosure of fees and expenses in participant-directed defined contribution plans, three types of plan information have to be disclosed:

- General plan information,
- Administrative expense information,
- Individual expense information.

General plan information deals with the plan's structure and mechanics (e.g., how to give investment instructions). The administrative expenses information explains the fees and expenses (e.g., legal, accounting, and recordkeeping fees) that can be charged to all individual accounts. Participants must also be informed of fees and expenses specific to their accounts, e.g., fees for plan loans or processing Qualified Domestic Relations Orders (QDROs). For each investment option under the plan, data about historic performance (one-, five-, and 10-year returns) and relevant indexes for comparing performance. Fees and expenses must be explained both as a percentage of assets and as dollar amounts per $1,000 invested.

In February 2012, EBSA published a final rule on disclosure obligations that plan service providers owe to fiduciaries. The definition of service providers includes registered investment advisors, certain broker-dealers, TPAs, and other providers who receive direct or indirect compensation from plan assets in the amount of $1,000 or more. There were some changes between the Interim Final Rule (IFR) and the final rules. The final rule applies to plans that are defined benefit or defined contribution plans as defined by ERISA, but not to SEPs, SIMPLE plans, 403(b) plans, IRA plans, or welfare benefit plans.

The information must be submitted, in writing, to the fiduciary responsible for the plan. Electronic means of disclosure are permitted as long as the disclosures are readily accessible to the fiduciary. EBSA strongly encourages service providers to furnish a summary or similar tool that helps fiduciaries locate all the required disclosures. Service providers can use Employee Benefits Security Administration (EBSA's) sample guide, published as an appendix to the final rule, as a model. Whenever the individual information changes, the service providers must disclose the change; in any event, disclosure is required within 60 days of the time the service provider learns of the change. Good-faith correction of errors is permitted within 30 days of discovery of an error or omission.

When a plan fiduciary or plan administrator requests, the service provider must divulge information (e.g., compensation) about the service arrangement. The final regulation is effective for both existing and new contracts as of July 1, 2012. Failure to comply with these requirements is a prohibited transaction for the fiduciary, whereas compliance secures a prohibited transaction exemption. The final rule requires plan fiduciaries to terminate service arrangements as soon as possible if a provider fails to respond to a fiduciary's request for information within 90 days. [DOL Fact Sheet, *Final Regulation Relating to Service Provider Disclosures Under Section 408(b)(2)*, <http://www.dol.gov/ebsa/newsroom/fs408b2 finalreg.html> (Feb. 2012) (last viewed Feb. 15, 2017)]

The general rule is that fiduciaries are forbidden to deal with plan assets in their own interest and, unless they qualify for a Prohibited Transaction Exemption, they cannot provide investment advice to participants if the advice results in higher fees for the fiduciaries or their affiliates. The PPA creates an exemption for advisers who receive fees for advice—under an eligible investment advice arrangement, with either level fees or advice generated by a certified, objective computer model. The DOL's 2011 final rule applies to banks, insurance companies, broker-dealers, registered investment advisers, and their affiliates, employees, representatives, and agents. A qualifying arrangement must be based on generally accepted investment theories and consider historical returns. Investments must be suitable for the individual investor, bearing in mind the fees and expenses of the investment. Computer models must also use generally accepted investment theories and analyze historic risks and returns. At least annually, the fiduciary advisor has to get an independent audit, and auditor has to issue a written report within 60 days of completing the audit. [76 Fed. Reg. 66637 (Oct. 27, 2011)]

T.D. 9484, 75 Fed. Reg. 27927 (May 19, 2010) contains the Final Regulations under Code § 401(a)(35)'s diversification requirement. Defined contribution plans that invest in publicly traded employer securities must give certain plan participants and beneficiaries (e.g., those who have at least three years of service) the right to change their investments in the plan out of employer securities. At least three diversified investment options other than the employer's stock must be offered, and covered employees and beneficiaries must be allowed to change their investment choices at reasonable intervals—at least once every quarter.

EBSA published a Final Rule in August, 2007, effective October 9, 2007, amending the ERISA § 502(c)(7) civil penalty rules (29 C.F.R. § 2560.502c-7) in light of the PPA. Civil penalties of up to $100 (later increased to $110, to $131, and subsequently to $133) per day can be assessed for violation of ERISA § 101(m), which obligates the administrators of individual account plans to notify participants and beneficiaries of their right to sell the employer stock in their accounts and reinvest, and to advise them of the importance of diversification. [EBSA Direct Final Rule, RIN 1210-AB23, 72 Fed. Reg. 44970 (Aug. 10, 2007). See 81 Fed. Reg. 42491 (June 30, 2016 and Conduent FYI, *DOL, PBGC and HHS Increase Penalties for Violations* (Feb. 10, 2017) (benefitslink.com) for the latest penalty increases.]

§ 11.05 NOTICES OF REDUCTION OF BENEFIT ACCRUALS

Under ERISA § 204(h), plan administrators are required to notify participants, alternate beneficiaries under QDROs, and any union representing the workers whenever a plan amendment significantly reduces future benefit accruals under any qualified plan that is subject to ERISA's minimum funding standards (e.g., defined benefit plans).

The Tenth Circuit has held that a wear-away period does not have to be explicitly disclosed as long as the notice provided by the employer provides sufficiently representative examples of the effects of a plan amendment. A wear-away period is a consequence of a change in the terms of a plan and does not have to be disclosed as a new eligibility requirement. The Tenth Circuit said that plaintiffs who were informed that their benefits would be frozen received adequate notice for § 204(h) purposes. The court said that it would not invalidate an SPD for failure to discuss a wear-away period unless the employer was guilty of deceit or failed to explain the benefit calculation. [*Tomlinson v. El Paso*, 653 F.3d 1281 (10th Cir. 2011); see also *Jensen v. Solvay Chems.*, 625 F.3d 641 (10th Cir 2010). The case was remanded; the district court held once again that the plaintiffs would only be entitled to recover lost benefits if the failure of notice was "egregious." The district court, affirmed by the Tenth Circuit in 2013, ruled that the employer's conduct was not egregious—there was no intention to violate employees' rights, only an unintentional error when drafting a complex notice: *Jensen v. Solvay Chems., Inc.*, 721 F.3d 1180 (10th Cir. 2013).]

If a plan "egregiously" fails to meet the notice requirement, then the affected participants and alternate payees will be entitled to receive whatever benefits they would have received if the plan had never been amended to cut back the benefits. An "egregious" failure is intentional refusal to provide notice, or simple failure to provide most of the affected individuals with most of the information they are entitled to receive.

An amendment reduces the rate of future benefit accrual if it can reasonably be expected that the annual benefit commencing at Normal Retirement Age (NRA) (or at the later actual retirement age) will decline because of the amendment. For example, if the plan provides a normal retirement benefit of 50% of the average pay for the highest five years multiplied by the number of years of participation and divided by 20, a change in either the numerator or the denominator of this fraction could produce a substantial reduction.

The required notice must be given in plain English, with enough information for participants and beneficiaries to understand the assumptions that will be used in future calculations, and the effect of the amendment on their benefit entitlement. In general, notice must be given at least 45 days before the effective date of the amendment, but advance notice can be reduced to 15 days if the plan has fewer than 100 participants, or if the amendment was made pursuant to a corporate merger or acquisition. Notice can be given after the effective date (as long as it is no more than 30 days after the effective date) if the amendment reduces or eliminates an early retirement benefit or retirement-type subsidy but does not substantially reduce the rate of future benefit accruals.

If there is an egregious failure (circumstances within the plan sponsor's control that either are intentional or lead to deprivation of information for most of those entitled to receive it), the amendment cannot be used to reduce benefits—affected individuals will continue to be entitled to receive the unreduced benefit as if there had been no amendment.

When a merger or acquisition transaction affects the surviving company's pension and benefit plans, it will probably be necessary to communicate with employees about the effect of the transition on their benefits. Notice will be required if a plan is terminated. A § 204(h) notice will probably be required if there is a potential reduction in benefits under a defined benefit plan or an individual account plan subject to minimum funding standards. In general, the notice must be furnished 45 days before the plan is amended, but a shorter, 15-day notice period is permitted in the mergers and acquisitions context. If restrictions are imposed on participants' ability to access their accounts, a blackout notice is required at least 30 but not more than 60 days before the restrictions take effect. [Principal Financial Group ThoughtCapital, *The Impact of Mergers, Acquisitions and Dispositions on Your Retirement Plan* (July 2010) (benefitslink.com)]

The PPA amended § 417(e)(3) to change the actuarial assumptions to be used in calculating the minimum present value of the accrued benefit. Because Rev. Rul. 2007-67, 2007-48 I.R.B. 1047, held that amendments to conform to the new requirements do not violate the anti-cutback rule, it is not necessary to provide a 204(h) notice if a lump-sum distribution from a defined benefit plan is reduced by conformity to the assumptions required by the PPA. See also IRS final regulations published November 24, 2009: A 204(h) notice is not required for amendments reflecting PPA requirements about interest rates and mortality assumptions. Nor is a 204(h) notice required to eliminate a benefit that is not a protected benefit or a protected benefit that can be eliminated or reduced in compliance with § 411(d)(6).

§ 11.06   OTHER NOTICES AND DISCLOSURES

There are many other circumstances under which the plan will be required to communicate with participants and beneficiaries, with the IRS, with the DOL, the PBGC—or all of them!

When an individual account plan is abandoned, 29 C.F.R. § 2578.1 explains how to terminate the plan and distribute benefits. [The Qualified Termination Administrator Special Terminal Report Instructions for Abandoned Plans U.S. Department of Labor <www.dol.gov/ebsa> (June 21, 2006); see also EBSA's Interim Final Rule, *Amendments to Safe Harbor for Distributions from Terminated Individual Account*. Plans for further rules about such distributions, reflecting PPA changes: 72 Fed. Reg. 7516 (Feb. 15, 2007).]

[A]   Notice of Deferred Benefits

Frequently, an employee will leave for one reason or another ("separation from service") at a time when he or she is entitled to a deferred vested benefit, but is not yet entitled to a retirement pension. The person in that situation is entitled to a notice containing:

- The name and address of the plan administrator;

- The nature, form, and amount of the person's deferred vested benefit;

- An explanation of any benefits that are forfeitable if the employee dies before a certain date.

The notice must be given no later than the date Schedule SSA is to be filed with the IRS. [Schedule SSA is the annual report that I.R.C. § 6057 requires of pension plans and other plans that are subject to the vesting requirements of ERISA Title I, Part 3] The IRS has the power to impose a penalty assessed per erroneous statement or willful failure to furnish a statement.

Not less than 30, or more than 90, days before the annuity start date of any benefit that is immediately distributable before the participant reaches 62 or normal retirement age, the participant must also be given notice of any right he or she has to defer distribution. [See Treas. Reg. § 1.411(a)–11(c)(2)]

[B]   Rollovers; Withholding Certificate

Not more than 180, and not less than 30, days before making a distribution, the plan administrator must notify the participant of the potential consequences of receiving a distribution that could be made the subject of a rollover. The notice should inform participants of their right to have the distribution deposited into an IRA, or to another qualified plan that will accept it.

Participants must be warned about the 20% withholding that will be imposed on all taxable distributions that are neither rolled over nor transferred—and that the sums that are received are taxable in the year of receipt. Participants must also be told that they can roll over the distribution within 60 days of its receipt to an IRA or another qualified plan. The notice must also provide information about capital gains treatment of lump sums, and the limited circumstances under which five-year averaging will be permitted. IRS Form 1099-R is used to report the taxable component of a designated distribution.

There is also a corresponding notice obligation before a plan makes a distribution that is *not* an eligible rollover distribution; the plan must send the participant IRS Form W-4P, Withholding Certificate for Pension or Annuity Payments. The W-4P informs the participant of the options he or she has with respect to withholding:

- Direct the plan not to withhold;

- Direct withholding based on marital status or the number of allowances;

- Increase withholding on periodic payments (for instance, if the participant has high outside income and might otherwise owe a large balance at the end of the tax year).

[C]   QJSA/QPSA/QOSA Notice

Thirty to 180 days before receipt of benefits, a plan that permits payouts in annuity form must provide all participants with a plain English statement. [All participants—vested or otherwise—are entitled to the statement. See I.R.C. § 417(a)(3), Treas. Reg. §§ 1.401(a)(11), and 1.417(e)-1(b)(3)] The notice should contain:

- The terms and conditions of the joint and survivor annuity;

- The participant's right to waive the annuity, including a description of the consequences of the waiver;

- Rights of the participant's spouse;

- Description of the right to revoke the election, and consequences of the revocation.

A comparable explanation must be given about the Qualified Preretirement Survivor Annuity (QPSA), although the timing requirement is more complicated. The notice is due by the latest of:

- The period that begins on the first day of the plan year in which the participant reaches age 32, and ends at the end of the plan year before the participant reaches 35;

- A reasonable time (deemed to mean no more than a year) after a person becomes a plan participant, if hired after age 35.

The plan can omit the notice of the right to waive the QPSA/QJSA if the benefit is fully subsidized by the plan, and the participant can neither waive the QPSA/QJSA nor name a nonspouse as beneficiary. The benefit is fully subsidized if not waiving neither lowers the benefit nor results in higher costs for the participant.

The Qualified Optional Survivor Annuity (QOSA) notice must also be given in the 30–180 day time frame before benefits are paid. A QOSA (see § 12.05) is a joint and survivor annuity where the survivor receives a reduced benefit after the first spouse dies. The notice explains the terms and condition of the QOSA, the effect of waiving it, and spousal rights. The spouse's consent is not required to waive the QOSA—if it is actuarially equivalent to the QJSA; but if the QOSA is actuarially less valuable than the QJSA, spousal consent is required. [See <http://www.irs.gov/Retirement-Plans/Retirement-Plan-Participant-Notices-Qualified-Joint-&-Survivor-Annuity-%28QJSA%29-Notice> (Aug. 18, 2016) (last accessed Feb. 16, 2017) for an explanation of the requirement for providing QJSA notices.]

A retroactive annuity starting date is allowable only if the plan provides for it and the participant specifically asks for the retroactive starting date. Benefits must be determined in a way that puts the participant in the same position as if he or she had received benefit payments starting on the retroactive annuity starting date. The participant must get a make-up amount to reflect any missed payments (and interest on those missed payments). Furthermore, although commentators requested that this provision should be extended to defined contribution plans, the Final Rule continues to limit the availability of a retroactive start date to defined benefit plans.

If the participant is married, the spouse must consent to the election of the retroactive start date if the survivor payments under the retroactive annuity are less than the QJSA with a start date after the provision of the QJSA explanation. This is true even if the actual form of the benefit elected is a QJSA. But consent is required only if the survivor annuity is less than 50% of the annuity payable during the life of the participant under a QJSA that does not commence retroactively.

As for lump sums, electing a retroactive annuity starting date cannot reduce the size of the lump sum. The distribution must not be smaller than the distribution resulting from applying the applicable interest rate and mortality table to the annuity form that was used determine the benefit amount as of the retroactive start date.

Participants must be notified whenever they receive a plan distribution that is eligible for rollover.

During the period 90 to 180 days of retirement or ceasing work, participants must be informed of the benefits they are entitled to, and what procedures are used to obtain benefits. [See IRS, *Retirement Topics-Notices*, <http://www.irs .gov/Retirement-Plans/Plan-Participant,-Employee/Retirement-Topics-Notices> (Jan. 30, 2017) (last accessed Feb. 16, 2017)]

[D]   QDRO Notices

The general rule is that no one can garnish or otherwise get hold of plan benefits before they are paid. The exception to the rule is that a plan administrator not only has the right, but has the obligation, to comply with valid court orders that direct part of the benefit to the participant's separated or divorced spouse. However, not every divorce-related order must be treated as a Qualified Domestic Relations Order (QDRO).

Once a plan receives a court order, I.R.C. § 414(p) obligates the administrator to review it to see if it is qualified. The plan participant and the alternate payee (nearly always the spouse) must be notified that the plan has received an order and what the plan will do to assess its qualification. Then the administrator carries out that procedure and sends another notice to the participant and alternate payee, if the order has been determined to be qualified and therefore must be obeyed by the plan. EBSA published a Final Rule reflecting PPA changes, clarifying that an order can be QDRO even if it is issued after another domestic relations order, if it revises another DRO, or even if it is issued after the employee spouse's death. [RIN 1210-AB15, 75 Fed. Reg. 32846 (June 10, 2010). For general guidance, see EBSA, *QDROS: The Division of Retirement Benefits Through Qualified Domestic Relations Orders*, <http://www.dol.gov/ebsa/publications/ qdros.html> (undated, last accessed Feb. 16, 2017); see § 12.08.]

[E]   Break-in-Service Notice

ERISA's break-in-service rules are complex and difficult for participants to understand. Participants have the right to make a written request (although only once a year) when they are separated from service, or have a one-year break in service. The notice defines their accrued benefits under the plan, and the percentage of the accrued benefits that is nonforfeitable.

[F]   "Saver's Credit"

One effect of the Economic Growth and Tax Relief Reconciliation Act (EGTRRA) was to increase substantially the amount that taxpayers can contribute to IRA accounts (or defer in 401(k) or 403(b) accounts). The "saver's credit" is an income tax credit under I.R.C. § 25B for low-income taxpayers who contribute to an IRA or pension plan. Although the Saver's Credit as originally enacted had a sunset date, it was made permanent by the PPA. Depending on the qualified person's income, the credit equals either 10%, 20%, or 50% of the person's contributions to an employer-sponsored retirement plan or IRA; the maximum credit is $4,000 for a married couple filing jointly, $2,000 for all other filing statuses.

For 2015, the adjusted gross income (AGI) limit for the saver's credit is $61,000 for joint returns, $45,750 for heads of household, and $30,500 for single persons and married persons filing separate returns. For 2016, the limit is $61,500 for joint returns, $46,125 for heads of household, and $30,750 for single persons and married persons filing separate returns. The 2017 limit is $62,000 for joint returns, $46,500 for heads of household, and $31,000 for single persons and separate returns of married persons. [IRS, IR-2015-118, *IRS Announces 2016 Pension Plan Limitations* (Oct. 21, 2015), <https://www.irs.gov/uac/newsroom/irs-announces-2016-pension-plan-limitations-401-k-contribution-limit-remains-unchanged-at-18-000-for-2016>; Notice 2016-62, 2016-46 I.R.B. 725]

[G] FASB Changes

The Financial Accounting Standards Board (FASB) requires employers to disseminate financial statements that accurately reflect their ongoing obligations relating to pension and retiree health plans. Since 2009, FASB documents are organized into about 90 topics. For retirement and health topics, see, e.g., 712, post-employment compensation other than retirement;

- 715, retirement benefits;
- 960, accounting for defined benefit plans;
- 962, accounting for defined contribution plans;
- 965, accounting for health and welfare benefit plans.

[CCH Pension & Benefits *FASB Announces New Codification Structure, Superseding All Existing Statements* (June 26, 2009) (benefitslink.com). See <http://www.fasb.org> for the full codification.]

[H] Notices About Funding Problems

Before the enactment of the PPA, ERISA § 4011 required the administrator to notify participants and beneficiaries of the funding standards—and of the fact that the PBGC did not guarantee payment of all the benefits that might have been payable absent a PBGC takeover of the plan. Every year, the PBGC published a

Model Participant Notice Form to be used for this purpose, and provided Technical Updates including a worksheet for determining whether notice was required. Technical Update 06-03 explains how to make interest rate calculations for the 2006 participant notice; in general, plans subject to the variable-rate PBGC premium for 2006 had to issue this notice.

For plan years beginning after 2006, PPA § 501 repeals ERISA § 4011. Disclosure is still required, but now it is under Department of Justice jurisdiction as prescribed by ERISA Title I. [FR Doc E7-761, 72 Fed. Reg. 2615 (Jan. 22, 2007).

Section 4010 requires notification to the PBGC if a plan fails the "gateway" test: that is, if its funding target attainment percentage drops below 80%. The notice alerts the PBGC to its potential liabilities if the plan terminates with substantial underfunding, although the rule has always granted some exceptions.

As with most pay planning requirements, this one continued to evolve. In July 2015, the PBGC proposed rules that would have obligated more sponsors to make § 4010 filings in 2016 and later years. Under this proposal, plans with 500 or more participants would have to report if they were less than 80% funded. However, this proposal waives reporting of statutory liens resulting from missed contributions over $1 million, or outstanding minimum funding waivers over $1 million, as long as the waivers or missed contributions are reported to the PBGC under § 4043 on a timely basis. [Jeffrey Kamenir, *Will More Corporations Need to File PBGC Form 4010 for Their Defined Benefit Pension Plans for the 2016 Fiscal Year?*, Retirement Town Hall (Jan. 6, 2016) (benefitslink.com)]

Not only the reporting requirements but also the practical financial status of many plans were affected by changes in interest rate calculations mandated by several federal statutes, including the Moving Ahead for Progress in the 21st Century Act (MAP-21), Highway Transportation and Funding Act of 2014 (HATFA), and the Bipartisan Budget Act of 2015 (BBA 2015).

The PBGC reversed its course in 2016, rewriting the requirements again in a way that reduces the number of plans required to make § 4010 reports. Under the March 2016 final regulations, reporting is waived if the aggregate funding shortfall for an employer is less than $15 million, but the shortfall is measured using the non-stabilized rates that prevailed before HATFA. Because of this requirement, the figures used for § 4010 reporting might be different from the ones used to prepare Form 5500.

The 2016 final regulations add three new funding waivers. One is for controlled groups that have fewer than 500 employees in all their plans (including exempt plans), no matter how great the underfunding. Reporting is also waived if there is a statutory lien of more than $1 million because of missed required contributions or because the plan's minimum funding waivers exceed $1 million— but this § 4010 waiver applies only if these events are disclosed to the PBGC as "reportable events." Note that the PBGC now refers to what was known as the FTAP (Funding Target Attainment Percentage) as the "4010 funding target attainment percentage." [81 Fed. Reg. 15432 (Mar. 23, 2016); see Xerox FYI, *PBGC*

Finalizes Changes to 4010 Annual Financial Reporting (Mar. 25, 2016) (benefitslink.com); Practicallaw.com, *PBGC Issues Final Regulations on Pension Plan Reporting Under ERISA Section 4010* (Mar. 29, 2016) (benefitslink.com)]

Notice 2012-46, 2012-30 I.R.B. 86 (effective November 1, 2012) explains the ERISA § 101(j) notice requirements for single-employer plans subject to benefit limitations under § 436 because of deficient funding status. The administrator must give the notice to participants and beneficiaries within 30 days of the time the plan's funding status falls below the required level. DOL regulations state that noncompliance can be penalized by up to $1,000 a day per participant entitled to notification. (For violations occurring after November 1, 2015, and assessed after August 1, 2016, the penalty increases to $1,632 per day: see 81 Fed. Reg. 42491 (June 30, 2016).) The notice must be understandable to the average plan participant. Notice must be in writing, but can be electronic if it is reasonably accessible to the recipients. The notice must include:

- Plan name;

- Plan number;

- EIN;

- General description of the payment limitations.

In mid-2014, the PBGC published final regulations on the phase-in period for guarantee of benefits contingent on occurrence of an unpredictable contingent event (UCE), such as plant shutdowns. The regulations reflect PPA requirements. When an employer establishes a new pension benefit or increases a current benefit, the PBGC's guarantee of the additional benefit is generally phased in over a five-year period. The period begins when the change is adopted or on the effective date of the plan amendment—whichever is later. However, the 2014 regulations provide that the phase-in rules apply as if the plan amendment creating a benefit for the UCE was adopted on the date of the UCE rather than the date of the amendment. That is to say, the guaranteed benefits are lower for a UCE within five years of termination than they would have been before the PPA. An Unpredictable Contingent Event Benefit (UCEB) is a benefit triggered solely by a UCE. The most common UCEB is a full retirement benefit granted earlier than it would have been available absent the UCE. The PPA required faster funding of ongoing plans. In most situations that created greater parity between employer funding and the PBGC phase-in. However, this was not true of UCEBs; the unpredictability of the event meant that employers could not pre-fund it. The 2014 final regulations give examples, such as a facility that engages in sequential layoffs or closes in a series of steps. Because this is a PPA-related provision, the regulations are effective for UCEBs payable as a result of UCEs occurring after July 26, 2005. [79 Fed. Reg. 25667 (May 6, 2014)]

Plan sponsors must file Form 200 with the PBGC when a single-employer defined benefit plan whose funding target attainment percentage is less than 100% fails to make required contributions to the plan, when the aggregate unpaid balance is more than $1 million resulting in a lien on all of the assets of the sponsor and its controlled group. Form 200 is a simple two-page form. The PBGC designed the form to call only for information that is relevant to protect plan participants, and that is not available from other sources (such as Form 5500 and SEC filings). Filing can be done by mail, commercial delivery service, or e-filing. The due date is 10 days of the date the payment should have been made. Failure to make a require contribution can also be a reportable event under § 4043, but filing Form 200 satisfies the § 4043 reportable event requirement. [PBGC *Form 200 Instructions*, <http://www.pbgc.gov/documents/Form-200-Instructions.pdf> (last accessed Feb. 16, 2017)]

[I]   Notice of Termination

Under ERISA §§ 4041, 4050 and 29 C.F.R. Parts 4041 and 4050, termination of a qualified defined benefit plan requires preparation and distribution of a number of documents. For standard termination of a single-employer defined benefit plan:

- Notice of Intent to Terminate, given to participants, beneficiaries, alternate payees, and any unions representing the participants; it is given 60–90 days before the proposed termination date.

- Standard Termination Notice (Form 500), given to the PBGC not more than 180 days before the proposed termination date.

- Notice of Plan Benefits, explaining each person's benefits, given to participants, beneficiaries, and alternate payees; must be given on or before filing of Form 500.

- Form 501 (Post-Distribution Certification), given to the PBGC within 30 days after completion of the distribution of plan assets has been completed; it certifies that distribution is complete and was done properly. Schedule MP (Missing Participants) is filed with the PBGC in conjunction with Form 501, listing participants and beneficiaries who could not be located.

For distress terminations, the reporting requirements are somewhat different:

- Form 600 (Notice of Intent to Terminate), filed with the PBGC 60–90 days (or longer, if approved by the PBGC) before the proposed termination date, explaining how the distress criteria have been met, and giving data about the plan sponsor and its controlled group.

- Notice of Intent to Terminate, given to participants, beneficiaries, alternate payees, and unions no later than the time Form 600 is filed with the PBGC.

- ERISA § 4041(c)(2) disclosure to participants, beneficiaries, alternate payees, and union, within 15 days of receipt of a request, disclosing the information it has submitted to the PBGC in connection with the distress termination.

- Notice of request to bankruptcy court to approve the termination; given to the PBGC when the request is made to the bankruptcy court.

- Form 601 (Distress Termination Notice) for single-employer plans, given the PBGC within 120 days after the proposed termination date.

- Form 602 (Post-Distribution Certification): similar to the Form 501; also includes Schedule MP. [EBSA, *Reporting and Disclosure Guide*, <http://www.dol.gov/ebsa/pdf/rdguide.pdf> (last accessed Feb. 16, 2017)]

[J] PPA Benefit Statement

The PPA obligates plan administrators to issue periodic benefit statements to participants and beneficiaries. All defined contribution plans must issue a statement approximately once a year, and quarterly statements are required for individual account plans (e.g., 401(k)s) whose participants can direct the investment of their account balances. The quarterly statement must disclose:

- The total account balance;

- The amount that is vested; if none is, the earliest vesting date for the participant;

- A breakdown of the value of each of the investments within the account;

- Whatever limitations or restrictions are placed on the right to direct investments by the terms of the plan;

- An explanation of why diversification is important;

- URL for the DOL Website containing investment information;

- (For profit-sharing plans integrated with Social Security) an explanation of plan integration.

A direct final rule published in March 2015 allows the disclosures, once mandated annually, to be given at least once per period of 14 months. [Direct Final Rule, 80 Fed. Reg. 14301 (Mar. 19, 2015); see EBSA News, *US Labor Department Announces Additional Flexibility to 401(k) Plans Furnishing Annual Investment Information to Workers*, <http://www.dol.gov/ebsa/newsroom/2015/ebsa031815.html> (Mar. 18, 2015) (last accessed Feb. 16, 2017)]

Employers can use the general DOL and IRS procedures for distributing statements in electronic rather than hard-copy form. The information can be provided on a secure Website as well as through individual e-mails. But if the sponsor chooses to use a Website to distribute the information, participants and beneficiaries must be given a written notice explaining how to access the information online—and that they can get a free paper copy if they prefer.

Disclosure requirements are similar, but simpler, for individual account plans that do not permit individuals to direct the investment of their accounts: for example, it is not necessary to discuss restrictions on investments or the value of diversification.

[K]   Health Plan Notices

See § 11.02[B] for discussion of the requirements for SPDs for health plans. Additional notices are required outside the context of the SPD:
Heath plans require ongoing communications:

- When a female beneficiary enrolls in a plan, and each year thereafter, she must receive a notice about availability of benefits available for mastectomy and reconstruction under the Women's Health and Cancer Rights Act (WHCRA); see <http://www.dol.gov/ebsa/publications/whcra .html>. If the health plan SPD is reissued each year, the notice can be included there. Otherwise, a separate notice should be included in the annual enrollment materials.

- Any employee or dependent who is covered by Medicare Part A or B and lives in the service area of a Part D plan must receive notice as to whether the employer's coverage is creditable (see § 9.10[B]). The article suggests that notice should automatically be sent to all participants by October 15, because it is easy for the employer to know which employees are Medicare-eligible, but harder to determine which dependents are Medicare-eligible.

- Employees must be notified once every three years of the right to obtain a copy of the HIPAA notice of privacy practices. This requirement can be satisfied in conjunction with open enrollment by informing employees each year that they can request this notice. The notice form should be updated to reflect the 2013 HITECH Act requirement that covered entities must notify affected individuals when there has been a data security breach involving health information.

- In states that offer a premium assistance subsidy under CHIPRA, employees are entitled to an annual notice even if they are not enrolled in a CHIPRA plan. The DOL site has model notice language. The rules published at 81 Fed. Reg. 42491 (June 30, 2016) increase the maximum penalty for failure to provide notice of Children's Health Insurance Program (CHIP) coverage opportunities from $100 per day to $110 per day, and each employee who does not receive the notice is treated as a separate violation. The penalty was increased slightly, to $112 a day, in early 2017: see Conduent FYI, *DOL, PBGC and HHS Increase Penalties for Violations* (Feb. 10, 2017) (benefitslink.com).

- As of 2014, under PPACA, the Summary of Benefits and Coverage must indicate if the plan provides minimum value and offers minimum essential coverage. Persons hired after October 1, 2013, must get a copy of this notice within 14 days of their start date. The June 2016 rule increases the maximum penalty for failure to provide the Summary of Benefits and Coverage to $1,087; the 2017 figure is $1,105.

- The DOL also has model language for disclosures in SPDs and other plan materials that the plan is grandfathered; notice is required to retain grandfathered status.

- Small employers that have Qualified Small Employer HRAs (QSE-HRAs) must inform their employees about the extent to which the employer's contributions to the plan could be taxable to the employee, and how QSEHRA coverage affects the employee's compliance with PPACA's individual mandate and ability to buy health insurance coverage from a PPACA Exchange. The notice must be given at least 90 days before the beginning of the year in which the QSEHRA takes effect. But there is a transition rule for 2017, the first year in which QSEHRAs were available: notice must be given within 90 days of the date when the IRS issues guidance. [Notice 2017-20, 2017-11 I.R.B. 1010; see Kenneth A. Mason, *IRS Extends Deadline for Providing Small-Employer HRA Notices*, Spencer Fane LLP (Feb. 28, 2017), available at Lexology.com]

In plans that are subject to HIPAA's privacy policies, either because the plan receives PHI or because the employer sponsors an FSA or HRA, all participants must receive notice when the policies are adopted. An explanation of how to obtain notice of the plan's privacy practices must be provided at least once every three years.

The Children's Health Insurance Program Reauthorization Act of 2009 (CHIPRA), signed February 4, 2009, subsidizes health coverage for children in low-income families. A state can either provide coverage to low-income families directly, or subsidize coverage provided by the employer. The subsidy, in turn, can be administered by the state making payments to either the employer or the employee, although employers have the right to opt out of receiving payments (for example, if they are concerned about the difficulties of administering the program).

The CHIPRA imposes notice requirements both on employees (they must inform the health plan within days of becoming eligible under CHIPRA) and on health plans. Plans must notify participants of the potential for premium assistance, and must notify the state of information from participants who disclose their eligibility for premium assistance. To obtain special enrollment, an employee must request coverage within 60 days of either the date of termination of Medicaid or SCHIP coverage or the date the qualifying child or parent is found eligible for assistance. Plan administrators must report to the state the information needed to determine employees' eligibility for premium assistance.

See § 18.19[K] for notice requirements under PPACA (health care reform).

Final rules about wellness programs, pursuant to the ADA, require notification to employees about the information the program collects, who has access to the information, how it is used, and the plan's provisions for privacy and confidentiality. A sample notice can be found at the EEOC Website. The notice obligation applies starting the first day of the first plan year beginning on or after January 1, 2017. [EEOC notice: <https://www.eeoc.gov/laws/regulations/ada-wellness-notice.cfm >. See Plansponsor staff, *EEOC Provides Sample Notice for Wellness Programs*, plansponsor.com (June 21, 2016)]

Employees are not usually allowed to "stack" all the leave available to them from various sources, including the Family and Medical Leave Act (FMLA), other laws, and the employer's policy. However, to prevent them from doing so, the employer must give advance notice that the other leave runs concurrently with FMLA leave. The employee handbook (if any) and the notice should state whether paid sick, personal, or vacation leave is deemed concurrent with FMLA leave. If employees are allowed to make up for time taken under the FMLA, it is permissible to count that time against their allotment of FMLA leave, as long as the policy explains clearly that employees will be paid for the make-up time but will not get extra FMLA leave. [HR Daily Advisor, *FMLA Notice Requirements: Substitution and "Make Up" Leave* (Nov. 17, 2016) (benefitslink.com)]

§ 11.07 DISCLOSURE ON REQUEST

In addition to disclosures that must be made, and documents that must be furnished, automatically to all plan participants and beneficiaries, ERISA and the Internal Revenue Code require certain disclosures to be made only if a participant or beneficiary requests them.

Materials that can be requested include:

- A complete copy of the plan's latest Form 5500;

- The plan instrument (that is, the Collective Bargaining Agreement or trust that actually creates the plan);

- The latest updated SPD;

- A report on plan termination;

- Statement of accrued benefits (but the administrator only has to furnish this once in every 12-month period);

- Percentage of vesting; and, for participants who are not fully vested, the schedule on which full vesting will occur.

If a request is made, the information should be mailed within 30 days to the last known address of the requester. The plan is allowed to impose a reasonable charge for the information, based on the least expensive available means of reproducing the documents.

The plan documents, plan description, and latest annual report must be kept on file for participants who want to inspect them, at the plan administrator's principal office. If there is a request to make them available there, copies of the documents must also be kept at the employer's principal office and at each of the employer's locations where 50 or more employees work.

The Department of Labor can impose penalties of up to $147 a day, subject to a maximum of $1,496 per request (2017 figures), for failure to furnish documents on request. The Secretary of Labor has the power to demand documents that were requested by, but not furnished to, plan participants and beneficiaries under 29 C.F.R. § 2520.104a-8.

According to the Sixth Circuit, a written request for ERISA plan documents must provide clear notice of which documents are requested. The Sixth Circuit used a "clear notice" standard: did the plan administrator know or should have known which documents had been requested? The Sixth Circuit said that it was not an abuse of discretion to award a penalty that was only half the statutory maximum penalty at the time, of $55 because the delay was not prejudicial to the plaintiff. [*Cultrona v. Nationwide Life Ins. Co.*,748 F.3d 698 (6th Cir. 2014)]

In late 2016, the District Court for the Eastern District of Pennsylvania ordered Reppert, Inc., to pay $15,959 in restitution to a 401(k) plan participant who did not get the plan documents he requested. The fine was imposed for the period between December 6, 2008 to October 2, 2009 (starting 31 days after initial document request) and for failure to provide a copy of the custodial agreement from May 17, 2012 to January 2015. The maximum penalty at that time was $110/day, so the penalty could have been $33,000. However, the district court ruled that a $50 penalty was appropriate because the documents were withheld intentionally, but not in bad faith. A nominal penalty of $1 a day was imposed for non-provision of a document that the employer reasonably believed it was not obligated to provide; the employer's duty was a close question. The district court also found that the 401(k) plan did not file the required audit data with Form 5500 for several years, and the failure to file could not be blamed on the plan's recordkeeper. [*Askew v. R.L. Reppert, Inc.*, No. 11-cv-04003, 2016 U.S. Dist. LEXIS 151275 (E.D. Pa. Nov. 1, 2016); see Plansponsor editors, *Court Imposes Hefty Penalty for Failure to Provide Documents*, plansponsor.com (Nov. 15, 2016)]

In mid-2016, the Ninth Circuit ruled that although the claims regulations, 29 C.F.R. § 2560.503-1, obligate plans to give claimants copies of relevant documents, these regulations do not make plan administrators liable for § 502(c)(1) penalties if the documents are not produced in timely fashion. The Ninth Circuit (joining the First, Second, Third, Sixth, Seventh, Eighth, and Tenth Circuits) applied the rationale that obligations under § 2560.503-1 are imposed on benefits plans, whereas § 502(c)(1) sets out duties for plan administrators. Therefore, a plan administrator that failed to fully comply with the claims regulations (a disability claimant's request for e-mails about denial of his claim were not produced) was not liable under § 502(c)(1). [*Lee v. ING Groep, N.V.,* No. 14-15848, 2016 U.S. App. LEXIS 13517 (9th Cir. July 25, 2016); see Dylan D. Rudolph, *Ninth Circuit Clarifies Remedies for Failure to Provide Documents Relevant to a Benefit Claim,* Trucker Huss Benefits Report (Aug. 2016) (benefitslink.com)]

§ 11.08   ELECTRONIC COMMUNICATIONS

The Taxpayer Relief Act of 1997 (TRA '97) [Pub. L. No. 105-34] ordered the IRS to create rules for integrating computer technology into plan administration and the disclosure process. Since that time, the IRS, DOL, PBGC, and other agencies have developed rules for using the Internet, e-mail, and other electronic means to communicate with plan participants and beneficiaries—and to file official documents. The basic principle is that the electronic communication must be at least as accessible and understandable as a paper copy, and in general, participants and beneficiaries must not only have the right to receive a hard copy without charge, but must be informed of this right.

Treasury Regulations provide that notices can be delivered electronically only if the consent requirement is met or if the plan qualifies for an exemption. Participants receiving an electronic notice must be informed, in a readily understandable manner, what the subject matter of the notice is and how to access it. The recipient must give explicit consent to electronic delivery and must be informed that he or she can request a paper copy at no charge and withdraw consent. Disclosure is also required about the scope of the consent, how to update contact information, and the hardware and software requirements for using the system. If the hardware/software requirements change, a new consent form is required. PINs or other security devices must be implemented to prevent unauthorized persons from accessing the system or inputting information into it. Electronic witness affidavits and notarizations are acceptable as long as a notary or plan representative physically witnesses the application of the signature.

The District Court for the Eastern District of New York refused to relax the conditions set by the DOL's rules for electronic distribution of SPDs. The employee lost Internet access when she had to stop working, so she could not access the SPD during the 12 months when she could have made the election to continue life insurance coverage by submitting proof of disability. The employer also failed to give her notice that the SPD was posted. The district court treated the failure to satisfy the disclosure requirements as failure to provide a copy of the SPD, making the denial arbitrary and capricious. [*Thomas v. CIGNA Grp. Ins.*, No. 09-CV-5029 (SLT) (RML), 2015 U.S. Dist. LEXIS 25232 (E.D.N.Y. Mar. 2, 2015)]

EBSA made electronic filing available starting in 2005. [70 Fed. Reg. 51542 (Aug. 30, 2005)]

The PBGC announced that both estimated flat-rate filings and comprehensive filings for plan years that begin in 2011 can be submitted electronically using MyPAA, the PBGC's online system. Only electronic, not paper, filing is acceptable. The actual payment of the premium can either be done electronically via MyPAA, by electronic funds transfer, or by check. [*Premium Payment Instructions and Addresses*, <http://www.pbgc.gov>]

T.D. 9294 is the IRS's Final Rule, explaining how, qualified plans should use electronic means to provide notices to participants and obtain their consent and elections. The rule also applies to notices provided under various welfare benefit plans (accident & health plans; cafeteria plans; educational assistance plans; qualified transportation fringe plans; Archer MSAs; and HSAs). However, T.D. 9294, as an IRS rule, does not apply to ERISA Title I or IV notices (dealing with, e.g., SPDs, COBRA notices, and notices of benefit suspension) because those documents are under DOL or PBGC jurisdiction. [T.D. 9294, RIN 1545-BD68, 4830-01-p, 2006-48 I.R.B. 980]

Proposed regulations by the DOL call for electronic filing of top hat plan notices via EBSA's web-based filing system, with the data made publicly available on the DOL Website. Although top hat plans are exempt from most ERISA requirements, the administrator must make a one-time filing of a notice with DOL, and must respond if the DOL asks for plan documents [Pamela Baker, Michael R. Maryn and Martin J. Moderson, *Department of Labor to Require Electronic Filing of Top Hat Plan Notices*, Dentons (Oct.1, 2014), available at Lexology.com]

DOL Technical Release 2011-03 allows information about fees in individual account plans to be distributed electronically, and Websites can be used subject to certain safeguards (e.g., those prescribed by the DOL's FAB 2006-03, which allows quarterly individual benefit statements to use the IRS electronic disclosure rules). As long as the plan follows the technical release, the DOL will not take enforcement action merely because fee disclosures were made electronically rather than on paper. There is a general safe harbor for making electronic disclosures, even if the participant has not affirmatively agreed to this, if using a computer or other electronic system is an integral part of the employee's duties.

Under this interim policy, investment information and disclosure of administrative and individual expenses can be included in quarterly benefit statements that are transmitted electronically using FAB 2006-03 standards. However, certain investment data (e.g., a comparative chart of performance data) can be sent under the DOL safe harbor or the alternative e-mail method, but not under FAB 2006-03.

Six conditions are required to justify the use of electronic delivery:

- The person entitled to the disclosures responds to an initial notice by voluntarily providing an e-mail address;

- The plan submits the request on a clear and conspicuous initial notice;

- The participant or beneficiary must receive an annual notice satisfying most of the initial content notice requirements;

- Electronic delivery uses a method that is reasonably calculated to actually be received;

- Personal information must be kept confidential;

- The notice must be drafted to be understandable to the average participant.

- The notice must explain the rights to receive a free paper copy and/or opt out of receiving notices electronically. [DOL Technical Release 2011-03, <http://www.dol.gov/EBSA/pdf/tr11-03.pdf> (Sept. 13, 2011) (last viewed Feb. 17, 2017). See Voya Financial Qualified Plan News No. QPN 2017-5 (Mar. 23, 2017) (benefitslink.com)] Marsh & McLennan Benefit Advisor, *Electronic Distribution Rules* (Apr. 2017) (benefitslink .com) explains these rules and includes a useful chart of the subject of various notices and how to provide them electronically.

Multi-employer plans are required to e-file certain documents, such as notices of termination, notices of insolvency and the level of insolvency benefits, and the application for financial assistance. The rule applies only to notices submitted to the PBGC, not those provided to participants. [80 Fed. Reg. 55742 (Sept. 17, 2015)]

An SPD can be posted to a company intranet site if the safe harbor is observed. Each recipient must be notified in writing that the SPD is available; the significance of the SPD; and that a paper copy is available without charge on request. The plan administrator must ensure that the posting leads to actual receipt of the SPD—for example, by linking the SPD on the intranet home page, periodically reviewing to see if notices are received, or using tools that give notice when e-mail cannot be delivered. People who lack computer access or access to the intranet at work, and non-employees entitled to notice (e.g., COBRA beneficiaries) must be given an explanation of what documents will be provided electronically, how to update their e-mail addresses, and how to withdraw their consent to receiving electronic notice. Once they have received the explanation, they must consent affirmatively if they are to be given notice electronically. The explanation and consent procedures must be repeated if there are significant changes in the hardware or software requirements for the system. [Gary B.

Kushner, *SPD Electronic Disclosure*, Kushner & Company, kushnerco.com (Sept. 15, 2016) (benefitslink.com)]

§ 11.09 DISCLOSURE OF DOCUMENTS TO THE DOL AND PBGC

The current version of ERISA § 104(a) requires plan administrators to respond to DOL requests by providing documents relating to an employee benefit plan—including the latest SPD, a summary of plan changes not reflected in the SPD, and the plan instrument.

However, the DOL sees its primary role in this arena as helping participants and beneficiaries get documents from the plan, so the DOL can ask for documents that participants or beneficiaries are entitled to, have requested, but have not received. But the DOL will not ask for documents that the participants and beneficiaries are not entitled to see.

If the plan administrator doesn't respond to the request within 30 days, the DOL has the power (under ERISA § 502(c)(6)) to impose civil penalties of up to $147 a day (but not more than $1,472 per request). Penalties will not be imposed if factors beyond the administrator's control prevent compliance.

Effective March 3, 2009, the DOL can assess penalties, under ERISA § 502(c)(4) as amended by the PPA, against plan administrators who fail to provide the notices required under the PPA dealing with subjects such as limitations on distributions from underfunded plans; responsibilities of employers that participate in or withdraw from multi-employer plans; and participants' rights and obligations under defined contribution plans that automatically enroll employees as participants.

The amount of the penalty depends on the degree of willfulness. Failing to notify each person entitled to notice constitutes a separate violation. Plan administrators are personally liable for the penalties, and if there are multiple responsible parties, they can be held jointly and severally liable. [Final Regs, 74 Fed. Reg. 17 (Jan. 2, 2009)] For example, the 2017 maximum penalty for failure to notify participants in a defined benefit plan that the plan is subject to benefit restrictions under § 436 is $1,659 a day; the maximum penalty for failure to furnish a required blackout notice or notice of the right to divest employer securities is $133 per day per recipient.

In September, 2015, the PBGC issued final rules for reportable events, continuing the trend of reducing requirements for reporting events, so that only plans or sponsors at the greatest risk of default will be required to report. Earlier rules only focused on funding levels; the new rules focus on the risk that the plan will not be able to continue making payments that are required. Historically, only 4% of plans each year had a reportable event, and the PBGC expects that the new rules will reduce this even further. See § 10.05[C] for more discussion of reportable events. [80 Fed. Reg. 54979 (Sept. 11, 2015)]

It should be noted that even partially or totally frozen plans are subject to ERISA § 4043's reporting rules; event reporting ceases to be required only after the plan has been fully terminated and all of its assets distributed. The § 4062(e) reporting (and liability) rules are triggered when there is a permanent substantial cessation of operations at any of the sponsor's facilities if the workforce is reduced by more than 15% of all eligible employees in the controlled group. [Vivian S. McCardell, *Pension Plan Sponsors: Whether Your Pension Plan Is Frozen, Partially Frozen or Freeze Dried, Don't Forget Those PBGC Reportable Events*, Morgan Lewis & Bockius LLP (Aug. 11, 2015), available at Lexology .com]

The Cromnibus bill, Pub. L. No. 113-235, makes major changes in ERISA § 4062(e). In mid-2014, the PBGC imposed a moratorium until the end of 2014 on all new or open § 4062(e) cases, although employers were ordered to continue reporting these case. Under the Cromnibus bill, however, plans with fewer than 100 participants are exempt from § 4062(e) requirements, as are plans that were 90% or more funded in the plan year before cessation of operations. Plans that are exempt under these rules do not have to report cessation of operations. However, for other employers, reporting becomes crucial, because the enforcement moratorium has ended. [PBGC, *Important Changes to ERISA Section 4062(e)* (undated, viewed Jan. 23, 2015) (benefitslink.com)]

§ 11.10   FORM 5500

Qualified plans must report each year to the IRS, DOL, and PBGC so that these agencies can monitor plan operations and see if the plans remain qualified, are financially sound, and are operated in accordance with all applicable requirements. The basic Form 5500 covers plans with 100 or more participants; single-participant plans can use the less complex Form 5500-EZ. For 2007 and later plan years, the threshold for filing Form 5500-EZ rises from $100,000 to $250,000. Only one filing is necessary—the IRS transmits the information to the DOL and PBGC.

Form 5500, like the Form 1040, consists of a basic form and various schedules that provide additional information. Form 5500 deals with four main subjects: the plan's financial statements, actuarial data, administrative data, and any benefits covered by insurance. The annual report is due at the end of the seventh month following the end of the plan year.

A "large plan" is one with 100 or more participants as of the beginning of the plan year, and a "small plan" has fewer. If the number of participants at the beginning of a plan year was 80 to 120 and a Form 5500 was filed for the previous plan year, the plan has the right to elect to complete the Form 5500 and the schedules using the same category as the previous year.

Although it is usually thought of in connection with pension plans, Form 5500 must be filed by welfare benefit plans if they are at least partially funded by premiums paid by the employer. Filing may also be required if the premiums are paid through a trust, even if there are fewer than 100 participants.

In mid-2016, DOL proposed changes in the Form 5500 requirements, to generate more data about plan compliance (and make the data easier to analyze). The changes generally apply to the 2019 plan year, but employers can voluntarily adopt them earlier. The proposal also requires defined contribution retirement plans to report more about their investment activities, such as whether they offer qualified default investment alternatives, have a Roth feature, or provide investment education for participants. All qualified plans must disclose if they hold difficult-to-value investments such as hedge fund interests and derivatives. Schedule E (ESOPs) was eliminated in 2009, but has been reinstated. [81 Fed. Reg. 47533 (July 21, 2016)]

These are the most common schedules that apply to pension plan Form 5500 filings. There is no Schedule B, D, E, but see above for restoration of Schedule E, or F.

- Schedule A (insurance information) must be filed by large or small plans that have insurance contracts

- Schedule C (service provider information) is required for large plans that paid a service provider over $5,000, or that fired an accountant or actuary

- Schedule G (financial schedules): required of certain large plans

- Schedule H (financial information) required of all large plans

- Schedule I (financial information): required of all small plans

- Schedule MB (actuarial information) required of large or small multiemployer defined benefit or money purchase pension plans that are subject to the minimum funding requirement

- Schedule R (pension plan information) required of all pension plans

- Schedule SB (actuarial information) required of single- or multiple-employer defined benefit plans that are subject to minimum funding standards

- Accountant's report: required of all large plans; most small plans are exempt

In mid-2016, the DOL proposed changes to Form 5500 and its schedules that affect ERISA Title I group health plans, especially small ones. The changes are generally effective for plan years beginning on or after January 1, 2019. Prior to this proposal, certain unfunded and/or fully insured plans that had fewer than 100 participants were exempt from filing Form 5500. The proposal, however, requires filing of Form 5500, including the new Schedule J, for all group health plans that are subject to ERISA Title I. The DOL estimated that the proposal would expand the number of small group health plans required to file Form 5500 from 6,200 to over two million.

Under the proposal, a fully insured small group health plan would only be required to complete part of Schedule J, providing information about participation, coverage, insurance companies, and basic benefits. The full schedule also requires reporting of the number of people receiving COBRA coverage under the plan; whether the plan covers employees, spouses, dependents, and/or retirees in addition to active employees; if it is a high-deductible plan; if it is a grandfathered plan for PPACA purposes; if the plan includes an FSA or HRA; if the plan has received rebates (e.g., a rebate because their insurer's medical loss ratio is not high enough); information about the contributions made by employees and the employer; amount of claims paid versus denied claims; the number of appeals and appeal outcomes. The sponsor must report whether it complied with federal laws, such as HIPAA, GINA, PPACA, and the mental health parity statute. [Jeffrey P. Cairns and Abigail Clark, *Proposed Form 5500 Changes & the new Schedule J: Big Changes for Small Group Health Plans*, Stinson Leonard Street LLP (July 26, 2016), available at Lexology.com]

Like many tax forms, automatic extensions of the time to file are available for Form 5500. The Surface Transportation and Veterans Health Care Choice Improvement Act of 2015, Pub. L. No. 114-41, signed July 31, 2015, added an extra month to the automatic extension period for Form 5500 for tax years starting after December 31, 2015. Under this legislation, the extension period was 3½ months rather than the 2½ months under prior law; for calendar-year plans, that made the form due on November 15 rather than October 15.

However, subsequent legislation, the Fixing America's Surface Transportation Act of 2015, Pub. L. No. 114-94, repeals the extension, so once again the automatic extension period is 2½ months. The change was suggested by Assistant Secretary of Labor Phyllis C. Borzi, who said that Pub. L. No. 114-41 extended the deadline for filing with the IRS but not the DOL, and that the DOL needs to obtain the information from Form 5500 more quickly. [Plansponsor staff, *Form 5500 Deadline Extension Repealed*, plansponsor.com (Dec. 7, 2015)]

In September 2015, IRS's Employee Plans Compliance Unit announced a new project to identify non-filers of Form 5500. The IRS compares payroll and plan data to DOL records. Letters are sent to plans that have apparently failed to file. The letter puts them on notice that they were informed of the potential penalties.

Non-filers can return to compliance by participating in the Delinquent Filer Program. The FAQ for DOL's delinquent filer program says that a plan that has received an IRS late-filer letter can participate in the Delinquent Filer program, but a plan that has received a DOL late-filer letter cannot do so. Penalties under this program are only $10 a day, subject to a cap. The level of the cap depends on the size of the plan and how long it went without filing, but the maximum cap is

$4,000 per plan ERISA penalties for late filing are $1,100 a day under ERISA plus penalties of $25 a day (capped at $15,000) to the IRS. [Christopher M. Allesee, *New IRS Project Sets Its Sights on Form 5500 Non-Filers*, Graydon Head & Ritchey LLP (Sept. 3, 2015), available at Lexology.com]

In May 2014, the IRS created a one-year pilot program offering amnesty to one-person plans that failed to file Form 5500-EZ; the program was made permanent on June 3, 2015. The program covers plans that only covered the business owner or the owner and spouse, or that covered partners in a partnership and their spouses. To participate, the plan must submit complete, signed paper returns for all of the missing years. The top margin of the return must be marked "Delinquent Return Submitted Under Rev. Proc. 2015-32, Eligible for Penalty Relief" in red. Form 14704 (transmittal schedule) must be included with the submission. A penalty of $500 per delinquent return, up to $1,500 per plan, is imposed; this penalty is fixed and does not depend on the number of days of delinquency. Applicants for relief can combine multiple returns for one plan in a single submission, but returns for multiple plans cannot be combined. If the plan had reasonable cause for the failure, it can also seek penalty relief on this basis—but if the request for relief is denied, the reduced penalties under Rev. Proc. 2015-32 will not apply. [Rev. Proc. 2015-32, 2015-24 I.R.B. 1064]

The DOL, the IRS, and the PBGC collaborated on the development of the EFAST system for electronic filing of the 5500 series of forms. It has been superseded by the EFAST2 system, which took effect starting with the 2009 plan year, and since early 2013, paper filings of Form 5500 have been discontinued. (However, plans that cover only the business owner continue to file Form 5500-EZ or 5500-SF on paper.)

[FAQs at <http://www.dol.gov/ebsa/faqs/faq_dfvc.html> (Jan. 28, 2015) (last accessed Feb. 16, 2017)] Under IRS proposed regulations published in mid-2013, the administrators of large (250 or more tax returns filed per year) 401(k) and other plans would have to file Form 5500 and Form 8955-SSA electronically or on specified magnetic media. The proposals do not deal with ERISA reporting requirements. For plan years beginning on or after January 1, 2014, failure to make a required electronic filing will be penalized as failure to file. Waivers are theoretically available for hardship cases, but the preamble to the proposal says that waivers will rarely be granted. In practical terms, the proposal does not greatly change the employers' obligations, because DOL already required e-filing of Form 5500 and 5500-SF, and IRS's FIRE system allows e-filing for Form 8955-SSA. However, the small number of companies that file Form 5500-EZ and also file at least 250 returns a year must e-file the Form 5500-EZ. [*Employee Retirement Benefit Plan Returns Required on Magnetic Media*, 26 C.F.R. Part 301, 78 Fed. Reg. 53704 (Aug. 30, 2013)]

Form 8955-SSA is the annual registration statement identifying separated participants with deferred vested benefits, reporting the information about such benefits required by Code § 6057(a) for 401(k)s and other retirement plans.

Unless there is an extension, Form SSA-8955 must be filed by the last day of the seventh month after the last day of the plan year: July 31 for a calendar year plan.

The DOL can assess civil penalties of up to $2,097 (2017) per day per annual report, running from the date of the failure or refusal to file and until a satisfactory report is filed, against plan administrators who fail or refuse to comply with the annual reporting requirements. A report that is rejected for failure to provide material information has not been "filed."

However, voluntary compliance is usually sought before penalties are imposed. The EBSA sends correspondence asking for additional information if data is omitted, or if the agency thinks corrections are necessary in light of the instructions or to be internally consistent with other data on the form.

The EBSA has discretion to waive all or part of the penalty based on submission of a timely statement showing reasonable cause for failure to file the complete report at the time it was due. Penalties are not assessed during the time when the DOL is considering the statement of reasonable cause.

CHAPTER 12

PLAN DISTRIBUTIONS

§ 12.01 INTRODUCTION

One of the major tasks of plan administration is to distribute benefits from the plan to participants and their designated beneficiaries—although sometimes determining the proper beneficiary is not as easy as it sounds. The plan administrator must communicate with participants and beneficiaries of their distribution options with respect to accrued benefits. The plan administrator has a duty to provide whatever forms are necessary to make an election.

The standard form of distribution is a single-life annuity for single participants and a Qualified Joint and Survivor Annuity (QJSA) for married participants. Before the Pension Protection Act (PPA: Pub. L. No. 109-280), plans were required to offer joint and 50% survivor annuities (i.e., the annuity payment is cut in half when one of the annuitants dies). The PPA requires plans to offer joint and 75% survivor annuities as well. The payments under a joint and 75% QJSA will be smaller than under a 50% survivor annuity, or under a single-life annuity covering only one spouse.

The plan must also provide for a Qualified Preretirement Survivor Annuity (QPSA) for married persons who die before their pension enters pay status.

But plans can permit other payment forms: lump sums and annuities offering other provisions (but not extending for a term longer than the life expectancy of the employee or the joint life expectancy of the employee and designated beneficiary). [See I.R.C. § 401(a)(9)(A)(ii)] It is up to the plan whether to offer these alternate forms, or just the standard annuities. [See §§ 12.03, 12.09]

When a corporation is acquired (see § 16.02[A]), one scenario is for the acquired corporation's plan to be terminated, with a distribution to all participants. All benefits become 100% vested when the plan is terminated. Participants must be given distribution election forms. They can take the fund in cash, make an Individual Retirement Arrangement (IRA) rollover or, if they have been hired by the acquiring corporation and the plan allows, they can make a rollover to the acquiror's plan. Under this model, when payments are completed, the acquired corporation files a final Form 5500 and the plan is terminated. [Beth Harrington, *Impact of Merger or Acquisition on Company Retirement Plans* (Mar. 5, 2014) (benefitslink.com)]

A plan can be disqualified if it makes distributions outside the range of permitted events related to separation from service. A defined benefit or money purchase plan can only make distributions when the participant reaches Normal Retirement Age or separates from service. The rules are different for 401(k) plans: distributions can be made at retirement, death, attainment of age 59, disability, severance from employment, or hardship. Termination of service means ceasing to work for any entity that is treated as the same employer under the Code § 411 rules. However, employers are not prohibited from rehiring a former employee who has received a 401(k) distribution, although the IRS may look to whether there was a true termination or if the so-called termination was merely pretextual.

The IRS might also accept distributions made to a person who is rehired for substantially different duties, and on a part-time rather than the previous full-time schedule, but there must have been an intervening period when the person was not employed by the employer.

See § 12.09[A] for a brief discussion of the extent to which financially failing multi-employer plans will be permitted by the Multi-Employer Pension Reform Act to suspend benefits without violating the anti-cutback rule.

The Heroes Earnings Assistance and Relief Tax Act (HEART Act; Pub. L. No. 110-245) allows reservists called for at least six months of active duty to take withdrawals from a 401(k) or other defined contribution plan before age 59½ without having to pay the 10% penalty. (The withdrawals are taxable income, however.) This provision was included in the Code; expired; and was revived and made permanent by the HEART Act. Differential pay provided to employees who have been called up (i.e., supplements that the employer provides to make up the difference between military pay and what the servicemember earned while working) must be taken into account when calculating pension benefits. The HEART Act also protects survivor benefits under qualified plans for the survivors of servicemembers killed in the line of duty. [Rebecca Moore, *Reservist Benefits Bill Signed into Law*, plansponsor.com (June 19, 2008)]

ERISA, at 29 U.S.C. § 1053(a), requires pension plans to provide that the right to normal retirement benefit is nonforfeitable at the Normal Retirement Age (NRA). The Supreme Court denied certiorari in *Fry v. Exelon*, 571 F.3d 644 (7th Cir. 2009), 559 U.S. 936 (Feb. 22, 2010). The Seventh Circuit ruled that, before the PPA, it was lawful to define NRA as five years' service rather than a particular age. [Rebecca Moore, *Supreme Court Lets Stand Alternate Definitions for Retirement Age*, plansponsor. com (Feb. 23, 2010) But see *Laurent v. PriceWaterhouseCooper*, 794 F.3d 272 (2d Cir. 2015), disapproving of using five years of service as an NRA.]

For many years (e.g., DOL Interpretive Bulletin 95-1, Advisory Opinion 2002-14A) the Department of Labor took the position that selecting an annuity provider is a fiduciary decision. In other words, failure to select the safest annuity available could lead to fiduciary liability.

Then, in September 2007, to make annuity distributions more attractive, the DOL announced new rules relieving defined contribution plans from the "safest annuity available" rule. PPA § 665 mandated the DOL to issue regulations exempting defined contribution plans from this rule. First the DOL amended Interpretive Bulletin 95-1, effective November 13, 2007, limiting its applicability to defined benefit plans. Under the interim final rules, fiduciaries must select annuity providers with due care and skill, using factors such as the cost of the annuity vis-à-vis the benefits and administrative services offered; the annuity provider's capital, surplus and reserves; its rating; and whether it is covered by a state guarantee program. [Interim final rules, 72 Fed. Reg. 52004 (Sept. 12, 2007); safe harbor for fiduciaries choosing annuity providers, 72 Fed. Reg. 52021 (Sept. 12, 2007)]

DOL final regulations on selection of annuity providers for individual account plans (such as 401(k) plans) were published in late 2008, effective December 8, 2008. The PPA limited the application of the Interpretive Bulletin 95-1 "safest available provider" rule to defined benefit plans, raising the question of what standard should be applied to defined contribution plans. To qualify for the safe harbor, the individual account plan fiduciary must perform an objective, thorough, and analytical search to select annuity providers. The selection must reflect a determination that the provider has the ability to make all future payments under the contract, and that the total cost of the annuity contract (including fees and commissions) is reasonable in light of the benefits the contract provides. [DOL Reg. § 2550.404a-4, 73 Fed. Reg. 58447 (Oct. 7, 2008); Amendment to Interpretive Bulletin 95-1, 73 Fed. Reg. 58445 (Oct. 7, 2008)]

DOL FAB 2015-02 says that the employer's fiduciary duty to monitor an insurer's solvency ends once annuities from that insurer cease to be a defined contribution plan distribution option. The prudence of selection and monitoring of annuity providers is based on information available at the time of selection or periodic review; hindsight about subsequent events is not applied. Circumstances determine how frequently prudence must be reviewed. However, there are two circumstances in which the DOL requires immediate review of the prudence of the selection: when the annuity provider's rating is downgraded by a major insurance rating service or when there are complaints from annuitants about a pattern of untimely payments, suggesting that the provider is unsound. [Puneet Arora and Lynn Cook, *DOL Clarifies Annuity Selection Safe Harbor Regulation for DC Plans*, TowersWatson.com (Aug. 7, 2015) (benefitslink.com)]

The Pension Benefit Guarantee Corporation (PBGC) is concerned about the accelerating level of pension buyouts because the more participants who cash out with lump sums and the more insurers that issue annuities, the smaller the PBGC's premium base. Furthermore, the companies that de-risk are often financially stable and unlikely to require PBGC guarantees, leaving only the less stable companies in the pool. [Maria P. Rasmussen and James P. McElligott Jr., McGuire Woods LLP, *PBGC Wants Reporting on Lump-Sum Pension Cash-Outs and Annuity Purchases* (Jan. 16, 2015) (benefitslink.com)]

The PBGC premium filing procedure has been revised to require defined benefit plans to report certain pension risk transfers using lump-sum windows and annuity purchases; the PBGC found that there was no comprehensive source of detailed risk transfer data. [Rebecca Moore, *PBGC to Begin Requesting Pension Risk Transfer Information*, plansponsor.com (Jan. 13, 2015)] The IRS has also taken steps to limit de-risking: see § 12.03, below.

The normal payment method for a profit-sharing plan or stock bonus plan is a lump sum, not a periodic payment. When a participant in one of these plans dies, the entire vested balance remaining in the account must go to the beneficiary designated by the participant. The spouse's consent is required if a married participant is to designate anyone other than the spouse as beneficiary.

In 2008, the Northern District of Illinois ruled that Verizon was bound by the language in a defined benefit plan document even if there was a drafting error (multiplying the cashout value of an interest in the former plan by a variable transaction factor twice rather than once), but the court ruled in 2009 that Verizon could correct the error and would not be required to provide a $1.67 billion windfall to participants. The 2009 decision treated the error as an honest mistake, and other actions in administering the plan reflected an intent to use the multiplication factor only once. Magistrate Judge Morton Denlow said that employers would be discouraged from adopting plans if they suffered unduly harsh penalties for mistakes. The Seventh Circuit affirmed this decision in August 2010. [*Young v. Verizon* (N.D. Ill. 2009), *aff'd*, *Young v. Verizon*, 615 F.3d 808 (7th Cir. 2010). The Supreme Court refused to hear the case (No. 10-765), denying certiorari on May 23, 2011 and rehearing on July 25, 2011.]

The First Circuit held that, if a company representative, using an online benefits calculator, tells an employee that his retirement benefits will be greater than they actually are, the employee is only entitled to benefits as properly calculated under the plan, not the greater amount calculated by mistake. [*Livick v. Gillette Co.*, 524 F.3d 24 (1st Cir. 2008)]

In 2016, the Seventh and Eighth Circuits decided very similar cases on the question of whether pension plans calculated benefits correctly when employees took early retirement from one plan, went to work for another employer, and received benefits from each. The plans called for offsetting the second pension with amounts received from the first employer. The question was whether the offset should reflect the reduced early retirement benefit, or the amount the plaintiff would have received by retiring at normal retirement age. The Seventh Circuit said that the higher offset (for full retirement benefits) was proper, because the two amounts were actuarially equivalent. The retiree would receive the same amount over the course of his life whenever he chose to retire. Using the lower offset would give him a windfall for retiring early. [*Cocker v. Terminal R.R. Ass'n of St. Louis Pension Plan*, 817 F.3d 337 (7th Cir. 2016); *Ingram v. Terminal R.R. Ass'n of St. Louis Pension Plan*, 812 F.3d 628 (8th Cir. 2016); see Ronald J. Kramer and Christopher Bussey, *Seventh Circuit Does the Math and Sides with Plan Administrator in Pension Calculation Dispute*, Seyfarth Shaw LLP (Mar. 21, 2016), available at Lexology.com]

The Seventh Circuit held that ERISA § 502 does not rule out enforcement of a pension plan's recoupment provisions (by suspending benefits to recover a past overpayment). The Collective Bargaining Agreement (CBA) said that pension and disability benefits were to be reduced by Social Security benefits payable to the employee, and that a grant of retroactive Social Security benefits would be treated as an overpayment that would trigger an obligation to reimburse the plan. The plaintiffs' argument was that the employer had to sue for equitable relief and could not enforce contract remedies, but the Seventh Circuit said that enforcing a contractual provision, like the CBA reimbursement requirement, is not "judicial relief," and employees can be held to clearly disclosed requirements to repay duplicative payments they have received. [*Northcutt v. GM Hourly Rate Emp. Pension Plan*, 467 F.3d 1031 (7th Cir. 2006)]

Under federal law, overpayments must be returned to the pension plan—but the law does not state who must make the payments. Usually, the payor stops or reduces the payments until the overpayments have been recovered. Recoupment is also subject to state trust law, which requires decisions to be made based on equity principles, including "laches" (i.e., if a plan waits too long to recover over-payments, it may be held to have waived the right to repayment). There is no ceiling on the amount a private plan can recoup from later payments, but a multi-employer plan can impose only a 25% reduction, and the PBGC can reduce a pension by only 10% and does not impose interest. [Ellen E. Schultz, *"Over-paid" Pensions Being Seized*, WSJ.com (Aug. 13, 2010)]

There are no regulations explaining what to do when a defined contribution plan settles a suit or is awarded damages. It is up to the plan administrator to decide how to get the funds to the participants. The first step is to create a hold-ing account where the funds are distributed. First, the settlement funds go to attor-neys' fees (generally 25%–30% of the settlement). Then the administrator allocates the funds to plan participants based on available information in their files. Usually the distribution reflects each person's balance at the time the funds are received. Suits take years to resolve, so some employees will have left by the time settlement funds are available; it then becomes the administrator's duty to find them. [Lee Barney, *How to Treat Lawsuit Awards and Settlements*, planspon-sor.com (Aug. 7, 2015)]

It was once common for plan sponsors to use the IRS letter forwarding ser-vice to locate the payees of benefits. However, effective for requests postmarked on or after August 31, 2012, the IRS no longer treats finding missing participants a "humane purpose." Plan sponsors will, therefore, have to use costlier and more laborious methods. DOL suggests using Internet search, credit reports, and com-mercial locater services to find missing participants. The Social Security Admin-istration's forwarding service is still available, but at a cost of $25 per forwarded letter; the IRS used to forward up to 50 letters without charge. A terminating pen-sion plan can use the PBGC missing participants program, paying the benefit to the PBGC, which will try to locate the participant. The PPA mandated the exten-sion of this program to terminating 401(k) plans, but the PBGC never issued regu-lations. The PBGC also helps participants locate missing benefits. [McDermott Will & Emery, *IRS Eliminates Use of Letter Forwarding Service to Find Missing Participants and Beneficiaries* (Sept. 27, 2012) (benefitslink.com)]

DOL FAB 2014-01 (Aug. 14, 2014) explains how fiduciaries should search for missing participants or beneficiaries in terminated defined contribution plans and how to distribute the account balances of missing participants so that the assets are no longer plan assets and the person is no longer a plan participant. At least four steps must be taken (certified mailing of notice of plan termination; seeking updated information in plan and employer records; asking the designated beneficiary for information about the participant's whereabouts; using free Internet search tools). Further steps may be required depending on the size of the account balance and the cost of additional search. If the participant still cannot be located, the fiduciary must distribute the account balance, preferably by direct rollover to an IRA or annuity. If direct rollover to an individual plan is not possible or there is a good reason to avoid it, the DOL allows the fiduciary to transfer the account balance to a federally insured bank account or the state unclaimed property fund. ERISA § 404(a) provides a safe harbor for fiduciaries who send a notice to a participant or beneficiary, if no distribution election is made within 30 days of the notice. The notice must give the name of the plan, the account balance, and the available distribution elections. [<http://www.dol.gov/ebsa/regs/fab 2014-1.html> (Aug. 14, 2014) (last viewed Feb. 17, 2017).]

Non-qualified deferred compensation (NQDC) is compensation paid, usually to a former executive, under a plan that does not qualify for favorable tax treatment. See Chapter 8. An initial election to defer compensation generally must be irrevocable before the year in which the compensation is earned begins. The initial election to defer payment of performance-based deferred compensation (for example, a sales bonus that is paid after the year in which the sales were made) can be made six months before the end of the performance period, but only if the performance period is at least 12 months long, the executive works throughout the entire performance period, and the amount of performance-based compensation is not readily ascertainable at the time the deferral election is made. Changes to the time or form of payment of NQDC must be made at least 12 months before the scheduled payment date and must delay the payment for at least five years. NQDC can be distributed only pursuant to a fixed date set at the time of deferral, or on the executive's death, disability, separation from service, change in control of the employer company, or hardship—terms that have specific, and sometimes idiosyncratic, definitions in § 409A. [Lori Jones, *Section 409A: Top 10 Rules for Compliant Non-Qualified Deferred Compensation,* Thompsoncoburn .com (July 28, 2016) (benefitslink.com)]

[A]   Disaster-Related Distributions

The Katrina Emergency Tax Relief Act of 2005 (KETRA), Pub. L. No. 109-73, provided that the 10% penalty on early withdrawals would not be imposed on a "qualified Hurricane Katrina distribution" of up to $100,000 withdrawn by a storm victim from a qualified retirement plan, 403(b) plan, or IRA, although the amounts would be treated as income, recognized over a three-year period. [IRS Publication 4492, *Information for Taxpayers Affected by Hurricanes Katrina, Rita and Wilma*]

Although qualified hurricane distributions were announced for Hurricanes Katrina, Rita, and Wilma, they were not announced for Hurricane Irene, despite the severe financial impact of that storm. [Keith R. McMurdy, *Employees May Be*

Eligible for Retirement Funds After Natural Disasters, Employee Benefit News (Sept. 9, 2011) (benefitslink.com)]

Nor was there a qualified hurricane distribution for Superstorm Sandy. But see IRS Announcement 2012-44, 2012-49 I.R.B. 663, relaxing the requirements for plan loans and hardship distributions for Sandy-related events. See also IR-2012-83 for Code § 7058A relief.

[B] Roth Distributions

The enactment of Roth IRAs and Roth 401(k)s (i.e., accounts that are not tax-advantaged when deposits are made, but permit tax-free withdrawals on appropriate conditions, including retention of the sums within the account for at least five years) created a need for specialized distribution rules.

Proposed regulations on the taxation of Roth 401(k) distributions say that the five-year holding period begins at the beginning of the tax year in which the first Roth 401(k) contribution is made and ends at the end of the fifth tax year. In a direct rollover, the holding period from the sending plan is considered under the receiving plan (this is known as "tacking"—i.e., the earlier holding period is tacked on). However, tacking is not applied if the participant makes an indirect rollover within the 60-day period. Only the taxable part of the distribution can be the subject of an indirect rollover.

Both qualified and nonqualified Roth 401(k) distributions that could otherwise be rolled over can be rolled over directly to another qualified plan that accepts Roth 401(k) contributions. Distributions to a participant can be rolled over to a Roth IRA, and the taxable part of the distribution can be rolled over to another plan that accepts Roth 401(k) funds. Even a person whose adjusted gross income (AGI) is too high to make a Roth IRA contribution can roll funds over into a Roth IRA.

If one Roth plan does a plan-to-plan rollover to another Roth plan, the sending plan must inform the receiving plan that the distribution is a qualified distribution or the amount of the participant's basis and the date the five-year "clock" began to run. Participants are entitled to disclosure of the same information if they receive a distribution.

Partial distributions from a Roth plan allocate taxable income pro rata; that is, if $1,000 in a $10,000 account is income on amounts deposited into the plan, and the account owner receives a nonqualified distribution of $4,000, 10% is attributed to income and therefore is taxable income for the recipient; $3,600 is a nontaxable return of deferred amounts. Only the amount contributed to the account (not earnings) can become a hardship distribution. [71 Fed. Reg. 4320 (Jan. 26, 2006)]

Final rules were published in April 2007, covering Roth 401(k) distribution issues. As in the proposed regulations, the central question is whether the distribution is a qualified distribution and thus excludable from the recipient's gross income. If the distribution is made to a beneficiary or an alternate payee, the participant's age, death, or disability status is the deciding factor, except for rollovers made by a surviving spouse or alternate payee to his or her own employer's Roth plan. Part of a Roth 401(k) distribution can be rolled over directly to a Roth 401(k) or Roth IRA, but a distribution from a designated Roth account can be rolled over only to a 401(k) plan or a 403(b) plan with a Roth feature. [T.D. 9324, RIN 1545-BF04, 72 Fed. Reg. 21103 (Apr. 30, 2007)]

See § 12.10 for Roth account rollover issues.

[C] PPA Rules

Although the main focus of the Pension Protection Act (PPA; Pub. L. No. 109-280) is on improving the funding mechanisms, and therefore the stability, of defined benefit plans (including special rules for at-risk plans), this legislation has an impact on many areas of plan operations.

The Pension Protection Act forbids amendments that increase benefits in certain underfunded defined benefit plans (see § 5.10) unless the plan sponsor makes additional contributions or provides security. (This requirement does not apply to a new plan in its first five years of operation.) The PPA limits benefits that can be paid in a lump sum or other alternate form of distribution when a single-employer defined benefit plan is underfunded. For example, if its Adjusted Funding Target Attainment Percentage (AFTAP) (percentage of funding) is between 60%–80%, the plan cannot make an accelerated distribution that is greater than 50% of the amount otherwise payable, or that exceeds the present value of the maximum PBGC guarantee for the participant—whichever of the two is lower. See Code § 463(d)(3) and ERISA § 206(g)(3)(C). The PBGC publishes present value tables every year for this purpose.

For annuity starting dates in 2017, the present value runs from $153,783 (age 25) to $352,104 at age 45, $579,776 at 55, and $913,208 at 65, to $6,321,974 at 85. [PBGC, *Present Value of PBGC Maximum Guarantee,* available online at <http://www.pbgc.gov/prac/mortality-retirement-and-pv-max-guarantee/present-guarantee.html#main-content>; <http://www.pbgc.gov/prac/mortality-retirement-and-pv-max-guarantee/present-guarantee.html#2017> (Dec. 2, 2016)]

When an underfunded plan terminates, additional benefit accruals cease and the PBGC's guarantee covers only amounts earned before termination. If the plan terminates when the employer is bankrupt, only the benefits earned before the bankruptcy filing date are guaranteed. The PBGC pays benefits according to the terms of the plan. Most participants will receive their full benefits, but if the benefits exceed the limit on the PBGC guarantee, the PBGC will make estimated benefit payments while it examines the plan records, reducing any benefits that exceed the guarantee. For 80% of participants, the estimated benefit equals the final benefit, but the PBGC will make a single payment (including interest) to catch up if the final benefit is higher than the estimate. Anyone who retired before the PBGC take-over continues to receive the form of benefit already elected. Those who retire after the take-over choose from among the PBGC's annuity options. A participant who is not yet receiving payments from a terminated plan can begin to collect benefits at the plan's Normal Retirement Age. Someone who has already satisfied all the requirements (such as years of service) for early retirement as of the date of plan termination, or the earlier date on which the sponsor filed for bankruptcy protection, can begin early retirement benefits at early retirement age—but only if he or she is no longer employed by the plan sponsor. [PBGC, *Maximum Monthly Guarantee Tables* <http://www.pbgc.gov/wr/benefits/guaranteed-benefits/maximum-guarantee.html> (no date, last accessed Mar. 20, 2016)]

In 2017, the monthly maximum PBGC-guaranteed benefit for a 65-year-old retiree receiving a single-life in a single-employer plan is $5,369.32, and the maximum guarantee of a joint and survivor annuity is $4,832.39. At age 60, the corresponding amounts are $3,480.06 and $3,141.05 a month. The amounts at age 55 are $2,416.19 and $2,174.57, respectively. [PBGC, *Maximum Monthly Guarantee Tables*, <http://www.pbgc.gov/wr/benefits/guaranteed-benefits/maximum-guarantee.html> (no date, last accessed Feb. 17, 2017)]

The IRS has essentially ended its program of providing determination letters on the qualified status of plans (see § 10.2). Instead, the IRS will publish a Required Amendments List, setting out the statutory and administrative changes in the requirements for operating a qualified plan that might require a plan amendment. When the first list was published, the only item it contained was restrictions on accelerated distributions from underfunded, collectively bargained, single-employer defined benefit plans maintained by bankrupt employers. [Notice 2016-80: 2016-52 I.R.B. 918 Haynes and Boone LLP, *IRS Publishes First Required Amendments List*, (Dec. 30, 2016), available at Lexology.com]

The PPA also changes the interest rate and mortality table for minimum lump sum benefits, by reducing mortality assumptions and by requiring interest rates to be based on corporate bond yields, which will reduce lump sums. Valuation issues, including limitations on distributions made by underfunded plans, are addressed by T.D. 9467, *Measurement of Assets and Liabilities for Pension Funding Purposes, Benefit Restrictions for Underfunded Pension Plans*. [T.D. 9467, 2009-50 I.R.B. 760]

The static mortality tables to be used for valuation dates in calendar year 2016 were published in mid-2015 in IRS Notice 2015-53. These tables are based on the Society of Actuaries' draft tables published in mid-2014. The tables reflect increased life expectancy, and some commentators said that the greater liabilities caused by longer lives would induce plan sponsors to terminate their defined benefit plans. [Notice 2015-53, 2015-33 I.R.B. 190; Amy Gentile, *Rising Interest Rates Will Offset Longer Life Expectancy in Pension Plans*, Findleydavies.com (date?) (benefitlink.com); Vipal Monga, *Moody's: IRS Mortality Decision to Save Corporate Pensions $18B in 2016*, WSJ.com (Sept. 2, 2015)]

Notice 2016-50, 2016-38 I.R.B. 384, updates the static mortality tables to be used for purposes of ERISA § 303(h)(3)(A) and Code § 430(h)(3)(a), for calculating items such as funding targets for valuation dates in calendar year 2017. The Notice also includes a modified unisex table for determining the minimum present value of distributions under ERISA § 205(g)(3)/Code § 417(e)(3). The tables have not changed significantly for 2017 and the tables continue to use 2000 as a base year for projecting mortality. However, in September 2016, the IRS gave advance notice of its intention to release a draft of 2018 tables shortly thereafter, signaling intention to make major changes at last, probably involving some form of the SOA RP-2014 tables. [Rebecca Moore, *IRS Updates DB Plan Mortality Tables for 2017,* plansponsor.com (Sept. 6, 2016); Matt Klein, *Mortality Table Update,* Finleydavies.com (Sept. 9, 2016) (benefitslink.com)]

At the end of 2016, the IRS released proposals for the mortality tables to be used for minimum funding purposes for plan years beginning in 2018. Plans whose funding percentages are close to the 80% or 60% level at which restrictions are imposed on distributions might become subject to restrictions on lump-sum distributions. The new tables are also expected to increase plans' accounting liabilities because plans that assume greater longevity will increase plan sponsors' obligations. The 2016 proposal updates the base mortality table to the RP-2014 version, with projected mortality improvements based on the MP-2016 scale. However, the IRS will permit sponsors to use plan-specific mortality tables if they obtain IRS approval. [P-Solve USA, *IRS Mortality Tables . . . Finally!* (Jan. 9, 2017) (benefitslink.com); Javier Simon, *IRS Releases Proposed Mortality Tables for DB Plans*, plansponsor.com (Dec. 29, 2016)]

In late 2011, the PBGC published a proposed rule for determining benefits in a hybrid plan such as a cash balance plan. When a plan terminates, the variable rate to be used to determine accrued benefits is the average of the interest rates used by the plan in the five years before the date of termination. Variable interest rates create problems for the PBGC when a plan terminates because a participant's exact benefit can only be determined when he or she starts collecting benefits—so it is hard for the PBGC to decide if the benefit is de minimis and can be cashed out in a lump sum. The PBGC will use the present value methodology if the plan uses the § 417(e) present value rules to calculate the value of the lump sum. [76 Fed. Reg. 67105 (Oct. 31, 2011)]

See also Notice 2016-67, 2016-47 I.R.B. 751, explaining the limitations on interest rates for Pension Equity Plans (PEPs), defined benefit plans that express the accumulated benefit as the current value of accumulated percentages of the participant's final average compensation, highest average compensation, or highest average compensation in a period of years. [Rebecca Moore, *IRS Clarifies Interest Crediting Rules for Pension Equity Plans*,plansponsor.com (Nov. 7, 2016)]

For plan amendments adopted and effective after November 8, 2012, plan sponsors who are bankruptcy debtors are permitted to amend single-employer defined benefit plans to eliminate certain optional forms of benefits without violating the anti-cutback rule. Under IRS regulations finalized in November 2012, optional forms of benefits, such as accelerated benefits that are greater than what the participant would have received as a single-life annuity, can be eliminated when the plan is not fully funded. The proposed regulations require the bankruptcy court rule that eliminating the optional benefit form is necessary to avoid an involuntary or distress termination. The PBGC's consent to terminate is required, based on the agency's conclusion that the plan is unable to provide the benefits guaranteed under ERISA § 404(d)(2). If the sponsor eliminates an optional form of benefit under these regulations and plan does not offer other options with substantial survivor benefits, the sponsor can add other options to provide those benefits as part of the amendment that eliminates the lump sum distribution option. The entire plan amendment is considered together in determining if the amendment can take effect in accordance with § 436(c). [77 Fed. Reg. 66915 (Nov. 8, 2012)]

Proposed regulations published in the fall of 2008 cover the PPA requirement that the notice of a participant's rights to defer an immediate distribution also explain the consequences of taking that distribution. A qualified plan cannot distribute benefits before the NRA without the consent of the participant, so rules are necessary to determine what constitutes valid and informed consent. There is no official format for the disclosures, but all of the information must be given together (e.g., in a list). However, if the required information is already available in other documents that the plan participant can obtain without charge, it is permissible to give cross-references to the other documents instead of repeating the information.

The regulations also deal with the increased period (rising from 90 to 180 days) for giving notice under Code §§ 402(f) [rollover notices], 411 [notice of the right to defer a distribution], and 417 [notice and election periods for 401(k) plans offering annuity distributions]. Cashouts of over $5,000 from a 401(k) plan require the consent of the plan participant, so the participant must be informed of the consequences of deferring versus receiving the distribution immediately (e.g., tax consequences; investment costs; other plan provisions such as availability of retiree health coverage that affect the decision).

PPA § 829 permits a non-spouse beneficiary to roll over a plan distribution to an IRA. [Prop. Treas. Reg. §§ 1.401(a)-13, 1.401(a)-20, 1.402(f)-1, 1.411(a)-11, 1.417(e)-1, 73 Fed. Reg. 59575 (Oct. 9, 2008); see EBIA Weekly, *IRS Proposes Regulations Addressing Notice of Participant's Right to Defer a Distribution and 180-Day Notice Period* (Oct. 9, 2008) (benefitslink.com)]

In a 2013 decision, the Seventh Circuit noted that a higher discount rate means a higher growth rate over the annuity period and a lower present value for lump sums, whereas a low discount rate means a higher lump sum. In a class action about the discount rates used by pension plans and top hat plans to convert a straight life annuity to lump sum, the Seventh Circuit upheld a grant of summary judgment for the plans. The pension plan used a segment rate of approximately 5.4%. The Seventh Circuit pointed out that the PPA allows retroactive increases in the discount rate, subject to a cap, so the change was not a cutback. While the plan forbade reduction in accrued benefits (the value of the straight life annuity), it did not prevent a retroactive reduction in the benefits of participants who opted for a lump sum. The top hat plan used a higher discount rate (7.5%) but that was permissible because it was a nonqualified plan and the PPA cap did not apply. The plan also permitted a 7.5% discount rate for any plan that is not tax-preferred, a category that includes top hat plans. [*Dennison v. MONY Life Ret. Income Sec. Plan*, 710 F.3d 741 (7th Cir. 2013)]

[D]   Hardship Distributions

IRS FAQs from 2015 explain that retirement plans, including 401(k) plans, are allowed (but not required) to permit hardship distributions. Plans that allow such distributions must define what constitutes a hardship, although the standards must be objective and non-discriminatory. "Hardship" means an immediate and heavy financial need of the employee, spouse, or dependent. Some expenses are presumed to be immediate and heavy, such as critical medical expenses, purchase of a principal residence, avoiding eviction from a principal residence, certain repairs (e.g., after a natural disaster), education costs, and funeral or burial expenses. But a plan distribution is not considered necessary if the employee, making use of spouses' and minor childrens' resources, has other resources to satisfy the need.

Before taking a hardship distribution, an employee must access all other currently available distributions and loans under all plans maintained by the employer. The employee must not make elective contributions or employee contributions to any plan for six months after taking a hardship distribution. The hardship distribution must not exceed the need (although this is measured taking into account the taxes and penalties on the distribution). The maximum amount of elective contributions that can be distributed from a 401(k) plan as a hardship distribution equals the employee's total elective contributions (including designated Roth contributions) minus any previously distributed elective contributions. All hardship distributions except designated Roth contributions are included in gross income. Employees who take hardship distributions cannot repay them (unlike plans loans), so taking a hardship distribution has the effect of permanently reducing the account balance. Employees are not allowed to roll over hardship distributions to IRAs or qualified plans. Unless special legislation is passed (as was done for Hurricane Katrina but not for Superstorm Sandy), the regular hardship distribution rules apply when employees take hardship distributions to carry out repairs to the principal residence that are necessary because of a natural disaster. [<http://www.irs.gov/Retirement-Plans/Retirement-Plans-FAQs-regarding-Hardship-Distributions> (Jan. 23, 2017) (last accessed Feb. 17, 2017)]

PPA § 826 allows a hardship distribution to be made based on the needs of a primary beneficiary who is not the participant's spouse and who has an unconditional right to receive part or all of the account balance when the participant dies. A § 409A plan can consider the needs of a beneficiary in determining if an emergency has occurred.

The recession has also led to more requests for hardship distributions. Participants in 401(k) plans can receive hardship distributions before age 59½ subject to limitations—but only if the plan provides for them. Plans can be disqualified for making improper distributions. Permissible distributions are made for an immediate and heavy financial need of the participant, determined based on all the facts and circumstances.

Rev. Rul. 2010-27, 2010-45 I.R.B. 620 lists examples of expenses that could qualify for an unforeseeable emergency distribution from a 409A plan—e.g., illness or accident affecting participant or spouse, dependents, or beneficiary; family funeral expenses; imminent foreclosure. Emergency distributions can only be made for expenses that cannot otherwise be met by insurance or by liquidating assets.

IRA distributions before age 59½ are generally penalized by 10% of the taxable amount of the distribution, but Congress allows exceptions when the funds are genuinely necessary. However, not everyone who qualifies for a disability benefit can satisfy this exception. In this context, disability means inability to perform any substantial gainful employment. Disability must be long-standing or of indefinite duration. The person taking the distribution must not be able to work at all. But for people who do qualify, there is no restriction on how the funds will be used. [Beverly DeVeny, *Disability and the Exception to 10% Early Distribution Penalty*, irahelp.com (Oct. 10, 2016) (benefitslink.com)]

§ 12.02 CASHOUT

Although it is burdensome for a plan to make periodic payments of a very small sum, and it would be convenient to simply close the books by making a one-time payment, participants cannot be forced to "cash out" (take a lump sum instead of a stream of payments) unless their vested balance is very small—$5,000 or less.

The Economic Growth and Tax Relief Reconciliation Act (EGTRRA) provides for automatic rollovers of cashouts from 401(k) plans in amounts between $1,000 and $5,000 to IRAs.

The calculation of the accrued benefit under I.R.C. § 411(a)(7)(B)(i) does not have to include any service with respect to which the employee has already been cashed out at a level below $3,500.

The 2002 technical corrections bill, the Job Creation and Worker Assistance Act of 2002 [Pub. L. No. 107-147] provides that employers can disregard rollovers when they determine whether or not the balance exceeds $5,000 and therefore whether or not it is subject to cashout. At press time in 2017, the $5,000 figure had still not been increased.

A qualified plan can include a provision cashing out distributions under $5,000; mandatory distributions that exceed $1,000 must be rolled over to an IRA set up by the plan for the participant, unless the recipient makes an affirmative election to roll over the money elsewhere or takes it in cash. Fiduciaries are deemed to have satisfied their duties with respect to rollovers if the plan satisfies the requirements of I.R.C. § 401(a)(31)(B). These rules apply to distributions made without consent of the participant, at normal retirement age or age 62 (whichever is later). An eligible rollover distribution that is a plan loan offset is not subject to the general rules on automatic rollovers. QDROs and distributions to participants' spouses are not covered.

§ 12.03 LUMP SUMS

There is no legal requirement that plans offer lump sum distributions, although it is very common for them to do so for the convenience of retirees who either need a lump sum (to pay the entrance fee to a Continuing Care Retirement Community, for example) or who believe that they can achieve better investment results than a qualified plan, subject to fiduciary requirements, can muster. Plans that engage in de-risking usually do so by distributing lump sums rather than by purchasing annuities.

The interaction between PPA funding requirements and the post-2008 recession made employers less willing to distribute balances, especially large balances, in lump-sum form. Since the stock market decline, the PPA's rules often prevent the 25 highest-compensated employees from taking lump sums, because top earners are forbidden lump sums if the plan assets fall below 110% of liabilities, or if the lump sum represents more than 1% of total plan assets. However, there are loopholes, such as the executive's promise to repay if the plan terminates when it is insufficiently funded, or setting aside funds in an escrow account. [Jilian Mincer, *Execs Finding It Harder to Get Lump Sums*, WSJ.com (May 12, 2009)] The Pension Protection Act says that if any defined benefit plan is severely underfunded, or if the plan is underfunded and the plan sponsor is bankrupt, all payouts must be in annuity form—lump sum distribution is forbidden.

According to AonHewitt, in 2014, only 12% had a lump-sum payout offer that was open to former employees, a proportion that rose to 44% in 2015 and 56% in 2016. [Heather Gillers, *Pension Plan Assets Fall as Payouts Rise*, WSJ .com (Sept. 7, 2016)]

Another issue is how employees should be paid if they go through phased retirement, transitioning from full-time to part-time work rather than from full-time work to full retirement. Transamerica's Aegon Center for Longevity and Retirement said that 55% of employees aged 55 and over prefer to retire gradually, but only 27% can do this in their current job. [Joanne Sammer, *Taking Phased Retirement Options to the Next Level*, shrm.org (Feb. 7, 2017) (benefitslink.com)]

The general rule is that the present value of any optional form of benefit from a defined benefit plan must be at least as great as the amount calculated by using the § 417(e) interest rates and mortality tables. But this general rule does not apply to a distribution that is an annual benefit that does not decrease during the participant's life or that decreases because of the death of a survivor annuitant or the reduction or termination of qualified disability benefits or supplements to Social Security benefits. But the mathematical factors used to calculate life annuities are usually simpler—and change less often—than the § 417(e) factors, so converting a single-life annuity to a 10-year-certain life annuity gives different results than using the § 417(e) factors.

In September 2016, the IRS finalized a 2012 proposal to allow participants to split their benefits between a lump sum and a stream of monthly annuity payments, rather than having to opt for one or the other. The IRS's position is that the split makes it less likely that participants will outlive their benefits. Under T.D. 9783, if a plan offers an accelerated distribution such as a single sum as an optional benefit in addition to the required QJSA, participants who take the accelerated distribution place themselves at longevity risk. The final rule amends the regulations under § 417(e) to clarify the treatment of distributions that are split between lump sum and annuity forms. The final rule amends the regulations under § 417(e) so that plans can simply the treatment of distributions split between lump sum and annuity. Distribution of a lump sum will be permitted as long as the rest of the accrued benefit conforms to the minimum requirements of T.D. 9783. The new rule applies to annuity starting dates in plan years beginning on or after January 1, 2017. [T.D. 9783, 81 Fed. Reg. 62359 (Sept. 9, 2016); see Sally P. Schreiber, *Defined Benefit Plan Participants Can Receive Lump Sum and Annuity Under New Rules*, J. of Accountancy (Sept. 2016) (benefitslink.com). Rebecca Moore, *IRS Issues Final Rule on Requirements for Partial Annuities in DB Plans*, plansponsor.com (Sept. 9, 2016); Lee Barney, *IRS Guidance Explains Annuity Taxation During Partial Retirement*, plansponsor.com (June 14, 2016)]

The final regulation permits two approaches to calculating the benefits. "Explicit bifurcation" applies the § 417(e) lump-sum calculation to a specified portion of the accrued benefit, as if it constituted the entire benefit, while the rest of the benefit is paid in a different form of distribution offered by the plan. The second option, "implicit bifurcation," calls for paying part of the benefit as a lump sum, with the rest being at least equivalent to the total accrued benefit in normal form minus the annuity actuarially equivalent to the lump sum as calculated with the § 417(e) rates and tables. Plans that provide early retirement benefits, retirement-type subsidies, optional benefit forms, or ancillary benefits that apply to only part of the benefit must identify the part of the benefit that is paid as a lump sum. Plans that eliminated an optional form but had to retain it for part of the benefit under the anti-cutback rule are required to use the explicit bifurcation method. [Octoberthree.com, *IRS Finalizes Partial Annuity Regulation* (Oct. 6, 2016) (benefitslink.com)]

In the fall of 2009, the Supreme Court heard arguments about treatment of lump sums received at the time of the first retirement by rehired employees. The plan had two provisions. The "non-duplication" provision called for offsetting the "floor" amount, based on total years of service with the company. The "phantom account provision" further reduced benefits at retirement. The Second Circuit refused to grant deference to the administrator's determination.

The Supreme Court announced its decision on April 21, 2010, strongly affirming the discretion of plan administrators, and holding that, as long as the plan gives administrators the discretion to interpret the plan, courts must defer to the administrators' decisions as long as they are reasonable. (Of course, this principle does not prevent plan participants from bringing suits that claim that the administrators made an unreasonable decision!) [*Conkright v. Frommert*, 559 U.S. 506 (2010)] The case returned to the Second Circuit, which remanded it for a third time in late 2013. The Second Circuit held that the plaintiffs' suit is meritorious: the proposed offset method was unreasonable, and the Summary Plan Description (SPD) was not accurate enough because did not say that the lump sum distribution will reduce the benefit, only that it might. [*Frommert v. Conkright*, 738 F.3d 522 (2d Cir. 2013); see Kevin McGuinness, *Appellate Court Remands Case on Offsetting Pension Benefits*, plansponsor.com (Dec. 31, 2013). Xerox was ordered to pay close to $4.9 million in attorneys' fees and costs to the plaintiffs—but this was only about half of the plaintiffs' fee request. *Frommert v. Conkright*, No. 6:00-cv-06311-DGL-JWF (W.D.N.Y. Dec. 12, 2016); see Carmen Castro-Pagan, *Xerox Must Pay $4.9M in Fees, Costs in Pension Benefits Case*, bna.com (Dec. 14, 2016)]

The GAO is concerned that employees are often deprived of the information they need to decide whether to take advantage of a "window" to take a lump-sum benefit. The GAO reviewed 11 information packets from lump-sum offers affecting close to 250,000 participants, finding them consistently deficient in information or unclear about important matters. For example, value of lump sum often was not compared to value of the lifetime monthly benefit and mortality assumptions and interest rates often were not explained. Even though many people interviewed by the GAO said they wanted a lump sum for fear that the plan sponsor would default, the PBGC guarantees (and loss thereof) were not explained clearly. The GAO recommended that the DOL and Treasury supervise lump-sum offers and that disclosure of eight categories of information be made mandatory. [GAO, *Participants Need Better Information When Offered Lump Sums That Replace Their Lifetime Benefits*, <http://www.gao.gov/products/GAO-15-74> (Jan. 27, 2015)]

Pension de-risking began in 2012–2013 when Ford used it to settle $3.4 billion in pension obligations. Usually, the employer amends its plans to offer non-actives a one-time option to take a lump sum in lieu of accrued benefits. The offer might be extended to people already receiving pensions, although this will not be the case if the employer is worried about adverse selection. Lump-sum recipients can roll over the lump sum to an IRA to avoid immediate taxation. The plan then purchases annuities from insurance companies to cover benefits that were not cashed out. In the current low-interest-rate environment, these transactions are very expensive. Opponents of de-risking say that there is risk that pensioners will take lump sums, which they will then not be able to manage effectively.

Pension Risk Transfer (PRT) became popular when several factors converged. Defined benefit plans were already on the decline; new mortality tables made maintaining the plan more expensive; and PBGC premiums increased significantly. In 2013, there were $3.8 billion in group pension buyouts, an amount that reached $8.5 billion in 2014, when 280 plans engaged in PRT activity.

The IRS announced a change in policy in mid-2015: the form or period of distribution cannot be changed once distributions begin. Plan amendments that provide a lump sum to persons who have already retired are invalid, but lump-sum windows are still allowed for participants whose pension is not yet in pay status. De-risking programs in effect on July 9, 2015, are exempt if they were required by a CBA; the amendment was adopted by a board or committee; the IRS issued a favorable PLR on the transaction; or participants received written communications about the intent to implement the de-risking program. The Notice does not explain whether the prohibition applies to participants who are getting pensions but have not yet reached age 70½, or whether it applies to terminating plans (some plans with only a few pensioners want to buy them out on termination instead of buying a small number of annuities). [Notice 2015-49 2015-30 I.R.B. 79]

The Fifth Circuit dismissed a class action about Verizon's amendment of a plan to transfer assets to an annuity contract to settle $7.4 billion in pension liabilities. The court held that the decision was a settlor function, not a fiduciary function, and the SPD disclosed that the employer had retained the right to amend the plan. [*Lee v. Verizon*, 623 Fed. Appx. 132 (5th Cir. 2015)]

In mid-2016, the Supreme Court agreed to hear the case, but then remanded it for reconsideration on the issue of whether a plan participant has standing to sue when the participant's rights under a federal statute have been violated—but there has been no concrete harm. [*Cert. granted sub. nom. Pundt v. Verizon*, No. 15-785 (May 23, 2016); see Rebecca Moore, *Supreme Court Revives Part of Verizon PRT Challenge*, plansponsor.com (May 23, 2016)]

The Fifth Circuit once again held that the plaintiff did not have standing to sue, as required by Article III of the constitution, because his benefits were not threatened and therefore he was not injured. So the Fifth Circuit reaffirmed its dismissal of the class action [*Lee v. Verizon Commc'ns, Inc.*, 837 F.3d 523 (5th Cir. 2016); see Jacklyn Wille, *Verizon Victory Not Changed by Recent Supreme Court*

Case, bna.com (Sept. 19, 2016) (benefitslink.com); Rebecca Moore, *5th Circuit Again Dismisses Verizon Pension Buyout Lawsuit*, plansponsor.com (Oct. 14, 2016)]

Pension risk transfer is expected to transform pension management by "slashing their exposure to the volatility of the stock and bond markets" and gives insurance companies a source of growth when some of their traditional businesses are doing badly. As interest rates rise, it's cheaper to do a risk transfer. Prudential is the leader; it has 10 jumbo deals covering over 320,000 people and $45 billion of corporate pension obligations. MetLife and the U.S. unit of Britain's Legal & General are also involved. There are still about 22,000 single-employer defined benefit plans covering 30 million people. An employer doing a transfer has to turn over assets to back the obligation plus a "mid-single-digit" percentage of liabilities to pay the insurer. State regulators require the insurer to set aside capital, usually 5%–10% of the transaction, in case the predictions are wrong. [Leslie Scism, *Your Pension Check May Soon Be Coming from an Insurance Company,* WSJ.com (Mar. 12, 2017)]

§ 12.04   ANTI-ALIENATION RULE

The underlying purpose of pension plans is to provide income to retirees and their families once the individual is no longer able to work. This purpose could not be satisfied if the pension became unavailable for some reason. Therefore, pension, annuity, stock bonus, and profit-sharing plans are subject to anti-alienation requirements under I.R.C. §§ 401(a)(13) and 404(a)(2). The benefits under such plans may not be assigned or alienated in advance. But, just as with any legal rule, there are certain exceptions to what seems to be a blanket prohibition.

Federal tax liens under I.R.C. § 6331 can be enforced; they are not considered to violate this provision. [Treas. Reg. § 1.401(a)-13(b)(2)] The anti-alienation provision does not prevent the IRS from proceeding against an interest in ERISA plan benefits. [*United States v. McIntyre*, 222 F.3d 655 (9th Cir. 2000)]

Once a benefit is in pay status, a participant or beneficiary can make a voluntary revocable assignment of up to 10% of any benefit payment. However, assignments of this type cannot be used to defray the costs of plan administration.

A plan loan is not an improper alienation if:

- The plan includes a specific loan provision;

- Loans are available to all participants on a nondiscriminatory basis;

- The loan is not a prohibited transaction;

- The plan imposes a reasonable interest rate on plan loans;

- The loan is secured by the accrued nonforfeitable benefit. [See I.R.C. § 4975(d)(1) and § 4.18]

The Supreme Court's decision in *Patterson v. Shumate* [504 U.S. 753 (1992)] holds that ERISA's anti-alienation provisions are "applicable non-bankruptcy law" under Bankruptcy Code § 541(c)(1). Therefore, benefits from an ERISA-qualified plan can be excluded from the employee's bankruptcy estate, and will not be available to the employee's creditors.

But because of an earlier Supreme Court decision, *Mackey v. Lanier Collection Agency & Service* [486 U.S. 825 (1988)], pension benefits are protected from creditors, but welfare benefits are not. Creditors are sometimes entitled (within limits) to garnish the wages of debtors, but they cannot garnish future pension benefits. If the plan itself is terminating, creditors cannot garnish employees' interests in the plan, even if one consequence of the termination is that they will receive a lump sum instead of ongoing annuity payments. In 2005, the Supreme Court ruled, in *Rousey v. Jacoway*, 544 U.S. 320, that IRAs are entitled to the same bankruptcy protection as qualified plans. Also in 2005, Congress increased the bankruptcy protection granted to IRAs and qualified plans, via Pub. L. No. 109-8, the Bankruptcy Abuse Prevention and Consumer Protection Act (BAPCPA). BAPCPA also makes it harder for bankrupt employers to modify their retiree health benefits.

Once the benefits are paid, the anti-alienation provision no longer applies. [See *Robbins v. DeBuono*, 218 F.3d 197 (2d Cir. 2000)] So, unless there is a state law that offers additional protection, the funds can be attached by creditors.

§ 12.05 QJSA/QOSA PAYMENTS

The normal method of paying pension plan benefits to married participants is the QJSA, payable for the lives of both the employee and his or her spouse. Once the first spouse dies, the plan can reduce the annuity payable to the survivor—although not more than 50% of the initial payment, for a joint and 50% survivor annuity. Employers can also choose to subsidize the survivor annuity at some level between 50% and 100% of the original payment, and the Pension Protection Act requires a joint and 75% survivor annuity to be offered as an option when a QJSA is required.

See <http://www.irs.gov/Retirement-Plans/Retirement-Plan-Participant-Notices-Qualified-Joint-&-Survivor-Annuity-%28QJSA%29-Notice> (Aug. 8, 2016) (last accessed Feb. 17, 2017) for an explanation of the requirement for providing QJSA notices.

In addition to the QJSA/QPSA, a plan can offer term annuities and/or life annuities, and life annuities can include term certain guarantee features.

Why would a couple be willing to waive the standard form and take a payment other than a QJSA? For one thing, the payments might be larger in the short run. The participant might be the first spouse to retire, with additional funds expected in the future from the other spouse's pension. If the spouse who is expected to survive will have ample funds (e.g., from personal assets and insurance on the life of the other spouse), then a reduced or absent survivor annuity may not create problems.

I.R.C. § 417(d) provides that QJSAs are required only if the participant was married for one year or more before plan payments begin, with an exception for participants who marry in the year before payments begin and remain married for one year. To avoid tracking problems, most plans simply offer QJSAs to all married participants whatever the duration of the marriage.

Because of a 1984 federal law, the Retirement Equity Act, the employee spouse cannot waive the QJSA without the written consent of the other spouse. There is a 60-day window for making the waiver, starting 90 days before the annuity start date (the first day of the employee spouse's first benefit period under the plan), ending 30 days before the annuity start date. However, the Small Business Job Protection Act [Pub. L. No. 104-188] amended the Internal Revenue Code to allow QJSA disclosures to be given even after the annuity starting date.

If an employee is married but does not want to name his or her spouse as beneficiary and cannot locate the spouse to get a waiver, it is not enough to say that the spouse is missing. The participant must document the use of a locator service to find the spouse, must file a missing persons report, or get a legal or administrative ruling that the spouse cannot be found. The participant can also obtain a legal separation, court order of abandonment, or a divorce. [Plansponsor staff, *(B) Lines Ask the Experts—Missing Spouses as Beneficiaries*, plansponsor.com (Nov. 18, 2014)]

A waiver of the right to receive the pension in QJSA form must be in writing, and must either be notarized or witnessed by a representative of the pension plan. [See Treas. Reg. § 1.417(e)-1(b)(3)] Furthermore, the waiver must be expressed in a document specifically related to the plan; a prenuptial agreement between the employee and his or her spouse would not work for this purpose. [Treas. Reg. § 1.401(a)-20, Q&A 28] The waiver binds only the spouse who signs it; if the employee and spouse divorce, any subsequent spouse is still entitled to a QJSA unless he or she waives it. [I.R.C. § 417(a)(4)]

As a result of *Obergefell v. Hodges,* 135 S. Ct. 1039 (U.S. 2015), all states must recognize same-sex marriage, so a same-sex surviving spouse is entitled to survivor benefits on the same terms as the survivor of a male/female marriage.

For tax qualification purposes, IRS Notice 2014-19, 2014-17 I.R.B. 979, says that as of June 26, 2013, the date of the *Windsor* decision, qualified retirement plans must treat same-sex marriages on a parity with mixed-sex marriages.

An antenuptial agreement did not waive the ex-wife's right to 401(k) funds. The plan participant married the same woman three times and divorced her twice; at the time of his death, a third divorce was in the works. They signed a prenuptial contract before the third wedding waiving all claims in the other's separate property. The agreement defined retirement benefits as separate property. The prenuptial agreement contemplated future execution of a waiver or consent to beneficiary change. Hr consent did not satisfy the requirement if acknowledgment of the effect of the change. ERISA waiver requirements must be strictly complied with. [*MidAmerican Pension & Emp. Benefits Plan Admin. Comm. v. Cox*, 720 F.3d 715 (8th Cir. 2013)]

A business owner was both the sole participant in a plan and the plan representative so the Seventh Circuit held that his spouse's written consent to waive the right to an annuity from the plan was valid, even though her signature was not witnessed. ERISA § 205(C)(2)(A)(iii) requires a spousal waiver of the right to a survivor annuity to be written—and witnessed by a notary or plan representative. After the husband died, the wife sought benefits under the plan. She admitted that she had signed the waiver of joint and survivor annuity, but said the document was invalid because it had not been witnessed. The Seventh Circuit upheld the waiver and awarded benefits to the husband's sons, saying that it would be absurd to invalidate the consent form; the husband obviously knew that his wife had signed the form. [*Burns v. Orthotek, Inc. Employees' Pension Plan & Trust*, 657 F.3d 571 (7th Cir. 2011)]

In this context, ERISA preempts community property law [*Boggs v. Boggs*, 520 U.S. 833 (1997)], so a spouse who waives the right to a QJSA, cannot later assert community property rights in those benefits.

The PPA mandates that plans that have to offer QJSAs must, for plan years beginning after December 31, 2007, offer Qualified Optional Survivor Annuities (QOSAs). A QOSA is a joint and survivor annuity where the survivor receives 75% of the original annuity level (if the QJSA would otherwise provide less) or 50% if the QJSA has a survivor percentage of 75% or more, actuarially equivalent to the single-life annuity payable at the same time. If the existing plan terms provide a joint and survivor annuity which satisfies the QOSA percentage requirements, it is not necessary to amend the plan to adopt a QOSA. The requirement is that the QOSA be actuarially equivalent to a single-life annuity; it doesn't have to be equivalent to a QJSA. If the QOSA is actuarially equivalent to the QJSA, the participant's spouse is not required to consent to the participant electing the QOSA. However, spousal consent is required to elect a QOSA which is less valuable than the QJSA. The PPA does not obligate plans to provide an option for the QOSA that works the same way as a qualified pre-retirement survivor annuity does for the QJSA. [Notice 2008-30, 2008-12 I.R.B. 638]

Internal Revenue Code § 417(a)(1)(A)(ii) allows the plan participant to revoke the waiver of QJSA payment at any time before payments begin. The spouse's consent is not required for the revocation, because it has the effect of increasing, not decreasing, the spouse's rights.

[A] Section 415 Regulations

Final Regulations under § 415, reflecting the PPA as well as interim changes since the previous set of Final Regulations issued in 1981, were published in the

Federal Register for April 5, 2007, effective for limitation years beginning on or after July 1, 2007. Section 415 governs the limitations on benefits that can be provided under defined benefit plans, as well as the contributions that can be made to 401(k) and other defined benefit plans. For most plans, which are operated on a calendar year, that meant that the new rules would take effect January 1, 2008. Plans can provide that payments in any limitation year will not exceed the § 415(b) limit as of the annuity starting date, and increased pursuant to § 415(d); if this is done, the plan does not require actuarial adjustments for automatic increases unless the benefit is subject to § 417(e)(3).

Under the PPA, compensation used to calculate the "high 3" years does not have to be earned while the employee is an active plan participant. In general, the "high 3" is calculated subject to the annual compensation limit of § 401(a)(17), but the Final Regulations allow grandfathering-in of some additional compensation based on plan provisions that were in effect before April 5, 2007. In general, money received after severance from employment is not considered § 415 compensation, but the Final Regulations allows inclusion of certain payments under bona fide sick or vacation leave plans—even if the payments are made more than 2½ months after severance from employment or the end of the year.

The final regulations allow some payments from nonqualified plans to be treated as § 415 compensation, as well as certain payments to disabled participants. The IRS announced its intentions to revise the rules covering multiple annuity starting dates. Various technical changes are made in the way that defined benefit payouts are adjusted when payment begins between ages 62 and 65. [Final Rule, 72 Fed. Reg. 16878 (Apr. 5, 2007)]

[B] QLACs

In early 2012, the Treasury proposed a rule, explained in a fact sheet, under which workers would have more options for lifetime income to cope with the potential for living to very old age. The proposal would allow employees who take a lump sum 401(k) distribution to transfer part of the sum to the employer's defined benefit plan (provided that the employer has a defined benefit plan and it accepts such contributions) in exchange for an actuarially fair annuity—perhaps a longevity annuity, a life annuity that begins payments at an advanced age such as 85. This option is referred to as a Qualified Longevity Annuity Contract, or QLAC.

Prior law disfavored longevity annuities by mandating minimum required distribution calculations based on distributing the entire sum over the person's actuarially predicted life expectancy—creating the risk of outliving one's assets.

The proposed regulations make it easier for a plan to offer split options by simplifying the calculation of the benefit. Prior law required the statutory interest rate and mortality assumptions to be used for both the lump sum and the annuity, preventing plans from using their own figures in annuity calculations. The proposal would allow the plan's regular conversion factors to be used for the partial annuity, while the statutory factors apply to the lump sum.

The 2012 proposal identifies certain plan and annuity terms that are deemed to protect spousal rights and for which spousal consent will not be required before the annuity begins. At the annuity start date, the insurer issuing the annuity would be responsible for compliance with the consent requirements. [Proposed Regulations, 77 Fed. Reg. 5443 and 5454 (Feb. 3, 2012)]

When the QLAC rules were finalized in mid-2014, the limit on the amount of the account balance that can be used to purchase the QLAC was changed, to the lesser of $125,000 or 25% of the balance. The QLAC annuity must not be indexed or variable, and must not include a cash surrender provision. Annuity payments must begin no later than the time the participant reaches age 85, but this age limit will be adjusted actuarially to reflect increases in lifespan. [T.D. 9673, 2014-30 I.R.B. 212; see Tara Siegel Bernard, *Longevity Insurance Joins the Menu of Retirement Plan Options*, NYTimes.com (July 1, 2014)]

§ 12.06 POST-DEATH PAYMENTS

The terms of the plan, and the fact situation, determine whether payments must continue after the death of the plan participant. For instance, if the employee was unmarried and received a life annuity, or if the employee was married and the employee and spouse validly waived the QJSA in favor of a life annuity, the plan will have no post-death obligations. Usually, however, the plan will be required to make a single or ongoing distributions to a beneficiary designated by the employee, or named as beneficiary under the terms of the plan.

Internal Revenue Code § 401(a)(9)(B) provides that if an employee dies when an annuity or installment pension with a survivorship feature is in pay status, the plan continues distributions in the same manner, but to the beneficiary rather than the retiree. The general rule is that the plan has five years from the death of the employee to complete distribution of the decedent's entire interest.

The five-year rule does not apply if the decedent's interest is payable to a designated beneficiary in life annuity form, or in installments that do not extend past the beneficiary's life expectancy. In this situation, the plan must begin the distributions no later than December 31 of the year following the date of the employee's death.

Qualified plans are required to provide Qualified Preretirement Survivor Annuities (QPSAs) if a vested plan participant dies before benefits begin. [I.R.C. § 401(a)(11)] The QPSA for a defined benefit plan participant who was eligible to retire at the time of death must be at least as great as what the spouse would have received if the employee had retired with the QJSA on the day before the actual date of death.

In the case of a person who was not yet retirement-eligible on the date of death, the defined benefit plan must calculate the survivor annuity that would have been available if the employee had separated from service on the date he or she died, and survived until the plan's earliest retirement date. The QPSA must be at least equivalent to the QJSA that would have been payable if the employee spouse had died the day after retiring with a QJSA on the plan's earliest retirement date.

In a defined contribution plan, the QPSA must be actuarially equivalent to at least 50% of the nonforfeitable account balance as of the time of death.

The designated beneficiary can also be an irrevocable trust that is valid under state law and has identifiable beneficiaries. It is the responsibility of the employee who wants to take this option to provide the plan with a copy of the trust.

According to I.R.C. § 401(a)(9)(B), if an employee dies once payment of an annuity or installment pension has begun, the plan simply continues the distributions in the same manner—unless, of course, they are supposed to stop at the employee's death.

Plans are allowed to reduce pension benefits to fund the QPSA. Therefore, participants (with the consent of the spouse of a married participant) have the right to waive the QPSA in order to prevent this reduction in the pension amount.

The plan must notify participants of the right to waive the QPSA. The notice must be given in the period that starts on the first day of the plan year in which the participant reaches age 32 and ends with the close of the plan year before the plan year in which the participant reaches age 35. [I.R.C. § 417(a)(3)(B)]

The notice must disclose the terms and conditions of the QPSA; what happens if it is waived; the participant's right to revoke the waiver and re-start the QPSA; and the spouse's right to invalidate the waiver by withholding consent.

The Tenth Circuit ruled in 2009 that the anti-cutback rule does not apply to a death benefit, or a plan feature that pays a lump sum at retirement that is the actuarial equivalent of a death benefit. The death benefit was not an accrued benefit, because the plan's definition of accrued benefit excluded death benefits. Nor was it a retirement-type subsidy, because that term is limited to benefits that continue after retirement. [*Kerber v. Qwest Pension Plan*, 572 F.3d 1135 (10th Cir. 2009). See *In re Lucent*, 541 F.3d 250 (3d Cir. 2008) for the proposition that the death benefit was not an accrued benefit.]

The First Circuit held in 2016 that it was not arbitrary and capricious for a retirement plan committee to deny 10 years of guaranteed annuity payments to the beneficiaries of a terminally ill employee who died after his last day of work—but eight days before the annuity starting date. The employee took the employer's advice and delayed retirement, but the First Circuit held that the plan terms implicitly conditioned receipt of approximately $500,000 in guaranteed benefits on the employee surviving until the annuity starting date. The decedent,

a 37-year UPS veteran, was diagnosed with terminal cancer in 2008 and planned
to retire at the end of 2009. However, he took the advice of the company's HR
supervisor and stayed on the payroll as long as he could by delaying his official
retirement date to use up seven weeks of accrued vacation and personal time. He
submitted an application for retirement on January 7, 2010, his last day at work,
but his annuity starting date was March 1, 2010 because of the vacation and personal time. He opted for a single-life annuity with a 10-year guarantee; the beneficiaries were his four children. The plan provided that, when a vested participant
dies prior to the annuity start date, the participant's spouse or domestic partner is
entitled to a preretirement survivor annuity. The decedent also opted for an early
retirement incentive program that paid one year of compensation in exchange for
a release of all claims that were in effect at the time of retirement. The plan committee told the four children that they were not entitled to annuity benefits but the
decedent's ex-wife could get a reduced preretirement survivor annuity ($315 a
month; the annuity payment would have been $4,117). The First Circuit held that
it was reasonable for the committee to conclude that the only benefit available for
death before the start date was the surviving spouse benefit. [*O'Shea v. UPS
Retirement Plan*, 837 F.3d 67 (1st Cir. 2016); see Wolters Kluwer Law & Business, *Guaranteed Benefits Denied to Beneficiaries of Terminally Ill Employee
Who Died Before Annuity Starting Date* (Oct. 21, 2016) (benefitslink.com)]

[A] Beneficiary Designation Case Law

Although the broad principle of ERISA preemption is well-settled, there is
still tension between federal regulation of pensions and benefits and the traditional state domination of the domestic relations field, so case continue to be
decided on issues such as beneficiary designations that have not been updated to
reflect the state of the plan participant's family at the time of his or her death.

Federal employees are covered by the Federal Employees' Group Life Insurance Act of 1954 (FEGLIA), which permits employees to name the beneficiary
of their life insurance. Death benefits accrue first to the named beneficiary, followed by others in the statutory line of precedence. A Virginia statute revokes the
beneficiary designation of a former spouse whenever there is a change in marital
status. Another Virginia statutory provision says that, if that provision is preempted by federal law, the ex-spouse will have to compensate the person who
would otherwise have received the benefits for the benefits that person lost. Hillman named his first wife Judy Maretta as beneficiary of his FEGLI policy. They
divorced and he remarried without changing the beneficiary designation. When
Hillman died, Maretta collected the proceeds, and second wife Jacqueline Hillman sued her. The Supreme Court ruled in mid-2013 that state laws are preempted to the extent of any conflict with a federal statute. The relevant federal
scheme gives highest priority to the beneficiary by the insured, which must be
respected. [*Hillman v. Maretta*, 133 S. Ct. 1943 (2013)]

Boggs and *Egelhoff* hold that the benefits of an ERISA plan pass under the plan's designated terms, and state law cannot be used to divert benefits from the designated beneficiary. *Kennedy* questioned whether "wresting" is allowed; *Hillman v. Maretta & Windsor* resolved the issue.

State laws, including trust and estate laws, can govern compensation that is accrued but unpaid at the employee's death that does not consist of ERISA benefits: for example, wages, commissions, and bonuses. But ERISA preempts state court requiring participant to make a beneficiary designation, or a beneficiary to waive or consent to waiver of benefits.

ERISA also preempts laws that revoke beneficiary designation on divorce. Waivers in domestic relations orders that are inconsistent with plan terms are invalid. Best practice is to draft beneficiary designations to explain what happens if a beneficiary dies before the plan participant, and to explain that federal law governs challenges to the effectiveness of the designation (e.g., allegations of fraud or undue influence). The DOL's position is that the plan should bring an interpleader action in QDRO cases if, after the plan makes a determination and its decision has been appealed, there is still conflict about benefit entitlement. But for other disputes, the plan must pay the benefit to the successful claimant, and then defend the denial decision just like any other benefit denial decision. [Albert Feuer, *Determining the Death Beneficiary Under an ERISA Plan and the Rights of Such a Beneficiary*, 54 Tax Management Memorandum 323 (Aug. 26, 2013) (abstract: benefitslink.com)]

IRS Employee Plans News announced in September 2013 that the IRS will no longer allow pre-approved plans to automatically revoke spousal beneficiary designation at legal separation. (Automatic revocation on divorce is still acceptable.) Legal separation only eliminates the requirement that the participant obtain spousal consent to waive spousal death benefit and substitute another beneficiary. The separated spouse will receive the spousal death benefit unless the plan participant waived the death benefit and specifically named a different beneficiary. Automatic revocation language in the plan will not, by itself, satisfy the waiver requirement. The IRS said that an individually designed plan must either eliminate such language or clarify that revocation does not affect the spouse's right to QPSA death benefit. [Rebecca Moore, *Certain Revocations of Spousal Beneficiaries Not Allowed*, plansponsor.com (Sept. 25, 2013)]

The Eighth Circuit held that a wife was not properly informed of her waiver of pension rights when she signed a prenuptial agreement. The agreement waived all rights with respect to her husband's separate property, and listed the husband's retirement plan account as an asset. When the husband died, with his parents named as beneficiaries, he had filed for divorce, but the divorce had not yet been finalized. The plan administrator asked the wife to sign a waiver so the benefits could go to the husband's parents. She refused, and the plan asked for court guidance about how to distribute the benefits. The district court awarded the benefits to the parents, but the Eighth Circuit reversed, holding that she prenuptial agreement was not sufficient to satisfy ERISA § 1055(c)(2)(A)(iii)'s requirement for a waiver—leaving the wife as the proper recipient of the benefits. The Eighth Circuit held that the prenuptial agreement did not clearly and expressly inform the wife that she would be entitled to survivor benefits that were waived by the agreement. [*MidAmerican Pension & Emp. Benefits Plan Admin. Comm. v. Cox*, 720 F.3d 715 (8th Cir. 2013)]

Asa Williams divorced in 2006. In 2007, 2008, and 2011 he phoned his pension plan to say that his son, not his ex-wife, was his beneficiary. However, he never returned a signed beneficiary designation form. When he died in 2011, his ex-wife claimed benefits under the plan. The trial court awarded the benefits to the ex-wife, because Williams did not complete the beneficiary designation. The Ninth Circuit reversed, granting effect to his verbal "undesignations." The plan documents did not forbid unmarried participants to designate beneficiaries by phone. The Ninth Circuit held that the beneficiary designation forms merely confirm the participant's intentions, and are not plan documents. In this reading, only the documents that provide information about the participant's standing with the plan (e.g., the SPD or trust agreements) operate as "governing documents" which the plan administrator must follow. [*Becker v. Williams*, 777 F.3d 1035 (9th Cir. 2015)] The case was remanded to the District Court for the Western District of Washington, which held that unmarried plan participants (i.e., those not subject to spousal consent requirements) could change beneficiary designations over the phone because the plan documents did not set out mandatory requirements for changes; the district court said "carrier pigeon or messages in a bottle" could be used to change beneficiaries. Nevertheless, the district court ruled in favor of the ex-wife and not the son, because the son failed to prove that it was his father rather than someone else who telephoned in the beneficiary change. Xerox made repeated efforts to get the employee to submit signed and dated beneficiary designation forms, but he never complied. The divorce decree, which was not a QDRO, did not alter the beneficiary designation or remove the ex-wife as beneficiary. [*Becker v. Williams*, No. 3:11-cv-05830-BHS, 2016 U.S. Dist. LEXIS 29709 (W.D. Wash. Mar. 8, 2016); see Plansponsor editors, *Lack of Documentation Trumps Verbal Designation*, plansponsor.com (Mar. 22, 2016)]

The Ninth Circuit required a pension trust to recognize a QDRO issued under Washington state law on behalf of a payee who was not married to the plan participant, but had a 30-year quasi-marital relationship with him. The Ninth Circuit gave effect to the court order giving her a 50% interest in the pension benefits, because she was his dependent and therefore an appropriate alternate payee. In this view, ERISA does not define marital property rights, but makes QDROs part of state domestic relations laws; Washington recognizes property divisions between quasi-marital partners. The pension would have been community property if the couple had been married, and a 50–50 division was consistent with state law. [*Owens v. Automotive Machinists Pension Trust*, 551 F.3d 1138 (9th Cir. 2009)]

Early in 2009, the Supreme Court held that DuPont correctly paid retirement benefits to a plan participant's ex-wife, even though she renounced her interest in his retirement benefits when they divorced. The plan participant named his daughter as the new beneficiary—but did not remove his wife's name from the beneficiary designation form. A QDRO was executed at the time of the divorce, but not submitted to the plan. The participant died in 2001, with $402,000 in his pension account. The participant's daughter sued the plan, but the plan followed the beneficiary designation. The Supreme Court ruled that the ex-wife did not attempt to direct her interest in the plan to the estate or another potential beneficiary, so her waiver was not the type of assignment or alienation barred by the Retirement Equity Act. The plan had a procedure for waiving benefits, but the ex-wife did not use it—so in the absence of a QDRO, the plan had to distribute benefits according to the beneficiary designation in its records. [*Kennedy v. DuPont*; 555 U.S. 285 (2009)]

Plan participant Dennis Hall named his son as the sole beneficiary of his insurance benefits under an ERISA plan. Subsequently, he filled out and signed—but did not submit—a form naming his wife Jane was sole beneficiary. Hall died in 2011, and his surviving spouse submitted his will as evidence that he intended her to be the beneficiary of the insurance. The Eighth Circuit held that the plan did not abuse its discretion by rejecting this evidence. The will did not expressly dispose of non-estate assets like his life insurance. The terms of the plan required signed beneficiary designation forms to be submitted to the plan within 30 days of the date of the signature, and Hall did not submit the designation form on time (or at all). Plan administrators have discretion to excuse technical errors in a beneficiary designation, but they can also insist on strict conformity to the terms of the plan. The Eighth Circuit held that the plan exercised its discretion reasonably. [*Hall v. Metropolitan Life Ins.*, 750 F.3d 995 (8th Cir. May 8, 2014)]

§ 12.07   THE REQUIRED BEGINNING DATE

[A]   Theory and Application

Congress' initial reasons for passing ERISA, and for allowing Individual Retirement Accounts (IRAs) revolved around providing current income for workers for the time period between retirement and their death. Not only was estate planning with qualified retirement benefits not considered important, it was not even considered a worthwhile objective—the benefits were supposed to be used up during the individual's lifetime. Therefore, distributions from qualified plans and IRAs were required to start no later than a Required Beginning Date (RBD). The RBD was defined as April 1 of the year after the year in which the individual reached age 70½. An excise tax penalty was imposed on the failure to make at least the Minimum Required Distribution (MRD) each year.

Over the years, theories in Congress and at the IRS have changed. Estate planning for benefits is now treated as a legitimate objective. Furthermore, although the RBD/MRD requirements remain in effect for IRAs, and for qualified plan participants who are corporate officers or directors, or who own 5% or more of the stock in the employer corporation, they have been abolished for rank-and-file employees. If plan participants choose to defer retirement and remain at work past age 70½, they will no longer suffer a tax penalty for doing so.

For plan years beginning on or after January 1, 1997, I.R.C. § 401(a)(9)(C) sets the RBD for a rank-and-file employee at the later of April 1 following the year in which the individual reached age 70½ or that person's actual retirement date. The plan must make actuarial adjustments to the pensions of persons who continue to work after age 70½.

The eventual pension must be at least the actuarial equivalent of the benefits payable as of the date the actuarial increase must begin, plus the actuarial equivalent of any additional benefits that accrue after the starting date, reduced by the actuarial equivalent of whatever retirement benefits are actually distributed after the annuity start date. Employees who stay at work after age 70½ can be given the option of suspending distributions from the plan until they actually retire.

[B] Excise Taxes

Distributions from a retirement plan that occur before the participant reaches age 59½ are considered "early" or "premature" distributions. They are subject to an excise tax of 10% (in addition to the income tax on the distribution) unless one of a number of exemptions is available:

- The distribution is made on account of the participant's death

- The distribution is made on account of the participant's total and permanent disability

- The participant has separated from service and is at least 55 years old (50 for certain public employees)

- The distribution goes to an alternate payee under a QDRO

- The distribution is a dividend pass-through from an ESOP

- The distribution is an in-plan Roth rollover, or the distribution is rolled over to an IRA or another retirement plan within 60 days of being withdrawn

- The distribution is made to a military reservist called up for active duty

- Funds are withdrawn in a series of substantially equal payments

- The distribution is made under an IRS levy on the plan

- The participant withdraws an amount equal to large, unreimbursed medical expenses; expenses are "large" if they exceed 10% of AGI for a person who has not reached age 65, or 7.5% for a person who has

- The participant was automatically enrolled in the plan, and takes distributions allowed by the plan

- The participant withdraws funds from the plan to correct an excess contribution or excess deferral; the earnings of the excess funds must also be withdrawn

[IRS, *Retirement Topics-Exceptions to Tax on Early Distributions*, <https://www.irs.gov/Retirement-Plans/Plan-Participant,-Employee/Retirement-Topics-Tax-on-Early-Distributions> (Jan. 30, 2017) (last accessed Feb. 17, 2017)]

Before 1996, plan participants could find themselves between a rock and a hard place. In addition to the penalty on premature withdrawals, penalties were imposed on excess lifetime withdrawals from a pension plan and also on excess accumulations of pension benefits within the estate, if withdrawals were not made and funds accumulated until the participant's death. The SBJPA suspended the tax on excessive distributions for the period 1996–1999, but retained the tax on excessive accumulation in the estate. The Taxpayer Relief Act of 1997 permanently repealed both excise taxes, greatly increasing the financial and estate planning flexibility available to plan participants.

[C]   Required Minimum Distributions

An IRS Proposed Regulation [66 Fed. Reg. 3928–3954 (Jan. 17, 2001)] covers required minimum distributions from qualified plans, IRAs, and I.R.C. § 403(b) and § 457 (government and nonprofit-organization) plans, substantially simplifying the 1987 Proposed Rules under Code § 401(a)(8). (The QLAC rules discussed at § 12.05[B], above, constitute a partial exception to the RMD requirements.)

The 2001 proposal enacts a single Minimum Distribution Incidental Benefit (MDIB) table, in Treas. Reg. § 1.401(a)(9)-2, to be used to calculate the RMD, with a single table usable whether the beneficiary is a natural person (spouse or non-spouse) or an entity such as a trust or charity. The MDIB table uses the same assumption in all cases: that the beneficiary is 10 years younger than the employee (no matter what their actual ages are). Distributions are made over the predicted life expectancy of a person 10 years younger than the employee. Even greater "stretch-out" is allowed if the beneficiary is the employee's spouse, and is actually more than 10 years younger than the employee, because in that case the calculation of the RMD can be based on the spouse's actual life expectancy. If the employee fails to designate a beneficiary, the RMD is calculated based on the employee's own life expectancy, reduced by one year every year.

The general rule for post-death distributions is that the benefits remaining when the employee dies must be distributed over the life expectancy of the designated beneficiary. The calculation is made in the year the employee dies. If more than one beneficiary is designated (for instance, two or more of the employee's children), then the beneficiary with the shortest life expectancy is treated as the designated beneficiary—whether the employee dies before or after the RBD. If the employee dies without designating a beneficiary, then distribution must be made to his or her intestate distributees, over a period of five years.

The 2002 final rule, Notice 2002-27, 2002-18 I.R.B. 814, makes it easier to distribute benefits to separate accounts with different beneficiaries, slightly simplifies the RMD calculation by eliminating some of the mathematical factors used in the calculation. To clarify that the distribution to beneficiaries must begin in the year of death, Notice 2002-27 requires the beneficiary of a decedent's account to be named by September 30 (rather than December 30) of the year of death. This last change was made to make it clear that distribution to the beneficiaries must start in the year of death.

To prevent abusive planning (e.g., choosing a grandchild as annuitant to stretch out payments), T.D. 9130, 69 Fed. Reg. 33288 (June 15, 2004) forbids use of a joint and survivor annuity with a 100% survivor benefit if the beneficiary is more than 10 years younger than the employee. Additional adjustments are required if the employee starts to receive benefits before age 70 (because the earlier start means that more payments will be made). For annuities with no life contingency, T.D. 9130 lets the recipient change the form that future distributions will take at any time. When a person retires, or when the plan terminates, the form of distribution can be changed prospectively. An employee who marries can change the annuity to a joint and survivor annuity. T.D. 9130 also allows certain payments to children, under Code § 401(a)(9)(F), to receive the same favorable tax treatment as payments to a spouse.

Another Pension Protection Act change allows a non-spouse beneficiary to roll over inherited benefits to an IRA; previously, only a spouse could do this. [See Notice 2007-7, 2007-5 I.R.B. 395]

In October 2008, the Department of Labor published final rules on distributions of 401(k) benefits in terminated plans, when the beneficiary is not the participant's spouse and cannot be located. The rules also cover selection of annuity providers and cross-trading of securities by ERISA plans. Under the PPA, certain retirement benefits of deceased participants can be rolled over into an inherited IRA even if the beneficiary is not the deceased participant's spouse. The new rule, which includes a Prohibited Transaction class exemption, requires rollovers into inherited IRAs when a terminated or abandoned defined contribution plan cannot find the non-spouse beneficiaries of a deceased participant. [73 Fed. Reg. 58445 (Oct. 7, 2008)]

Although reviewing retirement plans is part of the due diligence for an M&A transaction, it is often left until the end of the process, when there is little time for thorough consideration, especially of issues about terminated participants. The DOL launched an audit initiative in mid-2016, looking for plans that have any terminated vested participants who might be entitled to benefits. The tax code mandates that retired participants start to take required minimum distributions (RMDs) from the plan starting in the year after the year in which they reach age 70½ or face tax penalties. (Employees who remain at work at an advanced age do not have to begin distributions until they retire.) However, many plan participants are unaware of these requirements or forget that they have to take a distribution. It is also common for participants to move without notifying the plan, so they become lost participants. The DOL initiative looks at whether the sponsor has procedures in place to find and pay vested participants. [Earle W. Allen, *Terminated Participants: Out of Sight, Out of Mind—That Is the Problem*, cammackretirement.com (July 25, 2016) (benefitslink.com)]

RMD failures are reported to the IRS on Form 14568-H, Appendix C, Part II, Schedule 8, as an attachment to Form 14568. But Schedule 8 can only be used for affected participants. If beneficiaries of the plan (whether or not they are the participant's spouse) are also affected by the failure, reporting is required on Form 14568 Appendix C, Part I. Plan sponsors can use the latest version of the IRS's Employee Plans Compliance Resolution System (EPCRS; see § 15.19[B]) to voluntarily correct a failure to make RMDs to participants and beneficiaries, as required by § 401(a)(9). In certain situations, the Self-Correction Program (SCP) can be used to correct RMD failure even when plan is under examination by the IRS, but the excise tax imposed on beneficiaries by § 4974 cannot be waived under SCP. A § 4974 waiver can be requested under the Voluntary Correction Program (VCP). If the RMD failure subject to this excise tax is the only failure in the VCP submission, a discount on the compliance fee may be available. If the plan sponsor does not make the necessary RMD, and the plan sponsor does not correct the failure, the plan could be disqualified, affecting all the participants, and the participant who was supposed to but did not receive the RMD might be liable for an excise tax of 50% of the RMD that was not received. [IRS.gov, *Correcting Required Minimum Distribution Failures* (Sept. 27, 2016) (benefitslink .com)]

§ 12.08 DIVORCE-RELATED ORDERS

[A] QDROs and QMCSOs

For many couples, one spouse's interest in a retirement plan is a major marital financial asset. In fact, it may be the only significant marital financial asset. Given our society's high divorce rate, plan administrators are often confronted with court orders incident to an employee's separation or divorce—or are faced with conflicting claims after the death of an employee who divorced, remarried, and eventually died without having changed the beneficiary designation from the first to the second spouse.

Although the general rule is that plan benefits cannot be anticipated or alienated, there is an important exception for family law orders that fit the definitions of Qualified Domestic Relations Orders (QDROs) or Qualified Medical Child Support Orders (QMCSOs).

Technically speaking, welfare benefit plans are not required to have QDRO procedures, because the QDRO requirements appear in ERISA Title I, Part 2, which does not apply to welfare benefit plans. However, five of the Circuits (the Second, Fourth, Sixth, Seventh, and Tenth) have concluded (in cases about life insurance) that QDRO procedures are required because ERISA doesn't specially say that welfare benefit plans do not have to have QDRO procedures. (The issue for health plans is covered by the QMCSO procedure.)

The Second, Third, Fourth, Seventh, and Tenth Circuits have required top hat plans to enforce QDROs, and the District Court for the District of New Hampshire joined them in late 2009. [*Metropolitan Life v. Drainville*, 2009 U.S. Dist. LEXIS 63613 (D.R.I. July 23, 2009), *MetLife v. Hanson*, 2009 U.S. Dist. LEXIS 92044 (D.N.H. Oct. 1, 2009)] Once the administrator determines that a court order has the status of a QDRO, payments can legitimately be made to the alternate payee: i.e., the separated or divorced ex-spouse of an employee.

A QDRO is a court order based on a state domestic relations law (including community property law) dealing with child support, alimony, or marital property rights. No court is allowed to use a QDRO to order a plan to make payments in any type or form not allowed by the plan documents. A QDRO cannot force a plan to pay benefits that have already been assigned to someone else under an earlier QDRO, or to increase the actuarial value of benefits to be paid. The Department of Labor's introduction to the subject of plan administration of QDROs can be found at <http://www.dol.gov/ebsa/faqs/faq_qdro.html> (undated, last retrieved Mar. 23, 2015).

To be entitled to recognition by the plan, a QDRO must contain at least this much information:

- The recipient's right to plan benefits;
- The names and addresses of the parties;
- The amount or percentage of the plan benefit to be paid to the alternate payee named in the order;
- The time period or number of payments covered by the order;
- The plan(s) it applies to (the same employee might be covered by more than one plan).

Generally, the alternate payee does not receive distributions under the QDRO before the date the employee would be entitled to them. However, distributions can be made from any plan on the earliest date the participant could get the distribution after separation from service, or when the participant reaches age 50—whichever is later. If the plan is drafted to allow it, QDROs can require immediate distribution, or at a time that is not related to the age of the employee spouse.

For QDROs issued when the employee spouse is still working and has not retired, the payments are calculated based on the present value of the normal retirement benefits already accrued as of that time. Early retirement subsidies are not taken into account. The QDRO can provide for recalculation at the time of retirement, in case an early retirement subsidy is actually paid.

The PPA cleared up the question of whether a later, or even posthumous, court order can be a QDRO by holding that an otherwise qualifying court order must be accepted as a QDRO even if it modifies, or is later in time than, another court order: PPA § 1101. The DOL published an Interim Final Rule under PPA § 1001, which says that an order can be a QDRO even if it is later than another order or QDRO, or if it revises the other order. This is true even if the second order involves the same employee but a different alternate payee.

Therefore, a posthumous order, or an order issued after the participant's annuity start date, can be a QDRO. But even after the PPA, a QDRO can only divide benefits as provided by the plan, not require additional forms of benefits. As long as a DRO does not attempt to assign benefits that have already been assigned to a different alternate payee under a different QDRO, an order can be QDRO even if it is issued after, or revises, another DRO. An order can be a QDRO even if it is issued after the participant dies, or after the participant's annuity starting date. However, an order cannot be a QDRO if it orders a plan to provide a type or form of benefit that is not available under the plan. [RIN 1210-AB15, *Final Rule Relating to Time and Order of Issuance of Domestic Relations Orders*, 75 Fed. Reg. 32846 (June 10, 2010)]

The Second Circuit ruled in mid-2015 that posthumous nunc pro tunc court orders filed in Connecticut by the ex-spouse of a retirement plan participant were valid QDROs that could direct the distribution of the assets from three out of the decedent's four plans. The Second Circuit held that for three of the plans, the orders were valid QDROs. However, the orders did not clearly specify the fourth plan, so the orders did not determine distribution of funds from that plan. [*Yale New Haven Hosp. v. Nicholls*, 788 F.3d 79 (2d Cir. 2015)]

[B] QDRO Methodology

Under the "separate interest" method of distribution under a defined benefit plan, the alternate payee gets future payments based on his or her life expectancy, not that of the plan participant. [See, e.g., *In re Marriage of Shelstead*, 66 Cal. App. 4th 893 (1998)] The nonemployee wife was awarded a 50% community property interest in the employee husband's pension plan. The order said that, if the wife died before the husband, she would be able to designate a successor in interest to receive her community property share. But the California Court of

Appeals decided that, although this was a divorce-related order, it was not a QDRO because it did not settle the rights of an alternate payee, and she could leave her share to anyone, not just another acceptable alternate payee.

Under the "shared payment" method, the alternate payee gets a portion of each pension payment made to the plan participant, so both the participant and the alternate payee use the same timing schedule and form of annuity. The alternate payee gets to take advantage of any early retirement incentives elected by the participant. The enhanced benefit under an early retirement plan is actuarially reduced if the alternate payee is younger than the participant (this is often the case, especially if the participant is male and his ex-wife is younger than he is), but is not increased if the alternate payee is older than the participant.

[C] The Administrator's Response

When a plan administrator receives a court order, the first step is to determine whether the order is entitled to QDRO status. However, once ERISA compliance is determined, the administrator must comply with the QDRO, without inquiring as to its acceptability under state law.

If the administrator believes that a document described as a QDRO is a sham, or at least questionable, PWBA Advisory Opinion #99-13A [(Sept. 29, 1999), <http://www.dol.gov/ebsa/regs/AOs/ao1999-13a.html> (last accessed Feb. 17, 2017)] provides guidance.

Administrators are "not free to ignore" information casting doubt on the validity of an order. If the administrator finds that evidence credible, the administrator must make a case-by-case determination of the validity of each order, "without inappropriately spending plan assets or inappropriately involving the plan in the state domestic relations proceeding."

Appropriate action could include informing the court of the potential invalidity of the order; intervening in a domestic relations proceeding; or even bringing suit. However, an administrator who cannot get a response within a reasonable time from the agency that issued the order "may not independently determine that the order is not valid under state law." ERISA Opinion Letter 94-32A says that it is improper to charge either the participant or the alternate payee a fee for processing a QDRO.

This determination must be made within a reasonable time. The employee and the proposed alternate payee must be notified promptly that the order was received. The administrator must explain to them how the plan will determine the validity of the alleged QDRO. The funds in question must be segregated, and separately accounted for, until the determination has been made. There is an 18-month limit on keeping the funds in the segregated account. [See EBSA Advisory Opinion 2000-09A (July 12, 2000), <http://www.dol.gov/ebsa/regs/AOs/ao2000-09a.html> (last accessed Feb. 17, 2017), for a discussion of what to do when an alternate payee is named under a plan that limits beneficiary designations to spouses, minor children, and parents—but not former spouses.]

[D] QDRO Case Law: *Egelhoff* and After

The Supreme Court decided, in *Egelhoff v. Egelhoff* [532 U.S. 141 (2001)] that ERISA preempts a Washington State law that made all beneficiary designations (in life insurance as well as qualified plans) invalid when the employee or insured person divorced. The Supreme Court decided that the state law "relates to" ERISA plans, and therefore is preempted, because qualified plans can be regulated only by federal, and not state, law.

The message of the Supreme Court's 1997 ruling in *Boggs v. Boggs*, 520 U.S. 833 (1997) is that, although QDROs are saved from ERISA preemption, other domestic relations orders issued by state courts are preempted.

The Second Circuit required a defined contribution plan to distribute assets to a former participant that were wrongly transferred to his wife after they were divorced—even though the plan did not recover the funds from the wife. The plan erroneously transferred half of the plaintiff's pension account to his ex-wife, giving her about $764,000 more than the divorce settlement entitled her to receive. The plaintiff did not discover this for several years. The plan administrator told the ex-wife to return the excess funds; she refused, and the plan sued her. The Second Circuit held that defined contribution plans allocate the risk of investment instability or beneficiary longevity to the employee. In this analysis, plan assets only become benefits when they are distributed at retirement—before that point, no one has a claim to any particular assets in the plan trust. [*Milgram v. Orthopedic Assocs. DC Pension Plan*, 666 F.3d 68 (2d Cir. 2011)]

The consequences of errors can be severe. The tax court upheld disqualification of an Employee Stock Ownership Plan (ESOP). The sole participants in the plan were a chiropractor and his ex-wife. The divorce decree awarded each of them half of the plan sponsor's outstanding stock, without acknowledging that almost all of the stock belonged to the ESOP. Later, the ex-wife transferred her ESOP shares to her ex-husband's ESOP account. The tax court said that the transfer disqualified the plan because it was not made under a QDRO. Therefore, it violated the anti-alienation provision. The transfer also violated the ESOP's own provisions about distribution rights. Disqualification not only creates ERISA fiduciary liability, for the open years (usually three years), but render the income of the plan trust taxable. Participants are taxable on their vested undistributed benefits, rollovers become taxable, and the plan sponsor's deductions for contributions to the plan are disallowed or delayed. The Voluntary Correction Program (VCP) and Employee Plans Compliance Resolution System (EPCRS) programs may be available to reduce exposure for plan failures (see §§ 10.04[A], 15.19[B]), but there is no standard IRS correction procedure when a plan participant transfers a benefit without complying with the QDRO rules. [*Family Chiropractic*

Sports Injury & Rehab Clinic, Inc. v. Comm'r, T.C. Memo 2016-10, 111 T.C.M. (CCH) 1046 (Tax Ct. Jan. 19, 2016); see Raymond P. Turner, *Death and Taxes for Qualified Plans*, Jackson Lewis (Mar. 14, 2016) (benefitslink.com)]

[E] PBGC QDROs

An extensive document published at PBGC.gov explains how the Pension Benefit Guarantee Corporation (PBGC) handles QDROs in the plans under its trusteeship. The document covers subjects such as how to identify alternate payees, how and when to make payments to the alternate payees, and the rights of alternate payees when the employee spouse dies. The total values of the participant's portion and the alternate payee's portion cannot exceed what the PBGC would have paid to the participant if there had been no QDRO. The document includes two basic model QDROs and special orders for child support and surviving spouse benefits.

Courts often consider the percentage of the benefit earned before, during and after the marriage when they divide pension benefits. The PBGC can use this "marital portion" or "marital fraction" analysis for either a shared payment or a separate interest QDRO.

An original signed order, or a certificated or authenticated copy of the order, should be sent to the PBGC QDRO Coordinator, P.O. Box 151750, Alexandria, VA 22315-1750. (Electronic transmission is not acceptable because of the need for a physical signature.) If the PBGC states that an order is not a valid QDRO, the parties will be given 45 days to appeal, and payments to alternate payees will be suspended, and reinstated if the PBGC later determines that the order was a valid QDRO. The PBGC also informally reviews draft orders to see if they would qualify if submitted in that form. Parties must notify the PBGC Customer Contact Center, (800) 400-7242, if any event occurs that affects a benefit: for example, the death of a participant or alternate payee, or the occurrence of an event named in the order, such as a child's majority or the alternate payee's remarriage.

A valid order should:

- Clearly specify the pension plan to which it applies;

- Clearly identify (including Social Security numbers and mailing addresses) the persons to whom it applies; all alternate and contingent payees;

- Specify the start date and amount to be paid to each alternate payee and the duration of payment, and what amount or percentage of the participant's monthly benefit goes to each alternate payee;

- Mandate payment from the PBGC to the alternate payee, rather than the participant receiving payment and then transmitting it to the alternate payee;

- Explain whether shared payments to the alternate payee survive the participant's death;

- Grant the domestic relations court continuing jurisdiction over the order. [*The Division of Pensions Through Qualified Domestic Relations Orders*, <http://www.dol.gov/ebsa/publications/qdros.html> (last accessed Mar. 20, 2016), or by phone at the EBSA hotline, 1-866-444-EBSA (3272).]

§ 12.09   REDUCTION OF BENEFIT FORMS

Qualified plans must always offer payments in the form of QJSAs, QOSAs, and QPSAs. What if a plan originally adopts additional, optional forms of benefit payments, then later finds that some of them are unpopular or hard to administer? For years beginning after December 31, 2001, as a result of EGTRRA, I.R.C. § 411(d)(6) and ERISA § 204(g) have been amended to make it easier for defined contribution plans to cut back on the number of benefit options that they offer, especially in connection with plan mergers and other transitions.

A defined contribution plan will not be penalized for reducing participants' accrued benefits if the plan adopts amendments that reduce the number of benefit options—provided that the participant is always entitled to get a single-sum distribution that is based on at least as high a proportion of his or her account as the form of benefit that is being eliminated under the plan amendment. EGTRRA obligates the IRS to issue new regulations no later than December 31, 2003, to this effect, applying to plan years beginning after December 31, 2003 (or earlier, if the IRS so specifies).

Under regulations published at 69 Fed. Reg. 13769 (Mar. 24, 2004), redundant optional forms of benefit can be eliminated, as long as another form in the same "family" remains available (the proposal defines six families of optional benefit forms), and as long as the "core" options remain available. A plan amendment changing the availability of benefit forms cannot be effective for any distribution with an annuity start date within 90 days after adoption of the amendment.

The core options that must be preserved are the straight life annuity, the 75% joint and survivor annuity, life and 10-year certain annuity, and the most valuable option the plan provides for participants with a short life expectancy. As a general rule, lump sum payouts cannot be eliminated by making use of this proposal, and plan amendments eliminating non-core options do not apply to start dates within four years after adoption of the amendment. The proposal imposes additional requirements to protect participants when early retirement benefits and subsidies are altered.

T.D. 9472, 2009-51 I.R.B. 850, is a final rule governing notice requirements under 204(h) for plan amendments that reduce accrued benefits. Code § 4980F(e)(3) requires notice to be provided within a reasonable time before a plan amendment reducing or eliminating an early retirement benefit or subsidy takes effect. In general, this means 45 days before the effective date (15 days for small or multi-employer plans). Unpredictable contingent event benefits are limited if a plan's AFTAP is, or would be, under 60%, and amendments increasing the plan's liabilities because of a benefits increase are limited if the AFTAP would be under 80%. Certain payments are prohibited when AFTAP is in the 60%–80% range; the sponsor is in Chapter 11; and the plan's actuary cannot certify that AFTAP is at least 100%. Benefit accruals cease when AFTAP falls below 60%. [*IRS Issues Final Rule on Certain Notice Requirements*, plansponsor.com (Nov. 23, 2009). See also proposed regulations, 77 Fed. Reg. 37349 (June 21, 2012) for elimination of some optional benefits from single-employer defined benefit plans sponsored by employers that are bankruptcy debtors.]

Notice 2012-46, 2012-30 I.R.B. 86, effective November 1, 2012, gives the ERISA § 101(j) notice requirements for single-employer plans subject to benefit limitations under § 436. The notice must be understandable by the average participant, containing the plan name, EIN, plan number, and a general description of the payment limitation. The prohibited benefits must be described in detail. The notice must explain when the limitation will cease to apply (e.g., when the AFTAP rises to at least 80%). If the limit is no longer in effect and participants can access distributions that were formerly prohibited, the plan administrator must send a written § 101(j) notice to participants no later than 30 days after the limitations no longer apply. [McGuireWoods LLP, *IRS Provides Guidance on Notices for Funding-Related Pension Plan Benefit Limitations* (Aug. 28, 2012) (benefitslink.com)]

[A] Suspension of Benefits Under MPRA 2014

The focus of this book is on single-employer plans rather than multi-employer plans. However, the Multi-Employer Plan Relief Act of 2014 (MPRA 2014), part of the Consolidated and Further Continuing Appropriations Act (nicknamed the "Cromnibus" Act) a spending bill that funds the federal government through September 2015, makes very significant changes to the regulation of multi-employer plans, including an unprecedented mechanism for suspending benefits from certain plans that are in critical and declining status.

The suspension will not violate the anti-cutback rule. A plan is in critical and declining status if its funded percentage is under 65% and it is projected to become insolvent within 15 plan years, or within 20 plan years if there are more than two inactive to every active participant or the funded percentage is below 80%. If the plan has 10,000 or more participants, to suspend benefits, the plan must select a participant in pay status as an advocate for retired and deferred vested participants. The plan's actuary must certify that the plan is projected to avoid insolvency until the suspension of benefits expires. The plan's trustees must determine that, without the suspension, the plan would become insolvent.

However, no benefit can be reduced below the level of 110% of the PBGC-guaranteed monthly benefit as of the date of suspension. Suspensions are limited for participants who are between ages 75 and 80 at the effective date of the suspension and forbidden for participants who have reached age 80. Disability benefits cannot be suspended. The effects of the suspension must be distributed equitably based on life expectancy, time in pay status, amount and type of benefit, the extent to which the benefit is subsidized, the number of years to retirement for active employees, whether the actives will withdraw support for the plan (leading to increased employer withdrawals), and the extent to which benefits derive from service with an employer that did not pay withdrawal liability.

The trustees are obligated to give notice of the proposed suspension to the Department of the Treasury, the participants, employers, and unions. Suspension requires a Treasury determination that the suspension satisfies the requirements. The suspension must also be submitted to the participants for a vote. A plan is considered "systemically important" if the PBGC would have to spend more than $1 billion to take it over; if the vote on a systemically important plan is negative, suspension can only occur if the Secretary of the Treasury orders the suspension (in originally proposed or modified form). For plans that are not deemed systemically important, the suspension takes effect unless a majority of all participants vote to reject it. [*"Cromnibus Act" Changes for Multiemployer and Single-Employer Defined Benefit Pension Plans* (Dec. 26, 2014) (benefitslink.com)]

The IRS and PBGC issued Rev. Proc. 2015-34, comprising proposed, interim, and temporary regulations about MPRA benefits suspensions and partitions. Rev. Proc. 2015-34 explains how to apply for a suspension, and includes a model notice to participants. Plans can request approval of suspension immediately, but applications probably will not be approved until final regulations are issued, which might not happen until 2016. The PBGC expects that, in the next three years, fewer than 20 plans will qualify for partition, and less than $60 million in PBGC assistance will be required. The IRS provided additional procedural guidance in Rev. Proc. 2017-43, 2017-31 I.R.B. 153 about how to apply on or after September 1, 2017, for permission to suspend benefits. The IRS provided additional procedural guidance in Rev. Proc. 2017-43, 2017-31 I.R.B. 153 about how to apply on or after September 1, 2017, for permission to suspend benefits.

Participants, beneficiaries of deceased participants, and alternate payees have to be notified of suspension. The sponsor must make reasonable efforts to communicate the information; mailing to the last known address is not sufficient. If the request for suspension is approved, the sponsor must make an annual re-determination that all reasonable measures have been taken to avoid insolvency, and suspension remains necessary to avoid insolvency. If the re-determination is not done, the suspension expires at the end of the year.

Systemically important plans may have to submit individual participant data to the Department of Treasury. If the plan applies for partition as well as suspension, the suspension cannot take effect until the effective date of the partition.

Rev. Proc. 2015-34 includes a model notice to disclose estimates of individual effects of the proposed reduction, a submission checklist, and a sample power of attorney. Under ERISA § 4233, the PBGC will only authorize partition if the PBGC's costs will be reduced, and the plan can stay solvent. The PBGC must certify to Congress that the funds to pay guaranteed benefits from the partitioned part of the plan come only from the PBGC's multi-employer guarantee fund. A plan applying for partition must submit complete data about the plan, its finances, and projected financial condition; identify which participants will be removed from the plan; how they were chosen; and what it will cost the PBGC to provide their guaranteed benefits [Rev. Proc. 2015-34, 2015-27 I.R.B. 4]

Final MPRA regulations were published by the IRS in mid-2016, discussing suspension of benefits after the employer's withdrawal from the plan, payment of the full withdrawal liability, and assumption of responsibility for providing benefits equal to the benefits that were reduced due to the plan's financial status. [81 Fed. Reg. 27011 (May 5, 2016); see Steptoe & Johnson LLP, *IRS and Treasury Issue Regulations Regarding Suspension of Pension Benefits* (May 3, 2016), available at Lexology.com]

About 10 million people participate in multi-employer plans, generally in heavily unionized sectors of the economy such as trucking, construction, and retailing. Some of them have earned pensions much higher than the PBGC maximum guarantee.

The Central States Pension Fund, one of the largest Teamsters pension funds (a multi-employer plan large enough to be "systemically important") filed for reorganization, stating that it was battered by trucking deregulation, declining union membership, stock market declines, and population aging. Insolvency was predicted in 10 to 15 years. [Mary Williams Walsh, *Teamsters' Pension Fund Warns 400,000 of Cuts*, NYTimes.com (Oct. 7, 2015)]

Members of Cleveland Iron Worker Local 17 Pension Fund voted 2-1 to approve pension cuts under the MPRA, becoming the first union to approve cuts. The cuts took effect February 1, 2017. [Rebecca Moore, *First Multiemployer Plan to Make Benefit Cuts Under MPRA*, plansponsor.com (Jan. 27, 2017); Frank T. Mamat, *Union Retirees Cut Their Own Pension to Forestall Doomsday Scenario*, Foster Swift Collins & Smith PC (Feb. 6, 2017), available at Lexology .com]

The Treasury rejected more than a dozen applications before approving the United Furniture Workers Pension Fund's application in July 2017. The application calls for partitioning the plan, with the PBGC granting assistance to one of them. [<https://www.treasury.gov/services/Responses2/UFW%20 Notification%20Letter.pdf > (July 20, 2017); see David B. Brandolph, *Treasury Department Gives Thumbs Up to Second Pension Rescue*, bna.com (July 21, 2017) (benefitslink.com)]

The PBGC assumed benefit payments for the Road Carriers Local 707 Pension Fund after it had been unable to pay full benefits for a year. The PBGC provides funding to failed multi-employer plans, but does not directly administer them the way it administers single-employer plans. As of February 1, 2017, benefits were cut back to the PBGC guaranteed limit. Only 7% of retirees and beneficiaries of this plan will receive their full benefit; 42% will experience cuts of more than half the promised benefits. PBGC director Tom Reeder warned that the PBGC's multi-employer plan program is in severe financial trouble and is likely to run out of money by 2025. [PBGC.gov Press Release No. 17-02, *PBGC Provides Financial Assistance to Road Carriers Local 707 Pension Fund—Participants' Benefits Payments Cut to PBGC Guaranteed Levels* (Mar. 1, 2017) (benefitslink.com); Rebecca Moore, *Benefit Cuts Could Hit More Than One Million Multiemployer Plan Members,* plansponsor.com (Mar. 2, 2017)]

§ 12.10 ROLLOVERS

Because of termination of employment, or termination of a plan itself, a person of working age may become entitled to a plan distribution. If he or she does not need the funds immediately, and would encounter an unwelcome income tax liability, one solution is to "roll over" the funds by placing them into another qualified plan or an IRA within 60 days. Technically, a direct rollover moves funds from one qualified plan to another qualified plan or to an IRA; the payment goes to the trustee of the plan or IRA. A direct payment transfers IRA funds from one IRA to the trustee of a second IRA. A direct transfer sends funds from a qualified plan to the trustee or custodian of an IRA inherited after the death of the original owner. Failure to satisfy the rules for these varying devices can subject the recipient of the funds to negative tax consequences. [Vivian S. McCardell, *Rollover Roulette: Rollover, Direct Rollover, Direct Payment, Direct Transfer, or Transfer (Part 1: The Terms),* Morgan Lewis & Bockius LLP (Apr. 4, 2017), available at Lexology.com]

The funds that are rolled over are not available to be spent by the plan participant, and therefore the participant is not taxed.

■ **TIP:** Although employees have a right to roll over these funds, the qualified plan that is the intended recipient does not have an obligation to accept rollovers. So it makes sense for the distributing plan to require employees to submit a statement that the potential recipient is not only qualified to take rollover contributions, but is willing to do so. The recipient plan is allowed to impose conditions, such as the form in which it will accept rollovers and the minimum amount it will accept as a rollover. The recipient plan is also entitled to set its own distribution rules and does not have to follow the rules of the original plan.

A direct rollover is considered a distribution, not a transfer of assets. [Treas. Reg. § 1.401(a)(31)-1] Therefore, the participant and spouse may have to sign a waiver because plan benefits are not being paid in QJSA form.

Rollovers can be carried out either by the plan administrator of the first plan sending a check or wire transfer to the trustee or custodian of the transferee plan, or by giving the participant a check payable to the IRA, plan trustee, or custodian. The IRS has ruled that the 60-day rollover requirement does not apply to a check for a plan distribution that was made payable to the sponsor of a second plan. The check was mailed to the recipient of the distribution, but made payable to her new employer, but she could not have cashed the check; therefore, it was a direct rollover as defined by § 401(a)(31). Her Form 1099-R showed Code G in Box 7, showing a direct rollover with no withholding. The IRS said that the distribution was a direct rollover, so the 60-day rule did not apply, and she could deposit the check in the new employer's plan even after 60 days. [Plansponsor Staff, *60-day Rollover Requirement Doesn't Apply to Check Made to New Plan*, plansponsor.com (Apr. 1, 2010)]

A distribution to a spouse, or a QDRO distribution to an ex-spouse, can also be rolled over, but only to an IRA, not to a qualified plan.

PPA § 829(a) enacts Code § 402(c)(11) that permits non-spouse beneficiaries to roll over a distribution they receive from a qualified plan to an IRA.

The Small Business Jobs and Credit Act of 2010, Pub L. No. 111-240, permits employers to amend a 401(k) plan to allow an eligible rollover distribution (ERD) to be transferred to a designated Roth account within the plan. (The transfer is taxable, not tax-free.) Transfers can be made after September 27, 2010, from a non-designated Roth account in the same plan, and if other requirements are met. However, in-plan conversions can only be made from amounts that could be distributed under the terms of the plan. Participants who rolled over ERD to a designated Roth account could include half of the taxable amount in their 2011 gross income and half for 2012, or could include it all in their 2010 gross income, depending on which provided better tax results. The American Taxpayer Relief Act of 2012 authorizes in-plant Roth conversions of defined contribution accounts that are not otherwise distributable, with no income limitation. Under prior law, only amounts that were distributable (e.g., to a participant who had reached age 59½) could be converted to Roth form. Although the provision is effective January 1, 2013, prior account balances can be converted. [Rebecca Moore, *Fiscal Cliff Deal Extends Roth Conversions*, plansponsor.com (Jan. 3, 2013)]

The 402(f) notice must be given when a participant gets a distribution that is eligible to be rolled over to an IRA or another qualified plan. A participant can waive the 30-day minimum notice, but not the 180-day maximum notice requirement. The notice must explain the rollover rules, tax consequences of taking a lump sum, the options for direct rollover (e.g., automatic rollover), the mandatory 20% withholding requirement, and tax consequences of options. Notice 2009-68, 2009-39 I.R.B. 423 includes two updated safe harbor notices replacing the ones issued in 2003—one for designated Roth accounts, one for other accounts. (A participant who has both kinds of accounts must receive both notices.)

Before the September 2014 proposals on Roth 401(k) rollovers, when funds were deposited directly into a new plan or IRA (rather than via trustee to trustee transfers), a rollover that combined both pre-tax 401(k) contributions and Roth contributions had to allocate to each destination account a pro rata share of both types of funds. In practical terms, the individual either had to wait until he or she got a job with a plan that allowed Roth contributions; leave the funds in the former employer's plan; or perform a direct rollover. Then, Notice 2014-54, 2015-41 I.R.B. 670, and accompanying proposed regulations liberalized the rollover rules; the proposed regulations were finalized in substantially the same form, for distributions on or after January 1, 2016. [Winstead.com, *Simplified 401(k) Roth Rollover Rules Finalized* (May 19, 2016) (benefitslink.com)]

The PBGC published a final rule for transferring assets from a defined contribution plan to a defined benefit plan. The PBGC's intention is to encourage lifetime income by making it easier to move funds to a defined benefit plan without worrying that rollovers would be lost if the PBGC takes over the plan and the maximum guarantee would otherwise apply. The five-year phase-in rule says that if defined benefits increased in the five years before termination, the increased benefits must be phased in over five years after the termination. But this rule does not apply to rollovers that derive from employee contributions. The rollover contributions are treated as accrued benefits coming from mandatory employee contributions, which are a higher-priority claim. However, under the final rule, participants generally cannot get a lump sum representing return of mandatory employee contributions attributable to rollover amounts. [79 Fed. Reg. 70090 (Nov. 25, 2014)]

§ 12.11 WITHHOLDING

A designated distribution is any amount of $200 or more that the participant could roll over, but chooses not to. Under I.R.C. §§ 401(a)(3) and 3405(c), plan administrators have to withhold a mandatory 20% of any designated distribution.

All or part of an employee's balance in a qualified plan is eligible for rollover, except:

- A series of substantially equal periodic payments, made at the rate of at least one payment a year, over the life of the employee or the joint lives of the employee and designated beneficiary;

- Payments made for a term of at least 10 years [See I.R.C. § 402(c)(4)];

- The RMDs under I.R.C. § 401(a)(8) for officers, directors, and 5% stockholders.

In the case of a partial rollover, withholding applies only to the part that the employee withdraws from the plan, not the part that is rolled over.

For amounts that are neither annuities nor eligible rollover distributions, optional withholding can be done at a rate of 10%. The employee can direct the plan not to withhold. During the six months immediately preceding the first payment, and at least once a year once benefits are in pay status, the plan must notify participants of their right to make, renew, or revoke a withholding election. The employer can either include the withheld amounts in each quarterly Form 941 filing, or use Form 941E to report withholding.

Starting January 1, 2010, eligible rollover distributions paid directly to a non-spouse beneficiary are subject to 20% mandatory withholding, not 10% voluntary withholding for non-periodic payments, unless the funds are directly rolled over to an IRA.

The plan administrator is responsible for withholding unless the administrator directs that the insurer or other payer of benefits perform this task. [Treas. Reg. § 31.3405(c)-1]

Whenever designated distributions (i.e., those eligible for withholding) are made, the employer and plan administrator become responsible for making returns and reports to the IRS, participants, and beneficiaries.

A penalty of $50 per day is imposed by I.R.C. § 6704(b), up to a maximum of $50,000, for failure to maintain the required records, although the penalty can be waived if the plan has a good excuse for noncompliance. [See I.R.C. § 6047(b) for the required records reports by employers or plan administrators.]

§ 12.12   PLAN LOANS AS DEEMED DISTRIBUTIONS

The federal Website firstgov.gov includes FAQs about plan loans:

- Loans are permitted from qualified plans, but not from IRAs or related plans (SEP, SARSEP, or SIMPLE).

- In fact, taking a loan disqualifies the account from being an IRA, and its entire value must be included in the owner's income for the year of the loan.

- Qualified plans are allowed to, but not required, to offer loans. A plan can limit the size of loans.

- The maximum allowable loan is the smaller of A or B, where A is $50,000 and B is $10,000 or half of the participant's vested valance, whichever is greater.

- A participant can have more than one loan outstanding at a time, as long as the aggregate balance does not exceed the permitted maximum.

- Plans that allow loans must specify application procedures and repayment terms for loans.

- Other than loans for purchase of a principal residence, repayment must be completed within five years, via a series of substantially equal payments made at least quarterly and including both principal and interest.

- Loan repayments are not plan contributions: see Reg. § 1.72(p)-1.

- Loan repayment can be suspended for employees who are on active military duty, or during a leave of absence lasting up to one year. However, an employee returning from leave must make up the missed payments either by making a lump sum repayment or increasing the periodic payments so that the loan does not extend past the original five-year term.

- Plan loans are not dependent on hardship, the employee's reasons for wanting the money, or whether the employee could borrow from other sources.

- It is permissible to make loans to owner-employees as long as all participants have equal access to loans.

- A loan that is not repaid according to the plan's terms is taxed as a plan distribution (and cannot be rolled over to an eligible retirement plan), but there is no plan distribution if the repayment terms are followed.

- After a deemed distribution, a default can be remedied by making the missed payment, but the participant's tax basis in the plan is increased by late repayments.

Code § 72(p) sets out the rules under which plan loans that fail to conform to the requirements will be treated as taxable distributions from the plan, rather than as tax-neutral loans. Regulations on this issue were proposed in 2000 and finalized at the end of 2002. [67 Fed. Reg. 71821 (Dec. 3, 2002)] The Final Regulations apply to loans, assignments, and pledges made on or after January 1, 2004 (although plans can adopt the rules earlier). An exemption is available for loans made under an insurance contract that was in effect on December 31, 2003, that is obligated to offer loans to unsecured contract holders.

A loan will not be treated as a deemed distribution if the plan suspends loan repayment when the borrower is on leave of absence for active military service, even if the leave lasts more than a year, as long as repayments resume when the borrower returns from military service, and repayment is complete by the normal term plus the term of military service. Before these regulations were finalized, the Proposed Regulation imposed a limit of only two loans per plan participant; additional loans would be treated as deemed distributions. The Final Regulations remove the two-loan limit, and allow credit card loans to be secured by amounts in a participant's account. Also see the Servicemembers Civil Relief Act, Pub. L.

No. 108-189, which limits the interest on plan loans incurred by employees who later go on active military service.

Also note that, in early 2009, the Federal Reserve Board amended Regulation Z, so that, as of July 1, 2010, most plan loans are exempt under the Truth in Lending Act. The FRB's rationale is that plan loans are different from ordinary loans because there is no third-party creditor, and the principal and interest are reinvested in the participant's account, so participants are less vulnerable than ordinary borrowers. [Rebecca Moore, *Plan Loans Exempt from Truth-in-Lending Disclosure Requirements*, plansponsor.com (Mar. 13, 2009)]

CHAPTER 13

PROCESSING AND REVIEWING CLAIMS AND APPEALS

§ 13.01 INTRODUCTION

All pension and welfare benefit plans that are subject to the Employment Retirement Income Security Act (ERISA) Title I are required to maintain a "reasonable claims procedure." An appropriate claims procedure is one that is described in the Summary Plan Description (SPD): does not place undue restrictions or inhibitions on the processing of claims, and satisfies the relevant regulations about filing claims, reviewing submitted claims, and informing participants when a claim is denied. [DOL Reg. § 2560.503]

At the very least, the procedure must give claimants (or their authorized representatives) the right to apply to the plan for review, see the pertinent documents, and submit written comments and issues for resolution.

The plan must give a specific reason if it denies a claim. Claimants must be referred to the relevant plan provision. They must be given information about how to appeal the denial. One of the reasons why the Patient Protection and Affordable Care Act (PPACA) is so controversial is the extent to which it imposes additional requirements not only for communicating with plan participants about their claims, but also about the timing of claims processing and the addition of a new external claims review step.

Although most of the cases in this chapter are health plan cases, claims issues also arise in the context of retirement plans. The Ninth Circuit held in 2016 that the employer, not the employees, is in the best position to determine if the plaintiff's employer participated in the pension plan. If a claimant makes a prima facie case that he or she is entitled to benefits, but does not have information about corporate structures or hours worked that is needed to prove the claim, the Ninth Circuit said that if the defendant controls the information, the defendant has the burden of producing it. (When the plaintiff, Barton, reached age 65, he contacted the plan's recordkeeper to ask about benefits. The plan administrator said that there was no information about his employment. He said that he had worked for entities related to the employer; the administrator said that the documents did not prove that he had a vested pension benefit. He submitted documentation of employment and tax withholding; the administrator said that there were no records of his eligibility specifically belonging to the plan.) [*Estate of Barton v. ADT Security Servs. Pension Plan*, No. 13-56379 (9th Cir. Apr. 21, 2016); see Rebecca Moore, *Appellate Court Switches Burden of Proof for Benefits Claim*, plansponsor.com (Apr. 25, 2016)]

§ 13.02 THIRD-PARTY ADMINISTRATORS (TPAs)

About two-thirds of covered workers in the United States get their benefits from plans that use some degree of third-party administration instead of handling all plan administration in house.

A TPA is an outsourcing firm that handles administrative tasks. It could be a consulting firm or a broad-based benefits administration firm. There are no federal licensing rules for TPAs, although some states impose their own requirements.

If the plan has unexpectedly high claims, TPAs usually provide stop-loss protection with back-up insurance that benefits the plan itself (rather than the employees with high expenses). Having a stop-loss plan doesn't turn a self-insured plan into an insured plan for ERISA purposes.

A TPA can be considered an ERISA fiduciary as long as it satisfies the statutory requirement of holding "any authority or control," even if it does not have discretionary control over the assets of the health plan it administers. The Sixth Circuit held that a TPA's authority to write checks on the plan's account (which continued to be exercised to pay the TPA's fees even after the contract with the plan sponsor ended) provided the necessary degree of authority or control to impose liability after the sponsor company went bankrupt and many employees had unpaid medical bills. [*Briscoe v. Fine*, 444 F.3d 478 (6th Cir. 2006)]

The Sixth Circuit held in 2012 that a TPA becomes a fiduciary when it exercises practical control over the plan's funds. Therefore, a TPA that failed to pay claims under a self-insured ERISA health benefits plan (the TPA misappropriated the funds) violated its fiduciary duty to act solely in the best interests of participants, [*Guyan Int'l Inc. v. Professional Benefits Administrators Inc.*, 689 F.3d 793 (6th Cir. 2012)]

§ 13.03 HEALTH PLAN CLAIMS

The Department of Labor's Pension and Welfare Benefits Agency (PWBA; later renamed EBSA) published a wide-ranging final rule on claims procedures for health and disability plans, amending 29 C.F.R. § 2560.503-1. [See 65 Fed. Reg. 70246-70271 (Nov. 21, 2000); 66 Fed. Reg. 35887 (July 9, 2001)] The PPACA claims rules (see § 13.03[A], below) build on these rules and add more requirements.

The Final Rule draws a distinction between pre-service claims (advance approval of health care services) and postservice claims (where medical care has already been provided). The distinction is made because postservice claims are much less urgent. The employee has already been treated, so the question becomes who will pay the bill, not whether potentially necessary care will be available or not.

Plans are not allowed to impose any fees or costs for appealing a denial. The reviewer cannot be either the person who made the initial denial or someone who works for that person. Whenever there is an issue of medical judgment, such as when treatment is necessary, the plan must consult appropriate health care professionals. The reviewer must examine the claim de novo (from the beginning), not just to see if the initial decision involved an abuse of discretion. The employee is allowed to introduce new facts that they did not provide earlier—even if these facts would not be admissible as evidence in a suit. There can be either a single level of review of denials, or two sequential levels of review, but no additional time is allowed to decide the second level of review.

If a person makes a claim and is denied on the basis of non-eligibility for coverage, the claims procedure will apply because there has been a denial. But if a plan requires preauthorization or otherwise requires submission of pre-service claims, EBSA says that the plan may have to treat an inquiry as a claim that has not been properly filed—and may have to explain how to file the claim.

The Employee Benefit Security Administration (EBSA) says that the time for making an initial claims decision starts when the claim has been filed in accordance with the plan's reasonable filing procedures—even if the plan does not have all the information needed to decide the claim. Plans are not permitted to extend time limits by asserting that the claim is not a "clean claim" (i.e., that necessary information is missing). Plans must disclose the rules, guidelines, and protocols used to make adverse benefit determinations—even if the rule was developed by a third party that claims that proprietary information is involved. A plan can set a maximum period for filing initial benefit claims—as long as it is a reasonable limit that does not unduly hamper the right to make claims.

In plans where there are two levels of review of adverse benefit determinations, EBSA's position is that the same standards (including time limits) apply to both levels of review. Second-level review is de novo, and must be done by someone other than the first-level decision-maker or his or her subordinate. The EBSA says that there cannot be more than two mandatory levels of appeals—but it is legitimate for a plan to offer additional voluntary levels of appeal, such as Alternative Dispute Resolution. Claimants who choose to sue rather than use voluntary remedies have not failed to exhaust administrative remedies. Furthermore, the litigation statute of limitations will be tolled while claimants voluntarily pursue additional levels of appeals. [DOL EBSA, *FAQs About the Benefit Claims Procedure Regulation*, <http://www.dol.gov/ebsa/faqs/faq_claims_proc_reg.html> (undated, last accessed Mar. 31, 2017)]

See Section [A], immediately below, for PPACA's variations on this theme.

[A] PPACA Requirements

Interim final regulations to implement the claims requirements under PPACA (the health care reform bill) were published in July 2010 by DOL, HHS, and the Treasury. These regulations make insurance companies that provide policies for group health plans subject to the requirements to the same extent as EGHPs are. All plans must have an internal appeals process that grants full and fair review of denials (on an expedited basis, for urgent cases). Plan participants must be given detailed information about why claims were denied, and how to initiate an appeal.

Before these rules were published, most—but not all—states had requirements for independent external review of claims (44 states had such requirements), but there was no uniformity so some states offered much more protection to claimants than others. The new rules set standards for state external review procedures, and establish a federal external review procedure for people who are not covered by a state review process. Participants in self-insured plans are covered by the interim final rules.

PPACA requires all group and individual plans to comply with the ERISA claims/appeals procedure. However, certain plans, such as stand-alone vision plans and welfare benefit plans that are not health-related, are not subject to this requirement. As a result of PPACA, group and individual insured plans and self-insured plans must have both an internal claims/appeal process and an external review process.

Under PPACA, for covered plans, the appeal and review mandate applies to all adverse benefit determinations. Cancellation or discontinuance of coverage with retroactive effect can be appealed, even if there is no actual benefit denial because of the rescission. Claimants must be notified of the outcome of urgent care claims as soon as possible, considering medical exigencies. The pre-PPACA provision that the time limit is extended if the claimant fails to provide adequate information remains in effect.

Group plans must inform the claimant of any new or additional evidence that the plan used or considered in connection with a claim. Before an appeal can be denied on the basis of a new or additional rationale, the claimant must be informed (without charge) of the evidence supporting the rationale. The information must be provided as soon as possible, definitely early enough for the claimant to respond to it before the final date for submitting information. (The authors of this treatise suggest that a plan that has two levels of appeals might wish to eliminate one to increase the time available for claims processing.)

The plan must not make the compensation or promotion of people handling claims depend on their denial of a particular claim or a stated percentage of claims, and hiring cannot be based on a propensity to deny claims. If a plan fails to meet all the requirements for internal claims, the claimant is deemed to have exhausted the internal review process—and thus to be entitled to initiate external review or bring suit immediately. In suits under ERISA § 502(a), the case will be reviewed de novo without deference to the claims administrator's decision.

Notices of adverse benefit determinations must include:

- The date of the service
- The name of the health care provider
- Amount of the claim
- The diagnosis and treatment codes, and what they mean

- Other information needed to identify the claim

- The reason(s) for the adverse determination, including the denial code and its meaning, and the standards used by the plan to deny the claim.

In addition to the internal claims process (within the plan), PPACA requires group plans to provide for external review of the plan's claims decisions. If the state has a review process that HHS deems to be acceptable, the state will perform the external review; the federal process is used only in states where there is no adequate state process. PPACA imposes 16 requirements on state external review procedures. The external review decision is binding on the plan and the insurer, but binds the claimant only to the extent that there are no other remedies. In particular, a dissatisfied claimant can still bring a suit under ERISA § 502(a)(1)(B). [Patricia Eschbach-Hall, Jones Day, *Claims and Appeals Procedures: New Internal and External Review Requirements* (August 2010) (benefits link.com)]

DOL proposed additional rules in late 2015, revising the ERISA regulations for disability benefit plans (and pension plans that provide disability benefits) in light of PPACA. The proposal requires denial notices to give better explanations of the standards for denials. Access to claim files is expanded, and claimants must be allowed to present evidence during the claim process. A final denial cannot be based on new evidence or a new rationale unless the claimant is given a reasonable opportunity to respond. No one involved in claim determinations can be given financial motivation for denying claims (e.g., a bonus for reducing the percentage of claims granted would be forbidden). If a denial conflicts with a grant of benefits by the Social Security Administration or other third-party disability payor or with the treating physician's opinion, the denial letter must explain the reason for the disagreement. The claimant must receive copies of any internal guidelines or standards used in making the determination. If none were used the insurer must disclose that no standards were applied. Notices must be understandable to claimants in light of any cultural or linguistic barriers.

Except in the case of minor errors, when a violation of the claims regulation leads to a deemed denial, the claimant can bring suit and get de novo judicial review of the case. Judges will not give deference to plan decisions made without giving the claimants the required procedural protections.

Any decision that has retroactive effect is considered rescission of benefits, and is an adverse determination that triggers a right of review. [80 Fed. Reg. 72014 (Nov. 18, 2015)]

Individuals have four months after a final denial of an internal appeal to request external review. If the claim is urgent, the plan must decide immediately if external review appropriate; for non-urgent claims, the plan has five business days to make the decision. This stage is called "preliminary review." The plan is required to notify the individual of its decision, in writing, within one business day of finishing the preliminary review. The appeal must be referred to an Independent Review Organization (IRO). DOL Technical Release 2010-01 says that, to qualify for the safe harbor, a self-funded plan must rotate claims assignments among three IROs. [Christy Tinnes and Brigen Winters, *External Review: To Delete or Not Delegate?*, plansponsor.com (Oct. 18, 2011)]

June 2011 amendments change the standard for deciding urgent care claims to making a decision as soon as possible consistent with medical needs, but always within 72 hours—rather than the 24-hour limit previously mandated. The amendments say that, when an external reviewer orders benefits, the plan must provide the benefits without delay—even if it intends to seek judicial review. Under the amendments, the only claims eligible for federal external review are claims involving medical judgment or rescission of coverage—not how the participant's diagnosis is coded, or whether care from an out-of-network specialist should be covered. [*Group Health Plans and Health Insurance Issuers: Rules Relating to Internal Claims and Appeals and External Review Processes*, 76 Fed. Reg. 37208 (June 24, 2011)]

[B]   Disability Plans

The DOL proposed regulations on claims procedures for disability plans in November 2015, then finalized the regulations in December 2016, effective for all disability claims filed on or after January 1, 2018. No matter how the plan describes the benefit, and whether it is a health or retirement plan, a plan is considered a disability plan for this purpose if the availability of a benefit is contingent on a showing of disability. The regulation includes many terms that are similar to the PPACA claims rules.

To prevent conflicts of interest, the disability plan rules require decision-makers to be independent and impartial. The plan must not hire, promote, compensate, or otherwise favor decision-makers on the basis of their tendency to deny claims.

Additional disclosure is required in denial notices. If the plan disagrees with a Social Security Administration decision, the denial notice must explain the basis of the disagreement. Denials based on the plan's internal rules and guidelines must explain these rules. If a denial at the appeal level is based on new evidence, the claimant must be notified of this and given a chance to respond.

All denial notices must describe any reduction of the length of time allowed to pursue claims; DOL's position is that a plan does not offer full and fair review of denials if it imposes a contractual limitations period that ends before review has been completed.

Claimants will be deemed to have exhausted administrative remedies (and therefore will be allowed to pursue ERISA remedies) in a broader range of circumstances, such as when the plan fails to follow its own procedures or fails to provide a reasonable claims procedure. A de minimis exception is allowed for small errors that are not prejudicial to the claimant, where the error was beyond the plan's control. Rescinding disability coverage (other than for non-payment of premiums) is considered an adverse benefit determination. Claims notices must be provided in a manner that is linguistically and culturally appropriate for the recipient. [81 Fed. Reg. 92316 (Dec. 19, 2016); see Practical Law, *Final DOL Disability Claims Regulations Require Notice of Contractual Limitations Periods* (Dec. 20, 2016) (benefitslink.com)]

According to DOL, close to two-thirds of ERISA litigation involves disability plans. Although this final rule has similarities to the PPACA claims procedures, certain unique features of disability claims are retained, such as timelines, and the disability rule does not require there to be an external review process. The final rule applies only to plans that not only make disability benefit determinations, but are subject to the ERISA claims procedure. For example, short-term disability plans that are not fully insured or funded may be exempt from the claims procedure if they qualify as payroll practices regulated by state law. However, funded or insured short-term disability plans and almost all long-term disability plans are covered by the final rule. It is helpful for employers to ask their insurers for a contract provision that the insurer will comply with all applicable laws, including ERISA. In fact, some retirement plans may even be subject to the rules if their eligibility or service credit requirements are affected by disability determinations and if the plan makes its own determination of disability rather than relying on a determination made by the Social Security Administration or a related long-term disability plan. Non-qualified deferred compensation plans that are classified as top hat plans are subject to the ERISA claims procedure. [Haynes and Boone, *Which Plans Are Subject to the DOL's Final Rules for Disability Claims Procedures?* (Feb. 13, 2017) (benefitslink.com); Damian A. Myers and James R. Huffman, *Disability Claims Procedures Should Be Updated for New Regulations,* Proskauer Rose LLP (Aug. 1, 2017), available at Lexology.com]]

The Ninth Circuit joined the First, Second, Third, Sixth, Seventh, Eighth, and Tenth Circuits in holding that failure to follow the claims procedure of 29 C.F.R. § 2560.503-1, such as failure to provide plan documents requested by a disability claimant, does not expose a plan to penalties under ERISA § 502(c)(1). The Ninth Circuit's conclusion is that the regulations under § 2560.503-1 cover benefit plans. However, ERISA § 5 02(c)(1) sets out the responsibilities and potential liability of plan administrators; the two groups are not the same. [*Lee v. ING Groep, N.V.,* 829 F.3d 1158 (9th Cir. 2016); see Dylan D. Rudolph, *Ninth Circuit Clarifies Remedies for Failure to Provide Documents Relevant to a Benefit Claim,* Trucker Huss Benefits Report (August 2016) (benefitslink.com)]

§ 13.04 HIPAA EDI STANDARDS

One reason for high medical costs is that a lot of time and effort is devoted to processing, transmitting, and analyzing information. A number of different standards evolved for storing and displaying health information. To streamline this process, the Health Insurance Portability and Accessibility Act (HIPAA) requires a uniform set of Electronic Data Exchange (EDI) standards to be placed into effect for health and welfare funds.

HIPAA's EDI standards apply to insured and self-insured Employee Group Health Plans (EGHPs), health insurers and HMOs, but not to small, self-administered health plans with fewer than 50 participants. Employers are covered only if they administer their own health plans.

The Health Information Technology for Economic and Clinical Health (HITECH) Act, part of the economic stimulus bill (Pub. L. No. 111-5), takes effect February 17, 2010. The HITECH Act expands the privacy and security provisions of HIPAA, and includes a new regulatory structure for electronic medical records. Civil monetary penalties (CMPs) for HIPAA violations have increased; for the most egregious violations, the penalty can reach $1.5 million per year. Persons whose personal health information (PHI) has been disclosed improperly can collect a share of the civil penalties.

Business associates of HIPAA-covered entities are subject to the same privacy rules as the covered entities are, including criminal penalties for violations. HHS' Office of Civil Rights continues to enforce HIPAA compliance, but state Attorneys General have also been given the power to enforce HIPAA by bringing suit in federal district court. [Troutman Sanders LLP, *Keeping Up with Recent Legislation: Numerous Changes to Group Health Plans Required*, plansponsor. com (Feb. 27, 2009)]

HHS published extensive proposed regulations (covering more than 50 pages in the Federal Register) in July 2010, implementing the HITECH Act requirements for privacy, data security, compliance, and the imposition of penalties. [RIN 0991-AB57, 75 Fed. Reg. 40868 (July 14, 2010)] Additional rules were published in 2013 [78 Fed. Reg. 5566 (Jan. 25, 2013)], conforming to the Genetic Information Nondiscrimination Act (GINA).

In late 2016, HHS increased the penalties for violations of the HIPAA privacy and security rules by 10.02%, and the penalties will be adjusted annually for inflation in January every year. [81 Fed. Reg. 61538 (Sept. 6, 2016); see Mary Harrison and Leslye Laderman, *HHS Increases Penalties for HIPAA Violations*, HRC FYI (Nov. 29, 2016) (benefitslink.com)] The penalties were increased again, in February 2017. A HIPAA violation that has a reasonable cause and is not due to willful neglect can be penalized by $1,118 to $55,910 per violation, subject to a cap of $1,677,299 for all violations of one provision in a single year. But if the violation is due to willful neglect, and is not corrected in a timely fashion, then the maximum penalty is $55,910 per violation, capped at $1,677,299 for similar violations in a year. [Conduent FYI, *DOL, PBGC and HHS Increase Penalties for Violations* (Feb. 10, 2017) (benefitslink.com)]

See Chapter 19 for further discussion of health EDI.

§ 13.05 CASE LAW ON CLAIMS

[A] Generally

Many cases have been litigated over questions of the proper way to handle and process claims within a plan—and especially over the standard of review that courts should apply when reviewing the decisions of plan administrators. If review is *de novo*, the court can consider all aspects of the decision, including its reasonableness and correctness. In most cases, however, the plan sponsor drafted the governing documents to reserve discretion—in which case, the court can only determine if the decision-maker acted arbitrarily and capriciously.

The Eighth Circuit joined other circuits in allowing reformation and surcharge as equitable remedies for breach of fiduciary duty. Silva's claim for supplemental life insurance under his employer's plan was denied for failure to submit the evidence of insurability required by the plan. After Silva's claim was submitted, it was discovered that 200 other employees signed up for supplemental life insurance without submitting Statement of Health forms. The Eighth Circuit held that, under § 502(a)(1)(B), there were issues of material fact precluding a decision on whether MetLife abused its discretion. The plan did not describe what evidence of insurability was sufficient; the Statement of Health form was not mentioned; and the experience of the other 200 employees showed that there were notice issues. The plaintiff could seek equitable surcharge from plan administrator, for failure to provide an SPD that would have explained the Statement of Health requirement. At the early pleading stage, relief could be sought under both (a)(1)(B) and (a)(3), because it was too soon to tell if the claims were duplicative. [*Silva v. Metropolitan Life Ins. Co.*, 762 F.3d 711 (8th Cir. 2014)]

Although the claimant has primary responsibility for providing medical proof of disability, if there is no evidence in the record to refute the beneficiary's disability theory, then the claims administrator has a duty to get material records from treating professionals that the administrator knows about, or to inform the claimant about missing records. But if there is enough evidence in the record to refute the claimant's theory, the administrator has no duty to obtain records. [*Harrison v. Wells Fargo Bank*, 773 F.3d 15 (4th Cir. 2014)]

The Seventh Circuit held in 2017 that ERISA plans do not have a remedy to enforce insurance coordination of benefits clauses against other payers—even though the court acknowledged that participants could be harmed if the result was that covered claims were denied. The case arose when a self-funded health plan paid the claims of participants injured when taking part in youth sports programs. The plan participants were also covered by policies issued to the sponsors of the program. The health plan said that, as a result of coordination of benefits, the insurance companies rather than the plan should have paid the claims. The plan brought a suit under ERISA § 502(a)(3), seeking declaratory relief, an equitable lien, subrogation, and reimbursement. The plan's argument was that it had paid claims it was not responsible for and so was entitled to reimbursement from the insurers. The Seventh Circuit, however, held that only equitable remedies were available—and an equitable remedy is limited to specifically identifiable funds in the defendant's possession or traceable to such funds. In this case, the plaintiffs were asking for the legal remedy of monetary damages. The Seventh Circuit acknowledged that this ruling creates difficulties because ERISA plans usually can't assert state-law reimbursement or contribution claims because of ERISA preemption, but this ruling also prevents them from asserting ERISA remedies. [*Cent. States Se. & Sw. Areas Health & Welfare Fund v. American Int'l Grp.*, No. 15-2237 (7th Cir. 2016); see GKLaw.com, *Seventh Circuit Decision Holds That ERISA Does Not Authorize Contribution Suits Brought By Plans* (Feb. 24, 2017)(benefitslink.com)]

[B] Experimental Treatment

EGHPs typically refuse to cover experimental treatment, and new forms of treatment are very often more expensive than the ones they replace, creating a need to determine which treatments are already accepted by the medical community. In a Wisconsin case involving a clinical trial for specialized chemotherapy for a brain tumor, coverage was denied as experimental. The patient's parents exercised the option of having an independent review organization perform expedited review of the denial. The review organization characterized the proposed treatment as medically necessary and within the standard of care, but still experimental. The state trial court said that Phase II clinical trials were unambiguously excluded from coverage. The state court of appeals reversed, saying that the termination of benefits was arbitrary and capricious; the state supreme court agreed. The denial letter did not provide specific reasons for the denial; the specific plan provision supporting the determination; the review procedures and time limits (including the right to sue); and either an explanation of the scientific or clinical judgment that the treatment was experimental, or a statement that such information will be furnished at no charge on request [*Summers v. Touchpoint Health Plan Inc.*, 2008 WI 45 (Wis. 2008)]

[C] Other Exclusions

Courts are often asked to rule on whether the involvement of drugs or alcohol in an injury justifies denying the claim:

- The Sixth Circuit ruled that it was reasonable to conclude that death caused by grossly negligent drunk driving is not accidental, so Personal Accident Insurance benefits could be denied to the beneficiary of a plan participant who died as a result of drunk driving. [*Lennon v. MetLife Ins. Co.*, 504 F.3d 617 (6th Cir. 2007)]

- However, the Fourth Circuit held that a crash caused by driving with a BAC of. 289 was still an accident; most drunk drivers are not killed. [*Johnson v. American United Life Ins. Co.*, 716 F.3d 813 (4th Cir. 2013)]

Although a claims administrator's decisions are generally upheld if they are grounded in any reasonable basis, the Ninth Circuit applied a higher standard because of both structural conflict of interest and procedural irregularities. The claimant fell and fractured her jaw when she had a seizure. Her group health plan covered the initial surgeries but denied preauthorization of additional dental care. The Ninth Circuit found that the insurer did not inform the plaintiff of her rights under ERISA § 502(a), and there was a suggestion of abuse of discretion because the insurer did not consult an appropriate medical professional. The insurer repeatedly described the treatment as dental rather than medical, but did not consider the clinical evaluation of the claimant's dentist, and did not substantiate its decision. [*Yox v. Providence Health Plan*, **659 Fed. Appx. 941** (9th Cir. 2016); see Roy F. Harmon III, *Ninth Circuit Finds Abuse of Discretion Due to Procedural, Substantive, and Structural Flaws*, healthplanlaw.com (Sept. 13, 2016) (benefitslink.com)]

[D] Timing

A statute of limitations prescribes the latest date at which a claim can be filed—a date that, in some circumstances, can be extended. But the length of the statute of limitations is only part of the inquiry. One of the most significant questions in tort law is when a potential plaintiff can be expected to be aware that an injury has occurred—and, therefore, when the clock starts for determining whether a claim is timely.

The Ninth Circuit held that the 180-day period to appeal the denial of a long-term disability claim was extended to Monday when the last day to submit the appeal fell on a Saturday, because the Federal Rules of Civil Procedure usually extend deadlines until the next business day when a deadline falls on a weekend or legal holiday. [*LeGras v. AETNA Life Ins. Co.*, No. 12-56541 (May 28, 2015)]

Because ERISA § 502(a) has no statute of limitations, courts have allowed plan administrators to set their own deadlines for judicial review, as long as the chosen deadline is reasonable. For plans that do not set a deadline, the court applies the statute of limitations for the most nearly analogous state-law claim. The Third Circuit held that if the plan imposes a deadline on judicial review (in this case, one year), the notice of benefit denial must inform the claimant of this. The claimant in this case received a denial letter on August 12, 2010. The letter told Mirza he could bring an ERISA § 502(a) suit, but did not explain the statute of limitations; he did not sue for about 19 months. The Third Circuit applied New Jersey's six-year statute of limitations for breach of contract cases, so his suit was not time-barred. [*Mirza v. Insurance Administrator of Am., Inc.*, 800 F.3d 129 (3d

Cir. 2015). See also *Moyer v. Metropolitan Life Ins. Co.*, 762 F.3d 503 (6th Cir. 2014)]

If the disability for which benefits are sought (e.g., severe mental illness, by itself or in conjunction with physical illness) might preclude making a prompt application, failure to make a timely filing might be excused. [*Waskiewicz v. UniCare Life & Accident Health Ins. Co.*, 802 F.3d 851 (6th Cir. 2015)]

Sometimes claims administrators are asked to reopen a denied claim to consider additional information. If the statute of limitations has already run, the administrator does not waive the statute of limitations defense by agreeing to reopen the claim. Therefore, the Ninth Circuit held that when MetLife reopened an long-term disability (LTD) claim in 2009, five years after it was denied, a 2011 suit was time-barred because the 2004 statute of limitations defense applied. An ERISA claim accrues when benefits are denied, or when the insured has reason to know the claim has been denied: i.e., that there is a clear and continuing repudiation of the claimant's rights under the plan. [*Gordon v. Deloitte & Touche*, 749 F.3d 746 (9th Cir. 2014)]

Santaliz-Rios v. Metropolitan Life Insurance, 693 F.3d 57 (1st Cir. 2012) applies an insurance policy three-year statute of limitations rather than the Puerto Rico 15-year contract statute of limitations. [See EBIA Weekly, *Court Enforces Plan-Imposed Limitations Period for Benefits Claims* (Oct. 25, 2012) (benefitslink.com).]

In late 2013, the Supreme Court ruled that an ERISA plan's three-year contractual statute of limitation was enforceable, even if it elapsed before it was possible for the plaintiff to file her suit (because the final claim denial took so long to be rendered). The Supreme Court found the limitation reasonable and not contrary to ERISA. The plaintiff sued within three years of the final claim denial, but more than five years after her first assertion of the claim. The Supreme Court said that the ERISA regulations about claims generally result in claims being administered within 12–16 months, and it was not unreasonable to allow another 20–24 months to file suit; equitable remedies like tolling, waiver, and estoppel might be available when the claims process takes so long that the plaintiff cannot file a timely claim. [*Heimshoff v. Hartford Life*, 134 S. Ct. 604 (2013)]

The Tenth Circuit revived ERISA claims, and joined the Second Circuit in a split about the proper statute of limitations for ERISA fiduciary breach claims. ERISA § 413 requires that suits be brought within six years of the last alleged breach, or the last date on which the fiduciary could have cured the breach—whichever is earlier. But claims of "fraud or concealment" can be brought within six years of discovery of the breach. The *Fulghum* plaintiffs alleged that they filed their claims within six years of the plan amendment that led to discovery of the alleged fraud. The majority view, held by the First, Seventh, and Ninth Circuits, is that the six-year statute of limitations only applies if there has been concealment of the alleged breach. But the Second and Tenth Circuits hold that the exception applies when there is either a claim of fraud or a claim of concealment; it is not necessary that both be alleged. In this case, the plaintiffs did not allege concealment, so when the case was remanded, they would have to prove fraud. [*Fulghum v. Embarq Corp.*, 778 F.3d 1147 (10th Cir.), *cert. denied*, 136 S. Ct. 537 (2015)]

When the case was remanded, the district court held in June, 2015 that the plan documents did not provide a right to lifetime benefits. The plaintiffs' motion for summary judgment was denied; the defendants' motion for summary judgment was granted. [*Fulghum v. Embarq Corp.*, No. 07-2602-EFM (D. Kan. June 10, 2015). The Tenth Circuit denied en banc rehearing, but granted rehearing by the panel on certain issues, on April 27, 2015: see 785 F.3d 395 (10th Cir. 2015)]

[E] Other Issues

Health plan fiduciaries have a duty to consider all pertinent available information and to make a decision based on substantial evidence. The Eighth Circuit reversed the lower court's grant of summary judgment to the employer, because the plaintiff should have been permitted to respond to the independent medical examiner's report to offer evidence that her obesity, alone or in conjunction with post-polio syndrome, rendered her totally disabled.

Especially in a situation in which one party has more resources and more power and is able to draft a document which the other party is not in a position to negotiate, courts will often be faced with allegations that a document is ambiguous, and should be construed in favor of the less-powerful party: here, the plan participant rather than the plan, plan administrator, or insurer.

The general rule is that the reviewing court will look only at the documents themselves. However, if a document is ambiguous, "extrinsic" (outside) evidence can be used to aid in its interpretation.

Estoppel is another legal doctrine, one which holds that in certain circumstances, a party will be "estopped" (prevented) from asserting a right that would otherwise apply—e.g., an employer that prevents an employee from filing a timely claim will not be allowed to reject claims on the grounds that they are untimely.

The doctrines of ambiguity and estoppel are often raised in cases involving plan amendments limiting benefits for those who have already retired. See Chapter 9 for retiree health benefits in general, and Chapter 14 for a discussion of the implications of amending a plan.

A litigator started collecting disability benefits for leg and foot pain in 2003. Benefits were discontinued in 2006 because of a functional capacity assessment, two independent medical exams, and a surveillance video. The plaintiff, Truitt, appealed, and her benefits were reinstated. A former boyfriend gave defendant Unum 600 pages of e-mails, documents, and photos showing Truitt working and engaging in recreational activities inconsistent with her claim of disability.

Benefits were terminated again, and Truitt sued; Unum counterclaimed to recover $1 million in benefits. The Fifth Circuit held that the burden of generating evidence is not solely on the plan administrator. Unum did not abuse its discretion in using the materials submitted by the ex-boyfriend, because it concluded that the e-mails were authentic and not tampered with. [*Truitt v. Unum Life Ins. Co. of Am.*, 729 F.3d 497 (5th Cir. 2013)]

Claims administrators are entitled to consider new information and, when appropriate, change their minds. Records that document the change can help rebut allegations of conflict of interest. In a disability case, where Aetna was granted discretion, Aetna initially said that after 24 months, the claimant could not perform any occupation. However, after surveillance, medical review, and an analysis of transferable skills, Aetna decided that she could do sedentary work and accordingly terminated benefits. The Seventh Circuit affirmed summary judgment for the insurer: the decision involved relevant new information; independent physician review provided a safeguard against conflict of interest; and the claimant's doctors were allowed to see the surveillance video and express their opinions. Furthermore, benefits were eventually restored. [*Geiger v. Aetna*, 845 F.3d 357 (7th Cir. 2017); see Boom: The ERISA law blog, *ERISA (7th Circuit): Four Ways to Inoculate Claims Denials from Allegations That a "Conflict of Interest" Affected Your Decision* (Jan. 9, 2017) (benefitslink.com)]

§ 13.06   *GLENN* AND THE STANDARD OF REVIEW

If and when a plan participant sues in connection with plan benefits, one of the most important questions is the "standard of review" the court will use to assess the plan administrator's decision. The two possibilities are "de novo" review, under which the court considers the question as if it were a new case, or review to see if the administrator abused his or her discretion. Many more plan decisions will be reversed—and many more claimants will win their cases—if the court can look at all the factors underlying the matter, and not just to see if there was an abuse of discretion.

The basic rule, as set by the seminal case of *Bruch v. Firestone Tire & Rubber* [489 U.S. 101 (1989)], is that plan administrators' decisions will be reviewed on a de novo basis, unless the plan itself is drafted to give the fiduciaries discretion over the way the plan operates. If the plan sponsor reserved this discretion, the court's only role is to see whether the administrators abused their discretion.

The mid-2008 Supreme Court decision in *Metropolitan Life Insurance Co. v. Glenn*, 554 U.S. 105 (2008) reaffirms *Bruch*. Wanda Glenn, a Sears employee was diagnosed with heart disease, and received 24 months of disability benefits. The insurer, Metropolitan Life Insurance Co. (MetLife) encouraged Glenn to apply for Social Security disability benefits. The Social Security Administration concluded that Glenn was unable to work, and granted the benefits. MetLife, however, rejected Glenn's application for long-term disability benefits, because the insurer concluded that Glenn was capable of doing sedentary work.

Glenn challenged the denial of benefits. According to the Sixth Circuit, MetLife should not have denied benefits; it was unduly influenced by its conflict of interest (as both payor of the benefits and decision-maker about qualifications). The *Glenn* decision says that there are four principles that determine what standard of judicial review should be applied in ERISA § 1132(a)(1)(B) cases:

- Trust law principles should be applied, as if the plan administrator were a trustee carrying out fiduciary activities.

- The decision will be reviewed de novo unless the plan specifies review for abuse of discretion only.

- Deferential review is appropriate where the plan gives the plan administrator discretion to determine eligibility.

- If the decision-maker has a conflict of interest—such as a dual role in both granting or denying claims and paying claims that are granted—that is a factor in deciding whether there was an abuse of discretion by the decision-maker.

Glenn extends the conflict of interest analysis to insurers that administer plans, not just to plan sponsors, a step that the Supreme Court felt justified in taking because insurers that administer ERISA plans must act in the best interests of participants. (Furthermore, a sponsor that has a conflict of interest may act according to that conflict when selecting an insurance carrier.)

Procedural irregularities in denying a claim (e.g., the appeal decision is issued late) for ERISA benefits can impose de novo review—but, in the Tenth Circuit view, only if the claimant provides meaningful new evidence or raises significant new issues in the appeal. In a two-level appeal process, failure to provide a denial letter (in this case, because it was mis-addressed) can be irregular enough to require a remand. [*Messick v. McKesson*, No. 15-4019, 2016 U.S. App. LEXIS 2904 (10th Cir. Feb. 17, 2016); see D. Michael Reilly, *ERISA—10th Circuit: What Happens When a "Procedural Irregularity" Occurs in an Appeal Denial?*, Lane Powell PC (Feb. 22, 2016), available at Lexology.com]

The Second Circuit held that an administrator's failure to comply with the DOL claims regulations means that the claim determination will receive no deference in federal court—unless the administrator can show that the failure was inadvertent and harmless. Claimants cannot recover civil penalties for the administrator's failure to comply with these regulations, but if a claims determination is challenged in a suit, failure of compliance could allow the claimant to introduce additional evidence outside the administrative record. [*Halo v. Yale Health Plan*, 819 F.3d 42 (2d Cir. 2016); see Michael T. Graham, Anne S. Becker & Jacob Mattinson, *Second Circuit Applies Stricter Rules for a Plan Administrator's Noncompliance with Benefit Claims Regulations*, McDermott Will & Emery (May 19, 2016), available at Lexology.com]

Subsequently, the District Court for the Southern District of New York held that, as a result of *Halo,* administrators that fail to comply strictly with the claims regulations lose access to arbitrary and capricious review. The 2017 case considers what constitutes a special circumstance that will entitle an administrator to a 45-day extension of time to rule on the claim. The district court held that reviewing information in the file, when the file remains under physician and vocational review, is not a special circumstance. In this reading, the exception would not mean anything if mere volume of work was considered extenuating. Denial letters should give detailed reasons, and requests for an extension should explain why the review cannot be completed within the statutory time frame. [*Salisbury v Prudential Ins. Co. of Am.,* No. 15-cv-9799, 2017 U.S. Dist. LEXIS 27983, 2017 WL 780817 (S.D.N.Y. Feb. 28, 2017); see Richard J. Pautler, *In a Significant Change, 2nd Circuit Requires Strict Compliance With Department of Labor Claim Regulations,* Thompson Coburn (Mar. 7, 2017), available at Lexology.com]

Courts do not always defer to the opinions of treating physicians, but plans that contradict the doctor must explain why the opinion was rejected. If the same "independent" medical reviewers are used over and over, they lose credibility. It is not per se improper for a plan to base decisions purely on file review, but if the plan gives the administrator the right to conduct a physical examination, the absence of an examination can give rise to suspicion. The Sixth Circuit held that it was arbitrary and capricious to deny long-term disability benefits for chronic neck pain when the plan said there was no evidence of impairment. The Sixth Circuit held that MRI and EMG evidence, and the doctor's opinion, actually were ample evidence of disability, which the plan ignored. Selective review of evidence is arbitrary. [*Shaw v. AT&T Umbrella Ben. Plan No. 1,* 795 F.3d 538 (6th Cir. 2015)]

The Ninth Circuit held that the allegedly independent physician consultants handling an LTD claim were conflicted. The consultants did not examine the plaintiffs before finding that he was not credible, even though there was substantial evidence that the claimant suffered mental limitations caused by pain medication. The Ninth Circuit implied that discovery can be granted about the number of reviews done by outside medical reviewers and how much they earn, in a case where the standard of review is "arbitrary and capricious." [*Demer v. IBM Corp.,* 835 F.3d 893 (9th Cir. 2016); Stephen D. Rosenberg, *The Ninth Circuit Deems the Compensation of Outside Medical Reviewers Relevant in LTD Litigation, in Demer v. MetLife,* Boston ERISA Law Blog (Aug. 30, 2016) (benefitslink.com)]

[A] Statutes Regulating Discretionary Clauses

"Discretionary clauses" give administrators full authority to interpret the terms of the plan, thereby triggering a more deferential standard of review when a denial is challenged. In mid-2009, the Sixth Circuit and the District Court for the District of Colorado ruled that ERISA does not preempt state laws forbidding discretionary language in insurance policies in ERISA plans. The Sixth Circuit found that a Michigan law banning discretionary language is enforceable because it comes under the insurance savings clause; *Miller* says that a law "regulates insurance" if it directly controls the terms of insurance contracts. The Colorado case says that the state law is valid (because it dictates the conditions under which an insurer will pay for a risk that it has assumed) but it did not apply to the plaintiff's case, because the law was not retroactive. [*American Council of Life Insurers v. Ross*, 558 F.3d 600 (6th Cir. 2009)]

The Seventh Circuit, joining the Ninth Circuit, held in 2015 that the Illinois statute that forbids discretionary clauses in insured employee benefit plans is not preempted by ERISA, because it is a state law regulating insurance. [*Fontaine v. Metropolitan Life Ins. Co.*, 800 F.3d 883 (7th Cir. 2015)]

If the disability plan or policy is silent on discretion, review is de novo. Many state insurance regulators (e.g., in Washington) forbid "abuse of discretion" language in disability policies. Minnesota does not bar discretionary review. Brake worked in South Dakota; she filed for disability benefits. Her employer is based in Minnesota. The policy called for discretionary review and the plan had a choice of law provision saying the plan used Minnesota law. South Dakota forbids discretionary review clauses; Minnesota does not. The Eighth Circuit applied Minnesota law and the abuse of discretion standard: choice of law in an ERISA contract is followed if it is not unreasonable or fundamentally unfair. [*Brake v. Hutchinson Tech., Inc.*, 774 F.3d 1193 (8th Cir. 2014)]

The Eighth Circuit affirmed the grant of summary judgment for MetLife. In 1991, Dennis Hall designated his son as beneficiary of his employment-related life insurance policy. The policy gave MetLife discretion to interpret the plan terms. A beneficiary change requires a signed, dated request submitted within 30 days of the date of the signature. In May 2001, Dennis married Jane. In March 2010, Dennis was diagnosed with cancer. In November 2010, he filled out and signed a beneficiary designation in favor of Jane, but did not submit it. On January 26, 2011, when he knew he was dying, he signed a will calling for distribution of the life insurance benefits to Jane. He died that day. Jane informed MetLife that she was named as life insurance beneficiary in the will. MetLife informed her that wills do not control the disposition of insurance benefits under an ERISA plan, and she was not designated as beneficiary. The Eighth Circuit reviewed the decision for abuse of discretion (in light of MetLife's discretionary authority) and decided that the decision was reasonable and supported by substantial evidence. The designation form was completed but not submitted within 30 days. The surviving spouse argued that the SPD (which does not set a time limit on submitting the beneficiary designation) should prevail over the plan language, but the Eighth Circuit said that this is not the case when the plan has a specific provision and the SPD is silent. [*Hall v. MetLife*, 750 F.3d 995 (8th Cir. 2014)]

Three court of appeals cases were decided in 2013 on the issue of whether requiring proof to be satisfactory to the insurer is a discretionary clause that will permit review under the "arbitrary and capricious" standard. At first, the consensus was that merely using the words "satisfactory proof" would not confer discretion, because the phrase is ambiguous. Satisfactory proof could either be an objective standard, where the insurer had no discretion, or subjective (i.e., the insurer has discretion).

The Seventh, Eighth, and Tenth Circuits have decided cases saying "proof satisfactory to the insurer" was a discretionary clause because the insurer had the power to make a subjective determination as to whether the proof was satisfactory. The Sixth Circuit held that a requirement of "satisfactory proof" was discretionary. Dictum in a Second Circuit case states that the word "satisfactory" is not enough because no plan would grant benefits on the basis of proof it deemed inadequate. This became the dominant position between 2005 and 2011. The Third and Ninth Circuits said that "proof satisfactory to the insurer" is not clear enough to grant discretion, and the Seventh Circuit reversed itself and joined them. In 2013, *Gross v. Sun Life Assurance Co. of Canada*, 734 F.3d 1 (1st Cir. 2013) said that "satisfactory to insurer" does not grant discretion, so review was de novo, and the Fourth Circuit agrees: *Cosey v. Prudential Insurance Co. of America*, 735 F.3d 161 (4th Cir. 2013), but the Sixth Circuit disagreed in mid-2013: *Frazier v. Life Insurance Co. of North America*, 725 F.3d 560 (6th Cir. 2013). In subsequent proceedings, the First Circuit held that Gross had achieved some degree of success on the merits, the standard under *Hardt*, and therefore was entitled to an award of attorneys' fees. The *Hardt* court did not decide whether a remand order, by itself, is sufficient to justify a fee award. The Sixth Circuit, and district courts in California, Massachusetts, and Alabama have said that it is. But district courts in Colorado, Michigan, and Florida disagree. [*Gross v. Sun Life Assurance Co. of Canada*, 763 F.3d 73 (1st Cir. 2014)]

The Fifth Circuit's position, for more than 25 years, was that denials of health and disability claims based on factual determinations (for example, the medical necessity of the treatment) were reviewed for abuse of discretion, whether or not the plan included discretionary *Firestone* language. A Texas statute forbids discretionary clauses. In April 2017, the Fifth Circuit rejected the argument that this statute overrides the Fifth Circuit's line of cases. The Fifth Circuit held that the Texas law governs the language that can be included in an insurance contract, but does not mandate the standard of review. However, en banc rehearing was granted in July 2017, so the decision might be reversed. [*Ariana M. v. Humana Health Plan of Tex. Inc.*, No. 16-20174 (5th Cir. Apr. 21, 2017); see Robinson + Cole LLP, *Fifth Circuit Maintains Default Deferential Standard of Review in Denial of Benefit Claims, But Suggests It May Soon Be Overruled*, erisaclaimdefense.com (May 3, 2017) (benefitslink.com); for grant of rehearing, see Benefitslawadvisor.com, *The Full Fifth Circuit Will Re-Visit the Standard of Review in Denial of Benefits Cases* (Aug. 12, 2017) (benefitslink.com)]

§ 13.07 CASE LAW ON CLAIMS PROCEDURAL ISSUES

Janie Butler went to alcohol rehab; her husband's ERISA health plan denied the care as medically unnecessary. Outpatient treatment and Alcoholics Anonymous had been tried, unsuccessfully. The insurer approved partial hospitalization, but Janie refused and dropped out of treatment. Five months later, she agreed to a 30-day residential treatment program but the insurer said she required only two days of inpatient detox and outpatient treatment. The insurer told the outside physician reviewer to use restrictive guidelines, resulting in denial of treatment with no consideration of past treatment or explanation why Butler's treating physicians were wrong. After seven years of internal reviews followed by extensive litigation, the district court found the denial to be arbitrary and capricious and awarded benefits, prejudgment interest, and $99,000 in statutory penalties to her then-husband, who was the assignee of plan benefits. (The penalties were imposed because the insurer took two years to respond to the husband's request for a copy of the coverage guidelines.) On appeal, the Sixth Circuit affirmed the grant of benefits but reversed the penalty, because 29 U.S.C. § 1132(c)(1)(B) imposes penalties of up to $100 a day for an administrator's failure to comply with an information request—but the insurer was not the plan administrator. The plan did not designate an administrator, so the plan sponsor was the default administrator. Damages under § 1132 were also inappropriate because John alleged a violation of a regulation implementing § 1133, not a violation of § 1132. [*Butler v. United Healthcare of Tenn., Inc.*, 764 F.3d 563 (6th Cir. 2014)]

Subrogation (see § 18.17) is another issue that may be involved. It is the right of a party, such as an insurance company or benefit plan that advances money to an injured person to be repaid when the injured person collects damages from the party causing the injury.

In a 2013 Supreme Court case, a plan participant injured in an automobile accident received $100,000 from his own insurer and $10,000 from other sources when he was injured in an automobile accident. After paying his lawyer, he had $66,000 left. His health plan had paid $66,866 of medical expenses for him. He claimed that he was not required to reimburse the health plan, because that would mean that he was not "made whole" for his damages. The Supreme Court held that the SPD for the health plan gave the insurer a right of subrogation, and this right, under contract law, prevailed over McCutchen's equitable arguments about "make-whole" relief. However, the reimbursement provision did not explain how to handle attorneys' fees, so the Supreme Court held that it was possible to apply another equitable doctrine, the "common fund" doctrine to resolve this issue. (This doctrine allows a person who creates a common fund for the benefit of multiple parties to be paid for creating the fund.) [*US Airways, Inc. v. McCutchen*, 133 S. Ct. 1537 (2013)]

The Supreme Court took up subrogation again in early 2016. Montanile received a $500,000 settlement when he was injured by a drunk driver. His ERISA plan advanced $120,000 in expenses. When the plan tried to enforce the subrogation clause, Montanile said that the money had been spent and was no longer available. The Supreme Court held that if there is no identifiable fund because the judgment or settlement money was spent in a way not involving traceable items, then it does not constitute "appropriate equitable relief" under ERISA for the plan to seek reimbursement from the injured person's general assets (rather than a separate fund created by the judgment or settlement). [*Montanile v. Bd. of Trs. of the Nat'l Elevator Indus. Health Ben. Plan*, 136 S. Ct. 651 (2016)]

The Sixth Circuit held that an employee's written request for ERISA documents must give clear notice of which documents are requested, so the plan administrator will be aware of which documents are requested. Cultrona applied for accidental death benefits after her husband, the plan participant, died. When her claim was denied, she made a request on November 18, 2011, for all documents that the administrator asserted gave notice of the plan amendment, and all documents in the administrative record relative to or supporting the decision. The plan administrator furnished a copy of the accidental death policy on June 12, 2012. The district court imposed a penalty of $8,910 for the delay. The Sixth Circuit said that the delay was not prejudicial, so it was not an abuse of discretion for the district court to award a penalty of $55/day rather than the possible maximum of $110/day. [*Cultrona v. Nationwide Life Ins. Co.*, 748 F.3d 698 (6th Cir. 2014)]

The Ninth Circuit held that when a claimant makes a prima facie case of entitlement to benefits but does not have access to corporate information about the claimant's employer that is needed to substantiate the claim, the burden shifts to the employer defendant to produce the information. In this case, when the claimant requested documents, other documents were produced but the SPD was not. The Ninth Circuit held that, although the burden of proof is on the claimant in some ERISA cases (e.g., proving disability under an LTD plan) but, in this situation, the defendant was the only one in possession of information that the claimant had no other means of obtaining. [*Barton v. ADT Sec. Servs. Pension Plan*, 820 F.3d 1060 (9th Cir. 2016); en banc rehearing was denied in September 2016. See Practicallaw.com Employee Benefits & Executive Compensation, *In the Ninth Circuit, a New Burden of Proof for Employers in Benefits Litigation*, (Sept. 22, 2016) (benefitslink.com).]

The First Circuit held that it was not arbitrary and capricious for a retirement plan committee to refuse 10 years of guaranteed annuity payments to the beneficiaries of a terminally ill employee who died after last day of work, but eight days before the annuity starting date—even though the employee took the employer's advice and delayed his retirement. The First Circuit held that the terms of the plan implicitly conditioned receipt of about $500,000 of annuity benefits on the employee surviving until the annuity starting date. The participant named his four children as beneficiaries of the annuity. The plan refused to make the payment (of about $4,117 a month) to them, but paid a reduced pre-retirement survivor annuity of $315 a month to the employee's ex-wife. The First Circuit held that it was reasonable for committee to conclude that the only benefit for death before annuity start date was the surviving spouse benefit. [*O'Shea v. UPS Ret. Plan*, 837 F.3d 67 (1st Cir. 2016); see Wolters Kluwer Law & Business, *Guaranteed Benefits Denied to Beneficiaries of Terminally Ill Employee Who Died Before Annuity Starting Date* (Oct. 21, 2016) (benefitslink.com)]

The Second Circuit held that a district court's remand to the ERISA plan administrator was not a final order that could be appealed. (The suit challenged a denial of long-term disability benefits; the district court ordered the plan administrator to calculate the amount of benefits.) The First, Fourth, Sixth, Eighth, and Eleventh Circuits have held that an ERISA remand order is not an appealable final order because it contemplates further proceedings before the plan administrator and, thus, can only be appealed if the collateral order doctrine applies. The Third, Seventh, Ninth, and Tenth Circuits allow immediate appeals in some circumstances. The Second Circuit found that this order was not final because there would be further proceedings but would not say that such orders are never immediately appealable. [*Mead v. Reliastar Life Ins. Co.*, 768 F.3d 102 (2d Cir. 2014)]

[A] HMO and TPA Involvement in Claims

Yet another facet in the complex picture comes from the involvement of HMOs and TPAs in the claims process. The legal questions become much more complex than a simple relationship between employee/plan participant and employer/plan sponsor.

As a general rule, an ERISA plan is the proper defendant if a participant wants to sue for benefits. However, in mid-2013, the Seventh Circuit held that if a health insurer decides all benefit eligibility issues and is the party that legally has an obligation to pay the benefits, an ERISA § 502(a)(1)(B) suit for benefits can be brought against the insurer. In this case, the plaintiffs charged that six insurers violated state law by imposing copayments for chiropractic treatment. [*Larson v. United Healthcare Ins.*, 723 F.3d 905 (7th Cir. 2013). See also *Cyr v. Reliance Standard Life Ins.*, 642 F.3d 1202 (9th Cir. 2011), also permitting an ERISA § 502(a)(1)(B) suit against an insurer.]

A health plan subject to PPACA has a choice of establishing a direct contractual relationship with an IRO or having the TPA handle the transaction; TPAs frequently have existing IRO relationships. But if the agreement is delegated, the sponsor must ensure that the TPA's contract with the IRO satisfies the requirements of Technical Release 2010-01. The delegation document should spell out the relationship between the plan and the TPA, making it clear what claims are involved. If the TPA that processes medical benefit claims for the plan does not handle prescription drug claims, then the plan must either contract with three more IROs, or delegate the hiring to another party (for example, a pharmacy benefits manager). [Christy Tinnes and Brigen Winters, *External Review: To Delete or Not Delegate?*, plansponsor.com (Oct. 18, 2011)]

In the wake of the Supreme Court's consolidated decision in *Aetna Health Inc. v. Davila*, and *Cigna Healthcare of Texas, Inc. v. Calad*, 542 U.S. 200 (2004), note that plan participants who claim that they were improperly denied necessary health care by a Managed Care Organization will have to bring the cases in federal court. The Supreme Court ruled that ERISA § 502(a) completely preempts state laws purporting to regulate managed care decisions about whether or not to provide treatment.

In the Eleventh Circuit view, whenever an administrator delegates authority to a TPA that is not a fiduciary, the TPA's decisions must be reviewed de novo, but the Tenth Circuit allows the decisions to be reviewed for abuse of discretion. [*Geddes v. United Staffing Alliance Empl. Med. Plan*, 469 F.3d 919 (10th Cir. 2006)]

The Supreme Court denied review in a Ninth Circuit case about whether health plan claims administrators are proper defendants in ERISA benefits suits. There is a circuit split on this issue, with some courts holding that only the plan administrator, or perhaps the administrator and the plan sponsor, can be sued. [*Spinedex Physical Therapy USA v. United Healthcare of Ariz.*, 770 F.3d 1282 (9th Cir. 2015), *cert. denied sub nom. United Healthcare of Ariz. v. Spinedex Physical Therapy*, 136 S. Ct. 317 (2015)]

[B] Exhaustion of Remedies

Exhaustion of remedies is a traditional legal doctrine under which parties will not be permitted to litigate a claim until they have satisfied the applicable administrative requirements—whether that means filing a claim with a state or federal antidiscrimination agency or using the appeals procedures provided by a health or welfare benefit plan. This is an important doctrine for employers, who can eliminate many suits at their earliest stages if the employees had an obligation to access plan remedies but failed or refused to do so. However, a counterbalancing legal doctrine is that employees do not have to exhaust administrative remedies when doing so would be futile.

When the insurer already concluded that a claimant was ineligible for long-term disability benefits (on the grounds that he could perform the duties of his own occupation), it would have been futile for the claimant to ask for a determination that he could not perform the duties of any occupation in order to get a waiver of life insurance premiums. In other words, the insurer could not require a second exhaustion of administrative remedies when the grounds for denying both claims were similar. [*Dozier v. Sun Life Assurance Co. of Canada*, 466 F.3d 532 (6th Cir. 2006), Similarly, *Paese v. Hartford Life & Accident Ins. Co.*, 449 F.3d 435 (2d Cir. 2006) holds that a finding that someone is not totally disabled from his own occupation implies a determination that he is not totally disabled from any occupation.]

In 2017, the Sixth Circuit joined six other circuits (the Third, Fourth, Fifth, Ninth, Tenth, and D.C.—although the Seventh and Eleventh disagree) in ruling that beneficiaries of an ERISA plan do not have to exhaust administrative remedies before bringing a suit that asserts statutory violations rather than claims for benefits. The Sixth Circuit plaintiffs are former employees of Cumberland University and participants in its defined contribution plan. In 2009, the university adopted a practice of matching employee contributions up to 5% of their salary. But the plan was amended retroactively to make the level of the match discretionary with the university, which did not match contributions at all between 2013 and 2015. The plaintiffs brought a class action suit charging wrongful denial of benefits, violation of the anti-cutback provision, failure to give proper notice to participants and beneficiaries, and breach of fiduciary duty. The district court dismissed the case for failure to exhaust administrative remedies. The Sixth Circuit reversed, holding that futile administrative proceedings were not required. The plaintiffs alleged that the benefit was properly calculated but the amendment was illegal—a question within the court system's expertise. [*Hitchcock v. Cumberland Univ.*, 851 F.3d 552 (6th Cir. 2017); see gtlaw.com, *Sixth Circuit Joins Six Other Circuits in Ruling Exhaustion of Plan's Administrative Procedures Not Required When Asserting Statutory Violations* (Mar. 23, 2017) (benefitslink.com)]

CHAPTER 14

AMENDING A PLAN

§ 14.01 INTRODUCTION

It is very likely that, no matter how carefully a plan was drafted, amendments will be required over the course of time. The company's line of business or workforce may change. The business may suffer reverses. And it's more than likely that Employment Retirement Income Security Act (ERISA) and the tax code will change in ways that require corresponding amendments to the plan. Each new tax bill that requires amendments includes a schedule for when plans are required to make their conforming amendments. In recent years, there have been major changes in the law such as the passage of the Genetic Information Nondiscrimination Act (GINA), the Americans with Disabilities Amendments Act (ADAA), and the large-scale revision of the Family and Medical Leave Act (FMLA) rules. The Trump administration's planning priorities include adopting pro-business rules and reducing the volume of federal regulation. A legal sea change of this kind requires re-examination of the company's plans to see if once-acceptable provisions now violate a tax or other provision.

Plan amendments can be adopted either prospectively or retroactively. Retroactive amendments can be made until the last day (including extensions) for filing the income tax return for the year the plan was adopted.

The Department of Labor (DOL) must be notified whenever a plan is materially modified or the information called for by ERISA § 102(b) changes. The DOL must receive an updated SPD when the participants and beneficiaries do. The DOL can reject an incomplete submission, giving the plan administrator 45 days for corrections. The 5500-series form filed with the IRS also requires reporting of the plan amendments and changes in the plan description that occurred during the year.

Plans frequently require amendments to keep up with tax law changes. Traditionally, plans obtained determination letters from the IRS, which protected them from disqualification if the IRS later discovered design defects in the plan documents. However, as § 14.02 shows, the IRS is phasing out the determination letter process once a new plan begins operations. This immunity does not extend to operational defects, only to design defects. See § 14.02, below.

An "operational error" is a failure to comply with the terms of the plan. Often, this can be corrected without IRS involvement and without penalties to the plan. The sponsor must put the plan and its participants in the position they would have been in if there had been no error. However, if correction requires a plan amendment, then it will probably be necessary to use the Employee Plans Compliance Resolution System (EPCRS), as set out in various Revenue Procedures (e.g., Rev. Proc. 2015-28, 2015-16 I.R.B. 920), and to file under the Voluntary Correction Program (VCP). There are five situations under which a sponsor can use the Self-Correction Program (SCP) to adopt a retroactive corrective amendment without making a VCP filing:

- A hardship distribution was made from a plan that did not have a hardship distribution option;

- Making a plan loan where, once again, this option was not included in the plan;

- Letting an employee participate in the plan prematurely—before he or she satisfied the eligibility requirements;

- Allocating a contribution to correct a violation of the § 401(e)(17) compensation limit;

- Correcting an actual deferral percentage (ADP) failure by making a Qualified Nonelective Contribution (QNEC) that would not otherwise be available under the plan.

For many years, EPCRS relied on the determination letter program, so it has been amended to remove those references. Eligibility for the self-correction program is still dependent on having a determination letter but now it need not be a current letter; the surviving determination letters do not have an expiration date. Traditionally, the fees for the VCP were published in the latest iteration of the EPCRS Revenue Procedure—but the IRS announced that the fees will be published in the IRS's annual guidance on user fees instead. [Rev. Proc. 2016-51, 2016-42 I.R.B. 465; see Lois Wagman Colbert et. al., *IRS Provides Guidance for the Post-Determination Letter Era,* Kilpatrick Townsend (Oct. 19, 2016), available at Lexology.com]

The plan must comply with the requirements of Code §§ 401(a), 410(b), and 411(d)(6). If the correction is a retroactive amendment to allow hardship distributions or loans, the best practice is to make sure that enough non-highly compensated employees (NHCEs) had access to them to satisfy the nondiscrimination rules. Amendments to change eligibility dates should also predominantly benefit NHCEs. The IRS has not formally stated its standards for approving a retroactive amendment to correct plan errors but it appears that the IRS wants documentary evidence that the plan was operated in accordance with what the sponsor, participants, and TPA believed were the terms of the plan. The best evidence is an Summary Plan Description (SPD) provision authorizing a particular event or practice. Correspondence and e-mails could also be used to show how parties thought the plan was supposed to operate. [Raymond P. Turner, *The Retroactive Amendment Fix for Plan Operational Failures*, Jackson Lewis PC (July 15, 2015), available at Lexology.com]

Rev. Proc. 2015-27, 2016-16 I.R.B. 914, reduces the VCP fees for some corrections of participant loan failures, and clarifies that Rev. Proc. 2013-12 does not provide the only acceptable method of correcting certain types of overpayments.

Rev. Proc. 2016-8, 2016-1 I.R.B. 243, updates the user fees for letter ruling and determination letter requests, as well as user fees for VCP submissions under EPCRS. The new fees, which in many cases are lower than the previous fees, became effective February 1, 2016. The user fee for regular VCP submissions for qualified plans and 403(b) plans are $500 (20 or fewer participants in the plan), $750 (21–50 participants), $1,500 (51–100 participants), $5,000 (101–1,000 participants), $10,000 (1,000–10,000 participants) and $15,000 if there are more than 10,000 participants. [Christie Daly, *Changes to User Fees for Voluntary Correction Program VCP Submissions*, Bryan Cave Benefits and Executive Compensation Blog (Jan. 8, 2016) (benefitslink.com)]

However, the fees are cut in half for VCP submissions made by April 29, 2017, as long as the only failure in the submission is failure to restate plan documents to reflect the provisions of the Pension Protection Act (PPA) by April 30, 2016. [Meredith R. Fergus, *Did Your Company Fail to Adopt a New Preapproved Defined Contribution Plan by the April 30th Deadline? The IRS Has a Solution for You*, Jackson Lewis PC (May 22, 2016), available at Lexology.com]

Generally, an employee's enrollment in an Employee Group Health Plan (EGHP) through a cafeteria plan is irrevocable for the year, unless there has been a qualifying change in status event that affects the employee's, spouse's, or dependent's eligibility for coverage. Typical events are marriage, divorce, change from full- to part-time status, or the birth of a child. The IRS added more events in 2014, where the employee can drop health coverage even if the event does not affect eligibility under the EGHPs. Under PPACA, an employee is treated as full-time for the entire upcoming year if the employee averaged more than 30 hours of service per week in a previous year, if the employer uses the "lookback" method to determine full-time status. The employee usually retains eligibility for coverage even if hours fall below the 30-hour threshold. However, the 2014 rule allows an employee who is eligible to buy coverage on a marketplace to drop the employer's coverage. The employer does not have to permit employees to terminate coverage for these reasons—but if the employer does allow it, the cafeteria plan must be amended retroactively to conform. [Leigh C. Riley and Casey K. Fleming, *Don't Forget to Amend Cafeteria Plan for New Permitted Election Change Events*, Foley & Lardner LLP (Nov. 30, 2015), available at Lexology .com]

Under Notice 2014-1, 2014-2 I.R.B. 393, plans can be amended to let employees change their cafeteria plan elections mid-year, if they have same-sex spouses and their status has changed either because of the Supreme Court decisions on same-sex marriage or because marriage takes place mid-year. [Stephen A. Riga, *At Year End, IRS Issues Guidance on Cafeteria Plan Transitional Rules for Windsor*, Ogletree Deakins (Dec. 26, 2013), available at Lexology.com]

Notice 2014-19, 2014-17 I.R.B. 979, requires plans to be amended to conform to *Windsor;* generally, the amendment was required by December 31, 2014. Notice 2014-37, 2014-24 I.R.B. 1100 provides that a 401(k) plan remains qualified if it adopts a mid-year amendment to comply with Notice 2014-19, 2014-17 I.R.B. 979. Rev. Proc. 2007-44 provides that, when there are changes to plan qualification requirements that affect provisions of the plan document, adoption of an interim amendment is generally required by later of end of plan year when change takes effect or the due date of the employer's tax return for the tax year including the date the change takes effect. However, that could violate the restriction on mid-year amendments of safe harbor 401(k) plans. Therefore, Notice 2014-37 reassures employers that the plan does not fail to be qualified merely because of the adoption of the mid-year amendment. [Sally P. Schreiber, *Notice Clarifies Midyear Amendment of Certain Retirement Plans Post-Windsor*, AICPA (May 15, 2014) (benefitslink.com)]

In most cases, the Internal Revenue Code does not require that employees be notified in advance that the plan will be amended. So they don't have a right to comment on the proposed amendment (although they do have a right to comment on the plan's initial application for a determination letter). The exception is that advance notice is required if the amendment changes the vesting schedules of participants who have three years or more of plan participation, because they have the right to choose between the new and the old schedules. However, ERISA does impose a notice requirement. Once a plan is amended, ERISA §§ 102(a)(1) and 104(b)(1) require participants to get a Summary of Material Modifications (SMM) within 210 days of the end of the plan year in which the change is adopted.

See *Coffin v. Bowater Inc.*, 501 F.3d 80 (1st Cir. 2007), an ERISA plan amendment must be in writing; must be executed by someone authorized to amend the plan; the language must make it clear that the plan is being amended; and any other requirements for amendments set out in the governing documents must be observed. *Halliburton Co. Benefits Committee v. Graves*, 463 F.3d 360 (5th Cir. 2006) holds that, to amend an ERISA welfare benefit plan, the employer must provide a procedure for amendment, must identify who is authorized to amend, and amendments are effective only if they follow the plan procedure.

The Second Circuit, reversing its own earlier rulings, applied the Supreme Court's *Schoonejongen*, *Jacobson*, and *Spink* decisions to find that employers and plan sponsors are not acting as fiduciaries when they modify, adopt, or amend plans. This is also true of multi-employer plans, so ex-participants and beneficiaries of the Niagara-Gennessee & Vicinity Carpenters Local 280 Pension and Welfare Funds were unable to recover assets that they said were wrongfully depleted by improper plan amendments that, they alleged, violated fiduciary duties. [*Janese v. Fay*, 692 F.3d 221 (2d Cir. 2012)]

§ 14.02   FLEXIBILITY THROUGH AMENDMENT

Before 2005, amendments to retirement plans to comply with changes in the law were submitted to the IRS for approval at irregular intervals. The IRS was often confronted with too many submissions at one time. Therefore, in 2005, a cyclical system was implemented, dividing plans into two groups: pre-approved and individually designed.

Most pre-approved plans are either prototype plans or volume submitter plans. A prototype plan has a basic plan document and an adoption agreement. The employer can choose among several plan options offered. A volume submitter plan provides plan language (including some options) that, after approval by the IRS, is used to create plans. Volume submitter plans offer many choices, whereas prototype plans have very few choices and make it difficult to shift the plan to a new provider.

Standardized prototype plans were reviewed on a six-year cycle, the first of which ended on April 30, 2010, for pre-approved defined contribution plans and on April 30, 2012, for defined benefit plans. Individually designed plans were reviewed on a five-year cycle, with the year for filing depending on the last digit in the company's Employer Identification Number (EIN); the first six-year cycle for pre-approved defined contribution plans ended April 30, 2010. The six-year cycle for defined benefit plans ends April 30, 2012.

The IRS Cumulative List explains what the IRS considers when reviewing documents submitted for individually designed plans; the list includes the changes made by tax statutes and relevant court cases. The cumulative list of changes required for defined contribution plans in 2017 is available in Notice 2017-37, 2017-29 I.R.B. 89.

The well-established procedure for securing determination letters was decimated in 2015. The IRS announced that it no longer had the resources to administer the five-year determination letter cycle for individually designed plans. Effective January 1, 2017, individually designed plans will be reviewed only at the time of initial qualification and at the time of termination.

The IRS will no longer accept "off-cycle" applications for determination letters (applications submitted outside the regular time frame for the cycle). Some plans get transition relief: Cycle A plans can continue to submit determination letter applications between February 1, 2016 and January 31, 2017. The IRS will still audit plans for compliance; therefore, plans will have to be more vigilant than ever to keep up with changes in tax law, because they can no longer obtain determination letters from the IRS stating that their plans are compliant. [Announcement 2015-19, 2015-32 I.R.B. 154. See IRS, *Determination, Opinion and Advisory Letter for Retirement Plans—Staggered Remedial Amendment Cycles*, available at <https://www.irs.gov/Retirement-Plans/Determination-Opinion-and-Advisory-Letter-for-Retirement-Plans-Staggered-Remedial-Amendment-Cycles> (Dec. 29, 2016) (last accessed Feb. 19, 2017), for a summary of the remaining elements of the determination letter program.]

To make up for the reduction in the amount of guidance plans can receive (caused by the reduction in availability of determination letters), the IRS expanded its pre-approved plan program to include defined benefit plans with cash balance features, and defined contribution plans with an Employee Stock Option Plan (ESOP) features. However, union plans and Taft-Hartley multi-employer plans, target benefit plans, plans with 401(h) retiree health accounts, variable annuity plans, and defined benefits plans whose benefit accrual is based on the rate of return of identified assets cannot use pre-approved plans. [Announcement 2015-19, 2015-32 I.R.B. 157. The 2016 annual revision to the determination letter procedure appears at Rev. Proc. 2016-6, 2016-1 I.R.B. 200.]

Notice 2016-3, 2016-3 I.R.B. 278 provides guidance for sponsors of individually designed plans that are in controlled groups that previously made Cycle A elections (i.e., Rev. Proc. 2007-44 permission for controlled group to elect multiple plans having Cycle A as their five-year amendment cycle). If the election was made by January 31, 2012, the sponsors can submit determination letter applications in the Cycle A submission period, between February 1, 2016 and January 31, 2017. Notice 2016-3 voids the expiration dates on determination letters obtained before January 4, 2016.

An employer that wanted to convert an existing individually designed plan into a pre-approved defined contribution plan could apply for a determination letter between January 1, 2016 and April 30, 2017. [Haynes and Boone LLP, *Additional Guidance Regarding Determination Letter Program Changes* (Jan. 15, 2016) available at Lexology.com; Lori L. Shannon and Monica A. Novak, *But Wait . . . There's More . . . Additional Revisions to the Employee Plans Determination Letter Program*, Drinker Biddle & Reath LLP (Jan. 19, 2016), available at Lexology.com]

IRS Publication 794, *Favorable Determination Letter* (Nov. 2016) explains the ongoing role of determination letters in providing assurance that a plan is properly qualified. But determination letters generally do not contemplate—and cannot be relied on as proof—whether the plan satisfies the § 401(a)(4) nondiscrimination requirements or the § 410(b) minimum coverage requirements. However, a favorable determination letter proves whether the plan satisfies one of the Code's safe harbors for acceptable plan design. There are many topics on which determination letters will not be issued—for example, whether a plan is a governmental or church plan, or whether disability or medical benefits are subject to § 105 or § 106.

See Rev. Proc. 2016-37, 2016-29 I.R.B. 136 for guidance on the phase-out of the determination letter process. Although in general applications will only be granted for initial qualification or termination of a plan, the IRS might accept an application from an individually designed plan that takes a new approach to plan design or is unable to adopt a pre-approved plan. As of January 4, 2016, favorable determination letters do not have an expiration date and expiration dates in earlier letters are no longer operative. Except to the extent that there is a subsequent change in the law, plan sponsors can continue to rely on a favorable letter. For adoption dates on or after January 1, 2017, it is no longer necessary for sponsors of individually designed plans to adopt interim amendments.

A disqualifying provision is a provision (or lack of one) in a new plan, or an amendment to an existing plan, that makes the plan non-compliant with the Code or that falls afoul of a provision that the IRS designates as disqualifying. Rev. Proc. 2016-37 extends the remedial amendment period for disqualifying provisions identified in Rev. Proc. 2007-44 from December 31, 2016 to December 31, 2017.

The IRS announced that it will publish a Required Amendments List each year and will issue an annual Operational Compliance List to explain the changes in qualification requirements that took effect during the year. [Katuri Kaye, *Internal Revenue Service Provides Guidance on the Scope of the New Determination Letter Program for Individually Designed Plans*, Truckerhuss.com (Aug. 4, 2016) (benefitslink.com)]

The first Required Amendments List appears in Notice 2016-80, 2016-52 I.R.B. 918. This initial list contains only one item: restrictions on accelerated distributions from underfunded single-employer, collectively bargained defined benefit plans whose sponsor is bankrupt. [Haynes and Boone LLP, *IRS Publishes First Required Amendments List*, (Dec. 30, 2016), available at Lexology.com]

In mid-2017, the IRS indicated a new direction: the existing programs for master and prototype plans and for volume submitter plans are being combined into a PA (pre-approved plans) program. The IRS wants employers that maintain individually designed plans to transition them to PA plans, although this will not be practical in every case. The PA program is available to both defined contribution and defined benefit plans. The IRS particularly favors the use of standardized PA plans, where the employer adopts the IRS's model documents without alteration. Non-standardized plans are allowed, giving employers some flexibility in plan definitions and administration. New form PA documents can be submitted between October 2, 2017 and October 1, 2018. [Susan E. Stoffer et. al., *IRS Reorganizes Pre-Approved Plan Opinion Letter Program*, Nelson Mullins Riley & Scarborough LLP, July 12 2017, available at Lexology.com.]

An employer will be permitted to suspend or reduce safe harbor contributions to a 401(k) plan if it is running at a loss for the plan year—or if the annual safe harbor notice reserves the right to amend the plan to reduce or suspend the contributions. The notice must be given 30 days in advance, explaining the amendment and its consequences for plan participants. The plan must be amended to provide that nondiscrimination testing will be satisfied for the entire year of the suspension or reduction. [T.D. 9641, 78 Fed. Reg. 68735 (Nov. 15, 2013)]

Although most plan actions that require communication with the IRS are subject to user fees, Rev. Proc. 2012-8, 2012-1 I.R.B. 235 provides that there is no user fee required if a plan makes an automatic change in its accounting period or accounting method if the change is authorized by a revenue procedure, or if the plan adopts a model amendment word-for-word if the model is published in a revenue procedure that states that the amendment should not be submitted to the IRS. A user fee applies when the change in funding or account method is discretionary, not mandatory.

In addition to amendments required for tax purposes, amendments for business purposes are common. To preserve flexibility, it's a good idea for the sponsor to draft the plan reserving the right to amend the plan in the future. Plans can be amended to change or eliminate:

- Ancillary life insurance provided in connection with a pension plan;

- Accident or health insurance that is incidental to a pension plan;

- Some Social Security supplements;

- Availability of plan loans;

- Employees' ability to direct investment of their plan accounts or balances;

- The actual investment options available under the plan;

- Employees' ability to make after-tax contributions to the plan, or to make elective salary deferrals to a plan that is not a 401(k) plan;

- Administrative procedures for the plan (although even after the amendments, participants must have a right to fair redress of their grievances);

- Dates used to allocate contributions, forfeitures, earnings, and account balances.

But any amendment must take into account I.R.C. § 411(d)(6), which forbids amendments that reduce accrued benefits, including early retirement benefits and retirement-related subsidies—even if the employees affected by the change consent to it. Furthermore, the general rule is that protected benefits cannot be reduced or eliminated when a plan is merged or its benefits are transferred to another plan.

However, a plan that is subject to the I.R.C. § 412 minimum funding standard can be amended retroactively to reduce accrued benefits—as long as the plan sponsor can prove to the DOL that the sponsor is undergoing substantial business hardship that mandates a cutback in benefits. The amendments must be adopted within 2½ months of the end of the plan year. They must not reduce anyone's accrued benefit for plan years before the beginning of the first plan year that the amendment applies to. IRS approval is required for amendments of this type, and the DOL may have to be notified.

A plan can be amended to change its vesting schedule as long as no participant loses any nonforfeitable accrued benefits.

A defined benefit plan can lose its qualified status if it adopts an amendment that increases plan liabilities, if the result is that the funded current liability falls below 60% for the plan year. The employer can preserve the plan's qualification by posting "adequate" security. Either the corporation must place cash and securities in escrow, or it must obtain a bond from a corporate security company that is acceptable under ERISA § 412. [See I.R.C. § 401(a)(29) and ERISA § 307; poorly funded plans are also subject to requirements under the Pension Protection Act of 2006]

Plan amendments also are required when the law changes to permit novel forms of benefit plans and new types of plans (e.g., the introduction of Roth IRAs and Roth 401(k) plans). Notice 2013-74, 2013-52 I.R.B. 819 provides guidance on "in-plan Roth rollovers": i.e., a rollover within a 401(k) plan to a designated Roth account in the same plan. The deadline for amending a plan to provide for in-plan Roth rollovers is the last day of the first plan year for which the amendment is effective.

When a plan terminates (see Chapter 17), it must be amended to bring it up to date, if the plan is to retain its tax-qualified status and if participants who receive distributions can make a tax-free rollover to another plan. In mid-2016, the IRS published informal guidance, recommending that the list of required amendments be consulted, and amendments should be made for all changes in the law that the plan had to implement before its termination date. When a plan applies for a determination letter on its termination, the IRS will state whether any additional amendments are required. Plans have the option of filing Form 5310 (Form 5300 for multi-employer plans that are insured by the Pension Benefit Guaranty Corporation (PBGC) and partially terminating plans) to get an IRS determination of whether they will be deemed qualified at the time of termination. However, the necessary amendments must be made before applying for the letter. [John Manganaro, *IRS Emphasizes Amendments Required Before Termination* (plansponsor.com) (Aug. 1, 2016)]

§ 14.03   CHANGE IN PLAN YEAR

The request for change in a retirement plan's plan year is made on Form 5308. IRS approval is automatic as long as:

- No plan year is longer than 12 months. In other words, a year can be broken up into two short years, but two short years can't be consolidated into a long one;

- The change does not have the effect of deferring the time at which the plan becomes subject to changes in the law;

- The plan trust (if any) remains tax-exempt and does not have any Unrelated Business Taxable Income in the short year;

- Legal approval for the change is granted before the end of the short year;

- (Defined benefit plans) The deduction taken for the short year is the appropriate prorated share of the costs for the full year.

§ 14.04   REDUCTION IN FORMS OF DISTRIBUTION

Although it is not permitted to amend a qualified plan in any way that reduces any participant's accrued benefit, it is permissible to amend a plan to eliminate optional forms of benefits (such as periodic payments other than the required Qualified Joint and Survivor Annuity (QJSA)/Qualified Preretirement Survivor Annuity (QPSA)). EGTRRA provides that, for plan years beginning after December 31, 2001, defined contribution plans can eliminate certain forms of benefit payout. See § 12.09 for details.

In particular, if funds are transferred from one qualified plan to another (e.g., in connection with a merger or acquisition), the transferee plan will not be required to provide all the payment options that the transferor plan provided. [See I.R.C. § 411(d)(6)(D) and ERISA § 204(g)(4)] However, if payout forms are eliminated, the plan participants must be allowed to take their distributions in lump-sum form.

To encourage the provision of lifetime income, the PBGC published a final rule for transferring defined contribution plan accounts to defined benefit plans. The rules provide that rollovers will not be lost if the PBGC takes over the plan, even if the maximum guarantee would otherwise apply. Under the five-year phase-in rule, defined benefit increases in the five years prior to termination must be phased in over five years after termination. This rule exists to deter plans from increasing benefits when they know they are in trouble. However, the 2014 final rule exempts rollovers that derive from employee contributions from the five-year phase-in rule. [79 Fed. Reg. 70090 (Nov. 25, 2014)]

In 2004, the Supreme Court ruled [*Cent. Laborer's Pension Fund v. Heinz,* 541 U.S. 739 (2004)] that a plan amendment increasing the varieties of postretirement employment that would cause a suspension of benefit payments violated the anti-cutback rule.

This decision was reflected in final regulations published in 2005. [T.D. 9219, 2005-38 I.R.B. 538] A plan amendment that decreases accrued benefits or places greater restrictions on the right to receive a benefit protected under I.R.C. § 411(d)(6) is in violation of § 411(d)(6) even if the restriction or condition is acceptable under the § 411(a) vesting rules. However, plans can be amended to restrict the availability of benefits accruing after the date of the amendment.

Final and proposed regulations on hybrid defined benefit plans were released in September 2014. The proposed regulations deal with the situation when the plan's interest credit is higher than a market rate of return. A plan will fail § 411 if an amendment decreases a participant's accrued benefit. An amendment that has the effect of eliminating or reducing an early retirement benefit or optional form of benefit for service before the amendment is deemed to reduce the accrued benefit. The proposed regulations note that the rules about market rate of return conflict with the anti-cutback rules, and permit plans whose interest crediting rate is non-compliant to be amended with respect to accrued benefits, to bring the interest crediting rate into line. [T.D. 9693, 2014-41 I.R.B. 596]

In late 2015, the IRS adopted new rules for market rate of return for hybrid pension plans that use a lump-sum-based benefit formula (e.g., cash balance and pension equity plans). Tax law forbids defined benefit plans to use interest rate credits that are higher than a market rate of return. The sponsor of a plan that does not satisfy this requirement is allowed to adopt an acceptable rate without violating the anti-cutback rule. The new rules generally apply to amendments made between September 18, 2014, and the first day of the first plan year that begins on or after January 1, 2017. [T.D. 9743, 2015-48 I.R.B. 697 and 80 Fed. Reg. 70680 (Nov. 16, 2015); see John Manganaro, *Final Market Rate of Return Rules Adopted for Hybrid Plans*, plansponsor.com (Nov. 13, 2015); see Steptoe & Johnson LLP, *Final Transitional Rules for Hybrid Retirement Plans Released* (Nov. 13, 2015), available at Lexology.com; Morganlewis.com, *Treasury/IRS Publishes Final Hybrid Plan Regulations* (Nov. 2011) (benefitslink.com)]

Plans are not required to issue a 204(h) notice if they are amended to adopt the PPA's interest rates and mortality tables, even if the amendment has the effect of reducing the size of lump-sum distributions. In October 2014, the Society of Actuaries gave final approval to a new set of mortality tables, which were expected to increase the liabilities of the typical pension plan by 4–8% because the tables reflect increased longevity. Plans that adopted interim amendments in the time since the last set of tables was published will experience a smaller increase in their liabilities. [Rob Kozlowski, *Moody's: New Mortality Tables Will Increase Pension Liabilities By $110 Billion*, Pensions & Investments (Nov. 3, 2014) (benefitslink.com)]

Mortality tables are important—and controversial—because they are central to calculating the amount of the employer's contribution to a defined benefit plan. The IRS decided in mid-2017 to delay implementation of the Society of Actuaries' RP-2014 mortality tables until 2018. This was welcome news for sponsors, because it improved plans' funding status and somewhat reduced employer liability. But the auditors of some plans required the RP-2014 tables to be used in the plan's financial statements. [Greg Meila and Justin Teman, *Thought Mortality Was Dead? Considerations for Pensions Given the IRS's Delay in Implementing RP-2014*, Cambridgeassociates.com (June 1, 2017) (benefitslink.com); Michael Katz, *IRS' Delay in Implementing Mortality Tables Affects Pension Decisions*, ai-cio.com (June 15, 2017) (benefitslink.com)]

In mid-2015, the IRS adopted a new policy, forbidding "lump-sum windows" (offers of lump sums to employees or retirees who agree to accept the lump sums instead of getting an ongoing stream of pension payments) to retirees who are receiving pension payments and have reached age 70½. The new policy's effective date is July 9, 2015. The IRS says that sponsors who engage in "pension de-risking" by offering lump-sum windows (thereby eliminating the obligation to continue administering plan payments in the future) have treated the right to convert current annuity to immediate lump sum as an increase in benefits. But as of July 9 the IRS says the only permitted benefit increases are those that increase ongoing annuity payments, and acceleration of payments is forbidden. However, the new policy does not apply to lump sum risk-transfer programs that were in place before July 9, 2015. [Notice 2015-49, 2015-30 I.R.B. 79; see Rebecca Moore, *IRS Announces Halt to Certain Lump-Sum Offerings*, plansponsor.com (July 10, 2015)]

Because IRS regulations permit a plan to be amended to eliminate provisions permitting the transfer of benefits between and among defined benefit and defined contribution plans, both the First and Ninth Circuits have ruled that DHL did not violate the anti-cutback rule by forbidding transfers. A plaintiff claimed that the amendment should not have been allowed because the total benefit from both plans was lower than if he had been allowed to transfer funds from the defined contribution plan. The Ninth Circuit held that there was no violation because the amendment did not reduce accrued benefits in the profit-sharing plan. The amendment did not change the formula for calculating benefits, which has always been based on final average compensation and years of service. The accrued benefit of both the profit sharing and retirement income plan remained the same. The Ninth Circuit found that the amendment did not eliminate an optional form of benefit; although transfer from the profit-sharing plan is an optional form of benefit it was not modified by the amendment. Participants retained the right to transfer the profit-sharing account balance to any eligible plan—but the retirement income plan could not accept it. [*Andersen v. DHL Retirement Pension Plan*, 766 F.3d 1205 (9th Cir. 2014); *Tasker v. DHL Retirement Sav. Plan*, 621 F.3d 34 (1st Cir. 2010) is the First Circuit's interpretation of the same transaction.]

§ 14.05   EGTRRA, CHIPRA, AND PPACA CONFORMING AMENDMENTS

It is common for plans to require amendments to conform to changes in tax and labor law (or to take advantage of additional options that have opened up for employers). Because these rules are often complex, difficult, and expensive to administer, it is common for the IRS to publish rules giving plans additional time to comply.

PPA § 1107 says that a timely plan amendment that eliminates or restricts a protected benefit is not be considered a cutback if the benefit reduction was mandated by § 436. [CCH Pensions & Benefits, *IRS Issues Sample Plan Amendment to Satisfy Code Sec. 436 Rules* (Dec. 14, 2011) (benefitslink.com); Rebecca Moore, *IRS Provides Sample Plan Amendment for Underfunded Pension Plan Limitations*, plansponsor.com (Nov. 29, 2011)]

PPACA compliance, at least until the effective date of any repeal plan that becomes law, requires the adoption of a number of plan amendments:

- Enrollment of persons under 19 without pre-existing condition limitations;

- Coverage of employees' dependent children to age 26, whether or not they are students or married, and whether or not they are tax dependents of the employees;

- Elimination of lifetime limits on essential health benefits (guidance has not yet been issued to define "essential," so plans must use a good-faith reasonable interpretation of the term);

- Restrictions on annual limits on essential health benefits; since 2012, the limit must be at least $1.25 million;

- Elimination of retroactive terminations of coverage;

- Amending FSAs, HRAs, and HSAs to eliminate reimbursement of the cost of over-the-counter drugs unless the participant has a prescription.

Non-grandfathered plans must be amended to provide the following:

- Coverage of some preventive services without cost sharing;

- Free choice of primary care provider (who can be a pediatrician for children enrolled in the plan); women can see an OB/GYN without prior authorization or referral;

- Emergency services must be covered without prior authorization, and emergency services must receive the same coverage whether in or out of network;

- The new external claims review process;

- The requirement of not discriminating in favor of highly compensated employees.

[Christy Tinnes and Brigen Winters, *A 2011 Plan Amendment Checklist*, Groom Law Group, plansponsor.com (Oct. 12, 2010)]

§ 14.06   ERISA 204(h) NOTICE

The plan administrator has a duty to notify employees when a defined benefit plan (or any other plan that is subject to the minimum funding requirement) is amended in a way that significantly reduces the rate at which future benefits will accrue. In effect, this is an early warning system that signals to employees that their eventual pensions may be smaller than anticipated.

EGTRRA supplements the rules found at ERISA § 204(h) with a comparable Internal Revenue Code provision, I.R.C. § 4980F, which also imposes an excise tax on failure to make the required notification. See 67 Fed. Reg. 19714 for additional Proposed Regulations on this topic and T.D. 9052, 2003-19 I.R.B. 879 for final regulations.

The notice must be understandable to the average plan participant, and must give enough information for him or her to understand approximately how much his or her benefit entitlement will be reduced by the amendment. See also Proposed Regulations, 69 Fed. Reg. 13769 (Mar. 24, 2004) for eliminating redundant optional forms of benefits within a "family" of defined benefit payment options.

If the plan is significantly underfunded, and therefore is subject to restrictions on benefit accruals, payments, or shutdown benefits, the Pension Protection

Act of 2006 (Pub. L. No. 109-280; PPA) requires the plan administrator to give written or electronic notice to plan participants within 30 days of the point at which the restriction takes effect.

§ 14.07 AMENDMENTS TO A BANKRUPT SPONSOR'S PLAN

Under Bankruptcy Code § 522, funds held in a qualified plan are protected from the plan sponsor's creditors—but only if the plan had a favorable determination letter in effect at the time of filing of the bankruptcy petition.

The general rule is that plan benefits may not be increased while the plan sponsor is a bankruptcy debtor. [See I.R.C. § 401(a)(33)] Amendments are forbidden if the plan's liabilities rise because of the benefit increase, or because of a change in the rate of accrual or nonforfeitability of benefits. However, amendments that take effect after the effective date of the plan of reorganization are allowed. So are amendments to plans, whose funded current liability percentage is 100% or more, or amendments approved by the IRS, or amendments required to maintain compliance with tax law changes.

The Bankruptcy Abuse Prevention and Consumer Protection Act (BAPCPA), Pub. L. No. 109-8, the bankruptcy reform legislation adopted in 2005, alters the treatment of retirement plans in bankruptcy. Bankruptcy Code § 1114, as amended, prevents a Chapter 11 debtor from terminating or modifying retiree welfare benefits without negotiating with retiree representatives. Benefits must be maintained unless the bankruptcy court approves a change. In addition, the court can set aside amendments to a retiree benefit plan made within 180 days before a bankruptcy filing unless the court finds that it is clearly equitable to modify the plan. The Third Circuit required strict compliance with § 1114, so even though the employer retained the right to amend its plan, it could not terminate retiree health benefits while the company was pursuing a bankruptcy reorganization. [*IUE-CWA v. Visteon Corp.*, 612 F.3d 210 (3d Cir. 2010)]

Also note that, even if the plan's sponsor is not bankrupt, the Pension Protection Act of 2006 (PPA) restricts amendments that increase benefits at a time when the plan is significantly underfunded.

In March 2011, the PBGC proposed a rule to amend its regulation dealing with benefits payable in terminated single-employer plans. The rule implements PPA § 403, which says that the phase-in period for the guarantee of benefits that are contingent on an "unpredictable contingent event" (UCE; the regulation gives the example of a plant shut-down) begins no earlier than the date of the event itself. The rule was necessary because PBGC's guarantee of new pension benefits and benefit increases phases in over a five-year period starting with the later of the date of adoption or the effective date of the change. (This rule was adopted to protect the PBGC against obligations that would be created by plans that knew they were going to terminate adopting new benefits.) The PPA added a new section, ERISA § 4022(b)(8), phasing in the guarantee as if the amendment creating an unpredictable contingent event benefit was adopted on the date of the event, rather than the (usually earlier) date of the plan amendment. The net effect is that the guarantee for benefits that arise from unpredictable contingent events that occur within five years of plan termination is probably lower than the guarantee that would have been available under the pre-PPA law. [PBGC Proposed Rule RIN 1212-AB18, 76 Fed. Reg. 13304 (Mar. 11, 2011)]

In mid-2014, the PBGC published final regulations on the phase-in period for guarantee of benefits contingent on occurrence of a UCE, providing that the phase-in rules apply as if the plan amendment creating a benefit for the UCE was adopted on the date of the UCE rather than the date of the amendment. That is to say, the guaranteed benefits are lower for a UCE within five years of termination than they would have been before the PPA. A Unpredictable Contingent Event Benefit (UCEB) is a benefit triggered solely by a UCE. The most common UCEB is a full retirement benefit granted earlier than it would have been available absent the UCE. The 2014 final regulations give examples, such as a facility that engages in sequential layoffs or closes in a series of steps. Because this is a PPA-related provision, the regulations are effective for UCEBs payable as a result of UCEs occurring after July 26, 2005. [77 Fed. Reg. 25667 (May 6, 2014)]

Certain single-employer defined benefit plans can be amended, starting August 31, 2012, to eliminate some optional forms of benefits without violating the anti-cutback rule, if the plan sponsor is a bankruptcy debtor; the plan is not fully funded; and the bankruptcy court and the PBGC agree that the amendment is necessary. The benefit form can only be eliminated if the PBGC and bankruptcy court determine that, unless the optional form of benefit is eliminated, the plan will have to go through a distress or involuntary termination. The PBGC must also determine that the plan's assets are insufficient to pay guaranteed benefits. If the sponsor uses these regulations to eliminate an optional form of benefit and the plan does not offer other options that have substantial survivor benefits, the sponsor can add more options to provide survivor benefits, as part of the amendment that eliminates the lump-sum distribution option. The entire amendment will be considered in determining if the amendment complies with § 436(c) requirements. [T.D. 9601, 77 Fed. Reg. 66915 (Nov. 8, 2012)]

§ 14.08   ISSUES HIGHLIGHTED BY THE IRS

IRS's Retirement Plans division has identified a group of issues that frequently require plan amendments. These issues often prevent the IRS from closing a case until the issues are resolved to the agency's satisfaction:

- Plans that do not reflect the final regulations under § 415, see Notice 2007-3

- Plans that do not include the required language about age and form adjustments (e.g., actuarial adjustments) if a defined benefit plan's benefit begins before age 62 or after age 65, or if the benefit is not payable as a straight life annuity and the benefit does not conform to § 417(e)(3)

- Defined contribution plans that use the correction methods for excess annual additions as described in the 1981 regulations rather than the 2007 regulations

- Failing to treat some post-severance compensation as § 415 compensation

- Continuing to use plan language calling for placing excess annual additions into a suspense account—this language was removed by the 2007 regulations

- Plans that refer to "separation from service" instead of "severance from employment" when distributions are made to participants for reasons other than severance from employment, death, or disability when the top-heavy ratio is calculated

- (401(k) plans): eligibility for making catch-up contributions is defined by reaching age 50 during the "plan year"—the correct measure is the "taxable year"

- Incorrect calculations of corrections of ADP [anti-discrimination testing] failures

[See IRS, *Determination, Opinion and Advisory*, <https://www.irs.gov/Retirement-Plans/Recurring-Plan-Issues-Found-in-Determination-Case-Review> (revised Apr. 19, 2016) (last accessed Feb. 19, 2017)]

CHAPTER 15

ENFORCEMENT AND COMPLIANCE ISSUES FOR QUALIFIED PLANS

§ 15.01   INTRODUCTION

The underlying purpose of the Employment Retirement Income Security Act (ERISA), and of various later pieces of legislation, is to make sure that plan participants and their beneficiaries receive the promised benefits. Therefore, the focus of enforcement is to make sure that plans remain sound, and that participants and beneficiaries do not fall victim to outright fraud, mistake, negligence, poor administration, or declines in the sponsoring company's financial fortunes. Certain types of transactions are prohibited—although "prohibited transaction exemptions" can be obtained in cases where payment of benefits is not placed at real risk. [See § 15.15[C]]

Fiduciary conduct is examined on two levels. Fiduciaries must satisfy their affirmative obligations (to choose proper investments for the plan; to diversify investments unless diversification itself is imprudent; to maintain proper liquidity; to obtain a reasonable yield on plan investments; and to make proper administrative decisions). They are also forbidden to engage in prohibited transactions. In addition to private suits by participants and beneficiaries, the Department of Labor (DOL) and the IRS carry out administrative enforcement efforts and become involved in litigation about plan compliance and participant and beneficiary rights. At the end of the Obama administration, efforts were made to extend the categories of businesses that would be treated as fiduciaries. At the beginning of the Trump administration, efforts were made to reverse these rules.

A pension plan is a legal entity that can sue or be sued under ERISA Title I. [See ERISA § 502(d)] Unless somebody is found liable in an individual capacity, the plan is responsible for paying all money judgments.

An ex-executive at Booz Allen Hamilton sued to recover more than $21 million he claimed he would have received for selling his stock if he had not been forced to retire before a Booz Allen Hamilton division was sold to another company. The Ninth Circuit dismissed the suit, holding that the stock rights plan was not covered by ERISA: it was not designed to provide deferred or retirement income, its purpose was to meet the firm's capital needs and give executives an incentive to remain with the company. [*Rich v. Shrader*, 823 F.3d 1205 (9th Cir. 2016), *cert. denied*, 137 S. Ct. 627 (2017); see Carmen Castro-Pagan, *Booz Allen Executive's $21M ERISA Claim Gets Booted*, bna.com (May 25, 2016) (benefitslink.com). Rebecca Moore, *Court Finds Equity Compensation Plan Not an ERISA Plan*, plansponsor.com (June 30, 2016). The Third, Fifth, and Eighth Circuits have reached similar conclusions.]

Because the management of plan assets for the sole benefit of participants and beneficiaries is so central to plan operation, the identification, duties, and liabilities of fiduciaries are central to plan enforcement.

ERISA § 402(a)(1) requires all plans either to have a named fiduciary, or to explain in the plan document how fiduciaries will be selected. Under ERISA § 411, a convicted felon is not permitted to serve as plan administrator, fiduciary, officer, trustee, custodian, counsel, agent, consultant, or employee with decision-making authority for 13 years after his or her conviction or the end of his or her prison term, whichever comes later.

Asserting that someone has breached fiduciary duties depends on being able to characterize that party as a fiduciary. Furthermore, the party must have been acting in a fiduciary capacity at the time. In 1995, in a welfare benefit plan case, the Supreme Court said that plan sponsors are generally free to amend or terminate welfare plans. In 1999, the Supreme Court extended this principle to pension plans and made it clear that, when they amend a plan, sponsors are acting as the settlers of the plan trust and not as fiduciaries of the plan.

Citing these cases, the Second Circuit abrogated some of its former decisions and held that employers and plan sponsors are not acting as fiduciaries when they modify, adopt, or amend plans—including multi-employer plans. The suit was brought on behalf of ex-participants and beneficiaries of a union pension and welfare fund. The plaintiffs wanted to recover assets that they claimed were wrongfully depleted by improper plan amendments that violated fiduciary duty. [*Janese v. Fay*, 692 F.3d 221 (2d Cir. 2012); see *Curtiss-Wright v. Schoonejongen*, 514 U.S. 73 (1995); *Lockheed v. Spink*, 517 U.S. 882 (1999)]

Breach of fiduciary duty claims is a very active area of litigation. There are many arguments that the employer and other defendants can raise:

- ERISA preemption;
- Plaintiff's lack of standing to sue;
- Suing the wrong defendant(s);
- Bringing suit after the statute of limitations has run;
- Demand for improper relief—e.g., seeking legal relief when only equitable relief is available; seeking individual relief when relief must be sought on behalf of the plan as a whole.

Courts have come up with many different answers to the question of who is the proper defendant in an ERISA case. ERISA § 502(a)(1)(B) says that a civil action may be brought by a participant or beneficiary to collect benefits under the plan—but does not say who the participant or beneficiary can sue. Section 502(d)(2) says that a money judgment against a plan is enforced only against the plan, unless another person is individually liable. In cases of benefit denial, the plan administrator is the proper defendant. ERISA § 3(16) says that the plan sponsor is the plan administrator, unless the terms of the plan say otherwise. If the plan designates an administrator, then it may be necessary to sue the designated administrator and not the employer—unless the employer has actual control over the operations of the plan.

Depending on the court and the fact situation:

- Only the plan as entity can be sued;

- The plan can be sued, but so can other parties;

- The formal administrator of the plan can be sued;

- A "de facto" plan administrator can be sued, even if he, she, or it is not formally designated as plan administrator, on the basis of control over the plan;

- Plan fiduciaries, including administrators, can be sued;

- An insurer can be sued (perhaps only if there is no plan or plan administrator that could be held liable).

[Terry Price, *Federal Court Rulings Identify Employers as Liable Party in ERISA Benefits Action*, Employee Benefit News (Sept. 15, 2006) (benefitslink .com)]

There is a circuit split as to whether claims administrators can be sued to recover benefits. Some decisions say that only the plan, the plan administrator, and perhaps the sponsor can be sued. In late 2015, the Supreme Court refused to hear a Ninth Circuit case about whether health plan claims administrators are proper defendants in ERISA benefits suits. [*Spinedex Physical Therapy USA v. United Healthcare of Ariz.*, 770 F.3d 1282 (9th Cir. 2014), *cert. denied*, 136 S. Ct. 317 (2015)]

The Supreme Court ruled in favor of an employer, acting both as plan sponsor and administrator, that terminated pension plans by purchasing annuities for participants. The union representing the company's employees urged that, instead, the company's plans should be merged into the union's multi-employer plan. The Supreme Court ruled that a bankrupt company does not have a fiduciary duty to consider the merger option. It did not violate ERISA for the company to put the plan through a standard termination and then purchase annuities to cover the payment obligations: terminating the plan in that manner ended the applicability of ERISA to the plan's assets and the employer's obligations. [*Beck v. PACE Int'l Union*, 551 U.S. 96 (2007)]

See § 15.09[C] for the crucial 2011 decision in *Amara v. CIGNA*, discussing the remedies available under ERISA § 502.

The final regulations under Code § 415, published in the Federal Register on April 4, 2007 (72 Fed. Reg. 16878) state that annual additions to the plan, for purposes of computing the § 415 limit, do not include payments made to the plan to restore losses due to a fiduciary's action or failure to act that could have been penalized under ERISA or any other applicable law as breaches of fiduciary duty.

Note that the Pension Protection Act of 2006 imposes a penalty of up to $100,000 and/or 10 years' imprisonment for coercive interference with rights under ERISA.

Employee Benefits Security Administration, part of DOL, is empowered to take enforcement action for ERISA violations. DOL's fact sheet about EBSA's 2016 ERISA enforcement activities shows more criminal enforcement and less civil than in 2015. Informal complaint resolution was actively pursued, leading to two years in a row of increased monetary recoveries in 2015 and 2016. In fiscal 2016, DOL, in conjunction with the Department of Justice, closed 333 criminal investigations, 20% more than in 2015. Sixty-seven criminal investigations were closed with results in 2015, rising to 75 in 2016. But the numbers of civil investigations closed, and civil investigations closed with a result, declined in 2014, 2015, and 2016; there were 2,002 civil investigations closed in 2015, 1,356 with results. EBSA monetary recoveries were $91.2 million in 2015, immensely increasing to $81.2 million in 2015; about half of the monetary recovery was attributable to the informal complaint resolution system. [Eversheds Sutherland .com, *Legal Alert: 2016 in Review: ERISA Criminal Enforcement Rises, Civil Enforcement Falls* (Feb. 28, 2016) (benefitslink.com)]

In 2010, the Supreme Court ruled that ERISA plaintiffs who sue under § 502(g)(1) can be awarded attorneys' fees even if they are not the prevailing party in the suit, because that section of ERISA gives the district court discretion to award attorneys' fees to either party. (This is in contrast to § 502(g)(2), a suit alleging that contributions to a multi-employer plan are delinquent; § 502(g)(2) limits fee awards to plaintiffs who obtain a judgment in favor of the pension plan.) This decision makes it likely that more pension plans will have to pay attorneys' fees to plaintiffs who achieve a degree of success in challenges to the plan. [*Hardt v. Reliance Ins. Co.*, 560 U.S. 242 (2010)]

Hardt's five-factor test for awarding attorneys' fees to a plan participant who wins an ERISA case focuses on the degree of success on the merits; the extent to which the opponent was culpable or acted in bad faith; the opponent's capacity to pay a fee award; the deterrent effect that the award would have to prevent similar conduct by others; if the plaintiff established an important point of ERISA law or benefited all of the beneficiaries of the plan; and the relative strength of the parties' positions. The Second Circuit held that it was error for the district court to consider only the degree of the insurer's bad faith in denying a claim, rather than all the factors. [*Donachie v. Liberty Life Assurance Co. of Boston*, 745 F.3d 41 (2d Cir. 2014)]

The First Circuit held that a plaintiff had achieved some degree of success on the merits, the standard under *Hardt*, and, therefore, was entitled to an award of attorneys' fees. The *Hardt* court did not decide whether a remand order, by itself, is sufficient to justify a fee award. The Sixth Circuit, and district courts in California, Massachusetts, and Alabama have said that it is. But district courts in Colorado, Michigan, and Florida disagree. [*Gross v. Sun Life Assurance Co. of Canada*, 763 F.3d 73 (1st Cir. 2014)]

§ 15.02 WHO IS A FIDUCIARY?

In general legal terms, a fiduciary is anyone responsible for another party's money or property. Fiduciaries have a legal duty to behave honestly and conscientiously, and to avoid promoting their own self-interest at the expense of the owner of the assets.

Many types of people who deal with pension and benefit plans are considered fiduciaries under ERISA—including some people who do not think of themselves in that way or do not understand their responsibilities and potential liabilities.

Fiduciary liability extends far beyond embezzlement and other criminal acts. It is even possible for one fiduciary's mistake or wrongdoing to get a group of other fiduciaries into trouble.

An individual, business, or institution that deals with a plan becomes a fiduciary whenever, and to the extent that, he or she:

- Exercises any discretionary authority (i.e., is able to make decisions) or control over the management of the plan;

- Exercises any authority (even if it is not discretionary) over the management and disposition of plan assets. The distinction is made because the greatest potential for abuse exists when money is at stake;

- Receives direct or indirect compensation for giving the plan investment advice about its assets;

- Has any discretionary authority or responsibility for day-to-day plan administration (as distinct from plan management).

In other words, if a plan hires attorneys, accountants, or actuaries to provide advice, those professionals will usually not become fiduciaries of the plan, because they do not control the direction that the plan takes. They merely provide technical information that the administrator and other fiduciaries use to make decisions.

Just having custody of plan assets doesn't necessarily make the custodian a fiduciary, so a law firm did not become a fiduciary by acting as an escrow agent for funds belonging to one of its clients. (The issue arose when a partner in the law firm embezzled some of the money.) [*Burtch v. Ganz (In re Mushroom Trans. Co. Inc.*), 382 F.3d 325 (3d Cir. 2004)] A custodian that transfers retirement plan assets at the direction of plan trustees is not a fiduciary, and is not liable under ERISA for the plan's losses, merely because it had check-writing authority. The custodian did not exercise authority or control over the assets. [*Erickson v. ING Life Ins. & Annuity Co.*, 731 F. Supp. 2d 1057 (D. Idaho 2010)]

■ **TIP:** If a professional adviser is not a fiduciary, ERISA probably will not preempt state-law malpractice suits brought by the plan.

Similarly, a stockbroker who simply executes the fiduciaries' orders to adjust the plan's investment portfolio is not a fiduciary—but an investment manager who has a role in setting the plan's investment policy is very definitely a fiduciary.

The Ninth Circuit held that being a fiduciary for ERISA purposes does not necessarily entail being a fiduciary as defined by Bankruptcy Code § 523(a)(4), the Bankruptcy Code provision that prevents bankruptcy discharge of debts for fiduciary fraud. [*Hunter v. Philpott*, 373 F.3d 873 (9th Cir. 2004)]

ERISA says that if the employer responsible for maintaining a defined benefit plan is a member of a controlled group, all members of the group are jointly and severally liable for funding the plan. If the sponsor can no longer pay the benefits, the Pension Benefits Guaranty Corporation (PBGC) can terminate the plan and make the sponsor and its controlled group pay the unfunded benefit liabilities. Under ERISA, once the plan is terminated, all parties except the PBGC are limited in relief they can obtain from either the current or former controlled group. The PBGC can get legal or equitable relief against the controlled group for failure to fund the plan; any other party can only get equitable relief.

The Eleventh Circuit ruled that a corporate employer undergoing bankruptcy reorganization cannot pursue an action for the benefit of its bankruptcy estate (and its unsecured creditors) against the employer's former owner for liabilities arising from the termination of a pension plan. The Eleventh Circuit accepted the bankruptcy trustee's contention that the paper company's ex-owner's principal purpose for selling the company was evasion of liability if the PBGC terminated the pension plan. The Eleventh Circuit said that the owner and other members of the controlled group would be treated as members of the controlled group at the time the plan terminated on March 1, 2004.

A Third-Party Administrator (TPA) can be considered an ERISA fiduciary even if it does not have discretionary control over the assets of the health plan it administered; the statutory language is "any authority or control." The Sixth Circuit held that a TPA's authority to write checks on the plan's account (which continued to be exercised to pay the TPA's fees even after the contract with the plan sponsor ended) provided the necessary degree of authority or control to impose liability after the sponsor company went bankrupt and many employees had unpaid medical bills. [*Briscoe v. Fine*, 444 F.3d 478 (6th Cir. 2006)]; on remand, the Western District of Kentucky held that the administrative services contract made the employer, not the plan, responsible for paying the TPA's fee, so it was a breach of fiduciary duty for the TPA to pay itself out of plan assets. It was also a breach of fiduciary duty to submit the Comprehensive Omnibus Budget Reconciliation Act (COBRA) premiums and funded claims reserve to the employer, which the TPA knew was in bad financial shape and likely to appropriate the money—which belonged to the plan and the plan participants, not the employer. [*Briscoe v. Preferred Health Plan, Inc.*, Civil Action No. 3:02CV-264-S, 2008 WL 4146381 (W.D. Ky. Sept. 2, 2008)]

A TPA hired as a health plan claims administrator to pay medical providers misappropriated the money. Many claims were not paid. The TPA had agreements to pay claims under self-insured ERISA health benefit plans funded by both employer contributions and employee payroll deductions. An employer discovered that funds were not accounted for and claims were not paid and sued the TPA. The Sixth Circuit held that a TPA becomes a fiduciary when it exercises practical control over the funds of an ERISA plan, even if its contract disclaims fiduciary status. Misappropriating plan assets violates the duty to act solely in the interests of participants. [*Guyan Int'l Inc. v. Professional Benefits Adm'rs Inc.*, 689 F.3d 793 (6th Cir. 2012)]

The Seventh Circuit imposed successor liability for withdrawal from a multi-employer pension plan on the purchaser of a business, despite lack of specific notice of the liability or the amount of liability. Under general common-law successor liability principles, an asset purchaser is not liable for the seller's debts and liabilities. However, both the Supreme Court and the Seventh Circuit have imposed liability in employment contexts when the successor was aware of the claim prior to the acquisition and there was substantial continuity of business. Under the Multiemployer Pension Plan Amendments Act (MPPAA), when an employer withdraws from a multi-employer plan, the sponsor calculates the amount of withdrawal liability and informs the employer as soon as possible to request payment. If the employer withdraws from the plan before selling its assets, the extent of liability is known before the sale. The Seventh Circuit said that, in enacting the MPPAA, Congress intended to prevent the withdrawing employer's share of unfunded vested benefits from being shifted to the other employers in the plan. In this case, the purchaser could have negotiated a lower price to reflect the potential withdrawal liability payment. [*Tsareff v. ManWeb Servs., Inc*, 794 F.3d 841 (7th Cir. 2015)]

The Ninth Circuit agreed with the Seventh Circuit that a successor company can be liable for the predecessor's MPPAA withdrawal liability. The asset purchaser was found liable for the predecessor's ERISA withdrawal liability even though the asset purchase agreement expressly disclaimed liability. The Ninth Circuit implied that successor liability could apply outside the context of asset sales. The Ninth Circuit said that the most important factor is substantial continuity of business owners, as measured by revenue rather than by the number of customers who carried over to the new business. (In bankruptcy cases, Bankruptcy Code § 363 may provide some protection against claims of successor liability.) [*Resilient Floor Covering Pension Trust Fund Bd. of Trustees v. Michael's Floor Covering, Inc.*, 801 F.3d 1079 (9th Cir. 2015)]

[A]   2010 and 2015-2016 DOL Proposals

In late 2010, DOL proposed the first update to the definition of "fiduciary" since shortly after ERISA was enacted. DOL sought to restore the simple two-part test for fiduciary status, removing the requirements of a mutual under-standing; that advice be given on a regular basis; and that it be a primary basis for investment of the plan assets. Under the 2010 proposal, a fiduciary is a party that renders investment advice about any plan assets (or has any authority or respon-sibility to do so) and receives direct or indirect compensation for the advice. [FR Doc 2010-26236, 75 Fed. Reg. 65263 (Oct. 22, 2010)] These rules were extremely unpopular with commenters and were withdrawn.

The next attempt was made in mid-2015, when DOL issued a Notice of Pro-posed Rulemaking (NPRM) extending the definition of fiduciary with the inten-tion of protecting retirement savers from kickbacks, hidden fees, and conflicts of interest that reduce the value of their accounts. The DOL said that this NPRM is superior to the 2010 proposal because the 2015 rule reflects input from stake-holders. The 2015 proposal imposes a duty on all investment advisers (whether or not they are regulated by the SEC) to work under a fiduciary standard, acting with care, skill, and prudently, and to avoid or at least disclose conflicts of interest. Fiduciary failure to act in the client's best interest can be penalized by DOL enforcement action, and also by IRS excise taxes on transactions that were based on advice that was not objective. The proposal exempts taking purchase orders for securities; imparting generalized financial education; and giving sales pitches to other plan fiduciaries who are financially knowledgeable. [DOL, *Conflict of Interest Proposed Rule*, 80 Fed. Reg. 21927 (Apr. 20, 2015)]

When ERISA was adopted in 1975, fiduciary rules and a ban on self-dealing were included in the Internal Revenue Code, with the result that the DOL and the IRS had separate similar regulations. In 1978, an agreement was made to give the DOL jurisdiction to issue regulations covering both qualified plans and IRAs, under both ERISA and the Code. Between 1975 and mid-2016, the DOL used a five-part test deriving from ERISA § 3(21) to determine who was a fidu-ciary: for example, advice had to be given on a regular basis, with the mutual understanding that the advice is the primary basis for an investment decision. Early in this period, there were more defined benefit than defined contribution plans. The defined contribution plans that existed usually did not allow partici-pants to direct their investments—whereas this is now the norm.

The DOL published proposed regulations in April 2016 about who is a fidu-ciary when giving investment advice to retirement plan sponsors or participants, 81 Fed. Reg. 20945 (Apr. 8, 2016). The DOL issued rules for satisfying the Pro-hibited Transaction Exemption that allows a service provider to be paid for invest-ment advice. DOL's rationale was that IRA investors and plan participants need help to understand their relationships with investors.

Under the DOL final rule, a fiduciary relationship exists if someone recom-mends the purchase, sale, or retention of an investment or recommends how to handle IRA distributions, rollovers, or transfers. But there is only a fiduciary rela-tionship if this action is directed to a specific recipient or is based on the particu-lar needs of a plan, participant, or beneficiary and the recommender (or one of its affiliates) is directly or indirectly compensated for the recommendation or investment. The 2016 rule does not require a regular pattern of advice or a mutual understanding on how the advice will be used, and the advice does not have to be the primary basis for an investment decision for the recommender to be a fiduciary. Whether a communication constitutes a recommendation is assessed based on the facts and circumstances. Education and general communications not tailored to a particular recipient are not advice. Retirement income estimates and questionnaires can be provided without becoming a fiduciary, if the material assumptions behind the documents are disclosed.

The final regulations set out a BIC (Best Interest Contract) standard, which was intended to be phased in between April 10, 2017 and January 1, 2018. The DOL issued a new PTE for BICs, limited to financial institutions such as banks, insurance companies, broker-dealers, and registered investment advisors. A fiduciary is someone who wants to be paid by a third party (for example, under a revenue-sharing arrangement) or to get compensation that varies based on the action taken (e.g., commissions and 12b-1 fees) for retail advice. Retail advice means advice to participants of defined contribution plans who direct their own investments or can make decisions about distributions; it also applies to advice to IRA owners of beneficiaries, to plan fiduciaries who manage under $50 million in assets; or a plan sponsor that does not make investment decisions, or that sponsors a plan with under $50 million in assets. The BIC exemption imposes a "best interests of the client" standard. The BIC exemption requires a written contract. Every financial institution involved must not only adopt procedures to avert conflicts of interest, but must post them online. Specific disclosures are required about the service provider's services, fees, and compensation.

The written contract must include warranties by the financial institution that it will maintain policies to mitigate conflicts. The organization must forbid compensation that is unreasonable vis-à-vis the services provided. The financial institution cannot use bonuses or incentives that encourage advisors to make recommendations that are not in the investor's best interest. The customer must receive a contract or separate written disclosure statement at the beginning of the relationship. The institution's website must be updated at least quarterly and links must be provided to comprehensive disclosures online; fees or compensation must be disclosed, the customer must be given contact information to make complaints; and must be informed the extent to which recommendations are limited to proprietary products and/or products that pay fees to the advisor.

The requirement of a written contract opens up the potential for suits for breach of contract. (ERISA plans were already required to disclose fees, and there is a cause of action against plan fiduciaries even without a written contract.)

Investment contracts must not limit liability for breach, require arbitration in an inconvenient venue, or impose rules that unreasonably limit claims. Class action waivers are forbidden, but waivers of punitive damages are allowed.

The final rule does not directly affect employers that are plan sponsors, because they were already subject to fiduciary standards—but it was expected to alter the business practices of the financial services industry.

The rule was supposed to take effect on June 7, 2016, but DOL agreed to defer applicability of these controversial regulations—first until April 10, 2017 and then a further 60 days, until June 9, 2017. In April 2017, DOL solicited comments to help it review the rule, considering whether it should be modified or even eliminated. [Frost Brown Todd, *The DOL's New Fiduciary Rules: What They Will Mean for Retirement Plan Sponsors* (Sept. 6, 2016) (benefitslink.com); 82 Fed. Reg. 16902 (Apr. 7, 2017). See Lee Barney, *DOL Moves Forward With 60-Day Fiduciary Rule Delay,* plansponsor.com (Apr. 5, 2017)]

On August 9, 2017, DOL notified the District Court for the District of Minnesota that it had submitted amendments to the Office of Management and Budget calling for another year of delay (until July 1, 2019) of the BIC exemption and related prohibited transaction exemptions. [Shearman & Sterling LLP, *DOL Seeks Further Delay of "Fiduciary Rule" Exemptions,* (Aug. 10, 2017) (benefitslink.com)]

The DOL issued initial guidance, in the form of FAQs, in October 2016, noting that any broker-dealer or financial intermediary can become a fiduciary by giving advice about retirement investments, and individual financial advisers and registered representatives employed by financial institutions can become fiduciaries. [Hillel T. Cohn, *DOL Issues First Guidance on Fiduciary Rule*, Morrison & Foerster LLP (Oct. 28, 2016), available at Lexology.com]

Further guidance, on investor rights, accounts that generate commissions, and the responsibilities of advisers, was published on January 13, 2017. DOL said that advisers are not required to shift their clients from commission- to fee-based accounts. An adviser does not have to locate the single best product for their clients—but must employ professional standards of care based on the client's financial interests. [Lisa Beilfuss, *Fiduciary Rule Guidance Unveiled as Implementation Deadline Looms*, WSJ.com (Jan. 13, 2017)]

The April proposal was finalized at the very end of 2016. The old five-part test has been eliminated; it is not necessary that advice be offered on a regular basis for fiduciary obligations to be triggered. Advisers, plan sponsors, and service providers who hold retirement plan education meetings with participants are allowed to discuss the plan's investments (which was previously forbidden). But if a specific fund is mentioned, other comparable funds in the plan must be discussed, without telling participants which to invest in. Health and welfare plans are exempt from the final rule unless they have an investment component (for example, this is true of Health Savings Accounts), in which case a BIC with the plan sponsor or participant is required. [Plansponsor editors, *What Plan Sponsors Should Know About the Final Fiduciary Rule*, plansponsor.com (Dec. 30, 2016)]

In April 2016, the House of Representatives approved a resolution to eliminate the 2016 version of the fiduciary rule; the Senate passed a similar resolution in May. President Obama vetoed the resolution, and Congress did not have enough votes to override the veto. But see below: overturning the rule is an important objective of the Trump administration.

Several lawsuits were filed to challenge the rule by financial services industry groups, alleging that the DOL lacked the authority to promulgate the rule, and the rule harms advisers and their clients by increasing the cost of providing advice. The DOL said that it engaged in a thorough and careful rulemaking process, lasting close to six years, including public hearings, dozens of meetings with stakeholders, and consideration of 3,000 comment letters received on the proposed regulations. [Leslie Scism, *New Rules on Retirement Advice Challenged in Another Lawsuit*, WSJ.com (June 8, 2016); Russell L. Hirschhorn and Benjamin Saper, *Update on Lawsuits Challenging the U.S. Department of Labor's Fiduciary Rule*, Proskauer Rose LLP (Oct. 26, 2016), available at Lexology.com.]

Despite administration and congressional opposition, the rule prevailed in court. The District Court for the District of Kansas agreed with the DOL and denied a preliminary injunction to stop the fiduciary rule. The district court said that Congress gave the DOL the power to adopt the rule. [*Market Synergy Grp. v. DOL*, No. 16-cv-4083 (D. Kan. Feb. 17, 2017)]

On November 4, 2016, the District Court for the District of Columbia not only denied the National Association for Fixed Annuities' request for a preliminary injunction, it granted summary judgment for the DOL. The plaintiffs appealed to the D.C. Circuit, seeking an emergency motion to halt the implementation of the rule pending appeal. [*National Ass'n for Fixed Annuities v. Perez*, No. 16-cv-1035, 2016 U.S. Dist. LEXIS 162428 (D.D.C. Nov. 23, 2016) discussed in John Hilton, *Kansas Judge Rejects DOL Rule Injunction*, insurancenewsnet.com (Nov. 29, 2016) (benefitslink.com); Russell L. Hirschhorn and Benjamin Saper, *DOL Prevails in First Challenge to the Conflict of Interest Rule and Related Exemptions*, Proskauer Rose LLP (Nov. 18, 2016), available at Lexology.com; Jacklyn Wille, *Emergency Request to Halt Fiduciary Rule Filed in Appeals Court*, bna.com (Dec. 1, 2016) (benefitslink.com); John Manganaro, *DOL Fiduciary Rule Wins Another Court Victory*, plansponsor.com (Feb. 9, 2017); Employee Benefits Alert, *Kansas Court Again Upholds Fiduciary Rule as Department of Labor Seeks to Delay Implementation*, Millerchevalier.com (Feb. 22, 2017) (benefitslink.com)]

Early in 2017, the District Court for the Northern District of Texas held that the DOL had the authority under ERISA to implement the fiduciary rule, also holding that the adoption process did not violate the APA, and it was not impermissible to create a new private cause of action. [*Chamber of Commerce v. Hugler*, No. 16-1476, **2017 U.S. Dist. LEXIS 17619** (N.D. Tex. Feb. 8, 2017); see John Manganaro, *DOL Fiduciary Rule Wins Another Court Victory*, plan sponsor.com (Feb. 9, 2017); Daniel R. Kleinman et. al., *Update on DOL Fiduciary Rule Applicability Delay and Litigation*, Morgan Lewis & Bockius LLP (Feb. 10, 2017), available at Lexology.com. The *Hugler* decision was appealed on February 25. See Thinkadvisor.com, *Emergency Request to Block DOL Fiduciary Rule Filed in Texas Court* (Mar. 14, 2017) (benefitslink.com).]

President Trump issued a memorandum on the rule, directed to the Secretary of Labor, on February 3, 2017. The memorandum says that the administration's priorities are to empower Americans to make their own decisions to save for retirement. The memorandum says that the fiduciary rule could significantly alter the receipt of financial advice. The DOL is directed to examine whether the rule impairs access to retirement information and financial advice and to prepare an updated legal and economic impact analysis of the rule. If the Secretary of Labor finds that the rule is disruptive to the retirement services industry, is likely to lead to more litigation and higher prices, or otherwise is inconsistent with administration priorities, he is directed to publish a new rule revising or rescinding the fiduciary rule. [Presidential Memorandum (to Secretary of Labor) on fiduciary duty rule, (Feb. 3, 2017), available at <https://www.whitehouse.gov/briefing-room/disclosures>. See Spender Fane Blog (no title), (Feb. 6, 2017) (benefitslink.com); John Manganaro, *Trump Administration Hits Hurdle in Fiduciary Fight*, plansponsor.com (Feb. 28, 2017)] A commentator said that DOL's cost/benefit analysis was likely to show that implementing the fiduciary rule would increase litigation because the fiduciary rule permits investors to bring class action suits against brokers. Under previous rules, a customer who alleged a violation of the suitability standard (the requirement that brokers only recommend investments that are suitable for the particular client) probably had to arbitrate the claim using the FINRA arbitration system, and could not sue. [Lisa Beilfuss, *As Fiduciary Rule Gets Reviewed, Class-Action Provision Is Under Microscope*, WSJ.com (Mar. 15, 2017)]

DOL announced that it would not take enforcement action under the fiduciary rule during the "gap period" if the extension does not take effect, or if compliance with the rule occurred within a reasonable time. [DOL FAB 2017-01 (Mar. 10, 2017); see Andrew L. Oringer and K. Susan Grafton, *DOL Announces That It Will Not Take Enforcement Action in Regard to Compliance with the New Fiduciary Rule as Potential Repeal or Modification Remains Under Review*, Dechert LLP (Mar. 13, 2017), available at Lexology.com]

Congress did not take action, and the fiduciary rule took effect on June 9, 2017. [Lisa Beilfuss, *"Fiduciary" Rule To Take Effect June 9 With No Further Delay, Labor Secretary Says,* WSJ.com (May 22, 2017); Plansponsor editors, *No More Delays for DOL Fiduciary Rule,* plansponsor.com (May 24, 2017)]

§ 15.03 FIDUCIARY DUTIES

[A] ERISA Requirements

ERISA imposes four major duties on fiduciaries: loyalty, prudence, acting in accordance with the plan documents, and monitoring the performance of parties to whom fiduciary responsibility has been delegated.

The source of the duty of loyalty is the ERISA mandate that plan assets be held for the exclusive benefit of participants and beneficiaries. Once assets have been placed into the plan trust, or used to buy insurance, they can no longer be used for the benefit of the employer.

The duty of prudence requires fiduciaries to behave with the level of care, skill, prudence, and diligence that a hypothetical prudent person would use to handle the same tasks. This hypothetical prudent person is familiar with the plan and its situation—not the "man on the street" who lacks specialized knowledge.

Although trust law requires every asset within a trust to satisfy the prudent person test, DOL Reg. § 2550.404a-1(c)(2) allows the fiduciary to select assets by considering the relevant facts and circumstances, including the role of the individual investment within the portfolio. Relying on expert advice is encouraged, but it does not guarantee that an investment choice will be considered prudent.

ETIs are Economically Targeted Investments that use ESG standards (environmental, social or governance). DOL Interpretive Bulletin 2015-01 discusses the fiduciary process that plan committee (the plan's fiduciaries) should use to assess adding ETIs as plan investments. Although ETIs are not inherently suspect and do not require special scrutiny, DOL says that ESG features can be secondary factors used as tie-breakers in comparing equally prudent investment choices. However, fiduciaries must only select ETIs that are expected to perform as well as investments with similar risk categories. DOL says it's not prudent to accept a lower rate of return than other investments with commensurate rate of risk. [C. Frederick Reish, Bruce L. Ashton and Joshua J. Waldbeser, *"Socially Responsible" Investing Under ERISA: New DOL Guidance* Drinker Biddle (Nov. 18, 2015), available at Lexology.com]

In general, it will not be considered a breach of fiduciary duty to make a mistake in calculations. The Second Circuit rejected a former employee's argument that it was a breach of fiduciary duty for the administrator of a stock option plan to tell her that she could exercise her options after retirement. Not only were the communications not intentionally false, the Second Circuit said that the advice was not even really wrong. The court ruled that, even if there had been an unintentional misstatement about the consequences for non-ERISA stock option plan, of a retirement decision under an ERISA plan, there would not have been a violation of fiduciary duty. [*Bell v. Pfizer*, 626 F.3d 66 (2d Cir. 2010)]

The Ninth Circuit ruled that, in a case where the plaintiff asserted that he had enough years of service to qualify for retirement benefits, and the employer says that he did not have enough service with the employer or its affiliates, the claimant may have the burden of proof if he has at least equal access to the information (such as records of medical treatment to prove disability). But if the defendant has superior access to the data—as was true in this case—the burden shifts to the defendant to produce the evidence. [*Estate of Barton v. ADT Security Servs. Pension Plan*, No. 13-56379 (9th Cir. Apr. 21, 2016); see Rebecca Moore, *Appeals Court Switches Burden of Proof for Benefits Claim*, plansponsor.com (Apr. 25, 2016) Rehearing en banc was denied in September 2016: *Barton v. ADT*

Sec. Servs. Pension Plan, 2016 WL 1612755(9th Cir. Apr. 21, 2016); see Practi-callaw.com Employee Benefits & Executive Compensation, *In the Ninth Circuit, a New Burden of Proof for Employers in Benefits Litigation*, (Sept. 22, 2016) (benefitslink.com)]

The First Circuit held that the benefits sought by the plaintiff were not pro-vided by the terms of the plan document. The plaintiff decided to take early retire-ment based on an e-mail and a letter estimating his benefit at $2,372 a month, but when he actually retired, he was told that his pension was only $570.87. The First Circuit held that materials described as estimates were not plan amendments, and the plain terms of the plan rejected crediting his account with years of service for other employers. [*Guerra-Delgado v. Popular*, 774 F.3d 776 (1st Cir. 2015)]

The Third Circuit ruled that a woman who retired based on alleged misrep-resentations about the pension her husband would receive did not make out a case of breach of fiduciary duty. To prove detrimental reliance, there must be both injury and reasonableness. The plaintiff must have engaged in some action; merely expecting continued benefits is not enough. The wife was not a partici-pant in the plan and the couple's retirement decisions did not change their ben-efits in any way. [*Shook v. Avaya Inc.*, 625 F.3d 69 (3d Cir. 2010]

In mid-2016, the Tenth Circuit held that a pension plan consultant did not violate ERISA by giving the wrong amount when a participant asked how much his pension would be. The participant retired, relying on the $8,444.18 a month figure he was given. Later, the plan told him that he had been overpaid and had to give back $5,000 a month in overpayments. He could not live on the correct $3,653 monthly pension but could not find another job. The Tenth Circuit held that the consultant was not a fiduciary when she made the incorrect calculations: routine calculations carried out as part of a person's job are not discretionary con-trol over the plan, and DOL has issued an interpretive bulletin that plan consult-ants who do not have discretionary authority or provide investment advice are not fiduciaries. [*Lebahn v. Nat'l Farmers Union Uniformed Pension Plan*, No. 828 F.3d 1180 (10th Cir. 2016); see Rebecca Moore, *Consultant Off the Hook for Pro-viding Wrong Benefit Estimate*, plansponsor.com July 21, 2016]

Assets in a rabbi trust (see § 8.01[B][3]) are not protected against creditors' claims when the employer is bankrupt or insolvent. In 2008, when Chrysler was facing bankruptcy, it used $200 million in rabbi trust funds for company opera-tions, depleting the accounts of about 400 retired executives, including former chairman Lee Iacocca. Chrysler's reorganization proceedings did not give them any relief. The retirees sued State Street Bank, the trustee of the top hat plan for special retirement benefits for executives. The Sixth Circuit held that the plain-tiffs could not pursue state-law claims of fraud and fiduciary breach: the claims were preempted by ERISA. ERISA breach of fiduciary duty claims would be futile because the plan offered no bankruptcy protection. The Sixth Circuit held that the plan and trust operated in accordance with the plan documents. [Wilber H. Boies & Andrew C. Liazos, *Second Court of Appeals Win for State Street Bank* *in $200 Million Chrysler "Top Hat Plan" Class Action*, McDermott Will & Emery (Dec. 7, 2016), available at Lexology.com]

[B] Diversification

The general rule is that ERISA requires fiduciaries to diversify unless diversification is imprudent (the fiduciary has to prove this). There is an exception for Employee Stock Option Plans (ESOPs), which are designed to invest in employer stock. Consequently, ESOP fiduciaries do not have a duty to diversify. The non-ESOP fiduciary is supposed to select a balanced portfolio that is responsive to current conditions. The portfolio's liquidity and current return must be considered in light of anticipated needs for cash flow. Fiduciaries are not restricted to a "legal list" of investments, and are permitted to take a certain amount of risk, as long as the risk is reasonable in the context of the entire portfolio.

ERISA § 404(c) offers fiduciaries protection against liability. (It covers qualified defined contribution plans and the portions of defined benefit plans that allow direction of investment of individual accounts.) In general, fiduciaries have a duty to diversify and choose investments prudently, but 404(c) indemnifies them for losses in accounts where the participant exercises independent control over the investment of the account, after choosing from among a broad range of investments.

"Broad range of investments" is defined to mean that the participant has the chance to pick investments that will determine the return on the account, and can diversify to reduce risk. There must be at least three main diversified categories of investment choices offered, with materially different risk and return categories, so that the participant can assemble a portfolio with normal and appropriate risk and return characteristics. Employer stock cannot be made one of the core investments. Participants must be allowed to give investment instructions at least once per quarter—more frequently if market volatility requires.

The participant must have a reasonable opportunity to give instructions to an identified fiduciary, who is required to carry out the instructions as given. (Under limited circumstances, the fiduciary can ignore the instructions—for example, if the instruction would be a prohibited transaction or would subject the plan to taxable income.) Under this safe harbor provision, the fiduciary can hire a third-party service provider to carry out the instructions when it is prudent to do so. The participant is also considered to control the account when the fiduciary makes default investments under the default investment safe harbor—but if the plan does not qualify for the safe harbor, it can be held liable for losses in the value of default investments.

Plans that seek to use the safe harbor must disclose that the plan is using § 404(c) to relieve fiduciaries of liability; must describe the investment options and how to give investment directions; and that additional information is available on request (e.g., the annual operating expenses for each investment option, and how to get copies of prospectuses and financial statements). Item 8a of the Form 5500 asks if the plan or any portion of the plan intends to comply with § 404(c); the form must be signed under penalty of perjury.

Sponsors generally analyze funds into four categories: the default investment; core funds that allow participants to make basic asset allocation decisions; other funds; and special-purposes funds such as company stock or stable value funds. [Octoberthree.com, *The Fiduciary Duty to Monitor—401(k) Plan Investments* (Aug. 12, 2015) (benefitslink.com)] Enhanced diversification rights are mandated by the Pension Protection Act (PPA). In mid-2007, EBSA issued final regulations concerning penalties for plan administrators who fail to inform participants and beneficiaries of their right to diversify out of investments in employer securities. For plan years beginning after December 31, 2006, a civil penalty of up to $100 per day can be imposed under ERISA § 502(c)(7) for failure to provide the notice. [72 Fed. Reg. 44970 (Aug. 10, 2007). The corresponding DOL regulation appears at 72 Fed. Reg. 44991 (Aug. 10, 2007).]

On August 1, 2016, the penalty rose to $131 as a result of the Bipartisan Budget Act of 2015 and rose once again, to $133 as a result of the now-mandatory annual adjustments. [Conduent FYI, *DOL, PBGC and HHS Increase Penalties for Violations* (Feb. 10, 2017) (benefitslink.com)]

T.D. 9484 provides final regulations under Code § 401(a)(35), explicating the PPA's diversification requirements for defined contribution plans that hold publicly traded employer stock. For plan participants who have at least three years of service, their beneficiaries, and the beneficiaries of deceased participants, the plan must allow divestment of employer securities and re-investment in a reasonable menu of choices At least three varied options other than employer stock, each of them diversified, must be offered. Divestment opportunities must be provided at reasonable intervals, at least quarterly. Unless the restriction is required to comply with securities laws, the plan cannot impose conditions on re-investment of employer securities that are not imposed on other investments within the plan. [T.D. 9484, 75 Fed. Reg. 27927 (May 19, 2010)]

The Second Circuit held in 2016 that an investment company and its top manager were fiduciaries of two defined contribution plans maintained by a client. The investment manager was ordered to pay $9.7 million, including $5.3 million in prejudgment interest and disgorgement of $110,000 worth of fees. The court held that the manager breached his fiduciary duty by making an undiversified portfolio of energy stocks the sole assets placed in the plan trust. He did not explain to the sponsor's investment committee what had been transferred, and did not take steps to ensure ongoing prudent asset management. [*Severstal Wheeling Retirement Committee v WPN Corporation*, 659 Fed. Appx. 24 (2d Cir. 2016); see Plansponsor editors, *Investment Manager on the Hook for Poor Retirement Plan Diversification*, plansponsor.com (Sept. 30, 2016)]

[C] Stock-Drop Cases and Other Investment Issues

A "stock drop" suit charges a plan's fiduciaries with breach of duty because they retained employer stock as a plan investment without divulging to participants that the stock had declined in value or become risky (e.g., because of the plan sponsor's involvement in derivatives or other risky financial transactions). Another stock drop allegation is that the employer's stock represents too large a part of the plan's investments, and the plan should have been more diversified. Almost all stock drop cases are dismissed. Stock-drop cases frequently are associated with securities law cases, but ERISA cases are easier to bring because securities law requires proof of "scienter" (an enhanced form of intent). Courts of Appeals usually follow three principles:

- The amount of deference fiduciaries receive depends on the amount of discretion the plan design gives them;

- Mere fluctuations in the price of the employer's stock will not show that the fiduciaries were imprudent to keep the stock in the plan; something else has to be present;

- Possible liability factors include breaches of the duty of loyalty (misrepresenting or concealing material facts).

As of mid-2014, the Third, Fifth, Sixth, Ninth, and Eleventh Circuits had all adopted some version of the *Moench* presumption (named after *Moench v. Robertson*, 62 F.3d 553 (3d Cir. 1995)): that is, the fiduciaries of a plan were presumed to be prudent when they retained employer stock as a plan investment. A drop in the stock price was not enough to rebut the presumption. The courts differed in the stage of the case at which the presumption was applied, and what plaintiffs had to do to rebut the presumption.

However, in June 2014, the Supreme Court rejected the presumption of prudence. [*Fifth Third Bancorp et al. v. Dudenhoeffer*, 134 S. Ct. 2459 (2014). The case was settled in March 2016, for $6 million in benefits to participants. The employer stock fund was frozen, and participants who invested more than 20% of their account in that fund received notices about the importance of diversification. The District Court for the Southern District of Ohio granted preliminary approval of the settlement. *Dudenhoeffer v. Fifth Third Bancorp*, Case No. 1:08-CV-538 (Stipulation of settlement, S.D. Ohio Mar. 15, 2016); see Rebecca Moore, *Famous Fifth Third Stock Drop Suit Reaches Settlement*, plansponsor.com (Mar. 24, 2016).]

Although this is an ESOP case, the Supreme Court held that ESOP fiduciaries have the same duties as other fiduciaries, except that ESOP fiduciaries are not obligated to diversify plan investments, because ESOPs are intended to invest in employer securities. The Supreme Court said that the presumption makes it too difficult for plaintiffs to pursue their suits—and also said that the way for courts to determine the merits of a case is to examine the allegations of the complaint rather than presuming that fiduciaries acted prudently. If the complaint says that the fiduciaries had access to inside information that should have led them to divest the employer stock, the Supreme Court held that the plaintiff must allege an action that the fiduciaries could have taken without violating federal securities laws (which forbid trading on inside information). Sometimes it would be imprudent for fiduciaries to divest, if large sales of the employer's securities would disrupt the market and lead to further depression in the stock price.

At first, it was believed that *Dudenhoeffer* would make it easier to obtain damages in stock drop cases, because the presumption of prudence has been removed. However, this has not been the real-world result, because plaintiffs have seldom succeeded in pleading an alternative action that is considered better. For example, the D.C. Circuit rejected the argument that ESOP trustees failed to understand how risky it was to invest in JC Penney stock. The D.C. Circuit also rejected the argument that, based on publicly available information, the fiduciaries should have known that the price of the stock was so inaccurate that continuing to hold it was an imprudent risk. The D.C. Circuit requires claims of imprudence that rely on publicly available information to be accompanied by special circumstances, such as fraud. [*Coburn v. Evercore,* 844 F.3d 965 (D.C. Cir. 2016); see Plansponsor editors, *D.C. Appellate Court Affirms Employer Win in Stock Drop Suit,* plansponsor.com (Jan. 5, 2017). The Supreme Court refused (137 S. Ct. 583 (2016)) to hear an appeal of *Muehlgay v. Citigroup,* 649 Fed. Appx. 110 (2d Cir. 2016), a subprime mortgage market case where the Second Circuit held that the plaintiffs failed to show special circumstances. See Robert Steyer, *Citigroup 401(k) Stock-Drop Case Won't Be Heard By High Court,* Pionline.com (Dec. 6, 2016) (benefitslink.com).]

In the post-*Dudenhoeffer* environment, it is difficult for plaintiffs to win stock-drop cases. Lehman Brothers, J.P. Morgan Chase, Edison International, IBM, and British Petroleum have all won cases. The British Petroleum case involved the fall in BP's stock after the Deepwater Horizon oil spill. The Fifth Circuit held that stock-drop plaintiffs have the burden of proving an alternative course of action that is so clearly worthwhile that a prudent fiduciary would have to conclude that it would be more likely to help the fund than to harm it. The Fifth Circuit found the plaintiffs' suggestions (disclosing inside information; freezing trades in the employer stock) were inadequate because their probable effect would be to lower the stock price—an outcome that a prudent fiduciary would want to avoid. [*Whitley v. BP, PLC,* 650 Fed. Appx. 194, (5th Cir. 2016); see Jacklyn Wille, *BP Beats ERISA Challenge to Stock Drop in 5th Circuit,* bna.com (Sept. 28, 2016) (benefitslink.com); Rebecca Moore, *BP Stock Drop Suit Sent Back to Lower Court Again,* plansponsor.com Sept. 28, 2016; MorganLewis.com, *Stock-Drop Complaint Based on Insider Information Fails to State a Claim* (Nov. 3, 2016) (benefitslink.com)]

Another ESOP case was resolved in late 2015, when the Sixth Circuit used a "prudent process" standard to assess State Street Bank's handling of the ESOP portion of General Motors' 401(k) plan. Under this standard, a plaintiff calling an ESOP's investment in a publicly traded security imprudent must demonstrate special circumstances to survive a motion to dismiss. The Sixth Circuit found the process to be prudent because State Street repeatedly re-assessed the appropriateness of the investment, discussing it at 40 meetings in a period of less than nine months. [*Pfeil v. State Street Bank & Trust*, 806 F.3d 377 (6th Cir. 2015) Certiorari was denied: No. 15-1199 (June 27, 2016). See Rebecca Moore, *Court's Decision About State Street's Handling of GM Stock Stands*, plansponsor.com (June 27, 2016)]

The Second Circuit found that participants in the Lehman Brothers retirement plan did not prove that retaining employer stock in the plan was a breach of fiduciary duty. The Second Circuit said that, although ESOP fiduciaries are no longer entitled to a presumption of prudence, it is still necessary for plaintiffs to allege special circumstances that would have required fiduciaries to determine, from publicly available information, that the market under- or over-valued a stock. For claims based on non-public information, plaintiffs must plausibly allege an alternative action the fiduciaries could have taken that would have produced better results for the plan. In this case, the plaintiffs did not show that a prudent fiduciary would have thought the plan would benefit from disclosure of non-public information, or from ending purchases of employer stock. [*Rinehart v. Akers (In re Lehman Bros. Secs. & ERISA Litig.)*, 817 F.3d 56 (2d Cir. 2016); see Rebecca Moore, *Third Time's a Charm in Lehman Brothers Stock Drop Suit*, plansponsor.com (June 14, 2016). Certiorari was denied: see John Manganaro, *Lehman Stock Drop Suit Passed Over By Supreme Court,* plansponsor.com (Feb. 23, 2017)]

Despite the general lack of success for plaintiffs, there have been some multi-million-dollar settlements in stock drop cases. The *Dudenhoeffer* decision could have the effect of encouraging settlements, because it means that fewer cases will be dismissed at early stages, so plans and their fiduciaries may be willing to settle to avoid a prolonged, expensive trial. For example, a $9.7 million settlement was reached based on claims that, when Kodak filed for bankruptcy in January 2012, it failed to protect participants from financial loss. The plaintiffs claimed that the company's financial situation was so bad that retaining employer stock as an investment was imprudent. [*In re Eastman Kodak ERISA Litig.*, No. 6:12-CV-06051 (W.D.N.Y., settled 2016); see Rebecca Moore, *Kodak Settles Stock-Drop Suit for Nearly $10M*, plansponsor.com (May 2, 2016)]

Mass Mutual agreed to pay $30.9 million to settle a 2013 class action alleging mismanagement of the 401(k) plan. A proposed class of over 14,000 participants said the plan was subjected to excessive fees and paid too much for proprietary investment options, and the plan's fixed income option was too expensive and too risky. [*Gordan v. Mass. Mutual Life Ins. Co.*, No. 3:13-cv-30184, (D. Mass., motion for preliminary settlement approval filed June 15, 2016); see

Jacklyn Wille, *MassMutual Settles 401(k) Fee Lawsuit for $31M*, bna.com (June 17, 2016) (benefitslink.com)]

Early in 2017, preliminary approval was granted to a $4.5 million settlement under which J.C. Penney was alleged to retain company stock in the plan after this had ceased to be prudent. Penney did not admit liability. [Rebecca Moore, *J.C. Penney to Settle Stock Drop Suit*, plansponsor.com (Jan. 10, 2017)]

In 2008, the Ninth Circuit joined the First, Third, Fourth, Sixth, Seventh, and Eleventh Circuits in holding that former employees who have received a full distribution of their benefits under a defined contribution plan have standing to sue under ERISA to recover losses that they say were caused by breach of fiduciary duty. [*Vaughn v. Bay Envtl. Mgmt.*, 544 F.3d 1008 (9th Cir. 2008); see *Lanfear v. Home Depot, Inc.*, 544 F.3d 1008 (11th Cir. 2008); *Evans v. Akers*, 534 F.3d 65 (1st Cir. 2008); *In re Mutual Funds Inv. Litig.*, 529 F.3d 207 (4th Cir. 2008); *Bridges v. Am. Elec. Power Co.*, 498 F.3d 442 (6th Cir. 2007); *Graden v. Conexant Sys. Inc.*, 496 F.3d 291 (3d Cir. 2007); and *Harzewski v. Guidant Corp.*, 489 F.3d 799 (7th Cir. 2007).]

After *Dudenhoeffer*, the Ninth Circuit revised its *Harris v. Amgen* decision. Previously, the Ninth Circuit reversed dismissal of the case, using the presumption of prudence when investing in company stock. The November 2014 decision still reverses the dismissal and remands, but holds that there is no presumption of prudence for ESOP fiduciaries other than relief from the duty to diversify. The Ninth Circuit held that even though Amgen stock retained value, that did not mean that its value was not artificially inflated during the class period. The defendants argued that divestment would have caused the stock price to collapse, but the Ninth Circuit held that the fiduciaries could have removed the fund as an investment option without harming plan participants; the impact on the stock price was not certain, and removing the fund as a plan investment would not cause liquidation of the fund. [*Harris v. Amgen*, 770 F.3d 865 (9th Cir. 2014)] The Ninth Circuit denied en banc rehearing in *Harris v. Amgen*. Denial of en banc rehearing means that the case returns to the district court for reconsideration in light of *Dudenhoeffer*—and without applying a presumption of prudence. [*Harris v. Amgen*, No. 10-56014 (9th Cir. May 26, 2015); see John Manganaro, *9th Circuit Confirms Stock Drop Remand*, plansponsor.com (June 30, 2015)]

An early 2016 per curiam Supreme Court decision remanded *Amgen* once again, stating that the Ninth Circuit did not apply *Dudenhoeffer* properly. The Supreme Court did not find sufficient facts and allegations in the complaint to state a claim for breach of the duty of prudence, but said that it was up to the district court to decide if the complaint could be amended to satisfy the post-*Dudenhoeffer* standard. [*Amgen v. Harris*, 136 S. Ct. 994 (2016); see Jill Cornfield, *SCOTUS Again Remands Stock Drop Case*, plansponsor.com (Jan. 25, 2016); Plansponsor editors, *Key Recent Decisions in Employer Stock Plan Litigation*, plansponsor.com (Sept. 6, 2016)]

On a related issue, the Sixth Circuit ruled in mid-2012 that a stock-drop plaintiff did not have standing to sue because she could not demonstrate actual injury. She alleged that the company's stock price was artificially inflated because the company failed to disclose its inappropriate tax and lending practices. However, the plaintiff sold over 80% of her company stock holdings at a time when she charged the price was unfairly high—so if there was wrongdoing, she benefited from it rather than being harmed by it. [*Taylor v. KeyCorp.*, 680 F.3d 609 (6th Cir. 2012)]

"Reverse stock drop" suits are also a possibility. After the spinoff of the tobacco business from Nabisco's food business, the spinoff's new 401(k) plan maintained two Nabisco single-stock funds as frozen funds. Participants could retain their existing investments but could not add to them. Eventually, when Nabisco shares were at their lowest point, the funds were divested from the plan, followed by a takeover offer, a bidding war, and record-high stock prices. The fiduciaries were sued for breach of duty (disposing of the stock too quickly, forfeiting potential gains). The district court granted summary judgment for the plan and the fiduciaries, but the Fourth Circuit held that the defendants breached their duty of prudence because they could not show that they acted in the way a majority of prudent fiduciaries would act. The standard is whether fiduciaries perform an appropriate investigation of the value of an investment; apply reasoned processes consistent with what a prudent man acting in the same capacity would do; and monitor to determine whether the decision continues to be in the best interests of participants. [*Tatum v. RJR Pension Inv. Comm.*, 761 F.3d 346 (4th Cir. 2014) Certiorari was denied in mid-2015: No. 14-656, *cert. denied* (June 29, 2015).]

On remand from the Fourth Circuit, the District Court for the Middle District of North Carolina held that the fiduciaries were not personally liable for damages: a hypothetical prudent fiduciary would have divested Nabisco company stock funds from the plan. The district court held that Nabisco stock was depressed by "tobacco taint" and it was not foreseeable that the Nabisco funds' value would increase after the split. [*Tatum v. R.J. Reynolds Tobacco Co.*, No. 1:02CV00373, 2016 WL 660902 (M.D.N.C. Feb. 18, 2016); see Practical Law Employee Benefits & Executive Compensation, *On Remand, Plan Fiduciaries' Decision to Divest Nabisco Stock Fund Found Prudent* (Feb. 23, 2016) (benefit slink.com); see Rebecca Moore, *RJR Handed a New Win in Stock Divestment Decision*, plansponsor.com (Feb. 22, 2016)]

The case returned to the Fourth Circuit in 2017, and the fiduciaries prevailed once again. The Fourth Circuit held that the fiduciaries had breached the duty of procedural prudence, and that the fiduciaries had the burden of proof of causation. But the Fourth Circuit held that the district court had used the wrong legal standard, and sent the case back to the district court yet again to determine if a prudent fiduciary would (not could) have made the same decision as the actual fiduciaries. The Fourth Circuit applied the same standard to initial investment choices and divestment. [*Tatum v. RJR Pension Investment Committee*, 855 F.3d 553 (4th Cir. 2017); see John Manganaro, *RJR Wins Third Appellate Decision in ERISA Case*, plansponsor.com (May 2, 2017); Paul J. Ondrasik Jr. and Edward

Thomas Veal, *"Coulda, Woulda, Shoulda": Fourth Circuit Re-Revisits a Controversial Position on ERISA's Prudence Standard,* Steptoe & Johnson LLP (June 7, 2017), available at Lexology.com]

[D] Fiduciary Duties in Health Plans

ERISA's regulation of pension plans is extremely detailed, whereas its regulation of welfare benefit plans (a category that includes health plans) is limited. Nevertheless, ERISA often preempts state regulation, and the Supreme Court has frequently ruled in favor of plan administrators in health cases.

Welfare benefit plans, not just pension plans, must file Form 5500. Before mid-2016, the rule was that welfare benefit plans with fewer than 100 participants did not have to file Form 5500 unless they were operated through a trust or if they were uninsured or partially insured. However, in July 2016, the DOL, IRS, and PBGC jointly issued revisions to Form 5500, with compliance required starting with Form 5500 for the 2019 plan year. Under these rules, all group health plans that are subject to ERISA Title I are required to file Form 5500, whatever their size or insured status. Form 5500 Schedule J requires information about PPACA compliance, coverage of retirees and dependents, medical loss ratio rebates, and claims payments. [Frost Brown Todd, *Form 5500 Updates and Increased ERISA Penalties* (Oct. 5, 2016) (benefitslink.com)]

According to the Supreme Court, an HMO is not acting as a fiduciary when, acting through its doctors, it makes a "mixed" decision about medical treatment and health plan eligibility. [*Pegram v. Herdrich*, 530 U.S. 211 (2000)] Therefore, even if plan participants are right that the plan refused them necessary treatments in order to increase its profits, they have not stated a cause of action for breach of fiduciary duty.

The Supreme Court returned to the question of review of HMO coverage decisions in mid-2004: *Aetna Health Inc. v. Davila* and *CIGNA Healthcare of Texas, Inc. v. Calad*, 542 U.S. 200 (2004). One of the plaintiffs alleged harm caused by denial of coverage of an expensive arthritis drug; the other claimed that she was prematurely discharged from the hospital, leading to complications of surgery. They sued under a Texas state law dealing with HMO negligence. The Supreme Court held that ERISA completely preempts the state law, because ERISA covers all cases where someone claims that coverage was denied under a plan that is a welfare benefit plan for ERISA purposes. However, in this case, the Supreme Court clarified its earlier *Pegram* decision. In that case, HMOs were held not to be fiduciaries to the extent that they act through their physicians to make mixed eligibility and treatment decisions. The 2004 decision says that HMOs are fiduciaries when they make pure eligibility decisions. The consequence is that if patients sue in state court, claiming that they were wrongfully denied health benefits, the case is completely preempted by ERISA and can be removed to federal court.

Until early 2015, there was a lively conflict as to when a company that offered retiree health benefits must maintain them unchanged for the lifetime of the retirees (and, perhaps, retirees and spouses). These questions were put to rest when the Supreme Court permitted cuts in retiree benefits—reversing the Sixth Circuit holding that the benefits vested for life. The unanimous Supreme Court decision says that retiree health benefits are not deferred compensation, and the ambiguous provisions of the plan in question did not create a lifetime promise. The case was remanded for the Sixth Circuit to apply contract-law principles to see if the CBA granted free lifetime health benefits. The Supreme Court majority opinion said that when a contract is silent on the duration of retiree benefits, a court cannot draw an inference of lifetime vesting. [*M&G Polymers USA v. Tackett*, 135 S. Ct. 926 (2015)]

The Tenth Circuit ruled that retiree health and life insurance benefits are welfare benefit plans for ERISA purposes—not subject to the ERISA minimum vesting standard. Unless there is a contractual agreement to provide vested benefits, the employer can unilaterally modify or even eliminate such benefits. General contract law requires clear and express plan language, showing intent to vest. In this case, the documents (with the SPD treated as a plan document for this purpose) did not include express vesting language. [*Fulghum v. Embarq Corp.*, 778 F.3d 1147 (10th Cir. 2015) On remand, the District Court for the District of Kansas granted summary judgment for the defendants and denied summary judgment for the plaintiffs, on the grounds that the plan documents did not grant a right to lifetime benefits: *Fulghum v. Embarq Corp.*, No. 07-2602-EFM (D. Kan. June 10, 2015). En banc rehearing has been denied, but on April 27, 2015, the Tenth Circuit agreed to rehearing by the panel of certain issues: 785 F.3d 395 (10th Cir. 2015). At press time in 2017, the rehearing decision had not yet been announced.]

An FMLA plaintiff alleged that Aetna, acting as plan administrator, did not breach its fiduciary duty by telling the plaintiff's employer about his substance abuse history. The Tenth Circuit held that complying with its client's (i.e., the employer's) drug-free workplace policy could not be a breach of fiduciary duty. Aetna was entitled to discretion under the plan terms. When Aetna informed FedEx that the plaintiff had applied for disability benefits for alcohol or substance abuse after applying for FMLA leave for work-related stress, FedEx required return to duty testing and five years of follow-up drug tests, as required by the drug-free workplace policy. [*Williams v. FedEx Corp. Serv.*, 849 F.3d 889 (10th Cir., 2017); see Mike Reilly, *ERISA (10th Circuit): Does the ERISA Plan Breach Fiduciary Duties by Informing the Employer of an Employee/Disability Claimant's Substance Abuse Problem?*, boomerisablog.com (Feb. 27, 2017) (benefitslink.com)]

A claims administrator does not waive the statute of limitations defense by agreeing to reopen a denied claim in light of additional information, if the request for reopening occurs after the statute of limitations has run. MetLife reopened an LTD claim in 2009, five years after denying it, when the California Department of Insurance asked the company to permit submission of additional evidence about the claimant's depression. The Ninth Circuit held that a suit filed in 2011 was barred by the original 2004 statute of limitations defense; the statute of limitations was four years. The Ninth Circuit said that an ERISA claim accrues when benefits are denied or when the insured has reason to know there has been a clear and continuing repudiation of the claimant's rights under the plan. Reopening the claim did not waive the statute of limitations because California law does not permit an insurance company to waive an expired statute of limitations. [*Gordon v. Deloitte & Touche*, 749 F.3d 746 (9th Cir. 2014)]

See § 9.05[C] for more discussion of fiduciary issues in retiree health benefit plans.

§ 15.04 DUTIES OF THE TRUSTEE

Usually, pension and welfare benefit plans will be organized in trust form. Every trust must have at least one trustee. ERISA § 403(a) provides that the trustee can be named in the instrument itself, appointed under a procedure set out in the plan, or appointed by a named fiduciary.

The trustee has exclusive authority and discretion to manage and control the plan's assets. If there are multiple trustees, they must jointly manage and control, although ERISA § 403(a) permits them to delegate some duties. Certain fiduciary duties can be delegated—it depends on whether trustee responsibility or other duties are involved.

To implement the requirement that pension plans be operated solely in the interests of participants and beneficiaries, DOL ruled in late 2007 that it is improper for plan fiduciaries to use pension assets for political activities or furtherance of public debates, if the expenditures are not connected to increasing the value of the plan's investments. Fiduciaries who vote proxies must consider only factors that affect the value of plan investments, not general political or ethical factors. [DOL Advisory Opinion 2007-07A, <http://www.dol.gov/ebsa> (Dec. 21, 2007)] In an Interpretive bulletin dated October 17, 2008, the DOL held that pension funds subject to ERISA are not permitted to vote their proxies, and if they do vote, federal prosecution is possible. The DOL's rationale is that exercising fiduciary authority to promote legislative, regulatory, or public policy issues violates the "exclusive purpose" rule. This is a reversal of DOL's 1994 position that shareholders have a duty to vote proxies on the shares held in their portfolios. [John Richardson, *Americans Must Not Vote!* Global Investment Watch (Oct. 27, 2008) (benefitslink.com)]

A plan can be drafted to make its trustee subject to a named fiduciary who is not a trustee—for example, to make the trustee report to an administrative committee. If this is done, the trustee must comply with "proper" directions given by the named fiduciary, if they are in accordance with the plan's procedures and not contrary to law.

If there has been a proper appointment of an investment manager, the trustee does not have to manage or invest the assets placed under the investment manager's control. Crucially, the trustee will not be liable for the acts or omissions of the investment manager. The trustee has a duty to make sure that the manager charges reasonable fees; performance-based fees, rather than flat fees determined in advance, are allowed.

Another issue is the extent of liability—including personal liability of individuals who committed the wrongdoing—when there is a failure to remit amounts to a plan on schedule. For example, a company in financial trouble may succumb to the temptation to use insurance premiums or amounts that should be contributed to a pension plan to pay corporate creditors rather than for the specific purpose for which they should have been used.

The Fourth Circuit affirmed the theft convictions of two plan administrators (the company's president and its CFO) who did not deposit the contributions. Once due and payable, contributions become plan assets. An earlier Tenth Circuit ruling is that once an employer has paid wages or salaries to employees, it has a contractual duty to contribute to its ERISA plans; the contractual obligation itself is a plan asset. The defendants fell behind on vendor payments, made false financial statements, and borrowed money when the company was in financial trouble. They indicated on the Form 5500 that the contributions had been made to two pension plans and a health care plan, but in fact they used the money (over $329,000) to pay the company's bills. [*United States v. Jackson*, 524 F.3d 532 (4th Cir. 2008)]

The Seventh Circuit held that it was arbitrary and capricious for the trustees of a multi-employer plan to interpret "retirement" differently in two plan provisions to avoid paying $300 a month that the plaintiff participant was entitled to receive. One section of the plan defined retirement as cessation of covered employment. The participant received Worker's Compensation for an injury. Consistent with the Collective Bargaining Authority (CBA), his employer stopped contributing to the plan on his behalf in August 2009, but he continued working until the end of 2011. He said that his age and pension credits entitled him to a $2,900 monthly pension. The plan, however, said he was only entitled to $2,600 a month because he "retired" in August 2009. The Seventh Circuit said that it was unreasonable to deny the additional payment. The plan's definition was ambiguous, but it was unreasonable to apply the interpretation that reduced the participant's benefits. [*Schane v. International Bhd. of Teamsters Union Local No. 710 Pension Fund Pension Plan*, 760 F.3d 585 (7th Cir. 2014)]

Within three years after acquiring Anheuser-Busch Cos, resulting in a change in control, the company sold its entertainment division. Anheuser-Busch's pension plan said that a participant whose employment with the controlled group is involuntarily terminated within three years post-change in control would be entitled to enhanced pension benefit. The company asserted that employees at the entertainment division were not eligible for the extra benefits because they were still working for the successor. The Eight Circuit rejected the contention.

The plaintiffs were no longer employed by the controlled group, and it was an abuse of discretion not to comply with the terms of the plan. [*Knowlton v. Anheuser-Busch Cos. Pension Plan*, 849 F.3d 422 (8th Cir. 2017); see Haynes and Boone LLP, *Eighth Circuit Holds That Failure to Follow the Plain Language of the Plan Is Abuse of Discretion* (Mar. 1, 2017), available at Lexology.com]

§ 15.05 THE EMPLOYER'S ROLE

Although it might be predicted that the heaviest liability for plan misconduct would fall on the company that sponsors the plan, this is not always the case. The corporation might not be a fiduciary, or might not have a conflict of interest. ERISA §§ 403, 4042, and 4044 allow fiduciaries to perform certain actions without violating the duty to maintain the plan for the sole benefit of participants and beneficiaries. Employer contributions can be returned if:

- The contributions were made based on a mistake of fact;

- The plan is not qualified under I.R.C. §§ 401(a) or 403(a);

- The income tax deduction for part or all of the contribution is disallowed;

- The contribution could be treated as an excess contribution under I.R.C. § 4975.

Nor is there a conflict of interest if the fiduciary follows PBGC requirements for a distribution incident to a plan termination.

In mid-2008, the Supreme Court decided *Metropolitan Life Insurance Co. v. Glenn*, 554 U.S. 105 (2008), applying trust law principles to determine the standard of judicial review in ERISA § 1132(a)(1)(B) cases. If the plan administrator has the discretion to determine eligibility for benefits, deferential review will be applied, but if the decision-maker (whether an insurer or a plan sponsor) has a conflict of interest, that conflict of interest will be factored into deciding whether the decision was arbitrary and capricious. However, the mere fact that there is a conflict of interest will not prevent the court from applying a deferential standard of review to the administrator's decisions.

If a plan grants the decision-maker discretion to interpret the terms of the plan, a court reviewing the benefit denial uses the deferential "abuse of discretion" standard rather than the tougher de novo standard. In disability cases, if the plan or policy is silent on discretion review is de novo. Many state insurance regulators (e.g., in Washington) forbid "abuse of discretion" language in disability policies. Minnesota does not bar discretionary review. Brake worked in South Dakota; she filed for disability benefits. Her employer is based in Minnesota. The policy called for discretionary review and the plan had a choice of law provision saying the plan used Minnesota law. South Dakota forbids discretionary review clauses; Minnesota does not. The Eighth Circuit applied Minnesota law and the abuse of discretion standard: choice of law in an ERISA contract is followed if it is not unreasonable or fundamentally unfair. [*Brake v. Hutchinson Tech., Inc.*, 774 F.3d 1193 (8th Cir. 2014)]

The Tenth Circuit ruled that when procedural irregularities occur in denying a claim for ERISA benefits, de novo review is required only if the claimant's appeal provides meaningful new evidence or raises significant new issues. If the plan delayed in issuing a decision in an administrative appeal, the decision will still be reviewed for abuse of discretion, if the delay does not undermine the court's confidence in the integrity of the decision-making process and the claimant does not produce meaningful new evidence or raise meaningful new issues. [*Messick v. McKesson*, No. 15-4019, 2016 U.S. App. LEXIS 2904 (10th Cir. Feb. 17, 2016); see D. Michael Reilly, *ERISA—10th Circuit: What Happens When a "Procedural Irregularity" Occurs in an Appeal Denial?*, Lane Powell PC (Feb. 22, 2016), available at Lexology.com]

The District Court for the Southern District of New York ruled that an administrator's failure to strictly comply with all DOL claims regulations means that the claim will be reviewed de novo. This case involved DOL's deadline for ruling on an appeal from a denial of a claim for disability benefits (29 C.F.R. § 2560.503-1(b)). The regulation permits administrators to get a 45-day extension based on special circumstances that require more time to process the claim. The claim was denied after the deadline; the only reason given was "service not covered" although the regulations require denials to be specific and to reference the relevant plan provisions. The district court held that reviewing a file "which remains under physician and vocational review" was not a special circumstance, so the denial was reviewed de novo. [*Salisbury v. Prudential Ins. Co. of Am.*, No. 15-cv-9799, 2017 U.S. Dist. LEXIS 27983, 2017 WL 780817 (S.D.N.Y. Feb. 28, 2017); see Richard J. Pautler, *In a Significant Change, 2nd Circuit Requires Strict Compliance With Department of Labor Claim Regulations*, Thompson Coburn (Mar. 7, 2017), available at Lexology.com. See also *Halo v. Yale Health Plan*, 819 F.3d 42 (2d Cir. 2016)]

§ 15.06 INVESTMENT MANAGERS

[A] Qualified Managers Under ERISA

If the plan so permits, ERISA allows fiduciaries to delegate their investment duties to a qualified investment manager.

There are four categories of qualified investment managers:

- Investment advisers who are registered under the federal Investment Company Act—whether they are independent consultants or in-house employees of the plan;

- Trust companies;

- Banks;

- Qualified insurance companies.

ERISA requires the manager to acknowledge in writing that he, she, or it has become a fiduciary with respect to the plan.

DOL Reg. § 2510.3-21(c) explains who will be deemed qualified to render investment advice:

- Those who give advice about the value of securities or recommend investing, buying, or selling securities (or other property, such as real estate);

- Those who are given discretion to buy or sell securities for the plan;

- Those who give advice, on a regular basis, under an oral or written agreement, if the advice is intended to serve as a primary basis for investing plan funds.

As long as the fiduciaries were prudent when they chose the manager (and continued to review the manager's performance), the fiduciaries will not be liable for acts and omissions committed by the manager.

A broker-dealer, bank, or reporting dealer does not become a fiduciary if its only role is to take and execute buy and sell orders for the plan. [DOL Reg. § 2510.3-21(d)(1)] The investment manager is a fiduciary only as to whatever percentage of the overall investment he or she can influence (except in situations where ERISA § 405(a) makes the investment manager responsible for breaches by co-fiduciaries).

Investment managers, also known as "§ 3(38) managers," actually choose, remove, and replace investments from a plan. A fiduciary safe harbor is available if a plan sponsor or its plan committee is prudent in selecting an investment manager and then monitoring its performance. The safe harbor requires the manager to be a bank, registered investment adviser, or insurance company that has the power to manage, acquire, or dispose of plan assets—and that acknowledges its fiduciary status in writing. The fiduciary must engage in an objective process to discover the adviser's qualifications and manager's experience. The adviser's compensation must be reasonable and disclosed in the service agreement. (Information about advisers can be found on the Form ADV Part 2 that they file with the SEC, and the SEC can also state whether the manager has been disciplined for securities law violations.) The fiduciary should get a written description of the manager's investment process—e.g., whether generally accepted investment theories are used; whether the manager provides reports that can be used to monitor performance; how services will be tailored for the plan's needs; and whether the manager has enough liability insurance for the amount under management. [Fred Reish, *"Safe" Hows*, plansponsor.com (October 2011)]

In mid-2005, DOL and the SEC released suggestions for fiduciaries to help them choose and monitor investment consultants (complementing earlier DOL guidance about doing the same for employee benefit plan service providers such as recordkeepers). The SEC's concern is that investment consultants can experience conflicts of interest, especially in "pay to play" arrangements whereby the consultants are compensated by brokers or money managers for offering access to the consultant's plan clients.

The two federal agencies released a list of issues that a fiduciary must consider:

- Is the consultant registered as an investment adviser? If so, the fiduciary should review the disclosures on Part II of SEC's Form ADV.

- Get written acknowledgment that the consultant is a fiduciary and will comply with fiduciary obligations.

- Find out if the consultant or a related company has relationships with the money managers recommended and whether the consultant receives payments or trades by the money managers that the consultant recommends.

- Ask about the consultant's policy on conflicts of interest.

DOL suggests including questions on these topics in any request for proposals for a new consultant—and perhaps even seeking written answers from existing consultants. The RFP also can be used to obtain representations and warranties of compliance, collect information about the consultant's insurance coverage and willingness to indemnify the client. Plans should determine when the contract can be terminated either for cause or for the convenience of the parties; the plan's right to continue using materials developed by the service provider for the plan; liquidated damages for failure to satisfy contractual standards; and any pending litigation or complaints outstanding against the service provider. [McDermott Newsletters, *Recent Guidance on Selecting and Monitoring Service Providers* (June 27, 2005) (benefitslink.com)]

[B]   The Role of the Insurer

The Supreme Court's decision in *John Hancock Mutual Life Insurance v. Harris Trust* [510 U.S. 86 (1993)] holds that assets held in an insurer's general account and not guaranteed by the insurer are plan assets subject to ERISA's fiduciary requirements.

DOL issued interim regulations covering insurance contracts sold before December 31, 1998; later contracts are all covered by ERISA fiduciary rules. DOL's Interpretive Bulletin 95-1 says that a fiduciary who chooses annuities to distribute plan benefits has a fiduciary duty to choose the safest available contract, based on factors such as the insurer's size and reputation, the insurer's other lines of business, and the size and provisions of the proposed contracts.

§ 15.07 DUTY TO DISCLOSE

Employees have a right to information about their benefit options, and fiduciaries have a corresponding duty to make complete, accurate disclosure. Furthermore, they need information about the way the plan is expected to evolve, so they can make future plans. Both ERISA and the Internal Revenue Code impose extensive requirements for disclosures to plan participants.

The classic test, stemming from *Fischer v. Philadelphia Electric Co.* [96 F.3d 1533 (3d Cir. 1996)] is that plan participants who inquire must not only be informed about the current structure of the plan—they must be informed of proposals that are under "serious consideration" by management. [Some cases say that, although information must be provided to those who ask for it, it need not be volunteered if there is no request, e.g., *Bins v. Exxon Co.*, 220 F.3d 1042 (9th Cir. 2000); *Hudson v. General Dynamics Corp.*, 118 F. Supp. 2d 226 (D. Conn. 2000). But other cases say that there is a fiduciary duty to give information whenever silence could be harmful to beneficiaries' financial interests. See *Krohn v. Huron Mem. Hosp.*, 173 F.3d 542 (6th Cir. 1999)] The Fifth Circuit refused to adopt the "serious consideration" test [*Martinez v. Schlumberger Ltd.*, 338 F.3d 407 (5th Cir. 2003)], even though seven Courts of Appeals use this test. The Fifth Circuit assesses whether the information that was not given would have been material to a reasonable person's decision to retire.

The Seventh Circuit ruled in mid-2010 that an Health Management Organization (HMO) violated its fiduciary duty to plan participants by instructing participants to contact the call center for information—without telling them that they were not entitled to rely on statements from customer service representatives as to whether or not a procedure was covered by the plan. [*Kenseth v. Dean Health Plan Inc.*, 610 F.3d 452 (7th Cir. 2010). In subsequent proceedings, the Seventh Circuit held that compensation in money (the cost of the surgery) is not necessarily considered a legal rather than an equitable remedy, so it may be available under ERISA § 502(a)(3): *Kenseth v. Dean Health Plan, Inc.*, 722 F.3d 869 (7th Cir. 2013)]

According to the Second Circuit, ERISA § 104(b)(4) requires the plan administrator to provide copies of "plan documents" on request. In 2002, the Sixth Circuit held that affirmatively misleading employees about the continuation of health benefits, inducing them to retire early, is a fiduciary breach, even though not all the plaintiffs asked specific questions about future benefits. The appropriate test is whether the information is materially misleading, whether or not the employer intended to mislead or was negligent in providing the misleading information. [*James v. Pirelli Armstrong Tire Co.*, 305 F.3d 439 (6th Cir. 2002)]

The Fifth Circuit upheld an award of over $243,000 in damages and fees for the employer's failure to provide a copy of the SPD and rollover election forms. The plaintiff, Kujanek orally requested information about rolling over his plan balance (which was about $490,000 when he quit his job in 2007). The plan, relying on SPD language that all requests must be written, ignored his request. He did not receive a distribution until the value of the account had fallen to $306,000. The Fifth Circuit held that his request for a distribution triggered a fiduciary duty to provide the forms. [*Kujanek v. Houston Poly Bag*, 658 F.3d 483 (5th Cir. 2012)]

Nearly all the circuits (First, Second, Third, Sixth, Seventh, Eighth, Ninth, and Tenth) have ruled that ERISA § 502(c)(1) statutory penalties are not available for failure to follow the DOL claims procedure rule (see Chapter 13) or produce claims documents. The statutory penalties only apply to failures to produce documents in a party's role as plan administrator, whereas the claims rules impose duties on the plan, not its administrator. [*Lee v. ING Groep, NV,* No. 829 F.3d 1158 (9th Cir. 2016); see EBIA Staff, *Ninth Circuit Joins Others in Concluding Penalties Don't Apply to Requests for Claims-Related Documents*, Thomson Reuters Tax & Accounting (Aug. 26, 2016), available at Lexology.com; Dylan D. Rudolph, *Ninth Circuit Clarifies Remedies for Failure to Provide Documents Relevant to a Benefit Claim*, Trucker Huss Benefits Report (August 2016) (benefitslink.com)]

The Sixth Circuit held that an employee's written request for ERISA documents must give clear notice of which documents are requested; the standard is whether the plan administrator knew, or should have known, which documents were sought. In a case about accidental death benefits, the Sixth Circuit said that the plan administrator should have known that the policy was the correct document to furnish because it was the basis for the denial. The Sixth Circuit affirmed the penalty of $55 a day (half of the maximum at that time) because the claimant was not prejudiced by the delay. [*Cultrona v. Nationwide Life Ins. Co.*, 748 F.3d 698 (6th Cir. 2014)]

§ 15.08   PENALTIES FOR FIDUCIARY BREACH

A fiduciary that breaches the required duties can be sued by plan participants, plan beneficiaries, and/or the Department of Labor. Penalty taxes can be imposed for improper transactions involving the plan. Generally speaking, ERISA § 509 grants relief to the plan itself; participants and beneficiaries find their remedies under ERISA § 502(a)(3).

A large, overlapping, and potentially confusing variety of Civil Monetary Penalties (CMPs) can be imposed under various provisions of ERISA. The penalties are discussed in Chapter 35 of the Employee Benefits Security Administration's (EBSA's) Enforcement Manual, <http://www.dol.gov/ebsa/oemanual/cha35.html> (last accessed Feb. 20, 2017). The same action often violates several different sections, with penalties at least potentially assessed for each, such as:

- § 209(b) failure to furnish or maintain records;

- § 502(c)(1)(A) failure to notify participants of their rights to COBRA benefits;

- § 502(c)(1)(B) failure to provide required information on a timely basis;

- § 502(c)(2) failure or refusal to file an annual report;

- § 502(c)(3) failure to notify participants and beneficiaries when the plan fails to satisfy the minimum funding requirements; failure to give notice when excess pension assets are transferred to a 401(h) retiree health benefits account;

- § 503(c)(5) failure or refusal to file information required under ERISA § 101(g);

- § 503(c)(6) failure or refusal to comply with a participant's or beneficiary's request for information subject to disclosure under ERISA § 104(a)(6).

Most penalties are defined as a maximum amount per day. Courts hearing such cases have the discretion to reduce or even abate the penalty, based on factors such as the employer's inability to pay, its basic good faith, or extenuating factors such as destruction of records in circumstances beyond the employer's control.

The level of penalties remained more or less unchanged since 2003, so when inflation adjustments were required, the new penalties are much higher than the old ones. See 81 Fed. Reg. 29765 (May 12, 2016) and 81 Fed. Reg. 42491 (June 30, 2016) for adjustments to DOL civil penalties for violations of ERISA, as required by the Federal Civil Monetary Penalties Inflation Adjustment Act Improvements Act of 2015, which is a title of P. Law No. 114-74. Because the statute calls for annual inflation adjustments based on changes in the Consumer Price Index, penalties increased once again in 2017, for penalties assessed after January 13, 2017 for violations occurring after November 2, 2015.

For example, the penalty for failure to furnish reports such as pension benefit statements rises from $11 to $28 per employee (no change between 2016 and 2017). The ERISA § 502(c)(2) penalty for failure to file a Form 5500 annual report goes from $1,100 to $2,063 a day, and then to $2,097. Failure to notify participants of benefit restrictions when the plan is underfunded (ERISA § 502(c)(4)) goes from $1,100 to $1,632 a day to $1,659. The ERISA § 502(c)(6) penalty for failure to furnish information requested by the DOL goes from up to $110 per day, subject to a maximum of $1,100 per request, to up to $147 per day, capped at $1,472 per request. The 2017 amount is up to $149 a day, capped at $1.496 per request. The § 502(m) penalty for prohibited distributions rises from a maximum of $10,000 to a maximum of $15,909 per prohibited distribution, and then to a maximum of $16,169 per prohibited payment82 Fed. Reg. 8813 (Jan. 31, 2017); [DOL Fact Sheet, *Interim Final Rule Adjusting ERISA Civil Monetary Penalties for Inflation*, (June 30, 2016), available at <http://www.dol.gov/ebsa/pdf/fs-interim-final-rule-adjusting-erisa-civil-monetary-penalties-for-inflation.pdf> (last accessed

February 20, 2017); Conduent FYI, *DOL, PBGC and HHS Increase Penalties for Violations* (Feb. 10, 2017) (benefitslink.com)]

A fiduciary who is guilty of a breach of duty is personally liable to the plan and must compensate it for any loss in asset value caused by the violation. The fiduciary must also "disgorge" (surrender) any personal financial advantage improperly obtained: see ERISA § 409. However, there is liability only if there is a causal connection between a breach and the loss or the improper profits. Fiduciaries are not expected to guarantee that the plan will never lose money.

A plan can get a court order removing a faithless fiduciary from office. The removed fiduciary can be ordered to pay the plan's attorneys' fees plus interest on the sum involved. But plan participants cannot get an award of punitive damages, no matter how outrageous the fiduciary's conduct (although some courts will order punitive damages payable to the plan itself). In the most serious cases, a fiduciary can be subject to criminal charges instead of, or in addition to, civil penalties.

Plans can have "bad boy" clauses. For example, under ERISA § 206(d) and I.R.C. § 401(a)(13)(C) fiduciaries who are also plan participants can have their pensions reduced if they breach fiduciary duty, if they are convicted of crimes against the plan, or if they lose or settle a civil suit or enter into a settlement with the Department of Labor or PBGC.

The District Court for the Western District of New York ordered Xerox to pay almost $4.9 million in attorneys' fees and costs to plaintiffs who said that their pension benefits were miscalculated because a "phantom account" was used to offset lump sum payments previously received. However, this was only about half of the amount the plaintiffs requested. The judge allowed the use of billing rates from outside the district, but used 2011 billing rates, not later billing rates that the judge believed to be unreasonably high. Fees to the estate of one attorney who died while the suit was pending were cut in half because contemporary time records were not available. The same judge, in another ERISA case, held that billing rates of $250 to $950 an hour grossly exceeded reasonable hourly rates for the Western District of New York, but the Northern District of North Carolina accepted a $998 hourly rate for an experienced attorney. [*Frommert v. Conkright*, No.6:00-cv-06311-DGL-JWF, 2016 U.S. Dist. LEXIS 171471 (W.D.N.Y. Dec. 12, 2016); see Carmen Castro-Pagan, *Xerox Must Pay $4.9M in Fees, Costs in Pension Benefits Case*, bna.com (Dec. 14, 2016). The North Carolina case is *Kruger v. Novant Health*, No. 1:14cv00208 (N.D.N.C., settled Nov. 9, 2015)]

§ 15.09   ERISA § 502

[A]   Generally

ERISA § 502 gives participants and beneficiaries, the DOL, and fiduciaries many remedies against abuses and risks to the plan. In fact, an important part of litigation planning is deciding which subsection of ERISA § 502 to invoke—defendants can get a case dismissed if the wrong subsection is charged or if the plaintiff asks for remedies that are unavailable under that subsection.

Under ERISA § 502, "participant" means an employee or ex-employee who is or may become eligible to receive any benefit under the plan. "Beneficiary" either means someone eligible or potentially eligible to receive benefits under the plan terms, or as designated by a participant.

Participants and beneficiaries (but not the DOL, the employer, or the plan itself) can use ERISA § 502(a)(1)(B) to sue for benefits due under the terms of the plan, to enforce rights under the terms of the plan, or to clarify rights to future benefits under the terms of a plan.

Civil actions under ERISA § 502(a)(2) can be brought by participants, beneficiaries, or the DOL when a breach of fiduciary duty is alleged.

The DOL, participants, beneficiaries, or fiduciaries can sue under ERISA §§ 502(a)(3) and (5) to enjoin violations of ERISA Title I, to get equitable relief under Title I, or to impose penalties on PIIs for engaging in prohibited transactions. The remedies under ERISA § 502(a)(3) can include ordering return of misappropriated plan assets, plus the profits improperly earned on them—but this remedy is not available in situations where the defendant did not hold or profit from plan assets.

The Third Circuit dismissed a breach of fiduciary duty suit premised on excessive fees. According to the plaintiffs, John Hancock was a fiduciary because of its role as 401(k) plan service provider, and the excessive fees constituted a breach of duty. The Third Circuit held that the question was whether John Hancock acted as a fiduciary when the alleged wrongful acts were committed. The Third Circuit held that a service provider does not owe fiduciary duty to the plan if a plan trustee exercised final authority in deciding to accept or reject the terms offered by the service provider. Changing the fees required notice to the trustees, who could then terminate the contract. Hancock's ability to change the fees on its own funds was not closely enough related to the plaintiffs' fee claims to make Hancock a fiduciary. [*Santomenno v. John Hancock Life Ins. Co.*, 768 F.3d 284 (3d Cir. 2014). Certiorari was denied in mid-2015, 135 S. Ct. 1860 (2015); see EBIA Weekly, *U.S. Supreme Court Declines to Review Decision That Service Provider Was Not a Fiduciary in Setting Investment Fees* (May 28, 2015) (benefitslink.com)]

The question of what constitutes "appropriate equitable relief" is a difficult one, and many cases have been decided on this issue. In particular, the question of whether participants could sue for reduction in value of their own individual accounts—rather than the value of the plan as a whole—was an important litigation issue that was not resolved until 2008, when the Supreme Court ruled that ERISA § 502(a)(2) does not grant a remedy for individual remedies as distinct from injuries to the plan—but it does permit recovery for fiduciary breaches that impair the value of the assets in a particular account, because the goal of ERISA § 409 is to safeguard the benefits that participants are entitled to.

Although *Massachusetts Mutual Life Insurance v. Russell* [473 U.S. 134 (1985)] interprets ERISA § 502(a)(3) as limited to remedies for the plan as a whole, the plan in that case was a disability plan providing a fixed benefit, so administrator misconduct could not affect individual accounts unless the whole plan was at risk of default. The plaintiff in that case actually received the full benefit she was entitled to; she sued for damages for delay in claim processing. Furthermore, the Supreme Court read that case as involving a defined benefit plan in a benefits universe dominated by such plans. The *LaRue* case, in contrast, involved a defined contribution plan, for which a participant's entitlement can be reduced by fiduciary misconduct even if the plan as a whole remains solvent. The Supreme Court sent the case back to the district court, giving the plaintiff a chance to prove that the fiduciary was to blame for the decline in value of his account. Section 502(a)(2) carries out the purposes of ERISA § 409, which obligated fiduciaries to manage, administer, and invest plan assets properly so that participants and beneficiaries will eventually receive the benefits they were promised under the plan. In a defined benefit plan, fiduciary misconduct creates or increases the risk that the plan will default, so the previous decisions look at the effect of misconduct on the entire plan. In a defined contribution plan, misconduct can reduce the value of some but not all accounts—but the misconduct is still the type that ERISA § 409 is intended to deter or redress. [*LaRue v. DeWolff, Boberg & Assocs., Inc.*, 552 U.S. 248 (2008)]

Although technically the result was a victory for LaRue, after the Supreme Court remanded his case, James LaRue apparently ran out of money to continue litigating, so he settled with DeWolff, Boberg. The District of South Carolina's October 21, 2008 order approving the settlement said that the statute of limitations had expired on the events LaRue characterized as fiduciary breaches, so he could not refile later. The case was dismissed with prejudice, although he could bring a further suit for post-2002 events for which the statute of limitations had not run. [Fred Schneyer, *LaRue Bows Out of Legal Fight*, plansponsor.com (Oct. 30, 2008)]

The Seventh Circuit allowed a class of defined contribution plan participants to sue for relief under ERISA § 502, taking the position that the shift from defined benefit plans (the predominant plan type when ERISA was enacted) to defined contribution plans requires re-thinking the remedies available under § 502.

A 2008 Supreme Court decision allows individual defined contribution participants to seek relief; the Seventh Circuit extended this to a plaintiff class in a case alleging excessive fees. The Seventh Circuit held that a plan and its individual participants can be injured at the same time, if excessive fees are charged, or if imprudent choices are included in the plan's investment portfolio. However, the Seventh Circuit, while opening up the potential for class actions, said that the classes actually certified were improperly defined, because they did not have enough similarity because some class members were satisfied with their investment results. It would also be improper to certify a class that involved some fees that are fund-specific and other fees that are imposed equally on all plan partici-pants. [*Beesley v. International Paper Co./Spano v. Boeing*, 633 F.3d 574 (7th Cir. 2011)]

On remand from the Seventh Circuit, the District Court for the Southern District of Illinois certified a class of participants in Boeing's 401(k) plan who alleged breach of fiduciary duty: excessive administration fees; failure to disclose material information about the fees; and imprudent mutual fund investments. The district court approved of plaintiffs' designation of subclasses (one for each mutual fund at issue) and limitation of the class to participants during the time of the alleged breach. The Seventh Circuit had held that the original class of all past and future participants was excessively broad. [*Spano v. Boeing Co.*, 294 F.R.D. 114 (S.D. Ill. 2013)]

However, after *Dukes v. Wal-Mart* (see § 42.06[A]), all types of employ-ment class actions will be more difficult to maintain. *Dukes* creates problems for stock drop plaintiffs because the participants invested in the plan for differing periods of time, with different investment experiences.

In 2010, the Sixth Circuit joined the Second, Third, Fifth, Seventh, and Ninth Circuits in allowing equitable estoppel to be used for relief from harsh pen-sion plan provisions, even if the provisions are not inequitable. (Previously, the Sixth Circuit only applied equitable estoppel in the context of welfare benefits.) When a participant took early retirement after being told what his pension would be, he was told about two years later that he had been overpaid and had to return over $11,000 to the plan. He sued, arguing that the TPA made a contract to pay the amount of benefits originally stated. The Sixth Circuit allowed him to assert estoppel based on gross negligence that was severe enough to be tantamount to fraud. However, the Sixth Circuit rejected his ERISA § 502(a)(1)(B) claim, because the benefit election form was not a plan amendment, plan modification, or separate contract providing additional benefits; it merely stated the amount of the benefit. The Sixth Circuit also dismissed the plaintiff's fiduciary breach claim. [*Bloemker v. Laborers' Local 265 Pension Fund*, 605 F.3d 436 (6th Cir. 2010)]

An ERISA § 502(a)(3) suit for individual equitable relief can be maintained against a company that deceived its employees about benefit safety if they were transferred to a new division that was spun off by the company. The Supreme Court ruled that the corporation was acting as a fiduciary when it lied about ben-efit security. [*Varity Corp. v. Howe*, 514 U.S. 1082 (1996)]

A party in interest to a prohibited transaction with a plan can be liable under ERISA § 502(a)(3), even if the defendant is not a fiduciary [*Harris Trust v. Salomon Bros.*, 530 U.S. 238 (2000)]

In late 2016, the District Court for the Northern District of California allowed ERISA § 502(a)(3) to be used to enforce provisions of a top hat plan after a terminated executive signed an agreement that he was told did not affect his rights to non-qualified plan benefits. The district court found that appropriate equitable relief can include remedying inequities in waivers of plan rights. Top hat plans are subject to some (although not all) requirements of ERISA Title I, and the administrator of a top hat plan is immune from the fiduciary standard of care, but is not immune from § 502(a)(3) equitable remedies. Top hat plans are subject to equitable remedies for breach of the general standard of good faith imposed by contract law. [*Buster v. Mechanics Bank*, No. C16-01146 WHA, 2016 U.S. Dist. LEXIS 114994 (N.D. Cal. Aug. 26, 2016); see Plansponsor editors, *Court Finds ERISA Can Be Used to Enforce Top-Hat Plan Terms*, plansponsor .com (Nov. 9, 2016)]

ERISA § 502(a)(3) is also used by benefit plans to recover payments made on behalf of plan participants (e.g., when a participant is injured in an accident and later settles or wins a tort case about the accident). See § 18.17 for further discussion of subrogation.

Section 502(a)(6) authorizes civil actions by the DOL to collect the excise tax on prohibited transactions or the penalty tax on fiduciary violations. State governments (but NOT the DOL) can sue under § 502(a)(7) to enforce compliance with a Qualified Medical Child Support Order (QMCSO). The states have a role to play here because they have traditionally been empowered to deal with family law issues such as child support.

Funds from an insurance contract or annuity purchased in connection with termination of participant status can be secured by a suit under § 502(a)(9). Suit can be brought by the DOL, fiduciaries, or persons who were participants or beneficiaries at the time of the violation—but suit can only be brought if the purchase of the policy or annuity violated the terms of the plan or violated fiduciary obligations.

ERISA § 502(c) allows the Department of Labor to impose a penalty currently a maximum of $147 per day (dating from the date of failure or refusal to furnish the documents) against a plan administrator who doesn't comply with a participant's or beneficiary's request for plan documents within 30 days. Administrators can be penalized even if the failure is not deliberate—but not if it is due to matters beyond their reasonable control.

Both the federal and the state courts have jurisdiction under § 502(e) when participants or beneficiaries bring suit to recover benefits, clarify their rights to future benefits, or enforce rights under any plan that falls under ERISA Title I. Although ERISA does not rule out binding arbitration of claims, any other Title I claim can only be heard in a federal, not a state, court.

ERISA § 502(i) requires the DOL to impose a civil penalty on fiduciaries who violate the fiduciary responsibility provisions of Title I. A nonfiduciary who knowingly participates in a fiduciary violation can also be penalized under this section. The base penalty is 20% of the penalty that the court orders under ERISA § 502(a)(2) or (5). If the fiduciary or person who assisted the fiduciary in the breach settled with the DOL to avoid being taken to court, the base penalty is 20% of the amount of the settlement. The penalty can be reduced or even waived if the person acted reasonably and in good faith. Because the main objective of this section is to safeguard the plan, a reduction or waiver can also be obtained if the fiduciary or helper would not be able to reimburse the plan without severe financial hardship if the full penalty were assessed.

Section 502(k) permits plan administrators, fiduciaries, participants, and beneficiaries to sue the Department of Labor itself in district court in order to compel the agency to undertake an action required by ERISA Title I, to prevent the Department from acting contrary to Title I, or to review a final order of the Secretary of Labor.

Section 502 also permits fiduciaries to ask the court to remove another fiduciary from office, or to issue an injunction against anyone who has violated ERISA Title I or the plan's own terms.

It is mandatory for the DOL to impose civil penalties, under § 502(l), against a fiduciary who knowingly violates the Title I provisions on fiduciary responsibility, and also against anyone who knowingly participates in a violation. The basic penalty is 20% of the court order under §§ 502(a)(2) or (5), or the settlement with DOL in such a case. However, any penalty imposed under § 502(i), or any prohibited transaction excise tax, can be used to offset the § 502(l) penalty. The Secretary of Labor has discretion to reduce or waive the penalty in two circumstances: if the fiduciary acted reasonably and in good faith—or if waiver permits the fiduciary to reimburse the plan for its losses.

[B] Issues Under *Knudson, Sereboff,* and *McVeigh*

In 2002, the Supreme Court decided *Great-West Life & Annuity Insurance Co. v. Knudson.* [534 U.S. 204 (2002)] The Supreme Court ruled that a health plan and its administrator cannot sue under ERISA § 502(a)(3) when they claim that beneficiaries violate the terms of the plan by refusing to reimburse the plan for amounts the plan spent on the beneficiaries' medical care. The Supreme Court reached this conclusion because § 502(a)(3) refers to cases that traditionally came under the heading of "equity." Contract suits traditionally were considered suits at "law," not "equity."

After *Knudson*, plans faced three hurdles in bringing claims for restitution. First, the defendant (in many such cases, the plan participant, because the plan itself is the plaintiff) must have been unjustly enriched. In some cases, the defendant will have to have possession of specific property that really belongs to the plaintiff—and equitable relief must be appropriate.

In mid-2006, the Supreme Court revisited ERISA subrogation issues twice. In *Sereboff v. Mid Atlantic Medical Services Inc.* [547 U.S. 356 (2006)], the petitioners were covered by an ERISA plan that included a subrogation provision. The petitioners settled tort claims related to an automobile accident. Their insurer sued under ERISA § 502(a)(3) to recoup medical expenses paid on their behalf. The petitioners set aside part of the tort recovery, corresponding to the insurer's claim. The Supreme Court ruled that the insurer was entitled to recover the amount expended on the petitioners' medical care. The insurer acted as a fiduciary seeking "appropriate equitable relief" to enforce plan terms, as permitted by ERISA § 502(a)(3). Unlike *Knudson*, the disputed funds in this case were in the petitioners' possession and set aside in a separate account. The Supreme Court treated the insurer's claim as equitable not because it was a claim for subrogation, but because it was the equivalent of an action to enforce an equitable lien created by agreement.

A month later, in *Empire Healthchoice Assurance, Inc. v. McVeigh* [547 U.S. 677 (2006)], ruled that an insurer's attempt to recover health care costs paid on behalf of an injured federal employee had to be litigated in state court rather than federal court: there was no jurisdiction under 28 U.S.C. § 1331. Although the worker was covered under the Federal Employees Health Benefits Act, a statute that includes a provision that the terms of the federal plan's insurance contracts will preempt state or local law about health benefit plans, the Supreme Court held that the case for reimbursement does not "arise under federal law" and therefore there is no federal jurisdiction.

In 2013, the Supreme Court ruled in a case in which a plan participant received $110,000 in settlement funds after an automobile accident. He paid a 40% contingent fee to his lawyer, so he had $66,000 after that. His health plan sought to recover the $66,866 it had paid for his care. The plan participant, McCutchen, said that he was not obligated to reimburse the health plan, because if he did, he would not have received any compensation for the injuries he suffered. The Supreme Court ruled that the health plan's SPD clearly and explicitly gave the insurer a right of subrogation. This right, deriving from contract law, prevailed over McCutchen's equitable arguments about "make-whole" relief. However, the reimbursement provision did not explain how to handle attorneys' fees, so the Supreme Court held that it was possible to apply another equitable doctrine, the "common fund" doctrine to resolve this issue. (This doctrine allows a person who creates a common fund for the benefit of multiple parties to be paid for creating the fund.) [*US Airways, Inc. v. McCutchen*, 133 S. Ct. 1537 (2013)]

In early 2016, the Supreme Court resolved a circuit split about whether it is appropriate equitable relief for a plan to recoup money advanced to a plan participant when there is no specific fund (such as a trust holding judgment or settlement funds) against which to enforce subrogation. The Supreme Court ruled that an ERISA plan could not recover the $120,000 in medical bills it advanced to a participant who was injured by a drunk driver. The participant's tort case was settled for $500,000. The participant spent most of that money on non-traceable items; there was no fund to seize. The Supreme Court would not allow the plan to move against the participant's general assets. [*Montanile v. Bd. of Trs. of the Nat'l Elevator Indus. Health Benefit Plan*, 136 S. Ct. 651 (2016)]

Subrogation issues are also discussed in Chapter 18.

[C]   *Amara v. CIGNA*

CIGNA's conversion of its plan to cash balance form (discussed in Chapter 7) led to over a decade of litigation, with multiple appeals and remands. At the time of the conversion, CIGNA distributed summaries and an SPD stating that the new plan provided an overall improvement in retirement benefits; that participants' opening account balance equaled the full value of their accrued benefits; and the conversion did not save money for the employer. The employees contested these statements, arguing that the opening account balance was less than full value because it did not reflect the previous plan's early retirement subsidy. They also claimed that many participants were subject to wearaway, and that the employer saved $10 million a year by converting the plan. (CIGNA later conceded this point, but said that it spent the money on other benefit plans.)

The district court agreed with the plaintiffs that the plan materials were false and misleading, and ordered reformation of the plan to conform to the descriptions. The district court ruled that there was likely harm even without a showing of detrimental reliance by the plaintiffs (i.e., that they were harmed by relying on the employer's statements). The district court ordered the plan to give participants their pre-conversion frozen benefits, plus the cash balance benefits earned after the conversion, but did not order any compensatory damages, because it found that ERISA § 502(a)(3) provides only relief that is traditionally considered equitable.

In 2011, the Supreme Court held that the terms of an SPD are not part of the plan itself, and the SPD merely communicates about the plan. The plan's settlor determines the terms of the plan; the administrator provides the SPD. In effect, the Supreme Court overruled the line of decisions allowing enforcement of the terms of the SPD where it conflicts with the plan terms.

The Supreme Court also said that errors in an SPD cannot be enforced through a contractual claim for benefits under ERISA § 502(a)(1)(B). Merely showing likely harm to a class is not enough to support relief. The Supreme Court also held that courts do not have authority under § 502(a)(1)(B) to reform the terms of a plan. These parts of the holding are pro-employer.

But, with regard to what constitutes appropriate equitable relief under ERISA § 502(a)(3), the Supreme Court left open the possibility of obtaining reformation, equitable estoppel, and even surcharge (i.e., requiring the trustee to reimburse the plan). The Supreme Court said that a showing of detrimental reliance is usually not required in equitable proceedings for reformation or surcharges. Plaintiffs must show actual harm and causation—but actual reliance on the SPD would not have to be proved. The Supreme Court vacated the Second Circuit decision, and remanded the case for determination of the availability of equitable remedies. [*Amara v. CIGNA*, 131 S. Ct. 1866 (2011)]

On remand, the District Court for the District of Connecticut ordered reformation of CIGNA's cash balance plan, holding that both reformation and surcharge are appropriate equitable remedies. The district court used contract-law principles and ordered the plan to pay the class members all accrued benefits under both plans. The district court found that CIGNA ruled that CIGNA engaged in inequitable conduct. The defective notice caused employees to misunderstand the contract. CIGNA not only did not correct their misunderstanding, but also prevented employees from understanding the differences between the old and new plans and misled them into thinking their accrued benefits would be protected. [*Amara v. CIGNA Corp.*, 925 F. Supp. 2d 242 (D. Conn. 2012)]

When *Amara* returned to the Second Circuit, the appeals court agreed that the district court had discretion to reform the cash balance plan and agreed with the terms of the reformation, which conformed to the contract-law principles used by the Restatement of Trusts when consideration is involved in the creation of a trust. If one party induces the creation of a contract by fraud or intentional misrepresentation, the court can reform the contract to provide the victim with the terms as represented by the fraudulent party. The 2014 opinion found that CIGNA engaged in fraud or equivalent inequitable conduct: some terminated employees were misled about the risk of wearaway because of fluctuations in interest rates. [*Amara v. CIGNA*, 775 F.3d 510 (2d Cir. 2014); Rebecca Moore, *2nd Circuit Agrees with Reformation of CIGNA Cash Balance Plan*, plansponsor.com (Jan. 8, 2015)]

In early 2016, the District Court for the District of Connecticut ordered changes in the benefit calculations, even though the district court was aware that some overpayments would result. The 2016 decision forbids discounting opening account balances and changes the offset calculation for Social Security benefits. CIGNA was ordered to produce records to prove its contention that more than 9,000 class members were not entitled to any relief. [*Amara v. CIGNA Corp.*, No.3:01-cv-02361-JBA (D. Conn. Jan. 14, 2016); see Jacklyn Wille, *Judge Nixes Cigna's Pension Math in Long-Running Case*, BNA Pension & Benefits Daily (Jan. 19, 2016) (benefitslink.com)]

In mid-2016, the Ninth Circuit, relying on *Amara*, held that claims by retirement plan participants for equitable relief under ERISA are not duplicative of their benefit claims, and participants can seek equitable relief for breach of the fiduciary duty to disclose even in situations where the text of the plan is against them based on equitable factors such as misleading communications. The Second and Sixth Circuits also allow participants to seek reformation of the plan. [*Moyle v. Liberty Mut. Ret. Plan*, 823 F.3d 948 (9th Cir. 2016); see Rebecca Moore, *Court Allows Participants to Seek Plan Reformation Relief*, plansponsor.com (May 27, 2016)]

The Ninth Circuit enforced the less favorable terms of the plan document rather than the more generous terms of the SPD in a case where—unlike *Amara*—there was no evidence of mistake, fraud, duress, undue influence, or intent to deceive. Nor did the plaintiffs show that their position would have been different if they had received accurate SPDs. [*Skinner v. Northrop Grumman Retirement Plan B*, 673 F.3d 1162 (9th Cir. 2012)]

The Sixth Circuit found disgorgement (in this case, $3.8 million in profits constituting unjust enrichment to the insurer) to be an appropriate equitable remedy in an ERISA case about denial of long-term disability benefits. The Sixth Circuit joined the Eighth Circuit in holding that denial of benefits was an abuse of discretion, and permitted disgorgement in addition to benefit recovery. In the Sixth Circuit view, *Varity* (denying remedies under ERISA § 502(a)(3), a catch-all provision, if the plaintiff has a remedy for benefits under § 502(a)(1)(B)) did not apply in this case, because the plaintiff had two separate claims. [*Rochow v. Life Ins. Co. of N. Am.*, 737 F.3d 415 (6th Cir. 2013)] However, the case was reheard en banc and, in early 2015, the en banc court reversed, holding that § 502(a)(3) recovery is unavailable without a showing that § 502(a)(1)(B) does not provide an adequate remedy for denial of benefits. The en banc court was not willing to open up the potential for disgorgement of profits every time there was an arbitrary and capricious denial of benefits. [*Rochow v. Life Ins. Co. of N. Am.*, 780 F.3d 364 (6th Cir. en banc 2015)]

§ 15.10   ERISA § 510

ERISA § 510 makes it unlawful to interfere with ERISA rights, or to discharge or discriminate against a participant for exercising ERISA rights. The typical examples are firing an employee to prevent benefit accrual, or firing someone in retaliation for making a claim for plan benefits. As the number of layoffs increases, companies are at greater risk that laid-off employees will charge that they lost their jobs to cut benefit costs. Sometimes § 510 claims arise in the context of a wrongful discharge, Age Discrimination in Employment Act (ADEA), or whistleblower case. Section 510 is enforced under § 502, so the possible remedies are a grant of benefits, reinstatement, or injunctions—but not punitive or compensatory damages. Successful plaintiffs often receive attorneys' fees and costs. Back pay can be allowed as a form of restitution, but money damages are not allowed because § 502 offers only equitable relief.

ERISA preempts state-law wrongful termination claims when the former employee claims termination was motivated by interference with ERISA rights. [*Ingersoll-Rand v. McClendon*, 498 U.S. 133 (1990)] Section 510 applies to welfare benefit plans as well as pension plans. [*Inter-Modal Rail Employees v. Atchison, Topeka & Santa Fe R.R.*, 520 U.S. 510 (1997)] However, refusal to rehire laid off workers who have credited service, as part of a policy of reducing pension obligations, does not violate § 510 because the people who seek to be rehired have not yet been hired or promised benefits. [*Becker v. Mack Trucks Inc.*, 281 F.3d 372 (3d Cir. 2002)]

The Tenth Circuit held that a group of terminated employees who were not rehired after the sale of their employer's facility failed to prove a conspiracy between the employer and the purchaser to violate ERISA § 510 by selling the facility, getting rid of older employees, and depriving them of their pensions. The

Tenth Circuit concluded that the seller did not consider pension costs until after the sale. Both before and after the sale, most of the workers were over 40, but the percentage of over-40 workers rehired was lower than the pre-acquisition workforce. The Tenth Circuit held that § 510 is not violated if the employer is motivated by legitimate business reasons, even if the result is that some laid-off workers lose pension eligibility. [*Apsley v. Boeing Co.*, 691 F.3d 1184 (10th Cir. 2012)]

Pension risk transfer is the process under which a plan sponsor, to simplify administration and reduce future investment risks, makes a deal with a financial services firm, typically an insurer, under which the financial company is paid to administer the plan and make payments to the plan's beneficiaries. The employer transfers enough assets to back up the obligation, plus payment to the insurer (e.g., 5%-7% of the transferred assets). [Leslie Scism, *Your Pension Check May Soon Be Coming From an Insurance Company*, WSJ.com (Mar. 12, 2017)]

Verizon purchased an annuity from Prudential in a "de-risking" transaction to settle $7.4 billion in pension liabilities. The Fifth Circuit upheld dismissal of a class action challenging the transaction. The Fifth Circuit held that decisions to amend a plan and transfer assets to an annuity contract were settlor functions and not fiduciary functions because the decision to amend involves plan design, but the employer's fiduciary duties involve administration of the plan assets. In this case, the SPD disclosed that the right to amend the plan was reserved, and a timely Summary of Material Modifications was issued. The Fifth Circuit said that ERISA does not require the consent of plan participants before transferring obligations to an annuity. [*Lee v. Verizon,* 623 Fed. Appx. 132 (5th Cir. 2015); see Rebecca Moore, *Court Affirms Dismissal of Verizon Pension Risk Transfer Suit*, plansponsor.com (Aug. 21, 2015).] Under the name *Pundt v. Verizon*, the Supreme Court granted certiorari, vacated the case, and remanded it to determine if the plaintiffs have standing to sue when the only concrete harm they alleged was violation of a private right under a federal statute. [*Pundt v. Verizon*, No. 15-785, *cert. granted* (May 23, 2016); see Rebecca Moore, *Supreme Court Revives Part of Verizon PRT Challenge*, plansponsor.com (May 23, 2016)]

The Fifth Circuit reaffirmed its holding that the de-risking decision was lawful and that the class action was properly dismissed. The Fifth Circuit found that Pundt did not have standing under Article III of the U.S. Constitution because his benefits were not threatened, so he did not suffer actual injury. [*Lee v. Verizon Commc'ns, Inc.,* 837 F.3d 523 (5th Cir. 2016); see Jacklyn Wille, *Verizon Victory Not Changed by Recent Supreme Court Case*, bna.com (Sept. 19, 2016) (benefitslink.com); Rebecca Moore, *5th Circuit Again Dismisses Verizon Pension Buyout Lawsuit*, plansponsor.com (Oct. 14, 2016)]

When employees charge retaliation in violation of ERISA § 510, there is an important question as to whether the employee must have participated in a formal action or proceeding to be protected. The Second, Third, Fourth, and Sixth Circuits require a formal proceeding; the Fifth and Ninth say that unsolicited informal complaints are also covered. The Seventh Circuit held that, at least if a plan's anti-relation provision is ambiguous, doubts must be resolved in the employee's favor: § 510 applies as long as the employee's grievance is within the scope of § 510, even if the employer did not solicit information and if the employee suffered retaliation because of raising the issue. The employee must have a substantial complaint and a plausible grievance (although he or she does not have to be factually correct). [*George v. Junior Achievement of Central Indiana, Inc.*, 694 F.3d 812 (7th Cir. 2012); see also *Edwards v. Cornell & Son Inc.*, 610 F.3d 217 (3d Cir. 2010), *cert. denied*, 131 S. Ct. 1604 (2011)]

A single, unsolicited complaint to the employer about alleged violations of ERISA is not enough to support an ERISA § 510 claim if the employee is terminated. The Sixth Circuit said that there are two kinds of anti-retaliation clauses in federal law. One of them is an "opposition" clause that protects people who oppose violations of the law; the Consumer Financial Protection Act, Title VII, and the Fair Labor Standards Act are drafted this way. The other is a "participation" clause that forbids retaliation against people who participate in proceedings or hearings. The Sixth Circuit said that ERISA § 510 is a participation provision, so protection is triggered only by a proceeding or hearing. [*Sexton v. Panel Processing*, 754 F.3d 332 (6th Cir. 2014)]

A viable cause of action for retaliation under § 510 requires a strong linkage between the adverse action and the participant's request for benefits or attempt to protect benefits; most disputes do not rise to that level. However, the DOL recovered hundreds of thousands of dollars in back pay and other damages for three plan participants who were whistleblowers in a federal criminal case against a fiduciary who was guilty of malfeasance. She was put on administrative leave until her department was outsourced and then she was the only employee who was not retained by the new employer. [Stephen Rosenberg, *What Does Retaliation Under ERISA Look Like?*, ERISA Law Blog (Aug. 31, 2015) (benefitslink.com)]

§ 15.11 OTHER ENFORCEMENT ISSUES

[A] Generally

Criminal penalties can be imposed under ERISA § 511, making it a crime, punishable by up to one year's imprisonment and/or a fine of $10,000, to use or threaten force, fraud, or violence to restrain, coerce, or intimidate a participant or beneficiary, in order to interfere with or prevent exercise of any right under the terms of the plan or under Title I.

ERISA § 409(a) makes a breaching fiduciary personally liable to the plan to make up for losses caused by the breach (such as the difference between what the plan would have earned given appropriate investments, minus its actual earnings). The breaching fiduciary is also liable for any other legal and equitable remedies the plan chooses to impose.

However, in *Peacock v. Thomas* [516 U.S. 349 (1996)], the plaintiff won an ERISA case against his employer, but could not collect the judgment, allegedly because a corporate officer who was not a fiduciary misappropriated the funds that could have been used to satisfy the judgment. The plaintiff could not "pierce the corporate veil" and make the corporate officer personally liable, for various technical legal reasons. For one thing, the case was not closely enough related to ERISA for the federal courts to get involved. Anyway, a federal court cannot enforce a judgment against someone who was not liable for it in the first place.

The Department of Labor has authority under ERISA § 504(a)(2) to investigate whether a Title I violation has occurred so the employer might be ordered to submit books, papers, and records for DOL examination. This can be done only once per 12-month period unless the DOL has reasonable cause to believe that Title I was violated. The DOL also has subpoena power over books, records, and witnesses under § 504(c), but the subpoena can be enforced only if the agency shows that the investigation has a legitimate purpose, the inquiry is relevant to that purpose, and the government does not already have the information.

For purposes of compliance with a DOL investigative audit under ERISA § 504, the fiduciary exception to attorney-client privilege covers communications about plan administration between an ERISA trustee and the plan's attorney. Therefore, two multi-employer pension funds had to turn over plan administration materials about the decision to invest in entities related to Bernard Madoff. The funds asserted attorney-client and work-product privilege to avoid turning over the materials to the DOL. The fiduciary exception was created under trust law and holds that advice that trustees get about trust administration goes to the trust beneficiaries, not to the trustees. The funds were unsuccessful in asserting privilege because they did not provide privilege logs or say which litigation the documents were prepared for. [*Solis v. The Food Employers Labor Relations Ass'n*, 644 F.3d 221 (4th Cir. 2011)]

ERISA § 515 permits a civil action against an employer for delinquency in making contributions. This section does not have a statute of limitations, so most courts that have considered the issue use a six-year statute of limitations (typical for contract cases). The statute of limitations is clear under a similar provision, ERISA § 4003(e)(1) (which correlates with I.R.C. § 412(n)). If an employer fails to make a required contribution to the plan, at a time when the plan's funded current liability percentage is lower than 100% and the employer owes the plan more than $1 million (including interest), then all of the employer's real and personal property becomes subject to a lien in favor of the plan.

The plan that was supposed to, but did not, make the payment has an obligation to notify the PBGC within 10 days of the payment due date. The PBGC has six years from the date of the missed payment, or three years from the time it knew or should have known about the missed payment, to sue in federal District Court to enforce the lien. Fraud or concealment by the employer extends the statute of limitations to six years from the PBGC's discovery of the true state of affairs.

Excise taxes are imposed under § 4975 for the employer's failure to make timely payments of elective deferrals into the plan trust. (The excise tax is sent to the IRS with Form 5330.) Small (under 100 participant) plans are entitled to a safe harbor as long as employee contributions are deposited within seven business days of receipt. The safe harbor offers relief from the general rule that employers must deposit contributions as soon as they can be segregated from the employer's assets, but in any case within 15 business days of the end of the month of receipt. [73 Fed. Reg. 11072 (Feb. 29, 2008); see *EBSA Proposes Seven-Day Employee Contrib Safe Harbor*, plansponsor.com (Feb. 28, 2008)]

[B]   Sarbanes-Oxley Act and Dodd-Frank Act

The penalty for willful violation of reporting or disclosure rules [29 U.S.C. § 1311] was increased dramatically by the Sarbanes-Oxley Act. [Pub. L. No. 107-204] The maximum penalty under this provision (whether or not the violator is a publicly traded corporation) is $100,000 rather than $5,000 for an individual; 10 years rather than one year of imprisonment; and $500,000 rather than $100,000 if the violator is a corporation.

See the DOL final rule [68 Fed. Reg. 3729 (Jan. 24, 2003)] for the effects of the Sarbanes-Oxley Act on penalties. Although the main focus of this rule is on the penalties imposed pursuant to ERISA § 502(c)(7) for failure to provide proper notice of a blackout period, the Sarbanes-Oxley Act made several changes in penalty levels that apply to all ERISA violations, not just those involving corporate governance. At that time, the maximum penalty under ERISA § 502(c)(2) was $1,000 per day; starting on the date the plan administrator failed or refused to file the annual report. The maximum penalty under ERISA § 502(c)(5) was $1,000 per day (for violations occurring after March 24, 2003, the penalty can be up to $1,100 a day). [See 68 Fed. Reg. 2875 (Jan. 22, 2003)] Failure to furnish documents on request of plan participants, beneficiaries, or their designates could be penalized by up to $110 a day, subject to a maximum of $1,100 per request. At press time in 2017, the maximum penalty levels were $2,097 a day (§ 502(c)(2)); $1,527 a day (§ 502(c)(5)).

In all these cases, the plan administrator is entitled to notice and hearing before imposition of the penalty, and the administrator will be permitted to introduce evidence of why it would not be equitable to impose a penalty (e.g., the administrator acted in good faith and the non-compliance was due to factors beyond his or her control).

The Dodd-Frank Act, Pub. L. No. 111-203, regulating financial services, was passed after the 2008 stock market crash. It includes a bounty program under § 922: whistleblowers can receive 10–30% of fines and settlements garnered by enforcement actions triggered by their claims. The IRS also offers rewards of 15–30% of the proceeds of enforcement actions involving more than $2 million or involving taxpayers whose annual gross income exceeds $200,000. The IRS is not required to pay the whistleblower until the accused has exhausted all legal appeals and paid the IRS. Under the SEC and the Commodity Futures Trading Commission (CFTC) whistleblower programs, the minimum reward is $100,000, with no cap, if the tip leads to penalties of more than $1 million. Initially, the Dodd-Frank program was limited to insider trading, but now most kinds of investment fraud are covered. [Final rules, <http://www.sec.gov/rules/final/2011/34-64545.pdf> (May 25, 2011 ,) (last viewed Feb. 20, 2017)] See 79 Fed. Reg. 18630 (Apr. 3, 2014) for the Occupational Safety and Health Act's (OSHA's) interim final regulation explaining how whistleblowers can file a complaint of violations of Dodd-Frank Act § 1057.

A mid-2013 Fifth Circuit decision holds that a person who makes an internal complaint about wrongdoing (in this case, possible violations of the Foreign Corrupt Practice Act) is not a whistleblower for Dodd-Frank Act purposes, which requires providing the SEC with information about violations of the securities laws. Therefore, retaliation based on an internal complaint is not covered by the Dodd-Frank Act. [*Asadi v. G.E. Energy LLC*, 720 F.3d 620 (5th Cir. 2013)]

In 2014, the Supreme Court extended the definition of "whistleblower" under Sarbanes-Oxley to include employees of companies that are not publicly traded, but that are contractors for publicly traded companies. Mutual funds are generally operated as public companies without employees; advice is rendered and services are performed under contract with private companies. The whistleblowers in this case alleged mutual fund irregularities; they worked for a service provider company. Dodd-Frank's whistleblower provisions are not restricted to public companies, but were unavailable in this case because it arose before Dodd-Frank's effective date. [*Lawson v. FMR Inc.*, 134 S. Ct. 1158 (2014)]

In mid-2015, OSHA revised its procedures for whistleblower disputes. Under the regional ADR program, parties get help in reaching a settlement from a neutral OSHA representative with experience in whistleblower investigations. [<https://www.osha.gov/OshDoc/Directive_pdf/CPL_02-03-006.pdf> (last accessed Feb. 20, 2017)]

On January 15, 2016, the SEC announced an award of more than $700,000 to a person who was not a corporate insider, but who performed a detailed analysis that triggered a successful SEC enforcement action. SEC's 2015 Annual Whistleblower Report showed that about half the awards went to current or former employees, half to outsiders. [Harris M. Mufson and Andrew W. Schnitzel, *SEC Awards Whistleblower More Than $700,000*, Proskauer Rose LLP (Jan. 26, 2016), available at Lexology.com]

§ 15.12 LIABILITY OF CO-FIDUCIARIES

If a plan's assets are held by more than one trustee, the general rule is that all the trustees are jointly responsible for management, unless the plan's trust instrument either makes a specific allocation of responsibility, or sets up a procedure for allocating responsibility.

ERISA § 405(c)(1) allows a plan to make an explicit allocation of fiduciary responsibility (other than the responsibility of trustees) among the named fiduciaries. The plan can also have procedures for fiduciaries to designate a party other than a named fiduciary to carry out fiduciary responsibilities under the plan. In general, a fiduciary who designates someone else will not be responsible for the acts or omissions of the designee. The two major exceptions occur when making or continuing the designation violates the designor's duties under ERISA § 404(a)(1), or when ERISA § 405(a) makes the designor responsible for the co-fiduciary's breach.

Every trustee has a legal duty to use reasonable care to make sure the other fiduciaries do not breach their duties. Any fiduciary's misconduct implicates all the others. Fiduciaries are liable for the acts and omissions of their fellow fiduciaries if:

- They knowingly participate in, or knowingly conceal, a breach on another party's act;

- They facilitate someone else's breach by failing to perform their own fiduciary duties as stated by § 404(a)(2);

- They know about a breach by another fiduciary, but fail to take reasonable steps to remedy it.

In mid-2016, the Fifth Circuit affirmed a $6.5 million judgment about an ESOP's mis-handling of an $18.4 million stock purchase; the fiduciaries relied on an appraiser's inaccurate valuations. The Fifth Circuit found that the fiduciaries failed to investigate the appraiser's background (which included a fraud conviction), did not give him enough information about the company's risk factors, did not double-check the appraiser's conclusions, and ignored evidence of collusion with the company's attorney. [*Perez v. Bruister*, 823 F.3d 250 (5th Cir. 2016); see Jacklyn Wille, *Labor Secretary Wins 5th Circuit Battle Over Employer Stock*, bna.com (May 5, 2016) (benefitslink.com)]

Although ERISA makes all fiduciaries liable for breach of fiduciary duty, the statute does not explain how to apportion liability among fiduciaries, or specifically permit less-culpable fiduciaries to obtain contribution from more-culpable fiduciaries. In mid-2016, the Seventh Circuit held that § 502(a)(3) relies on trust concepts, so courts can order contribution or indemnification. ERISA § 405(b)(1)(B) permits fiduciaries to allocate responsibilities, and fiduciaries are not responsible for breaches of duties that have been allocated to a different fiduciary, so the Seventh Circuit held that courts should also be able to allocate blame. [*Chesemore v. Fenkell*, 829 F.3d 803 (7th Cir. July 21, 2016), *cert. denied* 137 S. Ct. 827 (2017); see Drinkerbiddle.com Fiduciary Liability Update, *Seventh*

Circuit Holds That ERISA Permits Indemnification or Contribution Among Fiduciaries (July 26, 2016) (benefitslink.com).]

Under a 1993 Supreme Court case, the plan can also get equitable remedies (but not damages) from a nonfiduciary who cooperated with a fiduciary who breached fiduciary duty. [*Mertens v. Hewitt Assocs.*, 508 U.S. 248 (1993)] Some courts have applied *Mertens* to prevent any claims by plans against nonfiduciaries. This only puts more pressure on the fiduciaries, because then they are the only possible defendants if something goes wrong. But fiduciaries cannot be liable for other fiduciaries' conduct occurring before they themselves became fiduciaries. Nor do they have a duty to remedy breaches that occurred before their tenure or after they cease to be fiduciaries.

A non-fiduciary who knowingly participates in a fiduciary's violation of the anti-kickback provision, ERISA § 406(b)(3), can be penalized under ERISA § 502(a)(3) even if the non-fiduciary is not a party in interest. The case involved a financial planner who signed up many of his clients in a tax avoidance scheme. [*National Security Sys., Inc. v. Iola*, 700 F.3d 65 (3d Cir. 2012)]

§ 15.13 BONDING

The basic rule set down by ERISA § 412(a) is that all fiduciaries, and plan officials who are not fiduciaries but who handle plan assets, must be bonded. Generally, the employer will maintain a single bond covering all of its plans that are subject to ERISA Title I. Recovery on behalf of one plan must not be allowed to reduce the amount available to the other plans below the minimum requirement.

The exceptions are some banks and insurance companies with assets over $1 million, and administrators, officers, and employees who deal with unfunded plans. (An unfunded plan is one whose assets come from the general funds of the employer or a union, even if the funds derive in part from employee contributions.) A bond is not required for amounts characterized as general assets of the employer until they are transferred to the insurers that pay the actual benefits.

Various forms of bonds are acceptable:

- Blanket bond (covering all the fiduciaries and everyone who handles the plan's money);
- Individual bond;
- Name schedule bond (covering a group of named individuals);
- Position schedule bond (covering whoever fills certain jobs or stands in certain relationships to the plan).

To be acceptable, the bond must not have a deductible, and must cover claims discovered after termination or cancellation of the bond. The amount of the bond must be large enough to cover the plan's potential losses caused by plan officials' dishonesty or fraud. Before the PPA, the bond was required to be 10% of the funds handled, with a minimum of $1,000 and a maximum of $500,000; the PPA increases the maximum to $1 million. If the DOL finds out that a plan does not have the required bond, it can order the company to get a bond; permanently bar the fiduciary from ever serving as an ERISA plan fiduciary; remove the plan administrator and appoint an independent trustee; or impose penalties. The bond must be issued by a surety or reinsurer listed in the Treasury Department Circular 570, a listing of approved institutions (e.g., Lloyds of London). Whether a plan should devote any assets to buying a bond that is larger than the amount required by ERISA is a fiduciary decision. [Nevin E. Adams, *5 Things People Get Wrong About ERISA Fidelity Bonds,* Napa-net (May 2, 2017) (benefitslink.com)] A fidelity bond is not the same thing as fiduciary liability insurance. ERISA § 412(a) requires bonding of all plan officials. The fidelity bond protects the plan against losses caused by an official's fraud or dishonesty. The fidelity bond carrier has a duty to report the amount of its coverage on the plan's Form 5500.

ERISA does not require fiduciary liability insurance. The insurance protects the plan against losses caused by breaches of fiduciary responsibility, but also protects the fiduciaries who are insureds under the policy from personal liability. Generally speaking, the fidelity bond is a plan expense that can be paid from plan assets, but fiduciary liability insurance premiums are not. [Carrie Byrnes and Tim Zehnder, *Fiduciary Bonds and Fiduciary Liability Insurance—Do You Need Both?,* Bryan Cave Benefits and Executive Compensation Blog (Mar. 13, 2014) (benefitslink.com)]

Coverage under a fiduciary liability policy is triggered when the claim is made, not when the alleged wrongdoing occurred. While the fiduciary liability policy is in force, it will cover claims reported during the policy period. But if a policy is cancelled or is not renewed, then future claims will not be covered even if they relate to acts that occurred before cancellation or nonrenewal. Extended reporting period (ERP) coverage is optional: in exchange for an additional premium, ERP coverage applies to claims filed during a specified period (usually 12 months post-policy expiration) relating to events while the policy was in force.

Standard ERP coverage will not provide complete protection in a merger or plan termination situation, because there is a possibility that fiduciary breaches will be alleged until the statute of limitations (which could be as long as six years) has elapsed since the merger or termination.

"Tail coverage" protects the trustees of merged or terminated plans. Insurers do not have to provide tail coverage under a basic policy; the purchaser must negotiate the terms of coverage and the premium. Insurers are often reluctant to offer as much coverage as the trustees want. It is wise to include a provision forbidding cancellation of the policy after the premium has been paid. According to Segal Select Insurance, the premium for a six-year tail policy is likely to be two or three times the premium for the underlying fiduciary liability insurance when the plan was in operation. Tail coverage is usually paid from the assets of the plan that is being merged or is terminating, so it is important to arrange and pay for the coverage before the plan assets have all been distributed.

Instead of tail coverage, the successor plan might obtain a "merged-plan" endorsement, but the merged plan must continue to renew the coverage every year until the statute of limitations has expired, and the insurer may change the available coverage and liability limits. [Segal Select Insurance Fiduciary Shield, *If a Plan Merger or Termination Is on the Horizon, Seek Tail Coverage* (Mar. 2014) (benefitslink.com)]

§ 15.14   INDEMNIFICATION

ERISA § 410 says that language in a plan, or in a side agreement with a fiduciary, is void as against public policy if it limits the fiduciary's liability for breach of fiduciary duty. However, the employer (as distinct from the plan) can permissibly indemnify the fiduciary or buy insurance covering the fiduciary. The fiduciary can also buy his or her own insurance coverage. [See § 43.08 for more discussion of fiduciary liability insurance.] The sponsor corporation can also agree to use corporate assets to indemnify the fiduciary. This is allowed by the Department of Labor, and it is not considered a prohibited transaction.

§ 15.15   PROHIBITED TRANSACTIONS

[A]   Generally

Objectivity is one of the most important fiduciary characteristics. ERISA bans certain types of transactions between a plan and parties who might lose objectivity because of those transactions. "Parties in interest" and "disqualified persons" are blocked from certain categories of transactions, even if a particular transaction is fair.

Title I of ERISA makes any one of these a prohibited transaction if it occurs between the plan and a party in interest:

- Sale, exchange, or lease of property, including the plan's assumption of a mortgage, or a mortgage placed on the property by a party in interest during the 10 years before the transfer of the property to the plan;

- Extensions of credit;

- Furnishing goods or services;

- Transfers or uses of plan assets for the benefit of a party in interest;

- Acquisition or holding of employer securities that are not qualified, or in excess of the normal limit (usually 10% of the fair market value of the plan assets);

- Use of plan income or assets by a fiduciary in her or her personal interest or for his or her own account;

- Payments to a fiduciary for his or her own account, made by anyone who deals with the plan;

- Conflict of interest: the fiduciary acts on behalf of a party, or representing a party, in any transaction representing the plan—if the interests of the party the fiduciary represents are adverse to the interests of the plan or of its participants and beneficiaries.

[B] Parties in Interest

ERISA § 3(14) defines "party in interest" (PII) very broadly:

- Any fiduciary or relative of a fiduciary;

- Plan employees or persons who provide counsel to the plan—or their relatives;

- The plan's service providers and their relatives;

- Any employer or employee organization (e.g., union) whose members are covered by the plan;

- Anyone who owns 50% or more of the employer corporation, whether ownership is direct or indirect; relatives of the 50% owner;

- A corporation, partnership, trust, or estate that is 50% or more controlled by anyone in one of the categories above (unless they are involved only as relatives of a person involved with the plan);

- Employees, officers, and directors of organizations in the list (or anyone with similar powers and responsibilities without the formal title);

- Employees, officers, and directors (or those with similar rights and duties) of organizations in the list;

- Employees, officers, and directors of the plan;

- Anyone who has a direct or indirect 10% share ownership in the plan or an organization closely related to the plan;

- Anyone with a direct or indirect 10% interest in the capital or profits of a partnership or joint venture with anyone on the list.

Any participant, beneficiary, or plan fiduciary can bring suit for "appropriate equitable relief" under ERISA § 406 when an individual or business that is a "party in interest" (e.g., the employees and service providers of the plan) enters into a prohibited transaction—even if this individual or business is not an ERISA fiduciary. [*Harris Trust & Sav. Bank v. Salomon Smith Barney*, 530 U.S. 238

(2000)] Therefore, the party in interest can be enjoined by a court, or required to make restitution to the plan, if the prohibited transaction results in financial losses to the plan.

A disqualified person who engages in a prohibited transaction can be required to pay an excise tax, even if he or she did not know the transaction was prohibited. The excise tax is 15% of the amount involved per year. An additional tax of 100% of the amount involved is imposed when the IRS notifies the disqualified person that the transaction is prohibited, but the transaction is not rescinded within 90 days of receipt of the notice. The excise tax is payable to the IRS. In addition, the Department of Labor can impose a civil penalty that is more or less equivalent to the excise tax if a plan that is not qualified under Title I engages in a prohibited transaction.

The rules for welfare benefit plans are slightly different: The excise tax, under ERISA § 502(i) and I.R.C. § 4975(f)(5), is 5% of the amount of the prohibited transaction, and this amount is cumulated if the prohibited transaction continues over several years. There is a 100% excise tax for failure to correct a prohibited transaction after receipt of notice from the IRS.

[C] Prohibited Transaction Exemptions

Because the prohibited transaction rules are so broad, the DOL has the power to grant "Prohibited Transaction Exemptions" (PTEs) for technically improper transactions that in fact are advantageous to the plan and benefit the plan's participants.

Exemptions fall into two main categories: the specific exemptions set out in ERISA § 408, and those granted by DOL and the Treasury based on a determination that the proposed exemption is administratively feasible; serves the best interests of participants and beneficiaries; and protects the rights of participants and beneficiaries.

To get an individual exemption, a plan must apply to the relevant agency or agencies, and also give notice to affected parties and publish a notice in the Federal Register, so affected parties can submit comments. Affected parties can place their comments (positive or negative) on the record. In some cases, a hearing will be required before the exemption is granted (e.g., when a fiduciary seeks permission to deal with the plan for his own account or to represent an adverse party).

ERISA includes statutory exemptions for loans to PIIs who are also plan participants or beneficiaries, as long as the loans are made on fair terms; for payment of reasonable compensation to PIIs for services they provide to the plan, rental of real estate to the plan at reasonable rates, and other deals that are the equivalent of arm's length transactions. There is also a statutory exemption for investing more than 10% of the plan's assets in qualifying employer securities and real property, as long as the plan purchases these items at a reasonable price and does not have to pay a commission to acquire them from the employer. Depending on the type of security, the plan will not be permitted to hold more than 25% to 50% of the entire issue.

"Class exemptions" have also been adopted for frequent transactions that are not harmful to the plan or its participants. Class exemptions have been granted, for instances, in connection with interest-free loans; mortgage loans to PIIs; and hiring PIIs to provide investment advice to the plan.

The Pension Protection Act of 2006 (Pub. L. No. 109-280) grants a Prohibited Transaction Exemption when fiduciaries provide investment advice to 401(k) plan participants after December 31, 2006—as long as the investment advice relies on an independently verified computer model, or the advisor's compensation is not dependent on the investments that the adviser suggests.

§ 15.16 PAYMENT OF PLAN EXPENSES

One of the EBSA's top enforcement priorities is to make plan sponsors reimburse plans for expenses that were paid out of plan assets but should have been paid by the sponsors themselves. The DOL said that its regional offices would be conducting more plan expense audits than before. If a violation is found, not only must the employer reimburse the plan, but anyone involved in the transaction is subject to a 20% penalty. The DOL can refer the case to the IRS for collection of the excise tax on prohibited transactions.

"Settlor functions" (decisions about establishing a plan or about plan design) are discretionary and not subject to the ERISA fiduciary requirements. Therefore, the expenses of performing settlor functions are not expenses of plan administration, and it is improper to use plan assets to pay them.

Plan-wide basic administrative services can be paid from the assets of an ERISA plan, because they are fiduciary rather than settlor expenses. For example, the plan can pay for recordkeeping, accounting, legal services dealing with fiduciary issues, trustee services, custodial services, annual or other periodic compliance audits, completion of legally mandated forms such as Form 5500, processing claims, and communicating with participants. Expenses for investment advice, educational seminars, and providing electronic access to plan information can also be paid out of plan assets. So can management fees and sales charges for plan investments.

However, settlor expenses that cannot be paid out of plan assets include, e.g., legal services for setting up a plan; costs of plan design; legal fees for plan termination; and most actuarial services used for planning.

Certain expenses related to fiduciary implementation of the settlor's decisions can be paid from plan assets: drafting legally required plan amendments, such as those required to maintain qualified status; nondiscrimination testing; applying for IRS determination letters; liability insurance covering plan fiduciaries; PBGC premiums (except for years when the plan is involved in distress or involuntary termination); fiduciary bonding. Sanctions and penalties can be paid out of plan assets if they were imposed on the plan—but not if they were imposed on a plan administrator in his personal capacity. Sanctions for late payment of PBGC premiums can be paid from plan assets (as long as the plan is not involved in a distress or involuntary termination)—but correction costs under the Voluntary Fiduciary Correction Program cannot be.

§ 15.17 SERVICE PROVIDERS

Part of the fiduciary's duty of prudence is intelligent and informed selection of service providers for the plan, followed by monitoring of the job that the service providers do. Although it is understandable that fiduciaries will think first of their friends, colleagues, or relatives in selecting a service provider, the baseline is that they must deal only with people who have at least the minimum qualifications and experience to do the tasks they are hired for. A thorough reference check should be performed.

In last decade, more than 75 suits have been filed alleging that defined contribution plans were charged excessive fees. The first suits involved large plans, then this type of litigation moved to smaller plans and non-profits. There are three major types of case. The first is the general excessive fee case where the plaintiffs allege that the plan sponsors chose investment options that were imprudent because they were too costly and performed worse than other available choices. The second type of general case is brought against plan service providers, treating them as "functional fiduciaries" whose revenue sharing activities allegedly constituted prohibited transactions. Finally, financial institutions that are also plan sponsors have often been sued for self-interest in using affiliated products in the plan. [<http://www.groom.com/media/publication/1636_401k_Fee_Cases-Detailed_Chart__September27_2016_.pdf>; see Groom Law Group, *Excessive Fee Litigation* (Oct. 26, 2016) (benefitslink.com)]

Compensation must be at least reasonably comparable to market rates for the same work. Selection by competitive bidding is helpful. Before retaining a service provider, it is vital to determine whether the fee that is quoted covers all the necessary services, or whether it is possible or likely that additional fees will be incurred, based on the predicted activities of the plan. The fiduciary doesn't always have to select the low bidder, but must be able to justify the selection as providing the best value on balance.

The Eighth Circuit upheld an award of $14.3 million against a 401(k) plan sponsor for breaching the fiduciary duty to control the costs of recordkeeping. The plaintiffs alleged that the sponsor breached its fiduciary duty by failing to monitor costs; paying above-market costs; and choosing investments that were more expensive than comparable investments. The Eighth Circuit found that it was acceptable to pay for recordkeeping through revenue sharing and bundled service agreements—but the fiduciaries failed to investigate adequately before incurring the costs. However, the Eighth Circuit remanded a separate award of $21.8 million in alleged financial losses that were calculated by comparing the investment results of one of the plan's investments in a mutual fund to the returns of a different mutual fund; the Eighth Circuit held that the hindsight calculation was too speculative. The Eighth Circuit also reversed $1.7 million against Fidelity, holding that income earned before plan assets were transferred between accounts did not constitute plan assets. [*Tussey et al. v. ABB*, 746 F.3d 327 (8th Cir. 2014). En banc rehearing was denied on May 20, 2014, and the Supreme Court denied certiorari: 135 S. Ct. 477 (2014).]

The case was remanded for the district court to examine issues about the extent of deference that plan decisions receive, and attorneys' fee issues. On remand, the District Court for the Western District of Missouri agreed with the plaintiffs that ABB breached its fiduciary duty in changing the investment selection, because the trustee and plan sponsor had a conflict of interest. Nevertheless, the defendant still prevailed, because the plaintiff made a crucial procedural error, failing to use the appropriate calculation of damages: *Tussey v. ABB*. [No. 2:06-cv-04305-NKL (W.D. Mo. July 9, 2015)]

Subsequently, however, the district court awarded $11.7 million in attorneys' fees and $2.28 million in costs and awards to the class representatives, finding that the case was valuable because it contributed to awareness of the need to monitor fees for recordkeeping, and the defendants were not merely negligent but acted with self-interest. [*Tussey v. ABB Inc.*, No. 2:06-cv-04305, 2015 U.S. Dist. LEXIS 164818 (W.D. Mo. Dec. 9, 2015)]

Litigation of the case continued. On remand, the district court held that the fiduciaries breached their fiduciary duty. The case went to the Eighth Circuit, which held that the district court erred by adopting a standard suggested by the Eighth Circuit. The Eighth Circuit said that the district court was supposed to evaluate several possible measures of damages, not unquestioningly adopt the Eighth Circuit's suggestion. [*Tussey v. ABB, Inc.*, 850 F.3d 951 (8th Cir. 2017); see Practicallaw.com, *Eighth Circuit Remands Tussey v. ABB, Inc. for a Second Time, Instructing District Court to Evaluate Methods of Measuring Plan Losses Caused by Fiduciary Breach* (Mar. 14, 2017) (benefitslink.com)]

The District Court for the Central District of California refused to certify a class action alleging excessive service provider fees. The plaintiffs said that the fees imposed on insurance company separate accounts that were offered to plans as investments were excessive because the accounts invested in publicly available mutual funds and the defendants did not provide any services on those accounts. The plaintiffs said the defendants should have used institutional leverage to get lower prices. The district court said that the suit did not satisfy class action requirements. A Rule 23(b)(1) class action is only available if there is a limited pool of money in dispute and one person's rights decrease the pool available to others: adjudication of one claim here would not affect all class members. A Rule (b)(3) class action was also unavailable, because the reasonableness of fees that each plan paid, compared to services received, was too unwieldy to be handled as a class action; class issues did not predominate over individual ones. [*Santomenno, et al. v. Transamerica Life Ins. Co., et al.*, 310 F.R.D. 451 (C.D. Cal. 2015)]

The DOL published a final rule February 3, 2012 about the disclosures a plan's service providers must give the fiduciaries, to show that providers' compensation paid out of plan assets does not exceed what is reasonable. For this purpose, providers include registered investment advisors, certain broker-dealers, TPAs, and others receiving $1,000 or more in direct or indirect compensation from plan assets. No form is prescribed for the disclosures (known as the "408(b)(2) notice"), although they must be in writing. Failure to comply with these requirements is a prohibited transaction for the fiduciary, whereas compliance entitles the fiduciary to a prohibited transaction exemption.

If the provider fails to respond to the fiduciary's request for information relating to future services within 90 days, the final rule requires the fiduciary to terminate the service arrangement as fast as it can. The final rule also permits providers to furnish a reasonable, good-faith estimate of compensation or costs that are difficult to itemize—as long as they disclose their calculation method. Disclosures of indirect compensation from third parties to service providers must also disclose the calculation method. [DOL Final Rule, 77 Fed. Reg. 5632 (Feb. 3, 2012); see § 6.07[B] for further discussion of fee disclosure.]

A Notice of Proposed Rulemaking was published in the *Federal Register* for March 12, 2014, proposing to require a guide to be provided to disclosures by covered service providers that appear in multiple or lengthy documents. The guide assists plan fiduciaries in locating specific items of information that relate to their contracts with the service provider—e.g., the services that will be provided, if the provider has fiduciary status, how much the service provider will be paid, plus required investment disclosures for fiduciary, brokerage, and recordkeeping services (e.g., total annual operating expenses). [FR Doc 2014-04868, 79 Fed. Reg. 13949 (Mar. 12, 2014); see DOL Fact Sheet, *Proposed Regulation to Require a Guide to Assist Plan Fiduciaries in Reviewing 408(b)(2) Disclosures* (March 2014), <http://www.dol.gov/ebsa/newsroom/fs408(b)(2)disclosures.html> (last viewed Feb. 21, 2017)]

A mid-2012 final rule revises the procedure for mailing or e-filing certain notices with DOL under the ERISA § 408(b)(2) rules for fiduciary-level fee disclosure. Fiduciaries must file these notices to get prohibited transaction relief. Relief is available if, when fiduciaries find out that there has been a discovery failure, they make a written request for the missing information to the service provider. If the service provider does not comply within 90 days, the fiduciary must notify the DOL, either mailing a written notice to DOL, EBSA Office of Enforcement, P.O. Box 75296, Washington, D.C. 20013, or using the link at <www.dol.gov/ebsa/regs/feedisclosurefailurenotice.html> (last accessed Feb. 21, 2017). The advantage of using the site is that it provides immediate electronic confirmation that notice is received. [Final Rule, DOL EBSA, *Amendment Relating to Reasonable Contract or Arrangement Under Section 408(b)(2)—Fee Disclosure*, 77 Fed. Reg. 41678 (July 16, 2012)]

Fiduciaries must assess the potential risk of loss, and the cost to the plan, if the service provider causes loss to the plan and is indemnified. Furthermore, indemnification or waiver of liability that relates to willful misconduct or fraud is void as against public policy, and it is neither prudent nor reasonable for fiduciaries to agree to such provisions.

ERISA and IRS rules forbid fiduciaries to deal with plan assets in their own interest. Unless a PTE is available, they cannot provide investment advice to participants if the advice increases the fees of the fiduciaries or their affiliates. The PPA created a PTE for advisers who give advice for a fee under an eligible arrangement—one that either has fees that are not affected by the specific advice given, or that are based on a certified, objective computer model. The DOL issued final rules about this PTE on October 24, 2011, effective December 27, 2011. These rules are also referred to as § 408(g) regulations. The DOL's fact sheet on the regulations estimates that 16,000 investment advisory firms will be subject to the exemption, and will offer investment advice to plans with about 17 million participants and beneficiaries, some 3.5 million of whom will access the advice.

The fiduciaries subject to the rule include banks; insurance companies; broker-dealers; registered investment advisers; and their affiliates, employees, representatives, and agents. A party that develops or markets computer programs for financial advice is also deemed to be a fiduciary adviser. The investment advice arrangement must be authorized by a plan fiduciary who is objective, and the fiduciary advisor must obtain an independent audit each year. Arrangements permitted under earlier guidance can still be used.

The final rule says that a fee-leveling arrangement must:

- be based on generally accepted investment theories that consider historic returns of different asset classes over a defined period of time;

- consider the fees and expenses of the recommended investments;

- reflect the adviser's knowledge of the participant or beneficiary's needs—such as age, life expectancy, distance from retirement age, other assets and income sources, and investment preferences; and

- not base the adviser's fees or compensation on the investment options chosen by the participant (although in some circumstances, compensation or bonuses based on the organization's overall profitability will be permitted).

Computer models must employ generally accepted investment theories that consider fees and expenses and historic risks and returns. [76 Fed. Reg. 66637 (Oct. 27, 2011)]

[A] Fees

Nature proverbially abhors a vacuum, and given the general lack of success with stock-drop suits, unhappy plan participants have sought other causes of action. In recent years, they have often alleged that the value of their accounts was impaired by payment of excessive fees.

In April 2013, the Seventh Circuit upheld American United Life Insurance's revenue-sharing practices in a suit brought by the trustee of a profit-sharing plan to which American United provided recordkeeping and administrative services. The trustee alleged that it was a breach of fiduciary duty for American United to receive revenue sharing payments from mutual fund providers that were not disclosed to clients. The plaintiff (and the Department of Labor) said that American United was a functional fiduciary under ERISA § 3(21)(A)(i) because of its authority to choose the mutual funds in which plan assets were invested. But the Seventh Circuit disagreed, holding that choice of mutual funds does not make a party a fiduciary; it would only be a fiduciary if the claim involved the way assets were handled, not revenue sharing. Certiorari was denied February 24, 2014. [*Leimkuehler v. American United Life Ins. Co.*, 713 F.3d 905 (7th Cir. 2013), *cert. denied*, 134 S. Ct. 1280 (2014)]

The plaintiffs alleged that Harris Associates LP charged twice as much for managing a fund family as it charged its independent clients for similar investment services. Harris said that its fees were at or only slightly above the median for comparable mutual funds. In 2010, the U.S. Supreme Court adopted the standard used by most federal courts, and held that the correct legal standard in an excessive fund fee case was whether the fees were so disproportionately large that they could not have been the product of arm's length bargaining. The case was remanded to the Seventh Circuit for reconsideration of its ruling that mutual fund managers can only be held liable if the allegedly excessive fees are fraudulent. [*Jones v. Harris*, 559 U.S. 335 (2010)]

The Supreme Court vacated an Eighth Circuit decision about whether mutual fund fees violated § 36(b) of the Investment Company Act. The Eighth Circuit had relied on the marketplace to prevent excessively high fees from being imposed. However, the U.S. Supreme Court remanded the case to comply with *Jones v. Harris*, where the standard is whether a fee is so unreasonably large that obviously there was no arm's length bargaining between the fund and its clients. [*Ameriprise Fin. Inc. v. Gallus*, 130 S. Ct. 2340 (2010)] The Eighth Circuit considered the case twice on remand, in March 2011 and April 2012. The 2012 decision held that the plaintiffs did not prove that the fees were so disproportionately large that they could not have been bargained for and could not be reasonable for the services rendered. [*Gallus v. Ameriprise*, 675 F.3d 1173 (8th Cir. 2012)]

The Seventh Circuit ruled in late 2011 that it is lawful for plan administrators to offer only retail mutual funds as investments, concluding that market competition will keep the fees down to a reasonable level. The Seventh Circuit held that fiduciaries do not have to find the least-expensive funds; their duty is to offer a range of funds. Furthermore, retail funds have greater liquidity than institutional funds, and retail funds do not necessarily charge higher fees. The Seventh Circuit found that ERISA does not impose a duty to make the plan more valuable to participants; it is legitimate for the employer to act in its own interests when deciding how much to contribute. [*Loomis v. Exelon*, 658 F.3d 667 (7th Cir. 2011)]

Since 2006, there have been numerous lawsuits about 401(k) plan fees, but no clear trend has emerged. These suits usually allege that a plan paid excessive fees, as a result of practices such as sharing fees with service providers, stocking the plan with actively managed funds instead of lower-fee index funds, and investing in more expensive share classes. The Ninth Circuit held that the six-year statute of limitations began when the decision was made to include the allegedly improper investment in the plan. Although fiduciaries have an ongoing duty to be prudent, the statute of limitations is six years rather than the three years under the "actual knowledge" standard. The *Moench* presumption was applied.

The Ninth Circuit held that fiduciaries can be liable based on selecting the plan's investment option; the § 404(c) safe harbor does not apply to designating investment options. Revenue sharing is not a prohibited transaction, because a PTE is available. It is not per se imprudent to include retail funds in the portfolio (rather than institutional funds only), and the portfolio can also include short-term funds. However, it was imprudent to include three particular retail funds because the plan failed to consider the differences between the retail funds and their institutional counterparts. Even though they used a consultant, the fiduciaries still had an obligation to consider all the available share classes for the fund. [*Tibble v. Edison*, No. 711 F.3d 1061 (9th Cir. 2013)] The Ninth Circuit denied rehearing in August 2013, amending the opinion but reaffirming the principle that the six-year statute of limitations applies. [729 F.3d 1110 (9th Cir. 2013)]

The Supreme Court reviewed only the issue of the proper statute of limitations for claims that it was imprudent to offer retail instead of lower-cost institutional funds. The Supreme Court ruled for the plan participants, holding that ERISA imposes a continuing duty of prudence that requires fiduciaries to monitor the plan's investments and remove imprudent investments. This duty is distinct from the duty of prudence in selecting investments for the plan's portfolio. Therefore, the statute of limitations does not necessarily start when an investment is added, and does not necessarily expire six years after the investment was added. [*Tibble v. Edison Int'l*, 135 S. Ct. 1823 (2015)]

However, the case was far from resolved. The case was remanded to the Ninth Circuit, which dismissed the suit on the grounds that the plaintiffs waived the argument that there was an ongoing fiduciary duty to monitor the continued appropriateness of investments, because the argument was not presented to the district court. Although that might seem to dispose of the matter for once and for all, en banc rehearing was granted on August 5, 2016. [*Tibble v. Edison Int'l*, 820 F.3d 1041(9th Cir. 2016); see Daniel Wiessner, *Edison International Wins Dismissal of U.S. Lawsuit Over 401(k)*, Reuters (Apr. 13, 2016) (benefitslink.com);

Jacklyn Wille, *Edison 401(k) Case Will Be Reheard by Ninth Circuit*, bna.com (Aug. 8, 2016) (benefitslink.com)]

In late 2016, the en banc court held that the argument that the fiduciaries had an ongoing duty to monitor the investments was not forfeited at the district court or Ninth Circuit level, and in fact the defendants themselves forfeited this argument by failing to raise it in time. The en banc Ninth Circuit applied trust law to determine the scope of the fiduciary duty to monitor and required periodic reevaluation of investments, especially when comparable products were available at lower cost. The en banc court sent the case back to the district court once again, with direction to reevaluate the award of costs and attorneys' fees in light of the Supreme Court decision and this decision. [*Tibble v. Edison,* 843 F.3d 1187 (9th Cir. 2016); see Jacklyn Wille, *Edison 401(k) Case Will Be Reheard by Ninth Circuit,* bna.com (Aug. 8, 2016) (benefitslink.com); John Manganaro, *Plaintiffs Still Pushing Tibble vs Edison Through Federal Courts,* plansponsor.com (Dec. 16, 2016)]

In August 2017, with the case back in the District Court for the Central District of California, it was held that investment in retail rather than institutional shares was imprudent, and there was an ongoing duty to monitor the continuing appropriateness of investments in the plans. The district court gave the parties four possible means of calculating the plaintiffs' damages, using the $7.5 million of profits lost by investment in retail shares as a starting point. The parties were told to attempt to agree on a damage figure; if they could not, they would have to return to the district court to argue for their preferred calculations. [*Tibble v. Edison Int'l,* No. CV 2007-0539-SVW-AGR, 2017 WL 3523737 (C.D. Cal. Aug. 16, 2017); see Nevin E. Adams, *Tibble's Trials Near the End With a Win,* NAPA Net (Aug. 17, 2017) (benefitslink.com)]

DOL's FAB 2015-02 says that the selection and monitoring of annuity providers is assessed based on the information available at the time of selection or periodic review, not with hindsight. Circumstances determine how often review must be done, but the FAB says immediate review is required in two situations: when a major insurance rating service downgrades the provider, or an annuitant complains about a pattern of late payments. [DOL FAB 2015-02; see Puneet Arora and Lynn Cook, *DOL Clarifies Annuity Selection Safe Harbor Regulation for DC Plans,* TowersWatson.com (Aug. 7, 2015) (benefitslink.com)]

The Fourth Circuit held that plaintiffs did not have standing to sue the Bank of America for investing defined benefit plan assets in funds affiliated with the bank. The plaintiffs did not allege any injury in fact because they did not say that they were deprived or benefits or likely to be deprived of them in the future, the Fourth Circuit said that participants in a defined benefit plan only have an interest in receiving their own future payments, not the fund's assets in general. [*David v. Alphin,* 704 F.3d 327 (4th Cir. 2013)]

The Eighth Circuit ruled that a participant in an overfunded defined benefit plan did not have standing to sue the plan for fiduciary breach. The plaintiff said that the plan engaged in prohibited transactions when it invested in funds offered by its subsidiaries and affiliates, resulting in abnormally high fees. The plan was always overfunded, and paid all the benefits owed to participants. The existence of the surplus meant that the plan's investment loss did not cause actual injury to the plaintiff's interest in the plan. The court said that a contrary ruling would allow participants to sue on behalf of the plan when they had not experienced injuries. [*McCullough v. Aegon*, 585 F.3d 1082 (8th Cir. 2009)]

§ 15.18   ERISA LITIGATION

[A]   Generally

The provisions of ERISA are enforced both by the federal government and by private litigation.

In ERISA litigation, as in many other types of cases involving plans, the basic questions include who can be sued, who is a proper plaintiff (especially in the class action context), the proper court for the case, when the suit must be filed to be timely, and what remedies can be ordered if the case is proved.

A late 2016 look at ERISA litigation trends showed that new theories were developed to attack the quality of the fiduciary process in plan administration: for example, not having enough investment options and not bargaining hard enough to reduce costs. Some cases targeted fee disclosures and the plans' arrangements with service providers. Failure of ongoing monitoring is a common theory—but participants now have the burden of proving that there was a strategy that fiduciaries could have used to improve the situation. Plaintiffs can no longer rely on allegations of ERISA violations to receive Article III standing automatically. [Plansponsor editors, *New Trends in ERISA Litigation Appeared in 2016*, plansponsor.com (Dec. 27, 2016)]

Seyfarth Shaw's 13th annual survey of workplace class action litigation showed many suits, but fewer filings and lower recoveries than in previous years. The monetary value of the top class action settlements was $1.87 billion in 2014, rising to $2.48 billion in 2015—but dropping precipitously to $1.75 billion in 2016. [Jane Meacham, *Settlement Amounts in DOL Enforcement Suits Declined Substantially in 2016*, Report Says, HR Daily Advisor (Feb. 15, 2017) (benefitslink.com)]

Jury trials are usually unavailable in ERISA § 502(a)(1)(B) and (a)(3) cases. Another possibility is that a jury will be empanelled in these cases, but it will only determine the part of the case relating to breach of contract. The judge in the case will decide claims of breach of fiduciary duty. However, *Knudson* treated the payment of a sum of money as a legal rather than an equitable remedy. *CIGNA v. Amara* has been followed by cases such as *Smith v. State Farm Group Long Term Disability Plan*, No. 12 C 9210, 2013 U.S. Dist. LEXIS 121572 (N.D. Ill. Aug. 27, 2013), denying jury trial. The Eastern District of Missouri did permit jury trial, but it is an outlier. [*Hellmann v. Cataldo*, No. 12-cv-02177-AGF, 2013 U.S. Dist. LEXIS 117676 (E.D. Mo. Aug. 20, 2013)]

By and large, ERISA cases are treated like contract cases. Therefore, the damages available to a winning plaintiff basically put the plaintiff in the position he or she would have been in if the contract had been complied with. "Extracontractual" damages (like damages for negligent or intentional infliction of emotional distress) will probably not be available. In most ERISA cases, punitive damages are also ruled out.

In any ERISA action brought by participants, beneficiaries, or fiduciaries, the winning side (whether plaintiff or defendant) can be awarded reasonable costs and attorneys' fees if the court thinks this is appropriate. Usually the attorneys' fee award starts out with the "lodestar" figure. This is the number of hours the winning lawyer spent on the case, multiplied by an hourly rate the court considers reasonable. In rare cases, the lodestar is reduced: if the court thinks the lawyer wasted time, for instance. Sometimes the fee award is greater than the lodestar amount, if the case was especially difficult, the lawyer broke new ground with innovative legal theories, or took on an unpopular case.

Thanks to a 2010 Supreme Court decision, § 502(g)(1) plaintiffs do not have to be the "prevailing party" to be awarded attorneys' fees, because that section (unlike § 502(g)(2)) gives the district court discretion to award attorneys' fees to either side. [*Hardt v. Reliance Ins. Co.*, 560 U.S. 242 (2010)]

The Sixth Circuit ruled in 2014 that forum selection clauses (designating where suits must be brought) are enforceable in ERISA plans. The Supreme Court declined to review the case. [*Smith v. AEGON Cos. Pension Plan*, 769 F.3d 922 (6th Cir. 2014), *cert. denied*, 136 S. Ct. 791 (2016). See Lauren A. Daming, *Supreme Court Declines to Review Validity of Forum Selection Clauses in ERISA Plans*, Greensfelder Hemker & Gale PC (Jan. 13, 2016), available at Lexology .com]

In late 2016, the Eighth Circuit enforced a plan's forum selection clause, so the appeal of a disability case would not be sent back to the District Court for the District of Arizona, where the plaintiff brought the case. The district court transferred the case to the Eastern District of Missouri. The district court held that the plaintiff was aware of the forum selection clause because it was in the SPD and the defendant did not act in bad faith when it transferred the case. [*In re Clause*, No. 16-2607, 2016 U.S. App. LEXIS 19390 (8th Cir. Oct. 26, 2016); see J. Robert Sheppard III, *Eighth Circuit Affirms Enforcement of ERISA Plan Forum Selection Clause*, Proskauer Rose LLP (Oct. 6, 2016), available at Lexology.com. Certiorari was denied, 137 S. Ct. 825 (2017); see Corey F. Schechter, *U.S. Supreme Court Denies Certiorari on Petition Requesting Review of Enforceability of Forum Selection Clauses In ERISA-Governed Benefit Plans*, Butterfield Schechter LLP (Feb. 23, 2017) (benefitslink.com)]

Several district courts have ruled recently on forum selection clauses:

- *Dumont v. PepsiCo, Inc.,* 192 F. Supp. 3d 209 (D. Me. 2016): the forum selection clause in a company retirement plan was invalid, because the plaintiff had limited opportunities to change his job (he was vested after working there for 31 years), did not negotiate plan terms or approve the clauses. ERISA lays venue where the plan is administered, where the breach occurred, or where the defendant can be found. The district court allowed the plaintiff to sue in Maine, concluding that the breach occurred where the benefits were paid.

- *Malagoli v. AXA Equitable Life Ins. Co.,* 2016 U.S. Dist. LEXIS 39112 (S.D.N.Y. Mar. 24, 2016): the case was transferred pursuant to the forum selection clause; the court found that forum selection clauses are not per se invalid.

- *Harris v. BP Corp. N. Am.,* 2016 U.S. Dist. LEXIS 89593 (N.D. Ill. July 8, 2016): the court refused to enforce the forum selection clause, holding that it violated ERISA's purpose of giving dissatisfied plan participants access to the court.

The Second Circuit held that a district court's remand to the ERISA plan administrator was not a final order that could be appealed. (The suit challenged a denial of long-term disability benefits; the district court ordered the plan administrator to calculate the amount of benefits.) The First, Fourth, Sixth, Eighth, and Eleventh Circuits have held that an ERISA remand order is not an appealable final order because it contemplates further proceedings before the plan administrator, and, thus, can only be appealed if the collateral order doctrine applies. The Third, Seventh, Ninth, and Tenth Circuits allow immediate appeals in some circumstances. The Second Circuit found that this order was not final because there would be further proceedings but would not say that such orders are never immediately appealable. [*Mead v. Reliastar Life Ins. Co.,* 768 F.3d 102 (2d Cir. 2014)]

[B] Preemption

In many instances, cases involving benefits will have to be brought in federal rather than state courts, because of ERISA preemption. In its *Aetna Health Inc. v. Davila,* and *CIGNA Healthcare of Texas, Inc. v. Calad,* 542 U.S. 200 (2004), decision, the Supreme Court ruled that ERISA completely preempts HMO participants' claims that they were improperly denied health care.

In general, ERISA will preempt state laws in cases requiring interpretation of plan documents. There is an exception to preemption for "the business of insurance"—so a number of cases deal with the question of whether federal or state courts should handle certain cases in which health or other insurance is involved in a benefit plan.

The preemption issue is very significant in these emotive cases, because if the case can be heard in state court, punitive damages could be available—and a sympathetic jury could impose heavy punitive damages.

The Illinois statute that forbids discretionary clauses in insured employee benefit plans is not preempted by ERISA, because it regulates insurance (it is specifically directed toward insurance entities, and it substantially affects risk pooling between the insurer and insured). [*Fontaine v. Metropolitan Life Ins. Co.*, 800 F.3d 883 (7th Cir. 2015) The Sixth and Ninth Circuits have ruled similarly.]

For cases filed after the February 18, 2005, effective date of the Class Action Fairness Act (Pub. L. No. 109-2), the federal system may be the only appropriate venue for certain class actions brought by health plan participants.

The Seventh Circuit held in early 2017 that ERISA plans cannot enforce coordination of benefits clauses against other payers—although the court acknowledged that this principle could harm plan participants whose covered claims are denied. A self-funded health plan paid claims to plan participants who were also covered by policies issued to the youth sports programs where the participants incurred injuries. The self-insured plan sued under § 502(a)(3), asking for declaratory relief, an equitable lien, and reimbursement. The Seventh Circuit held that they were seeking legal remedies, whereas only equitable remedies were available (i.e., recovery of specifically identifiable funds in the defendant's possession, or items traceable to such funds). However, ERISA plans generally cannot obtain reimbursement or contribution claims under state law, because the claims are preempted by ERISA—and the Seventh Circuit also ruled out ERISA reimbursement. [*Cent. States Se. & Sw. Areas Health & Welfare Fund v. American Int'l Grp.*, 840 F.3d 448 (7th Cir. 2016); see GKLaw.com, *Seventh Circuit Decision Holds That ERISA Does Not Authorize Contribution Suits Brought By Plans* (Feb. 24, 2017) (benefitslink.com)]

[C] Exhaustion of Remedies

The court system is supposed to handle major conflicts, not minor everyday disputes that can and should be addressed in less complex and less socially expensive ways. Therefore, plaintiffs often have a legal duty of "exhaustion of remedies." That is, they will not be permitted to bring court cases until they have pursued all the administrative remedies within the system they are challenging. ERISA requires every plan to have a system for pursuing claims and appealing claims denials. So the general rule is that would-be plaintiffs must go through these steps before filing suit. This is not stated in so many words in ERISA itself, but judges have looked to ERISA's legislative history and other labor laws to determine when this requirement should be implied.

Plaintiffs clearly have to exhaust their remedies within the plan when their case involves benefits. Courts are split as to whether ERISA § 510 plaintiffs (interference with protected rights; see above) are required to exhaust their remedies. Exhaustion of remedies will not be required if:

- Going through channels would be futile;

- It was impossible to pursue plan remedies because the defendant wrongfully denied the plaintiff access to the plan's claims procedures;

- Irreparable harm would ensue if exhaustion of remedies was required;

- Participants and beneficiaries did not know how to enforce their rights, because they were deprived of information about claims procedures.

Seven of the circuits have held that ERISA plan beneficiaries are not required to exhaust administrative remedies if their suit asserts statutory violations, not benefits claims. This is the position of the Third, Fourth, Fifth, Sixth, Ninth, Tenth, and D.C. Circuits. The Sixth Circuit reinstated a class action about a university's termination of the employer match under its defined contribution plan holding that pursuing administrative remedies would have been futile and the plaintiffs raised a question within the expertise of the court system (whether the plan's action was illegal). However, the Seventh and Eleventh Circuits do require exhaustion of remedies even in this circumstance. [*Hitchcock v. Cumberland Univ.*, 851 F.3d 552 (6th Cir. 2017); see gtlaw.com, *Sixth Circuit Joins Six Other Circuits in Ruling Exhaustion of Plan's Administrative Procedures Not Required When Asserting Statutory Violations* (Mar. 23, 2017) (benefitslink.com)]

[D]   Statute of Limitations

ERISA § 525 permits a civil action against an employer for delinquency in making contributions. This section does not contain an express statute of limitations; most courts use a six-year statute of limitations, treating the case as the equivalent of an action to enforce a written contract.

The statute of limitations for an ERISA § 409 case (breach of fiduciary duty) derives from ERISA § 413. The suit must be brought within three years of the time the plaintiff discovered the alleged wrongdoing, or six years from the date of the last breach or the last date on which the omission could have been cured—whichever is earlier.

The Tenth Circuit revived ERISA claims, and joined the Second Circuit in a split about the proper statute of limitations for ERISA § 413 fiduciary breach claims. ERISA § 413 requires that suits be brought within six years of the last alleged breach or the last date on which the fiduciary could have cured the breach—whichever is earlier. But claims of "fraud or concealment" can be brought within six years of discovery of the breach. The *Fulghum* plaintiffs alleged that they filed their claims within six years of the plan amendment that led to discovery of the alleged fraud. The majority view, held by the First, Seventh, and Ninth Circuits, is that the six-year statute of limitations only applies if there has been concealment of the alleged breach. But the Second and Tenth Circuits hold that the exception applies when there is either a claim of fraud or a claim of concealment; it is not necessary that both be alleged. In this case, the plaintiffs did not allege concealment so when the case was remanded, they would have to prove fraud. [*Fulghum v. Embarq Corp.*, 778 F.3d 1147 (10th Cir. 2015)]

On April 27, 2015, the Tenth Circuit once again held that the "fraud or concealment" exception applies when either one is present [785 F.3d 395 (10th Cir. 2015)], but en banc rehearing was denied. On remand, the District Court for the District of Kansas granted summary judgment for the defendants and denied summary judgment for the plaintiffs, on the grounds that the plan documents did not grant a right to lifetime benefits. [*Fulghum v. Embarq Corp.*, No. 07-2602-EFM (D. Kan. June 10, 2015)]

The Sixth Circuit held that a denial letter's failure to disclose time limits on suing the plan violated 29 U.S.C. § 1133. Therefore, the limitations period was unenforceable and the case was remanded for the district court to rule on its merits. An ERISA § 502(a)(1)(B) suit about termination of disability benefits was dismissed by the district court, which held that he had constructive notice of the limitations period because it was explained in plan documents that he could have requested. But the Sixth Circuit reversed, holding that not explaining the time limit was inconsistent with fair review. Note, however, that in 2014 alone, district courts in the Third, Ninth, and Eleventh Circuits have disagreed. [*Moyer v. Metropolitan Life Ins., Co.*, 762 F.3d 503 (6th Cir. 2014). See also *Santana-Diaz v. Metropolitan Life*, 816 F.3d 172 (1st Cir. 2016): a denial letter's failure to disclose the restricted statute of limitations made the limitation unenforceable; semble *Mirza v. Insurance Adm'r of Am.*, 800 F.3d 129 (3d Cir. 2015).]

The Third and Fifth Circuits start the statute of limitations running with knowledge that the facts constitute a breach of fiduciary duty; the Sixth, Seventh, Ninth, and Eleventh Circuits use the knowledge of the underlying facts; and the Second Circuit uses a hybrid test—knowledge of all the facts necessary to constitute a claim, including expert opinions and understanding of harmful consequences. [See, e.g., *Wright v. Heyne*, 349 F.3d 321 (6th Cir. 2003)]

In 2015, the Supreme Court ruled that the six-year statute of limitations does not always start when an investment is purchased for a plan's portfolio; plaintiffs can sue for violation of the ongoing duty of prudence, running from the point at which a prudent fiduciary would have detected that the investment had ceased to be appropriate and should have been divested. [*Tibble v. Edison Int'l*, 135 S. Ct. 1823 (May 18, 2015)] The Ninth Circuit dismissed the suit in April 2016, on the grounds that the argument about ongoing fiduciary duty to monitor investments was waived because it was not raised at the district court level. However, en banc rehearing was granted on August 5, 2016. [*Tibble v. Edison Int'l*, No. 10-56406 (9th Cir. Apr. 13, 2016), *en banc reh'g granted.*] The en banc court ruled in late 2016 that there was an ongoing duty to monitor—and it was the defendants, rather than the plaintiffs, who forfeited the argument by not raising it in time. The en banc Ninth Circuit applied trust law, however, to determine the scope of the fiduciary duty to monitor, and required periodic reevaluation of investments, especially when comparable products were available at lower cost. The en banc court sent the case back to the district court once again, with direction to reevaluate the award of costs and attorneys' fees in light of the Supreme Court decision and this decision. [*Tibble v. Edison,* 843 F.3d 1187 (9th Cir. 2016); see John Manganaro, *Plaintiffs Still Pushing Tibble vs Edison Through Federal Courts,* plansponsor .com (Dec. 16, 2016)]

The Eleventh Circuit applied *Tibble* to find a continuing duty to monitor the ongoing suitability of plan investments, so a suit is timely if filed at any time within six years of an alleged breach of this duty. [*Stargel v. Sun Trust Bank Inc.,* 791 F.3d 1309 (11th Cir. 2015)]

There is no explicit statute of limitations under § 510, so generally courts apply the state statute of limitations for the type of case most similar to the case. The Second Circuit deterred forum-shopping by applying the Pennsylvania statute (where the suit was untimely) and not the New York statute (which made the case timely) when plan participants living in Pennsylvania alleged that there was a partial termination of the plan, thus entitling them to collect their accrued benefits. [*Muto v. CBS Corp.,* 668 F.3d 53 (2d Cir. 2012)]

In a case that did not allege separate dishonest concealment, the Sixth Circuit rejected application of a six-year statute of limitations in a suit against a plan administrator and employer whose pension calculations were allegedly inaccurate. The plaintiffs sued for breach of fiduciary duty, for accounting, restitution, and other ERISA equitable relief; fraud; negligence; and promissory estoppel. The district court found all the claims to be time-barred. The plaintiffs obtained actual knowledge of the events in 2003, so their suit would be timely under a six-year but not under a three-year statute of limitations. The plaintiffs also sued their union, but the Sixth Circuit held that the plaintiffs did not prove that the union was an ERISA fiduciary. The Sixth Circuit held that the non-ERISA claims such as fraud and negligence were preempted by ERISA. [*Cataldo v. United States Steel Corp.,* 676 F.3d 542 (6th Cir. 2012)]

If the source of the suit is a fiduciary's omission rather than a wrongful action, the time limit is six years from the last date the fiduciary could have cured the problem.

In late 2013, the Supreme Court upheld an insurance policy provision requiring suits about an ERISA group disability plan to be filed within three years of the time proof of loss is due—even though its effect was to prevent the plaintiff from being able to sue at all. The administrative claims process was not completed within three years. The Supreme Court noted that claims are usually resolved within 12–16 months, so the three-year requirement was not unreasonable. The court said that, in the rare cases where the administrative process takes so long that suit is time-barred, equitable remedies such as tolling or estoppel might be available. [*Heimeshoff v. Hartford Life & Accident Ins. Co.*, 134 S. Ct. 604 (Dec. 16, 2013)]

The Eighth Circuit enforced a health plan's two-year deadline, and refused to apply the Missouri 10-year statute of limitations. The Missouri statute forbids parties from agreeing to a shorter period. But the Eighth Circuit held that the state statute was not controlling because parties do not have the power to choose state law to govern an ERISA plan. [*Munro-Kienstra v. Carpenters' Health & Welfare Trust Fund of St. Louis*, No. 14-1655, 2015 WL 3756712 (8th Cir. June 17, 2015)]

§ 15.19 CORRECTION PROGRAMS

[A] Plan Deficiency Aids

One of the central tenets of tax and ERISA enforcement for plans is that, wherever possible, plans should be encouraged to determine where they fall short of compliance, and to correct the problems before regulators detect them. The IRS publishes Alert Guidelines, Explanations, & Plan Deficiency Paragraphs [<https://www.irs.gov/retirement-plans/irs-checklists-for-retirement-plan-documents> (May 26, 2016) (last accessed Feb. 21, 2017)] so businesses can see the standards that IRS reviewers use when they review retirement plans for compliance. Each worksheet comes with explanatory text. The IRS Checksheets, also known as Plan Deficiency Paragraphs, are standardized text that plans can use to draft provisions that will satisfy IRS requirements.

[B] Voluntary Correction

The IRS has engaged in ongoing efforts to allow plans to correct failures without losing qualification. The Department of Labor encourages voluntary return to compliance by plan administrators.

The Employee Plans Compliance Resolution System (EPCRS) provides three levels of corrections of inadvertent errors that do not involve deliberate engagement in abusive tax strategies (e.g., inappropriate tax shelters):

- The Self-Correction Program (SCP) allows the least complex types of plans (403(b), SEPs, and SIMPLE IRAs) to correct minor operational failures. These corrections are performed purely in house, do not generate penalties, and need not involve or even be disclosed to the IRS.

- The Voluntary Correction Program (VCP) permits a plan sponsor who detects mistakes before an audit to correct those mistakes and pay a fee that is smaller than the penalties that would be imposed on deficiencies uncovered in an audit.

- The Correction on Audit Program (Audit CAP) permits correction in response to an audit, with sanctions reflecting the extent and seriousness of the deficiency.

EPCRS procedures are revised frequently.

Rev. Proc. 2015-27 modifies EPCRS, e.g., with respect to repayment of overpayments by plan participants. EPCRS allows sponsors to keep their plans tax-qualified by voluntarily correcting plan failures. Failures can be self-corrected without IRS approval under the SCP but IRS approval is required for corrections under VCP or Audit CAP. An overpayment is a mistaken payment by a plan: a participant receives too much because of a plan administration error or because the participant did not inform the plan of factors such as SSDI benefits that offset plan benefits. EPCRS requires sponsors to take reasonable steps to have overpayment repaid, with interest, unless it's under $100. Rev. Proc. 2015-27 clarifies that the plan sponsor is not required to seek repayment of all overpayments—for example, if the overpayment is the result of the plan's mis-calculation of the benefit.

The 2013 version of EPCRS was revised by Rev. Proc. 2015-28 (encouraging early correction of automatic contribution failures involving employee elective deferrals), and a new version of EPCRS was published in 2016, as Rev. Proc. 2016-51, 2016-42 I.R.B. 465. Because the determination letter process has been drastically curtailed (see § 10.02), Rev. Proc. 2016-51 eliminates references to favorable determination letters. The availability of the Self-Correction Program (SCP) for significant failures has changed. The IRS will no longer refund half the paid user fee when there is a disagreement about correction in Anonymous Submissions. Rev. Proc. 2016-51 also provides that user fees for VCP will be published in each year's Revenue Procedure updating user fees, rather than as part of EPCRS. Under the new version of EPCRS, sanctions under the Audit Closing Agreement Program are fact-based, but generally will be at least as great as the VCP user fee. Going forward, model VCP forms will only be available on the IRS Website; they will not be published in print in the IRS regulations. [IRS.gov, *Updated Retirement Plan Correction Procedures* (Oct. 3, 2016) (benefitslink .com); Robert B. Wynne, Katie M. Rak and Allison P. Tanner, *IRS Updates Correction Program for Retirement Plans*, McGuireWoods LLP (Oct. 6, 2016), available at Lexology.com; Matthew H. Hawes, R. Randall Tracht and Stefanie H. Ray, *Without Fanfare: IRS Issues New Revenue Procedure on EPCRS*, Morgan Lewis & Bockius LLP (Oct. 4, 2016), available at Lexology.com]

EPCRS can be used to voluntarily correct a failure to make required minimum distributions (RMDs) to participants and beneficiaries that are required by Code § 401(a)(9). If the plan sponsor does not comply, and the participant does not receive an RMD, the entire plan could be disqualified—affecting all the participants, not just the participant who may have to pay an excise tax of 50% of the RMD not received, under § 4974.

RMD failures are reported on Form 14568-H, Appendix C, Part II, Schedule 8, as an attachment to Form 14568. But Schedule 8 can only be used for affected participants; if beneficiaries are also involved, reporting is done on Form 14568 Appendix C, Part I, explaining whether the beneficiaries are spouses or not. If the failure is a § 401(a)(14) commencement of benefit failure, or any other failure, the proper form is also 14568 Appendix C, Part I.

In some cases, the Self-Correction Program (SCP) can be used to correct RMD failure even when plan is under examination. However the § 4974 excise tax owed by beneficiaries cannot be waived under SCP. A § 4974 waiver can be requested under the Voluntary Correction Program (VCP), and if the RMD failure subject to this excise tax is the only failure in the VCP submission, a discount on the compliance fee may be available. [IRS.gov, *Correcting Required Minimum Distribution Failures* (Sept. 27, 2016) (benefitslink.com)]

Sponsors have to pay a compliance fee to the IRS when a VCP correction is submitted; the fee is generally based on the number of plan participants. Effective February 1, 2016, new fees have been announced for VCP submissions under EPCRS. Unusually, most of the fees are lower than the previous fees. For plans with 20 or fewer participants, the fee has been reduced from $750 to $500. For 21–50 participants, it has been reduced from $1,000 to $750. For 51–100 participants, the reduction is from $2,500 to $1,500, but the fee for plans with 101–500 participants remains $5,000. Under the old rule, the maximum fee was $25,000 for plans with more than 10,000 participants; this has been greatly reduced, to $15,000. [Rev. Proc. 2016-8, 2016-1 I.R.B. 243; see Nancy S. Gerrie, Jacob Mattinson and Susan Peters Schaeffer, *IRS Announces Reduced VCP Compliance Fees*, McDermott Will & Emery (Jan. 21, 2016), available at Lexology.com]

Rev. Proc. 2015-27 allows reduced fees for certain minimum distribution failures (Code 401(a)(9)), as long as fewer than 300 participants are involved. Fees can also be reduced for participant loan failures corrected under EPCRS, if it is the only failure in the submission and not more than 25% of participants are affected by the failure. A corrective plan amendment must be adopted by 21 days after a favorable determination letter was issued or 150 days after the date of the IRS compliance statement—whichever is later. To be allowed to self-correct plan failures, the sponsor must maintain practices and procedures that are reasonably designed for Code compliance. Prior law said that this was true if excess annual additions were regularly corrected within 2½ months of the end of the limitation year. Rev. Proc 2015-27 extends that to 9½ months after the end of the limitation year.

Issues that cannot be handled under EPCRS might be appropriate for the sponsor to request a voluntary closing agreement under the IRS's Employee Plans Voluntary Compliance function. Sponsors can request these agreements to resolve tax issues about qualified plans. However, a request will not be approved if the plan sponsor is already being investigated by the IRS or has any pending tax appeals or Tax Court cases. Issues that could be resolved under VCP should use VCP. Voluntary closing agreements are not available if the IRS determines that the plan or plan sponsor was involved in an abusive tax avoidance transaction or where there has been a willful or intentional plan of tax evasion. Generally, the IRS will not negotiate about the amount of tax due or the interest on the tax due—but it is possible that the IRS will agree to abate penalties. If the plan is covered by ERISA Title I, the sponsor should use the DOL Voluntary Fiduciary Correction Program before applying for a closing agreement. The application should include an explanation of the problem, how it occurred, who is affected, and the amount of money involved, and an explanation of how taxes, penalties, and interest were calculated. The taxpayer must be able to show that the agreement is in the best interests of the IRS and that the taxpayer was not guilty of any intentional tax law violations. The sponsor must also complete all actions named in the closing agreement before the agreement is signed. A voluntary agreement cannot be used to seek guidance about, or address future events that could affect the plan's tax-qualified status. [IRS, *Employee Plans Voluntary Closing Agreements* (Jan. 12, 2016), available at <https://www.irs.gov/Retirement-Plans/Employee-Plans-Voluntary-Closing-Agreements> (updated Oct. 17, 2016) (last accessed Feb. 21, 2017)]

Once the sponsor and the IRS agree how to correct the failures disclosed in a VCP submission, the IRS issues a compliance statement. The statement is conditional on the sponsor actually completing the corrections by the end of the correction period. The usual period is 150 days, or longer for group submissions. The sponsor is required to seek out ex-employees and beneficiaries and revise its administrative procedures. A sponsor unable to meet the deadline should contact the VC specialist named on the compliance statement to explain why an extension is necessary; the specialist has discretion to grant an extension. If the sponsor fails to make full correction by the end of the correction period (as extended), it must make a second VCP statement, paying a second fee, and explain why the previous deadline was not met. A new VCP submission is also required to modify a compliance statement, but minor modifications can be made by making a written application to the IRS, which will issue a revised compliance statement if the change is accepted. [IRS.gov, *IRS Compliance Statement* (July 29, 2016) (benefitslink.com)]

The IRS is not the only agency to sponsor a correction program. DOL's EBSA oversees close to 681,000 retirement plans, about 2.3 million health plans, and about the same number of other welfare benefit plans (e.g., life insurance or disability plans) (October 2, 2015 figures). The plans covered approximately 143 workers and dependents, holding assets of more than $8.7 trillion. EBSA recovered $696.3 million for direct payment to plans and individuals: $265.3 million in plan assets restored and benefits recovered; $14.3 million through the Voluntary Fiduciary Correction Program (VFCP) and $13.9 million from the abandoned plan program. VFCP received 1,478 applications and there were 22,800 Delinquent Filer Voluntary Compliance Program (DFVCP) filings. Qualified Termination Administrators made 590 applications to wind up individual account plans abandoned by their sponsors: 207 applications were approved, and 205 plans distributed $13.8 million to participants.

In 2015, civil monetary recoveries were comparatively low (over the previous 15 years, the average was about $1.3 billion per year), but criminal investigations were unusually frequent.

In 2016, EBSA oversaw close to 681,000 retirement plans, about 2.3 million health plans, and over two million other welfare benefit plans (e.g., providing disability benefits or life insurance). In fiscal 2016, EBSA recovered a total of $777.5 million: almost half, $352.0 million, from enforcement actions, $9.5 million from the Voluntary Fiduciary Correction Program (VFCP), $21.8 million from the abandoned plan program, and $394.2 million from informal complaint resolution. EBSA closed 2,002 civil investigations in fiscal 2016, more than two-thirds of which—1,356 cases, 67.7%—resulting in corrective action for the plan. In fiscal 2016, 144 cases were referred to the solicitor of labor to be litigated, and DOL filed 62 civil suits in that year. EBSA's investigations resulted in 333 closed criminal cases; 96 people were indicted, and 75 investigations were closed by guilty fees or convictions. There were 1,490 VFCP applications received, and 22,070 Delinquent Filer Voluntary Compliance Program (DFVCP) filings received in fiscal 2016. [EBSA Fact Sheet, *EBSA Restores Over $777.5 Million to Employee Benefit Plans, Participants and Beneficiaries*, <http://www.dol.gov/ ebsa/newsroom/fsFYagencyresults.html> (undated, last viewed Feb. 21, 2017). See Sutherland.com, *Legal Alert: 2015 in Review: ERISA Civil Enforcement Recoveries Remain Low, Criminal Investigations Continue to Rise* (Feb. 2016) (benefitslink.com)]

DOL issues letters to plan sponsors who report failures to make timely 401(k) deposits on their annual return. DOL recommends making a VFCP filing to correct the issue and reduce risk of audit. Participant contributions become plan assets as of the date they can reasonably be segregated from the employer's general assets, whereas employer contributions become plan assets when they are actually contributed. Plans that have fewer than 100 participants at the beginning of the plan year qualify for a safe harbor if contributions are segregated within seven business days of the date they are withheld from wages or when voluntary after-tax contributions are received from employees. The correction for late transmittal is to transfer funds from the employer's general assets into the plan's trust as soon as possible after the error is corrected, preferably before Form 5500 is filed for the late deposits. Lost earnings on the late deposits must be made up. Unless corrected, delinquent deposits result in § 4975 prohibited transactions, subject to excise taxes (paid to the IRS on Form 5330). The employer becomes a disqualified person for using plan assets for its own business purposes. However, the VFCP sometimes waives excise taxes on delinquent deposits. DOL does not recommend audit for fiduciary breaches associated with delinquent deposits that have been reported under VFCP. ERISA requires DOL to impose a civil penalty for fiduciary breach equal to 20% of amount recovered in settlement or litigation, but this is waived if there is voluntary reporting and correction under VFCP.

Notice must be given to interest parties, including the EBSA regional office, within 60 calendar days after the VFCP submission. [Susan Quintanar, *Late Deposits—A Timely Topic*, Trucker Huss (Dec. 2015) (benefitslink.com)]

EBSA provides a model application form for filing VFCP applications. The plan sponsor reports the plan, the transaction that was corrected, amount of correction, who was involved, when the breach occurred, and how it was corrected. Late deposits of employee deferrals are a prohibited transaction, so they are subject to excise tax unless participants get notice. [Chris Ciminera, *The Voluntary Fiduciary Correction Program—How to File an Application*, Employeebenefit planaudit.belfint.com (July 23, 2015) (benefitslink.com)]

Rev. Proc. 2012-35, 2012-37 I.R.B. 341 states that, for requests postmarked on or after August 31, 2012, the IRS will no longer forward letters on behalf of retirement plan sponsors, administrators, or trustees of abandoned plans. The IRS changed its policy in light of the other options available to find missing participants. The change affects sponsors and administrators who want to use EPCRS to correct failures requiring payment of additional benefits, so future EPCRS guidance will give an extended correction period for those affected by the change. [Plansponsor staff, *IRS Stops Forwarding Letters for Missing Participants*, plan sponsor.com (Sept. 4, 2012)]

See <http://www.dol.gov/ebsa/actuarialsearch.html> (last accessed Feb. 21, 2017), for EBSA's online tools for employees and employers. When civil penalties are due for delinquent filings of annual reports, the tools permit plan administrators to return to compliance under the Delinquent Filer Voluntary Compliance Program by filing the overdue reports.

Plan administrators can use the DFVCP to reduce the civil penalties they may be subject to—as long as they make the required DFVCP filings before the DOL gives the administrator written notice of failure to file a timely annual report under ERISA Title I. (Form 5500-EZ filers and filers of Form 5500 for one-participant plans for business proprietors are not eligible for DFVCP because they are not covered by Title I.) An IRS late-filer penalty letter won't keep plan from participating in DFVCP, but a DOL Notice of Intent to Assess Penalty always does.

The EFAST2 FAQ explains how to file a delinquent Form 5500 under DFVCP, and the DOL has posted an online penalty calculator for DFVCP.

DFVCP penalties can be paid by check, sending the check and a paper copy of Form 5500, or Form 5500-SF, or the plan (without attachments or schedules) to DFVCP, P.O. Box 71361, Philadelphia, PA 19176-1361. The penalties can also be paid electronically at <https://www.askebsa.dol.gov/dfvcepay/calculator> (last accessed Feb. 21, 2017).

Failure to make a timely Form 5500 filing can be penalized by both the DOL and the IRS. DOL civil penalties are up to $ 2,097 per day (2017 figure). The IRS penalties, which apply in addition to the DOL penalties, can be as high as $25/day, subject to a cap of $15,000 per return. [Conduent FYI, *DOL, PBGC and HHS*

Increase Penalties for Violations (Feb. 10, 2017) (benefitslink.com)] Plan administrators are personally liable for ERISA § 502(c) civil penalties, and the penalties cannot be paid from the assets of an employee benefit plan.

IRS's Employee Plans Compliance Unit announced a new project to identify non-filers of Form 5500 by comparing payroll and plan data to DOL records. Letters are sent to companies that apparently failed to file. The letters operate as notice that they were informed of potential penalties, unless they clear their records by explaining why filing is not required. The Delinquent Filer Program has much lower penalties than the general ERISA penalties: $10 a day, capped at $750, $1,500, $2,000, or $4,000, depending on the size of the plan, versus the ERISA penalty for late filing of Form 5500. (The possible maximum penalty rose to $1,632 a day as of August 1, 2016 and $1,659 a day after January 13, 2017.)

DOL's FAQ says that a plan that receives an IRS late-filer letter can participate in the Delinquent Filer Program, but it is too late to participate once a DOL late-filer letter has been issued. [DOL EBSA, *Frequently Asked Questions: The Delinquent Filer Voluntary Compliance Program*, <http://www.dol.gov/ebsa/faqs/faq_dfvc.html> (last accessed Feb. 21, 2017)]

The PBGC's mission includes the early warning program (EWP) for single-employer defined benefit plans. The PBGC says that, in appropriate cases, termination of a plan can be averted by working with the sponsor to set up protective devices before a transaction that could increase the plan's losses. The PBGC regularly monitors businesses and markets, identifying about 300 events a year that could raise concerns. After deeper review, about 100 early warning cases are selected each year. Potential areas of concern are changes in a plan's controlled group or transfers of significantly underfunded pension liabilities. Sometimes the PBGC protects participants (and itself) by requiring higher plan contributions, or requiring the sponsor to obtain a letter of credit or a guarantor. Every year, the PBGC moves to terminate about five risky plans—less than 2% of those monitored. [Rebecca Moore, *PBGC Lists Triggers for Early Warning Program*, plansponsor.com (Jan. 17, 2017); Towerswatson.com, *PBGC Adds to List of Early Warning Factors* (Feb. 2017) (benefitslink.com)]

EBSA announced in early 2013 that migration to the fully electronic EFAST2 system is complete for all filing years and paper filings will no longer be accepted. See the DOL Website for an explanation of which version of the Form 5500/5500SF is required for your plan, and which schedules to use. The announcement, which primarily deals with the DFVC program, says that, although DFVC does not offer relief from late filing penalties under the Code or ERISA Title IV, the PBGC has agreed to provide some ERISA § 4071 penalty relief for delinquent filings of annual reports if the conditions of the DFVC program are satisfied. Relief from IRS penalties may be available if the DFVC and IRS requirements are satisfied. [Notice: RIN 1210-ZA 15 <http://www.dol.gov/find/20130128> (last viewed Feb. 21, 2017), FAQs at <http://www.dol.gov/ebsa/faqs/faq_dfvc.html> (last viewed Feb. 21, 2017). See Notice 2014-35, 2014-23 I.R.B. 1072.]

CHAPTER 16

EFFECT OF CORPORATE TRANSITIONS ON PENSION AND BENEFIT PLANS

§ 16.01 INTRODUCTION

A qualified plan can change its form for several reasons: by amendment, by termination, or as a response to a change in form in the corporation that sponsors the plan. The sponsoring corporation can merge with or be acquired by another company, and some or all of the first plan's employees can become employees of the new or surviving corporation. The transition may be primarily motivated by corporate needs or primarily to change the form or operation of the plan (e.g., combining several existing plans for ease of administration or to cut costs).

One of the most important questions in an M&A situation is how the surviving entity's benefits package should be structured and whether one company's package should be adopted. If the acquired business' benefits are a smaller percentage of payroll than the acquiror's, scaling up to the higher level would increase the cost of the acquisition. In some deals, each company retains a separate benefits package but it is much easier to administer a single plan, especially if the two companies are fully integrated. In a multi-national transaction, it may be necessary to conform to the country's rules that requires the highest benefits. [Joanne Sammer, *Managing Benefits in an M&A or IPO Deal*, shrm.org (Feb. 25, 2016) (benefitslink.com)]

Basic fiduciary principles continue to apply during a transition, and plans must still be maintained for the sole benefit of participants and beneficiaries. Therefore, the Supreme Court decided that plan participants and beneficiaries can sue under the Employment Retirement Income Security Act (ERISA) § 502(a)(3) to get equitable relief for themselves, when a company spun off its money-losing divisions to a new, financially unstable corporation and then lied to employees about the safety of their benefits if they transferred to the new corporation. [*Varity Corp. v. Howe*, 516 U.S. 489 (1996)]

However, because pension benefits vest but welfare benefits (including retiree health and insurance benefits) generally do not, ERISA fiduciary duty is not violated by transferring the obligation to pay nonpension retiree benefits to a new company spun off from the former employer. Nor will the courts hear an ERISA contract claim.

Code § 6058(b) requires filing of an actuarial statement at least 30 days before a merger, consolidation, or transfer of assets to another plan, even if the transfer is part of a spin-off. IRS Form 5310-A, Notice of Plan Merger or Consolidation, Spinoff, or Transfer of Plan Assets or Liabilities is filed to give notice of the combination of two or more plans into a single plan, splitting a plan into two or more spinoff plans, or a transfer of assets or liabilities to another plan. However, penalties will not be imposed for failure to file Form 5310-A in certain cases, such as when defined contribution plans are merged, but the sum of the account balances in each plan equals the fair market value of the plan assets; or two defined benefit plans are merged when the total liabilities of the smaller plan are less than 3% of the assets of the larger plan. [IRS Publication 794, *Favorable Determination Letter* (Nov. 2016), <http://www.irs.gov/pub/irs-pdf/p794.pdf>

(last viewed Feb. 23, 2017). This publication explains that, for terminating plans, the determination letter is based on the law in effect at the proposed termination date. See Rev. Proc. 2016-37, 2016-29 I.R.B. 136.]

The Sixth Circuit allowed claims by executives of Metaldyne about cancellation of their Supplemental Executive Retirement Plan (SERP) plan to be tried in state court. Metaldyne was once partially owned by the investment firm Heartland Industrial Partners, LP. In mid-2006, Heartland agreed to sell its Metaldyne stake to another investment firm. The SERP included change in control provisions under which Metaldyne would owe the plaintiffs about $13 million. To avoid having to make these payments, Metaldyne's board terminated the SERP. The SERP participants sued in state court for tortious interference with contractual relations. The Sixth Circuit found that these claims were not preempted by ERISA because the state court would not have to interpret the SERPs, just calculate damages if the plaintiffs proved that canceling them violated state law. [*Gardner v. Heartland Indus. Partners*, 715 F.3d 609 (6th Cir. 2013)]

Metaldyne was acquired by Asahi, a Japanese corporation, in 2007. The Pension Benefit Guarantee Corporation (PBGC) sought to make Asahi responsible for Metaldyne's underfunded pension plan. The District Court for the District of Columbia ruled that U.S. courts had personal jurisdiction over Asahi because of its activities directed at the United States (acquiring Metaldyne with knowledge of its pension liability issues). ERISA makes each member of a controlled group jointly and severally liable for pension liabilities in connection with termination of an underfunded plan or the employer's withdrawal from the plan. Even performing due diligence for a potential acquisition could be considered purposeful conduct that could subject a non-U.S. corporation to personal jurisdiction in the United States. If a non-U.S. corporation becomes part of a U.S. corporation's controlled group, any pension liabilities of the U.S. company might be deemed to arise out of the activities directed at the United States. However, it is unlikely that the PBGC would actually be able to collect a judgment from a non-U.S. corporation whose sole asset in the United States is a bankrupt subsidiary. The case was settled in late 2014. [Mark S. Chehi, *Japanese Acquirer Resolves Pension-Related Liabilities of US Subsidiary*, Skadden, Arps, Slate, Meagher & Flom LLP (Nov. 10, 2014) (benefitslink.com)]

Successful acquisitions often require retention of the target's essential employees. The acquiror and target company must decide who will be responsible for any change in control payments associated with the deal. Sometimes the buyer assumes the seller's employment agreements or negotiates new terms to take effect after the closing. A "pay to stay" retention agreement is a possibility, obligating key employees to remain employed for a stated period of transition. If this benefits both buyer and seller, they might be willing to share the cost. Paid time-off (PTO) and other credits under benefit plans are often dependent on length of service, so the seller might ask the buyer to give its employees credit under the buyer's benefit plans. It makes sense to restrict this to employees who are actually retained post-closing, and to stipulate that this provision does not obligate the buyer to hire the seller's employees. Another option is to pay off all accrued PTO at the closing and get a fresh start on the plan. [Beau Hurtig, *Employment Issues in the M&A Process*, Fredrikson & Byron PA (Mar. 2, 2015), available at Lexology.com]

See Chapter 43 for discussion of business-related liability insurance in general. Corporate and plan transitions can give rise to liability, with questions about who is responsible for actions at what time, so it is wise to have appropriate insurance coverage. Coverage under a fiduciary liability policy is triggered when the claim is made, not when the alleged wrongdoing occurred. While the fiduciary liability policy is in force, it will cover claims reported during the policy period. But if a policy is cancelled or is not renewed, then future claims will not be covered even if they relate to acts that occurred before cancellation or nonrenewal. Extended reporting period (ERP) coverage is optional: in exchange for an additional premium, ERP coverage applies to claims filed during a specified period (usually 12 months post-policy expiration) relating to events while the policy was in force.

Standard ERP coverage will not provide complete protection in a merger or plan termination situation, because there is a possibility that fiduciary breaches will be alleged until the statute of limitations (which could be as long as six years) has elapsed since the merger or termination.

"Tail coverage" protects the trustees of merged or terminated plans. Insurers do not have to provide tail coverage under a basic policy; the purchaser must negotiate the terms of coverage and the premium. Insurers are often reluctant to offer as much coverage as the trustees want. It is wise to include a provision forbidding cancellation of the policy after the premium has been paid. According to Segal Select Insurance, the premium for a six-year tail policy is likely to be two or three times the premium for the underlying fiduciary liability insurance when the plan was in operation. Tail coverage is usually paid from the assets of the plan that is being merged or is terminating, so it is important to arrange and pay for the coverage before the plan assets have all been distributed.

Instead of tail coverage, the successor plan might obtain a "merged-plan" endorsement, but the merged plan must continue to renew the coverage every year until the statute of limitations has expired, and the insurer may change the available coverage and liability limits. [Michael W. Huddleston, *Insurance Issues in Mergers and Acquisitions*, Munsch Hardt Kopf & Harr PC (Feb. 1, 2015), available at Lexology.com]

§ 16.02   CHOICE OF FORM

[A]   Generally

Companies considering a merger or acquisition must consider the plan design options that are available for the type of transaction selected. Nondiscrimination testing will probably be required, and there will be compliance requirements for the surviving plan. The presence or absence of golden parachutes, retiree health benefit obligations, and the Comprehensive Omnibus Budget Reconciliation Act (COBRA) obligations must be determined. Worker Adjustment and Retraining Notification Act (WARN) [29 U.S.C. § 2101 *et seq.*] notification may also be required if there is a significant reduction in the workforce after the corporate transition. [See § 30.10] Plan discrimination testing must also be repeated after a change of corporate organization. [See § 4.22] Changes in ownership or the form of ownership of a corporation sponsoring a plan may constitute "reportable events" of which the PBGC must be notified (in case the plan is unable to meet its payment obligations and the PBGC has to take over).

In a stock sale, the acquiror buys 100% of the target's shares. All assets or liabilities of the target thereby become assets or liabilities of the acquiror. Unless the target plan is terminated before the transaction, the acquiror becomes the sponsor of the target's retirement plans. This could be costly, especially for defined benefit and retiree health plans.

In an asset sale, the acquiror purchases all of the target's assets but the target's corporate existence continues. Usually the sale proceeds are used to satisfy the target's liabilities and then the target is shut down. But as long as the target continues in existence, it is still the plan sponsor. The plan could be continued for the benefit of its remaining employees. Terminated employees would be paid out of the target's plan. If the acquiror becomes the sponsor of the target's plan, it has three options:

- Maintain both plans, especially if the target is considered a separate division. The acquiror becomes the sponsor and administrator of the target's plan. Former employees of the target still have their salary deferrals deposited into the target's plan. However, the employees are now employed by the acquiror, so coverage, participation, and nondiscrimination testing are based on the combined group of employees. However, under this scenario, the acquiror must pay two sets of plan administration costs. There might be problems with the target's plan that are not immediately evident.

- Merge the plans, giving the target's plan participants the same vested benefits after as before the merger. The acquiror will be responsible for historical activities of the target's plan.

- Terminate the target's plan (the most common option). At termination, all benefits become 100% vested. The target must distribute benefits to the participants, who can take the funds in cash, carry out Individual Retirement Account (IRA) rollovers, or, if they have been hired by the acquiror and the plan allows, roll over the funds to the acquiror's plan. Once payouts are finished, the target's plan files a final Form 5500 and is terminated. If the acquiror chooses, it can amend its plan to provide that service with the target counts toward eligibility and/or vesting for the acquiror's plan. Otherwise, the target's ex-employees will be treated as new hires. [Beth Harrington, *Impact of Merger or Acquisition on Company Retirement Plans* (Mar. 5, 2014) (benefitslink.com)]

A recent article summarizes the risks that may be uncovered in the course of performing due diligence before a transaction. The author notes that it is easy to overlook liabilities for benefit plans other than defined benefit pension plans because they do not appear on the balance sheet. Of course an attorney skilled in ERISA issues should review plan documents, Form 5500 filings, plan audits, reports of funding and assets, and contracts with service providers to make sure that the plans are compliant. Due diligence review of health and welfare plans is often limited to determining that the proper 5500 forms have been filed, and there are no audits or lawsuits pending. But if the target's health plans are self-funded, supplemented by a stop-loss policy, reserves will be needed for "runoff claims" (i.e., incurred but not paid by the closing date).

If the buyer maintains the seller's business, the buyer will probably be a successor business for COBRA purposes, so it will have to offer continuation coverage to former employees of the seller who lose their jobs because of the transaction. In a stock transaction, the buyer assumes the obligations under the retiree health benefit plan, although, as Chapter 9 shows, it may be possible to reduce or terminate retiree health benefits. When employees are terminated, state law may require payment for accrued but unused vacation days. Withdrawal from a multi-employer plan can be quite costly.

In a stock sale, there will be no withdrawal liability if the purchaser assumes the Collective Bargaining Agreement (CBA), but an asset sale is likely to subject the buyer to withdrawal liability, which may be the equivalent of a large part of the purchase price. There is a safe harbor under ERISA § 4024: withdrawal liability is waived in a bona fide arm's length asset sale as long as the buyer is obligated to contribute to the plan, on behalf of approximately the same number of union members, as the seller did; the buyer purchases a bond protecting the plan for five years; and the contract of sale makes the seller secondarily liable for the withdrawal liability if the buyer withdraws from the plan in less than five years. [Mary L. Komornicka, *Looking Past Due Diligence for Benefit Plans in Mergers and Acquisitions*, Larkin Hoffman Daly & Lindgren (Third Quarter 2015) (benefitslink.com)]

[B] T.D. 8928

[1] Generally

T.D. 8928, 66 Fed. Reg. 1843 (Jan. 10, 2001), provides that, when a corporation makes an asset sale (of substantially all the assets of a trade or business, or an asset as substantial as a factory or a corporate division), it is treated as the successor employer if the seller entirely ceases to provide group health plans, and the buyer maintains business operations using the assets. A transfer (e.g., in bankruptcy) is considered an asset sale if it has the same effect as a sale would have.

The plans that the seller maintained before the transaction could be retained, frozen, or terminated. A buyer who adopts an existing plan could agree to assume liability only going forward, with the seller retaining liability for violations of the plan rules that occurred before the sale. As for plans maintained by the buyer before the transaction, the buyer's and seller's plans could merge. [See below for the anti-cutback rules and the requirement of crediting prior service to the new plan.]

Like all rules, this has exceptions. If the transaction is in effect a merger rather than an asset sale, liabilities will be characterized as they would be in a merger. If the buying corporation is a mere continuation of the selling corporation, or if the transaction is a fraud intended to escape liability, the transaction will be disregarded.

If only plan assets, and not the operating terms of the two plans, are merged, then the transaction is not considered a plan amendment that has the effect of reducing plan accruals. However, if the plans merge and one adopts the other's formulas and definitions, the original plan is deemed to have been amended. If benefits are reduced, notice must be given under ERISA § 204.

[2]   ERISA Issues

In most instances, duplicative plans are merged, or some of them are eliminated. The seller's plan generally transfers assets (and related liabilities) either to the buyer's existing plans or to a newly created plan. ERISA does not require employees to be represented in the negotiations; but once the deal is consummated, the surviving and new plans must be operated subject to fiduciary standards, and mandatory communications must be made to employees.

A corporation's decision to terminate or amend a plan, or to spin off part of a plan, is a discretionary "settlor" function, and the plan sponsor does not act as a fiduciary. The amount of assets to be assigned to a spun-off plan, or the decision to transfer employer securities to a new plan created as part of a spin-off, is not a fiduciary decision. However, the fiduciaries of the plan making the transfers must comply with the plan merger and asset transfer standards set out in ERISA § 208.

Many transactions are structured so that the buyer assumes the seller's responsibility for providing unfunded benefits, such as retiree health coverage. The seller's decision to transfer the liability, and the buyer's commitment to accept it, are also settlor functions and therefore cannot give rise to a claim for breach of fiduciary duty. However, ERISA § 208 does require that each participant receive at least as good a benefit package if the plan were terminated just after the transaction as he or she would have received if the plan had terminated just before the transaction. It should also be remembered that plan assets must not be used for purposes other than paying benefits.

A former Booz Allen Hamilton executive sued the company alleging that he lost $21 million that he would have received for selling his stock if he had not been forced to retire before his division was sold. The Ninth Circuit held that the stock rights plan in which he participated was intended to meet the firm's capital needs and encourage executives to remain employed. It was not an ERISA plan because it was not designed or intended to provide deferred or retirement income. [*Rich v. Shrader*, 823 F.3d 1205 (9th Cir. 2016), *cert. denied,* 137 S. Ct. 627 (2017); see Carmen Castro-Pagan, *Booz Allen Executive's $21M ERISA Claim Gets Booted*, bna.com (May 25, 2016) (benefitslink.com). The Third, Fifth, and Eighth Circuits have ruled similarly.]

Anheuser-Busch's pension plan said participant whose employment with the controlled group is involuntarily terminated within three years of a change in control would be entitled to enhanced pension benefits. The company argued that employees of the entertainment division were not eligible for the enhanced benefit because they continued to work for the successor that now owned the division. The Eighth Circuit disagreed, holding that although they were not unemployed, their employment with the controlled group had terminated. It was an abuse of discretion for the trustees to fail to follow the plain language of the plan. [*Knowlton v. Anheuser-Busch Cos. Pension Plan*, 849 F.3d 422 (8th Cir. 2017); see Haynes and Boone LLP, *Eighth Circuit Holds That Failure to Follow the Plain Language of the Plan Is Abuse of Discretion* (Mar. 1, 2017), available at Lexology.com]

The Multiemployer Pension Plan Amendments Act (MPPAA) provides that, when an employer withdraws from a multi-employer plan, the sponsor of the plan calculates the employer's liability and contacts the employer as soon as possible to obtain payment. The Seventh Circuit held that a purchaser was subject to successor liability for the withdrawal liability, because it was aware of the potential withdrawal liability (although the seller did not learn that it was deemed to have withdrawn from the multi-employer plan, owing $662,000 in withdrawal liability until after it sold its assets) and because there was substantial continuity of business. The Seventh Circuit said that Congress wanted to prevent the withdrawing employer's share of unfunded vested benefits from being shifted to other employers in the multi-employer plan. [*Tsareff v. ManWeb Servs., Inc*, 794 F.3d 841 (7th Cir. 2015)]

The Ninth Circuit joined the Seventh Circuit in holding that a successor employer can be liable for its predecessor's liability for withdrawing from an ERISA multi-employer pension plan and broadened the class of potential successors. The Seventh Circuit held an asset purchaser liable for the seller's ERISA withdrawal liability, even though the asset purchase agreement expressly disclaimed liability. The Ninth Circuit said that the critical factor is continuity of customer base. A flooring company went out of business and sold its equipment at a public auction. An ex-employee leased the store and warehouse, solicited the ex-employer's customers, and hired many of its employees. The Ninth Circuit remanded for the district court to carry out more fact-finding on successorship. In bankruptcy cases, Bankruptcy Code § 363 may provide some protection against successor liability claims. [*Resilient Floor Covering Pension Trust Fund Bd. of Trs. v. Michael's Floor Covering, Inc.*, 801 F.3d 1079 (9th Cir. 2015)]

When a single-employer defined benefit plan terminates without having enough assets to pay liabilities, the plan sponsor and any businesses sharing 80% or more common control are jointly and severally liable for the plan's unfunded liabilities. For at least 30 years, the PBGC took the position that buyers of a company's assets were not subject to this termination liability. Then, in 2016, the PBGC changed its position and argued that a buyer of assets was liable, as a successor, for the seller's unfunded defined benefit plan liabilities. Some courts have held that a buyer can be liable if it has notice of the liability and the buyer has substantial continuity of operations with the seller. However, the District Court for the Northern District of Ohio disagreed. The PBGC argued for applying federal common law. The district court refused, holding that ERISA has a specific statutory scheme which must be followed. If the termination liability arises in a bankruptcy situation, it is possible—but not guaranteed—that an asset purchaser will be able to use Bankruptcy Code § 363(f) to avoid successor liability for the payments required when withdrawing from a multi-employer plan. [*PBGC v. Findlay Indus., Inc.*, 2016 WL 7474404 (N.D. Ohio Dec. 29, 2016); see Eric Keller, *PBGC Attempts to Hold Asset Buyer Liable for Seller's Underfunded Single Employer Pension Plan Termination Liabilities*, Paulhastings.com (Feb. 2, 2017) (benefitslink.com)]

A group of terminated employees who were not rehired after their employer's facility was sold sued, alleging a conspiracy by the employer and the purchaser to violate ERISA § 510 by terminating older employees and depriving them of pension benefits. The Tenth Circuit ruled for the employer, holding that pension issues were not even considered until after the sale so they could not have motivated the sale. The Tenth Circuit held that there is no § 510 violation if the employer acted for legitimate business reasons, even if some laid-off employees lost pension eligibility. [*Apsley v. Boeing Co.*, 691 F.3d 1184 (10th Cir. 2012)]

[C] Labor Law Implications of Choice of Form

Labor law follows the basic rule that a merger or sale of stock obligates the acquiring company to assume the liabilities of the acquired or selling company. This includes the Collective Bargaining Agreement (CBA). But in an asset sale, the CBA is not assumed unless the purchaser voluntarily takes it on, or unless there is another reason to view the buyer as a successor or surrogate of the seller.

Yet even if the company is not fully bound by its predecessor's CBA, it could still have a duty to bargain in good faith with the existing union, based on continuity linking the old and new enterprises. If a transaction lacks real substance, the successor could be forced to assume the predecessor's labor-law obligations. The main test is whether there has been a significant practical change or whether operations continue despite a nominal change in ownership.

In addition to situations in which one entity replaces another, two or more enterprises can be treated as a "single employer" for labor-law purposes. One might be treated as an alter ego (surrogate) of the other. If a parent company and its subsidiary engage in the same line of business, the National Labor Relations Board (NLRB) will probably treat them as a single enterprise, not two. Furthermore, "joint employers" that are separate entities but share decision making about labor issues may be treated together by the NLRB.

Either a purchaser must be prepared to take on the predecessor's union contracts and other labor-law obligations, or must structure the transaction to be free of such obligations. Also note that a change in corporate ownership (even if corporate structure remains the same) can lead the state to revoke the privilege to self-insure against Worker's Compensation claims.

A new company that adopts an existing operation can unilaterally change the wage scale, unless it's "perfectly clear" that the new owner will hire all of the old employees. In a "perfectly clear" case where the new owner does not consult with the union and there is no evidence of what would have emerged if there had been negotiations, the employees are given the benefit of the doubt. It is assumed that the former wage rate would have continued and would not have been diminished. So new ownership in a "perfectly clear" case cannot lead to wage cuts unless the union agrees.

In its 1999 decision in *St. Elizabeth's Manor* [329 N.L.R.B. 341 (1999)], the NLRB created a "successor bar" rule under which an incumbent union would be given a reasonable amount of time, after a corporate takeover, to bargain with the successor employer without challenges to the union's majority status. However, the NLRB overruled this decision in mid-2002. Under the new rule, in a successorship situation the incumbent union is entitled to rebuttable presumption of continuing majority status—but if there is evidence to rebut the presumption, an otherwise valid challenge to majority status will be allowed to proceed. [*MV Transportation*, 337 N.L.R.B. 129 (2002)]

In an asset transaction, the NLRB's position is that the purchaser or new employer must recognize and bargain with the union representing the seller's employees, if the new employer continues the business in substantially unchanged form, and hires the employees of the previous employer as the majority of the workforce after the transaction closes. However, the new employer is not required to abide by the predecessor's the CBA if it informs the union and employees, either before or at the time of hiring, that it does not intend to be bound. In that situation, the new employer can establish new terms and conditions of employment that are different from the existing CBA and can bargain for a new agreement.

However, an asset buyer that communicates correctly can set terms and conditions of employment to be used as a starting point in bargaining, unless the asset purchase agreement includes an agreement to assume the CBA, making it perfectly clear that the purchaser is a successor employer. A 2016 NLRB decision makes it harder to avoid perfectly clear successor status. The NLRB asserts an obligation to bargain when the asset purchaser manifests an intention to retain the predecessor's employees without making it clear that continuing to work for the purchaser constitutes acceptance of new terms and conditions of employment. To avoid successorship, the new employer must announce the intention to set new conditions before, or at least at the same time as, expression of intent to hire the seller's employees. [*Nexeo Solutions, LLC*, 364 N.L.R.B. No. 44 (2016); see Keith J. Brodie, *Buyer Beware—NLRB Decision Creates New Risks for Purchasers of Union Operations*, Barnes & Thornburg LLP (Aug. 3, 2016), available at Lexology.com. Like all recent NLRB decisions, it is likely to be overturned as the composition of the agency shifts under the Trump administration.]

In mid-2016, the Eighth Circuit held that a business buyer was liable under the WARN Act to employees of the seller who were not offered jobs—even though the asset purchase agreement assigned all WARN Act liability to the seller. The asset purchase agreement required the seller to keep the people who were not offered jobs in employment status for 14 days after the closing of the deal. The seller did not give WARN Act notices; but the seller had no assets, so a group of 449 ex-employees sued the buyer. Under the WARN Act "sale of business" exception, the seller is responsible for providing notice for terminations up to the date of the sale, the buyer is responsible for subsequent terminations. The WARN Act treats the seller's employees as employees of the buyer immediately after the sale takes effect: see 29 U.S.C. § 2101(b)(1). In this case, the Eighth Circuit held that the buyer can remain liable for the seller's failure and that it is impossible to contract out of statutory responsibilities The Eighth Circuit found that the asset purchase agreement was binding only on the companies that signed it, not their employees. Because the buyer purchased everything essential to the business (e.g., the business name and customer lists), the Eighth Circuit treated the transaction as the sale of a going concern (with WARN Act obligations) rather than an asset sale (free of such obligations). [*Day v. Celadon Trucking Servs., Inc.*, 827 F.3d 817 (8th Cir. 2016); see Marc A. Mandelman, *8th Circuit Rules Parties to Corporate Transactions Cannot Contract Around The WARN Act Sale of Business Exception* (Aug. 3, 2016), available at Lexology.com; Tamara R. Jones, *Appellate Spotlight Be Forewarned: WARN Act Obligations Not Easily Avoided*, Constangy Brooks Smith & Prophete LLP (Aug. 10, 2016), available at Lexology.com]

The Eighth Circuit held in early 2014 that the purchaser of a business has the Uniformed Services Employment and Reemployment Rights Act (USERRA) obligations. The seller corporation's failure to list the plaintiff as an active employee when it sold its assets to another company violated USERRA by failing to treat the plaintiff, who was deployed on active military duty, on parity with other employees on leave. [*Dorris v. TXD Servs., LP*, 753 F.3d 740 (8th Cir. 2014)]

[D]   Transitions and Unemployment Insurance

Although it is a comparatively minor cost, the acquirer of a business may wish to take advantage of the amount of the Federal Unemployment Tax Act (FUTA) tax already paid by the transferor of the business for the part of the year before the transition. The successor employer can rely on wages paid (and therefore on FUTA payments made) by the predecessor if either one of two circumstances exists. The first is that the transferee acquires substantially all the property used in the transferor's entire trade or business (or in a separate unit of the trade or business). The other is that, whether or not the property was acquired, at least one employee from the old business remains employed immediately after the transfer.

> ■ **TIP:**   A multistate operation will usually be permitted to combine wages paid in the various states for FUTA purposes.

The IRS's view, for Federal Insurance Contributions Act (FICA) and tax withholding as well as FUTA purposes, is that, in a statutory merger or consolidation, the surviving corporation is the same taxpayer and the same corporation as the predecessor corporation(s). Of course, that means that the successor will have to pay any taxes due but unpaid by the predecessor—unless the successor gives the local administrative agency adequate written notice.

However, most state unemployment laws provide that companies remain subject to unemployment insurance laws for at least two years once they have acquired an experience rating—with the result that the transferor may remain liable in a year after it ceases operations, unless it applies to the local administrative agency for a determination that it is no longer an employer.

If the predecessor has acquired a good experience rating, the successor will probably be able to take over the experience rating with the rest of the operation, as long as operations remain more or less the same, at the original business location, and the workforce remains stable. Altering these important factors in effect creates a new enterprise, which will have to acquire its own experience rating.

[E]   COBRA Issues

Depending on the structure of the transaction, it is likely that some of the employees of one or both of the companies involved in a transition will lose their jobs. Perhaps as a result of the deal, some individuals will remain employed but will cease to be covered by an Employer Group Health Plan (EGHP). If a COBRA event occurs, unless the organization is too small to be covered, it will be necessary to provide COBRA notice. In the context of a corporate transition, that raises the question of who is responsible for providing the notice.

The crucial question is whether there has been a qualifying event. If there has, the structure of the transaction (stock sale versus asset sale) will determine the allocation of the notice burden. COBRA provides that an M&A qualified beneficiary may have a qualifying event if he or she was last employed by the acquired corporation (in a stock sale) or was last employed in connection with the assets being sold in an asset sale. However, a stock sale is not a COBRA qualifying event if the employee continues to be employed by the acquired organization after the transactions, even if the employee is no longer covered by an EGHP.

An asset sale results in a qualifying event for those whose employment is associated with the purchased assets, unless the buying corporation is a successor employer and the employee is employed by the buying corporation immediately after the sale. There is no COBRA event after an asset sale for people who retain their coverage under the selling corporation's EGHP. A successor employer is either a mere continuation of the former employer company; an entity that results from the merger or consolidation of the employer corporation; or a continuation of the business operations associated with the purchased assets.

[Kenneth W. Ruthenberg Jr., *Don't Pick up COBRA as Part of Your Next Deal—Negotiating COBRA Liability in Business Transactions*, <http://www .insurancethoughtleadership.com/articles/dont-pick-up-cobra-as-part-of-your-next-deal#axzz325WWYia4> (Aug. 30, 2011) (last accessed Feb. 23, 2017); Jefferson A. Holt, *An Oldie but a Goodie: Liability for COBRA Continuation Coverage in M&A Transactions*, Burr & Forman LLP (Oct. 18, 2016), available at Lexology.com]

[F] Bankruptcy as a Transition

When a bankrupt company operates as a Debtor in Possession under Chapter 11, the benefit plans will usually remain in operation during the reorganization process, but a Chapter 7 liquidating bankruptcy will probably lead to termination of the plans.

The Supreme Court's 2007 *Beck* decision made it clear that a bankrupt company does not have a fiduciary duty to consider the option of merging its pension plan into a union multi-employer plan rather than adopting the company's preferred alternative of carrying out a standard termination and buying annuities to satisfy payment obligations. The Supreme Court's rationale was that terminating a plan is a business decision made by the plan sponsor in its role as settlor of the trust that administers the plan. In this reading, this is not an administrative decision made by the plan's fiduciaries—even if they are the same people as those who carry out the settlor functions. Furthermore, ERISA's termination section (§ 4041) does not discuss mergers. [*Beck v. PACE Int'l Union*, 551 U.S. 96 (2007)]

In 2011, the Third Circuit became the first court of appeals to rule that a claim against a debtor for post-petition liability for withdrawing from a multi-employer pension plan receives administrative expense priority in the company's Chapter 11 bankruptcy case. The Multi-Employer Pension Plan Amendments of 1980 amended ERISA to make employers who withdraw from multi-employer plans liable for their pro rata share of unfunded, vested benefits as of the time of withdrawal.

The Third Circuit balanced Bankruptcy Code and ERISA objectives by apportioning the withdrawal liability between the pre- and post-petition time periods. The post-petition portion can be an administrative expense; the balance was deemed to be a general unsecured claim. The Third Circuit limited the size of the administrative expense claim to prevent the estate from being swallowed up by the withdrawal liability claim. [*In re Marcal Paper Mills, Inc.*, 650 F.3d 311 (3d Cir. 2011)]

The PBGC does not get involved in a standard termination because the plan has adequate assets to satisfy its obligations. If a distress termination occurs, the PBGC is required to pay the guaranteed benefits. The PBGC allows distress terminations in Chapter 11 bankruptcy cases if the bankruptcy court makes a determination, under ERISA § 1341(c), that the employer will not be able to pay all of its debts under a reorganization plan and will not be able to stay in business unless the pension plan is terminated.

The court has to decide whether there is any feasible reorganization plan that would preserve the pension plan; it is not restricted to considering the plan proposed by the debtor. An important question is whether financing could be obtained to continue the business—and if the parties that might provide the financing insist on termination of the pension plan. The company must explore alternatives, such as eliminating only some pension plans and maintaining others; exploring funding waivers; freezing future benefit accruals, but not terminating the plan; and looking for non-pension means of saving money.

The PBGC does not guarantee any benefits earned after the date of the bankruptcy filing, even if the plan does not terminate until later. The limitations on the PBGC guarantee also apply as of the date of the filing, not the (generally higher) limitations in a later year of plan termination. The filing date also determines who is entitled to benefits that fall in Priority Category 3. [PBGC, *How the Bankruptcy Date Rule Can Affect Your Benefits*, <http://www.pbgc.gov/about/pg/other/how-the-bankruptcy-date-rule-can-affect-your-benefits.html> (undated, last viewed Feb. 23, 2017)]

A corporation contemplating bankruptcy will have to determine the future of its plans, including who will serve as administrator and trustee before and after bankruptcy and how benefits will be distributed from a terminated plan.

Severance benefits usually come from the employer's assets, and may have the status of a priority claim in bankruptcy. The Bankruptcy Abuse Prevention and Consumer Protection Act (BAPCPA; Pub. L. No. 109-8), 2005's bankruptcy reform legislation, affects the treatment of pensions and employee benefits in several ways.

When an employer files for bankruptcy protection, wage and benefit claims for 180 days (rather than prior law's 90 days) are priority claims, and $10,000 per employee in wages and benefits (raised from the previous level of $4,000) counts as a third-priority claim. The $10,000 figure is indexed for inflation. The bankruptcy trustee can avoid transfers made to or for the benefit of corporate insiders during two years (rather than one) prior to the filing. Transfers made under an employment contract can be avoided by the trustee—whether or not the transfers caused the employer to become insolvent—if they occurred outside the ordinary course of business. BAPCPA also places limits on retention bonuses and severance benefits that can be paid to corporate insiders.

The employer's creditors are not permitted to reach amounts contributed by employees, or withheld from their wages for contribution, to a plan when the amounts are in the employer's hands because they have not yet been placed into the plan.

If the employer modified retiree welfare benefits (e.g., retiree health plans) within the 180 days before filing of the bankruptcy petition, any party of interest can apply for a court order. The modification will be enjoined unless the court rules that the balance of equities clearly supports the modification.

Usually conflicts arise when bankruptcy results in a reduction of benefits. The Third Circuit ruled that plan amendments adopted just before a Chapter 11 filing, which resulted in the doubling or even quintupling of pension benefits for certain participants (including corporate insiders), was invalid as a fraudulent conveyance. The court also criticized the introduction of the amendment to the board of directors as an "administrative formality" as evidence of bad faith and the use of a surplus in the union side of the pension accounts to fund the new benefits. [*Pension Transfer Corp. v. Beneficiaries Under Third Amendment to Fruehauf Corp. Ret. Plan*, 444 F.3d 203 (3d Cir. 2006)]

A later Third Circuit case holds that, even if a company has reserved the right to amend or terminate a plan (e.g., a retiree health plan), the company still must comply with the BAPCPA requirements for obtaining court approval for changes to the plan. [*IUE-CWA v. Visteon Corp.*, 612 F.3d 210 (3d Cir. 2010)]

See Chapter 19 for a discussion of the obligation to provide continuation coverage under COBRA (as modified by the American Recovery and Reinvestment Act (ARRA) subsidy program). Even if a health plan is terminated, outstanding claims will have to be satisfied. Under the Health Insurance Portability and Accessibility Act (HIPAA) (also discussed in Chapter 19) employees are entitled to certificates of creditable coverage showing their date of enrollment in the plan, so they can establish their entitlement to purchase individual coverage.

§ 16.03   THE ANTICUTBACK RULE

Internal Revenue Code § 411(d)(6) forbids amendments that reduce accrued benefits, including early retirement benefits and the availability of additional forms of payment over and above the required QJSA and QPSA. But according to *Board of Trustees of the Sheet Metal Workers National Pension Fund v. C.I.R.* [117 T.C. 220 (2001)], only employees, not retirees, can "accrue" benefits. Therefore, eliminating post-retirement Cost of Living Increases does not violate the anti-cutback rule, because the benefits were not "accrued."

In 2004, the Supreme Court ruled [*Cent. Laborer's Pension Fund v. Heinz*, 541 U.S. 739 (2004)] that an amendment increasing the varieties of post-retirement employment that would cause the suspension of benefit payments violated the anti-cutback rule. [See T.D. 9219, 2005-38 I.R.B. 538 and T.D. 9280, 72 Fed. Reg. 45379 (Aug. 9, 2006) for Final Regulations reflecting *Heinz*.]

If a plan is spun off, the spin-off plan is required to maintain the old plan's payment options as to benefits accrued before the spinoff.

In a merger, employees are permitted to retain their premerger pay-out options. In practice, this means that if a merged plan wants to have a single pay-out structure, it must improve the less-favorable plan to equal the options under the more-favorable plan.

Section 411(a)(10)(B) requires that individuals who had three years of service before the corporate transition will be entitled to keep the old vesting schedule, if it is more favorable to them than the newly adopted one. Employers have an obligation to inform employees of this option.

According to I.R.C. § 414(l), if plans (even plans maintained by the same employer) merge or consolidate, or if a plan's assets and liabilities are transferred to another plan, each participant's benefit immediately after the transition, calculated on a termination basis, must be at least as great as his or her benefit would have been if the plan had terminated immediately before the transition.

The regulations for this section say that a transfer of assets and liabilities from one plan to another will be treated as a spinoff followed by a merger. This usually means that Form 5310-A has to be filed at least 30 days before the merger, spinoff, or asset transfer.

Section 414(l) requires a plan's actuaries to make reasonable assumptions about expected retirement age, mortality, and interest rates before and after the asset transfer. The termination assumptions that the PBGC uses offer a safe harbor because using them is always deemed reasonable, but their use is not mandatory.

The Secretary of the Treasury has the power to enforce ERISA § 208, which is very similar to I.R.C. § 414(l). The Department of Labor has indirect enforcement powers under ERISA § 208, because of its enforcement powers over fiduciary conduct.

Internal Revenue Code § 414 has separate rules for merging two defined contribution plans; two defined benefit plans; and one plan of each type to make sure that participants' entitlement to benefits is not reduced as a result of the transaction. There are further requirements to be observed if one of the plans is fully funded but the other is underfunded. For defined benefit plans, this section serves two policy purposes. It avoids manipulation of funding by means of moving plan assets between the plans of a controlled group of corporations, and it prevents the dilution of benefits within the ERISA § 4044 priority order for categories of assets during a termination.

The priority order is as follows:

- Assets are allocated to benefits coming from participant contributions;
- Benefits going to individuals who were already getting benefits during the three years before the termination;
- Benefits to persons who could have been getting benefits during that three-year period;
- PBGC-guaranteed benefits;
- Other nonforfeitable benefits;
- Everything else.

The First Circuit ruled in 2010 that it was permissible for a plan to eliminate an option for participants to move assets from a defined contribution plan to a defined benefit rule, even though it had the effect of diminishing an accrued benefit. DHL acquired Airborne and merged its defined contribution and defined benefit plans into its own plan, eliminating the right to move balances between plans. The First Circuit, although decrying the unfairness of the result, held that, although Tasker's actual pension was only about half of what he had expected, DHL did not violate any of ERISA's statutory requirements. [*Tasker v. DHL Ret. Sav. Plan*, 621 F.3d 34 (1st Cir. 2010)] Subsequently, in a case involving the same plan, the Ninth Circuit agreed that it was not a cutback to eliminate the transfer provision. [*Andersen v. DHL Ret. Pension Plan*, 766 F.3d 1205 (9th Cir. 2014)]

In a case of first impression, the First Circuit held in 2013 that retroactively conferred benefits are "benefits attributable to service" that are considered accrued benefits under the anti-cutback rules. Banked hours are hours worked in a year over and above the number of hours needed to earn a full year of service credit. They are banked for purposes such as filling in during a year when the participant does not have a full year of credit. They are cashed in at retirement as additional pension credits. Four union locals merged, also merging their pension plans. All of the plans had different banked hour rules, so they were unified at the highest level. The result was that many participants, including the plaintiffs, received retrospective increases in the levels of banked hour credits after the merger. Eventually the merged pension trust got into financial trouble and wanted to reduce the retrospective banked hour benefits to the level each participant would have received under the original plan he belonged to before the merger. The First Circuit held that ERISA does not limit accrued benefits to those that were promised in advance. Although these benefits were conferred retroactively, they were nonetheless attributable to prior service. [*Bonneau v. Plumbers & Pipe-fitters Local Union 51 Pension Trust Fund*, 736 F.3d 33 (1st Cir. 2013)]

A new employer that purchased the old employer's business, told employees that they would receive past service credit in the new employer's plan for time worked for the predecessor. The Ninth Circuit held that the plain terms of the plan did not entitle the plaintiffs to past service credit. However, the Ninth Circuit permitted the plaintiffs' claims for § 1132(a)(3) equitable relief to go to trial; it was permissible for them to bring simultaneous claims under § 1132(a)(1)(B) (that were dismissed) and (a)(3). [*Moyle v. Liberty Mut. Ret. Ben. Plan*, 823 F.3d 948 (9th Cir. 2016)]

§ 16.04 NOTICE OF REDUCTION OF BENEFITS

ERISA § 204(h) requires notices of reductions in future benefits to be given before the effective date of any amendment that eliminates or reduces an early retirement benefit or early retirement subsidy. An excise tax is imposed on failure to provide proper notice.

T.D. 9472, 2009-51 I.R.B. 850, is a final rule governing notice requirements under § 204(h) for plan amendments that reduce accrued benefits. Code § 4980F(e)(3) requires notice to be provided within a reasonable time before the plan amendment takes effect. In general, that means 45 days before the effective date (15 days for small or multi-employer plans). However, for some amendments that took effect by December 31, 2008, notice is acceptable if given at least 30 days before the effective date. [T.D. 9472, 2009-51 I.R.B. 850]

§ 16.05 THE MINIMUM PARTICIPATION RULE

Initially, minimum participation rules were applied to both defined contribution and defined benefit plans. However, the Small Business Job Protection Act of 1996 [Pub. L. No. 104-188] eliminated this rule for defined contribution plans—now only defined benefit plans are required to have a minimum number or percentage of participants. This is significant in the context of corporate transitions because asset buyers often decline to adopt the seller's plan. If the plan is not adopted, there is a risk that the new plan will fail to cover the mandated number or percentage of employees.

Some relief is available under I.R.C. § 410(b)(6)(C), which allows one year after an acquisition or the disposition of a corporation to satisfy the minimum participation requirement. But after that, the plan is likely to become disqualified—unless it has been terminated in the interim.

A possible strategy is to freeze the plan. However, if too many participants choose to cash out, that creates difficulties. Two or more plans can be merged into a larger plan, offering a benefit structure at least as favorable as the most favorable of the merged plans, no later than the fifteenth day of the tenth month after the end of the plan year.

§ 16.06 IN-SERVICE DISTRIBUTIONS AND REHIRING

The underlying purpose of pension plans is to provide post-retirement financial security. Therefore, "in-service distributions" (distributions from the plan while the individual is still working) historically were severely discouraged by the Code. Although many government agency employers had phased retirement plans, few private-sector employers did so. There are some special rules governing taxation of in-service distributions during a transition. Treasury Regulation § 1.401-1(b)(1)(i) provides that defined benefit plans cannot make in-service distributions before the employee's retirement or termination of employment—unless the plan itself is terminated. But a defined contribution plan that is not a 401(k) plan can use the two-year/five-year rule. That is, contributions can be withdrawn from the plan after the contributions have been in the plan for two years, or the participant has five years of plan participation.

> ■ **TIP:** EGTRRA eliminates the "same desk" rule for 401(k) plans. In other words, when there is a merger consolidation, or liquidation, participants in a 401(k) plan will be entitled to take a distribution from the plan even if the successor company hires them and they have not separated from service. Congress intended to increase the portability of pensions in this situation.

Because of the abolition of the same desk rule, distributions can be made from the seller's plan in either an asset or a stock sale, to employees who go to work for the buyer or stay at the subsidiary that has been sold, as long as that subsidiary drops participation in the plan by the time of the sale. [*Cassidy v. Akzo Nobel Salt Inc.*, 308 F.3d 613 (6th Cir. 2002)] The termination plan defined release as permanent separation initiated by the employer for reasons such as lack of work, RIF, or unsatisfactory performance by the employee.

Under the Pension Protection Act, Pub. L. No. 109-280, employees who have reached age 62 can lawfully receive in-service distributions under a phased retirement plan (see § 9.06). See also T.D. 9235, 2007-24 I.R.B. 1386 (Final Regulations on the definition of Normal Retirement Age).

The Sixth Circuit held that ERISA does not require job loss or a period of unemployment before benefits can be enhanced based on a change of control. (In this case, employees were credited with five additional years of service if they lost their jobs within three years of a change in control.) [*Adams v. Anheuser-Busch Cos.*, 758 F.3d 743 (6th Cir. 2014)]

§ 16.07 TAX ISSUES

If, after a merger, liquidation, or reorganization, the surviving company maintains the predecessor corporation's qualified plan, I.R.C. § 381 generally provides that the original plans' tax attributes are passed on to the successor plan. If two qualified plans consolidate, the deductions taken by each employer before the consolidation will not be retroactively disqualified by the consolidation.

The acquiring corporation can keep up the plan for the benefit of those covered by it under the old ownership—with no obligation to cover the workers who were its own employees before the acquisition.

Asset purchases that result in the liquidation of the seller company or acquisition of its assets by the purchaser company, can create "orphan plans" (plans with no sponsor), which create tax problems. Once a plan loses its sponsor, it can lose tax-qualified status. There may also be ERISA fiduciary liability issues about managing, reporting, and distributing assets from the plan. The IRS's Employee Plans Compliance Resolution System (EPCRS; see § 15.19[B]) has a process for correcting errors of orphan plans. [Keith R. McMurdy, *Don't Let Your Plan Become an Orphan*, Fox Rothschild LLP Employee Benefits Legal Blog (Jan. 24, 2012) (benefitslink.com)]

The Sixth Circuit applied labor, not corporation, law to determine whether a company is subject to the Family and Medical Leave Act (FMLA), finding that it is irrelevant for this purpose whether there is a transfer of assets or a merger with the seller. The Sixth Circuit pointed out that the FMLA defines "employer" to include successors in interest, and the Regulations (29 C.F.R. § 825.107) adopt the Title VII standard for successorship in interest. [*Cobb v. Contract Transp., Inc.*, 461 F.3d 632 (6th Cir. 2006)]

The risk of acquisition or merger makes corporate recruitment more difficult, because top candidates have a realistic fear that they will lose their jobs during a shake-up. Employment agreements with prominent candidates often include "golden parachutes" (providing generous compensation if the job is lost because of a corporate transition) and "golden handcuffs" (retention bonuses that are forfeited if the individual quits shortly after being hired). Most of these programs only take effect when employees have involuntary job loss; some plans have a "window period" during which payments will be made even if the employee quits voluntarily. See § 1.01[B] for discussion of limitations on golden parachutes and other severance payments to top management of financial services companies receiving federal bail-out funds.

A "stay bonus" for remaining with the new owner is a fixed benefit (and therefore a fixed incremental cost for the business buyer). The bonus is paid after the employee has remained for a certain period of time. It could also be combined with a golden parachute. For instance, the executive could be offered two months' salary as a bonus for staying a year, or given a severance package of three months' salary and outplacement assistance if terminated without good cause within 18 months of the transition.

Internal Revenue Code § 280G does not allow corporations to deduct "excess parachute payments." Any "disqualified person" who receives an excess parachute payment is subject to a 20% excise tax, under I.R.C. § 4999. A parachute payment is a payment of compensation, contingent on a change in ownership, and equal to three times or more of the base amount (roughly speaking, the base amount is the individual's normal compensation). There are many ways to draft parachute agreements. A safe harbor cutback provides that payments will be reduced to equal the maximum amount that will not trigger the excise tax. A valley provision, also known as a better-off cutback, reduces the payment the same way, unless the executive would be better off financially by receiving the higher amount and paying taxes on it. A full gross-up reimburses the executive for the excise tax; this is very expensive for the payor corporation, especially because the gross-up payment is not deductible. Public companies must also consider the probable reactions of shareholders. A modified gross-up calls for limitation to the maximum amount that will not trigger excise tax. [PLC Employee Benefits & Executive Compensation, *Addressing Sections 280G and 4999 in Executive Employment Agreements* (Apr. 16, 2013) (benefitslink.com)]

Code § 409A is the IRS's attempt to control inappropriate deferral of nonqualified deferred compensation. (See § 8.02[D]) Section 409A potentially applies to many compensation arrangements in change of control situations: severance agreements, stock options, and incentive agreements, for example. Violating § 409A can lead to accelerated inclusion in income for the person receiving the compensation, and a 20% federal tax penalty. California imposes its own 20% penalty as well.

For § 409A purposes, merger or acquisition of a company's equity usually does not constitute a separation of service for employees who continue to be employed after the transaction. If there is an asset sale or transfer, someone who leaves the seller's employ and goes to work for the buyer generally does have a separation from service. But if the transaction is a transfer of substantial assets, such as substantially all of a business' assets, then the buyer and seller can make an election as to which employees who go to work for the buyer have a separation from the seller's service. The election must be set out in a written document created before the transaction closes, the document must be the product of bona fide, arm's-length negotiations, and all employees must be treated consistently for this purpose. [Will Fogleman and John McGuiness, *Separation Anxiety: Analyzing Separations from Service Under Section 409A*, Bloomberg BNA Pensions & Benefits Daily (Dec. 23, 2014) (benefitslink.com)]

A single-trigger arrangement provides benefits upon change in control, even if the executive is not terminated at the time of the acquisition. Double-trigger arrangements, which require an adverse employment action within a specified time of the change in control, are growing in popularity. Post-change in control severance usually is paid in a lump sum, because after the change, the restrictive covenants are less of a concern to the acquired company. The executive also wants to receive the funds in a lump sum to avoid being at the mercy of the acquiring company's CEO and management team.

One potential risk is that alternative payment methods under a double-trigger severance plan could fall under § 409A. The company might fail to recognize this because the pre- and post-change severance arrangements are specified in different documents—for example, the overall severance plan and an individual executive's change-in-control agreement. A double-trigger arrangement typically becomes subject to § 409A if the "good reason" payment trigger is excessively broad—say, if it allows the executive to resign and collect severance based on a minor reduction in pay or duties; if the installment payments exceed $490,000 (indexed for inflation), or the payments extend more than two years after separation from service. Because of economic uncertainty, "earn-outs" have become more popular in private company acquisitions. The earn-out provides for future payments to the seller of the acquired company if the company reaches certain business milestones—typically, within two to five years, although the period could be 10 years or even longer. A stock option cash-out or management incentive plan can be subject to an earn-out without violating § 409 as long as payments are made at the same time, and generally on the same terms and conditions, to payments to the shareholders as a whole. To qualify for this treatment, the earn-out payments generally must be made within five years of the transaction's closing date, although § 409A permits limited customized alternatives tailored to the situation of an earn-out that exceeds five years.

Earn-outs are speculative and difficult to value. There are risks: if the earn-out is overvalued, there will be penalties for a § 409A violation, but if it is undervalued, the option-holders will suffer economic harm. Some companies value the earn-out at the time of the assumption, whereas others use an "open transaction" approach, adjusting the options to reflect the earn-out only as it is paid. The issue could also be avoided by requiring option holders to exercise their options just before the transaction. [Juliano P. Banuelos, *Recent Compensation Trends in Mergers and Acquisitions and Section 409A*, Orrick Perspectives (Oct. 2011) (benefitslink.com)]

As well as their tax implications, golden parachutes have ramifications for corporate law and securities regulation. Exchange Act § 14A, enacted by the Dodd-Frank Act, requires a non-binding shareholder vote about golden parachute compensation. The vote cannot be used to overrule the Board of Directors' decision, change the board's fiduciary duties, or restrict the ability of shareholders to include their own proposals in the corporation's proxy materials. Proxy statements must include a separate resolution, subject to shareholder vote, to approve any compensation agreements—unless the shareholders have already approved the agreement through a "Say on Pay" vote. This provision is effective for shareholder meetings that occur after January 21, 2011. [Michael S. Melbinger, Winston & Strawn LLP, *Executive Compensation Blog* (Aug. 12, 2010) (benefitslink.com)]

§ 16.08   THE PBGC EARLY WARNING PROGRAM

The PBGC has consistently required reporting of plan conditions that might result in plan termination and, therefore, PBGC liability, but in recent years, the number of "reportable events," and the categories of employers that must report them, have been reduced significantly.

In December 2016, the PBGC Website was updated to add two new events to the list of transactions monitored by the PBGC: reduction in credit rating and downward trend in financial factors such as cash flow. The Early Warning Program identifies about 300 transactions a year where additional information is requested; about 100 transactions get deeper review, and in about five cases a year, the PBGC intervenes to terminate a risky plan. The PBGC can negotiate a settlement with the plan, under which the employer will contribute more to the plan than its minimum funding obligation, the employer gives the PBGC a letter of credit to cover its unfunded liabilities or future pension contribution obligations; the employer grants the PBGC a security interest in named corporate assets; or the employer submits a guarantee from a related corporation. [Harold J. Ashner and Deborah West, *PBGC Expands Scope of Early Warning Program,* Bloomberg BNA Pension & Benefits Daily (Jan. 10, 2017) (benefitslink.com); Rebecca Moore, *PBGC Lists Triggers for Early Warning Program,* plansponsor .com (Jan. 17, 2017); Towerswatson.com, *PBGC Adds to List of Early Warning Factors* (Feb. 2017) (benefitslink.com)]

The administrator of a single-employer plan is obligated to submit a "4063 notice" when an employer who is a contributing sponsor ends operations at a facility, resulting in job loss for more than 20% of the plan participants. A 4063 notice is also required if a substantial employer withdraws from a multiple employer plan. The 4063 notice does not replace any Reportable Event notice that is required by § 4043. At press time in 2015, there was no official PBGC form for the 4063 notice; employers who are required to report should send the notice within 60 days of the event—either by mail to the PBGC's Corporate Finance & Restructuring Department, 1200 K Street NW, Washington, DC 20005-4026, faxed to (202) 842-2643, or e-mailed to 4063.report@pbgc.gov. [PBGC, Section 4063 Notices, <http://www.pbgc.gov/prac/reporting-and-disclosure/section-4063-notices.html> (last viewed Feb. 23, 2017)]

There was a moratorium on § 4062(e) enforcement between 2012 and 2014. Then, in late 2014, the Consolidated and Further Continuing Appropriations Act, Pub. L. No. 113-235 (aka "Cromnibus"), made major changes in § 4062(e) reporting. Plans with fewer than 100 participants are no longer subject to § 4062(e). Plans are exempt if they had 90% or greater funding in the plan year before cessation. When operations at a facility terminate permanently, liability occurs when there is a 15% reduction in the total number of employees eligible to participate in any employee benefit plan, including 401(k) plans, that are maintained by members of the controlled group. (This replaces a test of 20% of participants in defined benefit plans.) Generally speaking, there is no § 4062(e) event unless participants actually lose their jobs—not merely go to work for a successor employer.

For employers that trigger the 15% level, the Cromnibus legislation permits a new, less expensive option for satisfying § 4062(e) liability. The employer can make installment payments over seven years, each on equal to one-seventh of the unfunded vested benefit multiplied by the percentage reduction in active participants. Each installment is capped at an amount by which the additional contributions increase the plan's minimum funding contributions. Employers can stop making installment payments if, in any year, the plan's unfunded vested benefits become 90% funded—even if the plan falls below the 90% level later. These rules apply to cessations of operations that occur on or after December 16, 2014. The PBGC must apply these rules to earlier cessations, unless a settlement agreement was entered into before June 1, 2014.

The PBGC's position is that, with these new rules in place, the moratorium is no longer required because obligations have been clarified. Cessation of operations does not have to be reported by plans with fewer than 100 participants, or that are at least 90% funded. (Although multi-employer plans are generally beyond the scope of this book, the Cromnibus legislation also takes the dramatic step of permitting certain failing multi-employer plans to reduce benefits.)

When a plan is terminated, the Code generally requires 100% vesting, and full vesting of participants affected by a partial termination (reduction of group of employees covered by a plan because of plan amendment or severance). However, the Code does not define the percentage at which a partial termination occurs. The *Matz* case spent almost 19 years in the Seventh Circuit, with five appeals. Dismissal of the case was finally affirmed in late 2014. In 2004, the Seventh Circuit adopted a rebuttable presumption that a reduction of 20% or more was a partial termination—but a reduction of less than 10% was conclusively not a partial termination. In Rev. Rul. 2007-43, the IRS adopted the 20% presumption but not the conclusive rule that a 10% reduction was not a partial termination. In 2014, the Seventh Circuit said that the length of time for aggregating reductions to determine if a partial termination occurred is generally one plan year. However, complex transactions are not always completed within a year, so related significant corporate events that occur over a multi-year period can be combined to measure the percentage reduction. The 2014 opinion says that employees of seven subsidiaries were terminated, but even if aggregated, the percentage reduction would be only 17%, and thus not conclusive. [*Matz v. Household Int'l Tax Reduction Inv. Plan*, 774 F.3d 1141 (7th Cir. 2014)]

§ 16.09   STOCK OPTIONS

During the late lamented Internet boom at the start of the twenty-first century, stock options were greatly cherished by employees because of the possibility of purchasing stock for a few dollars and being able to resell it at a much higher price—especially if the company was a start-up with the potential for a high-flying Initial Public Offering. Under current depressed stock market conditions, far fewer employees hold options that can be exercised profitably. However, in the hope that conditions will turn around again, the topic is worth discussing.

Mergers raise many questions about stock options, including:

- Do employees of the acquired company forfeit their outstanding options?

- Are their options bought out?

- Do they receive options in the acquirer company in exchange?

One of the factors fueling the economic boom of the late 1990s and early 2000s was the incentive to mergers and acquisitions offered by "pooling of interest" accounting. When pooling of interest was available, it allowed two companies to exchange equity securities and pool their bookkeeping and accounting thereafter. The net result was that the company's reported earnings would be higher, because there was no need to amortize goodwill as an expense. In contrast, if the transaction had to be accounted for under the purchase method, the acquirer would be deemed to purchase the acquired company, and the financial statements of the combined entity must reflect the fair value of the company's assets and liabilities. However, for most transactions initiated after June 30, 2001, pooling of interest accounting is unavailable—the purchase method must be used instead. For most plans, all outstanding stock options will vest upon a change in control; vested options can be exercised within a limited period, such as 30 or 60 days.

[See § 22.02 for further discussion of stock options]

Treatment of outstanding options is an important part of M&A planning. Whether vesting should be accelerated when there is a change in control is a business decision, separate from consideration of the transaction's effect on outstanding options. The board of directors should be allowed maximum flexibility to decide, at the time of a transaction, whether options that have not already been exercised should be canceled; if the options should be taken over or substituted by the acquiring corporation; or cashed out for the difference between the exercise price of the option and the price per share of the stock to be received in the transaction. One possibility is to cancel the out-of-the-money options without consideration, but to pay cash for the in-the-money options. The acquiring company may wish to assume the target company's options instead of substituting them; substitution could deplete the acquiror's equity incentive plan pool—or could have the inadvertent effect of modifying the awards in a way that triggers § 409A or makes the options non-qualified.

If the acquiring company is a public corporation, the stock exchanges allow the remaining shares under the target company's assumed plan pool to be issued without approval by the shareholders. But the acquiror may prefer to substitute rather than assuming the target's options, if the acquiror wants all of its options to have uniform terms and conditions. Shares underlying substituted options do not have to be registered; there is already a registration statement in effect (which is not true of assumed options). The acquiror may prefer not to assume the options if their terms, or the size of the class qualifying for options, is not consistent with the acquiror's corporate culture. An acquiror that does not pay cash for the underlying stock in the transaction may prefer not to cash out the stock options, so the plan must be flexible enough to permit termination of the options instead. If the options are canceled, the optionees can exercise their vested options until the transaction closes. Cashing out options benefits the acquiror because it does not have to administer the options after the closing; it does not incur a compensation expense; its shareholders' equity is not diluted; and employees can get cash for their equity without having to pay out-of-pocket to fund the exercise price. Holders of options in private companies like cash-outs because the optionees can receive liquidity without having to make an investment.

It must be decided (either when the options are granted in the first place, or when a corporate transition occurs) whether vesting should be accelerated if the transaction constitutes a change of control. The acceleration provisions can be embodied in the incentive plan, or in agreements outside the plan, such as the option award, executives' employment contracts, their severance, or retention agreements. In addition to the conventional single- and double-trigger arrangements, hybrid arrangements are possible, such as partial vesting on change of control, with additional vesting if a second triggering event occurs. Or, vesting might depend on the way the options are treated in the transaction. For example, vesting might be accelerated only if the awards are not assumed by the acquiror, which would mean that the optionee would not be able to vest at a later time, even if he or she remains employed. [Pamela B. Greene and Ann Margaret Eames, *Stock Options in Merger & Acquisition Transactions*, Corporate & Securities Advisory (June 6, 2011) (benefitslink.com)]

Many transactions involving grants of stock or other forms of compensation, outside the context of a qualified retirement plan, trigger the application of Code § 409A (see § 8.02[D]). Mid-2016 final and proposed regulations under § 409A tackle the situation where the parties to an acquisition transaction seek to change the payment terms of the target's incentive-based pay arrangements (especially those based on stock value) to align better with the treatment of shareholders who purchased their shares. The 2016 rules allow stock rights to be deemed compliant with § 409A as long as payments are not extended more than five years after the transaction and if the terms are the same as the terms for shareholders. However, stock rights cannot be restructured as unvested promises to cash out the award and cannot be converted to Restricted Stock Units that provide payments over the original vesting term of the award under terms that are not the same as those applying to shareholders. [Ropes & Gray LLP, *Updates to the 409A Rules* (June 27, 2016), available at Lexology.com]

CHAPTER 17

PLAN TERMINATION

§ 17.01 INTRODUCTION

When companies start a pension plan, they usually do so in good faith, and with the intention of keeping the plan in operation as long as it is necessary to provide benefits. However, ERISA and the Internal Revenue Code recognize that sometimes it will be necessary to terminate a pension plan—usually because the sponsoring corporation is ceasing operations, being absorbed by another company, or has financial difficulties so severe that it cannot continue to meet its obligations. There are even some rare circumstances under which the plan is *over* funded, and the employer is able to terminate the plan, distribute its assets, and retain the plan surplus for its own benefit.

Plan termination is usually voluntary, premised on the employer's decision to shut down the plan. However, courts, based on a determination that the economic security of plan participants is at risk, can order involuntary terminations. The legal system provides structures for winding up pension plans in an orderly way. Usually, the plan's assets are applied to purchase annuities that will pay participants' pensions as they become entitled to receive them.

Sponsors of frozen plans are especially likely to terminate plans or to consider terminating them in the future. The financial trade-off is the cost of purchasing annuities to replace the pensions or making lump-sum buyout payments, versus the book value of the plan and ongoing overhead costs. If the employer keeps up the plan, it must make pension payments as they accrue, plus administrative costs and the Pension Benefit Guaranty Corporation (PBGC) premiums. According to the *CFO Journal*, as of 2009, 21% of the Fortune 500 had frozen their pension plans—a proportion that rose to 39% in 2015. [Tatyana Shumsky, *CFOs Work to Freeze Defined Benefit Pensions,* WSJ.com (Aug. 20, 2016)]

Pension risk transfer is the practice of an employer entering into a contract with an insurer. The employer transfers enough assets to back up the obligations and compensate the insurer for its role; thereafter, the pension payments are made by the insurer, not by the plan. The employer benefits by eliminating the costs and risks associated with investing to cover the pension liabilities, and reducing exposure to volatile financial markets. State regulators impose capital requirements (e.g., 5%–10% of the transaction) that the insurer must retain in case its predictions about investment trends turn out be wrong. [Leslie Scism, *Your Pension Check May Soon Be Coming from an Insurance Company,* WSJ.com (Mar. 12, 2017)]

In 2016, there were $13.7 billion in single-premium pension buy-out transactions, about 1% higher than the 2015 level. [LIMRA.com, *U.S. Single Premium Pension Buy-Out Sales Top $13.7 Billion in 2016, LIMRA Secure Retirement Institute Reports,* (Mar. 1, 2017) (benefitslink.com)]

The LIMRA Secure Retirement Institute found that in the third quarter of 2016, there were more than a billion in pension buyouts, the fourth consecutive quarter in which this was true. LIMRA analyzed that pension buyouts are becoming more common—and involving smaller employers—because companies want to escape low interest rates and rising PBGC premiums. Pension buy-out activity increased 80% in the third quarter, and as of September 30, 2016, 17,165 buy-out contracts had been reported. By the end of the third quarter, the group annuity risk transfer market held $141 billion in assets. [LIMRA.com, *LIMRA Secure Retirement Institute Survey: Single Premium Pension Buy-out Sales Nearly $6 Billion in the Third Quarter 2016* (Nov. 29, 2016) (benefitslink.com); John Manganaro, *DB Pension Buyouts Reached a Milestone in Q1*, plansponsor.com (June 1, 2016)]

Under the relevant legal and tax rules, a plan termination can be either complete or partial. When a termination occurs, all accrued benefits vest immediately—including benefits that would not vest until later under the plan's normal vesting schedule. This requirement is imposed to reduce the temptation to terminate expensive and inconvenient plans!

Terminating a plan involves both the IRS and the Department of Labor (DOL). Both the Employment Retirement Income Security Act (ERISA) and the IRC must be consulted. There are forms to be filed, consents to be secured, and disclosure obligations to the participants and beneficiaries of the plan. Then, the plan's assets are distributed within an "administratively reasonable time" (generally defined as one year or less). But if the process continues for too long, the plan may be treated as if it had not terminated, and reports under I.R.C. §§ 6057–6059 will still be required. Section 6059 applies only to defined benefit plans.

A federal agency called the Pension Benefit Guaranty Corporation (PBGC) plays an important role in the termination of defined benefit plans. When a plan termination is contemplated, the plan notifies the PBGC, which has 60 days (or longer, if the plan consents to an extension) to review the proposed termination for any improprieties.

The PBGC also has the power to ask the federal court system to close down a pension plan (even if the employer has not sought to terminate the plan) and supervise the orderly distribution of its assets. The PBGC is not involved in the termination of defined contribution plans, because each participant in such a plan has an individual account that can be distributed to him or her.

There are certain exceptions to these general rules. Benefits are not guaranteed if they become nonforfeitable only because of the termination; nor does the agency guarantee benefits in full if the plan was in effect for less than 60 months before it terminated. If a benefit was scheduled to increase under a plan amendment that was either made or took effect within 60 months prior to the termination, the PBGC will not guarantee the increase.

The PBGC's guarantee applies only to benefits accrued before a plan terminates—and only to benefits accrued before the filing date if the employer is bankrupt when the plan terminates. In general, the PBGC pays benefits according to the terms of the plan, but if an individual's full benefit exceeds the PBGC's limit, the PBGC pays estimated benefits while it examines the plan records, and then reduces benefits to the limit. For about 80% of participants and beneficiaries, the estimated benefit is the same as the final benefit; but if the estimated benefits are lower than the actual benefit, the PBGC will make a single payment (including interest) to catch up. [PBGC, *PBGC's Guarantees for Single-Employer Pension Plans Fact Sheet*, <http://www.pbgc.gov/about/factsheets/page/guar-facts.html> (undated, last accessed Feb. 23, 2017)]

Terminating a plan requires bringing it into conformity with all legal and regulatory changes since the last update and there are usually several federal statutes each year requiring conforming amendments. Informal IRS guidance from mid-2016 says that a terminating plan must adopt final amendments, to ensure that the plan will retain its tax-favored status and that when participants receive distributions, they will be able to roll them over tax-free to other plans. The IRS directs administrators of terminating plans to consult the annual Cumulative List of tax-law changes for the period of the termination. When the plan applies for a determination letter approving its termination process, the IRS will advise whether any amendments are still required. Multi-employer plans insured by the PBGC, partially terminating plans, and plans whose status as part of an affiliated group is unclear can file Form 5310 or Form 5300 to obtain an IRS determination of qualified status as of the time of termination. [John Manganaro, *IRS Emphasizes Amendments Required Before Termination* (plansponsor.com) (Aug. 1, 2016)]

Coverage under a fiduciary liability policy is triggered when the claim is made. Extended reporting period (ERP) coverage is optional, at extra cost. It covers claims filed during a specified period (typically, one year after the policy expired), relating to events during the policy term. Standard ERP coverage will not provide complete protection when a plan terminates because fiduciary breaches might be alleged for up to six years (the longest statute of limitations likely to be applied) after the plan was terminated. "Tail coverage" protects the trustees of terminated plans. According to Segal Select Insurance, the premium for a six-year tail policy is likely to be two or three times as high as the underlying fiduciary liability insurance for the pre-termination period. Tail coverage is usually paid from the assets of the plan that is being merged or is terminating, so it is important to arrange and pay for the coverage before the plan assets have all been distributed. [Segal Select Insurance Fiduciary Shield, *If a Plan Merger or Termination Is on the Horizon, Seek Tail Coverage* (Mar. 2014) (benefitslink .com)]

[A] Changes Under the PPA

The Pension Protection Act of 2006, Pub. L. No. 109-280, affected most areas of pension and benefit law, and plan termination is no exception. The variable rate premium was capped for employers with 25 or fewer employees. To deter manipulation of employee censuses, the same participant count is used for both the flat- and variable-rate premiums. The PPA imposed a new category of premiums, a termination premium of $1,250 per participant per year for three years.

See <http://www.pbgc.gov/prac/prem/premium-rates.html> (last accessed Feb. 23, 2017) for the premium rates prevailing in 2017, reflecting subsequent legislation including the Moving Ahead for Progress in the 21st Century (MAP-21) Act, Pub. L. No. 112-140; Highway and Transportation Funding Act (HATFA), Pub. L. No. 113-159; the Multi-Employer Pension Act (MPRA), part of Pub. L. No. 113-235; and the Bipartisan Budget Act of 2015, Pub. L. No. 114-74.

Before the passage of HATFA, bankrupt sponsors were not permitted to make accelerated distributions (e.g., of lump sums). HATFA provides that the determination of the funding percentage for plans whose sponsor is in bankruptcy cannot use the higher interest rate under the 25-year-average rate.

The MPRA builds on the disclosures that defined benefit plans must make in their annual funding notices. Multi-employer plans that have terminated through mass withdrawal by employers have alternative means of giving notice. The Employee Benefit Security Administration (EBSA) final regulations, published in February 2015, state that the annual funding notice does not have to be provided in a plan year if the notice's due date occurs on or after the date on which PBGC Form 500 (standard termination notice) was filed. However, this relief is available only if the proposed termination date is on or before the due date of the funding notice.

Furthermore, the final distribution of assets to satisfy the plan's benefits liabilities must be carried out in accordance with ERISA § 4014(b). The notice includes information about the plan's assets and benefit payments; the PBGC guarantees, insolvency, and possible benefit reductions. Funding notices must be furnished to the PBGC and to each participant covered by the plan on the last day of the notice year, and to every beneficiary, alternate payee, and labor organization. Notice must also be given to every employer that is a party to the Collective Bargaining Agreements (CBAs) under which the plan is maintained—or who might otherwise be subject to ERISA withdrawal liability. The general rule is that notices must be furnished within 120 days of the end of the notice year. However, small plans (100 participants or fewer on each day of the previous year, whether it is a single- or multi-employer plan) have a deadline of the date the annual report is filed, or the date of any extensions granted, whichever is later. See Appendix A for model notices for single and multiple-employer plans, Appendix B for multi-employer plans. [80 Fed. Reg. 5625 (Feb. 3, 2015)]

The PPA enacted Code § 430, defining the minimum required contribution to a single-employer defined benefit plan as the target normal cost (expected benefit accruals during the year) plus the amount needed to amortize any shortfall in funding over a seven-year period. Employers that fail to satisfy the minimum funding standard are subject to an excise tax under Code § 4971. Proposed rules were issued in April 2008, and finalized in September 2015. The final regulation treats the plan year in which a plan is terminated as a short year, ending on the termination date. The target normal cost and amortization amount are prorated to reflect the short year. The minimum required contribution for the year of termination must be paid within 8½ months after the date of termination. If the plan is covered by PBGC termination insurance, the Code § 430 termination date is also the termination date under ERISA § 4048. For other defined benefit plans, the § 430 termination date is the last date on which all actions to terminate the plan (other than distribution of assets) have occurred. The assets must be distributed as soon as administratively feasible, including time needed to get an IRS determination letter approving the termination process. [T.D. 9732, 80 Fed. Reg. 54373 (Sept. 9, 2015)]

If a plan is at risk (see Chapter 5 for more discussion), it will be limited in its ability to provide shutdown benefits, unless the employer either makes additional contributions to strengthen the plan, or provides security for the benefits. Participants in at-risk plans are entitled to notification about the limits on distributions. Furthermore if a distress or involuntary termination occurs, the plan must inform the participants (within 15 days of the PBGC filing) of the information contained in the notice to the PBGC (new ERISA § 4041(c)(2)(D), 4042(c)(3)).

The D.C. Circuit held that shutdown benefits were not payable when Thunderbird Mining Corporation, a wholly owned subsidiary of Eveleth Mines, terminated its pension plan, because Thunderbird was not "shut down." The company was still trying to get new orders after production was stopped at its plant, although production had ceased and all except four hourly employees had been laid off. The bankruptcy court approved the sale of the Eveleth assets; the purchaser hired the hourly employees under a new CBA. [*United Steel Workers v. PBGC*, 707 F.3d 319 (D.C. Cir. 2013)]

In mid-2008, the PBGC proposed a rule under the PPA, to treat the termination date of a plan that ends when its employer is in bankruptcy as of the date of the filing of the bankruptcy petition, not the actual date of termination. The rule was finalized in mid-2011. The effect of this rule is that the benefits guaranteed by the PBGC will probably be somewhat smaller, because amounts earned by plan participants after the date of the bankruptcy filing will not be guaranteed by the PBGC. [76 Fed. Reg. 34590 (June 14, 2011), finalizing proposed rules at 73 Fed. Reg. 37390 (July 1, 2008).]

ERISA § 4062(e), the section dealing with substantial cessation of operations in single-employer plans, has been amended frequently. [For the history, see Harold J. Ashner and Deborah West, *Section 4062(e) Liability in Transition: Planning for an Uncertain Future*, Bloomberg BNA Pension & Benefits Daily (Aug. 27, 2014) (benefitslink.com)]

Certain business events are deemed to predict whether the plan is likely to terminate soon, while it is unfunded (and therefore likely to require the PBGC's expensive involvement). In mid-2010, the PBGC proposed rules defining such § 4062(e) events, drawing a distinction between contractions in operations and actual cessation of operations, placing the action level at a 20% reduction in the number of active participants. [PBGC, *Liability for Termination of Single-Employer Plans; Treatment of Substantial Cessation of Operations*, 75 Fed. Reg. 48283 (Aug. 10, 2010). The 2010 proposals were withdrawn, after industry protests that defaults were unlikely.]

Late in 2012, the PBGC relieved about 92% of plan sponsors of the obligation to provide guarantees. The PBGC said it would not take action against companies that were either small (fewer than 100 plan participants) or creditworthy. The policy continued to evolve, and a moratorium on § 4062(e) enforcement was called for the second half of 2014. [PBGC Press Release No. 14-09, *PBGC Issues Moratorium on 4062(e) Enforcement*, <http://www.pbgc.gov/news/press/releases/pr14-09.html?cid=CPAD01PRJUL0820141> (July 8, 2014)]

The "Cromnibus" legislation (the Consolidated and Further Continuing Appropriations Act) essentially restructures advance reporting of adverse events under ERISA § 4062(e). Under Cromnibus, plans with fewer than 100 participants are no longer subject to § 4062(e). Plans are exempt if they had 90% or greater funding in the plan year before cessation. When operations at a facility terminate permanently, liability occurs when there is a 15% reduction in the total number of employees eligible to participate in any employee benefit plan, including 401(k) plans, that are maintained by members of the controlled group. (This replaces a test of 20% of participants in defined benefit plans.) Generally speaking, there is no § 4062(e) event unless participants actually lose their jobs—not merely go to work for a successor employer.

For employers that trigger the 15% level, the Cromnibus legislation permits a new, less expensive option for satisfying § 4062(e) liability. The employer can make installment payments over seven years, each on equal to one-seventh of the unfunded vested benefit multiplied by the percentage reduction in active participants. Each installment is capped at an amount by which the additional contributions increase the plan's minimum funding contributions. Employers can stop making installment payments if, in any year, the plan's unfunded vested benefits become 90% funded even if the plan falls below the 90% level later. These rules apply to cessations of operations that occur on or after December 16, 2014. The PBGC must apply these rules to earlier cessations, unless a settlement agreement was entered into before June 1, 2014.

The PBGC's position is that, with these new rules in place, confusion has been dispelled and clear rules are in place, so the moratorium is no longer required. The PBGC nevertheless will not enforce § 4062(e) against financially sound companies (other than continuing to carry out the terms of a pre-June 1, 2014 settlement). Cessation of operations does not have to be reported by plans with fewer than 100 participants, or that are at least 90% funded. [PBGC, *Important Changes to ERISA Section 4062(e)*, <http://www.pbgc.gov/about/faq/pg/important-changes-to-erisa-section-4062%28e%29.html> (undated, last Feb. 25, 2017) (benefitslink.com)]

[B] Partition and Suspension Under MPRA

The PPA required underfunded multi-employer plans to increase contributions, reduce benefits, and pay surcharges and take a longer-term view of the plans' potential financial risks. Plans were analyzed as being in the "yellow zone" if endangered or the "red zone" if in critical status. Despite these measures for shoring up the plans, as of early 2015, one-tenth of multi-employer plans faced insolvency. The PBGC's 2014 annual report showed a 500% increase in the PBGC multi-employer plan's deficit.

According to Segal Consulting, most multi-employer plans are still in the green zone (64%), with 11% in the yellow zone and 25% in the red zone. Of plans in the red zone, 15% were in critical status, the remaining 10% in critical and declining status. In 2009, at the peak of the financial crisis, only 38% of multi-employer plans were in the green zone; the improvement is attributable to rehabilitation measures undertaken by plan trustees. However, about half of the plans currently in critical and declining status were in the red zone even in 2008 before the crash, and may need drastic measures to survive. [Plansponsor staff, *Multi-employer Plans' Zone Status Remains Stable*, plansponsor.com (Jan. 19, 2017)]

To combat these problems, the Multi-employer Pension Act (MPRA) allows plans in "critical and declining" status to suspend benefits for active or retired workers under certain circumstances. A plan is in critical and declining status when its funded percentage is below 65% and the plan is projected to become insolvent within 15 plan years. A plan is also deemed to be in critical and declining status if insolvency is predicted within 20 years and the plan has more than two inactive to every active participant, or the funded percentage is under 80%.

To suspend benefits, the plan's actuary must certify that the plan will not become insolvent as long as the suspension of benefits is in effect. The plan's trustees must determine that the plan would become insolvent if benefits cannot be suspended. Benefits cannot be reduced below 110% of the amount of the PBGC guarantee as of the date of suspension and participants aged 75–80, or who are disabled, are somewhat protected. Benefits cannot be suspended at all for recipients who have reached age 80. The proposal to suspend benefits must be disclosed to the U.S. Treasury, and put to a vote. However, if the plan is "systemically important" (i.e., if the PBGC might have to spend over $1 billion providing benefits) and if the employees vote against suspension, the Secretary of the Treasury must either permit the suspension or modify the suspension plan.

The MPRA gives the PBGC additional authority to partition failing multi-employer plans or to encourage plan mergers. [PBGC, *Important Changes to ERISA Section 4062(e)* <http://www.pbgc.gov/about/faq/pg/important-changes-to-erisa-section-4062%28e%29.html>, (undated, last viewed Feb. 24, 2017) (benefitslink.com)]

A PBGC final rule published in April 2016 explains the requirements for approving benefits, and provides additional details about the application process and the notice requirements. [81 Fed. Reg. 25540 (Apr. 28, 2016); see Rebecca

Moore, *IRS Issues Final Rules for Multiemployer Plan Suspension of Benefits*, plansponsor.com (Apr. 28, 2016).]

The IRS issued guidance in Rev. Proc. 2016-27, 2016-19 I.R.B. 725, but then replaced that Revenue Procedure with Rev. Proc. 2017-43, 2017-31 I.R.B. 153. Rev. Proc. 2017-43 provides that, if the Treasury finds an error in an application, it can ask the plan sponsor for supplementary information. The plan must break out the projected withdrawal liability payments attributable to prior withdrawals from those that are attributable to withdrawals that are expected to occur in the future. [Rebecca Moore, *IRS Updates Procedures for Applying for Suspension of Benefits,* plansponsor.com (July 13, 2017)]

According to the PBGC, there are five eligibility requirements for partition. The plan must be in critical and declining status. The employer must have taken (or be engaged in taking) all reasonable steps to avoid insolvency. The PBGC must decide that partitioning the plan is necessary to keep it solvent—and will reduce the financial risk to the PBGC. The PBGC must certify to Congress that the partition does not impair the PBGC's ability to assist other plans. The cost of partition will be paid exclusively from the PBGC's multiemployer fund.

A PBGC FAQ guidance document says that it is possible for partition to occur without suspension of benefits but this is unlikely: it could occur only if none of the participants or beneficiaries are entitled to benefit greater than 100% of the applicable PBGC guarantee.

Partition applications must be filed by the plan sponsor and signed by an authorized trustee. The partition application must include basic information about the plan, the proposal for partition, financial and actuarial information, data about the participants, and information about financial assistance.

First the PBGC performs an initial review to see if the application is complete; if not, it will ask the sponsor for the missing information. The PBGC has up to 270 days to review a complete application. The PBGC's partition order sums up its findings and conclusions; the effective date of approved partition; what the plan sponsor has to do to carry out the partition; and other appropriate information. The partition order creates a successor plan. The original plan must provide the "residual benefit" to participants whose benefits are transferred to the new plan. The residual benefit equals the difference between what it would have paid if partition had not occurred, and the amount the PBGC pays under the successor plan. [PBGC.gov, *Partition FAQs for Practitioners*, <http://pbgc.gov/prac/pg/mpra/partition-faqs-for-practitioners.html> (last accessed Feb. 24, 2017). See also PBGC's Final Rule, 80 Fed. Reg. 79687 (Dec. 23, 2015) making minor changes in information reporting, the timing of the PBGC's initial review of partition applications and a coordinated application process for both partition and suspension of benefits. The final rule applies to partition applications submitted on or after January 22, 2016. See Rebecca Moore, *PBGC Issues Final Rule for Multiemployer Plan Partitions*, plansponsor.com (Jan. 11, 2016)]

Under prior law, partition required the plan to be in bankruptcy. Participants' benefits were reduced to the PBGC guarantee level for multi-employer plans, which was usually quite low (typically, under $13,000 a year for 30 years' service). The MPRA increases the PBGC's power to partition plans, with the PBGC assuming some benefit liabilities to preserve a plan that otherwise would run out of money within 20 years. Benefits can be maintained at 110% of the PBGC guaranteed amount, but all participants must suffer benefit cuts. The PBGC's estimate is that some 1.5 million participants are covered by multi-employer plans that are likely to become insolvent. Suspensions could preserve payments to 600,000 of them and keep payments above the PBGC guarantee level for the rest. Most plans facing insolvency will require both suspension and partition. The best candidates for partition are plans that could not survive with benefit cuts alone. The PBGC's finances are perpetually troubled; it must certify that involvement in a partition will not impair its ability to help other multi-employer plans. In 2015, the PBGC estimated that it would take on up to $60 million in payments and process up to six applicants a year. [Hazel Bradford, *Multiemployer Funds, PBGC Face Hurdles with Partition*, Pionline.com (July 13, 2015) (benefitslink.com)]

Another possibility is merger under ERISA § 5231. The PBGC proposed a rule in mid-2016 to facilitate mergers. The PBGC has the power to intervene to promote a merger between two multi-employer plans by offering training, mediation, and technical assistance. To get involved, the PBGC must determine that the merger is in the best interests of the participants and beneficiaries of at least one of the plans involved in the merger, and the merger will not harm the overall interests of participants and beneficiaries of any plan involved in the merger. The PBGC can offer financial assistance if at least one of the plans is in critical and declining status, expected to become insolvent within 14–19 years. The funds that the PBGC devotes to this purpose must not impair the agency's other financial obligations. [81 Fed. Reg. 36229 (June 6, 2016); see Robert F. Schwartz and Alex E. Trabolsi, *Pension Benefit Guaranty Corporation Issues Proposed Rule for Multiemployer Plan Mergers and Transfers*, Truckerhuss.com (June 20, 2016) (benefitslink.com)]

Proposed regulations were published in early 2016, largely dealing with the specific situation of United Parcel Services' withdrawal from the Central States, Southeast and Southwest Pension Fund. [81 Fed. Reg. 7253 (Feb. 11, 2016); see Morganlewis.com, *Treasury Releases Proposed Regulations Clarifying the UPS Rule Under MPRA* (Feb. 2016) (benefitslink.com); Plansponsor editors, *Proposed Guidance Issued for Multiemployer Plan Suspension of Benefits*, plansponsor.com (Feb. 12, 2016)]

The first application to reduce benefits was made in early October 2015 by the Central States fund. The Treasury rejected this application, on the grounds that the proposal imposed the benefit cuts unevenly, the plan applied unreasonably optimistic assumptions about future investment returns, and the notices sent to participants and beneficiaries contained so much technical verbiage that they were incomprehensible. The average proposed reduction under the plan was 23%—but some members would face a 90% benefit cut. [David Moberg, *Central States*

Pension Fund Prepares to Slash Hundreds of Thousands of Workers' Pensions, NYTimes.com (Oct. 5, 2015); Timothy W. Martin, *Treasury Department Rejects Teamsters' Central States Proposal to Cut Retiree Benefits,* WSJ.com (May 6, 2016); Mary Williams Walsh, *Treasury Department Rejects Plan to Cut Pension Benefits for Teamsters,* NYTimes.com (May 7, 2016)]

After several applications were rejected, the first plan to obtain permission to cut benefits was the Iron Workers Local 17 Pension Fund in Cleveland. The fund had previously applied to cut benefits, but then withdrew the proposal in mid-2016. The local also became the first to vote to approve pension cuts; the cuts took effect February 1, 2017. [Stephen Koff, *Iron Workers Retirees Get Temporary Reprieve From Pension Cuts,* Cleveland.com (Aug. 5, 2016) (benefitslink .com); Hazel Bradford, *Treasury Approves First MPRA Application for Iron Workers Local 17,* pionline.com (Dec. 16, 2016) (benefitslink.com); Rebecca Moore, *First Multiemployer Plan to Make Benefit Cuts Under MPRA,* plan sponsor.com (Jan. 27, 2017); Frank T. Mamat, *Union Retirees Cut Their Own Pension to Forestall Doomsday Scenario,* Foster Swift Collins & Smith PC (Feb. 6, 2017), available at Lexology.com]

The second approved application was the United Furniture Workers Pension Fund A, approved by the Treasury in a July 20, 2017 letter to the fund, which was predicted to become insolvent in 2021 without assistance. Approval from the Treasury meant that the proposal could be submitted to the membership. [<https:// www.treasury.gov/services/Responses2/UFW%20Notification%20Letter.pdf>; see David B. Brandolph, *Treasury Department Gives Thumbs Up to Second Pension Rescue,* bna.com (July 21, 2017) (benefitslink.com)]

[C] Withdrawal Liability

An employer can withdraw from participation in a multi-employer plan, either by complete withdrawal (permanent end of the obligation to contribute, or by permanently leaving the kind of business operations covered by the plan) or by partial withdrawal (when the metric used to determine the employer's contribution to the multi-employer plan, such as hours worked or units of production, drops by 70% or more or when the obligation to contribute is reduced, e.g., when one of the employer's multiple CBAs expires). The plan will impose withdrawal liability on any employer to whom unfunded vested benefits are allocable.

Final regulations under the MPRA were published in mid-2016, explaining the situation in which the employer withdraws from the plan, pays the withdrawal liability in full, and assumes liability for providing benefits equal to the reduced benefits reflecting the plan's financial status. [81 Fed. Reg. 27011 (May 5, 2016); Rev. Proc. 2016-27, 2016-19 I.R.B. 725; see Steptoe & Johnson LLP, *IRS and Treasury Issue Regulations Regarding Suspension of Pension Benefits* (May 3, 2016), available at Lexology.com] There are also ERISA rules when all the contributing employers withdraw (which will result in termination of the plan), or a non-termination mass withdrawal (when substantially all employers withdraw). There are special rules for industries such as construction, entertainment, trucking, and retail food sales because of the high degree of mobility within these industries.

Generally speaking, an employer is deemed not to withdraw from a multi-employer plan as a result of an asset sale, subject to conditions set out in ERISA § 4204. ERISA § 4225 limits withdrawal liability if the employer sells all or substantially all of its operating assets, or if it is insolvent. [PBGC, *Withdrawal Liability*, <http://www.pbgc.gov/prac/multiemployer/withdrawal-liability.html> (last accessed Mar. 24, 2016)]

However, changes may be in store. On January 4, 2017, the PBGC issued a request for information (RFI), seeking public comments about whether plans should be allowed to use an alternative method of covering withdrawal liability. If adopted, this plan would provide for an "old" and "new" pool of withdrawal liability. The old pool would contain all of the unfunded liabilities of all the plans in the multi-employer plans. The new pool would consist of the future liabilities of some of the employers. The purpose of the proposal is to make multi-employer plans more attractive to new employers and to give employers already in the pool greater certainty about their possible liability exposure, making it less likely that they will withdraw. The proposal explains the conditions for moving to the "new" pool (e.g., paying frozen withdrawal liability and being absolved from other liabilities). [PBGC, *Request for Information: Two Pool Withdrawal Liability* (Jan. 4, 2017), available at <https://www.pbgc.gov/about/who-we-are/retirement-matters/post/2017/01/04/Request-for-Information-Two-Pool-Withdrawal-Liability.aspx>]

Some plans dramatically reduced the interest rate assumptions used in calculating withdrawal liability. Instead of using the plan's assumed rate of return (7%–8% is typical) to calculate withdrawal liability, they used the PBGC's long-term interest rate, which is about 3%. Changing the interest rate can double or even quadruple the amount of withdrawal liability. Plans can make these changes without notifying employers, which can lead to very unwelcome surprises. A 2015 article suggests that employers monitor the rates and contest unreasonable rate changes. [Kevin M. Williams, *Multiemployer Pension Plans: Withdrawal Liability is Mounting*, FordHarrison (July 28, 2015) (benefitslink.com)]

The Third Circuit ruled that withdrawal liability for a member of a multi-employer plan that is covered by more than one CBA is calculated using the highest rate for any of the CBAs. The surcharge imposed under the PPA when a plan is in critical status is not included in the withdrawal liability, unless the employer's payment is part of the highest contribution rate under any of the CBAs. [*Bd. of Trs. of the IBT Local 863 Pension Fund v. C&S Wholesale Grocers Inc.*, 802 F.3d 534 (3d Cir. 2015)]

Tiernan & Hoover did not receive notice that it was deemed to have withdrawn from the plan until after it sold its assets to ManWeb Services (a non-union company). The Seventh Circuit held that ManWeb Services became a successor employer, liable for the withdrawal liability, because there was substantial continuity of business and ManWeb was aware of the claim before the acquisition. The price of the assets could have been adjusted accordingly. The Seventh Circuit held that Congress' intent was to protect the multi-employer plan and not require the remaining employers in the plan to make up for withdrawals after asset sales. [*Tsareff v. ManWeb Servs., Inc*, 794 F.3d 841 (7th Cir. 2015)]

The Ninth Circuit also made a successor liable for the predecessor's withdrawal liability. The Ninth Circuit treated the most important factor in successorship analysis as substantial continuity in business operations, particularly whether the new employer took over the economically critical bulk of the predecessor's customer base. [*Resilient Floor Covering Pension Trust Fund Bd. of Trs. v. Michael's Floor Covering, Inc.*, No. 12-17675, 2015 WL 5295091 (9th Cir. Sept. 11, 2015)]

ERISA provides that when a single-employer defined benefit plan terminates without enough assets to pay its liabilities, the plan sponsors and other businesses that share 80% or more common control are jointly and severally liable for those unfunded liabilities. For about three decades, the PBGC's position was that buyers of corporate assets are not subject to termination liability, but the PBGC changed its position and argued for successor liability of an asset buyer. The District Court for the Northern District of Ohio rejected this contention, holding that there is a specific ERISA statutory scheme, and it, and not federal common law, must be followed. In a bankruptcy situation, it is possible (although not inevitable) that Bankruptcy Code § 363(f) can be used to insulate asset purchasers from successor liability for withdrawal liability from a multi-employer plan. [*PBGC v. Findlay Indus., Inc.*, 2016 WL 7474404 (N.D. Ohio Dec. 29, 2016); Eric Keller, *PBGC Attempts to Hold Asset Buyer Liable for Seller's Underfunded Single Employer Pension Plan Termination Liabilities*, Paulhastings.com (Feb. 2, 2017) (benefitslink.com)]

§ 17.02 TERMINATION TYPES

There are three kinds of termination that apply to single-employer plans. In a standard termination, the plan can pay all benefits without financial input from the PBGC. In a distress termination, the plan needs PBGC assistance, e.g., because it is unable to fund the pension plan and still stay in business. Standard and distress terminations are initiated by the company. The third type, involuntary termination, is initiated by the PBGC. [PBGC, *Pension Plan Termination Fact Sheet*, <http://www.pbgc.gov/about/factsheets/page/termination ›.html> (undated, last accessed Feb. 24, 2017). Generally, if a multi-employer plan is unable to pay benefits as they come due, the PBGC will provide funding assistance, but the plan will not be terminated.]

Once the decision to terminate the plan is made, the date of termination must be chosen. The corporation's Board of Directors will probably have to pass a resolution to this effect. Participants and beneficiaries are entitled to between 60 and 90 days' notice of the impending termination. Benefits will probably be distributed as annuities, lump sums, and/or transfers to Individual Retirement Arrangements (IRAs) and other qualified plans. If it is determined that the assets are sufficient to satisfy all benefit obligations, then the IRS and PBGC forms are prepared and submitted. The relevant forms include PBGC Form 500 and IRS Forms 5310, 6088, and 8717. Participants and beneficiaries are given an official Notice of Plan Benefits. They are also entitled to 45 days' notice of which insurer will provide the annuities for benefits distributed in this form.

After the forms have been filed, the PBGC has 60 days to raise any concerns it has. The IRS can take as long as 18 months to review filings and issue a determination letter. But once the determination letter has been issued, the funds must be distributed within 120 days.

The three most common funding strategies are:

- Contributing a minimum amount for an ongoing plan each year until termination, with a final contribution when the plan's assets are distributed—typically, 18–24 months after the termination date)

- Contributing a level amount each year until the year of planned termination—e.g., if termination is set for five years in the future, spread the cost evenly over the five-year period

- Fully funding the plan under the PPA rules for ongoing plans, using investment income to make up for the shortfall when the plan is terminated.

The first alternative is probably the most expensive, but it reduces the time frame until termination—and risk increases over time.

[A] Generally

There are two types of voluntary termination: standard and distress. See 29 C.F.R. Part 4041 for Regulations. A standard termination, governed by ERISA § 4041, is used by plans that have at least enough assets to pay the benefits guaranteed by the PBGC. All terminations are handled as standard terminations unless the PBGC permits a "distress termination," which imposes lower obligations on the plan.

Under ERISA § 4044, there are six priority categories of accrued benefits. When the plan's assets are distributed, all Category-1 claims must be paid, then all Category-2 claims, and so on, until the assets are exhausted. Therefore, in many instances some of the classes will go unpaid. The categories, in descending order of priority, are:

- Voluntary employee contributions made to the plan. (NOTE: These amounts are NOT guaranteed by the PBGC, because they fall outside the definition of "basic benefits.");

- Mandatory contributions that employees made to the plan, plus 5% interest;

- Annuity benefits that derive from employer contributions, if the annuity was or could have been in pay status three years or more before termination of the plan. ("Could have been" refers to the situation in which employees continue to work despite their eligibility for early retirement);

- All other PBGC-guaranteed benefits;

- All other nonforfeitable benefits;

- All benefits that are accrued but forfeitable.

Before a plan administrator can actually make any distributions, there is a legal obligation to determine the plan's ability to pay benefits at the level deemed appropriate by the PBGC. The plan administrator must notify the PBGC if the plan is unable to pay the guaranteed benefits. The PBGC makes its own determination and issues notices. If, on the other hand, the administrator determines that the PBGC-guaranteed benefits, but not all the guaranteed liabilities, can be paid, then the plan should distribute the assets but notify the PBGC.

If the PBGC affirms the administrator's characterization, it will issue a Notice of Liability resolving the issue of the plan's sufficiency. The plan administrator is obligated to provide a new valuation of the plan's liabilities and guaranteed benefits. An enrolled actuary must certify the valuation.

Hughes Aircraft Co. v. Jacobson [525 U.S. 432 (1999)], which involved several other pension issues, also affects plan termination. This case involves a plan partially funded by mandatory employee contributions. The employer suspended its own contributions at a time when the plan had a surplus. The employer created a new, noncontributory plan for new plan participants. Participants in the existing plan charged the employer with ERISA violations in connection with the amendment. The Supreme Court held that the employees were not entitled to an order terminating the plan voluntarily because the changes in plan structure did not constitute an ERISA § 4041(a)(1) voluntary termination. As long as a plan continues to provide benefits to participants and to accumulate funds for future payments, termination is not appropriate.

Under the Supreme Court's 2007 *Beck* ruling, it is not a violation of fiduciary duty for a bankrupt company to put the plan through a standard termination (and purchase annuities to satisfy the obligation to pay benefits) in lieu of merging the pension plan into a multi-employer union-run fund. [*Beck v. PACE Int'l Union*, 551 U.S. 96 (2007)]

Also note that the final regulations about nonqualified plans such as top-hat plans provide that terminating and then liquidating a nonqualified plan may be considered a prohibited acceleration of payments that results in the recipient being taxed under Code § 409A. There is an exception to this rule if the employer terminates all the plans of the same type, pays out benefits over a period of one to two years, and refrains from adopting new plans of the same type for three years. [Final Regulations, 73 Fed. Reg. 19234 (Apr. 17, 2007)]

[B] Standard Termination

The steps in a standard termination, as set out in Part 4041 of the PBGC regulations, are:

- File Form 500, Standard Termination Notice with the PBGC. This must be done on paper, because must be hand-signed by the plan administrator

- This is also true of Form 501, the Post-Distribution Certification.

- The plan's enrolled actuary must sign Schedule EA-S, the Standard Termination Certification of Sufficiency

- Interested parties other than the PBGC (the plan's participants, beneficiaries of deceased participants), must be issued Notice of Intent to Terminate, at least 60 and not more than 90 days before the proposed date of termination

- Participants, beneficiaries, and alternate payees must be given notice of plan benefits no later than the filing date for the Form 500

- Participants and beneficiaries must be given a Notice of Annuity Information not more than 45 days before the distribution date if any benefits will be distributed in annuity form

- Participants who receive annuity payments must be given a Notice of Annuity Contract within 30 days of the contract becoming available

- If the plan has any missing participants, Schedule MP must be submitted to the PBGC, listing them

- The PBGC has 60 days after receipt of Form 500 to review it and determine if the termination complies with the applicable legal requirements. The PBGC selects plans with fewer than 300 participants at random; all larger plans are audited. The PBGC audits all plans that distribute assets without filing Form 500

- Form 501, the Post-Distribution Certification, must be filed with the PBGC within 30 days of the date all plan benefits have been distributed.

If this is filed more than 90 days after the distribution deadline, the PBGC will assess a late filing penalty.

Generally speaking, all assets must be distributed by the later of 180 days after the PBGC completes its review, or, if the plan administrator applied for an IRS determination letter about the termination, the deadline is 120 days after a favorable determination letter has been received. [PBGC, *Standard Terminations* (last accessed Feb. 24, 2017), available at <http://www.pbgc.gov/prac/terminations/standard-terminations.html>]

When a plan goes through a standard termination, ERISA § 4050 provides for payment of a designated amount to the PBGC to cover claims from missing participants. The calculation usually depends on the most valuable annuity benefit payable under ERISA assumptions about missing participants, which use the Part 4044 interest assumptions, but with a different mortality table. Until 2007, the PBGC used the table in Rev. Rul. 95-6, but effective February 27, 2007, a blend of mortality rates for healthy males and healthy females (50% each) taken from Part 4044 will be used instead. [Mortality tables for 2017 valuation dates, <http://www.pbgc.gov/prac/mortality-retirement-and-pv-max-guarantee/erisa-mortality-tables/erisa-section-4044-mortality-table-for-2017-valuation-dates.html> (last accessed Feb. 24, 2017)]

To find missing participants, terminating plans can use the PBGC's missing participants program, paying the benefits to the PBGC, which then searches for the participants. The DOL's suggestions for finding missing participants include commercial locater services, Internet searches, and consulting credit reports.

A 2016 proposal calls for expanding this program to cover some defined benefit plans not already covered plus terminated defined contribution plans. The proposal would permit plans to transfer missing participants' benefits to the PBGC, which would retain the funds, add the participant to its database and periodically search for the participants. The PBGC planned to finalize the proposal and implement it in 2018. [91 Fed. Reg. 64699 (Sept. 20, 2016); see PBGC.gov, *Proposed Expanded Missing Participants Program* (Sept. 19, 2016) (benefitslink .com); Haynes and Boone LLP, *PBGC Missing Participant Program to Include 401(k) Plans and Certain Other Plans That Terminate After 2017*, (Sept. 30, 2016), available at Lexology.com]

Effective for requests postmarked on or after August 31, 2012, the IRS will no longer forward letters from plan sponsors who need to find the payees of benefits. Rev. Proc. 2012-35, 2012-37 I.R.B. 341 states that the IRS no longer considers finding missing participants a "humane purpose." The Social Security Administration's forwarding service is still available, but it costs $25 per letter. [McDermott Will & Emery, *IRS Eliminates Use of Letter Forwarding Service to Find Missing Participants and Beneficiaries* (Sept. 27, 2012) (benefitslink.com); Plansponsor staff, *IRS Stops Forwarding Letters for Missing Participants*, plan sponsor.com (Sept. 4, 2012)]

In August 2014, the DOL issued Field Assistance Bulletin 2014-01, explaining how to find missing participants and distribute their account balances, given that the IRS letter-forwarding service is no longer available. If notice cannot be given to participants through first-class mail or e-mail, the DOL says that the employer can use certified mail; check its records other than the records of the terminated plan (e.g., Employee Group Health Plan (EGHP) records, which may be more current); ask the beneficiary designated under the plan how to locate the participant; or use no-fee Internet tools like public record databases and Internet search mechanisms. If this is unavailing, the fiduciary may have to take additional steps, based on the size of the account balanced against the cost of additional searches (by hiring an investigator or paying to access credit reports). The DOL says that if a participant cannot be located, or does not give distribution instructions, fiduciaries should consider transferring the benefits into an IRA. As a last resort the funds may have to be deposited into a bank account for the participant, or transferred to the state unclaimed property fund. [DOL FAB 2014-01, <https://www.dol.gov/agencies/ebsa/employers-and-advisers/guidance/field-assistance-bulletins/2014-01> (Aug. 14, 2014) (last viewed Feb. 24, 2017)]

Within 120 days after the proposed termination date, the plan administrator must submit a Schedule EA-5 of the Form 500, a certificate prepared by a PBGC-enrolled actuary to the PBGC. The certificate estimates the value of the plan assets and the present value of plan liabilities, so that the actuary can certify that assets are adequate to satisfy the liabilities. The administrator must also furnish any other information the PBGC requests. The plan administrator must certify under penalty of perjury that the actuary's certificate is correct, and that the information given to the PBGC has been accurate and complete.

Once all the assets are distributed, the administrator must file PBGC Form 501 within 30 days of the final distribution, to prove that the assets were distributed; penalties are imposed for each day the filing is late. [See 29 C.F.R. § 4010.14] Late filing can also have the effect of creating a last, short plan year for the plan—thereby reducing the refund of the PBGC premium that the employer would otherwise be entitled to receive.

The ERISA § 204(h) notice of the amendment (including disclosure of its effective date) must be given. [See § 5.07 for further discussion of this issue.]

[C] Notification

The DOL's *Reporting and Disclosure Guide for Employee Benefit Plans* [<http://www.dol.gov/ebsa/pdf/rdguide.pdf> (Sept. 2014) (last accessed Feb. 24, 2017)] explains that voluntary standard termination of a single-employer plan that is insured by the PBGC and has enough assets to provide all plan benefits is a multi-step process:

- Choose the termination date

- Issue a Notice of Intent to Terminate (NOIT) to the affected parties (other than the PBGC); Appendix B of the Form 500 package includes a model NOIT. Generally, the NOIT is filed between 60 and 90 days before the proposed termination date

- Issue a Notice of Plan Benefits to participants and beneficiaries no later than the time Form 500, the Standard Termination Notice, is filed with the PBGC

- File the PBGC Form 500 no later than 180 days after the proposed termination date

- Distribute the plan assets needed to satisfy all plan benefits in time for the distribution deadline; the distribution deadline is 180 days after the 60-day PBGC review period ends, or 120 days after receipt of a favorable IRS determination letter, whichever is later (provided that the plan administrator requested the determination letter no later than the time Form 500 was filed with the PBGC)

- If there are any missing participants, use the procedure described in PBGC Schedule MP (Missing Participants). This form is filed with Form 501

- File Form 501, the Post-Distribution Certificate, with the PBGC within 30 days of distribution of all benefits. The PBGC's policy is that it will not impose penalties for late filing of Form 501 unless it is filed more than 90 days after the distribution deadline, including any extensions.

These requirements come from ERISA §§ 4041, 4050, and 29 C.F.R. (Parts 4041 and 4050).

ERISA § 4041(a)(2) requires that the NOIT must be given to plan participants; their beneficiaries; alternate payees under domestic relations orders; and the employees' collective bargaining representative (if the workplace is unionized). Anyone who becomes a beneficiary of a deceased participant or becomes an alternate payee (e.g., as a result of divorce) after the proposed termination date but before the plan's assets have been distributed is also entitled to a NOIT.

Items to be disclosed on the NOIT include:

- The sponsor's name and EIN

- The plan's name and plan number

- Name, address, and telephone number of a contact person

- The fact that the sponsor intends to carry out a standard termination

- Proposed termination date; this can be a Saturday, Sunday, or federal holiday

- A statement that another notice will be given if the termination does not occur, or the termination date changes

- A statement that the plan assets must be adequate to provide all plan benefits for a standard termination to occur

- The applicable statement about the end of benefit accruals (see below)

- A statement that everyone entitled to benefits will receive a written notification explaining benefits

- How to get a copy of the updated SPD; the plan administration can also include a copy of the SPD with each copy of the NOIT

- Disclosure that the PBGC guarantee ends when all the assets have been distributed

- For people whose benefits are already in pay status on the proposed termination date, either a statement that their benefits will not be affected by the termination, or an explanation of how they will be affected

- Notice of annuity information, unless the participant will be cashed out by receiving a lump sum; e.g., the name and address of all insurers from whom annuity contracts will be purchased, and the facts that the insurer becomes responsible for payment once the annuity is purchased, and that state guaranty associations back up this obligation

- If the transaction is a spin-off/termination, participants and beneficiaries of the original plan must be notified 60–90 days before the proposed termination date, receiving information about annuities furnished by the surviving plan.

There are three possibilities for cessation of benefit accruals: either they cease on the termination date (but continue if the plan does not terminate); a plan amendment is adopted, pursuant to ERISA § 204(h), cutting off benefit accruals as of a specified date; or benefit accruals have already ceased, pursuant to § 204(h), before the NOIT was issued.

The NOPB (Notice of Plan Benefits) explains who is the sponsor of the plan, who can be contacted for benefit questions, and the amount of the benefit. If the benefit is only estimated, that must be disclosed. For people already receiving benefits, the NOPB explains the amount and form of benefits payable as of the termination date; any benefits payable on the participant's death, and who they go to; and an explanation of any change in the benefit that has happened or is scheduled to happen after termination of the plan. For participants who will be cashed out involuntarily, the NOPB explains how much the benefit is; who the beneficiary is; and beneficiary's entitlement to death benefits. For lump sum benefits other than involuntary cashouts, the NOPB explains which mortality table will be used to value the lump sum, how interest rates are used in the calculation, and what the interest rates are. If the benefits will not be paid in a lump sum, the

NOPB explains how the payment will differ from the plan's normal retirement benefit. For people whose benefits are not yet in pay status, the NOPB explains the basic form of distribution at normal retirement age, alternative benefit forms, any benefits available before NRA, and information about lump-sum calculations.

The PPA enacted new ERISA sections, §§ 4041(c)(2)(D), 4042(c)(3), requiring plan participants to be given the same information about involuntary and distress terminations as the plan furnishes to the PBGC. The new requirement replaces the participant notice formerly required under ERISA § 4011. See <http://www.pbgc.gov/documents/500_instructions.pdf> for the Form 500 instructions (last accessed Feb. 24, 2017). Information about plan termination must also be provided in the Summary Plan Description (SPD) furnished to plan participants. Form 500 is filed with Schedule EA-S, which specifies that the plan's assets are sufficient to satisfy its obligations.

If the PBGC deems the Form 500 to be incomplete, or the plan fails to submit additional information requested by the PBGC, the PBGC has the power to issue a Notice of Noncompliance, which stops the standard termination process—and restores the plan to status as an ongoing plan. A Notice of Noncompliance can also be issued if the plan administrator fails to properly complete the distribution of all plan assets.

[D] Distress Termination

A plan that does not have enough assets to pay all the benefit liabilities can apply to the PBGC for a "distress" termination, which is available only if the plan's sponsors (and the other corporations that are part of a controlled group of corporations with the sponsor) can prove financial hardship, e.g., involvement in voluntary or involuntary bankruptcy or insolvency proceedings. See 29 C.F.R §§ 4041.41–4041.50, § 4050, and 29 C.F.R. Parts 4041 and 4050.

If a company makes a Chapter 11 filing, seeking bankruptcy reorganization, a distress termination will be permitted only if the bankruptcy court decides that terminating the plan is necessary, or that the company cannot remain in business and pay its debts if it maintains the plan.

When the PBGC takes over a plan in a distress termination, the employer is liable to the PBGC for the amount of underfunding, which in most cases will become a general unsecured claim. The PBGC is often one of the debtor's largest unsecured creditors, entitled to a pro rata share of the recovery for the class of general unsecured creditor. It is a basic fact of bankruptcy that the amount of influence a creditor has is proportionate to the size of its claim. The PBGC receives distributions under the debtor's reorganization plan—often in the stock of the reorganized debtor company, which the PBGC sells to recoup some funds. [Ronald Silverman and Scott Seamon, *The Unexpected Guest*, N.Y.L.J. (Dec. 13, 2010) (law.com)]

Distress termination might also be permitted if the sponsor proves to the PBGC that terminating the plan is essential to paying its debts and remaining in operation. A distress termination might also be available if pension costs have become intolerable only because of the decline in the covered workforce—loss of stock market value of the plans' assets would not be considered an acceptable rationale.

The documents required for a distress termination are:

- Form 600 (Distress Termination Notice of Intent to Terminate), given to the PBGC, including information about which "distress test" the plan satisfies. Form 600 must be filed 60–90 days before the proposed termination date;

- Termination notice submitted to the PBGC about the number of participants and the plan's assets and liabilities;

- Notice of Intent to Terminate (NOIT; given to all other interested parties, such as participants, beneficiaries, unions, and alternate payees); provided no later than the date the Form 600 is filed with the PBGC. The plan must also disclose whatever information was submitted to the PBGC within 15 days of a request, or whenever the plan updates the information given to the PBGC that was the subject of a previous request;

- Notice of request to bankruptcy court (given to the PBGC whenever the plan asks the Bankruptcy Court to approve plan termination as part of the bankruptcy process);

- Form 602 (post-distribution certification) furnished to the PBGC within 30 days of completion of the distribution process; here, too, the PBGC will not assess penalties if the form is furnished within 90 days of the end of the process;

- Schedule MP (Missing Participants), filed with Form 602;

- Starting on the proposed termination date, the plan reduces the benefits of participants who are already receiving benefits to the amount of the maximum PBGC guarantee.

The duty to notify participants is more or less the same for standard and distress terminations. The PBGC must be informed about participants and beneficiaries, within 120 days after the proposed termination date, or 30 days after the PBGC informs the plan that requirements for a distress termination have been satisfied—whichever is later. Form 601, *the Distress Termination Notice*, must be filed with the PBGC; the Schedule EA-D actuarial certification must be filed with it. [DOL, *Reporting and Disclosure Guide*, <http://www.dol.gov/ebsa/pdf/rdguide.pdf> (Sept. 2014) (last accessed Feb. 24, 2017)]

For a distress termination to be permitted, the PBGC must make a determination that the plan sponsor and any affiliated corporations all satisfy at least one financial distress test (different corporations can satisfy different tests), such as: a liquidating bankruptcy petition has been filed; a petition for bankruptcy reorganization has been filed, and the court approves plan termination because the reorganization would otherwise be impossible; the sponsor or an affiliate must terminate the plan to stay in business; or the cost of pension coverage has become unreasonably burdensome—but only because of the decline in the number of covered employees. [PBGC, *Distress Terminations*, http://www.pbgc.gov/prac/terminations/distress-terminations.html (undated, last accessed Mar. 23, 2016); *Pension Plan Termination Fact Sheet*, <http://www.pbgc.gov/about/factsheets/page/termination.html> (undated, last viewed Feb. 24, 2017)]

If the PBGC determines that the plan does not qualify for a distress termination, then it must remain in operation rather than terminating, and will be monitored by the PBGC.

If the plan has enough assets to pay the guaranteed benefits, the PBGC issues a "distribution notice." Within 15 days of receiving this notice, the plan administrator must give each participant and beneficiary a notice of impending distribution. Unless an extension has been granted, the distribution must begin within 60 days and be completed within 240 days. Then PBGC Form 602 (Post-Distribution Certification) must be filed within 30 days of the completion of distribution of the assets. If the plan does not have enough assets to satisfy all benefits liabilities, the plan sponsor and all members of its controlled group are jointly and severally liable to the PBGC for all unfunded benefit liabilities calculated under 29 C.F.R. 4022 Subpart D.

The Eleventh Circuit held that the bankruptcy trustee of a bankrupt sponsor cannot sue the former owner of the corporation on behalf of the estate and the unsecured creditors for liabilities from termination of the plan. ERISA provides that, once a plan is terminated, all parties except the PBGC are limited in the relief they can receive from either the current or former controlled group. The PBGC can obtain legal or equitable relief against the controlled group for failure to fund the plan, but all other parties can only obtain equitable relief. The bankruptcy trustee sued on behalf of non-PBGC parties. The district court held that the trustee sought a lump-sum amount, which is a legal remedy. The Eleventh Circuit, however, held in early 2014 that it was irrelevant whether the remedies were legal or equitable: the trustee does not have a cause of action to recover funds for the bankruptcy estate. ERISA does not make the controlled group's duty to pay unfunded benefit liability run to the plan sponsor. It runs to the beneficiaries of the plan, not the bankrupt sponsor's unsecured creditors. Furthermore, the statute of limitations had run, so the PBGC could no longer sue the controlled group for termination liability. [*Durango-Georgia Paper Co v. H.G. Estate LLC*, 739 F.3d 1263 (11th Cir. 2014)]

[E] Partial Termination

Partial termination is a concept that affects both the PBGC and the IRS. The definition has changed over time, and the definitions are not always consistent between the two agencies.

The IRS is pursuing both defined benefit and defined contribution plans that have experienced partial termination events. When a partial termination occurs, all affected participants become 100% vested, although usually they will not receive distributions except to the extent they are eligible because of termination of employment. The IRS Employee Plans Compliance Unit's Partial Termination/ Partial Vesting Project uses data from Form 5500 filings to discover partial termination events (involuntary removal of a group of employees from plan participation when there has been a significant reduction in the participant group). A partial termination could be caused by plant shutdown, layoffs, downsizing, restructuring, or a sale that excludes a group of participants from the plan. The determination that a partial termination has occurred is a fiduciary decision generally made by the plan administrator or administrative committee. Although there are IRS guidelines, the determination must be made based on the facts and circumstances of the case.

The IRS uses a rebuttable presumption that there has been a partial termination if there has been a 20% turnover rate within a short period of time. The turnover rate equals the number of participants whose severance from employment is initiated by the employer during the applicable period divided by the sum of the number of participants at the start of the applicable period and the participants added during the applicable period.

The IRS treats any separation from service other than death, disability, or retirement at normal retirement age as employer-initiated, unless the employer can verify that the employee chose to leave or was terminated for cause. Events outside the employer's control, such as economic conditions, are still considered employer-initiated. The employer's normal turnover rate is also a factor: if this year's rate is 22% but the historical rate is 10%, the IRS might be persuaded that the current turnover rate is really only 12%, so there has not been a partial termination. For 401(k) plans, all employees eligible to make elective deferrals are considered participants, whether or not they actually make deferrals. [Lisa B. Zimmer, *Partial Plan Termination . . . What's That?*, Warner Norcross & Judd LLP (Nov. 11, 2011) (benefitslink.com)]

The administrator of a single-employer plan is obligated to submit a "4063 notice" when an employer who is a contributing sponsor ends operations at a facility, resulting in job loss for more than 20% of the plan participants. (The name refers to ERISA § 4063.) A 4063 notice is also required if a substantial employer withdraws from a multiple-employer plan. The 4063 notice does not replace any Reportable Event notice that is required by § 4043. Employers who are required to report should send the notice within 60 days of the event—either by mail to the PBGC's Corporate Finance & Restructuring Department, 1200 K

Street NW, Washington, DC 20005-4026, faxed to (202) 842-2643, or e-mailed to 4063.report@pbgc.gov. [PBGC, *Section 4063 Notices*, <http://www.pbgc.gov/prac/reporting-and-disclosure/section-4063-notices.html> (last viewed Feb. 24, 2017)]. The PBGC's e-filing portal was launched on December 9, 2015; although primarily intended for Form 4010 events reporting, it can also be used for § 4043 reporting. [See 81 Fed. Reg. 54980 (Sept. 11, 2015).]

ERISA § 4043 requires plan sponsors and administrators to give the PBGC notice in advance if possible or after an event has occurred. The notice informs the PBGC of negative factors that might show that the plan or its sponsor is in financial trouble (e.g., reduction in the number of active participants; inability to pay benefits as they come due; liquidation of the sponsor or a member of its controlled group). The information helps the PBGC decide if an involuntary termination proceeding is warranted. ERISA § 303(k) and Code § 430(k) entitle the PBGC to place a lien on single-employer plans that are underfunded by more than $1 million, if any person fails to make a contribution when due. All property of the parties liable for the contributions (the plan sponsor and all members of its controlled group) is subject to the lien. The events are reported on Form 10 and Form 10-A (advance notice). Proposed regulations were issued on April 3, 2013, reducing the number of reportable events (see 78 Fed. Reg. 20039). [PBGC, *Reportable Events and Large Unpaid Contributions*, < http://www.pbgc.gov/prac/reporting-and-disclosure/reportable-events.html> (undated, last viewed Mar. 24, 2016).]

In recent years (see §§ 5.09, 11.09), the PBGC has reduced the extent to which vicissitudes in plan operations will be "reportable events" that must be disclosed to the PBGC. A September 11, 2015 final rule follows the trend of concentrating on the few plans or sponsors that are at greatest risk of default. Instead of focusing only on funding levels, the PBGC's current approach is to grant waivers based on whether or not there is a risk that the plan will not be able to be maintained. The PBGC's estimate is that only about 6% of plans and sponsors will be subject to most reporting requirements. [80 Fed. Reg. 54979 (Sept. 11, 2015)]

Frozen plans remain subject to § 4043 reporting rules; the rules only cease to apply when the plan is fully terminated and all assets distributed. Most of the reportable events could still occur in a frozen plan. [Vivian S. McCardell, *Pension Plan Sponsors: Whether Your Pension Plan Is Frozen, Partially Frozen or Freeze Dried, Don't Forget Those PBGC Reportable Events*, Morgan Lewis & Bockius LLP (Aug. 11, 2015), available at Lexology.com]

The Seventh Circuit rule is that events from more than one plan year can be used to determine if a partial termination has occurred, when an employee alleges that his balances should vest fully because of the termination. [*Matz v. Household Int'l Tax Reduction Inv. Plan*, 227 F.3d 971 (7th Cir. 2000); see also *Sea Ray v. Robinson*, 164 F.3d 981 (6th Cir. 1999)] The Sixth Circuit's rationale in this situation is that, if review was limited to a single year, employers would be able to escape liability by firing some employees in December, some in January. [*Sea Ray*, 164 F.3d 981]

On a related issue, the *Matz* court required counting of both vested and non-vested participants to determine whether a partial termination occurred. However, the Supreme Court ordered the court to reconsider its opinion because of *United States v. Mead Corp.* [533 U.S. 218 (2001)], a Supreme Court case about the extent to which courts have to abide by the rules of administrative agencies. This time, the Seventh Circuit decided that only nonvested participants should be counted in deciding if there has been a partial termination. [*Matz v. Household Int'l Tax Reduction Inv. Plan*, 265 F.3d 572 (7th Cir. 2001)] Litigation in the case continued, and in 2004 the Seventh Circuit adopted the IRS's formula, on the grounds that at-will employees have no reasonable expectation of receiving benefits before vesting occurs, because the at-will employees can be terminated at any time. The Seventh Circuit set 20% as the dividing line: there is a rebuttable presumption that there is no partial termination when reduction in plan participation is below 20%, and a rebuttable presumption of partial termination when plan participation drops by more than 20%. [*Matz v. Household Int'l Tax Reduction Inv. Plan*, 388 F.3d 570 (7th Cir. 2004). See also 441 F.3d 500 (7th Cir. 2006) for class certification issues in this litigation.]

A decade later, the case was still in the court system. When the *Matz* case returned to the Seventh Circuit, after close to nineteen years and five appeals, the Seventh Circuit affirmed the dismissal of the case. In Rev. Rul. 2007-43, the IRS adopted the 20% presumption but not the conclusive rule that a 10% reduction was not a partial termination. In 2014, the Seventh Circuit said that the length of time for aggregating reductions to determine if a partial termination occurred is generally one plan year. However, complex transactions are not always completed within a year, so related significant corporate events that occur over a multi-year period can be combined to measure the percentage reduction. The 2014 opinion says that employees of seven subsidiaries were terminated, but even if aggregated, the percentage reduction would be only 17%, and thus not conclusive. [*Matz v. Household Int'l Tax Reduction Inv. Plan*, 774 F.3d 1141 (7th Cir. 2014)]

[F] Orphan Plans

Although in most cases, termination will be performed by the plan sponsor, an "abandoned" or "orphan" plan is one which no longer has a plan sponsor, or whose sponsor has ceased to conduct business.

When an asset purchase results in the liquidation of the seller company, or when corporate assets are acquired by a buyer, some legacy retirement plans can become orphan plans if they are forgotten or abandoned. The lack of a sponsor may lead to the plan losing its tax-qualified status. There are also fiduciary issues about managing the plan's assets, reporting, and distributions. EPCRS (see § 15.19[B]) includes an orphan plan process. [Keith R. McMurdy, *Don't Let Your*

Plan Become an Orphan, Fox Rothschild LLP Employee Benefits Legal Blog (Jan. 24, 2012) (benefitslink.com)]

In March 2005, the DOL issued guidance for winding up of orphan plans by Qualified Termination Administrators (QTAs) who have the power to distribute the benefits from individual account plans when they deem the plan to be abandoned (e.g., there have been no contributions to, or distributions from, the plan over a 12-month period or the sponsor corporation has been liquidated in a Chapter 11 bankruptcy proceeding). A QTA must be a person or entity who could serve as an IRA trustee, such as a bank, insurer, or mutual fund.

The QTA must also notify the DOL that the plan is abandoned, that it intends to serve as QTA, the estimated value of the plan assets, and similar items. The DOL has issued a model notice that can be used for this purpose. There is a safe harbor for balances rolled over to IRAs.

The abandoned plan process requires the use of a QTA, a party eligible to serve as trustee or issuer of an individual retirement plan and who holds the abandoned plan's assets. The QTA must make a finding that the sponsor no longer exists, cannot be found, or can no longer maintain the plan. The plan is officially deemed terminated 90 days after EBSA's Office of Enforcement acknowledges receipt of the notice of plan abandonment.

In order to wind up an abandoned 401(k) plan, the QTA:

- Updates the plan records;

- Calculates benefits payable to each participant and beneficiary;

- Reports any delinquent contributions;

- Uses plan assets to pay the reasonable expenses of serving as QTA;

- Notifies the participants and beneficiaries of the upcoming termination. The notice must include the statement that actual benefits may be more or less than the estimate because of investment gains or losses and administrative expenses. The QTA must explain distribution options to the participants and beneficiaries, warning them that if they do not make an election within 30 days, the QTA will deposit the account balance in an IRA, a federally insured interest-bearing bank account, or send it to the unclaimed property fund of the state of the participant's last known address;

- Distributes the benefits;

- Files the Special Terminal Report for Abandoned Plans;

- Circulates a final notice.

In FY 2016, EBSA (part of DOL) received 663 applications from QTAs. EBSA approved 424 terminations and closed applications; those plans distributed $21.8 million to participants. [EBSA Fact Sheet, *EBSA Restores Over $696.3*

Million to Employee Benefit Plans, Participants, and Beneficiaries, <https://www.dol.gov/ebsa/newsroom/fsFYagencyresults.html> (last accessed Feb. 24, 2017)]

§ 17.03   THE PBGC'S ROLE

A great deal of work is required to terminate a plan and wind up its affairs. For most participants, it takes the PBGC about three years to process a termination and provide finalized benefits. Most employees are not subject to recoupment. However, the delays and uncertainty make it difficult for participants in a terminating plan to make financial plans.

The PBGC sends a letter to participants informing them that their plan has been terminated and the PBGC has taken over as trustee. Once the PBGC determines the benefit, it sends a "benefit determination letter" explaining the final benefit amount. The PBGC continues making payments to retirees, with any adjustments required to reflect the limits on the PBGC guarantee.

In the case of a single-employer plan, the PBGC guarantees payment of all nonforfeitable benefits. However, the PBGC guarantee is subject to a maximum limitation, with the result that some participants will not receive the full benefit they would have received had the plan not terminated.

Persons who were already retired before the PBGC takeover continue to receive the benefit form they elected. Those who retire later choose among the PBGC's retirement options. Most de minimis benefits (under $5,000) will be cashed out in a lump sum. Monthly benefits under $50 will be paid in a single annual check. Other benefits will be paid monthly. If the plan has adequate assets, some participants will receive more than the basic PBGC guarantee, usually if they retired, or could have retired, three years before the guarantees took effect.

A participant who has not yet commenced benefit payments from a terminated plan can begin benefits at the plan's normal retirement date. A person who has satisfied all requirements (such as years of service) for early retirement as of the date of plan termination (or bankruptcy filing date) can commence early retirement payments at early retirement age—but only if he or she no longer works for the employer.

For benefits already in pay status, the guarantee is based on age at the date the guarantee takes effect but for those not already receiving benefits, the guarantee is based on the age at which payments begin (with adjustments for disabled participants). The maximum guarantee is also adjusted for payment forms other than the single-life annuity. [PBGC.gov, *PBGC's Guarantees for Single-Employer Pension Plans Fact Sheet*] In a standard termination, a fully funded plan terminates; the PBGC does not become a trustee. In a distress termination, the sponsors must apply the limits themselves, so benefits are reduced as of the date of termination. The PBGC sometimes needs years to make the calculations for an involuntary termination.

In certain years, people receiving PBGC benefits are entitled to the Health Coverage Tax Credit (HCTC). The HCTC pays 72.5% of the qualified health insurance premium for people who receive PBGC (or Trade Adjustment Assistance) benefits. The HCTC expired on December 31, 2013 but was reinstated until December 31, 2019 by the Trade Preferences Extension Act of 2015, Pub. L. No. 114-27. [Segal Consulting Update, *Restoration of the Health Coverage Tax Credit* (Oct. 5, 2015) (benefitslink.com)]

It is unusual, but not impossible, for a company to take back control of plans that were taken over by the PBGC. For example, in 2016, for only the second time, a takeover was reversed. (The first reversal occurred in 1993 when three pension funds reverted to LTV Steel.)

The Renco Group Inc., took back two pension funds as of June 1, 2016. Renco pledged to pay all future benefits plus $35 million in shutdown benefits not covered by the PBGC. Renco also agreed to reimburse the PBGC for $15 million that it spent on benefits since the November 2012 PBGC takeover. Renco announced that it was leaving its controlled group; the PBGC sued the company for fraud in 2013, alleging that the principal purpose of the transaction was to avoid responsibility for the severely underfunded pension funds. The case was settled in December 2013. [Hazel Bradford, *Renco Group to Take Back 2 Plans from PBGC; Marks Second Time in Agency History*, Pionline.com (Mar. 4, 2016) (benefitslink.com)]

Although the PBGC administers single-employer plans that it takes over, under the multi-employer program, the fund's management remains the same but the PBGC provides funding. In fiscal 2016, the PBGC paid $113 million in financial assistance to 65 multi-employer plans that aggregate more than 86,000 participants. More than a million people are participants in multi-employer plans that are expected to run out of money in the next two decades.

A Teamster pension fund, the Road Carriers Local 707 Pension Fund, was taken over by the PBGC in early 2017 after the fund had been unable to pay full benefits for a year; the PBGC will pay more than $1.7 million a month for this purpose. As of February 1, 2017, benefits under the fund were cut back to the PBGC guarantee limit, so the average benefit will be $570 a month, whereas the average unreduced benefit was $1,313 a month. Only 7% of participants and beneficiaries will receive the full benefit they were promised; 42% will experience a reduction of more than half of the promised benefits. [Rebecca Moore, *Benefit Cuts Could Hit More Than One Million Multiemployer Plan Members,* plansponsor.com (Mar. 2, 2017)]

Two other Teamster local funds in New Jersey were also close to failure and the New York State Teamsters Pension Fund was also in very poor financial condition. Multi-employer plans were destabilized by trucking deregulation in the 1990s. Deregulation, changes in shipping equipment and techniques, and stock market losses caused a number of employers to go out of business—leaving fewer employers to fund the plans. [Meep, *When Multiemployer Pensions Fail: Teamsters Local 707,* Stump (Feb. 28, 2017) (benefitslink.com)]

[A] PBGC Guarantee

Defined benefit plans pay premiums to the PBGC annually, providing funds for the federal agency to supervise plan terminations and, if necessary, assume payment of a terminating or terminated plan's obligations to its participants. The PBGC guarantee is intended to protect the employees of the plan, not the sponsor corporation. If the assets of a terminating plan are not large enough to pay the benefits, the PBGC will make payments (subject to limitations on the amount it will pay) and then seek recoupment from the sponsoring corporation. However, an employer's liability to the PBGC is capped at 70% of its net worth, or 75% of the unfunded guaranteed benefits.

Since 2005, the premium has increased steadily, the objective being improving the financial soundness of the PBGC. Until the passage of the Deficit Reduction Act of 2005, Pub. L. No. 109-171, the single-employer premium had been stable at $19 per employee per year for many years. This legislation also implemented inflation indexing for the premium. There are various PBGC premiums: a flat-rate premium for single-employer plans, charged for each participant; a flat-rate premium for multi-employer plans; a variable-rate premium based on the extent of the plan's unfunded vested benefits; and a one-time premium for terminating plans ($1,250). The variable rate premium is subject to a cap.

The premium was altered by the Moving Ahead for Progress in the 21st Century Act (MAP-21, Pub. L. No. 112-140) and the Bipartisan Budget Act of 2013, Pub. L. No. 113-67. Reflecting the various modifications, for plan years beginning in 2015, the flat-rate premium is $57 for single-employer plans, $26 for multi-employer plans. (Originally, a $13 figure was announced, but the Cromnibus legislation, Pub. L. No. 113-235, doubled the premium as a trade-off for the relief the bill provides for financially distressed multi-employer plans.) The variable-rate premium (VRP) for single-employer plans is $24 per $1,000 of unfunded vested benefit. The Bipartisan Budget Act of 2013 increased the VRP by $10. The VRP is subject to indexing, but the statutory rounding rules were not triggered so there was no indexed increase. In 2017, premiums rose again: the per-participant flat-rate premium for single-employer plans is $69, the VRP is $34 The VRP for 2017 is capped at $517 per participant, which may be lower if the plan has fewer than 25 participants. The 2017 flat-rate premium for multi-employer plans is $28, There is no VRP for multi-employer plans. The scheduled increases for future years are $74 single-employer flat-rate premium in 2018, $80 in 2019. The VRP is projected to increase to $38/$1,000 UVB for 2018, $42 for 2019, with the cap remaining $517 for both years, and the mutli-employer flat rate remaining stable at $28. [<http://www.pbgc.gov/prac/prem/premium-rates.html> (last accessed Feb. 24, 2017)]

The due date for a terminating plan's final premium is the filing date for the post-distribution certificate. This rule was adopted because the final premium was sometimes forgotten in standard terminations when the due date was months after the plan closed its books. Furthermore, plans will generally be exempt from the variable rate premium for the year in which a standard termination is completed, and small plans may be exempt from the variable rate premium for the first year of coverage. [79 Fed. Reg. 13547 (Mar. 11, 2014); see Rebecca Moore, *PBGC Finalizes Premium Changes*, plansponsor.com (Mar. 10, 2014)]

In April 2009, the Second Circuit held that PBGC termination premiums are not contingent pre-petition claims that can be discharged under Chapter 11. Therefore, companies that terminate their plans post-filing may still have to pay the premium. The Second Circuit ruled that the PBGC's right to termination premiums does not arise until after the discharge, so there was no valid right before bankruptcy decided by non-bankruptcy law (the test of a dischargeable pre-petition claim). Certiorari was denied in late 2009. [*PBGC v. Oneida Ltd.*, 562 F.3d 154 (2d Cir. 2009)]

The PBGC guarantees "basic benefits." (The PBGC has legal authority to set up a separate trust fund to guarantee nonbasic benefits, but it has chosen not to do so.) The basic benefit guaranteed by the PBGC is a monthly life annuity that lasts for the participant's life. (This is in contrast to the joint and survivor annuity that is the normal payment form for a married participant to receive under an ongoing plan.) The annuity begins at age 65.

Benefits and increases that were not in effect for five years before the termination date/bankruptcy filing date receive only partial, phased-in protection: the PBGC guarantees 20% or $20 per month of the increase (whichever is larger) of the increase for each full year since the increase took effects. Shut-down benefits are phased in depending on the number of years since the plant closing or other shutdown event: a rule adopted to deter plans from increasing benefits, knowing that the obligation would be passed along to the PBGC. [PBGC.gov, *PBGC's Guarantees for Single-Employer Pension Plans Fact Sheet*]

However, the PBGC also wants to promote lifetime annuities, so it adopted a final rule in November 2014, making it easier to transfer assets from a defined contribution plan to a defined benefit plan, so that the eventual distributions will be made in annuity form. Under this final rule, the benefit based on the transferred amount is added to the PBGC's maximum guarantee for the single-employer plan, so participants will not lose protection by rolling over the benefits. The five-year phase-in requirement does not apply to the transferred amount. However, if the plan goes through a distress termination, participants probably will not be able to get a lump-sum distribution of mandatory employee contributions attributable to the rollover amounts. [PBGC Final Rule, RIN 1212-AB23, 79 Fed. Reg. 70090 (Nov. 25. 2014)]

The IRS noted that many defined benefit plans are closed to new hires, who are usually offered a defined contribution plan. In early 2016, the IRS proposed relief for employers who have both closed defined benefit plans and defined contribution plans. The proposed rules make it easier for the employer to pass non-discrimination testing. Without this relief, it would be increasingly difficult for the closed plan to satisfy the minimum coverage test (Code § 410(b)) as the grandfathered employees continue to accrue seniority and have higher salaries than the younger workers in the defined contribution plan. [81 Fed. Reg. 4976 (Jan. 29, 2016); Announcement 2016-16, 2016-18 I.R.B. 697. See Gregory L. Needles and Timothy Kennedy, *Proposed IRS Regulations Provide Relief to Sponsors of Closed Defined Benefit Plans*, Morgan Lewis & Bockius (Mar. 3, 2016), available at Lexology.com]

The IRS extended the temporary relief for an additional year (until plan years beginning after 2018) for plans that were soft-frozen by amendments adopted before December 13, 2013. The IRS did not think that it would complete the process of issuing new final regulations until 2018. [Notice 2016-57, 2016-40 I.R.B. 432; see Marjorie Martin & Joanne Jacobson, *IRS Extends Temporary Nondiscrimination Relief for Closed DB Plans Through 2017* (Sept. 19, 2016) (benefitslink.com); Rebecca Moore, *IRS Extends Nondiscrimination Relief for Closed DBs*, plansponsor.com (Sept. 21, 2016)]

The size of the maximum benefit the PBGC will guarantee for an individual depends on that person's age—and also if the payment is made in the form of a single-life annuity, a joint and survivor annuity where the benefits remain the same after the first annuitant's death, or a joint and 50% survivor annuity (i.e., the survivor benefit is half of the basic benefits). The table assumes that both spouses are the same age; adjustments are made if their ages are different. For example, using 2016 figures, at age 65, the maximum straight-life annuity guarantee is $5,011.36 a month, whereas the maximum joint and 50% survivor annuity guarantee is $4,961.25. At age 60, the monthly maximum guarantees are $3,257.38 and $2,931.64 respectively; at 55, $$2,255.11 and $2,029.60. For single-employer plans that fail in 2017, at age 65, the guarantee limits are $64,432 for a straight-life annuity, $57,989 for a joint and 50% survivor annuity; at age 60, the maximums are $41,881 and $37,693; at 55, the figures are $28,994 and $26,095. The guarantee is larger than most pensions, so the PBGC said that almost 85% of retirees who get their pensions from the PBGC receive the full amount. The PBGC pays benefits to about 1.5 millon people in failed pension plans, and covers close to 40 million people in private-sector plans. [PBGC, *Maximum Monthly Guarantee Tables*, <http://www.pbgc.gov/wr/benefits/guaranteed-benefits/maximum-guarantee.html> (last accessed Feb. 24, 2017). PBGC.gov, PBGC No. 16-16, *PBGC Guarantee Limit for Single-Employer Plans Increases for 2017* (Oct. 28, 2016) (benefitslink.com) Full table: <http://www.pbgc.gov/wr/benefits/guaranteed-benefits/maximum-guarantee.html?source=govdelivery&utm_medium=email&utm_source=govdelivery>]

The maximum guarantee did not change between 2015 and 2016 because increases are linked to the Social Security cost of living adjustment, and there was no Social Security COLA in 2016. The guarantee for the multi-employer program is not indexed, so it remains 100% of the first $2,640, and 75% of the next $7,920 (a total of $8,580) for 20 years' service; for 35 years' service, it is $15,015 a year (100% of the first $4,620 earned, 75% of the next $13,860).

For annuity dates starting in 2016 the present value of the PBGC's maximum guarantee depends on the plan participant's age: e.g., $228,314 at age 40, $364,612 at 50, $467,483 at 55, $604,988 at 60, $795,820 at 65, and $1,149,073 at 70. The present value figure is significant because certain underfunded defined benefit plans—those whose adjusted funding target attainment percentage falls between 60% and 80% may not make "prohibited payments." A prohibited payment is a payment that exceeds 50% of the amount that would be payable if the plan were not underfunded, or the present value of the payment recipient's maximum benefit guaranteed by the PBGC—whichever is less. The PBGC publishes a new table annually.

For annuity starting dates in 2017, the present value table runs from $153,783 at age 25, $362,104 at age 45, $579,776 at age 55, $913,208 at age 65; the highest figure on the table is $6,321,974 at age 85. [PBGC, *Present Value of PBGC Maximum Guarantee* <http://www.pbgc.gov/prac/mortality-retirement-and-pv-max-guarantee/present-guarantee.html#main-content>; <http://www.pbgc .gov/prac/mortality-retirement-and-pv-max-guarantee/present-guarantee.html #2017> (Dec. 2, 2016)]

When a plan is to be terminated, the PBGC:

- Determines if the benefit is nonforfeitable and payable in periodic installments; if so, it is a guaranteed basic benefit;

- Performs actuarial calculations to convert benefits in other forms to straight life annuities commencing at age 65.

The PBGC has the power to assess penalties if an employer was late in paying its PBGC premiums, or if the employer failed to provide the required notices to employees.

The PBGC adopted a rule in 2011, implementing PPA § 403. The rule makes the phase-in period for the guarantee of benefits contingent on an "unpredictable contingent event" begin no earlier than the event itself. (The PBGC's example of such an event is a plant shut-down.) The rule was necessary because PBGC's guarantee of new pension benefits and benefit increases phases in over a five-year period starting with the later of the date of adoption or the effective date of the change, and the PBGC wanted to protect itself against plans adopting new benefits when they knew they were going to terminate. The net effect is that the guarantee for benefits that arise from unpredictable contingent events that occur within five years of plan termination is probably lower than the guarantee that would have been available under the pre-PPA law. [76 Fed. Reg. 34590 (June 14, 2011)]

In mid-2014, the PBGC published final regulations on the phase-in period for guarantee of benefits contingent on occurrence of an unpredictable contingent event (UCE), such as plant shutdowns. The regulations reflect PPA requirements. When an employer establishes a new pension benefit or increases a current benefit, the PBGC's guarantee of the additional benefit is generally phased in over a five-year period. The period begins when the change is adopted, or the effective date of the plan amendment—whichever is later. However, the 2014 regulations provide that the phase-in rules apply as if the plan amendment creating a benefit for the UCE was adopted on the on the date of the UCE rather than the date of the amendment. That is to say, the guaranteed benefits are lower for a UCE within five years of termination than they would have been before the PPA. A Unpredictable Contingent Event Benefit (UCEB) is a benefit triggered solely by a UCE. The most common UCEB is a full retirement benefit granted earlier than it would have been available absent the UCE. The PPA required faster funding of ongoing plans. In most situations, that created greater parity between employer funding and the PBGC phase-in. However, this was not true of UCEBs; the unpredictability of the event meant that employers did not pre-fund it. The 2014 final regulations give examples, such as a facility that engages in sequential layoffs or closes in a series of steps. Because this is a PPA-related provision, the regulations are effective for UCEBs payable as a result of UCEs occurring after July 26, 2005. [79 Fed. Reg. 25667 (May 6, 2014)]

Variable interest rates create serious problems when the plan is terminated because a participant's exact benefit can only be determined at the time benefits begin—but the PBGC needs to know if the benefit amount is de minimis and, therefore, can be made in a single payment. A PBGC proposed regulation, implementing PPA § 2006, was published in late 2011.

The proposed regulation explains how to determine the benefits payable when a hybrid plan (e.g., cash balance or pension equity) terminates: a variable rate is used that is an average of rates used in the five years before termination. In a distress termination, the proposed termination date determines the benefits under the plan. If the proposed termination date is deferred, the benefits accrued between the proposed and actual termination dates are recalculated with the interest rate that would have applied before the final termination date. [Proposed Regulations, 76 Fed. Reg. 67105 (Oct. 31, 2011); see Deloitte's Washington Bulletin, *PBGC Proposes Rules on Determining Benefits in Terminating Hybrid Plans* (Nov. 7, 2011) (benefitslink.com)]

[B] Proposal on Payment Forms

Regulations proposed in 2000 and adopted, more or less intact, in 2002 [PBGC No. 02-14 (Dec. 22, 2000), 65 Fed. Reg. 81456 (Dec. 26, 2000), 67 Fed. Reg. 16949 (Apr. 18, 2002)] discuss payment options when the PBGC takes over a plan. Participants can select alternative annuity benefit forms—straight life, five, 10, or 15 years certain and continuous; joint and survivor annuities with various levels of benefits, and "pop-up" annuities that increase if the beneficiary dies before the participant. (Alternate payment forms require the consent of spouses of married participants.) The regulations also discuss inheritance of payments to a deceased participant.

Some changes were made in the definition of "earliest PBGC Retirement Date." The regulations define the "earliest PBGC Retirement Date" as the earliest date the plan participant could retire for the purposes of ERISA Title IV. Usually, this will mean either age 55 or the first date the participant could retire and collect an immediate annuity, whichever is later.

[C] Penalties and PBGC Enforcement

The PBGC, like the IRS, has the power to assess penalties if required documents are omitted, if documents are filed but are late, if payments are not made, or if payments are made but in an untimely fashion. The PBGC can waive penalties if the failure was due to factors outside the business' control. Penalties can be waived in full or in part, e.g., if there were factors preventing timely full compliance, but the plan was dilatory in getting back into compliance.

Penalties can be waived if payment would impose undue hardship on the business. "Reasonable cause" that might justify a waiver requires a showing that even ordinary business care and prudence would not have permitted full timely payment. Reasonable reliance on incorrect advice from a PBGC employee could give rise to a waiver—but reliance on the plan's own professional advisors will not. [PBGC Final Regulations, 71 Fed. Reg. 66867 (Nov. 17, 2006)]

The general increase in ERISA penalties announced in mid-2016, pursuant to the Federal Civil Monetary Penalties Inflation Adjustment Act Improvements Act of 2015 (part of Pub. L. No. 114-74) includes a number of increases relevant to troubled and terminating plans. For example, a multiemployer plan must certify when it is in endangered or critical status; failure to certify is treated as failure to file an annual report, and the new penalty can be as much as $2,063 a day. Failure to inform participants of benefit restrictions under Code § 436 can be penalized by $1,632 a day. An endangered multiemployer plan that fails to adopt a funding improvement plan, or a multiemployer plan in critical status' failure to adopt a rehabilitation plan, can be penalized by up to $1,296 a day—and failing to meet a benchmark in a funding improvement plan is subject to the same penalty. [81 Fed. Reg. 29765 (May 12, 2016); 81 Fed. Reg. 42491 (June 30, 2016)]

In early 2017, there were more increases, but not for penalties in general, only for two penalties. The penalty for violating ERISA § 4071 (not giving the PBGC required information) rose from $2,063 to $2,097 a day, and the failure to issue the multi-employer plan notices required by ERISA § 4302 rose from $275 to $279 a day. [82 Fed. Reg. 8813 (Jan. 31, 2017)]

The PBGC also maintains an Early Warning Program, where it scrutinizes employers and corporate transactions that could endanger stability. The PBGC concentrates on controlled groups (i.e., related corporations) whose plans, when aggregated, have 5,000 or more participants and/or $50 million or more in underfunding. In late 2016, the PBGC reorganized its Website, announcing that new FAQs about the Early Warning Program would be posted in 2017 and that the PBGC would be monitoring trends that could increase risks to plans and the PBGC's insurance program. The PBGC asks for information about events, the plan's controlled group, the financials of the sponsor and the other members of its group, and the most recent actuarial data about the plan.

Although it seldom takes this drastic step, the PBGC has the power under ERISA § 4042(a)(4) to involuntarily terminate a failed plan. This power gives the PBGC leverage to negotiate settlements with plan sponsors to stave off involuntary termination. Settlements require the employer to improve the financial stability of the plan, whether by increasing its cash contributions to the plan, giving the PBGC a security interest in employer assets to safeguard unfunded liabilities, or securing guarantees or letters of credit. [<http://www.pbgc.gov/prac/risk-mitigation.html>; see Harold J. Ashner and Deborah West, *PBGC Expands Scope of Early Warning Program,* Bloomberg BNA Pension & Benefits Daily (Jan. 10, 2017) (benefitslink.com)]

In mid-2017, the PBGC retreated somewhat from earlier guidance about this program. A May 10, 2017 update to the PBGC Website removed two risk factors (credit deterioration and downward trend in the company's economic metrics) from the list of warning factors. The PBGC said that the company's credit rating would still be a factor in that analysis, but would not trigger an investigation by itself. The guidance from May 2017 includes a sample information request. [Groom Law Group, *PBGC Walks Back Early Warning Program Expansion* (May 11, 2017) (benefitslink.com)]

[D]   QDROs in Plans Under PBGC Control

Qualified Domestic Relations Orders (QDROs) are discussed in detail at § 12.08. If the PBGC takes over a plan some of whose benefits must be paid to alternate payees (ex-spouses and separated spouses of participants), it issues two standard QDRO forms (Model Separate Interest; Model Shared Payment) for use by domestic relations courts. PBGC QDROs either specify or give the alternate payee discretion to control the time at which benefits begin, how the benefits are paid, the percentage of the pension payment going to the alternate payee, and how long the alternate payments begin. The Model Separate Interest Form is used when the order is issued before the benefits are in pay status. In effect, the pension account is divided into two, one for the participant, the other for the alternate beneficiary. The Shared Payment Form divides each payment, as it comes due, between participant and alternate beneficiary. [*The Division of Pensions Through Qualified Domestic Relations Orders,* <http://www.dol.gov/ebsa/publications/qdros.html> (undated, last accessed Mar. 23, 2016)]

§ 17.04 INVOLUNTARY TERMINATION

[A] Basic Procedure

ERISA § 4042 governs involuntary termination proceedings brought when the plan assets are less than the total of guaranteed benefits. The PBGC asks the appropriate federal district court to oust the plan administrator and appoint a trustee to wind up the plan. ERISA § 4062(b)(1) makes the employer liable to the PBGC for the total amount of unfounded plan liabilities on the termination date, plus interest starting on the termination date.

The PBGC is empowered to ask for involuntary termination if:

- The plan has failed to meet its minimum funding standards;

- The plan cannot pay current benefits when due;

- The plan has been required to report one or more distributions to a "substantial owner" (10% shareholder);

- The PBGC's losses are expected to increase "unreasonably" unless the plan is terminated.

If the plan does not even have enough assets to pay its current benefits, much less to keep paying benefits as they come due; or the plan has applied for a distress termination but lacks money to fund the guaranteed benefits, the PBGC has an obligation to seek involuntary termination. [PBGC, *Pension Plan Termination Fact Sheet*, <http://www.pbgc.gov/about/factsheets/page/termination .html> (last accessed Feb. 24, 2017)]

[B] The Role of the Trustee

If the district court appoints a trustee, the plan must be terminated. The PBGC can also force termination of a plan even without such an appointment. If a trustee is appointed, his or her duty is to keep the plan administrator, participants, beneficiaries, unions, and employers with potential ERISA liability informed about the progress of the termination. The trustee has the power to demand turnover of some or all of the plan's records and assets. The trustee has a choice of either continuing the pattern of benefit payments in place before the trustee's appointment, or limiting payment of benefits to the basic benefits.

Under ERISA § 4062(d), the employer is liable for the unpaid contributions to the trustee plan. The employer must provide the trustee with cash, or securities acceptable to the trustee, in an amount equal to:

- The accumulated funding deficiencies under I.R.C. § 412(a);

- Any funding deficiencies that the IRS waived under I.R.C. § 412(c) before the termination date;

- All decreases in the minimum funding standard permitted by I.R.C. § 412(e) before the termination date, plus interest running from the termination date.

Under certain circumstances outlined in ERISA § 4069(b), a successor corporation can become liable for such amounts, if the sponsor reorganizes; the purpose of the reorganization was to evade liability; and reorganization occurred within the five years before a plan termination that would have caused liability. In this context, reorganization means a merger, consolidation, or becoming a division of another company; changing identity, form, or place or organization; or the liquidation of a subsidiary into its parent.

Also note that ERISA § 4062(b) provides that when an employer ceases operations at a facility, leading to separation from service of 20% or more of the total number of plan participants, the employer either has to fund the guaranteed benefits immediately, or make provision for their funding.

[C] Calculations for Involuntary or Distress Terminations

Under 29 C.F.R. Part 4044, benefits under a plan going through an involuntary or distress termination are calculated based on a determination of the likelihood (low/medium/high) that the participant will retire early in various years. Then, once early retirement benefits are computed, the total value of benefits under the plan can be computed. The process uses the Unreduced Retirement Age, which is either the normal retirement age or the earliest age at which a pension can be paid without actuarial reduction—whichever is earlier.

Table I-17, Appendix D, is used to compute the value of early retirement benefits in an involuntary or distress termination whose valuation date is in 2017. For Unreduced Retirement Ages in 2018, the probability of early retirement is considered low if the total value of retirement benefits is under $631, medium if the value falls in the range of $631 to $2,665, and high if the value exceeds $2,665. The latest date on Table I-17 is 2027, when the probability is low for benefits under $774, medium for benefits between $774 and $3,268, and high for benefits over $3,268. [81 Fed. Reg. 83137 (Nov. 21, 2016); see Plansponsor editors, *PBGC Issues New Table for Use by Involuntarily Terminating DBs*, plansponsor.com (Nov. 22, 2016)] In this table, "year" means the year in which the unreduced benefit becomes payable. The "low" and "high" benefits are dollar amounts; the "medium" benefits are a range between the two figures.

The PBGC publishes mortality tables, updated annually, to calculate the present value of annuities in involuntary termination situations. [See Notice 2016-50, 2016-38 I.R.B. 344 for the mortality tables to be used in 2017. Matt Klein, *Mortality Table Update,* Finleydavies.com (Sept. 9, 2016) (benefitslink.com)]

§ 17.05 PLAN REVERSIONS

Before ERISA, it was legal for an employer to simply wind up a plan and take back its assets. But under current law, a plan provision that calls for reversion (or increased reversion) cannot become effective until the end of the fifth calendar year following the year of adoption. In other words, employers have to wait at least five years to take advantage of a reversion opportunity. Furthermore, if the plan called for mandatory contributions, once the benefits are paid off, assets must be allocated to mandatory contributions before the reversion occurs.

An employer that is entitled to a reversion must pay 50% of the reversion amount as an excise tax. However, if the employer establishes a qualified replacement plan or amends the terminating plan to increase benefits, the excise tax is reduced to 20%. IRS Form 5330 is used to pay the excise tax. It is due the last day of the month after the month in which the reversion occurred.

§ 17.06 EFFECT ON BENEFITS

[A] Forfeit of Benefits

Benefits become nonforfeitable when a plan terminates or partially terminates. A defined contribution plan's benefits become nonforfeitable if and when the employer completely ceases its contributions to the plan. If a defined benefit plan terminates within 10 years of its creation, I.R.C. § 411(d)(2) imposes limits on the benefits that can be paid to the 25 highest-compensated individuals covered by the plan. This rule prevails even if it results in the loss of some accrued benefits.

In the Seventh Circuit view, the employees of a bankrupt company raised a sufficient claim of breach of fiduciary duty by alleging that the company's executives failed to provide ongoing funding for a health plan that was terminated as part of the bankruptcy process. The executives were fiduciaries because of their control over the committee that invested the plan's assets. However, the Seventh Circuit dismissed claims of breach of fiduciary duty by not giving notice of the likelihood of plan termination, on the ground that there is no duty to disclose likely future termination unless plan participants are deliberately misled. [*Baker v. Kingsley*, 387 F.3d 649 (7th Cir. 2004)]

[B] The Anticutback Rule

Whether deliberately or inadvertently, employers sometimes make cutbacks in a plan, or scale it down. The effect can be inadvertent if the employer lacks the money to make a required deposit, or simply is ignorant of what the legal requirements are. The consequences are not always those intended by the employer. The worst-case scenario is that the plan will be treated as partially terminated, and then retroactively disqualified, obligating the employer to pay back taxes for prior plan years. Retroactive disqualification also harms employees, who are likely to owe back taxes. Furthermore, distributions from a disqualified plan cannot be rolled over to a qualified plan.

A plan is frozen if it is amended to keep the plan trust in existence, but without further contributions or accrual of benefits. A frozen plan is still subject to the top-heavy plan rules, and still has to provide Qualified Joint and Survivor Annuity (QJSAs) and Qualified Pre-Retirement Survivor Annuity (QPSAs) on the same terms as if it had not been frozen.

A frozen plan is a defined benefit plan that either has ceased benefit accruals for all employees, or accrues benefits for existing employees but does not accept new entrants. The sponsor of a frozen plan still encounters costs for maintaining the plan, including paying actuaries, accountants, and administrators. Various financial factors make it increasingly likely that plans will freeze plans: higher life expectancies, increasing PBGC premiums, and low interest rates that increase the amount that must be contributed to maintain the plan. [Jerry Kalish, *Frozen Pension Plans Becoming a High Maintenance Item*, Retirement Plan Blog (Feb. 3, 2015) (benefitslink.com)]

See 77 Fed. Reg. 37349 (June 21, 2012) for proposed regulations allowing plan sponsors in bankruptcy to amend their single-employer defined benefit plans to eliminate optional forms of benefit that are not permitted because the plan is underfunded. Under the conditions prescribed in the regulations (e.g., approval of the PBGC and bankruptcy court), eliminating the optional benefit forms will not violate the anti-cutback rule.

A recent article discusses some of the operational issues for frozen plans. Freezing a plan does not eliminate all of the management and reporting burden; nor does it entirely insulate the sponsor from the consequences of market fluctuations. The article calls for evaluation of the time horizon and cash requirements of the frozen plan; calculating the effect of ongoing funding or termination liability on the balance sheet; selecting investments to meet the funding target; and adjusting the financial strategy as the market changes. In a soft freeze, the plan will be maintained for longer, so management choices must be updated for a longer period. The article advocates using ALM (Asset/Liability Modeling) to set investment directions, not only maximizing total return but also considering how the plan's liabilities affect the metrics that apply to the plan. [Bank of America/Merrill Lynch Workplace Insights, *A Road Map for Effectively Managing a Frozen Pension Plan* (Apr. 2016) (benefitslink.com)]

§ 17.07 REPORTING AND COMPLIANCE

When a plan is terminated, IRS Form 5310 is used to request an IRS determination letter stating that the associated plan trust did not become disqualified or lose its exempt status. Form 6088 must be filed in conjunction with this form, listing up to 25 owners or 5% shareholders of the employer corporation who received any distribution from the plan during the preceding five years.

The general rule is that Form 5310-A must be filed 30 days or more before a transfer of plan assets to another qualified retirement plan because of a merger, consolidation, or change in ownership of assets or liabilities. When two defined contribution plans merge or a defined contribution plan is spun off, or a defined benefit plan engages in a merger or spinoff that has only minimal effects, the Form 5310-A filing is not required.

In the somewhat unlikely case that the trust of a terminating plan has more assets than are needed to pay all the plan benefits, and therefore the employer recovers those excess assets, Form 5319 must be filed by the last day of the month after the month in which the employer recouped the assets. This is also the form the employer uses to pay the excise tax on the recouped funds.

The Form 5500-series annual report must be filed for the year of the merger, consolidation, division, or termination. If a trust is frozen (the plan maintains its assets, although benefit accruals have stopped), the 5500-series filing is required in every year until all the assets have been distributed. Form 8955-SSA is submitted to the IRS to identify separated plan participants who are entitled to deferred vested benefits. For the 2016 instructions, see <http://www.irs.gov/pub/irs-pdf/i8955ssa.pdf>. The information used to be reported on Schedule SSA, but it was replaced by Form 8955-SSA for plan years beginning on or after January 1, 2009. Unless there is an extension, Form 8955-SSA must be filed by the last day of the seventh month after the last day of the plan year: July 31 for a calendar year plan. Generally speaking, the form will have to be e-filed with the IRS FIRE system, but see Rev. Proc. 2015-47, 2015-39 I.R.B. 419 for exemptions when e-filing would cause economic hardship to a plan.

Four penalties can be imposed for different kinds of failures in connection with Form 8955-SSA. If the failure falls under Code § 6652(d)(1), failure to file an annual registration statement, the penalty is $1 per participant per day of omission, up to $5,000. Failure to file notification of a change in plan status, such as termination of the plan or change in plan name or plan administrator (§ 6652(d)(2)), is also penalized $1/day, capped at $1,000, but there is no failure to file as long as the change in status is reported on Form 5500 or 5500-SF. Failure to furnish timely statements to participants, or furnishing a fraudulent statement (§ 6690) is penalized by $50 per statement. The § 6652(e) late filing penalty is $25 per day of failure for failure to file Form 8955-SSA as prescribed, unless there is a reasonable excuse for the failure. [IRS, *Penalties Related to the Filing of Forms 8955-SSA* (updated July 5, 2016), available at <https://www.irs.gov/retirement-plans/penalties-related-to-the-filing-of-forms-8955-ssa> (last accessed Feb. 24, 2017)]

§ 17.08 PAYMENT OF EXPENSES

It is appropriate for fiduciaries to use plan assets to pay the expenses of an ongoing plan. However, the decision to terminate a plan is a business decision made by the plan's settlor, and not a fiduciary decision. That means that some of the termination expenses relate to settlor functions—and it violates ERISA to use plan assets to pay settlor expenses. These expenses are considered fiduciary expenses that can properly be paid out of plan assets:

- Getting an audit;
- Preparing and filing the final annual report;
- Amending the plan to carry out the termination;
- Calculating benefits;
- Preparing benefit statements;
- Notifying participants and beneficiaries about their rights incident to termination.

However, the cost of maintaining the plan's tax-qualified status—including the cost of getting determination letters—is a settlor expense. Legal fees for plan termination are considered settlor expenses. The general rule is that PBGC premiums can be paid out of plan assets, because they are considered to relate to fiduciary implementation of settlor decisions. However, premiums for years when the plan is involved in a distress or involuntary termination cannot be paid out of plan assets. Similarly, sanctions for late payment of PBGC premiums can be paid from plan assets, except sanctions imposed when the plan was involved in a distress or involuntary termination. Plan assets can be used to pay sanctions and penalties that were imposed on the plan, but not those imposed on a plan administrator in his or her individual capacity. [Andree M. St. Martin and Jennifer E. Eller, *Paying Employee Benefit Plan Expenses Chart*, Practical Law Co. (undated) (benefitslink.com) (chart giving the source for the treatment of various items)]

Part IV
BENEFIT PLANS

CHAPTER 18

EMPLOYEE GROUP HEALTH PLANS (EGHPs)

§ 18.01   INTRODUCTION

Health insurance costs are a major planning factor for business. For many years, health care costs, and therefore insurance costs, rose much faster than inflation, until employers faced a heavy burden. In the 1970s and 1980s, there was a vast shift from indemnity insurance [see § 18.12] to some form of managed care. The promise of managed care was that eliminating waste and keeping employees healthier would reduce costs.

However, by the end of the twentieth century, managed care was a problem in and of itself. Insurers began to charge the kind of double-digit annual premium increases that caused so much pain in the 1970s. Many patients were dissatisfied with managed care, charging that they were often denied access to necessary care. Doctors were dissatisfied, with the restrictions on their freedom to prescribe, with the amount of paperwork they had to do, and with both the size and speed of their reimbursement from managed care organizations (MCOs).

Just as there has been a transition from defined-benefit to defined-contribution or employee-funded retirement plans, health plans have shifted from the once-predominant indemnity plan to a heavy dominance of some form of managed care. Some employers have always chosen to self-insure rather than purchase insurance; others have switched to self-insurance to cut costs. A new form that is emerging is the so-called defined contribution or consumer-driven health plan (CDHP).

The passage of health care reform legislation, the Patient Protection and Affordable Care Act, Pub. L. No. 111-148 (PPACA) is discussed below, in § 18.19. The legislation attracted a great deal of opposition, and implementation was marked by many challenges and many delays.

After the 2016 presidential election, PPACA repeal was an important policy objective of the new administration. At press time, the American Health Care Act (AHCA) was introduced into Congress, but was withdrawn when it appeared that it did not have enough votes to pass. The AHCA was not a full repeal of PPACA, but would have made major changes, such as eliminating the employer and individual mandates. The AHCA would also have changed the way in which subsidies were provided for low-income people to buy insurance. PPACA provides a tax deduction; the AHCA would have provided a refundable tax credit. PPACA subsidies vary based on the taxpayer's income, whereas the AHCA credit would vary based on the taxpayer's age. Older taxpayers would have received a larger tax credit than younger taxpayers—but insurers would also be allowed to charge premiums five times as high for the oldest as for the youngest insureds, whereas PPACA limits the premium differential to three times as high.

AHCA failed to gain votes both from congress members who thought it was too harsh and those who thought it did not do enough to eliminate Obamacare. A similar, but not identical, bill was introduced in the Senate as the Better Care Reconciliation Act, but it failed to get enough votes to pass in July 2017. It is likely that additional bills will be introduced from all parts of the political spectrum; the question is whether PPACA will remain in effect simply because it is too difficult to reach consensus on how to replace it, or whether a new statutory scheme will be adopted.

In mid-2012, the Supreme Court did not find PPACA unconstitutional. However, that did not end challenges to the validity of the statute as a whole or to the mandate that employer plans cover contraceptives (see § 18.19[N]).

The payment of federal subsidies to people who purchased health care coverage from the federal insurance exchange was challenged in the Supreme Court. The plaintiffs said that the statutory language refers only to subsidies for purchases of coverage on "an exchange established by the state." Most of the states refused to set up exchanges, leading many people to purchase insurance from the federal exchange. About 85% of exchange users qualify for subsidies, so the decision had great practical effect in allowing many low-income people to retain insurance coverage that they would not have been able to afford without subsidies. [*King v. Burwell*, No. 14-114 (U.S. June 25, 2015); see Adam Liptak, *Supreme Court Allows Nationwide Health Care Subsidies*, NYTimes.com (June 26, 2015)]

The Fourth Circuit ruled in 2013 that the employer mandate (that large employers provide insurance) does not violate the Commerce Clause of the Constitution, and also found the individual mandate constitutional. Certiorari was denied on December 2, 2013. [*Liberty Univ. v. Lew*, 732 F.3d 72 (4th Cir. 2013), *cert. denied*, 134 S. Ct. 683 (Dec. 2, 2013)]

In September 2016, private industry employers spent $2.44/hour worked (7.6% of total compensation costs) for health insurance: in establishments with 1–50 employees the figure was $1.94/hour, far less than the $2.77/hour (8.5% of compensation) for establishments with 50–99 workers, or $4.28/hour (9%) for establishments with more than 500 employees. $1.59/hour worked in 1–50 employee establishments, $1.94/hour for 50–99 workers, $2.77/hour 100–499 (8.5%), $4.28/hour (9.0%) for over 500. [BLS, *Health Insurance Costs 7.6 Percent of Total Compensation for Private Employers in September 2016* (Dec. 14, 2016) (benefitslink.com)]

In March 2017, 67% of workers in private industry had access to medical care benefits provided by the employer, and 49% of private industry workers participated in these plans, for a take-up rate of 72%. (The other 28% did not accept the benefits, for reasons such as having other forms of health care or not being able to afford the employee's share of the cost of the benefit.) Access and participation varied by occupation. Among professionals, 82% had access and 61% participated (a take-up rate of 74%) for production workers, access was 69%, participation 49%, and the take-up rate was 71%. Service workers had an access rate of 39%, a participation rate of 23%, and a take-up rate of 61%. The average private industry employer paid 79% of the premium for single coverage and 70% of the premium for family coverage—so the employee's share was quite substantial. [Bureau of Labor Statistics Economics Daily, *79 Percent of Managers and 39 Percent of Service Workers Offered Medical Benefits in March 2017* (July 27, 2017) (benefitslink.com)]

The Employee Benefits Research Institute (EBRI) reported that since the passage of PPACA, the proportion of self-insured plans in the private sector, and the number of workers covered by self-insured plans, increased. In 1996, 28.5% of private-sector businesses with health plans had at least one self-insured plan; this was true of 39% of businesses in 2015. The percentage of workers enrolled in self-insured plans rose from 58.2% to 60% between 2013 and 2015. [Rebecca Moore, *More Small and Mid-Sized Firms Using Self-Insured Health Plans*, plan sponsor.com (July 28, 2016)]

In mid-2016, HHS announced inflation adjustments for civil money penalties, including the Health Insurance Portability and Accessibility Act (HIPAA) violations, and the DOL increased penalties under its jurisdiction. The maximum penalty for failure to provide the Summary of Benefits and Coverage rose from $1,000 to $1,087. The maximum annual penalty for violation of PPACA's rules about reporting medical loss ratios and providing rebates if loss ratios were inadequate rose from $100 to $109. [81 Fed. Reg. 61538 (Sept. 6, 2016); see Practicallaw.com, *HHS Increases Penalties for HIPAA Noncompliance, Effective August 1* (Nov. 14, 2016) (benefitslink.com)]

Federal law makes the Employee Group Health Plan (EGHP) the primary payor and Medicare only the secondary payor for Medicare beneficiaries who continue to be employed. However, this provision is poorly enforced, and in many instances, Medicare ends up paying for health care for working elderly people, where the EGHP should have been the primary payor. One of the provisions of the Medicare, Medicaid & SCHIP Extension Act of 2007, Pub. L. No. 110-173 § 111, requires Medicare Insurers and self-funded EGHPs report to HHS on situations in which the EGHP had primary responsibility; failure to report is punished by civil money penalties. Reporting is also required for liability insurance (including self-insurance), automobile no-fault insurance, and Worker's Compensation claims made by Medicare beneficiaries. The penalty for such failures from $1,000 to $1,138, for violations occurring after November 2, 2015. [81 Fed. Reg. 61538 (Sept. 6, 2016)]

One of the most important differences between the Employment Retirement Income Security Act's (ERISA's) pension plan provisions and its welfare benefit plan provisions is that, by and large, welfare benefits do not vest, and can be altered or terminated if the plan document retains the sponsor's discretion to do so. However, in some situations, the employer will be deemed to have a contractual obligation to maintain the plan. In a unionized company, the Collective Bargaining Agreement (CBA) will impose further limitations on the employer's ability to alter the health plans it maintains. [For the requirements for Summary Plan Descriptions (SPDs) for health plans, see § 11.02[B].]

In mid-2013, the Supreme Court ruled that § 2 of the federal Defense of Marriage Act was unconstitutional, with the result that same-sex married couples became eligible for a variety of federal employment-related benefits.

Two years later, a 5-4 Supreme Court decision required all of the states to recognize same-sex marriage; see § 18.06. [*Obergefell v. Hodges*, 135 S. Ct. 2584 (June 26, 2015)]

§ 18.02 THE HEALTH CARE LANDSCAPE

Although initially the employer group health plan market was divided only between self-insured and indemnity insurance plans, today managed care is virtually universal. There are many types of managed care plans. At one time the Health Management Organization (HMO) was the dominant managed care form, but today its predominance is yielding to plans that provide somewhat more flexibility and provider choice for patients. The Consumer-Driven Health Plan (CDHP), such as the high-deductible health plan (HDHP) used in conjunction with a Health Savings Account (HSA) is gaining prominence (see § 18.18, below).

The Kaiser Family Foundation (KFF) reported that the percentage of employers providing coverage was much the same in 2015 and 2016 and employers' costs were also about the same, but the trend of shifting cost increases to employees continued. Premiums for family coverage rose an average of 3%, about the percentage of wage increases, reaching $18,142 a year. However, four-fifths of employees with health coverage are responsible for deductibles, and deductibles are about 50% higher than they were five years earlier. The average deductible for the entire insurance market is $1,500, but it is $2,100 for smaller companies. Employees' premiums have also risen, so that they now represent about one-third of the total cost of insurance. The average 2016 employee premium for family coverage was $5,277 a year. [Reed Abelson, *Workers Pay More for Health Care as Companies Shift Burden, Survey Finds*, NYTimes.com (Sept. 14, 2016); Anna Wilde Mathews, *Average Cost of Employer Health Coverage Tops $18,000 for Family in 2016* WSJ.com (Sept. 14, 2016)]

Voluntary benefits are used to fill gaps in traditional health insurance plans. Traditionally, voluntary benefits were offered for insurance (life, vision, dental, disability, critical illness, accident). Newer voluntary benefit plans provide benefits such as identity theft protection, financial counseling, or pet insurance. At one time, executives were sometimes offered individual medical plans but such plans are generally forbidden by PPACA.

ERISA provides a safe harbor for plans with minimal employer involvement, where the covered employee pays the full premium. Safe harbor plans must be completely voluntary, with the employer's involvement very minimal (the employer makes no contributions, does not endorse the plan, and receives nothing other than reasonable compensation for the tasks of collecting and remitting the premiums paid by the employees). The safe harbor does not apply if the employer negotiates plan terms, selects the insurer, assists employees with claims or disputes, or associates the plan with other plans it sponsors. Plans that do not qualify for the safe harbor must comply with all ERISA requirements, such as having a written plan document, filing Form 5500, and offering Comprehensive Omnibus Budget Reconciliation Act (COBRA) coverage. [Ascende.com, *When is a Voluntary Plan Truly a Voluntary Benefit Plan?* (Mar. 4, 2016) (benefitslink.com)]

As employee health care obligations rise, in the form of higher premiums and copayments, some employers offer "gap insurance," special policies to cover the out-of-pocket costs of hospital stays or unexpected treatment. Guardian Life and Aflac sell these policies; they are offered by employers as a voluntary benefit, paid for by employees (although the employer may offer a subsidy). Hospital-indemnity insurance covers hospital stays; accident insurance covers emergency room visits post-accident; and critical care insurance pays a lump sum such as $5,000 to $30,000 for a specific diagnosis such as cancer. The policies cost $5–$25 per two-week pay period, possibly varying by age and amount of coverage. [Rachel Emma Silverman, *For Cash-Strapped Workers, "Insurance on Insurance,"* WSJ.com (Dec. 6, 2016)]

On July 21, 2014, President Obama signed an executive order forbidding federal contractors to discriminate against transgender (or gay, lesbian, or bisexual) persons. The executive order does not exempt religious organizations. [Peter Baker, *Obama Calls for a Ban on Job Bias Against Gays*, NYTimes.com (July 21, 2014)]

In mid-2015, the Equal Employment Opportunity Commission (EEOC) reversed its policy; it now deems any employment action that is sex-based or based on gender, including actions based on sexual orientation, to constitute unlawful sex discrimination that violates Title VII. Therefore, employees anywhere in the United States (even if their state does not forbid sexual-orientation or gender-identity discrimination) can file Title VII complaints on these bases. [*Redacted v. Fox (Baldwin v. Dep't of Transportation)*, Appeal No. 0120133080 (EEOC July 16, 2015); see Roxana S. Bell, *New EEOC Ruling Says That Title VII Already Prohibits Sexual Orientation Discrimination*, Bingham Greenebaum Doll LLP (July 17 2015), available at Lexology.com; Allen Smith, *EEOC: Sexual Orientation Discrimination is Sex Discrimination*, SHRM (July 20, 2015) (benefitslink.com)] However, it is likely that this policy will be reversed once again, and the EEOC will no longer treat sexual orientation or gender nonconformity discrimination as a violation of Title VII.

According to the Movement Advancement Project, as of mid-2015, there were 20 states with employment discrimination laws forbidding discrimination on the basis of sexual orientation or gender identity: California, Colorado, Connecticut, Delaware, Hawaii, Illinois, Iowa, Maine, Maryland, Massachusetts, Minnesota, Nevada, New Jersey, New Mexico, New York, , Oregon, Rhode Island, Utah, Vermont, Washington (and the District of Columbia). New Hampshire and Wisconsin forbade discrimination on the basis of sexual orientation, but had no statutory provision about gender-identity discrimination. State laws in Arkansas and Tennessee forbid localities to adopt their own anti-discrimination laws about sexual orientation or gender identity. [For an online chart of laws banning discrimination against LGBT employees, see <http://www.lgbtmap.org/equality-maps/non_discrimination_laws> (last accessed Mar. 24, 2016).]

On April 9, 2015, the District Court for the Middle District of Florida approved a consent decree between the EEOC and Lakeland Eye Clinic about termination of an employee transitioning from male to female. The clinic agreed to pay the ex-employee $150,000 and provide a neutral letter of reference. The employer agreed to revise its discrimination and harassment policies to protect future transgender employees. [*EEOC v. Lakeland Eye Clinic,* No. 8:14-cv-2421-T35AEP (M.D. Fla., settled Apr. 19, 2015)]

The District Court for the Eastern District of Michigan ruled in favor of a funeral home that fired an employee for dressing as a woman as part of the transition process. The court applied the Religious Freedom Restoration Act (RFRA) to exempt the employer from Title VII, on the basis of a sincere religious belief that men should not dress as women. The EEOC appealed the loss to the Sixth Circuit. [*EEOC v. R.G. & G.R. Harris Funeral Homes,* 201 F. Supp. 3d 837 (E.D. Mich. 2016); see Robert G. Young, *"Least Restrictive Means?" Court Grants Employer Religious Exemption from Title VII in Gender Stereotyping Case,* Bowditch & Dewey (Sept. 8, 2016), available at Lexology.com; Robin E. Shea, *EEOC Appeals Loss in Detroit Transgender Case,* Constangy Brooks Smith & Prophete LLP (Oct. 17, 2016), available at Lexology.com]

In *Fabian v. Hospital of Central Connecticut,* 172 F. Supp. 3d 509 (D. Conn. Mar. 2016) the district court held that employment discrimination on the basis of transgender identity (in this case, a transwoman who applied for a job) is sex discrimination that violates Title VII. However, *Christiansen v. Omnicom Group, Inc.,* 167 F. Supp. 3d 598, (S.D.N.Y. 2016) held that, although sexual orientation discrimination is "reprehensible," it does not violate Title VII. OSHA's published position <https://www.osha.gov/Publications/OSHA3795.pdf> (undated; last accessed Feb. 26, 2017) is that employees should be permitted to use the restroom consistent with their gender identity, not their birth certificate identity. [Stefanie K. Vaudreuil, *Revisiting Transgender Employment Issues,* Liebert Cassidy Whitmore (June 2, 2016), available at Lexology.com] However, it is predictable that OSHA, as constituted and staffed under the Trump administration, will reverse this policy.

§ 18.03   BENEFITS MANDATES

[A]   Generally

One important characteristic of the health care reform legislation is that it phases in a standard package of required health care benefits. But even before the PPACA, there were both federal and state limitations on the principle that employers had complete discretion as to which benefits would be included in their plans.

At the federal level, the Children's Health Insurance Program Reauthorization Act of 2009, Pub. L. No. 111-3 (CHIPRA), requires employers to amend their EGHP and cafeteria plans to allow special enrollment of employees and dependents who either lose their Medicaid or SCHIP eligibility, or have become eligible to participate in the EGHP because the state will provide assistance with the employee's responsibility for health insurance premiums. [Troutman Sanders LLP, *Keeping up with Recent Legislation—Numerous Changes to Group Health Plans Required*, plansponsor.com (Feb. 27, 2009); Norbert F. Kugele, Warner Norcross & Judd LLP, *New Federal SCHIP Law Requires Cafeteria and Health Plan Amendments* (Feb. 10, 2009) (benefitslink.com)]

The HITECH Act (Health Information Technology for Economic and Clinical Health Act), part of the economic stimulus bill, expands HIPAA's privacy and security provisions. Business associates of covered entities are subject to the same privacy rules as the covered entities themselves, including criminal penalties. Business associates who discover a breach of the confidentiality or security rules by the covered entity are supposed to either take steps to cure the breach, or terminate their business relationship with the covered entity. Business associates must notify covered entities (who must then notify the affected individual participants) when there has been a breach of unsecured PHI. The covered entity is required to notify HHS—and the news media—if more than 500 people were affected by the breach.

Civil monetary penalties (CMPs) have been increased, and part of a CMP can be distributed to individuals whose PHI was improperly disclosed. The Office of Civil Rights retains its role in enforcing HIPAA compliance, but state attorneys general have been given enforcement powers through suits in federal district courts.

The HITECH Act includes many new regulations for electronic medical records; an accounting must be given of how the records were used and disclosed in the previous three years. The new requirements are generally effective February 17, 2010. [Troutman Sanders LLP, *Keeping up with Recent Legislation—Numerous Changes to Group Health Plans Required*, plansponsor.com (Feb. 27, 2009)]

[B] Maternity Stays

The Newborns' and Mothers' Health Protection Act of 1996 (NMHPA) [Pub. L. No. 104-204] and the Taxpayer Relief Act of 1997 [Pub. L. No. 105-35; Final Regulations, 73 Fed. Reg. 62410 (Oct. 20, 2008)] combine ERISA and tax code provisions to mandate that group health plans (both insured and self-insured, whatever the number of participants) provide at least a minimum hospital stay for childbirth. The minimum is 48 hours after a vaginal delivery, 96 hours after a Caesarian section, although earlier discharge is permitted if the mother wishes and her attending physician consents.

However, the plan is not allowed to offer financial incentives to the physician or the mother to shorten the stay. If the plan does not provide hospitalization benefits for childbirth, it is not required to add those benefits because of this legislation. State laws requiring a longer maternity stay are not preempted. On a related issue, in late 2011, California adopted legislation (SB 299/AB 592 and SB 222/AB 210) to enhance employment and insurance protection for pregnant women, requiring maintenance of at least the same level of insurance benefits during pregnancy-related leave that the employee had before taking leave, and requiring all individual policies to cover maternity services. The law covers all employers of five or more.

[C]   Women's Health and Cancer Rights Act (WHCRA)

The Women's Health and Cancer Rights Act (WHCRA) [Pub. L. No. 105-277], became law on October 21, 1998, effective for plan years beginning on or after that date. The Act provides that if an EGHP covers mastectomies, it must also cover reconstructive breast surgery if the patient wants it and her attending physician prescribes it. This includes reconstruction of the mastectomized breast; surgery on the other breast to balance the patient's appearance; prostheses; and treatment of physical complications of mastectomy. Deductibles and coinsurance for reconstructive surgery must be comparable to those imposed on other procedures.

EGHPs (and the insurers and HMOs that provide the medical and surgical benefits) have an ongoing obligation to notify new plan participants of their WHCRA rights, and to renew the notice annually. (It is not necessary for both the EGHP and insurer or HMO to furnish the notice, as long as one of them does.)

It did not violate the WHCRA (or ERISA) for a plan to limit reimbursement for bilateral breast reconstruction performed by non-network surgeons to 150% of the cost of unilateral reconstruction. Nor was the plan required to pay for private duty nurses, because the plan specifically excluded that service. Although plans that cover mastectomy must cover reconstruction "in a manner determined in consultation with the attending physician and the patient," deductibles and coinsurance can be imposed, and the plan can negotiate the level and type of reimbursement with the provider. [*Krauss v. Oxford Health Plans, Inc.*, 517 F.3d 614 (2d Cir. 2008)]

[D]   Contraceptives

Even before PPACA, there was authority for requiring EGHPs to cover contraception. A December 14, 2000, EEOC decision [available at <http://www.eeoc.gov/policy/docs/qanda-decision-contraception.html> (last accessed Apr. 11,

2016)] agrees with the charging parties, a group of female employees, that it violates Title VII for a plan to fail to cover prescription contraceptive drugs and devices when it covers other types of preventive medical care, and when it covers vasectomy and tubal ligation (permanent surgical methods of contraception). The EEOC treats the distinction as discrimination on the basis of sex (in that only women use birth control pills, diaphragms, and IUDs) and pregnancy. The EEOC ruled that the Pregnancy Discrimination Amendment forbids discrimination on the basis of potential as well as actual pregnancy.

PPACA's rules for preventive care require non-grandfathered health plans to cover all FDA-approved methods of contraception, with no deductible or other cost sharing from the employee. An HHS Interim Final Rule (IFR) gave religious employers an extra year to comply, and gave them the option of buying insurance without contraceptive coverage. A religious employer is defined as a nonprofit organization that primarily serves and employs people of a particular faith, and the organization's purpose is inculcating the religious values of that faith. [76 Fed. Reg. 46621 (Aug. 3, 2011)]

HHS issued new final rules in July 2015, adding an alternative means for religious nonprofit organizations to give notice of their objection to providing contraception coverage. Instead of completing DOL's opt-out form, organizations that say that completing the form makes them complicit in providing contraception, can give HHS written notice of their religious objection to providing contraceptive services to their employees. The final rules also allow some closely held for-profit businesses to use the same opt-out mechanism. [80 Fed. Reg. 41317 (July 14, 2015); see HHS Press Release, *Administration Issues Final Rules on Coverage of Certain Recommended*]

Challenges to the contraceptive mandate were also asserted by closely held businesses, which argued that being required to cover contraceptives (or contraceptives that they believed actually aborted a fertilized egg rather than preventing conception) violated the corporation's rights under RFRA.

In June 2014, the Supreme Court ruled that it violates the Religious Freedom Restoration Act (RFRA) to require closely held corporations to abide by contraception mandate, because corporations are "persons" as defined by the RFRA, and free exercise of religion is not restricted to nonprofit organizations. The Supreme Court held that the RFRA was enacted to protect business owners from having to choose between their religious convictions and complying with the law. [*Burwell v. Hobby Lobby*, No. 13-354/*Conestoga Wood Specialties v. Burwell*, 134 S. Ct. 2751 (2014)]

Zubik v. Burwell consolidates cases brought by several religious organizations. At that point, the Second, Third, Fifth, Sixth, Seventh, Tenth, Eleventh and D.C. Circuits had upheld the federal government's accommodation process for religious organizations as consistent with the RFRA. Only one Circuit, the Eighth, had found the accommodation invalid as an excessive burden on religious freedom.

Zubik was heard by the eight surviving Justices after Scalia's death. The Supreme Court did not make a definitive decision; it sent the case back to the lower court to work out a compromise. [Jess Bravin and Louise Radnofsky, *Supreme Court Sends Birth-Control Case Brought by Religious Employers Back to Lower Courts*, WSJ.com (May 16, 2016)] There is some precedent for rehearing 4-4 cases once the court is at full strength again. [*Zubik v. Burwell*, 136 S. Ct. 1557 (2016); *Eternal Word Television Network v. Sec'y of HHS*, 818 F.3d 1122 (11th Cir. 2016); see Timothy Jost, *Eleventh Circuit Upholds Religious Accommodation on Contraceptive Coverage*, healthaffairs.org (Feb. 19, 2016) (benefitslink.com)]

On January 9, 2017, the Trump administration issued FAQs announcing that it was not modifying the current accommodation offered to employers (notifying the insurer, plan administrator, or HHS of the objection to covering contraceptives, leading to the insurer or administrator becoming responsible for providing the coverage). [<https://www.dol.gov/sites/default/files/ebsa/about-ebsa/our-activities/resource-center/faqs/aca-part-36.pdf>; see Timothy Jost, *Administration Sticks With Current Accommodation For Employers Objecting To Contraceptive Coverage*, Healthaffairs.org (Jan. 10, 2017) (benefitslink.com)]

The Trump administration issued an Executive Order on May 4, 2017, directing federal agencies to consider exempting religious employers from the contraception mandate. The EO deals with organizations such as charities and universities that are not already exempt as religious institutions. The Office of Management and Budget announced that it was reviewing an interim final rule submitted by DHS, the DOL, and Treasury under which any non-government organization, including a for-profit business, could assert an objection to providing contraceptive coverage. [<https://www.whitehouse.gov/the-press-office/2017/05/04/presidential-executive-order-promoting-free-speech-and-religious-liberty> ; see Amy Gordon, *Executive Order Regarding Contraceptive Mandate Directed Toward Religious Employers,* McDermott Will & Emery (May 11, 2017), available at Lexology.com; Robert Pear, *White House Acts to Roll Back Birth-Control Mandate for Religious Employers,* NYTimes.com (May 29, 2017)]

On a related issue, the District Court for the District of Columbia held in mid-2015 that a non-religious, nonprofit employer can lawfully refuse to provide coverage of certain contraceptive methods based on an objection that is moral rather than religious. According to the district court, the exemption is not limited to objections based on a theistic religion. A moral philosophy about the sanctity of life is also entitled to exemption. [*March for Life v. Burwell*, 128 F. Supp. 3d 116 (D.D.C. 2015)]

However, the Third Circuit held that a non-religious organization that provides counseling on alternatives to abortion is not similarly situated to a religious organization, so it is subject to the contraception mandate. [*Real Alternatives v. HHS,* No. 16-1275 (3d Cir. Aug. 4, 2017); see Timothy Jost, *Appellate Ruling Deals Setback to Opponents of Contraceptive Coverage Mandate,* healthaffairs.org (Aug. 6, 2017)]

[E] Mental Health Parity

A very controversial 1996 federal statute, the Veterans' Affairs, Housing and Urban Development and Independent Agencies Appropriations Act [Pub. L. No. 104-204], imposed a requirement of parity in EGHPs with more than 50 participants. Under the parity provision, plans that did not impose lifetime or annual limits on medical and surgical benefits could not do so on mental health benefits, and plans that imposed limits had to apply the same limits to mental health as to medical/surgical benefits. In 1996, this requirement was made part of ERISA.

The Mental Health Parity Act was permitted to expire, and then was revived several times through short-term extensions, from Pub. L. No. 107-116, Pub. L. No. 107-147, Pub. L. No. 107-313, Pub. L. No. 108-197, Pub. L. No. 108-311, Pub. L. No. 109-151, and Pub. L. No. 109-432.

Mental health parity requirements were made permanent, as the Paul Wellstone and Pete Domenici Mental Health Parity and Addiction Equity Act (MHPAEA) by the Emergency Economic Stabilization Act, Pub. L. No. 110-343. Employers of 50 or more employees are covered. The MHPAEA extends the parity requirement to substance abuse treatment. The financial requirements and treatment limitations for mental health or substance abuse treatment cannot be more restrictive than the predominant requirements or limitations that apply to substantially all of the plan's medical and surgical benefits. It is now unlawful to impose separate treatment limitations on mental health/substance abuse treatment—e.g., frequency of treatment, number of visits, days of coverage. The criteria for determining the medical necessity of mental illness and substance abuse treatment must be disclosed on request to current or potential participants and beneficiaries of the plan, and to contracting providers. Participants and beneficiaries are entitled to request an explanation of denials of mental health and substance abuse benefits. Employers are entitled to exemption from the parity requirement if the cost of parity exceeds 2% of total plan costs (in the first year of the requirement) or 1% in later plan years [Interim final regulations: T.D. 9479, 75 Fed. Reg. 5410 (Feb. 2, 2010)]

In November 2013, DOL, HHS, and the Treasury published joint final rule on mental health parity to implement the MHPAEA by ensuring that features such as copayments, deductibles, and limits on visits are not more restrictive for mental health/substance abuse treatment than for medical/surgical treatment. [78 Fed. Reg. 68240 (Nov. 13, 2013)]

The Second Circuit permitted EGHP participants and an association of mental health providers to bring an ERISA suit against a self-insured health plan's Third-Party Administrators (TPA) for violating the parity requirements. The suit charged that the TPA only applied preauthorization and concurrent review policies to mental health claims, and used more restrictive guidelines for medical necessity of mental health claims. The Second Circuit ruled that the MHPAEA parity requirements can be enforced under ERISA § 502(a)(3), and the TPA was the appropriate defendant because it had complete control over benefit claims. [*N.Y. State Psychiatric Ass'n v. UnitedHealth Grp.*, 798 F.3d 125 (2d Cir. 2015)]

Principal Life Insurance, the insurer and claims administrator, denied many hospital charges for treatment of SW, a minor, for an eating disorder, on the grounds that the policy limits had been exceeded. The plan imposed a 10-day limit on inpatient mental health services, so it paid for 10 days of hospitalization in 2006 and only the first 10 days of a hospitalization in 2007. The Eighth Circuit held that there was insufficient evidence to treat the hospitalization as focused on SW's mental rather than her physical health. [*Wrenn v. Principal Life Ins. Co.*, 636 F.3d 921 (8th Cir. 2011)]

The Ninth Circuit held that insurance coverage of residential treatment for anorexia nervosa was not required by the Blue Shield policy—but was required by the MHPEA. California's mental health parity law requires coverage of medically necessary treatment of severe mental illness, and anorexia is considered a severe mental illness. It would be irrational to pay for 100 days of treatment in a skilled nursing facility that was not suitable for Harlick's condition while excluding suitable and effective care. [*Harlick v. Blue Shield of California*, 656 F.3d 832 (9th Cir. 2011), later proceedings 686 F.3d 699 (9th Cir. 2012)]

In mid-2015, Aetna Life and Health Insurance agreed to pay up to $4.5 million to settle claims that it failed to cover the diagnosis and treatment of disorders on the autism spectrum. But $1.5 million of the fine will be suspended if the company complies with the settlement and obeys the Missouri statute requiring coverage of Applied Behavioral Analysis, a costly autism therapy. Aetna also admitted to violating the autism mandate in 2012 and paid a $1.5 million fine, but did not perform the compliance audit required by the earlier settlement [Joe Harris, *Aetna Fined for Violating Autism Coverage Law*, Courthouse News Service (May 20, 2015) (benefitslink.com)]

[F] Other Inclusion Issues

EGHPs are forbidden to discriminate against employees or their dependents who suffer from end-stage renal disease (ESRD). Internal Revenue Code § 5000 imposes a heavy penalty: 25% of the employer's health care expenses (not just the amount that would have been paid for ESRD coverage in the absence of discrimination). Also note that ERISA § 609(d) requires plans to maintain their coverage of pediatric vaccines at least at the May 1, 1993 level.

In January 2003, the Second Circuit ruled that it is not a violation of Title VII for a plan to exclude coverage of surgical procedures to correct infertility that are performed only on women, because infertility affects male and female participants equally. The district court hearing this case applied the "equal access" standard often used in ADA cases, asking whether all employees have equal access to plan benefits. However, the Second Circuit held that this is not an appropriate standard in a Title VII case, in which the relevant standard is whether sex-specific conditions exist. If they do, the next inquiry is whether excluding coverage of those conditions results in a plan that has inferior coverage for one sex. The Second Circuit said that the Pregnancy Discrimination Act's ban on discrimination on the basis of pregnancy or related conditions does not extend to discrimination on the basis of infertility, because both men and women have reproductive capacity and can be infertile. [*Saks v. Franklin Covey Co.*, 316 F.3d 337 (2d Cir. 2003)]

PPACA requires coverage of adult children up to age 26; by the time it was passed, more than two-thirds of the states had already expanded the age to which dependent coverage would be available, sometimes extending coverage even more than the PPACA requirement; some states require coverage to age 30. These state laws do not apply to self-insured medical plans, but do apply to EGHPs and possibly to stand-alone insured dental and vision plans. (Extending the parent's policy was usually more affordable than buying a policy for the adult child—especially if the adult child had a pre-existing condition.) [Louise Radnofsky, *Millions of Young Adults Join Parents' Health Plans*, WSJ.com (June 8, 2012)]

The IRS definition of "dependent" is found in Code § 152. For tax purposes, a dependent is either the taxpayer's qualifying child or qualifying relative, which is significant if the EGHP covers tax dependents who are not the employee's spouse or child under age 27. [Haynes & Boone LLP, *IRS Proposed Regulations Clarify the Definition of Tax "Dependent,"* (Feb. 7, 2017), available at Lexology.com]

[G] State Mandatory Coverage

PPACA takes the approach of requiring both businesses and individuals to purchase health insurance coverage, or pay a fine—an approach that was already pioneered by several of the states, including California and Massachusetts. However, the Massachusetts mandate was repealed in 2014. [Kaiser Health News, *Mass. Employer Health Insurance Mandate Repeal Moves Forward*, <http://www.kaiserhealthnews.org/daily-reports/2013/july/12/health-reform-state-issues.aspx> (July 12, 2013)]

By mid-2007, Rhode Island, Connecticut, and Missouri had joined Massachusetts in requiring some employers to establish cafeteria plans qualifying under Code § 125, and Maine adopted a universal health plan, but it attracted few new subscribers, perhaps because many potential insured persons found the premiums unaffordable. [Sibson Consulting, *More States Enact Cafeteria Plan Mandates* (Aug. 10, 2007) (benefitslink.com); Pam Belluck, *Maine Learns Expensive Lesson as Universal Health Plan Stalls*, N.Y. Times, Apr. 30, 2007, at A1]

After three years, Vermont abandoned its Green Mountain Care (state-financed single payer) plan. The state's governor said that the taxes required to sustain the plan would have been too disruptive. There was supposed to be an 11.5% payroll tax on businesses, plus 9.5% assessment on people earning over

400% of FPL (the federal poverty line), with a lower tax on a sliding scale for people earning less. The state decided it was not going to get the federal funding it expected under a PPACA waiver. [Anthony Brino, *Vermont Abandons Single Payer, for Now*, Healthcare Payer News (Dec. 18, 2014) (benefitslink.com)] Mandates have also been adopted at the local level, e.g., by San Francisco.

Before PPACA, the general legal principle was that it was entirely up to employers to decide whether or not to offer insurance coverage. However, some attempts were made to require large employers to provide health insurance. Legislation was introduced in about 30 states. Maryland passed a bill, nicknamed the "Wal-Mart law," requiring a minimum level of health care spending by large employers. The governor vetoed it, but the state legislature overrode the veto. Early in 2007, the Fourth Circuit held that the statute was invalid—imposing Maryland-only requirements, contrary to ERISA's mandate of uniform national rules. [*Retail Industry Leaders Ass'n v. Fielder*, 475 F.3d 180 (4th Cir. 2007)] Although PPACA does not have provisions dealing specifically with the very largest employers, it does impose heavier requirements on "large employers" (those with 50 or more employees) than on smaller employers.

§ 18.04 DENTAL PLANS

Many medium-sized and large companies offer some form of dental coverage. As with most health-related benefits, the prevalence of the benefit increases directly with the size of the company.

Most dental plans offer fee-for-service coverage, although some plans use HMOs or PPOs.

The basic structure of a dental plan is a schedule of covered procedures and payments for each (which might be defined as dollar amounts or percentages). The dentist who renders the care is paid for each service to covered employees (in a fee-for-service plan) or receives capitated or other prearranged compensation under an HMO or PPO plan. There is an increasing trend to require advance approval of large nonemergency claims.

The general rule is that the percentage of coverage is inversely related to the expected cost of the service. Low-cost procedures like X-rays and examinations get a higher percentage of reimbursement than fillings, root canals, and dental surgery, with lowest levels of reimbursement for prosthetics and orthodontia. Dental plans typically exclude cosmetic dentistry, hospitalization for inpatient dental procedures, and amounts that would be covered by other insurance (including Worker's Compensation).

§ 18.05 PRESCRIPTION DRUG COVERAGE

Many companies' EGHPs provide at least some coverage of prescription drugs, as a complement to medical treatment. Some employers offer separate prescription drug plans with the objective of saving money by ordering in bulk. Some prescription drug plans also cover employees' dependents—often, with some degree of financial responsibility on the employee's part.

See Chapter 9 for a discussion of the effect of Medicare Part D (prescription drug coverage) on EGHP and retiree health plan operations. Group health plans that cover anyone eligible for Medicare Part D (whether as an active worker, a retiree, a spouse, or a dependent) and that cover prescription drugs must make an annual electronic filing with CMS, within 60 days of the start of each new plan year, disclosing whether the prescription drug coverage is creditable or noncreditable. The typical prescription drug plan covers only outpatient drugs; drugs taken by hospital patients come under the hospital care benefit. The usual plan imposes a copayment on each prescription (e.g., $5–$25). Overall dollar limitations on reimbursement per plan year are common. However, many plans are bedeviled by high increases, such as 15%–20% a year, in prescription drug costs.

In an effort to keep costs down, or at least to tamp down the speed of the rate of increase, plan sponsors are altering prescription drug plan design, incorporating features such as imposing higher copayments; imposing a coinsurance percentage instead of a flat amount; requiring doctors to get prior authorization for expensive drugs; requiring a trial of a less expensive drug before a more expensive one is prescribed ("step therapy"); raising the copayment on proprietary drugs when a generic formulation is available ("therapeutic focus"); excluding coverage of drugs prescribed for off-label uses; and having two or even three tiers with a $100 copayment in the highest tier and lower copayments for generics and less expensive branded drugs. [Bob Kalman, Buck Consultants, *How to Manage Pharmacy Benefits Plans: Part 1: Getting the Plan Design Right* (Feb. 2012) (benefitslink.com)]

In 2011, 56% of plans required step therapy; this rose to 69% in 2015. A new tactic for extremely expensive drugs for which there is no generic equivalent is the "split fill." Plan participants are given only a two-week rather than a one-month supply. The rest of the drug is only prescribed after a nurse confirms that the patient is doing well on the drug and has not stopped taking it because of side effects. [Peter Loftus, *Employers Battle Drug Costs*, WSJ.com (Dec. 18, 2015)]

§ 18.06 SAME-SEX MARRIAGE

[A] Current Trends

Until recently, same-sex marriage was almost unthinkable. After an epochal 2013 Supreme Court decision; a second Supreme Court decision was pending. 36 states recognized same-sex marriage before the Supreme Court decided another major same-sex marriage case in June 2015.

The federal Defense of Marriage Act (DOMA) provided that only marriages between a man and a woman are recognized for federal purposes. Some of the states adopted similar legislation or amendments to the state constitution. In June, 2013, the Supreme Court ruled that § 3 of the federal DOMA was unconstitutional: it violates due process and equal protection, because it does not serve any legitimate state purpose to disparage same-sex marriages in comparison to male/female marriages, and it deprives same-sex married couples of valuable protections. (Section 3 provides that a same-sex partner cannot be treated as a "spouse" under federal law.) The Supreme Court found that DOMA § 3 improperly interferes with the states' regulation of marriage. The Supreme Court upheld the lower court ruling that invalidates California's Proposition 8 (the referendum forbidding same-sex marriage), on the grounds that the plaintiffs did not have standing to sue when the state of California no longer defended the validity of Proposition 8. [*United States v. Windsor*, 133 S. Ct. 2675 (2013); *Hollingsworth v. Perry*, 133 S. Ct. 2652 (2013)]

The Supreme Court majority ruled that all the states must recognize SSM because DOMAs are unconstitutional on equal protection grounds. Therefore, they must permit same-sex couples to marry, and they must grant recognition to marriages performed in other states and countries. [*Obergefell v. Hodges*, 135 S. Ct. 2584 (June 26, 2015); see Adam Liptak, *Gay Marriage Upheld by Supreme Court in Close Ruling*, NYTimes.com (June 26, 2015)]

[B] Taxation of Same-Sex Spouses

Various retirement issues (such as whether a pension will be paid as a qualified joint and survivor annuity (QJSA)) are governed by federal law. One reason why the Supreme Court DOMA decisions were so significant is that many employment issues depend on whether another person is the employee's "spouse" or not. Spouses are allowed to file joint income tax returns; unmarried cohabitants are not, so the Supreme Court decisions makes it possible for married same-sex couples to file jointly.

On August 29, 2013 (i.e., after the *Windsor* decision but before *Obergefell*), the IRS enunciated the basic principle that same-sex married couples are married for federal tax purposes if they entered into a marriage that was legal where it was celebrated—whether or not they currently live in a state that recognizes same-sex marriage. This principle is set out in Rev. Rul. 2013-17, 2013-38 I.R.B. 201. After *Obergefell*, the IRS proposed regulations issued in October 2016 reaffirm the principle that same-sex marriages are treated the same way as mixed-sex marriages for federal income tax purposes. A marriage is recognized for federal tax purposes if it would be recognized by an U.S. state, possession, or territory. However, civil unions and registered domestic partnerships are not treated as marriages. [Notice 2015-86, 2015-52 I.R.B. 887 and 80 Fed. Reg. 64378 (Oct. 23, 2015)]

Marriage has implications for pension and benefit plans: e.g., qualified plans must provide a QJSA and Qualified Preretirement Survivor Annuity (QPSA) and spousal consent is required to waive the QJSA or QPSA. Minimum distribution rules and rollover rules give surviving spouses additional options not available to beneficiaries who are not spouses and there are Qualified Domestic Relations Order (QDRO) rules for allocating pensions on divorce. The IRS extended its general principle (that same-sex marriages are effective for federal law purposes if they were legal at the place of celebration) to these pension provisions.

In some circumstances, same-sex partners who were unable to marry will be treated as surviving spouses. On November 4, 2015, it was reported that the Veterans' Administration (VA) provided survivor benefits to the domestic partner of a deceased servicemember, even though they were not married when the servicemember died. (Connecticut automatically converted civil unions to marriages effective October 1, 2010; New Hampshire converted civil unions to marriages July 1, 2014, but prospectively only.) [Tara Siegel Bernard, *Gay Couples Are Eligible for Social Security Benefits, U.S. Decides*, NYTimes.com (Aug. 21, 2015)]

[C] Employer Responsibilities

The rule under *Windsor* is that, for purposes of federal benefits (including ERISA, the Family Medical Leave Act (FMLA), COBRA coverage, and income tax) same-sex marriage is treated on a par with male/female marriage. But family law is usually state law, with the definition of "spouse" left up to the states.

Certain fringe benefits (e.g., employee discounts, group term life insurance) are tax-free to employees and their spouses or dependents. When a same-sex partner is considered a spouse, the employer does not have to impute income on the value of health benefits provided to a same-sex spouse, or withhold income tax and pay the Federal Insurance Contributions Act (FICA) tax on this imputed income for same-sex married couples. The payroll system will probably require re-programming accordingly.

§ 18.07 TAX ISSUES IN EGHPs

For both the employer and the employee, the major EGHP tax issues fall under I.R.C. §§ 104–106. It is often in the best interests of both employer and employee for benefits to be provided under a plan of accident and health insurance (A&H). This result is desirable because the employer can deduct its costs of offering such a plan, and the employee does not have taxable income because the plan exists.

See § 18.19[B][6] for PPACA's rules on nondiscrimination in EGHPs. Section 104 provides that an employee does not have gross income when he or she receives A&H insurance benefits that the employee paid for, or that derive from employer contributions that have already been taxed to the employee. For years after 1996, amounts paid under other arrangements having the effect of A&H plans will be taxed as if they did, in fact, come from an A&H plan. Section 105 provides that amounts an employee receives from an A&H plan are taxable if they are paid by the employer or stem from employer contributions not already taxed to the employee. If the employer reimburses medical expenses incurred by the employee for him- or herself and family, if the expenses would be deductible under I.R.C. § 213 (medical diagnosis and treatment, rather than cosmetic or experimental procedures), and if they have not already been deducted by the employee, then the employee has no gross income as a result of the medical expense reimbursement.

The employee can rely on I.R.C. § 105 to exclude amounts that were not received from an insurance policy, as long as they were received under a "plan." For this purpose, a plan is a structured arrangement—although it need not be legally enforceable or even written. The purpose of the plan must be to provide benefits to common-law employees (not independent contractors or self-employed persons) in the event of personal injury or sickness. If the plan is not legally enforceable, Treas. Reg. § 1.105-5 imposes the additional requirement that it be communicated to employees before they encounter any covered health expenses.

The third section of the trilogy, I.R.C. § 106, provides that employees do not have gross income if their employers provide them with A&H insurance.

The IRS issued final regulations in May 2014, providing that, under Code § 402(a), starting with the 2015 tax year, amounts paid from a qualified retirement plan to pay accident or health insurance premiums will be taxable to the participants in the plan, unless an exemption is available. Amounts used to pay premiums for disability insurance that replaces retirement contributions when an employee becomes disabled qualify for an exemption. Retirees are not taxed on plan payments of medical benefits. To qualify for an exemption, the aggregate contribution for benefits cannot exceed 25% of total plan contributions. The plan must set up a separate account to fund those benefits. If unallocated contributions or forfeitures are used to pay accident or health premiums, this constitutes a taxable distribution. [T.D. 9665, 79 Fed. Reg. 26838 (May 12, 2014)]

On July 31, 2006, Final Regulations were published explaining comparability testing for employer contributions to HSAs. An employer who contributes to any employee's HSA has to make comparable contributions for all employees with HSAs. The employer's failure to do so is penalized under Code § 4980G by an excise tax of 35% of the aggregate employer contribution to all employee HSAs for the year. [Watson Wyatt Insider, *IRS Issues Final Regulations on Comparable Contributions to HSAs* (Sept. 2006) (benefitslink.com); Nevin E. Adams, *HSA Comparability Rules Published*, plansponsor.com (July 28, 2006)]

These excise taxes are reported on Form 8928. The excise tax, $100 per beneficiary per day, is also imposed for failure to comply with other requirements, such as rules about mental health parity and pre-existing condition limitations. [IRS Form 8928, <https://www.irs.gov/pub/irs-pdf/f8928.pdf> (revised May 2016) (last accessed Feb. 24, 2017)]

Small employers (with up to 25 employees and average wages up to $51,600) may be eligible for a tax credit, for two consecutive years in 2014 and later. The credit is highest when the average wage is under $25,900, and phases down until it is eliminated when average wages reach $51,600 (2016–2017 level; indexed for inflation). See Code § 45R and the Final Regulations at 79 Fed. Reg. 36640 (June 30, 2014). For 2010–2013, the maximum credit is 35% of the premium paid by an eligible small business (25% of premiums paid by an eligible tax-exempt organization). After that, the credit is defined as a maximum of 50% of the premium paid by an eligible small employer (35% of premiums paid by an eligible nonprofit employer). The credit is computed on Form 8941. [See § 18.19[C]; Final Regulations, 79 Fed. Reg. 36640 (June 30, 2014); IRS, *Small Business Health Care Tax Credit Questions and Answers*, <http://www.irs.gov/ uac/Small-Business-Health-Care-Tax-Credit:-Questions-and-Answers> (Nov, 2, 2016) (last accessed Feb. 24, 2017); IRS Health Care Tax Tip 2016-20 (Feb. 1, 2017), available at <https://www.irs.gov/Affordable-Care-Act/Employers/ Understanding-the-Small-Business-Health-Care-Tax-Credit> (last accessed Feb. 24, 2017)]

The PPACA requires self-insured plans and issuers of health insurance policies to make small payments, reported on IRS Form 720. For plan years ending on or after October 1, 2012 and before October 1, 2019, the fee is $1 per covered person for the first year, $2 per covered person for the second year, with inflation adjustments in subsequent years. The money is used for quality assurance activities. [77 Fed. Reg. 22691 (Apr. 17, 2012)] Health care FSAs and HRAs with employer contributions are considered to be self-funded group health plans, so they are subject to the fee. This fee, known as the "PCORI fee," is $2.08 for plan years where the last day occurred between October 2, 2014 and October 1, 2015, $2.17 for plan years ending between October 2, 2015 and October 1, 2016, and $2.26 for years ending between October 2, 2017 and October 1, 2018. [Gary B. Kushner, *It's PCORI Filing Time Again*, Kushner & Co. (June 10, 2016) (benefitslink.com)]

§ 18.08 HEALTH-BASED DISCRIMINATION

PPACA's ban on pre-existing condition limitations in health plans builds on a 2001 HHS/IRS interim regulation on discrimination based on health factors. This rule implements a HIPAA provision, Code § 9802/ERISA § 702, forbidding discrimination in health coverage. EGHPs and insurers are forbidden to discriminate against, or charge higher premiums to, individual participants or beneficiaries on the basis of individual health factors such as health status, claims experience, or medical history. Note that whether a plan provision complies with HIPAA doesn't determine whether or not it violates the Americans with Disabilities Act (ADA).

Certain plans are exempt from the interim final rule, such as benefits that are not covered by HIPAA (e.g., long-term care insurance); single-participant plans; and self-funded plans that elect under 45 C.F.R. § 146.180 to opt out of the nondiscrimination requirements.

HHS issued a proposed rule under PPACA § 1557 forbidding discrimination on the basis of race, color, national origin, sex, age, or disability in any health program that receives federal financial assistance. The rule does not apply directly to most EGHPs but might apply indirectly. The proposed rule defines "employee benefit programs" broadly to include fully insured and self-insured plans, wellness programs, and health clinics sponsored by an employer. However, most of these programs do not receive federal funding.

All health insurers participating in the PPACA health insurance Marketplace program must comply with the nondiscrimination requirements in all their products, including group policies sold outside the Marketplace.

HHS interprets sex discrimination to include discrimination based on orientation, sexual stereotyping, and gender identity, so coverage must not be denied because of gender identity. Coverage must be offered consistent with gender identity, but sex-specific treatments (such as Pap smears for a transman) cannot be denied because the person identifies as the other sex. HHS said that explicitly excluding all health services related to transition would be facially discriminatory, but the agency has also said that the proposed rule does not require coverage of any particular benefit or service. HHS sought comments about whether there should be a religious organization exemption. For individuals with disabilities, any covered entity must provide auxiliary aids and services like sign language interpreters. Covered entities have 90 days from effective date of requirement to post a notice explaining customers' rights and how to file a discrimination complaint with the Office of Civil Rights. [80 Fed. Reg. 54172 (Sept. 8, 2015); HHS Fact Sheet, <http://www.hhs.gov/civil-rights/for-individuals/section-1557/nondiscrimination-health-programs-and-activities-proposed-rule/index.html> (last accessed Feb. 25, 2017)] The rule was finalized, effective July 18, 2016. The final rule does not state directly whether or not sexual orientation discrimination violates § 1557, but the preamble says that HHS' policy favors a ban on sexual orientation discrimination, and HHS will continue to monitor legal developments.

Before PPACA, people with serious or chronic illnesses were often unable to get health coverage. Even after PPACA, some insurers design benefits in a way that discourages enrollment by people with major health needs. HHS' Office for Civil Rights received a complaint when four insurers in Florida used "adverse tiering" to put all drugs for treating HIV in the highest cost-sharing tier. HHS noted that one-fourth of insurers put all HIV drugs in the top tier, where patients must pay the most for medications. Section 1557 applies to the PPACA Marketplaces and to private health plans such as EGHPs, if the health insurer receives any federal financial assistance. Section 1557 forbids discrimination in insurance design, such as denials or claim limitations, imposing additional restrictions on coverage (such as higher cost-sharing) and discriminatory marketing practices and benefit designs. HHS said that adverse tiering is discriminatory unless it satisfies the recognized standards of care for a condition. It also violates § 1557 to impose age limits on services that are effective at all ages, requiring prior authorization for certain classes of medications, and imposing limitations and exclusions that are not based on clinical guidelines and medical evidence. [81 Fed. Reg. 31376 (May 18, 2016); see Douglas Jacobs & Wayne Turner, *Nondiscrimination and Chronic Conditions—The Final Section 1557 Regulation*, healthaffairs.org (July 20, 2016) (benefitslink.com)]

Note, however, that in early 2017, the District Court for the Northern District of Texas issued a nationwide preliminary injunction against enforcement of the § 1557 provisions forbidding discrimination on the basis of having an abortion or being transgender. Eight states and three private religious healthcare providers sued, opposing the inclusion of transgender status and abortion in the definition of discrimination "on the basis of sex," preferring to use the Title IX definition of sex as immutable binary differences between males and females. The district court agreed that Congress did not intend the ban on sex discrimination to cover gender identity or abortion and that § 1557 violates the Religious Freedom Restoration Act because it made it more expensive to uphold religious beliefs. However, the other parts of the rule dealing with, e.g., age, race, and disability took effect. [*Franciscan Alliance, et al. v. Burwell*, No. 7:16-cv-00108-O, **2016 U.S. Dist. LEXIS 183116** (N.D. Tex. Dec. 31, 2016); see Tabatha L. George, Alexa Greenbaum and Jaklyn Wrigley, *Federal Judge Blocks Transgender Protections*, Fisher Phillips (Jan. 3, 2017), available at Lexology.com. The case has been appealed to the Fifth Circuit, as No. 17-10135. On July 10, 2017, the district court issued a stay of the proceeding, pending HHS' reconsideration of the PPACA § 1557 final regulations. The district court kept the injunction in effect. [*Franciscan Alliance, Inc. v. Price*, No. 7:16-cv-00108 (N.D. Tex., stay granted July 10, 2017); see Haynes and Boone LLP, *Court Issues Stay on Proceedings in Challenge to ACA Section 1557 Nondiscrimination Regulations* (Aug. 3, 2017), available at Lexology.com]

The Genetic Information Nondisclosure Act (GINA, Pub. L. No. 110-233) was enacted on May 21, 2008 and took effect November 21, 2009. It forbids employers to require genetic testing or to consider genetic information for hiring, firing, or promotions, and also forbids health insurers to deny coverage or set premium or deductible levels on the basis of genetic test results. GINA restricts the extent to which employers and insurers can ask for family medical histories. It is unlawful for an EGHP to give financial incentives (e.g., rebates or reduced premiums) for completing family medical histories as part of a health risk assessment. However, an EGHP can request family medical history to determine if an employee should be placed in a wellness or disease management program, as long as the employee gives the information voluntarily, and the information is only requested after plan enrollment and is not used in underwriting.

The 2009 GINA regulations jointly published by the IRS, DOL, and CMS forbid adjusting premiums or contribution rates for an EGHP because of the genetic information of one or more group members. Even genetic information that is legitimately acquired cannot be used to discriminate, although a group premium can be increased based on a manifestation of a disease or disorder. Group rates do not have to be reduced by costs relating to benefits for genetic tests and counseling services that are permitted.

GINA Title II forbids employment discrimination based on genetic information, and limits the employer's use of genetic information. It is under the jurisdiction of the EEOC. [EBSA.gov, *FAQs on the Genetic Information Nondiscrimination Act* (Sept. 15, 2010) (benefitslink.com)]

The EEOC issued final regulations for GINA Title II, the employment title, effective January 10, 2011. Under the Title II final regulations, an employer is not liable for inadvertent acquisitions of genetic information, or if information is provided voluntarily (e.g., under a wellness program), if family history is obtained to comply with state or local law, as part of an FMLA certification, or some employer leave policies. Nor are employers liable if the information is publicly available, comes from genetic monitoring that is required by law or offered on a voluntary basis, or is acquired by a forensic lab for law enforcement purposes. However, employers must keep exempt genetic information confidential, separate from ordinary personnel records.

GINA Title I and Title II are considered separate, so an employer will not be subject to double liability for Title II claims involving matters enforced under Title I. But it is possible to violate both titles and be penalized, for example, for requiring submission of genetic information to participate in an EGHP. [GINA recordkeeping requirements: 77 Fed. Reg. 5396 (Feb. 3, 2012)]

On January 17, 2013, HHS published a final rule covering the application of the HIPAA privacy rule to Titles I and II of GINA. Genetic information is considered health information, which cannot be used for underwriting purposes (except for long-term care insurance policies). [Katherine Georger, *New HIPAA Final Rule Implements GINA Restriction on Use and Disclosure of Genetic Information for Underwriting Purposes*, Holland & Hart LLP News Update (Jan. 23, 2013) (benefitslink.com)]

Rulemaking continued in 2015 and 2016. The EEOC issued a Notice of Proposed Rulemaking and a fact sheet on October 30, 2015, explaining the relationship between wellness programs and GINA. A wellness program that is part of an EGHP can provide incentives in exchange for health information about the employee's spouse. The 2015 proposal allows limited incentives (not more than 30% of the total annual cost of coverage for the plan) for providing health status information about the employee's spouse as part of the employee's health risk assessment (HRAs). HRAs typically measure things like cholesterol and glucose levels. But it is not permitted to offer incentives for the spouse to provide his or her own genetic information, including genetic test results. [80 Fed. Reg. 66853 (Oct. 30, 2015)]

The proposed rules were finalized in mid-2016, with few changes. The final rules took effect on July 18, 2016. [ADA rule: 81 Fed. Reg. 31125 (May 17, 2016); GINA rule, 81 Fed. Reg. 31143 (May 17, 2016). See Rachel Emma Silverman, *EEOC Issues New Rules for Wellness Programs*, WSJ.com (May 16, 2016)]

The Fifth Circuit held in late 2015 that it did not violate GINA to place a fire department paramedic on alternate duty when he failed to comply with a mandatory wellness program that evaluated fitness for duty. Employees who were not certified as fit for duty or who did not take the examination were placed on alternate duty; after 60 days on alternate duty, they lost eligibility for overtime. The Fifth Circuit ruled that GINA does not forbid wellness programs that do not involve genetic information. [*Ortiz v. City of San Antonio Fire Dep't*, 806 F.3d 822 (5th Cir. 2015)]

§18.09 HEALTH SAVINGS ACCOUNTS (HSAs) AND ARCHER MSAs

Current health policy relies heavily on tax-favored accounts that combine a high-deductible health plan (HDHP) with an investment account. Within statutory limits, account holders are entitled to deduct contributions to the investment account and employers' contributions to the accounts are not taxable income for the employee. The intention is that the account, over time, will generate investment returns that, in conjunction with the original deposits, can be applied toward the account holder's medical expenses. There are several kinds of tax-favored health accounts; collectively, they are sometimes referred to as Consumer-Driven Health Plans (CDHPs).

According to United Benefit Advisors, in 2016, 26.4% of U.S. employees were enrolled in CDHP plans, 21.7% more than the year before and almost 70% more than five years earlier. About one-quarter of plans offered in 2016 (25.7%) were CDHP plans, a 14.2% increase over a five-year period. In 2015, CDHP plans were 5.6% cheaper than the average plan, a cost difference that fell to 3.5% in 2016. [Bill Olson, *Annual Survey Finds Enrollment in Consumer-Directed Health Plans Jumps 22 Percent Despite Increase in Plan Costs*, UBABenefits.com (Oct. 20, 2016) (benefitslink.com); S. Miller, *HSA Enrollment Rises but Misunderstanding Still Common*, shrm.org (June 1, 2017) (benefitslink.com)]

The tax rules governing HDHPs, Medical Savings Accounts (MSAs), as well as the PPACA rules, limit the amount of cost-sharing that plan participants will be responsible for; the out-of-pocket limit for family coverage is usually twice the limit for employee-only coverage.

[A] MSAs

In addition to imposing health insurance portability requirements, HIPAA enacted I.R.C. § 220, which adds a new type of health plan for taxable years that begin after December 31, 1996. The "Medical Savings Account" (MSA), started out as a small-scale pilot project for the years 1997–2000. The MSA account is tax-exempt, but account owners do not get a tax deduction when they withdraw funds from the account to pay medical expenses, because the contributions have already received favorable tax treatment. Funds taken from the account for any other purpose are not only taxable income but subject to an excise tax. The tax, formerly 15%, rose to 20% for distributions after 2010. [IRS Publication 969, *Health Savings Accounts and Other Tax-Favored Health Plans*, <http://www.irs.gov/pub/irs-pdf/p969.pdf> (last accessed Feb. 24, 2017), for 2016 returns.]

The Community Renewal Tax Relief Bill of 2000 (H.R. 5652), passed on December 15, 2000, renamed the account the Archer MSA (after Representative Bill Archer, Republican of Texas) and extended its lifetime for a further two years. Then the Job Creation and Worker Assistance Act of 2002 [Pub. L. No. 107-147], extended the availability of Archer MSAs until December 31, 2003.

The Archer MSA program was terminated at the end of 2005, but was retroactively reinstated in December 2006. [Announcement 2007-44, 2007-9 I.R.B. 1238]

MSAs are subject to limits. The 2016 MSA limits are an annual deductible of at least $2,250, but not more than $3,350 for single coverage; an annual deductible of $4,450–$6,700 for family coverage; and a limit on out-of-pocket expenses of $4,450 for single coverage and $8,150 for family coverage. [IRS, IR-2015-119, *In 2016, Some Tax Benefits Increase Slightly Due to Inflation Adjustments, Some Are Unchanged* (Oct. 21, 2015), available at <http://www.irs.gov/pub/irs-news/IR-15-119.pdf>]

For 2017, some figures remain the same but others increase slightly. The self-only coverage limitations remain the same, but the annual deductible for family coverage must be within the range of $4,500 to $6,750. The maximum out-of-pocket expense is $4,500 for single coverage, $8,250 for family coverage. [IR-2016-139, *In 2017, Some Tax Benefits Increase Slightly Due to Inflation Adjustments, Others Are Unchanged,* (Oct. 25, 2016), available at <https://www.irs.gov/uac/newsroom/in-2017-some-tax-benefits-increase-slightly-due-to-inflation-adjustments-others-are-unchanged>]

[B] HSAs Under MPDIMA

Division B of the Medicare Prescription Drug Improvement and Modernization Act of 2003 (MPDIMA; Pub. L. No. 108-173) is called the Health Savings and Affordability Act of 2003. MPDIMA provides for two new kinds of accounts: the Health Savings Security Account (HSSA) and the Health Savings Account (HSA). See § 9.10 for a discussion of the effect of MPDIMA's Medicare prescription drug plan on retiree health benefits and corporate accounting.

HSSAs are designed for uninsured persons or those who are covered only under a high deductible plan. This discussion focuses on the employment-related

HSA plan structure, which is much easier to understand in the context of Archer MSAs and other plans than when viewed in isolation.

Starting January 1, 2004, individuals under age 65 who have a qualified health plan can contribute to HSAs, with the maximum contribution limited to the HDHP's deductible. The limit is increased for persons aged 55–65, who are allowed to make catch-up contributions. If both spouses are 55 or over, a married couple is allowed to make two catch-up contributions. Eligible individuals (persons covered by an HDHP, and not covered by another plan that duplicates the HDHP's coverage) can receive a tax deduction.

An increasing number of employers have adopted HDHPs combined with HSAs; in many companies, this is the only health benefit offered. If employees are allowed to make pre-tax contributions to the HSA, the contributions plus the employer's contributions are subject to the Code § 125 anti-discrimination rules. If employees are not entitled to make pre-tax contributions, then the employer's contributions must be comparable between highly compensated employees and non-highly compensated employees. Only eligible individuals are permitted to make HSA contributions or have them made on their behalf by the employer. An eligible individual must be enrolled in an HDHP with no other coverage that provides medical benefits before the statutory minimum HDHP deductible has been satisfied.

Because it would pay benefits before the HDHP deductible has been satisfied, Medicare constitutes disqualifying coverage. Eligibility for Medicare (which occurs on the first day of the month in which the person reaches age 65) does not affect a person's status as eligible individual until the person has coverage in effect, at which time the person ceases to be HSA-eligible on the first day of the month when Medicare entitlement begins. A person becomes entitled to Medicare Part A benefits automatically when he or she applies for Social Security benefits—or by making a separate Medicare application (e.g., a person aged 65 or over who is still in the workforce). It is not permitted to waive Medicare Part A eligibility. To remain HSA-eligible, a person over 65 must withdraw the application for Social Security benefits, and repay any retirement or Medicare benefits already received. A person who does not understand these rules and continues to contribute to the HSA after losing eligibility could be subject to a 6% excise tax on excess contributions unless the excess is distributed in a timely fashion. [Leslye Laderman and Mary Harrison, *Older Workers and Retirees: Avoiding HSA Pitfalls*, Conduent FYI (Feb. 9, 2017) (benefitslink.com)]

The HSA itself is a trust created exclusively for the purpose of paying the qualified medical expenses of an eligible person. The term "qualified medical expenses" has the same definition as in Code § 220(d)(2). If funds are paid or distributed out of an HSA, and are used to pay the account beneficiary's qualified medical expenses, they do not constitute taxable income for the beneficiary. However, amounts that are distributed but are used for other purposes not only constitute gross income for the employee, but also are subject to a 15% excise tax penalty. The excise tax is waived if the distribution is made after the beneficiary's death; after the beneficiary becomes totally disabled; or after the beneficiary becomes eligible for Medicare.

The Eighth Circuit Bankruptcy Appeals Panel (BAP) held in mid-2013 that a Chapter 7 debtor could not protect his HSA from the claims of creditors. He described it as either exempt under the Bankruptcy Code's protection of health insurance plans regulated by state law or was a right to receive disability benefits or payments because of personal injury. The BAP said that an HSA is merely a trust account that gives the account holder unrestricted access to assets. It is not a health insurance plan merely because tax penalties are imposed for using the funds for non-health purposes. [*In re Leitch*, BAP No. 13-6009, 494 BR 918, 2013 WL 3722091 (B.A.P. 8th Cir. July 16, 2013)]

In early 2017, the Eleventh Circuit, after certifying a question to the Georgia Supreme Court, also held that HSAs are not exempt from inclusion in the Chapter 7 bankruptcy estate. The state supreme court held that HSAs are not exempt as disability, illness or unemployment benefits or as a pension or annuity plan. [*Mooney v. Webster (In re Mooney)*, No. 15-11229, 2017 U.S. App. LEXIS 1509 (11th Cir. per curiam Jan. 27, 2017); see Daniel Gill, *Health Savings Acct. Not Exempt in Georgia Bankruptcy,* bna.com (Feb. 2, 2017) (benefitslink.com)]

For 2016, the contribution limit for an individual with self-only coverage $3,350 (the same as the 2015 figure), but the family coverage limit increases to $6,750. The catch-up contribution remains $1,000, because this figure is not adjusted for inflation. The minimum deductible for an HSA-compatible HDHP plan remains $1,300 for individual, $2,600 for family, coverage. The 2016 out-of-pocket maximums are $6,550 for single, $13,100 for family, coverage. There is a new requirement for 2016: HSAs must limit the maximum out-of-pocket spending incurred by any one person to the single out-of-pocket limit for the plan, even if the individual is enrolled in family coverage. [Rev. Proc. 2015-30, 2015-20 I.R.B. 970; see Tiffany N. Santos, *Plan Year Changes for Group Health Plans for Year-End 2015 and 2016*, Trucker Huss APC (Sept. 3, 2015), available at Lexology.com]

Most of the limitations for 2016 and 2017 are the same. For 2017, the limitation on deductions for self-only HDHP coverage is $3,400 ($50 more than in 2016); the family limitation is $6,750 (unchanged in 2016–2017). A plan is an HDHP if the annual deductible is at least $1,300 for single, $2,600 for family coverage. The out-of-pocket maximum for both 2016 and 2017 is $6,500 for single coverage, $13,100 for family coverage. [Rev. Proc. 2016-28, 2016-20 I.R.B. 853]

Rev. Proc. 2017-37, 2017-21 I.R.B. 1252 gives the 2018 HSA limits. The maximum contribution is $3,450 (single) or $6,900 (family); the catch-up contribution remains limited to $1,000. The minimum deductible is $1,350 or $2,700, and the maximum amount that employees can be required to pay out of pocket is $6,650 (single), $13,300 (family). [Damian E. Myers, *IRS Announces HSA and HDHP Limitations for 2018*, Proskauer Rose Employee Benefits & Executive Compensation (May 5, 2017) (benefitslink.com)]

If an employee and his or her spouse have separate self-only HDHP coverage, each can contribute the single-person maximum to a separate HSA. If one spouse has family HDHP coverage, both spouses are considered to have family coverage, so the couple can contribute up to the family maximum, plus an additional $1,000 if one is over 55, $2,000 if both are over 55. Spouses can either establish separate accounts or share an HSA; contributions are allocated 50-50 to each account unless the spouses agree on a different allocation.

On the compliance front, MPDIMA adds a new Code § 106(e) that states that an employer's contributions to an HSA are considered to be contributions under an Accident & Health plan. The employer's contributions are not subject to FICA or Federal Unemployment Tax Act (FUTA)—but they must be shown on the employee's Form 1099. Failure to provide the mandated reports is penalized under Code § 6693(a). An employer that commits to making HSA contributions for employees, but fails to do so, is penalized under Code § 4980G.

[C] IRS Guidance on MSAs and HSAs

Shortly after MPDIMA was passed, the IRS provided guidance in Notice 2004-2, 2004-2 I.R.B. 269 and Notice 2004-50, 2004-33 I.R.B. 196.

A Medicare-eligible person who has not yet enrolled can maintain an HSA, but can no longer contribute to the HSA after enrolling in Medicare.

Another related tax-advantaged form is the Health Flexible Savings Account (Health FSA).

[D] Plan Comparisons

ERISA and the Internal Revenue Code make it possible for employers to offer a (potentially confusing) variety of tax-advantaged health insurance plans. By far the most popular arrangement is the Health Savings Account used in conjunction with a High-Deductible Health Plan, and this is the arrangement that is most favored under current tax law. (See § 18.10 below for Medical Expense Reimbursement Plans, § 18.11 for Flexible Spending Accounts (FSAs), and § 18.18 for Health Reimbursement Arrangement (HRA) plans.)

An HSA is an account established by an individual to pay his or her medical expenses, whereas an HRA is a benefit plan established by an employer. A Health FSA is also a benefit plan created by an employer; it reimburses employees for qualified medical expenses. An HSA must be coordinated with a High Deductible Health Plan (HDHP); health FSAs and HRAs can be coordinated but do not have to be. Only employees can contribute to HRAs, whereas HSAs and Health FSAs can include contributions from the employer and/or employee.

There is no contribution limit for HRAs, whereas HSA limits are adjusted each year. HSAs and Health FSAs can include pre-tax employee contributions, whereas HRAs are solely funded by the employer. HSAs are not covered by

COBRA; HRAs generally are; some Health FSAs are subject to COBRA. HSAs are portable, but the other two types of account are not, because the employee is not the owner of the account.

A chart published in early 2017 compares HSAs, FSAs, and HRAs. HSA contributions are tax-deductible; contributions made via payroll deductions are pre-tax. The interest and capital gains on investments in the plan are not taxed. Employees are not taxed if they make a withdrawal from the plan to pay qualified expenses. FSA contributions are pre-tax. Reimbursements from an HRA are free of income tax. Because all the funds in the HSA belong to the employee, unlimited carryovers from year to year are allowed. FSAs are primarily "use it or lose it" but employers can allow limited carryovers to the next year. Employers can allow unused HRA funds to roll over to the next year. HSA or FSA funds can be used for any medical expense that is qualified under Code § 213 and has been paid out of pocket and not otherwise reimbursed; the employer determines which § 213(d)-eligible expenses can be reimbursed from the plan. [Acclaris, *HSA/FSA/ HRA Comparison Chart,* available at <http://www.Acclaris_HSA_HRA_FSA_ CC_2017.pdf>]

§ 18.10   MEDICAL EXPENSE REIMBURSEMENT PLANS

Medical expense reimbursement plans usually reimburse employees directly for their medical expenses. Payment comes from the employer's resources, not from an insurance policy. Usually, the plan sets a maximum: e.g., only claims of $X per year will be covered. The plan can also be coordinated with insurance, so that the employer pays up to a certain amount, with insurance covering the rest.

The plan must cover employees, although it is not a legal requirement that it cover all employees. The plan can be informal. There is no legal requirement that the plan be in writing, unless it is a "welfare benefit plan" for ERISA purposes. In any case, employees must be given reasonable notice of the plan's existence and of how it operates.

For tax purposes, the most important question is whether the plan shifts risk to a third party (other than the employer and employee). A plan that uses a third-party administrator (TPA) to handle administrative or bookkeeping services does not shift risk to the TPA. The employer's costs of maintaining a self-insured plan will probably be deductible, as ordinary and necessary business expenses.

Internal Revenue Code § 105(h) governs self-insured medical expense reimbursement plans—those whose benefits are not payable exclusively from insurance. Plans of this type must satisfy coverage and nondiscrimination tests to qualify:

- The IRS issues a determination letter stating that the plan is nondiscriminatory;

- The plan covers at least 70% of all employees;

- At least 70% of all employees are eligible for the plan, and 80% or more of the eligible employees are actually covered.

The plan is not discriminatory if the benefits provided for highly compensated employees (HCEs) and their dependents are also provided for other employees. The plan can impose a dollar maximum on the benefits paid on behalf of any individual, but cannot set the maximum at a percentage of compensation, because that would improperly favor HCEs.

If a self-insured medical reimbursement plan is discriminatory, then the HCEs (but not the rank-and-file employees) will have taxable income equal to the employer's plan contributions on their behalf; the taxable income is subject to income tax withholding, but not FICA or FUTA. [See I.R.C. § 3121(a)(2)(B)]

Notice 2015-17 provides temporary relief from the § 4980D excise tax for programs that reimburse employees for the cost of buying health insurance in the individual market, including the Marketplace. Notice 2013-54 (Sept. 13, 2013) said that employer payment plans (EPPs; also known as opt-out payments) are group health plans that have to satisfy PPACA market reforms—but by their nature, the reimbursement plans do not comply with the ban on dollar limits or the requirement of free preventing services. Therefore, the IRS has held that the plans are subject to the $100 per person per day excise tax.

Notice 2015-17 allows employers that are too small to be Applicable Large Employers and that fund EPPs to escape the excise tax until June 30, 2015. The relief applies only to reimbursement of health premiums, not to standalone HRAs or other arrangements that compensate employees for medical expenses other than health insurance premiums. [Notice 2015-17, 2015-14 I.R.B. 845]

The IRS provided additional relief in December 2016. For 2017, opt-out payments are not counted as employee contributions in calculating whether a plan is affordable—provided that the opt-out arrangement was adopted before December 16, 2015. Proposed regulations issued in July 2016 took the position that the opt-out payment was really a salary reduction paid by the employee, which could make the coverage unaffordable and subject the employer to PPACA penalties. The proposed regulations said that opt-out payments did not have to be included in the affordability calculation until final regulations were issued and took effect. Originally, the IRS expected this to occur by January 1, 2017. However, in December 2016, the IRS was still considering how to treat opt-out payments. [81 Fed. Reg. 91755 (Dec. 19, 2016); see Jason T. Froggatt et. al., *Update #2: Relief Extended for "Opt-Out" Payments for Health Coverage*, Davis Wright Tremaine LLP (Jan. 23, 2017), available at Lexology.com]

§ 18.11   FLEXIBLE SPENDING ACCOUNTS (FSAs)

A Flexible Spending Account (FSA), also known as a medical flexible spending account or flex account, is an arrangement (either stand-alone or part of a cafeteria plan) under which an employer diverts some cash compensation into a separate account. The funds must be identified for a specific use: either for dependent care expenses, or for medical expenses that are not reimbursed by insurance or directly by the employer. The maximum amount of reimbursement that can be made "reasonably available" to a participant during a period of coverage is limited to 500% of the total premium for the coverage. FSA reimbursement must be made available at least monthly, or when the level of expenses reaches a reasonable minimum amount such as $50.

Funds targeted for medical care cannot be used for dependent care, and vice versa. A medical expense FSA must last at least twelve months, although a short first year, when the plan is initially adopted, is allowed. Premiums for other health coverage cannot be reimbursed by the FSA.

Before 2012, there was no limit on health FSAs, but PPACA imposes a $2,500 maximum. For 2015–2016, the maximum annual employee contribution to a health care FSA is $2,550; the 2017 limit is $2,600. [Rev. Proc. 2014-61, 2014-47 I.R.B. 860; Rev. Proc. 2015-53, 2015-44 I.R.B. 615; Rev. Proc. 2016-55, 2016-45 I.R.B. 707] To receive reimbursement, the FSA participant must submit a written statement from an independent third party (such as the doctor or medical office administrator) to confirm that a medical expense of $X has been incurred, and that this expense was neither reimbursed by nor eligible for reimbursement under any other plan. Since 2005, FSAs have been allowed to carry over unused amounts from one year to the next.

Initially, sums were forfeited to the extent they were not used for medical expenses during the plan year. Then the IRS permitted a grace period for reimbursement of expenses incurred in the two-and-a-half months after the end of the plan year. Notice 2013-71, 2013-47 I.R.B. 532, modifies the cafeteria plan "use it or lose it" rules by allowing a carryover of $500 to the next year. In light of the limit on FSA contributions, the Treasury saw less need to prevent excess sheltering of funds in FSA accounts. The plan must elect between allowing the two-and-a-half month grace period and the carryover; it cannot provide both. Even if there is no grace period, a "run-out" is allowed: using prior-year funds early in the next year to pay expenses incurred in the prior year. This differs from a grace period, which allows use of amounts from Year #1 to be used to pay Year #2 expenses. Notice 2013-71 says that carryforward coverage ends with the termination of employment unless COBRA is elected. Therefore, employees who have carryforward accounts must be offered the chance to make a COBRA election (see Chapter 19).

See Notice 2015-87: COBRA continuation coverage does not have to be offered for a health FSA unless, as of the date of the qualifying event, the amount that the qualified beneficiary is entitled to receive during the rest of the plan year exceeds the amount the health FSA is entitled to collect for continuation coverage for the rest of the plan year. The notice explains when COBRA has to be offered with respect to a health FSA that allows carryforwards. The carryforward is included to determine the size of the benefit that the qualified beneficiary can receive in the balance of the plan year. The maximum amount a health FSA can charge for continuation coverage does not include unused amounts carried over from previous years. [Notice 2015-87, 2015-52 I.R.B. 889]

The Heroes Earnings Assistance and Relief Tax Act (HEART Act, Pub. L. No. 110-245) allows employers to amend their FSA plans so that reservists called up for six months or more of active duty can take "Qualified Reservist Distributions," withdrawing their FSA balances as a taxable cash distribution. [IRS Notice 2008-82, 2008-41 I.R.B. 853]

Rev. Rul. 2010-23, 2010-39 I.R.B. 388, says that a tax-free arrangement can only reimburse OTC drugs if the drugs are prescribed by a physician.

§ 18.12   EGHP STRUCTURES

Originally, indemnity plans were the standard; now, that role is held by managed care plans of various types. Within the managed care category, HMOs were once dominant, but now must share the spotlight with other plan forms that offer greater choice of health care providers. Recently, attention has been given to defined contribution and voucher plans.

Usually, indemnity plans are divided into "basic" and "major medical" models. Basic coverage encompasses surgery, hospitalization, and care provided by physicians during a hospital stay. A major medical plan pays when other coverage is exhausted. A comprehensive major medical plan combines basic and major medical features, whereas a supplemental plan offers pure excess insurance.

The standard model for indemnity insurance calls for the patient to be responsible for paying a deductible each year (e.g., $X, or $X per family member) before the plan has any responsibility for payments. Most plans also impose a coinsurance responsibility: In an 80/20 plan, for example, once the deductible is satisfied, the patient is responsible for 20% of the bill—or 20% of the "schedule amount" that the plan pays for the service, plus the full difference between the actual charge and the schedule amount. It is also typical for indemnity plans to include a "stop-loss" provision that represents the maximum out-of-pocket spending an individual or family will incur under the plan. But the plan, in turn, usually limits its exposure by imposing overall limits on each employee's coverage, whether per year or over a lifetime.

Reimbursement to providers under indemnity plans is generally made on the basis of the table of "usual, customary and reasonable charges" promulgated by the insurer. These are either historical figures or a schedule of charges for various items.

§ 18.13   MANAGED CARE

[A]   Concepts and Models

Managed care was a response to the climate of the 1970s and 1980s, when employers were faced with explosive increases in insurance premiums.

Theoretically, managed care will encourage participants to adopt healthier lifestyles and, by deploying preventive care effectively, will detect disease early when it is more likely to be curable.

A common feature of managed care plans is utilization review. Patients may be required to consult a "gatekeeper" primary care physician before they can be referred to a specialist. Nonemergency procedures may have to be approved in advance by a claims reviewer. Patients' operations and hospital stays will be assessed for medical necessity.

In some managed care models, the employee is required to get all care within a closed network of providers; otherwise, reimbursement will not be available for out-of-network care (except in emergencies or when necessary care is not available within the network). But the trade-off is that the employee either gets care within the network at no additional charge, or pays only a small amount per visit, per prescription, or per service.

Managed care plans typically have their own payment schedules, which may be significantly lower than actual health care costs encountered in the community. The managed care plan's reimbursement to the patient may be defined in terms of this schedule, with the result that the patient has very significant copayment responsibilities. If a patient has satisfied the deductible and is charged $1,000 for a procedure and the health plan's schedule amount is $800; it pays 80% of the schedule amount, or $640, making the patient responsible for the remaining $360.

Generally, employees will be given one open enrollment period a year. During this time, employees who have just become eligible will be able to select one of the options available under the plan. Employees who have already selected a plan option will be able to change their selection. Once made, a decision is usually irrevocable until the next open enrollment period. Most open enrollment periods occur in the autumn, but this is by custom; it is not a legal requirement.

In 2003, the Supreme Court upheld state "any willing provider" laws (statutes requiring MCOs to accept all licensed health care providers who apply; about half the states have such laws). The MCOs' argument was that closed networks control costs by imposing lower fees, but the Supreme Court said that extending the freedom of health care providers to offer care, and making more options available to patients, should be accorded higher priority. [*Kentucky Ass'n of Health Plans v. Miller*, 538 U.S. 329 (2003)]

[B]   Health Maintenance Organizations

The Health Maintenance Organization, or HMO, is both a network of providers and a mechanism for financing health care. The theory is that participating providers are paid on a "capitated" basis. That is, they receive a fee "per head" covering all medical services under the plan for a particular employee or dependent of an employee. The theory is that, because providers do not receive more if their patients get additional health services, they will not be motivated to order unnecessary services for purely financial reasons.

In a "staff model" HMO the health professionals are salaried employees of the HMO. In the more prevalent Individual Practice Association (IPA) model HMO, the health professionals enter into contracts with the IPA, and the IPA negotiates with the HMO to set a reimbursement schedule for each service on the schedule.

Under the "group model," the HMO enters into contracts with independent group practices that are responsible for administrative tasks and are usually paid on a capitated basis. The "network model" HMO's doctors practice primarily in fee-for-service mode However, they also agree to provide certain services to HMO patients, once again generally in exchange for a capitation fee.

Federally qualified HMOs must provide an obligatory package of services, such as hospital care, physicians' services, and emergency medical treatment. Federally qualified HMOs can also provide additional, optional services such as long-term care, longer-term mental health treatment, dental and vision care; physical therapy; and prescription drugs. Optional services do not have to be provided on a capitated basis, and the HMO can impose fees on such services.

[C]   Preferred Provider Organizations (PPOs)

A PPO is an administrative structure under which health care providers become "preferred" by affiliating with the structure. Employers negotiate with the PPO to set the rate scale for specified health services. In 2007, the PPO was the managed care form with the most enrollees.

There is no set enrollment period for employees to join a PPO. Nor is there a single centralized entity that has complete financial responsibility for the enrollees' care. Sponsorship of PPOs is quite diverse: They might be created by a hospital or other health care provider, a health insurer, entrepreneur, or group of doctors.

United Benefits Advisors' 2016 Health Plan Survey reported that almost half of employees are enrolled in PPOs. The average health plan costs for employers maintaining a PPO declined a little in 2016, falling from $9,736 (2015) to $9,727 (2016). Out of the $9,727, employees contributed $3,378, slightly more than the $3,333 figure from 2015. The median PPO deductible for in-network care from $1,000 in 2015 to $1,500 in 2016. The deductible for out-of-network care rose 13.3%, to $3,400, and the median copayment was $300 in 2016, 20% higher than in 2015. [Bill Olson, *PPO Deductibles Increase Fifty Percent in 2016, Employer Costs Remain Steady*, ubabenefits.com (Aug. 24, 2016) (benefitslink.com)]

[D]   Point of Service (POS) Plans

A point of service plan is a hybrid of indemnity and HMO concepts. Participants can select their providers from a network, but they are not obligated to get their care within the network. If they do, their only copayment responsibility is a small amount per visit. Indemnity concepts such as an annual deductible and a coinsurance percentage apply when they choose out-of-network care. POS plans usually impose a high coinsurance percentage, such as 40%, on out-of-network care.

[E]   Managed Care Cost Reduction Techniques

Utilization review (UR) is a cornerstone of managed care cost-cutting. In traditional fee-for-service medicine, the health care provider determines which treatments will be used, and the payor reimburses for part or all of the care ordered by the provider.

Managed care adds "gatekeepers"—reviewers who determine whether a claim satisfies the requirements of the plan. In many instances, the plan will require prior approval of claims, and will deny or reduce claims for nonemergency services that did not receive this approval in advance. UR also includes concurrent review (e.g., reviewing the need for continued hospitalization while the patient is still in the hospital) and retrospective review (after treatment is completed).

Procedural controls are common. Most plans will pay for a second opinion prior to surgery, but will not pay for surgery unless the second opinion confirms the recommendation for surgery. Cost-cutting techniques also include adopting a fixed payment schedule, and favoring outpatient and home care over hospitalization.

A carve-out is a discount mechanism under which particular forms of medical expense, or high-cost conditions, are managed separately from the rest of the health plan.

[F]   Cost Trends

Managed care became popular because of undesirable increases in the cost of indemnity health plans. However, managed care has not lived up to its promise of reducing health care costs. Managed care premiums have always risen much faster than inflation. In response, employers often shifted much or all of the increase to employees, requiring them to pay premiums for the first time, or increasing their premiums, deductibles, and/or coinsurance. It also became common to impose surcharges on coverage of spouses who could obtain coverage elsewhere.

In addition to shifting more of the premium to employees, employers adopted cost-cutting measures such as having only high-deductible health plans; imposing a surcharge on spousal coverage if the spouse could be covered elsewhere; reducing the size of the network; and imposing extra fees for using certain doctors or hospitals. Other cost-control measures include imposing a formulary for prescription drugs, using a "tiered" system under which reimbursement is higher for generic than for brand-name drugs, restricting or eliminating family benefits, and performing audits to make sure that ineligible persons are not covered under the plan.

Between 2006 and 2015, the average deductible for employer-provided coverage rose from $303 to $1077. In addition to deductibles, some employees are responsible for copayments (dollar amounts, such as $10 per doctor visit) or coinsurance (a percentage of the cost of a health care service). Between 2004, the average copayment fell, but average deductibles and coinsurance rose much faster than the overall cost of covered benefits. In 2004, deductibles represented 24% of all cost-sharing, a proportion that rose to 47% in 2014. This trend probably reflects the growing dominance of HSAs, which are more likely to impose coinsurance than copayments for doctor visits. [Healthsystemtracker.org, *Payments for Cost Sharing Increasing Rapidly Over Time* (Apr. 14, 2016) (benefitslink .com)] Between 2001 and 2015, according to Willis Towers Watson, the cost of all employee benefits rose 24%—and the cost of health care benefits doubled, rising from 5.7% to 11.5% of pay for active employees. [Stephen Miller, *Employers' Benefit Costs Have Risen 24% Since 2001,* shrm.org (July 27, 2017) (benefitslink.com)]

Annual increases in health insurance costs for 2015–2017 were in the range of 7–9%, and the cost of health care benefits (including both the employer's and employee's share) averaged $13,000 (almost one-eighth of average pay). [Plansponsor staff, *Medical Cost Trends Continue to Outpace Inflation and Wages,* plansponsor.com (May 12, 2017)]

PPACA's shared responsibility mandate does not extend to employees' spouses, so it is lawful to reduce spousal benefits, such as refusing to cover spouses who have access to other coverage; imposing a surcharge on spouses who could be covered elsewhere; and giving employees monetary incentives for not enrolling their spouses. [Joanne Sammer, *"Carving Out" Spousal Benefits: Cost-Cutting, with Repercussions,* shrm.org (Nov. 9, 2015) (benefitslink.com)]

The American Health Policy Institute reported that 1.2% of plan participants who are high-cost claimants (those whose bills exceed $50,000 in one year) absorb 31% of total spending—almost 30 times as much as the average participant. The average high-cost claimant uses $122,382 in services per year. Half (53%) of costs associated with high-cost claimants are due to chronic conditions. [Rebecca Moore, *Managing High Cost Claimants Critical to Reducing Health Benefit Costs,* plansponsor.com (July 13, 2016)]

[G] Choosing a Managed Care Plan

Most employers can choose among several or many managed care plan vendors (although they will not be able to take advantage of this to bargain for low prices!). When an employer chooses a plan, cost considerations are important, but they don't tell the whole story. PPACA's Insurance Exchanges are intended to make the health insurance market more competitive, thus lowering premiums.

Employees may initially be glad to sign up with a plan that imposes low copayments, but they will be dissatisfied if they have to travel too far to find a network provider, or wait too long for appointments. Other possible sources of discontent are difficulties in getting referrals to specialists, and denial of access to prescriptions, tests, and treatments that the patients and/or doctors think are likely to be beneficial.

When an account representative approaches you, collect as much information as you can about the plan, its history, and its results (including references from other subscribers). You can find out how an HMO, PPO, or POS selects the physicians in its network, and how doctors in the network resolve problems among themselves—and with the managed care plan about preferred treatment methods.

Your state insurance department will probably have information about the plan's operations, loss ratios (percentage of premiums used to pay claims rather than profits or administrative expenses) and how complaints have been resolved in the past.

Factors to consider are:

- Number of health care providers in the network or participating in the plan;

- Qualifications of health care providers (board certification or eligibility; hospital affiliations; any past complaints or suits);

- How the provider pattern fits your employee census (Are there too many obstetricians and not enough cardiologists, or vice versa?);

- Quality of hospitals and other facilities involved with the plan;

- Utilization review and other cost-control measures;

- Availability of primary care physicians at off hours (to cut down on the number of emergency room visits);

- Use of claims management to coordinate treatment of serious illness and injury to promote rehabilitation;

- How premiums compare to those of other MCOs—however, a low premium may simply mean that you will face exceptionally large increases in the future;

- Measures the plan takes to promote consumer satisfaction (telephone help lines, clear explanations of claims procedures, swift resolution of claims disputes, periodic surveys to assess consumers' reactions to the plan).

[H] Self-Insured Plans

As insurance premiums increase, more and more employers adopt, or at least consider adopting, self-insured plans. However, a self-insured plan has a heavy administrative and disclosure burden. Reinsurance is vital, because even a young and healthy group of employees can incur catastrophically high claims if even one employee is in a serious accident or has a child with major health care needs. Furthermore, health care providers tend to shift costs onto self-payors.

One coping mechanism is to use a Blue Cross or other entity as a Third-Party Administrator (TPA), which could give your plan access to the insurer's discount structure.

In a specific stop-loss plan, the insurer agrees to reimburse the employer or other plan sponsor for any claim that exceeds a specified amount (the "retention"). An aggregate stop-loss plan covers all claims above the retention in a particular year. In effect, a stop-loss plan works like an insurance policy with a very high deductible. But from the insurer's viewpoint, a specified stop-loss plan is more favorable, because although the insurer collects premiums in either case, it has no direct liability to the employees covered by a stop-loss plan, and cannot be sued by them for allegedly improper denials of claims or refusals to pre-approve treatment. A stop-loss plan ends on a particular date, and the insurer is not responsible for claims that accrued by that date but have not yet been filed. In contrast, an insured plan is responsible for these "tail" or IBNR (Incurred But Not Reported) claims. [John Tozzi, *Small Business Makes a Risky Bet on Health Care*, Bloomberg Businessweek (Apr. 5, 2012) (benefitslink.com)]

For the years 2014–2016, PPACA provided a temporary reinsurance program to stabilize premiums after insurers are required to accept all applicants for individual coverage. Insurers and plan sponsors must pay into the stabilization fund; the fee is $63 per person per year. [77 Fed. Reg. 73118 (Dec. 7, 2012)]

§18.14 EMPLOYER LIABILITY FOR HEALTH PLAN ACTIONS

[A] Generally

The managed care relationship has three parts: the managed care organization (MCO) that provides care; the employer that enters into a contract with the MCO; and the employee or dependent that receives health care. When there is a bad result (whether or not malpractice occurred), the employee might want to sue the employer as well as the MCO.

Initially, employers usually avoided liability because the health plan provided the actual treatment (or claims denial). In many cases, plans escaped liability as well, because ERISA preempts state law but says virtually nothing about the plan's obligations. This state of affairs led to many demands for increased regulation (especially state regulation) to protect health care consumers. Many of these explosive issues are beyond the scope of this book, because they involve the employer and the EGHP only indirectly.

The Supreme Court has tackled some of these issues. *Humana Inc. v. Forsyth* [525 U.S. 299 (1999)] permitted EGHP members to bring a Racketeer Influenced and Corrupt Organizations Act (RICO) suit for insurance fraud when they alleged that they were overbilled as part of a conspiracy to force them to make excessive copayments. The significance of a RICO suit is that treble damages can be ordered. The defendant claimed that the McCarran-Ferguson Act [15 U.S.C. §§ 1011–1015] (which exempts "the business of insurance" from antitrust regulation) preempts the RICO suit. However, the Supreme Court held that RICO does not invalidate or supersede state insurance laws, so the McCarran-Ferguson Act does not bar the RICO suit.

The Supreme Court returned to EGHP ERISA issues in April 1999, finding in *UNUM Life Insurance Co. of America v. Ward* [526 U.S. 358 (1999)] that ERISA does not preempt state "notice-prejudice" laws. These laws prevent insurers from denying claims because they were filed late, unless the delay actually prejudiced the insurer's interests. This decision does not harm employers who administer EGHPs, because it says that although the employer is the insurer's "agent," the employer's role "relates to" an ERISA plan and therefore ERISA preempts suits against the employer with respect to this role.

In mid-2000, the Supreme Court decided, in *Pegram v. Herdrich* [530 U.S. 211 (2000)], that when an HMO, acting through its doctors, makes a mixed decision about medical treatment and health plan eligibility (rather than a purely medical decision about what kind of operation is proper for a particular diagnosis, or a purely financial decision), then the HMO is not acting as a fiduciary. Therefore, even if patients are correct that the HMO refused them necessary and medically valid treatment because the HMO wanted to increase its profits by cutting the amount of care available to subscribers, this would not state a cause of action for breach of fiduciary duty.

[B] ERISA Preemption Issues

In mid-2004, the Supreme Court ruled that ERISA completely preempts HMO participants' claims of improper denial of health benefits. Therefore, any such suits that are filed in state court can be removed to federal court. Only the ERISA remedies, and not state tort remedies such as punitive damages, will be available. In the Supreme Court's view, ERISA contains a complete set of remedies, which Congress intended to be exclusive. However, ERISA stands for

"Employee Retirement Income Security Act," and although the statute contains lengthy provisions about pension plans and their administration, it has far less to say about welfare benefit plans such as health plans—and nothing at all to say about the activities of health insurers—who are third parties in the employer/employee relationship anyway. [*Aetna Health Inc. v. Davila, Cigna Healthcare of Tex., Inc. v. Calad*, 542 U.S. 200 (2004)]

The Sixth Circuit held in 2012 that a TPA that is authorized to pay medical claims on behalf of employers is an ERISA fiduciary: a party is a fiduciary to the extent of exercising any discretionary authority or control over plan management, or any authority or control over the management or disposition of plan assets. [*Guyan Int'l Inc. v. Professional Benefits Admins., Inc.*, 689 F.3d 793 (6th Cir. 2012)]

One of the themes of this book is that the balance between state and federal law is critical to the entire subject of employment law. In many cases, plaintiffs who are seeking faster resolution or a greater breadth of remedies will file cases in state court. Often, the employer will then claim that the case can be heard (if at all) in the federal courts, because ERISA preempts the state-law cause of action.

The Supreme Court ruled in mid-2006 that certain claims must be litigated in state, not federal, court. [*Empire Healthchoice Assurance, Inc. v. McVeigh*, 547 U.S. 677 (2006)] The injured employee was covered by a plan subject to the Federal Employees Health Benefits Act (FEHBA). FEHBA says that the terms of insurance contracts insuring federal employees preempt state or local law about health benefit plans. Nevertheless, when an insurer sought reimbursement of amounts it spent on the care of a federal employee who received an automobile injury settlement, the Supreme Court required the case to be heard in state court. The Supreme Court ruled that there was no federal jurisdiction under 28 U.S.C. § 1331, because the claim for reimbursement did not arise under federal law, so federal jurisdiction could not be triggered.

§ 18.15   LABOR LAW ISSUES IN THE EGHP

A 1996 NLRB ruling holds that an employer's reservation of the right to "amend or modify" the health plan did not give the employer the power to replace the existing fee-for-service plan with a managed care plan. Such a change is so sweeping that the employer cannot implement it unilaterally without bargaining. [*Loral Defense Systems-Akron*, 320 N.L.R.B. No. 54 (Jan. 31, 1996), *aff'd*, 200 F.3d 436 (6th Cir. 1999)]

Although it deducted premiums from an employee's pay, a West Virginia employer failed to remit the premiums to the insurer of the health plan. The employee encountered a very large medical bill, which the insurer refused to pay. The employee sued the employer and its owners (in their role as administrators of the health plan) for breach of fiduciary duty. The Southern District of West Virginia held that the employer and owners were fiduciaries because of their discretionary authority over premium payment. Commingling plan assets (the premiums) with the employer's general assets and using the funds to pay the employer's operating expenses breached the duty of loyalty. Commingling also violated the duty to hold plan assets in trust, and the defendants were also culpable for failing to disclose circumstances that could affect the benefits available under the plan. [*Cook v. Jones & Jordan Eng'g, Inc.*, Civil Action No. 5:06-cv-00627, 2009 WL 37376 (S.D. W. Va. 2009)]

§ 18.16 QUALIFIED MEDICAL CHILD SUPPORT ORDERS (QMCSOs)

Divorce courts often issue orders explaining how to divide an employee spouse's retirement benefits with the divorcing non-employee spouse. These orders are called Qualified Domestic Relations Orders, or QDROs. [See § 12.08] The counterpart for the EGHP is the QMCSO, which supplements COBRA continuation coverage as an additional means of protecting children against loss of health care coverage as a result of their parents' divorce. [See § 12.08[A]] A QMCSO is a court order that requires a parent covered by an EGHP to take whatever steps are necessary to enroll the child ("the alternate recipient") in the health plan—whether that includes notifying the plan or paying insurance premiums.

A valid QMCSO must identify the plans it covers, the period of time of the order, the type of coverage each alternate recipient must receive, and the name and last known mailing address of the employee parent and all alternate recipients.

When a health plan receives a document described as a QMCSO, the plan has an obligation to review it to see if it is a valid order. Every health plan must have a written document setting out its procedure for reviewing QMCSOs. Courts do not have the power to order benefits that are not provided under the plan—so, for instance, if a plan does not offer dependent coverage, a QMCSO cannot create this coverage.

The plan administrator must notify the participant and the alternate recipients that the order has been received, and how the plan will analyze the order's validity. If, as usually happens, the plan approves the order as valid, then the participant and alternate recipients must be notified. Because the alternate recipients are children, they can designate a parent, stepparent, or attorney to receive copies of the notice on their behalf.

State governments (but NOT the DOL) can sue under I.R.C. § 502(a)(7) to enforce compliance with a Qualified Medical Child Support Order (QMCSO). The states have a role to play here because they have traditionally been empowered to deal with family law issues such as child support.

§ 18.17   THE EMPLOYER'S RIGHT OF SUBROGATION

Subrogation is a legal concept under which a party that advances expenses can recover them when the person who received the funds is reimbursed for those expenses. More specifically, if an EGHP covers the medical treatment of an injured employee, or dependent of an employee, the EGHP will have a legal right to part of the verdict or settlement that the employee receives from suing whoever caused the accident or manufactured the dangerous product.

In the typical subrogation case, a plan participant is injured, and the plan provides funds for treatment of his or her injuries. Then the injured person settles a case, or wins a judgment, against the person responsible for the injuries. In practical terms, that usually means a liability insurance company gets involved. The EGHP then attempts to recover the benefits from the injured person's tort recovery.

For the plan to have a right of subrogation, the plan language, or the insurance covering the plan, must provide this right explicitly. State law must also be consulted to see if limitations are imposed on subrogation—but even if they are, the federal courts may conclude that the state limitations are preempted by ERISA, e.g., *Levine v. United Healthcare Corp.* [402 F.3d 156 (3d Cir. 2005)] Some state laws facilitate subrogation: for instance, by requiring the participant to agree to subrogation as a condition of receiving benefits under the plan.

The Supreme Court decided a subrogation case. [*Great-West Life & Annuity Ins. Co. v. Knudson*, 534 U.S. 204 (2002)] In this case, the plan called for recovery from plan beneficiaries if they recovered any payments from third parties. The plan paid most of the $411,157.11 in medical expenses when a car crash rendered an employee quadriplegic. She settled her tort case; the settlement allocated only $13,828.70 to past medical expenses. The Supreme Court refused to allow the plan to sue under ERISA § 503(a)(3) (civil action to enjoin an act or practice violating the terms of the plan), or to obtain equitable relief to collect more of the funds it had advanced. The Supreme Court refused to permit the plan to bring such a suit, ruling that compelling payment of money due under a contract is not an "equitable" remedy.

The Supreme Court held that an insurer's civil action to recover amounts advanced for health care is "appropriate equitable relief" permitted by ERISA § 502(a)(3)(B), because injured plan participants were the equivalent of trustees because they agreed to set aside part of their tort recovery to reimburse the insurer. [*Mid Atl. Med. Servs., LLC v. Sereboff*, 547 U.S. 356 (2006)]

Subsequently, however, the Supreme Court ruled that it is not "appropriate equitable relief" to seek recovery against an injured person's general assets when the injured person spent the money on non-traceable items. Hence, the plan was unable to recoup the $120,000 it advanced in medical expenses after the injured employee settled his case against the drunk driver who injured him for $500,000: there was no identifiable fund from which to recover. [*Montanile v. Bd. of Trs. of the Nat'l Elevator Indus. Health Ben. Plan*, 136 S. Ct. 651 (2016)]

The "make-whole" doctrine also has to be considered in cases where the injured person has received a recovery, but less than an amount necessary to compensate for all injuries received. This doctrine absolves the injured person of having to reimburse the plan until he or she has been "made whole." Yet another factor is the "common fund" doctrine: whether the EGHP's right of recovery is reduced to account for attorneys' fees paid to the injured person's attorney. The rationale for this doctrine is that without the attorney, there would have been no "common fund" for the injured person and the plan to share, and therefore both of them should contribute toward the fees.

In 2013, the Supreme Court held that contract principles govern when a participant receives less than full compensation for injuries. The common fund doctrine is subject to the terms of an ERISA plan. In this case, the plan paid about $67,000 of medical expenses for the participant; he received $110,000 in tort damages. After paying his attorney, he had less than $66,000, and would have received no recovery if he reimbursed the plan. The Third Circuit held that the plan was not entitled to be reimbursed for all the funds advanced, because it would be inequitable to deprive the victim of any recovery. The Supreme Court vacated and remanded the case. However, because the plan did not specifically explain how attorneys' fees would be handled, the Supreme Court allowed the use of the common fund doctrine to prevent the victim from owing more to the plan than he actually received from his tort case. [*US Airways Inc. v. McCutchen*, 133 S. Ct. 1537 (2013)]

The Supreme Court held in 2017 that the Federal Employees Health Benefits Act preempts state laws that forbid subrogation, so when a federal employee is injured in an automobile accident, the private insurance plan that insures the employee and advances medical costs is entitled to recover from the amount the injured employee recovers from the driver. [*Coventry Health Care of Missouri, Inc. v. Nevils*, No. 16-149 (S. Ct. Apr. 18, 2017)]

§ 18.18   DEFINED CONTRIBUTION, CDHP, AND HRA PLANS

A defined contribution health plan, also known as a "consumer-driven" plan, is another way of limiting the employer's exposure to cost increases. The most popular form of CDHP is the Health Savings Account, separately or in tandem with a high-deductible health plan (HDHP).

The employer agrees to give the employee a fixed amount that can be applied to a menu of health care choices. The employer's exposure is limited and is not subject to health care price increases. In effect the voucher works like a defined contribution or 401(k) plan, shifting control to the employees—but also putting them at risk of bad or simply unlucky decisions. The rationale is that greater employee liability for health care costs will lead employees to become better informed and shop for more economical medical care.

In a fixed-dollar contribution plan, the employer offers a choice of health plans and gives each worker a certain amount of compensation to buy insurance. Employees who want a more expensive policy must use their own pretax dollars to pay the difference. In a fixed-percentage contribution plan, the employer's contribution is defined as a percentage of the premium, with the rest paid by the employee.

Employers could also combine a high deductible health plan with a funded or unfunded account for medical expenses. The employer might set up an account in which funds are accumulated on behalf of active employees, to be used for their eventual retiree health expenses.

Defined contribution plans are touted as means of improving employees' consumerism and health care shopping behavior, although that was also an argument used in favor of managed care, which is now failing to control costs.

If the arrangement constitutes a Flexible Spending Account, then Internal Revenue Code requirements will have to be satisfied. If the arrangement is trust-funded, it may become an ERISA welfare benefit plan, with additional requirements to meet. Very possibly, the IRS will treat the arrangement as a self-insured medical plan, in which case there may be nondiscrimination, Comprehensive Omnibus Budget Reconciliation Act (COBRA), and Health Insurance Portability and Accessibility Act (HIPAA) compliance obligations. Questions of dependent coverage will have to be worked out.

CDH plans can be combined with HRAs and the plan can be set up so that the employee is required to satisfy a deductible before accessing HRA funds. Another option is for the employer to cover up to 100% of preventive care services, or require employees to use HRA amounts for this purpose. The employer can also impose a cap, such as $3,000 a year, on the amount that can be rolled over from year to year within an HRA.

An HRA is a plan that is 100% funded by employer contributions and provides reimbursement for medical expenses incurred during the 12-month plan year (but not before). In fact, carryover of unused amounts is not only permitted, it is mandatory. The balance in the HRA may be used to provide coverage of medical expenses; and the balance must be used for this purpose if a COBRA event occurs. Distributions for any purpose other than paying medical expenses jeopardizes the exclusion from income of all distributed amounts. Notice 2002-45 says that any expense that qualifies under § 213(d) can be reimbursed from the HRA, including insurance premiums, with one major exception. Because of § 106(c), no amount that constitutes a "qualified long-term care service" under § 7702B(c) can be reimbursed because health FSAs are not allowed to cover long-term care.

IRS Notice 2013-54, 2013-40 I.R.B. 287 and DOL Technical Release 2013-03 took the position that HRAs and Health FSAs are group health plans subject to PPACA requirements—including the ban on annual dollar limits on essential health benefits and the requirement of providing certain preventive services without cost-sharing. Violations are subject to the § 4980D excise tax. Under this guidance, a traditional standalone HRA generally could not comply with PPACA and could not be used by employers to pay premiums for health insurance purchased individually by employees.

A standalone HRA, sometimes offered instead of an EGHP, is also known as an "employer payment plan" or "employer health care arrangement." under which employers reimbursed employees for the premiums on health insurance the employees obtained individually. In March 2015, the IRS announced a temporary relief provision for companies that are not Applicable Large Employers (ALEs): they will not be liable for the § 4980D excise tax merely for having an employer payment plan for any period before July 1, 2015. But after June 30, 2015, the excise tax will be applied even to small employers. This relief is limited to premium reimbursement arrangements, and does not apply to standalone HRAs or other arrangements that reimburse employees for medical expenses as distinct from insurance premiums. [Notice 2015-17, 2015-10 I.R.B. 722]

Subsequently, employers with fewer than 50 full-time employees that do not have health plans were authorized to offer Qualified Small Employer HRAs (QSEHRAs) by the 21st Century Cures Act, Pub. L. No. 114-255. The Cures Act suspended the excise tax once again, until December 31, 2016, and authorized QSEHRA plans. QSEHRAs are fully funded by the employer with no employee contributions. A QSEHRA can reimburse employees for medical care expenses (including their families' medical expenses if the plan allows it). The plan must cover all eligible employees but it is permitted to exclude employees who have not yet worked for the employer for 90 days; part-time or seasonal employees; some non-citizen employees; and some employees covered by a CBA.

For 2017, the reimbursement limit for a QSEHRA is $4,950 or $10,000 if the HRA reimburses family members' expenses. These limits are prorated for an employee who is covered by the QSEHRA for only part of the year. The benefits must be provided on the same terms to all eligible employees but the amount of benefits can be based on the cost of an Exchange policy, and those prices vary based on the employee's age and number and ages of family members. Most QSEHRAs will not be deemed to be EGHPs and are not subject to COBRA. [Jeffrey Herman, *New HRAs for Small Employers,* Employee Benefits & Executive Compensation Blog (Feb. 10, 2017) (benefitslink.com); Vorys, Sater, Seymour and Pease LLP, *21st Century Cures Act* (Dec. 16, 2016) (benefitslink.com); Alistair Nevius, *Congress Enacts Law Allowing HRAs Under The Affordable Care Act*, J. of Accountancy (Dec. 8, 2016) (benefitslink.com)]

Notice 2017-20 gives small employers additional time to comply with the QSEHRA's notice requirement. Employers seeking to implement a QSEHRA must notify employees about the effect of the QSEHRA's coverage on their obligations under PPACA's individual mandate, the extent to which the employer's QSEHRA contributions could be taxable income for the employees, and how QSEHRA participation affects the employee's ability to receive a tax credit for buying health coverage from an Exchange. Generally speaking, this notice must be given at least 90 days before the beginning of the year in which the QSEHRA becomes effective. But for 2017 only, there is a transition rule: instead of the notice being due by March 13, 2017, for 2017 QSEHRAs, notice can be given any time within 90 days after the IRS issues additional guidance. [Kenneth A. Mason, *IRS Extends Deadline for Providing Small-Employer HRA Notices*, Spencer Fane LLP (Feb. 28, 2017), available at Lexology.com]

§ 18.19 HEALTH CARE REFORM UNDER PPACA

[A] Introduction

In March 2010, Congress passed the Patient Protection and Affordable Care Act, Pub. L. No. 111-144. Almost immediately, a package of amendments was passed: the Health Care and Education Affordability Reconciliation Act of 2010, Pub. L. No. 111-152. For convenience, in this book the abbreviation "PPACA" will be used to refer to the main bill, as amended by the reconciliation bill.

The focus of the legislation is on extending insurance coverage to more Americans. This discussion focuses on employers' duties and entitlements under PPACA, although the law naturally has major impact on health care users and providers, on insurers, and on the Medicare and Medicaid programs. PPACA was designed to have as many people as possible covered by an EGHP or individual policy that provides "minimum essential coverage." The statutory objective is that the subsidies and tax incentives will lead to the creation of many new plans and coverage of a higher percentage of the employee population.

PPACA envisions the development of new "Marketplaces" for the purchase of insurance by people who are not covered by an EGHP, or who do not have access through employment to affordable coverage. (See below for SHOP Exchanges for small businesses to purchase coverage.) As originally conceptualized, the states would set up their own Marketplaces (aka Exchanges), with a federal Exchange as a fall-back. In practice, most of the states refused to set up a Marketplace, although there were some hybrid state-federal programs.

As of the beginning of 2016, the Commonwealth Fund reported that there were 18 federally facilitated marketplaces, state-run marketplaces in 12 states and the District of Columbia, with various hybrids in the other states. [Commonwealth Fund, Health Insurance Marketplaces by Type, <http://www.common wealthfund.org/interactives-and-data/maps-and-data/state-exchange-map> (last accessed Feb. 25, 2017)]

One of the impulses in passing PPACA was a perception that small businesses found it difficult to find insurance that they could afford. PPACA has provisions about creating a SHOP (Small Business Health Options) Exchange program to address these concerns—including small businesses that want to offer health insurance even though they are not subject to the "pay or play" penalty. However, the scheduled opening of the SHOP Exchange was delayed for a year because the rollout of PPACA in general was stressful and marked by massive computer problems. [Louise Radnofsky, *White House Opens Health-Insurance Portal to Small Businesses in Five States*, WSJ.com (Oct. 27, 2014)]

SHOP was not a popular program. As of January 2017, only 7,554 employers, with 38,749 employees, purchased coverage through the federally facilitated marketplace. State-based SHOP exchanges were more popular, enrolling 19,651 employers with 193,949 covered individuals.

On May 15, 2017, CMS announced that the federally facilitated SHOP Exchange would essentially be eliminated. HealthCare.gov would continue to make eligibility determinations for small employers to see if they qualify for the small employer tax credit, but would not enroll employers or employees or process premium payments. (The tax credit is limited to two years, so most qualifying employers have probably already exhausted their eligibility.) However, HealthCare.gov will bring small employers together with insurers that sell SHOP plans or with agents and brokers who have registered with CMS. State SHOP marketplaces could either enroll small employers online, or refer them to agents and brokers. [Timothy Jost, *CMS Announces Plans to Effectively End the SHOP Exchange,* Health Affairs (May 15, 2017), available at healthaffairs.org; Michelle Hackman, *White House Closes a Health-Care Enrollment Option,* WSJ.com (May 15, 2017)]

The FPL (federal poverty level) is an important concept for understanding PPACA. Many rights and responsibilities are determined based on whether an employee's household income falls below the FPL, or whether it exceeds 400% of the FPL. For 2017, the FPL for a one-person family is $12,060, so subsidies may be available up to $48, 240. For a two-person family, the corresponding figures are $16, 240 and $64,960. [82 Fed. Reg. 8831 (Jan. 31, 2017)] Before PPACA, there were important protections against loss of coverage under COBRA (Consolidated Omnibus Budget Reconciliation Act) (see § 19.02), and a 2009 statute, the American Recovery and Reinvestment Act (ARRA), Pub. L. No. 111-5, made it possible for some workers to receive a subsidy to help them afford COBRA coverage (see § 19.02[F]).

A person who loses health coverage because of termination of employment has two options: to make a COBRA election or to buy coverage from a PPACA Marketplace. It is common for employers to make pre-tax payments of COBRA premiums for a stated number of months. COBRA coverage is often more expensive than Marketplace coverage. Marketplace coverage is prospective; COBRA notices are often mailed several weeks after the employee's termination and the employee might have interim medical needs.

Marketplace coverage can only be purchased during the annual open enrollment period, running from November 15 to February 15, or during a special enrollment period. A special enrollment period is the 60 days after a qualifying life event such as loss of coverage, move to a new coverage area, or a change in premium tax credit eligibility. A person who elects COBRA to get retroactive coverage then drops it to substitute less expensive Marketplace coverage would have to wait until the open enrollment period because dropping coverage is not a qualifying event, and there might be a gap in coverage for which the employee is penalized. An employer's payment of COBRA premiums for a highly compensated employee might be discriminatory under Code § 105(h), leading to taxes on benefits for participants in self-insured plans or employer penalties if the plan is insured. The best practice is to give the employee a cash payment for the COBRA premium. This is not discriminatory, because § 105(h) does not apply to after-tax payment of premiums. That would give the employee the ability to opt for either COBRA or a Marketplace policy. The COBRA notice should explain this alternative. [Richard J. Birmingham, *What Everyone Needs to Know About the Coordination of Severance Benefits, COBRA, and the ACA*, Davis Wright & Tremaine (June 9, 2014) (benefitslink.com)]

PPACA also gave states the option of expanding Medicaid coverage, with the federal government paying the full cost of expansion for 2014 to 2016 and at least 90% of the cost afterward. However, for political reasons, some states rejected Medicaid expansion. [Louise Radnofsky, *In Medicaid, a New Health-Care Fight*, WSJ.com (Feb. 10, 2013)]

[B] Employer Mandates

Although there are a number of employer mandates that took effect as soon as PPACA was passed, or six months later, perhaps the most important PPACA provision is the requirement that employers (other than very small employers) offer either affordable coverage of a package of minimum basic benefits to their employees, or pay a penalty to the federal government (see § 18.19[H] below). As discussed below, the employer shared responsibility payments (aka "pay or play") were supposed to take effect January 1, 2014, but the effective date was postponed. See § 18.19[B][3] for discussion of the way in which some rules are relaxed for "grandfathered" plans—those already in existence when PPACA was enacted. At press time in 2017, the American Health Care Act (AHCA), which would have eliminated the employer mandate, was withdrawn before being voted on. Several repeal and repeal-and-replace measures were submitted to the Senate in mid-2017, but none of them passed.

[1] Mandates in General

Starting with the first plan year that begins six months after PPACA's enactment, health plans must cover participants' dependent adult children up to the age of 26 if the adult children are not eligible to enroll in another group plan.

CHIP (Children's Health Insurance Program) (see § 18.03[A]) was reauthorized for two years, until fiscal 2015. [Jennifer Steinhauer and Robert Pear, *House Approves Bill on Changes to Medicare*, NYTimes.com (Mar. 26, 2015)]

Plans must eliminate lifetime dollar limits and restrictive annual limitations on the essential health benefits. A group or individual insurer is permitted to rescind a policy if and only if there was fraud or intentional misrepresentation of material fact. The enrollee is entitled to prior notice of cancellation of coverage, which is allowed only for nonpayment of premium, plan termination, moving outside the plan's service area, not being in the association anymore if coverage is limited to association members, or discontinuation of that type of coverage (which requires 90 days' notice).

As of January 1, 2014, waiting periods of more than 90 days before a new hire can participate in the health plan are forbidden, and so are annual dollar limits on benefits a participant can receive under the health plan. [Workforce.com, *Understanding Key Provisions in Federal Health Care Reform Legislation* (Mar. 22, 2010) (benefitslink.com). Final regulations were published in 2014: 79 Fed. Reg. 10295 (Feb. 24, 2014).]

Additional regulations were published in mid-2014. An "otherwise eligible individual" cannot be required to wait more than 90 days before coverage takes effect. The February 2014 regulations allowed a bona fide orientation period. The subsequent regulations consider a period of up to one month to be a reasonable and bona fide orientation period. [79 Fed. Reg. 35942 (June 25, 2014)]

Starting January 1, 2014, pre-existing condition exclusions (PCEs) cannot be imposed on any enrollee in a non-grandfathered plan. That is, group health plans and insurers cannot use a person's pre-existing health condition to deny or limit coverage. Eligibility cannot be conditioned on a participant's, or dependent of a participant's, medical condition, claims experience, receipt of health care, medical history, genetic information, or disability. Premiums cannot be increased based on health factors.

All plans must offer preventive services without requiring any cost-sharing by employees: all the preventive services and immunizations recommended by the U.S. Preventive Services Task Force and the Centers for Disease Control, and the preventive services for children (e.g., immunization) recommended by the Health Resources and Services Administration.

Health plans must permit enrollees to choose any available participating primary care provider, including a pediatrician for children covered by the plan. Emergency services in a hospital Emergency Room have to be covered without prior authorization, even if the hospital is not part of the plan's network. Women must be allowed to receive obstetric and gynecological services without a referral from a primary care provider. This requirement is effective for plan years beginning on or after six months from PPACA's enactment date. (The enactment date is March 23, 2010, so six months later is September 23, 2010.)

As originally enacted, PPACA required that, as of January 1, 2014, employers with over 50 employees would have to provide "free choice" vouchers to employees with income below 400% of the FPL, and who would have high financial obligations under the employer's plan. However, this requirement was repealed in April 2011 as part of the negotiations to pass a budget bill. [Deloitte's

Washington Bulletin, *Budget Bill Cuts into PPACA: Free Choice Vouchers To Be Eliminated* (Apr. 18, 2011) (benefitslink.com)]

Group health plans and health insurers have to have an effective claims appeals process, including internal claims appeals and notification to employees. At a minimum, the process must include an internal appeal process for claims, notice to participants of appeals procedures, and must give enrollees the right to review their files, present evidence (including testimony) in the appeal, and retain their coverage pending appeal.

PPACA gives group health plans and insurers two options for external review: either comply with state external review requirements that include the protections of the NAIC (National Association of Insurance Commissioners) Uniform External Review Model Act, or if the state requirements are less protective or the plan is self-funded so those requirements do not apply, the plan must implement an external review process that satisfies the NAIC requirements. [Christine C. Rinn, *Health Insurance Reforms Under PPACA: The Future Is Now*, <http://www.crowell.com/PDF/events/hoops-2010/Health-Insurance-Market-Reforms-Under-PPACA.pdf> (last viewed Feb. 25, 2017)]

PPACA adds a new ERISA § 715(a), Code § 9815(a)(1) to apply the requirements of the Public Health Service Act (PHS) Part A, Title XXVII to EGHPs and health insurers. Section 2719 of the PHS provides the standards for internal claims and appeals and external review. In general, § 2719 requires an effective internal claims and appeals process, incorporating the DOL claims regulation (29 C.F.R. § 2560.503-1). See 75 Fed. Reg. 52597 (Aug. 26, 2010) for model notices for internal or external review.

In mid-2011, the IFR was amended. Instead of the IFR's absolute 24-hour deadline for deciding urgent care claims, the old standard (as soon as possible, definitely within 72 hours) was reinstated. Plan materials may have to be translated if over 10% of the population of the county speaks certain non-English languages. Benefits must be provided immediately if ordered by an external reviewer, even if the plan intends to seek judicial review. [*Group Health Plans and Health Insurance Issuers: Rules Relating to Internal Claims and Appeals and External Review Processes*, 76 Fed. Reg. 37208 (June 24, 2011)]

As originally enacted, PPACA amended § 18A of the Fair Labor Standards Act to require plans with over 200 employees to adopt automatic enrollment, under which newly hired full-time employees would be enrolled in the employer's plan, although they would be informed of this and given a chance to opt out (e.g., if they could not afford to pay their share of the premium). However, before the requirement was scheduled to take effect, the Bipartisan Budget Act of 2015, Pub. L. No. 114-74, repealed the automatic enrollment requirement. Some state wage laws forbid withholding from wages without the employee's affirmative election, but DOL's position [see <https://www.dol.gov/ebsa/regs/aos/ao2008-02a.html>] is that such laws are preempted by ERISA. [Joseph J. Lazzarotti, *ACA Auto-Enrollment Requirement Repealed*, Benefits Law Advisor (Nov. 2, 2015) (benefitslink.com)]

CMS published a final rule to prevent discrimination against persons with pre-existing conditions. Beginning in 2014, coverage cannot be denied based on pre-existing condition exclusions (PCEs) or other health conditions. Policies in the individual market will be guaranteed available and will be offered during open enrollment periods; policies in the group market will be continuously available year round. The only rating factors allowed in the individual/small group market are age (where premiums for the oldest enrollees cannot be more than three times those for the youngest), family size, geography, and tobacco use (1.5 times higher for tobacco users). There must be a single, statewide risk pool for the small group market and one for the individual market, unless insurers want a single pool for both. [CMS Final Rule, 78 Fed. Reg. 13406 (Feb. 27, 2013)]

Starting January 1, 2011, health insurers and the administrators of self-insured plans must report their "loss ratios" (percentage of premiums used to pay medical claims and not used for administrative expenses or profits) to Health and Human Services (HHS). The minimum required loss ratio for large-group plans (with 100 or more enrollees) is 85% loss ratio. Small-group plans must have an 80% loss ratio. State laws that require higher loss ratios are not preempted. However, HHS has discretion to adjust these percentages if an 80% loss ratio would destabilize the individual market. Health insurers that fail to satisfy the loss ratio standards must give each customer a pro rata rebate. This topic is discussed further at § 18.19[O][4], below.

It is illegal to retaliate against an employee who gets a tax credit, or who provides information about a violation of the employer's obligations under the Fair Labor Standards Act (e.g., automatic enrollment for companies with over 200 employees; providing notice about employees' rights to secure coverage under an Exchange) (see PPACA § 1558). Retaliation complaints are filed with OSHA; the deadline is 180 days after the retaliatory act. [Maureen Knight, James Coleman, and James Napoli, *Will 40 Be the New 30? The PPACA's 30-Hour Coverage Threshold May Lead to More Off-The-Clock Claims*, HR Magazine/SHRM (July 2014) (benefitslink.com)]

If the evidence shows retaliation, and settlement is not reached, OSHA orders the employer to reinstate the employee with back pay. OSHA findings become a final order of the DOL unless appealed within 30 days. The employee can seek district court review if a final DOL decision has not been rendered within 210 days of the filing date of the complaint, or 90 days after OSHA issued written findings. [OSHA Fact Sheet, *Filing Whistleblower Complaints under the Affordable Care Act*, <http://www.osha.gov/Publications/whistleblower/OSHAFS-3641.pdf> (Jan. 2014) (last accessed Feb. 25, 2017)]

PPACA amends the Fair Labor Standards Act to require employers to provide break time and a private place other than a restroom stall for employees who are breast-feeding to express and store milk. This PPACA provision does not preempt state laws that offer more protection to employees.

[2] The Essential Health Benefits Package

The essential health benefits package specifies the benefits, cost-sharing standards, and levels of coverage that must be offered for a plan to be PPACA-compliant. (Self-insured plans are not subject to the PPACA provisions dealing with essential health benefits.)

Qualified Health Plans have to provide coverage of essential benefits at Bronze, Silver, Gold, or Platinum levels. The difference among the plans is that the Bronze level provides benefits actuarially equivalent to 60% of the full actuarial value of benefits under the plan (i.e., participants can be required to pay 40% of the cost of care); Silver provides actuarial equivalent of 70% of the full actuarial value; Gold, 80% and Platinum, 90% (i.e., the participant pays only 10% of the cost of care). HHS will issue regulations explaining how to calculate actuarial value. At press time in 2017, there was some interest in Congress in cutting back on the requirements for minimum essential benefits, as a way to make insurance less expensive.

For plan years beginning on or after January 1, 2014, health insurers selling in the individual or small group market must ensure that their coverage includes the essential health benefits package, and that insured persons are not subjected to cost-sharing obligations greater than the permitted levels.

Starting in 2014, the minimum services are:

- Outpatient health care;
- Emergency services;
- Hospitalization;
- Maternity/newborn care;
- Mental health and substance abuse services;
- Prescription drugs;
- Services and devices for physical therapy and rehabilitation;
- Lab tests;
- Preventive and wellness services, including management of chronic disease;
- Pediatric services, including oral and vision care.

This is just a minimum list: plans are permitted to provide additional services. The scope of benefits must be equivalent to a typical employer-sponsored plan; PPACA required the DOL to conduct a survey to define the typical EGHP benefit package.

Essential health benefits must not be denied based on age, life expectancy, disability, degree of medical dependency, or quality of life. Benefit design (coverage, reimbursement rates) must not discriminate on the basis of age, disability, or predicted lifespan. Emergency Room services must be covered even if the facility is not in the insurer's provider network, and the patient's cost-sharing for emergency services cannot be higher than for an in-network facility.

Limitations are imposed on the annual deductible that can be imposed on an insured person in the small group market. The 2016 out-of-pocket (OOP) maximum for in-network care is $6,850 (individual coverage) and $13,700 for family coverage. A plan that imposes a family OOP maximum greater than $6,850 will have to calculate an individual maximum within the family coverage amount. For 2017, the OOP maximum is $7,150 for self-only coverage and $14,300 for family coverage. [CMS, *Fact Sheet on Final HHS Notice of Benefit and Payment Parameters for 2017*, <http://www.nationaldisabilitynavigator.org/wp-content/uploads/news-items/CMS_FactSheet-NBPP-Rule-2017.pdf>]

The 2018 limit is $7,350 for an individual and $14,700 for family coverage. The limits are different for HSA-compatible High Deductible Health Plans (HDHPs): a maximum of $6,550 for individual and $13,100 for family coverage. HDHPs are subject to both HHS and IRS limits, and must follow the more stringent one. [David M. Pixley, *HHS Issues Updated Out-of-Pocket Maximums for 2018*, Graydon Head & Ritchey LLP (Sept. 13, 2016), available at Lexology .com; Richard Stover and Kimberley Mitchell, *HHS Proposes 2018 OOP Maximums and Marketplace Guidance*, Xerox FYI (Sept. 8, 2016) (benefitslink.com)]

A recent article says that the out-of-pocket limits probably would not be affected by the initial attempts to repeal PPACA (or by renewed attempts later in 2017) because Congress plans to use the reconciliation process, a political tactic that can only be used for provisions that have a direct impact on the federal budget, which is probably not true of out-of-pocket limits. [Kimberley Mitchell, *HHS Finalizes the 2018 OOP Maximums*, Xerox FYI (Dec. 20, 2016) (benefitslink .com)]

Catastrophic plans (offering limited coverage for very high expenses, leaving the rest of the financial burden on the insured person) can be offered on the individual market only, not the group market, and only to people who are under age 30 or exempt from the individual requirement of maintaining minimum coverage. Catastrophic plans cover the essential benefit package, but only after the insured person has spent the HSA out-of-pocket limit on care.

[3] Grandfathered Plans

In order to pass the controversial health care reform package, it was necessary to promise plan participants that they would be able to keep their existing health insurance—which requires granting some additional leeway to plans that were in existence on March 23, 2010, when PPACA was enacted. PPACA applies to both insured and self-insured employer plans. However, there are some differences in the rules applied to grandfathered group health plans and new group health plans, with grandfathered plans exempt from some requirements. Grandfathered plans are deemed to provide minimum essential coverage for purposes of the mandate.

A plan continues to be treated as a grandfathered plan even if new employees and their families are allowed to enroll in the plan. Grandfathered plans are not required to provide the essential benefits without cost-sharing, so if they required deductibles and coinsurance for these benefits before PPACA, they can continue to do so. Nor do they have to offer preventive care services without cost-sharing. They are not required to allow participants to access emergency services without certification and without restriction to in-network providers. [See 75 Fed. Reg. 34537 (June 17, 2010) for HHS/DOL/IRS regulations about retaining grandfathered status when the plan's insurer is changed.]

"Grandmothered" plans that furnish some coverage but are not fully PPACA-compliant have received several extensions of relief, on the theory that they could furnish at least some coverage for people who cannot afford a compliant policy. A grandfathered plan is one that gets relief because it was in existence when PPACA was enacted; grandfathered plans can offer coverage indefinitely, as long as they are not amended in a way that removes their grandfathered status. Grandmothered plans, in contrast, are those that were purchased after PPACA was enacted but before market reforms took effect on January 1, 2014. In the fall of 2013, HHS allowed transitional relief allowing grandmothered plans to continue to be sold. It was extended for two further years in 2014, and for another year in 2016. CMS issued guidance on February 23, 2017, allowing grandmothered plans that are renewed before October 1, 2018, to continue to provide coverage until December 31, 2018. [Stephanie P. Hales, Dora Hughes and Laura R. Cohen, *Trump Administration Will Allow Certain Affordable Care Act Noncompliant Plans to Continue Through Dec. 31, 2018*, Sidley Austin LLP (Mar. 1, 2017), available at Leoxlogy.com]

[4] Cadillac Plans

The PPACA, as originally enacted, required a non-deductible, 40% excise tax will to be imposed under Code § 4980I on health coverage providers to the extent that the total value of employer-sponsored health coverage for a particular participant is greater than $10,200 (individual) or $27,500 (family coverage). This "Cadillac tax" allowed additional amounts for coverage of people in high-risk jobs like police and firefighters, and for non-Medicare-eligible retirees over 55. The Protecting Americans Against Tax Hikes (PATH Act; Pub. L. No. 114-113) delays the effective date of the Cadillac tax until 2020, and made the tax deductible as a business expense.

[5]   Self-Insured Plans

Most of the PPACA requirements apply to self-insured as well as insured group health plans. For example, discrimination on the basis of health status or pre-existing conditions is forbidden and, if the plan has dependent coverage, adult children must be covered to age 26. Plans cannot maintain annual or lifetime benefit limits and coverage must not be rescinded other than on the basis of the participant's fraud or intentional misrepresentation. But some requirements do not apply to self-insured plans: they do not have to offer PPACA's minimum benefits package and are not subject to the annual limitation on health plan deductibles.

[6]   Nondiscrimination Requirements

PPACA § 2716 makes fully insured group health plans subject to the Code § 105(h) nondiscrimination rules. Previously, only self-insured plans were subject to these rules. To comply, the plan must benefit 70% of all employees, or, if 70% of employees are eligible to participate, 80% of the eligible employees must participate. It is not considered unlawful discrimination to exclude employees with less than three years of service; those under 25; part-time or seasonal employees; employees covered under a CBA (Collective Bargaining Agreement); and non-resident aliens. [Nelson Mullins Riley & Scarborough, LLP, *The Odd Couple: Healthcare Reform and Executive Compensation* (Apr. 15, 2010) (benefitslink.com)]

The penalties under the nondiscrimination rules are considered excise rather than income taxes, so if an insured plan discriminates, the highly compensated employees are not taxed on their benefits, but the employer is subject to an excise tax penalty of $100 per day per participant (under Code § 4980D). Small employers—those with fewer than 50 employees—are exempt from the excise tax. The excise tax is capped at 10% of the aggregate amount the employer paid or incurred for the plan during the previous tax year, or $500,000, whichever is less. Excise tax liability is reported on Form 8928. The nondiscrimination requirement can be enforced by the Department of Labor, and participants and beneficiaries have the right to sue to enforce it. [Steven Friedman, Terri Solomon and Stephanie Kastrinsky, *Employers with Insured Health Plans Must Take Care in Providing Healthcare Subsidies to Departing Executives*, Littler Mendelson (Oct. 29, 2012) (benefitslink.com)]

[7]   Full-Time and Part-Time Employees

Employers (other than those exempt because of their small size) who do not offer compliant health coverage are subject to penalties if they do not offer at least minimum coverage to their full-time employees. PPACA uses a special definition of full-time employees, premised on working 30 rather than 40 hours a week.

Staffing firms' position with respect to PPACA is complex, especially in light of the many staffing models. If the IRS concludes that working for a staffing firm is a full-time payrolled position, the worker should not be treated as a variable-hour employee who is not entitled to benefits. [79 Fed. Reg. 8544 (Feb. 12, 2014)]

Reducing hours to prevent workers from being entitled to health care coverage could create problems with ERISA § 510 (the ban on interference with benefits). A class action has been filed in the Southern District of New York by about 10,000 employees who say their hours were cut to keep them from being full-time workers entitled to PPACA coverage. However, ERISA requires the employer have acted with specific intent to interfere with the employee's rights under a plan. [*Marin v. Dave & Buster's Inc.*, No. 1:15-cv-03608 (S.D.N.Y. pending)]

[C] Small Business Tax Credit

For tax years beginning after December 31, 2009, PPACA enacts a new Code § 45R, making a new tax credit available to certain small business employers. A small business, defined as one with 25 or fewer employees, whose average annual wages are under $50,000, is eligible for a tax credit that can be as much as 50% of the non-elective contributions made on behalf of employees for their health insurance premiums. To qualify for the credit, the employer must contribute at least half the premium for the coverage, and must make uniform payments on behalf of all employees. However, the credit will be limited if the employer pays an above-average premium for its coverage. [See FAQs at <https://www.irs.gov/uac/Small-Business-Health-Care-Tax-Credit:-Questions-and-Answers> (Nov. 2, 2016) (last accessed Feb. 25, 2017)]

The employer receives the maximum amount of credit if it has 10 or fewer employees, with average wages under $20,000 (this amount will be adjusted for inflation beginning in 2013; the 2016 figure is $25,900). Average wages are rounded down to the next $1,000—that is, a wage of $32,408 is treated as $32,000.

The credit phases down, but is not eliminated, if the employer has more than 10 but fewer than 25 Full-Time Equivalents (FTEs), and is eliminated once the number of FTEs reaches 25. It also phases down as the average wage increases, phasing out at $51,600 a year (2016 figure) or $52,000 (2017 figure). The number of FTEs is calculated by dividing the number of hours worked by 2,080. The credit can be claimed in only two consecutive taxable years in 2014 and beyond. [IRS Health Care Tax Tip 2016-20 (Feb. 17, 2016), available at <https://www.irs.gov/affordable-care-act/employers/understanding-the-small-business-health-care-tax-credit> (last accessed Feb. 25, 2017)]

This credit is a component of the general business credit under Code § 38(b)(36), claimed on Form 3800. Form 8941 is used to calculate the credit so it can be carried back one tax year and forward 20 tax years. The credit can also be claimed in full against both regular and AMT (Alternative Minimum Tax) liabilities.

Another credit, the Health Coverage Tax Credit (Code § 35), is payable with respect to was people aged 55 and over who receive their pensions from the PBGC, people who are eligible for Trade Adjustment Assistance (TAA); (see § 19.02[F]), and older workers who receive wage subsidies under the Alternative TAA program or the Reemployment TAA program. At various times, the credit ranged between 65% and 80% of the qualified premium. As a result of 2015 trade legislation, the HCTC, which had expired January 1, 2014, was restored for all eligibility coverage months occurring before January 1, 2020 as a refundable credit equal to 72.5% of insurance premiums (including COBRA premiums) paid by workers who lost their jobs as a result of foreign competition. [Trade Preferences Extension Act of 2015, Pub. L. No. 114-27]

[D] Extended Coverage of Participants' Children

Before PPACA, many plans offered family coverage: coverage not just of the employee participating in the plan, but of the employee's spouse and children. Traditionally, children were eligible for coverage only until they reached the age of majority or married. Then there was a trend toward covering adult "children" of plan participants. (See § 18.03[F] for a discussion of state laws requiring extended coverage, e.g., if the child was a full-time student.) The federal "Michelle's Law" also required extended coverage of adult offspring with disabilities.

There are two aspects to coverage of adult children under PPACA. PPACA requires group health plans (including self-insured plans) to allow participants to continue coverage of their children until the child turns age 26, even if the child is not a student and even if the child is married. But for plan years beginning after January 1, 2014, grandfathered group health plans do not have to extend adult dependent coverage if the child is eligible to enroll in another EGHP (e.g., because of the child's own employment or spouse's employment).

[T.D. 9482, 2010-22 I.R.B. 698; DOL, *Fact Sheet: Young Adults and the Affordable Care Act*, <http://www.dol.gov/ebsa/newsroom/fsdependentcoverage .html> (undated, last accessed Feb. 25, 2017)]

Also note that in several states (e.g., Connecticut, Florida, Illinois, Nebraska, New Jersey, New York, Ohio, Pennsylvania, South Dakota, and Wisconsin) coverage may have to be extended even past age 26. Such coverage is taxable unless the child is a "qualifying child" or "qualifying relative" for federal tax purposes. [Cynthia Lee, *Wisconsin Bill Passed to Conform State Tax Treatment of Coverage of Adult Children*, Beyond Health Care Reform Blog (Oct. 28, 2011) (benefitslink.com)]

[E] Retiree Issues

When it was first enacted, PPACA required a federal appropriation of $5 billion for employers to reimburse part of the costs of covering early retirees (aged 55–64) and their dependents for the gap period between retirement and Medicare eligibility. The program, known as the Early Retiree Reinsurance Program (ERRP), ran out of money and stopped accepting new applications on May 5, 2011; the program was formally terminated at the beginning of 2014. [78 Fed. Reg. 23936 (Apr. 23, 2013)]

PPACA does not eliminate the subsidy that employers receive for furnishing prescription drug coverage to retirees that is actuarially equivalent to Medicare Part D coverage (see § 9.10[B]). However, PPACA reduces the value of the tax break. Qualifying employers continue to receive the subsidy, and the subsidy is not taxable income. However, under pre-PPACA law, the subsidy was deductible to the employer, but starting in 2013 the deduction will no longer be available.

Plans that cover only retirees, not active employees, are exempt under ERISA § 732 from certain requirements that EGHPs are subject to. The District Court for the Southern District of California held that PPACA did not eliminate this rule; in fact, retiree-only plans are exempt from certain PPACA mandates, including the ban on lifetime dollar limits. [*King v. Blue Cross & Blue Shield of Illinois*, 2015 WL 2385684 (S.D. Cal. 2015); see EBIA Weekly, *Retiree-Only Health Plan Exempt from Lifetime Dollar Limit, Court Rules* (May 28, 2015) (benefitslink.com)]

[F] Cafeteria Plans, HSAs, HRAs, and FSAs

As a counterpart to SIMPLE IRAs (see § 4.06[G]), PPACA allows certain small employers to provide simple cafeteria plans, which are deemed to satisfy the nondiscrimination rules. For years beginning after December 31, 2010, an eligible employer is one who had an average of 100 or fewer employees in either of the two preceding years, if the employer was in existence throughout the year. If it was not, then the employer can be eligible if it reasonably expects to average 100 or fewer employees on business days during the current year. If the employee census later grows, the employer can maintain an existing Simple Cafeteria Plan as long as it has under 200 employees.

The employer contribution must be at least 6% of the employee's compensation for the year, or twice the employee's salary reduction contribution— whichever is less. Employees who worked for at least 1,000 hours in the previous year are eligible to participate, but employees can be excluded if they are covered by a CBA, are under 21, or have not performed at least one year of service for the employer. [Gary B. Kushner, Kushner & Co., *New Simple Cafeteria Plans* (Aug. 14, 2010) (benefitslink.com)]

Starting 2011, reimbursement under FSA, HRA, or HSA is limited to prescription drugs, and is not available for over-the-counter drugs. The additional tax imposed on distributions from an HSA or MSA not used for qualified medical expenses rises, to 20%.

As of January 1, 2013, contributions to an FSA for medical expenses are limited to $2,500 a year (a figure that will be adjusted for inflation). The 2015 amount is $2,550, which remains unchanged for 2016; the 2017 amount is $2,600. [Rev. Proc. 2015-53, 2015-44 I.R.B. 615; Rev. Proc. 2016-55, 2016-45 I.R.B. 707]

[G] Wellness Programs

For PPACA purposes, a wellness program is one that is offered by an employer to promote health or prevent disease. All similarly situated individuals must be allowed to participate in the program, and health status factors must not be used in deciding who qualifies for a rebate or premium discount.

Wellness programs must be reasonably targeted at improving health or preventing illness, and are not allowed to operate as a subterfuge to justify health status discrimination. A reasonable alternative standard must be offered for people whose medical condition keeps them from achieving a stated goal. Under PPACA, starting 2014, the discount can be 30% or even as much as 50%, with wellness discounts extended to the individual market with a 10-state demonstration project beginning July 2014. PPACA allows employees who meet health benchmarks to get waivers of copayments and deductibles and relief from surcharges. [Roni Caryn Rabin, *Will Health Overhaul Incentives also Penalize Some Workers?*, NYTimes.com (Apr. 12, 2010)]

Joint HHS, DOL, and Treasury rules on wellness programs can be found in T.D. 9620, 2013-27 I.R.B. 1. The rules support wellness programs, including participatory programs that are generally available without regard to the individual's health status, such as reimbursement of gym membership or payment for filling out a health risk survey. Programs that are contingent on health (i.e., the reward is triggered by meeting specific health standards such as giving up smoking) must be reasonably designed to promote health or prevent disease, and must not be overly burdensome on participants. Alternative means to qualify must be provided for employees who have a medical reason for being unable to satisfy the health-related standard. Potentially discriminatory underwriting practices are limited. There is an increasing trend of penalizing workers who do not sign up for wellness programs. Two-thirds of large companies have incentives for wellness program participation and almost one-quarter of those penalize employees who opt out. Financial incentives may be linked to specified goals such as glucose or blood cholesterol or weight. Most large employer self-insure, so medical costs come out of their revenues.

According to the Society on Human Resources Management (SHRM), many employers are terminating wellness programs, finding that the anticipated cost reductions did not materialize. In 2016, only about a third of survey respondents offered health coaching, versus almost half a year earlier. [Rachel Emma Silverman, *Employers Cut Down on Wellness Benefits*, WSJ.com (June 20, 2016)]

The Eleventh Circuit upheld a wellness program, calling for blood tests and an online risk assessment questionnaire, under the ADA safe harbor for insurance plans that engage in good faith in underwriting and classifying risks. [*Seff v. Broward Cnty.*, 691 F.3d 1221 (11th Cir. 2012)]

The EEOC was unable to get a court order to prevent Honeywell from penalizing employees for refusing to participate in biometric testing. Honeywell required employees (and their spouses, if the employee had family coverage) to submit blood test results or lose the employer's HSA contribution (potentially up to $1,500). Employees were also hit with a $500 surcharge and a $1,000 tobacco surcharge. The EEOC alleged violations of Title VII, the ADA, and GINA. The District Court for the District of Minnesota denied the request to block the surcharges. [*EEOC v. Honeywell*, No. 14-cv-4517, 2014 U.S. Dist. LEXIS 157945 (D. Minn. Nov. 6, 2014). However, in response to EEOC rules, Honeywell decided to cap the penalty for non-compliance at $1,500: Tara Siegel Bernard, *The Sticks and Carrots of Employee Wellness Programs*, NYTimes.com (Oct. 31, 2015).]

As part of its efforts to eliminate disability discrimination in the workplace, the EEOC published a Notice of Proposed Rulemaking (NPRM) on April 20, 2015, dealing with the application of ADA Title I to employee wellness programs that ask health questions or include medical examinations (e.g., cholesterol or high blood pressure screening). The EEOC's fact sheet says that it is reasonable to collect information on a health risk assessment to inform employees about their personal risks, or to aggregate information from many assessments to design programs targeting particular medical conditions. But it is not reasonable to collect information otherwise. Wellness programs must be voluntary. Employees must not be forced to participate, cannot be disciplined for nonparticipation, and they cannot be denied health insurance or given reduced health benefits. Employers must not interfere with the ADA rights of employees who do not want to participate. It is unlawful to coerce or threaten employees to get them to participate or to achieve specific health outcomes. Limited incentives for participation or reaching the targets are permissible—not exceeding 30% of the total cost of employee-only coverage. If the wellness program is part of an EGHP, complying with the HIPAA privacy rule (see § 19.05[F]) is generally adequate. Employers must offer reasonable accommodations so employees with disabilities can participate and earn incentives. [80 Fed. Reg. 21659 (Apr. 20, 2015). See 81 Fed. Reg. 31125 (May 17, 2016) for final HHS rules about wellness programs under the ADA, and 81 Fed. Reg. 31143 (May 17, 2016) for final HHS rules about genetic testing in wellness programs. See Rachel Emma Silverman, *EEOC Issues New Rules for Wellness Programs*, WSJ.com (May 16, 2016)]

The final ADA rules for wellness programs require employees to receive notice about what information the program collects, who gets the information, how it is used, and the plan's privacy and confidentiality provisions. Employers cannot require participation in wellness programs; cannot deny or restrict health coverage on the basis of nonparticipation, cannot retaliate for nonparticipation, and cannot use coercion or threats to induce employees to participate. The EEOC Website has a sample notice. The notice obligation is effective the first day of the first plan year beginning on or after January 1, 2017. [EEOC notice: <https:// www.eeoc.gov/laws/regulations/ada-wellness-notice.cfm>. See Plansponsor staff, *EEOC Provides Sample Notice for Wellness Programs*, plansponsor.com (June 21, 2016).]

The District Court for the Eastern District of Wisconsin denied summary judgment for the EEOC in a wellness program case. The EEOC argued that requiring employees who opted in to the employer's self-insured health plan to complete a health risk assessment violated the ADA. The EEOC also argued that an employee suffered retaliation when she complained about the requirement. The district court ruled that the program was voluntary, even though employees who did not complete the health risk assessment were responsible for 100% of the premium cost, and granted summary judgment for the employer. However, the retaliation claim proceeded to trial. However, the district court said that the retaliation claim had to be tried. [*EEOC v. Orion Energy Sys., Inc.*, No. 208 F. Supp. 3d 989 (E.D. Wis. 2016); see Russell Chapman, *Half a Loaf: Court Rejects ADA "Safe Harbor" But Approves Pre-Regulations Wellness Program as "Voluntary,"* Littler.com (Sept. 23, 2016) (benefitslink.com); Practical Law Employee Benefits & Executive Compensation, *EEOC Loses Again in Wellness Litigation* (Nov. 10, 2016) (benefitslink.com)]

The case was settled on April 5, 2017; Orion agreed to pay $100,000 to the terminated employee and revise its wellness program to reduce the incentives for participation and avoid medical examinations that are not considered voluntary under the ADA: see Heather C. Panick, *EEOC and Orion Energy Systems, Inc. Settle Wellness Case,* Jackson Lewis PC (Apr. 20, 2017), available at Lexology .com]

The EEOC's final regulation on wellness programs took effect January 1, 2017; the District Court for the District of Columbia denied the AARP's request to block implementation of the regulation pending a court decision on the merits. (The AARP argued that the incentives prevent the programs from being truly voluntary.) According to the AARP, the rules are arbitrary, capricious, and an abuse of EEOC discretion. The AARP said that the rules could lead employees' individual health care costs to double or even triple. The district court ruled that the AARP did not show either irreparable harm or likelihood of success on the merits. [*AARP v. EEOC,* No. 16-cv-2113, 2016 U.S. Dist. LEXIS 180612, 100 Empl. Prac. Dec. (CCH) P45,710 (D.D.C. Dec. 29, 2016); see Seth J. Safra & Laura M. Fant, *District Court Denies Preliminary Injunction in AARP Suit to Block Final Rules on Employee Wellness Programs*, Proskauer Rose LLP (Jan. 31, 2017), available at Lexology.com; Rebecca Moore, *AARP Sues for Injunction of EEOC Wellness Program Rules*, plansponsor.com (Oct. 25, 2016); Rachel Emma Silverman, *AARP Sues Over Wellness-Program Rules Set by Federal Government*, WSJ.com (Oct. 25, 2016); Reed Abelson, *AARP Sues U.S. Over Rules for Wellness Programs*, NYTimes.com (Oct. 25, 2016)]

In mid-2017, the district court held that the EEOC's decision to set the voluntariness level for incentives at 30% was poorly reasoned and not entitled to deference from the court. Instead of vacating the final regulations, the district court remanded them to the EEOC for reconsideration. [*AARP v. EEOC*, No. 16-cv-2113 (D.D.C. Aug. 22, 2017); see Pepper Hamilton LLP (Aug. 23, 2017) (benefitslink.com)]

When an employee lost EGHP coverage because he did not complete the health risk assessment and biometric medical examination required by his employer, the EEOC sued under the ADA's ban on involuntary medical examinations. The district court dismissed the suit. The Seventh Circuit affirmed, not on the merits, but because the relief sought was unavailable or moot. (The employer retroactively reinstated insurance after the employee gave in and had the tests; the employer later terminated the testing program, concluding that it was not cost-effective.) The employee did not pay any medical expenses that were not covered by the plan; he did not prove damages for emotional distress; and the employer did not act with malice or reckless indifference to his rights, so punitive damages would not be available. [*EEOC v. Flambeau, Inc.*, 846 F.3d 941 (7th Cir. 2017); see Kristin L. Bauer and Paul Patten, *Seventh Circuit Delivers Blow to EEOC Wellness Program Challenge, But Avoids Ruling on ADA Safe Harbor*, Jackson Lewis PC (Jan. 26, 2017), available at Lexology.com; Gerald L. Maatman, Jr. and John S. Marrese, *Seventh Circuit Declines to Address The EEOC's Challenge to the Legality of Employer's Wellness Plan*, Seyfarth Shaw LLP (Jan. 29, 2017), available at Lexology.com]

[H] Penalties for Failure to Offer Affordable Coverage

A large employer (one with over 50 employees) is subject to a fine (the "assessable payment") if it fails to offer its full-time employees and their dependents the opportunity to receive minimum essential coverage under a plan sponsored by the employer—but only if at least one full-time employee has enrolled in an Exchange and received a premium tax credit or cost-sharing reduction. Large employers can avoid the assessable payment by providing their employees vouchers for purchasing coverage from an Exchange. The IRS issued proposed regulations and an FAQ on the Code § 4980H "shared responsibility" (aka "pay or play") obligation at the beginning of 2013. [78 Fed. Reg. 217 (Jan. 2, 2013)]

The assessable payment was originally scheduled to begin January 1, 2014, but was postponed until January 1, 2015 for companies with 100 or more employees; in 2015, they must offer affordable coverage to at least 70% of their full-time employees; in 2016, this must rise to 95% or penalties will be assessed. [Robert Pear, *Further Delays for Employers in Health Law*, NYTimes.com (Feb. 10, 2014)]

As of January 1, 2015, employers with 100 or more full-time equivalent employees (2015) or 50 or more (2016 and subsequent years) have reporting obligations pursuant to the pay or play penalty. The penalty, which is indexed, starts at $2,000. However, for 2015 only, penalties were waived for the first 80 full-time equivalents (FTEs).

A different penalty, of $3,000 per employee as indexed, is imposed for each employee who obtains coverage on an Exchange because the coverage offered by the employers did not satisfy PPACA requirements, or was not affordable. These employer penalties are not tax-deductible.

According to Notice 2015-87, 2015-52 I.R.B. 889, the 2015 penalties are $2,080 for failure to offer coverage, and $3,120 for failure to offer affordable minimum-value coverage, and the 2016 figures are $2,160 and $3,240 respectively. The 2017 figures are $2,260 and $3,390. [Notice 2015-87, 2015-52 I.R.B. 889]

For 2015, employers must offer PPACA-compliant coverage to 70% of full-time employees; in 2016 and later, they must cover 95% of full-time employees. There are also reporting obligations for self-funded plans, to administer the individual mandate. A company with 50 or more full-time equivalent employees (those working 30 hours or more) is an ALE. Employees who average less than 30 hours a week are combined into an equivalent number of 30-hour employees to determine if there are 50 or more full-time equivalent employees. Employees of controlled groups and companies with 80% shared ownership are aggregated for this test.

For most PPACA purposes, large employers have more obligations, so large-employer status is undesirable. However, PPACA also imposes a number of requirements only on small, but not on large employers, such as using a single risk pool for setting premiums and providing 10 essential health benefits. PPACA called for employers with 51–100 employees to be treated as small employers for these purposes starting January 1, 2016. The intention was to improve the position of the SHOP Exchanges by bringing in a new group of customers.

The Protecting Affordable Coverage for Employees Act (PACE) Act of 2015, Pub. L. No. 114-60, repeals this "mandated small group expansion" although states are allowed to determine the size of the "small group market" under their insurance laws. California, Colorado, Maryland, New York, Virginia, Vermont, and the District of Columbia have laws or administrative regulations defining a small group as one covering fewer than 100 employees. It was anticipated that most states would continue to require groups with more than 50 employees to use community rating. [Craig Hasday, *Another Change to ACA: States Can Decide on Small Group Expansion*, frenkelbenefits.com (Oct. 8, 2015) (benefitslink.com)]

ALE employers report both pay or play and individual mandate information on Forms 1094C and 1095C. Insurers and non-ALE self-insured employers use Forms 1094B and 1095B. Reporting of information to employees, COBRA beneficiaries, and retirees can be done on Forms 1095B and 1095C but the employer can elect other formats for reporting. The due date for these forms is the same as for Form W-2, and statements to employees can be provided with the W-2. Reports to employees are due January 31 after the year of the events; reports to the IRS are due February 28 (if filed on paper) or March 31 (if e-filed). [Month by Month, *Employers Must Track Employees in 2015 for Required Reporting Under Health Reform Rules*, Brown Todd (Jan. 15, 2015) (benefitslink.com); Jackson Lewis PC, *Health Care Reform: Employers Should Prepare Now for 2015 to Avoid Penalties* (Aug. 8, 2014) (benefitslink.com)]

A 2015 statute, Trade Preferences Extension Act increases the base penalties for failure to issue information returns from $100 to $250 per return, capped at $3 million per employer. All penalties are doubled if both a payee statement and an information return submitted to the IRS are involved. If the failure reflects intentional disregard of the law, the penalty is $500 per return, and the cap does not apply. [Trade Preferences Extension Act, Pub. L. No. 114-27]

There was a slight inflation adjustment announced in mid-2014: for 2015, coverage is considered affordable if it does not cost more than 9.56% of the employee's household income for the relevant year. Thus, for 2015, a single person earning 300% of the poverty level ($35,010) must pay up to $3,347 (9.56% of income) for the second-lowest silver plan. A subsidy is available if he or she pays more. [Rev. Proc. 2014-37, 2014-33 I.R.B. 363]

For 2016, the required premium contribution rises to 9.66% of income ($3,411) for a person at 300% of poverty. [Jed Graham, *ObamaCare's Max Deductible to Hit $6,850 in 2016*, Investor's Business Daily (Feb. 23, 2013) (benefitslink.com)] For 2017, the percentage is 9.69%; see Rev. Proc. 2016-24, 2016-18 I.R.B. 677. The 2018 percentage returns to 9.56% of income: Rev. Proc. 2017-36, 2017-21 I.R.B. 1251.

[I]   The CLASS Act

The Community Living Assistance Services and Support (CLASS) Act was intended to facilitate saving by employees for the cost of home care. However, the program never took effect.

In October 2011, HHS announced that the CLASS Act program was financially unsustainable and would not be implemented. [Rebecca Moore, *Repeal of Long-Term Care Provision of Health Reform Heads to House*, plansponsor.com (Jan. 19, 2012)] At the beginning of 2013, as part of the "fiscal cliff" deal to resolve the budget crisis, the CLASS Act was formally repealed.

[J] PPACA Effects on Employees

The intention of PPACA is to provide most people with at least the minimum benefits package, with limits on employee payments responsibilities, through their employment. The health care reform legislation provides both "carrots" and "sticks"—many employees will be able to receive premium credits or vouchers to help them pay for insurance; temporary high-risk pools followed by Insurance Exchanges will be available to cover workers who do not receive employment-related insurance coverage.

[1] Premium Credits

PPACA allows workers with household income between 100% and 400% of the federal poverty level (FPL) to receive a refundable tax credit if their employer fails to offer creditable coverage and if the employees purchase coverage under an Exchange. The premium credit is defined as 2% of income for taxpayers whose income equals 100% of FPL, increasing to 9.5% of income for employees whose income is in the 300%–400% FPL range.

A taxpayer will not be eligible for the tax credit if he or she is eligible for "minimum essential coverage," including coverage under an eligible employer-sponsored plan that pays at least 60% of the cost of a plan that provides the minimum essential benefits. (A person who could enroll in an employer's plan, but chooses not to, does not qualify for the premium tax credit.)

See proposed regulations, 78 Fed. Reg. 4593 (Jan. 22, 2013) for HHS' procedure for verifying eligibility for the credit.

Opponents of PPACA brought several suits to challenge the legality of the subsidy, arguing that the subsidy could only be paid in states that have established their own Exchange, not in states that declined to set up an Exchange and where the federal Exchange is in operation. For 2014, subsidies are available to individuals with income under $45,960, and the amount increases with family size; the maximum for a four-person family is $94,200. Only 14 states have their own Exchanges; the federal Exchange covers about 4.5 million people, some of whom cannot afford health insurance without a subsidy. They will not be penalized for failure to maintain insurance coverage—but, of course, they will not be insured.

In mid-2015, the Supreme Court resolved a circuit split by ruling that the federal government can provide subsidies to qualifying persons whether they buy their insurance from a state marketplace, or from the federal marketplace in states that refused to set up exchanges of their own. (About 85% of people who buy coverage from an exchange qualify for the subsidy.) The plaintiffs argued that PPACA refers only to subsidies for purchases from "an exchange established by the state," but the Supreme Court rejected this argument. [*King v. Burwell*, No.

14-114 (U.S. June 25, 2015); see Adam Liptak, *Supreme Court Allows Nation-wide Health Care Subsidies*, NYTimes.com (June 26, 2015)]

Some Republican members of the House of Representatives filed suit in the District Court for the District of Columbia charging that it was unconstitutional for the Obama administration to pay $136 billion in subsidies to insurers without congressional approval. (Under PPACA, the federal government reimburses insurers when the insurers are required to reduce the deductibles and copayments for some people who buy coverage on an Exchange.)

The District Court for the District of Columbia dismissed part of the suit as a political dispute that cannot be handled by the courts, but allowed part of the suit to proceed on the grounds that it involves the role of the House of Representatives in safeguarding the expenditure of public funds. Subsequently, the district court held that HHS did not have the authority to spend the money to provide subsidies. [*House of Representatives v. Burwell*, No. 14-1967 (RMC) (D.D.C. May 12, 2016); Carl Hulse, *Judge Backs House Challenge to a Key Part of Health Law*, NYTimes.com (May 13, 2016)].

At the end of 2016, the D.C. Circuit placed the case on hold until February 21, 2017, to give the Trump administration time to consider how to handle the suit. [*U.S. House of Representatives v. Burwell*, No. 16-5202, 2016 U.S. App. LEXIS 23584 (D.C. Cir. Dec. 5, 2016); see Morningconsult.com, *Court Agrees to Temporary Delay of GOP Obamacare Lawsuit* (Dec. 5, 2016) (benefitslink.com). The case was renamed *U.S. House of Representatives v. Price* to reflect the incoming Secretary of HHS.]

A group of more than a dozen Democratic state Attorneys General moved to intervene in this suit; the D.C. Circuit granted the motion on August 1, 2017. The insurance industry advocates retention of the subsidies, arguing that if they are not continued, insurers will have to raise premiums or stop selling certain types of insurance. Many people would become uninsured, because they would not be able to afford insurance without the subsidies. [Ken Yood, Matthew J. Goldman and Jordan E. Grushkin, *ACA Cost-Sharing Reductions: An Uncertain Future*, Sheppard Mullin Richter & Hampton LLP (May 5, 2017), available at Lexology.com; Stephanie Armour, *Democratic Attorneys-General Seek to Preserve Affordable Care Act Subsidies*, WSJ.com (May 18, 2017). The states are California, Connecticut, Delaware, Hawaii, Illinois, Iowa, Kentucky, Maryland, Massachusetts, Minnesota, New Mexico, New York, Pennsylvania, Vermont, Washington (state and D.C.). For grant of the motion to intervene, see Ben Agatston, *AG Healey and Other AGs Win Right to Contest Trump Admin [sic] on "Cost Sharing Reduction" Payments*, A Healthy Blog (Aug. 2, 2017), available at hcfma.org.]

[2] Individual Penalties

Although PPACA provides rights for individuals, including greater access to health insurance because they cannot be turned down for coverage because of

PCEs, the law also imposes individual personal responsibility requirements. Starting in 2014, a "shared responsibility payment" is imposed for each month that a person fails to maintain minimum essential health coverage for themselves and their dependents. The penalty is imposed on the taxpayer, so in effect dependent children are exempt from the penalty. The coverage can be obtained either through an EGHP or by purchasing an individual policy; the Exchanges exist to make it easier to obtain individual coverage.

The penalty is the larger of a flat dollar amount per person, or a percentage of household income. For families, the penalty per child is half the individual penalty, subject to a cap amount no matter how large the family is. Married couples are jointly liable for the penalty. But the federal government will not bring criminal prosecutions or impose liens or levies for failure to pay it. The Individual Shared Responsibility payment is defined as the greater of a flat fee or a percentage of household income. The 2016–2017 flat fee is $695 per adult, $347.50 for a child; the penalty for a family is capped at $2,085. The percentage is 2.5% of household income in excess of the income threshold at which filing an income tax return is required. The payment is not imposed on Medicare beneficiaries, certain religious groups, or people who were not covered for a period of three months or less. Unpaid penalties are not subject to ordinary IRS collection methods, but the penalty (plus interest) can be deducted from tax refunds. [IRS.gov, *Individual Shared Responsibility Provision—Reporting and Calculating the Payment* (revised Nov. 30, 2016), available at <https://www.irs.gov/affordable-care-act/individuals-and-families/aca-individual-shared-responsibility-provision-calculating-the-payment> (last accessed Feb. 26, 2017)]

The Individual Shared Responsibility Payment is imposed under Code § 2000A(c)(1)(B), on taxpayers who do not have minimum essential coverage for one or more months in a taxable year, and who are not entitled to an exemption. The calculation depends on the average premium for a bronze plan, calculated each year. For the calculation method, see Rev. Proc. 2016-43, 2016-36 I.R.B. 316.

[3]   Taxes on High-Income Participants

Although the focus of this discussion of PPACA is on the employer's point of view, certain provisions affecting individuals are crucial to understanding PPACA. One of the ways that the health care reform program will be funded is through increasing the Medicare tax imposed on plan participants with especially high income.

Before PPACA, the FICA payroll tax was imposed on all earned income up to the FICA limit (for 2013, it is $113,700, for 2014, it is $117,000, for 2015–2016, it is $118,500, and for 2017 it is much higher: $127,200), and the

Medicare tax was imposed on all income without the limit. (For employees, the employer and employee each pay 1.45%; self-employed persons pay 2.9%.)

Starting in 2013, the 1.45% Medicare payroll tax rises to 2.35% for high-income persons. Only the employee's share, not the employer's share, rises. For this purpose, a high-income taxpayer is one with total earned income plus investment income greater than $250,000 (joint return) or $200,000 (other returns). Although in general self-employed persons can deduct half of the regular FICA tax, the additional Medicare tax is not deductible. Elective contributions are generally subject to FICA tax, but the additional Medicare tax does not apply to elective contributions or to earnings on qualified plans, including 401(k) plans. Tax-exempt bond interest and profits on the sale of the taxpayer's principal residence are not included in gross income, so they are not included in the Medicare tax base.

The reconciliation bill imposes an additional Medicare tax equal to 3.8% of certain investment income (the smaller of net investment income, or modified AGI minus $250,000 for joint returns, $125,000 for married persons filing separate returns, and $200,000 for other filing statuses). See T.D. 9645, 2013-51 I.R.B. 738 for final regulations on the additional Medicare tax enacted on high earners, e.g., how to withhold the additional tax and correct overpayments and underpayments. The employer must withhold the additional tax from wages over $200,000 paid to anyone, irrespective of the recipient's filing status or wages paid by other employers. The employer cannot modify its withholding of additional Medicare tax. However, a person who expects to owe more than the amount withheld by the employer can increase withholding on the W-4 (e.g., a joint return where neither spouse earns over $200,000, but the total is over $250,000).

If the American Health Care Act (AHCA) had passed, these taxes would have been eliminated, significantly reducing the income tax obligations of the wealthy.

[K] Recordkeeping, Reporting, and Disclosure

PPACA imposes many information requirements on health plans—communication with employees about their health plans and communication with regulators to ensure that employers satisfy their obligations (and also to claim the financial assistance they are entitled to).

Many of the provisions of PPACA require notices to be furnished, either to specific participants, or as a part of the plan's general benefits materials. Many plans include these notices in the annual enrollment package or the plan's SPD.

All plans, including grandfathered plans, must offer a one-time special enrollment period for adult children who were not covered because of age or who aged out of the plan, and for persons who lost coverage because they reached the plan's maximum coverage, and notice must be given of the special enrollment period.

PPACA also requires notices of:

- Grandfathered status;

- Patient Protection Model Notice: If the plan requires participants to designate a primary care provider, how to choose one; notice that female enrollees can see a OB/GYN without prior authorization or referral. (Not required for grandfathered plans);

- Explanation of the external review process; many plans include this in the SPD (Not required for grandfathered plans);

- Notice of internal adverse benefit determination;

- Advance notice that coverage will be cancelled or rescinded.

[Christy Tinnes and Brigen Winters, *What Notices Are Required by PPACA?*, plansponsor.com (Sept. 21, 2010)]

In addition to specific PPACA notices, many other notices are required of health plans (e.g., annual notice of rights under the Women's Health and Cancer Rights Act; this can be given in the health plan's SPD if it is reissued each year). Employees and their dependents who are eligible for Medicare must be informed if the employer's coverage is creditable or non-creditable (i.e., whether the coverage of prescription drugs is equal or better than the coverage offered under Medicare Part D). See § 9.10[B].

Participants must be notified every three years that they can obtain a copy of the HIPAA notice of privacy practices and the notice form must be updated to reflect the HITECH Act requirement of notice to people whose Protected Health Information has been compromised by a security breach. In states that have a CHIPRA (child health premium assistance) program, all employees must receive an annual notice about the premium subsidy, even if they are not enrolled in a CHIPRA plan, see the DOL Website for model notice language.

As a parallel to the Summary Plan Description for a pension plan (see § 11.02), the employer must give each employee a summary of health care benefits that explains the covered benefits, exclusions, cost sharing, and continuation coverage. For readability, the summary must be in 12-point or larger type. This document is referred to as the Summary of Benefits and Coverage (SBC). PPACA says that this explanation must be "culturally and linguistically appropriate" for the beneficiary who receives it. If the health plan changes, the employer must update the summary to reflect material modifications, at least 60 days before the change. Satisfying this requirement also satisfies the ERISA requirement of providing a Summary of Material Modification (SMM). The summary must be provided to job applicants when they apply, to enrollees before they enroll or re-enroll, and to the policyholder or certificate holder when the policy is issued or the certificate is delivered. The SBC can be furnished either on paper, or electronically as long as the DOL's electronic disclosure safe harbor (see 29 C.F.R.

§ 2520.104b-1) is satisfied. Willful failure to provide an SBC is subject to a fine of $1,000 per failure (each person affected constituting a separate offense) and is also subject to an excise tax of $100 per day per person affected under Code § 4980D.

The insurers of insured plans provide the SBC to the plan, and the plan and the insurer are jointly responsible for giving participants the SBC, but only one has to furnish the SBC, not both. The plan administrator is responsible for providing SBCs to participants of self-insured plans. Although grandfathered plans and HRAs are required to furnish the SBC, the requirement does not apply to retiree-only plans or plans such as stand-alone vision and dental plans that are exempt from HIPAA requirements.

The SBC must include:

- A uniform glossary of insurance and medical terms so that consumers may compare health coverage and understand the terms of (or exceptions to) their coverage;
- A description of the coverage, including cost sharing for each category of benefits;
- Exceptions, reductions and limitations on coverage;
- Cost-sharing provisions of coverage, including deductibles, coinsurance and copayment obligations;
- The renewability and continuation of coverage provisions;
- A "coverage facts label" that includes examples to illustrate common benefits scenarios;
- For coverage beginning on or after January 1, 2014, a statement of whether the plan provides minimum essential coverage and whether the plan pays at least 60% of the total cost of benefits;
- A statement that the SBC is only a summary and that the plan document, policy or certificate of coverage should be consulted to determine the governing contractual provisions of coverage;
- Contact information for questions and for obtaining a copy of the plan document or insurance policy, certificate or contract of insurance;
- For plans that maintain one or more provider networks, an Internet address for obtaining a list of network providers;
- For plans that use a prescription drug formulary, an Internet address for obtaining information on prescription drug coverage;
- An Internet address for obtaining the uniform glossary.

Further revisions were published in February 2016. The template was reduced from eight pages to five pages, and the text of certain questions was rewritten. Rather than being reduced, the uniform glossary was expanded to six pages, with definitions of 16 new terms such as "Marketplace" and "Maximum Out-of-Pocket Limit." [81 Fed. Reg. 9860 (Feb. 26, 2016) (HHS) and 81 Fed. Reg. 9887 (Feb. 26, 2016) (DOL); Cheiron, *Agencies Propose Revisions to Summary of Benefits and Coverage Template and Uniform Glossary* (Mar. 25, 2016) (benefitslink.com). See <http://www.dol.gov/ebsa/pdf/sbc-completed-sample-proposed-new.pdf> (last accessed Feb 25, 2017) for a sample of the proposed SBC for 2017, and <http://www.dol.gov/ebsa/pdf/sbc-uniform-glossary-proposed-new.pdf> (last accessed Feb. 25, 2017) for the glossary proposed for 2017.]

In April 2016, a new SBC template was issued, for plan years starting on or after April 1, 2017. This template is five pages long; there is a new introductory paragraph explaining the function of the SBC. Terms in the glossary are hyperlinked to definitions in the electronic version of the SBC. Disclosures about appeal rights and continuation coverage has been revised. The coverage examples now deal with diabetes care, childbirth, and treatment of a foot fracture. [EPIC Compliance Alert, *New Summary of Benefits and Coverage (SBC) for 2017* (Aug. 31, 2016) (benefitslink.com)]

PPACA § 9002 requires employers to disclose the aggregate cost of employer-sponsored coverage on Form W-2, whether the employee or employer pays. Only the total amount must be reported; an itemized breakdown is not required. Salary reduction contributions to FSAs under a cafeteria plan and contributions to MSAs or HSAs are not considered employer-sponsored coverage, so they do not have to be disclosed on the Form W-2. [Notice 2012-9, 2012-4 I.R.B. 315]

Final Regulations on the Code § 6055 requirements for minimum essential health coverage were published on March 10, 2014. The regulations explain the requirements imposed on companies with 50 or more full-time employees to report to the IRS and to employees about health care coverage available to employees. The requirements will be used by the IRS to enforce the pay-or-play mandate once it takes effect and to administer the tax credit that certain individuals will receive for buying health care coverage on an Exchange under Code § 36B. The penalty for not providing coverage will not be imposed on companies with 50–99 employees until 2016, but reporting under § 6056 is nonetheless required for 2015.

There are two ways that employers can satisfy their obligations under § 6056: either they can certify with respect to a particular full-time employee that the employee was offered affordable coverage, and minimum essential coverage was offered to the employee's spouse and dependents, or the employer certifies that affordable health coverage satisfying the minimum value requirements was offered to at least 98% of its full-time employees. There is a special transition rule for 2015 only for employers that made a qualifying offer of coverage to at least 95% of its full-time workforce.

Employers that offer a self-funded plan are required by § 6055 to make information reports to the IRS and employees when they provide minimum essential coverage. The reports are used to determine if the individual had the coverage required by the individual mandate. Employers that sponsor self-funded plans can use Form 1094-C to combine reporting for §§ 6055 and 6056.

Failure to satisfy these reporting requirements can be penalized under § 6721 (failure to file required information returns) and § 6722 (failure to provide payees with reports). However, if there is reasonable cause, § 6724 may offer relief by waiving penalties. There is a special transition rule for returns and statements filed in 2016 dealing with 2015 coverage: penalties will not be imposed for incorrect or incomplete information, but relief will not be granted if employers fail to make required reports, or if they do not attempt in good faith to comply.

Code § 6056 requires employers to report both to employees and the IRS. The IRS needs the information to administer the health care reform program; employees need the information to determine if they are entitled to a federal subsidy to help them with their share of health insurance premiums. [Chadron J. Patton, *Final Regulations Streamline ACA Reporting Rules*, Spencer Fane Britt & Browne (Mar. 13, 2014), available at Lexology.com]

A self-funded employer, even if it is not an ALE, must report each individual covered for each month of the calendar year. For fully insured plans, the insurance carrier must report individuals' coverage on a month by month basis. Individual mandate reporting is due in early 2016 for each month of 2015. ALE employers report both pay or play and individual mandate information on Forms 1094C and 1095C. Insurers and non-ALE self-insured employers use Forms 1094B and 1095B. Reporting of information to employees, COBRA beneficiaries, and retirees can be done on Forms 1095B and 1095C but the employer can elect other formats for reporting. Reports to employees are generally due January 31 after the year of the events; reports to the IRS are due February 28 (if filed on paper) or March 31 (if e-filed). [Month by Month, *Employers Must Track Employees in 2015 for Required Reporting Under Health Reform Rules*, Brown Todd (Jan. 15, 2015) (benefitslink.com)]

In late 2016, the IRS released the forms for reporting under §§ 6055 and 6056; there were few major changes from the previous editions of the form. Penalties for failure to file returns or furnish statements to employees rose to $260/violation, capped at $3,193,000/year (with a lower maximum for certain small businesses). [Chelkogroup.com, *Final Forms for ACA Reporting Released* (Oct. 4, 2016) (benefitslink.com)]

In mid-2016, the DOL, the IRS, and the PBGC jointly issued revisions to Form 5500, but compliance is not required until forms are filed for the 2019 plan year. All group health plans covered by ERISA Title I must file Form 5500. (Previous rules did not require a health or welfare plan with fewer than 100 participants to file if the plan was fully insured and/or unfunded.) The revisions add a new Schedule J to the form, for reporting on PPACA compliance, the number of people offered and the number receiving COBRA coverage; what kind of group health benefits are provided and how they are paid; if the plan is an HDHP, health FSA, or HRA. The penalty for failure to file Form 5500 increased from $1,100 per day to $2,063 a day. [Jeffrey P. Cairns & Abigail Clark, *Proposed Form 5500 Changes & the New Schedule J: Big Changes for Small Group Health Plans*, Stinson Leonard Street LLP (July 26, 2016), available at Lexology.com; Frost Brown Todd, *Form 5500 Updates and Increased ERISA Penalties* (Oct. 5, 2016) (benefitslink.com). The penalty for non-filing increased once again, to $2,097 a day: see 82 Fed. Reg. 8813 (Jan. 31, 2017).]

PPACA compliance requires the adoption of a number of plan amendments:

- Enrollment of persons under 19 without pre-existing condition limitations;

- Coverage of employees' dependent children to age 26, whether or not they are students or married, and whether or not they are tax dependents of the employees;

- Elimination of lifetime limits on essential health benefits

- Elimination of retroactive terminations of coverage;

- Amending FSAs, HRAs, and HSAs to eliminate reimbursement of the cost of over-the-counter drugs unless the participant has a prescription.

Non-grandfathered plans must be amended to provide:

- Coverage of some preventive services without cost sharing;

- Free choice of primary care provider (who can be a pediatrician for children enrolled in the plan); women can see an OB/GYN without prior authorization or referral;

- Emergency services must be covered without prior authorization, and emergency services must receive the same coverage whether in-network or out of network;

- The new external claims review process;

- The requirement of not discriminating in favor of highly compensated employees.

[L] Health Insurance Exchanges and High-Risk Pools

One of the main drivers behind the legislation was the perception that many individuals and small businesses found it difficult to buy and maintain health insurance. PPACA's response to this problem is the creation of health insurance exchanges: the SHOP Exchange (Small Business Health Options Program) and an individual exchange. For this purpose, a small employer is one that has between one and 100 employees. Starting in 2017, states also have the option to allow companies with more than 100 employees to purchase insurance from the SHOP Exchange. Starting in 2016, two or more states can join in a Health Care Choice Compact, offering at least two qualified health plans that are available in more than one state. The intention is that competition across state lines will be more vigorous and will result in lower premiums.

However, CMS announced on May 15, 2017, that most of the functions of the federally facilitated SHOP Exchange would end. Small employers could still use HealthCare.gov to get eligibility determinations about the small employer tax credit, but HealthCare.gov would not enroll employers. Instead, it would refer them to insurers, agents, and brokers that sell health plans. [Timothy Jost, *CMS Announces Plans to Effectively End the SHOP Exchange,* Health Affairs (May 15, 2017), available at healthaffairs.org; Michelle Hackman, *White House Closes a Health-Care Enrollment Option,* WSJ.com (May 15, 2017)]

At press time in 2017, when attempts were made to replace PPACA, there was a revival of interest in high-risk pools as a mechanism for making some degree of coverage available to people with a medical history requiring extensive care, and who would otherwise be shut out if insurers were no longer required to extend coverage to all applicants. Opponents of this proposal said that high-risk pools provide only limited coverage at prices that are too high for many people with serious health conditions to afford.

[M] Timeline

The original PPACA statute included a timetable for various activities. However, for reasons including political challenges and difficulties in setting up the computer system for enrollment, a number of delays and postponements were granted. Provisions taking effect in 2010 include:

- All individual and group policies must cover employees' adult children up to age 26;

- A temporary nationwide high-risk pool will be set up to cover people with pre-existing conditions; this pool will be replaced by the Exchanges in 2014;

- Lifetime maximums on coverage are forbidden, although, until 2014, annual maximums can be imposed, subject to limits set by HHS;

- EGHPs must provide coverage for preventive care, without imposing cost-sharing on plan beneficiaries: e.g., immunizations, preventive care for children, Pap smears, etc.;

- Insurers can only rescind coverage on the basis of fraud, not because the individual makes expensive claims;

- Health plans must report their loss ratios.

Provisions taking effect in 2011 include:

- If loss ratios are less than 85% (large group plans) or 80% (individual and small group plans), then the insurer must give rebates to consumers;

- HRAs and health FSAs can no longer cover over-the-counter drugs that are not prescribed by a doctor. HSAs and MSAs can still cover them, but not on a tax-free basis;

Provisions taking effect in 2012 include:

- New uniform rules for electronic funds transfers and health care payments take effect.

Provisions taking effect in 2013 include:

- The uniform rules on claims and eligibility verification take effect.

Provisions taking effect in 2014 include:

- The temporary high-risk pool and the temporary reinsurance program for employees over age 55 end; the American Health Benefit Exchanges go into operation;

- Employers can offer financial rewards to employees who participate in wellness programs;

- Persons whose income is below 133% of the federal poverty level are eligible for Medicaid (unless they live in a state that refused Medicaid expansion);

- Persons whose income does not exceed 400% of the federal poverty level are protected by a sliding scale of maximum out-of-pocket payments. An employee cannot receive the premium tax credit if the employer offered "affordable";

- Limits are imposed on waiting periods for coverage and deductibles for small-group health plans;

- Medicare tax rate increases to 2.35% for high-income taxpayers ($250,000 for joint returns, $200,000 for other returns). High-income taxpayers are also subject to a 3.8% assessment on their unearned income;

The key elements of the employer mandate for 2015 are the following:

- To avoid the shared responsibility penalty, minimum essential coverage must be offered to at least 70% of full-time employees (a special rule for 2015 only; after 2015, coverage must be offered to 95% of employees).

- Employees are considered "seasonal" employees only if their customary annual employment is six months or less.

- The final regulations include a list of factors for determining if a person is a variable-hour employee.

- The final regulations explain when a staffing firm's offer of coverage satisfies the client-employer's obligation to offer coverage. If a worker is not a common-law employee of the staffing firm, the offer of coverage is treated as made by the client-employer, but only if the fee charged to the client-employer is higher than the fee that would be charged if the employee did not enroll in health coverage.

[T.D. 9655, *Shared Responsibility for Employers Regarding Health Coverage*, 79 Fed. Reg. 8544 (Feb. 12, 2014), also available at 2014-9 I.R.B. 541]

Many provisions were delayed, such as the excise tax on "Cadillac plans" (plans with especially high costs), which was supposed to take effect in 2018 but was postponed until 2020.

[N] The Future of PPACA

The PPACA is an extremely controversial statute and its legality became the subject of many challenges. Its future became dubious after President Trump's election; the Republican-controlled Congress considered PPACA repeal an important political objective. When the 2018 edition of this book went to press in August 2017, the House of Representatives narrowly passed the American Health Care Act. Similar (but not identical) legislation, the Better Care Reconciliation Act, was introduced in the Senate, but was not passed before Congress recessed for the summer.

In mid-2012, the Supreme Court decided a case about the legality of the "individual mandate" (i.e., the requirement that individuals either maintain health insurance coverage—under an EGHP or by individual purchase—or pay a monetary penalty). The Supreme Court, although holding that the individual mandate violated the Commerce Clause, nevertheless upheld most of PPACA because it found the mandate to be a valid tax. One PPACA provision, the one imposing financial penalties on states that reject Medicaid expansion was found invalid. [*National Fed'n of Indep. Bus. v. Sebelius*, consolidated with *Dep't of HHS v. Florida*, and *Florida v. Dep't of HHS*, 132. S. Ct. 2566 (2012).]

King v. Burwell [No. 14-114 (U.S. June 25, 2015)] holds that people who buy insurance on an exchange can receive federal subsidies whether their state established an exchange, or they use the federal exchange that covers the states that do not have their own exchanges.

Shortly after his inauguration, President Trump issued an Executive Order (EO) directing federal agencies to use their maximum authority and discretion to waive, defer, grant exemptions from, or delay implementation of any PPACA provision that imposes a tax, fee, penalty, or regulatory burden on people, health insurers, purchasers of health insurance, or manufacturers of health care products. Sheryl Simmons of Maestro Health said that the EO does not rescind any existing regulations, it only applies to fiscal burdens. [Rebecca Moore, *ACA Executive Order Does Not Stop Plan Sponsor Actions*, plansponsor.com (Feb. 7, 2017)]

The IRS issued guidance in August 2017, making it clear that the employer and individual mandates continue to apply, and penalties will be assessed for non-compliance. The IRS also released draft forms for PPACA reporting on July 28, 2017. [IRS Office of Chief Counsel Information Letters 2017-0010, 2017-0017 (Apr. 14, 2017), available at <https://www.irs.gov/pub/irs-wd/17-0010> and <https://www.irs.gov/pub/irs-wd/17-0013.pdf>; see Winstead PC, *IRS Confirms ACA Tax Assessable Payments Still in Effect* (July 19, 2017) (benefitslink .com); Burnhambenefits.com, *Pay or Play Mandates, Employer Reporting, and Health Insurance Fee* (Aug. 16, 2017) (benefitslink.com)]

[O]   Implementing Regulations

In late 2015, the Treasury, DOL, and HHS published joint final regulations about many PPACA topics, such as preserving grandfathered status, the ban on pre-existing condition limitations and dollar limits, and dependent child coverage. The regulations make few changes from previous proposed and interim final regulations. The joint final regulations are generally effective for plan years beginning on or after January 1, 2017. [80 Fed. Reg. 72192 (Nov. 18, 2015)]

A health insurance company's loss ratio is the percentage of the premiums that it collects that it distributes in the form of benefits. The higher the loss ratio, the more of the premium is used to provide health care; the lower the ratio, the more of the premium that goes toward the insurer's operating costs and profits.

Rebates are required if the Medical Loss Ratio (MLR) falls below 85% (large group) or 80% (small group). Rebates can take the form of a premium credit, a check for a lump sum, or a lump-sum reimbursement to the account the enrollee used to pay the premium. A civil monetary penalty (CMP) of $100/day can be imposed for each individual affected by the violation of the reporting and rebate requirements. [75 Fed. Reg. 74864 (Dec. 1, 2010)]

CHAPTER 19

HEALTH INSURANCE CONTINUATION AND PORTABILITY (COBRA AND HIPAA)

§ 19.01   INTRODUCTION

The two dominant mechanisms for providing health insurance coverage in our society are employee group health plans (EGHPs) and the Medicare system for senior citizens and the disabled. However, there are many instances in which a person has lost coverage under one EGHP and is not (or is not yet) covered by another one, and is not eligible for Medicare. Individual health coverage is expensive—and furthermore, the ex-employee or a member of his or her family might have a medical condition that makes insurance harder to obtain or raises its cost even higher.

Two federal statutes, the Comprehensive Omnibus Budget Reconciliation Act (COBRA) and the Health Insurance Portability and Accessibility Act (HIPAA) work together to make the transition between EGHPs, or from EGHP coverage to individual health coverage, at least somewhat smoother. Both statutes impose responsibilities on the employer, so the health plan administrator must be aware of these duties. The health care reform act, the Patient Protection and Affordable Care Act (PPACA) (see § 18.19) creates a new paradigm under which, for the first time, employers have a duty to provide health insurance, and individuals have a duty to purchase health insurance.

As part of the ongoing attempt to stimulate the economy, Congress passed the ARRA, American Recovery & Reinvestment Act of 2009 [Pub. L. No. 111-5, Title III] early in 2009, providing subsidies for COBRA premiums. See § 19.02[F]. This was a temporary program that expired in 2010.

Not strictly in the COBRA context, but dealing with issues of continued coverage, the Children's Health Insurance Program Reauthorization Act of 2009 (CHIPRA; Pub. L. No. 111-3, signed February 4, 2009) requires employers to amend their plans to permit special enrollment of employees and dependents if they lose their Medicaid or SCHIP coverage—or if they become eligible under Medicaid or SCHIP for the state to assist them with paying EGHP premiums and other financial responsibilities. [CHIPRA, Pub. L. No. 111-3]

§ 19.02   COBRA CONTINUATION COVERAGE

Continuation coverage is the right of a "qualified beneficiary" (i.e., a former employee or his or her spouse and dependents) to maintain coverage under the employer's group health plan after a "COBRA event." Some of the important legal questions include which employers are subject to COBRA; which employees, ex-employees, and their family members are permitted to make a COBRA election; and what the employer's responsibilities are to furnish notice of COBRA rights.

[A]   Qualifying Events

A COBRA event is either personal or work-related and poses a threat to coverage under the ordinary circumstances:

- The employee is terminated or has hours reduced (unless termination is for gross misconduct);

- The employee divorces or becomes legally separated;

- The employee's dependent child ceases to be covered by the plan (usually because of "aging out");

- The employee's employer files for bankruptcy protection;

- The employee becomes Medicare-eligible (which entitles the employee's spouse to COBRA coverage);

- The employee dies (obviously, this is only a COBRA event for the survivors).

People who remain at work past 65 may be Medicare eligible at the time that they apply for COBRA coverage. COBRA is generally secondary to Medicare Parts A and B; Medicare covers 80% of cost, the COBRA policy pays 20%. Retirees who have not signed up for Medicare would have to pay 80% of the costs out of pocket. Therefore, an active employee's becoming entitled to Medicare is usually not a COBRA qualifying event.

There is a Medicare Special Enrollment Period (SEP) that lasts eight months after retirement—but people who fail to enroll during the SEP must wait until the next open enrollment period to sign up and their premium will be 10% higher (for late enrollment) for the rest of their lives. Because COBRA coverage lasts at least 18 months, there is a risk that some people will wait too long to enroll in Medicare. If the COBRA plan did not constitute Part D creditable coverage, they will also pay a penalty of 1% of the Part D premium for every month without creditable coverage.

If an EGHP terminates or reduces coverage because of Medicare eligibility, causing a loss of coverage for a retiree's spouse and dependents, the family members have a qualifying event entitling them to elect up to 36 months of continuation coverage from the date of Medicare entitlement. [Katy Votava, *COBRA Considerations When Medicare-Eligible*, Crain Investment News (Apr. 26, 2015) (benefitslink.com); Jennifer Carsen, *How COBRA Intersects with Medicare and Retiree Health Plans*, HR Daily Advisor (Dec. 27, 2016) (benefitslink.com)]

Although COBRA does not define "gross misconduct," the standard is probably the same as "willful misconduct"—substantial and willful disregard of the employer's best interests. The District Court for the District of Idaho ruled in mid-2014 that it was gross misconduct for a grocery store supervisor to tell a co-worker to take a stale cake from the "sales cart." The supervisor said that she was really fired for sex discrimination and everyone was allowed to take stale goods. The district court said that she provided no evidence of discrimination and termination for stealing is always misconduct, no matter how trivial the value of the stolen items, because it shows willful and intentional disregard for the employer's interests. [*Mayes v. WinCo Holdings*, No. 4:12-cv-00307-EJL-CWD (D. Idaho Apr. 23, 2014)] On appeal, the Ninth Circuit held that Mayes' termination might have been pretextual; she introduced evidence that taking "stales" was allowed, and that the real motivation was replacing her with a man as head of the freight crew. The Ninth Circuit reversed summary judgment for the employer on both the Title VII and COBRA counts; if her termination for misconduct was pretextual, then she could not be denied COBRA coverage on grounds of gross misconduct. [*Mayes v. WinCo, Holdings, Inc.*, 846 F.3d 1274 (9th Cir. 2017); see Manatt Phelps & Phillips LLP, *Termination for Cake Theft May Have Been Pretext, Ninth Circuit Rules* (Feb. 27, 2017), available at Lexology.com]

Two of the most common COBRA events are divorce or legal separation. As long as one spouse notifies the plan or the COBRA administrator within 60 days of the event, the plan will have obligations. For example, if the plan does not terminate spousal coverage based on legal separation, the non-employee spouse will remain covered, and there will be no need for COBRA. If the employee drops the non-employee spouse from coverage during the annual open enrollment period, the plan has no COBRA obligations because the loss of coverage is caused by the employee's election, which not a COBRA qualifying event. The COBRA regulations (although not the statute) include an "anticipation of divorce" rule: the plan must make COBRA coverage available to the non-participant spouse, even if he or she was not enrolled in the plan at the time of the divorce, if the participant eliminated coverage in anticipation of the divorce. The IRS has not issued regulations on this point, and there is no DOL model COBRA notice for it. The firm of Foley & Lardner recommends discussing this rule in the SPD and/or the COBRA election materials. If the plan administrator is uncertain why a spouse has been dropped, the administrator should ask the participant or the spouse. The 36-month COBRA period begins with the date of the divorce, not the date of termination of coverage, so claims do not have to be covered between the date coverage was dropped and the date of divorce or legal separation. [Foley & Lardner LLP, *"We Have To Offer COBRA, When?" The "In Anticipation Of Divorce" Rule* (Feb. 14, 2014) (benefitslink.com)]

Whenever a "qualifying event" occurs, anyone who performs services for the employer and is covered by the EGHP must be given COBRA rights—including partners, self-employed people who are allowed to participate in the plan, and eligible independent contractors.

Voluntary plans are used to supplement traditional health insurance plans by providing insurance coverage for such things as life, vision, disability, or dental. Voluntary plans are exempt from the Employment Retirement Income Security

Act (ERISA) requirement (e.g., having a written plan document; satisfying fiduciary duty rules) and are also exempt from COBRA. The ERISA safe harbor protects plans that are fully paid for by the employees and the employer's involvement is minimal, where the employer does not endorse plans or include COBRA language in the plan. Employee-pay-all programs are exempt from COBRA. However, COBRA requirements may be triggered if a voluntary plan provides medical care, or if individual policies fail the safe harbor and are deemed to be group medical plans. [Ascende.com, *When Is a Voluntary Plan Truly a Voluntary Benefit Plan?* (Mar. 4, 2016) (benefitslink.com)]

The District Court for the District of Kansas ruled that a long-term disability plan does not have to give COBRA notices; although it is a welfare benefit plan, it is not a "group health plan," because a group health plan provides medical care rather than benefits for persons who are unable to work. [*Ernisse v. L.L. & G., Inc.*, Case No. 07-2579-JAR, 2008 WL 4499974 (D. Kan. Sept. 29, 2008)]

When a person makes a COBRA election, health insurance coverage continues under the EGHP—but the employee, not the employer, pays the premium. (The employer can also agree to subsidize the COBRA premium, e.g., as an early retirement incentive.) The employer can impose an administrative charge of up to 2% of the premium, but no other fees or charges. The COBRA premium is set once a year, in advance.

In the mergers and acquisitions context, an employee is generally entitled to continuation coverage if there is a qualifying event. In a stock sale, there is a qualifying event if the employee loses his job. In an asset sale, there is a qualifying event if the employee loses his job or loses coverage under the selling company's EGHP and is not employed by the buyer acting as a successor employer after the closing of the deal. Merger or acquisition partners should consider how responsibility will be allocated if there is a qualifying event. If the seller maintains an EGHP post-transaction, its EGHP has to make COBRA coverage available. If not, the buyer might be a successor employer required to provide continuation coverage. Nevertheless, even if responsibility is allocated by contract, the statutorily responsible party will remain responsible, so it is sensible to include indemnification provisions in the contract. [Jefferson A. Holt, *An Oldie but a Goodie: Liability for COBRA Continuation Coverage in M&A Transactions*, Burr & Forman LLP (Oct. 18, 2016), available at Lexology.com]

During a Reduction in Force (RIF) or severance, the employer often wants to provide subsidized health coverage—but this can create COBRA problems. For example, imagine one severance program that provides six months of company-paid health premiums; the second program offers three months of "garden leave" before termination, with the employer paying health insurance premiums during the leave. COBRA entitlement dates from the qualifying event, even if coverage is not lost until later. However, many plans consider a terminating employee eligible for coverage until the end of the month of termination, with COBRA starting on the first day of the next month. In this situation, the employee might claim to be entitled to six months of paid premiums. A reduction in hours is only a qualifying event if it causes loss of coverage. The employer could specify that coverage ends on the last day worked and offer to subsidize the cost if the employee elects COBRA coverage. Or, the plan could have the COBRA period run concurrently with extended subsidized coverage—in which case, COBRA notice should be given of the qualifying event. An employer that provides more coverage than the minimum COBRA requirement may need consent of its insurer. [Michael Lane, *Did You Consider the COBRA Implications of Your Severance Arrangement?*, Thompson Coburn LLP (Nov. 2, 2016), available at Lexology.com]

There are three basic methods of structuring continuing coverage in a severance package. The "choice method" gives a choice between COBRA coverage and an alternative set out in the severance package; consecutive coverage offers a certain number of months of coverage as if the ex-employee were still active, followed by 18 months of COBRA coverage; or concurrent coverage (e.g., 12 months of coverage at the active rate, followed by six months of COBRA coverage, for a total of 18 months of continuation coverage). The plan and paperwork for the severance must make it clear how the coverage is structured.

See Notice 2015-87. COBRA continuation coverage does not have to be offered for a health FSA unless, as of the date of qualifying event, the qualified beneficiary is entitled to receive more during the rest of the plan year than the amount the health FSA can require as payment for continuation coverage for the balance of the year. Notice 2015-87 explains when COBRA has to be offered for health FSAs that allow the $500 carryover until the following year. The carryover amount is included in determining the amount of the benefit for the remainder of the plan year. But unused amounts carried over from earlier years are not included in calculating the COBRA premium. [Notice 2015-87, 2015-52 I.R.B. 889]

[B] Covered Businesses

Businesses are subject to COBRA if they have 20 or more employees on a typical workday, and if they maintain a group health plan (either insured or self-insured). Most of the states (all except Alabama, Alaska, Arizona, Hawaii, Idaho, Indiana, Michigan, Montana, Virginia, and Washington) have COBRA expansion statutes that require companies with fewer than 20 employees to provide the equivalent of the federal COBRA notice and continuation coverage rights.

The length of the required period of continuation coverage ranges from three months (Georgia) to 36 months (in California, Minnesota, Nevada, New Hampshire, North Dakota, South Dakota, and Texas). [Kaiser Family Foundation, *Expanded COBRA Continuation Coverage for Small Firm Employees, 2013*, see <http://kff.org/private-insurance/state-indicator/expanded-cobra-continuation-coverage-for-small-firm-employees/> (last accessed Feb. 25, 2017)]

The Sixth Circuit held, in mid-2007, that in rare cases it will be possible for an employer with fewer than 20 employees to be sued under COBRA—for example, if the employer's statements or behavior would lead a reasonable plaintiff to believe that he or she had COBRA coverage. But the actual plaintiff lost her case. She alleged that she overheard corporate managers talking about providing benefits to another employee; but even if this conversation did take place, no one said anything about COBRA coverage for the plaintiff. [*Thomas v. Miller*, 489 F.3d 293 (6th Cir. 2007)]

Self-insured plans are subject to COBRA, too. The "premium" for them is a reasonable estimate, using reasonable actuarial assumptions, of the cost of providing health coverage for employees similarly situated to the qualified beneficiary.

Continuation coverage must be the same as active employees receive, although continuation coverage can change as the underlying plan changes. If the employer terminates or reduces coverage in an EGHP, qualified beneficiaries must be allowed to elect coverage under whatever plan the employer continues to maintain for similarly situated active employees. The employer cannot condition continuation coverage on submission of evidence of insurability. [See I.R.C. § 4980B(f)(2)(D)]

[C] Family Rights

The employee's spouse and children may also have independent rights to maintain coverage: for instance, after a divorce, when the former employee dies, or when the former employee becomes eligible for Medicare. (In this situation, the former employee no longer has COBRA rights—but, because Medicare does not cover spouses or dependents, these family members have COBRA rights.)

The one-time employee can exercise the COBRA election on behalf of his or her spouse and children, and the spouse can exercise the election on behalf of the children. However, only plan participants, not their beneficiaries, are entitled to receive penalties if the plan administrator fails to provide COBRA notice. [*Wright v. Hanna Steel Corp.*, 270 F.3d 1336 (11th Cir. 2001)]

As a result of the Supreme Court's June, 2013 decision striking down part of the federal Defense of Marriage Act (DOMA; see § 18.06), same-sex married couples are entitled to spousal coverage under COBRA. Since mid-2015, the Supreme Court has ruled that all states must recognize same-sex marriage, reaffirming the principle that same-sex spouses have COBRA rights.

[D] Duration of Coverage

COBRA specifies minimum obligations that employers must meet; they always have discretion to provide additional coverage. The basic duration of COBRA continuation coverage for ex-employees is 18 months, starting with the qualifying event. In some instances, ARRA will increase the duration of coverage (see § 19.02[F]). However, if the ex-employee satisfies the Social Security

Administration definition of total disability (basically, is incapable of substantial gainful activity), the employee and family members are entitled to 29 months of continuation coverage, not 18. But for the 11 months after the end of the normal 18-month term, the employer can lawfully charge the employee 150% of the premium, not just the normal 102%.

Qualified beneficiaries can get 29 months of continuation coverage with respect to the same qualifying event if they are qualified with respect to a termination of employment or a reduction in hours; they became disabled within the first 60 days of COBRA continuation coverage; and they give the plan administrator a copy of the determination of disability within 60 days of the date it was issued and also within the initial 18-month COBRA period.

If the qualifying event is the ex-employee's becoming eligible for Medicare, his or her qualified beneficiaries are entitled to 36 months of continuation coverage. See Rev. Rul. 2004-22, 2004-10 I.R.B. 553, providing that Medicare entitlement is not a second qualifying event for a beneficiary who would not have lost coverage under the plan as a result of Medicare entitlement. If the plan does not terminate coverage for the employee's spouse, the spouse is entitled to only 18 months of continuation coverage because there has not been a second qualifying event.

However, COBRA entitlement ends if the EGHP for active employees is terminated without being replaced (i.e., there is no longer a plan whose coverage can be continued); the qualified beneficiary obtains coverage under another EGHP; the qualified beneficiary fails to pay the COBRA premium; or the employee becomes eligible for Medicare. (Family members of a Medicare-eligible person still have COBRA rights.)

[E] COBRA Regulations

The IRS published important Proposed Regulations at 63 Fed. Reg. 708 (Jan. 7, 1998), adopted as 26 C.F.R. § 54.4980B-1 to conform COBRA to HIPAA (see below), the Small Business Job Protection Act [Pub. L. No. 104-188], and various other statutes. As a result of these changes, qualified beneficiaries can get 29 months (rather than the basic 18 months) of COBRA coverage with respect to the same qualifying event if:

- They are all qualified with respect to a termination of employment or a reduction in hours;

- They became disabled (as defined by the Social Security Administration) within the first 60 days of COBRA continuation coverage;

- They gave the plan administrator a copy of the determination of disability within the initial 18-month COBRA period and also within 60 days of the date the determination was issued.

During the 11-month extension, the employer can charge a premium that is 150% of the applicable premium, whereas the employer is limited to charging 102% of the premium during the 18-month basic COBRA period. Charging 150% is not considered premium discrimination on the basis of health status, so I.R.C. § 9802(b) is not violated. If there is a second qualifying event during a disability extension, then COBRA coverage can last for 36 months, with the 150% premium charged until the end of the 36-month period.

HIPAA entitles children born to, or adopted by, covered employees during a period of COBRA coverage to be covered by COBRA. The child's maximum coverage period runs from the date of the employee's qualifying event, and not from the child's birth or adoption. The effect is that the child's COBRA coverage ends at the same time as the coverage of other family members.

[F] TAAP and ARRA Subsidy Programs

Acknowledging that the high cost of COBRA premiums can be burdensome on people who have lost their jobs, Congress has enacted two subsidy programs to reduce these costs.

The earlier program, the Trade Act of 2002 [Pub. L. No. 107-210] enacted a tax credit under Code § 35: workers who were displaced by factors such as overseas business or imports could qualify for a tax credit equal to 65% of the COBRA premium. The credit was refundable (i.e., persons with no tax liability could receive a refund). The credit could be submitted to the health plan, so the qualifying individuals would have to pay only 35% of the COBRA premium. The Trade Act credit applied only to persons not covered by other government or private insurance programs; aged 55–64 and receiving guarantee payments from the PBGC; or unemployed and entitled to Trade Adjustment Assistance benefits under the Trade Act. [Jerry Geisal, *Congress Extends Health Premium Subsidies*, work force.com (Oct. 1, 2008) (benefitslink.com)]

The Trade Adjustment Assistance Program (TAAP) was expanded in May 2009. Benefits include unemployment benefits, retraining, and 80% of the cost of medical insurance for workers who lost their jobs because of their employer's overseas move or foreign competition.

The economic stimulus plan enhanced TAAP so that displaced workers could receive as much as 156 weeks of training and up to 156 weeks of cash payments. The tax credit for health insurance premiums rises from 65% to 80%. Workers over age 50 could get wage subsidies for up to two years. Unemployment benefits were extended. [Jerry Geisel, *Obama Signs Extension of Health Insurance Tax Credit*, Business Insurance (Dec. 30, 2010) (benefitslink.com)] Congress did not take further action, so the credit reverted to the 65% level on February 13, 2011. [Jerry Geisel, *Health Insurance Subsidy Reverts to 65%*, Business Insurance (Feb. 22, 2011) (benefitslink.com)]

Pub. L. No. 112-40, the Trade Adjustment Assistance Extension Act of 2011 (Oct. 21, 2011), reauthorized the TAAP until December 31, 2013. Coverage for TAA/ATAA eligible individuals and people who receive pensions from the PBGC is extended until the later of their maximum COBRA period or January 1, 2014. However, it does not appear that terminated COBRA coverage is revived by this legislation.

For months beginning after February 12, 2011, this statute also increases the Health Coverage Tax Credit (HCTC); (see Code § 35) to 72.5% of the health insurance premiums of eligible individuals and their families. (The previous level was 65%, although for months before February 13, 2011, it was 80%). In general, the HCTC is available to persons eligible under TAA or the Alternative Trade Adjustment Assistance Program (ATAAP), and to retirees who receive their pensions from the PBGC and who have lost employer coverage. [See Allison Ullman, Seth Perretta, and Joel Wood, *Recently Enacted Trade Adjustment Assistance Extension Act of 2011 Affects Health Coverage Tax Credit and COBRA Continuation Coverage*, Crowell & Moring LLP (Nov. 10, 2011) (benefitslink .com)]

The HCTC expired January 1, 2014, but was restored by the Trade Preferences Extension Act of 2015, for all eligibility coverage months occurring before January 1, 2020. [Trade Preferences Extension Act of 2015, Pub. L. No. 114-27]

Pub. L. No. 111-5, the American Recovery and Reinvestment Act of 2009 (ARRA), created a temporary program to provide up to nine months of federally funded COBRA subsidies (later extended to 15 months by the Department of Defense Appropriations Act of 2010, Pub. L. No. 111-118). Employers advanced 65% of the COBRA premium and later claimed a payroll tax credit; the employees paid the other 35%. After two extensions, under the Temporary Extension Act of 2010 (TEA), Pub. L. No. 111-144 and the Continuing Extension Act of 2010, Pub. L. No. 111-157, the program expired in 2010.

§ 19.03   COBRA AND THE FMLA

Taking the Family and Medical Leave Act (FMLA) leave [see Chapter 38] is not in and of itself a COBRA-qualifying event. But if an employee who was covered by the EGHP before or during the FMLA leave fails to return to work after the FMLA leave, there is a qualifying event for this person (and any dependent at risk of losing health coverage) as of the last day of the FMLA leave. The employer is not allowed to make the ex-employee reimburse the employer for health premiums paid during the leave.

However, there is no qualifying event if, while the employee is on leave, the employer eliminates EGHP coverage for the entire group of workers the person on leave belonged to. The rationale is that the worker would have lost health coverage even if he or she had not taken leave.

The qualifying event for an employee who does not return to work occurs on the last day of the FMLA leave, and the regular COBRA notice must be given. The qualifying event occurs even if the employee had an obligation to pay health insurance premiums during the leave but failed to do so. State laws that require a longer leave than the 12-week FMLA period are disregarded in determining whether a qualifying event has occurred.

§ 19.04 COBRA NOTICE

[A] Generally

One of the most important tasks in COBRA administration is timely issuance of the proper notices, as provided by I.R.C. § 4980B(f)(6)(A) and ERISA § 606. There are three types of COBRA notice: one given to employees as soon as they become eligible for participation in the health plan (informing them of COBRA rights they might have in the future), the one given to a qualified beneficiary in connection with a COBRA event, and the notice of rights under ARRA. The employer has an obligation to notify the plan administrator when employment-related qualifying events occur, such as when an employee is terminated or laid off, or when the company files in Chapter 11 for bankruptcy protection. The responsibility for reporting personal qualifying events, such as divorce or separation, rests on the qualified beneficiary.

There are three timing requirements. The employee must give notice to the plan that a qualifying event has occurred within 60 days of the event. At that point, the employer has 30 days to notify the plan administrator that there has been a qualifying event for which COBRA notice must be provided; and the plan administrator has a further 14 days to actually issue the notice.

A COBRA notice should explain:

- Who can be a qualified beneficiary;
- What events trigger the right to continuation coverage;
- How and when to elect coverage;
- The right to reject the coverage (e.g., for financial reasons);
- Rights of the other qualified beneficiaries if one qualified beneficiary waives the election;
- Obligation to pay the premiums on time;
- How long the coverage will last;
- Events that will allow the employer to terminate continuation coverage;
- If the health plan satisfies PPACA's minimum coverage and affordability standards;

- How to purchase coverage on a health insurance Exchange;
- Eligibility criteria for premium tax credits under PPACA.

Notice must be furnished to covered employees and covered spouses on the earlier of two dates: 90 days from the first date of coverage (or the date on which the plan first becomes subject to COBRA, if that happens later), or the date on which the plan administrator has to provide a COBRA election notice.

The election notice must be furnished within 44 days of the qualifying event—or the date the qualified beneficiary ceases to be covered under the plan, if the plan's terms date the start of COBRA coverage from the loss of plan coverage.

Plans must provide notice when coverage is unavailable. The notice of unavailability must be given within 14 days of receiving notice of a qualifying event when the plan denies coverage—whether or not the notice was given in proper form. Termination notices must be given as soon as practicable after the plan administrator determines that continuation coverage is ending.

While PPACA is still in existence, an employee who loses health coverage because of termination can either make a COBRA election or buy coverage in a PPACA Marketplace. COBRA coverage can be more expensive than Marketplace coverage. Because the COBRA notice is often sent weeks post-termination, the employee might have medical needs in the interim. Marketplace coverage is prospective, and can only be purchased during the annual open enrollment period or within 60 days of a qualifying life event such as loss of coverage or change in premium tax credit eligibility. But dropping coverage is not a qualifying event, so an employee who makes a COBRA election to get retroactive coverage but wants to drop it might have to wait until the next open enrollment period to sign up. The employee might also be penalized for going without coverage. Employers often agree to make pre-tax payments of a certain number of months of COBRA premiums. Payment of premiums for a highly compensated employee might be discriminatory under Code § 105(h), with the result that a participant in a self-insured plan could be taxed on the benefits. If it is an insured plan, the employer might encounter PPACA penalties. The best practice is to give the employee a cash payment for the COBRA premium, which is not discriminatory: § 105(h) does not apply to after-tax payments of premiums. This permits the employee to decide whether to opt for COBRA or Marketplace coverage—alternatives that should be discussed in the COBRA notice. [Richard J. Birmingham, *What Everyone Needs to Know About the Coordination of Severance Benefits, COBRA, and the ACA*, Davis Wright & Tremaine (June 9, 2014) (benefitslink.com)]

A recurring issue is what must be done to demonstrate an adequate attempt to furnish notice.

Mailing to the employee's last known address is generally considered sufficient, at least if the Post Office does not return the notice. Even if the employee does not in fact receive the notice, the employer is not liable if a proper attempt to notify was made:

- A wrongful termination suit included a count of not providing a COBRA election notice. The plaintiff alleged that his ex-employer knowingly gave the wrong address to the TPA. The employee said that shortly after being terminated he submitted a change of address form and he had also given the employer the new address four years earlier, submitting a W-4 and mailings from the health insurer giving the new address. The employer told the TPA to send the notice to his old address. The court said that it is acceptable to send notice by first-class mail to employee's last known address—but the case went to trial, because there was a dispute as to whether the employer knowingly sent the notice to the wrong address. [*Newton v. Prator*, Civil Action No. 14-3116, 2016 WL 698170 (W.D. La. Feb. 18, 2016); see EBIA Weekly, *Former Employee Challenges Provision of COBRA Notice to Last-Known Address* (Mar. 10, 2016) (benefitslink.com)]

- The Eighth Circuit ruled against a former employee who said that he was not given COBRA notice. The employer created a presumption of receipt of the notice by submitting its log of notices, date-stamped by the Postal Service. The employer stated that whenever its TPA was notified of a COBRA qualifying event, it processed, printed, and mailed the election notice to the beneficiary, then showed the log to a USPS clerk who verified that the mailed items corresponded to the log entries. The employee's testimony that he did not receive the notice could not overcome the presumption of receipt. [*Hearst v. Progressive Foam Techs., Inc.*, 641 F.3d 276 (8th Cir. 2011)]

- An ex-employee charged her former employer, in its role as plan administrator, with COBRA notice failure. She said that she never received the notice because it used an unofficial abbreviation for the town where she lived. The District Court for the Southern District of New York ruled that the employer made a good-faith effort to comply. The notice had the correct address and zip code and the employee admitted receiving at least 18 other pieces of mail from the employer that were addressed in the same way. [*Vangas v. Montefiore Med. Ctr.*, No. 11 civ 6722, 2014 WL 5786720 (S.D.N.Y. Nov. 5, 2014)]

Department of Labor Advisory Opinion 99-14A allows the health plan to satisfy the notice requirement by sending a single notice to multiple beneficiaries living at the same address: e.g., one first-class letter covering the employee, spouse, and dependent children. But there must either be a separate election notice in the mailing for each qualified beneficiary, or an explanation of their independent rights to elect coverage. [See <http://www.dol.gov/ebsa/regs/AOs/ao1999-

14a.html> but an administrator who is on notice of the employee's divorce cannot treat notice to the employee as notice to his or her ex-spouse: *Phillips v. Saratoga Harness Racing Inc.*, 233 F. Supp. 2d 361 (N.D.N.Y. 2002).]

The Fifth Circuit ruled that an employer can have a COBRA election period of any length, as long as the period is at least 60 days. Participants in a plan that failed to set an election deadline could therefore make a COBRA election at any time during the 18 months following the qualifying event. [*Lifecare Hosps. Inc. v. Health Plus of La. Inc.*, 418 F.3d 436 (5th Cir. 2005)]

If an ex-employee needs only a certain number of months of COBRA coverage (usually the waiting period for eligibility in a new plan), COBRA does not permit the ex-employer's plan to require the ex-employee to pay for a full 18 months of retroactive coverage. [*Popovits v. Circuit City Stores Inc.*, 185 F.3d 726 (7th Cir. 1999)]

The first premium payment is not due until 45 days after the election. Qualified beneficiaries get an automatic grace period of at least 30 days, during which coverage cannot be terminated for nonpayment of premiums—even if the underlying EGHP has a shorter grace period. But if the plan provides a longer grace period, the employee must be permitted to take advantage of it.

[B] Penalties for Notice Failure

The Internal Revenue Code and ERISA § 502(g) impose a penalty of $110 per day per beneficiary for noncompliance, subject to a maximum of $220 per family per day. There is also a limit of the smaller of $500,000 or 10% of the amount the employer paid (or incurred obligations for) its EGHPs in the preceding year. Furthermore, a health plan that does not conform to COBRA does not generate I.R.C. § 162 "ordinary and necessary business expenses." Therefore, the employer is denied a deduction for health plan costs. Although many ERISA penalties were increased in 2016, and again in early 2017, this penalty does not seem to have been affected.

The penalty is imposed on the employer. It can also be imposed on the individuals responsible for administering the plan or providing benefits under it, if those individuals have contractual responsibility for running the plan. A third-party administrator (TPA) would fall into this category unless factors beyond the administrator's control prevented the notice from being given.

There is a cap of $2 million for all plans administered, for an administrator who fails to satisfy all the COBRA requirements, but who is not guilty of willful neglect and who did have reasonable support for his or her decisions.

The penalty can be reduced or waived if no one had reason to know that the appropriate notices were not given, or if the failure to notify was corrected within 30 days after a responsible person became aware of the failure.

The Eighth Circuit upheld summary judgment for the employer in a suit for statutory damages brought by an employee who said she was not notified of

COBRA rights. Awarding statutory damages is discretionary and the district court found that the employee was not harmed: the employer acted in good faith, and the unreimbursed medical bills were lower than the premiums the plaintiff would have paid. [*Cole v. Trinity Health Corp.*, 774 F.3d 423 (8th Cir. 2014)]

In addition to the statutory penalties, any person or organization can be sued under ERISA Title I by someone who lost coverage because of the defendant's actions or inaction.

In early 2015, a $1 million settlement was approved—among the largest, if not the largest average per-person recovery in any COBRA class action. The employer allegedly failed to distribute timely COBRA notices and notices about PPACA subsidies. About 70 members of the class received more than $5,000 each (a total of $375,000); the class representatives received a $12,000 "service award," and attorneys' and costs of $625,000 were awarded. [*Slipchenko v. Brunel Energy, Inc.*, No. 4:11-cv-10465, 2015 WL 338358 (S.D. Tex. Jan. 23, 2015)]

IRS Form 8928 must be filed to self-report any failure to satisfy the Code § 4980B requirements to provide COBRA continuation coverage. The form must be filed by any employer, group health plan, plan administrator, or plan sponsor that is subject to the excise tax for failure to provide continuation coverage. Form 8928 is due by the due date for the responsible party's federal income tax return. Interest is charged on taxes not paid by the due date (even if the responsible party obtained an extension of time to file by using Form 7004), and there are also penalties for late filing of returns and late payment of the tax. [Form 8928, <http://www.irs.gov/pub/irs-pdf/f8928.pdf> (revised May 2016) (last accessed Feb. 26, 2017)]

§ 19.05 HEALTH INSURANCE PORTABILITY

[A] Coverage

An important focus of the PPACA is to permit previously uninsured individuals, or individuals who once had insurance coverage but had to drop it, to resume their insured status. The PPACA also restricts the use of pre-existing condition exclusions (PCEs): denials or limitations of coverage based on the applicant's or insured person's health status. However, an earlier statute already tackled some of the same concerns, and may play a particularly important role if PPACA is repealed; at press time in 2017, it did not appear that congressional Republicans intended to repeal the Health Insurance Portability and Accountability Act (HIPAA).

The Health Insurance Portability and Accountability Act of 1996 [I.R.C. Chapter 100, §§ 9801–9806], also known as the Kennedy-Kassebaum Act, copes with the situation in which a person leaves employment with one employer, gets another job, and experiences health care bills before he or she is covered by the new employer's plan, or where the new plan might exclude coverage of the ailment as a pre-existing condition.

For plan years beginning after June 30, 1997, the HIPAA "creditable coverage" requirement in effect allows coverage to carry over from one plan to the other, as long as employees use COBRA (or other means) to make sure that there is never a gap of 63 days or more in coverage.

Although plans can control costs by imposing pre-existing condition limitations, the scope of the limitation is restricted. Under HIPAA, the most stringent definition of "pre-existing condition" that a plan can apply is a mental or physical condition for which medical advice, diagnosis, care, or treatment was sought during the six-month period before the enrollment date. In general, the maximum duration for a pre-existing condition limitation is 12 months from the enrollment date for the current health plan. The enrollment date is the earlier of the first day of the waiting period for enrollment or the date of actual enrollment. Late enrollees (who fail to enroll in the plan during the open enrollment period, or the first period of eligibility) can be subject to an 18-month rather than a 12-month pre-existing condition limitation.

The Genetic Information Nondiscrimination Act (GINA, Pub. L. No. 110-233) requires genetic testing information to be kept separate from other medical data.

"Creditable coverage" means coverage from another EGHP, from individual health insurance, from Medicare Part A or B, or from Medicaid. Health plan coverage ceases to be creditable, and therefore is not portable to a new plan, if there is a break of 63 days or more during which the employee is completely without health insurance. The so-called affiliation period (the waiting period after a new employee enrolls in a new health plan) is not considered a period of being uninsured.

The mental health parity requirement applies to HIPAA.

[B] Nondiscrimination Requirements

HIPAA forbids discrimination in benefits in health plans. (In this context, discrimination is closer to the Title VII sense than the pension plan sense of not favoring highly compensated employees.) Under HIPAA, it is unlawful for a plan to base its rules for eligibility or continued eligibility, or its definition of the waiting period, on an employee's or dependent's:

- Health status;
- Physical or mental health condition;
- Claims experience;
- Past receipt of health care;
- Medical history;
- Genetic information;

- Evidence of insurability;

- Disability.

None of these factors can be used to increase the premium or other contribution that an individual plan participant has to pay, when compared to other similarly situated participants. HIPAA does not limit the premiums or copayments that employers can require participants to pay. It is also legitimate to offer employees discounts, rebates, or reductions in their copayment obligations based on their participation in health promotion and disease prevention programs (such as smoking cessation or weight loss programs).

Almost six years after interim and proposed regulations were issued, DOL, HHS, and the IRS teamed up again to issue Final Regulations covering HIPAA's nondiscrimination rules for wellness programs. The Final Regulations, appearing in the *Federal Register* on December 13, 2006, permit employers to offer incentives under wellness plans. See § 18.19[G] for more discussion of wellness plans and incentives.

Further rules were promulgated by HHS, DOL, and the Treasury in mid-2013. These rules increase the maximum reward to 30% of total cost of coverage (50% for smoking cessation programs), but programs must not be overly burdensome on participants and must not discriminate on the basis of health status. [T.D. 9620, 2013-27 I.R.B. 1; see Peter K. Bradley et al., *New Guidance Regarding Preventive Services, Cost Sharing, and Wellness*, Hodgson Russ LLP (Mar. 31, 2014), available at Lexology.com]

HIPAA applies to workplace wellness programs offered as part of an EHGP. The employee's consent is required for the employer to use or disclose individual health information for employment-related actions without the consent of the employee. The employer must maintain firewalls to prevent unauthorized access to information. [Jocelyn Samuels, HHS director, Office For Civil Rights, *How HIPAA Applies to Certain Workplace Wellness Programs*, hhs.gov blog (Mar. 14, 2016) (benefitslink.com)]

The EEOC is also concerned about potential discrimination in health plans. The EEOC published a Notice of Proposed Rulemaking on April 20, 2015 about possible ADA issues raised when employee wellness programs collect health information from employees. [80 Fed. Reg. 21659 (Apr. 20, 2015); see EEOC, *Fact Sheet for Small Business: The EEOC's Notice of Proposed Rulemaking on the Americans with Disabilities Act and Employee Wellness Programs*, <http://www.eeoc.gov/laws/regulations/facts_nprm_wellness.cfm> (last accessed Apr. 2, 2017)]

See also 80 Fed. Reg. 54172 (Sept. 8, 2015), an HHS proposed rule forbidding discrimination on the basis of race, color, national origin, sex, age, or disability in any health program that receives federal financial assistance. [HHS Fact Sheet, <http://www.hhs.gov/civil-rights/for-individuals/section-1557/nondiscrimination-health-programs-and-activities-proposed-rule/index.html> (last accessed Apr. 2, 2017). The rule became final, with an effective date of July 18, 2016: 81 Fed. Reg. 31375 (May 18, 2016). See Julie LaVille Hamlet and Jennifer B. Van Regenmorter, *HHS Issues Final Rule Implementing PPACA Non-discrimination Provisions*, Foster Swift Collins & Smith PC (June 30, 2016), available at Lexology.com]

Part of § 1557 (the prohibitions on discrimination on the basis of gender identity or termination of pregnancy) has been enjoined nationwide by the District Court for the Northern District of Texas, so HHS' Office of Civil Rights will not enforce that portion of the rule—but will continue to enforce the rest of § 1557. [*Franciscan Alliance v. Burwell*, No. 7:16-cv-00108, 2016, 2016 U.S. Dist. LEXIS 183116 (N.D. Tex., temporary injunction issued Dec. 31). See HHS.gov, *Section 1557 of the Patient Protection and Affordable Care Act*, <https://www.hhs.gov/civil-rights/for-individuals/section-1557/index.html> (undated; last accessed Apr. 2, 2017).]

The case was stayed in mid-2017, for HHS to reconsider the § 1557 regulations. The injunction remained in effect pending resolution of the issue. (The caption changes to reflect the new Secretary of HHS.) [*Franciscan Alliance, Inc. v. Price*, No. 7:16-cv-00108 (N.D. Tex., stay granted July 10, 2017); see Haynes and Boone LLP, *Court Issues Stay on Proceedings in Challenge to ACA Section 1557 Nondiscrimination Regulations* (Aug. 3, 2017), available at Lexology.com]

It is common for executives' employment agreements to specify their entitlement to various kinds of payments on termination. When there is no agreement, the employer often provides severance benefits, including subsidized health care coverage, in exchange for release of employment-related claims. Sometimes the employer will continue to cover the ex-employee as if he or she were still an active employee for a certain number of months or years—often, as long as severance pay continues. When this coverage ends, the ex-employee is eligible to make a COBRA election.

Another approach is to subsidize COBRA coverage, usually by the employer making direct premium payments to the insurer. Before PPACA, self-insured employers had to be careful to avoid discrimination in favor of HCEs. If the company paid 18 months of premiums for HCEs but only one month for rank and file workers (or no payment at all for non-HCEs), the HCE might be taxed not only on the premiums but on all health benefits. To avoid this, employers often made cash severance payments that could, but did not have to be, used to pay COBRA premiums. Some employers "gross up" these amounts (increase the payment to account for the ex-employee's tax obligations). Pre-PPACA, the nondiscrimination rules did not apply to insured plans.

[C]   Insurers' Obligations

One of Congress's rationales in passing HIPAA was that employers, especially small companies, often had difficulty getting insurance—and once they had insurance, they often faced cancellation of coverage or at least excessively high rate increases.

HIPAA imposes obligations on insurers with respect to group health policies. The rules are different for "small employer" coverage (2–50 employees) and "large employer coverage" (groups of more than 50 employees). HIPAA's general requirement is that insurers who sell small employer coverage within a state must sell to all small employers who want to purchase the coverage, although there is no corresponding obligation to sell to would-be large-group buyers.

In either the small- or the large-group market, the insurer has an obligation to renew coverage or continue it in force as long as the purchase chooses, unless the purchaser:

- Stops paying the premiums;

- Commits fraud related to the policy;

- The insurer withdraws from the relevant market within the state;

- Plan enrollees move outside the service area for a network plan;

- (In a plan based on association membership) enrollees cease to be members of the association;

- The purchaser violates the rules on participation or contributions to the plan.

If an insurer discontinues one kind of group coverage but maintains others, all affected plan sponsors, participants, and beneficiaries are entitled to 90 days' notice of the discontinuance. The plan sponsor must be given the option to purchase the other coverage that the insurer offers in that market.

The insurer must act uniformly, without considering the existing or potential health problems of plan participants and beneficiaries, or the claims experience of the plan sponsor. An insurer that chooses to discontinue all of its coverage in the small- or large-group market must give state insurance regulators 180 days' notice of intent to discontinue. An insurer that withdraws will be barred from re-entering the market for five years. This requirement is imposed to prevent insurers from leaving and re-entering the market purely based on their own needs.

[D] Exceptions to the Portability Rule

Plans of certain types are not subject to the portability rules, because they are not deemed to be health benefit plans:

- Plans that offer accident and/or disability insurance;

- Liability insurance plans;

- Insured plans that provide medical benefits that are secondary or incidental to other benefits;

- Limited scope plans providing, e.g., dental, vision, or long-term care benefits;

- Coverage that is limited to a specified disease or illness;

- Fixed-indemnity plans (e.g., hospitalization insurance);

- Medicare Supplementary (Medigap) insurance.

Plans that cover only a single current employee are not subject to portability requirements.

PPACA adopted the HIPAA excepted benefits rule, with the result that HIPAA excepted benefits do not have to comply with the prohibition on annual limits, cover participants' children to age 26, provide mandated preventive care, or satisfy the limits on out-of-pocket spending.

[E] Penalties and Enforcement

Health plans are subject to a penalty tax, under I.R.C. Chapter 100, for failure to comply with the HIPAA portability rules.

The HITECH Act, which requires privacy and security in data use, provides that civil penalties for noncompliance due to willful neglect are distributed to HHS' OCR, to be used to enforce the law. The general penalty is $100 per violation, subject to a cap of $25,000 per year for violation of the same requirement or prohibition; higher tiers are penalized by $1,000 per violation, capped at $100,000 a year, $10,000 a violation, capped at $250,000 a year, and $50,000, capped at $1.5 million per year. [HIPAA Survival Guide, <http://www.hipaa survivalguide.com/hitech-act-13410.php> (last accessed Feb. 26, 2017)]

[F] Data Privacy and Security

As discussed in § 26.07, HIPAA also penalizes misuse of Protected Health Information (PHI). "Covered entities"—typically, an insurer or self-insured plan—are not permitted to use or disclose PHI without the consent of the subject of the information. [See 45 C.F.R. Parts 160 and 164.] The privacy rules are limited to health plans, not other welfare benefit plans (including disability plans), and PHI can lawfully be used for payment, treatment, or health care operations. In an insured EGHP, the insurer rather than the plan is the covered entity. The covered entity must provide privacy notices to plan members explaining their rights to data confidentiality.

The Health Information Technology for Economic and Clinical Health (HITECH) Act, part of the economic stimulus bill, took effect February 17, 2010, expanding HIPAA's privacy and security provisions and adding a new regulatory structure for electronic medical records. The HITECH Act increases the civil CMPs that can be imposed for violations and the individuals whose PHI has been disclosed improperly can collect a share of the civil penalties.

Business associates of HIPAA-covered entities are subject to the same privacy rules as the covered entities are, including criminal penalties for violations. A business associate that discovers that a covered entity with which it has a business relationship has breached the security or confidentiality rules is supposed to take steps to cure the breach—or terminate the contract. Notice must be given to individuals whose PHI was improperly disclosed; and if 500 or more people were affected by the breach, disclosure to HHS and the news media is also required. Covered entities and their business associates who use electronic health records are required to provide an accounting of how the electronic records were used and disclosed in the previous three years. HHS' Office of Civil Rights continues to enforce HIPAA compliance, but state Attorneys General have also been given the power to enforce HIPAA by bringing suit in federal district court. [Troutman Sanders LLP, *Keeping up with Recent Legislation: Numerous Changes to Group Health Plans Required*, plansponsor.com (Feb. 27, 2009)] On September 17, 2014, the HHS' OCR issued guidance on implementing *Windsor* in HIPAA privacy requirements. Same-sex spouses (as defined by the place where the marriage was celebrated) have the same privacy rights as male/female couples. Legally married same-sex spouses are covered by 45 C.F.R. § 164.510(b) (disclosure of PHI to family members when relevant to their involvement in care or payment, or notification of person's location, condition, or death). A same-sex spouse is a family member whose genetic information cannot be used under 45 C.F.R. § 164.502(a)(5)(i) (ban on using genetic information for underwriting purposes). [Denise Erwin and Sarah Sise, *HHS Guidance Recognizes HIPAA Privacy Rights of Same-Sex Spouses and Dependents*, Bryan Cave Benefits and Executive Compensation (Oct. 10, 2014) (benefitslink.com)]

Many courts have held that there is no private cause of action for violation of HIPAA's privacy rules: enforcement must come from the government—HHS for civil actions, the Department of Justice for criminal cases. [See, e.g., *Acara v. Banks*, 470 F.3d 569 (5th Cir. 2006); *Lester v. M&M Knopf Auto Parts*, 04-CV-850S, 2006 WL 2806465 99 (W.D.N.Y. Sept. 28, 2006)]

Data confidentiality protects the patient against improper disclosure of PHI by health care providers and insurers. The related subject of "data security" is tackled by a final rule appearing at 68 Fed. Reg. 8333 (Feb. 20, 2003). Covered entities are required to carry out technical, physical, and business procedures to protect PHI from unauthorized access (e.g., by hackers), and to have compliance programs so their employees carry out the program.

Ransomware is malicious software that infects a system to either destroy data or encrypt it so legitimate users cannot access it. OCR's July 2016 guidance for health care providers holds that there has been a HIPAA breach if electronic protected health information (ePHI) that has been encrypted on the entity's system is attacked by ransomware, even if there is not necessarily been access to the data. Covered entities have an obligation to prevent, detect, and respond to ransomware attacks. The OCR says the obligation is to have a strong security program that includes a risk assessment, staff training, and access controls. The health care provider must perform frequent data backups in case recovery is necessary, and must be able to activate response procedures when there is a security incident. [Dianne J. Bourque and Kate F. Stewart, *"Your Money or Your PHI"*: *OCR Releases Guidance on Ransomware*, Mintz Levin Cohn Ferris Glovsky and Popeo PC (July 12, 2016), available at Lexology.com]

The HHS' OCR announced it would do more investigations of HIPAA breaches affecting under 500 people, depending on size of breach; if unencrypted PHI was stolen or improperly disposed of; and whether there were multiple breach reports from the same entity. Breaches involving 500 or more are automatically investigated by OCR. [Haynes and Boone LLP, *OCR to Investigate HIPAA Breaches of Less Than 500 Individuals* (Sept. 2, 2016), available at Lexology.com]

In early 2013, HHS' OCR published an omnibus restatement of the HIPAA privacy and security rules, replacing interim final rules from 2009 and a 2010 NPRM reflecting the HITECH Act Amendments. Covered entities and their contractors and subcontractors are subject to civil and criminal penalties for violations of the privacy, security, and breach notification rules. Security breaches must be reported to HHS each year, and large-scale breaches must also be reported to the individuals involved and to the news media. There are requirements for using encryption and destruction of obsolete information to prevent unauthorized persons from accessing protected health information (PHI).

Penalties are imposed for failure to notify individuals of breach of their PHI, and failure to notify the media of a breach. The size of the penalty depends on circumstances such as whether the covered entity knew of the breach, or if it engaged in willful neglect. This rule makes some changes to conform HIPAA to the Genetic Information Nondiscrimination Act (GINA) Title I (health coverage) and Title II (employment). For example, GINA treats genetic information as health information and health plans must be informed that it is forbidden to use or disclose genetic information for underwriting purposes. (However, the information can be used for underwriting of long-term care insurance.) The final rule became effective on March 26, 2013 and covered entities must comply by September 23, 2013. [78 Fed. Reg. 5566 (Jan. 25, 2013)]

As a result of the Federal Civil Monetary Penalties Inflation Adjustment Act Improvements Act of 2015 (part of Pub. L. No. 114-74), GINA penalties increase significantly as of August 1, 2016. For example, the penalty imposed on EGHP sponsors and health insurers for violating ERISA requirements about genetic information rises from $100 to $110 per day. De minimis failures to satisfy the requirements about handling of genetic information that are not corrected before the Secretary of Labor issues a notice are subject to a minimum penalty of $2,745 (the previous minimum penalty was $2,500). Such failures that are not de minimis and are not corrected before notice from the DOL are subject to a $16,473 minimum penalty (formerly $15,000). The penalty for unintentional failures to satisfy ERISA's genetic information requirements is capped at $549,095 (previous cap: $500,000). [81 Fed. Reg. 29765 (May 12, 2016); 81 Fed. Reg. 42491 (June 30, 2016); see Practicallaw.com, *HHS Increases Penalties for HIPAA Noncompliance, Effective August 1* (Nov. 14, 2016) (benefitslink.com); Mary Harrison and Leslye Laderman, *HHS Increases Penalties for HIPAA Violations*, HRC FYI (Nov. 29, 2016) (benefitslink.com)]

Penalties increase every year, in January. See 82 Fed. Reg. 8813 (Jan 31, 2017) for 2017 figures. The maximum penalty for a privacy and security violation, where there was reasonable cause and the violation was not caused by willful neglect, ranges from $1,118 to $55,910 per violation, capped at $1,677,299 for violations of the same provision in a calendar year. The range is $11,182–$55,910, also with a $1,677,299 cap, for willful-neglect violations that are correct in a timely fashion (usually, this means within 30 days), and $55,910 per violation, capped at $1,677,299, for willful-neglect violations that are not timely corrected.

However, a bill has been introduced in the House of Representatives; the Preserving Employee Wellness Programs Act; if enacted, it would allow employers to gather health and genetic information (e.g., weight, blood pressure, information about cancer risks) from employees and their families, and would increase penalties for opting out of a wellness program. [Reed Abelson, *How Healthy Are You? G.O.P. Bill Would Help Employers Find Out*, NYTimes.com (Mar. 10, 2017)]

Although there is no comprehensive federal law requiring companies to notify individuals of data breaches, nearly all of the states have laws mandating data breach notification to individuals. (South Dakota and Alabama are the only holdouts, and legislation has been introduced in Alabama.) In March 2016, New Mexico became the 48th state requiring notification. Under the New Mexico statute, individuals must be notified as soon as possible and definitely within 30 days of the breach, unless the employer investigates and determines there is no significant risk of identity theft or fraud as a result of the breach. Individuals cannot sue to enforce this statute, but the state attorney general can sue on behalf of affected individuals for an injunction or damages for actual losses. Civil penalties of up to $25,000 can be imposed for knowing or reckless violation of the law (which also requires disposal of records that contain personal information once the records are no longer required for business purposes) and a penalty of $10 per failed notification, capped at $150,000, can be imposed for failure to notify. [Brian J. Willett, *And Then There Were Two—New Mexico Set to Become 48th State to Enact Data Breach Notification Law*, Reed Smith LLP (Mar. 21, 2017), available at Lexology.com]

Employers often pay health care providers to do drug tests, fitness for duty exams, and employment physicals. The results of these tests are PHI and the doctor is not allowed to disclose test or examination results to the employer without the patient's authorization. However, it is permissible for a health care provider to condition doing a test on the employee's consent to disclosure. Nor does it violate

HIPAA for the employer to make continued employment contingent on disclosing the test results. Data can also be disclosed to the employer if the examination was part of medical surveillance of the workplace and the employer needs the information to make a report about work-related injuries that is required by OSHA or state law. Health care providers can also disclose PHI when required by Worker's Compensation law. [Kim C. Stanger, *HIPAA: Disclosing Exam Results to Employers*, Holland & Hart LLP (Sept. 22, 2015), available at Lexology.com]

In a number of cases, security was compromised by the theft of computers that had PHI in unencrypted or otherwise insecure form. Heavy fines have been imposed in some of these cases.

The largest privacy breach settlement since 2003 was negotiated in mid-2014 when HHS' OCR ordered Columbia University and New York Presbyterian Hospital to pay $4.8 million to settle charges about a privacy breach involving almost 7,000 patient records that became searchable through Internet search engines when a networked server was deactivated. [Ann Mizner McKay, *Largest Privacy Breach Payment to Date Since HIPAA Enforcement in 2003*, WGA InsureBlog (May 30, 2014) (benefitslink.com)]

St. Elizabeth's Medical Center settled a breach case in 2015 for over $200,000; the facility failed to consider the risks of cloud-based storage and document sharing of documents containing PHI. Media such as Dropbox and Google Drive can be involved in privacy breaches. [Jennifer C. Archie, Susan Ambler Ebersole and Kasey P. Branam, *St. Elizabeth's Medical Center Pays $218,400 to Settle Alleged HIPAA Security Case Stemming from Use of Cloud-Based Document Sharing Service*, Latham & Watkins LLP (Sept. 2, 2015), available at Lexology.com]

Advocate Health Network agreed to settle with HHS' OCR for multiple violations under HIPAA about protected electronic information such as clinical information, patients' names, and their credit card numbers. The settlement is $5.55 million, the largest to date against a single entity. The penalty is so large because noncompliance was so extensive and went on for so long. [HHS.gov, *Advocate Health Care Settles Potential HIPAA Penalties for $5.55 Million* (Aug. 4, 2016) (benefitslink.com); Peter S. Vogel, *HIPAA Penalty of $5.5 Million Seems Like a Lot, But It's Only $1.375 Per Patient!*, Gardere (Aug. 15, 2016), available at Lexology.com]

The OCR settled with Care New England Health System, which owns hospitals and health care providers with regard to HIPAA violations. The settlement requires a payment of $400,000 and a corrective action plan. The system self-reported a breach to OCR after unencrypted back-up tapes containing PHI of over 14,000 people were lost. [Alessandra V. Swanson and Liisa M. Thomas, *OCR Reaches $400,000 HIPAA Settlement for Failure to Update Business Associate Agreement*, Winston & Strawn LLP (Oct. 4, 2016), available at Lexology.com]

MAPFRE Life Insurance Co. of Puerto Rico settled with the OCR for $2.2 million after an unencrypted USB device was stolen after being left unsecured overnight in the IT department. It had PHI of about 2200 people. OCR found lack of compliance with other HIPAA provisions, including lack of risk analysis or risk management plan. [Sean R. Baird, Rebecca L. Williams & Adam H. Greene, *The Price of PHI—A $2.2 Million USB Drive*, Davis Wright Tremaine LLP (Jan. 20, 2017), available at Lexology.com]

Children's Medical Center of Dallas was fined $3.2 million because the lack of a risk management plan, and the lack of encryption, meant that employees could use unencrypted mobile devices between 2007 and 2013. [Peter S. Vogel, *$3.2 Million HIPAA Fine For Violations Since 2006!* Gardere Information Technology & e-Discovery Blog (Feb. 3, 2017) (benefitslink.com)]

At the beginning of 2017, the OCR announced its first HIPAA enforcement action for lack of timely breach reporting. Operating room schedules containing 836 patients' PHI, were lost from Presence Health's surgery center. (The general rule is that reporting is required within 60 days of the breach—earlier, in some situations.) According to the OCR, Presence Health took 101 days to notify the OCR and 104 days to notify plan participants and the media. The settlement was $475,000, much lower than the average 2016 settlement of $2 million. [Sean R. Baird et. al., *Time Waits for No One: OCR Announces First HIPAA Settlement for Lack of Timely Breach Notification*, Davis Wright Tremaine LLP (Jan. 12, 2017), available at Lexology.com; Rebecca L. Williams, Adam H. Greene and Sean R. Baird, *Time Waits for No One: OCR Announces First HIPAA Settlement for Lack of Timely Breach Notification*, dwt.com (Jan. 12, 2017) (benefitslink.com); Gretchen E. Leach, *OCR Issues $475,000 Fine for Untimely Reporting of HIPAA Breach*, Nossaman LLP (Jan. 12, 2017), available at Lexology.com]

These are all administrative enforcement actions carried out by OCR. However, litigation against the health care institution by private plaintiffs is unlikely to succeed. The Fourth Circuit joined the Sixth, Seventh, and Ninth Circuits in holding that fear of future identity theft or other harm from a data breach is not, by itself, an injury in fact that confers standing to sue. In the Fourth Circuit case, two veterans sued the VA when their personal and medical information was compromised by data breaches (in one case, a laptop containing unencrypted patient records was stolen; in the other, four boxes of pathology reports were lost or stolen; a total of almost 10,000 people were affected by the breaches). The plaintiffs asked for damages for embarrassment, mental distress, and potential future identity theft and misuse of their personal information. The Fourth Circuit held that fear of future identity theft was too speculative to confer standing, because it depended on a chain of hypothetical actions by third parties acting independently of the defendants. [*Beck v. McDonald*, 848 F.3d 262 (4th Cir. 2017); see James M. Westerlind and Andrew Dykens, *Fourth Circuit Holds That Threat of Future Harm Is Insufficient to Satisfy Injury in Fact Requirement for Article III Standing,* Arent Fox LLP (Mar. 17, 2017), available at Lexology.com]

ProPublica found that hundreds of repeat HIPAA violators, including CVS Health, Walgreens, Wal-Mart, and the U.S. Department of Veterans Affairs, were not subjected to punitive action. The Department of Veterans Affairs is the worst violator but has never been sanctioned apart from a 2009 penalty for putting prescription bottles in unsecured dumpsters. ProPublica found that HHS' Office of Civil Rights seldom punishes small-scale privacy breaches, even if they caused lasting harm, although an offender's past record is supposed to be consulted in deciding whether to impose fines. There were close to 18,000 complaints to OCR in 2014, but the agency's Website shows fewer than 30 fines imposed since 2009. [Charles Ornstein, *Repeat Violators of Health Privacy Laws Often Go Unpunished*, NPR.org (Dec. 29, 2015) (benefitslink.com)]

CHAPTER 20

DISABILITY PLANS

§ 20.01 INTRODUCTION

Workers are at risk of becoming disabled by injury or illness—whether or not employment-related. Many employers either provide disability insurance under an Employment Retirement Income Security Act (ERISA) plan, or give employees the option to purchase disability coverage on their own, at a lower premium than they could find in the ordinary individual market.

A very frequent, and often underestimated, source of disability is mental illness. According to IBI, for every diabetic employee, there are three who suffer from depression or anxiety. Almost all diabetics have received treatment, whereas only about a quarter of depressed employees have been treated. The average diabetic misses three days of work a year; the average depressed person misses 4.7 days. [Sarah Courtney, *Mental Health Issues Account for 40% of All Disability Claims*, ClaimVantage (Sept. 23, 2015), available at Lexology.com]

There are both public (Social Security Disability Income; Worker's Compensation) and private systems for dealing with disability. The Supreme Court ruled that the Commissioner of Social Security reasonably construed the definition of disability to deny benefits to a claimant who was healthy enough to do her former job (elevator operator) even though that job no longer exists in significant numbers within the national economy. [*Barnhart v. Thomas*, 540 U.S. 20 (2003)] Some states require employers to provide disability benefits; in other states, employers often do this as an employee benefit. Benefits are analyzed as short-term disability (STD) or long-term disability (LTD), with separate standards for each.

Returning to the subject of disability in 2008, the Supreme Court upheld the Kentucky state retirement system's practice of calculating disability retirement benefits by including extra years of service for those who became disabled before normal retirement age, but not for those who were disabled after normal retirement age. The Supreme Court did not consider this to be age discrimination; depending on the age at hire, some younger workers did better than older workers, and some older workers did better than younger workers, under the system. The court held that, in drafting the Age Discrimination in Employment Act (ADEA), Congress considered it acceptable to consider age when setting disability benefit formulas. [*Kentucky Ret. Sys. v. EEOC*, 554 U.S. 135 (2008)]

A person entering the workforce in 2015 would have a one-third chance of dying or qualifying for disability benefits before retirement age. It is often asserted that Social Security Disability benefits are freely available. However, the conclusion of Center on Budget and Policy Priorities' 2015 policy brief on the Social Security system is that about 60% of applicants are denied. The most common reason for denial is not having enough work history. Benefits require having worked for a quarter or more of one's adult life, including five of the last 10 years. A qualifying disability must be severe and expected to last at least 12 months or cause the individual's death. More than half of the people who eventually got benefits were initially rejected and only received benefits on additional review. The death rate of people receiving disability benefits is three to six times as great as people in the same age cohort not receiving benefits, suggesting that most of the claims are legitimate. The age cohort 50–64 is growing, which tends to increase the number of persons receiving disability benefits. [<http://www.cbpp .org/research/chart-book-social-security-disability-insurance> (updated Aug. 23, 2016) (last accessed Feb. 26, 2017)]

Because disability claims are administered by the same insurance company that pays claims that are granted, the legal system had to determine the effect of this conflict of interest on the standard of review. Should a court review a claims decision deferentially, or only see if there was an abuse of discretion and sustain the decision if it was not arbitrary and capricious? This is discussed in *Metropolitan Life v. Glenn*, 554 U.S. 105 (2008). See § 20.07 for post-*Glenn* case law, and Chapter 13 for the subject of claims in general.

The Sixth Circuit affirmed an award of improperly denied LTD benefits and awarded $3.8 million in disgorgement of the insurer's profits for breach of fiduciary duty. The Sixth Circuit held that disgorgement was an appropriate equitable remedy to prevent unjust enrichment and did not constitute double recovery when coupled with an award of improperly denied benefits. However, the en banc Sixth Circuit reversed in March 2015, concluding that remedies under ERISA § 502(a)(3) are not available unless the plaintiff can prove that a recovery under § 502(a)(1)(B) for denial of benefits is inadequate to make the plaintiff whole. [*Rochow v. Life Ins. Co. of N. Am.*, 737 F.3d 415 (6th Cir. 2013), *rev'd*, 780 F.3d 364 (6th Cir. 2015); see Colter Paulson, *En Banc Court Overturns Prior ERISA Decision*, Squire Patton Boggs (Mar. 6, 2015), <http://www.sixthcircuitappellate blog.com/recent-cases/en-banc-court-overturns-prior-erisa-decision>]

In a non-disability case, the Supreme Court ruled in early 2016 that it is not "appropriate equitable relief" for a plan to attempt to recover against the general assets of person who received both advances for medical expenses and a settlement of the personal injury case. The injured employee spent most of the $500,000 settlement on non-traceable items, so there was no fund from which recovery could be sought. [*Montanile v. Bd. of Trs. of the Nat'l Elevator Indus. Health Ben. Plan*, 136 S. Ct. 651 (2016)]

The Sixth Circuit held that a long-term disability claimant who files for bankruptcy but fails to list the LTD claim in the bankruptcy estate will probably not be estopped from suing for wrongful denial of disability benefits. There was no evidence of intentional concealment, and Ohio exempts disability insurance proceeds from the debtor's estate, so there was no motive to conceal the claim. [*Javery v. Lucent Tech, Inc. Long Term Disability Plan*, 741 F.3d 686 (6th Cir. 2014)]

Under the Family and Medical Leave Act (FMLA), although the provisions about substituting paid for unpaid leave do not apply when an employee receives disability benefits during an FMLA leave, the employer and employee can, by agreement, supplement disability benefits by running paid leave concurrently with FMLA leave. (See Chapter 38.)

§ 20.02   EMPLOYMENT-BASED PLANS

Usually, a STD is defined either as one that lasts less than six months, or one that lasts less than a year. Long-term disability benefits typically terminate after a period of years (e.g., five years) or at age 65, when the employee would presumably be retiring anyway.

A typical arrangement is for the employer to self-insure for short-term disability, but to buy LTD insurance (possibly with the covered employees contributing part of the cost). It is also typical for STD and LTD plans to use different definitions of disability. The long-term plan has more restrictive definitions, because the employer's possible exposure is greater.

Using an "own occupation" definition (the person is disabled when unable to carry out the duties of the pre-disability occupation) makes it easier to qualify for benefits than using an "any occupation" definition (benefits stop as soon as the person is able to return to any work, or any work suitable to his or her education and training). Another frequent plan design is for the definition to start out as "own-occ" but switch after two years to inability to perform any occupation suitable to the individual's education and training.

Benefits from group disability plans are offset by Social Security Disability Income; benefits from individual policies are not.

Plaintiff Hannington's disability benefits under an ERISA plan were offset by his service-related disability compensation under the Veterans' Benefits Act (VBA), The First Circuit held that the VBA compensation should not have offset his disability benefits: the plan called for reduction for "other income" under the Social Security Act or "any other similar act or law." The First Circuit held that VBA benefits are not "similar" to the SSA benefits because they are based on military service rather than employment. [*Hannington v. Sun Life & Health Ins. Co.*, 711 F.3d 226 (1st Cir. 2013)]

LTD plans usually replace 60%–70% of pre-disability income; 60% is the most common level. The plan may also limit income replacement from all sources, including Worker's Compensation and Social Security, to a percentage such as 75% of pre-disability income. Many group plans offset (reduce) disability benefits to account for government benefits and damages received from tort suits or settlements (e.g., if the employee was injured in an accident or by a defective product), whereas individual policies generally do not require benefit offsets. The Ninth Circuit held that it was not an abuse of discretion for a plan to deduct SSDI (Social Security Disability Income) payments from the benefits paid by two LTD plans. The plain language of the plan explained the plan's right to be reimbursed for overpayments, and defined other sources of income (specifically including Social Security benefits) as overpayments. The Ninth Circuit also allowed a double offset of the SSDI benefit from two separate plans. [*Renfro v. The Funky Door LTD Plan*, 686 F.3d 1044 (9th Cir. 2012)]

Another cost-saving measure for a group plan is to have benefits start after a waiting period, so that the plan covers situations in which work ability is impaired for a long time, but not ordinary illnesses and minor injuries (which are probably covered by sick leave anyway).

A Taft-Hartley plan is a temporary disability plan jointly run by employers and a union. The plan's goal is to assist employees who are in financial need because of a disability, while also helping them return to work as soon as possible (if they can be rehabilitated adequately). A 2010 Second Circuit decision treats Taft-Hartley plan benefit decisions as inherently subject to a conflict of interest when they make benefit decisions. The Second Circuit ruled that the plan did not give enough weight to the testimony of the attending physician of an employee, injured in an automobile accident, who claimed ongoing pain and weakness. The court also said that the independent report should not have concluded that the worker was capable of performing three occupations. [*Durakovic v. Building Serv. 32 BJ Pension Fund*, 609 F.3d 133 (2d Cir. 2010)]

Highly compensated employees, who often experience crushing income loss after disability (because disability benefits are capped at a level far below their pre-disability income) can be good subjects for corporate disability buy-up policies—supplemental group disability plans providing additional income replacement.

The buy-up plan could be either employer paid, in which case the employer can deduct the premiums and the employee does not have taxable income because of the premium payments, but benefits will be taxable when received; or the employer sponsors the plan, allowing insurers to sign up employees who pay for their own coverage but can then receive benefits tax-free. The second approach is more popular. A disability buy-up can also be included in a cafeteria plan, so that premiums are paid with pre-tax dollars but benefits are taxable. In this case, the coverage will be portable, and employees can take it with them when they change jobs. In a hybrid plan, the employer pays the premiums for a select group of employees; other employees can participate by paying premiums.

Buy-up plans are structured with two tiers. The first tier is a guaranteed issue policy issued at standard rates without underwriting. The second tier has limited underwriting, which may lead to higher premiums or some coverage restrictions. [See Assurant Employee Benefits, *Long-Term Disability Glossary of Terms*, <http://www.assurantemployeebenefits.com/816/aebcom/xhtml_clip/disabilityedu/aeb_glossary.pdf> (last accessed Feb. 27, 2017)]

As an incentive for rehabilitation, the plan may continue benefits at a low level while the individual engages in a trial period of re-employment, or undertakes part-time or lower-level work in an attempt to re-enter the workforce. [See Chapter 37 for a discussion of the Age Discrimination in Employment Act (ADEA) (29 U.S.C. §§ 621 *et seq.*) implications of disability plans.]

Many insurance policies and ERISA plans exclude coverage of disabilities resulting from, or related to, voluntary intoxication or drug use. The District Court for the Northern District of Georgia ruled in mid-2016 that a 0.25 blood alcohol concentration is not enough to exclude a claim, especially when the employer failed to interview witnesses. The claimant was a lawyer who sustained a brain injury in a fall down stairs. He applied for LTD benefits because of memory defects. The district court said that the insurer should have obtained a blood test and a list of symptoms to be expected at various alcohol levels to determine if it was reasonable to link the injury to intoxication. [*Prelutsky v. Greater Georgia Life Ins. Co.*, No. 1:15-cv-628-WSD, 2016 WL 4177469 (N.D. Ga. Aug. 8, 2016); see D. Michael Reilly, *ERISA: "Key Evidence Needed to Prove the Intoxication Exclusion,"* Lane Powell PC (Aug. 15, 2016), available at Lexology.com]

§ 20.03   STATE MANDATES

In five states (California, Hawaii, New York, New Jersey, and Rhode Island), employers are required to provide TDI (Temporary Disability Insurance) coverage for between 26 and 52 weeks of non-occupational temporary disability for industrial and commercial workers. Either the state administers a fund from which employer contributions are distributed to disabled employees, or the state maintains a fund but gives employers the choice of self-insuring, buying insurance, or paying into a union-sponsored disability plan.

TDI benefits are offset (that is, reduced) by Worker's Compensation and unemployment benefits.

§ 20.04   COMPLIANCE ISSUES

[A]   ERISA Compliance

For ERISA purposes, most disability arrangements are welfare benefit plans, and therefore subject to disclosure, filing, and fiduciary requirements. Some disability plans, however, are top-hat plans that only cover executives, so the employer's disclosure obligations are more limited. If a plan is maintained only to comply with Worker's Compensation or state mandates, then ERISA § 4(b)(3) exempts the plan from ERISA compliance obligations. ERISA compliance is also excused in situations where an employer makes payments out of its general assets to an employee who is out of work for medical reasons. [See 29 C.F.R. § 2510.3-1(b)(2)]

If the employee pays all the premiums for LTD insurance, and the employer's only role is to administer the payments (without giving its approval of the policy), then ERISA does not preempt a suit by the employee against the insurer claiming bad faith termination of benefits. There are two tests for deciding whether ERISA preempts litigation about a disability policy:

- Was there a "plan, fund or program"? In this case, a plan was clearly present—but it was not an ERISA plan;

- Does the arrangement qualify for the ERISA safe harbor? The safe harbor is available if the employer does not make any contributions to the plan; the plan is completely voluntary; the employer does not profit from the plan (although it can legitimately receive a reasonable administrative fee); and the employer allows one or more insurers to publicize the availability of the program, but does not endorse or recommend it.

Wisconsin's FMLA requires employers to provide disability leave to new mothers if they provide paid disability leave at all (or to provide six weeks of unpaid leave if they do not have a disability plan). On September 30, 2014, the Sixth Circuit permanently enjoined enforcement of the law, finding it to be preempted by ERISA because it could require benefits for women who do not fit the plan's definition of short-term disability. [*Sherfel v. Newson*, 768 F.3d 561 (6th Cir. 2014); see EBIA Weekly, *Sixth Circuit: ERISA Preempts State Leave Law as Applied to Disability Plan* (Nov. 13, 2014) (benefitslink.com); Jacklyn Wille, *Divided Sixth Circuit Rules That ERISA Bars Wisconsin Law on Maternity Leave*, Bloomberg BNA (Oct. 1, 2014) (benefitslink.com)]

Most of the circuits (the First, Second, Third, Sixth, Seventh, Eighth, Ninth, and Tenth) have held that ERISA § 502(c)(1) statutory penalties are not available to requests for claims-related documents, or for failure to follow the claims procedure rule. In mid-2016, the Ninth Circuit held that the statutory penalties apply only to failure to produce documents in the role of plan administrator—whereas the claims rules impose requirements on the plan, not its administrator. [*Lee v. ING Groep, NV,* No.14-15848, 2016 U.S. App. LEXIS 13517 (9th Cir. July 25, 2016); see EBIA Staff, *Ninth Circuit Joins Others in Concluding Penalties Don't Apply to Requests for Claims-Related Documents*, Thomson Reuters Tax & Accounting (Aug. 26, 2016), available at Lexology.com]

Aetna, in its role of administrator of FedEx's STD plan, informed the employer that an employee had filed a substance-abuse-related disability claim. The notice was required by FedEx's drug-free workplace policy. The Tenth Circuit held that the district court was right to dismiss the employee's ERISA suit: furnishing accurate information to comply with its client's policy could not be a breach of Aetna's fiduciary duty. [*Williams v. FedEx Corp. Servs. & Aetna Life Ins. Co.*, 849 F.3d 889 (10th Cir. 2017); see Haynes and Boone LLP, *Disability Plan Can Disclose Disputed Substance Abuse Problem to Employer Without Violating ERISA* (Mar. 9, 2017), available at Lexology.com]

[B] Tax Issues

Whether an employer can get a tax deduction for the cost of its disability plan depends on satisfying I.R.C. § 162 (ordinary and necessary business expenses). The employer's contributions must also satisfy I.R.C. § 104.

From the employee's viewpoint, the key section is I.R.C. § 106, which excludes employer coverage under an accident and health insurance (A&H) plan from the employee's gross income. This section is usually interpreted to include the premiums that the employer pays to maintain an insured disability plan, as well as the value of coverage under a self-insured disability plan. After a disability occurs, the benefits received by the employee under A&H or disability insurance must be included in income to the extent that they are attributable to previously excluded employer contributions. Amounts paid directly by the employer to the employee are also includible in gross income.

However, benefits paid for permanent loss (or loss of use) of a body part or its function, or for disfigurement, are not included in the employee's income, as long as the benefit is computed without regard to absence from work.

A settlement in a retaliatory discharge case described the proceeds as compensation for emotional distress; in 2014, the Tax Court held that even if there are physical manifestations of emotional distress, that is not sufficient to make the settlement one for "physical injury" as set out in § 104(a)(2). [*Sharp v. Comm'r*, TCM 2013-90 (Dec. 20, 2013)]

T.D. 9665, 79 Fed. Reg. 26838 (May 12, 2014) makes it possible for LTD insurance to cover retirement plan contributions (e.g., to 401(k) plans), thus preserving benefits for workers with disabilities. Before the issuance of that T.D., defined benefit plans usually continued to accrue benefits for disabled employees—but defined contribution plans lacked comparable protections. Disability insurance covering plan contributions is considered an investment of the plan, so premiums and benefit payments are only taxed to the participant when they are withdrawn. Employers have three approaches to disability risks. First, they can self-insure by amending the 401(k) plan to continue contributions of behalf of disabled employees. They can either cover the risk within the plan, or buy coverage outside the plan. Only covering the risk within the plan conforms to T.D. 9665. The self-insured approach requires the employee to be totally disabled as defined by the SSA, which is a stricter definition than most private insurance policies.

Coverage outside the plan allows greater flexibility, but disability benefits cannot be contributed to the employee's 401(k) account and appreciation on assets received as benefits is taxable. The third option buys coverage within the plan, with benefits paid directly to the employee's defined contribution plan account. The plan allows a group (or, for very small plans, an individual) policy as an investment option. The participant elects to have part of his or her pre-tax deferrals, and perhaps employer contributions such as profit-sharing and matching funds, used to buy LTD coverage. If the employee becomes disabled, the insurer pays cash to the plan account; the employee receives the same payments as if he or she had not become disabled. [David C. Kaleda, Emily R. See and Matt Schoen, *Addressing the Risk of Long-Term Disability on Retirement Income*, 42 Journal of Pension Planning & Compliance No. 4 (Winter 2017) (benefitslink .com)]

[C]   ADA Compliance

It should also be noted that a disability plan that imposes lower limits for mental health care than for care of physical ailments may violate the Americans with Disabilities Act (ADA). The Mental Health Parity Act [42 U.S.C. § 300gg] makes it unlawful for employee group health plans to set lower limits for mental health care than for treatment of physical illnesses. This statute, however, is not applicable to disability plans.

ADA Title IV immunizes insurer and benefit plan decisions based on underwriting, classifying, or administering risk, as long as the decisions are not a subterfuge to escape ADA compliance. Decisions that have actuarial support are likely to qualify for this safe harbor.

The Ninth Circuit held that a teacher who applied for medical leave and disability benefits on the basis of total disability when her back condition worsened could sue under the ADA, alleging that she was denied reasonable accommodation. In the Ninth Circuit view, the ADA and disability claims were not necessarily inconsistent. The applications did not consider reasonable accommodation, future ability to work, or ability to perform other jobs. [*Smith v. Clark Cnty. Sch. Dist.*, 727 F.3d 950 (9th Cir. 2013)]

[D]   EEOC Compliance Manual

The Equal Employment Opportunity Commission (EEOC) directives do not have the force of law. Even Regulations promulgated by this agency have often been invalidated by court decisions. However, you should consult Section 3 of the EEOC's Compliance Manual, issued October 3, 2000 [<http://www.eeoc.gov/policy/docs/benefits.html> (last viewed Feb. 26, 2017)] for EEOC policy on what constitutes discrimination on the basis of age or handicap, and what "equal" benefits mean in the context of disability benefits.

The Compliance Manual permits employers to reduce long-term disability benefits to account for Social Security Disability Income, Worker's Compensation, and other non-age-based government benefits. LTD benefits paid to older workers can also be reduced by pension benefits that come from employer contributions, under two conditions. Either the employee voluntarily opts to receive the pension (at any age) or has reached age 62 of the plan's normal retirement age (whichever is later) and is eligible for a full, unreduced pension. In plans partially funded by employee contributions, the employer is only permitted to reduce benefits that can be traced back to its own contributions, not employee contributions.

The EEOC's position is that disability retirement benefits are not equal if they are calculated on the basis of the number of years the employee would have worked until Normal Retirement Age (NRA), because that approach favors younger employees. But disability benefits under government programs can legitimately be used to reduce disability benefits paid by the employer.

[E] Other Compliance Issues

Disability benefits are not considered "medical care," so when an employee is terminated, the right to Comprehensive Omnibus Budget Reconciliation Act (COBRA) continuation coverage [see Chapter 19] extends to the employee group health plan but not to the long-term disability plan.

The Eleventh Circuit ruled that Social Security Disability Income (SSDI) decisions (and information submitted by the claimant in his or her SSDI application) should be taken into account in determining whether a claimant satisfies the policy's definition of disability. If the SSDI decision is not rendered until after the claim denial but during the administrative appeal, the Eleventh Circuit apparently reduced a claimant's burden of proof. Even though the claimant refused to submit the evidence to the insurer that was submitted to the Social Security Administration, the Eleventh Circuit required the insurer to consider that evidence. The decision implies that the insurer might have to defer its determination until the SSDI process is complete or perhaps the administrator can approve a claim before the SSDI process is finished, but cannot deny it until then. [*Melech v. Life Ins. Co. of N. Am.*, 739 F.3d 663 (11th Cir. 2014)]

The Family and Medical Leave Act [Pub. L. No. 103-3; see Chapter 38] may entitle the employee to claim unpaid leave for personal medical needs, or the need to care for a sick family member.

The Supreme Court ruled in May 2010 that an employee, who applied for LTD benefits from a plan insured by Reliance Standard, was entitled to attorneys' fees when the trial court found that the benefit denial was an abuse of discretion. The court remanded to give Reliance 30 days to reconsider; if it did not, judgment would be entered for the plaintiff. Reliance granted the benefits, but argued that an attorneys' fee award was inappropriate because the plaintiff received only a remand, not court-ordered benefits. The Supreme Court held that the relevant ERISA section gives the district court discretion to award attorneys' fees to either side—fee awards are not limited to prevailing parties. [*Hardt v. Reliance Standard Life Ins.*, 560 U.S. 242 (2010); see also *Williams v. Metropolitan Life Ins. Co.*, 609 F.3d 622 (4th Cir. 2010), awarding attorneys' fees to a disability claimant who had a degree of success in arguing that she suffered ongoing pain and loss of function in her hands and wrists, and eventually received LTD benefits for carpal tunnel syndrome.]

The First Circuit held that a disability plan's Functional Capacity Evaluation does not have to be performed by a doctor to be valid. Nor was it an abuse of discretion to deny benefits to a claimant who failed to cooperate with the evaluation performed by a physical therapist. The terms of the plan required claimants to cooperate, and a video showed that the plaintiff did not perform lifting, pushing, pulling, or climbing activities and gave only "sub-maximal" effort to tasks during the evaluation. [*Ortega-Candelaria v. Johnson & Johnson*, 755 F.3d 13 (1st Cir. 2014)]

§ 20.05   CASE LAW ON "TOTAL DISABILITY"

In many instances, the question is not how to interpret the plan—the question is whether or not the claimant satisfies the plan's definition of "total disability." It may be inability to perform the applicant's own occupation, or any occupation for which his or her education and training qualifies him or her—or the definition may shift depending on the length of the period of disability.

Even if the question is ability to engage in "any gainful occupation," most courts will require consideration of the individual's earnings history and the availability of jobs in the relevant geographic area. The Second Circuit held that the fact that an employee continues to work does not prevent him from showing that he was disabled, if there is evidence that the disability was very severe. In this case, an office administrator who suffered a head injury experienced a decline in work performance and ability to interact with others, and was fired about a year after the accident. She was treated for headaches, mood changes, sleep disorder, and impaired memory. The Second Circuit rejected the insurer's conclusion, that the disability was only partial or temporary, for lack of evidence. [*O'Hara v. National Union Fire Ins.*, 642 F.3d 110 (2d Cir. 2011)]

Most policies do not allow mere diagnosis of a condition (such as fibromyalgia) to trigger disability benefits. The District Court for the District of Nevada granted summary judgment for the employer: the plaintiff's doctor did not specify any restrictions or limitations relating to her fibromyalgia diagnosis; she continued to work for a year after the diagnosis; and there was inadequate evidence that she met the policy's definition of disability. [*Decovich v. Venetian Casino Resort*, No. Case No. 2:11-CV-872 JCM (CWH), 2017 WL 388819 (D. Nev. Jan. 26, 2017), see Mike Reilly, *ERISA: Fibromyalgia—"[D]Iagnosis Is Not The Automatic Equivalent to A Finding Of Disability."* Boom: The ERISA Law Blog (Feb. 7, 2017) (benefitslink.com)]

§ 20.06   EFFECT OF PLAN AMENDMENTS

The Sixth Circuit held that it was not an abuse of discretion to amend a multi-employer pension plan to impose a two-year cap on occupational disability benefits: the plan did not provide vested welfare benefits. The plaintiff was injured at work in 1990, and began to receive disability benefits under the Indiana Laborer's Pension Fund. In 2001, he was informed that benefits under the Total and Permanent Disability Benefit category were canceled, but he would receive Occupational Disability benefits until the plan's early retirement age. The plan gave the trustees authority to determine benefit eligibility and amend the plan—but amendments reducing vested benefits were restricted. In 2004, the occupational disability benefit was amended to cut off benefits at early retirement age or December 31, 2006, whichever came first. The Sixth Circuit ruled that welfare benefits can be terminated at any time as long as termination is consistent with the terms of the plan. [*Price v. Bd. of Trs. of the Indiana Laborer's Pension Fund*, 707 F.3d 647 (6th Cir. 2013)]

According to a 2006 Second Circuit decision, the standard for judicial review of an administrator's benefit determination is the SPD that was in effect when the plaintiff became disabled—and not the amended SPD in effect when the application was denied. (The later SPD granted discretion to the plan administrator; the earlier one did not.) The right to benefits vested when the plaintiff became disabled, so the second SPD could not apply. [*Gibbs v. Cigna*, 440 F.3d 571 (2d Cir. 2006)]

§ 20.07 CLAIMS PROCEDURES AND THE STANDARD OF REVIEW AFTER *GLENN*

[A] Generally

See Chapter 13 for a discussion of claims procedures, including the additional requirements imposed by PPACA, the health care reform statute. Also see Chapter 11 for discussion of which documents (e.g., guidelines used in analyzing claims) participants are entitled to receive on request.

It is common for retirement plans to have disability features. Some defined benefit plans allow immediate payment of the claimant's accrued benefits on proof of disability; many of these plans do not reduce the benefit for early retirement. The plan may also provide for retirement benefits to continue to accrue during a period of disability, with the accrued benefits paid at a later time, such as the plan's early retirement date. Even 401(k) plans may permit special distributions on disability. Defined benefit plans typically impose special age and service eligibility requirements for collecting disability benefits (e.g., at least age 50 with 10 years of service).

DOL proposed regulations were published in late 2015, extending some of PPACA's procedural protections and safeguards for EGHPs participants to disability benefit plans and pension plans that offer disability benefits. The proposed regulations require plans to make sure that claims adjudicators are independent. No one involved in decision-making can have a financial interest in the outcome (e.g., qualifying for a bonus for the number of claims denied). Adverse benefit determinations must be provided in a manner that is linguistically and culturally appropriate.

When a claim is denied, the claimant must receive information about why the determination was adverse, such as why the plan disagreed with a Social Security disability determination. Claimants must be granted access to claim files and testimony during the review process. They must be given a chance to present written testimony and other evidence. A final denial cannot be based on new evidence or new rationales unless the claimant gets a reasonable chance to reply. If a plan fails to satisfy the claim processing rules, the claimant is deemed to have exhausted administrative remedies and therefore can sue. The 2015 proposal makes an exception for minor errors that are not prejudicial to the claimant, are attributable to good cause or were beyond the plan's control, and do not reflect a pattern of noncompliance. Under the proposal, rescission of disability coverage (retroactive cancellation or discontinuance of coverage not caused by non-payment) is treated as an adverse determination. In general, retirement plan disability provisions will be subject to the new claims rules, although the existing exemption from claims procedural rules for retirement plans that rely on disability findings by outside parties (e.g., the Social Security Administration) probably continues to apply. [80 Fed. Reg. 72014 (Nov. 18, 2015)]

The November 2015 proposed regulations were finalized in December 2016 applicable to all disability claims filed on or after January 1, 2018. DOL said that almost two-thirds of ERISA litigation involves disability plans; these rules are intended to improve claims review by expanding the procedural requirements. Under the final regulations, any plan (including a health or retirement plan) can be treated as a disability plan if the availability of a benefit depends on showing disability. However, many STD plans (e.g., plans that are not funded) are exempt because they are considered to be payroll practices regulated by state law.

Decision-makers must be independent and impartial. Denial notices must give full disclosure and claimants must receive notice and a chance to respond if the denial of an appeal is based on new evidence. Rescinding disability coverage is now considered an adverse benefit determination that triggers appeal rights. The plan must consider the claimant's response in its decision-making. Claimants must be notified that they are entitled to request a copy of the entire claim file, plus other relevant documents. All denial letters must describe any statute of limitations imposed by the policy, and when the period ends. If the claimant used a Social Security Administration determination to support the claim, and the plan disagreed, the reason for disagreement must be explained. Decision-makers such as claims adjudicators and medical experts must not be hired or fired or compensated based on the probability that they will deny claims.

The final regulation incorporates the stricter PPACA standard: remedies are deemed exhausted if the plan fails to set or follow reasonable claims procedures. [81 Fed. Reg. 92316 (Dec. 19, 2016); see Haynes and Boone, *Which Plans Are Subject to the DOL's Final Rules for Disability Claims Procedures?* (Feb. 13, 2017) (benefitslink.com)]; Hrishi Shah, *Department of Labor Finalizes Claims and Appeals Regulations for Disability Benefits,* Franczek Radelet PC (June 21, 2017), available at Lexology.com. At the end of July 2017, the DOL announced that it was reviewing the final regulations, sowing confusion among employers who are not sure what their compliance obligations are. A recent article suggests full compliance with the final regulations, because it is unlikely that DOL will completely eliminate these rules, and compliance can strengthen an employer's litigating position: see Mark L. Stember, *New Disability Regulations: Wait-and-See or Move Forward?*, Kilpatrick Townsend & Stockton LLP (Aug. 7, 2017), available at Lexology.com]

Even though primary responsibility for providing medical proof of disability falls on the claimant, the Fourth Circuit held that sometimes the administrator has an obligation to obtain medical records and information. If there is no evidence in the record to refute the beneficiary's disability theory, the claims administrator has a duty to obtain material records from whatever treating professionals the administrator is aware of—or inform the claimant which specific records are missing. But if the record contains enough evidence to refuse the claimant's theory, the administrator has no duty to obtain records. [*Harrison v. Wells Fargo Bank*, 773 F.3d 15 (4th Cir. 2014)]

[B]   De Novo or Abuse of Discretion?

When a case gets to court, the question is whether the plan administrator's decisions will be reviewed "de novo" (the court examines all aspects of the case for the first time) or whether the administrator's decisions will be valid.

Before the Supreme Court's 2008 decision in *Metropolitan Life v. Glenn*, 554 U.S. 105 (2008), the courts of appeals developed a number of different standards for reviewing claims decisions. In many cases, benefit claimants asserted that courts should perform de novo review of benefit determinations because the decision was made by an insurer that had a conflict of interest because it both made the claims decision and paid the benefits, so extending more benefits would reduce its profitability. However, in many of these cases, the plan was drafted to give the plan administrator discretion to make decisions—which would make the standard of review whether the decision-maker acted arbitrarily and capriciously.

Glenn involved a claimant who received 24 months of disability benefits for heart disease. The plan administrator, MetLife, had discretionary authority. MetLife encouraged Glenn to apply for SSDI benefits, which she received. Then MetLife concluded that Glenn was capable of working, and terminated her benefits. The Supreme Court found that MetLife's conflict of interest was one factor in reviewing the decision, but all facts and circumstances must be considered. *Glenn* applied the same analysis whether the plan was self-administered by the employer or was administered by an insurance company that had a financial interest in the outcome of its determinations.

After *Glenn*, conflict of interest is a factor in the decision, but decisions are not automatically reviewed de novo if there was a conflict of interest. The Fourth Circuit ruled that before *Glenn*, it used a modified abuse of discretion standard that reduced the amount of deference accorded to decision-makers who had a conflict of interest. After *Glenn*, its new test is whether the decision to terminate disability benefits was reasonable and whether there was an abuse of discretion.

After reconsidering a 2003 ruling, the First Circuit joined the Third, Seventh, and Ninth Circuits and held that a policy provision requiring proof of disability "satisfactory to Sun Life" did not confer enough discretionary authority for the insurer's decisions to be reviewed deferentially. The First Circuit found that the disability plan was an ERISA plan because it was a component of a unified plan that gave employees unified plan communications, with the employer receiving unified billing statements from providers. The program did not qualify for the safe harbor for voluntary plans: it was fully funded by the employer, so the safe harbor for plans without employer contributions was inapplicable. The case was remanded because de novo review found the plaintiff's medical evidence adequate to demonstrate entitlement to disability benefits—but the insurer's surveillance showed her performing activities inconsistent with her claim. [*Gross v. Sun Life Assurance Co. of Canada*, 734 F.3d 1 (1st Cir. 2013)]

Subsequently, Gross applied for attorneys' fees, arguing that she obtained some degree of success on the merits. The First Circuit agreed, finding that the earlier decision was enough to entitle her to a fee award because it reflected the court's judgment that the claim had at least some merit. The *Hardt* court did not decide whether a remand order is itself sufficient to justify a fee award. The Sixth Circuit and the District Courts for the Northern District of California, Massachusetts, and the Southern District of Alabama also say a remand order justifies a fee award, but the District Courts for Colorado, the Eastern District of Michigan, and the Southern District of Florida disagree. [*Gross v. Sun Life Assurance Co. of Canada*, 763 F.3d 73 (1st Cir. 2014)]

In suits for alleged unlawful denial of disability benefits, the first question is whether review is for abuse of discretion or de novo. If the plan or policy is silent on discretion, review is de novo. Many state insurance regulators (e.g., in Washington) forbid "abuse of discretion" language in disability policies. Minnesota does not bar discretionary review. Brake worked in South Dakota; she filed for disability benefits. Her employer is based in Minnesota. The policy called for discretionary review and the plan had a choice of law provision saying the plan used Minnesota law. South Dakota forbids discretionary review clauses; Minnesota does not. The Eighth Circuit applied Minnesota law and the abuse of discretion standard: choice of law in an ERISA contract is followed if it is not unreasonable or fundamentally unfair. [*Brake v. Hutchinson Tech., Inc.*, 774 F.3d 1193 (8th Cir. 2014)]

A recent article says that over half the states have statutes that forbid discretionary clauses. Several cases have held that ERISA does not preempt such statutes. [See, e.g., *Fontaine v. Metro. Life Ins. Co.*, 800 F.3d 883 (7th Cir. 2015); *Standard Ins. Co. v. Morrison*, 584 F.3d 837 (9th Cir. 2009). See Groom Law Group, *The Tide Is Turning Against Discretionary Authority and the Abuse-of-Discretion Standard of Review* (June 20, 2017) (benefitslink.com)] In mid-2017, the Ninth Circuit held that ERISA does not preempt California's ban on discretionary clauses. The California statute applied to a plan that was insured and administered by a TPA—in fact, it applied to a plan that was already in operation when the statute was passed, based on renewal of the insurance policy funding the plan after the statute took effect. [*Orzechowski v. Boeing Co. Non-Union Long-Term Disability Plan,* No. 14-55919 (9th Cir. May 11, 2017)]

A few months later, however, the Ninth Circuit held that ERISA preempts the California statute with respect to self-funded disability plans, because ERISA includes a "deemer" clause that says that ERISA employee benefit plans are not deemed to be insurance companies for purposes of state laws that regulate insurance. The upshot was that the Ninth Circuit held the proper standard for review of denial of short-term disability benefits was abuse of discretion. [*Williby v. Aetna Life Ins. Co.,* No. 15-56934, 2017 WL 3482390 (9th Cir. Aug. 15, 2017); see Michelle Roberts Bartolic, *ERISA Watch—ERISA Preempts California's Ban on Discretionary Clauses as It Applies to Self-Funded Disability Plans,* roberts-bartolic.com (Aug. 21, 2017) (benefitslink.com)]

Texas has a statute forbidding discretionary clauses. The Fifth Circuit's longstanding position was that disability claims denials based on factual determinations (e.g., whether the claim was for medically necessary treatment) were reviewed for abuse of discretion, whether or not the plan included discretionary *Firestone* language. In April 2017, the Fifth Circuit rejected the argument that this statute overrides the Fifth Circuit's line of cases—a three-judge panel of the Fifth Circuit held that the Texas law governs the language that can be included in an insurance contract, but does not set the standard of review. However, en banc rehearing was granted in July 2017, so the decision might be reversed. [*Ariana M. v. Humana Health Plan of Tex. Inc.,* No. 16-20174 (5th Cir. Apr. 21, 2017); see Robinson + Cole LLP, *Fifth Circuit Maintains Default Deferential Standard of Review in Denial of Benefit Claims, But Suggests It May Soon Be Overruled,* erisaclaimdefense.com (May 3, 2017) (benefitslink.com); for grant of rehearing, see Benefitslawadvisor.com, *The Full Fifth Circuit Will Re-Visit the Standard of Review in Denial of Benefits Cases* (Aug. 12, 2017) (benefitslink.com)]

A district court performing de novo review of a benefit denial must consider all the evidence to determine if there is a preponderance of evidence of entitlement. However, the Ninth Circuit uses a bright-line test that inability to sit for more than four hours a day constitutes inability to perform a sedentary occupation. Hence, a claimant whose doctor said he was limited to sitting for four hours, standing two hours, and walking two hours in an eight-hour day was not capable of carrying out his own occupation, which was classified as sedentary. [*Armani v. Northwestern Mutual Life Ins. Co.,* 591 Fed. Appx. 567 (9th Cir. 2016); see Sean P. Nalty, *Ninth Circuit Creates Bright-Line Rule, Finds Those Who Cannot Sit for More Than Four Hours Cannot Perform Sedentary Jobs,* Ogletree Deakins (Nov. 8, 2016), available at Lexology.com]

DOL sets deadlines, such as 45 days for ruling on an appeal of a denial of disability benefits (29 C.F.R. § 2560.503-1(b), -1(h)(3)(i)), although administrators can get a 45-day extension based on the administrator's determination that there are special circumstances that require additional processing time.

Historically, courts have applied the "arbitrary and capricious" standard of review as long as administrators substantially complied with the rules. But the rule in the Second Circuit is that administrators that do not strictly satisfy all requirements of the claims rule lose the protection of the arbitrary and capricious review and their decisions are reviewed de novo, unless the administrator can show that it operates under procedures that fully conform to the regulations, and the failure of compliance in processing the plaintiff's claim was inadvertent and harmless.

In a recent District Court for the Southern District of New York case, an LTD claim was denied after the 45-day period. The sole reason given for the denial was "service not covered" although the claims regulation also requires a specific reason for a denial, referencing specific plan provisions. Prudential said that it needed the extra 45 days to review information in the file "which remains under physician and vocational review." The district court ruled that that is not a special circumstance justifying an extension; the exception would be meaningless if merely being busy was enough to extend the time. When an extension is sought, information must be given explaining why the denial was beyond the administrator's control. [*Salisbury v Prudential Ins. Co. of Am.*, No. 15-cv-9799 (AJN), 2016 U.S. Dist. LEXIS 90289, 2017 WL 780817 (S.D.N.Y. Feb. 28, 2017) (S.D.N.Y. Feb. 28, 2017); see Richard J. Pautler, *In a Significant Change, 2nd Circuit Requires Strict Compliance With Department of Labor Claim Regulations*, Thompson Coburn (Mar. 7, 2017), available at Lexology.com. See also *Halo v. Yale Health Plan*, 819 F.3d 42 (2d Cir. 2016); *Montefiore Med. Ctr. v. Local 272 Welfare Fund*, No. 10-1451-cv (2d Cir. Dec. 2, 2016)]

[C]   The Treating Physician Rule

When the Social Security Administration decides whether an applicant is entitled to receive SSDI benefits, it uses the "treating physician" rule. In other words, the opinion of a physician who actually treats the claimant is given more weight than the opinion of a physician-reviewer who looks at the patient's medical file but doesn't actually examine the patient. There was a Circuit split as to whether this rule should be applied in the context of an ERISA plan.

The Supreme Court resolved the Circuit split through its May 2003 decision in *Black & Decker Disability Plan v. Nord*. [538 U.S. 822 (2003)] The Supreme Court ruled that the Social Security rule does not have to be followed in cases involving private ERISA plans rather than public benefits. The court ruled that it was not arbitrary and capricious for the plan to base its conclusion that the plaintiff was not disabled on the opinions of an independent neurologist and psychiatrist who reviewed the plaintiff's medical records. [*Whitaker v. Hartford Life & Accident Ins. Co.*, 404 F.3d 947 (6th Cir. 2005)]

The Sixth Circuit held that selective review of evidence is arbitrary and reversed a denial reflecting record review by a neurologist and pain management specialist who said the plaintiff was capable of sedentary work. The Sixth Circuit said that there was ample contrary evidence, which the plan simply ignored rather than confuting. The treating physician found disc herniation and a positive EMG and said that the plaintiff could only stand or sit for 30 minutes at a time. It is not necessary to defer to the opinions of the treating physician, but the plan must explain why those opinions were rejected. If the same "independent reviewers" are used all the time, they lose credibility. Although it is not per se improper to make decisions based on file review, if the plan gives the administrator the right to conduct a physical examination, it looks suspicious if no examination is performed. [*Shaw v. AT&T Umbrella Benefit Plan No. 1*, 795 F.3d 538 (6th Cir. 2015)]

The Ninth Circuit held in mid-2016 that it was an abuse of discretion to deny an LTD claim. The "independent" physician consultants who handled the claim had a conflict of interest. Although there was substantial evidence that the plaintiff's mental limitations were caused by pain medications, the consultants did not examine him before declaring that he was not credible. The opinion implies that, when the standard of review is whether the decision was arbitrary and capricious, evidence about the number of performed by the independent reviewers, and how much they earn, is discoverable. [*Demer v. IBM Corp.*, No. 13-17196, 2016 WL 4488006, 2016 U.S. App. LEXIS 15788 (9th Cir. Aug. 26, 2016); see Stephen D. Rosenberg, *The Ninth Circuit Deems the Compensation of Outside Medical Reviewers Relevant in LTD Litigation, in Demer v. MetLife,* Boston ERISA Law Blog (Aug. 30, 2016) (benefitslink.com)]

§ 20.08   APPEALS OF CLAIM DENIALS

The Ninth Circuit said that it was "illogical" and "implausible" to refuse to grant LTD payments to a Honda employee who was disabled by Chronic Fatigue Syndrome (CFS) and who qualified for Social Security disability payments. His claim was denied on the grounds that there were no objective physical findings substantiating his illness, although he submitted medical evidence of having an unusually severe case of CFS. The Ninth Circuit found an abuse of discretion: disregarding ample medical evidence and insisting on objective findings where there is no objective medical test available. [*Salomaa v. Honda*, 642 F.3d 666 (9th Cir. 2011)]

The Second Circuit held that subjective evidence must be weighed before rejecting a disability claim (in this case, based on tinnitus, hearing loss, headaches, and vertigo). The fact that evidence is subjective does not make it worthless. Furthermore, there is no accepted objective test for tinnitus, so the claimant could not have submitted objective evidence. [*Miles v. Principal Life Ins. Co.*, 720 F.3d 472 (2d Cir. 2013)]

The Ninth Circuit extended the 180-day period to appeal a denial of an LTD claim to Monday when the last day to submit the appeal was on a Saturday on the grounds that in federal litigation, deadlines that fall on Saturday, Sunday, or legal holidays are usually extended to the next business day. [*LeGras v. AETNA Life Ins. Co.*, 786 F.3d 1233 (9th Cir. 2015)]

The Sixth Circuit held that termination of LTD benefits was supported by substantial evidence. Guardian Life Insurance decided that a former CEO who had several operations for a herniated disk was able to return to work; was participating in a new venture; and, although he was not getting paid yet, had an employment agreement promising him a $115,000 salary. (His previous salary was $140,000.) The Sixth Circuit held that, to terminate LTD benefits, it is not necessary that the insured earn as much as before the disability, as long as he or she is able to perform the major duties of a consistent occupation. [*Schwalm v. Guardian Life Ins. Co. of Am.*, 626 F.3d 299 (6th Cir. 2010)]

LTD benefits were wrongfully denied when the claimant's doctors ordered indefinite restrictions forbidding the claimant to pinch with more than five pounds of force, kneel, or squat. The employer said that an indefinite restriction was not a permanent one, so she was not disabled. The Eighth Circuit ruled that the denial was an abuse of discretion, because in context, it was clear that the plaintiff had a permanent disability. It was not an abuse of discretion for the district court to award attorneys' fees to the plaintiff because this was not a close case—the employer obviously refused to give credence to the medical evidence. [*Rote v. Titan Tire Corp.*, 611 F.3d 960 (8th Cir. 2010)]

A Ford engineer applied for LTD benefits. The district court granted summary judgment for the insurer on the grounds that the plaintiff had been terminated by Ford before she applied for benefits. However, the Sixth Circuit reversed and remanded, holding that at the onset of disability (Type 1 diabetes; gender identity disorder; major depression), the plaintiff was a covered employee. Her failure to apply for benefits before being terminated could be attributed to severe mental illness. The Sixth Circuit gave her the opportunity to prove, on remand, that the failure to apply was caused by the disability for which benefits are sought. [*Waskiewicz v. UniCare Life & Accident Health Ins. Co.*, 802 F.3d 851 (6th Cir. 2015)]

Truitt, a litigator, claimed disability (leg and foot pain) and started getting benefits in 2003. Benefits were discontinued in 2006 because of a surveillance video, two Independent Medical Exams, and a functional capacity assessment. Benefits were reinstated after Truitt appealed. Her ex-boyfriend gave Unum 600 pages of e-mails, documents, and photos showing Truitt working and performing recreational activities inconsistent with her disability claim. Unum used this evidence to terminate benefits again. Truitt sued, saying her computer was hacked and the e-mails should not have been used. Unum counterclaimed for refund of $1 million in benefits. The Fifth Circuit held that the burden of generating evidence is not solely on the plan administrator, and Unum did not abuse its discretion by using the e-mails sent by the ex-boyfriend because it identified the evidence as supporting the benefit denial. The Fifth Circuit ruled that the e-mails were authentic and not tampered with and remanded for the district court to apply federal common law to reassess the reimbursement claim. [*Truitt v. Unum Life Ins. Co. of Am.*, 729 F.3d 497 (5th Cir. 2013)]

The Second Circuit held that a district court's remand to an ERISA plan administrator was not a final order that could be appealed. Mead applied for LTD; claims administrator Reliastar denied the claim; Mead sued. The district court ordered Reliastar to calculate the amount of benefits. Reliastar wanted to appeal this order. The First, Sixth, Eight, and Eleventh Circuits hold that a remand order is not an appealable final order because it anticipates further proceedings before the plan administrator. The Third, Seventh, Ninth, and Tenth Circuits allow immediate appeals of remand orders in some circumstances. The Second Circuit agreed that this particular order was not final because there would be further proceedings but refused to take a position that such orders are never immediately appealable. [*Mead v. Reliastar Life Ins. Co.*, 768 F.3d 102 (2d Cir. 2014)]

[A]   Statute of Limitations Issues

Heimeshoff, the Supreme Court case upholding a contractual three-year statute of limitations, is a disability case. Because ERISA has no statute of limitations, one must be borrowed; the Supreme Court held that the statute of limitations can be set by contract as long as the period is reasonable and does not conflict with another applicable statute of limitations. [*Heimeshoff v. Hartford Life & Accident Ins. Co.*, 134 S. Ct. 604 (2013)]

However, in late 2015, the District Court for the Eastern District of Wisconsin held that a fully-insured LTD plan could not establish a statute of limitations shorter than the state statute of limitations. The district court applied the three-year state statute of limitations, in light of the insurance exception to ERISA preemption. [*Lundsten v. Creative Cmty. Living Servs. LTD Plan*,126 F. Supp. 3d 1043 (E.D. Wis. 2015); see Benefitsnotes.com, *Not all Plans can Establish a Shortened Limitations Period for Filing Lawsuit* (Oct. 2015) (benefitslink.com)]

The Ninth Circuit held that the statute of limitations for filing an ERISA claim for denial of protected benefits is four years (for contract claims) even if the insurance plan or ERISA itself does not have an explicit time limit. An ERISA claim accrues either at the point of benefit denial or when the claimant had reason to know the claim was denied, in this case when the plaintiff's attorney was informed that the claim was denied.

When a claims administrator is asked to reopen a denied claim to consider additional information, the administrator does not waive the statute of limitations defense by agreeing to reopen the claim. Reopening the claim did not waive the statute of limitations because California law does not permit an insurance company to waive an expired statute of limitations. [*Gordon v. Deloitte & Touche*, 749 F.3d 746 (9th Cir. 2014)]

Witt filed a disability claim in 1997. Initially, the claim was approved but then benefits were terminated for lack of adequate medical records. Witt's administrative appeal was unsuccessful. Witt sued in 2012. The Eleventh Circuit said that, for ERISA benefits claims, the most analogous state-law statute of limitations is applied; here, that meant Alabama's six-year statute of limitations. A "courtesy review" of the claim in 2011 did not revive the claim. [*Witt v. Metropolitan Life Ins. Co.*, 772 F.3d 1269 (11th Cir. 2014)]

In 2014, the First Circuit joined the Second, Third, and Ninth Circuits in holding that, the cause of action to recover ERISA benefits starts to run as soon as the beneficiary learns that his or her claim has been rejected. Each payment does not start a new limitations period. [*Riley v. Metro. Life Ins. Co.*, 744 F.3d 241 (1st Cir. 2014)]

Because a denial letter did not provide the notice of the shortened statute of limitations required by 29 U.S.C. § 1133, the Sixth Circuit found the limitations period unenforceable and remanded to the district court for further proceedings. After two years of LTD, MetLife terminated Moyer's benefits, finding that he could work outside his own occupation. His administrative appeal was unsuccessful. He was informed of his right to sue but not of the contractual limitations period. The district court dismissed his ERISA § 502(a)(1)(B) suit, finding that he had constructive notice of the limitations period because it was stated in plan documents that he could have requested. The Sixth Circuit reversed, finding that failure to mention the time limits was inconsistent with fair review. The Sixth Circuit reads 29 C.F.R. § 2560.503-1 to require denial letters to explain the review process and time limits, including the right to sue. However, in 2014 alone, district courts in the Third, Ninth, and Eleventh Circuits rejected this interpretation. [*Moyer v. Metropolitan Life Ins. Co.*, 762 F.3d 503 (6th Cir. 2014)]

CHAPTER 21

INSURANCE FRINGE BENEFITS

§ 21.01   INTRODUCTION

In addition to plans in which insurance operates behind the scenes (health plans; pension plans funded by insurance contracts), some fringe benefit plans exist to provide insurance coverage to employees. This chapter covers life insurance and long-term care insurance (LTCI) fringe benefits.

Voluntary benefit plans are frequently used to supplement traditional health insurance plans by providing, e.g., insurance for life, vision, dental, disability, critical illness, or accidents; some companies even offer pet insurance. Voluntary plans must satisfy all of the Employment Retirement Income Security Act (ERISA) requirements including operating under a written plan document, filing Form 5500, and satisfying ERISA's financial responsibility rules. However, there is a safe harbor that exempts certain voluntary benefit plans from ERISA coverage. Plans are not covered by ERISA if the plan is completely voluntary; the employer does not endorse insurers, and the employer's sole role is to forward payments by employees (who pay the entire cost of the plan) to the insurers. Programs that are entirely paid for by employees are exempt from Comprehensive Omnibus Budget Reconciliation Act (COBRA), but COBRA may be triggered if a voluntary plan provides medical care, or individual policies that fail the safe harbor test are deemed to be group medical plans. Voluntary plans that reimburse for medical care are subject to the Health Insurance Portability and Accessibility Act (HIPAA) and must maintain procedures for protecting employees' health information, but certain plans, such as stand-alone vision and dental plans have a specific HIPAA exemption. [Ascende.com, *When is a Voluntary Plan Truly a Voluntary Benefit Plan?* (Mar. 4, 2016) (benefitslink.com)]

§ 21.02   LIFE INSURANCE FRINGE BENEFITS

Life insurance is a very popular benefit. Not only do many employers offer it, but also when it is available it is almost universally chosen. According to BLS' National Compensation Survey, in March 2016, 59% of private-industry workers had access to work-related life insurance benefits, and 57% participated (a take-up rate of 98%). Full-time workers were much more likely to be offered life insurance benefits (74% offered, 73% accepted, take-up rate of 98%) than part-time workers (12% offered, 11% accepted, 89% take-up rate). Union workers were much more likely than others to have access to life insurance benefits: the union access rate was 85%, the acceptance rate 83%, and the take-up rate 97%, compared to 54%, 53%, and 98% respectively for non-union workers. [BLS, *Table 5, Life Insurance Benefits: Access, Participation, and Take-Up Rates*, <http://www.bls.gov/news.release/ebs2.t05.htm> (July 28, 2016) (last accessed Feb. 27, 2017)]

[A]   Favorable Tax Treatment

The Internal Revenue Code authorizes several mechanisms under which employers can provide life insurance to employees at little or no income tax cost to the employees. (These mechanisms are distinct from the "key-person" insurance coverage that pays benefits to the corporation itself when it becomes necessary to replace a top executive or creative person.) The basic rule is that, if the employer pays the premiums and the insurance proceeds go to the beneficiary designated by the employee, the employee will have taxable income and the employer will be able to deduct the cost of providing the insurance. (The employer gets a deduction only for "ordinary and necessary business expenses.") However, the Code also provides certain relief measures that limit or eliminate the tax cost of these fringe benefits.

In mid-2005, the IRS issued T.D. 9223 to forbid abusive transactions involving "springing value" life insurance policies transferred to employees. The transactions are abusive because the purpose is to have an employee who has received a policy from a § 412(i) plan taxed at the cash surrender value of the policy, which is low. T.D. 9223 makes the employee taxable on the full fair market value (FMV) of the transferred life insurance contract. [*Final Regulations: Value of Life Insurance Contracts When Distributed from a Qualified Retirement Plan*, 2005-39 I.R.B. 591 (Aug. 26, 2005); see also Rev. Proc. 2004-16, 2004-10 I.R.B. 559, and Rev. Rul. 2004-20, 2004-10 I.R.B. 546]

An individual insurance contract plan is exempt from the minimum funding requirement of I.R.C. § 412 if it satisfies six requirements:

1. It is funded exclusively by the purchase of individual annuity and/or insurance contracts from a licensed life insurance company, although purchases can be made either directly by the employer or through a trust or custodial account.

2. The contract provides for level premium payments, either annual or more frequent.

3. The benefits under the plan equal benefits provided under each contract at the plan's Normal Retirement Age, guaranteed by the carrier to the extent premiums have been paid.

4. The premiums payable for the current and all previous plan years were paid before lapse (or the contract is reinstated).

5. There has never been a security interest at any time during the plan year affecting rights under the contract (although a security interest created after the distribution of the contract to the participant is permissible).

6. There are no policy loans outstanding at any time during the plan year prior to distribution of the policy.

The employer can deduct contributions used to pay premiums on the insurance contract if the plan holds the contract until the employee's death or until the contract is distributed or sold to the employee (e.g., at retirement).

The IRS targets plans involving specially designed life insurance policies whose cash surrender value is temporarily set far lower than the premiums paid. Such policies are distributed or sold to employees at the artificial cash surrender value; the "springing" feature then returns the value of the policy to something more commercially realistic.

Announcement 2005-80, 2005-46 I.R.B. 967, lists § 412(i) defined benefit plans and 20 other tax-saving devices that are deemed improper by the IRS. The § 412(i) programs targeted by the IRS include plans in which the life insurance death benefits are greater than the benefits specified in the plan documents, or those in which the rights of plan participants to buy life insurance contracts under the plan are extremely unequal.

[B] Employee-Owned, Employer-Paid Insurance

It is common for employers to pay the premiums for life insurance owned by the employees covered by the plan. Treas. Reg. § 1.1035-1 gives the employer an income tax deduction for the cost of the plan, provided that the employer is not the beneficiary, and also limited by the I.R.C. § 162 "ordinary and necessary" rule.

The premiums that the employer pays are taxable income for the employee, but the insurance proceeds are not taxable income for the beneficiary who receives them. [See I.R.C. § 101] If the employee borrows against the policy, interest on the loan (unlike most forms of personal interest) is deductible.

> ■ **TIP:** Employer-pay life insurance plans are not subject to nondiscrimination requirements, so it is perfectly legitimate for the employer to furnish insurance to the employees the employer particularly wants to motivate, without making the plan available to the whole workforce.

Most group life insurance policies include a "portability" (also known as "right of conversion") provision under which employees can convert their employment-related coverage to an individual policy. Employers have a responsibility to tell employees about the right to convert group to individual life insurance at termination of employment, and the right to apply for waiver of premium if the employees become disabled or are absent from work. Failure to give the required information can subject the employer to liability. The employer should inform the departing employee to contact the insurer as soon as possible, because the group plan may impose a deadline for conversion and submission of the first individual premium payment. [Ford & Harrison Practical Insights: *Liability for Termination of Group Life Insurance Coverage* (Oct. 2009) (benefitslink.com)]

In a case where a disabled doctor and his wife met with the employer's benefit representative to discuss means to continue welfare benefits as long as possible, the representative failed to explain how to convert the $750,000 life insurance policy to individual coverage. After the doctor's death, his widow sued the life insurance plan. The District Court for the Western District of Pennsylvania ruled in 2017 that the employer, as plan administrator, had committed a breach of fiduciary duty. Explaining benefits was a fiduciary function; the plan administrator should have known that the couple would not convert the policy to individual status without an adequate explanation; and the couple detrimentally relied on the misrepresentation. The right to convert had long since expired, so the insurer had no liability—but the employer was surcharged $750,000 to make up for the insurance coverage, plus interest, fees, and costs. [*Erwood v. Life Ins. Co. of N. Am.*, No. 14-1284, 2017 U.S. Dist. LEXIS 56348 (W.D. Pa. 2017); see S. Howard Kline, *Employer Liable for Failing to Provide Life Insurance Conversion Information to Disabled Employee*, Buchanan Ingersoll & Rooney PC (Apr. 20, 2017), available at Lexology.com]

[C] Company-Owned Life Insurance (COLI)

Under this variation, the policies are owned by the company itself, and can be used to finance death benefits paid under the employer's benefit plans. Cash-value insurance can be used to finance retirement benefits. The beneficiary of the plan, or the estate of the deceased employee, does have income under I.R.C. § 101(a), because the death benefits are deemed to be paid directly by the employer and not by an insurer.

When the employer owns the COLI policy and uses it only to fund the death benefit, the employee does not have taxable income during his or her life from either the policy's cash surrender value or the premium payments that the employer makes—as long as the employee's beneficiary is only an unsecured creditor with respect to the proceeds of the policy.

Usually, the corporation is not entitled to a deduction for the premiums it pays for COLI, because of the employer's interest as a beneficiary. However, there is an exception to this rule for premiums paid for certain annuity contracts used in connection with COLI plans.

Closely held corporations often use life insurance on the owner's life for succession planning: for example, to redeem the deceased owner's shares or to compensate for revenue lost as a result of the owner's death. Amounts received under a life insurance contract, either as a lump sum or stream of benefits, are not included in the recipient's taxable income. [See Code § 101(j)]. However, for a life insurance contract owned by a "person" in business (corporations are considered to be persons) who is a beneficiary of a contract that insures the life of the person's employee, the excluded amount is limited to the aggregate premiums and other amounts paid by the employer. The limitation does not apply if notice and consent requirements were satisfied before the contract was issued; the proceeds are paid to the employee's heirs or used to redeem the employee's interest in the employer company; or the insured was a director of the company, or was employed at any time in the 12 months before his or her death.

The notice and consent requirement is satisfied if, before the contract is issued, the employee (who can be a highly compensated employee and/or a 5% owner of the business) gets written notice of the employer's intent to insure the employee's life, plus the maximum face amount that might be written. The employee must give written consent to being insured, including maintenance of the policy after employment terminates. The employee must be notified in writing that the employer is the beneficiary of the death benefits. According to the IRS, the notices and consents must be given; actual knowledge is not a defense. The notice can be given in a shareholder agreement, LLC agreement, buy/sell agreement, or other corporate document. Generally speaking, the employer must include Form 8925 in its federal tax return for every year the insurance is in effect, and must retain records to support the data claimed on the form. [Mitchell W. Goldberg, *Beware of the Tax Traps of Employer-Owned Life Insurance Contracts*, Berger Singerman LLP (Sept. 7, 2016), available at Lexology.com; Steve Gorin, *How To Avoid Tax Traps in Life Insurance*, Thompson Coburn LLP (Jan. 10, 2017), available at Lexology.com]

One factor impelling Congress to regulate COLI was the belief that COLI carried the potential for abuse; this type of insurance is sometimes stigmatized as "janitor" or "dead peasant" insurance. In some instances, a corporation collects significant insurance benefits on the lives of low-paid workers who had little or no personal or company-provided insurance and whose families therefore were left poorly provided for. Insurance benefiting the company when non-key employees die was criticized as unfair, because the insurance is sometimes maintained on retirees and other ex-employees, so companies benefit by the death of persons who are no longer employees at all, much less key employees. (Initially, corporations were only deemed to have an insurable interest in the lives of key employees, but this rule was changed in the 1980s.)

This type of insurance can also be used by corporations for financial manipulation. Corporations can deduct the insurance premiums they pay for this purpose; and, because they are insurance policies, the buildup of cash value is not taxed, and increase in cash value can be used to improve the financial results on the company's books. The insurance proceeds are not taxable income, so the company can get a windfall if someone dies after a short period of employment. The insurance can also be used as collateral for loans, or policy loans can be taken against the insurance. A mid-2014 article describes COLI as "dubious in the extreme" because the death of non-executive employees or former employees does not damage the company and the employees do not obtain any benefits by supplying data used in the application—so the company is unjustly enriched. The article calls COLI "mainly a tool to allow companies to speculate in financial markets." The COLI market slowed down in 2006 after enactment of the PPA, which permits a company to insurance only the highest-paid 35% of employees and only with their consent. Nevertheless, one-third of the 1,000 largest corporations have COLI, and about $1 billion in new policy value is written each year—as much as 20% of all new life insurance sold each year. Corporations that own COLI say that they use the benefits they collect for employee benefits like long-term health care, pensions, and other deferred compensation but there is no obligation for them to use the money for this purpose; it is simply a source of tax-free cash. [Teresa Tritch, *What Are You Really Worth to Your Employer?*, NYTimes.com (June 25, 2014); David Gelles, *An Employee Dies, and the Company Collects the Insurance*, NYTimes.com (June 22, 2014)]

[D]   Section 79 (Group-Term Life)

Internal Revenue Code § 79 allows an employer to establish a written, nondiscriminatory plan to provide term life insurance policies to a group of employees. (Term life insurance is pure insurance, with no cash value.) Employees can receive up to $50,000 worth of coverage under the plan with no tax consequences to them. But if the employer provides coverage over $50,000, the employee does have taxable income. The calculation is based on an official IRS table. The excess coverage is subject to the Federal Insurance Contributions Act (FICA) tax but not the Federal Unemployment Tax Act (FUTA) tax or income tax withholding. [I.R.C. § 3121(a)(2)]

The table was revised effective July 1, 1999. [See 64 Fed. Reg. 29788 (June 3, 1999)] At press time in 2017, this table was still current.

Employee's Age	Prior Law	Revised Rates
Up to 25	.08	.05
25–29	.08	.06
30–34	.09	.08
35–39	.11	.09
40–44	.17	.10
45–49	.29	.15
50–54	.48	.23
55–59	.75	.43
60–64	1.17	.66
65–70	2.10	1.27
>70	3.76	2.06

A Section 79 plan must either be available to all employees, or to groups of employees defined in a way that does not allow selection of employees based on individual characteristics. So the plan can condition eligibility on factors related to age or employment, but not on the amount of the corporation's stock that the person owns. Nor can the amount of coverage be based on individual factors (although it can be proportionate to compensation). As a general rule, Section 79 plans must cover at least 10 employees.

To satisfy the nondiscrimination test, the plan must benefit at least 70% of the sponsoring company's employees, and not more than 15% of the participants may be key employees. If the group-term life insurance plan is part of a cafeteria plan, it must also satisfy the I.R.C. § 125 rules. If the plan fails the nondiscrimination test, then highly compensated employees will have to include the full cost of coverage (not just the coverage over and above $50,000) in income. [Marsh & McLennan Benefit Advisor, *Internal Revenue Code Section 79* (Nov. 2015) (benefitslink.com)]

The Moving Ahead for Progress in the 21st Century Act (MAP-21; Pub. L. No. 112-141) allows sponsors of over-funded defined benefit pension plans to use Code § 401(h) to transfer funds from the pension plan to an account to provide retiree benefits: either health benefits or group-term life insurance (generally limited to $50,000 per person). Section 401(h) was scheduled to expire on December 31, 2013, but MAP-21 not only extended its applicability until December 31, 2021 but also added group-term life to health benefits as a possible 401(h) benefit. The life insurance assets must be kept in a separate account within the 401(h) plan, segregated both from the general assets of the defined benefit plan and the retiree health benefit account. The 2015 statute that provides interim funding for the federal highway system also extends the authorization for 401(h) plans until 2025. [Surface Transportation and Veterans Health Care Choice Improvement Act, Pub. L. No. 114-41; see Pensions & Investments, *Use of Excess DB Plan Assets for Health Care Extended to 2025* (July 31, 2015) (benefitslink.com)]

[E] Split Dollar

A split dollar plan is a benefit arrangement that divides ownership, and possibly premium payments, between an employer and an employee. Each year the employer makes a contribution equal to the policy's increase in cash value for the year. Under the "endorsement method," the employer owns the policy. The policy is endorsed to allocate cash value and death benefit between employer and employee. Under the "collateral assignment" method, either the employee or a third party owns the policy and then assigns it to the employer. At the employee's death, the employer receives either the cash value of the policy or an amount representing the premiums paid; the rest of the benefits go to the employee's designated beneficiary. If the plan is an "equity split dollar plan," the employer is entitled to repayment of the premiums it paid, while the rest of the proceeds go to the designated beneficiary.

Split dollar plans became popular as a way to enhance the compensation of top executives without angering the shareholders by disclosing the full value of the compensation package, and while giving executives the security of benefits backed by the insurer's resources. [For historical perspective on split dollar, see, e.g., Theo Francis and Ellen E. Schultz, *Insurers Move to Protect Executive Policy*, Wall St. J., Dec. 30, 2002, at C1.]

However, beginning in 2001, the IRS launched an attack on split dollar as a compensation mechanism. Another factor was the Sarbanes-Oxley Act's ban on personal loans to the directors and officers of public corporations, a provision that brought new sales of corporate split dollar policies to a halt because of uncertainties as to whether split dollar arrangements would be treated as interest-free loans to executives.

Seven corporations created what they called a welfare benefit plan providing life insurance for employees. A mid-2015 Tax Court decision holds that a closely held corporation could not deduct payments on a life insurance plan that provided death, medical, and disability benefits to participating employees, who recognized income from the plan. The Tax Court held that the arrangement was actually split-dollar life insurance benefiting the owners of the companies. Policies were purchased in the name of the fringe benefit plan, paying benefits for employees who died while they were employed or after retirement. The corporations deducted the premiums as ordinary and necessary business expenses for funding a benefit plan. However, the policies were not group life insurance; underwriting standards were used that are not permitted under a group plan. The Tax Court said that the owner/employees were the true owners of the policies because they received benefits on death or retirement and their benefits were substantially greater than benefits for non-owners. Because most of the payments went toward benefits for owners, the plan was split-dollar, and the owners had compensation. The Code § 6662(a) accuracy-related penalty was applied because the owners did not perform due diligence about the so-called welfare plan; the transaction had already been flagged by the IRS as inappropriate. [*Our Country Home Enters., Inc. v. Comm'r*, 145 TC No. 1 (July 13, 2015)]

[F] Case Law on Life Insurance Fringe Benefits

Life insurance plans, like other employee benefit plans, often give rise to disputes about benefit eligibility and whether a survivor beneficiary has been properly designated.

Spradley, a 37-year veteran at Owens-Illinois, took early retirement at age 55 because of a disability. About nine months before his retirement, he submitted a claim stating that the Social Security Administration found him to be permanently and totally disabled as of March 1, 2008. Under the plan, PTD (permanent total disability) life insurance benefits are payable to persons who are unable to engage in substantial gainful activities because of a permanent and total disability commencing before age 65, and who file a claim within 12 months of leaving employment—or who are under 65 and receive SSDI (Social Security Disability

Income). Spradley received a denial letter that referred only to health insurance, not the PTD life insurance he applied for. He appealed the denial, which was upheld on the grounds that health insurance is available only to active employees. He brought an ERISA suit. The defendant argued that PTD life insurance is available only for temporary disability. The district court ordered payment of benefits. On appeal, the question was whether the plan administrator's denial was arbitrary and capricious. The Tenth Circuit found that the denial was inappropriate, and the district court should have entered judgment for the plaintiff based on the record instead of remanding for further proceedings—which would only give the plan a chance to fabricate more excuses. [*Spradley v. Owens-Illinois Hourly Emps. Welfare Benefit Plan*, 686 F.3d 1135 (10th Cir. 2012)]

Life insurance plans may be ERISA welfare benefit plans in which case there will be fiduciary obligations, and certain disclosures will be required. In a Fourth Circuit case, a life insurance/accidental death & disability plan was offered, with coverage for employees' children. The plaintiff, McCravy, filed a claim after her daughter died. The claim was denied, on the grounds that the daughter was no longer eligible for coverage after she reached age 19—but the plan continued to accept premiums for the coverage. The Fourth Circuit ruled that McCravy was entitled not only to a return of the premiums but also to a surcharge, as equitable relief under ERISA § 502(a)(3). [*McCravy v. MetLife*, 690 F.3d 176 (4th Cir. 2012)]

In a case where delays by the employer's HR department prevented conversion of a group life insurance policy to individual coverage, the District Court for the Northern District of Georgia rejected the employer's argument that *Varity v. Howe*, 516 U.S. 489 (1996) ruled out a § 502(a)(3) claim, because adequate relief was available under § 502(a)(1)(B). The District Court for the Northern District of Georgia denied the employer's motion to dismiss, holding that *Varity* requires both theories of recovery to be based on the same alleged conduct. In this case, the alleged wrongful conduct was not the Prudential benefit determination but the employer's failure to provide the application on time. The employer's alleged breach deprived the plaintiff of a § 502(a)(1)(B) claim under the terms of the policy, leaving § 502(a)(3) as the only potential source of recovery. The district court also held that *CIGNA v. Amara*, 131 S. Ct. 1866 (2011) specifically allows monetary make-whole relief, even if the fiduciary was not unjustly enriched by its improper conduct. [*Biller v. Prudential Ins. Co. & Six Continents Hotels, Inc.*, 2014 U.S. Dist. LEXIS 118577, 2014 WL 4230119 (N.D. Ga. Aug. 26, 2014)]

The Eighth Circuit joined other circuits in allowing reformation and surcharge as equitable remedies for breach of fiduciary duty. Silva's claim for supplemental life insurance under his employer's plan was denied for failure to submit the evidence of insurability required by the plan. After Silva elected the supplemental life insurance, the coverage appeared on his benefits election package on the employer's intranet and premiums were withheld from his paycheck. The employer said that he should have been prompted to complete and submit the Statement of Health form but there was no evidence of this prompt except the employer's testimony. After Silva's claim was submitted, it was discovered that 200 other employees signed up for supplemental life insurance without submitting Statement of Health forms. Under § 502(a)(1)(B), the Eighth Circuit found that there were issues of material fact precluding a decision on whether MetLife abused its discretion because the plan did not describe what evidence of insurability was sufficient and the Statement of Health form was not mentioned. The Eighth Circuit said that Silva should be allowed to pursue § 502(a)(3) equitable claims for breach of fiduciary duty; the other 200 employees showed that there were notice issues. The plaintiff could seek equitable surcharge from plan administrator, for failure to provide the Summary Plan Description (SPD) that would have explained the Statement of Health requirement, and the complaint could be amended to seek reformation and estoppel. At the early pleading stage, relief could be sought under both § 502(a)(1)(B) and (a)(3) because it was too soon to tell if the claims were duplicative. [*Silva v. Metropolitan Life Ins. Co.*, 762 F.3d 711 (8th Cir. 2014)]

There are only two elements to surcharge as a make-whole remedy: breach of fiduciary duty and resulting actual harm. These are high-value cases because the benefit might be over a million dollars. When there is failure to disclose the right to convert the policy to individual coverage, the employer rather than the insurance company, is liable for the failure. [*Brenner v. Metropolitan Life Ins. Co.*, Civil Action No. 11-12096-GAO, 2015 U.S. Dist. LEXIS 36044 (D. Mass. Mar. 3, 2015)]

Jane Hall said that it was an abuse of discretion for MetLife to deny her claim for the proceeds of her deceased husband's life insurance policy but the Eighth Circuit affirmed summary judgment for the insurer. In 1991, the decedent, Dennis Hall, designated his son as beneficiary of his employment-related life insurance policy. The plan requires beneficiary changes to be made by signed, dated request sent within 30 days of the signature. In May 2001, Dennis and Jane Hall married. In March 2010, Dennis was diagnosed with cancer. In November 2010, he filled out and signed a form designating Jane as beneficiary but did not submit it. On January 26, 2011, he was told that his death was imminent. He executed a will the next day, calling for distribution of his life insurance and other benefits to Jane, and died that day. On February 10, 2011, Jane wrote to MetLife to claim the insurance proceeds. MetLife said that insurance benefits from an ERISA plan cannot be transferred by will and it had not received a signed transfer form. The plan gave the administrator discretion, so the administrator's decision was reviewed for abuse of discretion (see § 13.06). The Eighth Circuit found that the administrator's decision was reasonable and supported by substantial evidence. It was reasonable to hold that the policy was not part of the decedent's estate and could not be disposed of by will. The surviving spouse argued that the SPD does not have a deadline so it should prevail, but the Eighth Circuit held that that argument is invalid if the plan includes a specific provision in an area where the SPD is silent. [*Hall v. MetLife*, 750 F.3d 995 (8th Cir. 2014)]

However, in many instances, the employer will have retained the right to amend the plan and modify or even eliminate benefits—in which case, the employer will probably win the case. For example, in 2015, the Tenth Circuit held that retirees' life insurance benefits were welfare benefits and, consequently, are not subject to the ERISA minimum vesting rules. The general rule is that the employer can unilaterally modify or even eliminate such benefits—unless, under general contract principles, the employer has entered into a contractual obligation to provide vested benefits. In this case, there was no clear and express vesting language in the plan. [*Fulghum v. Embarq Corp.*, 778 F.3d 1147 (10th Cir. 2015)]

§ 21.03 LONG-TERM CARE INSURANCE PLANS

Long-term care insurance (LTCI) is private insurance, sold by life and health insurers, that covers the cost of home and institutional care for the frail elderly and disabled. Some employers offer group long-term care insurance plans as an employee benefit—and to permit employees not only to purchase coverage for themselves and their spouses, but for their parents. Individual coverage for senior citizens can be difficult to find, and is often expensive when it is available. The justification usually given for including this benefit in the benefit package is that it relieves some of the stress of being a caregiver, allowing employees to be more productive. Since the coverage is paid for by the employees, it is a very inexpensive benefit for the employer.

Almost all policies are now individual; although at one time, employer-sponsored plans made up about a third of the LTCI market, it has declined to the point that Genworth is the only company continuing to focus on the employer-sponsored LTCI market. [Jill Cornfield, *Will Employers Respond to Long-Term Care Concerns?*, plansponsor.com (Feb. 6, 2014)]

The situation in 2017 was that many insurers had stopped selling LTCI policies, because they originally sold policies with "lapse-supported pricing" but discovered that many more purchasers than anticipated maintained their policies long enough to make claims. The insurers encountered a "triple whammy" of fewer lapses than expected, lower interest rates, and a slower buildup of reserves than anticipated. [Craig Hasday, *Employer Eldercare Assistance—Not a Bad Idea,* frenkelbenefits.com (Apr. 28, 2017) (benefitslink.com)]

Certain kinds of LTCI are tax-favored: for policies that satisfy federally prescribed criteria, LTCI premiums are tax-deductible (within limits), and a certain amount of benefits can be received under the policy even if the insured person has no taxable income. (If the policy is an indemnity policy that pays the full cost of care, then the entire amount is tax-free—but indemnity policies are rare.) The cost figures for this purpose are adjusted every year.

For 2017, the potentially deductible long-term care insurance premium is limited to $410 (person under 40), $770 (ages 40–50), $1,530 (ages 50–60), $4,090 (60–70), and $5,110 (over 70). The periodic payment that can be received under a long-term care insurance policy is $360. [Rev. Proc. 2016-55, 2016 I.R.B. 707i; see LTC Partner, *2017 Long-Term Care Insurance Tax Deduction,* <http:// longtermcareinsurancepartner.com/long-term-care-insurance/2017-long-term-care-insurance-tax-deduction> (last accessed Feb. 27, 2017), which says that half the states have some kind of provision for tax deductibility of long-term care insurance premiums: this is true in Alabama, Arkansas, California, Colorado, the District of Columbia, Hawaii, Idaho, Indiana, Iowa, Kentucky, Louisiana, Maine, Maryland, Minnesota, Mississippi, Missouri, Montana, Nebraska, New Jersey, New Mexico, New York, North Carolina, North Dakota, Ohio, Virginia, West Virginia, and Wisconsin.]

Starting in 2013, fewer taxpayers will be able to claim medical expense deductions, because even qualified medical expenses are deductible only to the extent that they exceed 10% of Adjusted Gross Income (AGI). Previously, qualified expenses over 7.5% of AGI were deductible. Senior citizens, who usually have higher medical expenses than younger people, get a relief provision: the 10% limit does not apply to persons aged 65 or over until 2017.

CHAPTER 22

OTHER FRINGE BENEFITS

§ 22.01 INTRODUCTION

This book has already dealt with issues of setting and administering current compensation (pay planning), deferred compensation (pension planning), and the provision of several of the major types of fringe benefits: health plans, disability coverage, and life insurance plans.

This chapter traces their tax, the Employee Retirement Income Security Act (ERISA), and state-law consequences. The availability of benefits tends to fluctuate based on employers' needs: when employees are hard to recruit, benefits often become more generous—especially if employers can put together a package of benefits that are low or moderate in cost, but highly valued by employees. However, the economic decline beginning in 2008 not only created something of a buyer's market for employment, but also reduced the amount of funds many corporations had available for benefits and other compensation.

For tax purposes, the most relevant sections include I.R.C. § 162 (allowing a deduction for all of the employer's ordinary and necessary business expenses, including the employer's contributions to unfunded welfare benefit plans) and I.R.C. §§ 419 and 419A, which set limits on the deductions.

In general, employers will be able to deduct direct payments of benefits or expenses. Employers can make contributions that bear a reasonable actuarial relationship to the amounts that will be needed to pay benefits in the future. In some circumstances, a statutory safe harbor allows deductible contributions.

If a funded welfare plan earns income (e.g., from investments), that income will probably be taxed to the employer that maintains the plan. Unrelated business taxable income (UBTI) earned by the plan will almost certainly be taxed to the employer. [See Chapter 1, §§ 1.08, 1.12 for a discussion of some of the issues of determining who is an "employee" who is or might be eligible for plan participation.]

IRS Form 8839 is used to claim the adoption credit and/or the exclusion for employer-provided adoption benefits. The maximum amounts for these credits in 2017 is $13,750, with the maximum benefit phasing down at modified adjustment gross income (MAGI) of $203,540 and phasing out at MAGI of $245,540. [Rev. Proc 2016-55, 2016-45 I.R.B. 707]

In a case of first impression, the District Court for the Southern District of Florida held that, to use the rules for children with special needs under Code §§ 23 and 137 (which allow the maximum tax benefit to be used for certain special needs adoptions, without consideration of actual adoption expenses or employer reimbursement), there must first be an individualized state determination that the adoptee does in fact have special needs. The taxpayers's argument (that it would be pointless to obtain an individual determination when it was obvious that the child met the statutory definition) failed. The district court said that the Code's use of the word "determined" implies a ruling by a decision-maker, not just application of a statute. [*Lahmeyer v. United States*, 2014 WL 3973152 (S.D. Fla. 2014)]

§ 22.02 STOCK OPTIONS

[A] Generally

Stock options give employees (either a broad base of employees, or top executives only) the right to purchase stock in the employer corporation at a particular price at a stated time. The intention is that the exercise price will be far below the market value of the shares. However, under current conditions, many options are "underwater" (see § 22.02[G])—that is, they are almost certain not to be exercised, because the holder of the option would have to pay far more than the market price to exercise the option.

For tax purposes, stock options are divided into statutory and non-statutory options. Statutory options are granted as part of an employee stock purchase plan or incentive stock option program; all other options are non-statutory. The distinction is significant because the two types of options are taxed differently. The IRS says that options granted under an Employee Stock Ownership Plan (ESOP) or an Incentive Stock Option (ISO) plan will generally be statutory options, whereas other options are non-statutory. A person receiving a grant of statutory options generally does not have income either at the time of the grant or when the option is exercised, although exercise of an ISO may be subject to Alternative Minimum Tax. See the instructions for Form 6251.

But when the stock obtained via the option is sold, the taxpayer's income or loss will be treated as a capital gain or capital loss (depending on whether the stock was sold for more or less than the option price). If the stock is sold before the holding period expires, then the income from the sale will be ordinary income. The employer must issue Form 3921 when an ISO is exercised, to give the employee the information needed to determine if any tax is payable because of an ISO-related transaction. The employer must issue Form 3922 when an employee sells or otherwise transfers stock acquired via an ESOP option.

For non-statutory options, the primary tax question is whether the fair market value of the option can be readily determined (e.g., if it is actively traded on an established market). The IRS says that most non-statutory options do not have a readily determined fair market value, so granting the option is not a taxable event—but the fair market value of the stock minus the amount paid for it constitutes taxable income when the option is exercised. The employee will have income or loss (generally capital rather than ordinary) on selling the stock obtained under the option. [IRS Topic 427, *Stock Options*, <http://www.irs.gov/taxtopics/tc427.html> (last updated Feb. 17, 2017) (last accessed Feb. 27, 2017). See IRS Publication 525, *Taxable and Nontaxable Income*, for guidance on classifying options.] For practical and tax reasons, the employer will probably want to impose some limitations on the options. A typical restriction is the employee's obligation to put (resell) the stock back to the corporation on termination of employment. An arrangement like this includes a method of calculating the put price (e.g., book value or a set P/E ratio).

A stock bonus plan is very similar to a profit-sharing plan from both the labor law and tax perspectives. However, distributions are generally made in the employer's common stock rather than in cash. Employees must be given put options obligating the employer to repurchase shares of stock that are not readily tradeable on an established market.

An ESOP is a stock bonus plan or a plan combining stock bonus and money-purchase features. ESOPs invest primarily in the employer's common stock. The Internal Revenue Code contains additional rules for leveraged ESOPs that borrow the funds used to purchase the stock. ESOPs are often adopted as a defense against hostile takeovers of the issuing corporation. Furthermore, because ESOPs are designed to invest in employer stock, fiduciaries of such plans are not vulnerable to "stock-drop" suits that are common in 401(k) plans when the value of the employer's stock has declined, and plan participants charge that fiduciaries should have removed the stock from the list of available plan investments, or at least diminished its importance.

Usually, an ESOP works by issuing options allowing participating employees to purchase employer stock. The employee makes an election to have a particular amount or a percentage of after-tax wages deducted from pay and accumulated. After the regular purchase period ends, the option is exercised and the shares are purchased at the option price. If the conditions under the Code are satisfied, the employee does not have income—and the employer does not have a compensation deduction—at the time the shares are acquired. The employee must be employed at the time of the grant, and up to three months before the exercise, and the employee must hold the shares for one year from the transfer of the shares, or two years from the grant of the option, whichever is later. (This is also true of ISOs.)

Under § 423 final regulations effective January 1, 2010, stock acquired under an Employee Stock Purchase Plan (ESPP) option receives favorable treatment if the statutory requirements are satisfied. Section 423 forbids employees to acquire shares at a rate exceeding $25,000 in fair market value of stock for each calendar year in which an option remains outstanding and exercisable, calculated the same way as the $100,000 limitation on ISOs.

The employee is not taxed (but the employer does not receive a deduction) when the option is exercised, if the purchase price is at least 85% of the Fair Market Value (FMV) of the stock when the option was granted or when it is exercised (whichever is less); the plan and the offering satisfy the § 423 requirements; and the employee holds the stock for at least two years from grant and one year from exercise of the option. For nonqualified options, the employee has ordinary income at the time of exercise, equal to any excess of fair market value over the exercise price.

An employer can make multiple, successive, or overlapping offerings, with different option terms. If an offering under an ESPP fails to satisfy the § 423 requirements, stock purchased in that offering does not receive favorable tax treatment, but it does not disqualify other offerings that comply with the rules. Most

ESPPs accumulate employees' contributions in an unfunded account that is used to buy the stock at a set price on a set date.

The plan, including the maximum number of shares available, must be approved by stockholders within 12 months before or after the adoption date of the plan. The regulations clarify some questions about which company's shareholders must approve the plan in a mergers and acquisitions context. Other than the four statutory exceptions, options must be granted to all employees of any corporation whose employees receive any options. Up to $25,000 worth of stock can be optioned for each year the option is outstanding, whether or not the option is exercisable. The exercise price must be at least 85% of the FMV at the time of grant or exercise.

An option is considered granted only when the maximum number of shares that can be purchased under the option is determinable. If the plan uses an open formula, where the number of shares depends on the share price and accumulation account at the date of exercise, the option is only considered granted when it is exercised—unless the overall maximum number of shares is stated from the outset. The plan must provide that options can be granted only to employees, not independent contractors, and anyone who owns 5% or more of the company's stock must not receive options under the plan. The plan cannot allow for redemption more than 27 months from the date of the grant (or five years, if the option price is at least 85% of the FMV at the date of exercise).

If the exercise price of options is not determinable on the grant date—for example, if it is based on the fair market value on a later date—then the participant's tax liability when the shares are sold may depend on the exercise price per share, determined as if the option had been exercised on the grant date. Therefore, Form 3922 requires the company to report information for this calculation.

Form 3921 (ISOs) reports:

- Grant and exercise date of the ISO;
- Exercise price per share;
- FMV of a share on the exercise date;
- Number of shares transferred in exercise of the ISO.

Form 3922 (ESOP shares) reports:

- Grant and exercise date of the option;
- FMV of a share on the grant date and exercise date;
- The price paid per share on the exercise date;
- Number of shares to which title was transferred;
- Date of the first transfer of title;

- (If the exercise price was not fixed or determinable on the grant date) Exercise price per share, calculated as if the option had been exercised on the grant date.

An option issuer's failure to make a timely Form 3921 or 3922 filing is penalized, under Code § 6721, by up to $50 per form (capped at $187,500 for small businesses, $536,000 for other businesses), if the return is correctly filed within 30 days of the due date. A small business is one with average gross receipts under $5 million in its three most recent calendar years. The penalty doubles to $100 per information return, up to a maximum of $536,000 for small businesses, $1,609,000 for others, if the return is filed more than 30 days late, but before August 1; and $260 per return if filed after August 1 or not at all, with a maximum penalty of $1,072,500 for small businesses, $3,218,500 a year for others. However, the penalty is $530 per return, with no maximum, if the non-filing is the result of intentional disregard of tax requirements. [IRS.gov, *2017 General Instructions for Certain Information Returns* (Jan. 11, 2017), available at <http://www.irs.gov/pub/irs-pdf/i1099gi.pdf> (last accessed Feb. 27, 2017)]

Stock appreciation rights (SARs) are really a form of cash compensation. The grantee of SARs gets money from the corporation, based on the price of the company stock. If, for instance, a corporate Vice President has SARs for 1,000 shares, the corporation will pay him or her the difference between the FMV of those shares at the time of exercise and the FMV at the time of grant. SARs are not usually issued by themselves, but to accompany stock options. (SARs issued in conjunction with stock options are called "tandem SARs.") A restricted stock plan grants stock outright, although with restrictions that defer taxation until the restrictions lapse. Phantom stock plans entitle the plan participant to receive cash and/or stock equal to the value of a hypothetical award of shares, although the participants do not actually receive ownership of the shares, only compensation equal to their value. The employee is taxed on SARs when the right to the benefit is exercised; the recipient has ordinary income equal to the value of the award, minus any consideration the employee paid for the SARs. (Usually, the employee did not have to pay for them.) The employer gets a tax deduction equal to the value of the award minus any consideration paid. If the employee receives stock instead of cash for the SARs, the amount of gain is taxable when the award is exercised, even if the shares are not sold at that time. However, any gain on eventual sale is capital gain, not ordinary income. [National Center for Employee Ownership, *Phantom Stock and Stock Appreciation Rights (SARS)*, available at <https://www.nceo.org/articles/phantom-stock-appreciation-rights-sars> (undated, last accessed Feb. 27, 2017)]

A stock grant agreement can claw back shares when the employee goes to work for a competitor, or restrain taking that job. Restrictive covenants can be included in agreements for stock options, restricted stock, and performance shares. Courts have been more likely to enforce restrictive covenant (especially covenants not to compete) if the remedy is the mere loss of compensation rather than the employee being prevented from earning a living.

A public company must satisfy the requirements under Code § 162(m) for restricted stock and restricted stock units (RSUs) to be fully deductible. Under § 162(m), the general rule is that a public company is limited to a $1 million compensation deduction apiece for its CEO and four other highest compensated officers. But there is an exception: the $1 million limit does not apply to qualified performance-based compensation that is only paid if the payee meets at least one objective performance goal that was set in advance. The performance-based compensation must have been ordered either by the company's board or a compensation committee consisting of outside directors and the terms of the plan are disclosed to, and approved by, the shareholders in advance. In mid-2012, the IRS issued guidance on whether dividends on restricted stock and the equivalent on RSUs must satisfy the § 162(m) requirements separately to be treated as fully deductible performance-based compensation: Rev. Rul. 2012-19, 2012-28 I.R.B. 16.

T.D. 9716, 80 Fed. Reg. 16970 (Mar. 31, 2015) provides that a plan under which an option or SAR is granted must state the maximum number of shares with respect to which options or SARs can be granted to "any individual." Prior law required disclosure of the maximum number of shares with respect to which stock options and SARs could be granted. T.D. 9716 adds restricted stock, restricted stock units, and other equity-based awards. If the corporation goes public, the § 162(m) deduction limit does not apply to RSUs that are paid—not just granted—before the earliest transition event listed in the IRS regulations.

Each year, the compensation committee must certify in writing that the performance goals were satisfied before the incentive compensation is paid. The performance goals must be set during the first 90 days of the performance period (i.e., by March 16 for calendar-year plans). IRS regulations say that compensation attributable to a stock option or SAR is performance-based if the grant is made by the compensation committee; the plan states the maximum number of shares that can be granted; and the exercise price of an option or base price for evaluating an SAR at least equals the fair market value of a share at the award date. The regulations provide that compensation is not performance-based if the committee has the power to increase the amount that would otherwise be due for meeting a goal or if part or all of the sum is payable whether or not the goal is met. However, compensation can be performance-based if the committee exercises "negative discretion," such as an "umbrella" plan that reduces the bonus from the maximum amount because the committee feels that less than the maximum should be paid. If the compensation committee sets actual targets that are used to set each year's awards, the performance criteria and the maximum amount that can be awarded must be approved by the stockholders every five years. [GTLaw.com, *Section 162(m): Actions That Should be Taken by March 30, 2016, and/or in This Year's Proxy to Avoid the $1,000,000 Deduction Limitation* (Mar. 22, 2016) (benefitslink.com)]

Restricted stock is company stock that is released based on a vesting schedule, whereas RSUs are a right to get vested stock in the future. Usually, restricted stock carries voting rights but RSUs do not. Some companies make "dividend equivalent" payments on RSUs: cash payments equivalent to the dividends on the restricted stock for the period between the grant and the vesting date. Rev. Rul. 2012-19 says that to qualify for exemption from the $1 million exemption, the dividends or dividend equivalents can only be payable if the payee meets performance goals. However, the performance goals for this purpose do not have to be the same ones for granting the underlying restricted stock or RSUs.

A company deciding whether to offer options or restricted stock must consider many factors, such as dilution of the interests of existing stockholders. To provide the same amount of compensation, a smaller amount of restricted stock can be issued versus stock options because the holder of restricted stock may have value that accrues on the grant date, whereas the holder of stock option does not have this value. [Hoon Lee, *Stock Options, Restricted Stock and Restricted Stock Units*, Hoon Lee Law PLLC (Jan. 17, 2017), available at Lexology.com]

Public corporations should not only review their stock compensation plans for compliance, they should check the tax consequences of other documents, such as severance plans and golden parachutes, involving employees who receive grants of restricted stock and/or RSUs. [Buck Consultants FYI, *IRS Clarifies Treatment of Performance-Based Restricted Stock and Restricted Stock Units* (Aug. 8, 2012) (benefitslink.com)]

As long as stock options are issued "at the money" rather than at a discount, they are not subject to Code § 409A (the tax provisions dealing with certain nonqualified plans).

Nor does I.R.C. § 409A apply to stock appreciation rights (SARs) that are issued by a public company if the rights are settled in employer stock; they are not discounted, and therefore do not have the effect of deferring compensation.

The IRS has consistently taken the position that discounted stock options are deferred compensation subject to § 409A. The § 409A exemption for nonqualified options requires an exercise price at least equal to the FMV of the underlying shares as of the grant date. If the grantee is entitled to dividend equivalence at the exercise price, the grant is considered to be issued at an exercise price below the FMV, so it is subject to § 409A. Public companies must calculate FMV using a reasonable method employing actual sales of its common stock; a private company must use valuation methods that are reasonable in light of the relevant facts, circumstances, and factors. An existing grant that is materially modified is treated as a new grant subject to § 409A, and repricing will probably be required. Violation of any requirement of § 409A renders the SARs or Nonqualified Stock Options (NQSOs) immediately taxable or taxable on vesting (the time at which the option is no longer subject to a substantial risk of forfeiture), and imposes a 20% penalty tax on the amount of compensation recognized for this purpose. [Peter Alwardt, *Discounted Stock Options are Subject to 409A*, Eisneramper.com (Oct. 22, 2015) (benefitslink.com)]

A junior stock plan is another motivational device. Executives are given the right to buy junior stock (stock in the employer corporation with reduced dividend rights and voting powers). Owners of junior stock can convert it to ordinary common stock by achieving specified performance goals.

In 2011, the Supreme Court of Texas held that it is lawful for an employer to require an employee to give a covenant not to compete in exchange for letting the employee exercise stock options—as long as the noncompete agreement is reasonable in time, geographic area, and scope of activity, whether or not the employee had access to confidential information. The state Supreme Court said that stock options that are reasonably related to goodwill or other protectable interests such as confidential information and trade secrets create the necessary connection between the noncompete clause and the business interests. In this case, the stock options were ancillary to the protection of goodwill, so the agreement could be legitimate. The case was remanded to the trial court to determine the reasonableness of the agreement. [*Marsh USA Inc. v. Cook*, 354 S.W.3d 764 (Tex. 2011)]

The Idaho Supreme Court ruled that stock options are not wages under state law—so it was not a violation of state law to fire an employee for intending to exercise his stock options. The court defined "wages" under state law to mean compensation for services rendered, determined on the basis of time, task, piecework, or commissions—categories that do not include stock options. Therefore, firing someone for reasons related to stock option exercise did not violate the public policy exception to employment at will, because "wages" meant only monetary compensation paid on a periodic basis, not non-monetary compensation paid in stock. [*Paolini v. Albertson's Inc.*, 143 Idaho 547 (2006)]

See § 1.01[A] for discussion of advisory "say on pay" votes that public corporations must hold as a result of the Dodd-Frank Act (Pub. L. No. 111-203), the extensive package of financial services regulatory legislation that was enacted in July 2010.

[B] Incentive Stock Options (ISOs)

Internal Revenue Code § 422 creates a specially tax-favored category of Incentive Stock Options (ISOs). An ISO plan is permitted to discriminate in favor of highly compensated employees. However, favorable tax consequences are available to the employee only if he or she retains the shares for at least one year from the exercise of the option and two years from the grant of the option.

Incentive Stock Options (ISOs) can only be granted to company employees and not to directors, consultants, or advisors who are not employees. The exercise price of an ISO must be at least equal to the FMV of the underlying security on the date of the grant. If the grantee owns 10% or more of the company's stock, the exercise price must be at least 110% of FMV at the date of the grant.

Employees themselves can only exercise ISOs, during their lifetimes. Employees are only allowed to transfer ISOs by will or in intestacy.

ISOs must be granted under a plan adopted by the issuing company's Board of Directors and approved by stockholders. The grant must be made within 10 years of the date the plan was adopted. ISOs must be exercised within 10 years of the grant (five years, if the grantee is a 10% stockholder), or three months after termination of employment, whichever is earlier. (An extension is available if employment terminates due to death or disability.) The aggregate FMV of underlying securities for any ISO first exercisable in a calendar year cannot exceed $100,000 determined at the time of the grant. If all these conditions are met, there is no taxable income for the employee at the time of the grant or when the option is exercised. However, the difference between the value of the security at the time of the exercise of the ISO and the exercise price is an adjustment item for alternative minimum tax purposes. If the underlying securities are held for at least one year after exercise, or two years after the grant, any gain or loss from disposition of the securities is considered a long-term capital gain or loss for the employee. But if the holding period requirements are not satisfied, then the options will generally be taxed as nonqualified stock options (NQSOs).

The practical implication is that the difference between ISOs and NQSOs is minimal if the option will only be exercised when the recipient expects to sell the stock quickly or when the option is "out of the money" when it is exercised. [IRS Tax Topic 427, *Stock Options*, <https://www.irs.gov/taxtopics/tc427.html> (updated Feb. 17, 2017) (last accessed Feb. 27, 2017); see Louis Barnett Barr, *Understanding the Differences Between U.S. Tax Qualified and Nonqualified Stock Options*, Schwell Wimpfheimer & Associates LLP (Feb. 17, 2016), available at Lexology.com]

Section 251 of the American Jobs Creation Act of 2004 (Pub. L. No. 108-357) amends I.R.C. § 3121(a), § 421(b), and § 423(c) to provide that the Federal Insurance Contributions Act (FICA) and the Federal Unemployment Tax Act (FUTA) "wages" do not include remuneration derived from exercising an Incentive Stock Option or an option to buy stock under an ESOP. (Nor does this remuneration count toward the person's future Social Security benefits.) The spread (the difference between the stock's FMV and the option price) is not income at the time of the exercise. However, if the statutory holding period is satisfied, it does constitute capital gain once the stock is disposed of. This treatment is effective for stock acquired through options exercised after the enactment of the American Jobs Creation Act (AJCA).

Code § 425 provides that an ISO loses its entitlement to favorable tax treatment if it is modified, unless the modified option meets the ISO requirements as of the date of the modification, or unless changes are made in connection with a corporate transaction. As long as the option itself provides for employer discretion (e.g., to pay a bonus or make a loan when an option is exercised), the exercise of discretion is not a modification of the option.

An out-of-the-money option has no economic value and, therefore, does not operate as an incentive to the option-holder. Therefore, in bad economic times, repricing is common: companies either reduce the exercise price of the employees' outstanding stock options to the current price or raise the exercise price to provide tax benefits for the holders of the options. Section 409A requires an ISO's exercise price to be at least equal to the stock price on the date of the option grant. For a private company, it must be at least equal to the fair market value of the stock, calculated by reasonably applying a reasonable valuation method reflecting the facts and circumstances at the date of valuation. Otherwise, discount stock options—those granted at an exercise price below the stock price on the grant date—are subject to ordinary income tax plus a 20% penalty tax when they vest, measured on the difference between the stock price at the time of vesting and the exercise price.

Employees must be given the choice of whether or not to take the repricing offer; if they refuse, the options continue to be treated as discount options. Accepting the offer provides the tax benefits of an ISO, but does not necessarily maximize the future profit that can be obtained from the option. [Jin Dong Park, *Upward Stock Option Repricing*, J. of Accountancy (Sept. 2011) (benefits link.com)]

[C] Nonqualified Stock Options (NQSOs)

An NQSO grants the right to purchase a certain number of shares at a predetermined exercise price. For tax reasons, this must be at least the fair market value (FMV) of the shares on the date of grant. An NQSO typically vests over time and/or when milestones are achieved. When it is exercised, the recipient has ordinary income equal to the FMV minus the exercise price. Tax is deferred because income is not recognized until the option is exercised. The employer company gets an equivalent deduction. But if the FMV drops below the exercise price, the option becomes essentially worthless.

A restricted stock award is a grant of shares subject to risk of forfeiture until conditions (such as passage of time or achievement of performance milestones) occur. For example, an employee could be entitled to receive 360 shares vesting over 36 months at 10 shares per month, if the employee remains employed. Restricted stock agreements often provide that unvested shares terminate automatically when employment ends, giving the company the right to repurchase the vested shares.

The tax consequences of restricted stock depend on whether a timely § 83(b) election was filed with IRS (i.e., filed within 30 days of issuance). If there is an election, the recipient has ordinary income of the FMV of the stock at the time of the award, minus any amount the recipient paid for the stock. There are no tax consequences for the recipient when the risk of forfeiture lapses. But there is tax at the time of lapse if no election was filed; the taxable amount of ordinary income is the value of the stock at time of vesting minus amount paid for the stock. The employer receives a compensation deduction at the same time, in the same amount. When the value of the company's stock is low, recipients probably prefer restricted stock; but as they value rises, they may prefer NQSOs. However, NQSOs can become valueless if the company's stock value falls below the NQSO exercise price. A restricted stock award makes the recipient a shareholder on the award date, even though some shares are subject to forfeiture. Therefore, unless the award clearly rules it out, there may be shareholder rights issues (dealing with voting, dividends, etc.) with respect to unvested shares. [Lindsey Day, entre-VIEW: *Non-qualified Stock Options or Restricted Stock Awards?* (Jan. 27, 2015) (benefitslink.com)]

For example, assume that a startup company that an employee 100,000 shares of stock, 25,000 of which vest at the end of each 12-month period after the grant date. The FMV of the shares is 5 cents per share on the grant date, rising to 25 cents after Year 1, 75 cents after Year 2, $2.00 a share after Year 3, and $5 a share after Year 4. Section 83(b) makes the equity grant taxable at the FMV of the shares of the vesting date. An employee whose effective federal income tax rate is 30% will pay $60,000 in federal income tax because of the grant. If the employee makes an § 83(b) election, however, the tax would be only $1,500 (100,000 × 5 cents × 30% tax rate). The § 83(b) election is irrevocable. If the employee forfeits the property, or its value falls, the employee cannot reverse the election or obtain a refund of the tax already paid. [Timothy E. Glasgow, *Taking Advantage of the Section 83(b) Election*, Bryan Cave LLP (Nov. 4, 2015), available at Lexology.com]

NQSOs can be granted to anyone, not just employees, and there are no pre-scribed exercise terms or price or transfer restrictions. However, if an NQSO's exercise price is below the FMV of the security at the grant date, it is subject to Code § 409A. If the holder is an employee of the company, withholding and employment taxes apply. [Foley & Lardner LLP, *ISO v. NQSO: The Difference or Lack Thereof*, Lexology.com (Sept. 6, 2013)]

The FMV of the stock at the time of the exercise of the option, minus the price of the option, is a preference item for Alternative Minimum Tax purposes.

The American Jobs Creation Act of 2004 (AJCA), Pub. L. No. 108-357, changed the tax effectiveness of discount stock options (non-qualified stock options with an exercise price lower than the stock's fair market value on the grant date). Under prior law, the question was whether the discount was so deep that the grant should be treated as direct issuance of the stock. For example, if options were granted to buy $10/share stock for a penny a share, that would be treated as a direct grant; but if the exercise price for the same stock were $8, the option feature would be recognized, and there would be a taxable event only at exercise of the option.

The AJCA subjects discount stock options to the I.R.C. § 409A deferred compensation rules (see Chapter 8). Deferred compensation can be paid only on the occurrence of specified events: death, separation from service, disability, change in control, unforeseen financial hardship, or the arrival of the date speci-fied in the plan. The taxable income equals the option spread (the exercise price minus the current FMV of the stock). The spread is also subject to a 20% excise tax penalty.

[D]   Option Taxation Under I.R.C. § 83

Internal Revenue Code § 83 governs all transfers of property in exchange for performance of services, so it is important to stock option taxation but also has broader applicability. Under I.R.C. § 83, the person who performs the services has taxable income, at ordinary income (not capital gains) rates at the time that the rights in the property become transferable or are no longer subject to a substantial risk of forfeiture.

The amount of ordinary income to be recognized equals the fair market value (FMV) of the property minus any amount the employee paid for it. The options can be made forfeitable if the employee leaves before a certain number of years of employment. That motivates the employee to stay longer by offering tax incentives: There is no taxable income until the restriction lapses.

The point at which an option becomes subject to I.R.C. § 83 depends on whether it has an ascertainable market value (for instance, if it is traded on an established market). If so, and if the option is vested, it is taxed as soon as it is granted—not at the later point when it is exercised. Options that have no ascer-tainable FMV do not become subject to I.R.C. § 83 until they are exercised, on the theory that an option with an FMV can be sold as a separate asset.

Therefore, the employee faces taxation at two stages. The first is when the option can be exercised and the stock purchased; the second is when the stock is sold. (Gains from the sale of stock are capital gains; they do not generate ordi-nary income.)

Stock options are vested when the stock is transferable and there is no longer a substantial risk of forfeiture. (Sometimes stock awarded to employees is endorsed on its face to prevent transfer.) Section 83 holds that property is subject to a substantial risk of forfeiture if the right to receive the property is conditioned on future performance of substantial services ("earn-out restriction").

There's no bright-line test for when services are substantial; it depends on factors such as the regularity with which services are supposed to be performed and the amount of time needed to perform them. A retiree whose consulting agree-ment allows him or her to keep the stock while failing to perform the services is not performing substantial services.

Under I.R.C. § 83, refraining from performing services (e.g., under a non-compete clause) can also give rise to a substantial risk of forfeiture.

For purposes of the Exchange Act of 1934's ban on "short-swing" profits earned by officers, directors, or 10% shareholders of public companies, Internal Revenue Code § 83(c)(3) provides that rights are not vested at any time that the person receiving stock options cannot sell the stock without violating the short-swing profit rules. That means that the insider who gets a stock option has no income either for six months or until the first day that the stock can be sold.

In early 2014, the IRS finalized regulations to clarify when there is a "substantial risk of forfeiture" on transfer of stock that is treated as employee compensation under § 83. The May 2012 proposals, published as REG-141075-09, were adopted with a few clarifications. Under the final rules, substantial risk of forfeiture can be established only through a service condition or a condition related to the purpose of the transfer (e.g., achieving a performance goal)—either performance or refraining from performance (e.g., under a noncompete agreement). In determining substantial risk based on a condition related to the purpose of the transfer, both the likelihood of the event occurring and the likelihood of the forfeiture being enforced must be considered. In general, transfer restrictions such as lock-ups, bans on insider trading, and blackout periods do not create a substantial risk of forfeiture. But if the stock cannot be sold because of Exchange Act § 16(b)'s short-swing profit rules, unless the taxpayer elects under § 83(b) to be taxed when the stock is issued, the stock is considered subject to a substantial risk of forfeiture. [T.D. 9659, 2014-12 I.R.B. 653]

IRS's § 83 regulations say that a provision calling for forfeiture of stock if the employee is discharged for cause or for committing a crime does not create a substantial risk of forfeiture. Nevertheless, in 2014 the Tax Court held that the discharge for cause provision in the taxpayer's employment agreement did create a substantial risk of forfeiture. The clause permitted termination for cause for several reasons, including failure to perform his duties diligently and adhere to the employment agreement. The Tax Court said that the regulations, as interpreted, focus on termination for committing a crime, which is unusual enough not to constitute a substantial risk. In this case, however, the Tax Court believed that the broader terms in the taxpayer's employment agreement did create a substantial risk of forfeiture. [*Austin v. Comm'r*, 141 T.C. No. 18 (2013)]

The health care reform law, PPACA, imposes additional taxes on high-income earners: AGI over $200,000 on a single return, $250,000 on a joint return. For these high earners, an additional Medicare tax of 0.9% is imposed on wages, self-employment income, and taxable fringe benefits. In addition, there is a 3.8% surtax on net investment income. The investment surtax applies to gains on non-qualified stock options when they are issued, and on restricted stock when it vests. Tax treatment of dividends on restricted stock depends on whether a § 83(b) election to accelerate income tax was made. If it was made, the 3.8% tax applies to the dividends, but if it was not made, then the dividends are subject to the 0.9% tax. If the American Health Care Act had passed, it would have eliminated these taxes. At press time in 2017, Republicans in Congress were working on tax reform, and it is possible that elimination of these taxes will be part of their tax reform proposal. [See T.D. 9645, 2013-51 I.R.B. 738 for final regulations on withholding, overpayments, and underpayment for the additional Medicare tax enacted on high earners by PPACA].

The employer must withhold the additional tax from wages over $200,000 paid to anyone, irrespective of the recipient's filing status or wages paid by other employers. The employer cannot modify its withholding of additional Medicare tax. However, a person who expects to owe more than the amount withheld by the employer can increase withholding on the W-4 (e.g., a joint return where neither spouse earns over $200,000, but the total is over $250,000). In the usual stock option situation, until the option vests, the corporation is still considered the owner of the stock. The dividends on the stock are considered additional compensation for the employee. On the other hand, the corporation can deduct these dividends (as employee compensation) even though under ordinary circumstances a corporation cannot deduct the dividends that it pays.

The employee has the right to elect immediate taxation in the year of the transfer of the property, even if I.R.C. § 83 would not otherwise impose tax. This is a reasonable choice where otherwise the appreciation on the stock would be taxed as compensation.

On July 17, 2015, the IRS proposed an amendment that would eliminate the requirement of submitting a copy of the § 83(b) election with the income tax return. The IRS's rationale is that the previous requirement prevented people in this situation from e-filing their returns, because commercial tax filing software has no way to attach the election. Under the proposal, the employee files the election with the IRS separately, within 30 days after the property is transferred to the employee. If the proposal is finalized, for transfers on or after January 1, 2016, the IRS will scan the election form, file, it and eventually link it with the tax return. [80 Fed. Reg. 42439 (July 17, 2015)] The proposal was finalized in July 2016, eliminating the requirement of filing a copy of the § 83(b) election with the tax return, thus facilitating e-filing of tax returns. [T.D. 9779, 2016-33_I.R.B_ 233; see Crescent Moran Chasteen, *IRS Simplifies Section 83(b) Election Process*, Nutter McClennen & Fish LLP (Aug. 3, 2016), available at Lexology.com]

> ■ **TIP:**   If the employee pays the tax right away and later has to forfeit the options (e.g., by quitting his or her job), the tax already paid is not refundable.

The employer can deduct the compensation that the employee includes in income under I.R.C. § 83 (as long as the compensation is reasonable). The deduction is taken in the employer's tax year that includes the year in which the employee includes the sum in his or her income. Nearly all employees pay taxes on a calendar-year basis, whereas most corporations operate on a fiscal year. The employer gets an immediate deduction if the property is vested as soon as it is transferred, or if the employee exercises the election to be taxed immediately.

To sum up the ISO/NQSO distinction, when an individual is granted NQSOs:

- (At time of grant) If there is no readily ascertainable FMV, there is no tax effect;

- (At time of grant) If there is an ascertainable FMV, § 83 governs taxation;

- (At time of exercise) The employee has taxable income equal to the FMV of the stock minus consideration paid for the option. However, if the stock received on exercise of the option is nontransferable and subject to a substantial risk of forfeiture, taxable income is not a factor until the condition lapses. At that point, gain is determined based on the FMV at the time of the lapse. If the employee actually sells the stock purchased under the option, then he or she will have capital gain or loss on the sale;

- The employer gets a deduction equal to the individual's gain.

If the employee gets ISOs instead of NQSOs:

- (At time of grant) The employee has no taxable income;

- (At time of exercise) The employee has no income;

- (At time of disposition of stock) The employee has capital gain or loss, with consequences depending on the length of the holding period;

- The employer does not get a deduction. [I.R.C. § 421(a)(2)]

If an employee disposes of shares obtained under an ISO within two years of the grant of the option or one year of exercising the option, any gain is ordinary income, and the employer is entitled to a tax deduction equal to this amount.

Taxpayers have often raised the argument that there is no taxable transfer of non-statutory options until the sale of the shares, if they financed the purchase with margin debt, because their own capital is not at risk until then. However, this argument has been rejected by the Tax Court and by the Fifth and Ninth Circuits, the Court of Federal Claims, and the Western District of Washington. [*Racine v. Comm'r*, 92 T.C.M. 100, 102 (2006); *Facq v. Comm'r*, 91 T.C.M. 1201 (2006), *Cidale v. United States*, 475 F.3d 685 (5th Cir. 2007); *United States v. Tuff*, 469 F.3d 1249 (9th Cir. 2006); *Facq v. United States*, 363 F. Supp. 2d 1288 (W.D. Wash. 2005); *Palahnuk v. United States*, 70 Fed. Cl. 87 (Fed. Cl. 2006)]

[E] Securities Law Issues for Stock Option Plans

Federal securities laws and state Blue Sky Laws must be consulted before offering stock options (or any other form of securities-based compensation). Public companies have an established obligation to disclose option transactions to their shareholders, and to reflect them in SEC filings and on proxy statements. The Exchange Act also forbids insiders to take short-swing profits.

For fiscal years ending on or after March 15, 2002, and for proxies for shareholder meetings or shareholder actions on or after June 15, 2002, the SEC has imposed additional disclosure requirements on reporting companies that offer stock compensation plans. Disclosure is now required of plans offering equity compensation, whether or not approved by security holders.

For each category, the reporting company must put a table in the Form 10-K (the annual report) and in the proxy statement whenever shareholders are asked to approve a compensation plan that includes securities. The table should have three columns:

- Number of securities to be issued on exercise of outstanding options, rights, and warrants;

- The weighted average exercise price for the outstanding options, rights, and warrants;

- Securities not reflected in the first column, still available to be issued in the future under equity compensation plans. The SEC adopted a final rule in late 2007 exempting certain stock options from registration under Exchange Act § 12(g). The rule provides one exemption for public companies that are required to file reports under the Exchange Act ("reporting companies"), another for non-reporting companies (e.g., smaller or private corporations). The exemption is limited to stock options issued as compensation, and does not extend to the underlying stock. [72 Fed. Reg. 69554 (Dec. 7, 2007)]

The SEC's 2006 final rule on disclosure of executive compensation requires public corporations to discuss stock options in the Compensation Discussion and Analysis disclosed to stockholders. Effective for fiscal years beginning on or after December 15, 2006, annual reports, proxy statements, and registration statements will have to give far more detail about option grants to and exercises by top management. A Summary Compensation Table is required, giving dollar amounts for stock awards and stock option awards (measured as of the grant date, using FAS 123R; see below). If the closing market price on the grant date is higher than the exercise price, the closing price must be disclosed. To prevent abusive backdating of options, the date that the decision to make the grant of options must be disclosed, if it is different than the stated grant date. If the exercise price of an option is different from the closing market price on the grant date, the methodology for calculating the price must be disclosed. [SEC Press Release, *SEC Votes to Adopt Changes to Disclosure Requirements Concerning Executive Compensation and Related Matters*, <http://www.sec.gov/news/press/2006/2006-123.htm> (July 26, 2006) (last accessed Feb. 27, 2017)]

The 2010 financial services reform package, the Dodd-Frank Act (Pub. L. No. 111-203) § 954, extends the availability of "clawback": i.e., funds that the corporation can recoup from executives who received stock options or other incentive compensation during the three years before the company had to restate erroneous financial statements. The SEC has proposed rules under Exchange Act § 10D to conform to this requirement.

In 2016, 737 public companies filed restatement disclosures, but not all of them were required to claw back compensation: clawback is only required if the restatement was caused by material noncompliance with securities law financial reporting requirements and the restatement was a "reissuance," not a minor revision restatement to correct immaterial errors. There were only 52 restatements requiring clawback. [Winston.com, *Clawbacks, Clawbacks Everywhere Nor any Moment to Think* (Oct. 18, 2016), available at Lexology.com]

In 2016, the Ninth Circuit held that Sarbanes-Oxley Act § 304 allows clawback of certain CEO and CFO compensation even if the officers were not personally at fault in the events triggering the clawback; the court held that corporate officers should not be allowed to profit from the misconduct of others within the company. [*SEC v. Jensen*, No. 14-55221 (9th Cir. Aug. 31, 2016); see Alexander Song, *Ninth Circuit Holds that SOX 304 Clawback Applies to Executives That Are Not at Fault*, Employment Matters blog (Sept. 14, 2016) (benefitslink.com)]

[F] Accounting Issues

Traditionally, the Financial Accounting Standards Board (FASB) did not require corporations to expense their stock options; the cost merely had to be reflected in the footnotes to the financial statement. Expensing means that the cost of the options is deducted in the year the option is offered. Although taxpayers usually want to increase their deductions to cut their tax bills, there is a countervailing pressure on corporations to report high earnings, so anything that depresses their earnings is unattractive.

This position has evolved since 2004, when FASB 123(R), *Share-Based Payment*, required expensing of stock options and other forms of share-based compensation beginning in July 1, 2005 (public corporations) and January 1, 2006 (non-public corporations). In mid-2009, FASB reorganized thousands of documents into a new classification of approximately 90 topics. Seven FASB statements about retirement and health plans (Nos. 35, 87, 88, 106, 112, 123(R), 158 were reorganized into five topics:

- 712, post-employment compensation other than retirement;
- 715, retirement benefits;
- 960, accounting for defined benefit plans;

- 962, accounting for defined contribution plans;

- 965, accounting for health and welfare benefit plans.

[CCH Pension and Benefits, *FASB Announces New Codification Structure, Superseding All Existing Statements* (June 26, 2009) (benefitslink.com). See <http://www.fasb.org> for the full codification.]

Accounting Standards Codification (ASC) Topic 718, *Stock Compensation*, sets out a general rule that equity awards granted to employees must be accounted for at fair value, measured at the time of grant (for awards settled in stock) and at the time of settlement or exercise (for awards settled in cash). Fair value is the same as the underlying value of the stock if it is a "full-value" award (e.g., restricted stock and performance shares). If it is an "appreciation" award, such as a stock option or stock appreciation rights, value is estimated under an option pricing model.

Subtopic 718-40 provides guidance for ESOP transactions; Subtopic 718-50 offers guidance for share-based payment transactions with Employee Stock Purchase Plans (ESPPs). Compensation cost for equity awards is based on award's fair value at grant, minus anything paid by the employee; the corporation makes a corresponding credit to its equity, usually paid-in capital. Estimates used in the option pricing model must be reasonable, supportable, and determined consistently between periods.

In 2016, FASB adopted some changes, in ASU 2016-09, effective for public company fiscal years that begin after December 15, 2016. Most of the general principles remain the same, but companies will be able to withhold shares for taxes in a way that reflects the highest individual tax rate in the relevant jurisdiction, not the minimum rate. The reason for the change is that the employee is likely to be in the top tax bracket—so a lower rate of withholding understates the employee's tax liability. [Winston.com, *FASB Changes the Accounting Rules for Equity Compensation*, (Apr. 7, 2016) (benefitslink.com); Wilson Sonsini Goodrich & Rosati, *FASB Updates Accounting Standards for Stock-Based Awards* (May 2, 2016) (benefitslink.com)]

The result is that the issuing company must take a compensation charge on its income statement as the employee's interest in the award increases, prorated over the term of the award. The value is adjusted each year to reflect changes in the stock price. If SARs or phantom stock awards are settled in shares rather than in cash, the company has to adopt a formula to estimate the present value of the award at the time of the grant, adjusted for expected forfeitures. [National Center for Employee Ownership, *Phantom Stock and Stock Appreciation Rights (SARs)*, available at <https://www.nceo.org/articles/phantom-stock-appreciation-rights-sars> (undated; last accessed Feb. 27, 2017)]

[G] Backdating; Coping with Underwater Options

An option is said to be "underwater" if the value of the stock on the open market declines below the exercise price given in the option. In that case, of course, the employee will not have any advantage from exercising the option. For example, if an employee is given the right to buy 5,000 shares of the company's stock for $50 a share on a specific date on the future, but on that date, the stock is worth only $30 a share, the option is essentially worthless. The corporation can take various measures to alter the options plan so that the grantee of the options will be able to exercise them at a gain. Generally speaking, the grantees will find this a more satisfying tactic than the corporation's shareholders will.

The conventional method of repricing options is to cancel the options and replace them with new options with a lower strike price—or amend the original options to change the strike price. However, in 2003, the New York Stock Exchange and NASDAQ changed their rules to require shareholder approval to reprice options. Another possibility is to cancel options and replace them with restricted stock units or phantom stock. Finally, some companies choose to calculate the current value of the underwater options, cancel them, and pay cash for the canceled vested options. [JP Morgan Compensation & Benefit Strategies, *Our Stock Options Are Underwater, We Might Re-Price Them* (Apr. 14, 2009) (benefitslink.com)]

One coping mechanism for price volatility, of doubtful legitimacy, is "backdating": deliberate alterations of grant dates to take advantage of lower stock prices that put options in the money when they're issued. Backdating is sometimes analyzed as breach of fiduciary duty by management. The Internal Revenue Code requires the FMV of options to be set in good faith. Allegations of backdating have been raised in many securities law cases, and some executives have been indicted—and a few convicted—on criminal charges such as fraud and criminal violations of the securities laws.

[H] Change of Control Issues

One of the numerous issues that has to be resolved in a merger or acquisition (see Chapter 16 for a general discussion) is what will happen to stock options in the transition. The problem is especially acute when only part of a company (for instance, a division or subsidiary) is sold, and there are arguments pro and con as to whether the plan's "change in control" threshold (which would lead to immediate vesting of options) has been reached. A common provision says that unvested options are forfeited when a person terminates employment other than in a change-of-control situation, and employees of the merged or acquired company are given a limited time (such as three months) to exercise their stock options; under the original option plan, they might have had as much as 10 years to exercise the options.

Many kinds of compensation arrangements in a change in control situation (e.g., stock options, severance arrangements, and incentive plans) can create problems under Code § 409A, the provision dealing with nonqualified plans. If § 409A is triggered, then the amounts must be included in income in the year they are paid even though the purpose of the arrangement was to defer taxation. Furthermore, there is a 20% federal tax penalty—plus an additional 20% penalty on transactions in California. Double-trigger plans often provide severance protection both before and after the change in control. Usually, severance before the change is paid in installments to coordinate with the imposition of restrictive covenants after the employee leaves the company. But after the change, restrictive covenants are of less concern, so severance is usually paid as a lump sum.

There are significant § 409A risks for double-trigger severance plans with alternative payment methods. Some companies fail to recognize this because the pre- and post-transaction severance provisions are in different documents—such as a company-wide severance plan and an individual change-in-control agreement with a top executive. This problem can be avoided by drafting both agreements with a consistent definition.

A double-trigger arrangement typically comes under § 409A if its "good reason" is excessively broad, allowing the executive to quit and collect severance when there has been only a minor reduction in pay or duties. Section 409A may also be triggered if the installment payments exceed $490,000 (as adjusted for inflation) or extend for more than two years after separation from service, if the definition of change in control falls afoul of the statutory definition in § 409A.

Stock options can be assumed in corporate transactions without § 409A penalties if the assumption satisfies the rules for assuming Incentive Stock Options (ISOs). In general, that means that the economics of the option must be preserved: valuing the consideration paid in the acquisition of the target company's stock, potentially including the earn-out. Because earn-outs are speculative, it's very possible that calculation assumptions will eventually be proved wrong, so there is a risk of future § 409A penalties if the transaction is over-valued. If it is under-valued, on the other hand, the option-holders will suffer economic detriment. Some companies value the earn-out at the time of the assumption, whereas others keep the transaction open and adjust the option to reflect the ongoing earn-out payments. The entire issue can be avoided by requiring option holders to exercise their options immediately before the transaction. [Juliano P. Banuelos, *Recent Compensation Trends in Mergers and Acquisitions and § 409A*, Orrick Perspectives (Oct. 2011) (benefitslink.com)]

If the options are cashed out, the acquiring company benefits by not having to administer them after the closing and employees can get money for their options without having to spend money to exercise options.

It is common for vesting of options to be accelerated if there is a change of control. Vesting provisions can be incorporated in the stock option plan itself or in other agreements, such as employment contracts, severance plans, and retention agreements. A single-trigger arrangement accelerates vesting and allows option awards to be exercised as soon as there is a change in control. A double-trigger arrangement requires something else to happen in addition, such as the optionee being fired without cause or resigning for good reason within a specified time after the transaction. [Pamela B. Greene and Ann Margaret Eames, *Stock Options in Merger & Acquisition Transactions*, Corporate & Securities Advisory (June 6, 2011) (benefitslink.com)]

§ 22.03 CAFETERIA PLANS

[A] Plan Characteristics

A cafeteria plan, as defined by I.R.C. § 125, is a written plan under which the employer offers a "menu" of benefits, permitting employees to choose between cash and a group of benefits. The plan must offer at least one taxable and one nontaxable benefit. Other than a 401(k) plan, the cafeteria plan may not offer any pension or deferred compensation benefits.

The I.R.C. § 125 requirements for a valid cafeteria plan are

- All plan participants are employees (although the Proposed Regulations allow ex-employees to be included in the plan, as long as it is not predominantly for their benefits). Spouses and children of employees can receive benefits under the plan, but cannot actively participate (e.g., by choosing the benefits);

- The participant chooses between cash and one or more benefits, although the amount of cash does not have to be as great as the entire cost of the nontaxable benefit [Prop. Reg. § 1.125-1];

- The plan does not discriminate in favor of highly compensated employees (HCEs);

- The benefits provided to HCEs do not exceed 25% of the total benefits for the year;

- The election to take benefits rather than cash must be made before the beginning of the plan year;

- Changes in the election must conform to the Regulations.

The allowable benefits include:

- Accident and health plans;

- Group-term life insurance;

- Disability coverage, including accidental death and dismemberment (ADD) plans;

- Dependent care assistance;

- Benefits that fail nondiscrimination tests and therefore are not part of a qualified plan;

- Vacation days;

- Group automobile insurance or other taxable benefit purchased by the employee with after-tax dollars.

Cafeteria plans are not permitted to include long-term care insurance. Neither can Flexible Spending Accounts (see § 18.11) because FSAs are not allowed to be used to pay insurance premiums.

For 2013 and 2014 plan years that begin on or after January 1, 2013, employee contributions to health FSAs that are made by salary reductions under a Code § 125 cafeteria plan are limited to $2,500 a year. This limitation does not apply to the employer's contribution to the plan, or to employee salary reduction contributions to a cafeteria plan that are used to pay the employee's share of health insurance premiums. For 2015, the Code § 125(i) limitation on voluntary employee salary reduction contributions to health FSAs increases to $2,550, which is also the 2016 level [Rev. Proc. 2014-61, 2014-47 I.R.B. 393]; the 2017 level rises to $2,600. [Rev. Proc. 2016-55, 2016-45 I.R.B. 707]

Initially, FSA balances were forfeited to the extent they were not used for medical expenses during the plan year. Recently, the IRS has permitted a grace period for reimbursement of expenses incurred in the two and a half months after the end of the plan year. In late 2013, the IRS allowed employers to choose between offering either this grace period or a $500 carryforward of unused funds at any time during the next plan year—but not both. Even plans that do not have a grace period can permit a "runout," i.e., prior-year funds can be used in the next year to pay expenses that were incurred but not paid in the prior year. This is different from a grace period, which allows prior-year funds to be used to pay current-year expenses. For the 2013 plan year, the deadline for adopting a grace period or carryforward amendment is December 31, 2014. [Notice 2013-71, 2013-47 I.R.B. 532]

The nontaxable benefits that can be included in a cafeteria plan are group-term life insurance, medical expense reimbursement, and accident and disability benefits as defined by I.R.C. § 106, dependent care assistance, and paid vacation days.

In a pretax premium plan, a "mini cafeteria" salary reduction plan is used to provide after-tax dollars for the employees to pay insurance premiums. The most common application is health insurance coverage for dependents, in plans where the employer covers employees but dependent coverage is on an "employee pay all" basis. The employer adopts a plan that allows the employee, before the start of the plan year, to elect a reduction in compensation sufficient to pay the employee's share of the premium. These salary reductions are not subject to the employer share of FICA.

If a cafeteria plan fails nondiscrimination testing, then the HCEs will have taxable income. The test for discrimination in benefits is whether contributions are made for each participant in a uniform relationship to compensation. If contributions for each participant are equal to the cost of coverage that the plan incurs for HCEs, or if contributions for each participant are at least equal to 75% of the cost for the similarly situated plan participant who has the highest cost of benefits, the plan satisfies the nondiscrimination tests.

Nontaxable cafeteria plan benefits are not subject to employer or employee FICA taxes. However, amounts placed into a 401(k) plan are subject to both employer and employee shares of FICA and FUTA.

Generally, participants will be given a 30-day period at the end of every year to make the election for the following year. The period might close a few days, or even a month, before the end of the year to give the plan administrators time to process the election request.

Cafeteria plans must be in writing, describe all benefits under the plan, apply uniformly to all participants, and be adopted on or before the first day of the plan's first plan year. Retroactive adoptions and amendments are forbidden.

The only permissible benefits for cafeteria plans are:

- Up to $50,000 group-term life insurance on the lives of employees;

- Accident and Health plans, including health Flexible Spending Accounts and payment of individual A&H premiums or COBRA premiums under an A&H plan;

- Contributions to a Health Savings Account (HSA distributions can be used to pay for long-term care or premiums of qualified long-term care insurance policies);

- Dependent care assistance;

- Adoption assistance;

- 401(k) contributions;

- Short- and long-term disability coverage

However, cafeteria plans are forbidden to offer:

- Scholarships;

- Tuition reduction;

- Employer-provided meals and lodging;

- Educational assistance;

- Long-term care insurance;

- Athletic facilities;

- Commuting benefits;

- Working condition fringe benefits;

- De minimis benefits;

- Employee discounts;

- Cell phones provided by the employer;

- MSA contributions;

- Group-term life insurance on non-employees (e.g., employees' parents).

The written plan document must explain how employees can make elections, the maximum salary reduction the plan will allow, the employer's contributions, and rules for any FSAs and HSAs included in the plan. The Proposed Regulations incorporate some of the safe harbor testing rules of Code § 410(b), with an objective test to determine when the actual election of benefits is discriminatory: when HCEs have higher benefits, measured as a percentage of compensation, than non-HCEs. [IRS Publication 15-B (for use in 2017, updated Dec. 16, 2016) <http://www.irs.gov/pub/irs-pdf/p15b.pdf> (last accessed Feb. 27, 2017)]

[B]   Cafeteria Plans After HIPAA

Proposed and Temporary Regulations for bringing cafeteria plans into conformity with HIPAA were published at 62 Fed. Reg. 60165 and 60196 (Nov. 7, 1997). Then, in March 2000, the IRS replaced the 1997 Temporary Regulations with T.D. 8878, 65 Fed. Reg. 15548, 2000-15 I.R.B. 857 (Mar. 23, 2000). These Regulations, which were supposed to be final, clarified the circumstances under which employees participating in cafeteria plans can change their elections in connection with accident, health, or group-term life insurance coverage. For example, a change might be needed when a Qualified Medical Child Support Order (QMCSO) is granted, or when the person gains or loses eligibility for Medicare or Medicaid.

At the beginning of 2001, the IRS revised this Treasury Decision. [See T.D. 8921, 66 Fed. Reg. 1837 (Jan. 10, 2001)] T.D. 8921 modifies the T.D. 8878 Final Regulations by allowing cafeteria plan participants to increase or decrease their coverage whenever they have a change-of-status event.

Changes were always allowed on the basis of marriage or divorce. Thanks to T.D. 8921, changes are also permitted when a dependent is born or adopted. An employee who decreases or cancels coverage under the cafeteria plan because of coverage under a spouse or dependent's plan has to certify that he or she is getting other coverage.

The cafeteria plan election can be changed to conform to a domestic relations order, but only if the spouse or former spouse actually provides coverage for the child; T.D. 8921 also allows elections to be changed when the employee's responsibility for payments under the plan increases or decreases significantly. The plan's payment for dependent care cannot be greater than what the employee earns.

The Simple Cafeteria Plan is a new plan form created by the health care reform statute. Small employers can set up Simple Cafeteria Plans starting in 2011. PPACA (the health care legislation) defines a small employer as one that averaged 100 or fewer employees in each of the previous two years. (For employers that have not been in business for two years, a reasonable estimate is used.) The advantage of the Simple Cafeteria Plan over a conventional cafeteria plan is that the employer is not subject to the requirements of nondiscrimination testing. All qualified employees must be eligible to participate if they had at least 1,000 hours of service in the previous plan year, but employees can be excluded if they are younger than 21 (or an even younger age stipulated by the plan), or if they are covered by a CBA. Highly compensated and key employees can participate in the Simple Cafeteria Plan, but the plan must not discriminate in their favor. All eligible employees must be allowed to elect any benefit in the plan under the same terms and conditions as all other participants. The employer sponsoring the plan must make at least a minimum contribution that the participant can apply toward any benefit within the plan. The minimum contribution for non-HCEs must equal or exceed the lesser of a uniform 2% of compensation (whether or not the employee contributes); a match equal to double the employee's contribution; or 6% of compensation. [Gary B. Kushner, Kushner & Co., *New Simple Cafeteria Plans* (Aug. 17, 2010) (benefitslink.com)]

§ 22.04   EDUCATION ASSISTANCE

Employers offer education assistance both because anything that employees consider a valuable benefit is a good motivator, and because a better-educated workforce promotes efficiency and productivity. However, the tax status of this benefit has fluctuated over the past decades.

There were no Code provisions allowing employees to receive educational assistance tax-free before I.R.C. § 127 was enacted in 1978, as a five-year pilot project. It was extended several times, and finally made permanent by the Economic Growth and Tax Relief Reconciliation Act (EGTRRA), which also removed the earlier limitation of the assistance to undergraduate-level education. Under I.R.C. § 127, employees can exclude from income up to $5,250 in benefits under an educational assistance program. [The version of Publication 970, Tax Benefits for Education, for calculating 2015 returns, is available at <http://www.irs.gov/pub/irs-pdf/p970.pdf> (last viewed Mar. 27, 2016)]

The "fiscal cliff" legislation, the American Taxpayer Relief Act of 2012, extends the educational assistance provision indefinitely. Up to $5,250 in employer assistance is not considered to be taxable income, and should not be reported on Form W-2. The educational assistance program must be in writing. If the benefits exceed $5,250, the excess should be included in form W-2, unless the amount constitutes a working condition fringe benefit (i.e., an amount the employee could have deducted, if he or she had paid it out of pocket). [See IRS guidance at <http://www.irs.gov/uac/Tax-Benefits-for-Education:-Information-Center> (updated Apr 15, 2016) (last viewed Feb. 27, 2017)]

In order to compete for workers, employers have to deliver the benefits that employees want, so student loan repayment benefits are gaining popularity. Three-quarters of survey respondents (76%) said that availability of loan repayment would be a major factor in the decision to take a job. Repayment plans can be structured as flat monthly amounts; a bonus at milestone anniversaries; or an option to split the employer's contribution between a 401(k) plan and the loan repayment. Note, however, that although tuition reimbursement can be tax-free for the employee (up to the $5,250 limit), the loan repayment is taxable income to the employee. [Bobbi Kloss, *A New Important Benefit Consideration: Student Loan Repayment,* The Institute for HealthCare Consumerism (Aug. 8, 2016) (benefitslink.com); Jared Bilski, *The Next 401(k)? Why Student Loan Repayment May Soon Be a Standard Benefit,* hrbenefitsalert.com (July 19, 2016) (benefitslink.com)]

§ 22.05 EMPLOYEE ASSISTANCE PROGRAMS (EAPs)

The purpose of the Employee Assistance Program (EAP) is to help employees cope with stress and other problems. The theory is that sympathetic listening, and referrals for whatever professional services are needed, will ease employees' anxieties and make them more productive. EAPs can offer any combination of one-on-one counseling, information and referral, hotlines and crisis intervention, and informational seminars.

EAPs typically deal with problems such as substance abuse, dependent care, and problems with spouses and children. Many companies have found that early intervention makes it possible to shorten the damage and amount of time that would otherwise be involved, for instance, when the employee "hits bottom" with a drug or alcohol problem, or when an untreated mental illness requires inpatient hospitalization in a crisis. Each dollar invested in EAP services is estimated to return anywhere from two to eight dollars in health and productivity savings.

EAPs also take a role in coordinating an employee's return to work after recuperating from an accident or illness (which may include a shortened or flexible schedule, intermittent FMLA leave, or other accommodations).

The services can be provided in house by the HR department, or contracted out to outside vendors. The second course is more expensive, but it may make the EAP more credible to employees, or may reassure employees that their confidentiality will be protected.

§ 22.06 MISCELLANEOUS FRINGES

Employees do not have taxable income if they receive certain minor fringe benefits provided by the employer on a nondiscriminatory basis to all employees. Under I.R.C. § 132, the benefits are not taxed to the employees. FICA, FUTA, and federal income tax withholding are not required, and the employer share of these taxes does not have to be paid. Generally, the employer will be able to deduct the cost of the program (which is supposed to be nominal, in any case) as long as it fits the definition of an ordinary and necessary business expense.

The categories of miscellaneous fringe benefits authorized under I.R.C. § 132 are:

- No-additional-cost services of the employer company (e.g., air travel for an airline employee; a simple will prepared by a law firm for a non-attorney staffer). The employee must gain access to services normally sold to customers, but the employer must not incur any substantial cost. In effect, the employees are given access to the business's excess capacity;

- Employee discounts; the discount must not exceed the gross profit percentage for goods, or 20% of the cost of services;

- De minimis fringe benefits, such as free beverages at work or small Christmas presents—anything too trivial to account for separately;

- Working condition fringe benefits—goods or services the employee could deduct if he or she paid for them personally. Typical examples are business travel and the use of company cars;

- An on-premises gym for the exclusive use of employees and their families;

- Reimbursement of employment-related moving expenses that would be deductible if the employee paid them directly (but have not in fact been deducted by the employee).

- An on-premises eating facility such as a low-cost cafeteria that prepares meals on premises for the convenience of the employer (because employees can take shorter meal breaks since the subsidized dining facility is available). The facility must be owned or operated by the employer, must generate revenue at least equal to its operating costs, and must provide meals during the workday or right before or right after it. It must also be in or near the workplace and must be operated by the employer (possibly through a contract with a third-party management company).

In some years, the transportation fringe benefit has been set at a different level depending upon whether the benefit covers parking or transit passes and vanpooling. At first, the mass transit benefit was lower than the parking benefit. The two were temporarily equalized between 2009 and 2013, but the equalization provision expired December 31, 2013. The parking benefit continued to rise because, by statute, it is indexed for inflation. [Andrew Grossman, *Mass-Transit Commuters Face a Tax Hit*, WSJ.com (Dec. 29, 2013)]

The Tax Increase Prevention Act of 2014 (TIPA), Pub. L. No. 113-295, increases the monthly transit benefit from $130 to $250, so the parking and mass transit benefits were equal for 2014. [Notice 2015-2, 2015-4 I.R.B. 334]

For 2015, Rev. Proc. 2014-61, 2014-47 I.R.B. 393 once again provides different amounts for the two benefits: $130 for transit passes and van pooling, $250 for parking.

The Protecting Americans Against Tax Hikes (PATH Act), Pub. L. No. 114-133, permanently equalizes the parking and mass transit benefits. The 2016 amount is $255 a month. [Rev. Proc. 2016-14, 2016-9 I.R.B. 365] The 2017 amount, under Rev. Proc. 2016-55, 2016-45 I.R.B. 707, remains $255 a month.

The Emergency Economic Stabilization Act, Pub. L. No. 110-343, added a new bicycle commuting benefit under Code § 132. Employers can provide employees with tax-free reimbursement of up to $20 a month for each month in which the employee regularly bicycles to work, starting with December 31, 2008. Reimbursable costs include buying a bicycle that is regularly used for commuting, and repairing and storing it. [Rebecca Moore, *Economic Stabilization Plan Includes Bicyclist Benefit*, plansponsor.com (Oct. 29, 2008); EBIA Weekly, *Bicycle Commuting Fringe Benefit Added to Code Section 132(f)* (Oct. 29, 2008) (benefitslink.com)]

IRS Information Letter 2013-0032 says that bicycle share programs are not qualified transportation fringe benefits as defined by Code § 132, so the employer's expenses for a bicycle share program cannot be excluded from the employee's gross income. A bicycle share program is not considered a transit pass because it does not involve mass transit. It does not qualify as bicycle commuting reimbursement because that is limited to employee costs of buying and repairing a bicycle to be used to travel between home and work. [PLC, *IRS: Bike Share Expenses Do Not Qualify for Favorable Fringe Benefit Tax Treatment* (Oct. 2, 2013) (benefitslink.com)]

Another Code section, I.R.C. § 119, governs meals and lodging furnished on premises for the convenience of the employer (e.g., a room for a hotel manager who must be around to handle problems as they arise. Such benefits are not taxable income for the employee).

§ 22.07   VOLUNTARY EMPLOYEE BENEFIT ASSOCIATIONS (VEBAs)

A Voluntary Employee Benefit Association (VEBA), as defined by I.R.C. § 501(c)(9), is a trust that is funded by employer contributions (with or without employee contributions) and is used to pay benefits to employees who voluntarily exercise the option to participate in the association. VEBAs provide life, sickness, accident, or similar benefits to employee members and their dependents and designated beneficiaries. Benefits that can be offered by a VEBA safeguard or improve health or protect against a contingency that threatens the employee's earning power. But VEBAs are not allowed to offer reimbursement of commuting expenses, profit sharing, or stock bonuses.

The trust itself is not a taxable entity, but VEBA benefits constitute taxable income to the employee unless they are specifically exempted.

The VEBA must be controlled by its employee membership, by a bank or other independent trustee, or by fiduciaries chosen by or on behalf of the membership. A VEBA is considered a welfare plan under ERISA, and therefore is subject to ERISA Parts 1 (notice and reporting), 4 (trust and fiduciary responsibility), and 5 (enforcement).

§ 22.08   FRINGE BENEFIT PLANS: TAX COMPLIANCE

[A]   Reporting Requirements

The reporting requirements for a fringe benefit plan are set out in I.R.C. § 6039D. The plan must report:

- Number of employees at the employer company;
- Number of employees eligible to participate in the plan;
- Number actually participating;
- Number of highly compensated employees in each of the above categories;
- The plan's total cost during the year;
- The employer's name, address, and Employer Identification Number;
- The nature of its business.

If any fringe benefits are taxable, the employer can either add them to the regular wages for a payroll period, or withhold federal income tax at the rate for supplemental wages. [The relevant IRS publication is 15-B, *Employer's Tax Guide to Fringe Benefits*.]

[B]   The Employer's Tax Deduction

When it comes to pensions, the tax rules are devised to make sure that the employer contributes enough to fund the plan. In contrast, when it comes to welfare benefits, the tax focus is preventing excessive prefunding of benefit plans. So the relevant Code sections (I.R.C. §§ 419 and 419A) specify a maximum funding level for welfare benefit trusts. If this level is exceeded, the trust is no longer tax-exempt.

Although the employer receives a tax deduction for maintaining a welfare benefit trust, the deduction is limited to the "qualified cost" of the benefit plans for the year. That means the direct cost of funding benefits, plus whatever amount I.R.C. § 419A permits to be added to the account for the year as a safety cushion.

Reference should also be made to I.R.C. § 4976, which imposes a 100% excise tax on disqualified benefit distributions made from funded welfare benefit plans. For instance, retiree health and life insurance benefits for highly compensated employees are supposed to be kept in a separate account from comparable contributions for rank-and-file employees.

Therefore, benefits paid to HCEs from the general account would be disqualified. VEBA benefits to HCEs that violate nondiscrimination requirements are also disqualified, as are amounts that revert to the employer. (An erroneous contribution which is withdrawn by the employer after a determination that it is not deductible is not considered a reversion.)

§ 22.09   ERISA REGULATION OF WELFARE BENEFIT PLANS

[A]   Creation and Administration

Although most of the attention goes to ERISA's regulation of pension plans, ERISA also covers welfare benefit plans—a category roughly equivalent to fringe benefit plans. An ERISA welfare benefit plan is created (generally by a corporate resolution passed by the Board of Directors and managed by the relevant corporate officials) and administered to provide one or more of these benefits to plan participants and their beneficiaries:

- Medical benefits;
- Health care;
- Accident insurance;
- Disability benefits;
- Death benefits;
- Supplemental unemployment benefits;
- Vacation benefits;

- Training (e.g., apprenticeship);

- Day care centers (but not dependent care spending reimbursement accounts);

- Scholarships;

- Prepaid legal services;

- Any benefit described in the Labor Management Relations Act § 302(c) [29 U.S.C. §§ 141–144, etc.] other than death benefits, pensions, or insurance coverage for pensions or death benefits.

The people receiving the benefits must be common-law employees and not independent contractors. For this purpose, employee status depends on agency principles such as who controls and supervises the person, and whether the person can recognize profit or loss from the work relationship. It does not depend on the "reasonable expectations" of the parties. [*Mut. Ins. Co. v. Darden*, 503 U.S. 318 (1992)]

Welfare benefit plans are subject to ERISA Title I. The Eleventh Circuit has ruled that a Title I plan exists if circumstances lead a reasonable person to ascertain the intended benefits, intended beneficiaries, financing sources, and procedure for receiving benefits under the plan. [*Donovan v. Dillingham*, 688 F.2d 1367 (11th Cir. 1982)] A plan can be deemed to exist even if the ERISA rules are not observed, and in fact, even if there is no written instrument.

Severance pay plans are sometimes treated as pension plans, but are more likely to be characterized as welfare benefit plans. DOL Advisory Opinion 84-12A says that a severance pay plan is not a pension plan if:

- Its benefits are not contingent on the employee's retirement;

- Total payments do not exceed twice the employee's compensation for the year before the termination;

- Payments are completed within 24 months after termination of service for the employer.

Under a similar analysis, bonus programs are not treated as pension plans for ERISA Title I purposes unless the payments are systematically deferred at least until termination of employment. DOL Reg. § 2510.3 says that an employer plan that supplements retirement benefits (e.g., until early retirees can qualify for Social Security benefits) can be either a pension or a welfare benefit plan, depending on its terms and how it is administered.

ERISA Title I does not apply to certain payroll practices, such as extra pay for non-standard working hours (overtime, shift, or holiday premiums); sick leave; paid vacation, sabbaticals, military leave, and other paid absences.

Under prior law, welfare benefit plans were not required to file Form 5500 if they had fewer than 100 participants. However, a July 2016 DOL proposal calls for increasing the amount of information the DOL gathers, and changing the form of the information to make it easier to analyze. The proposal requires all health and welfare benefits to file Form 5500, no matter how many participants they have, and would have to complete Schedule J to disclose enrollment data and their practices for paying claims, maintaining wellness programs, and requiring cost sharing from plan participants. Welfare benefit plans with fewer than 100 participants will not be permitted to use Form 5500-SF any longer. (Compliance is not required until Form 5500s are prepared for the 2019 plan year.) [81 Fed. Reg. 47533 (July 21, 2016); see Carly E. Grey, *DOL Proposes Major Changes to Form 5500*, Morgan Lewis & Bockius LLP (July 20, 2016), available at Lexology.com; Frost Brown Todd, *Form 5500 Updates and Increased ERISA Penalties* (Oct. 5, 2016) (benefitslink.com)]

[B] ERISA Case Law on Welfare Benefits

Where failure to make complete disclosure could be harmful to benefit participants, a benefit plan administrator had a fiduciary duty to give complete and accurate information about the plan. Until 2006, Menasha Corporation retirees and their spouses continued to receive health insurance from the company. Between ages 62–65, the company paid 80% of the premium; when retirees turned 65, the company paid 100% of the premium. In 2006, however, Menasha informed the plaintiffs that it was adopting a new health plan, and premiums would no longer be 100% covered. The plaintiffs sued alleging violations of the Labor Management Relations Act, 29 U.S.C. § 185, and ERISA, 29 U.S.C. § 1132. The district court ruled in the plaintiffs' favor as to employee coverage, but in favor of defendant as to spouses. The Sixth Circuit reversed in part, ruling for the plaintiffs. Although healthcare is a "welfare benefit," not entitled to the same ERISA protection as pension benefits, certain actions by employers will waive the employers' right to alter welfare benefits. In this case, Menasha waived the right to change the benefits by providing vested healthcare coverage to retired employees and spouses, and by agreeing that CBAs could only be modified with signed, mutual consent of the parties. [*Moore v. Menasha Corp.*, 690 F.3d 444 (6th Cir. 2013)]

The Tenth Circuit ruled that retiree health and life insurance benefits are welfare benefit plans for ERISA purposes—not subject to the ERISA minimum vesting standard. Unless there is a contractual agreement to provide vested benefits, the employer can unilaterally modify or even eliminate such benefits. General contract law requires clear and express plan language, showing intent to vest. In this case, the documents (with the SPD treated as a plan document for this purpose) did not include express vesting language. [*Fulghum v. Embarq Corp.*, 778 F.3d 1147 (10th Cir. 2015)]

PART V

THE HR FUNCTION

CHAPTER 23

HIRING AND RECRUITMENT

§ 23.01   INTRODUCTION

Efficient hiring practices benefit the company at all levels. Prompt, economical selection of the best person to do the job (whether from inside the company or brought in from outside) will keep operations running smoothly and encourage innovation that will keep the business competitive.

On the downside, bad hiring practices create many kinds of risks such as employment discrimination charges, or charges of negligent hiring or retention (if an employee commits a crime or sexual harassment). Or, a poorly chosen employee can be inefficient, make costly mistakes and have to be replaced, generating additional costs.

The Hiring Inventives to Restore Employment (HIRE) Act was enacted in March 2010, providing payroll tax incentives for hiring previously unemployed workers, in the form of a payroll tax credit equal to the employer's share of the Federal Insurance Contributions Act (FICA) tax. The credit expired on January 1, 2011, and was not renewed. [Rebecca Moore, *New Law Offers Tax Incentives for Hiring*, plansponsor.com (Mar. 18, 2010)]

However, the Tax Relief, Unemployment Insurance Reauthorization, and Job Creation Act of 2010 (TRUI; Pub. L. No. 111-312) provided a different kind of payroll tax cut: reduction of the employee (not the employer) share of FICA tax to 4.2%. The Middle Class Tax Relief and Job Creation Act of 2012, Pub. L. No. 112-96, extends the 4.2% payroll tax rate until the end of 2012, but it was not extended further. [Josh Mitchell and Naftali Bendavid, *Tax Bill Passed by Congress Broadens Jobless Program*, WSJ.com (Feb. 18, 2012)]

In November 2011, Congress passed the VOW to Hire Heroes Act of 2011, including a new tax credit for hiring veterans: up to $9,600 per veteran for for-profit companies, $6,240 for tax-exempt organizations. The maximum credit was granted for hiring veterans with service-connected disabilities. [Notice 2012-13, 2012-9 I.R.B. 421] This credit expired December 31, 2013.

Late 2015 legislation, the Protecting Americans From Tax Hikes (PATH) Act, Pub. L. No. 114-113, extends the Work Opportunity Tax Credit (WOTC) until December 31, 2019. This credit allows employers to reduce their federal income taxes by $2,400 to $9,600 for each person hired from a targeted group (such as qualified veterans and people from families receiving federal financial assistance).

§ 23.02   PRODUCTIVE HIRING

The recession has increased the number of applicants for most jobs, and gives many hiring managers a choice among many qualified (or overqualified) candidates—but when a company seeks to keep payroll manageable, it is important to select the right candidate.

Current employees can be a great starting point for recruitment (and many companies offer bonuses if a current employee recruits someone who is hired and completes a minimum period satisfactorily), but they should not be the only source of recruitment—especially if you want a diverse workforce.

College and graduate school recruitment should not be restricted to those nearby, or only to a small class of Ivy League schools. If nationwide recruitment is a cost problem, the Internet allows nationwide recruiting and low cost. However, resumes posted on the Internet are no more or less truthful than those delivered by traditional means, so reference checks are still required.

See § 25.02[C] for a discussion of recent cases about the effect of covenants not to compete on hiring. However, the opposite tack could also be problematic.

In 2010, the Department of Justice (DOJ) sued Adobe, Apple, Google, Intel, Intuit, Lucasfilm, and Pixar, and private class actions were filed alleging that these companies conspired to avoid bidding wars for high-priced talents. The plaintiffs charged the companies with refraining from recruiting each others' employees, and argued that "non-poaching" agreements are per se illegal under Sherman Act § 1. The cases were consolidated in the District Court for the Northern District of California. Three defendants settled: Lucasfilm/Pixar agreed to pay $9 million and Intuit agreed to pay $11 million. Cases remained pending against the other four defendants, with 92% of the potential class members. [*In re High-Tech Employee Antitrust Litig.*, No. 11-02509 (N.D. Cal., partially settled 2013)]

Apple, Google, Intel, and Adobe agreed to settle in May 2014, under a settlement calling for $324.5 million in damages for 64,000 plaintiffs. However, Judge Lucy H. Koh of the Central District of California rejected the settlement in August 2014, finding that not only was there extensive evidence of conspiracy, but also plaintiffs would receive only about $4,000 each. [Thomas M. McInerney, *National Implications from Settlement of High-Profile Employee Raiding Case*, Ogletree Deakins (Apr. 26, 2014), available at Lexology.com]

Apple, Google, Intel, and Adobe made a second agreement, this time to pay $415 million to 64,000 employees and ex-employees, an average of about $5,000 per person after fees. The original settlement yielded less than $4,000 per person. There is no acknowledgment of liability in this settlement offer either. The district court gave preliminary approval to the settlement in March 2015, with the final approval hearing set for July 9, 2015. [David Streitfeld, *Bigger Settlement Said to Be Reached in Silicon Valley Antitrust Case*, NYTimes.com (Jan. 14, 2015)]

On September 2, 2015, the District Court for the Northern District of California approved a $415 million settlement of the antitrust class action—$90 million more than the proposal rejected in August 2014 as inadequate. Two similar cases, one against Microsoft and one against Oracle, were dismissed by the Northern District of California on statute of limitations grounds. [*In re High-Tech Employee Antitrust Litig.*, Case No. 5:11-cv-02509, 2015 U.S. Dist LEXIS 118051 (N.D. Cal. Sept. 2, 2015). The dismissed cases are *Ryan v. Microsoft*

Corp., No. 14-CV-04634, 2015 U.S. Dist. LEXIS 158944 (N.D. Cal. Nov. 23, 2015) and *Garrison v. Oracle Corp.*, No. 14-CV-04592, 2016 U.S. Dist. LEXIS 13118 (N.D. Cal. Feb. 2, 2016): see Timothy F. Haley, *Wage Suppression Antitrust Class Allegations Against Oracle Dismissed as Untimely*, Seyfarth Shaw LLP (Feb. 11, 2016), available at Lexology.com]

On October 20, 2016, the FTC and DOJ issued joint antitrust guidelines for human resources. The DOJ will bring criminal cases for unlawful wage fixing and no-poach agreements. The guidelines define some "red flags" in employment practices: for example, formal or informal agreements to avoid soliciting or hiring a competitor's employees or fixing or limiting employee compensation. Exchange of compensation information can violate the antitrust laws if it has the effect of reducing competition. [DOJ/FTC joint guidance, *Antitrust Guidance for Human Resource Professionals,* available at <https://www.ftc.gov/system/files/documents/public_statements/992623/ftc-doj_hr_guidance_final_10-20-16.pdf>; see Ashley K. Laken and Timothy F. Haley, *HR Professionals Take Note: DOJ and FTC Issue Guidance Regarding Antitrust Laws in the Employment Context,* Seyfarth Shaw LLP (Oct. 21, 2016), available at Lexology.com; Maria Greco Danaher, *What the DOJ/FTC's Recent "Antitrust Guidance for Human Resource Professionals" Means for Employers*, Ogletree Deakins (Nov. 1, 2016), available at Lexology.com]

§ 23.03 ANALYZING JOB REQUIREMENTS

In many cases, poor hiring decisions are made because of lack of insight into the real demands of the job. A candidate is chosen who matches the formal, written job description, but there's a mismatch, because the real job isn't very much like the job description. Often, people are hired on the basis of technical skills, but those skills are seldom used on a day-to-day basis.

The job should be analyzed to see how much time is spent on various tasks, such as working with machinery, writing and analyzing reports, or supervising other workers.

It is important to understand the physical demands of the job, to see who can meet them without accommodation, and what accommodations can reasonably be made to the needs of individuals with disabilities. The American with Disabilities Act (ADA) cases frequently turn on whether a task that the plaintiff cannot perform is an essential function of the job. [See § 36.05 for a discussion of reasonable accommodation.]

The job must be identified as exempt or nonexempt for wage and hour purposes. Controversial DOL regulations finalized in mid-2016 greatly increase the number of employees who are not exempt from overtime. [See 81 Fed. Reg. 32391 (May 23, 2016)] Sometimes it makes economic sense to restructure job duties so that the job becomes exempt from overtime requirements. However, the change must be real, not just a meaningless title.

There should be a written job description indicating:

- Job title;

- When it has to be filled;

- Why the organization needs someone for that position at all (perhaps the duties could be delegated to existing employees, outsourced, or assigned to temporary or part-time employees);

- Required educational qualifications;

- Necessary skills;

- Standards for defining inadequate, satisfactory, good, and excellent performance; the educational qualifications, skills, and experience that are really needed to perform the job; and standards (as objective as possible) for defining inadequate, satisfactory, good, and excellent performance.

The job description should indicate reporting relationships (whom the job-holder reports to; who reports to him or her). It should explain the promotion potential for the job, including conditions (such as getting an MBA or meeting performance goals). If your company has a grading system, the job grade should be indicated. The job description should also include the salary range.

§ 23.04 RECRUITMENT

It is probably worthwhile to consider promoting existing employees to fill important positions, although sometimes it is necessary to look outside—or desirable to get new skills and viewpoints. Even a policy of promoting from within requires recruiting, to fill entry- and mid-levels that have been vacated by the promoted employees.

The web and social media (blogs, Facebook, LinkedIn, etc.) are gaining in importance as recruiting and hiring sources. Note, however, that some state laws forbid employers to demand that applicants or employees provide the user names or passwords for their personal e-mail and social media accounts.

Checking applicants' social media can be beneficial, but is also risky. Research can reveal the applicant's membership in a protected class and open the way to allegations of discrimination. But it can also reveal evidence that precludes hiring the applicant (for example, references to a DUI conviction when the job is safety-sensitive). A 2016 article suggests checking social media only after the decision has been made to extend a job offer, as part of the background check. The HR department, not the hiring manager, should do the review: they have a better grasp on what is allowed. But if social media is consulted, it should be done consistently, to rebut charges of discrimination. But research should be limited to public posts and avoid asking for passwords. [Jonathan A. Segal, *6 Ways to*

Lawfully Embrace Social Recruiting, Duane Morris LLP (Aug. 16, 2016), available at Lexology.com]

As of early 2017, half the states had enacted statutes providing social media privacy protection for employees: Arkansas, California, Colorado, Connecticut, Delaware, Illinois, Louisiana, Maine, Maryland, Michigan, Montana, Nebraska, Nevada, New Hampshire, New Jersey, New Mexico, Oklahoma, Oregon, Rhode Island, Tennessee, Utah, Virginia, Washington, West Virginia, and Wisconsin. With state-to-state variations, the laws generally forbid employers to require job applicants or employees to disclose the user names or passwords for the individual's personal social media account. Devices and networks provided by the employer are not subject to these requirements, and these statutes do not prevent employers from accessing social media information that is publicly available. [National Conference of State Legislators, *State Social Media Privacy Laws* (updated Jan. 11, 2017) (last accessed Feb. 27, 2017), available at <http://www.ncsl.org/research/telecommunications-and-information-technology/state-laws-prohibiting-access-to-social-media-usernames-and-passwords.aspx>]

However, an online-only recruitment effort may not be enough. In mid-2016, the FCC fined a cable company $11,000 for inadequate job recruiting because the company's sole recruitment methods were online. FCC rules require recruitment efforts to reach a significant proportion of the local population and the FCC's position is that the local newspaper is presumed to be the means of reaching the greatest number of groups within a community. The FCC said that close to a third of the people in the cable system's service area did not have Internet access, so they couldn't see the ads. The fine also penalized failure to complete one year's EEO report, which is required to be released to the public. David O. Oxenford, *$11,000 FCC EEO Fine for Recruiting Solely Through Online Sources—Time to Revisit the FCC Rules?*, Wilkinson Barker Knauer LLP (July 26, 2016), available at Lexology.com]

[See § 27.05 for more discussion of the HR implications of social media usage.]

Job postings may literally be posted on a bulletin board, remaining there for five to 10 days. This is especially true in unionized companies, where the Collective Bargaining Agreement (CBA) governs the requirements for posting jobs. More and more companies are using the corporate Intranet for this purpose. The posting should explain the nature of the job (although another advantage of recruiting from within is that the applicants will be fairly familiar with it already); the qualifications required; and whether there are any limitations. For instance, seniority is a very significant factor in promotions in a unionized workplace. Some companies have a policy that employees are not allowed to apply for internal vacancies unless they have held their current job for at least six months with satisfactory or better performance appraisals. The usual policy is to keep the application confidential from the applicant's immediate supervisor, until there is the possibility that the promotion will be offered.

The state employment service can be a good resource for low-level jobs, and even some higher-level technical jobs. Unemployment benefits are not available to workers who have voluntarily quit, or who were fired for wrongdoing, so workers receiving benefits are probably not unstable or a bad risk merely on account of being unemployed. Also, people who are employed but want a new job sometimes register with the state employment office because it has contacts with a wide range of employers and because it does not charge jobseekers a fee. To fill higher-level positions, if a local company has had a major downsizing recently, check with the company that handles their executive outplacement.

The New York City Human Rights Law makes it illegal for employers to discriminate based on unemployment. Over two dozen proposals to adopt similar laws are pending at the federal, state, and local level. The states of New Jersey and Oregon, and the City of Chicago forbid help-wanted advertisements that rule out applications from unemployed persons, and the District of Columbia makes it unlawful for an employment agency or employer to treat being unemployed as a factor in hiring or employment decisions. The New York City statute is the only one with a private right of action.

The New Jersey Appellate Division upheld NJSA § 34:8B-1, the state law that forbids job advertisements that say all applicants must be currently employed. (The law does not require employers to hire unemployed persons, interview them, or even consider their applications, as long as they are allowed to apply.) The court found that the law did not infringe on employers' First Amendment rights. The statute was treated as commercial speech, so legal restraints are viewed more indulgently than restraints on political speech. The court found that the law was narrowly tailored to advance the substantial government interest in promoting opportunity for the unemployed. [*New Jersey Dep't of Labor & Workforce Dev. v. Crest Ultrasonics et al.*, 434 N.J. Super. 34, 82 A.3d 258 (N.J. App. Div. 2014)]

If you hire someone who held a senior position at one of your competitors, it is possible that the individual had an employment contract with the company that contained a covenant not to compete. Another possibility is that, when his or her severance package was negotiated, a covenant not to compete was signed at that time. Therefore, it is important to find out if a job applicant is subject to such an agreement, and whether taking the job that is offered would violate it.

Even without a covenant not to compete, a competitor could charge that you hired its ex-employee to misappropriate the competitor's customer lists and trade secrets. If you recruited the ex-employee, you might be charged with interference with contractual relationships. So make it part of the interview process to make a record about the circumstances of the contact.

§ 23.05 SEARCH FIRMS

Businesses often retain search firms for top executive and professional positions, although this can be a costly option.

There are two main types of firms in the search professional. Contingency firms are usually used to find candidates for mid-level jobs; an executive search firm usually gets involved only with upper-level jobs. A search firm works directly for the company seeking to hire an executive. Usually, its contracts require the company to pay for its services whether or not a candidate is hired. In contrast, a contingency firm's clients include both job seekers and companies looking to hire someone, and the company pays a fee if and only if hiring results.

A search firm's fee can be anywhere from 25% to 100% of the first year salary. Contingency firms usually charge less, perhaps 20% to 33% of the first year's salary. Only cash compensation, not bonuses or stock options, is included in the calculation. Both kinds of firms often give refunds if the new hire leaves or has to be discharged during a probationary period such as 90 days.

Many companies are not familiar with search firms, so they do not know what to expect or how to assess the quality of the firm's performance. John Marra, president of the recruitment firm Marra Peters & Partners, has some suggestions:

- Be clear on the criteria you use to judge the firm's performance;

- Get references from past clients and follow them up;

- Tell the search firm what you expect the successful candidate to accomplish the first six months and the first year after hiring, and how you will assess the new hire's performance;

- Ask the search firm to send only candidates who are a good match with your requirements;

- Get the search firm's promise to keep working with you until the vacancy is satisfactorily filled (if necessary, after someone has been hired, terminated after a probationary period, and a new search performed).

Some of the provisions to look for in a recruitment contract are:

- Clarification that the firm does not have the authority to hire someone on behalf of your company, or to promise terms and conditions of employment—only your company's authorized agent can do that;

- A statement that your company is committed to equal employment opportunity principles;

- The firm's agreement that it will be responsible if it commits discrimination in referring candidates to you—and that it will indemnify your company for any liability resulting from its discriminatory referrals;

- A clear statement of the firm's responsibilities, including screening candidates and checking their references;

- Recruiting expenses that your company agrees to pay;

- Whether you have to pay if you hire a candidate obtained through another channel, or only if the recruiter sends the successful candidate to you;

- The recruiter's promise not to contact or solicit your new hire for a period of at least two years.

§ 23.06 JOB APPLICATIONS

Frequently, the first real contact between the corporation and the potential employee occurs when the applicant submits a formal job application. The application is a legal document that can have serious consequences: both as a source of promises that the employer can be held to, and as a source of information whose correctness the applicant can be held responsible for. For example, false statements on an application can constitute "after-acquired evidence" of wrongdoing that can limit the damages available to a successful employee plaintiff. [See § 42.10[C]]

It often makes sense to have a candidate fill out a job application even if he or she has submitted a resume. The resume only includes the information the candidate wants to disclose. The application form is standard, and resumes are very variable, so it is easier to compare applicants if you have the same information about each. The application might ask for:

- Positions held with the last three or four employers;

- Dates of employment;

- Job title;

- Salary;

- Name of immediate supervisor;

- Why the candidate left that job (unless he or she is still employed);

- Permission to contact the supervisor for a reference.

■ **TIP:** In several states (e.g., California, Delaware, Minnesota, Wisconsin), if you require applicants to sign their applications, the state privacy law also requires you to give them a copy of the completed application, or lets employees copy personnel files including job applications.

The application should make it clear that the form is a legal document that can have serious ramifications. It is important to require the applicant to state that all the information given on the application is complete and accurate—and that it will be grounds for discipline or dismissal if the applicant is hired and the employer later finds out that false information was given on the application.

There should be a separate signature line if the employer wants to get a credit report to indicate release of this information. Applicants should be informed when reference checks will be done. The form should clarify that application is being made for at-will employment. If the job offer is conditional on the applicant's passing a physical examination and/or drug and alcohol testing, this should be indicated on the application.

Check state law about which questions are permissible, and which are ruled out by antidiscrimination laws.

A growing trend is for states and cities to limit the extent to which employers can ask about applicants' salary history. (The theory is that past discrimination has influenced salary levels, and it is unfair for a person's past experience of wage discrimination to continue to limit compensation for later jobs.) Delaware, Massachusetts, and Oregon and cities including Boston, New York City, and Philadelphia do not allow employers to ask job applicants about salary history. Once a job offer is extended, the question can be asked, and the employer can check the accuracy of the new employee's statement. [Amanda Van Hoose Garofalo and Amy J. Traub, *Employers Will No Longer Be Permitted to Ask About Previous Pay in New York City,* Baker & Hostetler LLP (Apr. 16, 2017), available at Lexology.com; Cody Emily Schvaneveldt, *Oregon Enacts New Equal Pay Law That Includes Salary History Inquiry Restrictions,* Littler Mendelson PC (June 1, 2017), available at Lexology.com; Michael L. Stevens, *Delaware Becomes the "First State" to Enforce Ban on Employer Requests for Salary History,* Arent Fox LLP (June 29, 2017), available at Lexology.com; Alif Mia and Amber M. Rogers, *San Francisco Bans Employers From Asking Job Applicants About Salary History, 26 States Considering Similar Legislation,* Hunton & Williams LLP (July 20, 2017), available at Lexology.com; Daniel J. Clark and Michael C. Griffaton, *Delaware Becomes the Latest State to Ban Salary Inquiries,* Vorys Sater Seymour and Pease LLP (Aug. 9, 2017), available at Lexology.com]

Massachusetts and at least a dozen other states have statutes giving employees the right to discuss their compensation if they want to—e.g., to compare compensation with co-workers to get information the employees can use to negotiate salaries, bonuses, and benefits. [Stacy Cowley, *Illegal in Massachusetts: Asking Your Salary in a Job Interview,* NYTimes.com (Aug. 3, 2016)]

In mid-2017, the Ninth Circuit held that it is not unlawful discrimination to pay men more than women for the same work if the differential reflects their past earnings. But after that case was decided, California adopted AB 1676, a statute that expands the group that can be used as comparators in equal pay cases, making it easier for plaintiffs to prove sex discrimination in compensation. [*Rizo v. Yovino,* 854 F.3d 1161 (9th Cir. 2017); see James McDonald Jr., *An Old-School Approach to Equal Pay at 9th Circ.,* Fisher Phillips (May 26, 2017), available at Lexology.com]

See 70 Fed. Reg. 58,947 (Oct. 7, 2005) for DOL's Office of Federal Contract Compliance Programs' (OFCCP) Final Rule covering federal contractors' records maintenance obligations with respect to Internet-based job applications.

If possible, contractors should collect data on the gender, race, and ethnicity of applicants (including those who apply online). Contractors are required to maintain records of Internet-based expressions of interest that resulted in the contractor considering an applicant for a particular job. [Tresa Baldas, *New Web Hiring Rules Cause Corporate Consternation*, Nat'l L.J. (Dec. 7, 2005) (law.com)]

See 78 Fed. Reg. 58683 (Sept. 24, 2013) for OFCCP regulations under Rehab Act 503: federal contractors are required to collect information about applicants' disabilities pursuant to the OFCCP's goal of having federal contractors hire a specified percentage of persons with disabilities. [DOL Final Rule, *Affirmative Action and Nondiscrimination Obligations of Contractors and Subcontractors Regarding Individuals with Disabilities*, 78 Fed. Reg. 58683 (Sept. 24, 2013)]

§ 23.07 ESTABLISHING TERMS AND CONDITIONS

The interview should stress the at-will nature of employment if your company wants the flexibility to terminate employees without a formal structure. Train interviewers to avoid statements such as "If you do a good job, you'll be set for life here" or "We never lay anybody off, no matter how tough the economy gets." Interviewers should also avoid statements about corporate procedure ("We go through all the channels before anybody gets fired") unless they accurately reflect corporate policy and practice.

Interviewers are agents of the company, and even if the employee handbook says that the company is only obligated if there are written contracts, in fact the company is likely to be held accountable for promises made by the interviewer (for instance, about vacation terms, the availability of leave, and education benefits). Even if the interviewer is not a common-law employee of the company, the agency relationship is likely to create liability for the company if the interviewer is guilty of discrimination. [See, e.g., *Halpert v. Manhattan Apartments Inc.*, 580 F.3d 86 (2d Cir. 2009); see Mark Hamblett, *2nd Circuit: Employer May Be Held Liable for Contractor Age Bias*, N.Y.L.J. (Sept. 14, 2009) (law.com)]

Many companies set a salary range rather than an explicit pay rate for a particular job. Interviewers should understand whether or not they can negotiate a salary with a promising candidate, or if that matter will have to be referred to a higher-up. Interviewees should always be told clearly who else is involved in the interview process, what the powers are of each person, and who has the power to actually make a job offer.

§ 23.08 REFERENCE CHECKS

Reference checks have become much more common, as prices have fallen and employers have become more sensitive to potential problems and liability related to the hiring process.

Reference checks on employees (rather than applicants) can also be useful. A lack of candor can be a valid reason for denying a raise or promotion, and "after-acquired evidence" discovered as late as the preparation for a discrimination suit can be used to reduce the recovery a plaintiff can obtain.

Over half of hiring managers (58%) said that they have detected lies on resumes. One-third said academic credentials were the major area; "improved" job descriptions and dates of employment were even more common. Companies give more attention to checking criminal records and credit scores than academic credentials, particularly because it is difficult to monitor online education or technical certifications. However, services such as Parchment, which create secure digital transcripts and diplomas that are verifiable, are gaining in popularity. [Melissa Korn, *Soon, You'll Have to Tell the Truth on Your Resume*, WSJ.com (Sept. 20, 2014)]

In early 2011, the Supreme Court unanimously upheld the federal government's background check procedure for workers employed by federal contractors. Although the Ninth Circuit granted an injunction against enforcement of the procedure, finding that the questions about counseling and drug treatment were too broad, and persons listed as references were asked open-ended questions that were not detailed enough, the Supreme Court held that the process was reasonably related to security needs, and the Privacy Act controls inappropriate releases of information. [*NASA v. Nelson*, 562 U.S. 134 (2011)]

Close to one-third of adults in the United States, almost 80 million people, have entries in the FBI's criminal records file. Many of these notations are for arrests rather than convictions, but only half of the files show final dispositions—so dismissals will not be noted. The availability of expungement depends on state law. Some states make it difficult to expunge records even when an arrest was clearly wrongful. In the federal system, and in Alaska, Arizona, Maine, and Nebraska, records are effectively permanent. Since 2009, the FTC has brought eight suits against background screening companies for failing to maintain accurate records. Millions of dollars of settlements have been reached in private suits—but without admission of liability. [Joe Palazzolo and Gary Fields, *Fight Grows to Stop Expunged Criminal Records Living On in Background Checks*, WSJ.com (May 7, 2015)]

The Seventh Circuit held that an employer was not guilty of discrimination when it asked a legitimate question—and a job applicant persisted in lying about it. Sweatt had been a Union Pacific track worker for several years. When he was 54, he applied for a job as a security guard because he wanted a lighter-duty job. He had to complete a personal history statement. The form said that convictions were not always disqualifying, but lying about them was. Sweatt did not disclose a domestic violence arrest and stated specifically that he had never been arrested. He denied the arrest at least five times. When he was not considered for the security job, he sued the railroad for age and race discrimination. The Seventh Circuit upheld the employer's policy, noting that some people disclosed arrests and were hired. The inquiry was job-related, because security positions require honesty. [*Sweatt v. Union Pac. R.R. Co.*, 796 F.3d 701 (7th Cir. 2015)]

In March 2014, the Equal Employment Opportunities Commission (EEOC) and FTC jointly published guidance about background checks, warning employers that whenever background information (from any source) is used to make employment decisions, compliance with anti-discrimination laws (including Title VII, Genetic Information Nondiscrimination Act (GINA), the Age Discrimination in Employment Act (ADEA), and the Fair Credit Reporting Act (FCRA)) is mandatory. The EEOC warned that it is illegal to check background information only because of a person's race, national origin, color, sex, disability, age, or genetic status. "Special care" should be taken when there are problems that may be more common among members of certain groups (e.g., some ethnic groups have higher arrest rates than others).

The EEOC says that "except in rare circumstances" employers should not seek genetic information from applicants or employees, and medical questions should not be asked before a job offer has been made. The FTC says that the FCRA requires safeguards if an employer obtains a credit or criminal background report from a company that compiles background information. The applicant or employee must be given written notice that this information might be used in employment decisions and his or her written consent must be obtained. If an investigative report (based on personal interviews) is ordered, the applicant or employee must be informed of the right to information about the investigation. If adverse actions are taken based on information from a profiling company, the employer must give the applicant or employee a copy of the FTC's summary of FCRA rights, and must give contact information for the profiling company. [EEOC/FTC, *Background Checks: What Employers Need to Know*, <http://www1.eeoc.gov//eeoc/publications/background_checks_employers.cfm?> (undated; last viewed Feb. 27, 2017)]

Background checks are subject to federal requirements in addition to the rules for consumer credit reports, and California imposes additional requirements. Federal (and California) laws have additional requirements for background checks in addition to rules for consumer credit reports. California regulates background checks done in-house by employers as well as those performed by consumer reporting agencies. The federal FCRA defines an investigative consumer report as one including information from personal interviews about the subject's character, reputation, and the like. California regulates all third-party collection of information obtained in any way, not just personal interviews with persons acquainted with the subject.

In addition to California, the states of Colorado, Connecticut, Hawaii, Illinois, Maryland, Nevada, Oregon, Vermont, and Washington and the cities of Chicago, New York City, and Philadelphia have statutes restricting employers' access to and use of credit reports in making employment decisions. [Jennifer L. Mora, Philip L. Gordon and William J. Simmons, *Philadelphia Becomes the First Jurisdiction in 2016 to Restrict Employers from Using Credit Information in*

Employment Decisions, Littler Mendelson PC (June 20, 2016), available at Lexology.com]

Employers that obtain investigative consumer reports must disclose that the report will be obtained for information; that it may contain information about the subject's character and reputation; the scope of the investigation; contact information about the agency that will generate the report. Notice of the right to inspect the agency's file in person, get a summary over the telephone, or have a copy mailed must be given. The subject must be permitted to check a box to request a free copy of the report, which must be provided within three days of the time the employer receives it. In general, arrests, convictions, and indictments can be reported for only seven years and bankruptcies for only 10 years, but California law makes an exception when employers seek older records as required by a government regulatory agency (e.g., some securities or banking-related convictions debar a person from working in the industry for 10 years). [Pamela Q. Devata and Dana Howells, *Checking Out Applicants (Part 2): Using Consumer Reporting Agencies for Background Checks*, Seyfarth Shaw LLP (June 27, 2014), available at Lexology.com]

The EEOC opposes blanket refusals to hire based on criminal records (or credit reports) if the refusal has a disparate impact on minorities, a principle embodied in April 2012 guidance. [EEOC Enforcement Guidance, *Consideration of Arrest and Conviction Records in Employment Decisions Under Title VII of the Civil Rights Act of 1964*, <http://www.eeoc.gov/laws/guidance/arrest_conviction .cfm> (Apr. 25, 2012) (last accessed Feb. 27, 2017)]

The EEOC encourages employers to use a two-step process: first a targeted screen of criminal records that considers what the record was for and when it occurred; the nature of the job; and then how the individual candidate should be assessed. The EEOC does not believe that this process imposes significant costs on employers. [Ilyse Schuman, *EEOC Clarifies Guidance on Criminal Background Checks*, Littler Mendelson (Sept. 25, 2013), available at Lexology.com]

The EEOC has brought suits in Illinois and South Carolina, charging that the defendants' criminal background check policies violated Title VII because they adversely impacted minorities and were not justified by being job-related and consistent with business necessity. The EEOC was unsuccessful in at least two suits: the District Court for the District of Maryland granted summary judgment for the employer, finding that the EEOC's statistical expert was unreliable; the Sixth Circuit upheld the district court's sanctions of almost $752,000 imposed on the EEOC for continuing to litigate a case after it became evident that the defendant did not maintain an unlawful company-wide ban on hiring persons with felony records. [*EEOC v. Freeman*, 961 F. Supp. 2d 783 (D. Md. 2013); *EEOC v. PeopleMark*, 732 F.3d 584 (6th Cir. 2013)]

In mid-2016, the Fifth Circuit held that Texas had standing to challenge April 2012 EEOC enforcement guidelines about the use of arrest and conviction records, on the grounds that the guidance was a final agency action as defined by the Administrative Procedure Act, and the state said it would have to either change its hiring practices or incur significant costs. Texas brought suit in late 2013 to enjoin application of the guidance, arguing that it conflicts with state laws that forbid employing people with criminal records in certain jobs. [*State of Texas v. EEOC*, 827 F.3d 372 (5th Cir. 2016); see Jennifer P. Woodruff, *No Texas Hold 'Em: Fifth Circuit Allows Texas to Challenge the EEOC Enforcement Guidance*, Ogletree Deakins (July 7, 2016), available at Lexology.com]

A few months later, however, the Fifth Circuit withdrew this opinion and remanded the case to the District Court for the Northern District of Texas. In the meantime, the Supreme Court had decided an unrelated case, *Army Corps of Engineers v. Hawkins*, 136 S. Ct. 1807 (2016), defining the process a court must use in deciding if an action is a final agency action that is ripe for challenge. [*State of Texas v. EEOC,* 838 F.3d 511 (5th Cir. 2016); see Gustavo A. Suarez, *The Texas Two-Step: Fifth Circuit Withdraws Ruling That Allowed Texas to Proceed with EEOC Background Check Lawsuit*, Ogletree Deakins (Sept. 30, 2016), available at Lexology.com]

Some states,(e.g., Hawaii) say that employer can consider convictions only if they bear a rational relationship to the job duties and responsibilities. The Hawaii Supreme Court held that there was no rational relationship between a conviction for possession with intent to sell crystal meth and a job as radiology technician. The drugs that radiology technicians use are not controlled substances. The court also said that there is no reason for a blanket disqualification for working with the elderly or children because there is no necessary connection between drug convictions and child or elder abuse. [*Shimose v. Hawaii Health Sys. Corp.*, 345 P.3d 145 (Haw. 2015)]

Many cities and local governments have "ban the box" laws, forbidding questions about criminal convictions on initial job applications.

In August 2014, New Jersey became the 13th state to ban the box for public employees and the sixth with a ban the box law covering private employers. (The others are Hawaii, Illinois, Maryland, Massachusetts, and Rhode Island). The various statutes differ as to when employers can ask about convictions—it could be only when a person has been offered a job interview, after the initial interview, or perhaps when a conditional job offer has been extended. [Andria Ryan, *Understanding "Ban The Box" Laws*, Fisher & Phillips LLP (Dec. 1, 2014), available at Lexology.com]

Subsequently, Virginia "banned the box" for public employment only; Oregon adopted a comprehensive ban the box law. [Hunton & Williams LLP, *Virginia Becomes the Next State to "Ban the Box"* (Apr. 15, 2015), available at Lexology.com. Connecticut and Vermont adopted "ban the box" laws in 2016. As a result, in mid-2016, there were nine states with "ban the box" laws (Connecticut, Hawaii, Illinois, Massachusetts, Minnesota, New Jersey, Oregon, Rhode Island, and Vermont) and at least two dozen cities (e.g., New York City, Philadelphia, San Francisco, Los Angeles, Chicago, Austin, Texas). [Todd H. Lebowitz and Jeffrey C. Bils, *Los Angeles Joins Ban the Box Movement*, Baker &

Hostetler LLP (Dec. 27, 2016), available at Lexology.com; Tanya A. Bovee, Holly L. Cini and Sarah R. Skubas, *Connecticut Joins Ban the Box Movement*, Jackson Lewis PC (June 7, 2016), available at Lexology.com] According to Garen Dodge, *"Ban the Box" and Background Checks—Recent Trends and Movements,* Sheppard Mullin Richter & Hampton LLP (July 12, 2017), available at Lexology.com, more than two-thirds of the U.S. population lives in a state or city that "bans the box."]

California expanded its ban the box law, effective July 1, 2017. Under the new law, an employer with five or more employees can only ask about convictions, where the inquiry has an adverse impact on a suspect class, if the employer can show that the inquiry is job-related and consistent with business necessity. Business necessity is not a defense if the applicant or employee can offer an equally effective, non-discriminatory alternative. However, employers have a defense if they follow licensing laws that require screening, and certain convictions are prima facie relevant—for example, fraud convictions for a financial-services job. [Jennifer B. Rubin, *California Joins the Ban-the-Box Bandwagon,* Mintz Levin Cohn Ferris Glovsky and Popeo PC (July 5, 2017), available at Lexology.com]

Usually, a criminal-record check starts with a trace on the applicant's Social Security number, which generates a list of previous addresses. (Of course, this implies that the applicant was operating "on the books" and using his or her own name!) A complete search looks for outstanding wants and warrants (misdemeanors as well as felonies), motor vehicle reports, credit reports, academic qualifications, and verification of past employment.

A good criminal record check goes back at least seven years. Because many court systems have automated records going back only one to six years, it is often necessary for the research firm to do a manual search (which often costs extra). It is also common for misdemeanor and felony records to be kept in different places, which could also lead to higher fees for separate searches. [Merry Mayer, *Background Checks in Focus*, HR Magazine, Jan. 2002, at 59] Federal contractors, especially defense contractors, must also be alert to the question of which employees will require a security clearance.

§ 23.09 NONDISCRIMINATORY HIRING

Federal law bans discrimination in employment, which definitely includes hiring. Discrimination on account of age, sex, race, disability, religion, and/or national origin is banned. Note, however, that in mid-2016 the Seventh Circuit held that precedent in the Seventh Circuit required dismissal of a Title VII suit alleging sexual orientation discrimination. [*Hively v. Ivy Tech Comty. Coll.*, No. 15-1720 (7th Cir. July 28, 2016). See Michelle E. Phillips and Paul Patten, *Discrimination Based on Sexual Orientation Not Protected by Title VII, Federal*

Court Rules, Jackson Lewis (Aug. 4, 2016), available at <https://www.jackson lewis.com/publication/discrimination-based-sexual-orientation-not-protected-title-vii-federal-court-rules>]

Although previously it had taken the position that sexual orientation discrimination was not covered by Title VII, the EEOC reversed itself and, starting in mid-2015, has taken the position that sex- or gender-based employment actions, including actions based on sexual orientation, are unlawful sex discrimination that is forbidden by Title VII. The EEOC has sued employers for discrimination against transsexual employees, and settled two cases for over $100,000 each. [*EEOC v. Deluxe Fin. Servs. Inc.*, No. 0:15-cv-02646 (settled Jan. 21, 2016); see <http://www.eeoc.gov/eeoc/newsroom/release/1-21-16.cfm>. See also *Lusardi v. McHugh*, Appeal No. 0120133395 (EEOC). Barbara E. Hoey, *Company to Pay $115,000 to Settle Sex Discrimination Suit on Behalf of Transgender Employee*, Kelley Drye & Warren LLP (Feb. 1, 2016), available at Lexology .com]

See § 34.06[D] for further discussion of sexual orientation and gender identity discrimination. Note that it is likely that, under the Trump administration, the EEOC will change its approach to this issue.

However, even a company that strives to avoid deliberate prejudice can find it hard to eradicate "disparate impact"—apparently neutral practices that actually disadvantage members of one group more than others. For instance, a minimum height requirement screens out more women and certain ethnic groups than white males. That does not mean that employers cannot impose height requirements, as long as it really is necessary to be taller than a certain height to do the job properly.

Other potential sources of disparate impact include:

- Educational standards;

- Pre-employment testing;

- Requirements of military service;

- Referrals from your current workforce (who tend to know people of their own ethnic group);

- Rules about facial hair (which could disadvantage religious applicants, or black men who have ingrown hairs that make shaving painful);

- Refusing to hire anyone who has ever been arrested, filed for bankruptcy, or had a child out of wedlock.

Your attorney should review hiring practices to make sure that they are not discriminatory and that all requirements can be justified in terms of the practical needs of the business and skills that will actually be used on the job. For each position, you should also determine the physical capacities that are central to the job, those that are sometimes used but are peripheral, and those that are never invoked by the job.

If employees request flextime (for parenting needs, as an accommodation to disability, as a religious accommodation, or simply for convenience), you should either be able to grant the request or demonstrate a legitimate business reason why conventional business hours or standard shifts must be observed.

There are two important criteria for assessing interview questions:

- Do the questions relate to legitimate workplace issues, rather than just satisfying curiosity?

- Are they asked uniformly, rather than only to a group of people chosen on the basis of preconceived notions? For instance, it is discriminatory to ask a woman if her husband "lets" her travel on business, but not discriminatory to discuss the amount of travel required with all applicants, including the number of overnight or prolonged stays required, and to ask all candidates if they are able to travel that much.

Equal employment opportunity law assumes that many candidates will be interviewed for each opening, and there are many reasons why the successful candidate will be selected. There is no reason to collect a great deal of information about candidates who have no real chance of selection. Therefore, some questions are acceptable when a conditional job offer is made that would not be allowed at a first-stage interview.

For instance, marital status and having children are very relevant to participation in an employee group health plan, but irrelevant if the person is not going to get a job offer. So this information should either be requested only after hiring, or collected on a separate sheet of paper and not consulted until after hiring. [See § 36.09 for a discussion of acceptable and unacceptable pre-employment inquiries and tests in the disability context.]

It is not acceptable to ask an interviewee about his or her history of receiving Worker's Compensation benefits, but anyone who gets a conditional job offer can be asked about past injuries that may require accommodation.

There are also circumstances under which the company's commitment to equal employment opportunity must be put into writing: if the company is a federal contractor, for instance.

In 2017, Quest Diagnostics reported that the number of positive drug tests in 2016 was higher than at any time in the previous 12 years. In 2015, 4% of tests were positive for marijuana, rising to 4.2% in 2016. Marijuana was the most common drug. In Washington and Colorado, positive tests for marijuana rose by 9% and 11% respectively, probably because recreational marijuana is legal. On 2016, about ¼ of 1% of drug tests were positive for cocaine; post-accident tests were twice as likely to show cocaine as pre-employment tests. In 2016, 1.1% of tests were positive for amphetamines, which includes prescription drugs. But there were fewer tests positive for heroin in 2016 than in 2015. [Lauren Weber, *More American Workers Are Testing Positive for Drugs,* WSJ.com (May 16, 2017). A recent article, Nelson D. Schwartz, *Economy Needs Workers, but Drug Tests Take a Toll,* NYTimes.com (July 24, 2017) says that many employers are unable to recruit enough workers who can pass drug tests.] More than half the states (including Arkansas, Florida, Minnesota, New York, North Dakota, Ohio, Pennsylvania and West Virginia) permit medical marijuana, eight states (including Maine and Massachusetts) and the District of Columbia have decriminalized recreational use of marijuana. In these jurisdictions, there are issues about what constitutes improper employer conduct. Many of these statutes permit employers to discipline employees for using or being under the influence of marijuana at work or for having a positive drug test reflecting earlier off-premises use. They often make it clear that employers have no duty to accommodate medical marijuana use. In contrast, Maine makes it unlawful to refuse to employ, or otherwise penalize, a worker for using recreational marijuana away from the workplace. [Tawny L. Alvarez, *Maine Passes Recreational Marijuana Statute—What Does This Mean for Employers?,* Verrill Dana LLP (Nov. 9, 2016), available at Lexology.com and *Marijuana is Legal in Massachusetts . . . Now What,* Verrill Dana LLP (Nov. 9, 2016), available at Lexology.com; Todd M. Torres, *Right to Light? Maine's New Marijuana Law Prohibits Employers from Discriminating Against Recreational Users,* Ogletree Deakins (Jan. 26, 2017), available at Lexology.com]

The federal Drug Enforcement Administration (DEA) continues to uphold the federal-law ban on marijuana, which remains classified as a Schedule I (highly dangerous) substance. [Laurie M. Weinstein, *Medical Marijuana and the Workplace,* Akerman LLP (Jan. 10, 2017), available at Lexology.com]

In mid-2015, the Colorado Supreme Court held that it is lawful to fire a medical marijuana user for failing a drug test. Because marijuana use violates federal law, it is not protected by the state statute that forbids discrimination on the basis of a "lawful activity." [*Coats v. Dish Network,* No. 13 SC 394, 2015 CO 44 (Colo. June 15, 2015)]

However, several cases offer protection to users of legal marijuana. The Rhode Island Superior Court held that there is a private right of action (i.e., individuals can bring suits) under the state's medical marijuana statute, and refusal to hire someone because of medical marijuana use violates that statute and might also constitute disability discrimination under the Rhode Island Civil Rights Act. [*Callaghan v. Darlington Fabrics Co.,* No. PC-2014-5680 (R.I. Super. Ct. May 23, 2017); see Anthony S. Califano, Ariel D. Cudkowicz and Frederick T. Smith, *Refusal to Hire Medical Pot Users Just Got Riskier—At Least in Rhode Island,* Seyfarth Shaw LLP (July 25, 2017), available at Lexology.com]

Despite the federal law criminalizing marijuana, the Massachusetts Supreme Judicial Court held that the plaintiff stated a claim for disability discrimination when she was fired for using medical marijuana—but there is no private right of action for wrongful termination in violation of public policy. The disability discrimination claim is the only means of redress for plaintiffs fired for marijuana use. The court held that the employer must use an interactive process to seek reasonable accommodation: are there alternatives to medical marijuana for the plaintiff? If not, does the employee's marijuana use subject the employer to undue hardship? [*Barbuto v. Advantages Sales & Mktg., LLC,* No. SJC-12226 (Mass. Sup. Jud. Ct. July 17, 2017); see Amanda G. Orcutt and Paul G. Lannon, *Medical Marijuana Use May Be Reasonable Accommodation Under Massachusetts Law,* Holland & Knight LLP (July 18, 2017), available at Lexology.com]

The District Court for the District of Connecticut held in August 2017, that the federal Controlled Substances Act does not preempt the Connecticut law that forbids firing or refusing to hire someone who uses medical marijuana. The district court said that the federal law is not concerned with employment practices. [*Noffsinger v. SSC Niantic Operating Co.,* No. 3:16-cv-01938 (JAM) (D. Conn. Aug. 8, 2017); see Marjory D. Robertson, *Another Victory for Medical Marijuana Users at Work!,* Sun Life Financial Inc. (Aug. 10, 2017), available at Lexology.com]

§ 23.10 PRE-EMPLOYMENT TESTING

It is legitimate for an employer to test job applicants to see if they have relevant skills. Title VII permits the use of professionally developed ability tests that are not designed or administered with a discriminatory motive. A valid test is one that is neither explicitly nor implicitly discriminatory against protected groups; one that tests skills that are actually used in the job; and one that has been validated by psychologists or other experts so that it really offers insight into the issues needed for effective hiring.

A Supreme Court case, *Albemarle Paper Co. v. Moody* [422 U.S. 405 (1975)], holds that if a test has a disproportionate negative effect on a minority group, the test is permissible only if professionally accepted methods verify the test's ability to predict important elements of work behavior. As *Griggs v. Duke Power Co.* [401 U.S. 424 (1971)] says, the point of pre-employment testing is to measure the applicant's performance in the context of a specific job, not in the abstract. Even if the company's pre-employment test is valid, it is discriminatory to give the test only to minority-group members.

However, in 2009, another Supreme Court case (dealing with a promotional exam for firefighters) endorsed properly validated and professionally drafted tests. New Haven, Connecticut refused to certify the test or use the test results to make up a promotion list, because almost all of the highest scoring candidates were white, and the city was afraid of lawsuits from minority firefighters. However, a suit was filed by white firefighters who said they were improperly denied promotions. The Supreme Court said that refusing to certify the test constituted intentional discrimination against the higher scoring white and Hispanic firefighters. Even if it had been sued by minority firefighters, the city could have defended itself by citing the Title VII provision that allows the use of valid, job-related tests that are implemented as a matter of business necessity. [*Ricci v. DeStefano*, 557 U.S. 557 (2009)]

In May 2016, the Office of Federal Contract Compliance Programs (OFCCP) announced a $1.85 million settlement with Gordon Food Services (GFS) regarding a strength test that discriminated against women applying for jobs as laborers. GFS hired 300 men and only six women out of 900 women who applied. The OFCCP said the test was invalid because it was not performed by, or its results interpreted by, a health care provider. The standards came from the coal mining industry and were not specific to the laborer's job; in fact, they were more stringent than the actual requirements for the job. [Kristine Sims, *OFCCP Takes Contractors Back to School on Pre-Employment Testing,* Constangy Brooks Smith & Prophete LLP (Aug. 17, 2016), available at Lexology.com]

If your company adopts a pre-employment test and monitors the results, discovering that the test has an adverse impact on women and/or members of minority groups, then you should either get rid of the test, change it to remove the adverse impact, or do a validity study that confirms both that the test is a business necessity and that it accurately predicts the skills needed for successful job performance. The Civil Rights Act of 1991 [Pub. L. No. 102-166] says that it is not acceptable to grade minority applicants' tests on a "curve," or to have a lower passing grade for minorities.

Publications about psychological testing are good for finding out which tests have already been validated. Three types of validation are accepted:

- Criterion-related (the test is an accurate predictor of work behavior or other criteria of employee adequacy);

- Content-related (the test accurately duplicates the tasks that will actually be called for in the workplace);

- Construct-related (the test identifies general mental and psychological traits needed to do the job, such as the ability to remain cool under pressure and respond courteously to angry customers).

§ 23.11 IMMIGRATION ISSUES

NOTE: Immigration issues are central to Trump administration policies. In addition to crackdowns on illegal immigration, at press time in 2017, changes were contemplated to the H-1B and other employment-related visa programs.

President Trump's Executive Order (EO) 13769 (Jan. 27, 2017) suspended entry into the United States by citizens of Syria, Iran, Libya, Somalia, Yemen, Iraq, and Sudan. (A second executive order on March 6, 2017 removed Iraq from this list.) As a result, employers who had employees who are citizens of those countries were advised that those employees would not be able to enter the United States; if they were sent outside the United States on business, they would not be able to re-enter for a period of 90 days after the EO was issued. Immigrant employees in the United States seeking to extend their visas might also be affected. However, U.S. permanent residents who are citizens of these seven countries can enter the United States, after the EO was re-interpreted to permit them to travel. [Roger Y. Tsai, *Workplace Implications of the President's Immigration Executive Order,* Holland & Hart LLP (Jan. 30, 2017), available at Lexology.com] At press time in August 2017, the status of this EO (and a subsequent similar EO) was pending before the Supreme Court, which had previously upheld portions of the EOs on an interim basis.

However, multinational employers affected by the EOs might be accused of discrimination if they changed their travel assignments on the basis of citizenship. Coping mechanisms could include using webcasts or videoconferences instead of sending employees outside the United States, and telling all employees who travel for business about the EO, without singling out citizens from the seven countries named in the EO. [Baker McKenzie, *President Trump's Executive Order Suspending Entry to the US Raises Employment Law Considerations*, Baker McKenzie (Jan. 31, 2017), available at Lexology.com]

Immigration cases about employer sanctions, document fraud, and unfair employment practices relating to immigration are heard by ALJs working for the Department of Justice's Executive Office for Immigration Review (EOIR). Under 8 U.S.C. § 1324a, employers can be subject to civil penalties for knowingly hiring or continuing to employ aliens who are not authorized to work in the United States, or for failure to prepare and maintain proper documentation on employees' work authorization. There are also penalties for document fraud (8 U.S.C. § 1324c) and unfair practices (8 U.S.C. § 1324b) and discriminating against persons who do have authorization to work in the United States on the basis of their national origin or citizenship. The Department of Justice's Civil Rights Division, Office of Special Counsel for Immigration-Related Unfair Employment Practices handles cases of immigration-related employment discrimination. [DOJ Fact Sheet, *EOIR's Office of the Chief Administrative Hearing Officer*, <http://www.justice.gov/eoir/press/2012/OCAHOFactSheet05292012.pdf> (Oct. 1, 2013) (last viewed Feb. 27, 2017)]

The DOJ Office of Special Counsel for Immigration-Related Unfair Employment Practices enforces the INA anti-discrimination provisions. It is unlawful to treat workers differently in hiring or firing because they are not U.S. citizens, because of the worker's immigration status, or the country he or she is from, or appears to be from (e.g., discriminating against people from Saudi Arabia). Discrimination in completing Form I-9 and using eVerify is also forbidden. The flyer says that I-9 discrimination may occur when the employer demands specific documents from non-U.S. workers; demands documents that are not needed to complete the I-9; rejects valid documents submitted by non-citizens; or demands that a lawful permanent resident present a new green card when the previous card expires. Possible forms of eVerify discrimination are suspending or terminating non-U.S. workers when tentative non-confirmation occurs; interference with the non-confirmation resolution process; selective use of eVerify for pre-screening; using eVerify to confirm continuing authorization of workers who are not subject to recertification; or making non-U.S. citizen workers provide additional documentation to establish work authorization. Retaliation for asserting rights under the INA is also forbidden. [Brandon Davis, *DOJ Issues Guidance on Citizenship/Immigration Status and National Origin Discrimination in Employment*, Phelps Dunbar LLP (Aug. 26, 2014), available at Lexology.com]

Victor Guerrero came to the United States from Mexico as a child. When he was a teenager, he used a false Social Security Number (SSN) to get work. Later, he became a lawful permanent resident and then a naturalized citizen, with a legitimate SSN. In 2011, he applied to work as a corrections officer. During the investigation, he admitted using a false SSN and was not hired on the grounds that using a false SSN showed a lack of moral character precluding law enforcement work. Guerrero sued under Title VII, charging national origin discrimination. The District Court for the Northern District of California ruled that Latino applicants suffered a significant disparate impact from the policy of condemning past use of a false SSN and awarded $140,362 in back pay, $145,972 in expenses—and $1,196,307 in attorneys' fees. California has laws forbidding adverse treatment of people who submit a new SSN once they obtain one legitimately. [*Guerrero v. California Dep't of Corrections,* No. C 13-05671, 2016 U.S. Dist. LEXIS 78796 (N.D. Cal. June 16, 2016); see Robert Neale & Kim Kiel Thompson, *SSN Mistake Leads to Million Dollar Verdict*, Fisher Phillips (Aug. 1, 2016), available at Lexology.com]

Form I-140 is the employment-based immigration petition. The Second Circuit held in late 2015 that U.S. Citizenship and Immigration Services (USCIS) has an obligation to give advance notice to either the beneficiary of an I-140 petition that has been approved or the successor employer, if there is intent to revoke the petition. The Second Circuit relied on the American Competitiveness in the 21st Century Act, which allows I-140 entitlement to be "ported" to a new employer. The case deals with the situation in which an employer sponsors a foreign national for permanent residence, but then the employee gets a different job after an application to adjust status (i.e., to begin the process of becoming a U.S. citizen). The petitioning employer often initiates the revocation process when the employee quits. Before this decision, the USCIS only notified the petitioning I-140 employer of the intent to revoke, or even waited until revocation occurred to give notice. The Second Circuit held that after entitlement is ported, the interested parties to the I-140 are the worker and the new employer, and not the petitioning employer (the only party to receive notice under the old rules). [*Mantena v. Johnson*, No. 14-2476 (2d Cir. Dec. 30, 2015)]

The Seventh Circuit held that only the employer, not the employee, receives notice and information about USCIS' decisions on visa petitions. Musunuru's employer started a green card petition for him; he was an H-1B programmer ana-lyst. He was assigned a priority date of February 17, 2004, under the EB-3 cat-egory. (The priority date controls when an applicant can file Form I-485, Adjustment of Status, to complete the process of becoming a permanent resident; H-1B is a non-immigrant visa.) After Musunuru filed Form I-485 in 2007, he changed employers. He was able to transfer his green card application to Cres-cent Solutions, his new employer. Crescent filed a labor certification application and Form I-140; they were approved in EB-2, the employment-based second pref-erence category. But USCIS issued an amended Form I-40 with a later priority date, January 28, 2011, extending Musunuru's waiting time to apply for natural-ization by several years, because Musunuru's ex-employer pleaded guilty to H-1B fraud in a different case. USCIS presumed that all its visa applications were fraudulent. The ex-employer went out of business and did not respond to the noti-fication. Crescent and Musunuru only learned about these actions when Crescent was notified of intent to revoke Crescent's petition on the grounds that Musunu-ru's previous work experience was not legitimate. Musunuru sued, arguing that he should have been informed of the revocation of the earlier petition and given a chance to respond. The Seventh Circuit held that the regulations for transferring a petition only require notice to the employer, which is the only one entitled to a chance to respond. [*Musunuru v. Lynch*, 831 F.3d 880 (7th Cir. 2016); see Rajula Sati and Maria Fernanda Gandarez, *You've Got Mail . . . if You're an Employer: Seventh Circuit Rules Employees Are Not Entitled to Same Visa Revocation Notice*, Ogletree Deakins (Feb. 3, 2017), available at Lexology.com]

[A] Employment Requirement

If an alien wishes to enter this country on the basis of employment, he or she must not only have a definite job offer from a U.S. employer, but the employer must have "labor certification." That is, the Department of Labor must certify that the job is "open" because the company cannot recruit a qualified U.S. worker at the prevailing wages. The Department of Labor updates the Foreign Labor Certification Data Center Online Wage Library every July 1. This resource is used to file labor certification applications and non-immigrant petitions for H-1B workers. [Rosanna M. Fox, *DOL Online Wage Library-Prevailing Wages Will Change on July 1*, Greenberg Traurig LLP (June 17, 2016), available at Lexology.com]

First, the employer must use the State Employment Service and post and advertise the job opportunity. The employer must interview any applicants who come through that route, and must file a recruitment report with the DOL explain-ing why none of those applicants was suitable for the position.

However, certain occupations are considered "shortage" occupations because of a documented difficulty in filling the jobs: nursing, physical therapy, and people of demonstrated exceptional ability in business, science, or the arts.

Multinational executives, outstanding university-level teachers, researchers, and people whose jobs are in the national interest do not displace American workers, so labor certification will not be required for such jobs.

Immigration law is basically a federal area, as the Supreme Court pointed out in June 2012, when it struck down most of Arizona's immigration law. The Arizona law made it a misdemeanor for an illegal alien to apply for work, or to work as either an employee or as an independent contractor. The Supreme Court noted that Congress chose not to make it a crime for illegal immigrants to work in the United States. However, the Supreme Court did uphold the part of the Arizona statute that allows the police to check the immigration status of people who have been detained. [*Arizona v. United States*, 132 S. Ct. 2492 (2012) Alabama enacted a statute, the Beason-Hammond Alabama Taxpayer and Citizen Protection Act, with similar immigration provisions. The Eleventh Circuit held that federal immigration law preempts this statute, which made it a crime for unauthorized aliens to work in the United States: *United States v. Alabama*, 691 F.3d 1269 (11th Cir. 2012), rendering the law unenforceable.]

South Carolina's immigration laws were also held to be preempted by federal immigration law. [*United States v. South Carolina*, 720 F.3d 518 (4th Cir. 2013)]

[B] Immigration Categories

Employment-based immigration is regulated under the Immigration Act of 1990. [Pub. L. No. 101-649] There are various categories of employable immigrants, e.g.:

- Priority workers (individuals of extraordinary ability and/or vocational responsibility);

- Professionals with advanced degrees and/or exceptional ability;

- Other workers (skilled workers, professionals without advanced degrees; unskilled workers who have DOL certification that there is a shortage of U.S. workers with similar skills);

- Special immigrants (e.g., religious workers sent to the U.S. by a religious hierarchy);

- Immigrants who have the financial capacity to invest at least $1 million within the United States, employing at least 10 U.S. workers;

- H-1B "specialty occupation" workers who reside temporarily within the United States, and work here, but do not become citizens;

- H-2 temporary non-agricultural workers.

The DOL and USCIS enforce termination requirements for H-1B workers. It may be required that the worker be paid the cost of transportation to return to the worker's last country of residence—even if the employer knows or suspects the worker intends to remain in the United States. Under USCIS regulations, terminating an H-1B worker before the end of the period of authorized stay obligates the employer to pay the reasonable cost of transportation for the worker (although the employer is not required to pay the cost of transporting the worker's family or possessions). The DOL requires payment of full wages (even if there is no work for the employee) until "bona fide termination," which requires notifying USCIS to cancel the H-1B petition and certifying that transportation costs have been paid. Failure to pay transportation costs could result in a DOL award of back pay for the entire period from termination to the expiration date of the H-1B petition—the worst-case scenario, for termination early in the visa, is having to pay almost three years' salary. [Douglas A. Hass and Staci Ketay Rotman, *Lesser Known DOL Regulations: "Bona Fide" Terminations for H-1B Workers*, Franczek Radelet PC (Aug. 14, 2014), available at Lexology.com]

A draft of an executive order, "Protecting American Jobs and Workers by Strengthening the Integrity of Foreign Worker Visa Programs," which became available in early 2017, would change the work visa programs, targeting H-1B and L-1 visas. This order also covers B-1 temporary business visas, E-2 investor visas, and H-2A agricultural worker visas. The EO directs the Department of Homeland Security (DHS) to review all regulations about foreign workers and initiate rulemaking to rescind any regulations that DHS believes are not in the national interest. The EO implies that, to make the H-1B process more efficient, there will be a shift from the current lottery to a competitive merit-based approach. [Findlaw.com Employment Law News blog, *Draft EO Could Upend Worker Visa Programs, Panicking Some Companies* (Feb. 21, 2017), available at FindLaw.com]

A second EO, the "Buy American and Hire America" EO directs the relevant federal agencies to issue new rules and guidance to protect American workers by re-directing visas to the most-skilled or highest-paid petitioners. However, the statute requires distributing visas by lottery, so Congress would have to act to change this. [Jorge R. Lopez and Michelle A. White, *New Executive Order Addresses H-1B Visas*, Littler Mendelson PC (Apr. 19, 2017), available at Lexology.com]

USCIS issued a memo in late 2000, nicknamed the "Terry Way memo," treating most computer programming jobs as specialty occupations that would qualify for H-1B visas. However, in 2017 USCIS reversed this position, now holding that low-level computer jobs do not qualify. [Melissa B. Winkler, *Guidance Memo on H-1B Computer-Related Positions Rescinded*, Fakhoury Law Group PC (Apr. 21, 2017), available at Lexology.com]

Because of the popularity of the H-1B program with employers, it was predicted that changes the program would probably take the form of greater protection for U.S. workers' wages, and stricter labor market tests. Changing the number of visas available each year requires congressional action; the president cannot do this alone. [Elizabeth Laskey LaRocca, Dana Delott and Lynda S. Zengerle, *How Employers Can Prepare for Trump Era Immigration Changes*, Steptoe & Johnson LLP (Dec. 27, 2016), available at Lexology.com]

The L-1B visa permits a multi-national company to transfer personnel to the United States based on their specialized knowledge of the organization's business. On August 17, 2015, the USCIS issued guidance, effective August 31, 2015, defining the type of knowledge that will qualify. The knowledge does not have to be proprietary or unique to the employer. [Fakhoury Law Group PC, *USCIS Issues L-1B Final Policy Guidance Memorandum* (Sept. 11, 2015), available at Lexology.com]

[C] Employer Responsibilities: No-Match Letters and E-Verify

U.S. labor and immigration law places a burden on the employer (or on an agency that gets a fee for recruitment or making referrals) to determine whether job applicants are legally permitted to work in this country. No later than three business days after hiring, the employer must ascertain if the new hire is a U.S. citizen or a legal immigrant who is not only permitted to reside in this country but to work here. Presidential Executive Order 12989 [61 Fed. Reg. 6091 (Feb. 13, 1996)] debars federal contractors from getting further federal contracts after they have been caught knowingly hiring illegal aliens.

The employer responsibilities stem from the Immigration Reform and Control Act of 1986 (IRCA). [7 U.S.C. § 1324a] The employer is responsible for checking documents presented by potential new employees to demonstrate their identity and authorization to work within the United States. (There are people who are lawfully permitted to enter and reside in this country, but not to work here, so there is more to the matter than distinguishing illegal aliens from lawful immigrants.)

The information must be obtained in a way that is not discriminatory against dark-skinned people, or people whose first language is not English.

Both the USCIS and the DOL are entitled to inspect a company's immigration-related forms, but to enter a workplace they must either have a warrant or give 72 hours' notice.

Employment of immigrants requires the employer to work with both the DOL's Employment and Training Administration and the USCIS, which is part of the Department of Homeland Security. Employers can obtain permission to hire foreign workers on either a temporary (e.g., nurses; seasonal agricultural workers; specialized professional workers) or a permanent basis, depending on the facts of the case and the conditions within the U.S. labor market. The overarching policy is that employment of a foreign worker depends on proof that there is a shortage preventing the hiring of U.S. workers for the job. Furthermore, the law requires lawful immigrant workers to receive at least the prevailing wage for their jobs, so immigrant workers cannot be used to depress wages. The DOL's Wage and Hour Division investigates employers' compliance with the Fair Labor Standards Act and the requirements of the H-1B and H-2A visa programs. The relevant DOL regulations can be found at 20 C.F.R. Parts 655 and 656.

Labor certification is the process of petitioning DOL's Employment and Training Administration (ETA); the ETA certifies to the USCIS that permitting the person the employer wishes to hire is appropriate because no U.S. worker is available to fill the job. [The DOL's explanation of the process can be found at *Hiring Foreign Labor*, <http://www.dol.gov/dol/topic/hiring/foreign.htm> (last accessed Feb. 27, 2017). There is an overview at <http://www.foreignlaborcert.doleta.gov/hiring.cfm> (Oct. 21, 2015) (last accessed Feb. 27, 2017)]

This discussion centers around the H-1B program (temporary employment in specialty occupations requiring specialized knowledge), although there are other kinds of visas: H-1B1 for workers from Chile and Singapore employed in specialty occupations; E-3 for Australians working in specialty occupations; H-2 temporary agricultural workers, H-2B skilled or unskilled workers, O-1 aliens with extraordinary ability, etc.

The employer must submit a Labor Condition Application (LCA/ETA Form 9035E/9035 for H-1 workers; ETA 9142 for H-2A and H-2B workers) to the DOL to attest that the employer has complied with the requirements of the relevant visa program. The application must be submitted electronically, using the DOL's iCERT system (<https://icert.doleta.gov>), unless special permission is granted to file by mail. The LCA must be submitted not earlier than six months before employment begins. Then the employer must file a petition with USCIS and get a visa for the employee from the Department of State. [DOL Employment and Training Administration, *Overview of the H-1B, H-1B1 and E-3 Temporary Programs,* <http://www.foreignlaborcert.doleta.gov/h-1b.cfm> (Feb. 25, 2016) (last accessed Feb. 27, 2017)]

[From the USCIS perspective, see *Nonimmigrant-Based Employment,* <http://www.uscis.gov/sites/default/files/USCIS/About%20Us/Electronic%20 Reading%20Room/Customer%20Service%20Reference%20Guide/Nonimmigrant_ Empl.pdf> (last viewed Feb. 27, 2017)]

The employer must submit Form I-129, "Petition for Non-Immigrant Worker," on behalf of the employee. Form I-129 can also be used to request an extension of the visa period, or to change the status of certain non-immigrant employees. "Blanket petitions" covering multiple workers who come from a place with the same U.S. consulate, who will perform the same services in the same location, are permitted.

It is illegal to knowingly hire an ineligible person. Knowledge includes constructive knowledge (reasonable inferences from facts and circumstances, to the degree that a person acting with reasonable care would have to be aware). According to USCIS regulations [see 8 C.F.R. § 274a], these circumstances create an inference of constructive knowledge:

- The employer actually has some information that the person is not eligible for U.S. employment;

- The applicant refuses to complete the I-9 form, or does it improperly;

- The employer acts with "reckless and wanton disregard" of the consequences of hiring ineligible persons.

However, accent and appearance are not acceptable sources of constructive knowledge. Once the employer knows that the hiree is (or has become, because of a change of status) ineligible to work in the United States, continuing employment is unlawful. [See 8 U.S.C. § 1324a]

President Trump issued Executive Orders (EOs) in early 2017 dealing with both border enforcement and enforcement of immigration laws within the United States. In February, DHS secretary John Kelly issued two memos to implement these EOs. DHS widened the category of people targeted for deportation, and increased the authority of local and state agencies to enforce federal immigration law, including deputizing state and local law enforcement workers as immigration officers. Kelly's memo calls for DHS to execute immigration laws against all removable aliens (those convicted or charged with criminal offenses, or who have abused public benefit programs, or pose a risk of any kind to public safety and national security. All undocumented individuals are presumed to have committed the offense of improper entry, which is a crime under 8 U.S.C. § 1325. The president's January 25 EO says that visa holders who violate or overstay their visas present a threat to national security and public safety. Therefore, they are removable aliens, and DHS can make them a priority for deportation.

DHS directs Department of Immigration and Customs Enforcement (ICE), Customs and Border Protection, and USCIS to issue guidance the promulgate regulations to assess and collect all fines and penalties against undocumented immigrants and "those who facilitate their unlawful presence." That could mean employers and recruiters. Under 8 U.S.C. § 1324(a)(10)(A), it is a crime to conceal, harbor, or shield any illegal alien, including a person who entered the U.S. illegally but has lost legal status. Employers can be convicted of "harboring" if they act in reckless disregard of a worker's status—for example, altering records, telling workers to get false documents, or obstructing inspections. Under 8 U.S.C. § 1324a(b), it is illegal to hire anyone without complying with the I-9 requirements for verification of work authorization and record-keeping. Employers that knowingly hire, or continue to employ, people whom they know are unauthorized to work can be fined and/or prosecuted. Employers can also be debarred from future federal contracting and government benefits for knowing hiring or continued employment of unauthorized workers. [Rachel Perez, *Up Against the Wall: New Immigration Measures Impact Employers*, Akerman LLP (Mar. 3, 2017), available at Lexology.com; Luis Campos, *Employer Compliance in an Era of Heightened Immigration Enforcement: The IMAGE Program*, Haynes and Boone LLP (Mar. 16, 2017), available at Lexology.com]

The IRCA sets out the responsibilities of an employer that uses temporary labor, or outsources some functions to contractors. Under IRCA (see 8 U.S.C. § 1324a(4)), a business that uses a contract or subcontract to obtain the labor of a person who the business knows is not authorized to work in the United States is liable because the business is considered to have hired the alien. Sometimes ICE applies this provision during I-9 compliance investigations to impose liability on a business owner for its contractors' immigration violations. The Department of ICE considers failure to abide by the I-9 requirements to constitute constructive knowledge that there might be unauthorized workers on the premises. Agreements with contractors should be drafted to require contractors to comply with all federal and state requirements for verifying workers' authorization to work in the United States, perhaps by requiring the contractor or employment agency to participate in E-Verify or submit to third-party audits of E-Verify and I-9 compliance. [Anna L. Scully, *I-9 and E-Verify Compliance Practices for Temporary Labor and Contractors: Four Things to Do Now to Minimize Risk*, Burr & Forman LLP (May 19, 2015), available at Lexology.com]

On December 23, 2016, based on a finding that fees did not meet the costs, the DHS imposed its first fee increase since November 23, 2010, for petitions and applications filed on or after December 23, 2016. [Cassie M. Ramos, *Imminent USCIS Fee Increase and I-9 Implementation*, Mintz Levin Cohn Ferris Glovsky and Popeo PC (Dec. 8, 2016), available at Lexology.com]

The federal crime of "aggravated identity theft" (18 U.S.C. § 1028A(a)(1)) carries a mandatory two-year prison sentence if a person convicted of certain crimes committed the crime by knowingly using someone else's means of identification. In a mid-2009 Supreme Court case, the petitioner was a Mexican citizen who, to establish eligibility to work in the United States, gave his employer false Social Security and alien registration cards with his name and identification numbers that belonged to other people. He was arrested for immigration offenses and aggravated identity theft. His argument was that the numbers were chosen at random, and he did not know that they belonged to other people. The Supreme Court ruled that, to convict, the prosecution must show that the defendant knew the identification numbers belonged to someone else. [*Flores-Figueroa v. United States*, 556 U.S. 646 (2009)]

In mid-2016, the Ninth Circuit held that Arizona laws against identity theft in employment are not preempted by the federal statute Immigration Reform and Control Act of 1986 (IRCA), even though some of the Arizona provisions conflict with the comprehensive federal regulation of immigration. The case was remanded to determine which parts of the Arizona law survive preemption. [*Puente Arizona v. Arpaio*, No. 15-15211 (9th Cir. May 2, 2016)]

E-Verify is an electronic program for ascertaining employees' right to work in the United States. It began as a voluntary program, although several states (e.g., Alabama, Arizona, Georgia, Mississippi, North Carolina, South Carolina, Utah) passed laws requiring employers in those states to use E-Verify. [Rebecca Moore, *House Bill Would Extend Use of Federal E-Verify Program*, plansponsor.com

(Aug. 5, 2008)] Tennessee adopted a law requiring private employers with 50 or more employees to use E-Verify, as of January 1, 2016. [Donald D. Berner, *E-Verify Expansion*, Foulston Siefkin LLP (Apr. 22, 2016), available at Lexology.com. The article says that future federal immigration reform will require use of E-Verify, which is an incentive for employers to adopt it before it is required. See also David S. Jones, *Many Tennessee Employers Will Soon Be Required to Use E-Verify*, Fisher & Phillips LLP (May 5, 2016), available at Lexology.com]

The E-Verify home page <https://www.uscis.gov/e-verify> (last accessed Feb. 27, 2017), provides many tools and tutorials for working with the system, including webinars and videos. See <https://www.dhs.gov/how-do-i/verify-employment-eligibility-e-verify> (updated Aug. 8, 2016) (last accessed Feb. 27, 2017) for the SelfCheck tool that individuals can use to check their employment eligibility.

Starting August 1, 2016, E-Verify began to deactivate user IDs that had not been accessed for 270 days. To avoid deactivation, employers should make a practice of logging in at least once every 270 days. [Elizabeth Laskey LaRocca, *E-Verify to Deactivate User Accounts*, Steptoe & Johnson LLP (June 20, 2016), available at Lexology.com]

A California statute effective January 1, 2016 imposes civil penalties of up to $10,000 for misuse of E-Verify; each unlawful use is a separate violation. California does not require most employers to use E-Verify. The statute does not allow employers to use E-Verify before extending an offer of employment. If the employer is informed that the employee's information appears to be inaccurate, the employer must notify the employee as soon as possible to resolve the problem. [D. Andrew Quigley and Anna Suh, *California's New E-Verify Law—Get It Right or Pay the Price*, Hunton & Williams LLP (Feb. 4, 2016), available at Lexology.com]

In addition to E-Verify, there is a lesser-known project, IMAGE (Mutual Agreement Between Government and Employers). IMAGE is a certification program run by the ICE. Certified employers receive information and training on proper hiring practices. Fines will be waived if fewer than 50% of the employer's I-9 forms contain errors and fines will be reduced even if more than half the forms include errors. To participate, an employer must enroll in E-Verify, complete the IMAGE self-assessment questionnaire; maintain a written policy for verification of employment eligibility in hiring; have an I-9 inspection; and sign a partnership agreement. (After this initial inspection, participating employers will be exempt from I-9 inspection for two years.) [Luis Campos, *Employer Compliance in an Era of Heightened Immigration Enforcement: The IMAGE Program*, Haynes and Boone LLP (Mar. 16, 2017), available at Lexology.com] The E-Verify RIDE (Record and Information from DMV) program is a pilot program in which Arizona, Florida, Idaho, Iowa, Maryland, Mississippi, Nebraska, North Dakota, Wisconsin, and Wyoming participate. The validity of driver's licenses and ID cards (which represent 80% of the documents submitted as proof of identity in the I-9 process) is checked against state DMV records. [Linnea C. Porter, *Arizona, Maryland and Wyoming to Participate in E-Verify Ride Program,* Greenberg Traurig LLP (Aug. 3, 2017), available at Lexology.com]

The ICE has the power, at any time, to serve a subpoena called a Notice of Inspection (NOI) requiring the employer to provide I-9s for every employee within three days. Infosys accepted a $34 million fine to settle DOJ charges about I-9 violations and ICE fined a 43-person business $40,000 even though every employee was authorized to work in the United States, but the employer could not locate their I-9 forms. The ICE audit process includes verifying every employee's identity and work authorization, and ordering the employer to fire every worker on the Notice of Suspect Documentation list within 10 days, or be sanctioned for every unauthorized worker. Criminal charges are possible for continuing to employ more than one unauthorized worker [*United States v. Infosys*, No. 4:13-cv-00634 (E.D. Tex. Oct. 30, 2013). See Sarah Buffett, *"I Thought I-9 Was a Highway . . . ": The Dangers of Ignoring I-9 Due Diligence in M&A Transactions*, Bloomberg BNA (Oct. 27, 2014) (benefitslink.com)]

The American Immigration Lawyers Association Liaison Committee to the USCIS Vermont Service Center published tips for handling site visits from agency officers. The Administrative Site Visit and Verification Program (ASVVP) sends USCIS officers to verify employment of H-1B and L-1 workers. Visits are usually unannounced and take less than an hour. Employers have the right to have a lawyer present at the inspection—but the inspection will not be delayed for a lawyer to arrive. (If the lawyer cannot arrive in time, the employer should take notes and discuss them with the lawyer.) The USCIS officer verifies that it's a legitimate business operation, that the information in the H-1B or L-1 petition is valid, and that pay stubs or W-2s demonstrate compliance with the petition. Employers that do not have the full documentation can ask for extra time—but will suffer adverse consequences if they fail to provide documents by the extended deadline. [Kristin Aquino-Pham, *Tips to Employers for Handling Site Visits*, Greenberg Traurig LLP (Aug. 3, 2016), available at Lexology.com]

ICE said, in March 2017, that there is no directive calling for workplace raids; the last raid occurred in 2009. But ICE retains the power to make site visits. In response, employers must be ready not only to comply with requirements, but to document compliance with requirements for Form I-9, E-Verify, etc. ICE could visit a worksite when it wishes to question a particular person or take a particular person into custody. ICE may also want to inspect the company's base of I-9 forms, either in response to a credible tip of abuse or as part of an initiative to inspect companies involved in national security and infrastructure industries. Good practices for employers include training an employee to greet ICE agents in a courteous and cooperative manner. At least one manager should be designated as the ICE liaison. The designated manager should contact the company's legal counsel. The ICE agents should not be allowed past the reception area until the manager and legal counsel are available to talk to them and the manager should take down each agent's contact information. The agents should be asked to present the subpoena or warrant under which they are operating. The manager should state that the company intends to comply with the ICE investigation—but only acting on advice of counsel. Even if the company is under investigation, ICE agents can only enter non-public areas of the premises if the company consents or if ICE has a valid search warrant. If legal counsel cannot appear in person, perhaps they can speak to the agents by telephone or other electronic means. Even if ICE presents a subpoena and a Notice of Inspection, the company is entitled to three days to turn over I-9 forms and related documents; it is a bad idea to waive this period. ICE should provide a receipt and chain of custody information when documents are turned over. If possible, copies should be retained of all documents that are turned over. Everyone in contact with ICE personnel should be professional and cooperative—but no one should volunteer information; questions should be answered exactly as asked. The company may need to communicate with its workforce what ICE is looking for, and how it will affect the employees. [Dawn M. Lurie and Leon Rodriguez, *Quick Guidance: What to DO in the Event of a Visit by the DHS-ICE Agents,* Seyfarth Shaw LLP (Mar. 30, 2017), available at Lexology.com]

The penalties imposed by the DOL for violations of various provisions affecting the H-1B and H-2 programs increased August 1, 2016. For example, the penalty for improperly displacing a U.S. worker rose from $15,000 per worker per violation to $16,312 per worker per violation; violations of H-1B visa requirements can now be penalized by $1,782; a willful H-1B violation or discrimination against an employee can be penalized by $7,251; and a willful violation that displaces a U.S. worker can be penalized by $11,940 per violation. [Practical Law, *DOL Increases Civil Money Penalties, Effective August 1* (July 5, 2016) (benefitslink.com)] Penalties rose again in 2017: willful displacement of a U.S. worker during the period that runs from 90 days before to 90 days after an H-1B petition can be penalized by $50,578 per violation. [Jeanne Harrison, *Increased Civil Penalties for Employment Law Violations,* Smith Currie & Hancock (Feb. 24, 2017), available at Lexology.com]

The National Labor Relations Board (NLRB) ruled that Farm Fresh Company Target One, LLC was guilty of interference with union organizing when it fired four workers for union activity. The NLRB ordered them to be rehired unconditionally. The employer wanted to use E-Verify to determine their employment eligibility. The District Court for the District of Arizona ruled that, because state law mandates the use of E-Verify, it was unlawful to require unconditional rehiring. The employer applied for an attorneys' fee award under the Equal Access to Justice Act. The district court ordered the NLRB to pay $55,000 of the employer's fees that were incurred because of the NLRB's unjustified demand that the employees be reinstated without checking their work eligibility. The fee request was granted even though the NLRB obtained much of the relief it sought. [Jeffrey W. Toppel, Howard M. Bloom and Philip B. Rosen, *District Court Orders NLRB Regional Director to Pay Over $55,000 in Attorneys' Fees to Employer in § 10(j) Fight,* Jackson Lewis PC (Nov. 26, 2014), available at Lexology.com]

USCIS' web page on penalties says that failure to verify eligibility; failure to complete and retain Form I-9 as required; knowingly hiring or continuing to employ an unauthorized person; or discrimination on the basis of national origin, citizenship, or immigration status, can be penalized by civil fines, court orders mandating hiring or back pay, debarment from government contracts, or criminal penalties for a pattern or practice of violations.

The penalty for I-9 violations is a minimum of $216, a maximum of $2,156, for each form. Hiring or continuing to employ an unauthorized person is penalized by $539–$4,313 per worker for a first offense, $4,313–$10,781, for a second offense, and $6,469–$21,563 for a third offense. The penalty schedule for discrimination in hiring is $445–$3,563 for a first offense, $3,563–$8,908 for a second offense, and $5,345–$17,816 for a third offense. Penalties for document fraud range from $445–$3,563 per worker (first offense), $$3,563–$8,908 (second or third offense). The penalties for document abuse not tantamount to fraud are $178–$1,782, and are the same for first, second, and third offenses. For criminal violations, the fine is up to $3,000 per unauthorized alien and/or up to six months in prison (whether it is a first, second, or third offense). [USCIS, *Penalties*, <https://www.uscis.gov/i-9-central/penalties> (Feb. 15, 2017) (last accessed Feb. 27, 2017); see Anita M. Sorensen, *DHS to Issue New I-9 Form Following Recent Penalties*, Foley & Lardner LLP (Oct. 17, 2016), available at Lexology.com]

[D] Employment Verification Documents

Hired individuals prove their eligibility to work within the United States either by showing that they are U.S. citizens (e.g., showing a U.S. passport or birth certificate evidencing birth within the United States) or by showing that they have a so-called green card. (The document, Form I-551, is no longer actually green.)

Since 1997, the Immigration and Naturalization Service has issued Form I-766, a tamper-resistant card issued to aliens whose immigration status permits work within the United States. The I-766 is a List A Employment Authorization Document (EAD): that is, it establishes both the job applicant's identity and his or her entitlement to work.

There are three categories of documents. List A documents can be used to prove both identity and employability; List B documents prove identity only; List C documents prove employability only.

In a November 24, 2015 *Federal Register* notice, USCIS proposed changes in Form I-9 to make it easier to complete the form on a computer; computerization is intended to increase accuracy. Additional space is provided to enter multiple preparers and translators. There are on-screen instructions for each field, plus a dedicated area for extra info that employers had to put in the margins. There are buttons to access instructions electronically, print the form, or clear it to start over.

A QR code (barcode) is generated once the form is printed; it can be used to speed up audits. However, this is not an electronic form: the employer must still print hard copies of Form I-9, have them signed, and retain copies. If the employer uses E-Verify, the Form I-9 information must be entered into that system. [80 Fed. Reg. 73200 (Nov. 24, 2015); Robert Neale, *60 Day Comment Period on Proposed Changes to Form I-9 Ended on January 25, 2016*, Fisher & Phillips LLP (Feb. 2, 2016), available at Lexology.com]

A subsequent version of I-9 took effect January 22, 2017. It has some extra instructions and formatting and, to be easier to use, the instructions have been expanded from six to 15 pages. The new I-9 can be completed electronically and notifies users of errors before printing—but must still be printed out in hard copy and signed. Employers that cannot use the interactive PDF can print out the form and hand-write its contents. Under the previous rule, a foreign national authorized to work in the United States had to submit both Form I-94 and a foreign passport number; the new rule is that either will suffice. The employer must state whether or not a preparer or translator was involved in preparing the form. The new I-9 form has a drop-down list of acceptable documents to prove identity and work authorization; employers should be aware that the list is not comprehensive and other types of documents can be used. The employer has an obligation to review the documents, and must accept all documents that are legally permitted. [<https://www.uscis.gov/i-9>; see Gretchen M. Ostroff, *The New Form I-9: The Forgotten Immigration Law,* Vandeventer Black LLP (Jan. 31, 2017), available at Lexology.com] As of September 17, 2017, the latest version of the Form I-9 (Employment Eligibility Verification) must be used. The revised form allows Form FS-240, Consular Report of Birth Abroad, to be submitted as an identity document. New hires must sign and complete Section 1 no later than the first day of employment. [Victoria M. Garcia, *Latest I-9 Form Published Today,* Bracewell LLP (July 17, 2017), available at Lexology.com]

Although ICE imposed a $226,000 fine on the Employer Solutions Staffing Group for Form I-9 violations, the Fifth Circuit reversed the sanctions, holding that it was not unlawful for the employer to have one person inspect employees' original documents in Texas, while someone else completed the Section 2 employer attestation in Minnesota, based on photocopies sent from Texas. The Fifth Circuit held that the INA is unclear as to whether the attestation has to be completed by the same person who reviewed the documents, so it was reasonable to divide the job between two people. (Before the Fifth Circuit decision, ICE changed the Form I-9 instructions to require both steps to be performed by the same person.) [*Employer Solutions Staffing Grp. v. OCAHO,* 833 F.3d 480 (5th Cir. 2016); see Nicola Ai Ling Prall, *5th Circuit Throws Out I-9 Fines Against Employer for Alleged Section 2 Attestation Deficiencies,* Jackson Lewis PC (Aug. 15, 2016), available at Lexology.com]

[E]   H-1B, H-2A, and H-2B Visas

The H-1B visa is a non-immigrant visa for temporary workers in "specialty occupations." This means jobs that apply a highly specialized body of knowledge in both a theoretical and a practical way. Most H-1B visa holders work in high-tech businesses, such as software development. The initial duration of the visa is three years, although it can be extended for three more years. The worker must have at least a bachelor's degree in his or her specialty field, or must have equivalent qualifications and expertise. If the job requires a state license, the visa holder must have the license. H-1B workers must be paid either the salary the employer would otherwise pay for the job, or the prevailing wage in the area. This requirement is designed to prevent employers from hiring foreign workers simply to lower wage costs. Willful violation of this requirement or the layoff requirement can be penalized by a fine and three years' debarment from federal contracts.

Employers usually recruit workers from foreign students in the United States on student visas and about to graduate from a program that gives them the necessary specialized skills. However, there were indications that, in addition to stepping up deportation and limiting entry of undocumented persons into the United States, the federal government would also restrict H-1B visas, although visa holders are legally present in the United States and permitted to work.

In 2004, the H-1B Visa Reform Act added 20,000 extra H-1B visa slots for people who hold a Master's or higher degree from a U.S. institution.

New STEM OPT (Science, Technology, Engineering, Math/Optional Practical Training) rules were published March 11, 2016, effective May 10, 2016. The rules allow international students studying STEM subjects in the United States to remain in this country for three years of on-the-job training—seven months longer than the previous rule allowed, but they are not allowed to replace a U.S. worker. Visa holders can apply for H-1B visas under the extra 20,000 STEM slots. Advocates for U.S. workers have challenged the program, and the D.C. Circuit is scheduled to hear a case in May 2016. [81 Fed. Reg. 13039 (Mar. 11, 2016); see Liz Robbins, *New U.S. Rule Extends Stay for Some Foreign Graduates*, NY Times.com (Mar. 9, 2016)]

H-1B visa holders may not be hired until the employer has first attempted to recruit qualified U.S. workers, although a more qualified H-1B applicant can legitimately be preferred to a less-qualified U.S. citizen. Employers are also forbidden to terminate U.S. workers for the purpose of replacing them with H-1B workers. Temporary agencies and other suppliers of contingent workers are forbidden to make any placements of H-1B workers with any company that has displaced U.S. workers.

The DOL regulation not only protects U.S. jobs, but also it protects the H-1B workers from exploitation. They must be given benefits on the same basis as their U.S. counterparts. Whenever their employer places them in a nonproductive category (e.g., there is a temporary lull in work), they must be kept at full salary. It is unlawful for employers to require H-1B workers to reimburse them for the cost of filing the employment petition, or to penalize workers for terminating their work assignment prematurely.

To encourage reporting of misconduct, protection is extended to applicants, employees, and ex-employees who assist the Departments of Labor and Justice in their investigations. In fact, H-1B whistleblowers can be permitted to remain in the United States for up to six years.

The H-1B season for fiscal 2018, with a cap of 65,000 visas (6,800 reserved for citizens of Chile and Singapore) plus 20,000 visas for applicants with advanced degrees from U.S. institutions, began on April 3, 2017. (Nominally the season begins on April 1, but because that was a Saturday, it was delayed until the next business day.) In 2016, 346,000 petitions were made for the 85,000 slots and the filing period closed on April 7. The filing fee for Form I-129, Petition for a Non-Immigrant Worker, is $460, and the fee for Form I-539, Application to Extend/Change Non-Immigrant Status is $370. [Gregory A. Wald et. al., *USCIS to Accept Cap-Subject H-1B Specialty Occupation Visa Petitions on April 3, 2017*, Squire Patton Boggs (Feb. 15, 2017), available at Lexology.com; Matthew C. Morse, *Preparing for Upcoming H-1B Cap Season*, Fakhoury Law Group PC (Feb. 3, 2017), available at Lexology.com]

USCIS also announced that inspectors covering the H-1B program would be directed toward outsourcing companies, many of them in India, that recruit H-1B workers for U.S. corporations. Additional inspections will target companies with a high percentage of H-1B workers who work off-site at another location and companies whose business data is hard to verify by using standard sources. USCIS set up a new online "hotline" for reporting H-1B abuses. Legislation has also been introduced in Congress that would impose additional requirements on companies applying for H-1B visas that pay less than $100,000 a year. A complementary announcement by the DOJ's Civil Rights Division cautions employers against disfavoring U.S. workers by using the H-1B program to hire non-U.S. workers for jobs where qualified U.S. workers are available. [Laura Meckler, *Trump Administration Re-Opens H-1B Program, With a Twist*, WSJ.com (Apr. 3, 2017)]

Between October and December 31, 2016, DOL received 83,167 labor condition applications—68% were in one of five computer and software categories. About a quarter of the applications (23.9%) came from just one state, California. The top 10 H-1B employers were consulting companies such as Deloitte & Touche and Infosys. In the same time period, DOL got 35,281 applications for a prevailing wage determination for the permanent residence process; the most common occupations were also computer-related, and all of the top five employers were tech companies: Microsoft, Apple, Intel, Qualcomm, and Google. [Glenn M. Rissman, *Just Who is Using All those H-1B Visas?*, Stearns Weaver Miller Weissler Alhadeff & Sitterson PA (Mar. 3, 2017), available at Lexology.com]

In order to terminate an H-1B worker lawfully, several steps must be undertaken. Both the worker and USCIS must be notified of the termination. The DOL Labor Condition Application must be withdrawn and the worker must be offered payment of his or her fare home. The consequences of failure can be severe: for example, an ALJ ordered an employer to pay $183,000 in back wages, plus interest. An H-1B employee who had a three-year visa was fired after two months. He was awarded back pay for the two-and-a-half years between his termination and his departure from the United States, on the grounds that, because the procedure was not observed, there had been no bona fide termination. [Kramer Levin Naftalis and Frankel LLP, *H-1B Employer Found Liable for Substantial Back Wages After Failing to Notify USCIS of Termination* (Aug. 15, 2016), available at Lexology.com]

The U.S. employer is required to pay H-1B workers as long as they are employed, so the general rule is that they cannot be laid off or placed on unpaid leave. However, INS and the DOL agree that H-1B workers are entitled to take FMLA leave on the same terms as U.S. workers and are entitled to leave as an ADA reasonable accommodation. [Franczek Radelet, *Are Foreign Nationals on H-1B Work Visas Eligible for FMLA Leave?*, fmlainsights.com (Sept. 1, 2016) (benefitslink.com)]

The "50/50 Rule" requires companies that have at least 50 employees, at least 50% of whom hold H-1B or L-1 visas, to pay a fee of $4,000 for each H-1B petition and $4,500 for L-1 visa petitions. The rule was enacted by Pub. L. No. 111-230. It expired September 30, 2015, but was reinstated by the Fiscal Year 2016 Department of Homeland Security Appropriations Bill, which is part of the omnibus spending bill passed in December 2015. The additional filing fee is authorized until September 20, 2015; the money is used to enhance border security. Employers filing H-1B petitions should indicate if they are within the 50/50 category and, if so, pay the fee.

If the employer has not filed a labor condition application (LCA) in the period since 2008, the employer's Federal Employer ID Number (FEIN) must be validated with the DOL. This usually takes three business days. Some small companies do not have documents needed for verification; they can usually submit a letter from their bank verifying the FEIN and that the company has an account with the institution.

On November 18, 2016, the Department of Homeland Security (DHS) published a final rule, effective January 17, 2017, dealing with highly skilled non-immigrant foreign workers (such as H-1B visa holders) and employment-based immigrant workers with EB-1, -2, and -3 visas. Some holders of temporary work visas receive a 10-day grace period to enter the United States before starting work and, at the end of the visa period to change or extend their visa status or leave the United States. When employees holding temporary work visas lose their jobs and seek to file a new visa petition with a new employer, the 2016 rule gives them a 60-day grace period. Portability requirements for H-1B visas have been codified. The rule explains how H-1B workers can change jobs or employers, when a portability petition has been filed by a second employer. Workers are allowed to file "bridge petitions": successive portability petitions. H-1B workers who assist in investigations about Labor Condition Application violations may be protected by showing that their failure to maintain H-1B status was due to extraordinary circumstances.

Generally, an H-1B petition for a licensed occupation requires the worker to be licensed, but the final rule permits a temporary approval if there are technical reasons that preclude licensure before getting the H-1B. H-1B workers (and their H-4 dependents) who are being sponsored for status as legal permanent residents of the United States can extend non-immigrant stay beyond the regular six-year limit. The rule explains when an I-140 petition remains valid after the original petitioner withdraws the petition or goes out of business; the priority date can be transferred to a subsequent new petition. [81 Fed. Reg. 82398 (Nov. 18, 2016); see Susan J. Cohen, *Long-Awaited High Skilled Worker Regulations Published by the Department of Homeland Security*, Mintz Levin Cohn Ferris Glovsky and Popeo PC (Nov. 21, 2016), available at Lexology.com]

In 2015, the DHS issued an H-4 EAD rule under which certain spouses of H-1B visa holders could obtain Employment Authorization Documents (EADs) allowing them to work while awaiting permanent resident status. About 90% of H-4 visas are held by women; 80% of them are Indian. Typically, they are married to employees of tech companies.

A group of American tech workers, Save Jobs USA, brought a suit in the District Court for the District of Columbia in 2015, arguing that DHS lacked the authority to promulgate the rule. The district court granted summary judgment for the DHS. After the inauguration in 2017, the DOJ did not file a brief to support the DHS motion. The DOJ moved to hold the proceedings in abeyance for 60 days (until early April 2017) so the new staff could consider the policy. If the H-4 EAD is eliminated, it might result in fewer businesses being started, and fewer jobs being created. U.S. employers might also find it difficult to compete for H-1B workers who might prefer to work in another country, where their spouses can be employed. [*Save Jobs USA v. DHS*, 105 F. Supp. 3d 108 (D.D.C. 2015); the case has been appealed to the D.C. Circuit. See Matthew J. Martinez, *Future of H-4 Work Permits Uncertain*, Jackson Lewis PC (Mar. 23, 2017), available at Lexology.com]

Non-immigrant work visas (e.g., H-1B or L-1) can be revoked by the Department of State (DOS) on the basis of "derogatory information" about the visa holder—which could mean a DUI arrest even without a finding of guilt. The DOS has revoked some visas on this basis and told people within the United States that they must re-apply the next time they leave and re-enter the United States. Visa revocation does not necessarily mean that the person will be denied re-admission. [Maria Fernanda Gandarez and Matthew Kolodziej, *DUI Arrest Could Now Lead to Visa Revocation for Employees in U.S. Even Without a Conviction*, Ogletree Deakins Aug. 23, 2016, available at Lexology.com]

In 1986, the H-2 visa program for unskilled foreign workers was divided into H-2A and H-2B. H-2B permits temporary recruitment of unskilled non-agricultural workers for jobs no qualified U.S. worker will take. Non-immigrant visa petitions are now determined by the USCIS, an agency within the Department of Homeland Security. Homeland Security, in turn, designated DOL as the agency to advise it about whether H-2B petitions should be granted. In 2005, the DOL adopted the H-1B program's skill-based wage calculation method. [76 Fed. Reg. 3452 (Jan. 19, 2011); *Louisiana Forestry Ass'n Inc. v. Sec'y of Labor*, 745 F.3d 633 (3d Cir. 2014)]

The Ninth Circuit held that the Fair Labor Standards Act (FLSA) requires employers to reimburse H-2A temporary agricultural workers for their travel and immigration expenses; reimbursement is required in the first week of employment. [*Rivera v. Peri & Sons Farms*, 735 F.3d 892 (9th Cir. 2013)]

DOL's Wage and Hour Division (WHD) published new rules in 2015, updating 29 C.F.R. Part 503. The rules cover applications for Temporary Employment Certification, ETA Form 9142B, filed on or after April 29, 2015. The employer applies for a prevailing wage determination, then submits an H-2B registration form that certifies the need for immigrant workers for up to three years. Each season, the employer submits Form 9142B 75–90 days before the workers will be needed. The employer must demonstrate, not just attest, that it was unable to hire enough U.S. workers. The wage offered to H-2B workers must be at least equal to the prevailing wage or the federal, state, or local minimum wage and must be paid for the full term of employment. Employees must be paid at least once every two weeks. The employer must provide all necessary tools, supplies, and equipment at no charge to the workers. H-2B workers cannot be hired because of a strike or lockout and the employer cannot lay off any U.S. worker doing a similar job starting 120 days before the H-2B employment period and continuing throughout the whole period of H-2B employment. The employer must pay certain travel expenses (for inbound travel, for all workers who complete 50% of the job order) and outbound travel, even if the worker is dismissed before the end of the period. H-2B workers must not be placed in occupations or job locations outside those certified on the employer's H-2B application. Retaliation and discrimination are forbidden against workers who exercise job-related rights. Labor certifications can be revoked for offenses such as fraud, failure to cooperate with a DOL investigation, and failure to comply with DOL remedial orders. Civil money penalties of up to $10,000 subsequently raised to $11,940 per violation (including failure to pay workers properly and failure to abide by the terms of the labor certification can be imposed). Individuals who suffer damages from violations are entitled to back wages and make-whole relief.

However, the Tenth Circuit cast doubt on the entire H-2B labor certification and visa process by holding that DOL is not a subordinate agency of the Department of Homeland Security and, therefore, DOL does not have the power to issue H-2B regulations: only the Department of Homeland Security, which runs the Immigration and Naturalization Agency, has power to do so. [*G.H. Daniels III & Assocs. v. Perez*, 626 Fed. Appx. 205 (10th Cir. 2015)]

A provision of the 2016 Department of Labor Appropriations Act, Pub. L. No. 114-113, forbids the DOL to use FY 2016 funds to enforce certain of the provisions of the 2015 regulation, but the regulations remain in force, and DOL's position is that employers must obey them. [Department of Labor Wage and Hour Division (WHD), *H-2B Side-by-Side Comparison of the 2009 and 2012 Rules*, <http://www.dol.gov/whd/immigration/H2BFinalRule/H2BSideBySide.htm> (last accessed Feb. 27, 2017)]

In response to requests from industry, the DHS announced in June 2017 that it would make 15,000 additional H-2B visas, over and above the statutory limit of 66,000, available to businesses at risk of financial loss if they are unable to hire enough workers. [Laura Meckler, *Homeland Security Department to Issue More Visas for Summer Workers*, WSJ.com (June 21, 2017); Laura Meckler and Michael C. Bender, *U.S. to Offer More Visas to Temporary Seasonal Workers*, WSJ.com (July 17, 2017)]

[F] Case Law on Immigration Issues in Employment

Undocumented workers are entitled to some of the rights extended to people who have work authorization because a contrary result could encourage employers to hire undocumented people in order to underpay them and subject them to unlawful working conditions. However, undocumented people will probably not be entitled to remedies that are as extensive as those that documented workers can obtain.

Undocumented aliens are employees entitled to vote in union representation elections, even if their status has been challenged under the IRCA. [*NLRB v. Kolkka*, 170 F.3d 937 (9th Cir. 1999)] But an illegal alien is not an "employee" for Worker's Compensation purposes, and therefore cannot receive Comp benefits for an on-the-job injury [*Granados v. Windson Dev. Corp.*, 257 Va. 103, 509 S.E.2d 290 (1999)], or back pay in a suit alleging unfair labor practices. [*Hoffman Plastic Prods. Inc. v. NLRB*, 535 U.S. 137 (2002); *Palma v. NLRB*, 723 F.3d 176 (2d Cir. 2013)]

The Second Circuit permitted an award of lost earnings—using United States and not home country rates—to an undocumented worker crippled in a fall, because the injury was caused by the employer's violation of scaffolding requirements, not by the employee's ineligibility to work legally in the United States. [*Madeira v. Affordable Hous. Found. Inc.*, 469 F.3d 219 (2d Cir. 2006). See also *Majlinger v. Cassino Contracting Corp.*, 25 A.D.3d 4, 802 N.Y.S.2d 56 (2d Dept. 2005) allowing compensation for lost U.S. earnings at U.S. rates, holding that this does not conflict with IRCA; *Flores v. Limehouse*, 2006 U.S. Dist. LEXIS 30433 (D.S.C. May 11, 2006) holding that IRCA does not preempt claims by undocumented workers against their employers under RICO and federal and state labor law—even if the workers obtained employment fraudulently; *Rosa v. Partners in Progress, Inc.*, 868 A.2d 994 (N.H. 2005) (for undocumented worker to be able to make a tort claim, the employer must have known or have a duty to know the worker's employment was illegal).]

California Labor Code § 1171.5 says that immigration status is irrelevant to liability issues under the state's labor and employment laws. IRCA preempts state or local laws that impose criminal penalties for employing ineligible aliens, but does not preempt state Worker's Compensation laws. In this reading, the purpose of the Worker's Compensation (WC) law is remedial and humanitarian, not penal, and it does not impose penalties for employing aliens, so it does not conflict with and is not preempted by IRCA. Although WC benefits cannot be paid as a direct result of fraudulent misrepresentation, that principle is not applied where use of fraudulent documentation to obtain employment did not cause the physical injury. [*Farmers Bros. Coffee v. Workers' Comp. Appeals Bd. & Ruiz*, 133 Cal. App. 4th 533 (Cal. App. 2005)]

In 2011, in a suit alleging overtime violations and failure to pay for all hours worked, the District Court for the District of Massachusetts ordered the restaurant to answer written questions about potential class members, but denied the restaurant's motion for information about plaintiffs' immigration status. The district court ruled that allowing recovery by illegal aliens is compatible with federal immigration policy, and there is a consensus that FLSA recoveries are not discretionary—wages must be paid even if the worker is undocumented. [*Lin v. Chinatown Rest. Corp.*, No. 09-11510-GAO, 2011 U.S. Dist. LEXIS 30626 (D. Mass. Mar. 23, 2011). See also *NLRB v. Domsey Trading Corp.*, 636 F.3d 33 (2d Cir. 2011), holding that, in an NLRB compliance hearing about alleged unlawful termination of strikers, the employer has the right to cross-examine plaintiffs about their immigration status, and expert testimony about immigration is admissible.]

The California Supreme Court permitted an employee to pursue a discrimination suit even though he presented false work authorization documents to be hired. California took the position that employees and job applicants are entitled to the same protection against discrimination (in this case, termination allegedly for filing a Worker's Compensation claim) as legal workers, although their wage recovery is limited to wages earned before the employer learned of the misrepresentation. The court reached this result because federal law requires termination once an employer learns of an employee's lack of authorization to work in the United States. Illegal workers cannot be reinstated because federal law forbids it. [*Salas v. Sierra Chem. Co.*, 59 Cal. 4th 407 (Cal. 2014)]

The Eighth Circuit held in mid-2013 that unauthorized aliens could maintain a FLSA suit for willful violations (denial of minimum wage and overtime), on the grounds that employers cannot be entitled to profit from knowingly hiring people who are not authorized to work in the United States. [*Lucas v. Jerusalem Cafe LLC*, 721 F.3d 927 (8th Cir. 2013); see also *Vallejo v. Azteca Elec. Constr.*, No. CV-13-01207-PHX-NVW, 2015 U.S. Dist. LEXIS 11780 (D. Ariz. Feb. 2, 2015)]

Early in 2017, the NLRB, DOL's WHD, OSHA, EEOC, and OFCCP released a joint Fact Sheet, "Retaliation Based on the Exercise of Workplace Rights is Unlawful," reminding employers that retaliation is unlawful no matter the immigration status of the worker asserting legal rights. Workers are always entitled to be paid for work they have done, but undocumented workers' remedies are limited. For example, they cannot recover reinstatement or back pay under the National Labor Relations Act (NLRA). [Kimberly N. Dobson, Howard M. Bloom and Philip B. Rosen, *NLRB Joins Other Federal Agencies in Combatting Retaliation*, Jackson Lewis PC (Jan. 17, 2017), available at Lexology.com]

Although the remedies unauthorized workers can obtain from U.S. courts are limited, the Fourth Circuit upheld an EEOC subpoena to investigate charges of national origin discrimination filed by unauthorized workers who charged they were fired for complaining about discrimination against Hispanic workers. The Fourth Circuit said that Title VII gives the EEOC jurisdiction whenever there is a plausible or arguable basis to subpoena information, and Title VII does not explicitly forbid undocumented workers to file complaints. [*EEOC v. Maritime Autowash, Inc.*, No. 15-1947, 2016 WL 1622290 (4th Cir. Apr. 25, 2016); see Gerald L. Maatman, Jr., *Fourth Circuit Says EEOC Can Serve Subpoena on Employer*, Seyfarth Shaw LLP (Apr. 29, 2016), available at Lexology.com]

In 2004, the Seventh Circuit ruled that employees cannot state a RICO claim by alleging that the employer deliberately hired illegal aliens to keep wages down. In such a situation, the defendant company is the "enterprise," so there is no one for it to conspire with for RICO purposes. [*Baker v. IBP Inc.*, 357 F.3d 685 (7th Cir. 2004)] The Eleventh Circuit, however, disagreed, ruling that both RICO and state law claims were raised by allegations that the employer conspired with temporary agencies to hire illegal workers and use false documentation, with the objective of lowering wages and escaping Worker's Compensation responsibilities. The Supreme Court granted certiorari in December of 2005, but dismissed certiorari as improvidently granted in June 2006 and sent the case back to the Eleventh Circuit to resolve some minor issues. [*Williams v. Mohawk Indus. Inc.*, 411 F.3d 1252 (11th Cir. 2005), *cert. granted but dismissed as improvidently granted*, 547 U.S. 516 (2006)]

In September 2008, the Ninth Circuit upheld the Legal Arizona Workers Act, a 2007 Arizona state law penalizing employers who hire illegal aliens, by revoking their state business licenses. The Supreme Court upheld this law in mid-2011, holding that federal immigration law does not preempt the state law, because it is possible for employers to comply with both. IRCA forbids states to impose any criminal or civil sanctions for hiring illegal immigrants, other than through licensing and similar laws—but the Arizona statute is a licensing law because it is enforced by taking away the licenses of companies that hire undocumented workers. [*Chamber of Commerce v. Whiting*, 131 S. Ct. 1968 (2011)]

After almost a decade, Wal-Mart prevailed in an FLSA/RICO suit about the company's relationships with contract janitorial services that hire immigrants, allegedly including illegal immigrants. The Third Circuit held that there were too many differences among the plaintiffs to certify an FLSA class action because in order to certify the class, the district court must make a finding that the members of the collective action are similarly situated, but they worked for 70 contractors and subcontractors, in 180 stores in 33 states, and Wal-Mart did not directly set wages and hours. The Third Circuit held that there was no evidence that Wal-Mart itself trafficked or helped workers to stay in the United States illegally. [*Zavala v. Wal-Mart Stores Inc.*, 691 F.3d 527 (3d Cir. 2012)]

§ 23.12 ADA COMPLIANCE IN HIRING

Researchers from Rutgers and Syracuse Universities sent out fictitious resumes and cover letters for thousands of accounting jobs. "Candidates" who disclosed a disability got 26% less interest than those who did not (34% for experienced, 15% just out of college). In 2013, 34% of working-age people with disabilities were employed, as compared to 74% of those without disabilities. The researchers used two resumes, one for a well-qualified candidate with six years' experience, one for someone a year out of college. One cover letter did not refer to any disabilities; one referred to a spinal cord injury, and the third referred to Asperger's Syndrome. The negative results were about the same for physical and mental disabilities. [Noam Scheiber, *Fake Cover Letters Expose Discrimination Against Disabled*, NYTimes.com (Nov. 2, 2015)]

In the ADA context, the job description defines the essential functions of the job. Job postings must conform to the job description. For example, a job description that stipulates that the bulk of the job involves lifting could exempt the employer from having to accommodate an employee's lifting restrictions—unless it is contradicted by a job posting that mentions only functions that the employee with the limitation can handle. Job descriptions should include a blanket statement permitting managers to add more tasks to the position. Other relevant documents such as performance evaluations should cross-reference the job description. [Linda B. Hollinshead, *Do I Really Need to Update That Job Description? Failing to Do So May Complicate ADA Litigation*, Duane Morris LLP (Oct. 26, 2015), available at Lexology.com]

For ADA purposes, some pre-employment inquiries are simply unacceptable; others are permissible only after a conditional job offer has been made.

The EEOC's Technical Assistance Manual for implementation of the ADA defines these pre-hire questions as improper:

- Have you ever been treated for these diseases?

- Have you ever been hospitalized? Why?

- Are there any health factors that prevent you from doing the job you applied for? (However, if the inquiry is restricted to specific job functions, it is permissible to ask about ability to perform those particular functions, and about potential accommodations.)

- How much sick leave did you take last year?
- Are you taking any prescribed medications?
- Have you ever been treated for substance abuse?

When it comes to pre-employment testing, it is discriminatory to give a test in a form or manner that requires the use of an impaired sensory, speaking, or manual skill, unless the point of the test is the degree to which that skill is present. So an assembly-line job may legitimately require manual dexterity. But if the point is to test keyboarding speed, a hearing-impaired person may have to be given a test that includes nonverbal commands as to when to start and stop. It may be necessary to have a test read aloud to a blind or dyslexic person, or to have a sign language interpreter. Every effort should be made to administer the test in a room that is wheelchair-accessible.

> ■ **TIP:**   Tell applicants if there will be a test as part of the interview process. Then it is up to them to explain the nature of any accommodation they need to take the test.

Pre-employment medical examinations are allowed only if the candidate has already met the other criteria, and a conditional job offer has been extended. The examination must be required of everyone in that job category who gets a conditional offer. Once the offer has been made, it is acceptable to ask about past injuries and Worker's Compensation claims.

To avoid violating the Genetic Information Nondiscrimination Act (GINA), it is important to avoid asking about family medical history, because such inquiries can constitute requests for forbidden genetic information.

On January 17, 2013, HHS published a final rule covering the application of the Health Insurance Portability and Accessibility Act (HIPAA) privacy rule to Titles I (health coverage) and II (employment) of the Genetic Information Nondiscrimination Act (GINA). Genetic information is considered health information, which cannot be used for underwriting purposes (except for long-term care insurance policies). Covered entities must comply no later than September 23, 2013. [Katherine Georger, *New HIPAA Final Rule Implements GINA Restriction on Use and Disclosure of Genetic Information for Underwriting Purposes*, Holland & Hart LLP News (Jan. 23, 2013) (benefitslink.com). The EEOC has also published rules about GINA; for final rules about the application of GINA to wellness programs, see 81 Fed. Reg. 31143 (May 17, 2016), discussed in Rachel Emma Silverman, *EEOC Issues New Rules for Wellness Programs*, WSJ.com (May 16, 2016)] Wellness programs are also discussed at §§ 18.19[G], 19.05[B], and 36.10[D].

Post-offer medical examinations are considered nondiscriminatory, and therefore it is not necessary to provide proof of business necessity. But if the applicant with a disability is in fact qualified for the job, and the offer is withdrawn subsequent to the examination, the employer must show job-related business necessity for canceling the offer, and must also prove that reasonable accommodation to the disability could not be made without undue hardship.

For active employees, medical examinations and inquiries about the nature and severity of disability can be required only if they are job-related and consistent with business necessity: For instance, someone has been ill or injured, and the question is fitness to return to work.

The ADA also requires disability-related information to be kept confidential. In fact, it should be collected and maintained on separate forms, and even stored in files separate from general personnel information, although there are certain exceptions to the general rule of confidentiality: GINA also contains confidentiality requirements for genetic information, which must be kept separate from other health information.

- Supervisors and managers can be informed about work restrictions or accommodations that are needed;

- If emergency treatment might be required for a disabled employee (e.g., an epileptic might have a seizure; a diabetic might go into insulin shock or coma), first aid and safety personnel can be informed, so they will be prepared;

- A special post-September 11 rule allows collection of information about special needs for evacuation in an emergency;

- Government officials investigating ADA compliance are entitled to information about the number of employees with disabilities, and the nature of the disabilities.

The ADA forbids employers to ask about prescription drug use unless the workers have been seen to compromise safety or appear unable to function. (There is an ADA exception: public safety workers such as police and firefighters, who are required to report prescription drug use that could create a threat to public safety.) Even jobs that are subject to federal drug testing requirements (e.g., bus and truck drivers) are tested for only six categories of drugs, and powerful drugs like Xanax, Vicodin, and OxyContin are not included. Many states have drug-free workplace laws, but their provisions vary widely and tend to focus on illegal drugs.

On December 1, 2015, for World AIDS Day, the EEOC issued two documents about ADA issues for HIV/AIDS patients, explaining that job applicants and employees are protected from employment discrimination and harassment based on HIV status, and are entitled to reasonable accommodations at work. In most situations, the employee can keep HIV status private. [<http://www.eeoc .gov/eeoc/newsroom/release/12-1-15.cfm> (Dec. 1, 2015) (last accessed Feb. 27, 2017); see Matthew C. Luzadder and Janine N. Fletcher, *EEOC Issues Guidance*

Directed Specifically to HIV Positive Employees and Their Physicians, Kelley Drye & Warren LLP (Jan. 7, 2016), available at Lexology.com]

A 2010 Sixth Circuit case involves seven former employees of Dura Automotive Systems, who said that the company's drug testing policy (which led to terminations for taking prescription drugs) violated the ADA. The Sixth Circuit said that the relevant section of the ADA, 42 U.S.C. § 12112(a)(6), makes it unlawful to discriminate against a Qualified Individual with a Disability (QIWD) by using qualification standards that tend to screen out persons with disabilities—unless the standard is job-related and consistent with business necessity. The Sixth Circuit ruled that only a QIWD can sue under this section, although any employee can bring suit under other ADA sections. In this case, at least six of the seven plaintiffs were not disabled as defined by the ADA (the seventh might have had a record of disability), so they could not sue. The case arose before the ADAAA took effect (see § 36.03) so that law did not apply. [*Bates v. Dura Auto. Sys. Inc.*, 625 F.3d 283 (6th Cir. 2010)]

According to the Department of Veterans' Affairs, veterans aged 18–34 are a vulnerable population whose unemployment rate since 2005 is 20% higher than non-veterans of the same age. The unemployment rate for veterans 18–24 is 40% higher than people in the same age cohort who were not in the military. [Robert W. Goldfarb, *Veterans Battle for Jobs on the Home Front*, NYTimes.com (May 9, 2015)]

If an employee or a job applicant is a veteran and possibly disabilities may be service-related, then both the ADA and Uniformed Services Employment and Reemployment Rights Act (USERRA) (see § 1.18) may be involved. In fact, USERRA actually requires more of employers, by imposing a duty to assist veterans in becoming qualified for jobs, whereas the ADA just protects the rights of individuals with disabilities who are qualified for the job they hold or have applied for. Both statutes require employers to provide reasonable accommodation. The EEOC guidance says that an employer seeking to hire someone with a service-connected disability can ask if he or she is a disabled veteran—if the employer has an affirmative action obligation, or voluntarily seeks to benefit individuals with disabilities. It is also acceptable to recruit through organizations for veterans with disabilities. But before asking for applicants to voluntarily describe themselves as disabled veterans, the employer must explain that the information will only be used for affirmative action purposes, and will be kept confidential. Although the ADA does not require affirmative action for disabled veterans, it is acceptable for an employer to give a preference to disabled veterans. Recruiting material can be made handicap-accessible, and advertisements can state explicitly that disabled veterans are welcome to apply. [EEOC, *Veterans with Service-Connected Disabilities and the Americans with Disabilities Act (ADA): A Guide for Employers*, <http://www.eeoc.gov/eeoc/publications/ada_veterans_employers.cfm> (Feb. 29, 2008) (last viewed Feb. 27, 2017)]

The tax code provides various employer incentives, such as the § 44 disabled access credit, available for small businesses that make their premises accessible; and the § 190 barrier removal deduction for removing physical, structural, and transportation barriers on business premises. The § 190 deduction can be taken by any size business, but is not available for construction of new premises, only retrofitting; it is limited to $15,000 a year, but larger amounts can be depreciated.

To carry out the administration policy of promoting employment of veterans and workers with disabilities, the Office of Federal Contract Compliance Programs (OFCCP) issued final rules under Rehabilitation Act § 503 and Vietnam Era Veterans' Readjustment Assistance Act of 1974 (VEVRAA) in mid-2013, calling for affirmative action by federal contractors to hire these groups. The affirmative action requirements for veterans apply to contractors with federal contracts or subcontracts over $100,000; the requirements for persons with disabilities apply to all federal contractors holding federal contracts over $10,000. Federal contractors that already had to develop written affirmative action plans now must also set hiring benchmarks for veterans and persons with disabilities. Federal contractors are required to use a three-stage approach to self-identification, asking applicants to identify themselves if they are disabled or veterans. (The EEOC has informed the OFCCP that this inquiry does not violate the ADA.) Data on hiring and recruitment efforts must be retained for three years.

The final rules call for a hiring goal of 7% of the workforce (as adjusted) to consist of persons with disabilities, and 8% veterans, covering all groups and jobs. (A small contractor, with under 100 employees, can set a target of 7% employment of PWDs in its total workforce.) These are goals, not quotas, and there is no penalty for non-attainment—but federal contracts can be revoked if the contractor cannot show a legitimate effort to meet the target. [78 Fed. Reg. 58682 (Sept. 24, 2013)]

Since March 24, 2014, VEVRAA permitted federal contractors to either use OFCCP's national benchmarks, or set their own benchmarks. The national benchmark fell from 7.2% to 7.0% on April 21, 2015. The benchmark fell again in 2016, to 6.9%, reflecting the decline in the percentage of veterans in the civilian labor force. [Cara Yates Crotty, *Hiring Benchmark for Protected Veterans Is Down a Bit This Year*, Constancy Brooks Smith & Prophete (June 21, 2016), available at Lexology.com] The benchmark fell again: as of March 31, 2017 it is 6.7%. (The decline reflects the aging of the cohort of Vietnam veterans, which reduces their representation in the workforce.) [Stephanie Underwood, *Hiring Benchmark for Protected Veterans Is Reduced Again*, Constancy Brooks Smith & Prophete LLP (Apr. 5, 2017), available at Lexology.com. See <https://ofccp.dol-esa.gov/errd/VEVRAA.jsp> for the VEVRAA Benchmark Database.]

The OFCCP form explains why employers request self-identification, how the information will be used, that there will be no retaliation for self-identification, and that persons with a disability may be entitled to reasonable accommodation. The form expired January 31, 2017, but was renewed by the

OFCCP with a new expiration date of January 31, 2020. [<https://www.dol.gov/ofccp/regs/compliance/sec503/Self_ID_Forms/SelfIDForms.htm>; see Kelly Jennings Yeoman and Michael C. Griffaton, Labor and Employment Alert: *Federal Contractors Have an Updated Voluntary Self-Identification of Disability Form*, Vorys Sater Seymour and Pease LLP (Feb. 1, 2017), available at Lexology.com]

Veterans' preferences have been upheld as acceptable under Title VII § 712, and non-veterans do not have reverse discrimination claims under VEVRAA or Title VII. Many states authorize private employers voluntarily to implement veterans' preferences: Arizona, Arkansas, Florida, Idaho, Iowa, Kentucky, Maine, Massachusetts, Michigan, Montana, Nebraska, North Dakota, Oklahoma, Oregon, South Carolina, Virginia, Washington, and Utah. The EEOC is less positive about veterans' preferences, because veterans are predominantly male, so the preference could have a disparate impact on female job applicants. [Mickey Silberman, *Veteran Hiring and Veteran Preferences Gaining Steam*, Jackson Lewis PC (Apr. 23, 2015), available at Lexology.com]

§ 23.13   CREDIT REPORTING IN THE HIRING PROCESS

A federal law, the Fair Credit Reporting Act (FCRA) [15 U.S.C. §§ 1681a *et seq.*], as amended by the Consumer Credit Reporting Reform Act of 1996 (CCRRA) [Pub. L. No. 104-208], governs the use of credit reports and investigative credit reports not only for making loans and approving credit card applications, but in the employment context as well. [Kevin C. Donovan, *The Fair Credit Reporting Act: Misnamed But Mischievous*, Wilson Elser (Oct. 30, 2015), available at Lexology.com]

The FCRA provides that a consumer report is a written or oral communication from a consumer reporting agency, dealing with a consumer's entitlement to credit, "character, general reputation, personal characteristics, or mode of living."

An investigative credit report is different in that it involves personal interviews with people who have personal knowledge of the individual. The CCRRA requires employers to give job applicants a written disclosure statement, and to get their consent in writing, before requesting either a consumer report or an investigative consumer report. Furthermore, if the employer wants an investigative report, it must explain to the applicant (via a written disclosure mailed no later than three days after the report is requested) that this type of report covers matters like character and conduct.

The FCRA [see 15 U.S.C. § 1681b(3)(B)] says that "employment purposes" are legitimate reasons for requesting a credit report or investigative credit report. "Employment purposes" means "evaluating a consumer for employment, promotion, reassignment, or retention as an employee." Because the FCRA specifically authorizes the use of credit reporting information in the hiring process, doing so is not employment discrimination.

An "adverse action" includes "denial of employment or any other decision for employment purposes that adversely affects any current or prospective employee." When the credit report is negative, leading to adverse action, the employer must provide oral, written, or electronic (for instance, fax or e-mail) notice of the adverse action. It must also explain how to review the credit report file, correct errors (the negative report might refer to someone else with a similar name, or someone who has appropriated the job applicant's identity) and contest items that the consumer believes to be untrue. Notice must be given after the employer makes the decision, but before the adverse action is implemented.

The CCRRA also imposes an obligation on the employer. Before it gets any reports from a reporting agency, it must give the agency a statement that the employer complies with the various consumer protection requirements of credit reporting law.

As a result of a later statute, the FACTA (Fair and Accurate Credit Transactions Act of 2003; Pub. L. No. 108-159), 15 U.S.C. § 1681a has been amended to add a new subsection (x). Under the new law, a communication is not treated as a consumer report—and therefore is not subject to the FCRA requirements—if the purpose of the communication is job-related and not related to the person's creditworthiness.

To qualify for the FACTA exemption, the communication must be made to an employer as part of an investigation of suspected employment-related misconduct, or in compliance with laws or regulations (including the rules of a self-regulatory organization such as a stock exchange), or under the employer's pre-existing written policies. Reports of this type must not be disclosed to anyone except the employer or its agents, government officials, or self-regulatory organizations, unless disclosure is mandated by law. Furthermore, once the employer gets the information, if the information is the basis of any adverse action against the person, the employer must provide the person with a summary of the communication—but does not have to disclose the sources furnishing the information.

Effective July 21, 2011, the Dodd-Frank Act (Pub. L. No. 111-203) requires employers to disclose whenever credit scores have had an adverse effect on the employer's assessment of a job applicant.

In late 2010, the Third Circuit ruled that it does not violate the bankruptcy law provision 11 U.S.C. § 525(b) to avoid hiring a person because of his previous bankruptcy. (The situation would be different if someone who was already an employee was fired for filing a bankruptcy petition.) [*Rea v. Federated Investors*, 627 F.3d 937 (3d Cir. 2010)]

However, the EEOC's position is that discrimination on the basis of credit history is illegal, because of the disparate impact that such discrimination has on minorities. Employers who face Title VII disparate impact suits may be able to defend themselves by showing the procedure is job-related and consistent with business necessity. But even then, plaintiffs can still prevail by showing that there is an alternate practice that would achieve the same result without discriminatory impact.

In early 2017, the Ninth Circuit became the first court of appeals to consider several important issues in background check class actions. The Ninth Circuit held that including a liability release in the disclosure that a background check will be made not only violates the FCRA, it is a willful violation that creates concrete harm that gives aggrieved applicants standing to sue. The FCRA says that the background check disclosure statement must consist "solely" of the federally mandated language so adding a liability release—or anything else—violates the FCRA. [*Syed v. M-I, LLC,* 846 F.3d 1034 (9th Cir. 2017); see Gustavo A. Suarez, James R. Silvers and Jennifer P. Woodruff, *Ninth Circuit Breaks New Ground, Addresses Standing and Extraneous Content in Background Check Disclosure Forms/Screens,* Ogletree Deakins (Jan. 27, 2017), available at Lexology.com]

In 2014, the Sixth Circuit upheld a district court grant of summary judgment to employer Kaplan Higher Education Corp. The EEOC sued Kaplan, charging that its use of credit checks had a disparate impact on African-American applicants. Although the credit check vendor did not classify the race of applicants, the EEOC charged that a disproportionate number of African-American candidates were screened out because of their credit history. The Sixth Circuit ruled that the EEOC's expert witness identified African-American applicants by viewing their driver's license photographs—a "homemade methodology" that was not tested or validated, and could not be used to prove the case. Furthermore, the EEOC itself uses a credit check process similar to the challenged Kaplan process. [*EEOC v. Kaplan Higher Educ. Corp.*, 748 F.3d 749 (6th Cir. 2014). Certain jurisdictions, e.g., California, Colorado, Connecticut, Hawaii, Illinois, Maryland, Nevada, Oregon, Vermont, and Washington, and the cities of Chicago, New York, Philadelphia, and Madison, Wisconsin impose limits on the use of credit history in employment decision-making, although there may be exceptions for information that is substantially job-related, or when disclosures are made to applicants or employees that credit histories will be consulted. James D. Donathen et. al., *Recent New York City Legislation Will Prohibit Employers from Using Credit Checks to Screen Job Applicants*, Phillips Lytle LLP (Aug. 31, 2015)]

The Fourth Circuit affirmed dismissal of an EEOC nationwide pattern or practice suit; the court described the EEOC's expert analysis as "laughable." The EEOC said Freeman unlawfully relied on background checks with disparate impact on black, Hispanic, and male applicants. The Fourth Circuit said that the expert's report could not be relied on because it was laden with errors and logical fallacies. The sample analyzed only a limited number of background checks, ignoring a great deal of relevant data that were available for the period. [*EEOC v. Freeman*, 778 F.3d 463 (4th Cir. 2015)]

CHAPTER 24

RECORDKEEPING

§ 24.01 INTRODUCTION

[A] Employer Responsibility in General

Employee records are important in setting compensation, assuring that it is paid appropriately, and administering benefit plans. Proper records are necessary to handle insurance matters, comply with court orders, fill out tax returns and other government documents, and demonstrate EEO and immigration compliance. For a general introduction to federal requirements. [See the interactive *FirstStep Recordkeeping, Reporting & Notices Advisor*, <http://www.dol.gov/elaws/firststeprrn.htm> (last viewed Apr. 3, 2017)]

State law may require employees to be granted access (and perhaps to make copies) of their personnel files. For example, Connecticut defines personnel files as papers, documents, and reports about a particular employee, used to determine eligibility for employment, promotion, or discipline. But third-party references, records of stock option plans, security files, investigation reports about misconduct or crimes, and information required by the government and kept in separate files and documents prepared for litigation, are not considered personnel files. Delaware, Illinois, Maine, Massachusetts, Minnesota, Nevada, Oregon, Pennsylvania, and Washington also have laws regulating access to files. [Dabney D. Ware, *When a "Simple" Personnel File Request Is Not So Simple*, Foley & Lardner LLP (Sept. 9, 2013), available at Lexology.com; Susan Gross Sholinsky, *Take 5: Views You Can Use: Labor and Employment*, Epstein Becker Green (Nov. 12, 2013), available at Lexology.com]

In addition to determining its internal needs for gathering, processing, and deleting information, the company must be aware of legal requirements for record retention, and limitations on document destruction. Destroying documents that are subject to discovery in a court case is at least a civil offense, and may constitute contempt of court or even a criminal offense, depending on circumstances.

All documents in personnel files should be date-stamped when they are received, because it may be necessary to determine what was in the file at a particular time.

■ **TIP:** If it is legal and practical to destroy a document, make sure that all paper copies have been destroyed, as well as all computer files (including back-ups, copies on disks, and data uploaded to an Internet site for safekeeping). Just because someone has deleted a file does not mean that it has even been removed from that computer, much less from the entire network.

Whether the records are on paper or electronic, the goal of the corporate record retention policy should be to store and manage information on- and off-site in a systematic and cost effective manner. When necessary, the system must be able to handle litigation-related requests for documents, and managing risk.

The policy must satisfy the statutory and regulatory requirements for record retention, applicable statutes of limitations, and best practices for business. Publicly traded companies are subject to additional requirements imposed by the Sarbanes-Oxley Act (e.g., communications with the company's audit firm must be retained). The Public Company Accounting Oversight Board (PCAOB) requires accountants to retain audit work papers for at least seven years. Early in 2003, the SEC covered record retention issues in Exchange Act Release No. 47241.

Effective August 1, 2015, penalties for failure to furnish ERISA documents to plan participants and the DOL have increased. See 81 Fed. Reg. 29765 (May 12, 2016) and 81 Fed. Reg. 42491 (June 30, 2016). The increases were imposed under the Federal Civil Monetary Penalties Inflation Adjustment Improvement Act of 2015, which not only imposed major "catch-up" increases in penalties that had remained the same for about 15 years, but required annual inflation-based increases every January. As a result, the penalties increased once again, in January 2017: see 82 Fed. Reg. 8813 (Jan. 31, 2017).

A Sarbanes-Oxley provision enacted at 18 U.S.C. § 1519 calls for imprisonment of up to 20 years for knowing alteration, destruction, mutilation, falsification, or cover-up of records or documents with the intent to obstruct investigation of any matter under the jurisdiction of a federal department or agency. Even document destruction that occurred before a proceeding commenced can be prosecuted.

Courts have imposed major—even multi-million-dollar—sanctions on companies that destroyed key evidence in violation of court orders. Litigation parties that destroy evidence have also been precluded from introducing their own evidence as a penalty. It is increasingly clear that once litigation begins, a "litigation hold" should be placed on destruction of paper and electronic documents. Once the company becomes aware of impending litigation, employees should be informed of the possibility. They should receive copies of the relevant court orders, and be informed of the penalties for destruction of evidence.

However, if a company has a reasonable policy for when documents should be retained and when they should be destroyed, and the policy is consistently applied, then courts will probably find that it is unreasonable to expect the company to produce documents destroyed pursuant to the policy.

As Chapters 6 and 15 show, a current major litigation topic is whether defined contribution plans select the correct menu of investment options for plan participants—and whether the plan pays excessive fees for the investments in the plan or services to the plan. Even the cost of recordkeeping can create hazards for fiduciaries. In a Western District of Missouri class action, the plaintiffs were awarded $21.8 million against the plan's fiduciaries for failure to choose funds prudently and in accordance with the plan's published policies—and a further $13.4 million for failure to obtain rebates or monitor the cost of recordkeeping.

Although the exact form that it will take cannot be reliably predicted, it is likely that the Trump administration's pro-business and anti-regulatory stance will result in significant changes in both substantive and procedural requirements imposed on employers.

[B] 2002 DOL Final Rule

The Department of Labor published Final Rules Relating to Use of Electronic Communication and Recordkeeping Technologies by Employee Pension and Welfare Benefit Plans, updating 29 C.F.R. Part 2520, at 67 Fed. Reg. 17264 (Apr. 9, 2002). This document provides final rules under ERISA Title I for using electronic media to disclose benefit plan information to participants (a topic discussed in Chapter 27) and enacts a safe harbor for using electronic methods of disclosing and maintaining records. The final rule is effective October 9, 2002.

Under the Final Rule, 29 C.F.R. § 2520.107-1, electronic media can be used for maintenance and retention of records, if:

- The system has reasonable controls to ensure integrity, accuracy, authenticity, and reliability of the records.

- The records are maintained in reasonable order, in a safe and accessible place, so they can reasonably be inspected.

- The records can readily be converted into legible and readable hard copy from electronic form.

- The electronic data is labeled, securely stored, and backed up so it can be recovered if the main data repository is destroyed or corrupted.

- The employer retains paper copies of any data that cannot be seamlessly transferred to the electronic system.

The Final Rule permits destruction of paper records that have been transferred without error to the electronic system, unless there is a requirement (under the terms of the plan or an applicable law) that duplicate or substitute records be maintained in paper form.

See § 27.06 for more discussion of electronic media in pension and tax contexts.

[C] CHIPRA and ARRA Rules

The Children's Health Insurance Program Reauthorization Act (CHIPRA) of 2009, Pub. L. No. 111-3, which expands the state children's health insurance program, allows states to subsidize coverage provided by employers through their existing EGHPs. Plan administrators must report to the state the information needed to determine which plan participants are entitled to premium assistance from the SCHIP program. Employers therefore must create and maintain records about employees' eligibility for subsidy, and records for administering the subsidies. Employers must distribute the HHS model notice to inform employees about premium assistance. Failure to give notice is penalized by $100/day/ participant (increasing to $110/day on August 1, 2016 for failures occurring after November 2, 2015). [Norbert F. Kugele, Warner Norcross & Judd LLP, *New Federal SCHIP Law Requires Cafeteria and Health Plan Amendments* (Feb. 10, 2009) (benefitslink.com). The penalty rises to $112 per day, also for violations occurring after November 2, 2015, if the penalty is imposed after January 13, 2017: see 82 Fed. Reg. 8813 (Jan. 31, 2017)]

[D] PPACA (Health Care Reform) Requirements

At press time in 2017, congressional Republicans drafted a bill, the American Health Care Act, to repeal PPACA. The bill was withdrawn, because some congress members found it too severe and others not severe enough. When this book went to press in August 2017, Congress was in recess; PPACA repeal legislation had been introduced in the Senate but had not passed.

One reason that Patient Protection and Affordable Care Act (PPACA) is unpopular is because of the recordkeeping and notice burden. Participants must be notified of their right to keep their adult children in the plan until they reach age 27. The plan must keep track of the facts supporting its entitlement to grandfathered status—or causing loss of that status. When the health insurance exchanges are in operation, it will be necessary for employers to prove that they offer at least minimum required coverage or that they are exempt from the requirement. Otherwise, penalties will be imposed. [Christy Tinnes and Brigen Winters, *What Notices Are Required by PPACA?*, plansponsor.com (Sept. 21, 2010)]

PPACA requires the cost of providing Employee Group Health Plan (EGHP) coverage to be reported on employees' W-2 forms. Final regulations on the Code § 6055 requirements for minimum essential health coverage were published on March 10, 2014. The regulations explain the requirements imposed on companies with 50 or more full-time employees to report to the IRS and to employees about health care coverage available to them. The requirements will be used by the IRS to enforce the pay-or-play mandate, and to administer the tax credit that certain individuals will receive for buying health care coverage on an Exchange under Code § 36B. Information is reported to employees on Form 1095-C then transmitted to the IRS on Form 1094-C. The due date is the same as for Form W-2, and employee statements can be provided with the W-2 form. E-filing is mandatory for employers who are required to file 250 or more tax returns; the due date is March 31 for e-filing, but non-e-filed reports to the IRS are due February 28. The due date for information statements sent to employees is January 31, 2016. Notice to employees can be given electronically if the employees agree.

There are two ways that employers can satisfy their obligations under § 6056: either they can certify with respect to a particular full-time employee that the employee was offered affordable coverage, and minimum essential coverage was offered to the employee's spouse and dependents, or the employer certifies that affordable health coverage satisfying the minimum value requirements was offered to at least 98% of its full-time employees. There is a special transition rule for 2015 only for employers that made a qualifying offer of coverage to at least 95% of its full-time workforce.

Employers that offer a self-funded plan are required by § 6055 to make information reports to the IRS and employees when they provide minimum essential coverage. The reports are used to determine if the individual had the coverage required by the individual mandate. Employers that sponsor self-funded plans can use Form 1094-C to combine reporting for §§ 6055 and 6056.

Failure to satisfy these reporting requirements can be penalized under § 6721 (failure to file required information returns) and § 6722 (failure to provide payees with reports). However, if there is reasonable cause, § 6724 may offer relief by waiving penalties. There is a special transition rule for returns and statements filed in 2016 dealing with 2015 coverage: penalties will not be imposed for incorrect or incomplete information, but relief will not be granted if employers fail to make required reports, or if they do not attempt in good faith to comply. [79 Fed. Reg. 13220 (Mar. 10, 2014). Lois Mathis-Gleason, *Retirees Receiving Health Coverage: Must We Report Them?*, IFEBP.org (Aug. 18, 2015) (benefitslink.com); Healthcare-Attorneys.com, *Reporting Deadline for Form 1094-C and Form 1095-C Extended* (undated, last accessed Aug. 17, 2016) (benefitslink.com)]

Penalties for PPACA reporting violations were increased significantly by a 2015 statute, the Trade Preferences Extension Act. The penalties for information returns, including forms W-2, 1094-B and -C, and 1095-B and -C, are now $250 per return. The penalty is doubled if both a payee statement and an IRS information form are not properly submitted. The penalty is $500 per return if failure was caused by intentional disregard of the law, and the cap does not apply. [Trade Preferences Extension Act, Pub. L. No. 114-27]

In late July 2017, the IRS released draft forms for PPACA reporting, but warned not to use the drafts for filing purposes; taxpayers should only use finalized official IRS forms. [See, e.g., <https://www.irs.gov/pub/irs-dft/f1094b – dft-.pdf> (July 28, 2017)]

§ 24.02 OSHA RECORDS

[A] Injury and Illness Recordkeeping

Complying with the Occupational Safety and Health Act (OSHA) [see Chapter 31] keeping track of employees' injuries and occupational illnesses, and may require reporting to OSHA.

OSHA Forms 300 (Injury and Illness Log), 300A (Summary of Work-Related Injuries and Illnesses), and 301 (Incident Report) are used to report work-related injuries and illnesses. These forms are available at <https://www.osha.gov/recordkeeping/RKforms.html> (last accessed Mar. 29, 2016). Small employers (up to 10 employees) and low-risk "partially exempt industries" do not have to file these forms. Non-exempt employers must display Form 300A in the workplace each year, during the period between February 1 and April 30. Employees, ex-employees, and their representatives are entitled to view the injury and illness records, and on request, the employer must provide a copy of the relevant records by the end of the next business day. [OSHA, *OSHA'S Recordkeeping Page,* <https://www.osha.gov/recordkeeping/index.html> (last accessed Feb. 28, 2017)]

OSHA issued a final rule in September 2014, requiring reporting of all fatalities within eight hours. Lesser injuries (hospitalization, amputation, loss of an eye) must be reported within 24 hours. Small and low-risk businesses are exempt. [79 Fed. Reg. 56129 (Sept. 18, 2014). See OSHA, *Updates to OSHA's Reporting and Recordkeeping Rule: An Overview,* <https://www.osha.gov/recordkeeping2014/OSHA3744.pdf> (Sept. 2014) (last viewed Feb. 28, 2017)]

The reporting requirements took effect January 1, 2015, in states under federal OSHA jurisdiction. States that maintain their own OSHA programs get an additional year, until January 1, 2016, to implement the requirements. North Carolina, Iowa, Tennessee, and Indiana adopted and implemented the requirements with effective dates in 2015; Arizona, Minnesota, New Mexico, Oregon, Virginia, and Washington started the process of adopting implementing regulations. [Tressi L. Cordaro, *State Plans Slowly Adopt New Federal OSHA Reporting Requirements*, Jackson Lewis PC (Mar. 4, 2015), available at Lexology.com]

The reporting form became available online at the end of 2015. There are two reporting options. The employer can either make an online report, or telephone the local OSHA office or the agency's 24-hour central hotline, (800) 321-6742. The employer must give the business name, the names of the employees who were hurt, the location and time of the incident, including the cause if known, a brief description, the number of injuries and/or fatalities; if there were fatalities, hospitalizations, amputations, or loss of eyes; and the name and telephone number of the designated contact person. [<https://www.osha.gov/pls/ser/serform.html> (expiration date Jan. 31, 2018) (last accessed Feb. 28, 2017) ; see Valerie Butera, *OSHA Unveils Long Awaited Online Form for Reporting Work-Related Fatalities and Severe Injuries*, Epstein Becker Green (Jan. 8, 2016), available at Lexology.com]

OSHA published regulations in May 2016, under which employers with 250 or more employees must submit the Form 300 (log), Form 300A (summary of reports), and Form 301 (incident report) to OSHA each year, in electronic form, starting July 1, 2017 for Form 300A and July 1, 2018 for Forms 300A, 300, and 301. Employers in high-risk industries with between 20 and 249 employers must also e-file Form 300A each year. On May 17, 2017, OSHA announced that it would not accept electronic submissions of the 2016 injury and illness data. On

June 28, 2017, OSHA proposed a rule delaying the initial deadline for online post-ing of this information until December 1, 2017 as part of OSHA's reconsideration of whether to maintain, modify, or terminate the rule. [82 Fed. Reg. 29261 (June 28, 2017); see Michael C. Griffaton and Benjamin A. Shepler, *Labor and Employ-ment Alert: OSHA Delays Electronic Reporting Rule*, Vorys Sater Seymour and Pease LLP (May 18, 2017), available at Lexology.com; Elise C. Scott and John Fehrenbach, *OSHA Announces Electronic Recordkeeping App*, Winston & Strawn LLP (July 19, 2017), available at Lexology.com] The regulations say that some of the data (but with employee personal information redacted) will be posted to OSHA.gov. OSHA requires employers to establish and disseminate a reasonable reporting procedure that gives employees and their representatives (e.g., union officials) access to complete injury and illness records. The regulations also include provisions forbidding employers to retaliate against employees who report an injury or illness. [81 Fed. Reg. 29624 (May 12, 2016); 81 Fed. Reg. 31854 (May 20, 2016); see Bryan E. Keyt, Mitchell S. Allen and Erin L. Brooks, *What Employers Need to Know About OSHA's New Reporting and Anti-Retaliation Regulations*, Bryan Cave LLP (July 6, 2016), available at Lexology.com]

The regulations also include provisions forbidding employers to retaliate against employees who report an injury or illness. The effective date of the anti-retaliation provision was supposed to be May 11, 2016, but, after the regulation was challenged in a suit by the National Association of Manufacturers and seven other employer groups, OSHA announced that enforcement of the anti-retaliation provi-sion would be delayed until November 1, 2016. [*TEXO ABC/AGC, et. al. v. Thomas*, No. 3:16-cv-1998 (N.D. Tex., filed July 8, 2016); see Katherine Fechte, *Imple-mentation of OSHA Anti-Retaliation Rule Delayed Until November*, Greenfelder Hemker & Gale PC (Aug. 10, 2016), available at Lexology.com; Mark A. Lies, II, *OSHA Again Delays Enforcement Date for New Workplace Injury and Illness Reporting Rule*, Seyfarth Shaw LLP (Oct. 19, 2016), available at Lexology.com]

On November 28, 2016, the district court denied a temporary injunction to prevent the recordkeeping standard from taking effect, holding that the plaintiffs did not show irreparable harm. Consequently, the rule took effect on December 1, 2016. [See Edwin G. Foulke Jr., *Judge Rules That OSHA Can, FOR NOW, Start Enforcing Limits on Incentives and Drug Testing*, Fisher Phillips (Nov. 29, 2016), available at Lexology.com]

The Occupational Safety and Health Review Commission (OSHRC) heard oral arguments in November 2010 (the first oral arguments allowed in four years) on the issue of when a company can be cited for reporting violations. OSHA said the DOL has six months from the time it discovered or should have discovered the facts needed to issue a citation, whereas DOL argued that an inaccurate log entry is a violation until it has been corrected or the five-year record retention period has expired. OSHRC fined the company $13,300 for recordkeeping vio-lations, accepting the argument that failure to keep proper records is a continuing violation. [*Secretary of Labor v. AKM LLC dba Volks Constructors*, OSHRC No. 06-1990, 2011 WL 896347 (OSHRC Mar. 11, 2011)]

Then, however, the D.C. Circuit reversed OSHRC, and ruled that the statute of limitations for recordkeeping violations is only six months, not five years, because each violation charged was a separate event. [*Sec'y of Labor v. AKM LLC dba Volks Constructors*, 675 F.3d 752 (D.C. Cir. 2012)] In mid-2015, OSHA proposed a rule as a work-around to avoid this result for recordkeeping violations that are more than six months old. The proposal amends the recordkeeping regulations to make the duty to make and maintain injury and illness records an ongoing obligation that lasts five years after the time the record should have been made. As a result, employers can be cited for recordkeeping violations for up to six months after the end of the five-year record retention period. [80 Fed. Reg. 45116 (July 29, 2015)]

At the end of 2016, OSHA issued a final rule, effective January 18, 2017, amending the 29 C.F.R. Part 1904 record-keeping regulations. OSHA described the rule as a mere continuation of a 40-year-old policy. The 2016 final rule defines a continuing obligation to make and keep records of each recordable injury and illness; a citation for failure to record injuries properly can result in a citation for the entire five-year record retention period. [Michael T. Taylor and Darren A. Crook, *OSHA Announces Rule Clarifying Workplace Injury Reporting That Imposes "Continuing Obligation" on Employers to Maintain Injury Records for Five Years*, Baker & Hostetler LLP (Dec. 20, 2016), available at Lexology.com; George M. Macchia, *OSHA Amends Its Rule Requiring Employers to Keep and Maintain Records of Recordable Injuries and Illnesses for Five Years*, Epstein Becker Green (Jan. 11, 2017), available at Lexology.com]

However, the proper procedure would have been for OSHA to continue litigating the *Volks* case instead of adopting a new regulation. The Congressional Review Act, which allows Congress to overturn certain recent administrative regulations, was applied to invalidate OSHA's treatment of recordkeeping omissions as ongoing violations. The House of Representatives passed a resolution of disapproval, H.J. Res. 83, on March 1, 2017; the Senate passed it on March 22, 2017. [Arthur G. Sapper, *Quashing Lawlessness: Congress Votes on OSHA's Attempt to Avoid the Volks Decision*, Ogletree Deakins (Mar. 7, 2017), available at Lexology.com; Tressi L. Cordaro, *OSHA's Volks Rule Overturned by Congressional Review Act*, Jackson Lewis PC (Mar. 22, 2017), available at Lexology .com] President Trump signed the joint resolution into law on April 3, 2017. [Huu Nguyen and Sarah K. Rathke, *OSHA Rule Repealed by Trump Administration*, Squire Patton Boggs (Apr. 30, 2017), available at Lexology.com]

[B] Asbestos, Lead, and Noise Monitoring Records

If the workplace noise level is high, the employer not only must monitor exposure, but must maintain records for two years. Records of employees' hearing tests must be retained at least as long as they work for the employer. Exposure monitoring records and asbestos and lead medical surveillance records should be retained for at least 30 years after termination of employment of the individual monitored.

Asbestos monitoring records should indicate:

- Each monitored employee's name, Social Security number, extent of exposure;
- If a respirator was worn; if so, what kind;
- Date the asbestos level was monitored;
- The workplace operation or process that was monitored;
- How the samples were taken and evaluated;
- Evidence supporting the scientific validity of the sampling methodology;
- How long the sampling process lasted; number of samples taken; sampling results.

For each employee subject to medical surveillance, the record should give his or her name and Social Security number, the employee reports of asbestos-related medical conditions; and a written report from the doctor who performs the surveillance, indicating whether the employee actually is suffering effects of asbestos exposure.

For testing of lead rather than asbestos, the employer must maintain written records of tests determining whether the ambient lead level exceeds the Permissible Exposure Limit (PEL). The test record should indicate:

- Name and Social Security number of each monitored employee;
- Date of the test;
- Area that was monitored;
- Previous airborne lead readings taken at the same place;
- Employee complaints that might be related to lead exposure;
- Any other evidence suggestive of lead exposure.

[C] OSHA Postings

Employers must post a notice of OSHA rights, as mandated by 29 C.F.R. § 1903.2(a). Failure to post is subject to civil penalties. An employer who receives an OSHA citation must post a copy of the citation near each place where a violation occurred. The copy must be left in place for three working days or until the violation is corrected—whichever comes first. Posting is also required if the employer contests a citation or files a petition for modification of abatement. For violations occurring after November 1, 2015, and cited after August 1, 2016, the penalty for violations of the posting requirement can be as high as $12,471 per violation; they can reach $12,675 for violations occurring after January 13, 2017. [Practical Law, *DOL Increases Civil Money Penalties, Effective August 1* (July 5, 2016) (benefitslink.com); OSHA.gov, *Penalties,* available at <https://www .osha.gov/penalties/> (undated; last accessed Feb. 28, 2017)]

§ 24.03 TITLE VII RECORDKEEPING AND NOTICE REQUIREMENTS

The Equal Employment Opportunity Commission (EEOC) requires companies with 100 or more employees to file an annual report. The Employer Information Report (EEO-1) is a simple two-page form that tracks the composition of the workforce. The due date is September 30 of each year. A copy of the most recent report must be kept on file at every company required to file (either at the "reporting unit" or the company's or division's headquarters). The EEOC also has the right to require other reports about employment practices if the agency thinks additional reports are necessary to carry out Title VII or the Americans With Disabilities Act.

The federal Website GovDocs has been updated to incorporate the Genetic Information Nondiscrimination Act (GINA; see § 34.01[B]), and the EEOC released its GINA-compliant poster; see <http://www.eeoc.gov/employers/ upload/eeoc_self_print_poster.pdf> (last accessed Feb. 28, 2017).

The EEOC published a final rule on February 3, 2012 extending the Title VII and ADA recordkeeping requirements to entities covered by GINA. As of April 3, 2012, employers with 15 or more employees must retain all personnel and employment records for at least one year, and retain documents about any GINA charges until those charges have been disposed of. Documents include requests for accommodation, application forms, hiring, promotion, demotion, transfer, layoff, and termination data and records of pay, tenure, training, and apprenticeship. Records must be retained for at least a year after any employee's involuntary termination. [77 Fed. Reg. 5396 (Feb. 3, 2012)]

The Vietnam Era Veterans' Readjustment Assistance Act (VEVRAA) and Rehab Act § 503 require federal contractors to collect data and report on their success in recruiting and hiring veterans and persons with disabilities (PWDs). Federal contractors must ask job applicants to self-identify if they have a disability or are veterans. Hiring and recruiting data must be retained for three years, and federal contractors must review their success in recruiting veterans and PWDs each year. On January 31, 2017, the OMB renewed the disability self-identification form until January 31, 2020. The form explains why the request is made; how the information will be used; that it is unlawful to retaliate against people who self-identify, and that they may be entitled to reasonable accommodation. (Because this is an official OMB form, it must be used verbatim, not modified by the employer.)

As a result, federal contractors and subcontractors subject to Rehab Act § 503 (employers with 50 or more employees working on federal contracts over

$50,000) are required to ask applicants (before or after a job offer) to self-identify. Federal contractors with 100 or more employees must summarize employee responses in each of the job groups in the contractor's affirmative action plan. [<https://www.dol.gov/ofccp/regs/compliance/sec503/Self_ID_Forms/SelfIDForms.htm >; see Annette Tyman and Michael L. Childers, *OMB Renews Disability Self-ID Form Required for Federal Contractors and Subcontractors*, Seyfarth Shaw LLP (Feb. 1, 2017), available at Lexology.com; Kelly Jennings Yeoman & Michael C. Griffaton, *Labor and Employment Alert: Federal Contractors Have an Updated Voluntary Self-Identification of Disability Form*, Vorys Sater Seymour and Pease LLP (Feb. 1, 2017), available at Lexology.com]

On January 29, 2016, the EEOC announced a proposed major revision of the EEO-1. All companies with 100 or more employees must file the EEO-1 report disclosing demographic data, plus the new report on compensation and hours worked. Federal contractors and first-tier subcontractors who have 50–99 employees must file the demographic report but not the compensation report. Large employers would have to report the W-2 earnings and hours for all employees, analyzed by race/ethnicity and gender. The EEOC requirement would apply to all large employers, not just federal contractors. [Christine Hendrickson et. al., *Breaking News: New EEOC Pay Report Proposed for Employers in 2017*, Seyfarth Shaw LLP (Jan. 29, 2016), available at Lexology.com]

The EEOC published the first forms to be used for this purpose on February 1, 2016, but the filing deadline for 2017 was postponed from September 30, 2017 to March 31, 2018 because of the need to adopt new reporting methods. Employers must report all W-2 earnings, not just base pay. [81 Fed. Reg. 45479 (July 14, 2016); see Danielle M. Berti and Michael D. McGill, *EEOC Revises Contractor Pay Reporting Rule*, Hogan Lovells (July 13, 2016), available at Lexology.com; W. Carter Younger et.al., *EEOC's Revised Annual Collection of Pay Data on EEO-1 Forms*, McGuireWoods LLP (July 15, 2016), available at Lexology.com]

The acting chair of the EEOC, Victoria Lipnic, said in February 2017 that the agency was examining whether to maintain the EEO-1 requirement; but, at press time in 2017, no definitive steps had been taken. [David J. Goldstein, *Revised EEO-1 Report—Where Does It Stand?*, Littler Mendelson (July 31, 2017), available at Lexology.com]

If a discrimination charge is made, all records relating to the employment action involved in the charge must be retained until there has been a final disposition of the charge. According to 29 C.F.R. § 1602.14, this means that either the case is over, or the employee's time to sue has elapsed.

Users of pre-employment tests must maintain records about the validation of the test, including statistical studies to determine if the test has adverse impact on protected classes of applicants and employees.

Employers also have to make records that are relevant to charges of unlawful employment practices and maintain those records. [See 42 U.S.C. § 2000e-8(c)]

Employers are required to educate employees about their legal rights by displaying a number of posters issued by federal agencies. A general overview on posting requirements appears in the DOL's "eLaws Power Advisor," <http://www.dol.gov/compliance/topics/posters.htm> (last accessed Mar. 25, 2015). The posting requirements can be found at DOL's *Poster Page*, <http://www.dol.gov/oasam/boc/osdbu/sbrefa/poster/matrix.htm> (last accessed Mar. 29, 2016).

Other mandatory posters include:

- Employee Rights Under the Fair Labor Standards Act
- Job Safety and Health: It's the Law
- Employee Rights and Responsibilities under the Family and Medical Leave Act
- Equal Employment Opportunity Is the Law
- Migrant and Seasonal Agricultural Worker Protection Act Notice
- Employee Rights for Workers with Disabilities Paid at Special Minimum Wages
- Employee Polygraph Protection Act Notice
- Your Rights Under USERRA
- Genetic Information Nondiscrimination Act information

Posting is also required of minimum wage information. The DOL updated the 2017 minimum wage poster to include the Executive Order 13658 requirement that federal contractors pay a minimum wage of $10.20 per hour. [Revised poster: <http://www.dol.gov/whd/flsa/eo13658/App-B.pdf> (last accessed Feb. 28, 2017)]

In lieu of posting separate documents for each statute, employers can use the "Federal 6-in-1" poster, which has been revised in 2016 to reflect changes in the FLSA, FMLA, and Employee Polygraph Protection Act. [<https://www.dol.gov/whd/regs/compliance/posters/flsa.htm,https://www.dol.gov/whd/regs/compliance/posters/eppa.htm>, <https://www.dol.gov/whd/regs/compliance/posters/fmla.htm>; see Kenneth W. Gage, Jon A. Geier and Tammy R. Daub, *Federal 6-in-1 Poster Update,* Paul Hastings LLP (Sept. 22, 2016), available at Lexology.com]

In late 2010, the National Labor Relations Board (NLRB) announced that companies would be required to post notices on its bulletin boards to inform employees of their rights to unionize. [Notice of Proposed Rulemaking, 75 Fed. Reg. 80410 (Feb. 22, 2010)]

The posting requirement was supposed to take effect November 14, 2011, but it was delayed, first until January 31, 2012, then until April 30, 2012, in response to business criticisms. [Tara Cantore, *NLRB Postpones Required Date to*

Post Employee Rights, plansponsor.com (Dec. 27, 2011) and *NLRB Postpones Implementation Date for Notice Posting Rule*, plansponsor.com (Oct. 5, 2011)]

Two circuit courts (the Fourth and the D.C. Circuits) found the posting requirement inappropriate and unenforceable. The Fourth Circuit said that Congress intended the NLRB's powers to be limited, dealing only with Unfair Labor Practices and representation elections—and that the NLRB's powers are triggered only by a complaint or an election petition. In this analysis, posting requirements imposed by other agencies such as OSHA and the EEOC are based on statutory authorization from Congress, whereas the NLRB has not been given this power. Rather than uphold part of the posting requirement but remove the NLRB's power to treat failure to post as an Unfair Labor Practice, the Fourth Circuit struck down the entire regulation, concluding that the NLRB would not want to have a purely advisory rule that it was unable to enforce. [*Chamber of Commerce v. NLRB*, 721 F.3d 152 (4th Cir. 2013), *Nat'l Ass'n of Mfrs. v. NLRB*, 717 F.3d 947 (D.C. Cir. 2013)] Both the D.C. and Fourth Circuits denied rehearing, and the NLRB allowed the deadline for seeking certiorari to pass without seeking review. [Benjamin P. Glass, *NLRB Throws in the Towel on Notice Posting Rule*, Ogletree Deakins (Jan. 3, 2014), available at Lexology.com]

§ 24.04 FMLA RECORDS

Federal law does not impose any specific form for keeping the Family and Medical Leave Act (FMLA) records, so any paper or electronic method can be used to record the necessary information:

- Basic payroll data for each employee, such as hours worked; pay rate; supplemental wages or wage deductions; total compensation paid;

- Dates on which FMLA leave was taken;

- Hours of leave (if less than a day was taken);

- Copies of the employee's notice to the employer of impending leave;

- Copies of the employer's disclosure materials about FMLA rights;

- Documentation of the employer's leave policy;

- Records of payment of premiums for employee benefit plans;

- Records of any dispute about when employees are entitled to leave or reinstatement after a leave.

■ **TIP:** Because employee medical records, including certification of serious medical condition and fitness to return to work, are confidential, they should be kept physically separate from the employee's other records, to prevent unauthorized access to the data. [See § 26.07 about privacy requirements]

The required FMLA poster must be displayed in all business locations (or the information provided electronically) even if there are no FMLA-eligible employees at that location. The DOL stopped publishing the model forms as appendices to the FMLA regulations. Instead, they appear on the DOL site, making it possible for the agency to amend the forms without going through the Office of Management and Budget. The new regulations instruct employers about their GINA confidentiality obligations: it is permissible to disclose genetic information or family history that is consistent with the FMLA.

Employers are permitted to adapt the forms rather than using them unaltered, provided that the employer's version does not call for disclosure of more information by the employee or health care provider than the FMLA regulations permit.

The new forms added in 2013 are:

- WH-380-E certification of health care provider of serious health condition (employee);

- WH-380-F health care provider certification for family member's serious health condition;

- WH-381 notice of eligibility, rights, and responsibilities;

- WH-382 designation notice;

- WH-383 reserved;

- WH-384 certification of exigency of military family leave;

- WH-385 certification of serious injury or illness of a servicemember for military family leave;

- WH-385-V certification of serious injury or illness of a veteran for military caregiver leave.

[Airline Flight Crew Technical Corrections Act, Pub. L. No. 111-119]

Employers subject to the FMLA must post (on paper or electronically) a copy of the FMLA general notice in each location where the employer has an employees, regardless of whether anyone working at that location is FMLA-eligible, in a place visible to all employees and job applicants. If there are any eligible employees at the location, the general notice must be included in employee handbooks or other written information about benefits and leave. The mid-2016 edition of the poster is designed to be more user-friendly than the previous versions, but it does not make significant changes from the 2013 version. Employers are permitted to continue using the 2013 version, but it is no longer available on the DOL Website. [Burton D. Garland, Jr. *Attention—The DOL Has Made Its FMLA Poster More "Reader Friendly"!*, Ogletree Deakins (Aug. 25, 2016) (benefitslink.com)]

§ 24.05 IMMIGRATION RECORDS

The information collected to verify identity and eligibility to work in the United States [see § 23.11[D]] must be retained for three years after the date of hiring. Records should be retained for three years from the date of recruiting or referral with respect to applicants who were not hired or who did not accept a job offer. Certifications of employment eligibility furnished by state employment services must also be retained for three years. For former employees, the record-retention period is the later of three years after hiring, or one year after termination.

Under the National Archives and Records Administration's schedule for purging records, as of January 1, 2016, E-Verify transaction records more than 10 years old are automatically deleted from the E-Verify system. Therefore, employers will no longer have access to this information from this source. Employers can obtain some records of older cases from the Historic Records Report system, but the report is not available after December 31, 2015. [Amy L. Peck, *Government to Delete E-Verify Records After 10 Years*, Jackson Lewis PC (Nov. 18, 2015), available at Lexology.com]

Because illegal immigration is a very high enforcement priority for the Trump administration, employers should be especially careful to obtain proper documentation of employees' authorization to work in the United States, and should keep the records ready for inspection. There may be major changes in the H-1B program, which could affect hiring and retention of both employees and information.

§ 24.06 EMPLOYMENT TAX RECORDS

Newly hired employees should be asked to provide a W-4 (withholding exemptions) form, so the appropriate number of exemptions can be used to withhold income taxes. An employee about to retire should be asked for Form W-4P to determine whether pension withholding should be done, and if so, in what amount. Note that, in recent years, the FICA and FUTA payroll taxes have been adjusted several times, so it is essential to use the appropriate withholding tables for the pay period. IRS Publication 15, Employer's Tax Guide, requires at least the following information to be collected by the employer and made available for IRS review on request:

- Dates and amounts of all payments of wages and pensions;
- Fair market value of any wages paid other than in cash (e.g., in merchandise or services);
- Each employee's name, address, Social Security number, and job title;
- Dates each employee started and terminated employment;

- Dates and amounts of any payments made by the employer, or by an insurer or other third party, to employees who were out sick or injured;

- Copies of W-4 and W-4P forms;

- W-2 forms sent to employees but returned as undeliverable;

- Copies of all tax returns;

- Records of dates and amounts of tax deposits.

The Pension Protection Act of 2006, Pub. L. No. 109-280, adds a new section to the Internal Revenue Code, § 6039I, requiring the owners of employer-owned life insurance contracts issued after the PPA took effect to report to the IRS each year on the number of employees the company has, how many of them are covered by company-owned life insurance, the amount of insurance in force under those insurance policies, the nature of the company's business, and that all employees covered under the COLI program have consented to being covered (or the number of employees who are covered but did not provide a written consent form). Businesses with COLI programs are required to keep any records necessary for determining if the PPA COLI rules have been complied with.

For tax years ending on or after November 14, 2007, a policyholder owning employer-owned life insurance contracts issued after August 17, 2006 must attach Form 8925 to the income tax return. The form discloses the number of employees covered by employer-provided life insurance contracts; whether each one consented in writing, in advance, to be insured and for coverage to continue after employment ends. [Sutherland Asbill & Brennan LLP, *Legal Alert: IRS Issues Forms to Report Employer-Owned Life Insurance* (Feb. 7, 2008)]

In early 2017, the IRS updated its guide to reporting and disclosure. The new guide covers topics such as Form 5500, forms for documenting distributions from the plan; Form 5330, and safe harbor notices. This guide should be used in conjunction with DOL's Retirement Plan Reporting and Disclosure Guide and trouble-shooting documents. [<https://www.irs.gov/pub/irs-tege/irs_reporting_disclosure_guide.pdf>; the DOL documents are <http://www.dol.gov/ebsa/pdf/rdguide.pdf> and <http://www.dol.gov/ebsa/pdf/troubleshootersguide.pdf>. See John Manganaro, *IRS Updates Reporting Disclosure Guide*, plansponsor.com (Mar. 3, 2017)]

§ 24.07 UNEMPLOYMENT INSURANCE RECORDS

FUTA records must show the total amount of remuneration to employees in the calendar year, the amount of wages subject to tax, and the contributions made to the state unemployment insurance funds of each state in which the company does business. The records must be kept open to inspection by the IRS and state unemployment tax officials.

Records must be organized by pay period (dates the period starts and ends; total remuneration including commissions paid in the period) and by employee. The records to be kept for each worker include:

- Name;

- Social Security number;

- Date of hiring (or rehiring) and termination;

- Place of work;

- Wages for each payroll period;

- Wage rate;

- Date wages were paid;

- Amount of expense reimbursement granted;

- Time lost when worker was unavailable for work.

Although unemployment insurance information can be released to government agencies other than the employment security agency (e.g., child support enforcement agencies), in general the information is confidential and should not be disclosed to unauthorized parties.

§ 24.08 RECORD-RETENTION REQUIREMENTS

Various state and federal laws require retention of records (about individual employees and summaries reflecting the entire corporate experience). The enterprise should draft its record-retention policies to comply with statutory requirements:

- Title VII: Personnel and employment records as well as EEO-1 reports must be kept for six months. Records relating to a discrimination charge must be retained until the charge is disposed of;

- Equal Pay Act: Records of a pay differential imposed on the basis of sex must be kept for two years;

- FMLA: Records must be retained for three years;

- FICA/FUTA: Records of withholding and paying these taxes must be retained for four years;

- ERISA: There are two record retention provisions. Section 107 requires the filer or certifier of certain information (e.g., Form 5500) to maintain sufficient records to explain, corroborate, substantiate, or clarify the filing or certification. Relevant records might include plan documents, e-mails, work records, or spreadsheets. Such records must be maintained for six years after the date they were filed (including any amendments). But ERISA § 209 requires all such information to be retained for as long as it might be relevant to determining benefit entitlement—which is tantamount to requiring them to be retained indefinitely. Retention is the responsibility of the employer, not its TPA. Section 107 does not impose money penalties for violations and the § 209 civil penalty is small (as of August 1, 2016, $28 per affected employee, an amount that was not affected by the January 2017 round of increases), but failure to retain required information might be deemed a breach of fiduciary duty, or might embroil the employer in a costly suit over benefits. Failure to disclose documents requested by employees is subject to a penalty of $110 per day. [Melissa Travis, *Retention of Plan Documents: A Primer*, Pension Consultants, Inc. (Aug. 15, 2014) (benefitslink.com)] Federal contractors: Information about the employer's contractor status must be retained for three years;

- OSHA: The record-retention requirement for employee exposure to toxic substances is very long: 30 years;

- Tax records: The minimum retention period is four years.

- ADEA: 29 C.F.R. § 1627.3(b)(2) requires a benefit plan that is subject to the ADEA to be kept on file while the plan is in operation, and for at least one year after its termination.

The EEOC requires all personnel and employment records, such as job applications, promotion, demotion and layoff records, pay records, and requests for reasonable accommodation to be retained for one year from the date of the personnel action or the date the record was made (whichever is later). But if the record relates to involuntary termination of an employee, all of the employee's personnel or employment records must be maintained for a year from the date of termination. But, as noted above, all records relating to a discrimination charge must be retained until final disposition of the charge or lawsuit. If there has been a suit, final disposition means termination of the litigation; otherwise, it means the statute of limitations for filing a district court suit has run. [EEOC, *Summary of Selected Recordkeeping Obligations in 29 CFR Part 1602,* <http://www.eeoc.gov/employers/recordkeeping_obligations.cfm> (undated, last viewed Feb. 28, 2017)]

Joint guidance about background checks, published by the EEOC and FTC in March 2014, says that personnel or employment records, including job applications, must be kept for at least one year after the record was made, or the personnel action was taken (whichever is later). For federal contractors that have 150 or more employees, and federal contracts of at least $150,000, the DOL extends this retention requirement to two years. When a discrimination charge is made, employment records must be retained at least until completion of the case. The

FTC says that background reports can be discarded after record retention obligations have been satisfied—but they must be disposed of in a manner that preserves privacy (e.g., shredding or burning paper; deleting electronic files so that they cannot be retrieved). [EEOC/FTC, *Background Checks: What Employers Need to Know*, <http://www.eeoc.gov/eeoc/publications/background_checks_employers.cfm> (undated; last accessed Feb. 28, 2017)]

CHAPTER 25

CORPORATE COMMUNICATIONS

§ 25.01 INTRODUCTION

Communications within the corporation, and from the corporation to outsiders, have tremendous practical and legal consequences. To avoid trouble, everyone in a position to speak for the corporation should be aware of these potential ramifications and should be very careful about what is communicated and in what form. Corporations sometimes have obligations to disclose certain things; other things should not be said.

An emerging issue is the extent to which employers can adopt contract provisions that vary the timing rules under state law. In late 2013, the Supreme Court upheld a disability policy's contractual requirement that suits be filed within three years after proof of loss was due. In this case, the plaintiff sued within three years of the final claim denial, but more than five years after she first asserted her claim. The Supreme Court said that the contract provision was reasonable and enforceable. [*Heimeshoff v. Hartford Life & Accident Ins. Co.*, 134 S. Ct. 604 (2013)]

The district court dismissed an Fair Labor Standards Act (FLSA)/Equal Pay Act (EPA) suit against FedEx, brought by an employee who charged that she was paid less than co-workers. The claims were timely under the statutes, but the district court enforced the employment agreement, which required suits to be brought within six months. The Sixth Circuit held that reducing the statute of limitations was an unlawful waiver of the plaintiff's rights under the FLSA and, because the EPA is part of the FLSA, protection under that statute cannot be waived either. [*Boaz v. FedEx Customer Info. Servs., Inc.*, 725 F.3d 603 (6th Cir. 2013)]

The Third Circuit (joining the First and Sixth Circuits) held in mid-2015 that if a plan imposes deadlines on judicial review (in this case, one year, when the state statute of limitations for breach of contract claims was six years), the limitation must be stated in denial notices. Otherwise, the limitation will not be enforceable. [*Mirza v. Insurance Adm'r of Am., Inc.*, 800 F.3d 129 (3d Cir. 2015); see Duane Morris LLP, *Third Circuit Rules That Plan Must Give Notice of Limitations Period* (Aug. 27, 2015) (benefitslink.com)]

Forum selection and choice of law clauses in employment and noncompete agreements are also significant. The recent Supreme Court *Atlantic Marine* decision holds that contractual forum selection clauses will be enforced except in the more egregious cases. This is beneficial to employers that want to avoid involvement of states like California that disfavor noncompete agreements. [*Atlantic Marine Constr. Co., Inc. v. U.S. Dist. Ct. for the W. Dist. of Tex.*, 134 S. Ct. 568 (2013)]

The Defend Trade Secrets Act (DTSA; Pub. L. No. 114-153), gives employers a federal cause of action against employees who misappropriate trade secrets. But employers can only seek punitive damages and attorneys' fees under this statute if employees were notified, in a nondisclosure or noncompete agreement, that the DTSA allows disclosures by whistleblowers to government agencies or in sealed court papers. [Heather M. Muzumdar, Deborah S. Brenneman and Candice

S. Thomas, *It's Time to Update Noncompete Agreements & Confidentiality Policies*, Thompson Hine LLP (June 10, 2016), available at Lexology.com]

§ 25.02 EMPLOYMENT CONTRACTS

[A] Basic Considerations

Labor law aspects of Collective Bargaining Agreements (CBA) between an employer and a union are discussed in Chapter 30. For employees who are not union members, there are both advantages and disadvantages to entering into a written employment contract. The written contract reduces uncertainty, and that is good—but it also limits flexibility, and that can create problems. An individual written employment contract should cover issues such as:

- Duration of employment;

- Renewal provisions (including the amount of notice to be given);

- The duties the employee will perform;

- Promotion possibilities;

- Compensation and benefits, including contingent compensation— contingent on results and/or bonuses and stock options;

- Rights in inventions and other intellectual property developed by the employee during the contract term; treatment of intellectual property developed while the contract is in force but not during working hours, or not of the type the employee was hired to produce;

- Covenant not to compete with the employer, and agreement not to solicit its employees and customers, even after termination of employment. Even in a jurisdiction that is not opposed to these provisions (see § 25.02[C] below), to be enforceable, these agreements must be reasonable in both duration and geographic scope, and must not be so severe that they prevent the individual from earning a living;

- Severability: If any contract provision is invalid, that provision will be removed from the contract, and the rest of the contract will remain valid and enforceable;

- Alternative Dispute Resolution: Whether disputes about the contract will be resolved by an arbitrator, mediator, or other decision maker other than a court. If so, whether class arbitration will be permitted.

[B]   Employment Contract Case Law

Individual employment contracts are usually analyzed under the same rules as ordinary commercial contracts, so it is relevant whether there was a meeting of the minds; each side obtained consideration; and there was no mistake about the terms. (Relief for one or both parties may be available if there was a mistake, especially mutual mistake.) The Statute of Frauds is another fundamental contract rule, one that says that a contract that lasts a year or more can only be enforced if it is in writing.

The Fifth Circuit upheld the dismissal of state-law claims relating to William Sullivan's hiring as CEO of Leor Energy. An employment contract was drafted and never signed. Sullivan was fired after a brief time at Leor. The unsigned contract was not enforceable because of the Statute of Frauds. Texas law says that just because it is possible that a contract could be terminated within a year (Sullivan's contract allowed either side to terminate the agreement) does not mean it is not for a fixed term of over one year. Sullivan also asserted that the Statute of Frauds did not apply because he had partially performed the agreement, but the Fifth Circuit held that the "partial performance" exception only applies when not applying it would mean that fraud was tolerated. In this case, Sullivan was paid a salary for his work, so he was not defrauded. [*Sullivan v. Leor Energy LLC*, 600 F.3d 542 (5th Cir. 2010)]

Under New York common law, at-will employees cannot sue for wrongful discharge. In 2012, the New York Court of Appeals refused to make an exception for hedge fund compliance officers. The plaintiff said that he was fired for objecting to improper trading. The Court of Appeals ruled that state common law is not required to take a more active role merely because there are federal law compliance requirements. The plaintiff could not make use of federal whistleblower protection because there was no evidence that he told anyone outside the firm about the alleged misconduct. [*Sullivan v. Harnisch*, 19 N.Y.3d 259, 969 N.E.2d 758, 946 N.Y.S.2d 540 (2012)]

[C]   Noncompete Case Law

At one time, only major executives or employees with highly skilled knowledge jobs were required to sign noncompete agreements (aka covenants not to compete). However, Professor Orly Lobel of the University of San Diego School of Law noted that noncompete agreements are expanding beyond their conventional usage in high-skilled knowledge jobs and are now standard in many service jobs. [Steven Greenhouse, *Noncompete Clauses Increasingly Pop Up in Array of Jobs*, NYTimes.com (June 8, 2014)] Evan Starr, of the University of Maryland, found that in 2014, about 20% of employees at all levels were subject to noncompetes—a figure that had tripled since 2000. According to the Department of the Treasury, one-sixth of workers who do not have a college degree are covered by noncompete agreements; a total of 30 million employees of all kinds are covered. Research shows that salaries, especially tech-industry salaries, are significantly lower in states where noncompete agreements are strictly enforced. [Orly Lobel, *Companies Compete but Won't Let Their Workers Do the Same,* NYTimes.com (May 4, 2017); Conor Dougherty, *Signing Away the Right to Get a New Job,* NYTimes.com (May 13, 2017)]

A restrictive covenant is an employment contract provision imposing a limitation (such as time, scope, and/or geographic area) on the employee's ability to work in that occupation or profession when employment ends. A restraint is reasonable if it is reasonably limited in time and scope, is no greater than needed to protect the employer's legitimate interests, does not impose undue hardship on the employee, and is not harmful to the public.

Nearly all of the states (47) allow noncompete agreements under some circumstances. However, there are many state statutes forbidding or restricting noncompetes that apply only to certain categories of employees (e.g., lawyers and health care workers), reflecting public policies about access to services and free flow of information. Some states have quite idiosyncratic statutes. Bans are imposed for car salespersons (Louisiana), secretaries and clerical workers (Missouri), real estate brokers and barber and cosmetology students in Vermont. [Kathryn K. Conde, *Protected Occupations: Statutory Exemptions from Non-Competes for Employee Classes*, Nutter McClennen & Fish LLP (Jan. 14, 2016), available at Lexology.com; Mark Muro, *Why States Should Stop the Spread of Noncompete Pacts*, WSJ.com (May 23, 2016)]

Hawaii Act 158, effective July 1, 2015, forbids high-tech companies (those that derive a majority of their gross sales from software and/or information technology) to require their employees to sign noncompete and non-solicitation agreements as a condition of employment. In this context, non-solicitation means only solicitation of former co-workers; provisions against soliciting clients are acceptable. [Jackson Lewis PC, *Hawaii Bans Non-Compete and Non-Solicit Clauses in High-Tech Employment* (July 10, 2015), available at Lexology.com]

An Illinois statute, the Freedom to Work Act, prohibits employers from requiring low-wage workers (those earning less than $13 an hour) to sign noncompete agreements. Such agreements are deemed unreasonable and courts are not permitted to interpret them. The statute took effect January 1, 2017. Massachusetts considered, but did not adopt, a similar statute. [Robert W. Horton, *Non-Competition Agreements Under Fire: Who Should be Required to Sign?*, Bass, Berry & Sims PLC (Aug. 30, 2016), available at Lexology.com; Clifford R. Atlas, *Illinois Statute Bars Non-Competes for Low-Wage Workers*, Jackson Lewis PC (Aug. 25, 2016), available at Lexology.com; Peter A. Steinmeyer and Matthew Savage Aibel, *Illinois Passes Law Banning Noncompete Agreements for Low Wage Workers*, Epstein Becker Green (Sept. 1, 2016), available at Lexology.com; William A. Nolan, *Does New Illinois Law Signify a Third Frontier of Noncompete State-by-State Variations?*, Barnes & Thornburg LLP (Sept. 19, 2016), available at Lexology.com]

Laws limiting noncompete agreements were enacted in Utah, Connecticut, and Rhode Island in 2016, and bills have been introduced in Idaho, Maryland, Massachusetts, Nevada, and Washington either forbidding noncompete agreements for low-paid employees or restricting the permissible scope of agreements. [Jonathan L. Shapiro, *Which States Are Likely to Enact Laws Restricting Non-Compete Agreements in 2017?*, Epstein Becker Green (Mar. 23, 2017), available at Lexology.com]

Multi-state employers must consider the enforceability of noncompete agreements in different states. For example, North Dakota, by statute, forbids enforcement of noncompetes. The California Business and Professional Code makes most noncompetes unenforceable. In contrast, Oklahoma might enforce such provisions but on very restrictive conditions. A "red pencil" state may find the entire agreement unenforceable if there is one overbroad provision, whereas a "blue pencil" state would strike out the offending provisions but enforce the rest. (Provisions will only be removed, not added.) Most states are "purple pencil" states that might redraft provisions to render the agreement enforceable.

The Seventh Circuit, relying on the power to blue-pencil excessively broad agreements, affirmed a preliminary injunction enforcing a covenant not to compete. The Seventh Circuit found a two-year noncompete clause enforceable with respect to commercial roofing products; the court essentially added a geographic restriction to the agreement, enforcing non-solicitation as to the former employer's actual customers but not prospective customers. [*Turnell v. CentiMark Corp.*, 796 F.3d 656 (7th Cir. 2015)]

The Eighth Circuit held that an independent contractor salesman's noncompete agreement was unenforceable. The court found that, based on his relationship to customers, limited knowledge that could be used to pirate customers, and limited training offered by the company, it would be unfair to enforce a three-year noncompete. The Eighth Circuit held that the agreement was not reasonably necessary to protect the company's business. The salesman did not receive any special training or support, and it would be unreasonable to require him to give up the customer base that he developed himself. [*Ag Spectrum Co. v. Elder*, No. 16-3113, 2017 U.S. App. LEXIS 14128 (8th Cir. Aug. 2, 2017); see Jonathan L. Shapiro, *Eighth Circuit Finds Independent Contractor's Noncompete Unreasonable*, Epstein Becker Green (Aug. 7, 2017), available at Lexology.com]

The North Carolina Supreme Court ruled in 2016 that an unreasonable territorial restriction in a noncompete adopted in connection with an asset sale was unenforceable; the state supreme court said that the provision had to be stricken from the contract; the state courts do not have the power to blue-pencil the inappropriate provision. [*Beverage Sys. of the Carolinas, LLC v. Associated Beverage Repair, LLC*, No. 316A14 (N.C. Mar. 18, 2016); see Paul E. Freehling, *North Carolina Courts Are Forbidden to "Blue Pencil" an Unenforceable Non-Compete*, Seyfarth Shaw LLP (Apr. 4, 2016), available at Lexology.com]

The Nevada Supreme Court rejected the blue-pencil doctrine and held a casino's noncompete was unreasonable and therefore unenforceable. The non-compete forbade employees to work for any other gaming establishment within 150 miles for one year. The court said that this unfairly restricted employees' ability to work, and exceeded the scope of what was necessary to protect the employer's interests. On the grounds that courts cannot make private agreements, the court refused to rewrite the contract. [*Golden Road Motor Inn, Inc. v. Islam,* 376 P.3d 151 (Nev. 2016); see Salomon Laguerre, *All or Nothing: Nevada Supreme Court Refuses to Adopt "Blue Pencil" Doctrine for Non-Compete Agreements,* Seyfarth Shaw LLP (Aug. 4, 2016), available at Lexology.com]

However, Nevada enacted a statute, Assembly Bill 273, on June 3, 2017 to overrule this decision and to give courts the power to blue-pencil noncompetes, revising the agreements as necessary and enforcing the revised version. Under Assembly Bill 273, a noncompete agreement is void and unenforceable unless it is supported by valuable consideration; it does not impose more restraint than necessary to protect the employer; the restrictions are appropriate to the consideration the employee received for signing the agreement; and the agreement does not subject the employee to undue hardship. Noncompetes are only enforceable when the employer is either paying the employee's salary or providing equivalent compensation to a laid-off employee. Limitations are imposed on non-solicitation agreements that cover ex-employees. [Robert B. Milligan, *Nevada Enacts New Non-Compete Law,* Seyfarth Shaw LLP (July 6, 2017), available at Lexology .com]

Alabama adopted a new restrictive covenant statute, effective January 1, 2016, under which noncompete and non-solicitation covenants are allowed, but their restrictions must be reasonable. Restrictive covenants must be limited to the geographic area where the company operates a similar business. A temporal restriction of up to two years in an ordinary noncompete clause is presumed to be reasonable. When post-separation consideration is paid for the agreement, a temporal restriction of 18 months or the period over which the consideration is paid is presumed reasonable. The statute allows blue-penciling of restrictions that are too extensive—but an agreement that does not meet one of the six exceptions for restrictive covenants, including noncompete and nonsolicitation agreements, can be voided in its entirety. An agreement cannot be blue—penciled if it is designed to coerce payment of a debt, or to reduce the price at which the company's stock is redeemed. [Zachary C. Jackson, *A Dash Of Certainty—Alabama's New Restrictive Covenant Statute*, Epstein Becker Green (July 8, 2015), available at Lexology.com; James A. Patton, *Alabama's Restrictive Covenants Statute: New Insight on Retroactivity, Employee Training, and the Blue Pencil Rule,* Ogletree Deakins (Sept. 16, 2016), available at Lexology.com]

In a unionized workplace, the employer must consider the implications of the duty to bargain on the agreement. Minteq International Inc., had a CBA that ran from 2011 to 2014. In 2013, the employer unilaterally required newly hired employees to sign a noncompete agreement that also forbade disclosure of certain confidential information about the company. A mid-2016 NLRB decision says that the employer had the duty to bargain over imposing noncompetes. The CBA's management rights clause did not refer to the noncompete and nondisclosure provisions, so it did not waive employees' rights to collective bargaining. [*Minteq Int'l, Inc.*, 364 N.L.R.B. No. 63 (July 29, 2016); see Mark Theodore, *Non-Compete Agreement a Mandatory Subject of Bargaining, NLRB Rules*, Proskauer Rose LLP (Aug. 17, 2016), available at Lexology.com]

Post-employment restrictive covenants are disfavored in New York, where both state and federal courts recently refused to order even partial enforcement of unreasonable restrictive covenants. The courts would not blue-pencil excessively broad restrictions to make them enforceable, taking the position that employers should be aware when a restriction is excessive. [Neal H. Klausner and David Fisher, *Courts Put Down Their Blue Pencils*, N.Y.L.J. (Oct. 20, 2014), available at law.com. See also *Brown & Brown v. Johnson*, 115 A.D.3d 162 (N.Y. App. Div. 2014). New York's definition of reasonable restrictions comes from *BDO Seidman v. Hirshberg*, 93 N.Y. 382 (N.Y. 1999).]

Another area of state-to-state difference is when noncompetes can be signed. A 2012 New Hampshire statute says that a noncompete is void if it is not given to job applicants or promotion candidates before the job or promotion offer. In early 2014, the District Court for the Southern District of Alabama held that a noncompete agreement can only be signed after employment begins. However, Minnesota and Oregon have held that a restrictive covenant must be signed before employment starts for employment itself to constitute consideration. Oregon makes a noncompete agreement void unless the employer informs the employee, in a written offer of employment received at least two weeks before the first day of employment, that the noncompete is a required condition of employment—or the employer and employee enter into the agreement when the employee is promoted. This provision does not apply to confidentiality agreements or non-solicit or non-service agreements. [V. John Ella and Thomas A. Davis, *Should a Non-Compete Be Signed Before or After Employment Begins? Answer: It Depends*, Jackson Lewis PC (Jan. 19, 2014), available at Lexology.com]

The Illinois Court of Appeals ruled that, if there is no other consideration, a covenant not to compete requires at least two years of continued employment [see *Fifield v. Premier Dealer Servs., Inc.*, 2013 Ill App. (1st) 120327 (June 24, 2013)] but federal district courts in Illinois will not apply the two-year rule, using a fact-specific test instead. [See, e.g., *R.J. O'Brien & Assocs., LLC v. Williamson*, No. 14 C 2715, 2016 U.S. Dist. LEXIS 32350 (N.D. Ill. Mar. 10, 2016)]

Pennsylvania held that a post-employment covenant not to compete, signed after the start of employment, is void for lack of consideration even if the agreement recites the parties' intention to be legally bound, notwithstanding Pennsylvania's Uniform Written Obligations Act, which says that there is consideration for a written promise if the writing expressly states the intention to be bound. However, noncompetes can be valid if they are signed at commencement of employment or if the agreement is signed in connection with a promotion or pay raise.

Multi-state operations must consider the laws of other states in which ex-employees might compete; it might not be possible to enforce the preferred choice of law. Illinois and Kentucky have also refused to enforce noncompetes where there is no consideration other than continued employment. However, Wisconsin has taken the opposite approach, holding that the employer's forbearance in not firing an at-will employee provides consideration for the restrictive covenant. [Compare *Socko v. Mid-Atlantic Sys. of CPA, Inc.*, 126 A.3d 1266 (Pa. 2015) with *Runzheimer Int'l, Ltd. v. Friedlen, et al.*, 862 N.W.2d 879, 2015 WI 45 (Wis. 2015)] See also *Charles T. Creech, Inc. v. Brown*, 433 S.W.3d 345 (Ky. 2014) (continued employment is not consideration); *Emp't Staffing Grp., Inc. v. Little*, 777 S.E.2d 309, 314 (N.C. App. 2015) ($100 payment to a current employee is adequate consideration for a noncompete agreement)]

Reasonable choice of law provisions (determining where suits about the agreement would be heard) can be included. Choice of law provisions are generally enforced unless they violate local public policy or if a state that is chosen that has no connection with the employment relationship. The employer can also provide consideration such as cash, stock options, a raise, additional paid time off, severance benefits, or additional training. If this is done, the agreement should explain the consideration and that the employee acknowledges that it is adequate. [Peter A. Steinmeyer and Scarlett L. Freeman, *In Today's Environment, What Is "Adequate Consideration" for a Restrictive Covenant Signed by an Existing Employee?*, Epstein Becker Green (May 10, 2016), available at Lexology.com]

The Eighth Circuit allowed Ozark Mobile Imaging to assign confidentiality and noncompete agreements to Mobilex, the buyer of Ozark's assets. The Eighth Circuit ruled that the assignment did not materially change the employee's obligations and the agreements were not specific to Ozark. The agreements did not say whether or not they were assignable, so the Eighth Circuit considered whether a Missouri court would find them assignable, and decided that they were. [*Symphony Diagnostic Servs. No. 1 v. Greenbaum*, 828 F.3d 643 (8th Cir. 2016); see James P. Flynn et. al., *Assignment Lessons: 8th Circuit Finds Assigned Non-Competes Enforceable—Under Certain Facts*, Epstein Becker Green (Aug. 3, 2016), available at Lexology.com]

In mid-2015, the Seventh Circuit refused to enforce a standard restrictive covenant agreement against an ex-employee who opened a competing business and solicited former co-workers and customers of the ex-employer. Although the court conceded that she violated the restrictive covenant, the court said that the covenants did not protect any legitimate business interests of the ex-employer. She did not make use of confidential information; the clients she solicited were not necessarily loyal to the ex-employer and had no exclusive or long-term arrangements that were protectable; and there was a high turnover in employees even without solicitation. [*Instant Tech. LLC v. DeFazio*, 793 F.3d 748 (7th Cir. 2015)]

The "employee choice" doctrine says that if an employee has the choice between receiving contractual benefits and agreeing not to compete or competing but surrendering those benefits, the covenant not to compete will not be required to satisfy standards of reasonableness. However, a 2015 case reaffirms that the employee choice doctrine only applies when the employee resigns because that is the only situation in which a really free decision can be made. Covenants not to compete that are imposed on terminated employees must satisfy the reasonableness standard. The employee choice doctrine is also limited to situations in which the employer would be willing to continue employing the employee. In this case, the court found that a two-year time period for a noncompete was reasonable. [*IBM v. Smadi*, No. 14 CV 4694 (VB), 2015 U.S. Dist. LEXIS 27321 (S.D.N.Y. Mar. 2, 2015)]

The Eighth Circuit predicted that the Arkansas Supreme Court would probably adopt the majority rule: that a covenant not to compete can be assigned to the purchaser of a business, although some states say that a noncompete can only be assigned if the employee consents to the assignment. [*Stuart C. Irby Co., Inc. v. Tipton*, 796 F.3d 918 (8th Cir. 2015)]

Drafting suggestions for covenants not to compete that will be enforceable include:

- Describe the scope of prohibited activities in a way that will continue to apply if the employee's job responsibilities change.

- Make the covenant applicable to other activities the employee is involved in during his or her tenure.

- In states where the enforceable portions of a covenant will be enforced and the rest will be stricken, describe the restrictions broadly but include alternatives—if a covenant covering the entire state is stricken, the employer will have no protection, but a covenant limited to a certain number of miles or a particular geographic area might be limited by a court but otherwise upheld. The clause could also give a list of prohibited activities, but specify that the covenant applies only to activities the employee actually engages in during the term of the agreement.

- Specify liquidated damages, because, when an employer moves for a temporary restraining order (TRO) and preliminary injunction, it will be difficult to calculate the damages for violation of the covenant. The amount of liquidated damages must reflect reasonable assumptions about potential damages, and must not be punitive. One option is to call for a larger amount in the first month, on the theory that the initial violation may include disclosure of trade secrets or interference with goodwill that cannot be remedied even by a prompt injunction, plus smaller amounts for each month that the violations continue.

- Some employers permit the employee to buy out of the covenant by paying a significant sum before competing, to compensate the employer for lost income.

- A "fail-safe" clause states that both parties intend the covenant to be enforceable, and it was a significant factor in the hiring decision—so the employee agrees to pay a fixed amount to make up for non-enforcement of the covenant, if the employee leaves before the employer receives full consideration for the agreement.

- If state law allows, call for the employee to pay the employer's attorneys' fees for disputes about the covenant. [Lee A. Spinks, *Now That We Know the Basic Rules . . . Drafting Covenants Not to Compete to Maximize the Likelihood of Enforcement*, Poyner Spruill LLP (Nov. 11, 2013), available at Lexology.com]

Late in 2012, the Supreme Court held that the Oklahoma Supreme Court was wrong to hold that the noncompete provisions in two employment contracts were void because they violated public policy. The decision should have been left up to the arbitrator. The clause referred to any "dispute, difference or unresolved question." When two employees quit and went to work for a competitor, Nitro-Lift demanded arbitration. The ex-employees sued in Oklahoma state court to enjoin enforcement of the noncompete agreement, which they said was null and void. The Oklahoma Supreme Court asked the parties to show why the state law limiting the enforceability of noncompete agreements should not be applied. The Supreme Court held that the Federal Arbitration Act (FAA) applies in both federal and state courts and attacks on the validity of the contract (rather than on the validity of the arbitration clause) must be resolved by the arbitrator. The validity of the arbitration clause is determined by the court. If the arbitration clause is valid, then the validity of the rest of the contract is decided by the arbitrator. [*Nitro-Lift Techs., LLC v. Howard*, 133 S. Ct. 500 (2012)]

The First Circuit upheld the district court's issuance of a preliminary injunction preventing an ex-employee from doing business with his ex-employer's customers—even if the customers initiated the contact. The defendant was an account executive who worked under a non-solicitation/non-disclosure agreement. He went to work with a competitor, and dealt with some customers of his former employer. The employer obtained a preliminary injunction for one year dealing with these customers. The First Circuit held that there is no real distinction between soliciting business and merely "accepting" it. Non-solicitation agreements protect the ex-employer's accrued goodwill, no matter who makes the first contact. [*Corporate Techs., Inc. v. Harnett*, 731 F.3d 6 (1st Cir. 2013)]

In the past, it was simple to define solicitation: contacting customers in person or by telephone. But it is not yet clear whether e-mail and networking, updating a LinkedIn account, e-mailing an entire address book to report a job change, or disseminating the new employer's promotional materials on social media can be considered solicitation.

The First Circuit has held that an e-mail announcement of a new job to a targeted group of customers, 40% of whom were clients of the ex-employer, violated the non-solicitation agreement by piquing curiosity and inducing customers to contact the new employer. Massachusetts cases have held that updating a Facebook page to reflect a new job is passive, not active solicitation that violates a noncompete, and that merely updating a LinkedIn profile is not solicitation; the Connecticut Superior Court agreed with this proposition, because it was not targeted and there was not necessarily overlap between the old and new employer's clientele. [*Corporate Techs., Inc. v. Hartnett*, 731 F.3d 6 (1st Cir. 2013); *Invidia LLC v. DiFonzo*, 202 WL 5576406 (Mass. Super. Ct. Oct. 22, 2012) (passive solicitation); *KNF&T Staffing, Inc. v. Muller*, 31 Mass. L. Rep. 561 (Mass. Super. Ct. 2013) and *BTS USA Inc. v. Executive Perspectives LLC*, No. 10 CV 116010685, 2014 Conn. Super. LEXIS 2644 (Conn. Super. Ct. Oct. 6, 2014) (updating LinkedIn profile)]

California law actually forbids noncompete agreements, although, in the right case, California might agree with the many states that accept the "inevitable disclosure" doctrine—i.e., that an ex-employee can be enjoined from going to work for a competitor of the former employer, if the inevitable result would be disclosure of the ex-employer's trade secrets, even if the ex-employee does not intend to do so.

However, California has adopted the Uniform Trade Secrets Act, which allows protection of some information, including client lists. [*Edwards v. Arthur Andersen*, 44 Cal. 4th 937 (Cal. 2008); see Labor Code § 16600]

Also note that even though California law bars covenants not to compete, a California court does not have the power to issue an injunction forbidding the parties in a California suit from bringing suit in a different state to enforce the covenant not to compete. [*Advanced Bionics Corp. v. Medtronic Inc.*, 29 Cal. 4th 697, 59 P.3d 231, 128 Cal. Rptr. 2d 172 (2002)] The theory is that judges should respect the powers of other judges, especially those in other states.

New York considers noncompete agreements an unreasonable restraint on trade. To enforce one, the employer must show that the covenant is reasonable in duration and scope, does not harm the public interest, does not subject the employee to undue hardship, and is no broader than needed to protect the employer's protectable interests. An employee on "garden leave" (i.e., paid to remain at home and not take another job) is still subject to the duty of loyalty to the employer. The "employee choice" doctrine says that courts will not analyze the reasonableness of a covenant that gives an employee a choice between competing (and forgoing benefits) and not competing (and receiving benefits). It is common for employers to require job applicants to disclose terminations for cause. Failure to disclose could justify firing the new employee. In other words, it is often rational for employees to quit before they can be terminated for cause. [Alexandra

Wald and Nathaniel P.T. Read, *To Quit or Not to Quit?*, N.Y.L.J. (Nov. 13, 2012) (law.com)]

The general rule is that employees who are not bound by employment agreements or termination agreements containing noncompete clauses are free to compete with the employer after they leave. A top executive may be considered a fiduciary as to the employer. A principle of corporate law called the "corporate opportunity doctrine" imposes a duty on a current employee to disclose to the employer whenever a business opportunity arises that is appropriate for the corporation, and it is improper for an executive to take personal advantage of the opportunity at the corporation's expense.

§ 25.03 EMPLOYEE HANDBOOKS

[A] Generally

Employee handbooks are traditional in large corporations, as a means of creating a uniform culture and distributing information to what can be a large, diverse, and widely disseminated group of employees. Handbooks are useful in training new hires about the employer's expectations. They provide a ready reference about work rules—and employee discipline often revolves around claimed infractions of these rules, so employees must be informed of the rules.

Not all handbooks are printed; more and more companies are using the Web or an intranet to provide information. The employee handbook sets expectations, encourages employees to follow the rules, ensures consistent treatment for all, and bolsters the employer's position in unemployment cases. The handbook should detail procedures for requesting time off, complaining about harassment, maintaining time records, reporting theft or violence in the workplace, as well as setting policies such as dress codes and workplace drug/alcohol policies. It is less expensive to put the handbook online, and updates are easier—but the cautious employer will be sure to get an acknowledgment (on paper or electronic) that the employee received the handbook. [D. Albert Brannen, *Why Your Company Needs a Handbook*, Fisher & Phillips LLP (June 1, 2014), available at Lexology.com]

Handbooks are supposed to be written for employees, telling them the essential terms and conditions for the employment relationship. In addition to indicating the employer's compliance with anti-discrimination and wage and hour laws, the handbook should make it clear if employment is at-will. Employees should be informed about company policies about tuition reimbursement, vacation and sick leave over and above what is legally mandated, and how to use these policies. An argument could be made for writing the handbook to include only the policies employees need to know, with a separate procedure manual instructing supervisors how to carry out the policies, with citations to the relevant statutes and regulations. It is efficient for all supervisors to have a uniform reference point for employer policy. However, the procedure manual and the employee handbook should be compared to avoid conflicts. [Cecilia Romero, *Employee Handbook Versus Procedures Manual: Keeping Policies Consistent*, Holland & Hart LLP (Dec. 14, 2015), available at Lexology.com]

Employers who maintain employee handbooks should be aware that the National Labor Relations Board (NLRB) and the Equal Employment Opportunity Commission (EEOC) are giving handbooks more scrutiny than ever before, and challenging more provisions; handbooks should be updated in light of current legal issues such as same-sex marriage and accommodation of religious dress and pregnancy-related disability. [Tracey E. Diamond, *Updating Your Employee Handbook for 2016*, Pepper Hamilton LLP (June 20, 2016), available at Lexology.com]

A 2014 article challenges the conventional wisdom by arguing that employee handbooks are no longer useful. In this view, the handbook's social media policies are likely to be obsolete. Employees probably don't care about the company history and mission statement. Few employees will read all the work rules and in an at-will work environment, they can be terminated for work misconduct even if there are no published rules. The Employment Retirement Income Security Act (ERISA) requires distribution of non-handbook documents explaining benefits. The author of the article says that the only potentially useful content for a handbook could be a statement that employment is at will; an anti-harassment policy that will satisfy the employer's obligations; the 29 C.F.R. § 541.603 FLSA safe harbor notice; election options under the FMLA; and information about the Sarbanes-Oxley hotline for whistleblowers. [Kevin Connelly, *Employee Handbooks (1971–2014): R.I.P.*, DLA Piper (Feb. 4, 2014), available at Lexology.com]

Even if this is not the employer's intention, statements made in the handbook may be deemed to create a binding contract. Furthermore, once the employer is deemed to have created a contract, some courts will say that the employer can no longer amend that contract whenever it wants to, without providing additional consideration to the employees in return for the change. Although some courts say that the fact that the employee continues to work for the employer provides consideration, others require the employees to get some additional benefit if the employer wants to alter the contract.

The Sixth Circuit held that incorrect statements by the employer (that the plaintiff was eligible for the Family and Medical Leave Act (FMLA) leave) led to equitable estoppel. Thus, the employee had to be granted FMLA leave even though, but for the employer's statements, he would not have been eligible because the company was too small to be covered by the FMLA. When the plaintiff said that he needed time off to treat heart disease, the employer sent him FMLA paperwork, provided a form with "eligible for FMLA leave" checked off, and told him to have a doctor complete the certification. The employee handbook said that employees were eligible if they worked 1,250 hours the previous year and did not mention the 50- employee limit. The plaintiff was fired after a final written warning for failure to complete assignments. He said that the reason he did not complete the assignments was that he took time off, which he thought was FMLA leave. [*Tilley v. Kalamazoo Cnty. Road Comm'n*, 777 F.3d 303 (6th Cir. 2015)]

A "Woolley disclaimer" states that an employee handbook is not a contract. The District Court for the District of New Jersey refused to enforce an arbitration clause that was included in a manual with a Woolley disclaimer, finding that the arbitration clause was unenforceable because the employer could unilaterally modify any provision without notice to employees. The result is that in New Jersey, or a state with similar laws, a stand-alone arbitration agreement protects the employer's interests better. [*Raymours Furniture Co., Inc. v. Rossi*, No. 13-4440, 2014 U.S. Dist. LEXIS 1006 (D.N.J. Jan. 2, 2014)]

In a mid-2016 California Court of Appeal case, the handbook language gave the employer the power to unilaterally modify policies. The plaintiff said that this freedom made the provisions of the handbook illusory and unenforceable. But the court rejected this argument, stating that the handbook included separate language requiring the signatures of both parties to modify a contract and a unilateral right to modify is legitimate if it is subject to limitations such as requiring fairness and reasonable notice. [*Harris v. TAP Worldwide, LLC*, 248 Cal. App. 4th 373 (Cal. App. 2016); see Ronald W. Novotny, *California Court of Appeal Upholds Arbitration Agreement Despite Employee's Refusal to Sign It*, Atkinson Andelson Loya Ruud & Romo (July 6 2016), available at Lexology.com]

■ **TIP:**   Many federal and state statutes limit the policies that employers can adopt. For example, a policy against leaves of less than one day could violate the Family and Medical Leave Act, or might be a refusal to make a reasonable accommodation required by the Americans with Disabilities Act (ADA).

Typical subjects for coverage in the handbook include benefits, pension plans, stock options, vacation and leave policies, the drug-free workplace policy, and explanation of employees' rights under various federal statutes; what constitutes a disciplinary offense; and discipline policy (including grounds for termination).

[B]   At-Will Employment

For employees who are not unionized, and who do not have individual employment contracts, it is often a good idea to put a disclaimer in the handbook, informing employees that they are hired at will; can be fired without the employer having to demonstrate good cause for termination; and the handbook is not a contract and the information in it is provided for guidance only.

To be legally effective, a disclaimer must be clear and conspicuous. It cannot be buried in small print somewhere in the back of the book. In fact, the first page is an excellent location. When a disclaimer is issued, it does not apply to people who were already employees and working under the old policy.

The mere fact that the employer has a system of progressive discipline, spelled out in the handbook, does not mean that the employee is no longer an at-will employee. However, it makes sense to include a disclaimer explaining the function of the disciplinary system.

The more specific a provision is, the more likely that courts are to construe it as creating a formal contract. However, in order to win when they charge breach of this implied contract, employees may have to show detrimental reliance (i.e., that they relied on the provision, and this reliance was harmful for them). At the very least, employees will have to prove that they read the handbook, because it is hard to claim reliance on an unread provision.

[C]   Orientation Checklists

It is a good idea to provide orientation to train new hires. It is even better to standardize the orientation process, with standard documents for welcoming and instructing new employees. Both the employee and the supervisor handling the orientation should sign the document, so that later on the employee will not be able to claim that lifetime employment was promised if the document clearly states that employment is at will.

Subjects for the checklist include the company's equal employment opportunity policies; if there is a formal probation process, what its terms are; the new employee's job title, duties, and promotion path; compensation and benefits for the job; and work rules.

Even if the manual indicates the employees will be on probation for a certain length of time after being hired, they will still be entitled to good faith and fair dealing from the employer. In fact, some courts will allow probationary employees to sue for wrongful termination, if the employer did not offer them long-term employment after the end of the probation period.

[D]   Legal Consequences of Handbooks

The NLRB is vigilant about what it deems to be violations of NLRA § 7 in employee handbooks. Even some well-established policies have been held by the NLRB to impair employees' protected concerted activity. The NLRB published a memorandum on March 18, 2015 explaining which policies it considers unlawful. A confidentiality policy must not prevent employees from discussing the terms and conditions of employment—but discussion of trade secrets or customer information can be forbidden. The NLRA gives employees the right to criticize the company's labor policies or treatment of employees. A ban on disrespectful, negative, or rude conduct could be unlawful, but employers can require professional, respectful treatment of co-workers or customers. Threatening or coercing co-workers can be forbidden but vigorous discussion cannot be. In the NLRB view, employees have the right to communicate with the media and other third parties about the terms and conditions of employment. During break or non-work time, employees have the right to take photographs and make recordings related to protected concerted activities, but employers can forbid activities that could reveal trade secrets. Health care employers can forbid activities in patient areas that could lead to breach of confidentiality of patient information. [<http://static .ow.ly/docs/GC%2015_04%20Report%20of%20the%20General%20Counsel%20 Concerning%20Employer%20Rules.pdf_36Fc.pdf> (last accessed Feb. 28, 2017); see Jill K. Bigler, *Could This Be You? Your Employee Handbook Is on the NLRB's Radar*, Bricker & Eckler LLP (Aug. 3, 2015), available at Lexology.com]

The NLRB's position is that employees have the right to use the company e-mail system to discuss working conditions with co-workers, so employers should not forbid employees to use the e-mail system for all non-work purposes. [*Cellco P'ship d/b/a Verizon Wireless*, N.L.R.B. No. 28-CA-145221 (Sept. 18, 2015)]

The NLRB's interpretations sometimes prevail in court. The D.C. Circuit invalidated three work rules in Hyundai's employee handbook that could reasonably be interpreted to restrict activity protected by NLRA § 7. One rule forbade discussion of matters under investigation by the employer, a rule that the court said was overbroad and should have been limited to situations involving confidential information. The second forbade disclosure of any of the employer's electronic communications to unauthorized persons, which the court found invalid because of the potential chilling effect on discussion of employment conditions. A rule forbidding any non-work activities during working hours could also implicate protected union activities. [*Hyundai Am. Shipping Agency v. NLRB*, 805 F.3d 309 (D.C. Cir. 2015)]

In general, the NLRB opposes the use of broad or vague rules about, e.g., civility, respect, disparagement, or confidentiality—even if the policy has a saving clause about not restricting protected collective activity. The NLRB ruled that Chipotle violated the NLRA in its social media policy forbidding "false" and "misleading" posts, holding that posts can only be forbidden if they are malicious as well as false and misleading. The NLRB said that the policy against disclosure of confidential information was vague and undefined. Terminating an employee for asking co-workers to sign a petition against denial of work breaks was unlawful. [*Chipotle Servs. LLC & Pennsylvania Workers' Organizing Comm.*, No. 04-CA-1437314 (N.L.R.B. 2016); see Jackie S. Gessner, *Burrito Bowls, Guacamole, & . . . Tweets?*, Barnes & Thornburg LLP (Mar. 18, 2016), available at Lexology.com]

§ 25.04 WORK RULES

Some organizations are small enough, informal enough, or simple enough in operation that they do not need written work rules. But in the larger organization, or even a small operation where the work rules could become an issue, a written list of rules (in the handbook or set out separately) can be very useful.

The work rules document should make it clear that the employer is the only one to make work rules and that the employer has the right to modify them at any time. The rules themselves are not a contract with the employees that has to be negotiated, or that has to be maintained in its original form.

Work rules deal with issues such as workplace safety; emergency procedures; dress and grooming rules; when paid or unpaid leave is available and how to request leave; and bans on harassment, fighting, and weapons. Some employers have a no-fault absence policy, where the amount of time off is specified, and employees can take it for any reason, but they are disciplined for excessive absence. A paid leave bank allows unused days to be carried over or cashed out. Workplace leave policies must satisfy the legal rules for disability and FMLA leave. Many organizations forbid soliciting donations in the workplace, but any such rule must be clearly communicated; non-discriminatory; and uniformly applied.

For example, the Eleventh Circuit held that a policy forbidding employees to distribute non-work materials violated NLRA § 7. An employer can forbid distribution of non-work materials during working hours and employees who are not assigned to work can be prohibited from handing out non-work materials (e.g., union flyers) to employees who are at work. But the employer's policy was overbroad because it prevented employees from distributing materials in a mixed-use area of the plant, at times when neither the employees giving out the materials nor those receiving them were at work. [*Mercedes-Benz Int'l v. NLRB*, 838 F.3d 1128 (11th Cir. 2016); see Anne R. Yuengert, *Employers Hold Up on the Hand Out Policies: 11th Circuit Classifies Company Non-Solicitation Policy as Overbroad*, Bradley Arant Boult Cummings LLP (Oct. 6, 2016), available at Lexology.com]

> ■ **TIP:** Even though the work rules are not contractual in nature, it is a good idea to have employees sign a notice stating that they received a copy of the work rules and had a chance to read and become familiar with them. The notice may come in handy later if the employee claims that he or she never saw the rules or didn't understand them.

§ 25.05 SYSTEMS OF PROGRESSIVE DISCIPLINE

One approach to at-will employment is for the employer to take and maintain a consistent position that only the employer determines the quality of the employee's work performance. Employees can therefore be disciplined or fired based on the employer's sole determination that their work is unsatisfactory. In a unionized workplace, it is almost certain that the collective bargaining agreement will require a system of progressive discipline, where all the steps, from a verbal warning through levels of reprimands, must be followed before the employee can be fired.

There are various reasons why even a nonunion workplace might have a progressive discipline system. It could improve efficiency. Sometimes, employees really do not know that their work is below par, so it is better to show them how to improve instead of firing them. Also, if the employer voluntarily adopts a progressive discipline system, this could make employees less interested in unionizing.

The downside is that having specific rules to follow limits the employer's flexibility. Even in a nonunion setting, the disciplinary system may be treated by courts as a contractual obligation, so that once the system is set up, it has to be maintained in the future.

Usually, a system of progressive discipline begins with an oral warning explaining why the supervisor is dissatisfied with the employee's performance. The next step is a written warning. If performance is still unsatisfactory, discipline proceeds to a probationary period or suspension (usually unpaid, lasting three–five days), then demotion or termination.

All the steps, including oral warnings, should be documented in the employee's personnel record. The written warning should include a place for the employee's signature, indicating that the document has been read. The employee should be given a copy for reference. It is often helpful to let the employee include a brief written statement giving his or her side of the story.

It is important to monitor the reasons for an employee's lateness or absence. Discipline or discharge could constitute a violation of a statute if the employee has been injured (and qualified for Worker's Compensation), is disabled as defined by the ADA, or is taking care of a sick family member and therefore is entitled to FMLA leave.

All investigations should be documented, to show that the employer is acting on the basis of facts and not discrimination against members of a protected group.

An objective party should review all termination decisions. The best time is after tempers have had a chance to cool, but promptly enough to demonstrate the employer's efficiency and involvement. Before a termination, review the process to see that the employee received the appropriate warnings; the investigation gave enough weight to the employee's explanation; and the employee was treated fairly, objectively, and on a par with other similarly situated employees.

In general, employees who are discharged for cause are not entitled to severance pay (see Chapter 3). However, the employee handbook may have been written in such general terms that it constitutes a contract to pay severance benefits, even in connection with a discharge for cause. Severance policies that are written and communicated to workers may become welfare benefit plans subject to ERISA. If there is no formal plan, and the employer has not entered into an express or implied contract, then it is completely at the employer's discretion to grant or withhold severance benefits.

§ 25.06 EMPLOYEE EVALUATIONS

Regular evaluations of employee performance can be critical in making sure that the organization meets its goals. Employees who are not performing up to par can be identified and given the training, encouragement, or whatever they need to improve. When it's time to award merit raises and bonuses, the performance appraisal should identify the stars.

A well-done performance appraisal identifies real problems in employee performance and gives insights into solutions. Some of the basic issues for performance reviews include whether the employee's work was satisfactory in amount and quality; how well the employee knows the job; the employee's ability to acquire new skills; and areas in which improvement is needed.

At a minimum, the employee should be shown a written performance appraisal, be given an opportunity to discuss it, and should be asked to sign a statement that he or she has read the document. Some states make it a legal requirement that the employee must be allowed to add comments; it is a good idea anyway.

The modern form of appraisal is the "360-degree review," which has input from more than one person, including co-workers and customers. However, it can be hard to gather all the necessary information, and not everyone will be candid. An alternative might be to have more frequent but informal reviews: for instance, at the end of every project, or every quarter or twice a year.

§ 25.07 MANDATORY PREDISPUTE ARBITRATION PROVISIONS

Employers, faced with the delay, high costs, and significant risks of employment litigation, often seek to require in advance that employees will raise any discrimination claims using the arbitration process rather than litigation (see Chapter 40).

To have a chance of enforcement, a handbook provision must make it clear which statutes are covered, and clearly and explicitly indicate that arbitration is the sole remedy. It makes sense to have the employee sign a document when he or she receives the handbook—not only stating that the handbook has been received, but that the employee has read its contents and understands them.

In recent years, most cases have come down on the side of arbitration, even if it is compelled by a mandatory predispute arbitration clause (i.e., if employees had to agree to arbitrate their claims as a condition of being hired)—a proposition that was approved by the Supreme Court in *Circuit City v. Adams*. [532 U.S. 105 (2002)] The jurisdiction and the facts of the case will determine whether the fact that the employee continues to work after the arbitration requirement has been imposed constitutes acceptance of the terms of the arbitration provision.

The Supreme Court ruled in 2009 that a labor union could require arbitration of a grievance brought by workers who said they were demoted because of age discrimination—the Supreme Court rejected drawing a distinction between collective bargaining agreements (CBAs) and individual contracts that contain arbitration clauses. [*14 Penn Plaza LLC v. Pyett*, 556 U.S. 247 (2009)] Another Supreme Court decision—in a consumer protection rather than an employment case—has been read to mean that federal law supports arbitration so strongly that state rulings about the unconscionability of arbitration agreements will be preempted. [*AT&T Mobility LLC v. Concepcion*, 131 S. Ct. 1740 (Apr. 27, 2011). See also *American Express Co. v. Italian Colors Res.*, 133 S. Ct. 2304 (2013)]

In a decision covering all employees whose employers are engaged in interstate commerce (whether or not the company is unionized—about 25% of non-union workers are subject to arbitration clauses), the NLRB ruled in early 2012 that requiring employees to waive collective actions and class arbitration and arbitrate all employment disputes individually violates the NLRA.

The NLRB said that it was not bound by *AT&T Mobility* because that case does not apply to rights specifically guaranteed to employees by the NLRA. [*D.R. Horton & Michael Cuda*, 357 N.L.R.B. No. 184, Case 12-CA-25764 (Jan. 3, 2012)] In 2013, however, the Fifth Circuit held that it is permissible for an employer to impose a class action arbitration waiver; it is not inconsistent with the employees' legal right under the NLRA to pursue collective action. But the Fifth Circuit held that the arbitration agreement must clarify that employees do not waive the right to file NLRB complaints. [*DR Horton v. NLRB*, 737 F.3d 344 (5th Cir. 2013) *reh'g denied*, No. 12-60031 (5th Cir. Apr. 16, 2014)]

The NLRB once again asserted its opposition to waivers of class and collective actions—and once again, the Fifth Circuit upheld the validity of such waivers. [*Murphy Oil v. NLRB*, 808 F.3d 1013 (5th Cir. 2015)] In mid-2016, the Seventh Circuit created a circuit split by agreeing with the NLRB that forbidding class and collective actions violates the NLRA. [*Lewis v. Epic Sys.*, No. 15-2997 (7th Cir. May 26, 2016); see Jessica Silver-Greenberg and Noam Scheiber, *Court Rules Companies Cannot Impose Illegal Arbitration Clauses*, NYTimes.com (May 27, 2016)]

This position is distinctly out of phase with the numerous court decisions enforcing arbitration agreements that include class action waivers. [E.g., *Owen v. Bristol Care, Inc.*, 702 F.3d 1050 (8th Cir. 2013); *Parisi v. Goldman, Sachs & Co.*, 710 F.3d 483 (2d Cir. 2013); *Walthour v. Chipio Windshield Repair, LLC*, 745 F.3d 1326 (11th Cir. 2014) or holding that class relief is not available if the agreement does not explicitly permit class actions, e.g., *Reed Elsevier, Inc. v. Crockett*, 734 F.3d 594 (6th Cir. 2013); *Huffman v. The Hilltop Cos.*, LLC, 747 F.3d 391 (6th Cir. 2014).]

The existence of such a wide circuit split led, as predictable, to the Supreme Court granting certiorari on January 13, 2017 in a consolidated case covering the

Murphy Oil, Ernst & Young, and Epic Systems cases. When certiorari was granted, it was anticipated that the case would be heard in that term with a final decision being handed down by the end of June 2017. However, on February 8, 2017, the Supreme Court announced that the oral arguments would be scheduled during the 2017–2018 term (i.e., the term beginning in October 2017). Therefore, the decision would not be rendered until late 2017 or even 2018. It is also possible that the case would be sent back to the lower courts—leaving multi-state employers without clear direction. [Richard R. Meneghello, *Good Things Come to Those Who Wait? Supreme Court Delays Class Waiver Decision Until Next Term*, Fisher Phillips (Feb. 8, 2017), available at Lexology.com]

The Eighth Circuit agreed with the NLRB that it was reasonable for employees to think that a class or collective action waiver interfered with their right to file Unfair Labor Practices charges with the NLRB—but the Eighth Circuit nevertheless refused to hold that maintaining the arbitration agreement was an Unfair Labor Practice. [*Cellular Sales of Mo. LLC v. NLRB*, No. 15-1860 (8th Cir. June 2, 2016); *see* Howard M. Bloom and Philip B. Rosen, *Eighth Circuit Finds Class and Collective Action Waivers Lawful Under NLRA, Contrary to Seventh Circuit*, Jackson Lewis PC (June 3, 2016), *available at* Lexology.com]

In late 2016, the Sixth Circuit ruled that, under Kentucky law, continued employment constitutes assent. Therefore, plaintiffs who signed an electronic form acknowledging that they had received and understood the updated handbook, which included a class action waiver and mandatory arbitration clause, were required to bring individual arbitration cases rather than lawsuits. [*Aldrich v. University of Phoenix, Inc.*, 661 Fed. Appx. 384 (6th Cir. 2016); see Gail Jankowski, *Applying Kentucky Law, Sixth Circuit Finds Continued Employment Constitutes Assent to Arbitration Agreement*, Carlton Fields (Nov. 28, 2016), available at Lexology.com]

The Sixth Circuit has found certain agreements limiting FLSA rights to be unenforceable, finding that they are not covered by the FAA if they are part of an ordinary employment or severance agreement rather than an arbitration agreement. [*Boaz v. FedEx Customer Info Servs.*, 725 F.3d 603 (2013), *Killion v. KeHE Distributors, LLC*, 761 F.3d 574 (6th Cir. 2014)]

The Second Circuit upheld an arbitration agreement's waiver of class and collective actions in a case where the plaintiff alleged that she was wrongfully denied $1,867 in overtime. The plaintiff said that it would cost $200,000 in attorneys' fees, costs, and expert testimony to recover less than $2,000, but the Second Circuit held that it is lawful for an employer to rule out class and collective actions even if the practical effect is that small claims cannot be brought. [*Sutherland v. Ernst & Young*, 726 F.3d 290 (2d Cir. 2013)]

A mid-2014 presidential Executive Order, the Fair Pay and Safe Workplaces Executive Order, EO 13673, provided that if a federal contract is for $1 million or more, the contractor would not be permitted to impose a requirement of pre-dispute arbitration for Title VII, sexual harassment, or sexual assault cases. However, the Fair Pay and Safe Workplaces Executive order was not only challenged several times in court, but was eliminated by congressional action (H.J. Res. 37). Congress acted under the Congressional Review Act, which allows Congress to invalidate recently passed administrative rules, and to prevent the rules from being re-adopted by the federal agency in substantially similar form without congressional approval. Furthermore, President Trump issued an EO of his own, *Revocation of Federal Contracting Executive Orders,* which expressly revokes EO 13673 and related orders, 13738 and 13683.

The fact that a statute can be enforced through federal lawsuits does not rule out arbitration, so the Fifth Circuit upheld mandatory arbitration of the Uniformed Services Employment and Reemployment Rights Act (USERRA) claims brought by a Marine reservist who said he was harassed and eventually fired because of his military status. [*Garrett v. Circuit City Stores,* 449 F.3d 672 (5th Cir. 2006). See § 1.18 for more discussion of USERRA.]

The Fifth Circuit held in 2016 that it is better practice to have a separate arbitration agreement than to include the arbitration requirement in the employee handbook. In a case where the handbook said that the employer retained the right to amend its arbitration rules, the Fifth Circuit refused to compel arbitration of Title VII claims. The plaintiff alleged that he was fired 15 days after reporting harassment. The Fifth Circuit said that, under Texas law, changes to an arbitration agreement are valid only if the changes are prospective; apply equally to employer and employee claims; and the employee receives advance notice that the change will occur. Otherwise, the agreement is illusory and unenforceable. In this case, the Fifth Circuit found the agreement to be illusory because the arbitration provision took effect immediately, so it remanded the case for trial in the federal district court. [*Nelson v. Watch House Int'l LLC,* 815 F.3d 190 (5th Cir. 2016); see Hannah L. Hembree and Donna K. McElroy, *Texas Employers Requiring Mandatory Arbitration Must Review Their Arbitration Agreements Under New Fifth Circuit Opinion,* Dykema Gossett PLLC (Mar. 10, 2016), available at Lexology.com]

An employee handbook's statement that its provisions were not binding and did not create an employment contract led the Fourth Circuit to hold that the handbook's arbitration provision was unenforceable. Therefore, an employee could bring a federal collective action. [*Lorenzo v. Prime Commc'ns, LP,* 806 F.3d 777 (4th Cir. 2015)]

California has decided a number of cases in which arbitration agreements have been found unconscionable—but many of these cases have been reversed by the Supreme Court or the Ninth Circuit, and most other states have not followed California's example. In 2013, The California Supreme Court overturned its 2011 decision (that an employee could not be required to waive his or her right to a "Berman" wage claims hearing before the state Labor Commission). In 2013, the Supreme Court said that the FAA preempts the state law that forbids such a waiver. However, the case was remanded to determine if the arbitration clause itself was unconscionable; the court said that unconscionable arbitration clauses can be invalidated despite *Concepcion* and *Italian Colors*. [*Sonic-Calabasas A, Inc. v. Moreno*, 57 Cal. 4th 1109 (Cal. 2013)]

In mid-2014, California ruled that an employee's waiver of class arbitration is enforceable. However, employers cannot require employees to waive the right to bring Private Attorney General Act (PAGA) wage claims. [*Iskanian v. CLS Transp. Los Angeles LLC*, 59 Cal. 4th 348, 327 P.3d 129 (Cal. 2014)] Certiorari was denied on January 20, 2015, 135 S. Ct. 1155 (2015). As a result, employees can continue to bring PAGA suits, and an arbitration agreement that prevents employees from bringing such suits is unenforceable, even though employers can lawfully forbid class arbitration. The Ninth Circuit held in September 2015 that a waiver of representative PAGA claims cannot be enforced—but the other claims in an employment-law class action had to be arbitrated. [*Sakkab v. Luxottica Retail N.*, 803 F.3d 425 (9th Cir. 2015)]

However, the District Court for the Central District of California refused to utilize *Iskanian*, applying federal preemption. The district court ruled in mid-2014 that, under the FAA and *Concepcion*, state law cannot invalidate waivers of class or representative actions in arbitration agreements. The district court held that *Concepcion* overrules the right to bring PAGA collective actions and the FAA's policy of encouraging arbitration preempts state laws that forbid waivers of PAGA collective actions. [*Fardig v. Hobby Lobby Stores, Inc.*, SACV 14-00561JVS, 2014 WL 4782618 (C.D. Cal. Aug. 11, 2014)]

See § 40.07 for additional discussion of predispute arbitration mandates.

§ 25.08 DEFAMATION

A hostile or unflattering statement that a company or one of its agents makes about a job applicant, employee, or former employee could become the focus of charges, or even a lawsuit. However, there are several circumstances under which negative statements are legally protected. For one thing, the statements might have been demonstrably true. They might have been made without malice, or in a privileged context.

Slander is defined as communicating a defamatory statement orally or otherwise informally. Libel means communicating a defamatory statement more broadly ("publishing" it). A defamatory statement is one that attributes serious misconduct to someone else. The victim of slander or libel can sue and obtain tort damages, unless the statement was privileged in some way.

The basic rule is that a plaintiff not only has to prove that defamation occurred, but also that some actual damages were suffered because of the defamation. But there are some statements so negative that they are automatically presumed to damage the reputation of the person about whom they are made. A plaintiff who proves such "defamation per se" can win without proving actual damages (concrete injury attributable to the defamation).

To support a suit, the alleged slander or libel must be a statement of fact, not a mere opinion or a general, imprecise statement ("Marcia is hard to work with"; "Steve seems to be working through some problems in his life."). A pure opinion cannot be defamatory, because it is not a statement of fact, but a statement of fact backing up that opinion can be defamatory. A corporation is liable for the statements of its employees and agents, as long as they were acting within the scope of their employment.

Truth is always a defense to a defamation charge: For instance, it is not defamatory to say that an employee was fired for stealing office supplies if this is what actually happened. If the employer believes a statement is true, and the statement is communicated without malice, then the employer is entitled to a defense. The jury, not the judge, decides whether or not a statement was communicated with malice.

A statement has not been "published" to the extent that a libel charge can be made if it is communicated only to the plaintiff, or to someone who is acting on behalf of the plaintiff (including a friend or an investigator who calls to find out what the employer is saying about the employee). Courts take different positions about communications that stay within the employer corporation. Some courts say that this is so narrow that no publication has occurred, whereas others accept the plaintiff's argument that dissemination was broad enough to constitute libel.

Although employers are hesitant to communicate about employees, technology like e-mail, blogging, and social networking makes it easier to disseminate information—positive or negative—about employees. Not only references, but performance reviews, outplacement interviews, and written or electronic conversations can give rise to defamation suits. Former employees, who may feel that they have little chance of getting another job in the current economy, also have less to lose, may be more likely to file a defamation suit. More and more suits involve "defamation by conduct" such as subjecting an employee to an underserved investigation of alleged wrongdoing. Attorneys for employers suggest making sure that corporate policies are applied evenly (e.g., requiring all terminated employees to turn in their company laptops immediately) so no one can claim to have been singled out unfairly.

§ 25.09 PRIVILEGED STATEMENTS

[A] Generally

Some kinds of communication are essential to the operation of businesses and the legal system, so they are afforded special treatment. They are referred to as "privileged," and by definition cannot be defamatory.

In addition to absolute privilege, "qualified" privilege exists in some circumstances. A qualified privilege is one that can be taken away under some circumstances, whereas an absolute privilege survives all kinds of challenges. If the employer asserts a qualified privilege, it has the burden of proving that it is entitled to the privilege.

If a corporation has an audit committee, discussion of possible embezzlement or securities violations are probably entitled to qualified privilege as long as they remain within the committee, and are not disclosed (other than to law enforcement officials, which is the subject of another privilege). If there has been an investigation about workplace matters, disclosing the results of the investigation to the employees at large would probably also be privileged.

Even though they are not law enforcement officials, the Equal Employment Opportunity Commission (EEOC) and unemployment officials are close enough so that communications to them are privileged. There is at least a qualified privilege to make statements in the course of processing a union grievance or issuing dismissal letters required under a collective bargaining agreement. In fact, in some states (Michigan, New Mexico, Louisiana, Missouri) the privilege is absolute, not qualified.

California [Cal. Civ. Code § 47(c)] gives employers a qualified privilege for statements made without malice and on the basis of credible evidence. Alaska presumes [Alaska Stats. § 09.65.160] that employers act in good faith when they discuss their employees with other prospective employers. However, if the employer acts recklessly, maliciously, or contrary to the employee's civil rights, the privilege is no longer available.

In any state, employers are probably entitled to a qualified privilege when they make good-faith comments on employee performance to someone who has a legitimate right to the information. However, some degree of caution must be exercised. Not all co-workers necessarily have a legitimate interest in performance appraisals.

There is a qualified privilege to protect the safety of employees who might hurt themselves, or might be hurt by others. (Communications that are privileged in the context of a defamation suit are probably also privileged if the employee sues for violation of privacy instead of, or in addition to, defamation.)

However, even if a privilege initially exists, it can be sacrificed—most typically, by failure to act in good faith, or by making statements without proof and with reckless disregard as to whether or not they are true.

It was long assumed that employers could instruct employees to keep complaints and investigations confidential. However, the NLRB sometimes challenges confidentiality requirements on the grounds that they can violate NLRA § 8(a)(1) by suppressing discussion of ongoing investigations of employee misconduct.

- Banner Estrella Medical Center (358 NLRB No. 93 2012): it is a violation of NLRA § 8(a)(1) to impose a blanket confidentiality policy for internal workplace investigations. The NLRB said that the employer has the burden of proof that there is a legitimate business need for confidentiality in a particular situation (e.g., witness protection, a risk of destruction of evidence or fabricated testimony).

- Design Technology Group LLC (NLRB Apr. 19, 2013): a handbook rule forbidding employees to disclose their wages or compensation to third parties, including co-workers, violates the NLRA; it was unlawful to fire three employees for posting Facebook messages complaining about a supervisor who belittled their fears about working late in a dangerous neighborhood.

- Quicken Loans Inc. (NLRB June 21, 2013): the NLRB found an employment agreement invalid because employees were forbidden to disclose any proprietary or confidential information to anyone. Confidential information was defined to include personnel lists, contact information for workers, and employee handbooks; the ALJ said that it violates NLRA § 7 to forbid discussion of wages or benefits.

- Dish Network Corp. (NLRB 2013): the NLRB found a social media rule unlawful; it forbade disparaging or defamatory comments about the company, its products or services, customers, or employee, and it forbade employees to contact the media, talk to government agencies, or make public communications without permission. *Banner Estrella* and *Hyundai America Shipping Agency* were appealed to the D.C. Circuit.

The Fifth Circuit agreed with the NLRB that the employer's confidentiality policy violated NLRA § 8(a)(1) because it prevented employees from discussing wages. The policy forbade employees to copy or share confidential information, broadly defined to include personnel information and documents. In the Fifth Circuit view, employees have a right to discuss wages with co-workers; there was no evidence that employees used this information outside the company. The Fifth Circuit examined the written terms of the policy, not the way it was implemented, so it rejected the employer's argument that the policy was not used to suppress discussion of wages. [*FlexFrack Logistics v. NLRB*, 746 F.3d 205 (5th Cir. 2014). The employer raised a challenge based on *Noel Canning*, but the Fifth Circuit held that this argument was not raised on a timely basis.]

Federal contractors are forbidden to maintain or enforce pay secrecy policies. Under Executive Order 13665, *Non-Retaliation for Disclosure of Compensation Information* [see <https://www.whitehouse.gov/the-press-office/2014/04/08/executive-order-non-retaliation-disclosure-compensation-information> (Apr. 8, 2014) (last accessed Mar. 1, 2017)], it is unlawful for a federal contractor to discharge or otherwise discriminate against employees or job applicants for discussing their own or co-workers' compensation. Federal contractors are not allowed to maintain or enforce pay secrecy policies, or discharge or otherwise discriminate against employees or applicants for discussing their own or a co-worker's compensation. But employers can probably require confidentiality in appropriate cases if it is necessary to protect witnesses, avoid cover-ups, and prevent destruction of evidence. Employers should protect themselves by having formal policies. The complainant should be asked if he or she wants the investigation to remain confidential (and this is usually the case). The employer should protect itself by getting a written statement of this intent. [Catherine Dunn, *NLRB Rules on Keeping Employees from Discussing HR Investigations*, Corporate Counsel (Aug. 31, 2012) (law.com)]

[B] Attorney-Client Privilege

The term "privilege" is also applied to communications that are privileged in the sense of being protected from disclosure. To do a good job, lawyers must learn all the facts of the situation, not just the facts that put their clients in a favorable light. Certain information is privileged if a client communicates it to a lawyer. The lawyer cannot be required to disclose this information—in fact, in most instances, it is unethical for the lawyer to disclose the information without the client's consent.

The factors that determine the availability of attorney-client privilege include whether the contact with the lawyer was made specifically to seek legal advice (not business advice, or when the lawyer was acting as a corporate director); whether the communication dealt with the lawyer-client relationship; if the client intended the information to be confidential; and whether the client's deliberate or inadvertent act terminated the privilege (e.g., material distributed to non-lawyers is not privileged).

It can be hard to determine the status of corporate documents.

A report might be confidential only if it were drafted specifically as a confidential document for transmission to the attorney.

If the primary purpose of a communication is to get legal advice, a secondary business motive will not take away the privilege. But the privilege will be waived (that is, surrendered) if the corporation voluntarily distributes the document to non-attorneys, or discloses or allows the disclosure of a significant part of the document. For instance, if a corporation issues a press release about a development, or sends an employee to read a technical paper at an industry conference, it will not be able to argue that the press release or the technical paper is confidential.

However, a statement made by an employee who is not acting as an agent of the employer, but is simply an independent witness to an event probably will not be confidential, no matter why the statement was made.

In addition to the attorney-client privilege, the law of evidence contains a separate "work product" privilege. Work product is material prepared by attorneys and their employees as part of representing a client. Work product is also confidential and cannot become part of the discovery process before litigation.

The New Jersey Supreme Court ruled that the attorney-client privilege outweighs corporate policy about use of workplace computers. Therefore, a plaintiff suing her employer had a reasonable expectation that e-mails to and from her lawyer using her personal, password-protected Yahoo account, would be private even though they were sent on a laptop owned by the company. [*Stengart v. Loving Care Agency Inc.*, 990 A.2d 650 (N.J. 2010)]

[C] Self-Critical Analysis

When a company finds out that misconduct may have occurred and launches an investigation, the company has to decide if it should report any misconduct that it discovers to the authorities. If the company's stock is publicly traded, disclosure will probably be required by the securities laws and the company will be liable under the anti-fraud provisions of federal securities laws. Financial institutions are required to file a Suspicious Activities Report with the FinCEN (Financial Crimes Enforcement Network) when they become aware of potential illegalities. Federal regulations make government contractors subject to debarment or suspension for knowing failure to make timely disclosure of credible evidence of fraud, conflict of interest, bribery, or False Claims Act violations in connection with performance of a government contract.

If the corporation itself is clearly a victim (e.g., of embezzlement or theft of trade secrets) then self-reporting can result in help from the authorities. There are more advantages than disadvantages in reporting offenses committed by an employee with little corporate exposure (e.g., a criminal act carried out on company property, but not related to the criminal's employment). The stronger the evidence, the stronger the case for reporting—especially since the likelihood that regulators will discover the wrongdoing also increases. The Department of Justice Principles of Federal Prosecution of Business Organizations permit prosecutors to treat timely, voluntary disclosure of wrongdoing as a mitigating factor, and cooperation with the authorities can affect the decision of what crimes to charge. The DOJ's Antitrust Division offers amnesty to the first corporation to confess to an antitrust violation—and turn in the other co-conspirators. [Michael B. Mukasey and Andrew J. Ceresney, *Should Corporations Self-Report Wrong Doing?*, N.Y.L.J. (Oct. 1, 2010) (law.com)]

Companies that want to improve diversity and eliminate discrimination often make studies of their employment and HR practices. Can discrimination plaintiffs require the company to disclose those documents, and use them to prove that the company used discriminatory employment practices?

Several federal courts have recognized a "self-critical analysis privilege": in other words, that these reports are internal documents that should not have to be revealed to plaintiffs, because companies should be encouraged to be candid about their discrimination problems instead of suppressing what they know to avoid embarrassing disclosures in lawsuits.

The opposite view is that the documents were prepared as part of the company's Title VII compliance program, would eventually be reported to the EEOC, and therefore could not reasonably be described as privileged. Even under this argument, a distinction might be drawn between a self-critical analysis that a company originated voluntarily and one that is mandated by the EEOC or by federal contract regulators. Or the court might require the company to produce hard information like statistics about workplace diversity, but permit the analytical part of the report to remain confidential.

It also helps to control dissemination of sensitive documents. The fewer people who have access to the document, and the more they agree that the company needs to analyze its performance in order to improve, the less likely they are to disclose the document in a way that is harmful or embarrassing to the corporation.

§ 25.10 DUTY TO COMMUNICATE

Not only are there situations in which an employer becomes liable for defamation or other disclosures, but also sometimes the employer can get into trouble for failing to communicate. There might be a duty to disclose dangerousness, so that other employers will not hire someone who puts their other employees or customers at risk. A subsequent employer may sue if the first employer fails to reveal relevant information, such as a job applicant's dismissal for stealing or workplace drug dealing.

Employers have a legal duty to protect customers and co-workers. That makes them negligent if they know that someone is dangerous, but they still retain him or her as an employee. This is true even if the risk is of conduct outside the scope of employment. An employer who knows that an employee has violent tendencies can be liable because of workplace assaults committed by that person, even if the assaults are not only not part of the job, but are contrary to the employer's policy and work rules. However, if the injured person is a fellow employee, it is very likely that the employee's only remedy will be through the Worker's Compensation system. [See § 33.03 for the concept of WC exclusivity]

Employers can be sued for negligent hiring or negligent entrustment if they hire someone for a safety-critical job but fail to check that person's references. In some contexts (such as hiring workers for a nursing home or day care center) there may be a duty to consult a special database maintained by the state or by a licensing organization to list individuals who are ineligible for employment because they have been convicted of a crime.

An employer will probably be exempt from liability for negligent hiring if a thorough investigation is performed before hiring; but if an employer fails to discover information that would have been disclosed by an ordinary background check, liability is a possibility.

Discrimination plaintiffs sometimes add a negligent hiring claim to their complaints. Their theory is that the employer was negligent in hiring and/or retaining a supervisor who was racist, sexist, or otherwise prone to engage in discriminatory conduct. The advantage to the plaintiff is that, although the discrimination claim is subject to the Civil Rights Act of 1991 (CRA '91) cap on damages (see § 42.12[B]), the negligent hiring claim is not. Also, it is hard to introduce evidence into a discrimination case about acts of discrimination or harassment carried out against employees other than the plaintiff, but this is relevant evidence in a negligent hiring case.

The employer might also be liable for negligent supervision, if the court or jury accepts the argument that the supervisor would not have been able to carry out the act of discrimination or harassment if the employer had managed the facility better.

The Federal Trade Adjustment Assistance Extension Act of 2011 required all the states to adopt unemployment insurance integrity provisions dealing with recovery of erroneous benefit payments, no later than October 21, 2013. Employers and their agents must respond in timely fashion to state agencies' requests for information about overpayments. Compliance is especially difficult with respect to employees who have separation or settlement agreements under which the employer agrees not to challenge the ex-employee's unemployment benefit claim, so severance agreements should make it clear that the employer will respond to state requests. [Eric J. Janson and Marc R. Jacobs, *You (Don't) Have the Right to Remain Silent—How New Unemployment Insurance Integrity Laws May Affect Your Separation and Settlement Agreements with Departing Employees*, Seyfarth Shaw LLP (Nov. 12, 2013), available at Lexology.com]

§ 25.11 RESPONSES TO REFERENCE CHECKS

The employer has to steer between two hazards: neither committing defamation, nor failing to disclose information that must be divulged. One approach that often works is just to confirm the start and end dates of a former employee's employment, and then say that it is against company policy to discuss ex-employees. Another possibility is to disclose only information that is fully documented by HR files. See § 23.08 for discussion of "ban the box" laws that restrict inquiries about criminal records.

■ **TIP:** If your state gives employees the right to review their files and make their own comments, make sure that any response to an inquiry includes the employee's comments. For instance, "Ms. Jones was dismissed for excessive lateness and poor performance. However, she said that other people were late just as often, and we should have been more sympathetic about her performance because her mother had just died." That way, the questioner gets both sides of the story.

According to employment lawyer Wendy Bliss, it is perfectly legitimate for a former employer to provide information about the candidate's performance as a member of a work team, and the adequacy of his or her work habits. But information should be disseminated only if it is truthful, work-related, and can be supported by documentation. Bliss suggests that employers should have a written policy about what kind of information will be given in references—and who will be allowed to provide this information. Information should not be released without a signed consent and release form (including a liability waiver) from the employee.

If an employee's resignation or termination is being negotiated, one area of negotiation is what will be said in response to reference checks.

It may be easier to get reference check information by asking about a job candidate's strengths and accomplishments as an employee, rather than stating or implying that you want negative information. No one is going to sue for defamation for being described as "hard working," "effective," or "creative"!

The growing trend toward outsourcing functions opens new risks if background checks are omitted, but the law is not clear as to whether the employer or the staffing agency is responsible for performing the checks. Hence, employers who are concerned about liability risks should either perform or make sure that the staffing agency performs background checks on people working with children or vulnerable adults, anyone working in a customer's home, and anyone who has access to bank accounts or confidential information.

The employer's contract with the agency should include a warranty that the agency has performed background checks on all agency workers and certification that the check did not show anything precluding placement of the worker. The agency should warrant that background checks were performed in accordance with the Fair Credit Reporting Act (FCRA) and state laws. Employers should make sure that the agency maintains adequate liability insurance and should seek indemnification from the agency. [Tresa Baldas, *Outsourced Employees Triggering More Suits*, Nat'l L.J. (Feb. 22, 2006) (law.com)]

§ 25.12 NEGOTIATED RESIGNATIONS

In some cases, an employee has been guilty of misconduct so serious (securities fraud or embezzlement, for example) that immediate removal is needed to reduce the risk to the corporation. In other cases, it will be less clear that employment must be ended—situations that fall under the Hollywood euphemism "creative differences." In such a situation, both parties benefit if they negotiate a resignation. The employee will leave on a stipulated date, and will release the company from all claims of employment-related discrimination. [See Chapter 37, § 37.07[A] for the specific problems of drafting a release that will satisfy the provisions of the Older Workers Benefit Protection Act (OWBPA), Pub. L. No. 101-433.]

A resignation agreement is a contract and therefore is subject to the ordinary rules of contract law. For instance, if the employer deliberately misleads an employee, or subjects him or her to undue influence, the resignation agreement will be void and the employer will not be able to enforce it against the employee. The implications of the agreement are serious enough that first-line supervisors should not be allowed to negotiate. Either a trained HR staffer or an attorney should take on this role.

The agreement covers issues such as:

- The employee represents that he or she has not already filed any charges, or instituted litigation against the employer. If legal action is already in the works, settlement discussions or conciliation from the antidiscrimination agency is in order, but it is too late to negotiate a simple resignation agreement;

- The employee waives all claims against the employer. Drafting the proper, enforceable language is an intricate legal task;

- The employee agrees to treat the resignation as voluntary, and therefore not to apply for unemployment compensation;

- The employer should state that it does not admit liability of any kind, but is only using the agreement to clarify the issues;

- The employer should specify the kind of reference it will give the employee, and how it will handle reference checks from potential future employers;

- The employee should waive any merit-based bonuses that would otherwise be payable in the year of the resignation;

- The employee should agree to return all materials in his or her possession containing trade secrets or other proprietary materials of the employer, and should agree to refrain from using the employer's proprietary/trade secret information in any later employment;

- The employee should agree to keep the terms of the agreement confidential.

Similar issues are at play when the employee initiates resignation or an employee is terminated for cause or laid off. In these situations, for senior or highly compensated employees, it is likely that an executive separation agreement will be negotiated reflecting factors such as the following:

- Termination date—if there is a long time between firing and the last day of work, is the executive expected to keep working? (If so, the employer could be liable for the employee's actions between the signing of the separation agreement and the last day of work.) It could be worthwhile to obtain a second release on the actual last date of work, with benefit payments contingent on signing this second release;

- Would a later termination date permit vesting of any benefits or awards?;

- Some executive compensation packages include cash incentives. If the employee makes wage law claims, the separation agreement should indicate that there is a dispute, which has been compromised for an agreed-upon fixed payment. If state law requires payment of earned compensation on the last day of employment, this must be done;

- The separation form should discuss not merely the amount of severance, but the amount and timing of payments, and who is responsible for payments in a change of control situation. OWBPA requirements must be satisfied;

- Specify if the executive will receive any non-cash benefits, such as continuation of health benefits, outplacement services, or a positive or at least neutral recommendation;

- Post-termination restrictive covenants. If there is a prior agreement that includes restrictive covenants that continue after termination of employment, the company should not use an integration clause in the separation agreement that says the separation agreement constitutes the full agreement between the parties;

- Non-disparagement and confidentiality;

- Forum and choice of law—an important issue because state laws vary so much; and

- Dispute resolution, including the types of claims covered; if you wish to exclude class arbitration or collective actions, this is the place to do it. [Renee Inomata, *10 Most Overlooked Executive Separation Agreement Clauses—Part 2*, Burns & Levinson LLP (Sept. 9, 2014), available at Lexology.com]

§ 25.13 RELEASES

An employee who has already filed discrimination charges may be willing to settle those charges, receiving some consideration in exchange for releasing the employer from further threat of suit by that employee. (However, a suit brought by another employee, or by the EEOC, continues to be a risk.) During the negotiations before a resignation, the employer and employee could agree on a severance package that winds up their relationship, making it clear that the soon-to-be-ex-employee will not bring any discrimination charges.

A release is a contract, a legal agreement for surrendering claims that already exist. A release can be quite general, simply referring to "all claims" or quite specific, spelling out a whole laundry list of claims. A release of liability could be combined with reasonable covenants not to compete and provisions about the employer's intellectual property.

Courts might refuse to enforce a release that is too general, on the grounds that it is not specific enough to inform employees of their rights. But a release that is too detailed can put ideas into the heads of employees who had no real intention of bringing suit—or who didn't know the vast and exotic variety of ways in which they can make trouble for the employer!

Separation agreements usually include releases; these provisions are potentially controversial. During termination negotiations, the employer should make it clear that providing a release is a condition of getting severance pay. Severance pay could also be conditioned on returning the employer's property and documents or executing noncompete, nondisclosure, and/or non-solicitation agreements. Code § 409A compliance is also required, and can affect the timing of payments. (See § 8.02[D]). If the employee is over 40, the OWBPA must also be complied with. [Monica A. Kohles, William (Bill) J. Wortel and Carrie Elizabeth Byrnes, *Five Key Considerations When Drafting a Release*, Bryan Cave LLP (July 3, 2014), available at Lexology.com]

If an employee signs a release in exchange for severance but there is a prolonged period between the decision to end employment and the actual departure date, a "back-stop release," a second release covering the period between the initial release and the employee's departure, can be prudent for management. Generally speaking, employees can only release claims that have already accrued, not those that accrue in the future, so the back-stop release covers the "tail" period until the actual departure. [Neal T. Buethe, *The "Back-Stop" Release*, Briggs and Morgan (June 20, 2016), available at Lexology.com]

Before payments of pensions and benefits begin, the plan might require the potential participant or beneficiary to sign a release stating that the plan has computed the amounts of benefits correctly, or that the participant or beneficiary waives all claims against the plan except the right to receive benefits as specified by the plan.

Courts are split as to whether such mandatory releases are enforceable. If all plan participants and beneficiaries have to sign, the release becomes part of ordinary plan administration, and there is no additional consideration for it. The employer gets something (freedom from suits and other claims) but doesn't give up anything in return (the benefits would be available under the plan anyway).

All contracts require consideration to be enforceable. Each party must receive something under the contract. In a typical release situation, the employer provides additional benefits (e.g., extra severance pay; outplacement assistance; early retirement incentives) over and above normal severance. The employee offers the employer a release of all claims, thus sparing the employer the risk of having to defend against charges. If each party gets something of value, the court probably won't worry about exact equivalence, as long as the parties knew their rights and understood all the implications of the release.

The EEOC has attacked some standard language often used in releases. The EEOC's position is that it is implementing its 1997 Enforcement Guidelines about non-waivable rights. The EEOC objects to covenants not to sue that cover filing all kinds of charges; general release language that is applicable to all charges including discrimination charges; confidentiality and non-disparagement clauses that require a person to notify the ex-employer before disclosing information even in response to a subpoena. A mid-2014 article suggests that releases should have a "carve out" permitting the employee to file discrimination charges. The carve out can be drafted to require the employee to waive the right to monetary damages if charges are filed. If there is a confidentiality clause, it should make it clear that the employee can participate in a government investigation. [Tim K. Garrett. *Release Language Hazards and How to Fix Them*, Bass, Berry & Sims PLC (June 17, 2014), available at Lexology.com]

A general release covers all claims in existence at the time of the release; a limited release covers only the types of claims named in the release itself.

> ■ **TIP:** A release covering an injured worker who is entitled to Worker's Compensation is valid only if it is approved by a Worker's Compensation judge. Special care is required in drafting the release. If the worker releases claims relating to compensable physical injury, he or she will still have the right to bring suit on other grounds, such as claims that the employer acted in bad faith or intentionally inflicted emotional distress on the employee. [See, e.g., *Duncan v. Hartford Life &Accident Ins. Co.*, No. 2:11-cv-01536-GEB-CKD, 2013 WL 506465 (E.D. Cal. Feb. 7, 2013), holding that ERISA claims were not released by standard language in a WC release.]

The EEOC and the NLRB review severance agreements, with particular attention to waivers and releases of claims, confidentiality, and non-disparagement. The NLRB has challenged confidentiality and nondisparagement provisions as violations of NLRA §§ 7 and 8. The best practice is to limit the provision to actual non-public proprietary business information, rather than forbidding disclosure of any information about the company. The nondisparagement provision should forbid only false statements that are willful, malicious, or knowingly untrue. There should also be a savings provision permitting employees to exercise rights under the NLRA.

The agencies tend to oppose attempts to limit employees' rights to file administrative charges, communicate with regulators, or participate in agency investigations, so the agreements should carve out agency investigations of all kinds (perhaps in a bolded paragraph the carves out all agency investigations, with cross-references in the discussion of individual issues). Payment of severance should never be conditioned on withdrawal of a pending agency charge. However, the employee should be required to inform the agency of the agreement. [Debra A. Mastrian, *Tips for Drafting Severance Agreements to Avoid*

Scrutiny from the EEOC and NLRB, SmithAmundsen LLC (Oct. 7, 2015), available at Lexology.com]

The Fifth, Seventh, Eighth, and Ninth Circuits have ruled that employees do not waive their rights under the FLSA if they cash checks that are described as "full payment" for wages and overtime. Employees do not waive FLSA rights unless they are notified of the rights they waive. [*Beauford v. ActionLink, LLC*, 781 F.3d 396 (8th Cir. 2015)]

The Seventh Circuit ruled in early 2011 that Worker Adjustment and Retraining Notification (WARN) Act claims can be waived in a voluntary general release. The Seventh Circuit upheld the release because the release (and the severance agreements in connection with closing DHL Express shipping facilities) were negotiated by the union; were not ambiguous; and suggested consulting a lawyer before signing. [*Ellis v. DHL Express Inc. USA*, 633 F.3d 522 (7th Cir. 2011)]

However, as the FMLA regulations provide (see Chapter 38), the Department of Labor says that it is invalid for employees to give an advance release of claims that might arise under the FMLA in the future. But with respect to FMLA claims that have already arisen, it is legitimate for employers to offer—and employees to sign—a release of existing claims. Supervision by the Department of Labor, or by a court, is not required.

The fact that a departing employee had an outstanding request for FMLA leave when she accepted severance and signed a release did not mean that the release invalidly released prospective rights. The Eleventh Circuit held that prospective rights in this context are rights to take FMLA leave in the unspecified future; a prospective waiver is a waiver of an event that has not happened yet. In this case, Paylor validly released a claim that had already accrued. She received consideration for the release in the form of severance pay that would not otherwise have been available. [*Paylor v. Hartford Fire Ins.*, 748 F.3d 1117 (11th Cir. 2014)]

It is common for settlement agreements to include a confidentiality clause and a release of all claims. Generally, judicial approval will be required for FLSA settlements. Early in 2015, the District Court for the Southern District of New York rejected a proposed FLSA settlement, finding several serious defects. There was no estimate provided of the number of hours the plaintiff worked or his applicable wages. No sworn statements, affidavits, or declarations were submitted in the request for approval. The confidentiality provision purported to prevent the plaintiff from discussing the settlement with anyone except his attorneys, family, and financial planners. Then the agreement was re-submitted, without the confidentiality provision but requiring both parties to respond to inquiries by saying that the dispute was amicably resolved. The district court also rejected this formulation, saying that it was too much like a gag order, and public policy required permitting the plaintiff to describe the outcome as a victory.

However, *Picerni v. Bilingual Seit & Preschool Inc.* [925 F. Supp. 2d 368 (E.D.N.Y. 2013)], says that private FLSA settlements do not need court approval.

Other courts have found that approval is not if the parties have counsel and negotiated the settlement in an adversary proceeding [*Fernandez v. A–1 Duran Roofing, Inc.*, 2013 WL 684736 (S.D. Fla. Feb. 25, 2013)]—but these cases are outliers. [*Camacho v. Ess-A-Bagel, Inc.*, No. 1:14-cv-2592, 2015 U.S. Dist. LEXIS 2658 (S.D.N.Y. Jan. 9, 2015)]

The Second Circuit held in mid-2015 that FLSA settlements are unenforceable if they have not been approved by either the DOL or a judge. [*Cheeks v. Freeport Pancake House, Inc.*, 796 F.3d 199 (2d Cir. 2015)]

In light of the *Cheeks* case, the District Court for the Eastern District of New York ruled that Federal Rules of Civil Procedure 41(a)(1)(a) requires approval from either a court or the DOL to dismiss a Fair Labor Standards Act (FLSA) claim with prejudice. The district court said that the FLSA is a uniquely protective statute, and requiring supervision of dismissals fits in with the statutory objective. [*Martinez v. Ivy League Sch., Inc.*, No. 2:15-cv-07238-DRH-GRB (E.D.N.Y. June 18, 2016); see Robert S. Whitman, Howard M. Wexler and Meredith-Ann Berger, *District Court Turns the Other "Cheeks" on Parties' Proposed Stipulation of Dismissal*, Seyfarth Shaw LLP (July 11, 2016), available at Lexology.com] Similarly, a 2017 Southern District of New York case requires court approval to use a Federal Rules of Civil Procedure Rule 68 offer to settle an FLSA case: *Mei Xing Yu v. Hasaki Rest., Inc.*, No. 16-CV-6094 (JMF) (S.D.N.Y. Apr. 10, 2017); see Brett C. Bartlett and Samuel Sverdlov, *SDNY Pancakes Parties' Attempt to Bypass Cheeks: Requires Approval of Rule 68 Settlement*, Seyfarth Shaw LLP (May 1, 2017), available at Lexology.com]

Employment settlements typically require the employee's promise not to re-apply at the same company to preclude retaliation claims if the ex-employee is not re-hired. However, the Ninth Circuit has held that such a clause violates California public policy [see Cal. Bus. & Prof. Code § 16600], which is broader than just covenants not to compete, and deals with all issues of employee mobility and limitations on the right to practice one's profession. [*Golden v. California Emergency Physicians Med. Grp.*, 782 F.3d 1083 (9th Cir. 2015)]

The Tax Court agreed with the IRS: a settlement agreement between a university and a former professor who claimed that her colleagues created a hostile work environment that forced her out was taxable income for the professor. The Tax Court rejected the professor's contention that the funds were tax-exempt as an award for personal physical injuries under Code § 104(a)(2). The Tax Court held that settlement agreements are interpreted under their express language, and the agreement contained only one reference to its being conditioned on the plaintiff settling her Workers' Compensation claim. In the Tax Court view, the settlement could have reflected non-Workers' Compensation claims, and the plaintiff failed to prove that the settlement, described as for emotional distress, was for physical injury. Even if emotional distress has physical manifestations, that is not sufficient to exclude settlement proceeds from taxable income. [*Sharp v. Comm'r*, T.C. Memo 2013-290 (2013)]

In mid-2009, the EEOC published a guidance document (subsequently revised in April 2010) in Question & Answer form covering waivers of discrimination claims in severance agreements. The EEOC noted that older employees are often targeted because they earn more than less experienced, younger co-workers.

The document is intended for employees, and includes sample language and examples of adequate consideration and knowing and voluntary waivers. In general, it re-states existing principles rather than breaking new ground. To be valid, waivers must be knowing and voluntary, written clearly enough for employees to understand them, must not be induced by improper conduct on the employer's part, and the employee must be given access to counsel and given enough time to consider the terms. Employees must receive some additional consideration for signing the waiver that they would not otherwise receive. Waivers must not give up the right to pursue remedies for future acts of discrimination. Waivers should not limit employees' right to testify or participate in EEOC proceedings. [EEOC, *Understanding Waivers of Discrimination Claims in Employee Severance Agreements*, <http://www.eeoc.gov/policy/docs/qanda_severance-agreements .html> (July 15, 2009; Appendix B revised Apr. 2010) (last accessed Mar. 1, 2017). See *EEOC v. Watkins Motor Lines, Inc.*, 553 F.3d 593 (7th Cir. 2009): the EEOC can continue to investigate and pursue claims made by a person who signed a waiver.]

States take varying approaches about what can be covered by a general release. Some states say that they can cover all claims, known or unknown, but other states say that a general release is not effective for claims that the employee did not know about or suspect at the time the release was signed. Under this theory, people can only give up claims that they know about and decide are worth less than the benefits under the release.

The Fifth Circuit held that a broad, generic state-court settlement release did not prevent two ex-employees from suing for unpaid overtime—even though the wage claims were discussed during settlement negotiations, and the release included all claims arising out of employment. The employer sued several employees in Texas state court for breach of noncompete clauses. The suit was settled with a release covering all claims and causes of action related to or in any way arising from employment. Despite the release, the employees brought suit in federal district court for overtime violations under FLSA § 207. The district court ruled for the employer, but the Fifth Circuit reversed: the prior suit was not an FLSA suit and the parties did not negotiate the amount of overtime. Consequently, the settlement was not a valid FLSA waiver because it was not reached in a bona fide FLSA dispute. [*Bodle v. TXL Mortg. Corp.*, 788 F.3d 159 (5th Cir. 2015)]

The California Court of Appeal ruled that USERRA rights (see § 1.18) cannot be eliminated by a contract; 38 U.S.C. § 4302(b) says that USERRA supersedes any state law or contract that reduces, limits, or eliminates any rights under the statute. Therefore, a release of rights in a severance agreement was unenforceable to the extent that it dealt with allegations he was terminated because of his military status. Under California law, a general release does not cover claims that the releaser did not know about at the time of the release. [*Perez v. Uline*, 157 Cal. App. 4th 953 (Cal. App. 2007)]

However, a 2010 Sixth Circuit decision holds that a release under IBM's Individual Separation Allowance Plan prevented an ex-employee from asserting USERRA claims. The court found that the release was enforceable because it was knowing and voluntary; there was no evidence of fraud or overreaching; and the release form was not ambiguous. [*Wysocki v. IBM*, 607 F.3d 1102 (6th Cir. 2010)]

Although it is common for employment, change in control, and severance agreements to condition payment of severance or other compensation on the employee's signing a general release of all claims against the employer, the documents must be carefully drafted in light of Code § 409A. (See § 8.02[D]) In general, § 409A allows a severance agreement to permit payment at any time during the 90 days after the event—but only if the employee does not have a direct or indirect election about when to receive the benefits.

Executives can create problems for their former employers if they do not sign the release until the calendar year after employment ends. Problems can be averted by drafting releases to say that if benefits could be paid in two different tax years, depending on when the employee signs the release, benefits will automatically be paid in the later year, no matter when the release is signed.

A new rule took effect April 1, 2011. If the payment window between an event and the deadline for payment overlaps the end of a calendar year, generally payments cannot begin until the year in which the payment window ends. For most plans, problems did not start until the fourth quarter of 2011, because the payment window for § 409A plans is usually 90 days or less, so payments in the first three quarters will not overlap two calendar years. But some plans do allow payments to be made either in the year of the event or the following two-and-a-half months. Penalties will be imposed if payments that were supposed to be made in 2012 were made in 2011, unless a correction procedure is available. The rule allows the payment window to be shortened from 90 days to a shorter period (e.g., 30 or 45 days), which could be a good tax move although it increases the problems of administration.

A further complication is that the Age Discrimination in Employment Act (ADEA) releases generally require 45 days' notice, and employees must be given seven days after signing to revoke their consent. Therefore, severance payments are generally reserved until after the revocation period ends. [McGuireWoods LLP, *Employee Release Provisions Present Section 409A Trap for the Unwary* (Aug. 31, 2011)]

When Allstate transitioned its workforce from employees to independent contractors, over 6,200 agents were terminated. They were offered four severance options. Three of them required releasing claims, including ADEA claims, in exchange for compensation and other benefits. The remaining option, the "base option," did not require claims releases, but provided only 13 weeks of severance and required additional noncompete and non-solicitation agreements. More than 400 of the former agents brought ADEA suits. Allstate said that the claims were barred by valid ADEA releases. The court asked the jury to determine if the releases signed by the first ten plaintiffs were knowing and voluntary. The jury found that eight of the releases were not knowing and voluntary, so the suit was allowed to proceed. When asked to overturn the jury findings on voluntariness, the District Court for the Eastern District of Pennsylvania held that the Older Workers Benefit Protection Action (OWBPA) requirements (see § 37.07) are a minimum, not a maximum requirement, so an ADEA waiver can be invalidated even if it satisfies the OWBPA. The district court said that when a court finds that a release is OWBPA-compliant, it must carry out a separate analysis of the validity of the release with respect to the totality of the circumstances. The analysis uses factors such as how clear and specific the release's language is; the plaintiff's education and business experience; how much time for consideration before signing was given; if the terms could be negotiated; and whether the signer received additional consideration over and above benefits he or she was already entitled to. The court said that the waivers were not voluntary because the release terms were non-negotiable and the agents were forced to sign waivers to preserve their financial security. If they were fired, they would have lost their investment in their agencies. The district court also said that Allstate made misrepresentations that affected the voluntariness of the waivers, even if the employees did not rely on the misrepresentations. The court said that a representation or omission is material if a reasonable person would have considered it important to the decision. [*Romero v. Allstate Ins. Co., et al.*, 2016 WL 2619853 (E.D. Pa. May 4, 2016), Colton D. Long, *What Is Knowing and Voluntary? One Court's Take on the Enforceability of ADEA Waivers*, Ogletree Deakins (June 10, 2016), available at Lexology.com]

The SEC said that it has received reports about language in severance agreements that inhibits disclosure of the employer's improper activities. The Dodd-Frank Act gives the SEC the power to prosecute employers for retaliatory actions and conditions in employment or severance agreements that forbid reporting wrongdoing violate public policy. The risk is that employees, who need severance benefits and a good reference, will accept questionable terms such as agreeing to pay over any award to the company, or agreeing to notify the company before contacting the SEC or other enforcement agency. [Ben DiPietro, *Companies Trying to Contain Potential Whistleblowers*, WSJ.com (May 14, 2013)]

§ 25.14 SARBANES-OXLEY AND DODD-FRANK NOTICES

The Sarbanes-Oxley Act of 2002 [Pub. L. No. 107-204] became law in July 2002. It is a wide-ranging piece of legislation; many of the issues it covers are outside the scope of this book because they involve corporate governance and accuracy in accounting. The Sarbanes-Oxley Act sets rules about "blackout periods" in individual account plans such as 401(k) plans. Sarbanes-Oxley Act § 306(b) requires the corporation to give advance notice to plan participants if their ability to control their plan accounts will be limited during a blackout period, and to explain in plain English what their rights are. [See 68 Fed. Reg. 3715 (Jan. 24, 2003) for DOL's Final Rule on this subject.] The Sarbanes-Oxley and Dodd-Frank Acts were targeted by the Trump administration for repeal or reform, so changes can be expected with respect to securities regulation and related issues.

The general rule is that the notice must be given at least 30 days, but not more than 60 days, before the start of the blackout period, although exceptions are recognized if circumstances make it unfeasible to give the notice at the regular time. The notice must disclose the start and end dates of the blackout period and explain the extent to which participants' ability to change their plan investments or get distributions or loans from the plan will be affected. The notice must be written, rather than verbal, but it can be distributed electronically.

Civil money penalties of up to $131 per participant per day can be imposed on the plan administrators as individuals if the required notice is not given (although DOL also has discretion to suspend penalties if the imposition of penalties would be unjust). The civil penalty was increased by the Federal Civil Monetary Penalties Inflation Adjustment Act Improvements Act of 2015, Pub. L. No. 114-74, and increased once again, to $133 per participant per day, by regulations published at 82 Fed. Reg. 8813 (Jan. 31, 2017).

The notice must be in writing—so a speech to the workforce wouldn't count—but it can be handed to participants, mailed, or distributed electronically. [See 68 Fed. Reg. 3729 (Jan. 24, 2003) for the text of a model notice that can be used to comply with the disclosure requirement] The model notice ("Important Notice Concerning Your Rights Under the [Plan Title] Plan") includes when the blackout period starts and ends; the reason it was imposed; the extent of the restrictions a warning of the need to consider investment strategy in light of the restrictions; and contact information for questions.

Sarbanes-Oxley is one of several statutes giving protection to whistleblowers: persons who disclose corporate wrongdoing to law enforcement authorities. Corporations are forbidden to retaliate against whistleblowers.

The most recent form of whistleblower protection derives from PPACA § 1558, which amends the Fair Labor Standards Act to protect employees against retaliation for disclosing violations of PPACA Title I. [OSHA Fact Sheet, OSHAFS-3641.pdf?, *Filing Whistleblower Complaints Under the Affordable Care Act*, <https://www.osha.gov/Publications/whistleblower/OSHAFS-3641 .pdf> (Jan. 2014) (last accessed Mar. 1, 2017)]

Although it is predominantly aimed at preventing future stock market crashes, the Dodd-Frank Wall Street Reform and Consumer Protection Act, Pub. L. No. 111-203, has some implications for corporate governance and corporate communications. The Dodd-Frank Act and the SEC's final whistleblower rules affect three aspects of corporate internal investigations: informing employees of internal corporate controls, carrying out investigations, and dealing with regulators.

For almost a decade, internal investigations were based on Sarbanes-Oxley, including its requirement for internal controls such as "up the ladder" reporting requirements and the role of independent directors, especially the audit committee, in ensuring compliance. Both internal and outside investigators need strategies for handling the consequences of reporting violations to regulators before there has been an in-house investigation. Employees must learn to use the internal reporting mechanisms.

The possibility that employees will go straight to regulators in the hope of collecting rewards puts pressure on businesses to report their own violations, to achieve cooperation credit, and to avoid negative response from shareholders. If the whistleblower goes to the company first and the company itself gives the SEC information leading to a successful investigation, the whistleblower gets credit for all of the information provided by the company. But if the whistleblower interferes with the internal investigation, the reward for the whistleblower will be reduced. It is unlawful to penalize whistleblowers whether or not the SEC ever investigates the complaint if the reported conduct actually violated the law or the whistleblower received an award. However, if an employee's knowledge of potential investigations comes from an attorney during an interview in an internal investigation, Rule 21F-4(b)(4)(vi) says that the information is not original and cannot support a whistleblower complaint. [Final Regulations, 76 Fed. Reg. 34,300 (June 13, 2011)]

On April 1, 2015, the SEC announced its first enforcement action under Rule 21F-17, a Dodd-Frank whistleblower rule. The SEC alleged that KBR, Inc.'s confidentiality agreement that was applied to witness interviews in internal investigations impeded protected whistleblower activity. Employees were not allowed to discuss internal investigations with third parties without prior approval from the company's legal department. The SEC said that it is a violation to maintain an agreement that could stop employees from reporting securities law violations to the SEC, even if the agreement is not enforced. KBR paid a $130,000 fine to settle the case but did not admit liability. A recent article recommends that a corporate officer send a notice to the entire workforce to remind them that confidentiality agreements do not bar reporting of violations to appropriate government agencies. [Cleary Gottlieb Steen & Hamilton LLP, *Action Required: How to Update Employee Confidentiality Provisions in Light of Recent SEC Enforcement Action* (Apr. 20, 2015), available at Lexology.com; Sharon B. Bauman et.al., *SEC Not Keeping Quiet About Employee Confidentiality Agreements*, Manatt Phelps & Phillips (Oct. 2, 2015), available at Lexology.com]

On August 16, 2016, the SEC announced that HealthNet Inc., had agreed to a $340,000 settlement under Rule 21-F17 because of severance agreements that prevented employees from receiving SEC whistleblower awards. [<https://www.sec.gov/news/pressrelease/2016-164.html>; see Lloyd B. Chinn, Harris M.

Mufson and Esther Y. Pak, *SEC Continues to Scrutinize Separation Agreements*, Proskauer Rose LLP (Aug. 17, 2016), available at Lexology.com]

See Chapter 39 for further discussion of whistleblower issues, as they existed at press time in 2017. Note that the Trump administration has announced an intention to repeal the Dodd-Frank Act. Changes in the whistleblower rule are a particular focus.

CHAPTER 26

PRIVACY ISSUES

§ 26.01   INTRODUCTION

For the employee, a significant part of each working day is spent in the workplace. The employer takes on some of the roles of the government. Do employees have the same civil rights with respect to their employers as citizens have with respect to their governments? In some ways, the answer is "Yes," but in other ways, the legal system balances the employer's need for honesty, sobriety, and efficiency in the workplace against the employees' desire for privacy. Many (if not most) constitutional rights are limitations on government power, not the power of private entities such as employers.

Many of the topics in this book are either completely regulated by federal laws, or federal laws are dominant, but in the privacy arena, state laws are very significant. Most states have laws on access and copying of personnel files, so that employees can view and copy their own files, but access by outsiders is restricted.

Some states (e.g., Connecticut and Massachusetts), give employees and former employees the right to review their personnel files (e.g., paper and electronic documents about their work and character). [Dabney D. Ware, *When a "Simple" Personnel File Request Is Not So Simple*, Foley & Lardner LLP (Sept. 9, 2013), available at Lexology.com]

The Supreme Court ruled that a corporation does not have a right of "personal privacy," using the ordinary definition of "personal." The Freedom of Information Act (FOIA) mandates that federal agencies make their records and documents publicly available. However, there is an exception for law enforcement records whose disclosure could reasonably be deemed an unwarranted invasion of personal privacy. A competitor of AT&T made a FOIA request for documents that AT&T gave the FCC during an investigation. Although the Third Circuit agreed with AT&T that the corporation had a privacy right that could prevent disclosure of the documents, the Supreme Court reversed in March 2011—although a corporation has the legal status of a "person," the concept of "personal privacy" is limited to human beings, and has traditionally been applied only to individuals. [*FCC v. AT&T*, 131 S. Ct. 1177 (2011)]

In a case brought by a pilot who concealed his HIV status (the FAA would not issue medical certificates to HIV-positive people) and who was fired and indicted for making false statements to a government agency when his status was uncovered in a federal investigation of invalid Federal Arbitration Act (FAA) certifications, the Supreme Court held that the suit could not be maintained against the federal Department of Transportation. The Privacy Act sets standards for management of federal records and allows suits for actual damages when an intentional or willful violation affects an individual. The Supreme Court held that the Privacy Act does not unequivocally authorize damages for mental and emotional distress—so there was no clear waiver of sovereign immunity, and the plaintiff could not sue the federal agency. [*FAA v. Cooper*, 132 S. Ct. 1441 (2012)]

As of late 2015, the states of Alabama, Alaska, Arizona, Florida, Georgia, Illinois, Indiana, Kansas, Kentucky, Louisiana, Maine, Minnesota, Mississippi, Nebraska, North Dakota, Oklahoma, Tennessee, Texas, Utah, and Wisconsin had "bring your gun to work" laws balancing employers' rights to control the presence of guns against employees' rights to carry licensed weapons. The typical statute obligates employers to allow employees to keep guns in their own vehicles in the parking lot, but allows them to forbid guns on the premises otherwise. [Tawny L. Alvarez, *Guns at Work in the Mass Shooting Debates*, Verrill Dana LLP (Dec. 3, 2015), available at Lexology.com]

At the end of 2016, Ohio adopted S.B. 199, allowing holders of concealed carry permits to keep firearms in their cars in their employers' parking lots. [Rina R. Russo, *Governor Kasich Signs Bill Prohibiting Ohio Employers from Banning Employees from Bringing Firearms on Company Property*, Benesch Friedlander Coplan & Aronoff LLP (Dec. 20, 2016), available at Lexology.com]

Tennessee's 2013 statute was amended in April 2015. It provides that employers are not liable for violent acts committed by a person who stored a weapon in a car pursuant to the statute. [Phylinda Ramsey, Constangy Brooks Smith & Prophete LLP, *Tennessee's "Guns In Trunks" Law: What Employers Need to Know Now* (Aug. 27, 2015), available at Lexology.com]

After the 2016 presidential election, many workplaces became the scene of heated political debate and many employees became involved in political activities. A recent article says that whether an employer can take adverse action against an employee or implement a ban on future political activities is a factual inquiry. It depends on state law, if the employee's conduct is legal, and if the employee is covered by a CBA or an individual employment contract. Several states, such as California, Colorado, Connecticut, Louisiana, New York, South Carolina, and Utah, forbid employers to take adverse action based on lawful off-premises activity. However, some statutes provide an exemption for public or religious employers, or situations in which the employee's political activity creates a material conflict with the employer's business. California, Colorado, and Louisiana forbid policies that keep employees from participating in politics or running for office. Under NLRA § 7, even in a non-union workplace, employees have a right to engage in concerted activities for mutual aid or protection—so political advocacy (including contacting legislators, giving testimony, and demonstrating) is protected if it relates to labor or working conditions such as paid sick leave, the minimum wage, or immigration reform. [Zoe M. Argento, *Dear Littler: Can A Boss Fire Someone for Off-Duty Political Activities?*, Littler Mendelson PC (Jan. 20, 2017), available at Lexology.com]

§ 26.02 POLYGRAPH TESTING

There are many problems with using polygraphy ("lie detector tests") in the workplace setting. These tests are expensive and not very reliable. In essence, they detect whether the test subject is nervous, and a practiced liar may be far less nervous than a timid but honest employee.

There are outright bans on polygraph testing in the workplace in Massachusetts, Michigan, Minnesota, and Oregon. Alaska, Connecticut, Delaware, Hawaii, Maine, Nebraska, New Jersey, New York, Rhode Island, West Virginia, and Wisconsin forbid employers to require, request, or even suggest testing. In one of these states, it violates public policy to fire someone for refusing to take a polygraph test, because the test cannot be demanded as a condition of employment. In Illinois, Maine, Michigan, Nevada, New Mexico, and Virginia, testing is not forbidden, but polygraph operators have to be licensed.

The Federal Employee Polygraph Protection Act of 1988. [Pub. L. No. 100-347, 29 U.S.C. § 2001; EPPA] forbids most private employers from using polygraph tests for pre-employment screening. In the workplace itself, it is permissible to polygraph employees but only in the course of an ongoing investigation about economic loss or injury to the employer's business. (In this context, drug tests and written or oral "honesty tests" are not considered polygraph examinations.)

Under the federal law, an employee can be asked to submit to polygraph testing only if the employer reasonably suspects the employee's involvement; the employee has access to the property involved in the inquiry; and the employer provides a written disclosure statement before the examination.

The employer is required to keep these statements on file for three years after they are issued.

The employer must advise the employee of his or her rights to seek representation (e.g., by a lawyer or union representative); to refuse the test, or stop a test that has begun; to review the questions before the test; and to review the results before the employer takes adverse employment action based on the results.

The employee must be notified that test results may be turned over to prosecutors.

Before August 1, 2016, the maximum civil penalty for violating the EPPA by unlawfully requiring a polygraph test, taking adverse employment action against an applicant or employee for refusing to take an unlawful test, interfering with a DOL investigation, or other violations of 29 C.F.R. 801.42(a), the federal polygraph rules, was $10,000. After August 1, 2016, the maximum penalty rises to $19,787. The maximum penalty after January 13, 2017, is $20,111. [DOL Wage and Hour Division, *Employee Polygraph Protection Act (EPPA)*, available at <https://www.dol.gov/whd/polygraph/> (undated, last accessed Mar. 1, 2017)]

In an EPPA suit, the Fourth Circuit held that the polygraph does not have to be the sole reason for the discharge for EPPA to be violated, but the employer is automatically liable (unless an exception applies) if the polygraph was the sole reason for the discharge. There is an exception for ongoing investigations of economic loss or injury to the employer's business, when the employer reasonably suspects the employee is involved. There is a Department of Labor regulation, 29

C.F.R. § 801.4(c), that says that it violates EPPA for an employer to receive polygraph information from law enforcement, but the Fourth Circuit held that the regulation is invalid, because employers have to participate actively to be held liable. [*Worden v. Suntrust Banks Inc.*, 549 F.3d 334 (4th Cir. 2008)]

An Eleventh Circuit case arose when a bank branch manager was fired after $58,000 disappeared from two ATMs at the bank. Surveillance cameras showed the plaintiff and his four employees repeatedly violated the bank policy requiring two people to be present whenever cash was handled or secure areas were accessed. The ex-manager was fired after refusing to take a polygraph test. The bank said that he was fired for violating the two-person access policy, not for his refusal. The Eleventh Circuit affirmed summary judgment for the defendant on the polygraph claim, holding that an inventory shortage by itself is not enough to justify a polygraph but if there is additional evidence of theft and reasonable suspicion, it is lawful to ask for the test. Mere access or opportunity is not tantamount to reasonable suspicion, but other evidence (such as information from co-workers) can justify a polygraph request. [*Cummings v. Washington Mut.*, 650 F.3d 1387 (11th Cir. 2011)]

In 2006, the Eleventh Circuit ruled that a company did not violate the Employee Polygraph Protection Act by accepting the union's proposal that miners who were fired for theft be allowed to take a polygraph test so they could clear their names and be rehired. The company was not liable because the proposal was for the employee's own good, and there was no evidence that the company exerted pressure on the union to propose the testing. Nor was the union liable, because it acted on behalf of its members. [*Watson v. Drummond Co.*, 436 F.3d 1310 (11th Cir. 2006)]

§ 26.03   DRUG USE IN THE WORKPLACE

[A]   A Pervasive Problem

Drug use in the workplace, and the effects of off-premises drug use at work, are significant problems. Many employers, because of the nature of their business (e.g., public transportation and public safety) or because they are federal contractors, are subject to legal mandates to maintain a drug-free workplace.

Drug users (primarily users of illegal drugs, but sometimes of prescription drugs) are likely to be impaired during working hours. They may use or even deal drugs in the workplace. If they can't afford to pay for their drugs, they are very likely to steal, embezzle, or commit industrial espionage to get drug money. Employees who are already breaking the law by illegal drug use may lose their inhibitions against committing other crimes as well.

Another implication of widespread drug use is that it makes it difficult for employers who drug test applicants to find enough potential workers who can pass the test. A recent article says that some employers are having trouble filling good jobs—or even have to refuse customer orders because they do not have enough workers. [Nelson D. Schwartz, *Economy Needs Workers, but Drug Tests Take a Toll,* NYTimes.com (July 24, 2017)]

In 2017, Quest Diagnostics reported that the number of positive drug tests in 2016 reached the highest level in 12 years. The most commonly found drug was marijuana, especially in Washington and Colorado (where recreational marijuana is legal). However, the percentage of tests that were positive for heroin dropped between 2015 and 2016. [Lauren Weber, *More American Workers Are Testing Positive for Drugs,* WSJ.com (May 16, 2017)]

Federal law requires drug testing for some categories of workers, such as truckers and workers in environmental cleanup. These jobs require hard physical labor, with high turnover. Employers find that many applicants fail drug tests, especially tests for abuse of prescription drugs.

Federal Department of Transportation (DOT) rules require mass transit, aviation, rail, and motor carrier workers who fail a drug test (or refuse to take one) to successfully complete drug treatment and pass a series of urine tests before they can return to any safety-sensitive duties. In 2008, the regulations were amended to require the urine testing to be done by direct inspection (by a person of the same sex as the worker). The D.C. Circuit upheld the regulations, finding that they were not arbitrary and capricious. It was rational for the DOT to require direct inspection because cheating on drug tests is so widespread. It was not irrational to impose the direct inspection method for return-to-duty tests but not examinations after an accident, because of the differing likelihood of cheating. There is a compelling public interest in transportation safety, so the procedure falls under the Fourth Amendment exception for warrantless searches that promote a compelling public interest. [73 Fed. Reg. 62910 (Oct. 22, 2008); see *BNSF Ry. Co. v. United States Dep't of Transp.,* 566 F.3d 200, 1378 (D.C. Cir. 2009)]

In May 2016, OSHA published a rule about electronic reporting of workplace injuries and illnesses. The rule says that blanket policies requiring post-injury drug tests in all cases may deter employees from reporting accidents. This rule does not state that employers will be penalized for across-the-board drug testing rules, but advocates drug testing only when there is a reasonable possibility that drug use contributed to the injury—and only when the drug test accurately detects impairment. The rule does not affect post-accident testing that is permitted by a Worker's Compensation law or required by federal regulation. OSHA's position is that employers should not provide incentives (such as throwing a pizza party for employees in a month when no accidents are reported) that could discourage injury reporting. Instead, OSHA prefers positive incentives for following safety rules. [81 Fed. Reg. 31854 (May 20, 2016); see Aaron R. Gelb et. al., *OSHA Issues New Illness and Injury Recordkeeping Rule That Casts Doubt upon Commonplace Employer Drug Testing and Safety Incentive Policies,* Vedder Price PC (May 19, 2016), available at Lexology.com]

The OSHA rules were unpopular with industry, and there was a Congressional hearing. OSHA postponed enforcement of the rule until November 1, 2016. A suit was filed to challenge the reporting rules, alleging that OSHA exceeded its statutory authority and promulgated the rules without an adequate regulatory analysis. The plaintiffs charged that the rule impairs employers' ability to investigate accidents, and conflicts with state-law requirements of post-accident testing. [*TEXO ABC/AGC v. Thomas*, No. 3:16-cv-1998 (N.D. Tex. Nov. 28, 2016); see Jennifer L. Curry, *OSHA Postpones Its New Workplace Injury and Illness Reporting Rule in the Face of Scrutiny and a New Lawsuit*, Ober Kaler (July 15, 2016), available at Lexology.com]

The rule was supposed to take effect August 10, 2016, but was delayed until November 1, 2016, then delayed again until December 1, 2016. The District Court for the Northern District of Texas asked for additional time to consider a motion for a preliminary injunction and declaratory judgment that the rule was unlawful because OSHA exceeded its statutory authority and acted arbitrarily and capriciously. The court refused to grant a temporary injunction, holding that the plaintiffs failed to show irreparable harm. Consequently, the rule took effect on December 1, 2016. [Mark A. Lies, II, *OSHA Again Delays Enforcement Date for New Workplace Injury and Illness Reporting Rule*, Seyfarth Shaw LLP (Oct. 19, 2016), available at Lexology.com; Ronald W. Taylor, *OSHA Recordkeeping Goes Public*, Venable LLP (May 19, 2016), available at Lexology.com; Shontell Powell and Melissa A. Bailey, *OSHA Pushes Back Enforcement Date for Anti-Retaliation Provisions Again*, Ogletree Deakins (Oct. 18, 2016), available at Lexology.com]

In many states, the Worker's Compensation administration has designed a model drug-free program design. Drug-free programs (which should always be reviewed by counsel before implementation) should create a rebuttable presumption that if employees refuse to be tested after a workplace injury or if a test is positive for alcohol or specified drugs, the substance is the cause of the injury and the injury is not compensable by Worker's Compensation. If there is an official notice to this effect, it should be posted in the workplace, and employees should be trained. In a union workplace, management should bargain to have this provision included in the collective bargaining agreement (CBA). Supervisors and managers should be trained to investigate all accidents, especially those that result in injury, and document why a drug/alcohol test was requested. Witness affidavits should be taken. Samples must be taken promptly (alcohol tests within eight hours of the event; drug tests within 32 hours of the event), and specimens should be processed by certified labs with a medical review officer. [Tony Fiore, *Drug-Free Workplace Policy Best Practices Checklist*, Kegler Brown Hill + Ritter (Oct. 19, 2015), available at Lexology.com]

Several West Virginia court decisions have held that drug testing is an undue invasion of privacy except in safety-sensitive jobs, or unless justified by the employer's reasonable good-faith objective suspicion of drug use. This line of cases allows testing of job applicants, on the grounds that they have a lower expectation of privacy than employees. The West Virginia Safer Workplaces Act was signed April 26, 2017, effective July 7, 2017, to reverse these cases. The statute authorizes workplace drug testing and allows employers to impose adverse employment consequences on employees who fail the test. Drug or alcohol testing can be required as a condition of hiring or continued employment. The act specifically articulates a state public policy of permitting employers to adopt a written policy for testing of applicants and employees. The statute also permits an employer use a positive test as a rationale for refusal to hire, firing, or requiring an employee to go through rehab. [Nixon Peabody LLP, *West Virginia Employer's Right to Drug-Free Workplace Outweighs Employee's Right to Privacy in the Workplace* (May 9, 2017), available at Lexology.com]

The abuse of legal substances, such as alcohol and prescription drugs, also creates problems for employers. A 2010 Sixth Circuit case was brought by seven employees fired for failing drug tests for prescription drugs. The Sixth Circuit ruled that six out of the seven plaintiffs were not disabled for the Americans with Disabilities Act (ADA) purposes (the seventh one might have had a record of disability). The ADA forbids imposition of qualification standards that tend to screen out individuals with a disability, unless those qualifications are job-related and consistent with business necessity. [*Bates v. Dura Auto Sys. Inc.*, 625 F.3d 283 (6th Cir. 2010)]

Aetna, in its role as administrator of FedEx's short-term disability plan followed the terms of FedEx's drug-free workplace policy and informed FedEx when an employee filed a disability claim involving substance abuse. The employee sued, alleging that Aetna violated its duties under ERISA. The Tenth Circuit upheld the grant of summary judgment for Aetna. The court held that following its agreement with a client could not constitute a breach of fiduciary duty. [*Williams v. FedEx Corp. Servs. & Aetna Life Ins. Co.*, 849 F.3d 889 (10th Cir. 2017); see Haynes and Boone LLP, *Disability Plan Can Disclose Disputed Substance Abuse Problem to Employer Without Violating ERISA* (Mar. 9, 2017), available at Lexology.com]

Alcohol tests are considered medical examinations, and "do you drink regularly" or "have you ever gone to AA?" are disability-related questions that cannot be asked before a job offer has been made. A question about amount/frequency of alcohol intake could elicit information about alcoholism, so it is also improper. Once a job offer has been made, disability-related questions and alcohol testing are acceptable—but if testing is done, it should be uniform, not limited to people who divulged a problem with alcohol. A job offer can be revoked on the basis of test results if the reasons are job-related and consistent with business necessity (the employer reasonably concludes, on the basis of objective evidence, that the person is unable to perform the essential functions of the job or poses a direct threat that could not be controlled by reasonable accommodation). Employees can be tested if the test is job-related and consistent with business necessity. It is lawful to have a rule against being under the influence of alcohol in the workplace. Alcohol levels can be tested based on a reasonable belief that an employee is under the influence, or after an accident. State law determines if random testing is allowed. [M. Tae Phillips, *Alcoholism and the ADA: The Dos and Don'ts of Alcohol Testing in the Workplace*, Ogletree Deakins (Aug. 14, 2015), available at Lexology.com]

Employees can be disciplined under employee procedures if the employee is impaired at work, or legal activities outside work harm work performance. For employees who are not impaired in the workplace and whose performance is not impaired, state law may forbid discipline. In Illinois, Minnesota, Missouri, Montana, Nevada, North Carolina, Tennessee, and Wisconsin, employers are forbidden to discriminate against employees based on use of legal products. California, Colorado, New York, and North Dakota forbid discrimination on the basis of activities that are legal. On August 28, 2014, the EEOC issued an Informal Discussion Letter that says that it probably violates the ADA to require employees who are (or who are perceived to be) alcoholics to refrain from alcohol use permanently. Last chance agreements can be used to have an employee get treatment, and can mandate workplace testing, but the agreement should not forbid the employee to use alcohol outside the workplace. [Michael D. Wong, *Alcohol Use— Can You Regulate and/or Discipline an Employee for Using Alcohol Outside of Work?*, SmithAmundsen LLC (Nov. 5, 2015), available at Lexology.com]

With respect to alcohol, the Eleventh Circuit upheld the termination of a truck driver the week after his diagnosis of chronic alcoholism, finding that the diagnosis precluded his performing essential functions of the job and therefore also preventing him from being a qualified individual. The employer's policy was not to employ anyone with a diagnosis of alcoholism within the past five years. Department of Transportation (DOT) regulations forbid employment of drivers with a current diagnosis of alcoholism. The plaintiff said that he had received rehabilitation treatment, and his doctor cleared him to return to work. The Eleventh Circuit said that a seven-day-old diagnosis is "current" in terms of DOT compliance, but did not indicate how long a time must elapse for the diagnosis to cease to be current. [*Jarvela v. Crete Carrier Corp.*, 754 F.3d 1283 (11th Cir. 2015) *vacated, reh'g granted* (Jan. 28, 2015)]

The District Court for the Southern District of New York ruled that time that New York City municipal employees were required to spend going to alcohol counseling was not work. Even if it had been work, it would be a non-compensable postliminary activity. [*Gibbs v. City of New York*, No. 12-cv-8340 (RA), 2015 U.S. Dist. LEXIS 7960 (S.D.N.Y. Jan. 23, 2015)]

Under the Federal Drug-Free Workplace Act, [41 U.S.C. § 701] companies with federal procurement contracts over $25,000 (and many companies are federal contractors) must certify to the contracting agency that they will provide a drug-free workplace. The contract will not be awarded if they do not make the certification. Federal contractors must create a drug-free awareness program and order employees to follow the program and give notice if they are convicted of a drug offense. The employer must notify the federal agency within 10 days of receiving an employee report. All employees must be penalized if they are convicted of workplace-related drug violations, and the contractor must continue to make a good-faith effort to keep drugs out of the workplace.

If the employer is a defense contractor, it must do regular drug tests on employees in "sensitive positions," in other words, those with access to classified information.

As of early 2017, 28 states (most recently, Arkansas, Florida, Georgia, Illinois, New York, North Dakota, Ohio, Pennsylvania) and the District of Columbia allowed medical marijuana. They were joined by West Virginia, whose Medical Cannabis Act was signed April 19, 2017, with patient cards to be issued starting July 1, 2019, on the basis of medical certification of 16 specified conditions. [Michael C. Griffaton, *Labor and Employment Alert: West Virginia Becomes the 29th State to Permit Medical Marijuana*, Vorys Sater Seymour and Pease LLP (Apr. 20, 2017), available at Lexology.com; Kathryn J. Russo, *West Virginia Enacts Medical Marijuana Law*, Jackson Lewis PC (Apr. 28, 2017), available at Lexology.com] Recreational marijuana was decriminalized to some extent in eight states (including Maine and Massachusetts).

Many state statutes make it clear that employers have no duty to accommodate medical marijuana use. However, if the state does forbid adverse employment action against medical marijuana users, taking such action might justify an ADA claim. The federal Drug Enforcement Administration has not changed its position that marijuana is a dangerous drug, and it is still included in Schedule I. [Laurie M. Weinstein, *Medical Marijuana and the Workplace*, Akerman LLP (Jan. 10, 2017), available at Lexology.com; Todd M. Torres, *Right to Light? Maine's New Marijuana Law Prohibits Employers from Discriminating Against Recreational Users*, Ogletree Deakins (Jan. 26, 2017), available at Lexology.com; Christopher J. Lalak, *Drug-Testing Dilemma: How Ohio's Forthcoming Medical Marijuana Law and a New OSHA Rule Combine to Make Headache for Employers*, Benesch Friedlander Coplan & Aronoff LLP (June 3, 2016), available at Lexology.com; Tawny L. Alvarez, *Maine Passes Recreational Marijuana Statute—What Does This Mean for Employers?*, Verrill Dana LLP (Nov. 9, 2016), available at Lexology.com; Tawny L. Alvarez, *Marijuana is Legal in Massachusetts . . . Now What*, Verrill Dana LLP (Nov. 9, 2016), available at Lexology.com]

In 2003, the U.S. Supreme Court held that even in a state that permits medical marijuana, an employer can penalize an employee who tests positive for drugs, and in 2005 the Supreme Court permitted the federal government to enforce the Controlled Substances Act's prohibition of medical marijuana even if the usage conforms to state law. [See also *Roe v. TeleTech Customer Care Mgmt. (Colorado), LLC*, 171 Wash. 2d 736, 257 P.3d 586 (Wash. 2011) and *Emerald Steel Fabricators Inc. v. Bureau of Labor & Indus.*, No. BOLI 3004, LA A130422 (Or. 2010)]

In some cases, medical marijuana users, although not violating the law, will develop problems associated with marijuana use that require referral to the Employee Assistance Program or other mental health/substance abuse resources.

Many cases have permitted firing employees who test positive for marijuana, even if they are certified for medical marijuana and did not use the drug in the workplace. There are cases of this type from the Sixth and Ninth Circuits and the District Court for the District of New Mexico, and from California, Colorado, Michigan, Washington, Oregon, Montana, and California. [*Garcia v. Tractor Supply Co.*, No. CV 15-00735 WJ/WPL, 2016 U.S. Dist. LEXIS 3494 (D.N.M. Jan. 7, 2016); see Alyssa M. Smilowitz, *New Mexico Court Holds Employers Need Not Accommodate Medical Marijuana Use*, Jackson Lewis PC (Jan. 13, 2016), available at Lexology.com; *Swaw v. Safeway, Inc.*, Case No. C15-939 MJP 2015 U.S. Dist. LEXIS 159761 (W.D. Wash. Nov. 20, 2015)]

In a closely watched 2015 case, the Colorado Supreme Court held that it was lawful to fire a medical marijuana user (in this case, a quadriplegic who uses marijuana to control pain and muscle spasms) who failed a drug test. The court said that marijuana use does not qualify as a protected off-duty "lawful activity," because it violates federal law. [*Coats v. Dish Network*, No. 13 SC 394, 2015 CO 44 (Colo. June 15, 2015)]

However, subsequent cases in Rhode Island, Massachusetts, and Connecticut have ruled in favor of persons terminated for medical marijuana use. [See, e.g., *Callaghan v. Darlington Fabrics Co.*, No. PC-2014-5680 (R.I. Super. Ct. May 23, 2017), discussed in Anthony S. Califano, Ariel D. Cudkowicz and Frederick T. Smith, *Refusal to Hire Medical Pot Users Just Got Riskier—At Least in Rhode Island*, Seyfarth Shaw LLP (July 25, 2017), available at Lexology.com; *Barbuto v. Advantage Sales & Mktg., LLC*, No. SJC-12226 (Mass. Sup. Jud. Ct. July 17, 2017); see Amanda G. Orcutt and Paul G. Lannon, *Medical Marijuana Use May Be Reasonable Accommodation Under Massachusetts Law*, Holland & Knight LLP (July 18, 2017), available at Lexology.com; *Noffsinger v. SSC Niantic Operating Co*, No. 3:16-cv-01938 (JAM) (D. Conn. Aug. 8, 2017); see Marjory D. Robertson, *Another Victory for Medical Marijuana Users at Work!*, Sun Life Financial Inc. (Aug. 10, 2017), available at Lexology.com]

The Sixth Circuit held in mid-2016 that an employer's decision not to grant an apprenticeship to an employee who used prescription opioids was not disability discrimination and did not violate the FMLA. An employee who was hired in 1996 was injured at work, and received workplace accommodations for nine years. His own doctor removed his work restrictions, but the company doctor maintained them in light of evidence that the employee was addicted to opioid painkillers. The plaintiff alleged that he was regarded as disabled because it was believed that his drug use limited the major life activity of working. The Sixth Circuit held that inability to do a particular job is not a major life activity, and not letting him climb or work at heights did not show that he was regarded as disabled. [*Ferrari v. Ford Motor Co.*, 826 F.3d 885 (6th Cir. 2016); see Catherine A. Cano, *Employer's Honest Belief That Employee Could Not Perform Job Due to Use of Opioid Medications Did Not Constitute Disability Discrimination,* Jackson Lewis PC (June 29, 2016), available at Lexology.com]

However, employers do not always prevail in drug cases. The District Court for the Eastern District of California permitted a suit to go forward when an employee was fired based on use of medical marijuana for anxiety. The employer's policy said that it would not discriminate on the basis of valid medical use of marijuana. The court held that a reasonable jury could find that the policy would rule out firing the employee. However, the claim under California's anti-discrimination statute was dismissed, because California law does not protect employees against termination for using marijuana. [*Shepherd v. Kohl's Dep't Stores*, No. 1:14-cv-0190-DAD-BAM, 2016 U.S. Dist. LEXIS 101279 (E.D. Cal. Aug. 2, 2016); see Manatt Phelps & Phillips LLP, *California Employee Can Pursue Termination Claims Over Marijuana Use* (Oct. 11, 2016), available at Lexology.com]

The Connecticut Supreme Court ruled in mid-2016 that, even though there is a well-defined public policy against workplace drug use, termination is not mandatory for public employees caught smoking marijuana during working hours. The plaintiff worked at the University of Connecticut Health Center; campus cops saw him smoking in a state-owned van. He had two bags of marijuana in his possession. He was arrested, but eventually criminal charges were dismissed. He was fired, grieved his termination, and was reinstated by the arbitrator, subject to a six-month unpaid suspension and an agreement to accept random drug tests post-reinstatement. The state supreme court held that, by agreeing to arbitration, the employer agreed to accept arbitrators' judgment. The court held that reinstating the employee did not violate public policy, which does not mandate termination in every case, and the employee's inappropriate conduct did not endanger public safety. [*State of Conn. v. Connecticut Emps. Union Indep.*, 322 Conn. 713, 142 A.3d 1122 (2016); see Kelly M. Cardin & Marc L. Zaken, *Connecticut's Highest Court Reinstates State Employee Fired for Smoking Marijuana at Work*, Ogletree Deakins (Aug. 29, 2016), available at Lexology.com]

[B] Case Law on Drug Testing

Pre-employment drug testing is more likely to be upheld by the courts than testing of current employees, on the theory that employees have a legitimate right of privacy. (For example, in late 2003 West Virginia ruled that because of the lower expectation of privacy, it is permissible to require job applicants to take a drug test even though state law bars mandatory testing of employees.) [*Baughman v. Wal-Mart Stores Inc.*, 215 W. Va. 45 (W. Va. 2003)]

About 20 million people have paruresis (inability to urinate when observed), and perhaps a new hire or employee's claim of a medical condition that makes it impossible to provide a urine sample should be treated as a request for disability accommodation. In 2011, the EEOC announced its position that bladder functions are a major life activity. But a refusal to be tested without an assertion of medical reasons does not require accommodation. When medical claims are made, consider whether blood, saliva, or hair could be sampled instead for drug testing. There might also be conditions (such as a private restroom with the water running) that could permit the applicant to give a sample. [*Linkous v. Craft Master Mfg., Inc.*, No. 7:10-CV-00107, 2012 WL 2905598 (W.D. Va. July 16, 2012); *Kinneary v. City of New York*, 601 F.3d 151 (2d Cir. 2010)]

The District Court for the Southern District of Ohio rejected an ADA claim of paruresis in 2015. Even if the condition was ADA-protected, the terminated employee did not inform the company of his condition or ask for accommodations. The company had an honest belief that he committed misconduct by not providing a urine sample. [*Lucas v. Gregg Appliances, Inc.*, Case No. 1:14-cv-70, 2015 U.S. Dist. LEXIS 49660 (S.D. Ohio W. Div. Apr. 15, 2015)]

The EEOC has settled two suits about job applicants who were denied hiring because they had End Stage Renal Disease and could not provide urine samples for pre-employment drug tests. Kmart agreed to pay $102,000 to the job applicant in January 2015 and to revise its policy to reasonably accommodate drug testing without a urine specimen; Wal-Mart paid $72,500 in October 2014. [*EEOC v. Kmart Corp.*, No. GJH-13-CV-2576, 2014 WL 5320957 (D. Md. Oct. 15, 2014); *EEOC v. Wal-Mart Stores East, LP*, 14-cv-00862, 2014 WL 6608585 (D. Md. Oct. 21, 2014)]

Employers must consult state law to see what types of drug tests are permitted. In late 2013, the District Court for the District of Maryland held that state law forbids private employers to perform breath alcohol tests on employees: the statute allows only testing of blood, urine, hair, and saliva. However, the plaintiffs' claim for invasion of privacy was dismissed, because the district court held that employees had no privacy interest in the information gathered through breath testing. [*Whye, et al. v. Concentra Health Servs., Inc.*, No. 12-cv-3432 (ELH) (D. Md. Sept. 24, 2013)]

The Tenth Circuit held in early 2017 that it was not unconstitutional to fire an employee for having a positive random cocaine test. The plaintiff worked with children in a safety-sensitive position (lieutenant in a juvenile detention center), so the search was reasonable and the need to protect children outweighed his individual privacy interest. The county's drug testing policies did not create an implied contract or protectable property interest in continued employment. The county's random drug testing policy says that discipline must follow the county's HR guide. The guide recommends only a suspension for first-time drug offenses—but makes it clear that employees still work at will and the county can legitimately bypass the suggested disciplinary procedure. The handbook's at-will provision made it clear that the plaintiff did not have a property interest in continued employment. [*Washington v. Unified Gov't of Wyandotte Cnty., Kansas*, 847 F.3d 119 (10th Cir. 2017); see Michael Clarkson & KyraAnne Gates, *Tenth Circuit Upholds Discharge of Employee in Safety-Sensitive Position Who Tested*

Positive for Cocaine, Ogletree Deakins (Feb. 16, 2017), available at Lexology .com]

Current substance abuse is not a disability for ADA purposes (although it is unlawful to discriminate against someone who is now clean and sober because of a past history of substance abuse).

The ADA has a safe harbor [42 U.S.C. § 12114(b)] for people who have completed a rehab program. Just entering a program isn't enough; the safe harbor is for people with a history of staying clean.

The Sixth Circuit affirmed summary judgment for a hospital that refused to hire two nurses who had restrictions on their licenses after being fired from another hospital for stealing narcotics, and participating in a state-approved drug rehabilitation program. It did not violate the ADA to apply a neutral practice of not hiring nurses with past or present license restrictions, whether or not the license restrictions were disability-related. [*Lopreato v Select Specialty Hosp.*, No. 15-5011, 2016 U.S. App. LEXIS 1825 (6th Cir. Jan. 29, 2016)]

Courts have come to varying conclusions as to whether or not a person fired for failing a drug test will be entitled to unemployment benefits, or will be deemed to have been terminated for misconduct.

The Michigan Court of Appeals permitted unemployment benefits to be awarded to employees terminated for positive marijuana tests as long as they are covered by the medical marijuana act. The court treated their termination as a "penalty" forbidden by the state's medical marijuana law. There was no evidence of use or possession in workplace. One employee was tested after a workplace injury; another one was fired by a health facility after a patient complaint and after the employee openly discussed her marijuana use. A recent article suggests adopting saliva or blood tests that detect active marijuana in the employee's bloodstream at work. [*Braska v. Challenge Mfg. Co.*, 861 N.W.2d 289 (Mich. App. 2015)]

Michigan governor Rick Snyder signed a bill creating a one-year pilot program under which workers who fail drug tests administered by an employer will not be entitled to unemployment benefits. Businesses are not required to notify the state if applicants refuse to be tested, or if they fail a drug test, but if they convey the information, the unsuccessful applicants will lose UI eligibility. [AP, *Michigan: Failing Drug Test Could Imperil Jobless Pay*, NYTimes.com (Oct. 29, 2013)]

But if the drug-free workplace policy is not explicit enough [*Comer*, Unempl. Ins. Rep. (CCH) ¶ 8635 (Mo. App. 2006)], or if the employer fails to demonstrate the validity of the test itself [*Owen County*, Unempl. Ins. Rep. (CCH) ¶ 8607 (Ind. App. 2006)], then benefits might be available.

Under the Middle Class Tax Relief and Job Creation Act of 2012, states are allowed to require drug tests and deny benefits to unemployment benefit applicants who were fired for unlawful use of a controlled substance or who work in an occupation where drug testing is regularly performed. An Obama-era regulation, 20 C.F.R. § 620, set out only eight categories of occupation as being subject to regular testing. On March 14, 2017, the Senate approved J.R. 42, which had already passed in the house. J.R. 42 eliminates the limitation of drug testing to those eight occupations. The DOL will have to determine which occupations regularly conduct drug testing, but will not be able to reinstate the Obama-era regulation or issue a substantially similar one without Congressional approval. [Joshua D. Bortnick, *Congress Passes Resolution to Block Obama Administration Restrictions on Drug Testing Those Seeking Unemployment Benefits*, Ogletree Deakins (Mar. 17, 2017), available at Lexology.com]

Drug tests (and fitness for duty exams and employment physicals) create information that is Protected Health Information (PHI) for Health Insurance Portability and Accessibility Act (HIPAA) purposes. The doctor cannot disclose the test or exam results to the employer without the employee's consent. However, it is allowed for a provider to condition performing the test on the employee's consent to disclosing the results. It does not violate HIPAA for the employer to make continued employment contingent on disclosure of the results. HIPAA allows disclosure of the results if the examination is part of medical surveillance of the workplace, or to report to OSHA or state investigators about work-related injuries. HIPAA also allows health care providers to disclose PHI as needed to comply with Workers' Compensation laws. [Kim C. Stanger, *HIPAA: Disclosing Exam Results to Employers*, Holland & Hart LLP (Sept. 22, 2015), available at Lexology.com]

[C]   Tobacco Issues

Tobacco is a drug, albeit a legal one. Some employers are providing incentives to encourage employees to stop smoking (e.g., paying for smoking cessation classes or offering a bonus); others are imposing penalties on those who smoke (e.g., higher insurance premiums), even outside the workplace, or requiring nicotine testing as part of the pre-employment drug test. Many of the states have "lawful activities" statutes that protect employees who smoke away from the worksite from discrimination. However, some companies refuse to hire smokers; others fire employees who are found to smoke (even off-site), and sometimes employers deliberately refrain from asking job applicants because they assume smokers will lie. [Jeremy Smerd, *Smoker? Can't Work Here, More Firms Say*, workforce.com (Nov. 9, 2007) (benefitslink.com)]

§ 26.04   CRIMINAL RECORD AND CREDIT CHECKS

A federal law, the Fair Credit Reporting Act (FCRA), [15 U.S.C. § 1681] as amended by the Consumer Credit Reporting Reform Act of 1996, [Pub. L. No. 104-208] governs the access of businesses to credit reports. Although credit reports are most commonly used in the context of loans or merchandise sales, it is also fairly common for potential employers to run a credit check before making a job offer.

Under the FCRA, employers must notify applicants before they seek credit information as part of the application process. A civil penalty is imposed for ordering a credit check without the mandatory notification. The employer must also notify applicants and employees before any negative employment-related action is taken on the basis of an investigative credit report.

The FCRA allows credit reporting agencies to disclose the information they have gathered to companies that use the information for "employment purposes," i.e., evaluating the subject of the credit report for employment, promotion, retention as an employee, or reassignment. The reporting agency is allowed to furnish a report discussing the job applicant's or employee's creditworthiness, standing, character, and reputation.

The FTC and Equal Employment Opportunity Commission (EEOC) published joint guidance reminding employers that the FCRA requires safeguards if an employer obtains a credit or criminal background report from a company that compiles background information. The applicant or employee must be given written notice that this information might be used in employment decisions and his or her written consent must be obtained. If an investigative report (based on personal interviews) is ordered, the applicant or employee must be informed of the right to information about the investigation. If adverse actions are taken based on information from a profiling company, the employer must give the applicant or employee a copy of the FTC's summary of FCRA rights, and must give contact information for the profiling company. [EEOC/FTC, *Background Checks: What Employers Need to Know*, <http://www.eeoc.gov/eeoc/publications/background_checks_employers.cfm> (Mar. 2014)]

The Consumer Financial Protection Bureau (CFPB) took enforcement action against General Information Services and its affiliate, e-Background-checks.com, for violating the FCRA by failing to give applicants the legally required safeguards. The CFPB found that some reports contained inaccurate information and the companies did not follow FCRA requirements for protection against inaccuracies (screening out common names; using consumer dispute data to identify errors; removing judgments more than seven years old). The CFPB ordered the companies to make $10.5 million in restitution to affected consumers and pay a civil penalty of $2.5 million. [Donnelly L. McDowell, *CFPB Obtains $13M FCRA Settlement with Employee Background Screening Providers*, Kelley Drye & Warren LLP (Nov. 10, 2015), available at Lexology.com]

Federal (and California) laws have additional requirements for background checks in addition to the rules for consumer credit reports. California regulates background checks performed by an employer in-house in addition to those performed by a consumer reporting agency. The FCRA defines an investigative consumer report as one containing information that derives from personal interviews about the target's character or reputation; California law applies to all third-party collection of information obtained in any way. California employers seeking investigative consumer reports must disclose that the report will be obtained; that it may contain information about character and reputation; the scope of the investigation; how to contact the investigating agency; and a notice of the right to inspect the agency's file. The target is entitled to request a free copy of the report, which must be provided within three days of the time it is provided to the employer. [Pamela Q. Devata and Dana Howells, *Checking Out Applicants (Part 2): Using Consumer Reporting Agencies for Background Checks*, Seyfarth Shaw LLP (June 27, 2014), available at Lexology.com]

The EEOC lost a case against Kaplan Higher Education Corporation. The EEOC alleged that Kaplan's use of credit checks had a disparate impact on African-American applicants. However, the Sixth Circuit held that the methodology of the EEOC's expert witness for identifying the race of applicants was deficient, and lacked scientific accuracy and verification. Furthermore, the EEOC itself uses a similar credit check process for applicants for jobs with the agency. [*EEOC v. Kaplan Higher Educ. Corp.*, 748 F.3d 749 (6th Cir. 2014); semble *EEOC v. Freeman*, 951 F. Supp. 2d 783 (D. Md. 2013). The article says that the states of California, Colorado, Connecticut, Hawaii, Illinois, Maryland, Nevada, Oregon, Vermont, and Washington, and the cities of Chicago and Madison, Wisconsin have enacted restrictions on the use of credit history by employers. Some of these statutes permit exceptions for job-related information, or for situations when applicants and employees are informed that their credit histories will be consulted.]

As a result of the Dodd-Frank Act, Pub. L. No. 111-203, starting July 21, 2011, employers have been required to inform job applicants whenever the employer has obtained the applicant's credit scores, and those scores have had an adverse effect on the employer's decision on the application.

The 2003 legislation, the Fair and Accurate Credit Transactions Act (FACTA; Pub. L. No. 108-159) amends 15 U.S.C § 1681a, enacting a new subsection (x) under which a communication will not be treated as a consumer report (and therefore will not be subject to FCRA requirements) if it is a job-related communication not related to the creditworthiness of the individual. The communication must be made to the employer as part of an investigation of suspected workplace misconduct, or under the employer's pre-existing policies or under any law or regulation. To qualify for the exemption, the information must be disclosed only to the employer or to government officials or self-regulatory officials—unless broader disclosure is mandated by law. If the employer uses the information as the basis of any adverse action against the subject of the investigation, the subject must be furnished a summary of the information. The employer, however, is not obligated to disclose the sources of the information.

Under the Intelligence Reform and Terrorism Prevention Act of 2004, Pub. L. No. 108-458 (Dec. 17, 2004), private employers can access the FBI criminal records database to obtain information about employees or applicants for private security jobs. Section 6403 of the statute provides that, on the written consent of the employee or applicant, the employer can submit fingerprints or other means of identification to the state's investigative agency for a background check. (States can opt out of the background check system by passing a law, or if the state governor issues an order to this effect.) The state investigative agency will notify the employer if the applicant or employee has been convicted of a felony, an offense involving dishonesty, or a false statement in the previous 10 years, and whether there have been any unresolved felony charges in the previous year. The employer has an obligation to disclose the information to the employee. [See also § 23.08]

The Supreme Court unanimously upheld the standard background check procedure that the Department of Commerce requires of government contractors. The standard background check requires employees to answer whether they used, possessed, supplied, or manufactured illegal drugs in the past year. If so, they must provide information about any treatment or counseling received. Employees are also required to sign a release for personal information from schools and employers. The government submits a questionnaire to employees' references, asking about adverse information and reasons to question the employee's honesty or truthfulness. The Supreme Court found these inquiries reasonable, and the Privacy Act limits disclosure of the information to the public. [*NASA v. Nelson*, 562 U.S. 134 (2011)]

The EEOC's position is that a blanket refusal to hire based on the applicant's credit reports or criminal records is illegal if it has a disparate impact on racial minorities. [EEOC Enforcement Guidance, *Consideration of Arrest and Conviction Records in Employment Decisions Under Title VII of the Civil Rights Act of 1964*, <http://www.eeoc.gov/laws/guidance/arrest_conviction.cfm> (Apr. 25, 2012) (last viewed Mar. 29, 2016)]

At least two courts rejected the EEOC's litigating position on this subject. The District Court for the District of Maryland granted summary judgment for the employer, finding that the EEOC's statistical expert was unreliable; the Sixth Circuit upheld the district court's sanctions of almost $752,000 imposed on the EEOC for continuing to litigate a case after it became evident that the defendant did not maintain an unlawful company-wide ban on hiring persons with felony records. [*EEOC v. Freeman*, No. 09-CV-2573 (D. Md. Aug. 9, 2013); *EEOC v. PeopleMark*, 732 F.3d 584 (6th Cir. 2013); see Brian D. Hall, *EEOC's Campaign Against Criminal Background Checks Takes Recent Hits*, Porter Wright Morris & Arthur LLP (Oct. 10, 2013), available at Lexology.com; Joann Coston-Holloway, *EEOC Provides Clarification on Use of Criminal History Information in Hiring Decisions*, Baker Donelson Bearman Caldwell & Berkowitz PC (Jan. 16, 2014), available at Lexology.com]

Although the Third Circuit was uncomfortable with "bright-line" tests (refusal to hire any person with a criminal conviction), the court accepted the employer's business necessity defense because the plaintiff did not rebut testimony about risk due to hiring convicted persons. [*El v. Se. Penn. Transit Auth.*, 479 F.3d 232 (3d Cir. 2007)]

The Fifth Circuit ruled in mid-2016 that the EEOC's enforcement guidance on background checks is a "final agency rule" that can be challenged in court by the state of Texas (which alleged that the EEOC rule conflicts with Texas law forbidding hiring people with criminal records for certain types of jobs). The Fifth Circuit held that the state had standing to sue because state agencies' hiring is subject to the EEOC guidance, and increasing the regulatory burden on employers when they hire is an injury that can be redressed by the court system. [*Texas v. EEOC*, No. 14-10949 (5th Cir. June 27, 2016); see Gerald L. Maatman et. al., *Don't Mess with Texas: EEOC's Criminal Background Check Guidance Subject to Challenge*, Seyfarth Shaw LLP (June 28, 2016), available at Lexology.com] But this opinion was withdrawn, and the Fifth Circuit remanded the case to the District Court to the Northern District of Texas, reflecting an unrelated Supreme Court decision about the definition of "final agency action." [*State of Texas v. EEOC*, 838 F.3d 511 (5th Cir. 2016); see Gustavo A. Suarez, *The Texas Two-Step: Fifth Circuit Withdraws Ruling That Allowed Texas to Proceed with EEOC Background Check Lawsuit*, Ogletree Deakins (Sept. 30, 2016), available at Lexology.com. The Supreme Court case is *Army Corps of Engineers v. Hawkins*, 136 S. Ct. 1807 (May 31, 2016)]

A "ban the box" law forbids employers (depending on the statute, sometimes only public employers or both public and private employers) to ask questions about criminal convictions on initial job applications. See § 23.08 for more discussion of this issue.

By mid-2017, more than two-thirds of the U.S. population lived in places with ban the box laws. There were 27 states that forbade criminal-record inquiries in public employment. Ten states: California, Connecticut, Hawaii, Illinois, Massachusetts, Minnesota, New Jersey, Oregon, Rhode Island, and Vermont, and over two dozen cities forbade private employers to ask about convictions before a job offer is extended. [Garen Dodge, *"Ban the Box" and Background Checks—Recent Trends and Movements*, Sheppard Mullin Richter & Hampton LLP (July 12, 2017), available at Lexology.com; Jennifer B. Rubin, *California Joins the Ban-the-Box Bandwagon*, Mintz Levin Cohn Ferris Glovsky and Popeo PC (July 5, 2017), available at Lexology.com]

Depending on the terms of the statute, employers might be allowed to make criminal history inquiries after the initial application; after the applications have received an initial screening; after a person has been selected for a job interview; after the interview; or only after a conditional job offer has been made. [Philip L. Gordon and Zoe M. Argento, *San Francisco's Board Of Supervisors "Bans The Box" and Further Complicates Criminal History Checks by the City's Employers*, Littler Mendelson (Feb. 10, 2014), available at Lexology.com]

Some states, e.g., Hawaii, say that employer can consider convictions only if they bear a rational relationship to the job duties and responsibilities. Hawaii Supreme Court dealt with relationship of drug conviction to jobs. Shimose was denied a job as a radiology technician because he had a conviction for possession with intent to distribute crystal meth. The Hawaii Supreme Court denied summary judgment for the employer, finding a lack of proof of rational relationship between the offense and the job. The defendant said that radiology techs have access to drugs and syringes and could steal medication or sell drugs to patients but the court said that the drugs the patient would work with were not controlled. The court also said that there is no reason for a blanket disqualification for working with the elderly or children because there is no necessary connection between drug convictions and child or elder abuse. [*Shimose v. Hawaii Health Sys. Corp.*, 345 P.3d 145 (Haw. 2015)]

§ 26.05 GENETIC TESTING

In addition to a variety of state laws, Congress adopted protection against genetic discrimination in the Genetic Information Nondisclosure Act (GINA; Pub. L. No. 110-233). The statute forbids discrimination on the basis of genetic predisposition to disease, but not disease already manifested. Genetic discrimination cases require use of the Title VII process, including the requirement of a Right to Sue letter. Title I of GINA applies to group health plans maintained by private employers, as well as to unions, government employers, and insurers. Title II applies to entities covered by Title VII. GINA Title II prohibits the use of genetic information in employment and restricts the acquisition and disclosure of genetic information. The EEOC was empowered to issue regulations under Title II of GINA, and to enforce it, effective November 21, 2009, for employers of 15 or more employees.

The EEOC proposed regulations on March 2, 2009, clarifying the definition of "genetic information" and providing guidance on proper use of the information. A party subject to Title II of GINA is permitted to obtain genetic information only if it was:

- Acquired inadvertently (e.g., volunteered by the employee, or overheard);

- Aggregate information, not individually identifiable, stemming from genetic counseling at a wellness program;

- Information given to an employer to certify eligibility for leave;

- Information from genetic monitoring required by law (e.g., by OSHA);

- Voluntarily authorized in writing by the employee.

There is a limited exception for information obtained by law enforcement or the military to assist in genetic identification, and for publicly available information.

In order to prevent genetic markers for a disease being treated as preexisting conditions, the regulations define "manifestation of disease" as a condition that has been or reasonably could be diagnosed by a health care professional. Therefore, the presence of a genetic marker, even one that assures that the individual is certain to develop the disease in the future, is not a manifestation of disease.

However, even if the employer has obtained the information legitimately, the information must be kept confidential and must not be used to discriminate. Genetic information (except publicly available information) must be kept in a separate, confidential file rather than in an ordinary personnel file.

Genetic information can be disclosed only to the person it relates to; to an occupational health researcher carrying out research pursuant to federal regulations; or in response to a court order that specifically calls for information. However, information may not be disclosed in response to a discovery request that is not under a court order (e.g., a party in a lawsuit asks for the information). Disclosure is permitted to government officials assessing the company's GINA compliance, in connection with a request for leave, or to officials investigating contagious disease or an imminent hazard of death or life-threatening illness.

Employers should make sure that doctors avoid questions about family medical history in post-offer, pre-employment medical examinations and fitness for duty exams. Nor may genetic information be obtained in connection with the interactive process of establishing reasonable accommodation to disability.

■ **TIP:** The EEOC says that the best practice for an employer asking for documentation of disability is to state in the request that genetic information, including family medical history, should not be provided.

Employers were required to begin posting the official GINA information no later than November 21, 2009. [74 Fed. Reg. 9056 (Mar. 2, 2009)]

The EEOC published a final rule on recordkeeping requirements under GINA. As of April 3, 2012, companies with 15 or more employees must retain all personnel and employment records relating to GINA for at least one year. If charges are filed under GINA, relevant documents must be retained until final disposition of the case. If an employee is involuntarily terminated, records must be kept for a year after termination. The relevant documents in this context include requests for accommodation; application forms; records of hiring, promotion, demotion, transfer, layoff, and termination; and records about terms of employment, e.g., pay, training, and tenure. [77 Fed. Reg. 5396 (Feb. 3, 2012), finalizing the Notice of Proposed Rulemaking, 76 Fed. Reg. 31892 (June 2, 2011).]

On January 17, 2013, HHS published a final rule covering the application of the HIPAA privacy rule to GINA Titles I (health coverage) and II (employment). The final rule specifies that genetic information is considered health information, which cannot be used for insurance underwriting purposes other than for long-term care insurance policies. [Katherine Georger, *New HIPAA Final Rule Implements GINA Restriction on Use and Disclosure of Genetic Information for Underwriting Purposes*, Holland & Hart LLP News Update (Jan. 23, 2013) (benefitslink.com)]

The EEOC published final rules about the use of genetic information in wellness programs; the rules took effect July 18, 2016. Wellness programs that ask employees and their spouses for genetic information are allowed to request genetic information from employees' spouses in return for incentives, including financial incentives that do not exceed 30% of the cost of self-only insurance coverage. [81 Fed. Reg. 31143 (May 17, 2016). See Rachel Emma Silverman, *EEOC Issues New Rules for Wellness Programs*, WSJ.com (May 16, 2016); Corie Hengst, *EEOC Announces Final Rules for Wellness Programs*, plansponsor.com (May 16, 2016)]

As a result of the Federal Civil Monetary Penalties Inflation Adjustment Act Improvements Act of 2015 (part of Pub. L. No. 114-74), GINA penalties increase significantly as of August 1, 2016. For example, the penalty imposed on EGHP sponsors and health insurers for violating the ERISA rules dealing with genetic information rises from $100 to $110 per day. The minimum penalty for a minor failure to satisfy the requirements for securing genetic information is $2,745 if the violation is corrected before the DOL issued a notice. If the failure is more serious and is not corrected before notice from the DOL, the minimum penalty is $16,473. The penalty for all unintentional failures of GINA requirements is capped at $549,095. [81 Fed. Reg. 29765 (May 12, 2016); 81 Fed. Reg. 42491 (June 30, 2016)]

The EEOC's first GINA case, against Fabricut, alleging that employees were sent to a particular laboratory for physicals and were required to complete a family history questionnaire, was settled via a $50,000 consent decree.

§ 26.06 SEARCHES AND SURVEILLANCE

[A] Constitutional Limits on Employees

Although the Constitution puts limits on unreasonable searches and seizures, the focus is on the activities of public agencies such as the police and the military. Therefore, it is very unlikely that the actions of a private employer would have a constitutional dimension, or that the employee would be able to invoke the Fourth Amendment as protection against searches and seizures.

It is becoming more common for employers to use tracking devices (such as sensors that employees wear around their necks, or placed on furniture) to find out how employees work and what can be done to enhance productivity. Companies that use these devices handle privacy issues by letting employees opt out of tracking or by pointing out that employees' movements can already be tracked with smartphones and ID badges. Privacy issues could arise when GPS data is used to investigate workplace misconduct. Tracking of company vehicles is likely to pass scrutiny but there might be problems with tracking employees' personal vehicles used for work purposes. Two New York state cases have held that taxi drivers had no legitimate expectation of privacy in GPS data from cabs; even if there had been a privacy interest, the city had a legitimate interest in detecting overcharges. [*Tracking Sensors Invade the Workplace*, WSJ.com (Mar. 6, 2013); Karla Grossenbacher, *The Legality of Tracking Employees by GPS*, Seyfarth Shaw LLP (Feb. 16, 2016), available at Lexology.com]

Monitoring of employees' movements by GPS can be used to verify routes and locations (seeing that orders are delivered on time, for example) and to make sure that employees obey the speed limit and other traffic laws. Monitoring can check time records and overtime hours; locate stolen vehicles; and make sure that employees are not in places they ought not to be during working hours. To balance the employer's information needs against employees' right to privacy, GPS information should only be collected on topics relevant to job performance; tracking off-duty activity could be illegal. State law should be consulted. For example, California forbids the use of an electronic tracking device without the owner's consent, so tracking company vehicles is more likely to be upheld than tracking employees' smartphones.

A GPS tracking policy should explain the business benefits of the policy (for example, improved customer service and safety; better time records) and give clear notice of the employer's right to monitor employees' travels in company vehicles. The policy should explain how the employer will use and safeguard the data, forbid disabling GPS devices without permission, and get the employees' signed acknowledgment that they have received a copy of the policy. Employer best practices include monitoring only during working hours and refraining from collecting information about employees' private lives. Data must be stored securely. In a union workplace, depending on the language of the CBA and the course of dealing, it may be necessary to engage in collective bargaining before adopting GPS tracking. [Jennifer M. Holly, *There's An App for That: Considerations in Employee GPS Monitoring,* Seyfarth Shaw LLP (Jan. 26, 2017), available at Lexology.com]

However, an employer's surveillance activities might constitute an invasion of privacy, which could furnish grounds for a suit by an employee.

An employer can legitimately order a workplace search if there is a good reason in the first place (such as getting evidence of embezzlement, theft of products, or other work-related misconduct) and the scope of the search is appropriate to satisfying that purpose. But, because the employer controls the workplace but employees control their own personal possessions such as coats and handbags, get legal advice about how to handle a search.

Surveillance programs are most likely to survive legal challenge if:

• They are created in response to a real problem (e.g., inventory shrinkage) or a real threat (e.g., potential employer liability);

• Employees are accurately informed of the purposes and content of the program;

- Surveillance is restricted to the least intrusive method that is still effective.

Workplace video surveillance is governed by state privacy laws. Courts usually focus on nature of the intrusion on reasonable expectations of privacy, and if the employer had legitimate business justification for surveillance. The privacy expectation analysis involves factors such as the physical location that was surveilled and its relationship to the workplace as a whole. One end of the spectrum is an open, accessible space where work is performed in full view. The other end is a restricted-access, limited-view space for inherently personal activities, such as a bathroom or locker room. In between are employee common areas that are not open to the general public where there can still be an expectation of privacy, especially areas assigned to an employee, such as a cubicle or desk. Courts have rejected surveillance used for unprotected reasons, such as harassment or prurient curiosity, but usually support video surveillance for a reasonable objective, where information is restricted to those with a need to know. In union workplaces, surveillance is probably a term and condition of employment that cannot be changed unilaterally, and video surveillance must not impair employees' right to organize and improve working conditions. If the recording includes sound as well as video, federal and state eavesdropping/wiretapping laws apply, and consent of at least one party is probably required. [Kevin Koronka and Joel Bagby, *Cat's Away, Mice Will Play: Workplace Video Surveillance*, Husch Blackwell LLP (May 5, 2015), available at Lexology.com. See, e.g., *Consolidated Freightways v. Cramer*, 534 U.S. 1078 (2002); *Kline v. Sec. Guards Inc.*, 386 F.3d 246 (3d Cir. 2004) *Brewers & Maltsters v. NLRB*, 414 F.3d 36 (D.C. Cir. 2005); *Nat'l Steel Corp. v. NLRB*, 324 F.3d 928 (7th Cir. 2003)]

When employees take FMLA leave or make a disability claim, the employer may order video surveillance—e.g., to determine if employees are performing tasks that they claim are impossible because of job-related injuries. Such surveillance is usually upheld by the courts if the employer is deemed to have honest doubts about the validity of the leave request. For example, *Vail v. Raybestos*, 533 F.3d 904 (7th Cir. 2008) upheld surveillance of an employee who took leave for migraines and was found to run a lawn service on the side. In *Crouch v. Whirlpool*, 447 F.3d 984 (7th Cir. 2006), the Seventh Circuit upheld the validity of videotaping a suspected leave abuser, who was caught doing yard work and flying to Las Vegas when he was off work due to a knee injury. The Pennsylvania Superior Court ruled in mid-2010 that it was not an invasion of privacy to tape a WC claimant while he was praying at his mosque, given WC claimants' diminished expectation of privacy caused by the knowledge that they might be investigated. [*Tagouma v. Investigative Consultant Servs. Inc.*, 2010 Pa. Super. 147 (Pa. Super. 2010)]

The District Court for the Southern District of California dismissed all claims in a class action brought by 12,400 current and former Apple employees in California. Employees in all 52 retail stores in California were subject to mandatory checks of bags, purses, backpacks, and briefcases whenever they left the store. Employees could be disciplined for leaving the store without being searched. Employees said that they often had to wait to find someone to do the search. The district court dismissed FLSA claims because it was a security screening after employees had clocked out; it was not a compensable principal activity. The California state-law claims were dismissed; the court said that employees could avoid being searched by not bringing bags to work. [*Frlekin v. Apple Inc.*, No: 3:13cv03451, 2015 U.S. Dist. LEXIS 151937 (N.D. Cal. Nov. 7, 2015); see Shar Bahmani, *How Do You Like Them Apples? Apple, Inc. Wins Dismissal of Class Action Brought by Its Employees at Retail Stores in California*, Squire Patton Boggs (Nov. 11, 2015), available at Lexology.com]

[B] Wiretapping

Wiretapping, and other forms of interception of wire, oral, and electronic communications, including e-mail (or electronic or mechanical interception of conversations) are covered by the federal Omnibus Crime Control and Safe Streets Act of 1968. [18 U.S.C. §§ 2511 *et seq.*] Interceptions by the employer are regulated. Interceptions are prohibited only if the employee had a reasonable expectation that the communication would not be subject to interception.

For instance, if a telephone salesperson has known from the beginning of the job that contact with customers is subject to monitoring, there would be no reasonable expectation of privacy. But even if interception of calls is legitimate, the employer must cease the interception if it is clear that a particular call is personal and not business-related. One of the parties to a communication has a right to intercept it; so does anyone with explicit or implicit consent to intercept.

The federal statute imposes penalties for improper interception that can be as high as $10,000. Punitive damages can be imposed on an employer that acted wantonly, recklessly, or maliciously.

[C] Internet and E-Mail Monitoring

Apart from the fact that employees are supposed to use the company computer system for work, employee e-mails can subject the employer to liability (in the context of sexual or racial harassment, for example, or concealment of improprieties). See § 27.06 for discussion of the human resources implications of social networking. State and federal wiretap statutes typically include a "provider exception," under which the provider of communications is allowed to intercept messages on the system. An employer is clearly a provider when it owns the equipment on which the employees communicate.

Most employers have broad policies that warn employees that e-mails can be monitored, usually stated in the employee handbook or displayed on the log-in screen for the e-mail system. Software is now available to mechanize e-mail monitoring, so the IT department will not have to do so manually. E-mail monitoring usually begins only after there has been a problem, such as an allegation of harassment or misuse of proprietary information. Employees should probably be informed that their e-mail has been read, which has the effect of reinforcing the employer's e-mail policy. [Shannon Green, *When Should Employers Be Monitoring Employee Email?*, Corporate Counsel (Mar. 13, 2013) (law.com)]

In late 2007, the NLRB voted 3-2 to permit employers to restrict the use of the company e-mail system for union organizing campaigns and distributing union news, on the grounds that personal use of the e-mail system can be restricted. However, to be valid, a ban on personal use must be evenly applied, not limited to union applications. [*The Guard Publishing Company d/b/a The Register-Guard & Eugene Newspaper Guild, CWA Local 37194*. Cases 36–CA–8743-1, 36–CA–8849-1, 36–CA–8789-1, and 36–CA–8842-1] The D.C. Circuit upheld the NLRB's Unfair Labor Practice decision when a newspaper disciplined the union president for sending three union-related e-mails to co-workers. Although the newspaper's e-mail policy forbade using the system for commercial ventures, religious or political causes, or outside organizations, the NLRB found that personal e-mails were common and did not result in discipline. The D.C. Circuit said that the policy did not rule out sending union e-mails that merely clarified facts about a union rally and did not call for action. [*Guard Publ'g Co. v. NLRB*, 571 F.3d 53 (D.C. Cir. 2009)]

On December 11, 2014, the NLRB overturned its 2007 *Guard Publishing* decision from 2007 and ruled that an employer cannot forbid employees to use the company e-mail system, on their own time, for union organizing. The NLRB said that, in light of the universality of e-mail as a communications medium, the earlier decision was now obviously incorrect. The NLRB will permit employers to ban non-work use of e-mail based on showing that the ban is necessary for productivity or discipline. However, union e-mails must be allowed if other non-work e-mails are allowed. [*Purple Commc'ns*, 361 N.L.R.B. No. 126 (2014); see David A. Zetoony, *Employee Monitoring: A How-To Guide,* Bryan Cave (Feb. 27, 2017) (benefitslink.com)] The employer asked the NLRB to reconsider this ruling; in 2017, the NLRB reaffirmed its earlier position, ruling once again that it presumptively violates the NLRA to forbid all use of the company e-mail system for non-work time, because certain usage could constitute protected concerted activity. [*Purple Commc'ns,* 365 N.L.R.B. No. 50 (2017). See Daniel B. Pasternak, *NLRB Will Not Hack Into Prior Decision Regarding Employee E-Mail Use During Non-Work Time,* Squire Patton Boggs (Apr. 2, 2017), available at Lexology.com]

It is common for companies to forbid recording conversations or taking photographs or videos in the workplace. Even without an explicit rule, employees might be told to stop photographing or recording. In December 2015, the NLRB ruled that Whole Foods Markets' company-wide rules against recordings were unlawful because they could reasonably be interpreted as a ban on protected concerted activity. It might be necessary to document or communicate about activities such as picketing or conditions such as dangers in the workplace. [*Whole Foods Mkt., Inc.*, No. 01-CA-096965 (NLRB Dec. 24, 2015); see Stephen W. Lyman, *NLRB "Deletes" Employer's "No-Recordings" Rule*, Hall Render Killiam Heath & Lyman PC (Feb. 4, 2016), available at Lexology.com]

In June 2010, the Supreme Court made its first ruling on privacy issues related to workplace texting, resulting in a narrow ruling. It decided that it was reasonable, under the Fourth Amendment, for the city of Ontario to perform an audit of employees' messages on pagers owned by the city to determine if the city should upgrade to a plan giving employees more minutes on their pagers. The Supreme Court declined to decide the broader issue of whether the plaintiff, a police sergeant who sent private messages (some of them sexually oriented) on his work-issued pager, had a reasonable expectation of privacy in those text messages. Because the search was legitimate, work-related, and not excessive in scope, the employer prevailed. [*Ontario v. Quon*, 560 U.S. 746 (2010)]

Some cases hold that employees have a greater expectation of privacy when:

- The employer allows some personal use of the electronic network, but imposes imprecise standards such as "subject to the highest standards of morality" (e.g., *Bowman v. Butler Township Board of Trustees*, 2009 Ohio 6128 (Ohio App. 2009));

- The employer is a multi-national corporation, and reviews electronic communications of employees located in the European Union, even though they are protected by EU law (Directive 2002/58/EC);

- The employee was disciplined for communications not made during work hours, and not made on the employer's system (e.g., N.Y. Lab. Law § 201-d(2)(a); Cal. Lab. Code §§ 1101–1102);

- The company is subject to a collective bargaining agreement that limits electronic monitoring, and the employer fails to comply.

However, in some circumstances there might even be a duty to monitor—for example, if the employer is on notice of unlawful usage of the network that could be harmful to others such as accessing child pornography, or creating a hostile work environment by displaying pornography on the corporate computer system. See, e.g., *Doe v. XYC Corp.*, 887 A.2d 1156 (N.J. Super. 2005).

A number of states (including California, Colorado, and New York) have statutes that forbid employers from disciplining employees for lawful conduct that they engage in off company premises. However, there are exceptions for conduct reasonably related to the employee's job, or when the conduct creates a conflict of interest for the employer (for example, with respect to trade secrets) or impairs the employer's business interests. Several states (Connecticut, Louisiana, New

York, South Carolina, Washington, and the District of Columbia) forbid discipline on the basis of engaging in political activities or speech.

Since early 2012, approximately half the states have adopted some kind of password protection law (Arkansas, California, Colorado, Connecticut, Delaware, Illinois, Louisiana, Maine, Maryland, Michigan, Montana, Nevada, New Hampshire, New Jersey, New Mexico, Oklahoma, Oregon, Rhode Island, Tennessee, Utah, Virginia, Washington, West Virginia, and Wisconsin). These laws forbid employers to demand the passwords to accounts created by applicants or employees that are exclusively for personal use. Employers cannot require employees to friend the employer or retaliate against employees who refuse unlawful demands. These statutes do not apply to work-related accounts and may allow employers to require disclosure of a password when necessary for a law enforcement investigation, or an internal investigation of employee misconduct. [National Conference of State Legislators, *State Social Media Privacy Laws* (July 6, 2016), available at <http://www.ncsl.org/research/telecommunications-and-information-technology/state-laws-prohibiting-access-to-social-media-user names-and-passwords.aspx> (last accessed Feb. 27, 2017)]

A mid-2016 article surveys privacy laws in approximately half the states. In Arizona, employers generally are permitted to review and monitor employees' work spaces, computers, phones, and e-mail and Internet use. The District of Columbia does not forbid investigating or monitoring employees or their use of employer-owned devices and networks. Florida recognizes invasion of privacy claims, and private wire or electronic communications require consent of at least one party to intercept. Georgia forbids employers to commit state-law torts such as defamation and invasion of privacy. Illinois protects the privacy of employees' Social Security numbers. The Indiana Wiretap Act requires consent of at least one party of intercept employees' telephone or computer communications. Employees can use the Louisiana state civil code to sue their employers for invasion of privacy. Massachusetts entitles employees and job applicants to notice that their credit reports will be requested; adverse actions based on a credit report must be disclosed. Lie detector tests are illegal, and pre-employment medical examinations are limited. Employers are not allowed to use genetic information in employment decisions, cannot make HIV testing a condition of employment, and cannot ask job applicants if they have ever been in a mental institution. Minnesota employers are allowed to monitor employees' at-work use of computers, e-mail, and Internet, if employees are notified, consent, and if the employer follows a clear policy. Mississippi forbids secret recording of communications when no party is aware that a recording is being made. Montana's constitution guarantees personal privacy, and statutes forbid recording conversations and monitoring electronic communications unless all parties consent. Nevada employers have wide latitude to monitor workplace communications, especially if there are explicit policies. New Hampshire requires consent of all parties for eavesdropping or wiretapping. New York generally permits video recordings without sound, but it is an unfair labor practice to spy on employees engaging in protected concerted activities. North Carolina allows interception of oral or electronic communications on consent of one party; Ohio allows audio recordings on consent of one party. Pennsylvania protects employees from searches that unreasonably intrude on seclusion, but reasonable workplace surveillance is permitted. Utah requires one-party consent for monitoring. [Ogletree Deakins, *A Comparative Guide to Privacy in the Workplace in Over 20 States* (Aug. 8, 2016), available at Lexology.com]

Although the question is generally the employer's right to monitor e-mails, a recent Eleventh Circuit case involves unauthorized access by a co-worker. A corporate executive, Carmicle, reported concerns to his employer company about certain financial projections. He admitted that much of his information came from using a default password to access other employees' e-mails. The company found that his allegations were meritless and fired him for unauthorized access of the e-mails. The Eleventh Circuit held that Carmicle violated the federal Computer Fraud and Abuse Act (CFAA). Carmicle argued that a CFAA violation requires the employer to suffer a loss, and his ex-employer's computers were not damaged and service was not interrupted. The Eleventh Circuit rejected this argument: the company had to hire a consultant to assess the extent of the damage and restore the data. The company policy was that employees did not have an expectation of privacy and the company could monitor employee e-mails. According to Carmicle, that meant that his access was not unauthorized as defined by the CFAA, but the Eleventh Circuit held that it would be unreasonable to allow generic passwords to be exploited to access e-mails without consent of either the employer or the employee. [*Brown Jordan Int'l, Inc. v. Carmicle*, 846 F.3d 1167 (11th Cir. 2017); see Jeffrey M. Schlossberg, *Eleventh Circuit Upholds Company Claims Against Former Executive for Unlawful Access to Email*, Jackson Lewis PC (Mar. 9, 2017), available at Lexology.com]

The NLRB started coming to grips with social media issues in October 2010. Since then, a consensus has emerged: the NLRB will challenge employer conduct that impairs employees' ability to engage in concerted activity—including discussion of working conditions. However, purely personal communications, especially if malicious, will not be deemed protected.

In an important opinion, the Fourth Circuit ruled in September 2013 that "liking" something on Facebook (in this case, a deputy sheriff liking the candidate running against the deputy's boss) is free speech protected by the First Amendment. The court said it was the Internet equivalent of putting a sign on the lawn. The NLRB has also decided cases where it found that there was protected collective activity when co-workers liked or commented on a post. [*Bland v. Roberts*, 730 F.3d 368 (4th Cir. 2013)]

The District Court for the District of New Jersey ruled in mid-2013 that it can violate the Stored Communications Act to discipline employees based on non-public posts to their Facebook wall (the post is an electronic communication that is archived; friends-only pages are not publicly available). In this case, however, the court found that the employer was not liable, because it was alerted to the post by a co-worker who was friended and therefore authorized to view the post and who voluntarily reported it to the employer. [*Ehling v. Monmouth-Ocean Hosp. Serv. Corp.*, 961 F. Supp. 2d 659 (D.N.J. 2013)]

A police department social networking policy forbade dissemination of any information that would tend to discredit or reflect unfavorably on the department, the city, or its employees. Making negative comments about internal operations or conduct of co-workers and supervisors was forbidden if it affected public perception of the police department. The policy allowed officers to comment about matters of general or public concern if the comments were not disruptive and did not undermine public confidence in the police. Two police officers posted on Facebook criticizing the experience of police instructors and supervisors. The plaintiffs were reprimanded and placed on probation for six months but were told it would not affect their chances of promotion. A few weeks later, however, the rules were changed so that no one on probation could get a promotion, so the plaintiffs were not allowed to take the sergeants' exam. One of the plaintiffs quit when he was scheduled to be fired. The two officers sued under 42 U.S.C. § 1983, claiming retaliation. The Fourth Circuit held that the policy was overbroad: it prevented unfavorable comments about police department investigations, although this is a central area of public concern. The Fourth Circuit analyzed whether they spoke as citizens on a matter of public concern; whether their First Amendment rights outweighed the department's interest in efficiency; and whether protected speech was a substantial factor in the adverse employment action, and concluded that the plaintiffs' rights were violated. However, the Fourth Circuit dismissed the retaliation claims because there was a fair investigation and the plaintiffs were charged with other infractions. The case remanded to determine the city's liability under § 1983. [*Liverman v. City of St. Petersburg*, No. 15-2207, 2016 WL 7240179 (4th Cir. Dec. 15, 2016)]

The NLRB held that it violated the NLRA to fire two workers for having a discussion on Facebook about mistakes made by the employer in withholding state income tax. The NLRB found that the employer's Internet policy violated the NLRA. The employer's argument was that although the activity was concerted, it was not protected because the employees made defamatory and disparaging comments about the employer. The NLRB rejected the argument because there was no direct confrontation with management and using one curse word was not serious enough to remove the protection. The comments concerned the employer's personnel practices, not its products, and the employer did not show that the comments were knowingly false or that the employees did not care whether they were true or not. The second worker's "liking" the post was also protected. To the NLRB, a policy forbidding "inappropriate" discussions about the company or its management violated the NLRA, because it is so imprecise that it threatens protected communications. [*Triple Play Sports Bar & Grille*, 361 N.L.R.B. No. 31 (2014)]

Another issue is whether the employer is entitled to access e-mails sent on its system that the employee claims are entitled to attorney-client privilege (for example, when an employee communicates with his or her attorney about a Title VII suit against the employer). See, e.g., *Pure Power Boot Camp Inc. v. Warrior Fitness Boot Camp*, LLC, 587 F. Supp. 2d, 548 (S.D.N.Y. 2008), which holds that it violated the Stored Communications Act to access a former employee's Hotmail e-mails from the company computer without consent. Although the employee was on notice that company computers could be searched for evidence of personal use, he did not know that his Web-based e-mail accounts like Hotmail could be included. The court held that the company policy did not waive privacy rights in Web-based accounts.

§ 26.07 HIPAA PRIVACY RULES

Congress passed the Health Insurance Portability and Accessibility Act (HIPAA). [Pub. L. No. 104-191; final rule on enforcement, 71 Fed. Reg. 8390 (Feb. 16, 2006)], covering many issues related to health insurance and health care. The statute ordered Congress to issue federal health care privacy standards by August 21, 1999. However, Congress failed to meet this deadline, which gave the Department of Health and Human Services the right to draft regulations.

HIPAA enforcement relies largely on HHS investigation of complaints of violations and efforts to obtain voluntary compliance by conciliation. Civil monetary penalties are imposed only if conciliation fails. HHS also carries out compliance reviews independent of complaints.

The HITECH Act (Health Information Technology for Information and Clinical Health Act; part of the American Recovery and Reinvestment Act of 2009, Pub. L. No. 111-5), took effect February 17, 2010, strengthening the privacy and security provisions of HIPAA, and increasing civil monetary penalties for HIPAA violations.

On September 17, 2014, the HHS OCR (Office for Civil Rights) issued guidance on implementing *Windsor* in HIPAA privacy requirements. Same-sex spouses (as defined by the place where the marriage was celebrated) have the same privacy rights as male/female couples. Legally married same-sex spouses are covered by 45 C.F.R. § 164.510(b) (disclosure of PHI to family members when relevant to their involvement in care or payment, or notification of person's location, condition, or death). A same-sex spouse is a family member whose genetic information cannot be used under 45 C.F.R. § 164.502(a)(5)(i) (ban on using genetic information for underwriting purposes). [Denise Erwin and Sarah Sise, *HHS Guidance Recognizes HIPAA Privacy Rights of Same-Sex Spouses and Dependents*, Bryan Cave Benefits and Executive Compensation (Oct. 10, 2014) (benefitslink.com)]

HHS' Office of Civil Rights (OCR) published an omnibus restatement of the HIPAA privacy and security rules reflecting the HITECH Act Amendments in early 2013. Covered entities and their contractors and subcontractors are subject to civil and criminal penalties for violations of the privacy, security, and breach notification rules. Security breaches must be reported to HHS each year and large-scale breaches must also be reported to the individuals involved and to the news media. There are requirements for using encryption and destruction of obsolete information to prevent unauthorized persons from accessing protected health information (PHI). Penalties are imposed for failure to notify individuals and the news media when a breach of security of PHI occurs. [78 Fed. Reg. 5566 (Jan. 25, 2013)]

There is no private right of action for violation of the HIPAA privacy rules (i.e., employees cannot sue if they claim their PHI was improperly disclosed or used). Instead, enforcement is the province of government agencies—HHS in the civil context, the Department of Justice in the criminal arena. However, under the HITECH Act, aggrieved individuals can receive a share of civil penalties collected for privacy breaches involving their data. [See, e.g., *Acara v. Banks*, 470 F.3d 569 (5th Cir. 2006)] A HIPAA privacy rule violation could be admissible as evidence in a private civil suit for, e.g., RICO violations or negligent infliction of emotional distress. [See, e.g., *Acosta v. Byrum*, 638 S.E.2d 246 (N.C. App. 2006)]

If the EGHP is funded by insurance and the employer-plan sponsor has no access to PHI, the insurer has full responsibility for privacy compliance. Such EGHPs are not directly affected by the privacy rules. A plan sponsor that does have access to PHI has an obligation to amend the plan document to institute privacy procedures under which participants can inspect (and, if necessary, correct) their PHI and control disclosure of the PHI to others. The plan sponsor must give the plan a certificate of complying amendments and safeguards. The plan must have a privacy officer, and it must modify contracts with business associates to make sure that PHI is protected.

A self-insured or self-administered plan doesn't have an insurer in the picture to handle privacy concerns, so the plan document must be amended to control dissemination of PHI; privacy safeguards and certification are required; a privacy officer must be appointed; and business associates' access to PHI must be controlled.

■ **TIP:** The privacy rules apply only to health plans, not to other types of welfare benefit plans (for instance, short-term and long-term disability plans, Worker's Compensation, and sick pay) even though administering these plans requires insight into the health status of employees.

The individual who is the subject of the information must give specific authorization before a covered entity can use protected health information for any reason other than payment, treatment, or health care operations. A covered entity is a health plan, health care clearinghouse, or health care provider that ever transmits health information electronically. PHI means all individually identifiable information that is transmitted or maintained in any form by a covered entity. A fully insured group health plan is not required to issue the Notice of Privacy Practices to its plan participants. The HMO or issuer of the plan has this responsibility. However, a self-insured plan does have to provide the Notice. For people already in the group, notice is required as of the plan's compliance date (and within 60 days after a material revision). New participants get the notice at enrollment. The notice must be written in plain English or otherwise effectively communicate how PHI can be used, and explain when the individual must authorize disclosure of information about him- or herself.

Enforcing this Regulation is the responsibility of the Department of Health and Human Services' Office of Civil Rights, which handles a spectrum of tasks from providing technical guidance and doing compliance reviews to complaint investigations, assessing civil penalties, and making referrals for criminal prosecution.

A historic privacy breach settlement was negotiated in mid-2014, when HHS' Office of Civil Rights (OCR) ordered Columbia University and New York Presbyterian Hospital to pay $4.8 million to settle charges that almost 7,000 patient records became accessible via Internet search engines when a networked server was deactivated in September 2010. The hospital paid $3.3 million, Columbia University paid the balance. [Clint Boulton, *Patient Data Leak Leads to Largest Health Privacy Law Settlement*, WSJ.com (May 9, 2014)]

An even higher settlement, $5.5 million, was agreed to by Advocate Health Network in mid-2016. Multiple HIPAA violations were involved and noncompliance had gone on for a long period of time. [HHS.gov, *Advocate Health Care Settles Potential HIPAA Penalties for $5.55 Million* (Aug. 4, 2016) (benefitslink .com); Peter S. Vogel, *HIPAA Penalty of $5.5 Million Seems Like a Lot, But It's Only $1.375 Per Patient!*, Gardere (Aug. 15, 2016), available at Lexology.com] Children's Medical Center of Dallas was fined $3.2 million; it did not require encryption or have a risk management plan, so its employees used unencrypted mobile devices between 2007 and 2013. [Peter S. Vogel, *$3.2 Million HIPAA Fine for Violations Since 2006!*, Gardere Information Technology & e-Discovery Blog (Feb. 3, 2017) (benefitslink.com)] See § 19.05[F] for more discussion of HIPAA privacy requirements.

CHAPTER 27

THE ROLE OF THE COMPUTER IN HR

§ 27.01 INTRODUCTION

Corporate human resource functions have always been number-intensive, from calculating a payroll to preparing reports on the nature of the workforce. Therefore, the HR department was an "early adopter" of all kinds of technology, going as far back as tabulating machines, through mainframe computers using punched cards, to the desktop PC, to today's networked systems. (Ironically, computer networks have something in common with the old-style mainframe with "dumb terminals" linked to it.)

Not only are computers used within the business and functions such as payroll preparation and tax reporting compliance often outsourced by electronic means, but also computerized communications continue to gain in importance. The Internet provides vast information and calculation resources for the HR department.

In addition to functions performed on the employer's computer system, functions accessing the Internet and using mobile devices are extremely significant, both for their business potential and for the problems they might create—not least of which is the amount of work time that employees spend on personal computing and social media. In response to the age of social media, the National Labor Relations Board (NLRB) maintains its own Facebook page, YouTube channel, and Twitter feed.

Purchasing "cyber" coverage requires additional review over and above the normal process of assembling a business insurance portfolio. Insurers that sell policies that cover computer and online risks will want to know about the business' data retention policies and controls. Warranties of the conduct of third parties (such as cloud service providers) may have to be given. The policy triggers must be appropriate to the insured's business—some policies will cover any security incident, whereas others rule out coverage if the insured failed with respect to any security duties. A policy might only cover security breaches that have been confirmed—but investigating a potential breach can be costly. Many policies will pay benefits if the insured pays a ransom to prevent a breach, but some will not cover ransom for the return of data that has already been stolen. [Walter J. Andrews and Jennifer E. White, *Digital Due Diligence: Four Questions to Evaluate Cyber Insurance Coverage*, Hunton & Williams LLP (Mar. 1, 2017), available at Lexology.com]

A BYOD ("bring your own device") policy calls for employees to use their own electronic devices rather than using devices provided by the employer, with the company offering information storage. The benefit to the company is reduction in hardware costs and, because employees choose the devices, they do not resent being provided with devices they disfavor. But the policy can also create problems. Employees may want to take the phone number—and contact data—when they leave the company. They might apply for overtime compensation for time spent checking e-mails. If the employer remotely wipes devices belonging to a terminated employee, it is likely to cause ill-will, although perhaps it could be lawful if the employee received advance written notice of this possibility. It is unclear how litigation holds affect employees' personal devices.

Employers should inform employees that they will not be reimbursed for lost or damaged devices, or for damage to the device or the employee's data. Some companies provide data plans for BYOD equipment. The policy should require all devices used at work to be password-protected with a strong password. Employees should be warned that they do not have privacy rights in employer information on the devices and that the employer has the right to access the device physically or remotely. Employees should be instructed to report the loss or theft of such a device immediately, and not to permit third parties to use the device. Anti-harassment policies (e.g., not using work computers to access pornography) should be extended to devices as well. [Ben H. Bodzy, Lawrence S. Eastwood and Megan Sutton, *PCBYOD—Bring Your Own Device Policies*, Baker Donelson Bearman Caldwell & Berkowitz (Aug. 23, 2013), available at Lexology.com; Tina A. Syring-Petrocchi, *Five Things to Consider When Creating a Bring Your Own Device (BYOD) Policy*, Barnes & Thornburg LLP (Oct. 14, 2013), available at Lexology.com]

The IRS issued an alert on February 2, 2017, warning about the evolution of "phishing" schemes seeking W-2 information that can be used to steal the identity of employees, coupled with demands to wire money to the scammers' account. [IR-2017-20, *Dangerous W-2 Phishing Scam* (Feb. 2, 2017), available at <https://www.irs.gov/uac/dangerous-w-2-phishing-scam-evolving-targeting-schools-restaurants-hospitals-tribal-groups-and-others>]

Although GPS tracking of employees is often useful (e.g., for verifying where employees are during work hours, whether deliveries are made on time, and that employees properly record their time), these advantages must be balanced against employees' privacy rights. Employers should be careful only to track data that is related to job performance. Employees must be given clear warning that they can be monitored when using company vehicles, and must be informed how the data will be stored and secured. [Jennifer M. Holly, *There's an App for That: Considerations in Employee GPS Monitoring*, Seyfarth Shaw LLP (Jan. 26, 2017), available at Lexology.com]

[A] Reporting to Federal Agencies

Over time, more and more federal agencies are requesting or requiring that forms and documents that formerly were filed on paper be uploaded to the agency's site (which is also a source of information about agency regulations and guidance).

On November 7, 2013 OSHA issued a Notice of Proposed Rulemaking to improve tracking of workplace injuries and illnesses. The rule calls for employers with 250 or more workers to make a quarterly electronic report of the illness and injury data already submitted to OSHA; employers with 20 or more employees in high-risk industries such as construction, nursing facilities, and warehouses will have to submit data annually. The high-risk industry data would be posted on the OSHA site with personal identifying information stripped out. [78 Fed. Reg. 67253 (Nov. 8, 2013)]

OSHA published a final rule on electronic recordkeeping in mid-2016, with an effective date of July 1, 2017. Under the rule (which has become the subject of court challenges), an employer with 250 or more employees must make an annual electronic report to OSHA of Form 300 (injury and illness log), Form 301 (incident reports), and Form 300A (summary form). Employers in high-risk injuries must also make electronic reports if they have between 20 and 249 employees, but they are only required to e-file Form 300A. [81 Fed. Reg. 31854 (May 20, 2016); see Bryan E. Keyt, Mitchell S. Allen and Erin L. Brooks, *What Employers Need to Know About OSHA's New Reporting and Anti-Retaliation Regulations*, Bryan Cave LLP (July 6, 2016), available at Lexology.com]

On June 27, OSHA announced that the effective date was delayed until December 1, 2017, and that OSHA was reviewing the rule and might eliminate it. However, a web-based application for submitting 2016 injury and illness data went live on August 1, 2017, ready for the December deadline. [Announcement of delay: 82 Fed. Reg. 13550 (June 28, 2017); see Brad Hiles, *OSHA Further Delays Electronic Reporting*, Husch Blackwell LLP (June 27, 2017), available at Lexology.com; Elise C. Scott and John Fehrenbach, *OSHA Announces Electronic Recordkeeping App*, Winston & Strawn LLP (July 19, 2017), available at Lexology.com]

Another aspect of OSHA's online presence is that whistleblowers who are covered by any of the 22 statutes administered by OSHA, including Sarbanes-Oxley Act § 806, can file complaints online in addition to the existing procedures for mailing the complaint or calling or visiting an OSHA office. Tips and applications for SEC and Commodities Futures Trading Commission (CFTC) rewards under the Dodd-Frank Act can also be submitted online. [<http://www.whistle blowers.gov/complaint_page.html> (last accessed Mar. 2, 2017)]

The Equal Employment Opportunities Commission (EEOC) carried out a pilot project for digital filing of charges in May 2015, known as ACT Digital (Action Council for Transformation to a Digital Charge System). The project was considered a success so, as of January 1, 2016, all EEOC offices e-mail employers to notify them when EEOC charges are filed against them. Employers are encouraged to contact the local EEOC office (which can be located by accessing <http://www.eeoc.gov/field>) to provide a current e-mail address and designate a contact person. The EEOC e-mail tells employers how to access the EEOC Respondent Portal to read and download the charge, schedule mediation, submit a position statement and attachments, reply to EEOC requests for information, give contact information for the lawyer handling the charge, or request an extension of time to respond. A portal for charging parties is planned for later in 2016. [FAQ: <http://www.eeoc.gov/employers/act-digital-qanda.cfm> (Mar. 9,

2016) (last accessed Mar. 2, 2017); user guide <http://www.eeoc.gov/employers/respondent_portal_users_guide.cfm> (Jan. 28, 2016) (last accessed Mar. 2, 2017); see Leigh Anne Benedic, *The EEOC Enters the Digital Age with Electronic Notice of Charges*, Porter Wright Morris & Arthur LLP (Feb. 29, 2016), available at Lexology.com]

In a November 24, 2015 *Federal Register* notice, the United States Citizenship and Immigration Service (USCIS) proposed changes in Form I-9 to make it easier to complete the form on a computer; digital forms are believed to be more accurate. There are instructions on the screen for each field and a dedicated area to enter extra information that would have been written in the margins of paper forms. The new drop-down menus, field checks, and error messages verify the correctness of the form. The site has buttons to access instructions electronically or print the form. Once the form is printed, a QR code (Quick Response matrix barcode) is generated, which can be used to speed up audits. However, this is not a fully electronic form. The employer must print it out, sign the hard copy, and retain a copy. [80 Fed. Reg. 73200 (Nov. 24, 2015)] A new form I-9 took effect on January 22, 2017. See § 23.11[D].

On December 9, 2015, the Pension Benefits Guaranty Corporation (PBGC) announced the launch of a new portal for electronic filing of Form 4010 and filings under the Employment Retirement Income Security Act (ERISA) § 4043. To use the portal, practitioners must have an e-4010 account with the PBGC. The portal includes a module which must be used for certain notices and applications (e.g., ERISA notices of termination, insolvency, and applications for financial assistance), and can also be used to file some other documents. However, this is separate from the MyPAA portal used to pay PBGC premiums. [80 Fed. Reg. 55743 (Sept. 17, 2015); see PBGC, *What's New for Practitioners,* <http://pbgc.gov/prac/whatsnew.html?CID=COLA01AEDEC1120151&source=govdelivery&utm_medium=email&utm_source=govdelivery> (last accessed Mar. 2, 2017)]

§ 27.02   INTERNET RESEARCH

Experts at many law firms publish articles about evolving news and legal analysis. The free feed at Lexology.com collates such articles each weekday. Law .com also has a variety of free newsletters in subject areas relevant to the HR function. The benefitslink.com online newsletters (one on pensions and benefits, one which covers health and welfare plans), which have expanded to publish twice every weekday, are also free.

The best government sites, such as <http://www.irs.ustreas.gov> are full of useful forms, explanations, and news summaries, as well as offering the full text of new regulations. It is worth scheduling time to regularly review the Pension and Welfare Benefit Administration and Occupational Safety and Health Administration (OSHA) sites to monitor ongoing developments; to see if you want to post an official comment on a proposal or testify at a hearing; or if there are new forms and publications available. [The IRS's portal for retirement plans, with links to major topics, can be found at <https://www.irs.gov/retirement-plans> (updated Mar. 2, 2017).]

In mid-2016, the IRS debuted a new web page explaining tax compliance for the sharing economy (aka gig, on-demand, or access economy). The IRS recommends using IRS Direct Pay or Treasury's Electronic Federal Tax Payment System to pay, or having more withheld from conventional job. [<https://www.irs.gov/businesses/small-businesses-self-employed/sharing-economy-tax-center>; see IR-2016-110, *IRS Launches New Sharing Economy Resource Center on IRS.gov, Provides Tips for Emerging Business Area* (Aug. 22, 2016) (benefitslink.com)]

The Department of Labor (DOL) has an immense bank of information online. Their main site is <http://www.dol.gov>. The Bureau of Labor Statistics reports the relative strengths of various employment sectors and employment cost trends. [See <http://www.bls.gov>] It also disseminates statistics on occupational safety and health. [See <http://www.bls.gov/bls/safety.htm>. OSHA's home page is <http://www.osha.gov>]

Federal contracting compliance information is available from the Office of Federal Contract Compliance Programs (OFCCP), <http://www.dol.gov/ofccp/>. During the Obama administration, the OFCCP administered a number of major Executive Orders, but at press time in 2017 it was anticipated that these orders would be invalidated by the courts, reversed by subsequent Executive Orders, or disapproved by Congress. The DOL has revised its Employment Law Guide, explaining the major laws that it enforces, and helping small businesses to develop wage, benefit, health and safety, and anti-discrimination policies. The update covers increases in minimum wages and Family and Medical Leave Act (FMLA) expansions. The guide is a companion to the online FirstStep overview advisor, <dol.gov/elaws/firststep> (last accessed Mar. 2, 2017); the law guide is <dol.gov/compliance/guide/index.htm> (last accessed Mar. 2, 2017).

The DOL maintains a Website, the H-1B Advisor, to assist employers and potential H-1B visa holders in understanding the requirements of the program [<http://www.dol.gov/elaws/h1b.htm> (last accessed Mar. 2, 2017)], and a Disability Nondiscrimination Law Advisor (part of the eLaws series) for employers to make sure their policies do not discriminate against persons with disabilities. The Disability Advisor contains a series of questions; the employer's answers generate a list of federal anti-discrimination laws that are likely to apply. [<http://www.dol.gov/elaws/odep.htm> (last accessed Mar. 2, 2017)]

The Employee Benefits Security Administration (EBSA), a subagency of DOL, has its site at <http://www.dol.gov/ebsa>. For Worker's Compensation information, see <http://www.dol.gov/owcp/Regs/unifiedagenda/main.htm> (last accessed Mar. 2, 2017). The Wage and Hour Division's Web presence is <http://www.dol.gov/WHD/workers.htm> (last accessed Mar. 2, 2017). See <http://www.pbgc.gov> for coverage of the expansion of PBGC information technology.

The EEOC launched an online Small Business Resource Center in late 2016. Small businesses that are near the threshold are often confused about whether they're subject to EEO laws, and what they have to do. The site is in plain English and explains requirements concerning, for example, discrimination, reasonable accommodation for disability, pregnancy, religion, and, retaliation.[<https://www.eeoc.gov/employers/smallbusiness/>; Robin E. Shea, *EEOC Small Business Resource Center: Two Thumbs Up!*, Constangy Brooks Smith & Prophete LLP (Sept. 29. 2016), available at Lexology.com]

Note, however, that this is a time of fast-moving changes in federal laws and regulations dealing with HR topics and agency Websites are not always updated with the most current information—and documents previously available on the site may be removed. Some government documents are revised frequently, and have date stamps; others are not dated, so it is difficult to determine how current the information is and whether it reflects important recent developments in the law.

§ 27.03   RECRUITING VIA THE INTERNET

If your corporation has a Website, it's easy and inexpensive to add an area for posting job opportunities. You can include an electronic form so even candidates who do not have an electronic resume can submit their qualifications. The form can be used for initial screening of applicants.

Newspaper Help Wanted ads are largely being replaced by listings on online job boards, aggregators, and business-oriented sites like LinkedIn.

To an ever increasing extent, performing a Web search on candidates' names is becoming a normal part of recruitment and hiring—for example, to see if inconsistent resumes have been posted to help-wanted sites, or to check out the candidate's blog (which might, for instance, include indiscreet material about the candidate's current employer, or negative comments about a competitor or an industry as a whole). Corporations also establish and update their own blogs or encourage employees to do so.

Federal contractors who accept Internet-based job applications are subject to DOL's OFCCPs' Final Rule on record-keeping. The final rule covers jobs for which the contractor accepts expressions of interest via the Internet, e-mail, employer Websites, or resume databanks. Federal contractors are required, wherever possible, to obtain data on the sex, race, and ethnicity of their employees and job applicants—including those who apply over the Internet. An Internet applicant is one who uses the Internet or related technology to submit an expression of interest and who demonstrates at least basic qualifications for the position, who the federal contractor has considered for a particular position, and who never took him- or herself out of consideration for the job before an offer was made. The rule requires federal contractors to maintain records of Internet-based expressions of interest that resulted in the contractor considering the applicant for a particular job (the OFCCP decided it would be too burdensome to make them retain records of non-specific applications). It is acceptable for federal contractors to discard expressions of interest that do not relate to a particular position or that do not meet the contractor's standards for submitting applications. [70 Fed. Reg. 58,945 (Oct. 7, 2005)]

§ 27.04 BENEFITS MANAGEMENT ONLINE

There are many reasons to limit the corporate content that is publicly available on the Internet: Premature disclosure of confidential information could result in loss of privacy, premature release of corporate plans, exposure of trade secrets, securities law violations, or the like. Corporations also generate a tremendous amount of information that is not security-sensitive, but is not of interest outside the organization.

The cost of implementing an intranet depends on the scope of the project, and whether the project requires full-scale programming or can be implemented wholly or partially with off-the-shelf commercial software packages. Another important question is whether the in-house information technology staff can handle the job, or whether a consultant will be needed.

An ERISA plans' Summary Plan Description (SPD) can be posted to the company's intranet site if the DOL's safe harbor for electronic disclosures is satisfied. (See § 11.08.) Each recipient must be given a written notice explaining that the SPD is available, and its significance. The plan administrator must facilitate the SPD actually being received: for example, by linking the SPD on the intranet's home page or using features that notify the administrator when e-mail messages bounce. Recipients must affirmatively consent to getting electronic rather than paper disclosure documents. If the system's hardware or software requirements change significantly, a new round of explanations and consents is required. [Gary B. Kushner, *SPD Electronic Disclosure*, Kushner & Company, kushnerco .com (Sept. 15, 2016) (benefitslink.com)] For a recent summary of electronic distribution rules under ERISA, COBRA, the FMLA, and HIPAA, see Marsh & McLennan Benefit Advisor, *Electronic Distribution Rules* (Apr. 2017) (benefitslink.com)

The District Court for the Eastern District of New York refused to relax the conditions set by the DOL's rules for electronic distribution of Summary Plan Descriptions (SPDs) and reversed a denial of benefits to the survivors of an employee whose life insurance policy lapsed for non-payment of premiums. The court found that it was arbitrary and capricious to deny benefits when the employee was never informed of the option to waive premiums upon disability, because the employer failed to give proper notice when publishing the SPD online. [*Thomas v. CIGNA Grp. Ins.*, No. 1:09-cv-05029-1, 2015 U.S. Dist. LEXIS 25232 (E.D.N.Y. Mar. 2, 2015)]

Small businesses that do not have retirement plans, or have 401(k) plans with high fees, are increasingly turning to "robo-style" automated investment services for small businesses. The firms in this growing sector include ForUsAll Inc., Captain401Inc., and Dream Forward Financial LLC. The robo-advisors work online and provide lower-cost indexed investments, usually low-cost exchange traded funds and index funds. [Anne Tergesen, *New Online 401(k) Plans Disrupt Retirement Market*, WSJ.com (July 31, 2016)]

§ 27.05 LEGAL IMPLICATIONS OF E-MAIL AND SOCIAL MEDIA

The benefits of e-mail in providing a simple method of communications are obvious. However, unencrypted e-mail is not secure. It is much more like a postcard that can be read by anybody than it is like a sealed letter—much less a coded message. Merely clicking a "delete" icon does not remove a message completely and permanently from the entire computer system, network, or service provider that offers e-mail service. So a message that is embarrassing or worse (e.g., one involving racial epithets, sexual harassment, or evidence of corporate wrongdoing) can be found by hostile parties—including plaintiffs' lawyers.

In mid-2010, the Supreme Court decided a case involving text messaging on an older technology (pagers). However, the court refrained from making a broad ruling about employees' expectation of privacy in personal text messages sent from the workplace. Instead, the Supreme Court held that it did not violate the Fourth Amendment for the city of Ontario to perform an audit of employees' messages on city-owned pagers to determine if the city should upgrade to a plan giving employees more minutes on their pagers. The plaintiff was a police sergeant who alleged that it was an unlawful search for the city to examine personal messages that he sent on his city-owned pager. Finding that the search of the pagers was legitimate, work-related, and not excessive in scope, the Supreme Court ruled in favor of the city. [*Ontario v. Quon*, 560 U.S. 746 (2010)]

If a company provides e-mail access at work, it should inform employees of the company's policies with respect to e-mail. A reasonable e-mail policy might inform employees that the employer maintains the right to monitor employee e-mails. (Bear in mind, however, that employers can be penalized if they obstruct employees from engaging in protected concerted activity.) Employees might be instructed to restrict the company e-mail system to business use. It is possible to block non-work sites or install tracking software, although the gains in efficiency might be overbalanced by losses in morale. Employees should be warned not to discuss matters that might have legal consequences (e.g., communications that could constitute price-fixing or industrial espionage), and told not to use obscene or suggestive language or apply slurs to any group.

In 2007, in its *Register Guard* decision, the NLRB said that employers had the right to forbid employees to use the company's e-mail system for union organizing. In 2014, however, the *Purple Communications* [361 N.L.R.B. No. 126

(2014)], decision reversed *Register Guard,* holding that employers must bar all non-work usage of their e-mail systems if they want to forbid using the e-mail system for union organizing.

Purple Communications asked the NLRB to reconsider this ruling but the reconsideration, in early 2017, resulted in the NLRB reaffirming its earlier position. The NLRB ruled once again that it is a presumptive violation of the NLRA for an employer to forbid all use of the company's e-mail system during non-work time: some usage could be protected concerted activity. [*Purple Commc'ns,* 365 N.L.R.B. No. 50 (2017). See Daniel B. Pasternak, *NLRB Will Not Hack into Prior Decision Regarding Employee E-Mail Use During Non-Work Time,* Squire Patton Boggs (Apr. 2, 2017), available at Lexology.com]

The NLRB extended *Purple Communications* in September 2015, holding that it violates the National Labor Relations Act (NLRA) to impose broad prohibitions on employee use of the company e-mail system that keeps them from communicating at times when they are not actually working. [*Cellco P'ship d/b/a Verizon Wireless*, No. 28-CA-145221 (Sept. 18, 2015)]

In general, the NLRB opposes the use of broad or vague rules about, e.g., civility, respect, disparagement, or confidentiality—even if the policy has a saving clause about not restricting protected collective activity. In early 2016, the NLRB struck down overbroad Chipotle policies and held that it was unlawful to force an employee to delete social media posts critical of the employer. It was also unlawful to fire him for asking co-workers to sign a petition about working conditions (alleged denial of work breaks). The NLRB said that the social media policy forbidding "false" and "misleading" posts was inappropriate because posts can be forbidden only if they are maliciously motivated as well as false or misleading. The NLRB said that a ban on disclosure of "confidential information" was vague and undefined. The company's "ethical communications policy" forbidding "exaggeration, guesswork, and derogatory characterizations of people and their motives" was invalid because it could be interpreted to prevent employees from engaging in their right to criticize management actions, forbid criticism of Management decisions. [*Chipotle Servs. LLC & Pennsylvania Workers' Organizing Comm.*, No. 04-CA-1437314 (N.L.R.B. Mar. 14, 2016); see Maria L.H. Lewis and Dennis M. Mulgrew, *The NLRB Rules That Chipotle's Handbook Policies Violated the NLRA*, Drinker Biddle & Reath (Mar. 22, 2016), available at Lexology.com]

In some cases, the employee's use of the employer's e-mail system, or a company-supplied laptop, to communicate with his or her attorney will remove attorney-client privilege from the communications—especially if the employer has a policy of forbidding non-work related e-mails; monitors e-mails, and has warned employees that their communications are subject to examination.

The New Jersey Supreme Court ruled that the attorney-client privilege outweighs corporate policy about use of workplace computers. Therefore, a plaintiff suing her employer had a reasonable expectation that e-mails to and from her lawyer using her personal, password-protected Yahoo account would be private even though they were sent on a laptop owned by the company. The court said that although companies can monitor use of their computers to protect their assets, and employees can be disciplined or fired for excessive personal use during work time, there is no need to read the specific contents of employees' privileged personal communications. [*Stengart v. Loving Care Agency Inc.*, 201 N.J. 300 (N.J. 2010)]

[A] Social Media

Employers should draft and publicize social media policies, information employees that, for example, they can be fired for social media abuse, and warning them not to divulge confidential or trade secret information in their posts. Employees should be told not to go online during work hours for non-work purposes, and informed how to act if they might be perceived as spokespersons for the company. The policy should also explain the risk of charges of defamation, harassment, discrimination, and invasion of privacy if social media is misused.

Since early 2012, almost half the states have adopted some kind of password protection law. As of mid-2015, the states were Arkansas, California, Colorado, Connecticut, Delaware, Illinois, Louisiana, Maine, Maryland, Michigan, Montana, Nevada, New Hampshire, New Jersey, New Mexico, Oklahoma, Oregon, Rhode Island, Tennessee, Utah, Virginia, Washington, West Virginia, and Wisconsin. There are state-by-state violations but, in general, these laws forbid employers to demand the passwords to accounts created by job applicants or employees that are exclusively for personal use. It is unlawful for employers to require employees to "friend" the employer (which would give the employer access to personal posts). [See 26.06[C]] Retaliation against employees who refuse unlawful demands is also forbidden. These statutes apply to personal accounts, not work-related accounts. Employers may be permitted to demand disclosure of passwords in connection with law enforcement investigations, or internal investigations of alleged misconduct by employees. [Philip L. Gordon and Joon Hwang, *Trendsetter or Outlier? Oregon Adds New Twist to Password Protection Laws*, Littler Mendelson (June 18, 2015), available at Lexology.com; John M. Dickman and Sabreena El-Amin, *List of States Enacting Social Media Privacy Laws Applicable to Employers Continues to Grow*, Winston & Strawn LLP (Sept. 9, 2015), available at Lexology.com; Katharine H. Parker and Daniel L. Saperstein, *Delaware Adds to Growing Patchwork of Social Media Laws*, Proskauer Rose LLP (Aug. 10, 2015), available at Lexology.com; Melissa M. Crespo and Christine E. Lyon, *Employer Access to Employee Social Media: Applicant Screening, "Friend" Requests and Workplace Investigations* (July 17, 2015), available at Lexology.com]

The Fourth Circuit treated a Facebook "Like," in this case a deputy sheriff Liking his boss's electoral opponent, as free speech protected by the First Amendment. Clicking the button publishes a substantive statement of liking something—

what the court called the Internet equivalent of putting a sign in your front lawn. [*Bland v. Roberts*, 730 F.3d 368 (4th Cir. 2013)]

The Tenth Circuit ruled that an employee who charged that she was terminated for using Facebook to report that she was sexually harassed by her supervisor did not satisfy the requirement of reporting harassment so that the employer can correct it. A complicating factor was that the plaintiff initially denied making the post and refused to make a harassment complaint to the HR department. After she admitted making the post, she was terminated for dishonesty, inappropriate behavior, and disrupting the workplace. The Tenth Circuit held that her employer could not be liable for sexual harassment because even if the plaintiff had never denied making the post, it did not comply with the employer's procedure for reporting harassment. [*Debord v. Mercy Health Sys. of Kan., Inc.*, 737 F.3d 642 (10th Cir. 2013)]

It is prudent to include a social media provision in non-solicitation agreements, so that the former employee agrees not to use social media to solicit the ex-employer's customers or induce its workers to leave. Merely posting general information about a new job probably does not violate a non-solicitation agreement but a target e-mail, private Facebook message, or Facebook post might be considered solicitation. Even an e-mail announcement of a new job might be treated as solicitation if it goes only to a small number of recipients, most of whom are clients of the former employer. It is also significant who makes the first contact in offering a job or asking for business. [Alyssa S. Gonnerman, *The Parting Shot—Restricting Former Employees' Social Media Use*, Husch Blackwell LLP (Aug. 20, 2015), available at Lexology.com]

[1] NLRB Rulings

With respect to social media, the NLRB's question is whether the employer's social media policy impairs the protected right of engaging in concerted mutual aid activities. Employer policies must be reasonable. The NLRB also assessed whether the social media activity is concerted (multiple employees act together), whether the activity is protected (i.e., involves workplace terms and conditions), and whether the employee has forfeited protection (e.g., by making maliciously untrue statements or lying to customers about product quality). It is a defense for the employer that the action would have been taken even if there had been no protected concerted activity: for example, there was a valid, nondiscriminatory reason to discipline or terminate the employee. While the NLRB frequently rejects social media policies that it sees as overly broad, it has also upheld discipline imposed for inappropriate social media conduct. In 2013–2016, the NLRB continued to reject social media policies that it defined as overly broad, but also upheld discipline of employees for inappropriate social media conduct:

- It was unlawful to fire three employees who posted Facebook messages criticizing their supervisor for dismissing their fears of working late in a dangerous neighborhood (Design Technology Group LLC).

- However, profane comments about the company and a supervisor in a private group message on Facebook were unprotected (Tasker Healthcare Group). [Baker & McKenzie, *Labor Year in Review: NLRB Targets Non-Unionized Employers and Expands Worker Rights* (Dec. 21, 2013), available at Lexology.com]

- An NLRB ALJ found that it was concerted activity for two employees of a youth center to discuss workplace concerns on Facebook. But, when they were not rehired as a result, the ALJ recommended dismissal of their ULP charge, because comments showing intent to be insubordinate or uncooperative to the employer waived protection under the NLRA, and the remarks could jeopardize program funding and the safety of program participants. [*Richmond Dist. Neighborhood Ctr.*, Case: 20-CA-091748, JD(SF)–53–13 (Nov. 5, 2013)]

- An August 22, 2014 decision, *Triple Play Sports Bar & Grille* [361 N.L.R.B. No. 31] holds that it violated the NLRA to fire two employees because of their Facebook criticism of the employer's failure to withhold the correct state income tax from their paychecks. The NLRB said that the communications were not maliciously untrue, and the employees sought support for group action about working conditions. [George M. Patterson, *NLRB Continues Aggressive Crackdown on Social Media Policies*, Mintz Levin Cohn Ferris Glovsky and Popeo PC (Sept. 3, 2014), available at Lexology.com]

The Second Circuit agreed with the NLRB: an employee did not forfeit the protection of the NLRA by posting a derogatory comment, including profanity, about his supervisor in a Facebook post encouraging co-workers to vote for the union in an upcoming certification election. The Second Circuit said that although the post was vulgar, it was protected because it dealt with workplace issues and occurred on social media, not disrupting the workplace. The employee took down the post after three days when he learned the post was accessible to the public. [*NLRB v. Pier Sixty, LLC*, No. 15-1841 (2d Cir. Apr. 21, 2017); see J. Gregory Grisham, *Second Circuit Upholds NLRB Order Finding Derogatory Facebook Post Protected Under the National Labor Relations Act*, Ford & Harrison LLP (Apr. 27, 2017), available at Lexology.com]

§ 27.06 FEDERAL RULES ON DIGITAL COMMUNICATIONS

Many of the rules affecting HR functions were drafted before the heyday of the personal computer, when plan administration generated mounds and mounds of paper (but nothing but paper). Two trends coalesced in the 1980s: personal computing and the drive to make government more efficient and reduce unnecessary paperwork. Obviously, the often-proclaimed Paperless Office never arrived, but to an increasing extent, documents are not only being created on computers but also distributed and retained electronically.

Department of Labor regulations [29 C.F.R. § 2560.104b-1] create a safe harbor for using electronic methods of satisfying the obligation to give various notices to government agencies, plan participants, and beneficiaries under the plan. The overriding objective is finding a method that is reasonably calculated to make sure that the information actually gets into the hands of those who are entitled to it.

The electronic communication must use content, format, and style consistent with the requirements for paper documents. When documents are furnished electronically, participants and beneficiaries must also receive a notice (whether hard-copy or electronic) explaining the significance of the document if it is not immediately apparent. Recipients must also be advised that they have the right to request a paper copy of the document. Furthermore, electronic distribution is permitted only for plan participants who have effective computer access at work, and for participants and beneficiaries who have expressly consented (whether electronically or on a paper document) to receiving digital documents. Documents can properly be furnished online only to people who have provided an e-mail address, given affirmative consent, or confirmed consent electronically, in a manner that shows they can effectively access the means the plan will use to communicate the information.

A valid consent requires advance provision of a clear and conspicuous statement (digital or hard-copy) of the kind of documents covered by the consent; that consent can be withdrawn at any time without financial penalty; how to withdraw consent; how to get hard copies of electronic documents; and the hardware and software requirements for accessing digital documents.

The PBGC's Web-based MyPAA (My Plan Administration Account Authentication Records) system can be used, e.g., to make filings, pay premiums (see <https://www.pbgc.gov/prac/prem/online-premium-filing-with-my-paa.html>), make the reports of events required under 29 U.S.C. § 1343, or ask the PBGC questions. Premium filings can be prepared directly on the MyPAA data entry screens, which can be reached by clicking on "Online Premium Filing (MyPAA)" at <http://www.pbgc.gov>. Software approved by the PBGC can be used to prepare the filing offline then upload it. Payments can be made electronically with the MyPAA system, via electronic checks or electronic funds transfer. Employers can also mail paper checks or use the <http://www.pay.gov> site, which permits payments of many kinds of obligations to the federal government. Electronic filing of Form 5500 became mandatory starting with the 2009 plan year. [Seyfarth.com, *Mandatory Electronic Filing of 5500s to Begin in 2010* (Sept. 30, 2009) (benefitslink.com)] As of January 1, 2010, all Form 5500s and 5500-SFs must be filed with EFAST-2 approved third party software, or e-filed.

[<http://www.efast.dol.gov/welcome.html> (last accessed Mar. 21, 2015) is the Welcome page for Form 5500 e-filing.]

Regulations that became final on September 29, 2014, require an employer that files over 250 forms a year to use the FIRE system to file Form 8955-SSA (deferred vested participants). An employer that files more than 250 returns a year will be penalized $1 per participant per day for failure to file Form 8955-SSA electronically; the penalty is capped at $5,000 per year. In addition to IRS penalties for failure to file Form 5500, DOL penalties can be as much as $2,063 a day. A one-participant plan that is required to file electronically must use Form 5500-SF to file the EFAST2 information required by Form 5500-EZ; they are not required to attach Schedules SB or MB. The EFAST2 filings of this type are not posted on the DOL's public disclosure Website. The regulation is effective for plan years that begin on or after January 1, 2014 Form 5500-EZ on Form 5500-SF has to be filed electronically for plan years beginning on or after January 1, 2015, if the deadline without extensions is after December 31, 2015.

However, a delinquent Form 8955-SSA or 5500-EZ must be filed on paper, because the IRS still does not have the capacity to accept e-filing. [T.D. 9695, 79 Fed. Reg. 58256 (Sept. 29, 2014)] Rev. Proc. 2015-47, 2015-39 I.R.B. 419, explains how to get a hardship exemption from the requirements of e-filing Form 8955-SSA and Form 5500-EZ. The main factor in granting the exemption is the amount by which filing electronically exceeds cost of filing on paper. However, IRS anticipates granting waivers of electronic filing only in exceptional cases, because e-filing is normally not very expensive. [Plansponsor editors, *IRS Clarifies Rules for Hardship-Related eFiling Waivers*, plansponsor.com (Sept. 15, 2015) (benefitslink.com)]

T.D. 9294 is the IRS's Final Rule, explaining how, effective January 1, 2007, qualified plans should use electronic means to provide notices to participants and obtain their consent and elections. The rule also applies to notices provided under various welfare benefit plans (accident & health plans; cafeteria plans; educational assistance plans; qualified transportation fringe plans; Archer Medical Savings Accounts (MSAs); and Health savings Account (HSAs)). However, T.D. 9294, as an IRS rule, does not apply to ERISA Title I or IV notices (dealing with, e.g., SPDs, Comprehensive Omnibus Budget Reconciliation (COBRA) notices, and notices of benefit suspension) because those documents are under DOL or PBGC jurisdiction. [T.D. 9294, RIN 1545-BD68, 2006-48 I.R.B. 980] IRS Publication 1220 provides detailed specifications (the publication is 150-pages long) for e-filing Forms 1097, 1098, 1099, 3921, 3922, 5498, and W-2G. The latest edition, for tax year 2017, was released in August 2017. [<http://www.irs.gov/pub/irs-pdf/p1220>]

DOL's final rules on fee disclosure require disclosure of three types of plan information: general information, administrative expenses, and individual expenses. If the plan's quarterly benefit statements satisfy the timing requirements, they can be used to provide these disclosures. Participants and beneficiaries must also be given certain investment-related information (fees, expenses, and investment alternatives) in comparative format, no later than the first date they can direct investments and at least once a year afterward. Investment-related information that is not contained in a pension benefit statement can be provided using the DOL electronic disclosure safe-harbor method or its alternative e-mail method, but not under the IRS electronic disclosure rules.

The initial notice to participants must be delivered on paper unless the recipient is part of a group that has had an e-mail address on file and used that address for dealing with the plan in the 12 months before the initial notice. Annual notices must be delivered on paper unless there is evidence that the recipient interacted with the plan electronically during that time. [DOL Technical Release 2011-03, <http://www.dol.gov/EBSA/pdf/tr11-03.pdf> (Sept. 13, 2011) (last accessed Mar. 3, 2017).]

An employee's general consent to receive materials about employee benefit plans by e-mail is not considered consent to receiving Form 1095-C (the PPACA form reporting health plan coverage) online, or general consent to receiving SPDs, plan documents, or SARs online. Providing Form 1095-C online requires specific informed consent from the employee in a form that demonstrates that the employee can access the format in which the document will be provided. Consent to receiving the form from the employer's Website requires the employer to give notice (in person, by postal mail, or by e-mail) that Form 1095-C has been posted to the employer's site. The notice must say, in all caps, IMPORTANT TAX RETURN DOCUMENT AVAILABLE (in the subject line of e-mail notices). [Sarah L. Bhagwandin, Dipa N. Sudra and Kim Kaald, *Going Green: What Procedures Should You Consider for 2016 Electronic ERISA Disclosures?*, Davis Wright Tremaine LLP (Dec. 15, 2015), available at Lexology.com]

NLRB General Counsel Memorandum 15-08 (Sept. 1, 2015) allows signatures to be submitted electronically for a showing of interest in forming a union. The NLRB accepts e-mail exchanges and signups on the Internet or an intranet as electronic signatures for a showing of interest. A union can maintain a site for online authorization forms or send form e-mails to employees. The union must also submit a declaration of what technology was used and how identification is controlled. [Timothy C. Kamin, *"Click Here to Organize"—NLRB Now Accepts E-Signatures on Authorization Cards*, Ogletree Deakins (Nov. 9, 2015), available at Lexology.com]

[A] Data Security

The Fourth Circuit has joined the Sixth, Seventh, and Ninth Circuits in holding that mere threat of future harm from a data breach, taken by itself, is not an injury-in-fact that confers standing to sue as required by Article III of the Constitution. The case involves data breaches at the Veterans Administration affecting about 10,000 patients. The plaintiffs asked for damages for embarrassment, mental distress, and potential future identity theft and misuse of their personal information. The Fourth Circuit held that fear of future identity theft was too speculative to confer standing, because it depended on hypothetical actions taken by third parties who were not related to the defendant. [*Beck v. McDonald*, 848 F.3d 262 (4th Cir. 2017); see James M. Westerlind and Andrew Dykens, *Fourth Circuit Holds That Threat of Future Harm Is Insufficient to Satisfy Injury In Fact Requirement for Article III Standing*, Arent Fox LLP (Mar. 17, 2017), available at Lexology.com]

There were the Health Insurance Portability and Accessibility Act (HIPAA) interim final rules in 2009, and a 2010 Notice of Proposed Rulemaking in mid-2010 about privacy, security, and enforcement. Early in 2013, HHS' Office of Civil Rights (OCR) published an omnibus restatement of the HIPAA privacy and security rules, reflecting the Health Information Technology for Economic and Clinical Health (HITECH) Act Amendments. Covered entities and their contractors and subcontractors are subject to civil and criminal penalties for violations of the privacy, security, and breach notification rules. Security breaches must be reported to HHS each year and large-scale breaches must also be reported to the individuals involved and to the news media. Penalties for failure to notify individuals of breach of their PHI and failure to notify the media when required have increased.

See 82 Fed. Reg. 8813 (Jan. 31, 2017) for the latest penalty figures; penalties range from $112 to $55,819 per violation for violations of the privacy and security rules, where the covered entity did not know and could not have known of the violation with reasonable diligence. The penalty range increases to $1,118 to $55,910 a year, when there was a violation but there was reasonable cause for it and there was no willful neglect. When there was willful neglect but the violation was quickly corrected, the penalty runs from $11,892 to $55,910 per violation. The penalty amount is a flat $55,910 per violation, not a range, for willful violations that were not quickly corrected. For all categories of violations, there is a cap of $1,677,299 for all identical violations in a calendar year.

Ransomware is malicious software that infects a system to either destroy data or encrypt it so that legitimate users cannot access it. The OCR's position is that electronic protected health information (ePHI) that has been encrypted on the entity's system by a ransomware attacker, but not necessarily accessed by a hacker, is considered breached for HIPAA purposes, unless the covered entity can show that the probability that data was compromised is low. July 2016 guidance from OCR says that covered entities have an obligation to prevent or detect and respond to ransomware attacks. A strong security program includes a risk assessment that contemplates the risks of ransomware, training staff about it, and setting access controls. Recovery relies on frequent data backups. Note that HIPAA requires covered entities to maintain a contingency plan. [Dianne J. Bourque and Kate F. Stewart, *"Your Money or Your PHI": OCR Releases Guidance on Ransomware*, Mintz Levin Cohn Ferris Glovsky and Popeo PC (July 12, 2016), available at Lexology.com]

Security breaches can have serious financial consequences for companies that break the rules. A major privacy breach settlement was negotiated in mid-2014, when HHS' OCR ordered Columbia University and New York Presbyterian Hospital to pay $4.8 million to settle charges about a privacy breach when, in September 2010, close to 7,000 patient records became searchable through Internet search engines when a networked server was deactivated. The hospital paid $3.3 million, Columbia University paid the balance. [Clint Boulton, *Patient Data Leak Leads to Largest Health Privacy Law Settlement*, WSJ.com (May 9, 2014)]

MAPFRE Life Insurance Co. of Puerto Rico settled with the OCR for $2.2 million: an unencrypted USB device was stolen after being left unsecured overnight in the IT department. The device contained PHI of about 2,200 people. OCR found lack of compliance with other HIPAA provisions, including lack of risk analysis or risk management plan. [Sean R. Baird, Rebecca L. Williams and Adam H. Greene, *The Price of PHI—A $2.2 Million USB Drive*, Davis Wright Tremaine LLP (Jan. 20, 2017), available at Lexology.com]

After a phishing incident compromised ePHI of 3,200 people, the Metro Community Provider Network entered into a $400,000 HIPAA settlement with the OCR. [Drinker Biddle, *A Failure to Plan Is a Plan to Fail: $400,000 HIPAA Settlement Highlights the Importance of Risk Assessments and Management Plans* (Apr. 18, 2017) (benefitslink.com)]

On January 9, 2017, the HHS' OCR announced the first HIPAA enforcement action for failure to file a timely breach report. Presence Health agreed to pay $475,000 to settle the case. Although breach reporting is required within 60 days of discovery of a breach, Presence Health took 101 calendar days to notify OCR and 104 days to notify victims and the media. [Sean R. Baird et. al., *Time Waits for No One: OCR Announces First HIPAA Settlement for Lack of Timely Breach Notification*, Davis Wright Tremaine LLP (Jan. 12, 2017), available at Lexology.com]

It can be difficult to safeguard business data when employees are terminated. The Computer Fraud and Abuse Act (CFAA) gives employers a civil claim against former employees who seek competitive advantage through wrongful use of information from the employer's computer system. The former employee is liable for accessing a protected computer without authorization, or in excess of authorized access, if it is done knowingly and with intent to defraud, as long as the access furthers the intended fraud and the person obtains anything of value. If a civil violation of the CFAA is proven, then the court can award compensatory damages and/or equitable relief such as an injunction. The statute of limitations is two years from the date of the access or the date it was discovered. The CFAA does not define "without authorization," but 18 U.S.C. § 103(e)(6) defines "exceed authorized access" as using permission to access a computer to obtain or alter information in a way that the user is not allowed to do.

Courts have interpreted this definition differently. Some decisions (e.g., *LVRS Holdings LLC v. Brekka*, 581 F.3d 1127 (9th Cir. 2009)) narrowly interpret the statute and limit its application to situations in which the person accessing was an outsider who had no permission to access the system at all—so an employee who exceeds his or her authorized access would not be covered.

Employers can protect themselves against data misuse by:

- Setting up a security system that flags unauthorized access to, or use of, data;

- Having new hires sign a confidentiality agreement that specifically references data protection;

- Exploring the technical feasibility of preventing transmission of certain crucial data to PCs or electronic devices;

- Including discussion of what kinds of remote access are permitted in your firm's telecommuting policy;

- Enforcing the information security policy, and impose even-handed discipline on all detected violations of the policy;

- As soon as possible after a resignation or termination, revoking the individual's log-in privileges on your computer system.

[Compare *Int'l Airport Ctrs. LLC v. Citrin*, 440 F.3d 418 (7th Cir. 2006) with, e.g., *Shamrock Foods Co. v. Gast*, 535 F. Supp. 2d 962 (D. Ariz. 2008); *Lasco Foods Inc. v. Hall*, 600 F. Supp. 2d 1045 (E.D. Mo. 2009). *United States v. Mitra*, 405 F.3d 492 (2005) defined "computers" very broadly, so that wireless networking stations and cell phones might also be subject to the CFAA.]

The staffing firm Korn/Ferry has a proprietary database called Searcher that is a crucial part of its intellectual property. Employees' access to the database is terminated when they cease to work for Korn/Ferry. In 2012, the Ninth Circuit ruled that ex-employee Nosal did not violate the CFAA when he induced accomplices to access the Searcher database to give Nosal information that he used to set up a competing business. At that time, the Ninth Circuit said that the conduct did not violate the CFAA: the accomplices willingly turned over passwords. However, in 2016, the Ninth Circuit reversed its earlier decision, holding that unauthorized use of passwords by ex-employees is a criminal violation of the CFAA—a holding that would probably apply to civil cases as well. [*United States v. Nosal*, 676 F.3d 854 (9th Cir. 2012), *rev'd* No. 14-10037 (9th Cir. July 5, 2016); see Demetri Economou, *Why the Ninth Circuit's "Password Sharing" Decision Is Relevant for All Employers*, Kane Russell Coleman & Logan PC (July 12, 2016), available at Lexology.com]

The Fourth Circuit ruled in mid-2012 that it did not violate the CFAA for an employee to download proprietary information into his own computer then use it in a presentation to a potential customer—on behalf of a competitor of his ex-employer, three weeks after quitting his job. Although the CFAA does include a civil provision, it does not apply to misappropriation of trade secrets or violating an employer's usage policy at a time when the individual was entitled to access the computer. [*WEC Carolina Energy Solutions LLC v. Miller*, 687 F.3d 199 (4th Cir. 2012)]

The Eleventh Circuit held that an executive, who misused generic passwords to hack co-workers' e-mail accounts to gather evidence to report to the company about what he called dubious financial projections, violated the CFAA. The executive, Carmicle, was fired. He said that he did not violate the CFAA because that statute requires the employer to suffer a loss and the computers were not damaged and service was not interrupted. The Eleventh Circuit agreed with the employer: the need to hire a consultant to find out what had happened and restore the data was a loss for CFAA purposes. Even though the company had a policy warning employees that their e-mails were subject to monitoring and employees did not have a privacy interest in their e-mails, that did not make Carmicle's access "authorized" as defined by the Stored Communications Act, which does not authorize exploitation of generic passwords to access e-mails without authorization. [*Brown Jordan Intl, Inc. v. Carmicle,* No. 846 F.3d 1167 (11th Cir. 2017); see Jeffrey M. Schlossberg, *Eleventh Circuit Upholds Company Claims Against Former Executive for Unlawful Access to Email*, Jackson Lewis PC (Mar. 9, 2017), available at Lexology.com]

The California Court of Appeal held that applicability of California Penal Code § 502(c)(5) (disrupting or denying computer services to an authorized user) is not limited to unauthorized hackers; the section can be violated by an employee who locks the employer out of its own system. In this case, a network engineer tried to preserve his job by preventing anyone else from gaining administrative access to his employer's network. He was sentenced to four years in prison and $1.4 million in restitution. [*People v. Childs*, 220 Cal. App. 4th 1079, 164 Cal. Rptr. 3d 287 (Cal. App. 2013)]

The Fifth Circuit agreed with an employer that the company was justified in denying severance benefits to a terminated employee who deleted computer files from his company laptop after signing a severance agreement requiring that he return all company property in his possession. He said that he was concerned about security—whereas the employer said he destroyed the only copies of raw data that supported the employee's final assignments for the company. [*Gomez v. Ericcson, Inc.*, No. 15-41479, 2016 WL 3669965 (5th Cir. July 8, 2016); see Lorene D. Park, *ERISA Governed Severance Plan Which Properly Denied Benefits to Employee Who Didn't Return Property*, WK Workday Blog (July 12, 2016) (benefitslink.com)]

Although there is no general federal statutory requirement that companies notify individuals of data breaches, almost all the states (all except South Dakota and Alabama—and a bill has been introduced in the Alabama legislature) have their own statutes. On March 16, 2017, New Mexico became the 48th state to adopt a law mandating reports of data breaches. The New Mexico law obligates companies to securely dispose of records that contain personal information once the records are no longer reasonably required for business purposes. The company must give notice as soon as possible after a breach—definitely within 30 days—unless the company's investigation shows that there is no significant risk of ID theft or fraud due to the breach. Individuals whose data was stolen do have the right to sue, but the state attorney general can bring a suit on behalf of affected individuals seeking an injunction or damages for actual losses, including financial losses. The company involved can be fined $10 for every notification that should have been but was not given, capped at $150,000. Knowing or reckless violations can be penalized by a civil penalty of $25,000. [Brian J. Willett, *And Then There Were Two—New Mexico Set to Become 48th State to Enact Data Breach Notification Law*, Reed Smith LLP (Mar. 21, 2017), available at Lexology.com]

CHAPTER 28

WORK-FAMILY ISSUES

§ 28.01   INTRODUCTION

Employees who have children or who have care responsibilities for their parents seek to balance their roles at work and at home. Even employees who do not have family responsibilities seek work-life balance.

There are new kinds of families developing (single parents, same-sex parents, blended families, grandparents raising grandchildren). Greater involvement of fathers in hands-on child care also increases the demand for Family and Medical Leave Act (FMLA) leave or flexible hours for fathers; however, paternity leave has never really caught on. [See Chapter 38] For a general introduction to caregivers in the workplace, see Jeremy Nobel et. al., *The Caregiving Landscape: Challenges and Opportunities for Employers,* Northeast Business Group on Health (Mar. 2017), available at <www.nebgh.org/wp-content/uploads/.../ NEBGH-CaregivingLandscape-FINAL-web.pdf>.

A recent study in the American Journal of Public Health says proportion of women taking maternity leave in the United States has remained about the same for two decades, despite the passage of paid leave laws. Although the economy has expanded about 66% in constant dollars since 1994, Ohio State researcher Jay Zagorsky said that "none of those benefits have flowed to women on maternity leave." The DOL reported in 2015 that only 12% of private sector workers had access to paid family leave. Paternity leave has grown, but from a very low base. About 300,000 babies are born each month; 22,000 men take paternity leave for newborns, whereas about 273,000 new mothers take time off in a typical month. Only half of maternity leaves are paid; the rate of paid leave rises by one-quarter of a percent per year. [Shereen Lehman, *Maternity, Paternity Leave Rates in the U.S. Remain Low*, reuters.com (Feb. 3, 2017) (benefitslink.com)]

The SHRM's 2016 employee benefits survey found that 26% of organizations offered paid maternity leave, 21% paid paternity leave, 20% paid leave for adoption, 13% allowed paid leave for foster care, and 6% for having a child by surrogacy. In 2016–2017, some major corporations enhanced parental leave entitlement. American Express granted all salaried employees 20 weeks of paid parental leave (for both mothers and fathers). IKEA salaried and hourly workers could get up to 16 weeks' leave, depending on how long they had worked for the company. (Hilton also gives the same leave availability to salaried and hourly workers, but many companies provide more favorable leave eligibility for salaried workers.) American Express allowed six to eight weeks of additional paid leave for new mothers when medically necessary. American Express also provides up to 20 days of backup child care at home or at a day care center. [S. Miller, *American Express Pushes Paid Parental Leave to 20 Weeks for Moms and Dads*, shrm.org (Dec. 14, 2016) (benefitslink.com); Molly Bangs, *IKEA Is Right: Hourly Workers Need Paid Parental Leave, Too*, tcf.org (Dec. 8, 2016) (benefitslink.com)]

Although some well-known companies are expanding their paid parental leave programs, the average amount of parental and caregiving leave has not changed significantly since 2012. Over the past 11 years, the proportion of organizations providing at least some pay to women on maternity leave has risen from 46% to 58%. However, the proportion offering full pay has actually fallen, from 17% in 2005 to 10% in 2016. Of all companies with 50 or more employees, only 6% provide full pay for maternity leave. The percentage of companies offering flexibility for family emergencies (ability to take time off during the day) also dropped, from 87% in 2012 to 81% in 2016. SHRM's 2016 study reported that only about a quarter (23%) of companies make a real effort to communicate with workers about programs available to them. In 2012, one-third (33%) of survey respondents allowed at least some paid telework on a regular basis; this percentage rose to 40% in 2016. Availability of phased return to work after childbirth also increased, from 73% in 2012 to 81% in 2016. [HREOnline.com, *SHRM Study Finds Sad State of Parental Leave* (Mar. 13, 2017) (benefitslink.com)]

Most of the states, plus the District of Columbia, have laws forbidding discrimination on the basis of pregnancy. Many state and local laws mandate reasonable accommodation for pregnant employees and employees recovering from childbirth. This is true in California, Connecticut, Delaware, the District of Columbia, Hawaii, Illinois, Louisiana, Maryland, Minnesota, Nebraska, New Jersey, New York, North Dakota, Rhode Island, Utah, and West Virginia. Some laws forbid employers to require pregnant employees to take leave.

In addition to the universal requirement of accommodating disability caused by pregnancy, Illinois requires accommodation of common conditions related to pregnancy and childbirth. New York requires accommodation, as temporary disability, of pregnancy-related conditions that are medically demonstrated and affect bodily functions, even if the condition is not otherwise a disability. California requires accommodation of pregnancy-related medical conditions of employees who do not take disability leave. [Elizabeth N. Hall, Heather M. Sager and Jonathan A. Wexler, *No Pregnant Pauses Here: Workplace Laws Protecting Expectant Mothers Becoming the Norm Across the United States*, Vedder Price PC (June 7, 2016), available at Lexology.com]

The 2016 edition of the National Partnership for Women and Families' report, *Expecting Better,* notes that Colorado, Delaware, Nebraska, North Dakota, Rhode Island, and Utah have recently added provisions on pregnancy accommodation and Delaware, Nebraska, and Utah adopted provisions accommodating nursing. [National Partnership for Women and Families, *Expecting Better* (4th ed. Aug. 2016), available at <http://www.nationalpartnership.org/research-library/work-family/expecting-better-2016.pdf > (last accessed Mar. 3, 2017)]

In September 2015, Rhode Island enacted legislation making it unlawful under the state Fair Employment Practices Law to deny reasonable accommodation to medical conditions related to pregnancy or childbirth, including lactation. Reasonable accommodation can mean time off or a modified schedule, but the employer cannot force an unwilling employee to take leave when another reasonable accommodation is available. Reasonable accommodation is required even if it is not provided to employees with non-pregnancy-related conditions. [Todd M. Torres, *Employers' Bundle of Joy: the Rhode Island General Assembly Passes Mandatory Reasonable Accommodation Law for Pregnant and Nursing Women*, Ogletree Deakins (Sept. 24, 2015), available at Lexology.com]

The 2016 Colorado statute describes possible accommodations as more or longer breaks, better seating, lifting limitations, a temporary transfer to an available, less-strenuous position, and modified work schedules. However, employers are not obligated to hire additional employees, fire non-pregnant employees, or promote or transfer employees. An interactive process of seeking accommodation is required when an employee indicates a need for pregnancy-related accommodations. [Kristin Berger Parker, *Are you Ready for Colorado's Pregnant Workers Fairness Act?*, Stinson Leonard Street LLP (Aug. 4, 2016), available at Lexology.com; Stephen E. Baumann II and Erin A. Webber, *Pre- and Post-Partum Protection: Colorado Enacts a Pregnant Workers Fairness Act*, Littler Mendelson PC (June 8, 2016), available at Lexology.com]

In July 2017, Connecticut's Act Concerning Pregnant Women in the Workplace became law, forbidding termination for pregnancy, refusal to provide reasonable leave for disability related to pregnancy, and refusal reinstate after maternity leave. All conditions related to pregnancy and childbirth, such as lactation, are covered, so this statute is broader than the federal Pregnancy Discrimination Act (PDA). [Keisha-Ann G. Gray and Laura Fant, *Connecticut Expands Anti-Discrimination and Accommodation Protection for Pregnant Employees and Applicants*, Proskauer Rose LLP (July 15, 2017), available at Lexology.com]

Nevada's Pregnant Workers' Fairness Act covers private employers with 15 or more employees. It is also more protective than the federal PDA, requiring reasonable accommodation of needs relating to pregnancy (e.g., extra breaks, light duty, or a temporary transfer). Nevada has a separate statute requiring paid or unpaid break time for lactation. [Mark Ricciardi and Holly Walker, *Expecting a Big Change: Nevada's New Pregnant Workers' Fairness Act*, Fisher Phillips (July 25, 2017), available at Lexology.com]

The Massachusetts Fair Employment Practices Act has been amended, effective April 1, 2018, to require accommodation of pregnant employees—even if they have no medical complications of pregnancy. The employer must give notice of rights under this statute to new hires and employees who disclose a pregnancy or related condition. [Samia M. Kirman and Brian E. Lewis, *Massachusetts Strengthens Protection for Pregnant Workers*, Jackson Lewis PC (July 31, 2017), available at Lexology.com; David C. Henderson and Robin Morse, *Massachusetts Gives Birth to Pregnant Workers Fairness Act*, Massachusetts Lawyers Weekly (Aug. 14, 2017), available at Lexology.com]

Nor is child care the only issue. People in mid-life are sometimes called the "sandwich generation" because they have responsibilities for aging parents as well as growing children. Work-life programs have gained prominence since

2001, as hard-pressed companies looked for ways to motivate employees without burdening themselves with very high capital obligations.

The Equal Employment Opportunities Commission's (EEOC's) position is that employers cannot forbid pregnant employees to work based on stereotypes about what is good for fetuses. For example, the EEOC settled a Pregnancy Discrimination Act (PDA) case for $45,000, when a doughnut franchise forced an employee to take unpaid leave because the employer heard that she might be pregnant and would not allow her to work without a medical release that her pregnancy was not high-risk. She was fired after complaining about this treatment. The EEOC press release announcing the settlement says that pregnant or believed to be pregnant employees cannot be required to provide medical documentation of their ability to work unless the employee requested accommodation. Retaliation for complaints is also unlawful. [Richard B. Cohen, *Pregnant? We Are Placing You on Unpaid Leave for Your Own Good*, FisherBroyles (Sept. 1, 2016), available at Lexology.com]

The Supreme Court held that Peggy Young could pursue her case against UPS. The decision holds that workers with pregnancy-based disabilities are entitled to accommodation on the same terms as workers with non-pregnancy based disabilities, unless the employer can show that there is a non-discriminatory, non-pretextual rationale for treating them differently. Therefore, it is unlawful to cite costs or convenience as a rationale for refusing light duty assignments to pregnant workers. [*Young v. UPS*, No. 135 S. Ct. 1338 (2015)]

On January 28, 2015, the Office of Federal Contract Compliance Programs (OFCCP) issued a Notice of Proposed Rulemaking (NPRM) rescinding the existing sex discrimination guidelines, replacing them with guidelines that reflect existing case law under Title VII (for employers with 15 or more employees) and the FMLA (for employers with 50 or more employees). The NPRM also adds compliance obligations for smaller companies that are government contractors with respect to accommodations for pregnant workers and family leave for male employees. The NPRM incorporates the PDA, but says the final rule will reflect the Supreme Court's *Young v. UPS* decision—which specifically refused to grant deference to EEOC guidance on light duty requirements for pregnant workers. The NPRM's definition of sex discrimination includes stereotyping about whether a person will or will not want to have children, and the role that person will play in child care. [Janet V. Britton, *OFCCP Proposes New Rule Related to Sex Bias*, Verrill Dana LLP (Feb. 4, 2015), available at Lexology.com] However, it is predictable that this rule will be altered by the Trump administration.

In 2013, there was a $20,000 settlement between the EEOC and Reed Pierce's Sportsman's Grill (Southern District of Mississippi). Adventures in Learning Aurora Inc., settled a case in the Northern District of Illinois for $31,000 after forcing the plaintiff to quit her job in the fourth month of pregnancy. A Comfort Inn that fired a pregnant housekeeper settled for $2,500 in back pay and $25,000 in compensatory and punitive damages. In the Northern District of Mississippi, Landau Uniforms paid $80,000 to settle charges of unequal treatment culminating in termination of a pregnant employee. [Lily M. Strumwasser, *Not Without Warning: The EEOC Continues to File Barrages of Pregnancy Discrimination Lawsuits*, Seyfarth Shaw LLP (Sept. 19, 2013), available at Lexology .com]

In mid-2014, the EEOC released enforcement guidance on pregnancy discrimination, with a Q&A about the guidance and a fact sheet for small business. It was the first time that the EEOC comprehensively updated its rules since the original drafting of the Compliance Manual in 1983. It was re-issued in mid-2015, reflecting *Young v. UPS*. The 2014 guidance says that the Pregnancy Discrimination Act (PDA) applies not only to current pregnancy or lactation, but also discrimination based on past or potential pregnancy. The EEOC's position is that pregnant workers who are able to perform their jobs must not be forced to take leave. Light duty must be made available to pregnant employees in the same manner as to employees who require light duty for other reasons. If there is direct evidence that light duty was denied because of animus against pregnancy, the employee does not have to prove that another employee was treated more favorably. Disparate impact cases are also possible if the employer's light duty policy has a disparate impact on pregnant employees. The EEOC says that light duty assignments cannot be restricted to workers with job-related injuries, but if employer policy limits the number or duration of light duty assignments, pregnant workers can be subject to the same limits as non-pregnant workers. [*Enforcement Guidance: Pregnancy Discrimination and Related Issues*, <http://www.eeoc.gov/laws/guidance/pregnancy_guidance.cfm> (June 25, 2015) (last accessed Mar. 3, 2017)] This rule is also likely to be replaced or removed.

New York State passed a package of eight bills, the Women's Equality Act, effective January 1, 2016. The New York State Human Rights Law has been amended to forbid family-status discrimination; marital-status discrimination was already illegal. Under this law, employers are not allowed to ask questions about, or consider parental status in employment decisions such as hiring, firing, compensation, and promotion. Reasonable accommodation (e.g., breaks, time off for medical appointments, leaves of absence for pregnancy-related disability) is required, unless it would be an undue hardship to the employer. [Lauren Helen Leyden et al., *New Women's Equality Act Legislation Raises Bar for New York Firms*, Akin Gump Strauss Hauer & Feld LLP (Oct. 26, 2015), available at Lexology.com]

The Massachusetts Maternity Leave Act (MMLA) was signed January 7, 2015, and took effect on April 7, 2015. Under prior law, women workers in Massachusetts were entitled to eight weeks of job-protected leave for birth or adoption. The MMLA extends this entitlement to men. However, if both parents work for the same employer, they receive only eight weeks of parental leave in total. If the employer agrees to provide more than eight weeks of leave, the employee cannot be denied reinstatement unless, before the leave, the employer gave the employee written notice that extra leave could lead to denial of reinstatement.

[Jackson Lewis PC, *Massachusetts Enacts Parental Leave Law, Giving Leave Rights to Male Employees* (Jan. 14, 2015) (benefitslink.com)]

In a case about a pregnant employee's ability to telecommute, the trial court ruled for the employer. On appeal, the Second Circuit vacated the ruling in part (but upheld dismissal of the phase of the case involving New York State human rights law). The plaintiff, a bank executive, quit her job and moved from New York to Los Angeles when her husband got a new job. The plaintiff's supervisor suggested that she continue to work offsite, under the bank's alternative work schedule policy. This policy treats not resuming a traditional work schedule or location when an alternative arrangement is canceled as a voluntary quit. After the plaintiff began work in Los Angeles, the bank said that all remote assignments would be reviewed. The next day, she told her supervisor that she was pregnant. The bank decided that team leaders had to work at least two days a week at headquarters, in Buffalo, New York. The plaintiff submitted a doctor's note stating that she could not travel that much. Management said that there was not enough remote work for her, so she either had to return to Buffalo within 30 days, go on short-term disability leave, or be terminated with 11 weeks' severance. She rejected these proposals and hired a lawyer. The bank agreed to permit her to work remotely from Los Angeles for the rest of her pregnancy, but reinstatement was conditioned on releasing her claims for money damages. She sued for FMLA interference, also raising claims under Title VII and California and New York state anti-discrimination law. The Second Circuit vacated some of the claims, but remanded the case for further proceedings. [*Sheng v. M&TBank Corp.*, 848 F.3d 78 (2d Cir. 2017); see D. Sharmin Arefin, *2nd Cir. Reverses Judgment in Favor of Bank Employer on "Remote Work" Pregnancy Discrimination Claims*, Maurice Wutscher LLP (Feb. 27, 2017), available at Lexology.com]

According to the Hastings College of the Law Center for WorkLife Law, the first lawsuit under Family Responsibilities Discrimination (FRD) was brought in 1971. By 2015, Hastings' database included more than 4,000 FRD cases. [The Hastings study is called *Litigating the Maternal Wall: U.S. Lawsuits Charging Discrimination Against Workers with Family Responsibilities*; see Fred Schneyer, *Strong Rise Seen in Family Responsibilities Discrimination Suits*, plansponsor.com (July 10, 2006). The Center has published a work sheet on FRD: Center for WorkLife Law, *Family Responsibilities Discrimination: Work Sheet* <http://work lifelaw.org/pubs/FRD_Fact_Sheet.pdf> (undated, last viewed Mar. 3, 2017)]

The Center for WorkLife Law updated its study, analyzing more than 4,400 suits FRD claims. The study shows a major increase in the number of filings over the past decade. Plaintiffs are much more likely to succeed bringing FRD cases than other employment cases: plaintiffs won about 75% of FRD cases, but only about a third of other types of employment cases. About two-thirds of the cases (67%) involved pregnancy and maternity leave, with a further 11% about elder care and 15% about care of spouses or children. Over the previous decade, elder care allegations increased 650%, pregnancy accommodation cases rose by 315%, and there was an 800% increase in cases charging denial of accommodation of breast feeding. Association discrimination cases increased by 400%, and claims about paternity leave rose 336%, although most claims brought by men were under the FMLA, and the success rate was lower than cases brought by women. [<http://www.worklifelaw.org/pubs/FRDupdate2016.pdf> (last accessed Mar. 4, 2017); see Alison B. Asarnow, *Study Shows Spike in Family Responsibilities Discrimination Claims*, Katz Marshall & Banks LLP (May 27, 2016), available at Lexology.com]

Perhaps most common form of FRD is "maternal wall" bias against mothers. It usually is experienced when a woman announces her pregnancy, returns from maternity leave, or switches from full-time work to a flexible schedule. Some women experience "lack of fit" FRD: the employer assumes that mothers are not suitable for a particular job, so they are channeled into inferior jobs that the employer considers more suitable. FRD cases tend to be brought under Title VII alleging disparate treatment or impact, harassment, failure to promote, or retaliation. Gender stereotyping might also be asserted under Title VII. Some FRD plaintiffs assert adverse employment action based on the employer's beliefs about appropriate social roles for men and women: for example, that a childless unmarried man would be more available to work long hours. Mothers might also be subjected to tougher scrutiny than other employees; they might be given negative evaluations that make it easier for them to be fired for minor infractions. The case law differs on whether a Title VII FRD claim requires an opposite-sex comparator.

FRD claims have also been brought under the FMLA: for example, discriminating against an employee who returns from leave or using gender stereotypes in granting or denying leave. ADA cases are also possible, such as association discrimination cases when a family member has health problems, or if the employee perceives a pregnant employee as disabled. Another possibility is an ERISA case, when the plaintiff alleges that the employer tried to avoid heavy medical costs by denying health benefits. [Debra S. Katz, *Recent Developments: Sex Discrimination and Family Responsibility Claims*, Katz Marshall & Banks LLP (Nov. 24, 2016), available at Lexology.com; includes older cases.]

Out of more than 2,100 caregiver discrimination cases tracked by the Center for WorkLifeLaw, there were four verdicts or settlements over $10 million (two of them were class actions). Twenty-one cases had verdicts or settlements over $1 million, usually because of high punitive damages. The average verdict or settlement was $578,316. Nearly all (88%) of caregiver-discrimination plaintiffs were women, and female plaintiffs won 51.6% of their cases whereas only 41.9% of male plaintiffs were successful. The Center for WorkLifeLaw noted that many cases reflect the "new supervisor syndrome" (which also operates in other types of workplace discrimination cases): the plaintiff was doing fine and receiving adequate accommodations, until the new supervisor canceled the accommodations. Some caregiver discrimination plaintiffs say their work situation deteriorated when they became pregnant with twins or triplets, or when they were expecting a second child, and management decided that they were not committed to their jobs. Some plaintiffs have alleged preemptive elder care discrimination, charging that a supervisor tries to get rid of them before they devote too much time to caring for their parents. [Preventing Discrimination Against Employees with Family Responsibilities: A Model Policy for Employers, <http://www.work lifelaw.org/pubs/Model_Policy_for_Employers.pdf> (last accessed Mar. 3, 2017)]

[A] Paid Leave Requirements

Employers are required to provide paid sick leave in Arizona, California, Connecticut, Massachusetts, New Jersey, New York, Oregon, Rhode Island, Vermont, and Washington state. Generally, the laws stipulate a number of hours of paid leave that employees are entitled to accrue per week or longer unit of time and explain when the hours can be used. As of July 1, 2017, Georgia companies with 25 or more employees that provide paid sick leave are required to allow employees to take up to five days a year of paid leave to care for sick members of their immediate families (e.g., spouses, parents, and children). [Shella B. Neba and Blaze R. Douglas, *Georgia Enacts Kin Care Law,* Littler Mendelson PC (May 15, 2017), available at Lexology.com] A number of cities—changing too often to cover here—also require paid sick leave. However, many states (e.g., Alabama, Florida, Georgia, Kansas, Louisiana, Michigan, Mississippi, Missouri, North Carolina, Ohio, Oklahoma, Oregon, Tennessee, and Wisconsin) have adopted statutes forbidding local jurisdictions to adopt their own paid sick leave requirements. [Towerswatson.com, *Voters in Arizona and Washington Approve Paid Sick Leave Mandate* (Feb. 23, 2017) (benefitslink.com)]

A Mercer Absence and Disability Management Survey published at the end of 2016 fund that 63% of organizations had Paid Time Off (PTO) plans, compared with 38% in 2010 and 50% in 2013. But many employees do not take all the time off available to them. Almost half of survey respondents (44%) said that their employees took less than 80% of the PTO available to them. A quarter of respondents offered paid parental bonding leave and the same proportion offered paid parental leave for the non-birth parent. Generally, parental leave for the birth parent started after the expiration of any disability leave, whereas the other parent's leave generally was allowed starting at birth. The median duration of leave in companies with paid parental leave benefits was six weeks for birth parents, four weeks for the other parent, and the amount of pay was usually 100% of the employee's regular pay. [Wolters Kluwer Law & Business, *Use Of PTO Plans Continues to Increase* (Dec. 27, 2016) (benefitslink.com)]

Enhanced family benefits may have strings attached: the family might have to identify a primary caregiver to get the longer leave and other benefits. Only the primary caregiver qualifies for longer leave time and other benefits. Most self-identified primary caregivers are women, which can enforce traditional gender roles. For example, Nestle gives the primary caregiver 14 weeks of paid and 12 weeks of unpaid leave but the other parent gets only one week of paid leave and one of unpaid leave. Accenture gives 16 weeks of leave to new mothers, eight weeks to other primary caregivers, and two weeks to secondary caregivers. Some employees (male or female) feel that they have been stigmatized and earn less and get fewer promotions if they take primary caregiver leave. [Claire Cain Miller, *Parental Benefits Where One Parent Counts for More*, NYTimes.com (Sept. 3, 2015)]

It has traditionally been the employer's prerogative to decide whether leave will be paid or unpaid. The FMLA requires employers to grant leave, within limits, when an employee has a serious health condition or cares for a family member who does However, there is no requirement that the employer pay employees who have taken FMLA leave.

The Wisconsin version of the FMLA required employers to provide disability leave to new mothers if they provide paid disability leave at all. Employers without disability plans were required to provide six weeks of unpaid leave. However, in 2014, the Sixth Circuit permanently enjoined enforcement of the law. The court found that the state law was preempted by ERISA, because could require benefits for women who do not fit the plan's definition of short-term disability. [*Sherfel v. Newson*, 768 F.3d 561 (6th Cir. 2014)]

An increasing trend is for states and cities to pass laws requiring paid leave for certain health or family events. So far, these programs are funded by payroll taxes on employees so they do not impose a direct financial burden on employers but, nevertheless, it is inconvenient to have to replace the work of employees on leave and to do the paperwork associated with the paid leave program.

The National Partnership for Women and Families published its first edition of *Expecting Better* (survey of federal and state laws about pregnancy/parenting leave) in 2005; the fourth edition was published in 2016, after updates in 2012 and 2014. The report includes a state-by-state chart summarizing family-related statutes, and a "report card." Twelve states were rated F, because they had no pro-family protective statutes. California was the only state to receive a grade of A; New York and the District of Columbia were rated A-. Connecticut, Hawaii, New Jersey, Oregon, and Rhode Island scored B+, and Illinois, Massachusetts, and Vermont were graded B. The study found that low-income parents were much less likely to get parenting-related benefits: 12% of all workers were entitled to paid family leave, but only 5% of people in the lowest quarter of wages (earning $11.64 per hour or less) got paid leave. However, 23% of workers in the highest quarter ($27.89 per hour or more) had access to paid family leave. [National Partnership for Women and Families, *Expecting Better* (4th ed. Aug. 2016), available at <http://www.nationalpartnership.org/research-library/work-family/expecting-better-2016.pdf> (last accessed Mar. 3, 2017)]

Some states (Connecticut, Hawaii, Illinois, New York, Oregon, and Rhode Island) have laws protecting victims of domestic violence in the workplace: e.g., forbidding discrimination and/or requiring time off to make court appearances and otherwise deal with domestic violence. California requires reasonable accommodation, such as changing the employee's telephone number or office location to hinder stalking. [Susan Gross Sholinsky, *Take 5: Views You Can Use: Labor and Employment*, Epstein Becker Green (Nov. 12, 2013), available at Lexology .com]

[B]   Leave for Military Families

Also note that the National Defense Authorization Act, signed on January 28, 2008, extends the requirements of the FMLA for families of military service members. An employee can use up to 12 weeks of unpaid leave when his or her spouse, child, or parent is called up or is on active duty in the armed forces. If the service member is seriously injured, his or her family member can take up to 26 weeks of FMLA leave to care for the injured service member. [Fred Schneyer, *FMLA Expansion for Military Family Headed to White House Again*, plan sponsor.com (Jan. 23, 2008)]

The 2008 revision of the FMLA final regulations makes it clear that intermittent or reduced leave can be taken for military family leave. See § 38.01[A]. Military-related FMLA leave was further expanded by the Defense Department Fiscal Year 2010 authorization bill, also known as the National Defense Authorization Act, signed October 28, 2009. The expanded entitlement allows a worker whose spouse, parent, or child is a reservist to take FMLA leave for a qualifying exigency arising from deployment to a foreign country on active duty. There is also a new leave right when an employee's spouse, parent, or child who serves in the regular armed forces is deployed to a foreign country. A military caregiver can take up to 26 weeks of leave per 12-month period to care for a parent, spouse, child, or relative to whom the employee is next of kin, when the servicemember is under treatment for a serious injury or illness incurred in the course of service (or that began before active duty but was aggravated by active duty).

The same categories of relatives can take leave to care for an ill or injured veteran who was on active duty within the five years before the date of treatment.

Notice 2010-15, 2010-6 I.R.B. 390, provides guidance in question and answer form about the HEART Act of 2008. The survivor of a deceased servicemember can make a tax-free rollover of the military death benefit and life insurance to the survivor's Roth IRA or education savings account. All qualified plans must provide that the survivors of a person who dies on active service must receive whatever additional benefits would have been provided if the servicemember had returned to work and died while employed. Final regulations under the National Defense Authorization Act permit 15 (rather than the earlier limit of five) days of rest-and-recuperation FMLA leave to be taken by an eligible employee. [Jeff Nowak, *DOL Issues Final Rule Implementing FMLA Amendments Expanding Military Family Leave and Leave for Airline Flight Crew Members*, Franczek Radelet FMLA Insights (Feb. 7, 2013) (benefitslink.com)]

Some states, e.g., California, Illinois, Indiana, Maine, Minnesota, Nebraska, New York, Rhode Island, and Washington have their own states providing leave rights to the families of servicemembers. [Buck Consultants FYI, *Washington State Expands Employee Leave Entitlements* (May 19, 2008) (benefitslink.com); George P. Kostakos, Stephen T. Melnick, *New Rhode Island Law Grants Military Families Unpaid Leave*, Littler Mendelson Press Releases (July 2008) (benefits link.com)]

[C] EEOC Guidance on Best Practices About Caregivers

The EEOC defines "best practices" as "proactive measures that go beyond federal nondiscrimination requirements" to remove barriers to equal employment opportunity. In May 2007, the EEOC issued Enforcement Guidance on employers' responsibilities toward workers who are caregivers for family members.

Although discrimination against caregivers is not per se forbidden, the EEOC warns that in some situations, placing an employee caregiver in an unfavorable position could constitute unlawful disparate treatment that violates Title VII or the Americans With Disabilities Act's ban on discrimination for associating with a person with a disability. The EEOC said that the Guidance does not create a new protected category; it explains the EEOC's enforcement priorities when caregiving is an additional element in an allegation of discrimination, and warns against making employment decisions based on stereotypes—e.g., that women, but not men, will have caregiving responsibilities.

The document points out that African-American women are particularly likely to combine paid work and family responsibilities, and lower-income workers are likely to encounter times when they have care responsibilities but cannot afford to hire someone to take care of the child or elder. However, the EEOC notes that there will probably be no violation of Title VII if employment decisions reflect poor or declining work performance and not assumptions or stereotypes—even if the employee's work is sub-par because of caregiving responsibilities. [EEOC Enforcement Guidance: *Unlawful Disparate Treatment of Workers with Caregiving Responsibilities* Number 915.002 <http://www.eeoc.gov/policy/docs/caregiving.html> (May 23, 2007) (last viewed Mar. 4, 2017)]

The EEOC followed up with a 13-page document to help employers adopt work-life policies that will assist employees who are responsible for the care of vulnerable children, parents, and other dependents. The EEOC's suggestions include training managers about the applicable laws and about employer policies; avoiding stereotypes (that mothers are caregivers and fathers are not; that mothers are not committed to their careers); allow flexible schedules if consistent with operational needs; help employees maintain their skills (while on leave and return to the workforce post-leave). [EEOC, *Employer Best Practices for Workers with Caregiving Responsibilities*, <http://www.eeoc.gov/policy/docs/caregiver-best-practices.html> (Jan. 19, 2011) (last accessed Mar. 4, 2017)]

§ 28.02   EMPLOYER-PROVIDED DAY CARE

One option, perhaps the most appreciated by employees, is for the employer to maintain an on-site day care center. Calculating the costs and benefits of running a day care center can be difficult. Initial expenses can be high, but this perk is valuable in recruiting good employees and retaining employees who need quality care for their children.

On-site care is only feasible for large companies—and probably is more workable outside big cities because metropolitan rents are often prohibitive. An employer-sponsored day care center has to be licensed. It will be subject to ongoing inspections. The employer company could become liable if, for example, a child was injured on the premises, or several children developed a contagious illness. The standard Worker's Compensation insurance policy also excludes injuries that occur in an employer-operated day care center.

It can be convenient for the employer to contract out daily operations to an experienced provider of high-quality child care, although this adds further expenses. The employer can also co-sponsor a nearby child care center that offers care to employees of several companies.

The Society for Human Resources Management's 2016 benefits survey found that the percentage of employers providing subsidized child care centers has fallen significantly: 9% did so in 1996, dropping to 4% in 2012 and 2% in 2016. Cisco Systems found that its in-house child care center was only 60%–80% full, so it provides backup child care on an ad hoc basis. Although child care benefits are popular with employees, they are expensive, hard to administer, and create significant liability risks. Employers tend to prefer PTO banks, flexible scheduling, and paid parental leave. [Joanne Sammer, *Onsite Child Care Ebbs as Flexible Benefits Flow,* shrm.org (Nov. 9, 2016) (benefitslink.com)]

Home Depot runs one of the largest day care centers in Atlanta for its employees. Patagonia Inc. spends $1 million a year on a facility with a 28-person staff, and says that it recoups 90% of the costs each year from tax credits, reduced turnover, and increased employee engagement. [Rachel Feintzeig, *The Case for Day Care at the Office*, WSJ.com (Sept. 26, 2016)]

However, it is much more common for employers to reimburse employees for some of their child care expenses. [See § 28.07 for a discussion of child care fringe benefits and their tax implications. A smaller-scale program gives employees "I&R" (information and referral) to child care resources, but does not actually furnish services or funds.]

A child care credit, 25% of qualified child care expenditures plus 10% of child care information and referral expenditures, capped at $150,000 per year, was provided under the Tax Relief, Unemployment Insurance Reauthorization, and Job Creation Act of 2010, Pub. L. No. 111-312, but only until the end of 2012. The American Taxpayer Relief Act of 2012, Pub. L. No. 112-240, extended the availability of this credit once again. The credit is claimed on Form 8882.

§ 28.03   BREAST FEEDING IN THE WORKPLACE

Breast feeding for at least the first six months of life, and preferably a year, is the medical recommendation for newborn babies. So either new mothers must choose bottle feeding; delay their return to work until they are ready to stop breast feeding; or participate in a workplace lactation program that either allows them to feed their babies at the workplace or gives them an appropriate private place to pump and store breast milk.

Workplace lactation programs are a good value for employers, because they aid employee retention. Furthermore, breast-fed babies are often healthier than formula-fed babies, so their parents need less time off to deal with babies' illnesses. The demands of a lactation program are modest. Participating employees need a private, reasonably quiet and pleasant place to express breast milk and a refrigerator or cooler to keep it cool, plus a sink to wash up. Typically, employees will need two 30-minute, or three 20-minute, breaks to express milk.

A University of Minnesota study said that only 40% of working mothers had access to adequate break time and appropriate space to express milk. [<https://www.minnpost.com/second-opinion/2015/10/most-working-moms-dont-have-adequate-workplace-support-breastfeeding-u-m-stud> (last accessed Mar. 4, 2017)]

The PPACA enacts new 29 U.S.C. § 207(r)(1), requiring all employers subject to the Fair Labor Standards Act (FLSA) to provide reasonable breaks to express breast milk for mother of infants up to a year old. A private space other than a restroom must be provided. Even pre-PPACA, about half the states had already enacted workplace lactation laws.

Companies with fewer than 50 employees are exempt if the requirement would create undue hardship (significant difficulty or expense for the employer). Although in general, the FLSA requires pay for breaks of less than 20 minutes, the new federal requirement says the break time can be either paid or unpaid. The new law does not preempt state laws that give greater protection to employees. The Patient Protection and Affordable Care Act (PPACA) provision on breast-feeding amends the FLSA, with the result that employees who are exempt under the FLSA (as executives, professionals, administrative workers, outside salespersons, or computer professionals) are not covered. [DOL's Wage and Hour Division has a Fact Sheet, *Break Time for Nursing Mothers.* <http://www.dol.gov/whd/nursingmothers/faqBTNM.htm> (last accessed Mar. 4, 2017). Depending on the scope of PPACA repeal, this provision might be eliminated.]

The Fact Sheet says that the FLSA does not require pay for breaks taken to express milk—but if the employer already provides paid breaks, nursing mothers must be allowed to use their paid breaks to express milk. The general FLSA requirement—that employees must be paid for break time unless they are completely free from work duties—continues to apply in this context. On an average,

DOL expects that two to three breaks will be required in an eight-hour shift, including time to get to the lactation area (which must be located conveniently enough that the mother is not deterred from taking breaks), any waiting time if the area is full, time to get the breast pump and set it up. The employer must provide a place to store the pump and an insulated container to store the milk. The lactation area need not be reserved exclusively for use by nursing employees, as long as it is private and suitable for expressing breast milk.

Mid-2015 EEOC guidance, <http://www.eeoc.gov/laws/guidance/pregnancy_guidance.cfm> (last accessed Mar. 4, 2017), says that a manager's statement that an employee was demoted because of her schedule for breastfeeding creates an inference that the demotion was unlawful. Women must be allowed to change their schedules or use sick leave for lactation-related reasons if employees are allowed to do the same for other conditions. If employees are otherwise entitled to use breaks for personal business, nursing mothers must be allowed to use breaks for lactation. PPACA does not preempted state laws that give employees additional protection. PPACA requires employers to provide nursing mothers with breaks for one year after the baby is born; New York, Maine, and Vermont require breaks to be provided for the first three years. [Elisheva M. Hirshman, *Don't Cry Over Spilled Milk: Best Practices for Handling Nursing Employees*, DLA Piper LLP (Feb. 11, 2016), available at Lexology.com]

In May 2013, the Fifth Circuit became the first Court of Appeals to decide a case about lactation discrimination. The Fifth Circuit treated lactation as a medical condition related to pregnancy and childbirth because it was a physiological state caused by childbirth. The plaintiff did not ask for accommodation of lactation; she alleged that she was fired merely for saying that she wanted to express milk at work. The Fifth Circuit treated this as sex discrimination that violated Title VII. [*EEOC v. Houston Funding II*, 717 F.3d 425 (5th Cir. May 30, 2013)]

In 2011, the IRS reversed its previous holding and said that breast pumps and supplies to assist lactation qualify as medical care under Code § 213(d), because they affect a structure or function of the mother's body. Therefore, they can be deductible medical expenses. If an FSA, MSA, HRA, or HSA reimburses the cost of these items, the employee does not have taxable income. [IRS Ann. 2011-14, 2011-9 I.R.B. 532]

Concluding that working mothers are the fastest-growing segment of the workforce, the National Business Group on Health released a 71-page toolkit, "Investing in Workplace Breastfeeding Programs and Policies," in early 2011. The kit was developed in conjunction with HHS' Office on Women's Health and Health Resources Services Administration's Maternal and Child Health Bureau. The kit has 10 major sections, including the business case for workplace lactation programs, the available options, experience of major employers, and resources for communicating with employees. [<http://www.businessgrouphealth.org/pub/f2ffe4f0-2354-d714-5136-79a21e9327ed> (last accessed Mar. 4, 2017)]

§ 28.04 ADOPTION ASSISTANCE

Under I.R.C. § 137, as amended by Economic Growth and Tax Relief Reconciliation Act (EGTRRA), employers can establish a written adoption assistance program, providing benefits for employees who adopt children. More than 100,000 Americans adopt children each year, so the question is whether the company will offer adoption assistance, and whether employees will get paid leave for adoption.

The tax code provides for two types of assistance. Within limits, certain employees can receive adoption assistance payments from their employers without those benefits being subject to income taxes. There is also a tax credit for adopting a child. Under prior law, more favorable tax treatment was extended when the adoptee had special needs, but current law offers the same treatment whether or not the adoptee has special needs.

PPACA made the adoption credit a refundable credit (i.e., if the credit reduces the taxpayer's tax liability below zero, he or she can receive a tax refund).

The 2017 maximum adoption credit, whether or not the child has special needs, is $13,570. Availability of the credit phases down when the adoptive parent(s)' modified Adjusted Gross Income (AGI) is more than $203,540, and phases out complete at modified AGI of $243,540. [Rev. Proc. 2016-55, 2016-45 I.R.B. 707]

Adoption assistance can be offered under a cafeteria plan—a structure that provides tax benefits for employees with no direct cash outlay by the employer. Adoption assistance programs provided to members of the armed forces are automatically treated as qualified, even if they would not otherwise satisfy the § 137 rules. But illegal adoptions, adoptions involving surrogate mothers, adoption of a stepchild, or adoption of an adult do not qualify under § 137.

§ 28.05 CORPORATE ELDER CARE ACTIVITIES

Everybody knows that the U.S. senior citizen population is growing, and soon the huge Baby Boom generation will reach retirement age. The vast majority of care provided to assist elderly people with their illnesses and limitations imposed by aging is unpaid, informal care from family members and friends.

Many middle-aged women, often at the peak of their careers, have to leave the workforce to care for their elderly parents, resulting in the sacrifice not only of immediate wages, but also reduced or unavailable pensions and lower Social Security benefits as they age. Federal legislation, the National Alzheimer's Project Act, Pub. L. No. 111-375, calls for the creation of a national strategic plan to fight Alzheimer's Disease. The law sets up an advisory council from all federal agencies dealing with health, science, and aging, as well as a coordinated national plan to improve early diagnosis and coordination of care, and to research new

treatments. [Pam Belluck, *Caring for the Patient with Alzheimer's*, NYTimes
.com (Jan. 2, 2011)]

The DOL released research briefs on two studies of paid family leave programs in California, New Jersey, and Rhode Island. The researchers found that the growth of paid leave in California and New Jersey has been steady, but is generally taken to care for new babies, not sick family members. Nearly all (88%) of California claims in 2014 were for infant care. However, caregiving for the elderly is likely to become a greater focus; by 2030, one-fifth of the population will be age 65 or older.[Lucas Deloach, *An Aging America and the Future of Paid Family Leave*, Seyfarth Shaw LLP (Sept. 1, 2016), available at Lexology.com]

Deloitte, recognizing that not all caregivers take care of children, added up to 16 weeks of paid caregiving leave including elder care and care for a sick family member. Starting in May 2016, Nike allowed up to 8 weeks of paid leave to care for a sick relative. The AARP Public Policy Institute/National Alliance for Caregiving said that almost 17% of Americans over 18 (approximately 40 million people) are unpaid caregivers for an adult: see <http://www.caregiving.org/wp-content/uploads/2015/05/2015_CaregivingintheUS_Final-Report-June-4_WEB.pdf> (last accessed Mar. 5, 2017). [Rachel Emma Silverman, *Deloitte to Offer Paid Leave for Elder Caregiving*, WSJ.com (Sept. 8, 2016)]

§ 28.06   THE CORPORATE ELDER CARE ROLE

One problem with corporate elder care efforts is that they often use a child-care template that is not very effective—child care doesn't require tangling with the Medicare Part D labyrinth, for example! Another problem is that, in a time of soaring benefit costs, corporations are far more willing to provide low-cost Information & Referrals (I&R) than more costly benefits such as paying for geriatric care management or offering paid leave to employees with elder care problems. The I&R system could be limited in scope and could be poorly edited, so that obsolete listings remain, or poor-quality providers are not eliminated. Even if the I&R system is excellent, employees still face a lot of hard work in creating and managing the elder care plan.

Under an I&R plan, the HR department, Employee Assistance Program, or other relevant department maintains listings of nursing homes, home health agencies, government agencies for the aging, and other resources.

Other elder care resources that employers can provide include support groups for caregivers; seminars and hotlines about relevant topics; caregiver fairs; counseling from a psychologist or clinical social worker; emergency and respite care; and case management services provided by social workers or geriatric care managers who help set up and manage a complete elder care plan.

Hundreds of companies, including Home Depot, Hewlett-Packard, and Yahoo, with millions of employees, offer backup elder care. The mechanism is for the employer to subscribe to a call center, which sends a qualified aide to the elder. The aides are trained and subject to background checks. Typically, the employee can use the service for 10–20 days, paying about $6 an hour for the service, with the company assuming the rest of the cost. Bright Horizons and Care .com are the two largest suppliers of backup elder care. Care.com also offers care planning by licensed social workers, paid for by employers. [Paula Span, *A Way to Stay on the Job*, NYTimes.com (Dec. 18, 2013)]

Attempts have been made to offer favorably priced long-term care insurance policies covering employees and/or their parents as a voluntary benefit, but it never became popular, and very few insurers remain in this market. Rev. Proc. 2016-55, 2016-45 I.R.B. 707, defines the qualified long-term care insurance policy premiums that can be deducted for 2017 by individual taxpayers, ranging from $410 a year for people who have not reached age 40 to $5,110 for those who are 70 years or older. Up to $360 a day in benefits from a qualified policy can be received tax-free.

§ 28.07   DEPENDENT CARE ASSISTANCE PLANS

The Internal Revenue Code recognizes, and gives favorable tax treatment to, plans under which the employer makes direct payments to provide dependent care to employees, or the employer reimburses employees for certain dependent care expenses. [I.R.C. § 129] The employer is not obligated to pre-fund the plan. It can pay benefits as they arise, out of current income, with no need to maintain a separate account. However, the employer is required to provide reasonable notice to eligible employees that the program is in existence and how it operates.

Employees do not have taxable income because of participation in an I.R.C. § 129 plan. However, the plan cannot pay more for dependent care than the employee earns. (In other words, the plan can't be set up as a perk for employees who are, in essence, on parenthood leave and earn very little.) Furthermore, in effect the plan only assists employees who are single parents, or who are part of a two-career couple, because the employee will have taxable income if the I.R.C. § 129 benefits exceed the income of the employee's spouse, unless that spouse is a full-time student or disabled.

In addition to these limitations, the maximum employer contribution to an I.R.C. § 129 plan that can be excluded from income is $5,000 per employee. This is further reduced to $2,500 in the case of married employees who file separate returns. The § 129 amounts are not indexed for inflation, so those numbers remain current.

For this purpose, dependent care expenses are household services and other expenses that are incurred to permit the employee to hold a job outside the home. In the I.R.C. § 129 context, "dependents" means dependent children under age 15, or a spouse or other dependent (e.g., an aging parent) who is physically or mentally incapable of self-care.

The Code defines a qualified dependent care assistance plan as a written plan for the exclusive benefit of employees, subject to a classification created by the employer but approved as nondiscriminatory by the IRS. To be considered nondiscriminatory, not more than 25% of the contributions to the plan or benefits received from the plan may relate to shareholders, 5% owners, or their families. The average benefits provided under the plan to employees who are not highly compensated must be 55% or more of those provided to highly compensated employees.

If the plan fails to be qualified for this reason, then HCEs (but not other employees) will have taxable income as a result of plan participation. Every year, by January 31, employees must be given a written report of the amounts paid or expenses incurred by the plan for that employee's dependent care in the previous year. An employer-provided day care center is deemed to be a welfare benefit plan, but a dependent care plan that involves reimbursement of employees' dependent care expenses is not.

See the IRS *Tax Topic 602—Child and Dependent Care Credit,* <http://www.irs.gov/taxtopics/tc602.html> (Feb. 17, 2017) (last accessed Mar. 4, 2017) for a taxpayer's eye view of this credit.

CHAPTER 29

DIVERSITY IN THE WORKPLACE

§ 29.01 INTRODUCTION

It can no longer be assumed that all employees in an organization will be young, able-bodied, Anglo-Saxon males. Greater diversity within a workplace allows recruitment of the best available talent and the widest variety of viewpoints and inputs—but also creates potential for misunderstanding and conflict among employees.

The HR department's mission is to promote efficiency and cooperation—not to eliminate differences or even prejudices. A company's workforce doesn't have to worship together, enjoy the same sporting events, celebrate the same holidays, or even like each other. They do have to understand the factors shaping other peoples' behavior, strive to avoid offending others, be tolerant of unintended offensive remarks and actions, and work together harmoniously and productively.

See Chapters 18, 34, and 41 for the Equal Employment Opportunity Commission's (EEOC) changes in its stance. At one time, the agency's position was that discrimination on the basis of sexual orientation or gender identity was not covered by Title VII. Since 2012, however, the EEOC has brought several administrative proceedings and filed suit in support of employees on these issues. [Richard D. Tuschman, *EEOC Will Now Process Sexual Orientation Discrimination Claims*, Akerman LLP (Feb. 24, 2015), available at Lexology.com]

However, the Missouri Court of Appeals ruled that the Missouri Human Rights Act does not prohibit discrimination on the basis of sexual orientation. The statute forbids discrimination based on "sex," which is not defined; the terms "sexual orientation" and "sexual identity" are not in the statute. [Armstrong Teasdale LLP, *Appeals Court Rules Sexual Orientation Not Covered by the Missouri Human Rights Act* (Oct. 27, 2015), available at Lexology.com]

In mid-2016, a three-judge panel of the Seventh Circuit initially held that, although the court was sympathetic to the EEOC, it felt constrained by precedent to hold that Title VII does not cover sexual orientation discrimination. But just a few months later, in October, the Seventh Circuit reversed and vacated this decision, and agreed to re-hear the case en banc. The en banc court held, by a vote of 8-3, that sexual orientation is covered by Title VII. [*Hively v. Ivy Tech Cmty. Coll.*, 830 F.3d 698 (7th Cir. 2016) and 853 F.3d 339 (7th Cir. 2017); see Jennifer L. Garner, *7th Circuit Rehears Hively Case*, Bowditch & Dewey (Dec. 1, 2016), available at Lexology.com; Damon W. Suden, *Seventh Circuit Reverses Decision That Title VII Doesn't Protect Against Anti-Gay Discrimination and Agrees to Re-hear Employment Discrimination Case*, Kelley Drye & Warren LLP (Oct. 11, 2016), available at Lexology.com; Joe Palazzolo, *Court Says Gay Employees Can Sue Under 1964 Civil Rights Act*, WSJ.com (Apr. 4, 2017)]

If federal protection is revoked, advocates will give higher priority to state and local rules. The New York City Human Rights Law forbids discrimination against transsexual people. California's Fair Housing and Employment Act prohibits discrimination or harassment in employment on the basis of gender identity, gender expression, or sexual orientation. Illinois and the District of Columbia include gender identity as a protected class. New York State does not have a statutory ban but Governor Andrew Cuomo took executive action forbidding discrimination in employment based on gender identity, transgender status, or gender dysphoria. According to the Human Rights campaign, close to 20 states have statutory protection for trans people. [Jesse McKinley, *Cuomo Planning Discrimination Protections for Transgender New Yorkers*, NYTimes.com (Oct. 22, 2015); Editorial Board, *New York Leads the Way on Transgender Rights*, NYTimes.com (Oct. 24, 2015); Amy L. Bess et. al., *Gender Identity Discrimination Claims on the Rise at State and Federal Levels*, Vedder Price PC (Mar. 3, 2016), available at Lexology.com.]

The employer should make a plan to respond when an employee announces transition. The employer should designate specific contacts for all employees to discuss the issues. There should be a written open-door policy encouraging transitioning employees to consult their managers. The employer should ask what accommodations are sought, the timetable for transition, and the name the employee wants to use. Co-workers should be educated to create an atmosphere of tolerance and mutual respect. [Janet A. Hendrick, *A Workforce in Transition: Working with Transgender Employees*, Fisher & Phillips LLP (Sept. 1, 2015), available at Lexology.com]

OSHA's Best Practices guide for providing restroom access for transgender workers recommends allowing workers to use the restroom for the sex they are transitioning to, and opposes forcing transitioning employees to use special or separate restrooms. [<http://www.dol.gov/asp/policy-development/Transgender BathroomAccessBestPractices.pdf> (June 1, 2015) (last accessed Mar. 5, 2017)]

OSHA's published position <https://www.osha.gov/Publications/OSHA 3795.pdf> (undated; last accessed Feb. 26, 2017) is that employees should be permitted to use the restroom consistent with their gender identity, not their birth certificate identity.

The question of restroom access is extremely controversial, and has led to legislative and litigation action as well as administrative rulings. North Carolina passed a law in March 2016 requiring people to use public restrooms that conform to the gender noted on their birth certificates. The Department of Justice brought a suit in the District Court for the Middle District of North Carolina, alleging that the law violates Title VII by compelling public agencies to discriminate. The state of North Carolina countersued the Department of Justice. Suits were filed by 11 states in May 2016 to challenge the rules about usage of bathrooms, locker rooms, and hospitals. [Alan Blinder, Richard Pérez-Peña and Eric Lichtblau, *Countersuits over North Carolina's Bias Law*, NYTimes.com (May 10, 2016); Louise Radnofsky, *Antibias Rules Set Up Tricky Question Over Gay Rights*, WSJ.com (May 26, 2016)] The District Court for the Eastern District of Pennsylvania ruled in mid-2017 that gender dysphoria and other conditions related to transexuality could be covered by the ADA, a holding that could increase employment protection for transpeople in the workplace. [*Blatt v. Cabela's Retail, Inc.,* No. 5:14-cv-04822 (E.D. Pa. 2017); see Nathaniel M. Glasser and Kate B. Rhodes, *Federal Court Rules Gender Dysphoria May Be Disability Under ADA,* Epstein Becker Green (June 9 2017), available at Lexology.com] It is likely that this is an area in which the Trump administration's policy will differ from that of the previous administration.

The DOL started to collect data on employment of people with disabilities in 2009. In 2009, the DOL found that there were 5.2 million disabled people in the workplace—a figure that actually dropped, to 4.9 million, in 2016. In 2016, about 300,000 fewer people with disabilities in the age group 16–64 were employed or looking for work. Labor force participation for working-age men with disabilities was 37.9% in 2009, 33% in 2015, and 34.2% in 2016. Participation among working-age women with disabilities was 32.5% in 2009 and 28.3% in 2016. For both sexes, the unemployment rate is more than twice as high for people with disabilities than for the non-disabled. [Eric Morath, *Weak Job Prospects for Disabled Workers Show Labor Market Isn't Fully Healed,* WSJ .com (June 22, 2017)]

[A] Federal Agency Diversity Standards

Federal government procurement is a major driver of the economy, so standards for federal contractors, as enforced by the Office of Federal Contract Compliance Programs (OFCCP), are significant for businesses that hold federal contracts or are subcontractors of federal contractors. However, this is an area in which Trump-era changes can be expected.

The OFCCP published a final rule in mid-2013, implementing the Vietnam Era Veterans' Readjustment Assistance Act (VEVRAA) and Rehabilitation Act, § 503. The rule imposes new requirements for federal contractors' affirmative action plans. It also adds new requirements for job listings, changes in the wording of the EEO clause, and additional recordkeeping requirements. Under the final rule, federal contractors that already had an obligation to develop written affirmative action plans are now required to set hiring benchmarks for protected veterans and a hiring goal for Qualified Individuals With Disabilities (QIWDs). Veteran hiring can be compared to a benchmark of the percentage of veterans in the civilian labor force, as set out in the OFCCP Website's benchmark database. The employer can also set its own benchmark, based on the average percentage of veterans in the state's labor force; the number of veterans participating in the state's employment service delivery system; applicant and hiring ratios for the previous year; and the contractor's conclusion about the effectiveness of its outreach and recruitment efforts.

The latest Rehabilitation Act regulations set a goal of 7% of each job group in federal contractors' workforces to be QIWDs. If the actual percentage in a work group is lower, the employer must determine if there are impediments to equal employment, and carry out a corrective program. The employer is required to invite covered veterans and QIWDs to self-identify after they have been hired and before starting work. The final rules add a new opportunity to self-identify before a job offer is made, so the contractor can calculate its percentage of veterans and disabled applicants. The invitation to self-identify can be included in application materials, or with the invitation already used to gather information about gender, ethnicity, and race. The 2013 regulation requires contractors to perform a new disability survey in their workforce every five years.

Under VEVRAA, federal contractors must keep records of the number of applicants who are protected veterans; the number of job openings; number of applicants for all jobs; and number of jobs filled. Contractors must also keep records about their outreach and recruitment efforts. The Rehabilitation Act regulations require similar documentation of applications, jobs, and hiring. Job listings posted by federal contractors must indicate that they are federal contractors—e.g., by including "VEVRAA Federal Contractor" in the listing. Subcontracts must include an EEO clause—e.g., by citing 41 C.F.R. § 60-300.5(a) and adding, in bold type, "This contractor and subcontractor shall abide by the requirements of 41 C.F.R. § 60-300.5(a). This regulation prohibits discrimination against qualified individuals on the basis of disability, and requires affirmative action by covered prime contractors and subcontractors to employ and advance in employment qualified individuals with disabilities." [Winston & Strawn LLP, *OFCCP Announces Final Rule on Veterans and Employees with Disabilities*, Lexology.com (Aug. 29, 2013)]

As the cohort of Vietnam veterans ages, more and more of them retire, leading to ongoing reductions in the VEVRAA benchmark. As of March 31, 2017, the benchmark fell from 6.9% to 6.7%. [Stephanie Underwood, *Hiring Benchmark for Protected Veterans Is Reduced Again*, Constangy Brooks Smith & Prophete LLP (Apr. 5, 2017), available at Lexology.com. VEVRAA Benchmark Database: <https://ofccp.dol-esa.gov/errd/VEVRAA.jsp>]

President Obama signed an executive order on July 21, 2014. Executive Order 13672 prohibits discrimination by federal contractors on the basis of lesbian, bisexual, or transgender status. There is no exemption for religious employers. [Peter Baker, *Obama Calls for a Ban on Job Bias Against Gays*, N.Y. Times, July 21, 2014, *available at* NYTimes.com]

On January 30, 2017 the Trump White House announced that this Executive Order (EO) would remain in place, although it was possible that further EOs would be adopted, including one with a religious freedom provision that would permit religious-based discrimination against LGBT employees and customers. [Jeremy W. Peters, *Obama's Protections for L.G.B.T. Workers Will Remain Under Trump*, NYTimes.com (Jan. 30, 2017)]

The Fair Pay and Safe Workplaces EO has been rescinded, with one consequence being a reduction in federal contractors' reporting and disclosure obligations, which could make it more difficult for employees to obtain evidence to bolster their claims of discrimination.

An HHS rule, finalized as of July 18, 2016, forbids discrimination against transgender patients by health care providers and insurers. Medical treatments must be covered for transgender people they would be covered for cisgender people. The proposal applies to all insurance companies that sell health insurance on the Patient Protection and Affordable Care Act (PPACA) Exchanges. It also applies to federally funded programs such as Medicare and Medicaid. Health care facilities that accept federal funding are not allowed to discriminate against transgender people. [Anna North, *New Health Care Rule Offers Key Protections for Transgender Americans*, NYTimes.com (Sept. 4, 2015)]

The final rule does not state directly whether or not sexual orientation discrimination violates the PPACA anti-discrimination provision, but the preamble to the final rule says that it is HHS policy to forbid sexual orientation discrimination, and HHS will continue to monitor legal developments. As of March 5, 2017, the final rule was no longer available on the HHS Website. [<http://www.hhs.gov/sites/default/files/2016-06-07-section-1557-finalrule-summary-508.pdf>; see Julie LaVille Hamlet and Jennifer B. Van Regenmorter, *HHS Issues Final Rule Implementing PPACA Nondiscrimination Provisions*, Foster Swift Collins & Smith PC (June 30, 2016), available at Lexology.com] At press time in 2017, information about Section 1557 had been removed from HHS' official Website.

In early 2017, the District Court for the Northern District of Texas granted a nationwide preliminary injunction against enforcement of § 1557's provisions about discrimination against transgender people. The rule was supposed to take effect July 18, 2016, but for EGHPs and insurers required to change their plan designs, the effective date was supposed to be the first day of the first plan year on or after January 1, 2017. The suit was brought by eight states and three private religious providers of health care. They argued that "on the basis of sex" should be limited to immutable binary differences between male and female. They also argued that the Title IX religious exemption should protect them against having to deliver health care that violates their beliefs. The district court granted relief under the Religious Freedom Restoration Act (RFRA), holding that § 1557 imposed costs on the exercise of religious beliefs. [*Franciscan Alliance, et al. v. Burwell*, Civil Action No. 7:16-cv-00108-O,2016 U.S. Dist. LEXIS 183116 (N.D. Tex. Dec. 31, 2016); see Tabatha L. George, Alexa Greenbaum and Jaklyn Wrigley, *Federal Judge Blocks Transgender Protections*, Fisher Phillips (Jan. 3, 2017), available at Lexology.com. The case is now called *Franciscan Alliance v. Price*.]

On December 3, 2014, the OFCCP issued a final rule to implement Executive Order 13672 (adding sexual orientation and gender identity discrimination to Executive Order 11246, the basic ban on discrimination by federal contractors). The final rule forbids federal contractors to discriminate on the basis of sexual orientation or gender identity. The contractors must include the current version of the EEO clause in their new or modified subcontracts and purchase orders and must update the EEO language in their advertisements and notices. However, 41 C.F.R. Parts 60-2 and 60-4 [requirements for affirmative action and written affirmative action programs] still refers only to race, gender, and ethnicity; sexual orientation and gender identity are not included. [Barbara A. Duncombe and Josha D. Prentice, *OFCCP Issues LGBT Non-Discrimination Final Rule*, Taft Stettinius & Hollister LLP (Dec. 5, 2014), available at Lexology.com]

On January 28, 2015, the OFCCP issued a Notice of Proposed Rulemaking (NPRM) rescinding the agency's existing sex discrimination guidelines and replacing them with new guidelines, reflecting developments since the original guidelines were issued in 1970. However, as of March 5, 2017, information about this NPRM was no longer on the OFCCP Website.

The OFCCP issued a final rule in mid-2016, effective August 15, 2016. Under the OFCCP rule discrimination on the basis of sex includes discrimination on the basis of pregnancy, childbirth, sex stereotyping, gender identity, and transgender status. The OFCCP rule does not cover sexual orientation, because the OFCCP's position is that sexual orientation discrimination is forbidden by Executive Order 11246. The OFCCP final rule requires transitioning employees to be given access to restrooms and similar facilities based on the gender with which they identify. According to the OFCCP, it is unlawful to maintain a health plan that excludes health care services related to sexual dysphoria or gender transition. [81 Fed. Reg. 39107 (June 15, 2016); OFCCP fact sheet, *OFCCP's Sex Discrimination Final Rule*, <https://www.dol.gov/ofccp/SexDiscrimination/SexDiscrim FinalRuleFactSheet_JRFQA508c.pd> (undated; last accessed Mar. 5, 2017). *See* Cara Yates Crotty, *OFCCP Issues Final Rule on Sex Discrimination*, Constangy Brooks Smith & Prophete LLP (June 21, 2016), available at Lexology.com]

In 2016, the District Court for the District of Connecticut held that employment discrimination against a job applicant on the basis of transgender identity. The Southern District of New York held that, although it called sexual orientation discrimination "reprehensible," it held that it did not violate Title VII in 2016—only to be reversed by the Second Circuit in March of 2017. [*Fabian v. Hospital of Cen. Conn.*, No. 3:12-cv-01154-SRU (D. Conn. Mar. 18, 2016); *Christiansen v. Omnicom Grp., Inc.*, 852 F.3d 195 (2d Cir. 2017). See Stefanie K. Vaudreuil, *Revisiting Transgender Employment Issues*, Liebert Cassidy Whitmore (June 2, 2016), available at Lexology.com]

The District Court for the Eastern District of Michigan held that the RFRA made a funeral home exempt from a Title VII suit about firing an employee who did not conform to the dress code. The dress code required male employees to wear dark suits with trousers; the employee, who was transitioning from male to female, wore what the employer considered inappropriate female clothing that violated the employer's religious beliefs. The district court held that, to overcome an RFRA exemption claim, the EEOC must show that the law it sought to enforce was the least restrictive means of enforcing a compelling government interest and held that Title VII was not the least restrictive means. The EEOC appealed to the Sixth Circuit. [*EEOC v. R.G. & G.R. Harris Funeral Homes*, 201 F. Supp. 3d 837 (E.D. Mich. 2016); see Robert G. Young, *"Least Restrictive Means?" Court Grants Employer Religious Exemption from Title VII in Gender Stereotyping Case*, Bowditch & Dewey (Sept. 8, 2016), available at Lexology.com; Robin E.

Shea, *EEOC Appeals Loss in Detroit Transgender Case*, Constangy Brooks Smith & Prophete LLP (Oct. 17, 2016), available at Lexology.com.]

In early 2016, the EEOC issued a statement and guidance about discrimination against people who are or appear to be Muslim or Middle Eastern. [Q&As: <http://www.eeoc.gov/eeoc/publications/muslim_middle_eastern_employers.cfm> (last accessed Mar. 5, 2017) about hiring, harassment, background checks, and religious accommodation; <http://www.eeoc.gov/eeoc/publications/muslim_middle_eastern_employees.cfm> (last accessed Mar. 5, 2017) covering approximately the same topics, but intended for job applicants and employees.] The EEOC's position is that employment cannot be denied to women who wear hijabs on the basis that it makes customers uncomfortable, nor can a temporary agency comply with a client's request to either refer someone else to work there or make the employee remove her hijab. In some circumstances, employers must grant requests to use a conference room for prayers, unless the room is needed at that time for business purposes. [Michael T. Miller, *EEOC Seeks to Prevent Discrimination Against Muslim and Middle Eastern Employees*, Briggs and Morgan (Feb. 22, 2016), available at Lexology.com]

Later that year, the EEOC released guidelines on national origin discrimination, replacing § 13 of the compliance manual. The guidelines apply to employers with four or more employees, irrespective of the employee's immigration status. Foreign nationals outside the United States who apply to work in the United States are also covered. The guidelines define national origin as a person's or ancestors' place of origin, country, or geographic region. An ethnic group is a group sharing common characteristics such as language, culture, ancestry, or race. Under the guidelines, national origin discrimination includes discrimination on the basis of ethnicity (e.g., Hispanic) or physical, linguistic, or cultural traits such as dress or accent. Perception of origin and association with persons of a disfavored nationality are also covered. An adverse employment action or hostile work environment can constitute discrimination. [<https://www.eeoc.gov/laws/guidance/national-origin-guidance.cfm> (last accessed Mar. 5, 2017); see Kristin Aquino-Pham, *EEOC Issues Guidance on National Origin Discrimination That Applies to Foreign National Employees*, Greenberg Traurig LLP (Nov. 23, 2016), available at Lexology.com]

§ 29.02 THE GLASS CEILING

Unfortunately, some people are actively and consciously hostile to those different from themselves. They engage in whatever discriminatory actions they think they can get away with. However, overt hatred and resentment are not the only factors that block full advancement for qualified women and members of minority groups. There are other, subtler forces at work, sometimes affecting people who on a conscious level are objective and tolerant.

The prejudices of the past cast a long shadow. If law and business schools used to discriminate against minorities and women, then the supply of members of these groups with professional degrees, and with decades of business experience, will be limited. If a company hardly ever recruits women or members of minority groups for its training program, and if its policy is to promote from within, then it will look to its (overwhelmingly white male) middle managers when it's time to fill senior posts.

These subtler barriers to advancement are sometimes called the "glass ceiling": Advancement up to a point is reasonably easy, but there are invisible barriers to achieving the really top jobs. See the reports of a federal commission convened under the Glass Ceiling Act, a provision of the Civil Rights Act of 1999. [Pub. L. No. 102-166]

According to the main report, "Many judgments on hiring and promotion are made on the basis of a look, the shape of a body, or the color of skin." [A *Solid Investment: Making Full Use of the Nation's Human Capital*, <http://digital commons.ilr.cornell.edu/cgi/viewcontent.cgi?article=1117&context=key_work place> (last accessed Mar. 5, 2017)]

Although the Glass Ceiling report acknowledges that some factors (such as educational systems and social attitudes) are beyond corporate control, the report identifies some factors that business can control. For example, a business determines the extent of its outreach efforts, the extent to which new employees are assigned to central, line jobs with promotion potential or to marginal or staff jobs; if mentors are available; whether promotions and good assignments follow good performance. Help and support from colleagues and access to informal networking, the CEO's support for the program, and managers being accountable for the results of the diversity program also promote the program's success.

Women of color in the executive suite say they confront a ceiling that is not glass—but concrete. Data from McKinsey & Co. and LeanIn.Org suggests that women of color are the least represented group in the senior and upper ranks of corporate America. Women of color provide 12% of first-level managers; 45% of first-level managers are white males. In the "C suite" (chief officers) white men are 71% of the workforce; only 3% of C Suite officers are women of color. Minority female senior executives often feel frustrated by the lack of mentors and sponsors with similar backgrounds. [Jo Piazza, *Women of Color Hit a "Concrete Ceiling" in Business*, WSJ.com (Sept. 27, 2016)]

Civil rights leaders have criticized the large tech companies like Apple and Google for lack of diversity and concentration on white and Asian men. (The major tech companies have a workforce that is 70% male, with 2–7% black workers. At Intel, the percentages are 76% male, 4% black, 8% Hispanic.) Intel adopted a five-year plan to recruit at least 14% more women, blacks, Hispanics, and other groups to reflect the available talent pool. Intel also set up a $300 million fund to be used for three years to improve diversity, recruit more women and minorities for technical jobs and make the industry more hospitable. The money will go to historically black colleges and universities and set up engineering scholarships. Intel will also invest in recruiting more women in the gaming industry. [Nick Wingfield, *Intel Allocates $300 Million for Workplace Diversity*, NYTimes.com (Jan. 6, 2015)]

In 2014, a number of tech companies started to publish censuses of the racial and ethnic makeup of their workforces. Several of these companies published diversity reports for 2015. LinkedIn said that it has increased the share of women in leadership roles: 30% of director-level and higher positions are women, up from 25% the year before. Women hold 18% of tech positions, 1% higher than the year before; 43% of hires in the previous 12 months were women. Google said that it now has 22% women in leadership positions and 18% of tech jobs. [Rani Molla, *Tech Companies Cite Small Gains for Women in Updated Diversity Reports*, WSJ.com (June 10, 2015). The Wall Street Journal's Diversity in Tech interactive report is available at <http://graphics.wsj.com/diversity-in-tech-companies> (last updated Apr. 4, 2016) (last accessed Mar. 5, 2017).]

§ 29.03 DIVERSITY TRAINING

Corporations frequently attempt to defuse hostilities within the workplace by offering (or requiring) diversity training. Usually, it is provided by outside contractors. The training could be a voluntary initiative by management, part of a negotiated settlement with the EEOC or a state antidiscrimination agency, or part of the settlement of a court case. The mission of the training is to make employees examine their assumptions and to relate to other employees in a more professional manner.

The goals of diversity training include:

- Finding areas in which the organization is defective;

- Setting goals for improvement;

- Identifying specific steps for reaching the goals;

- Training employees to carry out those steps.

However, diversity training is not without risks and disadvantages. The program can wind up furnishing evidence for a Title VII or other discrimination suit. A well-intentioned program to promote understanding and harmony can worsen the anger and resentment already simmering below the surface. Employees can feel that discussion of other religions or lifestyles is an insult to their own deeply held beliefs. An attempt to reach out to traditionally disfavored groups could be construed as reverse discrimination. And, in any event, a diversity training program (which could be viewed as purely cosmetic) is no substitute for effective hiring or for making sure that no one is subjected to a hostile environment in the workplace.

SkillSurvey published a document, *Beat Your Hidden Hiring Biases* suggests that data-driven hiring can improve the quality of the workforce by selecting the best candidates—not just the best white male candidates with an upper-middle-class or upper-class background. A more diverse employee census helps a business connect with a more diverse customer base. Even if a company does not face EEOC charges, or if the charges are held to be unfounded or the employer prevails in the court system, negative social media about lack of diversity can harm a company's sales and bottom line. SkillSurvey identifies various kinds of biases that can impair sound hiring. "Sourcing bias" looks only at candidates from certain channels (e.g., alumni groups for the hiring executive's college). "Application bias" sorts out people who don't have online access or who are not good writers—even if the job does not require IT or writing skills. "Qualification bias" hires on the basis of qualifications that are not really relevant to good performance of the job. "Reference bias" gives too much weight to personal ties; referrers do not necessarily know what kind of worker a referee will be. "Interview bias" involves questions that are culturally insensitive or invalid—and may even be unlawful, subjecting the company to potential liability under anti-discrimination statutes. Data-driven hiring assesses where a company finds its candidates, how applications are handled, and who is offered a job. It can be especially illuminating to follow up on candidates who were offered jobs that they turned down; it can show that the company makes potential high performers feel too uncomfortable to work there. [SkillSurvey.com, <http://www.skillsurvey.com/resource/beat-hidden-hiring-biases-ebook/> (undated, last accessed Apr. 4, 2017)]

§ 29.04 DIVERSITY AUDITS

The prospect of performing a diversity audit raises a similar mix of questions. A company that has central-office commitment to diversity might have very different conditions at the shop-floor level. Furthermore, a multi-unit company can find it difficult to maintain uniform policies throughout.

A well-designed audit can pinpoint the problems and lead to their resolution. However, a badly designed survey does not generate any useful information, but it does generate data that could be damning if a plaintiff discovers it. Doing a diversity audit shows that management cares about the issue. However, that could backfire, if employees expect real change that doesn't come.

■ **TIP:** If a lawyer performs or supervises the audit, there is at least a possibility that potentially embarrassing material can be protected by attorney-client confidentiality. But don't forget that confidentiality is sacrificed if the information is publicized.

Labor lawyers Christine Amalfe and Heather Akawie Adelman give some suggestions for an effective diversity audit. They say the first step is consulting an experienced employment lawyer; collecting objective data, not subjective comments; marking the report "privileged and confidential"; keep it separate from other HR information; and control distribution to persons with a genuine need to know.

§ 29.05   ENGLISH-ONLY RULES

In many (if not most) workplace situations, the ability to speak and understand English fluently is a valid job qualification. However, a person can be fluent in English even though it is not his or her first language. He or she may be more comfortable speaking other languages. If the employer bans languages other than English in the workplace, it is easy for national-origin minority groups to show disparate impact.

In some contexts, it is also required that management communicate with workers in languages other than English: for example, the PPACA requires distribution of health plan communications in other languages based on the county population that is literate only in a non-English language.

Many states have enacted statutes making English the official language of the state. Given the nationalist emphasis of the Trump administration and the movement for removing undocumented immigrants from the workforce, it is likely that more such laws will be adopted.

Most of the states (31, in 2014, with bills introduced in Michigan, New Jersey, New York, Pennsylvania, and West Virginia) have designated English as the official language, although this is probably as purely ceremonial like designating an official state bird or flower. [Hunter Schwartz, *States Where English Is the Official Language,* Washington Post (Aug. 12, 2014), available at <https://www.washingtonpost.com/blogs/govbeat/wp/2014/08/12/states-where-english-is-the-official-language/?utm_term=.cf90d17a4a73>]

DOL's position is that an employer who imposes an English-only rule must be able to demonstrate job-relatedness and business necessity: for instance, that there is no other way to meet customer needs or communicate in an emergency. But it would be hard to establish business necessity for forbidding employees to converse in other languages during meals or breaks, or when they are in the restroom or a locker room. Before adopting an English-only rule, employers should consider alternatives that are just as effective in promoting safety and efficiency. [DOL fact sheet, *What Do I Need to Know About English-Only Rules,* available at <www.dol.gov/oasam/...FINALEnglish-Only-Rules-Fact sheet> (undated, last accessed Mar. 5, 2017)]

Where a high percentage of employees or customers speak languages other than English, or where the company does a good deal of business in non-English-speaking countries, bilingual employees (whether native speakers or those who have learned the language) can be invaluable. The question then becomes whether the pay rate should be higher for bilingual employees.

Similarly, the EEOC's position is that English-only rules are acceptable only if they are justified by business necessity, and must be limited to situations when it would impair the employer's ability to operate safely or efficiently to allow employees to communicate in their native language. The EEOC said that bans on speaking other languages during meals or breaks "will rarely be justified." Discrimination on the basis of accent is unlawful, unless the individual's accent materially interferes with his or her ability to communicate effectively in English—and if speaking English is material to the job (e.g., teaching, customer service, telemarketing). [*Immigrants' Employment Rights Under Federal Anti-Discrimination Laws,* <https://www.eeoc.gov/eeoc/publications/immigrants-facts .cfm> (undated; last accessed Apr. 4, 2017)]

The EEOC settled an "English only" national origin discrimination case for $450,000 plus injunctive relief. Under 29 C.F.R. § 1606.7 (Guidelines on Discrimination Because of National Origin), the EEOC treats forbidding employees to speak their native language in the workplace as loss of employment opportunities because of national origin. The EEOC recognizes a business necessity defense for English-only rules in some circumstances: emergencies; communicating with customers, supervisor, or co-workers who only speak English; and when supervision requires giving instructions in English. [*EEOC v. Mesa Sys., Inc.,* No. 2:11-cv-01201 (D. Utah 2013)]

Although this issue is usually pursued by the EEOC, the NLRB can also get involved. In March 2015, the NLRB held Valley Health System LLC's English-only rule to be invalid, focusing not on discrimination but on the potential for chilling protected concerted activity. Valley Health System LLC forbade speaking non-English languages while on duty, when patients were present or nearby, or on staff. The NLRB said this was so broad that it could forbid employees to discuss working conditions in their native language. [Susanna Knutson Gibbons, *Time to Revisit English-Only Rules,* Poyner Spruill LLP (Mar. 30, 2015), available at Lexology.com]

§ 29.06 PROMOTING DIVERSITY

The American Sociological Association concluded that the most racially diverse companies earn 15 times more revenue than the least diverse. Diversity promotes business development by broadening the customer base. Recruitment requires being proactive and networking with people and groups likely to have good candidates. Contact groups for, e.g., black, Hispanic, female, disabled professionals and participate in events. Consider offering internships to underrepresented groups. [Findlaw.com blogs, Employment Law, *Recruiting for Diversity in Your Law Firm* (Feb. 2016)]

Michelle Wimes, the director of professional development and inclusion at Ogletree Deakins law firm, discussed common challenges businesses encounter in creating an effective diversity program: connecting diversity to bottom-line results; making employees think of the diversity department as one that serves organizational needs and goals, not just a "party planner" in charge of events and sponsorships; and cultivating a strong pipeline to have plenty of excellent diverse candidates available when there is a job opening (e.g., by working with colleges on internships, coaching, and mentoring). Many organizations examine their vendors' commitment to diversity, so diversity and inclusion can help market to them. [Jathan Janove, *Overcoming Diversity Challenges—Interview with Director of Professional Development & Inclusion Michelle Wimes*, Ogletree Deakins (Dec. 26, 2013), available at Lexology.com]

DOL reminded employers that internships provide a pool of motivated individuals whose performance can be assessed before a permanent job is offered. The DOL's guide for inclusive internships explains how to make the environment, including software, accessible and includes an appendix of hiring resources. Employers now see diversity as part of doing business, not something separate, and strive to include all kinds of workers, including in internships. Physical and technological (e.g., usable software) environment must be accessible. Appendix A of Hiring resources include U.S. Chamber of Commerce Institute for a Competitive Workplace Employment of People With Disabilities, <https://www.uschamber.com/sites/default/files/documents/files/020709_DisabilityInclusion_final.pdf> (last accessed Mar. 5, 2017). [DOL, Office of Disability Employment Policy, *Inclusive Internship Programs: A How-to Guide for Employers*, available at <http://www.dol.gov/odep/pdf/InclusiveInternship Programs.pdf> (undated, last accessed Mar. 5, 2017)]

Entrepreneur Kedar Iyer established GapJumpers, a software company that sets up "auditions" for jobs with tasks similar to the job. The clients do not see resumes, just names, photographs, and test results. Iyer did this so that employers would not limit recruitment to candidates from prestigious schools. Then he changed his model to duplicate blind auditions for orchestras (where the judges cannot see the candidates, just hear them playing). Researchers found that blind auditions greatly increased hiring of female musicians, and many more women applied because of this. GapJumpers has done more than 1,400 "auditions." About one-fifth of applicants who were not white, male, able-bodied, and graduates of elite institutions got first-round interviews; with blind auditions, 60% of those applicants got interviews.

There are other Silicon Valley startups designed to promote diversity in hiring. Gild has software that finds code that the applicants published online, and takes out biographical information before making referrals. Textio scans job-listings to identify language that discourages applicants. For example, men are more likely to apply if the ad calls for a "rock star"; women are more likely to apply if the ad calls for a "passion for learning." A 2015 study found that made-up candidates with black-sounding names from elite universities did only as well as white-sounding candidates from less prestigious schools. Muslim, ex-offenders, mothers, disabled, and gay candidates are less likely to get call-backs even from employers that think they are doing everything they can to promote diversity. [Claire Cain Miller, *Is Blind Hiring the Best Hiring?*, NYTimes .com (Feb. 25, 2016)]

Some companies are appointing a CDO, a Chief Diversity Officer, to handle matters such as recruitment, ethics, and legal compliance to improve the diversity of the company's workforce. The CDO is also responsible for seeing that mentoring, good assignments, and leadership training are available to employees from groups that have been disadvantaged in the workplace. About a quarter of CDOs report directly to the CEO; the rest report to HR or another department. CDOs who report to the CEO probably have greater power and influence. [Leslie Kwoh, *Firms Hail New Chiefs (of Diversity)*, WSJ.com (Jan. 5, 2012)]

However, after President Trump's inauguration, companies began to re-evaluate whether their diversity programs actually achieved bottom-line results, and began to consider how to incorporate white men into their diversity efforts. Some diversity executives saw their new role as maintaining harmony in the workplace after a divisive election. [John Simons, *In Trump Age, Taking a Different Tack on Workplace Diversity*, WSJ.com (Feb. 14, 2017)]

Another area of concern is diversity on the board of directors. In early 2013, institutional investors filed shareholder resolutions with 20 major companies protesting the absence of women from the companies' boards. The Thirty Percent Coalition Institutional Investor Committee approached companies including Hartford Financial, Lowe's Companies, and Urban Outfitters Inc. Calvert Investments analyst Christine DeGroot said that female and minority directors help companies widen their customer base and add new perspectives to the board. Making a commitment to adding women and minority directors shows that a company recognizes the value of diversity. [The Thirty Percent Coalition's Website is <http://www.30percentcoalition.org> (last accessed Mar. 5, 2017). See also "Lionel," *It's Time for Companies to Try a New Gender-Equality Playbook*, 30percentcoalition.org (Feb. 2017), available at https://www.30percentcoalition.org/news/93-in-the-news/226-wall-street-mc-kinsey>, pointing out that women are much more likely than men to spend five years without a promotion in an entry-level position, and that, early in their careers, men get 30% more promotions than women. A survey of over 34,000 employees at 130 companies showed that employees do not think their organization is really committed to diversity, and they are afraid to challenge gender bias in the workplace for fear of retaliation.]

Less than 20% of directors of Standard & Poors 500 companies are female. According to the Wall Street Journal, female directors usually had better resumes than their male counterparts, but earned $7,000 a year less. A survey of almost 800 directors of public companies showed that only 39% believed that gender diversity on boards is very important. Male directors aged 55–60 said that they could not find qualified female board candidates; female directors in the same age group attributed this to the lack of diversity in recruiting. Some boards require female—but not male—candidates to have served on a board before, which perpetuates past discrimination. [Cydney S. Posner, *Some Successful Approaches to Increasing Board Gender Diversity*, Cooley LLP (Aug. 17, 2016), available at Lexology.com]

PART VI

EMPLOYEE RELATIONS

CHAPTER 30

LABOR LAW

§ 30.01 INTRODUCTION

NOTE: In view of the Trump administration's pro-business priorities, the decline in the number of union members and the increasing number of states with right to work laws (see § 30.06), this will be an especially fast-changing area of law, so be sure to keep up with developments after press time.

In the broadest sense, labor law covers the entire relationship between employers and employees. However, the term is usually used in a much narrower sense: to mean the body of law dealing with whether a union will be allowed to organize a workplace; union elections, challenges to elections, and decertification of a union that is guilty of misconduct or that no longer represents employee interests; negotiating a Collective Bargaining Agreement (CBA); interpretation of the CBA; and strikes. Labor law sets rules for conduct by both management and unions.

In most cases, labor law is a matter of federal law. Congress has preempted this issue, in the interest of creating a single, uniform body of law that prevails throughout the country.

The extent of union membership reached its lowest level ever in 2016, for both public- and private-sector workers. In 2015, 11.1% of workers were union members; only 10.7% were in 2016. Private-sector membership fell because of the replacement of blue-collar manufacturing jobs by service jobs. In 2016, public-sector workers represented approximately 15% of the workforce, but half of all union members. The federal hiring freeze in 2017 and contraction in government, are likely to reduce public-sector union membership further. [Eric Morath and Kris Maher, *Share of U.S. Workers in Unions Falls to Lowest Level on Record*, WSJ.com (Jan. 26, 2017)]

Although the Second Circuit held that employees could not be compelled to arbitrate their Age Discrimination in Employment Act (ADEA) claims, despite the arbitration clause in their CBA, the Supreme Court reversed, holding in the spring of 2009 that federal law mandates the enforcement of CBA clauses that unambiguously require union members to arbitrate their ADEA claims. [*14 Penn Plaza LLC v. Pyett*, 556 U.S. 247 (2009); the Supreme Court already held that ADEA claims are arbitrable, in *Gilmer v. Interstate/Johnson Lane Corp.*, 500 U.S. 20 (1991).] The Supreme Court returned to the question of arbitrability in 2010 on another labor law issue, this time deciding that when a CBA's no-strike clause had to be interpreted, it was up to the district court and not the arbitrator to decide when the CBA had been officially ratified. [*Granite Rock Co. v. Int'l Bhd. of Teamsters*, 561 U.S. 287 (2010)]

Early in 2014, the Supreme Court ruled that, in a unionized workplace, donning and doffing time (putting on and removing protective clothing in a steel mill) was not compensable work time. The court held that the Fair Labor Standards Act issues could have been resolved via collective bargaining. [*Sandifer v. U.S. Steel Corp.*, 134 S. Ct. 870 (2014)]

In March 2016, the Supreme Court ruled that it was proper to certify a class of employees who charged that they were not paid properly for donning and doffing time—and further ruled that the employees could assert their case based on representative evidence about average time spent on these tasks. The Supreme Court did not require proof of each employee's individual time when the employer had failed to keep adequate records. [*Tyson Foods, Inc. v. Bouaphakeo*, No. 14-1146 (U.S. Mar. 22, 2016)]

Early in 2012, the National Labor Relations Board (NLRB) held that it violates the National Labor Relations Act (NLRA) for an employer to require that employees waive class arbitration of grievances because employees always have the right to take collective action about grievances, whether in court or in arbitration. This decision covers all employers operating in interstate commerce, whether or not their employees are unionized. However, the NLRB did not decide whether an employer can require employees to arbitrate instead of litigating collective actions. [*D.R. Horton Inc. and Michael Cuda* (N.L.R.B. 2012); see Scott Graham, *AT&T Mobility Doesn't Apply in the Workplace, Says NLRB*, Corporate Counsel (Jan. 9, 2012) (law.com)]

The Fifth Circuit held that it is permissible for an employer to impose a class action arbitration waiver; it is not inconsistent with the employees' legal right under the NLRA to pursue collective action. However, the Fifth Circuit held that the arbitration agreement must clarify that employees do not waive the right to file NLRB complaints. [*D.R. Horton v. NLRB*, 737 F.3d 344 (5th Cir. 2013).]

The NLRB allowed the July 15, 2014 deadline for appealing *D.R. Horton* to the Supreme Court to pass. However, the NLRB contained to assert that NLRA § 7 provides a right to pursue class arbitration even though this position has been rejected by the Second, Fifth, and Eighth circuits. The NLRB's policy is that it is only obligated to follow Supreme Court decisions, not circuit court decisions it disagrees with. [David P. Phippen, *NLRB Decides Not to Take a Chance on Supreme Court Review of Its Position on Class Action Waivers in Arbitration Agreements*, Constangy Brooks & Smith LLP (Aug. 27, 2014), available at Lexology.com] The NLRB's late-2014 *Murphy Oil* decision continues to find class-action waivers invalid for impairing protected collective activity. [*Murphy Oil USA, Inc.*, 361 N.L.R.B. No. 72 (Oct. 28, 2014), but the Fifth Circuit held that it does not violate NLRA § 8(a)(1) for an employer to impose a waiver of class and collective actions: *Murphy Oil v. NLRB*, 808 F.3d 1013 (5th Cir. 2015)]

In mid-2016, the Seventh Circuit agreed with the NLRB that an arbitration clause that forbids class and collective actions violates the NLRA by discouraging workers' collective action—but the Eighth Circuit reiterated the majority opinion that bans on class and collective arbitration are permissible. [Compare *Lewis v. Epic Sys.*, No. 15-2997 (7th Cir. May 26, 2016) *with Cellular Sales of Mo. LLC v. NLRB*, No. 15-1860 (8th Cir. June 2, 2016); see Howard M. Bloom and Philip B. Rosen, *Eighth Circuit Finds Class and Collective Action Waivers Lawful Under NLRA, Contrary to Seventh Circuit*, Jackson Lewis PC (June 3 2016), *available at* Lexology.com]

As anticipated, on January 13, 2017, the Supreme Court agreed to resolve the circuit split, granting a consolidated appeal of *Murphy Oil, Lewis,* and *Ernst & Young v. Morris,* a Ninth Circuit case that held against class action waivers. [Christopher C. Murray and Ron Chapman, Jr., *Supreme Court Jumps Into Class Action Waiver Fight,* Ogletree Deakins (Jan. 13, 2017), available at Lexology .com] When the appeal was granted, it was expected that the Supreme Court would render a final decision by the end of June 2017. However, a few weeks after granting the appeal, the Supreme Court announced that oral arguments in the case would not be scheduled until the Supreme Court term beginning October 2017—which means that the decision will not be rendered until late 2017 or even 2018. Employers feared that, after the long delay, the Supreme Court would simply send the cases back to the lower courts without giving employers clear direction. [Richard R. Meneghello, *Good Things Come to Those Who Wait? Supreme Court Delays Class Waiver Decision Until Next Term,* Fisher Phillips (Feb. 8, 2017), available at Lexology.com]

After certiorari was granted, the Sixth Circuit joined the Seventh and Ninth Circuits in holding that class action waivers in mandatory arbitration programs violate NLRA § 7. [*NLRB v. Alternative Entm't,* No. 16-1385 (6th Cir. May 26, 2017); see David Pryzbylski, *A Growing Divide: Sixth Circuit Decision to Invalidate Class/Collective Action Waiver Widens Appellate Court Split,* Barnes & Thornburg LLP (May 31, 2017), available at Lexology.com]

An executive order, the Fair Pay and Safe Workplaces Executive Order (EO 13673), was signed in mid-2014 covering federal contracts over $500,000. To prevent the federal government from repeatedly entering into transactions with known labor law violators, contractors who are subject to the order must report violations, dating back three years, of 14 areas of federal and state law. The areas in question involve wages and hours, safety and health, family leave, civil rights, and collective bargaining. This EO was nicknamed the "contractor blacklisting rule" and was extremely unpopular with business.

The District Court for the Eastern District of Texas issued a preliminary injunction against the Fair Pay and Safe Workplaces Rule (EO 13673) and the Department of Defense's implementing final rule and final guidance from the DOL. The rules were scheduled to phase in beginning October 25, 2016, the day after the injunction issued. The plaintiffs challenged the requirement of reporting civil judgments, administrative determinations on the merits, and arbitration awards. EO 13673 required this information to be used by federal contracting officers in deciding whether a bidder is responsible enough to be awarded a government contract. The plaintiffs challenged the requirement of disclosing specified information on pay stubs and the ban on pre-dispute arbitration of Title VII and sexual harassment allegations made by employees. The district court held that the disclosure provisions exceeded DOL's statutory authority; were preempted by other federal laws; and placed contractors at risk of unfair disqualification based on actions other than final adjudications of wrongdoing. The district court held that contractors were also forced to engage in compelled speech, violating their

First Amendment rights. The ban on predispute arbitration was struck down because it conflicts with the Federal Arbitration Act. However, the paycheck transparency rule (required disclosures on pay stubs) was not enjoined. [*Associated Builders & Contractors, et al. v. Rung*, 2016 U.S. Dist. LEXIS 155232, 167 Lab. Cas. (CCH) P36,481, 100 Empl. Prac. Dec. (CCH) P45,671 (E.D. Tex. Oct. 24, 2016); see Roger V. Abbott, *Federal Court Repudiates the Most Significant Provisions of the New DOL Rules*, Mayer Brown LLP (Oct. 27, 2016), available at Lexology.com; James J. Murphy and Hera S. Arsen, *Contractor Blacklisting Rule Enjoined at the Last Minute*, Ogletree Deakins (Oct. 25, 2016), available at Lexology.com]

On February 2, 2017, the House of Representatives passed House Joint Resolution 37 to nullify the Fair Pay and Safe Workplaces Rule. An identical resolution was introduced in the Senate as S.J. Res. 12. The Senate passed the resolution, and President Trump signed it into law, so the Fair Pay and Safe Workplaces rule will be abrogated—furthermore, express Congressional authorization will be required for the DOL to issue a similar regulation in the future.

The House applied the Congressional Review Act, 5 U.S.C. §§ 801–808, a statute enacted in 1996 as part of the Small Business Regulatory Fairness Act. It gives Congress the authority to pass joint resolutions to reject any rule that was adopted within the 60 previous days when Congress was in session. If such a resolution is passed, it nullifies the regulation, including any portions that have already taken effect. In practical terms, this statute is seldom used because, if the president and Congress are of the same party, they will probably not want to reverse orders adopted by their own administrators. However, when President Trump was inaugurated, many Obama regulations that were unpopular with Congress were vulnerable to this procedure. [Richard W. Arnholt, *Congress Acts to Rescind the Already-Enjoined Fair Pay and Safe Workplaces Regulation and Other Last-Minute Obama Administration Rules,* Bass, Berry & Sims PLC (Feb. 6, 2017), available at Lexology.com]

It must be remembered that the NLRA entitles all workers—union and non-union—to engage in protected concerted activity and some interesting initiatives are being taken outside the union context. Two ex-employees of the Service Employees International Union set up the coworker.org Website to help employees organize to improve working conditions. The site lists hundreds of change initiatives at various companies. They are new models for giving workers organizational power in the workplace. For example, after 25,000 workers in 17 countries signed a petition, Starbucks' dress code was altered to permit visible tattoos. The site also has a petition for a supermarket chain to allow workers to wear beards, and one for TGI Fridays to reinstate automatic service charges for large parties. [David P. Phippen, *Is There an App for That? Well Maybe Not an App, But There Sure Is a Website*, Constangy Brooks Smith & Prophete LLP (Jan. 6, 2016), available at Lexology.com]

A number of businesses have non-union workers' committees that transmit employees' complaints to management. A group of car-wash workers in California organized a committee when an immigrants' rights group informed them about their NLRA rights. Six workers were fired after writing to their employer about off-the-clock work, exposure to toxic chemicals, and being insulted in front of customers. The NLRB found unfair labor practices and ordered the workers to be reinstated with $6,000 in back wages. The employer made a separate agreement to pay $60,000 to settle minimum wage and overtime claims. [Steven Greenhouse, *Workers Organize, but Don't Unionize, to Get Protection Under Labor Law* NYTimes.com (Sept. 7, 2015)]

[A] Challenges to the NLRB Itself

As long as the NLRB has been in operation, businesses and unions that object to NLRB decisions have been challenging the correctness, appropriateness, and validity of those decisions. However, in recent years, the NLRB has confronted significant challenges to the way that the organization is constituted and whether it has had the power to issue valid decisions at certain crucial time periods.

In January 2008, the appointment of two NLRB commissioners expired and no one was appointed to replace them, so the NLRB had two members rather than the statutorily prescribed level of five. More than 400 decisions were issued by the two-member NLRB. In mid-2010, the Supreme Court ruled that the NLRB did not have the authority to issue decisions when it had only two members, so all of these decisions were invalid. As a result, many cases were sent back to the NLRB for reconsideration after it once again had a quorum. [*New Process Steel v. NLRB*, 560 U.S. 674 (2010). For an example of a challenge based on the Supreme Court's decision, see *NLRB v. Talmadge Park*, 608 F.3d 913 (2d Cir. 2010).]

At the beginning of 2012, the NLRB swore in three new members: Richard Griffin, Sharon Block, and Terence Flynn. These were all recess appointments. [Melanie Trottman, *Labor Board Swears in New Members*, WSJ.com (Jan. 10, 2012)] Terence Flynn resigned on May 27, 2012 after allegations that he leaked internal NLRB information. Flynn denied wrongdoing. [Steven Greenhouse, *Labor Board Member Resigns Over Leak to G.O.P. Allies*, NYTimes.com, <http://www.nytimes.com/2012/05/28/business/gop-labor-board-member-terence-flynn-quits-over-leak.html?_r=1> (May 27, 2012)]

Throughout 2014, the NLRB had a fully constituted five-member board. Nancy Schiffer's term expired December 16, 2014. In December 2014, Lauren McFerran was confirmed to replace her. [David J. Santeusanio and Brian M. Doyle, *The National Labor Relations Board: 2014 Year in Review*, Holland & Knight LLP (Jan. 29, 2015) available at Lexology.com] An immensely significant D.C. Circuit decision from early 2013 holds that the recess appointments of Sharon Block, Terence Flynn, and Richard Griffin to the NLRB were unconstitutional.

Certiorari was granted, and the Supreme Court agreed with the D.C. Circuit: the appointments were invalid. They were made at a time when the Senate was not truly in recess, because it re-convened every three days for pro forma sessions. The Supreme Court held that valid recess appointments can be made only when a recess lasts 10 days or longer. [*NLRB v. Noel Canning*, 134 S. Ct. 2550 (2014). On August 4, 2014, the NLRB issued a press release announcing that the agency ratified all of the actions taken during the period of time covered by this decision: Tony Mauro, *NLRB Ratifies Actions Affected by Noel Canning*, Nat'l L.J. (Aug. 5, 2014), available at law.com.]

A "PAS position" is one that requires presidential nomination and Senate confirmation. In the late 1990s, about 20% of PAS positions were held by acting appointees who had not been nominated or confirmed for the job. Theoretically federal law limits how long a person can serve in an acting capacity, but in practice many appointees have served longer. In 1998, Congress passed the Federal Vacancies Reform Act of 1998 (FVRA), which authorizes several ways for the president to fill PAS vacancies. The default provision is for the first assistant to the job to take over as acting holder of the job. The president can also appoint, as acting official, either a senior employee at the same agency or an officer who has already been nominated and confirmed for a job at another federal administrative agency. However, the FVRA was drafted to reduce the risk that acting appointments would be misused. The FVRA invalidates certain actions taken by acting officers who were not validly appointed.

The general counsel of the NLRB resigned in 2010. Then-president Obama appointed Lafe Solomon, a senior employee at the NLRB, as acting general counsel. Six months later, Obama nominated Solomon to hold the job permanently, but the Senate did not act on the nomination. Eventually, Obama withdrew Solomon's nomination and made another nomination. The Senate confirmed the nominee, Richard Griffin, in November 2013. But Solomon's tenure as acting general counsel and the attempt to appoint him permanently, had significant consequences.

The District Court for the District of Alaska ruled that Lafe Solomon did not have authority to continue to serve as the NLRB's acting general counsel after President Obama nominated him as general counsel in early 2011. Nevertheless, the district court found that unfair labor practice (ULP) complaints that Solomon issued against a hotel management company were valid under the "de facto officer" doctrine. The defendant in a ULP case argued that the complaints were invalid because when they were issued, Solomon's appointment was not valid because the NLRB lacked a quorum. The district court held that the lack of a quorum was not determinative because the general counsel has independent statutory authority to issue complaints. The de facto officer doctrine makes actions valid if they were performed under color of official title, even if the appointment is subsequently found to be invalid. [*Hooks v. Remington Lodging & Hospitality, LLC*, No. 13-00213 (D. Alaska Mar. 18, 2014)]

The D.C. Circuit held, in mid-2015, that Solomon's appointment violated the Federal Vacancies Reform Act, so he was not empowered to issue ULP findings. That casts decisions between his January 5, 2011 appointment and his departure on November 4, 2013 into doubt. However, the court said that the case is not "Son of Noel Canning": employers waived the defense of the invalidity of Solomon's appointment unless they raised it in a timely fashion. [*SW Gen. Inc. v. NLRB*, 796 F.3d 67 (D.C. Cir. 2015). See Patrick L. Egan, Howard M. Bloom and Philip B. Rosen, *Supreme Court to Hear Appeal of NLRB's Former Acting General Counsel's Decisions Following Nomination*, Jackson Lewis PC (June 21, 2016), available at Lexology.com.]

The case reached the Supreme Court, whose early 2017 decision restricted the president's ability to make administrative appointments without Senate advice and consent. The Supreme Court held that a person nominated to fill an office permanently cannot hold the office as an acting official. The Supreme Court said that, even though since 1998, 112 acting officials have been nominated for permanent appointments, the fact that Congress did not protest did not show Congress' acquiescence. The decision is an important one in defining, and limiting, the president's power to make appointments. However, it will not have significant practical effect because the only labor law cases it affects are those where a party raised a timely challenge to Solomon's appointment as acting general counsel, and Solomon's action was not ratified by Griffin after his confirmation. [*NLRB v. SW General* 137 S. Ct. 929 (2017); see Corey J. Goerdt and Andrew J. Hoag, *Supreme Court Uses Labor Case to Again Stifle Presidential Power,* Fisher Phillips (Mar. 21, 2017), available at Lexology.com; Edel Cuadra, *Supreme Court Rules Appointment of NLRB General Counsel Violated the Law*, Phelps Dunbar LLP (Mar. 22, 2017), available at Lexology.com; David P. Phippen, *Has The Supreme Court Invalidated Almost Two Years of Actions by The NLRB Acting General Counsel? (Maybe, But Employers Shouldn't Get Too Excited)*, Constangy, Brooks Smith & Prophete (Mar. 23, 2017), available at Lexology.com]

Another argument is that at least 10 NLRB regional directors were named by the invalidly appointed NLRB members, so the regional directors' decisions should also be struck down. Approximately 600 NLRB decisions and orders have been issued since January 2012, and another 1,400 cases could be challenged if a 2010 recess appointment is found invalid. [Melanie Trottman and Kris Maher, *Companies Challenge Labor Rulings*, WSJ.com (Mar. 8, 2013). See, e.g., *NLRB v. Enterprise Leasing Co. Se. LLC*, 722 F.3d 609 (4th Cir. 2013), holding that NLRB orders in two refusal to bargain cases were invalid, because the NLRB lacked a quorum.]

Eventually, in August 2013, the Senate confirmed enough NLRB members to bring the Board up to its full strength of five members—the first time this had been true since August 21, 2003. Chairman Mark Gaston Pierce was confirmed for another five-year NLRB term. Four new members were added: Nancy Schiffer, a senior attorney for unions; Harry I. Johnson, III, formerly a partner in the law firm Arent Fox LLP; Kent Hirozawa, one-time chief counsel to Chairman

Pearce; and Philip A. Miscimarra, ex-partner in Morgan Lewis & Bockius LLP. Pearce's term lasts until August 27, 2018. Schiffer's term ends December 16, 2014. Johnson's ends August 27, 2015, Hirozawa's ends August 27, 2016, and Miscimarra's ends December 16, 2017. [NLRB Press Release, *The National Labor Relations Board Has Five Senate-Confirmed Members*, <http://www.nlrb. gov/news-outreach/news-story/national-labor-relations-board-has-five-senate-confirmed-members> (Aug. 12, 2013) (last accessed Mar. 6, 2017)]

On January 26, 2017, Miscimarra (a Republican) was named acting chairman, replacing Pearce. Pearce and the remaining member, McFerran, are Democrats. The NLRA requires vacancies to be filled in a way that gives the president's political party a majority, so the next appointments will be Republicans. [Harold P. Coxson, *President Names Miscimarra as Acting Chair of the National Labor Relations Board,* Ogletree Deakins (Jan. 26, 2017), available at Lexology.com] Miscimarra announced that he would leave the NLRB when his term expires at the end of 2017. President Trump nominated two Republicans to fill vacancies on the NLRB. Marvin Kaplan was confirmed by the Senate on August 2, 2017, resulting in a four-person board with two Democrats and two Republicans. William Emanuel's nomination was not voted on before the August 2017 recess, but his confirmation was expected. [Robin Shea, *Kaplan Confirmed to NLRB—We Now Have an "R-D" Tie,* Constangy Brooks Smith & Prophete LLP (Aug. 3, 2017), available at Lexology.com and *NLRB Chairman Miscimarra Is Leaving in December,* Constangy Brooks Smith & Prophete LLP (Aug. 3, 2017), available at Lexology.com]

§ 30.02 SOURCES OF LABOR LAW

[A] Generally

The NLRA was supplemented in 1947 by the Labor-Management Relations Act (LMRA) [29 U.S.C. §§ 141–144, etc.], popularly known as the Taft-Hartley Act. The LMRA extends the powers of the NLRB. It outlaws certain kinds of strikes, including jurisdictional strikes, strikes to enforce unfair labor practices (rather than strikes to protest them), and secondary boycotts. A secondary boycott is an attempt to pressure a neutral company to keep it from dealing with a company that the union has a dispute with.

The Landrum-Griffin Act, known as the Labor-Management Reporting and Disclosure Act of 1959 (LMRDA) [Pub. L. No. 86-257], forbids hot-cargo agreements (agreements not to carry the merchandise of a company involved in a labor dispute). It allows prehire agreements in the building and construction industries, and makes it an unfair labor practice to picket in order to force an employer to recognize or bargain with a union.

Although the LMRDA deals predominantly with union corruption and its best-known feature is the LM-2 form detailing union expenses, the LMRDA includes a lesser-known provision called the "persuader rule" about payments to consultants. Companies have to report payment for services like talking to workers about their NLRA rights. DOL wants companies, consultants, and lawyers to report any time they draft, revise, or provide speeches, materials presented to employees, train supervisors, or develop personnel policies. This rule is controversial because it could remove attorney-client confidentiality from some work done by management attorneys. [Matthew D. Austin, *Prepare for the Impending Persuader Rules*, Roetzel & Andress (Jan. 11, 2016), available at Lexology.com. Challenges to the validity of the rule were filed immediately: see below.]

The DOL Office of Labor-Management Standards published a 129-page final version of the persuader rule, entitled "Interpretation of the 'Advice' Exemption in § 203(c) of the Labor-Management Reporting and Disclosure Act," on March 24, 2016, governing disclosure of agreements with consultants. The general rule is that the employer must file the LM-10 Employer Report; the consultant must file the LM-20 Agreement and Activities Report. Reporting is not required if the "persuader" is only giving advice to the employer, not interacting with employees. [81 Fed. Reg. 15924 (Mar. 24, 2016)]

In June 2016, the District Court for the District of Minnesota held that, although aspects of the final persuader rule are likely to be found invalid (because they require companies to report advice that is exempt under LMRDA § 203(c), an injunction was not appropriate, because the plaintiffs did not show a risk of irrevocable harm. The district court was not persuaded by First Amendment or administrative law arguments against the rule. [*Labnet v. DOL*, No. 16-cv-0844 (PJS/KMM) (D. Minn. June 22, 2016); see Steven M. Swirsky, *Court Denies Injunction to Keep Amended Persuader Rule from Taking Effect-Finds DOL Exceeded Authority Under LMRDA*, Epstein Becker Green (June 23, 2016), available at Lexology.com]

But the District Court for the Northern District of Texas issued first a temporary and then a permanent injunction preventing the rule from taking effect nationwide. Ten states intervened on the plaintiffs' side, arguing that the rule prevented states from regulating the practice of law. The district court held that promulgating the rule exceeded the DOL's authority under the LMRDA. [*Nat'l Fed'n of Indep.Businesses et al. v. Perez*, No. 5:16-cv-66, 2016 U.S. Dist. LEXIS 89694,166 Lab. Cas. (CCH) P10,916 (N.D. Tex. June 27, 2016) and (Nov. 16, 2016). See Seth H. Borden et. al., *Federal Court Permanently Enjoins DOL Union "Persuader" Rule Enforcement*, McGuireWoods LLP (Nov. 16, 2016), available at Lexology.com; Melanie Trottman, *Judge Effectively Kills Rule Forcing Employers to Disclose Anti-Union Deliberations*, WSJ.com (Nov. 16, 2016). Other cases were filed to challenge the persuader rule. Because of the Texas injunction, Arkansas decided not to rule on an application for an injunction: see David P. Phippen, *U.S. Department Of Labor Appeals "Persuader Rule" Injunction to Fifth Circuit*, Constangy Brooks Smith & Prophete LLP (Oct. 24, 2016), available at Lexology.com]

After the presidential election, the Minnesota plaintiffs moved for a stay or a dismissal without prejudice because they predicted that the incoming administration would not try to defend the rule. The District Court for the District of Minnesota accepted that argument, particularly in light of the Northern District of Texas injunction, and stayed the action, ordering the parties to file a status report about the DOL's plans. [*Labnet, Inc. v. U.S. DOL,* 197 F. Supp. 3d 1159 (D. Minn. 2016)]

On May 22, Alexander Acosta, the new Secretary of Labor, announced that the DOL would withdraw the persuader rule. DOL published a Notice of Rulemaking to rescind the rule on June 12, 2017. On June 15, 2017, the Fifth Circuit stayed the appeal for a further six months, for the rule to be finalized. [Timothy J. Sarsfield et. al., *A Victory for Attorney-Client Confidentiality: DOL Takes Formal Steps to Rescind Confidential Persuader Regulation,* Thompson Coburn LLP (May 24, 2017), available at Lexology.com; David P. Phippen, *Court Delays Persuader Rule Appeal for Six Months While Waiting for Final Regulations Rescinding the Rule,* Constangy Brooks Smith & Prophete LLP (June 29, 2017), available at Lexology.com; Ashley K. Laken, *DOL Issues Notice of Proposed Rulemaking to Rescind Obama Administration's Final Persuader Rule,* Seyfarth Shaw LLP (June 21, 2017), available at Lexology.com]

Certiorari was granted in *Unite Here Local 355 v. Mulhall*, a case about LMRA § 302(a), which makes it a crime for an employer to give "anything of value" to a labor union that represents or seeks to represent its employees. The question before the Supreme Court was whether it is a violation for the employer a promise that it will stay neutral in the organizing process, will give the union access to non-public areas of the employer's premises; and will provide a list of names and contact information for employees. The Supreme Court originally was also going to consider whether it violates § 302(b) for a union to try to enforce the employer's promises. The Eleventh Circuit treated neutrality agreements as unlawful "things of value," although the Third and Fourth Circuits disagreed. Subsequently, however, the case was dismissed as improvidently granted. [*Unite Here Local 355 v. Mulhall*, 134 S. Ct. 594 (2013), dismissed Dec. 10, 2013]

The Norris-LaGuardia Act severely limits the situations in which an employer can secure an injunction against a union, but does not completely rule out all injunctions. Although federal law usually preempts state law in the labor arena, the states do have a limited role in protecting their own legitimate interests. They can pass certain labor laws that will not be federally preempted: For instance, there is a legitimate state interest in preventing violence, so states can regulate how and when picketing can be done. States can legislate in areas such as minimum wages, child labor, and employment discrimination.

States can also cope with issues that are only peripheral to the main purposes of the LMRA. This category includes defamation suits brought by employers against unions, suits dealing with continuation of welfare benefits during strikes, and internal union affairs. States are also allowed to legislate in the area of union security, for instance by passing right-to-work laws forbidding union shops and agency shops. [See § 30.06]

The National Labor Relations Board's (NLRB) jurisdiction is limited to work performed in the United States; the agency has no jurisdiction over temporary work assignments in Canada. [*Asplundh Tree Expert Co. v. NLRB*, 365 F.3d 168 (3d Cir. 2004)]

[B]   NLRA Section 7

The National Labor Relations Act of 1935 (NLRA), also known as the Wagner Act, is one of the bedrock federal labor statutes. The NLRA establishes the National Labor Relations Board (NLRB) as a kind of referee between management and unionized labor.

Section 7 of the NLRA says that employees have the right to engage in "protected concerted activities." In other words, they can act together to form a union, join a union, present grievances, bargain collectively, go on strike, and picket peacefully.

In 2014, an NLRB regional director held that Northwestern University football players on scholarship were employees of the university with the right to organize and bargain collectively. The controversial decision said that football players spend as much as 50 hours a week on football, and coaches have so much control over whether the players can retain their scholarships that it was inaccurate to describe the players as primarily students. [Ben Strauss and Steve Eder, *College Players Granted Right to Form Union*, NYTimes.com (Mar. 26, 2014)]

The NLRB's general counsel released a memo on January 31, 2017, classifying scholarship football players in the National Collegiate Athletic Association (NCAA) Division I Football Bowl Subdivision programs as employees who are covered by NLRA § 7. The memo says that the NLRA and several recent cases support extending employee rights to certain student-workers. The memo says that scholarship football players at schools in this subdivision are common-law employees because they perform services for the school by participating in lucrative football games. The NCAA exercises significant control over the players by prescribing rules and academic requirements. This memo might give rise to a two-tier system in which athletes in revenue-producing sports are allowed to unionize, while those in minor sports cannot. It would be more difficult for women athletes to organize because their teams seldom produce major revenue. [<https://www.nlrb.gov/reports-guidance/general-counsel-memos> (Jan. 31, 2017); see Michael L. Stevens, Alexandra M. Romero and Richard L. Brand, *Back in the Game: NLRB General Counsel Says That Scholarship Football Players at Private Universities Are Employees Under the NLRA,* Arent Fox LLP (Feb. 6, 2017), available at Lexology.com]

In 2016, the District Court for the District of Idaho dismissed a Fair Labor Standards Act (FLSA) suit brought by Samantha Sackos, a former soccer player at the University of Pennsylvania, against the NCAA and 100 Division I schools, alleging that student-athletes were actually employees entitled to be paid under the FLSA. The district court dismissed all claims against the university, finding that there was no employer-employee relationship. Claims against the NCAA were dismissed because the court did not find it had jurisdiction. The federal and state institutions that were sued were immune under the Eleventh Amendment. The district court cited a DOL handbook that says interscholastic athletics does not constitute "work" for FLSA purposes, and sports activity does not create an employer-employee relationship. The Seventh Circuit affirmed in late 2016. [*Berger v. NCAA et.al.*, No. 1:14-cv-01710-WTL-MJD, 2016 U.S. Dist. LEXIS 18194 (S.D. Ind. Feb. 16, 2016), *aff'd*, 843 F.3d 285 (7th Cir. Dec. 5, 2016); see Lisa Karen Atkins and John Richard Carrigan, *NCAA Sacks Sackos Suit: Why NCAA Student-Athletes Are Not Employees Under the FLSA*, Ogletree Deakins (Feb. 22, 2016), available at Lexology.com; William R. Pokorny, *Seventh Circuit Says Student Athletes Are Not Employees,* Franczek Radelet PC (Dec. 7, 2016), available at Lexology.com.]

The District Court for the Northern District of California also ruled that student-athletes (in this case, a former football player) are not employees, and the district court rejected drawing a distinction between sports on the basis of the revenue they produce for the university: *Dawson v. National Collegiate Athletic Ass'n,* No. 16-cv-05487-RS (N.D. Cal. Apr. 25, 2017). See Julie Badel, *California District Court Rules That Student Athletes Are Not Employees,* Epstein Becker Green (Apr. 27, 2017), available at Lexology.com]

There can be legitimate business reasons for asking employees to maintain the confidentiality of internal investigations: e.g., protecting witnesses, victims, and the subjects of investigations; suppressing rumors; and encouraging employees to testify. Sometimes government agencies mandate confidentiality of certain information: the Equal Employment Opportunity Commission (EEOC) not only requires protection of harassment complaints, but employees must be informed of the confidentiality requirement.

Several NLRB decisions find that overly broad confidentiality provisions imposed by employers are unlawful because they violate the NLRA by suppressing legitimate discussion of working conditions. The Fifth Circuit agreed with the NLRB that the employer's confidentiality policy violated NLRA § 8(a)(1) because it prevented employees from discussing wages. The policy forbade employees to copy or share confidential information, broadly defined to include personnel information and documents. In the Fifth Circuit view, employees have a right to discuss wages with co-workers; there was no evidence that employees used this information outside the company. The Fifth Circuit examined the written terms of the policy, not the way it was implemented, so it rejected the employer's argument that the policy was not used to suppress discussion of wages. [*FlexFrack Logistics v. NLRB*, 746 F.3d 205 (5th Cir. 2014)]

In 2017, the D.C. Circuit agreed with the NLRB that a confidentiality agreement prevented employees from sharing information about working conditions by forbidding discussion of any information that did not come from the employee whose work and compensation were involved. Employees could discuss salary and discipline information shared by a co-worker, but the court found that this was ambiguous and did not give enough protection to discussion of information obtained legitimately. However, the D.C. Circuit ruled that the NLRB did not have substantial evidence for holding that the employer committed a ULP by asking employees not to discuss workplace investigations. The D.C. Circuit did not explore the issues further and did not decide whether the NLRB properly balanced employees' rights against the employer's interest in confidentiality, and whether the NLRB was correct to require employers to make a case-by-case determination of whether confidentiality was really necessary. [*Banner Health Sys. v. NLRB*, 851 F.3d 35 (D.C. Cir. 2017); see Bryan Bienias, *NLRB Restrictions on Employer Requests of Confidentiality in Workplace Investigations Remain After D.C. Circuit Decision*, Seyfarth Shaw LLP (Apr. 3, 2017) (benefitslink.com)]

[C] Unfair Labor Practices

Either a union or an employer can be guilty of an "unfair labor practice" (ULP) as defined by the NLRA and the LMRA. The NLRB has the power to issue a "cease and desist" order if it deems that an unfair practice has occurred. The NLRB also has powers to order positive actions, such as ordering an employer to bargain with a union.

NLRA § 8 defines unfair labor practices to include:

- Refusal to engage in collective bargaining—whether the recalcitrant party is management or union;

- Employer domination of a union;

- Retaliation against employees for filing charges with the NLRB or testifying before the agency;

- Discrimination against employees based on either union activities or refusal to join a union. In this context, discrimination includes firing, refusal to hire, refusal to reinstate, demotion, discrimination in compensation, discrimination in work assignments etc. However, if a union security clause is in place, employees can be required to pay union dues or the equivalent of dues, but they cannot be required to actually join the union;

- Deliberately inefficient work practices that require the employment of excessive numbers of workers ("featherbedding");

- Certain practices occurring during strikes or picketing.

The LMRA penalizes unfair labor practices by unions, including:

- Restraining or coercing employees when they exercise their right to bargain collectively, choose a representative, or vote against unionization;

- Causing an employer to discriminate against any employee;

- Refusing to participate in collective bargaining, once the union becomes the authorized bargaining representative for the employees;

- Engaging in strikes or concerted activity for the purpose of boycotting one employer, forcing another employer to recognize an uncertified union, forcing any employer to recognize a particular union when a different union is actually the authorized bargaining representative, or when a determination of jurisdiction still has to be made;

- Requiring union members in a union shop to pay excessive initiation fees or excessive dues;

- Featherbedding.

A ULP is an employment decision that interferes with the right to organize or discourages union membership. The test of such a decision is whether or not the action was motivated by anti-union animus.

The NLRB considers it a ULP to promulgate work rules that are likely to chill exercise of § 7 rights—even if the rules are never enforced. A rule that explicitly restricts § 7 activity violates the NLRA, and so does a rule that an employee would reasonably construe to prohibit § 7 activity, if the rule was promulgated in response to union activity, or the rule has been applied to restrict the exercise of § 7 rights. The Seventh Circuit held that a hospital unlawfully interfered with nurses' rights to organize and discriminated against a union activist nurse by forbidding solicitation in "patient care areas"—including the breakroom. The NLRB conceded that bans on solicitation in patient areas are valid, but the Seventh Circuit ruled that it was improper to define the breakroom as a patient care area because it was across the corridor from patient rooms. The facially valid anti-solicitation rule was applied in a discriminatory fashion: union solicitation was forbidden, but charitable solicitations and product sales were permitted. [*St. Margaret Mercy Healthcare Ctrs. V. NLRB*, 519 F.3d 373 (7th Cir. 2008)]

The Eleventh Circuit held that Mercedes' non-solicitation policy violated § 7. The NLRB found a violation because, although distribution of non-work materials during working hours can be forbidden and employees who are not working at the time can be forbidden to distribute non-work-related materials to employees who are at work, employees cannot be forbidden to distribute materials in a mixed-use area when neither the distributors nor the receivers were working. [*Mercedes-Benz Intl v. NLRB*, 838 F.3d 1128 (11th Cir. 2016); see Anne R. Yuengert, *Employers Hold Up on the Hand Out Policies: 11th Circuit*

Classifies Company Non-Solicitation Policy as Overbroad, Bradley Arant Boult Cummings LLP (Oct. 6, 2016), available at Lexology.com]

In early 2017, the NLRB, in conjunction with several DOL agencies (the Wage-Hour Division, OSHA, EEOC, and Office of Federal Contract Compliance Programs (OFCCP)), released a joint Fact Sheet, "Retaliation Based on the Exercise of Workplace Rights is Unlawful," reminding employers that retaliation is unlawful even if someone is an undocumented alien or is not authorized to work in the United States. The fact sheet says that workers are always entitled to be paid for work actually done, but remedies may be limited for undocumented workers. For example, they cannot be awarded reinstatement or back pay under the NLRA. [Kimberly N. Dobson, Howard M. Bloom and Philip B. Rosen, *NLRB Joins Other Federal Agencies in Combatting Retaliation*, Jackson Lewis PC (Jan. 17, 2017), available at Lexology.com]

In recent years, the NLRB has closely scrutinized employee handbooks for conformity with § 7. The NLRB has held that even some long-established policies are invalid because they impede protected concerted activities. In early 2015, the NLRB issued a 30-page memorandum about what policies are inappropriate in handbooks. A confidentiality policy must not prevent employees from discussing the terms and conditions of their employment, but it is legitimate to forbid discussion of trade secrets or confidential client information. The NLRA allows employees to criticize the company's labor policies or treatment of employees, but only to the extent the criticism pertains to the terms and conditions of employment. A blanket ban on disrespectful, negative, or rude conduct could be unlawful, but it is permissible to require professional, respectful treatment of customers and colleagues. Threats or coercion of co-workers can be forbidden; vigorous discussion cannot. Employees have a right to communicate with third parties, including the media, about the terms and conditions of employment. [<http://static.ow.ly/docs/GC%2015_04%20Report%20of%20the%20General%20Counsel%20Concerning%20Employer%20Rules.pdf_36Fc.pdf> (last accessed Mar. 5, 2017)]

The Second Circuit said that, although it was at the very limit of protectability, an employee's Facebook post that insulted his supervisor and used profanity was nevertheless protected because it encouraged co-workers to vote for the union in an upcoming election. The post dealt with workplace issues, and the statements were made in social media, not in the workplace. Once the employee discovered that the post was visible to the public, he took it down promptly. [*NLRB v. Pier Sixty, LLC*, No. 15-1841 (2d Cir. Apr. 21, 2017); see J. Gregory Grisham, *Second Circuit Upholds NLRB Order Finding Derogatory Facebook Post Protected Under the National Labor Relations Act*, Ford & Harrison LLP (Apr. 27, 2017), available at Lexology.com]

"Weingarten rights" are the labor-law equivalent of Miranda warnings in criminal law. An employee has the right to refuse to participate in an investigatory interview that the employee reasonably believes may result in discipline without a union representative present. It violates the NLRA for an employer to demand that the meeting continue without representation. *Weingarten* applies only if the employee's fear of discipline is objectively reasonable and if the employee asks for representation. The representative must be a current employee who is not a supervisor; generally it is a shop steward or other union official. If, through no fault of the employer, the employee's chosen representative is not available, the employee may have to accept a different union representative. The representative's role is to help the employee bring the case, clarifying the issues and helping the employee to raise the relevant facts. However, the employee does not have the right to bring his or her own lawyer. *Weingarten* no longer applies once the employer has made a decision. Employees can voluntarily waive *Weingarten* rights, as long as the waiver is clear and unmistakable. At various times the NLRB has hinted that *Weingarten* applies in non-union workplaces, and this seems to be the stance of the current board. [Kevin C. Donovan, *"Round Up the Usual Suspects" and Violate the NLRA? The Implications of Extending Weingarten Rights to Nonunionized Workplaces*, Wilson Elser Employment & Labor Newsletter (Dec. 2015) (benefitslink.com)]

NLRB said that filing a FLSA collective action is protected concerted activity, so firing an employee-plaintiff violated § 8(a)(1) even if no one asked him to do so. The NLRB said that filing a suit and applying for class certification was an effort to induce group action. [*200 E. 81st Rest. Corp.*, 362 N.L.R.B. No. 152 (July 29, 2015); see Gerald F. Lutkus, *NLRB: Filing an FLSA Collective Action Is Protected Concerted Activity*, Barnes & Thornburg LLP (July 31, 2015), available at Lexology.com]

In the NLRB's 2016 fiscal year, the NLRB issued 335 contested case decisions, nearly all of them (295) in ULP cases, the balance in representation cases. The regional offices issued 1,272 complaints. Virtually all (93%) of ULP cases that the NLRB found meritorious were settled. In 89% of cases, the regional offices won (in whole or in part) before the ALJ and full NLRB. NLRB judges closed 208 cases, and got 500 settlements. The NLRB got 1,648 employees reinstated, and the NLRB recovered $52,718,775 for employees as back pay and fees. [NLRB.gov, *FY 2017 Performance and Accountability Report*, <https://www.nlrb.gov/sites/default/files/attachments/basic-p> (undated, last accessed Apr. 5, 2017)]

[D]   LMRA Preemption

Many cases turn on whether § 301 of the Labor-Management Relations Act (LMRA) should be applied. This section gives federal District Courts jurisdiction over suits for violations of a collective bargaining agreement, as well as suits by one union against another. This section is often applied to bring labor questions into the federal courts—and keep them out of state courts when issues such as wrongful termination and unfair employee discipline are raised.

The most important issue in deciding whether LMRA preemption exists is the relationship between the controversy and the collective bargaining agreement. State laws are preempted whenever it is necessary to interpret the CBA.

However, the Supreme Court decided in 1994 that a mere need to refer to the CBA is not enough to justify preemption. The underlying dispute must really involve searching out the meaning of the terms of the contract. [*Lividas v. Bradshaw*, 512 U.S. 107 (1994)]

If the CBA includes a contractual grievance or arbitration provision (and most do), then potential plaintiffs have to exhaust their remedies (complete the entire process) before bringing suit under § 301.

Preemption has been found in cases such as:

- Failure to rehire, negligent and intentional infliction of emotional distress (because deciding the case required interpretation of the CBA's seniority provisions);

- A claim that a worker was denied reinstatement after a period of disability in retaliation for filing a Worker's Compensation claim, because the issue here was the management's exclusive right to hire and fire under the CBA "management rights" clause;

However, preemption was not found in these situations, on the grounds that the court did not have to interpret the CBA to decide the case:

- Retaliatory discharge;

- Discharge of an employee for reasons violating public policy;

- False imprisonment (unreasonable detention of an employee by a security guard);

- Claims about oral contracts other than the CBA (for instance, a verbal promise of lifetime employment) or implied contracts;

- Claims under state antidiscrimination laws on issues that are not normally bargained away during contract negotiations;

In 2012, the Fifth Circuit held that LMRA preemption should not have been applied in a case where a group of former employees raised tort claims against their ex-employer based on hearing loss that they said was caused by failure to abate workplace noise. The plaintiffs raised only state-law tort claims and the charges could be resolved without interpreting the CBA at all. [*McKnight v. Dresser, Inc.*, 676 F.3d 426 (5th Cir. 2012)]

§ 30.03 EMPLOYEE STATUS

[A] Definition of Employee

The NLRA defines the rights of "employees," so an important basic question is who fits into this category. Independent contractors are not employees, but common-law employees under the employer's control in terms of hiring, firing, work methods and results, provision of tools and materials, and employee discipline, are also employees for NLRA purposes.

The NLRB ruled that FedEx Home Delivery drivers are employees, but the D.C. Circuit held in early 2017 that they are independent contractors and, therefore, not permitted to unionize. The D.C. Circuit treated the independent contractor determination as a pure common-law agency question, in which the NLRB has no special expertise that is entitled to deference. The D.C. Circuit said that the NLRB stressed the wrong factors in characterizing the workers. [*FedEx Home Delivery v. NLRB,* 849 F.3d 1123 (D.C. Cir. 2017); see Richard J. Reibstein, *FedEx Succeeds Again on Appeal of an NLRB Ruling on Independent Contractor Misclassification,* Pepper Hamilton LLP (Mar. 7, 2017), available at Lexology-.com; Steven M. Swirsky, *D.C. Circuit Rejects NLRB Finding That FedEx Drivers Are Employees, Not Independent Contractors and Raises Doubts as to Board's Joint Employer Test,* Epstein Becker Green (D.C. Cir. Mar. 10, 2017), available at Lexology.com]

Employee status is maintained during a temporary layoff, if the worker reasonably expects to be recalled in the future. A sick or injured worker continues to be an employee either until he or she takes another permanent full-time job, or is permanently unable to return to work for physical reasons.

Sometimes retirees who do not have a right or reasonable expectation of re-hiring will not be considered employees. In other instances, however, retirees will continue to be treated as members of the bargaining unit, on the theory that the union bargained for a compensation package covering both active workers and retirees. This is a particularly significant question in terms of retiree health benefits promised "for life" when the employer later claims that the promise expired with the CBA. See § 9.08.

In 2004, in *Brown University,* 342 N.L.R.B. 483 (2004), the NLRB held that university student assistants are not statutory employees. This decision was reversed in mid-2016 when the NLRB ruled that agency principles require treating undergraduate or graduate student teaching assistants as employees who can unionize and engage in collective bargaining. [*Columbia Univ.,* No. 02-RC-143012 (N.L.R.B. Aug. 23, 2016); see Christopher W. Kelleher, *NLRB Paves Way for Student Unionization,* Seyfarth Shaw LLP (Aug. 24, 2016), available at Lexology.com]

The NLRB also ruled that university Resident Advisors were employees and eligible to unionize, on the grounds that they are required to sign employment agreements that govern compensation, training, and work rules; they receive free housing and a cash stipend, rather than academic credit; and they can be terminated or otherwise disciplined if they do a poor job. [David M. Felper, *Resident Advisors Are Subject to Union Organizing,* Bowditch & Dewey (June 8, 2017), available at Lexology.com]

As of February 2017, there were about 35 collective bargaining units of graduate students at public universities and about 30,000 graduate students belong to the United Auto Workers. There were union efforts at some major private universities. Columbia and Loyola University Chicago graduate students unionized and the union obtained some success at Yale. New York University voluntarily recognized a union in 2013. The Harvard election went to the NLRB for determination because the result was too close to call. Several Yale departments unionized; other department votes were under NLRB review. [Melanie Trottman and Melissa Korn, *Graduate Students Can Unionize at Private Colleges, U.S. Labor Panel Rules,* WSJ.com (Aug. 23, 2016); Elizabeth A. Harris, *Columbia Graduate Students Vote Overwhelmingly to Unionize,* NYTimes.com (Dec. 9, 2016); Noam Scheiber, *Grad Students Win Right to Unionize in an Ivy League Case,* NYTimes.com (Aug. 23, 2016); Melissa Korn, *Graduate Students Push for Unions at More Private Colleges,* WSJ.com (Feb. 24, 2017)]

[B] Part-Time and Temporary Workers

Whether an employee is considered full-time or part-time will affect the worker's benefit entitlement and when employers have discretion over what benefits to offer, it is much more likely that full-time workers will have access to a given benefit. (see § 1.10). PPACA has a special definition of "full-time," requiring large employers to make health care benefits available to employees who work at least 30 hours a week.

Temporary or casual workers will probably not be considered employees for labor law purposes. Part-time workers are considered employees, although sometimes it is inappropriate to put them in a bargaining unit with full-timers, if their interests are adverse.

In August 2000, the NLRB ruled that temporary workers can be included in the same collective bargaining unit as permanent employees, as long as the characteristics of the job are similar. [*M.B. Sturgis Inc.*, 331 N.L.R.B. 173 (Aug. 25, 2000)]

In 2004, the NLRB reversed this decision. [*Oakwood Care Ctr.,* 343 N.L.R.B. 659 (2004)] Then, in mid-2016, the NLRB reversed again and re-adopted its *M.B. Sturgis* position. The issue is most likely to arise when some of the employees have only one employer and some are jointly employed (for example, by a staffing agency and the employer contracting for the work to be done). Another scenario is a company that subcontracts out some services but has staffers who share a community of interest with people employed by a subcontractor. The NLRB's 2016 position is that a unit with both joint and singly employed employees fits within NLRA § 9(b) when it makes sense and helps employees exercise their rights. [*Miller & Anderson, Inc.*, 364 N.L.R.B. No. 39 (July 11, 2016); see Michael J. Lebowich and Corinne M. Osborn, *Stuck With It: Labor Board Forces Employers to Recognize Bargaining Units That Contain*

Employees of Two or More Separate Employers, Proskauer Rose LLP (July 13, 2016), available at Lexology.com; Alan D. Berkowitz and J. Ian Downes, *NLRB Says Employer Consent Is Not Required for Bargaining Units of Solely and Jointly Employed Workers,* Dechert LLP (Aug. 16, 2016), available at Lexology .com]

The NLRB ruled that the union has the right to show that the two companies are really joint employers of the workers, because they both determine the terms and conditions of employment. However, the user employer can rebut the union's contention by showing that the supplier employer maintains the real control over the workers.

The Seventh Circuit held that seasonal employees at a factory were eligible for inclusion in the bargaining unit with permanent employees, based on shared interests and the seasonal workers' reasonable expectation of future employment. The seasonal workers constituted a large part of the workforce; they came from a definable, static group of workers (the local Hispanic population), and all new permanent hires came from the pool of seasonal workers. The Seventh Circuit reached this conclusion although the seasonal employees did not receive the same benefits as the permanent employees; and the employer did not try to recruit former seasonal workers when new workers had to be hired. [*Winkie Mfg. Co. v. NLRB*, 348 F.3d 254 (7th Cir. 2003)]

[C] Supervisors

The text of the NLRA [29 U.S.C. § 152] says that "supervisors" such as foremen and forewomen are not "employees," for the common-sense reason that supervisors promote management interests and therefore do not fit in well with rank-and-file workers, who have different and often opposing interests.

A supervisor is someone who has a formal job title indicating supervisory status, has been held out as a supervisor by management, or is perceived as a supervisor by rank-and-file workers. A supervisor makes independent, individual judgments, can reward or discipline employees (up to and including firing them) and has authority to adjust employee grievances.

To be a supervisor, someone must have supervisory authority on a consistent basis (whether or not it is exercised). Sporadic or limited authority, such as power to take over in an emergency, doesn't make a rank-and-file worker into a supervisor. Courts have expanded the statutory definition, so that managers are not considered employees either, because of their discretion and ability to set corporate policy.

In mid-2001, the Supreme Court resolved a conflict about the status of Registered Nurses in nursing homes. Because the RNs direct the activities of non-RN staff, they are supervisors and cannot be organized in the same unit as the other staffers. [*NLRB v. Kentucky River Cmty. Care Inc.*, 532 U.S. 706 (2001)]

In 2013, the Sixth Circuit, reversing the NLRB, held that Registered Nurses (RNs) at a nursing home were supervisors because of their power to use independent judgment to assign, direct, and discipline Certified Nurse Assistants at the facility. The Sixth Circuit held that merely reporting misconduct is not supervisory authority, but it is not necessary for a worker to have the power to hire and fire to be considered a supervisor. [*GGNSC Springfield v. NLRB*, 721 F.3d 403 (6th Cir. 2013)]

In late 2016, the Fourth Circuit reversed several of its earlier decisions and held that RNs and Licensed Practical Nurses (LPNs) at a South Carolina nursing home could unionize because they were not supervisors. The Fourth Circuit said that the RNs and LPNs were not supervisors as defined by *Kentucky River,* because they could not perform supervisory functions; they could not use independent judgment to exercise authority because they were subject to detailed employer policies that specified what they were supposed to do in every situation. [*Palmetto Prince George v. NLRB,* 841 F.3d 211 (4th Cir. 2016); see John T.L. Koenig, *Fourth Circuit Finds Nurses Are Not Supervisors—Could Unionize,* Barnes & Thornburg LLP (Nov. 3, 2016), available at Lexology.com]

[D] Union Organizers

A paid union organizer can qualify as a protected "employee" under the NLRA. The fact that he or she is paid a salary by the union does not deprive him or her of the protection of federal labor law. This concept has been extended to treat a volunteer union organizer who is not paid by the union as an employee. [*NLRB v. Town & Country Elec. Inc.*, 516 U.S. 85 (1995); *NLRB v. Fluor Daniel*, 102 F.3d 818 (6th Cir. 1996)]

In general, the LMRA prevents employers from making payments to any union representative, but this rule is not violated by continuing to provide full pay and benefits to a long-tenure employee who served as shop steward and worked full-time representing employees who had grievances. The Ninth Circuit held that it was in the employer's best interests to have grievances handled expeditiously. The shop steward was an employee of the company and not the union because the company controlled his work week; he reported to the company's HR director; and his workplace was the shop floor, not the union hall. [*International Ass'n of Machinists v. B.F. Goodrich*, 387 F.3d 1046 (9th Cir. 2004)]

In appropriate cases, the employer can assert the defense that the union "salts" who applied for jobs were not entitled to be hired because they had a disabling conflict with the employer's interests. However, according to the D.C. Circuit, the disabling conflict defense can only be asserted if a union organizer seeks work while engaged in an economic strike against the employer, or if what is described as protected union organizing activity is actually a cloak for unlawful conduct aimed at sabotage or driving the employer out of business. [*Casino Ready Mix v. NLRB*, 321 F.3d 1190 (D.C. Cir. 2003)] In this case, the union salts responded to an advertisement, and were clearly qualified for the job, so refusal to assign work to them was unlawful discrimination. However, in 2003 the Seventh Circuit held that a construction company's hiring system, which gave preference to former employees and referrals from trusted sources did not violate the LMRA. The union "salts" were not hired—but that was not because of their union affiliation, but because they were walk-ins, the lowest-priority category in the employer's classification. [*International Union of Operating Eng'rs, Local 150 v. NLRB*, 325 F.3d 818 (7th Cir. 2003)]

§ 30.04 ELECTIONS, CERTIFICATION, AND RECOGNITION

[A] Generally

To gain "certification," and thereby become the bargaining agent for the employees (whom the employer must deal with), a union has to win an election supervised by the NLRB. There is a one-year period after the certification election during which no rival union is allowed to seek certification.

A union organizing campaign begins with a petition for certification. Typically, the petition is filed by the union or by an individual employee who is a union supporter. Most organizing work is done by pro-union employees, because employers can and usually do bar non-employees from soliciting on business premises during working hours. [But see § 30.04[H] for exceptions to this rule.] If there are two or more unions trying to organize the same workplace, the employer is allowed to express a preference for one over the other.

A certification petition is valid only if at least 30% of the employees in the bargaining unit indicate their interest, on authorization cards, union membership cards, membership applications, signatures on a certification petition, or via a record of paying union dues.

NLRB General Counsel Memorandum 15-08 (Sept. 1, 2015) allows signatures for a showing of interest to be submitted electronically, by e-mail or online. The authorization must include the signer's name, e-mail address or social media account, phone number, the name of the employer, and an indication of agreement. [NLRB General Counsel GC 15-08, *Guidance Memorandum on Electronic Signatures to Support a Showing of Interest*]

It is a serious unfair labor practice for employers to retaliate against workers because of their union activism, so it is important to document good business reasons for any disciplinary action taken against less-than-optimal workers who also happen to be union activists.

The employer has the right to request a representation election when a majority of the employees have submitted signed authorization cards designating a particular union as their bargaining agent. However, an employer that engages in serious ULPs forfeits the right to call for an election, and can be compelled to bargain with the union, because an employer loses the right to call for an election if it engages in conduct that is likely to disrupt the election. [*NLRB v. Orland Park Motor Cars*, 309 F.3d 452 (7th Cir. 2002)]

In 2016, unions won 72% of all representation elections and 74% of elections with units of 49 or fewer workers. Unions often concentrate on micro-units because they are easier to organize than larger bargaining units. This was the highest percentage of success in four years. However, the number of workers organized was the lowest in four years: only 57,800 in 2016 versus 63,300 in 2015. The number of elections fell from 1,626 in 2015 to 1,381 in 2016. Decertification elections were also common: 970 between 2012 and 2016, and unions lost more than 60% of the elections (596 in total) if the unit was 49 workers or fewer—the highest percentage in four years. [Jessica M. Marsh, Howard M. Bloom and Philip B. Rosen, *Unions Winning More Elections, But Organizing Fewer New Workers,* Jackson Lewis PC (Mar. 21, 2017), available at Lexology .com]

On November 30, 2011, the NLRB passed a chairman's resolution that limits appeals of union organizing elections in order to speed up the election process by limiting litigation before the election to matters directly related to the election, and deferring appeals until after the election (because many disputes become moot once the election is held). [The rule was proposed at 76 Fed. Reg. 36812 (June 22, 2011) and finalized at 76 Fed. Reg. 80138 (Dec. 22, 2011).]

Then, in May 2012, the District Court for the District of Columbia found that this rule was invalidly promulgated because the NLRB did not have a quorum when the rule was adopted. The NLRB had three members at that time; two members (both Democrats) voted for the rule, the one Republican member did not vote at all. The district court said that without three actual votes being cast, there was no quorum. In response, the NLRB suspended implementation of the new rule. [<http://www.nlrb.gov/news/nlrb-suspends-implementation-representation-case-amendments-based-court-ruling> (May 15, 2012)] At the end of 2013, the NLRB announced that it would not appeal this decision. [79 Fed. Reg. 7318 (Feb. 6, 2014). See *Chamber of Commerce of the USA v. NLRB*, 879 F. Supp. 2d 18 (D.D.C. 2012) and No. 12-5250 (stipulation of dismissal Dec. 9, 2013).]

In February 6, 2014, the NLRB re-proposed representation election rules that are essentially the same as the previous "quickie" or "ambush election" rule. [NLRB, *Amendments to NLRB Election Rules and Regulations Fact Sheet*, <http://www.nlrb.gov/news-outreach/fact-sheets/nlrb-representation-case-procedures-fact-sheet> (last accessed Mar. 5, 2017) includes a table comparing the current rules to the NLRB proposal.]

The NLRB finalized the proposed rules on December 12, 2014, effective April 14, 2015. Under the previous rules, the median time from petition to election was 38 days; the new rule would make it 10–14 days. The 2014 rule permits election petitions to be submitted in person, by fax, by mail, or electronically and election notices and voter lists can also be e-mailed. The NLRB then gives the parties information about election procedures and a statement of position form that can be used to define the issues for a pre-election hearing. The NLRB expects the regional director to set the pre-election hearing 8 days after the hearing notice is received, and a post-election hearing 14 days after filing of any objections. The party that did not petition for the election must submit a statement of position on all the issues for the pre-election hearing at least one business day before the hearing opens. Any positions not included in the notice are waived. (Prior law did not require disclosure of positions before the hearing.) The new rule speeds up the time when the union receives the list of prospective voters ("Excelsior list"), and increases the amount of information the employer must provide about those voters. The list must be provided within two business days of the direction of election, or the regional director's approval of the election agreement; the previous requirement was seven days. Post-hearing, pre-election briefs can only be submitted if the regional director finds them necessary. There will be no automatic stay of election for the NLRB to consider requests for review of regional director decisions. [79 Fed. Reg. 74307 (Dec 15, 2014)]

The Fifth Circuit upheld the quickie election rules in mid-2016, holding that the rules did not violate the NLRA or the Administrative Procedure Act, and that the plaintiffs did not prove that disclosing employees' e-mail addresses and cell-phone numbers threatened greater harm to employees than the existing procedure for giving unions a contact list. [*Associated Builders & Contractors of Texas v. NLRB*, No. 15-50497 (5th Cir. June 10, 2016)]

On March 19, 2015, the House of Representatives voted to join the Senate in sending a resolution to President Obama to block the quickie election rule. On March 31, 2015, President Obama exercised his fourth veto since his election to reject the congressional resolution calling for elimination of the Ambush Election Rule. Because of the veto, the rule took effect as scheduled on April 14. The Republicans did not have enough votes in the Senate to override the veto. [Melanie Trottman, *Obama Veto Protects Labor Board Rule*, WSJ.com (Mar. 31, 2015)]

The rule's effect on union organizing is hard to interpret. The NLRB reported that there were 2,198 certification petitions filed in 2016—and only 2,029 were filed in 2016. The NRLB's fiscal year ends September 30, so the quickie election rule was in effect for nine months of fiscal 2016. There were 1,574 certification elections in 2016, falling to 1,396 in 2016. The percentage of union victories rose slightly, from 71.2% in 2015 to 72.6% in 2016, but in both years, many petitions were withdrawn or dismissed without an election. [Philip B. Rosen et. al., *Union kNOw January 2017*, Jackson Lewis PC (Jan. 24, 2017), available at Lexology.com]

However, Bloomberg BNA reported in mid-2017 that unions won about 67% of elections—and 82% of the fastest elections, those with less than two weeks between the petition and the vote. [Robert J. Guidotti, Howard M. Bloom and Philip B. Rosen, *In Fastest Elections, Union Victory Rate Soars,* Jackson Lewis PC (May 5, 2017), available at Lexology.com]

[B]   Consent Elections

The NLRB is responsible for determining the validity of the representation petition. If the employer does not oppose holding the election, the election is a consent election. The employer and union sign a contract permitting an election. The NLRB will probably have to accept the consent agreement's definition of the appropriate bargaining unit, unless it violates the law (for instance, by including guards in a mixed bargaining unit).

Within seven days of the time that the appropriate NLRB Regional Director approves a consent agreement, the employer has a duty to submit the "Excelsior List" to the Regional Director. This is a list of the names and addresses of every worker eligible to vote in the consent election. The Regional Director distributes the list to all interested parties. [The name comes from the NLRB case of *Excelsior Underwear Inc.*, 156 N.L.R.B. 271 (1986).]

[C]   NLRB Hearings

If the employer objects, but the NLRB finds that there is reasonable cause to believe that the union might be an appropriate representative for the employees, the NLRB holds a nonadversary hearing to determine if there is a question of representation. (Employers who are dissatisfied with the Regional Director's decision can appeal to the central NLRB for review.) This type of hearing cannot be used to raise claims of unfair labor practices by either side.

In most instances, the hearing will result in setting a date for a secret ballot election under NLRB supervision. The NLRB will then certify the result: whether or not the union has secured a majority vote.

A union will be certified as bargaining representative for the unit if it wins the votes of a majority of the voters (not a majority of those eligible to vote). But the election will not be valid unless a "representative number" of eligible employees actually voted. There is no bright-line test for whether the number of voters was representative. Many factors, such as the voter turnout, adequacy of the employees' notice of the election and opportunity to vote, and the presence or absence of unfair practices by the employer, are considered to see if there was a high enough turnout.

[D]   Election Procedure

Usually, the election will be held at the workplace, because that is accessible to all employees. However, if there is good cause shown for holding an election somewhere else, or for allowing voting by mail, the NLRB will supervise the out-of-plant election. Elections are held by secret ballot. The voters enter the voting location, have their employee status checked, and then mark their ballots in a closed booth where their selections are not visible. The ballots are collected for later tallying.

Voting can be done either manually, in a voting booth, or by mailing ballots to the NLRB regional office. The NLRB has ruled about when employers are allowed to hold mandatory captive audience meetings before an election. The *Peerless Plywood* rule is that, in manual voting cases, the employer must not hold a captive audience meeting within 24 hours of the start of the election. For mail ballots, *Guardsmark, LLC* requires a 24-hour period without speeches before mailing. [Melissa D. Sobota, *NLRB Continues to Tweak Its Election Procedures; Announces New "Captive Audience" Rule in Mail Ballot Cases*, Franczek Rade-let PC (Feb. 5, 2016), available at Lexology.com]

Before a certification or deauthorization election, the employer must post an election notice in a conspicuous place in the workplace. The notice must be up for at least three full working days before 12:01 a.m. of the day scheduled for the election. Failure to post the notice can result in the election results being set aside. The notice must give the date, time, and place of the election, and must show a sample ballot so employees will know how to mark it to indicate their choice.

If there are objections to the eligibility of certain voters, or to the mechanics of the election, either the employer or union can file an objection with the NLRB.

If an employer relies on the results of an invalid election to change policies within the workplace, the Ninth Circuit said that the appropriate remedy is to hold a new election. [*Gardner Mech. Servs. v. NLRB*, 89 F.3d 586 (9th Cir. 1996)] A bargaining order is improper unless there is proof that it would be impossible to hold a valid election.

A close election resulted in a union victory. The employer refused to bargain with the union, alleging that, during the post-election proceedings, the NLRB improperly revoked subpoenas issued by the employer. The employer asked for documents about the union's alleged threats to voters before the election; the employer charged the union with threats and coercion. The NLRB issued a bargaining order, deciding that it was important for employees to be able to keep their activities as union agents confidential. The D.C. Circuit refused to enforce the NLRB order, finding that the agency's reasoning was flawed, and the NLRB failed to balance the employees' interests in confidentiality against the company's need for the information. [*Ozark Auto. Distribs., Inc. v. NLRB*, 779 F.3d 576 (D.C. Cir. 2015)]

[E] Voter Eligibility

The simple answer is that all "employees" in the "bargaining unit" are entitled to vote in a representation election. However, it can be hard to determine the appropriate bargaining unit, and there are some questions about who retains employee status.

In 2008, the D.C. Circuit ruled that a bargaining unit member is presumed to remain a member of the unit while on sick leave, long-term disability, or worker's compensation, unless the employer proves that the person has resigned or been terminated. [*Abbott Ambulance of Ill. v. NLRB*, 522 F.3d 447 (D.C. Cir. 2008)]

For laid-off workers, the question is whether they have a reasonable expectation of recall (determined as of the date of the election, not the date of the NLRB pre-election hearing). A person who was lawfully fired before the date of the election is not eligible to vote, but someone who is unlawfully discharged for union activity retains employee status, and therefore is entitled to vote.

Economic strikers (see § 30.09[B] for characterization of strikes) who have not been replaced as to the date of the election are entitled to vote. During the 12 months after the beginning of an economic strike, economic strikers are still entitled to vote if they have been replaced—even if they are not entitled to immediate reinstatement after the strike ends. Employees who are on the preferential reinstatement list are also entitled to vote. But if the election is held more than 12 months after the beginning of a strike, replaced economic strikers are not entitled to vote, even if they still have a reasonable expectation of recall.

Replacement workers hired during an economic strike are entitled to vote in the election, but only if they were employed before the eligibility cutoff date for the election. Unlike economic strikers, unfair labor practice strikers are always eligible to vote in representation elections, but their replacements are never entitled to vote.

[F] Electioneering and Communications

During a certification campaign, both employer and union are entitled to communicate their viewpoints to employees. The employer is considered a "person" entitled to exercise free speech rights, subject to limitations of accuracy and fairness. If the employer overreaches, the election results will be set aside, and the employer will have to go through the whole process again, perhaps with more employee sympathy for the union. In egregious cases, the employer might have to answer charges of an unfair labor practice.

The "critical period" is the time between the filing of a representation petition and the election itself. (For a runoff or rerun election, the critical period begins at the first election, and even conduct occurring before the certification petition was filed might be considered relevant as to the fairness of the election.) The NLRB will observe the conduct of both sides, and has the power to invalidate elections, even if the misconduct is not serious enough to constitute an unfair labor practice. The employer is held responsible for the conduct of its agents, including its lawyers and labor relations consultants.

■ **TIP:**   An employer can avoid liability for an inappropriate statement by an agent if it repudiates the statement promptly, admitting that it was out of line, restating it in proper form, and giving at least as much publicity to the retraction as to the original communication.

Certification elections are supposed to provide "laboratory conditions" (i.e., pure and untainted) for workplace democracy. Employers are not allowed to conduct pre-election polls, or even ask employees their opinions about unionization, if the inquiry is too close to the time of the election. However, it is accepted labor law that employers can call a meeting of workers on company time for management to assert its arguments against unionization. If the union is permitted to solicit employees during meals and other breaks, the employer can call a mass meeting without giving the union equal time to reply.

During the 24-hour period just before the election, neither management nor union is allowed to make speeches to massed employees on company time. If the employer does this, it is not an unfair labor practice, but it could lead to invalidation of the election. The employer is allowed to distribute printed materials to workers during this time. The employer can also conduct antiunion meetings away from the workplace during the 24-hour period, as long as attendance is voluntary and employees choose to come in on their own time.

These are examples that have been found to constitute unfair labor practices by the employer:

- Announcing benefits on election day;

- Explicitly promising benefits if the union loses;

- Threatening to withhold benefits if the union wins;

- Announcing new benefits during the critical period to show that the employer offers a better deal than the union—unless the benefits were decided before the representation petition was filed, or there is economic justification for providing them at that time;

- Telling employees that unless they returned to work the next day without a union contract, the business would be closed down, and its equipment would be leased, was a threat (an unfair labor practice) and not just a permissible prediction of future events. It was a threat because it referred to events wholly within the employer's control;

However, these have been held not to be improper practices by the employer:

- Delaying pay raises until after the election, as long as timing is the only issue—raises will be paid no matter who wins the election;

- Distributing fact-based (not coercive or threatening) handbills during an organizing drive, saying that unionization would lead to long, bitter negotiations and possibly an ugly strike;

- Announcing two new floating holidays the day before the election. The timing of the announcement was logical within the company's fiscal year; it was just a coincidence that it was right before the election.

The NLRB refused to invalidate a union election victory even though the union gave away free holiday hams a few days before the election. The NLRB's rationale was that the distribution was an annual event; the value of the hams was only about $10; and they were distributed at a voluntary gathering that was not linked to the election. The NLRB said that an election even one day after a give-away can be upheld, as long as there was no tendency to unlawfully influence the outcome of the election. [*Nuverra Envtl. Solutions, Inc.*, No. 08-CA-164447 (July 8, 2016); see Robert Murphy, Howard M. Bloom and Philip B. Rosen, *Ham-Handed Tactic? NLRB Says Union Giveaway Not Grounds for Setting Aside Election Victory,* Jackson Lewis PC (July 25, 2016), available at Lexology.com]

The Eighth Circuit held in early 2016 that it did not violate the NLRA to give an employee a verbal warning for soliciting union membership at the plant. The company solicitation policy limited discussion "for or against unions or other organizations" to non-working times, and said materials could not be distributed during work time, or in work areas at any time. The employee in question gave three co-workers union authorization cards to sign. They did not submit the cards and, while they were working, the employee asked them again. They reported her to management. The Eighth Circuit said that the worker's actions were part of an overall series of interactions seeking support for the union, so she violated the anti-solicitation policy. However, the Eighth Circuit held that the letter that the employer posted about the policy was overly broad and misleading. Although solicitation can be forbidden during work time and in work areas, discussions about the union are not necessarily solicitation and employees might be misled into believing they cannot talk about the union at all. [*ConAgra Foods v. NLRB*, 813 F.3d 1079 (8th Cir. 2016); see Jennifer M. Holly, *8th Circuit Upholds Employer's Right to Discipline Workers Who Solicit During Working Time*, Seyfarth Shaw LLP (Mar. 2 2016), available at Lexology.com]

[G] Buttons and Insignia

The right to free speech extends to employees in the workplace to the extent that workers must be allowed to wear union buttons. They must be allowed to wear union buttons to the poll, even though blatant electioneering like this would not be allowed in a general election.

Wearing union insignia is protected by NLRA § 7, and interfering with this right violates § 8(a)(1), unless the union materials cause a real safety hazard, or there is a real risk of violence between union supporters and opponents. The mere possibility of violence is not enough.

There is a partial exception. Employees who work with the public, and who are required to wear a uniform, can be forbidden to wear all kinds of jewelry, including union buttons. They can be required to wear the standard uniform, not a union T-shirt. But the employer must be careful to communicate the uniform policy, and to enforce it across the board, not just against union insignia.

The Starbucks dress code actually required employees to wear a variety of buttons and badges. Two union activist employees were fired for dress code violations. The Second Circuit vacated one termination and remanded the other. Discharge was upheld for an employee who, in addition to dress code violations, frequently missed work and was not well informed about current products. Discharge was remanded for further proceedings in the case of an employee discharged after a profane outburst in a Starbucks store while the worker was off-duty. It was remanded because the outburst was about union matters, and the NLRB was instructed to consider whether protected collective activity is limited to situations in which employees wear their work uniforms. [*NLRB v. Starbucks Corp.*, 679 F.3d 70 (2d Cir. 2012)]

The First Circuit held that the NLRB had substantial evidence for concluding that a car dealer's blanket rule forbidding union pins, insignia, or "message clothing" violated NRLA § 8(a)(1). An employer must show special circumstances (potential risks to employee safety; possible damage to machinery or products; creation of workplace dissension) to forbid insignia, and the rule must be narrowly tailored. The First Circuit held that the employer failed to show how wearing unobtrusive union insignia would harm the company's professional image. [*Boch Imports, LLC v. NLRB,* 826 F.3d 558 (1st Cir. 2016); see Manatt Phelps & Phillips LLP *First Circuit Sides with NLRB on Dress Code* (June 30, 2016), available at Lexology.com; Christopher A. Johlie and Melissa D. Sobota, *Adventures in Buttonland: NLRB Rejects Employer Attempts to Ban Buttons at Work*, Franczek Radelet PC (July 22, 2016), available at Lexology.com]

[H] Access by Non-Employees

In mid-2016, the NLRB ruled that off-duty employees are entitled to picket their employer's premises, unless the employer can prove that picketing had to be banned for reasons such as safety or preventing disruption of patient care in a healthcare workplace. [*Capital Med. Ctr.*, 364 N.L.R.B. No. 69 (Aug. 12, 2016); see Roger P. Gilson Jr. et al., *Labor Board Rules Off-Duty Employees May Picket on Employer Premises*, Jackson Lewis PC (Sept. 27, 2016), available at Lexology.com]

In most instances, a workplace is private property, not a public space. Therefore, union organizers do not automatically have a right to leaflet or distribute literature at a location where they are not employees if this is contrary to the wishes of the employer or other owner of the property. An exception might occur in a "company town" situation, where in effect all property is owned by the employer, so there is no public space where the union can distribute literature. [See, e.g., *Lechmere v. NLRB*, 502 U.S. 527 (1991)] Another exception might be a place that is so remote geographically that the union has no reasonable means of communicating with employees outside the workplace.

California law protects reasonable speech in privately owned shopping centers, but does not require shopping centers to allow expressive activities that interfere with normal business opportunities. The D.C. Circuit couldn't figure out whether forbidding all expressive activities on the premises that did not have a permit violated the NLRA, so it sent the case to the California Supreme Court for a determination of whether a mall can impose a rule against urging customers to boycott any of the tenants of the mall. [*Fashion Valley Mall LLC v. NLRB*, 451 F.3d 241 (D.C. Cir. 2006)]

In late 2012, the California Supreme Court ruled that a supermarket's privately owned entrance area is not a "public forum" as defined by the California constitution. Therefore, union picketing in such an area did not have protection under the state constitution. However, two California labor laws protected picketing. This decision conflicts with the D.C. Circuit's decision in 2004 that one of those statutes, the Moscone Act (which forbids injunctions against peaceful picketing) is unconstitutional because it grants greater protection to labor speech than to other forms of speech. [*Ralphs Grocery Co. v. United Food & Commercial Workers Union Local 8*, 55 Cal. 4th 1083, 290 P.3d 1116, 150 Cal. Rptr. 3d 501 (2012)]

The Sixth Circuit found that it was an Unfair Labor Practice for a non-union nursing home to require employees distributing union literature to leave non-working areas of the premises. The court found that the rights of employees who worked at other sites to receive the information outweighed the employer's property rights. There was no proof that nursing home residents would be any more distressed by the presence of union organizers than any other stranger. [*First Healthcare Corp. v. NLRB*, 344 F.3d 523 (6th Cir. 2003)]

The Third Circuit has found that the NLRA is not violated when an employer denies access to its property to union representatives who want to distribute handbills accusing the employer of using underpaid nonunion labor. In this context, the employer's property rights clearly prevail over the union's free speech right—especially because general information aimed at the public, not an actual certification election, was involved. [*Metropolitan Dist. Council of Phila. v. NLRB*, 68 F.3d 71 (3d Cir. 1995)] In contrast, where employee interests outweighed the employer's security and property rights concerns, the D.C. Circuit ruled that off-site employees must be allowed to distribute pro-union handbills in the plant parking lot. [*ITT Indus. v. NLRB*, 413 F.3d 64 (D.C. Cir. 2005)]

Can a business located in a shopping mall forbid the distribution of union literature in that mall? The Eighth Circuit says that a business that is just a tenant (and therefore does not have exclusive rights to the corridor outside its business location) cannot forbid union handbilling. But the Sixth Circuit says that a mall owner can ban solicitation by union representatives who are not employed at the mall, even if other kinds of solicitation (e.g., for charity) are allowed. [*O'Neil's Mkts. v. United Food & Commercial Workers*, 95 F.3d 733 (8th Cir. 1996); *Cleveland Real Estate Partners v. NLRB*, 95 F.3d 457 (6th Cir. 1996); *Riesbeck Food Mkts. Inc. v. NLRB*, 91 F.3d 132 (4th Cir. 1996)] Reasonable restrictions on the time, place, and manner of expressive activities can be imposed. Courts give more scrutiny to content-based restrictions on expressive activities than to those that are content-neutral. [*United Bhd. of Carpenters & Joiners Local 848 v. NLRB*, 540 F.3d 957 (9th Cir. 2008)]

Picketing is a particularly confrontational practice and has the potential to create conflict and danger, especially when persons who wish to enter the premises are told not to cross the line. The Ninth Circuit ruled that the NLRB was not entitled to a preliminary injunction to prevent a union from putting "Labor Dispute" banners outside stores that hire nonunion contractors because banners do not threaten, coerce, or restrain employees or potential customers. [*Overstreet v. United Bhd. of Carpenters & Joiners of Am.*, 409 F.3d 1199 (9th Cir. 2005)]

The question of non-employee access can also arise in the context of workplace inspections. A February 21, 2013 OSHA interpretation letter permits union organizers or community activists who are not employees to represent the employees when OSHA inspects a non-union workplace. [See 29 U.S.C. § 657(e).] The OSHA regulations (§ 1903.8(c)) state that the authorized employee representative will normally be an employee but a non-employee such as a safety engineer or industrial hygienist can be the representative if the compliance officer finds it necessary. Employee representatives can join the compliance officer on the walkaround inspection, interview non-management employees, and participate in informal settlement conferences after citations are issued. OSHA's position is that the union representative can file a complaint on behalf of an employee, ask for an inspection, protest the abatement period in a citation, and participate in contest proceedings. Employers dislike this practice because they believe it gives the union direct access to employees and sites that would otherwise be unavailable. [Jackson Lewis PC, *Union Reps on OSHA Inspections Seen as a Concern*, Lexology.com (Apr. 16, 2014)]

OSHA's letter announcing this interpretation is called the "Fairfax Memo." (Fairfax was the deputy assistant secretary of labor.) The National Federation of Independent Business (NFIB) sued to challenge the policy, alleging that the letter allows union recruiters to enter premises contrary to the employer's intentions, and that OSHA exceeded its statutory authority and promulgated a new policy without the necessary notice and comment. OSHA said that the NFIB did not have standing because it did not have injury in fact; the memo was not a final agency action; and if the NFIB was entitled to a remedy, it could be obtained without a declaratory judgment. The district court held that the memo was a final agency action that was required to go through the formal APA process, but the district court also held that the memo did not exceed OSHA's statutory authority and was not inconsistent with the text of the OSH Act. However, on February 13 (i.e., post-inauguration), OSHA filed a motion for another 30 days to file an answer to the complaint, In fact, OSHA withdrew the memorandum, leading to voluntary dismissal of the case in April 2017. [*NFIB v. Dougherty,* No. 3:16-CV-2568-D (N.D. Tex., *dismissed* Apr. 27, 2017); see Jordan Rodriguez, *Employers Earn an Important Victory In "Union Walk-Around" Lawsuit,* Kelley Drye & Warren LLP (Feb. 14, 2017), available at Lexology.com; Epstein Becker Green, *Labor Department Backs Away from Permitting Unions at OSHA Safety Inspections* (Feb. 17, 2017), available at Lexology.com]

§ 30.05 THE APPROPRIATE BARGAINING UNIT

Even after winning an election, a union cannot be certified unless it is organized as the appropriate bargaining unit for the enterprise. NLRA § 9(b) gives the NLRB power to determine the appropriate bargaining unit. The basic standard is whether there is a community of interest among the unit members, not just employees in general (who can be expected to want higher wages and better benefits). Neither employer nor union can tell in advance what will be considered the appropriate unit, or how large the unit will be.

The appropriateness of a bargaining unit depends on the duties, skills, and working conditions of the employees who are supposed to have common interests. If there are competing proposed bargaining units for the same company, their relative popularity with employees is highly significant.

A union can be organized by employer, craft, or plan, or a subdivision of one of these categories. A union decision to organize as a craft unit is legally protected. The NLRB does not have the power to decide that a different unit would be more appropriate.

Employees and supervisors cannot be in the same bargaining unit. In fact, in many instances, supervisors cannot unionize at all, because they are considered a part of management. As a general rule, professionals and nonprofessionals cannot be included in a unit, but this rule can be waived if a majority of the professional employees vote to be included. (The nonprofessionals do not get veto power over inclusion of professionals.)

Determination of professional status does not depend entirely on job title. The factual determination is whether the work is predominantly intellectual, is not routine, requires discretion and independent judgment, mandates specialized knowledge, and cannot be standardized as to time. Professionals can still be unionized, but they must consent to inclusion in a nonprofessional bargaining unit instead of having their own.

If plant guards are unionized, they must have their own bargaining unit. They cannot be organized with other employees, because the employer would not feel very secure during a strike if several guards were union activists—much less if one of them was the shop steward!

The NLRB has taken the position that "micro-units," targeting small groups of pro-union workers, can be acceptable. To challenge a micro-unit, the employer must show an overwhelming community of interest between included and excluded workers. Previously, unions tended to favor broad "wall to wall" units such as all production and maintenance employees in a facility, but unions have had some success with micro-units. NLRA § 9 rules out some bargaining units (e.g., one including guards with other workers) but does not say what is appropriate, leaving the determination up to the NLRB. [William Ozier, *Micro-Units—What Are They and Why Should I Care?*, Bass, Berry & Sims PLC (Sept. 9, 2013), available at Lexology.com] [See *Specialty Healthcare & Rehabilitation Ctr. of Mobile*, 357 N.L.R.B. No. 83 (2011)] The Sixth Circuit upheld this NLRB ruling in 2013 [*Kindred Nursing Ctrs. East, LLC v. NLRB*, 727 F.3d 552 (7th Cir. 2013)] permitting a relatively small bargaining unit of employees with a sufficient community of interest even if the unit excludes employees doing similar work.

The NLRB's position is that if an employer challenges the appropriateness of a proposed unit of employees, the employer must show that the employees it wants to add to the unit share an overwhelming community of interest with the employees in the smaller unit. The Fourth, Fifth, Sixth, and Eighth Circuits have deferred to the NLRB, upholding the unit approved by the NLRB unless the NLRB's unit is clearly inappropriate—even if there are other potential units that are also appropriate. [*Macy's, Inc. v. NLRB*, No. 15-60022 (5th Cir. June 2, 2016); see Thomas M. Lucas et. al., *Another Court of Appeals Upholds NLRB's "Micro-Unit" Policy for Union Elections*, Jackson Lewis PC (June 20, 2016), available at Lexology.com]

A mid-2016 NLRB decision makes it much easier for a union to represent both permanent workers at a company and staffing agency employees assigned there, because the decision eliminates the requirement that both the employer and the staffing agency consent to the combined bargaining unit. Under this interpretation, the union decides whether to organize the two groups jointly or separately, unless there is an overwhelming showing that the two groups do not have sufficient community of interest to be in the same bargaining unit. [*Miller & Anderson* (N.L.R.B. July 11, 2016); see Thomas R. Chibnall, John P. Hasman and Robert A. Kaiser, *NLRB Clears Path for Unionizing Temporary Workers and Permanent Employees as One Group*, Armstrong Teasdale LLP (July 12, 2016), available at Lexology.com]

In a mid-2016 decision, the D.C. Circuit granted in part and denied in part review of an NLRB decision that transferring work changed the scope of the bargaining unit. The NLRB ordered the employees to be returned to their original unit. The D.C. Circuit defined the question as whether the decision to move material hauling from the construction division to the ready-mix division was a mere transfer of work or if it changed the scope of the bargaining unit. If relocating the driving jobs was a transfer of work, the union had a duty to bargain but, if impasse was reached, the company would be permitted to make changes unilaterally. If the transfer changed the scope of the unit, then the union would not have to bargain. The D.C. Circuit said that relocation of some drivers to a different unit was a red herring: the significant action was the company's proposal to transfer work from the construction side to the ready-mix side, which was separate from management's proposal to use the same drivers for the work. The court held that transferring work out of the unit did not change the scope of the unit, which was defined by job classification and not by work done. [*Aggregate Indus. v. NLRB*, 824 F.3d 1095 (D.C. Cir. 2016); see Kaitlyn F. Whiteside, *D.C. Circuit: Transfer of Work Not an Unfair Labor Practice*, Seyfarth Shaw LLP (June 17, 2016), available at Lexology.com]

§ 30.06 UNION SECURITY

[A] NLRA Prohibitions

Union security is the degree to which a union can require workers at a particular workplace to join the union and/or pay dues (or, for people with a religious objection to unionization, pay assessments in lieu of dues). Once a union becomes the collective bargaining representative a group of workers, it is required to represent all of them and they all benefit by provisions negotiated by the union. From the union point of view, then, union security prevents workers from being "free riders" who obtain the same benefits as union members without having to pay dues or conform to union rules.

Closed shops (where only union members can be hired) are illegal. The NLRA also forbids "preferential hiring" situations under which the employer is obligated to hire only union members unless the union is unable to fill all vacancies with qualified workers.

However, the LMRA authorizes "union shops," where all current employees must be union members, and new hires can be required to join the union after hiring (within seven days in the construction industry, within 30 days in other industries), and "agency shops," where payment of initiation fees and union dues is mandatory, but actual membership is optional. "Union security" measures are available to a union that is the bona fide bargaining representative of the employees in the bargaining unit and there has not been a deauthorization election certified in the year preceding the effective date of the union security agreement.

It is not a breach of a union's duty of fair representation for it to enter into a CBA that contains a union security clause that echoes the wording of NLRA § 8(3)(a). [*Marquez v. Screen Actors Guild*, 525 U.S. 33 (1998)] The plaintiff claimed that she should have been notified of her right not to join the union and to pay the union only for its representational activities.

If the union wants "automatic dues checkoff" (deduction of dues from the paycheck, so the union doesn't have to bill the member), it must have its members provide a written assignment lasting until the contract expires, or for one year, whichever comes first.

In 1962, the NLRB ruled, in the case of *Bethlehem Steel*, 136 N.L.R.B. 1500, that an employer can cancel dues check-off when the CBA expires. However, in mid-2015, the NLRB reversed its policy and held that an employer can bargain for the right to discontinue check-off after the expiration of a CBA, as long as the waiver is clear and unmistakable. But the union continues to receive dues check-off after the CBA ends unless an employee revokes the check-off authorization (e.g., when resigning from a union) or if there is a strike or lockout that prevents wages from being earned from which dues can be deducted. [*Lincoln Lutheran of Racine*, 362 N.L.R.B. No. 188 (Aug. 27, 2015)]

In 2011, the Second Circuit held that the Newspaper Guild's right to dues checkoff survived the expiration of the CBA—but so did the arbitration requirements of the CBA, so a dispute about checkoff had to be arbitrated, not litigated. [*Newspaper Guild CWA of Albany v. Hearst Corp.*, 645 F.3d 527 (2d Cir. 2011)]

Under the NLRA [29 U.S.C. § 169], employees who have a religious objection to unionization cannot be forced to join or support a union—even if the workplace is subject to a union security measure. However, to prevent financial windfalls, the employee can be required to contribute the equivalent of the initiation fee to a nonreligious charity of the employee's choice. *Communication Workers of America v. Beck* [487 U.S. 735 (1988)] says that employees who do not want to join a union, but who are subject to a union security clause in the CBA, can be charged fees that can be traced back to collective bargaining, contract administration, and pursuing grievances. But they can prevent the union from using their money for political or other "nonrepresentational purposes."

In June 2007, the Supreme Court ruled that it is permissible for a state to require unions that represent public employees to get affirmative consent from non-members of the union before using their agency fees for political purposes. (In other words, a state can forbid the union to use the agency fees this way unless the non-member employee opts out.) [*Davenport v. Washington Educ. Ass'n*, 551 U.S. 177 (2007)]

The Supreme Court returned to the subject of agency fees early in 2009. The CBA between the State of Maine and the union representing its employees requires non-member employees who are represented by the union to pay a "service fee" equal to the part of the union dues devoted to representational activities such as collective bargaining and contract administration. These funds cannot be used for politics, lobbying, or public relations. The Supreme Court ruled early in 2009 that the First Amendment permits a local union to charge non-members for the expense of national litigation that they could be required to pay for if it were local: i.e., the suit relates to collective bargaining rather than political issues, and the union local has a reasonable expectation that other locals will contribute. [*Locke v. Karass*, 555 U.S. 207 (2009)]

In 1977, the Supreme Court found agency shop agreements acceptable in the public sector [*Abood v. Detroit Bd. of Educ.*, 431 U.S. 209 (1977)], but the issue returned almost 40 years later. A group of California public school teachers challenged California laws that permit agency shop agreements as long as the agency fees are used only for activities germane to collective bargaining. Non-members of the union can opt out of the portion of the fee applicable to non-bargaining activities (e.g., union support of political issues). The *Friedrichs* plaintiffs brought a First Amendment challenge to both the agency shop and the opt-out procedure (free speech and association). They argued that *Abood* should be overruled on the grounds that collective bargaining is political speech, and there is no compelling state interest for forcing employees to subsidize it. [Stephen J. Kane, *First Amendment and Collective Bargaining—Validity of Agency-Shop Arrangements*, Mayer Brown LLP (June 30, 2015), available at Lexology.com]

After Justice Scalia's death, the Supreme Court issued a simple one-line per curiam order: "The judgment is affirmed by an equally divided court." This innocuous statement in fact has major implications. Because the court's vote was 4-4, the Ninth Circuit decision upholding the California statute was affirmed. [*Friedrichs v. California Teachers Ass'n*, 136 S. Ct. 1083 (Mar. 29, 2016); see Adam Liptak, *Victory for Unions as Supreme Court, Scalia Gone, Ties 4-4*, NYTimes.com (Mar. 30, 2016); Melanie Trottman, *Supreme Court Ruling Spurs Unions While Opponents Regroup*, WSJ.com (Mar. 29, 2016)]

A "Hudson notice" (the name comes from *Chicago Teachers Union v. Hudson* [475 U.S. 292 (1986)]) informs non-members of a union of the "fair share" fees that they are charged to cover their fair share of the union's cost of negotiating and enforcing the CBA. Courts disagree about what constitutes an adequate Hudson notice, and how the union must present the figures.

A June 2012 Supreme Court case deals with a special assessment imposed on non-Union employees in a public sector agency shop. The special assessment, a 25% increase in monthly dues and removal of the previous cap on dues to create a "fight-back" fund to oppose legislation disfavored by the Union, was held to violate the non-members' First Amendment rights by forcing them into association and speech they did not endorse. The Supreme Court ruled that a separate Hudson notice should have been given. The Supreme Court said that a compulsory subsidy for private speech is permissible only when the fees are a necessary part of the larger purpose that led to the creation of the association. It is unlawful to charge the fee to non-Union members unless they opt out: the charge can only be imposed on non-members who affirmatively opt in to paying it. [*Knox v. SEIU*, 132 S. Ct. 2277 (2012)]

Yet another Supreme Court agency fee case was decided in mid-2014. The Supreme Court ruled that workers who provided home care to Medicaid recipients in Illinois were partial public employees who had the right to refuse to pay fair share fees. The Supreme Court said that the home care aides primarily worked for the elderly and disabled people who received the care, not for the home health agency that employed them, and requiring them to pay agency fees violated their First Amendment rights. However, the Supreme Court did not expand this holding to a more general rule that conventional public employees are exempt from paying agency fees. [*Harris v. Quinn*, 134 S. Ct. 2618 (2014)]

During the Bush administration, Executive Order 13201 required federal contractors to post a "Beck notice" to inform employees that they are not obligated to join a union; that they can object to use of their money for non-representation purposes, and can seek a refund of money used in this manner. [69 Fed. Reg. 16375 (Mar. 29, 2004)]

Shortly after his inauguration, President Obama signed three orders to expand the union rights of employees of federal contractors, and to reverse Bush administration policies. The first order (E.O. 13496) revoked E.O. 13201. E.O. 13201 required posting a notice of the right not to join a union. E.O. 13496 requires posting of a balanced notice of employee rights under the NLRA. E.O. 13496 applies to companies that have more than $100,000 in federal contracts. The second order holds that, when a federal agency changes the contractors who provide services to a federal building, the incoming contractor must offer jobs to the outgoing contractor's non-supervisory employees. The third order denies reimbursement of money spent on supporting or deterring employees' rights to unionize or bargain collectively. [DOL Office of Labor-Management Standards, *Executive Order 13496 Notification of Employee Rights Under Federal Labor Law*, <http://www.dol.gov/olms/regs/compliance/EO13496.htm> (undated, last accessed Mar. 5, 2017)].

Another Obama administration move was the NLRB's publication of regulations requiring employers to display a poster about the right to unionize, bargain collectively, distribute union literature, and be free of retaliation for collective action to improve wages and working conditions. (In effect, this is the converse of the Beck notice.) Originally, the requirement was supposed to take effect November 14, 2011. [Steven Greenhouse, *N.L.R.B. Tells Companies to Ease Right to Unionize*, NYTimes.com (Aug. 25, 2011). In response to protests by business groups, the NLRB twice postponed the effective date of the notice-posting requirement.]

Both the D.C. and the Fourth Circuit ruled in 2013 that the posting requirement was invalid. The D.C. Circuit held that the posting rule violates employers' expressive rights. Instead of severing the provision that failure to post is a ULP, the D.C. Circuit invalidated the entire rule, concluding that the NLRB would not want to have a purely voluntary rule that it could not enforce. The Fourth Circuit stated that the NLRB's powers are limited, not extensive, and the NLRB has power to act only when triggered by a certification petition or an Unfair Labor Practices charge. According to the Fourth Circuit, other agencies such as the EEOC and OSHA derive their authority to require posting from their governing statutes, and the NLRA does not authorize a posting requirement. [*Chamber of Commerce v. NLRB*, 721 F.3d 152 (4th Cir. 2013); *Nat'l Ass'n of Mfrs. v. NLRB*, 717 F.3d 947 (D.C. Cir. 2013)] The NLRB's petitions for rehearing in the Fourth and D.C. Circuits were denied. The NLRB declined to file a petition for certiorari. [Benjamin P. Glass, *NLRB Throws in the Towel on Notice Posting Rule*, Ogletree Deakins (Jan. 3, 2014), available at Lexology.com]

The Ninth Circuit upheld California Gov't Code §§ 16645–16649 (forbidding companies that receive state grants over $10,000 from using the money to assist, promote, or deter union organizing). The court found that the statute does not violate the First Amendment, does not undermine federal labor policy, and is not preempted by the NLRA. [*Chamber of Commerce v. Lockyer*, 463 F.3d 1076 (9th Cir. 2006)] Certiorari was granted in late 2007. According to the United States Solicitor General, New York, Florida, Illinois, Maine, Massachusetts, Minnesota, North Dakota, Ohio, and Rhode Island have similar laws, and bills of this type have been introduced in New Jersey and Michigan. The Supreme Court ruled that the California law was preempted by federal labor law. According to the Supreme Court, federal labor law promotes wide-open debate on labor matters, as long as employers refrain from coercion. [*Chamber of Commerce v. Brown*, 554 U.S. 60 (2008)]

The converse of union security is a state "right to work" law that says that unwilling employees cannot be compelled to join unions or pay dues. The Taft-Hartley Act permits states to adopt right to work laws.

Starting in 2012, when there were 22 right to work states, a trend has developed of additional states adopting right to work laws. Indiana kicked off this trend in early 2012 by becoming the 23rd right to work state.

The International Union of Operating Engineers, Local 150 and the United Steelworkers Union filed two suits in state court. *Zoeller* found the right to work law unconstitutional under the Indiana constitution; *Steelworkers v. Zoeller* found the right to work law unconstitutional under Indiana's unusual constitutional ban on demanding services without compensation. [*Zoeller v. Sweeney*, 19 N.E.3d 749 (Ind. 2014)]

On appeal, however, the Indiana Supreme Court upheld the state's right to work law, finding that the law does not require the union to provide services for free to workers who do not pay dues. The Seventh Circuit also upheld the statute's constitutionality: (*Sweeney v. Pence*, 767 F.3d 654 (7th Cir. 2014), holding that the state can forbid CBA provisions that require payment of fees to the union).

In late 2012, Michigan became the 24th right to work state, as a result of a statute affecting hundreds of thousands of private and public sector union members. (However, the police and fire unions are not affected by the law.) The right to work law means that non-union workers are not required to pay union representation fees. [Matthew Dolan and Kris Maher, *Michigan Approves Union Curbs*, WSJ.com (Dec. 12, 2012); Kris Maher, Q&A: *How Michigan's "Right-to-Work" Law Will Work*, WSJ.com (Dec. 11, 2012)]

Wisconsin became the 25th state to pass a private-sector right to work law. (2011's Act 10 limited bargaining rights for most public employees and banned automatic dues check off but was not a full-scale right to work law.) The statute operates prospectively only, so existing union security clauses remain in effect until the CBA expires. [Michael J. Rybicki, *Wisconsin Poised to Become 25th "Right To Work" State*, Seyfarth Shaw LLP (Mar. 6, 2015), available at Lexology.com] The constitutionality of Act 10 was upheld by the Seventh Circuit. [*Laborers Local 236 v. Walker*, 749 F.3d 628 (7th Cir. 2014); *Madison Teachers, Inc. v. Walker*, 851 N.W.2d 337(Wis. 2014). However, the Dane County Circuit Court ruled in April 2016 that the right to work law violated the state constitution because it subjected unions to a "taking" without compensation when they were required to represent people who did not pay dues: *Int'l Ass'n of Machinists v. State of Wisconsin*, No. 2015CV000628 (Dane Cnty. Cir. Ct. Apr. 8, 2016); see Monica Davey and Julie Bosman, *In Victory for Unions, Law on Dues Is Struck Down in Wisconsin*, NYTimes.com (Apr. 9, 2016). The ruling was certain to be challenged, and many commentators expected the state Supreme Court to reverse this decision.]

The West Virginia legislature passed a right to work law early in 2016. The governor vetoed it, but the legislature overrode the veto, so the Workplace Freedom Act took effect July 1, 2016, with the result that the majority of the states (26) had right to work laws. [Stephen W. Lyman, *Now There Are Twenty-Six: West Virginia Adopts "Right to Work,"* Hall Render Killian Heath & Lyman PC (Feb. 15, 2016), available at Lexology.com] Enforcement of the Workplace Freedom Act was temporarily enjoined on August 10, 2016. The judge held that the union plaintiffs showed potential harm to workers. [Brennan W. Bolt, *West Virginia Judge Temporarily Enjoins Right-to-Work Law*, McGuireWoods LLP (Aug. 12, 2016), available at Lexology.com]

In early January 2017, Missouri and Kentucky became right to work states, bringing the total to 28. The Kentucky law limits dues checkoff for public employees and forbids strikes or work stoppages by public employees. Kentucky also repealed the state's prevailing wage act for public construction projects. (The law had required contractors to set hourly rates by job classification, based on the pay rates for similar work set out in union contracts.) The New Hampshire legislature was considering a right to work bill supported by the governor.

At the federal level, Representatives Joe Wilson (R-SC) and Steve King (R-Ia) introduced a law that would forbid requiring workers to support a union or pay dues as a condition of employment; the president favors right to work legislation. [W. Eric Baisden and Adam Primm, *"Right-to-Work" Momentum Building in 2017*, Benesch Friedlander Coplan & Aronoff LLP (Feb. 10, 2017), available at Lexology.com; Kris Maher, *Missouri Becomes 28th Right-to-Work State*, WSJ.com (Feb. 6, 2017); Gerald Lutkus, *Kentucky Doubles Down: Right to Work and No Prevailing Wage,* Barnes & Thornburg LLP (Jan. 9, 2017), available at Lexology.com; George Adams & Raymond Haley III, *Kentucky Becomes 27th Right-To-Work State*, Fisher Phillips (Jan. 11, 2017), available at Lexology .com]

The District Court for the Northern District of Georgia struck down the provision of Georgia's right to work law that allowed employees to withdraw from union membership and stop paying dues at any time. The district court found that this conflicts with federal law, which allows unions to make authorizations irrevocable for up to one year. [*Georgia State AFL-CIO v. Olens*, No. 1:13-cv-3745-WCO (N.D. Ga. July 7, 2016); see John T.L. Koenig, *Federal Court Strikes Down Part of Georgia's Right to Work Law*, Barnes & Thornburg LLP (July 13, 2016), available at Lexology.com]

The Sixth Circuit held in late 2016 that counties in Kentucky have the right to pass their own right to work ordinances—but two local ordinances, one about hiring halls and one forbidding dues checkoff, were preempted because those were areas already occupied by federal labor law. [*Autoworkers Local 3047 v. Hardin Cntyy*, 842 F.3d 407 (6th Cir. 2016); see Keith J. Brodie, *Sixth Circuit Court of Appeals Rules Local Subdivisions of Government Can Pass Right-to-Work Ordinances*, Barnes & Thornburg LLP (Nov. 21, 2016), available at Lexology.com. The Sixth Circuit refused to vacate this ruling: see Keith Brodie, *Sixth Circuit Refuses to Vacate; Lets Local Municipal Right-To-Work Decision Stand*, Barnes & Thornburg LLP (Mar. 16, 2017), available at Lexology.com]

In contrast, the District Court for the Northern District of Illinois ruled in early 2017 that laws passed by a political subdivision of a state rather than by the state itself do not qualify for the exemption of "state or territorial law" under NLRA § 14(b), so they are preempted by federal law. This ruling will probably be appealed to the Seventh Circuit, creating the potential for a circuit split that could be resolved by the Supreme Court. [*International Union of Operating Engineers, Local 399, AFL-CIO, et al. v. Village of Lincolnshire, et al*, No. 16 C 2395 (N.D. Ill. Jan. 7, 2017); see Kenneth A. Jenero, *Courts Disagree on Whether Locally Enacted "Right-to-Work" Laws Are Pre-empted by the NLRA*, Holland & Knight LLP (Jan. 11, 2017), available at Lexology.com; Jennifer A. Dunn and Patrick M. DePoy, *Federal Court Strikes Down Lincolnshire's "Right to Work" Ordinance*, Franczek Radelet PC (Jan. 13, 2017), available at Lexology.com]

[B] Hiring Halls

Under a union security option, the employer decides who to hire, but the union may be able to get hirees to join or pay dues. A hiring hall works differently. It is a mechanism under which the union selects workers and sends them to the employer, based on the employer's requisition (for six plasterers and two electricians, for example). The union decides which union or nonunion workers will be referred for the job.

An exclusive hiring hall is a relationship under which the employer gets all its workers through union referrals. This is not considered a union security arrangement, so it is legal in the right-to-work states. A nonexclusive hiring hall makes union referral only one of the ways in which the employer can find new workers.

The NLRA provides that it is unlawful for a union to give preference to union members over equally qualified nonmembers in the operation of a nonexclusive hiring hall. The operation and structure of a hiring hall is a mandatory bargaining subject.

In a situation in which union members testified that they often got work for themselves without union referral, the union was not operating an exclusive hiring hall. Therefore, it was a ULP for the union to pressure management to avoid hiring persons who were not referred by the union, or to fire employees for that reason. Enforcement of a hiring hall arrangement depends on the terms of the CBA. Therefore, once the NLRB shows discriminatory conduct that could have affected employee rights, the burden shifts to the employer or union to show that it acted in compliance with the CBA. [*NLRB v. Local 334, Laborers Int'l Union*, 481 F.3d 875, 1639, 1714 (6th Cir. 2007)]

§ 30.07   THE COLLECTIVE BARGAINING PROCESS

[A]   Basic Issues

Under the NLRA, the purpose of certifying a union is to provide an ongoing process of collective bargaining between employer and union on important work-related issues, leading to the adoption of a union contract, or Collective Bargaining Agreement (CBA). Even after a CBA is in place, it is still necessary to bargain on "mandatory" issues, and allowable to bargain on "permissive" issues. [See 29 U.S.C. § 158(a)(5).] There are some subjects on which it is illegal to bargain. For instance, it is illegal to implement a closed shop, even if both employer and union are willing.

Mandatory bargaining subjects include work rules; dues checkoff; drug testing; transferring work out of the bargaining unit; contracting out work done by bargaining unit employees (however, contracting out work done by non-union employees is not a mandatory bargaining subject) no-strike/no-lockout clauses.

Mandatory bargaining subjects are those that materially or significantly affect the terms or conditions of employment. Issues that have a remote or incidental effect on the work environment are permissible subjects of bargaining.

The NLRB's position is that, even before the first CBA is agreed to, the employer must bargain with the union before imposing serious discipline (demotion, suspension, discharge) on an employee. The NLRB treats discretionary discipline as a term and condition of employment, like pay rates and benefits. [*Total Security Mgmt. Illinois 1, LLC*, 364 N.L.R.B. No. 106 (Aug. 26, 2016); see Philip B. Rosen and Howard M. Bloom, *Newly Organized Employer Must Bargain Over Discretionary Employee Discipline Pre-First Contract, NLRB Rules*, Jackson Lewis PC (Sept. 6, 2016), available at Lexology.com]

The Eighth Circuit held in early 2016 that an electrical subcontractor violated the NLRA by unilaterally changing break policy without giving the union a chance to bargain over the changes. Eliminating specific 15-minute breaks and allowing policies to be adopted "as part of the jobsite expectations" required bargaining because the change in policy was material, substantial, and significant. [*ParsonsElec., LLC v. NLRB*, 812 F.3d 716 (8th Cir. 2016); see Igor Babichenko, *Electrical Subcontractor Cannot Catch a Break from the Eighth Circuit*, McGuireWoods LLP (Feb. 11, 2016), available at Lexology.com]

Where bargaining is required, the employer has a duty to meet with the union at reasonable times to confer over the terms and conditions of employment (such as wages and hours). Insisting that bargaining sessions be held during regular business hours and making negotiating committee members use paid leave to attend the sessions was a management ULP because it interfered with the right to bargain collectively. [*Ceridian Corp. v. NLRB*, 435 F.3d 352 (D.C. Cir. 2006)]

Refusal to bargain is an unfair labor practice. On the other hand, certain issues are established as managerial prerogatives that can be decided unilaterally, without bargaining. Issues of this kind include sale of an entire business; complete termination of operations; a partial closing motivated by business needs and not by anti-union animus. Managerial prerogative also extends to relocating bargaining unit work when the nature of the employer's obligations has changed, and the work at the new location is significantly different from work at the old location

The basic rule is that bargaining is required if a decision is undertaken to save labor costs, but not if the employer takes on a program of modernization or environmental compliance that costs more than the potential savings on labor costs. Even if the employer has the right to make a decision without union involvement, it has an obligation to engage in "effects bargaining": that is, it must notify the union that the decision has been made, and must bargain about the effects the change will have on union members.

Changing the methods of production is considered a managerial prerogative, although employees who believe that they are adversely affected by the change can file a grievance or seek effects bargaining about the change.

A *Gissel* bargaining order (stemming from *NLRB v. Gissel Packing Co.*) [395 U.S. 575 (1969)] is an order compelling management to bargain in good faith with a union. Early in 2003, the D.C. Circuit upheld an NLRB order requiring a movie theater chain to bargain with union locals before making the theaters "manager-operated" and firing the union projectionists. Although technological improvements have greatly reduced the amount (and skill level) of the work done by projectionists, eliminating a job classification does not come under the heading of "new or improved work methods" that can be introduced without bargaining. Transfer of work always requires bargaining if it results in loss of bargaining unit jobs. [*Regal Cinemas Inc. v. NLRB*, 317 F.3d 300 (D.C. Cir. 2003)]

Bargaining must be done in good faith. Neither side is obligated to make concessions or give in where it thinks surrender would be imprudent. If the bargaining process comes to an impasse—i.e., neither side is introducing new proposals or yielding on proposals already on the table—then the employer can lawfully cease negotiating and simply put its own proposals into place.

"Regressive bargaining"—withdrawing an offer if the union is unable to meet the employer's time frame—has been upheld by the NLRB in *White Cap, Inc.* [325 N.L.R.B 220 (1998)], unless it is done specifically for the purpose of avoiding a contract. Where the employer has a legitimate business reason for wanting to resolve the issue quickly, regressive bargaining is permissible.

After a collective bargaining agreement expires, there is nothing left to be enforced under contract law. But labor law [NLRA § 8(a)(5)] obligates the employer to maintain the status quo, at least until an impasse is reached and the employer can start implementing its own proposals unilaterally. The employer cannot take advantage of a bargaining impasse to unilaterally impose new provisions, or any provisions more favorable to its own cause than the provisions that were on the table during negotiations.

The Seventh Circuit has ruled (in a case involving a union's request for information about hidden surveillance cameras in the workplace) that the right to bargain about a mandatory bargaining subject can only be waived by a clear and unmistakable expression of an intention to waive. [*Nat'l Steel Corp. v. NLRB*, 324 F.3d 928 (7th Cir. 2003)] The cameras are mandatory bargaining subjects because, like drug and alcohol tests, they involve the terms and conditions of employment. Furthermore, the employer was merely ordered to bargain and provide the union with information about the cameras; it was not forbidden to use security cameras or ordered to make public disclosure of the location of the cameras. The deployment of hidden surveillance cameras was also treated as a mandatory bargaining subject by *Brewers & Maltsters v. NLRB*, 414 F.3d 36 (D.C. Cir. 2005), because subjects plainly germane to the work environment are mandatory bargaining subjects, unless they are at the core of entrepreneurial control of the workplace. (See § 26.06 for additional discussion of workplace surveillance.)

The NLRB's long-term position is that a union does not waive the right to bargain over a mandatory bargaining subject unless the CBA includes clear and unmistakable waiver language. However, the D.C. Circuit said that there is a waiver when a CBA covers a subject, because bargaining has already occurred on that subject. The D.C. Circuit ordered the NLRB to pay an employer's fees and costs (over $17,000) because the NLRB continued to litigate a case when the NLRB knew that the D.C. Circuit would support the employer's position. [*Heartland Plymouth Ct. MI v. NLRB*, 838 F.3d 16 (D.C. Cir. 2016); see David P. Phippen, *D.C. Circuit Awards Attorneys' Fees and Costs to Employer After NLRB Pursued "Clear And Unmistakable Waiver" Theory at Odds With Controlling Precedent*, Constangy Brooks Smith & Prophete LLP (Oct. 24, 2016), available at Lexology.com]

According to the NLRB, a management rights clause must be very specific before the agency will find that the union waived the right to bargain over an action. For example, a standard broad management rights clause in a CBA did not invoke a clear and unmistakable waiver, because it did not specifically reference work rules, attendance, or progressive discipline. [*Graymont PA, Inc.*, 364 N.L.R.B. No. 37 (June 29, 2016); Kathryn E. Siegel, *NLRB Requires Specificity in Management-Rights Clauses,* Littler Mendelson PC (July 28, 2016), available at Lexology.com]

In mid-2016, the NLRB held that there is a duty to bargain over asking newly hired employees to sign non-compete agreements that also forbade disclosure of confidential information about the company. The NLRB said that bargaining was required because the requirement involved the employment relationship and continued after the end of employment. The management rights clause did not refer to noncompete or nondisclosure agreements, so there was no waiver of the right to bargain over these issues. [*Minteq Int'l, Inc.*, 364 N.L.R.B. No. 63 (July 29, 2016); see Mark Theodore, *Non-Compete Agreement a Mandatory Subject of Bargaining, NLRB Rules,* Proskauer Rose LLP (Aug. 17, 2016), available at Lexology.com]

A growing issue (see §§ 26.06 and 27.05) is the extent to which employers can monitor employees' social media activities.

The NLRB began to confront social media issues in late 2010. Since then, what has emerged as the major question is whether employees use social media to discuss or protest working conditions (which constitutes protected activity) or whether they merely discuss personal issues (which is probably not protected, especially if there are issues of misuse of the employer's proprietary information.) In general, employer policies are tested for reasonableness: are they too broad or impermissibly vague? Do they prevent employees from exercising their rights under the NLRA? In general, employees will be protected if social media is part of collective activity about working conditions—but will not be protected if they are merely griping about personal issues, or their conduct violates reasonable rules of civility.

In general, the NLRB opposes the use of broad or vague rules about, e.g., civility, respect, disparagement, or confidentiality—even if the policy has a saving clause about not restricting protected collective activity.

The NLRB's position is that, to be for example, NLRB ALJs or the full board have:

- Held, in *Purple Communications*, 361 N.L.R.B. No. 126 (2014), that employers cannot completely bar the use of their e-mail systems for union organizing, unless all non-work usage is barred. The NLRB reversed its previous stance, expressed in *Register Guard* (2007), that employers had the right to forbid the use of the company e-mail system for this purpose. [The NLRB reaffirmed the *Purple Communications* decision in 2017: 365 N.L.R.B. No. 50 (Mar. 24, 2017); see Daniel B. Pasternak, *NLRB Will Not Hack into Prior Decision Regarding Employee Email Use During Non-Work Time,* Squire Patton Boggs (Apr. 2, 2017), available at Lexology.com]

- Employers should not impose broad prohibitions on employee communication via the company e-mail system; preventing communication when employees are not required to be actually at work violates the NLRA. [*Cellco P'ship d/b/a Verizon Wireless*, No.28-CA-145221 (Sept. 18, 2015), <*http://apps.nlrb.gov/link/document.aspx/09031d4581 defe4b*>]

- *Triple Play Sports Bar & Grille*, 361 N.L.R.B. No. 31 (Aug. 22, 2014): the NLRB decided that it was a violation of the NLRA to fire two employees because of a Facebook discussion criticizing the employer's failure to withhold the correct state income tax from their paychecks. The employer conceded that concerted activity took place but said it was not protected because of profane language and disloyalty to the employer. The NLRB said that the communications were not maliciously untrue, and were engaged in to support group action about working conditions.

- *Chipotle Services LLC*, 364 N.L.R.B. No. 72 (Aug. 18, 2016): an employee's tweets criticizing the employer were not protected, because they did not constitute concerted activity. [Mark Theodore, *Labor Day Wouldn't Be Labor Day Without New NLRB Decisions*, Proskauer Rose LLP (Sept. 2, 2016), available at Lexology.com]

- The NLRB ruled in December 2015 that Whole Foods Markets' rules against recording or taking photographs in the workplace must be rescinded. The NLRB said that the rules were overbroad and unenforceable because they could reasonably be treated as a ban on protected concerted activity. Protected activities could require documenting dangers in the workplace, publicizing discussions about the terms and conditions of employment, or transmitting images of protected picketing. The NLRB relied on management testimony that the rules applied even to protected activity, which made the rules overbroad and unenforceable. [*Whole Foods Mkt., Inc.*, No. 01-CA-096965 (N.L.R.B. Dec. 24, 2015)]

Finally, employers are entitled to a defense if they would have taken adverse action against the employee even without the protected concerted activity. [Baker & McKenzie, *Labor Year in Review: NLRB Targets Non-Unionized Employers and Expands Worker Rights* (Dec. 21, 2013), available at Lexology.com]

[B] Typical CBA Clauses

Although the actual contract that emerges from bargaining will reflect the individual needs of the business, and the comparative strengths of management and union, CBAs frequently address management rights; define the bargaining unit; set out the workday and workweek and overtime policies; and classify jobs. If the employer has a progressive discipline system, it will be explained here.

CBAs define benefits such as health insurance, sick leave, and paid time off. Employees are informed how to pursue a grievance, and whether workplace disputes must be arbitrated. Seniority is a crucial concept in the union workplace, so CBAs explain the seniority rules and what constitutes a break in service. CBAs set out the relationship between management and the union, explaining hiring halls, union security, subcontracting and transfers of work, plant closing, and the effect of successorship.

[C]   Bargaining on Modification, Termination

The employer has an obligation to notify the union whenever it intends to modify or terminate a CBA. The employer must also notify the Federal Mediation and Conciliation Service (FMCS) of the intended action. Sixty days before the contract is scheduled to expire (or 60 days before the intended modification or termination), the employer must notify the union, inviting it to negotiate a new or amended contract. Notice to the FMCS is due 30 days after the notice to the union. Failure to give the required notice is an unfair labor practice. [29 U.S.C. § 158(d)]

The 60-day notice period is referred to as the cooling-off period. The contract remains in effect during this period, and neither strikes nor lockouts are permitted.

Employers need not volunteer information, but they have a duty to provide the union with whatever information (other than confidential or privileged information) the union requests in order to represent the employees adequately. Information relating to wage rates and job descriptions is presumed relevant. The union has to show a specific need for access to the employer's nonpublic financial information—e.g., if the employer claims inability to afford a wage increase. [*Lakeland Bus Lines Inc. v. NLRB*, 347 F.3d 955 (D.C. Cir. 2003)]

Unions in RiverStone's three divisions were decertified (see § 30.08 below) in 2013. The Seventh Circuit held at the end of 2016 that an employer was required to continue contributing to pension and welfare funds until the CBA expired: it was a violation of ERISA to cease contributing after the union was decertified. Although decertification prevented the union from enforcing the CBA, the funds were entitled, as third-party beneficiaries of a contract, to continue receiving contributions—and to seek relief under ERISA and the MPPAA, which creates a cause of action to collect delinquent employer contributions owed under a CBA or the terms of a plan. [*Midwest Operating Eng'rs Welfare Fund v. Cleveland Quarry*, 844 F.3d 627 (7th Cir. 2016); see Marjorie Johnson, *Despite Union's Decertification, Employer Must Contribute to Welfare Funds Until CBA Expires*, Employment Law Daily (Dec. 22, 2016) (benefitslink.com)]

§ 30.08   ELECTIONS AFTER CERTIFICATION

Representation elections are not the only kind that can be ordered and supervised by the NLRB. Federal labor law allows a rerun or runoff election to be held to redress an improper election. Once a union is in place, employees can ask that it be deauthorized or decertified. The employer also has the right to challenge a union's majority status.

A rerun election is held if there were election improprieties, or if two unions competed for representation; the ballot included a "no union" choice, and "no union" got as many votes as the other alternatives. (If there is only one union on the ballot, a tie vote means that the union loses, because it failed to attract a majority of the voters.)

A runoff election is held if no choice gets a majority. Only one runoff election can be held, although there could be both a rerun and a runoff election in the same organizing campaign.

A deauthorization petition is filed by a group of employees who want to remove the union's authority to enter into a union shop contract. Therefore, there are no deauthorization petitions in right-to-work states, because there aren't any union shops either. When a majority of the bargaining unit (not just a majority of the voters) vote for deauthorization, the union remains the authorized bargaining representative for the employees, but the employees no longer have to pay union dues.

The purpose of a decertification petition is to remove the union's bargaining authority. The petition can be filed by an employee, a group of employees, or someone acting on behalf of the employees. The employer does not have the right to file a decertification petition, but it does have a free-speech right to inform employees of their right to remove a union that they feel has not represented them adequately.

A decertification petition requires a showing of interest by 30% of the employees in the bargaining unit. Most petitions that are filed get the necessary vote (a majority of actual voters, not eligible voters) and therefore result in decertification of the union.

Decertification petitions cannot be filed at certain times: one year after certification of a union; a reasonable time after an employer's voluntary recognition of a union; or within 12 months of another decertification petition.

The employer has the right to petition the NLRB to determine that the union has lost its majority status. The employer must offer objective evidence of the change, such as employee turnover so heavy that few of the original pro-union workers remain; the union's failure to process employee grievances; or a strike that yielded no benefits for employees. If an employer has information that leads it to doubt the union's majority status, it is an unfair labor practice to enter into a contract with this union and then try to disavow the contract based on those doubts. The appropriate action is to refuse the contract. [*Auciello Iron Works Inc. v. NLRB*, 517 U.S. 781 (1996)]

In a decertification situation, the employer must be careful if it seeks to withdraw recognition from a union based on the employer's belief that the union has lost majority support. As the D.C. Circuit recently held, the employer withdraws recognition "at its peril," because it will be liable for ULPs if it refuses to bargain with the union. In this case, the employer believed that the union lost majority support—but after the decertification petition was filed, the inactive union appealed to its members. Several of them revoked their signatures on the petition, so the union regained majority status—but did not inform management of this. The D.C. Circuit held that despite this "gamesmanship" by the union, management erred in refusing to bargain. However, the court denied the NLRB's request for a bargaining order, which it deemed to be appropriate only for flagrant bad faith. Instead, the court ordered a new election to resolve the question of whether the union once again had majority support. [*Scomas of Sausalito v. NLRB,* No. 15-1412 (D.C. Cir. Mar. 12, 2017); see Joshua M. Henderson, *Court Upholds ULP Finding Against Employer Despite Union "Gamesmanship,"* Seyfarth Shaw LLP (Mar. 23, 2017) (benefitslink.com)]

When a decertification petition is filed, the NLRB considers it acceptable for the employer to offer "ministerial aid" (such as answering an employee's questions about timing of the petition) but providing substantial aid will invalidate the petition. For example, the D.C. Circuit upheld the NLRB's finding that management was unduly involved when two supervisors asked employees how many signatures they had obtained on a decertification petition—and then told them to get more signatures before filing the petition with the NLRB. The D.C. Circuit held that this was unlawful. [*Enter. Leasing Co. d/b/a Alamo Rent-a-Car v. NLRB,* No. 15-1200 (D.C. Cir. Aug. 5, 2016); see David J. Pryzbylski, *Employers' Role in Decertification Efforts Continue to Receive Intense Scrutiny,* Barnes & Thornburg LLP (Aug. 8, 2016), available at Lexology.com]

The general rule, known as the CBA bar, is that no union election can be held while a collective bargaining agreement is in force. However, if there has been a substantial increase in personnel since the contract was signed, a new election may be proper if the union no longer represents a majority of the current workforce.

There have been many changes to the "successor bar" rule of *St. Elizabeth's Manor* [329 N.L.R.B. 341 (1999)], under which an incumbent union would be given a reasonable amount of time after a corporate takeover to bargain with the successor employer without challenges to its majority status. However, in 2002, the NLRB overruled that decision [*MV Transp.,* 337 N.L.R.B. 129 (July 19, 2002)] taking the position that the incumbent union gets a rebuttable presumption of continuing majority status, but that will not bar an otherwise valid challenge to majority status.

The 2011 case of *UGL-UNICCO Service Co.* [357 NLRB No. 76 (Aug. 26, 2011)] brought back the irrebuttable presumption, but limited it to six months (if the successor recognized the union, retaining the terms and conditions of employment) or 12 months (if the successor recognized the union, but unilaterally sets terms and conditions). This rule was applied by the First Circuit in an early 2017 case. The employer argued that the NLRB's changes of position showed that the agency's interpretations were not entitled to deference. However, the First Circuit held that a six-month bar was not unduly restrictive, and effectuated the NLRB's purposes of protecting employees' right to unionize and maintaining labor stability. The First Circuit said that an agency can legitimately change its position if it gives a reasoned explanation for the change—and the NLRB did this by citing increases in mergers and acquisitions as a reason for adopting a firm six-month presumption to deal with the large number of successorship situations. [*NLRB v. Lily Transp. Corp.,* No. 15-2398 (1st Cir. Mar. 31, 2017); see Steven S. Goodman, Philip B. Rosen and Howard M. Bloom, *Federal Court: NLRB Correct That Successor Employer Must Bargain With Existing Union Under Labor Law,* Jackson Lewis PC (Apr. 27, 2017), available at Lexology.com]

It violates federal labor law for an employer to withdraw recognition of a union prematurely, without engaging in bargaining for a reasonable period of time. (However, pursuing reasonable bargaining will remove the taint of an earlier refusal to bargain.) In this case, there were only five bargaining sessions, and apparently the parties were close to reaching agreement when recognition was withdrawn, so the D.C. Circuit upheld the NLRB's ruling against the employer. [*Lee Lumber & Bldg. Materials Corp. v. NLRB*, 310 F.3d 209 (D.C. Cir. 2002)]

§ 30.09 STRIKES

DOL data showed that there were fewer major work stoppages in the decade 2006–2016 that in each year between 1947 and 1981. Between 2007 and 2016, there were 143 strikes or lockouts involving over 1,000 workers. The 70-year annual average was 164 per year. The last year with more than 100 major work stoppages was 1981, when Reagan sent the air traffic controllers back to work. Since 2007, the average was 14 major stoppages a year (the 2016 figure of 15 was slightly above average). Unions seldom believe they can win a strike. Global companies can shift production outside the United States, and strikers can easily be replaced. [Eric Morath, *There Were Fewer Worker Strikes and Lockouts in the Past Decade Than Used to Happen Every Year,* WSJ.com (Feb. 10, 2017)]

[A] Right to Strike

The NLRA gives employees the right to engage in "protected concerted activities"—joining together to organize, protest, and otherwise assert their interests in a lawful manner. This includes going on strike if a new contract cannot be negotiated, or based on a union's claim that working conditions are bad enough to justify a strike.

A striking union's gamble is that the employer will need to maintain continuous operations and therefore will grant significant concessions before the employees lose too much income by stopping work. But at other times employers actually benefit from strikes, if they can save payroll for a while, shut down an unproductive location, relocate to a lower-cost area (in another state or even another country) or bringing in "striker replacements."

Violence, sabotage, and threats are not protected activity. If a threatened strike would imperil the national health or safety, the President of the United States can order the U.S. Attorney General to petition the appropriate federal court for an 80-day cooling-off period, during which the strike is enjoined.

Secondary strikes and secondary boycotts—actions taken against one employer to put pressure on another employer that does business with the first employer—are banned by NLRA § 8(b)(4). A company that is the victim of a secondary strike or boycott can sue for damages under LMRA § 303.

[B] Types of Strike

Employees can lawfully engage in a work stoppage in three situations: an economic dispute with the employer; a claim of unfair labor practices by the employer; and a claim that conditions in the workplace are so unreasonably dangerous that work should not continue.

An "unfair labor practices" strike is caused in whole or part by unfair labor practices. There must be a causal connection between the strike and the employer practices. If the practices are simply cost-related (such as shift changes), then the strike should be characterized as an economic strike. But a strike that begins as an economic strike can be converted to an unfair labor practices strike if the employer acts unfairly or refuses to accept legitimate offers for return to work.

The Seventh Circuit held that it was unlawful to fire an employee who briefly refused to work to protest what she thought was unfair treatment of a co-worker. In other words, even in non-union workplaces, a brief work stoppage can be protected concerted activity. A supervisor at Staffing Network sent one of Griselda Barrera's co-workers home for poor performance. Barrera and others spoke up in her favor and briefly stopped working. Barrera was sent home and told not to come to work the next day. She decided she had been fired, so she filed an unemployment claim and a ULP charge. The Seventh Circuit agreed with the NLRB: the worker's discharge for insubordination was not justified. [*Staffing Network Holdings, LLC v. NLRB*, 815 F.3d 296 (7th Cir. 2016); see Erin Fowler and Christopher A. Johlie, *Seventh Circuit Court of Appeals Defers to NLRB: Employer Unlawfully Discharged Employee for Brief Refusal to Work*, Franczek Radelet (Mar. 10, 2016), available at Lexology.com; Beverly Alfon, *Yep, That Non-Union Employee's Attitude Is Likely Protected*, SmithAmundsen LLC (Mar. 14, 2016), available at Lexology.com]

An NLRB ALJ ruled that it is unlawful to discipline non-unionized employees who strike, as long as there is a true strike rather than an intermittent work stoppage. (NLRA rights are not contingent on union membership and, in recent years, non-union workers have been an NLRB enforcement priority.) OUR Walmart (Organization United for Respect at Walmart) is a group advocating for better working conditions for Walmart employees. OUR Walmart is backed by the United Food and Commercial Workers International Union but neither of them is authorized as collective bargaining representative of Walmart employees. OUR Walmart coordinated several one to three-day strikes. Walmart did not discipline any participating workers, but counted the absences under the attendance policy. As a result, some workers were disciplined and some were terminated. OUR Walmart filed ULP charges under NLRA § 8(a)(1). The ALJ held that the strikes were protected and ordered expunction of discipline and reinstatement of fired workers with back pay. [Anne R. Yuengert, *Can Your Non-Union Workers Strike? Yes, They Can*, Bradley Arant Boult Cummings LLP (Jan. 28, 2016), available at Lexology.com]

The main difference between an economic strike and an unfair labor practices strike is the extent of employees' reinstatement rights after the strike ends and they want to go back to work. Some issues are areas of managerial prerogative, so employees cannot lawfully strike to challenge management's decisions in these areas.

29 U.S.C. § 143 makes it a protected concerted activity for employees to refuse to work if there is measurable, objective evidence of undue hazards (not just a subjective feeling that something is wrong). The employees must also articulate goals that the employer can respond to: replace a defective machine or install guard rails, for instance, not just "make the workplace safer." [See Chapter 31 for information about occupational safety and health.]

If the underlying strike is lawful, then a sympathy strike (workers outside the striking bargaining unit refuse to cross the picket line) is probably protected concerted activity as defined by the NLRA. A 2003 decision of the Ninth Circuit says that a no-strike provision in a CBA does not bar a sympathy strike for another bargaining unit within the same local union, because the CBA clause did not clearly and unmistakably waive the right to call a strike in support of fellow union members. [*Standard Concrete Prods. Inc. v. Gen. Truck Drivers Office, Food & Warehouse Union*, 353 F.3d 668 (9th Cir. 2003)]

In contrast to those protected activities, a sitdown strike (an illegal takeover of the employer's premises) is unlawful. A wildcat strike, called by the rank and file without authorization from the union, is not protected activity if the workers want to usurp the union's role as sole bargaining representative for the workers.

Intermittent strikes are not protected, but a walk-out over wages, hours, or working conditions might be protected concerted activity covered by the NLRA, in which case employees cannot be disciplined for participating. In early 2017, the NLRB held that a one-day walkout to support Fight for Fifteen (the campaign to raise the minimum wage to $15/hour) was not an intermittent strike, and was protected. The NLRB rescinded discipline against participants: the workers did not engage in any strike activity other than the scheduled one-day protest. [*EYM*

King of Mo., 365 N.L.R.B. No. 16 (Jan. 24, 2017); see Brian W. Bulger, *Disciplining February 17 General Strikers May Cause Problems for Employers*, Cozen O'Connor (Feb. 13, 2017), available at Lexology.com]

A collective bargaining agreement can lawfully be drafted to include a no-strike clause. It is not protected concerted activity to call an economic strike in violation of a no-strike clause. Therefore, the employer can legitimately fire the strikers and deny them reinstatement after the strike ends.

Because of the special risks involved, NLRA § 8(g) requires unions at health care facilities to give at least 10 days' notice before a strike, picket, or concerted refusal to work. The employer must be notified of the date and time the action will commence. The NLRB ruled that starting the strike four hours later than the time stated in the notice violates the notice requirement. Unions are not permitted to make unilateral extensions of strike notices. Therefore, it was not an unfair labor practice to fire nurses involved in the strike. [*Alexandria Clinic PA*, 339 N.L.R.B. No. 162 (Aug. 21, 2003)]

[C] Lockouts and Other Employer Activity

The lockout is the employer's counterpart to the union's strike. In a strike, the employees refuse to come to work. In a lockout, the employer refuses to let them in. An employer that undertakes a lockout for business reasons can hire replacement workers. It can enter into a temporary subcontract for the duration of the lockout. However, the employer is not allowed to use the lockout to permanently contract out work formerly performed by employees. Lockouts are lawful if and only if they have a business motivation, not if they are used to prevent the workers from organizing a union, or to avoid bargaining with an incumbent union. However, a lockout is a justified response to a strike that violates a CBA no-strike clause.

It is an unfair labor practice for an employer to institute a lockout that is inherently destructive of the rights of employees. It is also an unfair labor practice to institute a lockout without having legitimate economic business justification (not just the employer's convenience). The mere possibility of a strike if contract negotiations break down is not a sufficient justification for a lockout during collective bargaining; and it might be treated as an unlawful refusal to bargain. Lockouts are analyzed even more stringently outside the strike context, because the union's power is weaker and there is less need for the employer to counter-balance it.

Employers are allowed to close a business, or shut it down temporarily, with economic motivations. But doing it to harm the union is an unfair labor practice. A "runaway shop" (transferring work between existing locations or opening a new location) is an unfair labor practice if it is based on antiunion motivation rather than a desire to enhance profitability.

During a strike, the employer is not permitted to alter the terms and conditions of employment that affect strikers. However, once a CBA expires, the employer is allowed to change those terms as they affect striker replacements.

The Seventh Circuit agreed with the NLRB that it violated the NLRA for a non-union company to transfer work from Illinois to Mexico to retaliate against strikers. The Seventh Circuit upheld the NLRB's order mandating that the work be sent back to Illinois. [*Amglo Kemlite Labs., Inc. v. NLRB*, 833 F.3d 824 (7th Cir. 2016). Edward M. Graham, Howard M. Bloom and Philip B. Rosen, *Non-Union, Specialty Lights Maker Must Return Work from Mexico, Federal Appeals Court Rules*, Jackson Lewis PC (Sept. 13, 2016)]

[D]   Striker Replacements

During a strike, employers are entitled to keep their operations open by hiring replacements. Employers can always hire replacements for jobs that are described as temporary stopgaps until the strike ends. The question is whether the employer can hire permanent replacements, outsource functions formerly performed by employees, or keep the replacements and deny reinstatement to the strikers post-strike.

It is not an unfair labor practice to discharge strikers who have lost their employee status, and therefore their protection under the NLRA. The NLRA protects only lawful strikes that are conducted in a lawful manner, are called for a protected purpose, and are authorized by the bargaining unit representative (if there is one).

A strike is lawful if it occurs after the expiration of a CBA, if it is either an economic or an unfair labor practices strike, or if it demands concessions from the employer. Wildcat strikes, sitdown strikes, and strikes contrary to a CBA no-strike clause are not protected. Excessive violence removes employee status, although a minor instance of violence would not prevent the perpetrator from being considered an employee.

In an economic strike, the employer can permanently replace the strikers and keep the replacement workers after the end of the strike. However, strikers are entitled to reinstatement after the strike if they have not been replaced. Delay in reinstating them counts as an unfair labor practice. Even after being replaced, an economic striker is still considered an employee. If the former economic striker makes an unconditional application for reinstatement, the employer must reinstate him if the replacement worker quits or is terminated. If no jobs are available at the time of the application, the employer must reinstate the ex-striker when a job becomes available.

However, the former striker does not have to be reinstated if the striker obtains regular and substantial employment elsewhere; the job itself was eliminated (e.g., automated); or there is a legitimate business reason, such as strike violence, to deny reinstatement.

The NLRB's position, which has been upheld by the Seventh Circuit, is that the main issue is whether the replacement workers have a reasonable expectation of recall after being laid off. Strikers are entitled to reinstatement if the replacements did not have a reasonable expectation of recall—unless the employer can prove that the job is vacant or there is good cause not to rehire the striker. A "Laid-law vacancy," otherwise known as a "genuine job vacancy," occurs if the replacement worker cannot reasonably expect recall after layoff.

Unless there is a legitimate and substantial business reason to depart from the rule, a reinstated economic striker must be treated equally with nonstrikers and permanent replacements, with the same benefits, including paid vacations and accrual of seniority. Normally, reinstatement should return the worker to status quo, but he or she can be demoted for a legitimate business reason such as a risk of sabotage.

Traditionally, the employer's motivation for hiring permanent replacements was not considered, unless it could be proved that the employer violated labor laws in a manner not related to the strike. But, in mid-2016, the NLRB ruled that it violates the NLRA to hire permanent striker replacements if the motivation is to discriminate against employees who engaged in protected conduct, or to discourage future protected conduct. [*American Baptist Homes of the West* (N.L.R.B. 2016); see John W. Alden, *NLRB Holds That Hiring Permanent Strike Replacements Can Constitute an Unfair Labor Practice*, Kilpatrick Townsend & Stockton LLP (June 10, 2016), available at Lexology.com]

[E] Subcontracting

When a strike is imminent, employers who have a pressing business reason, and who are not acting out of antiunion animus, can legitimately subcontract out work that was performed by the bargaining unit, even though employees are displaced. NLRA § 8(a)(3), which penalizes employer actions that are intended to discourage union membership, can be invoked even if there is no direct proof of the employer's motivation—if the employer's action is inherently destructive of important rights of the employees. Subcontracting is a mandatory bargaining subject, so the employer can act unilaterally if a bargaining impasse has been reached.

§ 30.10 THE WARN ACT

The Worker Adjustment Retraining and Notice Act (WARN Act) [29 U.S.C. § 2101] requires employers of 100 or more full-time employees (or a combination of full- and part-timers adding up to at least 100 people and 4,000 work hours a week) to provide notice of a plant closing or mass layoff. At least 60 days' notice must be given to employees, unions, and the federal government.

The Act defines a plant closing as employment loss (termination, prolonged lay-off, serious cutback in work hours) affecting 50 or more workers during a 30-day period.

A mass layoff has a lesser effect on the individual workers (e.g., potential for recall) and affects 500 people or one-third of the workforce. Anyone rehired within six months, or anyone who elected early retirement, should not be counted in determining if a mass layoff has occurred.

A reduction in force (RIF) may require compliance with the WARN Act or a related state statute (e.g., in California, Connecticut, Hawaii, Illinois, Maine, New Hampshire, New Jersey, New York, Tennessee, and Wisconsin). Penalties imposed for non-compliance can wipe out the savings associated with reducing payroll.

Even employers who qualify for the faltering company exception or the unforeseen business circumstance exception still must give as much notice to employees as is practicable, and the notice itself must explain why the full 60 days of notice was not given.

The faltering company exception applies if the company proves that it was actively seeking capital or new business 60 days before the shutdown; there was a realistic chance of obtaining it; the financing would have been enough to avert shutdown; and giving the notice would have made it impossible to secure the financing.

The unforeseen business circumstances exception requires events that are beyond the employer's control—for example, sudden, dramatic, and unexpected conditions such as unexpected termination of an important contract, a major supplier goes on strike, or the government orders closing of a site without time to prepare. However, this exception is seldom applied when a company was simply in bad financial condition and its finances continued to deteriorate.

Companies that plan RIFs should consider implementing an ERISA severance plan. If there is a plan in place, employees must exhaust the internal claims procedure before suing, and the employer can reserve the discretion to construe the plan terms as long as the employer does not act arbitrarily and capriciously. The Employment Retirement Income Security Act (ERISA) claims can be removed to federal court—thus escaping tougher state laws on severance. Furthermore, claims under an ERISA plan can be removed to federal court, and states tend to have tougher laws on severance.

According to the Ninth Circuit, for WARN Act purposes, the "site of employment" for construction workers is the actual job site and not the company headquarters. Therefore, since the site did not have 50 or more workers, the WARN Act did not apply. (There were 33 employees at headquarters plus three outside administrators, and 162 construction workers at sites in seven states.) [*Bader v. Northern Line Layers*, 503 F.3d 813 (9th Cir. 2007)]

Although the WARN Act refers to a "group" of laid-off employees, employers cannot avoid the application of the act by performing layoffs one at a time. All economically motivated layoffs within a 90-day period are aggregated toward the 50-employee figure. [*Hallowell v. Orleans Reg'l Hosp.*, 217 F.3d 379 (5th Cir. 2000)]

The Sixth Circuit held that 194 employees fired from Vanderbilt University in mid-2013 could not pursue a class action. The plaintiffs said that they, as well as 279 other employees, did not receive WARN Act notice. The Sixth Circuit held that the two layoffs were too far apart for the affected employees to be aggregated into one group; the statutory period is 90 days. The second layoff was 79 days after the first—but the first group of laid-off workers continued to be paid for 60 days. The court accepted Vanderbilt's argument that they were on paid leave, not terminated; they kept their pay and benefits and were not eligible for unemployment. [*Morton v. Vanderbilt*, 809 F.3d 294 (6th Cir. Jan. 5, 2016)]

However, according to the Third Circuit, an employer is not liable under the WARN Act for failure to give notice if the employer was not aware that a mass layoff was, objectively, more likely than not. (This is the position already adopted by the Fifth, Sixth, Seventh, Eighth, and Tenth Circuits.) The employer was a bankruptcy debtor that ran out of cash while waiting for a Russian asset purchaser to get government approval of the deal, causing the employer to convert its bankruptcy from Chapter 11 to Chapter 7 and make what were intended as temporary furloughs into a mass layoff. The Third Circuit agreed that the eventual shutdown was not foreseeable until the company had run out of cash. [*Varela v. AE Liquidation, Inc.*, No. 16-2203, 2017 U.S. App. LEXIS 14359 (3d Cir. Aug. 4, 2017); see Elliot M. Smith, *Mass Layoffs When Section 363 Sales Fail and Cases Convert: Third Circuit Adopts Probability Standard for WARN Act Liability*, Squire Patton Boggs (Aug. 14, 2017), available at Lexology.com]

If the employer fails to give the required notice, each affected employee is entitled to up to 60 days' back pay (work days, not calendar days) and benefits. A federal civil penalty of up to $500 can also be imposed for every day that the failure to give notice continued. A union can sue for damages on behalf of its members.

The Second Circuit held that there is a material question of fact requiring trial of a WARN Act case as to whether HoldCo and its closely held subsidiary were a single employer for WARN Act purposes. The Second Circuit held that a lender is responsible for giving WARN Act notice if it is so entangled with the borrower that it is responsible for managing the borrower's business. However, the Second Circuit refused to extend this principle beyond lenders. The Second Circuit used the five non-exclusive factors from DOL regulations (20 C.F.R. § 639.3(a)(3)) to determine whether related entities constitute a single employer: e.g., common ownership, shared directors and/or officers, de facto control, unified personnel policies, and interdependent operations. [*Guippone v. BH Holdings LLC*, 737 F.3d 221 (2d Cir. 2013)]

The Eighth Circuit ruled in mid-2016 that the buyer of a business had WARN Act liability to employees of the seller company who were not offered jobs—even though the asset purchase agreement assigned all WARN Act liability to the seller. In effect, the court held that it is impossible to contract out of statutory responsibilities. The asset purchase agreement required the seller, Continental, to keep the employees who were not offered jobs in employment status for 14 days after the deal closed. When 449 ex-employees were fired without WARN Act notice, Continental had no assets, so the ex-employees sued the buyer, Celadon. The WARN Act deems the seller's employees to become employees of the buyer right after the effective date of the sale: see 29 U.S.C. § 2101(b)(1). The WARN Act's objective is to make sure that someone is obligated to give notice to people who will suffer actual loss of employment. The sale of business provision makes the seller responsible for providing notice of terminations up to the date of the sale. The buyer is responsible for notice of terminations after the date of the sale. The Eighth Circuit held that the buyer can remain liable for the seller's failure. [*Day v. Celadon Trucking Servs., Inc.*, 827 F.3d 817 (8th Cir. 2016); see Marc A. Mandelman, *8th Circuit Rules Parties to Corporate Transactions Cannot Contract Around the WARN Act Sale of Business Exception* (Aug. 3, 2016), available at Lexology.com; Tamara R. Jones, *Appellate Spotlight Be Forewarned: WARN Act Obligations Not Easily Avoided,* Constangy Brooks Smith & Prophete LLP (Aug. 10, 2016), available at Lexology.com]

The Eleventh Circuit ruled that a covered employer (in this case, a casino dependent on electronic gaming shut down by a government task force on illegal gambling) must provide WARN Act notice even if the unforeseeable business circumstances exception applies. 29 U.S.C. § 2102(b) obligates the employer to provide as much notice as practicable, and the notice must say why the period was reduced. The Eleventh Circuit said that the 60-day period can be reduced if necessary, but the employer cannot entirely avoid the notice requirement. [*Sides v. Macon Cnty. Greyhound Park Inc.*, 725 F.3d 1276 (11th Cir. 2013)]

DHL Express announced in late 2009 that five of its six Chicago-area facilities would close. To get severance benefits, employees had to waive all of their claims against the employer, including WARN Act claims. Two of the laid-off workers sued under the WARN Act. The district court held that the WARN Act was not applicable, ruling that there was no plant closing, because the five facilities were not a single site, and the layoffs did not reach 33% of the workforce. Although the plaintiffs alleged that employer pressure and extreme economic uncertainty negated voluntariness, the Seventh Circuit ruled that the severance package was voluntary. The agreements and release were negotiated by the union; were unambiguous; and suggested that employees consult a lawyer. The Seventh Circuit ruled that WARN Act claims can be waived by a voluntary general release. [*Ellis v. DHL Express Inc. USA*, 633 F.3d 522 (7th Cir. 2011)]

A company that provided payroll management services for other companies was not a WARN Act "employer" and could not be held liable for failure to provide notice, because it did not order the closing. [*Administaff Cos., Inc. v. New York Joint Bd. Shirt & Leisurewear Div.*, 337 F.3d 454 (5th Cir. 2003)]

A WARN Act event may result in "substantial cessation of operations" as defined by ERISA § 4062(e), which may require giving notice to the PBGC.

§ 30.11 LABOR LAW ISSUES OF SHARED LIABILITY

[A] Possible Scenarios

There are many situations in which more than one company may be deemed to be a particular person's "employer." Sometimes, both companies will be liable, or the actions of one will be attributed to the other, with respect to unfair labor practices, defining the appropriate bargaining unit, or enforcing a collective bargaining agreement.

Vested benefits under a collective bargaining agreement are transferable when the employer transfers employees to another one of its locations, which is covered by another CBA with another union. [*Anderson v. AT&T Corp.*, 147 F.3d 467 (6th Cir. 1998)]

When one company merges with or takes over another, it is common for many or all of the first company's employees to be retained. Whether the acquirer is now the employer, and whether it is bound by the former employer's CBA and other promises to its workers is a factual question, depending on whether or not real operational changes were made.

In connection with CBAs, a "successor company" is one that continues the same business and hires at least half of the old employees. A successor employer is not bound by the predecessor's contracts, but does have an obligation to recognize and consult with the union. The Supreme Court has ruled that a new company becomes a successor if it is clear that all the former employees will be retained. [*NLRB v. Burns Int'l Sec. Servs. Inc.*, 406 U.S. 272 (1972)] *Canteen Corp. v. NLRB* [103 F.3d 1355 (7th Cir. 1997)] holds that a company can also be treated as a successor employer if it fails to give employees enough information about the new wages and working conditions to make a meaningful choice about accepting a job offer from the new employer.

After a merger or the purchase of a business, a successor has a duty to bargain collectively and can be liable for unfair labor practices committed by the predecessor if there is "continuity of identity" with the ex-employer, such as using the same facility to produce identical products and services, using the same or substantially the same labor force, without changes in job description, working conditions, supervision, equipment, or production methods.

An alternate test is whether there is a new corporate entity to replace the predecessor, whether there is a hiatus in the enterprise's operations, and whether the employment relationship with the prior workforce was terminated. If it is perfectly clear under the *Burns International* standard that the new owner will hire the entire existing workforce, then the incoming employer has a duty to consult with the union about wage scales. It cannot unilaterally impose cuts. If there is no such consultation, it is presumed that the negotiations would have continued the prior wage scale.

The NLRB's successorship doctrine requires the purchaser in an asset transaction to recognize and bargain with the union representing the seller's employees if the new employer continues the business in substantially unchanged form and hires the former owner's employees as the majority of its workforce after the transaction closes.

But the new employer can reject the predecessor's CBA if, before or at the time the employees are hired, the new employer tells the union and employees that it does not intend to be bound by the CBA; it can then bargain for a new CBA. The NLRB held that GVS was a successor employer because it bought buildings that it knew were subject to a New York City ordinance requiring building service employees to be retained for at least 90 days after a sale. GVS fired and replaced enough people so that the old employees were no longer a majority of the workforce. The NLRB called GVS a successor employer because it measured the workforce at the beginning, not the end, of the 90-day retention period. [*GVS Props., LLC*, 362 N.L.R.B. No. 194 (Aug. 27, 2015)]

However, an asset purchaser that communicates correctly can set terms and conditions of employment and use them as a starting point for bargaining— unless the asset purchase agreement obligates the buyer to assume the CBA. The NLRB's position is that there is an obligation to bargain if an asset purchaser manifests and intention to retain the seller's employees without making it clear that continued employment constitutes acceptance of the new terms. To avoid treatment as a perfectly clear successor, the new employer must announce its intention to establish new conditions before or at the same time as it expresses the intention to hire the employees. [*Nexeo Solutions, LLC*, 364 N.L.R.B. No. 44 (2016); see Keith J. Brodie, *Buyer Beware—NLRB Decision Creates New Risks for Purchasers of Union Operations*, Barnes & Thornburg LLP (Aug. 3, 2016), available at Lexology.com]

Another possibility is that two or more enterprises might be deemed to be "alter egos" (substitutes) for one another, even if they are not formally under common control. Alter egos may be held liable for each other's unfair labor practices. The test is whether transferring business from one alter ego operation to another benefits the transferor by eliminating labor relations obligations. The alter ego theory became part of labor law to prevent "double-breasting": the practice of pairing commonly owned firms, one with a union and one nonunionized. If the double-breasted firms are actually alter egos, a federal district court can require the nonunion firm to abide by the union firm's labor agreements, even if there has been no NLRB determination of a single bargaining unit.

Two or more entities organized as legally separate entities might be treated as a "single employer" if there is an integrated enterprise. The factors that determine integration include common ownership, common management, integrated business operations, and centralized control of labor relations.

These tests are similar to the tests to see if companies are alter egos. The difference is that the two alter ego companies are not considered a single enterprise, so all their employees are not necessarily in the same bargaining unit.

A parent company and its subsidiary would probably be treated as a single employer if they were fundamentally in the same industry or business enterprise. This would be manifested by sharing supervisory, technical, and professional personnel; sharing workforce and equipment; having common officers and directors; and operating under the same labor relations policies.

The NLRB might group separate entities together as "joint employers" if they "codetermine" (i.e., make decisions jointly) about essential terms and conditions of employment. Under this theory, the crucial factor is not whether the companies have overlapping ownership, but whether they make joint decisions about hiring and firing, working conditions, compensation, and supervision of employees.

The NLRB's controversial mid-2015 *Browning-Ferris* decision finds BFI and Leadpoint to be joint employers. Leadpoint supplied workers to BFI to sort materials at a recycling plant. The contract named Leadpoint as the employer and Leadpoint managed hiring and payroll. The contract allowed BFI to set work hours and processes and to reject workers provided by Leadpoint. The NLRB rejected 30 years of precedents and returned to the traditional common-law test of joint employment: sharing or co-determining the essential terms and conditions of employment. The NLRB said that if a union won an election, both BFI and Leadpoint would have to bargain with it. NLRB decided 3–2 that BFI and Leadpoint were joint employers. This new standard could make a business a joint employer based on its contractual right of control, even if it is never exercised. [*Browning-Ferris Indus. of Cal., Inc.*, 362 N.L.R.B. No. 186 (Aug. 27, 2015)]

Browning-Ferris has been applied to claim that a business' corporate social responsibility policy, mandating that suppliers and affiliates comply with applicable laws and treat their employees fairly, makes them joint employers with the supplier. [Steven M. Swirsky and Daniel J. Green, *Does the NLRB's New Joint-Employer Standard Mean That a Corporate Social Responsibility Policy Can Turn a Customer into a Joint Employer?*, Epstein Becker Green (Aug. 30, 2016), available at Lexology.com]

A bill was introduced in Congress, the Protecting Local Business Opportunity Act, H.R. 3457/S 2015, to overturn *Browning-Ferris*. It would amend NLRA § 2(2) to provide that two or more entities are joint employers only if each shares and exercises actual, direct, and immediate control over the essential terms and conditions of employment. Some state laws on this issue have actually passed. Louisiana, Tennessee, Texas passed laws protecting franchisors from joint employer treatment. Bills were introduced in Michigan, Virginia, and Wisconsin. [Greensfelder Hemker & Gale PC, *State Legislatures React to NLRB's Broad Joint Employer Standard* (Dec. 28, 2015), available at Lexology.com]

The NLRB held that a construction company and a temporary agency were joint employers because of the potential for future joint projects. The construction company placed conditions on the hiring and characteristics of employees assigned to it; together, the two companies controlled all terms of employment. [*Retro Envtl., Inc./Green JobWorks, LLC*, 364 N.L.R.B. No. 70 (Aug. 16, 2016); see Kathleen M. Tinnerello, Howard M. Bloom and Philip B. Rosen, *NLRB Finds Joint Employers Despite Speculative Future Relationship*, Jackson Lewis PC (Sept. 6, 2016), available at Lexology.com]

Since 2013, the NLRB has become active in pursuing franchises as joint employers of employees at franchised stores because of the degree of control over operations. This is particularly true of McDonald's. Ninety percent of the more than 14,000 McDonald's restaurants in the United States are franchised. McDonald's denies that it is a joint employer, saying that wages and working conditions are set by franchisees.

A month after its McDonald's decision, the NLRB re-evaluated its standards for considering two or more companies to be joint employers, in the context of a case where a union wanted to negotiate with a company that uses subcontracted workers. Unions say that prime contractors control wages and working conditions but disclaim responsibility when there are problems, and the presence of a subcontracting tier creates a second class of workers who do the same work for less money and fewer benefits. For 30 years, McDonald's position has been that it is usually not a joint employer with its franchisees, unless there is direct control (sharing or co-determination in hiring, firing, and discipline). The NLRB said that McDonald's is a joint employer with franchisees who violated the rights of employees who participated in protests. [Melanie Trottman and Julie Jargon, *NLRB Names McDonald's as "Joint-Employer" at Its Franchisees*, WSJ .com (Dec. 19, 2014)]

The NLRB's position since late 2014 has been that franchisors can be joint employers based on even indirect control over working conditions (e.g., making recommendations to a supplier during collective bargaining; having a contractual right to provide general supervision of employees). In general, courts focus on the extent to which a franchisor controls terms and conditions of employment in franchise units, and the franchisor's degree of supervision of employees' day-to-day activities, so the NLRB has not always prevailed.

To avoid joint employer treatment, the franchisor can draft the franchise agreement to provide that decisions are based on the franchisee's conformity to quality standards; the franchisor's suggestions not related to the standards are optional. Franchisees can also be required to maintain insurance for employment discrimination claims, and to indemnify the franchisor. [Jeffrey S. Klein, Nicholas J. Pappas and Sarah Martin, *Claims Against Franchisors as Alleged "Employers,"* Weil Gotshal & Manges LLP (Oct. 22, 2014), available at Lexology.com. See, e.g., *Orozco v. Plackis*, 757 F.3d 445 (5th Cir. 2014); *Olvera v. Bareburger*

Grp., LLC, 2014 WL 3388649 (S.D.N.Y. July 10, 2014); *Cordova v. SCCF, Inc.*, 2014 WL 3512838 (S.D.N.Y. July 16, 2014)]

[B] Agents of the Employer

An employer company will be liable for the actions of any "agent" of the company acting in the employer's interest. For example, a labor consultant is considered the employer's agent, but a Chapter 7 bankruptcy trustee is not. The determination uses factors similar to those used in deciding if someone is a common-law employee. The employer's degree of control is crucial: the right to hire and fire the agent; furnishing tools and materials; prescribing what the agent will do and how to do it.

Someone can become an agent of the company either by actual agency (explicitly granted) or apparent agency (where a principal says that the agent can speak for it, or knowingly lets the agent exercise authority). An employer is responsible for the actions performed by a supervisor in the course of actual or apparent authority. Even if a supervisor acts without authority, the employer can become liable by ratifying the supervisor's action (i.e., offering support for it after the fact). In general, however, the employer will not be responsible for actions for someone who is not an employee, or perhaps not a supervisory employee, unless the employer initiates, promotes, or ratifies the conduct. If the agent's improper conduct was an isolated, unpremeditated act, or if the employer repudiates the conduct, it is possible that the employer will be relieved of liability.

In general, the NLRB will blame the employer for an unfair labor practice only if it was committed directly by the employer, or by the employer's agent. But in a representation proceeding, a finding of agency is not required to set aside an election if the election was unfair enough to prevent employees from exercising a rational, unforced choice.

§ 30.12 EMPLOYER DOMINATION

In Europe, "codetermination," where union representatives collaborate closely with management, and where joint management-labor committees play an important decision-making role, is well accepted. However, under U.S. law, employer domination of a labor organization is an unfair labor practice. [See NLRA § 8(a)(2)] Although this provision was originally enacted to bar "sweetheart unions" (formed or taken over by the employer), it has been applied more broadly.

To avoid NLRB characterization of a work team or quality circle as an unduly dominated "labor organization," the employer should consider holding meetings away from the workplace, in a neutral space; involve as many people as possible in the team; focus on productivity and workplace issues rather than compensation; and make sure the team is not used to avoid contract negotiations.

§ 30.13 NLRB JURISDICTION

The National Labor Relations Board has the power to get involved in a situation if:

- It is a labor dispute—i.e., there is any controversy about conditions of employment or representation of workers. Strikes, walkouts, picketing, and employer refusals to bargain are labor disputes;

- It affects interstate commerce. The threshold is so low that virtually any business will be deemed to affect interstate commerce;

- Employers and employees, rather than independent contractors and their clients, are involved;

- The dispute involves working conditions.

The NLRB cannot initiate proceedings on its own: it only has the power to respond to a representation petition or unfair labor practice (ULP) charge. When it has issued a complaint or filed an unfair labor practices charge, the NLRB can ask a federal District Court to issue a temporary injunction. In fact, the agency has an obligation to seek an injunction if it charges unlawful secondary activity (such as striking one employer to put pressure on another), some forms of improper activity, or certain boycotts. However, permanent injunctions are very rare, because of the Norris-LaGuardia Anti-Injunction Act.

Theoretically, the NLRB has jurisdiction over all unfair labor practice claims that require interpretation of a CBA that is still in effect. In practice, the NLRB often declines to exercise its jurisdiction, allowing the parties to use the contract's grievance arbitration machinery, to proceed with ongoing arbitration, or to enforce an arbitration award. However, it is up to the NLRB to intervene or stay out. The employer and union cannot deprive the NLRB of jurisdiction by agreeing to arbitrate.

Except in extraordinary circumstances, courts do not have jurisdiction over any issues that were not raised before the NLRB [*NLRB v. Saint-Gobain Abrasives, Inc.*, 426 F.3d 455 (1st Cir. 2005)]

The NLRB's 1955 *Spielberg* [112 N.L.R.B. 1080] ruling said that the NLRB will defer to arbitrators' decisions when the parties agreed to be bound by arbitration; the proceedings appear to have been fair and regular; and the decision was not clearly repugnant to the NLRB's purposes and policies. However, the NLRB announced a change in policy at the end of 2014. On NLRA § 8(a)(1) or (a)(3) issues, the NLRB will only defer to the arbitrator's ruling if the party seeking deferral (usually the employer) can prove that the arbitrator was explicitly authorized to decide an Unfair Labor Practices issue; was presented with the issue; considered it; and the award is reasonably compatible with labor law. [Matthew D. Austin, *National Labor Relations Board and Deferral: The Law Has Changed,*

Have You Kept Up?, Roetzel & Andress (Mar. 19, 2015), available at Lexology .com]

On February 23, 2017, the NLRB published a proposal to revise its rules and regulations, reflecting current technology. The proposal includes e-filing, removing requirements for hard copy submissions and removing references to telegrams. The amendments took effect March 7, 2017, 10 days after the initial publication; the NLRB said the rule was procedural, not substantive, so a public comment process was not needed. All e-filed documents must be received by 11:59 p.m. on the due date in the receiving office's time zone. In general, a request for extension of time must be filed on or before the due date, but can be filed after the due date if caused by circumstances that were not reasonably foreseeable in advance. The NLRB can serve any document by fax or e-mail, and subpoenas can be delivered by a private delivery service. Documents can be submitted to the NLRB with electronic signatures. [<http://www.management memo.com/files/2017/02/NLRB-Amended-Rules-Published-2_24_17.pdf>; see Steven M. Swirsky, *What's Really in The NLRB's New Amendments to Its Rules and Regulations and What Do These Changes Mean for Employers?*, Epstein Becker Green (Feb. 26, 2017), available at Lexology.com]

§ 30.14 LABOR LAW IMPLICATIONS OF BANKRUPTCY FILINGS

The general rule is that the "automatic stay" on litigation as soon as a bankruptcy petition is filed will protect the company that files from being sued. However, because the NLRB is considered a unit of the federal government exercising its regulatory powers, NLRB unfair labor practices hearings are exempt from the automatic stay. However, the bankruptcy court has the power to enjoin the NLRB from doing anything that would prevent the reorganization of the bankrupt company.

Part of the bankruptcy process is a decision about which executory contracts (i.e., contracts to be performed in the future) will be carried out by the reorganized company and which can and should be rejected. The company seeking bankruptcy protection can petition the court to allow it to assume or reject a CBA. The court's standard for granting a rejection request is whether it would be fair to reject the contract, or whether the union unreasonably refused to accept contract modifications proposed by the employer. The employer does not have to prove that the proposed plan of reorganization will fail unless the contract can be rejected.

However, if the collective bargaining agreement expires while bankruptcy proceedings are pending, the whole issue becomes moot, because there is nothing for the employer to either accept or reject.

The Bankruptcy Abuse Prevention and Consumer Protection Act of 2005, Pub. L. No. 109-8 (BAPCPA), includes various provisions not only extending the exemption of individual debtor's retirement accounts from the bankruptcy estate, but altering the treatment of retirement plans in corporate bankruptcy. The employer's bankruptcy estate does not include funds that the employer withheld or funds received by the employer from employee wages to be paid to ERISA plans, such as defined contribution plans or benefit plans. [See BAPCPA § 323]

Bankruptcy Code § 1114, as amended by BAPCPA § 1403, permits the bankruptcy court to set aside modifications of retiree health plans that the employer made within the 180 days before filing, unless the court finds that the balance of equities clearly supports the changes. (Section 1114 is the provision that requires Chapter 11 debtors to negotiate with retiree representatives rather than unilaterally modifying or terminating retiree welfare benefits. After a bankruptcy filing, the benefits must be maintained unless the bankruptcy court orders or permits modification.)

BAPCPA raises the amount of wages and benefits earned by an employee before the employer's bankruptcy filing, but not paid before the filing, that can be treated as a priority claim. The current amount entitled to preference is $12,850: see 81 Fed. Reg. 8748 (Feb. 22, 2016). BAPCPA also limits the amount of severance or retention bonuses that can be paid to insiders of a bankrupt company.

Although Bankruptcy Code § 1113 allows a Chapter 11 debtor to reject its CBA under defined circumstances, this potentially conflicts with the NLRA, which forbids employers from unilaterally changing the terms and conditions of a CBA even after it expires. In a case of first impression, the Third Circuit decided in early 2016 that § 1113 does not distinguish between expired and unexpired CBAs, so a debtor that otherwise meets the conditions can reject continuing terms and conditions after a CBA expires. [*In Re: Trump Entm't Resorts Unite Here Local 54*, 810 F.3d 161 (3d Cir. 2016) The Supreme Court declined to review this case: *UNITE Here Local 54 v. Trump Entm't Resorts*, No. 14-1286 (May 31, 2016)]

CHAPTER 31

OCCUPATIONAL SAFETY AND HEALTH

§ 31.01   INTRODUCTION

The federal Occupational Safety and Health Act and the agency that administers it, the Occupational Safety and Health Administration (both abbreviated OSHA) have as their mission protecting employees against unreasonably hazardous workplaces. All employers must satisfy the "general duty standard" of maintaining a workplace that is reasonably free of recognized dangers. Additional standards are imposed in some circumstances, particularly in the construction industry. **NOTE: In addition to developments reflected in the 2018 edition, it is predictable that the Trump administration will reduce regulation and maintain a pro-business stance that is highly likely to reduce the role of OSHA.**

OSHA also protects whistleblowers under a number of statutes, not just those concerned with conventional safety and health issues; see § 31.09[C] below. Employees are also entitled to whistleblower protection in the context of securities law.

Employers are not held to an impossible standard of a hazard-free workplace, but they must be prepared to deal with known hazards (including disease and chemical toxicity as well as accident). They must use the reasonably available methods and technology to keep the dangers within bounds.

The California Court of Appeal ruled in 2011 that Cal OSHA regulations apply only to employees, so an independent contractor air conditioning servicer could not use those standards to prove negligence per se. (He charged the owner of a condominium complex with negligence per se because the ladder from which he fell did not have the state-mandated safety mechanisms.) [*Iversen v. California Vill. HOA*, 194 Cal. App. 4th 107 (2011)]

The Bureau of Labor Statistics (BLS) reported that, between 2014 and 2015, the injury and illness rate in private industry declined, falling from 3.2 cases per 100 full-time equivalent workers in 2014 to 3.0 cases in 2015. Naturally, the injury/illness rate varied by industry: in 2015, it ranged from 1.4/100 in business services to 4.8 in transportation. [Catherine M. Wilmarth, *Private Industry Workplace Injury and Illness Rates Continue to Decline*, BLS Report Says, Kelley Drye & Warren LLP (Dec. 14, 2016), available at Lexology.com]

§ 31.02   OSHA POWERS

Under the OSH Act, OSHA has the authority to inspect workplaces, order correction of violations, and impose penalties if correction does not occur as mandated. It has been held that it is not a violation of the OSH Act, or the Fourth Amendment's ban on unreasonable searches and seizures, for an OSHA compliance officer to videotape a construction site from across the street before going to the site and presenting his credentials. The theory is that looking at a site (to determine if fall protection techniques were adequate) is not a "search," so no warrant is required. [*L.R. Willson & Sons Inc. v. OSHRC*, 134 F.3d 1235 (4th Cir. 1998)]

The OSH Act also requires employers to keep records of workplace injuries and to use this information to generate annual reports (which must be disclosed to the workforce as well as being submitted to OSHA).

All employers whose operations affect commerce among the states are subject to OSHA. There is no minimum number of employees. However, small-scale or low-risk enterprises are entitled to relaxation of some reporting requirements.

> ■ **TIP:** An employer who would be damaged by full compliance with OSHA requirements can petition the Secretary of Labor for a temporary or permanent "variance" that protects the company against noncompliance penalties. Variances are effective only for the company that applies for them. It is no defense against a charge of noncompliance that a variance was granted to a different company in a similar situation.

The OSH Act interacts with various other statutes. It is probably a violation of public policy to discharge a worker because he or she filed a Worker's Compensation claim after suffering an occupational injury; to retaliate against a whistleblower who reported unsafe conditions to OSHA; or to take steps against someone who cooperated in an OSHA investigation.

Federal labor law says that a walkout premised on unsafe working conditions will not be treated as a strike. Furthermore, it is a protected concerted activity for workers to complain about safety conditions in the workplace, and therefore the employer cannot use this as a premise for employee discipline. However, state courts will not necessarily consider an OSHA violation relevant evidence of neglect if the employer is sued.

§ 31.03 OSHA REGULATIONS

The main authority for federal regulation of workplace safety comes from the OSH Act itself. OSHA's agency rules appear in the Code of Federal Regulations. In addition to the General Duty Clause, OSHA enforces more specific guidance in the form of the General Industry Standards that cover most industrial workplaces, and the Construction Standards. General Industry Standards deal with topics such as noise control, radiation safety; proper handling of "hazmats" (hazardous materials such as toxic chemicals and toxic wastes); Personal Protective Equipment (PPE) such as respirators and hard hats, guarding machinery, fire prevention; and the condition of floors (the "walking/working" standard).

The Construction Industry Standards overlap with the General Industry Standards. The two rules sometimes treat the same topics, but the construction rules tend to be more stringent in this case. The construction standards also cover control of asbestos, welding and cutting, scaffolding, steel construction, and the use of masonry and concrete in construction. [<https://www.osha.gov/record keeping2014/index.html> (last accessed Mar. 7, 2017)]

OSHA Forms 300 (Injury and Illness Log), 300A (Summary of Work-Related Injuries and Illnesses), and 301 (Incident Report) are used to report work-related injuries and illnesses. These forms are available at <https://www.osha.gov/recordkeeping/RKforms.html> (last accessed Mar. 7, 2017). Small employers (up to 10 employees) and low-risk "partially exempt industries" do not have to file these forms. Non-exempt employers must display Form 300A in the workplace each year during the period between February 1 and April 30. Employees, ex-employees, and their representatives are entitled to view the injury and illness records and, on request, the employer must provide a copy of the relevant records by the end of the next business day. [OSHA, *OSHA'S Recordkeeping Page,* <https://www.osha.gov/recordkeeping/index.html> (last accessed Mar. 7, 2017)]

Under a September 2014 final rule, all fatalities must be reported to OSHA within eight hours. All injuries resulting in hospitalization, amputation, or loss of an eye must be reported within 24 hours. Businesses with 10 or fewer employees are exempt from keeping routine records. The 2014 rule increases the list of industries that are not required to maintain routine records because they are low-risk industries: e.g., broadcasting, accounting, appliance stores, clothing stores, and ISPs. [Final Rule: 79 Fed. Reg. 56129 (Sept. 18, 2014); see OSHA Fact Sheet, *Updates to OSHA's Recordkeeping Rule: Reporting Fatalities and Severe Injuries,* <https://www.osha.gov/recordkeeping2014/OSHA3745.pdf> (Sept. 2014) (last accessed Mar. 7, 2017)]

In mid-2016, OSHA adopted new regulations dealing with electronic reporting of work-related illnesses and injuries. The regulations also include controversial provisions protecting workers from retaliation.

The reporting requirement calls for companies that have 250 or more employees to submit the Form 300A (summary), Form 300 (log), and Form 301 (incident report) to OSHA in electronic form each year, beginning with reports about calendar 2016 to be submitted in 2017. Employers that have 20–249 employees but are in a high-risk industry must e-file Form 300A each year. OSHA's regulation does not preempt state laws, and in fact OSHA encourages states to adopt their own, stricter requirements. [81 Fed. Reg. 31854 (May 10, 2016); FAQ, <https://www.osha.gov/recordkeeping/finalrule/finalrule_faq.html> (last accessed Mar. 7, 2017); see Bryan E. Keyt, Mitchell S. Allen and Erin L. Brooks, *What Employers Need to Know About OSHA's New Reporting and Anti-Retaliation Regulations,* Bryan Cave LLP (July 6, 2016), available at Lexology.com.]

In mid-2017, OSHA announced that it was reconsidering the rules about electronic reporting of injuries and illnesses, and might eliminate the rules. The effective date of the reporting rule was delayed from the originally scheduled July 1, 2017 until December 1, 2017, because the web application was not ready on time. The site launched on August 1, 2017. On June 27, OSHA announced that the effective date was delayed until December 1, 2017, and that OSHA was

reviewing the rule and might eliminate it. In the meantime, the website for submitting 2016 injury and illness data went live on August 1, 2017, ready for the
December deadline. [<https://www.osha.gov/newsreleases/trade/07142017>;
announcement of delay: 82 Fed. Reg. 13550 (June 28, 2017); see Brad Hiles,
OSHA Further Delays Electronic Reporting, Husch Blackwell LLP (June 27,
2017), available at Lexology.com; Elise C. Scott and John Fehrenbach, *OSHA
Announces Electronic Recordkeeping App,* Winston & Strawn LLP (July 19,
2017), available at Lexology.com]

The regulations are intended to protect employees against retaliation for
reporting injuries or illnesses. Employers must maintain reporting requirements
that are reasonable and do not deter reporting, and must inform employees of their
right to report without fear of retaliation. The 2016 rules give OSHA the power to
issue a citation for violation of the anti-retaliation provision even if there has been
no complaint from a worker. OSHA told employers to reconsider incentive
programs that give rewards for going a certain number of days without an
accident—because the program could encourage employees to cover up
accidents. OSHA prefers that employers offer positive incentives for obeying
safety rules. [Megan P. Caldwell, *Final Rule Issued to Improve Tracking of Workplace Injuries and Illnesses,* Husch Blackwell LLP (July 8, 2016), available at
Lexology.com]

A suit was filed on July 8, 2016 to challenge the rules, alleging that OSHA
exceeded its statutory authority by imposing a rule without adequate regulatory
analysis. The suit also charges that the rule limits employers' ability to investigate accidents, and conflicts with state mandates for post-accident testing.

OSHA's position is that, because of privacy concerns and to prevent employees from being discouraged from reporting accidents, employers should limit
post-accident drug testing to instances in which the test can accurately identify
impairment and the circumstances make it likely that drug use contributed to the
accident. This position can cause quandaries for companies in states where medical and/or recreational marijuana are legal because the employer may want to test
to see if marijuana was a factor in the accident. Most statutes decriminalizing
marijuana (see §§ 23.09, 26.03[A]) state explicitly that employers do not have a
duty to accommodate the use of medical marijuana. [Chrisopher J. Lalak, *Drug-
Testing Dilemma: How Ohio's Forthcoming Medical Marijuana Law and a New
OSHA Rule Combine to Make Headache for Employers,* Benesch Friedlander
Coplan & Aronoff LLP (June 3 2016), available at Lexology.com]

The business groups that were the plaintiffs in the suit challenged the rule's
limits on safety incentive programs and the ban on mandatory post-accident drug
testing, arguing that OSHA exceeded its statutory authority and acted arbitrarily
and capriciously. In response to a request from the court considering whether a
preliminary injunction against the rule should be issued, OSHA delayed the effective date twice, once until November 1, 2016, then until December 1, 2016.

[*TEXO ABC/AGC v. Thomas*, No. 3:16-CV-1998,(N.D. Tex. July 8, 2016); see Shontell Powell and Melissa A. Bailey, *OSHA Pushes Back Enforcement Date for Anti-Retaliation Provisions Again,* Ogletree Deakins (Oct. 18, 2016), available at Lexology.com; Mark A. Lies, II, *OSHA Again Delays Enforcement Date for New Workplace Injury and Illness Reporting Rule*, Seyfarth Shaw LLP (Oct. 19, 2016), available at Lexology.com; Thomas M. Eden, III, *Enforcement Date of OSHA Rule Delayed Again—Until December 1*, Constangy Brooks Smith & Prophete LLP (Oct. 20, 2016), available at Lexology.com] (This suit does not challenge the electronic reporting provisions.)

An October 19, 2016 memo from OSHA clarifies its position: the agency will not issue citations under this rule if drug testing is carried out pursuant to a state Workers' Compensation law or other state or federal law or regulation. OSHA considers testing reasonable if the employer had a reasonable basis for believing drugs were involved in the injury. [<https://www.osha.gov/record keeping/finalrule/interp_recordkeeping_101816.html>; see Sarah J. Lis, *OSHA Clarifies Its "Just Say No" to Automatic Post-Accident Drug-Testing Position*, Akerman LLP (Oct. 26, 2016), available at Lexology.com]

In another move reflecting the political changes that affect regulatory requirements, on May 10, 2017, the DOL eliminated its rule limiting states' ability to mandate drug testing of applicants for unemployment benefits: see John S. Ho, *One DOL Drug Testing Rule Officially Gone—Is OSHA Next?*, Cozen O'Connor (May 15, 2017), available at Lexology.com]

Then the court denied a temporary injunction, holding that the plaintiffs did not demonstrate irreparable harm. Therefore, the anti-retaliation provisions finally took effect, on December 1, 2016. [*TEXO ABC/ABG v. Perez*, No. 3:16-cv-1998-L, 2016 U.S. Dist. LEXIS 163757; 2017 OSHD (CCH) P33,558 (N.D. Tex. Nov. 28, 2016); Edwin G. Foulke Jr., *Judge Rules That OSHA Can, FOR NOW, Start Enforcing Limits on Incentives and Drug Testing*, Fisher Phillips (Nov. 29, 2016), available at Lexology.com]

On April 25, 2017, OSHA's Director of Enforcement Programs, Thomas Galassi, formally withdrew a similar letter written in 2013 to the United Steelworkers of America. Galassi said that only a certified or recognized union representing the workers is entitled to be present at workplace inspections. [Thomas Benjamin Huggett, *OSHA Rights Its Course: Only Authorized Union Agents and Employees Can Participate During OSHA Inspections,* Littler Mendelson PC (May 1, 2017), available at Lexology.com]

§ 31.04 CONTROLLING PHYSICAL HAZARDS

Every year, OSHA publishes a "Top 10" list of the greatest hazards; the lists do not vary much from year to year; generally, the items are fall protection, hazard communication, scaffolding, respiratory protection, lockout/tagout, powered industrial trucks, ladders, electrical wiring, machine guarding, and general electrical requirements.

In late 2016, OSHA updated the general industry fall protection and walking/working surfaces rules in a massive (more than 500 pages) rule allowing new options for preventing slip, trip, and fall hazards. The rule covers seven million worksites and 112 million workers. A new Subpart I has been added to the PPE standard, with requirements for personal fall protection systems tailored to specific industries. Previously, guardrails were the primary fall protection method. Employers now have six options: guardrails, safety nets, ladder systems, positioning systems, travel restraint systems, and personal fall arrest systems. OSHA expected the new rules to prevent 29 fatalities and almost 6,000 injuries a year. OSHA expected the standards to cost about $305 million to implement, but expected savings due to prevention of death and injuries to total $614 million. In general, the rule took effect January 17, 2017, but certain requirements phase in later, or even much later. Employers get 20 years, until November 18, 2036, to replace cages and wells used for fall protection with ladder safety or personal fall arrest systems. [81 Fed. Reg. 82494 (Nov. 18, 2016); see Andi S. Kenney, *OSHA Issues Final Rule on Walking-Working Surfaces and Fall Protection,* Jenner & Block LLP (Nov. 30, 2016), available at Lexology.com; Avi Meyerstein and Amy L. Wachs, *New Slip, Trip and Fall OSHA Rule*, Husch Blackwell LLP (Nov. 18, 2016), available at Lexology.com]

In mid-2016, there was a global health emergency when Zika virus, which usually causes mild flu-like symptoms in adults, can cause severe birth defects if a fetus is exposed; adults can develop muscle weakness or even paralysis. It is spread by mosquitos; there is no evidence of person-to-person transmission by casual contact, so infected employees are probably not a direct threat in the workplace. OSHA issued interim guidance on protecting workers from occupational Zika exposure: see <https://www.osha.gov/zika/index.html> The CDC does not advocate a total ban on travel to Zika areas, but says that pregnant women should avoid traveling there, and women trying to become pregnant should consult their doctors about infection protection. [Katharine M. Parker and Laura M. Fant, *Zika Virus and the Workplace: What Employers Should Know*, Proskauer Rose LLP (Aug. 22, 2016), available at Lexology.com.]

OSHA published a fact sheet, Crowd Management Safety Guidelines for Retailers, about eliminating work hazards by managing crowds of holiday shoppers. The fact sheet does not impose any new compliance requirements, but it helps employers identify hazards in areas of planning, pre-event set-up, the event, and emergencies. OSHA advises businesses that expect large crowds to hire extra staff as needed; have police officers or trained security personnel present; create a staffing plan with a location designated for each worker; get any necessary permits; consult fire and police departments about safety requirements; post signs with information such as store hours and locations of entrances, exits, and restrooms; and have a rehearsal before the holiday. Well before the date, set up rope lines or barricades; set up communications between employees and emergency responders; place attractive sale items to avoid bottlenecks; and keep carts and other obstacles away from exits. Have first aid kits and defibrillators available, with trained employees. [<https://www.osha.gov/OshDoc/data_General_Facts/Crowd_Control.html> (Nov. 2012) (last accessed Mar. 7, 2017)]

[A] Personal Protective Equipment

An important part of the employer's duty of providing a safe workplace is to furnish protective equipment and to make sure that machinery is guarded and that, where appropriate, moving parts will stop before employees are injured.

The legal system treats PPE (Personal Protective Equipment) as essential to workplace safety. Wherever possible, employers should eliminate hazards directly, by reducing the likelihood of falls, falling objects, burns, chemical exposure, etc. But it is not always possible to remove the hazard, and even when it is physically possible, the cost may be prohibitive.

In such situations, the employer has a duty to provide PPE, and the employee has a complementary duty to use it. The employer must provide suitable equipment, in sizes that fit the workers, and must train them in how to use the equipment. The obligation exists whenever a reasonable person, familiar with workplace conditions and industry practices, would require PPE. The industry standard is not a defense, however, if the employer knew or should have known that dangerous conditions were present—for instance, if injuries had occurred in the past under similar circumstances.

A respiratory protection rule took effect October 5, 1998. The standard, known as 1910.134, covers respirator use in general industry, shipyards, longshore work, and construction, but not in agriculture. For guidance to employers, OSHA issued compliance directive CPL 2-0.120, explaining how to analyze workplace hazards, select respirators, when to change the chemical cartridges in respirators, and how to make sure respirators fit properly. [See <http://www.osha.gov>]

At last, final rules were published in November 2007, taking effect six months after publication. The rules require the employer to pay for almost all mandatory PPE (the exceptions being ordinary clothing, weather gear, logging boots, prescription safety glasses, and ordinary safety-toe boots). The rule does not create obligations for employers to provide PPE in any additional situations. [72 Fed. Reg. 65341 (Nov. 15, 2007)]

OSHA imposed what was then the maximum fine of $140,000 for safety violations that led to the fatal electrocution of a Verizon technician in Brooklyn in 2011. OSHA also issued 10 citations for failure to follow safety rules. Verizon did not provide life-saving equipment and did not require protective helmets and gloves to be used during dangerous tasks. Douglas Lalima's death was not reported as required, and the technicians were not adequately trained for working near high-voltage lines. Verizon denied any wrongdoing and said that it would appeal the finding. [Hannah Miet, *Verizon Fined $140,000 After Electrocution Death*, NYTimes.com (Mar. 19, 2012)]

[B] Lockout/Tagout

OSHA's lockout/tagout rule (29 C.F.R. § 1910.147) applies in nonconstruction workplaces where the machinery has potentially dangerous moving parts. The rule imposes obligations on employers to immobilize machinery while it is being serviced, cleaned, repaired, etc. The rule does not apply to normal operation of the machinery, because in those situations the equipment and work routines are supposed to prevent injuries due to moving parts.

To comply with the lockout/tagout rule, machinery could be equipped with a trip control ("panic button") so it can be shut down quickly in an emergency. Blades and other dangerous parts can be protected with guards that protect workers' bodies from contact and prevent scrap materials from becoming projectiles. If guards are impractical, machinery could be equipped with sensing devices that turn off the machine if a body part goes beyond the safe point. Machinery can also be designed to require two hands to operate, so that it will not work when a hand is within reach of moving parts.

[C] Bathroom Breaks

The OSHA general industry sanitation standard [29 C.F.R. § 1910.141] requires the presence of toilet facilities in the workplace. An April 6, 1998, letter from OSHA forbids employers to impose unreasonable restrictions on bathroom use. OSHA inspectors who receive complaints on this issue are directed to investigate the reasonableness of the employer's policy.

Female workers (especially pregnant women) need more bathroom breaks than male workers, although older male workers may need to use the restroom more often because of prostate enlargement.

Acting under the general industry sanitation standard, OSHA published a Best Practices guide in mid-2015 for restroom access for transgender workers. OSHA said that transgender workers should be permitted to use the restrooms consistent with the gender to which they are transitioning. [<http://www.dol.gov/asp/policy-development/TransgenderBathroomAccessBestPractices.pdf> (2015) (last accessed Mar. 7, 2017)]

The EEOC's position is also that employees should be permitted to use the restroom and locker room for the gender with which they identify. However, it is unlikely that this position will be pursued during the Trump administration.

§ 31.05   CONTROLLING EXPOSURE TO HAZARDOUS CONDITIONS

[A]   Generally

The employer must limit employees' exposure to hazardous materials (e.g., asbestos, lead) and conditions (e.g., potentially damaging noise levels). Hazardous substances must be stored properly. Employees must be warned about their presence and taught how to handle the materials safely.

Other laws, such as environmental laws and laws requiring notification to the community of the presence or accidental release of hazardous substances, are also triggered when dangerous materials are used in a workplace. The company must have an emergency-response plan that involves coordination with fire departments and other community resources. [Jesse Newman, *EPA Overhauls Rules for Pesticide Use on Farms*, WSJ.com (Sept. 28, 2015)]

OSHA expects employers to maintain a complete protection program: telling employees to rest in the shade and drink water as necessary; wear hats and light-colored, reflective clothing; acclimate gradually to working in heart; and know how to recognize a heat emergency and what to do.

Heat-related deaths are most likely to occur on an employee's first few days on the job, before employees learn to pace themselves and use proper hydration. Fatalities have dropped about 50% since OSHA launched an annual summer heat campaign in 2011. In 2013 (most recent available) there were 34 deaths versus 61 in 2011; the average for 2003-2013 is 36 per year. In 2013, 3106 people missed at least one day of work due to heat-induced illness. [OSHA mobile phone heat app: <www.osha.gov/SLTC/heatillness/heat_index/heat_app.html> (last accessed Mar. 7, 2017)]

In 2012, OSHA modified the Hazard Communication Standard at 29 C.F.R. § 1919.1200 to conform to the United Nations's Globally Harmonized System of Classification and Labeling of Chemicals (GHS). The OSHA Hazard Communication Standard requires manufacturers and importers of chemicals to evaluate the hazards of their chemicals, and to label them and use Material Safety Data Sheets (MSDS) to inform customers of the hazards. Employers that have hazardous chemicals in the workplace must label the chemicals, have MSDSs available to workers who might be exposed, and give training on chemical hazards. OSHA renamed the MSDS "labeling and safety data sheets." Chemicals are labeled with a signal word, e.g., "Danger," an image, and a statement of the hazards caused by that chemical. [77 Fed. Reg. 17574 (Mar. 26, 2012)]

OSHA's Process Safety Management (PSM) standard deals with prevention of releases of extremely hazardous chemicals and worker protection. Traditionally, retail establishments were exempt because of their limited amounts of hazardous materials. However, after 15 people died in an ammonium nitrate fire, OSHA issued an enforcement memo putting certain retail establishments, including agricultural dealers who sell anhydrous ammonia to farmers, under the PSM standard without requesting public comments. The D.C. Circuit held that implementing the rule without comments violated the OSH Act. [*Agriculture Retailers Ass'n v. DOL,* 837 F.3d 60 (D.C. App. 2016); see Daniel R. Birnbaum and Michael T. Taylor, *Regulated Industry Successfully Challenges New OSHA Process Safety Management Enforcement Policies,* Baker & Hostetler LLP (Sept. 26, 2016), available at Lexology.com]

After OSHA issued a citation when a supervising employee worked on a dangerous ledge without fall protection (violating 29 C.F.R. § 1926.501(b)(1)), the Administrative Law Judge (ALJ) upheld the citation and imposed a $5,000 penalty (plus $4,000 for incorrect usage of fall protection by other employees)—but the Fifth Circuit reversed, finding that the decision was based on an error of law. In the Fifth Circuit view, failure to comply with a specific regulation, even if there is substantial danger, is not enough to constitute a violation of the OSH Act. Employers are not strictly liable; they are liable only if they knew or should have known there was a violation. The Fifth Circuit does not impute the supervisor's knowledge of his own misconduct to the employer if the employer's safety policy, training, and discipline make it unforeseeable that the supervisor would break the rules. Employee misconduct is an affirmative defense, requiring proof that the employer not only made, but adequately communicated, work rules designed to prevent violations, and has taken steps to detect and correct violations if they do occur. [*W.G. Yates & Sons Constr. Co. Inc. v. OSHRC,* 459 F.3d 604 (5th Cir. 2006). Although the Sixth Circuit imputes a supervisor's knowledge of his own misconduct to the employer, the Third and Tenth Circuits disagree: see the cases cited in *Danis-Shook Joint Venture XXV v. Sec'y of Labor,* 319 F.3d 805 (6th Cir. 2003). The Fifth Circuit's analysis of the employee misconduct affirmative defense derives from *Frank Lill & Son, Inc. v. Sec'y of Labor,* 362 F.3d 840 (D.C. Cir. 2004).]

An employer can be charged with constructive knowledge of safety violations that supervisors know or should know about and the site superintendent was at the site several times an hour. [*P. Gioioso & Sons Inc. v. OSHRC,* 675 F.3d 66 (1st Cir. 2012)]

In late 2016, the California Supreme Court reversed its previous position and made employers and owners of work premises potentially liable for "take-home" toxic exposure cases (i.e., where a worker exposes his or her family to clothes contaminated with a dangerous substance, usually asbestos). Employers and premises owners have a duty to exercise ordinary care in managing asbestos, including preventing take-home exposure. If exposure of household members is reasonably foreseeable, then defendants have a duty to take reasonable care to prevent transmission. But the duty runs only to household members, not other people in contact with the exposed employee. This holding applies to all workers at the site, no matter who their employer is. However, at least eight states (e.g., Delaware and Illinois) hold that there is no liability to household members unless there was a special relationship. Maryland and Iowa said that public policy does not favor imposing a duty to family members of employees. Texas, Washington,

Kentucky, Oklahoma, and North Dakota say that family exposures are not fore-seeable, so the employer or premises owner is not liable. But New Jersey, Tennessee, Louisiana, Connecticut, and California say that it is reasonably fore-seeable that exposed workers can carry asbestos home on their clothing. [Consolidated cases: *Kesner v. Superior Court*, 384 P.3d 283 (Cal. 2016) and *Haver v. BNSF Ry. Co.*, No. S219919, 2016 Cal. LEXIS 10159 (Cal. Dec. 1, 2016); see Nicholas P. Martin and Molly Friend, *California Supreme Court Imposes Broad Liability for Employers and Premises Owners in "Take-Home" Toxic Exposure Cases,* Wilson Elser (Dec. 19, 2016), available at Lexology.com]

[B] PELs

A PEL, or Permissible Exposure Limit, is set for certain hazardous sub-stances such as asbestos and lead. A PEL is a level of contact with the substance that employees can encounter without becoming endangered. The employer has an obligation to monitor the plant environment to determine the level of the regu-lated substance, to provide appropriate safety equipment (e.g., face masks and res-pirators) and to train employees in safety techniques.

OSHA rules require that employees have access to showers, changing rooms, eye baths, first aid, and other measures for preventing long-term contami-nation. Where necessary, the employer must provide protective clothing and appropriate containers for collecting contaminated clothing for treatment or dis-posal. Employees must not be permitted to smoke or eat in any environment where asbestos, lead, etc., are present. Warning signs must be posted in danger areas.

The employer's basic job is to keep employee exposure below the PEL. In some instances, this is impossible. When exposure reaches the "action level" defined by OSHA, the employer must take additional steps, such as periodic medical testing of employees to see if they have suffered environmental injury or illness.

The current PELs are more than 40 years old. NIOSH and American Con-ference of Government Industrial Hygienists (ACGIH) levels are usually stricter than OSHA requirements. Industry points out that NIOSH and the ACGIH can adopt standards without public notice and comment, and do not have to consider technical feasibility. [Jackson Lewis LLP, *OSHA Recommends New Exposure Limits* (Nov. 22, 2013), available at Lexology.com]

OSHA issued new voluntary standards for workplace chemical exposure in late 2013, stating that the existing standards are not protective enough. OSHA asked employers to comply voluntarily with the new standards; only the old PELs are enforceable. However, it is likely that the new standards will be treated by plaintiffs' lawyers as the appropriate threshold in toxic tort cases. [OSHA tool-kit, <http://www.osha.gov/dsg/safer_chemicals/index.html> (last viewed Mar. 8,

2017) and annotated list of PELs at <http://www.osha.gov/dsg/annotated-pels/index.html> (last viewed Mar. 8, 2017).]

[C] Noise Levels

In workplaces where the noise level routinely exceeds 85 decibels per eight-hour shift, the employer has an obligation to create and maintain a comprehensive program for hearing conservation. The environmental noise level must be monitored; employees' hearing must be tested (with a baseline reading within six months of initial exposure to high occupational noise levels, and an annual checkup after that), and they must be trained to protect themselves against hearing loss. If any audiometric test shows that an employee's hearing has deteriorated, the employer's obligation is to notify that worker within 21 days and then make sure that the worker uses hearing protection devices in the future.

In the October 19, 2010 *Federal Register*, OSHA published a proposed interpretation of "feasible administrative or engineering controls" in the context of workplace noise. However, in January 2011, OSHA withdrew the document because of industry complaints about potential costs, saying that it is studying other approaches to abating noise hazards in the workplace. [Fred Schneyer, *OSHA Takes More Time on Noise Standard*, plansponsor.com (Jan. 19, 2011)]

The Fifth Circuit ruled that hearing-loss claims based on charges that the employer failed to monitor noise exposure or protect employees against excessive noise could be heard in state court. The claims were not subject to the Labor Management Relations Act (LMRA) § 301 preemption (i.e., the doctrine that cases about interpretation of a CBA must only be heard in the federal system) because the state (Louisiana) had a body of workplace law about the duty to protect employees from injury. The case could be resolved using these principles without even consulting the CBA. Furthermore, Louisiana forbids CBA provisions that eliminate rights to workplace safety. [*McKnight v. Dresser, Inc.*, 676 F.3d 426 (5th Cir. 2012)]

[D] Workplace Violence

Workplace violence can occur among co-workers or other persons entering the workplace (e.g., a domestic abuser or stalker). According to the Department of Justice, one-sixth of violent crimes occur in the workplace. Retail establishments are at especially high risks because of long hours and direct interaction with customers. The Bureau of Justice Statistics found that, while retail workers make up 9% of the workforce, they experience 13% of all workplace violence and 27% of workplace homicides. [Dennis A. Davis and Luther Wright, Jr., *Is Your Workplace Violence Plan Ready? 5 Essential Elements of a Comprehensive Plan*, Ogletree Deakins (Nov. 4, 2015), available at Lexology.com]

Late in 2004, the U.S. Supreme Court applied the intentional infliction of emotional distress cause of action against an employer who failed to provide a safe workplace. The employer assigned a woman to a remote location; she asked not to be assigned to places that made her vulnerable to the former lover against whom she had an order of protection. The woman was kidnapped and raped by the ex-lover. The Supreme Court dismissed her constitutional claims but upheld the intentional infliction of emotional distress element of the case because the employer's actions (granting access to the attacker; refusing to let her work in a safer location) inflicted distress over and above that suffered directly from the incident. Worker's Compensation exclusivity did not apply, because the employer's conduct was intentional rather than negligent. Furthermore, most states do not cap damages for intentional infliction of emotional distress. [*Gantt v. Security USA, Inc.*, 543 U.S. 814 (2004)]

A BLS news release reports that there were 409 workplace homicides in 2014, about the same number as in 2013. For female victims, 32% of homicides were committed by relatives or domestic partners; for male victims, the most common type of homicide was killing by robbers (33%). NIOSH reported that between 2000 and 2013, there were 160 active shooter incidents in the workplace: 46% in commercial situations, 24% in schools, 10% in government offices. [<http://www.bls.gov/news.release/cfoi.nr0.htm> ; see James L. Curtis and Craig B. Simonsen, *Wave of Shootings Puts Workplace Violence Back in the Spotlight,* Seyfarth Shaw LLP (July 26, 2016), available at Lexology.com]

OSHA identifies homicide as the fourth largest cause of fatal occupational injuries in the United States. OSHA has not set mandatory standards to prevent workplace violence, but does have voluntary guideline recommendations. [<https://www.osha.gov/Publications/osha3148.pdf> (last accessed Mar. 8, 2017)] The guidelines cover training and investigations, and provide checklists. To avert workplace violence, employers can add a zero-tolerance for violence policy to their employee handbooks. They can train employees in personal safety and violence prevention. Employees should be encouraged to report any harassment or threats, which the employer should investigate promptly. If an investigation takes a long time, an alleged perpetrator can be suspended (to protect other employees) but with pay (so no adverse job action has been taken). To avoid claims of pretext, the anti-violence policy must be enforced consistently. Even if an employee is mentally ill, it does not violate the American with Disabilities (ADA) to take action based on dangerousness. [Allison Oasis Kahn, *5 Workplace Safety Tips to Protect Employees from Violent Co-Workers (While Complying with Employment Laws)*, Carlton Fields Jorden Burt (Aug. 27, 2015) available at Lexology.com]

Another version of the essential elements in a prudent anti-violence plan are: set up a crisis management team; enact or review the anti-violence policy, including educating employees that violent incidents will lead to discharge and arrest; training managers to defuse conduct that could lead to violence; and having a crisis plan, just as the enterprise has a crisis plan for fires or weather emergencies.

[Dennis A. Davis and Luther Wright, Jr., *Is Your Workplace Violence Plan Ready? 5 Essential Elements of a Comprehensive Plan*, Ogletree Deakins (Nov. 4, 2015), available at Lexology.com]

Under the General Duty Clause, employers are required to provide a workplace free of recognized hazards. Employees injured in violent incidents might be entitled to Worker's Compensation, tort recovery based on failure to provide adequate security, tort liability to victims of negligent acts committed by persons under the employer's control, or negligent hiring and retention. See DHS' active shooter training materials, available at <https://www.dhs.gov/active-shooter-preparedness>. The conclusion is that employees should be trained to run if there is an accessible escape path; hide if they can't flee the premises, and fight only if there is no other option. Escape routes should be kept open and employees should be trained to find them. It is not recommended to train employees to go to one safe room—because the shooter might be an employee who is thereby enabled to kill many co-workers at once. [Mark J. Neuberger, *Even as They Lament the Horrific Reality of Mass Violence, Employers Must Consider How to Prevent It in Their Workplaces*, Foley & Lardner LLP (June 20, 2016), available at Lexology .com; Joseph W. Gagnon, *How Employers Should Prep for Active Shooter Situations*, Fisher Phillips (Aug. 4, 2016), available at Lexology.com]

If employees are affected by a mass shooting (or other disaster), the employer should explain to the employees the forms of leave and other benefits available to them, such as health insurance, FMLA leave, Employee Assistance Program services, life and disability insurance, and bereavement leave. Injured employees may be entitled to ADA accommodations—for example, if they develop PTSD. See <http://www.dol.gov/odep/index.htm> for DOL's Office of Disability Employment Policy's PTSD resources. [Mark T. Phillis et. al., *When Tragedy Strikes: How Employers Can Assist Employees Affected by Mass Shootings and Disasters*, Littler Mendelson PC (June 16, 2016), available at Lexology.com]

In 2005, the American Journal of Public Health noted that workplaces where guns were allowed were five times as likely to have a workplace death as companies that forbid weapons. [Sara Murrah, *Guns in the Parking Lot: A Delicate Workplace Issue*, WSJ.com (Oct. 15, 2013)]

As of mid-2016, the states of Alabama, Alaska, Arizona, Florida, Georgia, Illinois, Indiana, Kansas, Kentucky, Louisiana, Maine, Minnesota, Mississippi, Nebraska, North Dakota, Oklahoma, Tennessee, Texas, Utah, and Wisconsin had "bring your gun to work" laws balancing employers' rights to control the presence of guns against employees' rights to carry licensed weapons. The typical statute obligates employers to allow employees to keep guns in their own vehicles in the parking lot but allows employers to forbid guns on the premises otherwise. [Terry L. Potter and Robert J. Rojas, *Workplace Gun Laws Result in Compliance and Safety Concerns for Employers*, Husch Blackwell LLP (Jan. 7, 2016), available at Lexology.com]

The Fifth Circuit held that a Mississippi employee could sue for wrongful termination after being fired for keeping a gun in his truck. The Fifth Circuit certified a question to the Mississippi Supreme Court, which responded that it is unlawful to fire someone for a reason that has been declared legally impermissible; in Mississippi, the guns-in-trunks law is an exception to employment at-will. However, the Mississippi Supreme Court also held that employers are not liable for incidents involving armed employees and third parties. [*Swindol v. Aurora Flight Sciences Corp.,* 197 So.3d 847 (Miss. 2016) and 832 F.3d 492 (5th Cir. 2016); see Robert Scavone Jr., Roland M. Juarez and Juan C. Enjamio, *Employer Prohibited from Terminating Employee for Storing Gun in Trunk in Mississippi,* Hunton & Williams LLP (Aug. 26, 2016), available at Lexology .com; FindLaw Employment Law News, *5th Cir.: Mississippi's Gun Laws Trump Company Policy* (Dec. 29, 2016), available at FindLaw.com]

Tennessee's 2013 statute was amended in April 2015. It provides that employers are not liable for violent acts committed by a person who stored a weapon in a car pursuant to the statute. [Phylinda Ramsey, *Tennessee's "Guns In Trunks" Law: What Employers Need to Know Now,* Constangy Brooks Smith & Prophete LLP (Aug. 27, 2015), available at Lexology.com]

The Utah Supreme Court has ruled that self-defense can serve a clear and substantial public policy, so an employee cannot be fired for defending him- or herself in a situation where the employee cannot withdraw from the encounter and reasonably believes that force is necessary to defend against an imminent threat of serious bodily harm. Therefore, Wal-Mart was wrong to fire five employees who violated company policy that requires disengaging, withdrawing, and calling the police. (The employees disarmed suspected shoplifters). The state supreme court answered a certified question from the District Court for the District of Utah; after the state ruling, the case was remanded to the district court for trial. [*Ray, et. al. v. Wal-Mart Stores, Inc.,* 2015 UT 83 (Sept. 17, 2015)]

§ 31.06 ERGONOMICS

Ergonomics is the study of the mutual adaptation between tools and the human body. Ergonomically efficient tools will reduce the number, or at least the degree, of injuries associated with tool use.

OSHA has made several attempts to impose ergonomic requirements on industry. This has been an extremely controversial quest. Congress's appropriation bills for OSHA between 1996 and 1998 actually forbade the agency to adopt ergonomics standards.

The Occupational Safety and Health Review Commission (OSHRC) issued an April 1997 decision that was the first declaration that the Secretary of Labor can properly cite ergonomic hazards under the general duty clause. [*Sec'y of Labor v. Pepperidge Farm Inc.,* 65 L.W. 2725 (OSHRC Apr. 26, 1997). See also *Reich v. Arcadian Corp.,* 110 F.3d 1192 (5th Cir. 1997)]

In March 2001, both Houses of Congress used a little-known federal statute called the Congressional Review Act of 1996 (CRA) to repeal the ergonomics regulations and prevent OSHA from enacting substantially similar regulations in the future. [See Steven Greenhouse, *House Joins Senate in Repealing Rules on Workplace Injuries*, N.Y. Times, Mar. 8, 2001, at A19] The statute was deployed once again in 2017 to eliminate a number of Obama-era regulations.

In 2011, DOL withdrew a proposal that would have required more logging of workplace musculoskeletal disorders. OSHA also withdrew another proposal re workplace noise that would have required installing noise-abating equipment. [Melanie Trottman, *Labor Department Withdraws Recordkeeping Proposal*, WSJ .com (Jan. 25, 2011)]

§ 31.07 VARIANCES

The OSH Act permits employers to petition for variances that will excuse them from having to comply with requirements that are particularly onerous. A variance can only be granted if employees will not be exposed to undue risk or danger.

The C.F.R. includes rules for "national security variances" and "experimental variances," but most of the variances granted are classified as either "temporary" or "permanent."

Grounds for a temporary variance are that the company will eventually comply with a new regulation, but cannot do so by its scheduled effective date because of a shortage of staff, materials, or equipment. (Being unable to afford to comply is not considered good cause for a variance.) A temporary variance lasts up to one year. It can be renewed twice, for up to 180 days at a time. The application must demonstrate that the employer is doing everything it can to comply as soon as possible, and that employees are being protected from undue hazards in the meantime.

A permanent variance is granted to an employer whose work methods are unconventional but still provide at least as much protection for employees as the OSHA regulations do. A company asking for a permanent variance can also apply for an interim variance.

The original plus six copies of the variance application and supporting documents must be filed. The documents must be signed by an authorized representative of the company, such as a corporate officer or the corporation's attorney.

Employees are entitled to notice of the variance application. They can ask that a hearing examiner conduct a hearing on the application.

Variance applications are reviewed, and then granted or denied, by the Assistant Secretary of Labor of Occupational Health and Safety in Washington. Anyone affected by a variance after it is granted can petition for modification or revocation of the order granting the variance. After a temporary variance ends, the employer can petition to have it renewed or extended.

§ 31.08 DIVISION OF RESPONSIBILITY

For OSHA purposes, companies are responsible for the safety of their "employees." A company that has all its work done by leased employees or independent contractors will not be subject to OSHA unless the arrangements are only a subterfuge to avoid liability. What counts is the economic reality of the work relationship, including the degree of control over the work, who signs the paycheck, and whether payment is a regular salary or a per-project amount. The power to change working conditions or fire the employee is considered especially significant. If several employers are involved (e.g., a temporary employment agency and its clients), OSHA responsibilities will be allocated based on actual job performance and working conditions. The basic rule is that the general contractor has primary OSHA responsibility for a construction worksite.

OSHA liability of general contractors can derive from several theories: the general contractor's agreement, in a construction project, to provide safety equipment; the general contractor's control over conditions when it is in charge of the site; the general contractor being the sole party with specialized knowledge to abate the hazards; and its actual knowledge of hazards (by observation or on notice from a subcontractor) that creates a duty to abate the hazards.

In doubtful cases, OSHA cites all possibly responsible parties and then allows them to make arguments why they are not liable. However, both a company that creates a hazard and the actual employer of the employees exposed to the hazard (and who were not protected by their employer) can be found liable.

OSHA uses a two-step test to see whether the Construction Standard should be applied to nonconstruction companies: ability to direct or control trade contractors, plus a high degree of involvement in the activities used in the project.

On August 25, 2014, OSHA and NIOSH jointly published guidance for staffing agencies and host employers about treatment of temporary workers. OSHA takes the position that the staffing agencies and host companies are joint employers of temporary employees. [Tressi L. Cordaro, *OSHA, NIOSH Release Recommended Practices for Protecting Temporary Workers*, Jackson Lewis PC (Aug. 26, 2014), available at Lexology.com]

Since its April 2013 announcement of an initiative to protect temporary workers, OSHA has published three guidance bulletins when staffing agency and host employer are joint employers. The more recent bulletins are about personal protective equipment and protection of whistleblowers. OSHA's position is that they are jointly responsible, and neither is exempt if the other party did not carry out its obligations. If PPE is necessary, the employer must provide the equipment and train employees and must make sure the PPE is in good condition. But OSHA says the staffing agency has to monitor the host employer's compliance and must assess potential hazards on an ongoing basis. The whistleblower bulletin says temporary workers are protected against retaliation by either the staffing agency or the host employer. If a host employer wants a temporary worker removed from its site for raising health or safety concerns or reporting an injury, the staffing firm can be liable for retaliation. Temporary workers can file an OSHA retaliation complaint against the staffing agency and/or host employer. [OSHA Temporary Worker Initiative Page, <https://www.osha.gov/temp_workers/index.html> (undated; last accessed Mar. 8, 2017)]

OSHA's temporary employee initiative, launched in 2013, treats temporary staffing agencies and host employers as sharing control. Therefore, they are jointly responsible for the safety and health of temporary workers, and both must comply with OSHA. OSHA's multi-employer worksite citation policy allows an employer to be cited for hazards affecting employees of other employers, if the cited employer created, controlled, or had the responsibility to correct the hazard. [Valerie Butera, *New NLRB Joint Employers Test—Why It Matters for OSHA*, Epstein Becker Green (Sept. 3, 2015), available at Lexology.com.]

Generally, in OSHA cases foreman's knowledge of a subordinate's safety violation is imputed to the employer. Some courts make an exception when the citation is caused by a safety violation committed by the foreman and the employer says he went rogue. In Quinlan, both foreman and subordinate engaged in unsafe work practices, by working on a 15-foot wall without fall protection. The Eleventh Circuit rejected the "rogue employee" argument. The supervisor disregarded the subordinate's violation, so knowledge was imputed to the employer. [*Quinlan v. Sec'y of Labor*, 812 F.3d 832 (11th Cir. 2016); see Stan Martin, *Foreman's Own Safety Violation Is Imputed to the Employer; Thus, OSHA Liability*, Commonsense Construction Law LLC (Jan. 23, 2016), available at Lexology.com. See also *Comtran Grp. v. DOL*, 722 F.3d 1304 (11th Cir. 2013): a supervisor's improper conduct is not automatically attributed to the employer, so the DOL must provide additional evidence of the employer's knowledge to make the employer liable. But in *Quinlan*, the supervisor failed to remedy breaches of safety rules that he observed personally.]

§ 31.09   OSHA ENFORCEMENT

[A]   Generally

Unlike ERISA enforcement (where federal jurisdiction preempts the state role), OSHA enforcement is coordinated between the states and the federal government. States have discretion to shape the degree of their occupational safety enforcement involvement. They can draft regulatory plans; if the Department of Labor believes the plan does enough to protect worker safety, it becomes an "approved state plan."

There are 28 states that have approved state OSH plans; in the rest of the states, federal OSHA regulates workplaces. The states and territories that have approved state plans are Alaska, Arizona, California, Connecticut, Hawaii, Illinois, Indiana, Iowa, Kentucky, Maine, Maryland, Michigan, Minnesota, Nevada, New Jersey, New Mexico, New York, North Carolina, Oregon, Puerto Rico, South

Carolina, Tennessee, Utah, Vermont, the Virgin Islands, Virginia, Washington, and Wyoming. However, in Connecticut, New York, and the Virgin Islands, the state plans cover only public employees, not those in the private sector. [The reports themselves are available at <http://www.osha.gov/dcsp/osp/efame/index.html> (last accessed Apr. 2, 2016). See <OSHA-approved state plans: <https://www .osha.gov/dcsp/osp/approved_state_plans.html> (undated, last accessed Mar. 8, 2017) for information about state plans in general.]

In states that do not have an approved state plan, OSHA has primary responsibility for safety enforcement. State governments, however, are allowed to regulate issues that the OSH Act does not cover (such as boiler and elevator safety) as well as broader safety issues (such as fire protection in buildings that are open to the public).

A multi-state company is not necessarily insulated from prosecution for citations in a state-plan state for conduct that occurred in a federal-plan state, and vice versa. Federal OSHA policy is that a state plan citation will not be used to impose a repeat citation. However, a citation in another federal-OSHA state might be. The federal OSHA field operations manual says that a state plan citation can be used as proof of the employer's knowledge of the hazard and the standard that was violated when the employer is cited for a willful federal violation. OSHA tries to negotiate an enterprise-wide settlement agreement to resolve large citations. Only 25 such agreements have been reached since OSHA was enacted in 1970, and 23 of them were made since January 1, 2010. [Travis W. Vance, *There's More Enforcement Overlap Between Federal OSHA and State Plans Than You Think*, Fisher & Phillips LLP (Nov. 17, 2015), available at Lexology.com]

One important function of state OSH agencies is offering free on-site consultations about how to maintain a safer workplace. The consultation is a simulated inspection, but the inspector is only authorized to point out problem areas and suggest solutions, not to issue citations or penalize the company. The consultation begins with an opening conference with the employer, proceeds to a walk-through and identification of safety problems, and ends with a closing conference about how to solve those problems.

[B]   Inspections

Inspections are a central part of OSHA's enforcement function, because direct evidence about workplace conditions is necessary.

A "programmed inspection" takes place on a routine basis, when workplaces are chosen at random from a list of sites with above-average injury rates.

Inspections can also be made based on written complaints from employees, former employees, or their representatives, such as attorneys and union staff. Complaints are made to OSHA's area director or Compliance Officer (CO). OSHA investigates the complaint and sends a copy of the complaint to the employer. (The complainant can request that his or her name be suppressed on the employer's copy.) Depending on the nature of the complaint, OSHA will either send the employer a letter describing the hazard that has been charged and giving a date for abatement, or schedule an inspection. The inspection probably will be scheduled if the employer ignores a letter from OSHA or if there is evidence of other safety problems.

OSHA is supposed to respond to a complaint of imminent danger within one day, to an allegation of a serious hazard within five working days, or within 30 working days if the complaint is less serious. A serious hazard is one that creates a reasonable expectation that it could cause death or irreversible bodily injury.

Generally speaking, OSHA inspections are made on an unannounced basis. However, the employer is entitled to notice if an imminently dangerous situation is alleged (because abatement is more important than detecting violations), if special arrangements are needed for the inspection, or if the inspection will be made outside normal business hours.

The CO shows credentials at the workplace and asks for permission to inspect. If permission is refused, the CO cannot perform a search without an administrative search warrant granted by a court, based on OSHA's showing that it has reason to believe that violations of the General Duty Clause or a more specific standard have occurred. However, courts need far less proof to authorize an administrative search than a search in a criminal case.

The employer is entitled to an opening conference before the inspection begins. This is the most important part of the inspection because it permits the employer to find out why the inspection has been scheduled and to negotiate to narrow the scope of the inspection and the ground rules for conducting it. Possible rules include submission of documents only on written request, and the inspector's agreement to move through the facility only when accompanied by a management escort.

A February 21, 2013 OSHA interpretation letter, known as the Fairfax memo (Fairfax was a deputy assistant secretary of labor) allows non-employee union organizers or community activists to represent employees during OSHA inspections of non-union workplaces. OSH Act § 8 permits a representative authorized by employees to accompany the compliance officer during an inspection. OSHA regulations (at § 1903.8(c)) state that the representative should be an employee— but, if the compliance officer finds good cause shown, the representative can be a non-employee such as a safety engineer or industrial hygienist who is reasonably necessary to a thorough and effective inspection in that he or she can make a positive contribution to the inspection. OSHA's On rare occasions, OSHA has used this provision to bring in outside safety experts to deal with complex situations. The interpretation letter allows the employee representative to participate in the walk-around, interview non-management employees, and participate in the informal settlement conference after citations are issued. If OSHA seeks a warrant, it must consult the Office of the Solicitor of Labor; the employer's attorney should confer with the Solicitor of Labor. Employers must grant access to OSHA compliance officers, but can deny access to third parties. If OSHA produces a warrant, the employer can move in district court to quash it. [Shontell Powell and Melissa A. Bailey, *How to Be Prepared If a Non-Employee Union Agent Shows Up with OSHA at an Inspection*, Ogletree Deakins (May 5, 2014), available at Lexology.com]

The National Federation of Independent Business (NFIB) sued in the District Court for the Northern District of Texas, objecting to the memo's effect of allowing union recruiters to enter workplaces where the employer does not want them. The plaintiffs said that the memo exceeds OSHA's statutory authority and violates the Administrative Procedure Act because the memo was not made available for public comment. OSHA moved to dismiss the case for lack of subject matter jurisdiction, arguing that the NFIB did not have standing because it did not have an injury in fact; that the memo was not a final agency action; and the NFIB did not need declaratory relief to get an adequate remedy. The district court held that the memo was a final agency action and, therefore, should have been published on notice and comment. However, the district court also held that the memo did not exceed OSHA's statutory authority because it was not inconsistent with the text of the OSH Act. [*NFIB v. Dougherty,* No. 3:16-CV-2568-D (N.D. Tex., pending); see Jordan Rodriguez, *Employers Earn an Important Victory in "Union Walk-Around" Lawsuit*, Kelley Drye & Warren LLP (Feb. 14, 2017), available at Lexology.com; Epstein Becker Green, *Labor Department Backs Away from Permitting Unions at OSHA Safety Inspections* (Feb. 17, 2017), available at Lexology.com]

On April 25, 2017, OSHA's Director of Enforcement Programs, Thomas Galassi, formally withdrew a similar letter written in 2013 to the United Steelworkers of America. Galassi said that only a certified or recognized union representing the workers is entitled to be present at workplace inspections. [Thomas Benjamin Huggett, *OSHA Rights Its Course: Only Authorized Union Agents and Employees Can Participate During OSHA Inspections*, Littler Mendelson PC (May 1, 2017), available at Lexology.com]

The employer has the right to take its own photographs of whatever the OSHA Compliance Officer (CO) photographs. After an inspection, plaintiffs' attorneys, unions, and competitors may make FOIA requests for the contents of OSHA inspection files, so the employer should inform OSHA of any materials that are trade secrets or confidential business information entitled to protection. [Eric J. Conn, *What Are Employers' Rights During OSHA Inspections?*, Epstein Becker Green (Oct. 10, 2013), available at Lexology.com]

Most employers grant permission, so the CO explains the procedure during the opening conference. Next is the "walk-through" (employer and employee representatives are allowed to comment). At this stage, the CO makes notes on any hazardous or noncompliant conditions prevailing in the workplace. At this point, the inspector often points out trivial violations that can be corrected on the spot: mopping up a pool of water that could cause a slip, for instance. At this stage, the CO usually asks to see the business's logs, summary reports, exposure records, training records, and other safety-related paperwork.

If the inspection is based on a complaint, the employer has the right to review the complaint, and can instruct the CO to limit the inspection to the issues raised by the complaint. The last part of the inspection is the "closing conference" when the CO reveals findings about potential OSHA violations.

COs do not have the power to issue citations during an inspection. The CO must return to the OSHA office and confer with the Area Director about the level of citation (if any) that should be issued in response to each perceived deficiency.

The procedure is slightly different in the construction industry. A "targeted inspection" is a short-form inspection that concentrates on the major hazards to construction workers' safety: falls, falling objects, electrical hazards, and vehicle accidents. The CO decides whether to do a focused or a full inspection during the opening conference. At sites where the general or prime contractor has a workable safety plan and designates a representative to work with OSHA, only a focused inspection will be performed. In contrast to a nonconstruction inspection, citations can be issued during a focused inspection if there are serious violations, or nonserious violations that are not abated immediately.

Tips for managing OSHA inspections include:

- Train managers how to respond, and whom to call (such as the company's in-house counsel).

- Draft scenarios for responding to accidents, fatalities, vehicle accidents, workplace violence, and natural disaster.

- Ask the OSHA inspector why he arrived; employers are entitled to be notified of complaints.

- Attempt to limit the inspection to the scope of the complaint (although the inspector has the power to broaden the inspection if employees inform them about hazards, or if the inspectors observe hazards).

- Can the inspector establish that any employees were exposed to the condition or reasonably might be expected to be exposed in the course of business? Can the inspector show that the employer knew or should have known of the hazard by exercising reasonable diligence?

- Employers have a duty to provide OSHA 300 Form and hazardous chemicals documentation promptly, but are entitled to a reasonable amount of time to produce other materials. Identify materials that you believe are privileged or are attorney work product.

- Do not volunteer self-audits, insurance documents, or reports from consultants unless your lawyer says they must be provided.

- Did you offer any training or instruction to employees that could reduce the level of citations?

- OSHA's definition of "supervisor" entitled to bind the company is broader than the NLRB or wage and hour definition; provide counsel or sit in with interviews with supervisors.

- If citations are issued, attend the informal conference, and contest any citation for which there is a reasonable argument. [Howard A. Mavity, *How To Manage an OSHA Inspection*, Fisher & Phillips LLP (Nov. 5, 2013), available at Lexology.com]

■ **TIP:** A labor lawyer wrote that when he audits a facility to prepare its defense in an OSHA case, he looks at housekeeping: dirt and sloppiness imply compliance problems. If an OSHA inspector sees a dirty facility, he will take a closer look at lockout/tagout issues and handling of hazardous chemicals; failure to clean up suggests that exits are not kept clear and trip hazards are not removed either. [Howard A. Mavity, *When I Go Into a Workplace, the First Thing I Consider Is Housekeeping*, Fisher & Phillips LLP (Oct. 2, 2013), available at Lexology.com]

[C] Whistleblowers

OSHA is responsible for receiving and processing whistleblower complaints charging violations of a number of environmental statutes in addition to the OSH Act. [See Final Regulation, 69 Fed. Reg. 52,103 (Aug. 24, 2004)]

OSHA issued a new Whistleblower Investigation Manual in early 2016. The manual applies the standard of reasonable cause to believe a violation occurred, rather than the higher preponderance of the evidence standard that applies at hearings. The reasonable cause standard (that a reasonable finder of fact could rule in favor of the complainant) applies to all elements of a violation. [<https://www.osha.gov/OshDoc/Directive_pdf/CPL_02-03-007.pdf> (last accessed Mar. 8, 2017); see Matthew M. Linton, *OSHA Issues New Whistleblower Guidance*, Holland & Hart LLP (Feb. 8, 2016), available at Lexology.com]

OSHA issued a final rule (effective March 5, 2015) about whistleblower claims under Corporate Fraud Accountability Act § 806 (part of the Sarbanes-Oxley Act), implementing the Dodd-Frank Act's 180-day statute of limitations for filing a retaliation complaint. Even if a prima facie case is made out (the complainant shows that protected activity contributed to the adverse action), OSHA will not investigate if the employer provides clear and convincing evidence that it would have taken the action even without protected activity. After the investigation, OSHA issues a preliminary order, which the parties can object to. It can be reviewed by an ALJ, the ALJ by the Administrative Review Board, and judicial review is available for ARB final order. [80 Fed. Reg. 11865 (Mar. 5, 2015)] Be aware that the Trump administration seeks to modify or repeal the Dodd-Frank Act, so this rule may change in the future.

The Eighth Circuit held that the Sarbanes-Oxley Act only protects whistle-blowers if a reasonable person, with the same position, training, and experience, would believe that there was a reportable violation of securities law. The Eighth Circuit found that the would-be whistleblower should have known that changes in the company's reporting of revenue, which had a tiny impact on the company's financial results, were not reportable to the SEC, so he was not entitled to whistleblower protection. [*Beacom v. Oracle*, No. 825 F.3d 376 (8th Cir. 2016); see FindLaw Employment Law blog, *8th Cir. Adopts "Reasonable Employee" Standard for SOX Whistleblowing Claims* (June 21, 2016), available at FindLaw .com]

The Second Circuit held that it was lawful to fire an employee for refusing to participate in an internal investigation of an alleged bid-rigging conspiracy: refusal to obey a direct, unequivocal, reasonable order is just cause for termination. [*Gilman v. Marsh & McLennan Co., Inc.*, No. 15-0603 (2d Cir. June 16, 2016)]

As one might guess, it is imprudent to fire a person who reports safety hazards, especially if the firing occurs within days after OSHA issues penalties and citations for those violations after an inspection triggered by an employee complaint. The District Court for the District of Idaho ordered an employer to pay $979 in lost wages plus $100,000 punitive damages. The employee, Kramer, warned the employer about numerous dangerous conditions, including shock hazards from exposed wiring, fall hazards from open service bays, and lack of protective and first aid equipment, but the employer did not remediate the conditions. [*Perez v. Sandpoint Gas N Go & Lube Ctr.*, No.2:14-cv-357, 2015 U.S. Dist. LEXIS 178214 (D. Idaho Sept. 29, 2015)]

The OSHA Fact Sheet, *Your Rights as a Whistleblower*, requires complaints to be filed in writing or by telephone. For most statutes (the OSH Act, Clean Air Act, CERCLA, Federal Water Pollution Control Act, Safe Drinking Water Act, Solid Waste Disposal Act, and Toxic Substances Control Act), the complaint must be filed within 30 days of the incident. However, longer reporting periods are permitted for the International Safe Container Act (60 days), Asbestos Hazard Emergency Response Act and Sarbanes-Oxley Act (90 days) and 180 days under the Surface Transportation Assistance Act, Energy Reorganization Act, and Pipeline Safety Improvement Act. In general, if the state has a state OSH plan, retaliation complaints are supposed to be filed with the state agency, although dual filing with OSHA is acceptable. [OSHA, *Your Rights as a Whistleblower,* <https://www.osha.gov/OshDoc/data_General_Facts/whistleblower_rights.pdf> (Feb. 2013) (last accessed Mar. 8, 2017).]

In September 2016, OSHA revised its Whistleblower Investigations Manual and provided new guidance on how to settle whistleblower cases. A settlement agreement cannot be approved if it contains provisions that discourage future disclosures or forbids contact with the government. (The SEC also took a similar position.) Nor will OSHA approve a waiver of an employee's right to money awards, or provisions that require employees to notify the employer or ex-employer of contact with the government, or that require employees to share whistleblower rewards with the employer. OSHA will not approve a settlement agreement that imposes liquidated damages that are clearly disproportionate to the anticipated loss if a breach occurs. [<https://www.osha.gov/OshDoc/Directive_pdf/CPL_02-03-005.pdf>, see FindLaw Employment Law News, *OSHA Takes a Harder Tack on Whistleblower Settlement Agreements* (Oct. 4, 2016), available at FindLaw.com; Laura M. Fant and Harris M. Mufson, *OSHA Issues New Guidance Regarding Whistleblower Settlements*, Proskauer Rose LLP (Sept. 19, 2016), available at Lexology.com]

OSHA started a four-year pilot program in mid-2016, in the Kansas City region. It is known as W-SVEP, the Whistleblower Severe Violators Enforcement Program, targeting employers that have multiple severe whistleblower violations. [Fisher & Phillips LLP, *OSHA Rolls Out a New Severe Violators Enforcement Program, but for Whistleblower and Not Safety Violations* (June 5, 2016), available at Lexology.com; Lewis M. Csedrik, *OSHA Announces New Enforcement Program for Whistleblower Cases,* Morgan Lewis & Bockius LLP (June 22, 2016), available at Lexology.com]

In addition to hard-copy filings, OSHA solicited public comments on its proposal for online submission of retaliation complaints, then launched the form without final rulemaking or discussion of comments. The 30-section Notice of Whistleblower Complaint form can be used for electronic submission of complaints. [<https://www.osha.gov/whistleblower/WBComplaint.html> (revised Jan. 2013, expires Mar. 31, 2017) (last viewed Mar. 8, 2017)]

OSHA's online complaint form for retaliation cases collects information about the complainant and the complainant's employer; asks the complainant to describe the protected activity, how management learned about it, and what retaliatory action was taken. [William Walden, *OSHA Online Retaliation Complaint Form Is Live and Freely Available*, Quarles & Brady LLP Labor & Employment Law Update (Dec. 2013) (benefitslink.com)]

On October 12, 2016, OSHA published a final rule about handling claims of Patient Protection and Affordable Care Act (PPACA) retaliation, but these provisions could become moot if PPACA is eventually repealed or significantly amended. The OSHA rules call for OSHA to notify the employer of complaints against it; the employer has 20 days to submit a written position statement and/or seek a meeting with OSHA. To succeed, a PPACA retaliation complaint must make a prima facie case that protected activity was a contributing factor to the adverse action charged by the plaintiff. If OSHA upholds the complaint, it can award relief such as back pay, reinstatement, and restoration of benefits. [81 Fed. Reg. 70607 (Oct. 13, 2016); see Taylor E. White, *OSHA Issues Final Rule Regarding Retaliation Claims Under the Affordable Care Act* (Oct. 13, 2016), available at Lexology.com]

After operating an ADR pilot project in two regions in 2012 and 2013, OSHA concluded that the early resolution process is effective in streamlining disputes and reaching settlements. Therefore, on August 18, 2015, ADR was made available in all regions, covering all 22 statutes administered by the agency. OSHA issued procedures in mid-2015 for using OSHA's regional ADR program to resolve whistleblower disputes. Parties can have a neutral OSHA representative with experience in whistleblower investigations help them negotiate a settlement. The Administrative Dispute Resolution Act requires all federal agencies to have an ADR policy for resolving disputes and case management. [<http://www.osha.gov/OshDoc/Directive_pdf/CPL_02-03-006.pdf> (last accessed Mar. 8, 2017)]

OSHA announced an award of almost $1 million in damages ($243,916 back wages, $110,000 compensatory damages, $600,000 punitive damages) plus reinstatement for a foreman and two truck drivers. The three were fired in retaliation for filing OSHA complaints that they were required to violate the Department of Transportation's maximum hours for commercial truck drivers. [Ada W. Dolph and Craig B. Simonsen, *OSHA Orders Asphalt Paving Company to Pay Nearly $1 Million and Reinstate Foreman and Two Drivers in Whistleblower Complaints*, Seyfarth Shaw LLP (Sept. 3, 2014), available at Lexology.com]

§ 31.10 OSHA CITATIONS

[A] Categories of Violations

The CO's comments during an inspection are not official OSHA pronouncements, and the employer cannot be penalized for failing to respond to them. However, penalties can be imposed for failure to respond to a written citation from the OSHA Area Director that is sent within six months after the date of the alleged violation that is cited. The citation form lists the violations, classified by seriousness, imposes penalties, and sets a date for abating each violation. Usually, the citation will be Form OSHA-2, sent by certified mail, although other forms can be used.

OSHA violations are generally divided into four categories: de minimis (trivial), nonserious, serious, and other. Penalties are heavier on willful violations or repeat violations within a three-year period. Criminal penalties might be imposed in the very worst cases, such as the preventable death of an employee.

In 2000, OSHA announced that it would not issue citations based on an employer's own voluntary safety and health audit (although the agency has the power to request internal audit reports). OSHRC ruled in mid-2013 that OSHA intentionally violated this policy by making heavy use of an employer's audit reports to identify issues on which the employer was cited. OSHA used a voluntary audit commissioned by the employer from a third-party safety consultant. Although OSHA violated its own policy, the OSHA ALJ would not vacate the citation of violations self-identified by the employer in the report. [*Sec'y of Labor v. BP Prods. N. Am. Inc.* (OSHRC 2013)]

Most state Worker's Compensation rules hold that an employer is not immune from liability for intentional torts. The District Court for the Eastern District of Louisiana held in early 2017 that an OSHA willful violation citation does not prove that the employer consciously intended the injuries to occur. An employer was cited for multiple OSHA violations, some willful, when employees were overcome by fumes when they were assigned to clean a rail car containing hazardous chemicals. In 2016, Washington and Kentucky also held that an OSHA citation for willful violation does not remove Worker's Compensation immunity, but an Idaho district court allowed employees to pursue tort claims against their employer when they were sent to retrieve radioactive plates without proper PPE. [*Hernandez v. Dedicated TCS, LLC*, Civil Action No. 16-3621 SECTION: "E"(5), 2017 U.S. Dist. LEXIS 30260 (E.D. La. Mar. 3, 2017); see Steven M. Siros, *OSHA Violation Doesn't Abrogate Workers' Compensation Immunity*, Jenner & Block LLP (Mar. 8, 2017), available at Lexology.com]

[B] Penalties

Penalties are set under OSHA § 17 (29 U.S.C. § 666).

It's hard to predict what penalty will be imposed for any particular OSHA violation, because the penalty is set within a framework provided by the statute and regulations. There are many factors involved, primarily the gravity of the violation. However, the size of the business, the employer's past history of violations, and whether or not the employer acted in good faith are all important considerations. Both aggravating and mitigating factors can be applied to set the final amount of the penalty.

The schedule of penalties remained unchanged between 1990 (under OBRA '90, Pub. L. No. 101-508) and 2015. In 2015, the Bipartisan Budget Act (BBA) of 2015, Pub. L. No. 114-74, § 701 ordered OSHA to join other federal agencies in indexing its penalty levels each year to reflect inflation, as required by the Federal Civil Penalties Inflation Adjustment Act of 1990, Pub. L. No. 101-410. The BBA requires the increases to take effect no later than August 1, 2016. The BBA also requires OSHA to impose a one-time "catch-up" increase to make up for the long period without increases, but the increase must not exceed the rate of inflation during the gap period. One reason it took so long to update the penalty schedule is that the Debt Collection Improvement Act of 1996, Pub. L. No. 104-134 requires agencies to adopt regulations that adjust penalties to reflect inflation, but it exempts OSHA penalties from automatic increases. The BBA eliminates this exemption. Although the BBA increases apply only to states under federal OSHA jurisdiction, states with state plans will probably mandate similar increases. [Alexander J. Bandza, *OSHA Penalty Limits to Increase Almost 80% in the Next Year, with Annual Inflation Adjustments Authorized Thereafter*, Jenner & Block (Nov. 3, 2015), available at Lexology.com; Howard A. Mavity, *The*

November Surprise: OSHA Raises Penalties 82% and No One Notices, Fisher & Phillips LLP (Nov. 4, 2015), available at Lexology.com]

In mid-2016, OSHA announced that maximum penalties for other-than-serious or serious violations or failure to correct violations would rise from $7,000 to $12,471; repeat violations can be penalized by up to $124,709, not $70,000—and the minimum penalty is $8,908 (rather than $5,000). The maximum penalty for a posting violation is $12,471. DOL's position is that, to remain "as effective as" federal OSHA, states must adopt the same penalty increases. [John F. Martin, *OSHA Officially Increases Civil Penalties by 78 Percent*, Ogletree Deakins (July 1, 2016), available at Lexology.com]

Annual adjustments are now mandatory and the 2017 figures, about 1% higher than their 2016 counterparts, are $12,675 for posting, other than serious, or serious violations; $12,675 for failure to abate a violation; and a very broad range of $9,054 to $126,749 for willful or repeated violations: see 82 Fed. Reg. 8813 (Jan. 13, 2017). These amounts apply to penalties assessed after January 13, 2017. [Tressi L. Cordaro, *OSHA Penalties Go Up . . . Yes, Again*, Jackson Lewis PC (Jan. 18, 2017), available at Lexology.com]

State-plan OSHA penalties, in the states that have state plans that cover private-sector workers (some state plans are limited to public sector workers) can be significant. Since June 2015, nine states have imposed a total of approximately $6.1 million in six-figure penalties against 21 companies. For example, Illinois imposed $2.2 million in penalties on three construction firms and a railcar services company. One of the penalties was close to $1.8 million. A foundry in Michigan was fined $638,450. [Carla J. Gunnin, *State OSHA Programs Can Be Significant Source of Big Fines*, Jackson Lewis PC (Nov. 6, 2015), available at Lexology.com]

Civil penalties are payable to the Secretary of Labor for deposit into the U.S. Treasury; the United States can bring suit to recover penalties. The proper court is the district court for the district in which the violation is alleged to have happened, or where the employer is headquartered.

Failure-to-abate penalties are applied when a cited violation becomes a final order, and the employer fails to correct the violation.

The "unit of prosecution" issue is how many charges should be filed for multiple similar violations. The OSHA regulations were amended in 2008 to provide that failure to provide respirators or workplace training is considered a separate violation for everyemployee who was not trained or who did not receive a respirator. [29 C.F.R § 1910.9(a) and (b)] Thirty-three other standards were also amended the same way. The regulations were amended in response to *Chao v. OSHRC*, 401 F.3d 355 (5th Cir. 2005), which held that failing to train eleven employees, and to provide them with respirators, constituted two violations, not 22 (eleven respirator, eleven training). The amendment was challenged by three trade associations that claimed the Secretary did not have authority to issue the amendments, because OSHRC is the only body that has the jurisdiction to set units of prosecution. In 2010, the D.C. Circuit rejected this argument, because setting the unit of prosecution is up to the legislatures, not the courts, and the Secretary of Labor is Congress' stand-in for these matters. [*National Ass'n of Home Builders v. OSHA*, 602 F.3d 464 (D.C. Cir. 2010). For the 2008 amendments, see 73 Fed. Reg. 75568 and 75583 (Dec. 12, 2008).]

In 2011, OSHRC accepted the DOL's argument that failure to keep proper records can be treated as a continuing violation of OSHA's five-year record retention requirement. Therefore, penalties could be imposed for violations that occurred over four years before OSHA issued a citation, whereas the construction company defendant argued that OSHA had only six months to bring charges. In addition to the initial failure to log employees' injuries and illnesses as they occurred, OSHRC ruled that AKM LLC failed to meet its obligations to retain the records for five years. [*Secretary of Labor v. AKM LLC d/b/a Volks Constructors*, OSHRC No. 06-1990, 2011 WL 896347 (OSHRC Mar. 11, 2011)]

The following year, however, the D.C. Circuit reversed. The statute of limitations is six months after the "occurrence of any violation." OSHA treated it as a continuing violation. The D.C. Circuit rejected this theory, pointing out that there were separate violations, although it left open the possibility of tolling for a true ongoing violation such as requiring workers to use unsafe equipment [*Sec'y of Labor v. AKM LLC d/b/a Volks Constructors*, 675 F.3d 752 (D.C. Cir. 2012)]

OSHA adopted a rule to work around the D.C. Circuit's opinion. Regulations published in mid-2015 propose to amend the recordkeeping requirements to make the duty to make and maintain records of injuries and illnesses an ongoing obligation that continues for five years after the record should have been made. Therefore, OSHA can cite employers for recordkeeping violations for up to six months after the end of the five-year record retention period. [80 Fed. Reg. 45116 (July 29, 2015)]

Asserting that it merely clarified its 40-year-old policy, OSHA published a rule on December 16, 2016, imposing a continuing obligation to make/keep records of each recordable injury and illness. Logs, reports, and annual summaries must be retained for five years, and this information must be made available to employees. Citations for failure to record injuries properly can lead to a citation for up to the entire five-year record retention period. [Michael T. Taylor and Darren A. Crook, *OSHA Announces Rule Clarifying Workplace Injury Reporting That Imposes "Continuing Obligation" on Employers to Maintain Injury Records for Five Years*, Baker & Hostetler LLP (Dec. 20, 2016), available at Lexology .com; George M. Macchia, *OSHA Amends Its Rule Requiring Employers to Keep and Maintain Records of Recordable Injuries and Illnesses for Five Years*, Epstein Becker Green (Jan. 11, 2017), available at Lexology.com]

Congress invoked the Congressional Review Act to reverse this OSHA action, on the grounds that it was improper for OSHA to change its regulations to avoid the *Volks* ruling; the proper tactic would have been seeking en banc rehearing. H.J. Res. 83 was passed by the House on March 1, 2017, by the Senate on

March 22, and was signed by the President on April 3, 2017. Tressi L. Cordaro, *OSHA's Volks Rule Overturned by Congressional Review Act*, Jackson Lewis PC (Mar. 22, 2017), available at Lexology.com]; Louis Schotemeyer, *President Trump Nullifies "Volks Rule" Regarding Occupational Safety and Health Administration (OSHA) Recordkeeping Requirements*, Newmeyer & Dillion LLP (Apr. 18, 2017), available at Lexology.com]

At the end of 2016, the Fifth Circuit vacated OSHA citations against an oil refinery, because they were issued more than six months after the occurrence. The Fifth Circuit said that they were not continuing violations even though the company did not address the findings of the OSHA analyses. Continuing violations toll the statute of limitations in only two situations: when conduct (e.g., ongoing harassment that creates a hostile work environment through its cumulative nature) does not become a violation until it is repeated within the limitations period; or if the law imposes a continuing obligation to act or refrain from doing something. The Fifth Circuit held that the regulations did not impose a continuing obligation for employers to address OSHA findings. [*Delek Refining Ltd. v. OSHRC*, No. 15-60433 (5th Cir. Dec. 29, 2016); see Ronald A. Sarachan and Kathryn P. Bullard, *Fifth Circuit Enforces Six-Month Statute of Limitations in OSHA Violations Case*, Drinker Biddle & Reath LLP (Jan. 17, 2017), available at Lexology.com]

The Severe Violator Enforcement Program (SVEP) is designed to bring recidivists back into compliance, using serious punitive elements such as issuing press releases describing the company as a severe violator; including it in the Severe Violator Log; re-inspecting the violator's facilities and inspecting other facilities within the same corporate enterprise; and requiring additional terms in settlements with the company. A company can be released from the program (at the discretion of the OSHA regional administrator) by paying all final civil penalties, completing all abatement required by the citations or settlement, addressing any other settlement terms, and completing three full calendar years after final disposition without any related serious violations. [Eric J. Conn, *5 Questions We Would Ask OSHA About the Severe Violator Enforcement Program (SVEP)*, Epstein Becker Green (Oct. 23, 2013), available at Lexology.com] But employers that fail to abate all hazards, pay all penalties, and otherwise comply with settlements remain in SVEP for three years and then are re-evaluated. [Henry Chajet and Mark Savit, *OSHA Says SVEP Is A Success*, Jackson Lewis LLP (Nov. 11, 2013), available at Lexology.com]

As of March 2015, SVEP had handled 474 cases—about 25% of them involving fatalities. About 60% of SVEP cases are in construction. [Tressi L. Cordaro, *Recent OSHA Inspection Statistics and Enforcement Initiatives*, Jackson Lewis PC (Mar. 23, 2015), available at Lexology.com]

The number of SVEP sites added in 2014 was 23% greater than in 2013. As of July 1, 2014, 423 sites were listed; the 2013 figure was 343. An employer can be placed in the program because of two or more willful, failure to abate, or repeat citations dealing with major hazards such as falls and exposure to lead or combustible dust. A company can also be listed if there is a fatality or accident that causes at least three workers to be hospitalized, if the inspection uncovers at least one willful, repeat, or failure-to-abate violation. An egregious violator can also be listed. [Bradford T. Hammock, Henry Chajet, and Mark Savit, *More Sites Added to OSHA's Severe Violator Enforcement Program*, Jackson Lewis PC (Aug. 4, 2014), available at Lexology.com]

A second program, the W-SVEP, was launched in 2016 to deter retaliation against employees who act as whistleblowers under any of the 22 statutes enforced by OSHA. If it is found that the employer retaliated against a whistleblower who reported a death or egregious safety and health violations, or if the employer was the subject of three or more whistleblower cases in a three-year period, the employer will be placed on the W-SVEP Log, a public watch list, and OSHA will issue a press release about the employer's record. An employer can be removed from the log if it prevails in a whistleblower case; or, after it has been on the log for three years, it can ask for a follow-up inspection to be removed from the log. [Lewis M. Csedrik, *OSHA Announces New Enforcement Program for Whistleblower Cases*, Morgan Lewis & Bockius LLP (June 22, 2016), available at Lexology.com]

OSHA criminal prosecutions are extremely rare, even in cases of obvious disregard of worker safety. The OSH Act allows criminal charges in three kinds of cases: a willful violation of a standard, leading to an employee's death; giving advance warning of an OSHA inspection; or falsification of documents. In 2013, there were only three criminal referrals. In late 2015, the Departments of Labor and Justice entered into a Memorandum of Understanding (MOU) for better coordination of the agencies' efforts to ensure workplace safety. The MOU covers not only OSHA but the Mine Safety and Health Act and the Migrant and Seasonal Agricultural Worker Protection Act. In addition to the three categories of OSHA crimes, the DOJ could bring charges such as conspiracy and witness tampering. The MOU transfers DOJ's criminal enforcement of OSHA from the fraud section of the criminal division (which has limited legal resources) to the environmental crimes section of the environment/natural resources division, which has far more investigators and attorneys. [Taylor E. White, *OSHA's Stronger Enforcement Options in 2016*, Gardere (Feb. 18, 2016), available at Lexology.com; Sidley Austin LLP, *DOJ And DOL Expand Criminal Worker Endangerment Initiative* (Jan. 20, 2016), available at Lexology.com]

Although Worker's Compensation exclusivity (see § 33.03) bars most suits for workplace injuries, the OSH Act makes criminal penalties available when the cause of an employee's death is directly related to willful violations of safety and health regulations. Federal penalties are up to six months in jail or a fine of up to $250,000 for an individual and/or $500,000 for a corporation. The OSH Act only imposes criminal penalties if there is a fatality, and seldom does this. Since the OSH Act was adopted in 1970, there have been over 400,000 workplace fatalities, but only 88 criminal prosecutions up through 2015. [Daniel A. Kaplan, *One of Our Employees Died at Work—Am I Going to Jail?*, Foley & Lardner LLP (Feb. 27, 2017), available at Lexology.com]

Donald L. Blankenship, former CEO of Massey Energy Co. was convicted in December 2015 on one misdemeanor count of conspiracy to violate federal mine safety laws in connection with an April 2010 mine explosion that killed 29 miners. He was acquitted on more serious charges of lying to the SEC and investors. In April 2016, he was sentenced to 12 months in prison, the maximum penalty for the charge. Blankenship is believed to be first CEO of a major corporation to be convicted of safety charges after a fatal industrial accident. Three other ex-managers at Massey were imprisoned for lying to investigators and conspiring to violate safety laws. [Kris Maher, *Former Massey Energy CEO Sentenced to 12 Months in Prison*, WSJ.com (Apr. 6, 2016)]

An employee died in 2009 when he was struck on the head by a twelve-pound piece that flew off an unguarded lathe. At one time, the lathe had guards but the employer removed them. OSHA issued seven violations and imposed a fine of $70,000 for each of them. The employer appealed, asserting that OSHA applied a novel and unreasonable interpretation. The Eighth Circuit held that the agency's view was entitled to deference because it comported with the plain language of the statute, and it is not per se unreasonable for an agency to change its regulatory interpretation. However, the Eighth Circuit re-heard the case en banc in late 2015, and held that OSHA is only entitled to deference if both its interpretation and the announcement of the interpretation are reasonable, faithful to the text of the regulation, consistent with prior interpretations, and do not subject parties to unfair surprises. [*Perez v. Loren Cook Co.*, 750 F.3d 1006 (8th Cir. 2014), 803 F.3d 935 (8th Cir. 2015)]

A Houston jury awarded $54 million in early 2016 to the family of a man killed building a stadium. He used a loader with a 2,700-pound carrying capacity to hold a 3,340-pound concrete section while another worker cut it. The excess weight caused the loader to gall over the side of the stadium and the decedent, Garcia, fell about four stories. OSHA had issued two willful citations (a $56,000 citation for exceeding the loader's capacity; another contractor was penalized $63,000 for exposing workers to the risk of being struck by the skid-steer loader). The jury did not even know about the citations when it rendered the award. [Howard A. Mavity, *Startlingly Large Verdict Reminds Employers of the Perils of Workplace Safety Failings*, Fisher & Phillips LLP (Feb. 16, 2016), available at Lexology.com]

Harco Construction LLC was convicted of manslaughter, criminally negligent homicide, and reckless endangerment in June 2016 for the death of 22-year-old worker who died when a trench collapsed. Harco was fined the maximum penalty for a corporation found guilty of a felony in New York—which is only $10,000. [Corinne Ramey, *Construction Company Convicted of Manslaughter Fined $10,000*, WSJ.com (Dec. 20, 2016)]

The Department of Justice announced that scrap processor Behr Iron & Steel Inc. was sentenced to five years' probation and ordered to pay $350,000 restitution to the estate of a dead employee. The company had already been fined $520,000 in a related OSHA case. Employees were required to clean a pit every day to remove scrap from a shredding machine. The employee died when his arm was caught by an unguarded conveyor belt. The employer conceded that the belt did not have guards or an emergency shut-off, and employees were not adequately trained. [Andrew S. Boutros, Benjamin D. Briggs and Craig B. Simonsen, *Scrap Processor Sentenced on OSHA Criminal Violation Causing Death of Employee*, Seyfarth Shaw LLP (July 14, 2016), available at Lexology.com]

It does not constitute double jeopardy to impose administrative penalties on an employer after it has been convicted of criminal OSHA violations because the administrative penalties are clearly civil and cannot result in imprisonment. [*S.A. Healy Co. v. OSHRC*, 138 F.3d 686 (7th Cir. 1998)]

§ 31.11   OSHA APPEALS

Employers don't have to agree with an OSHA citation. There are several administrative steps that can be taken to protest—although these administrative remedies do have to be exhausted before filing suit.

If an employer challenges a citation, OSHA has to prove that the employer failed to live up to some applicable standard. The agency also has to prove that feasible corrective measures existed that could have brought the employer into compliance. If the standard has a time element (for example, the noise exposure standard does), then OSHA also has to prove that the condition existed long enough and intensely enough to constitute a violation.

OSHA has to prove that the employer knew about the condition or could have become aware by exercising due diligence. It is not necessary to prove that the employer was aware of the standard and deliberately chose to violate it. A supervisor's or foreman's knowledge will be attributed to the employer, unless the employer maintained work rules that satisfied the OSHA standard, communicated those rules to employees, and enforced the work rules.

OSHA is entitled to prove the employer's knowledge (and therefore does not have to prove actual knowledge) in some situations:

- Another employee has already been injured by the same hazardous conditions;

- Several written employee complaints have already been made to OSHA;

- The employer knows that employees habitually omit safety equipment, or otherwise allow hazardous conditions to be present in the workplace;

- The employer doesn't provide enough training;

- The employer doesn't enforce its own safety rules;

- The hazards would easily have been discovered if the employer had performed an adequate inspection.

An employer that receives an OSHA citation has 15 days to file a Notice of Contest, disputing that there was a violation, demanding a fair period of time to abate the violation, or challenging the size of the penalty. If the employer is not sure whether or not to contest, it can schedule an informal conference with the OSHA area director to discuss OSHA's position on workplace conditions and how to improve them. The 15-day limit is strictly applied: OSHRC does not have jurisdiction to review a notice of contest filed after the 15-day period expires. [*Chao v. Russell P. LeFrois Builder, Inc.*, 291 F.3d 219 (2d Cir. 2002)]

There is no official form for the Notice of Contest; it is simply a letter stating in plain English that the employer disagrees with the citation and wants to contest some or all of the violations, to ask for a smaller penalty, and/or ask for more time to comply. If the Notice of Contest is not filed within the required 15 days, the citation becomes final, and no court has the power to reverse it or even to review it.

■ **TIP:**   If an employer appeals in bad faith, knowing that the citation is valid, the whole period of time until the challenge is resolved is treated as a period of noncompliance, with additional penalties for each day.

The potential financial impact of an OSHA citation on a business determines the amount of resources needed to defend it. The effect of OSHA citations on collateral litigation (such as Worker's Compensation and wrongful death cases) and other regulatory inspections (e.g., EPA inspections of chemical plants, which use the OSHA inspection as a road map) must be considered. The company must consider whether there is a risk of repeat OSHA citations. If the violation is described as willful, there is a risk of punitive damages in other litigation. Note that bid documents for competitive bidding often ask if there were any willful, repeat, or serious safety violations in the past three years, so it might be worth contesting the citations to avoid ripple effects. [Mark S. Dreux, *Properly Evaluating an OSHA Citation: Should You Contest the Citation?*, Arent Fox LLP (Sept. 27, 2013), available at Lexology.com]

The Obama administration issued an Executive Order, the Fair Pay and Safe Workplaces Order, a presidential Executive Order, in mid-2014. It required applicants for federal contracts over $500,000 to disclose any violation of various federal statutes in the three-year period before the bid; OSHA is one of the statutes covered by the order. [Executive Order 13673, *Fair Pay and Safe Workplaces*, <http://www.whitehouse.gov/the-press-office/2014/07/31/executive-order-fair-pay-and-safe-workplaces> (July 31, 2014)]

The District Court for the Eastern District of Texas preliminarily enjoined the application of the rule and a related Department of Defense rule, finding that this "blacklisting" rule was arbitrary and capricious because companies could be debarred from government contracting based on government actions that did not involve a final adjudication of wrongdoing. [*Associated Builders & Contractors, et al. v. Rung*, Civil Action No. 1:16-CV-425, 2016 U.S. Dist. LEXIS 155232; 167 Lab. Cas. (CCH) P36,481 (E.D. Tex. Oct. 24, 2016); see Roger V. Abbott, *Federal Court Repudiates the Most Significant Provisions of the New DOL Rules*, Mayer Brown LLP (Oct. 27, 2016), available at Lexology.com]

Not only was the rule enjoined by the court system, but Congress used the Congressional Review Act, 5 U.S.C. §§ 801–808, to eliminate the "blacklisting" rule. After President Trump's inauguration, OSHA withdrew the memorandum, and the case was voluntarily dismissed on April 27, 2017. The CRA was enacted in 1996, as part of the Small Business Regulatory Fairness Act. Congress has the authority to pass joint resolutions to reject any rule adopted within 60 legislative days earlier. Passage and signing of a resolution nullifies the regulation, and any of its provisions already in effect are nullified. In practical terms, the CRA is seldom used because if the president and Congress are of the same party, they probably would not want to reverse their own administration's order. However, many Obama-era regulations were vulnerable. [Richard W. Arnholt, *Congress Acts to Rescind the Already-Enjoined Fair Pay and Safe Workplaces Regulation and Other Last-Minute Obama Administration Rules,* Bass, Berry & Sims PLC (Feb. 6, 2017), available at Lexology.com]

When a Notice of Contest is filed, an OSHA Administrative Law Judge (ALJ) will set a date for a hearing. Although the hearing is informal, it is still governed by the Federal Rules of Evidence. The ALJ's decision becomes final 30 days after it is rendered, unless it is contested.

All Notices of Contest, and all ALJ decisions, are automatically passed along to the Occupational Safety and Health Review Commission (OSHRC). OSHRC has the power to order review of part or all of an ALJ decision. The employer, or any other party adversely affected by the decision, can file a Petition for Discretionary Review. Although it has the power to raise the level of a violation, OSHRC usually doesn't do so.

The employer can raise many arguments to OSHRC:

- The CO got the facts wrong;

- The employer did not know, and had no duty to know, that the violation had occurred;

- The inspection itself was improper—for example, the inspection was really a search, requiring a warrant that had not been obtained;

- OSHA applied the wrong standard;

- The standard itself was invalid, because it was not properly promulgated, or was so vague that employers could not reasonably be expected to understand and comply with it;

- The real cause of the violation was misconduct by employees, beyond the employer's control; this misconduct is unlikely to recur;

- Complying with the OSHA requirement actually increased the hazards to employees rather than decreasing them, but the employer was unable to get a variance.

OSHRC issues an order after considering the employer's arguments and defenses. The employer has 60 days from the date of the OSHRC order to file a further appeal. The employer can now go to federal court, because administrative remedies have been appealed. In fact, the employer can bypass the District Court (the lowest tier in the federal court system, where federal cases normally begin) and appeal either to the Court of Appeals for the Circuit where the violation is alleged to have occurred, or to the District of Columbia Circuit.

OSHRC's obligation, under the OSH Act, is to impose a penalty under 29 U.S.C. § 666 for each willful violation. (See § 31.10[B] above for increases in the penalty amounts.) The ALJ found that two related companies committed many willful violations of 29 C.F.R. § 1904.2(a) by refusing to record work-related accidents and illnesses. However, the ALJ grouped the violations so that each company was treated as having committed one willful violation, and was assessed with one penalty of $70,000 rather than the $9,000 each for 82 violations, and $8,000 for each of 52 violations, sought by the DOL. The Fifth Circuit agreed with the DOL: ALJs can select a per-violation penalty from within the statutory range, but are not permitted to manipulate the number of violations. DOL can group willful violations at the charging stage—but OSHRC does not have the authority to group per-instance willful violations at the penalty stage. [*Chao v. OSHRC/Chao v. Jindal United Steel Corp.*, 480 F.3d 320 (5th Cir. 2007); the penalty statute is 29 U.S.C. § 666. The circuit courts review OSHRC penalty determinations for abuse of discretion: *Chao v. OSHRC*, 401 F.3d 355 (5th Cir. 2005)]

SHRM editor Roy Maurer provided some advice about reducing fines. One important measure is to request an informal conference, which can result in lower penalties, more time to abate hazards, and reclassification or even deletion of some citations. Fines can be reduced by up to 10% if the employer has not had any willful, serious, repeat, or failure-to-abate citations in the preceding five years.

But employers do not qualify for this "Clean History" relief if they have had any of these major citations at any worksite in the United States. Recently, OSHA updated its Field Operations Manual to make it harder for employers to get penalty reductions. The employer must have had an inspection within the previous five years—with no violations being noted at the inspection. Penalties can be reduced 15% under the "quick fix" program if the employer corrects hazards within 24 hours of the inspection. The violation must not have been worse than "moderate-gravity serious," and the employer must undertake substantial permanent corrective actions to qualify. Sometimes OSHA will reduce penalties further and/or structure an installment payment plan, if the employer can show financial hardship; there is no official definition of hardship, so negotiation may be possible. OSHA sometimes reduces penalties based on "Enhanced Abatement" (improvements are extended throughout the corporation, or an external auditor is consulted). Safety improvements can also trigger penalty reductions, although expensive engineering controls might be required. [Roy Maurer, *How to Contest and Reduce OSHA Fines,* <http://www.shrm.org/hrdisciplines/safetysecurity /articles/Pages/Contest-Reduce-OSHA-Fines.aspx> (Feb. 28, 2013) (last accessed Mar. 8, 2017)]

§ 31.12 ABATEMENT

Abatement—removal of hazardous conditions—is the rationale for the whole OSHA process. An uncontested citation, a citation for which the contest period has expired, and a citation where the employer's challenge was partially or wholly unsuccessful, all give rise to abatement responsibilities.

Employers are required to abate violations within the shortest reasonable interval for correction. The CO orders an abatement date. Ordinarily, this will not be more than 30 days, although the initial abatement date could be more than 30 days from the date of the inspection if structural changes are needed, or if abatement relies on components that take a long time to deliver. [See OSHA Field Inspection Reference Manual CPL 2.103, at <http://www.osha.gov>]

> ■ **TIP:**   If a citation notes several violations, only some of which are contested, the appropriate action is to correct the uncontested violations, notify the OSHA area director that correction has occurred, and pay the penalties for the uncontested violations. With respect to contested citations, abatement and payment of fines will be suspended until there is an OSHRC final order.

OSHA reinspects the premises. If the same conditions are detected, penalties of up to $1,000 a day can be imposed. The employer, however, can contest penalties in the same way as an original citation.

The employer is entitled to file a Petition for Modification of Abatement (PMA) with the OSHA Area Director, no later than the scheduled abatement date, if factors beyond the employer's control prevent abatement. The PMA explains what the employer has done to cure the problem, how much additional time is required and why, and what the employer will do to protect employees until full abatement is achieved. The PMA must be posted and served on the employer's workforce, because they have the right to contest it.

If the PMA is uncontested, the Secretary of Labor has the power to approve it. OSHRC holds a hearing on contested PMAs, to determine if the employer did in fact act in good faith and was really unable to achieve full compliance. The employer does not have to comply with the underlying citation during the time that the PMA is under consideration.

An OSHRC ALJ decided in late 2013 that the OSH Act § 20(c) (authorizing OSHRC to grant "other appropriate relief") does not authorize OSHRC to order enterprise-wide abatement (i.e., an order to abate the same or similar hazards at other worksites that were not part of the citation). OSHRC found there was no precedent for interpreting that provision so broadly. [*Delta Elevator Serv. Corp., d/b/a Delta Beckwith Elevator Co.*, No. 12-1446 (OSHRC 2013)]

§ 31.13 OSHA CONSULTATION

State OSH agencies, working under grants from the federal OSHA, offer free on-site consultation services to identify and eliminate potential safety problems before they become real ones. The consultants are also available by telephone for advice and discussion. On-site visits are followed up by a written analysis of workplace hazards and suggestions for correction.

The consultants do not have the authority to impose penalties, but participating employers must agree to take steps to correct whatever problems the program uncovered.

Consultations cannot take place while an OSHA inspection is already underway, but if a consultation is scheduled, there is a good chance that OSHA will cancel a scheduled inspection, unless it is investigating a fatality or serious accident, or it is suspected that employees are in imminent danger.

An employer that has completed a consultation, made corrections based on the recommendations, and who posts a notice of correction where employees can see it, is entitled to request one year's immunity from scheduled OSHA inspections.

OSHA gives priority to scheduling consultation in industries with high hazards. The names of companies engaging in consultation will not be disclosed to state or federal enforcers unless the employer refuses to correct imminent hazards that are discovered during the process. [See 29 C.F.R. § 1908.5; for a map of locations, see <http://www.osha.gov/dcsp/smallbusiness/consult_directory.html> (last accessed Mar. 8, 2017)]

§ 31.14 VOLUNTARY PROGRAMS

Under the title of Voluntary Protection Programs (VPP), OSHA has three incentive programs (Star, Merit, and Demonstration) for employers with good safety records, who are supposed to serve as examples for other companies. Participants qualify for participation by proving that they maintain safe workplace and provide ongoing safety training for workers. OSHA and state authorities do not do programmed inspections at participating companies, although inspections will still be made if a complaint is registered.

Employers can apply to OSHA for VPP certification. They must complete applications that demonstrate their qualifications for participation. OSHA sends an inspector to check the company's safety records and site conditions, and expects that participants will show continuous improvement in their safety performance.

VPP began in 1982. The Star Program is for sites that are at or below the national average injury rate for their industry. OSHA reviews accident rates every year, and re-evaluates the participants every three to five years. Merit sites have the potential to reach Star status within three years, but in the meantime, they need help with their safety management. OSHA evaluates the site every 18–24 months. The Star Demonstration program is for sites that have reached Star levels, to test alternative means of promoting safety in the workplace. OSHA evaluates Star Demonstration sites every 12–18 months. [OSHA, *All About VPP*, <http://www.osha.gov/dcsp/vpp/all_about_vpp.html> (undated, last accessed Mar. 8, 2017)]

CHAPTER 32

UNEMPLOYMENT INSURANCE

§ 32.01 INTRODUCTION

Unemployment compensation (UC also known as Unemployment Insurance, or UI) is a state-administered insurance system. Employers make contributions to a fund. The State Employment Security Agencies (SESAs) that administer the system receive federal funding. In exchange, they must perform investigations and other managerial tasks.

Each state creates an Unemployment Insurance Trust Fund from employer contributions. In a few states, employee contributions are also required. However, the Federal Insurance Contributions Act (FICA) tax imposes equal (and substantial) burdens on both employer and employee, but unemployment tax is almost exclusively a responsibility of the employer. The theory is that in good times, unemployment will be low, and the fund will accumulate a surplus that can be used in bad times to pay unemployment insurance claims.

The Department of Labor's unadjusted and seasonally adjusted data on the number of unemployment insurance claims can be found at <http://www.dol.gov/ui/data.pdf> (last accessed Mar. 9, 2017). A map with UI contact and other information is posted to <http://www.careeronestop.org/localhelp/unemployment benefits/unemployment-benefits.aspx> (last accessed Mar. 9, 2017)

A SUB plan is a severance plan to supplement the payments from state unemployment compensation. To receive SUB pay, an employee must apply for and receive state unemployment benefits, and must verify each week that he or she is still unemployed but is available to work. (Some employers offer a bonus employment incentive payment to encourage workers to find a new job faster.) SUB pay must be periodic (weekly or with each payroll) rather than providing lump sums. A traditional SUB plan terminates payments when the former employee gets a new job or otherwise loses state unemployment benefits. Offset plans (which some states require) reduce the amount the employer pays by the amount of state unemployment benefits. Unless state law forbids, SUB pay can be made from the employer's general assets. If state law does forbid, payments can be made from a trust, which can be but does not have to be a tax-exempt 501(c)(17) trust or a VEBA. SUB pay from an approved plan is not subject to state unemployment taxes. Termination benefits that are excluded from FICA probably will not affect the recipient's eligibility for state unemployment benefits. SUB plans are subject to requirements of state law, which are not necessarily identical to federal tax rules. Some states reserve the right to approve SUB plans—and, as state unemployment insurance trusts become depleted, approval is more likely to be denied. [Vicki M. Nielsen, *The Advantages of Offering Supplemental Unemployment Benefits Instead of Severance, Part I: FICA Taxes and More*, Ogletree Deakins (Aug. 26, 2013), available at Lexology.com]

In March 2014, the Supreme Court held that the severance payments constituted FICA wages. The Supreme Court held that severance payments are made only to employees, and they are made because of service to employers because "service" is defined broadly as the entire relationship between the employer and employee. The court noted that the FICA statute provides a list of exemptions from the general rule that all compensation constitutes FICA wages. One of the exemptions is for severance payments made for disability retirement. The Supreme Court said it would not be necessary to specify this exemption if severance pay in general did not constitute FICA wages. Code § 3401(a), dealing with income tax withholding, also has a broad definition of taxable wages, subject to a list of exemptions. The list says that Supplemental Unemployment Benefits are treated as if they were wages: see § 3402(o). Quality Stores interpreted this to mean that, although SUB payments are treated "as if" they were wages, they are not wages for this purpose or for FICA purposes. However, the Supreme Court traced this provision to the history of tax withholding, when Congress wanted to relieve terminated workers from the burden of year-end tax liability. [*United States v. Quality Stores Inc.*, 134 S. Ct. 1395 (2014)]

Some help-wanted advertisements stipulate that the company will not hire unemployed persons, only those who already have another job. The New York City Human Rights Law makes it illegal for an employer to discriminate against unemployed job applicants. More than two dozen federal, state, and local provisions are pending to adopt similar laws. The states Oregon and New Jersey and the city of Chicago, forbid job advertisements that require applicants to be employed. The District of Columbia makes it unlawful for an employer or employment agency to treat unemployment as a factor in employment and hiring decisions, but the New York City law is the only one that grants a private right of action. [Phillip H. Wang, *The Unemployed—A Protected Category Coming to a Jurisdiction Near You*, DLA Piper (Sept. 30, 2013), available at Lexology.com]

The New Jersey Appellate Division upheld NJSA 34:8B-1, a state law forbidding job ads that require all applicants to be currently employed, finding that the law was narrowly tailored to furthering the government interest in the rights of the unemployed, and did not infringe on employers' First Amendment rights. [*New Jersey Dep't of Labor & Workforce Dev. v. Crest Ultrasonics et al.*, 434 N.J. Super. 34, 82 A.3d 258 (N.J. App. Div. 2014)]

§ 32.02 ELIGIBILITY FOR BENEFITS

In addition to the main program and the federal extensions, the unemployment system also includes benefits for federal workers and former military servicemembers; both programs are administered by state UI agencies on behalf of the federal government. Unemployment Compensation for Federal Civilian Employees (UCFE) provides unemployment benefits to federal civilian workers under the same conditions and in the same amount as benefits for other workers. Unemployment Compensation for Ex-Servicemembers (UCX), provides benefits for honorably discharged ex-servicemembers who completed their first full term of service (although there are some exceptions permitted). Members of the reserves and National Guard need 90 days of continuous active service and separation under honorable conditions to qualify for UCX benefits. [*Unemployment Compensation: Federal-State Partnership*, <http://www.ows.doleta.gov/unemploy/pdf/partnership.pdf> (Apr. 2016) (last accessed Mar. 7, 2017)]

[A] Generally

Two of the most important determinants in entitlement are whether the employee worked long enough before termination to qualify for benefits; and the reason for termination. The "base period" is the period of time used to analyze whether the job continued long enough.

In most states, the base period is the first four of the preceding five completed calendar quarters. Some states allow the four most recent quarters of employment to be counted. The difference is whether the most recent months of employment (which might have higher earnings) will be counted. Theoretically, only persons who earned at least a minimum amount during the base period can collect UI benefits. In practice, these limits are so low that nearly all employees meet them.

As §§ 1.08 and 1.10 of this title show, there are important issues under the "gig economy" in determining whether people in nontraditional arrangements are employees. In August 2015, the California Employment Development Department ruled that an Uber driver was an employee, not an independent contractor, because Uber controlled every aspect of driving and could terminate the employee at will. Therefore, the employee (whose name was withheld) was entitled to unemployment benefits. [Douglas MacMillan, *Another Uber Driver in California Ruled an Employee, Not Contractor*, WSJ.com (Sept. 10, 2015)]

In late 2016, New York State regulators found two Uber drivers to be employees, not independent contractors, and found them eligible for unemployment. Note, however, that unemployment determinations are made on an individual basis and the facts might be different in other cases involving Uber drivers. In California, for example, some drivers have been deemed to be employees while others have been treated as independent contractors. [Noam Scheiber, *Uber Drivers Ruled Eligible for Jobless Payments in New York State*, NYTimes.com (Oct. 13, 2016); Richard R. Meneghello, *First Crack in the Wall? 2 New York Uber Drivers Awarded Unemployment*, Fisher Phillips (Oct. 14, 2016), available at Lexology.com]

The New York Court of Appeals held that a yoga studio did not have enough control over some instructors for them to be employees. Some classes at the studio were taught by staff members (employees), others by non-staff members. The court of appeals held that the studio did not have enough control over results or the means to achieve them for the non-staff instructors to be employees. They set their own schedule, determined if they would be paid by the hour or a share of the class fees; they were only paid if a certain number of students took the class; they were allowed to teach for other studios; and they were not required to take training or attend staff meetings. [*Yoga Vida NYC, Inc. v. Commissioner of Labor*, No. 130 (N.Y. Oct. 25, 2016); see Allan S. Bloom, Carolyn M. Dellatore and Guy Brenner, *Yoga Instructors Can Be Independent Contractors, Says NY Court of Appeals*, Proskauer Rose LLP (Oct. 28, 2016), available at Lexology .com]

The Connecticut Supreme Court ruled in early 2017 that a person can be an independent contractor as defined by the state's Unemployment Insurance Act even if the person provides services to only one business or entity. Therefore, companies seeking to show that they are not the person's statutory employer are not required to prove that the person worked for other companies as well. The Connecticut statute employs a three-pronged ABC Test: first, is the person under direction and control of the employer? Second, are the services provided outside the employer's usual course and/or place of business? Third, does the worker customarily engage in an independently established business of the same type of services performed for the company?

In a case about appraisers, the trial court held that, although the appraisers were allowed to work for other companies, they would not survive economically without assignments from the employer. The case was appealed, on the single issue of whether it is necessary for the employer to prove the lack of other work relationships. The Connecticut Supreme Court held that the lack of other clients was not dispositive. The supreme court used 10 factors, which it said were not exclusive. The factors include state licensure or specialized skills, if the worker uses media such as advertisements or business cards to hold him- or herself out as an independent contractor, if the worker maintains a separate place of business, if the worker maintains liability insurance; if the worker invested in equipment; and whether the services are performed under the worker's name or a business name. [*Southwest Appraisal Grp., LLC v. Administrator, Unemployment Compensation Act,* No. SC 19651 (Conn. Mar. 21, 2017); see Guy Brenner and Carolyn M. Dellatore, *Connecticut Supreme Court Issues Important Clarification for Independent Contractor Test*, Proskauer Rose LLP (Mar. 23, 2017), available at Lexology.com]

The rationale for the UI system is to provide benefits for employees who lose their jobs through "no fault of their own." But in this context, an employee will not be considered to be at fault even if the employer was justified in firing him or her—for instance, if an employee is fired for incompetence but there was no crime or wrongdoing. For example, in *Time Warner Cable*, Unempl. Ins. Rep. (CCH) ¶ 8314 (Miss. App. 2006), benefits were held to have been correctly paid to a claimant who was terminated for lack of knowledge and judgment needed in his job. Inefficiency, unsatisfactory conduct, and good-faith errors do not constitute misconduct.

In general, benefits will not be available to anyone who quit voluntarily without good cause. However, states vary as to whether employees who quit will be entirely denied UI benefits, or whether benefit eligibility will merely be delayed. If the employer's conduct has been so abusive as to constitute constructive discharge, then the employee will be deemed to have had good cause to resign. [See <www.unemploymentinsurance.doleta.gov/unemploy/pdf/uilawcompar/2016 /nonmonetary.pdf> (last accessed Mar. 9, 2017) for tables explaining state laws and regulations about when an employee is deemed to have good cause for leaving work. For example, most states say it was acceptable to leave work to accept other work (although some states say only if the other job is better) or when the employee experiences sexual or other harassment, when compulsory retirement is imposed, or when the individual is sick (some states require that the employee must have left after requesting but being denied accommodation).]

However, there are situations where the employee is considered to have acted with good cause, even if the employer was not at fault. Many states interpret quitting a job to follow a spouse who has gotten a job elsewhere to constitute good cause.

Yet another issue is the treatment of persons who have accepted severance packages (see Chapter 3 for more discussion of severance benefits). The Massachusetts Court of Appeals ruled in 2006 that benefits should have been awarded to claimants who took a voluntary separation package because they had an objectively reasonable belief that they would have been fired if they had not taken the packages. The employer neither announced that employees would be chosen randomly for RIF nor announced criteria for selecting RIF candidates, thus giving employees good cause to cut their losses by taking the package and leaving. [*State St. Bank & Tr. Co.*, Unempl. Ins. Rep. (CCH) ¶ 8487 (Mass. App. 2006); see also *Johnson v. Unemployment Compensation Bd. of Review* (Pa. Commonwealth 2005), discussed in Asher Hawkins, *Bought-Out Verizon Workers Denied Jobless Aid*, The Legal Intelligencer (Mar. 10, 2005) (law.com)]

Employees who took a voluntary separation plan were eligible for benefits, based on testimony from a company Vice President and e-mails from the HR department stating that the plan was implemented because of lack of work. [*Verizon North*, Unempl. Ins. Rep. (CCH) ¶ 10,203 (Ohio App. 2006)]

In contrast, however, an office manager was given the choice between staying on while she looked for a new job, or leaving immediately and receiving severance pay. When she opted to leave right away, she was ineligible for benefits, because she was the one who made the departure decision. [*Arrow Legal Solutions Grp. PXC*, Unempl. Ins. Rep. (CCH) ¶ 8354 (Utah App. 2006)]

Benefits are also denied to persons who are guilty of "misconduct detrimental to the best interests of the employer." This is interpreted in an industrial rather than moral light, so improper activities are likely to rule out UI benefit eligibility even if they are not criminal in nature. Poor job performance would not be treated as "misconduct," unless it demonstrated gross negligence or willful disregard of the employer's best interests.

Depending on the state, disqualifying misconduct might also have to be work-related. Excessive absence or insubordination might be treated as misconduct. Benefits were properly denied to a claimant who was terminated for excessive absences. On her first day at work, she signed an acknowledgment of receiving the company handbook, including the attendance policy. The claimant asserted that she misinterpreted the policy, so her actions could not be deemed willful or wanton, but the Delaware Superior Court ruled that denial of benefits was correct because the employer coached her about the policy and warned her that she was at risk of termination for continuing to violate it. [*Jackson*, Unempl. Ins. Rep. (CCH) ¶ 8317 (Del. Super. Ct. 2008)]

Being intoxicated on business premises would almost certainly be considered misconduct. A truck driver whose blood alcohol concentration exceeded the legal limit was guilty of disqualifying misconduct, even though he was not convicted of driving under the influence and did not lose his license; he should have known that duty to his employer precluded driving while impaired. [*Risk*, Unempl. Ins. Rep. (CCH) ¶ 8557 (Minn. App. 2003)] Being stopped for a non-work-related DUI, resulting in surrender of the driver's license when the claimant's job at a tire shop required a valid license, constituted disqualifying misconduct. [*Gummert*, Unempl. Ins. Rep. (CCH) ¶ 9126 (Iowa Dist. Ct. 2008)]

New York granted unemployment benefits to a Whole Foods Market employee who violated store policy by taking a sandwich out of the trash at the end of his shift. Employees are required to get their supervisors' consent before taking food; servings are usually sample-sized, and must be logged and accounted for. Initially, unemployment benefits were denied on grounds of misconduct. The employee said that his previous supervisor allowed employees to take damaged food that was going to be thrown out and written off. The Administrative Law Judge (ALJ) sided with the employee, because he had a good record, did not take the sandwich out of the store, and this was an isolated instance of poor judgment that should not be considered misconduct. [Rebecca Moore, *Reason for Denying Unemployment Benefits Sounded Fishy*, plansponsor.com (Mar. 20, 2009). See also Rebecca Moore, *Dillards Tries to Block Unemployment Benefits for Hot Dog "Thief,"* plansponsor.com (July 29, 2011); The Indiana Court of Appeals reversed disqualification of Nolan Koewler, who was fired for eating two hot dogs that were left over after a company picnic. The Review Board concluded that he had been fired for theft, but the Court of Appeals noted that although employees including Koewler were told to put the leftovers away, they were not aware that it was supposed to be saved for Labor Day. Furthermore, the food had been supplied for consumption by employees, and Koewler was not aware that employees were no longer supposed to consume food items. But see Tara Cantore, *Dumpster Diving Employee Can't Get Unemployment*, plansponsor.com (Aug. 25, 2011): An employee fired for taking soup from a dumpster, a violation of the store policy against employees taking anything from the store without paying for it, was terminated for misconduct and, therefore, did not qualify for unemployment benefits.]

The New Jersey Unemployment Compensation Act defines three levels of disqualifying misconduct (simple, severe, and gross), each of which reduces benefit eligibility to a different extent. In mid-2017, the New Jersey Appellate Division struck down the regulatory agencies' definition of "simple misconduct" as arbitrary and capricious. The court said that benefits must not be denied based on actions or inactions that constitute only simple negligence rather than intentional wrongdoing. The court directed the state's DOL six months to draft a better definition. [*In re N.J.A.C. 12:17-2.1,* No. A-4636-14T3 (N.J.A.D. May 1, 2017); see Patrick T. Collins, *New Jersey's Unemployment Compensation Act Definition of "Simple Misconduct" Deemed Arbitrary and Capricious,* Norris McLaughlin & Marcus PA (May 2, 2017), available at Lexology.com]

Continued eligibility requires the claimant to make a serious search for work. Benefits will be terminated if the claimant receives but rejects a legitimate job offer for suitable work. Benefits will not be paid in any week in which the claimant receives a pension, annuity, retirement pay, or any other private or government payment based on past work history. But benefits can be paid in a week in which the claimant receives a distribution from a profit-sharing plan, because that is not treated as compensation for work. Benefits can be paid based on job loss due to a material change in working conditions imposed by the employer, if the employee has a valid reason for being unable to work under the new conditions. (This is referred to as "voluntary with good cause attributable to the employer.") A published job description can be evidence of the original nature of the job, and therefore whether material change has occurred. If a job is described as a day-shift position, a change to a night or swing shift might well be considered material.

In mid-2003, the New York Court of Appeals ruled that the employee's physical presence is critical, not the location of the employer on whose behalf the work was done. So a worker who telecommuted from Florida could not collect New York unemployment benefits, even though her employer was located in Long Island and work was directed and controlled from New York. [*Allen v. Comm'r of Labor,* 100 N.Y.2d 282 (N.Y. 2003); see John Caher, *N.Y. Court First to Rule on Telecommuting,* N.Y.L.J. (July 3, 2003), <http://www.law.com>; Al Baker, *Telecommuter Loses Case for Benefits,* N.Y. Times, July 3, 2003, at B1]

Strikers were held to be entitled to benefits after the date that permanent replacements were hired. (The employment relationship is severed when employees have been notified that they have been replaced, or their positions are permanently filled by someone else.) [*M. Conley Co.,* Unempl. Ins. Rep. (CCH) ¶ 10,186 (Ohio 2006)] School district employees were properly denied benefits during a work stoppage. When CBA negotiations reached an impasse, the employer implemented its best and final offer, which was not so unreasonable that employees would feel constrained to strike. Therefore, the work stoppage was a strike, not a lockout, and benefits were unavailable. [*Tietz,* Unempl. Ins. Rep. (CCH) ¶ 10,178 (Ohio App. 2005)] Union members did not get benefits: their work stoppage was not caused by a lockout, and they had the opportunity to return to work when the employer hired permanent replacement workers. [*Magnode*, Unempl. Ins. Rep. (CCH) ¶ 10,195 (Ohio App. 2006)]

For applications on or after July 17, 2016, Illinois applicants for unemployment benefits are required to register for employment services and post at least one resume on the state's job search site, unless there is an exemption. Previously, the benefit application was separate from the registration requirement, but now they are associated. A person who does not register by the deadline will not be eligible for benefits in any week before the week in which the registration is completed. Registration must be done online, on the official site; applicants without home internet access are directed to use a library or other public connection. [Jennifer Cerven, *Posting a Resume Is Now Required in Illinois to Receive Jobless Benefits,* Barnes & Thornburg LLP (July 14, 2016), available at Lexology .com]

[B] BAA-UC

The Department of Labor created a program called BAA-UC (BAA stands for Birth and Adoption) [20 C.F.R. Part 604], through a Notice of Proposed Rulemaking at 64 Fed. Reg. 67972 (Dec. 3, 1999), finalized, without significant changes, at 65 Fed. Reg. 37209 (June 13, 2000). The program allowed new parents to receive unemployment benefits for a one-year period beginning with the week of birth or adoption, because they would be treated as being "able and available for work" during this time period. The DOL regulations gave states the ability to opt in to the program, but no state elected to do so.

A lawsuit [*LPA, Inc. v. Chao*, 211 F. Supp. 2d 160 (D.D.C. 2002)] challenged the BAA-UC program as inconsistent with federal law. Although the suit was dismissed on procedural grounds, it caused the DOL to re-think the program. After review, the DOL decided that the BAA-UC experiment was a bad decision and an invalid interpretation of the rules about availability for work. It would also put additional strain on already hard-pressed state unemployment insurance funds. Therefore, the DOL decided to terminate the experiment, publishing a Notice of Proposed Rulemaking for this purpose at 67 Fed. Reg. 72122 (Dec. 4, 2002).

[C] Federal Statutes Extending UI

A federal statute, 42 U.S.C. § 177(a), the Robert T. Stafford Disaster Relief and Emergency Assistance Act, establishes the Disaster Unemployment Assistance (DUA) program. Up to 26 weeks of benefits can be furnished after a major disaster declared by the President, for unemployment caused by that disaster for which no other benefits are available. DUA eligibility ceases when the state agency finds that unemployment is no longer directly traceable to the major disaster. The minimum weekly amount of benefit is 50% of the state's average UI benefit. The maximum is set by state law.

The DUA benefit is considered a UC benefit. It cannot exceed the maximum benefit payable under the state's UC law. Qualifications for DUA are that the claimant no longer has a job, cannot reach the place of work, is unable to start a promised job; is the household breadwinner; has become head of the household because the former head of the household died in the disaster; or is unable to work because of an injury caused by the disaster. [DOL, *Disaster Unemployment Assistance* fact sheet, <http://workforcesecurity.doleta.gov/unemploy/disaster.asp> (updated July 10, 2015) (last accessed Mar. 9, 2017)]

DUA benefits are limited to the immediate result of the disaster itself, not more remote consequences of a chain of events that was started or made worse by the disaster. Examples of direct results are unemployment caused by damage to or destruction of the physical worksite, lack of access to the worksite because the government has ordered it closed, or lack of work and lost revenues caused to a business that got the majority of its income from the premises that were damaged, destroyed, or shut down. But "ripple effects" (for instance, if an office building is closed, workers who can't come in to work don't stop at a coffee shop for snacks) are not covered. Beneficiaries can include, for example, workers at airports closed by government orders.

In 2016, after Hurricane Matthew, 23 counties in North Carolina were approved for federal DUA, and the state's governor suspended the normal one-week waiting period for benefits. [Robin E. Shea, *Disaster Unemployment Assistance Available for 23 counties in NC*, Constangy Brooks Smith & Prophete LLP (Oct. 17, 2016), available at Lexology.com]

In addition to this federal law, some states have state "optional trigger" laws that let them provide a 13-week extended benefit period for workers who have used up their regular benefits during a period of high unemployment, at the same rate as regular unemployment compensation. States have the option to provide the additional 13 weeks of EB if unemployment is high, but not as high as the level where EB is mandatory in states where unemployment is high and rising. The EB program generally was 50% state, 50% federally funded, but the American Recovery and Reinvestment Act (ARRA) included a provision under which the federal government temporarily took over 100% funding of EB. This provision was renewed by Pub. L. No. 111-312, the 2010 tax bill, until January 4, 2012 [DOL, *100% Federal Funding of Extended Benefits (EB) Extended to January 4, 2012*, <http://www.ows.doleta.gov/unemploy/supp_act_eb.asp>] Subsequently, the American Taxpayer Relief Act of 2012 (ATRA), Pub. L. No. 112-240, extended 100% federal funding of EB until December 31, 2013. [DOL, *100% Federal Funding of Extended Benefits (EB) Extended to December 31, 2013*, <http://workforcesecurity.doleta.gov/unemploy/supp_act_eb.asp> (Jan. 16, 2013)]

In February 2012, Congress chose not to update the EB program criteria and, beginning in mid-2012, states stopped offering EB benefits. According to the National Employment Law Project, as of December 2013, none of the states qualified for EB. [National Employment Law Project, *Share of Unemployed Receiving Jobless Aid Will Hit Record Low* (Dec. 2013), <http://www.nelp.org/page/-/UI/2013/Issue-Brief-Record-Low-Share-Unemployed-Receiving-Jobless-Aid-Renew-EUC.pdf?nocdn=1> (last accessed Apr. 2, 2016)]

A program of Temporary Extended Unemployment Compensation was established under the Job Creation and Worker Assistance Act of 2002 (JWCAA). [Pub. L. No. 107-147] The program was originally scheduled to end as of January 1, 2003. It was extended to June 1, 2003 by Pub. L. No. 108-1 (which doesn't have a short title), and once again to December 31 by Pub. L. No. 108-26 (The Unemployment Compensation Amendments of 2003 Act). However, that was the final extension, and the program ended December 2003.

Emergency Unemployment Compensation (EUC; also known as EUC08) was a federal temporary extension of benefits for people who collected all their regular state benefits. This program was entirely funded by the federal government. The program was created by Pub. L. No. 110-252, the Supplemental Appropriations Act of 2008, and was expanded several times in light of ongoing economic problems, by Pub. L. No. 110-449, the Unemployment Compensation Extension Act of 2008, the Worker, Homeownership, and Business Assistance Act of 2009, Pub. L. No. 111-92, ARRA, Pub. L. No. 111-5. There were subsequent extensions under the Department of Defense Appropriations Act, Pub. L. No. 111-118, the Temporary Extension Act of 2010, Pub. L. No. 111-144, Continuing Extension Act of 2010, Pub. L. No. 111-157, and the Unemployment Compensation Extension Act of 2010, Pub. L. No. 111-205. The Middle Class Tax Relief and Job Creation Act of 2012, Pub. L. No. 112-96 did not eliminate the program but limited the categories of people who could receive benefits and reduced the maximum duration of benefits from 99 weeks to 73 weeks (in states with high unemployment) or 66 weeks (other states).

EUC expired once again at the end of 2013, and this time was not reauthorized. The Middle Class Tax Relief and Job Creation Act of 2012, Pub. L. No. 112-96, includes many provisions dealing with UI. UI benefits were restricted to people able and available to work and actively seeking work; recovery of overpayments was made mandatory; states were allowed to require drug testing of applicants if they were fired for drug use, or if the only suitable work for them was in an industry with mandatory drug testing; and provisions about work-sharing programs. [Josh Mitchell and Naftali Bendavid, *Tax Bill Passed by Congress Broadens Jobless Program*, WSJ.com (Feb. 18, 2012)]

A DOL regulation under this statute, 20 C.F.R. § 620, defined only eight categories of occupations as regularly performing drug testing. This regulation was overturned in early 2017, by Congress' Joint Resolution 42. JR 42 was signed by President Trump on March 31, 2017. Because the regulation was overturned by using the Congressional Review Act, DOL will require the consent of Congress to adopt a new regulation that is too similar to the regulation that was removed.

[Joshua D. Bortnick, *Congress Passes Resolution to Block Obama Administration Restrictions on Drug Testing Those Seeking Unemployment Benefits,* Ogletree Deakins (Mar. 17, 2017), available at Lexology.com; Kathryn J. Russo, *President Trump Signs Measure That Will Allow Broader Drug Testing of Applicants for Unemployment Benefits,* Jackson Lewis PC (Apr. 3, 2017), available at Lexology.com] The DOL officially revoked the rule on May 10, 2017. [John S. Ho, *One DOL Drug Testing Rule Officially Gone—Is OSHA Next?,* Cozen O'Connor (May 15, 2017), available at Lexology.com]

The STC program (for Short-Time Compensation; also known as work-sharing) provides partial unemployment benefits to persons who are still working at the same job, but whose hours have been reduced from full-to part-time.

The Middle Class Tax Relief and Job Creation Act of 2012 encourages states to have STC programs, but the programs must be consistent with the federal definition. The federal government will reimburse up to 100% of certain state STC costs for up to three years. [DOL, *Comparison of State Unemployment Insurance Laws,* <http://www.unemploymentinsurance.doleta.gov/unemploy/comparison2016.asp> (last accessed Mar. 9, 2017), reporting that in 2016, there were STC programs in Arizona, Arkansas, California, Colorado, Connecticut, the District of Columbia, Florida, Illinois, Iowa, Kansas, Maine, Maryland, Massachusetts, Michigan, Minnesota, Missouri, Nebraska, New Hampshire, New Jersey, New York, Ohio, Oklahoma, Oregon, Pennsylvania, Rhode Island, Texas, Vermont, Washington, and Wisconsin. Table 4-6 in this document summarizes the duration of the approved plans, maximum benefits (usually 12 months), and the required reduction of work hours to participate.]

Self-Employment Assistance (SEA) programs allow a person who is permanently laid off and at risk of exhausting benefits to receive a weekly allowance while starting a small business to become self-employed. The allowance is paid at the same rate as the person's regular weekly unemployment benefit amount. The Middle Class Tax Relief and Job Creation Act of 2012 also extended the SEA program to help states work with the long-term unemployed. SEA programs have been authorized in Delaware, Maine, Mississippi, New Hampshire, New Jersey, New York (expiring Dec. 7, 2015), Oregon, Pennsylvania, Rhode Island, and Vermont. Louisiana passed a law authorizing a SEA program, but did not have an active program as of 2015. [*Comparison of State Unemployment Insurance Laws* (accessed Apr. 2, 2016; reflects laws in effect Jan. 1, 2015)]

Unemployment benefits, retraining, and health insurance subsidies are available under the Trade Adjustment Assistance Program (TAAP) to workers who lost their jobs when their employer moved outside of the United States, or because of foreign competition. A brochure available on the DOL Website (as updated through February 19, 2013) explains that benefits are triggered by filing a petition with DOL, either online or at an American Job Center. The petition can be filed either by an employer, a union official, a job center operator or partner (such as a state workforce agency), or by three or more workers from the same firm. DOL investigates to determine if the layoff is eligible (i.e., was caused by increased importation, outsourcing of production, loss of business from a customer that is also TAAP-eligible, or a declaration of trade injury made by the International Trade Commission). If the DOL certifies eligibility, the state will notify the eligible workers that they can apply for benefits, such as job training, relocation assistance, and help with health insurance premiums. [DOL brochure, *The Trade Adjustment Assistance Program: Back to Work After a Trade-Related Layoff*, <http://www.doleta.gov/tradeact/pdf/2011_brochure.pdf> (last accessed Mar. 9, 2017)]

Workers who lost their jobs as a result of foreign competition once again qualify for a Health Coverage Tax Credit; this credit expired, but was revived by the Trade Preferences Extension Act of 2015, until January 1, 2020. [Trade Preferences Extension Act of 2015, Pub. L. No. 114-27]

[D]   Case Law on Benefit Eligibility

There are a number of reasons why benefits will be denied: that the individual was not totally unemployed; that he or she voluntarily quit his or her past job rather than being involuntarily employed; that he or she was guilty of misconduct (which generally means something worse than sheer incompetence). In a number of situations, the employer will be justified in terminating the employee—but UI benefits will nevertheless be available.

A nurse working under an intermittent employment contract was not entitled to benefits after the contract expired: A person who chooses to work under a fixed-term contract is not involuntarily unemployed when the contract ends. [*Brinkman*, Unempl. Ins. Rep. (CCH) ¶ 10,179 (Ohio App. 2005)]

The Tennessee Supreme Court ruled that a licensed time-share salesperson was not entitled to unemployment benefits when her service agreement with the time-share company ended. She was a "licensed real estate agent" excluded from UI benefits. She was paid on a commission basis and was responsible for her own income and payroll taxes. The Tennessee Supreme Court said that time-share salespersons are real estate agents because they must be licensed, and are paid commissions for engaging in real estate activities. [*Westgate Smoky Mountains at Gatlinburg v. Phillips, et al.*, No. E2011-02538-SC-R11-CV, 2013 Tenn. LEXIS 1014, Unempl. Ins. Rep. (CCH) P8438 (Tenn. 2013); see James R. Mulroy, II and Donald E. Hayes, Jr., *Time-Share Salesperson Not Entitled to Unemployment Insurance Benefits, Tennessee Supreme Court Rules*, Jackson Lewis PC (Jan. 13, 2014), available at Lexology.com]

According to Louisiana's District Court, providing a false Social Security number and false information about one's criminal record constitutes material misconduct. The job was coordinator of environmental health and safety, so the employer had the right to expect honesty and integrity, and the employer's work rules spelled out a zero-tolerance policy for document falsification. [*Sheppard*, Unempl. Ins. Rep. (CCH) ¶ 9043 (La. Dist. Ct. 2002)]

Paratransit, Inc.'s CBA requires employees to sign all disciplinary notices presented to them, if the notice states that signing merely acknowledges receipt of the notice, not the accuracy of the notice or whether the employee is at fault. The plaintiff, Medeiros, was suspended for two days without pay for harassing a passenger. He refused to sign the disciplinary notice, saying that it would be an admission of guilt and asked for a union representative. The employer said that he was not entitled to a representative and refusing to sign would be insubordination, for which he would be fired. He said that the union president told him not to sign anything without a union representative. He was fired, and his UI application was denied. The California Supreme Court ruled in his favor. The state supreme court said that violating the employer's order because of a good-faith error in judgment does not rule out receiving UI. There must be deliberate, willful, intentional disobedience. Furthermore, a single act of disobedience, without prior warnings, usually will only be treated as misconduct if it is substantially detrimental to the employer's interests. Asking for a union representative does not interfere with the employer's business. [*Paratransit, Inc. v. Unemployment Ins. Appeals Bd.*, 327 P.3d 840 (Cal. 2014)]

The used car manager for a Chevrolet dealership got into an argument with the general sales manager, who thought Broyles had a bad attitude and was disrespectful to a customer. The manager said that if Broyles did not want to be there and did not want to change his attitude, he should go home. Broyles, cursing at the manager, left the workplace and was fired the next day. The Oklahoma Employment Security Commission, consulting precedents from other states, denied benefits. The factors included the severity of the language; if customers or co-workers overheard the altercation; if the manager provoked the incident; if the employee had already been warned; if cursing was combined with other disobedience; and if there was a threat of violence. In this case, at least two co-workers were present. [*Broyles v. Okla. Employment Sec. Comm'n*, 333 P.3d 266 (Okla. App. 2014)]

Accepting benefits for total disability without actually having the claimed physical limitations was a falsehood in disregard of the employer's interest and standards, and therefore disqualifying misconduct that precluded receipt of UI benefits. [*Downey*, Unempl. Ins. Rep. (CCH) ¶ 12,505 (Pa. Commw. 2006)]

The Minnesota Supreme Court held in early 2014 that it is not a violation of public policy to fire an employee for applying for unemployment benefits. (The plaintiff applied for benefits after a reduction in hours.) The plaintiff did not allege that she was required to commit any illegal acts and the court refused to expand the definition of public policy to include all undesirable actions by employers. However, a commentator noted that the plaintiff was likely to apply for benefits once again, and the benefit application would probably not be deemed to be disqualifying misconduct. Minnesota also makes it a misdemeanor for an employer to impede or obstruct an application for unemployment benefits. [*Dukowitz v. Hannon Sec. Servs.*, 841 N.W.2d 147, 164 Lab. Cas. (CCH) P61,435, 97 Empl. Prac. Dec. (CCH) ¶ 44,984 (Minn. 2014)]

The New Jersey Appellate Division ruled in favor of a terminated hospital employee (a registered nurse) who refused flu vaccine on secular grounds. The hospital required flu shots, but employees claiming a documented religious or medical exemption could opt out but would have to wear face masks during the flu season. The plaintiff agreed to wear a mask, but still was fired. The court found that refusing immunization is not "misconduct," which is defined in New Jersey as work-connected, improper, malicious activity that is within the employee's control, and either deliberately violates the employer's rules or disregards standards of behavior. [*Valent v. Bd. of Review*, No. A-4980-11T2 (N.J.A.D. June 5, 2014)]

The District of Columbia Court of Appeals found that a worker had good cause to quit when her boss yelled at her and habitually insulted her while she was working. Good cause is a fact determination based on the reactions of a reasonably prudent person under similar circumstances. Allegations of verbal abuse are assessed on the totality of circumstances: whether insults were habitual; if employees were insulted in front of others; how offensive the language was; and whether the employee tried to protest abusive conduct. [*Imperial Valet Servs., Inc. v. Alvarado*, 72 A.3d 165, Unempl. Ins. Rep. (CCH) ¶ 8371 (D.C. 2013)]

Especially with the growth of statutes decriminalizing marijuana, the unemployment system has to confront issues of benefit eligibility when a person has been terminated for drug usage. The Michigan Court of Appeals, in three consolidated cases, permitted employees to collect unemployment benefits after a positive marijuana test—as long as their usage was consistent with the state's medical marijuana Act. The court of appeals treated the terminations as penalties forbidden by the medical marijuana law. In effect, the court held that the medical marijuana law preempts state unemployment law. In these cases, there was no evidence that the employees possessed or used marijuana in the workplace. One of them was tested after a workplace injury; another openly discussed her marijuana usage at her health care workplace, and was fired after a patient complained. The court of appeals did not address the Sixth Circuit's conclusion in *Casias* that the statute does not apply to private employers. [*Braska v. Challenge Mfg. Co.*, 307 Mich. App. 340 (Mich. App. 2015)]

Missouri held that an employee was not disqualified from benefits when he was fired after a positive marijuana test. Because the company's drug-free workplace policy did not use the word "misconduct," the Missouri Court of Appeals held that he was not on notice that drug use would preclude receipt of benefits. However, the court remanded the case for determination under the general misconduct standard, and to apply the state law holding that an employer does not have to show a demonstrable impact of drug use on the employee's ability to do his or her job. [*Comer*, Unempl. Ins. Rep. (CCH) ¶ 8635 (Mo. App. 2006)]

§ 32.03 CALCULATION OF BENEFITS

[A] Basic Calculation

The actual benefit depends either on the claimant's average weekly wage, or the wage earned in the quarter of the base period when wages were highest. For partial weeks of unemployment, a reduced benefit is available, although the various states use different calculation methods.

Individual claimants are usually assigned a 52-week "benefit year," beginning when the claim is filed, although some states use the same benefit year for all claimants. Usually, a one-week waiting period is imposed before benefits become payable. Most states limit the payment of basic benefits to 26 weeks. In times of very high employment, "extended benefits" are available for another 13 weeks in some states, another 20 weeks in other states. Once claimants use up the basic benefit, they must wait until the next benefit year before starting another base period and therefore qualifying for unemployment benefits all over again. So someone who receives benefits in a particular benefit year will have to be re-employed and work for at least a second base period before qualifying for a second benefit period.

[B] Benefit Offsets

Benefit offsets may be applied in two situations: if the unemployment benefit is reduced because other income is received, or if the UI benefits offset other amounts that the person would otherwise be entitled to receive.

As noted above, payments (e.g., pension, IRA) reduce entitlement to unemployment compensation if they can be traced to work done by the employee in the past. The offset is applied only to a plan maintained or contributed to by the company that was the employer during the base payment period, or the employer that is chargeable with the unemployment claim. So if the pension was earned at Company A, but the worker became unemployed while working for Company A, pension will not offset the unemployment insurance benefit.

States differ in their treatment of rollovers. Some states (e.g., New York and North Carolina) require a reduction of unemployment benefits because of rollovers; the other states do not. The Department of Labor's interpretation is that rollovers should not reduce unemployment benefits, but each state is permitted to set its own unemployment rules; this is not an exclusively federal area of regulation. Furthermore, reduction is necessary only for amounts based on the claimant's own past work history, not when a person receiving benefits gets a distribution as a surviving spouse.

A claimant's failure to report part-time income was caused by mistake and bad communications, rather than fraudulent intent, so he was required to repay the overpayment but was not subject to fraud penalties. [*Orzel*, Unempl. Ins. Rep. (CCH) ¶ 8655 (N.J. Super. Ct. 2006)]

About half the states deny unemployment benefits in weeks in which Worker's Compensation benefits are also received, or consider the Comp benefit income that reduces the benefit. (There is also a question of whether someone whose condition is bad enough to justify Comp benefits is "ready and able" to work even if he or she wants to work.)

Vacation pay also generally offsets unemployment benefits although an exception might be made if the claimant is deemed to be on vacation involuntarily rather than choosing to take time off.

Back pay awarded in a Title VII case generally is not reduced by UI. However, some courts, like the Second Circuit, say that courts that hear Title VII cases have discretion to reduce the award to account for UI received.

§ 32.04   EXPERIENCE RATING

[A]   Determination of Rating

The unemployment insurance rate that employers pay to help fund the system is partially based on their "experience" (the number of claims against them). The more claims, the higher the insurance rate. Seasonal businesses in particular often have a regular pattern of laying off workers who rely on UI until they are rehired.

The standard rate is 5.4%, although many employers qualify for a more favorable experience rate because of their record of few discharges and layoffs. The treatment of new employers varies from state to state. Some states impose a higher initial rate, until the employer can demonstrate its compliance with filing and payment requirements and its low experience of unemployment. On the other hand, some states have a special low rate for new employers until and unless they demonstrate bad claims experience. Some states even allow a zero rate (no tax at all) on employers with especially good claims experience. But all employers may become subject to the standard rate, and perhaps even additional "subsidiary contributions" if the state as a whole has a high unemployment rate and consequently has a low balance in its UI fund. A few states (Alaska, New Jersey, Pennsylvania) also require employee contributions to the system.

Employers in over half the states owe billions of dollars to the federal government for UI benefits. Thirty-five of the states borrowed federal money because their UI trust funds were too small to cope with recession-related unemployment. Seven of them opted to cut benefits to unemployment claimants to repay the federal loan. One problem with the current system is that the wage bases are so low, making it difficult for states to collect significant amounts. In over half of the states, the base is $15,000 or less. Federal law merely requires the state base to be as high as the federal base, which has been unchanged (at $7,000) since 1983. In 1983, that was 40% of the average wage, but it is now less than 20% of the average wage, and a small fraction of the FICA base. In 2016, the wage base was $7,000 in Arizona and Florida; $7,700 in Louisiana; $8,000 in Alabama, Tennessee, and Virginia; $8,500 in Maryland, $9,000 in the District of Columbia, Michigan, Nebraska, Ohio, and Texas; $9,500 in Georgia, Indiana, and Pennsylvania; $10,200 in Kentucky; $10,700 in New York; $12,000 in Arkansas, Maine, and West Virginia; $12,200 in Colorado; $12,960 in Illinois; $13,000 in Missouri; $14,000 in Mississippi, Kansas, New Hampshire, South Carolina, and Wisconsin; $15,000 in Connecticut, Massachusetts, and South Dakota; $16,800 in Vermont; $17,500 in Oklahoma; $18,500 in Delaware; $22,000 in Rhode Island; $22,300 in North Carolina; $24,100 in New Mexico; $25,500 in Wyoming; $28,300 in Iowa; $30,500 in Montana; $31,000 in Minnesota; $32,200 in Utah; $32,600 in Nevada and New Jersey; $36,900 in Oregon; $37,200 in Idaho and North Dakota; $39,700 in Alaska; $42,200 in Hawaii; and $44,000 in Washington. [*Comparison of State Unemployment Insurance Laws,* <https://work forcesecurity.doleta.gov/unemploy/comparison2016.asp> (last accessed Mar. 7, 2017; reflects laws in effect Jan. 1, 2016); in many of these states, the figures are subject to various kinds of adjustments. Several states, e.g., South Carolina and South Dakota, have automatic indexing.]

There are four basic methods of experience rating:

- Variations in payroll over time (showing whether the workforce has increased or decreased);

- Reserve ratio;

- Benefit ratio;

- Ratio of benefits to wages.

Some states use hybrid methods. States often permit joint filing and risk pooling: joint payment by a group of employers who get a combined experience rate for the group as a whole. A further refinement is a distinction between "charging" and "noncharging" claims. Some claims are not charged against the last employer's experience rating: for instance, claims for very brief periods of unemployment, or cases where the employee spent very little time working for the last employer. In some states, the employer is not charged for benefits paid after a period of disqualification based on voluntary quitting or misconduct, or when benefits are terminated because of the claimant's failure to seek suitable work. The rationale is that employers should not be penalized for circumstances beyond their control.

Another question is whether all employers in the base period, or only the last one in the series, will be charged with the claim. If more than one employer is charged, they might be charged with the most recent employer charged first, or the charge might be divided proportionate to the amount of wages they paid during the base period.

[B]   Collateral Estoppel

Two related legal doctrines, collateral estoppel and res judicata, may come into play in contesting unemployment claims. An employer's unsuccessful contest of one worker's claim could harm the employer in later lawsuits. Legal advice is required as to the comparative risk of letting a claim go through without opposition (which will increase the employer's experience rating and therefore its rates) or contesting the claim but losing and being at a disadvantage when similar claims are made later.

The doctrine of res judicata refers to a matter that has already been tried. If one court has already dealt with a case, a higher court may handle an appeal of the matter, but a different court, which is not in the same line of authority, will not decide a matter that has already been decided. The doctrine of res judicata applies only to the same legal issues and the same or closely related parties. So if one employee sues his or her employer for race discrimination, the defense of res judicata will not be available if a different employee sues another employer for race discrimination. But Employee A's suit against Company B may have "collateral estoppel" effect on Employee C's suit against Company B, because Employee A's suit involves decisions on some basic issues about Company B's policies.

Either side can use collateral estoppel. In a later court case, the employer says that the administrative decision proves that the employee was guilty of misconduct, so terminating the employee was not wrongful. [See Chapter 39 for wrongful termination suits.] The employee might assert that having received unemployment benefits proves that he or she did not quit and was not guilty of misconduct. Usually, administrative decisions in an unemployment matter will be granted collateral estoppel effect—but some states say that only a court decision can have that effect.

According to the Third Circuit, the ALJ's holding of misconduct in his unemployment compensation hearing did not prevent the employee from bringing suit for wrongful discharge. The station agent says that he put $80 for a ticket change fee in a drawer near the boarding gate, but the money was not entered into the computer system. The passenger complained when he was charged again for the fee that he paid in cash. The ticket agent was fired for violating the airline's rules. The unemployment ALJ denied benefits for questionable conduct and violation of procedure. In the Virgin Islands, the rule is that an unemployment insurance finding of misconduct does not preclude a wrongful discharge claim, because the two laws have different objectives. The facts and issues are different, and the wrongful termination statute does not refer to misconduct, so finding that the employee was guilty of misconduct does not resolve the issue of wrongful termination. [*Gonzalez v. AMR*, 548 F.3d 219 (3d Cir. 2008)]

[C] Planning Steps to Reduce Unemployment Tax Liability

The unemployment insurance system is designed to stabilize employment, so it penalizes employers who dislocate workers unnecessarily. Terminated employees often find it much easier to get a new job if their employment record indicates that they quit instead of being fired. Agreeing to treat the termination as a resignation can benefit both employer and employee, if the employer's experience rate stays low. But employees must understand the effect that the characterization of the termination will have on their UI application.

Companies can take various steps to reduce their experience rating and therefore their liability for unemployment tax:

- Understanding the nature and interaction of the federal and state payroll taxes;

- Reducing FUTA payments appropriately to compensate for state tax payments;

- Making sure taxes are paid when due;

- Reviewing state experience records for correctness;

- Understanding the experience rating system and the claims appeal procedure;

- Transferring employees within the organization instead of terminating them, to reduce unemployment claims;

- Analyzing operations to see if they could be made more consistent, less seasonal (thus avoiding layoffs and terminations);

- Firing unsatisfactory employees quickly, before they become eligible for benefits;

- Holding exit interviews with employees who quit, with a view to resolving problems that lead to resignations;

- Scheduling layoffs for Fridays, not earlier in the week wherever possible, because all the states provide benefits for partial weeks of employment;

- Maintaining adequate documentation of misconduct (which will also be useful if the terminated employee makes discrimination or wrongful termination claims);

- Monitoring all benefit claims and appealing claims that the company believes to be unfounded (e.g., employees who quit asserting involuntary termination).

The laws in over half the states (Arizona, Arkansas, California, Colorado, Georgia, Indiana, Kansas, Kentucky, Louisiana, Maine, Massachusetts,

Michigan, Minnesota, Missouri, Nebraska, New Jersey, New Mexico, New York, North Carolina, North Dakota, Ohio, Pennsylvania, South Dakota, Texas, Washington, Wisconsin, West Virginia) allow employers to make intentional over-payments of unemployment insurance taxes resulting in a lower tax rate for the next tax period; sometimes the numbers work out so that a small voluntary con-tribution produces a large reduction in future liabilities. [Howard Perlman, *Voluntary Contributions May Help Lower Unemployment Insurance Taxes,* Bloomberg BNA Payroll Blog (July 14, 2016), available at <https://www.bna .com/voluntary-contributions-may-b73014444772/>]

§ 32.05   ADMINISTRATION AND APPEALS

Traditionally, states required in-person application for unemployment ben-efits; now virtually all the states permit claims to be filed remotely (e.g., via tele-phone or the Internet). If and when an ex-employee applies for UI benefits, the employer is asked for the reason for the termination. The employer is given a cer-tain number of days to contest the claim. Once this period elapses, the employer can no longer protest the granting of benefits. If the employer objects to the grant of benefits, the state agency that administers unemployment benefits will assess the matter. The decision can be appealed to an Administrative Law Judge, an administrative board, and finally through the state court system (the federal courts are not appropriate for these questions).

If the employer fails to meet its burden of proof about the employee's dis-qualification at the administrative hearing, the case will not be remanded to give the employer another chance—and a remand will probably not be granted to sub-mit additional evidence [*Holmes*, Unempl. Ins. Rep. (CCH) ¶ 8664 (La. App. 2001)], so it's important to prepare well for the initial administrative hearing.

The Unemployment Insurance Integrity Act, part of the Federal Trade Adjustment Assistance Extension Act of 2011, required all the states to adopt changes in their UI laws, including integrity provisions to reduce erroneous pay-ments. Congress wanted to deter employers from failing to respond to claim notices because they considered charges to their reserve accounts as a simple cost of doing business.

The states were given until October 21, 2013, to adopt laws penalizing employers and employers' agents, including TPAs, for failure to give timely and adequate responses to state requests for information about overpaid unemploy-ment claims.

Penalties are imposed for a pattern of failure to respond. Many of the state integrity laws include penalties and civil fines. The overpaid claim is charged to the employer's experience rating and cannot receive a refund. Although states probably will not treat a single failure to respond as a pattern, employers should review their separation and settlement agreements to see if the employer agrees not to challenge the separated employee's unemployment claim. Separation agreements should include clear language about what the employer will do when an information request is received. Employers should also make sure that their TPAs respond promptly to state requests. [Eric J. Janson and Marc R. Jacobs, *You (Don't) Have the Right to Remain Silent—How New Unemployment Insurance Integrity Laws May Affect Your Separation and Settlement Agreements with Departing Employees*, Seyfarth Shaw LLP (Nov. 12, 2013)]

New Jersey enacted legislation on August 19, 2013, implementing the Trade Adjustment Assistance Extension Act penalties on employers who fail to make a timely response to a state unemployment office's request for information. Similar laws in Minnesota, South Carolina, Wyoming, and Iowa require the employer to reimburse the state unemployment account for the overpayment, but the New Jersey law does not include this requirement. [Stacey D. Adams and Jessica R. Agarwal, *New Jersey Law Penalizes Employers for Failing to Timely Respond to Requests Regarding Unemployment Insurance*, Littler Mendelson (Aug. 29, 2013), available at Lexology.com]

Effective January 3, 2016, the Illinois statute was amended to make it much easier for employers to challenge unemployment claims. The statute defines misconduct as deliberate, willful violation of an employer's reasonable rule or policy about the employee's behavior in the performance of work, if the violation harmed the employer or co-workers, or was repeated despite warnings. The 2016 clarifies that eight specific circumstances constitute disqualifying misconduct: falsification of an employment application; failure to maintain licenses or certifications required for the job; attendance violations that continue after a written warning; gross negligence that damages the employer's property or creates a safety hazard; insubordination; using alcohol or drugs in the workplace; or coming to work under the influence.

A 2016 Illinois Supreme Court case holds that the statutory definition is not exclusive and employees are disqualified from receiving benefits if they knowingly break a rule, engage in illegal conduct, or commit a prima facie intentional tort. [*Petrovic v. The Dep't of Emp't Sec.*, 2016 IL 118562 (Ill. Feb. 4, 2016); see Peter A. Steinmeyer and Julie Badel, *Illinois Legislative Changes and a State Supreme Court Decision Substantially Help Employers Challenge Unemployment Claims*, Epstein Becker Green (Feb. 9, 2016), available at Lexology.com]

§ 32.06 FUTA COMPLIANCE

Employers (but not employees) have an obligation to make payments under the Federal Unemployment Tax Act (FUTA) to fund the federal program of unemployment insurance. The general rule is that the basic federal FUTA tax rate is 6.0%, but this tax is imposed only on the first $7,000 of wages. The effective rate for most employers is much lower, because they are entitled to a credit of 5.4%—so they pay only $42 per covered worker per year. When it was first enacted, FUTA tax was 1.0% of the worker's total wages. In 1940, it was 3.0% of wages up to $3,000. In 1985, the nominal rate was raised to 6.2%, The taxable wage base went from $3,000 to $4,200 in 1972, to $6,000 in 1978, and to $7,000 in 1983, but it has not been raised since then—despite significant economic changes.

The states set their own taxable wage bases. Starting with calendar 2010, the 6.2% FUTA rate drops to 6.0%. Most employers actually pay a lower rate, because they qualify for a 5.4% credit for state employment taxes they have already paid. This is sometimes referred to as the "normal credit" or "90% credit." Sometimes the company will qualify for an even lower FUTA rate if its experience rating is good. The additional credit equals the difference between the basic state rate of 5.4% and the employer's actual experience rate. However, the full credit can be claimed only in states that the Department of Labor certifies as compliant with federal requirements To qualify for the full credit, the employer must make all state contributions by January 31 (the due date for Form 940). For 2010 and later years, the effective tax rate therefore can be as low as 0.6%. [*Comparison of State Unemployment Insurance Laws*]

If the state has not repaid money borrowed from the federal government, it will be classified as a "credit reduction state." The state will not be entitled to the full credit, so employers in that state will have to pay more FUTA tax when they file Form 940. Schedule A of Form 940 is used to report wages paid in any credit reduction state (including by a multi-state employer that has employees in a credit reduction state).

In 2015, four states had their credit reduced because of outstanding loans and two states did in 2016; it was estimated that in 2017, California would be the only U.S. state with a credit reduction. In general, the amount of outstanding unemployment insurance debt has been reduced very significantly: in 2010, there was $42.18 billion in such debt, falling steadily since 2012. The 2016 level was only $11.05 billion. [*State Unemployment Insurance Trust Fund Solvency Report 2017*, <http://www.oui.doleta.gov/unemploy/docs/trustFundSolvReport2017.pdf> (Mar. 7, 2017)]

The employer reports its FUTA liability on IRS Form 940. See IRS Tax Topics, Topic 759 for an explanation of depositing FUTA taxes and filing Form 940. The due date for filing Form 940 is January 31, but filing can be deferred until February 10 if all FUTA taxes have been deposited when due. When FUTA tax for the year exceeds $500, the employer must make at least one quarterly payment. FUTA liability under $500 in a quarter is carried forward to the next quarter. But when cumulative liability reaches $500, a deposit must be made by the last day of month after the end of the quarter. If FUTA liability exceeds $500 for a quarter, the tax must be deposited electronically, generally by using the Electronic Federal Tax Payment System. If the total FUTA liability for the year is less than $500 (since most employers pay $42 per worker per year, this means that there are fewer than 12 workers) then the amount can either be deposited or paid with Form 940. [<http://www.irs.gov/taxtopics/tc759.html> (updated Feb. 27, 2017, last accessed Mar. 9, 2017)]

CHAPTER 33

WORKER'S COMPENSATION

§ 33.01   INTRODUCTION

The states administer the Worker's Compensation ("Worker's Compensation" or WC) system to provide income to individuals who are unable to work because of employment-related illnesses and injuries. WC benefits, like unemployment insurance benefits, are funded by insurance maintained by the employer.

The WC system balances the interests of employers and employees: the employees' need for continuing income; the employer's need to have claims resolved quickly, in an administrative system that is not prone to make large sympathy awards the way the jury system is. Employers have a duty to make a prompt report of all accidents to the agency that administers the WC system. If an employee claims job-related injury or illness, the claim is heard by a WC tribunal. Depending on the state, this may be referred to as a board or a commission. The tribunal decides if the claim is valid. If so, benefits are awarded: reimbursement of medical expenses, plus weekly income.

WC benefits do not begin until a waiting period (typically three to seven days) has elapsed. This serves to distinguish genuine temporary disability from minor incidents without lasting consequences. However, most state WC laws also provide that, if a disability continues for a period of time (set by the state at anywhere from five days to over seven weeks), retroactive payments dating back to the original date of the injury will be granted.

The weekly benefit is usually limited to half to two-thirds of the pre-accident wage, subject to fixed minimum and maximum payments (often keyed to the state's average income) and also subject to an overall limitation on payments. In some states, additional payments are available if the worker has dependent children—especially in cases where the work-related incident caused the death of the worker. A burial benefit is also paid in death cases. Depending on the state it ranges between $1,000 and $5,000.

In 1999, the Supreme Court decided a Worker's Compensation case, *American Manufacturers Mutual Insurance Co. v. Sullivan.* [526 U.S. 46 (1999)] Under Pennsylvania's WC Act, once liability is no longer contested, the employer (or its insurer) has an obligation to pay for all reasonable or necessary treatment. However, an insurer or a self-insured employer is permitted to withhold payment for disputed treatment pending utilization review by an independent third party. The Supreme Court ruled that private insurers doing utilization review are not "state actors" subject to the Due Process clause of the Constitution. Employees have no property rights until treatments have been found reasonable and necessary. Therefore, the insurer has no obligation to notify employees, or to hold a hearing, if it withholds benefits until review has been completed and a decision made in the employees' favor.

The Virginia Workers' Compensation Commission has always counted members of a corporation's board of directors (whether or not they earn a salary) as employees—and the Virginia Act applies to all companies with three or more employees regularly in service. Executive officers can exempt themselves from the Act, but this requires filing a formal notice with the commission. The commission has the power to issue an order to show cause to determine if an employer that does not have WC coverage should be fined. [Vandeventer Black LLP, *Employers Beware: Unpaid Officers and Directors May Count as Employees Under the Virginia Workers' Compensation Act* (Nov. 7, 2016), available at Lexology.com]

§ 33.02 CLASSIFICATION OF BENEFITS

[A] Type and Degree of Disability

If the initial tribunal accepts the contention that the worker is genuinely disabled, and the disability is in fact work-related, benefits are awarded based on the type and degree of disability.

There are four categories of disability: permanent total, permanent partial, temporary total, and temporary partial.

Permanent disability payments can be based on wage loss, earning capacity, physical impairment, or some combination. A "schedule injury" is loss of a finger, toe, arm, eye, or leg. The schedule determines the number of weeks of benefits payable for such an injury. Death benefits are also available to the survivors of persons killed in work-related incidents.

WC statutes take four basic approaches: (1) impairment rating; (2) assessment of loss of earning capacity; (3) a hybrid approach; and (4) wage loss. These systems set benefits based on published schedules and ratings rather than actual economic loss. About a dozen states, including Michigan, apply the wage loss approach as long as disability continues. [Michael D. Sanders, *Workers' Compensation Facilitation—The New Trial?*, Foster Swift Collins & Smith PC (Nov. 17, 2016), available at Lexology.com]

A Colorado state judge awarded $530 per week benefits for the life of the widow of oilfield worker Jim Freemyer. Freemyer was overcome by toxic gases while measuring the level of oil in a storage tank. The CDC identified at least nine sudden deaths caused by dense plumes of hydrocarbons. In the past, such deaths were sometimes attributed to "natural causes" and benefits were denied. However, in late 2014, the North Dakota Supreme Court granted death benefits to the survivor of another oil field worker overcome by fumes. [Alexandra Berzon, *Widow Awarded Benefits in Hydrocarbons Storage-Tank Death*, WSJ.com (July 16, 2015)]

For injuries such as back strains related to lifting, the tribunal must make a case-by-case determination of the number of weeks of disability that can be anticipated, and the seriousness of the disability.

The Ohio Supreme Court held that a worker whose retirement was involuntary can receive WC temporary total disability benefits even if there was no loss of earnings. Previous state cases held that if retirement is related to an injury, the worker can file for temporary total disability benefits without seeking other employment. [*State ex rel. Honda of Am. Mfg., Inc. v. Industrial Comm'n of Ohio, et al.*, 139 Ohio St. 3d 290 (Ohio 2014)]

The Virginia Supreme Court ruled that if an employee announces his or her retirement and is injured shortly before the effective date of retirement, temporary total wage loss benefits are payable, but temporary partial benefits are not. A retired worker who suffers total incapacity from a work-related injury does not have to prove that he or she had a pre-injury intent to re-enter the workforce. The court held that the employee is eligible for up to 500 weeks of wage-loss benefits, even though those wages would not have been earned absent the injury. [*McKellar v. Northrop Grumman Shipbuilding, Inc.*, Record No. 140999 (Va. Sup. Oct. 29, 2015)]

Benefits can be granted for either "disability" or "impairment." The difference is that disability is defined to mean loss of wages, whereas impairment is permanent partial disability that does not cause wage loss.

The concept of Maximum Medical Improvement (MMI) comes into play in the case of a temporary disability. MMI is a doctor's opinion that there is no reasonable medical probability of further improvement in function (as determined based on factors such as current and proposed treatment, history of improvement, and pre-existing conditions). Most states impose an obligation on the employer to notify the employee that MMI has been reached, and the employee is likely to lose benefits within 90 days unless he or she returns to work or finds other employment. Benefits can be extended past the MMI if the claimant makes an honest effort yet cannot find suitable work.

In mid-2016, the Florida Supreme Court held that the statutory 104-week cap on temporary disability benefits was unconstitutional, stating that benefits cannot be terminated for a person who is totally disabled and unable to work and has not yet reached MMI. The supreme court revived the previous limit of five years (260 weeks) but stressed that it was not ruling that the entire WC system was invalid. [*Westphal v. City of St. Petersburg*, **194 So. 3d 311** (Fla. 2016); see Amy O'Connor, *Florida Supreme Court Strikes Down State Cap on Temporary Disability Benefits*, insurancejournal.com (June 9, 2016) (benefitslink.com)]

In addition to making wage-based payments, the employer must provide the employee with reasonable and necessary medical treatment, continued as long as the injured employee's medical condition requires. Most states include chiropractic in the definition of medical care. Many include home health attendants as well.

A 2011 Georgia Court of Appeals decision permitted aggravation of an injured employee's condition by light duty work to be treated as a new injury because the job responsibilities changed and the claimant was not performing his normal or ordinary duties. The claimant was an assistant pressman who suffered a work-related neck and arm injury in October 2002. He had carpal tunnel surgery and received WC benefits, including permanent partial disability. He returned to light duty work (including quality control and fulfillment) in mid-2003 with a permanent restriction on lifting, pushing, or pulling over 15 pounds. He said that the work exceeded his medical restrictions 40% of the time but his supervisors refused to modify the assignment. He was laid off in April 2008 and had lumbar fusion surgery in October 2008. He filed a claim for medical and temporary total disability benefits, which was granted because he worked under strenuous new circumstances that exceeded his light duty restriction. [*R.R. Donnelley v. Ogletree*, 312 Ga. App. 475 (2011)]

[B] Compensable Injuries

Whether an incident is covered by WC depends on several factors, e.g., employee status and the connection between employment and the injury. The Maine Law Court ruled that the WC Board was correct to apply the presumption of compensability in a death case when an employee working at home died of a heart attack while using a treadmill. The cause of death is rebuttably presumed work-related, if there is other evidence showing a rational potential for work-relatedness. In this case, the decedent was under extraordinary strain from work. His employer let him use the treadmill at home because he could work while performing the exercise recommended by his doctor. The evidence was not sufficient to rebut the presumption. [*Estate of Sullwold v. Salvation Army*, 2015 ME 4, 108 A.3d 1265 (2015)]

Evidentiary problems are involved if an employee is injured while working at home: there probably won't be witnesses to the accident and the employer is unable to control the work environment. An employee working at home still must prove that the injury was incurred in the course of, and arising out of, employment. To minimize WC risks associated with telecommuting, the employer can define work hours (and breaks) in a written job description; require the employee to specify where work will be done; perhaps carry out a safety inspection of the work area; and investigate work-related injuries. [Caroline E. Diwik and Joan M. Verchot, *Protect Yourself from Telecommuters' Workers' Compensation Claims*, Dinsmore & Shohl LLP (June 20, 2016), available at Lexology.com]

It is significant whether the injured person is a common-law employee rather than an independent contractor. Early in 2002, California ruled that even a hirer of an independent contractor can be liable to the contractor (or employees of the contractor) if, for example, the hirer provides unsafe equipment or makes another affirmative contribution to the injury—merely controlling safety conditions at the site is not enough to impose liability. [*McKown v. Wal-Mart Stores Inc.*, 27 Cal. 4th 219, 38 P.3d 1094, 115 Cal. Rptr. 2d 868 (2002); *Hooker v. DOT*, 27 Cal. 4th 198, 38 P.3d 1081, 115 Cal. Rptr. 2d 853 (2002)]

Sometimes injuries occurring outside the workplace will be covered—e.g., if the employer sent the employee to make a delivery or perform an errand, and the injury occurred in that place or en route. Injuries occurring during employer-sponsored athletics, or at a company picnic or holiday party, are probably compensable. Injuries on company premises during scheduled breaks are probably compensable, but employees take unscheduled breaks at their own risk because such injuries are considered to occur outside working hours. If employees are engaged in work-related tasks, injuries occurring at home can be compensable. [*A.E. Clevite, Inc. v. Tjas*, 996 P.2d 1072 (Utah App. 2000) (worker who became a paraplegic when he slipped while salting down his driveway so it would be safe for the expected delivery of a work-related package)]

Whether an incident is covered by WC may also depend on whether it results from an "accident" (an unexpected occurrence with a definite time, place, and occasion) and whether there is any reason to remove the incident from coverage (e.g., the employee's substance abuse was a causative factor).

One of the most vital factors is the employer's degree of control over the employee's activities. A Missouri case [*Leslie v. School Servs. & Leasing Inc.*, 947 S.W.2d 97 (Mo. App. 1997)] holds that a job applicant injured during training had not become an "employee," and therefore was not covered by WC. In this case, the potential employer didn't require her to take the training, didn't control her activities during the training process, and in fact didn't even guarantee her a job if she completed the training successfully.

In 2004, the New Jersey Supreme Court ruled that injuries occurring during a recreational or social activity can come under WC provided that the employee believed that he or she was required to engage in the activity. [*Lozano v. De Luca Constr. Co.*, 178 N.J. 513, 842 A.2d 156 (N.J. Super. Ct. App. 2004). Note that N.J.S.A. § 34:15-7 allows payment of WC benefits for recreational injuries sustained through activities that are a regular incident of employment and produce benefit for the employer over and above improved employee fitness and morale.]

The North Carolina Court of Appeals found that a leg injury was compensable. It occurred during a game of laser tag at a mandatory out-of-town sales conference. The analysis used six factors: employer sponsorship; whether attendance was voluntary; encouragement for employees to attend the event; degree to which the employer funded the event; whether the employees considered the event an employee benefit to which they were entitled of right; and whether the event provided tangible benefits to the employer, such as opportunities to give speeches or present awards. In this case, the employer paid for the laser tag event, attendance was mandatory, and the employer benefited. Thus, the injury was work-related and compensable. [*Holliday v. Tropical Nut & Fruit Co.* 780 S.E.2d 563 (N.C. App. 2015)]

At-work assaults raise difficult questions. The general rule is that injuries caused by assaults are compensable if the job increases the risk of encountering dangerous people (e.g., convenience store clerks are at risk of being robbed). But if the assault occurred for personal reasons, for instance if an abusive spouse commits an assault at the victim's workplace, the fact that the assault occurred at work will not necessarily render the injury a compensable one, if it is not work-related in any way. The WC system is essentially a no-fault system, so it will not be necessary to decide if the employer was at fault in not having a better security system. Virginia refused to apply WC exclusivity in the case of a paramedic who had a seizure and died three days after a co-worker deliberately shocked her with live defibrillator paddles, because an assault or horseplay is purely personal and not attributable to the employer. [*Hilton v. Martin, Va.*, 275 Va. 176 (2008)]

The Delaware Supreme Court allowed an employee injured by horseplay to bring a personal injury suit against the co-workers who injured him. The court used the four-part "Larson Test" (named after the treatise Larson's Workers' Compensation Law): the scope and seriousness of the deviation of the conduct from employment activities; if the conduct was separate from work duties or commingled with them; if the nature of the job typically includes horseplay; and whether the employer tolerated horseplay. In this case, a pipefitter/welder sued three co-workers for wrapping him in duct tape; he had to have back and knee surgery and counseling after the injury. He sued the co-workers for more than $74,000 in medical expenses and $142,000 lost wages and also sought future medical expenses. The Delaware Supreme Court remanded the case for a determination of whether the prank fell outside the scope of employment. [*Grabowski v. Mangler*, 938 A.2d 637 (Del. 2007)] On remand, the Delaware Supreme Court upheld summary judgment for the defendants. The injuries occurred at a time when there was no work to be done; horseplay was so frequent as to be an accepted part of the workday; and the prank was performed quickly without substantial abandonment of duties. [*Grabowski v. Mangler*, 956 A.2d 1217 (Del. 2008)]

Schmidt v. Smith [155 N.J. 44, 713 A.2d 1014 (1998)] says that bodily injury caused by sexual harassment is covered by the employer liability section of the Worker's Compensation insurance policy, because this section of the policy is designed to make funds available to compensate employees for their work-related injuries, even those for which Worker's Compensation payments are not available.

The Pennsylvania Supreme Court, without really exploring the policy issues, upheld a lower court's determination to uphold an award of Worker's Compensation benefits to an illegal alien, on the grounds that the employer did not show that the injured person failed to satisfy the requirements of a section of the Worker's Compensation Act. However, if the employer applies for suspension of such benefits, the employer does not have to make a showing of job availability. [*Reinforced Earth Co. v. WC Appeals Bd. (Astudillo)*, 810 A.2d 99 (Pa. 2002)] In contrast, *Granados v. Windson Development Corp.* [257 Va. 103, 509 S.E.2d 290 (1999)], held that an alien who was hired after submitting forged immigration documents could not become a lawful employee entitled to Worker's Compensation, because no employment contract could be formed.

The Second Circuit approved an award of lost earnings to an undocumented alien worker after he was crippled in a fall attributed to violations of the scaffolding requirements for work sites. New York case law specifically rejects the concept that the damages should be limited on the basis of what the worker would earn in his or her home country. The jury awarded $638,671.63 in compensatory damages, including about $93,000 for incurred expenses, $46,000 for past pain and suffering, $40,000 for lost earnings, $230,000 for future pain and suffering over the plaintiff's predicted life expectancy, and $230,000 for 26 years of future lost earnings. [*Madeira v. Affordable Hous. Found. Inc.*, 469 F.3d 219 (2d Cir. 2006). See also *Majlinger v. Cassino Contracting Corp.*, 25 A.D.3d 4, 802 N.Y.S.2d 56 (2d Dept. 2005) allowing compensation for lost U.S. earnings at U.S. rates, holding that this does not conflict with the federal immigration statute, the Immigration Reform and Control Act (IRCA); *Flores v. Limehouse*, No. 2:04-1295-CWH 2006 U.S. Dist. LEXIS 30433 (D.S.C. May 11, 2006) holding that IRCA does not preempt claims by undocumented workers against their employers under RICO and federal and state labor law—even if the workers obtained employment fraudulently; *Rosa v. Partners in Progress, Inc.*, 868 A.2d 994 (N.H. 2005) (for undocumented worker to be able to make a tort claim, the employer must have known or have a duty to know the worker's employment was illegal).]

When an illegal alien worker was injured in a fall from a roof, the Louisiana Court of Appeal found three parties, including Vaughan Roofing, liable for providing WC benefits. When Vaughan Roofing appealed, the Supreme Court denied certiorari, refusing to decide whether I.R.C. preempts the state ruling that illegal workers are entitled to WC benefits. [*Rodriguez v. Integrity Contr.*, 38 So. 3d 511 (La. Ct. App. 2010), *cert. denied, Vaughan Roofing & Sheet Metal LLC v. Rodriguez*, 562 U.S. 1256 (2011)] Tennessee awarded survivor benefits to foreign nationals (Mexicans) who were dependents of a worker who died in a work-related accident, although the court found they were not wholly dependent on remittances from their son and therefore the case remanded to determine the correct benefit to be paid. [*Fusner v. Coop Constr. Co.*, 211 S.W.3d 686 (Tenn. Sup. 2007)]

If the incident is covered, the next question is whether WC exclusivity applies. [See § 33.03]

[C] Problems of Co-Employment

There are many reasons for employers to use temporary, contingent, part-time, or leased workers. In some cases, employee leasing results in lower WC costs. For employers who do not self-insure, the insurance rate has a lot to do with past experience. The smaller the workplace, the greater the impact that a few claims—especially a few very large claims—will have on its experience rating. That is one of the motivations for using leased workers to replace some or all of a company's common-law employees. [See § 1.09 for more about employee leasing.]

Although a large leasing company will not qualify for small business discounted rates, a leasing company can offer the services of a broad range of workers, some in low-risk occupations such as office work.

In its initial years, a leasing company will probably qualify for low rates, because there has not been enough time for many accidents to happen. Abuses of the system are possible, if companies dissolve and re-form to manipulate their experience rates. Just for this reason, some states (e.g., Arizona, California, Colorado, Florida, Nevada, New Hampshire, New Mexico, Oregon, South Carolina, Texas, and Utah) disregard the presence of leasing companies, and still require the underlying employer to buy WC insurance and maintain its own experience rating. California AB 1897, signed September 28, 2014, makes companies with more than 25 employees that use workers supplied by a labor contractor jointly liable with the labor contractor if there is a failure to obtain WC coverage. The law does not apply to workers who are exempt as administrative, executive, or professional employees—or to companies with fewer than six workers supplied by the staffing company at a given time. [Baker & McKenzie, *Certain California Employers Who Use Staffing Agencies and Contractors Statutorily Liable for Wage and Hour and Safety Violations* (Dec. 26, 2014), available at Lexology .com]

Furthermore, state courts may decide that the leasing company or temporary agency's client is the actual employer, because it has real control over the worker's activities and therefore is legally responsible for compensation for injuries. Both companies might also be treated as co-employers.

A recent report on temporary work argues that getting workers from temporary agencies rather than hiring full-time workers permits employers to game the Worker's Compensation system because if workers are hurt on the job, the employer can avoid having this reflected in its experience rating by treating the workers as if they were employed by the temp agency. "Piggybacking" is the temp agency's practice of paying artificially low premiums by creating a separate company with a lower experience rating. For example, in 1995—and again in 2012, Business Staffing, Inc., was found guilty of fraud for setting up a sham insurance company and failing to pay benefits to injured workers. In November 2011, a Massachusetts employment agency was convicted of paying more than $30 million of employee compensation in cash, "under the table," to avoid paying employment taxes and to artificially deflate its WC premiums. In 2009, a staffing company accountant in New York was convicted of insurance fraud by reporting asbestos workers (who do a hazardous job) as clerical workers to reduce WC premiums. [Rebecca Smith and Claire McKenna, *Temped Out: How the Domestic Outsourcing of Blue-Collar Jobs Harms America's Workers*, Nat'l Employment Law Project/National Staffing Workers Alliance, <http://www.nelp .org/page/-/Reports/Temped-Out.pdf?nocdn=1> (undated, last accessed Mar. 10, 2017)]

Another possibility is that, if the underlying employer takes the position that the leasing company is the true employer, the underlying employer might be treated as a third party that can be sued for tort claims and cannot assert WC exclusivity. The underlying employer might be sued for negligence or for violating established safety rules, and might be forced to pay damages (including punitive damages). Nor would the employee's WC benefits be used to offset the underlying employer's liability in this situation.

The National Association of Insurance Commissioners (NAIC) has drafted an Employee Leasing Registration Model Act under which leasing firms must register with the state before they purchase WC insurance. At the time of registration, they must disclose their ownership and their past WC history. Registration will not be permitted if the company has had its insurance policies terminated in the past for failure to pay premiums.

The "borrowed servant" doctrine says that if an employer lends an employee to someone else to perform a "special service," the recipient of the special service is considered the employer of the borrowed employee if the recipient can control the details of the work. According to the Eighth Circuit, this requires a contract for hire and the employee's consent to the special employment relationship—and the burden of proof is on the party citing the doctrine. Therefore, an employee of the Truck Crane Service Co., injured on a job site operated by Maguire Tank Inc., and who received WC benefits from Truck Crane, nevertheless could sue Maguire Tank. Maguire Tank did not direct or control the injured person's actions. He merely worked there for a day and was not instructed in how to do his job by Maguire Tank employees. In fact, the injury occurred after the job was finished and part of a crane that was being prepared for shipping fell and injured the plaintiff's arm. [*Lundstrom v. Maguire Tank Inc.*, 509 F.3d 864 (8th Cir. 2007)]

The Texas Supreme Court ruled that if a general contractor provides Worker's Compensation insurance to a subcontractor, the general contractor cannot be sued for negligence by the subcontractor's employees. A premises owner can be deemed a general contractor if it fits under the definition in the WC Act. [*Entergy v. Summers*, 282 S.W.3d 433 (Tex. 2009)]

The Connecticut Supreme Court ruled in mid-2016 that a WC insurer has a subrogation claim against third-party tortfeasors to recover money paid to an employer because of an employee's injury. Pacific Insurance, Reliable Welding's insurer, paid WC benefits to a Reliable employee who was injured in a fall at a construction site. Pacific sued several other parties working on the project, alleging that the injury was caused by their negligent failure to provide proper fall protection. The state supreme court ruled that insurers have a broad right to sue for subrogation after they make payments for a loss caused by a third party. Subrogation applies in the WC context because it serves public policy objectives like keeping down the cost of insurance and preventing unjust enrichment of third-party tortfeasors. [*Pacific Insurance Co. Ltd. v. Champion Steel LLC*, 2016 WL 503057 (Conn. Sept. 27, 2016); see Terence J. Brunau, *CT Supreme Court*

Permits a Workers' Compensation Insurer to Sue Third Parties for Reimbursement, Murtha Cullina LLP (Sept. 22, 2016), available at Lexology.com]

[D] How the WC System Handles Disease Claims

WC benefits are also available if an employee develops a work-related disease. However, occupational diseases create some difficult problems of analysis. Disease is covered only if there is a close connection between onset of the disease and the work environment. This is fairly clear for "brown lung" disease and cotton mills, but more difficult if the claim is that nonsmoking employees have been harmed by cigarette smoke exhaled by customers and co-employees who smoke.

Depending on the state, benefits may also be available if workplace conditions aggravate a disease that the individual already had. In California, Florida, Kentucky, Maryland, Mississippi, North Dakota, and South Carolina, WC benefits will be available but will be reduced to compensate for the pre-existing condition. If, for instance, the worker's condition was 25% due to workplace factors, 75% due to the preexisting condition, only 25% of the full benefit will be payable.

Occupational disease creates difficult questions involving "long tail" claims: claims made on the basis that it took years, or even decades, for the symptoms caused by occupational exposure to hazardous substances to manifest themselves. During this long period of time, the employee could have held several jobs (involving exposure to different hazards) and/or engaged in behavior such as smoking that is hazardous or compounds other hazards.

The general rule under the legal system is that claims are timely if they are filed within a reasonable time after the individual first experiences disability or symptoms, and could reasonably be expected to draw a connection between work exposure and illness.

Another question is whether the employee's exposure was extensive enough to trigger the claimed symptoms. The epidemiology (disease pattern) for similar exposures should be studied to see if the employee's alleged experience is typical. Furthermore, one disease claim by an employee could trigger a wave of related claims from other employees who actually are ill, believe themselves to be ill because they have developed psychosomatic symptoms, or who just hope for easy money.

Asbestos-related disease is "bodily injury by disease" rather than "bodily injury by accident" under WC and employer liability insurance policies. Asbestos exposure is not an accident because it is not violent and because it develops over a latency period rather than right away. [*Riverwood Int'l Corp. v. Employers Ins. of Wausau*, 420 F.3d 378 (5th Cir. 2005)]

Washington State's Worker's Compensation system is no-fault, with a narrow exception that allows employees to sue their employers for work-related injuries that result from the employer's deliberate intention of producing injury. For many years, the exception was applied only in cases of physical assault. A 1995 case extended the exception to certain (not merely likely) injuries where the employer knew the specific claimant would be injured (not just that someone would be). In 2014, the Washington Supreme Court found asbestos exposure claims to be WC-exclusive in a case where machine shop workers were allegedly denied access to PPE while asbestos was being removed in 1985. The state supreme court held that the exposure was not certain to cause mesothelioma, so the exception did not apply. [*Walston v. Boeing Co.*, 334 P.3d 519 (Wash. 2014). See also *Birklid v. Boeing*, 127 Wis. 2d 853, 904 P.2d 278 (1995).]

West Virginia's deliberate intent statute (Code § 23-4-2) provides that employers are not immune for work-related injuries if the employer acted with deliberate intent. Recent amendments to the statute make it more difficult for employees to prove a case. The employee either must prove that the defendant acted with a consciously and deliberately formed intention to cause the specific injury or death that the employee sufferent, or that all five of the statutory factors are present. The five factors are: (1) a specific unsafe working condition was present, creating a high degree of risk and strong probability of death or serious injury; (2) before the injury, the employer had actual knowledge of this condition; (3) the specific unsafe condition violated a state or federal safety statute, rule, or regulation, or safety standards well-known and accepted in the industry; (4) despite the presence of all these factors, someone with actual knowledge continued to expose the employee to that specific danger; and (5) serious compensable injury or death occurred as a direct and proximate result of the specific unsafe working condition.

A serious compensable injury is defined as one with a total whole person impairment level of at least 13%. The amended statute says that actual knowledge cannot be presumed, but can be shown by evidence of deliberate failure to conduct an inspection or assessment that was required by statute. Documentary or other credible evidence is required to prove a supervisor's or manager's knowledge of prior accidents, regulatory citations, or safety complaints. Plaintiffs can only rely on statutes, regulations, or rules that apply specifically to the work and the working conditions, not those imposing a general requirement of safe operations. The amendments apply to injuries occurring on or after July 1, 2015. [Nick Linn and Matthew B. Hansberry, *West Virginia's Amended Deliberate Intent Statute*, Littler Mendelson (July 21, 2015), available at Lexology.com]

The Wyoming Supreme Court explained when WC benefits are available if a worker suffers a heart attack after doing physical labor. Employment-related coronaries are compensable only if there is a direct causal connection between the work done and the cardiac condition. The exertion causing the condition must have occurred during an actual period of employment stress that was unusual or abnormal for the job—whether or not it was unusual or abnormal for the employee. Acute symptoms must have manifested within four hours of the exertion. Medical evidence is mandatory for benefits to be available. Scherf, a 68-year-old employee, died after an at-work heart attack while he was servicing a front-end loader. He was a smoker with chronic high blood pressure and kidney failure but was physically active and seemed to handle his work duties well. He felt sick at work. Co-workers called an ambulance and he was treated for a heart attack but died the next evening. A cardiology expert witness testified that the attack began when he was at work, caused by heavy exertion when straining to open an access panel that was stuck in the mud. The Wyoming court awarded death benefits to his widow, concluding that this type of exertion was abnormal for oilers. [*Scherf v. State ex rel. Dep't of Workforce Serv.*, 2015 WY 130, 360 P.3d 66 (2015)]

[E] Psychological Injuries

By and large, the WC system deals with palpable physical injuries and diseases, although in some circumstances mental and emotional illnesses can be compensable. Emotional and mental injuries are analyzed in three categories:

- Mental-physical—physical impact of mental conditions, such as chest pains and high blood pressure;

- Physical-mental—such as suffering a phobia after being involved in an accident or developing "AIDS-phobia" after a needle-stick incident;

- Mental-mental—injuries with no physical component.

In all the states, mental-physical and physical-mental injuries are compensable as long as a causal connection between the two is established. Compensability of mental-mental injuries is less clear-cut. Some states, including Alabama, Florida, Georgia, Kansas, Minnesota, Montana, Nebraska, Ohio, Oklahoma, and South Dakota refuse to compensate cases where there is no demonstrated physical involvement. In the other states, it may be necessary to prove a connection to a severe, unpredictable event, and compensability may depend on whether the onset was gradual or sudden.

The Nevada Supreme Court permitted survivors to file a WC claim if a suicide is closely enough connected to a workplace injury. To prevail, the survivors must show that the industrial injury caused a psychological ailment severe enough to override rational judgment, and that caused the suicide. In this case, a bartender suffered chronic back pain after a workplace fall, and one of his doctors testified that he committed suicide because of the pain. [*Vredenburg v. Sedgwick CMA*, 188 P.3d 1084 (Nev. Sup. 2008); suicide can be compensable, even if the worker suffered from pre-existing depression, as long as a work-related injury was at least a contributing cause of the suicide: *Altes v. Petrocelli Elec. Co.*, 270 A.D.2d 767 (N.Y. Sup. 2000).]

§ 33.03 WC EXCLUSIVITY

The WC system gives employers the protection of "worker's compensation exclusivity"; in other words, in the normal work-related injury or illness case, the employee's only remedy against the employer is to collect compensation benefits. Tort lawsuits are not permitted. However, exclusivity applies only against the employer. If the employee is injured by a product manufactured by the employer, the employee can sue the employer in its capacity as manufacturer. Suits against other manufacturers, or non-employer parties responsible for hazardous conditions at the workplace, are also a possibility. The employer itself can sue the third party in order to recover the medical benefits that the employer provided on behalf of the employee.

WC is essentially a no-fault system, so negligence by any party is usually irrelevant. However, in some states, a worker's failure to use safety equipment can reduce (but not eliminate) the benefits that would otherwise be payable after an accident. Sometimes, the employer's wrongdoing will take the case out of WC exclusivity. Some (but not all) courts would allow an ordinary tort suit against an employer that deliberately concealed information about workplace hazards.

Compensation benefits will be granted only if the employee has medical evidence to prove the connection between the job and the disabling condition. Furthermore, the employee must be incapacitated by the condition, so benefits will not be awarded to a person who stoically continues to work despite pain. Courts have reached different conclusions as to whether a person is permanently and totally disabled only if there is absolutely no job he or she can perform, or whether "human factors" such as job availability within a reasonable commuting distance must be considered.

An appellate court in New Jersey upheld a $7.5 million jury award to a former Exxon worker and his wife. The court found Exxon liable for Bonnie Anderson's mesothelioma not only because she worked there for 12 years but because she washed her husband's work clothes for 24 years. The court rejected Exxon's argument that her claim was barred by WC exclusivity because Exxon took on a separate, independent role with respect to Ms. Anderson's non-occupational exposure to asbestos. (Occupational exposure was ruled out because her work as an electrician did not involve contact with asbestos.) New Jersey's rule is that employers have a duty to protect the spouses of employees, as well as employees, from asbestos exposure. [*Anderson v. A.J. Friedman Supply Co. Inc.*, 416 N.J. Super. 46 (2010)]

The Seventh Circuit had to decide whether an employee's common-law negligence claim was a claim to satisfy the insuring agreement of an excess WC policy under the employer liability laws. A former employee of TKK died of mesothelioma. TKK was named as defendant in a negligence suit. TKK notified its excess WC carrier of the suit. TKK retained primary responsibility for defending, settling, and paying claims of up to $275,000 per occurrence. After incurring about $400,000 in legal fees, TKK settled the suit. Safety National denied coverage, treating the negligence claim as a common-law claim that was not covered by the policy and was not brought under WC or employer liability laws. In Illinois, the Workers' Occupational Disease Act (ODA) is the exclusive remedy for employees who are injured at work or contract occupational disease. The Seventh Circuit held that the ODA does not cover all potential common-law claims, so employer liability should not be defined only as ODA statutory claims. The Seventh Circuit affirmed the district court's finding that the definition of "employer liability law" was broad enough to include common-law claims, even groundless claims for which the employer had an affirmative defense. [*TKK USA, Inc. v. Safety Nat'l Cas. Corp.*, 727 F.3d 782 (7th. Cir. 2013)]

A late 2015 Illinois Supreme Court case holds that mesothelioma sufferers are subject to WC exclusivity and the 25-year statute of repose under the Workers' Occupational Diseases Act. Therefore, common-law claims against a former employer for asbestos-related disease claims are barred even if the disease does not manifest itself until after the statute of repose has expired. [*Folta v. Ferro Eng'g*, 2015 IL 118070 (Ill. Nov. 4, 2015). But see *Tooey v. AK Steel Corp.*, 81 A.3d 351 (Pa. 2013): claims for occupational disease with a long latency period—more than the statutory 300 weeks—are not covered by the WC Act, and therefore exclusivity does not apply.]

There are three categories of workplace assaults for WC purposes. There is an inherent connection if the assault is related to employment, e.g., occurs in connection with an employee's termination. An assault might occur in the course of an inherently private dispute not related to employment, such as violence committed by the employee's spouse or partner. A "neutral force" random assault is committed on an employee outside the employment relationship. Inherent connection assaults are compensable under WC; private dispute assaults are not; neutral force incidents might be depending on circumstances. The "street risk" doctrine requires proof either that employees were indiscriminately exposed to dangers from the public, or the employee was assaulted because of his or her connection with the employer. The Tennessee Supreme Court ruled that WC benefits were not available for the widow of an employee whose murder at the workplace remained unsolved. The decedent opened the store; when the store owner arrived at 6 a.m., he found the body. The court treated the death as a "neutral force assault." The "street risk" doctrine did not apply because the premises were not open to the public at the time of the killing; his job did not involve public contact; and there was no evidence that members of the public were more likely to be close to the store in the early morning than at other times. [*Padilla v. Twin City Fire Ins. Co.*, 324 S.W.3d 507 (Tenn. 2010)]

WC exclusivity applies, and the victim does not have the right to bring tort claims against the employer in cases of rape or robbery by an unknown assailant. The Florida Court of Appeals ruled that the parents of a 16-year-old store employee who charged that she was raped by her manager cannot pursue a negligence suit against the store. (Their theory was that the store was negligent in hiring the manager.) The court of appeals held that it was possible that the family had a WC claim, but that would preclude a civil suit. [*John & Jane Doe v. Footstar Corp.*, 980 So. 2d 1266 (Fla. App. 2008)]

A Workers' Compensation carrier can take a credit under New York's Workers' Compensation Law § 29(4) against the settlement proceeds of a civil suit brought by WC recipient against her employer. The carrier is entitled to offset the full amount of settlement proceeds. An aide at a juvenile detention center was assaulted, raped, and abducted by a resident; eventually she received WC benefits for permanent partial disability. She received a $650,000 personal injury settlement in a suit charging that the institution and three supervisors were aware that the resident was a threat to her. The WC carrier approved the settlement, reserving its right under § 29(4) to take a credit against her future benefits equal to the net recovery. As a result, benefits were stopped. Under § 29(1), an employee can sue for negligence or a wrongful act that is not committed by a co-worker; the carrier has a lien on the WC benefits. Section 29(4) permits crediting the proceeds of the lawsuit against the payment obligation. In this case, the carrier waived its lien, so § 29(4) applied. The New York Court of Appeals held that the proceeds here compensated for the physical and mental injuries that resulted in the WC award, no matter how the recovery was structured for tax purposes. [*In re Beth v. NYS Office of Children & Family Servs.*, 22 N.Y.3d 80 (N.Y. 2013)]

The Texas Supreme Court ruled that a drug sales representative was acting in the scope of her employment (and therefore entitled to WC benefits when she was severely injured in an automobile accident) when driving to a storage unit containing drug samples, after a dinner with clients. The representative usually worked out of her home, but kept samples in a storage unit provided by the employer near her home. [*Leordeanu v. Am. Prot. Ins. Co.*, 330 S.W.3d 239 (Tex. 2010)]

The New Jersey Appellate Division extended the "going and coming" rule to grant full WC benefits to an off-site employee who was seriously injured during a five-mile trip to the deli for coffee, because a coffee break is a minor deviation from employment that does not prevent payment of full benefits. An alternative argument was that he was on an authorized "mission" for the employer (going to the union hall to discuss plans for a new project) and was required to be away from the workplace on business. It was reasonable for him to take his coffee break instead of interrupting the union official or simply doing nothing, and in a secluded rural location, it was reasonable to drive five miles to find good coffee. [*Cooper v. Barnickel Enters. Inc.*, 411 N.J. Super. 343 (N.J. App. Div. 2010)]

According to the North Carolina Court of Appeals, injuries were not compensable when two employees of the State Highway Patrol attended a holiday lunch at a public restaurant a half-hour drive from their workplace. Attendance was not mandatory. After lunch, the plaintiffs hit a tree when driving back to work in a state-owned vehicle. Both were injured and applied for WC benefits. They were not authorized to use the vehicle for going to the luncheon. The "going and coming" rule means that injuries sustained to or from work are only compensable if the employer furnishes the means of transportation as an incident of the contract of employment or if the injuries were sustained on the employer's premises. The court of appeals found that the claimants were injured by a risk common to travel on public roads. Injuries at employer-sponsored events may be compensable, depending on factors such as whether the attendance was voluntary, whether the employer financed the event, if employees considered the event to be a benefit they were entitled to, and whether the employer benefited tangibly from the event. [*Graven, et al. v. N.C. Dept. of Public Safety-Division of Law Enforcement, et al.*, 762 S.E.2d 230 (N.C. App. 2014)]

A few states, such as New York, recognize the "dual purpose" doctrine, making injuries compensable if they occur during travel for mixed personal and business purposes. Ohio rejected the doctrine in 1951, but in 2014, the Ohio Supreme Court refused to apply this doctrine when a visiting nurse was injured while performing personal errands en route to an assignment. The case was remanded for trial as to whether the injury actually was in the course of employment and whether the totality of the circumstances established a causal connection between the injury and employment. [*Friebel v. Visiting Nurse Ass'n of Mid-Ohio*, No. 2013-0892 (Ohio Oct. 21, 2014)]

§ 33.04 ALTERNATIVES FOR INSURING WC

[A] Types of Available Insurance

Depending on state law and the employer's own financial status and risk category, there are several ways to cope with the obligation to provide benefits for injured employees.

- Buying insurance from a state-run fund that is the sole source of WC coverage within the state;

- Buying insurance from a commercial carrier. Nearly all privately purchased policies will follow the form of the "standard policy"—the Worker's Compensation and Employers' Liability Policy developed by the National Council on Compensation Insurance (NCCI);

- Buying insurance from a state fund that competes with commercial carriers;

- Self-insurance (most employers who take this option combine it with third-party administration, reinsurance, or both);

- Insurance through a captive insurer owned by the employer;

- Participating in an assigned risk pool (depending on circumstances, this can be either mandatory or voluntary).

The Supreme Court ruled in mid-2006 that in the context of Chapter 11 bankruptcy, premiums owed to a WC insurer are not unpaid contributions to an "employee benefit plan" and therefore are not accorded priority under 11 U.S.C. § 507(a)(5). [*Howard Delivery Serv. Inc. v. Zurich Am. Ins. Co.*, 547 U.S. 651 (2006)]

[B] State Funds

State funds can be "monopolistic," also known as "exclusive," if all employers must buy coverage from the state fund. (Some states allow employers to self-insure.) Exclusive state funds set their rates based on actuarial data; their costs are low because they are non-profit organizations with no marketing expenses. Competitive funds allow employers to choose between self-insurance, subscribing to a state fund, or buying private insurance. There are exclusive state funds in North Dakota and Wyoming. Ohio and Washington allow a choice between self-insurance and purchasing from the state fund. Arizona, California, Colorado, Hawaii, Idaho, Kentucky, Louisiana, Maine, Maryland, Minnesota, Missouri, Montana, New Mexico, New York, Oklahoma, Oregon, Pennsylvania, Rhode Island, South Carolina, Texas, and Utah allow self-insurance, private insurance, and state insurance. [American Association of State Compensation Insurance Funds, *Types,* available at <http://www.aascif.org/index.php?page=types> (last accessed Mar. 10, 2017)]

Texas allows employers to self-insure for WC, but they must be careful to provide benefits at least roughly comparable to the benefits that would be available under an insured plan. In *Reyes v. Storage & Processors Inc.* [995 S.W.2d 722 (Tex. App. 1999)], the court said that employers cannot require arbitration of claims for work-related injuries if the benefits they provide are substantially less generous than Comp benefits.

In a surprising development in 2017, the Ohio Bureau of Workers' Compensation announced a $967 million rebate (from a $9.6 billion fund) payable to employers participating in the state funds, as a result of several years of better-than-expected investment returns, successful workplace safety programs, and injured workers able to return to the workforce because of good case management. Checks were scheduled to start being sent out in mid-2017. Most private employers would receive a rebate of two-thirds of their premium for the policy year that ended June 30, 2016. [Philip B. Cochran and M. Scott Young, *Ohio BWC Proposes $1 Billion Workers' Comp Rebate*, Thompson Hine LLP (Mar. 23, 2017), available at Lexology.com]

[C] Assigned Risk Pools

In any situation in which people or organizations have a legal obligation to maintain insurance coverage, some of them will not be insurable under normal underwriting standards. Assigned risk pools are created to issue coverage. In the WC context, the NCCI administers the National Worker's Compensation Reassurance Pool. It covers about 25% of all employers, making it the largest single WC insurer in the United States.

This WC assigned risk pool has some unusual features. Commercial insurers have to support it by paying "residual market assessments" of approximately 14 cents on every premium dollar they receive. But because of this heavy assessment, commercial insurers are less willing to grant discounts to their insurable customers, thus driving more employers to see the assigned risk pool as an attractive alternative.

[D]   Self-Insurance and Captive Companies

In all the states except North Dakota and Wyoming (which have exclusive state funds), employers who satisfy certain criteria (e.g., being financially capable of paying all WC claims that arise in the course of operations; posting bond or establishing an escrow) can elect to self-insure.

> ■ **TIP:**   Self-insurance is considered a privilege. It can be revoked by the state if an employer fails to file the necessary reports, does not maintain the required amount of excess insurance, or otherwise fails to keep up its end of the bargain. A change in corporate ownership might also lead to revocation of the privilege, even if the corporate structure remains the same.

In practice, self-insurance is practical only for very large companies with six- or seven-figure WC premium obligations; about one-third of the WC market is now self-insured because some economic giants have taken this option.

More than half the states impose a requirement that self-insured companies maintain reinsurance (excess coverage). It is prudent for companies to do this even if it is not required. Self-insured employers generally must show that they have arranged for claims administration, employee communications, and safety programs. These functions are usually performed under a Third-Party Administration (TPA) arrangement. An effective TPA should have 24-hour-a-day claims service; low turnover (experienced representatives do a much better job than novices); a high proportion of employees who have obtained professional certification in loss control; quick settlement of claims; and a low average final cost per claim.

In a pure self-insurance arrangement, the employer sets up reserves and pays all WC claims from these reserves. In a group arrangement, several companies join forces. Each one is jointly and severally liable for all Comp claims within the group. Most of the states permit group self-insurance; nationwide, there are over 250 group self-insurance pools. In a limited self-insurance arrangement, the employer is responsible for the Self-Insured Retention (SIR), which is roughly equal to a deductible, and excess insurance pays the rest.

Excess coverage can be written on a per-occurrence or per-loss basis, covering an aggregate amount for the year or per accident per payment year. (The payment year is a relevant concept because the consequences of an injury might extend over several years.) Specific excess insurance limits the employer's liability for claims for any occurrence where the exposure exceeds the SIR. Aggregate excess insurance copes with the possibility of a bad year. The employer has to pay the amount in the aggregate retention or loss fund. This is usually expressed as a percentage, such as 125%, of the reinsurance premium for the year. Aggregate excess coverage usually stops at $1 million or $2 million, so the employer will be at risk once again if the exposure is greater. Specific excess insurance is both easier to obtain and less expensive than aggregate insurance.

To self-insure, the company must file an application with the state (this typically costs $100–$1,000). The employer may have to post a letter of credit as security, and the lending bank will impose fees. Excess insurance and TPA fees each costs about 8%–13% of the amount that would otherwise be the WC premium. States also impose taxes on self-insurance arrangements—about 1%–4% of the premium that would have been charged by an insurer, incurred losses, or paid losses.

Working through a captive insurance company (one that does business only with a company that is its sole shareholder, or a small group of cooperating companies) is another option. The advantage of this arrangement to the employer is the ability to keep the underwriting income (deposits that are the equivalent of premiums, plus investment income), but the company will also have to pay the expenses of the captive insurer.

[E] High-Deductible Plans

A high-deductible plan combines features of both insurance and self-insurance. To reduce its premiums, the employer agrees to accept a higher deductible. Usually, it falls between $100,000 and $1 million, but policies are available with deductibles up to $5 million. Any employer can purchase a high-deductible policy. Unlike self-insurance, there are no financial qualifications imposed by the state.

When a claim is made under a high-deductible plan, the insurer pays the full claim, then bills the policyholder for payments made that fell within the deductible. Bills are usually sent on a monthly basis. Employers who buy high-deductible policies are generally required to create an escrow fund equal to about three months' potential loss payments, and must submit a letter of credit in an amount equal to the deductible. At the end of the first year of high deductible coverage, the letter of credit is adjusted upward or downward to reflect experience. Paid losses are billed until all claims have been closed. The high-deductible insurer may require indemnification or a hold-harmless agreement offering remedies against the employer if, for instance, legislation is passed subjecting the insurer to increased losses that fall within the deductible.

§ 33.05 SETTING THE WC PREMIUM

There are 600 industry classifications, each identified by a four-digit number. An employer's basic WC premium is the "manual rate" for its industry classification. The manual rate is the average cost of WC coverage for the classification, based on the number of claims in the past three years for injuries serious enough to cause lost work time. The rate is sometimes expressed as a percentage of total payroll, but is usually defined as a number of dollars per $100 of payroll. Large employers may qualify for premium discounts, because the administrative expenses are fairly similar for policies of all sizes.

The manual rate is only one factor in setting an individual employer's rate. Experience rating (the employer's actual claims experience for the previous two years) can increase or decrease the base premium that will be imposed in the future. States can also adopt retrospective rating, under which past losses are used to adjust the premium already charged for a particular year, so that either the employer is entitled to a refund or will have to make additional payments.

WC policies have both general inclusions, which recur in many industries (for workers in employee cafeterias, and repair and maintenance crews, for instance) and general exclusions that are written out of ordinary industry classifications (for instance, construction activities performed by employees; running an employer-operated day care center).

§ 33.06 BAN ON RETALIATION

Nearly all the states have passed statutes making it illegal to retaliate against an employee, either specifically for filing a Worker's Compensation claim or for filing any "wage claim" or "wage complaint," a broad category that includes WC. The states are Alabama, Arizona, California, Connecticut, Delaware, Florida, Hawaii, Idaho, Illinois, Indiana, Kansas, Kentucky, Louisiana, Maine, Maryland, Mississippi, Michigan, Minnesota, Missouri, Montana, New Hampshire, New Jersey, New Mexico, New York, North Carolina, North Dakota, Ohio, Oklahoma, Rhode Island, South Carolina, South Dakota, Texas, Vermont, Virginia, Washington, West Virginia, Wisconsin, and Wyoming.

The Ohio Supreme Court held in mid-2016 that it is not necessary to prove a workplace injury to state a prima facie case of WC retaliatory discharge. The court said that employees must be able to exercise their rights without fear of retaliation, including applying for WC even if the claim is eventually rejected. [*Onderko v. Sierra Lobo, Inc.*, 69 N.E.3d 679 (Ohio 2016); see Patrick O. Peters and James M. Stone, *Proof of Workplace Injury Not Required for Workers' Compensation Retaliation Claim in Ohio*, Jackson Lewis PC (July 26, 2016), available at Lexology.com; David A. Campbell et. al., *Labor and Employment Alert: Workers' Compensation Retaliation Does Not Require a Workplace Injury Under Ohio Law*, Vorys, Sater, Seymour and Pease LLP (Aug. 2, 2016), available at Lexology.com]

Minnesota held in 2014 that plaintiffs in WC retaliation cases are entitled to jury trial. The court permitted the plaintiff to sue when he charged that his supervisor threatened to fire him if he filed a WC claim, even though no adverse action was actually taken. (The supervisor denied threatening him.) The employer was also held responsible for the supervisor's threat, even though there was a complaint reporting system that would have allowed the employer to investigate and take corrective action. The state supreme court ruled that, because WC retaliation claims are a type of wrongful discharge claim, there is an implied right to a jury trial. [*Schmitz v. U.S. Steel*, 852 N.W.2d 669 (Minn. 2014)]

Missouri adopted a new stance, reversing its previous position, in 2014. The new standard is that a terminated employee who alleges retaliation for filing a WC claim only needs to prove that the WC claim was a contributing factor, not the exclusive reason for discharge. Plaintiff Templemire was injured in 2006 when his foot was crushed by a metal beam. He returned to light duty and got WC but was fired for failing to perform assigned tasks. He said that one reason for discharge was his WC claim. The trial court and appellate court followed the precedent that exclusive motivation must be proved, but the state supreme court reversed. [*Templemire v. W&M Welding, Inc.*, 433 S.W.3d 371 (Mo. 2014)]

Even in the minority of states that do not have a statute, it is very likely that courts will treat retaliatory discharge as an illegal violation of public policy.

The Tenth Circuit found it likely that UPS retaliated against an injured worker by denying him the opportunity to return to work with lifting restrictions. However, because the plaintiff suffered only monetary harm, the Tenth Circuit found the $2 million district court judgment excessive. After a 2003 injury, the company doctor told plaintiff Jones that he could not lift more than 20 pounds over his head, and carriers must be able to lift 70 pounds routinely. In 2004, two doctors cleared Jones to lift 70 pounds, but a UPS occupational health manager told them not to remove the lifting restrictions. Jones said that UPS retaliated against him for filing a WC claim. The Tenth Circuit found the retaliation claim valid (the occupational health manager intentional interfered with the medical evaluations to prevent his return to work) and found punitive damages appropriate, but said that $2 million was excessive because the manager's conduct did not involve disregard for health or safety. The Tenth Circuit affirmed the $630,000 award of actual damages. [*Jones v. United Parcel Serv. Inc.*, 674 F.3d 1187 (10th Cir. 2011)]

The Ninth Circuit ruled that it is not retaliation to fire a worker for lying about previous occupational injuries on a questionnaire. Although the state's Right to Privacy in the Workplace Act forbids employers to ask prospective employees if they have ever filed a Worker's Compensation claim, it is permissible to ask about previous occupational injuries, time lost from work because of work-related injuries, or medical treatment for those injuries, even though it wouldn't be difficult to extrapolate from those disclosures that a Comp claim had been filed. [*Carter v. Tennant Co.*, 383 F.3d 673 (9th Cir. 2004)]

§ 33.07 ADMINISTRATION OF WC

[A] Generally

In most states, employers are required to participate in the WC system (although Texas and New Jersey allow private employers to opt out of the system entirely, as long as they notify the Compensation Commission and their employees that they have left the system). The tradeoff is that injured employees have the right to bring tort suits against employers who are outside the WC system, whereas in most cases workers who are injured in a WC-covered workplace will not be allowed to sue the employer.

Some states allow employees to opt out of WC coverage as long as they do so in writing, within a reasonable time after starting a new job, and before any accident or injury has occurred. Corporate officers are often given the option of leaving the WC system.

The insurance premium depends on the level of risk: A coal mine is much more likely to have occupational injury claims than a boutique. The nationwide average premium is about 2.5% of compensation.

The general rule is that employees are obligated to notify the employer within a short time (usually about five days) after an injury or the onset of an illness. Employers should encourage reporting, because such information is needed for WC and other purposes (OSHA reports, improving safety conditions).

In some WC systems, the employer notifies its WC insurer, which then files the report. In other systems, the employer (whether it has insurance or is self-insured) is responsible for notifying the compensation board. If the employer fails to make the necessary report, the employee will probably be given additional time to pursue his or her claim.

If the employer agrees that the injury or disease is work-related and accepts the employee's characterization of its seriousness, the claim is uncontested. Most states follow the "agreement system" under which a settlement is negotiated by the parties, or by the employee and the employer's WC insurer. In some states, the agency that administers WC claims must approve all settlements, even in uncontested cases. Most settlements involve payment of ongoing benefits at a continuing rate: either a percentage of the employee's pre-accident income, or a percentage of the state's average income. However, there is an increasing trend to settle WC cases for a lump sum.

However, some uncontested cases are treated as "direct payment" cases. Either the employer or the insurer initiates the process, by making the statutory initial installment payment to the employee. Under this option, the employee does not have to sign anything or agree to anything—unlike the agreement system, which results in a written agreement.

WC settlements cover only the matters specifically set out in the agreement, so agreements must be drafted carefully. Employers are allowed to settle claims that have already accrued, but not future claims (such as claims for future medical expenses), because employees cannot be required to give up future claims that are hard to quantify in advance.

Generally, any settlement between employer and employee will be final. However, there are grounds for which agreements can be set aside, such as fraud, mutual mistake of fact (both sides believe something about the employee's condition that turns out not to be accurate), or mistake of law (misinterpretation of the legal rules and their consequences). Usually, the mere fact that the employee did not have a lawyer is not enough to invalidate a settlement—unless, perhaps, the employer prevented the employee from seeking legal advice. Just to be on the safe side, employers should inform employees that they have the right to be represented by counsel.

Contested cases are heard and decided by the agency administering the system. However, there are comparatively few contested cases. In most cases, it is quite clear that there has been an injury. Because WC is a no-fault system, it is not necessary to apportion blame.

Wisconsin has recently adopted several pro-employer amendments to its WC Act. The statute of limitations for traumatic injury claims was reduced from 12 years to six. Death or disability benefits cannot be paid if there is a direct link of causation between the workplace injury and violation of the employer's drug or alcohol policy. (Prior law merely reduced the benefits by 15%, with a limit of $15,000.) An employee cannot collect temporary disability benefits while released to work with restrictions if he or she is suspended or discharged for work-related misconduct. Temporary disability benefits are also unavailable, even if there has been no misconduct, if the employee is suspended or fired for a substantial work-related fault within the employee's control. [Dean F. Kelley, *Several New Worker's Compensation Provisions Favorable to Wisconsin Employers*, Ogletree Deakins (Apr. 26, 2016), available at Lexology.com]

In some states, mediation is either an option that is available (but only if both sides agree); in other states, it is compulsory. In mediated cases, a neutral mediator has at least one informal meeting with the parties. Sometimes, the meeting is held off the record, so both sides can speak freely, without having to restrict what they say to things that would help their case in formal legal proceedings. If necessary, the mediator arranges more meetings, until the mediator is either able to facilitate a settlement, or it is clear that an impasse has been reached.

In some states, when mediation fails, binding arbitration can be applied; in other states, the case is sent to the Comp board for adjudication.

Michigan applied mediation in WC cases until 2011. Certain types of cases automatically went to a mediator employed by the WC agency: for example, when the claimant did not have a lawyer, only a medical bill was at stake, the employer did not have the required WC coverage, or the only issue in the case was vocational rehabilitation. Since the repeal of the statute in 2011, cases can still be mediated if the WC agency or Michigan Administrative Hearing System determines that the case can be resolved via mediation. If the mediator cannot resolve the case within 12 weeks of the plaintiff's request for mediation, the case goes to a magistrate for review and then for a hearing. Although a procedure called facilitation is not prescribed by statute, WC magistrates in Michigan require facilitation before trying a case. Facilitation is done in a courtroom, off the record; the hearing usually lasts 30 minutes to two hours. The facilitator asks if the injury was initially deemed compensable; what the proper weekly compensation rate is; whether benefits were paid for medical care or wage loss; and why they were discontinued. Each attorney presents the client's case, and 90%–95% of cases are resolved without trial. [Michael D. Sanders, *Workers' Compensation Facilitation—The New Trial?*, Foster Swift Collins & Smith PC (Nov. 17, 2016), available at Lexology.com]

Appeal rights are granted to dissatisfied employers and employees. Usually, parties get 30 days to file for an appeal, although the requirements of different states range from 10 days to one year. Grounds for appeal include improprieties in the process and changed circumstances (such as unpredictable improvement or deterioration in the employee's condition) that were unknown at the time of the award.

Many state laws entitle the employee to an additional payment of 10%–20% if the employer is late in making a required payment. Civil fines may also be imposed, and the unpaid amounts could operate as a lien on the employer's assets.

[B]   Responding to an Accident

Even before there have been any accidents, your workplace should have an effective procedure in place, and should hold regular drills to make sure everyone can handle the procedure. Make sure that employees learn first aid and CPR. Keep plenty of first aid kits around, with fresh supplies, in convenient locations. It's important to provide first aid for all minor incidents, and immediate medical care in more serious cases.

Somebody must be designated to take charge of taking the injured worker to a doctor's office or hospital emergency room, or to call an ambulance. Someone must be in charge of filing the initial accident report (and an OSHA incident report if necessary). [See § 24.02[A]] There is clear evidence that the earlier and more aggressively rehabilitation can be pursued, the more likely it is that the employee will be able to return to work (or at least to limited duties or a less strenuous job) instead of becoming permanently disabled.

In addition to immediate accident reports, some states require a yearly report of all workplace incidents, similar to the OSHA annual report. [See § 24.02[A]] Follow-up status reports may also be required on individual accidents. Employers who fail to make mandatory reports can be subject to fines; there may even be criminal penalties.

As Chapter 18 shows, managed care dominates the U.S. health care system. It also plays a role in WC cases. Some states such as Connecticut, Florida, and Ohio make managed care involvement in WC cases compulsory. Many other states have laws authorizing managed care as an option in WC cases: Arkansas, California, Georgia, Kentucky, Massachusetts, Minnesota, Missouri, Montana, Nebraska, Nevada, New Hampshire, New Jersey, New York, North Carolina, North Dakota, Oregon, Pennsylvania, Rhode Island, South Dakota, Utah, and Washington.

§ 33.08 WC IN RELATION TO OTHER SYSTEMS

Because WC cases involve physical injury, in an employment context, both health care and employment law can be implicated—for example, the Employment Retirement Income Security Act (ERISA) and the Americans with Disabilities Act (ADA).

The U.S. Supreme Court rejected an appeal of a decision that allowed employees with WC claims to pursue a Racketeer Influenced and Corrupt Organizations Act (RICO) case against their employer. Plaintiffs said that the self-insured Cassens Transportation relied on its claims adjuster and poorly qualified doctors to get medical examinations that would deny WC claims. The case was remanded to the trial court for further proceedings. Business groups wanted the decision reversed, because they saw it as opening the door for bringing WC claims (which are usually heard in state courts) into the federal court system. [*Brown v. Cassens Transp. Co.*, 546 F.3d 347 (6th Cir. 2009)]

Insurers do not have to indemnify employers who are found to have intentionally injured employees. Hoyle was injured in a 14-foot fall from a scaffold. He sued in intentional tort, alleging that the supervisor wouldn't let him use bolts and pins to secure the ladder jacks. The employer's insurer sought a declaratory judgment that it did not have to indemnify. Ohio allows a suit for compensatory and punitive damages against an employer if the employer's acts or omissions were committed with intent to injure, or with belief that injury was substantially certain to occur. The employer's Employment Practices Liability Insurance (EPLI) policy covered acts that were substantially certain to cause injury but barred coverage for acts committed with deliberate intent to injure. The Ohio Supreme Court said that indemnification was not required because an exclusion for acts committed with deliberate intent to injure precludes coverage for employer intentional torts. The statute includes a rebuttable presumption that an injury is caused intentionally if it was caused by deliberate removal of a safety guard or deliberate lying about the toxicity of a substance in the workplace. [*Hoyle v. DTJ Enters., Inc.*, 2015-Ohio-843 (2015)]

Most state WC regulations include an intentional tort exception: i.e., employers are not immune if they have committed intentional torts. The District Court for the Eastern District of Louisiana ruled in early 2017 that OSHA's penalizing the employer for a willful violation is not proof that the employer consciously intended employees to be injured. (In this case, employees were overcome by fumes after being assigned to clean a tank car containing hazardous chemicals.) Washington and Kentucky have ruled similarly—but a district court in Idaho allowed employees to maintain tort claims after being told to retrieve radioactive materials without proper protective equipment. [*Hernandez v. Dedicated TCS, LLC*, Civil Action No. 16-3621 SECTION: "E"(5), **2017 U.S. Dist. LEXIS 30260** (E.D. La. Mar. 3, 2017); see Steven M. Siros, *OSHA Violation Doesn't Abrogate Workers' Compensation Immunity*, Jenner & Block LLP (Mar. 8, 2017), available at Lexology.com]

The Longshore and Harbor Workers' Compensation Act (LHWCA) provides a compensation scheme for disability or death caused by injury on the navigable waters of the United States. Benefits for most disabilities are subject to a cap of twice the national average of weekly wage for the fiscal year of the initial award of benefits. In cases where the employer contests liability or the employee contests employer's actions, the dispute goes to the DOL Office of Workers' Compensation Programs (OWCP). The OWCP attempts conciliation; if there is no resolution, there is an ALJ hearing resulting in a compensation order. After Roberts was injured in 2002, his employer, Sea-Land, voluntarily paid benefits until 2005. Roberts filed an LHWCA claim, which was controverted. In FY 2007, the ALJ awarded benefits at the statutory maximum rate—for 2002. Roberts said that it should have been set at the 2007 rate, because that was when he was "newly awarded compensation." In 2012, the Supreme Court ruled that the date that counts is the date worker becomes disabled because this is when entitlement to benefits is triggered, no matter when—or even whether—a compensation order issues. [*Roberts v. Sea-Land Servs., Inc.*, 132 S. Ct. 1350 (2012)]

Tennessee, like Iowa, Kentucky, Ohio, Oklahoma, and Washington, held that a job applicant cannot sue for retaliatory failure to hire. The plaintiff was injured in 2010 and received WC benefits. She was released for full duty. She applied for a job with the defendant, which was not her original employer. The defendant company refused to hire her because it believed that she would be injured again and make another WC claim. However, even in these states, a retaliatory refusal would probably violate the ADA (whether or not the applicant is actually disabled) because it is against the ADA to ask applicants about their job-related injuries or WC claims. [*Yardley v. Hosp. Housekeeping Sys., Inc.* (Tenn. Sup. Ct. Aug. 21, 2015)]

The Medicare system is a secondary payor with respect to Worker's Compensation: that is, if a Medicare beneficiary also receives WC, the WC system is required to pay for the care first, with Medicare responsible only for amounts not covered by WC. Employers and insurers have a duty to report WC claims involving Medicare beneficiaries who have received a settlement, judgment, award, or other reimbursement of medical expenses on or after July 1, 2009 to the Center for Medicare and Medicaid Services.

A Worker's Compensation release that did not explicitly mention ERISA claims or the ERISA plan did not release the employer from an ERISA disability claim. Teresa Duncan received disability benefits under an ERISA long-term disability plan from 2005 to 2010. She settled her WC claim in 2008 and released all claims. The release form said she would not "be able to go back to the defendant for additional treatment or disability payments." The Eastern District of California held in early 2013 that the standard language in WC releases applies only to WC claims, not ERISA claims. [*Duncan v. Hartford Life & Accident Ins. Co.*, 2:11-cv-01536-GEB-CKD, 2013 WL 506465 (E.D. Cal. Feb. 8, 2013)]

An insurance company employee usually worked at home. When she was on FMLA leave, her employer notified her that she needed to submit documentation for her entitlement to leave. Documents she had sent in the past were not received or were mislaid by the employer. One Sunday evening, she hand-delivered the documents to an unattended reception desk outside the HR department. She fell on the staircase. When she filed a WC claim, the Industrial Commission and the trial court denied her WC claim, holding that the injury did not occur in the scope of employment. Injuries occurring when an employee is engaged in purely personal business are not compensable. The incident did not occur in the course of employment: the employer did not order her to hand-deliver the paperwork, in the past, she had used e-mail and fax, and the employer's policy called for mail, fax, or e-mail submission. (The plaintiff said that she had done this in the past without success.) The court said that if the plaintiff opted for hand delivery, it should have been done during normal working hours and consigned to a responsible person. [*Samuel v. Progressive Casualty Ins. Co.*, 2017-Ohio-388 (Ohio 2017); see Rebecca Kopp Levine, *Sunday Deliveries of FMLA Paperwork: A Recipe for Disaster*, Porter Wright Morris & Arthur LLP (Feb. 27, 2017), available at Lexology.com]

[A] Taxation of WC Benefits

Generally speaking, WC insurance premiums paid by employers, or WC benefits received by employees, are not taxable income for the employee. Therefore, the employer does not have to perform tax withholding on these amounts, or withhold or pay FICA or FUTA tax on them. However, in a limited range of situations, WC benefits will be taxable: e.g., if they are paid to a person who has returned to work in a light-duty position; if they reduce Social Security benefits; or if state law calls for payment of non-occupational disability benefits. [See Chapter 20 for the related topic of disability benefits provided under a fringe benefit plan.]

The amount that the employer pays in WC premiums is tax deductible. So are loss amounts paid by a self-insured employer. However, reserves maintained in order to satisfy the deductible under a WC policy are not tax-deductible.

The Tax Court held that emotional distress damages were taxable income for the recipient, a professor who said she was demoted to a secretarial position in retaliation for reporting missing equipment. She brought a WC claim and a separate suit for gross negligence, alleging that some colleagues conspired to force her out. The university agreed to pay three installments of $70,000 each for her emotional distress. The Tax Court adopted the IRS position that the plaintiff did not prove that the amounts were paid for settling a WC claim; the agreement had only one reference to the agreement being conditioned on settlement of the WC claim. The Tax Court said that the settlement could have reflected non-WC claims, and the plaintiff failed to prove that the settlement was for physical injury (see Code § 104(a)(2)); it was described as a settlement of emotional distress claims. The Tax Court cited cases to show that even if there are physical manifestations of emotional distress, that is not sufficient to exclude settlement proceeds from the recipient's income. [*Sharp v. Comm'r*, T.C. Memo 2013-290 (2013)]

[B] ERISA

The general tenor of court decisions on this subject is that WC benefits can legitimately be used to offset accrued benefits that derive from the employer's contribution to a pension plan—but only if a statute specifically provides this, or if the plan has been drafted to include this specific provision. ERISA preempts state WC laws to the extent that they "relate" to an ERISA plan.

In 1992, the Supreme Court decided that a state law relates to an ERISA plan if it refers to or has a connection with the plan, even if the effect is indirect, and even if the law was not designed to affect the plan. Therefore, a law requiring employers to provide health insurance to employees who received or were eligible for WC was preempted. [*District of Columbia v. Greater Wash. Bd. of Trade*, 506 U.S. 125 (1992)]

[C] The ADA

A person might claim disability discrimination and also claim eligibility for WC benefits, at the same time or at different times.

The employer's obligation to engage in the interactive process with employees with disabilities (see § 36.05[A]) continues even if the disability was caused by a workplace injury. The interactive process is triggered by notice from the WC carrier that the employee has temporary or permanent work restrictions. The interactive process determines if the employee's restrictions affect the ability to perform the essential functions of the job. Frequently, the employee's doctor will certify the employee's ability to perform regular, modified, or alternative work. If the employer intends to offer such work, the relevant statute may require the employer to make a written offer of regular, modified, or alternative work on an approved WC form within 60 days. This can reduce exposure to WC benefits, so it is a popular tactic for insurance carriers. However, the ADA does not require creating new jobs or eliminating essential functions of the injured employee's job. If there is no suitable work available, the employer notifies the insurance carrier; the employee may be entitled to higher permanent disability benefits. [Ann K. Smith, Timothy M. Wojcik and Allison M. Scott, *Employers Beware: An Employer's Obligation to Engage in the Interactive Process Applies to Workers' Compensation Claims*, Atkinson Andelson Loya Ruud & Romo (Aug. 15, 2016), available at Lexology.com]

[D] Second Injury Funds

Although they predate the ADA, in a way "second injury funds" serve the same purpose as the ADA: promoting the employment of people with disabilities. Second injury funds (which exist in, for example, California, Missouri, New Jersey, and Washington State) deal with the situation in which a permanent disability is compounded by a later injury to become either a permanent partial disability that is more serious than before, or a permanent total disability. In states that do not have these funds, an employer who hires someone whose pre-existing condition deteriorates because of occupational factors, would be responsible for all of the employee's WC benefits, even though the occupational factors may be comparatively less important than the pre-existing condition.

When there is a second injury fund in the picture, the employer is responsible only for the economic consequences of the later injury. The second injury fund, which is publicly funded, takes on the rest of the economic burden.

The first injury must have been serious enough to be compensable, but need not actually have come under the WC system. For instance, the second injury fund could get involved if a work-related injury aggravates an existing condition caused by a non-work-related automobile accident or a birth defect.

■ **TIP:** To collect from the fund, the employer may have to certify that it knew about the pre-existing condition at the time of hiring. This, in turn, requires asking questions in a way that does not violate the ADA.

[E] Social Security Disability Income

In many states, the Social Security Disability Income (SSDI) system is considered the primary payer whenever an employee is injured seriously enough to meet the Social Security Administration's stringent definition of total disability. The states in this category are Alaska, Arkansas, California, Colorado, Florida, Louisiana, Maine, Massachusetts, Michigan, Minnesota, Missouri, Montana,

Nevada, New Jersey, New York, North Dakota, Ohio, Oregon, Utah, Washington, and Wisconsin.

When SSDI is involved, the payments from the federal agency reduce the WC benefit dollar-for-dollar, until the combination of SSDI and WC reaches the level of 80% of the worker's pre-accident earnings. However, SSDI reduces only the part of the benefit that represents lost income, not the part that goes to medical care or legal fees.

§ 33.09   TECHNIQUES FOR LOWERING COMP COSTS

Employers can reduce their costs via good planning—sorting valid from invalid claims, and finding more economical ways to handle the valid claims. Companies have had some success by educating workers that everyone is responsible for reducing injuries and maintaining a safer workplace. Focusing on getting injured workers back to work as soon as possible also helps cut costs. Departments can be made responsible for their own injury rates, and be made responsible for keeping their rates at least as low as those for comparable operations.

HR policies that are associated with lower WC rates include:

- Increasing employee involvement (e.g., through the use of quality circles). The more employees get involved, the more careful they will be about identifying potentially dangerous conditions, finding ways to correct them—and the more motivation they will have to return to work quickly after an injury;

- Strengthening grievance and conflict resolution procedures if dangerous conditions are alleged, and to resolve claims;

- Reducing turnover: Experienced workers are less likely to get hurt than novices;

- Training workers better—especially in lifting and safe handling of hazardous materials;

- Using health maintenance and wellness programs.

The National Institute of Occupational Safety and Health (NIOSH) defines three areas in which employers can be proactive to cut Comp costs:

- Using engineering controls, such as workstation layout, choice of tools, work methods, to tailor the job to fit employee capabilities and limitations;

- Reducing risk exposure through administrative controls, such as more rest breaks, better training, task rotation;

- Supplying workers with Personal Protective Equipment (PPE), although scientific consensus has not been reached on which devices are effective.

An article in CCH's Worker's Compensation newsletter gives some useful tips for spotting claims that might be fraudulent:

- Delayed reporting of injury;

- Accidents of a type that might be staged;

- The worker claiming injury was on probation or has been identified as having a poor work record;

- The alleged injury is not consistent with the worker's assigned duties;

- The injury is reported just after a weekend or holiday—showing that the injury might have been incurred away from the workplace, or work might have exacerbated a non-work-based injury.

Sometimes, a WC insurance premium quote will be inaccurate, and the premium can be reduced simply by:

- Checking to see if payroll is stated accurately, because the higher the payroll, the higher the premium;

- Making sure that employees are assigned to the lowest risk classification that accurately reflects their duties;

- Having your insurance agent review the calculations.

Employee handbooks should set out a WC policy that mandates immediate reporting. All details of an incident should be documented. For example, if a claimant slipped and fell, the condition of the ground should be noted. Witness statements should be taken. Although retaliation for filing a claim is unlawful, any non-WC factors that justify demotion or termination should be documented. If the employee was hurt while engaging in clearly prohibited conduct, the "voluntary abandonment" theory may bar benefit eligibility. [Jacob Dobres, *Early Steps for Effective Workers' Compensation Claim Management*, Dinsmore & Shohl LLP (Mar. 14, 2016), available at Lexology.com]

PART VII

SUBSTANTIVE LAWS AGAINST DISCRIMINATION

CHAPTER 34

TITLE VII

§ 34.01 INTRODUCTION

NOTE: The transition from the Obama to the Trump administration can be expected to result in major changes in EEOC policy and enforcement.

Title VII, passed as part of the Civil Rights Act of 1964, is the main federal civil rights statute that bans discrimination in employment. It has been enacted at 42 U.S.C. §§ 2000e *et seq.* (By the time Title VII came around, the United States Code was pretty much "full-up," leading to some very odd section numbers. Title VII starts with just plain § 2000e, which is divided into subsections running from § 2000e(a) to 2000e(n). The next section is § 2000e-1, with additional sections up to § 2000e-17.)

Title VII is supplemented by other civil rights statutes: Sometimes other parts of the United States Code (such as 42 U.S.C. §§ 1981, 1983, and 1985) are invoked in employment discrimination suits. Disability discrimination is barred by the Americans with Disabilities Act. [See Chapter 36] Age discrimination is barred by the Age Discrimination in Employment Act. [See Chapter 37]

In a sense, the Family and Medical Leave Act, [29 U.S.C. §§ 2601 *et seq.*] discussed in detail in Chapter 38, is also an antidiscrimination statute as well as an employee benefits statute, because it prevents discrimination against individuals who are ill or who must cope with illness as part of their family responsibilities. Note that any federal, state, or local law that creates special rights or preferences for veterans continues in force and is not repealed by Title VII [42 U.S.C. § 2000e-11] a provision that is more prominent in the post-9/11 environment.

The areas of discrimination forbidden by Title VII are race, color, religion, sex, and national origin. These are known as "suspect classifications," because employers are not supposed to discriminate for reasons involving these classifications. Until recently, sexual orientation and gender identity (being transsexual) were not considered suspect classifications, but there is an emerging trend in some courts, and in some states statutes, to treat them that way. This will probably be a hotly contested subject in 2017 and after. It will also be difficult for employers to steer between avoiding national origin discrimination and being certain to avoid employing persons whose immigration status does not permit them to work in the United States. [See § 34.06[D]; for immigration issues, see § 23.11.]

Title VII forbids employers to undertake adverse action against an applicant or employee on the basis of a suspect classification, which raises the question of what constitutes an adverse action. In mid-2015, the Third Circuit joined the Second, Fourth, Fifth, Sixth, and Eighth Circuits in holding that paid suspension is not a Title VII adverse action. An employee who was suspended with pay while her employer investigated allegations of time sheet fraud sued for sex discrimination and sexual harassment. However, the Third Circuit ruled that the text of Title VII does not refer to paid suspensions, so they cannot be an adverse employment action. [*Jones v. SEPTA*, No. 14-3814 (3d Cir. Aug. 12, 2015)]

In late 2016, the DOL finalized a 2015 proposed rule forbidding discrimination in apprenticeship programs that are registered with the DOL or state apprenticeship agencies. Some provisions took effect January 18, 2017; others are phased in over two years. The final rule prohibits discrimination on the basis of race, color, religion, sex (including pregnancy and gender identity), national origin, age (i.e., persons aged 40 or over are nevertheless entitled to apprenticeship), sexual orientation, genetic information, or disability. If an employer discovers that some groups are under-utilized and sets a goal to eliminate discrimination, it is obligated to eliminate existing impediments to equal opportunity. [Susan M. Schaecher, *Labor Department Finalizes Apprenticeship Program Discrimination Rule,* Fisher Phillips (Dec. 20, 2016), available at Lexology.com]

At least six jurisdictions (California, Connecticut, Illinois, New York, Oregon, and Washington, D.C.) forbid discrimination against unpaid interns on bases such as race, religion, color, sex, and national origin, and sexual harassment and retaliation may also be forbidden. However, under the Connecticut statute, interns can only file an Equal Employment Opportunity Commission (EEOC) complaint or federal suit if they receive significant remuneration, such as pensions, insurance, or access to professional certification. Academic research and experience are not sufficient for this purpose. [Royal LLP, *Connecticut Adds Interns to Its Anti-Discrimination Laws* (Oct. 21, 2015), available at Lexology .com]

It is very common for Title VII suits to involve multiple allegations (e.g., that the plaintiff suffered discrimination and/or harassment because of sex and race, or national origin and religion). In many instances, employees who say they have been discriminated against also say that their employer or ex-employer retaliated against them for protesting the violation of Title VII. Many cases also combine Title VII allegations with allegations under other statutes (e.g., sex and age discrimination under the Age Discrimination in Employment Act (ADEA)).

Also see 42 U.S.C. § 2000e-2(h), which says that it is not an unlawful employment practice for an employer to abide by Fair Labor Standards Act (FLSA) § 6(d) [29 U.S.C. § 206(d)] which allows certain differences in the minimum wage.

Title VII enforcement has two aspects: public (governmental) and private (suits brought by employees, job applicants, ex-employees, or groups of people in these categories). Section 2000e-5 gives the Equal Employment Opportunities Commission (EEOC) the power "to prevent any person from engaging in any unlawful employment practice" that is banned by 42 U.S.C. § 2000e-2 or 2000e-3.

In April 2015, the Supreme Court resolved a circuit split about whether the EEOC's satisfaction of its conciliation obligations is subject to judicial review. The Supreme Court held that the adequacy of conciliation is reviewable by courts, but only to a limited extent; the EEOC's statement that it undertook adequate conciliation is entitled to some deference. [*Mach Mining, LLC v. EEOC*, 135 S. Ct. 1645 (2015).]

On remand from the Supreme Court, the District Court for the Southern District of Illinois denied the EEOC's motion for reconsideration or clarification of the previous discovery order, but partially granted the EEOC's motion to amend the complaint to add several new defendants who were notified of the plaintiffs' claims, and where conciliation had been attempted. The court only allowed the EEOC to obtain discovery from entities in the original determination letter. [*EEOC v. Mach Mining, LLC*, No. 11-CV-00879, 2016 U.S. Dist. LEXIS 111461 (S.D. Ill. Aug. 22, 2016); see Gerald L. Maatman, Jr. and Alex W. Karasik, *Mach Mining: Court Denies the EEOC's Motion for Reconsideration of Discovery Order,* Seyfarth Shaw LLP (Aug. 29, 2016), available at Lexology.com]

The underlying sex discrimination case (and a similar case involving Mach and 12 other companies) were settled in January 2017; Mach agreed to pay $4.25 million and provide other relief (e.g., hiring goals to improve female representation). [*EEOC v. Mach Mining, LLC*, No. 11-cv-00879 (S.D. Ill., settled Jan. 25, 2017); see Patrick Dorrian, *Mach Mining, EEOC Ink $4.25M Pact in Landmark Sex Bias Case*, bna.com (Jan. 27, 2017)]

With respect to the EEOC's investigations, the Supreme Court ruled that when the EEOC issues a subpoena in a case, and a district court either enforces the subpoena or quashes it, then if the district court's decision is appealed, the appellate court will analyze whether the district court abused its discretion. The validity of the decision will not be reviewed de novo. Decisions about subpoenas issued by other agencies, such as the NLRB, are also reviewed for abuse of discretion. [*McLane Co., Inc. v. EEOC*, 137 S. Ct. 1159 (2017)]

After the enactment of Title VII, state laws still remain in force, although state laws are not permitted to require or even allow anything that is treated as an unlawful employment practice under Title VII [42 U.S.C. § 2000e-7]

In early 2017, the EEOC issued proposed enforcement guidance about the employer's obligation to be proactive to combat known or obvious risks of harassment—not just sexual harassment, but harassment charges based on sex stereotyping, gender identity, sexual orientation, and pregnancy. The guidance says that the EEOC will accept complaints that a person was harassed on the basis of perceived membership in a protected class, even if the person does not actually belong to that class. Associational harassment (e.g., being married to a member of a group disfavored by the harasser) is also covered, as are acts of harassment outside the workplace. [<https://www.regulations.gov/docket?D=EEOC-2016-0009> (Jan. 10, 2017); see James Nicholas, *EEOC Issues New Harassment Guidance,* Foley & Lardner LLP (Feb. 13, 2017)]

A number of cases have been decided about employers' power to set appearance standards. Employees can challenge these rules for several reasons: on the grounds of sexism, racism, or religious discrimination, for example (bans on religious garb: see § 34.07[B], [C] below).

Like the Seventh and Ninth Circuits, and most district courts that have considered the issue, the Second Circuit held that filing EEOC charges does not toll the statute of limitations for state-law tort claims, even if the tort claims involve the same facts as the EEOC case. The plaintiff charged hostile work environment, offensive physical conduct, and racially and sexually hostile comments tantamount to constructive discharge. She brought a suit in November 2009, combining Title VII and state tort claims (assault, battery, and intentional infliction of emotional distress). The state law claims were dismissed because they were time-barred: the plaintiff filed them more than one year after her last day of work for the defendant. In the future, it is likely that some plaintiffs will file state tort claims as soon as they make an EEOC charge, and request that the state-law proceedings be stayed until completion of the EEOC investigation. [*Castagna v. Luceno*, 744 F.3d 254 (2d Cir. 2014)]

[A] The Ledbetter Act

In 2007, the Supreme Court decided the case *Ledbetter v. Goodyear Tire*, 550 U.S. 618 (2007); see § 42.05[A]. The Supreme Court dismissed Ledbetter's charge that she was the victim of sex discrimination in compensation, holding that to be timely it would have to have been filed within 180 days of the employer's adoption of the discriminatory pay practice.

The first legislation signed by President Obama after his inauguration was the Lilly Ledbetter Fair Pay Act of 2009, Pub. L. No. 111-2, legislation designed to reverse the effect of this Supreme Court decision. Congress found that the short time frame impaired the rights that Congress intended to provide for employees. Under the Ledbetter Act, a discrimination charge is timely if it is filed within 180 days (or within 300 days, in a state with a work-sharing agreement with the EEOC) of any of these events:

- Adoption of a discriminatory practice;

- Employee becomes subject to that practice;

- Employee is affected by application of the practice—including every paycheck reflecting discrimination.

The Ledbetter Act applies to Title VII, the Americans with Disabilities Act (ADA), the ADEA, and the Rehabilitation Act. An employee who succeeds in pursuing a pay discrimination claim under Title VII, the ADEA, or the Rehab Act can recover back pay for up to two years before the filing of the charge, if the compensation discrimination was similar or related to discriminatory acts during the charge filing period.

[B] GINA

The Genetic Information Nondiscrimination Act of 2008 (GINA; Pub. L. No. 110-233, signed May 21, 2008, effective November 21, 2009) extends the protective provisions of Title VII to discrimination based on genetic information. Employers are forbidden to deny hiring, discharge anyone, or discriminate in pay or working conditions on the basis of the results of genetic testing. Health insurers are not permitted to deny coverage or set premiums or deductibles based on genetic test results. The EEOC proposed regulations under GINA prohibit hiring, firing, or other personnel decisions based on genetic predisposition to a disease. Employers are forbidden to deliberately acquire genetic information from employees or job applicants. The "water cooler" exception immunizes a supervisor who inadvertently discovers an employee's condition from statements made by other employees, or if a doctor's note contains the information. Genetic information includes tests of an individual and the individual's medical history and family medical history—but does not include information about a current disease or condition. A person's sex, age, or drug or alcohol test results are not considered genetic information. [Neil Roland, *EEOC Proposes Rules to Bar Genetic Discrimination*, workforce.com (Feb. 26, 2009) (benefitslink.com)]

Unlike HIPAA, GINA does not exempt plans that have fewer than two participants who are current employees. The regulations under GINA Title I took effect January 1, 2010 for calendar-year plans. See 78 Fed. Reg. 5566 (Jan. 25, 2013) for final regulations on the interaction of HIPAA privacy rules with the employment and health insurance provisions of GINA.

Even pre-GINA, the Health Insurance Portability and Accessibility Act (HIPAA) forbade imposing Pre-Existing Condition Exclusions (PCEs) solely based on genetic information. HIPAA also forbade discrimination in eligibility, benefits, or premiums for individual policies based on health factors (including genetic information). GINA Title I (prohibiting discrimination in EGHP coverage) broadens the underwriting protection, and forbids insurers to demand genetic tests and restricts the collection of genetic information. The premiums for a plan or group of similarly situated individuals within a plan must not be changed based on the genetic information of one or more individuals in the group. However, premiums can be increased for the group based on an actual disease or disorder experienced by a person in the group. A health care provider treating an individual can legitimately request genetic tests. A plan or insurer can request genetic test results to determine if a claim is payable—but only the minimum amount of information needed to process the claim. [*FAQs on the Genetic Information Nondiscrimination Act*, <http://www.dol.gov/ebsa/faqs/faq-GINA.html> (Aug. 2010) (last accessed Mar. 10, 2017)]

The EEOC published a final rule on recordkeeping requirements under GINA. As of April 3, 2012, companies with 15 or more employees must retain all personnel and employment records relating to GINA for at least one year. If charges are filed under GINA, relevant documents must be retained until final disposition of the case. If an employee is involuntarily terminated, records must be kept for a year after termination. The relevant documents in this context include requests for accommodation, application forms, records of hiring, promotion, demotion, transfer, layoff, and termination; and records about terms of employment, e.g., pay, training, and tenure. [77 Fed. Reg. 5396 (Feb. 12, 2012)]

The EEOC has published final rules on implementing Title II of GINA in wellness programs. Employers can furnish limited incentives to encourage employees to provide information about their spouses' health as part of a health assessment. The total incentive must not exceed 30% of the total annual cost of coverage for the plan. [EEOC final rule, 81 Fed. Reg. 31143 (May 17, 2016); see Corie Hengst, *EEOC Announces Final Rules for Wellness Programs*, plan sponsor.com (May 16, 2016)]

The AARP challenged these regulations in October 2016, taking the position that the regulations were arbitrary and capricious because the incentives prevent the disclosure of information from being voluntary. The District Court for the District of Columbia upheld the regulations in December 2016. The court held that, although the AARP had associational standing to sue to challenge the regulations (because AARP members were at risk of disability discrimination), the organization failed to prove irreparable injury. The district court said that potential disclosure of health information is not "public" disclosure, and employers are forbidden to use the information to discriminate. That some employees must pay higher premiums constitutes only economic harm, which is not irreparable. [*AARP v. EEOC*, No. 16-2113 (JDB), 2016 U.S. Dist. LEXIS 180612, 100 Empl. Prac. Dec. (CCH) P45,710 (D.D.C. Dec. 29, 2016); see Joy P. Waltemath, *EEOC ADA and GINA Wellness Regs Survive AARP Challenge*, WK Employment Law Daily (Jan. 3, 2016) (benefitslink.com)]

But in mid-2017, the district court held that the EEOC's designation of 30% as the level for adjudging voluntariness was not entitled to deference. The EEOC said that it decision was intended to harmonize with HIPAA rules, but the district court said this was irrelevant, because the HIPAA rules were adopted to reduce insurance discrimination, not to assess voluntariness. The district court also criticized the EEOC for failure to consider the financial impact of the 30% level on employees, and whether low-income employees would feel coerced to participate. Despite its disapproval of the EEOC's decision process, the district court did not vacate the 2016 regulations, because many employers have made good-faith changes in their practices based on the regulations. The district court remanded, directing the EEOC to reconsider. [*AARP v. EEOC*, No. 16-cv-2113 (D.D.C. Aug. 22, 2017); see Pepper Hamilton LLP (Aug. 23, 2017) (benefitslink.com)]

The BNV Home Care Agency, Inc. settled an EEOC GINA suit by agreeing to pay $125,000 to a group of current employees. The agency had asked employees and job applicants unlawful genetic information questions about their family history of heart disease, diabetes, cancer, and mental illness. [Alana Stramowski, *Home Care Agency to Pay $125,000 Over "Genetic Discrimination" Charges*, Home Health Care News (Nov. 7, 2016), available at homehealthcarenews.com]

§ 34.02 TREATMENT/IMPACT

Title VII discrimination claims are divided into two categories, each of which has its own requirements for drafting complaints and proving the case, and its own defenses that the employer can assert to win its case.

The two categories are disparate treatment and disparate impact. A disparate treatment case alleges that persons were singled out for inferior treatment because of the group they belong to. A disparate impact case alleges subtler forms of discrimination.

For instance, an allegation that a police department refused to hire Hispanics would be a disparate treatment claim. A disparate impact claim might challenge the police department's requirement that all newly hired officers be over 5'10'' tall, on the grounds that more Hispanics than people from other backgrounds are unable to meet this requirement, and therefore a requirement that seems at first glance to be acceptable actually discriminates against members of a protected group.

Under Title VII's discrimination (but not its retaliation) provisions, a "mixed motive" case can be maintained. That is, if an employer has several motivations for making an employment decision or adopting an employment practice, Title VII forbids practices that are partially motivated by discrimination against a protected group, not just those where discrimination is the sole motivation. [See 42 U.S.C. § 2000e-2(m)] In mid-2013, the Supreme Court ruled that mixed-motive cases are proper for discrimination based on personal characteristics (race, color, religion, sex, or national origin) but not for retaliation. [*University of Tex. Sw. Med. Ctr. v. Nassar*, 133 S. Ct. 2517 (2013)]

Using *Nassar*'s but-for causation standard, the First Circuit affirmed summary judgment for the employer in a sexual harassment/retaliatory termination case. Co-workers said that new employee Ponte had unusually serious problems settling into the job, and was not prepared for meetings. Ponte said that her supervisor sexually propositioned her on two occasions. She did not report this to the employer until much later, and even then, she merely said that she felt uncomfortable with the supervisor, not that sexual harassment had occurred. Her performance review was poor, reflecting lateness, poor communications, and failure to satisfy the regional sales plan. Ponte was fired in mid-2011. The First Circuit held that the *Nassar* test is that protected activity was the but-for cause of the adverse employment action; Nassar's vague complaints did not set out a but-for cause. Her performance problems began before the alleged harassment, and her supervisor was not the only person to criticize her work. The employer had a legitimate, nondiscriminatory reason to fire her. [*Ponte v. Steelcase Inc.*, 741 F.3d 310 (1st Cir. 2014)]

In a discrimination and retaliation case brought by a professor who charged that she was victimized for supporting a colleague's discrimination claim, the jury awarded $613,368, including $300,000 in compensatory damages (the full cap amount) plus $213,368 in back pay, the amount calculated by the plaintiff's expert witness. The Sixth Circuit granted remittitur. The back pay award was eliminated on the grounds that back pay awards must reflect amounts the defendant would have paid and the plaintiff did not establish her entitlement to back pay with reasonable certainty. However, the Sixth Circuit joined the Fifth Circuit in *Nassar,* holding that salaries paid by other employers can enter into the proper calculation of back pay. [*Szeinbach v. The Ohio State Univ.,* 820 F.3d 814 (6th Cir. 2016); see Justin Jennewine, *Sixth Circuit Rules on $200,000 Back Pay Issue*, Squire Patton Boggs (Apr. 28, 2016), available at Lexology.com]

Under the Supreme Court's June 2003 decision [*Desert Palace, Inc. v. Costa,* 539 U.S. 90 (2003)], a Title VII plaintiff can obtain a mixed-motive jury instruction without necessarily showing direct evidence of discrimination, because the statute does not specifically require direct evidence. Therefore, the general rule of civil litigation—allowing proof by direct and/or circumstantial evidence—applies.

The Supreme Court pointed out that Title VII and the ADEA have different language and different requirements, deciding, in mid-2009, that mixed-motive ADEA cases require the plaintiff to prove, by a preponderance of the evidence, that age was the "but-for" cause of the unfavorable employment action: in other words, that the action would never have been taken but-for the plaintiff's being over 40. [*Gross v. FBL Fin. Servs., Inc.,* 557 U.S. 167 (2009)]

The Eleventh Circuit (like the Sixth Circuit) said that the *McDonnell-Douglas* analysis does not apply at the summary judgment stage in mixed motive cases. The plaintiff must show that the protected characteristic was a motivating factor (not necessarily the sole factor) in the employer's decision to take adverse employment action. The Eleventh Circuit held that a Title VII/§ 1983 mixed-motive case should not have been dismissed: the plaintiff provided enough evidence that her sex was a motivating factor in the decision not to renew her teaching contract. [*Quigg v. Thomas Co. Sch. Dist.,* 814 F.3d 1227 (11th Cir. 2016); see Patrick Mulligan, *Eleventh Circuit Finds the McDonnell Douglas Burden Shifting Test Inapplicable to "Mixed-Motive" Discrimination Claims*, Bressler, Amery & Ross PC (Feb. 24, 2016), available at Lexology.com; see also *White v. Baxter Healthcare Corp.,* 533 F.3d 381 (6th Cir. 2008)]

In a suit about a police promotional examination, the First Circuit held that the test did not have unlawful disparate impact. The First Circuit held that the district court applied the proper statutory provision, 42 U.S.C. § 2000e-2(k)(1)(A)(i), and accepting the defendant's expert testimony was not clearly erroneous. [*Lopez v. City of Lawrence, Massachusetts,* No. 14-1952 (1st Cir. May 18, 2016)]

§ 34.03   TITLE VII COVERAGE

Title VII bans "unlawful employment practices." Unlawful employment practices discriminate against an employee or job applicant on the basis of the individual's race, color, religion, sex, or national origin. [42 U.S.C. § 2000e-2(a)] The question of whether Title VII forbids sexual orientation discrimination is still unresolved but some applicable state and local statutes do.

A July 2014 Executive Order which applies to federal contractors (although not to employers who are not federal contractors) forbids job discrimination against gay, lesbian, bisexual, and transgender persons. [Peter Baker, *Obama Calls for a Ban on Job Bias Against Gays*, NYTimes.com (July 21, 2014)]

Unlawful employment practices on the part of the employer are defined by 42 U.S.C. § 2000e-2(a) as:

- To fail or refuse to hire;

- To discharge;

- To discriminate with respect to compensation, terms, conditions, or privileges of employment;

- To limit, segregate, or classify employees or job applicants in a way that deprives or tends to deprive them of employment opportunities, or otherwise adversely affects their status as employees.

Title VII also bans discriminatory practices by employment agencies and labor unions, but their activities are outside the scope of this book.

In late 1998, the Fourth Circuit joined the Third, Fifth, Seventh, Eighth, Tenth, Eleventh, and D.C. Circuits in ruling that only employer companies, and not individuals, can be held liable under Title VII. [*Lissau v. S. Food Serv.*, 159 F.3d 177 (4th Cir. 1998); see also *Fantini v. Salem State Coll.*, 557 F.3d 22 (1st Cir. 2009)]

An important—and growing—part of the employment discrimination caseload is the "retaliation" case. Section 2000e-3(a) makes it unlawful for an employer to discriminate against anyone who has opposed an unlawful employment practice or who has "made a charge, testified, assisted, or participated in any manner in an investigation, proceeding, or hearing" under Title VII. [See § 34.08 for more about retaliation cases]

It is also an unlawful employment practice to indicate "any preference, limitation, specification, or discrimination" based on race, color, religion, sex, or national origin in a help-wanted ad, unless belonging to a particular group is a Bona Fide Occupational Qualification (BFOQ). [See 42 U.S.C. § 2000e-3(b).]

It might be a BFOQ to be male or female (e.g., because of authenticity, for an actor or actress; for privacy, for a restroom attendant); to be under 40 (in a job where public safety depends on youthful reactions) or even to belong to a particular religion (e.g., to work in a kosher slaughterhouse). Race is never a BFOQ. In the disability context, it is a BFOQ not to pose a safety risk to oneself or others. Where safety or efficiency is involved, it may be possible to raise a "business necessity" defense for a discriminatory business practice.

In the twenty-first century, BFOQ cases are not very common. A July 2014 Ninth Circuit case is an interesting exception. The case was brought by male sheriff's deputies who alleged that they were discriminated against by not being allowed to supervise female prisoners. The county explained that the policy was adopted to deter sexual abuse of female inmates and protect privacy. The Ninth Circuit held that a BFOQ defense must be proved by a preponderance of the evidence, by showing that the qualification is reasonably necessary to the essence of the defendant's operations, and nearly all men are unqualified or it is impossible or highly impractical to test to see which men are qualified. The employer must show a high correlation between sex and the ability to perform job functions, and must show alternative approaches are not viable. The Ninth Circuit said that there are ways to prevent sexual abuse of prisoners other than by not hiring men. [*Ambat v. City & Cnty. of San Francisco*, 757 F.3d 1017 (9th Cir. 2014)] The Sixth Circuit has held that being female is a BFOQ for working as a correctional officer in a women's prison. [*Everson v. Mich. Dep't of Corrs.*, 391 F.3d 737 (6th Cir. 2004)]

§ 34.04 EXCEPTIONS TO TITLE VII COVERAGE

[A] Definition of Employer

Perhaps the most important exception is found in 42 U.S.C. § 2000e(b), which defines an "employer" as a natural person or business engaged in an industry affecting commerce—and having 15 or more employees for each work day in 20 or more weeks either in the year in question or the preceding calendar year. So a very small business will be exempt from Title VII. Possibly some businesses with even more than 15 employees will escape coverage because their business does not "affect commerce," but most businesses do sell or at least attempt to make interstate sales, so their business will be deemed to "affect commerce."

The 15-employee figure is calculated based on the number of people on the payroll, not the number of full-time employees. [*Walters v. Metro. Educ. Enters., Inc.*, 519 U.S. 202 (1997)]

The Seventh Circuit held that a doctor-shareholder who was a board member of a small medical professional corporation was an employer, not an employee of the corporation for Title VII purposes. The Seventh Circuit used a common-law analysis to determine that she was not an employee: her work was not supervised, all the doctors had equal votes and shared economically, so they all controlled the practice. [*Bluestein v. Cent. Wis. Anesthesiology*, 769 F.3d 944 (7th Cir. 2014)]

Whether a company has 15 employees or not is a substantive element of the Title VII claim (in this case, a sexual harassment charge), not a jurisdictional prerequisite. The practical significance of this 2006 Supreme Court ruling is that the number of employees is an issue that can be waived if it is not raised on time, whereas questions of subject matter jurisdiction can be raised at any time. The Supreme Court decided that the 15-employee requirement is not jurisdictional because it is not found within the part of the Title VII statute that grants jurisdiction to the federal courts. [*Arbaugh v. Y&H Corp.*, 546 U.S. 500 (2006)]

Suit could be brought under Title VII against a U.S.-based parent corporation, even though it had only six employees, because its wholly owned Mexican subsidiary had at least 50 employees. Even though the Mexican employees would not be protected by Title VII, the Ninth Circuit ruled in 2002 that they should be included in the count. [*Kang v. U Lim Am. Inc.*, 296 F.3d 810 (9th Cir. 2002)]

The Third Circuit held that a temporary employee sent to a company by a temporary staffing agency was an employee of the client company as well as the staffing agency. Therefore, the temporary worker could bring a Title VII suit against the client company. The temporary worker said that the manager accused him and other African-American workers of stealing and ordered them to work in the back of the store with the garbage. The Third Circuit used a test of the hiring party's right to control the manner and means by which work was done. The client company had ultimate control over who worked at the store, and managed the temporary workers the same way it managed its own employees. [*Faush v. Tuesday Morning, Inc.*, 808 F.3d 208 (3d Cir. 2015)]

As shown below, there is a "ministerial exception" to accommodate First Amendment freedom of religion (see § 34.07). Another exception is allowed under 42 U.S.C. § 2000e-2(e) if religion, sex, or national origin is a bona fide occupational qualification "reasonably necessary to the normal operation" of the business. Educational institutions sponsored by a religious organization (e.g., Notre Dame or Yeshiva University) or institutions "directed toward the propagation of a particular religion" are permitted to base hiring and other employment decisions on religion—parochial schools can, but do not have to, employ staffers of other religions.

A Massachusetts state court granted summary judgment for a plaintiff whose job offer was withdrawn after he listed his husband as his emergency contact. The school said that it expected employees to model the school's values, including its opposition to same-sex marriage. Although the school is under Catholic auspices, only some staff members are required to be Catholic; the job in question, director of food services, was not one of them. The school claimed exemption from the state anti-discrimination law because it is controlled by a religious organization. However, the court held that the school does not limit enrollment or admission to Catholics. The school has a non-discrimination policy that covers sexual orientation; the court rejected the argument that the plaintiff was denied employment not because he is gay, but because of his marriage. [*Barrett v. Fontbonne Acad.*, 33 Mass. L. Rep. 287 (Mass. Super. Ct. 2015)]

According to the Seventh and Eighth Circuits, Congress took a valid action in 1972 when it abrogated sovereign immunity and made the states subject to Title VII, so Title VII disparate impact suits can be brought against a state employer.

[*Nanda v. Bd. of Trustees of the Univ. of Ill.*, 303 F.3d 817 (7th Cir. 2002); *Okruhlik v. Univ. of Ark.*, 255 F.3d 615 (8th Cir. 2001)]

[B] Aliens

Section 2000e-1 provides that Title VII does not apply to the employment of "aliens." In August 1998, the Fourth Circuit reversed its earlier ruling. Now *Egbuna v. Time-Life Libraries, Inc.* [153 F.3d 184 (4th Cir. 1998)] holds that it is necessary to be a U.S. citizen or an alien holding a valid work visa, to be a "qualified" individual. So an alien who does not have legal worker status in the United States cannot make out a Title VII prima facie case.

Furthermore, an employer does not violate Title VII if it (or a corporation it controls) takes an action with respect to an employee in a foreign country that is necessary to avoid violating that country's law—even if the action would be barred by Title VII if it were taken in the United States. The factors in whether an employer controls a corporation include whether there is common management, ownership, or financial control, and whether the two organizations have related operations. See also § 23.11 on immigration and nationality issues in hiring.

42 U.S.C. § 1981 applies only to conduct within the United States, so this provision does not cover allegations of racial discrimination made by a non-U.S. citizen who was transferred to South African by his U.S. employer. However, he could use § 1981 to charge discrimination while he worked in the United States. [*Ofori-Tenkorang v. Am. Int'l Grp., Inc.*, 460 F.3d 296 (2d Cir. 2006)]

[C] National Security

42 U.S.C. § 2000e-2(g) enacts a national security exception. It does not violate Title VII to fire or refuse to hire someone who has not met, or no longer meets, security clearance requirements "in effect pursuant to or administered under any statute of the United States or any Executive order of the President."

Engineer Hossein Zeinali, who is of Iranian descent, sued Raytheon for terminating him after the Department of Defense denied him a security clearance. The district court dismissed the race/national origin discrimination charges, holding that the federal courts do not have jurisdiction over security clearance cases. The Ninth Circuit reversed and allowed Zeinali's suit to proceed, because he did not dispute the validity of the denial—only whether it was legitimate for Raytheon to require a security clearance. He produced evidence that non-Iranian engineers without security clearances were allowed to work, so he raised a triable issue about whether having a security clearance was a bona fide requirement for engineers. [*Zeinali v. Raytheon Co*, 636 F.3d 544 (9th Cir. 2011)]

In light of the focus of the Trump administration on national security issues, it is plausible that this will become a more active subject for litigation.

[D] Seniority Systems

Employers are permitted, under 42 U.S.C. § 2000e-2(h), to abide by "bona fide seniority or merit systems," or to base compensation on quantity or quality of production, or to pay different rates at different locations—even if the result is to provide different standards of compensation or different terms, conditions, or privileges of employment. However, employers are not allowed to impose such differences in treatment if they are "the result of an intention to discriminate" on the basis of race, color, religion, sex, or national origin.

Also see 42 U.S.C. § 2000e-5(e)(2), which says that the unlawful unemployment practice occurs, with respect to a seniority system that was adopted "for an intentionally discriminatory purpose," whether or not the purpose can be discerned from the face of the provision, either when the seniority system is adopted, when the potential plaintiff becomes subject to the seniority system, or when the seniority system is applied in a way that injures the potential plaintiff.

The Lilly Ledbetter Act, Pub. L. No. 111-2, was passed to reaffirm these statutory principles and to overturn a Supreme Court decision that restricted the time to file discrimination suits.

A 2009 Supreme Court decision [*AT&T Corp. v. Hulteen*, 556 U.S. 701 (2009)] holds that AT&T abided by the terms of a bona fide seniority system, and therefore was not guilty of sex discrimination even though the pensions of some female workers were reduced because, before the passage of the Pregnancy Discrimination Act (PDA), AT&T treated pregnancy leave less favorably than other forms of temporary disability leave. (Once the PDA took effect, AT&T changed its policies, so the question was the effect of past discrimination.)

Section 2000e-2(h) also allows employers to use validated pre-employment tests of ability, as long as testing is not designed, intended or used to discriminate. The subject of test scores is taken up again in 42 U.S.C. § 2000e-2(l), which states that it is an unlawful employment practice to adjust scores or use different cutoff scores in hiring or promotion tests, based on the race, color, religion, sex or national origin of the test taker.

Also in 2009, the Supreme Court ruled that a city should not have refused to certify a promotional test for firefighters. The city argued that, because certifying the test would make the city vulnerable to lawsuits from minority firefighters who scored poorly, the test should have been discarded. The Supreme Court, however, held that refusing to certify the promotion list discriminated against high-scoring firefighters (mostly white and Hispanic), so the employer should have relied on its properly validated test. [*Ricci v. DeStefano*, 557 U.S. 557 (2009). CNN reported that payouts to 20 firefighters (19 white, one Hispanic) finally began in 2011; the 20 received $2 million for back pay, attorneys' fees, and pension credits. See Rebecca Moore, *Award Finally Decided in Connecticut Firefighters Suit*, plansponsor.com (Aug. 3, 2011)]

The following year, the Supreme Court heard another challenge to a firefighters' promotional exam, this time brought by black and Hispanic firefighters.

The Supreme Court ruled that challenges to the test were not untimely, although they were brought a number of years after the original test—because, when an employer continues to use an employment practice with disparate impact on a protected group, each use of the practice (i.e., each time a class of firefighters is promoted based on the original test results) can be challenged. [*Lewis v. City of Chicago*, 559 U.S. 932 (2010)]

§ 34.05 RACIAL DISCRIMINATION

[A] Basic Protections

The first equal opportunity laws were bans on racial discrimination. The Civil Rights Act of 1866, enacted at 42 U.S.C. § 1981, was passed to give former slaves the same rights as "white citizens." There is no requirement of a minimum number of employees for a § 1981 suit, and the EEOC and state antidiscrimination procedures do not have to be invoked before bringing suit under this provision.

The Civil Rights Act of 1991 generally requires plaintiffs to proceed under § 1981 if they have claims of racial discrimination, before using Title VII. Compensatory and punitive damages are not available under Title VII for any plaintiff who can get such damages under § 1981.

There have been some major recent cases about race discrimination. The quest to have a completely race-neutral workplace is a difficult one, and claims have been raised both by majority and minority groups that their rights have been violated.

The Fifth Circuit denied a motion to dismiss; a city police department's restriction of a detective's responsibilities after he completed a disciplinary suspension could be an adverse action. Three detectives—the plaintiff, who is African-American, and two white detectives—were suspended for falsifying time sheets. All three were reinstated but the plaintiff was subjected to restrictions that were not imposed on the others. He was not allowed to work undercover or be the lead investigator on a case. The Fifth Circuit held that loss of job responsibilities is not automatically an adverse employment action, but it could be. [*Thompson v. City of Waco*, 764 F.3d 500 (5th Cir. 2014)]

In mid-2013, the Supreme Court used standards similar to those for sexual harassment cases (see § 35.02) in a case of racial harassment of an African-American employee. The Supreme Court held that the employer is strictly liable if harassment is committed by a supervisor and involves a tangible employment action (e.g., hiring, firing, reassignment) against the victim. If the harasser is a supervisor, but there is no tangible employment action, then the employer can assert an affirmative defense under *Faragher/Ellerth*: that the employer took reasonable care to prevent and correct harassment, but the plaintiff unreasonably failed to take advantage of this procedure. A supervisor is a person authorized to take tangible employment actions against the plaintiff. However, in this case, the harasser was a co-worker of the plaintiff's. In cases of co-worker harassment, the Supreme Court held that the employer is liable only if it was negligent in controlling working conditions. [*Vance v. Ball State Univ.*, 133 S. Ct. 2434 (2013)]

In late 2015, the Tenth Circuit required courts to focus on the "polluting effect" of discriminatory conduct that creates a hostile work environment, rather than on the intent. The plaintiff, the sole black employee in the office, charged that co-workers harassed her with comments like "we need to bring back lynching" and "get ghetto," and many employees used racial slurs. The plaintiff reported these incidents. Two co-workers were written up and given HR training, but the plaintiff said the harassment continued. The plaintiff was eventually fired, allegedly for attendance violations. [*Lounds v. Lincare, Inc.*, 812 F.3d 1208 (10th Cir. 2015)]

The Fourth Circuit permitted a wrongful termination suit, brought under Title VII and 42 U.S.C. § 1983 by an Arab-American Muslim woman, to go to a jury. She alleged that when she worked at a real estate office between 2007 and 2013, she was frequently subjected to racial and ethnic slurs. She complained about the discrimination in 2012, and was fired in 2013, allegedly for lack of work. The district court dismissed the case, finding that the harassment was not severe and she did not show that the reason for her termination was pretextual, but the Fourth Circuit reversed, finding that there were disputed facts requiring a jury trial. [*Gessous v. Fairview Prop. Invs.* No. 15-1055 (4th Cir. July 6, 2016); see FindLaw Employment Law blog, *Muslim Woman's Discrimination Suit Revived* (July 19, 2016), available at FindLaw.com]

Even a single racial slur by a supervisor in the presence of another supervisor can be severe enough to create a hostile work environment. [*Taylor v. Metzger*, 706 A.2d 685 (N.J. 1998), although a later case, *Jordan v. Alternative Res. Corp.*, 458 F.3d 332 (4th Cir. 2006), holds that a single racial slur uttered by a colleague (it was directed at a TV news report, not at the plaintiff) was not enough to create a hostile work environment. Therefore, the employee could not prove a retaliation case when his job was eliminated several months later: the incident was isolated and did not alter the terms and conditions of employment.]

In 2014, the Fourth Circuit found that allegations that a co-worker twice used a racial slur during a confrontation (the plaintiff was fired a week after the incident) did not alter working conditions enough to create a hostile work environment, but this ruling was reversed when the case was reheard en banc in 2015. The en banc court held that an isolated incident can create a hostile work environment if it is severe enough, and it is unlawful to retaliate against employees who report even isolated harassment that is physically threatening or humiliating. [*Boyer-Liberto v. Fountainebleau Corp.*, 752 F.3d 350 (4th Cir. 2014), *rev'd*, No. 13-1473 (4th Cir. en banc May 7, 2015)]

The Second Circuit used a four-part analysis to decide that a single racial epithet (in this case, used by a supervisor) could be serious enough to create a hostile environment. The factors are frequency of discriminatory conduct; its severity; if it consisted of offensive language, or if physical threats also occurred; and whether there was unreasonable interference with the victim's work performance. [*Daniel v. T&M Protection Resources, Inc.,* No. 15-560-cv (2d Cir. Apr. 25, 2017); see Michael Casey Williams, *With N Word, Once Is Enough, Second Circuit Rules on Hostile Environment Case,* Bradley Arant Boult Cummings LLP (May 4, 2017), available at Lexology.com]

The Eighth Circuit found that there was a racially hostile work environment when white co-workers refused to work with the plaintiffs (who are black); there were many racist graffiti in the workplace that remained for months without being removed; rail cars were spray-painted with racist threats; and co-workers displayed Confederate flags and even swastikas. The plaintiffs complained, but management did not help them. The plaintiffs also alleged that white co-workers falsely accused them of safety violations that could have gotten them fired, and that they were disciplined for infractions that white workers were not punished for. [*Watson v. CEVA Logistics, Inc.,* 619 F.3d 936 (8th Cir. 2010)]

There are difficult issues because it is possible that some employees call display of a Confederate flat racial harassment, whereas other say it is protected as a display of national origin or is a religious artifact. Federal courts have not found a protected right to display the flags at work on either theory because the flag is not an inherent part of anyone's religious identity. However, there have been findings such as *McDonald v. ST Aerospace Mobile, Inc.* [Civil Action No. 12-0313-CG-C, 2013 WL 1007712 (S.D. Ala. Apr. 4, 2013)], that the display, in and of itself, does not create a hostile work environment. But the display could be evidence of racial bias that supports a discrimination charge: *Gray v. City of Dothan*, Civil Action No. 1:14cv592-MHT (WO), 2015 WL 3849576 (M.D. Ala. June 22, 2015). A possible policy would be to forbid all harassing, demeaning, or intimidating symbols that disparage any protected group, specifically identifying the Confederate flag as such a symbol. [William Ozier, *Confederate Flags in the Workplace: How Should an Employer Respond?*, Bass, Berry & Sims PLC (Dec. 17, 2015), available at Lexology.com]

After Judges Carnes and Pryor decided that calling a black man "boy" could be racist, they were open to the possibility that bananas could be used for racial harassment, but had other questions about a racially hostile work environment case. Plaintiff Reginald Jones cited bananas being left in his truck as one instance of racial harassment; the site manager said that banana peels were probably garbage left by kids—but there were no banana peels or other garbage on any other driver's truck. Jones said that he had seen co-workers wearing Confederate insignia. UPS said that it responded promptly and appropriately and a manager urged Jones not to resign when he said he was considering it. The Northern District of Alabama granted summary judgment for the employer, denying that bananas had racial connotations and finding that the conditions were not severe and pervasive enough to create a hostile environment. The Eleventh Circuit vacated summary judgment and remanded the case, because a reasonable trier of facts could conclude that the work environment was racially hostile. [*Jones v. UPS Ground Freight*, 683 F.3d 1283 (11th Cir. 2012)]

A Native American woman who was fired after testing positive for marijuana sued her former employer, the Mohave County Public Works Department, for race/ancestry discrimination. The district court granted summary judgment for the employer. Her job required maintaining a commercial driver's license, which calls for random drug testing. The plaintiff first claimed to use medical marijuana by prescription and later admitted to recreational use. The court held that there was no evidence that she was treated more harshly than non-Native American employees. All 10 employees with positive drug tests quit or were fired. [*Yazzie v. County of Mohave*, No. CV-14-08153, 2016 U.S. Dist. LEXIS 93898 (D. Ariz. July 19, 2016); see Rayna H. Jones, *Consistent Enforcement of Drug Policies Key to Avoiding Disparate Treatment Claims*, Ogletree Deakins (Aug. 18, 2016), available at Lexology.com]

The often-cited case of *Herrnreiter v. Chicago Housing Authority* [315 F.3d 742 (7th Cir. 2002)] was brought by a white auditor who was transferred by his black supervisor from the agency's investigation division to its auditing division. The Seventh Circuit held that there was no actionable racial discrimination (even though the plaintiff preferred the investigator's job) because he was not demoted to an objectively inferior position or prevented from exercising his professional skills.

There have been a number of major settlements of racial discrimination and harassment cases (e.g., nooses or swastikas displayed in the workplace, hate graffiti, display of minority employees' names on a "hit list") and racially hostile work environments. Settlements usually included injunctions, training, posting of information about the settlement, and monitoring by the EEOC to prevent further offenses. In many of these cases, the employer denied wrongdoing, but stated that it wished to settle to avoid prolonged litigation.

A suit on behalf of hundreds of African-American brokers, charging Merrill Lynch with systematic channeling of business to white brokers, settled in late 2013 after more than eight years. The plaintiffs charged two policies with disparate impact on African-Americans: allowing brokers to choose their own teams and allocating the accounts of departed brokers based on past results. The Seventh Circuit held that the discretion permitted to managers led to class-wide discrimination. [D. Lucetta Pope, *Distinguishing Dukes: How Decentralized Decision-Making Led to a $160 Million Agreement to Settle Race Discrimination Claims Against Merrill Lynch*, Faegre Baker Daniels (Dec. 23, 2013), available at Lexology.com]

Although it is generally thought of as a statute that forbids discrimination by employers, Title VII also forbids unions to commit discrimination. The Seventh Circuit ruled in 2014 that unions are liable for discrimination (in this case, in a suit brought by a black school teacher who said the union refused to pursue his grievance while it helped white employees) whether or not the union's action violates CBA grievance provisions. The Seventh Circuit said that the standards for an FLSA hybrid action (see § 1.06[A]) do not apply to Title VII cases. [*Green v. Am. Fed'n of Teachers*, 740 F.3d 1104 (7th Cir. 2014)]

[B] Reverse Discrimination

Although most discrimination suits are brought by members of protected groups charging that they were discriminated against by members of the dominant group, a reverse discrimination suit is brought by members of the dominant group charging that they were discriminated against for being, e.g., white, male, or non-disabled. This issue is intimately related to the question of when, if ever, affirmative action is appropriate (see § 34.05[C], below). It is likely that reverse discrimination suits will become more frequent, and will be more positively viewed by courts.

The city of New Haven, Connecticut, gave an examination for firefighters to be promoted to the jobs of lieutenant and captain. Far more white than minority firefighters passed the exam. The city, fearing that it would be sued by minority candidates, discarded the exam and did not promote anyone. The city was sued by white and Hispanic firefighters alleging that their superior test scores entitled them to promotion. The Supreme Court held that the city violated Title VII by refusing to certify the test and make promotions based on the test results, intentionally discriminating against the white and Hispanic firefighters without evidence that it would be liable if it did not make up for past disparate impact. If it had been sued by minority firefighters who charged a violation of Title VII, the Supreme Court said the city could have asserted the Title VII provision allowing valid, job-related tests. [*Ricci v. DeStefano*, 557 U.S. 557 (2009)]

In a reverse discrimination case brought by a white, Italian-American employee who alleged he was denied a promotion that went to a less qualified candidate who was white and Hispanic because the town wanted to appoint its first Hispanic/Latino police chief, the Second Circuit held that Hispanic is a race for § 1981 purposes and someone can belong to more than one race. Section 1981 does not forbid discrimination on the basis of national origin (although Title VII does), so if being Hispanic is a national origin, the plaintiff would have to present separate arguments in a case comprising both Title VII and § 1981 counts. [*Vill. of Freeport v. Barrella*, 814 F.3d 594 (2d Cir. 2016); see Rebecca L. Torrey et. al., *Is "Hispanic" a Race? Second Circuit Answers Yes*, Manatt Phelps & Phillips LLP (Mar. 3, 2016), available at Lexology.com]

The Seventh Circuit allowed a reverse discrimination case to go to trial because of a factual dispute about the reason for the plaintiff's termination. He said that he was laid off because his employer failed to meet federally mandated goals for minority hiring in a construction project. The employer's CBA required increased opportunities for women and minorities. The Seventh Circuit held that if, as the plaintiff alleged, the project superintendant said that he had only 8%

minority workers and needed 13.9%, it would be direct evidence of reverse discrimination. The plaintiff also alleged that, when he picked up his last paycheck, a supervisor said "sorry to hear about this minority thing." [*Deets v. Massman Constr. Co.*, 811 F.3d 978 (7th Cir. 2016); see Connie N. Bertram and Emilie Adams, *Seventh Circuit Allows Reverse Racism Claims to Proceed Against Contractor*, Proskauer Rose LLP (Feb. 4, 2016), available at Lexology.com]

[C] Affirmative Action and Quotas

According to 42 U.S.C. § 2000e-2(j), Title VII does not require employers to grant preferential treatment to any individual or any group because the workforce is imbalanced in terms of the number or percentage of workers from groups that have been discriminated against in the past. In other words, employers do not have to use quotas in hiring, promotion, etc. In the Trump era, it is likely that courts will take a strong stance opposing quotas and affirmative action.

In 1977, the Supreme Court decided that it is unlawful to perpetuate the present effects of past discrimination, although bona fide seniority systems can be left in operation. [*Teamsters v. United States*, 431 U.S. 324 (1977)] Under this approach, preferential hiring of women and minorities might be acceptable to correct an imbalance in the workforce that results from past discrimination. It might also be acceptable to set goals to remove past discrimination and to remove the barriers that existed in the past to prevent racially neutral hiring, but the hiring system must not exclude white applicants.

Cases in the late 1990s say that employers should not set up affirmative action programs merely to enhance diversity within the workplace, but an affirmative action program might be an appropriate corrective measure if there is a history of racism in a particular industry. [*Johnson v. Transp. Agency of Santa Clara Cnty.*, 480 U.S. 616 (1987); *Eldredge v. Carpenters Joint Apprenticeship & Training Comm.*, 94 F.3d 1366 (9th Cir. 1996); *Schurr v. Resorts Int'l Hotel*, 196 F.3d 486 (3d Cir. 1999)]

[D] Rules for Federal Contractors

In the past two decades or so, affirmative action has been most prominent in the context of government contracts. In 1995, the U.S. Supreme Court decided that race-based preferences in government contracting are permissible only if the actual contractor has been the victim of discrimination—not merely that he or she belongs to a group that has historically been economically disadvantaged. [*Adarand Constructors Inc. v. Pena*, 513 U.S. 1108, and 515 U.S. 200 (1995)] The case continued to bounce up and down the court system with various decisions that had more to do with technical legal issues than with the rights and wrongs of affirmative action. The case was supposed to be reheard by the Supreme Court, but in November 2001, the Supreme Court dismissed certiorari as having been improvidently granted. [*Adarand Constructors v. Mineta*, 534 U.S. 103 (2001)]

Executive Order 11246 requires government contractors and contractors on federally assisted construction projects worth over $10,000 to have a policy of furthering equal employment opportunity. If the contractor or subcontractor has more than 50 employees, and the contract is worth over $50,000, the company must have a formal affirmative action program, which must be submitted to the Office of Federal Contract Compliance Programs (OFCCP) within 30 days of the OFCCP's request to see the program.

Contracts over $1 million require a pre-award audit of the affirmative action program. [See 41 C.F.R. Part 60.] There are separate, slightly different, rules for construction contractors.

The OFCCP adopted two rules, effective March 24, 2014, which expand affirmative action requirements for veterans and Persons With Disabilities (PWDs). Federal contractors (with federal contracts and subcontractors over $100,000, for veterans; over $10,000 for PWDs) are required to gather and retain data about the results of their efforts to recruit and hire veterans and PWDs. Subcontractors are covered if their products are eventually sold to the federal government. Covered contractors must set numeric hiring targets: at least 8% of new hires should be veterans, at least 7% should be PWDs. Applicants must be invited to self-identify as veterans or PWDs before a job offer is extended, and the invitation must be repeated when a job offer is made. Recruitment and hiring data must be retained for at least three years. Contractors are required to undertake annual review to analyze the results of their good-faith efforts to hire PWDs and veterans. For companies with an annual affirmative action plan in place on March 24, 2014, the new obligations take effect with the new affirmative action plan year. [78 Fed. Reg. 58682 (Sept. 24, 2013)]

The benchmark is adjusted regularly, and was reduced to 6.7% as of March 31, 2017. [Stephanie Underwood, *Hiring Benchmark for Protected Veterans Is Reduced Again,* Constangy Brooks Smith & Prophete LLP (Apr. 5, 2017), available at Lexology.com]

In mid-2016, the OFCCP issued a final rule about sex discrimination, encompassing the latest EEOC rulemaking. The OFCCP rule took effect on August 15, 2016. See § 34.06[A], [C], and [D], below, for more details. The 2016 guidance defines "sex" to include pregnancy, childbirth, sex stereotyping (e.g., that women should wear "feminine" clothes or that men should not be caregivers), gender identity, and transgender status. Federal contractors are forbidden to discriminate in compensation on the basis of sex. [81 Fed. Reg. 39107 (June 15, 2016); see Michael L. Stevens and Karen S. Vldeck, *DOL Implements New Sex Discrimination Rules for Federal Contractors*, Arent Fox LLP (June 15, 2016), available at Lexology.com; Cara Yates Crotty, *OFCCP Issues Final Rule on Sex Discrimination*, Constangy Brooks Smith & Prophete LLP (June 21, 2016), available at Leoxlogy.com]

In mid-2016, the OFCCP settled with Colonial Parking, Inc. on charges of discriminating against African-American applicants for project manager jobs. The company agreed to pay $180,000 in back pay and interest to rejected applicants, and to hire three of the applicants. The company also agreed to pay $67,800 to African-American valets who were paid less than comparable Hispanic workers. [Louise Davies, *Contractor Settles with OFCCP for More Than $250K*, Constangy Brooks Smith & Prophete LLP (Sept. 21, 2016), available at Lexology .com]

[E] National Origin Discrimination

NOTE: Avoiding national origin discrimination, while vigilantly conforming to laws against employment of unauthorized workers, will give rise to many difficult problems for employers.

The EEOC responded to the increasing threat of national origin discrimination by issuing guidance on national origin discrimination. National origin discrimination is often intertwined with other types of discrimination: e.g., based on religion and/or having a native language other than English.

According to the guidance document [EEOC, *National Origin Discrimination*, <http://www.eeoc.gov/laws/types/nationalorigin.cfm> (undated, last accessed Mar. 10, 2017); the EEOC issued a new § 13, "National Origin Discrimination," as part of the agency's manual, <www.eeoc.gov/policy/docs/national-origin.html>, but as of April 4, 2017, it had been removed from the EEOC's Website.]

Employers with four or more employees are covered, irrespective of the employee's immigration status. The guidance applies to foreign nationals outside the United States who apply to work in the United States. The guidance defines national origin as the place of origin (country, former country, or geographic region) of a person or that person's ancestors. It also refers to national origin group or ethnic group. An ethnic group is a group with common social characteristics such as language, culture, ancestry, or race. National origin discrimination includes discrimination based on ethnicity (e.g., being Hispanic) or physical, linguistic, or cultural traits such as dress or accent. Perception of origin and association with people of disfavored ethnicities are also covered. The guidance also applies to trafficking cases, where workers are coerced or exploited based on their national origin. [<https://www.eeoc.gov/laws/guidance/national-origin-guidance.cfm>; Kristin Aquino-Pham, *EEOC Issues Guidance on National Origin Discrimination That Applies to Foreign National Employees*, Greenberg Traurig LLP (Nov. 23, 2016), available at Lexology.com]

With respect to immigrants, the EEOC took the position that immigrants are entitled to freedom from any kind of discrimination that is forbidden by any law under the EEOC's jurisdiction. Discrimination on the basis of place of birth (or ancestors' place of birth), including "looks, customs or language" is unlawful.

Discrimination is unlawful even if it is based on incorrect factual assumptions—e.g., that a person is an immigrant or comes from a particular country when that is not true. Discrimination based on association with a person of a disfavored group is also forbidden. Physical or verbal conduct (e.g., ethnic slurs) is forbidden if severe or pervasive enough to create a hostile work environment. Unless it interferes with a person's ability to carry out the job, discrimination on the basis of accent is illegal. [EEOC, *Immigrants' Employment Rights Under Federal Anti-Discrimination Law*, <https://www.eeoc.gov/eeoc/publicaitons/immigrants-facts.cfm> (last accessed Apr. 4, 2017)]

The New Jersey Supreme Court upheld a $1.4 million jury award of emotional distress damages to two Hispanic brothers who suffered racial harassment and retaliatory discharge. The plaintiffs, real estate executives, said that their heritage was frequently demeaned—including "Latin lover" "jokes"—told by the HR director. One brother reported harassment to the firm's in-house counsel in 2007, was told to calm down then fired four days later even though he had just received a $10,000 raise for excellent work performance. The other brother was fired a month later for complaining about harassment and the discharge. The plaintiffs said that the racist remarks were emotionally damaging. The jury awarded back and front pay, punitive damages, and attorneys' fees on race discrimination claims under New Jersey anti-discrimination law. The jury also awarded one brother $800,000 in emotional distress damages and $600,000 to the other. The state Supreme Court upheld the emotional distress damages finding they were not excessive enough to shock the conscience and the award could be made based on the plaintiffs' testimony; expert testimony was not required. [*Cuevas v. Wentworth Grp.*, 144 A.3d 890 (N.J. 2016); see David J. Treibman, *New Jersey Court Ruling Raises Price Of Employment Discrimination*, Fisher Phillips (Sept. 21, 2016), available at Lexology.com]

A Muslim teacher born in Turkey could proceed with a charge of national origin discrimination by alleging that the school where she worked had a culture of racial and ethnic hostility. Unal, who has a Turkish accent, was the only foreign-born teacher at the school. She said that the new principal made hostile comments and allowed other employees to do the same and that insensitive remarks were made about other nationalities as well. The Tenth Circuit found that Unal's strongest evidence was about hostility toward Turks, but harassment of other nationalities could be considered. [*Unal v. Los Alamos Pub. Schs.*, No. 15-2055, 2016 U.S. App. LEXIS 1480 (10th Cir. Jan. 29, 2016); see Emily Hobbs-Wright, *Muslim Teacher May Proceed with National Origin Hostile Work Environment Claim*, Holland & Hart LLP (Mar. 16, 2016), available at Lexology.com]

An Egyptian Muslim who was terminated for tardiness and carelessness after a probationary period brought a hostile work environment suit. The Second Circuit reversed dismissal of her case and remanded for jury trial, holding that a reasonable jury could find severe and pervasive discrimination from, for example, constant demands to remove her hijab, insults to Muslims as a group, and demeaning her race, ethnicity, and religion. [*Ahmed v. Astoria Bank*, No. 16-1389 (2d Cir. May 9, 2017); see Dawn Reddy Solowey, *Anti-Muslim Rhetoric in the Workplace: An Employer's Guide to Risks & Prevention*, Seyfarth Shaw LLP (May 23, 2017), available at Lexology.com]

However, the District Court for the Southern District of New York rejected a suit by a worker of Guyanese Indian descent. He worked with the manager's nephew; they did not get along and the plaintiff was fired. He said that he was discriminated against because of his national origin, alleging insulting remarks and favoring of Albanians like the owner. The court held that "you people are only here to make trouble" is not evidence because it was not clear what "you people" meant, and it is not illegal to prefer family members over other employees. [*Hiralall v. Sentoascare, LLC*, No. 13 Civ. 4437 (GBD) 2016 U.S. Dist. LEXIS 35781 (S.D.N.Y. Mar. 18, 2016); see Andrew L. Satenberg et. al., *Title VII's Ban on National Origin Discrimination Doesn't Cover Nepotism*, Manatt Phelps & Phillips LLP (Apr. 12, 2016), available at Lexology.com]

Ethnic "jokes" have been penalized as hostile work environment discrimination: Rhino Energy (Bolt, West Virginia) agreed to pay $62,500 to settle a case about harassment of a Polish-American foreman, and a case is pending against True Form Collision Repair in Oregon, for anti-Russian harassment. In both cases, the employee was terminated for misconduct, but claims that the termination was retaliation for complaining about the harassment. [See Richard R. Menghello, *Is It OK to Tell Polish Jokes at Work? (Answer: NO)*, Fisher & Phillips LLP (Mar. 16, 2016), available at Lexology.com]

The EEOC's position is that "English-only" rules presumptively violate the TVII ban on national origin discrimination, unless, e.g., English is required to communicate with customers or co-workers who only speak English; for safety or efficiency, etc. Furthermore, these exceptions apply to employees when they are carrying out their job duties. It would be unlawful to forbid workers to speak a non-English language while they are on break or not performing job duties. It would be unlawful to single out a specific non-English language, e.g., forbidding the use of Spanish or Arabic in the workplace when other non-English languages are permitted. An English-only rule would also be unlawful if it were adopted with the intent of committing national origin discrimination. [See 29 C.F.R. § 16.06.7; DOL, *What Do I Need to Know About English-Only Rules?*, <http://www.dol.gov/oasam/...FINALEnglish-Only-Rules-FactSheet>]

In March 2015, the NLRB held an English-only rule invalid, focusing not on discrimination but with potential for chilling protected concerted activity. Valley Health System LLC forbade speaking non-English languages while on duty, when patients were present or nearby, or when on staff. The NLRB said this was so broad that it could forbid employees to discuss working conditions in their native language. [Jaklyn Wrigley, *English-Only Policies in the Age of Multiculturalism*, Fisher & Phillips LLP (June 6, 2016), available at Lexology.com. See also *EEOC v. Mesa Sys., Inc.*, No. 2:11-cv-01201 (D. Utah 2013). The case was settled on September 27, 2013, for $450,000. See *Mesa Systems to Pay*

$450,000 to Settle EEOC National Origin Discrimination Lawsuit (Sept. 30, 2013), available at <http://www.eeoc.gov/eeoc/newsroom/release/9-30-13a.cfm> (last accessed Mar. 12, 2017)]

The EEOC has discussed harassment and discrimination against Asians. [EEOC, *Questions and Answers About Employer Responsibilities Concerning the Employment of Muslims, Arabs, South Asians, and Sikhs* (July 16, 2002), <http://www.eeoc.gov/facts/backlash-employer.html> (modified Mar. 21, 2005, available at the EEOC site on Mar. 10, 2017)] The agency position is that it is impermissible to deny employment (e.g., to people who wear turbans, headscarves, or other religious dress) even if the employer believes that customers will be hostile to such workers. A manager or supervisor who learns about ethnic slurs or harassment in the workplace should tell the harassers to stop doing this, and discipline anyone who is found to have committed harassment. If employees ask for the use of space for prayer, the employer can turn down the request only if the space is legitimately required for business needs. (Employers have a duty of reasonable accommodation to religious practice, whereas they merely need to avoid discrimination on the basis of national origin.) Nor can background checks be made more stringent based on an applicant's country of origin.

The relevant factors in determining whether national origin harassment has occurred include whether physical threats were made or workers were intimidated; whether the conduct was hostile and patently offensive; the frequency of the conduct; the context in which it occurred; and whether management acted appropriately after learning of the conduct.

The Ninth Circuit ruled that a CEO's insistence on calling an employee "Manny" or "Hank" rather than his Arabic name, Mamdouh el-Hakem, constituted intentional hostile work environment discrimination forbidden by 42 U.S.C. § 1981, even in the absence of racial epithets. [*El-Hakem v. BJY Inc.*, 415 F.3d 1068 (9th Cir. 2005)]

In a case alleging national origin (and religious) discrimination, the Sixth Circuit held that a reasonable jury could conclude that the plaintiff was fired for engaging in protected activity. Starting in 2009, Yazdian noticed that his supervisor was prejudiced against Muslims and Iranians. Yazdian accused supervisor Sweatt of creating a hostile work environment, and told Sweatt's manager Scott Jackson that Sweatt was discriminating against him and creating a hostile work environment. Sweatt imposed a written warning on Yazdian for "behavioral issues." Yazdian was allowed to, and submitted a rebuttal with detailed responses to each charge of inappropriate behavior. He included references, e-mails, and performance evaluations, but no one reviewed the rebuttal. He was fired for violating the company conduct policy. He sued; the district court granted summary judgment for employer on discrimination and retaliation claims. The Sixth Circuit found that complaining about Sweatt was protected activity, putting the employer on notice that Yazdian believed there had been violations of the law. [*Yazdian v ConMed Endoscopic Tech., Inc.*, 793 F.3d 634 (6th Cir. 2015)]

[F] EEOC 2006 Guidance

In April 2006, the EEOC revised § 15 of its compliance manual with respect to race and color discrimination. Studies show that racial prejudice persists in hiring—for example, white people with criminal records were three times as likely to be offered employment as black people with similar records, temporary agencies preferred white to black applicants, and interviews were 50% more likely to be given based on the same resume if it showed a "white" rather than a "black" surname. [In *El-Hakem v. BJY, Inc.*, 415 F.3d 1068, 1073 (9th Cir. 2005), the Ninth Circuit held that names are often a proxy for race and ethnicity.]

Title VII does not define "race," and neither does the EEOC; federal race/ethnicity data is collected using the OMB's categories (American Indian/Alaska native; Asian; Black (African-American); Native Hawaiian or Other Pacific Islander; and White, plus the ethnic category of Hispanic/Latino). This guidance says that Title VII generally covers:

- Racial or ethnic ancestry; the EEOC notes that race and national origin can overlap, but are not the same thing;

- Perceived race, even if the perception is incorrect;

- Association with someone of a particular race;

- Subgroup or "race plus," e.g., treating black women who have pre-school children worse than white women with pre-school children;

- Physical characteristics associated with race, such as skin color, hair, facial features, height and weight;

- Race-linked illnesses (for example, sickle cell anemia and diabetes). An employer who applies facially neutral standards that exclude the treatment of conditions for which certain ethnic groups are disproportionately at risk must show that the standards are based on generally accepted medical criteria;

- Cultural characteristics related to ethnicity, such as name, dress and grooming practices, accent or manner of speech;

- Reverse discrimination. The EEOC does not require a heightened standard of proof when Caucasian employees raise reverse-discrimination claims, but the ultimate burden of persuasion always rests with the plaintiff.

The EEOC notes that color discrimination can be intra-racial, for example, a black manager's favoring lighter-skinned black subordinates over darker-skinned subordinates.

A complaint can involve any combination of race, color, and national origin; EEOC policy is for complaints to list all allegations that can reasonably be made. Discrimination is also forbidden if it is based on the intersection of two or more protected categories (e.g., Latinos with a disability).

The EEOC's position is that disparate impact analysis applies to all objective or subjective criteria for recruitment, hiring, promotion, or layoff, as well as grooming standards and education requirements. Proof of a disparate impact case begins with a statistical showing that the policy or practice causes significant disparate impact to a protected group. Then the employer has the burden of showing the practice is job-related and consistent with business necessity. Finally, the burden shifts to whether the person challenging the policy or practice can show a less discriminatory alternative method for satisfying the business need.

In assessing arrest records, the employer must evaluate not only the relationship between the charge and the job, but whether or not the arrested person was actually guilty. For conviction records, the employer must consider the nature and gravity of the offense(s); the length of time elapsed since the conviction or completion of the sentence; and the nature of the job. The EEOC considers a blanket refusal to hire anyone who has ever had a conviction of any kind to be inappropriate because it is not job-related or consistent with business necessity. [For the EEOC's most recent statement of these principles, see EEOC Enforcement Guidance, *Consideration of Arrest and Conviction Records in Employment Decisions Under Title VII of the Civil Rights Act of 1964* <http://www.eeoc.gov/laws/guidance/arrest_conviction.cfm> (Apr. 25, 2012) (last accessed Mar. 11, 2017)] See § 23.08 for discussion of potential discrimination in background checks, including "ban the box" laws that forbid asking about criminal records at early stages of the hiring process. However, this is yet another topic where the Trump-era EEOC will probably change the previous policy.

The EEOC says that appearance and grooming standards must be neutral, consistently applied, and adopted for nondiscriminatory reasons. Racial or ethnic attire that conforms to the dress code must be allowed. Employers can require hairstyles that are neat, clean and well-groomed, as long as racial differences in hair texture are respected, and the standards are equally applied. The EEOC's basic position is that employers may have to make exception to their "usual rules or preferences" to accommodate religious clothing (e.g., head coverings), avoidance of some clothing items (e.g., some denominations forbid women to wear pants), and grooming practices (e.g., wearing a full beard; dreadlocks or side curls). [EEOC, *Religious Garb and Grooming in the Workplace: Rights and Responsibilities*, <http://www.eeoc.gov/eeoc/publications/qa_religious_garb_grooming.cfm> (Aug. 21, 2014) (last accessed Mar. 11, 2017)]

The EEOC said it was racial bias for Catastrophe Management Solutions to rescind a job offer when Chastity Jones was offered work as a customer service representative but was told that the company's grooming policy forbids dreadlocks because of its requirement of a "professional and business-like image." EEOC sued, arguing that it violates Title VII to single out specific hairstyles that conflict with "normative standards for other races." However, the Eleventh Circuit ruled for the employer in mid-2016, holding that dreadlocks are not an immutable characteristic of black people. The Eleventh Circuit cited two appellate decisions and seven district court decisions stating that Title VII does not protect hairstyles culturally associated with a particular race. [*EEOC v. Catastrophe Mgmt. Solutions*, 837 F.3d 1156 (11th Cir.), revised 2016 WL 7210059 (11th Cir. Dec. 13, 2016); see FindLaw Employment Law blog, *Employers Can Ban Dreadlocks, 11th Cir. Rules* (Sept. 22, 2016), available at FindLaw.com]

EEOC guidance says that Title VII allows diversity outreach. Affirmative action is action to overcome past or present barriers to equal employment opportunity, and can be court-ordered after a discrimination finding, negotiated as a remedy in a consent decree or settlement agreement, or created pursuant to government regulation. Voluntary affirmative action plans are permitted, for example, to eliminate a manifest imbalance in a job category that has traditionally been segregated. Courts ruling on a voluntary affirmative action plan look at whether it involves a quota or inflexible goal; whether the plan is flexible enough to make each candidate compete against all other qualified candidate; if the plan is unnecessarily harmful to interests of third parties, and whether the plan is temporary and will end when the goal has been met.

Race-based conduct by a supervisor, co-worker, or non-employee who is nevertheless under the employer's control (e.g., a customer or business partner) can constitute unlawful harassment if unwelcome and severe or pervasive enough to alter terms and conditions of employment as viewed by a reasonable person in the victim's position. The more severe, the less pervasive it has to be, and vice versa, so a single incident would create an abusive environment only if very severe (e.g., physical).

Employers are generally liable for the acts of supervisors. However, in hostile environment cases when there was no tangible action against the victim, the employer can raise the affirmative defense that it used reasonable care to prevent harassing behavior, or that any harassment was promptly corrected—but the employee unreasonably failed to make use of these procedures. If the harasser is high enough in rank to serve as proxy for the employer (e.g., if the harasser is an owner, president, partner, or corporate officer) then the affirmative defense is not available even for a hostile environment claim. For harassment committed by co-workers or customers on the employer's premises, the employer is liable if it knew or should have known about the conduct and did not take prompt corrective steps. [See <http://www.eeoc.gov/policy/docs/race-color.html> (last revised Feb. 8, 2011) (last accessed Mar. 11, 2017). This link includes a note on *Vance v. Ball State Univ.*, 133 S. Ct. 2434 (2013), pointing out that this decision says that a "supervisor" is someone who is empowered to take adverse employment action.]

Additional guidance was proposed in 2016, forbidding discrimination based on ethnicity, physical, linguistic, or cultural traits (e.g., wearing traditional dress), or perception that someone comes from a place disfavored by the employer. It is unlawful to discriminate based on status as a U.S. citizen—but it is permissible, in fact required, to employ only people who are authorized to work in the United

States. The guidance says that English-only rules are presumptively illegal. The guidance defines discrimination against Native Americans, or on the basis of tribal membership, as national origin discrimination. Intersectional discrimination is also forbidden (e.g., adverse practices imposed on Asian women but not Asian men or non-Asian women). The EEOC's position is that it is not acceptable to request that a staffing agency or employment agency avoid referring people of a particular national origin. The EEOC recommends best practices for employers: drafting written guidelines containing objective criteria for assessing candidates and employees; basing discipline on objective, job-related criteria; use multiple methods of recruiting to get a broader range of applicants; and train employees that harassment will not be allowed. [<https://www.regulations.gov/docket?D=EEOC-2016-0004> (June 2, 2016) (last accessed Mar. 11, 2017); see Virginia Broughton Reeves, *What Is National Origin Discrimination Under Title VII? The EEOC Weighs In*, Bradley Arent Boult Cummings LLP (June 9, 2016), available at Lexology.com]

In both December 2015 and March 2016, the EEOC released guidance tools for both employers and employees about how to avoid discrimination against people of Middle Eastern origin, particularly where this overlaps with discrimination against Muslims. [Employer Q&A: <https://www.eeoc.gov/eeoc/publications/muslim_middle_eastern_employers.cfm> (undated, last accessed Mar. 11, 2017); see Susan Gross Sholinsky and Ann Knuckles Mahoney, *EEOC Targets Religious and National Origin Discrimination Against Individuals Who Are or Are Perceived to be Muslim or Middle Eastern*, Epstein Becker Green (June 28, 2016), available at Lexology.com]

[G] Association Discrimination

"Association discrimination" is the claim that persons of one group were subjected to workplace discrimination because of their association with persons of another group.

Early in 2011, the Supreme Court held that Title VII forbids retaliation against a discrimination complainant that takes the form of punishing an associate of that person. In this case, Miriam Regalado filed an EEOC sex discrimination charge against North American Stainless in 2002. Three weeks after the charge was filed, Regalado's then-fiancé (they subsequently married) was fired. The Supreme Court's majority opinion says that the Title VII anti-retaliation provision covers any action by an employer that would prevent a reasonable worker from making or pursuing a discrimination charge. There are no hard and fast lines, but firing a close family member is almost always covered by Title VII, a mild reprisal against an acquaintance is not covered, and courts must decide the intermediate cases. A suit can be brought by anyone within the "zone of interests" protected by the law. [*Thompson v. North Am. Stainless*, 562 U.S. 170 (2011)]

The Second Circuit allowed such a case to proceed, holding that Title VII can be violated by firing a white man for associating with a person of another race (in this case, his black wife). Taking adverse action because of an interracial relationship reflects discrimination because it embodies stereotypes about how white people should behave. [*Holcomb v. Iona Coll.*, 521 F.3d 130 (2d Cir. 2008)]

On a case brought by a white man who charged that he was fired because he lived with, became engaged to, and eventually married a black woman, the Second Circuit held that engagement to marry is intimate association protected by the First Amendment. (The employer said that he was fired for misconduct including blocking a security camera.) However, the Second Circuit reversed the finding of liability under 42 U.S.C. § 1983 against the individual defendants. It also reversed an award of punitive damages because the First Amendment right of intimate association was not clearly established law at the time of the events. [*Matusick v. Erie Cnty. Water Auth.*, 739 F.3d 51 (2d Cir. 2014)]

The Eighth Circuit assumed without deciding that Title VII discrimination and retaliation suits can be premised on association with a member of a protected class. (Association discrimination suits have also been permitted in the Second, Fifth, Sixth, and Eleventh Circuits.) A white former police chief succeeded in claiming that trying to promote a black woman to a supervisory position was protected conduct. However, he lost the suit because the Eighth Circuit found that he did not link this conduct to the decision to fire him. [*Hutton v. Maynard*, 812 F.3d 679 (8th Cir. 2016); see Erik Peters, *With a Little Help from my Friends: 8th Circuit Assumes Without Deciding That Associational Bias Claims Exist Under Title VII*, Verrill Dana LLP (Feb. 4, 2016), available at Lexology.com]

§ 34.06 SEX DISCRIMINATION

[A] Generally

Discrimination on account of sex is unlawful, except if there is a gender-based (bona fide occupational qualification) BFOQ. In 1983, the Supreme Court decided that it constitutes sex discrimination for a health plan to provide less comprehensive benefits to male employees and their wives than to female employees and their husbands. [*Newport News Shipbuilding v. EEOC*, 462 U.S. 669 (1983)] Note, however, that in mid-2009, the Supreme Court ruled that AT&T did not commit sex discrimination by failing to adapt its pension plan to correct pre-Pregnancy Discrimination Act discrimination in treatment of pregnancy leave. [*AT&T Corp. v. Hulteen*, 556 U.S. 701 (2009)]

For Women's History Month, 2017, the DOL posted some statistics about working women. At that point, women made up almost half of the U.S. workforce. More than 74.6 million women held civilian jobs. Seventy percent of women in the workforce are mothers of children under 18. Among households with minor children, working mothers are the sole or primary earner in 40% of the households. [Tina A. Syring, *By the Numbers: Women in the Workforce*, Barnes & Thornburg LLP (Mar. 3, 2017), available at Lexology.com]

On January 28, 2015, the OFCCP issued a Notice of Proposed Rulemaking (NPRM) rescinding its existing sex discrimination guidelines, replacing them with guidelines that incorporate case law. This is the first time the guidelines were updated since they were issued in 1970. The NPRM says that minimum height and weight qualifications that are not related to job performance are discriminatory if they have a disparate impact on women. A policy that operators of large equipment cannot use the restroom while working is also discriminatory because women use the restroom more often than men. Federal contractors are liable for all compensation practices, including performance reviews, that have an adverse impact on the grounds of sex. [Janet V. Britton, *OFCCP Proposes New Rule Related to Sex Bias*, Verrill Dana LLP (Feb. 4, 2015), available at Lexology.com]

The OFCCP finalized the sex discrimination rule in June 2016, effective August 1, 2016. The rule's broad definition of sex discrimination includes discrimination based on pregnancy, childbirth, gender identity, and sex stereotyping. [81 Fed. Reg. 39107 (June 15, 2016); see Michael L. Stevens and Karen S. Vldeck, *DOL Implements New Sex Discrimination Rules for Federal Contractors*, Arent Fox LLP (June 15, 2016), available at Lexology.com; Cara Yates Crotty, *OFCCP Issues Final Rule on Sex Discrimination*, Constangy Brooks Smith & Prophete LLP (June 21, 2016), available at Lexology.com]

Ellen Pao, once a partner in the venture capital firm Kleiner Perkins Caulfield & Byers sued the firm for sex discrimination and retaliation. She said that she was given inferior assignments, was denied promotion, and experienced retaliation when she complained. The jury found for Kleiner Perkins in March 2015. She did not appeal the loss and was ordered by the San Francisco Superior Court to pay Kleiner Perkins $276,000 in court costs [Jeff Elder, *Ellen Pao Won't Appeal Trial Loss in Case Against Kleiner Perkins*, Caufield & Byers WSJ.com (Sept. 10, 2015)]

Karla Gerner said that the county, her employer, offered her a less favorable severance package than comparable male employees. The district court dismissed, holding that there had been no adverse employment action because severance benefits could only create adverse employment action if there was a contract violation and, in any event, severance benefits are paid after termination and after the employment relationship is over. The Fourth Circuit reversed. Any benefit—even one that the employer is not legally obligated to provide—might be discriminatory. Gerner testified that she was fired only after rejecting the discriminatory severance package, so she was an employee at that time. [*Gerner v. Cnty. of Chesterfield*, 674 F.3d 264 (4th Cir. 2012). *Hishon v. King & Spalding*, 469 U.S. 69 (1984) stands for the proposition that discrimination must be avoided in all benefits in the employment relationship.]

On a showing of enough circumstantial evidence that women suffer more bullying and harassment than men, female employees can maintain a Title VII gender-based discrimination action, even if the harassment takes the form of shouting, screaming, foul language, and invading employees' personal space rather than a direct solicitation of sexual activity. [*EEOC v. Nat'l Educ. Ass'n Alaska*, 422 F.3d 840 (9th Cir. 2005); the Eleventh Circuit reached a similar conclusion in 2009, and affirmed that holding en banc in 2010, *Reeves v. C.H. Robinson*, 569 F.3d 1290 (11th Cir. 2009), *aff'd en banc*, 594 F.3d 798 (2010)]

A grocery store supervisor, Mayes, frequently gave cakes from the "stales" cart as an incentive to night shift workers. Mayes was fired for taking a cake from the cart. She brought a Title VII suit, alleging that she was replaced by a man without supervisory experience and with limited training because she claimed that there was resentment that a woman was in charge of the freight crew and served on the safety committee. The district court dismissed Mayes's suit but the Ninth Circuit reinstated it, holding that her termination might have been pretextual. The Ninth Circuit found that there was evidence that it was accepted practice for supervisors to give stale cake to employees and it was not credible that Mayes would be fired for doing something that was accepted. [*Mayes v. WinCo, Holdings, Inc.*, 846 F.3d 1274 (9th Cir. 2017); see Manatt Phelps & Phillips LLP, *Termination for Cake Theft May Have Been Pretext, Ninth Circuit Rules* (Feb. 27, 2017), available at Lexology.com]

The Fifth Circuit applied the continuing violation doctrine in a hostile work environment case, requiring the district court to consider conduct outside the 300-day Title VII limitations period. The conduct creating the hostile work environment often extends over a period of time, so the entire course of harassment can be considered in determining liability as long as at least one act of harassment occurred during the limitations period. The plaintiff, a college professor, said that her immediate supervisor had harassed her on account of sex since 2003, such as insulting her ability because she is a woman, and excluding her from meetings because she "talked too much for a woman." She initiated, but then dropped, a state-court suit in 2009. The plaintiff was on sabbatical for job-related stress in 2010 and 2011; she said the harassment continued when she returned to work and the university did not respond to her complaints. The Fifth Circuit held that, in deciding whether to apply the continuing violation doctrine, the court decides if the acts in the alleged series are related; if intervening acts by the employer separate the earlier from the later acts; and whether there are any equitable factors that preclude the court's considering all of the continuing conduct in the plaintiff's case. The Fifth Circuit concluded that there was a continuing violation and remanded the case to see if claims about post-2011 conduct could survive summary judgment. [*Heath v. Bd. of Supervisors*, 850 F.3d 731 (5th Cir. 2017); see Esteban Shardonofsky and John P. Phillips, *Fifth Circuit Warps Time in Decision on the Continuing Violation Doctrine*, Seyfarth Shaw LLP (Mar. 14, 2017), available at Lexology.com]

The Seventh Circuit upheld the termination of a man (the only male respiratory therapist out of seven) who was fired for accessing hacking sites and pornography on the office computer system. The plaintiff alleged that, as the only male, he was targeted for investigation when inappropriate sites were accessed.

The Seventh Circuit held that it was reasonable to suspect him because he was logged on to the computer when the inappropriate sites were accessed, and he even admitted accessing 17 of the 31 sites. (He denied going to the hacking sites, and said malware must have gotten loaded onto his computer accidentally.) He did not show that women were allowed to violate the hospital's acceptable computer use policy with impunity. [*Farr v. St. Francis Hosp. & Health Ctr.*, 570 F.3d 829 (7th Cir. 2009)]

Tax lawyer Todd Lenart said that he experienced sex discrimination and a hostile work environment when his female supervisor favored women in hiring and at work. His supervisor said she wanted a "girl power team." The District Court for the Southern District of New York dismissed his hostile work environment claim, but allowed his sex discrimination claims to go forward, based on the female empowerment message and the fact that Lenart was terminated (allegedly because the tax department had been reorganized) and replaced by a woman. The hostile work environment claim was dismissed because he did not allege severe and pervasive harassment. [*Lenart v. Coach, Inc.*, 131 F. Supp. 3d 61 (S.D.N.Y. 2015)]

The physical examination for FBI special agent trainees requires men to do 30 pushups; women only need to do 14 pushups. The Fourth Circuit upheld this requirement in a suit brought by a rejected male applicant. The court said that physiological sex differences affect physical fitness standards, and can be considered as long as an equal burden is imposed on both sexes. [*Bauer v. Lynch*, 812 F.3d 340 (4th Cir. 2016)]

It violates the Fourteenth Amendment's guarantee of Equal Protection to apply a facially neutral state law in a way that reflects sexual stereotyping. Therefore, a male state trooper should have been granted a 30-day parental leave when his child was born. (Leave was denied on the basis that only women can be primary caregivers for infants.) However, *Knussman v. Maryland* [272 F.3d 625 (4th Cir. 2001)] holds that an award of $375,000 in emotional distress damages was disproportionate to the actual damages that the trooper suffered.

According to the Sixth Circuit, a company's anti-nepotism policy (requiring one spouse to resign when two employees marry) was rational. However, firing someone for criticizing the policy could be a violation of the employee's right of freedom of thought. In *Vaughn v. Lawrenceburg Power System* [269 F.3d 703 (6th Cir. 2001)], the bride agreed to resign, then the groom was fired for agreeing with the statement, "I take it you do not fully agree with our policy." The Sixth Circuit said that antinepotism rules get heightened scrutiny under the First Amendment right of freedom of association if, but only if, they place a direct and substantial burden on the right to marry. [See also *Montgomery v. Carr*, 101 F.3d 1117 (6th Cir. 1996.)]

The First Circuit considered when an employer will be liable for sex discrimination for firing an employee whose job performance was maligned by a co-worker who was angry about being jilted by the plaintiff. The First Circuit held that the plaintiff made a plausible case that he was fired because the HR director (who was not in his supervisory chain) took revenge on him for rejecting her sexual advances. The First Circuit defined a three-part test: (1) A co-worker makes negative statements about the plaintiff for discriminatory reasons and with intent to get the plaintiff fired; (2) Those acts are the proximate cause of the plaintiff's termination; (3) The employer was negligent in firing the plaintiff when it knew or should have known of the co-worker's discriminatory motivation. [*Velázquez-Pérez v. Diversified Developers Realty Corp.*, 753 F.3d 265 (1st Cir. 2014); see Chapter 35, especially § 35.01 and 35.04, for more discussion of workplace sexual harassment.]

In a Title VII suit alleging nationwide practices of sex discrimination in pay and promotions, the Second Circuit reversed a grant of summary judgment for the employer. The Second Circuit held that the magistrate judge improperly reviewed whether the EEOC's investigation was adequate, when the question for review was merely whether there was an investigation. [*EEOC v. Sterling Jewelers, Inc.*, 801 F.3d 96 (2d Cir. 2015)]

Sterling reached a partial settlement with the EEOC on May 4, 2017, agreeing to change its policies, but no damages were imposed. However, two other cases, a class action brought by almost 70,000 female employees, and the other brought by stockholders who alleged that the company should have disclosed the seriousness of the allegations against it, remained pending. [*EEOC v. Sterling Jewelers Inc.*, No. 08-CV-0706-RJA-MJR (consent decree May 4, 2017); see Daniel Wiessner, *Sterling Jewelers Settles EEOC Gender Bias Claims but Class Action Still Possible,* Insurance Journal (May 9, 2017), available at www.insurancejournal.com]

In 2010, the Ninth Circuit certified the largest employment discrimination class ever, including over a million plaintiffs. A class of women charging Wal-Mart with sex discrimination was initially certified in 2004. Extensive litigation ensued about the composition of the class. The Ninth Circuit certified one of the larger classes, but a smaller class was remanded for further analysis.

In mid-2011, however, the Supreme Court issued a ruling that will make it far more difficult for employees of large companies to bring class action discrimination suits. The Supreme Court held that the would-be class members failed to prove that there was a common, company-wide policy of discrimination. In the Supreme Court view, although the plaintiffs alleged that the Wal-Mart corporate culture discriminated against women, the official policy of the chain was to give local managers significant discretion. The Supreme Court's majority opinion said that the plaintiffs complained of millions of employment decisions, not a single employment decision that could properly be addressed in a class action. The Supreme Court also criticized the demand for back pay, and ruled that Wal-Mart was entitled to individual determinations of back pay eligibility for class members, rather than extrapolation from a sample of employees. Some commentators suggested that companies could protect themselves against class actions by delegating to managers. [*Wal-Mart Stores Inc. v. Dukes*, 131 S. Ct. 2541 (2011)]

After the Supreme Court ruling, the plaintiffs re-filed a narrower suit, with over 90,000 plaintiffs, against Wal-Mart in the Central District of California, limited to California stores.

The Sixth Circuit reversed the District Court for the Western District of Tennessee. The Sixth Circuit allowed former plaintiffs in *Dukes* to pursue class certification for their sex discrimination claims. After the 2011 Supreme Court decision, various groups of plaintiffs amended their case to include a narrower and more targeted range of employees and ex-employees. The Sixth Circuit said that no court had denied a (b)(3) class of current and former female employees, and the Supreme Court did not rule out a (b)(2) certifying a regional class, only a nationwide one. Therefore, the former members of the *Dukes* class could continue to assert the class claims, because the plaintiff group had been reduced, and a new certification theory (under Rule 23(b)(3)) had been introduced. [*Phipps, et. al. v. Wal-Mart Stores, Inc.*, 792 F.3d 637 (6th Cir. 2015)]

Female store managers at Family Dollar persuaded the Fourth Circuit that their case is not controlled by *Dukes* because there were nationwide policies for salary structures, and high-level management discretion follows common patterns that favor men. But they were merely allowed to amend their complaint, and may not succeed in obtaining nationwide class status. [*Scott v. Family Dollar Stores, Inc.*, 733 F.3d 105 (4th Cir. 2013)]

EEOC Enforcement Guidance published in May 2007 stresses that, although the EEOC does not consider being a caregiver for family members to be a separate new protected category, sometimes discrimination on the basis of care-giving will violate existing protection under Title VII and/or the Americans With Disabilities Act. The EEOC says that it may take enforcement steps when a caregiver (male or female) is subjected to stereotyping in hiring or in the work environment. [EEOC Enforcement Guidance: *Unlawful Disparate Treatment of Workers with Caregiving Responsibilities* Number 915.002, <http://www.eeoc.gov/policy/docs/caregiving.html> (updated Feb. 8, 2011) (last accessed Mar. 11, 2017). In April 2009, the EEOC published additional guidance on this topic at <http://www.eeoc.gov/policy/docs/caregiver-best-practices.html> (Jan. 19, 2011) (accessed Mar. 11, 2017); see § 28.01[C].] The OFCCP's June 2016 guidance on sex discrimination states that discriminating against male caregivers constitutes unlawful discrimination on the basis of sex stereotyping. [81 Fed. Reg. 39107 (June 15, 2016)]

The New Jersey Appellate Division ruled in 2015 that enforcing a weight standard for cocktail waitresses ("BorgataBabes") did not violate state anti-discrimination laws. The court found that the beverage server's job requires promoting the casino's image and the employees had agreed to abide by personal appearance standards, which were consistent with casino industry standards and customer expectations. Both men and women were required to be physically fit and forbidden to gain more than 7% of their baseline weight (except in cases of pregnancy or illness). Over a five-year period, 25 of the 686 female Borgata Babes—and none of the 46 males—were suspended for this reason. The court said that the dress code was not facially discriminatory because the skimpy form-fitting outfits women were required to wear were important to the entertainment nature of the business. However, a hostile environment sexual harassment count was reinstated because of evidence of the way the policy was applied to women returning from medical or maternity leave. [*Schiavo, et al. v. Marina Dist. Dev. Co., LLC, d/b/a Borgata Casino Hotel & Spa*, 442 N.J. Super. 346 (App. Div. 2015)]

[B] The Pregnancy Discrimination Act (PDA)

Section 2000e contains vital definitions for understanding federal antidiscrimination law. Sex discrimination includes, but is not limited to, discrimination "because or on the basis of pregnancy, childbirth, or related medical conditions." [42 U.S.C. § 2000e(k)]

This part of Title VII is referred to as the Pregnancy Discrimination Act (PDA). Under the PDA, women "affected by pregnancy, childbirth, or related medical conditions" have to be treated the same way as "other persons" who are not affected by such conditions, but who are comparable in their ability or inability to work. In other words, the PDA does not treat pregnancy itself as a disability, but to the extent that a particular pregnant worker does encounter disability, the employer must treat it the same way as other non-occupationally related disability.

The PDA requires equal treatment for "all employment-related purposes," including fringe benefits—a category that includes the all-important health benefits. However, employers do not have to provide health coverage if they would not otherwise. Employers have the discretion to provide abortion benefits, and are required to cover medical complications of abortion, but do not have to cover elective abortions, only abortions in situations where the mother's life would be endangered by carrying the fetus to term.

As a threshold question, to succeed in alleging pregnancy discrimination, the plaintiff must be a common-law employee, not an independent contractor who controls the major aspects of the work. [See, e.g., *Alberty-Velez v. Corporacion de Puerto Rico Para La Difusion Publica*, 242 F.3d 418 (1st Cir. 2003); *Murray v. Principal Fin. Grp., Inc.*, 613 F.3d 943 (9th Cir. 2010); *Glascock v. Linn Cnty. Emergency Med. PC*, 698 F.3d 695 (8th Cir. 2012)]

In early 2017, the Second Circuit limited plaintiffs' ability to use statistical evidence of pay disparity between the sexes, by itself, to prove an EPA claim. However, New York's Achieve Pay Equity Act is more employee-friendly than the EPA, so plaintiffs might succeed where they would not have a triable federal case. The plaintiff was a veterinarian who charged that she was paid less than male counterparts. The Second Circuit held that they were not valid comparators, because, although the plaintiff held the title of department head, she was a general practitioner performing basic treatment, whereas the men were specialists to whom the plaintiff referred difficult cases. She also had a lower patient load and a limited research load and was not required to supervise interns. Because there were no valid male comparators, the Second Circuit would not allow statistical comparisons between female and male veterinarians in general as the sole premise for an EPA case. [*Chiaramonte v. The Animal Med. Ctr.*, No. 16-0478-cv, 2017 U.S. App. LEXIS 137 (2d Cir. Jan. 26, 2017); see Seth Kaufman, *2nd Circuit Reaffirms Limitations on Statistical Evidence in Pay Equity Cases*, Fisher Phillips (Feb. 16, 2017), available at Lexology.com]

In 2014, the fiftieth anniversary of Title VII, the EEOC published its first pregnancy guidance in 30 years. Under this guidance, it violates the PDA to refuse light duty or other accommodations to pregnant workers if they are available to similar non-pregnant workers. The EEOC's Strategic Enforcement Plan for FY 2013–2016 calls for an increased focus on investigating pregnancy discrimination allegations. The guidance was revised once again in mid-2015, reflecting the *Young* case (see below). [EEOC, *Enforcement Guidance on Pregnancy Discrimination and Related Issues*, <http://www.eeoc.gov/laws/guidance/pregnancy_guidance.cfm> (June 25, 2015) (last accessed Mar. 11, 2017)]

The 2015 guidance modifies the 2014 version by saying that policies can violate the PDA even if they are not facially discriminatory, if pregnant employees are subjected to a burden without justification. The EEOC says that parental leave must be offered to similarly situated men and women on the same terms. Biological mothers can be offered more leave than fathers only if the extra leave is medically necessary. In September 2015, CNN and Turner Broadcasting settled an EEOC charge brought by ex-correspondent Josh Levs, who said that the company policy discriminated against biological fathers. Biological fathers received only two weeks of paid leave; biological mothers and all adoptive parents were offered 10 weeks of paid leave. The settlement was not disclosed, but Time Warner changed the policy to give all parents six weeks of paid leave. Another six weeks of leave is available for unforeseen medical needs of biological mothers. [Cheryl D. Orr and Alejandra Lara, *Mom-Friendly Policies May Be a Nice Perk but Could Constitute Gender Discrimination*, Drinker Biddle & Reath LLP (Oct. 29, 2015), available at Lexology.com]

A 2015 Supreme Court decision allowed Peggy Young to pursue a case against UPS. She alleged disparate treatment: that UPS policies granted accommodations to employees with work-related disabilities or ADA disabilities, or who had lost their Department of Transportation certification, but denied accommodation to pregnancy-related disabilities. The Supreme Court held that *McDonnell-Douglas* can be used to assert disparate treatment through indirect evidence. The prima facie is that a worker was pregnant; was refused the accommodation she sought; and others who were similar in their ability to work did receive accommodation. The employer can defend itself by proffering a legitimate, nondiscriminatory reason but higher cost or inconvenience is not enough. But the Supreme Court rejected Young's contention that if the employer accommodates only a subset of workers with disabling conditions, pregnant workers with similar ability to work must get the same treatment, even if another class of nonpregnant workers does not get accommodation. The Supreme Court said that pregnant workers do not get most favored nation status. The Supreme Court vacated summary judgment for UPS, because Young created a genuine dispute about the treatment of similarly situated workers and whether UPS' explanation was pretextual. The Supreme Court refused to grant deference to the EEOC's 2014 guidance on the subject, finding that it lacked the consistency and thoroughness to be persuasive. Furthermore, it was promulgated after certiorari was granted in this case. [*Young v. UPS*, 135 S. Ct. 1338 (Mar. 25, 2015)]

A pregnant corrections officer was denied light duty by the Ulster County Sheriff's Department, which only provided light duty for work-related injury. The Second Circuit allowed her pregnancy discrimination case to go to the jury, based on the premise that 100% of the workers denied light duty for pregnancy (in this case, the plaintiff was the only one requesting this accommodation) were denied whereas it might be acceptable if only a small percentage of pregnant workers were refused light duty assignments. [*Legg v. Ulster Cnty.*, No. 14-3636 (2d Cir. Apr. 26, 2016); see Robin E. Shea, *Court Sheds Light on "Pregnancy Accommodation" Obligation After Young v. UPS*, Constangy Brooks Smith & Prophete LLP (Apr. 29, 2016), available at Lexology.com]

The EEOC's position is that an employer cannot forbid pregnant employees from working because of stereotypes about fetal health. The EEOC settled a PDA case against a doughnut franchise that forced an employee to go on unpaid leave when the employer heard that she might be pregnant. First she was not allowed to work without providing a medical release that she did not have a high-risk pregnancy then fired for complaining. The EEOC settled the case for $45,000. The EEOC press release warns employers not to force pregnant employees (or employees believed to be pregnant) to provide medical documentation of their ability to work unless they have requested accommodation. [Richard B. Cohen, *Pregnant? We Are Placing You on Unpaid Leave for Your Own Good*, Fisher-Broyles (Sept. 1, 2016), available at Lexology.com]

The EEOC settled a suit against a North Carolina furniture store for $55,000. The plaintiff was hired as an apprentice; the job required using chemicals to repair furniture. When she disclosed her pregnancy, she was fired after the regional manager showed her a can of lacquer thinner that had a pregnancy warning. [<http://www1.eeoc.gov/eeoc/newsroom/release/2-3-17a.cfm> ; Richard B. Cohen, *Employers Cannot Play "Father Knows Best" to Pregnant Employees*, FisherBroyles (Feb. 6, 2017), available at Lexology.com]

The OFCCP's January 28, 2015 NPRM on sex discrimination requires that federal contractors—even those with fewer than 15 employees—must accommodate pregnant workers and provide family leave for fathers as well as for mothers. [Janet V. Britton, *OFCCP Proposes New Rule Related to Sex Bias*, Verrill Dana LLP (Feb. 4, 2015), available at Lexology.com; Melanie Trottman, *Labor Department Proposes to Update Sex-Discrimination Rules*, WSJ.com (Jan. 28, 2015)]

The OFCCP's June 2016 rule on Discrimination on the Basis of Sex (see 81 Fed. Reg. 39107 (June 15, 2016)) reiterates that pregnancy, childbirth, and lactation are included in the definition of sex discrimination.

Almost all of the states, and the District of Columbia, have statutes forbidding discrimination on the basis of pregnancy. Statutes in many also require reasonable accommodation of pregnant employees and employees recovering from childbirth. Some of these statutes forbid employers to force pregnant employees to take unwanted leave. The obligation to accommodate might not be limited to pregnancy-related disability. Possible accommodations include extra breaks at work; better seating; limitations on lifting; light duty, if available, and temporary transfers to a less strenuous job.

For example, Illinois requires accommodation of common conditions related to pregnancy and childbirth. New York employers must accommodate, as a temporary disability, a pregnancy-related condition that is medically demonstrated and affects bodily functions, even if it is not otherwise a disability. California requires accommodation of pregnancy-related medical conditions other than pregnancy disability leave. [Elizabeth N. Hall, Heather M. Sager and Jonathan A. Wexler, *No Pregnant Pauses Here: Workplace Laws Protecting Expectant Mothers Becoming the Norm Across the United States*, Vedder Price PC (June 7, 2016), available at Lexology.com; Kristin Berger Parker, *Are You Ready for Colorado's Pregnant Workers Fairness Act?*, Stinson Leonard Street LLP (Aug. 4, 2016), available at Lexology.com; Stephen E. Baumann II & Erin A. Webber, *Pre- and Post-Partum Protection: Colorado Enacts a Pregnant Workers Fairness Act*, Littler Mendelson PC (June 8, 2016), available at Lexology.com. Accommodation of pregnancy is required of private-sector employers by statute in California, Connecticut, Delaware, the District of Columbia, Hawaii, Illinois, Louisiana, Maryland, Massachusetts, Minnesota, Nebraska, Nevada, New Jersey, New York, North Dakota, Rhode Island, Utah, and West Virginia.]

Massachusetts adopted a statute requiring accommodation of pregnancy (even absent medical complications) in mid-2017, effective April 1, 2018, and Connecticut amended its statute in July 2017 to enhance protection available to pregnant workers. Nevada adopted a Pregnant Workers' Fairness Act; like the Connecticut statute, it provides more protection than the federal PDA. Nevada also has a separate statute requiring employers to provide lactation breaks. [See Keisha-Ann G. Gray and Laura Fant, *Connecticut Expands Anti-Discrimination and Accommodation Protection for Pregnant Employees and Applicants*, Proskauer Rose LLP (July 15, 2017), available at Lexology.com; Mark Ricciardi and Holly Walker, *Expecting a Big Change: Nevada's New Pregnant Workers' Fairness Act*, Fisher Phillips (July 25, 2017), available at Lexology.com; Samia M. Kirman and Brian E. Lewis, *Massachusetts Strengthens Protections for Pregnant Workers*, Jackson Lewis PC (July 31, 2017), available at Lexology.com]

On May 18, 2009, The Supreme Court held that it was not a violation of the PDA for AT&T not to revise its plan retroactively. AT&T acted under a valid seniority system, and thereby qualified for an exception to Title VII. The Supreme

Court refused to apply the Ledbetter Act (§ 34.01[A]), because the original system of service credits was not discriminatory, and therefore employees were not "affected by application of a discriminatory compensation decision or other practice," as the Ledbetter Act says, and without such an effect, the Ledbetter Act does not apply. [*AT&T v. Hulteen*, 556 U.S. 701 (2009)]

If pregnant employees are covered by the plan, the pregnant wives of employees must be covered (in a plan with dependent coverage), and vice versa. However, it is permissible to exclude the pregnancy-related conditions of dependents other than the spouses of employees, as long as the exclusion is applied equally for male and female employees and their dependents.

Transferring a pregnant employee from traveling to offer computer technical support to the help desk was an adverse employment action because it reduced her pay, the work was less technical, and the job was considered a demotion. The plaintiff was fired, and the Eleventh Circuit found that her pregnancy was a motivating factor. The plaintiff's supervisor admitted that one reason for the transfer was concern about her pregnancy; she had suffered a previous miscarriage. However, the Eleventh Circuit said that even well-intentioned actions can violate the law. [*Holland v. Gee*, 677 F.3d 1047 (11th Cir. 2012)]

The First Circuit ruled that a job application was ambiguous as to whether people who applied but were not hired were subject to the arbitration clause. Therefore, the First Circuit refused to mandate arbitration in a case where a job applicant asserted pregnancy discrimination. The court concluded that there was a valid arbitration agreement—but the conditions under which it would come into play (the plaintiff being hired and having a dispute with her employer) never occurred. [*Gove v. Career Sys. Dev. Corp.*, 689 F.3d 1 (1st Cir. 2012)]

Either male or female employees using reproductive technology may need time off from work for fertility procedures. The PDA forbids discrimination on the basis of pregnancy or "related conditions" but it is not clear if whether infertility treatment will be deemed related. In 2008, the Seventh Circuit held [*Hall v. Nalco*, 534 F.3d 644 (7th Cir. 2008)] that an employee who was fired because of absences due to fertility treatment was fired for the gender-specific characteristic of childbearing capability, not the gender-neutral condition of infertility. But the Second and Eighth Circuit have held [*Saks v. Franklin Covey*, 316 F.3d 337 (2d Cir. 2003); *Krauel v. Iowa Methodist Med. Ctr.*, 95 F.3d 674 (8th Cir. 1996)] that both sexes are affected by infertility so denial of reimbursement is not sex discrimination. Similarly, the District Court for the District of Michigan has held that infertility is not related to pregnancy or childbirth. [*LaPorta v. Wal-Mart*, 163 F. Supp. 2d 758 (D. Mich. 2001). Jennifer Gonzalez, *Infertility Issues in the Workplace*, Hall Render Killian Heath & Lyman PC (Aug. 2, 2016), available at Lexology.com]

In mid-2013, the Fifth Circuit became the first Court of Appeals to rule on lactation discrimination. The Fifth Circuit held that discriminating against an employing for breast-feeding or expressing milk is unlawful sex discrimination. The plaintiff charged that she was fired merely for saying that she wanted to express milk at work. The Fifth Circuit ruled that lactation is a medical condition related to pregnancy and childbirth because it is a physiological state caused by childbirth. [*EEOC v. Houston Funding II*, 717 F.3d 425 (5th Cir. 2013), see § 28.03 for further discussion of workplace breastfeeding issues.]

[C]   The Equal Pay Act (EPA)

The Equal Pay Act [29 U.S.C. § 206] is related to the Title VII provisions that forbid sex discrimination, but it is not a part of Title VII. The EPA covers all employers with *two* or more employees. It forbids discrimination in compensation, including all forms of benefits, on the basis of sex—if the two jobs are of equal skill, effort, and responsibility and are performed under similar working conditions. In other words, the statute does not apply to "comparable worth" claims under which women claim that a typically female job is of greater value to society than a higher-paid but different job typically performed by men (e.g., child care workers and parking lot attendants). See § 34.06[B] for discussion of the Supreme Court's 2009 *Hulteen* decision, finding that it was not illegal for a pension plan to continue to reflect the effect of pre-Pregnancy Discrimination Act pay inequalities.

Cost-based defenses are not allowed under the EPA, [see 29 C.F.R. § 216(b)] which says that even if it costs more to provide benefits to women than to men, the employer must either eliminate the benefit or provide it to everyone.

The EPA imposes civil penalties on employers who violate it; even criminal penalties, as prescribed by Fair Labor Standards Act § 216(a), are a possibility. Punitive damages are not allowed, but double back pay is. A winning plaintiff can get costs and attorney's fees.

The OFCCP 2016 final rule on sex discrimination, which has often been cited in this chapter, also applies to pay discrimination. The OFCCP's test is whether similarly situated employees receive the same compensation. This is a fact-specific analysis that involves consideration of, e.g., the tasks performed, skills, effort, and responsibility of the job. The OFCCP's position is that employees do not have to be comparable in all respects to be similarly situated. Compensation practices are unlawful if they have an adverse impact on employees on the basis of sex, unless they are job-related and consistent with business necessity. However, the final rule does not address whether an employer can lawfully rely on market forces or past salary to pay women less than men. [81 Fed. Reg. 39107 (June 15, 2016); see Michael L. Stevens and Karen S. Vldeck, *DOL Implements New Sex Discrimination Rules for Federal Contractors*, Arent Fox LLP (June 15, 2016), available at Lexology.com; Cara Yates Crotty, *OFCCP Issues Final Rule on Sex Discrimination*, Constangy Brooks Smith & Prophete LLP (June 21, 2016), available at Leoxlogy.com]

The Second Circuit affirmed dismissal of a suit charging that female attorneys were paid less than their male counterparts. The Second Circuit said that the

EEOC failed to adequately plead the EPA claim because it did not plead specific facts comparing job duties and the skill, effort, and responsibility involved in allegedly comparable jobs. [*EEOC v. Port Auth. of N.Y. & N.J.*, 768 F.3d 247 (2d Cir. 2014)]

Qualcomm paid $19.5 million to settle claims of lower pay and limited promotion options for women; the settlement was reached before suit was filed. Less than 15% of the organization's senior leadership jobs are held by women. The settlement affects about 3,300 employees, who are expected to receive about $4,000 each, and the company agreed to improve its hiring practices. [Sara Randazzo, *Qualcomm to Pay $19.5 Million to Settle Claims of Bias Against Women*, WSJ.com (July 26, 2016)]

The EEOC brought an EPA suit charging Maryland Insurance Administration with failing to pay three female fraud investigators the same wages as comparable male co-workers. The District Court for the Eastern District of Maryland granted summary judgment for the defendant. The court said that, although there was a pay discrepancy, it could be explained by factors other than gender. The district court held that the comparators designated by the EEOC had different job duties. [Gerald L. Maatman, Jr., *Court Rejects EEOC's EPA Lawsuit Theory*, Seyfarth Shaw LLP (Oct. 23, 2016), available at Lexology.com]

In mid-2017, the Ninth Circuit held that the EPA is not violated if men and women receive different levels of pay for the same work, if their compensation is based on past earnings. The Ninth Circuit said that the employer can justify the differential by asserting reasonable application of a policy that carries out a business purpose. However, a California statute, AB 1676 took effect January 1, 2016. It allows plaintiffs to cite comparators that are substantially similar even if not identical, and can draw evidence from all of a corporation's operations, not just one location. However, the Ninth Circuit ruled in mid-2017 that it does not violate the EPA to pay men and women different amounts for the same work—if the differential is based on earnings in their former job. (Since this case was decided, California adopted AB 1676, which allows plaintiffs charging pay inequality to argue based on substantially similar comparators even if they are not completely identical, and allows the entire corporation, not just one establishment, to be analyzed). [*Rizo v. Yovino*, 854 F.3d 1161 (9th Cir. 2017); see James McDonald Jr., *An Old-School Approach to Equal Pay at 9th Circ.*, Fisher Phillips (May 26, 2017), available at Lexology.com]

In an EPA case, the Tenth Circuit rejected the employer's argument that a pay differential was justified because the plaintiff and her male counterpart (who was hired later, and trained by the plaintiff, and earned $15,000 more) did not have the same job. The Tenth Circuit said that the plaintiff and the newly hired male administrator performed the same tasks and the plaintiff was paid on the basis of the duties usually performed by administrative assistants, not the management work she actually did. [*Riser v. QEP Energy*, No. 776 F.3d 1191 (10th Cir. 2015). See also *Drum v. Leeson Elec. Corp.*, 565 F.3d 1071 (8th Cir. 2009), the issue was not whether the new hire was entitled to be paid a market rate—but the employer's failure to justify paying the plaintiff much less than the market rate for her job.]

Seventh Circuit precedent is that past wages are a "factor other than sex" that will justify pay differentials because federal courts are not entitled to set standards for business practices, and men's higher wages reflect the greater amount of time women spend on child-rearing, something that the Seventh Circuit did not interpret as discrimination. [*Wernsing v. DHS, State of Ill.*, 427 F.3d 466 (7th Cir. 2005). Other circuits, however, have held that past wages constitute a "factor other than sex" only if the employer has an acceptable business reason for using past wages to set starting pay for new hires: *Aldrich v. Randolph Cent. Sch. Dist.*, 963 F.2d 520 (2d Cir.), *cert. denied*, 506 U.S. 965 (1992); *EEOC v. J.C. Penney Co.*, 843 F.2d 249 (6th Cir. 1992); *Kouba v. Allstate Ins. Co.*, 691 F.2d 873 (9th Cir. 1982); *Glenn v. Gen. Motors Corp.*, 841 F.2d 1567 (11th Cir. 1988).]

The EEOC imposed a requirement that employers report the number of employees in each "pay band" (broad level of compensation). Reporting of pay bands on Form EEO-1 was supposed to start September 30, 2017, but the EEOC delayed the requirement to March 31, 2018. Many Fortune 500 companies have voluntarily pledged to monitor salaries to remediate pay inequalities. [Georgia A. Jolink, *Pay Equity: Everything Employers Need to Know*, Baker & McKenzie (Sept. 20, 2016), available at Lexology.com]

The EPA is a strict liability statute (the employer's motivation for unequal pay is irrelevant). The employer's exercise of business judgment is a defense in a Title VII case, but not an EPA case. Therefore, business judgment jury instructions are inappropriate in a pure EPA case, although they can be given in a case that combines EPA and Title VII violations. [*Bauer v. Curators of Univ. of Missouri*, 680 F.3d 1043 (8th Cir. 2012)]

Employers may also be subject to state equal pay requirements. Effective January 1, 2016, the California Fair Pay Act forbids paying members of one sex less than rate paid to other sex for substantially similar work. If there is a discrepancy, the burden is on the employer to show that it comes from seniority or a merit system, calculation of earnings by quantity or quality of production, or a bona fide factor other than sex. [Jennifer B. Rubin and Brent M. Douglas, *California Expands Gender-Based Wage Protections by Adopting "Substantially Similar" Test and Requiring Employers to Justify Wage Discrepancies*, Mintz Levin Cohn Ferris Glovsky and Popeo PC (Oct. 8, 2015), available at Lexology.com]

In New York State, eight bills comprising the Women's Equality Act took effect on January 16, 2016. If women are paid less than men, the New York Equal Pay Act requires the employer to prove a bona fide factor other than sex which is both job-related and consistent with business necessity. Like the California law, it forbids employers to limit discussion of compensation. Employers are not permitted to ask about or consider parental status in employment and compensation decisions. Reasonable accommodation is required for pregnancy-related conditions. [Lauren Helen Leyden et al., *New Women's Equality Act Legislation Raises*

Bar for New York Firms, Akin Gump Strauss Hauer & Feld LLP (Oct. 26, 2015), available at Lexology.com]

The Maryland Equal Pay Act forbids pay discrimination on the basis of sex or gender identity, and makes it unlawful to provide less favorable employment opportunities (e.g., career tracks, information about promotion opportunities) on the basis of sex or gender identity. It takes effect October 1, 2016. In March 2016, Nebraska amended its equal pay statute to cover employers with two or more employees, rather than 15 or more employees. [Matthew Durham et. al., *Maryland Enacts Pay Equity Legislation Joining Growing List of States Enacting Pay Fairness Laws*, Winston& Strawn LLP (June 13, 2016), available at Lexology.com]

Massachusetts already had an equal pay requirement, but legislation passed in July 2016 makes its coverage much wider. The law does not take effect until July 1, 2018; the prolonged effective date is intended to give employers time to adapt. The statute requires equal pay not only for equal work but for comparable work, defined to include work that is substantially similar in skill, effort and responsibility, performed under similar working conditions. It is lawful to vary pay based on shifts and different hazards. Compensation is permitted to vary by seniority, but pregnancy-related or family leave does not reduce seniority for this purpose. Compensation can also vary by merit system, productivity, education, training, experience, or travel regularly required as part of the job. Employers are not allowed to ask job applicants about their past earnings, because these might reflect past discrimination. Employers are entitled to an affirmative defense if they made a good-faith self-evaluation of their pay practices and can demonstrate progress being made toward greater pay equity. [Andrew M. Kaplan and Michael C. Griffaton, *New Massachusetts Pay Equity Law: Equal Pay for Comparable Work (But Not Until 2018)*, Vorys, Sater, Seymour and Pease LLP (Aug. 19, 2016), available at Lexology.com]

Statutes adopted in Delaware and Oregon, and in various cities (e.g., New York and Boston) restrict employers' ability to ask job applicants about their salary history—although the statutes may permit the employer to ask once a job offer has been made and accepted, and to research to see if the newly hired employee's representation checks out. [Amanda Van Hoose Garofalo and Amy J. Traub, *Employers Will No Longer Be Permitted to Ask About Previous Pay in New York City,* Baker & Hostetler LLP (Apr. 16, 2017), available at Lexology.com; Cody Emily Schvaneveldt, *Oregon Enacts New Equal Pay Law That Includes Salary History Inquiry Restrictions,* Littler Mendelson PC (June 1, 2017), available at Lexology.com; Michael L. Stevens, *Delaware Becomes the "First State" to Enforce Ban on Employer Requests for Salary History,* Arent Fox LLP (June 29, 2017), available at Lexology.com; Alif Mia and Amber M. Rogers, *San Francisco Bans Employers from Asking Job Applicants About Salary History, 26 States Considering Similar Legislation,* Hunton & Williams LLP (July 20, 2017), available at Lexology.com); Daniel J. Clark and Michael C. Griffaton, *Delaware*

Becomes the Latest State to Ban Salary Inquiries, Vorys Sater Seymour and Pease LLP (Aug. 9, 2017), available at Lexology.com]

[D] Sexual Orientation and Gender Behavior Discrimination

For many years, Title VII was interpreted to exclude sexual orientation and gender identity from protection. However, societal changes (including Supreme Court recognition of the constitutional dimensions of same-sex marriage) have been reflected in changes in anti-discrimination law.

In mid-2016, a three-judge panel of the Seventh Circuit held that precedent in the Seventh Circuit required dismissal of a Title VII suit alleging sexual orientation discrimination. [*Hively v. Ivy Tech Cmty. Coll.,* No. 15-1720 (7th Cir. July 28, 2016). See Michelle E. Phillips and Paul Patten, *Discrimination Based on Sexual Orientation Not Protected by Title VII, Federal Court Rules,* Jackson Lewis (Aug. 4, 2016), available at <https://www.jacksonlewis.com/publication/ discrimination-based-sexual-orientation-not-protected-title-vii-federal-court-rules>] Then the Seventh Circuit vacated its decision and agreed to re-hear the case en banc. The en banc court, by a vote of 8 to 3, decided that sexual orientation decision constitutes sex discrimination that violates Title VII. Therefore, Hively's case could proceed to trial. [Jennifer L. Garner, *7th Circuit Rehears Hively Case,* Bowditch & Dewey (Dec. 1, 2016), available at Lexology.com; Damon W. Suden, *Seventh Circuit Reverses Decision that Title VII Doesn't Protect Against Anti-Gay Discrimination and Agrees to Re-Hear Employment Discrimination Case,* Kelley Drye & Warren LLP (Oct. 11, 2016), available at Lexology.com; Matthew Haag and Niraj Chokshi, *Civil Rights Act Protects Gay Workers, Court Rules,* NYTimes.com (Apr. 4, 2017); Joe Palazzolo, *Court Says Gay Employees Can Sue Under 1964 Civil Rights Act,* WSJ.com (Apr. 4, 2017)]

In 2016, the District Court for the Southern District of New York held that, although it called sexual orientation discrimination "reprehensible," it does not violate Title VII. [*Christiansen v. Omnicom Grp., Inc.,* 167 F. Supp. 3d 598 (S.D.N.Y. 2016); see Stefanie K. Vaudreuil, *Revisiting Transgender Employment Issues,* Liebert Cassidy Whitmore (June 2, 2016), available at Lexology.com] But the Second Circuit reversed and remanded this decision in early 2017. [*Christiansen v. Omnicom Grp., Inc.,* 852 F.3d 195 (2d Cir. 2017)]

In 2017, the Second Circuit affirmed dismissal of a suit alleging Title VII discrimination in the form of firing an employee for being gay. At that point, the Second Circuit refused to overturn its precedent from 2000. But the following month, rehearing was granted on the issue of whether Title VII forbids sexual orientation discrimination. [*Zardsa v. Altitude Express,* No. 15-3775 (2d Cir. Apr. 28, 2017); en banc rehearing granted: see Robin Shea, *Full Second Circuit to Reconsider Whether Title VII Prohibits Sexual Orientation Bias,* Constangy Brooks Smith & Prophete LLP (May 26, 2017)]

The District Court for the Western District of Pennsylvania interpreted Title VII's "because of sex" to forbid sexual orientation discrimination. The case was brought by a gay man who alleged constructive discharge because repeated offensive comments caused a hostile work environment. [*EEOC v. Scott Med. Health Ctr., P.C.* No. 16-225, 2016 U.S. Dist. LEXIS 153744, 100 Empl. Prac. Dec. (CCH) P45,675 (W.D. Pa. Nov. 4, 2016); see Frank C. Morris, Jr., Nathaniel M. Glasser and Jonathan K. Hoerner, *Western District of Pennsylvania Bucks Recent Trend and Permits Sexual Orientation Discrimination Claim to Proceed*, Epstein Becker Green (Nov. 9, 2016), available at Lexology.com; Shar Bahmani, *U.S. District Court Judge Sides With EEOC, Holds That Title VII Prohibits Discrimination Based Upon Sexual Orientation*, Squire Patton Boggs (Nov. 8, 2016), available at Lexology.com]

A few months later, the Eleventh Circuit refused to extend Title VII to sexual orientation discrimination, but held that the plaintiff could maintain a suit for discrimination for failure to conform to gender norms (in this case, the plaintiff was a lesbian who did not satisfy her supervisor's conception of proper feminine appearance and behavior) . [*Evans v. Georgia Reg'l Hosp.*, 850 F.3d 1248 (11th Cir. 2017); see Janet A. Hendrick and Megan E. Walker, *Appeals Court Refuses to Extend Title VII Coverage to Sexual Orientation*, Fisher Phillips (Mar. 14, 2017), available at Lexology.com] En banc rehearing was denied on July 6, 2017: see W. Jan Pietruszka and Daniel R. Strader, *Eleventh Circuit Declines to Reconsider Sexual Orientation Discrimination Decision; Plaintiff Will Appeal to U.S. Supreme Court*, Shumaker Loop & Kendrick (July 24, 2017), available at Lexology.com]

Some employers have agreed to settle cases of sexual orientation discrimination. Wal-Mart settled Denise Cote's suit in the District Court for the District of Massachusetts. Cote alleged that denying spousal health benefits to Cote and her wife required the couple to spend $150,000 on cancer treatment for Cote's wife. Wal-Mart agreed to pay $7.5 million to employees in the United States and Puerto Rico who were denied health coverage for their same-sex spouses during the period between January 1, 2011 and December 31, 2013 (after which Wal-Mart changed its policies). [AiVi Nguyen, *Wal-Mart Settles Class Action That Alleged Denial of Same-Sex Spousal Benefits Violated Title VII*, Bowditch & Dewey (Dec. 8, 2016), available at Lexology.com]

A sexual orientation discrimination suit against Pallet Companies/IFCO Systems settled for $202,200: $182,200 payable to a lesbian former employee who was harassed and terminated, the rest to the Human Rights Campaign's Workplace Equality Program. [Robin E. Shea, *EEOC Sexual Orientation Lawsuit Settles for $200K Plus*, Constangy Brooks Smith & Prophete LLP (July 1, 2016) available at Lexology.com]

According to the Movement Advancement Project, as of early 2016, almost half the states forbade discrimination on the basis of sexual orientation and/or gender identity. Twenty states had employment discrimination laws covering gender identity as well as sexual orientation: Hawaii, Washington, Oregon,

California, Nevada, Utah, Colorado, New Mexico, Minnesota, Iowa, Illinois, Vermont, Maine, Massachusetts, New York, Rhode Island, Connecticut, New Jersey, Delaware, Maryland (and the District of Columbia). Another two states (New Hampshire, and Wisconsin) had laws forbidding discrimination on account of sexual orientation, but not gender identity. However, Arkansas, North Carolina, and Tennessee had states forbidding the enactment of local antidiscrimination laws. [See <http://www.lgbtmap.org/equality-maps/non_discrimination_laws> (last accessed Mar. 11, 2017), for an interactive chart of state laws.]

The Eleventh Circuit held that discrimination based on gender stereotyping is sex discrimination, so it reinstated a Title VII suit by an auto mechanic who transitioned from male to female. The employer said that the employee was fired for sleeping on the job. She admitted sleeping, but the Eleventh Circuit said she presented enough evidence for the jury to conclude that discrimination was a motivating factor in her termination; a manager testified that the company looked for reasons to fire the plaintiff. [*Chavez v. Credit Nation Auto Sales, LLC*, No. 14-14596, 2016 U.S. App. LEXIS 598 (11th Cir. Jan. 14, 2016); see Suzanne Newcomb, *Eleventh Circuit Resurrects Transgender Mechanic's Title VII Gender Discrimination Claim*, SmithAmundsen LLC (Feb. 1, 2016), available at Lexology.com]

In 2015, the EEOC took the position that that any actions that are based on sex or gender, including actions based on sexual orientation, constitute unlawful sex discrimination that violates Title VII. So employees anywhere in the United States could file EEOC charges of sexual orientation discrimination. The EEOC made this ruling in a case brought by a Department of Transportation air traffic control specialist who alleged that he was denied hiring as a front-line manager because he is gay. The EEOC decided that sexual orientation discrimination involves Title VII because it takes gender into account in employment decisions; constitutes association discrimination on the basis of sex; and discriminates based on gender stereotypes. [*Redacted v. Fox (Baldwin v. Dep't of Transp.)*, Appeal No. 0120133080 (EEOC July 16, 2015)] It is likely that the EEOC will change its position, however.

In April 2012, the EEOC's *Macy v. Holder* [Appeal No. 01201220821 (Apr. 20, 2012)] decision applied Title VII to discrimination on the basis of gender identity or transgender status, including having transitioned or intending to do so. In the fall of 2014, the EEOC filed its first Title VII suits by transgender employees, in Florida and Michigan, against an eye clinic and funeral home respectively, for firing employees transitioning from male to female. The U.S. Office of Special Counsel issued a determination that the Department of the Army engaged in frequent, pervasive, humiliating discrimination against a veteran and civilian software specialist who transitioned from male to female. In 2015, the EEOC settled the *Lakeland Eye Clinic* case, and the District Court for the Middle District of Florida approved the settlement, which called for the complainant to receive $150,000 in damages plus a neutral reference. [*EEOC v. Lakeland Eye*

Clinic, <http://www.workplaceclassaction.com/files/2015/04/Order-Approving-Consent-Decree.pdf>; see Gerald L. Maatman Jr. and Howard M. Wexler, *The EEOC Settles Its First Transgender Suit Filed Under Title VII*, Seyfarth Shaw LLP (Apr. 1, 2015), available at Lexology.com]

The EEOC sued a funeral home chain for discrimination against an employee who transitioned from male to female. The employer refused to settle, and moved in the District Court for the Eastern District of Michigan for summary judgment. The motion was granted. The judge found that gender identity discrimination does not violate Title VII, the EEOC did not have enough evidence to get to a jury on sex stereotyping; and the employer was entitled to reasonable accommodation of its religious beliefs about proper gender roles and behaviors. [*EEOC v. R.G. & G.R. Harris Funeral Homes*, No. 14-13710 (E.D. Mich. Aug. 18, 2016); see Robin E. Shea, *BREAKING: Detroit-Area Funeral Home Wins in EEOC Transgender Case*, Constangy Brooks Smith & Prophete LLP (Aug. 19, 2016), available at Lexology.com; Robert G. Young, *"Least Restrictive Means?" Court Grants Employer Religious Exemption from Title VII in Gender Stereotyping Case*, Bowditch & Dewey (Sept. 8, 2016), available at Lexology.com; Robin E. Shea, *EEOC Appeals Loss in Detroit Transgender Case*, Constangy Brooks Smith & Prophete LLP (Oct. 17, 2016), available at Lexology.com]

The District Court for the District of Connecticut held that employment discrimination against a transsexual job applicant is sex discrimination that violates Title VII. [*Fabian v. Hospital of Cen. Conn.*, 172 F. Supp (D. Conn. 2016); see Stefanie K. Vaudreuil, *Revisiting Transgender Employment Issues,* Liebert Cassidy Whitmore (June 2, 2016), available at Lexology.com]

A mid-2017 Eastern District of Pennsylvania decision says that gender dysphoria and other conditions related to Gender Identity Disorder might be covered by the ADA. [*Blatt v. Cabela's Retail, Inc.*, No. 5:14-cv-04822 (E.D. Pa. 2017); see Nathaniel Glasser and Kate B. Rhodes, *Federal Court Rules Gender Dysphoria May Be Disability Under ADA,* Epstein Becker Green (June 9, 2017), available at Lexology.com]

Starting in mid-2015, the EEOC filed a series of suits calling for bathroom access for transitioning employees, and use of the pronouns the employees prefer. [*EEOC v. Deluxe Fin. Servs. Inc.*, No. 0:15-cv-02646 (D. Minn., settled Jan. 21, 2016), settled for $115,000. *Lusardi v. McHugh*, EEOC (Apr. 1, 2015) holds that the employer should not have continued to refer to an employee as "he" after transition, and should not have required the employee to use a single-user restroom instead of the women's room. The EEOC said that co-worker's discomfort does not justify discrimination: <http://transgenderlawcenter.org/wp-content/uploads/2015/04/EEOC-Lusardi-Decision.pdf> (last accessed Mar. 11, 2017).]

A DOL final rule, published mid-2016, covers government contractors' obligations under Executive Orders 11246 and 13672. The DOL rule forbids discrimination against gay or transgender workers, and requires employers to allow employees to use bathrooms and locker rooms consistent with their gender identity rather than their official identification. It is a recommended best practice that employers provide single-user, gender-neutral restrooms, changing rooms, and showers, but this is not a legal requirement. [81 Fed. Reg. 39107 (June 15, 2016); see Michael L. Stevens and Karen K. Vldeck, *DOL Implements New Sex Discrimination Rules for Federal Contractors*, Arent Fox LLP (June 15, 2016), available at Lexology.com]

PPACA included anti-discrimination rules forbidding discrimination on the basis of transgender status in health programs or activities that receive HHS funding or that were created by PPACA Title I. This provision, § 1557, also forbids discrimination against women who have had an abortion.

Most health providers were covered by the ban. However, even before Congress started an attempt in early 2017 to draft and pass legislation repealing PPACA, eight states and three private religious healthcare providers brought a suit in the District Court for the Northern District of Texas. The district court issued a nationwide preliminary injunction against enforcement of the transgender discrimination provision of § 1557. The plaintiffs argued that the definition of "on account of sex" should be the one used in Title IX: immutable binary differences between males and females. The plaintiffs also asked to apply the Title IX religious exemption so they would not be forced to deliver healthcare services contrary to their beliefs. The district court ruled that Congress did not intend the ban on sex discrimination to include gender identity, and that the plaintiffs' rights under the Religious Freedom Restoration Act were violated because additional expenses were imposed on the practice of their religious beliefs. However, the injunction applies to only two parts of the rule: the gender identity rule and a ban on discrimination for having an abortion; the rule took effect to forbid discrimination in healthcare based on race, age, disability, or sex other than transgender status. [Final regulations under § 1557: 81 Fed. Reg. 31375 (May 18, 2016). *Franciscan Alliance, et al. v. Burwell*, No. 7:16-cv-00108, 2016 U.S. Dist. LEXIS 183116 (N.D. Tex. Dec. 31, 2016); see Tabatha L. George, Alexa Greenbaum and Jaklyn Wrigley, *Federal Judge Blocks Transgender Protections*, Fisher Phillips (Jan. 3, 2017), available at Lexology.com]; the proceedings were stayed on July 10, 2017 by the district court, to give HHS time to reconsider whether to maintain the § 1557 final regulations. The injunction remained in effect. [*Franciscan Alliance, Inc. v. Price*, No. 7:16-cv-00108 (N.D. Tex., stay granted July 10, 2017); see Haynes and Boone LLP, *Court Issues Stay on Proceedings in Challenge to ACA Section 1557 Nondiscrimination Regulations* (Aug. 3, 2017), available at Lexology.com]

OSHA says that employees should be allowed to use bathrooms consistent with their gender identity, although employers are allowed to provide single-occupancy gender-neutral facilities or multi-occupant facilities with single stalls with doors. [OSHA/National Center for Transgender Equality, "Guide to Restroom Access for Transgender Workers," <https://www.osha.gov/Publications/OSHA3795.pdf> (last accessed Mar. 11, 2017)]

At press time in 2017, the situation of state laws about bathroom access was evolving too quickly to cover.

As a result of Executive Order 13672 (July 21, 2014), adding sexual orientation and gender identity discrimination to the coverage already available under Executive Order 11246, federal contractors are forbidden to discriminate in employment against gay, lesbian, bisexual, and transgender people, and the Office of Federal Contract Compliance Programs has adopted a directive defining discrimination based on gender identity or transgender status as sex discrimination. [Peter Baker, *Obama Calls for a Ban on Job Bias Against Gays*, NY Times.com (July 21, 2014); DIR 2014-02, <http://www.dol.gov/ofccp/regs/compliance/directives/dir2014_02.html> (undated, last accessed Apr. 3, 2016)] Although many Obama-era EOs were reversed by the Trump administration, President Trump announced on January 31, 2017, that EO 13672's ban on sexual orientation/gender identity discrimination would continue to be enforced. However, the possibility remained that additional EOs would be issued limiting the rights of LGBT employees, e.g., based on the employer's assertion of religious freedom. [Jeremy W. Peters, *Obama's Protections for L.G.B.T. Workers Will Remain Under Trump*, NYTimes.com (Jan. 30, 2017); Damian Paletta, *White House Will Continue Enforcing 2014 Obama LGBTQ Workplace Order,* WSJ .com (Jan. 31, 2017)]

In some instances, the case revolves around whether a person suffered adverse employment action not because of sexual activities or sexual orientation, but because a male employee was perceived to lack masculinity or a female employee to be unfeminine. (As discussed below at § 34.06[E], however, the highly feminine behavior of a woman becoming a mother also gives rise to workplace litigation.)

Employee plaintiffs have asserted theories of gender non-conformity bias that derive from the discussion of sex stereotyping in *Price Waterhouse*, 490 U.S. 228 (1989). [*Nichols v. Azteca Rest. Enters. Inc.*, 256 F.3d 864 (9th Cir. 2001); *Higgins v. New Balance Athletic Shoe Inc.*, 194 F.3d 252 (1st Cir. 1999)] The Fifth Circuit, sitting en banc, held in late 2013 that harassment based on gender stereotypes can be actionable under Title VII as "because of sex." The plaintiff, an ironworker, suffered constant verbal and physical harassment, including indecent exposure and jokes about rape, because the supervisor didn't think the victim was manly enough. There was no evidence that the harasser wanted to have sex with the victim, and there was no evidence of hostility toward men in general, or that men and women were treated differently. The Fifth Circuit joined the Third, Seventh, Eighth, and Tenth Circuits in holding that those factors (which come from the Supreme Court's *Oncale* ruling on same-sex harassment) are illustrative, not all required to prove harassment. Therefore, the EEOC could make its case based on harassment for perceived lack of conformity with gender stereotypes (whether or not the victim actually was "manly.") [*EEOC v. Boh Bros. Constr. Co.*, 731 F.3d 444 (5th Cir. 2013). The case was subsequently settled by a consent judgment under which Boh Brothers agreed to pay compensatory damages of

$125,000; see Manatt Phelps & Phillips LLP, *Same-Sex Harassment Suits Yield Sizable Settlement* (Mar. 19, 2014), available at Lexology.com]

In mid-2016, the EEOC settled one of the first suits the agency had brought against a private employer. The EEOC said that a supervisor repeatedly harassed employee Yolanda Boone, telling her that he wanted her to "turn back into a woman" and wear dresses. Boone charges she was fired in retaliation for protesting the harassment. Boone received $182,200 in damages, and Pallet Companies was ordered to pay $20,000 to the Human Rights Campaign Foundation's workplace equality program. [*EEOC v. Pallet Cos.*, No. 1:16-cv00595-CCB (D. Md., settled June 28, 2016); The EEOC's *Fact Sheet: Recent EEOC Litigation Regarding Title VII & LGBT-Related Discrimination*, available at <https://www1.eeoc.gov//eeoc/litigation/selected/lgbt_facts.cfm?renderforprint=1> (updated July 8, 2016) (last accessed Mar. 11, 2017), summarizes the EEOC's involvement in suits on these topics.]

The Eighth Circuit held that a female-to-male transsexual who was turned down for a part-time job as a package handler did not prove that hiring was denied because of the plaintiff's membership in a protected group. There was no evidence that the interviewer knew that the plaintiff was transsexual. When it is not clear that a person belongs to a protected group, the plaintiff must prove that the defendant was aware of the plaintiff's status or thought that the plaintiff was a member of the protected group. The Eighth Circuit believed UPS' explanation that Hunter was not hired because of his poor work history and unimpressive interview performance. [*Hunter v. UPS Inc.*, 697 F.3d 697 (8th Cir. 2012)]

The Ninth Circuit held that a casino bartender, terminated after almost 20 years for refusal to wear makeup did not have a Title VII cause of action: she failed to show that the grooming policy imposed greater burdens on female than on male bartenders. In the Ninth Circuit, the rule is that employers can impose different grooming standards on men and women, as long as one sex is not burdened more than the other. [*Jespersen v. Harrah's Operating Co.*, 392 F.3d 1076 (9th Cir. 2004)] The case was reheard en banc and affirmed. [444 F.3d 1104 (9th Cir. 2006)]

A hotel desk clerk, whose new boss said she did not have the "pretty Midwestern girl look" that was required, was terminated for "thwarting the interview procedure" and hostility to company policy. The plaintiff had short hair, didn't wear makeup, and wore loose, unfeminine clothing. The Eighth Circuit reversed the grant of summary judgment for the defendant, and remanded the case for further proceedings, holding that women bringing Title VII suits do not have to provide evidence of being treated differently from similarly situated males. [*Lewis v. Heartland Inns of Am.*, LLC, 591 F.3d 1033 (8th Cir. 2010). On the issue of sex stereotyping, see also *Chadwick v. WellPoint, Inc.*, 561 F.3d 38 (1st Cir. 2009).]

The Eleventh Circuit ordered the Georgia General Assembly to reinstate Vandiver Elizabeth Glenn, a transgender woman who worked as an editor for the assembly but was fired after telling her supervisor that she would be changing her name and working dressed as a woman. The Eleventh Circuit said that discrimination on the basis of gender nonconformity is sex-based discrimination that is reviewed using heightened scrutiny under the Equal Protection clause of the Constitution. [*Brumby v. Glenn*, 663 F.3d 1312 (11th Cir. 2011)]

[E] "Sex-Plus" Discrimination

The sex-plus cause of action asserts that the plaintiff suffered discrimination on the ground of sex and other factors—e.g., motherhood. Title VII does not list parenthood as a protected category. The Pregnancy Discrimination Act and Family and Medical Leave Act are limited to pregnancy and childbirth, and do not forbid bias against women who act as primary caregivers of their children. In 2004, the District Court for the District of Connecticut ruled that child care is gender-neutral and hence not protected under Title VII. [*Guglietta v. Meredith Corp.*, 301 F. Supp. 2d 209 (D. Conn. 2004). However, in a failure to hire/failure to promote case, the same district treated interview questions about child care arrangements as evidence of bias: *Senuta v. Groton, Conn.*, 2002 U.S. Dist. LEXIS 10792 (D. Conn. Mar. 5, 2002)]

The first lawsuit for Family Responsibilities Discrimination (FRD) was brought in 1971, with only eight such cases in the 1970s. Between 1986 and 1995, the Hastings College of the Law Center for WorkLife Law found that there were 97 lawsuits alleging discrimination on the basis of family responsibilities. The number rose to 481 cases in the decade 1996–2005. About 93% of FRD plaintiffs are women. Most allege that they suffered discrimination because of their care needs as parents, but some are caregivers for parents. The largest award to a successful FRD plaintiff was $25 million, but the average award is about $100,000; employees get settlements or win at trial in about half of FRD cases. [The Hastings study is called *Litigating the Maternal Wall: U.S. Lawsuits Charging Discrimination Against Workers with Family Responsibilities*. The Center for WorkLife Law's fact sheet on the issue is found at <http://worklifelaw.org/pubs/FRD_Fact_Sheet.pdf> (undated, last accessed Mar. 11, 2017).]

Perhaps most common form of FRD is "maternal wall" bias against mothers. FRD usually manifests when a woman announces her pregnancy, returns from maternity leave, or adopts a flexible schedule instead of full-time work. There is also "lack of fit" FRD when an employer assumes that a particular job is inappropriate for mothers, so women are channeled into inferior jobs that are perceived to be appropriate for women. FRD cases are usually brought under Title VII, for disparate treatment, disparate impact, harassment, failure to promote, or retaliating against employees who seek accommodation. Some claims involve gender stereotyping: for example, a belief that an unmarried childless man is the best employee because of his greater availability. Mothers could also be targeted for heightened scrutiny or negative evaluations so they can be fired. Courts are divided as to whether an FRD claim requires a comparator of the opposite sex.

There can be FMLA FRD claims based on discrimination when an employee returns from leave or when grant of leave is based on gender stereotyping. ADA FRD cases are also possible: for example, based on association with a family member with health problems or if the employer perceives the employee as disabled because of pregnancy or family health conditions. ERISA FRD cases have also been brought premised on the employer's attempt to avoid high medical costs. [Debra S. Katz, *Recent Developments: Sex Discrimination and Family Responsibility Claims*, Katz Marshall & Banks LLP (Nov. 24, 2016), available at Lexology.com; includes older cases.]

Several Circuits, including the First, have ruled that adverse job action on the basis of being a mother is sex discrimination based on stereotyping. In this case, in effect the plaintiff was told that her work was completely satisfactory, but she would not be promoted because she had young children and was going to school part-time. The plaintiff brought suit after the "team leader" job went to a woman with less experience and a lower performance evaluation than the plaintiff (3.84 versus 4.40). [*Chadwick v. WellPoint Inc.*, 561 F.3d 38 (1st Cir. 2009)]

The New Jersey Supreme Court held that the New Jersey Law Against Discrimination forbids discrimination on the basis of marital status, which includes being separated, divorced, or in the process of getting a divorce. A plaintiff was fired for poor performance during a corporate reorganization. He was told that his "ugly divorce" (allegedly both spouses were unfaithful) could affect his job. The court held that it is unlawful to impose conditions that are not related to the job, and employees cannot be fired for life decisions about marriage. [*Smith v. Millville Rescue Squad*, 225 N.J. 373 (2016); see Amy Beth Dambeck, *New Jersey "Marital Status" Protection Applies to All Types of Marital Status, State Supreme Court Says*, Constangy Brooks Smith & Prophete LLP (July 5, 2016)]

§ 34.07 RELIGIOUS DISCRIMINATION AND REASONABLE ACCOMMODATION

Religious charges are a comparatively small, but fast-growing, portion of the EEOC's caseload, more than doubling in 15 years. In fiscal 2016, there were 3,825 religious discrimination charges received, and 3,827 resolutions: 266 settlements, 183 withdrawals with benefits, 551 administrative closures 2,706 determinations of no reasonable cause, and 121 reasonable cause findings. There were 54 successful conciliations, 67 unsuccessful conciliations, 570 merit resolutions, and monetary benefits of $10.1 million (slightly lower than the 2015 level of $10.8 million) obtained through the administrative process (i.e., not via litigation). [EEOC, *Religion-Based Charges, FY 1997-FY 2016*, <http://www.eeoc.gov/eeoc/statistics/enforcement/religion.cfm> (undated, last accessed Mar. 11, 2017)]

On the grounds that everyone is entitled to equality and tolerance at work, the EEOC issued two Q&A documents in February 2016 about discrimination against people who are or appear to be Muslim or Middle Eastern. <http://www

.eeoc.gov/eeoc/publications/muslim_middle_eastern_employers.cfm> (last accessed Mar. 11, 2017) deals with hiring, harassment, background checks, and religious accommodations, and is aimed at employers; similar topics are discussed for employees in <http://www.eeoc.gov/eeoc/publications/muslim_middle_eastern_employees.cfm> (last accessed Mar. 11, 2017). The EEOC's position is that hiring cannot be denied on the grounds that customers are uncomfortable with workers who wear head coverings. The EEOC says that if employees ask to use a conference room for prayers, the employer probably has to grant the request unless it is an undue hardship (e.g., the room is needed for business purposes). Employees can be required to make up time that they miss for prayers. [Michael T. Miller, *EEOC Seeks to Prevent Discrimination Against Muslim and Middle Eastern Employees*, Briggs and Morgan (Feb. 22, 2016), available at Lexology.com] However, it is likely that the EEOC will alter its position on this issue.

The EEOC's position is that Title VII, like the ADA, forbids discrimination when someone is perceived as belonging to a particular group. The District Court for the Eastern District of Michigan denied summary judgment for the employer in a case where a dark-skinned Iraqi charged discrimination based on the perception that he was a Muslim; his supervisor said his hat looked like a Muslim topi. His national origin discrimination claim could also go forward. [*Kallabat v. AT&T*, No. 2:2012cv15470, 2015 U.S. Dist. LEXIS 78944 (E.D. Mich. June 18, 2015)]

[A] Employer's Duties and Obligations

Although issues about Muslims have frequently been discussed in the news since the 2016 presidential election, employers may be required to accommodate workers who belong to a variety of faiths and hold a variety of religious beliefs. Religious issues can arise in the workplace in many contexts: employees' need for time off for prayer, or to observe a Sabbath or attend services or religious events; wearing of religious dress; men wearing beards for religious reasons; and religious objections to joining a union.

The EEOC issued a 97-page revised version of the Compliance Manual § 12 (religious discrimination) on July 22, 2008. The EEOC issued accompanying guidance online: Questions and Answers and a Best Practices document for employers.

The Compliance Manual says that Title VII forbids differential treatment of employees on the basis of their religious beliefs or practices, including atheism. Religious beliefs include moral and ethical beliefs, and are not required to reflect the concept of a deity. Religious harassment, including association-based harassment, is also forbidden. Employers must provide reasonable accommodation of needs based on an employee's sincerely held religious belief, unless the cost or burden to the employer would be more than minimal. As examples of required accommodation, the EEOC lists scheduling changes; changing the tasks assigned to a worker; and allowing religious dress and beard or hairstyles. Employers must not favor expressions of some religions over others. Retaliation is also forbidden. [Revised § 12 of the Compliance Manual, <http://www.eeoc .gov/policy/docs/religion.pdf> (last accessed Mar. 11, 2017); Questions and Answers: Religious Discrimination in the Workplace <http://www.eeoc.gov/ policy/docs/qanda_religion.html> (updated Jan. 31, 2011) (last accessed Mar. 11, 2017); Best Practices for Eradicating Religious Discrimination in the Workplace <http://www.eeoc.gov/policy/docs/best_practices_religion.html> (updated July 23, 2008) (last accessed Mar. 11, 2017)]

The EEOC's Fact Sheet and Best Practices say that religion includes beliefs even if new, unusual, not part of a formal church, or that seem odd. Non-theistic ethical beliefs can count, but personal social, political, or economic views do not. Wearing clothing or jewelry that reflects faith, or displaying religious artifacts at work, is not considered harassment unless it deprecates other religions. A recent article says that an employee seeking religious accommodation must inform the employer that accommodation is needed because of a conflict between a work requirement and the employee's religious beliefs. The article's example is "I think it's a sin to work on Sunday." [Robin E. Shea, *Hallelujah! 5 Things About Religion in The Workplace That You May Not Have Known*, Constangy Brooks Smith & Prophete LLP (July 26, 2016), available at Lexology.com]

"Onionhead," a/k/a Harnessing Happiness, has been held to be a religion for Title VII purposes. United Health Programs held Onionhead workshops with employees to change the corporate culture. The meetings included chanting and prayers, and the advisor asked participants for personal information and gave them advice about their personal lives. E-mails between management and the advisor referred to God, spirituality, demons, Satan, and miracles. The handouts referred to faith, the soul, heaven, and the Universal Plan. The EEOC sued on behalf of employees who were fired for refusing to participate in Onionhead programs. The employer said that it was not a religion, but a conflict-resolution tool. In late 2016, the District Court for the Eastern District of New York applied a two-part test: were the Onionhead beliefs sincerely held, and were they a religion to the believers? The court said that Onionhead was a religion, because beliefs do not have to be either traditional or widely held to be religious. [*EEOC v. United Health Prog*rams, 213 F. Supp. 3d 377 (E.D.N.Y. 2016); see Margaret Carroll Alli, *"Onionhead" Is a Religion Under Title VII: Court Finds in Favor of Employees in Reverse Religious Bias Case*, Ogletree Deakins (Nov. 2, 2016), available at Lexology.com]

A jury in the District Court for the Central District of Illinois awarded $240,000 to two Muslim employees who were fired for refusing to transport beer. Each of them received $1,500 in back pay, $20,000 for mental or emotional pain—and $100,000 in punitive damages. [*EEOC v. Star Transport Inc.*, No. 13-1240 (C.D. Ill., jury verdict submitted Oct. 21, 2015)]

The EEOC issued further guidance specifically dealing with religious dress in the workplace in March 2014. The EEOC's examples include wearing religious articles (such as cross or hijab), avoiding certain garments (women who will not wear pants or short skirts) and shaving/hair length requirements. The EEOC's position is that federal law requires employers to make exceptions to their usual rules or preferences to permit employees to observe religious dress and grooming practices. The EEOC reads Title VII to cover all aspects of religious observance, practice, and belief, whether based on theistic beliefs or non-theistic moral or ethical beliefs. Non-belief is also covered in cases in which the employer tries to make an employee wear religious articles or garb to which the employee objects on grounds of non-belief. However, personal preferences are not protected by Title VII. The EEOC says that a newly adopted observance can be sincere, and so can be a periodic observance (e.g., a Muslim employee who only wears a head covering during Ramadan). Customer preference is not a defense to a discrimination claim. The EEOC says that it is unlawful to assign a worker to a non-customer contact position because of actual or feared customer preference. [EEOC.gov, *Religious Garb and Grooming in the Workplace: Rights and Responsibilities*, <http://www.eeoc.gov/eeoc/publications/qa_religious_garb_grooming .cfm> (undated, last accessed Mar. 11, 2017)]

In recent years, religious headgear—generally involving Muslims but sometimes Sikhs or orthodox Jews—has been a litigation focus.

The Abercrombie & Fitch "Look Policy" governing employees' appearance at work, has been the subject of several religious discrimination cases because of its effect on Muslim employees who wear hijabs, culminating in a 2015 Supreme Court decision.

The Tenth Circuit ruled for Abercrombie & Fitch in a case where a job applicant who wore a hijab was not offered a job. The Tenth Circuit held that because religion is an individual, personal matter, the burden is on a job applicant or employee to request accommodation. The Supreme Court reversed, holding that Abercrombie & Fitch at least suspected that Elauf wore hijab for religious reasons, so desire to avoid accommodating her religious practice was enough to sustain a suit. The majority said that Title VII forbids adverse employment decisions that have a forbidden motivation—whether the employer acts on actual knowledge, suspicion, or just a hunch. [*EEOC v. Abercrombie & Fitch*, 135 S. Ct. 2028 (2015)] After the Supreme Court decision, Abercrombie & Fitch settled Elauf's suit for $25,670.53 in damages plus $18,983.03 in court costs. [Robin E. Shea, *EEOC, Abercrombie Settle Hijab Lawsuit*, Constangy Brooks Smith & Prophete LLP (July 21, 2015), available at Lexology.com]

After the United States' invasion of Afghanistan in 2001, a Muslim salesman (Mohommed Rafiq) charged that his managers, despite repeated protests, called him "Taliban" managers and co-workers told him to go back home and mocked his religious requirements for daily prayers and halal food. A supervisor ordered him to attend a United Way meeting and gave him a written warning for his "militant stance" and "acting like a Muslim extremist." Rafiq complained to the general manager after an argument with a finance manager and was fired. The EEOC brought a hostile work environment suit, which was dismissed by the district court for lack of evidence of severe and persistent harassment and failure to prove deterioration in quality of life caused by the severity of the harassment. The Fifth Circuit reversed, holding that the pattern of harassment alleged was explicitly based on religion and national origin, and was severe enough to impair daily life. [*EEOC v. WC&M*, 496 F.3d 393 (5th Cir. 2007)]

A Jewish police officer alleged repeated workplace harassment, including frequent anti-Semitic remarks. He was not allowed to wear a yarmulke because it violated the uniform policy, but another officer was allowed to wear Christian religious symbols on his uniform. A New Jersey jury found a hostile work environment but did not award damages, and ruled that the delay in the plaintiff's promotion to corporal was not discriminatory. Both sides appealed. The New Jersey Supreme Court applied the same test for a hostile environment based on religion as for one based on sex or race: whether a reasonable person would consider the antagonistic, degrading, or demeaning acts and comments in his or her presence to be severe or pervasive enough to alter the working conditions for the worse. In this case, the plaintiff was repeatedly subjected to humiliating anti-Semitic comments, not the mere "ribbing" that the defense characterized it as. [*Cutler v. Dorn*, 196 N.J. 419 (N.J. July 31, 2008)]

The Fifth Circuit held that it was permissible to fire an employee (an Evangelical Christian) who refused to pray the rosary with a nursing home resident. The court said that there was no evidence that the facility knew that the plaintiff's religious beliefs precluded this. Reading the rosary for residents was a regularly scheduled activity. The Fifth Circuit said that the important question was not what the employer knew about the employee's religious beliefs, but what motivated the employment decision. In this case, the Fifth Circuit said that the plaintiff was fired for refusing to perform a work assignment. [*Nobach v. Woodland Vill. Nursing Ctr., Inc.*, 799 F.3d 374 (5th Cir. 2015)]

The Sixth Circuit held that it was not religious discrimination to refuse to hire an applicant who refused to disclose his Social Security Number, which he characterized as the Mark of the Beast and hence contrary to his religion. [*Yeager v. FirstEnergy Generation Corp.*, cert. denied, 136 S. Ct. 40 (2015), below 777 F.3d 362 (6th Cir. 2015)]

However, another "Mark of the Beast" plaintiff (who refused to use his employer's biometric hand scanner to clock in) fared better. The Fourth Circuit affirmed a $586,860 jury award, holding that it would not have been unduly burdensome to the employer to offer reasonable accommodation to the employee's religious objection to using the scanner. [*EEOC v. Consol. Energy*, No. 16-1230 (4th Cir. June 12, 2017); see Richard B. Cohen, *Biometric Scanning and the Mark of the Beast: A Case of Accommodation of Religious Beliefs,* FisherBroyles LLP (June 13, 2017), available at Lexology.com]

The California Court of Appeal held that it does not constitute religious discrimination to refuse to hire a vegan who refused to be vaccinated with a vaccine grown in chicken embryos, because beliefs about harming animals are secular, not a religious philosophy, because they were deemed to lack a spiritual or otherworldly component. [*Friedman v. S. Cal. Permanente Med. Grp.*, 125 Cal. Rptr. 2d 663 (Cal. App. 2002)] In contrast, a 2011 case brought by a vegan employee of Cincinnati Children's Hospital, fired for refusing to take a flu shot containing animal products, was settled in October 2013. The employer's motion to dismiss was denied because the question was whether the employee's vegan beliefs were held as sincerely as traditional religious views. [George E. O'Brien Jr., *Hospital Settles Religious Bias Claim With Vegan*, Littler Mendelson (Oct. 9, 2013), available at Lexology.com]

Mandatory flu vaccination is an issue that frequently arises in hospital workplaces. A Boston hospital required flu vaccinations and allowed some medical exemptions but no religious exemptions. A Muslim employee refused to be vaccinated on the grounds that the vaccine contained pork products and many vaccines are contaminated. She refused even when offered a vaccine without pork products. On the deadline for being vaccinated, she asserted a serious allergy to vaccine and was given two weeks to seek medical exemption. The exemption was denied. The hospital tried to find her a job in a non-patient-care area where employees were not required to be vaccinated, but was unable to do so. She was eventually terminated but her departure was reported as a voluntary quit so she could look for another job. She sued under Title VII and Massachusetts law for religious discrimination. The District Court for the District of Massachusetts granted summary judgment for the employer on the basis that it made extensive efforts at accommodation and exempting the employee would be a hardship to the hospital. [*Robinson v. Childrens Hosp. Boston*, No. 14-10253(DJC), **2016** WL 1337255 (D. Mass. Apr. 5, 2016); see Norma W. Zeitler, *Court Says Mandatory Flu Vaccine for Hospital Worker Does Not Violate Title VII*, Barnes & Thornburg LLP (Apr. 18, 2016), available at Lexology.com. See also *Fallon v. Mercy Catholic Med. Ctr.*, 200 F. Supp. 3d 553 (E.D. Pa. 2016), discussed in A. Kevin Troutman, *Court Tosses Flu Shot Lawsuit*, Fisher Phillips (Sept. 7, 2016), available at Lexology.co: a health care worker's objections to vaccination (that vaccines were not as effective as claimed) was a personal, secular moral belief that did not qualify for a religious exemption.]

Saint Vincent Health Center (Erie, Pennsylvania) required flu vaccination for all employees unless they received an exemption and wore a face mask when in contact with patients. Fourteen exemptions were granted for medical reasons, but six employees who asked for religious exemptions were turned down and fired for refusing vaccination. The hospital settled EEOC charges for $300,000. [<https://www1.eeoc.gov/eeoc/newsroom/release/12-23-16.cfm>; see Richard B. Cohen, *$300,000 for A Flu Vaccine?* FisherBroyles (Dec. 30, 2016), available at Lexology.com]

Challenges to the sincerity of an employee's religious beliefs almost never succeed, but employers tend to prevail when the issue is what constitutes reasonable accommodation. An IRS employee, who had to pass a metal detector in the federal building, converted to the Sikh religion, which requires its followers to carry a ceremonial knife. Her Title VII claim was dismissed, because the court rejected her proposed accommodation (carrying a 3 inch dulled blade or working from home): guards cannot be expected to test the sharpness of weapons, and the plaintiff did not prove she could complete her duties from home. However, her RFRA claim was permitted to continue because that statute applies to federal policies, including access to federal buildings. [*Tagore v. United States*, 735 F.3d 324 (5th Cir. 2013)]

The Seventh Circuit reversed summary judgment for the employer, and permitted a Nigerian immigrant to pursue his religious discrimination claim when he was denied unpaid leave to return to Nigeria to perform funeral rites for his father. Adeyeye, who believed that his family's spiritual well-being depended on performance of the rites, took time off without authorization and was fired when he returned from the trip. The Seventh Circuit held that there were genuine questions of material fact precluding summary judgment; Adeyeye informed his employer that he sincerely believed in his funerary obligations, even if the beliefs, a mixture of Christian and animist, was not a conventional religion. Furthermore, the employer frequently hired temporary replacements when regular workers were unavailable, so granting the requested leave would not have imposed undue hardship on the employer. [*Adeyeye v. Heartland Sweeteners*, 712 F.3d 444 (7th Cir. 2013)]

Employers do not have an obligation to incur undue hardship to accommodate religious observance or practice: 42 U.S.C. § 2000e(j). In fact, a 1977 Supreme Court case holds that investing more than a minimal amount in accommodation can actually represent an illegal preference in favor of the employee who receives the accommodation. [*TWA v. Hardison*, 432 U.S. 63 (1977)]

Except in very limited cases (being a priest or minister, for example) religious beliefs are irrelevant to employment and cannot be used as a hiring criterion. Employers are not supposed to prefer one religion over another, or even to prefer organized religion over atheism or agnosticism.

The Supreme Court unanimously endorsed the ministerial exception (i.e., held that the First Amendment prevents courts from interfering when a church takes employment action against a minister). This was the first Supreme Court case on this issue, although all 12 Circuits have recognized the principle. The Court left open the possibility of suits for breach of contract or tortuous conduct. The Court said that the ministerial exception is not a jurisdictional bar but an affirmative defense: that is, an employer that asserts the defense has the responsibility for proving that it applies. [*Hosanna-Tabor Evangelical Lutheran Church v. EEOC*, 132 S. Ct. 694 (2012)]

Probably the most common religious accommodation issue involves work assignments when the employee is supposed to observe a Sabbath, attend religious services, study the scriptures, teach in a religious school, or the like. The consensus is that the employer has to accommodate activities (or non-activities, like avoiding work on the Sabbath) that are mandated by an organized religion, but not employee's personal wishes about religious observance.

For example, in 2014, the district court granted summary judgment for an employer that refused to give an employee time off to attend the ground-breaking ceremony for her church. The district court said that not every church-related activity is a protectable religious practice. However, the Fifth Circuit applied the court system's traditional reluctance to delve into professed religious beliefs and found that the employee was entitled to go to the jury on her accommodation claim (but not her retaliation claim—she did not show meaningful adverse employment action related to her religious beliefs). Davis cast doubt on the employer's undue hardship argument because at least one volunteer was available to substitute for her during the ceremony. Although it is unlikely that an employer would be required to accommodate one employee by forcing another employee into a permanent and unwanted shift swap, the situation is very different when it is a single occasion and a co-worker is willing to exchange the shift. [*Davis v. Fort Bend Cnty.*, 765 F.3d 480 (5th Cir. 2014). Certiorari was denied, 135 S. Ct. 2804 (2015) so the case was remanded for jury trial.]

The EEOC considers it unlawful discrimination to set overtime rates in a way that disadvantages employees who observe a Sabbath other than Sunday. [See Guidelines, 29 C.F.R. Part 1605] The EEOC considers acceptable accommodations to include voluntary substitution of one employee for another, swapping shifts, lateral transfers, changes of job assignment, and flextime (i.e., the employee makes up the time devoted to religious observance).

In mid-2016, a North Carolina company agreed to pay $42,500 to settle an EEOC religious discrimination suit involving a Seventh Day Adventist truck drivers whose beliefs preclude working on Saturday, which is designated as the Sabbath. The business' facilities were usually closed on Saturdays and employees were seldom required to work on Saturday, but the complainant was denied accommodation and then fired when he was told to work on a particular Saturday. [Richard B. Cohen, *Accommodate Religious Beliefs: Or Pay $42,500 to Settle*, FisherBroyles (Aug. 26, 2016), available at Lexology.com]

However, employers are not required to accommodate religious observance by violating the seniority rights of a nonobservant employee. In the view of the EEOC, it would be undue hardship for the employer to have to pay overtime to other employees to cover for the religious employee or to have an untrained or inexperienced person covering for the religious employee.

The Second Circuit reversed the lower court and ruled that offering a shift change on Sundays is not a reasonable accommodation to an employee's Sabbath observance. The proposed schedule change allowed him to attend church, but did not satisfy his religious mandate to avoid working at all on Sunday. [*Baker v. Home Depot*, 445 F.3d 541 (2d Cir. 2006).]

States are not allowed to pass laws that give employees an absolute right to get their Sabbath day as a day off—that would be an unconstitutional establishment of religion. [*Estate of Thornton v. Caldor, Inc.*, 472 U.S. 703 (1985)] However, an employee who is fired for refusing to work on the Sabbath is entitled to collect unemployment benefits. [*Hobbie v. Unemployment Appeals Comm'n of Fla.*, 480 U.S. 136 (1987)] Some state laws, including New York's Human Rights Law, make it clear that employees who get time off for religious observances must make up the time at another time that is religiously acceptable.

[B]   Steps Toward Religious Accommodation

Bulletin board postings or the corporation's online presence can be used to get volunteers to cover for workers taking prayer time or observing religious holidays. A diverse workforce really helps here—Christian employees can cover the holidays of non-Christian religions, and vice versa. Optional or floating personal days can be used for religious observance.

Because Islam requires five daily prayers, several occurring during the normal work day, it can be difficult to accommodate Muslim employees in a production line environment. Part of the prayer obligation is keyed to sundown, so it does not occur at the same time every day, making it harder to schedule prayers. The need for Muslims to wash their hands and feet before prayer can cause hazardous wet conditions in the washrooms (or hallways, if water is tracked). One simple solution is to install a special self-draining basin, or arrange to have the floors mopped more often.

The EEOC charged meat packer JBS with a pattern or practice of violating Title VII by not accommodating Muslim employees by letting them take unscheduled prayer breaks, or moving the meal break to cover the sunset prayer. The district court found that either of those accommodations would be an undue hardship because of more-than-de-minimis cost in terms of food safety, operational efficiency, and employee safety. They would also inconvenience non-Muslim co-workers who had to fill in. [*EEOC v. JBS USA, LLC*, 940 F. Supp. 2d 949 (D. Neb. 2013); at press time in 2017, the case was still ongoing.]

One hundred fifty Somali Muslim workers at Cargill Meat Solutions (Fort Morgan, Colorado) walked off their jobs when they said they were told their prayer breaks would be reduced. (The company denied announcing this.) They were fired for job abandonment. The employees said that there was a practice of asking their supervisors for one or two ten-minute prayer breaks during a shift. Cargill said that it accommodated the vast majority of prayer requests but sometimes, when the facility was short-staffed, the breaks had to be denied. Cargill offered reinstatement, but only ten workers returned. [Julie Turkewitz, *Prayer Dispute Between Somalis and Plant Reshapes a Colorado Town, Again* NY

Times.com (Mar. 8, 2016). See also Steven T. Collis, *Prayer Breaks Present Difficult Religious Accommodation Issue*, Holland & Hart LLP (June 8, 2016), available at Lexology.com, about Ariens Co.'s dispute with Muslim employees. The company changed the policy under which the 53 Muslim production workers were allowed to take prayer breaks; seven employees were fired for taking unauthorized breaks and seven quit.]

Although it is often impossible to arrange the menu in the employee cafeteria to conform to all dietary requirements, it is a reasonable gesture to provide some vegetarian alternatives, and to make sure that people whose religion bans the consumption of pork or beef will have other menu choices available.

A growing concern for many employers is how to balance some employees' desire to evangelize for their faith against the desire of other employees to maintain their existing religion (or lack thereof) and lifestyle. Cases have been brought alleging a religiously hostile environment caused by unwanted attempts at religious conversion.

Employees who are not allowed to preach in the workplace can invite co-workers to a church service, prayer meeting, Bible study group, etc., that meets outside the workplace, so their religious expression can be continued elsewhere. The Ninth Circuit permitted a government agency employer to restrict prayer meetings and displays of religious symbols in the workplace: employees were allowed to discuss religion with one another, but not with clients, and could display religious items but not where they would be visible to clients. Prayer meetings were permitted in the break room or outside the office, but not in the conference room, which could only be used for business purposes. The Ninth Circuit concluded that the employer had found an appropriate balance between employees' religious rights and the agency's duty of religious neutrality. [*Berry v. Dep't of Social Servs., Tehama Cnty.*, 447 F.3d 642 (9th Cir. 2006)]

[C] Case Law on Reasonable Accommodation

The Second Circuit ruled in 2003 that an employer's rejection of an employee's proposed accommodation of religious needs is a discrete act. Therefore, the statute of limitations is 300 days from the occurrence of the act; the statute of limitations does not restart with every scheduled prayer time that the employee was forced to work. Once an employer rejects a proposed accommodation, the facts to make the case are in existence; the decision is not re-implemented periodically. [*Elmenayer v. ABF Freight Sys. Inc.*, 318 F.3d 130 (2d Cir. 2003)]

The Fourth Circuit concluded that reasonable accommodation was provided to the religious beliefs of a worker with a Saturday Sabbath who was also forbidden to work on seven religious holidays. In this case, the seniority-based bidding system for work shifts operated as a significant accommodation in and of itself, as a neutral method of reducing the number of days that an employee must work when he or she prefers not to, whether for religious or any other reason. The plaintiff also had access to holidays and unpaid time off that could be used neutrally for any reason including religious observance. The plaintiff also failed to switch shifts with another employee. Employers are not required to violate the CBA or the seniority system to accommodate religious needs. [*EEOC v. Firestone Fibers & Textiles Co.*, 515 F.3d 307 (4th Cir. 2008)]

A petroleum company reached a $125,000 religious discrimination settlement with the EEOC after the company enforced its dress code and refused to let a Rastafarian employee wear the headwrap required by her religion. [Adrien Martin, *RaceTrac Settles Religious Discrimination Suit for $125,000*, plan sponsor.com (Jan. 22, 2007)]

The Seventh Circuit held that it did not constitute religious discrimination to fail to hire an applicant as a security guard because he wore dreadlocks, finding that he did not prove that he mentioned his religious beliefs or that the belief was the reason for the refusal to hire him. (The defendant said that it did not know that he wore dreadlocks for religious reasons.) [*Lord Osunfarian Xodus v. Wackenhut Corp.*, 619 F.3d 1109 (7th Cir. 2010)]

§ 34.08   RETALIATION

Section 8 of the EEOC Compliance Manual (used by EEOC offices), EEOC Directives Transmittal 915.003 (May 20, 1998), covers retaliation. There are three essential elements in a retaliation claim that the EEOC will pursue:

- The charging party engaged in protected activity, such as opposing discrimination or participating in the Title VII complaint process;

- The employer took adverse action against the charging party;

- There was a causal connection between the protected activity and the employer's adverse action.

A retaliation complaint might be proper if the charging party had a reasonable good-faith belief that the employer committed discrimination (even if this belief was incorrect), and the charging party used a reasonable means to protest this to the employer.

It is illegal to retaliate against a charging party if he or she, or someone closely associated with him or her, participated in any statutory enforcement proceeding. This includes any investigation, proceeding, hearing, or suit under any of the statutes enforced by the EEOC. It is unlawful for one employer to retaliate on the basis of a complaint against another employer.

In 2016, the EEOC updated its guidelines on retaliation for the first time since 1998. Retaliation is now the leading cause of action for discrimination: there were close to 40,000 retaliation charges in 2015, about 45% of all charges, 119% more than in 1998. The guidance applies to various laws that the EEOC enforces: Title VII, the ADEA, ADA, EPA, GINA, and § 501 of the Rehabilitation Act.

Retaliation is materially adverse action undertaken by an employer, such as threats, warnings, poor evaluations, and transfers—anything that could be enough to discourage employees from engaging in legally protected activity. Employees could experience retaliation based on their participation in an EEO process or opposition to the employer's violations of EEO law. Participation means making a claim or testifying at or participating in an investigation, hearing, or proceeding. Employees are entitled to protection against retaliation for participation even if the underlying charge is untimely or not meritorious, but false or bad-faith statements are considered in assessing the merits of the claim. Opposition means reasonable actions taken to oppose what is reasonably believed to be an EEO violation by the employer. The most usual form of opposition is to complain to a manager, but opposition could also take the form of communicating with lawyers or union officials—or even calling the police in extreme cases of workplace harassment. The EEOC treats internal complaints, such as those made to a manager, as constituting both participation and opposition. Illegal acts, such as fabricated charges or threats of violence, are not protected.

For an allegation of opposition to support a retaliation charge, it must be reasonable and reflect a good-faith belief that the employer's conduct is or could become unlawful. An employer is permitted to terminate or otherwise discipline an employee for legitimate, non-retaliatory, non-discriminatory reasons, even if the employee has engaged in protected activity. When a manager recommends adverse action against an employee who has engaged in protected activity, the employer can reduce the risk of retaliation by independently evaluating the appropriateness of the adverse action. The remedies for Title VII retaliation include compensatory and punitive damages, but subject to a cap ranging from $50,000 for defendants with 15–100 employees to $300,000 (500 or more employees); GINA remedies are the same as Title VII remedies. Under the EPA, compensatory and punitive damages are available for retaliation, and are not capped, even though such damages are not available for non-retaliation claims. [Notice 914.004 EEOC Enforcement Guidance on Retaliation and Related Issues (Aug. 25, 2016), available at <https://www.eeoc.gov/laws/guidance/upload/retaliation-guidance.pdf>; Q&A <https://www.eeoc.gov/laws/guidance/retaliation-qa.cfm>; small business fact sheet, <https://www.eeoc.gov/laws/guidance/retaliation-factsheet.cfm>; *see* Richard R. Meneghello, *10 Things You Need To Know About EEOC's New Retaliation Guidance*, Fisher Phillips (Aug. 31, 2016), *available at* Lexology.com; Derek G. Barella et. al., *EEOC Issues Final Guidance on Employer Retaliation*, Winston & Strawn LLP (Sept. 1, 2016), available at Lexology.com]

The Supreme Court resolved several questions about the retaliation cause of action in its June 22, 2006, decision in *Burlington Northern & Santa Fe Railway Co. v. White*, 548 U.S. 53 (2006). The Supreme Court ruled that retaliation against employees who engage in protected concerted activity is unlawful, whether or not the form the retaliation takes is employment-related. The Supreme Court reached this conclusion based on differences in the statutory language covering the substantive ban on discrimination and the anti-retaliation provision. However, to be actionable, the retaliatory measures must be severe enough that a reasonable employee might have been deterred from pursuing discrimination charges. In the case at bar, there was actionable retaliation because even though the petitioner's job classification did not change, she was assigned less attractive work (more arduous, dirtier, more strenuous) to punish her for complaining about workplace sexual harassment.

In 2013, the Supreme Court made it more difficult for employees to assert Title VII retaliation claims. As a result of this decision, to prevail, the plaintiff must prove that retaliation is the "but-for" cause of the adverse employment action that the employee complains about. It is not enough that retaliation is one of the factors supporting the employer's decision. The Supreme Court therefore mandated a higher standard of proof than the one used by the EEOC. It is also the ADEA standard of proof that the Supreme Court mandated in 2009, in its *Gross v. FBL Financial Services* decision.

The Supreme Court's rationale is that Title VII's retaliation provision is separate from the basic provision forbidding discrimination. Mixed-motive cases are acceptable in cases involving discrimination on the basis of the five personal characteristics listed in Title VII: race, color, religion, sex, and national origin. The Supreme Court majority found that the language of the Title VII retaliation provision has more in common with the ADEA than with the rest of Title VII. [*University of Tex. Sw. Med. Ctr. v. Nassar*, 133 S. Ct. 2517 (2013)]

"Cat's paw" theory makes an employer liable if the decisionmaker is manipulated by a biased person into taking adverse action against an employee. The Second, Third, Fifth, Sixth, Seventh, Eighth, and Tenth Circuits allow this theory to be used in Title VII retaliation cases to prove but-for causation of the adverse employment action. In a mid-2015 Fifth Circuit case, the plaintiff said that supervisors made retaliatory statements about him to Internal Affairs, resulting in the chief of police (who did not have retaliatory animus) taking adverse action. To avoid cat's paw liability, the decisionmaker must act on an independent review of all the available information rather than relying on one, possibly biased, person's input. [*Zamora v. City of Houston*, 798 F.3d 326 (5th Cir. 2015); *Vasquez v. Empress Ambulance Serv., Inc.*, No. 15-3239, 2016 WL 4501673 (2d Cir. Aug. 29, 2016); see Michael Marra and Richard R. Meneghello, *Cat's Paw Theory of Discrimination Adopted By 2nd Circuit*, Fisher Phillips (Aug. 30, 2016), available at Lexology.com]

The Second Circuit allowed a § 1983 suit for retaliation to be based on complaints of discrimination. The plaintiff was a bilingual high school teacher who alleged discrimination based on his Hispanic ethnicity. He said he was required to do additional work without compensation because he was assigned many students who are not fluent in English. He said that in retaliation for complaining about discrimination, he was assigned poor students, was not informed about curriculum changes, and he received his first negative performance review in 16 years. [*Vega v. Hempstead Union Free Sch. Dist.*, 801 F.3d 72 (2d Cir. 2015)]

A white female university professor, Patricia Hentosh, sued for retaliation when she was denied tenure. She claimed that the university ignored her complaints about an Asian professor because it discriminates against Caucasians. Hentosh filed an EEOC race discrimination charge on May 26, 2010, primarily citing discrete employment acts that occurred more than 300 days before the filing. The EEOC dismissed the charge and issued a right to sue letter on January 26, 2012. Her application for tenure was denied in the fall of 2011 when the EEOC investigation was in progress. On April 24, 2012, she sued for discrimination and retaliation alleging that the denial of tenure had discriminatory and retaliatory motives. The district court dismissed the case, holding that the filing was untimely so she did not exhaust her administrative remedies—so the district court did not have jurisdiction over the case because the denial of tenure claim was not within the scope of the EEOC charge or reasonably related to it. The employer's motion to dismiss the retaliation charge was denied because a retaliation claim can be raised for the first time in federal court, without a second EEOC charge being filed. The employer's motion for summary judgment on retaliation was granted because the district court held that the plaintiff did not prove that the desire to retaliate was the but-for cause of the adverse action. The Fourth Circuit affirmed in September 2014. [*Hentosh v. Old Dominion Univ.*, 767 F.3d 413 (4th Cir. 2014)]

The Second Circuit ruled that Title VII's retaliation provisions include both an "opposition" and a "participation" clause. It is unlawful for an employer to retaliate against an employee who opposes the employer's unlawful employment practices. But adverse job action imposed for participation in an employer's internal investigation of harassment charges, with no connection to a formal EEOC investigation, does not entitle the employee to maintain a Title VII retaliation suit. [*Townsend v. Benjamin Enters.*, 679 F.3d 41 (2d Cir. 2012)]

Many jurisdictions, such as the Fifth Circuit, apply a "manager rule": a manager's disagreement with the employer's policy, expressed in the course of work, is not considered Title VII protected activity in the retaliation context. The rule started in FLSA cases and was later applied to Title VII, to avoid large parts of the manager's job being treated as protected activity. However, the Fourth Circuit refused to apply the manager rule when a manager was fired, allegedly for telling an employee to file a sexual harassment suit. The Fourth Circuit's rationale was that a person's job title does not define what oppositional conduct is protected, and employees should not be discouraged from reporting sexual harassment. In the Fourth Circuit analysis, communication is protected if the employee communicates a belief to employer that the employer has committed discrimination, in an area that is either unlawful under TVII, or the employee reasonably believes it is. However, protection can be lost if the manager acts unreasonably. [*DeMasters v. Carilion Clinic*, 796 F.3d 409 (4th Cir. 2015)]

The EEOC might seek temporary or preliminary relief such as injunction if the retaliation places the charging party at risk of irreparable injury and there is a substantial likelihood that the retaliation claim will succeed. The compliance manual notes that all of the statutes enforced by the EEOC make both compensatory and punitive damages available to victims of retaliation.

Retaliation complaints under 42 U.S.C. § 1981 are cognizable. A defendant argued that it was not fair to apply § 1981 in the retaliation context, because it has a longer statute of limitations than Title VII and awards are not subject to the CRA '91 damage caps, but the Supreme Court held that this "end run" is allowed for discrimination claims and should also be allowed for retaliation. [*CBOCS West Inc. v. Humphries*, 553 U.S. 442 (2008)]

Although Title VII retaliation damages are subject to the statutory cap, there is no cap on ADEA or EPA damages.

CHAPTER 35

SEXUAL HARASSMENT

§ 35.01 INTRODUCTION

Sexual harassment is the subjection of an employee to unwanted sexual contact, propositions, or innuendoes. Sexual harassment occurs in two forms: either "quid pro quo" harassment, where an employee is threatened with job detriment for not complying with a sexual proposition or offered job benefits for compliance, or "hostile environment" harassment, where the atmosphere in the workplace is offensive.

Sexual harassment is considered a form of sex discrimination and therefore is forbidden by Title VII. The Equal Employment Opportunity Commission (EEOC) has adopted a two-part test. Conduct is unwanted if the employee did not solicit or initiate the conduct, and the employee finds it undesirable or offensive.

The Fourth Circuit refused to apply disparate impact analysis in sexual harassment cases, and ruled late in 2002 that the alleged sexual harassment was not actionable because co-workers would have subjected the plaintiff to the same offensive behavior and vulgar language if she had been male. [*Ocheltree v. Scollon Prods. Inc.*, 308 F.3d 351 (4th Cir. 2002), *on reh'g*, 335 F.3d 325 (4th Cir. 2003)] On rehearing, the court found that a reasonable jury could have found the conduct to be sexually discriminatory against the sole female worker, in the context of a pervasively harassing work environment. However, punitive damages were denied because of lack of proof of employer knowledge sufficient to support punitive damages.

The Ninth Circuit also permitted a gender-based harassment action to be maintained based on a showing that women were subjected to a greater degree of bullying, shouting, cursing, and invasion of personal space, even though the perpetrator was not attempting to solicit sexual activity from employees. [*EEOC v. Nat'l Educ. Ass'n Alaska*, 422 F.3d 840 (9th Cir. 2005)]

It is also possible that an employer will be held liable when a supervisor is harassed by a subordinate. Some courts use a hybrid standard, halfway between the reasonableness standard for harassment by co-workers and the much higher burden the employer must meet to avoid being held liable when a subordinate is harassed by a supervisor. [*Simmons v. DNC Hosp. Mgmt. of Okla., LLC*, 2015 WL 4430967 (D. Okla. July 20, 2015); *Knudsen v. Bd. of Supervisors of Univ. of La. Sys.*, 2015 WL1757695 (E.D. La. Apr. 16, 2015)]

The sexual harassment cause of action requires that the victim suffer tangible job action, not merely lack of friendliness or exclusions from workplace social activities. In a 2006 sexual harassment retaliation case, *Burlington Northern & Santa Fe Railway Co. v. White*, the Supreme Court ruled that retaliation liability is broader than liability for workplace discrimination: retaliation can be actionable even if the employee's job classification and compensation do not change, as long as the retaliatory measures are severe enough to be daunting to a reasonable employee. [548 U.S. 53]

In mid-2016, Fox News settled former anchor Gretchen Carlson's sexual harassment suit for $20 million—one of the largest single-plaintiff sexual harassment settlements ever reported. Carlson alleged that she was harassed by Roger Ailes, who was ousted as chairman of Fox News as a result of this case. Fox also settled with at least two other women who alleged harassment by Ailes. [Michael M. Grynbaum and John Koblin, *Fox Settles With Gretchen Carlson Over Roger Ailes Sex Harassment Claims*, NYTimes.com (Sept. 6, 2016)]

A California federal court ordered a food company to pay $1.47 million to a class of farmworkers under an EEOC sexual harassment suit. Multiple women were harassed and male employees who tried to defend them suffered retaliation. The EEOC also announced a similar settlement in the amount of $272,000, going to 20 employees of a large apple producer. [Richard B. Cohen, *From Farms to Swanky Resorts: EEOC Obtains Enormous Damages for Vulnerable Workers*, FisherBroyles (July 25, 2016), available at Lexology.com]

A 2014 article advises employers to avoid these mistakes:

- Maintaining an anti-harassment policy that covers only sexual harassment and omits race, religious, national origin, and other forms of harassment.

- Failing to implement an alternative procedure if the alleged harasser is in the reporting chain.

- Merely parroting statutory language, without explanation.

- Failing to train employees until a complaint has been made.

- Forcing accuser and accused to continue working together; it may be appropriate to suspend the alleged harasser (with pay) pending the investigation, or transfer one employee to prevent escalation of hostility.

- Failing to perform a complete investigation, with testimony from all witnesses; the HR department and legal counsel should be involved right away.

- Responding inappropriately for the level of alleged misconduct; in some cases, termination is excessive, whereas in other cases a reprimand is inadequate. [Robin E. Shea, *The "Dirty Dozen": Top 12 Employer Harassment Mistakes*, Constangy Brooks & Smith LLP (Aug. 8, 2014), available at Lexology.com]

Although one or more individuals may commit sexual harassment, it is the employer company that has the legal liability. The only way the employer can avoid liability is by carrying out appropriate investigations of allegations of harassment and by taking appropriate steps to deal with harassment accusations that are well founded.

§ 35.02   THE EMPLOYER'S BURDEN

In this context, two of the key cases are *Burlington Industries, Inc. v. Ellerth* [524 U.S. 742 (1998)] and *Faragher v. City of Boca Raton.* [524 U.S. 775 (1998)] If the action that the plaintiff complains of had adverse employment effect on the victim, the employer is absolutely liable. The employer is still liable even if no adverse employment effect occurred—unless the employer can assert as a defense that it maintained proper antiharassment and grievance policies.

The *Ellerth* case involved a sales representative who felt threatened by repeated remarks and gestures from a manager (not her immediate supervisor). She was not deprived of job benefits. Although she knew the company had an antiharassment policy, she did not complain about the harassment while it was occurring. She quit her job but did not attribute her resignation to harassment. Three weeks later, she sent a letter to the company explaining why she resigned.

The Supreme Court's decision was that the supervisor's threats of adverse job action created a hostile work environment. In such a situation, the employer becomes vicariously liable for the supervisor's conduct by:

- Failing to stop it after learning about it;

- Giving the supervisor apparent authority over the victim, thus making harassment possible;

- Allowing the supervisor to actually take adverse job action against the victim.

However, the other side of the coin is that the employer can be free of liability by taking reasonable care to maintain a workable complaint procedure, if the plaintiff fails to use the procedure.

In the *Faragher* case, a lifeguard sued her municipal employer and two supervisors for creating a hostile environment (including lewd touching of female employees). The employer did have an antiharassment policy, but it was not publicized to the employees. The employer didn't supervise the conduct of the supervisors themselves, and didn't create a procedure for reporting to someone other than the supervisor who committed the harassment. Therefore, the Supreme Court held that the employer was legally responsible for the hostile environment, because it failed to communicate the antiharassment policy and didn't track the conduct of supervisors.

In 2003, the Third Circuit (contrary to holdings in the Second and Sixth Circuits) held that the *Ellerth/Faragher* affirmative defense would not be available to employers in situations where the employee was able to prove constructive discharge. The Supreme Court reversed the Third Circuit in mid-2004. The Supreme Court settled a contentious point by holding that the test of constructive discharge is objective (whether a reasonable person would feel compelled to resign) rather than subjective (the individual employee's personal reaction to the situation). The Supreme Court also noted that, although firing an employee is always an official act (and therefore the affirmative defense is not available), constructive discharge is not always an official act of the employer company. Therefore, the company should be given the chance to assert and prove the affirmative defense. [*Suders v. Easton,* 325 F.3d 432 (3d Cir. 2003), *rev'd sub nom. Pa. State Police v. Suders,* 542 U.S. 129 (2004)]

The Second Circuit ruled in 2012 that the *Ellerth/Faragher* affirmative defense cannot be used where the alleged harasser is high enough in the corporate hierarchy to be considered a proxy or alter ego of the organization. In this case, the alleged harasser was a corporate executive and the husband of the company president. The president took over the investigation, hiring an outside HR consultant who said that the charges were unfounded. [*Townsend v. Benjamin Enters. Inc.,* 679 F.3d 41 (2d Cir. 2012)]

Plaintiff Pullen's supervisor allegedly verbally harassed her, touched her inappropriately, and showed her inappropriate pictures of other women. One of Pullen's co-workers did report harassment and said that Pullen was also victimized. The school board investigated, concluded the complaint was well-founded, and disciplined the supervisor. Pullen sued for hostile work environment harassment. The district court held that it was entitled to the *Faragher/Ellerth* defense because Pullen did not use the established complaint procedure, but the Fifth Circuit reversed, holding that summary judgment was inappropriate because the policy was not properly publicized. A copy of the policy was placed on a bulletin board in the office, but employees' testimony was conflicting as to whether or not they were aware of the policy. [*Pullen v. Caddo Parish Sch. Bd.,* 830 F.3d 205 (5th Cir. 2016); see Nicole Eichberger and Charles J. Stiegler, *Fifth Circuit Decision Reinforces the Importance of Clearly Communicating Anti-Harassment Policies,* Proskauer Rose LLP (July 26, 2016), available at Lexology.com]

It is not always simple to determine whether an individual accused of harassing conduct is a supervisor or not. In mid-2013, the Supreme Court decided a case about the definition of "supervisor" and the employer's burden. The case involved racial rather than sexual harassment, but it relied heavily on *Ellerth/Faragher,* so it will certainly be influential in sexual harassment cases. In a case of harassment by a supervisor, where there was tangible employment action taken against the plaintiff (such as firing or reassigning him or her) then the employer is strictly liable. If the harasser is a supervisor (defined as someone who has the authority to take tangible employment actions against subordinates) and there is no tangible employment action, the *Faragher/Ellerth* affirmative defense can be raised. But if, as in this case, the harasser is considered a co-worker rather than a supervisor, the employer is only liable if the hostile work environment can be attributed to the employer's negligence. [*Vance v. Ball State Univ.,* 133 S. Ct. 2434 (2013)]

In a Title VII retaliation case, an employee's demand that a supervisor stop harassing is protected conduct, even if there is no formal complaint to the employer. Three women were fired after complaining about harassment by a supervisor; a man who witnessed the harassment was also fired for talking to an investigator. The jury awarded $1.5 million to the plaintiffs. The Sixth Circuit held that the Title VII opposition clause prohibits retaliation for expansively defined opposition, including telling the supervisor to cease the harassment. [*EEOC v. New Breed Logistics*, 783 F.3d 1057 (6th Cir. 2015)]

The employer prevailed in a later Sixth Circuit case, because the court found that the harasser, a store manager, was not a supervisor. The Sixth Circuit held that, although the manager could hire new employees and write up employees for misconduct, he could not fire, promote, demote, or transfer employees. [*EEOC v. AutoZone, Inc.*, No. 16-6387 (6th Cir. June 9, 2017); see Laura J. Maechtlen and Gerald L. Maatman, Jr., *Sixth Circuit Shuts Down EEOC's Appeal in Sex Harassment Suit*, Seyfarth Shaw LLP (June 13, 2017), available at Lexology.com]

In an early 2015 decision, the New Jersey Supreme Court provided ammunition for both plaintiffs and defendants. The court clarified that the *Faragher/Ellerth* affirmative defense is available under New Jersey state anti-discrimination law—and also expanded the definition of "supervisor." A supervisor is someone who has the authority to take or recommend tangible employment action against the plaintiff—or has the power to direct the plaintiff's work on a day-to-day basis. Summary judgment for the employer was reversed, and the case was remanded. [*Aguas v. State of N.J.*, 107 A.3d 1250 (N.J. 2015); see Joseph Domenick Guarino, Brian Kaplan and Amanda Grace Tomney, *New Jersey High Court Decision Will Reshape Employer Liability in Sexual Harassment Cases*, DLA Piper LLP (Feb. 13, 2015), available at Lexology.com]

In a case of first impression, the First Circuit held in mid-2014 that if the harasser is not the complainant's supervisor (in this case of female-on-male harassment, the harasser was a non-manager—in the HR office, ironically enough), the employer is liable only if it was negligent in controlling the working conditions. The Supreme Court has not ruled on quid pro quo harassment by a co-worker (as distinct from hostile work environment harassment). The co-worker made advances to the plaintiff; when he rejected her, she complained about the quality of the plaintiff's work until he got fired. [*Velazquez-Perez v. Developers Diversified Realty Corp.*, 753 F.3d 265 (1st Cir. 2014)]

The Fourth Circuit set a nine-part test to determine if a customer company had enough control over a temp agency employee to be liable for damages to the temp worker. The plaintiff suffered repeated sexual harassment from a foreman. She complained to the temp agency and management at the customer company. The foreman who harassed her assigned her to work on a particular machine. She refused, saying she was tired from working too much overtime. She was sent home; the customer told the temp agency to replace her. The foreman allegedly said she could have her job back if she granted him sexual favors. She sued both companies. The district court dismissed, the Fourth Circuit reversed. The factors in joint employment are: (1) authority to hire and fire; (2) day to day supervision, incl. discipline; (3) if customer furnishes equipment and place of work; (4) responsibility for payroll and other employee records; (5) how long individual worked for the customer; (6) if customer trains the individual; (7) if individual's duties are similar to those of customer's employees; (8) whether the individual only works for the customer; and (9) if the parties intended to have an employment relationship. Control is the most important. The temp agency handled employment matters, and the temp employees wore different uniforms. The Fourth Circuit found joint employment based on the customer company's substantial control over the plaintiff's environment. [*Butler v. Drive Automotive Indus.*, No. 14-1348 (4th Cir. July 15, 2015)]

Although many cases involve the conduct of supervisors (because of their ability to affect working conditions), employers have also been held liable, in appropriate cases, for harassment committed by nonsupervisory, fellow employees, and by customers.

Another 2013 Supreme Court case also affects proof requirements. *University of Texas Southwestern Medical Center v. Nassar*, 133 S. Ct. 2517 (2013) is a Title VII retaliation case. The Supreme Court set a higher standard for proof of retaliation claims than for discrimination claims. In a retaliation case, the plaintiff must show that retaliation was the "but-for" cause of the adverse action; it is not enough that it be one of several motivating factors.

The First Circuit applied the *Nassar* but-for causation standard to affirm summary judgment for the employer in a sexual harassment/retaliatory termination case. The plaintiff was fired in mid-2011. She said that her supervisor propositioned her on two occasions but she did not inform the employer until much later; even then, she merely said she felt uncomfortable with the supervisor but did not charge sexual harassment. The employer said that she was fired for poor performance, tardiness, and ineffective communications. The First Circuit found that her vague complaints could not establish a but-for case. The employer had a legitimate nondiscriminatory reason to fire her. Her performance problems began before the alleged harassment and her supervisor was not the only person to criticize her work. [*Ponte v. Steelcase Inc.*, 741 F.3d 310 (1st Cir. 2014)]

The Fourth Circuit refused to require a heightened causation standard as a result of *Nassar*, holding that *Nassar* is a mixed-motive case that did not alter the standard of causation to be used for pretext claims. (In this case, the plaintiff was fired after complaining about co-worker harassment; management said that she was fired because she was not a team player, used too much leave time, and was unwilling to do extra work). [*Foster v. Univ. of Md.*, 787 F.3d 243 (4th Cir. 2015)]

In what could be the first case of its type, the New Jersey Court of Appeals ruled that a business owner who says that a customer insisted that she have sex with him or he would not place an order could use the New Jersey Law Against Discrimination to sue for discriminatory refusal to do business on the basis of gender. The court found that quid pro quo harassment in business unlawfully interferes with women's ability to earn a living. [*J.T.'s Tire Serv. v. United Rentals N. Am., Inc.*, 411 N.J. Super. 236 (N.J. App. Div. 2010)]

A male waiter charged harassment after he terminated his sexual relationship with a female supervisor. (The supervisor conceded that there had been a relationship, but denied that she harassed him in order to get him to resume the relationship.) The Seventh Circuit held that there was a material issue of fact about the hostile work environment, and remanded to see if there was a basis to find the employer liable. The Seventh Circuit held in early 2010 that the same rules apply for males alleging harassment by females as for females alleging harassment by males: if there was a consensual relationship in the past, the question is whether, by both subjective and objective standards, there was a hostile work environment. The Seventh Circuit found that dismissal six months after complaints to Turner's supervisors were not close enough in time to suggest retaliation—especially since Turner received a positive evaluation in the interim. However, he also received at least 10 reprimands for poor workplace behavior. [*Turner v. The Saloon, Ltd.*, 595 F.3d 679 (7th Cir. 2010)]

The employer's burden rests with the employer—harassed employees can't sue their unions for involvement in the employer's failure to redress sexual harassment. If one union member accuses another of harassment, the union has a duty to give both of them fair representation at the disciplinary hearing—but the union does not have an obligation to investigate or remedy discrimination. [*Thorn v. Amalgamated Transit Union*, 305 F.3d 826 (8th Cir. 2002)]

§ 35.03 APPROPRIATE EMPLOYER RESPONSES

[A] Statutory and Case Law

Most companies are aware of the potential risk of sexual harassment litigation. After the landmark *Ellerth* and *Faragher* cases, the employer must prevent severe, pervasive unwelcome physical and verbal conduct to prevent the development of a hostile, intimidating, or offensive environment. Supervisors and managers must be trained to recognize and report harassment. There must be a chain of command that can bypass an alleged harasser. Employees must believe that their complaints will be taken seriously. Top management must be involved, to prove that the company takes these matters seriously.

If customers commit the harassment, the Tenth Circuit analyzes the situation as if the harassers were co-employees (not supervisors). So the employer will not be strictly liable for the actions of customers, but will be liable if its negligence permitted the harassment to continue. [*Lockard v. Pizza Hut Inc.*, 162 F.3d 1062 (10th Cir. 1998)]

If the employer is negligent, it can be held liable for harassment by a non-employee. The Second Circuit held that the employer's response (stopping the harassing conduct; dismissing a player from the football team for harassing the plaintiff; ordering anti-harassment training for the entire athletics staff) was adequate. But the plaintiff's retaliation claim survived a defense motion for summary judgment. Temporal proximity between her complaints and her loss of a graduate assistant position and termination of her student employment privileges was enough to get to trial. [*Summa v. Hofstra Univ.*, 708 F.3d 115 (2d Cir. 2013)]

It is important to look behind supervisors' write-ups to make sure that the lateness, poor work habits, etc., actually occurred—and that one subordinate was not singled out for conduct that was not punished in employees who did not become sexual targets.

The Second Circuit ruled in mid-2016 that an employer can be liable for retaliatory actions taken by a co-worker, even if the co-worker is not a supervisor. The plaintiff was harassed by a co-worker; she reported the harassment to their employer, Empress Ambulance Services. The plaintiff said that the harasser interfered with the investigation by doctoring text messages to make it look like the plaintiff sent sexually oriented text messages to the co-worker. Empress fired both employees. The plaintiff sued; the district court dismissed the case on the grounds that the harasser did not have decision-making authority but the Second Circuit reversed, citing the agency law principle that a co-worker's retaliatory intent can be imputed to a negligent employer. [*Vasquez v. Empress Ambulance Serv.*, 835 F.3d 267; (2d Cir. 2016); see Casey C. Sullivan, *2nd Cir. Adds More Claws to Cat's Paw Discrimination Theory*, FindLaw Second Circuit blog (Sept. 1, 2016), available at FindLaw.com.]

Sexual harassment charges require conduct that was unwanted, but some courts weaken the employer's defense in consensual cases. A Seventh Circuit case was brought by a teenage store employee who filed an EEOC charge about inappropriate sexual advances from her 25-year-old shift supervisor, who was convicted of aggravated sexual abuse. The trial court rejected the claim, stating that she engaged in a consensual sexual relationship, but the Seventh Circuit permitted her lawsuit to advance because of her status as a minor. [*Jane Doe v. Oberweis Dairy*, 456 F.3d 704 (7th Cir. 2006)]

The district court made a similar ruling in a case in which a teenage fast-food worker was subjected to sexual harassment by a manager who had had sexual relations with several other employees. The manager fired her for missing a shift (after he re-scheduled her without notice), then rehired her and continued the harassment. The young woman complained repeatedly to shift supervisors and to an assistant manager, who repeatedly frustrated her attempts to file a formal complaint. When the worker's mother came to the restaurant to complain, she was fired again, this time permanently. The district court ruled for the employer, on the grounds that the worker did not invoke the company's complaint procedure, and retaliation for her mother's conduct was not actionable.

In this case, however, the Seventh Circuit reversed, ruling that the reasonableness of an employer's complaint mechanism only affects the employer's liability for damages, not a claim of unlawful termination. The age and sophistication of the complainant are very relevant to the determination of whether the complaint mechanism is adequate. Although employers do not have to have a tailored procedure for each individual, if the business plan is to hire teenage part-time workers, the complaint procedure should be comprehensible to them. At a minimum, employees should have been informed of a toll-free telephone number in the HR department to report complaints; the plaintiff here first was told there was no number to call, then given a wrong number. Furthermore, because a minor has to bring suit by means of a representative, retaliation based on the actions of a young worker's representative should be actionable. [*EEOC v. V&J Foods, Inc.*, 507 F.3d 575 (7th Cir. 2007)]

[B]   EEOC Enforcement Guidance

The EEOC's 20-page guidance on the employer's responsibilities, *Enforcement Guidance: Vicarious Employer Liability for Unlawful Harassment by Supervisors*, Number 915.002 (June 18, 1999), <http://www.eeoc.gov/policy/docs/harassment.html>, was updated to discuss *Vance v. Ball State* (see § 35.02 above) remained in force for more than 15 years.

In early 2017, the EEOC published a proposal, "Proposed Enforcement Guidance on Unlawful Harassment," seeking comments on the *Ellerth/Faragher* test. The proposal requires employers to act promptly and appropriately, unless the employee delays unreasonably in making a complaint. Under the 2017 proposal, the employer must maintain a program to combat known or obvious risks of harassment. Failure to do so forfeits the affirmative defense. The EEOC reaffirmed its position that employers have a duty to respond to conduct that is not yet violative, to prevent it from escalating to violate Title VII.

The EEOC affirmed core principles for preventing and addressing harassment: there must be committed and engaged leadership, consistent and demonstrated accountability, strong and comprehensive anti-harassment policies, an accessible complaint procedure that employees trust, and regular training.

The guidance says that the EEOC will consider harassment charges based on sex stereotyping, sexual orientation, gender identity, pregnancy, and violation of privacy of genetic information. The EEOC says it will take complaints with respect to perceived (even if incorrect) membership in a protected class; associational harassment; where harassment happened outside the workplace; or where the complainant was not the target. Victoria A. Lipnic, a co-author of the guidance, has been named as Acting Chair of the EEOC, so it is possible that the guidance will remain in effect and will not be struck down with other recent regulations. [<https://www.regulations.gov/docket?D=EEOC-2016-0009> (Jan. 10, 2017); Press release: <https://www.eeoc.gov/eeoc/newsroom/release/1-10-17a.cfm>; see Charles C. Warner, *EEOC Issues Proposed Guidance on Harassment*, Porter Wright Morris & Arthur LLP (Jan. 20, 2017), available at

Lexology.com; James Nicholas, *EEOC Issues New Harassment Guidance,* Foley & Lardner LLP (Feb. 13, 2017)]

Another federal agency, the Office of Federal Contract Compliance Programs (OFCCP), the part of the Department of Labor that supervises federal contractors, published a Final Rule on sex discrimination in mid-2016. The rule reiterates that sexual harassment, defined to include unwelcome sexual advances, requests for sexual favors "offensive remarks about a person's sex" and other physical or verbal conduct "of a sexual nature" is unlawful if it forms the basis of employment decisions, unreasonably interferes with the victim's work performance, or creates a hostile work environment. The 2016 Final Rule also forbids discrimination based on sex stereotyping (expectations about how men and women should look and act). [OFCCP Final Rule, *Discrimination on the Basis of Sex,* 81 Fed. Reg. 39107 (June 15, 2016)]

[C] Internal Investigations of Harassment Allegations

A recent article points out that a company's in-house counsel should not take the lead in investigating discrimination complaints—because the lawyer might have to testify at trial about the reasonableness of the employer's response to employee complaints. If the lawyer testifies, documents might become discoverable, including notes taken by in-house counsel when interviewing employees. In an Ohio case, mistrial was declared after the employer failed to produce the attorney's investigative notes from the internal investigation of allegations of discrimination, harassment, and retaliation. The employer was sanctioned by having to pay over $300,000 of the plaintiffs' attorney's fees because the house counsel had an ethical conflict of interest by performing the investigation. The article suggests having the investigation performed by HR personnel (trained to investigate) or outside consultants, although they should keep in-house counsel informed of the progress of the investigation. [*EEOC v. Spitzer,* 866 F. Supp. 2d 851 (N.D. Ohio 2013)]

In a harassment case, the employer said that it did not have to produce all of its documents from its investigation, because some of the documents were covered by work product or attorney-client privilege. The District Court for the District of Massachusetts said that privilege was waived for the investigation report and all of the documents, interviews, and notes that were part of the investigation, because the investigation was directed and controlled by the attorney. This decision does not say that privilege is waived whenever a lawyer's communications with an investigator merely further the investigation without the lawyer becoming part of it. The best practice to preserve privilege is that lawyers should give instructions to investigators, but then remove themselves from the investigation. [*Koss v. Palmer Water Dep't,* 977 F. Supp. 2d 28 (D. Mass. 2013)]

§ 35.04 HOSTILE WORK ENVIRONMENT HARASSMENT

[A] Generally

A hostile work environment is one where actions are taken to make an employee feel unwelcome. Harassment cases have been recognized dealing with race, religion, disability, and age, as well as cases in which women are made uncomfortable by, e.g., unwanted touching, crude propositions, dirty jokes, pin-ups, etc. Hostile work environment sexual harassment cases have been recognized for many years, dating back to the Supreme Court case of *Meritor Savings Bank v. Vinson.* [477 U.S. 57 (1986)]

A single act of harassment, if it is severe enough, can create a hostile work environment. The Seventh Circuit permitted a claim of co-worker harassment, who alleged unwelcome physical contact with intimate parts of her body, to proceed to trial. But she did not show that the alleged comments by her supervisor were severe or pervasive enough to create a hostile environment: the court said that she did not show that she felt humiliated or physically threatened, and she did not allege that her work performance was affected. [*Berry v. Chicago Transit Auth.*, 618 F.3d 688 (7th Cir. 2010)]

It can be difficult to predict what conduct will be considered sufficiently outrageous to create a hostile environment, because different courts have reached very different conclusions. There is often disagreement about the seriousness of conduct that constitutes harassment, how severe and prolonged it must be, and the extent of injuries that the complainant must suffer before having a sustainable case.

The Eleventh Circuit permitted a female sales representative to pursue a hostile work environment suit because of very frequent use of anti-female language ("bitch" "whore") even though it was not specifically directed at the plaintiff herself. The plaintiff also alleged that there was a lot of workplace discussion about sexual topics, and sexually suggestive radio shows were frequently played in the workplace. Ingrid Reeves resigned her job in 2004 and brought suit. The Northern District of Alabama granted summary judgment for the employer, finding that Reeves herself was not the individual target, so the harassment was not "based on" her sex. A three-judge panel of the Eleventh Circuit reversed this decision in 2008, and was upheld by an en banc panel (of all the judges on the court) in 2010. [*Reeves v. C.H. Robinson*, 594 F.3d 798 (11th Cir. 2010)]

A corrections officer brought a suit under Title VII and California law about unwanted kisses and hugs from the county sheriff, occurring more than 100 times over a 12-year period. According to the plaintiff, the sheriff hugged women but shook hands with men. The Ninth Circuit held that a reasonable juror could conclude that this was not a mere innocent difference in routine interactions. The case was remanded to determine if the plaintiff made out a case of hostile work environment. [*Zetwick v. County of Yolo,* 850 F.3d 436 (9th Cir. 2017); see Manatt

Phelps & Phillips LLP, *Ninth Circuit: Hugs from Supervisor Can Form Basis of Suit*,(March 10 2017), available at Lexology.com]

[B] Retaliation

As Chapter 34 discusses, allegations of retaliation for filing discrimination claims are in themselves a major litigation area.

The Supreme Court's 2009 *Crawford* decision, which holds that employees are protected against retaliation if they respond to questioning in an employer's internal investigation—not just if they volunteer information about illegalities in the workplace—began as a sexual harassment case. The plaintiff charged her employer with retaliating against her for testifying in an investigation of charges raised by another employee; Crawford said that she had also been harassed by the same supervisor. [*Crawford v. Metropolitan Gov't of Nashville & Davison Cnty., TN*, 555 U.S. 271 (2009)]

The First Circuit held that a reasonable jury could believe that the drug company manager plaintiff, Collazo, opposed sexual harassment when he helped a co-worker pursue harassment charges. Although the employer's internal inquiry cleared the alleged harasser, a plaintiff does not have to prove that the conditions he or she opposed actually violated Title VII—only that he or she had a good faith reasonable belief that they did. Management argued that Collazo was fired for performance problems, and because his job was eliminated in a reorganization, but the First Circuit refused to allow reorganization to be used as an excuse for discriminatory or retaliatory termination. Nor was he given any counseling or progressive discipline for the supposed performance problems. Although other employees were transferred, Collazo was the only person terminated, and the only person not given a chance to transfer. Collazo did not get any verbal or written warnings or counseling in the months before his termination, supposedly for deficient performance. [*Collazo v. Bristol-Myers Squibb Mfg. Inc.*, 617 F.3d 39 (1st Cir. 2010)]

§ 35.05 SAME-SEX HARASSMENT

For several years, courts were divided about whether sexual harassment of a male employee by a male supervisor, or a female employee by a female supervisor, was barred by Title VII. Perhaps this reflects a stereotype of sexual harassment as only something that is perpetrated by males against females. Questions were raised as to whether same-sex harassment could be described as occurring "on account of sex," because the harasser is of the same sex as the victim.

The uncertainty was resolved by the Supreme Court in *Oncale v. Offshore Servs. Inc.* [523 U.S. 75 (1998)], which brought same-sex harassment into the ambit of Title VII.

An oil rig worker said that a bisexual male co-worker harassed him by not only insisting on describing his sexual activities with women, but also propositioning the plaintiff and subjecting him to unwanted sexual touching. The Sixth Circuit held that the plaintiff failed to provide proof of the alleged harasser's sexual orientation, which was necessary to create the inference that the plaintiff was harassed "because of his sex." The Sixth Circuit requires proof of at least one of three elements in a same-sex harassment case: (1) credible evidence that the alleged harasser is homosexual; (2) clear evidence that the harasser is generally hostile to the presence of members of the plaintiff's sex in the workplace; or (3) in a mixed-sex workplace, with worse treatment by the harasser of one sex than the other. All of the oil rig workers were male and there was no evidence that the alleged harasser was hostile to males as a group. Therefore, the Sixth Circuit required proof of the alleged harasser's sexual orientation, and held that a suggestion that he was bisexual was not enough to prove the plaintiff's case. [*Wasek v. Arrow Energy Servs., Inc.*, 682 F.3d 463 (6th Cir. 2012)]

The Eighth Circuit held that a male supervisor's squeezing of a male employee's nipple, saying "This is sexual harassment," was not actionable because the crude and offensive conduct ceased when the employee complained. The Eighth Circuit said there was no evidence that grabbing the plaintiff's nipple or handing him a towel which the supervisor had rubbed on his crotch were based on sex or hostility to male workers, nor was the supervisor acting out of sexual desire. The plaintiff's Age Discrimination in Employment Act (ADEA) claim was also dismissed on the grounds that age-based comments were "simple teasing or offhand comments" that did not prove an objectively hostile work environment. [*Rickard v. Swedish Match N. Am., Inc.*, 773 F.3d 181 (8th Cir. 2014), *reh'g denied and reh'g en banc denied* (Jan. 16, 2015)]

On August 12, 2013, California Governor Brown signed SB 292, amending the Fair Employment and Housing Act (FEHA) to provide that sexual harassment plaintiffs do not have to prove that the harassing conduct was motivated by sexual desire. Under SB 292, the sexual orientation of the victim, or the sexual intent of the harasser is no longer relevant. [Susan W. Pangborn, *New California Law Expands the Concept of Sexual Harassment*, Kilpatrick Townsend & Stockton LLP (Aug. 14, 2013), available at Lexology.com. The legislation overrules *Kelley v. The Conco Cos.*, 196 Cal. App. 4th 191 (2011), which was interpreted to require a motivation of sexual desire in same-sex harassment cases.]

The Fifth Circuit, sitting en banc, held in late 2013 that harassment based on gender stereotypes can be actionable under Title VII as "because of sex." The ironworker plaintiff suffered constant verbal and physical harassment, including indecent exposure and jokes about rape, because the supervisor didn't think the victim was manly enough. There was no evidence that the harasser wanted to have sex with the victim and there was no evidence of hostility toward men in general, or that men and women were treated differently. The Fifth Circuit joined the Third, Seventh, Eighth, and Tenth Circuits in holding that those factors (which come from the Supreme Court's *Oncale* ruling on same-sex harassment) are illustrative, not all required to prove harassment. Therefore, the EEOC could make its case based on harassment for perceived lack of conformity with gender stereotypes (whether or not the victim actually was "manly.") [*EEOC v. Boh Bros. Constr. Co.*, 731 F.3d 444 (5th Cir. 2013). The case was subsequently settled by a consent judgment under which Boh Brothers agreed to pay compensatory damages of $125,000: see Manatt Phelps & Phillips LLP, *Same-Sex Harassment Suits Yield Sizable Settlement*, Lexology.com (Mar. 19, 2014).]

The Tenth Circuit, reversing the district court, held that it is possible for women to create a work environment that is hostile to other women (e.g., lewd jokes and offensive touching directed by lesbians against the heterosexual female plaintiff). However, the Tenth Circuit dismissed the retaliation claim because, at worst, there was one instance of discipline, in a situation that could be interpreted as management's attempt to prevent future harassment. [*Dick v. Phone Directories Co.*, 397 F.3d 1256 (10th Cir. 2005)]

The Eighth Circuit disagreed, affirming summary judgment for the employer in a case in which a heterosexual female employee said that another heterosexual female employee subjected her (and other women) to unwanted rude, vulgar, and sexually charged behavior, such as sexual innuendo and groping. The plaintiff said that co-worker also engaged in similar conduct toward male employees. The plaintiff said that she complained about 100 times to at least 12 managers, but management denied that she had complained and refused to transfer her out of the baking department. Because the co-worker treated males and females in the same vulgar and inappropriate way, the Eighth Circuit said that the plaintiff could not prove that the conduct was motivated by sexual desire, that harassment was motivated by general hostility to the presence of women—or men—in the workplace, or that the harasser targeted only one sex for harassment. [*Smith v. HyVee Inc.*, 622 F.3d 904 (8th Cir. 2010)]

§ 35.06 ORIENTATION AND PERCEIVED ORIENTATION

Bibby v. Philadelphia Coca-Cola Bottling Co., 260 F.3d 257 (3d Cir. 2001) says that three kinds of same-sex harassment are illegal: unwanted sexual advances made toward an employee of the same sex; harassment because the harasser believes that women or men do not belong in that type of workplace; or harassment for failure to behave with appropriate masculinity or femininity.

Some transsexual plaintiffs now raise claims that they are discriminated against because they present themselves as the "other" sex and do not conform to gender stereotypes.

Prior to general recognition of sexual orientation discrimination under Title VII, the Third Circuit permitted an effeminate gay man to pursue a Title VII claim of harassment based on his failure to conform to gender stereotypes. The Third Circuit said that the case should not have been dismissed, but should have gone to a jury, because it was uncertain whether the case involved sexual orientation or gender discrimination (but affirmed dismissal of his charge that he was harassed for not conforming to his co-workers' religious beliefs). [*Prowel v. Wise Business Forms Inc.*, 579 F.3d 285 (3d Cir. 2009)]

§ 35.07   WRONGFUL DISCHARGE CLAIMS

Employers often fear that they may be caught between two fires. If they do not respond to allegations, they face EEOC charges and/or lawsuits. But if they fire an alleged harasser, he or she may sue for wrongful termination. It is a delicate balance, but the employer can avoid liability by carrying out a thorough investigation in each case and taking proportionate steps against anyone found to have committed harassment. A complete "paper trail" is very important here (as in many other contexts).

When discriminatory discipline is charged, the question is whether different discipline is imposed for the same offense. A black female employee did not have a discrimination claim when she was fired for groping the genitals of male co-workers, when a white female was not fired for exposing her breasts on request, because the black female had engaged in conduct contrary to the wishes of its recipients, justifying a higher level of discipline. [*Wheeler v. Aventis Pharm.*, 360 F.3d 853 (8th Cir. 2004)]

Another implication of wrongful termination law is that in Maryland, an employee discharged for refusing to have sexual intercourse with a harasser can pursue a tort claim for abusive discharge in addition to the sexual harassment charges. The additional tort claim can be pursued because the state has a public policy against prostitution—and having sex to keep a job is, in effect, prostitution. [*Insignia Residential Corp. v. Ashton, Md.*, 755 A.2d 1080 (Md. 2000)]

§ 35.08   DAMAGE ISSUES

The Supreme Court has imposed a general rule, for all kinds of cases, that punitive damages should not be more than nine times compensatory damages. Late in 2003, the District of Columbia Court of Appeals struck down an award of $4.8 million in punitive damages in a sexual harassment retaliation case, finding it to be unconstitutionally excessive (26:1 ratio). The award was also improper because it reflected the defendant's nationwide conduct, not just its treatment of the individual plaintiff. Furthermore, the most relevant civil penalty under the local Human Rights Act was only $50,000 for multiple offenses. [*Daka Inc. v. McCrae*, 839 A.2d 682 (D.C. App. Dec. 24, 2003)]

A jury found Asarco liable for sexual harassment but found no compensatory damages, so it awarded $1 in nominal damages and $858,750 in punitive damages. The trial court reduced the award to $300,000 under the Title VII cap on damages. The Ninth Circuit, noting that an award of 300,000 times compensatory damages is impermissible, reduced the damages to $125,000, with the alternative of a new trial if Asarco would not accept the reduced damages. [*Arizona v. Asarco*, 733 F.3d 882 (9th Cir. 2013)] The Ninth Circuit reheard the case en banc and reinstated the $300,000 award. This time, the court said that reprehensibility was the most important factor in setting punitive damages and, by adopting the cap, Congress authorized the cap amounts as not offending due process. The jury was instructed that nominal damages were limited to $1, so they were not permitted to award higher nominal damages that, perhaps, would reduce the ratio of punitive to other damages. [*Arizona v. Asarco LLC*, 773 F.3d 1050 (9th Cir. 2014)]

Normally, the question is whether the defendant will have to pay the plaintiff's legal fees and costs—but, in rare cases, a prevailing defendant will be entitled to a fee award. The EEOC brought a suit on behalf of more than 200 female truck drivers who said that they suffered sexual harassment, including rape in some cases, by male drivers assigned as trainers by their employers, CRST Van Expedited Inc. The District Court for the Northern District of Iowa not only dismissed the EEOC suit but also ruled that the defendant was the prevailing party in the suit—so the EEOC would have to pay almost $5 million of CRST's legal fees and litigation expenses. The district court found that the EEOC completely mishandled the preparation of the case and entirely failed to prove its pattern-or-practice theory. The district court dismissed all of the plaintiffs' claims because the EEOC did not investigate or attempt conciliation in each individual case. The district court also said that the trainers were not supervisors, so CRST was not vicariously liable for any harassment that occurred.

The EEOC appealed to the Eighth Circuit, which upheld most of the district court's findings. However, the Eighth Circuit ruled that claims of two of the plaintiffs should not have been dismissed. Therefore, CRST was no longer a prevailing defendant, and the EEOC did not have to pay its fees and costs right away The Eighth Circuit held that the EEOC had an obligation to investigate thoroughly before filing suit and to attempt conciliation of each claim. [*EEOC v. CRST Van Expedited Inc.*, 679 F.3d 657 (8th Cir. 2012); *en banc reh'g denied* (June 8, 2012)]

The case was sent back to the Northern District of Iowa, which reinstated the finding that CRST was a prevailing defendant (because the EEOC's investigation was inadequate); the EEOC failed to attempt conciliation; and it did not have evidence to back up its pattern or practice claim. The fee award was also reinstated. [*EEOC v. CRST Van Expedited, Inc.*, No. 07-CV-95, 2013 U.S. Dist. LEXIS 107822 (N.D. Iowa Aug. 1, 2013)]

But the serial story took another twist. In late 2014, the Eighth Circuit reversed and remanded the district court order requiring the EEOC to pay attorneys' fees, narrowing the potential fees for litigation abuses. The Eighth Circuit said that the dismissal of 67 claims for failure to investigate or conciliate was not a ruling on the merits, so a fee award was unavailable on those claims. [*EEOC v.*

CRST Van Expedited, Inc., 774 F.3d 1169 (8th Cir. 2014). Rehearing and en banc rehearing were denied, No. 13-3159, 2015 U.S. App. LEXIS 2652 (8th Cir. Feb. 20, 2015). Certiorari was granted on the issue of whether the employer can receive an attorneys' fee award based on the EEOC's failure of conciliation: The Supreme Court ruled in mid-2016 that a party to a suit can be considered the prevailing party even if the case was decided purely on procedural grounds, and the merits of the case were not reached. The Supreme Court said that Congress enacts provisions for making one party pay the other side's attorneys' fees to discourage frivolous litigation, even if there has not been a ruling on the merits. But, instead of upholding or reversing the $4.7 million fee award that the EEOC had been ordered to pay, the Supreme Court sent the case back to the Eighth Circuit to determine if the EEOC was liable for the fees. *EEOC v. CRST Van Expedited*, 136 S. Ct. 1642 (May 19, 2016); see Gerald L. Maatman, Jr., Christina M. Janice and Alex W. Karasik, *U.S. Supreme Court Rejects the Government's Position in the Largest EEOC Fee Sanction Case Ever*, Seyfarth Shaw LLP (May 19, 2016), available at Lexology.com]

See also *EEOC v. Great Steaks, Inc.*, 667 F.3d 510 (4th Cir. 2012), the jury ruled for the defendant in an EEOC suit charging hostile environment sexual harassment. The Fourth Circuit held that the defendant was not entitled to an award of attorneys' fees under Title VII, the Equal Access to Justice Act, or the federal statute against "vexatious litigation." The Fourth Circuit held that, although a prevailing defendant does not have to prove the plaintiff's subjective bad faith to receive a fee award, the plaintiff must either have made a groundless, unreasonable, or frivolous claim, or must have prolonged the litigation after it was clear that the suit was inappropriate. In this case, even though the EEOC's case was not strong enough to win, it was not worthless.

§35.09   LIABILITY OF INDIVIDUALS

Sexual harassment charges are not really very similar to charges of, say, environmental pollution, commercial fraud, or tax evasion. Although a corporation is only an artificial person, so individuals must commit its wrongful acts, in some cases individuals who commit a tort or a crime are doing so on behalf of the corporation. People who commit sexual harassment may be echoing a corporate culture that tolerates such things, but they are not benefiting the corporation!

Nevertheless, the language of Title VII, like most antidiscrimination statutes, refers only to "employers," and with few exceptions, courts have ruled that only the employer corporation, and not the individual, is liable for harassment. [No individual liability: *Carrisales v. Dep't of Corrs.*, 90 Cal. Rptr. 2d 804 (Cal. 1999); *Smith v. Amedisys Inc.*, 298 F.3d 434 (5th Cir. 2002). But see *Speight v. Albano Cleaners*, 21 F. Supp. 2d 560 (E.D. Va. 1998), where the individual supervisor was held liable, but the corporation was not held liable.]

The New Hampshire Supreme Court held in 2016 that individual liability can be imposed for aiding and abetting workplace discrimination that violates the state's anti-discrimination and anti-retaliation statutes. The New Hampshire Supreme Court held that the state statute makes aiding and abetting harassment illegal, and does not limit liability to the employer. The statute's filing provisions allow a complaint to be filed against a "person," employer, labor organization, employment agency, or public accommodation, and the definition of "person" includes individuals. [*EEOC v. Fred Fuller Oil Co. Inc.*, 134 A.3d 17 (N.H. 2016); see Tawny L. Alvarez, *While There WAS No "I" in Defendant, There Is Now: New Hampshire Supreme Court Finds Individual Liability in State Anti-Discrimination and Anti-Retaliation Statutes*, Verrill Dana LLP (Feb. 26, 2016)]

§ 35.10 INTERACTION WITH OTHER STATUTES

It is a familiar theme throughout this book that legal concepts do not exist in isolation, and a single case may trigger many statutes and regulations.

According to the Kentucky Supreme Court, there is an exception to Worker's Compensation (WC) exclusivity for injuries occurring through the "deliberate intention" of the employer. Therefore, although a suit against the employer for the physical and psychological consequences of sexual harassment would not necessarily be barred by WC exclusivity, nevertheless plaintiffs must make a choice. Either they can bring a tort suit (for instance, for intentional or negligent infliction of emotional distress; battery) or file for Worker's Compensation benefits. Acceptance of the Comp benefits rules out a suit involving the same injuries. [*Am. Gen. Life & Accident Ins. Co. v. Hall*, 74 S.W.3d 688 (Ky. Sup. 2002)]

The Bankruptcy Abuse Prevention and Consumer Protection Act of 2005 (BAPCA; Pub. L. No. 109-8) denies a discharge in a Chapter 13 case for civil damages awarded against the debtor when the debtor's willful or malicious injury resulted in personal injury or death to a plaintiff.

CHAPTER 36

AMERICANS WITH DISABILITIES ACT (ADA)

§ 36.01 INTRODUCTION

Since its passage in 1990, the Americans With Disabilities Act (ADA) has been contentious and controversial. In recent years, the Supreme Court and the lower courts have greatly limited the scope of this Act, especially in the employment arena. Employers nearly always prevail in these cases, for a variety of reasons, such as lack of proof that the plaintiff was a Qualified Individual With a Disability (QIWD), suffered adverse employment action, sought reasonable accommodation, and/or that reasonable accommodation would have been possible without undue burden on the employer.

Perhaps the suit can be dismissed because it was brought against an employer who is not subject to the ADA, or on grounds of untimeliness.

The ADA starts at 42 U.S.C. § 12101 (regulations at 29 C.F.R. § 1630.1). Title I is the employment title; Title II deals with public services (i.e., provided by government); Title III with public accommodations, and Title IV with miscellaneous issues, some of which relate to employment.

Major legislation, the ADA Amendments Act of 2008, or ADAAA, was passed in 2008 to clarify some disputed ADA issues, and reverse some of the harsher effects of recent Supreme Court precedents. See § 36.03, below.

July 26, 2015 was the 25th anniversary of the ADA. For the first 15 years or so, litigation revolved around whether someone was a QIWD. In 2008, the ADAAA significantly expanded the class of QIWDs, shifting the emphasis to the interactive process. Employers are probably safer in assuming that an employee who mentions a condition affecting ability to work has a disability. The employer should be prepared to engage in an interactive process of looking for accommodations. The employer's actions must be documented; so must reasons why accommodation is not available. Employers must be flexible, considering individual needs. If an employee exhausts the Family and Medical Leave Act (FMLA) leave but is still unable to return to work, the employer should consider ADA issues before firing the employee. Additional leave, or a new job consistent with the employee's restrictions, might be a reasonable accommodation. Similar considerations come into play for employees injured at work who receive Workers' Compensation benefits and who have restrictions that prevent them from returning to their previous jobs. [Christopher G. Ward, *25 Years of the ADA: Five Tips for ADA Compliance*, Foley & Lardner LLP (Aug. 3, 2015), available at Lexology.com]

On December 1, 2015, for World AIDS Day, the Equal Employment Opportunity Commission (EEOC) issued two documents about ADA issues for HIV/AIDS patients. "Living With HIV Infection: Your Legal Rights in the Workplace Under the ADA," says that job applicants and employees are protected from employment discrimination and harassment based on HIV status and are entitled to reasonable accommodations at work. In most situations, the employee can keep HIV status private. Employers are forbidden to reject applicants, terminate employees, or deny promotion purely based on HIV status, and objective evidence is required to assert a defense of safety risk or inability to perform essential functions. The EEOC's examples of reasonable accommodation include changes in work and break schedules, unpaid time off, and working from home. [<http://www.eeoc.gov/eeoc/newsroom/release/12-1-15.cfm> (last accessed Mar. 13, 2017); see Matthew C. Luzadder and Janine N. Fletcher, *EEOC Issues Guidance Directed Specifically to HIV Positive Employees and Their Physicians*, Kelley Drye & Warren LLP (Jan. 7, 2016), available at Lexology.com]

§ 36.02   REACH AND RANGE OF ADA TITLE I

According to 42 U.S.C. § 12101, Congress went on record that the over 43 million employees with disabilities (a number that is increasing as the population ages) have a history of social alienation and discrimination in important areas such as work, housing, public accommodations, health services, and education. Congress declared that people with disabilities are a minority group that has suffered discrimination—and that our national goal in dealing with people with disabilities should be "to assure equality of opportunity, full participation, independent living, and economic self sufficiency." The legislative purpose is given as providing "clear, strong, consistent, enforceable standards addressing discrimination against individuals with disabilities."

A "covered entity," as defined by 42 U.S.C. § 12111(2), means an employer, an employment agency, a union, or a joint labor-management committee.

Only employers who have at least 15 employees in each working day in each of 20 or more weeks in the current or preceding year are subject to the ADA. [42 U.S.C. § 12111(5)]

In an April 22, 2003, decision, the Supreme Court ruled that four physicians who were shareholders and directors of a medical PC were probably not "employees," using the economic reality test. The doctors controlled business operations; they were not subject to the control of others. If so, the professional corporation had fewer than 15 "employees," and the PC's bookkeeper could not bring suit under the ADA, whether or not it was true that she was terminated because of disability. [*Clackamas Gastroenterology Assocs., PC v. Wells*, 538 U.S. 440 (2003)]

For ADA (and Rehab Act and Title VII) purposes, the Seventh Circuit held that a doctor who was a shareholder and board member of a small medical professional corporation was an employer, not an employee, of the corporation. The Seventh Circuit used six common-law factors related to control over the person's work to determine that she was not an employee. She was not supervised; all the doctors had equal voting power; and profits and losses were shared equally. [*Bluestein v. Cent. Wis. Anesthesiology*, 769 F.3d 944 (7th Cir. 2014)]

An employer with fewer than 15 employees, although exempt under the ADA, can be sued under the Rehabilitation Act. [*Schrader v. Fred A. Ray, MD PC*, 296 F.3d 968 (10th Cir. 2002)]

Individuals are nearly always exempt from being sued under antidiscrimination suits (only the employer company is liable). *Alberte v. Anew Health Care Services* [588 N.W.2d 298 (Wis. App. 1998)] permits an ADA suit against an individual who was president, administrator, and 47.5% shareholder in a company accused of disability discrimination. In this reading, the president was the company's agent and personally liable for both compensatory and punitive damages. But this ruling is an anomaly. Far more typically, in mid-2007, the Eleventh Circuit held that individuals cannot be sued for violating the ADA's ban on retaliation in employment, nor under the Florida state statute that forbids HIV/AIDS discrimination. [*Albra v. Advan, Inc.*, 490 F.3d 826 (11th Cir. 2007)]

A U.S. citizen who works outside the United States can count as an employee entitled to protection under the ADA. [42 U.S.C. § 12111(4)] However, it is not unlawful for a workplace outside the United States to comply with local law, even if the result is discrimination. Foreign operations of a foreign company that is not controlled by an American employer are exempt from the ADA. [42 U.S.C. § 12112(c)]

Section 12115 requires employers to post notices of ADA rights "in an accessible format" in the workplace.

The ADA does not invalidate or limit the remedies, rights, and procedures of any state or federal law that provides additional protection of the rights of individuals with disabilities. [42 U.S.C. § 12201]

"Mixed-motive" cases (where disability discrimination is alleged to be only one factor in the employer's decision) can be brought in some circuits, where it is not necessary for the plaintiff to allege that the employer was solely motivated by disability discrimination. [*McNely v. Ocala Star-Banner Corp.*, 99 F.3d 1068 (11th Cir. 1996)] However, the Sixth Circuit does not allow mixed-motive cases: to sue there, the plaintiff must allege that disability must have been the sole cause for the employment decision. [*Hedrick v. W. Reserve Care Sys.*, 355 F.3d 444 (6th Cir. 2004)] On the other hand, the Ninth Circuit does permit mixed-motive ADA cases. [*Head v. Glacier Nw.*, 413 F.3d 1053 (9th Cir. 2005)]

Most of the circuits allow hostile environment claims in the ADA context, because the ADA uses the same language as Title VII "terms, conditions and privileges of employment" so the concept of the hostile work environment has been extended to cover the ADA as well as Title VII. [*Shaver v. Indep. Stave Co.*, 350 F.3d 716 (8th Cir. 2003); *Flowers v. S. Reg'l Physician Servs. Inc.*, 247 F.3d 229 (5th Cir. 2001); *Fox v. Gen. Motors Corp.*, 247 F.3d 169 (4th Cir. 2001)]

To win a hostile environment suit, the plaintiff must show that he or she is a member of the protected group; that unwelcome harassment occurred; that it resulted from membership in the protected class; and it was severe enough to affect the terms, conditions, or privileges of employment. [*Reedy v. Quebecor Printing Eagle, Inc.*, 333 F.3d 906 (8th Cir. 2003)]

In the *Shaver* case, the plaintiff had severe epileptic seizures, and at least some of his colleagues treated him as stupid or mentally ill for that reason or because he had had brain surgery resulting in removal of part of his skull. There is evidence that he was taunted, but the Eighth Circuit concluded that the verbal harassment was not severe enough to rise to the level of an objectively hostile work environment. The plaintiff was upset, but not threatened or traumatized.

Much later, the Eleventh Circuit affirmed summary judgment for McDonald's in a hostile environment case, despite undisputed evidence that the manager joked about an employee's deformed eye "every day" and refused to stop calling him "cockeyed" despite the employee's protests. The manager said "if you don't like it, go home" and made him clock out. The employee complained to McDonalds' district manager. The Eleventh Circuit said that McDonald's was not liable, because its anti-discrimination policy strictly prohibited disability-based harassment and retaliation. The Eleventh Circuit said that the plaintiff failed to comply with the policy: the district manager was not designated to receive complaints. Because the manager was the harasser, a reasonable employee would have contacted the McDonald's HR department. [*Cooper v. CLP Corp.*, No. 16-10536, 2017 U.S. App. LEXIS 2300 (11th Cir. Feb. 9, 2017); see Marjory D. Robertson, *No ADA Hostile Environment Where Boss Made Fun of Employee's Lazy Eye*, Sun Life Financial (Feb. 14, 2017), available at Lexology.com]

Although Congress specifically stated in 42 U.S.C. § 12202 that states are NOT immune from ADA suits, the Supreme Court held in 2001 that Congress had no right to abrogate the states' "sovereign immunity" (freedom from being sued) with respect to ADA Title I cases that seek money damages rather than injunctions, because there was no documentation of a past history of disability discrimination perpetrated by the states themselves. [See *Bd. of Trs. of the Univ. of Ala. v. Garrett*, 531 U.S. 356 (2001)]

In 2002, the Supreme Court held that punitive damages are not available in a suit for discrimination against disability discrimination committed by a public body, or by an agency that receives federal funding. [*Barnes v. Gorman*, 536 U.S. 181 (2002)] The Fifth Circuit later ruled that Congress did not properly abrogate the states' sovereign immunity with respect to ADA Title II either [*Reickenbacker v. Foster*, 274 F.3d 974 (5th Cir. 2001)], and the Second Circuit agrees. [*Garcia v. SUNY Health Scis. Ctr.*, 280 F.3d 98 (2d Cir. 2001)] *Gibson v. Ark. Dep't of Corrs.* [265 F.3d 718 (8th Cir. 2001)] says that although the states themselves are immune from suits for damages under the ADA, state officials can be sued to get prospective injunctive relief. It has also been held that states can be held liable for retaliation against employees who exercise ADA rights. [*Roberts v. Pa. Dep't of Pub. Welfare*, 199 F. Supp. 2d 249 (E.D. Pa. 2002). See Shannon P. Duffy, *States Not Immune from ADA Retaliation Suits*, The Legal Intelligencer (Feb. 27, 2002) (law.com)]

However, the Fifth Circuit ruled that the Eleventh Amendment does not give the states immunity against ADA suits brought by the United States itself seeking victim-specific relief for individuals. In this situation, the individuals themselves would not be able to sue—but one consequence of a state ratifying the U.S. Constitution is consent to being sued by the United States itself and by other states. [*United States v. Miss. Dep't of Pub. Safety*, 321 F.3d 495 (5th Cir. 2003)]

§ 36.03   FORBIDDEN DISCRIMINATION

It is unlawful to discriminate against a qualified individual with a disability (QIWD) because of that person's disability, with respect to the terms, conditions, and privileges of employment: e.g., job application, hiring, promotion, discharge, compensation, and training. [See 42 U.S.C. § 12112.]

Section 12112 goes on to enumerate seven types of action that constitute disability discrimination:

- Limiting, segregating, or classifying applicants or employees in ways that affect their opportunities, because of disability;

- Entering into a relationship (for instance, with an employment agency) that results in disability discrimination;

- Using standards, criteria, or methods of administration that either discriminate or perpetuate discrimination by another party under the same administrative control (e.g., another division in the same company);

- Denying jobs or benefits to a qualified person who has a relationship or association with someone else who has a disability (e.g., refusing to hire someone merely because he or she is married to a person with a disability who has high medical bills that might result in higher employee group health plan (EGHP) premiums);

- Failing to make a reasonable accommodation to known physical or mental limitations of an employee or applicant who is a QIWD—unless the accommodation would work undue hardship on the employer; or denying employment opportunities to QIWDs if the denial is based on the need to accommodate;

- Using employment tests or other standards or criteria that screen out people with disabilities—but a defense is available for job-related measures that are consistent with business necessity;

- Using tests that are biased by an applicant's or employee's impairment (speech difficulties, for instance) and therefore fail to reflect the job aptitudes that the test is supposed to assess.

It is also unlawful to retaliate against anyone who opposed any act of disability discrimination, or who made a charge, testified, assisted, or participated in an investigation, administrative proceeding, or court case. It is unlawful to interfere with the ADA investigation process, or to "coerce, intimidate, threaten, or interfere with" anyone because of enforcement of ADA rights. [42 U.S.C. § 12203]

The ADA Amendments Act of 2008 (ADAAA; Pub. L. No. 110-325) was passed to reverse various Supreme Court decisions that made it very difficult for ADA claims to succeed because they ruled that a variety of impairments were not

ADA "disabilities." As a result of the ADAAA, the central question is not whether the plaintiff has a disability, but whether the employer reasonably accommodated disabled applicants and employees.

The ADAAA adds two lists of major life activities, although the statute specifies that these lists are illustrative, not comprehensive. Major activities of daily living include self-care, manual tasks, seeing, hearing, eating, standing, walking, sleeping, breathing, working, concentrating, thinking, learning, and communicating. The second list is of major body systems (e.g., circulatory, digestive, excretory, reproductive) whose impairment can constitute a disability. An impairment is considered a disability even if it is episodic or in remission, as long as it substantially limits a major life activity during a relapse.

The definition of being "regarded as" having a disability is expanded to forbid employers to discriminate based on their perception of a mental or physical impairment—whether or not the plaintiff can establish that the impairment actually limits or is perceived to substantially limit a major life activity. A "regarded as" claim cannot be based on a transitory impairment—one that actually lasts, or is expected to last, six months or less. Employers do not have a duty to provide reasonable accommodation for a perceived disability. Except for ordinary glasses and contact lenses, mitigating measures are not taken into account in determining whether a person has a disability. [EEOC Notice *Concerning the Americans with Disabilities Act (ADA) Amendments Act of 2008*, <http://www.eeoc.gov/ada/amendments_notice.html> (undated, but refers to EEOC regulations taking effect March 25, 2011; last accessed Mar. 13, 2017). See § 36.04[F] for EEOC guidance about the ADAAA.]

[A] Association

The ADA also forbids discrimination in fringe benefits on the basis of an employee's relationship to or association with a person who has a disability.

The EEOC says that the ADA association provisions forbid employers to discriminate based on stereotyping of people who associate with someone who has a disability: e.g., that a person whose child has a disability will take excessive time off work or that a person who worked or lives with HIV-positive people will develop AIDS. The relationship does not have to be familial, as long as the employer used the relationship to take adverse action. The EEOC does not treat the belief that the person's association with a person with a disability will increase the company's health insurance costs as a legitimate business motivation—but does not require employers to enhance their insurance program to make it more disability-friendly. Employees who seek leave to care for family members with a disability must be treated equally with employees who seek leave for other reasons. [EEOC, *Questions and Answers About the Association Provision of the Americans with Disabilities Act*, <http://www.eeoc.gov/facts/association_ada.html> (Feb. 2, 2011) (last accessed Mar. 13, 2017)]

Trujillo v. PacifiCorp., 524 F.3d 1149 (10th Cir. 2008), allowed an ADA association discrimination suit to proceed where a married couple were terminated, allegedly for falsifying their time records. According to the plaintiffs, they were fired because their son's terminal illness was very costly for the employer's self-insured medical plan.

EEOC Enforcement Guidance published in mid-2007 points out that, although employees who are caregivers for children or elderly or disabled family members are not entitled to separate protection against discrimination, subjecting a caregiver employee to negative employment actions could violate the ADA's ban on discrimination on the basis of association with a person with a disability. [EEOC Enforcement Guidance: *Unlawful Disparate Treatment of Workers with Caregiving Responsibilities* Number 915.002, <http://www.eeoc.gov/policy/docs/caregiving.html> (updated Feb. 8, 2011) (last accessed Mar. 13, 2017). See also EEOC, *Employer Best Practices for Workers with Caregiving Responsibilities*, <http://www.eeoc.gov/policy/docs/caregiver-best-practices.html> (Jan. 19, 2011) (last accessed Mar. 13, 2017).]

[B] Retaliation

As Chapters 34 and 41 show, retaliation charges represent a major portion of the EEOC's caseload and, in some instances, a plaintiff will succeed on a retaliation charge even though the underlying discrimination allegation is dismissed.

In mid-2016, the EEOC released Enforcement Guidance on Retaliation and Related Issues, superseding at last the provisions of the 1998 Compliance Manual. The guidance covers the ADA as well as many other discrimination statutes. The guidance also covers ADA interference, the coercion, threats, etc., deployed to prevent employees from exercising ADA rights. The ADA's interference provision is broader than the anti-retaliation provision, so it covers conduct that is not materially adverse enough to constitute retaliation. However, the EEOC says that the interference provision requires conduct that is reasonably likely to interfere with ADA rights: for example, a policy that limits the amount of leave an employee can take, with no exceptions in any circumstances. [<https://www.eeoc.gov/laws/guidance/retaliation-guidance.cfm?utm_content=&utm_medium=email&utm_name=&utm_source=govdelivery&utm_term=>. Derek G. Barella et. al., *EEOC Issues Final Guidance on Employer Retaliation*, Winston & Strawn LLP (Sept. 1, 2016), available at Lexology.com]

Two early 2017 retaliation cases were dismissed on the grounds that the employees failed to show that they were qualified individuals, either for failure to show disability or for failure to prove that a reasonable accommodation was available. This was a surprising result, because ADA plaintiffs more frequently prevail on retaliation than on discrimination charges:

- Summary judgment for the employer was upheld because the plaintiff failed to show that she was qualified or that accommodation was possible that would allow her to perform the essential functions of the job [*Bagwell v. Morgan Cnty. Comm'n,* No. 15-15274 , 2017 U.S. App. LEXIS 894 (11th Cir. Jan. 18, 2017);

- A retaliation claim was dismissed for failure to allege a "plausible disability." The plaintiff said that bulging disks, muscle spasms, and other symptoms caused chronic pain that limited her ability to work and exercise, but the district court held that it is not enough that the plaintiff's condition makes work more difficult. [*Smith v. Constellation Brands, Inc.,* No. 3:16-cv-04101, 2017 U.S. Dist. LEXIS 8368 (N.D. Cal. Jan. 19, 2017)]

For cases in which the plaintiff prevailed, see, for example:

- An ADA retaliation claim does not require that the plaintiff actually be disabled, if the plaintiff had a good-faith belief that he or she was disabled. *Foster v. Mountain Coal,* 830 F.3d 1178 (10th Cir. 2016); *Gavurnik v. Hope Properties,* No. 2:16-cv-00633. (E.D. Pa. Jan. 3, 2017); *Jones v Brennan,* Case No. 16-CV-0049-CVE-FHM, 2016 U.S. Dist. LEXIS 168309 (N.D. Okla. Dec. 6, 2016). But see *Madrigal v. Senior Aerospace SSP,* 2:16-cv-01883-CAS(SSx), 2016 U.S. Dist. LEXIS 105836 (C.D. Cal. Aug. 9, 2016), holding that actual disability may be required for retaliation claims under California law. [Marjory D. Robertson, *Can a Non-Disabled Employee Win on an ADA Retaliation Claim?,* Sun Life Financial Inc (Jan. 24, 2017), available at Lexology.com]

§ 36.04 DEFINING "DISABILITY"

[A] Generally

According to 42 U.S.C. § 12102, there are three forms of disability. The first is a physical or mental impairment that substantially limits an individual's major life activity(ies). The second is a record of such impairment. The third is being regarded as having such an impairment, even if this perception is inaccurate.

According to the statute, transvestism is not a disability [42 U.S.C. § 12209], nor are homosexuality, bisexuality, transsexualism, pedophilia, exhibitionism, gender identity disorders, compulsive gambling, kleptomania, pyromania, or current use of illegal drugs. [42 U.S.C. § 12211]

In 1989, when the ADA was adopted, so-called "immoral" behavior like "sexual behavior disorders," e.g., transexuality, was excluded from coverage. Kate Lynn Blatt, a transwoman who was fired by Cabela's, brought an ADA (and Title VII) suit, challenging the constitutionality of excluding transpersons from

ADA coverage. [Saranac Hale Spencer, *Transgender Woman Challenges Constitutionality of ADA Exclusion*, The Legal Intelligencer (Jan. 22, 2015), available at Lexology.com. In 2017, the employer's motion to dismiss the case was denied. Blatt argued that ADA § 12111's exclusion of sexual orientation and sexual identity from coverage deprived her of equal protection of the law. The District Court for the Eastern District of Pennsylvania decided to avoid constitutional questions about equal protection. The district court decided that the ADA is a remedial statute that should be interpreted broadly. The court narrowly read the § 12111 exclusion as limited to the fact of identifying with another sex. The district court ruled that the plaintiff's gender dysphoria might be covered by the ADA as a disability interfering with life activities such as work, reproduction, and interacting with other people. [*Blatt v. Cabela's Retail, Inc.*, No. 5:14-cv-04822 (E.D. Pa. May 18, 2017); see Nathaniel M. Glasser and Kate B. Rhodes, *Federal Court Rules Gender Dysphoria May Be Disability Under ADA*, Epstein Becker Green (June 9, 2017), available t Lexology.com] See § 34.06[D] for discussion of regulations and cases holding that gender identity is not only not a disability, but also it is a category about which discrimination is forbidden.]

A QIWD is defined by 42 U.S.C. § 12111(8) as one who can perform the essential functions of the job (with or without accommodation). The employer's determination about which functions of a job are essential is entitled to consideration. Written job descriptions used in advertising or job interviews are considered evidence of the essential functions of the job. In other words, these descriptions must be drafted with care! [Linda B. Hollinshead, *Do I Really Need to Update That Job Description? Failing to Do So May Complicate ADA Litigation*, Duane Morris LLP (Oct. 26, 2015), available at Lexology.com]

The Fifth, Sixth, Seventh, and Eighth Circuits have all held that it does not violate the ADA to fire a driver who is unable to provide a Department of Transportation (DOT) medical certification. A 2016 Fifth Circuit case involves a driver who fainted at home and then was diagnosed with a heart condition. DOT certification is required to be a commercial driver, so losing the certification means ceasing to be a qualified employee. [*Williams v. J.B. Hunt Trans., Inc.*, No. 15-20610 (5th Cir. June 20, 2016); see Michael C. Wilhelm, *Can a Driver Who Does Not Satisfy DOT Standards Win an ADA Claim?*, Briggs and Morgan (June 27, 2016), available at Lexology.com]

The EEOC's position is that determining which functions are essential to a job is a complex process involving several factors, e.g.:

- Expertise or skill needed to do that task;
- Other employees available to perform that function (as individuals or as a team);
- If that function is the entire rationale of the job;
- Time spent on that particular function;

- Qualifications of people who held the same job in the past;

- What would happen if the individual did not perform the function in question;

- What the Collective Bargaining Agreement (if there is one) says about the function as it relates to the job.

The Fourth Circuit held that even an impairment expected to last less than six months can be severely limiting (in this case, multiple leg fractures and tendon damage that kept the plaintiff from walking for seven months). The district court dismissed the case, on the grounds that the ADA does not cover temporary disabilities and he could have worked with a wheelchair. The Fourth Circuit reversed, stating that the district court should have considered whether the plaintiff was substantially limited before asking whether he could work with or without accommodation. [*Summers v. Altarum Inst.*, 730 F.3d 325 (4th Cir. 2014)]

The Ninth Circuit ruled that a police officer with ADHD did not have a disability as defined by the ADAAA. Although a federal jury awarded him more than $500,000 in compensatory damages, back pay, front pay, and attorneys' fees when he was placed on administrative leave after being fired for arrogance, bullying, and inability to work in a team, the Ninth Circuit reversed, holding that no reasonable jury could have found substantial limitation in Weaving's ability to work or interact. Mere trouble getting along with co-workers is not a substantial limitation, and the record showed the plaintiff's problems were almost entirely with co-workers and subordinates, not his supervisors. [*Weaving v. City of Hillsboro*, 763 F.3d 1106 (9th Cir. 2014)]

In contrast, the Fourth Circuit said Jacobs could take her ADA case to a jury. She was fired after disclosing that she had social anxiety disorder and asking for the accommodation of a reassigned with less direct interaction with the public. She was originally hired as an office assistant, and her job consisted mostly of filing and microfilming. After less than a month, she was promoted to be a deputy clerk in the criminal division, involving public interaction, but was fired when she disclosed her social anxiety disorder and said she did not want to work at the front desk. The Fourth Circuit agreed with the EEOC that interacting with other people is a major life activity. Jacobs was fired without any discipline, and there was no attempt at accommodation after she revealed her diagnosis. [*Jacobs v. N.C. Administrative Office of the Courts*, 780 F.3d 562 (4th Cir. 2015)]

An Autozone parts sales manager was terminated because of her permanent 15-pound lifting restriction. The Seventh Circuit ruled that a rational jury could have concluded that lifting (which was mentioned in the published job description) was an essential function. Other parts sales managers testified that lifting was required. The Seventh Circuit held that the EEOC was not entitled to a "team concept" jury instruction arguing that co-workers could have lifted heavy items for the plaintiff. [*EEOC v. Autozone, Inc.*, 809 F.3d 916 (7th Cir., 2016); see Gerald L. Maatman, Jr., and Howard M. Wexler, *Seventh Circuit Slams the "Brakes" on the EEOC's Appeal of AutoZone ADA Defeat*, Seyfarth Shaw LLP (Jan. 8, 2016), available at Lexology.com; Tina A. Syring, *Permanent Lifting Restrictions and the ADA*, Barnes & Thornburg LLP (Jan. 8, 2016), available at Lexology .com]

The Seventh Circuit reversed dismissal of an ADA suit and remanded to the jury. The plaintiff had had a hysterectomy and was cleared to return to work after eight weeks—but not to push more than 20 pounds (a limitation that was later increased to 50 pounds). She was a hairdresser in a nursing home and could no longer push the residents' wheelchairs to the beauty shop, which the facility deemed to be an essential function of the job. The plaintiff offered to transfer to the laundry department, but was not permitted to do so, so she quit. In an opinion that seemed to suggest that having another employee push wheelchairs could be a reasonable accommodation, the Seventh Circuit said that the jury had to decide fact issues such as the percentage of time spent transporting residents versus doing their hair; if transport was essential to being a hairdresser; and if assigning someone else to transport residents would create problems for the residents. [*Kauffman v. Petersen Health Care, d/b/a Mason Point*, 769 F.3d 958 (7th Cir. 2014)]

In another case involving a health worker (this time a nurse's aide), the District Court for the Northern District of Oklahoma held in mid-2017 that a pregnant plaintiff's 25-pound lifting restriction, taken by itself, did not establish a valid ADA claim when she did not plead that she had an abnormal or high-risk pregnancy. [*LaCount v. South Lewis SHOPCO, LLC*, No. 16-CV-0545-CVE-TLW (N.D. Okla. May 5, 2017); see Catherine A. Cano, *Oklahoma Case Serves as Reminder That Pregnancy Alone, Without More, Is Not an ADA Disability*, Jackson Lewis PC (May 11, 2017), available at Lexology.com]

In June 1999, the Supreme Court decided three major employment-related cases, concluding that an individual is not disabled if the condition has been corrected, e.g., through medication or an assistive device. [*Murphy v. United Parcel Serv.*, 527 U.S. 516 (1999); *Sutton v. United Air Lines*, 527 U.S. 471 (1999); *Albertsons v. Kirkingburg*, 527 U.S. 555 (1999)] The ADAAA, however, says that ordinary eyeglasses and contact lenses are the only ameliorative measure that can be considered in determining whether a person has an ADA disability.

Courts differ in their attitude toward obesity as a disability.

The Eighth Circuit held that it did not violate the ADA for a trucking company to require drivers whose Body Mass Index (BMI) is 35 or over to undergo sleep studies to see if they have sleep apnea—a condition that could make them fall asleep at the wheel. The requirement was adopted based on recommendations from two advisory committee to the Department of Transportation, who said that the program could reduce accident rates. The Eighth Circuit held that business necessity is present if the employer can show legitimate non-discriminatory reasons to doubt the plaintiff's ability to perform job functions. The plaintiff said that he had no documented sleep issues at work, but the Eighth Circuit's position was that his statement did not prove he did not have sleep apnea. [*Parker v. Crete*

Carrier Corp., 839 F.3d 717 (8th Cir. 2016); see Sarah Smith Kuehnel, Erin E. Williams and Andrew P. Burnside, *The Eighth Circuit & the ADA, Part I: Court Tips the Scale in Employer's Favor in Suit Challenging Sleep Test for Overweight Workers*, Ogletree Deakins (Oct. 31, 2016), available at Lexology.com]

EEOC regulations say that body weight that is above or below the normal range, or that is the product of a physiological disorder, can be an impairment, and has litigated on this basis. In 2006, the Sixth Circuit held, in *EEOC v. Watkins Motor Lines Inc.*, that a plaintiff who charged that he was fired because the employer perceived his weight was a disability did not identify an underlying physiological disorder that made him fat, so he could not show he was regarded as impaired.

The Eighth Circuit joined the Second and Sixth Circuits in holding that obesity in and of itself will not support an ADA claim or disability discrimination or "regarded as" discrimination. The plaintiff was not hired as a machinist because his Body Mass Index was at least 40.4 and the company policy was not to hire anyone with a BMI of 40 or more for this safety-sensitive position. The Eighth Circuit held that overweight is only an ADA impairment if it is not only outside the normal range but the result of a physiological disorder. [*Morriss v. BNSF Ry. Co.*, 817 F.3d 1104 (8th Cir. 2016); certiorari was denied in October; see Royal PC, *Supreme Court Declines to Hear Case on Whether Obesity Is Covered by the ADA* (Oct. 4, 2016), available at Lexology.com]

The District Court for the District of Arizona held in early 2017 that for a regarded-as claim, the plaintiff must allege that the employer wrongfully believed that the employee had an impairment that would constitute a covered disability and the plaintiff's knee and joint problems and trouble climbing and bending did not qualify. The employer had a legitimate, non-discriminatory reason to terminate the plaintiff: he falsely reported carrying out certain maintenance tasks that he could not handle because he was unable to climb. The plaintiff claimed ADA interference in that he had informed the employer that he would need surgery in several months, but the district court said that discharge for misconduct is permissible even if a person has requested leave. [*Valtierra v. Medtronic Inc.*, No. CV-15-865-PHX-SMM, 2017 U.S. Dist. LEXIS 15471(D. Ariz. Feb. 3, 2017); see Marjory D. Robertson, *Is Morbid Obesity a Disability Under the ADA? Courts Say No*, Sun Life Financial Inc (Feb. 7, 2017), available at Lexology.com]

[B] Attendance

The question is often raised whether predictable, regular attendance is a fundamental job qualification. If it is, then it does not violate the ADA to fire, refuse to hire, etc., a person who cannot satisfy attendance requirements because of disability. [See, e.g., *EEOC v. Yellow Freight Sys., Inc.*, 253 F.3d 943 (7th Cir. 2001) (granting an unlimited number of sick days is not a reasonable accommodation)] A person whose physical or mental condition precludes working more than 40 hours a week has been held not to be ADA disabled, [*Tardie v. Rehabilitation Hosp. of R.I.*, 168 F.3d 538 (1st Cir. 1999)] given that there are many jobs available that do not require a commitment of over 40 hours a week. Also see *Davis v. Florida. Power & Light* [205 F.3d 1301 (11th Cir. 2000)] finding that mandatory overtime was an essential function of the job, and it would violate the collective bargaining agreement to provide a no-overtime or selective-overtime arrangement for a disabled worker.

If a job requires especially long hours (e.g., 50–60 a week), this should be reflected in the job description. The Fourth Circuit held in 2012 that a maintenance engineer who was able to work eight hours a day, but could not work overtime or rotating shifts, was not disabled. He received long-term disability benefits from May to October 2004, then returned to work; his employer and the union negotiated a new day-shift job with base hours of eight hours a day rather than 10. The First, Third, Fifth, and Eighth Circuits have all ruled that an employee who can work 40 hours a week but not overtime is not substantially limited for ADA purposes. [*Boitnott v. Corning Inc.*, 669 F.3d 172 (4th Cir. 2012)]

The Second Circuit ruled in late 2013 that the defendant employer could not treat regular attendance as an essential job function in all ADA cases. Not only did the employer permit one-hour flextime at the beginning of the workday, but also for years the plaintiff had been given additional leeway in her start time, and she was willing to work late to make up for lost time. [*McMillan v. City of New York*, 711 F.3d 120 (2d Cir. 2013)]

The Sixth Circuit affirmed summary judgment for the employer in early 2017. A customer service representative who suffered from depression and anxiety requested various accommodations, such as a flexible start time, breaks during the day, and leave until she completed an eight-week treatment program. The Sixth Circuit ruled that attendance is an essential function, particularly for interactive jobs like being a customer service representative. The plaintiff admitted that she could not perform her job during an attack, so a flexible start time and multiple breaks would not be reasonable accommodations. The eight-week leave was unreasonable, even though her doctor estimated that she could return to work at that time. The doctor's return date was not probative, especially since the plaintiff had taken several leaves without her condition improving. [*Williams v. AT&T Mobility Servs.*, 847 F.3d 384 (6th Cir. 2017); see Marjory D. Robertson, *Employee with Depression & Panic Attacks Not Entitled to ADA Accommodations,* Sun Life Financial Inc. (Jan. 30, 2017), available at Lexology.com]

The Fifth Circuit held that working on-site was an essential part of a litigator's job [*Credeur v. State of La.,* No. 16-30658 (5th Cir. June 23, 2017); see George M. Patterson, *Fifth Circuit Holds Reporting to Work Regularly Is Essential Function of Attorney's Job Under the ADA,* Mintz Levin Cohn Ferris Glovsky and Popeo PC (July 12, 2017), available at Lexology.com]

The Tenth Circuit held that a temporary receptionist's request for indefinite leave was not a reasonable accommodation: the essential functions of the job included being present at the reception desk. It was legitimate for the employer to consider her status as a temporary worker. [*Punt v. Kelly Servs.,* No. 16-1026 (10th Cir. July 6, 2017); see Nina M. Markey and Marc D. Esterow, *Tenth Circuit Affirms Staffing Company Win in Reasonable Accommodation Suit,* Littler Mendelson PC (Aug. 3, 2017), available at Lexology.com]

[C] Infertility

A 1996 case says that reproduction is not a major life activity, but in 1997, the Northern District of Illinois disagreed, even though reproduction does not directly affect employment. [Compare *Krauel v. Iowa Methodist Med. Ctr.,* 95 F.3d 674 (8th Cir. 1996), with *Erickson v. Bd. of Governors, Nw. Ill. Univ.,* 911 F. Supp. 316 (N.D. Ill. 1997), *later proceedings,* 207 F.3d 945 (7th Cir. 2000)]

The plaintiff in *Saks v. Franklin Covey Co.* [117 F. Supp. 2d 318 (S.D.N.Y. 2000)] was covered by a self-insured health plan that excluded "surgical impregnation procedures." She sued under Title VII, the ADA, and the Pregnancy Discrimination Act. The court ruled that infertility might be a disability, because it interferes with the major life activity of procreation.

However, the ADA claim was dismissed because all employees got the same coverage; infertile employees were not singled out for inferior coverage of reproductive services. The plan also qualified for the safe harbor for bona fide employee benefit plans. The Title VII claim failed because both male and female infertility were excluded. Surgical procedures were excluded for both female employees and wives of male employees. The PDA claim failed because infertility treatments were equally unavailable to pregnant and nonpregnant employees and beneficiaries.

The Second Circuit affirmed the dismissal in 2003 [*Saks v. Franklin Covey Co.,* 316 F.3d 337 (2d Cir. 2003)], although using a slightly different rationale. The District Court looked at the question of whether all employees have equal access to plan benefits. The Second Circuit said that this standard, often used in ADA cases, was wrong because this was really a Title VII case. Therefore, the correct standard is whether sex-specific conditions exist. If they do, the question becomes whether excluding coverage for those conditions results in a plan with inferior coverage for one sex.

In 2008, the Seventh Circuit held that an employee terminated for excessive absences related to fertility treatment could assert a Title VII case because the employee was fired for a gender-specific characteristic of childbearing capacity, rather than the gender-neutral characteristic of infertility. [*Hall v. Nalco,* 534 F.3d 644 (7th Cir 2008); see Jennifer Gonzalez, *Infertility Issues in the Workplace,* Hall Render Killian Heath & Lyman PC (Aug. 2, 2016), available at Lexology.com]

According to the Northern District of Illinois, it did not violate the ADA to refuse to pay for infertility treatment for an employee's spouse, because the law does not extend to dependents of an employee if the dependents do not perform services for the employer. [*Niemeier v. Tri-State Fire Prot. Dist.*, 2000 U.S. Dist. LEXIS 12621 (N.D. Ill. Aug. 24, 2000)] Furthermore, non-employees can't sue the employer under Title VII or the PDA. The employee had standing (the legal right to pursue the PDA claim), but the claim itself was invalid, because the plan did not cover fertility treatment for either sex.

[D]   Psychiatric Disability

ADA regulations [29 C.F.R. § 1630.2(h)(2)] define mental impairment to include developmental disability, learning disabilities, organic brain syndrome, and neurological disease, as well as mental or psychological disorders. The examples given by the EEOC are major depression, bipolar disorder, panic disorder, obsessive-compulsive disorder, post-traumatic stress disorder, schizophrenia, and personality disorders.

The psychiatric profession's official compendium, the Diagnostic and Statistical Manual of Mental Disorders (DSM), is the first step in identifying mental disorders. However, certain disorders are included in the DSM but excluded from ADA coverage—for instance, current drug and alcohol abuse, compulsive gambling, certain sexual disorders, and kleptomania.

The EEOC reported that it received approximately 5,000 charges relating to mental health conditions in 2016, and mental health charges make up about 5% of charges. Its resource document, *Depression, PTSD, and Other Mental Health Conditions in the Workplace*, issued December 12, 2016, is a Q&A about employee rights. It deals with the definition of discrimination, the direct threat defense, essential functions of a job, and the privacy of mental health information. Possible accommodations include schedule changes, quiet office space, telecommuting, and changes in supervision. The EEOC's position is that employers should not ask about mental health unless the employee asks for accommodation; after a job offer has been made, but only if everyone in the same job category is asked the same question; if the employer has a disability affirmative action program; or if there is objective evidence that a current employee poses a safety risk or is unable to perform the job. The EEOC says a condition can be substantially limiting (thereby requiring accommodation) if it makes activities harder to perform or more time-consuming. [<https://www.eeoc.gov/eeoc/publications/mental_health.cfm>; Laura Lawless Robertson, *EEOC Issues New Guidance on the Rights of Applicants and Employees with Mental Health Conditions*, Squire Patton Boggs (Dec. 14, 2016), available at Lexology.com; Jessica A. Lordi and Janica Pierce Tucker, *EEOC Guidance on the Rights of Employees with Mental Health Conditions*, Taft Stettinius & Hollister LLP (Jan. 17, 2017), available at Lexology.com]

Guidance was also furnished on the role of mental health providers in the reasonable accommodation process. Under this approach, a mental health condition qualifies for accommodation if it substantially limits one or more major life activities, such as communicating, concentrating, eating, sleeping, regulating thoughts or emotions, self-care, or interaction with others. The EEOC's examples of disabilities include major depressive disorder, bipolar disorder, schizophrenia, post-traumatic stress disorder (PTSD), and obsessive-compulsive disorder. A condition can be substantially limiting even if it does not result in a high degree of functional limitation. A mental health provider can document a request for accommodation, giving the provider's professional qualifications, the nature of the employee's condition, and the functional limitations the employee would experience without treatment. Information relating to a request for accommodation is confidential, and it violates the ADA to take adverse action against an employee because of information provided with a request for accomodation. [<https://www.eeoc.gov/eeoc/publications/ada_mental_health_provider.cfm>; see Robert Sheridan, *EEOC Releases Guidance Concerning the Mental Health Provider's Role in ADA Reasonable Accommodation Requests*, Mintz Levin Cohn Ferris Glovsky and Popeo PC (Jan. 18, 2017), available at Lexology.com]

In an ADA/Rehab Act case, the employer accommodated the employee's anxiety disorder by permitting her to take a break at the onset of a panic attack. However, a supervisor allowed the plaintiff to take a break, heard screaming, and found her kicking and rolling on the lobby floor, with incisions in her wrist. The plaintiff was hospitalized, given FMLA leave, and terminated after an independent fitness for duty examination. The Seventh Circuit held that the employer was justified in getting an assessment of the likelihood that a disruptive incident might recur. The Seventh Circuit said that even if intolerable behavior is related to disability, it is a legitimate reason for termination. The Seventh Circuit discussed the difference between the issue of whether an employee is qualified, where the burden of proof is on the employee, and the "direct threat" defense (see § 36.06[A]), an affirmative defense placing the burden of proof on the employer. The direct threat defense does not apply when an employee has displayed actual dangerous conduct in the workplace: the threat is no longer potential, but actual. [*Felix v. Wisconsin Dep't of Transportation*, 828 F.3d 560 (7th Cir. 2016); see Jennifer Cerven, *Court Provides Roadmap for Managing "Intolerable" Behavior from Employee with Disabilities*, Barnes & Thornburg LLP (July 8, 2016), available at Lexology.com]

A special education teacher suffering from PTSD asked for a leave of absence and a transfer to another school because her deteriorating relationship with the principal caused a relapse. She was transferred to a program for children with learning disabilities. Her doctor recommended that she take another leave and then transfer to a less stressful environment. She was granted leave but the transfer was denied. She was fired for poor performance. The Seventh Circuit held that the school did not go far enough in accommodating the plaintiff's needs. Issues that could be disability-related cannot be used to justify termination. [*Lawler v. Peoria Sch. Dist. No. 150*, 837 F.3d 779 (7th Cir. Sept. 16, 2016)]

However, ADA claims (in a case that also involved FMLA claims) were dismissed. The plaintiff's supervisor noticed that his attendance and work performance had deteriorated and told the bank's medical director that the plaintiff might be depressed. The plaintiff was diagnosed with major depression; hospitalized; and after discharge, was assigned to a business trip. He stayed in a hotel and drove a company vehicle but did not work. He was placed on a performance improvement plan and subsequently terminated for leaving work without completing the plan. The Fourth Circuit held that even though the employee had a psychiatric disability, the employer was not required to disregard flagrant misconduct. [*Vannoy v. Federal Reserve Bank of Richmond*, 827 F.3d 296 (4th Cir. 2016); see Kathleen Kapusta, *No Evidence FMLA Notice Informed Employee of Job Restoration Right Interference Claim Revived*, WK WorkDay Blog (June 30, 2016) (benefitslink.com)]

Even misconduct might have to be accommodated, if it is caused by disability. A call center employee with bipolar disorder was fired for avoiding customer calls. The Wisconsin Court of Appeals ruled that a discharge caused by conduct that is a direct result of a disability is also assumed to be a direct result of the disability. [*Wisconsin Bell, Inc. v. Labor & Indus. Rev. Comm'n*, No. 2016AP355 (Wis. App. Mar. 28, 2017); see Brian M. Radloff and Mark A. Johnson, *Wisconsin Court Holds Discharge Employee Because of Misconduct Caused by Disability Can Be Discrimination*, Ogletree Deakins (Apr. 14, 2017), available at Lexology.com]

Furthermore, persons who are troubled but not classically mentally ill may seek treatment such as family therapy. Such individuals are not impaired for ADA purposes. A mental illness impairment may be present yet not covered by the ADA, if it is mild enough not to substantially limit the impaired person's ability to work and carry out other major life activities.

[E]   *Williams* and "Impairment"

Early in 2002, the Supreme Court decided *Toyota Motor Manufacturing, Kentucky, Inc. v. Williams.* [534 U.S. 184 (2002)] The court held that the plaintiff, who had carpal tunnel syndrome, was not disabled for ADA purposes. She was able to care for herself and perform ordinary daily tasks. In this view, merely having an impairment does not make a person disabled, nor does being unable to perform the tasks associated with that person's specific job, as long as the person can perform other tasks.

Williams is one of the cases that the ADAAA is designed to reverse.

The Lilly Ledbetter Fair Pay Act, Pub. L. No. 111-2, also applies to the ADA, so a suit can be brought within 180 days (or, if the state has an anti-discrimination agency, 300 days) of each time that an employee is subjected to discriminatory conduct under the ADA—even if the conduct is the result of a policy that was adopted much earlier.

[F]   EEOC Guidance

The EEOC proposed regulations in September 2009 to implement the ADAAA.

Under the proposal, actions based on an impairment include actions based on symptoms of an impairment. Reasonable accommodation is not required in "regarded-as" cases. An impairment that substantially limits one life activity does not have to be shown to limit others. For example, a diabetic whose endocrine system is substantially limited does not also have to show substantial limitation in eating; a person whose normal cell growth is limited by cancer doesn't have to show limitation in working. The examples of episodic or remitting impairments include epilepsy, hypertension, multiple sclerosis, asthma, cancer, depression, bipolar syndrome, and post-traumatic syndrome disorder.

The DOL lists certain impairments as consistently meeting the definition of disability: deafness, blindness, intellectual disability, amputations, use of a wheel-chair, autism, cancer, cerebral palsy, diabetes, epilepsy, multiple sclerosis, muscular dystrophy, and major mental illness. However, the EEOC's position is that the fact that a condition does not appear on the list does not mean it is not a disability. Some conditions are disabling for some people but not others, depending on their seriousness: for example, asthma, learning disabilities, back injuries.

The fact that a claimant got another job does not rule out that person's having a substantial limitation in working. Under the proposed regulations, a person with a disability can usually establish coverage by showing a limitation in major life activities other than working, so it will generally be unnecessary to consider whether there is a limitation in working. The new definition of "regarded as disabled" is an adverse action taken by an employer because of an actual or perceived impairment. The employee need not prove that the employer perceived him or her as substantially limited in the ability to perform a major life activity.

Effective October 11, 2016, DOJ updated the ADAAA rules for Title II and III (local and state government and places of public accommodation, respectively), adding new sections to the regulations about the meaning and interpretation of the definition of disability. [81 Fed. Reg. 53203 (Aug. 11, 2016); see Camille P. Toney, *DOJ Expands "Disability" Definition with New Final Rule Updating ADA,* Greensfelder Hemker & Gale PC (Aug. 26, 2016), available at Lexology.com]

Previously, in 2006, the EEOC issued FAQs about the ADA implications of deafness and hearing impairment in an aging population. The EEOC warns employers to assess hearing-impaired workers' abilities on a case-by-case basis, and not to assume that hearing impairment always means that the worker compromises workplace safety. Lip-reading and sign language interpretation are not considered mitigating measures, because they do not improve the person's hearing.

The EEOC says that it is inappropriate to ask questions about hearing tests, hearing aids, and occupationally caused hearing loss during pre-job-offer interviews. However, it is legitimate to direct all job applicants to information (e.g., an HR person; part of the company Website) about reasonable accommodations in the application process.

The EEOC lists sign language interpreters; special telephones; telephone headsets; vibrating or flashing emergency notifications; assistive software; writing notes; assistive listening devices; and devices that translate speech into writing as examples of reasonable accommodation for those with hearing loss. Changing the employee's work area (e.g., away from an area with ambient noises that interfere with a hearing aid) can also be a reasonable accommodation. In some instances, allowing an employee to trade an assignment with another employee to avoid a task that is a small part of the job, and that is difficult for a hearing-impaired person to perform, will be considered a reasonable accommodation. But a solution that deprives the hearing-impaired worker of real-time access to events (e.g., furnishing written minutes after a meeting) is not adequate. [EEOC, *Questions and Answers About Deafness and Hearing Impairments in the Workplace and the Americans with Disabilities Act*, <http://www.eeoc.gov/eeoc/publications/qa_deafness.cfm> (Mar. 2014) (last accessed Mar. 13, 2017)]

UPS policy did not provide interpreters for deaf employees at short meetings. A deaf worker sued, charging that it was not a reasonable accommodation to have someone give him written summaries of the meetings instead of having an interpreter. (The employee has limited reading skills; he repeatedly complained that he did not understand various written materials, but was merely told to look up difficult words in a dictionary.) The district court dismissed the suit but the Ninth Circuit reversed, saying that UPS did not provide effective accommodations. The case was settled in late 2011 for $95,000 plus three years of nonmonetary relief (appointing an ADA coordinator, investigating disability discrimination complaints promptly, and providing accommodation to deaf and hearing-impaired employees). [*EEOC v. UPS Supply Chain Solutions*, 620 F.3d 1103 (9th Cir. 2010) Settlement: *EEOC v. UPS Supply Chain Solutions*, No. CV 06-06210 ABC (Ex)]

In 2006, the Ninth Circuit ruled that excluding all deaf people from driving UPS package cars violated the ADA [*Bates v. UPS*, 465 F.3d 1069 (9th Cir. 2006)], but this decision was reversed after an en banc rehearing. The en banc panel held that UPS showed business necessity by citing the Department of Transportation hearing acuity requirements for drivers of large trucks. But the en banc decision requires UPS to prove business necessity to refuse to allow hearing-impaired people to drive trucks. The ADA has no equivalent of a Bona Fide Occupational Qualification (BFOQ) defense. Job-relatedness requires the employer to show that the standard fairly and accurately measures the individual's actual ability to perform essential functions of the job. [*Bates v. UPS*, 511 F.3d 974 (9th Cir. 2007)]

In May 2016, the EEOC issued a document (technically not official guidance, but valuable in revealing the EEOC's priorities) covering ADA leave as a reasonable accommodation. The EEOC's position is that employees requesting leave for reasons related to disability must have the same access to leave as employees whose requests are not disability-related. The EEOC says the employer must consider providing unpaid leave as an accommodation, even if FMLA or personal leave is no longer available, if this is not an undue hardship for the employer. The EEOC requires employers to make exceptions to their policies such as maximum leave and no-fault attendance, and grant additional leave, unless the exception would impose undue hardship. The obligation to engage in the interactive process is triggered when an employee asks for disability-related leave. The EEOC allows employers (with the employee's permission) to contact the employee's health care provider for information about the need for leave. The EEOC does not permit "100% healed" provisions that prevent an employee from returning to work until he or she is able to return to work without restrictions, if the employee can perform the job with or without reasonable accommodations. But there are exceptions to this general rule if the employee's return to work creates a significant risk of harm to the employee or others that cannot be eliminated via reasonable accommodation. The EEOC does not require employers to grant requests for indefinite leave: the employee must be able to estimate a date for return to work. The EEOC also requires employers to consider reassigning the employee to a vacant position for which the employee is qualified. [EEOC, *Employer-Provided Leave and the Americans With Disabilities Act*, <https://www.eeoc.gov/eeoc/publications/ada-leave.cfm> (May 9, 2016)(last accessed Mar. 13, 2017); see FMLA Insights, *EEOC Issues New Resource Document Addressing Leave as a Reasonable Accommodation Under the ADA. What's the Impact on Employers?* (May 10, 2016) (benefitslink.com); Duane Morris LLP, *EEOC Issues Guidance Relating to Leaves of Absence and the ADA* (May 16, 2016), available at Lexology.com]

The EEOC has settled several cases about denial of leave, or fixed leave policies that do not take into account the individual needs of employees. In June 2016, three automobile dealerships in Nevada agreed to pay $50,000 for firing an employee with multiple sclerosis who asked for leave after symptoms sent her to the emergency room. Lowes, a home improvement chain, paid $8.6 million for firing three employees with disabilities, refusing to provide them with reasonable accommodation when they needed more leave than the company's maximum permitted leave. The EEOC said that it violates the ADA to impose an arbitrary time limit. [Anat Maytal, *Drawing the Line on Leave Policies for Employees With Disabilities*, Baker & Hostetler LLP (Aug. 4, 2016), available at Lexology.com; Donna M. Glover, *EEOC and Lowe's Settle ADA Leave Accommodation Suit for $8.6 Million*, Ober Kaler (May 13, 2016)]

§ 36.05 REASONABLE ACCOMMODATION

[A] Employer's Obligation

Employers have an obligation to engage in an interactive process of reasonable accommodation, to permit employment or continued employment of qualified individuals with disabilities. However, it is not required that employers undergo undue hardship in making such accommodations.

The interactive process may have to begin even before employment does. In early 2016, the Fifth Circuit held that a job offer should not have been withdrawn as soon as the employer learned of a field engineer's severe rotator cuff injury. He could not drive a company vehicle, work with his hands above shoulder level, or lift more than 10 pounds. The Fifth Circuit said that there was a duty to find out if reasonable accommodation was possible. [*Cannon v. Jacobs Field Servs.*, 813 F.3d 586 (5th Cir. 2016); see Robin E. Shea, *Employers, the ADA Interactive Process Applies to Post-Offer Medical Examination, Too*, Constangy Brooks Smith & Prophete LLP (Jan. 15, 2016), available at Lexology.com]

Manning, a diabetic who quit when her employer rejected her suggested accommodation (assigning her to the steady day shift she worked before a corporate restructuring assigned her to unpredictable work hours) could not maintain an ADA suit. The court found that she did not participate in the interactive process in good faith. The employer said that she could not get a steady daytime schedule, but that it would discuss alternatives; she said that she had no choice but to quit, and refused to talk to the employer. [*EEOC v. Kohl's Dep't Stores, Inc.*, 774 F.3d 127 (1st Cir. 2014)]

The jury awarded close to $2 million to a pharmacist who was fired for refusing to give shots to customers. He suffered from trypanophia, a fear of needles severe enough to cause fainting. The Tenth Circuit reversed, holding that giving shots was an essential function of the job and removing an essential function is never required as a reasonable accommodation. [*Stevens v. Rite-Aid*, 851 F.3d 224 (2d Cir. 2017); see Richard B. Cohen, *Firing of Pharmacist with Trypanophobia Upheld: He Could Not Perform Essential Job Function*, Fisher-Broyles LLP (Mar. 23, 2017), available at Lexology.com]

The Seventh Circuit ruled that termination does not occur until an employee has unequivocal confirmation of the decision to terminate him or her. Once an employer is on notice that an employee has a disability, it has an obligation to engage in the interactive process. Therefore, it was unlawful to fire a narcoleptic employee who submitted medical documentation of her diagnosis (the employer said it was "just the doctor's opinion"). [*Spurling v. C&M Fine Pack, Inc.*, 739 F.3d 1055 (7th Cir. 2014)]

The regulations governing the interactive process appear at 26 C.F.R. Part 163. Best practices for the process include:

- Creating a policy, probably as part of the ADA policy, and preferably included in the employee handbook, to explain the process to employees. At a minimum, employees should be informed that if they request accommodation, their job description will be reviewed to consider the effect of disability on the essential functions of the job.

- Making sure that written job descriptions accurately describe the essential functions. Under the ADA regulations, a task is essential if the job exists to do that task; if it absorbs a high percentage of work time; if no or only a few other employees can do it; a worker was hired for specialized expertise; not performing the task would have serious consequences; the duty is required by the CBA; there is a history of people with that job title performance that function.

- Training supervisors to recognize requests for accommodation; an employee's verbal statement that problems at work are caused by medical needs is probably enough to trigger the process, but merely asking for a new piece of equipment without mentioning disability probably does not. However, supervisors should be trained not to ask questions about disability.

- Holding a personal meeting with the employee, supervisors, and a representative of the HR department to identify the problems and possible solutions, especially solutions suggested by the employee.

- Consulting your Worker's Compensation carrier if the employee was injured at work; there may be state-run programs to modify the workplace.

- Keeping the employee's identity confidential, consult experts such as vocational rehabilitation specialists.

- Requesting information from the employee's doctor—or having the employee obtain the information; be sure to include the GINA safe harbor language in the communication, and limit the request to information that is a business necessity.

- Continuing the process by making sure that accommodations are effective.

- Documenting the process [Patti C. Perez, *Your Compliance Toolbox: 7 Tips for a Successful Interactive Process*, Ogletree Deakins (Aug. 28, 2015), available at Lexology.com]

It is also worthwhile to implement a policy telling employees to consult the HR department, not their supervisors, if they seek accommodation; such a policy limits the amount of confidential information that supervisors receive. Supervisors should be trained to send accommodation requests to the HR department without asking the employee for more information. Only as much disability-related information as is needed to start the interactive process should be requested, and the information should not be shared with anyone except the relevant manager. [Kelly D. Gemelli, *Top 10 Mistakes to Avoid During the Reasonable Accommodation Process*, Jackson Lewis PC (Oct. 6, 2015), available at Lexology.com]

Section 12111(9) says that the category of reasonable accommodation may include making existing facilities readily accessible and usable by QIWDs. It can also include job restructuring, part-time or other altered work schedules, reassignment to a *vacant* position (in April 2002, the Supreme Court ruled that it is not in general "reasonable" to reassign an employee if the reassignment violated an established seniority system—but the employee can demonstrate that an exception should be made in his or her individual case: *US Airways v. Barnett*, 535 U.S. 391 (2002)). Other possible reasonable accommodations include acquiring or modifying equipment, providing training, making readers or interpreters available, etc.

The ADA does not set a specific time limit for leaves. The EEOC's position is that leave of absence may be a reasonable accommodation unless the employer shows that keeping the job open is an undue hardship. Most cases say that a leave of absence cannot be indefinite and it is not reasonable to request leave without specifying a return to work date. The Eighth Circuit held that a request for leave until at least a given date, with no return date, requires the employee to provide at least some information about return and demonstrate that he or she will be able to return to work eventually. The employer can ask for the anticipated return date when leave is taken, or during the interactive process of negotiating accommodation. Instead of automatically terminating the employee for missing the return to work date, the better practice is to make a written request for a new date and ask if the employee can return to work now with or without reasonable accommodation. The employee's inability to supply a return date or failure to respond, can justify termination (unless Worker's Compensation law or the FMLA precludes termination). [*Peyton v. Fred's Stores of Ark.*, 561 F.3d 900 (8th Cir. 2009)]

"Auxiliary aids and services" is defined by § 12102 to mean interpreters or other effective methods of communicating with hearing-impaired people, readers, taped texts, and other ways to deliver texts to the visually impaired, acquiring or modifying adaptive equipment or devices, or "other similar services and actions."

Asking for a free reserved parking space on site is a request for ADA accommodation even if it does not involve performance of essential job functions. (The plaintiff was a government lawyer who wanted the parking space because knee problems made it hard to walk.) The district court dismissed the case on the grounds that the plaintiff did not show that denial of on-site parking limited her ability to perform the essential functions of the job. However, the Fifth Circuit held that the employer has a duty to make facilities accessible and providing a parking space potentially does this. The case was remanded; the Fifth Circuit did not say whether providing the parking space would constitute a reasonable accommodation. [*Feist v. State of La.*, 730 F.3d 450 (5th Cir. 2013)]

A clear path of at least 36" wide is needed to maneuver a wheelchair through a hall or aisle. Turning requires either a 60" circle or a T-shaped area at least 60" long and 36" wide. Ramps should not be steeper than 1:20. Wheelchair-accessible counters should not be higher than 36". Wheelchair users find hard floors more convenient than carpeted floors, and lever-style knobs are easier to operate than round doorknobs or knobs with thumb latches. [Michael C. Wilhelm, *Tips for Making the Workplace Wheelchair Accessible*, Briggs and Morgan (Sept. 24, 2013), available at Lexology.com]

An undue hardship is an action that requires significant difficulty or expense. [42 U.S.C. § 12111(10)] This determination is made based on factors such as the cost of the accommodation and how it compares to the employer's budget.

The employer must retain records about requests for accommodation for one year after the request or personnel action, whichever is later. [29 C.F.R. § 1602.14]

[B]   EEOC Enforcement Guidance

On October 17, 2002, the EEOC released a major enforcement guidance. [*Enforcement Guidance: Reasonable Accommodation and Undue Hardship Under the Americans with Disabilities Act*, <http://www.eeoc.gov/policy/docs/accommodation.html> (last accessed Mar. 13, 2017)] The EEOC has retained this document on its Website, but warns that it should be interpreted in light of the ADAAA.

Under the Guidelines, employers need not eliminate essential job functions. Employers do not have to provide items used for both work and nonwork tasks; employees are responsible for furnishing their own prostheses, eyeglasses, and hearing aids.

Employees who want accommodation must make a clear request but need not use the term "reasonable accommodation," as long as it is clear what they mean. Employers must act on reasonable verbal requests but can ask to have them confirmed by a written memorandum.

The employer can demand reasonable documentation of, for instance, the nature, severity, and duration of the impairment, which activities are impaired, and the extent to which the employee's functional ability is limited. But documentation cannot be required if the disability and accommodation are obvious, or if the employee has already furnished adequate information. The employer can choose its preferred (usually the most cost-effective) reasonable accommodation, and need not follow the employee's suggestion.

Using accrued paid leave, or unpaid leave, is a reasonable accommodation, but employers do not have to offer additional paid leave to employees with a disability. Employees should be allowed to exhaust paid leave before taking unpaid leave. Unless it is an undue hardship, the employer must keep the job open during leave. A leave request need not be granted if the employer can keep the employee at work via a reasonable alternative accommodation.

The EEOC position is that employers should consider ADA and FMLA entitlement separately and then determine whether the two statutes overlap. The EEOC's example is an ADA-disabled person who needs 13 weeks of leave. The FMLA requires only 12 weeks of leave, but the EEOC says the ADA requires the employer to provide the 13th week unless that would be an undue hardship.

If there is a vacant position available for transfer, the employer does not have to train the person with a disability as an accommodation, unless training would be offered to a nondisabled employee. The EEOC position is that a transfer is a reasonable accommodation, so it must be offered even if the employer does not normally provide transfers. It is not enough to allow the disabled employee to compete for a vacant position; it should be offered to any QIWD who wants the transfer as an accommodation.

Final regulations about the ADAAA were published in the Federal Register on March 25, 2011. [76 Fed. Reg. 16977] Under these final regulations (which cover the "Appendix," also known as the Interpretive Guide), a disability is a physical or mental impairment substantially limiting one or more major life activities; a record or history of disability; or being regarded as having a disability. (These three potential litigation areas are sometimes referred to as the three "prongs" of the ADAAA.)

The regulations provide principles for determining whether a person has a disability. An impairment does not have to prevent or severely or significantly restrict performance of a major life activity to be considered a disability. The final regulations state that whether an impairment is a disability should be broadly construed to the maximum extent allowed by law. If an impairment is substantially limiting when it is active, then it is a disability even if it is episodic or in remission. Other than ordinary eyeglasses or contact lenses, mitigating measures are not taken into account in making disability determinations.

In order to focus on whether or not there was discrimination, and not whether the charging party fits within the definition of disability, the final regulations now forbid discrimination on the basis of disability, not discrimination against a QIWD.

Under the 2011 final regulations, major life activities include major bodily functions, such as the functions of the immune system; normal cell growth; and brain, neurological, and endocrine functions. Certain conditions, such as diabetes, epilepsy, bipolar disorder, and being HIV+ are considered to be impairments. The final regulations make it easier for employees to make out a case of regarded-as-disabled liability, because the focus has shifted from the employer's beliefs about the nature of impairment and to the way the employer treated the individual. It's also easier to establish regarded-as liability; now the focus is on treatment of the plaintiff and not on the employer's beliefs about the nature of the impairment. [The regulations, fact sheets, and Q&A can be found at <http://www.eeoc.gov/laws/statutes/adaaa_info.cfm> (last accessed Mar. 13, 2017).]

For general information about ADA and small business, see <http://www.eeoc.gov/eeoc/publications/adahandbook.cfm> (undated, last accessed Mar. 13, 2017). To find nearest Small Business Liaison, see <http://www.eeoc.gov/employers/contacts.cfm> (accessed Mar. 13, 2017).

[C]   Case Law

It is very common for summary judgment to be granted to the employer in ADA cases—often on the grounds that the plaintiff did not have a disability for ADA purposes, or that he or she was not qualified, but sometimes on the grounds that there was no reasonable accommodation possible, or that the employer either provided reasonable accommodation or attempted to do so, but the interactive process was frustrated by the employee. A number of cases, however, resulted in summary judgment at the district court level, which was then reversed by the court of appeals, and the case sent back to the district court for a full trial.

Employers are required to offer an effective accommodation, although not necessarily the one the employee prefers. The interactive process can be terminated after a reasonable accommodation has been offered.

For example, in mid-2015 the Second Circuit dismissed a suit by a deaf software engineer. He received onsite and remote interpreters, real-time online transcription, and video relay services. He said that the videos did not have on-screen translations and there were delays in getting transcripts. He asked for intranet videos in captioned form and transcripts of all audio files; IBM refused. The Second Circuit held that IBM met its obligations: the translations worked, even if not as fast as the plaintiff wanted. [*Noll v. IBM*, 787 F.3d 89 (2d Cir. 2015)]

Some courts say that the employee must take the first step by requesting accommodation. The Seventh Circuit decided that it does not violate the ADA to refuse a software engineer's request to work at home as an accommodation to the fatigue and pain caused by treatment for cancer. In fact, in the Seventh Circuit view, most jobs require supervision, teamwork, and interaction with others, so working at home will rarely constitute a reasonable accommodation. [*Rauen v. United States Tobacco Mfg. Ltd.*, 319 F.3d 891 (7th Cir. 2003); working at home was not a reasonable accommodation for an employee traumatized by witnessing a fatal workplace shooting incident: *Mason v. Avaya Commc'ns, Inc.*, 357 F.3d 1114 (10th Cir. 2004)]

Note, however, that the D.C. Circuit found in 2007 that revoking a disabled worker's previously given permission to work at home two days a week was discriminatory, because the telecommuting arrangement constituted a reasonable accommodation. [*Woodruff v. Peters*, 482 F.3d 521 (D.C. Cir. Apr. 6, 2007)]

The Sixth Circuit reversed summary judgment for Ford, and reinstated the EEOC's suit against Ford, holding that the plaintiff was otherwise qualified (because physical presence at the workplace was not required) or she requested reasonable accommodation for her disability of Irritable Bowel Syndrome. The plaintiff was a steel buyer. Ford argued that the job required face-to-face meetings and trips to supplier sites, so it refused her request to telecommute. Other accommodations were offered, such as moving her desk closer to the bathroom, or re-assigning her to a different job that would permit telecommuting. The plaintiff was fired after she was placed on a Performance Improvement Plan but her performance did not improve. The Sixth Circuit held that technology reduces the importance of the employee's presence in the workplace, so the vital question was not whether "attendance" is an essential job function but whether her presence was truly essential. [*EEOC v. Ford*, 752 F.3d 634 (6th Cir. 2014), *reh'g en banc granted*, No. 12-2484, 2014 U.S. App. LEXIS 17252 (Aug. 29, 2014)]

The en banc court reversed again, holding that the plaintiff was not a qualified employee, because working in the office all or at least most of the time was an essential part of the job; full-time telecommuting would not be adequate. [*EEOC v. Ford*, 782 F.3d 753 (6th Cir. en banc 2015)]

In mid-2015, the D.C. Circuit held that telecommuting was not a reasonable accommodation for a budget analyst who frequently missed work as a result of hypothyroidism, depression, and migraine. After she exhausting her FMLA leave, she asked to be allowed to start work at 11 a.m. (the other employees started between 6 and 8 a.m.) and to telecommute. The D.C. Circuit agreed with the employer that presence in the office and in-person interaction were essential. [*Doak v. Johnson*, 798 F.3d 1096 (D.C. Cir. 2015)]

A television station told an injured sports reporter that she could not return to work until she could carry the camera provided by the station. When she was ready to return, she was told that she had been replaced and there were no jobs open. The Eleventh Circuit held that photography was an essential function of the job and the plaintiff did not provide evidence that a lighter camera was available capable of satisfying the station's broadcast requirements. [*Tetteh v. WAFF Tel.*, 2016 WL 624393 (11th Cir. Feb. 17, 2016); see Franklin Corley, *The Americans with Disabilities Act; Sexual Harassment Under Title VII*, Sirote & Permutt PC (Mar. 2, 2016), available at Lexology.com]

The Eleventh Circuit held that indefinite extension of light duty is not a reasonable accommodation. The employer's procedure said that there was no such thing as permanent light duty, and required a medical due process hearing when employees spent 270 days on light duty in a two-year period. The plaintiff could not return to full duty after the 270 days elapsed, and it was uncertain if she could ever return to full duty, so it did not violate the ADA to terminate her. [*Frazier-White v. Gee*, 818 F.3d 1249 (11th Cir. 2016); see Keith Anderson, *Never Forever: Indefinite Extension of Light Duty Not Required Under ADA*, Bradley Arant Boult Cummings LLP (Apr. 14, 2016), available at Lexology.com]

The EEOC took the position that an employer must reassign a person with a disability to a vacant position for which he or she has the minimal qualifications, as a required accommodation. But the Eleventh Circuit rejected this position in late 2016, holding that a worker with a disability must compete with other workers for a vacancy. The plaintiff was a nurse who walked with a cane. The hospital said that the cane was a safety risk in the psychiatric ward where she worked. She was allowed to apply for other jobs at the hospital but was terminated when she was not selected for any of them. The Eleventh Circuit, like the Fifth, Sixth, and Eighth Circuits, held that reassignment is an available option, but not required when the employer has a policy of competitive appointments. However, the Seventh, Tenth, and D.C. Circuits agree with the EEOC: employers must offer preferential access to vacant positions as an accommodation. [*EEOC v. St. Joseph's Hosp.*, No. 15-14551, 2016 WL 7131479 (11th Cir. Dec. 7, 2016); see Brian D. Hall, *Eleventh Circuit Rejects EEOC Position Regarding Reassignment as A Reasonable Accommodation*, Porter Wright Morris & Arthur LLP (Dec. 12, 2016), available at Lexology.com]

§ 36.06 DEFENSES

[A] Primary Defense

The primary defense, under 42 U.S.C. § 12113, is that the employer's criterion, standards, or tests may screen out individuals with a disability, but are nevertheless appropriate because they are job-related and consistent with business necessity, and the employer cannot achieve the same goals via reasonable accommodation. Qualification standards can lawfully rule out employment of anyone who poses a direct threat to the health or safety of others. According to 42 U.S.C. § 12111(3), a "direct threat" is a significant risk to the health or safety of others that cannot be eliminated by reasonable accommodation.

The defense of "direct threat" is still usable now that the ADAAA is in force but the employer must rely on reasonable medical judgment, based on the most current medical knowledge and objective evidence about the employee's ability to work safely. For example, a mid-2013 case finds that the employer's doctor's opinion that an employee with a seizure disorder, who sometimes needed to be taken to the emergency room from work, was invalid because the doctor used improper methodology. [*EEOC v. Rexnord Indus., LLC*, 966 F. Supp. 2d 829 (E.D. Wis. 2013)]

An employee who makes serious and credible threats of violence toward co-workers is not ADA-qualified. Mayo worked as a welder for decades after his 1999 diagnosis of major depressive disorder. In 2010, he and some co-workers charged a supervisor with bullying them. Mayo started to make comments about coming to work with a shotgun and blowing off some heads, and "taking out" management. When a senior HR manager asked if he meant it, he said he couldn't guarantee he wouldn't do that. He was banned from the property, and the company contacted the police. He was hospitalized for six days, then took FMLA leave. Toward the end of leave, his psychologist released him to work, but the company terminated him when his leave ended. The Ninth Circuit said his comments were the product of his disability, so it was discrimination to fire him. The Ninth Circuit said the threats proved he couldn't handle an essential function of the job: working with people and managing stress in the workplace. [*Mayo v. PCC Structurals Inc.*, 795 F.3d 941 (9th Cir. 2015)]

The Sixth Circuit found it objectively reasonable for a police department to believe that a police officer posed a direct threat and was not qualified to do his job. After three operations for a brain tumor, his behavior changed and he started to abuse steroids, harass the chief of police, and spy on family members. It did not violate the ADA to prevent him from returning to work after the third surgery. [*Michael v. City of Troy Police Dep't*, 808 F.3d 304 (6th Cir. 2015); see Michael C. Wilhelm, *Can an Employee's Bizarre Behavior Support a Determination That He Poses a "Direct Threat" Under the ADA?*, Briggs and Morgan (Jan. 20, 2016), available at Lexology.com]

Two district courts in New York heard similar cases in mid-2016. In the Southern District case, the jury awarded over $250,000 to a plaintiff who was disqualified as a police officer because he had been hospitalized for a seizure and took anti-seizure medication. He submitted a letter from his neurologist that his seizure disorder was controlled and he could serve as a police officer. In the Eastern District case, a police officer was hospitalized in November 2009 for bipolar affective disorder. The following month, his psychiatrist cleared him to return to work without restrictions, but he was placed on restricted duty on the recommendation of the police psychiatrist. Eventually, the police psychiatrist cleared him to work without restrictions, in April 2010, but he was not allowed to return to full duty until December. The jury awarded him $80,000 for past economic damages and $49,500 for pain and suffering. [*Pesce v. City of New York*, 159 F. Supp. 3d 448 (S.D.N.Y. 2016); *Hoey v. County of Nassau*, No. 2:12-cv-04935 (E.D.N.Y. May 18, 2017); see Marjory D. Robertson, *Police Officers with Epilepsy and Bipolar Disorder Win in ADA Discrimination Jury Trials*, Sun Life Financial Inc (Mar. 12, 2017), available at Lexology.com]

The Tenth Circuit held that the district court gave improper jury instructions on the ADA direct threat defense; the instructions should have been more favorable to the employer. The plaintiff is legally blind. His job with the defendant was eliminated. He was offered a new job, but contingent on passing a physical examination. He did pass the exam but the doctor said that he would require accommodations to mitigate the risks of his visual impairment. The defendant decided it could not reasonably accommodate his condition and rescinded the job offer. The defendant's litigating position was that his impaired vision created a significant risk of harm to himself and others and there was no available reasonable accommodation. The Tenth Circuit said that that's the correct definition of direct risk. The Tenth Circuit said that the jury instruction should have conveyed that proof of an actual threat is unnecessary; the employer's reasonable belief is enough. The jury was told to consider whether the defendant's belief was reasonable—but not why they should consider this. [*EEOC v. Beverage Distributors Co., LLC*, 780 F.3d 1018 (10th Cir. 2015)]

In a late 2016 consent decree with the EEOC, the Georgia Power Company agreed to pay $1.6 million and change its policies about drugs, alcohol, and seizure disorders. Georgia Power fired or denied hiring based on perceived safety threats—but the EEOC said the company didn't assess their individual ability to carry out the tasks and ignored opinions of their treating physicians. Three employees were fired even though their physicians had cleared them to return to work. [*EEOC v. Georgia Power Co.*, No.1:13-cv-03225-AT (N.D. Ga., settled Nov. 15, 2016); see Heather C. Panick, *The EEOC Settles Its "Direct Threat" Lawsuit Against Georgia Power Co. for $1.6 Million*, Disabilityleavelaw.com (Nov. 17, 2016) (benefitslink.com)]

The Supreme Court greatly increased the applicability of this exception in a June 2002 decision [*Chevron USA Inc. v. Echazabal*, 536 U.S. 73 (2002)] by allowing employers to use it in the context of danger to a job applicant or employee whose own physical condition would be endangered by workplace conditions.

In 2012, the Supreme Court gave an expansive interpretation to the "ministerial exception" (the principle that courts will not intervene in a congregation's selection of religious ministers). Cheryl Perich, who taught at a religious school, argued that she was fired in retaliation for threatening to file an ADA suit. (Perich suffers from narcolepsy.) The Supreme Court accepted the employer's argument that Perich, as a "called" teacher (who led prayers and religious activities as well as teaching secular subjects) was a religious minister, so the exception applied. [*Hosanna-Tabor Evangelical Lutheran Church v. EEOC*, 132 S. Ct. 694 (2012)]

[B]   Drug and Alcohol Exception

Congress must have been concerned about the potential for claims of disability on the basis of substance abuse, because there are several statutory references. According to 42 U.S.C. § 12111(6), a "drug" is a controlled substance as defined by federal law, and "illegal use of drugs" means using controlled substances, but does not include drugs taken under the supervision of a licensed health professional.

Section 12114 says that an employee or job applicant who is currently engaging in the illegal use of drugs is not a QIWD. However, a person who is in rehab, has completed a rehab program, or otherwise stopped using drugs can be considered a QIWD. So can a person who is not in fact using illegal drugs, but who is incorrectly perceived to be.

However, a 2013 Fifth Circuit ruling permits enforcement of a corporate policy calling for termination of employees who reject treatment for drug or alcohol problems or who start but fail to complete a treatment program. Leave was granted for a factory worker to be treated for Vicodin addiction. He went through detox but left the program before receiving addiction treatment. The Fifth Circuit agreed with the district court: summary judgment for the employer was proper in the worker's ADA and FMLA suit. The safe harbor does not protect everyone who enters a treatment program—only those who remain drug-free for a significant amount of time. [*Shirley v. Precision Castparts Corp.*, 726 F.3d 675 (5th Cir. 2013)]

The plaintiff in the Supreme Court case of *Raytheon v. Hernandez* [540 U.S. 44 (2003)] was forced to resign after he tested positive for cocaine, thus violating a workplace conduct rule. More than two years later, after he said he had stopped using drugs, he applied to be rehired. Rehiring was denied, on the basis of a corporate policy against rehiring anyone who had been terminated for misconduct. The employee who rejected his application said that she did not know he was a former addict when she denied the application.

The Supreme Court held the no-rehire policy was neutral and satisfied the *McDonnell-Douglas* requirements. On remand, the Ninth Circuit found that there was a genuine issue of material fact as to whether the decision to refrain from rehiring him was disability-based, and therefore the Ninth Circuit reversed the grant of summary judgment for the defense. [362 F.3d 564 (9th Cir. 2004)]

Employers are allowed to forbid the use of alcohol or illegal drugs at the workplace, can enforce the requirements of the Drug-Free Workplace Act, can make a rule that employees not be under the influence of alcohol or drugs when they are at work (even if they used the substances outside the workplace), and can adopt reasonable procedures (including drug testing) to make sure employees are not currently abusing substances. Drug testing is not considered a "medical examination" for ADA purposes. Many of these provisions are repeated in 42 U.S.C. § 12210.

A "last chance" agreement, where reinstatement after rehab is conditional on continued good performance (and perhaps on passing periodic drug tests) has been upheld as a reasonable accommodation to the disability of alcoholism. [See, e.g., *Longen v. Waterous Co.*, 347 F.3d 685 (8th Cir. 2003)]

The Seventh Circuit affirmed summary judgment for the employer on ADA (and FMLA) claims brought by an employee who was already on a Last Chance Agreement and who was fired after coming to work drunk and failing a blood alcohol test. The Seventh Circuit ruled that she did not show that she had an alcoholism disability, because alcohol did not substantially limit her major life activities; she was fired for violating her employer's legitimate expectations by coming to work impaired. According to 42 U.S.C. § 12114(c)(4), alcoholic employees can be held to same qualifications standards as other employees, even if the unsatisfactory performance is related to alcoholism. The Seventh Circuit held that the employer did not fail to accommodate—in fact, it gave her time off for AA meetings. [*Ames v. Home Depot USA Inc.*, 629 F.3d 665 (7th Cir. 2011)]

The Sixth Circuit held in mid-2016 that an employer's decision not to grant an apprenticeship to a user of prescription opioids was not disability discrimination. The plaintiff was hired in 1996. After a work injury, he received accommodation for nine years. His doctor removed his work restrictions, but the company doctor maintained them because of evidence that plaintiff Ferrari was addicted to opioid painkillers. Before the apprenticeship physical, Ferrari submitted two doctor's notes. One said he was taking opioids; the other did not address the issue. He said he had been tapering off for three months. He submitted a doctor's note that the drugs did not affect his ability to work as an apprentice. An independent examination said that his medical records contradicted his representation that he had stopped taking the drugs three months earlier. The independent examiner said he could not work without restrictions while he used prescription opioids. His doctor maintained ladder and overhead work restrictions. The employer let him work a different job and said he could take up the apprenticeship once he ceased using the opioids. Ferrari said that the employer regarded him as disabled in the major life activity of working. The Sixth Circuit held that inability to perform a particular job is not limitation in a major life activity and forbidding him to climb or work at heights did not show that he was regarded as disabled. [*Ferrari v. Ford Motor Co.*, 826 F.3d 885 (6th Cir. 2016); see Catherine A. Cano, *Employer's Honest Belief That Employee Could Not Perform Job Due to Use of Opioid Medications Did Not Constitute Disability Discrimination,* Jackson Lewis PC (June 29, 2016), available at Lexology.com]

Courts in California, Colorado, Michigan, Oregon, New Mexico, and Washington have all held that it does not violate state law or public policy to fire a new hire who failed a drug test for using medical marijuana and there is no duty to accommodate medical marijuana use [*Garcia v. Tractor Supply Co.*, No. CV 15-00735 WJ/WPL, 2016 U.S. Dist. LEXIS 3494 (D.N.M. Jan. 7, 2016); see Alyssa M. Smilowitz, *New Mexico Court Holds Employers Need Not Accommodate Medical Marijuana Use,* Jackson Lewis PC (Jan. 13, 2016), available at Lexology.com. *Martin v. Estero Fire Rescue*, No. 2:13-cv-393-FtM-29DNF, 2014 WL 3400974 (M.D. Fla. July 11, 2014) holds that a firefighter's conditions of depression and anxiety were not ADA disabilities when he charged that firing him for testing positive for marijuana constituted disability discrimination.]

But there are also contrary holdings. In mid-2017, the Rhode Island Superior Court allowed individual employees to sue under the state's medical marijuana statute. The case also holds that refusing to hire an applicant because he or she uses medical marijuana not only violates the state medical marijuana law, but might also constitute disability discrimination under the state civil rights act. [*Callaghan v. Darlington Fabrics Co.,* No. PC-2014-5680 (R.I. Super. Ct. May 23, 2017); see Anthony S. Califano, Ariel D. Cudkowicz and Frederick T. Smith, *Refusal to Hire Medical Pot Users Just Got Riskier—At Least in Rhode Island,* Seyfarth Shaw LLP (July 25, 2017), available at Lexology.com]

The Massachusetts Supreme Judicial Court held that firing a person for using medical marijuana could be disability discrimination, but disagreed with Rhode Island by finding that Massachusetts employees have no private right to action for wrongful termination in violation of public policy. Their sole remedy is asserting a claim of disability discrimination. In this reading, employers who are informed of an employee's medical marijuana usage have an obligation to engage in the interactive process of accommodation, and are entitled to an undue hardship defense. [*Barbuto v. Advantages Sales & Mktg., LLC,* No. SJC-12226 (Mass. Sup. Jud. Ct. July 17, 2017); see Amanda G. Orcutt and Paul G. Lannon, *Medical Marijuana Use May Be Reasonable Accommodation Under Massachusetts Law,* Holland & Knight LLP (July 18, 2017), available at Lexology.com]

The District Court for the District of Connecticut held in August 2017 that the federal Controlled Substances Act does not preempt the Connecticut statute that makes it illegal to refuse to hire or to fire a person for using medical marijuana. The district court said that the Controlled Substances Act is a criminal law that does not govern employment practices. [*Noffsinger v. SSC Niantic Operating Co,* No. 3:16-cv-01938 (JAM) (D. Conn. Aug. 8, 2017); see Marjory D. Robertson, *Another Victory for Medical Marijuana Users at Work!,* Sun Life Financial Inc. (Aug. 10, 2017), available at Lexology.com] See § 23.09 for more discussion of medical marijuana in the workplace.

■ **TIP:** A substance abuser entering a rehab program (at least if it is an inpatient program) may be entitled to FMLA leave. Reasonable ADA accommodation may require providing additional leave after the 12 weeks of FMLA leave have been used up.

§ 36.07 "REGARDED AS" LIABILITY

The ADA covers qualified individuals who actually do not have a disability, but who are discriminated against because of the perception that they do. The ADAAA expands the definition of "regarded as" to forbid discrimination on the basis of the employer's perception of a mental or physical impairment—whether or not the plaintiff can prove that the impairment actually limits or is perceived to limit a major life activity. However, a "regarded as" claim can only be based on a long-lasting impairment, not one that lasts or is expected to last for less than six months. The ADAAA resolved a circuit split by holding that reasonable accommodation is not required in "regarded-as" cases.

A "100% healed" policy forbids employees to return to work unless they are free from all medical restrictions; employees who have restrictions are terminated. The Seventh Circuit held in 2011 that 100% healed policies are a per se ADA violation. [*Powers v. USF Holland, Inc.*, 667 F.3d 815 (7th Cir. 2011); *Kotwica v. Rose Packing Co. Inc.*, 637 F.3d 744 (7th Cir. 2011)]

According to the Second Circuit, a trucking company did not violate the ADA by refusing to hire drivers who used prescription drugs with side effects that could impair their driving ability. According to the Second Circuit, the trucking company did not perceive such persons as disabled. Furthermore, the EEOC's regulation, 29 C.F.R. § 1630.2(j)(3)(i) says that inability to perform a particular job is not the equivalent of a substantial limitation in the activity of working; being a truck driver is not a class of job or a broad range of jobs. The fact that the defendant company did not have any less demanding driving jobs to offer (that might have been performed safely by prescription medication users) does not prove that the defendant regarded the applicants as unfit for any driving position at all. [*EEOC v. JB Hunt Transp.*, 321 F.3d 69 (2d Cir. 2003)]

§ 36.08 DISABILITY AND THE BENEFIT PLAN

[A] Employer's Obligations and Challenges

Under the ADA, employers are permitted to make benefit plan decisions that are consistent with underwriting, reasonable risk classifications, or actual or reasonably anticipated experience. If the employer does not normally provide health benefits, it has no obligation to provide special insurance coverage for the disabled or to adopt a plan that covers both disabled and nondisabled employees.

Three Circuit Courts (the Sixth, Seventh, and Eleventh) have ruled that a totally disabled retiree or ex-employee is not "qualified" (because he or she is unable to perform job functions) and therefore cannot sue for fringe-benefit discrimination. [*Morgan v. Joint Admin. Bd. Ret. Plan*, 268 F.3d 456 (7th Cir. 2001); *EEOC v. CAN Ins. Cos.*, 96 F.3d 1038 (7th Cir. 1997); *Parker v. Metro. Life Ins. Co.*, 99 F.3d 181, *aff'd*, 121 F.3d 1006 (6th Cir. 1997); *Gonzalez v. Garner Food Servs., Inc.*, 89 F.3d 1523 (11th Cir. 1996)]

The Eighth Circuit dismissed ADA claims by an employee with multiple sclerosis who was fired the day after her employer learned that its health premiums were going to increase by about 30%. The Eighth Circuit held that she did not prove that the employer's explanation—her poor job performance—was pretextual. The Eighth Circuit found that there was no evidence that the manager who fired the plaintiff was even aware that the premium had increased, much less that he blamed the plaintiff for the additional costs. [*Libel v. Adventure Lands of Am.*, 482 F.3d 1028 (8th Cir. 2007)]

[B] EEOC Compliance Manual

In 2000, the EEOC redrafted its Compliance Manual Section 3, which can be found at <http://www.eeoc.gov/policy/docs/benefits.html>. As of press time in 2017, the EEOC had not issued a new version of this document. The employer must provide "equal" benefits for all employees, irrespective of disability. However, benefits can be "equal" even if there are certain distinctions drawn on the basis of disability. The employer is entitled to employ practices that reflect sound actuarial principles or are related to actual or reasonably anticipated experience.

The employer can rebut charges of disability discrimination by proving that disparate treatment is necessary to maintain the solvency of the plan, because covering the disabilities at issue would cost enough to threaten the fiscal soundness of the plan, and there is no way to change the plan without affecting disabilities.

In the EEOC view, it violates the ADA to:

- Exclude an employee from participation in a service or disability retirement plan because of disabilities;

- Have a different length of participation requirement in the same plan because of disability;

- Provide different levels of types of coverage within a plan (although coverage levels can be lower in disability than in service retirement plans).

Service retirement benefits can legitimately be denied to any employee who voluntarily took disability retirement.

§ 36.09 QUESTIONS AND MEDICAL TESTS

The general ADA rule is that employers are not permitted to ask job applicants or perform medical exams to find out if the applicant has a disability or to discover the nature and severity of the disability. However, it is permissible to tell the applicant what the job entails and ask about ability to perform these tasks. So "have you ever had any back problems?" is not a legitimate question, but "This job involves lifting 25-pound weights several times an hour, and sometimes involves lifting up to 100 pounds—can you handle that?" is acceptable.

Once the company decides to extend a job offer, then it is permissible to require a medical examination, as long as all employees (whether or not they have a disability) are subject to this requirement, and the results of the examination are kept in separate medical files and kept confidential, disclosed only to persons with a genuine work-related need to know.

Furthermore, any medical examination or inquiries must be job-related and consistent with business necessity. Voluntary medical examinations (including taking medical histories) are allowable if they are part of a program available to all employees at a work site, and an employer can ask about an employee's ability to perform job-related functions. [42 U.S.C. § 12112(d)]

The Sixth Circuit held that psychological counseling an employee was required to undergo (her supervisor thought she might be depressed) could be considered a medical examination, so she could maintain a 42 U.S.C. § 12112(d)(4)(A) claim (the ban on requiring a medical examination to see if an employee has a disability). The factors include whether the examination was performed by a health care professional, and whether it was designed to find mental impairments. [*Kroll v. White Lake Ambulance Auth.*, 691 F.3d 809 (6th Cir. 2012)]

The EEOC's enforcement guidance on disability-related inquiries (2000) allows the employer to make inquiries, including sending employees for medical examinations, as long as the inquiries are job-related and consistent with business necessity. Inquiries made can be based on the employer's reasonable belief, founded on objective evidence, that the employee's medical condition impairs his or her ability to perform essential job functions, or leads the employee to pose a direct threat. The Seventh Circuit has held that it is not wrongful termination to fire an employee who does pose a direct threat, based on an individualized assessment, reflecting reasonable medical judgment about the nature and seriousness of the threat. [*Felix v. Wisconsin DOT*, 828 F.3d 560 (7th Cir. 2016); see Alan M. Kaplan, *Disabilities—The Direct Threat Defense: A Tool in The Employer's Tool Box*, Masuda Funai Eifert & Mitchell Ltd. (Aug. 11, 2016), available at Lexology.com]

A related issue is when genetic information reveals disability or the potential to develop a disability. Title I of the Genetic Information Nondiscrimination Act (GINA; Pub. L. No. 110-233) applies to the group health plans of private employers, and to unions, government employers, and insurers. Title II applies to entities covered by Title VII. The EEOC is the agency in charge of enforcing GINA, and it proposed regulations on March 2, 2009 clarifying the rules for acquiring and disseminating genetic information.

See 29 C.F.R. Part 1635 for final regulations, effective January 10, 2011, under GINA Title II.

GINA defines manifestation of disease to mean a condition that has been, or reasonably could be, diagnosed by a health professional. Merely testing positive for a genetic trait is not considered a manifestation, even if the person tested is certain to develop the disease eventually—a requirement that was adopted to prevent positive markers being classified as preexisting conditions. Employers that require a medical examination after a job offer has been made and before the new hire starts work should make sure that the doctors administering the physicals do not ask about family medical history unless the GINA requirements are satisfied. The same is true of fitness for duty examinations. The EEOC says that the best practice is, when an employee is asked to provide documentation of disability, the request should tell the employee not to provide genetic information (including family medical history). [RIN 3046-AA84, 74 Fed. Reg. 9056 (Mar. 2, 2009)] May 2016 EEOC final rules dealing with GINA's effects on wellness programs are discussed at § 36.10[D] below.

The EEOC's first settlement of a suit about genetic information involved an applicant who was not hired for a clerical job because the employer regarded her as likely to develop carpal tunnel syndrome because of family medical history information that she disclosed in response to an improper inquiry. The employer, Fabricut, Inc., agreed to pay $50,000 and provide other relief. [*EEOC v. Fabricut, Inc.*, No. 13-CV-248-CVE-PJC (N.D. Okla., settled May 7, 2013); see EEOC Press Release, *Fabricut to Pay $50,000 to Settle EEOC Disability and Genetic Information Discrimination Lawsuit*, <http://www.eeoc.gov/eeoc/news room/release/5-7-13b.cfm> (May 7, 2013)]

§ 36.10 INTERACTION WITH OTHER STATUTES

In 2003, the Supreme Court held that, in a suit under the Federal Employers Liability Act (FELA), damages for mental anguish (fear of developing cancer after exposure to asbestos) can be recovered if the plaintiff has already suffered another actionable injury (e.g., asbestosis). Pain and suffering associated with physical injury is actionable, even though independent claims for negligent infliction of intentional distress often are not. Here, the plaintiffs did not seek damages for the increased risk of future cancer. Instead, they sought compensation for their current injuries, which include experiencing fear. However, to win a case of this type, the plaintiff must prove that the alleged fear is genuine and serious. Although this case deals specifically with a federal employment statute, it's an important indication of the Court's thinking on these topics. [*Norfolk & W. Ry. Co. v. Ayers*, 538 U.S. 135 (2003)]

On February 28, 2012, the EEOC released two guidance documents protecting veterans with disabilities. The unemployment rate for post-911 veterans is about 12%, 3% higher than the overall rate. The ADAAA requires reasonable accommodation to the impairments of veterans, including traumatic brain injuries and PTSD. Revised guidance for employers explains how the ADA treats recruitment, hiring, accommodation of veterans' disabilities, and the differences in coverage between the ADAAA and Uniformed Services Employment and Reemployment Rights Act (USERRA). The revised Guide for Wounded Veterans explains to injured veterans the rights and protections they are entitled to. [CCH Employment Law Daily, *Revised EEOC Guidance Clarifies Interplay Between ADA and USERRA for Employers, Explains Rights to Veterans with Service-Related Disabilities* (Mar. 2012) (benefitslink.com)]

Office of Federal Contract Compliance Programs (OFCCP) regulations under Rehab Act § 503 and the Vietnam Era Veterans' Readjustment Assistance Act (VEVRAA) took effect March 24, 2014, expanding affirmative action requirements for persons with disabilities (PWDs) and veterans. Federal contractors with $10,000 or more in contract value are covered. Subcontractors and sub-subcontractors are covered if their products or services are eventually sold to the federal government. Contractors' affirmative action plans must set a target of 7% disabled employees in each job group, although a contractor with fewer than 100 employees can use a target of 7% employment of PWDs in the total workforce. However, this is a goal, not a quota, and no penalties will be imposed for failure to meet it. The benchmark is adjusted annually; starting as of March 4, 2016, it is 6.9%. [OFCCP, *Annual VEVRAA Benchmark Effective Dates,* <https://www.dol.gov/ofccp/regs/compliance/AnnualVEVRAABenchmark EffectiveDates.htm> (last accessed Mar. 13, 2017)]

The latest benchmark, applicable as of March 31, 2017, is 6.7%. [Stephanie Underwood, *Hiring Benchmark for Protected Veterans Is Reduced Again,* Constangy Brooks Smith & Prophete LLP (Apr. 5, 2017), available at Lexology.com. See <https://ofccp.dol-esa.gov/errd/VEVRAA.jsp> for the VEVRAA Benchmark Database.]

Contractors are required to gather data about their recruitment and hiring efforts, with a three-year retention requirement. The OFCCP said that the ADA's exception for affirmative action permits self-identification before a job offer. Employers are now required to ask employees to voluntarily self-identify every five years, and must inform employees that they can change their disability status at any time. (See the form on the OFCCP Website.) Federal contractors are required to review the results of their diversity efforts annually. [79 Fed. Reg. 58683 (Sept. 24, 2013)]

The DOL's Veterans' Employment and Training Service (VETS) finalized its Notice of Proposed Rulemaking about VEVRAA in late 2014. The mandated report is now called VETS-4212 Report. Contractors must report the total number of employees and new hires who are protected veterans but it is not required that they report disabled veterans, active duty wartime veterans, medal winners, or recently separated veterans. [Linda Cavanna-Wilk and Karen M. Tyner, *VETS Publishes Final Rule on VEVRAA Reporting Requirements*, Ford & Harrison LLP (Oct. 1, 2014), available at Lexology.com]

On the grounds that health care costs can be a proxy for age, the Eighth Circuit reversed summary judgment for the employer and reinstated an ADEA discrimination and retaliation claim, based on evidence that the employer asked its health insurer for a rate reduction because it laid off the "older and sicker" employees. However, the Eighth Circuit upheld dismissal of the plaintiff's ADA claims because the plaintiff did not prove that her having knee surgery affected the decision to lay her off—or even that any employment decision-maker knew about the surgery. [*Tramp v. Associated Underwriters, Inc.*, 768 F.3d 793 (8th Cir. Oct. 7, 2014)]

[A]   The Rehabilitation Act

The ADA is a successor statute to the Rehabilitation Act of 1973 (29 U.S.C. §§ 793 *et seq.*; "Rehab Act"). There are many circumstances in which the HR department will have to apply the ADA in conjunction with other laws—typically, the FMLA and ERISA.

The Rehab Act applies to federal contractors and subcontractors whose government contract involves more than $2,500, and to federal programs and federal grantees. It does not apply to businesses that are not involved in government contracting.

Rehab Act § 503 protects qualified handicapped applicants against discrimination in employment practices. However, one reason that the ADA was passed is that the Rehab Act does not contain a private right of action. In other words, handicapped persons who charge that they were victims of discrimination cannot sue the alleged discriminators. Another section, § 504, does carry a private right of action, but only for discrimination solely on account of handicap in a federally financed program or activity.

Rehab Act § 503 imposes an affirmative action requirement. Federal contractors must have goals for hiring and promotion of qualified handicapped individuals. However, the Department of Labor does not have the power to enforce this requirement by bringing administrative prosecutions against companies that violate it.

The Fifth and Ninth Circuits have held that the Rehab Act protects independent contractors as well as common-law employees. The Fifth Circuit held in early 2016 that Rehab Act § 504's ban on discrimination is very broadly worded, and any federally funded program (not just the plaintiff's employer) can be sued. [Jonathan R. Tung, *Contractor Doctors Can Sue Under 1973 Rehab Act*, FindLaw 5th Circuit Court of Appeals Opinion Summaries Blog <http://blogs.find law.com/fifth_circuit/> (Feb. 4, 2016); *Fleming v. Yuma Reg'l Med. Ctr.*, 587 F.3d 938 (9th Cir. 2009)]

A Kansas State University assistant professor sued the school, alleging disability discrimination and retaliation when an extension of her six-month leave of absence was denied (Professor Hwang suffered from cancer). She was granted long-term disability benefits, terminating her employment. The Tenth Circuit held that the Rehabilitation Act was not violated. The plaintiff did not show that she was able to perform the essential functions of the job, and extending the leave and keeping the job open was not a reasonable accommodation. Hwang said that having an inflexible policy limiting leave to six months was discriminatory, but the Tenth Circuit said that even the EEOC's policy manual describes a six-month leave as more than a reasonable time. [*Hwang v. Kansas State Univ.*, 753 F.3d 1159 (10th Cir. 2014)]

The Fourth Circuit ruled that there were genuine issues of material fact as to whether a blind employee of a government agency received reasonable accommodation. The agency got new software, which was not compatible with the screen reader that the plaintiff used. Management said that it would have cost $200,000 to retrofit the software to accommodate the screen reader. She was reassigned to another unit, at the same grade, salary, and benefits but she alleged that she received only limited assignments, not full-time work. The Fourth Circuit said that the plaintiff offered suggestions for making her screen reader compatible and that other call centers accommodated blind employees. The court held that she was denied opportunity by being transferred out of full-time work. [*Reyazuddin v. Montgomery Cnty., Md.*, 789 F.3d 407 (4th Cir. 2015)]

Under OFCCP regulations, federal contractors and subcontractors who are subject to Rehab Act § 503 must invite employees and job applicants to self-identify if they have a disability. The covered employers are those who have 50 or more employees working on federal contracts over $50,000. A contractor with 100 or more employees must summarize employee responses in each job group created under their affirmative action plan, and compare their performance to the OFCCP's 7% (as adjusted) goal of hiring a significant number of employees with disabilities.

The official OFCCP form (which must be used verbatim, without modifications by the employer) explains why the request is made, how the information will be used, and reassures employees that they will not suffer retaliation for self-identifying and they may be entitled to reasonable accommodation if they do. The existing form expired on January 31, 2017, but was renewed by the Office of Management and Budget (OMB) with an expiration date of January 31, 2020. [<https://www.dol.gov/ofccp/regs/compliance/sec503/Self_ID_Forms/SelfIDForms.htm>; see Kelly Jennings Yeoman and Michael C. Griffaton, *Labor and Employment Alert: Federal Contractors Have an Updated Voluntary Self-Identification of Disability Form*, Vorys Sater Seymour and Pease LLP (Feb. 1, 2017), available at Lexology.com; Annette Tyman and Michael L. Childers, *OMB Renews Disability Self-ID Form Required for Federal Contractors and Subcontractors*, Seyfarth Shaw LLP (Feb. 1, 2017), available at Lexology.com]

[B] The ADA and Disability Benefits

A February 12, 1997, EEOC Notice No. 915.002, sets out the EEOC's position that employees can legitimately make ADA claims (based on the assertion that they are qualified to perform essential job functions) at the same time that they apply for disability benefits (which are premised on inability to do gainful work).

This position was adopted by the Supreme Court. [*Cleveland v. Policy Mgmt. Sys. Corp.*, 526 U.S. 795 (1999)] According to *King v. Herbert J. Thomas Memorial Hospital* [159 F.3d 192 (4th Cir. 1998)], actually receiving disability benefits (as distinct from just applying for them) prevents an age-discrimination plaintiff from claiming she was able to perform the job at the time of her discharge.

Applying for Social Security Disability Insurance (SSDI) does not automatically preclude an ADA suit, a plaintiff who has sworn to his or her inability to work will be required to reconcile that with the position taken in the ADA suit that he or she is qualified to work. [*Gilmore v. AT&T*, 319 F.3d 1042 (8th Cir. 2003); *Lane v. BFI Waste Sys. of N. Am.*, 257 F.3d 766 (8th Cir. 2001)]

On a related issue, late in 2003 the Supreme Court decided that it was reasonable for the Commissioner of Social Security to use that agency's definition of "disability" to deny benefits to a claimant who had recovered to the point of being healthy enough to do her former job—as an elevator operator—even though that job no longer exists in significant numbers within the national economy. [*Barnhart v. Thomas*, 540 U.S. 20 (2003)]

The Ninth Circuit held in 2013 that an elementary school employee's FMLA and insurance disability claims (paid based on an application stating she was totally disabled) were not inconsistent with her ADA claim that she was denied the reasonable accommodation of being permitted to transfer to a less demanding job. The Ninth Circuit held that FMLA and insurance disability applications did not consider her future ability to work, the possibility of doing other jobs, or reasonable accommodation. [*Smith v. Clark Cnty. Sch. Dist.*, 727 F.3d 950 (9th Cir. 2013)]

However, the Second Circuit affirmed partial summary judgment for the defendant in an ADA case (that also raised ADEA and Title VII claims) because the plaintiff failed to explain why filing an SSDI application that said he was not able to work did not estop his claim of discriminatory discharge. [*Kovaco v. Rockbestos-Suprenant Cable Corp.*, 834 F.3d 128 (2d Cir. 2016)]

[C]   The FMLA

A person with a "serious health condition" (as defined by the FMLA) may also be a QIWD. An FMLA "serious health condition" causes at least three sick days and at least one visit to a doctor, with a follow-up plan of care. An ADA disability causes a substantial limitation in a major life activity.

FMLA leave, although unpaid, is easier to obtain than medical leave as a reasonable ADA accommodation, because employers with 50 or more employees have to grant FMLA leave to eligible employees. Reinstatement after FMLA leave is automatic, but ADA reinstatement requires showing of ability to perform essential work tasks (with or without reasonable accommodation).

If the employee qualifies for FMLA leave and has a disability, FMLA leave should not be denied for reasons such as lack of sufficient notice of a predictable event or failure to document the need for leave. [Vonbriesen.com, *Dancing with the Devil: Balancing FMLA and ADA Obligations* (Oct. 19, 2015) (benefitslink .com)]

It is unclear how much leave must be provided, after FMLA leave is exhausted, as a reasonable accommodation under the ADA. Once an employee has exhausted all leave provided by the employer, including FMLA leave, the employer must assess if the employee is covered by the ADA. If so, the employer must engage in the interactive process, and may have to reassign the employee to a vacant job as a reasonable accommodation.

When an employee applies for FMLA leave, the employer can offer light duty as an alternative so that the employee will be able to continue to draw a paycheck. However, the right to elect FMLA leave is absolute when the employee cannot carry out the current job because of a serious health condition, so the employee has the right to take FMLA leave if he or she prefers. If the employee opts for light duty instead of FMLA leave, the time in light duty job does not reduce the amount of FMLA leave available. For ADA purposes, the employer is not required to create light duty work, but can create a temporary position as part of the interactive process of accommodation. [Jeff Nowak, *Don't Be Tripped Up by Light Duty Obligations Under the FMLA and ADA: A Discussion of Employer Best Practices*, FMLA Insights (Oct. 3, 2014) (benefitslink.com)]

The Fifth Circuit treated FMLA and ADA requests as antagonistic, interpreting a request for FMLA leave as a claim that a serious health condition precludes the employee from carrying out the essential functions of the job, whereas a request for ADA accommodation asserts the employee's ability to do the job with suitable accommodation. [*Acker v. General Motors LLC*, No. 16-11174 (5th Cir. Apr. 10, 2017); see Wolters Kluwer Legal & Regulatory, *GM Didn't Violate FMLA by Suspending Electrician Who Failed to Follow Union-Negotiated Policy for Calling in Absences* (May 19, 2017) (benefitslink.com)]

It has been held that it is lawful to terminate an employee who cannot provide a reasonable estimate of when he or she will be able to resume all of the essential functions of the job. In a case brought by a supervisor of released felony offenders, the written job description listed 18 essential functions, including fieldwork at supervisees' homes. The court said that to show that a request for a leave of absence is reasonable, the employee must provide an estimated date for resuming essential duties, with reassurance that the employee can perform all the essential functions in the near future. [*Robert v. Bd. of Comm'rs of Brown Cnty.*, 691 F.3d 1211 (10th Cir. 2012)]

Neither having a disability nor taking FMLA leave will protect an employee from performance issues or consequences of misconduct. An insulin-dependent diabetic took FMLA leave. She hung up on at least two customers during a shift as a consumer service representative; she was already on a last chance agreement for performance issues. She said her blood sugar was low and she did not remember hanging up. The employer took the position that hanging up is an intentional action, there was no evidence of a low blood sugar episode other than her assertion; and she only discussed the medical issue when it became apparent that she was going to be fired. The Tenth Circuit held that, absent contrary evidence, the employer's honest, good-faith belief that the employee committed misconduct will overcome a discrimination or retaliation claim—even if it turns out that the employer was wrong or made a bad business decision. The Tenth Circuit said that requests for ADA accommodation are prospective in nature; asking to forgive misconduct in the past is not an accommodation. [*DeWitt v. Southwestern Bell Tel. Co.*, No. 14-3192, 2017 U.S. App. LEXIS 843 (10th Cir. Jan. 18, 2017); see David T. Wiley, *Employee's "Alternative Facts" Can't Overcome Summary Judgment for Employer*, Jackson Lewis PC (Jan. 23, 2017), available at Lexology.com]

The Tenth Circuit revived ADA (and FMLA) claims in a case where it was possible that the plaintiff was fired for taking a large amount of leave, not for the employer's explanation that he committed a safety violation and argued with a co-worker about it. The Tenth Circuit held that a reasonable jury could find that the plaintiff, who had chronic pain caused by a degenerative neck injury, had an ADA disability because of serious limitations on his ability to sleep, even though he took pain and sleep medications. [*Smothers v. Solvay Chems., Inc.*, No. 12-8013 (10th Cir. Jan. 21, 2014)]

The EEOC's position is that it violates the duty of reasonable accommodation to terminate employees who are unable to return to work or unable to return to full duty at the end of the FMLA leave. This is not necessarily the position that the courts will take, but there have been a number of settlements on this issue, and some employers have agreed to drop policies requiring termination after a certain amount of leave. The employer may be able to show undue hardship because of the cost of giving extended leave (although this argument is harder to sustain when leave is unpaid) or the operational difficulties of changing work schedules or hiring temporary employees to fill in. COBRA allows employers to provide COBRA notice to an employee on extended leave after FMLA leave has been used up, shifting the premium payment obligation to the employee.

The EEOC position is that the employer must hold the job open as an accommodation unless this is an undue hardship. It may also be required to hold open a vacant equivalent position the employee is qualified for, or even vacant non-equivalent jobs the employee is qualified for. However, if the employee fails to apply or reapply for extended leave, it may be possible to terminate the employee for job abandonment. There may also be medical information that justifies denial of further leave. If there is a need to replace an employee who is on extended leave, the employer should document the reasons why this is necessary.

Chemical Transportation Inc., settled an EEOC suit in late 2015, agreeing to pay $300,000 for ADA violations (not allowing employees to return to work when they had any medical restrictions; firing those who could not return to full unrestricted duty after 12 weeks of leave). [Luke P. Breslin, *Trucking Company to Pay $300,000 to Settle EEOC ADA Accommodation Suit*, Jackson Lewis PC (Oct. 11, 2015), available at Lexology.com]

A 2011 article recommends that if an employee's mental or physical condition precludes performing the essential functions of the job with or without reasonable accommodation, the employee should be placed on leave. An FMLA notice should be issued to anyone who misses three or more days at work. Before FMLA or other legally guaranteed leave ends, or when an employee who is not eligible for guaranteed leave applies for leave, the employer should engage in the interactive process to determine if reasonable accommodations are available to return the employee to work. The article suggests requiring that employees re-apply for extended leave at intervals (perhaps every three, six, or twelve months, depending on administrative convenience) but employees should not be terminated for failure to return to work unless they have also failed to apply for extended leave. Employers can tell employees that they must either return to work or be considered to have abandoned the job, if the medical evidence shows that the employee is able to perform the job. But extended leave is a reasonable accommodation if the employee cannot currently perform the essential functions of the job but might be able to do so in the future. Extended leave would not be required if the medical evidence shows that the employee will never be able to return to work, or if the employee has applied for LTD benefits on the basis of permanent total disability.

If the employee has applied for SSDI, the employer should document the interactive process and that the employee is unable to return to work because some courts have held that it is not inconsistent to apply for SSDI and also raise an ADA claim, because SSDI focuses on what the employee is unable to do, whereas the ADA focuses on ability to work with reasonable accommodation. [Kerry Notestine and Kelley Edwards, *Recent EEOC Lawsuits Highlight Impor-tance of Adopting Comprehensive Procedures for Managing Employee Leaves*, Littler Mendelson Insights (Feb. 2011) (benefitslink.com)]

The First Circuit ruled that an employee's seven-week trip to the Philip-pines with her seriously ill husband, for a faith healing pilgrimage, was not cov-ered by the FMLA. The employee also raised a claim of association discrimination under the ADA, which also failed: it did not violate the ADA to demand verification of her husband's condition, and a paperwork requirement is not an adverse employment action for ADA purposes. [*Tayag v. Lahey Clinic Hosp.*, 632 F.3d 788 (1st Cir. 2011)]

[D]   HIPAA and Wellness Programs

Under HIPAA, a plan may not discriminate among similarly situated per-sons based on their health status, so differences in costs or premiums are forbid-den. However, "adherence to programs of health promotion and disease prevention" (i.e., wellness programs) can lawfully give rise to premium discounts or reduced payment responsibilities. Wellness programs can include, for example, assessment of the health risks affecting individual employees, health screening, integration with the corporate attendance program, and diet or exercise plans.

DOL, HHS, and the IRS published final HIPAA regulations about wellness programs in the December 13, 2006 Federal Register. The three agencies issued a second set of joint final rules for wellness programs in mid-2013, reaffirming the agencies' belief in the value of these programs in alleviating chronic illness and keeping health care costs in check. The rules permit participatory wellness programs that are available to employees without regard to health status (e.g., rewards for taking health information seminars or completing a health question-naire; paying for health club memberships). The program can offer rewards for meeting a health goal (for example, quitting smoking; meeting a target for weight or blood cholesterol) but the rewards must not discriminate against employees with health problems. [T.D. 9620, 2013-27 I.R.B. 1]

2014 FAQs provide additional detail. For example, if an employee's doctor says that the outcome-based wellness program is not medically appropriate for the employee, the plan must provide a reasonable alternative standard such as an activity-only program (e.g., a weight-loss program). [FAQs, <http://www.dol.gov/ebsa/faqs/faq-aca18.html> (Jan. 9, 2014) (last accessed Apr. 4, 2016)] The Patient Protection and Affordable Care Act (Pub. L. No. 111-148), the health care reform program adopted in 2010, encourages wellness programs, so this will con-tinue to be a significant issue. See § 18.19[G].

In mid-2016, the EEOC issued final rules about the application of ADA Title I to wellness programs that require employees and their spouses to provide health information. The rules, issued in mid-2016, permit employers to use medical questionnaires, health risk assessments, and biometric screenings to determine the employee's health risks as part of a voluntary wellness program that offers incen-tives that do not exceed 30% of the total cost of self-only coverage. [81 Fed. Reg. 31125 (May 17, 2016); see Corie Hengst, *EEOC Announces Final Rules for Well-ness Programs*, plansponsor.com (May 16, 2016); Rachel Emma Silverman, *EEOC Issues New Rules for Wellness Programs*, WSJ.com (May 16, 2016)]

The final ADA rules for wellness programs require employees to receive notice about what information the program collects, who gets it, how it is used, and the plan's privacy and confidentiality provisions. Under these final rules, employers cannot require participation in the program; cannot deny or restrict health coverage for employees who refuse to participate; cannot retaliate against non-participating employees; and cannot use coercion or threats to force partici-pation. The EEOC Website includes a sample notice, to be used for issuing notices no later than the first day of the first plan year beginning on or after January 1, 2017. [EEOC notice: <https://www.eeoc.gov/laws/regulations/ada-wellness-notice.cfm>. See Plansponsor staff, *EEOC Provides Sample Notice for Wellness Programs*, plansponsor.com (June 21, 2016)]

The EEOC has investigated several wellness programs and brought several suits starting in August 2014.

Flambeau's self-funded health plan was only open to employees who par-ticipated in health risk assessments and biometric screening (although participa-tion did not depend on the result). The EEOC brought a suit under ADA § 12112(d)(4)(A), which forbids employers to require any medical examination unless the exam is job-related and consistent with business necessity. The com-pany prevailed at the district court level, successfully relying on the ADA safe harbor provision (§ 11202(c)(2)), which says that employers are not liable for acts based on underwriting or administering the terms of a plan that is based on underwriting, classifying, or administering risks. [*EEOC v. Flambeau, Inc.*, 131 F. Supp. 3d 849 (W.D. Wis. 2015)]

In early 2017, the Seventh Circuit affirmed dismissal of the suit, not on the merits, but because the relief sought by the plaintiff was unavailable or moot. The company reinstated the plaintiff's coverage retroactively, once he underwent the tests and paid his share of the premium. Furthermore, before the 2014 benefit year, plaintiff Flambeau had discontinued the assessment and testing as not cost-effective. A claim can be mooted if the allegedly unlawful activity ends before the suit, as long as the employer can show the discontinuance was not litigation-related. [*EEOC v. Flambeau, Inc.*, 846 F.3d 941 (7th Cir. 2017); see Gerald L. Maatman, Jr. and John S. Marrese, *Seventh Circuit Declines to Address the EEOC's Challenge to the Legality of Employer's Wellness Plan*, Seyfarth Shaw LLP (Jan. 29, 2017), available at Lexology.com; Kristin L. Bauer and Paul Patten, *Seventh Circuit Delivers Blow to EEOC Wellness Program Challenge, But Avoids Ruling on ADA Safe Harbor*, Jackson Lewis PC (Jan. 26, 2017), available at Lexology.com]

The District Court for the Eastern District of Wisconsin denied the EEOC's motion for summary judgment in a case about a wellness program. The EEOC charged that requiring employees to complete a health risk assessment if they wanted coverage under the employer's self-insured plan violated the ADA. The EEOC said that an employee who refused to fill out the health assessment and wrote an e-mail complaining about the policy, was terminated a few days after sending the e-mail. The district court said that the safe harbor for insurance plans did not apply to this plan because it was not used to underwrite or classify risk. However, the court said that the employer was entitled to summary judgment on the ADA discrimination claim because the program satisfied the statutory definition of a voluntary program. Even the possibility that the employees would have to pay 100% of the health insurance premium (if they did not complete the health assessment) did not make the program involuntary. However, the district court refused to dismiss the retaliation claim, and ordered it to be tried. [*EEOC v. Orion Energy Sys., Inc.*, 208 F. Supp. 3d 989 (E.D. Wis. 2016); see Russell Chapman, *Half a Loaf: Court Rejects ADA "Safe Harbor" But Approves Pre-Regulations Wellness Program as "Voluntary,"* Littler.com (Sept. 23, 2016) (benefitslink .com); Practical Law EE Benefits & Executive Compensation, *EEOC Loses Again in Wellness Litigation* (Nov. 10, 2016) (benefitslink.com)] The EEOC and Orion reached a settlement in April 2017. Orion agreed to pay $100,000 to the terminated employee and avoid posing disability-related inquiries or requiring medical examinations that do not satisfy the ADA's definition of voluntariness. Orion also agreed to restrict incentives to 30% of the cost of employee-only coverage. [Heather C. Panick, *EEOC and Orion Energy Systems, Inc. Settle Wellness Case*, Jackson Lewis PC (Apr. 20, 2017), available at Lexology.com]

Although the commoner type of suit has the EEOC suing an employer, a 2017 decision involves a suit by the AARP against the EEOC to challenge the 2016 final regulations. The District Court for the District of Columbia upheld the regulations at the end of 2016. The court held that, although the AARP had associational standing to sue, (its mission is advocating for the elderly), the organization failed to prove irreparable injury and thus could not obtain an injunction. The district court said that potential disclosure of the health information does not constitute public disclosure and employers are forbidden to use the information to discriminate. If employees must pay higher premiums, this is economic harm, which is not irreparable. [*AARP v. EEOC*, No. 16-2113 (JDB), 2016 U.S. Dist. LEXIS 180612; 100 Empl. Prac. Dec. (CCH) P45,710 (D.D.C. Dec. 29, 2016); see Joy P. Waltemath, *EEOC ADA and GINA Wellness Regs Survive AARP Challenge*, WK Employment Law Daily (Jan. 3, 2016) (benefitslink.com); Seth J. Safra and Laura M. Fant, *District Court Denies Preliminary Injunction in AARP Suit to Block Final Rules on Employee Wellness Programs*, Proskauer Rose LLP (Jan. 31, 2017), available at Lexology.com]

In August 2017, the District Court for the District of Columbia refused to grant deference to the EEOC's decision that wellness programs are voluntary if the incentives do not exceed 30%. The district court found that the EEOC did not have an adequate rationale for selecting this figure. However, although the court could have vacated the regulations, it chose not to do so. The regulations were sent back to the EEOC for reconsideration. [*AARP v. EEOC*, No. 16-cv-2113 (D.D.C. Aug. 22, 2017); see Pepper Hamilton LLP (Aug. 23, 2017) (benefitslink .com)]

§ 36.11   ADA ENFORCEMENT

The EEOC has enforcement power over the ADA. [42 U.S.C. § 12111(1)] The remedies available for disability discrimination are also available in retaliation cases. [42 U.S.C. § 12203(c)] ADA charges must be filed with the EEOC or the state agency. [See § 41.03 for an explanation of the process.] The charge must be filed within 180 days of the last discriminatory act (in nondeferral states) or within 300 days of the last act (in deferral states). The Title VII investigation and conciliation procedures will be followed, and the ADA remedies are equivalent to Title VII remedies, with the distinction that reasonable accommodation can be ordered as an ADA remedy.

The EEOC and the federal courts have discretion to make an attorneys' fee award to the prevailing party. If the United States loses a case, it can be required to pay attorneys' fees—but if the United States wins, the other party cannot be required to compensate the government for the costs of the case. [See 42 U.S.C. § 12205.]

§ 36.12   THE ADA PRIMA FACIE CASE

In 2016, the Fourth Circuit joined the Sixth and Seventh Circuits in holding that ADA claims must be proved using the stringent "but-for" standard, and not the less demanding "motivating factor" test. A housekeeper was injured at work; her Worker's Compensation claim was settled by mediation and she was fired a month later. The employer said that she was terminated as part of a cost-cutting restructuring plan, but the EEOC had rebuttal evidence. The jury found for the plaintiff on her WC retaliation and tortious interference claims, but for the defendant on other counts. The Fourth Circuit said that the Title VII standard that discrimination is "a" motivating factor does not apply in ADA cases. Instead, the "but-for" standard (that the adverse action would not have occurred but for discrimination) under the ADEA applies because the statutory language of the ADA is closer to the ADEA than to Title VII. [*Gentry v. E.W. Partners Mgmt. Co., Inc.*, 816 F.3d 228 (4th Cir. 2016); see Paul Holscher, *Fourth Circuit Adopts "But For" Standard for Proof of Discrimination Under Americans with Disabilities Act*, Jackson Lewis PC (Mar. 21 2016), available at Lexology.com. The "but-for" standard comes from *Gross v.FBL Fin.*, 557 U.S. 167 (2009).]

In contrast, the Eighth Circuit says that claims can proceed if the adverse employment action had both permissible and impermissible motives. [*Oehmke v. Medtronic, Inc.*, 844 F.3d 748(8th Cir. 2016); see Jody Kahn Mason, *Eighth Circuit Leaves Open the Question of Whether a "Mixed-Motive" or "But-For" Causation Standard Should Be Applied to Disability Discrimination Claims Under the ADA*, Jackson Lewis PC (Dec. 28, 2016), available at Lexology.com]

The Fifth Circuit ruled that, even after the ADAAA has taken effect, plaintiffs are still required to prove that they have a disability before they prove discrimination, rejecting the plaintiff's argument that the focus is on the existence of discrimination rather than the presence of a disability. [*Neely v. PSEG*, 736 F.3d 242 (5th Cir. 2013)]

§ 36.13   DAMAGES

Although, in the vast majority of cases, employers prevail in ADA cases, there is still the risk that high damages will be awarded in the few cases in which plaintiffs win. The Fourth Circuit upheld a jury award of $8,000 in compensatory and $100,000 in punitive damages to a deaf former package handler at FedEx who was denied reasonable accommodation. Despite numerous requests, he was denied sign language interpreters at employee meetings and training sessions. In the court's view, his supervisors' indifference to the need to accommodate his disability meant that his safety, and perhaps the safety of others, was jeopardized. [*EEOC v. Federal Express Corp.*, 513 F.3d 360 (4th Cir. 2008)]

Although the Second, Eighth, and Tenth Circuits have upheld jury verdicts granting compensatory and punitive damages, the Seventh Circuit interpreted the Civil Rights Act of 1991 to allow compensatory and punitive damages for ADA claims only if they fall under §§ 12112 or 12112(b)(5). Retaliation claims are provided for by § 12203—and therefore the remedies are limited to the equitable relief provided by 42 U.S.C. § 2000e-5(g)(1). Because the plaintiff was only entitled to equitable remedies, she had no right to a jury trial. [*Kramer v. Banc of Am. Sec., LLC*, 355 F.3d 961 (7th Cir. 2004)]

§ 36.14   ARBITRATION OF ADA CLAIMS

Wright v. Universal Maritime Service Corp. [525 U.S. 70 (1998)] involves an injured stevedore who was denied employment because potential employers deemed him to be permanently disabled. The plaintiff sued under the ADA without first filing a grievance or going through arbitration under the collective bargaining agreement.

The lower federal courts dismissed his case because of his failure to exhaust grievance remedies, but the Supreme Court unanimously reversed. Although ADA claims are subject to compulsory arbitration under the U-4 (securities industry employment agreement), the Supreme Court treated this case differently because Wright's claims arose under a statute, not a contract. Contract claims are presumed to be subject to arbitration, but statutory claims are not.

For a CBA to rule out litigation of a claim under an antidiscrimination statute, *Wright* says that the CBA must be very clear on that point. A generalized arbitration clause that fails to specify the antidiscrimination statutes that it covers will not be enough to keep disgruntled employees out of the court system.

According to *EEOC v. Waffle House Inc.* [534 U.S. 279 (2002)], the EEOC can pursue an ADA case, including victim-specific relief, even though the employee him- or herself was covered by a mandatory predispute arbitration requirement and would not have been able to sue the employer because of this requirement. [See Chapter 40 for fuller discussion of arbitration and ADR.]

CHAPTER 37

AGE DISCRIMINATION IN EMPLOYMENT ACT

§ 37.01 INTRODUCTION

The Age Discrimination in Employment Act (ADEA), unlike Title VII and the ADA, is found in Title 29 of the United States Code starting at Section 621. (Title VII and the ADEA are in Title 42). In other words, Congress considered the ADEA to be labor law instead of civil rights law. [See § 41.06[A] for a discussion of Equal Employment Opportunities Commission (EEOC) procedure for filing discrimination charges, and § 42.11 for a discussion of procedural issues arising in private ADEA lawsuits filed by an employee or class of employees.]

Congress defined its purpose in passing the ADEA as protecting older people who want to stay in the workforce and are still capable of working from discrimination involving "arbitrary age limits." The ADEA's aim is to "promote employment of older persons based on their ability rather than age; to prohibit arbitrary age discrimination in employment; to help employers and workers find ways of meeting problems arising from the impact of age on employment." [29 U.S.C. § 621]

A researcher concluded that women over age 40 face the worst workplace discrimination. Lauren Stiller Rikleen wrote in the Harvard Business Review that 40,000 dummy applications were sent to online job posting sites. Middle-aged women applying for sales jobs got the lowest level of callbacks. [Ashley S. O'Neill, *The Inbox—Dissing the Qualified*, Zuckerman Spaeder LLP (Mar. 15, 2016), available at Lexology.com; Harriet Torry, *Ageism Thwarts Policies to Boost the Senior Workforce, Study Finds*, WSJ.com (Mar. 2, 2017)]

The EEOC's position is that it is not per se illegal for an interviewer to ask for an applicant's birth date, or date of high school graduation, or to ask for college transcripts to be submitted, but the employer's motivation in asking will be considered if there is an ADEA suit. It is probably impractical for candidates to vocally protest when an improper inquiry is made, but perhaps they can say "My most recent experience is the most relevant to this job." Interviewers should avoid telling applicants that they are overqualified or have too much experience because these sound like proxies for age discrimination. [Dana Wilkie, *When Interviewers Press for Birth Dates and Grad Dates, Is It Discriminatory?*, Nelson Mullins Riley & Scarborough (Mar. 8, 2016), available at Lexology.com]

The basic rule is that anyone over age 40 is protected by the ADEA [29 U.S.C. § 631], so the protected group is not restricted to senior citizens. In a limited range of situations, being under 40 is a bona fide occupational qualification (BFOQ). In other cases, adverse employment action against an older person could be legally justified by a Reasonable Factor Other than Age (RFOA). State age discrimination suits have been upheld when young people are deprived of employment opportunities because of their youth because this, too, is discrimination "on account of age." [*Bergen Commercial Bank v. Sisler*, 157 N.J. 188 (N.J. 1999); *Zanni v. Medaphis Physician Servs. Corp.*, 240 Mich. App. 472 (2000)]

In fiscal 2016, the EEOC received 20,857 ADEA charges, and reduced its backlog somewhat by clearing 22,594 cases. The resolutions included 1,445 settlements; 1,252 withdrawals with benefits; and 3,729 administrative closures. The EEOC made 620 reasonable cause determinations, and 15,548 no-reasonable-cause determinations. Conciliation was successful in 339 cases, but, in 281 cases, conciliation was attempted but failed. There were 3,317 merit resolutions. The agency reported $88.2 million in monetary benefits obtained without litigation (much lower than the previous year's figure of $99.1 million). [EEOC, *Age Discrimination in Employment Act FY 1997-FY 2016,* <http://www.eeoc.gov/eeoc/statistics/enforcement/adea.cfm> (last viewed Mar. 15, 2017)]

According to the ABA Journal, the EEOC filed only two age discrimination cases in 2016, because the cases are difficult and costly for the agency to litigate. The Supreme Court's 2009 *Gross v. FBL Financial Services* decision (see § 37.03[B], below) made ADEA litigation much more difficult by requiring age discrimination to be the prime or motivating reason for the adverse employment action, rather than just one factor in the employer's decision. The EEOC made no-probable-cause determinations in more than two-thirds of ADEA charges (68.8%), whereas only 3.4% of harassment charges resulted in no-probable-cause findings. [FindLaw InHouse blog, *EEOC Rarely Files Suits for Age Bias* (Aug. 15, 2017), available at FindLaw.com]

See § 7.04 for discussion of cases considering whether cash balance plans are inherently discriminatory against older employees; nearly all cases have held that they are not, for various rationales (e.g., that the asserted favoritism toward younger employees merely reflects the economic principle of the time value of money).

The Pension Protection Act of 2006, Pub. L. No. 109-280, amends ADEA § 4(i) (29 U.S.C. § 623(i)). For post-PPA time frames, a plan is not guilty of age discrimination if the participant's accrued benefit is at least as great as the benefit of a similarly situated younger individual who is either a plan participant or potential plan participant. Two participants are considered to be similarly situated if they are the same as to date of hire, period of service, position, compensation, work history, etc., and differ only in their age. In making this determination, the subsidized part of any available early retirement benefit is disregarded. The accrued benefit can be expressed as an annuity payable at Normal Retirement Age (NRA) , the current value of the accumulated percentage of the employee's final average compensation (the measure used by many defined benefit plans) or the balance of a hypothetical account (i.e., a cash balance plan).

The Lilly Ledbetter Fair Pay Act, Pub. L. No. 111-2 (signed Jan. 29, 2009), amends the ADEA (as well as Title VII, the ADA, and the Rehabilitation Act), to reverse the Supreme Court's *Ledbetter v. Goodyear Tire & Rubber,* 550 U.S. 618 (2007) ruling about the timing of discrimination suits. The Ledbetter Act adds a new ADEA § 7(d)(3), providing that an unlawful employment practice is deemed to occur when it is initially adopted; when a person first becomes subject to the practice—or each time the person is affected by the practice, e.g., every time he or she receives a paycheck that is unfairly low because of discrimination. Depending on whether or not the state has a work-sharing agreement with the EEOC, suit must be brought either within 180 days or 300 days of the last act covered by the Act. A successful plaintiff can recover back pay for up to two years before the date the charge was filed. The Act became effective as if it had become law the day before the Supreme Court *Ledbetter* decision—with the result that any cases that were pending on May 28, 2007, or have been filed since then, can take advantage of the statute's timing rules.

The EEOC Compliance Manual § 2-IVC.4, Compensation Discrimination, has been amended to allow suit 180 or 300 days after receipt of compensation affected by a discriminatory practice, and says the time frames apply to "all forms of compensation, including the payment of pension benefits," but the EEOC "strongly encourages" suit within 180 or 300 days of retirement to make sure that the suit is timely.

In 2005, the Supreme Court ruled that disparate impact ADEA claims are allowed—opening the door to challenges to allegedly age-neutral policies that plaintiffs deem to have unfair effects on older workers. [*Smith v. City of Jackson*, 544 U.S. 228 (2005)]

§ 37.02 ADEA EXCEPTIONS

The ADEA bars job discrimination, so a discharge for good cause will not violate the ADEA. As is true of many other labor and anti-discrimination laws, the ADEA exempts very small businesses. The definition of "employer" is limited to industries affecting commerce and having 20 or more employees for each workday in each of 20 or more weeks in the current or previous year. [29 U.S.C. § 630(b)]

The ADEA applies to employees of the United States branch of a foreign corporation that has 20 or more employees worldwide; there need not be 20 employees at the U.S. branch. [*Morelli v. Cedel*, 141 F.3d 39 (2d Cir. 1998)] The number of employees at several small affiliates of a larger corporation can be aggregated for the 20-employee test if the parent company directed the discriminatory act or policy; the original larger enterprise was split up to avoid liability; and the corporate veil can be pierced (i.e., the parent can be held liable for the subsidiaries' debts, torts, and breaches of contract). [*Papa v. Katy Indus. Inc.*, 166 F.3d 937 (7th Cir. 1999)]

According to a 2017 Ninth Circuit decision, a political subdivision of a state is deemed to be an employer for ADEA purposes whether or not it has 20 employees. However, the Sixth, Seventh, Eighth and Tenth Circuits have found the ADEA text to be ambiguous, so context is required to interpret it. [*Guido v. Mount Lemmon Fire Dist.*, No. 15-15030 (9th Cir. June 19, 2017); see Daniel B. Pasternak, *Ninth Circuit Court of Appeals: Public Employers with Less Than 20*

Employees Are Covered by the ADEA, Squire Patton Boggs (June 26, 2017), available at Lexology.com]

Although the general rule under the ADEA is that no one can be compelled to retire simply because of that person's age, there is an important exception. Under 29 U.S.C. § 631, a person who has been a "bona fide executive or high policy maker" for two years just before retirement, can lawfully be compelled to retire at 65, as long as he or she is entitled to aggregate retirement benefits that are the equivalent of an annuity of $44,000 a year or more. EEOC Guidelines [29 C.F.R. § 1625.12(d)] define a bona fide policymaker as the manager of an entire enterprise, or at least a customarily recognized department or subdivision. He or she must direct the work of at least two employees, and must hold a job that regularly involves the exercise of discretionary power. At least 80% of work time (or at least 60% in a retail or service business) must be spent on managing the business rather than on routine tasks. The Higher Education Amendments of 1998 [H.R. 6 (Oct. 7, 1998)] reinstate a traditional ADEA exception. Under the Amendments, it is lawful to require tenured faculty members to retire solely on the basis of age. Although this act affects a small group of individuals, it is significant in showing a possible trend toward restricting the scope of the ADEA and other civil rights legislation.

§ 37.03 FORBIDDEN PRACTICES

[A] Statutory Prohibitions

Under 29 U.S.C. § 623, employers are forbidden to:

- Discriminate because of age (by firing or failing or refusing to hire, or in any other way) against anyone in connection with "compensation, terms, conditions, or privileges of employment";

- Use age to "limit, segregate, or classify" employees that reduce employment opportunities or "otherwise adversely affect" status as an employee;

- Reduce any employee's wage rate to comply with the ADEA;

- Discriminate against an employee or job applicant because of that person's protests about age discrimination, or in retaliation for that person's bringing an ADEA charge or involvement in someone else's ADEA charge;

- Publish Help Wanted ads that indicate "any preference, limitation, specification, or discrimination, based on age."

Section 623 also forbids age discrimination perpetrated by employment agencies and unions, but those provisions are outside the scope of this book.

The EEOC has ruled that the ADEA applies to apprenticeship programs. Early in 2005, the Fourth Circuit upheld this rule as valid and not contrary to the Congressional intent in passing the ADEA. [*EEOC v. Seafarers Int'l Union*, 394 F.3d 197 (4th Cir. 2005)]

Only significant employment actions will support a suit.

The Eighth Circuit affirmed dismissal of an ADEA suit, finding that a small reduction in hours, negative performance reviews, and allegations of differential treatment as compared to younger employees (e.g., he claimed that younger workers were given advance notice of inspections) were inadequate to constitute adverse employment actions [*Baucom v. Holiday Cos. Inc.*, 428 F.3d 764 (8th Cir. 2005)]

In a case of first impression for the Circuit, the Fifth Circuit ruled in 2011 that a hostile work environment suit can be brought under the ADEA. The plaintiff, Dediol, established that: he was over 40; subjected to harassment; it was severe enough to create an objectively intimidating, hostile, or offensive work environment; there was a rationale for imposing liability on the employer. He was also permitted to pursue constructive discharge and religiously hostile work environment claims after being denied permission for time off for a church event. [*Dediol v. Best Chevrolet Inc.*, 655 F.3d 435 (5th Cir. 2011)]

Unlike the ADA, the ADEA does not require employers to provide reasonable accommodation. For example, the Eighth Circuit granted summary judgment for the employer when a 63-year-old employee's job was eliminated when the staff was streamlined. The court held that the employer had no obligation to find her another job within the company. [*Haggenmiller v. ABM Parking Servs., Inc.*, No. 15-3107, 2016 WL 4791860 (8th Cir. Sept. 14, 2016); see Bruce J. Douglas, *Minnesota Employer Had No Duty to Find New Position for Older Worker, Eighth Circuit Holds*, Ogletree Deakins (Oct. 10, 2016), available at Lexology.com]

An Alameda County judge approved age discrimination claims of 130 employees laid off by the Lawrence Livermore National Laboratory, finding that they provided adequate evidence of disproportionate termination of employees older than age 40 and reassignment of their duties to younger workers. The ex-employees had an average age of 54 and an average tenure of 20 years at the laboratory. This decision affects a group of consolidated suits filed in 2009 after the lab was privatized. [Shelley Eades, *Judge OKs Age Bias Claims Against Lawrence Livermore Lab*, The Recorder (Oct. 17, 2012) (law.com)]

But, in the second phase of the trial, an Oakland jury found for the defense, holding that 2008 mass layoffs did not have an adverse impact on older workers. In May 2013, a jury awarded $2.8 million in economic damages on findings that the lab illegally breached the plaintiffs' employment contracts, but the second jury rejected the disparate impact age claims, rejecting the request for $25 million in emotional distress damages. [*Andrews v. Lawrence Livermore*, No. C 11-3930 CS (Cal. Super. May 10, 2013)]

The third trial in the case, a jury trial, involved 10 out of the original 130 plaintiffs; the 10 are scientists and engineers laid off in 2008 when the lab was privatized. The Phase 1 trial in early 2013 resulted in more than $2.7 million in breach of contract damages for five plaintiffs. At the Phase 2 trial in late 2013, a different jury found that the layoff did not have a disproportionate impact on employees aged 40 and over. On January 20, 2015, however, a continuance was announced for the case to be mediated. After months of mediation, the case was settled in late 2015 for $37.3 million, with no admission of liability. [*Andrews, et. al. v. Lawrence Livermore National Sec., LLC*, No. RG09453596 (settled 2015)]

In 2015, the Eleventh Circuit, unlike the Fifth, Seventh, Eighth, and Tenth Circuits allowed a disparate impact suit by a job applicant (as distinct from a current employee). But in late 2016, the Eleventh Circuit reversed its earlier opinion and joined the other circuits. The 49-year-old plaintiff applied to work at a company that was looking for people two or three years out of college. [*Villarreal v. RJ Reynolds,* 839 F.3d 958 (11th Cir. 2016); see J. William Manuel, *Can a Job Applicant File a Disparate Impact ADEA Claim? No—According to the Eleventh Circuit,* Bradley Arant Boult Cummings LLP (Oct. 11, 2016), available at Lexology.com; Casey C. Sullivan, *11th Circuit Deals a Major Blow to Age Discrimination Suits,* FindLaw InHouse blog (Oct. 18, 2016), available at FindLaw .com]

As in many other types of litigation, settlements are common in ADEA cases, and can be quite costly to the employer:

- Rental Pro, a Kentucky company that rents miscellaneous equipment, agreed to pay $37,000 to settle a suit about terminating 52-year-old Ronald Johnson. The company's owner mentioned "young blood" and "younger and peppier employees." [*EEOC v. Rental Pro*, No. 6:15-cv-00154-GFVT (E.D. Ky., settled 2016); see EEOC Press Release, *Rental Pro to Pay $37,000 to Settle EEOC Age Discrimination Lawsuit* (Feb. 2, 2016) (benefitslink.com)]

- Popeye's Louisiana Kitchen agreed to pay $36,000 (i.e., full back pay with liquidated damages) to settle EEOC ADEA charges. Leroy Keasley, 40, Kevin Bryant, 58, and Lula Wright-Hill, 54 were denied hiring; Wright-Hill and Bryant were also veterans. EEOC said that manager asked Wright-Hill and Keasley how old they were and told them they were too old to work in the restaurant. The job application was revised to eliminate the requirement of stating age or date of birth. [Plansponsor staff, *Restaurant Manager Accused of Rejecting "Too Old" Job Candidates*, plansponsor.com (Jan. 22, 2016)]

- Seymour Midwest (a tool manufacturing company) agreed to pay $100,000; the EEOC charged that the company asked applicant Steve Maril if he was within the company's "ideal range" of 45–52, and refused to hire him when they discovered he was 58. [Rebecca Moore, *Firm Ordered to Stop Asking Applicants Age Before Job Offer* (plansponsor .com) (Jan. 8, 2016)]

- Texas Roadhouse agreed to pay $12 million to settle charges that persons aged 40 and over were denied jobs as servers, hosts, server assistants, and bartenders, pursuant to a nationwide policy of age discrimination. The EEOC sued Texas Roadhouse in September 2011. There was a trial that lasted almost a month, resulting in a hung jury. Retrial was scheduled for May 15, 2017, but the case was settled in March. [*EEOC v. Texas Road-house,* No. 1:11-cv-11732-DJC (D. Mass., settled Mar. 31, 2017); see Amanda Umpierrez, *Texas Roadhouse to Pay $12 Million in Age Dis-crimination Lawsuit,* plansponsor.com (Apr. 3, 2017)]

In mid-2016, the EEOC released Enforcement Guidance on Retaliation and Related Issues, superseding the provisions in the 1998 Compliance Manual pro-visions. The guidance covers the ADEA as well as several other anti-discrimination statutes. Retaliation means any action that could deter a reasonable person from engaging in legally protected activity. Both "participation" and "opposition" are legally protected. The EEOC says that internal complaints made before a charge is filed constitute participation, which is defined as mak-ing a charge, testifying, or otherwise being involved in a proceeding or investi-gation. Opposition means opposing alleged discrimination by the employer. Three is a reasonableness requirement for opposition, but not for participation. [<https://www.eeoc.gov/laws/guidance/retaliation-guidance.cfm?utm_content= &utm_medium=email&utm_name=&utm_source=govdelivery&utm_term=>; Derek G. Barella et. al., *EEOC Issues Final Guidance on Employer Retalia-tion*, Winston & Strawn LLP (Sept. 1, 2016), available at Lexology.com]

[B] Supreme Court Precedents

A Supreme Court case, *Public Employees Retirement System of Ohio v. Betts* [492 U.S. 158 (1989)], held that the ADEA did not apply to employee ben-efits. In 1990, Congress amended the statute, adding a new § 630(l), extending the ADEA ban on age discrimination in "compensation, terms, conditions, or privi-leges of employment" to cover "benefits provided pursuant to a bona fide employee benefit plan."

To win, the ADEA plaintiff does not have to show that he or she was replaced by someone under 40; it may even be possible to win by showing age-motivated replacement by another person over 40 (for instance, choosing some-one who will retire soon, thus removing two older workers from the workplace). [*O'Connor v. Consol. Coin Caterers Corp.*, 517 U.S. 308 (1997)]

The Tenth Circuit refused to impose a bright-line test (where an age differ-ence of five years or less would rule out age discrimination), and permitted an

ADEA action to proceed when a 62-year-old was replaced by a 57-year-old. The small gap in ages would make it harder for the plaintiff to prevail, but it was only one factor for the jury to consider. [*Whittington v. Nordam Grp. Inc.*, 429 F.3d 986 (10th Cir. 2005)]

In 2004, the Supreme Court ruled that one group of over-40 workers could not use the ADEA to charge they were the victims of discrimination in favor of another group of over-40 workers who were older than they were. (This was a retiree health benefits case about grandfathered benefits.) The Supreme Court concluded that the ADEA permits employers to favor their oldest group of workers, even at the expense of younger workers who are nevertheless over 40 and covered by the ADEA. [*General Dynamics Land Sys., Inc. v. Cline*, 540 U.S. 581 (2004); see also *Lawrence v. Town of Irondequoit*, 246 F. Supp. 2d 150 (W.D.N.Y. 2002), permitting employers to enhance retiree health benefits for persons over 80.]

The EEOC adapted its ADEA regulations to conform to *Cline* and provide that it is lawful to favor the oldest employees over younger, but still, ADEA-eligible, employees. The agency revised § 1625.2 so that its caption is "discrimination prohibited by the Act," rather than "Discrimination between individuals protected by the Act." Asking for a date of birth or age on a job application is not a per se violation, but will be closely scrutinized by the EEOC because it could have the effect of discouraging older applicants.

The final rule, published in mid-2007, states that employers are not required to prefer older individuals, and applicable state or local laws forbidding preferences for older individuals remain valid. [72 Fed. Reg. 36873 (July 6, 2007)]

The Third Circuit ruled in early 2017 that workers in their 50s can be characterized as a subgroup of ADEA plaintiffs, if the employer's policies place them at a disadvantage versus other workers over 40. The Third Circuit allowed subgroup comparisons as proof of a disparate impact claim, but the Second, Sixth, and Eighth Circuits have rejected subgroup claims. [*Karlo v. Pittsburgh Glass Works, LLC*, No. 15-3435, 2017 WL 83385 (3d Cir. Jan. 10, 2017); see Evandro C. Gigante, Third *Circuit Permits ADEA "Subgroup" Claims,* Proskauer Rose LLP (Feb. 16, 2017), available at Lexology.com; John M. O'Connor, *50 Really Is the New 40,* Epstein Becker Green (Jan. 17, 2017), available at Lexology.com; Michael D. Mandel et. al., *Old and Older: 3rd Circuit Validates Age Discrimination Subgroup Theory,* McGuireWoods LLP (Jan. 13, 2017), available at Lexology.com]

A group of Mississippi police officers objected to a plan that gave higher percentage raises to police officers with *fewer* than five years' service. Because the veteran officers tended to be older than those with shorter tenure, they alleged that the practice had a disparate impact on older officers, even though it did not explicitly categorize them on the basis of age. The U.S. Supreme Court ruled in the spring of 2005 that the plaintiffs did not have a valid claim—but the Court clarified that, under the right circumstances, disparate-impact ADEA cases can be valid, because the ADEA's statutory language is very close to that of Title VII.

However, employers who are charged with disparate impact age discrimination can raise a defense that the disputed practice is based on reasonable factors other than age (RFOA), whereas there is no similar defense in race or sex discrimination cases.

The plaintiffs in this case were unsuccessful because they failed to identify the specific aspect of the pay plan that harmed the interests of older workers. The defendant, on the other hand, had a reasonable explanation for its adoption of the practice: to retain the newer officers, their compensation had to be brought closer to market norms. [*Smith v. City of Jackson, Miss.*, 544 U.S. 228 (2005)]

In mid-2009, the Supreme Court decided, in *Gross v. FBL Financial*, that in order to win, a mixed-motive ADEA plaintiff must prove by a preponderance of the evidence that age was the "but-for" cause of the challenged employment action: that it would never have occurred but-for the plaintiff's age. The burden of persuasion is always on the plaintiff, and can be met by either direct or circumstantial evidence. The burden of persuasion never shifts to the defendant. This is not the same standard applied in Title VII, but the Supreme Court stressed the difference in wording and legislative history between the ADEA and Title VII. [*Gross v. FBL Fin. Servs., Inc.*, 557 U.S. 167 (2009)]

St. Mary's Honor Center v. Hicks [509 U.S. 502 (1993)] says that the plaintiff always has the "ultimate burden of persuasion." So if the judge or jury (whichever is responsible for determining the facts of the case) does not believe the employer's explanation of the reasons behind its conduct, the plaintiff could still lose—if he or she fails to provide adequate evidence. The *Hicks* standard is sometimes called "pretext-plus": The plaintiff has to do more than show the defendant's excuses are a mere pretext for discrimination.

Although the ADEA statute explicitly waives sovereign immunity, permitting suits by state employees, the Supreme Court ruled that Congress violated the Eleventh Amendment by abrogating sovereign immunity without demonstrating a history of violations of this type committed by state employers. [*Kimel v. Florida Bd. of Regents*, 528 U.S. 62 (1999)]

The Ninth Circuit ruled in mid-2016 that the ADEA does not rule out First Amendment retaliation claims under the civil rights statute 42 U.S.C. § 1983. Therefore, public-sector employees can use § 1983 to sue a state or local government entity or official for age-based retaliation, even though state actors are immune from ADEA claims. In this reading, a public employee who alleges retaliation for making age discrimination complaints can sue under § 1983, but cannot sue for the underlying age discrimination. [*Stilwell v. City of Williams*, 831 F.3d 1234 (9th Cir. 2016); see Billie D. Wenter, *Ninth Circuit Holds Section 1983 First Amendment Retaliation Claim Not Necessarily Precluded by Age Discrimination in Employment Act,* Littler Mendelson PC (Aug. 9, 2016), available at Lexology .com]

The Supreme Court's June 2000 decision in *Reeves v. Sanderson Plumbing Products Inc.* [530 U.S. 133 (2000)] is a narrow procedural one. It holds that an ADEA plaintiff can defeat a motion for judgment as a matter of law (a procedural technique for terminating a lawsuit without a full trial) by establishing a prima facie case plus enough evidence for a reasonable court or jury to find that the employer's defense is merely pretextual. It is not required that the plaintiff introduce any further evidence at this stage, unless a rational finder of fact would not be able to find the defendant's conduct discriminatory. However, *Reeves* had little practical impact on the litigation climate, it certainly didn't issue in a new pro-plaintiff era.

The Supreme Court permitted an ADEA suit to proceed, after the complainant filed a Form 283 intake questionnaire with the EEOC, but did not file the official Form 5 (charge). The EEOC did not carry out informal dispute resolution with the employer. The Supreme Court held that a valid ADEA charge requires only a few items of information (the name of the charging party, the nature of the allegation, and a request that the EEOC settle a dispute or take remedial action). In this case, the employer was aware that the plaintiff and 13 other employees had alleged age discrimination. The Court remanded the case to the district court, holding that the lower court can make up for the deficiency by attempting to reconcile the parties in a settlement. (The EEOC stated that it has improved its procedures to make sure the same problem will not recur.) [*Federal Express Corp. v. Holowecki*, 552 U.S. 389 (2008); see also *Holender v. Mutual Indus. N. Inc.*, 527 F.3d 352 (3d Cir. 2008), in which the Third Circuit allowed a suit to proceed based on the filing of a two-page document, including an EEOC Form 5 ("Charge of Discrimination"). The Third Circuit deemed the document to be a valid charge because it contained the information required by the regulations.]

In February 2008, the Supreme Court did not really resolve the question of whether testimony of bias exhibited by a different supervisor is admissible to show a corporate culture of discrimination. The Court did not adopt the district court's outright ban on testimony by employees of other supervisors, but neither did it adopt the Tenth Circuit's position that such testimony should always be admitted. The Supreme Court required a fact-based inquiry based on balancing relevance against prejudice, and stated that, in general, the courts of appeals should defer to the district court's determination (because the district court hears all of the testimony instead of just seeing the record on appeal). Instead of reversing, the Tenth Circuit should have sent the case back to the district court. Because the two statutes use similar language, the ruling also applies to "different-supervisor" testimony in Title VII cases. The likely result of this decision is that employers will have to fully litigate more cases: fewer cases will be disposed of at the summary judgment stage, because plaintiffs will be able to offer a broader range of evidence at the early stages. [*Sprint/United Mgmt. Co. v. Mendelsohn*, 552 U.S. 379 (2008)] Before the Supreme Court decision, Sprint settled ADEA charges brought by 1,700 employees laid off between October 2001 and March 2003 for $57 million; the employees were expected to receive between $4,226 and $35,738 each. The company denied wrongdoing but wanted to reduce its legal fees by settling the case. [Rebecca Moore, *Sprint Settles Age Discrimination Suits for $57M*, plansponsor.com (Sept. 18, 2007)]

The Supreme Court also ruled in 2008 that Federal employees can use the counterpart of the ADEA that covers federal workers to assert age-based retaliation claims., [*Gomez-Perez v. Potter*, 553 U.S. 474 (2008)] and that the employer always has the burden of production and the burden of proof when it comes to the affirmative defense of reasonable factors other than age (RFOA). [*Meacham v. Knolls Atomic Power Labs*, 554 U.S. 84 (2008)]

[C] Employee Status

ADEA cases are limited to the employment context, not all aspects of economic life. Therefore, it could not be an ADEA violation to use age to refuse an automobile dealership to an applicant; dealers are contractors, not employees. [*Mangram v. GM Corp.*, 108 F.3d 61 (4th Cir. 1997)]

Salespersons who are independent contractors are not covered by the ADEA. [*Oestman v. Nat'l Farmers Unions Inc.*, 958 F.2d 303 (10th Cir. 1992)] The Eighth Circuit ruled in 2010 that it was not a violation of the ADEA to fire an independent contractor marketing representative and replace her with a younger employee. [*Ernster v. Luxco, Inc.*, 596 F.3d 1000 (8th Cir. 2010); see CCH Pensions and Benefits, *Independent Contractors Are Not Protected by ADEA When Terminated* (Mar. 19, 2010) (benefitslink.com)]

The critical test of employee status is whether the economic realities of that person's situation are more like employment or more like another relationship (such as being a partner in a partnership). [*EEOC v. Sidley Austin Brown & Wood*, 315 F.3d 696 (7th Cir. 2002)] The shareholders in a professional corporation are not counted in determining if the PC has 20 "employees" for business purposes. [*Schmidt v. Ottawa Med. Ctr. PC*, 322 F.3d 461 (7th Cir. 2003)]

■ **TIP:** In April 2003, the Supreme Court ruled (although in an ADA rather than an ADEA case, and a case brought by someone who was an ordinary employee rather than by a shareholder-director) that doctors-shareholders in medical PCs are NOT employees, and are not counted in determining if the business has enough employees to be subject to an anti-discrimination statute. [*Clackamas Gastroenterology Assocs., PC v. Wells*, 538 U.S. 440 (2003); a later ADA case also finds that a medical Professional Corporation doctor/shareholder was not an employee: *Bluestein v. Cent. Wis. Anesthesiology*, 769 F.3d 944 (7th Cir. 2014)]

The Eighth Circuit affirmed summary judgment for the employer in a Minnesota civil rights case. The plaintiff, Nash, was hired as an intern when he was 54. Although he was not considered a very good worker, he was hired full-time at age 55. He was fired for poor performance in less than six months. The Eighth Circuit held that Nash failed to rebut the employer's legitimate rationale for firing him. He was replaced by younger employees, but they were interns too and were replaced at the end of their internship. [*Nash v. Optomec, Inc.*, 849 F.3d

780 (8th Cir. 2017); see Andrew E. Tanick, *Eighth Circuit Methodically Rejects Plaintiff's Allegations of Pretext in Age Discrimination Case*, Ogletree Deakins (Mar. 9, 2017), available at Lexology.com]

[D] Occupational Qualifications and RFOAs

Being under 40 can be a bona fide occupational qualification (BFOQ) for a narrow range of jobs, usually involving public safety (e.g., the strength, agility, and quick reaction time required of police officers and firefighters), [see 29 U.S.C. § 623(f)(1)] but most ordinary private sector jobs will not give rise to a BFOQ defense. The First Circuit held that forced retirement of police officers in Puerto Rico did not violate the ADEA, and the older officers were not entitled to keep their jobs by passing a skills test. [*Correa-Ruiz v. Fortuno*, 573 F.3d 1 (1st Cir. 2009)]

Reasonable factors other than age (RFOA) can offer a defense, as long as the employer used objective, job-related criteria to make the employment decision, and applied those criteria uniformly. Courts have often accepted arguments that the employer's decision was not really age-based, but was inspired by factors that merely tend to go along with age: for instance, the tendency of salaries to rise with experience. Employers in search of cost cutting might discharge higher-paid older workers in order to replace them with lower-paid workers.

The RFOA is an affirmative defense—i.e., one that the employer has to prove, not one that the plaintiff must disprove, and the employer has the burden of production and the burden of proof on the RFOA defense. [*Meacham v. Knolls Atomic Power Labs*, 554 U.S. 84 (2008)]

The EEOC Regulations say that, if the RFOA has a disparate impact on over-40 workers, the employer must prove that it has a business necessity for the action. The EEOC issued an NPR on March 31, 2008, in response to the *Smith v. City of Jackson* decision. Based on the comments received, the EEOC decided to issue further guidance, and about two years later, in February 2010, the EEOC published a Notice of Proposed Rulemaking (NPR) to define "reasonable factors other than age" under the ADEA. The determination of whether an employment practice is based on RFOA is made based on the facts and circumstances, and whether the employer responded prudently to the facts of the case.

RFOAs must be objectively reasonable (assessed from the point of view of a reasonable employer acting under similar circumstances), and the employer must manifest prudence and awareness of responsibilities under the ADEA. A reasonable factor is one that an employer that uses reasonable care to avoid limiting the employment opportunities of older persons would use. Reasonableness is affected by the design of the practice, which must be reasonably administered to further a legitimate business purpose. The NPR permits consideration of job performance, skill sets, and flexibility in deciding who will be affected by a RIF—as long as the employer has made reasonable efforts to be accurate and fair, and has taken steps to ameliorate avoidable harm.

In 2012, the EEOC issued a Q&A, explaining what employers must do to use a Reasonable Factors Other Than Age (RFOA) defense when practices that are neutral on their face but might have disparate impact on older workers are challenged. The employer is only required to prove an RFOA after an employee has identified a specific business practice with disparate impact on older workers. An RFOA is reasonably designed when administered to achieve a legitimate business purpose—for example, a physical test for police patrol officers.

Whether the factors are indeed reasonable depends on, e.g.,

- Their relation to the employer's stated business purpose;

- The extent to which the factor is accurately defined and fairly and accurately applied (application includes training managers and supervisors);

- Limits on supervisors' discretion, especially when the criteria are vulnerable to negative age-based stereotypes;

- The extent to which the employer assessed the adverse impact of the practice on older workers;

- The degree of harm to workers over 40—not just the number of people affected and the extent of the injury, but the employer's measures to reduce harm, balanced against the burden of the actual and potential measures

The EEOC stresses that these are not elements that all employers must prove in every case, merely characteristics of reasonable practices.

The EEOC said that, unlike an employment test that has been challenged under Title VII, it is not necessary for the employer to produce a validation study about the RFOA.

The EEOC says it is not unreasonable to use subjective decision-making (e.g., ranking an applicant or employee's qualities such as flexibility and willingness to learn new things), but it is useful to give supervisors evaluation criteria to help them avoid age-based stereotypes. The EEOC said that employers are not obligated to discover and use the least discriminatory method of achieving the purpose—but attempts to limit harm to older persons are not irrelevant. [EEOC, *Questions and Answers on EEOC Final Rule on Disparate Impact and "Reasonable Factors Other Than Age" Under the Age Discrimination in Employment Act of 1967*, <http://www.eeoc.gov/laws/regulations/adea_rfoa_qa_final_rule.cfm> (last accessed Mar. 15, 2017)]

It is a defense to an age discrimination charge if an employer follows the provisions of "a bona fide seniority system that is not intended to evade" the ADEA's purposes. [29 U.S.C. § 623(f); 29 C.F.R. § 1625.8] However, even a valid seniority system cannot be used to impose involuntary retirement on an employee who is capable of working and wants to continue. Furthermore, older seniority systems (and retirement plans) are not "grandfathered in." Section 623(k) requires all seniority systems and benefit plans to comply with the ADEA, no matter when they were adopted.

§ 37.04 IMPLICATIONS FOR BENEFIT PLANS

[A] Generally

At one time, it would have been accurate to say that the ADEA covered only hiring, firing, and salary, but not employee benefits, based on a Supreme Court decision. [*Public Employees Ret. Sys. of Ohio v. Betts*, 492 U.S. 158 (1989)] In 1990, however, Congress passed a statute, the Older Workers Benefit Protection Act (OWBPA) to make it clear that the ADEA covers all of the terms and conditions of employment, including the full compensation package. Therefore, in the current legal environment, it is important to discover how the ADEA interacts with Employment Retirement Income Security Act (ERISA), insurance laws, and other laws affecting compensation and benefits.

Section 623(i) takes up the question of how the ADEA interacts with employee benefit plans. Employers are forbidden to "establish or maintain" a pension plan that requires or even permits age-based termination or reduction of pension credits. In a defined benefit plan, benefits must continue to accrue at the same rate. In a defined contribution plan, the employer's allocations must be made to all employees' accounts on the same basis, irrespective of their ages. [29 U.S.C. § 623(i)(1)] People who count as "highly compensated employees" for tax purposes are not entitled to this protection. [See 29 U.S.C. § 623(i)(5)]

The ADEA provides various defenses and safe harbors for employers. Voluntary early retirement plans are allowable as long as they are consistent with the ADEA's purpose of protecting employment rights for older workers. [29 U.S.C. § 623(f)(B)(2)]

It is permissible for a plan to put an upper limit on the amount of benefits a plan can provide to anyone, or to limit the number of years of employment that can be taken into account, as long as these provisions are imposed without regard to age. [29 U.S.C. § 623(i)(2)] For instance, if the plan does not permit crediting of more than 30 years of service, this is an allowable age-neutral provision because it applies to employees with more than 30 years' tenure whether they started working for the company at age 18 or age 40.

Once an employee has reached the plan's Normal Retirement Age (NRA) and has started to receive a pension, then the employer's obligation to continue accruing benefits is satisfied by the actuarial equivalent of the pension benefits themselves. [29 U.S.C. § 623(i)(3)(A)]

Section 623(i)(3)(B) says that, for employees who have reached NRA but have not started to draw a pension (typically, employees who defer their retirement and are still working), and whose benefits have not been suspended pursuant to ERISA § 203(a)(3)(B) or I.R.C. § 411(a)(3)(B), the employer's obligation to keep accruing benefits is satisfied by making an actuarial adjustment to the pension that the employee eventually receives, so that he or she gets a larger pension because of deferred retirement.

Final and proposed IRS regulations were published in September 2014 about hybrid defined benefit plans. (A hybrid defined benefit plan expresses the accrued benefit as the balance of a hypothetical account or the current value of the accumulated percentage of the participant's final average compensation.) For plan years that begin on or after January 1, 2016, the final regulations provide that, if the annual benefit payable to a participant before NRA is greater than the annual benefit for a corresponding form of benefit for any similarly situated older person who is or could be a participant and who is at or before NRA, then the excess benefit is not part of the subsidized portion of an early retirement benefit. It will not be disregarded for age discrimination purposes.

An amendment that decreases a participant's accrued benefit causes the plan to fail Code § 411 testing. The September 2014 proposed regulations explain when a hybrid plan fails to satisfy § 411(b)(1)(H), the rules that forbid reduction of benefit accrual because the employee has attained a particular age, if the plan's interest credit for any plan year is higher than a market rate of return. An amendment that has the effect of eliminating or reducing an early retirement benefit or an optional form of benefit for service performed before the amendment is deemed to reduce the accrued benefit. The proposed regulations note that the rules about market rate of return conflict with the anti-cutback rules. Therefore, the IRS will permit a plan whose interest crediting rate is noncompliant to be amended with respect to benefits already accrued, to bring the interest crediting rate into conformity with the rules. [T.D. 9693, 2014-41 I.R.B. 596]

The 2014's "Cromnibus" legislation provides that if, on or before December 8, 2014, a defined benefit plan's NRA was an age allowed by law or the age when at number of years of service of at least 30 was completed (whichever is earlier), the plan is not disqualified merely because the NRA applies only to certain participants, or only to the employees of certain employers.

Because the ADEA covers persons over age 40, the protected group includes many people who will voluntarily elect early retirement. Section 623(l) says that it does not constitute age discrimination for a pension plan to set a minimum retirement age as a condition for being eligible for either early or normal retirement.

A defined benefit plan can lawfully provide early retirement subsidies, or supplement the Social Security benefits of retirees who get a reduced benefit because they retire before the plan's NRA. [29 U.S.C. § 623(l)(1)(B). With respect to retiree health benefits, also see 29 U.S.C. § 623(l)(2)(D).]

There is no ADEA violation if a departing employee's severance pay is reduced to account for the value of retiree health benefits, and/or the value of additional pension benefits that are made available because of a contingency that is not based on age to a person who is already eligible for a full retirement benefit. [29 U.S.C. § 623(l)(2)] For this purpose, severance pay is defined to include certain supplemental unemployment insurance benefits. [See 29 U.S.C. § 613(l)(2)(C) and I.R.C. § 501(c)(17).]

■ **TIP:**   If the employer says that retiree health benefits will be provided, and reduces severance pay accordingly, but fails to provide retiree health benefits, 29 U.S.C. § 623(l)(2)(F) lets employees sue for "specific performance" (i.e., to make the employer provide the benefits). This is an additional right, over and above any other remedies the individual has.

In mid-2003, the EEOC reversed its earlier position and proposed Regulations under which employers would be allowed to coordinate retiree health benefits with Medicare: i.e., it would not be considered an ADEA violation to reduce or even eliminate retiree health benefits at the point at which the ex-employees become eligible for Medicare; the rule was finalized in 2004. [68 Fed. Reg. 41542 (July 14, 2003)] The EEOC's authority to promulgate this rule was upheld by the Third Circuit (and certiorari was denied) based on a 2005 Supreme Court administrative law decision requiring deference to an agency's reasonable interpretation of statutes within the agency's scope of operations. [*AARP v. EEOC*, 489 F.3d 558 (3d Cir. 2007), *appeal dismissed*, 128 S. Ct. 1733 (Mar. 28, 2008). The administrative law case is *National Cable & Telecomm. Ass'n v. Brand X Internet Servs.*, 545 U.S. 967 (2005).]

In December 2007, the EEOC issued a Final Rule reflecting the Third Circuit's decision. Employers are allowed to limit health benefits to retirees who are not yet eligible for Medicare or to supplement Medicare coverage but without offering coverage identical to coverage offered to non-Medicare-eligible retirees. Prescription drug coverage does not have to be identical for both groups of retirees. The rule applies only to ADEA issues, not other issues. [72 Fed. Reg. 72938 (Dec. 26, 2007)]

The Seventh Circuit granted summary judgment for the employer in an ADEA case. The court held that the plaintiffs were terminated because the employer made a rational business decision to terminate them to preserve supplemental insurance coverage. The employer was a cash-strapped county in Indiana. The county offered early retirement incentives to reduce its payroll. Some employees accepted early retirement packages, retired, and then were rehired as part-time, at-will employees. In 2013, the county's Medicare Supplementary (Medigap) insurer said that current employees are ineligible for Medigap insurance, and the plan would lose its federal exemption if the rehired employees remained in the plan. The result would be much higher premiums. The county fired the rehired retirees who were covered by Medicare and Medigap insurance.

The rehired retirees alleged that their ADEA and equal protection rights were violated. The Seventh Circuit's conclusion was that being over 65 was not the but-for cause of their termination. The decisional factor was not their age, but the combination of employment and Medigap insurance. According to the Seventh Circuit, the plaintiffs could not prevail, because they did not show they received less favorable treatment than younger employees. Nor did they show disparate impact, because there was no specific allegedly age-neutral employment practice that operated to their disadvantage. The equal protection argument was also unsuccessful, because the plaintiffs did not identify a suitable group of comparators. Even if they had, the county's cost-cutting actions would have been justified by the county's poor financial status. [*Carson v. Lake Cnty., Ind.,* No. 16-3665 (7th Cir. July 26, 2017); see Greg Grisham and Frank Day, *Seventh Circuit Holds Distressed County Did Not Violate ADEA When It Terminated Rehired Retirees to Preserve Supplemental Health Coverage and Avoid Additional Costs,* Fordharrison.com (July 26, 2017) (benefitslink.com)]

[B] Case Law on Pension and Benefit Issues

Another of 2008's many Supreme Court age discrimination rulings held that it was not age discrimination for a public retirement system to add years to the disability retirement formula (resulting in a higher benefit) only for employees who became disabled before Normal Retirement Age, not for those—like the plaintiff—who continued to work after Normal Retirement Age, and subsequently became disabled. The Supreme Court held that the difference in treatment was not motivated by age, because age and pension status are distinct. [*Kentucky Ret. Sys. v. EEOC,* 554 U.S. 135 (2008)]

The Seventh Circuit ruled in mid-2010 that a cash balance plan provision that cut off interest credits when a participant reached age 55 did not discriminate against older workers. According to the Seventh Circuit, the interest credits, which were designed to reverse the 8.5% annual discount applied to opening account balances, were not benefit accruals, so discontinuing them did not violate ERISA's ban on age-related cuts in accruals. The plan offered a lump sum cash balance, so it was not an "eligible cash balance plan" under the Treasury regulations. [*Walker v. Monsanto Co. Pension Plan,* 614 F.3d 415 (7th Cir. 2010)]

The Eighth Circuit used the familiar rationale that correlation is not causation to hold that plan contributions to a frozen plan on behalf of airline pilots were not reduced "on account of age," although the contributions were based on projected final average earnings for the plaintiffs, and the projected earnings could not be calculated without considering the pilot's age. Many factors, not just age, could reduce projected final average earnings: for example, seniority and position, the number of annual pay increases the pilot had received, and benefits under the frozen plan. [*Northwest Airlines, Inc., v. Phillips,* 675 F.3d 1126 (8th Cir. 2012)]

§ 37.05 HEALTH BENEFITS

If the employer maintains a group health plan, the plan must cover over-65 employees on equal terms with younger employees. Either the cost per employee must be the same, irrespective of age, or the employer must offer equal benefits.

Under ADEA § 3(f)(2), an employer can abide by the terms of a bona fide employee benefit plan without violating the ADEA or the OWBPA. A bona fide plan is one which:

- Existed before the challenged employment action occurred;

- The terms of the plan are observed;

- The plan is not used to force anyone into involuntary retirement;

- (Except for voluntary early retirement plans) the costs incurred, or the benefits paid, are equivalent for older and younger employees.

For EEOC regulations on this subject, see 29 C.F.R. § 1625.10.

Under ADEA § 4(f)(2), the employer is allowed to compare costs quoted on the basis of five-year age brackets (e.g., employees aged 30–35). Comparisons must be made using adjacent age brackets: not the costs of employees 65–70 versus those of employees aged 20–25, for instance.

ADEA § 4(l)(3)(B) allows long-term disability benefits to be reduced by pension benefits for which the individual is eligible at age 62 or normal retirement age. Also see Regulations at 29 C.F.R. § 1625.10(f)(1)(ii). The EEOC says it will not pursue an ADEA claim in situations where disability benefits stop at 65 for disabilities occurring before 60, or stop five years after a disability that occurred after age 60.

The Eighth Circuit reversed summary judgment for the employer and reinstated claims of discrimination and retaliation under the ADEA. The day before her scheduled knee surgery, the plaintiff was laid off; so were three other employees, aged 72, 38, and 39. The Eighth Circuit found that there was evidence that the employer asked its health insurer for reduced rates because it had laid off its "older and sicker" employees and disciplined the plaintiff for poor performance after she opted for the company medical plan instead of Medicare. The Eighth Circuit held that health care costs can be a proxy for age if the employer assumes the two factors are correlated and engages in age discrimination by acting accordingly. The Eighth Circuit said *Hazen Paper Co. v. Biggins*, 507 U.S. 604 (1993) did not apply: that is a pension case, and health cases are different because the employer's perception of premiums is related to age in a way that pensions and age are not. [*Tramp v. Associated Underwriters, Inc.*, 768 F.3d 793 (8th Cir. 2014)]

§ 37.06 PROVING THE ADEA CASE

The Tenth Circuit ruled that in order to exhaust their administrative remedies, private-sector employees have a duty to cooperate with the EEOC's investigation of their age bias charges before they file suit. [*Shikles v. Sprint/United Mgmt. Co.*, 426 F.3d 1304 (10th Cir. 2005)]

The Eleventh Circuit ruled in early 2013 that the "cat's paw" theory of liability (developed in the context of USERRA: see § 1.18) is not applicable in ADEA cases. "Cat's paw" liability (also known as "subordinate bias theory") is the principle that the employer can be liable if the actual decision-maker was manipulated by someone else who had a discriminatory intent against the plaintiff. The Eleventh Circuit held that this concept is not applicable to ADEA cases because the ADEA requires but-for causation, whereas USERRA plaintiffs can win by showing that discrimination against servicemembers was one of several motivating factors in the adverse employment decision. [*Sims v. MVM, Inc.*, 704 F.3d 1327 (11th Cir. 2013)]

The Ninth Circuit affirmed summary judgment for the employer in an ADEA case brought by a 66-year-old and a 47-year-old laid off by a television station. However, the court ruled that plaintiffs can make out a prima facie case of disparate-treatment age discrimination purely by statistics, by showing a stark pattern that cannot be explained by anything other than discrimination. In this case, the television station had to cut its budget, and persuaded the court that it was necessary to lay off general-assignment reporters based on the dates their contracts expired—and that on-camera news anchors, whatever their age, had to keep their jobs so viewers would not know that the station was financially troubled. The station also benefited by the "same-actor" inference: i.e., the plaintiffs were laid off by the person who hired them, must have known their ages, and presumably would not have hired them if he objected to working with people over 40. [*Schechner v. KPIX TV CBS*, 686 F.3d 1018 (9th Cir. 2012)]

Age, race, and sex discrimination claims by a 52-year-old African-American security guard failed. She was fired after an incident with an uncooperative patient at the psychiatric hospital where she worked. She was fired and replaced by a 39-year-old African-American woman. The Sixth Circuit held that her case was untenable because she was replaced by another African-American woman, not someone outside the protected class. But the Sixth Circuit held that the district court erred by conflating the qualification prong with the hospital's non-discriminatory rationale for termination. The Sixth Circuit held that Loyd's 25-year tenure showed that she met the minimum qualifications for the job. Loyd made a prima facie case, but the defendant showed a legitimate non-discriminatory reason for termination: a major infraction committed when she was already at the final written warning level. [*Loyd v. Saint Joseph Mercy Oakland*, 766 F.3d 580 (6th Cir. 2014)]

In an ADEA/breach of contract case, the Second Circuit affirmed the grant of summary judgment for the employer The plaintiff was RIFed when he was 56, the oldest person in his work group, and the only person to be terminated. However, 419 other employees were RIFed; he was the lowest-ranked salesperson in his group, one of the lowest-ranked in the organization, and had received a negative performance review in mid-2010. The Second Circuit agreed that age was not the but-for cause of his termination because there was genuine evidence of deterioration in his performance. [*Delaney v. Bank of Am.*, 766 F.3d 163 (2d Cir. 2014)]

The Eighth Circuit held in mid-2015 that a supervisor's use of the terms "historically" and "old school" did not constitute direct evidence of age discrimination. The supervisor told the plaintiff to think of his work differently from how he had considered it "historically," and said he should tell clients that a book he had published was relevant to clients' problems and was not "old school." The Eighth Circuit said that, considered in context, the words did not refer to the plaintiff and were not evidence of discrimination. [*Wagner v. Gallup*, Inc., 788 F.3d 877 (8th Cir. 2015)]

Although hurtful age-related jokes were frequent and supervisors allowed the plaintiff to be caricatured as a decrepit, aged "carry-out" (i.e., one who would work until he dropped in his tracks), and the plaintiff alleged that he was replaced by a much younger woman, the District Court for the Southern District of New York ruled that the 67-year-old plaintiff's allegations were merely conclusory and he did not give enough detail to create a plausible inference that he was terminated as a result of age bias. [*Franchino v. The Roman Catholic Archdiocese of N.Y.*, No. 15 CV 6299 (VB), 2016 U.S. Dist. LEXIS 78559 (S.D.N.Y. June 15, 2016); see Richard B. Cohen, *67-Year Old Employee a "Carry Out"—He Will Pass Away on the Job*, FisherBroyles (June 23, 2016), available at Lexology .com.]

The Ninth Circuit applies a rebuttable presumption that, if the replacement employee is within 10 years of the plaintiff's age, the age difference is not substantial. The plaintiff, a 54-year-old Homeland Security agent, was turned down for promotion. The four successful candidates were 44, 45, 47, and 48. The Ninth Circuit held that he was not turned down in favor of a "substantially younger person"—but nevertheless found that the plaintiff rebutted the presumption by introducing the employer's statements that younger, less experienced agents were preferred and the employer's urging that the plaintiff retire. [*France v. Johnson*, No. 13-15534, 2015 U.S. App. LEXIS 17915 (9th Cir. Aug. 3, 2015)]

However, the Eleventh Circuit found that a seven-year age gap (a 49-year-old was replaced by a 42-year-old, i.e., someone in the protected class) was substantial. Although the district court said that the plaintiff did not show that he was qualified for his position, the Eleventh Circuit said that holding the job for nine years out of his 30-year career demonstrated qualification. [*Liebman v. Metropolitan Life*, 808 F.3d 1294 (11th Cir. 2015)]

A mid-2015 article advises employers to learn from another employer's mistakes. Calling an employee and his colleagues "old farts" is inadvisable, especially just before firing them. It told against the employer that the plaintiff was given three or four warnings on the day he was terminated (for poor performance and insubordination), when he had been given only one, first-level, warning previously. Like many cases, this arose when a new supervisor made changes in the workplace. The employer argued that the plaintiff, as an at-will employee, was not entitled to progressive discipline, but the Fifth Circuit held that an employer that chooses to adopt a progressive discipline policy must apply it to all employees, and failure to follow the policy can be evidence of an unlawful or discriminatory motive. [*Goudeau v. National Oilwell Varco*, 793 F.3d 470 (5th Cir. 2015)]

[A] Damage Issues

The Tenth Circuit allows a plaintiff in a race/age discrimination case to receive the statutory maximum damages on a Title VII compensatory damage claim (see § 42.12[B] for discussion of the CRA '91 damage cap), plus ADEA back pay and liquidated damages. On the issue of front pay, both Title VII and the ADEA make this available as a remedy. Reinstatement is the preferred remedy, but this is not always practical—particularly since in this case, the defendant corporation's financial condition was deteriorating, so any job might be short-lived. Furthermore, where there is a hostile environment that renders reinstatement inappropriate, even an unconditional offer of reinstatement in a comparable job does not prevent an award of front pay as an alternative to reinstatement. [*Abuan v. Level 3 Commc'ns, Inc.*, 353 F.3d 1158 (10th Cir. 2003)]

The Fifth Circuit has ruled that front and back pay are available in ADEA discrimination and retaliation cases—but punitive damages and damages for pain and suffering, are not. However, the Fifth Circuit permitted a suit under state anti-discrimination statutes, which usually allow recovery of emotional distress and punitive damages. [*Vaughan v. Anderson Reg'l Med. Ctr.*, No. 16-60104, 2016 WL 7365629 (5th Cir. Dec. 16, 2016); W. Stephen Cockerham and Leslie Brockhoeft, *Are Pain and Suffering and Punitive Damages Recoverable Under the ADEA and FLSA? The 5th Circuit Issues Inconsistent Decisions*, Husch Blackwell LLP (Jan. 13, 2017), available at Lexology.com; Esteban Shardonofsky, *Fifth Circuit Protects 40-Year-Old Case and Affirms ADEA Limits on Recoverable Damages*, Seyfarth Shaw LLP (Jan. 3, 2017), available at Lexology.com; the precedent is *Dean v. Am. Sec. Ins. Co.*, 559 F.2d 1036 (5th Cir. 1977).

There is a circuit split: the Seventh Circuit allows compensatory and punitive damages for ADEA retaliation claims: see Patrick J. Maher, *Fifth Circuit Denies Punitive and Compensatory Damages for ADEA Retaliation Claims, Creates Circuit Split*, Ogletree Deakins (Feb. 21, 2017), available at Lexology.com]

A mid-level manager was awarded $51.4 million in a case in the District Court for the District of New Jersey—about five times as high as any previous New Jersey award, possibly the largest U.S. jury award in any single-plaintiff age discrimination case. The plaintiff, Braden, was RIFd in 2012, at age 66, after 28 years. Six months later, he brought an EEOC age discrimination charge because he was the oldest of six employees in his unit and the only one RIFed. Forty-two-year-old and 38-year-old employees with the same title were retained. The jury awarded almost $50 million in punitive damages for reckless disregard of discrimination laws, plus $520,000 in lost wages and benefits and an equal amount for emotional distress. Although this is an unpublished decision, it is worth considering because it shows how high the stakes can be. [*Braden v. Lockheed Martin Corp.*, No. 14-4215-RMB-JS , 2017 U.S. Dist. LEXIS 10668 (D.N.J. Jan. 26, 2017) (unpublished) ; see Lynne Anne Anderson, *Jury Awards $51 Million to an Age Discrimination Plaintiff: What Can We Learn?*, Drinker Biddle & Reath LLP (Jan. 31, 2017), available at Lexology.com]

The Second Circuit held that a $250,000 settlement of an ADEA suit constituted FICA wages. The agreement permitted the employer to make all legally required deductions and withholding, but did not characterize the $250,000. The Second Circuit held that the remedies under the ADEA are lost wages, liquidated damages, and equitable relief, plus costs, attorneys' fees, and prejudgment interest. ADEA remedies do not include recovery for pain and suffering or emotional distress (which would probably not be treated as wages). [*Gerstenbluth v. Credit Suisse*, 728 F.3d 139 (2d Cir. 2013)]

As Chapter 40 shows, arbitration is involved for an ever-increasing proportion of employment disputes—although the court's caseload continues to be increased by cases examining the question of whether a particular dispute should be litigated or arbitrated.

In April 2009, the Supreme Court extended its line of pro-arbitration decisions by ruling that federal law mandates enforcement of a CBA clause that clearly and unmistakably obligates union members to arbitrate their ADEA claims. [*14 Penn Plaza LLC v. Pyett*, 556 U.S. 247 (2009); the Supreme Court already held that ADEA claims are arbitrable, in *Gilmer v. Interstate/Johnson Lane Corp.*, 500 U.S. 20 (1991)]

The issue recurred in 2017. Employees who were RIFd from General Mills in 2012, and who took severance packages, signed releases of claims about the termination, and agreed to pursue any future disputes through individual arbitration. The District Court for the District of Minnesota permitted the suit to continue, citing ADEA § 626(f)(1), which refers to disputes about waivers being decided by "a court of competent jurisdiction." But the Eighth Circuit reversed, holding that the ADEA is not the type of federal statute that provides such clear entitlement to a trial in court that arbitration clauses are unenforceable. The Eighth Circuit read § 626(f)(1) as defining procedural rights that are not immutable and can be waived. [*McLeod v. General Mills, Inc.*, No. 15-3540, 2017 WL 1363797 (8th Cir. Apr. 14, 2017); see Liz Kramer, *8th Circuit Finds ADEA Does*

Not Preclude Arbitration, Stinson Leonard Street LLP (Apr. 28, 2017), available at Lexology.com]

§ 37.07   WAIVERS OF ADEA RIGHTS

[A]   Requirements for Valid Waiver

It makes sense for employers to make it part of the severance process to request that terminating employees sign a waiver of their rights to bring suit for discrimination allegedly occurring in the course of the employment relationship. However, in order to be valid and enforceable, a waiver of ADEA rights must be strictly tailored to satisfy the requirements of the Older Workers Benefits Protection Act, a 1990 statute that has been enacted as 29 U.S.C. § 626(f)(1). Furthermore, waivers do not prevent the EEOC from carrying out an age discrimination investigation or bringing suit against the employer. It is unlawful for ADEA waivers to prohibit employees from filing charges with the EEOC or participating in EEOC investigations.

A waiver is not valid if it is not "knowing and voluntary" on the part of the employee. No one can surrender legal rights without receiving full disclosure of the implications of the document he or she signs. The ADEA provides a definition of what is required before a waiver will be considered knowing and voluntary:

- The agreement that contains the waiver must be written in understandable terms;

- The waiver specifically mentions ADEA rights or claims;

- Only claims that have already arisen are waived—not claims that might arise in the future;

- The employee receives something in return for the waiver; it is not enough that the employee receives severance or other benefits that would be provided even if there had been no waiver;

- The document includes a written warning that the employee should consult a lawyer before signing the agreement;

- The employee gets at least 21 days to think over the employer's severance offer. If the agreement is offered to an entire group (e.g., in connection with a layoff or incentives for voluntary departure) then the offer must remain open for at least 45 days;

- When incentives are offered to a group, everyone in the group must get an understandable notification of the features of the program: who can participate; eligibility factors; time limits; and the ages and job titles of everyone eligible or chosen for the program, vis-à-vis the ages of workers in the organizational unit or job classification who were not eligible or selected. (This was included in the law to make it easier for potential plaintiffs to decide if age was an improper factor in selecting employees for the program.)

Waivers are also used when charges have been filed, and then the employer and employee agree on a settlement. In this case, the waiver is only considered knowing and voluntary if all the rules noted above have been observed, and the employee has been given a reasonable time to consider the offer.

Getting a waiver does not provide complete protection for the employer. Sometimes the employee will go to court and sue anyway, claiming that the lawsuit is permissible because the waiver was defective in some way. Section 626(f)(3) provides that it is up to the employer to prove that the waiver satisfied the various requirements and therefore was knowing and voluntary. The employee is not required to prove that the waiver was invalid.

[B] EEOC Rules

The EEOC's rule on waivers, can be found at 29 C.F.R. § 1625.22. A valid ADEA waiver must:

- Be embodied in a written document that contains the entire agreement (the agreement cannot be written but supplemented by oral discussion);
- Be written in plain English, appropriate to the signer's educational level;
- Information about exit incentives must also be understandable;
- Be honest and accurate, not misleading;
- Specify that it relates to ADEA claims;
- Advise the employee to consult an attorney before signing.

In general, waivers can release existing claims but not those that might arise in the future. However, the Final Rule allows an otherwise valid waiver to include the signer's agreement to retire, or otherwise terminate employment at a specified future date.

For the waiver to be valid, the signer must receive consideration specific to the waiver, which he or she would not receive otherwise. Therefore, normal severance pay is not adequate to support a waiver. Nor does it constitute valuable consideration if the employer restores a benefit that was wrongfully terminated in the past. However, the Final Rule says that it is not necessary to give greater consideration to over-40 employees who sign waivers than to under-40 employees, even though the older employees waive an additional range of claims (those arising under the ADEA).

Despite the existence of waivers, a certain number of employees will nevertheless bring age discrimination claims against the employer, claiming that the waivers were invalid and therefore did not constitute a knowing and voluntary waiver of the right to sue.

The Supreme Court's decision in *Oubre v. Entergy Operations Inc.* [522 U.S. 422 (1988)] says that such a person can bring suit under the ADEA even without tendering back (returning) the severance pay received under the agreement that included the allegedly invalid waiver. The rationale is that the defective waiver does not qualify for ratification by the ex-employee, so it is not necessary to return the consideration to avoid ratification.

The EEOC published Final Regulations to implement *Oubre*. [See 29 C.F.R. Part 1625 as amended by 65 Fed. Reg. 77438 (Dec. 11, 2000), effective January 1, 2001], and published guidance in mid-2009 in Question and Answer form, *Understanding Waivers of Discrimination Claims in Employee Severance Agreements*, <www.eeoc.gov/policy/docs/qanda_severance-agreements.html> (July 15, 2009; appendix B, a sample waiver, was revised in April 2010) (last accessed Mar. 15, 2017). The EEOC's position is that the existence of a valid waiver is an affirmative defense for the employer. That means that the employer has the burden of proving the validity, but the employee can produce evidence that the waiver was not knowing and voluntary. The EEOC analyzes covenants not to sue in the same way as waivers, and in fact believes they may be even more damaging to employee rights because employees might be deterred from bringing suit with respect to wrongdoing occurring after the covenant was signed.

According to the agency, ordinary contract principles about ratification and tender-back do not apply to employment waivers, because ex-employees might not be able to afford to give back the consideration even if they have a valid claim against the former employer.

Tender-back is not required even if the waiver seems to be lawful, and even if the employee does not allege fraud or duress. Once the case is resolved, the trial court may have to determine the employer's entitlement to restitution, recoupment or set-off. However, the employer can only recover the amount of consideration paid for the waiver, or the amount the plaintiff is awarded for winning the case—whichever is lower. Employees who file suit in bad faith can also be required to pay the employers' attorneys' fees.

The guidance points out that waivers cannot be used to limit an employee's right to testify or participate in any EEOC proceedings. It is not acceptable for an employer to cure a defective waiver by subsequently providing the information that was omitted, then re-starting the period of time to sign the waiver. The EEOC did not take a position as to whether employers must disclose the criteria under which employees were selected for RIF, although some lower courts have required this: see § 37.07[C], below.

[C]   Case Law on ADEA Waivers

Oubre, and EEOC's regulations issued in response, make it clear that ADEA waivers and releases can be enforceable—but only if they satisfy all of the requirements of the OWBPA. If restrictions are imposed on the employee's right to sue—including challenges to the validity of the release itself—it is possible that the release will be deemed to violate the OWBPA. The release must be understandable.

Cases on these issues include:

- At first the District Court for the District of Colorado invalidated the waiver of ADEA claims that the plaintiff signed when he was RIFed. The district court held that the waiver did not satisfy the Older Workers Benefit Protection Act (OWBPA) because it did not properly advise the employee of his right to counsel since it merely said he had been given an opportunity to consult an attorney The district court reconsidered, then reversed, agreeing with the employer that the release language had been accepted by other courts and otherwise satisfied OWBPA requirements. [*Foster v. Mountain Coal Co. LLC*, No. 12:cv-03341-LTD-MJW (D. Colo. May 16, 2014)]

- The District Court for the Northern District of California found releases to be satisfactory under the OWBPA. Mid-level managers in a "career planning" initiative received only 21 days' notice and were not informed of the identity of other employees who were RIFed. They said that this was a group termination program entitling them to 45 days to consider the offer, and information about others also RIFed. The court held that there was no group program because the terminations occurred at different times over a period of several months, with termination decisions made by different decision-makers. The plaintiffs were fired for failure to meet goals under Performance Improvement Programs. [*Barnes v. The Hershey Co.*, No. 3:12-cv-01334-CRB, 2015 U.S. Dist. LEXIS 89947 (N.D. Cal. July 9, 2015)]

- A collective action was allowed to proceed despite a valid arbitration agreement requiring individual actions because the OWBPA states that a worker challenging the validity of an ADEA waiver has the burden of proof "in a court of competent jurisdiction" that the waiver was knowing and voluntary. The District Court for the District of Minnesota said that this requirement prevails over the Federal Arbitration Act principle that employers can impose waivers of class or collective actions. [*McLeod v. General Mills*, 140 F. Supp. 3d 843 (D. Minn. 2015)]

When Allstate reclassified its agents as independent contractors rather than employees, more than 6,200 agents were terminated. They were permitted to choose among four severance options, three of which required releases of claims, including ADEA claims. The fourth option did not require a release but did require additional noncompete and nonsolicitation options, and severance pay was limited to 13 weeks. Over 400 of the ex-agents brought an ADEA suit. Allstate said that the claims were barred by the releases signed. The jury found that eight out of the 10 releases they examined were not knowing and voluntary. The District Court for the Eastern District of Pennsylvania ruled that the statutory factors are not necessarily sufficient to establish knowledge and voluntariness. The OWBPA sets a baseline that is a minimum, not a maximum, requirement.

The district court held that a court that finds that an ADEA release satisfies the statutory minimum requirements still must carry out a separate analysis of the totality of the circumstances to determine the release's validity. The factors to be considered include the clarity and specificity of the language of the release, the plaintiff's education and business experience, the time the plaintiff was given to consider the release before signing; if the plaintiff had—or was encouraged to obtain—legal counsel; if the plaintiff had the ability to negotiate terms; and whether the waiver provided additional consideration over and above what the employee was already entitled to. In this case, the district court held that the release was non-negotiable, so the time to consider was meaningless.

The court found that the severance options forced the agents to sign waivers to ensure their financial security, so the waivers were not voluntary. Agents who refused to sign would have been fired, losing the money they had invested in their agencies. The district court also found that Allstate misrepresented the transaction in a way that affected voluntariness, whether or not an individual employee actually relied on the misrepresentation when signing the waiver. The court defined a material misrepresentation or omission as one that a reasonable person would have considered important in making the decision. [*Romero v. Allstate Ins. Co., et al.*, 2016 WL 2619853 (E.D. Pa. May 4, 2016); Colton D. Long, *What Is Knowing and Voluntary? One Court's Take on the Enforceability of ADEA Waivers*, Ogletree Deakins (June 10, 2016), available at Lexology.com]

CHAPTER 38

THE FAMILY AND MEDICAL LEAVE ACT (FMLA)

§ 38.01 INTRODUCTION

The Family and Medical Leave Act (FMLA) was enacted on February 3, 1993, as 29 U.S.C. §§ 2601–2654. Congress stated an intention to aid families in which both parents, or the single parent, work outside the home, and to minimize sex discrimination by making leave available in a gender-neutral manner.

The FMLA focuses on two subjects: health care (whether for the employee's own serious health condition or for a family member for whom the employee is a caregiver) and parenting a newborn or newly adopted child. 29 U.S.C. § 2601(a)(2) says that "it is important for the development of children and the family unit that fathers and mothers be able to participate in early childrearing and the care of family members who have serious health conditions."

Under appropriate circumstances, qualifying employees can take up to 12 weeks of leave a year, whether the leave is taken all at once, in several blocks, or intermittently in small units. FMLA leave can be important for preserving the job (and benefits) of someone who has used up all of his or her sick days and is too sick to maintain a normal work schedule, but not sick enough to obtain disability benefits or file for disability retirement.

Employers have the option of providing paid leave under these circumstances, but it does not violate the federal statute for the employer to provide only unpaid FMLA leave. [See § 38.06[G] for state-law developments.]

Leave can be taken, under 29 U.S.C. § 2612, for a total of 12 weeks in any 12-month period (not necessarily a calendar year), when the employee has or adopts or fosters a child (but this leave can only be taken during the first year after the child's birth or after the adoption or foster care placement) or for a serious health condition suffered by the employee or his or her spouse, parent, or child. If the employee is the sick person, the serious health condition must prevent the employee from performing the functions of the job. The FMLA also includes provisions for leave for family members of military personnel.

The employer must give employees at least 60 days' notice of changes in the method of calculating the leave year. [29 C.F.R. § 825.200(d)] The 12-week limit applies per year, not per illness. Therefore, an employee who uses up the allowance is not entitled to additional leave based on events later in the same leave year.

As defined by 29 U.S.C. § 2611(9), a reduced leave schedule is a partial leave under which the employee does work, but for less than the usual number of hours per workday or workweek.

It is unlawful for employers to interfere with employees' exercise of FMLA right or to discriminate or retaliate against them for exercising such rights, charging the employer with FMLA violations, or participating in an investigation. [29 U.S.C. § 2615]

The FMLA does not modify federal or state antidiscrimination laws. [See 29 U.S.C. § 2651(a)] Employers always have a legal right to set up their own policies that are *more* generous than the FMLA: § 2653, and the federal statute does not preempt state and local laws that require employees to offer even more leave than the FMLA does. [29 U.S.C. § 2651(b)] Employers do not have the power to draft their benefit plans or programs to limit FMLA rights, nor can a Collective Bargaining Agreement be used to cut back FMLA rights. [See 29 U.S.C. § 2652(b).]

The DOL published a 20-page FMLA guide in 2012, and updated it in mid-2015, "Need Time? The Employee's Guide to the Family and Medical Leave Act," to explain FMLA rights—and obligations—to employees. [<http://www .dol.gov/whd/fmla/employeeguide.pdf> (June 2015) (last accessed Mar. 16, 2017)]

The 2018 edition went to press during Hurricane Harvey, a catastrophic storm that brought various FMLA concepts into play. A recent article says that FMLA leave is not required when employees are coping with physical results of a natural disaster, e.g., going through a flooded house to discard ruined belongings. However, natural disasters frequently cause serious health conditions (e.g., storm-related injuries, hypertension) in employees or their families. When the business is shut down by a disaster, and employees are off work for one or more weeks, that time does not reduce the employee's future entitlement to FMLA leave. [FMLAinsights.com, *Hurricane Harvey and the FMLA: Are Your Employees Eligible for Leave During a Natural Disaster?* (Aug. 29, 2017) (benefitslink .com)]

FMLA Title I covers private employment. The statute also has a Title II, covering federal employees. Although the Supreme Court has ruled that Congress exceeded its power when it made state government employers subject to the Americans with Disability Act (ADA) and the Age Discrimination in Employment Act (ADEA), the Supreme Court reached the opposite conclusion with respect to the FMLA provisions permitting leave to care for a sick family member, finding that Congress validly abrogated state sovereign immunity when it comes to family leave. [*Nevada Dep't of Human Resources v. Hibbs*, 538 U.S. 721 (2003)]

In March 2012, a divided (5-4) Supreme Court held that the states have not waived sovereign immunity and cannot be sued for monetary damages under the FMLA "self-care" provision (i.e., leave taken to care for the employee's own serious health condition). The Supreme Court held that Congress could not remove states' immunity from suit because there was no widespread evidence of sex discrimination or sex stereotyping that prevented women from taking leave to care for their own illnesses. [*Coleman v. Court of Appeals of Md.*, 132 S. Ct. 1327 (2012)]

According to a late 2016 Third Circuit decision, Montclair State University could not be sued under the FMLA. As an arm of the state (because the state treasury would be responsible if a judgment were ordered against the university), it is immune under the Eleventh Amendment. [*Maliandi v. Montclair State Univ.,*

845 F.3d 77 (3d Cir. 2016); see Wolters Kluwer Law & Business, *State University Is an Arm of the State, Immune from FMLA Suit* (Feb. 6, 2017) (benefitslink .com)]

[A] 2008–17 Changes

By 2008, it was clear that the FMLA was in need of clarification and amplification.

Additional protection was added to the FMLA for the families of military servicemembers—the first extension of the FMLA's requirements in the 15 years the law had been in effect. The extension provides up to 12 weeks of unpaid leave when an employee's spouse, child, or parent is called up or is on active duty in the armed forces, and up to 26 weeks when a child, parent, or spouse is injured seriously enough during military service to be unable to continue his or her duties. Employee Benefit Security Administration (EBSA) proposed revisions in early 2008, and then issued final regulations that took effect on January 16, 2009. [DOL, EBSA, Notice of Proposed Rulemaking to Amend the FMLA (RIN 1215-AB35) (Feb. 11, 2008)]

The definition of family members under the military family leave benefit is broader than in the FMLA in general; the military provision includes siblings and cousins. Family members are also entitled to 12 weeks of FMLA leave when a servicemember, Reservist, or National Guard member is called up or released to civilian life. Entitlement to this leave is certified on Form WH-384.

To make it easier to administer FMLA leave, the 2008 rules allow the employer to require notice within two days of the absence, or within five days of the leave request. The HR department is permitted to contact the health care provider.

The previous rules allowed employers to demand a fitness for duty exam before the employee returned to work; the final rule obligates the employer to notify employees if an exam is required before returning; the notice must list the essential functions of the employee's job (to show that the employee has recuperated enough to perform them).

The DOL's position is that prospective waivers of FMLA claims are invalid, but employees can voluntarily agree to settle an FMLA claim that has already matured without DOL supervision or court approval.

New hires must be given a written notice of FMLA rights when they are hired, unless there is an employee handbook that covers this subject. The notice can be posted electronically by satisfying the general electronic notice requirements—but paper copies must be posted where employees who do not have computers can see them.

The employer is permitted to require a new medical certification for each new leave year. If the employee asserts a continuing, open-ended condition, the employer can require recertification of the need for leave every six months (the previous rule was that recertification could be required when the minimum duration specified by the employee had elapsed). If circumstances (the seriousness of the condition, or frequency or duration of absences) change, recertification can be required more often.

The previous regulations required employees to try to schedule their intermittent or reduced schedule leave in a way that did not disrupt the employer's operations; now employees are required to "make a reasonable effort" to avoid undue disruption. The general rule is that the employer is not permitted to reduce the employee's leave entitlement by more than the amount of leave actually taken. However, sometime it is impossible to start or stop part-way through a shift, in which case the entire period the employee must be away from work counts against his or her FMLA entitlement. The revised rules permit temporary transfer of employees who need intermittent or reduced schedule leave, if the need for leave is foreseeable (based on planned medical treatment) or if such leave is permitted for the birth or adoption of a child. However, employers are not allowed to impose temporary transfers when employees have frequent and unpredictable absences caused by a chronic condition.

When an employee is ready to return to work after FMLA leave, the employer can ask for more than a simple statement of ability to return to work. If reasonable safety considerations are involved, the employer can ask for a fitness for duty certificate for intermittent leave.

Although the provisions about substituting paid for unpaid leave do not apply when an employee receives disability benefits during an FMLA leave, the employer and employee can, by agreement, supplement disability benefits by running paid leave concurrently with FMLA leave; this is also true for Worker's Compensation benefits. The employer can consider FMLA leave when awarding bonuses for perfect attendance.

The Defense Department Fiscal Year 2010 Authorization Bill expands FMLA entitlement for military families. After the expansion, an employee whose spouse, parent, or child is a reservist can take FMLA leave for a qualifying exigency arising from deployment to a foreign country on active duty, with a new right to leave based on the deployment of the employee's spouse, parent, or child who serves in the regular armed forces to a foreign country.

Military caregiver leave has been expanded to 26 weeks per 12-month period in order to care for a parent, spouse, child, or relative to whom the employee is next of kin. Leave can also be taken when the family member is a veteran being treated for a qualifying illness or injury when the veteran was on active duty during the five years before the date of treatment.

A February 23, 2015 DOL final rule amends the FMLA to implement *Windsor*, defining "spouse" to include most same-sex married couples. Effective March 27, 2015, a couple is deemed married for FMLA purposes if their marriage was valid at the place of celebration, even if it is not valid where they live. [80 Fed. Reg. 9989 (Feb. 25, 2015)]

The forms were replaced by substantially similar forms, labeled as valid until May 2018. [The updated forms are available at <http://www.dol.gov/whd/fmla/2013rule/militaryForms.htm> (last accessed Mar. 16, 2017).] Some of the medical certification forms include Genetic Information Nondiscrimination Act (GINA) safe harbor language: warnings not to provide information about genetic tests or certain family heath history data. Employers can avoid penalties by warning employees and healthcare providers to refrain from disclosing genetic information. [Luke A. Wingfield, *New FMLA Forms Address GINA Safe Harbor*, McBrayer McGinnis Leslie & Kirkland PLLC (Nov. 11, 2015), available at Lexology.com] DOL no longer prints model forms in the appendices to the FMLA regulations: they are posted on the DOL Website, so they can be changed without obtaining the approval of the Office of Management and Budget. DOL has developed a new certification form for leave occasioned by the serious injury or illness of an eligible veteran. Employers are permitted to adapt the forms rather than using them as published by DOL—as long as the employer's version does not call for disclosure of more information than the standard forms require. The updated regulations confirm that employers have obligations to keep genetic information confidential. The new forms are:

- WH-380-E, health care provider's certification of an employee's serious health condition;

- WH-380-F, the counterpart for a family member's serious health condition;

- WH-381, notice of eligibility, rights, and responsibilities;

- WH-382, designation notice;

- WH-384, certification of need for military family leave (number WH-383 is reserved);

- WH-385, certification of servicemember's serious injury or illness;

- WH-385-V, the counterpart for a veteran's serious injury or illness.

[Airline Flight Crew Technical Corrections Act, Pub. L. No. 111-119]

§ 38.02 FMLA ELIGIBILITY ISSUES

Like most federal employment discrimination laws, the FMLA exempts very small employers. The FMLA applies only to employers engaged in interstate commerce or activities affecting commerce (but most employers fit into this category)—and only if, in the current year or the previous calendar year, there were at least 50 employees on each workday of 20 or more workweeks. Furthermore, the FMLA does not apply when there are fewer than 50 people at that worksite and the total number of employees at all of the employer's sites within a

75-mile radius is less than 50. Anyone who acts on behalf of the employer, whether directly or indirectly, also counts as an employer. So does the successor in interest of a past employer. [29 U.S.C. § 2611(4)]

According to the Fifth Circuit, the definition of an eligible employer subject to the FMLA (at least 50 employees within 75 miles of the worksite) is not a jurisdictional requirement of an FMLA case. The Fifth Circuit remanded a case to see if the employer would be forbidden to raise the defense that it was not covered by the FMLA if the employee was told by the company that she was covered by the Act and relied on this statement. [*Minard v. ITC Deltacom Commc'ns Inc.*, 447 F.3d 352 (5th Cir. 2006)]

The 75-mile requirement was interpreted by the Tenth Circuit as surface miles, not linear miles as the crow flies, so in this case, the surface measurement was 75.6 miles so the employer was not subject to the FMLA. [*Hackworth v. Progressive Cas. Ins. Co.*, 468 F.3d 722 (10th Cir. 2006)]

In mid-2016, the District Court for the Eastern District of Louisiana held that the 50-employee threshold was met because the plaintiff, a telecommuter who worked several states away, reported to an office that had at least 50 employees within 75 miles. If an employee does not have a fixed work site, the 75-mile radius is calculated from the home base where work is assigned, or where the employee reports. However, state rules may be different: for example, the Louisiana Employment Discrimination Law requires 20 employees within the state for coverage. [*Donahoe-Boehne v. Brinkmann Instruments,* No. 16-2766 (E.D La. June 15, 2016); see E. Adrienne Jackson and Alan J. Marcuis, *Telecommuting Employees Entitled to FMLA If Office to Which They Report Meets 50-or-More Employee Threshold*, Hunton & Williams LLP (July 28, 2016), available at Lexology.com; Dave Straufseld, *For Telecommuter Fmla 50 Employee Threshold Measured By Office To Which She Reported*, WK WorkDay Blog (June 23, 2016) (benefitslink.com)]

The Sixth Circuit held, in mid-2006, that whether a company is subject to the FMLA is measured under labor rather than corporate law, and it is irrelevant whether a company transfers its assets or merges with another company. [*Cobb v. Contract Transp., Inc.*, 452 F.3d 543 (6th Cir. 2006). The FMLA regulations, at § 825.107, use the Title VII test for liability of successor employers.]

The Seventh Circuit held that a person can be jointly employed by companies with distinct labor forces (here, Trans States and GoJet negotiated CBAs separately). The two leading factors are whether the employers agree to share the employee's services, and whether one employer directly or indirectly acts in the interests of the other. The question is whether an employee has a need for medical leave when it is requested, not whether the employee could have stayed healthy by being more prudent. [*Cuff v. Trans States Holdings, Inc.*, 768 F.3d 605 (7th Cir. 2014)]

Even after it is established that an employer is covered, not all employees are entitled to take FMLA leave. Eligibility is limited to an employee who not only has worked for the employer for at least 12 months, but put in at least 1,250 hours for that employer in the preceding year. [See 29 U.S.C. § 2611(2)(A).]

The 1,250 hours are counted back from the time the employee went on FMLA leave, not from the time the employer fired the employee or took other adverse action. Therefore, a plaintiff who took three leaves that she claimed satisfied FMLA requirements, and therefore did not work 1,250 hours during the year before her discharge, was still entitled to bring an FMLA suit. [*Butler v. Owens-Brockway Plastic Prods. Inc.*, 199 F.3d 314 (6th Cir. 1999)]

For purposes of the 1,250-hour eligibility requirement, overtime hours are treated as hours worked. The FMLA can be used to protect leave during what would otherwise be overtime, including a request not to work overtime. The FMLA regulations say that if the employee on FMLA leave missed voluntary overtime, it cannot be counted against the person's FMLA leave entitlement. But if the employee would normally have been required to work the overtime, the time the employee missed is considered intermittent FMLA leave. The DOL defines overtime as voluntary if the employee would have been required to work it except for taking the FMLA leave. Required overtime hours must be included in the FMLA entitlement calculation because they increase the amount of leave the person is entitled to. For example, someone who has to work 48 hours a week and takes eight hours of leave has taken only one-sixth of a week of FMLA leave. [Christy Phanthavong and Carrie Byrnes, *Quirky FMLA Counting Rules: Overtime*, Bryan Cave (Oct. 1, 2014) (benefitslink.com)]

The Eleventh Circuit ruled in 2012 that the FMLA protects a request made before eligibility is achieved for leave to be taken post-eligibility. The plaintiff was fired after requesting FMLA leave for upcoming childbirth. She was fired after taking time off when her doctor ordered bed rest. The Eleventh Circuit cited 29 C.F.R. § 825.110(d)(4), which says that FMLA eligibility is determined when leave begins and the plaintiff would have been FMLA-eligible when the baby was due. The court also pointed out that FMLA policy is for employees to give employers notice of health events that can be announced in advance (e.g., elective surgery, childbirth), and removing FMLA protection would give employees an incentive not to provide notice—leading to additional inconvenience for employers. [*Pereda v. Brookdale Senior Living Communities Inc.*, 666 F.3d 1269 (11th Cir. 2012)]

A Seventh Circuit plaintiff sued under the FMLA after being fired for receiving more than eight points under the no-fault attendance policy. She said that two of the absences were actually FMLA leave, for which she could not be penalized. However, she was not employed for 1,250 hours during the preceding 12 months, unless she was allowed to toll the 12-month period by adding in time worked during 56 days that preceded the time period, when she was on FMLA leave. The Seventh Circuit ruled that she was not entitled to tolling; the 1,250 hour requirement must be applied strictly. With respect to alleged FMLA retaliation (absenteeism points were not removed under the company's rolling no-fault policy), the court held that although removal of points is an employment benefit, it did not accrue before the leave commenced—and the FMLA itself says that employment benefits do not accrue while a person is on leave. [*Bailey v. Pregis Innovative Packaging, Inc.*, 600 F.3d 748 (7th Cir. 2010)]

In *Ragsdale v. Wolverine Worldwide* [535 U.S. 81 (2002)], the Supreme Court ruled that the DOL regulation [29 C.F.R. § 825.700(a)] is invalid to the extent that it requires employers to disclose the relationship between FMLA leave and the employer's own leave policies. The revised regulations reflect this decision: see § 38.01[A], above.

U.S. employers must pay their H-1B workers as long as they are employed (see § 23.11[E]); they cannot be "benched" or otherwise placed on unpaid leave. However, the DOL and Immigration and Naturalization Service take the position that H-1B workers are entitled to FMLA leave on the same terms as U.S. workers. [Franczek Radelet, *Are Foreign Nationals on H-1B Work Visas Eligible for FMLA Leave?*, fmlainsights.com (Sept. 1, 2016) (benefitslink.com)]

Another issue is the ambit of relatives for whom FMLA leave may be taken. In an Eleventh Circuit case from 2013, an employee requested FMLA leave to help her father while he dealt with his brother's terminal illness. The request was granted verbally by a supervisor, and Dawkins took the leave. However, FMLA leave is not available to care for a terminally ill uncle. While Dawkins was away, her temporary promotion was rescinded. Dawkins sued for FMLA retaliation, and asserted equitable estoppel when the employer defended by arguing that she was ineligible for leave. The Eleventh Circuit held that it was not reasonable to rely on the supervisor's approval of the leave. Dawkins knew, from past instances of FMLA leave, that paperwork had to be completed. She also asked for FMLA forms to be sent to her uncle's address, indicating that she was going to take time off anyway. [*Dawkins v. Fulton Cnty. Gov't, Case*, 733 F.3d 1084 (11th Cir. 2013)]

Leave that is granted to an employee who is not eligible under the FMLA is not FMLA leave and cannot be counted against the 12-week allocation if the employee subsequently becomes eligible. A 2014 article explains that, while employers can provide non-required leave, the leave does not thereby become FMLA leave. Employers can maintain non-FMLA leave policies; provide leave as an ADA accommodation; or handle special situations on a case-by-case basis. [Christy Phanthavong and Chris Rylands, *Quirky FMLA Counting Rules: Leave Prior to Eligibility*, Bryan Cave (Oct. 15, 2014) (benefitslink.com)]

Note, however, that the Sixth Circuit applied equitable estoppel, and found an otherwise ineligible employee entitled to FMLA leave because of the employer's misstatement that he was eligible. (The company did not have 50 workers within a 75-mile radius.) In the court's view, the employer misrepresented a material fact on which the employee reasonably relied, to his detriment. When the employee said he needed time off to treat a heart ailment, the employer sent him FMLA paperwork, including a form marked "eligible for FMLA leave." The employee handbook said employees were eligible on the basis of working 1,250 hours in the preceding year, and did not mention the 50-worker limit. Tilley was fired after a final written warning for failure to complete assignments on time; he said that he could not complete the assignments because he took leave that was described as FMLA leave. [*Tilley v. Kalamazoo Cnty. Road Comm'n*, 777 F.3d 303 (6th Cir. 2015)]

Under most anti-discrimination statutes, the suit must be brought against the employer corporation, and not against individual decision-makers.

However, in 2016, the Second Circuit ruled that a company's HR director could be individually liable for FMLA violations. In this reading, the HR director's control over the employee's job and the termination decision made the director an "employer." The Second Circuit noted that the definition of "employer" is very similar to the Fair Labor Standards Act (FLSA) definition, where individual liability has been found based on degree of control [*Graziadio v. Culinary Inst. of Am.*, 817 F.3d 415 (2d Cir. 2016); see Erin Dougherty Foley and Craig B. Simonsen, *Second Circuit Court Holds HR Director Is Individually the "Employer,"* Seyfarth Shaw (Mar. 22, 2016) (benefitslink.com)]

Similarly, the District Court for the District of Massachusetts ruled that FMLA interference and retaliation charges could be pursued against a corporate chief procurement officer who allegedly unfairly criticized the plaintiff's performance and placed him on a Performance Improvement Plan when he was on FMLA leave. [*Eichenholz v. Brink's Inc.*, No. 16-cv-11786-LTS (D. Mass. May 9, 2017); see HR Daily Advisor, *Can an Individual Supervisor Be Liable Under the FMLA?* (Aug. 30, 2017) (benefitslink.com)]

§ 38.03   WHEN LEAVE IS AVAILABLE

An eligible employee can take FMLA leave for his or her own serious health condition or the serious health condition of an eligible family member.

The statute itself defines "serious health condition" as an "illness, injury, impairment, or physical or mental condition" that requires either inpatient care (in a hospital, nursing home or hospice) or at least continuing treatment by a health care provider. [29 U.S.C. §§ 2611(6) and (11)]

Under DOL regulations (§ 825.114), a serious health condition includes one that requires "inpatient" care, which in turn is defined as an "overnight stay"—a term that is not defined. The Third Circuit defined an "overnight stay" for FMLA purposes as a substantial period of time running from one calendar day to the next, based on admission and discharge. A period of at least eight hours would be considered substantial. In a case where a plaintiff suffered chest pains at work, arrived at the hospital just before midnight, was admitted just after midnight, and discharged in the evening of the day of admission, the Third Circuit found that there had not been an overnight stay, because he did not remain in the hospital from one calendar day to the next. [*Bonkowski v. Oberg Indus., Inc.*, 787 F.3d 190 (3d Cir. 2015)]

Qualifying family members are spouse (husband or wife only—not cohabitant), child (including adopted or foster child) who is either under 18 years old or mentally or physically disabled, or parent (biological parent or someone who played a parental role—but NOT a mother- or father-in-law, even though many individuals become caregivers for their in-laws). [See 29 U.S.C. §§ 2611(7) and (12)]

FMLA leave may be available to care for a grandparent who was in loco parentis to the employee. The Second Circuit held that an employee who was fired after taking time off to care for his seriously ill grandfather had a triable case of FMLA interference. The district court said that the employee was at fault for not pointing out that his grandfather had raised him, but the Second Circuit said that the employer had an obligation to ask for additional information needed to determine the availability of leave. [*Coutard v. Municipal Credit Union*, 848 F.3d 102 (2d Cir. 2017); see Ronald Miller, *Employer Must Inquire Further When Employee Seeks FMLA Leave to Care for Ailing Grandparent*, Employment Law Daily (Feb. 14, 2017) (benefitslink.com); Jeffrey Rhodes, *Employee Denied FMLA Leave for Sick Grandparent Can Go to Jury*, shrm.org (Mar. 15, 2017) (benefitslink.com)]

The District Court for the Western District of Kentucky ruled that FMLA leave cannot be taken when a non-marital partner is ill (in this case, with complications of pregnancy) nor can leave be taken to care for a "child" who is still unborn. [*Lukudu v. JBS USA, LLC*, CIVIL ACTION NO. 3:12-CV-00704-TBR, 2014 U.S. Dist. LEXIS 33351 (W.D. Ky. Mar. 14, 2014)]

An African-American teacher's contract was not renewed after he took extensive absences for his own diabetes and care of his son with sickle-cell anemia. His FMLA claims went to trial, but the Seventh Circuit upheld dismissal of claims for race discrimination and disability discrimination and retaliation. The Seventh Circuit said that he was not a Qualified Individual With a Disability, did not request accommodation, and did not produce evidence of similarly situated co-workers who received better treatment. But his FMLA claims of interference and retaliation were supported by comments from his principal that he would be disciplined if he took more time off to care for his son. The principal said that sickle cell disease was not serious enough to justify taking time off. The Seventh Circuit said that FMLA interference could be inferred because most of the plaintiff's absences qualified under the FMLA. [*Preddie v. Bartholomew Consolidated Sch. Corp.*, 799 F.3d 806 (7th Cir. 2015)]

Travel time to care for an out-of-state family member is an FMLA gray area. If it is clear that an employee will be needed to care for a family member on a certain date, then travel to arrive by that time is probably part of protected leave. The line seems to be drawn between direct care (covered by the FMLA) and indirect care (e.g., fixing up a relative's house; not covered). [Jeff Nowak, *Does Travel Time Count as FMLA Leave?*, Franczek Radelet FMLA FAQ (Feb. 23, 2011) (benefitslink.com)]

The Eleventh Circuit held that it was permissible to fire an employee who was out of work for four weeks (after being given two weeks' leave) to assist her daughter, who was having a baby. The leave request did not mention either the FMLA or pregnancy complications. Pregnancy in and of itself is not a serious health condition, so a valid FMLA request must assert the need for a caregiver as a result of complications. [*Cruz v. Publix Super Mkts. Inc.*, 428 F.3d 1379 (11th Cir. 2005)]

The Seventh Circuit upheld dismissal of FMLA (and ADA) claims brought by an employee who tested positive for alcohol. The employee was on a last chance agreement after ongoing alcohol problems and a drunk driving arrest. She was tested for alcohol because she appeared to be under the influence of alcohol at work. The plaintiff did not prove she was entitled to FMLA leave. Although substance abuse is considered a serious health condition, this is true only if the employee receives inpatient treatment or is under continuing care from a health care provider. The plaintiff's FMLA retaliation claim failed because she did not show a connection between her alleged request for leave and a materially adverse action. The blood alcohol test could not have been retaliatory, because it was permitted by the Last Chance Agreement, and she was terminated for violating that agreement. [*Ames v. Home Depot USA Inc.*, 629 F.3d 665 (7th Cir. 2011)]

If both spouses work for different employers, each one is entitled to 12 weeks of leave when a child is born or adopted, but if they work for the same employer, the employer can legally require them to split a single 12-week leave period, or to share the 12 weeks when they are caring for the same sick parent. [See 29 U.S.C. § 2612(f)] Pregnancy-related medical complications do not reduce the total, because they are taken for the employee's own health condition. The DOL says that unmarried couples with the same employer do not have to split the 12-week allotment; each can take the full 12 weeks. For other types of FMLA leave, such as care for a seriously ill child, each parent can take 12 weeks of leave. Eligible spouses who have the same employer can also take a combined 26 weeks of leave in 12 months if they are military caregivers. [Jeff Nowak, *The FMLA Marriage Penalty: When Spouses Work for the Same Employer*, FMLA Insights (Oct. 9, 2015) (benefitslink.com)]

On October 11, 2015, California amended the "kin care" provision of Labor Code § 233, which allows employees to use half of their accrued sick leave to care for a family member (broadly defined to include grandparents, grandchildren, and siblings as well as spouse, domestic partner, or children). Caregiver leave can be taken for preventive care as well as diagnosis and treatment, and for certain events related to domestic violence. [Angie Brown, *California Kin Care Amendment Effective January 1st, 2016*, ClaimVantage (Nov. 10, 2015), available at Lexology.com]

Georgia employers with 25 or more employees are also obligated to give employees who are entitled to paid sick leave up to five annual "kin care" days. [Shella B. Neba and Blaze R. Douglas, *Georgia Enacts Kin Care Law*, Littler Mendelson PC (May 15, 2017), available at Lexology.com]

Moonlighting by people on FMLA leave seems to peak in last months of year. Employers tend to think this justifies discipline or termination for FMLA abuse. However, the employer should investigate whether the employee is unable to work at his or her regular job, but is able to handle the moonlighting job. For example, an employee's bad back may rule out manual labor, but not clerical work. The FMLA statute and regulations do not explicitly prohibit employees on FMLA leave to work, unless the employer has a generally applied policy against moonlighting by employees on equivalent types of leave. DOL's Wage & Hour Division permits consistent no-moonlighting policies to be applied to people on FMLA leave because workers on FMLA leave are still employed. However, state law might forbid restrictions on lawful off-duty conduct. WHD says you can apply a consistent no-moonlighting policy to an employee on FMLA leave because people on FMLA leave still have an employment relationship. If you do have a policy, remind employees about it when they go on leave. But check state law, which might forbid restrictions on lawful off-duty conduct. [Kristen E. Michaels, *Tis The Season for Moonlighting: FMLA Leave and Secondary Employment*, McDermott Will & Emery (Dec. 22, 2015) (benefitslink.com)]

§ 38.04 THE EMPLOYER'S OBLIGATION

It is the employer's responsibility to determine if the FMLA applies, so when an employee calls in sick it is necessary to find out if the employee is likely to miss more than three consecutive days of work, if the employee has a chronic condition that manifests intermittently, if he or she is caring for a family member with a serious health condition, or has pregnancy complications.

To avoid discrimination, there should be a standard list of questions that are asked of everyone who calls in sick: for example, the specific reason for the absence, which job duties the person cannot perform, if he or she has already taken leave for the same condition and when; if he or she is seeing a doctor; when he or she discovered the need for time off; and when he or she will return to work. If FMLA leave has already been taken for the same condition, find out if recertification is appropriate; if there seems to be a pattern of abuse (e.g., an excessive number of Monday and Friday absences); 29 C.F.R. § 825.308(e) permits the employer to check with the employee's doctor to see if three-day weekends are consistent with the medical need for leave. [Jeff Nowak, *Suffering from Super Bowl-Induced FMLA Leave?*, Franczek Radelet FMLA Insights (Feb. 7, 2011) (benefitslink.com)]

Nowak counsels, in the situation where a leave request is denied (particularly at holiday time) and then, at the last minute, the employee requests FMLA leave for a flare-up of a chronic condition, that the employer send a cover letter to the employee. The letter should explain that the FMLA request covers time for which leave was denied, so the employer requires confirmation of the medical need for leave in light of the employee's pattern of leave use. If the employee fails to provide certification, or the certification is dubious, it is legitimate for the employer to ask for clarification or a second opinion. If there is already a certification on file, asking for FMLA leave on days when leave was denied could be considered a significant change in circumstances justifying a recertification request. [Jeff Nowak, *An Employee Requests and Is Denied Vacation Leave but Later Takes FMLA Leave for the Same Time Period. What Recourse Does an Employer Have?*, Franczek Radelet FMLA Insights (Jan. 8, 2013) (benefitslink .com)]

The FMLA regulations state that if there is a temporary cessation of one week or more (e.g., a school vacation) then those days that employer activity has ceased do not count against the FMLA entitlement—even if the employee would not have been healthy enough to work. With respect to holidays, if an employee observes a holiday that falls on Friday or Monday and takes the whole week off, the whole workweek should be counted as a full week of FMLA leave. However, if the employee works any part of the workweek, then the holiday cannot be counted as FMLA leave. [See 29 C.F.R. § 825.200(h)] This section also applies to calculation of FMLA leave when the operation is shut down by a natural disaster. If the employer is shut down for a week or more, the lost days do not reduce the employee's FMLA leave entitlement, even if it is obvious that the employee would not have been able to work during the downtime. [Jeff Nowak, *FMLA FAQ: How Do Snow Days Affect FMLA Leave?*, Franczek Radelet FMLA Insights (Jan. 22, 2016) (benefitslink.com)]

[A] Benefits

The employer must reinstate the employee after leave, and must maintain all employee benefits during leave. [See 29 U.S.C. § 2615(c) for health coverage requirements] However, the employee does not accrue seniority or additional benefits. FMLA leave is not considered a break in service when pension eligibility is determined.

"Benefits" means all of the employer's benefits (not just those offered under Employment Retirement Income Security Act (ERISA) plans), e.g., "group life insurance, health insurance, disability insurance, sick leave, annual leave, educational benefits, and pensions." [29 U.S.C. § 2611(5)]

When employees are on FMLA leave, the employee group health plan (EGHP) must maintain their coverage at the original level. If employees are required to pay part of the EGHP premium under normal circumstances, the plan can require them to continue contributing during FMLA leave. Furthermore, if the employee is more than 30 days late paying the premium, health insurance coverage can legitimately be terminated. If coverage is terminated in this manner, but the employee returns to work and is reinstated, then he or she is entitled to immediate reinstatement in the EGHP, with no need to satisfy plan requirements a second time.

If the employee quits instead of returning from leave, the employer is entitled to recover the health premiums expended on the employee's behalf during the leave period. But if the employee files a health claim for treatment during the leave period, a claim that would otherwise be allowable cannot be denied because the employee later terminates employment.

Nowak warns that a policy of recovering health insurance premiums only from new mothers who do not return from maternity leave, but not from other non-returning employees, could violate the PDA. [Jeff Nowak, *When Employee on FMLA Leave Indicates They Will Not Return from FMLA Leave, What Should an Employer Do?*, Franczek Radelet FMLA Insights (June 22, 2012) (benefits link.com)]

Employees on FMLA leave must receive holiday pay, if employees on other kinds of leave are paid for the holiday. Entitlement to benefits (other than the EGHP) for employees on FMLA leave depends on the employer's treatment of other kinds of leave. For example, if an employee using vacation leave gets holiday pay for the vacation day before the holiday, employees on FMLA leave must be allowed the same treatment. But if employees are not paid for the holiday if they are absent on unpaid leave the day before the holiday, it is permissible not to pay employees on FMLA leave for the day. FMLA expert Jeff Nowak suggests adopting policy language as follows: "consistent with the company's leave policy, no vacation or other benefits accrue during unpaid FMLA leave, and you will not be paid for holidays during the leave." The period of FMLA leave is considered continuous service and there is no break in service with respect to vesting and eligibility for retirement plan participation. [Jeff Nowak, *FMLA FAQ: Am I Required to Pay My Employee for Holidays Occurring During FMLA Leave?*, Franczek Radelet FMLA Insights (May 29, 2014) (benefitslink.com)]

If a bonus is based on achieving a goal, DOL regulations say [see 29 C.F.R. § 825.215(c)] that the employers are not required to pay the bonus to someone who missed the goal because of taking FMLA leave—unless the bonus is paid to people who took equal amounts of non-FMLA leave. The DOL defines "goal-based" broadly. Bonuses (e.g., holiday bonuses) that are paid to all employees are not goal-based but attendance, safety, sales, and production bonuses are considered goal-based. The regulations do not state whether bonuses have to be prorated. [Jeff Nowak, *FMLA FAQ: Is An Employer Required to Pay a Prorated Amount of Annual Bonus After Employee Takes FMLA Leave?* (Dec. 23, 2014) (benefitslink.com)]

If an employee who has received health coverage during leave says that he or she will not return to work after leave, or who returns to work but only for less than 30 days, the employer will generally be entitled to recoup the cost of EGHP coverage for any unpaid portion of the FMLA leave period. An employer maintaining a self-insured plan can only recoup its share of allowable COBRA premiums, not including the 2% administration fee. The self-insured employer is nevertheless required to pay health claims incurred during the FMLA leave.

However, recoupment is not permitted if the employee is unable to return because of the onset, continuation, or recurrence of a serious health condition (of the employee or family member) or other circumstances beyond the employee's control (e.g., a need to care for a person with a serious health condition who is not a member of the immediate family; the employee's spouse gets a work transfer of more than 75 miles; the employee was laid off while on leave). The employer is entitled to demand certification of the serious health condition from a health care provider. If 30 days elapse without the certification being provided, the employer can recover the contributions. The cost of coverage cannot be recouped from certain key employees who are not entitled to reinstatement.

The recoverable premiums are considered a debt owed by the non-returning employee. The premiums can be deducted from amounts owed to the employee, such as wages or profit-sharing distributions (although there may be limits under other federal laws, or under state law). The employer can also sue the ex-employee for the amounts owed. [HR.CCH.com, *Can Employer Recover Health Coverage Costs If Employee Doesn't Return From FMLA Leave?* (Dec. 5, 2016) (benefitslink.com)]

[B]   Reinstatement

Section 2614 takes up the subject of reinstatement in more detail. It provides that an employee who returns from leave not only must not lose any benefits because of taking leave, but must be reinstated either in the old job or an equivalent new one. The second job is equivalent to the first if it provides equivalent terms and conditions of employment (benefits, pay, etc.) The right to be rehired in one's former position is not absolute; an employee can be fired if his job has been eliminated when a number of positions were consolidated. [*Yashenko v. Harrah's N.C. Casino Co.*, 446 F.3d 541 (4th Cir. 2006)]

A person who is unable to perform an essential function of the job is not entitled to reinstatement, although rights may be available outside the FMLA context under the ADA, state leave law, or a CBA. The FMLA allows restoration to be delayed until the employee provides a fitness for duty certificate (if the leave was taken for the employee's own serious health condition, not as a family caregiver)—as long as the employer asked for certification before the leave began. An employee who would have been laid off or fired even if no leave had been taken can still be laid off or fired. Reinstatement is not required if the employee unequivocally stated that he or she would not return post-leave. Reinstatement is forfeited if the employee took leave fraudulently, or violated a uniformly enforced policy against moonlighting.

The FMLA creates an exception for employees earning in the top 10% of the employer's workforce. It is not necessary to reinstate them after leave if reinstatement would cause "substantial and grievous economic injury" to the employer, and the employer promptly notifies the employee that reinstatement will be denied. The statute does not define this, but the regulations say that the standard is more rigorous than the ADA "undue hardship" standard. If reinstatement is denied on the basis of substantial and grievous injury, the employer must give the employee written notice of the effect on health benefits. Failure to give this notice means that reinstatement will be required. [HR Daily Advisor, *Mastering Tough FMLA Issues: Employees Who Don't Have Restoration Rights* (Mar. 3, 2017) (benefitslink.com)]

However, taking FMLA leave does not entitle any employee to anything he or she would not have been entitled to by remaining at work without taking leave.

For example, the Fourth Circuit held in mid-2017 that it was legitimate to give the plaintiff a different, but equivalent, job after he returned from leave, and then to RIF him when the company failed to get a government contract. The burden was on the plaintiff to show that the stated reason (failure to get the contract) was pretextual; it was not up to the employer to show he would have been terminated even if he had not taken FMLA leave. [*Waag v. Sotera Defense Solutions, Inc.*, No. 15-2521 (4th Cir. May 16, 2017); see Salomon Laguerre and Louisa J. Johnson, *Fourth Circuit Decision Reiterates That Filling Employee's Position During Leave and Re-Assigning Employee to a Different But Equivalent Position After Leave Is OK Under the FMLA*, Seyfarth Shaw LLP (May 31, 2017), available at Lexology.com]

An employee who returns from FMLA leave and is ready to work is entitled, in the Sixth Circuit view, to immediate reinstatement, not reinstatement a month later. The statute does not provide the employer with additional time to adjust to the employee's return. Therefore, insisting that an employee take a longer leave than the employee could certify to be medically necessary could be treated as interference with FMLA rights. [*Hoge v. Honda of Am. Mfg. Inc.*, 384 F.3d 238 (6th Cir. 2004)]

The Eleventh Circuit held that a jury could conclude that reassignment to an inferior position immediately after returning from FMLA leave for childbirth and infant care was prejudicial. The trial court had to consider the plaintiff's claim for reinstatement as injunctive relief, even if there were no monetary damages. [*Evans v. Books-a-Million*, 762 F.3d 1288 (11th Cir. 2014)]

The Third Circuit refused to dismiss an interference/retaliation case based on evidence of denial of reinstatement. The job of a hospital credentialing assistant consisted of about 60% typing. The plaintiff broke a bone in her hand in a non-work-related incident and took a leave of absence, returning after several weeks with a splint on her hand. The hospital kept her on leave until she could return to full duty, and got someone else to fill her job after she had been on leave for 12 weeks. An employer demanding certification of an employee's ability to perform the essential functions of the job must furnish a list of essential functions at the time FMLA leave is approved. If the employer believes the certification is inadequate, it should ask the employee for permission to ask the health care provider for clarification. [*Budhun v. Reading Hosp. & Med. Ctr.*, 765 F.3d 245 (3d Cir. 2014)]

The Fourth Circuit upheld dismissal of charges of ADA violations and FMLA retaliation (because of clear evidence that he was terminated for misconduct). However, the Fourth Circuit vacated summary judgment for the employee on the FMLA interference count, holding that he would have structured his leave differently if he had received proper notice of his right to reinstatement after leave. [*Vannoy v. Federal Reserve Bank of Richmond*, 827 F.3d 296 (4th Cir. 2016); see Kathleen Kapusta, *No Evidence FMLA Notice Informed Employee of Job Restoration Right Interference Claim Revived*, WK WorkDay Blog (June 30, 2016) (benefitslink.com)]

Although it is not forbidden for employers to require a fitness for duty certification before reinstating an employee who has taken FMLA leave, the employer must maintain a uniform policy requiring certification, and must inform the employee of the requirement as soon as leave is designated as FMLA leave. [*Casagrande v. OhioHealth Corp.* , 666 Fed. Appx. 491 (6th Cir. 2016); see *FMLA Notice Failure Is FMLA Interference,* Wagner Law Group Health and Welfare Law Alert (Feb. 1, 2017) (benefitslink.com)]

The Tenth Circuit held that it was lawful to discharge an employee who refused to cooperate with the FMLA process, submitting forms more than seven weeks after her employer's initial request and after there had been several reminders, because termination was for lack of cooperation, not for exercising FMLA rights. [*Dalpiaz v. Carbon Cnty.*, 760 F.3d 1126 (10th Cir. 2014)]

Employee Agee submitted a doctor's note that imposed an indefinite restriction on her ability to work overtime. The employer gave her the choice of either applying for FMLA leave or being terminated. When she failed to complete the FMLA paperwork, she was fired. The Eleventh Circuit upheld the termination: mandatory overtime was established as an essential function of the job, so inability to work overtime showed she was not a qualified individual with a disability for ADA purposes. It was also legitimate to fire her for failure to submit the FMLA forms. [*Agee v. Mercedes Benz*, No. 15-11747, 2016 WL 1248507 (11th Cir. Mar. 30, 2016); see Ryan M. Bates and Thomas P. Murphy, *Eleventh Circuit Nixes Disability Discrimination Claim Due to Employee's Inability to Work Overtime*, Hunton & Williams LLP (Apr. 7, 2016), available at Lexology.com]

In most states (although California is an exception), employers can defend against FMLA charges by alleging an honest belief that the employee was abusing leave, even if the belief turns out to be incorrect. However, a complete investigation is required. Tools for fighting abuse include medical certification and recertification and requiring second or even third opinions. If the employee will have an ADA disability after FMLA leave ends, the interactive process (see § 36.05) should begin during the leave. Employers who claim that the leave request is an undue hardship must be able to document the hardship—for example, by showing loss of productivity, lower morale because workers are overburdened, lost sales, or deterioration in customer service. [Jeff Nowak, *Best Practices for Employers When Administering FMLA Leave: A Recap of Our Webinar*, Franczek Radelet FMLA Insights (Dec. 12, 2012) (benefitslink.com)]

The Third Circuit joined the Seventh, Eighth, and Tenth Circuits in holding that even if the employee made out a prima facie case of FMLA retaliation, summary judgment was properly granted for the employer because the employer had an honest belief that the employee was misusing FMLA leave. (He had DUI court dates coinciding with days he took intermittent FMLA leave.) There was no evidence of denial of benefits he was entitled to, so his FMLA retaliation charge was dismissed. Although a request for intermittent FMLA leave could also be a request for an ADA accommodation, there was no evidence in this case that the employee requested, but was denied, accommodation for his hip condition. [*Capps v. Mondelez Global, LLC*, 847 F.3d 144 (3d Cir. 2017); see Lorene D. Park, *Honest Belief Employee Was Abusing FMLA Leave Defeats Retaliation Claim*, Employment Law Daily (Feb. 1, 2017) (benefitslink.com); Jody Kahn Mason, *Third Circuit Says "Last Call" for Employee Terminated After Caught Drinking While on FMLA "Bed Rest,"* Jackson Lewis PC (Feb. 3, 2017), available at Lexology.com]

Anyone who is on FMLA leave can be laid off during a RIF, if he or she would have been laid off anyway. [*O'Connor v. PLA Family Health Plan Inc.*, 200 F.3d 1349 (11th Cir. 2000)]

[C] Interference and Retaliation

Employees on FMLA leave cannot be asked to work—a proposition that requires a definition of "work." According to the District Court for the Northern District of Ohio, making frequent work-related calls to a person on leave from surgery could constitute FMLA interference, although workers on leave can be asked to close out assignments or provide information about passwords or colleagues who can take over tasks from them. [*Vess v. Select Med. Corp.*, No. 3:11 CV 2549 (N.D. Ohio Mar. 15, 2013)]

Requiring substantial work during leave would be interference, but asking workers on leave to answer occasional inquiries about projects or making a few phone calls as a professional courtesy, is not. The employer should give employees on leave written notice they should not work while they are on leave, other than simple ministerial tasks like updating the status of their pre-leave assignments. [*Smith-Schrenk v. Genon Energy*, No. H-13-2902, 2015 U.S. Dist. LEXIS 3007 (S.D. Tex. Jan. 12, 2015). See also *Reilly v. Revlon*, 620 F. Supp. 2d 524 (S.D.N.Y. 2009); *Kesler v. Barris*, 482 F. Supp. 2d 886 (E.D. Mich. 2007), expecting employee to take occasional calls is not interference.]

The Tenth Circuit revived FMLA (and ADA) claims because a terminated employee was treated more harshly than co-workers who did not take extensive FMLA leave. The employer said that Smothers was fired for a safety violation and arguing with a co-worker about the violation; he charged FMLA retaliation. Smothers had degenerative disc disease resulting from a neck injury. He had three operations but still had chronic pain and frequently took FMLA leave. He was pressured to change shifts but refused, because it would cut his income by $7,000 a year. An HR representative told Smothers's supervisor that forcing him to change shifts would violate the FMLA. [*Smothers v. Solvay Chems., Inc.*, 740 F.3d 530 (10th Cir. 2014)]

The Seventh Circuit held that a former employee's trip to Las Vegas with her terminally ill mother could be considered family care leave. The Seventh Circuit held that the plaintiff provided the same kind of assistance (bathing, dressing, giving medication, etc.) during the trip that she gave her mother at home. However, the First and Ninth Circuits require active participation in a family member's health treatment to justify FMLA leave. [*Ballard v. Chicago Park Dist.*, 741 F.3d 838 (7th Cir. 2014)]

Although intent is not required for an interference claim, the Tenth Circuit found that termination two days after a request for FMLA leave was justified by the employee's lack of improvement after receiving mixed feedback in his performance review. The retaliation claim required circumstantial evidence of a retaliatory motive, which the plaintiff could not provide. [*Brown v. ScriptPro LLC*, 700 F.3d 1222 (10th Cir. 2012)]

It is not retaliation to terminate an employee if termination would have been justified even if no leave had been taken, e.g., when an employee failed a Performance Improvement Plan before taking FMLA leave. [*Ross v. Gilhuly*, 755 F.3d 185 (3d Cir. 2014)]

A commercial motor vehicle driver who was fired when his employer discovered that he had been diagnosed as an alcoholic. He asked for leave to get treatment. His request for FMLA leave was approved. After about a month of leave, he wanted to return to work; his employer determined that he was not qualified to work (Department of Transportation regulations do not allow anyone with a current diagnosis of alcoholism to drive a commercial vehicle) and fired him. He sued for FMLA interference and retaliation. (He also brought ADA claims, which were also dismissed.) The Eleventh Circuit dismissed the FMLA interference claim because he would have been fired because of his alcoholism diagnosis whether or not he took leave. The retaliation claim was dismissed because he could not show that his termination was leave-related. [*Jarvela v. Crete Carrier Corp.*, 754 F.3d 1283 (11th Cir. June 18, 2014), *vacated and reh'g granted*, 776 F.3d 822 (11th Cir. 2015)]

Plaintiff Wink was granted intermittent FMLA leave to take her autistic son to appointments. In February 2012, the child was excluded from day care because of autism-related aggression. Wink was allowed to work at home two days a week, with time at home spent caring for her son treated as intermittent FMLA leave. However, the employer company ran into financial trouble and terminated remote work arrangements. Wink was told that, starting in three days, she would have to work at the office 40 hours a week. She said she could not arrange for child care that quickly. The HR department incorrectly told her that she could not use FMLA leave for child care. She reported to the office and said she did not have child care for the day; she was told that failure to work the full day would be treated as a voluntary quit. In her suit for FMLA interference and retaliation, the jury found for the plaintiff on retaliation only. The Seventh Circuit affirmed the finding of retaliation.

The Seventh Circuit also upheld the liquidated damages award; the employer was not acting in good faith when it told Wink she could not take FMLA leave to care for a family member. The Seventh Circuit decided not to reduce the jury's award of attorneys' fees. Although only the retaliation claim was successful, it was reasonable for the attorney to assert the interference claim as well and the unsuccessful claim did not increase the costs of the suit enough to justify a reduction in the fee. [*Wink v. Miller Compressing Co.*, 845 F.3d 821 (7th Cir. 2017); see Katrin Schatz, *A Cautionary Tale: How Sudden Changes to Intermittent FMLA Can Cost You*, Jackson Lewis PC (Jan. 17, 2017), available at Lexology.com]

§ 38.05   INTERMITTENT LEAVE

Section 2612(b) governs intermittent leave and leave that produces a reduced work schedule. The FMLA provides the equivalent of 12 weeks of work: up to 480 hours a year for full-time workers, and an equivalent prorated amount for part-time workers, such as 240 hours a year for someone who works a half-time schedule. The FMLA regulations [see 29 C.F.R. § 825.205(b)] refer to the actual number of hours the employee usually works in a week; or in an average week, if the schedule varies. Therefore, a person who is exempt from receiving overtime benefits but who typically works longer than 40 hours a week can get additional intermittent leave because of this work history.

For intermittent leave or reduced schedule leave, only the amount of leave actually taken counts toward leave entitlement. The calculation is based on the regular workweek, so someone who works four days a week, eight hours a day is entitled to 384 hours of FMLA leave (12 weeks at 32 hours/week). The regulations say that if the employee's schedule varies, the calculation should be based on a weekly average of hours scheduled during the 12 months before the leave, including hours for which any kind of leave was taken. [Jeff Nowak, FMLA FAQ: *How Do I Calculate FMLA Leave Where My Employee's Work Schedule Varies from Week to Week?* (Jan. 8, 2015) (benefitslink.com)]

Employers are not obligated to grant intermittent leave for cosmetic procedures. The general rule is that leave to care for a newly born or adopted child must be taken in a block of time off, and not on an intermittent or reduced schedule—unless the employer agrees to the special schedule. Intermittent leave for parents can be denied unless the child has a serious health condition, or unless a pregnant employee has severe morning sickness or needs time off for prenatal care. Leave premised on a serious health condition can be taken intermittently or on a reduced schedule when it is medically necessary.

It is permitted for the employer to use health-related intermittent/reduced leave to offset birth or adoption leave taken by the employee in the same year, but only to the actual extent of intermittent or reduced leave that was taken.

When a health-related intermittent leave can be predicted, based on scheduled medical treatment, the employer can lawfully transfer the employee to an available alternative position—as long as:

- The employee is qualified for the position;

- The two jobs are equivalent in pay and benefits;

- The second job provides a better accommodation to the changed work schedule than the first job did;

- Once the need for intermittent leave ends, the transferred employee must be offered reinstatement in the former job or a comparable job. It violates the FMLA for employers to use transfers deliberately to discourage the use of FMLA leave or to retaliate against employees who take or request leave.

The Seventh Circuit held that employers should not summarily deny intermittent FMLA leave when an employee takes more leave than the estimate in the certification form—although it is legitimate to ask for recertification if the circumstances have changed. The Seventh Circuit also held that the plaintiff does not have to present expert testimony to prove he was incapacitated each day for which FMLA leave was requested. For a chronic condition like depression, medical evidence is needed to establish the serious health condition but expert testimony is not required to show incapacitation by the condition. The intermittent leave regulations allow leave even if the employee does not receive treatment during the absence. [*Hansen v. Fincantieri Marine Grp.*, 763 F.3d 832 (7th Cir. 2014)]

A social worker used intermittent leave to care for her sick elderly mother. Several requests were approved between mid-2013 and early 2014. In March 2014, the plaintiff's mother was seriously ill; the plaintiff asked for and received five days of intermittent leave. But when she got back, she was warned that "any other" company would have fired her. A new head of HR ordered her to provide travel receipts or receipts from a health care provider for any future leave taken on less than 30 days' notice. The employer warned employees whose Paid Time Off (PTO) balance was low that they could get into trouble by using their PTO and taking time off—and did not exempt FMLA leave. The plaintiff sued after her mid-2014 termination for poor performance. The Eleventh Circuit held that she had enough evidence to defeat summary judgment: a reasonable jury could believe that the documentation requirement prevented her from taking leave. The requirement seemed to have been created just for the plaintiff. [*Diamond v. Hospice of Florida Keys, Inc.*, No. 15-15716, 2017 U.S. App. LEXIS 1483 (11th Cir. Jan. 27, 2017); see Marjory D. Robertson, *Employers Beware: Asking For Receipts and Making Comments About Time Off Can Be Unlawful FMLA Interference*, Sun Life Financial Inc. (Jan. 30, 2017), available at Lexology.com]

An employer that is dubious about the authenticity of a certification can ask the health care provider if he or she prepared the certification, and what it means. The employer can also ask for a second opinion—and, if it conflicts with the initial opinion, can ask for a third opinion to resolve the conflict. However, the employer must pay for the second and third opinions, and the third opinion is binding. [Daniel Cafaro, *7 Best Practices in FMLA Intermittent Leave Administration*, Smart HR (Apr. 12, 2013) (benefitslink.com)]

§ 38.06 RELATING FMLA LEAVE TO OTHER LEAVE

[A] Generally

The simplest example is in the case of an employer that does not offer any form of paid leave. If the employer is subject to the FMLA, it must offer unpaid leave to FMLA-eligible employees. More difficult issues arise when the employee is entitled both to FMLA leave and to some form of paid leave (e.g., vacation; sick leave).

The general rule is that employers are not required to allow employees to accrue vacation and sick leave when they are on FMLA leave—but employers must use the same accrual policy for FMLA leave as for other types of leave. [HR Daily Advisor, *Ask the Expert: Should Weeks of FMLA Be Used to Calculate Vacation Benefits?* (Sept. 22, 2016) (benefitslink.com)]

In general, employees will not be entitled to "stack" all the leave available to them from the FMLA, other laws, and the employer's policies. However, to prevent stacking, the employer must notify employees in advance that the other leave runs concurrently with FMLA leave. Employees are entitled to more leave than the FMLA provides, if this is required by state law, policy, or a CBA. It would be interference with FMLA rights to force employees to make up time taken for FMLA leave to receive a full paycheck—or to forbid them from making up time taken for other kinds of leave. If employees are allowed to make up the time taken under the FMLA, the time can still be counted against their FMLA allowance—as long as they are warned that if they get paid for time, it will not extend their entitlement to FMLA leave. [HR Daily Advisor, *FMLA Notice Requirements: Substitution and "Make Up" Leave* (Nov. 17, 2016) (benefitslink .com)]

In a controversial 2007 decision, the Seventh Circuit ruled that it violates the FMLA to make an employee use paid sick and vacation leave, even if the employee was also receiving disability benefits under a multi-employer plan. (See

29 C.F.R. § 825.207(d)(1).) Therefore, the Seventh Circuit allows an employee who takes FMLA leave to extend the 12 week allotment under the FMLA by any other paid leave offered by the employer. The employer's theory was that the regulation applies only to benefits under the employer's own temporary disability plan, not a third-party plan, but the Seventh Circuit held that the regulation does not distinguish based on the type of disability plan. [*Repa v. Roadway Express*, 477 F.3d 938 (7th Cir. 2007)]

The Ninth Circuit held that it is not mandatory that employees take FMLA leave whenever they qualify for it; they can affirmatively decline to use FMLA leave, perhaps to save it for later. Therefore, it did not violate the FMLA to fire a worker who asked for vacation, rather than FMLA leave, to care for her sick father in Guatemala. The employer's policy required unpaid FMLA leave to run concurrently with paid vacation time, creating an incentive for employees to use their paid time first. The Ninth Circuit rejected Escriba's contention that allowing her to decline FMLA leave was an unlawful waiver: the Ninth Circuit drew a distinction between surrendering a right completely and not using it immediately. However, the Ninth Circuit rejected the employer's application for an award of court costs as a prevailing party. The plaintiff had limited financial resources, the case involved important issues and levying costs against her would discourage other low-income workers from pursuing their rights. [*Escriba v. Foster Poultry Farms, Inc.*, 743 F.3d 1236 (9th Cir. 2014)]

An employee can be required to take leave if the employee's doctor imposes restrictions (e.g., based on known mental health issues) and there are no available positions that fit the restrictions. In the unusual case when the employer insists on leave but the employee wants to work, the employee will only have a sustainable FMLA interference claim if he or she later seeks FMLA leave that is denied because the previously, allegedly improper leave used up the employee's leave allowance. [*James v. Hyatt*, 707 F.3d 775 (7th Cir. 2013); *Tracy v Trinity Marine Prods.*, 721 F.3d 542 (8th Cir. 2013)]

State law may require employers to provide intermittent leave on more generous terms than the FMLA does. If the employee is also a qualified person with a disability as defined by the ADA, then it may be necessary to grant even more than the equivalent of 12 weeks' intermittent leave as a reasonable accommodation.

Sometimes it is hard to distinguish between leave taken because of complications of pregnancy and leave taken to prepare for parenting. Under Wage and Hour Division regulations, FMLA leave is not available after the employee has taken a disability leave for pregnancy-related complications. However, if there is a post-delivery period when the mother is physically unable to work, that period can be counted as a leave for serious illness, even though it also represents parenting leave. This is especially significant if both parents work for the same employer and would otherwise have to split a single 12-week leave period.

If the state has a law obligating employers to provide paid or partially paid maternity leave, employees are entitled to unpaid FMLA law in addition to the paid leave required by state law. Furthermore, if the state has an FMLA-type law that extends coverage in circumstances that the federal law does not provide for (e.g., taking care of a friend or parent-in-law), the state-required leave is treated as if it were taken for non-FMLA purposes and therefore does not reduce the 12-week FMLA allowance.

A late 2010 article says that it is an open question whether intermittent FMLA leave is available for fertility treatment, because the statute and regulations are silent and there is no clear judicial rule. Only one, unpublished, Circuit Court decision has ruled that infertility is a serious health condition for FMLA purposes. Even in this outlier case, the Sixth Circuit upheld the plaintiff's termination for lack of evidence that the employee took time off for an FMLA-covered reason. [*Culpepper v. BlueCross BlueShield of Tenn.*, 321 Fed. Appx. 491 (6th Cir. 2009) (unpublished); see Jennifer Gonzalez, *Infertility Issues in the Workplace*, Hall Render Killian Heath & Lyman PC (Aug. 2, 2016), available at Lexology .com] It is possible that denying the leave might be considered to violate the ADA or PDA. If the employee is covered by the FMLA, then taking intermittent leave for fertility treatment cannot be used as a negative factor in hiring, promotion, or discipline. If leave is requested after a miscarriage or the death of a newborn, some decisions hold that bereavement leave is not covered by the FMLA, unless the bereaved employee has a serious health condition as a result of bereavement. [Keisha-Ann G. Gray, *Procreation Problems*, Human Resource Executive Online (Nov. 2, 2010) (benefitslink.com)]

OSHA announced in late 2014 that the FMLA's confidentiality provision, 29 C.F.R. § 825.500(g), outweighs the OSHA rules. Therefore, if an employee provides certification of the need for leave due to a workplace injury or illness, the employer is not obligated to record the event on its OSHA log. [*Sec'y of Labor v. USPS*, No. 08-1547 (OSHRC Sept. 29, 2014)]

A seven-week trip to the Philippines, accompanying a seriously ill husband who consulted a faith healer, was not covered by the FMLA, so it was lawful to fire the employee for taking unapproved leave. The retaliation claim failed because the plaintiff not merely obtained FMLA leave when her husband received conventional medical care, but also because a pilgrimage to a spiritual healing center (much less tourism) is not protected by the FMLA. [*Tayag v. Lahey Clinic Hosp. Inc*, 632 F.3d 788 (1st Cir. 2011)]

Statutes governing medical leave typically define the amount of medical leave that must be granted. Conditions that require long-term absences are often severe enough to trigger protection against disability discrimination. Worker's Compensation might also be involved if the illness or injury is work-related.

Many companies maintain a formal policy that sets a maximum length of available medical leave (e.g., six months or a year), with termination for employees who are unable to return to work after exhausting their leave allowance. Multi-state companies must make sure that the policy is acceptable under the laws of all the states in which they do business. Calendar-year employers might face situations in which an employee succeeds in taking 12 weeks' leave in each of two calendar years.

[B]   ADA Interface

FMLA leave is available for the employee's "serious health condition"; if the condition is also an ADA disability, the employer must engage in the interactive process to see if reasonable accommodation can be made. The two statutes use different definitions. The FMLA considers whether the employee is sick for at least three days, consulting a doctor at least once, with a follow-up plan of care; whereas the ADA considers whether the person has a substantial limitation in a major life activity. For employees who have ADA disabilities, the employer should not deny FMLA leave based on the lack of notice of a predictable event or failure to document the need for leave, because the FMLA leave might be a reasonable accommodation. However, the employee should be required to provide medical certification, a clear return-to-work date, and achievable work restrictions. An employee who qualifies for FMLA leave can be offered the chance to work at home or go on light duty, but it is up to the employee and the employer cannot mandate these measures. If the employee accepts this alternative, the employer should get the employee's written consent to using the assignment in lieu of FMLA leave. [Vonbriesen.com, *Dancing with the Devil: Balancing FMLA and ADA Obligations* (Oct. 19, 2015) (benefitslink.com)]

An employer can satisfy both the FMLA and the ADA by offering a reduced work schedule to a disabled employee until he or she has used the 12 weeks of FMLA leave. After FMLA leave, employees are entitled to reinstatement in a job equivalent to the original job. The FMLA permits the employer to demand a physical exam to determine if a worker can be reinstated after a health-related FMLA leave. To satisfy the ADA as well, the examination must be job-related, not a comprehensive inventory of all physical conditions.

Although the two statutes were designed to accomplish different goals, workers sometimes find that FMLA leave is more accessible than taking time off as an ADA reasonable accommodation. Remember, FMLA leave is available when the employee is the sick person—not just when the employee is a caregiver.

Furthermore, if the company employs at least 50 people and the employee has put in the necessary 1,250 hours in the previous 12 months, entitlement to FMLA leave is automatic. The employer's discretion as to what constitutes a reasonable accommodation is not a factor. The right to reinstatement is also automatic. Employers can raise a defense of unreasonable hardship in ADA cases—but not in FMLA cases. [D.C. Bar Labor &Employment Law Section seminar (June 11, 2013)]

Absences that qualify under the FMLA or ADA should not be counted against an employee's record under a no-fault attendance policy.

Worker's Compensation defines disability in terms of specific injuries, such as the loss of hands or feet. The Worker's Compensation laws do not make explicit provision for leaves of absence, but denying reasonable time off could be interpreted as illegal retaliation for filing a Comp claim. However, it is lawful to fire someone who receives Worker's Compensation benefits as long as there is a legitimate non-retaliatory reason for the termination. Recipients of Worker's Compensation benefits are not guaranteed reinstatement if they recover from their injuries. If a work-related injury is also a disability, reasonable accommodation may be required under the ADA.

The EEOC's Enforcement Guidance on Reasonable Accommodation and Undue Hardship specifically says that no-fault leave policies that make termination automatic after a certain amount of leave has been taken violate the ADA.

However, some courts have ruled that indefinite leave is not required as a reasonable accommodation. A 2012 case permits terminating an employee who is unable to give a reasonable estimate of when he or she will be able to resume all essential functions of the job. The written job description listed 18 essential functions, including home visits to clients. A caseworker who used a wheelchair was terminated when, after surgery because she was unable to return to work at full capacity. She brought an ADA failure to accommodate/FMLA retaliation suit. The Tenth Circuit held that a request for a leave of absence is reasonable only if the employee can estimate when he or she can resume essential duties. [*Robert v. Board of Comm'rs of Brown Cnty.*, 691 F.3d 1211 (10th Cir. 2012)]

The Second Circuit reversed a $541,000 damage award under the New York Human Rights Law to a cancer patient who was fired after she said she did not know when she could return to work after exhausting the FMLA leave plus additional leave granted by the employer. The Second Circuit said that indefinite leave is not available as an accommodation, and she was unable to perform the essential functions of her job at the time she was terminated. [*Vangas v. Montefiore Med. Ctr.*, 823 F.3d 174 (2d Cir. 2016); see Manatt Phelps & Phillips LLP, *Indefinite Leave Not Required, Second Circuit Rules* (June 17, 2016), available at Lexology.com]

It is well-settled that having a disability or taking FMLA leave will not protect an employee from the consequences of misconduct or performance issues. A customer service representative who is an insulin-dependent diabetic took FMLA leave. When she was on a last chance agreement for performance, she hung up on at least two customers in a shift. She said she didn't remember doing it because she had low blood sugar at the time. The employer fired her, concluding that she must have intentionally hung up on customers because it's difficult to hang up accidentally; there was no evidence to support the assertion that she had a blood sugar episode; and she did not mention medical issues until it appeared that she was going to be fired. The Tenth Circuit affirmed summary judgment for the employer in her ADA and FMLA suit. Her only request for ADA accommodation was a request that her misconduct be overlooked, but the Tenth Circuit said that requests for accommodation are prospective only. [*DeWitt v. Southwestern Bell*

Tel. Co., No. 14-3192, 2017 U.S. App. LEXIS 843 (10th Cir. Jan. 18, 2017); see David T. Wiley, *Employee's "Alternative Facts" Can't Overcome Summary Judgment for Employer,* Jackson Lewis PC (Jan. 23, 2017), available at Lexology .com]

[C] COBRA and HIPAA

An IRS Final Rule, published starting at 64 Fed. Reg. 5160 (Feb. 3, 1999), provides that merely taking FMLA leave is not a COBRA qualifying event. However, a qualifying event does occur with respect to an employee (and any dependents of the employee who are at risk of losing health coverage) who fails to return to work at the end of the FMLA leave. The typical example is a new mother who does not return to work after the end of maternity leave.

Under the Final Rule, the Comprehensive Omnibus Budget Reconciliation Act (COBRA) qualifying event occurs on the last day of the FMLA leave. The employer is not allowed to condition the COBRA election on the employee paying the employee group health plan (EGHP) back for premiums paid on his or her behalf during the leave. However, if the employer has actually terminated coverage under the group plan for the whole class of employees that the employee belonged to before the FMLA leave, continuation coverage does not have to be offered to employees who do not return from leave. HIPAA's protection ends if the individual goes for 63 days or more without "creditable coverage." A joint Treasury/DOL/HHS rule holds that a period of FMLA leave when the person on leave has not continued group health coverage does not count toward the 63-day period for the person on leave or his or her dependents. [69 Fed. Reg. 78800 (Dec. 30, 2004)]

[D] Cafeteria Plans

The IRS published final regulations, effective October 17, 2001, applicable for cafeteria plan years beginning on or after January 1, 2002, explicating the FMLA obligations of cafeteria plans. [See T.D. 8966, R.I.N. 1545-AT47, 66 Fed. Reg. 52676.]

The employer must offer coverage under any group health plan as long as the employee is on paid or unpaid leave, on the same conditions as coverage would have been provided if the employee had continued to work during the leave period.

When the employee is on unpaid FMLA leave, the employer must either allow the employee to revoke the coverage or continue coverage but stop contributing premiums to the plan. The employer can then maintain the coverage by taking over both the employer and the employee share of the premium. The employer can recover the employee share of contributions when the employee returns from the leave. If the employee does not return, 29 C.F.R. § 825.213(a) permits the employer to recover both the employer and the employee shares of the premium from the employee. However, an employee who directed that premium payments be discontinued cannot be required to make contributions until after the end of unpaid leave.

[E]   Fair Labor Standards Act

A 1998 Opinion Letter from the Department of Labor [Opinion Letter #89 (1998)] says that salaried workers who are exempt from the FLSA (and therefore are not entitled to overtime pay) are not entitled to FLSA protection merely because their employer docks their paychecks to reflect unpaid FMLA leave, even though pay deductions for absence are more characteristic of FLSA-covered wage workers than of "exempts."

[F]   USERRA

Under the Uniformed Services Employment and Reemployment Rights Act [38 U.S.C. §§ 4301 *et seq.*] (USERRA), the Department of Labor indicated in mid-2002 that National Guard members and reservists who are called to active duty, and then released from active duty and return to their civilian jobs, are entitled to count their active duty service toward the 1,250 hour "work" requirement for FMLA eligibility. [HR Daily Advisor, *Coordinating FMLA with USERRA* (Apr. 7, 2017) (benefitslink.com)] See § 1.18[A]. See § 38.01[A] for discussion of FMLA rights of the families of servicemembers: leave may be available either to assist the servicemember with deployment or return to civilian life, or to care for a sick or injured servicemember.

[G]   State and Local Paid Leave Laws

There is no general federal requirement that employers provide paid leave for employees who are sick, taking care of a sick family member, or who have a new baby or have just adopted a child. However, Executive Order 13706, signed on Labor Day, 2015, taking effect in 2017, requires federal contractors to accrue at least one hour of paid sick leave for every 30 hours worked. See DOL's paid leave resources page, <www.dol.gov/featured/paidleave>. [Ilyse W. Schuman, *President Signs Executive Order Mandating Paid Sick Leave for Federal Contractors, Says DOL Final Rule on Contractor Pay Transparency Is Imminent*, Littler Mendelson (Sept. 8, 2015), available at Lexology.com]

But there is an increasing trend for states and localities to require paid leave.

Paid sick leave requirements have been enacted in the states of Arizona, California, Connecticut, Massachusetts, Oregon, and Vermont, Washington State, and in Washington, D.C. [Evandro C. Gigante and Laura M. Fant, *Arizona and*

Washington Become Latest States to Require Paid Sick Leave, Proskauer Rose LLP (Nov. 16, 2016), available at Lexology.com; Adam T. Pankratz, *Washington State Approves Paid Family and Medical Leave: What Employers Need to Know*, ogletree.com (July 7, 2017) (benefitslink.com)]

In addition to these state laws, more than a dozen cities, many of them on the East or West Coasts, have paid sick leave laws: e.g., New York City, Newark, Philadelphia, San Francisco, San Diego, Oakland, Portland (Oregon). See § 1.06 for more discussion of paid leave laws.

Wisconsin's state FMLA requires employers to permit employees to substitute any type of paid or unpaid leave provided by the employer for part of the statutory family or medical leave. The state civil rights agency said that an employer violated the state law by not permitting plaintiff Sherfel to substitute short-term disability benefits for part of her baby bonding leave. The employer said that Sherfel was not disabled and the state FMLA was preempted by ERISA to the extent that it allowed non-disabled employees to access disability benefits. The Sixth Circuit held that the state law was preempted. Preemption did not impair the federal FMLA (which does not require substitution of leave), and failure to apply preemption would impair ERISA enforcement by confusing employers. [*Sherfel v. Newson*, 768 F.3d 561 (6th Cir. 2014)]

§ 38.07 NOTIFYING THE EMPLOYER

No one schedules an emergency, of course. However, treatment for some serious health conditions is scheduled in advance (e.g., elective surgery). Section 2612(e) requires the employee to give at least 30 days' notice before leave based on the expected due date of a baby, or the expected placement date for adoption or foster care. If the date of birth or placement is less than 30 days from the time the employee decides to apply for FMLA leave, the employee must give as much notice as is practicable.

The FMLA imposes a duty on employees taking leave based on planned medical treatment to make reasonable efforts to schedule the treatment in the way that causes the least disruption to the employer (as long as this does not endanger the sick person's health). The employee should provide at least 30 days' notice before the leave is scheduled to begin—but if the need for the treatment becomes known less than 30 days in advance, the employee must provide as much notice as is practicable.

Nursing home employee Suzan Gienapp was granted leave to take care of her daughter, who was undergoing treatment for thyroid cancer; she did not say when she expected to return. Gienapp returned in 12 weeks, but her employer, expecting that she would not return, had hired a replacement. The employer said that she was caring for her grandchildren, which is not covered by the FMLA, However, the Seventh Circuit held that Gienapp was not required to give a return date when she requested unforeseen event leave and her efforts related to her sick daughter. [*Gienapp v. Harbor Crest*, 756 F.3d 527 (7th Cir. 2014); see Jeff Nowak, *Did a Court Just Allow an Employee FMLA Leave to Care for Her Grandchild?*, FMLA Insights (July 11, 2014) (benefitslink.com). See 29 C.F.R. § 825.303, if employees do not know how much unforeseen leave they need, they do not have to tell the employer how much leave is required. They must comply with the employer's policy, which Gienapp did by satisfying the employer's monthly call-in requirement.]

In 2017 alone, employers prevailed in at least five cases where employees did not follow the employer's procedures for requesting leave . [See, e.g., *Acker v. General Motors*, No. 16-11174 (5th Cir. Apr. 10, 2017); *Alexander v. Kellogg USA*, No. 2:15-cv-02049 (6th Cir. Jan. 14, 2017); *Duran v. Stock Bldg. Supply W., LLC*, No. 15-55536 (9th Cir. Jan. 12, 2017); *McKenzie v. Seneca Foods Corp.*, No. 16-cv-49-jdp (W.D. Wis. Mar. 27, 2017); *Scales v. FedEx Ground Package Sys.*, No. 15C50038 (N.D. Ill. Jan. 24, 2017). These cases are discussed in Marjory D. Robertson, *The Trend Continues: Courts Uphold FMLA Call-In & Notice Requirements to Outsourced Providers*, Sun Life Financial Inc. (Apr. 12 2017), available at Lexology.com; Wolters Kluwer Legal & Regulatory, *GM Didn't Violate FMLA by Suspending Electrician Who Failed to Follow Union-Negotiated Policy for Calling in Absences* (May 19, 2017) (benefitslink.com)]

§ 38.08   CERTIFICATION OF HEALTH CARE LEAVE

Employers have the right, under 29 U.S.C. § 2613, to require employees to prove that their request for medical leave is supported by a health care provider. This process is called certification. Employees have a duty to furnish the employer with a copy of the certification document, in a timely manner.

DOL regulations provide that the employee is solely responsible for getting medical certification of need for FMLA leave, and the employer does not have to pay for it: see 29 C.F.R. § 825.305(d).

FMLA regulations require the employee to return the medical certification form to the employer within 15 calendar days of receiving the blank form, unless there are circumstances that prevent the employee from submitting the form despite diligent good faith efforts: see 29 C.F.R. § 825.305(b). Before taking adverse action against the employee based on failure to return the certification, the employer must make sure that it has notified the employee of the need to return the form and has inquired if anything prevented the return. FMLA expert Jeff Nowak recommends sending a letter to the employee as soon as the fifteenth calendar day passes, offering assistance if the employee needs help completing the form and setting a firm seven-day deadline to receive the form. A telephone call (documented by the employer) should follow if the form is not received. If the employee fails to provide the certification, FMLA leave can be denied after the fifteenth day until certification is received, and days after Day 15 can be treated as unexcused absences. 29 C.F.R. § 825.313(b) says that leave is not

FMLA leave if the employee never returns the certification; Nowak reads this to mean that the entire absence, from the first day, is not FMLA leave. [Jeff Nowak, *FMLA FAQ: How Do Employers Count Unexcused Absences When FMLA Medical Certification Is Not Returned?*, Franczek Radelet FMLA Insights (Oct. 11, 2012) (benefitslink.com)]

The Third Circuit said that regulations are enforced strictly against employers, and employees get the benefit of the doubt. In this reading, the FMLA requires employers to give employees a chance to correct an inadequate medical certification before firing them. Plaintiff Hansler asked for two days a week of leave for about a month; her certification was not adequate to determine her eligibility because it failed to state the nature or duration of her medical condition. Leave can only be denied on the basis of inadequate certification if the employee is given at least seven calendar days to correct it (longer, if it could not be fixed by then despite the employee's diligent good-faith efforts. [*Hansler v. Lehigh Valley Hosp. Network*, No. 14-1772, 2015 WL 3825049 (3d Cir. June 22, 2015)]

The FMLA regulations say that the requirement of "continuing treatment by a health care provider" can be satisfied with at least three days of incapacitation, but they do not indicate whether medical testimony is required. A 2010 Third Circuit case holds that the employee's own testimony about the length of incapacitation, in conjunction with medical evidence, can be used to prove eligibility. The Third Circuit held that some medical evidence is required; the employee's unsupported testimony is not enough. The plaintiff was fired for violating the employer's policy requiring a call-in on sick days. The employer said that she did not qualify for FMLA leave because of the lack of proper notice, and because she did not prove three days of incapacitation. The Third Circuit remanded the case to the district court for further proceedings. [*Schaar v. Lehigh Valley Health Servs., Inc.*, 598 F.3d 156 (3d Cir. 2010)]

§ 38.09 DISCLOSURE TO EMPLOYEES

In April 2016, the DOL issued a new FMLA guide for employers, including a flow chart for handling FMLA requests. A new FMLA poster was also issued; it must be posted even in locations that do not have any FMLA-eligible employees. If there are any eligible employees, the general notice must be included in employee handbooks and other written materials about benefits and leave provisions. [Poster: <https://www.dol.gov/whd/regs/compliance/posters/fmlaen.pdf>; Guide: <http//www.dol.gov/whd/fmla/employerguide.htm> (last accessed Mar. 16, 2017); see Franczek Radelet, *DOL Requires Employers to Use New FMLA Poster, Publishes Guide to Help Employers Administer FMLA*, FMLA Insights (Apr. 25, 2016) (benefitslink.com); Burton D. Garland, Jr., *Attention—The DOL Has Made Its FMLA Poster More "Reader Friendly"!*, Ogletree Deakins (Aug. 25, 2016) (benefitslink.com)]

One of the many penalties that increased in mid-2016 is the penalty for violation of the FMLA posting requirement (29 U.S.C. § 2619(b), 29 C.F.R. 825.300(a)(1)); as of August 1, 2016, it rose from $110 per offense to $163 per offense. [81 Fed. Reg. 42491 (June 30, 2016)] It was increased again, to $166 per offense, as of January 18, 2017. Employers who employ a significant number of people who are literate in a language other than English must also post a translation of the notice into that language.

Plaintiff Bellone asked for leave. He was given a medical certification form and told to return it within 15 days. He had his doctor complete it and submitted the document. The employer waited until Bellone's 12 weeks of FMLA leave were used, then waited another four weeks to send a designation notice retroactively designating the 12 weeks as FMLA leave. Bellone was fired shortly afterward for reasons not directly related to the leave. He sued his former employer alleging that, if he had known that his absence would be treated as FMLA leave, he would have planned his leave to have some time left over. However, the First Circuit ruled that lack of proper notice did not harm Bellone. He received 16 weeks of leave and did not prove that he was actually able to return sooner, or would have handled his absence differently if he had received the correct notice. [*Bellone v. Southwick-Tolland Reg'l Sch. Dist.*, 748 F.3d 418 (1st Cir. 2014)]

The Tenth Circuit excused an employer for not advising an employee of her FMLA rights because she had taken multiple FMLA leaves in the past. Under the regulations, an employee who seeks leave for the first time does not have to explicitly mention the FMLA to be entitled to leave, but the Tenth Circuit held that calling in sick without providing further information does not trigger FMLA rights—particularly if the employee is well-acquainted with the proper procedure. The court held that an employee can be fired for not complying with the procedure for giving notice of absences, even if the improperly reported notices were FMLA-eligible. (The employee was caring for her seriously ill mother.) The plaintiff was on a final warning for coming to work drunk, so her termination was lawful. [*Branham v. Delta Airlines*, No. 16-4092, 2017 U.S. App. LEXIS 1965 (10th Cir. Feb. 3, 2017); see Marjory D. Robertson, *Good News For Employers: FMLA Frequent Fliers May Have Tougher Notice Obligations*, Sun Life Financial Inc. (Feb. 5, 2017), available at Lexology.com]

For many years, the federal courts followed the "mailbox rule"—a presumption that a letter that was sent to the correct address, with appropriate postage attached, would be delivered. The Third Circuit cast doubt on this rule in a mid-2014 case. A college instructor who was suffering from depression filled out a request form for personal leave. Shortly thereafter, the plaintiff gave her employer medical certification that complied with the FMLA requirements. The request for personal leave was converted to FMLA leave. The college mailed her a notice that her absence would be treated as FMLA leave. She was out on leave for 14 weeks, then provided medical certification of her ability to return to work without restrictions. Then she was informed that she had been terminated for failure to return to work after her 12 weeks of FMLA leave ended. The plaintiff brought suit, alleging that she had not known that her absence was treated as FMLA leave—an allegation that made the issue of whether she received the notices central to the case. The Third Circuit held that, although there is a strong presumption that certified mail will be received, there is a weak presumption that first-class mail is received, and the presumption disappears if the addressee denies receiving it. The court suggested using a form of delivery that provides a verifiable receipt. [*Lupyan v. Corinthian Colls.*, 761 F.3d 314 (3d Cir. 2014)]

Companies that have employee handbooks must include FMLA information in the handbook. Even if there is no handbook, employees who actually request leave are entitled to a written explanation of their rights. Employees must be notified, e.g.,

- That the requested leave reduces the employee's "bank" of FMLA leave for the year;

- Whether the employer requires medical certification of the serious health condition; consequences if the certification is not provided;

- The fact that employees who are entitled to paid leave have a right to substitute paid leave for FMLA leave; the conditions under which the employer will substitute paid leave on its own initiative;

- The employee's right to be reinstated in a comparable job after returning from leave;

- The method for the employee to pay health premiums while he or she is on FMLA leave;

- Disclosure of the employee's obligation to reimburse the employer for premiums if the employee does not return to work after the leave;

- Any requirements for proving fitness for duty before returning to work;

- (For key employees) limitations on the right to reinstatement.

§ 38.10 ADMINISTRATIVE REQUIREMENTS

The Department of Labor's investigative authority under the FMLA is the same as its authority under FLSA § 11(a), including subpoena power. Employers have a duty to make and retain records showing FMLA compliance. The general rule is that the DOL can only require employers and employee plans to submit books and records once a year, unless the DOL is investigating a charge made by an employee, or has reason to believe that there has been an FMLA violation. [29 U.S.C. § 2616]

Not only do employers face FMLA suits from employees or groups of employees, but they can also be sued by the DOL, which can sue on behalf of employees to recover the same kind of damages employees would get. If the DOL wins an FMLA case, the damages go to the employee, not to the government agency (unless it is impossible to locate the employees within three years). [See 29 U.S.C. § 2617(b).] The secretary of labor has the power to investigate and try to resolve complaints of FMLA violations, to the same degree as investigations and resolutions of violations of FLSA §§ 6 and 7. But employees are no longer allowed to bring FMLA suits once the DOL starts a suit. [29 U.S.C. § 2617(a)(4)]

§ 38.11   FMLA ENFORCEMENT

[A]   Litigation and Arbitration

It is very common for employment discrimination plaintiffs to charge retaliation, either as their sole cause of action, or because they say that the employer retaliated against them for making an internal complaint or filing charges with an anti-discrimination agency. The FMLA is no exception.

The FMLA ban on retaliation can be invoked by a worker who claims he or she suffered retaliation for asking for FMLA leave; it is not required that leave was actually granted. The Third Circuit said that employers should not be given an incentive to fire employees for exercising their legal rights. The Third Circuit sent the case back to the District Court, for a jury to determine whether the defendant had constructive notice of the hours that the plaintiff worked at home (and which put her over the 1,250 hour mark for eligibility under the FMLA). But the court rejected the plaintiff's argument that she would be entitled to FMLA leave if the employer failed to advise her about the eligibility rules, because that argument was based on a DOL regulation that was rejected by the courts and that the agency had to revise. [*Erdman v. Nationwide Ins. Co.*, 582 F.3d 500 (3d Cir. 2009)]

The Seventh Circuit allowed an FMLA retaliation case to proceed to the jury when the AMA changed its plan to eliminate one job for budgetary reasons and instead eliminated the job of a veteran employee who had applied for FMLA leave. The Seventh Circuit held that referring to FMLA leave in an e-mail recommending the employee's termination could be deemed retaliation and a reasonable jury could conclude that he was fired for requesting leave. [*Shaffer v. AMA*, 662 F.3d 439 (7th Cir. 2011)]

See also *Richardson v. Monitronics International*, 434 F.3d 327 (5th Cir. 2005) holding that although mixed-motive retaliation cases are possible—if the employer's action was at least partially motivated by retaliation for exercise of FMLA rights—the employer can win by showing that there was cause to fire the employee even if FMLA rights had never been used. *Mauder v. Metro. Transit Authority* [446 F.3d 574 (5th Cir. 2006)] holds that it was not retaliation to terminate an employee who was already on a corrective action plan, and Type II diabetes and medication side effects causing uncontrollable diarrhea did not constitute a "serious health condition."

The "cat's paw" theory is that a prejudiced person influences the employer to take adverse action against a plaintiff. The Sixth Circuit not only applied this theory in the FMLA context, but permitted a multi-level cat's paw, where a supervisor influences members of management, who then get the company to take adverse action against an employee who exercises rights under the FMLA. However, the Sixth Circuit dismissed the plaintiff's FMLA retaliation claim, because the plaintiff was granted the leave she requested and was reinstated as team leader after her leave. [*Marshall v. Rawlings Co. LLC,* No. 16-5614 (6th Cir. Apr. 20, 2017); see Kathleen Kapusta, *Cat's Paw Theory Applies to FMLA Retaliation Claims,* Employment Law Daily (Apr. 24, 2017) (benefitslink.com)]

The Seventh Circuit held in late 2015 that the two-year FMLA statute of limitations began when three contested absences (the employee said they were covered by the FMLA) were held to be unauthorized, not when she was fired several years later for absenteeism. The plaintiff argued that this position would prevent FMLA enforcement in workplaces with no-fault absenteeism policies because no one would sue if the only consequence of missing work was a reprimand and an entry in the employee's record, but the Seventh Circuit said that the FMLA includes judicial and administrative remedies and the DOL's Wage and Hour Division can investigate alleged abuses. [*Barrett v. Illinois Dep't of Corrs.,* 803 F.3d 893 (7th Cir. 2015); see Wolters Kluwer Law & Business, *Limitations Period Starts When Absence Classified Non-FMLA, Not When Fired Years Later for Too Many Absences* (Nov. 13, 2015) (benefitslink.com)]

FMLA claims can become the subject of arbitration as well as litigation. The Seventh Circuit found that where a Collective Bargaining Agreement included broad anti-discrimination language, the arbitrator did not exceed his powers by interpreting the FMLA as well as the CBA. [*Butler Mfg. Co. v. United Steelworkers,* 336 F.3d 629 (7th Cir. 2003)]

[B] Releases

The 2009 revision of the FMLA rules provides that, while employees cannot waive FMLA claims that arise in the future, if a claim has already arisen, a release does not require DOL or court supervision to be valid. Previously, the Fifth Circuit held that public policy favors enforcement of waivers, and an employee who keeps the money paid for a release ratifies the release. [*Faris v. Williams WPC-I, Inc.,* 332 F.3d 316 (5th Cir. 2003)], whereas the Fourth Circuit required DOL supervision of all FMLA releases, whether retrospective or prospective. [*Taylor v. Progress Energy Inc.,* 493 F.3d 454 (4th Cir. 2007)]

An employee who received a poor performance evaluation after taking extensive FMLA leave was given a choice between a Performance Improvement Plan (under which she would be terminated if she failed to meet the plan's goals) and 13 weeks of severance benefits in exchange for a release of FMLA claims. She accepted the severance, and then joined two other plaintiffs in a suit charging FMLA interference and retaliation. She argued that she did not waive her FMLA rights, because 29 CFR § 825.220 forbids prospective waivers of FMLA rights. The Eleventh Circuit, however, held that a prospective right is the right to take FMLA leave in the future, whereas the plaintiff (Paylor) released a claim that had already accrued. The Eleventh Circuit found the release to be valid and enforceable; it was signed voluntarily by an adult with business experience; she was given 21 days to consider the deal; and she received consideration for the release in the form of severance benefits that would not otherwise have been available. [*Paylor v. Hartford Fire Ins.*, 748 F.3d 1117 (11th Cir. 2014)]

[C] Damages

If the employees win, 29 U.S.C. § 2617(a) provides that the court can order damages equal to the wages and benefits that the employee lost as a result of the violation. Even employees who have not lost compensation can receive damages to compensate them for financial losses (such as costs of hiring someone to care for sick relatives), but damages of this type are limited to 12 weeks' salary for the employee-plaintiff.

Furthermore, winning FMLA plaintiffs can receive double damages: their damages (plus interest) and also an equal amount of liquidated damages. However, if the employer can prove that it acted in good faith and reasonably believed that it was in compliance with the FMLA, the court has discretion not to order double damages.

In a case of first impression, the Ninth Circuit ruled that FMLA front pay, which is awarded either in lieu of reinstatement, or to make up for compensation that was lost between the court's judgment and the plaintiff's reinstatement, is an equitable remedy. Therefore, the amount is determined by the judge, not the jury, and the judge also decides if reinstatement is practical. (The Fourth, Fifth, and Tenth Circuits had already ruled that the judge determines if front pay is available and, if so, how much.) Under the FMLA, liquidated damages are mandatory unless the employer proves both its good faith and that it had reasonable grounds for believing it acted lawfully. However, liquidated damages are not automatically payable in every case in which front pay is ordered, because it is possible for an employer to act in good faith, but for reinstatement to be impractical because of the friction caused by the plaintiff's extensive usage of FMLA leave. [*Traxler v. Multnomah Cnty.*, 596 F.3d 1007 (9th Cir. 2010)]

Plaintiff Jackson, a welder, used his accrued paid sick leave when he had gallbladder surgery. Then he took FMLA leave, which was extended by a month. He was still unable to return to work and was terminated. When he was finally released to work, he re-applied, and had the highest score of any interviewee, but was not hired. At trial, he prevailed on FMLA, ADA, and state-law claims. His employer appealed, saying that he failed to show that he could perform the essential functions of the job or that there was a causal link between FMLA and the failure to rehire. The Eighth Circuit held that he demonstrated ability to carry out essential functions and causal connection. The Eighth Circuit said that Jackson could get liquidated damages if the employer failed to show that it acted in good faith—but emotional distress damages are not available under the FMLA. [*Jackson v. City of Hot Springs*, 751 F.3d 855 (8th Cir. 2014)]

A district court jury awarded $1.2 million in damages and attorneys' fees to Pat Hurley, who was fired after informing his employer that he would need time off to deal with depression. However, the Eleventh Circuit reversed the award in 2014, holding that the FMLA only protects leave for incapacity that has already occurred, not conditions that are likely to occur in the future. [*Hurley v. Kent of Naples*, 746 F.3d 1161 (11th Cir. 2014)]

An employee who has received an FMLA back pay award is not precluded from receiving liquidated damages for retaliation. The Tenth Circuit held that wages that are temporarily lost but restored after a significant delay must be treated as "lost or denied" for purposes of calculating FMLA liquidated damages. [*Jordan v. U.S. Postal Serv.*, 379 F.3d 1196 (10th Cir. 2004)]

An employee obtained summary judgment in her FMLA interference and retaliation claims; she charged that she was fired because the company failed to accommodate her need for a 20-hour work week during pregnancy. The employer argued that she was not eligible under the FMLA because she had been employed for less than a year, but the last day she worked, and the date of the termination letter, was November 16, 2009, and she was hired November 17, 2008. The Eighth Circuit found that she promptly submitted a doctor's note explaining her need for a reduced schedule because of pregnancy complications. However, the Eighth Circuit vacated and remanded the award of $49,769 in back pay, $30,876 in pre-judgment interest, and $80,645 in liquidated damages, because the Eighth Circuit said the jury rather than the district court should have set the damages. [*Wages v. Stuart Mgmt. Corp.*, 798 F.3d 675 (8th Cir. 2015)]

A federal jury in Connecticut awarded more than $500,000 to nurse Connie Sue Summerlin for FMLA violations. The verdict included $197,507.19 in back pay, doubled as liquidated damages, plus attorneys' fees and costs. Summerlin's suit alleged that she was injured outside a patient's home in February 2010, an injury that was aggravated in April by work-related lifting. After FMLA leave, she was cleared to return to full duty on March 8, 2011, But she was not reinstated because she was told that her job and been eliminated and was offered only per-diem assignments. She charged that she was denied reinstatement in retaliation for filing a Worker's Compensation claim. The district court judge reduced the damages to $462,000 back pay. The judge gave Summerlin a choice between reduction of damages that the judge called excessive, and a new trial; she accepted the reduction. [Mary Kate Nelson, *Judge Reduces Almost Family FMLA Penalty to $500,000*, homehealthcarenews.com (Dec. 6, 2015), available at   <http://homehealthcarenews.com/2015/12/judge-reduces-almost-family-fmla-penalty-to-500000/>]

Although most of the remedies are equitable ones, the Southern District of Georgia allows jury trials in FMLA cases, because they are allowed in Fair Labor Standards Act cases, and the two statutes contain many similar provisions. [*Helmly v. Stone Container Corp.*, 957 F. Supp. 1274 (S.D. Ga. 1997)] So does the Sixth Circuit. [*Frizzell v. Southwestern Motor Freight*, 154 F.3d 641 (6th Cir. 1998)]

In addition to money damages, courts in FMLA cases can award the appropriate equitable relief for the case, including hiring, reinstatement, and promotion. FMLA winners are entitled to receive reasonable costs, defined to include attorneys' fees and expert witness fees. Section 2617(a)(3) makes this automatic for plaintiffs who win, not a matter of discretion for the court.

This is not true of all federal statutes. Some of them do not allow attorneys' fee awards at all, others allow a fee award to any prevailing party (plaintiff or defendant) or leave it up to the court whether an award should be made, or limit fee awards to cases in which the losing party's conduct has been outrageous.

PART VIII

PROCEDURE FOR HANDLING DISCRIMINATION CHARGES

CHAPTER 39

WRONGFUL TERMINATION AND AT-WILL EMPLOYMENT

§ 39.01 INTRODUCTION

Employees always have the right to quit their jobs, no matter how inconvenient their departure may be for the employer (although employment contracts can require a certain amount of notice, can obligate the employee to compensate the employer for economic loss caused by a resignation, and can impose reasonable restrictions on re-employment and use of the employer's proprietary information).

The employer's right to fire an employee is not so simple and clear-cut. Some employees have written contracts that specify the conditions under which they can be terminated. Unionized employees are covered by collective bargaining agreements (CBAs). In CBAs or individual employment contracts, if the agreement sets out a termination procedure (such as a warning, then a chance for the employee to respond to charges, a suspension, and then termination), then it is a breach of contract to terminate the employee without following the procedure.

Employers may also find that they are subject to responsibilities under implied contracts. The employer's written documents that it issues such as the employee handbook or even its oral statements are deemed to constitute a legally enforceable contract, then the employer will have to abide by that contract.

A supervisor is a representative of the employer when he or she is acting in the scope of his or her job, in a situation in which he or she is authorized to act. The supervisor's conduct will then have legal implications for the employer. A supervisor's negligence or outrageous conduct (such as abusive treatment of an employee that results in emotional distress) can be imputed to the employer. In many instances, the supervisor will *not* be personally liable, e.g., under federal and state antidiscrimination statutes or for inducing a breach of contract.

Even if termination is justifiable, however, it must be carried out in a reasonable manner, avoiding intentional infliction of emotional distress. The employer must also avoid both actionable defamation (destructive false statements) and depriving another employer of the accurate information needed to make a rational hiring decision.

There are also several statutes (e.g., the Sarbanes-Oxley and Dodd-Frank Acts) that protect whistleblowers—employees who expose wrongdoing on the part of the employer—from retaliation. See § 39.04[B] below. Workers' Compensation claimants are also protected against retaliation: see § 39.04[C].

"Constructive discharge" is the legal concept that an employee who responds to intolerable conditions by quitting is entitled to be treated as if he or she had been fired, because the employer's conduct was the equivalent of a discharge. To prove constructive discharge, the employee does not have to prove that the employer intended to force a resignation, only that it was reasonably foreseeable that a reasonable employee would quit under the same circumstances. The Supreme Court's mid-2004 decision, *Pennsylvania State Police v. Suders* [542 U.S. 129 (2004)] makes it clear that the test of constructive discharge is objective, not subjective, based on the behavior of the hypothetical reasonable employee rather than the personal reactions of the plaintiff. In a pregnancy discrimination/FMLA case, the Sixth Circuit ruled that a threat of demotion coupled with other factors can constitute constructive discharge. [*Saroli v. Automation & Modular Components, Inc.*, 405 F.3d 446 (6th Cir. 2005)]

There is a special rule for federal employees: they are required to consult an equal opportunity counselor within 45 days of an alleged act of discrimination. Green, a postal employee, complained that he was denied a promotion because of his race. His supervisor accused him of the crime of delaying mail. Green and the United States Postal Service (USPS) entered into a settlement agreement where he agreed to retire in exchange for the USPS dropping the criminal charges. Green submitted his resignation on February 9, 2010, effective March 31. Forty-one days after submitting the resignation paperwork, and 96 days after the agreement, Green made a complaint of constructive discharge to a USPS EEO counselor. Green then brought a race discrimination suit in district court. The district court dismissed the complaint as untimely, and the Tenth Circuit affirmed, holding that the suit was untimely because he did not contact the EEO counselor within 45 days of the settlement agreement. However, the Supreme Court reversed, in a mid-2016 decision. The Supreme Court said that, in a constructive discharge case, the alleged act of discrimination is the date the employee gives notice of resignation, so that is when the statute of limitations starts to run—not the effective date of the resignation. Requiring the complaint to be filed before the resignation ignores the fact that an employee might have to give notice and would not be able to leave work immediately. [*Green v. Brennan*, 136 S. Ct. 1769 (2016)]

The fact situation is not one that is likely to be repeated frequently, but it should be noted that at the end of 2004, the U.S. Supreme Court ruled that it did not violate a police officer's First Amendment or Fourteenth Amendment rights to fire him for selling videos (and police paraphernalia) on the Internet. The videos featured the officer in police-related pornographic scenarios. The Supreme Court held that he was not expressing himself on matters of public concern or commenting on police department operations. [*City of San Diego v. John Roe*, 543 U.S. 77 (2004)]

The vast majority of employees do not have a written contract. They are legally defined as "at-will" employees who work "at the will of the employer." However, at-will employers are not permitted to discharge employees for reasons that violate an antidiscrimination statute, or for reasons contrary to public policy.

Employees who want to bring suit under federal antidiscrimination laws (Title VII, the ADA, the Age Discrimination in Employment Act (ADEA), and the Family and Medical Leave Act (FMLA) have to satisfy elaborate procedural requirements. [See Chapters 40 and 41] Employees who charge the employer with wrongful termination merely have to go to state court and file a complaint. This is much easier to do, so employers may find themselves fighting on two fronts, or may be able to raise the argument that a wrongful termination case should be dismissed because the employee was required—but failed—to use the procedure for a discrimination suit.

The Second Circuit held in mid-2016 that it is not unlawful to fire an employee for refusing to participate in an internal investigation (in this case, charges of a bid-rigging conspiracy). The Second Circuit applied Delaware law, because that was the state where the employer company was incorporated, and ruled that refusal to obey a direct, unequivocal, reasonable order is grounds for termination. [*Gilman v. Marsh & McLennan Co.*, 826 F.3d 69 (2d Cir. 2016); see Michael D. Hynes et. al., *Second Circuit Affirms Employer's Right to Terminate Employees Who Fail to Cooperate with Internal Investigations*, DLA Piper LLP (July 1, 2016), available at Lexology.com]

§ 39.02 EMPLOYEE TENURE

Some state court cases consider it an implied promise of continuing employment once an employee has worked for the employer for a long time (say, a decade or more), and a number of states impose an implied covenant of good faith and fair dealing in the employment context.

The Connecticut Court of Appeals ruled that it is permissible to terminate an at-will employee even before work begins: either side can terminate the relationship at any time for any reason, not conditioned on work actually beginning. (The plaintiff was hired for a sales job and asked to submit references; when he reported for work, he was told that there were issues about his references.) He sued, claiming a breach of the employment contract and the contract to hire him, charging that the offer letter constituted negligent misrepresentation. [*Petitte v. DSL.net, Inc.*, 102 Conn. App. 363 (Conn. App. 2007); see Rebeca Moore, *Court Upholds Firing Before Work Commenced*, plansponsor.com (Aug. 22, 2007)]

New York's highest court ruled that an at-will employee can be fired at any time unless there is a statutory ban, an express limitation in an individual employment contract, or the firing reflected a constitutionally impermissible rationale. Therefore, a group of five financial services money managers who claimed fraudulent inducement because they were not informed of the merger that led to their termination could not sustain a fraudulent inducement claim. [*Smalley v. Dreyfus Corp.*, 10 N.Y.3d 55 (2008)]

Under Virginia law, unless there is an employment contract that specifies duration, either party can terminate the employment relationship on reasonable notice of intention to terminate. The Virginia Supreme Court said that all that is required is effective notice, making it clear that employment has ended. The fact that the plaintiff had worked at the job for 17 years did not entitle her to notice prior to termination; she remained an at-will employee. [*Johnson v. William E. Wood & Assocs.*, No. 151160, 2016 Va. LEXIS 67 (Va. 2016); see Michael C. Griffaton, *Labor and Employment Alert: Yes, Virginia, At-Will Employment Ends With or Without Advance Notice*, Vorys, Sater, Seymour and Pease LLP (June 6,

2016), available at Lexology.com; Neil S. Lowenstein, *Virginia Supreme Court Confirms Employee Firings on the Spot,* Vandeventer Black LLP (June 23, 2016), available at Lexology.com]

The New York Court of Appeals held in mid-2012 that a hedge fund compliance officer who was fired after confronting his boss about allegedly improper trades was an at-will employee not entitled to common-law protection against wrongful termination. Compliance was only part of his job, and the court held that his regulatory and ethical obligations as compliance officer were not so intertwined with his employee responsibilities for separation to be impossible. [*Sullivan v. Harnisch*, 19 N.Y.3d 259 (N.Y. 2012)]

Months before Weiss was scheduled to receive a $60,000 bonus, he was terminated, allegedly for failure to supervise an employee who took kickbacks and was guilty of other financial misconduct. Weiss sued in state court to recover the bonus. The case was removed to federal court on diversity grounds. The jury ruled for Weiss on his breach of contract claim. The employer appealed to the First Circuit, which held that the plan gave a management committee the power to decide if an employee was terminated for good cause and thereby forfeited the bonus. [*Weiss v. DHL Express Inc.*, 718 F.3d 39 (1st Cir. 2013)]

In a Title VII case, the district court dismissed the case, but the Ninth Circuit reversed, holding that the plaintiff's termination might have been a pretext for gender discrimination. The plaintiff, a grocery store supervisor, was fired for giving cakes from the "stales" cart to night shift workers. She said that it was common and permitted for supervisors to distribute stale cakes. She was denied COBRA coverage and credit for her accrued vacation days on the grounds that she was fired for gross misconduct. She said that the real motivation was to substitute a man, with much less training and experience, as leader of the freight crew. She cited sexist remarks about women in the freight crew and safety committee. The Ninth Circuit found direct evidence of gender discrimination as well as indirect evidence: many employees testified about the practice of distributing leftover cakes. [*Mayes v. WinCo Holdings, Inc.*, 846 F.3d 1274 (9th Cir. 2017); see Manatt Phelps & Phillips LLP, *Termination for Cake Theft May Have Been Pretext, Ninth Circuit Rules* (Feb. 27, 2017), available at Lexology.com]

A doctor sued two colleagues for tortious interference with his employment contract, alleging that he was fired because of their statements to the clinic's board of directors. The Seventh Circuit held that, under Wisconsin law, tortious interference with contract requires that the defendant was not justified in interfering. Giving truthful information is privileged. Saying that the plaintiff coerced and intimidated co-workers was true, even if the proof showed only intimidation. Saying that co-workers "filed complaints" against him was substantially true, even if the complaints were made orally. [*Wesbrook v. Ulrich*, 840 F.3d 388 (7th Cir. 2016); see Ryan N. Parsons, *Seventh Circuit Recognizes "Substantial Truthfulness" Defense to Tortious Interference Claims Under Wisconsin* Law, Foley & Lardner LLP (Nov. 8, 2016), available at Lexology.com]

§ 39.03   PROMISSORY ESTOPPEL

The theory of "promissory estoppel" is sometimes decisive in employment cases. The theory is that the employer's promise to the employee estops (precludes) the employer from disavowing that promise, often because the employee has "undergone detrimental reliance" (suffered in some way after relying on a statement or implication from the employer).

The classic example is a top executive recruited from another company, who gives up a high salary and stock options, has expenses of relocation, and then is fired shortly after taking up the new job. However, employees who allege oral promises of permanent employment may find that their claims are barred by a legal doctrine, the Statute of Frauds that requires contracts lasting a year or more to be in writing if they are to be enforceable.

§ 39.04   PUBLIC POLICY

[A]   Generally

A whole line of cases permits employees to sue when they are fired for a reason contrary to the public policy of the state. In other words, it is unlawful to fire an employee for doing something that is acceptable or even admirable. For instance, no matter how inconvenient the timing is for the employer, it is not permitted to fire an employee for serving jury duty.

The First Circuit ruled that for a safety engineer to inform his supervisors about potential overtime violations with respect to the security guards he supervised was part of his job duties. Doing so was not protected activity under the Fair Labor Standards Act, so firing him for raising the issue could not be retaliation in violation of the Fair Labor Standards Act (FLSA). [*Claudio-Gotay v. Becton Dickinson Caribe Ltd.*, 375 F.3d 99 (1st Cir. 2004)]

It violates ERISA § 510 to fire an employee merely to prevent access to pension or welfare benefits. [See Chapter 15]

Certiorari was denied in a Third Circuit decision holding that it did not violate ERISA § 510 to fire an HR director for her unsolicited comments to management about what she perceived to be ERISA violations (such as misrepresentation) in the company health plan. The Second and Fourth Circuits have ruled similarly—that protection under § 510 is limited to testimony in a formal inquiry such as a federal investigation. However, the Fifth and Ninth Circuits agree with the DOL, that informal, unsolicited comments are protected. [*Edwards v. A.H. Cornell & Son, Inc.*, 610 F.3d 217 (3d Cir. 2010), *cert. denied*, 131 S. Ct. 1604 (2011)]

In 2014, the Sixth Circuit held that in theory unsolicited complaints can give rise to an ERISA § 510 cause of action, but, in the particular case, held that a single complaint is not enough. The plaintiff e-mailed the corporation's Chairman of the Board, threatening to report ERISA violations in the election for the board. The Sixth Circuit drew a distinction between two kinds of federal anti-retaliation laws: an "opposition clause" protecting people who oppose violations of the law, and "participation clauses" that limit protection to people who have participated in a formal proceeding. According to the Sixth Circuit, ERISA's anti-retaliation provision is a participation clause (as are the ADA, FMLA, and PPACA protective provisions), whereas Title VII and the FLSA have opposition clauses. [*Sexton v. Panel Processing,* 754 F.3d 332 (6th Cir. 2014)]

A 2010 Sixth Circuit case was brought by an employee who charged that he was fired for refusing to participate in a market allocation conspiracy in the packaged ice industry. (His former employer plead guilty to antitrust charges and agreed to pay a $9 million fine, and three executives plead guilty to individual charges.) He said that he was blackballed and was unable to find another job since exposing the conspiracy. The Sixth Circuit ruled that he was not covered by the Crime Victims' Rights Act: although preventing a person from getting a job may be the subject of a civil action, it is neither inherently criminal nor an inherent part of the antitrust conspiracy. The plaintiff filed a separate Racketeer Influenced and Corrupt Organizations Act (RICO) suit alleging that he was fired for refusing to participate in the scheme, and because he cooperated with federal authorities. [*In re McNulty,* 597 F.3d 344 (6th Cir. 2010)]

Public policy arguments can also be raised to justify termination. A groundskeeper sued his employer and the union that represented him, calling himself a whistleblower against the union president, who resigned after being convicted of embezzlement. The Ninth Circuit held that the plaintiff created a hostile work environment by harassing and making racist, sexist, and homophobic statements about his co-workers, so it was legitimate to fire him. The union did not breach its duty of fair representation: it investigated the plaintiff's termination grievance and negotiated a settlement, which the plaintiff refused to accept. The union was not obligated to pursue arbitration of what it reasonably believed to be a meritless claim. [*Gazzano v. Stanford Univ.,* 649 Fed. Appx. 610 (9th Cir. 2016); see Susan T. Ye, *Ninth Circuit Issues Pro-Employer and Pro-Union Ruling Against Worker with a Long History of Harassing Comments,* Ogletree Deakins (Aug. 31, 2016), available at Lexology.com]

Medical marijuana is the majority of the states (and recreational marijuana is legal in several states: see § 26.03[A]) but courts consistently permit firing employees who test positive for marijuana, even if they are certified for medical marijuana and did not use the drug in the workplace. There are cases of this type from the Sixth and Ninth Circuits and from Colorado, Michigan, Washington, Oregon, Montana, and California. [*Swaw v. Safeway, Inc.,* Case No. C15-939 MJP, 2015 U.S. Dist. LEXIS 159761 (W.D. Wash. Nov. 20, 2015)]

Although some medical marijuana statutes forbid employers to penalize a medical marijuana cardholder or registered qualifying patient for having a positive drug test (e.g., Arizona, Connecticut, Delaware, Maine, Nevada, and Rhode Island), they permit employers to ban use, possession, and impairment by marijuana during working hours. Other laws permit the employer to conclude that a positive test is proof of workplace impairment, which would justify firing even a cardholder. Federally regulated employers are required to observe drug-free workplace laws. [Kathryn J. Russo and Dona Vetrano Pryor, *Demystifying Employer Drug Policies in Medical Marijuana States*, Jackson Lewis LLP (Oct. 31, 2013), available at Lexology.com]

Kohl's policy said that there would be no discrimination against valid medical users of marijuana. The plaintiff was nevertheless fired when his medical marijuana use (for anxiety) was revealed by a post-injury drug test. He sued for breach of implied contract and the covenant of good faith and fair dealing. The District Court for the Eastern District of California permitted the suit to proceed because a reasonably jury could conclude that the employer's policy would preclude discrimination against marijuana users. The implied contract and covenant of good faith claims could also proceed because these are fact-intensive inquiries inappropriate for summary judgment. However, the claim under the Fair Employment and Housing Act (FEHA), the California civil rights law, was dismissed: California law does not prevent termination of employees who use marijuana, whatever their reason. [*Shepherd v. Kohl's Dep't Stores*, No. 1:14-cv-0190-DAD-BAM, 2016 U.S. Dist. LEXIS 101279 (E.D. Cal. Aug. 2, 2016); see Manatt Phelps & Phillips LLP, *California Employee Can Pursue Termination Claims over Marijuana Use* (Oct. 11, 2016), available at Lexology.com]

The Tenth Circuit held that it was not unconstitutional to fire an employee whose random drug test was positive for cocaine. The test was not an unreasonable search because he was in a safety-sensitive position (lieutenant in a juvenile detention center). His job involved working with children, which outweighed his individual privacy interest. The county drug testing policies did not create an implied contract or a protectable property interest in continued employment. The county's random drug testing policy says failing a test is cause for discipline including discharge, but says that discipline has to follow the HR guide. The guide recommends a suspension for first-time drug offenses, but notes that the employees still work at-will and the county had the right to bypass the suggested disciplinary procedure. [*Washington v. Unified Gov't of Wyandotte Cnty., Kansas*, 847 F.3d 1192 (10th Cir. 2017); see Michael Clarkson and KyraAnne Gates, *Tenth Circuit Upholds Discharge of Employee in Safety-Sensitive Position Who Tested Positive for Cocaine*, Ogletree Deakins (Feb. 16, 2017), available at Lexology.com]

Utah's disciplinary rules for attorneys require in-house counsel to report illegal activity to corporate management. The Utah Supreme Court rejected a wrongful termination suit by an in-house attorney who said he was fired for reporting illegal activity. The court said that the disciplinary rule was not a clear and substantial public policy that will prevent discharge of an at-will employee. Even if it was a public policy, the employer's countervailing interest in regulating the workplace might outweigh it. [*Pang v. Int'l Documents Servs*, 2015 UT 63 (Utah 2015)]

On opposition to sexual harassment, see *DeMasters v. Carillion Clinic*. [796 F.3d 409 (4th Cir. 2015)] DeMasters was fired for acting contrary to the company's best interests by encouraging an employee to pursue sexual harassment charges, including a suit that was settled. The Fourth Circuit refused to apply the "manager rule" (protests against employer policies are not protected if the employee is a manager required to uphold those policies), holding that it an FLSA rule that is inappropriate in the Title VII context. The Fourth Circuit held that communications are protected when the employee informs the employer that it has committed discrimination under Title VII, as long as the employee's belief is reasonable and the employee acts reasonably. Utah says that self-defense can be a clear and substantial public policy, so an employee cannot be fired for engaging in self-defense if the employee cannot withdraw from the encounter and reasonably believes force is necessary to defend against an imminent threat of serious bodily harm. Wal-Mart policy calls for employees to disengage, withdraw from conflict, and call the police. Five plaintiffs were fired for disarming suspected shoplifters. The district court hearing the case certified a question to the Utah Supreme Court, which was asked to assume that the employees could not safely disengage from confrontation. The case returned to the District Court for the District of Utah to decide whether it was actually true that the employees could not safely withdraw. [*Ray, et. al. v. Wal-Mart Stores, Inc.*, 2015 UT 83 (Sept. 17, 2015)]

On a certified question from the Fifth Circuit, the Mississippi Supreme Court ruled in March 2016 that it is unlawful to terminate an employee for keeping a gun in his car in the company parking lot. The Mississippi legislature adopted a statute modifying the employment at-will doctrine to forbid firing an employee for keeping a gun in the trunk at work. Accordingly, the Fifth Circuit permitted the employee to sue for wrongful termination. [*Swindol v. Aurora Flight Scis. Corp.*, No. 2015-FC-01317-SCT, 2016 Miss. LEXIS 131, 2016 WL 1165448 (Miss. Mar. 24, 2016) and No. 14-60779,2016 WL 419136 (5th Cir. Aug. 8, 2016); see J. William Manuel, *More Guns in Trunks—Mississippi Supreme Court Amends Wrongful Discharge Doctrine*, Bradley Arant Boult Cummings LLP (Mar. 29, 2016), available at Lexology.com; Robert Scavone Jr., Roland M. Juarez and Juan C. Enjamio, *Employer Prohibited from Terminating Employee for Storing Gun in Trunk in Mississippi,* Hunton & Williams LLP (Aug. 26, 2016), available at Lexology.com; Robin Banck Taylor, *Fifth Circuit Broadens Exceptions to At-Will Employment,* Ogletree Deakins (Aug. 17, 2016), available at Lexology.com. States with similar gun laws include Alabama, Alaska, Arizona, Florida, Georgia, Illinois, Indiana, Kansas, Kentucky, Louisiana, Maine, Minnesota, Nebraska, North Dakota, Oklahoma, Tennessee, Texas, Utah, and Wisconsin.]

[B] Whistleblower Employees

The case of the "whistleblower" employee is more complex. Employees (often those who are dissatisfied for other reasons) go to the press, or file complaints with enforcement agencies, about some aspect of corporate conduct they find unsatisfactory. In some instances, firing (or taking other adverse employment action) against whistleblowers violates public policy, because in appropriate cases, whistleblowers are exposing violations of law or other improprieties.

At the end of 1998, the Supreme Court held that an action under 42 U.S.C. § 1985 (damage to person or property) can be maintained by an at-will employee who alleges that he was fired for assisting a federal criminal investigation of the employer company. [*Haddle v. Garrison*, 525 U.S. 121 (1998)]

Whistleblower issues frequently appear before the Supreme Court. The Supreme Court ruled in 2010 that a whistleblower cannot bring a False Claims Act suit based on information that has already been disclosed in county or state reports. (Previous law said that information in congressional, federal administrative, or GAO reports is already known, and therefore cannot form the basis of a "qui tam" whistleblower action.) [*Graham Cnty. Soil & Water Conservation Dist. v. United States ex rel. Wilson*, 559 U.S. 280 (2010). See *Rockwell Int'l Corp. v. United States*, 549 U.S. 457 (2007) for the principle that the whistleblower must be the original source of the information, having direct and independent knowledge of the facts of the case. The Supreme Court extended this principle in 2011. *Schindler Elevator Corp. v. United States ex rel. Kirk*, 131 S. Ct. 1885 (2011), ruling that releasing documents pursuant to a FOIA request is a "report" that makes the documents public, so the information in the documents will not support a whistleblower award.]

Government employees cannot be fired for testifying about government corruption. Generally speaking, government employee whistleblowers are only held to have enforceable First Amendment rights when they speak as citizens, on a matter of public interest, not when they speak as employees. In this case, however, the Supreme Court held that the plaintiff, a state community college employee laid off after testifying at a federal trial about a state legislator's no-show job at the institution, was subpoenaed. He had a legal obligation to testify, and therefore was considered a citizen speaking on a matter of public concern entitled to First Amendment protection. [*Lane v. Franks*, 134 S. Ct. 2369 (2014)]

The U.S. Supreme Court found that an air marshal (MacLean) was protected by the federal Whistleblower Protection Act when he went public about his concerns that budget cuts could make it easier for terrorists to smuggle weapons onto planes. When members of Congress saw the news reports, they got the travel policy reversed. MacLean was fired for disclosing sensitive information without authorization. He appealed under the Whistleblower Protection Act, which forbids retaliation for disclosing a substantial and specific danger to public health or safety. Although disclosures "specifically prohibited by law" are not protected, the Supreme Court ruled that agency regulations are not considered "laws" for this purpose. [*Dep't of Homeland Sec. v. MacLean*, 135 S. Ct. 913 (2015)]

The health care reform act, the Patient Protection and Affordable Care Act (PPACA), Pub. L. No. 111-148, deals with the subject of whistleblower protection. It says that only federal, and not state or local disclosures, will rule out a False Claims Act qui tam action. PPACA § 1558 amends the Fair Labor Standards Act to provide that it is unlawful to discharge or discriminate (in compensation or working conditions) against anyone who has given information to the federal government or a state attorney general, testified or is about to testify, or assisted in a proceeding involving an alleged violation of the health care reform law. OSHA interim final rules were published February 22, 2013 covering complaints made by employees who say they suffered retaliation for receiving a subsidy or tax credit in connection with using a health insurance Exchange (rather than being covered by an EGHP). The general OSHA whistleblower procedures apply in this situation. [<http://www.dol.gov/find/20130222/OSHA2013.pdf> (last accessed Mar. 17, 2017)] However, if PPACA is eliminated, this will no longer be an issue; if it is significantly amended, it is uncertain at press time whether the replacement bill will include a similar provision.

Damages in whistleblower cases can be quite substantial. OSHA ordered an aviation company in Alaska to reinstate an employee who repeatedly raised safety concerns (about recordkeeping and inadequate drug testing) and pay more than $400,000 in back pay plus $100,000 for the employee's pain, suffering, and mental distress. In January 2016, OSHA ordered a trucking company in New York to pay $32,642 in lost wages, $10,000 in punitive damages, and $3,060 in attorneys' fees for violating the Surface Transportation Assistance Act whistleblower provision. OSHA also sued in a New York district court in early 2016 for lost wages, compensatory, and punitive damages for firing an employee who reported safety concerns about damage to the floor in the work area.

OSHA's Whistleblower Investigations Manual, <https://www.osha.gov/OshDoc/Directive_pdf/CPL_02-03-007.pdf> was updated in January 2016 (last accessed Mar. 17, 2017). It says that compensatory damages are appropriate whenever a complainant has objective manifestations of distress, which can be proved with evidence from complaint or statements from friends, family, or co-workers. The manual says OSHA investigators should consider punitive damages if the employer's actions were particularly egregious or if the employer acted with knowledge that its actions were illegal. The number of whistleblower complaints increases each year; between 2014 and 2015, there was a 6% increase. OSHA's budget request asked for a 23% increase in funding to handle whistleblower cases. [Keller and Heckman LLP, *Potential Damages in Whistleblower Cases* (Mar. 1, 2016), available at Lexology.com]

A company that fired an employee who reported safety hazards, just a few days after OSHA issued citations and penalties for those violations, was ordered to pay $979 in back pay—and $100,000 in punitive damages. The employee informed the business owner about shock hazards, exposed wires, fall hazards, and lack of protective equipment. When the employer refused to respond, the employee complained to OSHA. [*Perez v. Sandpoint Gas N Go & Lube Ctr.*, Case No. 2:14-CV-00357-BLW, 2015 U.S. Dist. LEXIS 178214 (D. Idaho Sept. 29, 2015)]

OSHA ordered CSX to pay $5,000 in punitive damages, and expunge a suspension from an employee's record. An employee, who was also a union official, was suspended for five days, allegedly because of a safety infraction. OSHA found that the suspension was imposed in retaliation for raising concerns about safety hazards. [Sam Kramer, *OSHA Orders Employer to Pay Damages to FRSA Whistleblower*, Katz Marshall & Banks LLP (June 7, 2016), available at Lexology.com]

OSHA revised its regional ADR program procedures so that parties to a whistleblower dispute can negotiate a settlement with help from a neutral OSHA representative with experience in whistleblower investigations. [<https://www.osha.gov/OshDoc/Directive_pdf/CPL_02-03-006.pdf> (last accessed Mar. 17, 2017)]

For investigations, the 2016 edition of the Whistleblower Investigation Manual uses a standard of reasonable cause to believe a violation occurred, rather than the higher preponderance of evidence standard that applies at hearings. This standard applies to all elements of a violation—i.e., that a reasonable judge could find in favor of the complainant. [<https://www.osha.gov/OshDoc/Directive_pdf/CPL_02-03-007.pdf> (last accessed Mar. 17, 2017); Matthew M. Linton, *OSHA Issues New Whistleblower Guidance*, Holland & Hart LLP (Feb. 8, 2016), available at Lexology.com]

In late 2016, OSHA revised its Whistleblower Investigations Manual again. Like the SEC, OSHA is opposed to severance provisions that could prevent employees from reporting violations of the law to the government. OSHA will not approve a settlement agreement that includes a "de facto gag order" (i.e., which discourages whistleblowing) even if there is no outright ban. OSHA will not approve a provision that limits a person's ability to provide information to the government or cooperate in investigations; if the employee must notify the employer before communicating with the government; if the employee must affirm that he or she has not given information to the government; or a waiver of the right to collect a whistleblower award. Nor will OSHA approve a settlement where liquidated damages for breaching the agreement are clearly disproportionate to the anticipated loss that can be predicted as a result of the breach. [<https://www.osha.gov/OshDoc/Directive_pdf/CPL_02-03-005.pdf>, see FindLaw Employment Law News, *OSHA Takes a Harder Tack on Whistleblower Settlement Agreements* (Oct. 4, 2016), available at FindLaw.com; Laura M. Fant and Harris M. Mufson, *OSHA Issues New Guidance Regarding Whistleblower Settlements*, Proskauer Rose LLP (Sept. 19, 2016), available at Lexology.com]

The recordkeeping rules at 29 C.F.R. Part 1904 include an anti-retaliation provision. The provisions were supposed to take effect August 10, 2016, but they were delayed, first until November 1, 2016 then until December 1, at the request of the Northern District of Texas, which was considering a challenge to the regulations brought by industry groups. [Shontell Powell and Melissa A. Bailey, *OSHA Pushes Back Enforcement Date for Anti-Retaliation Provisions Again,* Ogletree Deakins (Oct. 18, 2016), available at Lexology.com]

Significant penalties have been imposed on companies that retaliated against employees who reported safety violations:

- OSHA ordered $50,000 in compensatory damages, $150,000 in punitive damages, and over $22,000 in back pay, interest, and attorneys' fees in a Federal Railroad Safety Act case about an apprentice electrician who was seriously injured at work. OSHA's investigation revealed information about prior unrelated workplace injuries. The company terminated the electrician, concluding that he was dishonest about his past injuries. [Ada W. Dolph and Craig B. Simonsen, *Railroad Ordered to Pay $225,000 in Whistleblower Action Where Employee Allegedly Lied About Prior Injuries,* Seyfarth Shaw LLP (Oct. 27, 2014), available at Lexology.com]

- OSHA ordered almost $1 million in damages ($243,916 in back pay, $110,000 in compensatory damages, $600,000 in punitive damages) plus reinstatement for a foreman and two truck drivers who were fired in retaliation for filing OSHA complaints. They said that they were required to violate the Department of Transportation's maximum hour requirement for commercial truck drivers. [Ada W. Dolph and Craig B. Simonsen, *OSHA Orders Asphalt Paving Company to Pay Nearly $1 Million and Reinstate Foreman and Two Drivers in Whistleblower Complaints,* Seyfarth Shaw LLP (Sept. 3, 2014), available at Lexology.com]

- OSHA ordered RCL Wiring LP to pay $154,749 in back wages, $177,720 in punitive damages and attorneys' fees and to reinstate the terminated employee who reported a work-related injury. OSHA found that the employee was forced to file an additional injury report, and threatened with discipline for late filing. [Punam Kaji and Brendan Fradkin, *OSHA Assesses $332,000 in Sanctions and Compels Rehire in Wrongful Termination Action,* Haynes and Boone LLP (Feb. 2, 2016), available at Lexology.com]

In 2015, OSHA received over 3,000 whistleblower complaints. Resolving a complaint can take months, or even years; to speed up the process, OSHA launched an expedited case processing pilot project in its western region, comprising California, Nevada, Arizona, and Hawaii. A whistleblower who has filed a complaint can ask OSHA to put its investigation on hold and issue expedited findings that will be reviewed by a DOL Administrative Law Judge (ALJ). Cases can be moved to an ALJ if they are based on a statute that permits de novo review by an ALJ; either 30 or 60 days (depending on the statute) have elapsed since the complainant's initial filing with OSHA; federal investigators determine that the basic elements of the retaliation claim have occurred; both sides had a chance to submit witness statements and written responses and meet with an OSHA investigator; and the employee is able to respond to the employer's submission. OSHA either issues merit findings as soon as possible, refuses to expedite the case, or dismisses the claim (which then entitles the employee to appeal to an ALJ). [Harini Srinivasan, *OSHA Announces Pilot Program to Expedite Whistleblower Claims,* Katz Marshall & Banks LLP (Sept. 22, 2016), available at Lexology .com]

In addition to its workplace safety responsibilities, OSHA is responsible for enforcing several federal whistleblower statutes, although the Sarbanes-Oxley Act is the only one that deals with financial wrongdoing rather than health and safety.

The federal Sarbanes-Oxley Act [Pub. L. No. 107-204] (also discussed in this book in connection with 401(k) plans and corporate communications— notices to employees about "blackout" periods that restrict their abilities to trade their plan accounts) includes two provisions to protect whistleblowers.

In 2013, the Second Circuit clarified the standard for analyzing Sarbanes-Oxley whistleblower retaliation claims (18 U.S.C. § 1514A). The Second Circuit said that the plaintiff had to prove by a preponderance of the evidence that he was engaged in protected activity; that the employer knew it; and that the protected activity was a contributing factor in the adverse employment action. The employer can rebut with clear and convincing evidence it would have done the same thing without protected activity. [*Bechtel v. Admin. Review Bd.,* 710 F.3d 443 (2d Cir. 2013)]

In mid-2016, the Eighth Circuit held that the Sarbanes-Oxley Act only protects whistleblowers if a reasonable person, with the same position, training, and experience, would believe that there was a reportable violation of securities law. In this case, the Eighth Circuit concluded that the employee should have known that the changes in the way the company reported revenue, that had only a minimal effect on the corporation's books, were not improprieties that had to be reported to the SEC. Therefore, he was not entitled to whistleblower protection. [*Beacom v. Oracle,* 825 F.3d 376 (8th Cir. 2016); see FindLaw Employment Law blog, 8th *Cir. Adopts "Reasonable Employee" Standard for SOX Whistleblowing Claims* (June 21, 2016), available at FindLaw.com]

Before 2010, when the Dodd-Frank Act created a private civil cause of action, whistleblower claims went to the DOL's Administrative Review Board (ARB). The ARB required whistleblowers to have a reasonable belief that there had been a violation of each element of the cause of action for the fraud that the whistleblower reported. This "definitively and specifically" standard for claims was adopted by the First, Second, Fourth, Fifth, and Ninth Circuits, in deference to the ARB's rulemaking authority. But the more recent trend, adopting by the Sixth Circuit, is to require only a subjective belief that is objectively reasonable in light of the whistleblower's experience and training. Then, in 2011, ARB changed its rule to a "reasonable basis" standard, which was followed by the Second and Third Circuits. [*Rhinehimer v. U.S. Bancorp Inv., Inc.*, 787 F.3d 797 (6th Cir. 2015)]

When a Sarbanes-Oxley claim is filed with OSHA, then withdrawn, the statute of limitations is four years: the catch-all statute of limitations under 28 U.S.C. § 1658(a) applies. Sarbanes-Oxley includes a "kickout" provision permitting charging parties to withdraw a complaint from OSHA if it remains unresolved after 180 days. In this case, the CFO of a video game publisher was fired; she said it was because she said that the company misstated figures in an SEC filing. The district court jury awarded more than $500,000 in back pay and damages for emotional distress. The suit was filed almost two years after the kickout and almost three years after the plaintiff's termination. The Fourth Circuit held that emotional distress damages are available in Sarbanes-Oxley retaliation cases because the statute provides for all relief needed to make the plaintiff whole. [*Jones v. SouthPeak Interactive Corp. of Del.*, 777 F.3d 658 (4th Cir. 2015); *Halliburton, Inc. v. Admin. Review Bd.*, 771 F.3d 254 (5th Cir. 2014), and *Lockheed Martin Corp. v. ARB*, 717 F.3d 1121 (10th Cir. 2013) also allow the award of emotional distress damages in this context.]

Under the Corporate Fraud Accountability Act, § 806 of the Sarbanes-Oxley Act, 18 U.S.C. § 1514A is amended to provide that publicly traded companies are forbidden to "discharge, demote, suspend, threaten, harass, or in any other manner discriminate against an employee in the terms and conditions of employment" because the employee has engaged in any lawful act to provide information to the government or participate in an investigation of securities fraud or corporate wrongdoing. (The lawful acts condition is important—whistleblowers are not protected if they commit burglaries or hack computer systems to get this information, for example.)

Someone who believes that he or she has been discriminated against for whistleblowing can file a complaint with the Secretary of Labor; if, after 180 days, the Secretary has not issued a final decision, the whistleblower can sue in federal district court (even if the amount in controversy is below the $75,000 usually required to get to federal court). The Sarbanes-Oxley Act provides for whatever relief is necessary to make a successful whistleblower claimant whole—i.e., compensatory damages, reinstatement with whatever seniority the person would have had without discrimination, back pay plus interest, and compensation for special damages such as attorneys' fees, expert witness fees, and costs.

Sarbanes-Oxley § 1107 (18 U.S.C. § 1513(e)) makes it a crime for "any person" to retaliate against a whistleblower; this provision is not limited to public corporations. It also applies to a whistleblower's truthful disclosures of any violation (not just criminal violations) of any federal law (not just securities laws). A criminal Sarbanes-Oxley case requires proof that action was knowingly taken with intent to retaliate; the retaliation harmed the whistleblower; and retaliation was motivated by cooperation with law enforcement. In this context, harm to the whistleblower includes not just termination or demotion, but threats, harassment, or disparagement of the person to potential employers. A criminal Sarbanes-Oxley action can also be a predicate act for RICO purposes. [Anthony R. Petruzzi and Adrienne B. Kirshner, *Beware of Potential Criminal Implications for the Improper Handling of a Whistleblower Investigation*, Tucker Ellis (Oct. 21, 2015), available at Lexology.com; *United States v. Camick*, 796 F.3d 1206, (10th Cir. 2015) holds that a conviction can be upheld if there are multiple reasonable inferences that could be drawn from the evidence.]

OSHA issued a final rule (effective March 5, 2015) under § 806 of the Corporate Fraud Accountability Act, reflecting the Dodd-Frank amendments to the Sarbanes-Oxley Act. Complaints can be made orally or filed online. OSHA investigates and dismisses the complaint unless the complainant shows that the protected activity was a contributing factor to the adverse action. Even if a prima facie is made out, OSHA will not investigate if the employer provides clear and convincing evidence that it would have taken the action even without protected activity. After the investigation, OSHA issues a preliminary order, which the parties can object to. It can be reviewed by an ALJ, the ALJ by the Administrative Review Board (ARB), and judicial review is available for ARB final orders. [80 Fed. Reg. 11865 (Mar. 5, 2015)]

The Third Circuit affirmed the dismissal of Sarbanes-Oxley whistleblower retaliation claims. The plaintiff, an accounts payable manager, asserted that he raised internal concerns about the reporting of expenses for company events. He was terminated; the company said it was because other employees complained about him, including sexual harassment allegations. The Third Circuit held that he did not show a causal connection between his discharge and protected activity. There was a time gap (10 months between reports and termination); the HR investigators were not even aware of the reports; and the employer showed that he would have been fired even absent protected activity. [*Wiest v. Tyco Elec. Corp.*, 812 F.3d 319 (3d Cir. 2016); see Steven J. Pearlman and Andrew M. Schnitzel, *3rd Circuit Affirms Dismissal in Long-Running Wiest SOX Whistleblower Case*, Proskauer Rose LLP (Feb. 8, 2016), available at Lexology.com] Also see Sarbanes-Oxley Act § 1107, which provides for fines and/or up to 10 years' imprisonment, for knowing harmful actions, taken with intent to retaliate against someone who provided truthful information about Sarbanes-Oxley violations to any law enforcement officer. This provision covers all actions, including interference with any person's lawful employment or livelihood.

Companies can take steps to encourage employees to report internally rather than immediately contacting outside agencies. The company should have a clear reporting chain, and make sure that information is transmitted to the proper decision-maker. The reporting mechanism should be easy to use and should be explained to employees. Reports should be encouraged, because they can be instrumental in saving the company's reputation by solving problems before they become untenable. In some cases, it is worth allowing customers, suppliers, and consultants to report internally because their outsider perspective can be useful—and they might otherwise be encouraged to seek bounties. [Alexandra Wrage, *8*

Ways to Encourage Whistleblowers to Report Internally, Compliance Insider (May 10, 2012) (law.com)]

"W-SVEP" (Severe Violator Enforcement Program) is a four-year OSHA pilot program to detect and punish retaliation against employees who are whistle-blowers under any of the 22 statutes that OSHA enforces. The program began May 31, 2016, in several states in the Midwest. OSHA places companies that retaliate against whistleblowers who reported a death or severe safety violations on the W-SVEP Log, which is a public watch list, and issues a press release about the employer. Employers are also placed on the log if they have been the subject of three or more whistleblower cases over a three-year period. Employers are removed from the log if they win the whistleblower case. Even if they lose, after three years they can ask for a follow-up inspection to be removed from the log. [Lewis M. Csedrik, *OSHA Announces New Enforcement Program for Whistle-blower Cases*, Morgan Lewis & Bockius LLP (June 22, 2016), available at Lexology.com]

The Second Circuit held that whistleblower claims under the Sarbanes-Oxley Act are arbitrable, rejecting the plaintiff's arguments that arbitration does not provide adequate accountability or transparency and does not furnish infor-mation that would encourage other employees to make meritorious claims of their own. [*Guyden v. Aetna Inc.*, 544 F.3d 376 (2d Cir. 2008)]

Mutual funds are usually organized as publicly traded companies that do not have any employees. Instead, they enter into contracts with private (non-publicly traded) companies that do have employees to provide advice and other services to the mutual funds. In early 2014, the Supreme Court held that Sarbanes-Oxley Act protection against retaliation covers employees of private companies that are con-tractors for public corporations. The 6-3 majority reached this result because the law was passed in response to the Enron scandal, and such coverage would meet the legislative objective. The plaintiffs were employees of a private subcontractor that advised Fidelity mutual funds; Jackie Lawson and Jonathan Zang (the plain-tiffs) were terminated for informing bosses and SEC of their suspicions that Fidel-ity violated securities laws. (They could not use the Dodd-Frank whistleblower provisions because their actions occurred before Dodd-Frank took effect.) [*Lawson v. FMR Inc.*, 134 S. Ct. 1158 (2014)]

The Dodd-Frank Wall Street Reform and Consumer Protection Act of 2010, Pub. L. No. 111-203, includes an incentive provision for whistleblowers, even if the claim involves a privately held corporation not subject to Sarbanes-Oxley. If whistleblowers voluntarily provide information that leads the federal government to recover more than $1 million for a violation of the federal securities laws (including the Foreign Corrupt Practices Act, abbreviated as FCPA), the SEC has discretion to award them between 10% and 30% of the part of the recovery over and above $1 million. Awards are only available for providing original informa-tion, not already available through existing investigations or reports—and that the SEC did not already have. The SEC issued final rules about the whistleblower program in May 2011. The rules enhance rewards for employees who go through channels within their company before approaching the SEC; those who go directly to the SEC, without giving the employer a chance to correct the problem, get lower rewards. Employees have up to 120 days after making an internal complaint to go to the SEC. Whistleblowers can get credit if they report a minor violation that would not otherwise qualify for a bounty, if their complaint leads to an internal investigation that uncovers additional wrongdoing that the company discloses to the SEC. [76 Fed. Reg. 34300 (June 13, 2011)]

SEC's implementing rules for the whistleblower program treat the date of an internal report as the date of the SEC report, as long as the whistleblower contacts the SEC within 120 days. This is an incentive for companies to investigate allegations of misconduct and make voluntary disclosures before the employee goes to the SEC. [Robert R. Stauffer and William L. Von Hoene, *Dodd Frank Whistleblower Provisions—A 5-Year Update*, Jenner & Block (July 8, 2015), available at Lexology.com]

In its 2016 annual report about the Dodd-Frank whistleblower program, the SEC Office of the Whistleblower said that, over the life of the program, over $111 million had been awarded to 34 whistleblowers. FY 2016 awards, $57 million, were greater than the awards for all previous years put together. Out of the ten largest awards ever made, six—including one that was more than $30 million by itself—were made in FY 2016. [<http://www.sec.gov/whistleblower/reportspubs/annual-reports/owb-annual-report-2016.pdf> (last accessed Mar. 17, 2017)]

Since the Dodd-Frank whistleblower program started in 2011, the agency has paid out $111 million to 34 whistleblowers. (In 2016 alone, there were 13 awards aggregating more than $57 million). The SEC has received 18,334 tips (4,200 of them in 2016). Twenty-two percent of tips dealt with corporate disclosures and financials; 15% with fraud in offerings, and 11% with market manipulation. [Harris M. Mufson, *Highlights of SEC's 2016 Annual Whistleblower Report*, Proskauer Rose LLP (Dec. 19, 2016), available at Lexology.com]

The first SEC Dodd-Frank whistleblower award during the Trump administration, in the amount of close to $4 million, was announced on April 25, 2017. [<https://www.sec.gov/news/press-release/2017-84>; see Lloyd B. Chinn and Harris M. Mufson, *SEC Announces First Whistleblower Award During Trump Era*, Proskauer Rose LLP (Apr. 26, 2017), available at Lexology.com]

In mid-2014, the SEC resolved its first Dodd-Frank retaliation case (as distinct from making awards to whistleblowers who reported improprieties). The head trader at a hedge fund reported that the fund engaged in transactions that violated the Investment Advisers Act of 1940. The fund took adverse employment action, and the trader eventually resigned. The fund agreed to pay more than $2.1 million to settle the SEC charges, including a $300,000 civil penalty. It was not disclosed what proportion of those amounts reflected the retaliation charge rather than the underlying Investment Advisers Act violations. [Sutherland Asbill & Brennan LLP Legal Alert, *SEC Launches First Whistleblower Retaliation Case Under Dodd-Frank* (June 20, 2014) (benefitslink.com)]

A Sarbanes-Oxley whistleblower was awarded $2.7 million in front pay, plus $1.6 million in back pay and other compensatory damages—one of the largest retaliation awards ever made. The jury held that he suffered retaliatory termination for opposing fraud committed by a publicly traded pharmaceutical company. Reinstatement was considered impractical so he was awarded front pay from his current age, 58, to the age of 66½, which was considered his projected retirement date. [*Perez v. Progenics Pharm.*, 204 F. Supp. 3d 528 (S.D.N.Y. 2016); see Matthew LaGarde, *SOX Whistleblower Awarded $2.7 Million in Front Pay*, Katz Marshall & Banks LLP (Oct. 3, 2016), available at Lexology.com]

The SEC's whistleblower rules under the Dodd-Frank Act affect three aspects of corporate internal investigations: informing employees about internal corporate controls, carrying out the investigation itself, and dealing with regulators.

Dodd-Frank protects whistleblowers whether or not the SEC actually investigates the complaint, if it found any violations, or the whistleblower actually received an award. However, if the employee does not learn about the potential violation that he or she reported from a corporate attorney in the course of a corporate investigation, Rule 21F-4(b)(4)(vi) says that the whistleblower is not the source of the information, and therefore cannot receive an award. [Steven S. Sparling and Arielle Warshall Katz, *Internal Investigation Strategies in a Post Dodd-Frank World*, N.Y.L.J. (Aug. 11, 2011) (law.com)]

The District Court for the District of Nebraska ruled that a report to the SEC is not required for protection against retaliation (although it is required to collect a bounty). The district court ruled that disclosing the results of her internal investigation to FINRA was the equivalent of complying with an SEC rule, because the SEC must approve all FINRA rules and is entitled to amend them. [*Bussing v. COR Clearing, LLC* 20 F. Supp. 3d (D. Neb. 2014)]

The Tenth Circuit held that protection is not limited to reporting fraud against shareholders. Retaliation against any SEC rule is covered—in this case, charging a Lockheed Martin executive with ethics violations in operating a pen pal program for soldiers in Iraq. [*Lockheed Martin Corp. v. Admin. Review Bd.*, 717 F.3d 1121 (10th Cir. 2013)]

The Fifth Circuit held in mid-2013 that it is necessary to contact the SEC with information about securities law violations to be a Dodd-Frank whistleblower. A person who charges retaliation for filing an internal complaint (in this case, alleged violations of the Foreign Corrupt Practice Act) is not a whistleblower and not protected under the Dodd-Frank Act. [*Asadi v. G.E. Energy LLC*, 720 F.3d 620 (5th Cir. 2013)] Probably in response to *Asadi*, the SEC issued a rule interpretation that whistleblowers who make internal reports of irregularities are entitled to the same protection as those who report to the SEC. [<http://www.sec.gov/rules/interp/2015/34-75592.pdf> (last accessed Mar. 17, 2017)]

The Second Circuit agrees with the SEC (and disagrees with the Fifth Circuit) that an internal whistleblower, who does not report to the SEC, can pursue a Dodd-Frank retaliation claim under Rule 21-F2. [*Berman v. Neo@Ogilvy LLC &*

WPP Grp. USA, Inc., 801 F.3d 145 (2d Cir. 2015); see Sullivan & Cromwell LLP, *Dodd-Frank Whistleblower Provision* (Sept. 11, 2015), available at Lexology .com] The Ninth Circuit joined the Second Circuit in early 2017, holding that internal reports are protected under Dodd-Frank. [*Somers v. Digital Realty Trust*, 850 F.3d 1045 (9th Cir. 2017). See Gary M. Gansle et.al., *Ninth Circuit Expands Reach of Dodd-Frank Anti-Retaliation Protections*, Squire Patton Boggs (Mar. 9, 2017), available at Lexology.com]. Certiorari was granted on June 26, 2017, as No. 16-1276. See Joseph Fazioli and Argia J. DiMarco, *Supreme Court to Clarify Definition of "Whistleblower" Under the Dodd-Frank Act*, Dechert LLP (June 27, 2017), available at Lexology.com]

The District Court for the Eastern District of Tennessee dismissed a Dodd-Frank retaliation claim brought by a former financial advisor who claimed that he was fired for helping the FBI investigate insider trading at the firm. The district court held that the Dodd-Frank provision is only triggered by reporting directly to the SEC. The case was appealed to the Sixth Circuit, which did not decide this question, but affirmed dismissal of the case on the grounds that the plaintiff failed to plausibly allege that he engaged in protected activity. It is not settled law whether Dodd-Frank covers assistance in FBI investigations. One argument is that Dodd-Frank incorporates Sarbanes-Oxley, which refers to federal regulatory and law enforcement agencies. However, another Dodd-Frank provision defines a whistleblower as a person who reports securities law violations to the SEC. The SEC's position is that Dodd-Frank whistleblowers are protected no matter where they make their disclosures, but not all courts will defer to the SEC. Since the *Berman* decision, three district courts have adopted the Fifth Circuit's restrictive *Asadi* position: *Puffenbarger v. Engility Corp.*, 151 F. Supp. 3d 651 (E.D. Va. 2015); *Deykes v. Cooper-Standard Auto., Inc.*, No. 2:16-CV-11828, 2016 WL 6873395 (E.D. Mich. Nov. 22, 2016); and *Lamb v. Rockwell Automation Inc.*, No.15-CV-1415-JPS, 2016 WL 4273210 (E.D. Wis. Aug. 12, 2016).

Dodd-Frank protection of whistleblowers is much broader than Sarbanes-Oxley's. The Sarbanes-Oxley statute of limitations is six months; the Dodd-Frank statute of limitations is three years. Sarbanes-Oxley claims must be submitted to OSHA first and can only go to federal court if the DOL fails to issue a final decision within 180 days.

A Dodd-Frank Act suit can be brought right away and its remedies (including doubled back pay) are more extensive than the Sarbanes-Oxley remedies. [*Verble v. Morgan Stanley Smith Barney*, LLC, No. 15-6397, 2017 WL 129040 (6th Cir. Jan. 13, 2017), *cert. denied*, 137 S. Ct. 1348 (2017); see Matthew LaGarde, *Sixth Circuit Sidesteps Whether Whistleblowers Need to Tip Off Regulators to Receive Protections Under Dodd-Frank*, Katz Marshall & Banks LLP (Mar. 20, 2017), available at Lexology.com; Harris M. Mufson and Edward C. Young, *U.S. Supreme Court Passes on Opportunity to Address Scope of Dodd-Frank "Whistleblower" Provision*, Proskauer Rose LLP (Mar. 23, 2017), available at Lexology.com]

This issue could become moot if Sarbanes-Oxley and/or Dodd-Frank are repealed or substantially modified by Congress or Executive Order.

The Third Circuit ruled that all a whistleblower needs is a reasonable belief that the employer has violated or will violate a securities law; the complainant does not have to show that he or she identified a specific statute when making an internal complaint. [*Bechtel v. U.S. DOL*, 710 F.3d 443 (2d Cir. 2013) (Sarbanes-Oxley claim requires whistleblower to prove by a preponderance of the evidence that protected activity was a contributing factor in the adverse employment action; the employer can defend itself with clear and convincing evidence it would have taken the same action without the protected activity—a much higher standard than Title VII, which merely requires a legitimate, nondiscriminatory reason); *Wiest v. Lynch*, 719 F.3d 121 (3d Cir. 2013)]

The District Court for the Eastern District of Wisconsin ruled in mid-2016 that the plaintiff, a former CEO who complained to the board of directors, could not maintain a Sarbanes-Oxley whistleblower claim. His complaints did not involve securities violations or fraud and the disclosures were not protected because he was complaining about the board itself. The plaintiff charged that the company was being mismanaged, for example, by overpaying for legal work, and acted unethically in a suit brought by a former employee. The plaintiff, who had signed Form 10-Qs in the past, said that he would not sign the next form because of issues that he said were concealed from the SEC. The board tried to remove him as CEO, accusing him of poor performance and improperly retaining money advanced to him to pay his divorce lawyer. In the district court's view, the fraud he alleged was merely ordinary corporate issues, and the board did not make any material misrepresentations. An e-mail to the board, complaining about the board, could not be considered a protected whistleblower complaint because he did not contact anyone else. [*Verfuerth v. Orion Energy Sys., Inc.*, No. 14-cv-352 (E.D. Wis. Aug. 25, 2016); see Matthew R. Engel and Steven J. Pearlman, *E.D. Wisconsin: SOX Does Not Protect Whistleblower Complaints Based on Immaterial, Routine Events*, Proskauer Rose LLP (Sept. 23, 2016), available at Lexology .com]

Nielsen, a fire engineering manager responsible for ensuring that engineering plans met safety standards, was terminated. He said that this was part of a cover-up of approval of inadequate designs. According to the Second Circuit, complaints must include enough facts to state a plausible claim: enough for there to be more than speculation that the plaintiff is entitled to relief. The Second Circuit said that Nielsen merely said that one employee's review of fire safety designs was inadequate. There was no allegation of violation of securities or fraud laws; the designs were not subject to federal standards, and there was no connection to financial markets. [*Nielsen v. Aecom Tech. Corp.*, 762 F.3d 214 (2d Cir. 2014)]

The Second Circuit, agreed with a district court in Texas: the Dodd-Frank retaliation provision, 15 U.S.C. § 78u-6(h)(1)(a), does not cover conduct outside the United States. The Southern District said that, although non-U.S. citizens working for non-U.S. subsidiaries can qualify for whistleblower bounty awards, that does not mean that they are covered by the retaliation provision. (The similar Sarbanes-Oxley anti-retaliation provision does not apply extraterritorially either.) Furthermore, the report involved violations of the Foreign Corrupt Practices Act, which is not covered by Sarbanes-Oxley § 806. [*Liu v. Siemens A.G.*,763 F.3d 175 (2d Cir. 2014)]

Nevertheless, as of late 2014, the SEC had made four awards to people living outside the United States—including the record-breaking award in the $30-$35 million range, paid to an unnamed foreign resident. The SEC finds enough territorial nexus if information leads to successful enforcement, in the United States, of U.S. securities laws even if the claimant is not a U.S. citizen, lives in another country, or even if the violation of U.S. law occurred entirely overseas. [Jennifer L. Farer, *SEC Announces Record-Breaking Award for Foreign Whistleblower in the Wake of Liu v. Siemens*, McGuireWoods LLP (Oct. 7, 2014), available at Lexology.com]

In January 2016, the SEC announced that it had awarded more than $700,000 to a company outsider who gave the SEC a detailed analysis that resulted in a successful enforcement action. Eric Scott Hunsader, owner of a market data firm, later revealed that he was the tipster. Hunsader said that the discovered that traders violated SEC regulations by using an NYSE data feed. [Bryan B. House, Lisa M. Noller and Courtney Worcester, *SEC Pays First Whistleblower Award to "Company Outsider,"* Foley & Lardner LLP (Apr. 12, 2016), available at Lexology.com. For other awards, see Lloyd B. Chinn, Harris M. Mufson and Anthony DiBenedetto, *SEC Issues Another Multi-Million Dollar Whistleblower Award*, Proskauer Rose LLP (Sept. 22, 2016), available at Lexology.com;

In April 2015, the SEC carried out its first enforcement action based on a confidentiality agreement; KBR, Inc., paid a $130,000 fine to settle the SEC's case but did not admit liability. The SEC said that KBR's policy, under which employees could be disciplined or fined for discussing an internal investigation with a third party without prior approval from the legal department, violated SEC Rule 21F-17. The SEC's action was based on potential chilling effects of the rule, not on a known violation. Best practice is to send a notice, signed by a corporate officer to the company's employees informing them that confidentiality agreements do not prevent reporting of violations to the appropriate government agencies. [Sharon B. Bauman et.al., *SEC Not Keeping Quiet About Employee Confidentiality Agreements*, Manatt Phelps & Phillips (Oct. 2, 2015), available at Lexology.com; Cleary Gottlieb Steen & Hamilton LLP, *Action Required: How to Update Employee Confidentiality Provisions in Light of Recent SEC Enforcement Action* (Apr. 20, 2015), available at Lexology.com]

In mid-2016, BlueLinx agreed to pay $265,000 to settle SEC charges about requiring departing employees to waive the right to SEC whistleblower awards. [Brian P. Morrissey and Benjamin M. Mundel, *SEC Fines Company That Used Severance Agreements to Discourage Whistleblowing*, Sidley Austin LLP (Aug. 15, 2016), available at Lexology.com.]

The False Claims Act (FCA), 31 U.S.C. § 3729–3733, is the federal statutory version of the ancient equitable form of suit, the "qui tam" action, under which a "relator" sues on behalf of the government to recover funds paid as a result of fraud or other wrongdoing. A successful relator is entitled to collect an award of part (15%–25%) of the government's recovery, which is often very high not only because of the large amounts involved, but because treble damages may be available.

To get an award, the relator must be the original source of the information. The Third, Seventh, Eighth, Tenth, and Eleventh Circuits have held that a relator's second-hand knowledge of an employer's billing practices prevent the person from receiving an award. The plaintiff alleged that his employer violated the FCA by billing the federal government for medications that it got for free. The plaintiff was not directly involved in the billing process. His qui tam action was based on what his managers told him and what he saw in company reports. A three-part test applies: first, have the plaintiff's allegations been publicly disclosed? Second, is the suit based on this information? Third, is the plaintiff an original source of the information? The Eleventh Circuit upheld the grant of summary judgment for the employer because being told about, or reading about, billing practices is merely indirect knowledge. [*Saldivar v. Fresenius Med. Care Holdings, Inc.*, 841 F.3d 927 (11th Cir. 2016); see Jeff Gibson, *Eleventh Circuit Holds Secondhand Knowledge Does Not Make Relator an Original Source*, Bass, Berry & Sims PLC (Nov. 15, 2016), available at Lexology.com]

Suppression of material information could constitute fraud against the government. The Implied False Certification Theory says that it violates the FCA to make a claim for government payments that does not disclose that the defendant has violated a material requirement of the government program which makes the payments. A unanimous Supreme Court held in mid-2016 that in some circumstances, this theory gives rise to liability—as long as the non-disclosure is significant enough that disclosure could have prevented the federal payment from being made. (In this case, claims were made for Medicaid reimbursement without disclosing that certain staff members were not licensed or qualified.) The decision also holds that conditions of compliance can be material even if the government did not previously identify them as such. [*Universal Health Servs., Inc. v. United States ex rel. Escobar,* 136 S. Ct. 1989 (2016); see Adam Herzog, *SCOTUS Ruling May Increase FCA Whistleblower Claims,* Katz Marshall & Banks LLP (July 26, 2016), available at Lexology.com]

The Eighth Circuit upheld summary judgment for the employer on an FCA retaliation claim [31 U.S.C. § 3730(h)]. The Eighth Circuit held that the FCA requires the plaintiff to show that the alleged retaliatory act was solely motivated by protected activity; a mixed-motive case is not available. The plaintiff, a doctor, alleged that the Mayo Holding Company made false statements about his work in review and termination meetings. He charged that he was fired for reporting two instances of substandard care, because he refused to transfer a patient who was not stabilized, and because he complained about unlicensed care and unlawful billing. The Eighth Circuit held that he failed to show that the stated reason for his termination, poor work, was pretextual. He was a probationary employee, and hospital staff said that he was hard to work with and did not complete paperwork on time. [*Elkharwily v. Mayo Holding Co.*, 823 F.3d 462 (8th Cir. 2016); see John P. Bueker et. al., *Eighth Circuit Affirms That Retaliation Under False Claims Act Requires Showing That Retaliation Was Motivated Solely by Plaintiff's Protected Activity*, Ropes & Gray LLP (Dec. 7, 2016), available at Leoxlogy.com]

The Seventh Circuit held that, in an FCA whistleblower retaliation case, the test is whether a reasonable employee would believe that the employer was defrauding the government. Violation of a self-imposed requirement that was not part of the government contract will not support an FCA case. [*United States ex rel. Uhlig v. Fluor Corp.*, 839 F.3d 628 (7th Cir. 2016); see John P. Bueker, Kirsten Mayer and Alexandra Roth, *Seventh Circuit Rejects False Claims Act and Retaliation Claims Premised on Purported Breach of Contract,* Ropes & Gray LLP (Nov. 30, 2016), available at Lexology.com]

According to the Sixth Circuit, the retaliation provisions of the False Claims Act and the Energy Reorganization Act cannot be used by a job applicant because he or she is not an "employee." (The plaintiff charged that he was denied hiring because he reported environmental violations at a previous job.) [*Vander Boegh v. EnergySolutions, Inc.*, 772 F.3d 1056 (6th Cir. 2014)]

In addition to federal statutes, employers risk large verdicts under state statutes, which may have idiosyncratic definitions of "whistleblower." For example, Florida and New Jersey have comprehensive laws that protect employees of private companies who object to unlawful activities, report such activities to government agencies, or participate in government investigations. New York's law is narrower, banning only retaliation for disclosure or threatened disclosure of health care fraud or conduct that substantially endangers public health or safety.

In at least two states (Indiana and Utah), state securities regulators give rewards to whistleblowers for tips about violations of state statutes. An Indiana informant who knew about JPMorgan Chase's failure to disclose conflicts of interest to its clients received a $95,000 award under a program, created in 2011, where up to 10% of the monetary sanction against a company can be paid to a whistleblower. Utah awards can be as high as 30%, and there have been 15 successful prosecutions under this program since 2011. [Gretchen Morgenson, *To Crack Down on Securities Fraud, States Reward Whistle-Blowers*, NYTimes.com (Aug. 22, 2016)]

Maine plaintiffs alleged that firing them violated the state's whistleblower protection and human rights laws. The district court granted summary judgment for the employer on the grounds that employees are not protected if they complain about conditions that are part of their job duties. The First Circuit, however, reversed, finding that there is no job duties exception in either statute. [*Pippin v. Boulevard Motel Corp.*, 835 F.3d 1363 (1st Cir. 2016)]

In late 2015, the Connecticut Supreme Court expanded employers' potential exposure to whistleblower damage claims. Connecticut General Statutes § 31-51q provides a damage remedy if a public or private employee is subjected to adverse consequences for exercising constitutionally guaranteed free speech rights. Since 2006, Connecticut courts read this to exclude statements that were made as part of the employees' official duties—a rule that was changed in 2015, protecting an employee's right to free speech about matters of public interest, even if the matters are part of the employee's job duties. [*Trusz v. UBS Realty Invs. LLC*, No. SC 19323 (Conn. Oct. 13, 2015)]

A mental health counselor brought suit under Sarbanes-Oxley and the Florida whistleblower act. She alleged that she was fired for reporting child abuse and fraud to management of the company where she worked. The district court not only granted summary judgment for the defendant on all counts, it awarded attorneys' fees and costs to the defendant. Florida law authorizes a fee award to a prevailing defendant, whereas Sarbanes-Oxley does not. The plaintiff argued that the state provision was preempted by the federal law, but the Eleventh Circuit ruled in mid-2014 that it was not: it is possible to comply with both statutes, and Sarbanes-Oxley is merely silent and does not forbid fee awards to prevailing defendants. [*Smith v. Psychiatric Solutions, Inc.*, 750 F.3d 1253 (11th Cir. 2014)]

Before 2013, the California Labor Code forbade employers to impair employees' right to report what they reasonably believed to be violations of state or federal law, if reports were made to a government or law enforcement agency. As of January 1, 2014, however, the law extends protection to employees who report illegal behavior internally to a supervisor, to another employee with the power to investigate and cure the violation, or externally to any public body engaged in an investigation.

The New Jersey Law Against Discrimination has been amended to forbid retaliation for requesting employment information to investigate discrimination or sue for compensation discrimination. (The law does not require the employer actually to provide the information, only to refrain from retaliation.) Minnesota amended its whistleblower law to clarify that the law is a broad one that forbids penalties against employees for good-faith reporting of a violation, suspected violation, or planned violation of law. [*Mooney v. Atlantic City*, No. L00204710 (N.J. Super. Ct. Law Div. Oct. 17, 2013); *Cadwell v. City of Highland Park*, 2013 WL 3971570 (Mich. Cir. Ct. Feb. 25, 2013)]

Employees of Department of Defense (DOD) prime contractors had partial protection under the Defense Contractor Whistleblower Act, 10 U.S.C. § 2409, and under the False Claims Act's anti-retaliation provisions. But protection was limited to disclosure of information about mismanagement of DOD grants or contracts, dangers to public health or safety, or violations of law relating to the DOD contract or grant. Disclosures were only protected if made to a member of Congress, the Inspector General, or certain DOD or DOJ officials. Additional protection is provided by National Defense Authorization Act of 2013, § 827, the Enhancement of Whistleblower Protections for Contractor Employees of the

Department of Defense, which took effect January 1, 2013. Protection now extends to employees of DOD subcontractors, not just prime contractors, whatever the size of the contract, and a broader range of reporting is covered. The Department of Defense published regulations on September 30, 2013 implementing this statute. Contracting officers must include notice of the whistleblower clause in all solicitations and contracts issued on or after September 30, 2013. [Mary E. Pivec and Igor M. Babichenko, *DOD Publishes Emergency Interim Final Rule Protecting Whistleblowers Employed Under a DOD Contract or Subcontract*, Williams Mullen (Oct. 11, 2013), available at Lexology.com]

A maintenance manager raised a claim under the Energy Reorganization Act, but the Ninth Circuit held that he did not engage in any protected activity. He claimed that he objected to an internal report about safety procedures. The Ninth Circuit held that the plaintiff had no independent knowledge of possible safety violations. He only complained about the reporting procedure, with no connection to a concrete, ongoing safety concern. Furthermore, the company was already aware of the situation and was correcting it. (The company said that the manager was fired for improperly approving payments to a member of his family.) [*Sanders v. Energy Northwest*, 812 F.3d 1193 (9th Cir. 2016); see Steven J. Pearlman and Jeremy M. Mittman, *9th Circuit Dismisses ERA Whistleblower Retaliation Claim*, Proskauer Rose LLP (Feb. 19, 2016), available at Lexology .com]

The IRS also has a whistleblower program: someone who reports a case involving over $2 million in unpaid taxes can collect up to 30% of the IRS's recovery, and up to 15% of the IRS's recovery can be awarded in small cases. The IRS has handled about 40 large cases since 2010. In FY 2014, over 14,000 tips were submitted to the IRS but most were rejected. The IRS awarded $11.6 million to a whistleblower in September 2015 and said that as many as 10 more large payouts might be made in fiscal 2015 based on reports of massive tax cheating. The IRS is particularly interested in unlawful repatriation of foreign earnings, and in multi-year corporate cases (because the case can still continue after the statute of limitations for a particular year expires). [Laura Saunders, *Blowing the Whistle on Tax Cheats*, WSJ.com (Sept. 4, 2015)]

The Commodity Futures Trading Commission (CFTC) made its first whistleblower award, in the amount of $240,000, in mid-2014. Its second award of about $290,000 was announced in September 2015. Awards are available, under the Dodd-Frank Act, for information that leads to enforcement action resulting in more than $1 million in monetary sanctions for abuses in the commodities market. The whistleblower receives 10%–30% of the sanctions. Dodd-Frank allows the CFTC to sue employers that retaliate against whistleblowers; under previous law, the whistleblower's only method of redress was a suit against the employer in federal court. [CFTC press release PR 7254-15, *CFTC to Issue Whistleblower Award of Approximately $290,000* (Sept. 29, 2015) (benefitslink. com); 81 Fed. Reg. 59551 (Aug. 30, 2016); see Aaron D. Blacksberg,

Whistleblowers Are Getting Much-Needed Help from the CFTC, Katz Marshall & Banks LLP (Oct. 13, 2016), available at Lexology.com]

In May 2017, the CFTC amended its whistleblower rules, increasing protection for whistleblowers and reiterating the CFTC's power to bring enforcement actions in retaliation cases. The CFTC can bring a retaliation action against the employer even if the whistleblower employee did not qualify for an award. Corporate agreements such as confidentiality agreements and arbitration agreements must not be drafted to prevent employees from contacting the CFTC about potential violations of the Commodity Exchange Act. [Stephen M. Quinlivan, *CFTC Revises Whistleblower Rule to Enhance Anti-Retaliation Provision,* Stinson Leonard Street LLP (May 22, 2017), available at Lexology.com; Paul M. Architzel, Gail C. Bernstein and Yevedzo Chitiga, *CFTC Increases Anti-Retaliation Protections for Whistleblowers,* Wilmer Cutler Pickering Hale and Dorr LLP (May 24, 2017), available at Lexology.com]

[C] WC Claimants

Retaliation against employees who have filed Worker's Compensation claims is unlawful, because public policy favors injured employees receiving income to replace the income lost when they are injured.

Minnesota permits termination for dishonest behavior, including filing a false Worker's Compensation (WC) claim. However, WC law forbids retaliatory discharge for applying for WC benefits. The District Court for the District of Minnesota ruled that summary judgment was unavailable in the case of an employee who said that she was injured by slipping in the company parking lot during breaks. The video from the parking lot did not show her falling. Her insurance claim was denied and she was fired for filing a false claim. The district court held that the employer's investigation was incomplete. The video was of poor quality, and some footage had been deleted; the plaintiff could also have been outside camera range when she fell. The employer did not ask the plaintiff's doctor if her injuries were consistent with her account of the fall. [*Schaefer v. BioLife Plasma LLC*, Civil No. 11-3468, 2013 U.S. Dist. LEXIS 133343 (D. Minn. Sept. 18, 2013)]

Reversing its previous position, the Missouri Supreme Court adopted a new standard: an employee who alleges retaliatory termination for filing a Worker's Compensation claim need only prove that the claim was a contributing factor, not the exclusive reason for his discharge. Plaintiff Templemire was injured in 2006, when his foot was crushed by a metal beam. He returned to light duty and received WC benefits, but was fired for failing to perform assigned work. He said that his WC claim was one reason for his discharge. The trial court and intermediate appellate court used the old standard, but the Missouri Supreme Court ruled in his favor. [*Templemire v. W&M Welding, Inc.*, 433 S.W.3d 371 (Mo. 2014)]

The Minnesota Supreme Court ruled in mid-2014 that Worker's Compensation retaliation cases are a kind of wrongful termination claim, and, therefore, jury trial is available. The employee can sue if his or her supervisor threatened termination if the employee made a WC claim, even if no adverse action was actually taken. The employer is liable for the supervisor's threat even if there was a reporting system for employee complaints. [*Schmitz v. U.S. Steel*, 852 N.W.2d 669 (Minn. 2014)]

Continental Tire fired a 22-year veteran trucker who refused to take a mandatory drug test after being involved in an accident. He brought a suit for retaliatory termination for filing a Worker's Compensation claim. The Seventh Circuit held that there was no evidence that the employer's explanation—that he was fired for refusing to be tested—was not true. Nor could he prove that requiring post-accident drug testing discouraged employees from filing Worker's Compensation claims. [*Phillips v. Continental Tire The Americas LLC*, 743 F.3d 475 (7th Cir. 2014)]

The Ohio Supreme Court ruled in mid-2016 that it is not necessary to prove that a workplace injury occurred in order to state a prima facie case of Worker's Compensation retaliatory discharge. The plaintiff was prescribed painkillers for a knee injury, although there was a dispute as to whether the injury occurred at work. The employee sought but was turned down for light duty work and filed a WC claim, which was denied as non-work-related. At the end of 2012, he was fired for filing a fraudulent claim and sued for retaliatory termination. The Ohio Supreme Court held that the purpose of the statute is for employees to be able to exercise their rights without fear of retaliation, and that filing fraudulent (rather than merely unviable) claims is a crime. [*Onderko v. Sierra Lobo, Inc.*, Slip Op. No. 2016-Ohio-5027 (Ohio July 21, 2016); see Patrick O. Peters and James M. Stone, *Proof of Workplace Injury Not Required for Workers' Compensation Retaliation Claim in Ohio*, Jackson Lewis PC (July 26, 2016), available at Lexology.com]

In mid-2011, the Ohio Supreme Court held that a machine shop worker who was fired within an hour of reporting a workplace injury—but before he could apply for WC benefits—could sue his ex-employer under the state law forbidding retaliation for making WC claims. [*Sutton v. Tomco*, 950 N.E.2d 938 (Ohio 2011)]

§ 39.05 PREEMPTION ARGUMENTS

Preemption is the legal doctrine under which passage of a federal law limits or eliminates the state's power to regulate that subject. ERISA preempts state wrongful termination claims based on alleged termination to avoid paying pension benefits. All such claims must be brought in federal court, under ERISA § 510, and not in state court.

The Family and Medical Leave Act preempts common-law claims of retaliatory discharge when an employee says he or she was fired as punishment for taking FMLA leave. [*Hamros v. Bethany Homes*, 894 F. Supp. 1176 (N.D. Ill. 1995)]

The Sixth Circuit upheld the dismissal of a wrongful termination suit brought by a former Whirlpool executive. Lewis charged that he was fired, in violation of public policy, because he refused to commit the Unfair Labor Practice of firing employees for engaging in union activism. The Sixth Circuit held that Lewis' claim was preempted by the NLRA, so he should have raised his claim before the NLRB. (In fact he did, but the NLRB found that his charge was without merit.) Supervisors are generally excluded from coverage under the NLRA, but there is a cause of action for termination or other discipline for refusing to commit Unfair Labor Practices—but the NLRB has exclusive jurisdiction over such claims. [*Lewis v. Whirlpool Corp.*, 630 F.3d 484 (6th Cir. 2011)]

However, National Labor Relations Act §§ 7 and 8 do not so completely preempt state wrongful discharge claims that the state claims can be removed to federal court. In 2005, the Fourth Circuit held that preemption depends on a preexisting federal cause of action, and the wrongful discharge case was not based on the right to bargain collectively or the ban on unfair labor practices. [*Lontz v. Tharp*, 413 F.3d 435 (4th Cir. 2005)]

Preemption arguments can also be used in state court. If the employee is covered by a state antidiscrimination law that is not preempted by federal law, the employer may be able to get a wrongful termination suit dismissed, because the employee should have sued for discrimination. From the employer's viewpoint, the best-case scenario is that the employee waited too long, so the discrimination charges must be dismissed.

The Michigan Whistleblower Protection Act (WPA) preempts common-law claims of discharge in violation of public policy, which creates problems for employees because the WPA statute of limitations is only 90 days, a short deadline that employees might easily miss. An employee who charged that she was fired for reporting that a co-worker planned to use state grant money for personal purposes was not protected by the WPA because that statute requires a violation to have occurred already. [*Pace v. Edel-Harrelson*, No. 151376 (Mich. Sup. Feb. 1, 2016); see Emory D. Moore, *The Whistleblower Protection Act Does Not Protect an Employee Who Reports a Future Violation of Law, but Public Policy Might*, Foster Swift Collins & Smith PC (Mar. 11 2016), available at Lexology .com; Leigh M. Schultz, *Whistleblower Claims Cannot be Based on Future or Planned Acts in Michigan*, Miller Canfield PLC (Feb. 22, 2016), available at Lexology.com]

CHAPTER 40

ARBITRATION AND ADR

§ 40.01   INTRODUCTION

For many years, arbitration was a minor and somewhat disfavored part of the legal system. Today, after a long series of pro-arbitration Supreme Court decisions, it is a central part of employer-employee relations (as well as business-consumer relations and commercial arbitration, which are beyond the scope of this book). Arbitration is no longer limited to cases involving unions and unionized employees, and it is very common for employers to require employees to arbitrate work-related disputes, including discrimination charges, rather than litigating them.

Alternative Dispute Resolution (ADR) methods are supposed to be informal, governed more by justice and fairness than by strict rules of legal procedure. Depending on the ADR method, either one person or a panel of people will either assist the parties to work out their own solution (mediation) or will make a decision (arbitration).

Both unionized and nonunionized companies often find mediation or arbitration a superior alternative to litigation when employees make claims that they have suffered employment discrimination. In fact, employers often use various methods to make sure that all claims will have to go through arbitration. The question is when and how it is legitimate to impose an arbitration requirement on employees. If the employees freely choose arbitration over litigation, this problem does not arise, but nevertheless, the employer will still have to find a way to present its case effectively to the arbitrator.

The "first principles" of arbitration are that arbitration should be independent of the court system and should provide flexibility and respect the rights of the parties.

The federal statute known as the Railway Labor Act was enacted to resolve labor disputes. It requires minor disputes to be arbitrated before two labor and two industry representatives, plus a neutral referee to break tie votes. First, the parties must engage in "on-property proceedings" (going through the full grievance procedure under the Collective Bargaining Agreement (CBA)), and try to get a settlement "in conference." If they cannot agree, either side can refer the matter to the National Railroad Adjustment Board (NRAB) for arbitration. An arbitrator's order can be reviewed by the courts for failure to comply with the requirements of the Railway Labor Act, for not confining itself to matters within the jurisdiction of the Board, or for fraud or corruption. There was a circuit split over whether NRAB proceedings can also be reviewed for due process violations as well as these statutory grounds for review. In late 2009, the Supreme Court ruled that statutory and not Constitutional analysis should be applied. As long as a respondent does not seek to modify the Board's judgment, it can cite any information that appears in the record to support the Board's judgment. The Supreme Court held that the requirement to "conference" the dispute is not jurisdictional, so it is not necessary to prove that the dispute was conferenced before the Board hears a dispute. [*Union Pac. R.R. Co. v. Brotherhood of Locomotive Eng'rs*, 558 U.S. 67 (2009)]

As an option for the whistleblower complaints Occupational Safety and Health Administration (OSHA) receives under the almost two dozen statutes it administers, OSHA operated a pilot project for ADR in two regions in 2012 and 2013. The project was deemed a success and was made available nationwide in mid-2015.

A neutral OSHA representative with experience in whistleblower investigations helps the parties reach settlement. Both sides must agree to ADR. If an investigation has already begun, it is stayed. ADR is handled by a regional ADR coordinator, who is not allowed to share info with the OSHA investigative staff. State programs are encouraged to adopt this or a similar ADR process for whistleblower claims. [OSHA, *Alternative Dispute Resolution (ADR) Processes for Whistleblower Protection Program*, <https://www.osha.gov/OshDoc/Directive_pdf/CPL_02-03-006.pdf> (last accessed Mar. 19, 2017)]

§ 40.02 GRIEVANCES AND DISCIPLINE

[A] "Progressive Discipline"

The typical CBA for a unionized company spells out a system of "progressive discipline" under which employees whose work performance is unsatisfactory will be warned, offered guidance and training, and given a series of escalating penalties before being fired. Progressive discipline is sometimes used in nonunionized environment, although less frequently.

The system must make it clear to employees what the employer's expectations are and what the employer intends to do if the rules are violated. Once employees have been told what they are doing wrong, they should be given a reasonable amount of time to correct it. There should be a monitoring process to sort out the employees who have made adequate progress from those who have not. The time period should probably be between 30 and 90 days: Too long a period may make the arbitrator believe that the employer is stringing together isolated, unrelated incidents to make a case.

Employees who have been subject to discipline are likely to feel that they were unfairly singled out—and in some cases, this will result in discrimination or wrongful termination charges. An important HR function is creating a legally sustainable system of progressive discipline, and making sure that supervisors understand the system and apply it objectively.

A legally sustainable disciplinary system should be:

- Consistent—not only must discrimination be avoided but employees should not be subjected to supervisors' whims or penalized when the supervisor has a bad day;

- Well documented—an arbitrator or court should be able to see that each step reflects the employer's own rules;

- Clear—employees should know that if they fail to meet X goals in Y days, they will be put on probation, lose wages, or be terminated;

- Appropriate—the degree of the sanction should reflect the severity of the error or misconduct;

- Reciprocal—employees should get a chance to give their side of the story to an objective decision maker who isn't already committed to management's viewpoint.

Arbitrators will examine the "step formula" under the system and see if it was followed. For example, if the first step results in a determination that the employee was at fault, then he or she might be verbally admonished, whereas by the fourth step, dismissal could be appropriate. If the step formula is not followed, the arbitrator is likely to reverse the decision or substitute a lesser penalty, and there's a good chance that the courts will uphold the arbitrator.

Presenting grievances to the employer is one of the clearest cases of concerted activity protected by the NLRA, whether or not the employees are unionized. However, they must in fact act in concert, or one employee must present a shared grievance. One person pressing his or her own agenda is not protected under the National Labor Relations Act (NLRA). For NLRA purposes, a grievance must be something that relates directly to the terms and conditions of employment.

Once they have made a complaint, employees are required to return to work within a reasonable time. In fact, one of the bywords of labor arbitration is "obey now, grieve later."

[B] Grievance Records

It makes sense to buy or design standard forms for keeping track of employee grievances, although there is no specific federal requirement for making such records or keeping them for a particular length of time. The grievance form should contain:

- Identification of the CBA that creates the grievance procedure and the specific clause of that contract that has to be interpreted;

- Date the grievance was submitted;

- Grievance case number;

- Name, department, shift, and job title of the employee who submits the grievance;

- What the employee says is wrong;

- Records of statements by witnesses;

- Documentary evidence relevant to the grievance;

- Whether the employee was represented (e.g., by the shop steward or a fellow employee);

- Written decisions by the first-level supervisor or others involved in processing the grievance;

- A signed statement by the union representative as to whether the union considers the grievance to be adequately resolved;

- Signatures of the employee and all decision makers.

It can be very helpful to analyze past grievances to see how patterns change over time.

[C] NLRB Deference

Although the National labor Relations Board (NLRB) has the power, under the NLRA § 10(a), to prevent unfair labor practices, the NLRB will defer to grievance arbitration (i.e., will not interfere) if several criteria are satisfied. The dispute must have arisen during an ongoing collective bargaining relationship; interpreting the CBA is central to resolving the dispute; the employees do not claim that the employer deprived them of all their rights under labor law; and the arbitration clause is broad enough to cover the existing dispute.

Once the arbitrator issues a decision, the question is whether it can be enforced. In 1955, the NLRB's *Spielberg* ruling said that NLRB defers to arbitrators' decisions when proceedings appear to have been fair and regular; parties agreed to be bound; and decision wasn't clearly repugnant to the NLRB's purposes and policies. But at the end of 2014, the NLRB changed its policy toward deferral, saying that it would only defer on an NLRA § 8(a)(1) or (3) issue if the party seeking deferral (which is usually the employer) can prove the arbitrator was explicitly authorized to decide the Unfair Labor Practice (ULP) issue; the arbitrator was presented with the statutory issue, and considered it; and the award is reasonably permitted by labor law. [Matthew D. Austin, *National Labor Relations Board and Deferral: The Law Has Changed, Have You Kept Up?*, Roetzel & Andress (Mar. 19, 2015), available at Lexology.com]

§ 40.03 MEDIATION

A mediator is a neutral third party who listens to both sides and helps the parties themselves work out a solution that is acceptable to both of them.

The American Arbitration Association has a set of uniform Employment Mediation Rules. Parties can trigger this procedure by writing a request to the American Arbitration Association (AAA) for mediation, or by filing a Submission to Mediation form, also with the AAA.

One reason that the procedure for filing discrimination charges is so elaborate is that part of the EEOC's job is to attempt mediation of the charge. [See Chapter 41]

The District Court for the Southern District of New York has had a program to mediate employment discrimination cases since 2011. As of October 3, 2016, the wage and hour cases assigned to certain Southern District of New York judges will go directly to mediation under a pilot program for the (Fair Labor Standards Act) FLSA mediation. If the parties reach a settlement, they must draft a joint statement explaining the settlement, why it is fair and reasonable, The district judge assigned to the case has to approve the mediation settlement, because the Second Circuit's position is that all private FLSA settlements must be approved by the district court or the DOL. [Cindy Schmitt Minniti, *New York Federal Court Pilots Mandatory Mediation Program for FLSA Cases*, Reed Smith LLP (Oct. 17, 2016), available at Lexology.com. The approval requirement comes from *Cheeks v. Freeport Pancake House*, 796 F.3d 199 (2d Cir. 2015).]

§ 40.04   ARBITRATION VS. LITIGATION

Opponents of mandatory arbitration state that the process is pro-employer, not only because it restricts discovery and limits the remedies available to a successful plaintiff, but also because there is a risk that arbitrators will (consciously or unconsciously) favor employers. Employers are much more likely to need to choose arbitrators in the future than employees, who typically are involved in only one case.

Many cases have arisen in the court system because one party wants to litigate a dispute and the other says that arbitration is required. Complex and ever-evolving technical legal principles are involved in determining not only if a dispute must be arbitrated, but which questions are to be resolved by courts and which by arbitrators. The Supreme Court has weighed in on this question many times.

In a 2010 case, about a race discrimination and retaliation suit brought by a one-time account manager, the employer pointed to an employment agreement imposing mandatory arbitration. The plaintiff, Jackson, said that the agreement was unconscionable under state law and, therefore, unenforceable. The arbitration agreement gave the arbitrator sole authority to resolve disputes about the interpretation, applicability, enforceability, or formation of the agreement. The Supreme Court ruled that when the arbitration agreement includes a "delegation clause" that gives the arbitrator the power to resolve disputes about the agreement, then it is up to the arbitrator, not the court system, to decide the unconscionability of the entire agreement. In this case, however, the Supreme Court said that Jackson used a mistaken strategy. He challenged the validity of the agreement as a whole, and did not challenge the validity of the delegation clause until his case had reached the Supreme Court, by which time it was too late to raise a new argument. [*Rent-a-Center West v. Jackson*, 561 U.S. 63 (2010)]

Another 2010 case, about whether a strike violated the CBA's no-strike clause and was therefore unlawful, required determining when the CBA took effect. The Supreme Court said that determining if the CBA had been officially ratified was up to the district court, not the arbitrator. The parties agreed to arbitrate that type of dispute—including resolving any issues about the validity of the arbitration clause. Because the federal system favors arbitration, there is a presumption of arbitrability—but it applies only if there is a valid arbitration agreement and a question about whether the agreement covers the actual dispute between the parties. The Supreme Court said that in that situation, the court should order arbitration only if the presumption of arbitrability has not been rebutted by the party seeking to litigate the dispute. [*Granite Rock Co. v. Int'l Bhd. of Teamsters*, 561 U.S. 287 (2010)]

Although it is not an employment decision (it involves consumers who wanted to bring a class arbitration about sales tax charged on "free" cell phones), the 2011 Supreme Court decision in *AT&T Mobility LLC v. Concepcion*, 563 U.S. 333 (2011) has often been interpreted to mean that the federal policy in favor of arbitration is so strong that state rulings that arbitration agreements are unconscionable will be preempted.

After *Concepcion*, Nordstrom revised its employee handbook to state that most arbitration class actions were forbidden. When an employee nevertheless filed a class action alleging violation of a number of federal and state employment laws, the Ninth Circuit held that the revision constituted a valid arbitration agreement, and remanded to the district court to order individual arbitration. [*Davis v. Nordstrom, Inc.*, 755 F.3d 1089 (9th Cir. 2014)]

In a late 2012 summary ruling, the Supreme Court held that the Oklahoma Supreme Court was wrong to hold that the noncompete provisions in two employment contracts were void for violating the state's public policy against noncompete clauses. The Supreme Court said that the decision should have been made by the arbitrator. The employment contracts included an arbitration clause covering "any dispute, difference or unresolved question." The two plaintiffs quit their jobs and went to work for a competitor. Their former employer Nitro-Lift demanded arbitration. The plaintiffs sued in Oklahoma state court to enjoin enforcement of the noncompete clauses, which they alleged were null and void. The trial court ordered arbitration, but the Oklahoma Supreme Court asked the parties to show why the state law limiting enforceability of noncompete agreements should not apply. The Supreme Court held that federal substantive law under the FAA applies in both state and federal courts. If an arbitration clause is severable, then its validity is determined by the court system. But attacks on the validity of the contract, not just the validity of the arbitration clause, are resolved by an arbitrator. If the arbitration clause is valid, the validity of the rest of the contract is decided by the arbitrator. [*Nitro-Lift Techs., LLC v. Howard*, 133 S. Ct. 500 (2012)]

Many arbitration clauses include a requirement that grievances be arbitrated individually, even if multiple employees make similar claims and want to bring a class or collective action. The NLRB's position is that these "class action waivers" are unlawful, because filing a class or collective action about wages, hours, or working conditions is protected concerted activity, whether it occurs in court or before an arbitrator. The NLRB has maintained this position in a series of rulings, but the courts disagree, and will enforce class action waivers. [*D.R. Horton Inc. and Michael Cuda*, Case No. 12-CA-25764 (N.L.R.B. Jan. 3, 2012)]

In 2013, the Fifth Circuit held that the NLRB was wrong: it is permissible for an employer to impose a class action arbitration waiver; it is not inconsistent with the employees' legal right under the NLRA to pursue collective action. But the Fifth Circuit held that the arbitration agreement must clarify that employees do not waive the right to file NLRB complaints. [*D.R.Horton v. NLRB*, 737 F.3d 344 (5th Cir. 2013), *reh'g denied* No. 12-60031 (Apr. 16, 2014).] The NLRB's *Murphy Oil* decision rejects holdings in the Second, Fifth, and Eighth Circuits and continues to take the position that class action waivers are invalid because they impair protected collective activity. [Daniel J. McCoy and Saundra L. M. Riley, *Amidst Widespread Scrutiny, NLRB Reaffirms D.R. Horton and Invalidates Arbitral Collective Action Waivers*, Fenwick & West LLP (Nov. 25, 2014), available at Lexology.com; once again, the Fifth Circuit held that the NLRB was wrong, and class and collective action waivers are lawful: *Murphy Oil v. NLRB*, 808 F.3d 1013 (5th Cir. 2015).

The Fifth Circuit reaffirmed its position in mid-2016, although in an unpublished case: *Citi Trends, Inc. v. NLRB*, No. 15-60913, 2016 WL 4245458 (5th Cir. Aug. 10, 2016); see Barry Leigh Weissman, *Fifth Circuit Follows D.R. Horton and Murphy Oil Precedent, Ruling That an Arbitration Agreement Prohibiting Employee Class or Collective Actions Is Permissible*, Carlton Fields (Sept. 6, 2016), available at Lexology.com]

A Second Circuit non-precedential summary order from mid-2016 merely maintains the status quo, saying that, until the Second Circuit's *Sutherland* is overruled, class action arbitration waivers do not violate the NLRA. [*Patterson v. Raymour's Furniture Co.*, 659 Fed. Appx. 40 (2d Cir. 2016); see Brian J. Stair, *Second Circuit Reluctantly Maintains Status Quo on Class Waiver Provisions, But Hints at Future Change in Law*, Husch Blackwell LLP (Sept. 12, 2016), available at Lexology.com. The *Sutherland* case is *Sutherland v. Ernst & Young*, 726 F.3d 290 (2d Cir. 2013).]

The circuit split widened in 2016. The Eighth Circuit held that the NLRB was wrong: it was lawful for an employer to maintain and enforce an arbitration agreement that forbade employees to bring class or collective actions. The Eighth

Circuit made this ruling even though it agreed with the NLRB that the provision could make employees think that they would not be allowed to file Unfair Labor Practices charges with the NLRB. [*Cellular Sales of Missouri LLC v. NLRB*, 824 F.3d 772 (8th Cir. 2016); see Howard M. Bloom and Philip B. Rosen, *Eighth Circuit Finds Class and Collective Action Waivers Lawful Under NLRA, Contrary to Seventh Circuit*, Jackson Lewis PC (June 3, 2016), available at Lexology.com]

However, this decision was issued shortly after a Seventh Circuit decision, and shortly before a Ninth Circuit decision, both of which accepted the NLRB's theory that class and collective action waivers violate the NLRA by preventing employees from exercising their rights to protected collective activity. [*Lewis v. Epic Sys.*, 823 F.3d 1147 (7th Cir. 2016); see Jessica Silver-Greenberg and Noam Scheiber, *Court Rules Companies Cannot Impose Illegal Arbitration Clauses*, NYTimes.com (May 27, 2016); *Morris v. Ernst & Young*, 834 F.3d 975 (9th Cir. 2016); see Lonnie Giamela, Christopher C. Hoffman and Richard R. Meneghello, *Mandatory Class Waivers Struck Down by 9th Circuit*, Fisher Phillips (Aug. 22, 2016), available at Lexology.com; Lonnie Giamela et. al., *Mandatory Class Waivers Struck Down By 9th Circuit*, Fisher Phillips (Aug. 22, 2016), available at Lexology.com]

On January 13, 2017, the Supreme Court granted certiorari in a consolidated case, No. 16-285, including *Lewis, Ernst & Young,* and *Murphy Oil*. At the time certiorari was granted, a final decision was expected by June 2017. However, just a few weeks after the grant of certiorari, on February 8, 2017, the Supreme Court announced that the case would be scheduled for oral argument in the 2017–2018 term that begins in October 2017. Therefore, three would be no decision until late 2017 or perhaps 2018. [Richard R. Meneghello, *Good Things Come to Those Who Wait? Supreme Court Delays Class Waiver Decision Until Next Term*, Fisher Phillips (Feb. 8, 2017), available at Lexology.com]

Subsequently, the Sixth Circuit joined the group of jurisdictions holding that class action waivers in mandatory arbitration programs violate NLRA § 7. [*NLRB v. Alternative Entm't,* No. 16-1385, 2017 WL 2297620 (6th Cir. May 26, 2017); see David Pryzbylski, *A Growing Divide: Sixth Circuit Decision to Invalidate Class/Collective Action Waiver Widens Appellate Court Split,* Barnes & Thornburg LLP (May 31, 2017), available at Lexology.com]

The federal statute UETA (the Uniform Electronic Transactions Act) says that an electronic signature is attributable to a person if the "signature" was that person's act. In a California Court of Appeal case, the plaintiff said that he never saw the arbitration clause and would not have signed it immediately. The Court of Appeal held that the electronic signature was the plaintiff's act because the employer proved that he carried out the steps for signing the agreement. The employee was sent an e-mail linked to a home page. Accessing the page requires a private, unique user name and password. The employee has to create a new password on logging on and the new password is required to access the document. The employee is prompted to type in his or her name after clicking an "I Accept" box. This data is stored electronically with the date, time, and IP address of the signature. [*Espejo v. Southern California Permanente Med. Grp.*, 246 Cal. App. 4th 1047, 201 Cal. Rptr. 3d 318 (Apr. 22, 2016); see Alexandra Aurisch, *Employee's Electronic Signature on Arbitration Agreement Is Authentic*, Wilson Elser (June 6, 2016), available at Lexology.com]

§ 40.05 LABOR ARBITRATION

[A] Grievance Arbitration and Contract or Interest Arbitration

Arbitration and mediation have a long history as means to settle disputes between labor and management without a strike and without litigation. By agreeing to arbitrate an issue, in effect the union agrees not to strike over that issue. The employer agrees not to take unilateral action.

The two main types of labor arbitration are grievance arbitration (also known as rights arbitration), used when there is a disagreement about interpretation of an existing contract, and contract or interest arbitration, invoked when the parties are not sure which provisions should be included in a new, renewed, or reopened CBA. However, this promotes a somewhat different mind-set from the type of arbitration discussed later in this chapter, where the focus is not on avoiding a strike dealing with an entire bargaining unit, but a court case involving one person's discrimination charge.

Nearly all collective bargaining agreements allow for an in-house grievance procedure, but if that does not resolve the problem, then final, binding arbitration, resulting in a decree that can be enforced by the court system, is the last part of the procedure.

Organizations such as the AAA and the Federal Mediation and Conciliation Service (FMCS) maintain lists of qualified arbitrators, who are familiar both with the conditions in a particular industry and with arbitration rules and practices. If there will be only one arbitrator, then both sides will have to agree on an acceptable arbitrator. If there are three arbitrators, usually each side selects one arbitrator, and the two arbitrators select the third.

As a preliminary step, the employer and union try to agree on a statement of the issues involved in the grievance. If they cannot even agree on that, the arbitrator may have to draft the statement.

> ■ **TIP:** If the employer wants to discharge or discipline an employee, it will proceed first in arbitration; in other matters, the union usually proceeds first.

[B] Arbitrability

If it is not clear whether a company has agreed to submit a particular issue to arbitration, then the issue is arbitrable. This principle comes from "The

Steelworkers' Trilogy," three cases decided by the Supreme Court in 1960. [*Steelworkers v. American Mfg. Co.*, 363 U.S. 564 (1960); *United Steelworkers of Am. v. Warrior Gulf Navigation Co.*, 363 U.S. 574 (1960); *United Steelworkers of Am. v. Enter. Wheel & Car Corp.*, 363 U.S. 593 (1960)] If a CBA contains both an arbitration clause and a no-strike clause, any dispute that involves the application and interpretation of the CBA is arbitrable unless arbitration is specifically ruled out by the terms of the contract.

Under the Steelworkers' Trilogy, the language of the CBA is the first thing the arbitrators consult, but this is not the only factor in the analysis. The "law of the shop" (practices that have evolved in that particular operation) can be considered. Factors such as the effect of the arbitrator's decision on productivity, morale, and workplace tensions are also legitimate considerations. Courts can't review the merits of an arbitration decision or whether a different resolution would have been more sensible. All the court can do is decide whether the arbitration award "draws its essence" from the arbitration agreement.

However, because of a later Supreme Court case [*First Options of Chicago, Inc. v. Kaplan*, 514 U.S. 938 (1995)], the court system rather than the arbitrator decides whether a party agreed to arbitrate a particular type of dispute, if there is no clear, unmistakable evidence of the parties' intentions. There is no right to re-arbitrate an issue already considered by the NLRB in an unfair labor practice proceeding.

When Cooper Tire & Rubber signed a CBA, it also signed a side letter limiting its contributions to retiree health benefits. When a dispute arose about one of the terms of the side letter, the union went to federal court to compel arbitration of the retiree's grievance about the benefits. Management's position was that the side letter covering retiree health benefits did not have an arbitration clause. The Sixth Circuit analyzed the case using a "scope" test: that is, unless the parties agreed to the contrary, disputes about a side agreement are arbitrable if the subject matter of the side agreement falls within the scope of the arbitration clause in the CBA. Therefore, the union had standing to arbitrate on behalf of retirees and their survivors. However, the Sixth Circuit vacated the order certifying a class action, because the district court should have required the union to get the consent of the class members to being represented by the union. [*United Steelworkers of Am. v. Cooper Tire & Rubber Co.*, 474 F.3d 271 (6th Cir. 2007)]

The "scope" test is also used in the Third, Seventh, and Ninth Circuits. Other courts have used different formulas: in the Second, Fourth, and Eighth Circuits, if the side agreement deals with matters that are not similar to the subject matter of the CBA, then the side agreement is merely collateral to the CBA and is not covered by its arbitration clause. But if the subject matter of the side agreement is integral to the CBA, then side-agreement disputes are arbitrable. [See, e.g., *United Steelworkers v. The Duluth Clinic, Ltd.*, 413 F.3d 786, 788 (8th Cir. 2005)]

[C] Potentially Arbitrable Issues

Many issues have been found potentially arbitrable. In fact, because collective bargaining and arbitration are complementary processes, the list is similar to the list of issues that are mandatory bargaining subjects. Arbitrable issues include sale of a business, relocation of its operations, contracting out bargaining unit work, discharging an employee, layoffs and post-layoff recalls, assignments of supervisors to bargaining unit work, and the scheduling and classification of work. Compensation and benefits, seniority systems, and no-strike clauses are also suitable subjects for arbitration.

[D] The Process of Labor Arbitration

In most instances, when management and union hit a deadlock over a grievance or dispute, resort to arbitration will be automatic. However, depending on needs and comparative bargaining power, the arbitration clause might be drafted to allow only the union to invoke arbitration. Employees might also be given the right to invoke arbitration in situations where the union declines to press an employee grievance.

> ■ **TIP:** Even if the CBA does not include a formal arbitration clause, management and union can sign a "submission agreement" agreeing to be bound by the arbitration decision on a one-time basis.

Arbitration clauses usually call for the involvement of either the Federal FMCS or the AAA. However, the parties can agree on other ways to resolve disputes if they so choose.

Arbitration begins with a "demand": Either side invokes the CBA arbitration clause and notifies the appropriate agency. The FMCS can be called in by either management or union to assist in the negotiating process. The FMCS can also offer its services, but cannot demand to be made part of the process. FMCS will not mediate a dispute that has only minor effect on interstate commerce if there are other conciliation services (e.g., state agencies) available. The FMCS can also refuse to intervene on behalf of parties who have a record of noncooperation with arbitration, including failure to pay arbitration fees.

Once an arbitration award is rendered, it is usually final, binding, and not subject to judicial review by any court. In other words, agreeing to submit to arbitration is a very significant decision that cannot be undertaken casually. It will probably be impossible to get any kind of review or have the decision set aside. However, a serious irregularity in the process, such as proof that the arbitrator was not impartial, may justify setting aside the award.

The mission of the Federal Mediation and Conciliation Service (FMCS) is to assist in contract negotiation disputes between employers and their unionized employees. The FMCS also assists in mediation of discrimination cases and grievances before they reach the arbitration stage. Parties can request an arbitrator online, at <http://www.fmcs.gov> or can download request forms from the site and then fax them or mail them to the FMCS. [The FMCS' FAQ is at <http://www.fmcs.gov/internet/faq.asp?categoryid=336> (last viewed Mar. 17, 2017)].

[E] Case Law on Labor Arbitration

In late 2000, the Supreme Court decided that, in a unionized workplace, an arbitrator's decision is enforceable by the court system as long as the arbitration award draws its essence from the Collective Bargaining Agreement (CBA). So, unless the arbitrator's decision actually violates a statute or regulation, it must be enforced—even if it violates public policy. [*E. Associated Coal Corp. v. UMW*, 531 U.S. 57 (2000)]

Arbitration awards are quite hard to overturn. For example, a court cannot overturn an award merely because it believes the arbitrator made the wrong decision, or misinterpreted the facts of the case. One of the rare cases in which an award was overturned involved a new zero-tolerance drug policy adopted by an oil refining company for all its facilities nationwide. The policy was challenged by the union, which claimed that it was impermissible to adopt such a policy unilaterally, without bargaining. One arbitrator upheld the policy. The other arbitrator upheld most of the policy, but disapproved of the potential for firing employees immediately, without a chance for rehabilitation. The employer sought to have the district court vacate the award, but the district court upheld. The Third Circuit reversed the district court, finding that the arbitrator exceeded his discretion by attempting to substitute his own discretion in an area of legitimate management prerogative. The Third Circuit held that the award did not draw its essence from the collective bargaining agreement. [*Citgo Asphalt Refining Co. v. Paper, Allied-Industrial Chem., & Energy Workers Int'l Union Local No. 2-991*, 385 F.3d 809 (3d Cir. 2004)]

[F] Just Cause

One of the distinctive features of a collective bargaining agreement is that it means that employees no longer work at the will of the employer. Therefore, they cannot be discharged, or even subjected to lesser forms of discipline, without just cause. So the arbitrator's task becomes to determine whether the employer did, indeed, act with just cause. The arbitrator must determine if the employee really did whatever the employer claims he or she did; whether the employer offered the employee due process before imposing discipline; and whether the discipline was reasonable and not out of proportion to the offense. Usually, arbitrators divide offenses into very serious offenses such as assaulting someone at work, stealing, or creating a safety hazard (which will justify dismissal) and less serious rules, which are appropriate for progressive discipline such as admonition, notations in the permanent record, or suspension with or without pay.

Despite the explicit public policy against workplace drug use, the Connecticut Supreme Court held in mid-2016 that termination is not mandatory for a public employee caught smoking marijuana during working hours. The plaintiff worked at the University of Connecticut Health Center. Campus cops saw him smoking marijuana and seized two bags of marijuana. He was arrested but criminal charges were dismissed. The union representing the employee took the case to arbitration. The arbitrator ruled that termination was excessive and was not required by the facility's drug-free workplace policy. The arbitrator found it to be a mitigating factor that the employee used marijuana as therapy for anxiety and depression. The state supreme court held that, by requiring arbitration, the employer agreed to accept the arbitrator's decision. The award did not violate public policy because the court said that public policy does not require termination in every case, and the employee's conduct, although inappropriate, did not endanger public safety. [*State of Conn. v. Conn. Employees Union Indep.*, No. 19590 (Conn. Aug. 30, 2016); see Kelly M. Cardin and Marc L. Zaken, *Connecticut's Highest Court Reinstates State Employee Fired for Smoking Marijuana at Work,* Ogletree Deakins (Aug. 29, 2016), available at Lexology.com]

[G] Contract Interpretation

When arbitrators interpret a contract, their job is to find out what the parties meant. If the language of the contract is plain, clear, and unambiguous, the arbitrator has to follow it—even if the arbitrator doesn't think that the contract as written is very sensible or fair. In fact, if the arbitrator doesn't follow this "plain meaning rule," a court is likely to decide that the arbitrator's award is invalid and not entitled to be enforced by the court system.

In fact, if a contract (any kind of contract, not just a CBA) is supposed to represent the whole agreement between the parties, a legal principle called the "parol evidence rule" says that evidence of anything said or written before or during the negotiations cannot be introduced to contradict the written contract or vary its terms. ("Parol" is an archaic term for "word" or "speech.") However, parol evidence can be used to explain terms that are unclear or ambiguous.

§ 40.06 ARBITRATION OF EMPLOYMENT DISCRIMINATION CLAIMS

[A] Employer-Imposed Clauses

The reputation of arbitration has had its ups and downs. A Supreme Court case, *Alexander v. Gardner-Denver* [415 U.S. 36 (1974)] allowed an employee to litigate after pursuing arbitration remedies, on the grounds that the arbitration provision in the plaintiff's CBA did not offer enough protection for statutory claims—i.e., claims that arise under Title VII, the Americans With Disabilities Act, or other antidiscrimination law.

In 1991, however, the Supreme Court took a different tack. The important case of *Gilmer v. Interstate/Johnson Lane Corp.* [500 U.S. 20 (1991)] allowed an employer to impose mandatory arbitration (under the U-4 securities industry employment agreement) for Age Discrimination in Employment Act (ADEA) claims. The Supreme Court said that it wasn't really contradicting the earlier *Gardner-Denver* decision, because that involved a union contract that the plaintiff was subject to along with all the other union members, whereas Gilmer signed the U-4 agreement as an individual.

Under *Gilmer*, an arbitration clause can be valid as long as the process provides a written award rendered by a neutral arbitrator, and as long as discovery and adequate remedies are available under the arbitration process.

In April 2009, the Supreme Court extended its line of pro-arbitration decisions by holding that an arbitration clause in a CBA prevented employees from litigating ADEA claims when building service employees were re-assigned to lower-paid jobs as porters and cleaners. The union withdrew age discrimination charges because it had consented to the new contract under which the reassignments were made. The individual workers affected by the reassignments filed ADEA charges with the Equal Employment Opportunity Commission (EEOC), and received right to sue letters. The Second Circuit refused to compel arbitration, taking the position that a CBA provision cannot be enforced if it prevents ADEA suits. The Supreme Court reversed, finding that federal law favors arbitration, mandating enforcement of a CBA provision that clearly and unmistakably obligates union members to arbitrate claims. In the Supreme Court view, the ADEA does not contradict the general federal policy of supporting arbitration. [*14 Penn Plaza LLC v. Pyett*, 556 U.S. 247 (2009)]

The *Gilmer* case was the "opening bell" for recognition of employers' right to impose predispute arbitration requirements: That is, employees would be covered by employment agreements, job handbooks, or other means of ensuring that they would have to arbitrate discrimination claims instead of litigating them.

In another case where the employer permitted employees to opt out of the arbitration requirement, a plaintiff who did not opt out filed a class action charging failure to pay required overtime. The plaintiff said that it was an Unfair Labor Practice to offer employees a benefit to persuade them to avoid engaging in protected concerted activity (i.e., suing the employer in a class action). The Ninth Circuit rejected this creative argument, holding that the plaintiff was unable to prove that arbitration gave employees an immediate benefit. [*Johnmohammadi v. Bloomingdales, Inc.*, 755 F.3d 1072 (9th Cir. 2014)]

The Eighth Circuit ruled in mid-2016 that an employer's inconsistent conduct cost it the right to compel arbitration. Plaintiff Messina had a two-year employment contract and a separate arbitration agreement. He was fired after six months. He sued for wrongful termination in Minnesota state court; the case was removed to federal court. The defendant asserted 24 affirmative defenses and recommended mediation, but did not mention arbitration. Several months later, the employer asked the plaintiff's lawyer to stipulate for arbitration but the plaintiff refused. Another month later, the defendant moved to compel arbitration. The Eighth Circuit held that the employer waived the right to demand arbitration by its inconsistent conduct that prejudiced the plaintiff. [*Messina v. North Central Distributing, Inc.*, 821 F.3d 1047 (8th Cir. May 10, 2016); see FindLaw Eighth Circuit blog, *8th Circuit Clarifies When a Party Loses Arbitration Rights* (May 18, 2016), available at FindLaw.com; Barry Leigh Weissman, *Eighth Circuit: Delay in Asserting Right to Arbitrate and Using Litigation Machinery Results in Waiver*, Carlton Fields (May 23, 2016), available at Lexology.com]

The Civil Rights Act of 1991 and the Americans with Disabilities Act (ADA) both include language favoring arbitration and other forms of Alternative Dispute Resolution (ADR) as means of handling discrimination charges. For the ADA provision, see 42 U.S.C. § 12212: Wherever it is lawful and appropriate, ADR (including settlement negotiations, conciliation, facilitation, mediation, fact-finding, mini-trials, and arbitration) is "encouraged" when ADA charges are asserted. Similarly, in 2004 the Fifth Circuit ruled that there is no reason why arbitration of Fair Labor Standards Act claims cannot be compelled. [*Carter v. Countrywide Credit Indus., Inc.*, 362 F.3d 294 (5th Cir. 2004)] The Fifth Circuit agreed with the District Court that the contract provision requiring the employer and employee to split the costs of arbitration was invalid—but also agreed with the District Court that the proper remedy was to sever this invalid provision and enforce the rest of the agreement.

The two main ADR methods are arbitration (a trusted person or panel renders a decision) and mediation (a trusted person helps the parties reach a mutually acceptable decision).

> ■ **TIP:** If an employer offers to arbitrate, and the employee refuses, this could be treated as evidence of the employer's good faith—preventing the employee from collecting damages for breach of the covenant of good faith and fair dealing.

A "Woolley disclaimer" states that an employee manual is not a contract. The District Court for the District of New Jersey refused to enforce an arbitration clause because it was included in a manual with the Woolley disclaimer. The court said that the arbitration clause was unenforceable because the non-contract status of the manual meant that the employer could unilaterally modify the provision without notice to employees. [*Raymours Furniture Co., Inc. v. Rossi*, No. 13-4440, 2014 U.S. Dist. LEXIS 1006 (D. N.J. Jan. 2, 2014)]

Where the handbook included a disclaimer that it was not binding and did not create an employment contract, the Fourth Circuit found the handbook's arbitration provision was not enforceable and did not prevent an employee from bringing a collective action in federal court. [*Lorenzo v. Prime Commc'ns, LP*, 806 F.3d 777 (4th Cir. 2015)]

However, the Ninth Circuit applied the FAA to compel arbitration of a dispute resolution policy in the company policy manual, which was separate from the employee's signed acknowledgment of receiving the manual. The Ninth Circuit held that the employee knowingly waived the right to bring Title VII claims in court. [*Ashbey v. Archstone Property Mgmt., Inc.*, 785 F.3d 1320 (9th Cir, 2015)]

In mid-2015, the Second Circuit said that an at-will employee was required to arbitrate claims because continued employment after the handbook was amended to adopt the mandatory arbitration requirement constituted acceptance of the new terms. In addition, the plaintiff electronically accepted the modified handbook several times after it was amended, further demonstrating consent. [*McAllister v. East*, No. 11-4696 (2d Cir. May 5, 2015)]

The First Circuit ruled that a job application was ambiguous as to whether people who applied but were not hired were subject to the arbitration clause. Therefore, the First Circuit refused to mandate arbitration in a case where a job applicant asserted pregnancy discrimination. The court concluded that there was a valid arbitration agreement—but the conditions under which it would come into play (the plaintiff being hired and having a dispute with her employer) never occurred. [*Gove v. Career Sys. Dev. Corp.*, 689 F.3d 1 (1st Cir. 2012)]

Employees challenging arbitration requirements frequently argue that the agreement is unenforceable because of substantive and/or procedural defects that render it unconscionable. Until recent years, there were a number of California cases finding unconscionability—but even in California it is very common for arbitration agreements to be upheld despite unconscionability challenges.

In 2013, The California Supreme Court overturned its 2011 decision (that an employee could not be required to waive his or her right to a "Berman" wage claims hearing before the state Labor Commission). In 2013, the California Supreme Court said that the FAA preempts the state law that forbids such a waiver. However, the case was remanded to determine if the arbitration clause itself was unconscionable; the court said that unconscionable arbitration clauses can be invalidated despite *Concepcion* and *Italian Colors*. [*Sonic-Calabasas A, Inc. v. Moreno*, 57 Cal. 4th 1109 (Cal. 2013)]

A few weeks later, the Ninth Circuit found an arbitration clause unconscionable because job applicants had to agree to arbitration when they applied, but did not get a copy of the arbitration agreement for weeks later; the procedure for selecting arbitrators favored the employer; and employees could not recover their share of arbitration costs if they won the case, making it impractical to pursue many small claims. However, on the same day the Ninth Circuit also decided that claims for public injunctive relief from arbitration are no longer allowed because of *Concepcion*. [*Chavarria v. Ralphs Grocery Store*, 733 F.3d 916 (9th Cir. 2013); *Ferguson v. Corinthian Coll. Inc.*, 733 F.3d 928 (9th Cir. 2013)]

In mid-2014, the California Supreme Court ruled that, although an employee's waiver of the right to arbitrate on a class basis is enforceable, employers cannot require employees to waive the right to bring Private Attorney General Act (PAGA) claims about wage-and-hour claims. [*Iskanian v. CLS Transp. Los Angeles LLC*, 59 Cal. 4th 348 (Cal. 2014)] Certiorari was denied on January 20, 2015. [135 S. Ct. 1155 (2015)] As a result, employees can continue to bring PAGA suits and an arbitration agreement that prevents employees from bringing such suits is unenforceable, even though employers can lawfully forbid class arbitration.

A February 2017 case involved a PAGA claim brought by a class of employees who alleged that they were misclassified as exempt from overtime. The arbitration agreement, which included a severability clause, forbade collective, representative, and class action claims. The district court found the arbitration clause unconscionable and unenforceable, but the Ninth Circuit reversed. In the Ninth Circuit views, the only severable aspects of the clause were the waiver of representative PAGA claims and allowing only the employer, not employees, to seek an injunction or equitable relief in court. Therefore, the case had to be arbitrated. [*Poublon v. C.H. Robinson Co.,* No. 15-55143, 2017 WL 461099 (9th Cir. Feb. 3, 2017): see Liz Kramer, *3 Class Actions, 3 Motions to Compel Arbitration, 1 Class Action Survives,* Stinson Leonard Street LLP (Feb. 10, 2017), available at Lexology.com]

In a case that deals with California law, but is not an employment case, the Supreme Court held at the end of 2015 that the FAA preempts a California statute that forbids class action waivers in arbitration. The contract included a severability clause providing that the waiver would not be enforceable if it violated a state law banning class action waivers. However, the Supreme Court ruled that this savings clause would apply only to a valid state law. The Supreme Court said that the California law was invalidated by *Concepcion.* [*DirecTV v. Imburgia*, 136 S. Ct. 463 (Dec. 14, 2015)]

The Ninth Circuit held that a waiver of representative claims under PAGA cannot be enforced because the FAA did not preempt the *Iskanian* decision. However, the plaintiffs' non-PAGA claims had to be arbitrated rather than litigated. [*Sakkab v. Luxottica Retail N.*, 803 F.3d 425 (9th Cir. 2015). In a similar case, however, the Nevada Supreme Court ruled that *Concepcion* means that class action waivers are enforceable: *Tallman v. Eighth Judicial Dist. Ct. of Nev.*, 359 P.3d 113 (Nev. 2015)]

The District Court for the Central District of California ruled in mid-2014 that, under the FAA and *Concepcion, supra,* state law cannot invalidate waivers of class or representative actions in arbitration agreements. The case was brought by non-exempt employees who argued that California law precluded enforcement of the agreement, because the broad language forbidding joint claims, class and collective actions violated *Gentry* [see *Gentry v. Superior Ct. of L.A. Cnty.*, 42 Cal. 4th 443 (2007)] and their right to bring PAGA suits. The district court held that *Concepcion* overrules *Gentry*, and the FAA's policy of encouraging arbitration preempts state laws that forbid waivers of PAGA collective actions. Because of the federal preemption issue, the district court did not follow *Iskanian*. [*Fardig v. Hobby Lobby Stores*, Inc., SACV 14-00561JVS, 2014 WL 4782618 (C.D. Cal. Aug. 11, 2014)]

A subsequent Executive Order, the Fair Pay and Safe Workplaces Executive Order, issued in July, 2014, forbade federal contractors that had contracts of $1 million or more to require predispute arbitration of Title VII, sexual harassment, or sexual assault cases—but not wage and hour claims. However, this order was struck down in early 2017. [See Michael J. Schrier, *Fair Pay and Safe Workplaces Regulations and Executive Orders Are Rescinded,* Duane Morris LLP (Mar. 28, 2017)]

[B] AAA Arbitration

The American Arbitration Association (AAA) has long been respected for its work in dispute resolution. The AAA's National Rules for the Resolution of Employment Disputes (promulgated in 1993; amended in 1995 to increase due process protection for employees) cover about three million workers.

The due process standards for fair arbitration require that the employer and employee have an equal role in selecting the arbitrator or arbitration panel. Both sides have a right to counsel. The arbitrator can order whatever discovery he or she thinks is necessary. The arbitrator must explain the decision in a written decision. Arbitration remedies must be equal to remedies that could be obtained by litigating. Attorneys' fees will be awarded in the interests of justice, so it is not necessary to be the prevailing party.

> ■ **TIP:** The employer can indicate in employment applications, the employee handbook, and/or employment contracts that employment disputes will be resolved under AAA rules.

Since 1996, AAA arbitrators have had the power to order discovery. Either employers or employees can be ordered to produce documents, answer written lists of questions, or appear and answer questions posed by an attorney. Under the 1996 rules, any party can be represented by an attorney. The arbitrator has a duty to make a decision and render a written award within 30 days of the end of the hearing. The arbitrator has the power to render whatever award he or she thinks is just, including ordering one side to pay the attorneys' fees and costs of the other side.

The arbitrator gets paid a fee for working on the case, and the AAA itself is entitled to an administration fee. The AAA fee depends on the size of the claim or counterclaim, determined at the time it is filed, not by any later amendments.

The AAA's general policy is that it will administer arbitration even if the employer unilaterally imposed the arbitration requirement as a condition of employment. However, the organization reserves the right to refuse to enforce unfair arbitration policies—policies that fail to provide basic due process protection to employees.

In late 2014, California passed AB 802, which requires AAA, JAMS, and other major arbitration providers to publish on their websites, at least quarterly, details on arbitrations handled, including the name of the employer, the employee's annual wage, the amount of the claim, who won, the size of the award, who the arbitrator was and what fees the arbitrator received, and the total number of times the employer has been involved in arbitration or mediation with the same provider. [Robin E. Largent, *California Enacts New Laws Attacking Arbitration and Arbitration Agreements*, Carothers DiSante & Freudenberger LLP (Oct. 1, 2014), available at Lexology.com]

The Fourth Circuit refused to vacate an arbitration award that used the opt-out class certification rules under the AAA Supplementary Rules for Class Arbitration, and not the Fair Labor Standards Act opt-in class certification rules. (The case was brought by three former managers charging that the ex-employer violated the Fair Labor Standards Act (FLSA) by failing to pay overtime.) The AAA Class Rules permit the arbitrator to decide if a case should proceed as a class. The Fourth Circuit ruled that the arbitrator rendered a reasoned award, and the arbitration agreement gave the arbitrator the power to render any relief that a court could provide. [*Long John Silver's Rests. v. Cole*, 514 F.3d 345 (4th Cir. 2008)]

[C] Securities Industry Arbitration

Workers in the securities industry have to sign a standard employment agreement called the U-4 as a condition of working in the industry. It was the only industry to have a uniform mandatory arbitration requirement, so it served as a kind of "test bed" for studying legal issues about arbitration.

As of August 7, 1997, the National Association of Securities Dealers (NASD) voted to eliminate mandatory arbitration of employment discrimination claims brought by registered brokers under federal and state antidiscrimination statutes.

The New York Court of Appeals ruled in early 2007 that a securities industry employer cannot be sued for defamation in connection with the contents of a NASD U-5 statement (reasons for termination of an employee). The forms are as absolutely privileged as ethics complaints against an attorney, because public policy calls for candor. [*Rosenberg v. MetLife*, 8 N.Y.3d 359 (2007)]

The Second Circuit held in early 2016 that FINRA Rule 13200 does not forbid a pre-dispute waiver of arbitration in FINRA, so five former employees were required to arbitrate their claims in a non-FINRA forum. [*Credit Suisse Secs., LLC v. Tracy*, No. 15-0345 (2d Cir. Jan. 28, 2016)]

The Second Circuit also found that FINRA's arbitration rules, including the rule forbidding arbitration of putative or collective class actions, were incorporated into JP Morgan's employment agreement. When former financial advisers sued JP Morgan for violation of the overtime laws, Morgan moved to compel arbitration under the employment contract. However, the Second Circuit held that FINRA forbids arbitration of collective claims. Even though the FINRA rule was amended, the Second Circuit said that referring to FINRA rules in an employment agreement places the employer at risk that the rules might change. [*Lloyd v. JP Morgan Chase*, 791 F.3d 265 (2d Cir. 2015)]

[D] Getting Ready for Arbitration

To be prepared for arbitration, you should:

- Review how the dispute arose, and what has already been done to resolve it;

- Check all relevant work rules and policies and how they were applied, both to the grievant and the other employees;

- Makes copies of all relevant documents for your own file, for the employee, and for the arbitrator;

- Inform the employee of documents in the employee's possession that you want copies of, and that you want copies sent to the arbitrator;

- If necessary, ask the arbitrator to subpoena necessary documents that you have not been able to get by informal means;

- Make sure all the witnesses sound accurate and articulate, but not mechanical or coached;

- Anticipate questions that will be asked during cross-examination, and prepare the witnesses to answer them;

- Make a list of points that you want each witness's testimony to put into the record;

- Review collections of published arbitration decisions, because even though arbitrators don't absolutely have to follow past precedents, they will often be swayed by interpretations that other arbitrators have reached in similar cases.

The first stage in an arbitration hearing is the opening statement. Usually, in a case where the employer's termination or discipline is being challenged, the employer will present its case first, because the employer has to prove the justification for its actions. In other types of cases, the employee usually gives the first opening statement. Next comes the other opening statement, and then the side that goes first introduces the testimony of its witnesses; the other side has the right to cross-examine. Then, the parties sum up their cases, and it is up to the arbitrator to decide.

[E] Appeals

In general, the court system tries to get involved with arbitration as little as possible, although arbitration awards can be enforced by the court system, and sometimes disputes about arbitrability or arbitration process are litigated.

Early in 2004, the Ninth Circuit tackled the question of whether the federal courts can hear appeals of arbitration awards in the employer's favor—in other words, whether an employee can challenge an award of $0. The Ninth Circuit said no: when it comes to deciding whether the amount in controversy is the $75,000 required for diversity jurisdiction (jurisdiction based on the parties being citizens of different states), the amount in controversy is the amount actually awarded in the arbitration proceeding, not the amount that the employee claimed he or she was entitled to. [*Luong v. Circuit City Stores Inc.*, 356 F.3d 1188 (9th Cir. 2004)] Later in the year, however, another panel of the Ninth Circuit allowed a $0 arbitration award to be judicially reviewed if the amount at stake in the underlying dispute satisfies the amount in controversy requirement. [*Theis Research Inc. v. Brown & Bain*, 386 F.3d 1180 (9th Cir. 2004, amended Feb. 18, 2005)]

The Ninth Circuit held in late 2013 that courts have taken two approaches to non-appealability clauses. One way, adopted by the Third, Seventh, and Eleventh Circuits, is to construe a requirement of binding, non-appealable arbitration to rule out federal court review of the merits of the decision—but to allow review on the grounds set out in FAA § 10 for vacating an arbitration award (e.g., fraud or the arbitrator's partiality). The other option is that no appellate review will be permitted at all. The Supreme Court's *Hall Street* decision says that the FAA § 10 criteria for vacating an award are the only criteria that can be used to set aside an award, and parties cannot add more grounds by private contract. The Ninth Circuit interpreted this decision to mean that not only is it impossible to add more grounds for vacating arbitration awards, you cannot eliminate the § 10 grounds either, because the purpose of the FAA is to allow limited judicial review of arbitration awards. [*In re Wal-Mart Wage & Hour Employment Practices Litig.*, 737 F.3d 1262 (9th Cir. 2013)]

The AAA's Optional Appellate Arbitration Rules took effect November 1, 2013. Arbitration awards can be reviewed by a panel of arbitrators (or by a single arbitrator, if this is what the parties request). Appellate arbitrators consider allegations that an award was based on a clearly erroneous factual determination and/or material, prejudicial errors of law. [Katharine H. Parker et al., *AAA Adopts Optional Appellate Arbitration Process*, Proskauer Rose LLP (Nov. 12, 2013), available at Lexology.com]

§ 40.07 MANDATORY PREDISPUTE ARBITRATION CLAUSES

[A] "Predispute" vs. "Postdispute" Clauses

There are many ways to draft an arbitration provision. Predispute arbitration clauses specify in advance that future disputes, if they occur, will be arbitrable. Such a provision can be either voluntary or mandatory. If voluntary, arbitration is just one option available for resolving disputes. If mandatory, the employee is blocked from suing the employer. Postdispute arbitration clauses are an agreement between employer and employee after a claim has been raised, and the best way to handle it is via arbitration.

In 1998, the Supreme Court resolved some difficult issues in *Wright v. Universal Maritime Service Corp.* [525 U.S. 70 (1998)] In this case, an injured stevedore was denied employment because companies that might have employed him considered him permanently disabled. He sued under the ADA without filing a grievance or going through arbitration under the CBA. The district court dismissed his case because he did not exhaust his grievance remedies. The Fourth Circuit upheld the district court.

However, the Supreme Court reversed the Fourth Circuit. The *Gilmer* case permits compulsory arbitration of an ADA claim, but the Supreme Court ruled that a contract claim must be treated differently from a statutory claim. Contract claims are presumed arbitrable, but statutory claims are not. A CBA must be very explicit to prevent litigation of a claim under a civil rights statute. A general arbitration clause that does not list the civil rights statutes that are covered will not prevent litigation under those statutes.

Early in 2002, the Supreme Court returned to the subject of predispute arbitration mandates. The ruling in *EEOC v. Waffle House Inc.* [534 U.S. 279 (2002)] is that the EEOC can pursue employment discrimination litigation (in this case, involving the Americans with Disabilities Act) even if the employees themselves would be required to submit their disputes to arbitration. The decision is very important as an indicator of legal thinking about arbitration, but it will not have much practical effect, because the EEOC doesn't take on many cases a year, and not all of them involve companies with mandatory arbitration requirements.

On September 25, 2016, a California statute was signed, forbidding agreements that force a California-based employee to litigate or arbitrate California-based employment claims in a different state. The statute covers contracts entered into, modified, or extended on or after January 1, 2017. Employees must not be required, as a condition of employment, to adjudicate their claims outside California, and employers cannot deprive employees of the substantive protections of California law with respect to any California dispute. [Susan W. Pangborn et. al, *California Prohibits Employers from Requiring Out-of-State Litigation and Arbitration*, Kilpatrick Townsend & Stockton LLP (Sept. 28, 2016), available at Lexology.com]

Accenture account executive Armand Santoro's employment contract required arbitration of all employment-related disputes, including Title VII and ADEA discrimination claims. Santoro was terminated at age 66, during a cost-cutting campaign, and replaced by a younger man. He brought a suit against his ex-employer under the ADEA, FMLA, and ERISA. Santoro cited the Dodd-Frank Act provision that whistleblowers' right to sue their employers can only be altered by mandatory predispute arbitration requirements if the arbitration clause has an explicit "carve-out" of Dodd-Frank claims. The Fourth Circuit held that this provision is limited to whistleblower claims, and does not prevent enforcement of arbitration clauses in other employment contexts. [*Santoro v. Accenture Fed. Servs.*, 748 F.3d 217 (4th Cir. 2014)]

The Second Circuit affirmed an order compelling arbitration of Title VII and ADA claims. The plaintiff argued that the arbitration clause was invalid because its six-month statute of limitations did not give him a chance to exhaust his administrative remedies. The Second Circuit held that it is not settled law that Title VII and the ADA require exhaustion of administrative remedies before arbitration (although they do before litigation). The Second Circuit also held that the clause could be construed to waive the requirement of exhaustion of remedies and prevent employers from citing it as a defense. Furthermore, that was a threshold issue to be determined by the arbitrator. [*Virk v. Maple-Gate Anesthesiologists, P.C.*, No. 15-513, 2016 WL 3583248 (2d Cir. July 1, 2016); see Joshua S. Wirth, *Second Circuit Rejects Argument That Arbitration Clause Was Void Due to Inability to Vindicate Rights Under Title VII and ADA*, Carlton Fields (July 28, 2016), available at Lexology.com]

In 2016, the Fifth Circuit indicated that it is better to have a separate arbitration agreement than to put the arbitration requirement in the employee handbook. A plaintiff brought a Title VII suit charging race and religious discrimination and association discrimination for being in an interracial relationship. He alleged that he was fired 15 days after reporting harassment. The arbitration agreement in the employee handbook reserved the employer's right to amend the agreement. The Fifth Circuit held that, under Texas law, changes to an arbitration agreement are prospective only, must apply equally to employer and employee claims, and the employee must receive advance notice that a change will be made. Otherwise, the agreement is illusory and unenforceable. In this case, because the arbitration provision took effect immediately, the Fifth Circuit found that the agreement was illusory, and, therefore, the plaintiff could proceed with his federal suit. [*Nelson v. Watch House Int'l LLC*, 815 F.3d 190 (5th Cir. 2016); see Hannah L. Hembree and Donna K. McElroy, *Texas Employers Requiring Mandatory Arbitration Must Review Their Arbitration Agreements Under New Fifth Circuit Opinion*, Dykema Gossett PLLC (Mar. 10, 2016), available at Lexology.com; Lawrence J. McNamara and Allyn Jacque Lowell, *Fifth Circuit Decision May Endanger Many Texas Arbitration Agreements*, Ford & Harrison LLP (Mar. 4, 2016), available at Lexology.com]

The Third Circuit held that, although the Dodd-Frank Act forbids enforcement of predispute arbitration agreements in certain whistleblower cases, none of those cases applied to the plaintiff's retaliation suit. The plaintiff informed his supervisor that a product was priced contrary to the relevant regulations, and recommended changing the price. He said that changing the price would cost the company more than a million dollars, but would save customers $2 million. He was terminated, allegedly for a billing irregularity (the plaintiff denied this accusation). The Third Circuit held that mandatory predispute arbitration is not allowed for the Sarbanes-Oxley whistleblower provision, but this case was brought under the Dodd-Frank whistleblower provision, which is structured differently and does not forbid pre-dispute arbitration requirements. [*Khazin v. TD Ameritrade Holding Corp.*, 773 F.3d 488 (3d Cir. 2014). See also *Murray v. UBS Sec., LLC*, No. 12 Civ. 5914(KPF), *2014 OSHD (CCH) P33,356*, 2014 WL 285093 (S.D.N.Y. Jan. 27, 2014), *appeal denied* 2014 WL 1316472 (Apr. 1, 2014), holding Dodd-Frank Act whistleblower claims to be arbitrable.]

The Fifth, Sixth, Ninth, and Eleventh Circuits have ruled that Uniformed Services Employment and Reemployment Rights Act (USERRA) claims are subject to arbitration. *Garrett v. Circuit City Stores*, 449 F.3d 672 (5th Cir. 2006) holds that USERRA's preemption provision does not show that Congress intended to rule out arbitration, because arbitration does not waive any of the substantive rights protected by USERRA. *Landis v. Pinnacle Eye Care*, 537 F.3d 559 (6th Cir. 2008) uses a similar analysis; its concurring opinion says that Congress did not use the kind of unambiguous language that would be necessary to rule out arbitration. [Howard S. Suskin and Benjamin J. Wimmer, *Arbitrability of USERRA Claims: Battle on the Home Front*, special to law.com (Oct. 15, 2008); *Ziober v. BLB Resources,* No. 14-56374, U.S. App. LEXIS 18516, 2016 WL 5956733 (9th Cir. Oct. 14, 2016); see Kimberlee W. DeWitt, *Ninth Circuit Joins Sister Circuits in Holding That Employees May be Required to Arbitrate USERRA Claims*, Hunton & Williams LLP (Nov. 4, 2016), available at Lexology.com]

The Eleventh Circuit enforced an arbitration clause even though some of its provisions violated USERAA. USERRA's non-waiver provision says that the statute supersedes any contract that reduces, limits, or eliminates USERRA rights. Plaintiff Bodine's employment contract imposed a six-month statute of limitations and allowed the arbitrator to apportion costs and attorneys' fees. There is no statute of limitations under USERRA, and the statute forbids imposing court costs or fees on USERRA plaintiffs. The Eleventh Circuit compelled arbitration after severing the invalid provisions, holding that the FAA allows reformation of arbitration agreements, in this case, to conform to another statute. [*Bodine v. Cook's Pest Control Inc.*,830 F.3d 1320 (11th Cir. 2016); see Robert Scavone Jr. & Juan C. Enjamio, *Eleventh Circuit: Arbitration Agreement Enforceable Despite Terms That Violate USERRA*, Hunton & Williams LLP (Aug. 18, 2016), available at Lexology.com]

[B] Claims Other Than Discrimination

Mandatory predispute arbitration clauses are not limited to use in connection with discrimination claims. Five of the federal Circuit Courts have ruled that arbitration can be a proper way to handle ERISA claims. [*Bird v. Shearson Lehman/American Express*, 926 F.2d 116 (2d Cir. 1991); *Pritzer v. Merrill Lynch*, 7 F.3d 1110 (3d Cir. 1993); *Kramer v. Smith Barney*, 80 F.3d 1080 (5th Cir. 1996); *Amulfo P. Sulit, Inc. v. Dean Witter Reynolds, Inc.*, 847 F.2d 475 (8th Cir. 1988); *Williams v. Imhoff*, 203 F.3d 758 (10th Cir. 2000)]

Some courts are beginning to enforce clauses that forbid ERISA class actions and require individual arbitration of such claims. [E.g., *Tenet Healthsystem Phila., Inc. v. Rooney*, No. 12-mc-58, 2012 U.S. Dist. LEXIS 116280 (E.D. Pa. Aug. 14, 2012); *Luchini v. Carmax, Inc.*, No. CV F 12-0417 LJO DLB, 2012 U.S. Dist. LEXIS 102198 (E.D. Cal. July 23, 2012)] DOL regulations (see 29 C.F.R. § 2560.503-1) impose certain conditions for an arbitration clause to be enforceable: benefit claimants cannot be subjected to arbitration costs, a mandatory arbitration provision must not prevent claimants from exercising their statutory remedies or keep them from going to court to appeal an arbitrator's decision. The new AAA appellate panels, staffed by ex-judges, can be used to assert a claim that the arbitration award reflects clearly erroneous fact determinations and/or material, prejudicial errors of law. [James Baker, *A Sea Change for ERISA Litigation*, Baker & McKenzie (Dec. 2013) (benefitslink.com). See *Owen v. Bristol Care, Inc.*, 702 F.3d 1050 (8th Cir. 2013), and *Quilloin v. Tenet Health Sys. Phila., Inc.*, 673 F.3d 221 (3d Cir. 2012).]

Retirees from Honeywell International filed at least three suits challenging the termination, as of January 2017, of their retiree health and prescription drug coverage. Several district courts held that the employees could not compel arbitration of the dispute. The District Court for the Southern District of Ohio held that Honeywell only agreed to arbitrate with unions and employees—not with retirees or ex-employees. [*Fletcher v. Honeywell Int'l, Inc.*, **207 F. Supp. 3d 793** (S.D. Ohio 2016); see Jacklyn Wille, *Honeywell Won't Have to Arbitrate Retiree Health Cuts*, bna.com (Sept. 16, 2016) (benefitslink.com). The others are *Cooper v. Honeywell*, No. 1:16 cv 00471 (D. Mich.) and *Kelly v. Honeywell*, No. 3:16 cv 00543 (D. Conn), which remain pending.]

The Eleventh Circuit held that the right to bring FLSA collective actions is not a substantive right that can never be waived. Therefore, it upheld an arbitration agreement forbidding FLSA class claims. The Eleventh Circuit did not find any Congressional intention under the FLSA to overrule the FAA's strong support of arbitration. [*Walthour v. Chipio Windshield Repair*, 745 F.3d 1326 (11th Cir. 2014). The Second, Fourth, Fifth, and Eighth Circuits had already taken this position. For example, *Parisi v. Goldman, Sachs & Co.*, 710 F.3d 483 (2d Cir. 2013) finds that the arbitration agreement clearly did not provide for class-wide arbitration.]

Russell brought a class action against his employer, Citigroup, at a time when the arbitration agreement did not mention class claims. He charged the company with failure to pay call center workers for time spent logging in and out of their computers. He was later rehired, at a time when the arbitration agreement had been updated and did cover class claims. Citigroup moved to compel arbitration, but the Sixth Circuit held that the new arbitration agreement did not cover lawsuits that were already in progress when the arbitration agreement was signed because the language of the agreement was prospective, so the Sixth Circuit refused to compel arbitration of a claim that was embodied in a suit already in progress. [*Russell v. Citigroup, Inc.*, 748 F.3d 677 (6th Cir. 2014)]

Plaintiffs in a 2014 Sixth Circuit case were mortgage loan officers who were not paid overtime because they were classified as independent contractors. They filed a class/collective action under the FLSA and the Ohio Minimum Fair Wage Standards Act. The Sixth Circuit held that the employer could compel individual arbitration, even after the expiration of the plaintiffs' employment contracts. The contracts contained an arbitration clause but did not specify whether class arbitration was available, so the Sixth Circuit held that class-wide arbitration is available only if the agreement specifically permits it. [*Huffman v. The Hilltop Cos.*, 747 F.3d 391 (6th Cir. 2014) It was already clear that CBA disputes must be arbitrated even after the expiration of the CBA: *Litton Fin. Printing v. NLRB*, 501 U.S. 190 (1991). See also *Reed Elsevier, Inc. ex rel. LexisNexis Div. v. Crockett*, 734 F.3d 594 (6th Cir. 2013): when the contract is silent on the issue of class arbitration, class arbitration is not available.]

However, for FLSA cases that are not covered by the FAA, the Sixth Circuit may hold that agreements that reduce the statute of limitations, or otherwise limit the right to bring a timely lawsuit, are not enforceable if they are part of a severance agreement or ordinary employment contract rather than in an arbitration agreement. [*Boaz v. FedEx Customer Info. Servs.*, 725 F.3d 603 (6th Cir. 2013); *Killon v. KeHE Distributors*, 761 F.3d 574 (6th Cir. 2014)]

The Eighth Circuit held that ERISA does not apply to executive's employment contracts that are not part of an ERISA plan—even if the amount to be paid is determined by reference to terms of an ERISA plan. Therefore, a terminated CEO was allowed to arbitrate his claims that he was deprived of benefits to which he was entitled when he was terminated in anticipation of a merger. Although usually employers favor arbitration and employees favor litigation, in this case the employer argued that the dispute involved an ERISA plan and, therefore, had to be litigated in federal court. The Eighth Circuit's decision that it was a pure contract dispute over a free-standing agreement meant that the ex-CEO could arbitrate his claims, including state-law claims for double damages. Because his contract was not part of an ERISA plan, his state-law claims were not preempted. [*Dakota, Minn. & E. R.R. Corp. v. Schieffer*, 715 F.3d 712 (8th Cir. 2013)]

Missouri now holds that continued employment does not constitute sufficient consideration to enforce an arbitration provision. In this case, the arbitration agreement was signed when the employee was promoted from hourly work to a salaried management job. The Missouri Supreme Court held that the agreement was not a condition of initial employment or employment for a defined term; the employee could still quit or be fired at any time. The arbitration agreement gave the employer discretion to revoke or modify the agreement on 30 days' notice. The state supreme court found that this made the promise to arbitrate illusory because the employer could change the agreement at any time. [*Baker v. Bristol Care*, 450 S.W.3d 770 (Mo. 2014)]

As a general rule, a biased arbitration panel is not a ground for refusing to arbitrate, because it is possible to use the bias to overturn the arbitrator's decision once it is rendered. However, the Sixth Circuit applied a different analysis to this situation in which the process of selecting the arbitrator was fundamentally unfair, because it prevented the arbitral forum from being an adequate substitute for the court system. In this instance, the fees paid by the defendant were a major source of revenue for the arbitration provider, causing an obvious conflict of interest. [*Walker v. Ryan's Family Steak Houses, Inc.*, 400 F.3d 370 (6th Cir. 2005)]

The Third Circuit asserted an objective theory of contract formation to hold that a Spanish-speaking worker was bound by the arbitration clause in the English contract he signed—although the bilingual employee who translated the contract for him admitted that he did not translate the arbitration clause. The result was that, when the Spanish-speaking worker was fired and tried to sue for wrongful termination, the Third Circuit required the claim to be arbitrated instead. [*Morales v. Sun Constructors Inc.*, 541 F.3d 218 (3d Cir. 2008)]

In contrast, six years later the California Court of Appeal found an arbitration agreement so permeated with unconscionability that it was completely unenforceable; the court refused to sever and enforce the acceptable provisions. A car wash required newly hired employees to sign an employment agreement. The plaintiffs were Spanish speakers who did not read English. The document was partially in English, partially in Spanish. The plaintiffs thought that they were signing work applications. The manager did not explain the documents or tell the plaintiffs that they waived the right to sue. The court said that there was no mutuality: the employer could sue, but the employees were required to arbitrate. The agreement included a provision presuming that breach of the confidentiality provision would cause immediate irreparable harm but there were no presumptions in the employees' favor; only the employer could recover fees and costs; and employees were obligated to discuss disputes with the management before consulting third parties—giving the employer a "free peek" at the arbitration issues. [*Carmona v. Lincoln Millennium Car Wash, Inc.*, 226 Cal. App. 4th 74 (Cal. App. 2014)]

[C] Arbitration Costs

American Express Co. v. Italian Colors, 133 S. Ct. 2304 (2013) is not an employment case (it is an antitrust case about disputes between American Express and merchants who accept credit cards), but it is immensely significant to arbitration of employment cases. The Supreme Court ruled that the FAA does not permit a court to invalid a contract's waiver of class arbitration on the grounds that the cost of arbitrating small individual claims would outweigh the potential recovery that could be obtained.

The Second Circuit upheld an arbitration agreement's waiver of class and collective actions in a case where the plaintiff alleged that she was wrongfully denied $1,867 in overtime. The plaintiff said that it would cost $200,000 in attorneys' fees, costs, and expert testimony to recover less than $2,000. The Second Circuit followed *Italian Colors:* arbitration can be compelled even if the cost would greatly outweigh the potential recovery. [*Sutherland v. Ernst & Young,* 726 F.3d 290 (2d Cir. 2013)]

A class of massage therapy students sued their school for violating the FLSA by not paying them for massaging clients. The school moved to compel arbitration under their enrollment agreement. However, the Tenth Circuit ruled that the arbitration clause was unenforceable because the prospect of having to pay the arbitrators' fees deprived the students of the chance to vindicate their statutory rights. The Tenth Circuit made this ruling even though the students could have opted out of the arbitration clause when they enrolled. [*Nesbitt v. FCNH, Inc.,* 811 F.3d 371 (10th Cir. 2016); see Howard S. Suskin, *"Effective Vindication" Exception Invalidates Arbitration Clause,* Jenner & Block LLP (Feb. 29, 2016), available at Lexology.com]

The Eleventh Circuit enforced a clause requiring arbitration of all employment-related claims, even though the employee said that he could not afford to arbitrate. The agreement did not allocate the costs of arbitration for people who opted not to be represented by the union; the employer said that the employee would have to pay half the costs. The Eleventh Circuit held that the effective vindication doctrine does not apply to arbitration agreements under the U.N. convention on foreign arbitral awards. (The plaintiff is Nicaraguan; he brought a suit in Florida state court alleging that his work injuries were due to his employer's negligence.) The plaintiff did not submit evidence about how high the fees would be—and the court pointed out that he could have obtained arbitration without charge by using the union lawyer. [*Suazo v. NCL (Bahamas), Ltd.,* 822 F.3d 543 (11th Cir. 2016); see Jodi A. Pandolfi, *Arbitration. Effective Vindication. Eleventh Circuit Affirms Order Compelling Arbitration Where Employee Failed to Establish That the Cost of Arbitration Would Effectively Deny Him Access to the Arbitral Forum,* Baker & McKenzie (Sept. 26, 2016), available at Lexology .com]

[D]   Class Arbitration and Waivers

Throughout the legal system, there has been a trend for decades (encompassing both statutes and court decisions) to limit the availability of class actions.

A number of compulsory arbitration agreements required by employers also require employees to waive the option of bringing employment-related claims as class arbitrations—so the court system has also had to determine the validity of such clauses. As of the 2018 edition, the clear legal trend favored the validity of waivers of class arbitration.

The Third Circuit decided in 2014 that the question of whether an arbitration agreement authorizes class arbitration is a "substantive question of arbitrability." The practical result is that the decision must be made by the court system, not by an arbitrator. [*Opalinski v. Robert Half*, 761 F.3d 326 (3d Cir. 2014). Subsequently, the district court dismissed the action, holding that the arbitration clause did not permit class arbitration. The case went back to the Third Circuit, which held once again that the court system decides the availability of class arbitration and, in this case, the arbitration clause did not manifest an agreement to permit class arbitration: *Opalinski v. Robert Half Int'l*, 2017 WL 395968 (3d Cir. Jan. 30, 2017). See Liz Kramer, *3 Class Actions, 3 Motions to Compel Arbitration, 1 Class Action Survives* Stinson Leonard Street LLP (Feb. 10, 2017), available at Lexology.com]

The California Supreme Court required a case-by-case determination of who decides the availability of class claims in arbitration. The determination is based on the terms of the agreement; any ambiguities are resolved against the drafter of the agreement. In a mid-2016 case, the California Supreme Court ruled that class arbitration was available because the agreement broadly required arbitration of all employment-related disputes. The agreement did not state whether the arbitrator could decide the availability of class arbitration; the court treated this as an ambiguity to be resolved against the employer, and in favor of class arbitration. [*Sandquist v. Lebo Automotive, Inc.*, 1 Cal. 5th 233, 376 P.3d 506; 205 Cal. Rptr. 3d 359 (2016); see David L. Cheng, *Who Decides Whether Arbitration Will Include Class Claims? California High Court Says Ambiguous Agreements May Be Decided in Favor of Workers*, Ford & Harrison LLP (Aug. 1, 2016), available at Lexology.com]

A recent article suggests that, when FLSA class claims are raised, the employer should move quickly to enforce arbitration requirements, before the process of class certification begins. Agreements should be drafted with a delegation clause. In a Fifth Circuit case, a former bank teller asserted a putative class FLSA claim that bank tellers were wrongfully denied overtime.

The article suggests, for FLSA class claims, move fast to enforce arbitration clause before process of class certification begins and make sure the agreement has a delegation clause. Reyna, an ex-bank teller, alleged failure to pay overtime to tellers in a putative class FLSA claim. The first stage of an FLSA class action is considering whether the claims are similar enough to notify potential class members nationwide. The second stage, after discovery, rules on similarity of claims to continue in a single action. The bank's dispute resolution policy had an arbitration provision, which allowed class actions only on agreement of all the parties. The bank moved to compel arbitration when class certification was being considered. The district court denied the motion, saying it should wait until the second stage, but the Fifth Circuit reversed: the issue should be decided long before nationwide notification. The Fifth Circuit said that the arbitration clause's delegation clause gave the arbitrator authority to decide gateway questions of arbitration, including whether the agreement covers a particular controversy and gave arbitrator sole authority to resolve disputes about interpretation or formation of the arbitration policy. [*Reyna v. Int'l Bank of Commerce*, 839 F.3d 373 (5th Cir. 2016); see Daniel S. Klein, *Fifth Circuit Holds Bank Overtime Claims Should Be Arbitrated, Providing Guidance on Employer-Friendly Delegation Clauses*, Kane Russell Coleman & Logan PC (Oct. 13, 2016), available at Lexology.com]

In an FLSA case seeking overtime payments, the Fifth Circuit held that the evidence showed that the parties intended the arbitrator to resolve disputes about arbitrability—including the availability of class or collective arbitration. A former employee of J&K Administrative Management Services was unable to arbitrate collective claims. She filed a complaint and motion to compel arbitration, seeking the arbitrator's decision about whether collective arbitration was available. The Fifth Circuit held that usually, "gateway" disputes (about whether a dispute is arbitrable in the first place) are resolved by courts, and procedural questions are resolved by the arbitrator. However, gateway questions can be arbitrated if the agreement clearly and unmistakably provides for arbitration and the agreement can also provide for arbitration of the availability of class arbitration. [*Robinson v. J&K Admin. Mgmt. Servs.*, 817 F.3d 193 (5th Cir. 2016); see John B. Lewis, *The Fifth Circuit Addresses an Issue That Refuses to Die: Who Determines Whether Class or Collective Arbitration Is Available?*, Baker & Hostetler LLP (Mar. 23, 2016)]

Ex-employees of a pizzeria brought an FLSA collective action. The defendant implemented an arbitration policy covering current employees that forbade active employees to join the collective action. The district court enjoined the employer from enforcing the arbitration agreement against active employees who chose to join the suit—but the Eighth Circuit reversed, finding that the ex-employees did not have standing to challenge the arbitration agreement affecting the current employees. [*Conners v. Gusano's Chicago Style Pizzeria*, 779 F.3d 835 (8th Cir. 2015)]

The issue of waiver also arises when an employee or group of employees brings a suit; the employer answers the complaint and participates in litigation; and subsequently attempts to terminate the lawsuit by moving to compel arbitration. The plaintiff(s) then argue(s) that the employer's participation in the suit waived its ability to compel arbitration.

In a 2013 Ninth Circuit case, the district court held that a wage and hour defendant waived arbitration by not asserting it in two similar cases that were consolidated with the plaintiff's case. The Ninth Circuit reversed, citing *Italian Colors* for the principle that waiver of arbitration is not favored, and the plaintiff did not show prejudice from the employer's delay in seeking arbitration. The Ninth Circuit also upheld the agreement's waiver of class arbitration. [*Richards v. Ernst & Young, LLP*, 734 F.3d 871 (9th Cir. 2013)]

The District Court for the District of Minnesota allowed an Age Discrimination in Employment Act (ADEA) collective action to proceed despite a valid arbitration agreement mandating individual suits. The court noted that the Older Workers' Benefit Protection Act says that a plaintiff who challenges the validity of an ADEA waiver has the burden of proof "in a court of competent jurisdiction" that the waiver was invalid. This reference to a court was considered enough to override FAA considerations. [*Mcleod v. Gen. Mills*, 140 F. Supp. 3d 843 (D. Minn. 2015); see Liz Kramer, *"Older Workers" Do Not Have to Arbitrate Statutory Employment Claim*, Stinson Leonard Street LLP (Nov. 1, 2015), available at Lexology.com]

But the Eighth Circuit reversed in April 2017, holding that the ADEA does not fall within the category of statutes that create a clear entitlement to having the case heard in the court system. According to the Eighth Circuit, the ADEA does not mandate an absolute right to trial by jury; it simply defines various procedural rights that can be waived by an individual. [*McLeod v. General Mills, Inc.*, No. 15-3540, 2017 WL 1363797 (8th Cir. Apr. 14, 2017); see Liz Kramer, *8th Circuit Finds ADEA Does Not Preclude Arbitration*, Stinson Leonard Street LLP (Apr. 28, 2017), available at Lexology.com]

§ 40.08   FACTORS THAT PROMOTE ADR SUCCESS

Most successful ADR systems embody several steps, including in-house procedures for resolving grievances before outside parties get involved. In-house resolutions can be quick and inexpensive. Using a mediator or arbitrator always involves some degree of delay and expense, even if it is far less than the ruinous effort of litigation.

Any ADR system should specify whether the matter will be heard by one mediator or arbitrator or by a panel. Panels usually have three members; it's definitely better to have an odd number to prevent 2–2 or 3–3 splits.

The ADR policy should specify not only the number but the qualifications of the decision makers. It should be clear which employees will be allowed to use ADR to settle disputes—and which ones will be compelled to use it. The policy should clarify which disputes are involved: All employment-related disputes? All federal statutory discrimination claims? Only certain federal claims? Only claims that would otherwise go to state court?

An appropriate policy is fair to employees, providing them with as much due process protection as litigation would offer. They should have an adequate opportunity to assert claims, get evidence about what the employer did, and receive adequate remedies if the mediator or arbitrator decides in their favor.

The American Bar Association's "Due Process Protocol" sets out these standards for fairness in mandatory arbitration matters:

- The employee is aware of the arbitration requirement and accepts it voluntarily;

- The employee can be represented at arbitration (e.g., by a lawyer or union representative);

- The employee has access to a full range of remedies;

CHAPTER 41

EEOC AND STATE ENFORCEMENT OF ANTIDISCRIMINATION LAWS

§ 41.01   INTRODUCTION

NOTE: At press time in 2017, it was anticipated that the Trump-era EEOC would make major changes in policy and enforcement priorities.

The Equal Employment Opportunity Commission (EEOC) is in charge of enforcing Title VII and the Americans with Disabilities Act (ADA). It also enforces the Equal Pay Act (EPA) and Age Discrimination in Employment Act (ADEA), although the enforcement provisions for these acts are slightly different because they reflect their derivation from the Fair Labor Standards Act. EPA complainants do not have to file an EEOC charge; the rules for ADEA charges are found in 29 C.F.R. § 1626.4.

The EEO-1 report is an annual survey filed each year by businesses with more than 100 employees and by federal contractors with 50 or more employees and that have $50,000 or more in federal contracts. The EEOC uses information from this report to analyze employment patterns, and the Office of Federal Contract Compliance Programs (OFCCP) uses the data to select employers for compliance review. The EEOC's reporting portal is at <www.eeoc.gov/employers/eeo1survey/index.cfm> (last accessed Mar. 20, 2017). To use it, the employer must go to <https://egov.eeoc.gov/eeo1/get_password.jsp> (last accessed Mar. 20, 2017) to obtain a password and log-in credential. [Laura A. Mitchell, *EEO-1 Reporting Portal Now Open: Changes Unveiled*, Jackson Lewis PC (Aug. 26, 2015), available at Lexology.com]

On January 29, 2016, the Obama administration issued rules requiring federal contractors with 100 or more employees to report to the federal government about pay, analyzed by race, gender, and ethnicity on the EEO-1. EEOC said that the information would "inform our investigations." [81 Fed. Reg. 5113 (Feb. 1, 2016); see Julie Hirschfeld Davis, *Obama Moves to Expand Rules Aimed at Closing Gender Pay Gap*, NYTimes.com (Jan. 29, 2016)]

In 2017, however, the entire Fair Pay and Safe Workplaces rule, including the pay disclosure provisions was eliminated by Joint Resolution 37, which was passed by both houses of Congress in early 2017, and signed by President Trump on March 27, 2017. The president also signed an EO, *Revocation of Federal Contracting Executive Orders*. [Michael J. Schrier, *Fair Pay and Safe Workplaces Regulations and Executive Orders Are Rescinded*, Duane Morris LLP (Mar. 28, 2017), available at Lexology.com]

On August 29, 2017, the Office of Management and Budget announced that large employers would no longer be required to submit data about W-2 compensation and hours worked as part of the EEO-1, because the data collection and reporting burden was deemed too burdensome. However, employers must still complete the rest of the report. [Ted Mann, *White House Won't Require Firms to Report Pay by Gender, Race,* WSJ.com (Aug. 29, 2017); Annette Tyman, Lawrence Z. Lorber and Michael L. Childers, *Revised EEO-1 "Component 2" Stayed Effective Immediately; Component 1 Still in Effect,* Seyfarth Shaw LLP (Aug. 29, 2017), available at Lexology.com.

The EEOC's basic enforcement scheme is that people who believe they have been discriminated against file charges with the EEOC. The EEOC works with state antidiscrimination agencies, using methods ranging from informal persuasion to litigation to get employers to comply with the law and eliminate any discriminatory practices occurring in the workplace.

The EEOC can intervene in a suit brought by an employee or can bring its own lawsuits against employers. The EEOC has the power to collect data, investigate allegations of discrimination, view conditions in the workplace, and inspect records. It can also advise employers about how to comply with the law. The EEOC has the power to subpoena witnesses and documents, bring suits, and supervise the collection of damages that courts have ordered or that employers have agreed to pay under a settlement.

The EEOC launched an online Small Business Resource Center in late 2016. Small businesses are often confused about which EEO laws cover them and what their obligations are. The site is written in plain English and explains employers' obligations in connection with, e.g., discrimination, disability accommodation, pregnancy, religion, and the ban on retaliation. [<https://www.eeoc.gov/employers/smallbusiness/>; Robin E. Shea, *EEOC Small Business Resource Center: Two Thumbs Up!*, Constancy Brooks Smith & Prophete LLP (Sept. 29. 2016), available at Lexology.com]

The EEOC's subpoena power is granted by 29 C.F.R. § 1601.16. The time to raise objections to an EEOC subpoena is very short. A petition to seek revocation or modification of a subpoena must be mailed to the issuing director (or the general counsel, if the subpoena was issued by the commissioner) within five business days after service of the subpoena. The petition must identify every part of the subpoena being challenged and the rationale for the challenge. The EEOC is required to rule on the petition (granting it and revoking or modifying the subpoena, or denying it) within eight calendar days after receipt, or "as soon as practicable." [Michael C. Wilhelm, *Why Employers Need to Respond to EEOC Subpoenas as Soon as Possible*, Briggs and Morgan (Sept. 16, 2013), available at Lexology.com]

The Fourth Circuit upheld an EEOC enforcement subpoena in April 2016, holding that the EEOC can investigate employers even if a national origin discrimination/retaliation charge was filed by employees who are not legally authorized to work in the United States. (However, remedies available to undocumented workers are limited.) The Fourth Circuit said that Title VII grants jurisdiction to the EEOC if there is a plausible or arguable basis for a subpoena (in this case, the employer did not cooperate with EEOC requests for information), and does not specifically prevent undocumented workers from filing complaints. [*EEOC v. Maritime Autowash, Inc.*, No. 15-1947 (4th Cir. Apr. 25, 2016); see Gerald L. Maatman, Jr. and Alex W. Karasik, *Investigating Illegal Aliens' Charges: Fourth Circuit Says EEOC Can Serve Subpoena on Employer*, Seyfarth Shaw LLP (Apr. 29, 2016), available at Lexology.com]

The Tenth Circuit held that it was not an abuse of discretion for the district court to refuse to enforce a broad EEOC administrative subpoena related to one employee's ADA and PDA charge. The EEOC wanted information about many employees over a period of several years. When the plaintiff asked for changes in her work duties and schedule when she said pregnancy made her rheumatoid arthritis worse, the employer fired her because it believed she could not safely carry out the essential functions of the job. The EEOC sought a complete list of employees asking for disability accommodation and a list of all pregnant employees and whatever accommodations they received. The Tenth Circuit held that the EEOC must demonstrate a realistic expectation that the information will advance its investigation. [*EEOC v. TriCore Reference Labs.*, No. 849 F.3d 929 (10th Cir. 2017); see Gerald L. Maatman, Jr., Chrstopher J. DeGroff and Alex W. Karasik, *No Subpoena For You!—Tenth Circuit Says EEOC's Subpoena Out of Line* Seyfarth Shaw LLP (Mar. 2, 2017), available at Lexology.com]

The Ninth Circuit ruled in late 2015 that the EEOC's subpoena powers extend to nationwide personnel information, including Social Security numbers. In a pregnancy discrimination case, the EEOC asked for information about all of the defendant company's locations throughout the United States. The Ninth Circuit held that information about the names, SSNs, addresses, and phone numbers of employees who were given strength tests had to be disclosed, with information about why certain employees were fired. The court held that the EEOC's broad enforcement authority is not limited by strict requirements of relevancy and the EEOC might need the information to contact other employees who had relevant information. The case was remanded to consider whether disclosure of information about terminations would unduly burden the employer. [*EEOC v. McLane Co., Inc.*, 804 F.3d 1051 (9th Cir. 2015)]

Certiorari was granted in this case, but on the single issue of the appropriate standard of review of EEOC subpoenas issued during investigation of discrimination charges, and the amount of deference to be granted to district court decisions about enforcement of investigatory subpoenas. In its April 3, 2017 decision, the Supreme Court held that the proper standard is whether the EEOC abused its discretion. The stricter, de novo, standard of review does not apply. [137 S. Ct. 1159 (2017). See Jennifer Cerven, *Should Appeals Courts Give Deference to Lower Courts in EEOC in Subpoena Enforcement Actions? U.S. Supreme Court Agrees to Take on the Issue*, Barnes & Thornburg LLP (Sept. 30, 2016), available at Lexology.com]. On remand, the Ninth Circuit vacated the district court's order denying enforcement of the subpoena. The Ninth Circuit found that denial was an abuse of discretion, because the information was relevant to the EEOC investigation—learning about other job applicants and employees who took the strength test might be helpful: *U.S. EEOC v. McLane Co., Inc.*, No. 13-15126 (9th Cir. May 24, 2017). See Gerald L. Maatman, Jr., Christopher J. DeGroff and Alex W. Karasik, *Following U.S. Supreme Court review, Ninth Circuit Remands EEOC Subpoena Case,* Seyfarth Shaw LLP (May 25, 2017), available at Lexology.com]

Hispanic employees at a poultry processing plant alleged that they were sub-jected to sexual harassment and physical abuse. The employer denied the allega-tions, which it said were fabricated so the workers could get U visas for assisting in a government investigation. The District Court for the Southern District of Mis-sissippi allowed the company to take discovery about the visa applications—but the Fifth Circuit vacated the discovery order and remanded for the district court to find a way to handle discovery that does not discourage abuse reporting. The Fifth Circuit held that the EEOC did not have to produce U Visa information, but the plaintiffs did, because they did not have an obligation of confidentiality. [*Cazorla v. Koch Foods of Miss.*, LLC, 838 F.3d 540 (5th Cir. 2016); see Gerald L. Maatman, Jr., *Fifth Circuit Green Lights Discovery Over Immigration Status in EEOC Litigation,* Seyfarth Shaw LLP (Oct. 3, 2016), available at Lexology .com]

The EEOC plays a dual role: investigating charges brought by employees (some of whom go on to file suits), and also litigating as a plaintiff. The theory is that the EEOC acts as plaintiff to preserve the rights of all the employees within the workplace. The EEOC always has a right to investigate and, where it believes a cause of action exists, to litigate. So employees' waivers and releases, or their settlement of claims against the employer, can prevent those employees from suing their employers, but will not prevent a suit by the EEOC. Furthermore, waivers and releases are void as against public policy if they try to prevent employees from assisting in an EEOC investigation.

Similarly, the EEOC can pursue an ADA case (including seeking specific relief for an individual) even if the individual employee was covered by a man-datory predispute arbitration agreement (see § 40.07) and therefore could not sue the employer. [*EEOC v. Waffle House*, 534 U.S. 279 (2002)]

EEOC investigators assign cases to classifications of A (the most serious), B, and C. In an A-1 case, the EEOC itself may pursue the case as plaintiff. An A-2 case is likely to result in a finding of good cause, but no litigation by the EEOC itself. It's a bad sign if the EEOC sends out a questionnaire to potential plaintiffs; asks the defendant for a statement of its position; if the EEOC does not ask the employer to mediate; or if it's a deferral state (see below) but the first con-tact comes from the federal EEOC.

It is often helpful to demonstrate good faith by offering unconditional rein-statement to a charging party. There are many cases indicating that if the charging party rejects such an offer, he or she will not be eligible for various kinds of relief (back pay, front pay, possibly even court-ordered reinstatement).

The Department of Labor also has the right to sue federal contractors for remedies, including punitive damages, if the contractors are guilty of race, sex, or religious discrimination. Employees of federal contractors get a choice of filing their complaints with the EEOC or the DOL. The EEOC and DOL have a work-sharing plan.

It is often predicted that a poor economic climate will increase the number of discrimination charges filed because unemployed workers are willing to bring charges and risk getting reputations as troublemakers.

In a 2015 decision, the Supreme Court ruled that pregnant plaintiffs can use the *McDonnell-Douglas* method of proof to show denial of accommodation when non-pregnant employees with similar restrictions obtained accommodation. However, the Supreme Court said that pregnant workers do not get "most favored nation" status that would automatically guarantee accommodation. [*Young v. UPS*, 135 S. Ct. 1338 (2015). See EEOC guidelines updated to reflect this decision: <http://www.eeoc.gov/laws/guidance/pregnancy-guidance.cfm> (June 2015) (last accessed Mar. 20, 2017)]

For the fiscal year ended September 30, 2016, the EEOC received 91,503 charges and resolved 97,443 charges, leaving a backlog of 73,508 charges. 15,800 charges were settled before litigation. The EEOC filed 86 new discrimination suits (58 individual, 29 with multiple charging parties or policies). At the end of the year, EEOC was still actively prosecuting 165 suits; 47 are systemic discrimination cases, 32 are multiple-victim cases. The EEOC obtained over $482 million for victims of discrimination in private and public workplaces. [<https://www.eeoc.gov/eeoc/newsroom/wysk/2016_highlights.cfm>; see Giselle Madrigal, *The EEOC Rings Out 2016 with End of the Year Stats*, Stearns Weaver Miller Weissler Alhadeff & Sitterson PA (Dec. 29, 2016), available at Lexology.com]

The EEOC's Fiscal Year 2016 Performance Report showed that there were more charges filed in 2016 than in 2015, but recoveries from mediation, conciliation, and settlement fell (from $356.6 million in 2015 to $347.9 million in 2016). The number of merits suits filed dropped from 142 to 85, and litigation recoveries also fell, from $65.3 million (2015) to $52.2 million (2016). [Robin Shea, *EEOC Performance in FY 2016: Is the Agency "Mellowing"?*, Constangy Brooks Smith & Prophete LLP (Nov. 18, 2016), available at Lexology.com]

[A]   Recent Settlements

The EEOC has settled cases about the various statutes it enforces, and often multiple issues are resolved in multiple cases under the same statute. EEOC settlements usually require payment of a sum (possibly quite substantial), and often require injunctive relief, training, and monitoring by the EEOC for a period of years to prevent future violations.

For recent examples of EEOC settlements, see, e.g., the following:

- Under a November 15, 2016 consent decree with the EEOC, the Georgia Power Company agreed to pay $1.6 million and change its policies about seizure disorders, drugs, and alcohol. The company failed to hire, or fired, people based on perceived safety threats, but the EEOC said the company failed to make individual assessments of their ability to work and ignored the opinions of their treating physicians. [*EEOC v. Georgia Power Co.*, No.1:13-cv-03225-AT (N.D. Ga., settled Nov. 15, 2016); see Heather C. Panick, *The EEOC Settles its "Direct Threat" Lawsuit Against Georgia Power Co. for $1.6 Million*, Disabilityleavelaw.com (Nov. 17, 2016) (benefitslink.com)]

- EEOC sued Chemical Transportation, Inc., in September 2013, charging that it violated the ADA by forbidding employees to work with any medical restriction and firing them if they could not return to full unrestricted duty after 12 weeks of leave. EEOC said they denied disabled employees transfers to open positions they were qualified for. CTI agreed to pay $300k and provide other relief, e.g., eliminating those policies. [Luke P. Breslin, *Trucking Company to Pay $300,000 to Settle EEOC ADA Accommodation Suit*, Jackson Lewis PC (Oct. 11, 2015), available at Lexology.com]

- A "Hebrew Pentecostal" (a Christian whose denomination forbids work between sunset on Friday and sunset on Saturday) was told, about two weeks after he was hired as a bookkeeper for the National Federation of the Blind, that he would have to work on Saturdays. He was denied accommodation (e.g., working Sundays or working late on other nights) and fired. The case was settled for $25,000. [<http://www1.eeoc.gov/eeoc/newsroom/release/2-8-16.cfm>; see Richard B. Cohen, *Why Doesn't This Administration Help Victims of Religious Discrimination?*, FisherBroyles (Feb. 16, 2016), available at Lexology.com]

- A national origin discrimination/sexual harassment/retaliation suit was settled for $1.02 million when Mexican immigrants were targeted by a manager for sexual harassment, including attempted rape. Victims were threatened with firing and deportation. [*EEOC v. Vail Run Resort Cmty. Ass'n, Inc. d/b/a Vail Run Resort, et al.*, No. 1:15-cv-01592-RPM (D. Colo., settled 2016); see EEOC press release, *Vail Condo Association Will Pay Over $1 Million to Settle EEOC National Origin Discrimination and Sexual Harassment Lawsuit* (Feb. 12, 2016), available at <http://www1.eeoc.gov/eeoc/newsroom/release/2-12-16.cfm?renderfor print=1>.]

- The EEOC's suit against Pallet Companies/IFCO Systems, for sexual orientation discrimination (a lesbian employee was harassed and terminated in retaliation for complaints), settled for $202,200: $182,200 to the ex-employee, and the balance to the Human Rights Campaign's Workplace Equality Program. [Robin E. Shea, *EEOC Sexual Orientation Lawsuit Settles for $200K Plus*, Constangy Brooks Smith & Prophete LLP (July 1, 2016) available at Lexology.com]

- BNV Home Care Agency, Inc. (New York City) agreed to pay $125,000 to current employees to settle a Genetic Information Nondiscrimination

Act (GINA) suit the EEOC filed in September 2014 (but without admission of wrongdoing). Employees and job applicants were asked unlawful genetic information questions about their family history of heart disease, diabetes, cancer, etc. [Alana Stramowski, *Home Care Agency to Pay $125,000 Over "Genetic Discrimination" Charges*, Home Health Care News (Nov. 7, 2016), available at homehealthcarenews.com]

- Saint Vincent Health Center (Erie, Pennsylvania) agreed to pay $300,000 to settle a case about its refusal to accommodation religious beliefs against vaccination. The hospital granted 14 exemptions for health reasons but denied religious accommodation to six employees, who were fired. [<https://www1.eeoc.gov/eeoc/newsroom/release/12-23-16.cfm>; see Richard B. Cohen, *$300,000 for A Flu Vaccine?*, FisherBroyles (Dec. 30, 2016), available at Lexology.com]

- In mid-2016, the EEOC settled for almost $9 million with three companies (car dealerships in Nevada; a home improvement chain) that violated the ADA by discriminating against employees who asked for leave or exhausted their allotment of medical leave. The EEOC's position is that it violates the ADA to impose an arbitrary time limit without considering individuals' need for leave. [Anat Maytal, *Drawing the Line on Leave Policies for Employees With Disabilities*, Baker & Hostetler LLP (Aug. 4, 2016), available at Lexology.com]

[B] Recent Litigation

Samantha Elauf charged Abercrombie & Fitch with religious discrimination because, when she applied to work in a store, she was not hired. She said it was because she wears hijab. Abercrombie & Fitch said that she did not request religious accommodation; she did not explain why she wears a head covering during the interview. The Tenth Circuit, unlike the Seventh, Eighth, Ninth, and Eleventh Circuits, held that an employee or applicant must specifically request religious accommodation. The Supreme Court ruled for Elauf, holding that Abercrombie & Fitch at least suspected that Elauf wore hijab for religious reasons, so desire to avoid accommodating her religious practice was enough to sustain a suit. [*EEOC v. Abercrombie & Fitch*, 135 S. Ct. 2028 (June 1, 2015)] After the Supreme Court decision, Abercrombie & Fitch settled Elauf's suit for $25,670.53 in damages plus $18,983.03 in court costs. [Robin E. Shea, *EEOC, Abercrombie Settle Hijab Lawsuit*, Constangy Brooks Smith & Prophete LLP (July 21, 2015), available at Lexology.com]

In companies with Muslim employees, especially if they are assembly-line workers who have limited control over their work time, questions arise about providing breaks for the daily prayers. The EEOC charged meat packer JBS USA with a pattern or practice of violating Title VII by not permitting Muslim employee to take unscheduled prayer breaks or moving the meal break to cover the sunset prayer. In 2013, the District Court for the District of Nevada held that those were not reasonable accommodations: they would have a more than de minimis cost in terms of food and employee safety and operational activities, and would inconvenience non-Muslim employees who would have to cover for Muslim co-workers. [*EEOC v. JBS USA, LLC*, 940 F. Supp. 2d 949 (D. Neb. 2013)]

After the 2013 case, the EEOC pursued JBS again in another facility, this one located in Colorado, in connection with prayers at or near sundown during Ramadan 2008. The company and its workforce were unable to reach agreement on this issue, and many Muslim employees were fired for job abandonment. In mid-2010 the EEOC brought a religious discrimination/retaliation suit. JBS moved for summary judgment on the pattern or practice, discrimination, and retaliation claims. The EEOC argued that it could argue the issue of undue hardship even though the Nebraska case had already found that the proposed accommodations were an undue hardship. The district court allowed the undue hardship issue to be litigated in Colorado because the plants had different staffing levels, different CBAs, and the workers made different requests for accommodation. [*EEOC v. JBS USA, LLC*, 115 F. Supp. 3d 1203 (D. Colo. 2015)] Another Colorado company, Cargill Meat Solutions, also fired a group of Muslim workers for job abandonment in connection with prayer breaks; although the employer offered reinstatement, only 10 out of 150 workers returned to work. [Julie Turkewitz, *Prayer Dispute Between Somalis and Plant Reshapes a Colorado Town, Again*, NYTimes.com (Mar. 8, 2016)]

The EEOC issued a statement and guidance about discrimination against people who are, or appear to be, Muslim or Middle Eastern, and also issued two Q&As. [<http://www.eeoc.gov/eeoc/publications/muslim_middle_eastern_employers.cfm> (last accessed Mar. 20, 2017) about hiring, harassment, background checks, and religious accommodation; <http://www.eeoc.gov/eeoc/publications/muslim_middle_eastern_employees.cfm> (last accessed Mar. 20, 2017) about the same topics but aimed at applicants and employees. Michael T. Miller, *EEOC Seeks to Prevent Discrimination Against Muslim and Middle Eastern Employees*, Briggs and Morgan (Feb. 22, 2016), available at Lexology.com] Note, however, that these are Obama-era initiatives that may be altered in the Trump administration.

There is a circuit split as to whether an employer has an obligation to assign a person with a disability to a vacant position for which he or she has the minimum qualifications as a reasonable accommodation. The EEOC's position is that the employer is obligated to do so, and the Seventh, Tenth, and D.C. Circuits agree—but the Fifth, Sixth, Eighth and Eleventh Circuits say that workers with a disability must compete for the vacancy, and the employer is justified in selecting the best-qualified worker. [*EEOC v. St. Joseph's Hosp.*, No. 15-14551, 2016 WL 7131479 (11th Cir. Dec. 7, 2016); see Brian D. Hall, *Eleventh Circuit Rejects EEOC Position Regarding Reassignment as a Reasonable Accommodation*, Porter Wright Morris & Arthur LLP (Dec. 12, 2016), available at Lexology.com]

The EEOC has filed several challenges to employers' wellness programs (which provide financial incentives for healthy behavior like smoking cessation, exercise, and weight loss—and usually impose penalties for failure to meet goals). HIPAA authorizes employers to impose penalties of 30%–50%, depending on circumstances.

An ADA suit filed in the Eastern District of Wisconsin in mid-2014 alleges that the program was not truly voluntary because the employee who refused to participate had to pay $400 a month for health coverage, plus a $50 a month penalty, and was later fired. A decision was announced in September 2016. The district court held that the program did not violate the ADA when it required employees to pay 100% of the premium if they did not complete a health risk assessment at the beginning of the plan year. The assessment included a history questionnaire, screening, and a blood test, although blood samples were analyzed anonymously to determine the ailments present in the workforce as a whole. The EEOC alleged that the employer violated the ADA and unlawfully retaliated against the plaintiff, The district court held that the ADA safe harbor did not apply because the wellness program was independent of the health plan and was not used to underwrite or classify risk. However, the financial incentive did not exceed 30% of the cost of self-only coverage, so the program satisfied the definition of voluntariness. The court said that requiring employees to pay the full premium if they opted out of the wellness program was merely an incentive, not a compulsion, and employees had a choice even if it was a bad one, so the employer got summary judgment on the ADA count. The retaliation claim went to trial because of the disputed facts of the circumstances of her termination. [*EEOC v. Orion Energy Sys.*, No. 1:14-cv-01019 (E.D. Wis. Sept. 19, 2016); see Practical Law Employee Benefits & Executive Compensation, *EEOC Loses Again in Wellness Litigation* (Nov. 10, 2016) (benefitslink.com)]. Orion agreed on April 5, 2017, to pay $100,000 to the terminated employee to settle the case. Orion also agreed to reduce the incentives for participation, and to avoid mandating medical examinations when the requirement violates the ADA. See Heather C. Panick, *EEOC and Orion Energy Systems, Inc. Settle Wellness Case,* Jackson Lewis PC (Apr. 20, 2017), available at Lexology.com]

In late 2016, the American Association of Retired Persons (AARP) sued to enjoin the EEOC's final wellness program rules, characterizing them as arbitrary, capricious, an abuse of discretion, and unlawful. The AARP said that some employees' individual health costs could double or even triple. The suit also said that GINA forbids employers to ask for medical data, because such requests are correlated with discrimination. [*AARP v. EEOC,* No. 16-cv-2113 (D.D.C. ,filed Oct. 24, 2016); see Rebecca Moore, *AARP Sues for Injunction of EEOC Wellness Program Rules,* plansponsor.com (Oct. 25, 2016); Rachel Emma Silverman, *AARP Sues over Wellness-Program Rules Set by Federal Government,* WSJ.com (Oct. 25, 2016); Reed Abelson, *AARP Sues U.S. Over Rules for Wellness Programs,* NYTimes.com (Oct. 25, 2016)]

The EEOC continued its scrutiny of this issue, publishing a notice of proposed rulemaking (NPRM) in the spring of 2015 dealing with the application of the ADA to employer wellness programs. The rule focuses on avoiding discrimination and protecting privacy. The EEOC said that the ADA permits health questions and exams that are voluntary and part of a health program, but the program must be reasonably likely to promote health or prevent disease to ask the questions. If medical information is sought via health risk assessment, the employer must either provide feedback about risk factors or use aggregate information to improve the program. Employers must not mandate participation, or limit or deny health coverage for non-participation. The maximum incentive or penalty for non-participation is 30% of total cost of employee-only coverage (not just the employee's share). Reasonable accommodation must be offered so persons with disabilities (PWDs) can participate and earn incentives. Employees must be notified as to what information will be collected, how it will be used, who gets to see it, and how confidentiality will be preserved. [80 Fed. Reg. 21659 (Apr. 20, 2015); see the EEOC's fact sheet for small business, <http://www.eeoc.gov/laws/regulations/facts_nprm_wellness.cfm> (last accessed Mar. 20, 2017)]

The EEOC finalized the NPRM in mid-2016, without making significant changes. The effective date of the final rule is July 18, 2016. [ADA provisions: 81 Fed. Reg. 31125 (May 17, 2016); genetic information disclosure provisions, 81 Fed. Reg. 31143 (May 17, 2016). See Rachel Emma Silverman, *EEOC Issues New Rules for Wellness Programs*, WSJ.com (May 16, 2016)]

The District Court for the District of Columbia upheld the regulations in December 2016; the AARP sued to challenge the regulations, arguing that the regulations are arbitrary and capricious because employees are forced to disclose health information to avoid a significant financial penalty. The court held that the AARP did not suffer irreparable harm because the information was kept within the plan, not disclosed to the public. Although some people would experience financial harm by having to pay higher insurance premiums, the court said that this is economic harm, which is not considered irreparable. [*AARP v. EEOC*, No. 16-2113 (JDB), 2016 U.S. Dist. LEXIS 180612 (D.D.C. Dec. 29, 2016); see Joy P. Waltemath, *EEOC ADA and GINA Wellness Regs Survive AARP Challenge*, WK Employment Law Daily (Jan. 3, 2016) (benefitslink.com)]

But when there was a full trial in district court, the court held, in mid-2017, that the EEOC's adoption of a 30% level to determine whether incentives are voluntary was not entitled to deference, because it was not based on sound reasoning. Nevertheless, the court did not vacate the final regulations: it sent them back to the EEOC, ordering reconsideration. [*AARP v. EEOC*, No. 16-cv-2113 (D.D.C. Aug. 22, 2017); see Pepper Hamilton LLP (Aug. 23, 2017) (benefitslink.com)]

Another EEOC wellness program case featured the EEOC as plaintiff rather than defendant. The EEOC challenged a wellness program, calling it an involuntary medical examination for ADA purposes [see 42 U.S.C. § 12112(d)(4)]. The program required employees to have a health risk assessment and biometric screening to participate in the EGHP. The Seventh Circuit dismissed the EEOC's case, holding that whether the wellness program was an involuntary medical examination for ADA purposes was moot. The 2016 regulations, taking the position that denial of benefits to non-participants renders a program involuntary, were issued after the suit was filed. The Seventh Circuit held that the case was moot because the EEOC complainant no longer worked at the company, and the employer terminated the requirements after finding that they did not save money. [*EEOC v. Flambeau, Inc,* 846 F.3d 941 (7th Cir. 2017); see Kristin L. Bauer and Paul Patten, *Seventh Circuit Delivers Blow to EEOC Wellness Program Challenge, But Avoids Ruling on ADA Safe Harbor,* Jackson Lewis PC (Jan. 26, 2017), available at Lexology.com]

The EEOC's Fact Sheet and Best Practices say that religion includes beliefs even if they are new, unusual, not part of a formal church, or that seem bizarre to the mainstream. Non-theistic ethical beliefs can attain the status of religious beliefs, but personal social, political, or economic views cannot. Wearing clothing or jewelry that reflects faith, or displaying religious artifacts at work, is not considered harassment unless it deprecates other religions. Making fun of the beliefs of others and workplace proselytizing to co-workers who are not interested, are not protected religious expression (although employers are not required to prevent all religious discussion within the workplace). An employee seeking religious accommodation must state that accommodation is needed to resolve a conflict between a work requirement and the employee's religious beliefs: e.g., "I can't work on the Sabbath, because that is sinful." [Robin E. Shea, *Hallelujah! 5 Things About Religion in the Workplace That You May Not Have Known,* Constangy Brooks Smith & Prophete LLP (July 26, 2016), available at Lexology .com]

The EEOC prevailed at trial, but the Tenth Circuit reversed in a legally blind plaintiff's ADA suit. When his job was eliminated, he was offered a promotion but the offer was rescinded when the doctor said that he required accommodation to mitigate the risks from his impaired vision. The EEOC sued; the employer litigated based on the direct threat defense. The Tenth Circuit held that the jury instructions about the "direct threat" standard were incorrect. The Tenth Circuit said the defendant should not have been found liable if it reasonably believed the job would entail a direct threat; proof of actual threat is not required. [*EEOC v. Beverage Distributors Co., LLC,* 780 F.3d 1018 (10th Cir. 2015)]

The EEOC sued on behalf of Chastity Jones, who was offered a call center job if she cut her dreadlocks. The employer's policy required professional-looking hair styles that are not "excessive" or in "unusual colors." The EEOC said that dreadlocks are culturally associated with black people, so the policy was not really race-neutral. The Eleventh Circuit ruled for the employer, holding that dreadlocks are not an immutable characteristic of black people. The Eleventh Circuit found that the EEOC failed to show intentional discrimination to support its disparate treatment theory. The court cited two Court of Appeals and seven district court decisions holding that hairstyles culturally associated with a particular race are not protected by Title VII. [*EEOC v. Catastrophe Mgmt. Solutions,* 837

F.3d 1156 (11th Cir. 2016); see FindLaw Employment Law blog, *Employers Can Ban Dreadlocks, 11th Cir. Rules* (Sept. 21, 2016), available at FindLaw.com]

A significant emerging issue is the scope of the EEOC's duty to conciliate—and what will happen to the case if the EEOC's conciliation efforts are deficient.

The Supreme Court resolved a circuit split by holding, in April 2015, that the EEOC's compliance with its conciliation obligations is subject to judicial review. The Supreme Court said that there is a strong presumption that Congress intends the actions of administrative agencies to be subject to judicial review. The presumption can be rebutted if the statute's language shows an intention to make the agency self-policing, but that is not true here. The Supreme Court held that the EEOC must attempt conciliation before filing a suit. At a minimum, the EEOC must notify the employer of the claim and give it a chance to discuss. The scope of court review is limited: the court only determines if this minimal standard has been satisfied. The EEOC's affidavit is enough to show satisfaction of the requirement, but if the employer contests this, the court has to engage in factfinding. If it agrees with the employer, the remedy is to order the EEOC to conciliate. [*Mach Mining, LLC v. EEOC*, 135 S. Ct. 1645 (2015)]

The Supreme Court sent the case back to the Seventh Circuit, which remanded it to the district court for proceedings consistent with the Supreme Court ruling. On remand, the District Court for the Southern District of Illinois partially granted the EEOC's motions to strike with respect to evidence of communications during conciliation. The EEOC said that striking the information was necessary to prevent disclosure of confidential information about the EEOC's procedures. The district court also granted partial summary judgment for the EEOC on the defense of failure to conciliate. The district court said that the EEOC's September 17, 2010 letter to the company, Mach, met the first requirement for conciliation because it described the alleged offenses and identified the aggrieved individuals. The district court held that the EEOC also gave proper notice and communicated with Mach to give it a chance to remedy its practices. The district court concluded that Mach merely said that the EEOC failed to provide all the information that Mach requested—not that the EEOC failed to satisfy its statutory obligations to disclose. [*EEOC v. Mach Mining, LLC*, Case No. 11-cv-00879-JPG-PMF, 2016 U.S. Dist. LEXIS 5918 (S.D. Ill. Jan. 19, 2016); see Gerald L. Maatman, Jr., Christina M. Janice and Alex W. Karasik, *Mach Mining Part 3: Supreme Court Gem Resurfaces in Southern District Of Illinois*, Seyfarth Shaw LLP (Jan. 25, 2016), available at Lexology.com]

In mid-2016, the District Court for the Southern District of Illinois denied the EEOC's motion for reconsideration or clarification of the prior discovery order, with the result that the EEOC could only get discovery from entities named in the determination letter. However, the court allowed the EEOC to amend its complaint to add two new defendants, because they had been notified and conciliation was attempted. [*EEOC v. Mach Mining, LLC*, Case No. **11-cv-00879-**JPG-PMF, 2016 U.S. Dist. LEXIS 111461 (S.D. Ill. Aug. 22, 2016), ; see Gerald L. Maatman, Jr. and Alex W. Karasik, *Mach Mining: Court Denies the EEOC's*

Motion for Reconsideration of Discovery Order, Seyfarth Shaw LLP (Aug. 29, 2016), available at Lexology.com]

In early 2017, Mach Mining and affiliated companies agreed to a $4.25 million settlement of sex bias claims. Mach also agreed to hiring goals that were expected to add 34 women in coal production jobs and be supervised by a female HR consultant. A separate suit was filed in 2016 against 13 companies, including Mach Mining, about exclusion of women from non-office jobs. The monetary relief is divided into $1,550,000 in the 2011 suit and $4.25 million in the multi-party 2016 suit. [*EEOC v. Mach Mining, LLC*, No. 11-cv-00879 (S.D. Ill., settled Jan. 25, 2017); see Patrick Dorrian, *Mach Mining, EEOC Ink $4.25M Pact in Landmark Sex Bias Case*, bna.com (Jan. 27, 2017)]

The Ninth Circuit reinstated an EEOC pattern or practice suit, finding that the class claims received adequate conciliation efforts. The Ninth Circuit held that it is not required that the EEOC identify each aggrieved employee and try to conciliate individually before it brings a pattern or practice action because a requirement of individual conciliation would deny recovery to class members who were not identified when the EEOC filed its suit. But this was not entirely a victory for the EEOC: the Ninth Circuit held that the EEOC's investigation must be reasonably related to the suit, not a "fishing expedition." The court also held that the 300-day limitations period starts when the first aggrieved employee files an EEOC charge, so all members of the group are protected as long as someone makes a timely claim. The Ninth Circuit held that this applies to EEOC suits; it was already the rule in suits brought by private plaintiffs. Additional agency charges do not have to be filed in a pattern or practice case if acts occur after the EEOC makes a reasonable cause determination, as long as those claims are like the original charge or are reasonably related to it. [*Arizona ex rel. Horne v. The Geo Grp.*, 816 F.3d 1189 (9th Cir. 2016); see Julie G. Yap and Alison Hong, *Conciliation Made Easy? The Ninth Circuit Reinstates EEOC Pattern or Practice Action in Light of Mach Mining*, Seyfarth Shaw LLP (Apr. 4, 2016), available at Lexology.com]

In late 2015, the Seventh Circuit rejected the EEOC's attempt to bring a suit without engaging in conciliation—or even alleging discrimination or retaliation. When a CVS manager was fired in 2011, he signed the company's standard separation agreement, which includes a release of all Title VII claims in exchange for severance pay. The EEOC did not allege discrimination against this employee; instead, it filed a separate suit against the employer, without filing a discrimination charge or seeking conciliation, alleging that the separation agreement was unenforceable because it interfered with the employee's rights to file EEOC charges and participate in investigations. The EEOC sued under Title VII § 707(a), which forbids any pattern or practice that limits full enjoyment of Title VII rights. The EEOC's position was that conciliation is not required for § 707(a) suits, but the Seventh Circuit said that the conciliation requirement applies. The Seventh Circuit found that the separation agreement was valid: it did not interfere with employees' rights to file charges or participate in EEOC investigations, suggested that employees consult an attorney, and included the employee's acknowledgment that acceptance of the agreement was knowing and voluntary. [*EEOC v. CVS Pharmacy, Inc.*, 809 F.3d 335 (7th Cir. 2015)]

The Fifth Circuit also permitted a pattern or practice suit alleging discrimination against black and Hispanic employees under Title VII § 706, rejecting the argument that the EEOC can only bring pattern or practice suits under § 707. The Fifth Circuit said that it is legitimate for the EEOC to use statistical and anecdotal evidence rather than evidence about specific employees at the investigation stage, and does not have to identify any aggrieved individual by name to satisfy the conciliation requirement. [*EEOC v. Bass Pro Outdoor World*, No. 15-20078 (5th Cir. June 17, 2016). See Manatt Phelps & Phillips LLP, *EEOC Victory on Pattern or Practice Suits* (July 15, 2016), available at Lexology.com] However, in January 2017, the District Court for the Southern District of Texas denied the EEOC's motion to include additional plaintiffs who had not applied for work at Bass Pro before conciliation occurred. [*EEOC v. Bass Pro Outdoor World*, No. Civil Action No. 4:11-CV-3425, 2017 U.S. Dist. LEXIS 495 (S.D. Tex. Jan. 3, 2017); see Gerald Maatman, Jr., Christopher J. DeGroff and Alex W. Karasik, *No Means No—Judge Limits the EEOC's Claims in Bass Pro Case (Again)*, Workplace Class Action Blog (Jan. 6, 2017), available at <http://www.workplaceclassaction.com/2017/no-means-no-judge.lim[...]>]

The EEOC suffered defeat several times in its case against trucking company CRST Van Expedited Inc.—but it has also experienced victory at several stages of this complex case. The EEOC sued CRST, charging serious sexual harassment, including rape in some cases, of more than 200 female truck drivers by male drivers assigned to train them. The District Court for the Northern District of Iowa not only dismissed the EEOC's case, but also ordered the EEOC to pay more than $4.467 million in fees and expenses to CRST as the prevailing party. After a female driver filed EEOC charges, the EEOC approached more than 2,700 female ex-employees, recruiting more than 200 potential class members. The district court criticized the EEOC for an improper attempt at pursuing a pattern or practice case without producing evidence. The district court eliminated many other potential plaintiffs for various reasons (e.g., they did not allege severe and pervasive harassment; they did not list the potential recovery from the suit in their bankruptcy petitions; they did not complain to CRST and give the company a chance to eliminate the harassment). The district court reduced the plaintiff class to 67, then dismissed all those claims for the EEOC's failure to investigate or attempt conciliation of each individual claim. The district court also held that the trainers were not supervisors, so CRST would not be vicariously liable if harassment occurred. The Eighth Circuit upheld most of the district court's findings, but ruled that two plaintiffs had viable claims. The Eighth Circuit held that, because CRST was no longer a prevailing defendant, the EEOC did not have to pay CRST's attorneys' fees immediately.

The Eighth Circuit agreed with the district court that the EEOC failed to meet its obligation to attempt conciliation of each claim. What the EEOC should have done was to investigate thoroughly before filing suit, and attempt conciliation of each claim uncovered during the investigation. The case was remanded to the district court, which once again held that CRST was the prevailing defendant, and once again ordered the EEOC to pay almost $5 million to CRST. [*EEOC v. CRST Van Expedited Inc.*, 679 F.3d 657 (8th Cir. 2012); *en banc reh'g denied* (June 8, 2012). *EEOC v. CRST Van Expedited, Inc.*, No. 07-CV-95, 2013 U.S. Dist. LEXIS 107822 (N.D. Iowa Aug. 1, 2013)]

Then, in late 2014, the Eighth Circuit reversed and remanded the district court's previous order requiring the EEOC to pay CRST's attorneys' fees, narrowing the potential fees for litigation abuse. The Eighth Circuit held that dismissal of 67 claims for failure to investigate or conciliate was not a merits ruling, so CRST was not entitled to a fee award on those claims. The case was remanded once again for a ruling on why any of the remaining individual claims were frivolous, unreasonable, or groundless. The Eighth Circuit held that the EEOC's presuit obligations are non-jurisdictional preconditions, not elements of the claim. [*EEOC v. CRST Van Expedited, Inc.*, 774 F.3d 1169 (8th Cir. 2014) Certiorari was granted, as 136 S. Ct. 582 (2015), on December 4, 2015; arguments were heard in the case on March 28, 2016.]

In mid-2016, the Supreme Court ruled that it is possible to be the prevailing party in a case where there has never been a ruling on the merits, because Congress enacts fee-shifting statutes to discourage frivolous or unreasonable lawsuits and litigation conduct. However, the Supreme Court did not decide if the CRST case fits in that category. The Supreme Court remanded the case yet another time to the Eighth Circuit, to determine whether the EEOC will finally have to pay the $4.7 million sanction or not. [*EEOC v. CRST Van Expedited*, 136 S. Ct. 1642 (2016); see Gerald L. Maatman, Jr., Christina M. Janice and Alex W. Karasik, *U.S. Supreme Court Rejects the Government's Position in the Largest EEOC Fee Sanction Case Ever*, Seyfarth Shaw LLP (May 19, 2016), available at Lexology .com]

In a disability discrimination case, the jury found for the defendant on all counts. The EEOC moved for a new trial, but the district court denied the motion and the Seventh Circuit affirmed. The jury found that the EEOC failed to prove, by a preponderance of the evidence, that the plaintiff was a Qualified Individual With a Disability. The EEOC argued that the verdict was against the manifest weight of the evidence because the medical evidence showed that the employee was disabled as a matter of law and the jury instructions were confusing. However, the Seventh Circuit held that a rational jury could have concluded that lifting was essential to the job and the EEOC was not entitled to a "team concept" instruction arguing that co-workers could have helped with lifting. The EEOC could have made this argument in its closing statement, but chose not to do so. [*EEOC v. Autozone, Inc.*, 809 F.3d 916 (7th Cir. 2016); see Gerald L. Maatman, Jr., and Howard M. Wexler, *Seventh Circuit Slams the "Brakes" on the EEOC's Appeal of AutoZone ADA Defeat*, Seyfarth Shaw LLP (Jan. 8, 2016), available at Lexology.com]

The Second Circuit held that the EEOC did not adequately plead EPA claims in a case alleging that female attorneys were paid less than their male counterparts, so the court affirmed dismissal of the suit. This was a major loss for the EEOC, which considers equal pay enforcement an important objective. The EEOC's argument was that all attorneys are comparable, but the Second Circuit said that proving the case would require discussion of the comparative skill, effort, and responsibility involved in various jobs. [*EEOC v. Port Auth. of N.Y. & N.J.*, 768 F.3d 247 (2d Cir. 2014)]

The Seventh Circuit held that a company under common ownership with a defendant can be liable as a successor entity if the defendant cannot pay the judgment in a federal employment action and there is continuity between the operations and their workforces. The Seventh Circuit said that successor liability is the default assumption in enforcing federal labor and employment laws. The Seventh Circuit used a five-factor test: (1) Did the successor have knowledge of the pending suit? (2) Could the predecessor have provided the relief before the sale or dissolution? (3) Could the predecessor have provided the relief after the dissolution? (4) Can the successor(s) provide the relief? and (5) Is there continuity of operations and workforce between the predecessor and successor(s)? [*EEOC v. Northern Star Hospitality, Inc.*, 777 F.3d 898 (7th Cir. 2015)]

The EEOC prevailed in the "hand scanner" case. Before the trial, both sides agreed to delay resolution of certain damage issues. The collateral source rule provides that damages are not reduced by funds from an outside (collateral) source. The District Court for the Southern District of West Virginia found that pension benefits are a collateral source that do not reduce discrimination damages. The employer said that damages should be reduced because the plaintiff did not mitigate his damages (improve his financial situation by, e.g., getting another job). The plaintiff said that he made only limited efforts to find a job because he did not want to lose his pension. The district court held that, in light of his pension eligibility, his age, and limited education and the scarcity of jobs in the coal industry, he reasonably mitigated his damages. The plaintiff was awarded about $587,000 in economic damages. The district court issued a permanent injunction under which employees with a religious objection must be offered an alternative to the hand scanner. [*EEOC v. Consol Energy, Inc.*, Civil Action No. 1:13CV215, 2015 U.S. Dist. LEXIS 110728 (S.D. W.Va. Aug. 21, 2015)]

Subsequently, the district court held that the plaintiff's sincere belief that using the time clock meant pledging allegiance to the Antichrist was entitled to accommodation—disabled employees who were unable to use the scanner were accommodated. The district court ruled in early 2016 that wholesale denial of reasonable accommodation can constitute constructive discharge. [*U.S. EEOC v. Consol Energy, Inc.*, Case No. 1:13-cv-00215, 2016 U.S. Dist. LEXIS 15475 (N.D. W.Va. Feb. 9, 2016); see Andrew D. Peters, *Refusal to Exempt Employee from "Mark Of The Beast" Hand Scanner Proves Damning for Company,* Barnes & Thornburg LLP (Feb. 16, 2016), available at Lexology.com]

The Fourth Circuit upheld the jury verdict: *EEOC v. Consol. Energy,* No. 16-1230 (4th Cir. June 12, 2017). See Richard B. Cohen, *Biometric Scanning and the Mark of the Beast: A Case of Accommodation of Religious Beliefs,* FisherBroyles LLP (June 13, 2017), available at Lexology.com; Mark S. Kittaka, *Fourth Circuit Upholds "Mark of the Beast" Jury Verdict,* Barnes & Thornburg LLP (June 22, 2017), available at Lexology.com]

[C] EEOC Guidance Documents

NOTE: Many guidance documents were revised in 2016, at the end of the Obama administration. Be aware that changes in EEOC policy, to be embodied in later documents and probably withdrawal of existing documents, can be expected under the Trump administration.

The EEOC issued enforcement guidance about arrest and criminal records in April 2012. [EEOC enforcement guidance, *Consideration of Arrest and Conviction Records in Employment Decisions Under Title VII of the Civil Rights Act of 1964* (Apr. 25, 2012), <http://www.eeoc.gov/laws/guidance/arrest_conviction .cfm> (last accessed Mar. 20, 2017)]

In March 2014, the EEOC and FTC jointly published guidance about background checks, warning employers that whenever background information (from any source) is used to make employment decisions, compliance with anti-discrimination laws (including Title VII, GINA, the ADEA, and the Fair Credit Reporting Act—FCRA) is mandatory. The EEOC warned that it is illegal to check background information only because of a person's race, national origin, color, sex, disability, age, or genetic status. "Special care" should be taken when there are problems that may be more common among members of certain groups (e.g., some ethnic groups have higher arrest rates than others). The FTC said that the FCRA requires safeguards if an employer obtains a credit or criminal background report from a company that compiles background information. The applicant or employee must be given written notice that this information might be used in employment decisions and his or her written consent must be obtained. If an investigative report (based on personal interviews) is ordered, the applicant or employee must be informed of the right to information about the investigation. If adverse actions are taken based on information from a profiling company, the employer must give the applicant or employee a copy of the FTC's summary of FCRA rights, and must give contact information for the profiling company. [EEOC/FTC, *Background Checks: What Employers Need to Know,* <http://www .eeoc.gov/eeoc/publications/background_checks_employers.cfm> (Mar. 2014) (last viewed Mar. 20, 2017)]

In addition to EEOC involvement in this issue, there are federal and state "ban the box" requirements that control the inquiries employers are permitted to make about arrests and convictions; see § 23.08.

The Fourth Circuit affirmed the dismissal of an EEOC nationwide pattern or practice suit about background checks; the court said that the EEOC's expert analysis was "laughable." The EEOC said that the defendant unlawfully relied on background checks that had a disparate impact on African-American, Hispanic, and male applicants. But the Fourth Circuit said that the expert's report used only a limited number of background checks and ignored a great deal of relevant data; the report had so many errors and logical fallacies that it could not be relied on. [*EEOC v. Freeman*, 778 F.3d 463 (4th Cir. 2015)]

The Fifth Circuit ruled in mid-2016 that the state of Texas had standing to challenge the arrest/conviction records guidance, holding that the guidance is a final agency action for Administrative Procedure Act purposes: it is an action determining rights or obligations, or creating legal obligations. The Fifth Circuit held that the state is an employer that is subject to the guidance, giving it presumptive constitutional standing to challenge it. The state suffered concrete injury because the guidance forced it to either change its hiring practices or incur significant costs. In this reading, increased regulatory burden is injury in fact (an argument that is likely to be heard many times in the future). The Fifth Circuit agreed with the state that it had to change its state laws, so the EEOC overrode the state's interest in excluding felons from certain jobs. [*State of Tex. v. EEOC*, 827 F.3d 372 (5th Cir. 2016); see Jennifer P. Woodruff, *No Texas Hold 'Em: Fifth Circuit Allows Texas to Challenge the EEOC Enforcement Guidance*, Ogletree Deakins (July 7, 2016), available at Lexology.com]

In March 2014, the EEOC released guidance on proper handling of religious garb under corporate dress codes. The examples given include wearing religious articles (e.g., cross or hijab), prohibition on certain garments (women not wearing pants or short skirts), and shaving/hair length requirements. The EEOC's position is that federal law requires employers to make exceptions to their usual rules or preferences if required for employees to observe religious dress and grooming practices. The EEOC says that Title VII covers all aspects of religious observance, practice, and belief whether they are based on belief in God or non-theistic moral or ethical beliefs. Nor can employers require employees to wear religious garb or articles if they object on the basis of their non-belief. However, personal preferences that are not religion-based are not protected. An employee's newly adopted practice can be considered sincere even if it is recent, and wearing religious dress only during sacred periods (e.g., a Muslim employee who wears a scarf only during Ramadan) does not mean that the employee does not hold a sincere belief. Customer preference is not a defense to a discrimination claim, and the EEOC says it is unacceptable to assign an employee to a non-customer-contact position because of actual or feared customer preferences. The EEOC position is that, once an employer becomes aware that religious accommodation is needed, it must accommodate sincere religious beliefs, practices, or observances that conflict with work requirements, unless accommodation imposes an undue hardship on the employer. The need for accommodation is triggered when an employee cites a religious reason for not conforming to employer policy. The employer can require a religious item or attire to be covered when at work—but only if the employee can do so without violating his or her religious beliefs. The EEOC's examples include permitting employees to wear beards (although beard covers can be required for sanitary reasons), wearing yarmulkes, and carrying kirpans (Sikh ritual knives) as long as they are not sharp. [EEOC, *Religious Garb and Grooming in the Workplace: Rights and Responsibilities*, <http://www.eeoc.gov/eeoc/publications/qa_religious_garb_grooming.cfm> (Mar. 6, 2014) (last viewed Mar. 20, 2017). See also the EEOC's fact sheet, <http://www.eeoc.gov/eeoc/publications/fs_religious_garb_grooming.cfm> (Mar. 6, 2014) (last accessed Mar. 20, 2017).] See § 41.01[B] for cases about Islamic religious dress.

The EEOC says that some standard language in releases is invalid under the EEOC's 1997 Enforcement Guidance on non-waivable rights. The EEOC objects to covenants not to sue that cover all kinds of charges; general release language that applies to discrimination charges. The agency also objects to non-disparagement or confidentiality clauses that require the ex-employee to inform the employer before discussing information, even in response to a subpoena. The author of the article suggests including a carve-out in releases that allow the employee to file charges but waives the right to monetary damages on those claims. The confidentiality clause should make it clear that the employee can participate in an investigation. [Tim K. Garrett. *Release Language Hazards and How to Fix Them*, Bass, Berry & Sims PLC (June 17, 2014), available at Lexology .com]

The EEOC continued to issue guidance in 2016. In March 2016, the EEOC issued Q&As for employers and employees forbidding discrimination against Muslims and people of Middle Eastern origin, reminding employers that customer preference does not justify discrimination. [Susan Gross Sholinsky and Ann Knuckles Mahoney, *EEOC Targets Religious and National Origin Discrimination Against Individuals Who Are or Are Perceived to Be, Muslim or Middle Eastern*, Epstein Becker Green (June 28, 2016), available at Lexology.com]

For the first time since 2002, the EEOC updated its guidance on national origin discrimination. The 2016 proposed enforcement guidance defines national origin discrimination to include discrimination based on a perception of the country a person comes from, as well as discrimination based on physical, linguistic, or cultural characteristics (such as traditional dress), or because of association with someone of a disfavored national origin. Discrimination against Native Americans or members of a particular tribe is considered national origin discrimination. Except where federal law requires employees to be U.S. citizens, it is unlawful to impose a U.S. citizenship requirement, and the guidance reiterates the EEOC's position that English-only requirements can contribute to a hostile work environment. The EEOC said that national origin discrimination is often intersectional—

that is, it overlaps with other forms of discrimination. For example, it would be unlawful to impose worse treatment on Asian women than on non-Asian women or Asian men. The EEOC does not allow employers to direct employment agencies or staffing firms not to send workers from specified ethnic groups. The EEOC says that "promising practices" that it recommends to employers include using multiple methods of recruiting to reach more than one group; having objective criteria for assessing job applicants and employees, set down in written guidelines; using objective-job related criteria to discipline employees; and training employees that harassment is not acceptable in the workplace. [Proposed guidance available at <http://www.franczek.com/assets/htmldocuments/Proposed%20Enforcement%20Guidance%20on%20National%20Origin%20Discrimination.pdf> (June 2, 2016) (last accessed Mar. 20, 2017); see Gwendolyn B. Morales and William R. Pokorny, *EEOC Releases Draft Guidance Regarding National Origin Discrimination*, Franczek Radelet (June 28, 2016), available at Lexology.com.]

In late 2016, the EEOC redrafted § 13 of the compliance manual with further guidance about national origin discrimination, covering all employers with more than four employees. The guidance applies whatever the employee's immigration status may be. It also covers foreign nationals outside the United States who apply to work in the United States. The revised § 13 defines national origin as a person's place of origin (or his or her ancestors'); country, former country, or geographic region. The guidance also refers to national origin groups and ethnic groups. An ethnical group shares social characteristics such as race, language, culture or ancestry. The EEOC considers discrimination on the basis of ethnicity (e.g., Hispanic) or physical, linguistic, or cultural traits to be unlawful. Perceived origin and association are also covered. The guidance also applies to trafficking cases where coercion or exploitation is imposed because of national origin. [Notice 915.005 (Nov. 18, 2016), available at <https://www.eeoc.gov/laws/guidance/national-origin-guidance.cfm>; see Kristin Aquino-Pham, *EEOC Issues Guidance on National Origin Discrimination that Applies to Foreign National Employees*, Greenberg Traurig LLP (Nov. 23, 2016), available at Lexology.com]

The EEOC issued guidance on May 9, 2016 about providing ADA leave as reasonable accommodation. The EEOC's position is that disabled employees who request leave must have equal access to leave as employees who request leave for reasons not related to disability. The EEOC expects employers to consider providing additional leave after personal and Family and Medical Leave Act (FMLA) leave are used up, unless giving extra leave would be an undue hardship on the employer. When an employee says he or she needs disability-related leave, the employer is obligated to engage in the interactive process of discussing potential accommodations. The EEOC forbids "100%-healed" policies that do not let employees return to work unless they are free of all restrictions. [<https://www.eeoc.gov/eeoc/publications/ada-leave.cfm> (last accessed Mar. 20, 2017). See Duane Morris LLP, *EEOC Issues Guidance Relating to Leaves of Absence and the ADA* (May 16, 2016), available at Lexology.com; Anat Maytal, *Drawing the*

Line on Leave Policies for Employees with Disabilities, Baker & Hostetler LLP (Aug. 4, 2016), available at Lexology.com]

A late 2016 resource document covers the ADA rights of workers with mental health conditions. About 5% of EEOC charges received each year involve allegations of mental-health-based discrimination or harassment. Under the guidance, employees and applicants may be entitled to reasonable accommodation of mental health-related disability, such as schedule changes, a quiet office space, changes in how they are supervised, and/or telecommuting. The guidelines also assist mental health providers in drafting documentation of the employees' need for reasonable accommodation. [<https://www.eeoc.gov/eeoc/publications/mental_health.cfm> (last accessed Mar. 21, 2017); see Laura Lawless Robertson, *EEOC Issues New Guidance on the Rights of Applicants and Employees with Mental Health Conditions*, Squire Patton Boggs (Dec. 14, 2016), available at Lexology.com]

On June 20, 2016, the EEOC's Select Task Force on the Study of Harassment in the Workplace released its final report. The EEOC said that harassment remains a persistent problem and often goes unreported. It is not enough for employer merely to provide anti-harassment training; there must be a broader prevention effort. The report called for collaboration between the EEOC and NLRB to harmonize federal anti-discrimination laws with the NLRA. Workplace civility rules may have to be amended if they discourage employees from criticizing the employer, for example. Online harassment of co-workers must be discouraged, without violating the NLRA's requirement of free access to online media to discuss terms and conditions of employment. [Report: <http://www.eeoc.gov/eeoc/task_force/harassment/upload/report.pdf> (last accessed Mar. 20, 2017). See Christopher J. DeGroff et. al., *A Call For Harmony Between the EEOC and NLRB's Rules for Prevention and Investigation of Workplace Harassment*, Seyfarth Shaw LLP (June 21, 2016), available at Lexology.com]

Based on the task force report, the EEOC issued proposed guidance on harassment in early 2017. The EEOC asked for comments on the *Faragher/Ellerth* test (whether the employer should be relieved of liability because it acted promptly and appropriately, and the employee unreasonably delayed complaining about the alleged harassment). This guidance might be allowed to survive because the new EEOC commissioner Lipnic is a co-author of the guidance. [<https://www.eeoc.gov/eeoc/newsroom/release/1-10-17a.cfm> ; see Charles C. Warner, *EEOC Issues Proposed Guidance On Harassment*, Porter Wright Morris & Arthur LLP (Jan. 20, 2017), available at Lexology.com]

The EEOC released its Enforcement Guidance on Retaliation and Related Issues on August 29, 2016—18 years after the previous guidance was issued. In the interim, not only has the number of retaliation claims soared, but retaliation makes up a much larger share of the caseload (about 45% of all charges).

There are two kinds of retaliation charges. The "opposition clause" claims that an employee suffered retaliation for opposing an unlawful practice committed by the employer. The "participation" clause says that retaliation occurred because the employee participated in a case against the employer by filing a charge, participating in an investigation, or testifying at a hearing. The EEOC guidance says that the participation clause can be satisfied whether or not underlying discrimination allegation is reasonable—but the opposition clause only applies if the employee objects to practices that the employee reasonably believed to be unlawful. The EEOC disagrees with some federal courts.

The EEOC says that participation includes internal complaints whether or not a formal charge is ever filed with the EEOC or a local anti-discrimination agency. The EEOC also rejects the "manager rule" (which says that a manager has to step outside his or her management role and take a position adverse to the employer for the activity to be protected). The EEOC says that the manager rule discourages supervisors from obeying their duty to report harassment and participate in internal investigations.

The EEOC also takes a broad view of what constitutes a retaliatory adverse action—for example, making false reports to government authorities; disparaging someone in the media; threatening to reassign them; scrutinizing their work more severely; unfairly lowering a performance appraisal or giving a poor referral; physical or verbal abuse. The EEOC says that an employee can prove that the employer would not have taken the adverse action but for the protected activity by introducing a "convincing mosaic" of circumstantial evidence that demonstrates retaliatory animus (written or verbal statements, suspicious timing of actions, falsity of proffered reasons, evidence about comparators).

The mid-2016 guidance covers Title VII, the ADEA, ADA, EPA, GINA, and Section 501 of the Rehabilitation Act. Retaliation means a materially adverse action such as threats, warnings, bad evaluations, or other actions that could discourage a reasonable employee from protesting. In light of *Nassar,* the EEOC says that certain facts can defeat a retaliation claim: for example, poor performance, the employee's lack of qualifications, bad references, misconduct, or a Reduction in Force.

The EEOC says that employees are protected by the participation clause against retaliation if they make internal complaints before a charge is filed, or if they participate in an investigation or proceeding—whether or not the underlying allegations are valid. However, there is a distinction between the protection available for employees who oppose employer actions (which must be based on a reasonable good-faith belief that unlawful discrimination has occurred) and those who participate in proceedings. Illegal acts (e.g., threats of violence) and fabricated charges are not protected.

The EEOC's suggested practices for employers include having a written anti-retaliation policy, training all supervisors to follow it, giving advice and support to complainants, following up after protected activity has occurred, and reviewing compliance. [Notice 914.004, <https://www.eeoc.gov/laws/guidance/retaliation-guidance.cfm> (Aug. 29, 2016); see Richard R. Meneghello, *10 Things You Need to Know About EEOC's New Retaliation Guidance*, Fisher Phillips (Aug. 31, 2016), available at Lexology.com. See also Q&A, <https://www.eeoc

.gov/laws/guidance/retaliation-qa.cfm> and the small business fact sheet: <https://www.eeoc.gov/laws/guidance/retaliation-factsheet.cfm>; see Derek G. Barella et. al., *EEOC Issues Final Guidance on Employer Retaliation*, Winston & Strawn LLP (Sept. 1, 2016), available at Lexology.com]

The EEOC's long-term position is that being HIV-positive is a disability. Guidance about workplace HIV issues was published in late 2015, in connection with World AIDS Day. The EEOC says that HIV-positive people have workplace privacy rights, are entitled to protection against discrimination and harassment, and may be entitled to reasonable accommodation. (Discrimination and harassment also violate the ADA.) Employers are not permitted to terminate a person or reject him or her for hiring or promotion merely on the basis of HIV status, and employers asserting inability to perform job duties or safety risk must have objective evidence. There are situations in which employers are permitted to ask medical questions (for example, when an employee requests accommodation), but the information must be kept confidential and not divulged to co-workers unnecessarily. The accommodations that might be required include additional breaks, modified work schedules or time off for medical treatment, and telecommuting. However, an employee's illness or medication side effects are not an excuse for poor performance. [EEOC, *Living with HIV Infection: Your Legal Rights in the Workplace Under the ADA*, <http://www.eeoc.gov/eeoc/publications/hiv_individual.cfm> (last accessed Mar. 20, 2017)]

§ 41.02   EEOC ADR

At times, the EEOC itself will engage in ADR with employers and employees as an alternative to normal charge processing methods. The EEOC issued two policy statements on these subjects in 1997, although formal regulations were not issued at that time.

Under these policy statements, the EEOC said ADR was not appropriate in some cases. The agency did not treat ADR as fair or appropriate in important test cases where the EEOC wishes to establish policy or set a precedent; where the EEOC would have to maintain an ongoing presence to monitor compliance; charge—for instance, other employees and other companies in the same or different industries.

The EEOC took the position that ADR was fair and appropriate if it is voluntarily elected, not compelled; the EEOC assists employees with the process; the mediator or arbitrator is truly neutral proceedings are confidential; and the process results in an enforceable written agreement.

The EEOC's home page for mediation can be found at <http://www.eeoc.gov/eeoc/mediation/index.cfm> (last accessed Mar. 20, 2017), containing a number of resources, including a video about the advantages of mediation. EEOC mediation involves not only EEOC personnel trained in-house and outside contract mediators, but volunteers as well. Mediation is offered as an option early in the process of handling a discrimination charge, but mediation is not provided after the EEOC determines that a charge is without merit, unless the parties request it. The EEOC has entered into 1,573 Universal Agreements to Mediate (UAM)s with local employers and 214 UAMs with regional or national employers. These agreements expedite the mediation process by setting up an ongoing relationship between the company and the EEOC. [EEOC, *History of the EEOC Mediation Program*, <http://www1.eeoc.gov//eeoc/mediation/history.cfm> (last accessed Apr. 7, 2016)]

In fiscal 2014, the EEOC said that 10,421 mediations were conducted, leading to 7,846 resolutions, a resolution rate of over three-quarters (76.7%). There were fewer mediations conducted, and benefits were lower than in 2013 or 2012, but resolutions were faster an average of 96 days in 2014, versus 98 days in 2013 and 101 days in 2011–2012. In FY 2014, Monetary benefits of $144.6 million were obtained for 7,391 persons and 455 people received non-monetary benefits as a result of EEOC mediation. [EEOC, *EEOC Mediation Statistics FY 1999 Through FY 2014*, <http://www.eeoc.gov/eeoc/mediation/mediation_stats.cfm> (undated, last accessed Mar. 30, 2017) (Later were not available at that time)]

A late 2016 article predicted that the EEOC would place a greater emphasis on mediation in the Trump era. In fiscal 2016, the mediation program provided the largest share of awards secured for charging parties. [Allen Smith, *Expect More EEOC Mediation Under Trump Administration,* shrm.org (Dec. 20, 2016), available at <https://www.shrm.org/resourcesandtools/legal-and-compliance/employment-law/pages/eeoc-mediation.aspx>]

§ 41.03   TITLE VII ENFORCEMENT

Both the EEOC and state antidiscrimination agencies have a role in investigating an employee's allegations of discrimination. Initial charges can be filed with either the EEOC or the state or local agency.

However, if the employee goes to the EEOC first, it generally "defers" to the state or local agency. That is, it sends the paperwork to the state or local agency, and gives it a 60-day deferral period to resolve the complaint. [See 29 C.F.R. § 1601.74 for a list of state and local agencies that are deemed to have enough enforcement power to handle a discrimination charge.] Furthermore, some agencies (listed in 29 C.F.R. § 1601.80) are "certified" by the EEOC, based on a track record of at least four years as a deferral agency, during which time the EEOC found its work product to be acceptable.

On February 18, 2016, the EEOC announced that it had adopted new nationwide procedures, effective for all requests for position statements made on or after January 1, 2016. The EEOC will give the respondent (employer)'s position statement and any non-confidential attachments to the charging party on request, and the charging parties have 20 days to respond to the employer's position statement. However, the charging party's response goes only to the EEOC, not the respondent. This policy was controversial because employers often disclose very sensitive materials, such as confidential information about comparators, and they may give the EEOC protected commercial and trade materials. However, the policy change is not entirely negative for employers: some charging parties might drop their complaints if they see that the employer's case is very strong. [<http://www.eeoc.gov/eeoc/newsroom/release/position_statement_procedures .cfm> (last accessed Mar. 20, 2017); see Christopher J. DeGroff, Gerald L. Maatman, Jr., and Howard M. Wexler, *Opening The Vault—The EEOC's New Position on Handing Over Position Statements to Charging Parties*, Seyfarth Shaw LLP (Feb. 21, 2016), available at Lexology.com]

Title VII and ADA charges must be filed within the EEOC within 180 days of the time of the alleged discrimination (if there is no deferral agency in the picture) or within 300 days of the alleged discrimination, or 30 days of the time the deferral agency terminates processing of the charge (if a deferral agency is involved).

However, these timing requirements are tricky and provide many opportunities for the employer to get cases dismissed. In a case involving a deferral agency, the filing period is really only 240 days, because of the 60-day period when the EEOC steps aside and lets the deferral agency handle the matter. However, most deferral agencies have what is called "work sharing" agreements with the EEOC. In the jurisdiction of those agencies, an employee's complaint is timely if it is made more than 240, but less than 300, days after the alleged discrimination occurred.

Many cases involve statute of limitations issues and call for determining timing issues of when a discriminatory act occurred. The Supreme Court ruled, in May 2007, that a Title VII pay discrimination charge must be filed within 180 days of the time the discriminatory employment decision was made and communicated to the employee. It is not acceptable to treat discriminatory pay as a continuing violation, for which a charge can be filed within 180 days of any paycheck. The Supreme Court said that if an employer engages in a series of intentionally discriminatory acts, each of which could support a separate charge, then each act counts as a new violation. But continuing to pay a female employee less than a comparable male reflects later effects of past discrimination—so the clock does not start again with each paycheck. [*Ledbetter v. Goodyear Tire & Rubber Co.*, 550 U.S. 618 (2007)]

The first law signed by President Obama after his inauguration was the Lilly Ledbetter Fair Pay Act to reverse this ruling. The Ledbetter Act covers cases that had been filed or were pending on the day before the Supreme Court decision. As a result of the Ledbetter Act, a claim is timely if it is filed within 180 days (or 300 days, if applicable) of the adoption of a pay practice; when the worker becomes subject to the policy—or each time the policy is applied to an employee. Therefore, each new paycheck (or payment of benefits) can start the clock running. See also *Green v. Brennan*, 136 S. Ct. 1769 (2016): in a constructive discharge case, the allegedly discriminatory action is the plaintiff's resignation, so that is the starting point for the statute of limitations—not the earlier actions that motivated the employee to feel he or she was compelled to resign.

The EEOC is also the agency responsible for enforcement of Title II of the Genetic Information Nondiscrimination Act of 2008 (GINA; Pub. L. No. 110-233, codified at 42 U.S.C. § 2000ff). Proposed Regulations were published at 74 Fed. Reg. 9056 (Mar. 2, 2009). However, OSHA is responsible for enforcing the laws protecting whistleblowers.

A February 3, 2015 EEOC internal memo said that the EEOC will process and investigate claims of discrimination because of sexual orientation, transgender status, and gender identity as Title VII sex discrimination claims. [Richard D. Tuschman, *EEOC Will Now Process Sexual Orientation Discrimination Claims*, Akerman LLP (Feb. 24, 2015), available at Lexology.com] At press time in 2017, it was not known whether this position would continue in the Trump era.

In mid-2015, the EEOC amplified this position and held that any action that is sex-based or based on gender, including actions based on sexual orientation, constitutes sex discrimination that is forbidden by Title VII. This decision is binding on all federal departments and agencies, including the EEOC's field offices nationwide. Therefore, irrespective of whether they live in a state that bans sexual orientation discrimination, employees anywhere in the United States can file EEOC charges of sexual orientation discrimination. The complainant, a Department of Transportation supervisory air traffic control specialist, charged that he experienced workplace hostility and was denied a promotion because he is gay. The EEOC decided that sexual orientation discrimination involves Title VII because it takes gender into account in employment decisions; constitutes association discrimination on the basis of sex; and discriminates based on gender stereotypes. [*Redacted v. Fox (Baldwin v. Dep't of Transp.)*, Appeal No. 0120133080 (EEOC July 16, 2015); see Roxana S. Bell, *New EEOC Ruling Says That Title VII Already Prohibits Sexual Orientation Discrimination*, Bingham Greenebaum Doll LLP (July 17, 2015), available at Lexology.com; Allen Smith, *EEOC: Sexual Orientation Discrimination Is Sex Discrimination*, SHRM (July 20, 2015) (benefitslink.com)]

In March of 2016, the EEOC went beyond administrative hearings and filed its first two lawsuits charging sexual orientation discrimination (one in the Western District of Pennsylvania, the other in the District of Maryland). [Daniel Kitzes, *EEOC Files First—and Second—Sexual Orientation Discrimination Lawsuits*, Squire Patton Boggs (Mar. 1, 2016), available at Lexology.com] In the Pennsylvania suit, the district court denied the employer's motion to dismiss, holding that sexual orientation discrimination is forbidden by Title VII. [*EEOC v. Scott Med. Health Ctr., P.C.*, 217 F. Supp. 3d 834 (W.D. Pa. 2016); see Shar Bahmani, *U.S. District Court Judge Sides with EEOC, Holds That Title VII Prohibits Discrimination Based Upon Sexual Orientation*, Squire Patton Boggs (Nov. 8, 2016), available at Lexology.com]

In late 2014, the EEOC filed its first cases of transgender discrimination, including a suit against a Florida eye clinic. [*EEOC v. Lakeland Eye Clinic* (D. Fla. filed 2014); *EEOC v. RG & GR Harris Funeral Homes* (D. Mich., filed 2014); see Sandra R. King et. al., *EEOC Sues Over Transgender Discrimination*, Manatt Phelps & Phillips LLP (Oct. 17, 2014), available at Lexology.com] At press time in 2015, the EEOC had settled the *Lakeland Eye Clinic* case, and the District Court for the Middle District of Florida approved the settlement, which called for the complainant to receive $150,000 in damages plus a neutral reference. [*EEOC v. Lakeland Eye Clinic*, <http://www.workplaceclassaction.com/files/2015/04/Order-Approving-Consent-Decree.pdf>]

The EEOC sued a funeral home chain for discrimination against an employee who transitioned from male to female. The employer refused to settle, and moved in the District Court for the Eastern District of Michigan for summary judgment. The motion was granted. The judge found that gender identity discrimination does not violate Title VII, the EEOC did not have enough evidence to get to a jury on sex stereotyping; and the employer was entitled to reasonable accommodation of its religious beliefs about proper gender roles and behaviors. [*EEOC v. R.G. & G.R. Harris Funeral Homes*, No. 14-13710 (E.D. Mich. Aug. 18, 2016); see Robin E. Shea, *The EEOC's Defeat in Detroit: Pants, Skirts, Gender Identity, and Religion*, Constangy Brooks Smith & Prophete LLP (Aug. 26, 2016), available at Lexology.com; Robert G. Young, *"Least Restrictive Means?" Court Grants Employer Religious Exemption from Title VII in Gender Stereotyping Case*, Bowditch & Dewey (Sept. 8, 2016), available at Lexology.com] In October, the case was appealed to the Sixth Circuit. [Robin E. Shea, *EEOC Appeals Loss in Detroit Transgender Case*, Constangy Brooks Smith & Prophete LLP (Oct. 17, 2016), available at Lexology.com]

The EEOC's position is that employers have an obligation to provide bathroom access for employees going through transition consistent with the workers' preferred gender identity. [EEOC Fact Sheet, <https://www.eeoc.gov/eeoc/publications/fs-bathroom-access-transgender.cfm> (last accessed Mar. 20, 2017); see Shar Bahmani, *EEOC Warns US Employers That State Law Cannot Be Used to Justify Transgender Discrimination*, Squire Patton Boggs (May 5, 2016), available at Lexology.com].

In mid-2015, the EEOC filed a Title VII hostile environment suit against an employer who would not allow a transwoman employee to use the women's restroom: *EEOC v. Deluxe Financial Services Inc.* [No. 0:15-cv-02646 (D. Minn., settled Jan. 21, 2016)] The company insisted that the employee complete surgery before it would change her name or gender in the company's records and the company did not stop co-workers' derogatory behavior. An EEOC decision, *Lusardi v. McHugh*, Appeal No. 0120133395, reaches a similar result against the U.S. Army. [<http://www.eeoc.gov/eeoc/newsroom/release/1-21-16.cfm> (last accessed Mar. 20, 2017); see Barbara E. Hoey, *Company to Pay $115,000 to Settle Sex Discrimination Suit on Behalf of Transgender Employee*, Kelley Drye & Warren LLP (Feb. 1, 2016), available at Lexology.com; Nikki D.

Kessling and Mark D. Temple, *Transgenderism at Work: How Employers Can Stay Off the EEOC Radar Screen*, Reed Smith LLP (June 13, 2015), available at Lexology.com]

§ 41.04 EEOC INVESTIGATION

The EEOC's electronic complaint program, ACT Digital (Action Council for Transformation to a Digital Charge System) began as a pilot project in May 2015, in 11 out of the EEOC's 53 field offices. When a charge has been made, the EEOC e-mails the employer informing it of the charge with a link to the online portal. (This makes it particularly important for businesses to supply the EEOC with the e-mail address of the designated contact; if the EEOC does not have an e-mail address, it sends the notice by paper mail with charge information and instructions for accessing the portal.) The employer can download the charge, submit its position statement, respond to the invitation to mediate, and otherwise communicate with the EEOC.

The pilot was successful, so as of January 1, 2016, all EEOC offices use the system to notify employers of new charges. [ACT Digital information: <http://www.eeoc.gov/employers/act-digital-phase-1.cfm> (last accessed Mar. 20, 2017); Q&A <http://www.eeoc.gov/employers/act-digital-qanda.cfm> (last accessed Mar. 20, 2017); user's guide to the portal, <http://www.eeoc.gov/employers/respondent_portal_users_guide.cfm> (revised Jan. 28, 2016) (last accessed Mar. 20, 2017); see Leigh Anne Benedic, *The EEOC Enters the Digital Age with Electronic Notice of Charges*, Porter Wright Morris & Arthur LLP (Feb. 29, 2016), available at Lexology.com]

For charges filed with the EEOC on or after September 2, 2015, the EEOC's Online Charge Status System is available to both charging parties and respondents. They can log in with the EEOC charge number and the charging party's zip code (the employer's zip code, if different, will not work for this purpose) to get the current status of the charge and contact information for the EEOC staffer assigned to the case. [<http://www.eeoc.gov/employees/charge_status.cfm> (last accessed Mar. 20, 2017); see <http://www.eeoc.gov/eeoc/newsroom/release/3-23-16.cfm> last accessed Mar. 20, 2017, discussed in Michael T. Miller, *EEOC Implements New Online Charge Status System*, Briggs and Morgan (May 11, 2016), available at Lexology.com]

If the EEOC cannot settle a charge informally, its next step is to investigate the facts and determine if there is reasonable cause to believe that the employee's complaint is well-founded. If it makes such a "reasonable cause" determination, it has an obligation to attempt to conciliate: to get the employer to improve its equal opportunity policies, sign a compliance agreement, and compensate the employee for past discrimination. The EEOC cannot close its case file until it has evidence of the employer's actual compliance with the conciliation agreement.

An employer that receives an EEOC discrimination charge can either agree to immediate mediation or to offer a position statement giving its side of the story. Mediation usually happens before EEOC has made a merits determination, but conciliation occurs after a for-cause determination. The EEOC sometimes implies or threatens that it will sue if the employer refuses to conciliate, but seldom carries out the threat. In fiscal 2014, for example, the EEOC successfully conciliated 1,031 cases but filed suits in less than 8% of cases with for-cause determinations. If the employer agrees to conciliate, the EEOC lists its desired remedies (such as reinstatement, back pay, posting notices about statutory requirements, training employees about their rights, and a promise not to retaliate against the complainant). The focus is on remedies, because the EEOC has already made a for-cause determination. Under 42 U.S.C. § 2003-5(b), the EEOC is not permitted to publicize statements made during conciliation, and written consent is required to introduce the statements into evidence in subsequent proceedings. [Angus H. Macaulay, *How Conciliatory Should You Be?*, Nexsen Pruet (Aug. 4, 2016), available at Lexology.com]

If the EEOC believes that the employer is blocking the process, it sends a written notice demanding compliance. Title VII § 706(c) gives the EEOC discretion to sue the employer if an acceptable conciliation agreement cannot be reached within 30 days after the end of the period when the EEOC defers to state agency jurisdiction, or 30 days of the date a charge is filed with the EEOC. There is no statute of limitations for suits brought directly by the EEOC: They can sue even for events in the distant past.

If and when the EEOC concludes that there is no reasonable cause to believe that the facts are as charged by the employee, the EEOC will inform the charging party of this determination. In Title VII and ADA cases (but not Equal Pay Act or ADEA cases), the charging party can still sue the employer in federal court, but must get a "right to sue" letter from the EEOC indicating that the case has been closed. Usually, the EEOC gets 180 days to attempt conciliation, but the employee can ask for earlier termination of the EEOC's involvement, and earlier issuance of the right-to-sue letter. However, the employee cannot bypass the conciliation process entirely.

Once the right-to-sue letter is issued, the employee has only 90 days to file the federal suit. If the 90 days pass without commencement of a suit, the EEOC can still bring suit, on the theory that the potential private plaintiff's inaction has reinstated the agency's own powers.

A major sex discrimination suit involving about 44,000 female employees of the largest retail specialty jeweler in the United States was dismissed because the EEOC failed to prove that it undertook a nationwide investigation before bringing charges, and for attempting to introduce evidence that was not provided during discovery. The EEOC's Buffalo office investigated and the EEOC sued in 2008 alleging unlawful employment practices nationwide (sex discrimination in pay and promotions). The defendant moved for summary judgment, saying that there could not be nationwide allegations without a nationwide investigation; the magistrate judge agreed, stating that the EEOC had the burden of proving that it satisfied all conditions for filing a claim, including a full investigation. [*EEOC v. Sterling Jewelers*, No. 09-cv-00706 (W.D.N.Y., dismissed 2014)] However, in 2015, the Second Circuit reversed the grant of summary judgment, holding that it was improper for the magistrate judge to review whether the evidence uncovered by the EEOC's investigation was sufficient. The magistrate judge's task was only to determine if there was an investigation. [*EEOC v. Sterling Jewelers, Inc.*, 801 F.3d 96 (2d Cir. 2015). At press time in 2017, a class action involving 69,000 current and former employees was in arbitration: Susan Antilla, *Sterling Jewelers Suit Casts Light on Wider Policies Hurting Women*, NYTimes.com (Mar. 6, 2017). A class was certified; Sterling appealed the certification. The class action was set down for trial in early 2018. Sterling settled part of the case in mid-2017, agreeing to adopt anti-discrimination policies, but not offering to pay any damages. Sterling did not admit liability. [*EEOC v. Sterling Jewelers*, No. 1:08-cv-00706 (W.D.N.Y., settled May 5, 2017); see Reuters, *Sterling Jewelers Settles U.S. Agency's Sex Bias Claims*, Usnews.com (May 5, 2017), available at <https://www.usnews.com/news/us/articles/2017-05-05/sterling-jewelers-settles-us-agencys-sex-bias-claims>]

The EEOC's investigative powers generally end as soon as a right-to-sue letter has been issued. The exception is the case in which the EEOC thinks its investigation goes beyond the litigation, in which case it can intervene in the employee's private suit or file its own charges. However, the EEOC will not intervene in a suit, or bring a suit, if it makes a "no reasonable cause" determination.

In a case of first impression, the District Court for the Eastern District of Kentucky ruled in 2016 that the EEOC has the authority to conduct a warrantless search of commercial property, even without the employer's consent, to investigate a disability discrimination claim. The district court held that Title VII gives the EEOC access to "any evidence of any person being investigated or proceeded against" and an administrative warrant is not required. The courts have read the Fourth Amendment to permit federal agencies to perform warrantless searches if the statute provides safeguards roughly equivalent to those provided by a warrant. The district court treated the subpoena as the equivalent of an administrative warrant. It gave the parties access to the courts before the inspection, and the court could determine whether the search was related to the violation alleged in the complaint. The district court found the site visit relevant and not unduly burdensome because it provided information about the actual duties of the job. However, the district court found the subpoena to be overbroad, and limited the scope of the inspection to the parts of the workplace relevant to the job. [*EEOC v. Nucor Steel Gallatin, Inc.*, 184 F. Supp. 3d 561 (E.D. Ky. 2016); see Daniel R. Long, *Federal Court Allows the EEOC to Conduct Investigation on Employer's Premises Without Employer Consent or a Warrant*, Mintz Levin Cohn Ferris Glovsky and Popeo PC (May 24, 2016), available at Lexology.com]

Suits with the EEOC as plaintiff are limited to matters investigated as a result of a charge, not matters outside the scope of the matter for which the EEOC attempted to conciliate. In other words, the EEOC's efforts to conciliate one charge won't make the employer vulnerable to a host of other charges. Furthermore, because of the burden of its workload, the EEOC files only a few hundred suits a year.

§ 41.05 ADEA ENFORCEMENT

The rules for ADEA cases are similar, but not identical, to those for Title VII cases, so you should check to see if ADEA plaintiffs have violated any of the requirements for that type of suit. For example, in 2009, the Supreme Court ruled that the differences between the statutory language and case law of Title VII and the ADEA mean that ADEA plaintiffs who allege mixed motive discrimination (a combination of valid and illicit motivations for the adverse employment action) can win only if they prove, by a preponderance of the evidence, that the adverse action would never have been taken but for the plaintiff's age falling within the ADEA protected group. [*Gross v. FBL Fin. Servs., Inc.*, 557 U.S. 167 (2009)] The Ledbetter Act (see above) also applies to the ADEA.

In addition to suits brought by employees who charge that they have been subjected to age discrimination, the ADEA statute provides for enforcement by the Secretary of Labor; 29 U.S.C. § 26 gives the Secretary the power to investigate ADEA charges, including subpoenaing witnesses and inspecting employers' business records. (The DOL has delegated this power to the EEOC.)

Even criminal penalties can be imposed against anyone who "shall forcibly resist, oppose, impede, intimidate or interfere with" a DOL representative engaged in enforcing the ADEA. [See 29 U.S.C. § 629] The criminal penalty is a fine of up to $500 and/or up to one year's imprisonment, although imprisonment will be ordered only in the case of someone who has already been convicted of the same offense in the past.

Although the EEOC can become an ADEA plaintiff, it seldom does so. The cases it selects are usually large-scale, involving egregious practices, many employees, or a pattern or practice of discrimination. The EEOC can bring a suit even if no employee of the company has filed timely charges of age discrimination.

If the EEOC files suit after an employee has already sued based on the same conduct on the employer's part, the earlier individual suit can proceed. However, an individual who wants back pay or other monetary relief cannot file suit after the EEOC starts its own suit, because the EEOC litigates on behalf of all affected employees.

However, if the EEOC complaint covers a pattern or practice of discrimination lasting "up to the present time," this means the date when the EEOC filed its complaint, so an individual can file a private suit charging the employer with committing discrimination after the filing of the EEOC complaint.

The EEOC doesn't need written consent from employees to file a suit on their behalf. The EEOC can seek relief for all employees on the basis of a charge filed by one employee who only reported discrimination against him- or herself. The EEOC can also undertake a single conciliation effort for multiple charges, as long as the employer is notified that the charge involves more than one complainant.

No employee who has already sued the employer can get back pay or other individual relief as part of an EEOC suit involving the same facts. However, if an employee tried to sue, but the case was dismissed on the basis of untimely filing, then the EEOC can bring a suit to get an injunction against the employer, even if the EEOC's case is based on the same facts as the suit that was dismissed.

■ **TIP:** The general rule is that a company that files for bankruptcy protection is entitled to an automatic stay—a period of time during which suits against the company cannot proceed. However, a suit by the EEOC is considered an exercise of the government's regulatory, policing function, and therefore can proceed even while the automatic stay is in place.

In a case about the extent to which other employees will be permitted to "piggyback" their own charges in an ADEA case where another employee answered the EEOC questionnaire and made a statement (Form 283) but did not file a formal charge (Form 5), the Supreme Court held that employees should not be penalized for the EEOC's mistakes. The Court held that a valid ADEA charge requires only certain information (an allegation; the name of the charging party; and a request that the EEOC take remedial action or settle a dispute), and the intake questionnaire contained enough information to be adequate for this purpose. Although the informal dispute resolution procedure never occurred, the Supreme Court remanded the case to the district court to attempt to facilitate a settlement. [*Holowecki v. Federal Express*, 552 U.S. 389 (2008)]

For recent ADEA settlements, see, e.g.,

- Seymour Midwest, a tool manufacturing company, agreed to pay $100,000 to settle charges that applicant Steve Maril was asked if he was within the company's "ideal range" of ages 45–52; they wouldn't hire him when they found out he was 58. [Rebecca Moore, *Firm Ordered to Stop Asking Applicants Age Before Job Offer*, plansponsor.com (Jan. 8, 2016)]

- Rental Pro (in Kentucky) agreed to pay $37,000 to settle a suit about terminating 52-year-old Ronald Johnson. The company's owner mentioned "young blood" and "younger and peppier employees." [*EEOC v. Rental Pro*, No. 6:15-cv-00154-GFVT (E.D. Ky., settled 2016); see EEOC Press

Release, *Rental Pro to Pay $37,000 to Settle EEOC Age Discrimination Lawsuit* (Feb. 2, 2016) (benefitslink.com)]

- Popeye's Louisiana Kitchen agreed to pay $36,000 in back pay and liquidated damages. Leroy Keasley, 40, Kevin Bryant, 58, and Lula Wright-Hill, 54 were denied hiring; Wright-Hill and Bryant were also veterans. EEOC said that manager asked Wright-Hill and Keasley how old they were and told them they were too old to work in the restaurant. The company's job application was revised to eliminate the requirement of stating age or date of birth. [Plansponsor staff, *Restaurant Manager Accused of Rejecting "Too Old" Job Candidates*, plansponsor.com (Jan. 22, 2016)]

- In April 2017, the Texas Roadhouse restaurant chain agreed to pay $12 million to settle ADEA allegations referring to denial of "front of the house" (e.g., servers, bartenders) to persons over age 40, during the period January 1, 2007 and December 31, 2014. The settlement resolves a suit brought by the EEOC in September 2011. The settlement also included a three-and-a-half year compliance plan calling for monitoring and supervision by a diversity director. [*EEOC v. Texas Roadhouse*, No. 1: 11-cv-11732-DJC (D. Mass., settled 2017); see Amanda Umpierrez, *Texas Roadhouse to Pay $12 Million in Age Discrimination Lawsuit*, plansponsor.com (Apr. 3, 2017)]

§ 41.06 THE FEDERAL-STATE RELATIONSHIP

[A] ADEA Interaction

Unlike ERISA, which preempts whole classes of state laws dealing with certain retirement and employee benefit issues, the ADEA specifically provides for a joint working relationship between the federal government and state antidiscrimination agencies; 29 U.S.C. § 625(b) gives the Secretary of Labor the power to cooperate with state and local agencies to carry out the purposes of ADEA.

Section 633(a) provides that state agencies retain their jurisdiction over age-discrimination claims. However, federal ADEA suits supersede state age-discrimination enforcement efforts. A potential age-discrimination plaintiff has to go through enforcement procedures at both the state and the federal level. However, if the federal charge is filed on time, the complainant doesn't have to complete the state enforcement process—only to file a charge within the state system.

The federal ADEA provides that, if a state has a statute against age discrimination and has an enforcement agency, then potential plaintiffs have to file charges within both systems. The federal-state enforcement relationship revolves around the concepts of "referral" and "deferral."

Referral means that a state has a work-sharing arrangement with the EEOC, as provided by 29 C.F.R. § 1616.9. When an age-discrimination complaint is made to the state agency, the state agency refers it to the EEOC. If the state charge is dismissed, the EEOC has the power to conduct an independent investigation. Originally, the EEOC Regulations listed states that were identified as "referral" states because they had age discrimination laws. However, in August 2002, the EEOC proposed a set of regulations for ADEA litigation procedures: see 67 Fed. Reg. 52431 (Aug. 12, 2002), finalized at 68 Fed. Reg. 70150 (Dec. 17, 2003). The EEOC says that because most of the states now have laws to forbid age discrimination, it is no longer necessary to maintain these lists. The EEOC will simply make referrals to the state agencies as appropriate.

An additional group of states (Arizona, Colorado, Kansas, Maine, Ohio, Rhode Island, South Dakota, and Washington) are "conditional referral" states. They do have antidiscrimination statutes, but the terms of these state laws are quite different from the federal ADEA. This situation creates the possibility that employees will bring claims that are covered by the state law, but not by the federal law. In such instances, the state-only claims will not be referred to the EEOC. Claims that are covered only by federal law must be filed directly with the EEOC, within 180 days of the discriminatory act.

The deferral concept means that the EEOC defers to the state and does not process the charge for a period of 60 days after the referral, so that the state agency can take action.

Except in a deferral state, the charge must be filed no later than 180 days after the discriminatory act, or the latest act that forms part of a pattern. In a deferral state, the last permissible filing date is either 300 days after the discriminatory act (or last discriminatory act in a series) or 30 days after the state agency dismisses its charge and notifies the complainant of the dismissal—whichever comes earlier. Unlike Title VII plaintiffs, ADEA plaintiffs do not have to get a right-to-sue letter.

If a state has a law against age discrimination, 29 U.S.C. § 633(b) provides that employees may not bring ADEA suits in that state until they have waited 60 days for the state to resolve the charges. If state charges have been dismissed in less than 60 days, the employee doesn't have to wait for the full 60-day period to end. The 60-day period is imposed to allow for conciliation of the charge. [See 29 U.S.C. § 626(d)]

During this period, the EEOC's task is to decide if it has a "reasonable basis to conclude that a violation of the Act has occurred or will occur." If the answer is "yes," the EEOC makes a "good cause" or "reasonable cause" finding—i.e., that the employee had good cause to complain. Then the EEOC will probably issue a Letter of Violation. However, the mere fact that no letter is issued does not prove that the EEOC did not detect any violations.

Courts have reached different conclusions about what to do if the plaintiff does not wait 60 days as required. The Sixth Circuit says that the case should be dismissed (but without prejudice, so it can be refiled later). On the other hand, the Eighth Circuit says that the case should not be dismissed, only suspended pending the administrative disposition of the complaint. [Compare *Chapman v. City of Detroit*, 808 F.2d 459 (6th Cir. 1986), with *Wilson v. Westinghouse Elec. Co.*, 838 F.2d 286 (8th Cir. 1988)] The Final Rule calls for the EEOC to issue a Notice of Dismissal or Termination when the agency finishes processing a charge. A complainant can file suit in federal or state court at any time after 60 days have passed since the filing of the age discrimination charge—whether or not the EEOC has issued its Notice of Dismissal or Termination. But once the Notice is issued, the complainant has only 90 days from the date of the notice to bring suit; otherwise, the suit will be dismissed as untimely.

Next, the EEOC tries to get the company into compliance by informal persuasion. If the company and the EEOC reach an agreement that the agency believes will eliminate the discrimination, then the agreement will be written down and signed by the EEOC representative, a company representative, and the employee who charged the discrimination. If the charging party is not satisfied, he or she can withdraw the charge. The EEOC still has independent authority to settle on behalf of other employees affecting the discrimination.

On the other hand, if conciliation fails and no agreement is reached, possibly because there has been no discrimination, and therefore, the employer is unwilling to admit culpability and "admit" discrimination that never occurred in the first place, the EEOC and/or the charging party can sue. The charging party's suit must be brought no later than 90 days after receipt of notice from the EEOC that conciliation has failed, but it is not necessary to get a right-to-sue letter.

See 67 Fed. Reg. 52431 (Aug. 12, 2002) and 68 Fed. Reg. 70150 (Dec. 17, 2003). The notices inform the charging party that he or she has a right to sue the alleged perpetrator of age discrimination, but the right expires 90 days after the issue date of the NDT. Each aggrieved person will receive an individual NDT, but for multi-person charges, the NDT will not issue until proceedings end as to all of them.

Despite similarities, the NDT does not work in exactly the same way as a Title VII Right to Sue letter. A potential ADEA plaintiff can file suit at any time once 60 days have passed since the filing of the charge with the administrative agency, whether or not the NDT has issued. However, suit is untimely once 90 days have passed since the NDT date. To prevent confusion, the EEOC amended 29 C.F.R. § 1626.12 to clarify the difference between the notice that is issued when an EEOC conciliation attempt fails and this new type of notice.

The EEOC can terminate further processing of a charge if it discovers that a suit has been filed against the respondent of the charge, unless the agency determines that continued charge processing furthers the aims of the ADEA. However, the EEOC has the authority to investigate age discrimination cases and bring suit even if there is no individual charge filed. This is not true in Title VII or ADA Title I cases. When several people are involved in a charge, the EEOC will not issue an NDT until all the charges have been processed. The agency concluded that issuing a separate NDT to each charging party as his or her case was finished would lead to inefficient multiplication of court proceedings.

[B]   State Laws Against Age Discrimination

Most of the states have some kind of law prohibiting age discrimination in employment. These laws may differ from the federal laws, in terms of coverage (e.g., they may cover employers too small to be subject to federal anti-discrimination laws).

Although the procedure varies from state to state, usually a person who claims to be a victim of age discrimination begins the state enforcement process by filing a charge with the state human rights/equal employment opportunity agency, within the time frame set out by the statute. Depending on the statute, this could be anywhere from 30 days after the alleged discriminatory practice to one year plus 90 days of the time the complainant discovered the employer acted illegally.

Most of the states, like the federal government, have a dual system of agency enforcement and private litigation. The agency investigates the charge and issues either a finding of good cause or a no-cause finding. If the agency deems that the charge is well-founded, then it tries to conciliate or sues the employer. On the other hand, if it makes a no-cause finding, or cannot resolve the matter promptly, the employee has the right to bring suit in state court, under the state antidiscrimination law. However, in some states, there is no agency enforcement, so employers are only at risk of private suit. Other states, however, give complainants a choice between going straight to state court without making an agency charge or filing an administrative complaint—but they must choose one or the other.

The Seventh, Ninth, and more recently Second circuits have held that filing EEOC discrimination charges does not toll the statute of limitations for state-law tort claims even if the facts are the same. The plaintiff filed an EEOC charge after quitting her job as an accountant, claiming that racial and sexual comments and offensive physical contact constituted constructive discharge. She received a Right to Sue letter and filed a federal suit in November 2009, also raising state-law claims for assault, battery, and intentional infliction of emotional distress. The Second Circuit found that the state claims were time-barred because they were filed more than a year after employment ended. The Second Circuit rejected the plaintiff's judicial economy argument (that it was wasteful to bring a state case while the EEOC was reviewing the claims). The practical implication is that plaintiffs should file any state-law claims they have simultaneously with the EEOC charge and ask that the state tort proceedings be stayed until the EEOC completes its investigation. [*Castagna v. Luceno*, 744 F.3d 254 (2d Cir. 2014)]

CHAPTER 42

DISCRIMINATION SUITS BY EMPLOYEES: PROCEDURAL ISSUES

§ 42.01   INTRODUCTION

When it comes to litigating discrimination claims, it's understandable that both employers and employees feel vulnerable. Employers often feel that, no matter how little substance there is to a charge of discrimination, the employer will still have to fight the charge (which can be time-consuming and expensive) and might be ordered to pay immense damages. Employees feel that they are at the mercy of employers—that the only means of redress is complex and takes many years, by which time memories will have faded.

The Supreme Court held, in March 2011, that the "cat's paw" theory of liability, i.e., the allegation that an unbiased decision-maker acts on biased reports submitted by lower-level managers who are biased against the plaintiff, is viable. This decision reverses the Seventh Circuit, which had limited the employer's cat's paw liability to situations in which the biased supervisor exercised such singular influence over the decision-maker that the decision-maker engaged in blind reliance. This ruling was made in a Uniformed Services Employment and Reemployment Rights Act (USERRA) case, but this interpretation of cat's paw liability is likely to apply to Title VII cases as well, because USERRA and Title VII use similar language about "motivating factors" for employment discrimination. However, the Age Discrimination in Employment Act (ADEA) is drafted differently so this decision might not apply. [*Staub v. Proctor Hosp.*, 131 S. Ct. 1186 (2011). See also *Thomas v. Berry Plastics Corp.*, 803 F.3d 510 (10th Cir. 2015): in a cat's paw case, a thorough termination review process involving independent decision-makers can break the causal connection between one person's racial animus and the ultimate action against the plaintiff.]

Cat's paw theory has been applied in Title VII cases by the Second, Third, Fifth, Sixth, Seventh, and Eighth Circuits. The Second Circuit adopted the theory in a mid-2016 case in which an Emergency Medical Technician was sexually harassed by a co-worker. She reported the harassment to her supervisor, who told her to file a formal complaint. The harasser then fabricated evidence that the complainant, Vasquez, was harassing him. The Second Circuit held that the employer was liable if its negligence allowed the co-worker's retaliatory intent to be carried out. [*Vasquez v. Empress Ambulance Serv., Inc.*, No. 15-3239, 2016 WL 4501673 (2d Cir. Aug. 29, 2016); see Michael Marra and Richard R. Meneghello, *Cat's Paw Theory Of Discrimination Adopted By 2nd Circuit*, Fisher Phillips (Aug. 30, 2016), available at Lexology.com; Casey C. Sullivan, *2nd Cir. Adds More Claws to Cat's Paw Discrimination Theory*, FindLaw Second Circuit blog (Sept. 1, 2016), available at FindLaw.com.]

The Sixth Circuit held that the cat's paw theory applies in the FMLA context, and even allowed a multi-level cat's paw argument to be raised, where the prejudiced supervisor influences management members who induce the company to take adverse action against an employee who has exercised rights under the FMLA: *Marshall v. Rawlings Co. LLC,* No. 16-5614 (6th Cir. Apr. 20, 2017); see

Kathleen Kapusta, *Cat's Paw Theory Applies to FMLA Retaliation Claims,* Employment Law Daily (Apr. 24, 2017) (benefitslink.com)

Early in 2010, the Supreme Court ruled that a corporation's principal place of business is its executive office, and not where its products are sold. The case was brought in California state court by Hertz employees who said they were wrongfully denied overtime and vacation pay. Hertz, which is headquartered in New Jersey, wanted the suit tried in federal court as a diversity case. The Ninth Circuit rejected this argument, finding that Hertz does most of its business in California, so the case was not diverse. The Supreme Court reversed and remanded. The effect of this ruling is that more cases will go to federal court—which is more hostile to class actions than state courts. [*Hertz v. Friend,* 559 U.S. 77 (2010)]

The Ninth Circuit held that a clause in an arbitration agreement that forbids all federal court review of the award, including review permitted by FAA § 9, is not enforceable. The Ninth Circuit said that non-appealability clauses have been construed in two ways. The Third, Seventh, and Eleventh Circuits have held that binding, non-appealable arbitration precludes federal court review of the merits of the decision, but does not eliminate appeals under the circumstances permitting an award to be vacated under FAA § 10. The other possibility is that a non-appealability clause eliminates court review entirely. The Ninth Circuit concluded that the FAA's concept of due process in arbitration includes limited judicial review. [*In re Wal-Mart Wage & Hour Employment Practices Litig.,* 737 F.3d 1262 (9th Cir. 2013)]

The Supreme Court held, in March 2016, that a Fair Labor Standards Act (FLSA) class action about donning/doffing time can be based on statistical evidence (expert witness' analysis of videotapes of workers preparing for and leaving work). The workers should not be penalized for the skimpiness of the records kept by the employer. The Supreme Court found that the employees all did similar work in the same facility and were paid under the same policies, so the statistical evidence was adequate. [*Tyson Foods, Inc. v. Bouaphakeo,* 136 S. Ct. 1036 (2016); see Adam Liptak, *Supreme Court Upholds Worker Class-Action Suit Against Tyson,* NYTimes.com (Mar. 23, 2016); Jess Bravin, *Supreme Court Upholds Employee Class Action Against Tyson Foods,* WSJ.com (Mar. 23, 2016)]

§ 42.02 CAUSES OF ACTION

In legal parlance, a cause of action is something for which someone can be sued. Employees can charge employers with various kinds of wrongdoing, and the same suit can combine discrimination charges with other causes of action, such as:

- Violation of Title VII of the Civil Rights Act of 1964 (discrimination on the grounds of race, sex, nationality, or color—sexual harassment is considered a type of sex discrimination);

- Violation of the Pregnancy Discrimination Act (PDA), an addition to Title VII, which forbids treating a qualified pregnant employee on less favorable terms than a comparably situated, non-pregnant employee;

- Violation of the Age Discrimination Act (discriminating against an individual who is age 40 or over, in any term or condition of employment, including hiring, firing, promotion, and benefits);

- Violation of 42 U.S.C. § 1981, the Civil War-era statute that gives all citizens the same right to make contracts as "white citizens." Four Circuits allow § 1981 suits by at-will employees who claim they were discharged on the basis of racial prejudice—even though they had no written employment contracts. [*Lauture v. IBM*, 216 F.3d 258 (2d Cir. 2000); *Perry v. Woodward*, 199 F.3d 1126 (10th Cir. 1999); *Spriggs v. Diamond Auto Glass*, 165 F.3d 1015 (4th Cir. 1999); *Fadeyi v. Planned Parenthood*, 160 F.3d 1048 (5th Cir. 1998)] In 2009, the Third Circuit joined the First, Seventh, and Eleventh Circuits in applying 42 U.S.C. § 1981 to independent contractors, in a case involving alleged racist insults and cancellation of a black trainee's contract as a sales representative. [*Brown v. J. Kaz Inc. d/b/a Craftmatic of Pittsburgh*, 581 F.3d 175 (3d Cir. 2009)]

- Wrongful refusal to re-employ a military veteran, violating USERRA;

- Violation of the Equal Pay Act: paying women less than men for the same job. This federal law does not permit "comparable worth" claims that allege that a typically female job is more valuable than a different and higher-paid job that is typically performed by men (although a few states do require equal pay for comparable work);

- Retaliation against an employee who filed a discrimination claim (or exercised other legal rights, e.g., in connection with unemployment benefits or Worker's Compensation) or cooperated in an investigation;

- Any act of wrongful termination for other reasons (e.g., discharging someone who "blew the whistle" on corporate wrongdoing);

- Violation of labor law (e.g., retaliating against someone for protected activity such as supporting the union or asserting a grievance against the employer). Nearly all labor law claims must be brought in federal, not state, court, because the federal statute the Labor Management Relations Act (LMRA) preempts state regulation—in other words, this is considered purely a federal matter;

- Breach of contract (either an explicit, written contract such as an employment contract or a collective bargaining agreement, or an implied contract);

- Defamation (in the context of an unfavorable reference or unfavorable statements in the press, and if the employer cannot assert a defense of truth);

- Interference with contractual relations, e.g., the employer prevents an ex-employee from getting a new job or establishing a business;

- Infliction of emotional distress (either negligent or intentional).

In mid-2013, the Supreme Court ruled on the important question of who is a "supervisor." The actual case involved a racially hostile workplace, although this concept is most often invoked in sexual harassment cases. The Supreme Court held that the employer is strictly liable if harassment is committed by a supervisor and involves a tangible employment action (e.g., hiring, firing, reassignment) against the victim. If the harasser is a supervisor, but there is no tangible employment action, then the employer can assert an affirmative defense under *Faragher/Ellerth*: that the employer took reasonable care to prevent and correct harassment, but the plaintiff unreasonably failed to take advantage of this procedure. The Supreme Court defined a supervisor as a person authorized to undertake tangible employment actions against the plaintiff. Therefore, the Supreme Court rejected the Equal Employment Opportunity Commission's (EEOC) broader definition of a supervisor as someone who either can undertake tangible employment actions, or exercises significant direction over the plaintiff's work. The narrower the definition of supervisor, the fewer cases in which the employer will be strictly liable or will be required to raise the *Faragher/Ellerth* affirmative defense. In this case, the alleged harasser was a co-worker of the plaintiff's, so the Supreme Court held that the employer would be liable only if it was negligent in controlling working conditions. [*Vance v. Ball State Univ.*, 133 S. Ct. 2434 (2013)]

The Sixth Circuit held, in a mid-2017 sexual harassment decision, that the alleged harasser, a store manager, was not a supervisor because he did not have the authority to undertake tangible employment actions. Three employees charged him with making lewd comments. The employer promptly investigated the allegations and fired the supervisor; the Sixth Circuit held that the company's action was appropriate to relieve it of liability for co-worker harassment. [*EEOC v. AutoZone, Inc.*, No. 16-6387 (6th Cir. June 9, 2017); see Laura J. Maechtlen and Gerald L. Maatman, Jr., *Sixth Circuit Shuts Down EEOC's Appeal in Sex Harassment Suit*, Seyfarth Shaw LLP (June 13, 2017), available at Lexology.com]

Although the focus of this chapter is on Title VII and the ADEA, note that six of the circuits (the Second, Third, Seventh, Ninth, Eleventh, and D.C. Circuits) have held that a Rule 23 class action under state law can be maintained in the same proceeding as a FLSA collective action. The text of the FLSA says that the collective action cannot coexist with a suit brought by the DOL but does not say that a class action is unavailable. [*Calderone, et. al. v. Scott*, 838 F.3d 1101 (11th Cir. 2016); see Stephanie L. Adler-Paindiris, *11th Circuit Holds Rule 23*

Class Actions Can Proceed in Same Suit as FLSA Collective Actions, Jackson Lewis PC (Sept. 30, 2016), available at Lexology.com]

For other federal statutes under which discrimination claims can be raised, see, e.g., Chapter 36 (ADA) and 38 (FMLA).

Although litigation about employment discrimination is usually federal, state-law issues continue to arise. In a gender-based hostile environment case brought under state equal employment opportunity law, the Ninth Circuit held that the district court was wrong to hold that the employee's state-law claim was pre-empted by Labor-Management Relations Act § 301. [*Matson v. United Parcel Serv., Inc.*, 840 F.3d 1126 (9th Cir. 2016)]

§ 42.03 STATISTICS ABOUT CHARGES AND RESULTS

More than 90,000 charges were received by the EEOC in fiscal 2016 (91,503), with retaliation charges the most common type (42,018 charges, 45.9% of the total). About a third of the charges (32,309; 35.3%) involved race discrimination. The other types of charges asserted were 28,073 disability charges (30.7%), 26,934 sex discrimination charges (29.4%), age charges 20,857 (22.8%), 9,840 national origin discrimination charges (10.8%), 3,825 religious discrimination charges (4.2%), 3,102 charges of color discrimination (3. 4%), 1,075 Equal Pay Act charges (1.2%), and 238 GINA (genetic information) charges (0.3%). [*Charge Statistics (Charges filed with EEOC) FY 1997 through FY 2016*, <https://www.eeoc.gov/eeoc/statistics.enforcement/charges.cfm> (last accessed Mar. 22, 2017)]

In fiscal 2016, the EEOC filed 114 suits: 86 of them were merits suits. There were 46 suits with Title VII claims, 36 with ADA claims, two each with ADA and GINA claims, and five with EPA claims. There were 171 resolutions in 2016, 139 of merits suits, and 32 subpoena and preliminary relief actions. The EEOC obtained $52.2 million in monetary benefits (much less than in the record-breaking year of 2015, when benefits were $65.3 million), most of it ($36.8 million) under Title VII, $12.1 million under the ADA, and small amounts under other statutes. [*EEOC Litigation Statistics, FY 1997 through FY 2016*, <https://www.eeoc.gov/eeoc/statistics/enforcement/litigation.cfm> (last accessed Mar. 22, 2017)]

See Chapter 41 for more discussion of EEOC statistics on case filings and dispositions.

§ 42.04 TITLE VII PROCEDURE

[A] Complaining Party

Federal antidiscrimination laws include extremely complicated procedures for bringing a complaint, and one of the employer's main lines of defense is that the potential plaintiff has failed to satisfy the procedural requirements.

42 U.S.C. § 2000e(l) defines "complaining party" in a Title VII case as either the private person who brings a case or the EEOC or the U.S. Attorney General.

[B] The Charging Process

Nearly every phrase or term in this section has already been extensively litigated. Individuals who think they have experienced an unlawful employment practice cannot simply go to the relevant federal court and file a complaint. Instead, they must file a written, sworn document called a "charge" with an administrative agency. Would-be plaintiffs cannot go to court until there has been an administrative investigation and attempts to settle the matter without getting the court system involved.

The EEOC notifies the employer of the charge within 10 days, disclosing the date, place, and circumstances of the allegedly unlawful practices, and then starts an investigation to see if there is reasonable cause for the charge. The EEOC's duty is to complete the investigation as soon as possible—and within 120 days of the filing of the charge (or the referral date) "so far as practicable." (The EEOC has a big backlog and often misses the 120-day deadline.)

After a successful pilot program, the EEOC expanded its ACT Digital (Action Council for Transformation to a Digital Charge System) program as of January 1, 2016 to cover all 53 EEOC field offices. The EEOC e-mails employers to alert them that a charge has been filed. The employer uses the EEOC's employer portal to download the charge, submit its position statement, respond to the invitation to mediate, and otherwise communicate with the EEOC. [ACT Digital information: <http://www.eeoc.gov/employers/act-digital-phase-1.cfm> (last accessed Mar. 21, 2017); Q&A <http://www.eeoc.gov/employers/act-digital-qanda.cfm> (last accessed Mar. 21, 2017); user's guide to the portal, <http://www.eeoc.gov/employers/respondent_portal_users_guide.cfm> (revised Jan. 28, 2016) (last accessed Mar. 21, 2017)]

In another early 2016 change of procedure, the EEOC announced that, for all requests made on or after January 1, 2016, the EEOC will allow charging parties to request copies of the employer's position statement about the case, plus any non-confidential attachments to the position statement. The charging parties have 20 days to respond to the employer's position statement. The response is disclosed only to the EEOC, not the employer. [<http://www.eeoc.gov/eeoc/news room/release/position_statement_procedures.cfm> (last accessed Mar. 21, 2017); Christopher J. DeGroff, Gerald L. Maatman, Jr. and Howard M. Wexler, *Opening The Vault—The EEOC's New Position on Handing over Position Statements to Charging, Parties* Seyfarth Shaw LLP (Feb. 21 2016), available at Lexology .com]

Both charging parties and respondents can use the EEOC's Online Charge Status System to research charges that were filed with the EEOC on or after

September 2, 2015. By using the EEOC charge number and the charging party's (not the employer's) zip code, they can find out who the EEOC staffer assigned to the case is, and learn about the current status of the charge. [<http://www.eeoc.gov/employees/charge_status.cfm> (last accessed Mar. 21, 2017); see <http://www.eeoc.gov/eeoc/newsroom/release/3-23-16.cfm> (last accessed Mar. 21, 2017)]

A major sex discrimination suit involving about 44,000 female employees of the largest retail specialty jeweler in the United States was dismissed because the EEOC failed to prove that it undertook a nationwide investigation before bringing charges and for attempting to introduce evidence that was not provided during discovery. The magistrate judge agreed with the defendant that nationwide allegations mandate a nationwide investigation, stating that the EEOC had the burden of proving that it satisfied all conditions for filing a claim, including a full investigation. [*EEOC v. Sterling Jewelers*, No. 09-cv-00706 (W.D.N.Y., dismissed 2014); see John Caher, *Judge Faults EEOC for Probe Into Discrimination Claim*, N.Y.L.J. (Mar. 13, 2014), available at law.com] But the Second Circuit reinstated the case in 2015, holding that the magistrate judge used the wrong standard. Instead of reviewing whether the EEOC uncovered sufficient evidence, the question was whether the EEOC performed an investigation at all. [*EEOC v. Sterling Jewelers, Inc.*, 801 F.3d 96 (2d Cir. 2015).

Sterling has also been named in a class action, brought by 69,000 current and former employees, alleging discrimination in pay and promotion and sexual harassment; the case is being arbitrated pursuant to a mandatory arbitration requirement. See Susan Antilla, *Sterling Jewelers Suit Casts Light on Wider Policies Hurting Women*, NYTimes.com (Mar. 6, 2017)] A class was certified (Sterling appealed the certification), with trial scheduled for early 2018. Part of the case was settled, but with no admission of liability and no damages, only the employer's agreement to adopt anti-discrimination policy, in mid-2017: *EEOC v. Sterling Jewelers*, No. 1:08-cv-00706 (W.D.N.Y., settled May 5, 2017); see Reuters, *Sterling Jewelers Settles U.S. Agency's Sex Bias Claims*, Usnews.com (May 5, 2017), available at <https://www.usnews.com/news/us/articles/2017-05-05/sterling-jewelers-settles-us-agencys-sex-bias-claims>

Grievance procedures under a Collective Bargaining Agreement (CBA), or company-sponsored grievance procedures in a nonunion company, have no effect on Title VII suits. So the employee doesn't have to use those procedures before filing a charge with an antidiscrimination agency. On the other hand, ongoing grievances under the CBA won't prevent or delay a Title VII suit.

If the Equal Employment Opportunity Commission (EEOC) does not believe that the charge is supported by reasonable cause, it dismisses the charge, and the employee then has the right to sue. In fact, it is not even held against the employee that the EEOC made a "no-cause" finding. A no-cause determination does not prevent the employee from suing. It does not limit the suit, what the employee can try to prove, or even the remedies he or she can receive. The judge or jury makes its own independent inquiry into the facts and is not influenced by the EEOC investigation.

But if the EEOC does believe that the charge is supported, then the EEOC's job is to try to use "informal methods of conference, conciliation, and persuasion" to get the employer to change the employment practice. The conciliation process is confidential, and statements made during the process can only be publicized or used as evidence in litigation based on the written consent of the person making the statement. Violating this confidentiality can be punished by as much as $1,000 fine and/or a year in prison.

According to Seyfarth Shaw's analysis for charges that are eventually litigated, the EEOC spends an average of just over two months in conciliation (72 days). Once the EEOC says conciliation has failed, it spends an average of three months working on the case before filing suit. However, patterns differ among district offices. Conciliation moves fast in Baltimore, Washington, D.C., Little Rock, and Detroit, but is slow in Miami, Birmingham, Memphis, and Phoenix. [Gerald L. Maatman Jr., Andrew L. Scroggins and Christopher J. DeGroff, *New Study of EEOC Enforcement: Demystifying EEOC Determination, Conciliation & Litigation Timeline,* Seyfarth Shaw LLP (May 23, 2017), available at Lexology .com]

The Supreme Court resolved a circuit split by holding, in April 2015, that courts have the power to review whether the EEOC has satisfied its obligation of conciliation. The Supreme Court said that there is a strong presumption that Congress intends the actions of administrative agencies to be subject to judicial review. The presumption can be rebutted if the statute's language shows an intention to make the agency self-policing, but the Supreme Court did not find any such Congressional intent. The Supreme Court held that the EEOC must attempt conciliation before filing a suit. At a minimum, the EEOC must notify the employer of the claim and give it a chance to discuss. The scope of court review is limited: the court only determines if this minimal standard has been satisfied. The EEOC's affidavit is enough to show satisfaction of the requirement, but if the employer contests this, the court has to engage in factfinding. If it agrees with the employer, the remedy is to order the EEOC to conciliate. [*Mach Mining, LLC v. EEOC*, No. 13-1019 (U.S. Apr. 29, 2015)]

Subsequently, the case was remanded to the Seventh Circuit—which remanded it to the District Court for the Southern District of Illinois. The district court granted several motions for the EEOC, finding that the EEOC's conciliation efforts were adequate. [*EEOC v. Mach Mining, LLC,*. Case No. 11-cv-00879-JPG-PMF, 2016 U.S. Dist. LEXIS 5918 (S.D. Ill. Jan. 19, 2016); see Gerald L. Maatman, Jr., Christina M. Janice and Alex W. Karasik, *Mach Mining Part 3: Supreme Court Gem Resurfaces in Southern District of Illinois,* Seyfarth Shaw LLP (Jan. 25, 2016), available at Lexology.com] Later, the district court denied the EEOC's motion for reconsideration or clarification of the previous discovery order, but partially granted the EEOC's motion to amend the complaint to add new defendants—because the defendants had been notified, and conciliation with them had been attempted. [*EEOC v. Mach Mining*, LLC, No. 11-CV-00879, 2016 U.S. Dist. LEXIS 111461 (S.D. Ill. Aug. 22, 2016); see Gerald L. Maatman, Jr. and Alex W. Karasik, *Mach Mining: Court Denies the EEOC's Motion for Reconsideration of Discovery Order,* Seyfarth Shaw LLP (Aug. 29, 2016), available at Lexology.com]

In early 2015, the Ninth Circuit reinstated an EEOC pattern or practice suit. The Ninth Circuit held that it is not required that the EEOC identify each aggrieved employee and try to conciliate individually before it brings a pattern or practice action because a requirement of individual conciliation would deny recovery to class members who were not identified when the EEOC filed its suit. However, the Ninth Circuit required the EEOC investigation to be reasonably related to the suit, not a comprehensive "fishing expedition." The Ninth Circuit held that additional EEOC charges do not have to be filed in a pattern or practice case when additional acts occur after the EEOC makes a reasonable cause determination, as long as the new claims are like the original charge, or reasonably related to it. [*Arizona ex. rel. Horne v. The Geo Grp.*, 816 F.3d 1189 (9th Cir. 2016); see Julie G. Yap and Alison Hong, *Conciliation Made Easy? The Ninth Circuit Reinstates EEOC Pattern or Practice Action in Light of Mach Mining*, Seyfarth Shaw LLP (Apr. 4, 2016), available at Lexology.com]

If the discrimination charges involve multiple employees, it may be necessary for the EEOC to attempt conciliation with respect to each employee. The agency lost a major case, [*EEOC v. CRST Van Expedited Inc.*, 679 F.3d 657 (8th Cir. 2012), on remand, No. 07-CV-95, U.S. Dist. LEXIS 107822 (N.D. Iowa Aug. 1, 2013)] for failure to attempt conciliation at the individual level. [See § 41.01[B]] and the employer received an attorney's fee award against the EEOC. But the case continued and, in late 2014, the Eighth Circuit reversed and remanded the district court's fee order. The Eighth Circuit held that dismissal of 67 claims for failure to investigate or conciliate was not a merits ruling so CRST was not entitled to a fee award on those claims. The case was remanded once again for a ruling on why any of the remaining individual claims were frivolous, unreasonable, or groundless. The Eighth Circuit held that the EEOC's pre-suit obligations are non-jurisdictional preconditions, not elements of the claim. [*EEOC v. CRST Van Expedited, Inc.*, 774 F.3d 1169 (8th Cir. 2014); see Gerald L. Maatman, Jr. and Jennifer A. Riley, *The CRST Saga Continues: Eighth Circuit Overturns $4.7 Million Fee Award Against EEOC and Remands*, Seyfarth Shaw LLP (Dec. 23, 2014), available at Lexology.com. Rehearing and rehearing en banc were denied (No. 13-3159) in Feb. 20, 2015.]

In May 2016, the Supreme Court said that Congress' intent in allowing awards of attorneys' fees is to discourage frivolous or unreasonable lawsuits, so it is possible for a litigant to be a prevailing party in a suit that has been resolved on purely procedural grounds, without a ruling on the merits. But, instead of deciding whether CRST was the prevailing party, the Supreme Court sent the case back to the Eighth Circuit again for the Eighth Circuit to decide whether the EEOC will have to pay $4.7 million in fees. [*EEOC v. CRST Van Expedited*, 136

S. Ct. 1642 (2016); see Gerald L. Maatman, Jr., Christina M. Janice and Alex W. Karasik, *U.S. Supreme Court Rejects the Government's Position in the Largest EEOC Fee Sanction Case Ever*, Seyfarth Shaw LLP (May 19, 2016), available at Lexology.com]

The EEOC's powers to investigate a charge include having access "at all reasonable times" to all evidence that is relevant to the charges, and the EEOC also is entitled to make copies. [42 U.S.C. § 2000e-8(a)]

In 2017, the Supreme Court held that when a district court's decision to grant or deny enforcement of an EEOC subpoena is appealed, the proper standard for the court of appeals to use is abuse of discretion. The appellate court does not approach the review de novo. In a case where a worker was fired after failing a fitness for duty exam after maternity leave, the employer refused to give the EEOC information about other employees who were evaluated. On remand, the Ninth Circuit said that the district court was wrong to deny enforcement of the EEOC's subpoena: the information that the EEOC sought was relevant to the investigation, because information about other employees and applicants who took the strength test could be useful. The case was sent back to the district court again. [*McLane Co. v. EEOC,* 137 S. Ct. 1159 (2017); on remand, *U.S. EEOC v. McLane Co.,* No. 13-15126 (9th Cir. May 24, 2017). See Amber S. Healy and Shawn Ogle, *The US Supreme Court Limits Appellate Review of District Court's Refusal to Enforce Subpoenas Issued By the EEOC,* Atkinson Andelson Loya Ruud & Romo (May 19, 2017), available at Lexology.com; Gerald L. Maatman, Jr., Christopher J. DeGross and Alex W. Karasik, *Following U.S. Supreme Court Review, Ninth Circuit Remands EEOC Subpoena Case,* Seyfarth Shaw LLP (May 25, 2017), available at Lexology.com]

Unless there is a reason to excuse the requirement, plaintiffs must exhaust their remedies by pursuing EEOC charges. A Title VII plaintiff has not exhausted administrative remedies if a suit refers to time frames, discriminatory conduct, or perpetrators different from the ones raised in the administrative charges. The district court dismissed a Title VII retaliation claim for failure to exhaust EEOC administrative remedies, but the Sixth Circuit reinstated the case. Adamov charged that an executive made discriminatory comments about Adamov's Azerbaijani origin; Adamov also complained about failure to be promoted. The company fired Adamov, stating that he made a loan to a friend contrary to company ethics policy. He sued the bank and individual supervisors for discrimination and retaliation. Adamov submitted a draft EEOC charge, which was unsigned and undated, and asserted only a Title VII national origin discrimination claim. Before the court ruled on the defense motion to dismiss, Adamov filed a second charge, including a retaliation allegation and the defendant moved to dismiss once again. The district court dismissed the retaliation claim for failure to exhaust administrative remedies, but the Sixth Circuit reversed: the administrative exhaustion requirement of Title VII is not essential to the court's jurisdiction, and the defendant forfeited the exhaustion defense by not raising it before the district court. [*Adamov v. U.S. Nat'l Bank Ass'n,* 726 F.3d 851 (6th Cir. 2013)]

The Second Circuit made it easier to maintain Title VII cases in mid-2015, when it ruled that exhaustion of administrative remedies is a necessary condition for suing—but is not a jurisdictional prerequisite. The practical difference is that cases are not automatically dismissed for failure to exhaust and the employee can assert equitable defenses to excuse the failure. The plaintiff, Fowlkes, was transgender. He charged his union with discrimination and retaliation against him for filing an earlier suit. Fowlkes filed EEOC charges in the first suit, but not in the second. The district court held that it did not have jurisdiction over the second suit because the EEOC filing had not been made. The Second Circuit, however, held that the failure was not jurisdictional and remanded to give Fowlkes a chance to assert defenses. For example, exhaustion might have been futile because, at the time the second suit was filed, the EEOC's position was that Title VII did not cover discrimination on the basis of gender identity. (The EEOC has since changed its position: see § 34.06[D].) Fowlkes might also be able to show that the second case was reasonably related to the first case, where administrative remedies had been exhausted. [*Fowlkes v. Ironworkers Local 40*, 790 F.3d 378 (2d Cir. 2015)]

[C]   State Agencies

In a Fifth Circuit case, procedural failures required dismissal of an age-discrimination judgment in favor of the plaintiff. He filed a complaint with the EEOC and did not check the box on the form indicating that he wanted the charge filed with both the EEOC and the Texas Commission on Human Rights. Therefore, he failed to go through the mandatory step of filing a state charge—and his federal lawsuit was invalid. [*Jones v. Grinnell Corp.*, 235 F.3d 972 (5th Cir. 2001)] Although Texas has a work-sharing agreement, this merely means that a single filing can cover both state and federal requirements—not that the state procedure can be ignored, even in a case where the charging party asserts only federal claims.

However, a 2010 case (where the plaintiff, Rodriguez, filed charges with both the state agency and the EEOC) held that a federal suit was timely when it was brought within 90 days of the date of the federal right to sue letter, even though it was filed more than 90 days after the state right to sue letter was issued. Colorado has a work-sharing agreement with the EEOC, but the agreement does not give the state agency the power to act on behalf of the EEOC. Furthermore, the state right to sue letter did not inform Rodriguez of her federal rights, and referred only to the state case. Therefore, Rodriguez' federal suit was timely because it was filed within 90 days of the date of the federal right to sue letter. [*Rodriguez v. Wet Ink, LLC*, 603 F.3d 810 (10th Cir. 2010)]

§ 42.05   TIMING REQUIREMENTS

[A]   Generally

Section 2000e-5(c) says that if the state where the alleged unlawful employment practice occurred has a state antidiscrimination law, then EEOC charges may not be filed until 60 days have passed since commencement of state antidiscrimination charges. If the EEOC itself files a charge, it has an obligation to notify the appropriate state authority and give it sixty days to enforce the local law and eliminate the unlawful employment practice.

The basic rule is that, to avoid being dismissed as untimely, EEOC charges must be filed within 180 days of the date of the wrongful action. Then papers must be served on the employer within 10 days. However, if the state has an antidiscrimination agency, the employee has 300 days from the date of the wrongful action to file with the EEOC. There is an additional requirement that the employee not wait more than 30 days after the state or local agency has dismissed a state charge to file with the EEOC. [42 U.S.C. § 2000e-5(e)(1)]

The charge has to be verified (the charging party has to state under penalty of perjury that the statements in the charge are true). [42 U.S.C. § 2000e5(b)] In March 2002, the U.S. Supreme Court upheld an EEOC regulation, 29 C.F.R. § 1601.12(b), that allows "relation back." That is, if a charge is made within the 300-day period but verified later, it will still be timely because the verification "relates back" to the timely charge. The Supreme Court ruled in *Edelman v. Lynchburg College* [535 U.S. 106 (2002)] that Title VII requires both filing within 300 days and verification, but the two need not occur at the same time.

The Tenth Circuit held that verification of an EEOC charge is not jurisdictional, although it is a condition precedent to filing a Title VII suit. The employer must raise this defense when it first responds to the complaint; otherwise, it is waived. The Tenth Circuit gave some leeway to Title VII plaintiffs, who may be proceeding pro se. However, it is bad strategy for the employer to respond too soon: EEOC regulations allow a charging party to correct technical defects and verify the charge after the time to file has expired. [*Gad v. Kansas State Univ.*, 787 F.3d 1032 (10th Cir. 2015)]

The Supreme Court resolved another timing issue. If the plaintiff's claim is for only one act of discrimination or retaliation, or for several separate acts, then the claim must meet the 180-day or 300-day requirement to be timely. However, if the plaintiff charges a number of acts that he or she claims made up part of the same practice creating a hostile work environment, then the claim is timely as long as there was at least one act in the series that occurred during the 180-day or 300-day period. [*National R.R. Passenger Corp. v. Morgan*, 536 U.S. 101 (2002)]

Constructive discharge is the situation in which an employee resigns, but has really been forced out of the job by intolerable conditions. In mid-2015, the Supreme Court held that the timing period for constructive discharge filings (in this case, the special 45-day period for federal employees) begins when the employee resigns, not at the earlier period when conditions deteriorated to the point that the employee decided that quitting was necessary. The constructive discharge claim accrues when the employee gives notice of resignation, not on the effective date when the employee actually leaves. [*Green v. Brennan*, 136 S. Ct. 1769 (2016)]

Five years later, the Supreme Court ruled that a Title VII pay discrimination charge must be filed within 180 days of the time the discriminatory employment decision was made and communicated to the employee. It is not acceptable to treat discriminatory pay as a continuing violation, for which a charge can be filed within 180 days of any paycheck. The Supreme Court said that if an employer engages in a series of intentionally discriminatory acts, each of which could support a separate charge, then each act counts as a new violation. But continuing to pay a female employee less than a comparable male reflects later effects of past discrimination—so the clock does not start again with each paycheck. [*Ledbetter v. Goodyear Tire & Rubber Co.*, 550 U.S. 618 (2007)]

Legislation was passed and signed in 2009 to reverse this result for Title VII, the ADA, the ADEA, and the Rehabilitation Act: The Lilly Ledbetter Fair Pay Act of 2009, Pub. L. No. 111-2. The Ledbetter Act provides that a charge is timely if filed within 180 days (or 300 days, in certain instances) of the adoption of a discriminatory practice; the employee's becoming subject to that practice; or the employee being affected by the application of the practice. Every paycheck that reflects discrimination can start the time running anew. A successful plaintiff can recover back pay for up to two years before the date of filing of the charge, for similar or related discriminatory acts during the filing period. The Ledbetter Act is retroactive for all cases that were pending on the day before the Supreme Court's decision, but not for cases that were already complete at that time.

The Fifth Circuit applied the continuing violation doctrine (i.e., the entire period of harassment can be considered in determining liability, as long as there was at least one unlawful act during the limitations period) even if the harassment was severe enough to put the employee on notice of the duty to make a complaint. A college professor said that she was harassed on account of sex by her immediate supervisor since 2003. The harassment was not sexual, but consisted of derogating her abilities because she was a woman, and excluding her from meetings because she "talked too much for a woman." The plaintiff, Heath, filed a state-court discrimination suit in 2009 but dropped it. She took a sabbatical for job-related stress from 2010 to 2011. She alleged that the harassment resumed when she returned to work. According to the plaintiff, she complained about this treatment in 2009 and 2012, but the university ignored her complaints. The Fifth Circuit held that the date on which the plaintiff first becomes aware of having an actionable Title VII claim is no longer relevant. When a court decides whether to apply the continuing violation doctrine, the Fifth Circuit identified the factors as whether the acts are related; whether intervening acts by the employer separated the earlier from the later acts; and whether it would be inequitable for the court to consider all of the ongoing conduct as a series. The Fifth Circuit concluded that there was a continuing violation in this case, and remanded it to see if allegations about post-2011 conduct could survive summary judgment. [*Heath v. Bd. of Supervisors*, 850 F.3d 731 (5th Cir. 2017); see Esteban Shardonofsky and John P. Phillips , *Fifth Circuit Warps Time in Decision on the Continuing Violation Doctrine*, Seyfarth Shaw LLP (Mar. 14, 2017), available at Lexology.com]

In 2010, the Supreme Court ruled that discrimination charges brought by Chicago firefighters were not untimely. Although the promotion exam that allegedly had a disparate impact on black and Hispanic firefighters was given many years in the past, the Supreme Court ruled that the unlawful practice could be challenged every time it is used—i.e., every time a new promotion list is issued based on the allegedly biased examination. [*Lewis v. City of Chicago*, 559 U.S. 932 (2010)] In 2011, 19 white firefighters and one Hispanic firefighter began receiving payments under this decision; they will receive a total of $2 million in back pay, pension credits, and attorneys' fees. [Rebecca Moore, *Award Finally Decided in Connecticut Firefighters Suit*, plansponsor.com (Aug. 3, 2011)]

In 2008, the Second Circuit said that, for statute of limitations purposes, a claim of discriminatory loss of seniority occurred on the date when an airline clerk learned he had lost seniority, not on the later date when he was fired: discharge was only the delayed, neutral effect of an alleged earlier act of discrimination. [*Alleyne v. American Airlines*, 548 F.3d 219 (2d Cir. 2008)]

The EEOC has 30 days after filing of a charge, or 30 days after the expiration of the period for referring charges from state agencies, to negotiate with the employer to produce a conciliation agreement that ends the unlawful employment practice. If the 30-day period expires without a conciliation agreement, the EEOC has the power to sue the employer in federal court.

On the other hand, if the EEOC makes a "no-cause" finding about the charge, or 180 days have passed since the charge was filed with the EEOC or referred from the state agency, and the EEOC has not filed suit and there has been no conciliation agreement, then the EEOC will notify the charging party. This is known as a "right-to-sue letter," because it enables the charging party to bring a federal suit.

Some employers draft their job applications to include a limitation on the time within which employees can bring employment-related claims (e.g., six months, rather than the state's statute of limitations, which is likely to be longer). Some courts have upheld these limitations, on the theory that signing the application and taking the job obligates the employee to abide by the limitation. [See, e.g., *Thurman v. DaimlerChrysler, Inc.*, 397 F.3d 352 (6th Cir. 2004)]

In an Equal Pay Act (EPA)/Fair Labor Standards Act (FLSA) case, the district court enforced FedEx's employment agreement, which required actions to be brought within six months. (The suit was timely under federal law.) The Sixth Circuit reversed, finding that the shortened statute of limitations was an unlawful waiver of the plaintiff's rights under the FLSA; because the EPA is part of the FLSA, the Sixth Circuit did not permit waiver of the EPA claim either. [*Boaz v. FedEx Customer Info. Servs., Inc.*, 725 F.3d 603 (6th Cir. 2013)]

The New Jersey Supreme Court ruled in mid-2016 that employers cannot shorten the two-year statute of limitations for filing claims under the state's Law Against Discrimination. In this case, the employer's job application said that all suits must be filed within six months, but the state supreme court refused to enforce this provision because it conflicts with the state's public policy that employees should have a longer period to bring suit. [*Rodriguez v. Raymours Furniture Co. Inc.*, No. A-27-14 (N.J. June 15, 2016); see Rosemary S. Gousman and Richard R. Meneghello, *N.J. Employers No Longer Able to Shrink Lawsuit Time Limits*, Fisher Phillips (June 16, 2016), available at Lexology.com]

In late 2013, the Supreme Court upheld a contractual three-year limitation on bringing suits about an Employment Retirement Income Security Act (ERISA) disability plan. Although this was an ERISA case, it is likely to be influential in employment discrimination cases as well. [*Heimeshoff v. Hartford Life & Accident Ins. Co.*, 134 S. Ct. 604 (2013)]

The District Court for the District of Columbia held that, unless a statute forbids it, a contract can reduce the statute of limitations as long as the reduced statute of limitations is reasonable. The district court enforced a reduced (six-month) statute of limitations for 42 U.S.C. § 1981 claims but not for Title VII claims. The court found that a six-month limitation is reasonable under § 1981, not only because there is no proof that Congress intended a longer statute of limitations, but because there are no administrative requirements that make it impractical to file suit quickly. But Title VII is different: plaintiffs are required to exhaust their administrative remedies, and might not be able to do so within six months [*Njang v. Whitestone Grp., Inc.*, 2016 U.S. Dist. LEXIS 65370 (D.D.C. May 18, 2016); see Jose M. Jara et. al., *Worth Covering: News, Tips and Thoughts for Professional Liability Carriers,* FisherBroyles (Aug. 30, 2016), available at Lexology .com]

The New Jersey Supreme Court decided a case of first impression in mid-2016: whether the two-year statute of limitations under state anti-discrimination law can be reduced by contract. (The state law does not include an explicit statute of limitations, so the two-year statute of limitations for personal injury cases is applied.) The defendant's job application said that all employment-related claims had to be brought within six months. The plaintiff was injured at work and fired two days after his return to work, allegedly as part of a company-wide RIF. Almost seven months later, he brought a suit for disability discrimination. The lower courts upheld the provision as clear and unambiguous, but the state supreme court reversed, holding that the purpose of the statute is to combat discrimination. The state has a Division on Civil Rights, where complaints can be filed within six months of the accrual of a cause of action, as an alternative forum for discrimination cases. Enforcing the employer's restriction on filing claims would significantly curtail access to the Division. [*Rodriguez v. Raymours Furniture*, 138 A.3d 528 (N.J. 2016); see Maja M. Obradovic, *NJ Supreme Court Holds That Statute of Limitations to Sue Under NJ Law Against Discrimination*

Cannot Be Contractually Shortened, Greenbaum, Rowe, Smith & Davis LLP (July 20, 2016), available at Lexology.com]

In nearly all cases, the appropriate defendant is the employer company— there are virtually no situations in which Title VII suits can appropriately be brought against an individual person who is alleged to have performed discriminatory acts. For example, in 2007 the Eleventh Circuit held that individuals cannot be sued under either the ADA provision against retaliation in employment, or the Florida statute forbidding HIV/AIDS discrimination. The court held that the language of the employment provisions of the ADA is similar to that of Title VII and the ADEA, where individual suits have been ruled out; the Southern District of Florida has forbidden suits against individuals under the state HIV/AIDS statute. [*Albra v. Advan, Inc.*, 490 F.3d 826 (11th Cir. 2007)]

In rare cases, individual liability may exist under other federal statutes (e.g., the FLSA, EPA, or FMLA). In 2007, the First Circuit ruled that the president of a hotel was personally liable for wage and hour violations, because he had ultimate control over operations, and was instrumental in causing the corporation to violate the FLSA. [*Chao v. Hotel Oasis Inc.*, 493 F.3d 26, 42 Cal. 4th (1st Cir. 2007)] The Fifth Circuit held that a supervisor can be personally liable for retaliation in an FMLA wrongful discharge case. [*Modica v. Taylor*, 465 F.3d 174 (5th Cir. 2006)]. A much later case, *Eichenholz v. Brink's Inc.*, No. 16-cv-11786-LTS (D. Mass. May 9, 2017) allows FMLA retaliation and interference charges to be pursued against the employer corporation's chief procurement officer. See HR Daily Advisor, *Can an Individual Supervisor Be Liable Under the FMLA?* (Aug. 30, 2017) (benefitslink.com).

State courts may be more hospitable; even in a state that applies the concept of employment at will, it is possible that a supervisor would be held liable for discriminatory practices. [See, e.g., *Trau-Med of Am. Inc. v. All State Ins. Co.*, 71 S.W.3d 691, 703 (Tenn. 2002). Individual liability under New Hampshire's anti-discrimination and anti-retaliation statutes was found: the statute makes aiding and abetting unlawful, without limitation to who commits it, and a complaint can be filed against a "person," which includes individuals: *EEOC v. Fred Fuller Oil Co. Inc.*, 134 A.3d 17 (N.H. 2016); see Tawny L. Alvarez, *While There WAS No "I" in Defendant, There Is Now: New Hampshire Supreme Court Finds Individual Liability in State Anti-Discrimination and Anti-Retaliation Statutes*, Verrill Dana LLP (Feb. 26, 2016).]

Section 2000e-5(f)(3) provides that the suit can be filed in any federal District Court in the state where the alleged unlawful employment practice occurred. (The number of federal judicial districts in a state ranges from one to four.) The suit can also be brought in the judicial district where the relevant employment records are kept, or in the district where the plaintiff would have worked if there had been no unlawful employment practice. Finally, if the defendant company can't be found in any of those districts, the plaintiff can sue the defendant company in the judicial district where the company's principal office is located.

There is no explicit statute of limitations in 42 U.S.C. § 1981 (the federal law guaranteeing all persons within the jurisdiction of the United States the same rights to make and enforce contracts that "white citizens" have). Therefore, there was a circuit split on the proper statute of limitations to apply in § 1981 wrongful discharge cases. The split was resolved by the Supreme Court's May 2004 ruling: the statute of limitations is four years, because the current version of § 1981 was enacted by the Civil Rights Act of 1991 (CRA '91). Under federal law, the statute of limitations for all federal laws enacted after December 1, 1990, is four years, so that applies to CRA '91. [*Jones v. R.R. Donnelley & Sons Co.*, 541 U.S. 401 (2004)]

When there is no evidence of actual date on which a complainant received a right to sue letter, it will be presumed that delivery occurred three days after mailing—hence a suit, 98 days after issuance of the letter, was untimely, although the presumption can be rebutted by evidence of delayed receipt. Merely calling mail delivery unreliable is not enough. [*Payan v. Aramark Mgmt. Servs.*, 495 F.3d 1119 (9th Cir. 2007)]

[B]   Tolling

In a limited group of circumstances, the statute of limitations can be tolled (suspended) when it would be unjust to insist on strict compliance. Tolling may be permitted if:

- The employer was guilty of deception or some other wrongdoing that prevented the employee from asserting Title VII rights;

- The employee tried to file a timely lawsuit, but the pleading was rejected as defective;

- The employee filed in time, but in the wrong court.

Tolling is usually considered a defense, which means that it is up to the plaintiff to prove that it was available, and not up to the defendant to prove that it was not.

The term "tolling" is sometimes used to cover two different but related concepts. "Equitable tolling" allows a delayed case to continue because, even though the plaintiff's excusable ignorance or oversight caused the delay, the defendant is not prejudiced (harmed) by the delay.

"Equitable estoppel" prevents the defendant from complaining about a delay that was caused in whole or part by the defendant's deceit or other conduct prejudicial to the plaintiff's interests, e.g., if the employee is afraid to approach the EEOC and endanger the internal investigation and grievance procedure that was being carried out. [*Currier v. Radio Free Europe*, 159 F.3d 1363 (D.C. Cir. 1998)]

Note, however, that in 2014 the Second Circuit joined the Seventh and Ninth Circuits and the majority of district courts in holding that filing EEOC discrimination charges does not toll the statute of limitations for state-law tort claims, even if the same facts are involved in both cases. The plaintiff filed an EEOC charge after quitting her accounting job. She said that she suffered constructive discharge because of offensive physical contact and racial and sexual comments. In November 2009, she filed a federal suit and included state-law claims of assault, battery, and intentional infliction of emotional stress. The Second Circuit agreed that the state claims were time-barred and rejected the plaintiff's argument that judicial efficiency rules out bringing a state case while the EEOC is still reviewing the case. As a result, in these circuits, plaintiffs should file state-law claims at the same time as the EEOC charge, and ask that the state tort suit be stayed until the EEOC completes its investigation. [*Castagna v. Luceno*, 744 F.3d 254 (2d Cir. 2014)]

§ 42.06   CLASS ACTIONS

Class actions are governed by Rule 23 of the Federal Rules of Civil Procedure, especially Rule 23(b). The various subsections of Rule 23 create several alternative methods of litigating a class action, but each method has its own procedural requirements that must be satisfied. The requirements relate to what the plaintiffs want (money damages, or just an injunction?) and how people become members of the class (are they automatically included unless they opt out, or do they have to opt in?). It can also be difficult and expensive for the potential plaintiffs to give the required notice to everyone who might want to join the class.

Discrimination cases focusing on monetary damages can be hard to certify as class actions. Rule 23(b)(2) requires not only a common injury but uniform remedies for the whole class. Would-be plaintiffs who can't use Rule 23(b)(2) may have to fall back on Rule 23(b)(3), which requires them to prove that class-wide issues are more important in the case than individual issues. They must also prove that a class action is better than other methods of resolving the dispute. In some cases, a "hybrid" class action will be allowed. First a class is certified under Rule 23(b)(2) to decide if the employer is liable. If it is, damages are determined under Rule 23(b)(2). In recent years, many class actions have been denied certification, or have been certified and then de-certified, based on court findings that each claimant's assertions must be handled individually on a case-by-case basis.

Sometimes employees subject to an arbitration clause want to bring a class arbitration against an employer. To an increasing extent, employers are drafting arbitration clauses to require claims to be arbitrated individually—a practice that the National Labor Relations Board (NLRB) held to be unlawful. However, the Fifth Circuit permitted employers to require waivers of class arbitration, finding that the waiver is not inconsistent with the right to pursue collective action—as long as the arbitration agreement informs employees that the right to file an

NLRB complaint is not waived. [*D.R. Horton v. NLRB*, 737 F.3d 344 (5th Cir. 2013)] En banc rehearing was denied. The NLRB continues to make rulings that class arbitration waivers violate the National Labor Relations Act (NLRA), and courts continue to rule against the NLRB. [See, e.g., *Murphy Oil v. NLRB*, 808 F.3d 1013 (5th Cir. 2015)]

This issue was active in mid-2016, when the Eighth Circuit upheld the validity of class and collective action waivers [*Cellular Sales of Mo. LLC v. NLRB*, 824 F.3d 772 (8th Cir. 2016); see Howard M. Bloom and Philip B. Rosen, *Eighth Circuit Finds Class and Collective Action Waivers Lawful Under NLRA, Contrary to Seventh Circuit*, Jackson Lewis PC (June 3, 2016), available at Lexology.com], and the Second and Eleventh Circuit held that class action waivers do not violate the NLRA, although the Second Circuit decision is unpublished. [*Patterson v. Raymour's Furniture Co.*, 659 Fed. Appx. 40 (2d Cir. 2016); see Brian J. Stair, *Second Circuit Reluctantly Maintains Status Quo on Class Waiver Provisions, But Hints at Future Change in Law*, Husch Blackwell LLP (Sept. 12, 2016), available at Lexology.com] But the Seventh and Ninth Circuit agreed with the NLRB: forbidding employees to sue or arbitrate as a class impairs their ability to engage in collective activity that is protected by the NLRA. [*Lewis v. Epic Sys.*, 823 F.3d 1147 (7th Cir. 2016) and *Morris v. Ernst & Young*, 834 F.3d 975 (9th Cir. 2016); see Lonnie Giamela, Christopher C. Hoffman and Richard R. Meneghello, *Mandatory Class Waivers Struck Down by 9th Circuit*, Fisher Phillips (Aug. 22, 2016), available at Lexology.com]

On January 13, 2017, the Supreme Court agreed to hear a consolidated case on the issue of class and collective action waivers. However, in February the Supreme Court announced that it would not hear arguments until the term beginning in October 2017. [*Murphy Oil*, No. 16-307; *Morris v. Ernst & Young*, No. 16-300; *Lewis v. Epic Sys.*, No. 16-285; see Christopher C. Murray & Ron Chapman, Jr., *Supreme Court Jumps into Class Action Waiver Fight*, Ogletree Deakins (Jan. 13, 2017), available at Lexology.com] After the Supreme Court's announcement, the Sixth Circuit became another jurisdiction that adopts the NLRB's position that class action waivers in mandatory arbitration programs violate NLRA § 7. [*NLRB v. Alternative Entm't*, No. 16-1385, 2017 WL 2297620 (6th Cir. May 26, 2017); see David Pryzbylski, *A Growing Divide: Sixth Circuit Decision to Invalidate Class/Collective Action Waiver Widens Appellate Court Split*, Barnes & Thornburg LLP (May 31, 2017), available at Lexology.com]

On the question of availability of class arbitration in Fair Labor Standards Act cases, see, e.g., *Walthour v. Chipio Windshield Repair* [745 F.3d 1326 (11th Cir. 2014) (joining the Second, Fourth, Fifth, and Eighth Circuits, the Eleventh Circuit held that the right to bring an FLSA collective action is not a substantive legal right that can never be waived, so an arbitration agreement forbidding class claims was upheld); *Walton v. The Rose Grp.*, No. 13-1674 (E.D. Pa. Dec. 11, 2013) (clause forbidding class arbitration was enforced, even though the judge said it was unfair).]

[A]   The *Dukes* Case and Its Implications

In mid-2011, the Supreme Court held that the massive sex discrimination class action against Wal-Mart was improperly certified. The plaintiffs alleged that Wal-Mart's broad corporate culture discriminated against women in pay and promotions, creating a company-wide discriminatory policy. In the view of the Supreme Court majority, Wal-Mart gave store managers a significant amount of discretion, so the existence of sex discrimination would have to be assessed at the individual store level.

The Supreme Court majority opinion held that the plaintiffs failed to show a single policy rather than numerous acts of alleged discrimination against individuals, so there was no common employment decision that could be challenged under Rule 23(a)(2).

Nor could the plaintiffs use Rule 23(b)(2) to seek back pay, even if they called the back pay claims incidental to claims for injunctive relief. The Supreme Court held that Wal-Mart would be entitled to individual determinations of back pay eligibility—it would not be appropriate to determine a class-wide back pay award by extrapolating from a small sample.

Some commentators suggested that the lesson large companies can take from this is that if they establish an overall anti-discrimination policy but delegate significant power to regional managers, they will be able to use the *Wal-Mart* decision to defend themselves—possibly in contexts extending beyond discrimination cases. [*Wal-Mart v. Dukes*, 131 S. Ct. 2541 (2011)]

In the subsequent years, *Dukes*-related litigation continued. The Sixth Circuit reversed the District Court for the Western District of Tennessee. The Sixth Circuit held that *Dukes* plaintiffs' class claims were not time-barred, so they could pursue class certification of sex discrimination allegations. Wal-Mart plaintiffs amended their California case to narrow the class to current and former women employees who were discriminated against in California. Suits were also filed in Tennessee, Texas, Florida, and Wisconsin. The Sixth Circuit held that a class action can be tolled after a previous denial of class certification. The Sixth Circuit said that *Dukes* did not rule out a (b)(2) action: this was the first attempt to certify a regional class in Wal-Mart's Region 43. Because of the new certification theory and the more narrowly tailored plaintiff group, the Sixth Circuit allowed class claims to proceed. [*Phipps, et. al. v. Wal-Mart Stores, Inc.*, 792 F.3d 637 (6th Cir. 2015)]

Female store managers employed by Family Dollar Stores persuaded the Fourth Circuit that *Dukes* did not prevent them from pursuing a class action: there were nationwide policies for salary structures and management discretion followed common patterns favoring men. However, although the plaintiffs were allowed to amend their complaint, it was not clear that they would obtain nationwide class status. The case was remanded to the district court for further development of the record. [*Scott v. Family Dollar Stores, Inc.*, 733 F.3d 105 (4th Cir. 2013), *reh'g denied*, 743 F.3d 886 (4th Cir. 2013)]

The Seventh Circuit certified a class of African-American teachers in Chicago, saying that even if the legality of final employment decisions cannot be decided on a class-wide basis because there were individual exercises of discretion, sometimes the legality of intermediate decisions can be resolved for a class. About a quarter of Chicago tenured teachers were African-American, but schools that were selected for "turnaround" had 51% African-American tenured teachers. The Seventh Circuit held that, before the final, discretionary step was reached, there could have been disparate impact discrimination against African-American teachers. In this reading, a company-wide practice where some actions can be exercised by managers who have discretion may be a suitable subject for a class action. [*Chicago Teachers Union, Local No. 1, Am. Fed'n of Teachers, AFL-CIO v. Bd. of Educ. of the City of Chicago*, No. 14-2843 (7th Cir. Aug. 7, 2015)]

A class of steelworkers charged systemic racial discrimination in promotion and a racially hostile work environment. The district court refused to certify a class, but was reversed by the Fourth Circuit in 2009. After *Wal-Mart*, the district court decertified the class in the promotions part of the case but, on appeal, the Fourth Circuit reversed once again, holding that statistics showed that promotions were partially racially based. There was substantial anecdotal evidence of promotions discrimination in several departments. There was also evidence of a racially hostile work environment, so the case was remanded once again for recertification of the class. [*Brown v. Nucor Corp.*, 785 F.3d 895 (4th Cir. 2015)]

The EEOC lost a high-profile case in the Southern District of New York. The case began in 2007, when the EEOC filed a systemic pattern or practice pregnancy discrimination suit about 78 discriminatees against Bloomberg L.P. The district court granted summary judgment for Bloomberg on the class allegations, holding that a reasonable fact-finder could not conclude that Bloomberg maintained a practice of decreasing the pay or responsibilities of pregnant workers. The EEOC then asserted individual claims of pregnancy discrimination on behalf of 29 claimants who had not intervened in the suit, plus six more intervenors. Because of inadequacies in the EEOC's investigation and conciliation efforts, the district court dismissed the claims of the non-intervenor plaintiffs. The court found that the conciliation attempt was inadequate because it focused on excessively broad systemic claims, not individual claims. All claims about the intervenors were dismissed except for one count of pregnancy discrimination involving one employee. [*EEOC v. Bloomberg L.P.*, 967 F. Supp. 2d 802, 816 (S.D.N.Y. Sept. 9, 2013)]

After eight years and two Supreme Court appeals, a suit by a class of 700 black brokers against Merrill Lynch was settled in mid-2013. The class received $160 million, the largest race discrimination settlement to date. It was possible to certify a class in this case because Merrill Lynch imposed a system of uniform operations and strict centralized controls. *Dukes* means that if local supervisors have discretion, class members only have the same injury if the managers exercise discretion the same way, showing the same bias. The plaintiffs said that, even post-*Dukes*, a class should be certified because of two nationwide policies with disparate impact on African-American brokers: a policy allowing brokers to choose their own teams, and an account distribution policy that allocated a departing broker's accounts to other brokers based on their past results. According to the plaintiffs, the teams excluded black brokers, so their compensation and access to new accounts were limited. The Seventh Circuit certified a (b)(2) class for the limited purpose of deciding whether Merrill's practices violated federal law; if so, mini-trials would be held on individual damages. [*McReynolds v. Merrill Lynch*, 672 F.3d 482 (7th Cir. 2012)]

§ 42.07   THE DISCRIMINATION COMPLAINT

Once the case is cleared for litigation in federal court, the plaintiff must draft a complaint to inform the defendant and the court system of the nature of the allegations against the defendant.

Late in 2001, the Eleventh Circuit adopted a position already held by the Third, Seventh, and Eighth Circuits: An EEOC intake questionnaire constitutes a "charge" if it is verified and has the information a charge would contain, and a reasonable person would consider the questionnaire to manifest an intent to seek Title VII remedies. [*Wilkerson v. Grinnell Corp.*, 270 F.3d 1314 (11th Cir. 2001)]

A similar issue went to the Supreme Court in the ADEA context. The Court permitted an ADEA suit to proceed, after the complainant filed a Form 283 intake questionnaire with the EEOC, but did not file the official Form 5 (charge). The EEOC did not carry out informal dispute resolution with the employer. The Court held that a valid ADEA charge requires only a few items of information (the name of the charging party, the nature of the allegation, and a request that the EEOC settle a dispute or take remedial action). In this case, the employer was aware that the plaintiff and thirteen other employees had alleged age discrimination. The Court remanded the case to the district court, holding that the lower court can make up for the deficiency by attempting to reconcile the parties in a settlement. (The EEOC stated that it has improved its procedures to make sure the same problem will not recur.) [*Federal Express Corp v. Holowecki*, 552 U.S. 389 (2008)]

A 2008 Third Circuit case finds that a two-page document, including EEOC Form 5, constituted a charge. The first page gave the plaintiff's date of birth and contact information for the charging party and his employer. The complainant checked the box alleging age discrimination and cross-referenced the second sheet. He signed it in two places, but did not check the box for dual filing with the state agency, and did not have the signatures notarized. The second page, described as an affidavit, described improper questions asked at the interview, leading the plaintiff to believe that he was not offered a job because of his age (59). The EEOC regulations provide that a charge should contain identifying information for charging party and defendant, a statement of the facts allegedly constituting discrimination, how many employees the employer has, and whether or not the charging party has already initiated state proceedings.

About two months later, the EEOC wrote to the plaintiff's attorney asking for more information, stating that the plaintiff would have to provide the information within 33 days. But, instead of submitting the information to the EEOC, the plaintiff brought suit 80 days after submitting the document to the EEOC. The defendant moved to dismiss the case for failure to exhaust administrative remedies; the Third Circuit accepted the two-page document as a charge because it gave notice of the nature of the plaintiff's allegations. [*Holender v. Mutual Indus. N. Inc.*, 527 F.3d 352 (3d Cir. 2008)]

Although the defendant in a sexual harassment suit argued that the case should be dismissed for failure to exhaust administrative remedies, the Tenth Circuit held in 2017 that the sparsity of details in the plaintiff's EEOC charge did not require dismissal. The plaintiff wrote "see attached" for many questions asking for detailed information, but did not give the EEOC an attachment. The EEOC failed to ask for one. The plaintiff submitted a six-paragraph statement alleging that he was fired for rejecting his supervisor's sexual advances, and naming two witnesses and describing a co-worker as a comparator who received better treatment. The Tenth Circuit said that Congress did not provide much guidance as to what constitutes an adequate charge, and in this case the charge form gave a general description of the alleged discrimination. [*Jones v. Needham*, No. 16-6156 (10th Cir. May 12, 2017); see Manatt Phelps & Phillips LLP, *Lack of Detail in EEOC Charge Doesn't Mandate Dismissal of a Lawsuit* (June 5, 2017), available at Lexology.com; John P. Rodgers, *6 of One, Half a Dozen of the Other: 10th Circuit Rules Quid Pro Quo and Hostile Work Environment Harassment Theories Aren't So Different After All,* Bradley Arant Boult Cummings LLP (May 23, 2017), available at Lexology.com]

The Supreme Court held in 2014 that federal pleading rules merely require a short and plain statement of the claim. Therefore, a complaint cannot be dismissed for failure to state a claim merely because it did not invoke 42 U.S.C. § 1983, the statute under which damages were sought. An imperfect statement of legal theory does not justify dismissal. [*Johnson v. City of Shelby*, 135 S. Ct. 346 (2014)]

§ 42.08   MEETING BURDENS

In legal parlance, "the burden of production" means having to provide evidence to prove a particular point, and "the burden of proof" is the standard used to determine if adequate evidence has been supplied.

Section 2000e(m) says that "demonstrates" means "meets the burdens of production and persuasion." This covers the extremely important legal issue of who has to provide evidence of what. It is always easier to wait for the other party to produce evidence and then show that this evidence is incorrect, incomplete, not technically satisfactory, or inadequate to prove the case, than to have to submit independent evidence of one's own viewpoint.

Section 2000e-2(k) explains what the plaintiff has to prove in order to win a disparate-impact case. The complaining party must show that the employer's challenged employment practice has a disparate impact on a protected group. At this stage, the employer has a chance to prove that the employment practice is valid because it is job-related and consistent with the needs of the employer's business. However, if the employer demonstrates that the employment practice does not cause disparate impact, it is not necessary to prove business necessity for that practice. On the other hand, business necessity is only a defense against disparate impact claims, not against claims of intentional discrimination.

Another route for proving disparate impact is for the complaining party to demonstrate disparate impact and also show that the employer refused to adopt an alternative employment practice that would eliminate the disparate impact.

According to the Ninth Circuit, the 1991 amendments to Title VII, allowing proof of violation when discrimination was a motivating factor for the employer (rather than the sole motivating factor) does not require proof of the impermissible factor by direct evidence, because the statutory language does not include the phrase "direct evidence." A year later, the Supreme Court affirmed. [*Costa v. Desert Palace Inc.*, 299 F.3d 838 (9th Cir. 2002), *aff'd*, 539 U.S. 90 (2003)]

On a related issue, the Fifth Circuit ruled in late 2013 that, even after the ADAAA has taken effect, plaintiffs are still required to prove disability before they prove discrimination, rejecting the plaintiff's argument that the new focus is whether discrimination occurred, not whether the employee has a disability. The jury still must find the plaintiff to be a qualified individual with a disability (QIWD) as a predicate to finding disability discrimination. [*Neely v. PSEG*, 735 F.3d 242 (5th Cir. 2013)]

The Eleventh Circuit joined the Sixth Circuit in holding that, at the summary judgment stage of a mixed-motive discrimination case, the plaintiff's burden is to show that the protected characteristic was a (not necessarily the) motivating factor in the adverse employment action. Therefore, Title VII and § 1981 mixed-motive claims should not have been dismissed because the plaintiff provided enough evidence that her sex was a motivating factor in the decision not to renew her contract. The plaintiff was not required to prove that the employer's asserted reason for the adverse action was false. [*Quigg v. Thomas Co. Sch. Dist.*, 814 F.3d 1227 (11th Cir. 2016); see Patrick Mulligan, *Eleventh Circuit Finds the McDonnell Douglas Burden Shifting Test Inapplicable to "Mixed-Motive" Discrimination Claims*, Bressler, Amery & Ross PC (Feb. 24, 2016), available at Lexology.com; see *also White v. Baxter Healthcare Corp.*, 533 F.3d 381 (6th Cir. 2008); Akerman LLP, *Eleventh Circuit Announces New Standard for Employers to Win Cases on Summary Judgment* (Mar, 4, 2016), available at Lexology.com]

A Native American woman who was fired after testing positive for marijuana sued her former employer, the Mohave County Public Works Department, for race/ancestry discrimination and FMLA violations. The plaintiff's job required her to maintain a commercial driver's license, which requires random drug testing, and the employer imposed clear rules under which all safety-sensitive employees were subject to immediate dismissal for a positive drug or alcohol test. The plaintiff, Yazzie, at first said she used medical marijuana but later admitted to recreational use. The court found no evidence for her allegation of disparate treatment of Native American employees: all 10 employees who tested positive were fired or quit, and failing the test was a legitimate, non-discriminatory reason to fire her. [*Yazzie v. County of Mohave*, No. CV-14-08153, 2016 U.S. Dist. LEXIS 93898 (D. Ariz. July 19, 2016); see Rayna H. Jones, *Consistent Enforcement of Drug Policies Key to Avoiding Disparate Treatment Claims*, Ogletree Deakins Aug. 18, 2016, available at Lexology.com]

§ 42.09 RETALIATION CHARGES

A high percentage of discrimination cases also involve charges of retaliation. Indeed, in some cases, the judge or jury has ruled that the original charge of discrimination was not supported by adequate evidence—but there was enough evidence of retaliation for making the charge to subject the employer to retaliation liability.

Under a 2006 Supreme Court decision, liability for retaliation is broader than liability for underlying workplace discrimination, and a retaliation case can be sustained even if the employee is not demoted and his or her compensation remains the same—as long as the retaliation is severe enough that a reasonable employee would take it into consideration in deciding whether or not to pursue a discrimination complaint. [*Burlington N. & Santa Fe Ry. Co. v. White*, 548 U.S. 53 (2006)]

However, in 2013, on another issue, the Supreme Court found that retaliation liability is narrower than Title VII liability in general. The 2013 case was brought by a Muslim professor, who alleged that his supervisor harassed him because of his religion and Middle Eastern national origin, and that his employer retaliated against him by interfering with a job opportunity to punish him for making discrimination charges. The Supreme Court required retaliation plaintiffs to prove that retaliation was the "but-for" cause of the adverse employment action taken against them: i.e., that they would not have been fired, demoted, etc. without a retaliatory motive. This is the same standard used in Age Discrimination in Employment Act (ADEA) cases, but is more restrictive than non-retaliation Title VII cases, where the plaintiff can prevail by showing that discrimination was one of several motivations used by the employer. The Supreme Court held that mixed-motive cases are only proper in cases involving the five criteria based on personal characteristics specified in Title VII: race, color, religion, sex, and national origin. The Supreme Court noted that Title VII's retaliation provisions are in a separate section from the basic protection against discrimination, and considered the language of the retaliation section to be more like the ADEA, hence justifying applying the higher ADEA standard in retaliation cases. [*University of Tex. Sw. Med. Ctr. v. Nassar*, 133 S. Ct. 2517 (June 24, 2013)]

The First Circuit used *Nassar*'s "but-for" causation standard to affirm summary judgment for the employer in a Title VII sexual harassment/retaliatory termination case. The *Nassar* test is that protected activity is the but-for cause of adverse employment action. In this case, the plaintiff's performance problems began before the alleged harassment by her supervisor; she did not make a complaint of sexual harassment to the employer; and co-workers said that her work performance was substandard. Therefore, the employer had a legitimate, nondiscriminatory reason to fire her. [*Ponte v. Steelcase Inc.*, 741 F.3d 310 (1st Cir. 2014)]

In a case charging retaliatory termination for complaining about sexual harassment, the university's defense was that the plaintiff was fired because she was inflexible about working hours, abused her paid time off, and was not a team player. A supervisor said that her continued anger about the harassment incident kept her from being a good fit in the department. After *Nassar* was decided, the district court granted summary judgment for the employer, holding that the plaintiff did not prove but-for causation in her retaliation case. The Fourth Circuit reversed, holding that *Nassar* did not completely eliminate *McDonnell-Douglas* analysis. [*Foster v. Univ. of Maryland-Eastern Shore*, 787 F.3d 243 (4th Cir. 2015)]

The Supreme Court's 2009 *Crawford* decision holds that employees are protected against retaliation based on their answering questions during an internal investigation; it is not necessary for the employee to have volunteered the information or initiated the investigation, because participating in an investigation can constitute the type of active and consistent opposition to an unlawful practice that triggers entitlement to protection against retaliation. [*Crawford v. Metropolitan Gov't of Nashville & Davison Cnty., TN*, 555 U.S. 271 (2009)]

The Supreme Court ruled in early 2011 that Title VII forbids retaliation against someone who has filed a discrimination complaint if the retaliation takes the form of reprisals against a person who associates with the complainant. (In this case, it was the complainant's then-fiance who eventually became her husband.) The opinion says that Title VII's ban on retaliation extends to any action that would prevent a reasonable worker from making or pursuing a discrimination charge. Although it is difficult to draw firm lines, firing a close family member is very likely to be deemed retaliation; mild reprisal against an acquaintance is very unlikely to be; courts must find the balance in the intermediate areas. On the question of who is allowed to sue for retaliation, the Supreme Court said that as well as the person engaging in the protected activity, a suit can be brought by anyone within the zone of interests protected by Title VII. [*Thompson v. North Am. Stainless*, 562 U.S. 70 (2011)]

The Supreme Court did not give hard and fast rules for defining the zone, but suggested a sliding scale: firing a close family member is almost certainly a sustainable claim, whereas a lesser degree of action against an acquaintance almost certainly will not.

The Eighth Circuit assumed, without deciding, that suits can be brought under Title VII for discrimination or retaliation based on association with a member of a protected class. (The Second, Fifth, Sixth, and Eleventh Circuits have also allowed association discrimination claims). The Eighth Circuit held that it was protected conduct for a white former police chief to attempt to promote a black woman to a supervisory position. However, the Eighth Circuit also held that he could not connect this conduct to the decision to terminate him. [*Hutton v. Maynard*, 812 F.3d 679 (8th Cir. 2016); see Erik Peters, *With a Little Help from My Friends: 8th Circuit Assumes Without Deciding That Associational Bias Claims Exist Under Title VII*, Verrill Dana LLP (Feb. 4, 2016), available at Lexology .com]

The "cat's paw" theory can be used in retaliation suits in the Fifth, Sixth, Eight, and Tenth Circuits: that is, the plaintiff can prevail by showing but-for causation between one person's retaliatory animus and an adverse employment action done by someone else. A Fifth Circuit jury awarded $150,000 in compensatory damages where supervisors made retaliatory statements against the plaintiff to the police department's Internal Affairs division, resulting in adverse job action. The chief of police, the actual decision-maker, did not have retaliatory animus against the plaintiff. The take-away for employers is that investigators should not be allowed to recommend personnel actions, and the decision-maker must perform an independent review of the results of an investigation. [*Zamora v. City of Houston*, 798 F.3d 326 (5th Cir. 2015)]

The Second Circuit reversed a grant of summary judgment for the employer in a Title VII retaliation case because only three weeks elapsed between the plaintiff's complaint to her supervisor that male peers were paid more than she was and her termination. The employer gave several explanations of why the plaintiff was terminated, and there were inconsistencies between the employer's position statement to the EEOC and the evidence submitted in discovery and litigation. [*Kwan v. Andalex Grp., LLC*, 737 F.3d 834 (2d Cir. 2013)]

The Third Circuit ruled early in 2006 that retaliation claims can be premised on a hostile work environment. Most of the circuits allow retaliation claims premised on retaliation that takes the form of severe or pervasive harassment, but the Fifth and Eighth Circuits require an ultimate employment decision to sustain a retaliation claim. [*Jensen v. Potter*, 435 F.3d 444 (3d Cir. 2006)]

The anti-retaliation provisions of Title VII protect a person who is named as a voluntary witness in a Title VII case, even if he or she is not called to testify at the trial. [*Jute v. Hamilton Sundstrand Corp.*, 420 F.3d 166 (2d Cir. 2005)] In mid-2010, the Second Circuit rejected an original theory put forward by a plaintiff. The court ruled that declining to investigate an employee's complaint of workplace discrimination (in this case, race discrimination) does not constitute retaliation for making the charge. [*Fincher v. Depository Trust & Clearing Corp.*, No. 08-5013-cv (2d Cir. May 14, 2010)]

The Fifth Circuit dismissed a retaliation case in which the plaintiff said she questioned certain potentially discriminatory actions and a more senior employee threatened to reduce her salary. She resigned, citing the threat as her reason. The next day, the company president apologized and said that the manager did not have the authority to cut her pay. The Fifth Circuit ruled for the employer, holding that a reasonable employee would not have been deterred from opposing discrimination by a threat from someone outside her chain of command. [*Brandon v. The Sage Corp.*, 808 F.3d 266 (5th Cir. 2015)]

§ 42.10   TITLE VII LITIGATION

[A]   Three-Step Process

A Title VII case is very different from other civil cases, because so much revolves around questions of intentions and statistics, not just the proof of simple facts.

The basic Title VII case is a three-step process. The plaintiff establishes a prima facie case: the basic facts that are suggestive of discrimination. This is sometimes referred to as "McDonnell-Douglas burden-shifting analysis" after the Supreme Court case that established this technique.

After the plaintiff submits a prima facie case, the defendant can ask the court to dismiss the case at that stage (summary judgment), if the prima facie case would not be good enough for the plaintiff to win if the defendant did not submit a case of its own.

On the other hand, if the prima facie case is strong enough to keep the case going, the defendant employer gets a chance to rebut the plaintiff's charge of discrimination. The employer can do this by proving a legitimate, nondiscriminatory reason for the job action against the plaintiff. The employer can also prevail by proving that its action was impelled by business necessity. If summary judgment is not granted, then there will have to be a full trial. The jury (or the judge, if there is no jury in the case) will have to decide the facts.

The third step is the plaintiff's again. At this stage, the plaintiff gets to show "pretextuality": that the employer's allegedly nondiscriminatory reasons are fabricated to hide its discriminatory motive.

Whether a company actually has 15 employees is a substantive element of the Title VII case, not a jurisdictional prerequisite. Therefore, if the issue is not raised in a timely fashion, it is waived. The Supreme Court held early in 2006 that the 15-employee requirement is not jurisdictional because it does not appear in the part of the Title VII statute that grants jurisdiction to the federal courts. The court's lack of subject matter jurisdiction can be raised at any point in the case. [*Arbaugh v. Y&H Corp.*, 546 U.S. 500 (2006); similarly, *Minard v. ITC Deltacom Commc'ns Inc.*, 447 F.3d 352 (5th Cir. 2006) for the FMLA. See also *Solander v. South Ponderosa Stables*, No. CV-14-02081-PHX-DGC, 2015 U.S. Dist. LEXIS

89212 (D. Ariz. July 9, 2015); see William A. Nolan, *Employee Can't Count to 15 Under ADA Using Volunteers or Other Companies' Employees*, Barnes & Thornburg LLP (July 27, 2015), available at Lexology.com: an ADA suit was dismissed because there were fewer than 15 employees. The court refused to count volunteers toward the total: they were not formally trained. Nor could two other companies with the same owner be aggregated, because there was no common management of employee relations.]

The U.S. Supreme Court reaffirmed this three-step process in a disparate treatment Pregnancy Discrimination Act (PDA) case against UPS. The plaintiff, Young, brought a disparate impact PDA case against UPS alleging that the employer refused to accommodate the needs of pregnant workers to the same extent as other employees in need of leave. The Supreme Court held that *McDonnell-Douglas* can be used to assert disparate treatment through indirect evidence. The prima facie case is that the worker is pregnant; sought but was denied accommodation; and other workers with similar ability to work were granted accommodation. The employer can defend itself by offering a legitimate, nondiscriminatory reason for its action, but the Supreme Court said that it is not enough to say that the desired accommodation is too expensive or inconvenient. The Court vacated the grant of summary judgment to UPS because Young created a genuine dispute about the treatment of similarly situated workers and whether UPS' explanation was pretextual. However, the Supreme Court rejected Young's contention that if the employer accommodates only a subset of workers with disabling conditions, pregnant workers with similar ability to work must get the same treatment, even if another class of nonpregnant workers does not get accommodation. The Supreme Court said that pregnant workers do not get most favored nation status: pregnant workers are not entitled to favoritism. [*Young v. UPS*, 135 S. Ct. 1338 (2015)]

[B] Elements of the Prima Facie Case

The kind and amount of evidence that the plaintiff has to introduce to make a prima facie case depends on the kind of case (sex discrimination, sexual harassment, age discrimination, racial discrimination, etc.) and whether the plaintiff charges disparate treatment or disparate impact. Disparate treatment is a practice of intentional discrimination against an individual or group, whereas disparate impact is a practice that seems to be neutral and nondiscriminatory, but that has a heavier negative impact on some groups than others.

Furthermore, if the plaintiff charges that an employment practice has a disparate impact, and the employer responds by showing business necessity for that practice, the plaintiff can nevertheless win by proving that there was an alternative practice that would also have satisfied business necessity, but the employer refused to adopt that practice.

If a workplace decision involves many factors (for instance, promotion could be based on educational attainment, objective measures such as sales performance or departmental productivity, written tests, interviews, and assessments from supervisors), and the plaintiff challenges more than one of those criteria, the plaintiff has to be able to prove that each of those factors had harmful disparate impact on the plaintiff. If the various elements can't be separated and analyzed individually, then the whole decision-making practice can be treated as a single employment practice.

The "mixed motive" case works somewhat differently. It arises out of the situation in which several motivations influence the employer's decision. Some of them are lawful, others are discriminatory. The plaintiff can win a mixed motive case by showing that the discriminatory motive was influential. It is not necessary to prove that there were no legitimate motives involved. However, if the employer would have done the same thing even without a discriminatory motive being present, then the remedies available to the plaintiff will be reduced.

To establish the prima facie case, the plaintiff must show membership in a protected group; in discriminatory failure to hire cases, the plaintiff must show that he or she had the necessary qualifications for the job. In a discharge or failure to promote case, the plaintiff must show that work performance was adequate.

While disparate treatment cases usually depend on direct or indirect evidence of explicit discrimination, disparate impact cases usually turn on statistics about matters such as job applications and the composition of the workforce.

In mid-2003, the Supreme Court's *Desert Palace, Inc. v. Costa* decision [539 U.S. 90 (2003)] resolved a Circuit split. The First, Fourth, Eighth, and Eleventh Circuits had ruled that once the defendant meets its burden by articulating a legitimate nondiscriminatory reason for the job action, the plaintiff can get a jury instruction on mixed motive only by showing direct evidence. But the Supreme Court sided with the Ninth Circuit and allowed the instruction to be given on the basis of circumstantial evidence. In this case, the plaintiff, a truck driver, said that the employer's stated reason for firing her (a fight with another employee) was another instance of being treated more harshly than male co-workers for the same conduct. She also alleged that she was discriminated against when overtime work was available, and that supervisors were aware of and tolerated sex-based slurs against her.

Many jurisdictions, such as the Fifth Circuit, apply a "manager rule," under which a manager's disagreement with the employer's policy, expressed in the course of his or her work, is not a protected activity for a Title VII retaliation case. This began as an FLSA rule and was adopted in some Title VII cases. However, the Fourth Circuit refused to apply this rule in a case where a manager alleged that he was fired for helping an employee pursue a sexual harassment complaint. The Fourth Circuit held that the Title VII statutory language does not limit protection based on a person's job title. [*DeMasters v. Carilion Clinic*, 796 F.3d 409(4th Cir. 2015)]

In a race discrimination case under Title VII, § 1981, and § 1983 (see § 34.05[A]), the plaintiff said that she was subjected to a hostile work environment, demoted, transferred to another department, and replaced by a less-qualified white woman. The Second Circuit said that to survive a motion to dismiss, the plaintiff had to plead facts that gave plausible support to show the employer's discriminatory intent. Alleging replacement by a less-qualified white woman was enough to plead a disparate treatment claim. The Second Circuit held that making internal complaints of discrimination before filing her EEOC charge was not protected conduct under Title VII because there was no ongoing investigation for her to participate in. However, the Second Circuit rejected the manager rule: it is protected opposition activity if an employee (even one whose job duties include investigating complaints of discrimination) actively supports other employees in asserting their Title VII rights or personally criticizes the employer's discriminatory practices. Therefore, the plaintiff adequately pleaded opposition activity. The Second Circuit upheld the district court's dismissal of the hostile work environment claim, because she did not show adverse actions that were severe and pervasive enough to trigger Title VII. [*Littlejohn v. City of New York*, 795 F.3d 297 (2d Cir. 2015)]

The Second Circuit permitted a 42 U.S.C. § 1983 suit for retaliation, where the plaintiff, a bilingual high school teacher, charged both discrimination based on his Hispanic ethnicity and retaliation under Title VII and § 1983. He alleged that he was not compensated for being required to do additional preparation work and teach in both English and Spanish because he was assigned many students with limited English fluency. He filed an EEOC charge in August 2011 and amended it twice in 2012 to include retaliation for filing the initial charge. The Second Circuit held that § 1983 can be used to allege retaliation for a complaint of discrimination and that a state employee can sue a supervisor who acts under color of law to commit retaliation. [*Vega v. Hempstead Union Free Sch. Dist.*, 801 F.3d 72 (2d Cir. 2015)]

A First Circuit case highlights the difference between litigating disparate treatment and disparate impact cases. In mid-2015, the First Circuit held that former employees of a federal government call center could not pursue Title VII location-based claims of disparate impact and retaliation. The plaintiffs charged that a safety overhaul of their workplace (which was eventually closed) was discriminatory. They claimed that they suffered discrimination because of their Puerto Rican national origin and they were treated worse than mainland employees. They brought a pure disparate impact claim, not a disparate treatment claim. Initially, the First Circuit dismissed the claim because Title VII (at 42 U.S.C. § 2000e-2(h)) has a safe harbor provision for treating employees in different locations differently, as long as there is no intentional discrimination. The First Circuit also ruled that the agency had a legitimate business justification for rotating employees to maintain services while a facility is shut down. Repairing rather than closing the facility would have been too expensive. The retaliation claim was also dismissed because the plaintiffs failed to show a causal connection to any

protected activity. [*Abril-Rivera v. Johnson*, 795 F.3d 245 (1st Cir. 2015)] However, later in 2015, the First Circuit withdrew that opinion and replaced it with a
narrower but still pro-employer opinion. The amended opinion does not discuss
the safe harbor, and bases the decision only on the legitimate, non-discriminatory
business justification for re-assigning the workers. [*Abril-Rivera v. Johnson*, 806
F.3d 599 (1st Cir. 2015)]

A unanimous Supreme Court endorsed the "ministerial exception" in early
2012, holding that the First Amendment prevents courts from intervening when a
minister is fired. All 12 of the circuits have recognized this exception, although
this was the first time the Supreme Court dealt with the issue. The Court said that
the ministerial exception is not a bar to a court's jurisdiction; it is an affirmative
defense that has to be proved by the defendant raising it. The Supreme Court said
that ministers can still sue for tortious conduct or breach of contract. The plaintiff, Cheryl Perich, alleged that she was fired in retaliation for threatening to file
an ADA suit (she suffers from narcolepsy). The Sixth Circuit ruled for Perich,
holding that she spent 45 minutes a day teaching religion and the rest of the time
teaching secular subjects. The Supreme Court found this unpersuasive: all ministers have secular duties. [*Hosanna-Tabor Evangelical Lutheran Church v.
EEOC*, 132 S. Ct. 694 (2012)]

The Supreme Court ruled in favor of Samantha Elauf, a Muslim who wears
a head covering. She applied unsuccessfully for a job at Abercrombie & Fitch.
The Tenth Circuit ruled for the employer, on the grounds that Elauf did not
request accommodation. The Supreme Court reversed, holding that Abercrombie
& Fitch must at least have suspected that Ms. Elauf wore a head covering for religious reasons. The employer's apparent desire to avoid accommodating her religious practice was enough to sustain a suit. Title VII forbids adverse employment
decisions that have a forbidden motivation—whether the employer acts on actual
knowledge, suspicion, or even a mere hunch. [*EEOC v. Abercrombie & Fitch*, 135
S. Ct. 2028 (2015)] After the Supreme Court decision, Abercrombie & Fitch
settled Elauf's suit for $25,670.53 in damages plus $18,983.03 in court costs.
[Robin E. Shea, *EEOC, Abercrombie Settle Hijab Lawsuit*, Constangy Brooks
Smith & Prophete LLP (July 21, 2015), available at Lexology.com]

[C] Evidence

Not only can each side introduce evidence about the course of the plaintiff's
employment with the defendant company; in appropriate cases, the employer can
introduce evidence about the plaintiff that the employer did not have at the time
of the employment action.

The basic case on the use of after-acquired evidence is *McKennon v. Nashville Banner Publishing Co.* [513 U.S. 352 (1995)] In this case, the employer was
allowed to introduce, at the trial, negative evidence about the plaintiff that the
defendant learned after the employment action. Although the after-acquired

evidence couldn't have motivated the employer, it was still relevant to the plaintiff's qualifications and credibility, so it can be introduced at trial.

In many cases, the plaintiff introduces statistics to show a pattern of discrimination by the employer. To prevail, a plaintiff must identify a specific employment practice that discriminates, not just rely on bottom-line numbers about the employer's work-force. The plaintiff must present statistical evidence of a kind and degree adequate to show that the practice has caused denial of promotion because of the applicants' membership in a protected group. When read in conjunction with the other evidence, adequate statistics must be of a kind and degree that reveals a causal relationship between the allegedly discriminatory practice and the disparity between actual promotions of group members, and the promotions that could be expected if there had been no discrimination.

In deciding whether to admit expert evidence at the class certification stage of an employment discrimination case, courts focus on whether the expert opinion meets the test of scientific validity. In employment discrimination cases, the plaintiffs usually want to introduce expert testimony consisting of statistics that show that there has been disparate impact or a pattern or practice of discrimination. [Elise M. Bloom and Amanda D. Haverstick, *Class Actions After "Dukes,"* N.Y.L.J. (Oct. 24, 2011) (law.com)]

The Fourth Circuit affirmed the dismissal of an EEOC nationwide pattern or practice suit about background checks; the court said that the EEOC's expert analysis was "laughable." The EEOC said that the defendant unlawfully relied on background checks that had a disparate impact on African-American, Hispanic, and male applicants. But the Fourth Circuit said that the expert's report used only a limited number of background checks, and ignored a great deal of relevant data; the report had so many errors and logical fallacies that it could not be relied on. [*EEOC v. Freeman*, 778 F.3d 463 (4th Cir. 2015)]

The Seventh Circuit ruled that a plaintiff does not have to present a "convincing mosaic" of direct or indirect evidence to avoid summary judgment—as long as the plaintiff's evidence as a whole allows the finder of fact to decide that the adverse employment action was caused by discrimination. The "convincing mosaic" concept is a mental image, not a test. The Seventh Circuit said that trying to characterize evidence as direct or indirect shifts the focus away from the significant question: whether the adverse action is a product of discrimination. [*Ortiz v. Werner Enters.*, 840 F.3d 760 (7th Cir. 2016); see Abigail Cahak, *"Convincing Mosaic" Busted: Seventh Circuit Shatters Summary Judgment Standard for Discrimination Claims,* Seyfarth Shaw LLP (Sept. 9 2016), available at Lexology.com]

[D] Admissible and Inadmissible Evidence

The Second Circuit ruled that racist comments by a white employee can be used to show that the work environment was hostile to black people, even if the remarks were made after the black plaintiff resigned. [*Whidbee v. Garzarelli Food Specialties*, 223 F.3d 62 (2d Cir. 2000)] But testimony by four of the plaintiff's co-workers (that a supervisor's treatment of the demoted black employee was racially motivated) should not have been admitted. [*Hester v. BIC Corp.*, 225 F.3d 178 (2d Cir. 2000)] The witnesses could testify about their observations, but because they didn't know how good or bad the plaintiff's work performance actually was, they couldn't testify about the supervisor's motivation.

In mid-2011, the California Court of Appeal held that the trial court should have admitted "me too" evidence in a sexual harassment hostile work environment case. In other words, evidence that the defendant harassed other women should have been admitted because excluding it was prejudicial to the plaintiff's case. The court of appeal said that the evidence tended to show the defendant's bias against women and tended to disprove the legitimacy of his stated reason for firing the plaintiff. [*Pantoja v. Anton*, 198 Cal. App. 4th 87 (Cal. App. 2011)]

In an Equal Pay Act case, the Second Circuit limited the plaintiffs' ability to use statistical evidence of pay disparity between the sexes, by itself, to prove an EPA claim. However, New York's Achieve Pay Equity Act is more employee-friendly and forbids unequal pay for work requiring equal skill, effort, and responsibility performed under similar working conditions. The plaintiff is a veterinarian who alleged that she was paid less than male counterparts. But the Second Circuit ruled that they were not valid comparators. Even though the plaintiff's job title was department head, she was a general practitioner doing basic treatments. The men in question were specialists heading specialty departments. The plaintiff referred especially difficult cases to them. She had a lower patient load, did not do much research, and did not supervise interns, although the men cited as comparators did. The plaintiff wanted to introduce evidence of discriminatory pay across the board, but the Second Circuit said that even if female veterinarians are paid less than male veterinarians, it would not prove that the plaintiff as an individual was paid less because of her sex. Without valid male comparators, the plaintiff could not use statistical compilations as the sole factor in an EPA claim.

[*Chiaramonte v. The Animal Med. Ctr.*, No. 16-0478-cv, 2017 U.S. App. LEXIS 1371 (2d Cir. Jan. 26, 2017); see Seth Kaufman, *2nd Circuit Reaffirms Limitations on Statistical Evidence in Pay Equity Cases*, Fisher Phillips (Feb. 16, 2017), available at Lexology.com]

[E] Other Litigation Issues

If the plaintiff files suit in state court, the employer often tries to get the case removed to federal court. State courts usually have less crowded calendars, so cases can be decided faster. Sometimes, state law permits the employee to assert additional causes of action, or to get remedies that would not be available in federal court. Sometimes, too, a particular action is subject to state but not federal law. For example, some states ban discrimination in workplaces that are too small to be covered by the federal law. Sexual-orientation discrimination is not covered by Title VII, but is covered by certain state or local laws.

In many cases, federal law preempts state law. In other words, certain matters, such as most of labor law and benefit law, are covered by federal law, and the states cannot interfere. Therefore, if a plaintiff's state-court claims operate in one of these preempted areas, the employer has a strong argument for getting the case removed to federal court, or even dismissed.

As Chapter 40 shows, in many instances, a would-be plaintiff is subject to a mandatory arbitration clause that requires arbitration of all discrimination claims. The general principle is that pre-dispute arbitration requirements (i.e., an agreement to arbitrate disputes that arise in the future) will be enforceable even if the plaintiff charges a violation of rights under federal anti-discrimination laws.

Filing of the initial complaint is not the only point in the case at which time limits must be observed. A former high school teacher (Banks) brought a Title VII suit against the Chicago Board of Education. The district court granted the employer's motion for summary judgment. Banks moved under Federal Rules of Civil Procedure 59(e) to alter the judgment—but the motion was filed one day after the 28-day deadline. The Seventh Circuit does not entirely disregard untimely Rule 59(e) motions, but it treats them as Rule 60(b) motions. But a Rule 60(b) motion does not toll the time to file an appeal under FRAP 4(a)(1)(A). The Seventh Circuit held that the district court did not abuse its discretion by granting the motion. [*Banks v. Chicago Bd. of Educ.*, 750 F.3d 663 (7th Cir. 2014)]

As § 1.11 shows, it is often important to determine which enterprise(s) can be treated as the plaintiff's employer(s). The Third Circuit held that a worker assigned by a temporary agency to a client was an employee of both companies for Title VII purposes. A group of African-American temporary employees complained that they were accused of stealing, sent to work in the back of the store handling garbage, subjected to a racial slur, and were fired. The Third Circuit decided that the client was their employer, based on the client's right to control the manner and means by which work was done. The client had ultimate control over who worked at its store and controlled daily activities for both temporary and permanent employees. [*Faush v. Tuesday Morning, Inc.*, 808 F.3d 208 (3d Cir. 2015)]

The Fifth Circuit adopted the Seventh Circuit's test for joint liability: a staffing company is liable for discrimination (in this case, disability discrimination) committed by a client if the staffing company either participated in the discrimination, or knew or should have known about the discrimination but failed to take corrective measures. [*Burton v. Freescale Semiconductor Inc. & Manpower of Tex., LP*, 798 F.3d 222 (5th Cir. 2015)]

It is a good idea for companies that have been sued to determine if the plaintiff has recently filed a Chapter 7 bankruptcy petition. (This can be determined by using PACER, the Public Access to Court Electronic Records system or by accessing bankruptcy court records.) An employee who files such a petition but does not list the EEOC charge or potential claims against the employer as assets of the bankruptcy estate might be precluded from pursuing the claim. If the charge is not disclosed, the employee is no longer the real party in interest and cannot pursue the claim because it belongs to the bankruptcy estate, and only the bankruptcy trustee can pursue it. It might even be held that failure to list the claim even prevents the trustee from pursuing the claim. [Megan T. Muirhead, *An Employee's Bankruptcy Can Assist New Mexico Employers Defend Against the Employee's Claims*, Modrall Sperling (Oct. 26, 2015), available at Lexology.com]

§ 42.11 ADEA SUITS

[A] Generally

It is clear that the ADEA creates a private right of action—i.e., individuals can bring suit if they claim to have been subjected to age discrimination in employment. [See 29 U.S.C. § 626(c)] The statute is not very detailed. It says only that individuals can sue for "such legal or equitable relief as will effectuate the purposes" of the ADEA. However, a suit brought by the Secretary of Labor will terminate the rights of individuals to bring their own lawsuits involving their ADEA claims.

Under 29 U.S.C. § 626(d), would-be ADEA plaintiffs have to file their charges within 180 days of the alleged unlawful practice. In a "referral" state (a state whose antidiscrimination agency has a work-sharing agreement) the charge has to be filed within 300 days of the alleged unlawful practice. If the state-law proceedings are terminated, the potential plaintiff must file the charge within 30 days of the termination of the state proceeding.

When a charge is filed, all potential defendants are notified. In both the Title VII and ADEA contexts, the Secretary's duty is to "promptly seek to eliminate any alleged unlawful practice by informal methods of conciliation, conference, and persuasion."

In the federal system, whether a case can be heard by a jury (instead of just a judge) depends on several factors, including the preferences of the litigants and the nature of the suit itself. The basic rule is that juries are more appropriate for cases seeking money damages than those asking for purely equitable remedies such as injunctions or reinstatement. However, ADEA plaintiffs can demand a jury trial whenever they seek money damages, even if there are also equitable claims in the same suit.

When third parties, including independent contractors, are authorized to make hiring decisions on behalf of an employer, the Second Circuit held that the employer can be liable under the ADEA if the third party commits discrimination. General agency principles are used to assess the third party's authority. This is a fact inquiry, so summary judgment is not appropriate. [*Halpert v. Manhattan Apartments Inc.*, 580 F.3d 86 (2d Cir. 2009)]

The Third Circuit held in early 2017 that workers in their fifties can be characterized as a "sub-group" of plaintiffs if the employer's policies place them at a disadvantage versus other workers over 40. The Third Circuit allows sub-group comparisons to prove a disparate impact claim. However, the Second, Sixth, and Eighth Circuits ruled that sub-group ADEA claims are not allowed. [*Karlo v. Pittsburgh Glass Works, LLC*, No. 15-3435, 2017 WL 83385 (3d Cir. Jan. 10, 2017); see Evandro C. Gigante, Third *Circuit Permits ADEA "Subgroup" Claims*, Proskauer Rose LLP (Feb. 16, 2017), available at Lexology.com]

In the Ninth Circuit view, the ADEA does not preclude a First Amendment retaliation claim under 42 U.S.C. § 1983; public-sector employees can bring a suit under that statute for age-based retaliation against a state or local government entity or an official, even though the Supreme Court has held that state actors are immune from ADEA claims under the Eleventh Amendment. However, the ADEA is the sole source of remedies for age-based discrimination (as distinct from retaliation)—so Eleventh Amendment immunity would apply. [*Stilwell v. City of Williams*, 831 F.3d 1234 (9th Cir. 2016); see Billie D. Wenter, *Ninth Circuit Holds Section 1983 First Amendment Retaliation Claim Not Necessarily Precluded by Age Discrimination in Employment Act,* Littler Mendelson PC (Aug. 9, 2016), available at Lexology.com]

[B] Timing Issues for ADEA Suits

The EEOC will dismiss (as untimely) charges filed more than 180 days after the discriminatory act—or more than 300 days in a referral jurisdiction. Extra time may be available if the charging party has a valid claim to waiver, estoppel, or equitable tolling.

The EEOC has a statutory obligation to try to eliminate alleged unlawful practices by means of informal conciliation. If the EEOC tries to conciliate but fails, it will give the charging party a notice—but the notice will be clearly labeled to distinguish it from the Notice of Dismissal or Termination, which is issued in ADEA cases as a rough parallel to the Right to Sue letter in other discrimination cases.

An age discrimination charging party does not have to wait until the NDT is issued to sue—as long as he or she waits at least 60 days after the charge was filed. But once the NDT is issued, the complainant has only 90 days to file suit (which can be filed in either federal or state court), or the case will be dismissed as untimely.

It is in the employer's best interest for the court to rule that the cause of action "accrued" earlier, i.e., that the clock started ticking when the employee had to file suit. The earlier the cause of action accrues, the more likely it is that a claim can be dismissed as untimely.

If the alleged discriminatory act is firing the employee, there is a single act of discrimination. Most cases hold that the discriminatory act occurs on the date the plaintiff is unambiguously informed that he or she will be fired. The important date is the date of this notice, and not the first warning the plaintiff receives of impending termination, and not the last day the employee works for the employer or the last date he or she is on the payroll. The notice does not have to be formal, or even written, but it must be a definite statement that a final decision has been made to terminate the employee.

It is harder to place other discriminatory acts on a time continuum. It has been held that a claim of failure to promote accrues when the employees know or should have known about the facts that support the claim—probably, that a younger individual received the promotion that the plaintiff wanted.

If there is only a single employment decision, there is only a single act that might be discriminatory. However, some courts allow a plaintiff to argue that there was a continuing violation lasting over a period of time—for example, that the plaintiff kept his or her job, but was denied promotions he or she deserved because of age discrimination. In a case where the court accepts the continuing violation theory, the cause of action accrues with the last discriminatory act in the series. A filing that is timely for one act of discrimination will be timely for all acts of discrimination in the same series.

A bad performance appraisal that makes an employee more vulnerable to being laid off or RIFed (but that is not an actual threat of dismissal unless performance improves) is generally not considered an employment action that could give rise to an ADEA claim.

For discriminatory layoff charges, courts reach different conclusions as to when the cause of action accrues. One theory is that accrual occurs on the actual date of layoff. The other is that the cause of action accrues later, when the possibility of reinstatement ends because the employer has filled the last job for which the plaintiff might have been recalled.

[C] Tolling the ADEA Statute of Limitations

The statute of limitations can be tolled (suspended), giving employees additional time to litigate, in various circumstances—usually as a result of deception or other misconduct on the part of the employer. However, certain circumstances have been held not to be wrongful conduct, and will not toll the statute of limitations:

- Putting an employee on "special assignment" until termination takes effect;

- Offering a severance benefits package. However, offering a lavish severance package, but preventing employees from discussing it, was held to discourage employees from vindicating their legal rights, and therefore to toll the statute of limitations.

■ **TIP:**   The statute of limitations is not tolled during the employer's in-house grievance procedure. However, a collective bargaining agreement provision is invalid if it terminates the employee's right to pursue a grievance once he or she files age discrimination charges with the EEOC or the local antidiscrimination agency. The clause is void because it punishes employees for exercising their legal rights.

Even if tolling occurs, it probably cannot last beyond the point at which an employee who took reasonable steps to investigate would have been aware of discrimination.

The Eleventh Circuit created a circuit split by its decision in an ADEA disparate impact suit. Villareal, who was 49 years old, got no response to his job application. After about two years, he brought an ADEA class action, charging unlawful age-related tactics such as preferring candidates only two to three years out of college; "staying away" from candidates with more than eight years of experience. The district court held that only current employees could bring a disparate impact suit. The Eleventh Circuit reversed, holding that the statutory ban on "depriv[ing] any individual of employment opportunities" is broad enough to cover job applicants. The Eleventh Circuit also granted equitable tolling because the plaintiff did not learn about the age-related recruiting practices until after the statute of limitations had expired. The Eleventh Circuit said that tolling does not require that the employer committed misrepresentation; the question is whether a reasonably prudent plaintiff would have learned the facts earlier. However, the Fifth, Seventh, Eighth, and Tenth Circuits have held that job applicants cannot bring disparate impact ADEA suits. [*Villareal v. R.J. Reynolds*, 806 F.3d 1288 (11th Cir. 2015)]

Remember that 29 U.S.C. § 627 requires the employer to post a notice of ADEA rights. The EEOC and Department of Labor distribute free copies of the mandatory notice; posters can also be purchased from many publishers. If the notice is duly posted, then the court will presume that the employee could have read the poster and become aware of at least basic ADEA rights.

However, if the information is not posted, the court may conclude that the employer deprived the employee of access to information about ADEA rights, thus tolling the statute of limitations. Yet some courts say that the real test is whether the employee actually was aware of what the ADEA says. Given actual knowledge, the court may decide that the absence of a poster in the workplace does not justify extending the time to bring suit.

[D]   The ADEA Plaintiff's Burden of Proof

The *McDonnell-Douglas* pattern applies in ADEA cases. That is, first the plaintiff introduces evidence of a prima facie case of discrimination. If the evidence (taken at face value) is inadequate, the defendant employer can get summary judgment—that is, can have the case dismissed because of this inadequacy.

If, however, the case is good enough to survive a motion for summary judgment, it is the employer's turn at bat. By and large, proof is up to the plaintiff, but a Bona Fide Occupational Qualification (BFOQ) is an affirmative defense, which means that the employer has the burden of proving it. [*W. Air Lines Inc. v. Criswell*, 472 U.S. 400 (1985)] In non-BFOQ cases, the employer can rebut the prima facie case by showing a legitimate, nondiscriminatory reason for the conduct challenged by the employee. Then the employee gets another chance, to demonstrate that the employer's justification is actually a pretext for discrimination. *Meacham v. Knolls Atomic Power Labs* [554 U.S. 84 (2008)], similarly holds that the reasonable factors other than age (RFOA) defense is also an affirmative defense.

It is not necessary in all cases for the plaintiff to prove that he or she was replaced by someone under 40 (i.e., outside the protected group). [*O'Connor v. Consol. Coin Caterers Corp.*, 517 U.S. 308 (1997)] It is possible, although difficult, for the plaintiff to win a case in which he or she was replaced by another person over 40, as long as improper age-related motives are shown.

In 1993, the Supreme Court set a new standard for proving ADEA cases based on age-related factors rather than on age itself. For instance, a 30-year-old cannot have 30 years' employment experience, but a 38-year-old employee might have worked for the company for 20 years, and therefore have more seniority than a 50-year-old hired only 10 years earlier. In that example, the allegedly age-related factors of higher salary and benefits would actually make the 38-year-old the more expensive employee.

The key case on this issue is *Hazen Paper Co. v. Biggins* [507 U.S. 604 (1993)] which requires the plaintiff to prove that the employer's decision was influenced by age, not merely by age-related factors.

In 2009, the Supreme Court agreed to hear a mixed motive age discrimination case, to determine the burden of proof. The Supreme Court ruled that, in order to win, a mixed-motive ADEA plaintiff must prove by a preponderance of the evidence that age was the "but-for" cause of the challenged employment action: that it would never have occurred but-for the plaintiff's age. The burden of persuasion is always on the plaintiff, and can be met by either direct or circumstantial evidence. The burden of persuasion never shifts to the defendant. This is not the same standard applied in Title VII, but the Supreme Court stressed the difference in wording and legislative history between the ADEA and Title VII [*Gross v. FBL Fin. Servs., Inc.*, 557 U.S. 167 (2009)]

The Fourth, Sixth, and Seventh Circuits have applied the "but-for" test in ADA cases, because the ADA's statutory language is closer to the ADEA than to Title VII. [*Gentry v. E.W. Partners Mgmt. Co.*, Inc., 816 F.3d 228 (4th Cir. 2016); see Paul Holscher, *Fourth Circuit Adopts "But For" Standard for Proof of Discrimination Under Americans with Disabilities Act*, Jackson Lewis PC (Mar. 21, 2016), available at Lexology.com]

In a case under the ADA and Minnesota law, the Eighth Circuit, noting that the Fourth, Sixth, and Seventh Circuits extend *Gross'* analysis from the ADEA to the ADA, the Eighth Circuit nevertheless applied a mixed-motive causation standard. The Eighth Circuit allowed the claim to proceed if the adverse employment action was based on both permissible and impermissible motives. [*Oehmke v. Medtronic, Inc.*, No. 16-1052, 2016 WL 7404779 (8th Cir. Dec. 22, 2016); see Jody Kahn Mason, *Eighth Circuit Leaves Open the Question of Whether a "Mixed-Motive" or "But-For" Causation Standard Should be Applied to Disability Discrimination Claims Under the ADA*, Jackson Lewis PC (Dec. 28, 2016), available at Lexology.com]

The Third Circuit held in 2017 that DOL's FMLA regulations justify a mixed-motive instruction in FMLA retaliation cases, and plaintiffs do not need to produce direct evidence of FMLA retaliation. [*Egan v. Delaware River Port Auth.*, No. 16-1471, 2017 U.S. App. LEXIS 4993 (3d Cir. Mar. 21, 2017)] A few months later, the Second Circuit joined the Third Circuit in holding that the standard of proof in FMLA retaliation cases is whether taking leave was a motivating factor in the adverse employment action. The stricter but-for standard of Title VII and ADEA retaliation cases does not apply. [*Woods v. START Treatment & Recovery Ctrs., Inc.*, No. 16-1318 (2d Cir. July 19, 2017). See Nathaniel M. Glasser and Maxine Adams, *Second Circuit Adopts "Motivating Factor" Causation Standard for FMLA Retaliation Claims,* healthemploymentandlabor.com (July 24, 2017) (benefitslink.com).]

Early in 2008, the Supreme Court did not fully resolve the question about whether ADEA plaintiffs can prove a corporate culture of discrimination by introducing testimony of employees who did not have the same supervisor as the plaintiff. The Court would not entirely rule out the use of such testimony, requiring instead that in each case, the facts should be examined to see if the probative value of the testimony outweighed the risk of possible prejudice. The Court ruled that, in general, the district court's determination is entitled to a high measure of deference, because the lower court hears testimony rather than merely relying on the record on appeal. The relevant provision of the ADEA is drafted similarly to Title VII, so the same principle should also apply in Title VII cases. [*Sprint/United Mgmt. Co. v. Mendelsohn*, 552 U.S. 379 (2008)]

Direct evidence of age discrimination is hard to find—especially since even employers who do practice discrimination usually have enough sophistication to conceal it. As a practical matter, then, most ADEA cases will be based on statistical evidence in support of the allegation, with or without evidence about statements made by executives and supervisors. Statistics are especially prominent in disparate impact cases.

However, the legal trend has been to reduce the credence given to statistics. In *St. Mary's Honor Center. v. Hicks* [509 U.S. 502 (1993)], the court held that the plaintiff always has the "ultimate burden of persuasion." So if the fact-finder (which will be the jury or the judge in a nonjury case) doesn't believe the employer's explanation of why its conduct was legitimate, the plaintiff can still lose—if the plaintiff simply fails to offer enough evidence. The *Hicks* standard is sometimes called "pretext-plus": The plaintiff has to do more than just show that the defendant's excuses are a mere pretext for discrimination.

The Fifth Circuit rule is that punitive damages and damages for pain and suffering are not available in ADEA cases. However, the Fifth Circuit also wants to interpret the ADEA consistently with the FLSA because the ADEA's statutory language about remedies derives from the FLSA. Two separate Fifth Circuit panels reached different conclusions. One said that pain and suffering and punitive damages are unavailable in ADEA discrimination or retaliation cases; less than two weeks later, the other allowed emotional distress damages for FLSA retaliation. [Compare *Vaughan v. Anderson Regional Med. Ctr.*, No. 16-60104, 2016 WL 7365629 (5th Cir. Dec. 6, 2016) with *Pineda v. JTCH Apartments, LLC*, No. 843 F.3d 1062 (5th Cir. 2016); W. Stephen Cockerham & Leslie Brockhoeft, *Are Pain and Suffering and Punitive Damages Recoverable Under the ADEA and FLSA? The 5th Circuit Issues Inconsistent Decisions*, Husch Blackwell LLP (Jan. 13, 2017), available at Lexology.com]

[E] The ADEA Prima Facie Case

The basic prima facie (initial) case for an ADEA lawsuit is:

- The plaintiff belongs to the protected group—that is, is over 40;

- The plaintiff was qualified for the position he or she held or applied for;

- The plaintiff was not hired, discharged, demoted, deprived of a raise, or otherwise disfavored because of age;

- (In appropriate cases) The plaintiff was replaced—especially by someone under 40, although it is not absolutely required that the replacement come from outside the protected age group. If the charge is a discriminatory RIF, plaintiffs must show that age was a factor (although not necessarily the only factor) in targeting them for termination, or at least that the employer was not age-neutral in implementing the RIF program. Employers can defend against an accusation of a discriminatory RIF by showing good economic reason for cutting back; it isn't necessary to show that the company would be at the brink of bankruptcy without the reductions.

Depending on the type of case, the court where it is heard and the individual facts, the plaintiff may have to prove that his or her own qualifications and/or job performance were satisfactory, or may have to prove that they were superior to those of the person who replaced him or her.

In 2012, the EEOC issued a Q&A explaining what employers must do to use a Reasonable Factors Other Than Age (RFOA) defense when practices that are neutral on their face but might have disparate impact on older workers are challenged. The employer is only required to prove an RFOA after an employee has identified a specific business practice with disparate impact on older workers. An RFOA is reasonably designed and administered to achieve a legitimate business purpose—for example, a physical test for police patrol officers.

Whether the factors are indeed reasonable depends on, e.g.:

- Their relation to the employer's stated business purpose;

- The extent to which the factor is accurately defined and fairly and accurately applied (application includes training managers and supervisors);

- Limits on supervisors' discretion, especially when the criteria are vulnerable to negative age-based stereotypes;

- The extent to which the employer assessed the adverse impact of the practice on older workers;

- The degree of harm to workers over 40—not just the number of people affected and the extent of the injury, but the employer's measures to reduce harm, balanced against the burden of the actual and potential measures.

- The EEOC stresses that these are not elements that all employers must prove in every case, merely characteristics of reasonable practices.

The EEOC said that, unlike an employment test that has been challenged under Title VII, it is not necessary for the employer to produce a validation study about the RFOA.

The EEOC says it is not unreasonable to use subjective decision-making (e.g., ranking an applicant or employee's qualities such as flexibility and willingness to learn new things) but it is useful to give supervisors evaluation criteria to help them avoid age-based stereotypes. The EEOC said that employers are not obligated to discover and use the least discriminatory method of achieving the purpose—but attempts to limit harm to older persons are not irrelevant. [EEOC, *Questions and Answers on EEOC Final Rule on Disparate Impact and "Reasonable Factors Other Than Age" Under the Age Discrimination in Employment Act of 1967*, <http://www.eeoc.gov/laws/regulations/adea_rfoa_qa_final_rule.cfm> (last accessed Mar. 22, 2017)]

A 52-year-old African-American female security guard was fired after an incident with a truculent patient at the psychiatric hospital where she worked. She sued for age, race, and sex discrimination. The hospital said that she committed a major violation of disciplinary policy (telling the patient that she could leave if she had been admitted for substance abuse rather than psychiatric indications) when she was already on final written warning. She was replaced by a 39-year-old African-American woman. The Sixth Circuit said that she was not replaced by someone outside the protected class. However, the Sixth Circuit held that she made out an ADEA prima facie case: her 25 years of employment showed that she met the minimum qualifications for the job—but the employer provided a legitimate non-discriminatory justification for firing her. [*Loyd v. Saint Joseph Mercy Oakland*, 766 F.3d 580 (6th Cir. 2014)]

[F] ADEA Class Actions

Sometimes, an employee contends that he or she is the only person to suffer discrimination. Sometimes, however, it is alleged that the company engages in a pattern or practice of discrimination, affecting many people, and it becomes necessary to determine whether it is appropriate to certify a class action (i.e., to allow employees to combine their claims and present a single body of evidence).

The question of timing in class actions was addressed in *Armstrong v. Martin Marietta Corp.* [138 F.3d 1374 (11th Cir. 1998)] Certain employees were dismissed as plaintiffs from a pending ADEA class action. They brought their own suits. The Eleventh Circuit held that the statute of limitations is tolled (suspended) while a class action is pending, but starts all over again as soon as the district court issues an order denying class certification.

Would-be plaintiffs who are thrown out of a class action because they are not similarly situated to the proper plaintiffs must file their own suits within 90 days of being removed from the class. Equitable tolling (i.e., permitting an action that would otherwise be too late to continue, on the grounds of fairness) can be granted only if the EEOC actually misinformed the plaintiffs about the statute of limitations, not if the plaintiffs simply failed to consider this issue or made an incorrect determination of how long they had to bring suit.

§ 42.12   TITLE VII REMEDIES

[A]   Fundamental Remedies

Once the case gets to court and is tried to a conclusion (many cases are either settled along the way, or are dismissed before a full trial has occurred), and if the plaintiff wins (most employment discrimination cases are won by the employer), then the question becomes what remedies the court will order. Remedies are governed by 42 U.S.C. § 2000e-5(g).

The fundamental remedies under this section are equitable: hiring or reinstatement (plus up to two years' back pay for the time the plaintiff would have been working absent discrimination). Furthermore, the amount that the plaintiff earned in the meantime—or could have earned by making reasonable efforts—is offset against the back pay. In other words, plaintiffs have a duty to mitigate their damages. They have an obligation to use their best efforts to earn a living, instead of relying on the hope the defendant employer will eventually be ordered to pay up.

If the plaintiff further succeeds in proving disparate treatment (as distinct from facially neutral practices that have a disparate impact on the group the plaintiff belongs to), then compensatory damages can be awarded to the plaintiff as reimbursement for costs (such as job hunting or therapy) incurred directly as a result of the discrimination.

However, in cases of racial discrimination, the plaintiff must look to the Civil Rights Act of 1866 [42 U.S.C. § 1981], and not to Title VII, for compensatory and punitive damages. If the alleged discrimination consists of failing to accommodate a disability, the employer will not have to pay compensatory damages if it made a good-faith effort at reasonable accommodation, even if the offer of accommodation was later deemed inadequate.

If the court finds that the employer engaged in the unlawful employment practice that the plaintiff charged, it can enjoin the respondent from continuing that abusive practice. The court can order the defendant to take remedial steps, including but not limited to hiring an applicant or reinstating an ex-employee.

Employers cannot be ordered to hire, reinstate, or promote anyone, or pay back pay to him or her, if the employment action was taken "for any reason other than discrimination on account of race, color, religion, sex, or national origin" or unlawful retaliation. [42 U.S.C. § 2000e-5(g)(2)(A)]

In a mixed-motive case where the defendant demonstrates that, although a discriminatory motive was present, it would have taken the same action (e.g., fired or refused to promote the plaintiff) purely on the basis of the other motivations even if there had been no discrimination, then the court can grant a declaratory judgment (a declaration that the employment practice was unlawful), enjoin its continued use, or award attorneys' fees that can be traced directly to the mixed-motive claim. But, because the employer would have taken the same action even without discrimination, the court cannot award damages to the plaintiff or order the defendant to hire, rehire or promote the plaintiff. [42 U.S.C. § 2000e-5(g)(2)(B)]

The court has discretion, under 42 U.S.C. § 2000e-5(k), to order the loser—whether plaintiff or defendant—to pay the winner's attorneys' fees (including fees for expert witnesses, which can be very high) and court costs. However, losing defendants can't be ordered to pay fees to the EEOC. If the EEOC sues a company and loses, it can be ordered to reimburse the defendant for its fees and costs for the suit.

Also note that 42 U.S.C. § 2000e-2(n) provides that employees usually cannot challenge employment practices that were adopted based on a court order or to carry out a consent decree in an employment discrimination case, if the employees knew about the case and either had their interests represented or had a chance to voice their objections. However, employees who actually were parties in the case can enforce their rights under the order or settlement, and judgments and orders can be challenged on the grounds of fraud or the court's lack of jurisdiction over the case.

One important factor in analyzing employment cases is what claim(s) the employee raises. Some employment discrimination claims fit into the "breach of contract" category, but most of them are more like "tort" claims. The importance of the tort/contract distinction is that the remedies are different for the two categories. If a plaintiff proves breach of contract, the court's job is to put the plaintiff back in the position he, she, or it would have been in if the contract had been carried out. In the context of an employment contract, or implied employment contract, that probably means earnings and fringe benefits that were lost because of the breach, possibly plus out-of-pocket expenses for finding a new job. (The doctrine of mitigation of damages requires plaintiffs to do whatever they can to limit the amount of damages they suffer—which definitely includes finding a new job if at all possible, pending resolution of the claims against the former employer.)

Back pay is not limited to simple salary. It includes benefits, overtime, shift differentials, merit raises, and the like. However, if the employer can prove that the employee would have been laid off, or was unavailable for work, back pay will not be available for the time the employee would not have been working anyway.

Fringe benefits are valued at the cost the employee would have to pay to replace them, not the (probably lower) cost the employer incurred to offer them.

Amounts earned in the new job reduce what the ex-employer will have to pay in damages. On the other hand, to the extent that the plaintiff proves that the employer committed one or more torts, the successful plaintiff can be awarded back pay, front pay (moving from the end of the trial forward), lost earnings, medical expenses, and value of pain and anguish, and emotional distress. The plaintiff's spouse might be granted an award for loss of consortium (marital services that were not rendered because of the employer's wrongdoing). In most states, interest on the judgment, running from the time the case is decided, can also be ordered—which mounts up quickly if the award is in six or seven figures.

Sometimes, front pay and reinstatement can be combined, i.e., if the remedies don't overlap, chronologically or economically. Front pay can be awarded to get the plaintiff to the "point of employability," at which point he or she can be reinstated.

The equitable remedy of front pay can be denied to an employee whose conduct after termination renders her ineligible for reinstatement. This case involved a sexual harassment plaintiff who got another job at a bank, who was fired for attempting to process an unauthorized loan application. The case was remanded to determine if her misconduct in the second job would preclude reinstatement in the first job. [*Sellers v. Mineta*, 358 F.3d 1058 (8th Cir. 2004)]

A mid-2016 appeal of a retaliatory discharge case reverses the district court's grant of equitable remedies of front pay and reinstatement. The Ninth Circuit held that the jury's award of front pay for the same events rendered the equitable award a violation of the Seventh Amendment right of jury trial. [*Teutscher v. Riverside Sheriffs' Ass'n*, No. 13-56411 (9th Cir. Aug. 26, 2016)]

Many discrimination cases can be brought by the plaintiff in federal court, because there is a federal question (alleged violation of a federal statute). If the plaintiff chooses to sue in state court instead, the issue arises of whether the defendant can get the case removed to federal court. Further issues arise when the reason for going to federal court is "diversity" (the plaintiff and defendant are citizens of different states). Federal courts have jurisdiction in diversity cases if, and only if, the amount in controversy is at least $75,000.

[B]   CRA '91 Cap on Damages

The Civil Rights Act of 1991 (CRA '91) [Pub. L. No. 102-166] imposes a cap on total damages that can be awarded to a successful Title VII plaintiff: The amount depends on the size of the corporate defendant, not the number or seriousness of the charges. The cap applies to punitive damages and most compensatory damages (but not to medical bills or other monetary losses that the plaintiff incurred before the trial).

Companies with fewer than 15 employees are exempt from Title VII, so the cap calculation begins at the 15-employee level. The damage cap is $50,000 for a company with 15–100 employees. The cap is set at $100,000 for companies with 101–200 employees, $200,000 for 201–500 employees, and $300,000 for companies with over 500 workers.

The First Circuit ruled in mid-2011 that the number of employees for purposes of the CRA '91 damage cap is determined at the time of the discrimination, not at the time the court renders its decision. The District Court for the District of Puerto Rico awarded $300,000 in a sexual harassment case. The trial judge reduced this award to $50,000. On appeal, the First Circuit increased the compensatory damages to $200,000. The size of the employer's workforce had fallen dramatically between 2004 (when the alleged discrimination occurred) and the 2008 verdict. The First Circuit also held that the number of employees is an affirmative defense that has to be proved by the employer. [*Hernandez-Miranda v. Empresas Diaz Masso Inc.*, 651 F.3d 167 (1st Cir. 2011)]

In mid-2011, the Third Circuit reduced a $10 million jury award for racial discrimination received by three former police officers to $900,000. The officers brought only federal claims, so the $300,000 cap on damages applied. (If they had brought and prevailed on claims under Pennsylvania law, damages for those claims would not have been capped.) The plaintiffs, who are white, alleged that they suffered retaliation for protesting mistreatment of black co-workers. One of the plaintiffs was told that if he filed an EEOC charge, his supervisor would make his life "a living nightmare." In a separate opinion, $208,000 in back pay was awarded to one of the plaintiffs. [*McKenna v. Philadelphia*, 649 F.3d 171 (3d Cir. 2011)]

A federal jury in Ohio awarded $613,368 (including the cap amount, $300,000, in compensatory damages and $213,368 in back pay, the amount calculated by the plaintiff's expert witness). The plaintiff charged that she suffered discrimination and retaliation for supporting a university colleague's discrimination claim. The Sixth Circuit granted the defendant's motion for remittitur. The Sixth Circuit eliminated the back pay award, on the grounds that the plaintiff did not establish with reasonable certainty that she was entitled to back pay. However, like the Fifth Circuit in *Nassar,* the Sixth Circuit held that the calculation of back pay can include salaries paid by other employers. [*Szeinbach v. The Ohio State Univ.*, 820 F.3d 814 (6th Cir. 2016); see Justin Jennewine, *Sixth Circuit Rules on $200,000 Back Pay Issue*, Squire Patton Boggs (Apr. 28, 2016), available at Lexology.com].

In a case of race-based harassment and retaliatory discharge, the New Jersey Supreme Court upheld a jury award of $1.4 million in emotional distress damages to two brothers who were executives for the Wentworth Group. The jury also awarded back and front pay, punitive damages, and attorneys' fees. The plaintiffs said their heritage was frequently demeaned, and the "Latin lover" "jokes" were made by the HR director. One of the brothers charged that he reported the harassment to the company's in-house counsel in 2007, was told to calm down and was fired four days later—even though he had just received a $10,000 raise based on performance. His brother complained about the termination and was fired himself a month later. The plaintiffs sued the company and a key executive under New Jersey anti-discrimination law. They alleged that the racist remarks were emotionally damaging (although neither sought medical treatment)—especially since the remarks were made by or in the presence of senior executives, so they had no means of redress. The state supreme court denied the defendant's motion for remittitur of the emotional distress damage award, holding that it was not high enough to shock the conscience, and the award could be based on the plaintiffs' testimony, without expert witnesses. [*Cuevas v. Wentworth Grp.*, 144 A.3d 890 (N.J. 2016); see David J. Treibman, *New Jersey Court Ruling Raises Price of Employment Discrimination*, Fisher Phillips (Sept. 21, 2016), available at Lexology.com]

[C] Punitive Damages

One of the most controversial questions is the matter of punitive damages. Theoretically, punitive damages are supposed to be quite rare, ordered only in those cases when the defendant's conduct has been worse than merely negligent or improper.

A defendant that has acted maliciously, or at least with reckless indifference to the plaintiff's rights, can be ordered to pay punitive damages. The employer's conduct need not be "egregious" for punitive damages to be available. [*Kolstad v. Am. Dental Ass'n*, 527 U.S. 526 (1999)]

The general rule in the federal system—not just in employment discrimination cases—is that "double digit" punitive damages (i.e., more than 10 times the compensatory damages) are inappropriate, and that it is also inappropriate to impose punitive damages in a particular case because of the defendant's wrongful conduct in other cases or other states. According to the Fourth Circuit, it was permissible to award $100,000 to a wrongfully demoted employee who was not awarded any compensatory damages on her sex discrimination claim. The Fourth Circuit deemed the judge's award of $410,000 in back pay and interest to justify the punitive damage award, because the loss of income she suffered was actionable harm, the lost back pay was roughly equivalent to compensatory damages, and there is no explicit statutory condition under CRA '91 that punitive damages are dependent on compensatory damages. [*Corti v. Storage Tech. Corp.*, 304 F.3d 336 (4th Cir. 2002)]

Mine worker Angela Aguilar alleged constructive discharge after she was subjected to sexual harassment, retaliation, and intentional infliction of emotional distress. The state of Arizona sued the employer under the state civil rights act for harassment, disparate treatment, and retaliation; the suit was consolidated with Aguilar's Title VII suit and removed to federal district court. The jury ruled for Aguilar on the sexual harassment charge, but not on constructive discharge or retaliation. The jury did not find any compensatory damages, so it awarded $1 in nominal damages and $858,750 in punitive damages. The trial court applied the Title VII cap to reduce the damages to $300,000. The Ninth Circuit found that 300 times compensatory damages was unacceptable, so it ordered either retrial or a further reduction of the damages to $125,000. However, the case was re-heard en banc and, at the end of 2014, the en banc court reinstated the district court award. The en banc court identified reprehensibility as the most important factor in awarding punitive damages. In this reading, Congress adopted the cap to set the maximum amount that can be awarded without offending due process—so an award that does not exceed the cap is acceptable even if it far exceeds the 10:1 ratio. [*Arizona v. Asarco*, 733 F.3d 882 (9th Cir. 2013), *rev'd*, 773 F.3d 1050 (9th Cir. 2014)]

In 2014, the Second Circuit took the opposite view, finding that not only is a 10:1 ratio presumptively acceptable but also sometimes a 2:1 ratio is the maximum that will not be allowed. In a case alleging that a steelworker suffered racial harassment from a co-worker and that the employer failed to respond adequately, the jury awarded $1.25 million in emotional distress compensatory damages and $24 million in punitive damages. The district court found the punitive damages excessive and ordered remittitur to $5 million. The Second Circuit held in late 2014 that even as remitted, the punitive damages were excessive, and the district court exceeded the (narrow) scope of discretion it is allowed. Although the Second Circuit agreed that the evidence supported the district court's characterization of the employer's conduct as egregious, the disparity between compensatory and punitive damages was questionable. In a case with very high compensatory damages, the Second Circuit said that a 4:1 ratio is not predictable or proportionate. The Second Circuit said that where the compensatory award is fairly subjective (e.g., where emotional damages rather than easily calculated back pay is involved) a 2:1 ratio is the maximum that can be permitted. [*Turley v. ISG Lackawanna, Inc.*, 774 F.3d 140 (2d Cir. 2014)]

In ADA cases, recovery for combined compensatory and punitive damages is capped at $50,000 (if the employer has 15–100 employees), $100,000 (101–200 employees), $100,000 (100–200 employees), $200,000 (201–500 employees) or $300,000 (501 or more employees). The damage caps are applied per plaintiff. Although a Northern District of Alabama jury awarded $10,5 million against the Norfolk Southern Railway for disability discrimination ($2.5 million for emotional pain and mental anguish, $8 million in punitive damages, and $96,000 in lost wages), the final judgment was only $396,521 once the caps were applied. [*Whitted v. Norfolk S. Ry. Co., Inc.*, No. 2:13-cv-01550 (N.D. Ala. Jan. 29, 2016); see Christina A. Pate, *Statutory Damage Caps Save Companies Millions*, Squire Patton Boggs (Feb. 23, 2016), available at Lexology.com]

An unpublished district court case upholds an award of $51.4 million to an ADEA plaintiff who lost his job in a Reduction in Force. This is about five times the previous highest New Jersey award, possibly the largest jury award anywhere in the United States in a single-plaintiff ADEA case. The jury awarded almost $50 million in punitive damages based on the employer's reckless disregard of anti-discrimination laws, plus $520,000 each in lost wages and emotional distress. [*Braden v. Lockheed Martin Corp.*, No. 14-4215-RMB-JS (D.N.J. Jan. 26, 2017) (unpublished) ; see Lynne Anne Anderson, *Jury Awards $51 Million to an Age Discrimination Plaintiff: What Can We Learn*? Drinker Biddle & Reath LLP (Jan. 31, 2017), available at Lexology.com]

There are not many instances in which very large punitive damages have actually been paid. Such awards are vulnerable to being reduced on appeal. Or the plaintiff may feel both emotionally vindicated and sick of litigating the case, and may settle the case post-trial for much less than the theoretical award. Nevertheless, even if the order is never carried out, it can be a real public relations disaster for a company to be ordered to pay millions of dollars as a punishment.

The EEOC's Compliance Manual lists appropriate factors for deciding whether the employer acted with malice or reckless indifference. The factors include how unacceptable the conduct was; how much harm the complainant suffered; how long the practice continued; whether there was an extensive pattern of past discrimination, or just a few isolated instances; whether the employer tried to remedy the situation—or made it worse by concealment or retaliation.

[D] Attorneys' Fees and Costs

Under appropriate circumstances, a court can award attorneys' fees and costs to the "prevailing party"—and there has been a good deal of litigation, inside and outside the employment discrimination context, on the issue of who has been successful enough to receive a fee award.

In 2010, the Supreme Court ruled that a specific section of ERISA (§ 502(g)(1)) gives the district court discretion to award attorneys' fees to either party, not necessarily to the "prevailing" party. (In contrast, ERISA § 502(g)(2), about delinquent contributions to a multi-employer plan, limits fee awards to the prevailing party.) Therefore, it was not an abuse of discretion to grant attorneys' fees to a claimant who proved that denial of benefits was an abuse of discretion and obtained a remand for the insurer to reconsider the denial. The Supreme Court ruled that the statutory language does not require the party seeking fees to have prevailed. [*Hardt v. Reliance Ins. Co.*, 560 U.S. 242 (2010)]

Shortly thereafter, the Fourth Circuit applied this case to award attorneys' fees to a claimant who was granted summary judgment when the district court found that she was entitled to long-term disability benefits for carpal tunnel syndrome. The Fourth Circuit found that there was no inherent bias in the termination of long-term disability benefits after two years—but the denial was not supported by substantial evidence, because the plaintiff's pain and loss of function continued. [*Williams v. Metropolitan Life Ins. Co.*, 609 F.3d 622 (4th Cir. 2010); see Plansponsor Staff, *4th Circuit Upholds Award of Benefits and Attorneys' Fees in LTD Case*, plansponsor.com (July 2, 2010)]

It is rare but not unheard-of for an employer to receive a fee award as a prevailing defendant: for example, when the EEOC's investigation lasted more than six years; many remedies were unavailable (plants where discrimination allegedly occurred had closed); and the defendant was prejudiced by the delay (old personnel records had been routinely destroyed), the Fourth Circuit upheld an award of approximately $193,000 against the EEOC. [*EEOC v. Propak Logistics Inc.*, 746 F.3d 145 (4th Cir. 2014)]

The California Supreme Court ruled that, to get an award of costs in a California state discrimination case, a prevailing employer must prove that the suit was objectively groundless. The award of costs is discretionary. To avoid plaintiffs from being discouraged from pursuing civil rights cases, the California Supreme Court said that prevailing plaintiffs should get attorneys' fees and costs unless the special circumstances of the case would make that unjust, whereas prevailing defendants should only be awarded fees and costs if the suit was objectively unreasonable, or if the plaintiff continued to pursue a case after it was obvious that the plaintiff could not win. [*Williams v. Chino Valley Indep. Fire Dist.*, 347 P.3d 976 (Cal. 2015)]

The Second Circuit joined the Seventh, Tenth, and Eleventh Circuits in holding that, in a class action for unpaid wages and overtime filed by five ex-employees, expert witness fees cannot be recovered under the FLSA. The Second Circuit said that a district court can only make an award of expert fees if the statute explicitly provides for it; the case was remanded to determine if the New York Labor Law explicitly authorizes such an award. [*Gortat v. Capala Bros., Inc.*, 621 Fed. Appx. 19 (2d Cir. 2015)]

§ 42.13 SETTLEMENT OF A DISCRIMINATION SUIT

[A] Generally

Suits can be settled at any time before a verdict or judicial decision is rendered. In fact, they can even be settled after the judge and jury have spoken. As long as there are appeal rights that could be exercised, the case is still open for negotiation. The objective of any settlement is to provide something for both parties: for the defendant employer, the chance to dispose of the case expeditiously and to eliminate the risk of a huge jury verdict; for the plaintiff, the chance to get at least some money quickly instead of many years later. At a very early stage, the matter might be resolved by an agreement to let the employee resign instead of being fired and receive severance pay, and perhaps some other benefits, in exchange for releasing the employer from all liability. Both sides must agree on how the matter will be treated for unemployment insurance purposes (based on counsel from a lawyer).

In a situation where the employer acknowledges that the plaintiff has a valid case, or at least that the claims have some validity, the employer may want to settle early to limit its possible liability exposure and bad publicity.

Even if the employer thinks the plaintiff's claims are fabricated, exaggerated, or legally invalid, it still might be prudent to settle the case because of the sheer cost and effort involved in litigating a major suit, even if the final result is victory for the employer.

Usually, cases are settled somewhere around halfway between the plaintiff's demand and the defendant's counter-offer. Of course, both sides know this, and it influences the amounts they suggest at the negotiating table. No one should ever engage in negotiations without authority actually to settle the case, and without a range of acceptable settlement figures.

> ■ **TIP:** Cases that are settled quickly are also often settled within the policy limits of the employer's liability insurance policy. Therefore, the insurer will assume the entire cost of settlement. Moreover, if the employer does a prompt investigation of the allegations, negotiates in good faith, and does not unduly delay the settlement, the employer has not acted outrageously and has not violated the norms of public policy. Therefore, there will probably be no grounds for assessing punitive damages against the employer.

When a settlement is reached, there are two major legal documents to be prepared. The first is a court order dismissing the case with prejudice (i.e., in a way that prevents it from being refiled later) and a release containing the terms of the settlement. It is usually prudent to try to provide the text of the release, in order to control the basic form of its terms. The 2009 Family and Medical Leave Act regulations (see Chapter 38) make it explicit that, while prospective waivers are forbidden (i.e., employees cannot give up the right to bring suit for violations that might occur in the future), employees can settle FMLA claims that have already accrued without court approval or the supervision of the Department of Labor.

Mid-2009 EEOC guidance includes a section on Older Workers Benefit Protection Act (OWBPA) waivers. A waiver covering a group or class of employees carries additional disclosure requirements. There are seven factors under the OWBPA for determining whether an ADEA waiver is knowing and voluntary. It must be written in a manner that can be clearly understood; must specifically mention ADEA rights or claims; must inform employees of the right to consult a lawyer; must give the employee at least 21 days to consider the offer and seven days to revoke acceptance; the waiver cannot cover claims to arise in the future; and the employee must receive some consideration for the waiver that would not otherwise be available. A waiver is invalid if obtained by fraud or undue influence, or if there has been a material mistake, omission, or misstatement. [EEOC, *Understanding Waivers of Discrimination Claims in Employee Severance Agreements*,   <http://www.eeoc.gov/policy/docs/qanda_severance-agreements .html> (July 15, 2009; Appendix B modified Apr. 2010) (last accessed Mar. 22, 2017)]

The EEOC says that some standard language in releases is invalid under the EEOC's 1997 Enforcement Guidance on non-waivable rights. The EEOC objects to covenants not to sue that cover all kinds of charges; general release language that applies to discrimination charges. The agency also objects to non-disparagement or confidentiality clauses that require the ex-employee to inform the employer before discussing information, even in response to a subpoena. The author of the article suggests including a carve-out in releases that allow the employee to file charges but waives the right to monetary damages on those claims. The confidentiality clause should make it clear that the employee can participate in an investigation. [Tim K. Garrett. *Release Language Hazards and How to Fix Them*, Bass, Berry & Sims PLC (June 17, 2014), available at Lexology .com]

A settlement can be offered without admitting culpability. Also, under 29 C.F.R. § 1601.20(a), the EEOC has the power to dismiss an employee's discrimination charge if the employee rejects a written settlement offer from the employer that is a legitimate offer of "full relief" (i.e., adequate compensation for the discrimination suffered by the employee). The EEOC sends the employee a strongly worded form letter that gives him or her only two choices: to accept the settlement offer promptly, or have the EEOC charge dismissed. (This only means that the EEOC will not be involved in the case, not that the employee is prevented from suing.)

Full relief means that the employee gets full back pay, plus any out-of-pocket expenses related to discrimination (such as moving expenses after a wrongful termination, or psychological counseling for a stressed-out employee). Compensation must also be included for nonmonetary losses such as loss of sleep, anxiety, and indigestion.

However, the employer must be aware that settling with one employee is not necessarily the end of the problem. It is against public policy (and a court might issue an injunction forbidding this) to include a provision in a settlement agreement that forbids a current or former employee to cooperate with an EEOC investigation. A settlement can prevent a person from pursuing his or her own claims against the employer, but the EEOC's right to investigate workplace conditions, and pursue claims on its own behalf (and on behalf of other employees) continues.

[B]   Tax Factors in Settling Discrimination Cases

The plaintiff's objective is to wind up with the best after-tax result from pursuing or settling a case. In some instances, appropriate structuring of the settlement can produce a better after-tax result for the plaintiff while reducing the cash-flow impact on the defendant.

Damages for breach of contract are taxable income for the plaintiff, because they are treated as delayed payment of compensation that the employee would have received earlier if there had been no breach of contract.

The treatment of tort damages is more complex. Damages are not taxable if they are payable because of the plaintiff's "personal injury." The Supreme Court has ruled that Title VII damages and ADEA damages are not received for personal injury, because they are not similar enough to the damages received in traditional tort cases (car crashes, for instance). [*United States v. Burke*, 504 U.S. 229 (1992); *Comm'r of Internal Revenue v. Schleier*, 515 U.S. 323 (1995)] Nevertheless, in 2006 the D.C. Circuit held that compensatory damages for emotional distress and loss of reputation are not taxable, and it was unconstitutional to apply section 104(a)(2) [the definition of "personal physical injury"] to the plaintiff, because compensation for non-physical personal injury should not have to be included in income if it is unrelated to lost earnings. [*Murphy v. IRS*, 460 F.3d 79 (D.C. Cir. 2006)]

Later, this anomalous result was reversed. The IRS asked for rehearing en banc (i.e., by all of the judges of the D.C. Circuit, not just a panel consisting of some of them). Instead of granting en banc rehearing, the original three-judge panel re-heard the case and reversed its earlier holding. This time around, the D.C. Circuit joined the other Circuits in treating the amount as taxable income. [*Murphy v. CIR*, 493 F.3d 170 (D.C. Cir. 2007)]

The Small Business Job Protection Act of 1996 clarified the application of I.R.C. § 104(a)(2), the provision on taxation of damages. Starting August 21, 1996, damages received for "personal physical injuries" and physical illness are received free of tax—for instance, if the employer's wrongful conduct makes the employee physically ill. Damages for emotional distress are taxable except to the extent of medical expenses for their treatment.

Taxable damages that are wage replacements (under the FLSA, NLRA, Title VII, and ADEA, for example) may be FICA wages and may be subject to withholding. But see *Newhouse v. McCormack & Co.* [157 F.3d 582 (8th Cir. 1998)], where front and back pay awarded under the ADEA to a job applicant who was not hired was not considered "wages" subject to tax withholding. The Second Circuit held that settlement proceeds in an ADEA suit were wages subject to FICA. The agreement expressly permitted the employer to deduct and withhold all sums subject to withholding under applicable laws and regulations, but did not state how the $250,000 settlement proceeds would be treated for tax purposes. A court analyzing a settlement payment looks first to the nature of the claim that was settled, then remedies under governing law, then the parties' intention. In ADEA cases, the remedies are lost wages, liquidated damages, and equitable relief—but not pain and suffering or emotional distress damages (which would probably not be treated as wages). [*Gerstenbluth v. Credit Suisse*, 728 F.3d 139 (2d Cir. 2013)]

In a Title VII retaliation case, the Tax Court reaffirmed that emotional distress damages are taxable income for the person who receives them. The plaintiff, Sharp, was a professor who charged that she was demoted to a secretarial position in retaliation for reporting missing equipment. She said that she became depressed and suffered associated physical symptoms as a result of the stressful, hostile work environment. Her suit was settled; the university agreed to make three $70,000 installment payments to compensate her for emotional distress. She did not report the first installment as taxable income, deeming it to be damages for personal physical injury, exempted by Code § 104(a)(2). The IRS assessed tax on the funds. Sharp went to the Tax Court, which ruled in the IRS's favor and held that an accuracy-related penalty was due. The Tax Court said that the settlement agreement had only one reference to being conditioned on settling her Worker's Compensation claim. The settlement was for emotional distress, rendering the proceeds taxable income for the plaintiff. [*Sharp v. Comm'r*, No. 2013-290 (T.C. Dec. 23, 2013)]

A longstanding circuit split was resolved by the U.S. Supreme Court's January 2005 decision in *Commissioner v. Banks*, 543 U.S. 426 (2005). A judgment or settlement paid to a winning plaintiff's attorney under a contingent fee agreement must be included in the plaintiff's gross income, irrespective of whether state law gives the attorney special rights (over and above normal contract law rights) over amounts awarded to prevailing plaintiffs.

Section 703 of the American Jobs Creation Act (Pub. L. No. 108-357) makes attorneys' fees in employment discrimination cases an above-the-line deduction, although this is not true of attorneys' fees in other types of cases. *Banks* was decided after the enactment of this legislation, but the law is not retroactive.

The Second Circuit held that a Title VII award of back and front pay was subject to deductions of federal and state taxes, because the judgment replaced wages that the plaintiff lost due to discrimination and he would have had to pay taxes if there had been no discrimination and he had earned his ordinary salary. [*Noel v. New York State Office of Mental Health Cent. New York Psychiatric Ctr.*, 697 F.3d 209 (2d Cir. 2012)]

The Third Circuit held that prevailing plaintiffs in employment discrimination cases (in this case, the winner of an ADA suit) can receive an additional award to make up for the negative tax consequences of receiving a back pay award in a lump sum. The Third Circuit's rationale was that anti-discrimination statutes seek to make the plaintiff whole for the losses suffered, and the tax problems are a result of the underlying discrimination. The Tenth Circuit has ruled similarly, but the D.C. Circuit has held that plaintiffs are never entitled to a supplemental award to improve their tax position. [*Eshelman v. Agere Sys., Inc.*, 554 F.3d 426 (3d Cir. 2009); *Sears v. Atcheson, Topeka & Santa Fe R.R*, 749 F.3d 1451 (10th Cir. 1984) and *Dashnaw v. Pena*, 12 F.3d 1112 (D.C. Cir. 1994)]

CHAPTER 43

INSURANCE COVERAGE FOR CLAIMS AGAINST THE EMPLOYER

§ 43.01 INTRODUCTION

It is only prudent for a company to maintain insurance against significant risks. However, although the potential risk exposure in a discrimination, harassment, or wrongful termination suit is quite large, it can be difficult to buy insurance that will fully cover these claims—or even cover them at all. In addition, the collapse of the financial markets beginning in 2008 has given rise to a wide variety of securities-related claims, including those brought by employees whose pensions were jeopardized.

A basic principle of insurance law is that you can't buy insurance to protect yourself against the consequences of your own intentional wrongdoing. The current interpretation of this rule is that it does not violate public policy for companies to buy insurance covering employment-related liability, because this enhances the winning plaintiffs' chances to collect. This benefit is deemed to outweigh the risk that companies will be more willing to engage in improper employment practices if they know they are protected by insurance.

A related policy question is whether insurance can cover punitive damages. About two-thirds of the states that have decided cases about this say yes. However, punitive damages for intentional wrongdoing cannot be covered, and most punitive damages are imposed precisely because of the intentionality of the defendant's wrongful conduct.

The principle of "contra proferentem" is that ambiguous policy language is applied in favor of the insured, on the theory that the insurer could have drafted the policy more clearly. However, to make use of this principle, the insured must be able to convince the court that the language actually is ambiguous.

One hundred twenty days before current coverage expires, insured companies should analyze their liability insurance portfolio, and confer with an insurance agent, the general counsel, and the risk manager to create a current risk profile for the company and determine what coverage is available at what cost to insure against this risk. Insurers issue Conditional Notice of Non-Renewal Letters about 90 days before a policy expires, indicating that they do not wish to renew a policy but that they might offer terms on receipt of additional information about the insured company. The outcome of the strategy meeting should assist the company in negotiating renewals where non-renewal has been threatened—or in seeking alternative coverage. [DeAndre Salter and Karen Kutger, *As Prices Rise on Executive Liability Coverage, Strategy and Negotiations Enter Tough Terrain*, N.Y.L.J. (Mar. 26, 2009) (law.com)]

As computers become more and more dominant in business and the economy, they also are involved in an increasing number of crimes, and special "cyber" insurance and policy provisions come into play. To select the correct cyber coverage, a business must be certain to give the insurer accurate information about its data retention policies, computer controls, and other security measures. It might be necessary to warrant the conduct of third parties such as the business' cloud service providers. Renewal applications should always be reviewed carefully; interim changes in situation might make some of the insured's representations untrue, and courts allow policies to be rescinded for omissions, even inadvertent ones. The correct policy trigger should be chosen. Some policies will cover any security incident, whereas others ask whether the insured failed in any of its security duties. The practical benefit of the policy depends on whether the trigger is discovery or occurrence; a well-hidden breach could take a long time to detect. An investigation can cost almost as much as the breach itself, so coverage of suspected or alleged breaches is helpful. If there are gaps in coverage for cyber risk, other policies or endorsements might be able to fill the gap. Many cyber policies cover ransoms to prevent a breach—but exclude ransoms for returning information that has already been stolen. For example, in 2016 P.F. Chang sought coverage for payment card industry security standard assessments, but had to pay $2 million in fees and assessments because it couldn't prove that it had coverage. Some gaps can be filled by crime policies, but the insured might not be able to collect if the loss is blamed on the insured's negligence in failing to investigate fraud schemes. [Walter J. Andrews and Jennifer E. White, *Digital Due Diligence: Four Questions to Evaluate Cyber Insurance Coverage*, Hunton & Williams LLP (Mar. 1, 2017), available at Lexology.com]

Cyber coverage is not the same as E&O insurance. Cyber coverage is limited to third-party intrusions into files and databases, whereas E&O deals with mistakes by consultants and software developers. [Jose M. Jara et. al., *Worth Covering: News, Tips and Thoughts for Professional Liability Carriers,* Fisher-Broyles (Aug. 30, 2016), available at Lexology.com]

§ 43.02   COMMERCIAL GENERAL LIABILITY

[A]   Use of the CGL Policy

Most businesses get their basic liability coverage under the Commercial General Liability (CGL) policy. In fact, for most companies, this is the only liability insurance.

The CGL has two basic aims. The first is to provide a defense (i.e., supply a lawyer who will investigate, negotiate, and settle or try the case). The second is to pay whatever settlement or judgment the defendant company would otherwise have to pay to a successful plaintiff. The insurer's obligation is subject to the insured's obligation to pay a deductible. The insurer is not required to pay more than the limits of the policy. CGL policies are not really uniform. The Insurance Standards Organization (ISO) has published a very influential model policy, but insurers have the option of tailoring the model as they see fit.

Furthermore, the insurer must only pay for covered claims, not excluded ones. ISO has drafted an "employment-related practices exclusion," and the trend is for recent policies to follow this and simply exclude all claims related to a plaintiff's employment by a defendant. Even this is not as simple as it seems. For instance, a court might rule that the real injury to the plaintiff occurred after he or she was fired and therefore ceased to be an employee.

Even if the policy doesn't exclude all employment-related claims, there may be other factors that prevent the employer from collecting benefits under the policy.

[B]   Bodily Injury and Personal Injury

Coverage A of the CGL provides liability insurance when the insured becomes liable to someone who has suffered "bodily injury." It's rare for employment plaintiffs to claim that they suffered physically. Usually, they assert that they lost economic benefits (such as salary and pension) because of the employer's wrongful conduct. CGL Coverage A will *not* apply to charges of breach of contract or other economic consequences.

For this and other reasons, plaintiffs often ask for damages based on their emotional suffering. Their complaints allege pain and suffering, intentional infliction of emotional distress, or negligent infliction of emotional distress. (The availability of these causes of action varies between the federal and state systems, and from state to state.)

Most courts that have dealt with this question say that there is no "bodily injury" in an emotional suffering case unless the plaintiff can prove that there was at least some physical consequence of the emotional injury: an ulcer or high blood pressure, for instance. Even if there are physical consequences, they could be considered basically economic and therefore outside the scope of Coverage A.

The CGL's Coverage B deals with liability that the insured encounters for "personal injury" (such as libel or slander) or advertising injury (such as defaming another company's products in your ads). Coverage B might get involved in an employment-related case if, for instance, the plaintiff claims that the employer not only fired him or her, but blacklisted him or her and used a campaign of lies to prevent the ex-employee from getting another job or establishing business relationships.

Sometimes businesses find that they are not covered for advertising injury under their commercial liability coverage. Vitamin Health was sued by Bausch & Lomb when Vitamin Health advertised its supplement as "AREDS 2-compliant" (containing the vitamins recommended by the National Eye Institute's Age-Related Eye Disease Study). Bausch & Lomb alleged that Vitamin Health changed the formulation of the product so that it was no longer compliant with the standard. Vitamin Health's liability policy covered personal and advertising injury, defined as material that slanders or libels a person or organization or disparages someone's goods, products, or services. The policy excludes suits that allege infringement of intellectual property. It also excludes advertising injury arising out of a failure of goods, products, or services to conform to statements in the advertisement. Vitamin Health's insurer said that the advertisement did not disparage Bausch & Lomb products, and furthermore the two companies were involved in a patent infringement dispute. In a declaratory judgment suit about the duty to defend and indemnify Vitamin Health, the District Court for the Eastern District of Michigan ruled that there was no disparagement because the disputed advertisement was about Vitamin Health's product, not Bausch & Lomb's. The Bausch & Lomb suit was based on failure to conform to a statement about compliance; and the false advertising claim was part of a patent infringement suit. Vitamin Health settled the case in late 2016. [*Vitamin Health v. Bausch & Lomb*, No. 5:15-cv-12669 (E.D. Mich., settled Dec. 16, 2016); see Randall K. Miller and Kevin Weigand, *Insurance Coverage for "Advertising Injury" May Still Leave Businesses on the Hook for False Advertising Claims*, Venable LLP (Feb. 21, 2017) available at Lexology.com]

The First Circuit found the word "contractor" to be ambiguous, so a general contractor was covered when a house painter hired by the architect of a home renovation project was injured. The First Circuit said it was unclear whether a "contractor" meant anyone with a contract or anyone who had a contract with the insured. An employee of the house painter used a ladder on top of scaffolding allegedly erected by employees of the architect, but the architect blamed the employer of the injured painter. The general contractor, Benchmark, applied for CGL coverage, which was denied based on the bodily injury exclusion for employees, contractors, and subcontractors. The First Circuit said that the clause "injury to any employee of any contractor arising out of rendering services for which any insured may become liable" was ambiguous as to whether insured could be liable for bodily injury or for services, so it was construed in the favor of the insured. [*United States Liab. Ins. Co. v. Benchmark Constr. Servs., Inc.*, 797 F.3d 116 (1st Cir. 2015)]

[C] CGL Case Law

Under liability insurance and Worker's Compensation insurance policies, asbestos-related disease is "bodily injury by disease" and not "bodily injury by accident." Asbestos exposure is not an accident because of its non-violent nature and because injuries develop over a latency period rather than manifesting immediately. [*Riverwood Int'l Corp. v. Employers Ins. of Wausau*, 420 F.3d 378 (5th Cir. 2005)]

After a corporate transition, the liability policy might not cover the newly converted company. For example, automatic coverage under the liability policy might be limited to a certain number of days after which time it must be changed, reflecting the new corporate entity. In Texas, unlike many other states, insurance does not follow the business when there is a merger, asset sale, or other corporate transition and anti-assignment clauses (forbidding assignment of insurance without the carrier's consent) will probably be enforced. During an acquisition, the acquiror must make sure there is enough coverage for the potential insurable liability. The acquiror's existing general liability policies probably will not cover claims involving the acquired company because the acquiror is the named insured and the alleged bodily injury or property damage might not have happened during the policy period. If the acquiree is part of an industry that uses claims-made policies (e.g., if it has professional liability coverage), the acquiror should spend the extra money needed to buy a new policy with a retro date that at least matches the date of the acquiree's policies. If the target has large-scale exposure, for example, for toxic torts, the acquiror should compare the coverage to the potential liability, and try to get the acquiree's policy assigned. Injury claims against the acquiree for pre-transfer industry that pre-date the addition to the policy will not be covered without a special manuscript endorsement. If the acquiree's policy cannot be assigned, the acquiror can seek contractual indemnification from the owners of the acquiree, as part of the transaction, but coverage for indemnity is unlikely if the injury occurred before the indemnity agreement was entered into. The target company's preferred strategy is not to assign the policy but to get the carrier's consent to add the new entity as an additional named insured. [Michael W. Huddleston, *Insurance Issues in Mergers and Acquisitions*, Munsch Hardt Kopf & Harr PC (Feb. 1, 2015), available at Lexology.com]

When an employee of a subcontractor died in a fall, the employee's estate sued the subcontractor, general contractor, and property owner for wrongful death. The general contractor applied for CGL coverage, asserting a sum that it had to pay for bodily injury. The policy required defense of all suits, but excluded damages for injuries to the general contractor's employees. The general contractor reached a settlement with the decedent's estate and assigned its claim to the CGL insurer. The settlement said that the estate was only entitled to collect from the CGL insurer, not from the general contractor. The estate accordingly sued the CGL insurer, charging it with wrongful refusal to defend and indemnify the general contractor. The trial court granted summary judgment for the insurer, finding the claim to be excluded by the "employee exclusion" clause. Florida law provides that a contractor has a statutory employment relationship with the subcontractor's employees, making the general contractor the statutory employer of the decedent. The Eleventh Circuit affirmed. [*Stephens v. Mid-Continent Cas. Co.*, 749 F.3d 1318 (11th Cir. Apr. 24, 2014)]

The Third Circuit affirmed summary judgment for a CGL insurer: it had no obligation to defend or indemnify the insured for a Telephone Consumer Privacy Act consumer class action settlement for sending unsolicited faxes; this activity was not covered by the policy. [*Auto-Owners Ins. Co. v. Stevens & Ricci Inc.*, 835 F.3d 388 (3d Cir. 2016)]

A CGL policy covered "directors," defined as executive officers and directors. The Eighth Circuit ruled in mid-2014 that a supervisor's acts were not covered by the policy—he was not a director. The case arose when an injured worker sued the company and his supervisor, charging that the supervisor was negligent in allowing the worker to drive a truck that the supervisor knew was defective.

The Eighth Circuit interpreted "director" to mean "member of the board of directors," rather than "someone who directs the work of other employees." [*United Fire & Cas. v. Thompson*, 758 F.3d 959 (8th Cir. 2014)]

§ 43.03   OCCURRENCES AND THE PROBLEM OF INTENTION

Coverage under Coverage A depends on there being an "occurrence," which is defined as an accident that was neither intended nor expected by the insured. Coverage B does not have an occurrence requirement, but it does exclude coverage of personal injuries that stem from a willful violation of the law, committed by or with the consent of the insured company.

At first glance, it would seem that employment cases could never be covered under the CGL, because the plaintiff accuses someone of deliberately injuring him or her. The picture is far more complex. Some discrimination charges allege "disparate treatment" (roughly speaking, intentional discrimination), while others claim "disparate impact" (subtle negative effects on a protected group of employees). An employer's actions in adopting a policy or publishing an employee manual could have unintended consequences, which could possibly be treated as CGL "occurrences."

However, intentional discrimination would not be. Courts often treat some conduct (e.g., sexual harassment) as being so likely to have bad consequences for their victims that the consequences are presumed to have been intended, or at least expected, by the insured company.

Employment discrimination plaintiffs usually want the insurance company to be involved, because they know that liability insurance is another potential source of payment if they settle or win the case. In this instance, they are on the same side as the employer. They both want the CGL to cover the employee's claim. One simple strategy is for plaintiffs to add claims of negligent supervision by the employer, or negligent infliction of emotional distress, in the hope that these charges of negligence will be classified as covered "occurrences." The CGL exclusion of "intentional" conduct does not apply to conduct that is negligent, or even grossly negligent. However, this tactic usually fails because the negligence charges are treated as purely incidental to more important charges of intentional conduct.

In most instances, termination of an employee, even wrongful termination, does not involve the intention or expectation of harm, so the insurer will probably have a duty to defend. CGL personal injury coverage often excludes damage resulting from the willful violations of a penal statute or ordinance, committed by the insured or with the knowledge of the insured. Civil rights laws are not considered "penal statutes" for this purpose. Even if actions are "willful" for Title VII purposes, the criminal law exclusion will not be triggered.

Some CGL policies offer an endorsement or rider (at additional cost over the basic premium) that covers discrimination and harassment claims, often by broadening the underlying policy's definition of personal injury.

CGL policies typically exclude bodily injury to employees, arising out of and in the course of employment, whether the employer is liable as an employer or in other capacities. But that provision is probably included in the policy simply for coordination with Worker's Compensation. The employee could succeed in arguing that the tort claims they make do not arise out of or in the course of the employment relationship, because supervisors are not employed to commit discrimination or harassment. The insurer may have at least a duty to defend. Furthermore, occupational injuries could be treated as a known risk that employees are aware of, whereas discrimination and harassment are not risks of the same category.

§ 43.04   EMPLOYMENT PRACTICES LIABILITY INSURANCE

Because of the gaps in CGL coverage of employment matters, a separate form of policy, Employment Practices Liability Insurance (EPLI) evolved as of about 1990. The EPLI policy is designed to cover damages, judgments, settlements, defense costs, and attorneys' fee awards in the employment liability context (suits, proceedings, or written demands seeking to hold the employer civilly liable). Events included under the EPLI are discrimination, sexual harassment, hostile work environment harassment, wrongful termination, retaliation, defamation, false imprisonment, and negligent supervision, but not "golden parachutes" (payments to top managers who lose their jobs because of corporate transitions) or contractual obligations to make payments to terminated employees. The EPLI policy generally excludes criminal charges, fines, punitive damages, retaliation, and any amounts that are uninsurable because of a relevant state law.

Hiscox, an insurer provider estimated, in late 2015, that the average cost of defending or settling an employee discrimination charge was $125,000. Hiscox studied about 500 claims reported by companies with fewer than 500 employees. The average time to resolve the case was 275 days. The average deductible for companies with EPLI was $35,000. Only 19% of cases reported both defense costs and a settlement, suggesting that 80% of claims washed out. However, for the comparatively few cases that went to trial, and where the plaintiff won, the median judgment (not included defense costs) was $200,000. [Michael C. Wilhelm, *How Much Does an Employee Charge of Discrimination Cost?*, Briggs and Morgan (Nov. 4, 2015), available at Lexology.com]

The usual EPLI policy coverage limit is $1 million–$5 million, but some insurers offer "jumbo" policies of up to $100 million in coverage.

EPLI owners can benefit even if they are never sued, because insurers require insured parties to audit their HR functions, improve their procedures, and add new procedures to minimize the risk of suit. The policy may offer access to valuable low-cost consulting services, and compliance advice that would otherwise carry a high price tag.

Unlike CGL policies (which typically have occurrence coverage, triggered at the time of occurrence, which may be years before the claim is asserted), EPLI policies usually are written on a claims-made basis. A claims-made policy is one that provides coverage when claims are made while the insured still has coverage, but not for claims made after coverage expires, even if the allegedly wrongful conduct occurred while the policy was still in force. The ISO EPLI form modifies this by covering claims made during the 30 days after policy expiration, unless another insurer is already in the picture. If the same employee makes multiple claims, they are all considered to have arisen on the date of the first claim, so coverage will be continuous, and it will not be necessary to figure out whether the initial or the later insurer is responsible. Sometimes, it is a false economy to replace a liability insurance policy if the new policy has a waiting period, creating a gap in coverage. Claims-made insurance is cheaper because the insurer is exposed to liability for a shorter time, but the insured must report claims promptly.

Generally, EPLI policies define "claim" as a suit or demand made by a past, present, or prospective employee. Most policies include both lawsuits and administrative claims such as EEOC charges in the definition of "suit," whereas a demand is any written request for monetary or other relief. Employers often handle administrative charges and demand letters without notifying their insurance carriers, either because they do not consider them to be claims or they are afraid that reporting the claims will increase their premiums. However, this is a mistake, because failure to give timely notice can lead to denial of defense and indemnification. [Christopher J. Carney, *The Importance of Timely Reporting Claims Under an Employment Practices Liability Policy*, Brouse McDowell (Oct. 14, 2015), available at Lexology.com]

EPLI policies always provide that the insurer is not responsible for expenses incurred without express written consent, which means that attorneys' fees and litigation expenses, and settlement amounts, will not be covered if they are incurred before the claim is made. Many policies provide that an insured that reports circumstances that is aware might lead to a claim, subsequent claims about the same circumstances will be treated as if reported at the time of the initial report. This is beneficial to the insured because it preserves the policy limit in effect at that time, and allows some later claims to "read back" and accordingly be covered. In practical terms, the simplest tactic is to submit claim information to the business' insurance broker with a request to tender the claim under all applicable policies; the broker will be aware of each carrier's requirement for submission. [Christopher Andre, *Avoid Common Mistakes That Can Jeopardize Coverage Under an Employment Practices Liability Insurance Policy*, Atkinson Andelson Loya Ruud & Romo (May 5, 2017), available at Lexology.com]

EPLI claims-made issues are often complicated by the way discrimination claims are handled. Before suing, the claimant has to file a charge with the EEOC or other administrative body. The charge could be made in one policy period, the suit in a later one. Most EPLI policies trigger coverage by a claim for a wrongful act which is first made during the policy period. Both the administrative charge and the suit are usually treated as "claims." The District Court for the Northern District of Illinois held that coverage was triggered in the policy period because of an ambiguity in the policy. A claimant (in this case, an employee of a law school) has to make an EEOC (or other admin body) charge, so the charge could be in one policy period, the suit in a later one. Most EPLI policies trigger coverage by claim for a wrongful act which is first made during policy period. Both the administrative charge and the suit are usually treated as "claims," so there could be a dispute about when the claim was first made. An employee filed an EEOC charge on October 30, 2013; the right to sue letter was received about a week later. The law school's EPLI policy became effective November 13, 2013. The plaintiff sued on December 21, 2013. AIG denied coverage, saying the EEOC charge was a claim first made before the policy period. The district court said that both the EEOC charge and the suit satisfied the definition of "claim." If they constituted a single claim, then there would be no coverage because that "claim" was before the policy period. The law school said that they were separate—the policy used "or" between each alternate definition; the disjunctive "or" meant each definition was separate. The insurer argued that there can be no suit without an EEOC charge, so they must be the same claim. The court agreed but said that the policy language did not include a "deemer" clause (that any claims from the same facts or transactions were the same claim), and several clauses suggested that there could be separate claims with shared facts. The district court said it was reasonable to treat the two claims as separate and the suit was a claim first made during the policy period. The insurer asked for a ruling that it did not have a duty to defend; a clause said that the insurer has no duty to defend, but the court pointed to additional language imposing a duty to defend if claim for defense was asserted within 30 days of a claim being made. The district court said there was a duty to defend under Illinois law. Illinois law says that liability insurer either has to defend the insured with reservation of rights, or seek declaratory relief with respect to its obligations. If the insurer doesn't do either, and is found to have breached the duty to defend, it can't assert coverage defenses to indemnity—allowing the law school to argue that AIG is estopped from raising indemnity defenses. It's not clear why insurer didn't seek indemnity relief; it's not clear whether there was an earlier policy, and, if so, why the law school didn't give notice under that one. [*John Marshall Law Sch. v. Nat'l Union Fire Ins. Co. of Pittsburgh, PA*, No. 16 C 5753, 2016 WL 7429221 (N.D. Ill. Dec. 26, 2016). Lowndes Christopher Quinlan, *Law School Wins First Round in Fight Under EPLI Policy*, McGuireWoods LLP (Feb. 3, 2017), available at Lexology.com]

An HR blog looks at five main issues in researching and comparing EPLI policies:

Coverage—are only the standard issues (wrongful discharge, employment discrimination, harassment) covered, or are additional issues, such as negligent hiring, defamation, and infliction of emotional distress covered as well? Are claims covered only if asserted by full-time permanent employees, or are claims from independent contractors, part-time, temporary, seasonal, and temporary workers covered too?

Exclusions—all EPLI policies exclude punitive damages, and most of them list the statutes for which coverage will not be available, e.g., the Fair Labor Standards Act (FLSA), Worker Adjustment and Retraining Notification (WARN) Act, National Labor Relations Act (NLRA), Occupational Safety and Health Act (OSHA), or the Americans with Disability Act (ADA). The impact of an exclusion depends on the relevance of the topic to the company's business. Multi-state corporations may face a variety of risks under the different state laws, so it may be necessary to pay for coverage in multiple states to be protected against risks generated by individual state laws.

Deductibles, policy limits—these are usually applied on a per-claim as well as an aggregate basis, e.g., $250,000 per claim subject to a cap of $1 million on all claims. Accepting greater risk, by buying a policy with a higher deductible and/or lower cap, can be a cost-saving measure, but it leaves the insured vulnerable to more of the same risks that motivated buying the policy in the first place.

Timing issues—most EPLI policies are written on a "claims made" basis (i.e., to be covered, a claim must relate to conduct within the coverage period) and reported to the insurer during the prescribed reporting period. It is often necessary, even after discontinuing an EPLI policy, to purchase "long tail" coverage to account for claims that developed in earlier years but were not asserted until later. In some instances, long-simmering claims will be barred by statute of limitations and EEOC filing issues—but there are instances in which a claim covering many years of employment practices will be valid and will have to be defended. And, even if the claim itself is valid and requires a defense, if the insured fails to give timely notice to the insurer, the insurer may be relieved of responsibility.

Defense counsel, defense costs, and settlement—Generally, legal costs are included within the policy limit. If the claim is resolved in the employer's favor, this is not a problem, but if the employee prevails, amounts expended on defense are no longer available to pay the settlement or judgment awarded to the plaintiff or plaintiff class. Be aware that it is common for insurers to want to settle cases when the employer wants to fight to the last ditch, perhaps to clear its name and promote its good reputation. The policy might be drafted to give the insurer the right to settle even over the employer's objections. "Hammer clauses" are also common: i.e., the employer retains control over settlement—but if the employer rejects a settlement offer, insurance will not cover any discrepancy between the eventual settlement or judgment and the amount for which the employer could have settled the case. [Michael Moore, *Employment Practices Liability Insurance: Five Things Every HR Generalist Should Know*, <http:// www.paemploymentlawblog.com/2008/02/articles/employer-liability/[. . .]> (Feb. 12, 2008)]

Two commentators suggest the following questions for evaluating an EPLI policy:

- Does it cover all employees? What about the liability consequences of actions of leased employees and independent contractors?

- Are former employees covered?

- Are claims for breach of explicit or implied employment contract covered by or excluded from the policy?

- Does the insurer have to provide you with a defense in administrative (e.g., EEOC and local antidiscrimination agencies) proceedings, or only at trial? (Only a small percentage of discrimination charges make it to the trial stage, but the investigative stage can be very unpleasant for the employer.)

- Are retaliation claims (including retaliation for filing Worker's Compensation claims) covered? (This is a large and growing part of the discrimination caseload.)

- Are injunctive and declaratory relief covered, or only money damages?

- Is the deductible imposed on a per-year or per-claimant basis? (If the latter is true, an insured employer might end up having to pay several deductibles a year.)

[Stephanie E. Trudeau and William Edwards, Employment Law Letter, archived at <http://www.ulmer.com>]

§ 43.05   OTHER INSURANCE

The business insurance portfolio could also include other types of insurance, such as excess liability (supplementing the CGL), umbrella coverage (with a broader definition of "personal injury"), Worker's Compensation insurance (see Chapter 33 for more detailed consideration of WC issues) and Directors' and Officers' (D&O) coverage.

In late 2016, the District Court for the Eastern District of North Carolina held that the employee theft coverage in a crime policy was ambiguous, so the contract terms were construed in favor of the insured. The insured filed a claim after the principals of a company hired to handle the insured's payroll and taxes embezzled money. The policy covered loss of money "resulting from theft or forgery committed by an employee,"

"Employee" was defined to include "contractual independent contractor." Because the phrase "acting on behalf of" was ambiguous, the court construed it to mean that, because the corporation existed to facilitate embezzlement by its principals, the corporation acted on behalf of the principals when it contracted with the insured. Therefore, the principals were contractual independent contractors, and hence employees, so the monetary loss was covered as employee theft. [*Colony Tire Corp. v. Fed. Ins. Co.*, 2016 WL 6683590 (E.D. N.C. Nov. 14, 2016); see George B. Hall, Jr., *Federal Court in North Carolina Finds "Employee Theft" Insuring Clause Ambiguous*, Phelps Dunbar LLP (Dec. 5, 2016), available at Lexology.com]

The Eleventh Circuit held that Georgia law made an insurer responsible for harm caused by an intoxicated employee's vehicle use. The appellant was in an accident with a drunk driver who was driving a company vehicle with the employer's permission. The appellant was awarded $1 million. The employer's insurance company brought a declaratory judgment suit seeking a finding that the driver was not covered under the policy because he was not a permissive user: he violated the employer's internal policy by driving drunk. The Eleventh Circuit held that, in Georgia, inquiries into permissive use are limited to whether the vehicle was used for an approved purpose; violating the employer's policy did not alter this status. [*Great Am. Alliance Ins. Co. v. Anderson*, 847 F.3d 1327 (11th Cir. 2017); see Erin Dougherty Foley and Craig B. Simonsen, *Eleventh Circuit Finds Insurance Carrier Responsible in Georgia for Harm Intoxicated Employee*, [sic] Seyfarth Shaw LLP (Mar. 21, 2017), available at Lexology.com]

[A] Excess Liability and Umbrella Coverage

Every CGL policy has limits: maximum amounts of coverage obtainable under particular circumstances. If your company already has maximum CGL coverage, but feels that more is necessary, there are two ways to supplement it.

The first is "follow-form" excess liability insurance, which increases the dollar amount of coverage available under your CGL, Worker's Compensation, and Business Automobile Liability coverage, but subject to the same terms and exclusions. For many companies, an "umbrella" policy is a better choice, because it is more broadly defined and may cover situations that were excluded by the underlying policy. This kind of "gap" coverage is generally subject to a "retained limit," another term for "deductible."

Umbrella policies offer coverage in more situations because their definition of "personal injury" is broader than Coverage A or Coverage B of the standard CGL. A typical provision includes both bodily injury and mental injury, mental anguish, shock, sickness, disease, discrimination, humiliation, libel, slander, defamation of character, and invasion of property. Therefore, many employment-related claims would be covered.

[B] Worker's Compensation

Specialized Worker's Compensation (WC) coverage is available to deal with the employer's obligation to pay benefits to employees who are injured in job-related situations. Of course, because of WC exclusivity, the employer does not have to worry about ordinary liability suits from injured workers, although there may be special situations in which suit can be brought (against the employer or another party, such as the manufacturer of unsafe factory machinery) even though Worker's Compensation is involved. In a WC employment liability policy, Worker's Compensation is Coverage A; the employment liability (e.g., bodily injury that is not subject to WC exclusivity) is Coverage B.

California AB 1897, signed September 28, 2014, makes companies with more than 25 employees that use workers supplied by a labor contractor jointly liable with the labor contractor if there is a failure to obtain WC coverage. The law does not apply to workers who are exempt as administrative, executive, or professional employees—or to companies with fewer than six workers supplied by the staffing company at a given time. [Baker & McKenzie, *Certain California Employers Who Use Staffing Agencies and Contractors Statutorily Liable for Wage and Hour and Safety Violations* (Dec. 26, 2014), available at Lexology .com]

The Seventh Circuit had to decide whether an employee's common-law negligence claim against his employer was a "claim under employer liability laws" to satisfy the insuring agreement of an excess Worker's Compensation policy. The employee died of mesothelioma, and TKK was sued for negligence. TKK gave timely notice of suit to its excess WC carrier. TKK retained primary responsibility for defending, settling, and paying claims of up to $275,000 per occurrence. TKK settled the suit, incurring more than $400,000 in legal fees. The excess insurer, Safety National, denied coverage, on the grounds that the suit was for common-law negligence and was not brought under WC or employer liability laws. In Illinois, the Workers' Occupational Diseases Act is the exclusive remedy for employees who are injured at work or contract occupational disease. It bars common-law claims, so it offered a defense to the negligence claims, although TKK did not raise it as an affirmative defense. Safety National said that, because the Occupational Diseases Act was the sole means of recovery for the claims but it was not mentioned in the suit, the costs of defense and settlement were not covered by the policy as WC or employer liability claims. TKK said that the policy covered claims that were groundless, or even fraudulent. The Seventh Circuit held that the Occupational Diseases Act did not cover all potential common-law claims, so "employer liability laws" meant more than statutory claims under the Occupational Diseases Act. The Seventh Circuit affirmed the district court, which held that "employer liability law" was broad enough to include groundless common-law claims for which the employer had an affirmative defense. [*TKK USA, Inc., v. Safety Nat'l Cas. Corp.*, 727 F.3d 782 (7th Cir. 2013)]

A long-tail occupational disease claim is one that involves disease that does not manifest itself for many years after the exposure. Some decisions from Pennsylvania and Illinois allow employees to sue their former employers in the tort system rather than being limited to WC. However, in late 2015, the Illinois Supreme Court held that a mesothelioma claim was WC-exclusive, even though the injuries manifested after the end of the 25-year statutory period to file claims. WC exclusivity does not apply if an injury was not accidental, not received during the course of employment, or was not compensable under WC. The Illinois Supreme Court held that the 25-year period is a statute of repose that absolutely bars later claims against the employer, although it is possible that the employee would be able to sue someone other than the employer. [*Folta v. Ferro Eng'g*, 43 N.E.3d 108 (Ill. 2015)]

[C] Directors' and Officers' Liability (D&O)

D&O insurance covers the situation in which a corporation' directors and officers get not only themselves but the corporation into trouble. Frequently, executives will not agree to serve as directors or officers unless the corporation first promises them indemnification, i.e., that the corporation will pay the executive whatever amount he or she has to pay because of liability incurred while acting as a director or officer.

D&O insurance, in turn, reimburses the corporation for whatever it spends on indemnification, subject to a deductible and up to the limit of the policy.

In a case of first impression, the Second Circuit ruled in late 2010 that it is unlawful for a company to agree to indemnify its CEO or CFO for compensation or proceeds of stock sales that they are required to disgorge under Sarbanes-Oxley § 304 (the "clawback" provision that requires CEOs and CFOs to reimburse their employers for incentive compensation received or stock sale profits recognized in the 12 months after the filing of a financial statement that had to be restated due to misconduct). In 2006, the corporation's CFO and Chief Operation Officer were charged with civil accounting fraud as well as criminal charges. In 2007, the company restated its financial statements for the years 2003–2005. A derivative and class action suit against the company was settled in 2008; the indemnification occurred at this time. After the federal prosecutor appealed, the Second Circuit overturned the settlement, agreeing that indemnification was inappropriate. Because there is no private right to sue under Sarbanes-Oxley § 304, all enforcement is done by the SEC, so indemnification was an attempt to relieve the CEO and CFO of their burdens under Sarbanes-Oxley. The SEC might make similar arguments against indemnification re Dodd-Frank Act clawbacks—

although it is not clear if the Dodd-Frank clawback provision allows private suits. [*Cohen v. Viray*, 622 F.3d 188 (2d Cir. 2010)]

A line of Delaware cases, such as *Trascent Management Consulting, LLC v. Bouri,* require companies to abide by promises, such as those in employment contracts and LLC agreements, to advance legal fees and expenses when the provision is invoked by a director, officer, or employee. The employer cannot avoid its obligation by claiming that the promise was induced by the employee's fraud. [See, e.g., *Trascent Mgmt. Consulting, LLC v. Bouri,* 152 A.3d 108 (Del. 2016); Andrew N. Goldfarb, *Can an Employer Back out of a Promise to Provide Advancement by Claiming That the Employee Committed Fraud?*, Zuckerman Spaeder LLP (Dec. 8, 2016), available at Lexology.com]

[D]   Errors & Omissions (E&O)

Errors and Omissions insurance pays, on behalf of the insured, all loss for which the insured person is not indemnified by the insured organization if the person is liable because of any wrongful act he or she committed or attempted. In general, committing disparate treatment discrimination will be considered a wrongful act that can be covered under the policy, unless the policy definition covers only negligent, and not intentional, acts and omissions.

In many companies, E&O insurance is complemented by D&O insurance that covers the company for losses it incurs when it indemnifies directors and officers acting in that capacity.

An important issue is whether or not administrative actions (such as state agency and EEOC proceedings, subpoenas, and federal grand jury target letters) are considered "claims or suits" for insurance purposes. Businesses also often encounter expenses for their own administrative or internal investigations. The insurer is likely to make the argument that back pay awarded to a prevailing plaintiff is equitable relief and not "damages" that could be covered under the policy.

However, many courts have rejected this argument and required liability insurers to handle back-pay awards against their policyholders. E&O insurers may also resist paying back pay if the policy excludes amounts owed under a "contractual obligation," but here again, the insured will probably prevail if a back pay award is made. D&O or E&O coverage for subpoena or investigation compliance must be negotiated before your company becomes a target. If the policy specifically refers to an indictment, a Grand Jury subpoena would probably not be treated as a "claim." Other decisions say that an investigation in and of itself is not a request for relief, but subpoenas and investigative demands have been found to be claims when the insured was required to produce testimony and documents as part of an ongoing investigation of the corporation. [Joseph D. Jean and Rachel M. Wrightson, *Ensuring Coverage for Actions in Response to Investigations*, N.Y.L.J. (July 10, 2009) (law.com)]

Another insurance form covers plans, administrators, and trustees against allegations of impropriety. Many employment-related claims involve ERISA allegations, so the employer should at least consider adding this coverage to its insurance portfolio.

[E] Crime Policies

Crime policies protect the insured against certain losses resulting from crimes: e.g., employee dishonesty, computer fraud, kidnap and ransom, forgery or alteration, and computer fraud. However, coverage must be carefully selected and tailored to the business' needs and the nature and scope of risks it encounters.

The Fourth Circuit held that a policy covering loss from "employee dishonesty" was not ambiguous and, therefore, could not be construed against the insurer. The insured had several years of consecutive crime policies issued by different insurers. The insured sought recovery under the 2004 policy for losses caused by employee fraud starting in 1999 (when a different policy was in place). The insured relied on an endorsement to the 2004 policy that covered losses discovered during the policy period but sustained during the period of "any prior insurance." The Fourth Circuit held that the provision referred to the immediately preceding policy, not any earlier policy in effect at any time. [*EMCOR Grp., Inc. v. Great Am. Ins. Co.*, 636 Fed. Appx. 189 (4th Cir. 2016); see George B. Hall, Jr., *Fourth Circuit Refuses to Find Commercial Crime Policy Ambiguous*, Phelps Dunbar LLP (Mar. 7, 2016), available at Lexology.com]

In late 2016, the Fifth Circuit held that, because social engineering fraud endorsements were available, a social engineering fraud loss was not covered by a traditional commercial crime policy. An employee of the insured, Apache, received a call from someone purporting to be a representative of one of Apache's vendors. The caller told Apache to change the vendor's bank account information. The Apache employee said that a formal request was required. The next week, the accounts payable department received an e-mail that appeared to come from the vendor, with a signed letter on the vendor's letterhead, and two Apache employees called to confirm. About $7 million was transferred to the new account. A few weeks later, the vendor asked for payment. Apache was able to recoup some of the funds, but lost about $2.4 million. Apache claimed under the computer fraud provision of its crime protection policy, which did not have a social engineering fraud provision. The Fifth Circuit held that computer fraud requires an unauthorized transfer of funds, not merely any transfer where both a computer and fraud are present; there were events in the chain other than computer use responsible for the loss. [*Apache Corp. v. Great Am. Ins. Co.*, 2016 WL 6090901(5th Cir. Oct. 18, 2016); see David S. Wilson and Christopher McKibbin, *Apache Corporation: Fifth Circuit Holds that Commercial Crime Policy's Computer Fraud Coverage Does Not Extend to Social Engineering Fraud Loss* (Oct. 24, 2016), available at Lexology.com. See also *Pestmaster Servs. v.*

Travelers, No. 14-56294 (9th Cir. July 29, 2016) (holding that a crime policy is not a general fraud policy)]

Similarly, the Ninth Circuit held that a business management/accounting firm was not covered for funds that it was induced to wire by a social engineering fraud. The district court held that the insured did not show direct loss. The Ninth Circuit's rationale for its holding was different: that the company failed to show that the loss fit under any of the forgery, computer fraud, or funds transfer fraud provisions of the policy. The firm, Taylor & Lieberman, kept its clients' funds in separate bank accounts at City National Bank. Taylor & Lieberman's clients gave the firm power of attorney allowing transactions to be carried out. A criminal gained control of a client's e-mail account and sent two e-mails to Taylor & Lieberman, one directing $94,280 to be sent to an account in Malaysia, the second directing $98,485 to be sent to an account in Singapore. Taylor & Lieberman complied and sent confirming e-mails to the client's account indicating that the transfers had been made. The employee got a third e-mail, from a different e-mail address, and telephoned the client, discovering that all three e-mails were fraudulent. Taylor & Lieberman recovered some of the disbursements, but had to reimburse its client almost $100,000. Taylor & Lieberman filed claims under its forgery, computer fraud, and funds transfer fraud insurance, but the claims were denied because the insurer said that Taylor & Lieberman, as insured, had not suffered the direct loss that was covered by the policy. The Ninth Circuit held that the fraudulent e-mails were not financial instruments, so coverage for forgery or alteration of a financial instrument was not available. The Ninth Circuit said that the policy referred to items such as checks and drafts, not invoices or wire instructions. The computer fraud coverage required an unauthorized entry into the computer system; the Ninth Circuit said that sending an e-mail was not an unauthorized entry. The policy also required "introduction" of instructions that propagate themselves through the computer system (e.g., deliberately transmitting a virus), and the court said that this did not occur. The funds transfer fraud coverage was also unavailable because it applied only to fraudulent directions to make payments without the insured's knowledge or consent—whereas the insured carried out the wire transfers, and Taylor & Lieberman was not a "financial institution" that was directed to make payments pursuant to fraudulent instructions. According to a recent article, the moral of this story is that businesses should consider purchasing the separate social engineering fraud coverage that is now available. [*Taylor & Lieberman v. Federal Ins. Co.*, No. 15-54102, 2017 WL 929211 (9th Cir. Mar. 9, 2017); see David S. Wilson and Christopher McKibbin, *Taylor & Lieberman: Ninth Circuit Finds No Coverage Under Crime Policy for Client Funds Lost in Social Engineering Fraud*, Blaney McMurtry LLP (Apr. 3, 2017), available at Lexology.com]

The Seventh Circuit held that a company's vice president of major accounts was not an employee as defined by a crime policy. (She was supposed to remove old equipment and sell it to salvagers—but she kept $5.2 million in sales proceeds for herself.) The vice president's services were provided under a series of consulting agreements. She was fired and eventually was convicted of wire fraud and tax evasion. The Seventh Circuit held that her contracts were with a business entity she owned, not a "labor leasing firm." [*Telamon Corp. v. Charter Oak Fire Ins. Co.*, 2017 WL 942656 (7th Cir. Mar. 9, 2017); see David S. Wilson and Christopher McKibbin, *Telamon: Seventh Circuit finds Insured's Vice-President to be Independent Contractor Falling Outside Crime Policy's Employee Theft Coverage*, Blaney McMurtry LLP (Mar. 13, 2017)]

§ 43.06 DUTY OF THE INSURANCE CONTRACT

[A] Duty to Defend

A lesser-known, but perhaps more important, part of the liability insurance policy is the insurer's duty to defend. That is, whenever a claim is made against the employer, the insurer has to provide a lawyer and take care of the case. However, usually the insurer is in control of the litigation, and decides how vigorously to defend the case and when to settle (although some policies return control of litigation to the insured). Most policies are drafted so that, if the insured company settles the case without consent and participation of the insurer, the insured company will not be able to recover any part of the settlement costs from the insurer.

The insurer's duty to indemnify is the duty to pay on the insured's behalf when the insured settles or loses a lawsuit. The duty to defend is much broader. If the allegations against an insured company are invalid, or can't be proved, then the liability insurer's role is to get the charge dismissed, even though there is no liability to indemnify. In general, if the charges combine claims that are covered by liability insurance with others that are not, the insurer has a duty to defend against all the charges, not just the covered ones.

Usually, the insurer's duty to defend is triggered by a "claim" made against the insured employer. This is usually interpreted as filing a complaint with a court. EEOC or local agency proceedings are not generally considered "claims," so an insured company is on its own for a significant part of the process before the duty to defend begins.

The Eleventh Circuit held early in 2017 that a law firm's professional liability insurer had no duty to defend against claims for sanctions and non-pecuniary relief. The law firm was held in contempt and sanctioned for violating a protective order by using privileged information. The firm was sued for breach of contract, breach of the covenant of good faith, and declaratory relief. The insurer refused to defend, taking the position that the policy applied only to claims for damages, defined as "compensatory judgments, settlements or awards" and did not cover sanctions or other penalties. The Eleventh Circuit held that the attorneys' fees and costs the firm had to pay as punishment for contempt were sanctions, not claims for damages. [*Jones, Foster, Johnston & Stubbs, P.A. v. Prosight-Syndicate 1110 at Lloyd's*, 2017 WL 586450 (11th Cir. Feb. 14, 2017); see George

B. Hall, Jr., *Eleventh Circuit Affirms Ruling that Professional Liability Policy Does Not Cover Claims for Sanctions and Non-Pecuniary Relief*, Phelps Dunbar LLP (Mar. 6, 2017), available at Lexology.com]

[B]   Duties of the Insured

Insurance companies are relieved of their obligation to pay claims if the insured company fails to satisfy its obligations. The most obvious duty is paying premiums. Liability policies also require the insured to notify the insurer as soon as possible whenever a "claim" is made. Therefore, legal advice is necessary to determine which allegations have the legal status of a claim.

As government investigations (e.g., dealing with the Foreign Corrupt Practices Act) become more common, it is important to know when an investigation triggers coverage. The Eastern District of Virginia followed the Second Circuit in holding that search warrants and investigatory subpoenas can trigger insurance coverage. PSI was a NASA contractor; its D&O coverage applied to the company and individuals. NASA issued a warrant and subpoena. A few months later, the U.S. Attorney's Office notified PSI that a civil investigation was underway dealing with its participation in an SBA program. PSI sought defense costs from its insurer, which denied coverage, stating that there was no "claim." The district court disagreed: the policy's definition of "claim" was broad enough to encompass all written demands for relief as well as judicial, administrative, and regulatory proceedings. The insurer had a duty to defend because the warrant was a written demand for non-monetary relief: production of documents.

> ■ **TIP:**   Companies that receive investigative letters, warrants, or subpoenas, even without a formal demand or claim, should contact their D&O insurance carrier as soon as possible. [*Protection Strategies, Inc. v. Starr Indem. & Liab. Co.*, Civil Action No. 1:13-CV-00763 (E.D. Va. 2014). See *MBIA Inc. v. Federal Ins. Co.*, 652 F.3d 152 (2d Cir. 2011)]

§ 43.07   QUESTIONS OF TIMING

Liability policies are divided into "occurrence" and "claims-made" policies. If there is an "occurrence" covered by the policy (see above), all the occurrence policies in force at that time must make payments. But the insured doesn't get five times the amount of the liability. Coverage is coordinated (divided among them) to prevent windfalls.

A claims-made policy works differently. It covers only claims that are made during the policy term with respect to events that happened during the policy term. Because this can be a difficult standard to meet, claims-made policies are often extended to cover events after the policy's "retroactive date." There may also be an "extended reporting period" after the policy expires, where events are covered if they occurred while the policy was still in force, but were reported later.

Coverage under a fiduciary liability policy is triggered when the claim is made, not when the alleged wrongdoing occurred. While the fiduciary liability policy is in force, it will cover claims reported during the policy period. But if a policy is cancelled or is not renewed, then future claims will not be covered even if they relate to acts that occurred before cancellation or nonrenewal. Extended reporting period (ERP) coverage is optional: in exchange for an additional premium, ERP coverage applies to claims filed during a specified period (usually 12 months post-policy expiration) relating to events while the policy was in force.

Standard ERP coverage will not provide complete protection in a merger or plan termination situation because there is a possibility that fiduciary breaches will be alleged until the statute of limitations (which could be as long as six years) has elapsed since the merger or termination.

"Tail coverage" protects the trustees of merged or terminated plans. Insurers do not have to provide tail coverage under a basic policy; the purchaser must negotiate the terms of coverage and the premium. Insurers are often reluctant to offer as much coverage as the trustees want. It is wise to include a provision forbidding cancellation of the policy after the premium has been paid. According to Segal Select Insurance, the premium for a six-year tail policy is likely to be two or three times the premium for the underlying fiduciary liability insurance when the plan was in operation. Tail coverage is usually paid from the assets of the plan that is being merged or is terminating, so it is important to arrange and pay for the coverage before the plan assets have all been distributed.

Instead of tail coverage, the successor plan might obtain a "merged-plan" endorsement, but the merged plan must continue to renew the coverage every year until the statute of limitations has expired, and the insurer may change the available coverage and liability limits. [Segal Select Insurance Fiduciary Shield, *If a Plan Merger or Termination Is on the Horizon, Seek Tail Coverage* (Mar. 2014) (benefitslink.com)]

The Louisiana Supreme Court allocated defense costs pro rata, when the CGL provided coverage for part of the time of exposure in a long-latency disease case involving noise-induced hearing loss. The court held that the insured's defense costs should be allocated among the insurers and the insured, reflecting coverage and self-insurance periods. The latency period was 60 years; the policy covered only 26 months. The trial court required the employer to pay all defense costs for the suit because there was an allegation of exposure to harmful conditions during the policy period. But the state supreme court reversed: Louisiana law permits proration of the duty to indemnify among carriers, because the occurrence triggering coverage is the plaintiff's exposure to harmful conditions within the policy period. With respect to indemnification for occurrences when there is no insurer on the risk, the insured is considered responsible for a pro rata share. In this case, the policy language limits bodily injury coverage to damage occurring during the policy period. The Louisiana Supreme Court held that adopting joint and several liability would treat the insured the same way no matter how many years it maintained coverage; businesses should have incentives to remain insured. In this reading, the proper formula is based on the time of risk assessment, not the policy limits because the duties of defense and indemnification are separate. The employer's exposure for defense costs was limited to 3% of the total alleged period of exposure. [*Arceneaux v. Amstar Corp.*, No. 2015-C-0588, 2016 La. LEXIS 1675 (La. Sept. 7, 2016); see Nicholas C. Cramb and Lavinia M. Weizel, *Louisiana Supreme Court Adopts Pro Rata Allocation of Defense Costs Among Insurers and Insured*, Mintz Levin Cohn Ferris Glovsky and Popeo PC (Sept. 20, 2016), available at Lexology.com]

§ 43.08 FIDUCIARY LIABILITY INSURANCE

A fidelity bond makes a plan whole when it suffers losses from dishonest or fraudulent acts by employees who handle plan participants' money or securities. All qualified plans must maintain an ERISA fidelity bond in the amount of 10% of the amount handled (see ERISA § 412). "Plan officials" must be bonded; not only plan fiduciaries but also anyone who handles property of the plan is considered an official. The typical duration of a fidelity bond is three years, and the amount must be adjusted each year to make sure the 10% requirement is satisfied. The PPA increases the maximum amount of the fidelity bond required for plans that hold employer stock, for plan years beginning after January 1, 2007, from $500,000 to $1 million. If the DOL discovers that the plan does not have the necessary bond, it can order the company to get a bond; permanently bar the fiduciary from ever serving as an ERISA plan fiduciary; remove the plan administrator and appoint an independent trustee; or impose penalties. The fidelity bond carrier must report the amount of its coverage on the plan's Form 5500.

In contrast, fiduciary liability insurance protects the plan sponsor and its officers, directors, and employees from common-law, ERISA, and other statutory liability. ERISA does not require plans to maintain fiduciary liability insurance. Generally speaking, the fidelity bond is a plan expense that can be paid from plan assets, but fiduciary liability insurance premiums are not. [Carrie Byrnes and Tim Zehnder, *Fiduciary Bonds and Fiduciary Liability Insurance—Do You Need Both?*, Bryan Cave Benefits and Executive Compensation Blog (Mar. 13, 2014) (benefitslink.com); Nevin E. Adams, *5 Things People Get Wrong About ERISA Fidelity Bonds,* Napa-net (May 2, 2017) (benefitslink.com)]

Where the policy covers the plan itself, the insurer can sue the fiduciary to recover the amount it had to pay out because of the fiduciary's conduct. Fiduciary liability insurance is usually available only in limited amounts, on a claims-made basis.

The rule of thumb for fidelity bond coverage is 10% of assets. The maximum bond is $500,000 per plan, or $1 million for plan officials who hold employer securities. IRS's analysis of Form 5500 filings shows that failure to maintain an adequate fidelity bond is one of the two most common plan compliance issues. There is no specific requirement for the amount of coverage under a fiduciary liability insurance policy because ERISA does not require this type of insurance, but most plans do have it. Insurance agents can advise about the coverage carried by similar plans, and every renewal is a chance to reconsider the amount of coverage if any factors have changed [John Carl, *Case of the Week: ERISA Fidelity Bond vs. Fiduciary Liability Insurance*, napa-net.org (Aug. 3, 2016) (benefitslink.com); see PlanSponsor editors, *(b)lines Ask the Experts— Coverage Amount for Fiduciary Liability Insurance*, plansponsor.com (Sept. 6, 2016)]

Fiduciary insurers do not cover attorneys' fees when the DOL gives notice of an investigation because there is often a gap between the time when fiduciary consults an attorney and the time when the insurer recognizes its duty to defend. The insurer may require a written allegation of wrongdoing to find that a claim has been made. However, the DOL usually waits until after requesting documents or interviews to file written allegations. A VC (voluntary charging) letter sets out findings of violations and says the DOL has finished its investigation. If the insurer refuses to cover legal fees during the investigation, the fiduciary must seek payment of fees from the plan or plan sponsor. But for ESOPs and multi-employer plans, DOL's position is that it is inappropriate for the plan to indemnify the fiduciary or advance fees. One possible solution is to purchase an insurance endorsement for the gap, known as "pre-claim investigation" coverage of defense costs; at least two insurers sell this coverage. [Stephen M. Saxon, *Saxon Angle: How to Close the Gap*, plansponsor.com (Feb. 11, 2014)]

Other than banks, insurance companies, and broker-dealers, ERISA § 412 requires every fiduciary and every person who handles property of an employee benefit plan to be bonded. All plan trustees are fiduciaries; others can become fiduciaries through their relationship to a plan (discretionary authority or control over management of the plan—or any authority or control, discretionary or otherwise, over plan assets). Anyone who provides investment advice to the plan is also a fiduciary. DOL has required bonding of anyone whose duties involve receiving, keeping, or disbursing plan funds, having access to plan funds, or having the capacity to cause losses to the plan through fraud or dishonesty. Section 412 makes it illegal for any plan official to permit another plan official handle the plan's property without being bonded. In other words, anyone who has an obligation to be bonded must enforce this requirement on everyone else who has to be bonded. Several forms of fiduciary bond are available, so the plan must select the right form—and, if necessary, increase the bonding if the existing bond does not cover all the fiduciaries of the plan. [Joe Faucher, Reish & Reacher ERISA Controversy Report, *ERISA Fidelity Bonds—Who Needs Them, and Who is Responsible for Securing Them?* (Feb. 2011) (law.com)]

Fiduciary liability insurance is an asset of the plan, but also protects trustees' personal assets. Furthermore, a fiduciary who breaches his or her duty may not be able to afford to reimburse the plan for its full losses.

For the policy to be truly useful, the definition of the "insured" should include the plan and/or trust, all past, present and future trustees and employees, and their successors. Coverage for the spouse of an insured if named as an additional defendant should also be included. The general rule is that most fiduciary liability policies don't cover third-party administrators or service providers who act as fiduciaries, although it may be possible to add them to the policy under an endorsement.

The definition of "loss" should include defense costs (including costs for investigators and expert witnesses) settlements, judgments, and pre- and post-judgment interest. Although liability insurance typically excludes coverage of fines and penalties, IRS Employee Plans Compliance Resolution System (EPCRS) penalties and amounts paid to the DOL when it wins or settles an ERISA § 502(l) case are usually either included in the basic coverage or added by endorsement.

> ■ **TIP:**   The entire policy has to be examined to see if there are additional limitations—for instance, the definition of "loss" may exclude fines and penalties.

Most fiduciary liability policies are claims-made policies. At each anniversary date, the insured can evaluate and adjust the policy limits and scope of coverage, bearing affordability in mind. Once a policy is purchased, it is hard to change carriers, because the application requires a warranty that there are no known claims or circumstances that would be excluded by the new insurer if they were fully disclosed—and it's very common for companies to face claims of this type!

A mid-2011 article points out some common misconceptions that fiduciaries often have about fiduciary liability insurance:

- That an ERISA fidelity bond protects their personal assets; the purpose of the fidelity bond is to protect the plan and its participants against misconduct by the fiduciary;

- That employee benefit liability policies cover fiduciaries fully; their errors and omissions in administration of the benefit plan itself are covered, but other aspects, such as investment of plan assets, are not necessarily covered;

That D&O policies cover fiduciaries; this is true only with respect to activities in their capacity as directors and officers, not in their capacity as fiduciaries, and ERISA claims are usually excluded by D&O policies; Fiduciaries will be entitled to indemnification of all personal liabilities; this is not necessarily true, because ERISA prevents plans from indemnifying fiduciaries for breach of fiduciary duty. [Jerry Kalish, *Four Misconceptions About Fiduciary Liability Insurance*, Retirement Plan Blog (June 7, 2011) (benefitslink.com)]

A mid-2016 article, after discussing the increase in DOL penalties under the Federal Civil Penalties Inflation Adjustment Act Improvements Act of 2015 (penalties which increased subsequently, reflecting a mandatory annual inflation adjustment for 2017), says that the most important questions for trustees of employee benefit plans are the types of insurance they require, and the appropriate amount of insurance. The article notes that professional liability policies usually exclude taxes, fines, and penalties unless they are specifically covered by the policy. Fiduciaries can be held personally liable under ERISA and other statutes, and this liability cannot be paid out of plan assets.

In response to these developments, insurers have created "first-party" coverages, such as expenditures for compliance programs created voluntarily and not because a third-party claim has been asserted. Typical fiduciary policies cover not only voluntary compliance programs, but also penalties imposed under ERISA § 502(c), (i), and (l). For example, IRS's EPCRS and DOL's VFCP allow potentially liable parties to correct plan mistakes and apply for reduction or elimination of penalties. Generally speaking, plan assets may not be used to pay to correct many violations, unless the cost would otherwise be payable by the plan, and the plan documents allow assets of the plan trust to be used to pay reasonable and necessary expenses. A fiduciary policy can provide payment for the cost of correction programs, whose filing fees more or less operate as penalty equivalents.

The article says that fiduciary liability insurance may also be available to handle penalties under HIPAA, PPACA, and Code § 4975 (which allows the IRS to impose excise taxes on prohibited transactions such as failure to remit plan contributions on a timely basis). A typical fiduciary policy covers the full DOL statutory penalty under ERISA § 502(i) and (l) but limits will probably be imposed, such as $25,000 to $250,000, for voluntary compliance fees and HIPAA, PPACA, § 4975, and ERISA § 502(c) penalties. An excess insurance carrier might offer higher limits. Fiduciaries should also consider the possibility that new penalties will be created; some insurers sell a miscellaneous/other penalties endorsement that covers future types of penalties. Another option is for the fiduciary to remain aware of legal developments, and seek coverage if the possible forms of liability increase.

A large pension or benefit fund, with assets over $1 billion, might need $500,000 in coverage of penalties; a smaller plan would probably want $100,000–$250,000 of penalty coverage. An "umbrella" endorsement, which comes into play after other coverage is exhausted, might also be worthwhile. [The Euclid Perspective, *The Department of Labor Increases Civil Monetary Penalties* (July 25, 2016), available at <http://www.Euclid-Perspective-DOL-Increases-Civil-MonetaryPenalties_072516.pdf/> (last accessed Apr. 8, 2017)]

INDEX

References are to section number.

A

AAA (American Arbitration Association), 40.06[B]

Abandoned plans, 17.02[F]

Abatement, OSHA, 31.12

"ABC test" of employee status, 1.12[C]

Ability to work requirement in unemployment insurance, 32.02[D]

Absenteeism, 1.14[D]

Accent, and job performance, 34.05[E]

Access to records, 24.01

Accidental workplace injuries, 33.03

"Accountable plan" rules
income tax withholding, 2.03[A]

Account balance plans and Section 409A, 8.02[D]

Accounting
MPDIMA, 9.10[C]
PBGC, 5.08[C]
pension plans, 11.06[G]
"pooling of interest" accounting, 16.09
retiree health benefits, 9.10[C]
stock options, 22.02[F]

Accrual of benefits in defined benefit plans, 5.06, 5.07

Acquisitions. *See* Corporate transitions

ACT Digital, 27.01[A]

Actions
arbitration compared, 40.04
class actions. *See* Class actions
COBRA, 19.04[B]
discrimination. *See* Discrimination actions by employees
ERISA, 15.11[A], 15.18
FLSA, 1.06[A]
FMLA, 38.11[A]
qui tam, 39.04[B]
removal to federal court, 42.10[E]
"stock-drop" suits, 4.06, 22.02[A]

ADA Amendments Act of 2008 (ADAAA), 14.01, 36.01, 36.03
central question, 36.03
correction of condition, effect of, 36.04[A]
"disability" vs. impairment, 36.03, 36.04[A]
impairment vs. disability, 36.04[E]
major activities of daily living, 36.03
major body systems, 36.03
"regarded as" claims, 36.03, 36.04[F]

ADA (Americans With Disabilities Act)
alcohol exception, 36.06[B]
Alzheimer's Disease, 36.04[D]
arbitration
of claims, 36.14
language, 40.06[A]
association with disabled person, 36.03[A]
attendance, 36.04[B]
auxiliary aids and services, 36.05[A]
carpal tunnel syndrome, 36.04[E]
case law, 36.05[C]
compliance in hiring, 23.12
correction of condition, effect of, 36.04[A]
covered entities, 36.02
damages, 36.13
defenses, 36.06
disability
attendance, 36.04[B]
benefits, 20.04[C], 36.10[B]
carpal tunnel syndrome, 36.04[E]
defining, 36.03, 36.04
forms of, 36.04[A]
impairment vs., 36.03, 36.04[E]
infertility, 36.04[C]
plans, 20.04[C]
psychiatric, 36.04[D]
discrimination, 36.03, 36.10[B], 41.01
drug exception, 36.06[B]
drug testing, 26.03[B]

Records and recordkeeping (*cont'd*)
  office of federal contract compliance
    programs (OFCCP), 24.03
  OSHA. *See* OSHA records
  persons with disabilities (PWDs),
    24.03
  PPACA requirements, 24.01[D], 18.19[K]
  pre-employment tests, 24.03
  retention requirements, 24.01, 24.08
  Title VII requirements, 24.03
  Vietnam Era Veterans' Readjustment
    Assistance Act (VEVRAA), 24.03
Recruitment
  blogs, 23.04
  within company, 23.04
  internal transfers and promotions, 23.04
  Internet recruitment, 23.04, 27.03
  search firms, 23.05
  social media, 23.04
Reduction of benefit accruals
  communications, 11.05
  defined benefit plans, 5.07
  notice, 11.05
Reduction of benefits
  anti-cutback rule and, 16.04
  corporate transitions, 16.04
  distributions, 12.09
  proposed regulations, 12.09
Reductions in force (RIFs), 1.04
  described, 1.04
  ERISA severance plan, implementation of,
    30.10
  WARN Act, compliance with, 30.10
    faltering company exception, 30.10
    unforeseen business circumstances
      exception, 30.10
Reference checks, 23.08, 25.11
"Regarded as" liability, 36.03, 36.04[F],
  36.07
Regressive collective bargaining, 30.07[A]
Regulation Z, 6.02
Rehabilitation Act
  ADA and, 36.02, 36.10[A]
  Ledbetter Act and, 34.01[A], 42.05[A]
  timeliness of claim, 34.01[A]
Rehiring, 16.06
Reinstatement
  ADEA, 37.06[A]
  FMLA, 38.04[B]
  USERRA, 1.18
Releases, 25.13

Religion, what constitutes, 34.07[A]
Religious discrimination. *See* Discrimination;
    Discrimination actions by employees
Religious harassment, 34.07[A]
  association-based, 34.07[A]
Religious objections to unions, 30.06[A]
Remedies
  damages. *See* Damages
  enforcement and compliance for qualified
    plans, 15.09[A]
  exhaustion of remedies, 13.07[B], 15.18[C],
    42.04[B], 42.05[B]
Removal to federal court, 42.10[E]
Replacements, strike, 30.09[D]
Reportable events, 5.09, 10.05[A]
  active participant base, 10.05[A]
  early warning program (EWP), 5.09
Reports
  PPACA, 18.19[K]
  Special Terminal Report for Abandoned
    Plans, 17.02[F]
  taxes, 22.08[A]
  termination of plan, 17.07
Required beginning date (RBD)
  application, 12.07[A]
  excise taxes, 12.07[B]
  rules, 12.07[C]
  theory, 12.07[A]
Required minimum distributions (RMDs),
  12.07[C]
Reservists, 1.18. *See also* USERRA
  distributions to, 1.18[A], 2.01[A], 18.11
  pension benefits for, 12.01
  withdrawal from 401(k) or other defined
    contribution plan, 6.06[A], 12.01
Resignations, negotiated,
  factors, 25.12
Res judicata, 32.04[B]
Responding to accidents, 33.07[B]
Retaliation
  ADA, 36.03
  "Cat's paw" theory, 34.08, 42.09
  discrimination, 34.03, 34.08
  discrimination actions by employees,
    42.09
  FMLA (Family and Medical Leave Act),
    ban on, 38.04[C], 38.11[A]
  FLSA (Fair Labor Standards Act), ban on,
    42.09
  investigations, responses to questioning in,
    35.04[B]

S

Z